Random House Webster's

Modern Office Dictionary

RANDOM HOUSE
NEW YORK

Random House Webster's Modern Office Dictionary

Copyright © 1999 by Random House, Inc.

This book is available for special purchases in bulk by organizations and institutions, not for resale, at special discounts. Please direct your inquiries to the Random House Special Sales Department, toll-free 888-591-1200 or fax 212-572-4961.

Please address inquiries about electronic licensing of this division's reference products, for use on a network or in software or on CD-ROM, to the Subsidiary Rights Department, Random House Reference, fax 212-940-7370.

Library of Congress Cataloging-in-Publication Data
Random House Webster's modern office dictionary.-- 1st ed.
      p.   cm.
      ISBN 0-375-40517-8 (hc)
      1. Office practice Dictionaries.   2. Management Dictionaries.
  3. Commerce Dictionaries.   4. English language Dictionaries.
  I. Title: Webster's modern office dictionary.
  HF5547.5.R32   1999
  651'.03--dc21   99-26279
                                        CIP

Random House Webster's Modern Office Dictionary was compiled, edited, and composed by the dictionary staff of Random House Reference, a division of Random House, Inc.

Visit the Random House Reference Web site at www.randomwords.com

Typeset and printed in the United States of America

First Edition
0 9 8 7 6 5 4

September 2000
ISBN: 0-375-40517-8

New York   Toronto   London   Sydney   Auckland

Contents

Preface

Random House Webster's Modern Office Dictionary is a unique language reference, combining five dictionaries in one convenient volume:

The *General Dictionary*, with over 40,000 entries, is based on the authoritative *Random House Webster's College Dictionary*. It features clear and concise definitions, pronunciations, and word histories. Its thorough, up-to-date coverage of basic vocabulary is supplemented by hundreds of new words and meanings.

The *Business Dictionary* defines over 3,500 words, phrases, and abbreviations from all areas of business. It covers key terms in fields as diverse as personal finance, economics, insurance, manufacturing, retailing, and more. The executive, the student, the job seeker, the consumer—all are affected by the world of business, and all need to know its specialized vocabulary.

The *Computer Dictionary*, with over 3,000 entries, explains the latest terminology of personal computers and the Internet in clear, simple language. The widespread presence of computers at home and in the workplace has made it necessary for everyone to be computer-literate. This dictionary has been written for a wide audience, from the experienced "hacker" to the "newbie" who is confused by "computerese." As an added feature, most of the definitions provide abundant cross references leading to more information on a particular topic.

The *Legal Dictionary* provides a basic understanding of over 3,000 of the most common and important terms used in contemporary American law. It is often difficult to assign precise definitions to legal terms because of the changes, nuances, and variations in legal concepts. However, the objective of this dictionary is to explain the central meaning of a concept, the meaning that is understood and shared by members of the legal profession.

The *Abbreviations Dictionary* gives the expanded form of over 10,000 shortened forms commonly encountered in newspapers, magazines, advertising, and daily conversation. Included are shortened forms in everyday use, as well as those used in science and other specialized fields. All types of shortened forms are listed in this dictionary: abbreviations, such as "Dr." and "etc."; pronounceable acronyms, such as "NASA" and "scuba"; initialisms, such as "CIA" and "FDR"; and symbols, such as those for the chemical elements.

The *Ready Reference Guide* contains a wealth of information that will be useful in today's business environment. This reference section includes World and U.S. Time Differences, Forms of Address, Distances Between U.S. Cities, and more.

Random House Webster's Modern Office Dictionary will serve the needs of office professionals who need to look up information in the course of their workday, yet can be used by anyone who wants easy access to a comprehensive all-in-one reference.

v

Pronunciation Key

STRESS

Pronunciations are marked for stress to reveal the relative differences in emphasis between syllables. In words of two or more syllables, a primary stress mark (ˊ), as in *mother* (**muth′ər**), follows the syllable having greatest stress. A secondary stress mark (ˊ), as in *grandmother* (**grand′muth′ər**), follows a syllable having slightly less stress than primary but more stress than an unmarked syllable.

ENGLISH SOUNDS

a	act, bat, marry	oi	oil, joint, joy
ā	age, paid, say	o͝o	oomph, book, tour
â(r)	air, dare, Mary	o͞o	ooze, fool, too
ä	ah, part, balm	ou	out, loud, cow
b	back, cabin, cab	p	pot, supper, stop
ch	beach, child	r	read, hurry, near
d	do, madder, bed	s	see, passing, miss
e	edge, set, merry	sh	shoe, fashion, push
ē	equal, bee, pretty	t	ten, matter, bit
ēr	ear, mere	th	thin, ether, path
f	fit, differ, puff	th	that, either, smooth
g	give, trigger, beg	u	up, sun
h	hit, behave	ûr	urge, burn, cur
hw	which, nowhere	v	voice, river, live
i	if, big, mirror	w	witch, away
ī	ice, bite, deny	y	yes, onion
j	just, tragic, fudge	z	zoo, lazy, those
k	keep, token, make	zh	treasure, mirage
l	low, mellow, bottle (bot′l)	ə	used in unaccented syllables to indicate the sound of the reduced vowel in alone, system, easily, gallop, circus
m	my, summer, him		
n	now, sinner, button (but′n)		
ng	sing, Washington		
o	ox, bomb, wasp	ᵊ	used between i and r and between ou and r to show triphthongal quality, as in fire (fīᵊr), hour (ouᵊr)
ō	over, boat, no		
ô	order, ball, raw		

NON-ENGLISH SOUNDS

A	as in French **ami** (A mēˊ)		sound, including a trill or flap in Italian and Spanish and a sound in French and German similar to KH but pronounced with voice]
KH	as in Scottish **loch** (lôKH)		
N	as in French **bon** (bôN) [used to indicate that the preceding vowel is nasalized]		
		Y	as in French **tu** (tY)
Œ	as in French **feu** (fŒ)	ᵊ	as in French **Bastogne** (bA stônˊyᵊ)
R	[a symbol for any non-English r		

General Dictionary

G uide to the G eneral D ictionary

ENTRIES: WHERE AND HOW TO FIND THEM

MAIN ENTRIES AND THEIR VARIANTS

All **main entries,** whether they are single words, phrases, abbreviations, proper names, prefixes, or suffixes, are shown in one vocabulary listing in strict letter-by-letter alphabetical order. They appear in **large boldface type,** even with the left margin of the column.

Alternate forms are common alternatives to the entry term, having only minor spelling differences or a difference in suffix. They follow the main entry, in the same **large boldface type,** and are introduced by "or" or "also."
Examples: **medieval; elegiac**

Variants that are more substantially different in form are shown for some nouns. They appear in **smaller boldface type,** introduced by the words "Also called."
Example: **goose flesh**
Any variants that do not apply to the entire entry are shown either at the portion of the entry to which they apply or at the end of the entry, with numbers indicating the definitions for which they are appropriate alternatives.
Example: **ammonia** (def. 2)

HOMOGRAPHS

Homographs are identically spelled terms that differ in derivation. They are given separate main entries, each marked with a small superscript number.
Example: **cuff**[1], **cuff**[2]

GUIDE WORDS

Guide words, which are shown at the top left of even-numbered pages and the top right of odd-numbered ones, give the range of main entries covered on that page.

RUN-ONS

Run-ons are words closely related to the main entry, but having a different grammatical function. Preceded by a lightface dash (—), these words appear at the end of an individual entry.
Run-ons are typically formed by adding a suffix. Although a run-on is not explicitly defined, its meaning can be understood by combining the senses of its root word and suffix, taking into account the part of speech. Thus the adverb **elaborately,** run-on to the adjective **elaborate,** is understood to mean "in an elaborate manner."
Some run-ons are formed in other ways, for example by deleting or changing a suffix.

HIDDEN ENTRIES

Hidden entries are parenthesized boldface terms shown in the context of a definition, where the sense of the hidden entry is made clear.
Example: **intestine**

PHRASAL VERBS

Phrasal verbs, like **back off, clear up,** and **stand by** follow all other verb senses in an entry. In any entry showing two or more such phrases, the first is spelled out completely, while those that follow show a swung dash (~) replacing the entry verb in the phrase.

IDIOMS

Idioms, like **make one's mark,** are expressions whose meanings cannot be predicted from the usual meanings of their components. Idioms appear in a labeled group as the final definitions in an entry.

ENTRIES: HOW THEY ARE SHOWN

SYLLABIFICATION

All single-word entries of more than one syllable are **syllabified.** That is, they are divided into syllables by boldface centered dots. These dots indicate possible hyphenation points, places where a word may break at the end of a line in printed or typed text.

STRESS

Primary and secondary stress marks replace centered dots at some syllable breaks. These marks serve as an aid to pronunciation by indicating the relative differences in emphasis between syllables. A primary stress mark (ˊ) follows the syllable with greatest emphasis and a secondary stress mark (ˊ) follows one with lesser emphasis.

Entries consisting of two or more words are not fully syllabified, but are shown with a pattern of stress that reveals the relationship of each word to the others. Example: **physical therapy**

PRONUNCIATION

Pronunciations are shown in parentheses immediately following the entry form, using a system of diacritical marks over vowels. Use the "Pronunciation Key" in this book.

Many entries show full pronunciations. Entries that are not pronounced fully are similar in pronunciation to nearby related entries or have component parts pronounced elsewhere in the dictionary. In these cases, the word is syllabified and stressed, with either no pronunciation or with a pronunciation for only that portion of the word that changes significantly.

MAJOR PARTS OF THE ENTRY

PARTS OF SPEECH

Italicized **part-of-speech** labels, usually abbreviated, are given for main entries, run-ons, and list words to show their grammatical function in a sentence. Thus a main entry that is commonly used as a noun would receive the label *n.* (Trademarks, however, defined as such, are capitalized and labeled *Trademark.*)
Example: **min′eral wa′ter,** *n.*

If a main entry has more than one grammatical function, a part-of-speech label precedes each group of definitions given for that part of speech. Such an entry also includes a summary of all its parts of speech with inflected forms if appropriate.
Example: **net′tle,** *n., v.* **-tled, -tling.**—*n.* **1.** a plant with stinging hairs.—*v.t.* **2.** to irritate or annoy.

INFLECTED FORMS

Inflected forms are, typically, plurals of nouns, past tenses and participles of verbs, and comparatives and superlatives of adjectives and adverbs.

Such forms regarded as "regular" are not shown in the dictionary for the following:
1. **nouns** whose plural is formed by the simple addition of *-s* or *-es,* as *dogs* or *classes.*
   Nor are plurals shown for "mass nouns," nouns that would not be pluralized.
2. **verbs** whose past tense and past participle is formed by the addition of *-ed* and whose present participle is formed by the addition of *-ing,* with no alteration of the spelling (as in *talk, talked, talking*).

This dictionary does show inflected forms for:

1. nouns that form their plurals irregularly.
2. nouns ending in a vowel, where even if the plural is regular, some confusion about its form might exist.
3. nouns whose plurals require pronunciation.
4. verbs with irregular inflections.
5. adjectives and **adverbs** that form the comparative and superlative with an internal change in form or by adding -er and -est. The comparative and superlative are not shown for adjectives and adverbs that, by definition, cannot be compared or for those forming their inflections with *more* and *most*.

Inflected forms for verbs are shown in the following order: past tense, past participle (where this differs from the past tense), and present participle.

DEFINITIONS

Definitions within an entry are individually numbered in a single sequence, regardless of their groupings according to part of speech. In general, the most common part of speech is listed first, as is the most frequent meaning within the part-of-speech group.

Closely related definitions may be grouped together and sequentially marked with boldface letters under the same boldface definition number.

Plural forms of singular main entries are spelled out, while a change in typeface from roman to italics, or a change in capitalization, is shown by means of an italicized label.

Examples: **card**¹ (def. 3); **democrat** (def. 2)

USAGE AND OTHER LABELS

Entries that are limited to a particular region, time, subject, or level of usage are marked with appropriate labels, as *Brit., Archaic, Law, Slang,* and *Informal.*

CROSS REFERENCES

Definitions that serve as **cross references** to another part of the alphabet, where the entry with the full definition is shown, are displayed in small capital letters.

Examples: **crape; rubella**

Variants of main entries are given their own alphabetical main entries when they would otherwise be difficult to find.

ETYMOLOGIES

Etymologies, or word histories, appear in square brackets after the definitions. The following symbols appear in the etymologies:

< This symbol, meaning "from," is used to show descent from one language or group of languages to another.

<< This symbol, meaning "goes back to," is used to show descent from one language to another but with an intermediate stage omitted.

= This symbol, meaning "equivalent to," is used to show that a word is made up of the words or elements that follow it.

A word displayed in small capital letters is a cross reference to another entry where further information can be found.

A language label is shown without an accompanying italicized form when there is no significant difference in form or meaning between the word in the given language and the preceding word in the etymology, or the main-entry word itself.

A, a (ā), *n., pl.* **As** or **A's, as** or **a's.** the first letter of the English alphabet, a vowel.

a¹ (ə; *when stressed* ā), *indefinite article.* **1.** any one (used before a singular noun): *a new car.* **2.** one: *a dozen eggs.* **3.** the same: *two at a time.* **4.** any single: *not a one.*

a² (ə; *when stressed* ā), *prep.* per: *fifty cents a ride.*

A 1. ampere. **2.** angstrom. **3.** answer.

A *Symbol.* **1.** the first in order or in a series. **2.** a grade or mark indicating excellence or superiority. **3.** a major blood group.

a-¹, a prefix meaning: on (*afoot*); in (*abed*); to (*ashore*); at (*aside*).

a-², a prefix meaning: of (*akin*); from (*anew*).

a-³, a prefix meaning: not (*atypical*); without (*amorality*).

A. 1. America. **2.** American. **3.** April.

a. 1. about. **2.** acre. **3.** adjective. **4.** alto. **5.** answer.

AA 1. administrative assistant. **2.** Alcoholics Anonymous. **3.** antiaircraft.

A.A. Associate of Arts.

aard•vark (ärd′värk′), *n.* a large burrowing African mammal that feeds on ants and termites. [< Afrik < D, = *aarde* earth + *varken* pig]

AB Alberta.

AB *Symbol.* a major blood group.

ab. about.

A.B. 1. able-bodied seaman. **2.** Bachelor of Arts. [< L *Artium Baccalaureus*]

a.b. *Baseball.* (times) at bat.

A.B.A. American Bar Association.

a•back (ə bak′), *adv.* **1.** toward the back. —*Idiom.* **2. taken aback,** surprised; startled; disconcerted.

ab•a•cus (ab′ə kəs), *n., pl.* **-cus•es, -a•ci** (-ə sī′, -kī′). a device for making arithmetic calculations, consisting of a frame set with rods on which beads are moved.

ab•a•lo•ne (ab′ə lō′nē), *n.* an edible mollusk with a flat, oval shell that is a source of mother-of-pearl.

a•ban•don¹ (ə ban′dən), *v.t.* **1.** to leave completely; desert: *to abandon a sinking ship.* **2.** to give up; discontinue: *to abandon a project.* —**a•ban′don•ment,** *n.*

a•ban•don² (ə ban′dən), *n.* a complete surrender to natural impulses; freedom from constraint.

a•ban′doned *adj.* lacking in moral restraint; shameless or wicked. —**a•ban′doned•ly,** *adv.*

a•base (ə bās′), *v.t.,* **a•based, a•bas•ing.** to humble or degrade. —**a•base′ment,** *n.*

a•bash (ə bash′), *v.t.* to embarrass; disconcert. —**a•bash′ed•ly,** *adv.* —**a•bash′ment,** *n.*

a•bate (ə bāt′), *v.,* **a•bat•ed, a•bat•ing.** —*v.t.* **1.** to reduce in amount, degree, or intensity. **2.** *Law.* to stop or suppress (an action, nuisance, etc.). —*v.i.* **3.** to diminish in amount, degree, or intensity. —**a•bate′ment,** *n.*

ab•at•toir (ab′ə twär′, ab′ə twär′), *n.* a slaughterhouse.

ab•bé (a bā′, ab′ā), *n.* a title of respect for a French ecclesiastic or clergyman.

ab•bess (ab′is), *n.* the superior of a convent of nuns.

ab•bey (ab′ē), *n., pl.* **-beys. 1.** a monastery or convent. **2.** the church of an abbey.

ab•bot (ab′ət), *n.* the superior of a monastery. [< L < Gk < Aram *abbā* father]

abbr. or **abbrev.,** abbreviation.

ab•bre•vi•ate (ə brē′vē āt′), *v.t.,* **-at•ed, -at•ing. 1.** to shorten (a word or phrase) by omitting letters. **2.** to make briefer. —**ab•bre′vi•a′tion,** *n.*

ABC *n., pl.* **ABC's, ABCs. 1.** the alphabet. **2.** (*pl.*) basics.

ab•di•cate (ab′di kāt′), *v.t., v.i.,* **-cat•ed, -cat•ing.** to give up or relinquish (a throne, right, power, or responsibility), esp. in a formal way. —**ab′di•ca′tion,** *n.*

ab•do•men (ab′də mən, ab dō′-), *n.* **1.** the part of the body between the thorax and the pelvis; belly. **2.** the posterior segment of the body of an arthropod. —**ab•dom′i•nal** (-dom′ə nl), *adj.*

ab•dom′i•nals *n.pl.* the muscles of the abdomen. Also called **abs.**

ab•duct (ab dukt′), *v.t.* to carry off (a person) by force, esp. to kidnap. —**ab•duc′tion,** *n.* —**ab•duc′tor,** *n.*

a•bed (ə bed′), *adv.* in bed.

ab•er•ra•tion (ab′ə rā′shən), *n.* **1.** deviation from what is usual, normal, or right. **2.** mental unsoundness or disorder. **3.** a disturbance of the rays of a light such that they can no longer be brought to a sharp focus or form a clear image. —**ab•er′rant** (ə ber′ənt, ab′ər-), *adj.* —**ab′er•ra′tion•al,** *adj.*

a•bet (ə bet′), *v.t.,* **a•bet•ted, a•bet•ting.** to encourage or support, esp. in wrongdoing. —**a•bet′tor, a•bet′ter,** *n.*

a•bey•ance (ə bā′əns), *n.* temporary inactivity, cessation, or suspension: *to hold a question in abeyance.*

ab•hor (ab hôr′), *v.t.,* **-horred, -hor•ring.** to regard with repugnance or aversion; detest. —**ab•hor′rence,** *n.* —**ab•hor′rer,** *n.*

a•bide (ə bīd′), *v.,* **a•bode** or **a•bid•ed, a•bid•ing.** —*v.i.* **1.** to remain; stay. **2.** to dwell; reside. —*v.t.* **3.** to put up with; tolerate. **4. abide by, a.** to comply with; submit to. **b.** to remain faithful to; keep. —**a•bid′ance,** *n.*

a•bid′ing *adj.* enduring; steadfast. —**a•bid′ing•ly,** *adv.*

a•bil•i•ty (ə bil′i tē), *n., pl.* **-ties. 1.** power or capacity to do or act. **2.** a talent, skill, or aptitude.

ab•ject (ab′jekt, ab jekt′), *adj.* **1.** miserable or wretched. **2.** contemptible; despicable. —**ab•jec′tion,** *n.* —**ab•ject′ly,** *adv.*

ab•jure (ab joor′, -jûr′), *v.t.,* **-jured, -jur•ing. 1.** to repudiate or retract; recant. **2.** to renounce under oath. **3.** to refrain from. —**ab′ju•ra′tion** (-jə rā′shən), *n.* —**ab•jur′a•to′ry,** *adj.* —**ab•jur′er,** *n.*

ab•la•tive (ab′lə tiv), *adj.* **1.** designating a grammatical case that marks the starting point of an action and, in Latin, indicates manner, instrument, or agent. —*n.* **2.** the ablative case.

a•blaze (ə blāz′), *adj.* **1.** on fire. **2.** gleaming. **3.** excited; ardent.

a•ble (ā′bəl), *adj.,* **a•bler, a•blest. 1.** having the necessary power, skill, or resources. **2.** having or showing intelligence, skill, or talent. —**a′bly,** *adv.*

-able a suffix meaning: able to be (*readable*); tending to (*changeable*); worthy of (*lovable*).

a′ble-bod′ied *adj.* physically fit.

ab•lu•tion (ə bloo′shən), *n.* a cleansing of the body, esp. as a religious ritual.

ab•ne•gate (ab′ni gāt′), *v.t.,* **-gat•ed, -gat•ing.** to deny (rights, comforts, etc.) to oneself; renounce. —**ab′ne•ga′tion,** *n.*

ab•nor•mal (ab nôr′məl), *adj.* not normal, average, typical, or usual. —**ab′nor•mal′i•ty,** *n., pl.* **-ties.** —**ab•nor′mal•ly,** *adv.*

a•board (ə bôrd′), *adv., prep.* **1.** on, in, or into (a ship, train, airplane, etc.). **2.** alongside.

a•bode¹ (ə bōd′), *n.* **1.** a residence; home. **2.** a stay; sojourn.

a•bode² (ə bōd′), *v.* a pt. and past part. of ABIDE.

a•bol•ish (ə bol′ish), *v.t.* to do away with; put an end to.

ab•o•li•tion (ab′ə lish′ən), *n.* **1.** the act of abolishing or state of being abolished. **2.** (*sometimes cap.*) the legal termination of slavery in the U.S. —**ab′o•li′tion•ism,** *n.* —**ab′o•li′tion•ist,** *n., adj.*

A-bomb (ā′bom′), *n.* ATOMIC BOMB.

a•bom•i•na•ble (ə bom'ə nə bəl), *adj.* **1.** repugnantly hateful; detestable. **2.** very bad or unpleasant. —**a•bom'i•na•bly,** *adv.*

a•bom'i•nate' (-nāt'), *v.t.,* -nat•ed, -nat•ing. **1.** to loathe intensely. **2.** to dislike strongly. —**a•bom'-i•na'tion,** *n.*

ab•o•rig•i•nal (ab'ə rij'ə nl), *adj.* **1.** of aborigines. **2.** native; indigenous. **3.** (*usu. cap.*) of the Aborigines of Australia. —*n.* **4.** ABORIGINE.

ab'o•rig'i•ne (-nē), *n., pl.* -nes. **1.** one of the original or earliest known inhabitants of a country or region. **2.** (*usu. cap.*) a member of any of the peoples who are the aboriginal inhabitants of Australia. [< L *ab origine* from the origin]

a•bort (ə bôrt'), *v.i., v.t.* **1.** to undergo or cause to undergo abortion. **2.** to terminate (a missile flight, a mission, or a procedure) before completion. —*n.* **3.** the termination of a missile flight, a mission, or a procedure before completion. —**a•bor'tive,** *adj.* —**a•bor'tive•ly,** *adv.*

a•bor'tion *n.* **1.** the expulsion of an embryo or fetus from the uterus, esp. to end a pregnancy. **2.** something that fails to develop, progress, or mature. —**a•bor'tion•ist,** *n.*

a•bound (ə bound'), *v.i.* **1.** to occur or exist in great quantities or numbers. **2.** to be well supplied (usu. fol. by *in*). **3.** to be filled; teem (usu. fol. by *with*).

a•bout (ə bout'), *prep.* **1.** in regard to; concerning. **2.** in connection or association with. **3.** close to; near. **4.** on every side of. **5.** on the verge of. —*adv.* **6.** approximately. **7.** nearly; almost. **8.** not far off; nearby. **9.** on every side. **10.** in the opposite direction. —*adj.* **11.** moving around; astir.

a•bove (ə buv'), *adv.* **1.** in or to a higher place. **2.** overhead, upstairs, or in the sky. **3.** higher in rank, authority, or power. **4.** before or earlier, esp. in a text. —*prep.* **5.** in or to a higher place than; over. **6.** greater in quantity or number than. **7.** superior in rank or standing to. **8.** of too fine a character for. —*adj.* **9.** said, mentioned, or written above. —*n.* **10.** something that is above. —*Idiom.* **11.** above all, most importantly; principally.

a•bove'board' *adv., adj.* without tricks, concealment, or disguise.

ab•ra•ca•dab•ra (ab'rə kə dab'rə), *n.* **1.** a mystical word once used as a magical means of warding off misfortune. **2.** meaningless talk; gibberish.

a•bra'sion (ə brā'zhən), *n.* **1.** a wearing or rubbing away. **2.** a scraped area on the skin. —**a•brade',** *v.t.,* **a•brad•ed, a•brad•ing.**

a•bra•sive (ə brā'siv, -ziv), *adj.* **1.** causing abrasion. **2.** tending to annoy. —*n.* **3.** a material, as sandpaper, used for grinding, polishing, or smoothing. —**a•bra'sive•ly,** *adv.* —**a•bra'sive•ness,** *n.*

a•breast (ə brest'), *adv., adj.* **1.** side by side. **2.** informed; aware.

a•bridge (ə brij'), *v.t.,* **a•bridged, a•bridg•ing. 1.** to shorten while retaining the substance. **2.** to diminish or curtail. [≪ ML *abbreviāre* to shorten] —**a•bridg'ment, a•bridge'ment,** *n.*

a•broad (ə brôd'), *adv.* **1.** in or to a foreign country. **2.** out of doors. **3.** in general circulation. **4.** over a large area; far and wide.

ab•ro•gate (ab'rə gāt'), *v.t.,* -gat•ed, -gat•ing. to abolish formally or officially; annul. —**ab'ro•ga'-tion,** *n.* —**ab'ro•ga'tor,** *n.*

ab•rupt (ə brupt'), *adj.* **1.** sudden or unexpected. **2.** curt or brusque, as in speech. **3.** lacking in continuity or smoothness. **4.** steep; precipitous. —**ab•rupt'ly,** *adv.* —**ab•rupt'ness,** *n.*

ab•scess (ab'ses), *n.* a localized accumulation of pus in body tissues. —**ab'scessed,** *adj.*

ab•scond (ab skond'), *v.i.* to depart suddenly and secretly, esp. to avoid capture and legal prosecution. —**ab•scond'er,** *n.*

ab•sent (*adj., prep.* ab'sənt; *v.* ab sent', ab'sənt), *adj., v.,* -sent•ed, -sent•ing, *prep.* —*adj.* **1.** not present at a given time; away. **2.** not in existence; lacking. **3.** not attentive; preoccupied. —*v.t.* **4.** to take or keep (oneself) away. —*prep.* **5.** in the absence of; without. —**ab'sent•ly,** *adv.*

ab'sen•tee' (-tē'), *n., pl.* -tees. a person who is

absent, esp. from work or school. —**ab'sen•tee'-ism,** *n.*

ab'sent-mind'ed *adj.* preoccupied so as to be unaware or forgetful of other matters. —**ab'sent-mind'ed•ly,** *adv.* —**ab'sent-mind'ed•ness,** *n.*

ab•so•lute (ab'sə lōōt'), *adj.* **1.** being fully as indicated; complete or perfect. **2.** free from restriction, limitation, or exception. **3.** outright; unqualified. **4.** not limited by laws or a constitution. **5.** not comparative or relative. **6.** positive; certain. **7.** not mixed; pure. **8.** relatively independent syntactically in relation to other elements in a sentence. **9.** *Physics.* pertaining to a system of units based on some primary units, esp. of length, mass, and time. —**ab'so•lute'ly,** *adv.*

ab'solute ze'ro *n.* the temperature of − 273.16°C (− 459.69°F), the hypothetical point at which all molecular activity ceases.

ab'so•lu'tion *n.* **1.** the act of absolving. **2.** a remission of sin as effected by a priest in the sacrament of penance.

ab•solve (ab zolv', -solv'), *v.t.,* -solved, -solv•ing. **1.** to free from guilt or blame. **2.** to release from a duty, obligation, or responsibility. **3.** to grant remission of sins to. —**ab•solv'a•ble,** *adj.*

ab•sorb (ab sôrb', -zôrb'), *v.t.* **1.** to take up or drink in (a liquid); soak up. **2.** to take in and assimilate; incorporate. **3.** to occupy or fill fully; engross. **4.** to take in without echo, recoil, or reflection: *to absorb sound.* —**ab•sorb'en•cy,** *n.* —**ab•sorb'ent,** *adj.*

ab•stain (ab stān'), *v.i.* to refrain voluntarily. —**ab•stain'er,** *n.* —**ab•sten'tion** (-sten'shən), *n.*

ab•ste•mi•ous (ab stē'mē əs), *adj.* sparing or moderate, esp. in eating and drinking; temperate.

ab•sti•nence (ab'stə nəns), *n.* **1.** forbearance from indulgence of an appetite. **2.** avoidance of alcoholic liquors or of particular kinds of foods. —**ab'sti•nent,** *adj.*

ab•stract (*adj.* ab strakt', ab'strakt; *n.* ab'strakt; *v.* ab strakt' *for 7, 8,* ab'strakt *for 9*), *adj.* **1.** thought of apart from concrete realities or specific objects. **2.** expressing a quality apart from any specific object or instance. **3.** not applied or practical; theoretical. **4.** (in art) emphasizing line, color, and nonrepresentational form. —*n.* **5.** a summary, as of an article. **6.** something abstract, as an idea or term. —*v.t.* **7.** to take away; remove. **8.** to draw away the attention of. **9.** to summarize. —**ab•stract'ly,** *adv.*

ab•stract'ed *adj.* lost in thought; preoccupied.

ab•strac'tion *n.* **1.** an abstract idea or term. **2.** the act or process of abstracting. **3.** absentmindedness; inattention. **4.** an abstract work of art.

ab•struse (ab strōōs'), *adj.* hard to understand; recondite. —**ab•struse'ly,** *adv.* —**ab•struse'ness,** *n.*

ab•surd (ab sûrd', -zûrd'), *adj.* contrary to all reason or common sense; laughably foolish. —**ab•surd'i•ty,** *n., pl.* -ties. —**ab•surd'ly,** *adv.* —**ab•surd'ness,** *n.*

a•bun'dance (ə bun'dəns) *n.* a plentiful supply. —**a•bun'dant,** *adj.* —**a•bun'dant•ly,** *adv.*

a•buse (*v.* ə byōōz'; *n.* ə byōōs'), *v.,* **a•bused, a•bus•ing,** *n.* —*v.t.* **1.** to use wrongly or improperly; misuse. **2.** to treat in a harmful way. **3.** to insult; revile. —*n.* **4.** wrong, improper, or harmful use; misuse. **5.** harshly or coarsely insulting language. **6.** bad treatment; maltreatment. —**a•bu'sive** (-siv), *adj.* —**a•bu'sive•ly,** *adv.* —**a•bu'sive•ness,** *n.*

a•but (ə but'), *v.,* **a•but•ted, a•but•ting.** —*v.i.* **1.** to touch or join at the border. —*v.t.* **2.** to border on.

a•but'ment *n.* a mass, as of masonry, supporting and receiving the thrust of an arch or vault.

a•bys•mal (ə biz'məl), *adj.* **1.** of or like an abyss; immeasurably deep. **2.** extremely bad; dreadful. —**a•bys'mal•ly,** *adv.*

a•byss (ə bis'), *n.* **1.** an immeasurably deep, vast chasm. **2.** something profound or infinite. **3. a.** the primal chaos before Creation. **b.** hell.

Ab'ys•sin'i•an (ab'ə sin'ē ən) *adj.* **1.** from ancient Ethiopia. —*n.* **2.** a type of cat.

AC 1. air conditioning. **2.** Also, **ac, a.c., A.C.** alternating current.

Ac *Chem. Symbol.* actinium.

a/c account.

a•ca•cia (ə kā′shə), *n., pl.* **-cias. 1.** a small tree or shrub with clusters of small yellow flowers. **2.** the locust tree.

ac•a•dem•ic (ak′ə dem′ik), *adj.* **1.** of a school or college. **2.** pertaining to areas of study that are not vocational or applied. **3.** not practical or directly useful; theoretical. —**ac′a•dem′i•cal•ly,** *adv.*

a•cad•e•my (ə kad′ə mē), *n., pl.* **-mies. 1.** a secondary school, esp. a private one. **2.** a school or college for special instruction or training. **3.** an association for the advancement of arts, sciences, or letters. [< L < Gk *akadēmeia* name of the garden where Plato taught]

a cap•pel•la (ä′ kə pel′ə), *adv., adj.* without instrumental accompaniment.

ac•cede (ak sēd′), *v.i.,* **-ced•ed, -ced•ing. 1.** to give one's consent; agree. **2.** to assume an office, title, or dignity.

ac•cel•er•ate (ak sel′ə rāt′), *v.,* **-at•ed, -at•ing.** —*v.t.* **1.** to increase the speed of. **2.** to hasten the occurrence of. —*v.i.* **3.** to move or go faster. —**ac•cel′er•a′tion,** *n.*

ac•cel′er•a′tor *n.* **1.** a foot pedal used to control the speed of a motor vehicle. **2.** a device, as a cyclotron, that produces high-energy particles.

ac•cent (*n.* ak′sent; *v. also* ak sent′), *n.* **1.** prominence of a syllable in terms of differential loudness or pitch. **2.** degree of prominence of a syllable within a word or of a word within a phrase. **3.** a mark indicating stress or vowel quality. **4.** a characteristic or distinctive mode of pronunciation. **5.** greater emphasis on one musical tone than on surrounding tones. —*v.t.* **6.** to pronounce with prominence. **7.** to give emphasis to.

ac•cen•tu•ate (ak sen′chōō āt′), *v.t.,* **-at•ed, -at•ing. 1.** to give emphasis to. **2.** to pronounce with an accent. —**ac•cen′tu•a′tion,** *n.*

ac•cept (ak sept′), *v.t.* **1.** to receive willingly or with approval. **2.** to answer affirmatively to. **3.** to undertake the duties, responsibilities, or honors of. **4.** to admit formally, as to a club. **5.** to regard as true. **6.** to agree to pay, as a draft.

ac•cept′a•ble *adj.* **1.** capable or worthy of being accepted. **2.** barely adequate or satisfactory. —**ac•cept′a•bil/i•ty,** *n.* —**ac•cept′a•bly,** *adv.*

ac•cept′ance *n.* **1.** the act of accepting or state of being accepted or acceptable. **2.** a pledge to pay an order, draft, or bill of exchange.

ac•cept′ed *adj.* generally approved.

ac•cess (ak′ses), *n.* **1.** the ability or right to enter, approach, or use. **2.** a way or means of approach. **3.** a sudden outburst, as of rage. —*v.t.* **4.** to gain access to. **5.** to locate (data) for transfer from one part of a computer system to another.

ac•ces•si•ble *adj.* easy to approach, enter, use, or obtain. —**ac•ces′si•bil/i•ty,** *n.* —**ac•ces′si•bly,** *adv.*

ac•ces′sion (-sesh′ən), *n.* **1.** the act of acceding to an office, title, or dignity. **2.** an increase by addition. **3.** something added.

ac•ces′so•ry (-ses′ə rē), *n., pl.* **-ries,** *adj.* —*n.* **1.** a supplementary part or object. **2.** *Law.* one who, although absent, assists another in committing a felony. —*adj.* **3.** supplementary; subsidiary. **4.** *Law.* giving aid as an accessory.

ac•ci•dent (ak′si dənt), *n.* **1.** an unintentional and unfortunate happening. **2.** something that happens unexpectedly. **3.** chance; fortune. —**ac′ci•den′tal** (-den′tl), *adj.* —**ac′ci•den′tal•ly,** *adv.*

ac′ci•dent-prone′ *adj.* inclined to have accidents.

ac•claim (ə klām′), *v.t.* **1.** to greet or salute with loud approval. —*n.* **2.** loud approval.

ac•cla•ma•tion (ak′lə mā′shən), *n.* **1.** a loud demonstration of welcome or approval. —*Idiom.* **2. by acclamation,** by a majority voice vote or applause.

ac•cli•mate (ak′lə māt′, ə klī′mit), *v.t., v.i.,* **-mat•ed, -mat•ing.** to accustom or become accustomed to a new climate or environment. —**ac′cli•ma′tion,** *n.*

ac•co•lade (ak′ə lād′, -läd′), *n.* an award, honor, or laudatory notice.

ac•com•mo•date (ə kom′ə dāt′), *v.t.,* **-dat•ed, -dat•ing. 1.** to do a favor for. **2.** to provide with something needed or wanted. **3.** to provide with lodging. **4.** to have or make room for. **5.** to adapt or adjust.

ac•com′mo•dat′ing *adj.* eager to help or please.

ac•com′mo•da′tion *n.* **1.** the act of accommodating or state of being accommodated. **2.** adjustment or reconciliation. **3.** something that supplies a need or want. **4.** Usu., **-tions. a.** lodging. **b.** space, as a seat or berth, on a public conveyance.

ac•com•pa•ni•ment (ə kum′pə ni mənt, ə kump′-ni-), *n.* **1.** something added, as for ornament. **2.** a musical part supporting the principal part.

ac•com′pa•ny *v.t.,* **-nied, -ny•ing. 1.** to go, exist, or occur with. **2.** to perform an accompaniment to or for. —**ac•com′pa•nist,** *n.*

ac•com′plice (ə kom′plis), *n.* a person who helps another in a crime.

ac•com′plish (ə kom′plish), *v.t.* to bring to a successful conclusion.

ac•com′plished *adj.* **1.** successfully completed. **2.** skilled; expert.

ac•com′plish•ment *n.* **1.** the act of accomplishing. **2.** something accomplished; achievement. **3.** a social grace or skill.

ac•cord (ə kôrd′), *v.i.* **1.** to agree. —*v.t.* **2.** to make agree or correspond. **3.** to grant; bestow. —*n.* **4.** agreement; harmony. —*Idiom.* **5. of one's own accord,** voluntarily.

ac•cord′ing•ly *adv.* **1.** in accordance. **2.** therefore; so.

accord′ing to′ *prep.* **1.** in accord with. **2.** as stated by.

ac•cor•di•on (ə kôr′dē ən), *n.* **1.** a portable musical instrument with a keyboard and a bellows for forcing air through reeds. —*adj.* **2.** having folds like the bellows of an accordion: *accordion pleats.*

ac•cost (ə kôst′, ə kost′), *v.t.* to approach, esp. with a greeting, question, or remark.

ac•count (ə kount′), *n.* **1.** a report of events or situations. **2.** an explanatory statement. **3.** reason or basis. **4.** importance or worth. **5.** an amount of money deposited with a bank. **6.** a statement of financial transactions. **7.** a business relation in which credit is used. —*v.i.* **8.** to give an explanation. —*v.t.* **9.** to consider as; regard. —*Idiom.* **10. on account,** as partial payment. **11. on account of,** because of. **12. on no account,** absolutely not. **13. take into account,** to take into consideration.

ac•count′a•ble *adj.* **1.** responsible; answerable. **2.** explicable. —**ac•count′a•bil/i•ty,** *n.*

ac•count′ant *n.* a person whose profession is accounting.

ac•count′ing *n.* the organizing, maintaining, and auditing of financial records.

ac•cred•it (ə kred′it), *v.t.* **1.** to certify as meeting official requirements. **2.** to provide with credentials. **3.** to attribute; credit. —**ac•cred′i•ta′tion,** *n.*

ac•crue (ə krōō′), *v.i.,* **-crued, -cru•ing. 1.** to result from natural growth. **2.** to be added as a periodic gain, as interest on money. —**ac•cru′al,** *n.*

ac•cul′tur•ate′ (ə kul′chə rāt′) *v.,* **-ated, -ating.** to adopt the cultural traits of another group. —**ac•cul′tur•a′tion,** *n.*

ac•cu•mu•late (ə kyōō′myə lāt′), *v.t., v.i.,* **-lat•ed, -lat•ing.** to gather or collect, esp. by degrees; amass or mount up. —**ac•cu′mu•la′tion,** *n.*

ac•cu•rate (ak′yər it), *adj.* **1.** free from error. **2.** carefully precise. —**ac′cu•ra•cy, ac′cu•rate•ness,** *n.* —**ac′cu•rate•ly,** *adv.*

ac•curs•ed (ə kûr′sid, ə kûrst′) also **ac•curst′** (ə kûrst′), *adj.* **1.** under a curse. **2.** damnable.

ac•cu•sa•tive (ə kyōō′zə tiv), *adj.* **1.** designating a grammatical case that indicates the object of a verb or preposition. —*n.* **2.** the accusative case.

ac•cuse (ə kyōōz′), *v.t.,* **-cused, -cus•ing. 1.** to charge with a fault, offense, or crime. **2.** to blame. —**ac•cu•sa′tion** (ak′yōō zā′shən), *n.* —**ac•cus′er,** *n.*

ac•cused′ *n.* a person tried in court.

ac•cus•tom (ə kus′təm), *v.t.* to familiarize by custom or use; habituate.

ac•cus′tomed *adj.* customary; habitual.

ace (ās), *n., v.,* **aced, ac•ing.** —*n.* **1.** a playing card with one spot. **2.** a point, as in tennis, made on a serve that an opponent fails to touch. **3.** a fighter pilot who downs a number of enemy planes. **4.** an expert. —*v.t.* **5.** to score an ace against (an opponent). **6.** *Slang.* to defeat (usu. fol. by *out*). **7.** *Slang.* to receive a grade of A in or on.

a•cer•bic (ə sûr′bik), *adj.* **1.** sour or bitter in taste. **2.** sharp or bitter, as in expression. —**a•cer′bi•ty,** *n.*

a•ce•ta•min•o•phen (ə sē′tə min′ə fən), *n.* a crystalline substance used to reduce pain or fever.

ac•e•tate (as′i tāt′), *n.* **1.** a salt or ester of acetic acid. **2.** a synthetic material derived from the acetic ester of cellulose.

a•ce•tic (ə sē′tik), *adj.* of or producing vinegar or acetic acid.

ace′tic ac′id *n.* a pungent liquid, the essential constituent of vinegar.

ac•e•tone (as′i tōn′), *n.* a volatile, flammable liquid used as a solvent.

a•cet•y•lene (ə set′l ēn′), *n.* a colorless gas used for lighting and in welding.

ache (āk), *v.,* **ached, ach•ing,** *n.* —*v.i.* **1.** to have a continuous dull pain. **2.** to yearn; long. —*n.* **3.** a continuous dull pain. —**ach′y,** *adj.,* **-i•er, -i•est.**

a•chieve (ə chēv′), *v.t.,* **a•chieved, a•chiev•ing. 1.** to bring to a successful end. **2.** to get by hard work or effort. —**a•chieve′ment,** *n.* —**a•chiev′er,** *n.*

A•chil′les (or **A•chil′les′**) **heel′** (ə kil′ēz), *n.* a weak or vulnerable spot.

ac•id (as′id), *n.* **1.** a compound usu. having a sour taste and capable of neutralizing alkalis and turning blue litmus paper red. **2.** a substance with a sour taste. **3.** *Slang.* the drug LSD. —*adj.* **4.** of an acid. **5.** sour to the taste. **6.** sharp, biting, or ill-natured; caustic. —**a•cid•ic** (ə sid′ik), *adj.* —**a•cid′i•ty,** *n.*

ac′id rain′ *n.* rain containing acid-forming chemicals, resulting from the release into the atmosphere of industrial pollutants.

ac•knowl•edge (ak nol′ij), *v.t.,* **-edged, -edg•ing. 1.** to admit to be real or true. **2.** to show recognition or realization of. **3.** to recognize the authority or claims of. **4.** to express appreciation for. **5.** to make known the receipt of. —**ac•knowl′edg•ment, ac•knowl′edge•ment,** *n.*

ac•me (ak′mē), *n., pl.* **-mes.** the highest point or stage; peak.

ac•ne (ak′nē), *n.* a disorder of the sebaceous glands characterized by pimples, esp. on the face.

ac•o•lyte (ak′ə līt′), *n.* **1.** an altar attendant in public worship; altar boy. **2.** an attendant or assistant.

a•corn (ā′kôrn, ā′kərn), *n.* the typically ovoid fruit or nut of an oak.

a•cous•tic (ə kōō′stik) also **-ti•cal,** *adj.* **1.** pertaining to hearing, sound, or the science of sound. **2.** designed for controlling sound: *acoustic tile.* **3.** sounded without electric or electronic enhancement: *an acoustic guitar.* —**a•cous′ti•cal•ly,** *adv.*

a•cous′tics *n.* **1.** (*used with a sing. v.*) the branch of physics that deals with sound and sound waves. **2.** (*used with a pl. v.*) the qualities of a room, auditorium, etc., that determine the audibility of sounds in it.

ac•quaint (ə kwānt′), *v.t.* **1.** to make familiar or aware. **2.** to provide with knowledge; inform.

ac•quaint′ance *n.* **1.** a person whom one knows casually. **2.** personal knowledge. —**ac•quaint′ance•ship′,** *n.*

ac•qui•esce (ak′wē es′), *v.i.,* **-esced, -esc•ing.** to comply silently or without protest. —**ac′qui•es′cence,** *n.* —**ac′qui•es′cent,** *adj.*

ac•quire (ə kwīr′), *v.t.,* **-quired, -quir•ing. 1.** to get possession of. **2.** to gain through one's efforts. —**ac•quir′a•ble,** *adj.* —**ac•quire′ment,** *n.*

ac•qui•si•tion (ak′wə zish′ən), *n.* **1.** the act of acquiring. **2.** something acquired.

ac•quis•i•tive (ə kwiz′i tiv), *adj.* tending or seeking to acquire, often greedily. —**ac•quis′i•tive•ness,** *n.*

ac•quit (ə kwit′), *v.t.,* **-quit•ted, -quit•ting. 1.** to declare not guilty of a crime or offense. **2.** to conduct (oneself); behave. **3.** to release from an obligation. —**ac•quit′tal,** *n.*

a•cre (ā′kər), *n.* a unit of land measure equal to 43,560 square feet.

ac•rid (ak′rid), *adj.* **1.** harshly or bitterly pungent in taste or smell. **2.** sharply stinging or bitter; caustic: *acrid remarks.* —**a•crid•i•ty** (ə krid′i tē), **ac′rid•ness,** *n.* —**ac′rid•ly,** *adv.*

ac•ri•mo•ny (ak′rə mō′nē), *n.* sharpness, harshness, or bitterness of nature, speech, or disposition. —**ac′ri•mo′ni•ous,** *adj.*

ac•ro•bat (ak′rə bat′), *n.* a performer of gymnastic feats requiring agility, balance, and coordination. —**ac′ro•bat′ic,** *adj.*

ac′ro•bat′ics *n.* (*used with a pl. v.*) **1.** the feats of an acrobat. **2.** any feats requiring great agility: *verbal acrobatics.*

ac•ro•nym (ak′rə nim), *n.* a word, as *laser,* formed from the initial letters or groups of letters of words in a name or phrase.

ac•ro•pho•bi•a (ak′rə fō′bē ə), *n.* a pathological fear of heights.

a•cross (ə krôs′, ə kros′), *prep.* **1.** from one side to the other of. **2.** on or to the other side of. **3.** into contact with, usu. by accident. **4.** transversely over; crosswise of. —*adv.* **5.** from one side to another. **6.** on the other side. **7.** crosswise; transversely.

across′-the-board′ *adj.* **1.** applying to all members or categories. **2.** (of a bet, esp. in a horse race) covering win, place, and show.

a•cryl•ic (ə kril′ik), *n.* **1.** a paint with an acrylic resin as the vehicle. **2.** any of a group of synthetic textile fibers, as Orlon. **3.** ACRYLIC RESIN.

acryl′ic res′in *n.* any of a group of thermoplastic resins used to make paints, plastics, etc.

act (akt), *n.* **1.** something done; deed. **2.** the process of doing. **3.** a law, decree, edict, or statute. **4.** one of the main divisions of a play or opera. **5.** a short performance in a variety show. **6.** a display of insincere behavior. —*v.i.* **7.** to do something; carry out an action. **8.** to carry out a particular function; serve. **9.** to produce an effect. **10.** to conduct oneself; behave. **11.** to pretend or feign. **12.** to perform as an actor. —*v.t.* **13.** to perform (a dramatic role) on a stage. **14. act up, a.** to malfunction. **b.** to behave willfully.

act′ing *adj.* **1.** serving temporarily, esp. as a substitute during another's absence. —*n.* **2.** the art, profession, or activity of an actor.

ac•tin•i•um (ak tin′ē əm), *n.* a radioactive, silver-white metallic element. *Symbol:* Ac; *at. no.:* 89; *at. wt.:* 227.

ac•tion (ak′shən), *n.* **1.** the process of acting or the state of being active. **2.** an act or deed. **3.** actions, behavior; conduct. **4.** energetic activity. **5.** effect or influence. **6.** the mechanism by which something, as a gun, is operated. **7.** military combat. **8.** an event or series of events that form a literary or dramatic plot. **9.** a legal proceeding. —**ac′tion•less,** *adj.*

ac′tion•a•ble *adj.* furnishing grounds for a lawsuit.

ac•ti•vate (ak′tə vāt′), *v.t.,* **-vat•ed, -vat•ing. 1.** to make active. **2.** *Physics.* to induce radioactivity in. **3.** to aerate (sewage) in order to accelerate decomposition. **4.** to place (a military unit) on an active status. —**ac′ti•va′tion,** *n.*

ac•tive (ak′tiv), *adj.* **1.** engaged in action or activity. **2.** being in existence, progress, or motion. **3.** giving rise to action or change. **4.** agile; nimble. **5.** characterized by current activity, participation, or use. **6.** noting the voice of a verb having a subject that performs the action. —*n.* **7.** the active voice. —**ac′tive•ly,** *adv.*

ac′tiv•ism *n.* the doctrine or practice of vigorous action to achieve political or social goals. —**ac′tiv•ist,** *n., adj.*

ac•tiv•i•ty (-i tē), *n., pl.* **-ties. 1.** the state or quality of being active. **2.** energetic action; animation. **3.** a specific deed, action, occupation, or sphere of action.

ac•tor (ak′tər), *n.* a person who acts in stage plays or motion pictures.

ac′tress (-tris), *n.* a woman who acts in stage plays or motion pictures.

ac•tu•al (ak′chōō əl), *adj.* **1.** existing in fact or reality. **2.** existing at the present time. —**ac′tu•al′i•ty**, *n., pl.* **-ties.** —**ac′tu•al•ly,** *adv.*

ac•tu•ar•y (ak′chōō er′ē), *n., pl.* **-ies.** a person who computes insurance premium rates, risks, etc. —**ac′tu•ar′i•al,** *adj.*

ac′tu•ate′ (-āt′), *v.t.,* **-at•ed, -at•ing. 1.** to incite to action. **2.** to put into action. —**ac′tu•a′tion,** *n.* —**ac′tu•a′tor,** *n.*

a•cu•i•ty (ə kyōō′i tē), *n.* sharpness of perception.

a•cu•men (ə kyōō′mən), *n.* keen insight; shrewdness.

ac•u•punc•ture (ak′yōō pungk′chər), *n.* a Chinese medical practice that treats illness or relieves pain by the insertion of needles at specified sites of the body. —**ac′u•punc′tur•ist,** *n.*

a•cute (ə kyōōt′), *adj.* **1.** sharp or severe: *acute pain.* **2.** extremely serious; critical. **3.** (of disease) brief and severe. **4.** penetrating in insight or perception. **5.** extremely sensitive: *acute eyesight.* **6.** (of an angle) less than 90°. —**a•cute′ly,** *adv.* —**a•cute′ness,** *n.*

ad (ad), *n.* an advertisement.

A.D. or **AD,** in the year of the Lord (used with dates): *Charlemagne was born in* A.D. 742. [< L *annō Dominī*]

ad•age (ad′ij), *n.* a traditional saying; proverb.

a•da•gio (ə dä′jō, -zhē ō′), *adv., adj., n., pl.* **-gios.** —*adv.* **1.** *Music.* slowly. —*adj.* **2.** *Music.* slow. —*n.* **3.** *Music.* an adagio movement. **4.** a technically demanding ballet duet or trio. [< It, for *ad agio* at ease]

ad•a•mant (ad′ə mənt), *adj.* **1.** utterly unyielding; inflexible. —*n.* **2.** a legendary stone of impenetrable hardness. —**ad′a•mant•ly,** *adv.*

Ad′am's ap′ple (ad′əmz), *n.* a projection of the thyroid cartilage at the front of the neck.

a•dapt (ə dapt′), *v.t., v.i.* to adjust or become adjusted to new requirements or conditions. —**a•dapt′a•ble,** *adj.* —**a•dapt′a•bil′i•ty,** *n.* —**ad•ap•ta•tion** (ad′əp tā′shən), *n.*

add (ad), *v.t.* **1.** to unite or join so as to increase in number, quantity, size, or importance. **2.** to find the sum of. **3.** to say or write further. —*v.i.* **4.** to perform arithmetic addition. **5.** to be or serve as an addition. **6. add up,** to seem reasonable. **7. ~ up to,** to amount to; signify.

ADD attention deficit disorder.

ad•den′dum (-dəm), *n., pl.* **-da** (-də). **1.** an addition. **2.** an appendix to a book.

ad•der (ad′ər), *n.* **1.** the common European viper. **2.** a snake resembling the viper.

ad•dict (*v.* ə dikt′; *n.* ad′ikt), *v.t.* **1.** to cause to become physiologically dependent on a drug. **2.** to abandon (oneself) to something compulsively or obsessively. —*n.* **3.** one who is addicted, esp. to a drug. —**ad•dic′tion,** *n.* —**ad•dic′tive,** *adj.*

ad•di•tion (ə dish′ən), *n.* **1.** the act or process of adding. **2.** the process of uniting numbers to find their sum. **3.** something added. —*Idiom.* **4. in addition,** besides; also. **5. in addition to,** as well as; besides. —**ad•di′tion•al,** *adj.* —**ad•di′tion•al•ly,** *adv.*

ad•di•tive (ad′i tiv), *n.* **1.** a substance added to another to alter or improve its quality. —*adj.* **2.** characterized or produced by addition.

ad•dle (ad′l), *v.t., v.i.,* **-dled, -dling.** to make or become confused.

ad•dress (*n.* ə dres′, ad′res; *v.* ə dres′), *n.* **1.** the place where a person or organization is located. **2.** the location and name of the intended recipient indicated on a piece of mail. **3.** a formal speech. **4.** skillful management. **5.** a code that designates the location of information stored in computer memory. —*v.t.* **6.** to direct a speech or statement to. **7.** to use a specified form or title in speaking or writing to. **8.** to put the directions for delivery on. **9.** to direct the energy or efforts of (oneself).

ad•dress•ee (ad′re sē′, ə dre-), *n., pl.* **-ees.** one to whom mail is addressed.

ad•duce (ə dōōs′, ə dyōōs′), *v.t.,* **-duced, -duc•ing.** to bring forward, as in evidence.

ad•e•noids (ad′n oidz′), *n.pl.* a mass of tissue between the back of the nose and the throat.

a•dept (*adj.* ə dept′; *n.* ad′ept, ə dept′), *adj.* **1.** very skilled; expert. —*n.* **ad•ept 2.** a skilled person; expert. —**a•dept′ly,** *adv.* —**a•dept′ness,** *n.*

ad•e•quate (ad′i kwit), *adj.* **1.** fully sufficient for a requirement or purpose. **2.** barely sufficient or suitable. —**ad′e•qua•cy** (-kwə sē), *n.* —**ad′e•quate•ly,** *adv.*

ad•here (ad hēr′), *v.i.,* **-hered, -her•ing. 1.** to stick fast; cling. **2.** to hold closely or firmly. **3.** to be devoted in support or allegiance. —**ad•her′ence,** *n.* —**ad•her′ent,** *n., adj.*

ad•he′sive (-siv, -ziv), *adj.* **1.** coated with a sticky substance. **2.** tending to adhere; sticky. —*n.* **3.** an adhesive substance or material.

ad hoc (ad hok′, hōk′), *adj., adv.* for a particular purpose or end: *an ad hoc committee.*

a•dieu (ə dōō′, ə dyōō′), *interj., n., pl.* **a•dieus,** **a•dieux** (ə dōōz′, ə dyōōz′). good-bye. [< MF, = *a* (< L *ad* to) + *dieu* (< L *deus* god)]

ad in•fi•ni•tum (ad in′fə nī′təm), *adv.* without limit; endlessly.

adj. 1. adjective. **2.** adjustment. **3.** adjutant.

ad•ja•cent (ə jā′sənt), *adj.* lying near or contiguous; nearby or adjoining. —**ad•ja′cen•cy,** *n.* —**ad•ja′cent•ly,** *adv.*

ad•jec•tive (aj′ik tiv), *n.* a word functioning as a modifier of a noun. —**ad′jec•ti′val** (-tī′vəl), *adj.* —**ad′jec•ti′val•ly,** *adv.*

ad•join (ə join′), *v.t.* **1.** to be close or next to. —*v.i.* **2.** to be close or in contact. —**ad•join′ing,** *adj.*

ad•journ (ə jûrn′), *v.t.* **1.** to suspend to a future time, another place, or indefinitely. —*v.i.* **2.** to postpone, suspend, or transfer a proceeding. **3.** to go to another place. —**ad•journ′ment,** *n.*

ad•judge (ə juj′), *v.t.,* **-judged, -judg•ing. 1.** to award judicially. **2.** to decide by judicial procedure. **3.** to deem; consider.

ad•ju•di•cate (ə jōō′di kāt′), *v.t.,* **-cat•ed, -cat•ing.** to settle or determine (an issue or dispute) judicially. —**ad•ju′di•ca′tion,** *n.* —**ad•ju′di•ca′tive** (-kā′tiv, -kə tiv), *adj.* —**ad•ju′di•ca′tor,** *n.*

ad•junct (aj′ungkt), *n.* something added to another but not essential to it.

ad•just (ə just′), *v.t.* **1.** to change so as to fit, correspond, or conform. **2.** to put in working order or in a proper state. **3.** to settle satisfactorily. **4.** to determine the amount to be paid in settlement of (an insurance claim). —*v.i.* **5.** to adapt oneself. —**ad•just′a•ble,** *adj.* —**ad•just′er, ad•jus′tor,** *n.* —**ad•just′ment,** *n.*

ad•ju•tant (aj′ə tənt), *n.* **1.** a military staff officer who assists a commanding officer. **2.** an assistant.

ad lib (ad lib′, ad′-), *n.* **1.** something improvised in speech, music, etc. —*adv.* **2.** at one's pleasure; without restriction. **3.** as needed; freely.

ad-lib (ad lib′, ad′-), *v.,* **-libbed, -lib•bing,** *adj.* —*v.t., v.i.* **1.** to improvise (words, music, etc.). —*adj.* **2.** impromptu; extemporaneous.

Adm. or **ADM, 1.** admiral. **2.** admiralty.

adm. 1. administration. **2.** administrative. **3.** administrator.

ad•man (ad′man′, -mən), *n., pl.* **-men.** a person whose profession is writing, designing, or selling advertisements.

ad•min•is•ter (ad min′ə stər), *v.t.* **1.** to direct or manage. **2.** to give out, esp. formally; dispense. **3.** to give remedially. **4.** to tender (an oath). **5.** *Law.* to manage or dispose of (an estate).

ad•min′is•tra′tion *n.* **1.** management, as of a government or business. **2.** (*often cap.*) the executive branch of a government. **3.** the period during which an administrator or body of administrators serves. **4.** *Law.* the management of an estate. **5.** the act of administering. —**ad•min′is•tra′tive,** *adj.*

ad•min′is•tra′tor *n.* **1.** a person who

administers. **2.** *Law.* a person appointed to administer an estate.

ad•mi•ra•ble (ad′mər ə bəl), *adj.* worthy of admiration. —**ad′mi•ra•bly,** *adv.*

ad•mi•ral (ad′mər əl), *n.* **1.** the commander in chief of a fleet. **2.** a naval officer of the second-highest rank.

ad′mi•ral•ty *n., pl.* **-ties. 1.** the department of state having charge of naval affairs, as in Great Britain. **2.** a court dealing with maritime questions.

ad•mire (ad mī°r′), *v.t.* **1.** to regard with pleasure, approval, and often wonder. **2.** to regard highly; respect. —**ad′mi•ra′tion** (-mə rā′shən), *n.* —**ad•mir′er,** *n.* —**ad•mir′ing•ly,** *adv.*

ad•mis•si•ble (ad mis′ə bəl), *adj.* capable of being admitted or allowed. —**ad•mis/si•bil′i•ty,** *n.*

ad•mis′sion *n.* **1.** the act of admitting. **2.** right or permission to enter. **3.** the price paid for entrance. **4.** confession of a charge, error, or crime.

ad•mit′ (-mit′), *v.,* **-mit•ted, -mit•ting.** —*v.t.* **1.** to allow to enter. **2.** to permit to exercise a particular function. **3.** to concede as valid. **4.** to acknowledge; confess. **5.** to have capacity for. —*v.i.* **6.** to offer opportunity; allow: *It admits of no other interpretation.* —**ad•mit′tance,** *n.*

ad•mit′ted•ly *adv.* without doubt.

ad•mon•ish (ad mon′ish), *v.t.* **1.** to caution or advise against something. **2.** to reprove, esp. in a mild manner. —**ad•mo•ni•tion** (ad′mə nish′ən), *n.* —**ad•mon′i•to′ry** (-mon′i tôr′ē), *adj.*

ad nau•se•am (ad nô′zē əm), *adv.* to a sickening or disgusting degree.

a•do (ə dōō′), *n.* bustling activity; fuss.

a•do•be (ə dō′bē), *n., pl.* **-bes. 1.** sun-dried brick made of clay and straw. **2.** a silt or clay used to make bricks. **3.** a building constructed of adobe. [< Sp < Ar *al-ṭub* the brick]

ad•o•les•cence (ad′l es′əns), *n.* the transitional period between puberty and adulthood; youth. —**ad′o•les′cent,** *n., adj.*

a•dopt (ə dopt′), *v.t.* **1.** to take and use as one's own. **2.** to become the legal parent of (the child of another). **3.** to vote to accept. —**a•dopt′a•ble,** *adj.* —**a•dop′tion,** *n.* —**a•dop′tive,** *adj.*

a•dorn (ə dôrn′), *v.t.* **1.** to decorate with or as if with ornaments. **2.** to enhance. —**a•dorn′ment,** *n.*

ad•re•nal (ə drēn′l), *adj.* **1.** of or produced by the adrenal glands. **2.** situated near or on the kidneys.

adre′nal gland′ *n.* one of a pair of ductless glands located above the kidneys.

ad•ren′al•in (ə dren′l in) *n.* an adrenal secretion that increases heart rate, blood pressure, etc.

a•drift (ə drift′), *adj., adv.* **1.** floating without anchor or mooring. **2.** without aim or direction.

a•droit (ə droit′), *adj.* **1.** manually dexterous. **2.** cleverly skillful or resourceful. —**a•droit′ly,** *adv.* —**a•droit′ness,** *n.*

ad′u•la′tion (aj′ə lā′shən), *n.* excessive praise. —**a•du•late′,** *v.t.,* **-lat•ed, -lat•ing.**

a•dult (ə dult′, ad′ult), *adj.* **1.** having attained maturity. **2.** of, befitting, or intended for adults. —*n.* **3.** a person who has attained maturity or legal age. **4.** a full-grown animal or plant. —**a•dult′hood,** *n.*

a•dul′ter•ate′ *v.t.* **-at•ed, -at•ing.** to make impure by adding inferior, alien, or less desirable materials or elements. —**a•dul′ter•a′tion,** *n.*

a•dul′ter•y (ə dul′tə rē), *n., pl.* **-ies.** voluntary sexual intercourse between a married person and someone other than the spouse. —**a•dul′ter•er,** *n.* —**a•dul′ter•ess,** *n.* —**a•dul′ter•ous,** *adj.*

adv. 1. advance. **2.** adverb. **3.** adverbial. **4.** advertisement.

ad•vance (ad vans′, -väns′), *v.,* **-vanced, -vanc•ing,** *n., adj.* —*v.t.* **1.** to move, send, or bring forward. **2.** to present for consideration; propose. **3.** to further the development, progress, or prospects of. **4.** to raise in rank; promote. **5.** to raise in rate or amount; increase. **6.** to supply (money or goods) on credit. —*v.i.* **7.** to go forward; proceed. **8.** to make progress; improve. **9.** to rise, as in importance or status. —*n.* **10.** a forward movement. **11.** progress; improvement. **12.** a promotion. **13.** Usu., **-vances.** attempts made to form an acquaintanceship, reach

an agreement, or gain favor. **14.** a rise in price or value. **15.** something, as money, furnished on credit. —*adj.* **16.** going or placed before. **17.** made, given, or issued ahead of time. —*Idiom.* **18.** in advance, beforehand. —**ad•vance′ment,** *n.*

ad•vanced′ *adj.* **1.** beyond the beginning, elementary, or intermediate: *advanced mathematics.* **2.** far along in progress, development, or time.

ad•van•tage (ad van′tij, -vän′-), *n.* **1.** a circumstance favorable to success. **2.** benefit; gain. **3.** a position of superiority. **4.** the first point in tennis scored after deuce. —*Idiom.* **5.** take advantage of, a. to make good use of. b. to impose upon, esp. by exploiting a weakness. —**ad′van•ta′geous** (-vən tā′jəs), *adj.* —**ad′van•ta′geous•ly,** *adv.*

ad•vent (ad′vent), *n.* **1.** an arrival; a coming. **2. a.** (*usu. cap.*) the coming of Christ. **b.** (*cap.*) the period beginning four Sundays before Christmas.

ad•ven•ti•tious (ad′vən tish′əs), *adj.* **1.** not inherent; extrinsic. **2.** appearing in an abnormal place, as a root on a stem. —**ad′ven•ti′tious•ly,** *adv.*

ad•ven•ture (ad ven′chər), *n., v.,* **-tured, -tur•ing.** —*n.* **1.** an exciting and unusual experience. **2.** an uncertain and usu. risky undertaking. **3.** a commercial or financial venture. —*v.t., v.i.* **4.** to risk or hazard. —**ad•ven′tur•ous,** **ad•ven′ture•some,** *adj.* —**ad•ven′tur•ous•ly,** *adv.*

ad•verb (ad′vûrb), *n.* a word that modifies a verb, an adjective, or another adverb. —**ad•ver′bi•al,** *adj.*

ad•ver•sar•y (ad′vər ser′ē), *n., pl.* **-ies.** an opponent; enemy. —**ad′ver•sar′i•al,** *adj.*

ad•verse (ad vûrs′, ad′vûrs), *adj.* **1.** unfavorable or antagonistic. **2.** opposed to one's interests. —**ad•verse′ly,** *adv.*

ad•ver′si•ty (-vûr′si tē), *n., pl.* **-ties** for 2. **1.** adverse fortune; misfortune. **2.** an adverse event or circumstance.

ad•ver•tise (ad′vər tīz′), *v.,* **-tised, -tis•ing.** —*v.t.* **1.** to describe or announce (a product or service) publicly, esp. in order to promote sales. **2.** to call public attention to. —*v.i.* **3.** to seek something or offer goods or services through advertisements. —**ad′ver•tis′er,** *n.* —**ad′ver•tis′ing,** *n.*

ad•ver•tise•ment (ad′vər tīz′mənt, ad vûr′tis-mənt, -tiz-), *n.* a public announcement intended to advertise something.

ad•vice (ad vīs′), *n.* **1.** an opinion offered as a guide to action. **2.** a communication containing information.

ad•vis•a•ble (ad vī′zə bəl), *adj.* wise, as a course of action; prudent. —**ad•vis′a•bil′i•ty,** *n.*

ad•vise (ad vīz′), *v.t.,* **-vised, -vis•ing. 1.** to give advice to. **2.** to recommend as desirable or prudent. **3.** to give information or notice to. —**ad•vis′er, ad•vi′sor,** *n.*

ad•vis′ed•ly *adv.* after careful consideration; deliberately.

ad•vi′so•ry *adj., n., pl.* **-ries.** —*adj.* **1.** giving advice. **2.** having the power or duty to advise. —*n.* **3.** a report on existing or predicted conditions, often with advice for dealing with them.

ad•vo•cate (*v.* ad′və kāt′; *n.* -kit, -kāt′), *v.,* **-cat•ed, -cat•ing,** *n.* —*v.t.* **1.** to support or urge by argument, esp. publicly. —*n.* **2.** a person who speaks or writes in support of a cause. **3.** a person who pleads for or in behalf of another. [< L *advocātus* legal counselor] —**ad′vo•ca•cy** (-kə sē), *n.*

adz or **adze** (adz), *n.* an axlike tool with a curved head used esp. for dressing timbers.

ae•gis (ē′jis), *n.* **1.** sponsorship; auspices. **2.** protection; support.

ae•on (ē′ən, ē′on), *n.* EON.

aer•ate (âr′āt, ā′ə rāt′), *v.t.,* **-at•ed, -at•ing. 1.** to expose to or supply with air. **2.** to charge or treat with air or a gas, esp. with carbon dioxide. —**aer•a′tion,** *n.* —**aer′a•tor,** *n.*

aer•i•al (âr′ē əl), *adj.* **1.** of, in, produced by, or done in the air. **2.** inhabiting or frequenting the air. **3.** growing in the air, as the adventitious roots of some trees. **4.** of aircraft. —*n.* **5.** a radio or television antenna. —**aer′i•al•ly,** *adv.*

aer•ie (âr′ē, ēr′ē), *n., pl.* **-ies.** the lofty nest of an eagle or other bird of prey.

aero- or **aer-,** a combining form meaning air or aircraft (*aerodynamics*).

aer•o•bic (â rō′bik), *adj.* **1.** (of an organism or tissue) requiring oxygen to sustain life. **2.** of aerobics.

aer•o′bics *n.* (*used with a sing. or pl. v.*) exercises, as jogging, designed esp. to stimulate and strengthen the heart.

aer•o•dy•nam•ics (âr′ō dī nam′iks), *n.* the study of the motion of gases and of the effects of such motion on bodies in the gas. —**aer′o•dy•nam′ic,** *adj.* —**aer′o•dy•nam′i•cal•ly,** *adv.*

aer′o•naut′ (âr′ə nôt′) *n.* a pilot.

aer•o•nau•tics (âr′ə nô′tiks, -not′iks), *n.* the science or art of flight. —**aer′o•nau′ti•cal,** *adj.*

aer•o•plane (âr′ō plān′), *n. Brit.* AIRPLANE.

aer•o•sol (âr′ō sôl′, -sol′), *n.* **1.** a system of colloidal particles dispersed in a gas. **2.** a liquid substance sealed under pressure and released as a spray or foam.

aer•o•space (âr′ō spās′), *n.* **1.** the atmosphere and the space beyond. —*adj.* **2.** pertaining to missiles, spacecraft, etc., designed for use in aerospace.

aes•thete (es′thēt), *n.* a person who has or affects refined sensitivity toward the beauties of art or nature.

aes•thet′ic (-thet′ik), *adj.* **1.** pertaining to a sense of beauty or to aesthetics. **2.** having a sense or love of beauty. —**aes•thet′i•cal•ly,** *adv.*

aes•thet′ics *n.* the branch of philosophy dealing with beauty in nature and art.

a•far (ə fär′), *adv.* from, at, or to a distance.

af•fa•ble (af′ə bəl), *adj.* warm and friendly; pleasant. —**af′fa•bil′i•ty,** *n.* —**af′fa•bly,** *adv.*

af•fair (ə fâr′), *n.* **1.** something requiring action. **2. affairs,** matters of commercial or public interest. **3.** a private or personal concern. **4.** an amorous relationship. **5.** a notorious incident. **6.** a social gathering.

af•fect[1] (ə fekt′), *v.t.* **1.** to produce an effect on. **2.** to impress the mind or move the feelings of.

af•fect[2] (ə fekt′), *v.t.* **1.** to pretend or feign. **2.** to assume pretentiously or for effect. **3.** to use or adopt by preference.

af•fec•ta•tion (af′ek tā′shən), *n.* artificiality of manner, attitude, behavior, or appearance; pretension.

af•fect•ed (ə fek′tid), *adj.* **1.** characterized by affectation or pretension. **2.** assumed artificially; feigned.

af•fec•tion (ə fek′shən), *n.* fond devotion; love. —**af′fec′tion•ate** (-shə nit), *adj.* —**af•fec′tion•ate•ly,** *adv.*

af•fi•da•vit (af′i dā′vit), *n.* a written declaration made under oath before an authorized official. [< ML: (he) has declared on oath]

af•fil•i•ate (*v.* ə fil′ē āt′; *n.* -it, -āt′), *v.,* **-at•ed, -at•ing,** *n.* —*v.t.* **1.** to bring into close association or connection. —*v.i.* **2.** to associate oneself; be united. —*n.* **3.** an affiliated person or organization. —**af•fil′i•a′tion,** *n.*

af•fin•i•ty (ə fin′i tē), *n., pl.* **-ties. 1.** a natural liking or attraction. **2.** relationship, esp. by marriage; kinship.

af•firm (ə fûrm′), *v.t.* **1.** to assert positively; declare. **2.** to confirm or ratify. —*v.i.* **3.** to state something solemnly but without oath. —**af•fir•ma′tion** (ar mā′shən), *n.*

af•firm•a•tive (ə fûr′mə tiv), *adj.* **1.** affirming that something is true, valid, or a fact. **2.** expressing agreement or consent. —*n.* **3.** something, as a reply, that indicates assent. **4.** the side, as in a debate, that defends a proposition. —**af•firm′a•tive•ly,** *adv.*

affirm′ative ac′tion *n.* a policy to increase opportunities for women and minorities, esp. in employment.

af•fix (*v.* ə fiks′; *n.* af′iks), *v.t.* **1.** to fasten, join, or attach. **2.** to add on; append. —*n.* **3.** something affixed. **4.** a prefix or suffix.

af•flict (ə flikt′), *v.t.* to distress with mental or bodily pain. —**af•flic′tion,** *n.*

af•flu•ent (af′lōō ənt), *adj.* **1.** wealthy; rich. **2.** abundant; copious. —**af′flu•ence,** *n.* —**af′flu•ent•ly,** *adv.*

af•ford (ə fôrd′), *v.t.* **1.** to be able to do or bear without serious consequence. **2.** to be able to meet the expense of. **3.** to furnish; supply. —**af•ford′a•ble,** *adj.*

af•fray (ə frā′), *n.* a public fight; noisy brawl.

af•front (ə frunt′), *n.* **1.** a deliberate insult. —*v.t.* **2.** to insult deliberately.

Af•ghan (af′gan, -gən), *n.* **1.** a native or inhabitant of Afghanistan. **2.** (*l.c.*) a soft knitted or crocheted blanket. **3.** Also called **Af′ghan hound′.** a hound with a long head and long, silky fur.

Af•ghan•i•stan (af gan′ə stan′), *n.* a republic in SW Asia, between Pakistan and Iran.

a•field (ə fēld′), *adv.* **1.** away from home. **2.** off the subject or mark. **3.** in or to the field.

a•fire (ə fīʳr′), *adj.* on fire.

a•flame (ə flām′), *adj.* on fire; ablaze.

AFL-CIO American Federation of Labor and Congress of Industrial Organizations.

a•float (ə flōt′), *adv., adj.* **1.** floating on the water. **2.** on board a ship; at sea. **3.** covered with water; flooded.

a•foot (ə fŏŏt′), *adv., adj.* **1.** on foot. **2.** in progress; astir.

a•fore′said′ *adj.* said previously.

a•fraid (ə frād′), *adj.* **1.** feeling fear; apprehensive. **2.** feeling regret. **3.** feeling reluctance; disinclined.

a•fresh (ə fresh′), *adv.* once more; anew.

Af•ri•ca (af′ri kə), *n.* a continent S of Europe and between the Atlantic and Indian oceans.

Af′ri•can *adj.* **1.** of Africa. —*n.* **2.** a native or inhabitant of Africa, esp. black Africa. **3.** a person of African ancestry, esp. a black.

Af′ri•can-A•mer′i•can *n.* **1.** a black American of African descent. —*adj.* **2.** of African-Americans.

Af•ri•kaans (af′ri käns′, -känz′), *n.* an official language of South Africa, developed from 17th-century Dutch.

Af•ri•ka•ner (-kä′nər, -kan′ər) *n.* a white South African who speaks Afrikaans.

Af•ro (af′rō), *adj., n., pl.* **-ros.** —*adj.* **1.** of African-Americans or their culture, etc. —*n.* **2.** a full, bushy hairstyle.

Af′ro-A•mer′i•can *n., adj.* AFRICAN-AMERICAN.

aft (aft, äft), *adv.* **1.** at, close to, or toward the stern of a ship or tail of an aircraft. —*adj.* **2.** situated toward or at the stern or tail.

af•ter (af′tər, äf′-), *prep.* **1.** behind in place or position. **2.** later in time than. **3.** below in rank or estimation. **4.** in imitation of: *fashioned after Raphael.* **5.** in pursuit or search of: *I'm after a better job.* **6.** concerning; about: *They asked after you.* —*adv.* **7.** behind. **8.** afterward. —*adj.* **9.** later: *in after years.* **10.** located close to the rear, esp. to the stern or tail. —*conj.* **11.** subsequent to the time that: *after the boys left.*

af′ter•birth′ *n.* the placenta and fetal membranes expelled from the uterus after childbirth.

af′ter•care′ *n.* the care and treatment of a convalescent patient.

af′ter•ef•fect′ *n.* a delayed or secondary effect.

af′ter•glow′ *n.* the glow frequently seen in the sky after sunset.

af′ter•life′ *n.* life after death.

af′ter•math′ (-math′), *n.* **1.** a result, esp. a calamitous one; consequence. **2.** a new growth of crop, esp. grass.

af′ter•noon′ *n.* the time from noon until evening.

af′ter•thought′ *n.* **1.** a later thought. **2.** something, as a part, added later.

af′ter•ward (-wərd) also **-wards,** *adv.* at a later time; subsequently.

a•gain (ə gen′), *adv.* **1.** once more; another time. **2.** moreover; besides. **3.** on the other hand. —*Idiom.* **4.** again and again, repeatedly; often. **5.** as much again, twice as much.

a•gainst (ə genst′), *prep.* **1.** in opposition to; contrary to. **2.** in resistance to, defense from, or preparation for: *protection against mosquitoes.* **3.** in an opposite direction to. **4.** in or into contact with; upon. **5.** in competition with.

a•gape (ə gāp′), *adv.*, *adj.* with the mouth wide open, as in wonder.

ag•ate (ag′it), *n.* **1.** a variegated chalcedony with colored bands. **2.** a playing marble of agate or glass.

agcy. agency.

age (āj), *n.*, *v.*, **aged, ag•ing** or **age•ing.** —*n.* **1.** the length of time during which a being or thing has existed. **2.** a period of human life. **3.** the time of life at which a person becomes qualified or disqualified for something. **4.** old age. **5.** (*often cap.*) a historical or geological period. **6.** Usu., **ages.** a long time. —*v.i., v.t.* **7.** to grow or cause to grow old. **8.** to mature, as wine. —*Idiom.* **9. of age,** having reached adulthood, esp. as specified by law.

-age a suffix meaning: action or process (*coverage*); result of (*wreckage*); residence of (*parsonage*); aggregate (*coinage*); charge (*postage*).

a•ged (ā′jid *for 1, 3;* ājd *for 1, 2*), *adj.* **1.** of advanced age; old. **2.** of the age of. —*n.* **3. the aged,** (*used with a pl. v.*) old people collectively.

age•ism *n.* discrimination against older persons. —**age′ist,** *adj., n.*

age′less (-lis), *adj.* **1.** not appearing to age. **2.** lasting forever.

a•gen•cy (ā′jən sē), *n., pl.* **-cies. 1.** an organization, company, or bureau representing or doing business for another. **2.** a government bureau. **3.** the duty, function, or office of an agent. **4.** a means of accomplishing something; instrumentality.

a•gen•da (ə jen′də), *n., pl.* **-das.** a list of things to be done.

a•gent (ā′jənt), *n.* **1.** a person or business authorized to act for another. **2.** one that acts. **3.** a means; instrument. **4.** an official or representative of a government agency.

ag•glom•er•ate (*v.* ə glom′ə rāt′; *n.* -ər it, -ə rāt′), *v.*, **-at•ed, -at•ing,** *n.* —*v.t., v.i.* **1.** to gather into a cluster or mass. —*n.* **2.** a mass of things clustered together. **3.** rock composed of volcanic fragments. —**ag•glom′er•a′tion,** *n.*

ag•gran•dize (ə gran′dīz, ag′rən dīz′), *v.t.,* **-dized, -diz•ing.** to make great or greater, as in power. —**ag•gran′dize•ment** (-diz mənt), *n.*

ag•gra•vate (ag′rə vāt′), *v.t.,* **-vat•ed, -vat•ing. 1.** to make worse or more severe; intensify. **2.** to annoy; irritate. —**ag′gra•va′tion,** *n.*

ag•gre•gate (*adj., n.* ag′ri git, -gāt′; *v.* -gāt′), *adj., n., v.,* **-gat•ed, -gat•ing.** —*adj.* **1.** formed by the collection of particulars into a whole. —*n.* **2.** a sum, mass, or assemblage. —*v.t., v.i.* **3.** to collect into one sum, mass, or body. —**ag′gre•ga′tion,** *n.*

ag•gres•sion (ə gresh′ən), *n.* **1.** an unprovoked attack. **2.** offensive action in general. **3.** hostile behavior. —**ag•gres′sor,** *n.*

ag•gres•sive (ə gres′iv), *adj.* **1.** characterized by or tending toward aggression. **2.** vigorously energetic, esp. in the use of initiative. **3.** using daring or forceful methods: *aggressive treatment of infection.* —**ag•gres′sive•ly,** *adv.* —**ag•gres′sive•ness,** *n.*

ag•grieve (ə grēv′), *v.t.,* **-grieved, -griev•ing. 1.** to wrong grievously. **2.** to afflict with pain or distress. —**ag•grieve′ment,** *n.*

a•ghast (ə gast′, ə gäst′), *adj.* struck with shock, amazement, or horror.

ag•ile (aj′əl, -īl), *adj.* quick and well-coordinated; nimble. —**ag′ile•ly,** *adv.* —**a•gil•i•ty** (ə jil′i tē), *n.*

ag•i•tate (aj′i tāt′), *v.,* **-tat•ed, -tat•ing.** —*v.t.* **1.** to shake or move briskly. **2.** to disturb emotionally; perturb. —*v.i.* **3.** to arouse or try to arouse public interest. —**ag′i•ta′tion,** *n.* —**ag′i•ta′tor,** *n.*

ag•nos•tic (ag nos′tik), *n.* **1.** a person who holds that the existence of the ultimate cause, as God, is unknown and unknowable. —*adj.* **2.** of agnostics. —**ag•nos′ti•cism** (-tə siz′əm), *n.*

a•go (ə gō′), *adj.* **1.** gone by; past. —*adv.* **2.** in the past.

a•gog (ə gog′), *adj.* highly excited, as in anticipation.

ag•o•nize (ag′ə nīz′), *v.i., v.t.,* **-nized, -niz•ing.** to

suffer or cause to suffer extreme pain or anguish. —**ag′o•niz′ing•ly,** *adv.*

ag′o•ny (-nē), *n., pl.* **-nies. 1.** extreme mental or physical suffering. **2.** the struggle preceding death.

ag•o•ra•pho•bi•a (ag′ər ə fō′bē ə), *n.* abnormal fear of being in open areas. —**ag′o•ra•pho′bic,** *adj., n.*

a•grar•i•an (ə grâr′ē ən), *adj.* **1.** of land or land tenure. **2.** of farmers or agricultural interests. —*n.* **3.** one who favors the equal division of landed property. —**a•grar′i•an•ism,** *n.*

a•gree (ə grē′), *v.,* **a•greed, a•gree•ing.** —*v.i.* **1.** to be in accord in opinion or feeling. **2.** to give consent; assent. **3.** to arrive at a settlement or understanding. **4.** to be consistent; correspond. **5.** to be suitable or beneficial: *The climate did not agree with him.* **6.** to correspond in case, number, gender, or person. —*v.t.* **7.** to concede; grant: *I agree that he is the ablest of us.*

a•gree′a•ble *adj.* **1.** to one's liking; pleasing. **2.** willing or ready to agree. **3.** suitable; conformable. —**a•gree′a•bly,** *adv.*

a•gree′ment *n.* **1.** the state of being in accord; harmony. **2. a.** an arrangement accepted by all parties. **b.** a document setting forth such an arrangement.

ag•ri•busi•ness (ag′rə biz′nis), *n.* the businesses collectively associated with the production, processing, and distribution of agricultural products.

ag′ri•cul′ture *n.* the science, art, or occupation of cultivating land and raising crops and livestock; farming. —**ag′ri•cul′tur•al,** *adj.* —**ag′ri•cul′tur•al•ly,** *adv.*

a•gron•o•my (ə gron′ə mē), *n.* the science of farm management and the production of field crops. —**ag•ro•nom•ic** (ag′rə nom′ik), *adj.* —**a•gron′o•mist,** *n.*

a•ground (ə ground′), *adv., adj.* on or onto the ground beneath a body of water.

ah (ä), *interj.* an exclamation of pain, surprise, joy, etc.

a•head (ə hed′), *adv.* **1.** in, at, or to the front. **2.** forward; onward. **3.** into or for the future. **4.** onward toward success: *to get ahead in the world.* —*Idiom.* **5. ahead of,** before or further than.

a•hoy (ə hoi′), *interj.* a call used at sea to hail a ship.

aid (ād), *v.t., v.i.* **1.** to help; assist. —*n.* **2.** help; assistance. **3.** a helper; assistant.

aide (ād), *n.* **1.** an assistant. **2.** AIDE-DE-CAMP.

aide-de-camp (ād′də kamp′), *n., pl.* **aides-de-camp** (ādz′-). a military officer acting as a confidential assistant to a superior.

AIDS (ādz), *n.* a disease of the immune system characterized by increased susceptibility to opportunistic infections, certain cancers, etc. [*a(cquired) i(mmune) d(eficiency) s(yndrome)*]

ail (āl), *v.,* **ailed, ail•ing.** —*v.t.* **1.** to cause pain or trouble to. —*v.i.* **2.** to be ill.

ai•ler•on (ā′lə ron′), *n.* a movable surface on an aircraft wing, used to control roll.

ail′ment *n.* a physical disorder, esp. a minor one.

aim (ām), *v.t.* **1.** to direct (a gun, punch, remark, etc.) so as to hit. —*v.i.* **2.** to direct a gun, punch, etc. **3.** to direct one's efforts: *I aim at perfection.* —*n.* **4.** the act of aiming. **5.** the direction in which something is aimed. **6.** something intended; purpose. —*Idiom.* **7. take aim,** to aim a weapon.

aim′less *adj.* being without purpose. —**aim′-less•ly,** *adv.* —**aim′less•ness,** *n.*

ain't (ānt), **1.** *Nonstandard except in some dialects.* am not; are not; is not. **2.** *Nonstandard.* have not; has not.

air (âr), *n.* **1.** the mixture of nitrogen, oxygen, and minute amounts of other gases that surrounds the earth. **2.** a light breeze. **3.** general character or appearance; aura. **4. airs,** affected manners. **5.** a tune; melody. **6.** aircraft as a means of transportation. **7.** the medium through which radio waves are transmitted. **8.** *Informal.* air conditioning. —*v.t.* **9.** to expose to the air; ventilate. **10.** to bring to public notice; publicize. **11.** to broadcast or televise. —*Idiom.* **12. in the air,** in circulation; current. **13.**

off the air, not broadcasting. **14. on the air,** broadcasting. **15. up in the air,** not decided; unsettled.

air′ bag′ *n.* a bag that inflates automatically on impact to cushion automobile passengers.

air′borne′ *adj.* **1.** carried by the air. **2.** in flight.

air′brush′ *n.* **1.** an atomizer for spraying paint. —*v.t.* **2.** to paint using an airbrush.

air′ condi′tioning *n.* a system for reducing the temperature and humidity of air.

air′craft′ *n.*, *pl.* **-craft.** a machine, as an airplane, glider, or helicopter, supported for flight in the air.

air′field′ *n.* a level area on which airplanes take off and land.

air′ force′ *n.* the military unit of a nation charged with carrying out air operations.

air′head′ *n. Slang.* a scatterbrained or stupid person.

air′lift′ *n.* **1.** a system for transporting persons or cargo by aircraft, esp. in an emergency. —*v.t.* **2.** to transport by airlift.

air′line′ *n.* a system or company furnishing air transport, usu. scheduled.

air′lin′er *n.* a passenger aircraft operated by an airline.

air′mail′ or **air′ mail′,** *n.* **1.** the system of sending mail by airplane. **2.** mail sent by airmail. —*v.t.* **3.** to send by airmail.

air′man *n.*, *pl.* **-men. 1.** an aviator. **2.** *U.S. Air Force.* an enlisted person of one of the three lowest ranks (**air′man ba′sic, airman, air′man first′ class′**).

air′plane′ *n.* a heavier-than-air aircraft kept aloft by the upward thrust exerted by the passing air on its fixed wings and driven by propellers or jet propulsion.

air′port′ *n.* a facility for the landing, takeoff, and repair of aircraft, esp. one used for transporting passengers and cargo.

air′ raid′ *n.* a raid by enemy aircraft.

air′ship′ *n.* a self-propelled, lighter-than-air aircraft; dirigible.

air′sick′ness *n.* nausea from motion in air travel. —**air′sick′,** *adj.*

air′space′ *n.* the space above a nation over which the nation has jurisdiction.

air′tight′ *adj.* **1.** preventing the entrance or escape of air or gas. **2.** having no weak points: *an airtight contract.*

air′waves′ *n.pl.* the medium of radio and television broadcasting.

air′y *adj.,* **-i•er, -i•est. 1.** open to the air; breezy. **2.** of or like air. **3.** light and thin; delicate. **4.** insubstantial; unreal. **5.** high in the air; lofty. —**air′i•ly,** *adv.* —**air′i•ness,** *n.*

aisle (īl), *n.* a passage between or along sections of seats or shelves, as in a theater or department store.

a•jar (ə jär′), *adj., adv.* partly open.

AK Alaska.

a.k.a. also known as.

a•kim•bo (ə kim′bō), *adj., adv.* with hand on hip and elbow bent outward.

a•kin (ə kin′), *adj.* **1.** related by blood. **2.** allied by nature or inclination.

-al¹, an adjective suffix meaning: of or pertaining to (*tribal*); characterized by (*typical*).

-al², a noun suffix meaning act or process (*refusal*).

AL 1. Alabama. **2.** Anglo-Latin.

Al *Chem. Symbol.* aluminum.

à la or **a la** (ä′ lä, ä′ lə), *prep.* in the manner or style of.

Ala. Alabama.

al•a•bas•ter (al′ə bas′tər, -bä′stər), *n.* a finely granular variety of gypsum, often white and translucent, used for ornamental objects or work.

a•lac•ri•ty (ə lak′ri tē), *n.* **1.** cheerful readiness. **2.** liveliness; briskness.

a•larm (ə lärm′), *n.* **1.** sudden fear caused by danger. **2.** a warning of approaching danger. **3.** a device that gives a warning signal. **4.** a call to arms. —*v.t.* **5.** to make fearful; frighten. **6.** to warn of danger. —**a•larm′ing•ly,** *adv.*

alarm clock *n.* a clock with a device to awaken a sleeper.

a•las (ə las′, ə läs′), *interj.* an exclamation of sorrow, pity, etc.

Alas. Alaska.

Al•ba•ni•a (al bā′nē ə), *n.* a republic in S Europe, NW of Greece. —**Al•ba′ni•an,** *adj., n.*

al•ba•tross (al′bə trôs′, -tros′), *n., pl.* **-tross•es** or, for 1, **-tross. 1.** a large, web-footed bird of S and tropical oceanic waters. **2.** a burden.

al•be•it (ôl bē′it), *conj.* even if; although.

al•bi•no (al bī′nō), *n., pl.* **-nos.** a person, animal, or plant deficient in pigmentation, esp. a person with pale skin, white hair, and pinkish eyes. —**al′bi•nism,** *n.*

al•bum (al′bəm), *n.* **1.** a book with blank pages for displaying a collection, as of photographs. **2.** a phonograph record or set of records containing musical selections or a complete musical work.

al•bu•men (al byōō′mən), *n.* **1.** the white of an egg. **2.** ALBUMIN.

al•bu′min (-mən), *n.* any of a class of water-soluble proteins found in egg white, milk, blood, and animal and vegetable tissue.

al•che•my (al′kə mē), *n.* chemistry of the Middle Ages, concerned chiefly with attempts to turn base metals into gold. —**al′che•mist,** *n.*

al•co•hol (al′kə hôl′, -hol′), *n.* **1.** a colorless, volatile, flammable liquid produced by yeast fermentation of carbohydrates or synthetically: used chiefly as a solvent and in beverages and medicines. **2.** an intoxicating liquor containing alcohol. [< NL < ML < Ar *al-kuḥl* the powdered antimony]

al′co•hol′ic *adj.* **1.** of, containing, or caused by alcohol. **2.** suffering from alcoholism. —*n.* **3.** a person suffering from alcoholism.

al′co•hol•ism *n.* a chronic disorder characterized by dependence on and excessive use of alcoholic beverages.

al•cove (al′kōv), *n.* **1.** a recess opening out of a room. **2.** a recessed space in a wall, as for a bed.

al•der (ôl′dər), *n.* a shrub or tree of the birch family that grows in moist places in colder regions.

al′der•man *n., pl.* **-men.** a member of a municipal legislative body.

ale (āl), *n.* a malt beverage like but more bitter than beer.

a•lert (ə lûrt′), *adj.* **1.** fully aware and attentive; observant. **2.** quick to understand or respond; perceptive. **3.** watchful; vigilant. —*n.* **4.** a warning or alarm of danger. **5.** the period during which an alert is in effect. —*v.t.* **6.** to warn, as to prepare for an attack. —*Idiom.* **7. on the alert,** vigilant. —**a•lert′ly,** *adv.* —**a•lert′ness,** *n.*

al•fal•fa (al fal′fə), *n., pl.* **-fas.** a plant of the legume family that is widely cultivated for forage.

al•fres•co or **al fres•co** (al fres′kō), *adv., adj.* in the open air.

al′ga (al′gə) *n., pl.* **-gae** (-jē). a water plant; seaweed. —**al′gal,** *adj.*

al•ge•bra (al′jə brə), *n.* a branch of mathematics that utilizes symbols, as letters, to represent specific numbers, values, or vectors. [< ML < Ar *al-jabr* restoration] —**al′ge•bra′ic** (-brā′ik), *adj.* —**al′ge•bra′i•cal•ly,** *adv.*

Al•ge•ri•a (al jēr′ē ə), *n.* a republic in NW Africa. —**Al•ger′i•an,** *adj., n.*

Al•gon•qui•an (al gong′kē ən, -kwē ən) also **-ki•an** (-kē ən), *n.* **1.** a widespread family of North American Indian languages. **2.** a member of an Algonquian-speaking people.

al•go•rithm (al′gə riŧħ′əm), *n.* **1.** a set of rules for solving a problem in a finite number of steps, as for finding the greatest common divisor. **2.** a sequence of steps designed for programming a computer to solve a specific problem.

a•li•as (ā′lē əs), *n., pl.* **-as•es,** *adv.* —*n.* **1.** an assumed name. —*adv.* **2.** otherwise called.

al•i•bi (al′ə bī′), *n., pl.* **-bis,** *v.,* **-bied** (-bīd′), **-bi•ing.** —*n.* **1.** the defense by an accused person of having been elsewhere when an offense was committed. **2.** an excuse. —*v.i.* **3.** to give an excuse.

al•ien (āl′yən, ā′lē ən), *n.* **1.** a foreign-born resident who has not been naturalized. **2.** a creature from outer space. —*adj.* **3.** not naturalized. **4.** foreign; strange. **5.** opposed; hostile: *ideas alien to modern thinking.*

al′ien•ate′ (-nāt′), *v.t.*, **-at•ed, -at•ing. 1.** to cause to be indifferent or hostile. **2.** to transfer (title, property, etc.) to another. —**al′ien•a′tion,** *n.*

a•light¹ (ə līt′), *v.i.*, **a•light•ed** or **a•lit, a•light•ing. 1.** to dismount, as from a horse, or descend, as from a vehicle. **2.** to settle after descending.

a•light² (ə līt′), *adv., adj.* **1.** lighted up. **2.** burning.

a•lign (ə līn′), *v.t.* **1.** to arrange in a straight line. **2.** to adjust for coordinated functioning, as the wheels of a car. **3.** to ally (oneself) with a particular group, cause, etc. —*v.i.* **4.** to be in or fall into line. —**a•lign′ment,** *n.*

a•like (ə līk′), *adv.* **1.** in the same manner. **2.** to the same degree. —*adj.* **3.** similar or comparable.

al′i•men′ta•ry (-men′tə rē), *adj.* of, pertaining to, or providing nourishment.

alimen′tary canal′ *n.* a tubular passage functioning in the digestion of food and extending from the mouth to the anus.

al•i•mo•ny (al′ə mō′nē), *n.* an allowance paid to a spouse or former spouse for maintenance following a divorce or legal separation.

a•live (ə līv′), *adj.* **1.** having life; living. **2.** in existence or operation; active. **3.** full of energy and spirit; lively. —*Idiom.* **4. alive to,** alert or sensitive to. **5. alive with,** filled with.

al•ka•li (al′kə lī′), *n., pl.* **-lis, -lies. 1.** any of various bases that neutralize acids to form salts and turn red litmus paper blue. **2.** a mixture of soluble salts present in arid soils and detrimental to farming. —**al′ka•line′** (-līn′), *adj.* —**al′ka•lin′i•ty** (-lin′-i tē), *n.*

al•ka•loid′ *n.* any of various bitter-tasting nitrogen-containing compounds common in plants and including caffeine, nicotine, and quinine.

all (ôl), *adj.* **1.** the whole of: *all the cake.* **2.** the whole number of: *all students.* **3.** the greatest possible: *with all speed.* **4.** any whatever: *beyond all doubt.* **5.** nothing but: *The coat is all wool.* —*pron.* **6.** the whole number, quantity, or amount: *Did you eat all of the peanuts?* **7.** everything: *Is that all you've got to say?* —*n.* **8.** one's whole interest, energy, or property: *Give it your all.* —*adv.* **9.** wholly; completely: *all alone.* **10.** each; apiece: *The score was one all.* —*Idiom.* **11. all but,** very nearly; almost. **12. all in all,** everything considered. **13. at all, a.** in the slightest degree. **b.** for any reason. **c.** in any way.

Al•lah (al′ə, ä′lə), *n. Islam.* the Supreme Being; God.

all′-Amer′ican *adj.* **1.** selected as the best in the U.S., as in a sport. **2.** typically American. —*n.* **3.** an all-American player or team.

all′-around′ *adj.* **1.** able to do many things; versatile. **2.** comprehensive.

al•lay (ə lā′), *v.t.* **1.** to put (fear, doubt, etc.) to rest; calm. **2.** to lessen or relieve; alleviate.

al•lege (ə lej′), *v.t.*, **-leged, -leg•ing. 1.** to assert without proof. **2.** to offer as a reason or excuse. —**al•leged** (ə lejd′, ə lej′id), *adj.* —**al•leg′ed•ly,** *adv.*

al•le•giance (ə lē′jəns), *n.* loyalty to a government, sovereign, person, group, or cause.

al•le•go•ry (al′ə gôr′ē), *n., pl.* **-ries.** a narrative in which the actions of characters represent abstract ideas or moral principles. —**al′le•gor′i•cal** (-gôr′i-kəl, -gor′-), *adj.* —**al′le•gor′ist,** *n.*

al•le•gro (ə lā′grō, ə leg′rō), *adj., adv. Music.* brisk and rapid in tempo.

al•le•lu•ia (al′ə loo′yə), *interj.* HALLELUJAH.

al•ler•gen (al′ər jən, -jen′), *n.* a substance that induces an allergic reaction. —**al′ler•gen′ic,** *adj.*

al′ler•gy (-jē), *n., pl.* **-gies. 1.** an overreaction of the immune system to an ordinarily harmless substance, resulting in symptoms such as skin rash or sneezing. **2.** *Informal.* an aversion. —**al•ler•gic** (ə lûr′jik), *adj.*

al•le•vi•ate (ə lē′vē āt′), *v.t.*, **-at•ed, -at•ing.** to make easier to endure; ease. —**al•le′vi•a′tion,** *n.*

al•ley (al′ē), *n., pl.* **-leys. 1.** a narrow street or passage behind or between buildings. **2.** a bowling alley. —*Idiom.* **3. up one's alley,** compatible with one's interests or abilities.

al′ley cat′ *n.* a domestic cat, esp. of unknown parentage.

al•li•ance (ə lī′əns), *n.* **1.** a formal agreement, esp. between two or more nations, to cooperate for specific purposes. **2.** the persons or entities in an alliance. **3.** close relationship, as that created by marriage.

al•lied (ə līd′, al′īd), *adj.* **1.** joined by treaty or common cause. **2.** related; kindred.

al•li•ga•tor (al′i gā′tər), *n.* a large reptile with a shorter and broader snout than the crocodile. [< Sp *el lagarto* the lizard < L *lacertus* lizard]

all′-in•clu′sive *adj.* comprehensive.

al•lit•er•a•tion (ə lit′ə rā′shən), *n.* repetition of the same sound at the beginning of two or more stressed syllables. —**al•lit′er•a′tive,** *adj.*

al•lo•cate (al′ə kāt′), *v.t.*, **-cat•ed, -cat•ing.** to set apart for a particular purpose. —**al′lo•ca′tion,** *n.*

al•lot (ə lot′), *v.t.*, **-lot•ted, -lot•ting. 1.** to set apart or distribute as a portion. **2.** to allocate. —**al•lot′ment,** *n.*

all′-out′ *adj.* using all one's resources.

al•low (ə lou′), *v.t.* **1.** to permit. **2.** to let have. **3.** to acknowledge; concede: *I had to allow that he was right.* **4.** to set apart; allocate. —*v.i.* **5.** to permit as a possibility; admit. **6.** to make provision: *to allow for breakage.* —**al•low′a•ble,** *adj.*

al•low′ance (-əns), *n.* **1.** an amount or share allotted. **2.** a sum of money allotted on a regular basis or for a particular purpose. **3.** a reduction in price, as for damage. —*Idiom.* **4. make allowance(s) for,** to excuse.

al•loy (*n.* al′oi, ə loi′; *v.* ə loi′), *n.* **1.** a substance composed of two or more metals intimately mixed, as by fusion. **2.** something added that reduces quality or purity. —*v.t.* **3.** to mix so as to form an alloy.

all′ right′ *adv.* **1.** very well; yes. **2.** satisfactorily. **3.** without fail; certainly. —*adj.* **4.** safe; sound. **5.** acceptable; passable. **6.** reliable; good.

All′ Saints′/ Day′ *n.* a church festival celebrated Nov. 1 in honor of saints.

all′spice′ *n.* a spice made from the berries of an aromatic tropical American tree of the myrtle family.

all′-star′ *adj.* **1.** consisting entirely of star performers. —*n.* **2.** a player on an all-star team.

all′-time′ *adj.* never equaled or surpassed.

al•lude (ə lood′), *v.i.*, **-lud•ed, -lud•ing.** to refer casually or indirectly.

al•lure (ə loor′), *v.*, **-lured, -lur•ing,** *n.* —*v.t., v.i.* **1.** to tempt with something desirable. —*n.* **2.** the capacity to allure; fascination or charm. —**al•lure′ment,** *n.* —**al•lur′ing,** *adj.*

al•lu•sion (ə loo′zhən), *n.* **1.** a casual or indirect reference to something. **2.** the act of alluding. —**al•lu′sive** (-siv), *adj.* —**al•lu′sive•ly,** *adv.* —**al•lu′-sive•ness,** *n.*

al•lu•vi•um (ə loo′vē əm), *n., pl.* **-vi•ums, -vi•a** (-vē ə). sedimentary matter, as sand or mud, deposited by flowing water. —**al•lu′vi•al,** *adj.*

al•ly (*n.* al′ī, ə lī′; *v.* ə lī′), *n., pl.* **-lies,** *v.*, **-lied, -ly•ing.** —*n.* **1.** a nation, group, or person united with another for a common purpose. —*v.t., v.i.* **2.** to unite or become united formally, as by treaty, league, or marriage.

al•ma ma•ter (äl′mə mä′tər; al′mə mā′tər), *n.* a school, college, or university at which one has studied.

al•ma•nac (ôl′mə nak′), *n.* a publication containing statistical information, astronomical or meteorological data, and other useful facts.

al•might•y (ôl mī′tē), *adj.* **1.** having unlimited power; omnipotent. **2.** having very great power. —*n.* **3. the Almighty,** God.

al•mond (ä′mənd, am′ənd), *n.* **1.** the nutlike kernel of the fruit of a tree of the rose family. **2.** the tree itself.

al•most (ôl′mōst, ôl mōst′), *adv.* very nearly; all but.

alms (ämz), *n.* (*used with a sing. or pl. v.*) something, as money or food, given to the poor or needy.

a•loft (ə lôft′, ə loft′), *adv.* **1.** high up in the air. **2.** on, to, or in the upper rigging of a ship.

a•lo•ha (ə lō′ə, ä lō′hä), *n., pl.* **-has,** *interj.* **1.** hello. **2.** farewell. [< Hawaiian: lit., love]

a•lone (ə lōn′), *adj., adv.* **1.** apart from others. **2.** without another person. **3.** only. **4.** without equal. —*Idiom.* **5.** let alone, **a.** to refrain from bothering or interfering with. **b.** not to mention.

a•long (ə lông′, ə long′), *prep.* **1.** over the length or direction of. **2.** in the course of. —*adv.* **3.** parallel in the same direction. **4.** so as to progress; onward. **5.** in company; together. **6.** as a companion. **7.** from one person or place to another. **8.** as an accompanying item. —*Idiom.* **9.** all along, from the start. **10.** be along, *Informal.* to arrive at a place.

a•long′side′ *adv.* **1.** along or at the side. —*prep.* **2.** by the side of. **3.** alongside of, beside; alongside.

a•loof (ə lōōf′), *adj.* **1.** reserved or reticent in feeling or manner. —*adv.* **2.** at a distance in feeling or manner. —**a•loof′ness,** *n.*

a•loud (ə loud′), *adv.* **1.** with the normal speaking voice; vocally. **2.** loudly.

al•pac•a (al pak′ə), *n., pl.* **-as. 1.** a domesticated South American hoofed mammal related to the llama and having long, soft, silky fleece. **2. a.** the fleece of the alpaca. **b.** a yarn or fabric made of it.

al•pha (al′fə), *n., pl.* **-phas.** the first letter of the Greek alphabet (A, α).

al•pha•bet (al′fə bet′, -bit), *n.* the letters of a language, esp. in their customary order. [< LL < Gk *alphábētos = alpha + bēta* first two letters of the Greek alphabet] —**al′pha•bet′i•cal, al/pha•bet′ic,** *adj.* —**al′pha•bet′i•cal•ly,** *adv.*

al′pha•nu•mer′ic also **-mer′i•cal,** *adj.* utilizing both letters and numbers. —**al′pha•nu•mer′i•cal•ly,** *adv.*

al•pine (al′pīn, -pin), *adj.* **1.** of or like a lofty mountain. **2.** (*cap.*) of the Alps. **3.** native to the heights above the timberline.

al•read•y (ôl red′ē), *adv.* **1.** prior to a specified time; previously. **2.** so soon; so early.

al•so (ôl′sō), *adv.* in addition; besides.

alt. 1. alteration. **2.** alternate. **3.** altitude. **4.** alto.

al•tar (ôl′tər), *n.* a mound or platform at which religious rites are performed or on which sacrifices are offered.

al•ter (ôl′tər), *v.t.* **1.** to make different, as in size or style. **2.** to castrate or spay. —*v.i.* **3.** to become different. —**al′ter•a′tion,** *n.*

al•ter•ca•tion (ôl′tər kā′shən), *n.* a heated or angry dispute.

al′ter e′go, *n.* **1.** an intimate friend. **2.** a second self.

al•ter•nate (*v.* ôl′tər nāt′; *adj.,* *n.* -nit), *v.,* **-nat•ed, -nat•ing,** *adj.,* *n.* —*v.i.* **1.** to happen or bring about by turns. **2.** to shift or cause to shift back and forth, as between states or actions. —*adj.* **3.** occurring by turns. **4.** being every second one of a series. —*n.* **5.** a substitute. —**al′ter•nate•ly,** *adv.* —**al′ter•na′tion,** *n.*

al′ternating cur′rent *n.* an electric current that reverses direction at regular intervals.

al•ter′na•tive (-tûr′nə tiv), *n.* **1.** a choice limited to one of two or more possibilities. **2.** one of the possibilities that can be chosen. —*adj.* **3.** affording a choice. **4.** nontraditional or unconventional, as in ideas or methods. —**al•ter′na•tive•ly,** *adv.*

al′ter•na′tor (-tər nā′tər), *n.* a generator of alternating current.

al•though (ôl thō′), *conj.* in spite of the fact that; though.

al•tim•e•ter (al tim′i tər, al′tə mē′tər), *n.* a device used to measure altitude.

al•ti•tude (al′ti tōōd′, -tyōōd′), *n.* **1.** the height of a thing above a given reference plane, esp. above sea level. **2.** the angular distance of a heavenly body above the horizon. **3.** the perpendicular distance from the vertex of a geometric figure to the side opposite the vertex. —**al′ti•tu′di•nal,** *adj.*

al•to (al′tō), *n., pl.* **-tos. 1.** CONTRALTO. **2.** COUNTERTENOR.

al•to•geth•er (ôl′tə geth′ər, ôl′tə geth′ər), *adv.* **1.** wholly; entirely. **2.** with everything included. **3.** with everything considered; on the whole.

al•tru•ism (al′trōō iz′əm), *n.* unselfish concern for the welfare of others. —**al′tru•ist,** *n.* —**al′tru•is′tic,** *adj.* —**al′tru•is/ti•cal•ly,** *adv.*

al•um (al′əm), *n.* a crystalline double sulfate of aluminum and potassium, used as an astringent and styptic.

a•lu•mi•num (ə lōō′mə nəm), *n.* a silver-white metallic element, light in weight, ductile, and malleable, used in alloys. *Symbol:* Al; *at. wt.:* 26.98; *at. no.:* 13.

a•lum•na (ə lum′nə), *n., pl.* **-nae** (-nē, -nī) a female graduate or former student of a school, college, or university.

a•lum′nus (-nəs), *n., pl.* **-ni** (-nī, -nē) a graduate or former student of a school, college, or university.

al•ways (ôl′wāz, -wēz), *adv.* **1.** on every occasion; every time. **2.** all the time; continuously. **3.** forever. **4.** in any event; if necessary.

Alz′hei•mer's disease′ (älts′hī mərz, ôlts′-), *n.* a disease marked by progressive memory loss and mental deterioration associated with brain damage. [after A. *Alzheimer* (1864–1915), German neurologist]

am (am; *unstressed* əm, m), *v.* 1st pers. sing. pres. indic. of BE.

AM 1. amplitude modulation: a method of impressing a signal on a radio carrier wave by varying its amplitude. **2.** a system of broadcasting using AM.

Am *Chem. Symbol.* americium.

Am. 1. America. **2.** American.

A.M. Master of Arts. [< L *Artium Magister*]

a.m. or **A.M., 1.** before noon. **2.** the period from midnight to noon. [< L *ante merīdiem*]

A.M.A. American Medical Association.

a•mal•gam (ə mal′gəm), *n.* **1.** an alloy of mercury with another metal, used as a dental filling. **2.** a mixture or combination.

a•mal′ga•mate′ (-gə māt′), *v.t.,* *v.i.,* **-mat•ed, -mat•ing.** to mix, merge, or unite. —**a•mal′ga•ma′tion,** *n.*

am•a•ret•to (am′ə ret′ō, ä′mə-), *n., pl.* **-tos.** an almond-flavored liqueur.

am•a•ryl•lis (am′ə ril′is), *n.* a bulbous plant with large red or pink flowers resembling lilies.

a•mass (ə mas′), *v.t.* to collect; accumulate.

am•a•teur (am′ə chōōr′, -chər, -tər), *n.* **1.** a person who engages in an activity for pleasure rather than financial benefit. **2.** a person who lacks experience or skill. —*adj.* **3.** of, being, or engaged in by an amateur. —**am′a•teur′ish,** *adj.* —**am′a•teur•ism,** *n.*

am•a•to•ry (am′ə tôr′ē), *adj.* pertaining to or expressive of love.

a•maze (ə māz′), *v.t.,* **a•mazed, a•maz•ing.** to overwhelm with surprise or wonder; astonish. —**a•maze′ment,** *n.* —**a•maz′ing,** *adj.* —**a•maz′ing•ly,** *adv.*

Am•a•zon (am′ə zon′, -zən), *n.* **1.** a river in N South America. 3900 mi. (6280 km) long. **2.** (in ancient Greek legends) a member of a nation of female warriors. **3.** (*often l.c.*) a tall, powerful woman. —**Am′a•zo′ni•an** (-zō′nē ən), *adj.*

am•bas•sa•dor (am bas′ə dər, -dôr′), *n.* a diplomatic official of the highest rank, sent by one sovereign or state to another. —**am•bas′sa•do′ri•al,** *adj.* —**am•bas′sa•dor•ship′,** *n.*

am•ber (am′bər), *n.* **1.** a yellow, red, or brown translucent fossil resin of coniferous trees that is used for jewelry. **2.** the yellowish brown color of amber.

am•ber•gris (am′bər grēs′, -gris), *n.* an ash-colored secretion of the sperm whale intestine, used in perfumery.

am•bi•dex•trous (am′bi dek′strəs), *adj.* able to use both hands equally well. —**am′bi•dex•ter′i•ty,** *n.* —**am′bi•dex′trous•ly,** *adv.*

am•bi•ence or **-ance** (am′bē əns) *n.* surroundings; atmosphere. —**am′bi•ent,** *adj.*

am•big′u•ous (-big′yōō əs), *adj.* **1.** having several possible meanings or interpretations. **2.** doubtful or uncertain. —**am•big′u•ous•ly,** *adv.*

am•bi•tion (am bish′ən), *n.* **1.** an earnest desire for achievement, distinction, wealth, or power. **2.** the object of ambition. —**am•bi′tious,** *adj.*

am•biv′a•lent (-biv′ə lənt) *adj.* with conflicting emotions. —**am•biv′a•lence,** *n.*

am•ble (am′bəl), *v.,* **-bled, -bling,** *n.* —*v.i.* **1.** to go at a slow, easy pace. —*n.* **2.** a slow, easy pace. —**am′bler,** *n.*

am•bro•sia (am brō′zhə), *n.* **1.** the food of the ancient Greek and Roman gods. **2.** something that has a delicious taste or smell. —**am•bro′sial,** *adj.*

am•bu•lance (am′byə ləns), *n.* a vehicle equipped for carrying sick or injured people.

am′bu•la•to′ry (-lə tôr′ē), *adj., n., pl.* **-ries.** —*adj.* **1.** of or capable of walking. **2.** moving about. —*n.* **3.** the covered walk of a cloister.

am•bush (am′bŏŏsh), *n.* **1.** an act or instance of lying concealed so as to attack by surprise. **2.** the concealed position itself. —*v.t., v.i.* **3.** to attack from or lie in ambush. —**am′bush•er,** *n.*

a•me•ba (ə mē′bə), *n., pl.* **-bas, -bae** (-bē). a one-celled protozoan with a mass of cytoplasm that changes in shape as the organism moves and engulfs food. —**a•me′bic,** *adj.* —**a•me′boid,** *adj.*

a•mel•io•rate (ə mēl′yə rāt′), *v.t., v.i.,* **-rat•ed, -rat•ing.** to make or become better; improve. —**a•mel′io•ra′tion,** *n.* —**a•mel′io•ra′tive,** *adj.*

a•men (ā′men′, ä′men′), *interj.* so be it (used after a formal statement, esp. a prayer, to express solemn ratification or agreement). [< LL ≪ Heb *āmēn*]

a•me•na•ble (ə mē′nə bəl, ə men′ə-), *adj.* **1.** ready or willing to agree or yield. **2.** liable to be called to account; answerable. —**a•me′na•bil′i•ty,** *n.* —**a•me′na•bly,** *adv.*

a•mend (ə mend′), *v.t.* **1.** to modify or rephrase (a bill, law, etc.) by formal procedure. **2.** to improve. **3.** to remove faults; correct. —**a•mend′a•ble,** *adj.*

a•mend′ment *n.* **1.** the act of amending or state of being amended. **2.** an alteration of or addition to a bill, law, etc.

a•mends′ *n.* (*used with a sing. or pl. v.*) reparation for loss, damage, or injury.

a•men•i•ty (ə men′i tē, ə mē′ni-), *n., pl.* **-ties. 1.** an agreeable act or manner; courtesy or civility: *social amenities.* **2.** a feature that provides comfort, convenience, or pleasure.

Am•er•a•sian (am′ə rā′zhən), *n.* a person of mixed American and Asian descent.

A•mer•i•can (ə mer′i kən), *adj.* **1.** of the United States or its inhabitants. **2.** of North or South America. —*n.* **3.** a citizen of the United States. **4.** a native or inhabitant of the Western Hemisphere.

Amer′ican In′dian *n.* a member of any of the indigenous peoples of North and South America.

A•mer′i•can•ism *n.* a custom, trait, or language feature peculiar to the United States or its citizens.

A•mer′i•can•ize′ *v.t., v.i.,* **-ized, -iz•ing.** to make or become American in character. —**A•mer′i•can•i•za′tion,** *n.*

Amer′ican plan′ *n.* a system of paying a fixed hotel rate that covers room, service, and meals.

am••e•thyst (am′ə thist), *n.* a purple or violet quartz used as a gem.

a•mi•a•ble (ā′mē ə bəl), *adj.* having or showing agreeable personal qualities; pleasant and friendly. —**a′mi•a•bil′i•ty,** *n.* —**a′mi•a•bly,** *adv.*

am•i•ca•ble (am′i kə bəl), *adj.* friendly; peaceable. —**am′i•ca•bil′i•ty,** *n.* —**am′i•ca•bly,** *adv.*

a•mid (ə mid′) also **a•midst** (ə midst′), *prep.* in the middle of; among.

a•mi•go (ə mē′gō, ä mē′-), *n., pl.* **-gos.** a male friend.

a•mi′no ac′id (ə mē′nō, am′ə nō), *n.* any of a class of organic compounds that are the building blocks from which proteins are constructed.

a•miss (ə mis′), *adv.* **1.** out of the right or proper course or order. —*adj.* **2.** wrong or improper.

am•i•ty (am′i tē), *n.* peaceful relations, as between nations; friendship.

am•me•ter (am′mē′tər), *n.* an instrument for measuring current in amperes.

am•mo (am′ō), *n. Informal.* ammunition.

am•mo•nia (ə mōn′yə), *n., pl.* **-nias. 1.** a colorless, pungent gaseous compound used in the manufacture of chemicals and reagents. **2.** Also called **ammo′nia wa′ter.** ammonia dissolved in water.

am•mu•ni•tion (am′yə nish′ən), *n.* **1.** projectiles, esp. bullets or shells, fired by guns. **2.** a means of offense or defense.

am•ne•sia (am nē′zhə), *n.* complete or partial loss of memory. —**am•ne′si•ac′** (-zhē ak′, -zē-), **am•ne′sic** (-sik, -zik), *adj., n.*

am•nes•ty (am′nə stē), *n., pl.* **-ties,** *v.,* **-tied, -ty•ing.** —*n.* **1.** a general pardon for offenses against a government. —*v.t.* **2.** to grant amnesty to.

am′ni•o•cen•te′sis (-sen tē′sis), *n., pl.* **-ses** (-sēz). the surgical procedure of withdrawing a sample of fluid from the uterus of a pregnant woman for genetic diagnosis of the fetus.

a•mok (ə muk′, ə mok′), *adj., adv.* AMUCK.

a•mong (ə mung′), *prep.* **1.** in, into, or through the midst of. **2.** with a share for each of. **3.** in the class or group of. **4.** by the joint or reciprocal action of.

a•mongst (ə mungst′), *prep.* AMONG.

a•mor•al (ā môr′əl, ā mor′-), *adj.* **1.** neither moral nor immoral. **2.** lacking or indifferent to moral principles. —**a•mo•ral•i•ty** (ā′mə ral′i tē), *n.* —**a•mor′al•ly,** *adv.*

am•o•rous (am′ər əs), *adj.* **1.** inclined to love, esp. sexual love. **2.** being in love; enamored. **3.** expressing or pertaining to love. —**am′o•rous•ly,** *adv.* —**am′o•rous•ness,** *n.*

a•mor•phous (ə môr′fəs), *adj.* **1.** lacking definite form. **2.** of no particular kind or character; indeterminate. **3.** not crystalline. —**a•mor′phous•ly,** *adv.* —**a•mor′phous•ness,** *n.*

am•or•tize (am′ər tīz′, ə môr′tīz), *v.t.,* **-tized, -tiz•ing.** to liquidate or extinguish (a debt or other liability), esp. by periodic payments. —**am′or•ti•za′-tion,** *n.*

a•mount (ə mount′), *n.* **1.** the total of two or more quantities or sums. **2.** quantity; measure. —*v.i.* **3.** to yield a sum or total; add up. **4.** to be equal in value, effect, or extent.

a•mour (ə mŏŏr′), *n.* a love affair, esp. an illicit one.

am•per•age (am′pər ij, am pēr′-), *n.* the strength of an electric current measured in amperes.

am•pere (am′pēr), *n.* a unit of electric current equal to the steady current produced by one volt acting through a resistance of one ohm.

am•per•sand (am′pər sand′), *n.* a symbol (& or ·) for *and.* [contr. of *and per se and* lit., (the symbol) & by itself (stands for) and]

am•phet•a•mine (am fet′ə mēn′, -min), *n.* a drug that stimulates the central nervous system: used chiefly to counteract depression.

am•phib•i•an (am fib′ē ən), *n.* **1.** an amphibious cold-blooded vertebrate, as a frog. **2.** an amphibious airplane or military vehicle. —*adj.* **3.** AMPHIBIOUS.

am•phib•i•ous (am fib′ē əs), *adj.* **1.** capable of living or operating on land and in water. **2.** pertaining to military operations by both land and naval forces. —**am•phib′i•ous•ly,** *adv.*

am•phi•the•a•ter (am′fə thē′ə tər, -thēə′-), *n.* an oval or round building or room with tiers of seats around a central open area. Often, **am′phi•the′a•tre.**

am•ple (am′pəl), *adj.,* **-pler, -plest. 1.** fully sufficient for a purpose or need. **2.** large; roomy. —**am′-ply,** *adv.*

am′pli•fy′ *v.,* **-fied, -fy•ing.** —*v.t.* **1.** to make larger, greater, or stronger. **2.** to expand or clarify by expanding. **3.** to increase the amplitude of. —*v.i.* **4.** to discourse at length. —**am′pli•fi•ca′tion,** *n.*

am′pli•tude′ (-tōōd′, -tyōōd′), *n.* **1.** ample breadth or width; largeness. **2.** large measure or quantity. **3.** range, scope, or capacity, as of intellect. **4.** the absolute value of the maximum displacement during an oscillation. **5.** the maximum deviation of an alternating current from its average value.

a•muck (ə muk′), *adj.* **1.** being in a murderous frenzy. —*adv., Idiom.* **2.** **run** or **go amuck, a.** to rush about in a murderous frenzy. **b.** to be out of control. [< Malay]

am•u•let (am′yə lit), *n.* a charm worn to ward off evil.

a•muse (ə myōoz′), *v.t.*, **a•mused, a•mus•ing. 1.** to occupy pleasantly; divert. **2.** to cause to laugh. —**a•muse′ment,** *n.*

amuse′ment park′ *n.* a park equipped with recreational devices such as a Ferris wheel or roller coaster.

an[1] (ən; *when stressed* an), *indefinite article.* the form of A[1] before an initial vowel sound (*an arch; an honor*).

an[2] (ən; *when stressed* an), *prep.* the form of A[2] before an initial vowel sound: *55 miles an hour.*

-an[1], an adjective suffix meaning of, belonging to, or resembling (*American*).

-an[2], a noun suffix meaning: one belonging to or residing in (*Hawaiian*); one skilled in (*artisan*).

a•nach•ro•nism (ə nak′rə niz′əm), *n.* **1.** an error in which a person, object, or event is assigned an incorrect date or period. **2.** a thing or person that belongs to another, esp. an earlier, time. —**a•nach′-ro•nis′tic,** *adj.*

an•a•con•da (an′ə kon′də), *n., pl.* **-das.** a South American boa that often grows to more than 25 ft. (7.6 m).

an•a•gram (an′ə gram′), *n.* a word or phrase formed from another by rearranging its letters.

a•nal (ān′l), *adj.* of or near the anus. —**a′nal•ly,** *adv.*

an′al•ge′sic (an′əl jē′zik) *n.* **1.** a drug for relieving pain. —*adj.* **2.** pain-relieving.

a•nal•o•gy (ə nal′ə jē), *n., pl.* **-gies. 1.** a similarity between like features of unlike things on which a comparison may be based. **2.** a form of reasoning in which one thing is inferred to be similar to another thing in a certain respect on the basis of known similarities in other respects. —**an•a•log•i•cal** (an′l oj′i kəl), *adj.*

a•nal′y•sis (-sis), *n., pl.* **-ses** (-sēz′). **1.** separation of a material or abstract entity into its constituent elements, esp. as a method of studying its nature or determining its essential features. **2.** a presentation, usu. in writing, of the results of analysis. **3.** PSYCHO-ANALYSIS. —**an•a•lyt•ic** (an′l it′ik), **an′a•lyt′i•cal,** *adj.* —**an′a•lyt′i•cal•ly,** *adv.*

an′ar•chy (-kē), *n.* **1.** a state of society without government or law. **2.** confusion; disorder. —**an•ar′chic** (-är′kik), **an•ar′chi•cal,** *adj.* —**an•ar′chi•cal•ly,** *adv.*

a•nath•e•ma (ə nath′ə mə), *n., pl.* **-mas. 1.** a person or thing detested or loathed. **2.** a person or thing condemned to damnation. **3.** a formal ecclesiastical curse of excommunication.

a•nat•o•my (ə nat′ə mē), *n., pl.* **-mies. 1.** the science dealing with the structure of animals and plants. **2.** the structure of an animal or plant. **3.** a minute examination; analysis. —**an•a•tom•i•cal** (an′ə tom′i kal), **an′a•tom′ic,** *adj.*

an•ces•tor (an′ses tər), *n.* **1.** a person from whom one is descended; forebear. **2.** the form or stock from which an organism has descended. **3.** something serving as a prototype or forerunner. —**an•ces′tral,** *adj.*

an•chor (ang′kər), *n.* **1.** a heavy device thrown overboard to restrict the motion of a ship. **2.** something that gives support or stability. **3.** a broadcaster, as on a news program, who coordinates the reports of other broadcasters. **4.** a TV program that attracts many viewers who are likely to stay tuned to the network for the programs that follow. **5.** a well-known store that attracts customers to the shopping center in which it is located. —*v.t.* **6.** to hold fast by or as if by an anchor. **7.** to serve as a radio or television anchor for. —*v.i.* **8.** to lie at an-

chor. —*Idiom.* **9. at anchor,** kept in place by an anchor.

an′chor•man′ or **-wom′an** or **-per′son,** *n., pl.* **-men** or **-wom•en** or **-per•sons.** a person who anchors a program of news, sports, etc.; anchor.

an•cho•vy (an′chō vē, -chə-), *n., pl.* **-vies.** a small herringlike fish that is used in cooking.

an•cient (ān′shənt), *adj.* **1.** of or belonging to times long past, esp. before the end of the Western Roman Empire. **2.** very old; aged. —*n.* **3.** a person who lived in ancient times, esp. a Greek or a Roman. **4.** a very old person. —**an′cient•ness,** *n.*

an•cil•lar•y (an′sə ler′ē), *adj.* **1.** subordinate. **2.** auxiliary.

and (and; *unstressed* ənd, ən, n), *conj.* **1.** as well as; in addition to. **2.** added to; plus. **3.** then. **4.** at the same time. **5.** *Informal.* to: *Try and do it.*

an•dan•te (än dän′tā), *adj., adv. Music.* moderately slow.

and′i′rons (and′ī′ərnz) *n.pl.* metal supports for logs in a fireplace.

an•dro•gen (an′drə jən, -jen′), *n.* a substance, as testosterone, that promotes male characteristics.

an•drog•y•nous (an droj′ə nəs), *adj.* having both masculine and feminine characteristics. —**an•drog′-y•ny,** *n.*

an•droid (an′droid), *n.* an automaton in the form of a human being.

an•ec•dote (an′ik dōt′), *n.* a short account of an interesting, often biographical incident. —**an′ec•do′tal,** *adj.* —**an′ec•dot′ist,** *n.*

a•ne•mi•a (ə nē′mē ə), *n.* a reduction in the hemoglobin of red blood cells with consequent deficiency of oxygen, leading to weakness and pallor. —**a•ne′mic,** *adj.*

a•nem•o•ne (ə nem′ə nē′), *n., pl.* **-nes. 1.** a plant of the buttercup family, with petallike sepals in a variety of colors. **2.** SEA ANEMONE.

an•es•the•sia (an′əs thē′zhə), *n.* general or localized insensibility to pain or other sensation. —**an′-es•thet′ic** (-thet′ik), *n., adj.* —**an•es•the•tist** (ə nes′thi tist), *n.* —**an•es′the•tize′,** *v.t.* **-tized, -tiz•ing.**

a•new (ə nōo′, ə nyōo′), *adv.* **1.** once more. **2.** in a new form or manner.

an•gel (ān′jəl), *n.* **1.** a celestial attendant of God. **2.** a conventional representation of an angel, in human form, with wings. **3.** a messenger, esp. of God. **4.** a very kind person. **5.** *Informal.* a financial backer, as of a play. [< LL < Gk *ángelos* messenger] —**an•gel•ic** (an jel′ik), **an•gel′i•cal,** *adj.*

an′gel food′ cake′ *n.* a light, white cake made with stiffly beaten egg whites.

an•ger (ang′gər), *n.* **1.** a strong feeling of displeasure and belligerence. —*v.t., v.i.* **2.** to make or become angry.

an•gi•na pec•to•ris (an jī′nə pek′tə ris), *n.* a sensation of crushing pressure in the chest, caused by inadequate blood flow to the heart muscle. Also called **an•gi′na.**

an•gle[1] (ang′gəl), *n., v.,* **-gled, -gling.** —*n.* **1. a.** the space within two lines diverging from a common point. **b.** a figure so formed. **c.** the amount of rotation needed to bring one line into coincidence with another. **2.** a projecting corner. **3.** a point of view; standpoint. **4.** *Informal.* a secret motive or plan. —*v.t., v.i.* **5.** to move or bend at an angle. **6.** to hit or direct at an angle. **7.** to write from a particular or biased viewpoint.

an•gle[2] (ang′gəl), *v.i.,* **-gled, -gling. 1.** to fish with hook and line. **2.** to attempt to get something by sly or artful means. —**an′gler,** *n.*

An′gle *n.* a member of a Germanic people who migrated to England in the 5th century A.D.

An•gli•can (ang′gli kən), *adj.* **1.** of the Church of England. **2.** of England or its inhabitants. —*n.* **3.** a member of the Church of England. —**An′gli•can•ism,** *n.*

An′gli•cize′ (-sīz′), *v.t., v.i.,* **-cized, -ciz•ing.** to make or become English in form or character. —**An′gli•ci•za′tion,** *n.*

An•glo-Sax•on (ang′glō sak′sən), *n.* **1.** a member of any of the Germanic peoples who invaded and

occupied England in the 5th and 6th centuries A.D. **2.** OLD ENGLISH. **3.** a person of English ancestry. —*adj.* **4.** of the Anglo-Saxons.
An•go•la (ang gō′lə), *n.* a republic in SW Africa. —**An•go′lan,** *adj., n.*
An•go•ra (ang gôr′ə), *n., pl.* **-ras. 1.** a cat, goat, or rabbit with long, silky hair. **2.** (*often l.c.*) a yarn or fabric made from the hair of the Angora goat or rabbit.
an•gry (ang′grē), *adj.,* **-gri•er, -gri•est. 1.** feeling or showing anger. **2.** inflamed, as a sore. **3.** exhibiting characteristics associated with anger or danger: *an angry sea.* —**an′gri•ly,** *adv.* —**an′gri•ness,** *n.*
angst (ängkst), *n.* a feeling of dread, anxiety, or anguish.
an•guish (ang′gwish), *n.* **1.** acute suffering or pain. —*v.i., v.t.* **2.** to suffer or cause to suffer anguish. —**an′guished,** *adj.*
an•gu•lar (ang′gyə lər), *adj.* **1.** having, consisting of, or forming an angle. **2.** measured by an angle. **3.** bony, lean, or gaunt. **4.** moving awkwardly; stiff. —**an′gu•lar′i•ty,** *n.*
an•i•mad•vert (an′ə mad vûrt′), *v.i.* to comment unfavorably or critically. —**an′i•mad•ver′sion,** *n.*
an•i•mal (an′ə məl), *n.* **1.** a multicellular organism that can move voluntarily and can actively acquire food and digest it internally. **2.** an animal other than a human being. **3.** a brutish or beastlike person. —*adj.* **4.** of or derived from animals. **5.** pertaining to the physical rather than the spiritual or intellectual nature of human beings.
an′i•mate (*v.* -māt′; *adj.* -mit), *v.,* **-mat•ed, -mat•ing,** *adj.* —*v.t.* **1.** to give life to. **2.** to give zest to. **3.** to move or stir to action. **4.** to prepare or produce as an animated cartoon. —*adj.* **5.** possessing life; alive. **6.** of or relating to animal life. —**an′i•mat′ed,** *adj.* —**an′i•ma′tion,** *n.* —**an′i•ma′tor,** *n.*
an•i•mism (an′ə miz′əm), *n.* the belief that natural objects and phenomena possess souls. —**an′i•mist,** *n., adj.* —**an′i•mis′tic,** *adj.*
an•i•mos•i•ty (an′ə mos′i tē), *n., pl.* **-ties.** a feeling of ill will; hostility.
an′i•mus (-məs), *n.* strong dislike; animosity.
an•ise (an′is), *n.* **1.** a Mediterranean plant of the parsley family that yields aniseed. **2.** ANISEED.
an′i•seed′ (-ə sēd′), *n.* the aromatic seed of the anise, used in medicine and in cooking.
an•kle (ang′kəl), *n.* **1.** the joint between the foot and leg. **2.** the slender part of the leg above the foot.
an′klet (-klit), *n.* **1.** a sock that reaches just above the ankle. **2.** an ornament worn around the ankle.
an•nals (an′lz), *n.pl.* **1.** a record of events, esp. a yearly record, in chronological order. **2.** historical records; chronicles.
an•neal (ə nēl′), *v.t.* **1.** to free (glass, metal, etc.) from internal stress by heating and gradually cooling. **2.** to toughen or temper.
an•nex (*v.* ə neks′, an′eks; *n.* an′eks), *v.t.* **1.** to attach or append, esp. to something larger. **2.** to incorporate (territory) into the domain of a state. —*n.* **3.** something annexed. **4.** a subsidiary building or an addition to a building. —**an′nex•a′tion,** *n.*
an•ni•hi•late (ə nī′ə lāt′), *v.t.,* **-lat•ed, -lat•ing.** to reduce to utter ruin or nonexistence; destroy utterly. —**an•ni′hi•la′tion,** *n.* —**an•ni′hi•la′tor,** *n.*
an•ni•ver•sa•ry (an′ə vûr′sə rē), *n., pl.* **-ries. 1.** the yearly recurrence of the date of a past event. **2.** the celebration or commemoration of an anniversary.
an•no•tate (an′ə tāt′), *v.t.,* **-tat•ed, -tat•ing.** to supply (a text) with critical or explanatory notes. —**an′no•ta′tion,** *n.* —**an′no•ta′tive,** *adj.* —**an′no•ta′tor,** *n.*
an•nounce (ə nouns′), *v.,* **-nounced, -nounc•ing.** —*v.t.* **1.** to make known publicly. **2.** to state the approach or arrival of. —*v.i.* **3.** to serve as an announcer, esp. of a broadcast. **4.** to declare one's candidacy, as for a political office. —**an•nounce′ment,** *n.* —**an•nounc′er,** *n.*
an•noy (ə noi′), *v.t.* to disturb or bother, esp. persistently; irritate. —**an•noy′ance,** *n.* —**an•noy′ing,** *adj.* —**an•noy′ing•ly,** *adv.*

an•nu•al (an′yoo əl), *adj.* **1.** pertaining to a year. **2.** occurring or recurring once a year. **3.** (of a plant) living only one growing season. **4.** performed during a year. —*n.* **5.** an annual plant. **6.** a publication issued once a year. —**an′nu•al•ly,** *adv.*
an•nu′i•ty *n., pl.* **-ties. 1.** an amount of money payable at stated intervals, usu. annually. **2.** the right to receive an annuity.
an•nul (ə nul′), *v.t.,* **-nulled, -nul•ling. 1.** to declare void or null; invalidate. **2.** to reduce to nothing; obliterate. —**an•nul′ment,** *n.*
An•nun•ci•a•tion (ə nun′sē ā′shən), *n.* **1. a.** the angel Gabriel's announcement to the Virgin Mary of her conception of Christ. **b.** the church festival, March 25, in memory of this. **2.** (*l.c.*) an act or instance of announcing.
an•ode (an′ōd), *n.* **1.** an electrode with a positive charge. **2.** the negative terminal of a battery.
a•noint (ə noint′), *v.t.* **1.** to apply oil to by rubbing or sprinkling. **2.** to consecrate by applying oil. —**a•noint′er,** *n.* —**a•noint′ment,** *n.*
a•nom•a•ly (ə nom′ə lē), *n., pl.* **-lies. 1.** a deviation from the common type, rule, arrangement, or form. **2.** someone or something abnormal, unusual, or irregular. —**a•nom′a•lous,** *adj.*
a•non (ə non′), *adv.* **1.** soon. **2.** at another time.
anon. 1. anonymous. **2.** anonymously.
a•non•y•mous (ə non′ə məs), *adj.* **1.** of unknown or unacknowledged origin. **2.** not named or identified. **3.** lacking individuality or distinction. —**an•o•nym•i•ty** (an′ə nim′i tē), *n.* —**a•non′y•mous•ly,** *adv.*
an′o•rak′ (an′ə rak′), *n.* a hooded jacket; parka.
an•oth•er (ə nuth′ər), *adj.* **1.** being one more of the same; additional. **2.** of a different kind; distinct. —*pron.* **3.** an additional one. **4.** a different one. **5.** a person other than oneself or the one specified.
an•swer (an′sər, än′-), *n.* **1.** a reply, as to a question or request. **2.** an action serving as a reply or response. **3.** a solution to a problem, as in mathematics. —*v.i.* **4.** to speak, write, or act in response. **5.** to be responsible or accountable. **6.** to be satisfactory or serve. **7.** to conform; correspond. —*v.t.* **8.** to speak, write, or act in response to. **9.** to serve or fulfill. **10.** to conform or correspond to. **11.** answer back, to reply impertinently.
an′swer•a•ble *adj.* **1.** able to be answered. **2.** responsible.
an′swering machine′ *n.* a device that answers telephone calls with a recorded message and records messages from callers.
ant (ant), *n.* any of numerous small insects, usu. wingless, that live in highly organized colonies.
ant- var. of ANTI-.
-ant a suffix meaning: one that performs or promotes (*pollutant*); performing, promoting, or being (*pleasant*).
ant•ac•id (ant as′id), *adj.* **1.** neutralizing or counteracting acidity. —*n.* **2.** an antacid agent.
an•tag•o•nism (an tag′ə niz′əm), *n.* **1.** active hostility or opposition. **2.** an opposing force, principle, or tendency. —**an•tag′o•nis′tic,** *adj.*
ant•arc•tic (ant ärk′tik, -är′tik), *adj.* **1.** of, at, or near the South Pole. —*n.* **2. the Antarctic,** the Antarctic Ocean and Antarctica.
an•te (an′tē), *n., pl.* **-tes,** *v.,* **-ted** or **-teed, -te•ing.** —*n.* **1.** (in poker) a stake put into the pot by each player before the deal. **2.** the price or cost of something. —*v.t., v.i.* **3.** (in poker) to put (one's ante) into the pot. **4.** to produce or pay (one's share).
ante- a prefix meaning: happening before (*antediluvian*); in front of (*anteroom*).
ant′eat′er *n.* any of several tropical New World mammals having a long snout and feeding on ants and termites.
an•te•bel•lum (an′tē bel′əm), *adj.* existing before a war, esp. the American Civil War.
an•te•ced•ent (an′tə sēd′nt), *adj.* **1.** preceding; prior. —*n.* **2.** a preceding circumstance or event. **3.** antecedents, ancestors. **4.** a word, phrase, or clause referred to by a pronoun. —**an′te•ced′ence,** *n.*
an′te•cham′ber (an′tē-), *n.* a room that serves as a waiting room and entrance to a larger room.

an•te•di•lu•vi•an (an′tē di lōō′vē ən), *adj.* **1.** of the period before the Biblical Flood. **2.** out of date; antiquated.

an•te•lope (an′tl ōp′), *n., pl.* **-lopes, -lope. 1.** any of several ruminants, chiefly of Africa and Asia, having permanent unbranched horns. **2.** PRONGHORN.

an•ten•na (an ten′ə), *n., pl.* **-ten•nas** for 1, **-ten• nae** (-ten′ē) for 2. **1.** a conductor by which electromagnetic waves are sent out or received; aerial. **2.** one of the movable, sensory appendages occurring in pairs on the heads of insects and most other arthropods.

an•te•ri•or (an tēr′ē ər), *adj.* **1.** situated before or in front. **2.** preceding in time; earlier.

an•te•room (an′tē rōōm′, -rŏŏm′), *n.* ANTECHAMBER.

an•them (an′thəm), *n.* **1.** a hymn of praise, devotion, or patriotism. **2.** a piece of sacred vocal music.

an•ther (an′thər), *n.* the pollen-bearing part of a stamen.

an•thol•o•gy (an thol′ə jē), *n., pl.* **-gies.** a collection of selected writings. —**an•thol′o•gist,** *n.* —an•thol′o•gize′, *v.i., v.t.,* **-gized, -giz•ing.**

an•thra•cite (an′thrə sīt′), *n.* a hard coal that burns with little smoke. —**an′thra•cit′ic** (-sit′ik), *adj.*

an•thrax (an′thraks), *n.* an infectious bacterial disease of cattle, sheep, and other mammals that can be transmitted to humans.

an•thro•poid (an′thrə poid′), *adj.* **1.** resembling a human. —*n.* **2.** ANTHROPOID APE.

an′thropoid ape′ *n.* an ape resembling a human, as a gorilla or chimpanzee.

an′thro•pol′o•gy (-pol′ə jē), *n.* the science that deals with the origins, development, characteristics, and customs of humankind. —**an′thro•po•log′i• cal** (-pə loj′i kəl), *adj.* —**an′thro•pol′o•gist,** *n.*

an′thro•po•mor′phic (-pə môr′fik), *adj.* ascribing human form or attributes to a nonhuman thing or being. —**an′thro•po•mor′phism,** *n.*

an•ti (an′tī, an′tē), *n., pl.* **-tis.** a person who is opposed, as to a policy.

anti- a prefix meaning: against or opposed to (*antislavery*); preventing or counteracting (*anticoagulant*); opposite or contrary to (*antihero*); rivaling (*Antichrist*).

an•ti•bi•ot•ic (an′ti bī ot′ik), *n.* a substance, as penicillin, produced by a microorganism, capable of inhibiting or destroying other microorganisms, and used to treat infectious diseases.

an′ti•bod′y *n., pl.* **-ies.** a protein produced by the body that combines with a foreign antigen, as of a virus or bacterium, and disables it.

an•tic (an′tik), *n.* **1.** a playful prank. **2.** a ludicrous gesture or act. —*adj.* **3.** ludicrous; funny.

an•tic•i•pate (an tis′ə pāt′), *v.t.,* **-pat•ed, -pat• ing. 1.** to realize beforehand; foresee. **2.** to look forward to, esp. with pleasure. **3.** to prevent or thwart by acting in advance; forestall. —**an•tic′i• pa′tion,** *n.* —**an•tic′i•pa•to′ry** (-pə tôr′ē), *adj.*

an•ti•cli•max (an′tē klī′maks, an′tī-), *n.* **1.** an event, conclusion, or statement that is far less important or powerful than expected. **2.** a disappointing or inglorious descent. —**an′ti•cli•mac′tic,** *adj.*

an′ti•de•pres′sant *n.* a drug used to relieve mental depression.

an•ti•dote (an′ti dōt′), *n.* **1.** a remedy for counteracting the effects of a poison. **2.** something that counteracts injurious or unwanted effects.

an•ti•freeze (an′ti frēz′, an′tē-), *n.* a liquid used in the radiator of an internal-combustion engine to lower the freezing point of the cooling medium.

an•ti•gen (an′ti jən, -jen′), *n.* a substance that stimulates the production of antibodies. —**an′ti• gen′ic,** *adj.*

an′ti•his′ta•mine′ *n.* any of various drugs that block the action of histamines and are used esp. for treating allergies.

an′ti•knock′ *adj.* of or being a substance added to the fuel of an internal-combustion engine to minimize knock.

an•ti•mat•ter (an′tē mat′ər, an′tī-), *n.* matter composed only of antiparticles.

an•ti•mo•ny (an′tə mō′nē), *n.* a brittle, lustrous, white metallic element used chiefly in alloys. *Symbol:* Sb; *at. no.:* 51; *at. wt.:* 121.75.

an•ti•par•ti•cle (an′tē pär′ti kəl, an′tī-), *n.* a particle whose properties are identical in magnitude to those of a specific elementary particle but are of opposite sign.

an•ti•pas•to (an′ti pä′stō, än′tē-), *n., pl.* **-pas•tos, -pas•ti** (-pä′stē). an appetizer course in an Italian meal.

an•tip•a•thy (an tip′ə thē), *n., pl.* **-thies. 1.** a natural repugnance; aversion. **2.** an object of antipathy.

an•ti•per•spi•rant (an′ti pûr′spər ənt), *n.* an astringent preparation for reducing perspiration.

an•tip•o•des (an tip′ə dēz′), *n.pl.* places diametrically opposite each other on the globe. —**an•tip′o• dal,** *adj.*

an•ti•quar•i•an (an′ti kwâr′ē ən), *adj.* **1.** of antiquaries or antiquities. —*n.* **2.** an antiquary. —**an′• ti•quar′i•an•ism,** *n.*

an′ti•quar′y (-kwer′ē), *n., pl.* **-ies.** an expert on or collector of antiquities.

an′ti•quat′ed (-kwā′tid) *adj.* old or obsolete.

an•tique (an tēk′), *adj., n., v.,* **-tiqued, -ti•quing.** —*adj.* **1.** of, belonging to, or dating from a period long ago. **2.** in the tradition or style of an earlier period. **3.** old-fashioned; antiquated. —*n.* **4.** a piece of furniture, work of art, etc., produced in a former period. —*v.t.* **5.** to finish or treat so as to give an antique appearance. —*v.i.* **6.** to shop for antiques.

an•tiq′ui•ty (-tik′wi tē), *n., pl.* **-ties. 1.** the quality of being ancient. **2.** ancient times. **3.** **antiquities,** things, as relics, remaining from ancient times.

an•ti-Sem•ite (an′tē sem′īt, an′tī-), *n.* a person hostile toward Jews. —**an′ti-Se•mit′ic,** *adj.* —**an′• ti-Sem′i•tism,** *n.*

an•ti•sep•tic (an′tə sep′tik), *adj.* **1.** destroying certain germs. **2.** exceptionally clean. —*n.* **3.** an antiseptic agent. —**an′ti•sep′ti•cal•ly,** *adv.*

an•ti•so•cial (an′tē sō′shəl, an′tī-), *adj.* **1.** unwilling to associate in a normal or friendly way with others. **2.** detrimental to society. —**an′ti•so′cial•ly,** *adv.*

an•tith•e•sis (an tith′ə sis), *n., pl.* **-ses** (-sēz′). **1.** opposition; contrast. **2.** the direct opposite. —**an′ti• thet′i•cal** (-tə thet′i kəl), **an′ti•thet′ic,** *adj.* —**an′• ti•thet′i•cal•ly,** *adv.*

an•ti•tox•in (an′ti tok′sin), *n.* **1.** a substance formed in the body that counteracts a specific toxin. **2.** the antibody formed in immunization with a given toxin.

ant•ler (ant′lər), *n.* one of the solid horns, usu. branched, of an animal of the deer family.

an•to•nym (an′tə nim), *n.* a word opposite in meaning to another.

a•nus (ā′nəs), *n., pl.* **a•nus•es.** the excretory opening at the lower end of the alimentary canal.

an•vil (an′vil), *n.* a heavy iron block on which heated metals are hammered into desired shapes.

anx•i•e•ty (ang zī′i tē), *n., pl.* **-ties. 1.** mental uneasiness caused by fear, as of danger. **2.** a state of apprehension and psychic tension occurring in some forms of mental disorder.

anx•ious (angk′shəs, ang′-), *adj.* **1.** uneasy in the mind; worried. **2.** earnestly desirous; eager. —**anx′• ious•ly,** *adv.* —**anx′ious•ness,** *n.*

an•y (en′ē), *adj.* **1.** one or more without specification: *Pick out any six you like.* **2.** whatever it may be: *at any price.* **3.** some: *Do you have any butter?* **4.** every; all: *Any schoolchild would know that.* —*pron.* **5.** anybody; anyone. **6.** an unspecified quantity or number. —*adv.* **7.** to whatever degree or extent; at all.

an′y•how′ *adv.* **1.** in any way whatever. **2.** in any case; at all events.

an′y•place′ *adv.* ANYWHERE.

an′y•time′ *adv.* at any time; whenever.

an′y•where′ *adv.* **1.** in, at, or to any place. **2.** to any extent or degree. —*Idiom.* **3. get anywhere,** to achieve success.

A one or **A-1** or **A 1** (ā′ wun′), *adj.* first-class; excellent.

a·or·ta (ā ôr′tə), *n., pl.* **-tas, -tae** (-tē). the main artery of the mammalian circulatory system, conveying blood from the heart. —**a·or′tic,** *adj.*

a·pace (ə pās′), *adv.* with speed; quickly.

A·pach·e (ə pach′ē), *n., pl.* **A·pach·e, A·pach·es.** a member of a group of American Indian peoples of the U.S. Southwest.

a·part (ə pärt′), *adv.* **1.** into pieces or parts. **2.** separately in place, time, or motion. **3.** to or at one side; aside. —*adj.* **4.** having unique characteristics. —*Idiom.* **5.** apart from, besides.

a·part′heid (-hāt, -hīt), *n.* a former rigid policy of segregation of the nonwhite population in the Republic of South Africa.

a·part′ment (-mənt), *n.* a room or group of rooms used as a dwelling.

ap·a·thy (ap′ə thē), *n., pl.* **-thies. 1.** absence of emotion. **2.** lack of interest or concern. —**ap′a·thet′ic** (-thet′ik), *adj.*

ape (āp), *n., v.,* **aped, ap·ing.** —*n.* **1.** a tailless anthropoid primate with long arms and a broad chest. **2.** a monkey. **3.** an imitator; mimic. **4.** a clumsy or coarse person. —*v.t.* **5.** to imitate; mimic. —**ape′like′,** *adj.*

a·pé·ri·tif (ə per′i tēf′), *n.* an alcoholic drink taken to stimulate the appetite before a meal.

ap·er·ture (ap′ər chər), *n.* an opening, as a hole, slit, or gap.

a·pex (ā′peks), *n., pl.* **a·pex·es, a·pi·ces** (ā′pə-sēz′, ap′ə-). **1.** the highest point; peak. **2.** the tip or point.

a·phid (ā′fid, af′id), *n.* a tiny, soft-bodied insect that sucks sap from plants.

aph·o·rism (af′ə riz′əm), *n.* a terse saying embodying a general truth. —**aph′o·ris′tic,** *adj.* —**aph′o·ris′ti·cal·ly,** *adv.*

aph·ro·dis·i·ac (af′rə dē′zē ak′, -diz′ē ak′), *adj.* **1.** arousing sexual desire. —*n.* **2.** an aphrodisiac drug, food, etc.

a·pi·ar·y (ā′pē er′ē), *n., pl.* **-ies.** a place in which bees are kept. —**a′pi·a·rist** (-ə rist), *n.*

a·piece (ə pēs′), *adv.* for each one; each.

a·plen·ty (ə plen′tē), *adj., adv.* in generous amounts.

a·plomb (ə plom′, ə plum′), *n.* self-possession; poise.

a·poc·a·lypse (ə pok′ə lips), *n.* **1.** (*cap.*) REVELATION (def. 3). **2.** a prophetic revelation, esp. of a cataclysm in which good triumphs over evil. —**a·poc′a·lyp′tic** (-lip′tik), *adj.*

a·poc·ry·pha (ə pok′rə fə), *n.* (*used with a sing. or pl. v.*) **1.** (*cap.*) a group of books not found in Jewish or Protestant versions of the Old Testament but included in the Septuagint and the Vulgate. **2.** writings of doubtful authorship or authenticity.

a·poc′ry·phal *adj.* **1.** (*cap.*) of the Apocrypha. **2.** of doubtful authorship or authenticity.

ap·o·gee (ap′ə jē′), *n., pl.* **-gees. 1.** the point farthest from the earth in the orbit of the moon or a satellite. **2.** the highest point; climax.

a·po·lit·i·cal (ā′pə lit′i kəl), *adj.* not involved or interested in politics.

a·pol·o·get·ic (ə pol′ə jet′ik), *adj.* containing or expressing an apology. —**a·pol′o·get′i·cal·ly,** *adv.*

a·pol·o·gist (ə pol′ə jist), *n.* a person who defends an idea, faith, cause, or institution.

a·pol′o·gize′ *v.i.,* **-gized, -giz·ing.** to make an apology.

a·pol′o·gy *n., pl.* **-gies. 1.** an expression of regret, as for having been rude. **2.** a defense, as of a cause.

ap·o·plex·y (ap′ə plek′sē), *n.* STROKE¹ (def. 3). —**ap′o·plec′tic,** *adj.*

a·pos·ta·sy (ə pos′tə sē), *n., pl.* **-sies.** renunciation or abandonment of a previous loyalty, as to one's religious faith.

a·pos′tate (-tāt, -tit), *n.* a person who commits apostasy. —**a·pos′ta·tize′** (-tə tīz′), *v.i.,* **-tized, -tiz·ing.**

a posteriori (ā′ pō stēr′ē ôr′ī, -ôr′ē), *adj.* **1.** from particular instances to a general principle. **2.** based on observation or experiment.

a·pos·tle (ə pos′əl), *n.* **1.** (*sometimes cap.*) one of Christ's original 12 disciples. **2.** a pioneer of a reform movement.

a·pos·tro·phe¹ (ə pos′trə fē), *n.* the sign (') used to indicate the omission of one or more letters from a word, the possessive case, or plurals of abbreviations and symbols.

a·pos·tro·phe² (ə pos′trə fē), *n.* a rhetorical digression to address someone not present or a personified object or idea.

a·poth·e·car·y (ə poth′ə ker′ē), *n., pl.* **-ies.** a druggist; pharmacist.

a·poth·e·o·sis (ə poth′ē ō′sis, ap′ə thē′ə sis), *n., pl.* **-ses** (-sēz, -sēz′). **1.** elevation to the rank of a god. **2.** the ideal example; epitome.

ap·pall (ə pôl′), *v.t.* to fill with consternation; dismay. —**ap·pall′ing,** *adj.*

ap·pa·rat·us (ap′ə rat′əs, -rā′təs), *n., pl.* **-tus, -tus·es. 1.** a combination of instruments or materials having a particular function. **2.** a complex mechanism for a particular purpose. **3.** the means by which a system functions.

ap·par·el (ə par′əl), *n., v.,* **-eled, -el·ing** or (*esp. Brit.*) **-elled, -el·ling.** —*n.* **1.** clothing, esp. outerwear; garments. —*v.t.* **2.** to dress; clothe.

ap·par·ent (ə par′ənt, ə pâr′-), *adj.* **1.** readily seen; open to view. **2.** easily understood; obvious. **3.** according to appearances; ostensible. —**ap·par′ent·ly,** *adv.*

ap·pa·ri·tion (ap′ə rish′ən), *n.* **1.** a ghost. **2.** something making a strange or incongruous appearance.

ap·peal (ə pēl′), *n.* **1.** an earnest plea; entreaty. **2.** a request to an authority, as for help or a decision. **3.** an application for review by a higher court. **4.** the power or ability to attract. —*v.i.* **5.** to make an earnest plea. **6.** to apply for review of a case to a higher court. **7.** to exert an attraction. —*v.t.* **8.** to apply for review of (a case) to a higher court. —**ap·peal′ing,** *adj.*

ap·pear (ə pēr′), *v.i.* **1.** to come into sight. **2.** to have the appearance of being. **3.** to be or become obvious. **4.** to come before the public. **5.** to come before a court.

ap·pear′ance (-əns), *n.* **1.** the act or process of appearing. **2.** outward look; aspect. **3.** outward show; semblance. —*Idiom.* **4.** put in an appearance, to attend a gathering, esp. for a short time.

ap·pease (ə pēz′), *v.t.,* **-peased, -peas·ing. 1.** to bring to a state of calm; pacify. **2.** to satisfy; relieve. **3.** to yield to the demands of, esp. at the expense of one's principles. —**ap·pease′ment,** *n.* —**ap·peas′er,** *n.*

ap·pel·late (ə pel′it), *adj.* **1.** of appeals. **2.** (of a court) having the authority to review and decide appeals.

ap·pend (ə pend′), *v.t.* **1.** to add as a supplement. **2.** to affix.

ap·pend·age (ə pen′dij), *n.* **1.** a subsidiary part, as a limb, that diverges from a central or principal structure. **2.** something appended.

ap·pen·dec·to·my (ap′ən dek′tə mē), *n., pl.* **-mies.** surgical removal of the appendix.

ap·pen·di·ci·tis (ə pen′də sī′tis), *n.* inflammation of the appendix.

ap·pen·dix (ə pen′diks), *n., pl.* **-dix·es, -di·ces** (-də sēz′). **1.** supplementary material at the end of a text. **2.** a tube, closed at the end, extending from the cecum of the large intestine.

ap·per·tain (ap′ər tān′), *v.i.* to belong as a rightful attribute or part; pertain.

ap·pe·tite (ap′i tīt′), *n.* **1.** a desire for food. **2.** a desire to satisfy a need or craving.

ap′pe·tiz′er (-tī′zər), *n.* a portion of food or drink served before a meal to stimulate the appetite.

ap·plaud (ə plôd′), *v.i., v.t.* **1.** to clap the hands in approval or appreciation (of). **2.** to praise. —**ap·plaud′er,** *n.* —**ap·plause′,** *n.*

ap·ple (ap′əl), *n.* **1.** the rounded, edible, usu. red fruit of a tree of the rose family. **2.** a tree that bears apples.

ap′ple·jack′ *n.* a brandy distilled from fermented cider.

ap′ple·sauce′ *n.* apples stewed to a pulp.

ap•pli•ance (ə plī′əns), *n.* a device used esp. in the home to carry out a specific function, as toasting bread.

ap•pli•ca•ble (ap′li kə bəl, ə plik′ə-), *adj.* capable of being applied; relevant. —**ap′pli•ca•bil′i•ty,** *n.* —**ap′pli•ca•bly,** *adv.*

ap′pli•cant (-kənt), *n.* a person who applies.

ap′pli•ca′tion (-kā′shən), *n.* **1.** the act of applying. **2.** the use to which something is put. **3.** appropriateness; relevance. **4.** a petition; request. **5.** a form to be filled out by an applicant. **6.** persistent attention. **7.** a salve or ointment. **8. a.** a specific kind of task, as database management, that can be done using an application program. **b.** APPLICATION PROGRAM.

applica′tion pro′gram *n.* a computer program used for a specific kind of task, as word processing.

ap′pli•ca′tor *n.* a device for applying a substance, as medication.

ap•pli•qué (ap′li kā′), *n.*, *v.*, **-quéd, -qué•ing.** —*n.* **1.** a cutout design of one material applied to another. —*v.t.* **2.** to decorate with appliqué.

ap•ply (ə plī′), *v.*, **-plied, -ply•ing.** —*v.t.* **1.** to make use of. **2.** to assign to a specific purpose. **3.** to employ diligently. **4.** to bring into contact; lay or spread on. —*v.i.* **5.** to be pertinent or suitable. **6.** to make an application or request. —**ap•pli′er,** *n.*

ap•point (ə point′), *v.t.* **1.** to name or assign officially. **2.** to fix; set. **3.** to equip; furnish.

ap•point•ee (ə poin tē′), *n.*, *pl.* **-ees.** a person who is appointed.

ap•poin′tive *adj.* pertaining to or filled by appointment.

ap•point′ment *n.* **1.** an agreement to meet; engagement. **2.** the act of appointing. **3.** an office or position to which a person is appointed. **4.** Usu. **-ments.** equipment or furnishings.

ap•por•tion (ə pôr′shən), *v.t.* to distribute or allocate proportionally. —**ap•por′tion•ment,** *n.*

ap•po•site (ap′ə zit, ə poz′it), *adj.* suitable; apt. —**ap′po•site•ly,** *adv.* —**ap′po•site•ness,** *n.*

ap•praise (ə prāz′), *v.t.*, **-praised, -prais•ing. 1.** to determine the value of. **2.** to estimate the quality or importance of. —**ap•prais′al,** *n.* —**ap•prais′er,** *n.*

ap•pre•ci•a•ble (ə prē′shē ə bəl, -shə bəl), *adj.* sufficient to be readily perceived or estimated. —**ap•pre′ci•a•bly,** *adv.*

ap•pre′ci•ate′ (-shē āt′), *v.*, **-at•ed, -at•ing.** —*v.t.* **1.** to be thankful for. **2.** to value or regard highly. **3.** to be fully conscious of. —*v.i.* **4.** to increase in value. —**ap•pre′ci•a′tion,** *n.* —**ap•pre′cia•tive** (-shə tiv), **ap•pre′ci•a•to′ry** (-ə tôr′ē), *adj.*

ap•pre•hend (ap′ri hend′), *v.t.* **1.** to take into custody; arrest. **2.** to grasp the meaning of; understand. **3.** to anticipate with anxiety or fear.

ap′pre•hen′sion (-hen′shən), *n.* **1.** anxiety or fear, esp. of future trouble. **2.** the faculty or act of understanding. **3.** the act of arresting; seizure.

ap′pre•hen′sive (-siv), *adj.* anxious or fearful, esp. about something that might happen. —**ap′pre•hen′sive•ly,** *adv.* —**ap′pre•hen′sive•ness,** *n.*

ap•pren•tice (ə pren′tis), *n.*, *v.*, **-ticed, -tic•ing.** —*n.* **1.** a person who works for another in order to learn a trade. **2.** a learner; novice. —*v.t.*, *v.i.* **3.** to place as or serve as an apprentice. —**ap•pren′tice•ship′,** *n.*

ap•prise (ə prīz′), *v.t.*, **-prised, -pris•ing.** to give notice to; inform.

ap•proach (ə prōch′), *v.t.* **1.** to come nearer to. **2.** to come within range, as for comparison. **3.** to begin work on; set about. —*v.i.* **4.** to come nearer. —*n.* **5.** an act or instance of approaching. **6.** a means of access. **7.** the method used or steps taken in setting about a task. —**ap•proach′a•ble,** *adj.*

ap•pro•ba•tion (ap′rə bā′shən), *n.* approval.

ap•pro•pri•ate (*adj.* ə prō′prē it; *v.* -āt′), *adj.*, *v.*, **-at•ed, -at•ing.** —*adj.* **1.** particularly suitable; fitting. —*v.t.* **2.** to set apart for a specific purpose or use. **3.** to take possession of, esp. without permission. —**ap•pro′pri•ate•ly,** *adv.* —**ap•pro′pri•ate•ness,** *n.* —**ap•pro′pri•a′tor,** *n.*

ap•pro•pri•a′tion (-ā′shən), *n.* **1.** the act of ap-

propriating. **2.** money officially authorized to be paid from a public treasury.

ap•prov•al (ə prōō′vəl), *n.* **1.** the act of approving. **2.** permission; consent. —*Idiom.* **3. on approval,** subject to being rejected if not satisfactory.

ap•prove′ *v.*, **-proved, -prov•ing.** —*v.t.* **1.** to speak or think favorably of. **2.** to confirm or sanction formally; ratify. —*v.i.* **3.** to have a favorable view. —**ap•prov′ing•ly,** *adv.*

approx. approximate.

ap•prox•i•mate (*adj.* ə prok′sə mit; *v.* -māt′), *adj.*, *v.*, **-mat•ed, -mat•ing.** —*adj.* **1.** nearly exact but not perfectly accurate. —*v.t.* **2.** to come near to in quantity, quality, or condition. —**ap•prox′i•mate•ly,** *adv.* —**ap•prox′i•ma′tion,** *n.*

ap•pur•te•nance (ə pûr′tn əns), *n.* **1.** something subordinate to another. **2.** a legal right belonging to and passing with a principal property. **3. appurtenances,** accessories. —**ap•pur′te•nant,** *adj.*

Apr or **Apr.,** April.

ap•ri•cot (ap′ri kot′, ā′pri-), *n.* **1.** the downy, yellowish orange, peachlike fruit of a tree of the rose family. **2.** the tree itself.

A•pril (ā′prəl), *n.* the fourth month of the year, containing 30 days.

a pri•o•ri (ä′ prē ôr′ī, -ôr′ē), *adj.* **1.** from a general law to a particular instance. **2.** existing in the mind independent of experience. [< L]

a•pron (ā′prən), *n.* **1.** a garment covering the front of the body and worn to protect the clothing. **2.** a paved area where airplanes are parked. **3.** the part of a stage floor in front of the curtain line.

ap•ro•pos (ap′rə pō′), *adv.* **1.** by the way; incidentally. —*adj.* **2.** being appropriate and timely. —*Idiom.* **3. apropos of,** with reference to.

apse (aps), *n.* a usu. vaulted recess in a building, esp. at the end of a church.

apt (apt), *adj.* **1.** having a tendency; likely. **2.** being quick to learn; bright. **3.** suited to a purpose or occasion. —**apt′ly,** *adv.* —**apt′ness,** *n.*

apt. apartment.

ap•ti•tude (ap′ti tōōd′, -tyōōd′), *n.* **1.** innate ability; talent. **2.** readiness or quickness in learning. **3.** suitability; fitness.

Aq′ua•lung′ *Trademark.* an underwater breathing device.

aq′ua•ma•rine′ *n.* **1.** a transparent light blue or greenish blue gem. **2.** a light blue-green or greenish blue.

a•quar•i•um (ə kwâr′ē əm), *n.*, *pl.* **-i•ums, -i•a** (-ē ə). **1.** a glass-sided container in which aquatic animals or plants are kept. **2.** a place in which aquatic animals or plants are kept for exhibit.

a•quat•ic (ə kwat′ik, ə kwot′-), *adj.* **1.** living or growing in water. **2.** taking place or practiced on or in water. —*n.* **3. aquatics,** aquatic sports. —**a•quat′i•cal•ly,** *adv.*

aq•ue•duct (ak′wi dukt′), *n.* **1.** a conduit or channel for conducting water from a distance. **2.** a bridgelike structure that carries an aqueduct across a valley or over a river.

a•que•ous (ā′kwē əs, ak′wē-), *adj.* of, like, or containing water; watery.

aq•ui•line (ak′wə līn′, -lin), *adj.* **1.** of or resembling an eagle. **2.** curved like an eagle's beak.

AR Arkansas.

Ar *Chem. Symbol.* argon.

A/R accounts receivable.

Ar•ab (ar′əb), *n.* **1.** a member of an Arabic-speaking people. **2.** a member of a Semitic people inhabiting Arabia, SW Asia, and N Africa.

Ar•a•bic (ar′ə bik), *n.* **1.** a Semitic language spoken over much of N Africa, the Sahara, and SW Asia. —*adj.* **2.** of Arabic, the Arabs, or Arabia.

Ar′abic nu′meral *n.* any of the numerical symbols 0, 1, 2, 3, 4, 5, 6, 7, 8, and 9.

ar•a•ble (ar′ə bəl), *adj.* capable of producing crops by being plowed or tilled. —**ar′a•bil′i•ty,** *n.*

a•rach•nid (ə rak′nid), *n.* any of numerous arthropods, including spiders and scorpions, characterized by a body with eight appendages.

A•rap′a•ho′ or **-hoe′** (ə rap′ə hō′) *n.*, *pl.* **-hos** or

-hoes or **-hoe.** a member of a North American Indian people.

ar•bi•ter (är′bi tər), *n.* a person empowered to decide matters at issue; judge.

ar′bi•trage′ (-träzh′), *n.* the simultaneous purchase and sale of the same security in different markets to profit from price differences. —**ar′bi•trag′er,** **ar′bi•tra•geur′** (-trä zhûr′), *n.*

ar′bi•trar′y (-trer′ē), *adj.* **1.** subject to individual will or judgment without restriction. **2.** dictatorial; despotic. **3.** capricious; unreasonable. —**ar′bi•trar′i•ly,** *adv.* —**ar′bi•trar′i•ness,** *n.*

ar′bi•trate′ (-trāt′), *v.,* **-trat•ed, -trat•ing.** —*v.t.* **1.** to decide as arbitrator. **2.** to submit to or settle by arbitration. —*v.i.* **3.** to act as arbitrator.

ar•bi•tra•tion (är′bi trā′shən), *n.* the hearing and determination of a dispute or the settling of differences between parties by a person or persons chosen or agreed to by them. —**ar′bi•tra′tor,** *n.*

ar•bor (är′bər), *n.* **1.** a leafy, shady recess. **2.** a latticework bower intertwined with vines.

ar•bo′re•al (-bôr′ē əl), *adj.* **1.** of or like trees. **2.** living in trees.

ar•bo•re′tum (är′bə rē′təm), *n., pl.* **-tums, -ta** (-tə). a parklike area where trees or shrubs are grown for study or display.

arc (ärk), *n., v.,* **arced** or **arcked, arc•ing** or **arck•ing.** —*n.* **1.** an unbroken part of a curved line. **2.** a luminous bridge formed in a gap between two electrodes. **3.** something curved like an arc. —*v.i.* **4.** to form or move in an arc.

ar•cade (är kād′), *n.* **1.** a series of arches supported on columns. **2.** a covered passageway, usu. with shops on each side. **3.** an establishment for coin-operated games.

ar•cane (är kān′), *adj.* known or understood only by those with special knowledge; secret.

arch¹ (ärch), *n.* **1.** a curved construction spanning an opening and supporting weight. **2.** an archway. **3.** something resembling an arch. —*v.i., v.t.* **4.** to form or form into an arch.

arch² (ärch), *adj.* coyly roguish or mischievous. —**arch′ly,** *adv.* —**arch′ness,** *n.*

arch- a combining form meaning: principal (*archenemy*); extreme or ultimate (*archfiend*).

-arch a combining form meaning ruler (*monarch*).

arch. **1.** archaic. **2.** archipelago. **3.** architect; architecture.

ar•chae•ol•o•gy or **ar•che•ol•o•gy** (är′kē ol′ə jē), *n.* the scientific study of past peoples and cultures by analysis of physical remains, as artifacts. —**ar′chae•o•log′i•cal** (-ə loj′i kəl), *adj.* —**ar′chae•ol′o•gist,** *n.*

ar•cha•ic (är kā′ik), *adj.* **1.** marked by the characteristics of an earlier period; antiquated. **2.** (of a linguistic form) commonly used in an earlier time but rare in present-day usage. —**ar•cha′i•cal•ly,** *adv.*

arch•an•gel (ärk′ān′jəl), *n.* a chief or principal angel.

arch•bish•op (ärch′bish′əp), *n.* a bishop of the highest rank.

arch′di′o•cese′ *n.* the diocese of an archbishop. —**arch′di•oc′e•san** (-os′ə sən), *adj.*

arch′duke′ *n.* a prince of the former ruling house of Austria.

arch′en′e•my *n., pl.* **-mies.** a chief enemy.

arch•er (är′chər), *n.* a person who shoots with a bow and arrow.

ar•che•type (är′ki tīp′), *n.* an original pattern or model from which all things of the same kind are copied or on which they are based; prototype. —**ar′che•typ′al** (-tī′pəl), **ar′che•typ′i•cal** (-tip′i-kəl), *adj.*

ar•chi•pel•a•go (är′kə pel′ə gō′), *n., pl.* **-gos, -goes.** **1.** a group of islands. **2.** a large body of water with many islands.

ar•chi•tect (är′ki tekt′), *n.* **1.** a person who engages in the profession of architecture. **2.** planner or designer.

ar′chi•tec′ture (-tek′chər), *n.* **1.** the profession of designing buildings, communities, etc. **2.** the character or style of building. **3.** the design or structure of something. —**ar′chi•tec′tur•al,** *adj.* —**ar′chi•tec′tur•al•ly,** *adv.*

ar′chives (är′kīvz) *n.pl.* **1.** documents. **2.** a place for documents.

arch•way (ärch′wā′), *n.* **1.** an entrance or passage under an arch. **2.** an arch over a passage.

arc•tic (ärk′tik, är′tik), *adj.* **1.** (*often cap.*) of, at, or near the North Pole. **2.** extremely cold; frigid. —*n.* **3.** (*often cap.*) the region lying north of the Arctic Circle. [≪ Gk *arktikós* northern, lit., of the Bear (constellation)]

ar•dent (är′dnt), *adj.* **1.** characterized by intense feeling; fervent. **2.** fiercely bright. **3.** fiery; hot. —**ar′dent•ly,** *adv.*

ar•dor (är′dər), *n.* **1.** great intensity of feeling; fervor. **2.** intense heat. Also, *esp. Brit.,* **ar′dour.**

ar•du•ous (är′jōō əs; *esp. Brit.* -dyōō-), *adj.* requiring or marked by great exertion; laborious. —**ar′du•ous•ly,** *adv.* —**ar′du•ous•ness,** *n.*

are¹ (är; *unstressed* ər), *v.* pres. indic. pl. and 2nd pers. sing. of BE.

are² (âr, är), *n.* a surface measure equal to 100 square meters.

ar•e•a (âr′ē ə), *n., pl.* **-as.** **1.** an extent of space or surface. **2.** a geographical region. **3.** extent; scope. **4.** field; sphere. **5.** the quantitative measure of a plane or curved surface. —**ar′e•al,** *adj.*

ar′ea code′ *n.* a three-digit code that identifies one of the telephone areas into which the U.S. and certain other countries are divided.

a•re•na (ə rē′nə), *n., pl.* **-nas.** **1.** a space or building used for sports or other entertainments. **2.** a field of competition or activity.

aren′t (ärnt, är′ənt), contraction of *are not.*

Ar•gen•ti•na (är′jən tē′nə), *n.* a republic in S South America. —**Ar′gen•tine′** (-tēn′, -tīn′), **Ar′gen•tin′e•an** (-tin′ē ən), *n., adj.*

ar•got (är′gō, -gət), *n.* a specialized vocabulary peculiar to a particular group of people.

ar•gue (är′gyōō), *v.,* **-gued, -gu•ing.** —*v.i.* **1.** to present reasons for or against a thing. **2.** to contend orally; dispute. —*v.t.* **3.** to present reasons for or against. **4.** to persuade or compel by reasoning. —**ar′gu•a•ble,** *adj.* —**ar′gu•a•bly,** *adv.*

ar•gu•ment (är′gyə mənt), *n.* **1.** an oral disagreement; quarrel. **2.** a discussion involving differing points of view; debate. **3.** a statement or fact for or against a point. **4.** discourse intended to persuade.

ar′gu•men′ta•tive (-tə tiv), *adj.* given to argument; disputatious.

ar•gyle (är′gīl), *n.* (*often cap.*) a diamond-shaped knitting pattern of two or more colors.

a•ri•a (är′ē ə), *n., pl.* **-as.** an elaborate vocal solo with accompaniment, as in an opera.

ar•id (ar′id), *adj.* **1.** barren or unproductive due to lack of moisture. **2.** lacking vitality or imagination. —**a•rid′i•ty** (ə rid′i tē), *n.*

a•right (ə rīt′), *adv.* to rights; correctly.

a•rise (ə rīz′), *v.i.,* **a•rose, a•ris•en** (ə riz′ən), **a•ris•ing. 1.** to get up, as from a sitting position. **2.** to move upward; ascend. **3.** to come into being; spring up.

ar•is•toc•ra•cy (ar′ə stok′rə sē), *n., pl.* **-cies. 1.** the hereditary nobility. **2.** government by an aristocracy, elite, or privileged upper class. **3.** a class or group regarded as superior.

a•rith•me•tic (*n.* ə rith′mə tik; *adj.* ar′ith met′ik), *n.* **1.** the method or process of computation with figures. —*adj.* **ar•ith•met•ic 2.** Also, **ar′ith•met′i•cal.** of arithmetic. —**ar′ith•met′i•cal•ly,** *adv.*

Ariz. Arizona.

ark (ärk), *n.* **1.** the boat built by Noah for safety during the Biblical Flood. **2.** a chest containing tablets inscribed with the Ten Commandments, kept in the Biblical Tabernacle. **3.** a cabinet in a synagogue for the Torah scrolls.

Ark. Arkansas.

arm¹ (ärm), *n.* **1.** an upper limb of the human body. **2.** an armlike part or attachment. **3.** a combat branch of a military service. **4.** power; authority: *the long arm of the law.* —**Idiom. 5.** at **arm's length,** at a distance.

arm² (ärm), *n.* **1.** Usu., **arms.** weapons, esp.

firearms. **2. arms,** heraldic devices, as of a family. —*v.i.* **3.** to make ready for war. —*v.t.* **4.** to equip with weapons. —**Idiom. 5. up in arms,** provoked; indignant. —**armed,** *adj.*

ar•ma•da (är mä′də, -mā′-), *n., pl.* **-das. 1.** a fleet of warships. **2.** a large group of vehicles, airplanes, etc.

ar•ma•dil•lo (är′mə dil′ō), *n., pl.* -los. a burrowing mammal covered with jointed plates of bone and horn.

Ar•ma•ged•don (är′mə ged′n), *n.* **1.** the place where the final battle between good and evil will be fought. **2.** a final and decisive battle.

ar•ma•ment (är′mə mənt), *n.* **1.** military weapons and equipment. **2.** Usu., **-ments.** military strength collectively. **3.** the process of arming for war.

arm′chair′ *n.* a chair with supports for the arms.

armed′ forc′es *n.pl.* military, naval, and air forces.

Ar•me•ni•a (är mē′nē ə), *n.* a republic in W Asia, W of Azerbaijan: formerly a part of the USSR. —**Ar•me′ni•an,** *adj., n.*

ar•mi•stice (är′mə stis), *n.* a temporary suspension of hostilities by agreement of the warring parties; truce.

ar•mor (är′mər), *n.* **1.** any covering that serves as a protection or defense, as against weapons. **2.** the armored divisions of an army. —*v.t.* **3.** to cover or equip with armor. Also, *esp. Brit.,* **ar′mour.** —**ar′mored,** *adj.*

ar′mor•y (-mə rē), *n., pl.* **-ies. 1.** a storage place for weapons. **2.** a National Guard headquarters and drill center. **3.** a place where arms and armor are made.

arm′pit′ *n.* the hollow under the arm at the shoulder.

ar•my (är′mē), *n., pl.* **-mies. 1.** the military forces of a nation trained to fight on land. **2.** a body of persons trained and armed for war. **3.** a large or organized group.

a•ro•ma (ə rō′mə), *n., pl.* **-mas.** a distinctive, usu. agreeable odor; fragrance. —**ar•o•mat•ic** (ar′ə mat′-ik), *adj.*

a•ro′ma•ther′a•py *n.* **1.** the use of fragrances to affect or alter a person's mood or behavior. **2.** treatment of facial skin by the application of fragrant floral and herbal substances.

a•round (ə round′), *adv.* **1.** in a circle or ring. **2.** on all sides. **3.** in all directions. **4.** in circumference. **5.** in or to another or opposite direction. **6.** in the vicinity; nearby. —*prep.* **7.** on all sides of; encircling. **8.** on the edge or border of. **9.** in all or various directions from. **10.** in the vicinity of; near. **11.** here and there in. **12.** on or to the other side of.

a•rouse (ə rouz′), *v.t.,* **a•roused, a•rous•ing. 1.** to stir up; excite. **2.** to awaken from sleep. —**a•rous′al,** *n.*

ar•raign (ə rān′), *v.t.* **1.** to bring before a court to answer an indictment. **2.** to accuse or charge. —**ar•raign′ment,** *n.*

ar•range (ə rānj′), *v.,* **-ranged, -rang•ing.** —*v.t.* **1.** to place in proper, desired, or convenient order. **2.** to come to an agreement regarding. **3.** to adapt (a musical work) for particular instrumentation. —*v.i.* **4.** to make plans or preparations. **5.** to come to an agreement. —**ar•range′ment,** *n.* —**ar•rang′er,** *n.*

ar•ray (ə rā′), *v.,* **-rayed, -ray•ing,** *n.* —*v.t.* **1.** to place in order; marshal. **2.** to clothe, esp. in finery. —*n.* **3.** order, as of troops drawn up for battle. **4.** a large and impressive group. **5.** fine attire.

ar•rear (ə rēr′), *n.* **1.** Usu., **arrears.** the state of being late in repaying a debt. **2.** Often, **arrears.** an unpaid debt.

ar•rest (ə rest′), *v.t.* **1.** to seize (a person) by legal authority. **2.** to catch and hold; engage: *A noise arrested our attention.* **3.** to check the course of; stop. —*n.* **4.** the taking of a person into legal custody. **5.** the act of stopping or state of being stopped.

ar•rest′ing *adj.* attracting or capable of attracting attention or interest.

ar•ri•val (ə rī′vəl), *n.* **1.** the act of arriving. **2.** a person or thing that arrives.

ar•rive (ə rīv′), *v.i.,* **-rived, -riv•ing. 1.** to reach one's destination. **2.** to come: *The moment has arrived.* **3.** to attain a position of success. **4. arrive at,** to reach in a process or course.

ar•ro•gant (ar′ə gənt), *adj.* characterized by or proceeding from overbearing superiority or self-importance. —**ar′ro•gance,** *n.* —**ar′ro•gant•ly,** *adv.*

ar′ro•gate′ (-gāt′), *v.t.,* **-gat•ed, -gat•ing.** to claim or appropriate without right. —**ar′ro•ga′tion,** *n.*

ar•row (ar′ō), *n.* **1.** a slender feathered and pointed shaft shot from a bow. **2.** a figure with a wedge-shaped end used to indicate direction.

ar′row•head′ *n.* the pointed tip of an arrow.

ar′row•root′ *n.* **1.** a tropical American plant whose fleshy tubers yield an edible starch. **2.** the starch of the arrowroot.

ar•roy•o (ə roi′ō), *n., pl.* **-os.** (chiefly in the southwestern U.S.) a watercourse or gulch that is usu. dry except after heavy rains.

ar•se•nal (är′sə nl), *n.* **1.** a military establishment for producing and storing weapons. **2.** a supply; collection.

ar•se•nic (är′sə nik), *n.* a grayish white element having a metallic luster and forming poisonous compounds. *Symbol:* As; *at. wt.:* 74.92; *at. no.:* 33.

ar•son (är′sən), *n.* the malicious burning of property. —**ar′son•ist,** *n.*

art[1] (ärt), *n.* **1.** the production, expression, or realm of what is beautiful. **2.** objects subject to aesthetic criteria, as paintings. **3.** a field or category of art. **4.** illustrative or decorative material. **5.** skill in conducting a human activity. **6.** a branch of learning, esp. one of the humanities. **7.** skilled workmanship or execution.

art[2] (ärt), *v. Archaic.* 2nd pers. sing. pres. indic. of BE.

-art var. of -ARD: *braggart.*

art′ dec′o (dek′ō), *n.* (*often caps.*) a style of decorative art developed in the 1920s and marked chiefly by geometric motifs.

ar•te•ri•o•scle•ro•sis (är tēr′ē ō sklə rō′sis), *n.* abnormal thickening and loss of elasticity in the arterial walls.

ar•ter•y (är′tə rē), *n., pl.* **-ies. 1.** a blood vessel that conveys blood away from the heart. **2.** a main channel or highway. —**ar•te′ri•al** (-tēr′ē əl), *adj.*

ar•thri•tis (är thrī′tis), *n.* inflammation of one or more joints. —**ar•thrit′ic** (-thrit′ik), *adj., n.*

ar•thro•pod (är′thrə pod′), *n.* any of a group of invertebrates with a segmented body and jointed limbs, including insects, spiders, and crustaceans.

ar•ti•choke (är′ti chōk′), *n.* **1.** a thistlelike plant with an edible flower head. **2.** the flower head.

ar•ti•cle (är′ti kəl), *n.* **1.** a factual piece of writing, usu. on a single topic, appearing in a publication. **2.** an individual item. **3.** a word, as *a, an,* or *the,* that is linked to a noun and identifies the noun as a noun. **4.** a separate clause or section in a document, as a statute.

ar•tic•u•late (*adj.* är tik′yə lit; *v.* -lāt′), *adj., v.,* **-lat•ed, -lat•ing.** —*adj.* **1.** uttered clearly. **2.** capable of speech. **3.** capable of, expressed with, or marked by clarity and effectiveness of language. **4.** having joints or segments. —*v.t.* **5.** to pronounce clearly and distinctly. **6.** to give clarity or coherence to. **7.** to unite by joints. —*v.i.* **8.** to speak clearly. **9.** to form a joint. —**ar•tic′u•late•ly,** *adv.* —**ar•tic′u•late•ness,** *n.* —**ar•tic′u•la′tion,** *n.*

ar•ti•fact (är′tə fakt′), *n.* an object made by human beings, esp. one belonging to an earlier time or cultural stage.

ar•ti•fice (är′tə fis), *n.* **1.** a clever trick; stratagem. **2.** trickery; guile. **3.** cleverness; ingenuity.

ar′ti•fi′cial (-tə fish′əl), *adj.* **1.** produced by humans and not by nature. **2.** not real; simulated. **3.** not natural; forced or affected. —**ar′ti•fi′ci•al′i•ty** (-fish′ē al′i tē), *n.* —**ar′ti•fi′cial•ly,** *adv.*

artifi′cial respira′tion *n.* the stimulation of natural respiratory functions in a person whose breathing has failed by forcing air into and out of the lungs.

ar•til•ler•y (är til′ə rē), *n.* **1.** mounted projectile-firing guns or missile launchers. **2.** the branch of an army using artillery. —**ar•til′ler•y•man,** *n., pl.* -men.

ar•ti•san (är′tə zən), *n.* a person skilled in an applied art.

art•ist (är′tist), *n.* **1.** a person who practices one of the fine arts, esp. painting or sculpture. **2.** a person proficient in a performing art, as a musician. —**ar•tis′tic,** *adj.* —**ar•tis′ti•cal•ly,** *adv.*

art′less *adj.* **1.** free from deceit or cunning; ingenuous. **2.** not artificial; natural. **3.** lacking art, knowledge, or skill. —**art′less•ly,** *adv.* —**art′less•ness,** *n.*

art′y *adj.,* -i•er, -i•est. *Informal.* pretentiously artistic. —**art′i•ness,** *n.*

as (az; *unstressed* əz), *adv.* **1.** to the same degree or extent; equally. **2.** for example. **3.** thought to be: *the square as distinct from the rectangle.* —*conj.* **4.** to the same degree or extent that: *to run quick as a rabbit.* **5.** in the same manner that. **6.** while; when. **7.** since; because. **8.** though: *Strange as it seems, it is so.* **9.** that the result is. —*pron.* **10.** that, who, or which. **11.** a fact that. —*prep.* **12.** in the role or function of. —*Idiom.* **13.** as for or to, with respect to; about. **14.** as if or though, as it would be if. **15.** as is, just the way it exists or appears. **16.** as it were, so to speak. **17.** as of, beginning on; from.

As *Chem. Symbol.* arsenic.

ASAP (ā′sap), *adv.* without delay; promptly.

A.S.A.P. or **a.s.a.p.** as soon as possible.

as•bes•tos (as bes′təs, az-), *n.* a fibrous mineral formerly used for making fireproof articles and in building insulation.

as•cend (ə send′), *v.i.* **1.** to move upward; rise. —*v.t.* **2.** to succeed to: *The prince ascended the throne.* —**as•cent′,** *n.*

as•cend′an•cy or **-en•cy,** *n.* the state of being in the ascendant.

as•cend′ant or **-ent,** *n.* **1.** a position of dominance. —*adj.* **2.** ascending; rising. **3.** superior; dominant.

as•cen•sion (ə sen′shən), *n.* **1.** the act of ascending. **2. the Ascension,** the bodily ascending of Christ to heaven. **3.** (*cap.*) ASCENSION DAY.

Ascen′sion Day′ *n.* the 40th day after Easter, commemorating the Ascension of Christ.

as•cer•tain (as′ər tān′), *v.t.* to find out definitely. —**as′cer•tain′a•ble,** *adj.* —**as′cer•tain′ment,** *n.*

as•cet•ic (ə set′ik), *n.* **1.** a person who practices self-denial, esp. for religious reasons. —*adj.* **2.** rigorously abstinent; austere. —**as•cet′i•cism,** *n.*

ASCII (as′kē), *n.* a standardized code in which characters are represented for computer storage and transmission by the numbers 0 through 127. [*A(merican) S(tandard) C(ode) for) I(nformation) I(nterchange)*]

a•scor′bic ac′id (ə skôr′bik), *n.* a water-soluble vitamin occurring in citrus fruits, green vegetables, etc., essential for normal metabolism.

as•cot (as′kət, -kot), *n.* a tie or scarf with broad ends looped to lie flat one upon the other.

as•cribe (ə skrīb′), *v.t.* -cribed, -crib•ing. to credit to a cause or source; attribute. —**a•scrib′a•ble,** *adj.* —**a•scrip•tion** (ə skrip′shən), *n.*

a•sep′sis (ā sep′sis, ā sep′-) *n.* the absence of certain harmful bacteria. —**a•sep′tic** (-tik), *adj.*

a•sex•u•al (ā sek′shōō əl), *adj.* **1.** having no sex or sexual organs. **2.** independent of sexual processes, esp. not involving the union of male and female germ cells. —**a•sex′u•al′i•ty,** *n.* —**a•sex′u•al•ly,** *adv.*

ash[1] (ash), *n.* **1.** the powdery residue of matter that remains after burning. **2.** finely pulverized lava thrown out by a volcano during eruption. **3. ashes,** mortal remains, esp. after cremation.

ash[2] (ash), *n.* any of various trees of the olive family with tough, straight-grained wood.

a•shamed (ə shāmd′), *adj.* **1.** feeling shame; embarrassed. **2.** unwilling because of fear of shame, ridicule, or disapproval. —**a•sham′ed•ly,** *adv.*

ash•en (ash′ən), *adj.* **1.** ash-colored; gray. **2.** extremely pale; pallid.

a•shore (ə shôr′), *adv.* to or onto the shore.

ash′tray′ *n.* a receptacle for tobacco ashes.

A•sia (ā′zhə), *n.* a continent bounded by Europe and the Arctic, Pacific, and Indian oceans.

A′sian *adj.* **1.** of Asia or its inhabitants. —*n.* **2.** a native or inhabitant of Asia.

A•si•at•ic (ā′zhē at′ik, ā′shē-), *adj., n. Sometimes Offensive.* ASIAN.

a•side (ə sīd′), *adv.* **1.** on, to, or toward one side. **2.** away, as from one's thoughts. **3.** in reserve: *to lay money aside.* —*n.* **4.** something spoken by an actor to the audience and supposedly not heard by others on stage. —*Idiom.* **5. aside from, a.** apart from; besides. **b.** except for.

as•i•nine (as′ə nīn′), *adj.* silly; stupid. —**as′i•nine′ly,** *adv.* —**as′i•nin′i•ty** (-nin′i tē), *n.*

ask (ask, äsk), *v.t.* **1.** to put a question to. **2.** to request information about. **3.** to put into words; utter. **4.** to request or request of. **5.** to set a price of. **6.** to invite. —*v.i.* **7.** to make inquiry; inquire. **8.** to make a request or petition. —**ask′er,** *n.*

a•skance (ə skans′), *adv.* **1.** with a side glance. **2.** with suspicion; skeptically.

a•skew (ə skyōō′), *adv.* **1.** to one side; awry. —*adj.* **2.** crooked; awry.

a•sleep (ə slēp′), *adv.* **1.** in or into a state of sleep. —*adj.* **2.** sleeping. **3.** dormant; inactive. **4.** numb. **5.** dead.

a•so•cial (ā sō′shəl), *adj.* **1.** not sociable or gregarious; antisocial. **2.** selfish.

asp (asp), *n.* any of several venomous Eurasian snakes.

as•par•a•gus (ə spar′ə gəs), *n.* **1.** a plant of the lily family cultivated for its edible shoots. **2.** these shoots.

as•pect (as′pekt), *n.* **1.** appearance to the eye or mind; look. **2.** a way in which something may be regarded. **3.** a phase, as of a problem. **4.** a side or surface facing a given direction.

as•pen (as′pən), *n.* any of various poplars having leaves that tremble in the slightest breeze.

as•per•i•ty (ə sper′i tē), *n.* **1.** harshness or sharpness of temper or manner. **2.** roughness, as of surface.

as•per•sion (ə spûr′zhən, -shən), *n.* **1.** a damaging or slandering remark. **2.** the act of slandering; defamation.

as•phalt (as′fôlt), *n.* **1.** a mixture of dark-colored, bituminous substances with gravel or crushed rock, used esp. for paving. —*v.t.* **2.** to cover or pave with asphalt.

as•phyx•i•a (as fik′sē ə), *n.* lack of oxygen and excess of carbon dioxide in the blood, as from suffocation, that causes unconsciousness or death.

as•phyx′i•ate′ *v.,* -at•ed, -at•ing. —*v.t.* **1.** to produce asphyxia in. —*v.i.* **2.** to become asphyxiated. —**as•phyx′i•a′tion,** *n.*

as•pire (ə spīr′), *v.i.,* -pired, -pir•ing. to long, aim, or seek ambitiously, esp. for something great or of high value. —**as•pi•ra•tion** (as′pə rā′shən), *n.*

as•pi•rin (as′pər in, -prin), *n., pl.* -rin, -rins. **1.** a white, crystalline derivative of salicylic acid used to relieve pain and fever. **2.** a tablet of aspirin.

ass (as), *n.* **1.** a long-eared domesticated mammal related to the horse. **2.** a stupid, foolish, or stubborn person.

as•sail (ə sāl′), *v.t.* **1.** to attack vigorously or violently. **2.** to attack verbally. —**as•sail′a•ble,** *adj.* —**as•sail′ant,** *n.*

as•sas•sin (ə sas′in), *n.* a murderer, esp. one who kills a politically prominent person. —**as•sas′si•nate′,** *v.t.,* -nat•ed, -nat•ing. —**as•sas′si•na′tion,** *n.* [< ML *assassinī* (pl.) < Ar *ḥashshāshīn* lit., eaters of hashish]

as•sault (ə sôlt′), *n.* **1.** a sudden violent attack. **2.** an unlawful attempt or threat to do bodily harm. **3.** RAPE[1] (def. 1). —*v.t.* **4.** to make an assault upon.

as•say (*v.* a sā′; *n.* as′ā, a sā′), *v.t.* **1.** to examine or analyze. **2.** to analyze (an ore, alloy, etc.) to determine the presence of metal, as gold. **3.** to analyze (a drug) to determine potency or composition. —*n.* **4.** an analysis of the composition, characteristics, or strength of a substance. —**as•say′er,** *n.*

as•sem•blage (ə sem′blij; *for 3 also Fr.* A sän-blazH′), *n.* **1.** a group of persons or things;

assembly. **2.** the act of assembling. **3.** a sculpture made up of a group of unrelated objects.

as•sem•ble (ə sem′bəl), *v.*, **-bled, -bling. —v.t. 1.** to bring together into one place, body, or whole. **2.** to put together the parts of. —*v.i.* **3.** to come together. —**as•sem′bler,** *n.*

as•sem′bly *n., pl.* **-blies. 1.** a group of persons gathered together. **2.** (*usu. cap.*) a legislative body, esp. the lower house of a legislature. **3.** a bugle call summoning troops to fall into ranks. **4.** the putting together of parts, as of complex machinery.

as•sem′bly•man or **-wom′an,** *n., pl.* **-men** or **-wom•en.** a member of a legislative assembly.

as•sent (ə sent′), *v.i.* **1.** to agree or concur; acquiesce. —*n.* **2.** agreement or concurrence; acquiescence.

as•sert (ə sûrt′), *v.t.* **1.** to state positively; declare. **2.** to maintain or defend (claims, rights, etc.). —*Idiom.* **3.** **assert oneself,** to claim one's rights or declare one's views insistently. —**as•ser′tion,** *n.*

as•ser′tive *adj.* confidently aggressive or self-assured. —**as•ser′tive•ly,** *adv.* —**as•ser′tive•ness,** *n.*

as•sess (ə ses′), *v.t.* **1.** to estimate the value of (property) for tax purposes. **2.** to determine the amount of (damages, a fine, etc.). **3.** to impose a tax or other charge on. **4.** to judge the value or character of; evaluate. —**as•sess′ment,** *n.* —**as•ses′sor,** *n.*

as•set (as′et), *n.* **1.** a useful and desirable thing or quality. **2.** a single item of ownership having exchange value. **3. assets, a.** the total resources of a person or business, as cash or real estate. **b.** property available for the payment of debts.

as•sid•u•ous (ə sij′oo̅ əs), *adj.* **1.** constant; unremitting. **2.** working diligently at a task; industrious. —**as•si•du•i•ty** (as′i doo̅′i tē, -dyoo̅′-), **as•sid′u•ous•ness,** *n.* —**as•sid′u•ous•ly,** *adv.*

as•sign (ə sīn′), *v.t.* **1.** to allocate; allot. **2.** to give out as a task. **3.** to appoint, as to a post or duty. **4.** to name; specify. **5.** to ascribe; attribute. **6.** *Law.* to transfer (property, rights, etc.). —**as•sign′a•ble,** *adj.* —**as•sign′er;** *Chiefly Law,* **as•sign•or** (ə sī-nôr′), *n.* —**as•sign′ment,** *n.*

as•sig•na•tion (as′ig nā′shən), *n.* an appointment for a meeting, esp. a secret rendezvous or tryst.

as•sim•i•late (ə sim′ə lāt′), *v.,* **-lat•ed, -lat•ing.** —*v.t.* **1.** to take in and incorporate as one's own. **2.** to bring into conformity with the customs and traditions of a dominant culture. **3.** to absorb (food) and incorporate it into the body. —*v.i.* **4.** to be or become assimilated. —**as•sim′i•la′tion,** *n.*

as•sist (ə sist′), *v.t., v.i.* **1.** to aid; help. —*n.* **2.** a play helping a teammate to score or put out an opponent. **3.** a helpful act. —**as•sis′tance,** *n.*

as•sis′tant *n.* **1.** a person who assists; helper. —*adj.* **2.** assisting; helpful. **3.** subordinate.

assn. or **Assn.,** association.

as•so•ci•ate (*v.* ə sō′shē āt′, -sē-; *n., adj.,* -it, -āt′), *v.,* **-at•ed, -at•ing,** *n., adj.* —*v.t.* **1.** to connect in thought, feeling, or memory. **2.** to commit (oneself) as a companion, partner, or colleague. **3.** to unite; combine. —*v.i.* **4.** to join together as partners, companions, or colleagues. —*n.* **5.** a partner or colleague. **6.** a companion; comrade. —*adj.* **7.** connected or joined, esp. as a companion or colleague. **8.** having subordinate status. —**as•so′ci•a′tion,** *n.*

as•so•nance (as′ə nəns), *n.* **1.** similarity of sounds in words or syllables. **2.** rhyme in which the same vowel sounds are used with different consonants. —**as′so•nant,** *adj.*

as•sort (ə sôrt′), *v.t.* to distribute or arrange according to kind or class; classify.

as•sort′ed *adj.* consisting of various kinds; miscellaneous.

as•sort′ment *n.* **1.** the act of assorting. **2.** a mixed collection.

asst. assistant.

as•suage (ə swāj′, ə swäzh′), *v.t.,* **-suaged, -suag•ing. 1.** to make less severe; ease. **2.** to appease; satisfy.

as•sume (ə soo̅m′), *v.t.,* **-sumed, -sum•ing. 1.** to take for granted without proof; suppose. **2.** to take

upon oneself. **3.** to take over the duties or responsibilities of. **4.** to pretend to have or be; feign.

as•sump•tion (ə sump′shən), *n.* **1.** something taken for granted; a supposition. **2.** the act of assuming. **3. a.** (*cap.*) the bodily taking up into heaven of the Virgin Mary. **b.** a feast commemorating this, celebrated on August 15. —**as•sump′tive,** *adj.*

as•sure (ə shoor′, ə shûr′), *v.t.,* **-sured, -sur•ing. 1.** to declare positively or confidently to. **2.** to make (a future event) sure; guarantee. **3.** to give confidence to; reassure. **4.** *Chiefly Brit.* to insure against loss. —**as•sur′ance,** *n.* —**as•sured′,** *adj., n.* —**as•sur′ed•ly,** *adv.* —**as•sur′er, as•su′ror,** *n.*

as•ta•tine (as′tə tēn′, -tin), *n.* a rare element of the halogen family. *Symbol:* At; *at. no.:* 85.

as•ter (as′tər), *n.* any of various plants with white, pink, or blue rays around a yellow disk. [< L < Gk *astḗr* star]

as•ter•isk (as′tə risk), *n.* a starlike symbol (*) used in writing and printing as a reference mark or to indicate an omission.

a•stern (ə stûrn′), *adv.* **1.** behind a ship or aircraft. **2.** in a backward direction.

as•ter•oid (as′tə roid′), *n.* any of the thousands of small, solid bodies that revolve about the sun in orbits mostly between Mars and Jupiter.

asth•ma (az′mə), *n.* an often allergic respiratory disorder characterized by wheezing and difficulty in breathing. —**asth•mat′ic** (-mat′ik), *adj., n.*

a•stig•ma•tism (ə stig′mə tiz′əm), *n.* a defect of the eye or of a lens in which rays of light do not converge on a single focal point. —**as•tig•mat•ic** (as′tig mat′ik), *adj.*

a•stir (ə stûr′), *adj.* **1.** moving or stirring. **2.** out of bed.

as•ton•ish (ə ston′ish), *v.t.* to fill with sudden surprise or wonder; amaze. —**as•ton′ish•ing,** *adj.* —**as•ton′ish•ing•ly,** *adv.* —**as•ton′ish•ment,** *n.*

as•tound (ə stound′), *v.t.* to overwhelm with amazement. —**as•tound′ing,** *adj.* —**as•tound′ing•ly,** *adv.*

as•tral (as′trəl), *adj.* of, from, or like the stars.

a•stray (ə strā′), *adv., adj.* **1.** off the correct path or route. **2.** in or into error.

a•stride (ə strīd′), *adv.* **1.** with a leg on either side. **2.** with legs apart. —*prep.* **3.** with a leg on each side of. **4.** on both sides of.

as•trin•gent (ə strin′jənt), *adj.* **1.** causing constriction of soft tissue. **2.** harshly biting; caustic. —*n.* **3.** an astringent substance. —**as•trin′gen•cy,** *n.*

as•trol•o•gy (ə strol′ə jē), *n.* the study that assumes and attempts to interpret the influence of the heavenly bodies on human affairs. —**as•trol′o•ger,** *n.* —**as•tro•log•i•cal** (as′trə loj′i kəl), *adj.*

as•tro•naut (as′trə nôt′, -not′), *n.* a person engaged in or trained for spaceflight.

as′tro•nau′tics *n.* the science and technology of spaceflight, including interplanetary and interstellar flight. —**as′tro•nau′tic, as′tro•nau′ti•cal,** *adj.*

as•tro•nom•i•cal (as′trə nom′i kəl) also **-nom′ic,** *adj.* **1.** of astronomy. **2.** extremely large; enormous. —**as′tro•nom′i•cal•ly,** *adv.*

as•tron•o•my (ə stron′ə mē), *n.* the science that deals with the material universe beyond the earth's atmosphere. —**as•tron′o•mer,** *n.*

as•tro•phys•ics (as′trō fiz′iks), *n.* the branch of astronomy that deals with the physical properties of celestial bodies. —**as′tro•phys′i•cist** (-ə sist), *n.*

as•tute (ə stoot′, ə styoot′), *adj.* **1.** keenly perceptive or discerning. **2.** shrewd; crafty. —**as•tute′ly,** *adv.* —**as•tute′ness,** *n.*

a•sun•der (ə sun′dər), *adv., adj.* **1.** in or into separate parts. **2.** widely separated; apart.

a•sy•lum (ə sī′ləm), *n.* **1.** (esp. formerly) an institution for the care of ill or needy persons. **2.** a place of refuge; sanctuary. **3.** protection granted by a government to political refugees.

a•sym′me•try (ā sim′i trē) *n.* lack of symmetry. —**a′sym•met′ric** (ā′sə me′trik), **a′sym•met′ri•cal,** *adj.*

at (at; *unstressed* ət, it), *prep.* **1.** (used to indicate a point or place in space): *stood at the door.* **2.** (used to indicate a location or position, as in time): *at age 65.* **3.** (used to indicate amount, degree, or rate): *at great speed.* **4.** (used to indicate a direction or objective): *Look at that.* **5.** (used to indicate involvement): *at play.* **6.** (used to indicate a condition): *at ease.* **7.** (used to indicate a cause): *annoyed at their carelessness.* **8.** (used to indicate relative value): *at cost.*

At *Chem. Symbol.* astatine.

at•a•vism (at′ə viz′əm), *n.* the reappearance in an individual of characteristics of a remote ancestor that have been absent in intervening generations. —at′a•vist, *n.* —at′a•vis′tic, *adj.*

ate (āt; *Brit.* et), *v.* pt. of EAT.

-ate¹, a suffix meaning: of, having, or resembling (*compassionate*); to become or cause to become (*agitate*); to produce (*ulcerate*); to treat with (*aerate*).

-ate², a suffix meaning a salt of an acid (*sulfate*).

-ate³, a suffix meaning office, rule, or function (*consulate*).

at•el•ier (at′l yā′), *n.* a workshop or studio, esp. of an artist.

a•the•ism (ā′thē iz′əm), *n.* the doctrine or belief that there is no God. —a′the•ist, *n.* —a′the•is′tic, *adj.*

ath•lete (ath′lēt), *n.* a person trained or gifted in exercises or contests involving physical agility, stamina, or strength. —ath•let′ic (-let′ik), *adj.* —ath•let′i•cal•ly, *adv.*

ath′lete's foot′ *n.* ringworm of the feet.

at•las (at′ləs), *n.* a bound collection of maps.

At•las (at′ləs), *n.* a Titan condemned by Zeus to support the sky on his shoulders.

ATM an electronic machine that provides banking services when activated by insertion of a plastic card. [*a(utomated)-t(eller) m(achine)*]

at•mos•phere (at′məs fēr′), *n.* **1.** the gaseous envelope surrounding a heavenly body, esp. the earth; air. **2.** a conventional unit of pressure, the normal pressure of the air at sea level, about 14.7 pounds per square inch. **3.** a pervading environment or influence. **4.** a dominant mood or tone, as of a work of art. —at′mos•pher′ic (-fer′ik), *adj.* —at′mos•pher′i•cal•ly, *adv.*

at•oll (at′ôl, -ol, -ōl), *n.* a ring-shaped coral reef enclosing a lagoon.

at•om (at′əm), *n.* **1.** the smallest component of an element having the properties of that element, consisting of a nucleus of neutrons and protons surrounded by electrons. **2.** something extremely small; speck. —a•tom•ic (ə tom′ik), *adj.* —a•tom′i•cal•ly, *adv.*

atom′ic (or **at′om**) **bomb′**, *n.* a bomb whose explosive force comes from a chain reaction based on nuclear fission.

at•om•iz•er (at′ə mī′zər), *n.* an apparatus for reducing liquids to a fine spray, as for cosmetic application.

a•ton•al (ā tōn′l), *adj. Music.* lacking tonality. —a′to•nal′i•ty, *n.*

a•tone (ə tōn′), *v.i.*, **a•toned, a•ton•ing.** to make amends, as for an offense or sin. —a•tone′ment, *n.*

a•top (ə top′), *adj.*, *adv.* **1.** on or at the top. —prep. **2.** on the top of.

a•tri•um (ā′trē əm), *n.*, *pl.* **a•tri•a** (ā′trē ə), **a•tri•ums. 1. a.** an often skylighted court in a public building, as a hotel. **b.** the main or central room of an ancient Roman house. **2.** either of the two upper chambers of the heart that receive blood from the veins. —a′tri•al, *adj.*

a•tro•cious (ə trō′shəs), *adj.* **1.** extremely wicked, cruel, or brutal. **2.** shockingly bad; abominable. —a•tro′cious•ly, *adv.* —a•tro′cious•ness, *n.* —a•troc′i•ty (ə tros′i tē), *n.*, *pl.* **-ties.**

at•ro•phy (a′trə fē), *n.*, *v.*, **-phied, -phy•ing.** —n. **1.** a wasting away of the body or of a bodily organ or part. —v.t., v.i. **2.** to affect with or undergo atrophy.

at•ro•pine (a′trə pēn′, -pin), *n.* a poisonous alkaloid obtained from belladonna and used esp. to dilate the pupil of the eye.

at•tach (ə tach′), *v.t.* **1.** to fasten or join; connect. **2.** to assign or attribute. **3.** to bind by emotional

ties, as of affection. **4.** to take (property) by legal authority. —v.i. **5.** to become attached. —at•tach′a•ble, *adj.*

at•ta•ché (at′ə shā′), *n.*, *pl.* **-chés.** a diplomatic official or military officer assigned to an embassy, esp. in a technical capacity.

at•tach•ment (ə tach′mənt), *n.* **1.** the act of attaching or state of being attached. **2.** an emotional tie, as of affection. **3.** a fastening or tie. **4.** an additional or supplementary device. **5.** seizure of property by legal authority.

at•tack (ə tak′), *v.t.* **1.** to set upon in a forceful, violent, hostile, or aggressive way. **2.** to abuse verbally. **3.** to go to work on vigorously. —v.i. **4.** to make an attack. —n. **5.** the act of attacking. **6.** an onset of disease or illness. —at•tack′er, *n.*

at•tain (ə tān′), *v.t.* **1.** to achieve or accomplish, esp. by effort. —v.i. **2.** to arrive at or succeed in reaching or obtaining something. —at•tain′a•ble, *adj.* —at•tain′a•bil′i•ty. —at•tain′ment, *n.*

at•tempt (ə tempt′), *v.t.* **1.** to make an effort at; try. —n. **2.** an effort made to accomplish something. **3.** an attack or assault.

at•tend (ə tend′), *v.t.* **1.** to be present at. **2.** to go with; accompany. **3.** to take care of; minister to. **4.** to wait upon; serve. —v.i. **5.** to take care or charge. **6.** to apply oneself. **7.** to pay attention. **8.** to be present.

at•tend′ant *n.* **1.** a person who attends another, as to perform a service. —adj. **2.** being present or in attendance; accompanying.

at•ten′tion (-shən), *n.* **1.** the act or faculty of concentrating the mind on a single object, thought, or event. **2.** observant care or consideration. **3.** civility or courtesy. **4.** a military position with eyes to the front, arms to the sides, and heels together. —at•ten′tive, *adj.* —at•ten′tive•ly, *adv.* —at•ten′tive•ness, *n.*

at•ten′u•ate′ (-yōō āt′), *v.*, **-at•ed, -at•ing.** —v.t. **1.** to reduce in force, intensity, effect, or strength; weaken. **2.** to make slender or fine. —v.i. **3.** to become attenuated. —at•ten′u•a′tion, *n.*

at•test (ə test′), *v.t.* **1.** to affirm as correct, accurate, or genuine, esp. in writing. **2.** to give proof or evidence of; manifest. —v.i. **3.** to testify or bear witness. —at•tes•ta•tion (at′es tā′shən), *n.*

at•tic (at′ik), *n.* the part of a building, esp. of a house, directly under the roof.

at•tire (ə tīr′), *v.*, **-tired, -tir•ing,** *n.* —v.t. **1.** to dress or array. —n. **2.** clothes or apparel.

at•ti•tude (at′i tōōd′, -tyōōd′), *n.* **1.** manner, disposition, or feeling with regard to a person or thing. **2.** position or posture of the body. **3.** the inclination of the three principal axes of an aircraft relative to a reference point, as the ground. **4.** *Slang.* a testy, uncooperative disposition. —at′ti•tu′di•nal, *adj.*

attn. attention.

at•tor•ney (ə tûr′nē), *n.*, *pl.* **-neys.** a person legally authorized to act for another, esp. a lawyer. [< AF *attourne* lit., (one who is) turned to]

attor′ney gen′eral, *n.*, *pl.* **attorneys general, attorney generals.** the chief law officer of a country or state and head of its legal department.

at•tract (ə trakt′), *v.t.* **1.** to draw or pull by a physical force. **2.** to draw by appealing to the emotions or senses or by stimulating interest. —v.i. **3.** to possess attraction.

at•trac′tion *n.* **1.** the act, power, or property of attracting. **2.** an attractive quality or feature. **3.** a person or thing that attracts or entices. **4.** an electric or magnetic force that tends to draw oppositely charged bodies together.

at•trac′tive (-tiv) *adj.* **1.** providing pleasure; charming. **2.** arousing interest. **3.** having the power to attract. —at•trac′tive•ly, *adv.* —at•trac′tive•ness, *n.*

at•trib•ute (*v.* ə trib′yōōt; *n.* a′trə byōōt′), *v.*, **-ut•ed, -ut•ing,** *n.* —v.t. **1.** to regard as caused by, created by, or belonging to a specified person or thing. —n. **at•tri•bute 2.** a quality, characteristic, or property of a person or thing. —at•trib′ut•a•ble, *adj.* —at′tri•bu′tion, *n.*

at•tri•tion (ə trish′ən), *n.* **1.** a reduction in a work force without firing of personnel, as when workers retire and are not replaced. **2.** a wearing down or away by or as if by friction. —**at•tri′tion•al,** adj.

at•tune (ə to̅o̅n′, ə tyo̅o̅n′), v.t., **-tuned, -tun•ing.** to bring into accord, harmony, or sympathetic relationship.

atty. attorney.

ATV a small motor vehicle with treads, wheels, or both, capable of going over any nonroad surface including water. [a(ll)-t(errain) v(ehicle)]

a•typ•i•cal (ā tip′i kəl), adj. not typical; irregular. —**a•typ′i•cal•ly,** adv.

Au Chem. Symbol. gold. [< L aurum]

au•burn (ô′bərn), n. **1.** a reddish brown color. —adj. **2.** of the color auburn.

auc•tion (ôk′shən), n. **1.** a public sale at which property or goods are sold to the highest bidder. —v.t. **2.** to sell at auction. —**auc′tion•eer′,** n.

au•da•cious (ô dā′shəs), adj. **1.** bold; daring. **2.** insolent; brazen. —**au•da′cious•ly,** adv. —**au•dac•i•ty** (ô das′i tē), n.

au•di•ble (ô′də bəl), adj. capable of being heard. —**au′di•bil′i•ty,** n. —**au′di•bly,** adv.

au•di•ence (ô′dē əns), n. **1.** a group of spectators or listeners. **2.** the persons reached by a book, broadcast, film, etc.; public. **3.** an opportunity to be heard. **4.** a formal interview, as with a sovereign.

au•di•o (ô′dē ō′), adj. **1.** of or used in the transmission, reception, or reproduction of sound. **2.** of frequencies in the audible range. —n. **3.** the audio elements of television or films. **4.** the transmission, reception, or reproduction of sound.

au′di•ol′o•gy (-ol′ə jē), n. the study and treatment of hearing disorders. —**au′di•o•log′i•cal** (-ə loj′i kəl), adj. —**au′di•ol′o•gist,** n.

au′di•om′e•ter (-om′i tər), n. an instrument for gauging and recording acuity of hearing.

au′di•o•tape′ (ô′dē ō-), n. magnetic tape on which sound is recorded.

au′di•o•vis′u•al adj. of, involving, or directed at both hearing and sight.

au•dit (ô′dit), n. **1.** an official examination and verification of financial accounts and records. —v.t. **2.** to make an audit of. **3.** to attend (a course) as an auditor.

au•di•tion (ô dish′ən), n. **1.** a trial hearing or viewing, esp. of a performer seeking employment. —v.t., v.i. **2.** to give an audition (to).

au•di•tor (ô′di tər), n. **1.** a person authorized to audit financial accounts. **2.** one who attends an academic course to listen but not receive credit. **3.** a hearer; listener.

au′di•to′ri•um (-tôr′ē əm), n. **1.** a room set apart for an audience, as in a school. **2.** a building or hall for public gatherings.

au′di•to′ry adj. of hearing, the sense of hearing, or the organs of hearing.

Aug or **Aug.,** August.

au•ger (ô′gər), n. a tool for boring holes.

aught¹ (ôt), n. anything whatever: for aught I know.

aught² (ôt), n. a cipher (0); zero.

aug•ment (ôg ment′), v.t., v.i., to make or become larger; enlarge. —**aug′men•ta′tion,** n.

au•gur (ô′gər), n. **1.** a soothsayer; prophet. —v.t. **2.** to predict, as from omens. **3.** to serve as an omen of; foreshadow. —v.i. **4.** to be a sign; bode. —**au•gu•ry** (ô′gyə rē), n., pl. **-ries.**

au•gust (ô gust′), adj. inspiring reverence or admiration; majestic. —**au•gust′ly,** adv. —**au•gust′ness,** n.

Au•gust (ô′gəst), n. the eighth month of the year, containing 31 days.

auk (ôk), n. a diving bird of northern seas, with webbed feet and small wings.

auld lang syne (ôld′ lang zīn′), n. fondly remembered times.

aunt (ant, änt), n. **1.** the sister of one's father or mother. **2.** the wife of one's uncle.

au pair (ō pâr′), n. a person, usu. a young foreign visitor, who performs household tasks in exchange for room and board.

au•ra (ôr′ə), n., pl. **-ras. 1.** a distinctive and per-

vasive quality surrounding a person or thing. **2.** a light or radiance claimed to emanate from the body.

au•ral (ôr′əl), adj. of the ear or the sense of hearing. —**au′ral•ly,** adv.

au•re•ole (ôr′ē ōl′), n. a halo.

au re•voir (ō Rə vwАr′; Eng. ō′ rə vwär′), interj. French. good-bye; until we see each other again.

au•ri•cle (ôr′i kəl), n. **1.** the outer ear. **2.** (loosely) the atrium of the heart.

au•ro•ra (ə rôr′ə), n., pl. **-ras.** a display of bands of light sporadically seen in night skies of both hemispheres.

aus•pice (ô′spis), n., pl. **aus•pic•es** (ô′spə siz′). **1.** Usu., **-pices.** patronage; sponsorship. **2.** Often, **-pices.** a sign, esp. a favorable one; portent.

aus•pi′cious adj. **1.** promising success; favorable. **2.** favored by fortune; fortunate. —**aus•pi′cious•ly,** adv. —**aus•pi′cious•ness,** n.

aus•tere (ô stēr′), adj. **1.** severe, as in manner; forbidding. **2.** severely moral; ascetic. **3.** without ornament or adornment. —**aus•tere′ly,** adv. —**aus•ter′i•ty** (ô ster′-), n.

Aus•tral•ia (ô strāl′yə), n. **1.** a continent SE of Asia, between the Indian and Pacific oceans. **2.** a nation consisting of this continent and the island of Tasmania. —**Aus•tral′ian,** adj., n.

Aus•tri•a (ô′strē ə), n. a republic in central Europe. —**Aus′tri•an,** adj., n.

au•then•tic (ô then′tik), adj. **1.** not false or copied; genuine; real. **2.** entitled to acceptance or belief because of agreement with known facts or experience; trustworthy. —**au•then′ti•cal•ly,** adv. —**au′•then•tic′i•ty** (-tis′i tē), n.

au•thor (ô′thər), n. **1.** the composer of a literary work; writer. **2.** one who creates or originates something. **3.** the writer of a software program. —v.t. **4.** to be the author of. —**au′thor•ship′,** n.

au•thor•i•tar•i•an (ə thôr′i târ′ē ən, ə thor′-), adj. **1.** favoring or requiring complete obedience to authority. **2.** of or being a government in which authority is centered in a person or group not accountable to the people. —n. **3.** one who favors or acts according to authoritarian principles. —**au•thor′i•tar′i•an•ism,** n.

au•thor′i•ta′tive (-tā′tiv), adj. **1.** having the sanction or weight of authority. **2.** supported by evidence and accepted by most authorities. —**au•thor′i•ta′tive•ly,** adv. —**au•thor′i•ta′tive•ness,** n.

au•thor′i•ty n., pl. **-ties. 1.** the power to control, command, or determine. **2.** a power or right delegated or given. **3.** a person or body of persons in whom authority is vested. **4.** Usu., **-ties.** government. **5. a.** an accepted source of information, advice, or substantiation. **b.** a quotation or citation from such a source. **6.** an expert on a subject. **7.** persuasive force; conviction.

au•thor•ize (ô′thə rīz′), v.t., **-ized, -iz•ing. 1.** to give authority or official power to. **2.** to give approval for; sanction. **3.** to justify. —**au′thor•i•za′•tion,** n.

Au′thorized Ver′sion n. KING JAMES VERSION.

au•tism (ô′tiz əm), n. a developmental disorder characterized by extreme self-absorption, and detachment from reality. —**au•tis′tic,** adj.

au•to (ô′tō), n., pl. **-tos.** an automobile.

auto- a combining form meaning self or same (autograph).

au•to•bi•og•ra•phy (ô′tə bī og′rə fē, -bē-), n., pl. **-phies.** a history of a person's life written by that person. —**au′to•bi•o•graph′i•cal** (-ə graf′i kəl), adj.

au•toc•ra•cy (ô tok′rə sē), n., pl. **-cies.** government in which one person has unlimited authority.

au•to•crat (ô′tə krat′), n. **1.** a ruler with unlimited power. **2.** an authoritarian or domineering person. —**au′to•crat′ic,** adj. —**au′to•crat′i•cal•ly,** adv.

au•to•di•dact (ô′tō dī′dakt), n. a self-taught person.

au•to•graph (ô′tə graf′, -gräf′), n. **1.** a person's signature. **2.** something, esp. a manuscript, written in a person's own hand. —v.t. **3.** to write one's signature on or in.

au•to•im•mune (ô′tō i myo̅o̅n′), adj. of or

pertaining to the immune response of an organism against any of its own components.

au′to•mat′ (ô′tə mat′) *n.* a restaurant with coin-operated service.

au•to•mate (ô′tə māt′), *v.t., v.i.,* **-mat•ed, -mat• ing.** to operate by or undergo automation.

au′to•mat′ic (-mat′ik), *adj.* **1.** capable of operating independently of human intervention. **2.** involuntary; reflex. **3.** done unconsciously or from force of habit; mechanical. **4.** (of a firearm) capable of continuous operation. —*n.* **5.** an automatic machine or device, esp. a pistol. —**au′to•mat′i•cal•ly,** *adv.*

au′tomat′ic pi′lot *n.* an electronic control system, as on an aircraft, that automatically maintains a preset heading and attitude.

au′to•ma′tion (-mā′shən), *n.* the technique or system of operating or controlling a mechanical process by automatic means, as by electronic devices.

au•tom′a•ton′ (-ton′, -tn), *n., pl.* **-tons, -ta** (-tə). **1.** a robot. **2.** a person who acts in a mechanical manner.

au•to•mo•bile (ô′tə mə bēl′), *n.* a passenger vehicle typically having four wheels and an internal-combustion engine.

au′to•mo′tive (-mō′tiv), *adj.* **1.** of motor vehicles, esp. automobiles. **2.** propelled by a self-contained motor or engine.

au•ton′o•my (ô tun′ə mē) *n.* self-government. —**au•ton′o•mous,** *adj.*

au•top•sy (ô′top sē), *n., pl.* **-sies,** *v.,* **-sied, -sy• ing.** —*n.* **1.** examination of a body after death, as for determination of the cause of death. —*v.t.* **2.** to perform an autopsy on.

au•tumn (ô′təm), *n.* the season between summer and winter; fall. —**au•tum•nal** (ô tum′nl), *adj.*

aux•il•ia•ry (ôg zil′yə rē, -zil′ə-), *adj., n., pl.* **-ries.** —*adj.* **1.** additional; supplementary. **2.** used as a reserve in case of need. **3.** subsidiary; secondary. —*n.* **4.** an auxiliary person, thing, or group. **5.** AUXILIARY VERB.

auxil′iary verb′ *n.* a verb, as *be* or *have,* used with a main verb to express distinctions of tense, voice, etc.

a•vail (ə vāl′), *v.t., v.i.* **1.** to be of use, advantage, or value (to). —*n.* **2.** use or advantage. —*Idiom.* **3.** avail oneself of, to make use of.

a•vail′a•ble *adj.* **1.** ready for use; at hand. **2.** readily obtainable; accessible. —**a•vail′a•bil′i•ty,** *n.*

av•a•lanche (av′ə lanch′, -länch′), *n.* **1.** a large mass of snow, ice, etc., sliding down a mountain slope. **2.** an overwhelming quantity.

a•vant-garde (ə vänt′gärd′, av′änt-), *n.* **1.** the advance group in a field, esp. in the arts, whose works are unorthodox and experimental. —*adj.* **2.** characteristic of or belonging to the avant-garde.

av•a•rice (av′ər is), *n.* insatiable greed for riches. —**av′a•ri′cious** (-ə rish′əs), —**av′a•ri′cious• ly,** *adv.*

ave. avenue.

a•venge (ə venj′), *v.t.,* **a•venged, a•veng•ing. 1.** to take vengeance or exact satisfaction for. **2.** to take vengeance on behalf of. —**a•veng′er,** *n.*

av•e•nue (av′ə nyōo′, -nōo′), *n.* **1.** a wide street or main thoroughfare. **2.** a means of access or attainment.

a•ver (ə vûr′), *v.t.,* **a•verred, a•ver•ring.** to assert with confidence; declare.

av•er•age (av′ər ij, av′rij), *n., adj., v.,* **-aged, -ag• ing.** —*n.* **1.** an arithmetic mean. **2.** a typical or usual amount, rate, or level. —*adj.* **3.** of or forming an average. **4.** not unusual; common. —*v.t.* **5.** to find an average value for. **6.** (of a variable quantity) to have as an arithmetic mean. **7.** to do, be, or have typically. —*v.i.* **8.** to have or be at an average. —*Idiom.* **9. on the average,** usually; typically.

a•verse (ə vûrs′), *adj.* having a strong feeling of antipathy or repugnance.

a•ver•sion (ə vûr′zhən), *n.* **1.** a feeling of repugnance for something and a desire to avoid it. **2.** a cause or object of aversion.

a•vert (ə vûrt′), *v.t.* **1.** to turn away or aside. **2.** to ward off; prevent.

avg. average.

a′vi•ar′y (-er′ē), *n., pl.* **-ies.** a place, as a large cage, in which birds are kept. —**a′vi•a•rist** (-ar-ist), *n.*

a•vi•a•tion (ā′vē ā′shən), *n.* the design, development, production, operation, or use of aircraft. [< F, = L *avi(s)* bird + *-ation*] —**a′vi•a′tor,** *n.*

av•id (av′id), *adj.* **1.** enthusiastic; keen. **2.** keenly desirous; eager. —**a•vid•i•ty** (ə vid′i tē), *n.* —**av′id•ly,** *adv.*

av•o•ca•do (av′ə kä′dō, ä′və-), *n., pl.* **-dos. 1.** a pear-shaped fruit with soft, light green pulp. **2.** the tropical American tree that bears avocados.

av•o•ca•tion (av′ə kā′shən), *n.* something done in addition to a principal occupation, esp. for pleasure; hobby. —**av′o•ca′tion•al,** *adj.*

a•void (ə void′), *v.t.* **1.** to keep clear of; shun. **2.** to prevent from happening. —**a•void′a•ble,** *adj.* —**a•void′a•bly,** *adv.* —**a•void′ance,** *n.*

av•oir•du•pois (av′ər də poiz′), *n.* **1.** AVOIRDUPOIS WEIGHT. **2.** *Informal.* bodily weight, esp. excess heaviness.

avoirdupois′ weight′ *n.* the system of weights based on a pound of 16 ounces, used in Great Britain and the U.S.

a•vow (ə vou′), *v.t.* to declare frankly or openly. —**a•vow′al,** *n.* —**a•vowed′,** *adj.* —**a•vow′ed•ly,** *adv.*

a•wait (ə wāt′), *v.t.* **1.** to wait for; expect. **2.** to be in store for. —*v.i.* **3.** to wait.

a•wake (ə wāk′), *v.,* **a•woke** or **a•waked, a•woke** or **a•waked** or **a•wo•ken, a•wak•ing,** *adj.* —*v.t., v.i.* **1.** to rouse or emerge from sleep. **2.** to make or become active or alert. —*adj.* **3.** not sleeping. **4.** vigilant; alert.

a•wak′en *v.t., v.i.* to awake; waken. —**a•wak′ en•ing,** *adj., n.*

a•ward (ə wôrd′), *v.t.* **1.** to give as due or merited. **2.** to assign by judicial decree. —*n.* **3.** something awarded. **4.** a decision, as of an arbitrator.

a•ware (ə wâr′), *adj.* **1.** having knowledge or realization; conscious. **2.** informed. —**a•ware′ness,** *n.*

a•wash (ə wosh′, ə wôsh′), *adj., adv.* **1.** washed by waves or water. **2.** covered with water. **3.** covered, filled, or crowded.

a•way (ə wā′), *adv.* **1.** from this or that place. **2.** to another place or in another direction. **3.** to or at a distance; far. **4.** out of one's possession or use: *to give money away.* **5.** out of existence or notice: *to fade away.* **6.** incessantly or relentlessly. **7.** without hesitation: *Fire away.* —*adj.* **8.** absent. **9.** distant in place or time.

awe (ô), *n., v.,* **awed, aw•ing.** —*n.* **1.** a feeling of reverence, fear, and wonder. —*v.t.* **2.** to inspire or fill with awe.

awe•some (ô′səm), *adj.* **1.** inspiring or characterized by awe. **2.** *Slang.* very impressive. —**awe′ some•ly,** *adv.* —**awe′some•ness,** *n.*

awe′struck′ or **-strick′en,** *adj.* filled with awe.

aw•ful (ô′fəl), *adj.* **1.** extremely bad or unpleasant. **2.** inspiring fear. **3.** inspiring awe. **4.** *Informal.* very great. —*adv.* **5.** *Informal.* very; extremely. —**aw′ ful•ness,** *n.*

aw′ful•ly *adv.* **1.** very badly. **2.** *Informal.* very.

a•while (ə hwīl′, ə wīl′), *adv.* for a short time.

awk•ward (ôk′wərd), *adj.* **1.** lacking skill or dexterity; clumsy. **2.** lacking grace or ease. **3.** hard to use or handle; unwieldy. **4.** hard to deal with; difficult. **5.** embarrassing or inconvenient. —**awk′ ward•ly,** *adv.* —**awk′ward•ness,** *n.*

awl (ôl), *n.* a pointed instrument for piercing holes, as in leather.

awn (ôn), *n.* any of the bristles on a spike of a grass plant.

awn•ing (ô′ning), *n.* a rooflike shelter, as of canvas, that provides protection from the sun or rain.

AWOL (*pronounced as initials or* ā′wôl, ā′wol), *adj., adv.* **1.** absent without leave. —*n.* **2.** a person, esp. a soldier, who is absent without leave.

a•wry (ə rī′), *adv., adj.* **1.** askew. **2.** amiss; wrong.

ax or **axe** (aks), *n., v.,* **axed, ax•ing.** —*n.* **1.** a chopping tool with a blade on a handle. —*v.t.* **2.** to chop or split with an ax. **3.** to dismiss or remove, esp. brutally or summarily. **—Idiom. 4. have an ax to grind,** to have a particular personal or selfish motive.

ax•i•om (ak/sē əm), *n.* **1.** a self-evident truth that requires no proof. **2.** a proposition assumed without proof for the sake of studying its consequences. **—ax/i•o•mat/ic,** *adj.*

ax•is (ak/sis), *n., pl.* **ax•es** (ak/sēz). **1.** the line about which a rotating body turns. **2. a.** a central line that bisects a body or figure and in relation to which symmetry is determined. **b.** a line used as a reference for determining the position of a point or series of points. **3.** the main support of a plant or inflorescence. **—ax/i•al,** *adj.*

ax•le (ak/səl), *n.* a spindle or shaft on which a wheel or pair of wheels rotates.

a•ya•tol•lah (ä/yə tō/lə), *n.* a title for an Islamic religious leader with advanced knowledge of Islamic law. [< Pers < Ar *āyat allāh* sign of God]

aye¹ or **ay** (ī), *adv., n., pl.* **ayes. —adv. 1.** yes. **—n. 2.** an affirmative vote or voter.

aye² or **ay** (ā), *adv.* Archaic. ever or always.

a•zal•ea (ə zāl/yə), *n., pl.* **-eas.** a shrub of the heath family, with variously colored flowers.

Az•er•bai•jan (az/ər bī jän/), *n.* a republic in W Asia, N of Iran: formerly a part of the USSR.

AZT Trademark. an antiviral drug used in the treatment of AIDS.

Az•tec (az/tek), *n.* a member of an American Indian people whose empire in Mexico was conquered by Spaniards in 1521. **—Az/tec•an,** *adj.*

az•ure (azh/ər), *n.* **1.** the blue of a clear or unclouded sky. **—adj. 2.** of or having the color azure.

a B c d e f g h i j k l m n o p q r s t u v w x y z

B, b (bē), *n., pl.* **Bs** or **B's, bs** or **b's.** the second letter of the English alphabet, a consonant.

B Symbol. **1.** the second in order or in a series. **2.** a grade or mark indicating good but not excellent quality. **3.** a major blood group. **4.** Chem. boron. **5.** a designation for a low-budget motion picture.

b. 1. bachelor. **2.** bass. **3.** born.

Ba Chem. Symbol. barium.

B.A. Bachelor of Arts.

bab•ble (bab/əl), *v.,* **-bled, -bling,** *n. —v.i.* **1.** to utter sounds or words indistinctly. **2.** to talk irrationally or excessively. **3.** to make a murmuring sound. **—v.t. 4.** to utter in a foolish or meaningless fashion. **5.** to reveal thoughtlessly. **—n. 6.** the act or sound of babbling. **—bab/bler,** *n.*

babe (bāb), *n.* **1.** an infant; baby. **2.** a naive person. **3.** Slang (sometimes disparaging). a girl or woman.

ba•boon (ba bōōn/, bə-), *n.* a large monkey of Africa and Arabia with a doglike muzzle.

ba•by (bā/bē), *n., pl.* **-bies,** *adj., v.,* **-bied, -by•ing. —n. 1.** an infant or very young child. **2.** the youngest member of a family or group. **3.** a childish person. **4.** Informal. **a.** Sometimes Disparaging. a girl or woman. **b.** something that elicits one's special attention or pride. **—adj. 5.** of, for, or like a baby. **6.** smaller than the usual. **—v.t. 7.** to pamper. **—ba/by•hood/,** *n.* **—ba/by•ish,** *adj.*

ba/by boom/ *n.* a period of increase in the birthrate, as that following World War II. **—ba/by boom/er,** *n.*

ba/by car/riage *n.* a conveyance for pushing a baby about, resembling a basket set on four wheels.

ba/by-sit/ *v.,* **-sat, -sit•ting. —v.i. 1.** to take charge of a child while the parents are temporarily away. **—v.t. 2.** to baby-sit for (a child). **—ba/by-sit/ter,** *n.*

bac•ca•lau•re•ate (bak/ə lôr/ē it, -lor/-), *n.* **1.** BACHELOR'S DEGREE. **2.** a sermon delivered at a commencement.

bac•cha•nal (bak/ə nal/), *n.* an occasion of drunken revelry. **—bac/cha•na/li•an** (-nä/lē ən, -nāl/yən), *adj., n.*

bach•e•lor (bach/ə lər), *n.* **1.** an unmarried man. **2.** a person with a bachelor's degree. [< OF < VL *baccalār(is)* farmhand] **—bach/e•lor•hood/,** *n.*

bach/elor's degree/ *n.* a degree awarded by a college or university to a person who has completed undergraduate studies.

ba•cil•lus (bə sil/əs), *n., pl.* **-cil•li** (-sil/ī). any of several rod-shaped bacteria that produce spores. **—bac•il•lar•y** (bas/ə ler/ē), *adj.*

back¹ (bak), *n.* **1.** the rear part of the human body, from the neck to the end of the spine. **2.** the corresponding part of an animal's body. **3.** the part that forms the rear or reverse of any object or structure. **4.** the backbone. **5.** a football player stationed in the backfield. **—v.t. 6.** to support, as with authority or money: *to back a candidate.* **7.** to bet on. **8.** to cause to move backward. **—v.i. 9.** to go or move backward. **10. back down,** to abandon an argument or position. **11. ~ off,** to move back from something; retreat. **12. ~ out,** to fail to keep an engagement or promise. **13. ~ up, a.** to move backward. **b.** to support. **c.** to accumulate or become clogged due to a stoppage. **d.** to copy (a computer file or program) as a precaution against failure. **—adj. 14.** situated at or in the rear. **15.** pertaining to the past. **16.** in arrears: *back pay.* **17.** moving backward. **—Idiom. 18. behind one's back,** without one's knowledge, esp. treacherously or secretly. **19. (in) back of,** at the rear of; behind. **—back/er, n. —back/ing,** *n.*

back² (bak), *adv.* **1.** at, to, or toward the rear. **2.** in or toward the past. **3.** at or toward the original starting place or condition. **4.** in direct payment or return: *to answer back.* **5.** in a state of restraint or retention. **—Idiom. 6. back and forth,** backward and forward. **7. go back on,** to fail to keep: *to go back on a promise.*

back/bite/ *v.t., v.i.,* **-bit, -bit•ten** or **-bit, -bit•ing.** to slander (an absent person). **—back/bit/er,** *n.*

back/board/ *n.* **1.** a board placed at or forming the back of anything. **2.** Basketball. the vertical board to which the basket is attached.

back/bone/ *n.* **1.** the spinal column; spine. **2.** strength of character. **3.** a major support.

back/break/ing *adj.* demanding great effort, endurance, etc.

back/drop/ *n.* **1.** the rear curtain of a stage setting. **2.** the background of an event; setting.

back/field/ *n.* the football players stationed behind the line.

back/fire/ *v.,* **-fired, -fir•ing,** *n. —v.i.* **1.** (of an internal-combustion engine) to have a premature explosion in the intake manifold. **2.** to bring a result opposite to that planned or expected. **—n. 3.** a premature, explosive ignition of fuel in an engine.

back/gam/mon (-gam/ən), *n.* a game for two persons in which pieces are moved around a board in accordance with throws of the dice.

back/ground/ *n.* **1.** the parts, as of a scene, situated in the rear. **2.** one's origin, education, experience, etc. **3.** the antecedents or causes of an event or condition. **—adj. 4.** of or serving as a background: *background noise.*

back/hand/ *n.* **1.** (in tennis, squash, etc.) a stroke made with the back of the hand facing the direction of movement. **2.** handwriting that slopes toward the left. **—adj. 3.** backhanded. **—adv. 4.** in a backhanded way. **—v.t. 5.** to hit with a backhand.

back/hand/ed *adj.* **1.** performed with the back of the hand turned forward. **2.** sloping in a downward direction from left to right. **3.** oblique or ambiguous in meaning.

back/lash/ *n.* **1.** a sudden, forceful backward

movement; recoil. **2.** a strong negative reaction, as to social change.

back′log′ *n.*, *v.*, **-logged, -log•ging.** —*n.* **1.** an accumulation, as of unfinished tasks. —*v.i.* **2.** to accumulate in a backlog.

back′pack′ *n.* **1.** a pack of supplies carried on one's back, sometimes supported on a frame. —*v.i.* **2.** to hike with a backpack. —*v.t.* **3.** to carry in a backpack. —**back′pack′er,** *n.*

back′-ped′al *v.i.*, **-aled, -al•ing** or (*esp. Brit.*) **-alled, -al•ling.** **1.** to retard the motion of a bicycle by pressing backward on the pedal. **2.** to retreat from or reverse one's previous stand.

back′side′ *n.* the rump; buttocks.

back′slide′ *v.i.*, **-slid, -slid** or **-slid•den, -slid•ing.** to relapse into bad habits or sinful behavior. —**back′slid′er,** *n.*

back′stage′ *adv.* **1.** behind the proscenium in a theater, esp. in the wings or dressing rooms. —*adj.* **2.** located or occurring backstage. **3.** pertaining to secret activities. **4.** pertaining to the private lives of entertainers.

back′stroke′ *n.* a swimming stroke performed in a supine position.

back′ talk′ *n.* an impudent response.

back′track′ *v.i.* **1.** to return over the same course or route. **2.** to withdraw from an undertaking, position, etc.

back′up′ *n.* **1.** a person or thing that supports or reinforces another. **2.** an accumulation due to a stoppage. **3.** an alternate kept in reserve. **4.** a copy of a computer file or program kept in case the original is damaged or lost.

back′ward (-wərd), *adv.* Also, **back′wards. 1.** toward the rear. **2.** with the back foremost. **3.** in the reverse of the usual way. **4.** toward the past. —*adj.* **5.** directed toward the back or past. **6.** reversed or returning. **7.** behind in progress or development. **8.** bashful or hesitant. —*Idiom.* **9. bend over backward,** to exert oneself to the utmost. —**back′ward•ness,** *n.*

back′wa′ter *n.* **1.** water held or forced back, as by a dam or flood. **2.** a place or state of stagnant backwardness.

back′woods′ *n.* **1.** (*often used with a sing. v.*) wooded or sparsely settled districts. **2.** any remote or isolated area. —*adj.* **3.** of or like the backwoods.

ba•con (bā′kən), *n.* **1.** the back and sides of a hog, salted and dried or smoked. —*Idiom.* **2. bring home the bacon, a.** to earn a living. **b.** to succeed.

bac•te•ri•a (bak tēr′ē ə), *n.pl.*, *sing.* **-um** (-əm). any of numerous groups of one-celled organisms, various species of which are involved in infectious diseases, fermentation, etc. —**bac•te′ri•al,** *adj.*

bac•te′ri•ol′o•gy (-ē ol′ə jē), *n.* the science that deals with bacteria. —**bac•te′ri•o•log′i•cal** (-ə loj′i-kəl), *adj.* —**bac•te′ri•ol′o•gist,** *n.*

bad (bad), *adj.*, **worse, worst,** *n.*, *adv.* —*adj.* **1.** not good in any manner or degree. **2.** wicked. **3.** disobedient or naughty. **4.** of inferior quality. **5.** inaccurate or faulty. **6.** suffering from ill health. **7.** spoiled or rotten. **8.** harmful or detrimental. **9.** disagreeable; unpleasant. **10.** severe. **11.** regretful or upset. **12.** unfortunate or unfavorable. **13.** (of a debt) uncollectible. —*n.* **14.** something bad. —*adv.* **15.** *Informal.* badly. —*Idiom.* **16. not bad,** somewhat good. **17. too bad,** unfortunate or disappointing. —**bad′ness,** *n.*

bad′ blood′ *n.* unfriendly relations; enmity.

badge (baj), *n.* **1.** an emblem worn as a sign of membership, authority, etc. **2.** any distinctive mark.

badg•er (baj′ər), *n.* **1.** a burrowing, carnivorous mammal of North America, Europe, and Asia. **2.** its fur. —*v.t.* **3.** to harass persistently; nag.

bad′ly *adv.*, **worse, worst,** *adj.* —*adv.* **1.** in a bad way or manner. **2.** greatly or very much. —*adj.* **3.** in ill health; sick. **4.** sorry; regretful.

bad•min•ton (bad′min tn), *n.* a game played on a rectangular court with light rackets used to volley a shuttlecock over a net.

bad′-mouth′ or **bad′mouth′** (-mouth′, -mouᵺ′), *v.t.* to criticize, often disloyally.

baf•fle (baf′əl), *v.*, **-fled, -fling,** *n.* —*v.t.* **1.** to be-

wilder or perplex. **2.** to frustrate or thwart. —*n.* **3.** an artificial obstruction for checking or deflecting the flow of sounds, light, gases, etc. —**baf′fle•ment,** *n.* —**baf′fler,** *n.* —**baf′fling,** *adj.*

bag (bag), *n.*, *v.*, **bagged, bag•ging.** —*n.* **1.** a pliant container capable of being closed at the mouth. **2.** a piece of luggage. **3.** a purse. **4.** something hanging in a loose, pouchlike manner. **5.** BASE¹ (def. 4b). **6.** a hunter's total amount of game taken. **7.** *Slang.* a person's avocation or hobby. **8.** *Slang.* an unattractive woman. —*v.i.* **9.** to hang loosely. **10.** to swell or bulge. —*v.t.* **11.** to put into a bag. **12.** to kill or catch. **13.** to cause to swell. —*Idiom.* **14. in the bag,** *Informal.* virtually certain.

bag•a•telle (bag′ə tel′), *n.* a trifle.

ba•gel (bā′gəl), *n.* a doughnut-shaped roll of dough that is simmered in water and baked.

bag•gage (bag′ij), *n.* trunks, suitcases, etc., used in traveling.

bag′gy *adj.*, **-gi•er, -gi•est.** hanging loosely; bulging. —**bag′gi•ly,** *adv.* —**bag′gi•ness,** *n.*

bag′pipe′ *n.* Often, **-pipes.** a reed instrument consisting of pipes protruding from a bag into which air is blown. —**bag′pip′er,** *n.*

bah (bä, ba), *interj.* an exclamation of contempt or annoyance.

Ba•ha•mas (bə hä′məz), *n.* a country comprising a group of islands (**Baha′ma Is′lands**) in the W Atlantic Ocean, SE of Florida. —**Ba•ha′mi•an** (-hā′-, -hä′-), *n.*, *adj.*

Bah•rain or **-rein** (bä rān′, -rīn′, bə-), *n.* a sheikdom in the Persian Gulf, consisting of a group of islands. —**Bah•rain′i,** *n.*, *pl.* **-is,** *adj.*

bail¹ (bāl), *n.* **1.** money given as surety that a person released from legal custody will return at an appointed time. **2.** the state of release upon being bailed. **3.** one who provides bail. —*v.t.* **4.** to obtain the release of (an arrested person) by providing bail. **5.** to assist in escaping a predicament (usu. fol. by *out*).

bail² (bāl), *n.* the semicircular handle of a kettle or pail.

bail³ (bāl), *v.t.*, *v.i.* **1.** to dip (water) out of a boat, as with a bucket. **2. bail out,** to parachute from an airplane. —*n.* **3.** a container used for bailing.

bail•iff (bā′lif), *n.* **1.** an officer, similar to a sheriff, employed to keep order in the court, make arrests, etc. **2.** (in Britain) **a.** the chief magistrate in a town. **b.** an overseer of a landed estate.

bail•i•wick (bā′lə wik′), *n.* **1.** the district of a bailiff. **2.** a person's area of skill, knowledge, authority, etc.

bail′out′ *n.* a rescue from financial problems.

bait (bāt), *n.* **1.** food or some substitute, used as a lure in fishing or trapping. **2.** anything that lures; enticement. —*v.t.* **3.** to prepare (a hook or trap) with bait. **4.** to lure, as with bait. **5.** to set dogs upon (an animal) for sport. **6.** to torment, esp. with malicious remarks.

bake (bāk), *v.*, **baked, bak•ing.** —*v.t.* **1.** to cook by dry heat, as in an oven. **2.** to harden by heat, as pottery. —*v.i.* **3.** to prepare food by baking it. **4.** to become baked. —**bak′er,** *n.*

bak′er's doz′en *n.* a dozen plus one; 13.

bak′er•y *n.*, *pl.* **-ies.** a place where baked goods are made or sold. Also called **bake′shop′.**

bak′ing pow′der *n.* a leavening agent used in baking, consisting of sodium bicarbonate, an acid substance, and a starch.

bak′ing so′da *n.* SODIUM BICARBONATE.

bal•ance (bal′əns), *n.*, *v.*, **-anced, -anc•ing.** —*n.* **1.** a state of equilibrium. **2.** something used to produce equilibrium. **3.** steadiness of the body or emotions. **4.** an instrument for determining weight, usu. one having pans suspended from both ends of a bar. **5.** the remainder or rest. **6. a.** equality between the total debits and total credits of an account. **b.** the difference between these totals. —*v.t.* **7.** to bring to or hold in equilibrium. **8.** to be equal or proportionate to. **9.** to add up the two sides of (an account) and determine the difference. **10.** to weigh in a balance. **11.** to estimate the relative weight or importance of. **12.** to counteract or offset.

—*v.i.* **13.** to be in equilibrium. **14.** to be equal. **15.** to be in a state wherein debits equal credits. —*Idiom.* **16. in the balance,** with the outcome in doubt.

bal•co•ny (bal′kə nē), *n., pl.* **-nies. 1.** a railed platform projecting from the wall of a building. **2.** a gallery in a theater.

bald (bôld), *adj.* **1.** having little or no hair on the scalp. **2.** destitute of some natural growth or covering. **3.** plain or undisguised: *a bald lie.* **4.** having white fur or feathers on the head. —*v.i.* **5.** to become bald. —**bald′ness,** *n.*

bal•der•dash (bôl′dər dash′), *n.* nonsense.

bale′ful *adj.* menacing or malign; threatening evil. —**bale′ful•ly,** *adv.*

balk (bôk), *v.i.* **1.** to refuse curtly and firmly (usu. fol. by *at*). **2.** to stop short and refuse to go on. —*v.t.* **3.** to hinder or thwart. —*n.* **4.** an illegal motion made by a baseball pitcher, allowing runners to advance to the next base. **5.** a check or hindrance. —**balk′er,** *n.*

balk′y *adj.,* **-i•er, -i•est.** given to balking; stubborn.

ball¹ (bôl), *n.* **1.** a spherical or approximately spherical body. **2.** a round or roundish body for use in games. **3.** a game played with a ball, esp. baseball. **4.** a pitched ball in baseball that is not swung at by the batter and is not a strike. **5.** a spherical projectile for a weapon. **6.** a part of the body that is rounded or protuberant. —*v.t., v.i.* **7.** to form into a ball. **8. ball up,** to make into a mess; confuse. —*Idiom.* **9. on the ball, a.** alert or watchful. **b.** efficient; competent.

ball² (bôl), *n.* **1.** a large formal party featuring social dancing. **2.** *Informal.* a very good time.

bal•lad (bal′əd), *n.* **1.** a simple narrative poem, esp. of folk origin, adapted for singing. **2.** a simple song. **3.** a slow, romantic popular song. —**bal′lad•eer′,** *n.* —**bal′lad•ry,** *n.*

bal•last (bal′əst), *n.* **1.** any heavy material carried on a ship or vehicle to provide stability. **2.** gravel or broken stone placed under the ties of a railroad. —*v.t.* **3.** to furnish with ballast.

ball′ bear′ing *n.* **1.** a bearing consisting of hard balls running in a ring-shaped groove on which a shaft turns. **2.** any of the balls so used.

bal•le•ri•na (bal′ə rē′nə), *n., pl.* **-nas.** a female ballet dancer.

bal•let (ba lā′), *n.* **1.** a dance form characterized by graceful movements and conventionalized steps and gestures. **2.** a theatrical performance of such dancing and its accompanying music. **3.** a company of ballet dancers. —**bal•let′ic** (-let′ik), *adj.*

ballis′tic mis′sile *n.* a missile that travels to its target unpowered and unguided after being launched.

bal•lis•tics (bə lis′tiks), *n.* the science or study of the motion of projectiles. —**bal•lis′tic,** *adj.*

bal•loon (bə lōōn′), *n.* **1.** an inflatable rubber bag used as a toy. **2.** a fabric bag filled with heated air or a gas lighter than air, designed to rise and float and often having a gondola for passengers or instruments. —*v.i.* **3.** to ride in a balloon. **4.** to puff out. **5.** to increase rapidly. —*v.t.* **6.** to inflate or distend. —*adj.* **7.** puffed out like a balloon. —**bal•loon′ist,** *n.*

bal•lot (bal′ət), *n.* **1.** a sheet of paper or the like on which a vote is registered. **2.** the method or act of voting. **3.** the right to vote. **4.** the whole number of votes recorded. —*v.i.* **5.** to vote by ballot. —**bal′lot•er,** *n.*

ball′park′ *n.* **1.** a stadium where ball games, esp. baseball, are played. —*adj.* **2.** being an approximation.

ball′point′ pen *n.* a pen laying down ink with a small ball bearing.

ball′room′ *n.* a large room for dancing.

bal•ly•hoo (bal′ē hōō′), *n., pl.* **-hoos,** *v.,* **-hooed, -hoo•ing.** —*n.* **1.** a clamorous attempt to win customers or advance a cause. —*v.t., v.i.* **2.** to promote with ballyhoo.

balm (bäm), *n.* **1.** a fragrant gum resin or ointment used in perfumery or medicine. **2.** any of various

aromatic plants. **3.** anything that heals or soothes pain. [< OF *basme* < L *balsamum* balsam]

balm′y *adj.,* **-i•er, -i•est. 1.** mild and refreshing; soothing. **2.** *Informal.* crazy; foolish. —**balm′i•ness,** *n.*

ba•lo•ney (bə lō′nē), *n.* **1.** *Slang.* foolishness; nonsense. **2.** BOLOGNA.

bal•sa (bôl′sə, bäl′-), *n., pl.* **-sas. 1.** a tropical American tree yielding a very light wood. **2.** the wood.

bal•sam (bôl′səm), *n.* **1.** a fragrant resin exuded from certain trees. **2.** any of various trees yielding a balsam. **3.** any aromatic ointment for ceremonial or medicinal use.

bal•us•ter (bal′ə stər), *n.* any of a number of closely spaced supports for a railing.

bal′us•trade′ (-strād′), *n.* a railing with its supporting balusters.

bam•boo (bam bōō′), *n., pl.* **-boos.** a tall, treelike tropical grass with woody, hollow stems, used for making furniture, poles, etc.

bam•boo•zle (bam bōō′zəl), *v.t.,* **-zled, -zling.** to deceive by trickery; hoodwink.

ban (ban), *v.,* **banned, ban•ning,** *n.* —*v.t.* **1.** to prohibit, esp. by official authority. —*n.* **2.** the act of prohibiting by law. **3.** an informal denunciation, as by public opinion. **4.** a formal ecclesiastical condemnation.

ba•nal (bə nal′, -näl′, bān′l), *adj.* hackneyed; trite. —**ba•nal′i•ty,** *n., pl.* **-ties.** —**ba•nal′ly,** *adv.*

ba•nan•a (bə nan′ə), *n., pl.* **-as. 1.** a tropical plant, certain species of which are cultivated for their nutritious fruit. **2.** the fruit, having a yellow or reddish rind. [< Sp < Pg < a West African language]

band¹ (band), *n.* **1.** a company of persons, animals, or things acting together. **2.** a group of musicians, usu. using brass, woodwind, and percussion instruments. —*v.t., v.i.* **3.** to unite in a group or company.

band² (band), *n.* **1.** a thin strip of material, as for binding or trimming. **2.** a stripe, as of color. **3.** a segment of a phonograph record on which sound is recorded. **4.** a specific range of frequencies, as in radio. —*v.t.* **5.** to mark or furnish with a band.

band•age (ban′dij), *n., v.,* **-aged, -ag•ing.** —*n.* **1.** a strip of material used to bind up a wound, sprain, etc. —*v.t.* **2.** to bind or cover with a bandage.

Band′-Aid′ 1. *Trademark.* an adhesive bandage with a gauze pad in the center, used for minor abrasions and cuts. —*n.* **2.** (*often l.c.*) a makeshift aid or solution.

ban•dan•na or **-dan•a** (ban dan′ə), *n., pl.* **-dan•nas** or **-dan•as.** a large, usu. figured handkerchief often worn as a head scarf.

ban•dit (ban′dit), *n.* a robber, esp. a member of a marauding band. —**ban′dit•ry,** *n.*

band′stand′ *n.* a platform for a band or orchestra.

band′wag′on *n.* **1.** a large, ornate wagon for carrying a musical band, as in a circus parade. —*Idiom.* **2. climb** or **jump on the bandwagon,** to join a cause, movement, etc., that appears to have popular support.

ban•dy (ban′dē), *v.,* **-died, -dy•ing,** *adj.* —*v.t.* **1.** to trade or exchange. **2.** to throw or strike to and fro. **3.** to circulate freely. —*adj.* **4.** (of legs) curved outward; bowed.

bane (bān), *n.* **1.** a person or thing that ruins or spoils: *Gambling was the bane of his existence.* **2.** a deadly poison (often used in combination, as in the name of poisonous plants). —**bane′ful,** *adj.*

bang¹ (bang), *n.* **1.** a loud, sudden, explosive noise. **2.** a resounding blow. **3.** *Informal.* thrill; excitement. —*v.t.* **4.** to strike or beat resoundingly; pound. —*v.i.* **5.** to strike violently or noisily. **6.** to make a loud, explosive noise. **7. bang up,** to damage. —*adv.* **8.** abruptly or violently. **9.** directly; precisely.

bang² (bang), *n.* Often, **bangs.** a fringe of hair cut to fall over the forehead.

Ban•gla•desh (bäng′glə desh′, bang′-), *n.* a republic in S Asia, N of the Bay of Bengal. —**Ban′gla•desh′i,** *n., pl.* **-is,** *adj.*

ban•gle (bang′gəl), *n.* a rigid bracelet.

bang′-up′ *adj. Informal.* excellent; extraordinary.

ban•ish (ban′ish), *v.t.* **1.** to condemn to exile. **2.** to send, drive, or put away. —**ban′ish•ment,** *n.*

ban•is•ter (ban′ə stər), *n.* **1.** a handrail and its supporting posts, esp. on a staircase. **2.** a handrail, esp. on a staircase.

ban•jo (ban′jō), *n., pl.* **-jos, -joes.** a stringed musical instrument having a circular body covered in front with stretched parchment. —**ban′jo•ist,** *n.*

bank¹ (bangk), *n.* **1.** a long pile or heap. **2.** a slope; incline. **3.** the slope bordering a river, lake, etc. **4.** a broad elevation of the sea floor. **5.** the inclination of the bed of a banked road or track. **6.** the lateral inclination of an aircraft during a turn. —*v.t.* **7.** to border with or like a bank. **8.** to form into a heap. **9.** to build (a road or track) with an upward slope at a curve. **10.** to incline (an airplane) laterally. **11.** to cover (a fire) with ashes or fuel to make it burn slowly.

bank² (bangk), *n.* **1.** an institution for receiving, lending, and safeguarding money. **2.** a storage place for reserves: *a blood bank.* —*v.i., v.t.* **3.** to deposit in a bank. **4. bank on,** to depend on. —**bank′a•ble,** *adj.* —**bank′ing,** *n.*

bank³ (bangk), *n.* **1.** an arrangement of objects in a line or in tiers. —*v.t.* **2.** to arrange in a bank.

bank′er *n.* a person employed by a bank, esp. as an executive.

bank′roll′ *n.* **1.** money in one's possession. —*v.t.* **2.** to finance.

bank′rupt (-rupt), *n.* **1.** a person who is adjudged insolvent by a court and whose property is divided among creditors. **2.** a person lacking in a particular thing or quality. —*adj.* **3.** subject to legal process because of insolvency. **4.** lacking something. —*v.t.* **5.** to make bankrupt. —**bank′rupt•cy** (-rəpt sē, -rəp-), *n., pl.* **-cies.**

ban•ner (ban′ər), *n.* **1.** a flag or an ensign bearing some device, motto, or slogan. **2.** a headline extending across a newspaper page. —*adj.* **3.** leading or foremost.

banns (banz), *n. (used with a pl. v.)* notice of an intended marriage, given in a parish church.

ban•quet (bang′kwit), *n.* **1.** a lavish meal. **2.** a ceremonious public dinner. —*v.t.* **3.** to entertain with a banquet. —**ban′quet•er,** *n.*

ban•shee (ban′shē), *n., pl.* **-shees.** (in Irish folklore) a female spirit whose wailing is a sign that a loved one is about to die. [< Ir *bean sídhe* lit., woman of a fairy mound]

ban•tam (ban′təm), *n.* **1.** a chicken of very small size. **2.** a small and quarrelsome person. —*adj.* **3.** diminutive; tiny.

ban•ter (ban′tər), *n.* **1.** an exchange of light, playful remarks. —*v.i.* **2.** to use banter.

ban•yan (ban′yən), *n.* an East Indian fig tree whose branches send roots to the ground that become new trunks.

bap•tism (bap′tiz əm), *n.* **1.** a ceremonial immersion in water, or application of water, as an initiatory sacrament of the Christian church. **2.** any ceremony of initiation. —**bap•tis′mal,** *adj.*

Bap′tist (-tist), *n.* a member of a Protestant denomination that baptizes believers by immersion.

bap•tize (bap tīz′, bap′tīz), *v.t.,* **-tized, -tiz•ing. 1.** to administer baptism to. **2.** to give a name to at baptism. **3.** to initiate by purifying. —**bap•tiz′er,** *n.*

bar (bär), *n., v.,* **barred, bar••ring,** *prep.* —*n.* **1.** a relatively long piece of metal or wood, used as a guard or obstruction or for a mechanical purpose. **2.** an oblong piece of any solid material: *a bar of soap.* **3.** a long ridge of sand or other material near the surface of a body of water, often obstructing navigation. **4.** any obstacle or barrier. **5.** a counter or place where beverages, esp. liquors, or light foods are served. **6. a.** the legal profession. **b.** a railing in a courtroom separating the public from the judges, jury, attorneys, etc. **7.** a band or stripe. **8. a.** the line marking the division between two measures of music. **b.** the unit of music between two bar lines; measure. —*v.t.* **9.** to equip or fasten with a bar. **10.** to block by or as if by bars. **11.** to

exclude. **12.** to mark with bars. —*prep.* **13.** except; but: *bar none.* —**Idiom. 14. behind bars,** in jail.

barb (bärb), *n.* **1.** a point projecting backward from a main point, as of a fishhook or arrowhead. **2.** an unpleasant or carping remark. —*v.t.* **3.** to furnish with a barb. —**barbed,** *adj.*

Bar•ba•dos (bär bā′dōz, -dōs), *n.* a country on an island in the E West Indies. —**Bar•ba′di•an,** *adj., n.*

bar•bar•i•an (bär bâr′ē ən), *n.* **1.** a person regarded as savage, primitive, or uncivilized. **2.** a person without culture or education. —*adj.* **3.** uncivilized; crude; savage. —**bar•bar′i•an•ism,** *n.* —**bar•bar•ic** (-bâr′ik), *adj.*

bar′ba•rism (-bə riz′əm), *n.* **1.** a primitive or uncivilized condition. **2.** a barbarous act. **3.** a word or construction felt to be nonstandard.

bar•bar′i•ty (-bâr′i tē), *n., pl.* **-ties. 1.** brutality; cruelty. **2.** an act of cruelty. **3.** crudity of style, expression, etc.

bar′ba•rous (-bər əs), *adj.* **1.** uncivilized; wild; savage. **2.** savagely cruel or harsh. **3.** not conforming to accepted usage, as language. —**bar′ba•rous•ly,** *adv.*

bar•be•cue or **-que** (bär′bi kyōō′), *n., v.,* **-cued** or **-qued, -cu•ing** or **-qu•ing.** —*n.* **1.** meat or poultry roasted over an open fire. **2.** an outdoor meal at which foods are so cooked. —*v.t.* **3.** to roast over an open fire. **4.** to cook in a piquant sauce of tomatoes, vinegar, and sugar. [< Sp *barbacoa* < Taino (West Indian language): raised frame of sticks]

bar•ber (bär′bər), *n.* **1.** a person whose occupation is to cut hair, shave beards, etc. —*v.t.* **2.** to cut the hair or beard of. —*v.i.* **3.** to work as a barber.

bar•bi•tu•rate (bär bich′ər it, bär′bi tōōr′āt, -tyōōr′-), *n.* any of a group of derivatives of a crystalline powder **(bar′bitur′ic ac′id),** used as sedatives and hypnotics.

bar′ code′ *n.* a series of contiguous lines coded by width and applied to a consumer item for identification by a computerized scanner.

bard (bärd), *n.* **1.** an ancient Celtic bard. **2.** any poet. —**bard′ic,** *adj.*

bare (bâr), *adj.,* **bar•er, bar•est,** *v.,* **bared, bar•ing.** —*adj.* **1.** without covering or clothing; naked. **2.** without the usual furnishings. **3.** unadorned; plain. **4.** scarcely sufficient: *bare necessities.* —*v.t.* **5.** to reveal or divulge. —**bare′ness,** *n.*

bare′back′ or **-backed′,** *adv., adj.* without a saddle.

bare′faced′ *adj.* **1.** with the face uncovered. **2.** without concealment; boldly open.

bare′ly *adv.* **1.** scarcely; no more than. **2.** without disguise or concealment. **3.** scantily; meagerly.

bar•gain (bär′gən), *n.* **1.** an advantageous purchase acquired at less than the usual cost. **2.** an agreement between parties settling the terms of a transaction. **3.** something acquired by bargaining. —*v.i.* **4.** to discuss the terms of a bargain; negotiate. **5.** to conclude a bargain. **6. bargain for** or **on,** to expect; anticipate. —**bar′gain•er,** *n.*

barge (bärj), *n., v.,* **barged, barg•ing.** —*n.* **1.** a flat-bottomed vessel, pushed or towed in transporting freight. **2.** a large boat used in pageants or state ceremonies. —*v.i.* **3.** to move aggressively and clumsily. **4.** to intrude rudely: *They barged into the room.* —*v.t.* **5.** to transport by barge.

bar•i•tone (bar′i tōn′), *n.* **1.** a male voice or voice part between tenor and bass. **2.** a singer with such a voice.

bar•i•um (bâr′ē əm, bar′-), *n.* an active metallic element occurring in combination. *Symbol:* Ba; *at. wt.:* 137.34; *at. no.:* 56.

bark¹ (bärk), *n.* **1.** the abrupt, explosive cry of a dog or other animal. **2.** a short, explosive sound. —*v.i.* **3.** to utter or produce a bark. **4.** to speak sharply or gruffly. —*v.t.* **5.** to utter gruffly. —**Idiom. 6. bark up the wrong tree,** to misdirect one's thoughts or efforts.

bark² (bärk), *n.* **1.** the external covering of the woody stems, branches, and roots of plants. —*v.t.* **2.** to scrape the skin of. **3.** to strip the bark from.

bark′er *n.* a person who stands at the entrance to

a show, as in a carnival, calling out its attractions to passersby.

bar•ley (bär'lē), *n.* **1.** a cereal plant. **2.** the grain of this plant, used as food and in making beer and whiskey.

bar mitz•vah (bär mits'və), *n.* (*often caps.*) **1.** a ceremony for admitting a boy of 13 as an adult member of the Jewish community. **2.** the boy participating in this ceremony.

bar•na•cle (bär'nə kəl), *n.* a marine crustacean that attaches itself to ship bottoms and floating timber. —**bar'na•cled,** *adj.*

barn'storm' *v.i., v.t.* to tour (rural areas) giving political speeches, theatrical performances, etc. —**barn'storm'er,** *n.*

ba•rom•e•ter (bə rom'i tər), *n.* **1.** an instrument that measures atmospheric pressure. **2.** anything that indicates changes. —**bar•o•met•ric** (bar'ə me'-trik), *adj.* —**bar'o•met'ri•cal•ly,** *adv.*

bar•on (bar'ən), *n.* **1.** a member of the lowest grade of nobility. **2.** a powerful, wealthy man in some industry or activity. —**ba•ro•ni•al** (bə rō'nē-əl), *adj.*

bar•on•et (-ə nit, -net'), *n.* a member of a British hereditary order of honor, ranking below the barons. —**bar'on•et•cy,** *n., pl.* **-cies.**

ba•roque (bə rōk'), *adj.* (*often cap.*) **1.** of a style of architecture and art of the 17th to mid-18th century, characterized by elaborate and grotesque forms and ornamentation. **2.** of the musical period following the Renaissance, extending roughly from 1600 to 1750.

bar•racks (bar'əks), *n.* (*used with a sing. or pl. v.*) a building or group of buildings for lodging soldiers.

bar•ra•cu•da (bar'ə kōō'də), *n., pl.* **-das, -da.** any of several elongated, predaceous marine fishes.

bar•rage (bə räzh'), *n., v.,* **-raged, -rag•ing.** —*n.* **1.** a heavy barrier of artillery fire. **2.** an overwhelming quantity. —*v.t.* **3.** to subject to a barrage.

bar•rel (bar'əl), *n., v.,* **-reled, -rel•ing** or (*esp. Brit.*) **-relled, -rel•ling.** —*n.* **1.** a cylindrical wooden container with slightly bulging sides and flat ends. **2.** the standard capacity of a barrel, 31.5 gallons of liquid. **3.** any large quantity. **4.** the tubelike part of a gun. —*v.i.* **5.** to travel or drive very fast.

bar•ren (bar'ən), *adj.* **1.** not producing offspring; sterile. **2.** unproductive; unfruitful. **3.** without capacity to interest or attract. **4.** bereft; lacking: *barren of compassion.* —*n.* **5.** Usu., **-rens.** level or slightly rolling land, usu. infertile. —**bar'ren•ness,** *n.*

bar•rette (bə ret'), *n.* a clasp for holding a woman's hair in place.

bar•ri•cade (bar'i kād', bar'i kād'), *n., v.,* **-cad•ed, -cad•ing.** —*n.* **1.** a hastily constructed defensive barrier. **2.** any barrier. —*v.t.* **3.** to obstruct or shut in with a barricade.

bar•ri•er (bar'ē ər), *n.* **1.** anything that bars passage, as a fence. **2.** anything that obstructs or limits.

bar•ring (bär'ing), *prep.* excepting; except for.

bar•ris•ter (bar'ə stər), *n.* (in England) a lawyer who has the privilege of pleading in the higher courts.

bar•row[1] (bar'ō), *n.* a handbarrow or wheelbarrow.

bar•row[2] (bar'ō), *n.* an artificial mound, esp. over a grave.

bar'tend'er *n.* a person who mixes and serves alcoholic drinks at a bar.

bar•ter (bär'tər), *v.i.* **1.** to trade by exchange of commodities rather than by use of money. —*v.t.* **2.** to exchange in trade. —*n.* **3.** the act of bartering. **4.** items or an item for bartering. —**bar'ter•er,** *n.*

ba•salt (bə sôlt', bā'sôlt), *n.* the dark, dense, igneous rock of a lava flow. —**ba•sal'tic,** *adj.*

base[1] (bās), *n., adj., v.,* **based, bas•ing.** —*n.* **1.** a bottom support; the part on which a thing rests. **2.** a fundamental principle; basis. **3.** the principal element or ingredient. **4. a.** any of the four corners of a baseball diamond. **b.** a canvas sack marking first, second, or third base. **5.** a military headquarters or supply installation. **6. a.** the lower side or surface of a geometric figure. **b.** the number that serves as

a starting point for a numerical system. **7.** a chemical compound that reacts with an acid to form a salt. **8.** the part of a complex word to which affixes may be added. —*adj.* **9.** serving as or forming a base. —*v.t.* **10.** to form a base for. **11.** to establish, as a conclusion. —*Idiom.* **12. off base, a.** (in baseball) not touching a base. **b.** badly mistaken.

base[2] (bās), *adj.,* **bas•er, bas•est. 1.** morally low; meanspirited. **2.** of little or no value. **3.** debased or counterfeit. —**base'ly,** *adv.* —**base'ness,** *n.*

base'ball' *n.* **1.** a game involving the batting of a ball, played by two teams on a diamond formed by four bases. **2.** the ball used in this game.

base'board' *n.* a board or molding forming the foot of an interior wall.

base' hit' *n. Baseball.* a fair ball enabling the batter to reach base safely without an error in the field or with no runner forced out.

base'less *adj.* having no base or foundation; groundless.

base'line' or **base' line',** *n.* **1.** the area on a baseball diamond within which a runner must keep when running between bases. **2.** the line at each end of a tennis court. **3.** a basic standard or level; guideline.

base'ment *n.* a story of a building, partly or wholly underground.

base' on balls' *n., pl.* **bases on balls.** *Baseball.* the awarding of first base to a batter to whom four balls have been pitched.

bash (bash), *v.t.* **1.** to strike with a crushing blow. **2. a.** to assault physically. **b.** to abuse verbally. —*n.* **3.** a crushing blow. **4.** a lively social event.

bash'ful *adj.* easily embarrassed; shy. —**bash'-ful•ly,** *adv.* —**bash'ful•ness,** *n.*

ba•sic (bā'sik), *adj.* **1.** of or forming a base or basis; fundamental. **2. a.** pertaining to a chemical base. **b.** alkaline. —*n.* **3.** Often, **-sics.** an essential ingredient, principle, procedure, etc. —**ba/si•cal•ly,** *adv.*

BASIC (bā'sik), *n.* a high-level computer programming language that uses English words, punctuation marks, and algebraic notation.

bas•il (baz'əl, bā'zəl), *n.* an aromatic herb whose leaves are used in cooking.

ba•sil•i•ca (bə sil'i kə), *n., pl.* **-cas. 1.** an early Christian church having a nave, aisles, and vaulted apses. **2.** one of the seven main churches of Rome, or another Roman Catholic church accorded the same religious privileges. [< L < Gk *basilikē̂* (*oikía*) royal (house)]

ba•sin (bā'sən), *n.* **1.** a shallow, circular container, used chiefly to hold water. **2.** the quantity held by a basin. **3.** a sheltered area along a shore. **4. a.** a depression in the earth's surface. **b.** an area drained by a river.

ba•sis (bā'sis), *n., pl.* **-ses** (-sēz). **1.** a bottom or base; foundation. **2.** a fundamental principle. **3.** the principal constituent.

bask (bask, bäsk), *v.i.* **1.** to lie in pleasant warmth. **2.** to take great pleasure: *to bask in royal favor.*

bas•ket (bas'kit, bä'skit), *n.* **1.** a container made of twigs, straw, etc., woven together. **2.** the amount contained in a basket. **3.** the goal on a basketball court, an open net suspended from a metal hoop.

bas'ket•ball' *n.* **1.** a game played by two teams who score points by tossing a ball through a goal on the opponent's side of the court. **2.** the ball used in this game.

bas-re•lief (bä'ri lēf'), *n.* relief sculpture in which the figures project slightly from the background.

bass[1] (bās), *adj.* **1.** of the lowest pitch or range. **2.** of the lowest part in harmonic music. —*n.* **3.** the bass part. **4.** a bass voice, singer, or instrument. **5.** DOUBLE BASS.

bass[2] (bas), *n., pl.* **bass•es, bass.** any of numerous edible, spiny-finned, freshwater or marine fishes.

bas'set hound' (bas'it), *n.* one of a breed of short-legged hounds with a long body and long, drooping ears.

bas•si•net (bas'ə net'), *n.* a basket with a hood over one end, for use as a baby's cradle.

bas•soon (ba sōōn', bə-), *n.* a large woodwind

instrument of low range, having a double-reed mouthpiece. —**bas•soon′ist,** *n.*

bas•tard (bas′tərd), *n.* **1.** an illegitimate child. **2.** a mean, despicable person. —*adj.* **3.** illegitimate in birth. **4.** made or done in imitation; spurious; false.

baste¹ (bāst), *v.t.,* **bast•ed, bast•ing.** to sew with long, loose, temporary stitches.

baste² (bāst), *v.t.,* **bast•ed, bast•ing.** to moisten (meat or other food) with drippings, butter, etc., while cooking.

baste³ (bāst), *v.t.,* **bast•ed, bast•ing. 1.** to beat with a stick. **2.** to denounce or scold vigorously.

bas•tion (bas′chən), *n.* **1.** a projecting portion of a fortification. **2.** a fortified place. **3.** anything seen as preserving or protecting some quality, condition, etc. —**bas′tioned,** *adj.*

bat¹ (bat), *n., v.,* **bat•ted, bat•ting.** —*n.* **1.** the wooden club used in certain games, as baseball and cricket, to strike the ball. **2.** a heavy stick or club. **3.** a blow, as with a bat. —*v.t.* **4.** to hit with or as if with a bat. —*v.i.* **5.** to take one's turn as a batter.

bat² (bat), *n.* a nocturnal flying mammal with large wings made of membranes.

bat³ (bat), *v.t.,* **bat•ted, bat•ting. 1.** to blink; wink; flutter. —*Idiom.* **2. not bat an eye,** to show no surprise or other emotion.

batch (bach), *n.* **1.** a quantity or number coming at one time or taken together; group; lot. **2.** the quantity of bread, dough, etc., made at one baking. **3.** a group of jobs, data, programs, or commands treated as a unit for computer processing.

bat′ed (bā′tid) *adj.* (of breath) held back in suspense.

bath (bath, bäth), *n., pl.* **baths** (bathz, bäthz, baths, bäths). **1.** a washing or immersing of the body in water, steam, etc. **2.** a quantity of water or other liquid used for this purpose. **3.** BATHTUB. **4.** BATHROOM. **5.** BATHHOUSE (def. 2). **6.** Usu. **baths.** a spa. **7.** a preparation, as an acid solution, in which something is immersed.

bathe (bāth), *v.,* **bathed, bath•ing.** —*v.t.* **1.** to immerse in water or other liquid, as for cleansing or refreshment. **2.** to give a bath to. **3.** to apply water or other liquid to. **4.** to wash over or against, as by the action of the sea. **5.** to cover or surround: *sunlight bathing the room.* —*v.i.* **6.** to take a bath. **7.** to swim for pleasure. —**bath′er,** *n.*

bath′house′ *n.* **1.** a structure, as at the seaside, containing dressing rooms for bathers. **2.** a building having bathing facilities.

bath′ing suit′ *n.* a garment worn for swimming.

ba•thos (bā′thos, -thōs), *n.* **1.** a ludicrous descent from the lofty to the commonplace. **2.** insincere pathos; sentimentality. **3.** triteness or triviality. —**ba•thet•ic** (bə thet′ik), *adj.*

bath′robe′ *n.* a loose, coatlike garment worn before and after a bath and over sleepwear.

bath′room′ *n.* a room with a bathtub or shower and usu. a sink and toilet.

bath′tub′ *n.* a tub to bathe in.

ba•tik (bə tēk′), *n.* **1.** a technique of dyeing fabric using wax to cover those parts not to be dyed. **2.** a fabric so decorated.

bat mitzvah (bät mits′və), *n.* (*often caps.*) **1.** a ceremony for a girl of 12 or 13, paralleling the bar mitzvah. **2.** the girl participating in this ceremony.

ba•ton (bə ton′), *n.* **1.** a wand with which a conductor directs an orchestra or band. **2.** a metal rod twirled by a drum major or majorette. **3.** a staff serving as a mark of office or authority.

bat•tal•ion (bə tal′yən), *n.* **1.** a military unit comprising a headquarters and two or more companies. **2.** an army in battle array. [< MF *bataillon* < It *battaglione* large body of troops]

bat•ten (bat′n), *n.* **1.** a strip of wood used for various building purposes, as to cover joints between boards. —*v.t.* **2.** to furnish or bolster with battens.

bat•ter¹ (bat′ər), *v.t.* **1.** to beat or pound repeatedly. **2.** to subject (a person, esp. a wife or child) to repeated beating or other abuse. **3.** to damage by beating or rough usage. —*v.i.* **4.** to pound steadily.

bat•ter² (bat′ər), *n.* a mixture typically of flour,

milk or water, and eggs, used to make cakes, pancakes, etc.

bat•ter³ (bat′ər), *n.* a player whose turn it is to bat, as in baseball or cricket.

bat•ter•y (bat′ə rē), *n., pl.* **-ies. 1.** a cell or combination of cells for producing electric energy. **2.** two or more pieces of artillery used for combined action. **3.** a group of guns on a warship. **4.** any group or series of similar or related things: *a battery of tests.* **5.** *Law.* an unlawful attack upon another person, esp. by beating. **6.** a baseball pitcher and catcher considered as a unit.

bat•tle (bat′l), *n., v.,* **-tled, -tling.** —*n.* **1.** a hostile military encounter. **2.** any fight, conflict, or struggle. —*v.t., v.i.* **3.** to fight. —**bat′tle•field′,** *n.* —**bat′tler,** *n.*

bat′tle•ment *n.* Often, **-ments.** a parapet of a fortification, with open spaces for shooting. —**bat′tle•ment′ed,** *adj.*

bat′tle•ship′ *n.* any of a class of warships with the heaviest armor and most powerful guns.

bat•ty (bat′ē), *adj.,* **-ti•er, -ti•est.** *Slang.* crazy or eccentric.

bau•ble (bô′bəl), *n.* a cheap, showy trinket.

baud (bôd) *n.* a unit used to measure the speed of a signal or data transfer, as in computers.

baux•ite (bôk′sīt, bō′zīt), *n.* a claylike rock that is the principal ore of aluminum.

bawd•y (bô′dē), *adj.,* **-i•er, -i•est.** indecent; lewd; obscene. —**bawd′i•ly,** *adv.* —**bawd′i•ness,** *n.*

bawl (bôl), *v.i.* **1.** to cry or wail lustily. —*v.t.* **2.** to shout out. **3. bawl out,** *Informal.* to scold vigorously. —*n.* **4.** a loud shout. **5.** a loud weeping. —**bawl′er,** *n.*

bay¹ (bā), *n.* a body of water forming an indentation of the shoreline.

bay² (bā), *n.* **1.** a recess in a wall, usu. containing a window. **2.** a compartment, as in an aircraft or ship, set off by walls or bulkheads.

bay³ (bā), *n.* **1.** a deep, prolonged howl, as of a hound. **2.** the situation of a cornered animal or fugitive forced to face and resist pursuers: *a stag at bay.* —*v.i.* **3.** to howl.

bay⁴ (bā), *n.* LAUREL (def. 1).

bay⁵ (bā), *n.* **1.** a reddish brown horse or other animal. **2.** a reddish brown. —*adj.* **3.** reddish brown.

bay′ber′ry *n., pl.* **-ries. 1.** an aromatic shrub bearing a waxy berry. **2.** the berry.

bay′ leaf′ *n.* the dried leaf of the laurel, used in cooking.

bay•o•net (bā′ə net′, bā′ə nit), *n., v.,* **-net•ed** or **-net•ted, -net•ing** or **-net•ting.** —*n.* **1.** a daggerlike weapon attached to the muzzle of a gun for hand-to-hand combat. —*v.t.* **2.** to stab with a bayonet. [< F *baïonnette,* after *Bayonne,* France, where first made or used]

bay•ou (bī′ōō), *n., pl.* **-ous.** (in the southern U.S.) a marshy inlet or outlet of a lake, river, etc., usu. sluggish or stagnant.

ba•zaar (bə zär′), *n.* **1.** a shopping quarter, esp. in the Middle East. **2.** a sale of miscellaneous articles to benefit a charity.

ba•zoo•ka (bə zōō′kə), *n., pl.* **-kas.** a tube-shaped, portable weapon that fires an armor-penetrating missile.

BB (bē′bē′), *n.* a size of shot, 0.18 in. (0.46 cm) in diameter, fired from an air rifle (**BB gun**).

B.C. or **BC, 1.** before Christ (used with dates): *Cleopatra was born in 69 b.c.* **2.** British Columbia.

B.C.E. before the Common (or Christian) Era (used with dates).

be (bē; *unstressed* bē, bi), *v.* and *auxiliary v., pres. sing. 1st pers.* **am,** *2nd* **are,** *3rd* **is,** *pres. pl.* **are;** *past sing. 1st pers.* **was,** *2nd* **were,** *3rd* **was,** *past pl.* **were;** *pres. subj.* **be;** *past subj. sing. 1st, 2nd, and 3rd pers.* **were;** *past part.* **been;** *pres. part.* **be•ing.** —*v.i.* **1.** to exist or live. **2.** to occur. **3.** to occupy a position. **4.** to continue as before. **5.** (used to connect the subject with its predicate adjective or nominative): *He is tall.* **6.** (used to introduce or form interrogative or imperative sentences): *Is that right? Be quiet!* —*auxiliary verb.* **7.** (used with the present participle of another verb to form progressive tenses): *I am waiting.* **8.** (used with the infinitive or participle of another verb to indicate a command, arrangements, or future action): *He is to see me today.* **9.** (used with the past participle of another verb to form the passive voice): *The date was fixed.* **10.** (used in archaic constructions with some intransitive verbs to form perfect tenses): *He is come.*

Be *Chem. Symbol.* beryllium.

be- a prefix meaning: about or around (*besiege*); all over (*bedaub*); to provide with (*bejewel*); at or regarding (*bewail*); to make (*befriend*).

beach (bēch), *n.* **1.** an expanse of sand or pebbles along a shore. —*v.t.* **2.** to haul or run onto a beach.

beach′comb′er *n.* **1.** a person who lives by gathering salable jetsam or refuse from beaches. **2.** a vagrant who lives on the seashore.

beach′head′ *n.* the area that is the first objective of a military force landing on an enemy shore.

bea•con (bē′kən), *n.* **1.** a guiding or warning signal, as a light or fire. **2.** a tower or hill used for such purposes. **3.** a radio transmitter that sends out a signal as a navigational aid for ships and aircraft.

bead (bēd), *n.* **1.** a small, usu. round object of glass, wood, etc., pierced for stringing. **2. beads, a.** a necklace of beads. **b.** a rosary. **3.** any small globular body: *beads of sweat.* **4.** the front sight of a gun. **5.** a reinforced area of a rubber tire. —*v.t.* **6.** to ornament with beads. —*v.i.* **7.** to form in beads. —*Idiom.* **8. count** or **say one's beads,** to pray using rosary beads. **9. draw a bead on,** to take careful aim at.

bea•gle (bē′gəl), *n.* a small hound with drooping ears.

beak (bēk), *n.* **1.** the bill of a bird. **2.** any horny or stiff projecting mouthpart of an animal, fish, or insect. —**beaked** (bēkt, bē′kid), *adj.*

beak′er *n.* **1.** a large drinking cup with a wide mouth. **2.** a cuplike container with a pouring lip, used in a laboratory.

beam (bēm), *n.* **1.** a long piece of metal or wood, used as a rigid part of a structure or machine. **2.** the extreme width of a ship. **3.** the crossbar of a balance from which the scales are suspended. **4.** a ray of light or other radiation. **5.** a group of nearly parallel rays. **6.** a radio signal used to guide pilots. **7.** a radiant smile. —*v.t.* **8.** to emit in or as if in beams. **9.** to transmit (a radio or television signal) in a particular direction. —*v.i.* **10.** to emit beams, as of light. **11.** to smile radiantly.

bean (bēn), *n.* **1.** the edible seed or pod of various plants of the legume family. **2.** a plant producing beans. **3.** any other beanlike seed or plant, as the coffee bean. **4.** *Slang.* a person's head. —*v.t.* **5.** *Slang.* to hit on the head, esp. with a baseball. —*Idiom.* **6. spill the beans,** *Informal.* to disclose a secret.

bear¹ (bâr), *v.,* **bore, borne** or **born, bear•ing.** —*v.t.* **1.** to hold up or support. **2.** to give birth to. **3.** to produce by natural growth. **4.** to sustain or be capable of. **5.** to conduct (oneself, one's body, etc.). **6.** to suffer; endure. **7.** to warrant: *It doesn't bear repeating.* **8.** to carry; bring. **9.** to give: *to bear testimony.* **10.** to exhibit; show: *to bear a resemblance.* —*v.i.* **11.** to tend in a direction; go: *to bear left.* **12.** to be situated. **13.** to bring forth young or fruit. **14. bear down, a.** to press down. **b.** to strive harder. **15. ~ down on, a.** to press down on. **b.** to move toward rapidly. **16. ~ on,** to be relevant to. **17. ~ out,** to confirm. **18. ~ up,** to endure. **19. ~ with,** to be patient with. —**bear′a•ble,** *adj.* —**bear′er,** *n.*

bear² (bâr), *n.,* *pl.* **bears, bear,** *adj.* —*n.* **1.** a large, stocky, omnivorous mammal with thick, coarse fur. **2.** a gruff, clumsy, or rude person. **3.** a person who believes that stock prices will decline. —*adj.* **4.** marked by declining prices, esp. of stocks. —**bear′ish,** *adj.*

beard (bērd), *n.* **1.** hair growing on the lower part of a man's face. **2.** a similar growth on the chin of some animals. **3.** an awn, as on wheat. —*v.t.* **4.** to oppose boldly. **5.** to supply with a beard.

bear′ hug′ *n.* a forcefully tight embrace.

bear′ing *n.* **1.** the manner in which one conducts

or carries oneself. **2.** the act, capability, or period of bringing forth. **3.** reference or relation. **4.** the support and guide for a rotating or sliding shaft, pivot, or wheel. **5.** Often, **-ings.** direction or relative position.

beast (bēst), *n.* **1.** any nonhuman animal. **2.** a cruel, coarse person.

beast′ly *adj.,* **-li•er, -li•est. 1.** of or like a beast; bestial. **2.** nasty; disagreeable. —**beast′li•ness,** *n.*

beat (bēt), *v.,* **beat, beat•en** or **beat, beat•ing,** *n., adj.* —*v.t.* **1.** to strike forcefully and repeatedly. **2.** to thrash or flog in punishment (often fol. by *up*). **3.** to dash against. **4.** to flutter or flap (wings). **5.** to sound, as on a drum: *to beat a tattoo.* **6.** to stir vigorously. **7.** to make (a path) by repeated treading. **8.** to mark (time) with the hand or a metronome. **9.** to scour (the forest, grass, or brush) to rouse game. **10.** to overcome; defeat. **11.** to be superior to. **12.** *Informal.* to baffle. **13.** *Slang.* to escape or avoid (blame or punishment). —*v.i.* **14.** to strike repeatedly; pound. **15.** to throb. **16. beat down,** to subdue. **17. ~ off,** to ward off; repulse. —*n.* **18.** a stroke or blow. **19.** a throb or pulsation. **20.** one's regular path or habitual round. **21.** the marking of the metrical divisions of music. **22.** the accent or stress in a rhythmical unit of poetry. **23.** (*often cap.*) BEATNIK. —*adj.* **24.** *Informal.* exhausted; worn out. **25.** (*often cap.*) of or characteristic of beatniks. —*Idiom.* **26. beat it,** *Informal.* to go away. —**beat′a•ble,** *adj.* —**beat′er,** *n.*

be•a•tif•ic (bē′ə tif′ik), *adj.* **1.** bestowing bliss. **2.** blissful; saintly. —**be′a•tif′i•cal•ly,** *adv.*

be•at′i•tude′ (-tōōd′, -tyōōd′), *n.* **1.** supreme blessedness or happiness. **2.** (*often cap.*) any of the declarations of blessedness pronounced by Jesus in the Sermon on the Mount.

beat′nik (-nik), *n.* a disillusioned young person, esp. of the 1950s, rejecting conventional behavior, dress, etc.

beau (bō), *n.,* *pl.* **beaus, beaux** (bōz). a girl's or woman's sweetheart.

beau•te•ous (byōō′tē əs), *adj.* beautiful. —**beau′te•ous•ly,** *adv.*

beau•ti′cian (-tish′ən), *n.* a person who works in a beauty parlor.

beau′ti•ful (-tə fəl), *adj.* **1.** having beauty; aesthetically pleasing. **2.** wonderful; remarkable. —**beau′ti•ful•ly,** *adv.*

beau′ti•fy′ (-fī′), *v.t., v.i.,* **-fied, -fy•ing.** to make or become beautiful. —**beau′ti•fi•ca′tion,** *n.* —**beau′ti•fi′er,** *n.*

beau′ty *n.,* *pl.* **-ties. 1.** the quality in a person or thing that gives intense aesthetic pleasure. **2.** a beautiful person or thing.

beau′ty par′lor *n.* an establishment where women go for haircuts, manicures, etc. Also called **beau′ty shop′.**

bea•ver (bē′vər), *n.,* *pl.* **-vers, -ver. 1.** a large amphibious rodent with sharp incisors, webbed hind feet, and a flattened tail. **2.** its fur.

be•cause (bi kôz′, -koz′, -kuz′), *conj.* **1.** for the reason that. —*Idiom.* **2. because of,** by reason of; due to.

beck (bek), *n.* **1.** a beckoning gesture. —*Idiom.* **2. at someone's beck and call,** subject to someone's every wish.

beck′on (-ən), *v.t., v.i.* **1.** to signal or summon by a gesture of the head or hand. **2.** to lure; entice.

be•cloud (bi kloud′), *v.t.* **1.** to darken or obscure with clouds. **2.** to make confused.

be•come (bi kum′), *v.,* **-came, -come, -com•ing.** —*v.i.* **1.** to come, change, or grow to be. —*v.t.* **2.** to befit; suit. —*Idiom.* **3. become of,** to happen to.

bed (bed), *n., v.,* **bed•ded, bed•ding.** —*n.* **1.** a piece of furniture upon which a person sleeps. **2.** an area of ground in which plants are grown. **3.** the bottom of a lake, river, etc. **4.** a foundation or base. **5.** a layer of rock; stratum. —*v.t.* **6.** to provide with a bed. **7.** to put to bed. **8.** to plant in a bed. **9.** to place in layers. **10.** to embed. —*v.i.* **11.** to have sleeping accommodations. **12.** to form layers.

bed′bug′ *n.* a flat, wingless, bloodsucking bug that infests houses and esp. beds.

bed′clothes′ *n.pl.* coverings for a bed, as sheets and blankets.

bed′ding *n.* BEDCLOTHES.

be•dev•il (bi dev′əl), *v.t.,* **-iled, -il•ing** or (*esp. Brit.*) **-illed, -il•ling. 1.** to torment maliciously. **2.** to confuse; confound. —**be•dev′il•ment,** *n.*

bed′fel′low *n.* **1.** a person who shares one's bed. **2.** an associate or collaborator.

bed•lam (bed′ləm), *n.* a scene or state of wild uproar and confusion.

Bed•ou•in or **-u•in** (bed′ōō in), *n., pl.* **-in, -ins.** a traditionally tent-dwelling Arab of the deserts of SW Asia and N Africa.

bed′pan′ *n.* a shallow pan used as a toilet by persons confined to bed.

be•drag′gled (bi drag′əld) *adj.* soiled and wet.

bed′rid′den *adj.* confined to bed.

bed′rock′ *n.* **1.** unbroken solid rock, overlaid by soil. **2.** any firm foundation or basis.

bed′room′ *n.* a room used for sleeping.

bed′sore′ *n.* a skin ulcer on the body of a bedridden person, caused by immobility and prolonged pressure.

bed′spread′ *n.* a decorative outer covering for a bed.

bed′stead′ (-sted′, -stid), *n.* the framework of a bed supporting the springs and mattress.

bee (bē), *n.* **1.** any of a large group of four-winged hairy insects, some species of which produce honey. **2.** a social gathering to work together or to compete: *a quilting bee.*

beech (bēch), *n.* **1.** a tree having a smooth, gray bark and bearing small, edible, triangular nuts. **2.** its wood.

beef (bēf), *n., pl.* **beeves** (bēvz) for 1; **beefs** for 4, *v.* —*n.* **1.** an adult cow, steer, or bull raised for its meat. **2.** its meat. **3.** *Informal.* muscular strength. **4.** *Slang.* a complaint. —*v.i.* **5.** *Slang.* to complain. **6. beef up,** to strengthen; reinforce.

bee′line′ *n.* a direct course or route.

been (bin), *v.* pp. of BE.

beep (bēp), *n.* **1.** a short, usu. high-pitched tone produced by an automobile horn, electronic device, etc. —*v.i., v.t.* **2.** to make or cause to make such a sound.

beep′er *n.* a pocket-size electronic device whose signal notifies the person carrying it of a telephone message.

beer (bēr), *n.* **1.** an alcoholic, fermented beverage made from malt and hops. **2.** any of various beverages made from plants, as root beer.

beet (bēt), *n.* **1.** a plant with a fleshy red or white root. **2.** its edible root.

bee•tle¹ (bēt′l), *n.* an insect with hard, horny forewings that cover and protect the membranous flight wings.

bee•tle² (bēt′l), *adj., v.,* **-tled, -tling.** —*adj.* **1.** projecting; overhanging. —*v.i.* **2.** to project or overhang.

be•fall (bi fôl′), *v.t., v.i.,* **-fell, -fall•en, -fall•ing.** to happen (to), esp. by chance or fate.

be•fit (bi fit′), *v.t.,* **-fit•ted, -fit•ting.** to be appropriate for; suit; fit.

be•fore (bi fôr′), *prep.* **1.** previous to; earlier than. **2.** in front or ahead of. **3.** awaiting. **4.** in preference to. **5.** in precedence of, as in order or rank. **6.** in the presence or sight of. **7.** under the consideration or jurisdiction of: *summoned before a magistrate.* —*adv.* **8.** previously. **9.** earlier or sooner. **10.** in front; in advance. —*conj.* **11.** previous to the time when: *See me before you go.* **12.** rather than: *I will die before I submit.*

be•fore′hand′ *adv., adj.* in advance; ahead of time.

be•friend (bi frend′), *v.t.* to act as a friend to.

be•fud•dle (bi fud′l), *v.t.,* **-dled, -dling.** to confuse thoroughly. —**be•fud′dle•ment,** *n.*

beg (beg), *v.t., v.i.,* **begged, beg•ging. 1.** to ask for (alms or charity). **2.** to ask humbly or earnestly. **3. beg off,** to request release from an obligation. —*Idiom.* **4. beg the question, a.** to assume the truth of the point in question. **b.** to evade the issue.

---

c. to raise the question. **5. go begging,** to remain unused or unwanted.

be•get (bi get′), *v.t.,* **be•got, be•got•ten** or **be•got, be•get•ting. 1.** to be the father of. **2.** to cause; produce as an effect. —**be•get′ter,** *n.*

beg•gar (beg′ər), *n.* **1.** a person who lives by begging. **2.** a penniless person. —*v.t.* **3.** to impoverish. **4.** to cause to seem inadequate: *The place beggars description.*

beg′gar•ly (-lē), *adj.* **1.** like or befitting a beggar. **2.** meanly inadequate. —**beg′gar•li•ness,** *n.*

be•gin (bi gin′), *v.i., v.t.,* **be•gan, be•gun, be•gin•ning. 1.** to perform the first or earliest part of (something). **2.** to come or bring into existence. —**be•gin′ner,** —**be•gin′ning,** *n.*

be•gone (bi gôn′, -gon′), *v.i.* to go away; depart (usu. used in the imperative).

be•go•nia (bi gōn′yə), *n., pl.* **-nias.** a tropical plant cultivated for its ornamental leaves and flowers.

be•grudge (bi gruj′), *v.t.,* **-grudged, -grudg•ing. 1.** to envy the pleasure or good fortune of. **2.** to be reluctant to give or allow. —**be•grudg′ing•ly,** *adv.*

be•guile (bi gīl′), *v.t.,* **-guiled, -guil•ing. 1.** to influence by guile; delude. **2.** to charm or divert. **3.** to pass (time) pleasantly. —**be•guile′ment,** *n.* —**be•guil′er.** —**be•guil′ing•ly,** *adv.*

be•half (bi haf′, -häf′), *n.* **1.** interest; support. —*Idiom.* **2. in** or **on behalf of,** as a representative of.

be•have (bi hāv′), *v.,* **-haved, -hav•ing.** —*v.i.* **1.** to act or react in a particular way. **2.** to act properly. —*v.t.* **3.** to conduct (oneself) in a proper manner.

be•hav•ior (-yər), *n.* **1.** one's manner of behaving or acting. **2.** the action or reaction of a material, machine, etc., under given circumstances. Also, *esp. Brit.,* **be•hav′iour.** —**be•hav′ior•al,** *adj.*

be•head (bi hed′), *v.t.* to cut off the head of.

be•hest (bi hest′), *n.* **1.** a command; directive. **2.** an earnest request.

be•hind (bi hīnd′), *prep.* **1.** at or toward the rear of. **2.** later than; after. **3.** in the state of making less progress than. **4.** beyond. **5.** promoting or supporting. **6.** hidden or unrevealed by: *Malice lay behind her smile.* —*adv.* **7.** at or toward the rear. **8.** in a place or stage already passed. **9.** in arrears. **10.** slow; late. —*n.* **11.** *Informal.* the buttocks.

be•hold (bi hōld′), *v.,* **-held, -hold•ing, -beholding, interj.** —*v.t.* **1.** to look at; see. —*interj.* **2.** look! see! —**be•hold′er,** *n.*

be•hold′en *adj.* obligated; indebted.

be•hoove (bi hōōv′), *v.t.,* **-hooved, -hoov•ing.** to be necessary or proper for: *It behooves us to reconsider.*

beige (bāzh), *n.* **1.** a light grayish brown. —*adj.* **2.** of the color beige.

be•ing (bē′ing), *n.* **1.** the fact of existing; existence. **2.** essential substance or nature. **3.** a living person or thing.

be•la•bor (bi lā′bər), *v.t.* **1.** to explain, worry about, or work at unduly. **2.** to assail, as with ridicule. **3.** to beat; pummel.

Be•la•rus (byel′ə rōōs′, bel′-), *n.* a republic in E Europe, N of Ukraine: formerly a part of the USSR.

be•lat•ed (bi lā′tid), *adj.* late or delayed. —**be•lat′ed•ly,** *adv.*

belch (belch), *v.i., v.t.* **1.** to expel (gas) noisily from the stomach through the mouth. **2.** to gush forth: *Smoke belched from the chimney.* —*n.* **3.** an act or instance of belching.

be•lea•guer (bi lē′gər), *v.t.* **1.** to surround with military forces. **2.** to beset, as with difficulties.

bel•fry (bel′frē), *n., pl.* **-fries. 1.** a bell tower. **2.** the part of a steeple in which a bell is hung.

Bel•gium (bel′jəm), *n.* a kingdom in W Europe. —**Bel′gian,** *n., adj.*

be•lie (bi lī′), *v.t.,* **-lied, -ly•ing. 1.** to show to be false; contradict. **2.** to misrepresent. **3.** to be false to or disappoint: *to belie one's faith.*

be•lief (bi lēf′), *n.* **1.** something believed; opinion; conviction. **2.** confidence; faith; trust. **3.** a religious creed or faith.

believe to **berth**

be•lieve (bi lēv′), v., **-lieved, -liev•ing.** —v.i. **1.** to accept the truth, existence, reliability, or value of something. —v.t. **2.** to accept as true or real. **3.** to have confidence in the assertions of (a person). **4.** to suppose; think. —**be•liev′a•ble,** adj. —**be•liev′er,** n.

be•lit•tle (bi lit′l), v.t., **-tled, -tling.** to regard or portray as less impressive or important; disparage. —**be•lit′tle•ment,** n.

Be•lize (bə lēz′), n. a country in N Central America. —**Be•li′ze•an** (-zē ən), adj., n.

bell (bel), n. **1.** a hollow, cup-shaped metal instrument that rings when struck. **2.** the sound of a bell. **3.** something having the form of a bell. **4.** any of the half-hour units of nautical time rung on the bell of a ship. —v.t. **5.** to put a bell on. —v.i. **6.** to have the form of a bell.

bel•la•don•na (bel′ə don′ə), n., pl. **-nas. 1.** a poisonous plant with purplish red flowers and black berries. **2.** ATROPINE.

belle (bel), n. a woman or girl admired for her beauty and charm.

bell′hop′ n. a person employed, esp. by a hotel, to carry luggage and run errands.

bel•li•cose (bel′i kōs′), adj. inclined or eager to fight or quarrel. —**bel′li•cos′i•ty** (-kos′i tē), n.

bel•lig•er•ent (bə lij′ər ənt), adj. **1.** engaged in warfare. **2.** aggressively hostile. —n. **3.** a state or nation at war. **4.** a belligerent person. —**bel•lig′er•ence, bel•lig′er•en•cy,** n. —**bel•lig′er•ent•ly,** adv.

bel•low (bel′ō), v.i. **1.** to emit the loud hollow cry typical of a bull. **2.** to roar; bawl. —v.t. **3.** to utter in a loud deep voice. —n. **4.** a bellowing sound.

bel•lows (bel′ōz, -əz), n. (used with a sing. or pl. v.) **1.** a device for producing a strong current of air, consisting of a chamber that can be expanded and contracted. **2.** something resembling a bellows.

bell pepper n. a plant yielding a mild, bell-shaped pepper.

bell•weth•er (bel′weth′ər), n. **1.** one that leads or marks a trend. **2.** a sheep wearing a bell and leading a flock.

bel•ly (bel′ē), n., pl. **-lies,** v., **-lied, -ly•ing.** —n. **1.** the abdomen or underpart of an animal. **2.** the stomach with its adjuncts. **3.** the deep interior of something: a ship's belly. —v.t., v.i. **4.** to swell out.

bel′ly•ache′ n., v., **-ached, -ach•ing.** —n. **1.** a pain in the abdomen. —v.i. **2.** Informal. to complain.

be•long (bi lông′, -long′), v.i. **1.** to be properly placed. **2.** to be appropriate or suitable. **3. belong to, a.** to be the property of. **b.** to be a part or adjunct of: That cover belongs to this jar. **c.** to be a member of.

be•long′ings n.pl. possessions; personal effects.

be•lov•ed (bi luv′id, -luvd′), adj. **1.** greatly loved. —n. **2.** a person who is beloved.

be•low (bi lō′), adv. **1.** in or toward a lower place. **2.** on, in, or toward a lower deck or floor. **3.** on earth. **4.** in hell. **5.** at a later point in a text. **6.** in a lower rank or grade. —prep. **7.** lower down than. **8.** too undignified to be worthy of.

belt (belt), n. **1.** a band of flexible material, as leather, for encircling the waist. **2.** any encircling band or strip. **3.** an extended region having distinctive characteristics. **4.** an endless band passing about pulleys, used to transmit motion or convey objects. **5.** Slang. **a.** a hard blow. **b.** a swallow of liquor. —v.t. **6.** to gird or furnish with a belt. **7.** to sing loudly. **8.** Slang. to hit; strike. —**Idiom. 9. below the belt,** unfair or unfairly.

belt′way′ n. a highway around the perimeter of an urban area.

be•moan (bi mōn′), v.t. to express distress or grief over.

be•mused′ (bi myōozd′) adj. lost in thought; preoccupied.

bench (bench), n. **1.** a long, hard seat for several people. **2.** a seat occupied by a judge. **3. a.** the office or dignity of a judge. **b.** judges collectively. **4.** the seat on which the players of a team sit while not playing in a game. **5.** WORKBENCH. —v.t. **6.** to

seat on a bench. **7.** to remove (a player) from a game.

bench′mark′ or **bench′ mark′,** n. a standard or reference by which others can be measured or judged.

bend (bend), v., **bent, bend•ing,** n. —v.t. **1.** to force from a straight form into a curved or angular one. **2.** to guide in a particular direction. **3.** to cause to submit. —v.i. **4.** to become curved or bent. **5.** to assume a bent posture; stoop. **6.** to turn or incline in a particular direction. **7.** to yield; submit. —n. **8.** the act of bending. **9.** something bent. —**bend′a•ble,** adj.

be•neath (bi nēth′, -nēth′), adv. **1.** in or to a lower position; below. **2.** underneath. —prep. **3.** below; under. **4.** below the level or dignity of: behavior beneath contempt.

ben•e•dic•tion (ben′i dik′shən), n. the invocation of a blessing, esp. the short blessing at the close of a religious service.

ben′e•fac′tor, n. **1.** a kindly helper. **2.** a person who makes a bequest or endowment, as to an institution.

be•nef•i•cent (bə nef′ə sənt), adj. doing good or causing good to be done; charitable. —**be•nef′i•cence,** n. —**be•nef′i•cent•ly,** adv.

ben•e•fi•cial (ben′ə fish′əl), adj. conferring benefit; advantageous. —**ben′e•fi′cial•ly,** adv.

ben′e•fi′ci•ar′y (-fish′ē er′ē, -fish′ə rē), n., pl. **-ies. 1.** one that receives benefits. **2.** a recipient of funds or other property under a will, trust, etc.

ben′e•fit (-fit), n. **1.** something that is advantageous or good. **2.** a payment made by an insurance company, public agency, etc. **3.** a social event or a performance to raise money for a cause. —v.t. **4.** to be advantageous to. —v.i. **5.** to derive benefit.

be•nev•o•lent (bə nev′ə lənt), adj. **1.** characterized by goodwill. **2.** desiring to help others; charitable. **3.** established for good works. —**be•nev′o•lence,** n. —**be•nev′o•lent•ly,** adv.

be•night•ed (bi nī′tid), adj. **1.** ignorant. **2.** overtaken by darkness or night.

be•nign (bi nīn′), adj. **1.** having a kindly disposition. **2.** favorable; propitious. **3.** not malignant. —**be•nign′ly,** adv.

be•nig′nant (-nig′nənt), adj. **1.** benign; gracious. **2.** beneficial.

Be•nin (be nēn′), n. a republic in W Africa. —**Be•ni′nese,** adj., n., pl. **-nese.**

bent (bent), adj. **1.** curved; crooked. **2.** determined; resolved. —n. **3.** a predilection; talent.

be•numb (bi num′), v.t. **1.** to make numb. **2.** to make inactive; stupefy.

ben•zene (ben′zēn, ben zēn′), n. a colorless, flammable liquid obtained chiefly from coal tar: used in chemicals and as a solvent.

be•queath (bi kwēth′, -kwēth′), v.t. **1.** to dispose of (property or money) in a will. **2.** to hand down.

be•quest (bi kwest′), n. **1.** the act of bequeathing. **2.** something bequeathed.

be•rate (bi rāt′), v.t., **-rat•ed, -rat•ing.** to scold; rebuke.

be•reaved′ (bi revd′) adj. suffering a loved one's death. —**be•reave′, v.t., -reaved** or **-reft, -reav•ing.** —**be•reave′ment,** n.

be•reft′ (-reft′) adj. deprived of something.

be•ret (bə rā′), n. a soft, visorless cap.

ber•i•ber•i (ber′ē ber′ē), n. a disease caused by lack of vitamin B_1, leading to paralysis and emaciation.

ber•ry (ber′ē), n., pl. **-ries,** v., **-ried, -ry•ing.** —n. **1.** any small, usu. stoneless, juicy fruit, as the strawberry. **2.** a dry seed or kernel, as of wheat. —v.i. **3.** to gather or produce berries. —**ber′ry•like′,** adj.

ber•serk (bər sûrk′, -zûrk′), adj. violently or destructively frenzied. [< ON berserkr frenzied warrior = ber- bear + serkr shirt]

berth (bûrth), n. **1.** a shelflike sleeping space, as on a ship or train. **2.** a space allotted for a ship to dock or lie at anchor. **3.** a job; position. —v.t. **4.** to allot a berth to. —v.i. **5.** to come into a berth.

—*Idiom.* **6. give a wide berth to,** to keep a careful distance from.

ber•yl (ber′əl), *n.* a mineral, varieties of which are valued as gems: the chief ore of beryllium.

be•ryl•li•um (bə ril′ē əm), *n.* a hard, light metallic element used chiefly in copper alloys to reduce fatigue. *Symbol:* Be; *at. wt.:* 9.0122; *at. no.:* 4.

be•seech (bi sēch′), *v.t., v.i.,* **-sought** or **-seeched, -seech•ing.** to beg or ask eagerly (for). —**be•seech′er,** *n.* —**be•seech′ing•ly,** *adv.*

be•set (bi set′), *v.t.,* **-set, -set•ting. 1.** to attack on all sides; harass. **2.** to surround.

be•side (bi sīd′), *prep.* **1.** by or at the side of; near. **2.** compared with. **3.** apart from: *beside the point.* **4.** BESIDES (defs. 4, 5). —*Idiom.* **5. beside oneself,** frantic; distraught.

be•sides′ *adv.* **1.** moreover; furthermore. **2.** in addition. **3.** otherwise; else. —*prep.* **4.** in addition to. **5.** other than; except: *no one here besides me.*

be•siege (bi sēj′), *v.t.,* **-sieged, -sieg•ing. 1.** to lay siege to. **2.** to crowd around. **3.** to importune, as with requests. —**be•sieg′er,** *n.*

be•smirch (bi smûrch′), *v.t.* to soil; sully.

be•sot′ted (bi sot′id) *adj.* **1.** drunk. **2.** infatuated.

be•speak (bi spēk′), *v.t.,* **-spoke, -spo•ken** or **-spoke, -speak•ing. 1.** to reserve beforehand. **2.** to show; indicate.

best (best), *adj., superl. of* **good** *with* **better** *as compar.* **1.** of the highest quality or standing. **2.** most advantageous or suitable. **3.** largest: *the best part of a day.* —*adv., superl. of* **well** *with* **better** *as compar.* **4.** most excellently. **5.** in or to the highest degree. —*n.* **6.** someone or something that is best. **7.** salutations: *Give them my best.* —*v.t.* **8.** to get the better of; beat or surpass. —*Idiom.* **9. at best,** even under the most favorable circumstances. **10. get the best of, a.** to gain the advantage over. **b.** to defeat; subdue. **11. make the best of,** to cope with; accept.

bes•tial (bes′chəl, bēs′-), *adj.* **1.** of or having the form of a beast. **2.** brutal or inhuman. —**bes′ti•al′i•ty** (-chē al′i tē), *n.* —**bes′tial•ly,** *adv.*

be•stir (bi stûr′), *v.t.,* **-stirred, -stir•ring.** to rouse to action.

best′ man *n.* the chief attendant of the bridegroom at a wedding.

be•stow (bi stō′), *v.t.* to present as a gift; confer. —**be•stow′al,** *n.*

bet (bet), *v.,* **bet** or **bet•ted, bet•ting,** *n.* —*v.t.* **1.** to pledge (money, etc.) as a forfeit if one's forecast of a future event is wrong. **2.** to maintain as in a bet. —*v.i.* **3.** to make a bet. —*n.* **4.** a pledge made in betting. **5.** a thing pledged. **6.** something bet on. **7.** a person or thing considered a good choice.

be•take (bi tāk′), *v.t.,* **-took, -tak•en, -tak•ing.** to cause (oneself) to go.

bête noire (bāt′ nwär′, bet′), *n., pl.* **bêtes noires** (bāt′ nwärz′, bet′). a person or thing disliked or dreaded. [< F]

be•tide (bi tīd′), *v.t., v.i.,* **-tid•ed, -tid•ing.** to happen (to).

be•to•ken (bi tō′kən), *v.t.* **1.** to give evidence of; indicate. **2.** to portend.

be•tray (bi trā′), *v.t.* **1.** to deliver or expose to an enemy by treachery. **2.** to be unfaithful or disloyal to. **3.** to reveal (something meant to be hidden). **4.** to seduce and desert. —**be•tray′al,** *n.* —**be•tray′er,** *n.*

be•troth (bi trōth′, -trôth′), *v.t.* to promise to give in marriage. —**be•troth′al,** *n.*

bet•ter (bet′ər), *adj., compar. of* **good** *with* **best** *as superl.* **1.** of superior quality or excellence. **2.** of superior suitability; preferable. **3.** larger; greater. **4.** improved in health. —*adv., compar. of* **well** *with* **best** *as superl.* **5.** in a more excellent manner. **6.** more completely. **7.** more: *lives better than a mile away.* —*v.t.* **8.** to make better; improve. **9.** to surpass or exceed. —*n.* **10.** something that is preferable. **11.** Usu., **-ters.** those superior to oneself. —*Idiom.* **12. get the better of,** to prevail against.

bet′ter•ment *n.* the act of bettering; improvement.

bet′tor or **bet′ter,** *n.* one who bets.

be•tween (bi twēn′), *prep.* **1.** in the space separating. **2.** intermediate to in time, quantity, or degree. **3.** linking; connecting. **4.** by the common participation of: *Between us, we can finish the job.* **5.** distinguishing one from the other in comparison. **6.** existing confidentially for: *We'll keep this between ourselves.* —*adv.* **7.** in the intervening space or time.

be•twixt′ (-twikst′), *prep., adv.* **1.** between. —*Idiom.* **2. betwixt and between,** in a middle position.

bev•el (bev′əl), *n., v.,* **-eled, -el•ing** or (*esp. Brit.*) **-elled, -el•ling.** —*n.* **1.** the inclination or angle that one line or surface makes with another when not at right angles. **2.** an adjustable tool for laying out or measuring angles. —*v.t.* **3.** to cut at a bevel. —*v.i.* **4.** to slant; incline.

bev•er•age (bev′ər ij), *n.* any drinkable liquid, esp. other than water. [< AF, = *bevre* to drink (< L *bibere*) + *-age*]

bev•y (bev′ē), *n., pl.* **-ies. 1.** a group of birds, esp. quail. **2.** a large group or collection.

be•wail (bi wāl′), *v.t.* to express deep sorrow for; lament.

be•ware (bi wâr′), *v.t., v.i.* to be wary, cautious, or careful (of).

be•wil•der (bi wil′dər), *v.t.* to confuse or puzzle completely. —**be•wil′der•ment,** *n.*

be•witch (bi wich′), *v.t.* **1.** to affect by witchcraft or magic. **2.** to charm; fascinate. —**be•witch′ing•ly,** *adv.* —**be•witch′ment,** *n.*

be•yond (bē ond′), *prep.* **1.** on, at, or to the farther side of. **2.** more distant than. **3.** outside the limits or reach of. —*adv.* **4.** farther on or away.

Bhu•tan (bōō tän′), *n.* a kingdom in the Himalayas, NE of India. —**Bhu•tan•ese** (bōōt′n ēz′, -ēs′), *n., adj.* **-ese,** *adj.*

Bi *Chem. Symbol.* bismuth.

bi- a combining form meaning: twice (*biannual*); two (*bilateral*).

bi•an•nu•al (bī an′yōō əl), *adj.* occurring twice a year; semiannual. —**bi•an′nu•al•ly,** *adv.*

bi•as (bī′əs), *n., adv., v.,* **bi•ased, bi•as•ing** or (*esp. Brit.*) **bi•assed, bi•as•sing.** —*n.* **1.** a diagonal line running across a woven fabric. **2.** a particular tendency or inclination; prejudice. —*adv.* **3.** in a diagonal manner. —*v.t.* **4.** to cause partiality in; prejudice.

bi•ath•lon (bī ath′lon), *n.* **1.** an athletic contest combining cross-country skiing with rifle shooting. **2.** an athletic contest comprising any two consecutive events.

bib (bib), *n.* **1.** a shield of cloth, paper, etc., tied under the chin to protect the clothing during a meal. **2.** the upper front part of an apron, overalls, or the like.

Bib. 1. Bible. **2.** biblical.

Bi•ble (bī′bəl), *n.* **1.** the sacred writings of the Christian religion, comprising the Old and New Testaments. **2.** the sacred writings of the Jewish religion; Old Testament. **3.** (*l.c.*) a reference work esteemed for its usefulness and authority. [< OF < ML < Gk *biblíon* book, papyrus roll, der. of *býblos* papyrus, after *Býblos*, Phoenician port known for export of papyrus] —**Bib•li•cal, bib•li•cal** (bib′li-kəl), *adj.*

bib•li•og•ra•phy (bib′lē og′rə fē), *n., pl.* **-phies.** a list of writings compiled upon some common principle, as authorship or subject. —**bib′li•og′ra•pher,** *n.* —**bib′li•o•graph′ic** (-ə graf′ik), **bib′li•o•graph′i•cal,** *adj.*

bi•cam•er•al (bī kam′ər əl), *adj.* having two branches, as a legislative body. —**bi•cam′er•al•ism,** *n.*

bi•car′bo•nate of so′da (bī kär′bə nit, -nāt′), *n.* SODIUM BICARBONATE.

bi′cen•ten′ni•al *adj.* **1.** lasting 200 years. **2.** occurring every 200 years. —*n.* **3.** a 200th anniversary.

bi′ceps (-seps), *n., pl.* **-ceps, -ceps•es** (-sep siz). a muscle with two points of origin, as the muscle at the front of the upper arm.

bick•er (bik′ər), *v.i.* **1.** to engage in peevish argument. —*n.* **2.** a peevish quarrel. —**bick′er•er,** *n.*

bi•cus•pid *adj.* **1.** having two cusps or points, as certain teeth. —*n.* **2.** PREMOLAR (def. 1).

bi•cy•cle (bī′si kəl), *n., v.,* **-cled, -cling.** —*n.* **1.** a vehicle with two wheels in tandem, propelled by pedals and having handlebars for steering. —*v.i.* **2.** to ride a bicycle. —**bi′cy•clist,** *n.*

bid (bid), *v.,* **bade** or **bid, bid•den** or **bid, bid•ding,** *n.* —*v.t.* **1.** to command; order. **2.** to say as a greeting or wish. **3.** to offer (a sum) as the price one will charge or pay. **4.** to enter a bid of (a given quantity or suit at cards). —*v.i.* **5.** to make a bid. —*n.* **6.** the act of bidding. **7.** (in card games) **a.** an offer to make a specified number of points or tricks. **b.** the amount bid. **c.** a turn to bid. **8.** an invitation. **9.** an attempt to attain some goal or purpose. —**bid′der,** *n.*

bide (bīd), *v.i.,* **bid•ed** or **bode, bid•ed, bid•ing. 1.** to wait; remain. —*Idiom.* **2. bide one's time,** to wait for a favorable opportunity.

bi•det (bē dā′, bi det′), *n.* a low, basinlike bathroom fixture used for bathing the genital and perineal areas.

bi•en•ni•al (bī en′ē əl), *adj.* **1.** happening every two years. **2.** lasting for two years. **3.** (of a plant) living for two years, blooming and forming seeds in the second year. —*n.* **4.** an event occurring once in two years. **5.** a biennial plant. —**bi•en′ni•al•ly,** *adv.*

bier (bēr), *n.* a frame on which a corpse or coffin is laid before burial.

bi•fo•cal (bī fō′kəl, bī′fō′-), *adj.* **1.** (of an eyeglass lens) having two portions, one for near and one for far vision. —*n.* **2. -cals,** eyeglasses with bifocal lenses.

big (big), *adj.,* **big•ger, big•gest,** *adv.* —*adj.* **1.** large in size, amount, etc. **2.** important. **3.** grown-up; mature. **4.** magnanimous: *a big heart.* **5.** boastful. **6.** loud: *a big voice.* **7.** pregnant. —*adv.* **8.** boastfully. **9.** successfully. —**big′ness,** *n.*

big•a•my (big′ə mē), *n.* the act of marrying one person while still being legally married to another. —**big′a•mist,** *n.* —**big′a•mous,** *adj.*

big′ bang′ the′ory *n.* a theory that the universe began with an explosion of a dense mass of matter and is still expanding.

big′horn′ *n., pl.* **-horns, -horn.** a wild sheep of the Rocky Mountains with large, curving horns.

bight (bīt), *n.* **1.** a loop or slack part in a rope. **2.** a curve in the shore of a sea or river. **3.** a bay or gulf.

big•ot (big′ət), *n.* a person who is extremely intolerant of another's creed, belief, or opinion. —**big′ot•ed,** *adj.* —**big′ot•ry,** *n.*

big′ shot′ *n. Informal.* an important or influential person.

bike (bīk), *n., v.,* **biked, bik•ing.** —*n.* **1.** a bicycle, motorbike, or motorcycle. —*v.i.* **2.** to ride a bike. —**bik′er,** *n.*

bi•ki•ni (bi kē′nē), *n., pl.* **-nis. 1.** a very brief two-piece bathing suit for women. **2.** a very brief bathing suit for men. **3.** underwear briefs fitted low on the hip.

bi•lat•er•al (bī lat′ər əl), *adj.* **1.** having two sides. **2.** of or involving two or both sides, factions, or the like. —**bi•lat′er•al•ly,** *adv.*

bile (bīl), *n.* **1.** a bitter yellow or greenish liquid, secreted by the liver, that aids in digestion of fats. **2.** ill temper.

bilge (bilj), *n.* **1.** the lowest interior part of a ship's hull. **2.** Also called **bilge′ wa′ter.** seepage accumulated in bilges. **3.** *Slang.* foolish or worthless talk or ideas.

bi•lin•gual (bī ling′gwəl), *adj.* **1.** able to speak two languages. **2.** expressed in, involving, or using two languages. —**bi•lin′gual•ism,** *n.*

bil•ious (bil′yəs), *adj.* **1.** pertaining to bile. **2.** suffering from or attended by trouble with the liver. **3.** peevish; irritable. —**bil′ious•ness,** *n.*

bilk (bilk), *v.t.* to defraud; cheat. —**bilk′er,** *n.*

bill¹ (bil), *n.* **1.** a statement of money owed for goods or services supplied. **2.** a piece of paper money. **3.** a draft of a statute presented to a legislature. **4.** a public notice or advertisement. **5.** any written statement of particulars. **6.** a written statement, usu. of complaint, presented to a court. **7.** entertainment scheduled for presentation; program. —*v.t.* **8.** to send a bill. **9.** to enter (charges) in a bill. **10.** to advertise by bill or public notice. —*Idiom.* **11. fill the bill,** to fulfill a particular purpose or need.

bill² (bil), *n.* **1.** the parts of a bird's jaws that are covered with a horny or leathery sheath; beak. —*v.i.* **2.** to join bills, as doves. —*Idiom.* **3. bill and coo,** to kiss or fondle and whisper endearments.

bill′board′ *n.* a flat board, usu. outdoors, on which large advertisements are posted.

bil•let (bil′it), *n.* **1.** lodging for a soldier in a nonmilitary building. **2.** an official order directing the addressee to provide such lodging. **3.** a job; position; appointment. —*v.t.* **4.** to provide lodging for; quarter.

bil•let-doux (bil′ā dōō′), *n., pl.* **bil•lets-doux** (bil′ā dōōz′, -dōō′). a love letter. [< F]

bill′fold′ *n.* WALLET.

bil•liards (bil′yərdz), *n.* a game played with hard balls that are driven with a cue on a cloth-covered table. —**bil′liard,** *adj.*

bil•lion (bil′yən), *n., pl.* **-lions, -lion.** a cardinal number represented in the U.S. by 1 followed by 9 zeros, and in Great Britain by 1 followed by 12 zeros. —**bil′lionth,** *adj., n.*

bil′lion•aire′ (-âr′), *n.* a person with assets worth a billion or more dollars, pounds, etc.

bill′ of sale′ *n.* a document transferring title in personal property from seller to buyer.

bil•low (bil′ō), *n.* **1.** a great wave or surge of the sea. **2.** any surging mass: *billows of smoke.* —*v.i.* **3.** to rise, roll, or swell in billows. —**bil′low•y,** *adj.*

bil′ly goat′ *n.* a male goat.

bim′bo (bim′bō), *n., pl.* **-bos, -boes.** *Slang.* an unintelligent young woman with loose morals.

bi•month•ly (bī munth′lē), *adj., adv., n., pl.* **-lies.** —*adj.* **1.** occurring every two months. **2.** occurring twice a month; semimonthly. —*n.* **3.** a bimonthly publication.

bin (bin), *n.* a box or enclosed place for storing grain, coal, etc.

bi•na•ry (bī′nə rē), *adj., n., pl.* **-ries.** —*adj.* **1.** consisting of, indicating, or involving two. **2.** of or being a system of numerical notation to the base 2, in which each place of a number, expressed as 0 or 1, corresponds to a power of 2. **3.** of or involving a choice between two alternatives. —*n.* **4.** a whole composed of two.

bind (bīnd), *v.,* **bound, bind•ing,** *n.* —*v.t.* **1.** to fasten or encircle with a band, cord, etc. **2.** to bandage (often fol. by *up*). **3.** to fix in place by girding. **4.** to cause to cohere. **5.** to constrain or obligate, as by oath or law. **6.** to secure (a book) within a cover. **7.** to cover the edge of, as for protection or ornament. **8.** (of clothing) to chafe or restrict (the wearer). **9.** to constipate. —*v.i.* **10.** to cohere. **11.** to be obligatory. —*n.* **12.** something that binds. **13.** a difficult situation or predicament. —**bind′er,** *n.*

bind′ing *n.* **1.** anything that binds. **2.** the covering within which the leaves of a book are bound. —*adj.* **3.** having power to bind; obligatory.

binge (binj), *n., v.,* **binged, bing•ing.** —*n.* **1.** a bout of excessive indulgence, as in eating or drinking. —*v.i.* **2.** to go on a binge.

bin•go (bing′gō), *n.* a game of chance similar to lotto, usu. played by a large number of persons in competition for prizes.

bin•na•cle (bin′ə kəl), *n.* a stand or housing for a nautical compass.

bin•oc′u•lars (bə nok′yə lərz, bī-) *n.pl.* field glasses.

bio- a combining form meaning life or living organisms (*biodegradable*).

bi•o•chem•is•try (bī′ō kem′ə strē), *n.* the study of the chemical substances and processes of living matter. —**bi′o•chem′i•cal,** *adj.* —**bi′o•chem′ist,** *n.*

bi•o•de•grad′a•ble *adj.* capable of decaying

through the action of living organisms: *biodegradable paper.* —bi•o•de•grad′a•bil′i•ty, *n.*

bi′o•en′gi•neer′ing *n.* **1.** application of engineering principles to problems in biology and medicine. **2.** application of biological principles to manufacturing or engineering processes.

bi′o•eth′ics *n.* a field concerned with the ethical implications of certain medical procedures, as genetic engineering.

bi′o•feed′back′ *n.* a method of learning to modify a particular body function, as blood pressure, by monitoring it with the aid of an electronic device.

bi•og•ra•phy (bī og′rə fē), *n., pl.* **-phies.** a written account of another person's life. —bi•og′ra•pher, *n.* —bi′o•graph′i•cal (-ə graf′i kəl), *adj.*

bi′o•haz′ard *n.* anything used in or produced in biological research that poses a health hazard.

biol. **1.** biological. **2.** biologist. **3.** biology.

biolog′ical clock′ *n.* **1.** an innate mechanism of the body that regulates its rhythmic and periodic cycles. **2.** such a mechanism perceived as marking the passage of one's ability to bear children.

biolog′ical war′fare *n.* the wartime use of pathogenic organisms or toxins to destroy resources or human lives.

bi•ol•o•gy (bī ol′ə jē), *n.* **1.** the scientific study of life or living matter in all its forms and processes. **2.** the biological phenomena characteristic of an organism. —bi•o•log′i•cal (-ə loj′i kəl), *adj.* —bi′o•log′i•cal•ly, *adv.* —bi•ol′o•gist, *n.*

bi•on•ics (bī on′iks), *n.* the design of electronic devices and mechanical parts that perform tasks after the manner of humans and animals. —bi•on′ic, *adj.*

bi•op•sy (bī′op sē), *n., pl.* **-sies.** the removal for diagnostic study of a piece of tissue from a living body.

bi′o•rhythm (bī′ō-), *n.* an innate periodicity in an organism's physiological processes, as sleep and wake cycles.

bi′o•sphere′ (bī′ə-), *n.* the part of the earth's crust, waters, and atmosphere that supports life.

bi′o•tech•nol′o•gy (bī′ō-), *n.* the use of living organisms in the manufacture of drugs or other products or for environmental management.

bi•par•ti•san (bī pär′tə zən), *adj.* representing, characterized by, or including members from two parties or factions. —bi•par′ti•san•ship′, *n.*

bi•par′tite (-pär′tīt), *adj.* **1.** divided into or consisting of two parts. **2.** shared by two; joint.

bi′ped (-ped), *n.* a two-footed animal.

birch (bûrch), *n.* **1.** a tree with a smooth, laminated outer bark and close-grained wood. **2.** the wood itself. **3.** a bundle of birch twigs used for whipping.

bird (bûrd), *n.* **1.** a warm-blooded, egg-laying vertebrate having feathers and forelimbs modified into wings. —*Idiom.* **2. birds of a feather,** people with similar attitudes or interests. **3. for the birds,** *Informal.* worthless.

bird′ie *n.* a score of one stroke under par on a golf hole.

bird′s′-eye′ *adj.* **1.** seen from above; panoramic: *a bird's-eye view of the city.* **2.** superficial; general. **3.** having markings resembling birds' eyes: *bird's-eye tweed.*

birth (bûrth), *n.* **1.** an act or instance of being born. **2.** the act of bringing forth offspring. **3.** lineage; descent. **4.** any coming into existence. —*Idiom.* **5. give birth to, a.** to bear (a child). **b.** to originate. —birth′day′, *n.* —birth′place′, *n.*

birth′ control′ *n.* regulation of the number of children born through control or prevention of conception.

birth′mark′ *n.* a minor disfigurement or blemish on a person's skin at birth.

birth′rate′ *n.* the number of births in a place in a given time, usu. expressed as a quantity per 1000 of population.

birth′right′ *n.* any right or privilege to which a person is entitled by birth.

bis•cuit (bis′kit), *n.* **1.** a small, soft, raised bread, usu. leavened with baking powder or soda. **2.**

Chiefly Brit. a cracker or cookie. [< MF *biscuit* seamen's bread, lit., twice cooked]

bi•sect (bī sekt′), *v.t.* **1.** to cut or divide into two equal parts. **2.** to intersect or cross. —*v.i.* **3.** to split into two, as a road; fork. —bi•sec′tor, *n.*

bish•op (bish′əp), *n.* **1.** a prelate who supervises a number of local churches or a diocese. **2.** one of two chess pieces that may be moved any unobstructed distance diagonally. [< LL *episcopus* < Gk *epískopos* overseer]

bish′op•ric (-rik) *n.* the see, diocese, or office of a bishop.

bis•muth (biz′məth), *n.* a brittle, grayish white metallic element used in the manufacture of fusible alloys and in medicine. *Symbol:* Bi; *at. wt.:* 208.980; *at. no.:* 83.

bi•son (bī′sən), *n., pl.* **-son.** a North American buffalo, having a large head and high, humped shoulders.

bis•tro (bis′trō, bē′strō), *n.* a small, modest, European-style restaurant or café.

bit[1] (bit), *n.* **1.** the mouthpiece of a bridle. **2.** a removable drilling or boring tool for use in a brace, drill press, etc.

bit[2] (bit), *n.* **1.** a small piece or quantity of something. **2.** a short time. **3.** a stereotypic set of behaviors, attitudes, or actions associated with a particular role, situation, etc.: *the whole Wall Street bit.* **4.** a very small role, as in a movie. **5.** *Informal.* an amount equivalent to 12½ cents: *two bits.* —*Idiom.* **6. a bit,** somewhat: *a bit sleepy.* **7. bit by bit,** gradually. **8. do one's bit,** to contribute one's share to an effort.

bit[3] (bit), *n.* a single, basic unit of computer information, valued at either 0 or 1 to indicate the choice made between two alternatives. [*b(inary)* + *(dig)it*]

bitch (bich), *n.* **1.** a female dog. **2.** a female of canines generally. **3.** *Slang.* a malicious, unpleasant, selfish woman. —*v.i.* **4.** *Slang.* to complain; gripe. —bitch•y, *adj.,* -i•er, -i•est.

bite (bīt), *v.,* **bit, bit•ten** or **bit, bit•ing,** *n.* —*v.t.* **1.** to cut, wound, or tear with the teeth. **2.** to grip with the teeth. **3.** to sting, as an insect. **4.** to cause to sting or smart. **5.** to corrode. —*v.i.* **6.** to attack with the jaws, bill, sting, etc. **7.** (of fish) to take bait. **8.** to accept a deceptive offer or suggestion. **9.** to take a firm hold. —*n.* **10.** the act of biting. **11.** a wound made by biting. **12.** a cutting, stinging, or nipping effect. **13.** a small meal. **14.** a morsel of food. **15.** an exacted portion: *the tax bite.*

bit′ing *adj.* **1.** nipping; keen. **2.** cutting; sarcastic.

bit•ter (bit′ər), *adj.,* -ter•er, -ter•est. **1.** having a harsh, acrid taste. **2.** hard to bear; grievous. **3.** causing sharp pain: *a bitter chill.* **4.** characterized by intense hostility or resentment. **5.** experienced at great cost: *a bitter lesson.* —bit′ter•ly, *adv.* —bit′ter•ness, *n.*

bit•tern (bit′ərn), *n.* any of several wading birds of the heron family that inhabit reedy marshes.

bit′ter•sweet′ *adj.* **1.** both bitter and sweet to the taste. **2.** both pleasant and painful. —*n.* **3.** a climbing or trailing plant with scarlet berries. **4.** a climbing plant bearing orange capsules opening to expose red-coated seeds.

bi•tu•men (bī tōō′mən, -tyōō′-), *n.* any of various natural substances, as asphalt, consisting mainly of hydrocarbons. —bi•tu′mi•nous, *adj.*

bitu′minous coal′ *n.* a coal rich in volatile hydrocarbons and burning with a yellow, smoky flame.

bi•va•lent (bī vā′lənt, biv′ə-), *adj.* having a valence of two.

bi′valve′ *n.* a mollusk, as the oyster or clam, having two shells hinged together.

biv•ou•ac (biv′ōō ak′), *n., v.,* -acked, -ack•ing. —*n.* **1.** a military encampment made with tents or improvised shelters. —*v.i.* **2.** to assemble in a bivouac.

bi•week′ly (bī-), *adj.* **1.** occurring every two weeks. **2.** occurring twice a week; semiweekly.

bi•zarre (bi zär′), *adj.* markedly unusual; strange; odd. —bi•zarre′ly, *adv.*

blab (blab), v., **blabbed, blab•bing.** —v.t. **1.** to reveal indiscreetly and thoughtlessly. —v.i. **2.** to chatter indiscreetly or thoughtlessly.

black (blak), adj., **-er, -est,** n., v. —adj. **1.** lacking hue and brightness; opposite to white. **2.** enveloped in darkness. **3.** (sometimes cap.) **a.** of or belonging to any of the dark-skinned peoples of Africa, Oceania, and Australia. **b.** AFRICAN-AMERICAN (def. 2). **4.** soiled or stained. **5.** gloomy; dismal. **6.** sullen or hostile. **7.** evil or wicked. —n. **8.** the color opposite to white, absorbing all wavelengths of light. **9.** (sometimes cap.) **a.** a member of any of various dark-skinned peoples of Africa, Oceania, and Australia. **b.** AFRICAN-AMERICAN (def. 1). **10.** black clothing, esp. as a sign of mourning. —v.t., v.i. **11.** to make or become black. **12. black out,** to lose consciousness. —Idiom. **13. in the black,** operating at a profit. —**black′ish,** adj. —**black′ness,** n.

black′-and-blue′ adj. discolored, as by bruising.

black′ball′ v.t. **1.** to vote against. **2.** to ostracize. —n. **3.** a negative vote.

black′ber′ry n., pl. **-ries. 1.** the black or dark purple fruit of certain brambles. **2.** a plant bearing blackberries.

black′bird′ n. any of several American birds with black or mostly black plumage.

black′board′ n. a sheet of smooth, hard material, esp. dark slate, used for writing on with chalk.

black′en v.t. **1.** to make black; darken. **2.** to defame; slander. —v.i. **3.** to grow black. —**black′en•er,** n.

black•guard (blag′ärd, -ərd), n. a contemptible person; scoundrel.

black′head′ n. a small, black-tipped fatty mass in a skin follicle, esp. of the face.

black′ hole′ n. a theoretical object in space, perhaps a collapsed star, whose gravitational field is so intense that no light can escape.

black′jack′ n. **1.** a short, leather-covered club with a flexible handle. **2.** a card game in which the winner gets more points than the dealer, but not more than 21. —v.t. **3.** to beat with a blackjack.

black′list′ n. **1.** a list of persons who are under suspicion, disfavor, or censure. —v.t. **2.** to put on a blacklist.

black′ mag′ic n. sorcery.

black′mail′ n. **1.** a payment extorted by intimidation, as by threats of injurious revelations. —v.t. **2.** to subject to blackmail. [black + mail rent, tribute (now dial.) < ON] —**black′mail′er,** n.

black′ mar′ket n. the illicit buying and selling of goods in violation of price controls, rationing, etc.

black′out′ n. **1.** the extinguishing or concealment of lights, as from a power failure or as a precaution against air raids. **2.** a temporary loss of consciousness. **3.** a stoppage or suppression: a news blackout.

black′ sheep′ n. a person who causes shame or embarrassment to his or her family.

black′smith′ n. **1.** a person who makes horseshoes and shoes horses. **2.** a person who forges objects of iron.

black′thorn′ n. a thorny shrub with white flowers and small plumlike fruits.

black′top′ n., v., **-topped, -top•ping.** —n. **1.** a bituminous paving substance, as asphalt. —v.t. **2.** to pave with blacktop.

black′ wid′ow n. a venomous black spider of warm regions, including the U.S.

blad•der (blad′ər), n. **1.** a saclike organ serving as a receptacle for liquids or gases, esp. urine. **2.** an inflatable object resembling a bladder.

blade (blād), n. **1.** the flat cutting part of an implement, as a knife. **2.** SWORD. **3. a.** the leaf of a plant, esp. grass. **b.** the broad part of a leaf. **4.** the metal part of an ice skate in contact with the ice. **5.** a thin, flat part of something, as of an oar. **6.** a dashing young man.

blame (blām), v., **blamed, blam•ing,** n. —v.t. **1.** to hold responsible. **2.** to find fault with; censure. **3.** to place the responsibility for (a fault, error, etc.). —n. **4.** censure; reproof. **5.** responsibility for anything deserving of censure. —**blam′a•ble, blame′-**

a•ble, adj. —**blame′less,** adj. —**blame′less•ly,** adv.

blanch (blanch, blänch), v.t. **1.** to whiten; bleach. **2.** to boil (food) briefly, as to facilitate removal of skins. **3.** to make pale, as with fear. —v.i. **4.** to turn pale.

bland (bland), adj., **-er, -est. 1.** pleasantly gentle or agreeable. **2.** not highly flavored. **3.** insipid; dull. —**bland′ly,** adv. —**bland′ness,** n.

blan′dish•ment (blan′dish mənt) n. coaxing.

blank (blangk), adj., **-er, -est,** n., v. —adj. **1.** not written or printed on. **2.** not filled in. **3.** unrelieved by ornament. **4.** void of interest. **5.** expressionless. **6.** complete; utter. —n. **7.** a place or space where something is lacking. **8.** a printed form containing such spaces. **9.** a cartridge containing powder only, without a bullet. —v.t. **10.** to keep (an opponent) from scoring in a game. **11. blank out,** to cross out or delete. —**blank′ly,** adv. —**blank′ness,** n.

blan•ket (blang′kit), n. **1.** a large piece of soft fabric used esp. as a bed covering for warmth. **2.** any extended covering: a blanket of snow. —v.t. **3.** to cover with a blanket. **4.** to interrupt; obstruct. —adj. **5.** covering a large group of things, conditions, etc.

blare (blâr), v., **blared, blar•ing,** n. —v.i., v.t. **1.** to sound or exclaim loudly. —n. **2.** a loud, raucous noise.

blar•ney (blär′nē), n. flattery; cajolery.

bla•sé (blä zā′), adj. indifferent or bored, as from an excess of worldly pleasures.

blas•pheme (blas fēm′), v., **-phemed, -phem•ing.** —v.t. **1.** to speak irreverently of (God or sacred things). **2.** to speak evil of; slander. —v.i. **3.** to speak blasphemy.

blas′phe•my (-fə mē), n., pl. **-mies.** impious utterance or action concerning God or sacred things. —**blas′phe•mous,** adj.

blast (blast, bläst), n. **1.** a violent gust of wind. **2.** the blowing of a trumpet, whistle, etc. **3.** a loud, sudden sound. **4.** a vigorous criticism. **5.** an explosion. **6.** a blight. —v.t. **7.** to make a loud noise in; blow. **8.** to blight or wither. **9.** to shatter by or as if by an explosion. **10.** to criticize vigorously. —v.i. **11.** to produce a loud, blaring sound. **12.** to detonate explosives. **13. blast off,** (of a self-propelled rocket) to leave a launch pad. —Idiom. **14. (at) full blast,** at or with full volume or speed.

blast′ fur′nace n. a furnace into which air is forced to increase the rate of combustion.

blast′off′ n. the launching of a rocket, guided missile, or spacecraft.

bla•tant (blāt′nt), adj. **1.** brazenly obvious: a blatant error. **2.** offensively noisy or loud. —**bla′tan•cy,** n. —**bla′tant•ly,** adv.

blaze¹ (blāz), n., v., **blazed, blaz•ing.** —n. **1.** a bright fire. **2.** a bright, hot glow. **3.** a vivid display. **4.** a sudden, intense outburst, as of fury. —v.i. **5.** to burn brightly. **6.** to shine like flame. **7.** to burst out suddenly or intensely.

blaze² (blāz), n., v., **blazed, blaz•ing.** —n. **1.** a mark made on a tree to indicate a trail or boundary. **2.** a white area on the face of a horse, cow, etc. —v.t. **3.** to mark with blazes.

blaze³ (blāz), v.t., **blazed, blaz•ing.** to make known; proclaim.

blaz′er n. a sports jacket usu. with metal buttons.

bldg. building.

bleach (blēch), v.t., v.i. **1.** to make or become whiter or lighter in color. —n. **2.** a bleaching agent.

bleach′ers n.pl. tiers of spectators' seats.

bleak (blēk), adj., **-er, -est. 1.** bare, desolate, and windswept. **2.** cold and raw. **3.** without hope or encouragement. —**bleak′ly,** adv. —**bleak′ness,** n.

blear•y (blēr′ē), adj., **-i•er, -i•est. 1.** (of the eyes or sight) blurred or dimmed. **2.** indistinct; unclear. —**blear′i•ness,** n.

bleat (blēt), n. **1.** the cry of a sheep or goat, or a similar sound. —v.i. **2.** to utter a bleat.

bleed (blēd), v., **bled** (bled), **bleed•ing.** —v.i. **1.** to lose blood. **2.** to exude sap, resin, etc. **3.** to run, as a dye. **4.** to feel pity, sorrow, or anguish. —v.t. **5.**

to cause to lose blood. **6.** to drain sap, water, etc., from. **7.** to extort money from.

bleep (blēp) *v.t.* to delete (sound, esp. speech) from a broadcast.

blem•ish (blem′ish), *v.t.* **1.** to destroy or diminish the perfection of. —*n.* **2.** a defect or flaw.

blend (blend), *v.t.* **1.** to mix smoothly and inseparably. **2.** to prepare by mixing varieties: *to blend tobacco.* —*v.i.* **3.** to mix or mingle. **4.** to fit or relate harmoniously. **5.** to have no perceptible separation: *Sea and sky seemed to blend.* —*n.* **6.** something produced by blending.

blend′er *n.* **1.** a person or thing that blends. **2.** an electrical appliance that chops, liquefies, or mixes foods.

bless (bles), *v.t.,* **blessed** or **blest, bless•ing. 1.** to make or pronounce holy. **2.** to request divine favor for. **3.** to bestow some benefit upon. **4.** to extol as holy. **5.** to make the sign of the cross over.

blight (blīt), *n.* **1.** any of various diseases that wither or destroy plants. **2.** any cause of impairment or frustration. —*v.t.* **3.** to cause to wither. **4.** to destroy; ruin.

blimp (blimp), *n.* a small, nonrigid airship or dirigible.

blind (blīnd), *adj.,* **-er, -est,** *v.,* *n.* —*adj.* **1.** unable to see. **2.** not characterized by control: *blind chance.* **3.** not based on reason or intelligent judgment: *blind faith.* **4.** hidden from immediate view: *a blind corner.* **5.** having no outlets: *a blind passage.* **6.** done by instruments alone: *blind flying.* **7.** of or for blind persons. —*v.t.* **8.** to make sightless. **9.** to deprive of reason or judgment. **10.** to outshine; eclipse. —*n.* **11.** something that obstructs vision. **12.** a window covering. **13.** a structure in which hunters conceal themselves. **14.** a decoy or subterfuge. —**blind′er,** *n.* —**blind′ly,** *adv.* —**blind′ness,** *n.*

blind′ date′ *n.* a prearranged date between two people who have not met.

blind′fold′ *v.t.* **1.** to cover the eyes of, as with a cloth. —*n.* **2.** a cloth or bandage for covering the eyes. —*adj.* **3.** done with the eyes covered. **4.** rash; unthinking.

blind′side′ *v.t.,* **-sided, -siding.** to hit someone unawares.

blink (blingk), *v.i.* **1.** to open and close the eye, esp. involuntarily. **2.** to flash; twinkle. —*v.t.* **3.** to cause (the eyes or something else) to blink. **4. blink at,** to ignore. —*n.* **5.** the act of blinking. **6.** a gleam; glimmer. —*Idiom.* **7. on the blink,** not working properly.

blip (blip), *n.* a spot of light on a radar screen indicating the position of an object.

bliss (blis), *n.* **1.** supreme happiness. **2.** heaven; paradise. —**bliss′ful,** *adj.* —**bliss′ful•ly,** *adv.* —**bliss′ful•ness,** *n.*

blis•ter (blis′tar), *n.* **1.** a thin swelling on the skin containing watery matter, as from a burn. **2.** any similar swelling. —*v.t.* **3.** to raise a blister on. **4.** to rebuke severely. —*v.i.* **5.** to become blistered.

blithe (blīth, blīth), *adj.,* **blith•er, blith•est. 1.** lighthearted; cheerful. **2.** carefree; heedless. —**blithe′ly,** *adv.* —**blithe′some,** *adj.*

blitz (blits), *n.* **1.** a sudden and overwhelming military attack, esp. an aerial bombing. **2.** any swift, vigorous attack or barrage. —*v.t.* **3.** to attack with a blitz. [shortening of *blitzkrieg,* < G, = *Blitz* lightning + *Krieg* war]

bliz•zard (bliz′ərd), *n.* a heavy and windy snowstorm.

bloat (blōt), *v.t.* **1.** to expand or distend, as with air or water. —*v.i.* **2.** to become swollen.

blob (blob), *n.* **1.** a small lump or drop of a glutinous substance. **2.** a shapeless mass.

bloc (blok), *n.* a group, as of nations or legislators, united to further common interests.

block (blok), *n.* **1.** a solid mass of wood, stone, etc., usu. with one or more flat faces. **2.** a piece of wood used in making woodcuts or wood engravings. **3.** a platform for an auctioneer. **4.** a frame enclosing one or more pulleys. **5.** an obstacle or hindrance. **6.** an obstruction in a physiological or mental process. **7.** a quantity or section taken as a unit: *a block of theater tickets.* **8.** a section of a city enclosed by intersecting streets, or the length of one side of such a section. —*v.t.* **9.** to obstruct or hinder. **10.** to mount or shape on a block. **11. block out,** to sketch or outline roughly. —**block′age,** *n.*

block•ade (blo kād′), *n.,* *v.,* **-ad•ed, -ad•ing.** —*n.* **1.** the closing off of a port, city, etc., by ships or troops to prevent entrance or exit. **2.** any obstruction of passage. —*v.t.* **3.** to subject to a blockade.

block′bust′er *n.* a highly successful motion picture, novel, etc.

block′head′ *n.* a stupid person.

blond (blond), *adj.,* **-er, -est,** *n.* —*adj.* **1.** having light-colored hair and skin. **2.** light-colored: *blond curls; blond wood.* —*n.* **3.** a blond person. —**blond′ness,** *n.*

blonde (blond), *adj.* **1.** (of a female) blond. —*n.* **2.** a blond woman or girl.

blood (blud), *n.* **1.** the red fluid that circulates in the vascular system of vertebrates. **2.** the vital principle; life. **3.** a person or group regarded as a source of vitality: *The company needs new blood.* **4.** bloodshed; slaughter. **5.** the sap of plants. **6.** temperament. **7.** descent from a common ancestor. —*Idiom.* **8. in cold blood,** with merciless lack of feeling.

blood′ count′ *n.* the number of red and white blood cells in a specific volume of blood.

blood′cur′dling *adj.* arousing terror; horrifying.

blood′hound′ *n.* a large hound with an acute sense of smell, used in tracking humans.

blood′mo•bile′ (-mə bēl′), *n.* a small truck with medical equipment for receiving blood donations.

blood′ pres′sure *n.* the pressure of the blood against the inner walls of the blood vessels.

blood′shed′ *n.* destruction of life, as in war.

blood′shot′ *adj.* (of the eyes) red because of dilated blood vessels.

blood′stream′ *n.* the blood flowing through the circulatory system.

blood′suck′er *n.* any animal that sucks blood, esp. a leech. —**blood′suck′ing,** *adj.*

blood′thirst′y *adj.* **1.** eager to shed blood; murderous. **2.** indicating a desire for violence. —**blood′thirst′i•ness,** *n.*

blood′ ves′sel *n.* an artery, vein, or capillary.

blood′y *adj.,* **-i•er, -i•est,** *v.,* **-ied, -y•ing.** —*adj.* **1.** stained with blood or bleeding. **2.** characterized by bloodshed. **3.** bloodthirsty. —*v.t.* **4.** to stain with blood. **5.** to cause to bleed. —**blood′i•ness,** *n.*

bloom (blōōm), *n.* **1.** the flower of a plant. **2.** flowers collectively. **3.** the state of flowering. **4.** the time of greatest beauty, vigor, or freshness. **5.** a glowing indicative of health, or youth. **6.** a whitish, powdery coating on certain fruits and leaves. —*v.i.* **7.** to produce blossoms. **8.** to flourish. **9.** to be in a state of beauty and vigor. —**bloom′er,** *n.*

bloo•mers (blōō′mərz), *n.* (*used with a pl. v.*) loose trousers gathered at the knee, formerly worn by women for sports or as an undergarment. [after A. *Bloomer* (1818–1894), U.S. social reformer and advocate of the costume]

bloop•er (blōō′pər), *n.* **1.** an embarrassing mistake, as something said on television. **2.** *Baseball.* a fly ball that carries just beyond the infield.

blos•som (blos′əm), *n.* **1.** the flower of a plant. **2.** the state of flowering. —*v.i.* **3.** to produce blossoms. **4.** to develop successfully; flourish. —**blos′som•y,** *adj.*

blot (blot), *n.,* *v.,* **blot•ted, blot•ting.** —*n.* **1.** a spot or stain, esp. of ink on paper. **2.** a blemish on a person's reputation. —*v.t.* **3.** to spot or stain. **4.** to dry or remove with absorbent paper or the like. —*v.i.* **5.** to make a blot. **6.** to become blotted. **7. blot out,** to destroy completely; obliterate.

blotch (bloch), *n.* **1.** a large, irregular spot or blot. **2.** a skin blemish. —*v.t.* **3.** to mark with blotches. —**blotch•y,** *adj.,* **-i•er, -i•est.**

blot′ter *n.* **1.** a piece of blotting paper. **2.** a book in which events are recorded as they occur: *a police blotter.*

blouse (blous, blouz), *n., v.,* **bloused, blous•ing.** —*n.* 1. a garment for women and children, covering the body from the neck to the waistline. 2. a single-breasted military jacket. —*v.i.* 3. to puff out in a drooping fullness.

blow[1] (blō), *n.* 1. a sudden, hard stroke with a hand, fist, or weapon. 2. a sudden shock, calamity, etc. 3. a sudden attack. —*Idiom.* 4. **come to blows,** to begin to fight.

blow[2] (blō), *v.,* **blew, blown, blow•ing.** —*v.i.* 1. (of the wind or air) to be in motion. 2. to move along, carried by or as if by the wind. 3. to produce a current of air, as with the mouth. 4. to give out sound by blowing or being blown. 5. (of horses) to pant. 6. to brag. 7. (of a whale) to spout. 8. (of a fuse, tire, etc.) to stop functioning or be destroyed. —*v.t.* 9. to drive by means of a current of air. 10. to clear by forcing air through. 11. to shape (glass, smoke, etc.) with a current of air. 12. to cause to sound by blowing: *to blow a horn.* 13. to cause to explode. 14. to melt (a fuse). 15. *Informal.* to squander (money). 16. *Informal.* to bungle. 17. **blow over,** to pass away; subside. 18. ~ **up, a.** to explode. **b.** to lose one's temper. —*n.* 19. a blast of air or wind. 20. a violent windstorm. 21. the act of blowing. —*Idiom.* 22. **blow off steam,** to release tension, as by loud talking. —**blow′er,** *n.*

blow′-by-′blow′ *adj.* precisely detailed: *a blow-by-blow account.*

blow′out′ *n.* 1. a sudden bursting of an automobile tire. 2. a lavish party or entertainment.

blow′torch′ *n.* a small apparatus that gives an extremely hot gasoline flame.

blow′up′ *n.* 1. an explosion. 2. a violent outburst of temper. 3. an enlargement of a photograph.

blub•ber (blub′ər), *n.* 1. the fat of whales or other large marine mammals. 2. a noisy weeping. —*v.i.* 3. to weep noisily. —**blub′ber•y,** *adj.*

bludg•eon (bluj′ən), *n.* 1. a short, heavy club with one end heavier than the other. —*v.t.* 2. to strike with a bludgeon. 3. to coerce; bully.

blue (bloo), *n., adj.,* **blu•er, blu•est,** *v.,* **blued, blu•ing** or **blue•ing.** —*n.* 1. the pure color of a clear sky. 2. something having a blue color. 3. **the blue, a.** the sky. **b.** the sea. —*adj.* 4. of the color blue. 5. (of the skin) discolored. 6. depressed or melancholy. 7. puritanical. 8. indecent; suggestive. —*v.t., v.i.* 9. to make or become blue. —*Idiom.* 10. **out of the blue,** suddenly and unexpectedly. —**blu′ish,** *adj.*

blue′ber′ry *n., pl.* **-ries.** 1. the edible, usu. bluish berry of various shrubs. 2. any of these shrubs.

blue′bird′ *n.* any of several North American songbirds, the male of which is predominantly blue.

blue′ blood′ *n.* an aristocrat or noble. —**blue′-blood′ed,** *adj.*

blue′ chip′ *n.* a common stock issued by a company with a reputation for financial strength and regular dividend payments. —**blue′-chip′,** *adj.*

blue′-col′lar *adj.* of or designating factory workers or other manual laborers.

blue′ jay′ *n.* a common crested jay with a bright blue back and gray breast.

blue′ jeans′ *n.* (*used with a pl. v.*) trousers of blue denim.

blue′ law′ *n.* any puritanical law that forbids certain practices, as doing business, on Sunday.

blue′print′ *n.* 1. a photographic print, esp. of architectural drawings, using white lines on a blue background. 2. a detailed plan of action. —*v.t.* 3. to make a blueprint of.

blue′ rib′bon *n.* the highest award or distinction, as first prize in a contest.

blues *n.* 1. **the blues,** (*used with a pl. v.*) depressed spirits; melancholy. 2. (*used with a sing. v.*) a genre of jazz and popular music comprising songs of woe and yearning.

bluff[1] (bluf), *adj.,* **-er, -est,** *n.* —*adj.* 1. good-naturedly blunt or frank. 2. presenting a nearly perpendicular front. —*n.* 3. a cliff or hill with a broad, steep face.

bluff[2] (bluf), *v.t., v.i.* 1. to mislead (someone) by

feigning confidence. —*n.* 2. the act of bluffing. 3. a person who bluffs. —**bluff′er,** *n.*

blu′ing or **blue′ing,** *n.* a substance used to whiten clothes or give them a bluish tinge.

blun•der (blun′dər), *n.* 1. a gross or stupid mistake. —*v.i.* 2. to move or act clumsily or stupidly. 3. to make a mistake, esp. through stupidity. —*v.t.* 4. to bungle; botch. —**blun′der•er,** *n.*

blunt (blunt), *adj.,* **-er, -est,** *v.* —*adj.* 1. having a dull edge or point. 2. abrupt in manner. 3. slow in perception. —*v.t., v.i.* 4. to make or become blunt. —**blunt′ly,** *adv.* —**blunt′ness,** *n.*

blur (blûr), *v.,* **blurred, blur•ring,** *n.* —*v.t., v.i.* 1. to make or become indistinct. 2. to blot or smear. 3. to make or become dull. —*n.* 4. a smudge that obscures. 5. a blurred condition or thing. —**blur′ry,** *adj.,* **-ri•er, -ri•est.**

blurb (blûrb), *n.* a brief advertisement, as on a book jacket.

blurt (blûrt), *v.t.* to utter impulsively or inadvertently (usu. fol. by *out*).

blush (blush), *v.i.* 1. to redden, as from embarrassment. 2. to feel shame or embarrassment. —*n.* 3. a reddening, as of the face. 4. a rosy tinge. —*Idiom.* 5. **at first blush,** at first glance.

blush′er *n.* 1. a person who blushes. 2. a cosmetic used to color the cheeks.

blus•ter (blus′tər), *v.i.* 1. to roar and be tumultuous, as wind. 2. to be noisy or swaggering. —*n.* 3. boisterous noise and violence. 4. noisy, empty threats or protests. —**blus′ter•er,** *n.* —**blus′ter•y,** *adj.*

blvd. boulevard.

bo•a (bō′ə), *n.* 1. a nonvenomous, chiefly tropical snake, as the boa constrictor. 2. a scarf or stole, usu. of feathers or fur.

bo′a constric′tor *n.* a large snake of tropical America able to suffocate prey by coiling around it.

boar (bôr), *n.* 1. the uncastrated male swine. 2. a wild Old World swine.

board (bôrd), *n.* 1. a rectangular piece of sawed wood. 2. a flat piece of wood or other stiff material for a specific purpose: *a cutting board.* 3. a group of persons who direct some activity: *a board of directors.* 4. daily meals, esp. as provided for pay: *room and board.* 5. the side of a ship. 6. **a.** a piece of fiberglass or other material upon which an array of computer chips is mounted. **b.** CIRCUIT BOARD. —*v.t.* 7. to cover or close with boards (often fol. by *up*). 8. to furnish with meals, or meals and lodging, esp. for pay. 9. to get on (a ship, train, etc.). —*v.i.* 10. to take one's meals at a fixed price. —*Idiom.* 11. **on board,** on or in a ship, plane, etc. —**board′er,** *n.*

board′ing•house′ *n.* a house at which meals and lodging may be obtained for payment.

board′walk′ *n.* a promenade of wooden boards, usu. along a beach.

boast (bōst), *v.i.* 1. to speak with excessive pride; brag. —*v.t.* 2. to speak of with excessive pride. 3. to be proud in the possession of: *The town boasts two new schools.* —*n.* 4. a thing boasted of. 5. exaggerated speech; bragging. —**boast′er,** *n.* —**boast′ful,** *adj.* —**boast′ful•ly,** *adv.*

boat (bōt), *n.* 1. a vessel for transport by water. 2. a boat-shaped serving dish. —*v.i.* 3. to go in a boat. —*Idiom.* 4. **in the same boat,** in similar difficult circumstances. —**boat′ing,** *n.*

boat•swain (bō′sən), *n.* an officer on a ship in charge of rigging, anchors, etc.

bob[1] (bob), *n., v.,* **bobbed, bob•bing.** —*n.* 1. a short, jerky motion. —*v.i., v.t.* 2. to move quickly down and up. 3. **bob up,** to appear unexpectedly.

bob[2] (bob), *n., v.,* **bobbed, bob•bing.** —*n.* 1. a short, caplike haircut. 2. a dangling object, as the weight on a pendulum. 3. a float for a fishing line. —*v.t.* 4. to cut short.

bob•bin (bob′in), *n.* a reel or spool on which thread is wound.

bob′by pin′ *n.* a flat, springlike metal hairpin.

bob′cat′ *n., pl.* **-cats, -cat.** a North American lynx having a brownish coat with black spots.

bob′o•link′ (-ə lingk′) *n.* a meadow-dwelling songbird.

bob′sled′ *n., v.,* **-sled•ded, -sled•ding.** —*n.* **1.** a long sled having two pairs of runners, a brake, and a steering mechanism. —*v.i.* **2.** to ride on a bobsled. —**bob′sled′der,** *n.*

bob′tail′ *n.* **1.** a short tail. **2.** an animal with such a tail.

bob′white′ *n.* any of several small New World quails.

bode¹ (bōd), *v.t., v.i.,* **bod•ed, bod•ing.** to portend.

bode² (bōd), *v.* a pt. of BIDE.

bod•ice (bod′is), *n.* the part of a dress covering the body above the waist.

bod•y (bod′ē), *n., pl.* **-ies. 1. a.** the physical structure and substance of an animal or plant. **b.** the trunk or torso. **c.** a corpse. **2.** the main or central mass of a thing. **3.** a separate physical mass. **4.** *Informal.* a person. **5.** a collective group: *the student body.* **6.** substance; consistency. —**bod′i•ly,** *adj.*

bod′y•guard′ *n.* a person employed to guard an individual from bodily harm.

bod′y lan′guage *n.* nonverbal communication through gestures, facial expressions, etc.

bod′y pierc′ing *n.* the piercing of a part of the body, as the navel, in order to insert an ornamental ring or stud.

bog (bog, bôg), *n., v.,* **bogged, bog•ging.** —*n.* **1.** wet, spongy ground. —*v.t., v.i.* **2.** to sink in or as if in a bog. —**bog′gy,** *adj.,* **-gi•er, -gi•est.**

bog•gle (bog′əl), *v.,* **-gled, -gling.** —*v.t.* **1.** to overwhelm or bewilder, as with complexity. —*v.i.* **2.** to be overwhelmed or bewildered. **3.** to hesitate or waver. **4.** to start with fright.

bo•gus (bō′gəs), *adj.* not genuine; counterfeit.

bo•gy or **-gie** (bō′gē, bō○′ē, bō○′gē), *n., pl.* **-gies. 1.** a hobgoblin. **2.** anything that haunts, frightens, or harasses.

Bo•he•mi•a (bō hē′mē ə), *n.* a region in the W part of the Czech Republic: formerly a kingdom.

Bo•he′mi•an *n.* **1.** a native of Bohemia. **2.** (*usu. l.c.*) a person who lives an unconventional life, as a writer or artist. —*adj.* **3.** of Bohemia or its inhabitants. **4.** (*usu. l.c.*) of or characteristic of a bohemian.

boil¹ (boil), *v.i.* **1.** to change from a liquid to a gaseous state, as a result of heat, producing bubbles of gas. **2.** to reach the boiling point. **3.** to be in an agitated state. **4.** to be deeply angry. **5.** to undergo cooking in boiling water. —*v.t.* **6.** to cause to boil. **7.** to cook in boiling water. **8. boil down, a.** to reduce by boiling. **b.** to shorten; abridge. —*n.* **9.** the act or state of boiling. —**boil′er,** *n.*

boil² (boil), *n.* an inflammation of the skin with a pus-filled core.

bois•ter•ous (boi′stər əs), *adj.* **1.** rough and noisy. **2.** turbulent and stormy. —**bois′ter•ous•ly,** *adv.* —**bois′ter•ous•ness,** *n.*

bok′ choy′ or **bok′-choy′** (bok′ choy′), *n.* an Asian plant whose leaves are used as a vegetable.

bold (bōld), *adj.,* **-er, -est. 1.** courageous and daring. **2.** scorning or ignoring the rules of propriety. **3.** flashy; showy: *a bold pattern.* **4.** steep; abrupt. —**bold′ly,** *adv.* —**bold′ness,** *n.*

bo•le•ro (bə lâr′ō, bō-), *n., pl.* **-ros. 1.** a lively Spanish dance in triple meter. **2.** the music for this dance. **3.** a waist-length jacket, worn open in front.

Bo•liv•i•a (bə liv′ē ə), *n.* a republic in W South America. —**Bo•liv′i•an,** *adj., n.*

boll (bōl), *n.* a rounded seed pod of a plant, esp. of flax or cotton.

boll′ wee′vil *n.* a snout beetle that attacks the bolls of cotton.

bo•lo•gna (bə lō′nē), *n.* a cooked and smoked sausage usu. made of beef and pork. [after *Bologna,* Italy, where first made]

Bol•she•vik (bōl′shə vik, -shē-, bol′-), *n., pl.* **-viks, -vik•i** (-vik′ē, -vē′kē). **1.** a member of the group of radical Russian Marxists who seized control of the government in 1917. **2.** a member of any Communist Party. —**Bol′she•vism** (-viz′əm), *n.* —**Bol′she•vist,** *n., adj.*

bol•ster (bōl′stər), *n.* **1.** a long, often cylindrical cushion for a bed, sofa, etc. —*v.t.* **2.** to support with or as if with a bolster.

bolt¹ (bōlt), *n.* **1.** a strong fastening rod, usu. threaded to receive a nut. **2.** a movable bar used to lock a door. **3.** the part of a lock that is manipulated by the action of the key. **4.** a sudden dash. **5.** a roll of woven goods. **6.** a short, heavy arrow for a crossbow. **7.** a thunderbolt. —*v.t.* **8.** to fasten with or as if with a bolt. **9.** to break with: *to bolt a political party.* **10.** to say impulsively. **11.** to swallow (food) hurriedly. —*v.i.* **12.** to make a sudden flight or escape. **13.** to break away, as from one's party. —*Idiom.* **14. bolt upright,** stiffly or rigidly erect. —**bolt′er,** *n.*

bolt² (bōlt), *v.t.* to sift.

bomb (bom), *n.* **1.** a case filled with a bursting charge and exploded by a detonating device or by impact. **2.** an aerosol can and its contents. **3.** *Slang.* an absolute failure. —*v.t.* **4.** to attack with bombs. —*v.i.* **5.** *Slang.* to fail decisively.

bom•bard (bom bärd′), *v.t.* **1.** to attack with artillery fire. **2.** to assail vigorously. **3.** to direct high-energy particles or radiation against. —**bom•bard′ment,** *n.*

bom•bast (bom′bast), *n.* pompous oratory or pretentious writing. —**bom•bas′tic,** *adj.* —**bom•bas′ti•cal•ly,** *adv.*

bomb•er (bom′ər), *n.* **1.** an airplane equipped to drop bombs. **2.** a person who drops or sets bombs.

bomb′shell′ *n.* **1.** a bomb. **2.** something or someone having a sensational effect.

bo•na fide (bō′nə fīd′ fī′dē), *adj.* **1.** in good faith; without deception or fraud. **2.** genuine; real.

bo•nan•za (bə nan′zə), *n. pl.* **-zas. 1.** a rich mass of ore. **2.** a source of great and sudden wealth.

bon•bon (bon′bon′), *n.* a small piece of candy, usu. chocolate-coated.

bond (bond), *n.* **1.** something that binds, fastens, or confines. **2.** something that binds a person to a certain line of behavior: *the bond of matrimony.* **3.** something, as an agreement, that unites individuals or peoples. **4.** any written obligation under seal. **5.** the state of dutiable goods stored without payment of duties. **6.** an interest-bearing certificate of debt due to be paid by a government or corporation to an individual holder. **7. a.** a surety agreement. **b.** the money deposited as surety. **8.** a substance that causes particles to adhere. **9.** the attraction between atoms in a molecule. **10.** BOND PAPER. —*v.t.* **11.** to put on or under bond. **12.** to connect or bind.

bond•age (bon′dij), *n.* slavery or involuntary servitude.

bond′man or **-wom′an,** *n., pl.* **-men** or **-wom•en. 1.** a slave or serf. **2.** a person bound to service without wages.

bond′ pa′per *n.* a superior variety of paper usu. with high cotton fiber content.

bonds′man *n., pl.* **-men. 1.** a person who by means of a bond becomes surety for another. **2.** BONDMAN.

bone (bōn), *n., v.,* **boned, bon•ing.** —*n.* **1. a.** one of the structures composing the skeleton of a vertebrate. **b.** the hard connective tissue forming these structures. **2.** any of various similarly hard or structural animal substances, as whalebone. **3.** something resembling such a substance. —*v.t.* **4.** to remove the bones from. **5. bone up,** *Informal.* to study intensely; cram. —*Idiom.* **6. have a bone to pick with,** to have cause for reproaching. **7. make no bones about,** to act or speak openly about.

bon′er *n. Slang.* a stupid mistake.

bon′fire′ *n.* a large fire built in the open air.

bon•go (bong′gō, bông′-), *n., pl.* **-gos, -goes.** one of a pair of tuned drums, played by beating with the fingers.

bon•kers (bong′kərz), *adj. Slang.* crazy.

bon•net (bon′it), *n.* a hat, tied under the chin, worn formerly by women but now mostly by children.

bo•nus (bō′nəs), *n., pl.* **-nus•es.** something given or paid over and above what is due.

boo (bōō), *n., pl.* **boos,** *v.,* **booed, boo•ing.** —*n.* **1.** a sound made to express contempt or disapproval. —*v.i., v.t.* **2.** to cry "boo" (at).

boo′-boo′ *n., pl.* **-boos.** *Slang.* a stupid mistake.

boo•by (bōō′bē), *n., pl.* **-bies.** a stupid person. Also called **boob.**

boo′by prize′ *n.* a prize given to the worst player in a contest.

boo′by trap′ *n.* any hidden trap set for an unsuspecting person.

book (bŏŏk), *n.* **1.** a long printed work, on sheets of paper bound together within covers. **2.** a division of a literary work. **3. the Book,** the Bible. **4.** a libretto. **5. books,** financial records. **6.** a bound packet of tickets, checks, stamps, etc. —*v.t.* **7.** to enter in a book or list. **8.** to engage (rooms, transportation, or entertainment) beforehand. **9.** to enter a charge against (an arrested person) in a police register.

book′end′ *n.* a support at each end of a row of books to hold them upright.

book′ie *n.* BOOKMAKER.

book′ing *n.* an engagement of a professional entertainer.

book′ish *adj.* **1.** fond of reading; studious. **2.** stilted; pedantic.

book′mak′er *n.* a person who makes a business of accepting bets, esp. on horse races. —**book′mak′ing,** *n., adj.*

book′mark′ *n.* something placed between the pages of a book to mark a place.

book′worm′ *n.* **1.** a person who spends much time reading. **2.** any of various insects that feed on books.

boom¹ (bōōm), *v.i., v.t.* **1.** to make or cause to make a deep, resonant sound. **2.** to flourish or cause to flourish vigorously. —*n.* **3.** a deep, resonant sound. **4.** a rapid increase in sales, worth, etc. **5.** a period of rapid economic growth.

boom² (bōōm), *n.* **1.** a spar projecting from a ship's mast and used to extend sails. **2.** a chain, cable, etc., used to obstruct navigation. **3.** a beam projecting from the mast of a derrick for supporting objects to be lifted. **4.** a beam on a mobile crane for holding a microphone.

boo•mer•ang (bōō′mə rang′), *n.* **1.** a curved piece of wood that can be thrown so as to return to the thrower. **2.** a scheme, argument, etc., that injures the originator. —*v.i.* **3.** to act as a boomerang.

boon¹ (bōōn), *n.* a blessing; benefit.

boon² (bōōn), *adj.* jovial; convivial: *boon companions.*

boon′docks′ *n.* **the,** (*used with a pl. v.*) **1.** a backwoods or marsh. **2.** a remote rural area.

boon′dog′gle (-dog′əl, -dô′gəl), *n., v.,* **-gled, -gling.** —*n.* **1.** work of little value done merely to keep or look busy. —*v.i.* **2.** to do such work. —**boon′dog′gler,** *n.*

boor (bŏŏr), *n.* a rude, unmannerly person. —**boor′ish,** *adj.* —**boor′ish•ly,** *adv.*

boost (bōōst), *v.t.* **1.** to lift by pushing from below. **2.** to aid by speaking well; promote. **3.** to increase; raise. —*n.* **4.** an upward shove or lift. **5.** an increase. **6.** an act or remark that helps one's progress, morale, etc.

boot¹ (bōōt), *n.* **1.** a covering of leather, rubber, etc., for the foot and part of the leg. **2.** any sheathlike protective covering. **3.** a U.S. Navy or Marine Corps recruit. **4.** a kick. **5. the boot,** *Slang.* a dismissal. —*v.t.* **6.** to kick. **7.** to put boots on. **8.** to start (a computer) by loading the operating system. **9.** *Slang.* to dismiss.

boot² (bōōt), *n.* **1.** *Archaic.* something given into the bargain. —*Idiom.* **2. to boot,** in addition; besides.

booth (bōōth), *n., pl.* **booths** (bōōthz, bōōths). **1.** a stall for the sale or display of goods. **2.** a small compartment: *a telephone booth.* **3.** a partly enclosed compartment, as in a restaurant.

boot′leg′ *n., v.,* **-legged, -leg•ging,** *adj.* —*n.* **1.** something, esp. liquor, that is unlawfully made, sold, or transported. —*v.t., v.i.* **2.** to deal in (liquor

or other goods) unlawfully. —*adj.* **3.** made, sold, or transported unlawfully. —**boot′leg′ger,** *n.*

boot′less *adj.* unavailing; useless.

boo•ty (bōō′tē), *n., pl.* **-ties. 1.** plunder taken in war. **2.** something seized by violence and robbery.

booze (bōōz), *n., v.,* **boozed, booz•ing.** *Informal.* —*n.* **1.** liquor. —*v.i.* **2.** to drink liquor excessively. —**booz′er,** *n.*

bop¹ (bop), *n., v.,* **bopped, bop•ping.** —*n.* **1.** jazz marked by dissonant harmony, eccentric rhythms, and melodic intricacy. —*v.i.* **2.** *Slang.* to move, go, or proceed.

bop² (bop), *v.,* **bopped, bop•ping,** *n. Slang.* —*v.t.* **1.** to hit. —*n.* **2.** a blow.

bo•rax (bôr′aks), *n.* a white crystalline substance used as a cleansing agent, in glassmaking, etc.

bor•del•lo (bôr del′ō), *n., pl.* **-los.** a brothel.

bor•der (bôr′dər), *n.* **1.** the edge of a surface or area that forms its outer boundary. **2.** the line that separates one country, state, etc., from another. **3.** an ornamental design around an edge. —*v.t.* **4.** to make a border around. **5.** to form a border to. **6.** to adjoin. **7. border on,** to verge on; approach.

bore¹ (bôr), *v.,* **bored, bor•ing,** *n.* —*v.t.* **1.** to pierce (a solid substance), as with a drill. **2.** to make (a hole or passage) by drilling or digging. —*v.i.* **3.** to make a hole, as with a drill. —*n.* **4.** a hole made or enlarged by boring. **5.** the inside diameter of a hole or cylinder, as a gun barrel.

bore² (bôr), *v.,* **bored, bor•ing,** *n.* —*v.t.* **1.** to weary by dullness. —*n.* **2.** a dull, tiresome person or thing. —**bore′dom,** *n.*

bore³ (bôr), *v.* pt. of BEAR¹.

born (bôrn), *adj.* **1.** brought forth by birth. **2.** possessing from birth the quality stated: *a born musician.* —*v.* **3.** a pp. of BEAR¹.

born′-again′ *adj.* recommitted to faith through an intensely religious experience: *a born-again Christian.*

bo•ron (bôr′on), *n.* a nonmetallic element used in alloys and nuclear reactors. *Symbol:* B; *at. wt.:* 10. 811; *at. no.:* 5.

bor•ough (bûr′ō, bur′ō), *n.* **1.** an incorporated municipality smaller than a city. **2.** one of the five administrative divisions of New York City.

bor•row (bor′ō, bôr′ō), *v.t., v.i.* **1.** to obtain (something) with the promise to return it. **2.** to appropriate (an idea, etc.) from another source. —**bor′row•er,** *n.*

Bos•nia and Her•ze•go•vi•na (boz′nē ə; hûr′tsə gō vē′nə), *n.* a republic in SE Europe: formerly part of Yugoslavia.

bos•om (bŏŏz′əm, bōō′zəm), *n.* **1.** the breast of a human being. **2.** the breast conceived of as the center of feelings. **3.** a state of enclosing intimacy: *the bosom of the family.* —*adj.* **4.** intimate or confidential.

boss¹ (bôs, bos), *n.* **1.** a person who employs or supervises workers. **2.** a politician who controls the party organization. **3.** a person who is in charge. —*v.t.* **4.** to direct; control. **5.** to order about. —*adj.* **6.** *Slang.* first-rate. [< D *baas* master] —**boss′y,** *adj.,* **-i•er, -i•est.** —**boss′i•ness,** *n.*

boss² (bôs, bos), *n.* **1.** an ornamental protuberance of metal, ivory, etc. —*v.t.* **2.** to ornament with bosses. [< AF *boce* lump]

bot•a•ny (bot′n ē), *n.* the science that deals with plant life. —**bo•tan•i•cal** (bə tan′i kəl), **bo•tan′ic,** *adj.* —**bot′a•nist,** *n.*

botch (boch), *v.t.* **1.** to bungle. **2.** to patch clumsily. —*n.* **3.** a poor piece of work. —**botch′er,** *n.*

both (bōth), *adj., pron.* **1.** one and the other; two: *I met both sisters. Both of them were ill.* —*conj.* **2.** (used before words or phrases joined by *and* to indicate that each of the joined elements is included): *I am both ready and willing.*

both•er (both′ər), *v.t., v.i.* **1.** to annoy (someone). **2.** to trouble or inconvenience (oneself). —*n.* **3.** something or someone troublesome or annoying. —**both′er•some,** *adj.*

Bot•swa•na (bot swä′nə), *n.* a republic in S Africa.

bot•tle (bot′l), *n., v.,* **-tled, -tling.** —*n.* **1.** a glass or plastic container for liquids, having a neck and mouth. **2.** the contents of such a container. —*v.t.* **3.** to put into or seal in a bottle. **4. bottle up,** to repress or restrain. —*Idiom.* **5. hit the bottle,** *Slang.* to drink alcohol to excess. —**bot′tler,** *n.*

bot•tle•neck′ *n.* **1.** a narrow entrance or passageway. **2.** a place or stage at which progress is impeded.

bot•tom (bot′əm), *n.* **1.** the lowest part of anything. **2.** the under or lower side. **3.** the ground under any body of water. **4.** the seat of a chair. **5.** *Informal.* the buttocks. **6.** the cause; origin. —*v.i.* **7. bottom out,** to reach the lowest state or level. —*adj.* **8.** lowest: *bottom prices.* **9.** fundamental. —*Idiom.* **10. at bottom,** fundamentally.

bot′tom•less *adj.* **1.** without bottom. **2.** without limit.

bot′tom line′ *n.* **1.** the last line of a financial statement, showing net profit or loss. **2.** the ultimate result or consideration.

bot•u•lism (boch′ə liz′əm), *n.* a sometimes fatal disease of the nervous system caused by a toxin in spoiled foods.

bou•doir (boo′dwär, -dwôr), *n.* a woman's bedroom or private sitting room. [< F: lit., a sulking place]

bouf•fant (boo fänt′), *adj.* puffed out; full: *a bouffant hairdo.*

bough (bou), *n.* a large branch of a tree.

bouil•lon (bool′yon, -yən, boo′-), *n.* a clear broth.

boul•der (bōl′dər), *n.* a large and rounded or worn rock.

boul•e•vard (bool′ə värd′), *n.* a broad avenue, often lined with trees.

bounce (bouns), *v.,* **bounced, bounc•ing,** *n.* —*v.i.* **1.** to strike a surface and rebound. **2.** to move in a lively, energetic manner. **3.** (of a check) to be refused due to insufficient funds in the account. —*v.t.* **4.** to cause to bounce. **5.** *Slang.* to expel or dismiss promptly or forcibly. —*n.* **6.** a bound or rebound. **7.** a sudden spring or leap. **8.** ability to rebound; resilience. **9.** vitality; energy. **10. the bounce,** *Slang.* a dismissal. —**bounc′y,** *adj.,* **-i•er, -i•est.**

bounc′ing *adj.* stout, strong, or vigorous.

bound¹ (bound), *v.* **1.** pt. and pp. of BIND. —*adj.* **2.** tied; in bonds. **3.** made fast as if by a bond. **4.** secured within a cover, as a book. **5.** under obligation. **6.** destined or certain: *It is bound to happen.* **7.** determined or resolved.

bound² (bound), *v.i.* **1.** to move by leaps. **2.** to rebound; bounce. —*n.* **3.** a jump. **4.** a bounce.

bound³ (bound), *n.* **1.** Usu., **bounds.** limit or boundary: *within the bounds of reason.* **2. bounds,** territories on or near a boundary. —*v.t.* **3.** to limit. **4.** to form the boundary or limit of. **5.** to name the boundaries of. —*Idiom.* **6. out of bounds, a.** beyond prescribed limits. **b.** prohibited. —**bound′less,** *adj.* —**bound′less•ly,** *adv.*

bound⁴ (bound), *adj.* going or intending to go: *bound for Denver.*

bound•a•ry (boun′də rē, -drē), *n., pl.* **-ries.** something that indicates bounds or limits.

boun•te•ous (boun′tē əs), *adj.* **1.** giving generously. **2.** plentiful; abundant. —**boun′te•ous•ly,** *adv.* —**boun′te•ous•ness,** *n.*

boun′ty *n., pl.* **-ties. 1.** a premium or reward. **2.** a generous gift. **3.** generosity.

bou•quet (bō kā′, boo- for 1; boo kā′ for 2), *n.* **1.** a bunch of flowers. **2.** a characteristic aroma, esp. of a wine.

bour•bon (bûr′bən), *n.* a whiskey distilled from a mash having 51 percent or more corn. Also called **bour′bon whis′key.**

bour•geois (boor zhwä′), *n., pl.* **-geois.** —*n.* **1.** a member of the bourgeoisie or middle class. —*adj.* **2.** of or characteristic of the middle class. **3.** overly concerned with respectability or success.

bour•geoi•sie′ (-zē′), *n.* **1.** the middle class. **2.** (in Marxist theory) the capitalist class in conflict with the proletariat.

bout (bout), *n.* **1.** a contest, as of boxing. **2.** a period; spell.

bou•tique (boo tēk′), *n.* a small shop that sells fashionable items.

bo•vine (bō′vīn, -vēn), *adj.* **1.** of or resembling an ox or cow. **2.** stolid; dull. —*n.* **3.** a bovine animal.

bow¹ (bou), *v.i.* **1.** to bend the body or head, as in reverence or salutation. **2.** to yield; submit. —*v.t.* **3.** to bend (the body or head). **4.** to subdue; crush. —*n.* **5.** an inclination of the body or head in reverence, salutation, etc. —*Idiom.* **6. take a bow,** to stand up to receive applause, etc.

bow² (bō), *n.* **1.** a flexible strip of wood, bent by a string stretched between its ends, for shooting arrows. **2.** a bend or curve. **3.** a readily loosened knot having two projecting loops. **4.** a flexible rod strung with horsehairs used for playing an instrument of the violin family. —*adj.* **5.** curved: *bow legs.* —*v.t., v.i.* **6.** to bend; curve. **7.** to play (a stringed instrument) with a bow.

bow³ (bou), *n.* the forward end of a ship or boat.

bow•el (bou′əl, boul), *n.* **1.** Usu., **-els.** the intestine. **2. bowels,** the interior parts: *the bowels of the earth.* —*Idiom.* **3. move one's bowels,** to defecate.

bow•er (bou′ər), *n.* a leafy shelter; arbor.

bowl¹ (bōl), *n.* **1.** a deep, round dish. **2.** the contents of a bowl. **3.** a rounded, hollow part. **4.** an amphitheater; stadium.

bowl² (bōl), *n.* **1.** a ball used in lawn bowling. **2. bowls,** LAWN BOWLING. **3.** a delivery of the ball in bowling. —*v.i.* **4.** to play at bowling. **5.** to move along smoothly and rapidly. —*v.t.* **6.** to roll (a ball) in bowling. **7. bowl over,** to surprise greatly. —**bowl′er,** *n.*

bow′leg′ged (bō′leg′id) *adj.* having the legs curved outward.

box¹ (boks), *n.* **1.** a container or case, usu. having a lid. **2.** the quantity contained in a box. **3.** a compartment for a small group of people, as in a theater. **4.** a small enclosure in a courtroom. **5.** a small shelter: *a sentry's box.* **6.** any of the spaces on a baseball diamond marking the positions of the pitcher, batter, etc. —*v.t.* **7.** to put into a box. **8.** to enclose or confine (often fol. by *in* or *up*).

box² (boks), *n.* **1.** a blow with the hand or fist. —*v.t.* **2.** to strike with the fist. **3.** to fight against (someone) in a boxing match. —*v.i.* **4.** to participate in a boxing match.

box³ (boks), *n.* an evergreen shrub used for ornamental borders and hedges.

box′car′ *n.* a completely enclosed railroad freight car.

box′ing *n.* the act, technique, or profession of fighting with the fists.

box′ of′fice *n.* an office, as in a theater, at which tickets are sold.

boy (boi), *n.* **1.** a male child. **2.** a man, esp. when referred to familiarly. —*interj.* **3.** an exclamation of wonder, displeasure, etc. —**boy′hood,** *n.* —**boy′ish,** *adj.* —**boy′ish•ly,** *adv.* —**boy′ish•ness,** *n.*

boy•cott (boi′kot), *v.t.* **1.** to abstain from dealing with or buying, as a means of protest or coercion. —*n.* **2.** the act of boycotting. [after C. C. *Boycott* (1832–97), English estate manager, first victim]

boy′friend′ *n.* **1.** a favored male companion, sweetheart, or lover. **2.** a male friend.

boy′ scout′ *n.* (*sometimes caps.*) a member of an organization of boys (**Boy′ Scouts′**) that emphasizes self-reliance and service to others.

bra (brä), *n.* BRASSIERE. —**bra′less,** *adj.*

brace (brās), *n., v.,* **braced, brac•ing.** —*n.* **1.** something that holds parts together or in place. **2.** anything that imparts rigidity or steadiness. **3.** a device for holding and turning a bit. **4.** Usu., **braces.** an oral appliance for straightening irregularly arranged teeth. **5.** an orthopedic appliance for supporting a weak joint or joints. **6. braces,** *Chiefly Brit.* SUSPENDERS. **7.** a pair; couple. **8.** one of two characters, { or }, used to enclose words or lines to be considered together. —*v.t.* **9.** to fasten or strengthen with a brace. **10.** to steady (oneself), as against a shock. **11.** to stimulate or invigorate.

brace•let (brās′lit), *n.* an ornamental band for the wrist or arm.

brack•et (brak′it), *n.* **1.** a supporting piece projecting from a wall or the like. **2.** a shelf so supported. **3.** one of two marks, [or] , used to enclose written or printed material. **4.** a class or grouping: *the low-income bracket.* —*v.t.* **5.** to furnish with brackets. **6.** to place within brackets. **7.** to associate or class together.

brack•ish (brak′ish), *adj.* **1.** salty or briny. **2.** distasteful; unpleasant. —**brack′ish•ness,** *n.*

brad (brad), *n.* a slender wire nail with a small, deep head.

brag (brag), *v.,* **bragged, brag•ging,** *n.* —*v.i., v.t.* **1.** to boast. —*n.* **2.** a boast or vaunt. **3.** one who boasts. —**brag′gart,** *n.* —**brag′ger,** *n.*

braid (brād), *v.t.* **1.** to weave together three or more strands of. **2.** to trim with braid, as a garment. —*n.* **3.** a braided length or plait, esp. of hair. **4.** a plaited band of material, used as trimming.

Braille (brāl), *n.* (*often l.c.*) a system of writing for the blind, using combinations of raised dots. [after L. *Braille* (1809–52), French deviser of system]

brain (brān), *n.* **1.** the part of the central nervous system enclosed in the cranium of vertebrates, serving to control mental and physical actions. **2.** Sometimes, **brains.** intelligence. —*v.t.* **3.** to smash the skull of. —**brain′less,** *adj.*

brain′ death′ *n.* complete cessation of brain function: sometimes used as a legal definition of death. —**brain′-dead′,** *adj.*

brain′ drain′ *n.* a loss of trained professional personnel to another company, nation, etc.

brain′storm′ *n.* a sudden inspiration or idea.

brain′wash′ *v.t.* to subject to brainwashing.

brain′wash′ing *n.* a method for changing attitudes or beliefs, esp. through torture or psychological-stress techniques.

braise (brāz), *v.t.,* **braised, brais•ing.** to cook in fat and then simmer in a small amount of liquid.

brake (brāk), *n., v.,* **braked, brak•ing.** —*n.* **1.** a device for slowing or stopping a vehicle or mechanism. —*v.t., v.i.* **2.** to slow or stop by or as if by a brake.

bram•ble (bram′bəl), *n.* a prickly shrub of the rose family, as the blackberry. —**bram′bly,** *adj.,* **-bli•er, -bli•est.**

bran (bran), *n.* the partly ground husk of wheat or other grain, separated from the flour by sifting.

branch (branch, bränch), *n.* **1.** a division of the stem or axis of a tree or shrub. **2.** any section or subdivision of a body or system. **3.** a local operating division of an organization. **4.** a division of a family. **5.** a tributary stream. —*v.i.* **6.** to spread in branches. **7.** to diverge: *The road branches off to the left.* **8. branch out,** to expand or extend, as business activities. —**branched,** *adj.* —**branch′like′,** *adj.*

brand (brand), *n.* **1.** kind, grade, or make: *the best brand of coffee.* **2.** a mark made by burning or other means, to indicate kind, ownership, etc. **3.** a stigma. **4.** an iron for branding. **5.** a burning or partly burned piece of wood. —*v.t.* **6.** to mark with a brand. **7.** to stigmatize. —**brand′er,** *n.*

bran•dish (bran′dish), *v.t.* to shake or wave threateningly, as a weapon. —**bran′dish•er,** *n.*

brand′-new′ (bran′-, brand′-), *adj.* entirely new.

bran•dy (bran′dē), *n., pl.* **-dies,** *v.,* **-died, -dy•ing.** —*n.* **1.** a spirit distilled from wine or fermented fruit juice. —*v.t.* **2.** to flavor or preserve with brandy. [short for *brandywine* < D *brandewijn* burnt (i.e., distilled) wine]

brash (brash), *adj.,* **-er, -est. 1.** impudent; tactless. **2.** rash; impetuous. —**brash′ly,** *adv.* —**brash′ness,** *n.*

brass (bras, bräs), *n.* **1.** a metal alloy consisting mainly of copper and zinc. **2.** Often, **brasses.** the brass instruments of a band or orchestra. **3.** high-ranking officials, esp. military officers. **4.** impudence; effrontery. —*adj.* **5.** made of brass. —**brass′y,** *adj.,* **-i•er, -i•est.**

bras•siere (brə zēr′), *n.* a woman's undergarment for supporting the breasts.

brass′ tacks′ *n.pl.* the most fundamental considerations; essentials.

brat (brat), *n.* a spoiled or impolite child. —**brat′-ty,** *adj.,* **-ti•er, -ti•est.**

brat•wurst (brat′wûrst, -vŏŏrst′, brät′-), *n.* a sausage made of pork, spices, and herbs.

bra•va•do (brə vä′dō), *n., pl.* **-does, -dos.** an ostentatious display of courage.

brave (brāv), *adj.,* **brav•er, brav•est,** *n., v.,* **braved, brav•ing.** —*adj.* **1.** possessing or exhibiting courage. **2.** making a fine appearance. —*n.* **3.** a warrior, esp. among North American Indians. —*v.t.* **4.** to meet or face courageously. **5.** to defy; challenge. —**brave′ly,** *adv.* —**brav′er•y,** *n.*

bra•vo (brä′vō, brä vō′), *interj., n., pl.* **-vos.** —*interj.* **1.** well done! good! —*n.* **2.** a shout of "bravo!"

brawl (brôl), *n.* **1.** a noisy fight or quarrel. —*v.i.* **2.** to quarrel angrily and noisily. —**brawl′er,** *n.*

brawn (brôn), *n.* **1.** well-developed muscles. **2.** muscular strength. —**brawn′y,** *adj.,* **-i•er, -i•est.** —**brawn′i•ness,** *n.*

bray (brā), *n.* **1.** a harsh cry, as of a donkey. —*v.i.* **2.** to utter a bray.

bra•zen (brā′zən), *adj.* **1.** shameless or impudent. **2.** made of brass. **3.** like brass, as in sound, color, or strength. —**bra′zen•ly,** *adv.*

bra•zier¹ (brā′zhər), *n.* a metal receptacle for holding live coals.

bra•zier² (brā′zhər), *n.* one who makes articles of brass.

Bra•zil (brə zil′), *n.* a federal republic in South America. —**Bra•zil′ian,** *adj., n.*

Brazil′ nut′ *n.* the three-sided, edible seed of a South American tree.

breach (brēch), *n.* **1.** an infraction or violation, as of a law. **2.** a gap made in a wall, fortification, etc. **3.** a severance of friendly relations. —*v.t.* **4.** to make a breach in.

bread (bred), *n.* **1.** a baked food made of a dough containing flour or meal and usu. a leavening agent. **2.** livelihood. —*v.t.* **3.** to coat with breadcrumbs. —*Idiom.* **4. break bread,** to eat a meal.

bread′crumb′ *n.* a crumb of bread, either dried or soft.

breadth (bredth, bretth), *n.* **1.** the measure of the side-to-side dimension; width. **2.** freedom from narrowness, as of viewpoint. **3.** extent; scope.

bread′win′ner *n.* a person who earns a livelihood to support dependents.

break (brāk), *v.,* **broke, bro•ken, break•ing,** *n.* —*v.t.* **1.** to split into pieces; smash. **2.** to make useless by or as if by smashing. **3.** to crack or fracture. **4.** to violate (a law, promise, etc.). **5.** to rupture the surface of: *to break the skin.* **6.** to disrupt the regularity, uniformity, or continuity of. **7.** to end. **8.** to solve or decipher. **9.** to escape from. **10.** to better (a score or record). **11.** to disclose or reveal, as news. **12.** to bankrupt. **13.** to wear down the spirit or resistance of. **14.** to reduce in rank. **15.** to weaken the force of: *to break a fall.* **16.** to train to obedience. **17.** to train away from a habit. —*v.i.* **18.** to split into parts or fragments. **19.** to become useless or inoperative. **20.** to become disassociated: *to break with the past.* **21.** to move suddenly. **22.** to interrupt an activity. **23.** to appear or begin suddenly: *the storm broke.* **24.** (of the heart) to be overwhelmed with sorrow. **25.** (of the voice) to change tone abruptly. **26. break down, a.** to cease to function. **b.** to have a physical or mental collapse. **27. ~ in, a.** to enter property by force. **b.** to train or initiate. **c.** to begin to use. **d.** to interrupt. **28. ~ off,** to stop suddenly. **29. ~ out, a.** to begin abruptly. **b.** to manifest a skin eruption. **c.** to escape. **30. ~ up, a.** to separate; scatter. **b.** to end a personal relationship. **c.** to laugh or make laugh. —*n.* **31.** a crack or opening made by breaking. **32.** the act of breaking. **33.** an interruption of continuity. **34.** a brief rest, as from work. **35.** a beginning: *the break of day.* **36.** an abrupt change. **37.** a sudden dash; escape. **38.** a stroke of luck. —**break′a•ble,** *adj.*

break′down′ *n.* **1.** a breaking down. **2.** a mental or physical collapse. **3.** a classification; analysis.

break'er *n.* **1.** one that breaks. **2.** a wave that breaks into foam.

break•fast (brek'fəst), *n.* **1.** the first meal of the day. —*v.i.* **2.** to eat breakfast.

break'-in' *n.* an illegal forcible entry into a home, office, etc.

break'neck' *adj.* reckless or dangerous, esp. because of excessive speed.

break'through' *n.* **1.** a significant advance, as in scientific knowledge. **2.** an act of surmounting an obstruction or restriction.

break'up' *n.* **1.** a dispersal or disintegration **2.** the ending of a personal relationship.

break'wa'ter *n.* a barrier that breaks the force of waves, as before a harbor.

breast (brest), *n.* **1.** either of the pair of mammary glands on the chest of primates, esp. of the postpubertal female. **2.** the upper, front part of the body; chest. **3.** the bosom conceived of as the center of emotion. —*v.t.* **4.** to meet or oppose boldly.

breast'bone' *n.* STERNUM.

breast'stroke' *n.* a swimming stroke in which the arms move forward, outward, and rearward while the legs kick outward.

breath (breth), *n.* **1.** the air inhaled and exhaled in respiration. **2.** respiration. **3.** life; vitality. **4.** the ability to breathe easily. **5.** a single inhalation. **6.** a slight suggestion. **7.** a light current of air. —*Idiom.* **8.** out of breath, gasping for breath. **9.** under one's breath, in a whisper. —**breath'less,** *adj.* —**breath'less•ly,** *adv.* —**breath'less•ness,** *n.*

breathe (brēth), *v.i., v.t.,* breathed, breath•ing. **1.** to inhale and exhale (air) in respiration. **2.** to pause, as to rest. **3.** to live; exist. **4.** to whisper. —**breath'a•ble,** *adj.*

breath•er (brē'thər), *n.* **1.** a pause, as for breath. **2.** a person who breathes.

breath'tak'ing (breth'-), *adj.* astonishingly beautiful, remarkable, exciting, etc. —**breath'tak'ing•ly,** *adv.*

breech•es (brich'iz), *n.* (*used with a pl. v.*) **1.** knee-length trousers for men. **2.** *Informal.* TROUSERS.

breed (brēd), *v.,* bred, breed•ing, *n.* —*v.t.* **1.** to produce (offspring). **2.** to give rise to; engender. **3.** to bring up; rear. **4.** to raise (cattle, etc.) —*v.i.* **5.** to produce offspring. **6.** to be produced. —*n.* **7.** a stock; strain. **8.** sort; kind; group. —**breed'er,** *n.*

breed'ing *n.* **1.** the producing of offspring. **2.** the improvement of livestock or plants by selection. **3.** training; nurture. **4.** good manners.

breeze (brēz), *n., v.,* breezed, breez•ing. —*n.* **1.** a light wind. **2.** an easy task. —*v.i.* **3.** to proceed quickly and easily. —**breez'y,** *adj.,* **-i•er, -i•est.** —**breez'i•ly,** *adv.* —**breez'i•ness,** *n.*

breeze'way' *n.* an open-sided roofed passageway for connecting two buildings.

breth•ren (breth'rin), *n.pl.* **1.** fellow members. **2.** *Archaic.* brothers.

bre•vi•ar•y (brē'vē er'ē, brev'ē-), *n., pl.* **-ies.** a book containing the divine office of the Roman Catholic Church.

brev•i•ty (brev'i tē), *n.* shortness of duration.

brew (brōō), *v.t.* **1.** to make (beer, ale, etc.) by steeping, boiling, and fermenting malt and hops. **2.** to prepare (tea or coffee) by boiling, steeping, etc. **3.** to contrive or bring about. —*v.i.* **4.** to make beer or ale. **5.** to form: *Trouble was brewing.* —*n.* **6.** a brewed beverage. —**brew'er,** *n.* —**brew'er•y,** *n., pl.* **-er•ies.**

brew'er•y *n., pl.* **-ies.** a place for brewing beer or other malt liquors.

bri•ar (brī'ər), *n.* **1.** BRIER[1]. **2.** BRIER[2].

bribe (brīb), *n., v.,* bribed, brib•ing. —*n.* **1.** anything given to persuade or induce, esp an illicit payment. —*v.t.* **2.** to give or promise a bribe to. —**brib'er,** *n.* —**brib'er•y,** *n.*

bric-a-brac (brik'ə brak'), *n.* (*used with a sing. or pl. v.*) small articles collected for their decorative or other interest; knickknacks.

brick (brik), *n.* **1.** a block of clay hardened by heat and used for building, paving, etc. —*v.t.* **2.** to pave or build with brick.

brick'bat' *n.* **1.** a piece of broken brick used as a missile. **2.** a caustic criticism.

bride (brīd), *n.* a newly married woman or one about to be married.

bride'groom' *n.* a newly married man or one about to be married.

brides'maid' *n.* a woman who attends the bride at a wedding ceremony.

bridge[1] (brij), *n., v.,* bridged, bridg•ing, *adj.* —*n.* **1.** a structure spanning and providing passage over a river, road, etc. **2.** a connection or transition between two adjacent elements, conditions, etc. **3.** a raised platform from which a ship is navigated. **4.** the ridge of the nose. **5.** an artificial replacement for a missing tooth or teeth. —*v.t.* **6.** to make a bridge or passage over. —*adj.* **7.** (esp. of clothing) less expensive than a manufacturer's most expensive products.

bridge[2] (brij), *n.* a card game in which one partnership plays to fulfill a certain declaration against an opposing partnership.

bridge'work' *n.* a dental bridge or bridges.

bri•dle (brīd'l), *n., v.,* -dled, -dling. —*n.* **1.** the head harness of a horse, including bit and reins. **2.** a restraint; curb. —*v.t.* **3.** to put a bridle on. **4.** to restrain; curb. —*v.i.* **5.** to show resentment.

brief (brēf), *adj.,* -er, -est, *n., v.* —*adj.* **1.** lasting a short time. **2.** concise. —*n.* **3.** a memorandum of points of fact or of law for use in conducting a case. **4.** a summary or synopsis. **5.** briefs, close-fitting legless underpants. —*v.t.* **6.** to make a summary of. **7.** to instruct by a brief. —**brief'ing,** *n.* —**brief'ly,** *adv.*

brief'case' *n.* a flat rectangular case for carrying books, papers, etc.

bri•er[1] (brī'ər), *n.* a prickly plant or shrub.

bri•er[2] (brī'ər), *n.* a white heath, the woody root of which is used for making tobacco pipes.

brig (brig), *n.* **1.** a two-masted sailing vessel square-rigged on both masts. **2.** a military prison.

bri•gade (bri gād'), *n.* **1.** a military unit consisting of a headquarters and two or more regiments, squadrons, etc. **2.** a group organized for a particular purpose.

brig•a•dier' (brig'ə dēr'), *n.* a military officer of the rank between colonel and major general. Also called **brigadier general.**

brig•and (brig'ənd), *n.* a bandit, esp. one of a roving band. —**brig'and•age,** *n.*

bright (brīt), *adj.,* -er, -est. **1.** radiating much light. **2.** vivid or brilliant. **3.** quick-witted or intelligent. **4.** cheerful or lively. **5.** favorable or auspicious. **6.** illustrious or glorious. —**bright'ly,** *adv.* —**bright'ness,** *n.*

bril•liant (bril'yənt), *adj.* **1.** shining brightly. **2.** distinguished; outstanding. **3.** having great intelligence, talent, etc. —**bril'liance, bril'lian•cy,** *n.* —**bril'liant•ly,** *adv.*

brim (brim), *n., v.,* brimmed, brim•ming. —*n.* **1.** the upper edge of anything hollow. **2.** a projecting edge, as of a hat. —*v.i., v.t.* **3.** to be full or fill to the brim. —**brim'less,** *adj.*

brim'stone' *n.* (not in technical use) SULFUR.

brin•dle (brin'dl), *n.* **1.** a brindled coloring. —*adj.* **2.** BRINDLED.

brin'dled *adj.* gray or tawny with darker streaks or spots.

brine (brīn), *n.* **1.** water saturated with salt. **2.** the sea or ocean. —**brin'y,** *adj.,* -i•er, -i•est. —**brin'i•ness,** *n.*

bring (bring), *v.t.,* brought, bring•ing. **1.** to cause (someone or something) to come with, to, or toward the speaker. **2.** to cause to occur or exist. **3.** to persuade or compel. **4.** to sell for. **5.** bring about, to accomplish; cause. **6.** ~ forth, to produce. **7.** ~ off, to accomplish. **8.** ~ out, a. to reveal. b. to publish. **9.** ~ up, a. to rear. b. to mention for consideration. c. to vomit. d. to stop quickly or abruptly. —**bring'er,** *n.*

brink (bringk), *n.* **1.** the edge of a steep place or of land bordering water. **2.** any extreme edge.

bri•quette or **-quet** (bri ket'), *n.* a small block of compressed coal dust or charcoal used for fuel.

general

brisk (brisk), *adj.*, **-er**, **-est**. **1.** quick and active; lively. **2.** sharp and stimulating. —**brisk′ly**, *adv.* —**brisk′ness**, *n.*

bris•ket (bris′kit), *n.* **1.** the breast of an animal. **2.** a cut of meat from the brisket.

bris•tle (bris′əl), *n.*, *v.*, **-tled**, **-tling**. —*n.* **1.** a short, stiff hair of certain animals, esp. hogs. **2.** anything resembling these hairs. —*v.i.* **3.** to stand or rise stiffly. **4.** to become rigid with anger. **5.** to be thickly filled. —**bris′tly**, *adj.*, **-tli•er**, **-tli•est**.

britch•es (brich′iz), *n.* (*used with a pl. v.*) BREECHES.

Brit•ish (brit′ish), *adj.* **1.** of Great Britain or its inhabitants. —*n.* **2.** (*used with a pl. v.*) the people of Great Britain.

Brit′ish ther′mal u′nit *n.* the amount of heat required to raise the temperature of 1 lb. (0.4 kg) of water 1°F. *Abbr.:* Btu, BTU

Brit•on (brit′n), *n.* **1.** a native or inhabitant of Great Britain, esp. in England. **2.** a member of a Celtic-speaking people inhabiting ancient Britain.

brit•tle (brit′l), *adj.*, **-tler**, **-tlest**. having hardness and rigidity but breaking readily. —**brit′tle•ness**, *n.*

broach (brōch), *n.* **1.** a tapered tool for shaping and enlarging holes. —*v.t.* **2.** to mention for the first time. **3.** to tap or pierce. —**broach′er**, *n.*

broad (brôd), *adj.*, **-er**, **-est**. **1.** of great breadth. **2.** of great extent. **3.** open; full: *in broad daylight.* **4.** of extensive range or scope. **5.** liberal; tolerant. **6.** not detailed; general: *a broad outline.* **7.** plain or clear: *a broad hint.* —**broad′ly**, *adv.* —**broad′ness**, *n.*

broad′cast′ *v.*, **-cast** or **-cast•ed**, **-cast•ing**, *n.*, *adv.* —*v.t.*, *v.i.* **1.** to transmit (programs) by radio or television. **2.** to scatter or spread widely. —*n.* **3.** something broadcast. **4.** a radio or television program. —*adv.* **5.** over a wide area. —**broad′cast′er**, *n.*

broad′cloth′ *n.* a closely woven fabric of cotton, rayon, or silk, having a soft finish.

broad′en *v.i.*, *v.t.* to widen.

broad′ jump′ *n.* LONG JUMP.

broad′loom′ *n.* any carpet woven on a wide loom.

broad′-mind′ed *adj.* free from prejudice or narrowness; tolerant. —**broad′-mind′ed•ness**, *n.*

broad′side′ *n.* **1.** the side of a ship above the water line. **2.** a simultaneous discharge of all guns on one side of a warship. **3.** a concerted verbal attack. —*adv.* **4.** directly in the side: *The truck hit the fence broadside.* **5.** at random.

broad′-spec′trum *adj.* (of an antibiotic) effective against a wide range of organisms.

bro•cade (brō kād′), *n.*, *v.*, **-cad•ed**, **-cad•ing**. —*n.* **1.** fabric woven with a raised design. —*v.t.* **2.** to weave with a raised design.

broc•co•li (brok′ə lē), *n.*, *pl.* **-lis**. a plant resembling the cauliflower, with edible green flower heads.

bro•chure (brō shŏŏr′), *n.* a pamphlet or leaflet.

brogue[1] (brōg), *n.* an Irish accent in the pronunciation of English.

brogue[2] (brōg), *n.* a durable, low-heeled shoe.

broil (broil), *v.t.*, *v.i.* **1.** to cook by direct heat. —*n.* **2.** something broiled. —**broil′er**, *n.*

broke (brōk), *v.* **1.** pt. of BREAK. —*adj.* **2.** without money. **3.** bankrupt.

bro•ken (brō′kən), *v.* **1.** pp. of BREAK. —*adj.* **2.** fragmented or fractured. **3.** not functioning properly. **4.** infringed or violated. **5.** interrupted or disconnected. **6.** tamed; subdued. **7.** imperfectly spoken: *broken English.* **8.** disunited or divided: *broken families.* **9.** overwhelmed with sorrow. **10.** ruined; bankrupt. —**bro′ken•ly**, *adv.* —**bro′ken•ness**, *n.*

bro′ken-heart′ed *adj.* suffering from great sorrow or disappointment.

bro′ker *n.* **1.** an agent who buys or sells for others on commission. **2.** a mediator who negotiates agreements or contracts.

bro•mide (brō′mīd *or, for 1*, **-mid**), *n.* **1.** a compound containing bromine. **2.** potassium bromide, formerly used as a sedative. **3.** a trite saying. —**bro•mid′ic** (**-mid′ik**), *adj.*

bro•mine (brō′mēn, **-min**), *n.* a reddish, toxic liq-

uid element used in antiknock compounds, pharmaceuticals, etc. *Symbol:* Br; *at. wt.:* 79.909; *at. no.:* 35.

bron•chi•al (brong′kē əl), *adj.* pertaining to the bronchi.

bron•chi′tis (**-kī′tis**), *n.* inflammation of the membrane lining of the bronchial tubes.

bron′chus (**-kəs**), *n.*, *pl.* **-chi** (**-kē, -kī**). either of the two branches of the trachea.

bron•co (brong′kō) *n.*, *pl.* **-cos.** a wild or untamed range pony or mustang of the western U.S.

bronze (bronz), *n.*, *v.*, **bronzed**, **bronz•ing**, *adj.* —*n.* **1.** an alloy of copper and tin. **2.** a metallic brownish color. —*v.t.* **3.** to give the appearance of bronze to. —*adj.* **4.** made of or coated with bronze.

brooch (brōch), *n.* an ornamental clasp or pin.

brood (brōōd), *n.* **1.** a number of young hatched at one time. **2.** all the children in a family. —*v.i.* **3.** to sit upon eggs to be hatched. **4.** to dwell on a subject morbidly. —*adj.* **5.** kept for breeding.

brook[1] (brŏŏk), *n.* a small natural stream of fresh water.

brook[2] (brŏŏk), *v.t.* to bear; tolerate.

broom (brōōm, brŏŏm), *n.* **1.** a long-handled implement for sweeping, with a brush of straw or similar material. **2.** a flowering shrub of the legume family.

broom′stick′ *n.* the long slender handle of a broom.

bros. or **Bros.**, brothers.

broth (brôth, broth), *n.* a thin soup made by boiling meat, vegetables, or fish in water.

broth•el (broth′əl, brô′thəl), *n.* a house of prostitution.

broth•er (bruth′ər), *n.* **1.** a male sibling. **2.** a male numbered in the same kinship group, nationality, etc., as another. **3.** (*often cap.*) a man who devotes himself to the duties of a religious order without taking holy orders. —**broth′er•hood′**, *n.* —**broth′er•ly**, *adj.*

broth′er-in-law′ *n.*, *pl.* **broth•ers-in-law. 1.** the brother of one's spouse. **2.** the husband of one's sister. **3.** the husband of one's spouse's sister.

brou•ha•ha (brōō′hä hä′), *n.*, *pl.* **-has**. an uproar.

brow (brou), *n.* **1.** the ridge over the eye. **2.** an eyebrow. **3.** the forehead. **4.** the edge of a steep place.

brow′beat′ *v.t.*, **-beat**, **-beat•en**, **-beat•ing**. to intimidate by overbearing looks or words.

brown (broun), *n.*, *adj.*, **-er**, **-est**, *v.* —*n.* **1.** a dark color with a yellowish or reddish hue. —*adj.* **2.** of the color brown. **3.** sunburned or tanned. —*v.t.*, *v.i.* **4.** to make or become brown. **5.** to fry, roast, etc., to a brown color. —**brown′ish**, *adj.*

brown′-bag′ *v.t.*, **-bagged**, **-bag•ging**. to bring (one's lunch) to work or school, usu. in a small brown paper bag. —**brown′-bag′ger**, *n.*

brown•ie (brou′nē), *n.* **1.** an elf who secretly helps with chores. **2.** a square piece of chewy chocolate cake. **3.** (*cap.*) a Girl Scout between the ages of 6 and 8.

brown′out′ *n.* a curtailment of electric power to prevent a blackout.

browse (brouz), *v.*, **browsed**, **brows•ing**, *n.* —*v.t.*, *v.i.* **1.** to eat or nibble at (foliage, berries, etc.). **2.** to look through casually. —*n.* **3.** tender shoots or twigs as food for cattle. —**brows′er**, *n.*

bruise (brōōz), *v.*, **bruised**, **bruis•ing**, *n.* —*v.t.* **1.** to injure and discolor without breaking the skin. **2.** to hurt slightly, as with an insult. **3.** to crush (drugs or food) by pounding. —*v.i.* **4.** to bruise body tissue. **5.** to become bruised emotionally. —*n.* **6.** an injury due to bruising.

bruis′er *n.* *Informal.* a strong, tough man.

brunch (brunch), *n.* a meal that serves as both breakfast and lunch.

Bru•nei (brōō nī′, -nā′), *n.* a sultanate on the NW coast of Borneo. —**Bru•nei′an**, *adj.*, *n.*

bru•net′ (brōō net′) *adj.* dark brown, esp. of skin or hair.

bru•nette (brōō net′), *adj.* **1.** (of a female) having dark hair and, often, dark eyes and complexion. —*n.* **2.** a girl or woman with such coloration.

brunt (brunt), *n.* the main force or impact, as of an attack or blow.

brush[1] (brush), *n.* **1.** an implement consisting of bristles and a handle, used for painting, grooming, etc. **2.** the bushy tail of an animal, esp. a fox. **3.** a light, stroking touch. **4.** a close encounter. —*v.t.* **5.** to sweep, paint, etc., with a brush. **6.** to touch lightly in passing. **7.** to remove by brushing. —*v.i.* **8.** to skim with a slight contact. **9. brush off,** to rebuff. **10. ~ up on,** to review (studies, a skill, etc.).

brush[2] (brush), *n.* **1.** a dense growth of bushes, shrubs, etc. **2.** BRUSHWOOD.

brush′-off′ *n.* an abrupt rebuff.

brush′wood′ *n.* branches broken from trees.

brusque or **brusk** (brusk), *adj.* abrupt in manner or speech. —**brusque′ly,** *adv.* —**brusque′ness,** *n.*

Brus′sels sprouts′ (sprout′), *n.* a plant with small, cabbagelike, edible heads along the stalk.

bru•tal (brōot′l), *adj.* **1.** savage; cruel. **2.** harsh; severe. —**bru•tal′i•ty,** *n.,* *pl.* **-ties.** —**bru′tal•ly,** *adv.*

bru′tal•ize′ *v.t.,* **-ized, -iz•ing. 1.** to make brutal. **2.** to treat with brutality. —**bru′tal•i•za′tion,** *n.*

brute (brōot), *n.* **1.** an animal; beast. **2.** an insensitive or crude person. —*adj.* **3.** animallike. **4.** irrational. **5.** savage; cruel. —**brut′ish,** *adj.* —**brut′ish•ly,** *adv.*

B.S. Bachelor of Science.

Btu or **BTU,** British thermal unit.

bu. bushel.

bub•ble (bub′əl), *n.,* *v.,* **-bled, -bling.** —*n.* **1.** a spherical body of gas in a liquid. **2.** a globule of gas in a thin liquid envelope. **3.** anything that lacks firmness, substance, or permanence. **4.** a transparent dome. —*v.i.* **5.** to form or produce bubbles. **6.** to flow with a gurgling noise. —**bub′bly,** *adj.,* **-bli•er, -bli•est.**

buc•ca•neer (buk′ə nēr′), *n.* a pirate. [< F *boucanier* lit., barbecuer]

buck[1] (buk), *n.* **1.** the male of the deer, antelope, etc. **2.** BUCKSKIN. **3.** an impetuous man or youth.

buck[2] (buk), *v.i.* **1.** to leap with arched back so as to dislodge a rider. **2.** to resist or oppose something obstinately. —*v.t.* **3.** to throw (a rider) by bucking. **4.** to resist or oppose obstinately.

buck[3] (buk), *n.* **1.** a sawhorse. **2.** a leather-covered block used in gymnastics for vaulting.

buck[4] (buk), *n.* **1.** ultimate responsibility. —*Idiom.* **2. pass the buck,** to shift responsibility or blame to another person.

buck[5] (buk), *n. Slang.* a dollar.

buck•et (buk′it), *n.* **1.** a deep, semicircular container with a semicircular handle. **2.** a scoop, as on a steam shovel. **3.** the amount a bucket can hold. —*Idiom.* **4. drop in the bucket,** a small, inadequate amount. **5. kick the bucket,** *Slang.* to die.

buck•le (buk′əl), *n.,* *v.,* **-led, -ling.** —*n.* **1.** a clasp used for fastening two loose ends, as of a belt. **2.** a bend, bulge, or warp, as in a board. —*v.t.,* *v.i.* **3.** to fasten with a buckle. **4.** to bend or warp. **5. buckle down,** to set to work with determination.

buck′ler *n.* a round shield held by a grip.

buck•ram (buk′rəm), *n.* a stiff cotton fabric for interlinings, book bindings, etc.

buck′shot′ *n.* a large size of lead shot used for hunting game.

buck′skin′ *n.* **1.** a strong, soft leather, orig. made from deerskins, now usu. from sheepskins. **2.** **-skins,** clothes or shoes made of buckskin.

buck′tooth′ *n.,* *pl.* **-teeth.** a projecting front tooth. —**buck′toothed′,** *adj.*

buck′wheat′ *n.* **1.** any of several plants cultivated for their edible triangular seeds. **2.** the seeds of this plant, made into flour or a cereal.

bu•col•ic (byōo kol′ik), *adj.* **1.** of shepherds; pastoral. **2.** of or suggesting an idyllic rural life. —**bu•col′i•cal•ly,** *adv.*

bud (bud), *n.,* *v.,* **bud•ded, bud•ding.** —*n.* **1.** any of the small terminal bulges on a plant stem, from which leaves or flowers develop. **2.** an undeveloped person or thing. —*v.i.* **3.** to put forth buds. **4.** to begin to develop. —*Idiom.* **5. in the bud,** in an undeveloped, early stage. —**bud′der,** *n.*

bud•dy (bud′ē), *n.,* *pl.* **-dies.** *Informal.* a friend; comrade.

budge (buj), *v.t.,* *v.i.,* **budged, budg•ing. 1.** to move slightly: *The car wouldn't budge.* **2.** to yield or cause to yield.

budg•et (buj′it), *n.* **1.** an estimate of expected income and expenses. **2.** a plan of operations based on such an estimate. **3.** a limited stock or supply. —*v.t.* **4.** to allot (funds, time, etc.). —**budg′et•ar′y** (-i ter′ē), *adj.*

buff (buf), *n.* **1.** a soft, thick, light yellow leather. **2.** a brownish yellow color. **3.** a devotee of some activity or subject. **4.** *Informal.* the bare skin: *in the buff.* —*adj.* **5.** of the color buff. **6.** made of buff. **7.** *Slang.* physically attractive; muscular. —*v.t.* **8.** to clean or polish with a buffer.

buf•fa•lo (buf′ə lō′), *n.,* *pl.* **-loes, -los, -lo,** *v.,* **-loed, -lo•ing.** —*n.* **1.** any of several large wild oxen, as the bison or water buffalo. —*v.t. Informal.* **2.** to puzzle or baffle. **3.** to intimidate. [< Pg < LL *būfalus* << Gk *boúbalos*]

buff′er[1], *n.* **1.** anything used for absorbing shock, as during a collision. **2.** a temporary storage area that holds data until the computer is ready to process it. **3.** any substance capable of neutralizing both acids and bases in a solution.

buff′er[2], *n.* a leather-covered stick, block, or wheel used for polishing or buffing.

buf•fet[1] (buf′it), *n.* **1.** a blow or violent shock. —*v.t.* **2.** to strike, as with the fist. **3.** to strike against or push repeatedly: *The wind buffeted the house.*

buf•fet[2] (bə fā′, bŏo-), *n.* **1.** a cabinet for holding china, linen, etc. **2.** a meal laid out so that guests may serve themselves. **3.** a counter for food or refreshments.

buf•foon (bə fōon′), *n.* a person who amuses others by jokes, pranks, etc. —**buf•foon′er•y,** *n.* —**buf•foon′ish,** *adj.*

bug (bug), *n.,* *v.,* **bugged, bug•ging.** —*n.* **1.** any of a group of insects with sucking mouthparts. **2.** (loosely) any insect. **3.** *Informal.* any microorganism, esp. a virus. **4.** a defect, as in computer software. **5.** a hidden electronic eavesdropping device. —*v.t.* **6.** to install a secret listening device in or on. **7.** *Informal.* to annoy or pester.

bug′bear′ *n.* any source, real or imaginary, of fright or fear.

bug•gy (bug′ē), *n.,* *pl.* **-gies. 1.** a light, horse-drawn carriage with a single seat. **2.** BABY CARRIAGE.

bu•gle (byōo′gəl), *n.,* *v.,* **-gled, -gling.** —*n.* **1.** a brass wind instrument like a cornet but usu. without valves. —*v.i.* **2.** to sound a bugle. —**bu′gler,** *n.*

build (bild), *v.,* **built, build•ing,** *n.* —*v.t.* **1.** to construct by joining parts or materials. **2.** to establish or base. **3.** to form or create. —*v.i.* **4.** to engage in building. **5.** to increase in intensity, tempo, etc. **6. build up, a.** to develop or increase. **b.** to praise or promote. —*n.* **7.** physique: *a strong build.* —**build′er,** *n.*

build′ing *n.* **1.** any relatively permanent structure with a roof and walls. **2.** the act or business of constructing houses or other buildings.

build′up′ or **build′-up′** *n.* **1.** an increase in number, strength, etc. **2.** extravagant praise or publicity.

built′-in′ *adj.* **1.** built as part of a larger construction: *built-in bookcases.* **2.** inherent.

built′-up′ *adj.* **1.** built or enlarged by adding something. **2.** filled in with buildings.

bulb (bulb), *n.* **1. a.** a swollen, underground stem with fleshy leaves, as in the onion or daffodil. **b.** a plant growing from such a stem. **2.** any round, enlarged part. **3.** an incandescent lamp or its glass housing. —**bul′bous,** *adj.*

Bul•gar•i•a (bul gâr′ē ə, bŏol-), *n.* a republic in SE Europe. —**Bul•gar′i•an,** *n., adj.*

bulge (bulj), *n.,* *v.,* **bulged, bulg•ing.** —*n.* **1.** a rounded projection or protruding part. —*v.i.,* *v.t.* **2.** to swell or cause to swell outward. —**bulg′y,** *adj.,* **-i•er, -i•est.**

bu•lim•i•a (byōo lim′ē ə, -lē′mē ə, bŏo-), *n.* an eating disorder marked by excessive eating binges followed by self-induced vomiting. **—bu•lim′ic**, *adj., n.*

bulk (bulk), *n.* **1.** magnitude in three dimensions, esp. when great. **2.** the main mass or body. **—adj. 3.** being or involving material in bulk. **—v.i. 4.** to increase in size or importance. **—bulk′y**, *adj.*, **-i•er, -i•est. —bulkiness**, *n.*

bulk′head′ *n.* **1.** a wall-like construction inside a ship for forming watertight compartments. **2.** a re-taining structure for shore protection. **3.** a boxlike structure covering a stairwell.

bull¹ (bŏŏl), *n.* **1.** the male of a bovine animal or of certain other large animals, as the elephant and moose. **2.** a speculator who believes that stock prices will increase. **—adj. 3.** male. **4.** marked by rising prices, esp. of stocks: *a bull market.*

bull² (bŏŏl), *n.* a formal papal document.

bull³ (bŏŏl), *n.* exaggerations; lies; nonsense.

bull′dog′ *n.* **1.** a shorthaired, muscular dog with prominent, undershot jaws. **2.** a stubbornly persist-ent person. **—adj. 3.** like a bulldog; stubborn.

bull′doz′er *n.* a large, powerful tractor having a vertical blade at the front end for moving earth, rocks, etc.

bul•let (bŏŏl′it), *n.* a small metal projectile for fir-ing from small arms.

bul•le•tin (bŏŏl′i tn, -tin), *n.* **1.** a brief public statement, as of late news. **2.** a periodical publica-tion issued by an organization.

bull′fight′ *n.* a traditional spectacle, as in Spain and Mexico, in which a bull is fought and killed by a matador. **—bull′fight′er**, *n.* **—bull′fight′ing**, *n.*

bull′frog′ *n.* a large North American frog with a deep voice.

bull′head′ed *adj.* stubborn.

bul•lion (bŏŏl′yən), *n.* gold or silver in bars or in-gots.

bul•lock (bŏŏl′ək), *n.* a castrated bull; steer.

bull′pen′ *n.* **1.** a place where relief pitchers warm up during a baseball game. **2.** *Informal.* a cell for the temporary detention of prisoners.

bull′s-eye′ *n., pl.* **-eyes. 1.** the circular spot at the center of a target. **2.** a shot that hits this.

bul•ly (bŏŏl′ē), *n., pl.* **-lies**, *v.*, **-lied, -ly•ing. —n. 1.** person who habitually intimidates weaker people. **—v.t. 2.** to intimidate. **—v.i. 3.** to be loudly arro-gant.

bul•rush (bŏŏl′rush′), *n.* any of various rushes of the sedge family and the cattail family.

bul•wark (bŏŏl′wərk, -wôrk), *n.* **1.** a defense wall; rampart. **2.** a protection or defense. **3.** Usu., **-warks.** a wall enclosing the perimeter of a ship's deck.

bum (bum), *n., v.*, **bummed, bum•ming**, *adj.* **—n. 1.** a loafer; idler. **2.** a tramp, hobo, or derelict. **3.** *Informal.* an enthusiast: *a ski bum.* **—v.t. 4.** *Infor-mal.* to borrow without expectation of returning. **—v.i. 5.** to live as a bum. **—adj. Slang. 6.** of poor quality. **7.** false or misleading: *a bum rap.* **8.** lame.

bum•ble (bum′bəl), *v.*, **-bled, -bling. —v.i. 1.** to blunder. **2.** to stumble. **—v.t. 3.** to bungle or botch. **—bum′bler**, *n.*

bum′ble-bee′ or **bum′ble bee′**, *n.* any of sev-eral large, hairy social bees.

bum•mer (bum′ər), *n. Slang.* any unpleasant ex-perience, esp. with a hallucinogenic drug.

bump (bump), *v.t., v.i.* **1.** to strike or collide (with). **2.** to bounce along with jolts. **3. bump into,** to meet by chance. **4. ~ off,** *Slang.* to murder. **—n. 5.** a collision; blow. **6.** a swelling from a blow. **7.** a small area higher than the surrounding surface. **—bump′y**, *adj.*, **-i•er, -i•est.**

bump′er *n.* **1.** a metal guard for protecting the front or rear of an automobile, truck, etc. **—adj. 2.** unusually abundant: *a bumper crop.*

bump•kin (bump′kin), *n.* an awkward, simple rus-tic; yokel.

bun (bun), *n.* **1.** a bread roll, either plain or slightly sweetened. **2.** hair gathered into a round coil.

bunch (bunch), *n.* **1.** a connected group; cluster: *a bunch of grapes.* **2.** a group of people or things. **—v.t., v.i. 3.** to gather into a bunch.

bun•dle (bun′dl), *n., v.*, **-dled, -dling. —n. 1.** a

quantity of material gathered or bound together. **2.** a package. **3.** a group of things; bunch. **4.** *Slang.* a great deal of money. **—v.t. 5.** to tie or wrap in a bundle. **6.** to send away hurriedly. **7. bundle up,** to dress warmly.

bun•ga•low (bung′gə lō′), *n.* a small house, usu. one-storied.

bun•gle (bung′gal), *v.*, **-gled, -gling**, *n.* **—v.t., v.i. 1.** to do or work clumsily or inadequately. **—n. 2.** something bungled. **—bun′gler**, *n.*

bun•ion (bun′yən), *n.* an inflammation of the bursa of the big toe.

bunk¹ (bungk), *n.* **1.** a built-in platform bed, as on a ship. **2.** BUNKHOUSE. **—v.i. 3.** to occupy a bunk. **—v.t. 4.** to provide with a place to sleep.

bunk² (bungk), *n. Informal.* BUNKUM.

bun•ker (bung′kər), *n.* **1.** a large bin or receptacle. **2.** a partially underground bomb shelter or fortifica-tion. **3.** *Golf.* any obstacle constituting a hazard. **—adj. 4.** characterized by or given to extreme measures to avoid defeat: *a bunker mentality.*

bunk′house′ *n.* a rough building housing ranch hands, campers, etc.

bun•kum (bung′kəm), *n.* insincere or empty talk. [after a pointless speech in Congress by F. Walker, who explained that he was expected to make a speech by his constituents in *Buncombe*, county in North Carolina]

bun•ny (bun′ē), *n., pl.* **-nies.** a rabbit, esp. a young one.

bunt (bunt), *v.t., v.i.* **1.** to push (something) with the horns or head. **2.** to tap (a pitched baseball) close to home plate. **—n. 3.** a push with the head or horns. **4.** a bunted baseball. **—bunt′er**, *n.*

bun•ting¹ (bun′ting), *n.* **1.** a coarse, open fabric for flags, etc. **2.** flags collectively.

bun•ting² (bun′ting), *n.* a small, seed-eating song-bird.

bun•ting³ (bun′ting), *n.* a hooded sleeping gar-ment for infants.

bu•oy (bŏŏ′ē, boi), *n., pl.* **-oys**, *v.* **—n. 1.** an an-chored float used as a marker or mooring. **2.** a ring-like life preserver. **—v.t. 3.** to keep afloat. **4.** to mark with buoys. **5.** to sustain or encourage.

buoy′ant (boi′ənt, bŏŏ′yənt) *adj.* **1.** tending to float. **2.** cheerful. **—buoy′an•cy**, *n.*

bur (bûr), *n.* **1.** a rough prickly case around the seeds of certain plants. **2.** any bur-bearing plant. **3.** BURR¹ (defs. 1, 2).

bur•den¹ (bûr′dn), *n.* **1.** that which is carried; load. **2.** that which is borne with difficulty; onus. **—v.t. 3.** to load heavily. **4.** to load oppressively; trouble. **—bur′den•some**, *adj.*

bur•den² (bûr′dn), *n.* **1.** a repeated main point or idea. **2.** a musical refrain; chorus.

bur•dock (bûr′dok), *n.* a coarse broad-leaved weed bearing prickly heads of burs.

bu•reau (byŏŏr′ō), *n., pl.* **bu•reaus, bu•reaux** (byŏŏr′ōz). **1.** a chest of drawers. **2.** a government department or administrative unit. **3.** a business of-fice or agency.

bu•reauc•ra•cy (byŏŏ rok′rə sē), *n., pl.* **-cies. 1.** government by a rigid hierarchy of administrators and officials. **2.** a body of officials and administra-tors. **3.** administration characterized by excessive red tape and routine. **—bu•reau•crat** (byŏŏr′-ə krat′), *n.* **—bu′reau•crat′ic**, *adj.* **—bu′reau• crat′i•cal•ly**, *adv.*

bur•geon (bûr′jən), *v.i.* **1.** to grow or develop quickly. **2.** to begin to grow, as a bud.

burg•er (bûr′gər), *n.* a hamburger.

bur•glar (bûr′glər), *n.* a thief who breaks and enters. **—bur′glar•ize′**, *v.t., v.i.*, **-ized, iz•ing. —bur′glar•y**, *n., pl.* **-glar•ies.**

Bur•gun•dy (bûr′gən dē), *n., pl.* **-dies.** (*often l.c.*) any of the red or white wines orig. produced in Burgundy, a region in central France.

bur•i•al (ber′ē əl), *n.* the act or ceremony of bury-ing.

Bur•ki•na Fa•so (bər kē′nə fä′sō), *n.* a republic in W Africa.

bur•lap (bûr′lap), *n.* a coarse fabric of jute or hemp.

bur•lesque (bər lesk′), *n., v.,* **-lesqued, -lesqu•ing.** —*n.* **1.** a parody or caricature. **2.** a stage show featuring bawdy comedy and striptease acts. —*v.t., v.i.* **3.** to mock by burlesque.

bur•ly (bûr′lē), *adj.,* **-li•er, -li•est.** large in bodily size; sturdy. —**bur′li•ness,** *n.*

burn (bûrn), *v.,* **burned** or **burnt, burn•ing,** *n.* —*v.i.* **1.** to be on fire. **2.** to give off light. **3.** to be hot. **4.** to be injured, damaged, or destroyed by fire, heat, or acid. **5.** to feel strong emotion. —*v.t.* **6.** to cause to be consumed by fire. **7.** to use as fuel. **8.** to sunburn. **9.** to injure, damage, or destroy with or as if with fire. **10.** to produce with fire: *to burn a hole.* **11.** to cause a stinging sensation in. **12. burn down,** to burn to the ground. **13. ~ out,** to exhaust or become exhausted through overwork and stress. **14. ~ up,** *Informal.* to make or become angry. —*n.* **15.** an injury caused by burning. **16.** the process or result of burning. —**burn′a•ble,** *adj.*

burn′er *n.* the part of a gas or electric fixture or appliance from which flame or heat issues.

bur•nish (bûr′nish), *v.t.,* **1.** to polish (a surface) by friction. —*n.* **2.** brightness; luster. —**bur′nish•er,** *n.*

burn′out′ *n.* **1.** the termination of effective combustion in a rocket engine, due to exhaustion of propellant. **2.** fatigue and frustration resulting from prolonged stress and overwork.

burp (bûrp), *Informal.* —*n.* **1.** a belch. —*v.i.* **2.** to belch. —*v.t.* **3.** to cause (a baby) to belch.

burr¹ (bûr), *n.* **1.** a ragged edge raised on metal during drilling, shearing, etc. **2.** a hand-held rotary power tool used to cut small recesses. —*v.t.* **3.** to form a rough edge on.

burr² (bûr), *n.* **1.** the pronunciation of (r) as a trill, as in Scottish speech. **2.** a whirring noise.

bur•ro (bûr′ō, boŏr′ō, bur′ō), *n., pl.* **-ros.** a donkey.

bur•row (bûr′ō, bur′ō), *n.* **1.** a hole dug in the ground by an animal. **2.** a place of retreat. —*v.i.* **3.** to dig a burrow. **4.** to lodge or hide in a burrow. **5.** to proceed by or as if by digging. —*v.t.* **6.** to dig a burrow into. **7.** to make by burrowing. —**bur′row•er,** *n.*

bur•sa (bûr′sə), *n., pl.* **-sae** (-sē), **-sas.** a sac containing lubricating fluid, as between a tendon and a bone.

bur•sar (bûr′sər, -sär), *n.* a treasurer, esp. of a college.

bur•si•tis (bər sī′tis), *n.* inflammation of a bursa.

burst (bûrst), *v.,* **burst, burst•ing,** *n.* —*v.i.* **1.** to break apart with sudden violence. **2.** to issue forth suddenly. **3.** to give sudden expression to emotion. **4.** to be extremely full. **5.** to appear suddenly. —*v.t.* **6.** to cause to burst. —*n.* **7.** an act or instance of bursting. **8.** a sudden display of intense activity. **9.** a sudden expression of emotion. **10.** a rapid sequence of shots.

Bu•run•di (boŏ roŏn′dē), *n.* a republic in central Africa. —**Bu•run′di•an,** *adj., n.*

bur•y (ber′ē), *v.t.,* **-ied, -y•ing. 1.** to put in the ground and cover with earth. **2.** to put (a corpse) in the ground or a vault. **3.** to plunge in deeply. **4.** to conceal from sight. **5.** to involve (oneself) deeply.

bus¹ (bus), *n., pl.* **bus•es, bus•ses,** *v.,* **bused** or **bussed, bus•ing** or **bus•sing.** —*n.* **1.** a large motor vehicle for many passengers. **2.** a circuit that connects the CPU with other devices in a computer. —*v.t.* **3.** to transport by bus. —*v.i.* **4.** to travel by bus. [short for *omnibus*]

bus² (bus), *v.i., v.t.,* **bused** or **bussed, bus•ing** or **bus•sing.** to work as a busboy.

bus′boy′ *n.* a waiter's helper in a restaurant.

bush (boŏsh), *n.* **1.** a low plant with many branches. **2.** something resembling this, as a shaggy head of hair. **3.** a large uncleared area. —*v.i.* **4.** to spread like a bush. —*Idiom.* **5. beat around the bush,** to avoid talking about a subject directly. —**bush′y,** *adj.,* **-i•er, -i•est.**

bushed *adj. Informal.* exhausted; tired out.

bush•el (boŏsh′əl), *n.* **1.** a unit of dry measure equal to 4 pecks, 2150.42 cubic inches, or 35.24 liters. **2.** a large, unspecified amount.

bush′ league′ *n.* a secondary baseball league. —**bush′-league′,** *adj.* —**bush′ lea′guer,** *n.*

busi•ness (biz′nis), *n.* **1.** an occupation, profession, or trade. **2.** a profit-seeking enterprise or concern. **3.** trade or patronage. **4.** a person's principal concern. **5.** affair; matter. —*adj.* **6.** of or suitable for business. —*Idiom.* **7. mean business,** to be in earnest.

busi′ness•like′ *adj.* showing attributes prized in business, as practicality and efficiency.

bus•ing or **bus•sing** (bus′ing), *n.* the transporting of students by bus to schools outside their neighborhoods, esp. to achieve racial balance.

bust¹ (bust), *n.* **1.** a representation of the head and shoulders of a human subject. **2.** a woman's bosom.

bust² (bust), *Informal.* —*v.i.* **1.** to burst. **2.** to go bankrupt. —*v.t.* **3.** to burst or break. **4.** to ruin financially. **5.** to demote. **6.** to tame: *to bust a bronco.* **7.** to arrest. **8.** to hit. —*n.* **9.** a failure. **10.** a hit; punch. **11.** an economic depression. **12.** an arrest.

bus•tle¹ (bus′əl), *v.,* **-tled, -tling,** *n.* —*v.i.* **1.** to move or act with great energy. —*n.* **2.** energetic activity. —**bus′tler,** *n.*

bus•tle² (bus′əl), *n.* a pad formerly worn to expand the back of a woman's skirt.

bus•y (biz′ē), *adj.,* **-i•er, -i•est,** *v.,* **-ied, -y•ing.** —*adj.* **1.** actively engaged in work. **2.** not at leisure. **3.** full of activity. **4.** (of a telephone line) in use. **5.** cluttered with fussy details. —*v.t.* **6.** to make or keep busy. —**bus′i•ly,** *adv.* —**bus′y•ness,** *n.*

bus′y•bod′y *n., pl.* **-ies.** a person who meddles in the affairs of others.

but (but; *unstressed* bət), *conj.* **1.** on the contrary: *He went, but I did not.* **2.** and yet; nevertheless: *strange but true.* **3.** except; save: *did nothing but complain.* **4.** without the circumstance that: *It never rains but it pours.* **5.** otherwise than: *There is no hope but by prayer.* **6.** that: *I don't doubt but you'll do it.* **7.** that … not: *No leaders ever existed but they were optimists.* —*prep.* **8.** other than; except: *nothing but trouble.* —*adv.* **9.** only; just: *There is but one answer.* —*Idiom.* **10. but for,** were it not for.

bu•tane (byoō′tān), *n.* a colorless, flammable gas, used as fuel.

butch (boŏch), *adj. Slang.* **1.** (of a woman) having traits usu. associated with males. **2.** (of a male) exaggeratedly masculine.

butch•er (boŏch′ər), *n.* **1.** a dealer in meat. **2.** a person who slaughters or dresses animals for food. **3.** a brutal murderer. —*v.t.* **4.** to slaughter or dress (animals) for market. **5.** to kill brutally. **6.** to bungle; botch. —**butch′er•y,** *n., pl.* **-ies.**

but•ler (but′lər), *n.* the chief male servant of a household.

butt¹ (but), *n.* **1.** the thicker or larger end of anything: *a rifle butt.* **2.** an unused end or remnant. **3.** *Slang.* the buttocks.

butt² (but), *n.* **1.** an object of ridicule. **2.** a target. —*v.t., v.i.* **3.** to set end to end.

butt³ (but), *v.t., v.i.* **1.** to strike or push with the head or horns. **2. butt in,** to intrude or meddle. —*n.* **3.** a push or blow with the head or horns.

butt⁴ (but), *n.* a large cask for wine, beer, or ale.

but•ter (but′ər), *n.* **1.** a fatty solid that separates from milk or cream when it is churned. **2.** any substance of butterlike consistency. —*v.t.* **3.** to put butter on or in. **4. butter up,** to flatter. —**but′ter•y,** *adj.*

but′ter•cup′ *n.* a plant with glossy yellow flowers.

but′ter•fin′gers *n., pl.* **-gers.** a person who drops things; a clumsy person.

but′ter•fly′ *n., pl.* **-flies.** any of numerous insects with a slender body and broad, often conspicuously marked wings.

but′ter•milk′ *n.* the sour liquid remaining after butter has been separated from milk.

but′ter•nut′ *n.* **1.** the edible oily nut of an American tree of the walnut family. **2.** the tree itself.

but′ter•scotch′ *n.* a flavoring or a hard, brittle taffy made with butter, brown sugar, etc.

but•tock (but′ək), *n.* **1.** either of the two fleshy protuberances forming the human rump. **2.** **buttocks,** the human rump.

but•ton (but′n), *n.* **1.** a small disk or knob used as a fastener, as on clothing. **2.** anything resembling a button. —*v.t., v.i.* **3.** to fasten or be fastened with a button or buttons.

but′ton-down′ *adj.* **1.** (of a collar) having buttonholes with which it can be buttoned to the garment. **2.** conventional; unimaginative.

but′ton-hole′ *n., v.,* **-holed, -hol•ing.** —*n.* **1.** the slit through which a button is passed. —*v.t.* **2.** to accost and detain in conversation.

but•tress (bu′tris), *n.* **1.** a projecting support built into or against a wall. **2.** any prop or support. —*v.t.* **3.** to support or prop up.

bux•om (buk′səm), *adj.* (of a woman) fullbosomed.

buy (bī), *v.,* **bought, buy•ing,** *n.* —*v.t.* **1.** to acquire by paying money; purchase. **2.** to acquire by exchange or concession. **3.** to bribe. **4.** *Informal.* to accept or believe. —*v.i.* **5.** to be or become a purchaser. **6. buy off,** to bribe. **7.** ~ **out,** to purchase all the business shares belonging to. **8.** ~ **up,** to buy as much as one can of. —*n.* **9.** something bought. **10.** a bargain.

buy′back′ *n.* a repurchase by a company of its own stock.

buy′out′ *n.* the purchase of all or a controlling percentage of the shares in a company.

buzz (buz), *n.* **1.** a low, humming sound, as of bees. **2.** *Informal.* a phone call. —*v.i.* **3.** to make a low, humming sound. **4.** to be filled with such a sound, as a room. **5.** to whisper; gossip. —*v.t.* **6.** to signal with a buzzer. **7.** *Informal.* to telephone. **8.** to fly a plane low over.

buz•zard (buz′ərd), *n.* **1.** any of several broadwinged Old World hawks. **2.** any of several New World vultures, esp. the turkey vulture.

buzz′er *n.* a signaling apparatus that produces a buzzing sound.

buzz′word′ *n.* a word or phrase that has come into vogue in a particular profession.

by (bī), *prep.* **1.** near or next to: *a home by a lake.* **2.** by way of; via: *She came by air.* **3.** beyond; past: *We drove by the church.* **4.** during: *by day.* **5.** not later than: *I′ll be done by noon.* **6.** to the extent or amount of: *taller by three inches.* **7.** according to: *by*

law. **8.** through the agency of: *issued by the government.* **9.** from the hand or mind of: *a poem by Keats.* **10.** on behalf of: *to do well by one′s children.* **11.** after; next after: *piece by piece.* **12.** the number of times specified by a multiplier or divisor: *Multiply 18 by 57.* **13.** with another dimension of: *10 by 12 feet.* **14.** in terms or amounts of: *sold by the bushel.* **15.** to, into, or at: *Come by my office.* —*adv.* **16.** at hand; near: *The school is close by.* **17.** past: *The car drove by.* **18.** aside; away: *to put money by.* **19.** past; over: *in times gone by.* —*Idiom.* **20. by and by,** before long. **21. by and large,** in general.

by- a combining form of BY: *by-product; bystander.*

bye (bī), *n.* (in a tournament) the status of a player not paired with a competitor in an early round and thus advanced to the next round.

by′-elec′tion *n.* a special election held between general elections to fill a vacancy.

by′gone′ *adj.* **1.** former; past. —*n.* **2.** something in the past. —*Idiom.* **3. let bygones be bygones,** to forget past disagreements.

by′law′ *n.* a rule governing the internal affairs of a corporation or society.

by′line′ *n.* a line in a newspaper or magazine article giving the author′s name.

by′pass′ *n.* **1.** a road enabling motorists to avoid a city or to drive around an obstruction. **2.** a surgical procedure in which a diseased or obstructed organ is circumvented. —*v.t.* **3.** to avoid by following a bypass. **4.** to neglect to consult.

by′-prod′uct *n.* **1.** a secondary or incidental product, as in a manufacturing process. **2.** the result of another action.

by′-road′ *n.* a side road.

by′stand′er *n.* a person present but not involved.

byte (bīt), *n.* a group of adjacent bits, usu. eight, processed by a computer as a unit. [perh. alteration (influenced by BIT³) of BITE]

by′way′ *n.* a little-used road.

by′word′ *n.* **1.** a proverb. **2.** a person regarded as the embodiment of some quality. **3.** an object of scorn.

Byz•an•tine (biz′ən tēn′, -tīn′), *adj.* **1.** of the Byzantine Empire or its ornate style of architecture. **2.** (*sometimes l.c.*) **a.** very complex or intricate. **b.** characterized by intrigue.

a b C d e f g h i j k l m n o p q r s t u v w x y z

C, c (sē), *n., pl.* **Cs** or **C′s, cs** or **c′s.** the third letter of the English alphabet, a consonant.

C *Symbol.* **1.** the third in order or in a series. **2.** a grade or mark indicating fair or average quality. **3.** the Roman numeral for 100. **4.** Celsius. **5.** Centigrade. **6.** *Chem.* carbon.

c 1. circa. **2.** curie. **3.** cycle.

C. 1. Calorie. **2.** Catholic. **3.** College.

c. 1. calorie. **2.** carat. **3.** *Baseball.* catcher. **4.** cent. **5.** centimeter. **6.** century. **7.** chapter. **8.** circa. **9.** cognate. **10.** copyright. **11.** cubic. **12.** cycle.

CA California.

Ca *Chem. Symbol.* calcium.

ca or **ca.,** circa.

cab (kab), *n.* **1.** a taxicab. **2.** a horse-drawn vehicle for public hire. **3.** the enclosed part of a locomotive, truck, etc., where the operator sits.

ca•bal (kə bal′), *n.* **1.** a small group of secret plotters, as against a government. **2.** secret plots and schemes.

ca•ban•a (kə ban′ə, -ban′yə), *n., pl.* **-as.** a small structure for use as a bathhouse at a beach or swimming pool.

cab•a•ret (kab′ə rā′), *n.* a restaurant providing musical entertainment.

cab•bage (kab′ij), *n.* a vegetable with leaves

formed into a compact, edible head. [< OF « L *caput* head]

cab•in (kab′in), *n.* **1.** a small house or cottage of simple design and construction. **2.** the enclosed space for the passengers, pilot, or cargo in an air or space vehicle. **3.** an apartment or room in a ship.

cab•i•net (kab′ə nit), *n.* **1.** a piece of furniture with shelves, drawers, etc., for holding or displaying items. **2.** a wall cupboard. **3.** the case enclosing a radio, television, etc. **4.** (*often cap.*) a council advising a sovereign or a chief executive.

ca•ble (kā′bəl), *n., v.,* **-bled, -bling.** —*n.* **1.** a heavy, strong rope of fiber or metal wire. **2.** an insulated electrical conductor, often in strands. **3.** CABLEGRAM. **4.** CABLE TELEVISION. —*v.t.* **5.** to send (a message) by cable. **6.** to send a cablegram to. **7.** to fasten with a cable. —*v.i.* **8.** to send a message by cable.

ca′ble•gram′ *n.* a telegram sent by underwater cable.

ca′ble tel′evision *n.* a system of televising programs to private subscribers by means of coaxial cable.

ca•boose (kə bōōs′), *n.* a car for the crew at the rear of a freight train.

ca•ca•o (kə kä′ō, -kā′ō), *n., pl.* **-os. 1.** a small

tropical American evergreen tree. **2.** the seeds of this tree, the source of cocoa and chocolate.

cache (kash), *n.*, *v.*, **cached, cach•ing.** —*n.* **1.** a hiding place for food, treasures, etc. **2.** anything hidden in a cache. —*v.t.* **3.** to hide in a cache.

ca•chet (ka shā′), *n.* **1.** an official seal, as on a document. **2.** an official sign of approval. **3.** superior status; prestige. **4.** a design, slogan, etc., printed on an envelope for philatelic purposes.

cack•le (kak′əl), *v.*, **-led, -ling,** *n.* —*v.i.* **1.** to utter a shrill, broken cry, as of a hen. **2.** to laugh in a shrill, broken manner. —*n.* **3.** the act or sound of cackling. —**cack′ler,** *n.*

ca•coph•o•ny (kə kof′ə nē), *n.*, *pl.* **-nies.** harsh, discordant sound. —**ca•coph′o•nous,** *adj.*

cac•tus (kak′təs), *n.*, *pl.* **-ti** (-tī), **-tus•es, -tus.** a desert plant with succulent, leafless stems usu. bearing spines.

cad (kad), *n.* a man who behaves dishonorably toward women. —**cad′dish,** *adj.* —**cad′dish•ness,** *n.*

ca•dav•er (kə dav′ər), *n.* a corpse, as for dissection.

CAD/CAM (kad′kam′), *n.* computer-aided design and computer-aided manufacturing.

cad•die (kad′ē), *n.*, *v.*, **-died, -dy•ing.** —*n.* **1.** a person hired to carry a golfer's clubs. —*v.i.* **2.** to work as a caddie.

ca•dence (kād′ns), *n.* **1.** rhythmic flow, as of sounds or words. **2.** the beat or measure of any rhythmic movement. **3.** modulation of the voice in speaking. —**ca′denced,** *adj.*

ca•det (kə det′), *n.* a student at a military or naval academy.

cadge (kaj), *v.t.*, *v.i.*, **cadged, cadg•ing.** to obtain (something) by begging or by sponging on another. —**cadg′er,** *n.*

cad•mi•um (kad′mē əm), *n.* a white, ductile metallic element, used in plating and in making alloys. Symbol: Cd; *at. wt.:* 112.41; *at. no.:* 48.

ca•dre (kad′rē, kä′drā), *n.* a core group of trained workers around which an expanded organization can be built.

Cae•sar•e•an (si zâr′ē ən), *n.* (*sometimes l.c.*) CESAREAN.

ca•fé (ka fā′, kə-), *n.*, *pl.* **-fés. 1.** a restaurant, usu. small and unpretentious. **2.** a barroom or nightclub. [< F: lit., coffee]

caf•e•te•ri•a (kaf′i tēr′ē ə), *n.*, *pl.* **-as.** a restaurant in which patrons select food at a counter and carry it to tables.

caf•feine (ka fēn′), *n.* a bitter alkaloid, usu. derived from coffee or tea, used as a stimulant.

caf•tan (kaf′tan, kaf tan′), *n.* a long coatlike garment with wide sleeves, worn in the Middle East.

cage (kāj), *n.*, *v.*, **caged, cag•ing.** —*n.* **1.** an enclosure with wires, bars, etc., for confining birds or animals. **2.** a similar enclosure, as for a cashier. —*v.t.* **3.** to put or confine in or as if in a cage.

cag′ey or **cag′y,** *adj.*, **-i•er, -i•est.** cautious; shrewd. —**cag′i•ly,** *adv.* —**cag′i•ness,** *n.*

cais•son (kā′son, -sən), *n.* **1.** a pressurized, watertight chamber for use in underwater construction. **2.** a two-wheeled wagon, used for carrying ammunition.

ca•jole (kə jōl′), *v.t.*, *v.i.*, **-joled, -jol•ing.** to persuade by flattery or promises. —**ca•jol′er,** *n.* —**ca•jol′er•y,** *n.*

Ca•jun (kā′jən), *n.* **1.** a native of Louisiana descended from French immigrants from E Canada. **2.** the form of French spoken by the Cajuns.

cake (kāk), *n.*, *v.*, **caked, cak•ing.** —*n.* **1.** a sweet, baked, breadlike food. **2.** a thin baked or fried mass of batter or minced food. **3.** a shaped, hard mass: *a cake of soap.* —*v.t.*, *v.i.* **4.** to form into a crust or compact mass. —*Idiom.* **5. piece of cake,** something that can be done easily. **6. take the cake,** to win the hypothetical prize.

Cal. California.

cal. 1. caliber. **2.** calorie.

cal•a•bash (kal′ə bash′), *n.* **1.** the large, gourdlike fruit of a tropical American tree. **2.** a container or utensil made from its shell.

ca′la•ma′ri (kal′ə mär′ē, kä′lə-) *n.* cooked squid.

cal•a•mine (kal′ə mīn′), *n.* a pink powder consisting of zinc and iron oxides, used in skin lotions.

ca•lam•i•ty (kə lam′i tē), *n.*, *pl.* **-ties. 1.** a great misfortune. **2.** grievous affliction; misery. —**ca•lam′i•tous,** *adj.*

cal•ci•fy (kal′sə fī′), *v.t.*, *v.i.*, **-fied, -fy•ing.** to harden by the deposit of calcium salts. —**cal′ci•fi•ca′tion,** *n.*

cal•ci•um (kal′sē əm), *n.* a silver-white metal, occurring in combination in chalk, limestone, etc., and also found in bones and shells. Symbol: Ca; *at. wt.:* 40.08; *at. no.:* 20.

cal•cu•late (kal′kyə lāt′), *v.*, **-lat•ed, -lat•ing.** —*v.t.* **1.** to determine by using mathematics; compute. **2.** to determine by reasoning; estimate. **3.** to make fit for a purpose: *The remarks were calculated to inspire confidence.* —*v.i.* **4.** to make a calculation. **5.** to count or rely. —**cal′cu•la•ble,** *adj.* —**cal′cu•la′tion,** *n.*

cal′cu•lat′ing *adj.* **1.** shrewd. **2.** selfishly scheming.

cal′cu•la′tor *n.* **1.** an electronic or mechanical device that performs calculations. **2.** a person who calculates.

cal′cu•lus *n.*, *pl.* **-li** (-lī′), **-lus•es. 1.** a method of calculation by a special system of algebraic notations. **2.** a stone formed in the gallbladder, kidney, etc. [< L: pebble, small stone (used in calculating)]

cal′dron (kôl′drən) *n.* cauldron.

cal•en•dar (kal′ən dər), *n.* **1.** a table with the days of each month and week in a year. **2.** a system of reckoning the beginning, length, and divisions of the year. **3.** a schedule of appointments, cases to be tried in court, etc. —*v.t.* **4.** to enter in a calendar.

calf[1] (kaf, käf), *n.*, *pl.* **calves. 1.** the young of the domestic cow or other bovine animal. **2.** the young of certain other mammals, as the elephant or whale. **3.** calfskin leather.

calf[2] (kaf, käf), *n.*, *pl.* **calves.** the fleshy back part of the human leg below the knee.

cal•i•ber (kal′ə bər), *n.* **1.** the diameter of a circular section, esp. the inside of a tube. **2.** the diameter of the bore of a gun. **3.** degree of competence. Also, *esp. Brit.,* **cal′i•bre.**

cal′i•brate′ (-brāt′), *v.t.*, **-brat•ed, -brat•ing. 1.** to mark (a thermometer or other instrument) with indexes of degree or quantity. **2.** to determine the correct range for (a gun, mortar, etc.). —**cal′i•bra′tion,** *n.* —**cal′i•bra′tor,** *n.*

cal•i•co (kal′i kō′), *n.*, *pl.* **-coes, -cos,** *adj.* —*n.* **1.** a plain-woven cotton cloth printed with a figured pattern. —*adj.* **2.** mottled or variegated in color: *a calico cat.*

cal•i•per (kal′ə pər), *n.* **1.** Usu., **-pers.** an instrument for measuring thicknesses and diameters, consisting usu. of a pair of adjustable pivoted legs. —*v.t.*, *v.i.* **2.** to measure with calipers.

ca•liph (kā′lif, kal′if), *n.* a former title for a religious and civil ruler of the Islamic world. —**cal•iph•ate** (kal′ə fāt′, -fit), *n.*

cal•is•then•ics (kal′əs then′iks), *n.* (*used with a sing. or pl. v.*) gymnastic exercises for health. —**cal′is•then′ic,** *adj.*

calk (kôk), *v.t.*, **calked, calk•ing,** *n.* CAULK.

call (kôl), *v.t.* **1.** to cry out in a loud voice. **2.** to summon. **3.** to telephone. **4.** to waken. **5.** to convene: *to call a meeting.* **6.** to name (someone) as. **7.** to designate as something specified: *She called me a liar.* **8.** to demand payment of (a loan). —*v.i.* **9.** to speak loudly. **10.** to make a short visit. **11.** to telephone. **12.** (of a bird or animal) to utter its characteristic cry. **13. call for,** to come to get. **b.** to demand. **14. ~ off,** to cancel (something planned). **15. ~ up, a.** to remember. **b.** to telephone. **c.** to summon for action, esp. military service. —*n.* **16.** a cry or shout. **17.** the vocal sound of a bird or other animal. **18.** the act of telephoning. **19.** a short visit. **20.** a summons or invitation. **21.** fascination or appeal: *the call of the sea.* **22.** a need or occasion: *no call for panic.* **23.** a demand or claim: *a call on one's time.* —**call′er,** *n.*

call′ girl *n.* a female prostitute with whom appointment can be made by telephone.

cal·lig·ra·phy (kə lig′rə fē), *n.* fancy penmanship or the art of writing beautifully. —**cal·lig′ra·pher,** *n.*

call′ing *n.* **1.** a vocation or profession. **2.** a strong impulse or inclination.

cal·lous (kal′əs), *adj.* **1.** thickened and hardened, as skin. **2.** insensitive; unsympathetic. —**cal′lous·ness,** *n.*

cal·low (kal′ō), *adj.* immature or inexperienced. —**cal′low·ness,** *n.*

cal·lus (kal′əs), *n., pl.* **-lus·es. 1.** a hardened or thickened part of the skin. —*v.i., v.t.* **2.** to form a callus (on).

calm (käm), *adj.,* **-er, -est,** *n., v.* —*adj.* **1.** without rough motion. **2.** not windy. **3.** tranquil; serene. —*n.* **4.** freedom from motion or disturbance. **5.** absence of wind. **6.** serenity; tranquillity. —*v.t., v.i.* **7.** to make or become calm. —**calm′ly,** *adv.* —**calm′ness,** *n.*

ca·lor·ic (kə lôr′ik, -lor′-), *adj.* **1.** of calories. **2.** of heat.

cal·o·rie (kal′ə rē), *n.* **1.** the amount of heat necessary to raise the temperature of one gram of water by 1°C **(small calorie),** or of one kilogram of water by 1°C **(large calorie). 2.** a unit equal to the large calorie, used to express the heat output of an organism and the energy value of food.

ca·lum·ni·ate (kə lum′nē āt′), *v.t.,* **-at·ed, -at·ing.** to make false and malicious statements about; slander. —**ca·lum′ni·a′tion,** *n.* —**cal′um·ny,** *n.*

calve (kav, käv), *v.i., v.t.,* **calved, calv·ing.** to give birth to (a calf).

ca·lyp·so (kə lip′sō), *n., pl.* **-sos.** a musical style of West Indian origin, influenced by jazz.

ca·lyx (kā′liks, kal′iks), *n., pl.* **ca·lyx·es, cal·y·ces** (kal′ə sēz′, kā′lə-). the outermost group of floral parts; the sepals collectively.

cam (kam), *n.* an irregularly shaped disk or cylinder that gives a rocking motion to any contiguous part.

ca·ma·ra·de·rie (kä′mə rä′də rē, kam′ə-), *n.* comradeship; good-fellowship.

cam·ber (kam′bər), *v.t., v.i.* **1.** to arch slightly; curve upward in the middle. —*n.* **2.** a slight arching, upward curve, or convexity.

Cam·bo·di·a (kam bō′dē ə), *n.* a republic in SE Asia. —**Cam·bo′di·an,** *adj., n.*

cam·bric (kām′brik), *n.* a thin cotton or linen fabric.

cam·cord·er (kam′kôr′dər), *n.* a hand-held television camera with an incorporated VCR.

came (kām), *v.* pt. of COME.

cam·el (kam′əl), *n.* either of two large, humped ruminants of the Old World. [< L *camēlus* < Gk *kámēlos* < Semitic; cf. Heb *gāmāl*]

ca·mel·lia (kə mēl′yə, -mē′lē ə), *n., pl.* **-lias.** a shrub with glossy evergreen leaves and roselike flowers. [after G. J. *Camellus* (1661–1706), Jesuit missionary who brought it to Europe]

cam·e·o (kam′ē ō′), *n., pl.* **-os. 1.** a jewel with a head in profile carved or set in relief. **2.** an effective literary sketch or small dramatic scene. **3.** a small but notable part in a film or play.

cam·er·a (kam′ər ə), *n., pl.* **-as. 1.** a photographic device with an aperture that opens to admit light: focused by a lens, the light forms an image on a light-sensitive film or plate. **2.** the device in which a picture to be televised is formed before it is changed into electric impulses. —**Idiom. 3. in camera,** privately.

Cam·e·roon (kam′ə rōōn′), *n.* a republic in W equatorial Africa. —**Cam′e·roon′i·an,** *adj., n.*

cam·i·sole (kam′ə sōl′), *n.* a short garment worn underneath a sheer bodice.

cam·o·mile (kam′ə mīl′, -mēl′), *n.* CHAMOMILE.

cam·ou·flage (kam′ə fläzh′), *n., v.,* **-flaged, -flag·ing.** —*n.* **1.** the disguising of elements of a military installation to conceal it from the enemy. **2.** a disguise or deception. —*v.t.* **3.** to disguise or deceive by means of camouflage. —**cam′ou·flag′er,** *n.*

camp¹ (kamp), *n.* **1. a.** a place where a group of persons is lodged in tents or other temporary shelters. **b.** such shelters collectively. **c.** the persons so sheltered. **2.** a group of people favoring the same ideals, doctrines, etc. **3.** a recreation area in the country, esp. one for children. —*v.i.* **4.** to establish a camp. **5.** to live in or as if in a camp: *They camped out by the stream.* [<< L *campus* field]

camp² (kamp), *n.* **1.** something that provides amusement by virtue of its being contrived, overdone, or tasteless. —*adj.* **2.** campy. [origin uncertain]

cam·paign (kam pān′), *n.* **1.** a series of military operations for a specific objective. **2.** a systematic course of aggressive activities: *a sales campaign; a campaign for mayor.* —*v.i.* **3.** to conduct a campaign. —**cam·paign′er,** *n.*

cam·phor (kam′fər), *n.* a white, pleasant-smelling substance used chiefly as a moth repellent.

cam·pus (kam′pəs), *n., pl.* **-pus·es.** the grounds, often including the buildings, of a college or other school.

camp′y *adj.,* **-i·er, -i·est.** characterized by camp: *a campy spoof of romantic operetta.*

cam′shaft′ *n.* an engine shaft fitted with cams.

can¹ (kan; *unstressed* kən), *auxiliary v., pres.* **can,** *past* **could. 1.** to be able to: *She can solve the problem.* **2.** to know how to: *I can play chess.* **3.** to have the power to: *a dictator who can impose harsh laws.* **4.** to have the right to: *He can say whatever he wishes.* **5.** may; have permission to: *Can I speak to you?* **6.** to be likely to: *A coin can land on either side.*

can² (kan), *n., v.,* **canned, can·ning.** —*n.* **1.** a sealed metal container for food, beverages, etc. **2.** a receptacle for garbage, ashes, etc. —*v.t.* **3.** to preserve by sealing in a can, jar, etc. **4.** *Slang.* to dismiss; fire. —**can′ner,** *n.*

Can. 1. Canada. **2.** Canadian.

Can·a·da (kan′ə də), *n.* a nation in N North America. —**Ca·na·di·an** (kə nā′dē ən), *adj., n.*

ca·nal (kə nal′), *n.* **1.** an artificial waterway for navigation, irrigation, etc. **2.** a tubular passage for food, air, etc., in an animal or plant.

can·a·pé (kan′ə pē, -pā′), *n., pl.* **-pés.** a cracker or piece of bread topped with savory food.

ca·nar·y (kə nâr′ē), *n., pl.* **-ies. 1.** a yellow finch of the Canary Islands, bred as a cage bird. **2.** a light yellow.

can·cel (kan′səl), *v.t.,* **-celed, -cel·ing** or (*esp. Brit.*) **-celled, -cel·ling. 1.** to make void. **2.** to call off. **3.** to mark (a postage stamp, ticket, etc.) so as to render invalid for reuse. **4.** to compensate for; neutralize. **5. a.** to eliminate (a common factor) from a denominator and numerator. **b.** to eliminate (equivalent terms) on opposite sides of an equation. **6.** to cross out with lines. —**can′cel·la′tion,** *n.*

can·cer (kan′sər), *n.* **1.** a malignant growth or tumor that tends to spread. **2.** any evil that spreads destructively. **3.** (*cap.*) the fourth sign of the zodiac. —**can′cer·ous,** *adj.*

can·de·la·brum (-brəm), *n., pl.* **-bra** (-brə), **-brums.** a branched holder for more than one candle.

can·did (kan′did), *adj.* **1.** frank; outspoken. **2.** informal; unposed: *a candid photo.* —**can′did·ly,** *adv.* —**can′did·ness,** *n.*

can·di·da (kan′di də) *n.* a disease-causing fungus.

can·di·date (kan′di dāt′, -dit), *n.* a person who seeks or is nominated for an office, honor, etc. [< L *candidātus* clothed in white (in reference to the white togas worn by those seeking office)] —**can′di·da·cy** (-də sē), *n., pl.* **-cies.**

can·dle (kan′dl), *n., v.,* **-dled, -dling.** —*n.* **1.** a long, slender piece of tallow or wax with an embedded wick, burned to give light. —*v.t.* **2.** to examine (eggs) for freshness by holding up to a light. —**can′dler,** *n.* —**can′dle·stick′,** *n.*

can·dor (kan′dər), *n.* **1.** the state or quality of being candid. **2.** freedom from bias. Also, *esp. Brit.,* **can′dour.**

can·dy (kan′dē), *n., pl.* **-dies,** *v.,* **-died, -dy·ing.** —*n.* **1.** a confection made of sugar or syrup, combined with flavoring, fruit, etc. —*v.t.* **2.** to cook in sugar or syrup, as yams. **3.** to preserve by cooking in heavy syrup, as fruit. **4.** to reduce (sugar, syrup, etc.) to a crystalline form. [ME *sugre candi* candied sugar < MF < Ar *qandī* ≪ Skt *khaṇḍakaḥ* sugar candy] —**can′died,** *adj.*

cane (kān), *n., v.,* **caned, can•ing.** —*n.* **1.** a short stick used as a support in walking. **2.** a long, jointed woody stem, as that of bamboo. **3.** a plant having such a stem. **4.** split rattan. **5.** a rod used for flogging. —*v.t.* **6.** to flog with a cane. **7.** to make with cane: *to cane chairs.* —**can′er,** *n.*

ca•nine (kā′nīn), *adj.* **1.** of or like a dog. **2.** of the four pointed teeth next to the incisors. —*n.* **3.** a dog or member of the dog family. **4.** one of the four pointed teeth of the jaws.

ca′nine tooth′ *n.* one of the four pointed teeth next to the incisors.

can•is•ter (kan′ə stər), *n.* a small box or can for holding tea, sugar, etc.

can•ker (kang′kər), *n.* **1.** a gangrenous or ulcerous sore, esp. in the mouth. Also called **can′ker sore′.** —**can′ker•ous,** *adj.*

can•na•bis (kan′ə bis), *n.* **1.** the hemp plant. **2.** the flowering tops of the plant.

canned *adj.* **1.** preserved in a can or jar. **2.** recorded or prerecorded: *canned laughter.*

can′ner•y *n., pl.* **-ies.** a factory where foodstuffs are canned.

can•ni•bal (kan′ə bəl), *n.* **1.** a person who eats human flesh. **2.** an animal that eats its own kind. —*adj.* **3.** of or like cannibals. —**can′ni•bal•ism,** *n.* —**can′ni•bal•is′tic,** *adj.*

can′ni•bal•ize′ *v.t., v.i.,* **-ized, -iz•ing.** to take from one thing, as a part from a machine, for use on or in another.

can•non (kan′ən), *n., pl.* **-nons, -non.** a mounted gun for firing heavy projectiles.

can′non•ade′ (-ə nād′), *n., v.,* **-ad•ed, -ad•ing.** —*n.* **1.** a continued discharge of cannon. —*v.t., v.i.* **2.** to attack with or discharge cannon.

can•not (kan′ot, ka not′, kə-), *v.* **1.** a form of *can not.* —**Idiom. 2. cannot but,** to have no choice but to.

can•ny (kan′ē), *adj.,* **-ni•er, -ni•est. 1.** careful; prudent. **2.** astute; shrewd. —**can′ni•ly,** *adv.* —**can′ni•ness,** *n.*

ca•noe (kə nōō′), *n., v.,* **-noed, -noe•ing.** —*n.* **1.** a slender, open boat propelled by paddles. —*v.i.* **2.** to paddle or go in a canoe. —**ca•noe′ist,** *n.*

can•on¹ (kan′ən), *n.* **1.** a rule or law enacted by a church council. **2.** the body of ecclesiastical law. **3.** a principle or rule. **4.** the books of the Bible officially recognized by any Christian church. **5.** the works of an author accepted as authentic.

can•on² (kan′ən), *n.* a member of the clergy who serves in a cathedral.

can′on•ize′ *v.t.,* **-ized, -iz•ing. 1.** to declare officially as a saint. **2.** to glorify or exalt. —**can′on•i•za′tion,** *n.*

can•o•py (kan′ə pē), *n., pl.* **-pies,** *v.,* **-pied, -py•ing.** —*n.* **1.** a covering suspended above a bed, throne, etc. **2.** an awning stretching from a doorway to a curb. **3.** a rooflike projection or covering. —*v.t.* **4.** to cover with a canopy.

cant¹ (kant), *n.* **1.** insincere statements, esp. pious platitudes. **2.** the private language of the underworld. **3.** the vocabulary of a particular class, profession, etc. —*v.i.* **4.** to talk piously or hypocritically.

cant² (kant), *n.* **1.** a salient angle. **2.** a slanting or tilted position. **3.** an oblique line or surface. —*v.t., v.i.* **4.** to tilt or tip.

can't (kant, känt), contraction of *cannot.*

can•ta•loupe or **-loup** (kan′tl ōp′), *n.* a muskmelon having a rough rind and pale-orange edible flesh.

can•tan•ker•ous (kan tang′kər əs), *adj.* quarrelsome; irritable. —**can•tan′ker•ous•ly,** *adv.* —**can•tan′ker•ous•ness,** *n.*

can•ta•ta (kən tä′tə), *n. pl.* **-tas.** a choral composition resembling a short oratorio.

can•teen (kan tēn′), *n.* **1.** a small container for carrying water. **2.** a cafeteria or snack bar, as at a military base. **3.** a place where free entertainment is

provided for military personnel. [< F *cantine* < It *cantina* cellar]

can•ter (kan′tər), *n.* **1.** an easy gallop. —*v.i., v.t.* **2.** to move or cause to move at a canter.

can•ti•cle (kan′ti kəl), *n.* a hymn or chant, chiefly from the Bible, used in church services.

can•ti•le•ver (kan′tl ē′vər, -ev′ər), *n.* **1.** any rigid structural member projecting from a vertical support, used as a structural element of a bridge, dam, etc. —*v.t.* **2.** to construct with a cantilever.

can•to (kan′tō), *n., pl.* **-tos.** one of the main divisions of a long poem.

can•ton (kan′tn, kan ton′), *n.* a small territorial district, esp. one of the states of Switzerland.

can•tor (kan′tər), *n.* a synagogue official who sings certain prayers designed as solos. —**can•to′ri•al** (-tôr′ē əl), *adj.*

can•vas (kan′vəs), *n.* **1.** a closely woven, heavy cloth used for tents, sails, etc. **2.** a painting on canvas. **3.** tents or sails collectively.

can′vas•back′ *n., pl.* **-backs, -back.** a North American duck with a whitish back.

can•vass (kan′vəs), *v.t., v.i.* **1.** to solicit votes, opinions, sales, etc. from (a district or group of people). —*n.* **2.** a soliciting of votes, opinions, etc. —**can′vass•er,** *n.*

can•yon (kan′yən), *n.* a deep valley with steep sides. [< MexSp < Sp *cañón* a long tube, a hollow]

cap (kap), *n., v.,* **capped, cap•ping.** —*n.* **1.** a close-fitting covering for the head, sometimes having a visor. **2.** anything resembling a cap in shape or use: *a bottle cap.* **3.** a maximum limit. **4.** a noise-making device for toy pistols. —*v.t.* **5.** to put a cap on. **6.** to outdo.

CAP computer-aided publishing.

cap. 1. capital. **2.** capital letter.

ca•pa•ble (kā′pə bəl), *adj.* **1.** having ability; competent. **2. capable of, a.** having the ability for. **b.** predisposed to: *capable of murder.* —**ca′pa•bil′i•ty,** *n., pl.* **-ties.** —**ca′pa•bly,** *adv.*

ca•pa•cious (kə pā′shəs), *adj.* spacious or roomy. —**ca•pa′cious•ly,** *adv.* —**ca•pa′cious•ness,** *n.*

ca•pac•i•tor (kə pas′i tər), *n.* a device for accumulating and holding a charge of electricity.

ca•pac′i•ty *n., pl.* **-ties. 1.** the ability to receive or contain. **2.** cubic contents or volume. **3.** mental ability. **4.** the ability to do something. **5.** a position; function: *to serve in an advisory capacity.*

cape¹ (kāp), *n.* a sleeveless garment fastened at the neck and falling loosely from the shoulders. —**caped,** *adj.*

cape² (kāp), *n.* a piece of land jutting into a large body of water.

ca•per¹ (kā′pər), *v.i.* **1.** to leap about in a sprightly manner. —*n.* **2.** a playful leap. **3.** a prank.

ca•per² (kā′pər), *n.* a shrub of Mediterranean regions whose flower bud is pickled and used for seasoning.

Cape′ Verde′ (vûrd), *n.* a republic consisting of a group of islands in the Atlantic, W of Senegal in W Africa.

cap•il•lar•y (kap′ə ler′ē), *n., pl.* **-ies,** *adj.* —*n.* **1.** one of the minute blood vessels that connect the arteries and veins. **2.** a tube with a small bore. —*adj.* **3.** pertaining to capillaries or capillarity. **4.** like hair.

cap•i•tal¹ (kap′i tl), *n.* **1.** a city that is the seat of government of a country, state, etc. **2.** CAPITAL LETTER. **3.** the wealth, as in money or property, owned or used in business. —*adj.* **4.** pertaining to financial capital. **5.** principal; primary. **6.** of or being the seat of government. **7.** excellent or first-rate. **8.** punishable by death. [< AF < L *capitālis* of the head]

cap•i•tal² (kap′i tl), *n.* the distinctively treated upper end of an architectural column. [≪ LL *capitellum* little head]

cap′ital gain′ *n.* profit from the sale of assets, as bonds or real estate.

cap′ital goods′ *n.pl.* machines and tools used in the production of other goods.

cap•i•tal•ism *n.* an economic system in which the means of production and distribution are privately owned. —**cap′i•tal•ist,** *n.* —**cap′i•tal•is′tic,** *adj.*

cap′i•tal•ize′ *v.t.*, **-ized**, **-iz•ing. 1.** to write in capital letters or with an initial capital. **2.** to convert into or use as capital. **3.** to supply with capital. **4.** **capitalize on**, to take advantage of. —**cap′i•tal•i•za′tion**, *n.*

cap′ital let′ter *n.* a letter of the alphabet that differs from its corresponding lowercase letter in form and height.

cap′i•tal•ly *adv.* excellently.

cap′ital pun′ishment *n.* punishment by death for a crime.

Cap•i•tol (kap′i tl), *n.* **1.** the building in Washington, D.C., in which the U.S. Congress meets. **2.** (*often l.c.*) a building occupied by a state legislature.

ca•pit•u•late (kə pich′ə lāt′), *v.i.*, **-lat•ed**, **-lat•ing. 1.** to surrender on stipulated terms. **2.** to give up resistance. —**ca•pit′u•la′tion**, *n.*

cap•let (kap′lit), *n.* an oval-shaped pharmaceutical tablet that is coated to facilitate swallowing.

ca•pon (kā′pon, -pən), *n.* a cockerel castrated to improve its flesh for use as food.

cap•puc•ci•no (kap′ə chē′nō, kä′pə-), *n.*, *pl.* **-nos.** espresso coffee mixed with foaming steamed milk and sprinkled with cinnamon.

ca•price (kə prēs′), *n.* **1.** a sudden, unpredictable change. **2.** a tendency to change one's mind without motive. —**ca•pri′cious** (-prish′əs), *adj.* —**ca•pri′cious•ly**, *adv.* —**ca•pri′cious•ness**, *n.*

cap•size (kap′sīz, kap sīz′), *v.i.*, *v.t.*, **-sized**, **-siz•ing.** to turn bottom up; overturn.

cap•stan (kap′stən, -stan), *n.* a windlass rotated in a horizontal plane, for winding in ropes, cables, etc.

cap•sule (kap′səl, -sōōl, -syōōl), *n.*, *v.*, **-suled**, **-sul•ing**, *adj.* —*n.* **1.** a gelatinous case enclosing a dose of medicine. **2.** a dry fruit composed of two or more carpels. **3.** a pressurized cabin in a spacecraft. **4.** a concise report. —*v.t.* **5.** to enclose in a capsule. **6.** to summarize. —*adj.* **7.** short and concise. —**cap′su•lar**, *adj.*

capt. captain.

cap•tain (kap′tən, -tin), *n.* **1.** a person in authority over others. **2.** an army officer ranking above a first lieutenant. **3.** a naval officer ranking above a commander. **4.** the commander of a merchant vessel. **5.** the pilot of an airplane. **6.** the field leader of a sports team. —*v.t.* **7.** to command as a captain. —**cap′tain•cy,** *n.*

cap•tion (kap′shən), *n.* **1.** an explanation for a picture or illustration. **2.** a motion-picture or television subtitle. —*v.t.* **3.** to supply a caption for.

cap•tious (kap′shəs), *adj.* **1.** faultfinding. **2.** designed to ensnare or perplex. —**cap′tious•ly**, *adv.* —**cap′tious•ness**, *n.*

cap•ti•vate (kap′tə vāt′), *v.t.*, **-vat•ed**, **-vat•ing.** to attract intensely; enchant. —**cap′ti•va′tion**, *n.* —**cap′ti•va′tor**, *n.*

cap′tive (-tiv), *n.* **1.** a prisoner. —*adj.* **2.** unable to avoid listening to something: *a captive audience.* —**cap•tiv′i•ty**, *n.*, *pl.* **-ties.**

cap′ture (-chər), *v.*, **-tured**, **-tur•ing.** —*v.t.* **1.** to take by force or stratagem; seize. **2.** to record in lasting form: *a movie that captures Berlin in the 1930s.* **3. a.** to enter (data) into a computer for processing or storage. **b.** to record (data) in preparation for such entry. —*n.* **4.** the act of capturing. —**cap′tor**, *n.*

car (kär), *n.* **1.** an automobile. **2.** a vehicle running on rails, as a streetcar. **3.** the part of a conveyance, as an elevator, that carries the passengers or freight. **4.** any wheeled vehicle. [< AF < L *carra* < Celtic]

ca•rafe (kə raf′, -räf′), *n.* a bottle for holding wine, coffee, or other beverages.

car•a•mel (kar′ə məl, -mel′, kär′məl), *n.* **1.** burnt sugar, used for coloring and flavoring food. **2.** a chewy candy made from sugar, butter, milk, etc.

car•at (kar′ət), *n.* **1.** a unit of weight in gemstones, 200 milligrams. **2.** KARAT.

car•a•van (kar′ə van′), *n.* **1.** a group traveling together for safety, as through a desert. **2.** a large van. [< It *carovana* < Pers *kārwān*]

car•a•way (kar′ə wā′), *n.* **1.** a plant of the parsley family. **2.** the aromatic, seedlike fruit of this plant used in cooking.

car•bide (kär′bīd, -bid), *n.* a compound of carbon with another element or group.

car•bine (kär′bēn, -bīn), *n.* a light, gas-operated semiautomatic rifle.

car•bo•hy•drate (kär′bō hī′drāt, -bə-), *n.* any of a class of organic compounds composed of carbon, hydrogen, and oxygen, including starches and sugars.

car•bol′ic ac′id (kär bol′ik), *n.* PHENOL.

car•bon (kär′bən), *n.* **1.** a nonmetallic element found combined with other elements in all organic matter and in a pure state as diamond and graphite. *Symbol:* C; *at. wt.:* 12.011; *at. no.:* 6. **2.** Also called **car′bon cop′y.** a duplicate made with carbon paper. **3.** a sheet of carbon paper. —**car•bon•if′er•ous**, *adj.*

car•bon•ate (*n.* -bə nāt′, -nit; *v.* -nāt′), *n.*, *v.*, **-at•ed**, **-at•ing.** —*n.* **1.** a salt or ester of carbonic acid. —*v.t.* **2.** to charge with carbon dioxide. —**car′bon•a′tion**, *n.*

car′bon diox′ide *n.* an incombustible gas present in the atmosphere and formed during respiration.

car′bon monox′ide *n.* a colorless, odorless, poisonous gas produced when carbon burns with insufficient air.

car′bon pa′per *n.* paper faced with a preparation of carbon or the like, used to make copies of typed or written material.

car•bun•cle (kär′bung kəl), *n.* a skin inflammation of deep interconnected boils. —**car•bun′cu•lar** (-kyə lər), *adj.*

car•bu•re•tor (kär′bə rā′tər, -byə-), *n.* a device for mixing vaporized fuel with air to produce an explosive mixture, as for an internal-combustion engine.

car•cass (kär′kəs), *n.* **1.** the dead body of an animal. **2.** a framework or shell.

car•cin•o•gen (kär sin′ə jən), *n.* any substance that tends to produce a cancer. —**car′cin•o•gen′ic**, *adj.* —**car′ci•no•ge•nic′i•ty** (-jə nis′i tē), *n.*

car•ci•no′ma (-sə nō′mə), *n.*, *pl.* **-mas**, **-ma•ta** (-mə tə) a malignant tumor.

card[1] (kärd), *n.* **1.** a piece of stiff paper, thin pasteboard, or plastic for various uses, as to record information. **2.** one of a set of thin pieces of cardboard used in playing various games. **3. cards**, a game played with such a set. **4.** a folded piece of thin cardboard printed with a message of holiday greeting, congratulations, etc. **5.** POSTCARD. **6.** a piece of fiberglass or other material upon which an array of computer chips is mounted. **7.** an amusing or witty person. —*Idiom.* **8. put** or **lay one's cards on the table,** to be completely straightforward.

card[2] (kärd), *n.* **1.** a machine for combing fibers of cotton, flax, wool, etc. —*v.t.* **2.** to dress (wool or the like) with a card. —**card′er**, *n.*

card′board′ *n.* a thin, stiff pasteboard, used for signs, boxes, etc.

car•di•ac (kär′dē ak′), *adj.* of or near the heart.

car′diac arrest′ *n.* the abrupt cessation of heartbeat.

car•di•gan (kär′di gən), *n.* a sweater or jacket that opens down the front. [after the Earl of *Cardigan* (1797–1868), British hero in Crimean War]

car•di•nal (kär′dn l), *adj.* **1.** of prime importance. **2.** deep red. —*n.* **3.** a high ecclesiastic appointed by the pope and standing next in rank. **4.** a bright red North American songbird. **5.** a deep, rich red color. —**car′di•nal•ly**, *adv.*

car′dinal num′ber *n.* any of the numbers that express amount, as *one, two, three.*

cardio- a combining form meaning heart (*cardiogram*).

car•di•o•graph (kär′dē ə graf′, -gräf′), *n.* ELECTROCARDIOGRAPH.

car′di•ol′o•gy (-ol′ə jē), *n.* the study of the heart and its functions. —**car′di•o•log′i•cal** (-ə loj′i kəl), *adj.* —**car′di•ol′o•gist**, *n.*

car′di•o•pul′mo•nar′y *adj.* of the heart and lungs.

car′di•o•vas′cu•lar *adj.* of the heart and blood vessels.

general

card′sharp′ *n.* a person who cheats at card games. Also called **card′ shark′.**

care (kâr), *n., v.,* **cared, car•ing.** —*n.* **1.** a troubled state of mind. **2.** a cause of concern. **3.** serious attention: *devoted great care to his work.* **4.** protection; charge. —*v.i.* **5.** to be concerned. **6.** to make provision: *Will you care for the children?* —*v.t.* **7.** to feel concern about. **8.** to desire; like: *Would you care to dance?*

ca•reen (kə rēn′), *v.i., v.t.* to lean or cause to lean over to one side.

ca•reer (kə rēr′), *n.* **1.** an occupation followed as one's lifework. **2.** a person's general course of action through life. **3.** a swift course. —*v.i.* **4.** to go at full speed.

care′free′ *adj.* without worry.

care′ful *adj.* **1.** cautious in one's action. **2.** done with accuracy or caution. —**care′ful•ly,** *adv.* —**care′ful•ness,** *n.*

care′giv′er *n.* a person who cares for a child or for someone who is sick or disabled.

care′less (-lis), *adj.* **1.** not paying enough attention to what one does. **2.** not exact or accurate. **3.** heedless; unconsidered. **4.** unconcerned. —**care′less•ly,** *adv.* —**care′less•ness,** *n.*

ca•ress (kə res′), *n.* **1.** a light stroking gesture expressing affection. —*v.t.* **2.** to stroke lightly and affectionately.

car•et (kar′it), *n.* a mark (^) made in written or printed matter to indicate where something is to be inserted. [< L: (there) is lacking]

care′tak′er *n.* **1.** a person in charge of maintaining a building, estate, etc. **2.** a person or group that temporarily performs the duties of an office. **3.** a person who takes care of another.

car′fare′ *n.* the cost of a ride on a subway, bus, etc.

car•go (kär′gō), *n., pl.* **-goes, -gos.** the load of goods carried by a ship, plane, etc.; freight.

car•i•bou (kar′ə bōō′), *n., pl.* **-bous, -bou.** the reindeer of North America. [< CanF < Algonquian *γalipu* shoveler, referring to its habit of scraping aside snow to find food]

car•i•ca•ture (kar′i kə chər), *n., v.,* **-tured, -tur•ing.** —*n.* **1.** a ludicrously exaggerated depiction of a person or thing. **2.** an imitation so inferior as to be ludicrous. —*v.t.* **3.** to make a caricature of. —**car′i•ca•tur•ist,** *n.*

car•ies (kâr′ēz), *n., pl.* **-ies.** decay, as of bone or teeth.

car•il•lon (kar′ə lon′, -lən), *n.* a set of stationary bells in a tower, sounded by manual or pedal action or by machinery.

car•jack•ing (kär′jak′ing), *n.* the forcible stealing of a vehicle from a motorist. —**car′jack′er,** *n.*

car•mine (kär′min, -mīn), *n.* a crimson or purplish red color.

car•nage (kär′nij), *n.* the slaughter of many people, as in battle.

car′nal (-nl), *adj.* **1.** of the flesh or body; sensual. **2.** not spiritual; worldly. —**car•nal′i•ty,** *n.* —**car′nal•ly,** *adv.*

car•na•tion (kär nā′shən), *n.* a cultivated plant with fragrant flowers in a variety of colors.

car•ni•val (kär′nə vəl), *n.* **1.** a traveling amusement show with sideshows and rides. **2.** a festival. **3.** the period of merrymaking immediately before Lent. [< It *carnevale,* OIt *carnelevare* taking meat away]

car•ni•vore (kär′nə vôr′), *n.* **1.** an animal that eats flesh. **2.** a plant that eats insects. —**car•niv′o•rous,** *adj.*

car•ob (kar′əb), *n.* **1.** a tree bearing long pods. **2.** pulp from the pods, used as a chocolate substitute.

car•ol (kar′əl), *n., v.,* **-oled, -ol•ing** or (*esp. Brit.*) **-olled, -ol•ling.** —*n.* **1.** a song of joy or praise. **2.** a Christmas song. —*v.i., v.t.* **3.** to sing joyously. —**car′ol•er, car′ol•ler,** *n.*

car•om (kar′əm), *n.* **1.** a shot in billiards in which the cue ball hits two balls in succession. **2.** any hit and rebound. —*v.i.* **3.** to make a carom. **4.** to hit and rebound.

ca•rot•id (kə rot′id), *n.* **1.** either of two large arteries, one on each side of the neck, that carry blood to the head. —*adj.* **2.** pertaining to a carotid artery.

ca•rouse (kə rouz′), *v.,* **-roused, -rous•ing,** *n.* —*v.i.* **1.** to engage in a drunken revel. —*n.* **2.** a noisy or drunken gathering; revel. —**ca•rous′er,** *n.*

car•ou•sel (kar′ə sel′), *n.* **1.** MERRY-GO-ROUND (def. 1). **2.** a revolving conveyor on which items are placed: *a baggage carousel.*

carp¹ (kärp), *v.i.* to find fault unreasonably; cavil. —**carp′er,** *n.*

carp² (kärp), *n., pl.* **carps, carp.** a large freshwater food fish.

carpal tunnel syndrome chronic wrist pain associated esp. with repetitive movements, as at a keyboard.

car•pel (kär′pəl), *n.* a simple pistil or a single member of a compound pistil.

car•pen•ter (kär′pən tər), *n.* a person who builds or repairs wooden structures. —**car′pen•try,** *n.*

car•pet (kär′pit), *n.* **1.** a heavy woven fabric for covering floors. **2.** any covering resembling a carpet. —*v.t.* **3.** to cover with a carpet. —*Idiom.* **4.** **on the carpet,** reprimanded. —**car′pet•ing,** *n.*

car′pool′ *n.* an arrangement among automobile owners by which each in turn drives the others to and from a designated place.

car′port′ *n.* a roof projecting from the side of a building for sheltering an automobile.

car•pus (kär′pəs), *n., pl.* **-pi** (-pī). **1.** the wrist. **2.** the wrist bones collectively.

car•rel or **-rell** (kar′əl), *n.* a cubicle or desk partitioned off for private study in a library.

car•riage (kar′ij), *n.* **1.** a horse-drawn vehicle for conveying persons. **2.** BABY CARRIAGE. **3.** a movable part, as of a machine, designed for carrying something: *a typewriter carriage.* **4.** bearing of the head and body.

car•ri•on (kar′ē ən), *n.* dead and putrefying flesh.

car•rot (kar′ət), *n.* **1.** a plant widely cultivated for its edible orange root. **2.** this root. **3.** something offered as an incentive.

car′rou•sel′ (kar′ə sel′) *n.* CAROUSEL.

car•ry (kar′ē), *v.,* **-ried, -ry•ing,** *n., pl.* **-ries.** —*v.t.* **1.** to move while supporting or holding; transport. **2.** to wear, hold, or have around one. **3.** to serve as a medium for the transmission of. **4.** to transfer to a subsequent time, page, or column. **5.** to bear the weight or burden of. **6.** to hold (the body or head) in a certain manner. **7.** to bear (oneself) in a specified manner. **8.** to secure the passage of (a motion or bill). **9.** to gain a majority of votes in (a district). **10.** to have as a consequence: *Violation carries a stiff penalty.* **11.** to keep in stock. —*v.i.* **12.** to act as a bearer or conductor. **13.** to be transmitted or sustained. **14. carry away,** to stir strong emotions in. **15. ~ on, a.** to manage. **b.** to persevere. **c.** to be disruptive. **16. ~ out, a.** to execute. **b.** to accomplish; complete. **17. ~ over,** to postpone. —*n.* **18.** range, as of a gun. **19.** a portage. —**car′ri•er,** *n.*

car′ry-out′ *adj., n.* takeout.

car′sick′ *adj.* ill with motion sickness during automobile travel.

cart (kärt), *n.* **1.** a two-wheeled vehicle drawn by a horse, ox, etc. **2.** any small vehicle pulled by hand. —*v.t.* **3.** to haul, as in a cart or truck. —**cart′age,** *n.* —**cart′er,** *n.*

carte blanche (kärt′ blänch′, blänsh′), *n.* full discretionary power. [< F: lit., blank document]

car•tel (kär tel′), *n.* an international syndicate formed to control prices and output in some field of business.

car•ti•lage (kär′tl ij), *n.* a firm, elastic type of connective tissue. —**car′ti•lag′i•nous** (-tl aj′ə nəs), *adj.*

car•tog•ra•phy (kär tog′rə fē), *n.* the production of maps. —**car•tog′ra•pher,** *n.* —**car′to•graph′ic** (-tə graf′ik), *adj.*

car•ton (kär′tn), *n.* a large cardboard or plastic box.

car•toon (kär tōōn′), *n.* **1.** a drawing caricaturing some action or subject. **2.** COMIC STRIP. **3.** a motion picture consisting of a sequence of drawings that seem to move. —*v.t., v.i.* **4.** to draw a cartoon (of). —**car•toon′ist,** *n.*

car•tridge (kär′trij), *n.* **1.** a cylindrical case for holding a charge of powder and usu. a bullet for a firearm. **2.** a compact container, as for magnetic tape or a roll of film.

cart′wheel′ *n.* **1.** a handspring done to the side. —*v.i.* **2.** to roll forward end over end.

carve (kärv), *v.,* **carved, carv•ing.** —*v.t.* **1.** to cut so as to form something. **2.** to form by or as if by cutting: *to carve a statue out of stone.* **3.** to cut into slices, as meat. **4.** to decorate with designs cut on the surface. —*v.i.* **5.** to form designs by carving. **6.** to carve meat. —**carv′er,** *n.* —**carv′ing,** *n.*

cas•cade (kas kād′), *n., v.,* **-cad•ed, -cad•ing.** —*n.* **1.** a waterfall descending over a steep, rocky surface. **2.** anything flowing or falling in abundance; torrent. —*v.i., v.t.* **3.** to fall or cause to fall in a cascade.

case[1] (kās), *n.* **1.** a specific instance or example. **2.** the actual state of things: *That is not the case.* **3.** a patient or client. **4.** a specific matter requiring discussion, decision, or investigation. **5.** a statement of facts in support of an argument. **6.** a suit or action at law. **7.** a category in the inflection of nouns or pronouns, noting their syntactic relation to other words. —*Idiom.* **8. in any case,** anyhow. **9. in case of,** in the event of.

case[2] (kās), *n., v.,* **cased, cas•ing.** —*n.* **1.** a container for enclosing something. **2.** an outer covering. **3.** a box with its contents: *a case of soda.* **4.** a surrounding frame, as of a door. —*v.t.* **5.** to put in a case. **6.** *Slang.* to examine (a house, bank, etc.), esp. in planning a crime.

ca•sein (kā′sēn, -sē in), *n.* a protein precipitated from milk, forming the basis of cheese and certain plastics.

case′ment *n.* a window sash opening on side hinges.

cash (kash), *n.* **1.** money in the form of coins or banknotes. **2.** money or an equivalent paid at the time of purchase. —*v.t.* **3.** to give or obtain cash for (a check, money order, etc.). **4. cash in,** to turn in and get cash for.

cash•ew (kash′ōō, kə shōō′), *n.* the small, kidney-shaped, edible nut of a tropical American tree.

cash•ier[1] (ka shēr′), *n.* **1.** an employee, as in a market, who collects payment for purchases. **2.** an executive who superintends the financial transactions of a company.

cash•ier[2] (ka shēr′), *v.t.* to dismiss from a position of trust, esp. with disgrace.

cash•mere (kazh′mēr, kash′-), *n.* **1.** a fine, downy wool from goats of Kashmir and Tibet. **2.** a fabric made from this wool.

cash′ reg′ister *n.* a business machine that records and totals receipts and has a money drawer.

cas′ing *n.* **1.** a case or covering. **2.** a framework, as around a door. **3.** the outer covering of an automobile tire. **4.** the skin of a sausage or salami.

ca•si•no (kə sē′nō), *n., pl.* **-nos. 1.** a place for gambling. **2.** a card game for two, three, or four players.

cask (kask, käsk), *n.* **1.** a container resembling a barrel but larger and stronger. **2.** the quantity such a container holds.

cas•ket (kas′kit, kä′skit), *n.* **1.** a coffin. **2.** a small chest or box, as for jewels.

cas•sa•va (kə sä′və), *n., pl.* **-vas. 1.** a tropical American plant with tuberous roots. **2.** a starch from the roots, the source of tapioca.

cas•se•role (kas′ə rōl′), *n.* **1.** a baking and serving dish of glass, pottery, etc. **2.** food baked in such a dish.

cas•sette (kə set′, ka-), *n.* a case in which audiotape or videotape runs between two reels.

cas•sock (kas′ək), *n.* a long, close-fitting garment worn by clerics.

cast (kast, käst), *v.,* **cast, cast•ing,** *n.* —*v.t.* **1.** to throw or hurl. **2.** to direct (the eye, a glance, etc.). **3.** to send forth: *to cast light.* **4.** to shed or drop: *The snake cast its skin.* **5.** to deposit (a ballot or

vote). **6.** to select (performers) for (a play or role). **7.** to form (an object) by pouring into a mold. —*v.i.* **8.** to throw. **9. cast about,** to seek. **10. ~ away** or **aside,** to reject; discard. **11. ~ off, a.** to discard. **b.** to let loose, as a ship from a mooring. —*n.* **12.** the act of throwing. **13.** a throw of dice. **14.** the performers in a play, motion picture, etc. **15.** something made in a mold. **16.** a rigid surgical dressing, as for a broken limb. **17.** sort; kind. **18.** a hue; shade. —**cast′ing,** *n.*

cas•ta•net (kas′tə net′), *n.* a handheld percussion instrument consisting of two wooden shells clicked together, esp. to accompany dancing.

cast′a•way′ *n.* **1.** a shipwrecked person. **2.** anything thrown away. —*adj.* **3.** shipwrecked. **4.** thrown away.

caste (kast, käst), *n.* **1.** any of the hereditary social divisions of traditional Hindu society. **2.** any rigid system of social distinctions. **3.** social position: *to lose caste.*

cast′er *n.* **1.** a small wheel on a swivel, set under a piece of furniture to facilitate moving it. **2.** a bottle or cruet for holding a condiment.

cas•ti•gate (kas′ti gāt′), *v.t.* **-gat•ed, -gat•ing.** to criticize severely. —**cas′ti•ga′tion,** *n.* —**cas′ti•ga′-tor,** *n.*

cast′ i′ron *n.* a hard, brittle alloy of carbon and other elements. —**cast′-i′ron,** *adj.*

cas•tle (kas′əl, kä′səl), *n.* **1.** a fortified residence, as of a noble in feudal times. **2.** a strongly fortified stronghold. **3.** *Chess.* the rook. [< L *castellum* fortress]

cas′tor oil′ *n.* a colorless or pale oil from the bean of a tropical plant, used as a lubricant and cathartic.

cas•trate (kas′trāt), *v.t.* **-trat•ed, -trat•ing.** to remove the testes of; emasculate. —**cas•tra′tion,** *n.*

cas•u•al (kazh′ōō əl), *adj.* **1.** happening by chance. **2.** offhand or cursory. **3.** indifferent; apathetic. **4.** appropriate for informal occasions. **5.** irregular; occasional. —**cas′u•al•ly,** *adv.* —**cas′u•al•ness,** *n.*

cas•u•al•ty (kazh′ōō əl tē), *n., pl.* **-ties. 1.** a member of the armed forces lost through death, wounds, etc. **2.** one who is injured or killed in an accident. **3.** a serious accident.

cas•u•ist•ry (kazh′ōō ə strē), *n., pl.* **-ries.** adroit, specious argument. —**cas′u•ist,** *n.* —**cas′u•is′tic,** *adj.*

cat (kat), *n.* **1.** a small domesticated carnivore popular as a pet. **2.** any related carnivore, as the lion, tiger, or leopard. **3.** a woman given to malicious gossip. —*Idiom.* **4. let the cat out of the bag,** to divulge a secret.

cat•a•clysm (kat′ə kliz′əm), *n.* any violent upheaval. —**cat′a•clys′mic,** *adj.*

cat•a•comb (kat′ə kōm′), *n.* an underground cemetery, esp. one consisting of tunnels with recesses for tombs.

cat•a•log (kat′l ôg′, -og′), *n.* **1.** a systematic list, as of items for sale or courses at a university, often including descriptive material. **2.** a book or pamphlet that contains such a list. **3.** a list of the contents of a library. —*v.t., v.i.* **4.** to make a catalog (of). —**cat′a•log′er,** *n.*

cat•a•logue (kat′l ôg′, -og′), *n., v.t., v.i.,* **-logued, -logu•ing.** CATALOG. —**cat′a•logu′er,** *n.*

ca•tal•pa (kə tal′pə), *n., pl.* **-pas.** a tree with white flower clusters and long, beanlike seed pods.

cat•a•lyst (kat′l ist), *n.* **1.** a substance that causes or speeds a chemical reaction without itself being affected. **2.** anything that precipitates an event. —**cat′a•lyt′ic,** *adj., n.*

cat•a•ma•ran (kat′ə mə ran′), *n.* **1.** a sailboat whose frame is set on two parallel hulls. **2.** a raft formed of logs lashed together.

cat′a•mount′ *n.* cougar.

cat•a•pult (kat′ə pult′, -pŏolt′), *n.* **1.** an ancient military engine for hurling stones, arrows, etc. **2.** a device for launching an airplane from the deck of a ship. —*v.t., v.i.* **3.** to hurl or be hurled from or as if from a catapult.

cat•a•ract (kat′ə rakt′), *n.* **1.** a large waterfall. **2.**

a. an abnormality of the eye characterized by opacity of the lens. **b.** the opaque area.

ca•tarrh (kə tär′), *n.* inflammation of a mucous membrane, esp. of the respiratory tract.

ca•tas•tro•phe (kə tas′trə fē), *n., pl.* **-phes. 1.** a sudden and widespread disaster. **2.** a fiasco. —**cat•a•stroph•ic** (kat′ə strof′ik), *adj.*

cat′bird′ *n.* a North American songbird with catlike vocalizations.

cat′call′ *n.* **1.** a shrill sound or raucous shout expressing disapproval. —*v.t., v.i.* **2.** to sound catcalls (at).

catch (kach), *v.,* **caught, catch•ing,** *n.* —*v.t.* **1.** to seize or capture. **2.** to trap or ensnare. **3.** to take and hold: *to catch a ball.* **4.** to surprise in some action. **5.** to receive or contract: *to catch a cold.* **6.** to be in time to get aboard (a train, boat, etc.). **7.** to lay hold of; clasp: *He caught her in an embrace.* **8.** to entangle. **9.** to attract: *to catch our attention.* **10.** to see or hear. **11.** to comprehend. —*v.i.* **12.** to become gripped or entangled. **13.** to take hold. **14.** **catch at,** to grasp at eagerly. **15.** ~ **on, a.** to become popular. **b.** to understand. **16.** ~ **up, a.** to overtake something moving. **b.** to do enough so that one is no longer behind. —*n.* **17.** the act of catching. **18.** anything that catches, as a door latch. **19.** any tricky or concealed drawback. **20.** a momentary break in the voice. **21.** something caught, as a quantity of fish. **22.** one that is worth getting. **23.** a fragment: *catches of a song.* —**catch′er,** *n.*

Catch-22 (kach′twen′tē too′) *n.* frustrating situation involving contradictions.

catch′ing *adj.* **1.** contagious. **2.** attractive.

catch′up *n.* ketchup.

catch′word′ *n.* a word or phrase repeated so often that it becomes a slogan.

catch′y *adj.,* **-i•er, -i•est. 1.** pleasing and easily remembered. **2.** likely to attract attention. **3.** tricky; deceptive.

cat•e•chism (kat′i kiz′əm), *n.* a summary of the principles of a Christian religion, in the form of questions and answers. —**cat′e•chist,** *n.* —**cat′e•chize′** (-kīz′), *v.t.,* **-chized, -chiz•ing.**

cat•e•gor•i•cal (kat′i gôr′i kəl, -gor′-), *adj.* **1.** unconditional; absolute. **2.** belonging to a category. —**cat′e•gor′i•cal•ly,** *adv.*

cat′e•go′ry (-gôr′ē), *n., pl.* **-ries.** any division in a system of classification. —**cat′e•go•rize′,** *v.t.,* **-rized, -riz•ing.**

ca•ter (kā′tər), *v.i.* **1.** to provide food and service. **2.** to provide what is desired: *to cater to popular demand.* —*v.t.* **3.** to provide food and service for: *to cater a reception.* —**ca′ter•er,** *n.*

cat′er-cor′nered (kat′i-, kat′ē-, kat′ər-), *adj.* **1.** diagonal. —*adv.* **2.** diagonally.

cat•er•pil•lar (kat′ə pil′ər, kat′ər-), *n.* the larva of a butterfly or moth, resembling a worm.

cat•er•waul (kat′ər wôl′), *v.i.* **1.** to utter long wailing cries, as cats in rutting time. —*n.* **2.** such a cry.

cat′fish′ *n., pl.* **-fish, -fish•es.** a scaleless fish with barbels around the mouth that resemble a cat's whiskers.

cat′gut′ *n.* a strong cord made from dried intestines, as of sheep.

ca•thar•sis (kə thär′sis), *n., pl.* **-ses** (-sēz). **1.** the purging of the emotions, esp. through a work of art. **2.** purgation of the bowels. —**ca•thar′tic,** *adj.*

ca•thar′tic *adj.* **1.** effecting a catharsis. **2.** evacuating the bowels. —*n.* **3.** medicine doing this.

ca•the•dral (kə thē′drəl), *n.* the principal church of a diocese, containing the bishop's throne.

cath•e•ter (kath′i tər), *n.* a thin tube inserted into a bodily passage, as to allow fluids to pass into or out of it. —**cath′e•ter•ize′,** *v.t.,* **-ized, -iz•ing.**

cath•ode (kath′ōd), *n.* **1.** the negative electrode of an electrolytic cell. **2.** the positive terminal of a battery. **3.** the negative electrode of an electron tube. —**ca•thod′ic** (kə thod′ik), *adj.*

cath′ode ray′ *n.* a narrow beam of electrons emanating from a cathode.

cath′ode-ray′ tube′ *n.* a vacuum tube generating a beam of electrons directed at a screen, used to

display images on a television receiver or computer monitor.

cath•o•lic (kath′ə lik, kath′lik), *adj.* **1.** universal in extent. **2.** broad-minded. —**cath′o•lic′i•ty** (-lis′i tē), *n.*

Cath′o•lic *adj.* **1.** of the Roman Catholic Church. —*n.* **2.** a member of the Roman Catholic Church. —**Ca•thol•i•cism** (kə thol′ə siz′əm), *n.*

cat•kin (kat′kin), *n.* a spike of flowers with scaly bracts and no petals, as on the willow.

cat′nap′ *n., v.,* **-napped, -nap•ping.** —*n.* **1.** a short, light nap. —*v.i.* **2.** to sleep briefly; doze.

cat′nip′ *n.* a plant of the mint family, having aromatic leaves that are a cat attractant.

CAT′ scan′ (kat), *n.* **1.** an examination employing beams of x-rays in two planes at various angles to produce computerized cross-sectional images of the body. **2.** an image so produced. [C(OMPUTERIZED) A(XIAL) T(OMOGRAPHY)] —**CAT′ scan′ner,** *n.*

cat′s′-paw′ *n.* a person used by another as a dupe.

cat•sup (kat′səp, kech′əp, kach′-), *n.* KETCHUP.

cat′tail′ *n.* a tall, reedlike marsh plant with cylindrical clusters of minute brown flowers.

cat•tle (kat′l), *n.* (*used with a pl. v.*) bovine animals, as cows and steers. —**cat′tle•man,** *n., pl.* **-men.**

cat′ty *adj.,* **-ti•er, -ti•est. 1.** slyly malicious. **2.** like a cat. —**cat′ti•ly,** *adv.* —**cat′ti•ness,** *n.*

cat′walk′ *n.* a narrow walkway high above the surrounding area.

Cau•ca•sian (kô kā′zhən), *adj.* **1.** of or designating one of the traditional racial divisions of humankind, marked by minimum skin pigmentation. **2.** of the Caucasus. —*n.* **3.** a person belonging to the Caucasian race. **4.** a native of the Caucasus.

cau•cus (kô′kəs), *n., pl.* **-cus•es,** *v.* —*n.* **1.** a meeting of the members of a political party to nominate candidates, determine policy, etc. —*v.i.* **2.** to hold a caucus.

caul•dron (kôl′drən), *n.* a large kettle.

cau•li•flow•er (kô′lə flou′ər, kol′ē-), *n.* **1.** a cultivated plant whose flower cluster forms a compact, whitish head. **2.** this head, used as a vegetable.

caulk (kôk), *v.t.* **1.** to fill (seams) of (a window, ship's hull, etc.) to make watertight or airtight. —*n.* **2.** a material used to caulk. —**caulk′er,** *n.*

cause (kôz), *n., v.,* **caused, caus•ing.** —*n.* **1.** one that produces a result. **2.** a reason or motive. **3.** a ground of legal action. **4.** an ideal or goal to which a person is dedicated. —*v.t.* **5.** to be the cause of. —**caus′al,** *adj.* —**cau•sa′tion,** *n.* —**caus′a•tive,** *adj.*

cause cé•lè•bre (kôz′ sə leb′; *Fr.* kōz sā leb′ʀ°), *n., pl.* **causes cé•lè•bres** (kôz′ sə leb′; *Fr.* kōz sā-leb′ʀ°). a controversy that attracts great public attention. [< F]

cause′way′ *n.* a raised road, as over wet ground.

caus•tic (kô′stik), *adj.* **1.** capable of burning or corroding living tissue. **2.** severely critical or sarcastic. —*n.* **3.** a caustic substance. —**caus′ti•cal•ly,** *adv.* —**caus•tic′i•ty** (-stis′i tē), *n.*

cau•ter•ize (kô′tə rīz′), *v.t.,* **-ized, -iz•ing.** to burn with a hot iron, a caustic, etc., esp. for curative purposes. —**cau′ter•i•za′tion,** *n.*

cau•tion (kô′shən), *n.* **1.** alertness and prudence in a hazardous situation. **2.** a warning. —*v.t., v.i.* **3.** to warn. —**cau′tion•ar′y,** *adj.* —**cau′tious,** *adj.* —**cau′tious•ly,** *adv.* —**cau′tious•ness,** *n.*

cav•al•cade (kav′əl kād′, kav′əl kād′), *n.* a procession, as of automobiles.

cav•a•lier (kav′ə lēr′), *n.* **1.** an armed horseman; knight. **2.** a courtly gentleman. —*adj.* **3.** haughty; disdainful. **4.** casual; lighthearted. [< MF: horseman ≪ LL caballārius groom] —**cav′a•lier′ly,** *adv.*

cav•al•ry (kav′əl rē), *n., pl.* **-ries. 1.** troops that serve on horseback. **2.** troops that ride in armored motor vehicles. —**cav′al•ry•man,** *n., pl.* **-men.**

cave (kāv), *n., v.,* **caved, cav•ing.** —*n.* **1.** a hollow in the earth, esp. one opening into a hill or mountain. —*v.i., v.t.* **2. cave in, a.** to collapse or cause to collapse. **b.** to yield; surrender.

ca•ve•at (kav′ē ät′, kä′vē-, kā′-), *n.* a warning or caution.

cave′ man′ *n.* **1.** a cave dweller, esp. of the Stone Age. **2.** a rough, brutal man.

cav•ern (kav′ərn), *n.* a large cave that is mostly underground. —**cav′ern•ous,** *adj.*

cav•i•ar (kav′ē är′), *n.* the roe of sturgeon, salmon, etc.

cav•il (kav′əl), *v.,* **-iled, -il•ing** or (*esp. Brit.*) **-illed, -il•ling,** *n.* —*v.i.* **1.** to raise trivial objections. —*n.* **2.** a trivial and annoying objection. —**cav′il•er;** *esp. Brit.,* **cav′il•ler,** *n.*

cav•i•ty (kav′i tē), *n., pl.* **-ties. 1.** any hollow place. **2.** a hollow in a tooth, produced by decay.

ca•vort (kə vôrt′), *v.i.* **1.** to caper about. **2.** to make merry.

caw (kô), *n.* **1.** the harsh call of a crow. —*v.i.* **2.** to utter this cry.

cay•enne (kī en′, kā-), *n.* a hot condiment composed of the ground pods and seeds of a pepper plant.

CB citizens band: a band of radio frequencies used for short-distance private communications.

Cb *Chem. Symbol.* columbium.

cc 1. carbon copy. **2.** cubic centimeter.

CCU coronary-care unit.

CD 1. certificate of deposit. **2.** Civil Defense. **3.** compact disc.

Cd *Chem. Symbol.* cadmium.

CD-ROM (sē′dē′rom′), *n.* a compact disc on which a large amount of digitized read-only data can be stored.

cease (sēs), *v.,* **ceased, ceas•ing,** *n.* —*v.i., v.t.* to stop; discontinue. —*n.* **2.** cessation. —**cease′less,** *adj.* —**cease′less•ly,** *adv.*

cease′-fire′ *n.* a temporary cessation of hostilities.

ce′cum (sē′kəm), *n., pl.* **-ca** (-kə). an anatomical blind pouch, in which ihe large intestine begins. —**ce′cal,** *adj.*

ce•dar (sē′dər), *n.* **1.** any of several coniferous trees. **2.** the wood of these trees.

cede (sēd), *v.t.,* **ced•ed, ced•ing. 1.** to surrender formally. **2.** to grant or transfer, as by a will. —**ced′er,** *n.*

ceil•ing (sē′ling), *n.* **1.** the overhead interior surface of a room. **2.** an upper limit: *a price ceiling.* **3.** the height above ground level of clouds covering more than half the sky.

cel•e•brate (sel′ə brāt′), *v.,* **-brat•ed, -brat•ing.** —*v.t.* **1.** to observe or commemorate with festivities. **2.** to perform with appropriate rites. —*v.i.* **3.** to have a good time. —**cel′e•brant** (-brənt), *n.* —**cel′e•brat′ed,** *adj.* —**cel′e•bra′tion,** *n.* —**cel′e•bra′tor,** *n.*

ce•leb•ri•ty (sə leb′ri tē), *n., pl.* **-ties. 1.** a famous person. **2.** fame.

ce•ler•i•ty (sə ler′i tē), *n.* swiftness; speed.

cel•er•y (sel′ə rē, sel′rē), *n.* a plant with stiff, edible leafstalks.

ce•les•tial (sə les′chəl), *adj.* **1.** of the sky. **2.** heavenly; divine. —**ce•les′tial•ly,** *adv.*

cel•i•ba•cy (sel′ə bə sē), *n.* **1.** abstention from sexual relations. **2.** the state of being unmarried. —**cel′i•bate** (-bit, -bāt′), *n., adj.*

cell (sel), *n.* **1.** a small room, as in a prison. **2.** a small compartment forming part of a whole. **3.** a plant or animal structure containing nuclear material; the basic unit of all organisms. **4.** a small unit of an organization. **5.** a device that converts chemical energy into electricity. **6.** a device for producing electrolysis, consisting of the electrolyte, its container, and the electrodes. —**celled,** *adj.*

cel•lar (sel′ər), *n.* an underground room or rooms, usu. beneath a building.

cel•lo (chel′ō), *n., pl.* **-los.** the second largest member of the violin family. —**cel′list,** *n.*

cel•lo•phane (sel′ə fān′), *n.* a transparent, paperlike material used for wrapping.

cel′lular phone′ *n.* a mobile telephone using a system of radio transmitters and computers for switching calls. Also called **cell′ phone′.**

cel•lu•lite (sel′yə līt′, -lēt′), *n.* (not used scientifically) lumpy fat deposits, esp. in the thighs and buttocks.

cel•lu•loid (sel′yə loid′), *n.* a tough, flammable thermoplastic.

cel•lu•lose (sel′yə lōs′), *n.* the chief constituent of the cell walls of plants, used to make paper, textiles, etc.

Cel•si•us (sel′sē əs), *adj.* of or noting a temperature scale in which 0° represents the freezing point of water and 100° the boiling point; Centigrade. [after A. *Celsius* (1701–44), Swedish astronomer who devised the scale]

Celt (kelt, selt), *n.* **1.** a member of any of a group of Indo-European peoples inhabiting the British Isles and areas of W and central Europe in antiquity. **2.** a speaker of a Celtic language.

Celt′ic *n.* **1.** a branch of the Indo-European language family, including Irish and Welsh. —*adj.* **2.** of the Celts or their languages.

ce•ment (si ment′), *n.* **1.** a mixture of clay and limestone, mixed with water, sand, and gravel to form concrete. **2.** any sticky substance that makes things adhere. —*v.t.* **3.** to unite by or as if by cement. **4.** to cover with cement. —*v.i.* **5.** to become cemented.

cem•e•ter•y (sem′i ter′ē), *n., pl.* **-ies.** a burial ground for the dead.

cen•o•taph (sen′ə taf′, -täf′), *n.* a monument commemorating a dead person whose body is buried elsewhere.

Ce•no•zo•ic (sē′nə zō′ik, sen′ə-), *adj.* noting or pertaining to the present era, beginning 65 million years ago and characterized by the ascendancy of mammals.

cen•ser (sen′sər), *n.* a container in which incense is burned.

cen•sor (sen′sər), *n.* **1.** an official who examines books, films, etc., to suppress anything objectionable. —*v.t.* **2.** to act upon as a censor. —**cen′sor•ship′,** *n.*

cen•so′ri•ous (-sôr′ē əs), *adj.* severely critical. —**cen•so′ri•ous•ly,** *adv.*

cen′sure (-shər), *n., v.,* **-sured, -sur•ing.** —*n.* **1.** strong disapproval. —*v.t., v.i.* **2.** to criticize harshly. —**cen′sur•a•ble,** *adj.*

cen•sus (sen′səs), *n., pl.* **-sus•es.** an official enumeration of the population, with details as to age, sex, occupation, etc.

cent (sent), *n.* a coin and monetary unit of the U.S., equal to $1/100$ of a dollar. [< L *centēsimus* hundredth]

cent. century.

cen′taur (sen′tôr), *n.* a race of creatures in Greek myth having the head and upper torso of a man and the body of a horse.

cen•ten•ar•y (sen ten′ə rē, sen′tn er′ē), *adj., n., pl.* **-ar•ies.** —*adj.* **1.** of a centennial. **2.** of a century. —*n.* **3.** a centennial. **4.** a century. —**cen′te•nar′i•an,** *n.*

cen•ten′ni•al (-ten′ē əl), *adj.* **1.** of a 100th anniversary. **2.** lasting 100 years. —*n.* **3.** a 100th anniversary or its celebration.

cen•ter (sen′tər), *n.* **1.** the point within a circle equally distant from all points of the circumference. **2.** a pivot or axis. **3.** the middle of something. **4.** the source of an influence, action, or force. **5.** a focus of interest or concern. **6.** a principal point, place, or object: *a shipping center.* **7.** (*usu. cap.*) a group holding political views intermediate between those of the Right and Left. **8.** a player who plays primarily in the center. —*v.t.* **9.** to place in a center. **10.** to focus. —*v.i.* **11.** to be at or come to a center.

cen′ter•fold′ *n.* **1.** a pair of facing pages, or a large page that folds out, at the center of a magazine. **2.** a photograph of a nude person appearing on a centerfold.

cen′ter•piece′ *n.* an ornamental object placed on the center of a dining table.

Cen•ti•grade (sen′ti grād′), *adj.* CELSIUS.

cen′ti•gram′ *n.* $1/100$ of a gram.

cen′ti•li′ter (-lē′tər) *n.* $1/100$ of liter.

cen′ti•me′ter (sen′tə-), *n.* $1/100$ of a meter, equivalent to 0.3937 inch.

cen′ti•pede′ (-pēd′), *n.* a segmented arthropod with a pair of legs on each segment.

cen′tral (sen′trəl), *adj.* **1.** of or forming the center. **2.** in, at, or near the center. **3.** constituting something from which things proceed or upon which they depend: *a central office.* **4.** principal; dominant. —**cen′tral•ly,** *adv.*

Cen′tral Af′rican Repub′lic *n.* a republic in central Africa.

cen′tral•ize′ *v.,* **-ized, -iz•ing.** —*v.t.* **1.** to gather about a center. **2.** to bring under one control. —*v.i.* **3.** to form a center. —**cen′tral•i•za′tion,** *n.*

cen′tral nerv′ous sys′tem *n.* the part of the nervous system comprising the brain and spinal cord.

cen•trif′u•gal (-trif′yə gəl, -ə gəl), *adj.* **1.** directed outward from the center. **2.** operated by centrifugal force.

cen′tri•fuge′ (-fyo͞oj′), *n.* an apparatus that rotates at high speed and separates substances of different densities.

cen•trip′e•tal (-trip′i tl), *adj.* directed toward the center.

cen′trist (sen′trist), *n.* (*sometimes cap.*) a person with moderate political views.

cen•tu•ry (sen′chə rē), *n., pl.* **-ries. 1.** a period of 100 years. **2.** one of the successive periods of 100 years reckoned forward or backward from A.D. 1.

CEO chief executive officer.

ce•ram•ic (sə ram′ik), *adj.* **1.** of products made from clay and similar materials, as pottery and brick. —*n.* **2.** ceramic material. —**ce•ram′ics,** *n.*

ce•re•al (sēr′ē əl), *n.* **1.** any plant of the grass family, as wheat or rye, yielding an edible grain. **2.** the grain itself. **3.** some edible preparation of it.

cer•e•bel•lum (ser′ə bel′əm), *n., pl.* **-bel•lums, -bel•la** (-bel′ə). the portion of the brain that coordinates movement and balance. —**cer′e•bel′lar,** *adj.*

ce•re•bral (sə rē′brəl, ser′ə-), *adj.* **1.** of the cerebrum or brain. **2.** characterized by the use of the intellect.

cere′bral cor′tex *n.* the outer layer of the cerebrum associated with the higher brain functions, as learning.

cere′bral pal′sy *n.* a condition marked by difficulty in coordinating voluntary movement, owing to brain damage.

ce•re•brum (sə rē′brəm, ser′ə-), *n., pl.* **-brums, -bra** (-brə). the forward and upper part of the brain, involved with voluntary movement and conscious processes.

cer•e•mo•ny (ser′ə mō′nē), *n., pl.* **-nies. 1.** the formalities observed on some solemn occasion. **2.** a solemn rite. **3.** any meaningless formal act. **4.** strict adherence to conventional forms. —*Idiom.* **5. stand on ceremony,** to behave in a formal manner. —**cer′e•mo′ni•al,** *adj., n.* —**cer′e•mo′ni•ous,** *adj.*

ce•rise (sə rēs′, -rēz′), *adj., n.* moderate to deep red.

cer•tain (sûr′tn), *adj.* **1.** free from doubt or reservation. **2.** quite sure. **3.** inevitable. **4.** established as true. **5.** fixed; agreed upon. **6.** definite but not specified: *certain persons.* **7.** trustworthy. **8.** some though not much: *a certain reluctance.* —*Idiom.* **9. for certain,** without a doubt. —**cer′tain•ly,** *adv.* —**cer′tain•ty,** *n.*

cer•tif•i•cate (sər tif′i kit), *n.* a document providing evidence of status or qualifications.

cer•ti•fy (sûr′tə fī′), *v.t.,* **-fied, -fy•ing. 1.** to attest as certain. **2.** to guarantee; endorse. **3.** to guarantee (a check) as to sufficiency of funds to cover payment. **4.** to license. —**cer′ti•fi′a•ble,** *adj.* —**cer′ti•fi•ca′tion,** *n.*

cer′ti•tude′ (-to͞od′, -tyo͞od′), *n.* freedom from doubt.

ce•ru•le•an (sə ro͞o′lē ən), *adj., n.* deep blue; azure.

cer•vix (sûr′viks), *n., pl.* **cer•vix•es, cer•vi•ces** (sûr′və sēz′, sər vī′sēz). a necklike part, esp. the constricted lower end of the uterus. —**cer′vi•cal** (-vi kəl), *adj.*

Ce•sar•e•an (si zâr′ē ən), *n.* (*sometimes l.c.*) the delivery of a baby by incision through the walls of the abdomen and uterus. Also called **Cesar′ean sec′tion.**

ces•sa•tion (se sā′shən), *n.* a temporary or complete stopping.

ces•sion (sesh′ən), *n.* **1.** the act of ceding, as by treaty. **2.** something ceded, as territory.

cess•pool (ses′po͞ol′), *n.* **1.** a reservoir for receiving the sewage from a house. **2.** a place of filth or immorality.

Cf *Chem. Symbol.* californium.

cf. compare. [< L *confer*]

cg. centigram.

ch. or **Ch.,** **1.** chapter. **2.** church.

Cha•blis (sha blē′), *n.* a dry, white Burgundy wine, orig. produced in Chablis, France.

Chad (chad), *n.* a republic in N central Africa. —**Chad′i•an,** *n., adj.*

chafe (chāf), *v.,* **chafed, chaf•ing.** —*v.t.* **1.** to wear away or make sore by rubbing. **2.** to irritate; annoy. **3.** to warm by rubbing. —*v.i.* **4.** to rub. **5.** to become annoyed.

chaff[1] (chaf, chäf), *n.* **1.** the husks of grains separated during threshing. **2.** worthless matter.

chaff[2] (chaf, chäf), *v.t., v.i.* **1.** to tease; banter. —*n.* **2.** good-natured teasing.

chaf′ing dish′ (chā′fing), *n.* a metal pan mounted atop a heating device for cooking or warming food at the table.

cha•grin (shə grin′), *n., v.,* **-grined** or **-grinned, -grin•ing** or **-grin•ning.** —*n.* **1.** a feeling of vexation produced by disappointment or humiliation. —*v.t.* **2.** to cause to feel chagrin.

chain (chān), *n.* **1.** a series of metal rings passing through one another. **2. chains, a.** shackles or fetters. **b.** bondage; servitude. **3.** a series of things following in succession: *a chain of events.* **4.** a range of mountains. **5.** a number of stores or other establishments under one ownership. **6.** a distance-measuring device used by surveyors. —*v.t.* **7.** to fasten with a chain. **8.** to confine or restrain.

chain′ reac′tion *n.* **1.** a nuclear or chemical reaction in which the reaction products in turn trigger additional reactions. **2.** a series of events in which each event is the result of the preceding one.

chain′ saw′ *n.* a portable power saw having teeth set on an endless chain. —**chain′-saw′,** *v.t., v.i.*

chair (châr), *n.* **1.** a seat for one person with a rest for the back. **2.** a position of authority. **3.** a chairman or chairwoman. —*v.t.* **4.** to seat in a chair. **5.** to preside over as chairman or chairwoman.

chair′man or **-wom′an** or **-per′son,** *n., pl.* **-men** or **-wom•en** or **-per•sons.** the presiding officer of a meeting, committee, etc., or the head of a board or department. —**chair′man•ship′,** *n.*

chaise longue′ (lông′) *n., pl.* **chaise longues, chaises longues** (shāz′ lông′). a chair with a seat long enough to form a complete leg rest.

cha•let (sha lā′, shal′ā), *n.* **1.** a wooden Alpine house with wide eaves and decorative carving. **2.** any dwelling built in this style.

chal•ice (chal′is), *n.* **1.** a cup for the wine of the Eucharist. **2.** a goblet.

chalk (chôk), *n.* **1.** a soft, white, powdery limestone. **2.** a piece of chalk or chalklike substance for writing on a blackboard. —*v.t.* **3.** to mark or rub with chalk. **4. chalk up, a.** to score or earn. —**chalk′board′,** *n.*

chal•lenge (chal′inj), *n., v.,* **-lenged, -leng•ing.** —*n.* **1.** a summons to engage in a contest or duel. **2.** a demand to explain, justify, etc. **3.** a stimulating or demanding situation, undertaking, etc. **4.** the demand of a sentry for identification. **5.** a formal objection to the qualifications of a juror. —*v.t.* **6.** to subject to a challenge. —*v.i.* **7.** to issue a challenge. —**chal′leng•er,** *n.*

cham•ber (chām′bər), *n.* **1.** a room, esp. a bedroom. **2. a.** a legislative, judicial, or deliberative body. **b.** a room housing such a body. **3. chambers,** a place where a judge hears matters not requiring action in open court. **4.** an enclosed space: *a chamber of the heart.* **5.** a receptacle for cartridges in a firearm. —**cham′bered,** *adj.*

cham′ber•maid′ *n.* a maid who cleans bedrooms, as in a hotel.

cham′ber mu′sic *n.* music for performance by a small ensemble in a room or a small concert hall.

cha•me•le•on (kə mē′lē ən, -mēl′yən), *n.* any of various lizards having the ability to change color. [< MF < L < Gk *chamailéōn* lit., dwarf lion]

cham•ois (sham′ē; *for 1 also* sham wä′), *n., pl.* **-ois, -oix** (-ēz; *for 1 also* -wä′) **1.** an agile goat antelope of high mountains of Europe. **2.** a soft, pliable leather from any of various animal skins dressed with oil.

cham•o•mile (kam′ə mīl′, -mēl′), *n.* a plant with scented foliage and daisylike flowers used medicinally and as a tea.

champ¹ (champ, chomp), *v.t., v.i.* to chew vigorously or noisily.

champ² (champ), *n. Informal.* a champion.

cham•pagne (sham pān′), *n.* a sparkling white wine, esp. one from the region of Champagne in France.

cham•pi•on (cham′pē ən), *n.* **1.** one who has placed first among all competitors. **2.** one who fights for or defends a person or cause. —*v.t.* **3.** to defend; support. —*adj.* **4.** first among all competitors. —**cham′pi•on•ship′,** *n.*

chance (chans, chäns), *n., v.,* **chanced, chanc•ing,** *adj.* —*n.* **1.** the unpredictable element of an occurrence. **2.** luck: *a game of chance.* **3.** a possibility or probability. **4.** an opportunity. **5.** a risk or hazard. **6.** a ticket in a lottery. —*v.i.* **7.** to happen by chance. —*v.t.* **8.** to risk. **9. chance on** or **upon,** to meet accidentally. —*adj.* **10.** accidental. —*Idiom.* **11. by chance,** accidentally. **12. on the (off) chance,** counting on the (slight) possibility.

chan•cel (chan′səl, chän′-), *n.* the space around the altar of a church for the clergy and choir.

chan′cel•ler•y (-sə lə rē, -slə rē, -səl rē), *n., pl.* **-ies. 1.** the position or department of a chancellor. **2.** a building occupied by a chancellor's department.

chan•cel•lor (-sə lər, -slər), *n.* **1.** the chief minister of state in some parliamentary governments. **2.** the chief administrative officer in some American universities. —**chan′cel•lor•ship′,** *n.*

chan•cer•y (-sə rē), *n., pl.* **-cer•ies. 1.** CHANCELLERY (def. 1). **2.** an office of public records. **3.** a court of equity. **4.** the administrative office of a diocese.

chan•cre (shang′kər), *n.* the initial lesion of syphilis and certain other infectious diseases.

chan•cy (chan′sē, chän′sē), *adj.,* **-i•er, -i•est.** risky; uncertain.

chan•de•lier (shan′dl ēr′), *n.* a decorative light fixture suspended from a ceiling.

chan•dler (chand′lər, chänd′-), *n.* **1.** a person who makes or sells candles or soap. **2.** a dealer in supplies, esp. for ships.

change (chānj), *v.,* **changed, chang•ing,** *n.* —*v.t.* **1.** to make different. **2.** to exchange: *to change places.* **3.** to give or get foreign money in exchange for. **4.** to remove and replace the coverings or garments of: *to change a baby.* —*v.i.* **5.** to become different. **6.** to make an exchange. **7.** to transfer between conveyances. **8.** to put on different clothes. **9. change off,** to take turns. —*n.* **10.** the act or result of changing. **11.** a variation or deviation. **12.** the substitution of one thing for another. **13.** a fresh set of clothes. **14.** variety or novelty. **15.** the money returned when the sum offered in payment is larger than the sum due. —**change′a•ble,** *adj.* —**change′a•bil′i•ty,** *n.*

change′ of life′ *n.* MENOPAUSE.

change′o′ver *n.* a conversion from one condition or system to another.

chan•nel (chan′l), *n., v.,* **-neled, -nel•ing** or (*esp. Brit.*) **-nelled, -nel•ling.** —*n.* **1.** the bed or deeper part of a river or other waterway. **2.** a wide strait, as between a continent and an island. **3.** a groove or furrow. **4.** a route through which anything passes. **5. channels,** the official course of communication. **6.** a frequency band used by a radio or television station. **7.** a tubular passage for liquids or fluids. —*v.t.* **8.** to convey through a channel. **9.** to direct: *to channel one's interests.*

chant (chant, chänt), *n.* **1.** a simple melody, esp. the traditional monodic intonation of the Christian Churh. **2.** a psalm or canticle for chanting. **3.** a phrase or slogan repeated rhythmically, as by a crowd. —*v.t., v.i.* **4.** to sing or utter in a chant. —**chant′er,** *n.*

chant•ey or **chant•y** (shan′tē, chan′-), *n., pl.* **-eys** or **-ies.** a sailors' song, esp. one sung in rhythm to work.

Cha•nu•kah (кнä′nə kə, hä′-), *n.* HANUKKAH.

cha•os (kā′os), *n.* utter confusion or disorder. —**cha•ot′ic** (-ot′ik), *adj.*

chap¹ (chap), *v.,* **chapped, chap•ping,** *n.* —*v.t.* **1.** to crack and redden (the skin). —*v.i.* **2.** to become chapped. —*n.* **3.** a fissure or crack in the skin.

chap² (chap), *n. Informal.* a fellow; guy.

chap. chapter.

chap•el (chap′əl), *n.* **1.** a private or subordinate place of worship, as in a hospital. **2.** a separate part of a church, used for special services.

chap•er•on or **-one** (shap′ə rōn′), *n., v.,* **-oned, -on•ing.** —*n.* **1.** a person, usu. an older woman, who, for propriety, accompanies young unmarried couples. —*v.t., v.i.* **2.** to act as chaperon (for). —**chap′er•on′age** (-rō′nij), *n.*

chap•lain (chap′lin), *n.* an ecclesiastic associated with a chapel, military unit, etc. —**chap′lain•cy,** *n.*

chaps (chaps, shaps), *n. (used with a pl. v.)* leather leggings worn over work pants, typically by cowboys and cowgirls.

chap•ter (chap′tər), *n.* **1.** a main division of a book, treatise, etc. **2.** a branch of a society, fraternity, etc. **3.** an assembly of the canons of a church.

char (chär), *v.t., v.i.,* **charred, char•ring. 1.** to reduce to charcoal. **2.** to burn slightly.

char•ac•ter (kar′ik tər), *n.* **1.** the aggregate of features and traits that form the individual nature of a person or thing. **2.** a trait or characteristic. **3.** moral quality or integrity. **4.** reputation. **5.** an eccentric or unusual person. **6.** a person represented in a drama, story, etc. **7.** a symbol used in a system of writing.

char′ac•ter•is′tic (-tə ris′tik), *adj.* **1.** distinctive; typical. —*n.* **2.** a distinguishing feature or quality. —**char′ac•ter•is′ti•cal•ly,** *adv.*

char′ac•ter•ize′ *v.t.,* **-ized, -iz•ing. 1.** to be a characteristic of. **2.** to describe the character of. —**char′ac•ter•i•za′tion,** *n.*

cha•rades′ (shə rādz′) *n.pl.* miming game.

char′broil′ *v.t.* to broil over a charcoal fire.

char′coal′ *n.* a black, carbon-containing material obtained by heating an organic substance, as wood, in the absence of air.

chard (chärd), *n.* a variety of beet with leafstalks that are used as a vegetable.

Char′don•nay′ (shär′dn ā′) *n.* dry white wine.

charge (chärj), *v.,* **charged, charg•ing,** *n.* —*v.t.* **1.** to ask as a price. **2.** to defer payment for (a purchase) until a bill is rendered. **3.** to hold liable for payment. **4.** to attack by rushing violently against. **5.** to accuse. **6.** to lay a command or injunction upon. **7.** to fill or load, as with bullets. **8.** to supply with a quantity of electrical energy. **9.** to suffuse, as with emotion. —*v.i.* **10.** to attack or rush violently. **11.** to require payment. —*n.* **12.** an expense or cost. **13.** an impetuous attack, as of soldiers. **14.** a duty or responsibility. **15.** care, custody, or superintendence. **16.** someone or something committed to one's care. **17.** a command or injunction. **18.** an accusation or indictment. **19.** the quantity that an apparatus is fitted to hold at one time: *a charge of coal for a furnace.* **20.** the quantity of electricity in a substance. —*Idiom.* **21. in charge,** in command; having the care or supervision. —**charge′a•ble,** *adj.*

charg′er *n.* **1.** a person or thing that charges. **2.** a horse ridden in battle.

char•i•ot (char′ē ət), *n.* a light, horse-drawn, two-wheeled vehicle of the ancient world, used in warfare, races, etc. —**char′i•ot•eer′** (-ə tēr′), *n.*

cha•ris•ma (kə riz′mə), *n., pl.* **-ma•ta** (-mə tə). personal magnetism that enables an individual to attract or influence people. —**char′is•mat′ic,** *adj.*

char·i·ta·ble (char′i tə bəl), *adj.* **1.** generous to the needy. **2.** kindly or lenient. **3.** concerned with charity. —**char′i·ta·bly,** *adv.*

char′i·ty *n., pl.* **-ties. 1.** generosity toward the needy. **2.** a charitable act or work. **3.** a charitable fund or institution. **4.** leniency in judging others. **5.** Christian love.

char·la·tan (shär′lə tn), *n.* a quack; fraud.

char′ley horse′ (chär′lē), *n.* a cramp or a sore muscle, esp. in the leg.

charm (chärm), *n.* **1.** a power of pleasing or attracting, as through personality. **2.** a trinket on a bracelet or necklace. **3.** an amulet. **4.** a formula or action credited with magical power. —*v.t., v.i.* **5.** to delight or please by attractiveness. **6.** to act (upon) with a magical force. —**charm′er,** *n.* —**charm′ing,** *adj.* —**charm′ing·ly,** *adv.*

char′nel house′ (chär′nl), *n.* a place where the bodies of the dead are deposited.

chart (chärt), *n.* **1.** a sheet giving information in tabular or diagrammatic form. **2.** a graph. **3.** a map, esp. a marine map. —*v.t.* **4.** to make a chart of. **5.** to plan.

char·ter (chär′tər), *n.* **1.** a governmental document outlining the conditions under which a business, city, or other corporate body is organized. **2.** a document defining the formal organization of a corporate body; constitution. **3.** an authorization from a central organization to establish a new branch, chapter, etc. **4.** a temporary lease of a ship or aircraft. —*v.t.* **5.** to establish by charter. **6.** to hire for exclusive use.

char·treuse (shär trōōz′, -trōōs′), *n.* a clear, yellowish green.

char′wom′an (chär′-), *n., pl.* **-en.** a woman hired to do general cleaning.

char·y (châr′ē), *adj.,* **-i·er, -i·est. 1.** careful; wary. **2.** sparing; frugal. —**char′i·ly,** *adv.* —**char′i·ness,** *n.*

chase¹ (chās), *v.,* chased, chas·ing, *n.* —*v.t.* **1.** to pursue in order to seize. **2.** to hunt. **3.** to devote attention to with the hope of attracting. **4.** to expel forcibly: *to chase the cat out of the room.* —*v.i.* **5.** to follow in pursuit. **6.** to rush; hasten. —*n.* **7.** the act of chasing. **8.** an object of pursuit. —*Idiom.* **9. give chase,** to pursue. —**chas′er,** *n.*

chase² (chās), *v.t.,* chased, chas·ing. to ornament (metal) by engraving or embossing.

chasm (kaz′əm), *n.* **1.** a deep cleft in the earth's surface; gorge. **2.** any gap or break.

chas·sis (chas′ē, shas′ē), *n., pl.* chas·sis (chas′ēz, shas′-). **1.** the frame, wheels, and machinery of a motor vehicle. **2.** a frame for mounting the circuit components of a radio or television set.

chaste (chāst), *adj.,* chast·er, chast·est. **1.** refraining from unsanctioned sexual activity. **2.** celibate. **3.** decent and modest. **4.** simple; unadorned. —**chaste′ly,** *adv.* —**chas·ti·ty** (chas′ti tē), *n.*

chas·ten (chā′sən), *v.t.* **1.** to inflict punishment upon to humble or improve. **2.** to restrain; subdue.

chas·tise (chas tīz′, chas′tīz), *v.t.,* **-tised, -tis·ing. 1.** to discipline, esp. by corporal punishment. **2.** to criticize severely. —**chas′tise·ment** (chas′tiz-, chas tīz′-), *n.* —**chas·tis′er,** *n.*

chat (chat), *v.,* chat·ted, chat·ting, *n.* —*v.i.* **1.** to converse informally. —*n.* **2.** an informal conversation.

châ·teau (sha tō′), *n., pl.* **-teaus** (-tōz′), **-teaux** (-tōz′, -tō′). **1.** a castle in France. **2.** a large country house or estate, esp. in France.

chat·tel (chat′l), *n.* a movable article of personal property.

chat·ter (chat′ər), *v.i.* **1.** to talk rapidly, continuously, and pointlessly. **2.** to utter rapid, speechlike sounds, as a monkey. **3.** to make a rapid clicking noise by striking together: *teeth chattering from the cold.* —*n.* **4.** rapid, pointless talk. **5.** the act or sound of chattering. —**chat′ter·er,** *n.*

chat′ter·box′ *n.* an excessively talkative person.

chat′ty *adj.,* **-ti·er, -ti·est. 1.** characterized by a friendly, informal style. **2.** given to chatting. —**chat′ti·ness,** *n.*

chauf·feur (shō′fər, shō fûr′), *n.* **1.** a person employed to drive a private automobile. —*v.t., v.i.* **2.** to serve as a chauffeur (for); drive.

chau·vin·ism (shō′və niz′əm), *n.* **1.** zealous and aggressive patriotism. **2.** biased devotion to any group, attitude, or cause. —**chau′vin·ist,** *n.* —**chau′vin·is′tic,** *adj.*

cheap (chēp), *adj.,* **-er, -est,** *adv.* —*adj.* **1.** inexpensive. **2.** shoddy or inferior. **3.** costing little labor or trouble: *Talk is cheap.* **4.** mean or contemptible. **5.** of little value: *Life was cheap.* **6.** stingy; miserly. —*adv.* **7.** at a low price. —**cheap′en,** *v.t., v.i.* —**cheap′ly,** *adv.* —**cheap′ness,** *n.*

cheap′skate′ *n. Informal.* a stingy person.

cheat (chēt), *v.t.* **1.** to defraud; swindle. **2.** to elude; escape: *to cheat death.* —*v.i.* **3.** to practice fraud or deceit. **4.** to violate rules or agreements. **5.** to be sexually unfaithful. —*n.* **6.** a person who cheats. **7.** a fraud or swindle. —**cheat′er,** *n.*

check (chek), *v.t.* **1.** to stop the motion of suddenly. **2.** to restrain; control. **3.** to verify the correctness of. **4.** to inquire into, search through, etc. **5.** to inspect the performance, safety, etc., of. **6.** to mark so as to indicate choice, correctness, etc. **7.** to leave in temporary custody: *Check your coats at the door.* **8.** to surrender (baggage) for conveyance. **9.** (in chess) to place (an opponent's king) under direct attack. —*v.i.* **10.** to correspond accurately. **11.** to make an inquiry or investigation. **12. check in,** to register or report one's arrival, as at a hotel or airport. **13. ~ out, a.** to leave a hotel, hospital, etc., officially. **b.** to verify or become verified. —*n.* **14.** a written order directing a bank to pay money. **15.** a bill at a restaurant. **16.** a ticket showing ownership. **17.** an inquiry or examination. **18.** a mark (✓) to indicate approval, verification, etc. **19.** a sudden stoppage. **20.** a means of stopping or restraining. **21.** a test or inspection. **22.** a pattern formed of squares. **23.** (in chess) the exposure of the king to direct attack. —*Idiom.* **24. in check,** under restraint.

check′er¹, *n.* **1.** a small, usu. red or black disk used in playing checkers. **2. checkers,** a game played by two persons, each with 12 playing pieces, on a checkerboard.

check′er², *n.* **1.** one that checks. **2.** a cashier, as in a supermarket. **3.** a checkroom employee.

check′er·board′ *n.* a board marked into 64 squares of two alternating colors, used in checkers or chess.

check′ered *adj.* **1.** marked by numerous changes: *a checkered career.* **2.** marked by dubious episodes: *a checkered past.* **3.** marked with squares.

check′list′ *n.* a list of items for comparison, verification, or other checking purposes.

check′mate′ (-māt′), *n., v.,* **-mat·ed, -mat·ing.** —*n.* **1. a.** (in chess) the maneuvering of the opponent's king into a check from which it cannot escape, thus winning the game. **b.** this position. **2.** a thwarting or defeat. —*v.t.* **3.** to put in checkmate. **4.** to defeat.

check′out′ *n.* **1.** the act of vacating and paying for one's hotel room. **2.** the time by which a hotel room must be vacated. **3.** a counter where customers pay for purchases.

check′point′ *n.* a place, as at a border, where travelers are stopped for inspection.

check′up′ *n.* a comprehensive physical examination.

ched·dar (ched′ər), *n.* a hard, smooth cheese that varies in flavor from mild to sharp as it ages.

cheek (chēk), *n.* **1.** either side of the face below the eye and above the jaw. **2.** impudence or effrontery.

cheer (chēr), *n.* **1.** a shout of encouragement, approval, etc. **2.** a state of feeling or spirits: *Be of good cheer.* **3.** gladness; gaiety. —*interj.* **4. cheers,** to your health (used as a toast). —*v.t.* **5.** to encourage or salute with cheers. **6.** to raise the spirits of: *The good news cheered her up.* —*v.i.* **7.** to utter cheers. **8.** to become cheerful. —**cheer′ful,** *adj.* —**cheer′less,** *adj.* —**cheer′y,** *adj.* **-i·er, -i·est.**

cheese (chēz), *n.* a food prepared from the curds of milk separated from the whey, often pressed and allowed to ripen. [< L *cāseus*]

cheese′burg′er *n.* a hamburger topped with melted cheese.

cheese′cake′ *n.* **1.** a firm, custardlike cake made with sweetened cream cheese or cottage cheese. **2.** *Informal.* photographs of scantily clothed, attractive women.

cheese′cloth′ *n.* a lightweight cotton gauze of loose weave.

chee•tah (chē′tə), *n.* a swift, long-legged, black-spotted cat of SW Asia and Africa.

chef (shef), *n.* a cook, esp. the chief cook in a restaurant.

chem•i•cal (kem′i kəl), *n.* **1.** a substance produced by or used in chemistry. —*adj.* **2.** of, used in, produced by, or concerned with chemistry or chemicals. —**chem′i•cal•ly,** *adv.*

chem′ical war′fare *n.* warfare with asphyxiating, poisonous, or corrosive gases, oil flames, etc.

che•mise (shə mēz′), *n.* **1.** a woman's loose-fitting, shirtlike undergarment. **2.** a dress with an unfitted waist.

chem•is•try (kem′ə strē) *n.* **1.** the science that studies the composition, properties, and activity of substances and various elementary forms of matter. **2.** rapport. —**chem′ist,** *n.*

che•mo•ther•a•py (kē′mō ther′ə pē), *n.* the treatment of disease by means of chemicals. —**che′mo•ther′a•peu′tic** (-pyoo′tik), *adj.*

cheque (chek), *n. Brit.* CHECK (def. 14).

cher•ish (cher′ish), *v.t.* **1.** to regard or treat as dear. **2.** to cling fondly to: *to cherish a memory.*

Cher•o•kee (cher′ə kē′), *n.,* *pl.* **-kee, -kees.** a member of an American Indian people of the Carolinas and Tennessee, living today in Oklahoma and North Carolina.

cher•ry (cher′ē), *n.,* *pl.* **-ries. 1.** a pulpy, globular fruit containing one smooth pit. **2.** the tree bearing such a fruit. **3.** the wood of this tree. **4.** a bright red.

cher•ub (cher′əb), *n.,* *pl.* **-u•bim** (-ə bim, -yōō-bim) for 1, 2; **-ubs** for 3. **1.** *Bible.* a celestial being. **2.** a member of the second order of angels, often represented as a winged child. **3.** a child with a chubby, innocent face. —**che•ru•bic** (chə rōō′bik), *adj.*

chess (ches), *n.* a game played on a chessboard by two people, each with 16 pieces.

chest (chest), *n.* **1.** the portion of the body enclosed by ribs. **2.** a large, heavy box with a lid. **3.** a set of drawers in a frame, as for holding clothes. **4.** a small cabinet, esp. one hung on a wall, for storage of toiletries and medicines.

chest′nut′ *n.* **1.** any of several trees of the beech family, bearing edible nuts. **2.** the nut of these trees. **3.** the wood of these trees. **4.** reddish brown. **5.** a stale joke, anecdote, etc.

chev•i•ot (shev′ē ət), *n.* a woolen fabric in a coarse twill weave, used for coats, suits, etc.

chev•ron (shev′rən), *n.* a badge of V-shaped stripes on the sleeve of a uniform, indicating rank, length of service, etc.

chew (chōō), *v.t., v.i.* **1.** to crush or grind with the teeth. **2. chew out,** *Slang.* to scold harshly. —*n.* **3.** an act or instance of chewing. **4.** something chewed or intended for chewing. —*Idiom.* **5. chew the fat** or **rag,** *Informal.* to have a chat. —**chew′er,** *n.*

chew′y *adj.,* **-i•er, -i•est.** (of food) not easily chewed. —**chew′i•ness,** *n.*

Chey•enne (shī en′, -an′), *n.,* *pl.* **-enne, -ennes.** a member of an American Indian people of the western plains, living today in Montana and Oklahoma.

Chi•an•ti (kē än′tē, -an′-), *n.* a dry red wine of Italy.

chic (shēk), *adj.,* **-er, -est,** *n.* —*adj.* **1.** fashionable; stylish. —*n.* **2.** style and elegance, esp. in dress.

chi•can•er•y (shi kā′nə rē, chi-), *n.,* *pl.* **-er•ies. 1.** trickery or deception. **2.** a trick.

Chi•ca•no (chi kä′nō, -kan′ō), *n.,* *pl.* **-nos.** a Mexican-American.

chick (chik), *n.* **1.** a young chicken or other bird. **2.** *Slang (often offensive).* a young woman.

chick•a•dee (chik′ə dē′), *n.,* *pl.* **-dees.** a North American bird of the titmouse family, with a dark-colored throat and cap.

Chick•a•saw (chik′ə sô′), *n.,* *pl.* **-saw, -saws.** a member of an American Indian people of Mississippi, later removed to Oklahoma.

chick•en (chik′ən), *n.* **1.** the common domestic fowl. **2.** the young of this bird. **3.** the flesh of the chicken, used as food. **4.** *Slang.* a coward. —*adj.* **5.** *Slang.* cowardly. —*v.* **6. chicken out,** *Slang.* to withdraw because of cowardice.

chick′en•pox′ *n.* a viral disease, commonly of children, characterized by fever and the eruption of blisters.

chick′pea′ *n.* **1.** a plant of the legume family, bearing edible, pealike seeds. **2.** its seed.

chic•o•ry (chik′ə rē), *n.,* *pl.* **-ries. 1.** a plant with toothed oblong leaves used for salad. **2.** the root of this plant, used in or as a substitute for coffee.

chide (chīd), *v.t., v.i.,* **chid•ed** or **chid** (chid), **chid•ed** or **chid** or **chid•den** (chid′n), **chid•ing.** to scold or reproach.

chief (chēf), *n.* **1.** a head or leader. —*adj.* **2.** most important; principal. —**chief′ly,** *adv.*

chief′tain (-tən), *n.* the chief of a clan or a tribe.

chif•fon (shi fon′, shif′on), *n.* **1.** a sheer fabric of silk, nylon, or rayon. —*adj.* **2.** made of chiffon. **3.** having a light, fluffy texture, as from beaten egg whites.

chif′fo•nier′ (shif′ə nēr′) *n.* tall chest of drawers.

chig•ger (chig′ər), *n.* the bloodsucking larva of a mite parasitic on humans and other mammals.

chil′blains′ (chil′blānz′) *n.pl.* inflammation caused by overexposure to cold, etc.

child (chīld), *n.,* *pl.* **chil•dren. 1.** a boy or girl. **2.** a son or daughter. **3.** an infant. —*Idiom.* **4. with child,** pregnant. —**child′birth′,** *n.* —**child′hood,** *n.* —**child′ish,** *adj.* —**child′ish•ly,** *adv.* —**child′ish•ness,** *n.* —**child′less,** *adj.* —**child′like′,** *adj.*

child′proof′ *adj.* designed to prevent child from being hurt.

Chil•e (chil′ē), *n.* a republic in SW South America. —**Chil′e•an,** *adj., n.*

chil•i or **chil•e** (chil′ē), *n.,* *pl.* **-ies** or **-es. 1.** the pungent pod of a red pepper, used in cooking. **2.** a highly seasoned dish of beef, chilies, and often tomatoes and beans.

chill (chil), *n.* **1.** a moderate but penetrating coldness. **2.** a sensation of cold, usu. with shivering. **3.** a depressing influence or feeling. —*adj.* **4.** moderately cold. —*v.i., v.t.* **5.** to become or make cold. —**chill′ness,** *n.* —**chil′ly,** *adj.* **-i•er, -i•est.**

chime (chīm), *n., v.,* **chimed, chim•ing.** —*n.* **1.** Often, **chimes. a.** a set of bells producing musical tones when struck. **b.** the musical tones thus produced. **2.** harmonious sound in general. —*v.i.* **3.** to sound chimes. **4.** to harmonize; agree. —*v.t.* **5.** to announce by chiming: *Bells chimed the hour.* **6. chime in, a.** to interrupt a conversation. **b.** to harmonize. —**chim′er,** *n.*

chi•me•ra (ki mēr′ə, kī-), *n.,* *pl.* **-ras** for 2. **1.** (*cap.*) a monster of classical myth, with a lion's head, goat's body, and serpent's tail. **2.** a fancy or dream; an imagining.

chim•ney (chim′nē), *n.,* *pl.* **-neys. 1.** a structure containing a flue by which the smoke, gases, etc., of a fire or furnace are carried off. **2.** a glass tube surrounding the flame of a lamp.

chim•pan•zee (chim′pan zē′, chim pan′zē), *n.,* *pl.* **-zees.** a large anthropoid ape of equatorial Africa.

chin (chin), *n., v.,* **chinned, chin•ning.** —*n.* **1.** the lower extremity of the face, below the mouth. —*v.t.* **2.** to grasp an overhead bar and pull (oneself) up until the chin is level with the bar.

Chin. or **Chin, 1.** China. **2.** Chinese.

chi•na (chī′nə), *n.* **1.** porcelain or a similar translucent ceramic material. **2.** porcelain or ceramic tableware.

Chi′na *n.* **1. People's Republic of,** a country in E Asia. **2. Republic of,** TAIWAN.

chin•chil•la (chin chil′ə), *n.,* *pl.* **-las. 1.** a small South American rodent raised for its silvery gray fur. **2.** this fur. **3.** a woolen coat fabric with a curly nap.

Chi·nese (chī nēz′, -nēs′), *n., pl.* **-nese,** *adj.* —*n.*
1. a native or descendant of a native of China. **2.** a
language or language family of China, comprising a
wide variety of speech forms. —*adj.* **3.** of China, its
people, or their language.

chink[1] (chingk), *n.* **1.** a crack, as in a wall. —*v.t.* **2.**
to fill up chinks in.

chink[2] (chingk), *v.i., v.t.* **1.** to make or cause to
make a short, sharp, ringing sound. —*n.* **2.** a chink-
ing sound.

chi·no (chē′nō), *n., pl.* **-nos. 1.** a twilled cotton
cloth used for uniforms, sportswear, etc. **2.** Usu.,
-nos. trousers of this cloth.

Chi·nook (shi nŏŏk′, -nōŏk′, chi-), *n., pl.* **-nook,
-nooks.** a member of an American Indian people
orig. inhabiting Oregon.

chintz (chints), *n.* a cotton fabric, usu. glazed and
printed in bright patterns.

chintz′y *adj.,* **-i·er, -i·est. 1.** like chintz. **2.** cheap
or gaudy.

chip (chip), *n., v.,* **chipped, chip·ping.** —*n.* **1.** a
small piece, as of wood, separated by chopping or
breaking. **2.** a small piece of food: *chocolate chips.*
3. a flaw made by the breaking off of a small piece.
4. a small disk used in gambling games as a
counter. **5.** a tiny slice of semiconducting material
on which a transistor or an integrated circuit is
formed. —*v.t.* **6.** to break a fragment from. —*v.i.* **7.**
to break off in small pieces. **8. chip in,** to contribute money, time, etc. —*Idiom.* **9. chip on one's
shoulder,** a readiness to quarrel.

chip·munk (chip′mungk), *n.* a small, striped
North American or Asian ground squirrel.

chip·per (chip′ər), *adj.* being in sprightly good humor and health.

chi·rop·o·dy (ki rop′ə dē, kī-; *often* shə-), *n.* PODI-
ATRY. —**chi·rop′o·dist,** *n.*

chi′ro·prac′tor (kī′rə prak′tər) *n.* one who
practices therapy based upon adjusting body structures. —**chi′ro·prac′tic,** *n.*

chirp (chûrp), *n.* **1.** the short, sharp sound made by
small birds. **2.** any similar sound. —*v.i., v.t.* **3.** to
make or express with such a sound.

chis·el (chiz′əl), *n., v.,* **-eled, -el·ing** or (*esp. Brit.*)
-elled, -el·ling. —*n.* **1.** a wedgelike, sharp-edged
tool for cutting or shaping wood, stone, etc. —*v.t.,
v.i.* **2.** to cut or work with a chisel. **3.** *Slang.* **a.** to
cheat or swindle (someone). **b.** to get by trickery.
—**chis′el·er;** *esp. Brit.,* **chis′el·ler,** *n.*

chit·chat (chit′chat′), *n.* light conversation; casual
talk.

chiv·al·ry (shiv′əl rē), *n.* **1.** the qualities expected
of a knight, including courage, generosity, and courtesy. **2.** the institution of medieval knighthood.
—**chiv′al·rous, chi·val·ric** (shi val′rik), *adj.*

chive (chīv), *n.* a plant related to the onion, having
slender leaves used as a flavoring.

chlo·ri·nate (klôr′ə nāt′), *v.t.,* **-nat·ed, -nat·ing.**
to combine or treat with chlorine, esp. for disinfect-
ing. —**chlo′ri·na′tion,** *n.*

chlo·rine (klôr′ēn, -in), *n.* a greenish yellow, poisonous, gaseous element, used to purify water and
to make bleaching powder and various chemicals.
Symbol: Cl; *at. wt.:* 35.453; *at. no.:* 17.

chlo·ro·form (klôr′ə fôrm′), *n.* **1.** a colorless volatile liquid used as a solvent and formerly as an anesthetic. —*v.t.* **2.** to administer chloroform to.

chlo′ro·phyll (-fil), *n.* the green pigment of plant
leaves, essential to photosynthesis.

chock (chok), *n.* **1.** a wedge for filling in a space,
holding an object steady, etc. —*v.t.* **2.** to furnish
with chocks. —*adv.* **3.** as tight as possible.

choc·o·late (chô′kə lit, chok′ə-, chôk′lit, chok′-),
n. **1.** a preparation of the seeds of cacao, often
sweetened and flavored. **2.** a candy or beverage
made from such a preparation. **3.** a dark brown
color. —*adj.* **4.** made or flavored with chocolate. **5.**
having the color of chocolate. —**choc′o·lat·y,
choc′o·lat·ey,** *adj.*

Choc·taw (chok′tô), *n., pl.* **-taw, -taws.** a member
of an American Indian people of Mississippi, later
removed to Oklahoma.

choice (chois), *n., adj.,* **choic·er, choic·est.** —*n.* **1.**
the act of choosing. **2.** the right or opportunity to
choose. **3.** the person or thing chosen. **4.** an alternative. **5.** a variety from which to choose. **6.** the
best part. —*adj.* **7.** excellent; superior. **8.** carefully
selected. —**choice′ness,** *n.*

choir (kwīʳr), *n.* **1.** a group of singers, as in a
church. **2.** the part of a church occupied by a choir.
[< OF *cuer* < L *chorus* chorus]

choke (chōk), *v.,* **choked, chok·ing,** *n.* —*v.t.* **1.** to
stop the breath of by obstructing the windpipe. **2.**
to obstruct; clog. **3.** to suppress or hinder. **4.** to enrich the fuel mixture of (an internal-combustion engine) by diminishing the air supply to the carburetor. —*v.i.* **5.** to become suffocated. **6.** to become
obstructed. **7. choke up,** to become speechless, as
from emotion. —*n.* **8.** the act or sound of choking.
9. a device in an automotive engine that controls
the flow of air.

chol·er·a (kol′ər ə), *n.* a severe, contagious infection of the small intestine, commonly transmitted
through contaminated drinking water.

cho·les·ter·ol (kə les′tə rōl′, -rôl′), *n.* a fatty,
crystalline substance abundant in animal fats, meat,
and eggs.

chomp (chomp), *v.t., v.i.* CHAMP[1].

choose (chōōz), *v.,* **chose, cho·sen, choos·ing.**
—*v.t.* **1.** to pick by preference; select. **2.** to decide
or desire. —*v.i.* **3.** to make a choice. —**choos′er,** *n.*

choos′y *adj.,* **-i·er, -i·est.** hard to please; particular. —**choos′i·ness,** *n.*

chop[1] (chop), *v.,* **chopped, chop·ping,** *n.* —*v.t.* **1.**
to cut with quick, heavy blows. **2.** to cut into small
pieces. —*v.i.* **3.** to make quick, heavy strokes, as
with an ax. —*n.* **4.** an act or instance of chopping.
5. a short downward blow or stroke. **6.** a cut of
lamb, pork, veal, etc. **7.** a short, irregular motion of
waves.

chop[2] (chop), *n.* Usu., **chops. 1.** the jaw. **2.** the
lower part of the cheek; the flesh over the lower
jaw.

chop′per *n.* **1.** one that chops. **2.** *Informal.* a helicopter.

chop′py *adj.,* **-pi·er, -pi·est. 1.** (of the sea, a lake,
etc.) forming short, broken waves. **2.** uneven in
style or quality. —**chop′pi·ly,** *adv.* —**chop′pi·
ness,** *n.*

chop′sticks′ *n.pl.* sticks used in eating, esp. in
some Asian countries.

chop′ su′ey (sōō′ē), *n.* a Chinese-style dish of
meat, bean sprouts, etc., served with rice.

cho·ral (kôr′əl), *adj.* of a chorus or a choir.
—**cho′ral·ly,** *adv.*

cho·rale (kə ral′, -räl′), *n.* **1.** a hymn, esp. one
with strong harmonization. **2.** a group of singers
specializing in church music.

chord[1] (kôrd), *n.* **1.** a feeling or emotion. **2.** the
line segment between two points on a given curve.

chord[2] (kôrd), *n.* a combination of three or more
musical tones sounded simultaneously. —**chord′al,**
adj.

chore (chôr), *n.* **1.** a small or routine task. **2.** a
hard or unpleasant task.

cho·re·og·ra·phy (kôr′ē og′rə fē), *n.* **1.** the art
of composing ballets and other dances. **2.** the
movements, steps, and patterns composed for a
dance, show, piece of music, etc. —**cho′re·og′ra·
pher,** *n.* —**cho′re·o·graph′ic** (-ə graf′ik), *adj.*

chor·is·ter (kôr′ə stər, kor′-), *n.* a singer in a
choir.

chor·tle (chôr′tl), *v.,* **-tled, -tling,** *n.* —*v.i.* **1.** to
chuckle gleefully. —*n.* **2.** a gleeful chuckle. [b. of
chuckle and *snort;* coined by Lewis Carroll in
Through the Looking-Glass (1871)] —**chor′tler,** *n.*

cho·rus (kôr′əs), *n., pl.* **-rus·es,** *v.* —*n.* **1. a.** a
group of persons singing in unison. **b.** a piece of
music for singing in unison. **2.** a part of a song that
recurs at intervals; refrain. **3.** a simultaneous utterance by many people, birds, etc. **4.** the sounds so
uttered: *a chorus of jeers.* —*v.t., v.i.* **5.** to sing or
speak simultaneously. —*Idiom.* **6. in chorus,** in
unison.

chow (chou), *n. Slang.* food.

general

chow·der (chou′dər), *n.* a thick soup of clams, fish, or vegetables, usu. with potatoes and milk.

chow′ mein′ (mān), *n.* a Chinese-style dish of vegetables, chicken, etc., served with fried noodles.

Christ (krīst), *n.* Jesus of Nazareth, held by Christians to be the Messiah prophesied in the Old Testament. [< L *Chrīstus* < Gk *Chrīstós* lit., anointed]

chris·ten (kris′ən), *v.t.* **1.** to receive into the Christian church by baptism; baptize. **2.** to give a name to, esp. at baptism. —**chris′ten·ing,** *n.*

Chris·ten·dom (kris′ən dəm), *n.* **1.** Christians collectively. **2.** the Christian world.

Chris·tian (kris′chən), *adj.* **1.** of Jesus Christ or His teachings. **2.** of or adhering to the religion based on the teachings of Jesus Christ. **3.** of Christians. —*n.* **4.** an adherent of Christianity.

Chris′ti·an′i·ty (-chē an′i tē), *n.* **1.** the Christian religion. **2.** the state of being a Christian. **3.** CHRISTENDOM.

Christ·mas (kris′məs), *n.* an annual Christian festival commemorating Jesus' birth, celebrated on December 25.

chro·mat·ic (krō mat′ik, krə-), *adj.* **1.** pertaining to color. **2.** progressing by semitones. —**chro·mat′i·cal·ly,** *adv.*

chro·mi·um (krō′mē əm), *n.* a lustrous metallic element used in alloy steels for hardness. *Symbol:* Cr; *at. wt.:* 51.996; *at. no.:* 24.

chro·mo·some (krō′mə sōm′), *n.* one of a set of threadlike structures that are composed of DNA and a protein and that carry the genes. —**chro′mo·so′mal,** *adj.*

chron·ic (kron′ik), *adj.* **1.** habitual or longstanding: *a chronic liar.* **2.** continuing a long time or recurring frequently, as a disease. —**chron′i·cal·ly,** *adv.*

chron·i·cle (kron′i kəl), *n., v.,* **-cled, -cling.** —*n.* **1.** a chronological record of events. —*v.t.* **2.** to record in a chronicle. —**chron′i·cler,** *n.*

chrono- a combining form meaning time (*chronometer*).

chro·nol·o·gy (krə nol′ə jē), *n., pl.* **-gies.** **1.** an arrangement according to the order in which things occur. **2.** a table or list so arranged. **3.** the science of arranging time in periods and ascertaining the dates of past events. —**chron·o·log·i·cal** (kron′l oj′i kəl), *adj.* —**chron′o·log′i·cal·ly,** *adv.*

chro·nom·e·ter (krə nom′i tər), *n.* a timepiece designed for the highest accuracy.

chrys·a·lis (kris′ə lis), *n., pl.* **chrys·a·lis·es, chry·sal·i·des** (kri sal′i dēz′). the hard-shelled pupa of a moth or butterfly.

chrys·an·the·mum (kri san′thə məm), *n.* **1.** any of many cultivated varieties of plants with showy flowers. **2.** the flower.

chub·by (chub′ē), *adj.,* **-bi·er, -bi·est.** round and plump. —**chub′bi·ness,** *n.*

chuck¹ (chuk), *v.t.* **1.** to toss; throw. **2.** to throw away. **3.** to resign from. **4.** to pat lightly, as under the chin. —*n.* **5.** a light pat. **6.** a toss; pitch.

chuck² (chuk), *n.* **1.** the cut of beef between the neck and the shoulder blade. **2.** a device for clamping work in a lathe or other machine tool.

chuck·le (chuk′əl), *v.,* **-led, -ling,** *n.* —*v.i.* **1.** to laugh softly. —*n.* **2.** a softly moderated laugh.

chum (chum), *n., v.,* **chummed, chum·ming.** —*n.* **1.** a close friend. —*v.i.* **2.** to associate closely. —**chum′my,** *adj.,* **-mi·er, -mi·est.**

chump (chump), *n. Informal.* a foolish or gullible person.

chunk (chungk), *n.* **1.** a thick mass or lump of anything. **2.** a substantial amount.

chunk·y *adj.,* **-i·er, -i·est.** **1.** thick or stout; stocky. **2.** full of chunks. —**chunk′i·ness,** *n.*

church (chûrch), *n.* **1.** a building that is used for public Christian worship. **2.** a religious service. **3.** (*sometimes cap.*) **a.** the body of Christian believers. **b.** a Christian denomination. **4.** religious authority as distinguished from the state. [≪ Gk *kyrī(a)kón* (*dôma*) the Lord's (house)]

churl (chûrl), *n.* **1.** a rude or surly person. **2.** a peasant; rustic. —**churl′ish,** *adj.* —**churl′ish·ness,** *n.*

churn (chûrn), *n.* **1.** a container in which cream or milk is agitated to make butter. —*v.t.* **2.** to agitate (cream or milk) in a churn. **3.** to make (butter) in a churn. **4.** to shake or agitate. **5.** (of a stockbroker) to trade (a customer's securities) excessively. —*v.i.* **6.** to operate a churn. **7.** to move or shake in agitation. **8. churn out,** to produce mechanically and in abundance. —**churn′er,** *n.*

chute¹ (shōōt), *n.* an inclined trough or shaft for conveying water, grain, etc., to a lower level.

chute² (shōōt), *n.* a parachute.

chut·ney (chut′nē), *n.* a sweet and sour relish of Indian origin.

chutz·pa or **-pah** (кнōōt′spə, hōōt′-), *n. Slang.* nerve; gall. [< Yiddish *chutspe* < Heb *ḥūṣpā*]

CIA Central Intelligence Agency.

ci·ca·da (si kā′də, -kä′-), *n., pl.* **-das, -dae** (-dē). a large insect, the male of which produces a shrill sound.

ci·der (sī′dər), *n.* the juice pressed from apples, used for drinking or for making vinegar.

ci·gar (si gär′), *n.* a roll of cured tobacco wrapped in a tobacco leaf for smoking.

cig·a·rette (sig′ə ret′), *n.* a short roll of finely cut tobacco wrapped in paper for smoking.

cinch (sinch), *n.* **1.** a strong girth for securing a pack or saddle. **2.** *Informal.* something sure or easy. —*v.t.* **3.** to gird or bind firmly. **4.** *Informal.* to make sure of.

cin·der (sin′dər), *n.* **1.** a partially burned piece of coal, wood, etc. **2. cinders,** any residue of combustion; ashes.

cin·e·ma (sin′ə mə), *n., pl.* **-mas.** **1. the cinema,** motion pictures, as an art or industry. **2.** a motion-picture theater. —**cin′e·mat′ic** (-mat′ik), *adj.* —**cin′e·mat′i·cal·ly,** *adv.*

cin′e·ma·tog′ra·phy (-tog′rə fē), *n.* the art or technique of motion-picture photography. —**cin′e·ma·tog′ra·pher,** *n.* —**cin′e·mat′o·graph′ic** (-mat′ə graf′ik), *adj.*

cin·na·mon (sin′ə mən), *n.* the aromatic inner bark of an East Indian tree, used as a spice.

ci·pher (sī′fər), *n.* **1.** ZERO (def. 1). **2.** a nonentity. **3.** a secret method of writing, as by code. **4.** the key to a secret method of writing. —*v.i.* **5.** to use numerals arithmetically.

cir·ca (sûr′kə), *prep.* about: used before approximate dates.

cir·cle (sûr′kəl), *n., v.,* **-cled, -cling.** —*n.* **1.** a closed plane curve consisting of all points at a given distance from the center. **2.** the portion of a plane bounded by such a curve. **3.** any circular object, formation, etc.: *a circle of dancers.* **4.** a realm or sphere: *a circle of influence.* **5.** a series forming a connected whole; cycle. **6.** a number of persons bound by a common tie. —*v.t.* **7.** to enclose in a circle. **8.** to rotate or revolve around. —*v.i.* **9.** to move in a circle. —**cir′cler,** *n.*

cir′cuit (-kit), *n.* **1.** the act of moving around. **2.** a circular journey. **3.** a periodic journey from place to place, as by judges, ministers, etc. **4.** the line bounding any area or object. **5.** the complete path of an electric current, including the generating apparatus, etc. **6.** a chain of theaters, nightclubs, etc. —*v.t.* **7.** to make the circuit of. —*v.i.* **8.** to go in a circuit.

cir′cuit board′ *n.* a sheet of fiberglass or other material on which electronic components are installed.

cir′cuit break′er *n.* a device for interrupting an electric circuit to prevent excessive current.

cir·cu·i·tous (sər kyōō′i təs), *adj.* roundabout; not direct. —**cir·cu′i·tous·ly,** *adv.* —**cir·cu′i·tous·ness, cir·cu′i·ty,** *n.*

cir′cu·lar (-kyə lər), *adj.* **1.** having the form of a circle; round. **2.** moving in or forming a circle. **3.** circuitous; indirect. —*n.* **4.** a letter or advertisement for general circulation. —**cir′cu·lar′i·ty,** *n.*

cir′cu·late′ (-lāt′), *v.,* **-lat·ed, -lat·ing.** —*v.i.* **1.** to move in a circle or circuit. **2.** to pass from place to place, from person to person, etc. —*v.t.* **3.** to disseminate; distribute. —**cir′cu·la·to′ry** (-lə tôr′ē), *adj.*

cir′cu·la′tion *n.* **1.** an act or instance of circulating. **2.** the continuous movement of blood through the heart and blood vessels. **3.** the distribution of copies of a periodical among readers.

circum- a prefix meaning around or about (*circumnavigate*).

cir•cum•cise (sûr′kəm sīz′), *v.t.*, **-cised, -cis•ing.** to remove the foreskin of (a male), esp. as a religious rite. —**cir′cum•ci′sion** (-sizh′ən), *n.*

cir•cum•fer•ence (sər kum′fər əns), *n.* **1.** the outer boundary of a circular area. **2.** the length of such a boundary.

cir•cum•flex (sûr′kəm fleks′), *n.* a mark (ˆ or ˜) placed over a vowel to indicate length, nasalization, etc.

cir•cum•lo•cu′tion (-lō kyōō′shən), *n.* a roundabout or indirect way of speaking.

cir′cum•nav′i•gate′ *v.t.*, **-gat•ed, -gat•ing.** to sail or fly completely around. —**cir′cum•nav′i•ga′-tion,** *n.*

cir′cum•scribe′ (-skrīb′), *v.t.*, **-scribed, -scrib•ing. 1.** to draw or trace a line around; encircle. **2.** to enclose within bounds; restrict. —**cir′cum•scrip′tion** (-skrip′shən), *n.*

cir′cum•spect′ (-spekt′), *adj.* cautious; prudent. —**cir′cum•spec′tion,** *n.*

cir′cum•stance′ (-stans′), *n.* **1.** a condition or attribute that accompanies or determines a fact or event. **2.** Usu., **circumstances.** the existing conditions or state of affairs. **3. circumstances,** the condition of a person with respect to material welfare: *a family in reduced circumstances.* **4.** an incident or occurrence. **5.** ceremonious display: *pomp and circumstance.* —**Idiom. 6. under no circumstances,** never.

cir′cum•stan′tial (-stan′shəl), *adj.* **1.** of or derived from circumstances. **2.** incidental. **3.** detailed; particular. —**cir′cum•stan′tial•ly,** *adv.*

cir′cum•vent′ (-vent′), *v.t.* to avoid by artfulness; elude. —**cir′cum•ven′tion,** *n.*

cir•cus (sûr′kəs), *n., pl.* **-cus•es. 1.** an entertainment featuring performing animals, clowns, acrobats, etc. **2.** (in ancient Rome) an amphitheater for chariot races, public games, etc. **3.** a display of rowdy sport or wild activity.

cir•rho•sis (si rō′sis), *n.* a chronic disease of the liver in which fibrous tissue replaces normal tissue.

cir•rus (sir′əs), *n., pl.* **cir•ri** (sir′ī). a high-altitude cloud composed of ice crystals and characterized by thin white bands.

cis•tern (sis′tərn), *n.* a reservoir or tank for storing water.

cit•a•del (sit′ə dl, -ə del′), *n.* a fortress for defending a city.

cite (sīt), *v.t.*, **cit•ed, cit•ing. 1.** to quote (a book, author, etc.), esp. as an authority. **2.** to mention in support or proof. **3.** to summon to appear in court. **4.** to commend, as for outstanding service. —**ci•ta′-tion,** *n.*

cit•i•zen (sit′ə zən, -sən), *n.* a native or naturalized member of a state or nation who owes allegiance to its government and is entitled to its protection. —**cit′i•zen•ry,** *n., pl.* **-ries.** —**cit′i•zen•ship′,** *n.*

cit′ric ac′id (si′trik), *n.* a white powder occurring in citrus fruits, used chiefly in flavorings.

cit•ron (si′trən), *n.* **1.** a pale yellow fruit resembling the lemon but larger. **2.** the candied rind of this fruit.

cit•ron•el•la (si′trə nel′ə), *n.* **1.** a fragrant, S Asian grass. **2.** a pungent oil distilled from this grass, used in perfumes and insect repellents.

cit•rus (si′trəs), *n., pl.* **-rus•es,** *adj.* —*n.* **1.** any tree or shrub of the genus that includes the lemon, lime, orange, etc. **2.** the fruit of any of these trees or shrubs. —*adj.* **3.** Also, **cit′rous.** of such trees or shrubs.

cit•y (sit′ē), *n., pl.* **-ies. 1.** a large or important town. **2.** an incorporated municipality, usu. governed by a mayor and council. **3.** the inhabitants of a city collectively. [< AF, OF *cite(t)* < L *cīvitātem,* acc. of *cīvitās* citizenry]

civ•ic (siv′ik), *adj.* of a city, citizenship, or citizens.

civ′ics *n.* the study of civic affairs and the privileges and obligations of citizens.

civ•il (-əl), *adj.* **1.** of citizens. **2.** of the ordinary life of citizens, as distinguished from military and ecclesiastical life. **3.** civilized. **4.** polite. —**ci•vil′i•ty,** *n., pl.* **-ties.** —**civ′il•ly,** *adv.*

ci•vil•ian (si vil′yən), *n.* **1.** a person not on active duty with a military, police, or firefighting organization. —*adj.* **2.** of civilians.

civ•i•li•za•tion (siv′ə lə zā′shən), *n.* **1.** an advanced state of human society, in which a high level of culture, science, and government has been reached. **2.** those people or nations that have reached such a state. **3.** the type of culture of a specific place, time, or group.

civ′i•lize′ *v.t.*, **-lized, -liz•ing.** to bring out of a savage, uneducated state; enlighten or refine. —**civ′i•lized′,** *adj.*

civ′il lib′erty *n.* a fundamental right, as freedom of speech, guaranteed to an individual by the laws of a country.

civ′il rights′ *n.pl.* the rights to personal liberty and to legal, economic, and social equality, established by amendments to the U.S. Constitution and by certain Congressional acts.

civ′il serv′ant *n.* a civil-service employee.

civ′il serv′ice *n.* those branches of public service concerned with governmental administrative functions outside the armed services.

civ′il war′ *n.* **1.** a war between factions in the same country. **2.** (*caps.*) the war in the U.S. between the North and the South, 1861–65.

Cl *Chem. Symbol.* chlorine.

claim (klām), *v.t.* **1.** to demand as a right. **2.** to assert as a fact. **3.** to require as due or fitting. —*n.* **4.** a demand for something as due. **5.** an assertion of something as a fact. **6.** a right to claim or demand. **7.** something that is claimed. —**claim′ant, claim′er,** *n.*

clair•voy•ant (klâr voi′ənt), *adj.* seeing beyond physical vision. —**clair•voy′ant,** *n.* —**clair•voy′-ance,** *n.*

clam (klam), *n., v.,* **clammed, clam•ming.** —*n.* **1.** any of various usu. edible bivalve mollusks. —*v.i.* **2.** to dig for clams. **3. clam up,** *Informal.* to refuse to talk.

clam•ber (klam′bər, klam′ər), *v.t., v.i.* to climb with difficulty, using both feet and hands.

clam•my (klam′ē), *adj.* **-mi•er, -mi•est.** cold and damp. —**clam′mi•ness,** *n.*

clam•or (klam′ər), *n.* **1.** a loud uproar, as from a crowd of people. **2.** a vehement expression of desire or dissatisfaction. —*v.i.* **3.** to make a clamor. —**clam′or•ous,** *adj.*

clamp (klamp), *n.* **1.** a device for holding or fastening objects together. —*v.t.* **2.** to fasten with a clamp. **3. clamp down,** to impose more strict control.

clan (klan), *n.* **1.** a group of families, as among the Scottish Highlanders, whose heads claim descent from a common ancestor. **2.** a group of people of common descent. —**clan′nish,** *adj.* —**clan′nish•ness,** *n.*

clan•des•tine (klan des′tin), *adj.* stealthy or surreptitious. —**clan•des′tine•ly,** *adv.*

clang (klang), *v.i., v.t.* **1.** to make or cause to make a loud, resonant sound, as that produced by a large bell. —*n.* **2.** a clanging sound.

clank (klangk), *n.* **1.** a sharp, hard, nonresonant sound. —*v.i., v.t.* **2.** to make or cause to make such a sound.

clap (klap), *v.* **clapped, clap•ping,** *n.* —*v.t.* **1.** to strike (one's hands) together, as in applauding. **2.** to strike with a light slap, as in greeting. **3.** to strike with an abrupt, sharp sound. **4.** to put or place quickly or forcefully. —*v.i.* **5.** to applaud. **6.** to make an abrupt, sharp sound. —*n.* **7.** the act or sound of clapping. **8.** a resounding slap. **9.** a loud and explosive noise. —**clap′per,** *n.*

clap•board (klab′ərd, klap′bôrd′), *n.* **1.** a thin board, thicker along one edge than the other, used in covering the outer walls of buildings. —*v.t.* **2.** to cover with clapboards.

clap′trap′ *n.* pretentious and insincere language intended to win applause.

clar•et (klar′it), *n.* a dry red table wine.

clar·i·fy (klar′ə fī′), v.t., v.i. -fied, -fy·ing. to make or become clear or intelligible. —clar′i·fi·ca′tion, n.

clar·i·net (klar′ə net′), n. a single-reed woodwind instrument in the form of a cylindrical tube. —clar′i·net′ist, clar′i·net′tist, n.

clar′i·on (-ē ən), adj. clear and shrill: the trumpet's clarion call.

clar′i·ty (-i tē), n. the state or quality of being clear.

clash (klash), v.i. 1. to collide with a loud, harsh noise. 2. to conflict; disagree. —v.t. 3. to strike with a loud, harsh noise. —n. 4. a loud, harsh noise. 5. a conflict, esp. of views or interests. 6. a battle or fight.

clasp (klasp, kläsp), n. 1. a device for fastening things or parts together. 2. a firm grasp or grip. 3. a tight embrace. —v.t. 4. to fasten with a clasp. 5. to grasp with the hand. 6. to hold in a tight embrace.

class (klas, kläs), n. 1. a number of persons or things regarded as belonging together because of common attributes or traits. 2. a. a group of students studying together with a teacher. b. a meeting of such a group. 3. a group of students graduated in the same year. 4. a social stratum whose members share the same social position. 5. any division of persons or things according to rank or grade. 6. Informal. elegance, as in dress and behavior. 7. any of several grades of passenger accommodations. —v.t. 8. to classify. —class′less, adj.

class′ ac′tion n. a legal proceeding brought by one or more persons representing the interests of a larger group.

clas·sic (klas′ik), adj. 1. of the highest class or rank. 2. serving as a standard or model. 3. CLASSICAL (defs. 1, 2). 4. of enduring interest, quality, or style. 5. traditional or typical: a classic comedy routine. —n. 6. an author or a literary work of the first rank. 7. the classics, the literature of ancient Greece and Rome. 8. a typical or traditional event.

clas′si·cal adj. 1. of or characteristic of ancient Greece and Rome. 2. conforming to ancient Greek and Roman models in literature or art. 3. of or being music of the European tradition marked by sophistication of structural elements. 4. versed in the ancient classics: a classical scholar. 5. accepted as standard and authoritative: classical physics. —clas′si·cal·ly, adv. —clas′si·cism, n.

clas′si·fied′ (klas′ə fīd′) adj. limited to authorized persons.

clas·si·fy (klas′ə fī′), v.t., -fied, -fy·ing. 1. to arrange or organize in classes. 2. to limit the availability of (information, a document, etc.) to authorized persons. —clas′si·fi′a·ble, adj. —clas′si·fi·ca′tion, n.

class′y adj., -i·er, -i·est. Informal. stylish; elegant. —class′i·ness, n.

clat·ter (klat′ər), v.i., v.t. 1. to make or cause to make a loud, rattling sound. —n. 2. a clattering sound. 3. a noisy disturbance; din.

clause (klôz), n. 1. a syntactic construction containing a subject and predicate. 2. a distinct article or provision in a document. —claus′al, adj.

claus·tro·pho·bi·a (klô′strə fō′bē ə), n., pl. -as. an abnormal fear of being in enclosed or narrow places. —claus′tro·pho′bic, adj.

clav·i·chord (klav′i kôrd′), n. an early keyboard instrument whose strings are struck by metal blades.

clav·i·cle (klav′i kəl), n. either of two slender bones that connect the sternum and the shoulder blades.

claw (klô), n. 1. a sharp, curved nail on the foot of an animal. 2. a pincerlike appendage of a lobster, crab, etc. —v.t. 3. to tear, scratch, etc., with or as if with claws.

clay (klā), n. 1. a natural earthy material that is plastic when wet, used for making bricks, pottery, etc. 2. earth; mud. 3. the human body. —clay′ey, adj., clay·i·er, clay·i·est.

clean (klēn), adj. and adv., -er, -est, v. —adj. 1. free from dirt or stains. 2. free from foreign matter

or pollutants. 3. free from irregularity: a clean cut. 4. trim: the clean lines of a ship. 5. complete: a clean break with tradition. 6. morally pure. 7. fair: a clean fight. 8. made without difficulty or interference: a clean getaway. 9. habitually clean or neat. 10. empty; bare: a clean sheet of paper. —adv. 11. in a clean manner. 12. wholly; completely. —v.t., v.i. 13. to make or become clean. 14. clean up, a. to tidy up. b. to finish. c. to make a large profit. —Idiom. 15. come clean, Slang. to admit one's guilt. —clean′ness, n.

clean·ly (adj. klen′lē; adv. klēn′-), adj., -li·er, -li·est, adv. —adj. 1. habitually clean or neat. —adv. 2. in a clean manner. —clean′li·ness (klen′-), n.

cleanse (klenz), v.t., cleansed, cleans·ing. to clean or purify. —cleans′er, n.

clear (klēr), adj. and adv., -er, -est, v. —adj. 1. free from darkness or cloudiness. 2. transparent: clear water. 3. easily seen; sharply defined. 4. easily heard. 5. easily understood. 6. evident; plain. 7. free from confusion. 8. free from blame or guilt: a clear conscience. 9. free from obstructions. 10. free from entanglement or contact. 11. without limitation or qualification. 12. free from debt. 13. net: a clear profit of $1000. —adv. 14. in a clear manner. 15. entirely; completely. —v.t. 16. to remove (people or things) from (a place or surface): Please clear the table. 17. to make clear or transparent. 18. to make free of confusion or doubt. 19. to make understandable. 20. to make (a path) by removing obstructions. 21. to relieve (the throat) of phlegm. 22. to free from suspicion or accusation. 23. to pass by or over without contact or entanglement: The ship cleared the reef. 24. to pass (commercial paper) through a clearinghouse. 25. to gain as profit. 26. to receive authorization for. 27. to authorize. —v.i. 28. to become clear. 29. clear away, to leave. 30. ~ out, a. to remove the contents of. b. to go away, esp. quickly. 31. ~ up, to make clear; explain. —clear′ly, adv. —clear′ness, n.

clear′ance n. 1. the act of clearing. 2. the distance between two objects; an amount of clear space. 3. a formal authorization permitting access to classified material.

clear′-cut′ adj. 1. having clearly defined outlines. 2. completely evident; definite.

clear′ing n. a tract of land, as in a forest, that contains no trees or bushes.

cleat (klēt), n. a piece of wood, metal, etc., fastened to a surface to serve as a support or to give a foothold.

cleav·age (klē′vij), n. 1. the act of splitting or state of being cleft. 2. a split or division.

cleave¹ (klēv), v.i., cleaved, cleav·ing. 1. to adhere closely; cling (usu. fol. by to). 2. to remain faithful: to cleave to one's principles.

cleave² (klēv), v.t., v.i., cleft or cleaved or clove, cleft or cleaved or clo·ven, cleav·ing. to split or divide by or as if by a cutting blow.

cleav′er n. a heavy knife or long-bladed hatchet, esp. one used by butchers.

clef (klef), n. a sign at the beginning of a musical staff to show the pitch of the notes.

cleft (kleft), n. a space or opening made by cleavage; a split.

cleft′ lip′ n. a congenital defect in which there is a vertical fissure in the upper lip.

cleft′ pal′ate n. a congenital defect of the palate in which a longitudinal fissure exists in the roof of the mouth.

clem·a·tis (klem′ə tis, kli mat′is), n. a vine of the buttercup family having showy flowers.

clem·ent (klem′ənt), adj. 1. lenient; compassionate. 2. (of the weather) mild or temperate. —clem′en·cy, n., pl. -cies.

clench (klench), v.t. 1. to close (the hands, teeth, etc.) tightly. 2. to grasp firmly. —n. 3. a tight hold; grip.

cler·gy (klûr′jē), n., pl. -gies. the body of ordained persons in a religion.

cler·ic (kler′ik), n. a member of the clergy.

cler′i·cal adj. 1. of or pertaining to an office clerk. 2. of or characteristic of the clergy or a cleric.

clerk (klûrk), *n.* **1.** a person employed to perform general office tasks. **2.** a salesclerk. **3.** a person who keeps the records of a court, legislature, etc. —*v.i.* **4.** to serve as a clerk. —**clerk′ship,** *n.*

clev•er (klev′ər), *adj.,* **-er•er, -er•est. 1.** mentally bright. **2.** superficially skillful or witty; facile. **3.** ingenious. —**clev′er•ly,** *adv.* —**clev′er•ness,** *n.*

CLI or **cli,** cost-of-living index.

cli•ché (klē shā′, kli-), *n., pl.* **-chés.** a trite, stereotyped expression. —**cli•chéd′,** *adj.*

click (klik), *n.* **1.** a slight, sharp sound: *the click of a latch.* —*v.i.* **2.** to make a click or series of clicks. **3.** *Informal.* **a.** to succeed. **b.** to function well together. **4.** *Computers.* to depress and release a mouse button rapidly, as to select an icon. —*v.t.* **5.** to cause to click.

cli•ent (klī′ənt), *n.* **1.** a person who uses the professional services of a lawyer, accountant, etc. **2.** a person receiving the benefits or services of a social or government agency. **3.** a customer.

cli•en•tele′ (-ən tel′), *n.* a body of clients and customers.

cliff (klif), *n.* a high, steep rock face; precipice.

cliff′-hang′er or **cliff′hang′er,** *n.* **1.** a melodramatic adventure serial in which each installment ends in suspense. **2.** a suspenseful situation or contest.

cli•mate (klī′mit), *n.* **1.** the prevailing weather conditions of a region. **2.** a region characterized by a given climate. **3.** a prevailing attitude, atmosphere, or condition. —**cli•mat′ic** (-mat′ik), *adj.*

cli•max (klī′maks), *n.* **1.** the highest or most intense point in the development of something. **2.** a decisive moment in the plot of a dramatic or literary work. **3.** an orgasm. —*v.t., v.i.* **4.** to bring to or reach a climax. —**cli•mac′tic,** *adj.*

climb (klīm), *v.i.* **1.** to move upward or toward the top of something. **2.** to slope upward. **3.** to ascend by twining, as a plant. **4.** to move by using the hands and feet. —*v.t.* **5.** to ascend or get to the top of, esp. by the use of the hands and feet. —*n.* **6.** an act or instance of climbing. **7.** a place to be climbed. —**climb′a•ble,** *adj.* —**climb′er,** *n.*

clinch (klinch), *v.t.* **1.** to settle (a matter) decisively. **2.** to secure (a nail, screw, etc.) in position by beating down the protruding point. —*v.i.* **3.** to engage in a clinch in boxing. **4.** *Slang.* to embrace passionately. —*n.* **5.** the act of clinching. **6.** an act or instance of a boxer holding an opponent about the arms to prevent punching. **7.** *Slang.* a passionate embrace. —**clinch′er,** *n.*

cling (kling), *v.i.,* **clung, cling•ing. 1.** to adhere closely. **2.** to hold tight, as by embracing. **3.** to remain attached, as to an idea. —**cling′er,** *n.*

clin•ic (klin′ik), *n.* **1.** a place for the medical treatment of outpatients. **2.** a place where physicians, dentists, etc., practice together. **3.** a group convening for instruction or remedial work: *a reading clinic.* **4.** the instruction of medical students by treating patients in their presence. [≪ L *clīnicus* < Gk *klīnikós* pertaining to a sickbed] —**clin′i•cal,** *adj.* —**clin′i•cal•ly,** *adv.* —**cli•ni•cian** (kli nish′ən), *n.*

clink¹ (klingk), *v.i., v.t.* **1.** to make or cause to make a light, sharp, ringing sound. —*n.* **2.** a clinking sound.

clink² (klingk), *n. Slang.* a jail.

clink′er¹, *n.* **1.** a mass of incombustible matter fused together, as in the burning of coal. **2.** a hard Dutch brick.

clink′er², *n. Slang.* a mistake or error.

clip¹ (klip), *v.,* **clipped, clip•ping,** *n.* —*v.t.* **1.** to cut, cut off, or trim, as with shears. **2.** to cut the hair or fleece of; shear. **3.** to cut short. **4.** *Informal.* to hit with a quick, sharp blow. **5.** *Slang.* to swindle. —*v.i.* **6.** to clip something. **7.** to move swiftly. —*n.* **8.** the act of clipping. **9.** anything clipped off. **10.** *Informal.* a quick, sharp blow. **11.** rate; pace: *at a rapid clip.*

clip² (klip), *n., v.,* **clipped, clip•ping.** —*n.* **1.** a device that grips and holds tightly. —*v.t., v.i.* **2.** to fasten with or as if with a clip.

clip′per, *n.* **1.** Often, **-pers.** a cutting tool, esp.

shears. **2.** a swift sailing ship, esp. a three-masted one.

clique (klēk, klik), *n.* a small, exclusive group of people. —**cli′quish,** *adj.* —**cli′quish•ly,** *adv.* —**cli′quish•ness,** *n.*

clit•o•ris (klit′ər is), *n., pl.* **clit•o•ris•es, cli•to•ri•des** (kli tôr′i dēz′). the erectile organ of the vulva. —**clit′o•ral,** *adj.*

cloak (klōk), *n.* **1.** a loose outer garment, as a cape or coat. **2.** a disguise; pretense. —*v.t.* **3.** to cover with a cloak. **4.** to hide; conceal.

cloak′-and-dag′ger *adj.* pertaining to espionage or intrigue.

clob•ber (klob′ər), *v.t. Informal.* **1.** to batter severely. **2.** to defeat decisively.

clock¹ (klok), *n.* **1.** an instrument, normally larger than a watch, for measuring and recording time. —*v.t.* **2.** to time with a stopwatch.

clock² (klok), *n.* an embroidered or woven design on the side of a sock or stocking.

clock′wise′ *adv.* **1.** in the direction of the rotation of the hands of a clock. —*adj.* **2.** directed clockwise.

clock′work′ *n.* **1.** the mechanism of a clock. —*Idiom.* **2. like clockwork,** with perfect regularity.

clod (klod), *n.* **1.** a lump, esp. of earth or clay. **2.** a stupid person. —**clod′dish,** *adj.*

clog (klog, klôg), *v.,* **clogged, clog•ging,** *n.* —*v.t.* **1.** to hinder or obstruct. —*v.i.* **2.** to become clogged. —*n.* **3.** anything that impedes movement. **4.** a shoe with a thick sole of wood, cork, etc.

clois•ter (kloi′stər), *n.* **1.** a covered walk having an open arcade and opening onto a courtyard. **2.** a place of religious seclusion, as a monastery or convent. —*v.t.* **3.** to confine, as in a cloister.

clone (klōn), *n., v.,* **cloned, clon•ing.** —*n.* **1. a.** an organism that is genetically identical to the individual from which it was asexually derived. **b.** a group of such organisms. **2.** a person or thing that closely resembles another in appearance, function, etc. —*v.i., v.t.* **3.** to grow or cause to grow as a clone.

close (*v.,* n. klōz; *adj.,* adv. klōs), *v.,* **closed, clos•ing,** *adj.,* **clos•er, clos•est,** *adv., n.* —*v.t.* **1.** to block or bar an opening in or passage through; shut. **2.** to stop or obstruct (a gap, aperture, etc.). **3.** to bring together; join: *Close up ranks!* **4.** to bring to an end. —*v.i.* **5.** to become closed. **6.** to unite. **7.** to come to an end. **8.** to reach an agreement. **9. close down,** to terminate the operation of. **10. ~ in on,** to approach stealthily, as to capture. **11. ~ out, a.** to reduce the price of (merchandise) for quick sale. **b.** to liquidate. —*adj.* **12.** compact; dense. **13.** being in or having proximity in space or time. **14.** similar in degree, action, etc.: *Dark pink is close to red.* **15.** near in kind or relationship: *a close relative.* **16.** intimate; dear. **17.** left flush with the surface or very short. **18.** strict; minute: *close investigation.* **19.** not deviating from a model. **20.** nearly even or equal: *a close contest.* **21.** without opening. **22.** confined; narrow. **23.** stuffy. **24.** secretive; reticent. **25.** parsimonious; stingy. **26.** scarce, as money. —*adv.* **27.** in a close manner. **28.** near; close by. —*n.* **29.** the act of closing. **30.** the end or conclusion. —**close′ly** (klōs′-), *adv.* —**close′ness** (klōs′-), *n.*

close′ call′ (klōs), *n.* a narrow escape from danger.

closed′-cap′tioned *adj.* (of a television program) broadcast with captions visible only with the use of a decoding device.

closed′ shop′ *n.* a business establishment in which union membership is a condition of employment.

close′out′ (klōz′-), *n.* a sale on merchandise at greatly reduced prices.

clos•et (kloz′it), *n.* **1.** a small room or cabinet for storing clothing, utensils, etc. —*v.t.* **2.** to shut up in a private room for a conference, interview, etc.

close′up′ (klōs′-), *n.* **1.** a photograph taken at close range. **2.** an intimate view of anything.

clo•sure (klō′zhər), *n.* **1.** the act of closing or state

of being closed. **2.** a conclusion or end. **3.** something that closes. **4.** CLOTURE.
clot (klot), *n., v.,* **clot•ted, clot•ting.** —*n.* **1.** a semisolid mass, as of coagulated blood. —*v.i., v.t.* **2.** to form into clots.
cloth (klôth, kloth), *n., pl.* **cloths** (klôᵗʰz, kloᵗʰz, klôths, kloths), *adj.* —*n.* **1.** a fabric made by weaving, felting, or knitting and used for garments, upholstery, etc. **2.** a piece of such a fabric for a particular purpose: *an altar cloth.* **3. the cloth,** the clergy. —*adj.* **4.** made of cloth.
clothe (klōᵗʰ), *v.t.,* **clothed** or **clad, cloth•ing. 1.** to provide with clothing. **2.** to cover.
clothes (klōz, klōᵗʰz), *n.pl.* garments for the body.
clo•ture (klō′chər), *n.* a closing of legislative debate in order to bring the question to a vote.
cloud (kloud), *n.* **1.** a visible collection of particles of water or ice suspended in the air. **2.** any similar mass, esp. of smoke or dust. **3.** anything that causes gloom, trouble, etc. **4.** a great number of insects, birds, etc., flying together. —*v.t.* **5.** to cover with clouds. **6.** to make gloomy. **7.** to make obscure. **8.** to place under suspicion, disgrace, etc. —*v.i.* **9.** to grow cloudy. —*Idiom.* **10. have one's head in the clouds, a.** to be lost in reverie. **b.** to be impractical. **11. under a cloud,** in disgrace; under suspicion. —**cloud′less,** *adj.* —**cloud′y,** *adj.,* -i•er, -i•est.
clout (klout), *n.* **1.** a blow, esp. with the hand. **2.** *Informal.* the ability to influence decisions, esp. those made by public figures. —*v.t.* **3.** to hit or cuff.
clove[1] (klōv), *n.* the dried flower bud of a tropical tree, used whole or ground as a spice.
clove[2] (klōv), *n.* a small section of a bulb, as of garlic.
clo•ver (klō′vər), *n.* any of various plants with leaves of three leaflets and dense flower heads.
clown (kloun), *n.* **1.** a comic performer, esp. in a circus, who entertains by pantomime, tumbling, etc. **2.** a prankster. **3.** a boor or fool. —*v.i.* **4.** to act like a clown. [perh. akin to ON *klunni* boor] —**clown′ish,** *adj.* —**clown′ish•ly,** *adv.* —**clown′ish•ness,** *n.*
cloy (kloi), *v.t., v.i.* to weary by excess, as of sweetness.
club (klub), *n., v.,* **clubbed, club•bing.** —*n.* **1.** a heavy stick, suitable for use as a weapon. **2.** a stick used in various games, as golf. **3. a.** a group of people organized for a social, literary, or other purpose. **b.** its meeting place. **4.** any of a suit of playing cards bearing black trefoil-shaped figures. —*v.t., v.i.* **5.** to beat with or as if with a club. **6.** to unite; join together.
club′foot′ *n., pl.* -**feet.** a congenitally deformed foot. —**club′foot′ed,** *adj.*
club′ so′da *n.* SODA WATER.
cluck (kluk), *v.i.* **1.** to utter the cry of a hen brooding or calling her chicks. —*n.* **2.** a clucking sound.
clue (klōō), *n., v.,* **clued, clu•ing.** —*n.* **1.** a guide in the solution of a problem, mystery, etc. —*v.t.* **2.** to direct by a clue.
clump (klump), *n.* **1.** a cluster, esp. of trees or other plants. **2.** a lump or mass. **3.** a heavy, thumping step, sound, etc. —*v.i.* **4.** to walk heavily and clumsily. **5.** to gather or be gathered into clumps. —**clump′y,** *adj.*
clum•sy (klum′zē), *adj.,* -si•er, -si•est. **1.** awkward in movement or action. **2.** awkwardly done: *a clumsy apology.* —**clum′si•ly,** *adv.* —**clum′si•ness,** *n.*
clus•ter (klus′tər), *n.* **1.** a group of persons or things close together. —*v.t., v.i.* **2.** to gather into or form a cluster.
clutch (kluch), *v.t.* **1.** to seize or grasp with or as if with the hands or claws. —*v.i.* **2.** to try to seize or grasp. —*n.* **3.** power or control: *fell into the clutches of the enemy.* **4.** a tight grip. **5.** a mechanism for engaging or disengaging a shaft that drives a mechanism or is driven by another part. **6.** a critical moment.
clut•ter (klut′ər), *v.t.* **1.** to fill or litter with things in a disorderly manner. —*n.* **2.** a disorderly heap or assemblage; litter. **3.** echoes on a radar screen that do not come from the target.
Cm *Chem. Symbol.* curium.

cm or **cm.,** centimeter.
CO 1. Colorado. **2.** Commanding Officer.
Co *Chem. Symbol.* cobalt.
co- a prefix meaning: together (*cooperate*); joint or jointly (*coauthor*); equally (*coextensive*).
Co. or **co., 1.** Company. **2.** County.
c/o care of.
coach (kōch), *n.* **1.** a large, horse-drawn, four-wheeled carriage. **2.** a public motorbus. **3.** the least expensive class of airline accommodations. **4.** a person who trains an athlete or team. **5.** a private tutor. —*v.t.* **6.** to instruct as a coach. —*v.i.* **7.** to work as a coach.
co•ag•u•late (kō ag′yə lāt′), *v.i., v.t.,* -lat•ed, -lat•ing. to change from a fluid into a thickened mass. —**co•ag′u•lant** (-lənt), *n.* —**co•ag′u•la′tion,** *n.*
coal (kōl), *n.* **1.** a black combustible mineral used as a fuel. **2.** an ember. —*Idiom.* **3. rake** or **haul over the coals,** to reprimand severely.
co•a•lesce (kō′ə les′), *v.i.,* -lesced, -lesc•ing. to grow together or unite into one body. —**co′a•les′-cence,** *n.*
co′a•li′tion (-lish′ən), *n.* an alliance, esp. a temporary one between factions, parties, etc.
coarse (kôrs), *adj.,* **coars•er, coars•est. 1.** composed of relatively large parts or particles. **2.** lacking in fineness of texture, structure, etc. **3.** harsh; grating. **4.** lacking refinement; crude. —**coarse′ly,** *adv.* —**coars′en,** *v.t., v.i.* —**coarse′ness,** *n.*
coast (kōst), *n.* **1.** the land next to the sea. **2.** a slide down a hill, as on a sled. —*v.i.* **3.** to descend a hill on acquired momentum. **4.** to progress or move with little or no effort. —**coast′al,** *adj.*
coast′er *n.* **1.** one that coasts. **2.** a small dish or mat for placing under a glass.
Coast′ Guard′ *n.* a U.S. military service charged with enforcing maritime laws, saving lives and property at sea, etc.
coat (kōt), *n.* **1.** an outer garment covering at least the upper part of the body. **2.** a natural covering, as hair, fur, or bark. **3.** a layer of anything that covers a surface: *a coat of paint.* —*v.t.* **4.** to cover or provide with a coat.
coat′ing *n.* outer layer.
coat′ of arms′ *n.* a full display of the armorial insignia of a person, family, or corporation, usu. on a shield.
co•au•thor (kō ô′thər, kō′ô′-), *n.* **1.** one of two or more joint authors. —*v.t.* **2.** to be a coauthor of.
coax (kōks), *v.t., v.i.* to attempt to influence (a person) by gentle persuasion, flattery, etc. —**coax′er,** *n.* —**coax′ing•ly,** *adv.*
co•ax•i•al (kō ak′sē əl), *adj.* having a common axis or axes.
cob (kob), *n.* **1.** CORNCOB. **2.** a short-legged, thick-set horse.
co•balt (kō′bôlt), *n.* a hard, ductile element occurring in compounds that produce blue coloring substances. *Symbol:* Co; *at. wt.:* 58.933; *at. no.:* 27.
cob•ble (kob′əl), *v.t.,* -bled, -bling. **1.** to mend (shoes, boots, etc.). **2.** to put together clumsily. —**cob′bler,** *n.*
cob′ble•stone′ *n.* a naturally rounded stone formerly used in paving.
COBOL (kō′bôl), *n.* a high-level computer language for writing programs to process large files of data. [*co(mmon) b(usiness)-o(riented) l(anguage)*]
co•bra (kō′brə), *n., pl.* -bras. a venomous Old World snake able to flatten the neck into a hood.
cob′web′ *n.* **1.** a web spun by a spider. **2.** anything finespun, flimsy, or insubstantial.
co•caine (kō kān′, kō′kān), *n.* a white alkaloid obtained from the leaves of a South American shrub, used as a local anesthetic and illegally as a stimulant.
cock[1] (kok), *n.* **1.** a rooster or other male bird. **2.** a hand-operated valve or faucet. **3. a.** the hammer of a firearm. **b.** its position preparatory to firing. —*v.t.* **4.** to draw back the hammer of (a firearm).
cock[2] (kok), *v.t.* **1.** to turn up or to one side, often in a jaunty manner. —*n.* **2.** the act of turning up or to one side.

cock•ade (ko kād′), *n.* a rosette or the like, worn on the hat as an indication of rank.

cock•a•too (kok′ə tōō′, kok′ə tōō′), *n.*, *pl.* **-toos.** a crested parrot of the Australian region.

cock′eyed′ *adj.* **1.** cross-eyed. **2.** *Slang.* **a.** tilted to one side. **b.** foolish; absurd. **c.** drunk.

cock•le (kok′əl), *n.* **1.** a bivalve mollusk with heart-shaped valves. **—Idiom. 2. cockles of one's heart,** the place of one's deepest feelings.

cock•ney (kok′nē), *n.*, *pl.* **-neys.** (*sometimes cap.*) **1.** a native of the East End district of London, England. **2.** the dialect of this population.

cock′pit′ *n.* **1.** an enclosed space in an airplane containing the flying controls, instrument panel, and seats for the pilot and copilot. **2.** a pit or enclosed place for cockfights.

cock′roach′ *n.* an insect characterized by a flattened body, rapid movements, and nocturnal habits: a common household pest.

cock′tail′ *n.* **1.** a chilled, mixed drink of liquor and juice or other flavorings. **2.** an appetizer: *shrimp cocktail.*

cock′y *adj.*, **-i•er, -i•est.** saucy and arrogant; conceited. **—cock′i•ly,** *adv.* **—cock′i•ness,** *n.*

co•coa (kō′kō), *n.* **1.** a powder made from roasted cacao seeds. **2.** a beverage made by mixing cocoa powder with hot milk or water and sugar. **3.** yellowish or reddish brown.

co•co•nut (kō′kə nut′, -nət), *n.* the large, hardshelled seed of the coconut palm, containing a white edible meat and a milky liquid.

co•coon (kə kōōn′), *n.* the silky envelope spun by the larvae of many insects, as silkworms, serving as a covering while they are in the pupal stage.

cod (kod), *n.*, *pl.* **cods, cod.** a food fish of cool, N Atlantic waters.

C.O.D. or **c.o.d.,** cash, or collect, on delivery.

co•da (kō′də), *n.*, *pl.* **-das.** a concluding passage of a musical movement following the last formal section.

cod•dle (kod′l), *v.t.*, **-dled, -dling. 1.** to pamper. **2.** to cook (eggs, fruit, etc.) in water just below the boiling point.

code (kōd), *n.*, *v.*, **cod•ed, cod•ing. 1.** a system of signals for communication by telegraph. **2.** a system used for brevity or secrecy of written communication. **3.** a systematically arranged collection of existing laws. **4.** the symbolic arrangement of statements or instructions in a computer program or the set of instructions in such a program. **5.** any system of rules and regulations: *a code of behavior.* **—***v.t.* **6.** to put into code.

co•deine (kō′dēn), *n.* an alkaloid obtained from opium, used chiefly as an analgesic and cough suppressant.

codg•er (koj′ər), *n.* an eccentric man, esp. one who is old.

cod•i•cil (kod′ə səl), *n.* a supplement to a will, containing an addition, modification, etc.

cod•i•fy (kod′ə fī′, kō′də-), *v.t.*, **-fied, -fy•ing. 1.** to reduce (laws, rules, etc.) to a code. **2.** to make a systematic arrangement of. **—cod′i•fi•ca′tion,** *n.* **—cod′i•fi′er,** *n.*

co•ed (kō′ed′, -ed′), *adj.* **1.** serving both men and women; coeducational. **2.** of a coed. **—***n.* **3.** a female student in a coeducational institution.

co′ed•u•ca′tion *n.* the education of both sexes in the same classes. **—co′ed•u•ca′tion•al,** *adj.*

co•ef•fi•cient (kō′ə fish′ənt), *n.* **1.** a number or quantity multiplying another quantity, as *3* in the expression *3x.* **2.** *Physics.* a constant that is a measure of a property of a substance, body, or process: *coefficient of friction.*

co•erce (kō ûrs′), *v.t.*, **-erced, -erc•ing. 1.** to compel or bring about by force or intimidation. **2.** to dominate or control. **—co•er′cion** (-ûr′shən), *n.* **—co•er′cive** (-siv), *adj.*

co•ex•ist (kō′ig zist′), *v.i.* **1.** to exist simultaneously. **2.** (esp. of nations) to exist together peacefully. **—co′ex•ist′ence,** *n.* **—co′ex•ist′ent,** *adj.*

cof•fee (kô′fē, kof′ē), *n.* **1.** a beverage made from the roasted, ground seeds (**cof′fee beans′**) of certain coffee trees. **2.** the seeds themselves. **3.** a trop-

ical tree that yields coffee beans. **4.** medium to dark brown.

cof•fer (kô′fər, kof′ər), *n.* **1.** a box or chest, esp. one for valuables. **2. coffers,** a treasury, as of an organization.

cof•fin (kô′fin, kof′in), *n.* the box in which a corpse is buried.

cog (kog, kôg), *n.* **1.** a gear tooth. **2.** a person who plays a minor part in an organization.

co•gent (kō′jənt), *adj.* convincing; believable. **—co′gen•cy,** *n.* **—co′gent•ly,** *adv.*

cog•i•tate (koj′i tāt′), *v.i.*, *v.t.*, **-tat•ed, -tat•ing.** to think hard (about); ponder. **—cog′i•ta′tion,** *n.*

co•gnac (kōn′yak, kon′-, kôn′-), *n.* **1.** (*often cap.*) the brandy produced near the French town of Cognac. **2.** (loosely) any good brandy.

cog•nate (kog′nāt), *adj.* **1.** related by birth. **2.** descended from the same language or form. **3.** similar in nature. **—***n.* **4.** a cognate person or thing. **5.** a cognate word.

cog•ni′tion (-nish′ən), *n.* **1.** the act or process of knowing. **2.** something known or perceived.

cog′ni•zance *n.* **1.** awareness or realization. **2.** judicial notice as taken by a court in dealing with a cause. **—cog′ni•zant,** *adj.*

co•gno•scen•ti (kon′yə shen′tē, kog′nə-), *n.pl.*, *sing.* **-te** (-tā, -tē). those who have superior knowledge of a particular field, as in the arts.

co•hab•it (kō hab′it), *v.i.* to live together as husband and wife without being legally married. **—co•hab′it•ant,** *n.* **—co•hab′i•ta′tion,** *n.*

co•here (kō hēr′), *v.i.*, **-hered, -her•ing. 1.** to stick together. **2.** to be logically connected.

co•her′ent (-hēr′ənt, -her′-), *adj.* **1.** logically connected; consistent. **2.** cohering; sticking together. **—co•her′ence,** *n.* **—co•her′ent•ly,** *adv.*

co•he′sion (-hē′zhən), *n.* **1.** the act or state of cohering. **2.** the molecular force between particles within a body or substance that acts to unite them. **—co•he′sive** (-siv), *adj.* **—co•he′sive•ly,** *adv.* **—co•he′sive•ness,** *n.*

co•hort (kō′hôrt), *n.* **1.** a companion or associate. **2.** a group, esp. of warriors or soldiers.

coif•fure (kwä fyŏŏr′), *n.* a style of arranging the hair.

coil (koil), *v.t.*, *v.i.* **1.** to wind into rings one above or around the other. **—***n.* **2.** a series of spirals or rings into which something is wound: *a coil of rope.* **3.** a single such ring. **4.** an electrical conductor, as a copper wire, wound up in a spiral or other form.

coin (koin), *n.* **1.** a piece of metal issued by a government as money. **2.** a number of such pieces. **—***v.t.* **3.** to make (coins) by stamping metal. **4.** to create or invent (a word or phrase). **—coin′age** (koi′nij), *n.* **—coin′er,** *n.*

co•in•cide (kō′in sīd′), *v.i.*, **-cid•ed, -cid•ing. 1.** to occupy the same location or time period. **2.** to correspond exactly.

co•in′ci•dence (-si dəns), *n.* **1.** a striking occurrence by mere chance of two or more events at one time. **2.** the fact of coinciding. **—co•in′ci•den′tal** (-den′tl), *adj.* **—co•in′ci•den′tal•ly,** *adv.*

co•i•tus (kō′i təs), *n.* sexual intercourse, esp. between a man and a woman. **—co′i•tal,** *adj.*

coke¹ (kōk), *n.* the solid product obtained by destructive distillation of coal, used as a fuel.

coke² (kōk), *n.* *Slang.* cocaine.

col- var. of com- before *l.*

Col. 1. Colonel. **2.** Colorado.

co•la (kō′lə), *n.*, *pl.* **-las.** a carbonated soft drink containing an extract made from kola nuts.

COLA (kō′lə), *n.* an adjustment in wages or social-security payments to offset fluctuations in the cost of living. [*C(ost) O(f) L(iving) A(djustment)*]

col•an•der (kul′ən dər, kol′-), *n.* a container with a perforated bottom and sides, for draining foods.

cold (kōld), *adj.*, **-er, -est,** *n.*, *adv.* **—***adj.* **1.** having a low or lower than normal temperature. **2.** feeling a lack of warmth. **3.** lacking in passion, enthusiasm, etc. **4.** not affectionate or friendly. **5.** lacking sensual desire. **6.** unconscious, as from a blow. **7.** lifeless; dead. **—***n.* **8.** the absence of heat. **9.** cold weather. **10.** a respiratory viral infection characterized by sneezing, sore throat, etc. —*adv.* **11.** thoroughly: *He knew his speech cold.* **12.** without preparation. —*Idiom.* **13. catch cold,** to become infected with a cold. **14. (out) in the cold,** neglected. —**cold′ly,** *adv.* —**cold′ness,** *n.*

cold′-blood′ed *adj.* **1.** designating animals, as fishes and reptiles, whose blood temperature varies with that of the surrounding medium. **2.** without emotion or feeling.

cold′ cream′ *n.* a cosmetic for cleansing or soothing the skin.

cold′ feet′ *n. Informal.* a lack of confidence or courage.

cold′ shoul′der *n.* a deliberate show of indifference.

cold′ tur′key *Informal.* —*n.* **1.** abrupt and complete withdrawal from the use of a narcotic drug or nicotine. —*adv.* **2.** without preparation; impromptu.

cold′ war′ *n.* intense rivalry between nations just short of armed conflict.

cole·slaw (kōl′slô′), *n.* a salad of finely chopped raw cabbage. [< D *koolsla* = *kool* cabbage + *sla* salad]

col·ic (kol′ik), *n.* **1.** acute pain in the abdomen or bowels. **2.** a condition of unknown cause in young infants characterized by prolonged crying. —**col′-ick·y,** *adj.*

col·i·se·um (kol′i sē′əm), *n.* a large building for sporting events, exhibitions, etc.

co·li·tis (kə lī′tis, kō-), *n.* inflammation of the colon.

col·lab·o·rate (kə lab′ə rāt′), *v.i.,* **-rat·ed, -rat·ing. 1.** to work with another, as on a literary work. **2.** to cooperate with an enemy nation. —**col·lab′o·ra′tion,** *n.* —**col·lab′o·ra′tive,** *adj.* —**col·lab′o·ra′tor,** *n.*

col·lage (kə läzh′), *n.* a work of art made by pasting various materials on a surface.

col·lapse (kə laps′), *v.,* **-lapsed, -laps·ing,** *n.* —*v.i.* **1.** to fall or cave in. **2.** to fold up, as for storage. **3.** to break down; fail utterly. **4.** to fall unconscious, as from exhaustion. —*v.t.* **5.** to cause to collapse. —*n.* **6.** a falling in, down, or together. **7.** a breakdown. —**col·laps′i·ble,** *adj.*

col·lar (kol′ər), *n.* **1.** the part of a shirt, coat, etc., around the neck. **2.** anything worn around the neck. **3.** a band or a chain fastened around the neck of an animal as a means of restraint or identification. —*v.t.* **4.** to put a collar on. **5.** to seize or detain.

col′lar·bone′ *n.* CLAVICLE.

col·lat·er·al (kə lat′ər əl), *n.* **1.** security pledged for the payment of a loan. —*adj.* **2.** accompanying; auxiliary. **3.** additional: *collateral evidence.* **4.** secured by collateral. **5.** secondary or incidental. **6.** (of a relative) descended from the same stock, but in a different line. **7.** situated or running side by side; parallel.

col·league (kol′ēg), *n.* a fellow worker or fellow member of a profession.

col·lect (kə lekt′), *v.t.* **1.** to gather together. **2.** to gather as a hobby: *to collect stamps.* **3.** to demand and receive payment of. **4.** to regain control of (oneself). —*v.i.* **5.** to assemble or accumulate. —*adj., adv.* **6.** requiring payment by the recipient: *a collect phone call.* —**col·lect′i·ble, collect′a·ble,** *adj.* —**col·lec′tion,** *n.* —**col·lec′tor,** *n.*

col·lec′tive *adj.* **1.** formed by collection. **2.** combined: *collective assets.* **3.** characteristic of a group: *collective wishes.* —*n.* **4.** a collective body or organization, as a farm. —**col·lec′tive·ly,** *adv.*

collec′tive bar′gaining *n.* negotiation between a union and employer for determining wages, working conditions, etc.

col·lec′tiv·ism *n.* the socialist principle of state control of all means of production. —**col·lec′tiv·ist,** *n., adj.* —**col·lec′ti·vize′,** *v.t.,* **-vized, -viz·ing.** —**col·lec′ti·vi·za′tion,** *n.*

col·lege (kol′ij), *n.* **1.** a degree-granting institution of higher learning. **2.** a constituent unit of a university. **3.** an institution for specialized instruction: *a barber college.* **4.** an organized association of persons with certain powers and rights: *the electoral college.* —**col·le·giate** (kə lē′jit, -jē it), *adj.*

col·lide (kə līd′), *v.i.,* **-lid·ed, -lid·ing. 1.** to strike one another with forceful impact; crash. **2.** to clash; conflict. —**col·li′sion** (-lizh′ən), *n.*

col·lie (kol′ē), *n.* a large dog with a long, narrow head, raised orig. for herding sheep.

col·lier (kol′yər), *n.* **1.** a ship for carrying coal. **2.** a coal miner.

col·loid (kol′oid), *n.* a substance made up of minuscule particles dispersed in a continuous gaseous, liquid, or solid medium. —**col·loi·dal** (kə loid′l), *adj.*

col·lo·qui·al (kə lō′kwē əl), *adj.* characteristic of ordinary or familiar conversation or writing rather than formal speech or writing. —**col·lo′qui·al·ism,** *n.* —**col·lo′qui·al·ly,** *adv.*

col·lo·qui·um (-kwē əm), *n., pl.* **-qui·ums, -qui·a** (-kwē ə). a conference at which experts discuss a specific topic.

col·lo·quy (kol′ə kwē), *n., pl.* **-quies. 1.** a dialogue. **2.** a conference.

col·lu·sion (kə lōō′zhən), *n.* a conspiracy for fraudulent purposes. —**col·lude′** (-lōōd′), *v.i.,* **-lud·ed, -lud·ing.**

Colo. Colorado.

co·logne (kə lōn′), *n.* a mildly perfumed toilet water.

Co·lom·bi·a (kə lum′bē ə), *n.* a republic in NW South America. —**Co·lom′bi·an,** *adj., n.*

co·lon[1] (kō′lən), *n., pl.* **-lons.** a punctuation mark (:) used in a sentence to indicate that what follows is an explanation, summation, etc.

co·lon[2] (kō′lən), *n., pl.* **-lons, -la** (-lə). the part of the large intestine extending from the cecum, where the large intestine begins, to the rectum. —**co·lon·ic** (kō lon′ik, kə-), *adj.*

colo·nel (kûr′nl), *n.* a commissioned military officer ranking above lieutenant colonel. —**colo′nel·cy,** *n., pl.* **-cies.**

co·lo·ni·al (kə lō′nē əl), *adj.* **1.** of a colony or colonies. **2.** (*often cap.*) pertaining to the 13 British colonies that became the United States of America, or to their historical period. —*n.* **3.** an inhabitant of a colony. —**co·lo′ni·al·ly,** *adv.*

co·lo′ni·al·ism *n.* the policy by which a nation seeks to extend its authority over other territories. —**co·lo′ni·al·ist,** *n., adj.*

col·on·nade (kol′ə nād′), *n.* a series of columns usu. supporting one side of a roof. —**col′on·nad′ed,** *adj.*

col·o·ny (kol′ə nē), *n., pl.* **-nies. 1.** a group of people who form a settlement in a new land that is subject to the parent nation. **2.** the region so settled. **3.** any territory separated from but subject to a ruling power. **4.** a group of people with the same nationality, interests, etc., living in a particular locality: *a colony of artists.* **5.** a group of like organisms living or growing in close association. —**col′o·nist,** *n.* —**col′o·nize,** *v.t., v.i.,* **-nized, -niz·ing.**

col·or (kul′ər), *n.* **1.** the quality of an object or substance with respect to light reflected by it. **2.** the natural hue of the skin. **3.** a vivid or distinctive quality. **4.** a pigment; dye. **5. colors, a.** a badge, ribbon, or uniform worn to signify allegiance, membership, etc. **b.** attitude; personality: *showed his true colors.* **c.** a flag or ensign. **6.** outward appearance: *a lie with the color of truth.* —*v.t.* **7.** to give or apply color to. **8.** to cause to appear different from the reality. **9.** to give a special character to: *The author's feelings color his writing.* —*v.i.* **10.** to take on or change color. **11.** to flush; blush.

col·o·ra·tu·ra (kul′ər ə tŏŏr′ə, -tyŏŏr′ə, kol′-), *n., pl.* **-ras. 1.** runs, trills, and other florid decorations in vocal music. **2.** a soprano specializing in such music.

col′or-blind′ *adj.* **1.** unable to distinguish one or more chromatic colors. **2.** showing or characterized by freedom from racial bias. —**col′or blind′ness,** *n.*

col′ored *adj.* **1.** having color. **2.** *Often Offensive.* belonging to a race other than the white, esp. to the black race. **3.** influenced or biased.

col′or·ful *adj.* **1.** abounding in color. **2.** having vivid, striking elements. —**col′or•ful•ly,** *adv.* —**col′or•ful•ness,** *n.*

col′or•less *adj.* **1.** without color. **2.** drab; lackluster. —**col′or•less•ness,** *n.*

co•los•sal (kə los′əl), *adj.* gigantic; huge. —**co•los′sal•ly,** *adv.*

co•los′sus (-los′əs), *n., pl.* **-los•si** (-los′ī), **-los•sus•es. 1.** a gigantic statue. **2.** anything gigantic or very powerful.

colt (kōlt), *n.* a young male animal of the horse family. —**colt′ish,** *adj.*

col•umn (kol′əm), *n.* **1.** a decorative pillar with a capital and usu. a base. **2.** any columnlike object, mass, or formation: *a column of smoke.* **3.** a vertical row or list. **4.** a vertical arrangement on a page of horizontal lines of type. **5.** a feature article that appears regularly in a newspaper or magazine. **6.** a long, narrow file of troops. —**co•lum•nar** (kə lum′nər), *adj.*

col′um•nist (-əm nist, -ə mist), *n.* a person who writes a newspaper or magazine column.

com- a prefix meaning: with or together (*commingle*); completely (*commit*).

co•ma (kō′mə), *n., pl.* **-mas.** a state of prolonged unconsciousness from which it is impossible to rouse a person.

Co•man•che (kə man′chē, kō-), *n., pl.* **-che, -ches.** a member of an American Indian people of the S Great Plains, living today in Oklahoma.

com•a•tose (kom′ə tōs′, kō′mə-), *adj.* **1.** affected with or characterized by coma. **2.** lacking vitality or alertness.

comb (kōm), *n.* **1.** a toothed strip of plastic, metal, etc., used to untangle or arrange the hair. **2.** the fleshy outgrowth on the head of certain roosters. **3.** a honeycomb. **4.** a machine for separating long cotton or wool fibers from short ones. —*v.t.* **5.** to arrange (the hair) with a comb. **6.** to search everywhere in: *to comb the files.* **7.** to separate (textile fibers) with a comb.

com•bat (*v.* kəm bat′, kom′bat; *n.* kom′bat), *v.,* **-bat•ed, -bat•ing** or (*esp. Brit.*) **-bat•ted, -bat•ting,** *n.* —*v.t., v.i.* **1.** to fight (against). —*n.* **2.** active fighting with enemy forces. **3.** any struggle or controversy. —**com•bat•ant** (kəm bat′nt, kom′bə tənt), *n.* —**com•bat′ive,** *adj.*

com′bat fatigue′ *n.* a mental disorder characterized by anxiety, nightmares, etc., occurring among soldiers in active and usu. prolonged combat.

com•bi•na•tion (kom′bə nā′shən), *n.* **1.** the act of combining or state of being combined. **2.** something formed by combining. **3.** an alliance of persons, parties, etc. **4.** the series of numbers dialed to open a special lock without a key.

com•bine (*v.* kəm bīn′; *n.* kom′bīn), *v.,* **-bined, -bin•ing,** *n.* —*v.t., v.i.* **1.** to join into a close union or whole; unite. —*n.* **2.** a combination of persons or groups to further their interests, as a syndicate or cartel. **3.** a harvesting machine for cutting and threshing grain in the field. —**com•bin′er,** *n.*

com•bo (kom′bō), *n., pl.* **-bos.** *Informal.* **1.** a small jazz or dance band. **2.** a combination.

com•bus•ti•ble (kəm bus′tə bəl), *adj.* capable of catching fire and burning. —**com•bus′ti•bil′i•ty,** *n.*

com•bus′tion (-chən), *n.* **1.** the act or process of burning. **2.** rapid oxidation accompanied by heat and usu. light.

come (kum), *v.i.,* **came, come, com•ing. 1.** to move toward someone or something. **2.** to arrive: *The train is coming.* **3.** to move into view. **4.** to extend; reach: *The dress comes to her knees.* **5.** to occur; happen. **6.** to be available: *Toothpaste comes in a tube.* **7.** to issue; be derived. **8.** to result: *This comes of carelessness.* **9.** to enter into a specified state: *to come into popular use.* **10.** to do or manage. **11. come about,** to happen. **12. ~ across** or **upon,** to encounter, esp. by chance. **13. ~ along, a.** to accompany someone. **b.** to proceed. **c.** to appear. **14. ~ around** or **round, a.** to revive. **b.** to change one's mind or decision. **15. ~ by,** to obtain; acquire. **16. ~ down with,** to become afflicted with (an illness). **17. ~ into, a.** to acquire. **b.** to inherit. **18. ~ off, a.** to happen. **b.** to acquit oneself.

c. to be effective. **19. ~ out, a.** to be revealed or published. **b.** to make a debut. **c.** to end. **20. ~ through, a.** to endure successfully. **b.** to fulfill demands. **21. ~ to, a.** to recover consciousness. **b.** to total. **22. ~ up,** to be referred to. **23. ~ up with,** to produce; supply.

come′back′ *n.* **1.** a return to a former higher status, prosperity, etc. **2.** a clever retort.

co•me•di•an (kə mē′dē ən), *n.* **1.** a professional entertainer who amuses an audience, as by telling jokes. **2.** an actor in comedy.

co•me′di•enne′ (-en′), *n.* a woman who is a comic entertainer or actress.

com•e•dy (kom′i dē), *n., pl.* **-dies. 1.** a humorous play, movie, etc., with a cheerful ending. **2.** any comic incident or incidents. —**co•me•dic** (kə mē′dik), *adj.*

come′ly (kum′lē), *adj.,* **-li•er, -li•est.** attractive; good-looking. —**come′li•ness,** *n.*

com•er (kum′ər), *n.* a person or thing that is very promising.

com•et (kom′it), *n.* a celestial body, consisting of a central solid mass and a tail of dust and gas, that orbits the sun along a highly eccentric course.

com•fort (kum′fərt), *v.t.* **1.** to soothe or console. —*n.* **2.** consolation; solace. **3.** a person or thing that consoles. **4.** a state of ease and satisfaction of bodily wants.

com•fort•a•ble (kumf′tə bəl, kum′fər tə-), *adj.* **1.** affording physical comfort or ease. **2.** contented and at ease. **3.** adequate or sufficient. —**com′fort•a•ble•ness,** *n.* —**com′fort•a•bly,** *adv.*

com′fort•er *n.* **1.** one that comforts. **2.** a thick, quilted bedcover.

com•ic (kom′ik), *adj.* **1.** pertaining to comedy. **2.** humorous; funny. —*n.* **3.** a comedian. **4. comics,** comic strips. —**com′i•cal,** *adj.* —**com′i•cal•ly,** *adv.*

com′ic strip′ *n.* a sequence of drawings relating a comic incident, an adventure, etc., often serialized in daily newspapers.

com•ma (kom′ə), *n., pl.* **-mas.** a punctuation mark (,) used to indicate a division in a sentence.

com•mand (kə mand′, -mänd′), *v.t.* **1.** to direct with authority; order. **2.** to demand. **3.** to deserve and receive (respect, attention, etc.). **4.** to dominate by reason of location. **5.** to be master of. —*v.i.* **6.** to have authority. —*n.* **7.** the act of commanding or ordering. **8.** an order given by one in authority. **9.** the possession of controlling authority. **10.** expertise; mastery. **11.** a signal, as a keystroke, instructing a computer to perform a specific task.

com•man•dant (kom′ən dant′, -dänt′), *n.* a commanding officer.

com′man•deer′ (-dēr′), *v.t.* to seize (private property) for military or other public use.

com•mand•er (kə man′dər, -män′-), *n.* **1.** a person who commands. **2.** an officer in the U.S. Navy or Coast Guard ranking below a captain and above a lieutenant commander.

com•mand′ment *n.* **1.** a command or mandate. **2.** (*sometimes cap.*) *Bible.* any of the Ten Commandments.

com•man•do (kə man′dō, -män′-), *n., pl.* **-dos, -does. 1.** a member of a specially trained military unit used for surprise destructive raids. **2.** a member of an assault team trained to operate against terrorist attacks.

com•mem•o•rate (kə mem′ə rāt′), *v.t.,* **-rat•ed, -rat•ing. 1.** to serve as a memorial of. **2.** to honor the memory of by some observance. —**com•mem′o•ra′tion,** *n.* —**com•mem′o•ra′tive,** *adj.*

com•mence (kə mens′), *v.i., v.t.,* **-menced, -menc•ing.** to begin; start.

com•mence′ment *n.* **1.** a beginning. **2.** the ceremony of conferring degrees or diplomas at a school.

com•mend (kə mend′), *v.t.* **1.** to mention as worthy of confidence, attention, etc. **2.** to entrust. **3.** to cite with special praise. —**com•mend′a•ble,** *adj.* —**com•mend′a•bly,** *adv.* —**com•men•da•tion** (kom′ən dā′shən), *n.* —**com•mend′a•to′ry** (-men′də tôr′ē), *adj.*

com•men′su•rate (-it), *adj.* **1.** having the same

general

measure. 2. corresponding in amount, magnitude, or degree. —**com•men′su•rate•ly,** *adv.*

com•ment (kom′ent), *n.* **1.** a remark; observation. **2.** gossip; talk. **3.** a criticism or interpretation: *The play is a comment on modern society.* **4.** an annotation to a text. —*v.i., v.t.* **5.** to make a comment or comments (on).

com′men•tar′y (-ən ter′ē), *n., pl.* **-tar•ies. 1.** a series of comments. **2.** an explanatory essay or treatise. **3.** anything serving to illustrate or exemplify.

com′men•ta′tor (-tā′tər), *n.* a person who discusses news or other topics on television or radio.

com•merce (kom′ərs), *n.* an interchange of goods between different countries or between areas of the same country; trade.

com•mer•cial (kə mûr′shəl), *adj.* **1.** pertaining to commerce. **2.** produced, marketed, etc., for profit. —*n.* **3.** a paid advertisement on radio or television. —**com•mer′cial•ly,** *adv.*

com•mer′cial•ize′ *v.t.,* **-ized, -iz•ing.** to make commercial in character, methods, etc. —**com•mer′cial•i•za′tion,** *n.*

com•min•gle (kə ming′gəl), *v.t., v.i.,* **-gled, -gling.** to mix or mingle together.

com•mis•er•ate (kə miz′ə rāt′), *v.,* **-at•ed, -at•ing.** —*v.t.* **1.** to feel or express sorrow or sympathy for. —*v.i.* **2.** to sympathize (usu. fol. by *with*). —**com•mis′er•a′tion,** *n.* —**com•mis′er•a′tive,** *adj.*

com•mis•sar•y (kom′ə ser′ē), *n., pl.* **-sar•ies. 1.** a store selling food and supplies, esp. in a military post. **2.** a dining room or cafeteria, esp. in a motion-picture studio.

com•mis•sion (kə mish′ən), *n.* **1.** the act of committing. **2.** an authoritative order. **3.** authority granted for a particular action or function. **4.** a document conferring authority, esp. one issued to military officers. **5.** the rank of a military officer. **6.** a group of persons authoritatively charged with particular functions. **7.** a sum or percentage allowed to agents, sales representatives, etc., for their services. —*v.t.* **8.** to give a commission to. **9.** to authorize. **10.** to order (a ship) to active duty. —*Idiom.* **11. in** (or **out of**) **commission,** in (or not in) operating order.

com•mis′sion•er *n.* **1.** a member of a commission. **2.** a government official in charge of a department. **3.** an official chosen by an athletic association to exercise broad authority.

com•mit (kə mit′), *v.t.,* **-mit•ted, -mit•ting. 1.** to give in trust or charge. **2.** to bind or obligate, as by pledge. **3.** to do; perform; perpetrate. **4.** to consign, as to a mental institution. —**com•mit′ment,** *n.* —**com•mit′tal,** *n.*

com•mit•tee (kə mit′ē), *n.* a group of persons chosen to investigate or act on a matter. —**com•mit′tee•man,** *n., pl.* **-men.** —**com•mit′tee•wom′an,** *n., pl.* **-wom•en.**

com•mode (kə mōd′), *n.* **1.** a low, highly ornamented chest of drawers. **2.** a stand containing a chamber pot or washbasin. **3.** TOILET (def. 1).

com•mo•di•ous (kə mō′dē əs), *adj.* spacious; roomy.

com•mod•i•ty (kə mod′i tē), *n., pl.* **-ties. 1.** an article of trade or commerce. **2.** something of use, advantage, or value. **3.** any unprocessed good, as a grain or a precious metal.

com•mo•dore (kom′ə dôr′), *n.* (formerly) a commissioned officer in the U.S. Navy or Coast Guard ranking above a captain.

com•mon (kom′ən), *adj.,* **-er, -est,** *n.* —*adj.* **1.** belonging to or shared by all in question. **2.** belonging equally to an entire community, nation, or culture: *a common language.* **4.** widespread; general. **4.** usual; familiar. **5.** of mediocre or inferior quality. **6.** coarse; vulgar. **7.** noting a noun, as *woman* or *pen,* that is not the name of any particular person or thing. —*n.* **8.** Often, **commons.** land owned or used by the residents of a community. **9. commons,** the common people. **10. commons,** (*used with a sing. v.*) a large dining room at a college. —*Idiom.* **11. in common,** shared equally. —**com′mon•ly,** *adv.*

com′mon•er *n.* a person without a title of nobility.

com′mon law′ *n.* the system of law originating in England, based on custom or court decision rather than civil or ecclesiastical law.

com′mon•place′ *adj.* **1.** ordinary. **2.** dull or platitudinous. —*n.* **3.** a trite or uninteresting saying. **4.** anything common or ordinary.

com′mon sense′ *n.* sound practical judgment; normal native intelligence. —**com′mon•sense′,** *adj.*

com′mon•weal′ *n.* the common welfare; public good.

com′mon•wealth′ *n.* **1.** the people of a nation or state; the body politic. **2.** a republican or democratic state. **3.** (*cap.*) a federation of states: *the Commonwealth of Australia.*

com•mo•tion (kə mō′shən), *n.* **1.** tumultuous activity; agitation. **2.** disturbance or upheaval.

com•mu•nal (kə myōōn′l, kom′yə nl), *adj.* **1.** shared by everyone in a group. **2.** of, by, or belonging to a community. **3.** pertaining to a commune. —**com•mu′nal•ly,** *adv.*

com•mune¹ (kə myōōn′), *v.i.,* **-muned, -mun•ing.** to talk together intimately.

com•mune² (kom′yōōn), *n.* **1.** a small group of persons living together and sharing possessions, work, income, etc. **2.** the smallest administrative division in France, Italy, etc.

com•mu•ni•ca•ble (kə myōō′ni kə bəl), *adj.* capable of being communicated or transmitted: *a communicable disease.* —**com•mu′ni•ca•bil′i•ty,** *n.*

com•mu′ni•cate′ *v.,* **-cat•ed, -cat•ing.** —*v.t.* **1.** to make known. **2.** to give to another; transmit. —*v.i.* **3.** to give or interchange thoughts, information, etc. **4.** to be connected, as rooms. —**com•mu′ni•ca′tor,** *n.*

com•mu′ni•ca′tion *n.* **1.** the act of communicating. **2.** something communicated. **3. communications,** a means of sending messages, orders, etc., as telephone or telegraph. —**com•mu′ni•ca′tive,** *adj.*

com•mun•ion (kə myōōn′yən), *n.* **1.** (*often cap.*) HOLY COMMUNION. **2.** a religious denomination. **3.** interchange of thoughts or emotions.

com•mu•ni•qué (kə myōō′ni kā′), *n., pl.* **-qués.** an official bulletin.

com•mu•nism (kom′yə niz′əm), *n.* **1.** a system of social organization based on the holding of all property in common. **2.** (*often cap.*) a political doctrine based on Marxism, seeking the creation of a classless society. **3.** (*often cap.*) a system of social organization in which all economic and social activity is controlled by a totalitarian state. [< F < L commūnis common + -ism] —**com′mu•nist,** *n., adj.*

com•mu•ni•ty (kə myōō′ni tē), *n., pl.* **-ties. 1. a.** a group of people who reside in a specific locality and share government. **b.** such a locality. **2.** a group sharing common interests: *the business community.* **3.** joint possession or ownership. **4.** similar character; agreement: *community of interests.*

com•mute (kə myōōt′), *v.,* **-mut•ed, -mut•ing,** *n.* —*v.t.* **1.** to change (a prison sentence or other penalty) to a less severe form. **2.** to exchange for something else. —*v.i.* **3.** to travel regularly over some distance, as between a suburb and a city. —*n.* **4.** a trip made by commuting. —**com•mu•ta•tion** (kom′yə tā′shən), *n.* —**com•mut′er,** *n.*

Com•o•ros (kom′ə rōz′), *n.* a republic in the Indian Ocean comprising three islands.

com•pact¹ (*adj.* kəm pakt′, kom-, kom′pakt; *v.* kəm pakt′; *n.* kom′pakt), *adj.* **1.** joined or packed closely together. **2.** small in size. **3.** pithy; terse. —*v.t.* **4.** to join or pack closely together. **5.** to form by close union. —*n.* **6.** a small case containing a mirror and face powder. **7.** a small automobile. —**com•pact′ly,** *adv.* —**com•pact′ness,** *n.*

com•pact² (kom′pakt), *n.* a formal agreement between two or more parties, states, etc.

com′pact disc′ *n.* an optical disc on which music, data, or images are digitally recorded for playback.

com•pac•tor (kəm pak′tər, kom′pak-), *n.* an appliance that compresses trash into small bundles.

com•pan•ion (kəm pan′yən), *n.* **1.** a person who frequently associates with another. **2.** a person in an intimate relationship with another. **3.** a person employed to accompany, assist, or live with another. **4.** a mate or match for something. —**com•pan'ion•ship'**, *n.*

com•pa•ny (kum'pə nē), *n., pl.* **-nies. 1.** a group of people. **2.** a guest or guests. **3.** companionship. **4.** a number of persons united for joint action, esp. for business. **5.** a basic unit of troops. —*Idiom.* **6. keep company,** to associate with, as in courtship. **7. part company,** to cease association.

com•par•a•tive (kəm par'ə tiv), *adj.* **1.** pertaining to comparison. **2.** relative: *to live in comparative luxury.* **3.** designating the intermediate degree of comparison of adjectives and adverbs, as *smaller* and *more carefully.* —*n.* **4.** the comparative degree. —**com•par'a•tive•ly,** *adv.*

com•pare (kəm pâr'), *v.*, **-pared, -par•ing,** *n.* —*v.t.* **1.** to examine for similarities and differences. **2.** to liken. **3.** to form the degrees of comparison of (an adjective or adverb). —*v.i.* **4.** to be worthy of comparison. **5.** to make comparisons. —*n.* **6.** comparison: *a beauty beyond compare.* —**com•pa•ra•ble** (kom'pər ə bəl), *adj.* —**com•par'er,** *n.* —**com•par'i•son** (-par'ə sən), *n.*

com•part•ment (kəm pärt'mənt), *n.* **1.** a space that is partitioned off. **2.** a separate room, section, etc. —**com•part•men'tal** (-men'tl), *adj.* —**com•part•men'tal•ize',** *v.t.*, **-ized, -iz•ing.** —**com•part•men'tal•i•za'tion,** *n.*

com•pass (kum'pəs), *n.* **1.** an instrument for determining directions, as by a magnetized needle that points north. **2.** an instrument with two hinged, movable legs for drawing circles, measuring distances, etc. **3.** the enclosing limits of an area. **4.** extent; range. **5.** due or proper limits. —*v.t.* **6.** to go or move around. **7.** to surround; encircle. **8.** to attain or achieve. **9.** to contrive; plot.

com•pas•sion (kəm pash'ən), *n.* a feeling of sympathy for another's misfortune. —**com•pas'sion•ate** (-ə nit), *adj.* —**com•pas'sion•ate•ly,** *adv.*

com•pat•i•ble (kəm pat'ə bəl), *adj.* **1.** capable of existing together in harmony. **2. a.** (of software) able to run on a specified computer. **b.** (of hardware) able to work with a specified device. —**com•pat'i•bil'i•ty,** *n.* —**com•pat'i•bly,** *adv.*

com•pa•tri•ot (kəm pā'trē ət; *esp. Brit.* -pa'-), *n.* a fellow countryman or countrywoman.

com•pel (kəm pel'), *v.t.*, **-pelled, -pel•ling.** to force or secure by force.

com•pel'ling *adj.* **1.** forceful. **2.** demanding attention.

com•pen•di•ous (kəm pen'dē əs) *adj.* containing the substance of a subject in a concise form.

com•pen•di•um (kəm pen'dē əm), *n., pl.* **-di•ums, -di•a** (-dē ə) a summary or abridgment.

com•pen•sate (kom'pən sāt'), *v.*, **-sat•ed, -sat•ing.** —*v.t.* **1.** to recompense; pay. **2.** to counterbalance; offset. —*v.i.* **3.** to make amends. —**com'pen•sa'tion,** *n.* —**com•pen•sa•to•ry** (kəm pen'sə tôr'ē), *adj.*

com•pete (kəm pēt'), *v.i.*, **-pet•ed, -pet•ing.** to strive to outdo another; vie.

com'pe•tent *adj.* **1.** having suitable skill, experience, etc., for some purpose. **2.** adequate but not exceptional. **3.** legally qualified as to age, soundness of mind, etc. —**com'pe•tence,** *n.* —**com'pe•tent•ly,** *adv.*

com•pe•ti•tion (kom'pi tish'ən), *n.* **1.** the act of competing. **2.** a contest for some prize, honor, etc. —**com•pet•i•tor** (kəm pet'i tər), *n.* —**com•pet•i•tive** (kəm pet'i tiv), *adj.*

com•pile (kəm pīl'), *v.t.*, **-piled, -pil•ing. 1.** to put together (documents, data, etc.) in one book or work. **2.** to make of materials from various sources: *to compile an anthology of plays.* **3.** to gather together; amass. —**com•pi•la•tion** (kom'pə lā'shən), *n.* —**com•pil'er,** *n.*

com•pla•cen•cy (kəm plā'sən sē) also **-cence** (-səns), *n., pl.* **-cen•cies** also **-cenc•es.** a feeling of quiet pleasure or security, often while unaware of unpleasant possibilities. —**com•pla'cent,** *adj.* —**com•pla'cent•ly,** *adv.*

com•plain (kəm plān'), *v.i.* **1.** to express dissatis-

faction, pain, etc. **2.** to make a formal accusation. —**com•plain'ant,** *n.* —**com•plain'er,** *n.*

com•plaint' *n.* **1.** an expression of discontent, pain, etc. **2.** a cause of discontent, pain, etc. **3.** an ailment; malady. **4.** (in a civil action) a formal accusation.

com•plai•sant (kəm plā'sənt, -zənt), *adj.* inclined or disposed to please. —**com•plai'sance,** *n.* —**com•plai'sant•ly,** *adv.*

com•ple•ment (*n.* kom'plə mənt; *v.* -ment'), *n.* **1.** something that completes or perfects. **2.** the amount that completes anything: *a full complement of packers.* **3.** any word or words used to complete a grammatical construction, esp. in the predicate. **4.** the quantity by which an angle or an arc falls short of 90°. —*v.t.* **5.** to form a complement to. —**com'ple•men'ta•ry,** *adj.*

com•plete (kəm plēt'), *adj., v.*, **-plet•ed, -plet•ing.** —*adj.* **1.** whole; entire. **2.** finished; concluded. **3.** thorough; unqualified. —*v.t.* **4.** to make whole. **5.** to bring to an end. —**com•plete'ly,** *adv.* —**com•plete'ness,** —**com•ple'tion,** *n.*

com•plex (*adj.* kəm pleks', kom'pleks; *n.* kom'pleks), *adj.* **1.** composed of interconnected parts. **2.** complicated or involved. —*n.* **3.** an intricate assemblage of related parts, units, etc. **4.** a cluster of interrelated, emotion-charged ideas and impulses that influences behavior. —**com•plex'i•ty,** *n., pl.* **-ties.**

com•plex•ion (kəm plek'shən), *n.* **1.** the color, texture, etc., of the skin, esp. of the face. **2.** aspect; character.

com•pli•cate (kom'pli kāt'), *v.t.*, **-cat•ed, -cat•ing.** to make complex or difficult. —**com'pli•ca'tion,** *n.*

com•pli•cat•ed *adj.* **1.** composed of elaborately interconnected parts. **2.** difficult to analyze, understand, or explain.

com•plic•i•ty (kəm plis'i tē), *n., pl.* **-ties.** partnership or involvement in wrongdoing.

com•pli•ment (*n.* kom'plə mənt; *v.* -ment'), *n.* **1.** an expression of praise or admiration. **2.** a formal act of respect or regard. —*v.t.* **3.** to pay a compliment to.

com'pli•men'ta•ry *adj.* **1.** of, conveying, or expressing a compliment. **2.** given free as a gift or courtesy.

com•ply (kəm plī'), *v.i.*, **-plied, -ply•ing.** to act in accordance with requests, requirements, etc. —**com•pli'ance,** *n.* —**com•pli'ant,** *adj.*

com•po•nent (kəm pō'nənt, kom-), *n.* **1.** a constituent part; element. **2.** a part of a mechanical or electrical system. —*adj.* **3.** being or serving as an element in something larger.

com•port (kəm pôrt'), *v.t.* **1.** to bear or conduct (oneself); behave. —*v.i.* **2.** to be in agreement. —**com•port'ment,** *n.*

com•pose (kəm pōz'), *v.*, **-posed, -pos•ing.** —*v.t.* **1.** to make up; constitute. **2.** to make by combining things, parts, etc. **3.** to create (a musical or literary work). **4.** to calm; settle. **5.** to set (type). **6.** to set type for (an article, book, etc.). —*v.i.* **7.** to create a musical or literary work.

com•posed' *adj.* calm or tranquil.

com•pos'er *n.* writer, esp. of music.

com•pos•ite (kəm poz'it), *adj.* **1.** made up of separate elements. **2.** belonging to a family of plants, as the daisy, in which the florets are borne in a close head. —*n.* **3.** something composite. **4.** a composite plant. —**com•pos'ite•ly,** *adv.*

com•po•si•tion (kom'pə zish'ən), *n.* **1.** the combination of parts to form a whole. **2.** makeup; constitution. **3.** the act of composing. **4.** something composed, as a piece of music or a short essay.

com•post (kom'pōst), *n.* a mixture of decaying organic matter, used for fertilizing soil.

com•po•sure (kəm pō'zhər), *n.* a self-controlled manner; calmness.

com•pote (kom'pōt), *n.* **1.** fruit stewed in a syrup. **2.** a stemmed dish for nuts, candy, etc.

com•pound¹ (*adj.* kom'pound, kom pound'; *n.* kom'pound; *v.* kəm pound', kom'pound), *adj.* **1.** composed of two or more parts or ingredients. —*n.* **2.** something formed by combining parts, elements, etc. **3.** a substance composed of two or more elements whose chemical composition is constant. **4.** a word composed of two or more parts that are also words. —*v.t.* **5.** to combine. **6.** to make by combining parts, elements, etc. **7.** to add to, esp. so as to worsen. **8.** to agree, for a consideration, not to prosecute (a crime or felony). **9.** to pay (interest) on the accrued interest as well as the principal.

com•pound² (kom′pound), *n.* an enclosure containing residences or other buildings.

com•pre•hend (kom′pri hend′), *v.t.* **1.** to understand. **2.** to include; comprise. —**com′pre•hen′si•ble** (-hen′sə bəl), *adj.* —**com′pre•hen′si•bly**, *adv.* —**com′pre•hen′sion** (-shən), *n.*

com′pre•hen′sive (-hen′siv), *adj.* wide in scope or content. —**com′pre•hen′sive•ness**, *n.*

com•press (*v.* kəm pres′; *n.* kom′pres), *v.t.* **1.** to press together and force into less space. **2.** to condense or shorten. —*n.* **3.** a pad held on the body to supply moisture or medication. —**com•pres′sion**, *n.* —**com•pres′sor**, *n.*

com•prise (kəm prīz′), *v.t.*, **-prised, -pris•ing. 1.** to include or contain. **2.** to form or constitute.

com•pro•mise (kom′prə mīz′), *n.*, *v.*, **-mised, -mis•ing.** —*n.* **1.** a settlement of differences by mutual concessions. **2.** something intermediate between different things. —*v.t.* **3.** to settle by compromise. **4.** to make vulnerable to danger, scandal, etc. —*v.i.* **5.** to make a compromise.

comp•trol•ler (kən trō′lər), *n.* CONTROLLER (def. 1).

com•pul•sion (kəm pul′shən), *n.* **1.** the act of compelling or state of being compelled. **2.** a strong, irresistible impulse.

com•pul′sive *adj.* due to or acting on inner compulsion. —**com•pul′sive•ly**, *adv.* —**com•pul′sive• ness**, *n.*

com•pul′so•ry (-sə rē), *adj.* **1.** required; mandatory. **2.** compelling; constraining.

com•punc•tion (kəm pungk′shən), *n.* uneasiness arising from guilt.

com•pute (kəm pyo͞ot′), *v.*, **-put•ed, -put•ing.** —*v.t.* **1.** to determine by arithmetical calculation. —*v.i.* **2.** to reckon; calculate. **3.** to use a computer or calculator. —**com•pu•ta•tion** (kom′pyo͞o tā′shən), *n.*

com•put′er *n.* **1.** a programmable electronic device that performs prescribed operations on data at high speed. **2.** one that computes.

com•put′er•ize′ *v.t.*, **-ized, -iz•ing. 1.** to control, process, or store by means of a computer. **2.** to automate by computers: *to computerize a business.* —**com•put′er•i•za′tion**, *n.*

com•rade (kom′rad, -rid), *n.* **1.** a companion or friend. **2.** a fellow member of a fraternal group, political party, etc. —**com′rade•ship′**, *n.*

con¹ (kon), *adv.* **1.** against. —*n.* **2.** the argument or vote against something.

con² (kon), *adj.*, *v.*, **conned, con•ning.** —*adj.* **1.** involving abuse of confidence. —*v.t.* **2.** to swindle. **3.** to persuade by deception.

con³ (kon), *n. Informal.* a convict.

con- var. of COM-.

con•cave (kon kāv′, kon′kāv), *adj.* curved inward like the inside of a circle.

con•ceal (kən sēl′), *v.t.* **1.** to hide. **2.** to keep secret. —**con•ceal′er**, *n.* —**con•ceal′ment**, *n.*

con•cede (kən sēd′), *v.*, **-ced•ed, -ced•ing.** —*v.t.* **1.** to acknowledge as true, just, or proper. **2.** to grant as a right or privilege. —*v.i.* **3.** to make a concession.

con•ceit (kən sēt′), *n.* **1.** an excessively favorable opinion of one's own ability, importance, etc. **2.** a whim; fanciful notion. —**con•ceit′ed**, *adj.*

con•ceive (kən sēv′), *v.*, **-ceived, -ceiv•ing.** —*v.t.* **1.** to form (a notion, purpose, etc.). **2.** to imagine. **3.** to become pregnant with. —*v.i.* **4.** to form an idea; think. **5.** to become pregnant. —**con•ceiv′a• ble**, *adj.* —**con•ceiv′a•bly**, *adv.*

con•cen•trate (kon′sən trāt′), *v.*, **-trat•ed, -trat• ing**, *n.* —*v.t.* **1.** to direct toward one point; focus. **2.** to put or bring into a single place, group, etc. **3.** to make denser, stronger, or purer. —*v.i.* **4.** to bring all efforts, faculties, etc., to bear on one objective. —*n.* **5.** a concentrated product. —**con′cen•tra′tion**, *n.*

concentra′tion camp′ *n.* a guarded compound for the confinement of political prisoners, minorities, etc.

con•cen•tric (kən sen′trik), *adj.* (esp. of circles or spheres) having a common center. —**con•cen′tri• cal•ly**, *adv.*

con•cept (kon′sept), *n.* a general notion or idea. —**con•cep•tu•al** (kən sep′cho͞o əl), *adj.* —**con• cep′tu•al•ly**, *adv.*

con•cep•tion (kən sep′shən), *n.* **1.** the act of conceiving or state of being conceived. **2.** the formation of a zygote from the union of sperm and egg; fertilization. **3.** a concept. **4.** origination; beginning.

con•cep′tu•al•ize′ (-cho͞o ə līz′), *v.*, **-ized, -iz• ing.** —*v.t.* **1.** to form a concept of. —*v.i.* **2.** to think in concepts. —**con•cep′tu•al•i•za′tion**, *n.*

con•cern (kən sûrn′), *v.t.* **1.** to affect; involve. **2.** to relate to. **3.** to trouble; disturb. —*n.* **4.** something that relates to a person. **5.** a matter that engages one's attention or affects one's welfare. **6.** solicitude or anxiety. **7.** a commercial company.

con•cerned′ *adj.* **1.** interested or affected. **2.** troubled or anxious.

con•cern′ing *prep.* relating to; regarding; about.

con•cert (kon′sûrt, -sərt), *n.* **1.** a public performance of music. **2.** accord or harmony. —*Idiom.* **3. in concert**, jointly.

con•cert•ed (kən sûr′tid), *adj.* **1.** planned together. **2.** performed together or in cooperation. —**con•cert′ed•ly**, *adv.*

con•cer•ti•na (kon′sər tē′nə), *n.*, *pl.* **-nas.** a small musical instrument resembling an accordion.

con•cer•to (kən cher′tō), *n.*, *pl.* **-tos, -ti** (-tē). a musical composition for one or more principal instruments and orchestra.

con•ces•sion (kən sesh′ən), *n.* **1.** the act of conceding or yielding. **2.** the thing or point yielded. **3.** something conceded by a government or a controlling authority, as a grant of land or a franchise.

conch (kongk, konch), *n.*, *pl.* **conchs** (kongks), **con• ches** (kon′chiz). **1.** a marine gastropod mollusk with a spiral shell. **2.** the shell of a conch. [< L < Gk *kónchē* shell]

con•cil•i•ate (kən sil′ē āt′), *v.*, **-at•ed, -at•ing.** —*v.t.* **1.** win over; placate. **2.** to win or gain (goodwill, regard, or favor). —**con•cil′i•a′tion**, *n.* —**con• cil′i•a′tor**, *n.* —**con•cil′i•a•to′ry** (-ə tôr′ē), *adj.*

con•cise (kən sīs′), *adj.* expressing much in few words. —**con•cise′ly**, *adv.* —**con•cise′ness**, *n.*

con•clave (kon′klāv, kong′-), *n.* **1.** a private or secret meeting, esp. of cardinals to elect a pope. **2.** an assembly or gathering, esp. one with special authority.

con•clude (kən klo͞od′), *v.*, **-clud•ed, -clud•ing.** —*v.t.* **1.** to bring to an end. **2.** to bring to a settlement. **3.** to deduce; infer. **4.** to determine or resolve. —*v.i.* **5.** to come to an end. —**con•clu′sion**, *n.*

con•clu′sive (-siv), *adj.* serving to settle or decide a question; decisive. —**con•clu′sive•ly**, *adv.* —**con• clu′sive•ness**, *n.*

con•coct (kon kokt′, kən-), *v.t.* **1.** to prepare by combining ingredients. **2.** to devise; contrive. —**con•coc′tion**, *n.*

con•com•i•tant (kon kom′i tənt, kən-), *adj.* **1.** accompanying; concurrent. —*n.* **2.** a concomitant quality or thing. —**con•com′i•tant•ly**, *adv.*

con•cord (kon′kôrd, kong′-), *n.* **1.** agreement; harmony. **2.** peace; amity.

con•cord•ance (kon kôr′dns, kən-), *n.* **1.** concord; harmony. **2.** an alphabetical index of the words of a book, as of the Bible, with a reference to the passage in which each occurs.

con•cor•dat (kon kôr′dat), *n.* **1.** an official agreement. **2.** an agreement between the pope and a secular government regarding the regulation of church matters.

con•course (kon′kôrs, kong′-), *n.* **1.** an assemblage; gathering. **2.** a broad thoroughfare. **3.** a large open space for crowds, as in a railroad station.

con•crete (kon′krēt, kong′-, kon krēt′, kong′-),

adj., n., v., **-cret•ed, -cret•ing.** —*adj.* **1.** constituting an actual thing or instance; real; perceptible. **2.** particular as opposed to general. **3.** made of concrete. —*n.* **4.** a stonelike building material made by mixing cement with sand or gravel. —*v.t., v.i.* **5.** to treat with concrete. **6.** to make or become solid; harden. —**con•crete′ly,** *adv.* —**con•crete′ness,** *n.*

con•cu•bine (kong′kyə bīn′, kon′-), *n.* **1.** a woman who cohabits with a man to whom she is not married, esp. a woman regarded as subservient. **2.** (among polygamous peoples) a secondary wife, usu. of inferior rank.

con•cur (kən kûr′), *v.i.,* **-curred, -cur•ring. 1.** to agree. **2.** to work together. **3.** to occur at the same time. —**con•cur′rence,** *n.* —**con•cur′rent,** *adj.* —**con•cur′rent•ly,** *adv.*

con•cus•sion (kən kush′ən), *n.* **1.** an injury to the brain from a blow, fall, etc. **2.** a shock caused by the impact of a collision, blow, etc.

con•demn (kən dem′), *v.t.* **1.** to express strong disapproval of. **2.** to sentence to severe punishment. **3.** to pronounce guilty. **4.** to force into a specified, usu. unhappy state: *Lack of education condemned him to a life of poverty.* **5.** to pronounce to be unfit for use or service: *to condemn an old building.* **6.** to take over (land) for a public purpose. —**con′dem•na′tion,** *n.* —**con•dem•na•to•ry** (-nə tôr′ē), *adj.*

con•dense (kən dens′), *v.,* **-densed, -dens•ing.** —*v.t.* **1.** to make more dense or compact. **2.** to shorten; abridge. **3.** to reduce to another and denser form, as a vapor to a liquid. —*v.i.* **4.** to become condensed. —**con•den•sa•tion** (kon′den sā′shən, -dən-), *n.* —**con•den′ser,** *n.*

condensed′ milk′ *n.* whole milk reduced by evaporation to a thick consistency, with sugar added.

con•de•scend (kon′də send′), *v.i.* **1.** to behave as if one is descending from a superior position. **2.** to stoop or deign to do something: *He would not condescend to misrepresent the facts.* —**con′de•scend′-ing•ly,** *adv.* —**con′de•scen′sion** (-sen′shən), *n.*

con•di•ment (kon′də mənt), *n.* something used to flavor food, as ketchup, mustard, or a spice.

con•di•tion (kən dish′ən), *n.* **1.** a particular state or situation of a person or thing. **2.** state of health. **3.** social position. **4.** a modifying circumstance: *It can happen only under certain conditions.* **5.** a prerequisite. **6.** Usu., **conditions.** existing circumstances: *poor living conditions.* **7.** a bodily disorder. —*v.t.* **8.** to put in a fit state. **9.** to accustom. **10.** to impose a condition on. **11.** to make (something) a condition. —**con•di′tion•er,** *n.*

con•di′tion•al *adj.* **1.** imposing, containing, or depending on a condition. **2.** involving or expressing a condition, as the first clause in the sentence *If it rains, we won't go.* —**con•di′tion•al•ly,** *adv.*

con•dole (kən dōl′), *v.i.,* **-doled, -dol•ing.** to express sympathy with a person suffering sorrow, misfortune, or grief: *to condole with a friend whose father has died.* —**con•do′lence,** *n.*

con•dom (kon′dəm, kun′-), *n.* a thin rubber sheath worn over the penis during intercourse to prevent conception or infection.

con•do•min•i•um (kon′də min′ē əm), *n.* **1. a.** an apartment house or office building, the units of which are individually owned. **b.** a unit in such a building. **2. a.** joint sovereignty over a territory by several states. **b.** the territory itself.

con•done (kən dōn′), *v.t.,* **-doned, -don•ing.** to disregard (something illegal, objectionable, etc.). —**con•don′a•ble,** *adj.*

con•dor (kon′dər, -dôr), *n.* either of two New World vultures: the largest flying birds in the Western Hemisphere.

con•du•cive (kən dōō′siv, -dyōō′-) *adj.* tending (to).

con•duct (*n.* kon′dukt; *v.* kən dukt′), *n.* **1.** personal behavior; deportment. **2.** direction or management. —*v.t.* **3.** to behave (oneself). **4.** to manage or carry on. **5.** to direct, as an orchestra. **6.** to lead or guide. **7.** to serve as a medium for (heat, electricity,

etc.). —*v.i.* **8.** to act as conductor. —**con•duc′tion,** *n.* —**con•duc′tive,** *adj.* —**con′duc•tiv′i•ty,** *n.*

con•duc′tor *n.* **1.** the person in charge of a train. **2.** a person who directs an orchestra or chorus. **3.** a substance or device that conducts heat, electricity, etc.

con•duit (kon′dwit, -dōō it, -dyōō -), *n.* **1.** a channel for conveying fluids. **2.** a structure containing ducts for electrical conductors or cables.

cone (kōn), *n.* **1.** a solid with a circular base and a plane curve tapering uniformly to a vertex. **2.** anything shaped like a cone. **3.** the cone-shaped multiple fruit of the pine, fir, etc. **4.** one of the cone-shaped cells in the retina of the eye.

con•fec•tion (kən fek′shən), *n.* a sweet preparation, as a candy or preserve. —**con•fec′tion•er,** *n.* —**con•fec′tion•er′y,** *n., pl.* **-ies.**

con•fed•er•a•cy (kən fed′ər ə sē), *n., pl.* **-cies. 1.** an alliance. **2. the Confederacy,** the group of 11 Southern states that seceded from the U.S. in 1860-61.

con•fed•er•ate (*adj., n.* kən fed′ər it; *v.* -ə rāt′), *adj., n., v.,* **-at•ed, -at•ing.** —*adj.* **1.** united in an alliance. **2.** (*cap.*) of the Confederacy. —*n.* **3.** an ally. **4.** an accomplice. **5.** (*cap.*) a supporter of the Confederacy. —*v.t., v.i.* **6.** to unite in an alliance. —**con•fed′er•a′tion,** *n.*

con•fer (kən fûr′), *v.,* **-ferred, -fer•ring.** —*v.i.* **1.** to consult or discuss something together. —*v.t.* **2.** to bestow upon as a gift, honor, etc. —**con•fer′ral, con•fer′ment,** *n.*

con•fer•ence (kon′fər əns), *n.* **1.** a meeting for discussion. **2.** an association of athletic teams, schools, or churches.

con•fess (kən fes′), *v.t., v.i.* **1.** to acknowledge or reveal (a fault, crime, etc.). **2.** to declare (one's sins) to a priest. **3.** (of a priest) to hear the confession of (a person).

con•fes′sion (-fesh′ən), *n.* **1.** acknowledgment; admission. **2.** acknowledgment of sin to a priest to obtain absolution. **3.** something confessed. **4.** an organized religious group sharing the same beliefs.

con•fes′sion•al *adj.* **1.** characteristic of confession. —*n.* **2.** a place set apart for the hearing of confessions by a priest.

con•fes′sor *n.* **1.** a person who confesses. **2.** a priest authorized to hear confessions.

con•fet•ti (kən fet′ē), *n.* small bits of paper thrown at festive events.

con•fi•dant (kon′fi dant′, -dänt′) or **con′fi•dante′,** *n.* a person to whom secrets are confided.

con•fide (kən fīd′), *v.,* **-fid•ed, -fid•ing.** —*v.i.* **1.** to impart secrets trustfully. —*v.t.* **2.** to tell in assurance of secrecy. **3.** to entrust.

con•fi•dence (kon′fi dəns), *n.* **1.** full trust; reliance. **2.** self-confidence; self-reliance. **3.** certitude; assurance. **4.** a confidential communication. —**con′fi•dent,** *adj.* —**con′fi•dent•ly,** *adv.*

con′fi•den′tial (-den′shəl), *adj.* **1.** secret. **2.** indicating confidence or intimacy. **3.** entrusted with private affairs: *a confidential secretary.* —**con′fi•den′-ti•al′i•ty,** *n.* —**con′fi•den′tial•ly,** *adv.*

con•fig•u•ra•tion (kən fig′yə rā′shən), *n.* **1.** the arrangement of the parts of a thing. **2.** external form. **3. a.** a computer plus the equipment connected to it. **b.** the act of configuring a computer system.

con•fine (*v.* kən fīn′; *n.* kon′fīn), *v.,* **-fined, -fin•ing,** *n.* —*v.t.* **1.** to enclose or keep within bounds. **2.** to shut up, as in prison. —*n.* **3.** Usu., **-fines.** a boundary or bound.

con•fined′ *adj.* **1.** limited or restricted. **2.** kept from leaving a place by illness, imprisonment, etc. **3.** being in childbirth.

con•fine′ment *n.* **1.** the act of confining. **2.** the state of being confined.

con•firm (kən fûrm′), *v.t.* **1.** to establish the truth, accuracy, etc., of; verify. **2.** to sanction; ratify. **3.** to make firm. **4.** to administer the rite of confirmation to.

con•fir•ma•tion (kon′fər mā′shən), *n.* **1.** the act of confirming or state of being confirmed. **2.** something that confirms; corroboration. **3.** a ceremony of admission to full membership in a religious community.

con•firmed' *adj.* **1.** made certain as to truth, accuracy, etc. **2.** habitual; inveterate: *a confirmed bachelor.*

con•fis•cate (kon'fə skāt'), *v.t.,* **-cat•ed, -cat•ing. 1.** to seize, by way of penalty, for public use. **2.** to seize by or as if by authority. —**con'fis•ca'tion,** *n.* —**con'fis•ca'tor,** *n.*

con•fla•gra•tion (kon'flə grā'shən), *n.* a large and destructive fire.

con•flict (*v.* kən flikt'; *n.* kon'flikt), *v.,* **-flict•ed, -flict•ing,** *n.* —*v.i.* **1.** to clash; disagree. —*n.* **2.** a battle or struggle. **3.** antagonism or opposition. **4.** incompatibility or interference. **5.** a mental struggle.

con•flu•ence (kon'flŏō əns), *n.* **1.** a flowing together of streams, rivers, etc. **2.** their place of junction. **3.** a crowd or throng. —**con'flu•ent,** *adj.*

con•form (kən fôrm'), *v.i.* **1.** to act in accordance; comply. **2.** to act in accord with the prevailing standards, attitudes, etc., of a group. **3.** to be or become similar in form or character. —*v.t.* **4.** to make similar in form or character. **5.** to bring into agreement. —**con•form'er,** *n.* —**con•form'ism,** *n.* —**con•form'ist,** *n., adj.* —**con•form'i•ty,** *n., pl.* **-ties.**

con•found (kon found', kən-; *for 3 usu.* kon'found'), *v.t.* **1.** to perplex or amaze. **2.** to throw into confusion. **3.** to damn (used in mild oaths): *Confound it!* —**con•found'er,** *n.*

con•found'ed *adj.* **1.** bewildered. **2.** damned.

con•front (kən frunt'), *v.t.* **1.** to face in hostility. **2.** to present for acknowledgment, contradiction, etc. **3.** to stand or come in front of. —**con•fron•ta•tion** (kon'frən tā'shən), *n.* —**con'fron•ta'tion•al,** *adj.*

con•fuse (kən fyōōz'), *v.t.,* **-fused, -fus•ing. 1.** to perplex or bewilder. **2.** to make unclear or indistinct. **3.** to fail to distinguish between. —**con•fus'ed•ly,** *adv.* —**con•fus'ing•ly,** *adv.* —**con•fu'sion,** *n.*

con•fute' (-fyōōt'), *v.t.,* **-fut•ed, -fut•ing. 1.** to prove to be false, invalid, or defective; disprove. **2.** to prove (a person) to be wrong by argument or proof. —**con•fu•ta•tion** (kon'fyōō tā'shən), *n.*

Cong. 1. Congregational. **2.** Congress. **3.** Congressional.

con•geal (kən jēl'), *v.t., v.i.* **1.** to change from a fluid to a solid state, as by cooling. **2.** to coagulate. —**con•geal'ment,** *n.*

con•gen•ial (kən jēn'yəl), *adj.* **1.** agreeable or suitable in nature. **2.** suited in tastes, temperament, etc. —**con•ge'ni•al'i•ty** (-jē'nē al'i tē), *n.* —**con•gen'ial•ly,** *adv.*

con•gen•i•tal (kən jen'i tl), *adj.* present or existing at the time of birth: *a congenital abnormality.* —**con•gen'i•tal•ly,** *adv.*

con•gest (kən jest'), *v.t.* **1.** to fill to excess; overcrowd or overburden; clog. **2.** to cause an unnatural accumulation of blood or other fluid in (a body part or blood vessel): *The cold congested her sinuses.* —**con•ges'tion,** *n.* —**con•ges'tive,** *adj.*

con•glom•er•ate (*n., adj.* kən glom'ər it, kəng-; *v.* -ə rāt'), *n., adj., v.,* **-at•ed, -at•ing.** —*n.* **1.** anything composed of heterogeneous elements. **2.** a corporation consisting of a number of subsidiary companies in unrelated industries. **3.** a rock consisting of pebbles or the like cemented together. —*adj.* **4.** consisting of heterogeneous elements. **5.** clustered. **6.** of a corporate conglomerate. —*v.t., v.i.* **7.** to collect or cluster together. —**con•glom'er•a'tion,** *n.*

Con•go (kong'gō), *n.* **1. People's Republic of the,** a republic in central Africa, W of the Democratic Republic of the Congo. **2. Democratic Republic of the,** a republic in central Africa. —**Con'go•lese'** (-gə lēz', -lēs'), *adj., n., pl.* **-lese.**

con•grat•u•late (kən grach'ə lāt'), *v.t.,* **-lat•ed, -lat•ing. 1.** to express pleasure to (a person), as on a happy occasion. **2.** to feel satisfaction or pride in (oneself) for an accomplishment or good fortune: *She congratulated herself on her narrow escape.* —**con•grat'u•la'tion,** *n.* —**con•grat'u•la•to'ry** (-lə tôr'ē), *adj.*

con•gre•gate (kong'gri gāt'), *v.i., v.t.,* **-gat•ed, -gat•ing.** to come or bring together in a crowd; assemble. —**con'gre•gant** (-gənt), *n.*

con•gre•ga'tion (kong'gri gā'shən), *n.* **1.** an assembly of people for religious worship. **2.** an assemblage; gathering.

con•gre•ga'tion•al *adj.* **1.** of a congregation. **2.** (*cap.*) pertaining to a form of Protestant church government in which each local church is self-governing. —**con'gre•ga'tion•al•ism,** *n.* —**con'gre•ga'tion•al•ist,** *n.*

con•gress (kong'gris), *n.* **1.** (*cap.*) the legislature of the U.S., consisting of the Senate and the House of Representatives. **2.** the legislature of a nation. **3.** a formal meeting or conference. —**con•gres•sion•al** (kən gresh'ə nl, kong-), *adj.* —**con'gress•man,** *n., pl.* **-men** —**con'gress•per'son,** *n.* —**con'gress•wom'an,** *n. fem., pl.* **-wom•en.**

con•gru•ent (kong'grōō ənt, kən grōō'-), *adj.* **1.** agreeing or corresponding. **2.** (of geometric figures) coinciding at all points when superimposed. —**con'gru•ence,** *n.*

con•gru•i•ty (kən grōō'i tē, kon-), *n., pl.* **-ties. 1.** agreement; harmony. **2.** the quality of being geometrically congruent. —**con•gru•ous** (kong'grōō əs), *adj.*

con•ic (kon'ik) also **-i•cal,** *adj.* having the form of, resembling, or pertaining to a cone.

co•ni•fer (kō'nə fər, kon'ə-), *n.* an evergreen tree or shrub that bears both seeds and pollen on dry scales arranged as a cone. —**co•nif•er•ous** (kō nif'ər əs, kə-), *adj.*

con•jec•ture (kən jek'chər), *n., v.,* **-tured, -tur•ing.** —*n.* **1.** the formation of an opinion without sufficient evidence. **2.** an opinion so formed. —*v.t., v.i.* **3.** to conclude from insufficient evidence. —**con•jec'tur•al,** *adj.*

con•join (kən join'), *v.t., v.i.* to join together. —**con•join'er,** *n.* —**con•joint'** (-joint'), *adj.* —**con•joint'ly,** *adv.*

con•ju•gal (kon'jə gəl), *adj.* of marriage or the relation of husband and wife. —**con'ju•gal•ly,** *adv.*

con•ju•gate (*v.* kon'jə gāt'; *adj.* kon'jə git, -gāt'), *v.,* **-gat•ed, -gat•ing,** *adj.* —*v.t.* **1.** to give the inflected forms of (a verb) in a fixed order. **2.** to join together, esp. in marriage. —*adj.* **3.** joined together, esp. in a pair. **4.** (of words) having a common derivation. —**con'ju•ga'tion,** *n.*

con•junc'tion *n.* **1.** a word functioning as connector between words, phrases, clauses, or sentences, as *but* and *unless.* **2.** union; association. **3.** a combination of events or circumstances. —**con•junc'tive,** *adj.*

con•junc•ti•vi•tis (kən jungk'tə vī'tis), *n.* inflammation of the mucous membrane that covers the exposed portion of the eyeball and the inner surface of the eyelid.

con•jure (kon'jər, kun'-), *v.,* **-jured, -jur•ing.** —*v.t.* **1.** to summon by or as if by invocation or spell. **2.** to produce by or as if by magic. **3.** to bring to mind. —*v.i.* **4.** to summon a devil or spirit by invocation or spell. **5.** to practice magic. —**con'jur•a'tion,** *n.* —**con'jur•er, con'ju•ror,** *n.*

conk¹ (kongk, kôngk), *Slang.* —*v.t.* **1.** to strike on the head. —*n.* **2.** a blow on the head.

conk² (kongk, kôngk), *v. Slang.* **conk out, 1.** to break down, as an engine. **2.** to go to sleep.

Conn. Connecticut.

con•nect (kə nekt'), *v.t., v.i.* **1.** to join or link together. **2.** to associate mentally. —**con•nec'tor, con•nect'er,** *n.* —**con•nec'tive,** *adj.*

con•nec'tion *n.* **1.** a connecting or being connected. **2.** anything that connects. **3.** association; relationship. **4.** Usu. **-tions.** influential or powerful associates. **5.** a transfer by a passenger from one conveyance to another. **6.** a relative, esp. by marriage.

con•nive (kə nīv'), *v.i.,* **-nived, -niv•ing. 1.** to cooperate secretly; conspire. **2.** to aid wrongdoing by forbearing to act or speak. [< L *co(n)nīvēre* to wink, turn a blind eye to] —**con•niv'ance,** *n.* —**con•niv'er,** *n.*

con•nois•seur (kon'ə sûr', -soor'), *n.* **1.** an expert judge in an art or in matters of taste. **2.** a discerning judge of the best in any field.

con•note (kə nōt′), *v.t.*, **-not•ed, -not•ing. 1.** to suggest (certain meanings, ideas, etc.) in addition to the explicit meaning. **2.** to involve as an accompaniment: *Injury connotes pain.* —**con•no•ta•tion** (kon′ə tā′shən), *n.* —**con•no•ta•tive** (kon′ə tā′tiv, kə nō′tə-), *adj.*

con•nu•bi•al (kə nōō′bē əl, -nyōō′-), *adj.* of marriage; conjugal.

con•quer (kong′kər), *v.t.* **1.** to win in war. **2.** to overcome by force. **3.** to win by effort, personal appeal, etc. **4.** to surmount. —*v.i.* **5.** to be victorious. —**con′quer•or,** *n.*

con•quest (kon′kwest, kong′-), *n.* **1.** the act of conquering. **2.** the winning of favor or affection. **3.** anything acquired by conquering.

con•quis•ta•dor (kong kwis′tə dôr′, -kēs′-), *n.*, *pl.* **-quis•ta•dors, -quis•ta•do•res** (-kēs′tə dôr′ēz, -āz). one of the 16th-century Spanish conquerors of the Americas.

con•science (kon′shəns), *n.* the sense of what is right or wrong in one's conduct or motives. —**con′science•less,** *adj.*

con•sci•en•tious (kon′shē en′shəs), *adj.* **1.** meticulous; careful. **2.** governed by or done according to conscience. —**con′sci•en′tious•ly,** *adv.* —**con′sci•en′tious•ness,** *n.*

conscien′tious objec′tor *n.* a person who refuses to serve in the armed forces for moral or religious reasons.

con•scious (kon′shəs), *adj.* **1.** aware of one's own existence, sensations, etc. **2.** having the mental faculties fully active. **3.** known to oneself. **4.** intentional: *a conscious effort.* —**con′scious•ly,** *adv.* —**con′scious•ness,** *n.*

con•script (*v.* kən skript′; *n.* kon′skript), *v.t.* **1.** to draft for military service. —*n.* **2.** a drafted recruit. —**con•scrip′tion,** *n.*

con•se•crate (kon′si krāt′), *v.t.*, **-crat•ed, -crat•ing. 1.** to make sacred. **2.** to dedicate to some purpose. **3.** to ordain to a sacred office. —**con′se•cra′tion,** *n.*

con•sec•u•tive (kən sek′yə tiv), *adj.* following in uninterrupted order; successive. —**con•sec′u•tive•ly,** *adv.*

con•sen•sus (kən sen′səs), *n.*, *pl.* **-sus•es. 1.** solidarity of opinion. **2.** general agreement or harmony.

con•sent (kən sent′), *v.i.* **1.** to agree to or comply with what is done or proposed by another. —*n.* **2.** agreement; compliance.

con•se•quence (kon′si kwens′, -kwəns), *n.* **1.** the result of an earlier occurrence. **2.** importance or significance.

con′se•quent′ *adj.* following as an effect or result. —**con′se•quent•ly,** *adv.*

con′se•quen′tial (-kwen′shəl), *adj.* **1.** consequent. **2.** important.

con•ser•va•tion (kon′sər vā′shən), *n.* **1.** the act of conserving. **2.** the preservation and protection of natural resources. —**con′ser•va′tion•ism,** *n.* —**con′ser•va′tion•ist,** *n.*

con•serv•a•tive (kən sûr′və tiv), *adj.* **1.** disposed to preserve existing conditions, institutions, etc., and to limit change. **2.** cautiously moderate. **3.** traditional in style or manner. —*n.* **4.** a conservative person. —**con•serv′a•tism,** *n.* —**con•serv′a•tive•ly,** *adv.*

con•serv′a•to•ry (-tôr′ē), *n.*, *pl.* **-ries. 1.** a school of music. **2.** a greenhouse.

con•serve (*v.* kən sûrv′; *n.* kon′sûrv, kən sûrv′), *v.*, **-served, -serv•ing,** *n.* —*v.t.* **1.** to prevent injury, decay, waste, or loss of. **2.** to preserve (fruit). —*n.* **3.** a jam made from a mixture of fruits.

con•sid•er (kən sid′ər), *v.t.* **1.** to think carefully about. **2.** to think, believe, or suppose. **3.** to bear in mind. **4.** to show consideration for.

con•sid′er•a•ble *adj.* **1.** large or great. **2.** worthy of consideration; important. —**con•sid′er•a•bly,** *adv.*

con•sid′er•ate (-it), *adj.* showing kindly regard for the feelings of others. —**con•sid′er•ate•ly,** *adv.*

con•sid′er•a′tion (-ə rā′shən), *n.* **1.** careful thought or attention. **2.** something kept in mind in making a decision. **3.** thoughtful or sympathetic regard. **4.** a recompense or payment. —*Idiom.* **5. take into consideration,** to take into account.

con•sid′er•ing *prep.* **1.** in view of. —*conj.* **2.** taking into consideration that.

con•sign (kən sīn′), *v.t.* **1.** to hand over or deliver. **2.** to entrust. **3.** to relegate. **4.** to ship (goods), esp. for sale. —**con•sign•ee′,** *n.*, *pl.* **-ees.** —**con•sign′or, con•sign′er,** *n.* —**con•sign′ment,** *n.*

con•sist (kən sist′), *v.i.* **1.** to be made up or composed: *Bread consists largely of flour.* **2.** to be inherent; exist or lie: *Our strength consists in unity.*

con•sist′en•cy (-sis′tən sē), *n.*, *pl.* **-cies. 1.** degree of density or firmness. **2.** steadfast adherence to the same principles, course, etc. **3.** agreement among parts. —**con•sist′ent,** *adj.* —**con•sist′ent•ly,** *adv.*

con•sole¹ (kən sōl′), *v.t.*, **-soled, -sol•ing.** to give solace or comfort to. —**con•so•la•tion** (kon′sə lā′shən), *n.* —**con•sol′ing•ly,** *adv.*

con•sole² (kon′sōl), *n.* **1.** a television, phonograph, or radio cabinet that stands on the floor. **2.** a desklike structure containing the keyboards, pedals, etc., of an organ. **3.** the control unit of a computer or of a mechanical, electrical, or electronic system. **4.** a storage tray between automobile bucket seats.

con•sol•i•date (kən sol′i dāt′), *v.t.*, *v.i.*, **-dat•ed, -dat•ing. 1.** to unite or combine into a single whole. **2.** to make or become firm or secure. —**con•sol′i•da′tion,** *n.* —**con•sol′i•da′tor,** *n.*

con•som•mé (kon′sə mā′, kon′sə mā′), *n.*, *pl.* **-més.** a clear soup made from rich stock.

con′so•nant *n.* **1.** a speech sound produced by obstructing the flow of air from the lungs. **2.** a letter representing such a sound. —*adj.* **3.** in accord: *behavior consonant with his character.* —**con′so•nan′tal** (-nan′tl), *adj.* —**con′so•nant•ly,** *adv.*

con•sort (*n.* kon′sôrt, *v.* kən sôrt′), *n.* **1.** a spouse, esp. of a reigning monarch. —*v.i., v.t.* **2.** to associate.

con•sor′ti•um (kən sôr′shē əm, -tē-), *n.*, *pl.* **-ti•a** (-shē ə, -tē ə). a combination, as of corporations, for carrying out a business venture.

con•spic•u•ous (kən spik′yōō əs), *adj.* **1.** easily seen or noticed. **2.** attracting special attention. —**con•spic′u•ous•ly,** *adv.* —**con•spic′u•ous•ness,** *n.*

con•spire (kən spī°r′), *v.i.*, **-spired, -spir•ing. 1.** to agree together, esp. secretly, to do something wrong, evil, or illegal. **2.** to act or work together toward the same goal. —**con•spir′a•cy** (-spir′ə sē), *n.*, *pl.* **-cies.** —**con•spir′a•tor** (-spir′ə tər), *n.* —**con•spir′a•to′ri•al** (-tôr′ē əl, -tōr′-), *adj.*

con•sta•ble (kon′stə bəl), *n.* **1.** a small-town peace officer. **2.** *Chiefly Brit.* a police officer.

con•stab•u•lar•y (kən stab′yə ler′ē), *n.*, *pl.* **-lar•ies. 1.** the body of constables of a district. **2.** a body of peace officers organized on a military basis.

con•stant (kon′stənt), *adj.* **1.** not changing; invariable. **2.** continuing without pause. **3.** regularly recurrent. **4.** steadfast; faithful. —*n.* **5.** something that does not change or vary. —**con′stan•cy,** *n.* —**con′stant•ly,** *adv.*

con•stel•la•tion (kon′stə lā′shən), *n.* **1.** any of various groups of stars that have been named. **2.** a group of related ideas, qualities, etc.

con•ster•na•tion (kon′stər nā′shən), *n.* a sudden, alarming amazement or dread.

con•sti•pate (kon′stə pāt′), *v.t.*, **-pat•ed, -pat•ing.** to cause difficult evacuation of the bowels. —**con•sti•pa′tion,** *n.*

con•stit′u•ent (-ənt), *adj.* **1.** serving to make up a thing; component. **2.** having power to frame or alter a political constitution. —*n.* **3.** a component. **4.** a voter in an electoral district. —**con•stit′u•en•cy,** *n.*, *pl.* **-cies.**

con•sti•tute (kon′sti tōōt′, -tyōōt′), *v.t.*, **-tut•ed, -tut•ing. 1.** to compose; form. **2.** to appoint. **3.** to establish, as a law. **4.** to give legal form to.

con′sti•tu′tion *n.* **1.** makeup; composition. **2.** the physical character of the body: *a strong constitution.* **3. a.** the system of fundamental principles according to which a nation, corporation, etc., is governed. **b.** the document embodying these principles. —con′sti•tu′tion•al, *adj.* —con′sti•tu′tion•al•ly, *adv.* —con′sti•tu′tion•al′i•ty (-shə nal′i tē, -tyo̅o̅′-), *n., pl.* **-ties.**

con•strain (kən strān′), *v.t.* **1.** to compel. **2.** to confine. **3.** to repress or restrain. —con•strained′, *adj.* —con•straint′, *n.*

con•strict (kən strikt′), *v.t.* to make narrow, as by squeezing. —con•stric′tion, *n.* —con•stric′tive, *adj.*

con•struct (*v.* kən strukt′; *n.* kon′strukt), *v.t.* **1.** to build by putting together parts. —*n.* **2.** something constructed. —con•struc′tion, *n.* —con•struc′tor, *n.*

con•struc′tive (-tiv), *adj.* **1.** helping to improve. **2.** pertaining to construction. —con•struc′tive•ly, *adv.*

con•strue (kən stro̅o̅′), *v.t.,* **-strued, -stru•ing. 1.** to explain or interpret. **2.** to analyze the grammatical structure of, esp. combined with translating.

con•sul (kon′səl), *n.* **1.** an official appointed by a government to look after its commercial interests and the welfare of its citizens in another country. **2.** either of the two chief magistrates of the ancient Roman republic. —con′su•lar, *adj.*

con•sult (kən sult′), *v.t.* **1.** to seek guidance or information from. **2.** to have regard for in making plans; consider. —*v.i.* **3.** to take counsel; confer: *to consult with a doctor.* —con•sult′ant, *n.* —con•sul•ta•tion (kon′səl tā′shən), *n.*

con•sume (kən so̅o̅m′), *v.t.,* **-sumed, -sum•ing. 1.** to expend by use; use up. **2.** to eat or drink up; devour. **3.** to destroy, as by burning. **4.** to spend (money, time, etc.) wastefully. **5.** to absorb; engross: *consumed with curiosity.* —con•sum′a•ble, *adj.*

con•sum′er *n.* **1.** a person or thing that consumes. **2.** a person who uses a commodity or service.

con•sum′er•ism *n.* a movement for the protection of the consumer against defective products, misleading advertising, etc.

con•sum•mate (*v.* kon′sə māt′; *adj.* kan sum′it, kon′sə mit), *v.,* **-mat•ed, -mat•ing,** *adj.* —*v.t.* **1.** to bring to completion or fulfillment. **2.** to complete (a marriage) by sexual intercourse. —*adj.* **3.** perfect; superb. —con•sum′mate•ly, *adv.* —con′sum•ma′tion, *n.*

con•sump•tion (kən sump′shən), *n.* **1.** the act of consuming. **2.** the amount consumed. **3.** the using up of goods and services. **4.** progressive wasting of the body, esp. from tuberculosis. —con•sump′tive, *adj.*

cont. continued.

con•tact (kon′takt), *n.* **1.** a touching or meeting. **2.** immediate proximity or association. **3.** the state of being in communication. **4.** a person through whom one can gain information, favors, etc. **5.** CONTACT LENS. —*v.t.* **6.** to put into contact. **7.** to communicate with. —*v.i.* **8.** to enter into contact.

con′tact lens′ *n.* a small plastic disk placed over the cornea to correct vision defects.

con•ta•gion (kən tā′jən), *n.* **1.** the communication of disease by contact. **2.** a disease so communicated. **3.** the transmission of an idea, emotion, etc. —contagious, *adj.*

con•ta′gious *adj.* **1.** transmitted by contact, as a disease. **2.** carrying a contagious disease. **3.** spreading from person to person: *contagious fear.* —con•ta′gious•ly, *adv.*

con•tain (kən tān′), *v.t.* **1.** to hold within its volume or area. **2.** to have capacity for. **3.** to prevent or limit the advance, spread, or influence of. —con•tain′er, *n.* —con•tain′ment, *n.*

con•tam•i•nate (kən tam′ə nāt′), *v.t.,* **-nat•ed, -nat•ing.** to pollute; taint. —con•tam′i•nant (-nənt), *n.* —con•tam′i•na′tion, *n.*

contd. continued.

con•tem•plate (kon′təm plāt′, -tem-), *v.,* **-plat•ed, -plat•ing.** —*v.t.* **1.** to observe thoughtfully. **2.** to consider thoroughly. **3.** to intend. —*v.i.* **4.** to consider deliberately. —con′tem•pla′tion, *n.* —con′tem•pla′tive, *adj.*

con•tem′po•rar′y (-rer′ē) *adj., n., pl.* **-ies.**

—*adj.* **1.** existing, occurring, or living at the same time. **2.** of the present time. **3.** of about the same age or date. —*n.* **4.** a person or thing belonging to the same time period as another. **5.** a person of the same age as another.

con•tempt (kən tempt′), *n.* **1.** a feeling of disdain for anything considered mean or worthless. **2.** the state of being despised. **3.** open disrespect for the rules of a court or legislative body. —con•tempt′i•ble, *adj.* —con•temp′tu•ous, *adj.*

con•tend (kən tend′), *v.i.* **1.** to struggle; compete. **2.** to dispute; argue. —*v.t.* **3.** to assert earnestly. —con•tend′er, *n.*

con•tent¹ (kon′tent), *n.* **1.** Usu., **-tents. a.** something that is contained. **b.** the subjects covered in a book, document, etc. **2.** significance or meaning. **3.** the amount contained.

con•tent² (kən tent′), *adj.* satisfied with what one has. —*v.t.* **2.** to make content. —*n.* **3.** satisfaction; contentment. —con•tent′ed, *adj.* —con•tent′ly, *adv.*

con•ten′tion (-shən), *n.* **1.** strife; conflict. **2.** dispute; controversy. **3.** a point contended for in controversy. —con•ten′tious, *adj.*

con•test (*n.* kon′test; *v.* kən test′), *n.* **1.** a competition, as for a prize. **2.** a struggle. **3.** a dispute. —*v.t.* **4.** to fight for, as in battle. **5.** to dispute; challenge. —con•test′a•ble, *adj.* —con•test•ant (kən tes′tant), *n.*

con•text (kon′tekst), *n.* **1.** the parts before and after a statement that can influence its meaning. **2.** the circumstances that surround a particular event, situation, etc. —con•tex•tu•al (kən teks′cho̅o̅ əl), *adj.*

con•tig•u•ous (kən tig′yo̅o̅ əs), *adj.* **1.** touching; in contact. **2.** near. —con•ti•gu•i•ty (kon′ti gyo̅o̅′i-tē), *n.*

con′ti•nent *n.* **1.** one of the seven main landmasses of the globe. **2. the Continent,** the mainland of Europe, as distinguished from the British Isles. —*adj.* **3.** characterized by self-restraint, esp. in sexual activity. **4.** able to control urinary and fecal discharge. —con′ti•nen′tal, *adj.*

con•tin•gen•cy (kən tin′jən sē), *n., pl.* **-cies. 1.** dependence on chance. **2.** a chance event.

con•tin′gent *adj.* **1.** dependent on something not yet certain. **2.** possible. **3.** fortuitous; accidental. —*n.* **4.** a quota of troops. **5.** one of the groups composing an assemblage.

con•tin•u•al (kən tin′yo̅o̅ əl), *adj.* **1.** often repeated; very frequent. **2.** continuous in time. —con•tin′u•al•ly, *adv.*

con•tin′ue *v.,* **-ued, -u•ing.** —*v.i.* **1.** to go on without interruption. **2.** to resume. **3.** to last or endure. **4.** to remain in a particular state, capacity, or place. —*v.t.* **5.** to go on with. **6.** to carry on from the point of interruption. **7.** to extend; prolong. **8.** to retain, as in a position. **9.** to postpone, as a legal proceeding.

con•ti•nu•i•ty (kon′tn o̅o̅′i tē, -tn yo̅o̅′-), *n., pl.* **-ties. 1.** the state of being continuous. **2.** a continuous whole. **3.** a motion-picture scenario.

con•tin•u•ous (kən tin′yo̅o̅ əs), *adj.* uninterrupted; going on without stop. —con•tin′u•ous•ly, *adv.*

con•tin′u•um (-yo̅o̅ əm), *n., pl.* **-u•a** (-yo̅o̅ ə). a continuous extent, series, or whole.

con•tort (kən tôrt′), *v.t., v.i.* to twist or become twisted out of shape. —con•tort′ed, *adj.* —con•tor′tion, *n.*

con•tor′tion•ist *n.* a person who performs gymnastic feats involving contorted postures.

con•tour (kon′to̅o̅r), *n.* **1.** the outline of a figure or body. —*v.t.* **2.** to shape to fit a certain form. —*adj.* **3.** shaped to fit a particular form.

contra- a prefix meaning against, opposite, or opposing (*contradict*).

con•tra•band (kon′trə band′), *n.* **1.** anything prohibited by law from being imported or exported. **2.** goods imported or exported illegally.

con′tra•cep′tion (-sep′shən), *n.* the deliberate prevention of conception or impregnation. —con′-tra•cep′tive, *adj., n.*

con•tract (*n., v. 6, 8* kon′trakt; *v.* kən trakt′), *n.* **1.** an agreement, esp. one enforceable by law. —*v.t.* **2.** to draw the parts of together: *to contract a muscle.* **3.** to shorten (a word, phrase, etc.) by omitting some elements. **4.** to get, as by exposure to contagion. **5.** to incur, as a debt. **6.** to assign (a job, project, etc.) by contract. —*v.i.* **7.** to become smaller; shrink. **8.** to enter into a contract. —**con•trac′-tu•al,** *adj.*

con•trac′tion (-shən), *n.* **1.** the act of contracting or state of being contracted. **2.** a shortened form of a word or phrase, as *isn't* for *is not*. **3.** the shortening of a muscle, esp. of a uterine muscle during childbirth.

con•trac•tor (kon′trak tər, kən trak′tər), *n.* one who contracts to furnish supplies or perform work, esp. in construction.

con•tra•dict (kon′trə dikt′), *v.t.* **1.** to assert the contrary of. **2.** to imply a denial of: *His lifestyle contradicts his principles.* —*v.i.* **3.** to utter a contrary statement. —**con′tra•dic′tion,** *n.* —**con′tra•dic′to-ry** (-dik′tə rē), *adj.*

con•tral•to (kən tral′tō), *n., pl.* **-tos. 1.** the lowest female voice, intermediate between soprano and tenor. **2.** a singer with such a voice.

con•trap′tion (kən trap′shən), *n.* a contrivance; gadget.

con•trar•y (kon′trer ē; *for 3 also* kən trâr′ē), *adj., n., pl.* **-trar•ies,** *adv.* —*adj.* **1.** opposite in character, direction, etc. **2.** unfavorable or adverse. **3.** stubbornly opposed or willful. —*n.* **4.** something that is opposite. —*adv.* **5.** oppositely; counter. —*Idiom.* **6. on the contrary,** in opposition to what has been stated. **7. to the contrary,** to the opposite effect. —**con′trar•i•ly** (kon′trer ə lē, kən trâr′-), *adv.* —**con′trar•i•ness,** *n.* —**con′trar•i•wise′,** *adv.*

con•trast (*v.* kən trast′, kon′trast; *n.* kon′trast), *v.t.* **1.** to compare in order to show differences. —*v.i.* **2.** to exhibit unlikeness on comparison. —*n.* **3.** the act of contrasting or state of being contrasted. **4.** a striking exhibition of unlikeness. **5.** a person or thing that is strikingly unlike in comparison.

con′tra•vene′ (-vēn′), *v.t.,* **-vened, -ven•ing. 1.** to deny or oppose. **2.** to go or act against; violate. —**con′tra•ven′tion** (-ven′shən), *n.*

con•trib•ute (kən trib′yo͞ot), *v.t., v.i.,* **-ut•ed, -ut•ing. 1.** to give (money, assistance, etc.) together with others. **2.** to furnish (an article, drawing, etc.) for publication. —*Idiom.* **3. contribute to,** to be a factor in. —**con•tri•bu•tion** (kon′trə byo͞o′shən), *n.* —**con•trib′u•tor,** *n.* —**con•trib′u•to′ry** (-tôr′ē), *adj.*

con•trite (kən trīt′), *adj.* caused by or showing sincere remorse. —**con•trite′ly,** *adv.* —**con•trite′-ness,** *n.* —**con•tri′tion** (-trish′ən), *n.*

con•trive (kən trīv′), *v.t.,* **-trived, -triv•ing. 1.** to plan with ingenuity. **2.** to bring about by a scheme. —**con•triv′ance,** *n.* —**con•triv′er,** *n.*

con•trol (kən trōl′), *v.,* **-trolled, -trol•ling,** *n.* —*v.t.* **1.** to exercise restraint or direction over. **2.** to hold in check. **3.** to test (a scientific experiment) by a standard of comparison. —*n.* **4.** the act or power of controlling. **5.** a check or restraint. **6.** a device for operating a machine. —**con•trol′la•ble,** *adj.*

con•trol′ler *n.* **1.** a government or corporate officer who superintends finances. **2.** a person or device that regulates.

con•tro•ver•sy (kon′trə vûr′sē), *n., pl.* **-sies. 1.** a usu. prolonged public dispute. **2.** an argument. —**con′tro•ver′sial,** *adj.* —**con′tro•ver′sial•ly,** *adv.*

con•tro•vert (kon′trə vûrt′, kon′trə vûrt′), *v.t.* **1.** to dispute; deny. **2.** to argue about; debate. —**con′-tro•vert′i•ble,** *adj.*

con•tu•ma•cious (kon′to͞o mā′shəs, -tyo͞o-), *adj.* stubbornly disobedient. —**con′tu•ma′cious•ly,** *adv.* —**con′tu•ma•cy** (-mə sē), *n., pl.* **-cies.**

con•tu•me•ly (kon′to͞o mə lē, -tyo͞o-; kən to͞o′mə-lē, -tyo͞o′-), *n., pl.* **-lies.** an insulting display of contempt. —**con′tu•me′li•ous** (-mē′lē əs), *adj.*

con•tu•sion (kən to͞o′zhən, -tyo͞o′-), *n.* a bruise. —**con•tuse′** (-to͞oz′, -tyo͞oz′), *v.t.,* **-tused, -tus•ing.**

co•nun•drum (kə nun′drəm), *n.* **1.** a riddle whose answer involves a pun. **2.** anything that puzzles.

con•ur•ba•tion (kon′ər bā′shən), *n.* a large, continuous group of cities or towns that retain their separate identities.

con•va•lesce (kon′və les′), *v.i.,* **-lesced, -lesc•ing.** to recover health after illness. —**con′va•les′cence,** *n.* —**con′va•les′cent,** *adj., n.*

con•vec•tion (kən vek′shən), *n.* the transfer of heat by the movement of the heated parts of a liquid or gas.

con•vene (kən vēn′), *v.i., v.t.,* **-vened, -ven•ing.** to assemble or cause to assemble, esp. for a meeting.

con•ven•ient (kən vēn′yənt), *adj.* **1.** suitable to the needs or purpose. **2.** at hand; accessible. —**con•ven′ience,** *n.* —**con•ven′ient•ly,** *adv.*

con•vent (kon′vent, -vənt), *n.* **1.** a community, esp. of nuns, devoted to religious life. **2.** the building occupied by such a community.

con•ven•tion (kən ven′shən), *n.* **1.** an assembly, as of delegates, to act on matters of common concern. **2.** an agreement; compact. **3.** an accepted usage, standard, or custom. —**con•ven′tion•al,** *adj.*

con•verge (kən vûrj′), *v.i.,* **-verged, -verg•ing.** to tend to meet in a point or line. —**con•ver′gence,** *n.* —**con•ver′gent,** *adj.*

con•ver•sant (kən vûr′sənt, kon′vər-), *adj.* familiar by use or study.

con•ver•sa•tion (kon′vər sā′shən), *n.* **1.** informal oral communication between people. **2.** an instance of this. —**con′ver•sa′tion•al,** *adj.* —**con′ver•sa′-tion•al•ist,** *n.* —**con′ver•sa′tion•al•ly,** *adv.*

con•verse¹ (*v.* kən vûrs′; *n.* kon′vûrs), *v.,* **-versed, -vers•ing.** —*v.i.* **1.** to talk informally with another. —*n.* **2.** conversation.

con•verse² (*adj.* kən vûrs′, kon′vûrs; *n.* kon′vûrs), *adj.* **1.** opposite or contrary in direction, action, etc. —*n.* **2.** something opposite or contrary. —**con•verse′ly,** *adv.*

con•vert (*v.* kən vûrt′; *n.* kon′vûrt), *v.t.* **1.** to change into a different form. **2.** to cause to adopt a different religion, political doctrine, etc. **3.** to obtain an equivalent value for in an exchange or calculation, as money or units of measurement. **4.** to assume unlawful rights of ownership of (personal property). —*v.i.* **5.** to become converted. —*n.* **6.** a person converted, as to a religion. —**con•ver′sion** (-vûr′zhən), *n.* —**con•vert′er,** *n.*

con•vert′i•ble *adj.* **1.** capable of being converted. —*n.* **2.** an automobile or boat with a folding top. **3.** a sofa that folds out for use as a bed.

con•vex (kon veks′, kən-), *adj.* curved or rounded outward like the outside of a circle. —**con•vex′i•ty,** *n.*

con•vey (kən vā′), *v.t.* **1.** to take from one place to another. **2.** to communicate; impart. —**con•vey′a•ble,** *adj.* —**con•vey′or, con•vey′er,** *n.*

con•vey′ance *n.* **1.** the act of conveying. **2.** a means of transporting, esp. a vehicle.

con•vict (*v.* kən vikt′; *n.* kon′vikt), *v.t.* **1.** to prove guilty of an offense, esp. after a legal trial. —*n.* **2.** a person serving a prison sentence.

con•vic′tion *n.* **1.** a firm belief. **2.** the act of convicting or state of being convicted.

con•vince (kən vins′), *v.t.,* **-vinced, -vinc•ing.** to persuade by argument and evidence. —**con•vinc′-ing,** *adj.* —**con•vinc′ing•ly,** *adv.*

con•viv•i•al (kən viv′ē əl), *adj.* **1.** friendly; agreeable. **2.** fond of feasting, drinking, and merry company. **3.** festive. —**con•viv′i•al′i•ty,** *n.*

con•voke (kən vōk′), *v.t.,* **-voked, -vok•ing.** to summon to meet or assemble.

con•vo•lut•ed (kon′və lo͞o′tid), *adj.* **1.** twisted; coiled. **2.** complicated; intricately involved.

con′vo•lu′tion *n.* **1.** a coiled condition. **2.** a coiling together.

con•voy (kon′voi; *v. also* kən voi′), *n.* **1.** a ship accompanied by a protecting escort. **2.** a group of vehicles traveling together. **3.** the act of escorting. —*v.t.* **4.** to escort, usu. for protection.

con•vulse (kən vuls′), *v.t.,* **-vulsed, -vuls•ing. 1.** to shake violently. **2.** to cause to shake violently with laughter, pain, etc. —**con•vul′sion,** *n.* —**con•vul′sive,** *adj.*

coo (kōō), *v.i.* **1.** to utter or imitate the murmur of doves. **2.** to murmur fondly or amorously. —*n.* **3.** a cooing sound.

co•in′ci•dence (-si dəns), *n.* **1.** a striking occurrence by mere chance of two or more events at one time. **2.** the fact of coinciding. —**co•in′ci•den′tal** (-den′tl), *adj.* —**co•in′ci•den′tal•ly,** *adv.*

co•in′ci•dence (-si dəns), *n.* **1.** a striking occurrence by mere chance of two or more events at one time. **2.** the fact of coinciding. —**co•in′ci•den′tal** (-den′tl), *adj.* —**co•in′ci•den′tal•ly,** *adv.*

cook (kŏŏk), *v.t.* **1.** to prepare (food) by the use of heat. —*v.i.* **2.** to prepare food by the use of heat. **3.** (of food) to undergo cooking. **4. cook up,** *Informal.* to concoct or contrive. —*n.* **5.** a person who cooks. —**cook′book′,** *n.* —**cook′er,** *n.* —**cook′er•y,** *n.*

cook′ie *n.* a small, flat, sweet cake.

cook′out′ *n.* an outdoor gathering at which food is cooked and consumed.

cool (kōōl), *adj.,* **-er, -est,** *n., v.* —*adj.* **1.** moderately cold. **2.** permitting relief from heat: *a cool dress.* **3.** not excited; calm. **4.** lacking in cordiality. **5.** calmly audacious. **6.** unresponsive; indifferent. **7.** *Slang.* **a.** great; excellent. **b.** highly skilled. **c.** socially adept. —*n.* **8.** a cool part, place, or time: *the cool of the evening.* **9.** calmness; composure. —*v.i., v.t.* **10.** to become or make cool. —**cool′ant,** *n.* —**cool′er,** *n.* —**cool′ly,** *adv.* —**cool′ness,** *n.*

coo•lie (kōō′lē), *n.* an unskilled laborer hired at low wages, esp. formerly in the Far East.

co-op (kō′op), *n.* a cooperative enterprise, building, or apartment.

coop (kōōp, kŏŏp), *n.* **1.** an enclosure or pen, as for poultry. —*v.t.* **2.** to place in or as if in a coop.

co•op•er•ate (kō op′ə rāt′), *v.i.,* **-at•ed, -at•ing.** to work or act together for a common purpose or benefit. —**co•op′er•a′tion,** *n.* —**co•op′er•a′tor,** *n.*

co•op′er•a•tive (-ər ə tiv, -ə rā′tiv), *adj.* **1.** cooperating or willing to cooperate. —*n.* **2.** an enterprise providing goods or services, owned and operated by its members. **3. a.** a building owned and managed by a corporation in which shares are sold, entitling shareholders to occupy individual units. **b.** an apartment in such a building. —**co•op′er•a•tive•ly,** *adv.*

co-opt (kō opt′), *v.t.* **1.** to choose as a fellow member. **2.** to win over into a larger group.

co•or•di•nate (*adj., n.* kō ôr′dn it, -dn āt′; *v.* -āt′), *adj., n., v.,* **-nat•ed, -nat•ing.** —*adj.* **1.** of the same order, rank, or degree. **2.** of or involving coordination or coordinates. —*n.* **3.** a coordinate person or thing. —*v.t.* **4.** to place in the same order or rank. **5.** to place in proper order or relation. —**co•or′di•na′tor,** *n.*

co•or′di•na′tion *n.* **1.** the act of coordinating or state of being coordinated. **2.** harmonious combination or interaction.

coot (kōōt), *n.* **1.** any of various swimming or diving birds. **2.** *Informal.* a foolish or crotchety person.

cop[1] (kop), *v.t.,* **copped, cop•ping.** *Slang.* **1.** to steal; filch. **2. cop out, a.** to renege. **b.** to give up or back out.

cop[2] (kop), *n. Informal.* a police officer.

co•pay (kō′pā′), *n.* a small fixed amount required by a health insurer to be paid by the insured for each outpatient visit or drug prescription. Also called **co•pay•ment** (kō′pā′mənt).

cope[1] (kōp), *v.i.,* **coped, cop•ing.** **1.** to struggle, esp. successfully. **2.** to deal with responsibilities or problems.

cope[2] (kōp), *n.* a long mantle worn by an ecclesiastic, esp. in processions.

cop•i•er (kop′ē ər), *n.* **1.** one that copies. **2.** an office machine for making instant copies of printed material.

co•pi•lot (kō′pī′lət), *n.* a pilot who is second in command of an aircraft.

cop•ing (kō′ping), *n.* the top covering of an exterior masonry wall.

co•pi•ous (kō′pē əs), *adj.* abundant; plentiful. —**co′pi•ous•ly,** *adv.* —**co′pi•ous•ness,** *n.*

cop•per (kop′ər), *n.* **1.** a metallic element having a reddish brown color: used as an electrical conductor

and in the manufacture of alloys. *Symbol:* Cu; *at. wt.:* 63.54; *at. no.:* 29. **2.** a reddish brown. **3.** a copper or bronze coin. [< L *cuprum*] —**cop′per•y,** *adj.*

cop′per•head′ *n.* a North American pit viper with a copper-colored head.

copse (kops) also **cop•pice** (kop′is), *n.* a thicket of small trees or bushes.

cop•u•late (kop′yə lāt′), *v.i.,* **-lat•ed, -lat•ing.** to engage in sexual intercourse. —**cop′u•la′tion,** *n.*

cop•y (kop′ē), *n., pl.* **-ies** for 1, 2, *v.,* **-ied, -y•ing.** —*n.* **1.** an imitation, reproduction, or transcript of an original. **2.** one of the various specimens of the same book, engraving, or the like. **3.** matter to be reproduced in printed form. **4.** the text of a news story, advertisement, etc. —*v.t., v.i.* **5.** to make a copy or copies (of). **6.** to imitate.

cop′y•cat′ *n.* a person or thing that imitates another.

cop′y•right′ *n.* **1.** the exclusive right to use a literary, musical, or artistic work, protected by law for a specified period of time. —*v.t.* **2.** to secure a copyright on.

co•quette (kō ket′), *n.* a woman who flirts insincerely. —**co•quet′tish,** *adj.*

cor•al (kôr′əl, kor′-), *n.* **1.** the hard skeleton secreted by certain marine polyps. **2.** such skeletons collectively, forming reefs, islands, etc. **3.** a yellowish red or pink. —*adj.* **4.** of or like coral.

cord (kôrd), *n.* **1.** a string or thin rope made of several strands twisted or woven together. **2.** a small, flexible, insulated electrical cable. **3.** a ribbed fabric, esp. corduroy. **4.** a rib on the surface of cloth. **5.** a cordlike structure: *the spinal cord.* **6.** a unit of volume used for fuel wood, equal to 128 cubic feet (3.6 cubic meters). —*v.t.* **7.** to fasten with a cord.

cor•dial (kôr′jəl), *adj.* **1.** courteous and gracious. —*n.* **2.** a liqueur. —**cor•dial′i•ty** (-jal′i tē, -jē al′-), *n.* —**cor′dial•ly,** *adv.*

cord′less *adj.* (of an electrical appliance) having a self-contained power supply.

cor•don (kôr′dn), *n.* **1.** a line of police, warships, etc., guarding an area. **2.** a cord or ribbon worn as an ornament. —*v.t.* **3.** to surround with a cordon.

cor•do•van (kôr′də vən), *n.* a soft, smooth leather.

cor•du•roy (kôr′də roi′), *n.* **1.** a cotton-filling pile fabric with lengthwise cords. **2. corduroys,** trousers made of this fabric.

core (kôr), *n., v.,* **cored, cor•ing.** —*n.* **1.** the central part of a fleshy fruit, containing the seeds. **2.** the central or most essential part. —*v.t.* **3.** to remove the core of. —**cor′er,** *n.*

co•ri•an•der (kôr′ē an′dər), *n.* an herb of the parsley family whose seeds are used as a flavoring.

cork (kôrk), *n.* **1.** the thick lightweight layer of a Mediterranean oak used for making floats, bottle stoppers, etc. **2.** a piece of cork or the like used as a stopper. —*v.t.* **3.** to stop with or as if with a cork. —*Idiom.* **4. blow** or **pop one's cork,** *Informal.* to lose one's temper.

cork′screw′ *n.* **1.** a spiral instrument with a sharp point, used for drawing corks from bottles. —*adj.* **2.** spiral. —*v.t., v.i.* **3.** to move in a spiral course.

cor•mo•rant (kôr′mər ənt), *n.* a diving seabird with a long neck and a throat pouch for holding fish.

corn[1] (kôrn), *n.* **1. a.** a cereal plant bearing kernels on large ears. **b.** the kernels of this plant, used as food. **c.** the ears of this plant. **2.** *Informal.* old-fashioned, trite, or sentimental material. —*v.t.* **3.** to preserve and season with brine.

corn[2] (kôrn), *n.* a horny growth of tissue formed over a bone, esp. on the toes.

corn′ bread′ or **corn′bread′,** *n.* a bread made with cornmeal.

corn′cob′ *n.* the elongated woody core in which the grains of an ear of corn are embedded.

cor•ne•a (kôr′nē ə), *n., pl.* **-as.** the transparent part of the external coat of the eye covering the iris and pupil. —**cor′ne•al,** *adj.*

cor•ner (kôr′nər), *n.* **1.** the meeting place of two converging lines or surfaces. **2.** the angle so formed. **3.** the point where two streets meet. **4.** any narrow or secluded place. **5.** an awkward position from which escape is impossible. **6.** a monopoly on a stock or commodity. **7.** region; quarter. —*adj.* **8.** on, at, or for a corner. —*v.t.* **9.** to place in or drive into a corner. **10.** to gain control of (a stock, commodity, etc.). —*Idiom.* **11. cut corners,** to reduce costs or care in execution.

cor'ner•stone' *n.* **1.** a stone representing the starting place in the construction of a building, usu. carved with the date. **2.** something that is essential or basic.

cor•net (kôr net'), *n.* a valved wind instrument of the trumpet family.

cor•nice (kôr'nis), *n.* a projecting molded feature surmounting a wall, doorway, or building.

corn'meal' *n.* meal made from corn.

corn'starch' *n.* a starchy flour made from corn, used for thickening gravies, sauces, etc.

cor•nu•co•pi•a (kôr'nə kō'pē ə, -nyə-), *n., pl.* **-as.** **1.** a horn containing food and drink in endless supply. **2.** an abundant supply. [< LL, = L *cornū* horn + *cōpiae* of plenty]

corn'y *adj.,* **-i•er, -i•est.** *Informal.* old-fashioned, trite, or sentimental.

co•rol•la (kə rol'ə, -rō'lə), *n., pl.* **-las.** the inner whorl of floral leaves of a flower.

cor•ol•lar•y (kôr'ə ler'ē, kor'-), *n., pl.* **-ies. 1.** *Math.* a proposition that is incidentally proved in proving another proposition. **2.** a natural consequence.

co•ro•na (kə rō'nə), *n., pl.* **-nas, -nae** (-nē). **1.** a circle of light seen around a luminous body, esp. the sun or moon. **2.** an envelope of ionized gas around the sun, visible during a total solar eclipse. —**co•ro'nal,** *adj.*

cor•o•nar•y (kôr'ə ner'ē, kor'-), *adj., n., pl.* **-ies.** —*adj.* **1.** of the heart. **2.** of the arteries that originate in the aorta and supply the heart muscle with blood. —*n.* **3.** a heart attack, esp. a coronary thrombosis.

cor•o•na•tion (kôr'ə nā'shən, kor'-), *n.* the act of crowning a sovereign.

cor•o•ner (kôr'ə nər, kor'-), *n.* a public officer whose chief function is to investigate any death not clearly resulting from natural causes.

cor•o•net (kôr'ə net', kor'-), *n.* **1.** a small crown worn by nobles or peers. **2.** a crownlike ornament for the head.

corp. or **Corp.,** corporation.

cor•po•ral¹ (kôr'pər əl), *adj.* of the human body; physical: *corporal punishment.*

cor•po•ral² (kôr'pər əl), *n.* a noncommissioned officer ranking just below a sergeant.

cor'po•ra'tion (kôr'pə rā'shən), *n.* an association of individuals, created by law and existing as an entity with powers and liabilities independent of those of its members. —**cor'po•rate** (-pər it, -prit), *adj.*

cor•po•re•al (kôr pôr'ē əl), *adj.* **1.** of the nature of the physical body. **2.** material; tangible.

corps (kôr, kōr), *n., pl.* **corps** (kôrz). **1. a.** a military organization of officers and enlisted personnel or of officers alone. **b.** a combat unit comprising two or more divisions. **2.** a group of persons associated or acting together.

corpse (kôrps), *n.* a dead body, usu. of a human being.

cor'pu•lent (kôr'pyə lənt) *adj.* fat; portly.

cor•pus (kôr'pəs), *n., pl.* **-po•ra** (-pər ə). **1.** a large or complete collection of writings. **2.** a body, esp. when dead.

cor•pus•cle (kôr'pə səl, -pus əl), *n.* **1.** an unattached cell, esp. a blood or lymph cell. **2.** any minute particle.

cor•ral (kə ral'), *n., v.,* **-ralled, -ral•ling.** —*n.* **1.** a pen for horses, cattle, etc. —*v.t.* **2.** to confine in or as if in a corral. **3.** *Informal.* to seize; capture.

cor•rect (kə rekt'), *v.t.* **1.** to set or make right. **2.** to point out or mark the errors in. **3.** to rebuke or punish. **4.** to counteract the effect of (something hurtful). —*adj.* **5.** true; accurate. **6.** in accordance with an acknowledged standard; proper. —**cor•**

rect'a•ble, *adj.* —**cor•rec'tion,** *n.* —**cor•rec'tive,** *adj., n.* —**cor•rect'ly,** *adv.* —**cor•rect'ness,** *n.*

cor•re•late (kôr'ə lāt', kor'-), *v.t.,* **-lat•ed, -lat•ing.** to bring into mutual or reciprocal relation. —**cor're•la'tion,** *n.*

cor•re•spond (kôr'ə spond', kor'-), *v.i.* **1.** to be in agreement or conformity; match. **2.** to be similar or analogous. **3.** to communicate by letters. —**cor're•spond'ence,** *n.* —**cor're•spond'ing,** *adj.*

cor're•spond'ent *n.* **1.** a person who communicates by letters. **2.** a person employed by a newspaper, television network, etc., to report news from a distant place. **3.** a thing that corresponds. —*adj.* **4.** similar or analogous.

cor•ri•dor (kôr'i dər, -dôr', kor'-), *n.* **1.** a hallway. **2.** a narrow tract of land forming an outlet through foreign territory. **3.** a densely populated region with major transportation routes.

cor•rob•o•rate (kə rob'ə rāt'), *v.t.,* **-rat•ed, -rat•ing.** to make more certain; confirm. —**cor•rob'o•ra'tion,** *n.* —**cor•rob'o•ra'tive** (-ə rā'tiv, -ər ə tiv), *adj.* —**cor•rob'o•ra'tor,** *n.*

cor•rode (kə rōd'), *v.,* **-rod•ed, -rod•ing.** —*v.t.* **1.** to eat or wear away gradually, esp. by chemical action. —*v.i.* **2.** to become corroded. —**cor•ro'sion** (-zhən), *n.* —**cor•ro'sive** (-siv), *adj.*

cor•ru•gate (kôr'ə gāt', kor'-), *v.,* **-gat•ed, -gat•ing.** —*v.t.* **1.** to bend into folds or alternate furrows and ridges. —*v.i.* **2.** to become corrugated. —**cor'ru•ga'tion,** *n.*

cor•rupt (kə rupt'), *adj.* **1.** guilty of dishonest practices, as bribery. **2.** debased in character. —*v.t., v.i.* **3.** to make or become corrupt. —**cor•rupt'i•ble,** *adj.* —**cor•rup'tion,** *n.* —**cor•rupt'ly,** *adv.*

cor•sage (kôr säzh'), *n.* a small bouquet worn by a woman, as at the shoulder.

cor•sair (kôr'sâr), *n.* a pirate or pirate ship, esp. formerly of the Barbary Coast.

cor•set (kôr'sit), *n.* a close-fitting, stiffened undergarment worn to shape and support the torso.

cor•tege or **-tège** (kôr tezh', -tāzh'), *n.* **1.** a procession, esp. a ceremonial one. **2.** a train of attendants; retinue.

cor•tex (kôr'teks), *n., pl.* **-ti•ces** (-tə sēz'). **1. a.** the outer layer of a body organ or structure. **b.** CEREBRAL CORTEX. **2.** the portion of a plant stem between the epidermis and the vascular tissue. —**cor'ti•cal** (-ti kəl), *adj.*

cor•ti•sone (kôr'tə zōn', -sōn'), *n.* an adrenal hormone used chiefly in the treatment of autoimmune and inflammatory diseases.

cor•vette (kôr vet'), *n.* **1.** a sailing warship smaller than a frigate. **2.** a lightly armed ship used esp. as a convoy escort.

cos•met•ic (koz met'ik), *n.* **1.** a preparation for beautifying the skin, hair, etc. —*adj.* **2.** imparting beauty. **3.** superficial. —**cos•met'i•cal•ly,** *adv.*

cos•mic (koz'mik), *adj.* **1.** of the cosmos. **2.** vast. —**cos'mi•cal•ly,** *adv.*

cos•mol•o•gy (-mol'ə jē), *n.* the study of the origin and general structure of the universe. —**cos'mo•log'i•cal** (-mə loj'i kəl), *adj.*

cos•mo•pol•i•tan (koz'mə pol'i tn), *adj.* **1.** composed of people or elements from many parts of the world. **2.** worldly; sophisticated. **3.** widely distributed. —*n.* **4.** a cosmopolitan person.

cos'mos (-məs, -mōs), *n., pl.* **-mos, -mos•es** for 2. **1.** the universe regarded as an orderly system. **2.** any complete, orderly system. [< Gk *kósmos* order, form, arrangement]

cost (kôst, kost), *n., v.,* **cost, cost•ing.** —*n.* **1.** the price paid to acquire or accomplish anything. **2.** a sacrifice or penalty. —*v.t.* **3.** to require the payment of. **4.** to result in the loss or injury of. —*Idiom.* **5. at all costs,** by any means necessary. —**cost'ly,** *adv.*

Cos•ta Ri•ca (kos'tə rē'kə, kô'stə, kō'-), *n.* a republic in Central America. —**Cos'ta Ri'can,** *n., adj.*

cost'-effec'tive *adj.* producing optimum results for the expenditure.

cost' of liv'ing *n.* the average that a person or

family pays for such necessities as food, clothing, and rent.

cos•tume (kos′tōōm, -tyōōm), *n., v.,* **-tumed, -tum• ing.** —*n.* **1.** the style of dress peculiar to a nation, historical period, etc. **2.** the clothing of another period, place, etc. **3.** an outfit; ensemble. —*v.t.* **4.** to furnish with a costume. —**cos′tum•er,** *n.*

co•sy (kō′zē), *adj.,* **-si•er, -si•est,** *n., pl.* **-sies.** cozy.

cot (kot), *n.* a light portable bed, esp. one of canvas on a folding frame.

cote (kōt), *n.* a coop or shed for sheep, pigeons, etc.

co•te•rie (kō′tə rē), *n., pl.* **-ries.** a group of people who associate closely. [< F, MF: an association of tenant farmers]

co•til•lion (kə til′yən, kō-), *n.* **1.** a formal ball, esp. for debutantes. **2.** a formalized dance for a large number of people.

cot•tage (kot′ij), *n.* **1.** a small house. **2.** a modest vacation house.

cot′tage cheese′ *n.* a soft, mild-flavored cheese made from skim-milk curds.

cot•ton (kot′n), *n.* **1.** a soft, white substance consisting of the fibers attached to the seeds of certain plants of the mallow family. **2.** the plant itself. **3.** cloth, thread, a garment, etc., of cotton. —*v.i.* **4.** to take a liking: *He doesn't cotton to strangers.* —**cot′ton•y,** *adj.*

cot′ton gin′ *n.* a machine for separating the fibers of cotton from the seeds itself.

cot′ton•mouth′ *n.* a pit viper of southeastern U.S. swamps.

cot′ton•seed′ *n., pl.* **-seeds, -seed.** the seed of the cotton plant, yielding an oil (**cot′tonseed oil′**) used in cooking, medicine, etc.

couch (kouch), *n.* **1.** a long piece of upholstered furniture for sitting or reclining. —*v.t.* **2.** to express, esp. indirectly.

couch′ pota′to *n. Informal.* a person whose leisure time is spent watching television.

cou•gar (kōō′gər), *n., pl.* **-gars, -gar.** a large, tawny wildcat of North and South America.

cough (kôf, kof), *v.i.* **1.** to expel air from the lungs suddenly with a harsh noise. —*v.t.* **2.** to expel by coughing. **3. cough up,** *Informal.* to relinquish, esp. reluctantly. —*n.* **4.** the act or sound of coughing. **5.** an illness characterized by frequent coughing.

cough′ drop′ *n.* a lozenge for relieving a cough, sore throat, etc.

could (kŏŏd; *unstressed* kəd), *auxiliary v.* **1.** pt. of CAN[1]. **2.** (used to express politeness): *Could you open the door, please?* **3.** (used to express doubt): *That could never be true.*

coun•cil (koun′səl), *n.* **1.** an assembly of persons convened for deliberation or advice. **2.** a group chosen to act in an advisory, administrative, or legislative capacity. —**coun′ci•lor, coun′cil•lor,** *n.*

coun•sel (koun′səl), *n., pl.* **-sel** for 3, *v.,* **-seled, -sel•ing** or (*esp. Brit.*) **-selled, -sel•ling.** —*n.* **1.** advice. **2.** consultation; deliberation. **3.** a lawyer or lawyers. —*v.t.* **4.** to give advice to. **5.** to recommend. —*v.i.* **6.** to give or take advice. —**coun′se•lor, coun′sel•lor,** *n.*

count¹ (kount), *v.t.* **1.** to check over one by one to determine the total. **2.** to name the numerals up to. **3.** to take into account. **4.** to consider or regard. —*v.i.* **5.** to name numerals in order. **6.** to have a specified numerical value. **7.** to have merit, value, etc. **8. count on** or **upon,** to rely on. —*n.* **9.** the act of counting. **10.** the total. **11.** an accounting. **12.** a separate charge in a legal indictment.

count² (kount), *n.* (in some European countries) a nobleman equivalent in rank to an English earl.

count′down′ *n.* the backward counting from the initiation of a project, as a rocket launching, with firing designated as zero.

coun•te•nance (koun′tn əns), *n., v.,* **-nanced, -nanc•ing.** —*n.* **1.** appearance, esp. facial expression. **2.** the face. **3.** approval. —*v.t.* **4.** to tolerate. **5.** to approve.

count•er¹ (koun′tər), *n.* **1.** a table on which goods

can be shown, business transacted, food served, etc. **2.** anything used to keep account, esp. a small object used in games. —*Idiom.* **3. over the counter, a.** (of the sale of stock) through a broker's office rather than through the stock exchange. **b.** (of the sale of medicinal drugs) without requiring a prescription. **4. under the counter,** in a clandestine manner, esp. illegally.

coun•ter² (koun′tər), *adv.* **1.** in the reverse direction. **2.** in opposition. —*adj.* **3.** opposite; contrary. —*n.* **4.** something opposite or contrary to something else. —*v.t., v.i.* **5.** to oppose.

counter- a prefix meaning: against or thwarting (*counterintelligence*); in response to (*counterattack*); opposite (*counterclockwise*); complementary (*counterbalance*).

coun′ter•act′ *v.t.* to act in opposition or a contrary way to.

coun′ter•at•tack′ *n.* **1.** an attack made as an offset or reply to another attack. —*v.t., v.i.* **2.** to make a counterattack (against).

coun•ter•bal•ance (*n.* koun′tər bal′əns; *v.* koun′-tər bal′əns), *n., v.,* **-anced, -anc•ing.** —*n.* **1.** a weight balancing another weight. **2.** an equal power or influence acting in opposition. —*v.t., v.i.* **3.** to act as a counterbalance (to).

coun′ter•clock′wise′ *adj., adv.* in a direction opposite to that of the normal rotation of the hands of a clock.

coun′ter•cul′ture *n.* the culture of those people who reject the dominant values of society.

coun•ter•feit (koun′tər fit′), *adj.* **1.** made in imitation with intent to deceive; forged. **2.** pretended; unreal. —*n.* **3.** an imitation intended to be passed off as genuine. —*v.t., v.i.* **4.** to make a counterfeit of (money, stamps, etc.). **5.** to feign. —**coun′ter•feit′er,** *n.*

coun′ter•in•tel′li•gence *n.* the activity of thwarting the intelligence-gathering efforts of a foreign power.

coun′ter•mand′ (-mand′, -mänd′), *v.t.* to revoke or reverse (an order).

coun′ter•part′ *n.* **1.** a person or thing closely resembling another. **2.** a copy or duplicate.

coun′ter•point′ *n.* the technique of composing two or more melodies that combine harmoniously.

coun′ter•pro•duc′tive *adj.* thwarting the achievement of an intended goal.

coun′ter•sign′ *n.* **1.** a secret sign necessary for admission to a guarded area. —*v.t.* **2.** to sign (a document signed by someone else), esp. in authentication. —**coun′ter•sig′na•ture,** *n.*

coun′ter•ten′or *n.* **1.** a tenor who can approximate the vocal range of a female alto. **2.** a voice part for a countertenor.

count•ess (koun′tis), *n.* **1.** the wife or widow of a count or earl. **2.** a woman with the rank of count or earl in her own right.

count′less *adj.* too numerous to count; innumerable.

coun•try (kun′trē), *n., pl.* **-tries,** *adj.* —*n.* **1.** a state or nation. **2.** the territory of a nation. **3.** the people of a nation. **4.** the land of one's birth or citizenship. **5.** rural districts. **6.** a territory demarcated by topographical conditions: *mountainous country.* —*adj.* **7.** rural.

coun′try•side′ *n.* a rural area.

coun•ty (koun′tē), *n., pl.* **-ties.** the largest local administrative division in most U.S. states.

coup (kōō), *n., pl.* **coups** (kōōz; *Fr.* kōō). **1.** a successful, unexpected act. **2.** COUP D'ÉTAT.

coup d'é•tat (kōō′ dā tä′), *n., pl.* **coups d'é•tat** (kōō′ dā täz′, -tä′). a sudden overthrow of a government by force.

coupe (kōōp), *n.* a closed, two-door car.

cou•ple (kup′əl), *n., v.,* **-pled, -pling.** —*n.* **1.** a combination of two of a kind; pair. **2.** a grouping of two persons, as a husband and wife. —*v.t., v.i.* **3.** to join; connect; unite. —*Idiom.* **4. a couple of,** a few. —**cou′pling,** *n.*

cou•plet (kup′lit), *n.* a pair of successive, rhyming lines of verse.

cou•pon (kōō′pon, kyōō′-), *n.* **1.** a certificate or

ticket entitling the holder to a gift or discount, or for use as an order blank, a contest entry form, etc. **2.** a detachable certificate calling for a periodic interest payment on a bond.

cour•age (kûr′ij, kur′-), *n.* the quality of mind that enables a person to face difficulty, danger, etc., without fear; bravery. **—cou•ra•geous** (kə rā′jəs), *adj.* **—cou•ra′geous•ly,** *adv.*

cour•i•er (kûr′ē ər, koŏr′-), *n.* a messenger, usu. bearing packages, diplomatic messages, etc.

course (kôrs), *n., v.,* **coursed, cours•ing.** **—n. 1.** a direction or route taken. **2.** a path, route, or channel. **3.** advance in a particular direction. **4.** a particular manner of proceeding. **5.** a regular or natural order of events: *the course of a disease.* **6.** a systematized series. **7.** a program of instruction, as in a college. **8.** a part of a meal served at one time. **—v.i. 9.** to run or race. **—Idiom. 10. in due course,** in the proper or natural order of events. **11. of course,** certainly.

court (kôrt), *n.* **1. a.** a place where legal justice is administered. **b.** a judicial tribunal that hears cases. **c.** a session of a judicial assembly. **2.** an open area surrounded by buildings, walls, etc. **3.** a short street. **4.** a quadrangle on which to play tennis, basketball, etc. **5. a.** the residence of a sovereign. **b.** a sovereign's retinue. **c.** a formal assembly held by a sovereign. **6.** devoted attention in order to win favor. **—v.t. 7.** to try to win the favor of. **8.** to woo. **9.** to act so as to cause: *to court disaster.* **—v.i. 10.** to woo a person.

cour•te•ous (kûr′tē əs), *adj.* showing good manners; polite. **—cour′te•ous•ly,** *adv.*

cour•te•san (kôr′tə zən, kûr′-), *n.* a prostitute associating with noblemen or men of wealth.

cour•te•sy (kûr′tə sē), *n., pl.* **-sies. 1.** polite behavior. **2.** a polite act or expression.

court′house′ *n.* **1.** a building housing law courts. **2.** a county seat.

cour•ti•er (kôr′tē ər), *n.* an attendant at a royal court.

court′ly *adj.,* **-li•er, -li•est.** polite, refined, or elegant.

court′-mar′tial *n., pl.* **courts-mar•tial, court-mar•tials,** *v.,* **-tialed, -tial•ing** or (*esp. Brit.*) **-tialled, -tial•ling. —n. 1.** a military court for trying armed forces personnel charged with infractions of military law. **2.** a trial by such a court. **—v.t. 3.** to try by court-martial.

court′room′ *n.* a room in which a court of law is held.

court′ship′ *n.* the wooing of one person by another.

court′yard′ *n.* a court open to the sky, esp. one enclosed on all sides.

cous•in (kuz′ən), *n.* the child of an uncle or aunt.

cou•tu•ri•er (koō toŏr′ē ər, -ē ā′), *n.* a designer of fashionable, custom-made clothes for women.

cove (kōv), *n.* a small indentation in a shoreline.

cov•en (kuv′ən, kō′vən), *n.* an assembly of witches.

cov•e•nant (kuv′ə nənt), *n.* **1.** a formal agreement. **2.** the conditional promises made to humanity by God, as revealed in Scripture. **—v.i. 3.** to enter into a covenant. **—v.t. 4.** to promise by covenant.

cov•er (kuv′ər), *v.t.* **1.** to extend over. **2.** to place something over or upon. **3.** to clothe. **4.** to hide from view. **5.** to deal with or provide for: *The rules cover working conditions.* **6.** to offset (an outlay, loss, etc.). **7.** to travel over. **8.** to report (a news event). **9.** to insure against risk or loss. **10.** to shelter; protect. **11.** to aim at, as with a pistol. **—v.i. 12.** to substitute for someone who is absent. **13.** to provide an alibi. **14. cover up,** to keep secret. **—n. 15.** something that covers, as the lid of a container. **16.** protection; shelter. **17.** anything that screens from sight: *under cover of darkness.* **18.** an assumed identity, occupation, etc. **19.** COVER CHARGE. **—Idiom. 20. take cover,** to seek shelter or safety. **21. under cover,** clandestinely; secretly.

cov′er•age (-ij), *n.* **1.** protection against risks specified in an insurance policy. **2.** the reporting of news.

cov′er charge′ *n.* a fee charged by a restaurant or nightclub for providing entertainment.

cov′er•let (-lit), *n.* a bed quilt that does not cover the pillow.

co•vert (adj. kō′vərt, kuv′ərt; *n.* kuv′ərt, kō′vərt), *adj.* **1.** secret; disguised. **—n. 2.** a thicket giving shelter to wild animals or game. **—co′vert•ly,** *adv.*

cov′er-up′ *n.* any stratagem or other means of concealing an illegal activity, blunder, etc.

cov•et (kuv′it), *v.t., v.i.* to desire (another's property) wrongfully. **—cov′et•ous,** *adj.*

cov•ey (kuv′ē), *n., pl.* **-eys.** a small group of game birds, esp. partridges or quail.

cow[1] (kou), *n.* **1.** the mature female of a bovine animal. **2.** the female of various other large animals, as the whale.

cow[2] (kou), *v.t.* to intimidate.

cow•ard (kou′ərd), *n.* a person who lacks courage. **—cow′ard•ice** (-ər dis), *n.* **—cow′ard•ly,** *adj., adv.* **—cow′ard•li•ness,** *n.*

cow′boy′ or **-girl′,** *n.* a person who herds cattle.

cow•er (kou′ər), *v.i.* to crouch in fear.

cowl (koul), *n.* **1.** a hooded garment worn by monks. **2.** the hood itself.

cow′lick′ *n.* a tuft of hair that grows in a direction different from the rest of the hair.

cow′slip′ *n.* an English primrose with fragrant yellow flowers.

cox•swain (kok′sən, -swān′), *n.* a person who steers a boat or racing shell.

coy (koi), *adj.,* **-er, -est.** artfully shy; coquettish. **—coy′ly,** *adv.* **—coy′ness,** *n.*

coy•o•te (kī ō′tē, kī′ōt), *n., pl.* **-tes, -te.** a carnivorous, wolflike mammal of North America. [< MexSp < Nahuatl *coyotl*]

coz•en (kuz′ən), *v.t., v.i.* to cheat; deceive. **—coz′en•age,** *n.*

co•zy (kō′zē), *adj.,* **-zi•er, -zi•est,** *n., pl.* **-zies. —adj. 1.** snugly warm and comfortable. **—n. 2.** a padded covering for a teapot to retain the heat. **—co′zi•ly,** *adv.* **—co′zi•ness,** *n.*

CPA certified public accountant.

CPI consumer price index.

CPR cardiopulmonary resuscitation.

CPU central processing unit: the key component of a computer system.

crab[1] (krab), *n.* a crustacean with a wide, flattened body and four pairs of legs.

crab[2] (krab), *n., v.,* **crabbed, crab•bing. —n. 1.** an ill-tempered person. **—v.i., v.t. 2.** to find fault (with).

crab′ ap′ple *n.* a small, tart apple.

crab′by *adj.,* **-bi•er, -bi•est.** ill-tempered; grouchy.

crack (krak), *v.i.* **1.** to break without separation of parts. **2.** to make a sudden, sharp sound, as in breaking. **3.** (of the voice) to break abruptly and discordantly. **4.** *Informal.* to break down, esp. under severe pressure. **—v.t. 5.** to cause to make a sudden, sharp sound. **6.** to cause to break without separation of parts. **7.** to strike forcefully. **8.** to tell: *to crack jokes.* **9.** to cause to make a cracking sound: *to crack one's knuckles.* **10.** to solve. **11.** *Informal.* to break into (a safe, vault, etc.). **12. crack down,** to become strict; take severe measures: *to crack down on drug pushers.* **13. ~ up,** *Informal.* **a.** to suffer a mental or physical breakdown. **b.** to crash, as in a vehicle. **c.** to laugh unrestrainedly. **—n. 14.** a break without separation of parts. **15.** a slight opening. **16.** a sudden, sharp noise. **17.** a resounding blow. **18.** a witty or cutting remark. **19.** a break in the tone of the voice. **20.** a chance; try. **21.** *Slang.* highly addictive, purified cocaine in the form of pellets. **—adj. 22.** first-rate; excellent. **—Idiom. 23. crack a smile,** *Informal.* to smile, esp. hesitantly. **24. get cracking,** to get moving; hurry up: *Let's get cracking.*

crack′down′ *n.* the stern enforcement of laws.

crack′er *n.* **1.** a thin, crisp biscuit. **2.** a firecracker.

crack•le (krak′əl), *v.,* **-led, -ling,** *n.* **—v.i. 1.** to make slight, sharp noises, rapidly repeated. **—n. 2.** a the act or sound of crackling. **3.** a network of fine cracks, as in some glazes. —**crack′ly**, *adj.*

crack′pot′ *Informal.* —*n.* **1.** an eccentric person. —*adj.* **2.** eccentric.

crack′up′ *n.* **1.** a crash; collision. **2.** a breakdown in health, esp. a mental breakdown.

cra•dle (krād′l), *n.*, *v.*, **-dled, -dling.** —*n.* **1.** a small bed for an infant, usu. on rockers. **2.** a support for an object set horizontally, as for the receiver of a telephone. **3.** a place of origin: *Athens is the cradle of democracy.* —*v.t.* **4.** to place or rock in or as if in a cradle. **5.** to nurture during infancy.

craft (kraft, kräft), *n.*, *pl.* **crafts** or, for 5, **craft,** *v.* —*n.* **1.** a trade or occupation requiring manual skill. **2.** skill; dexterity. **3.** cunning; deceit. **4.** the membership of a guild. **5.** a ship or other vessel. **6.** ships, aircraft, etc., collectively. —*v.t.* **7.** to make (an object) with great skill and care. —**crafts′man,** *n.*, *pl.* **-men.** —**crafts′man•ship′**, *n.* —**crafts′wom′an,** *n.*, *pl.* **-wom•en.**

craft′y *adj.* **-i•er, -i•est.** cunning; deceitful.

crag (krag), *n.* a steep, rugged rock. —**crag′gy** *adj.*, **-gi•er, -gi•est.**

cram (kram), *v.*, **crammed, cram•ming.** —*v.t.* **1.** to fill (something) with more than it can easily hold. **2.** to force or stuff. **3.** to overfeed. —*v.i.* **4.** to eat to excess. **5.** to study intensively for an examination at the last minute.

cramp¹ (kramp), *n.* **1.** an involuntary, painful muscle spasm. **2. cramps,** painful abdominal contractions. —*v.t.*, *v.i.* **3.** to affect or be affected with a cramp.

cramp² (kramp), *v.t.* to restrict or hamper.

cramped (krampt), *adj.* **1.** spatially confined or limited. **2.** (of handwriting) small and crowded.

cran•ber•ry (kran′ber′ē, -bə rē), *n.*, *pl.* **-ries. 1.** the sour red berry of a trailing plant, used to make a sauce, relish, or juice. **2.** the plant itself.

crane (krān), *n.*, *v.*, **craned, cran•ing.** —*n.* **1.** a large wading bird with long legs, bill, and neck. **2.** a device for lifting and moving heavy weights. —*v.t.*, *v.i.* **3.** to stretch (the neck).

cra•ni•um (krā′nē əm), *n.*, *pl.* **-ni•ums, -ni•a** (-nē ə). **1.** the skull of a vertebrate. **2.** the part of the skull that encloses the brain. —**cra′ni•al,** *adj.*

crank (krangk), *n.* **1.** an arm or lever for imparting motion to a rotating shaft. **2.** *Informal.* an ill-tempered person. **3.** an unbalanced person who is overzealous in advocating a private cause. —*v.t.* **4.** to start or rotate by turning a crank.

crank′y *adj.* **-i•er, -i•est. 1.** ill-tempered; grouchy. **2.** eccentric; erratic. —**crank′i•ness,** *n.*

cran•ny (kran′ē), *n.*, *pl.* **-nies.** a narrow opening in a wall, rock, etc.

crap (krap), *n.* *Slang (sometimes vulgar).* **1.** nonsense; drivel. **2.** junk; litter. —**crap′py,** *adj.* **-pi•er, -pi•est.**

crape (krāp), *n.* CREPE (defs. 1, 2, 3).

craps (kraps), *n.* a gambling game in which two dice are thrown.

crash (krash), *v.i.* **1.** to make a loud, clattering noise. **2.** to fall or break into pieces noisily. **3.** to strike, go, or collide violently and noisily. **4.** to land in such a way that damage is unavoidable. **5.** to collapse suddenly, as a financial enterprise. **6.** (of a computer) to fail suddenly because of a hardware malfunction or software bug. —*v.t.* **7.** to cause to break into pieces violently and noisily. **8.** to cause (a moving vehicle) to crash. **9.** to enter without invitation or payment. —*n.* **10.** an act or instance of crashing. **11.** a sudden loud noise. **12.** a sudden collapse, as of a business. —*adj.* **13.** characterized by speed and intensive effort: *a crash diet.*

crass (kras), *adj.*, **-er, -est.** without refinement or sensitivity. —**crass′ly,** *adv.* —**crass′ness,** *n.*

crate (krāt), *n.*, *v.*, **crat•ed, crat•ing.** —*n.* **1.** a slatted wooden box for packing, shipping, etc. —*v.t.* **2.** to pack in a crate.

cra•ter (krā′tər), *n.* **1.** the cup-shaped depression marking the orifice of a volcano. **2.** a similar depression formed by the impact of a meteoroid. **3.** the hole in the ground where a bomb has exploded. [< L < Gk *krātḗr* mixing bowl]

cra•vat (krə vat′), *n.* NECKTIE.

crave (krāv), *v.t.*, **craved, crav•ing. 1.** to long for; desire eagerly. **2.** to require; need.

cra•ven (krā′vən), *adj.* **1.** contemptibly timid. —*n.* **2.** a coward. —**cra′ven•ly,** *adv.*

crav′ing *n.* a great desire; yearning.

crawl (krôl), *v.i.* **1.** to move with the body close to the ground or on the hands and knees. **2.** to move slowly or laboriously. **3.** to behave in a cringing manner. **4.** to be, or feel as if, overrun with crawling things. —*n.* **5.** the act of crawling. **6.** a slow rate of progress. **7.** a swimming stroke in a prone position. —**crawl′er,** *n.*

cray•fish (krā′fish′), *n.*, *pl.* **-fish, -fish•es.** a freshwater crustacean resembling a small lobster.

cray•on (krā′on, -ən), *n.* **1.** a pointed stick of colored wax, used for drawing or coloring. —*v.t.* **2.** to draw or color with crayons.

craze (krāz), *v.*, **crazed, craz•ing,** *n.* —*v.t.*, *v.i.* **1.** to make or become insane. **2.** to make or become minutely cracked, as a ceramic glaze. —*n.* **3.** a fad. **4.** a minute crack or pattern of cracks in the glaze of a ceramic object.

cra•zy (krā′zē), *adj.*, **-zi•er, -zi•est,** *n.*, *pl.* **-zies.** —*adj.* **1.** mentally deranged. **2.** impractical; foolish. **3.** intensely enthusiastic. **4.** infatuated. —*n.* **5.** *Slang.* a crazy person. —**cra′zi•ly,** *adv.* —**cra′zi•ness,** *n.*

creak (krēk), *v.i.* **1.** to make a sharp, squeaking sound. —*n.* **2.** a creaking sound. —**creak′y,** *adj.*, **-i•er, -i•est.**

cream (krēm), *n.* **1.** the fatty part of milk. **2.** a soft solid preparation applied to the skin for cosmetic or therapeutic purposes. **3.** a food made with cream or having a creamy consistency. **4.** the best part of anything. **5.** a yellowish white. —*v.t.* **6.** to work into a creamy consistency. **7.** to prepare with cream or a cream sauce. **8.** to add cream to. **9.** *Slang.* to beat up or defeat decisively. —*Idiom.* **10. cream of the crop,** the best or choicest. —**cream′y,** *adj.*, **-i•er, -i•est.** —**cream′i•ness,** *n.*

cream′er•y *n.*, *pl.* **-er•ies.** a place where milk and cream are processed or where butter and cheese are produced.

crease (krēs), *n.*, *v.*, **creased, creas•ing.** —*n.* **1.** a ridge produced in anything by folding, striking, etc. **2.** a wrinkle. **3.** a sharp, vertical edge pressed into the front and back of trousers. —*v.t.* **4.** to make a crease in. —*v.i.* **5.** to become creased.

cre•ate (krē āt′), *v.t.*, **-at•ed, -at•ing. 1.** to cause to come into being. **2.** to arrange or bring about.

cre•a′tion *n.* **1.** the act of creating. **2.** something created. **3. the Creation,** the original bringing into existence of the universe by God. **4.** the universe.

cre•a′tive (-tiv), *adj.* **1.** having the quality or power of creating. **2.** resulting from originality of thought; imaginative. —**cre•a′tive•ly,** *adv.* —**cre•a′tive•ness,** *n.* —**cre′a•tiv′i•ty,** *n.*

cre•a′tor *n.* **1.** a person who creates. **2. the Creator,** God.

crea•ture (krē′chər), *n.* **1.** an animal. **2.** a human being.

cre•dence (krēd′ns), *n.* belief as to the truth of something.

cre•den•tial (kri den′shəl), *n.* Usu., **-tials.** evidence of entitlement to rights, privileges, or the like.

cre•den•za (kri den′zə), *n.*, *pl.* **-zas.** a sideboard, esp. one without legs.

cred•i•ble (kred′ə bəl), *adj.* **1.** capable of being believed. **2.** effective or reliable. —**cred′i•bil′i•ty,** *n.* —**cred′i•bly,** *adv.*

cred•it (kred′it), *n.* **1.** commendation given for some action, quality, etc. **2.** a source of pride or honor. **3. credits,** the names of all who contributed to a motion picture or television program. **4.** trustworthiness; credibility. **5. a.** permission to pay for goods at a later date. **b.** reputation for paying bills when due. **6.** official acceptance of the work completed by a student in a course. **7.** an entry of payment received on an account. **8.** any sum of money against which a person may draw. —*v.t.* **9.** to believe or trust. **10.** to give credit for or to. —*Idiom.* **11. on credit,** by deferred payment.

cred•it•a•ble *adj.* deserving credit or esteem. —**cred′it•a•bly,** *adv.*

cred′it card′ *n.* a card entitling a person to make purchases on credit.

cred′i•tor *n.* a person or firm to whom money is due.

cred′it un′ion *n.* a cooperative group that makes loans to its members at low interest rates.

cred•u•lous (krej′ə ləs), *adj.* willing to believe or trust too readily. —**cre•du•li•ty** (kri dōō′li tē, -dyōō′-), *n.* —**cred′u•lous•ly,** *adv.*

creed (krēd), *n.* **1.** an authoritative statement of the chief articles of Christian belief. **2.** an accepted system of religious or other belief. [< L *crēdō* I believe]

creek (krēk, krik), *n.* **1.** a small stream. —*Idiom.* **2. up the creek,** *Slang.* in a difficult situation.

Creek (krēk), *n., pl.* **Creek, Creeks.** a member of a loose confederacy of American Indian peoples that formerly occupied the greater part of Georgia and Alabama.

creep (krēp), *v.,* **crept, creep•ing,** *n.* —*v.i.* **1.** to move slowly with the body close to the ground. **2.** to approach or advance slowly or stealthily. **3.** to grow along the ground, a wall, etc., as a plant. —*n.* **4.** an instance of creeping. **5.** *Slang.* a repellent or obnoxious person. **6. the creeps,** a sensation of anxiety, disgust, etc. —*Idiom.* **7. make one's flesh creep,** to cause one to be frightened or repelled. —**creep′er,** *n.*

creep′y *adj.,* **-i•er, -i•est.** having or causing a sensation of horror or fear. —**creep′i•ly,** *adv.* —**creep′i•ness,** *n.*

cre•mate (krē′māt), *v.t.,* **-mat•ed, -mat•ing.** to reduce (a dead body) to ashes by fire. —**cre•ma•tion** (kri mā′shən), *n.*

Cre•ole (krē′ōl), *n.* **1. a.** a member of the French-speaking population of Louisiana that claims descent from the earliest French and Spanish settlers. **b.** a person of mixed black and Creole ancestry. **2.** (*l.c.*) a pidgin that has become the native language of a speech community. —*adj.* **3.** (*usu. l.c.*) made with tomatoes, peppers, onions, and spices.

cre•o•sote (krē′ə sōt′), *n.* an oily liquid distilled from coal and wood tar, used as a wood preservative and an antiseptic.

crepe or **crêpe** (krāp; *for 4 also* krep) *n., pl.* **crepes** or **crêpes** (krāps; *for 4 also* kreps *or* krep). **1.** a lightweight fabric of silk, cotton, etc., with a crinkled surface. **2.** a black piece of crepe, worn as a token of mourning. **3.** Also called **crepe′ pa′per.** a thin, wrinkled paper used for decorating. **4.** a thin, light pancake.

cre•scen•do (kri shen′dō), *n., pl.* **-dos, -di** (-dē). **1.** a gradual increase in loudness. **2.** a musical passage characterized by such an increase.

cres•cent (kres′ənt), *n.* **1.** the figure of the moon in its first or last quarter, resembling a segment of a ring tapering to points at the ends. **2.** any crescent-shaped object.

cress (kres), *n.* a plant, esp. the watercress, having pungent-tasting leaves often used for salad.

crest (krest), *n.* **1.** the highest part of a hill or mountain range. **2.** the highest point or level. **3.** the foamy top of a wave. **4.** a growth on the top of an animal's head, as the comb of a rooster. **5.** a heraldic device. —*v.i.* **6.** to form or rise to a crest. —**crest′ed,** *adj.*

crest′fall′en *adj.* dejected; discouraged.

cre•tin (krēt′n), *n.* **1.** a person affected with cretinism. **2.** a stupid, obtuse, or boorish person.

cre•vasse (krə vas′), *n.* a deep cleft in glacial ice, the earth's surface, etc.

crev•ice (krev′is), *n.* a crack forming an opening.

crew (krōō), *n.* **1.** a group of persons working together. **2.** the team that rows a racing shell. —**crew′man,** *n., pl.* **-men.**

crew′ cut′ *n.* a haircut in which the hair is very closely cropped.

crib (krib), *n., v.,* **cribbed, crib•bing.** —*n.* **1.** a child's bed with enclosed sides. **2.** a manger for fodder. **3.** a bin for storing grain. **4.** *Informal.* an illicit aid used by students while taking exams. —*v.t.*

5. to plagiarize. **6.** to confine in a crib. —*v.i.* **7.** *Informal.* to use a crib during exams.

crib•bage (krib′ij), *n.* a card game in which points for certain combinations of cards are scored on a small pegboard.

crick (krik), *n.* a sharp, painful spasm of the muscles, as of the neck.

crick•et[1] (krik′it), *n.* a jumping insect, the male of which makes a chirping sound by rubbing the forewings together.

crick•et[2] (krik′it), *n.* **1.** an outdoor game, popular esp. in England, that is played by two teams using bats, balls, and wickets. **2.** fair play; honorable conduct: *It's not cricket to ask such questions.* —**crick′et•er,** *n.*

cri•er (krī′ər), *n.* **1.** one who cries. **2.** an official who makes public announcements.

crime (krīm), *n.* an action that is legally prohibited.

crim•i•nal (krim′ə nl), *adj.* **1.** guilty of crime. **2.** dealing with crime or its punishment. —*n.* **3.** a person convicted of a crime. —**crim′i•nal′i•ty,** *n.* —**crim′i•nal•ly,** *adv.*

crimp (krimp), *v.t.* **1.** to press into small regular folds. **2.** to curl (hair). —*n.* **3.** the act of crimping. **4.** a crimped condition or form. —*Idiom.* **5. put a crimp in,** to hinder.

crim•son (krim′zən, -sən), *adj.* **1.** deep purplish red. —*n.* **2.** a crimson color. —*v.t., v.i.* **3.** to make or become crimson.

cringe (krinj), *v.i.,* **cringed, cring•ing.** to shrink or crouch, esp. in fear or servility.

crin•kle (kring′kəl), *v.,* **-kled, -kling,** *n.* —*v.t., v.i.* **1.** to wrinkle; ripple. **2.** to rustle. —*n.* **3.** a wrinkle or ripple. —**crin′kly,** *adj.,* **-kli•er, -kli•est.**

crin•o•line (krin′l in), *n.* **1.** a stiff, coarse fabric used as interlining in garments, hats, etc. **2.** a hoop skirt.

crip•ple (krip′əl), *n., v.,* **-pled, -pling.** —*n.* **1.** *Sometimes Offensive.* **a.** a lame or physically disabled person or animal. **b.** a person who is disabled in any way: *a mental cripple.* —*v.t.* **2.** to make a cripple of. **3.** to disable; impair.

cri•sis (krī′sis), *n., pl.* **-ses** (-sēz). **1.** a turning point for better or for worse. **2.** a condition or period of instability, difficulty, etc. **3.** the point in a serious disease at which a decisive change occurs.

crisp (krisp) also **crisp′y,** *adj.,* **-er, -est** also **-i•er, -i•est.** **1.** brittle. **2.** firm and fresh. **3.** decided; clear. **4.** lively; pithy. **5.** bracing; invigorating. **6.** curly. —**crisp′ly,** *adv.* —**crisp′ness,** *n.*

criss•cross (kris′krôs′, -kros′), *v.t.* **1.** to move back and forth over. **2.** to mark with crossing lines. —*v.i.* **3.** to pass back and forth. —*adj.* **4.** having many crossing lines. —*n.* **5.** a crisscross mark, pattern, etc. —*adv.* **6.** crosswise.

cri•te•ri•on (krī tēr′ē ən), *n., pl.* **-te•ri•a** (-tēr′ē ə), **-te•ri•ons.** a standard of judgment or criticism.

crit•ic (krit′ik), *n.* **1.** a person who judges literary or artistic works. **2.** a person who tends to make harsh judgments.

crit′i•cal *adj.* **1.** inclined to find fault or judge severely. **2.** requiring skillful judgment. **3.** of critics or criticism. **4.** of the nature of or constituting a crisis. **5.** crucial. —**crit′i•cal•ly,** *adv.*

crit′i•cism (-siz′əm), *n.* **1.** the act of criticizing. **2.** faultfinding or censure. **3.** the art of judging the merits of anything. **4.** a critique.

crit′i•cize *v.i., v.t.,* **-cized, -ciz•ing. 1.** to find fault (with). **2.** to evaluate.

cri•tique (kri tēk′), *n., v.,* **-tiqued, -ti•quing.** —*n.* **1.** an article evaluating a literary or other work; review. —*v.t.* **2.** to analyze critically.

crit•ter (krit′ər), *n. Dial.* a creature.

croak (krōk), *v.i.* **1.** to utter a low-pitched, harsh cry, as that of a frog. **2.** *Slang.* to die. —*n.* **3.** a croaking sound.

Cro•a•tia (krō ā′shə), *n.* a republic in SE Europe: formerly part of Yugoslavia. —**Cro′at** (-at, -ät), *n.* —**Cro•a′tian,** *adj., n.*

cro•chet (krō shā′), *n., v.,* **-cheted** (-shād′), **-chet•ing** (-shā′ing). —*n.* **1.** needlework done with a hooked needle for drawing yarn through intertwined loops. —*v.i.* **2.** to do this needlework. —*v.t.* **3.** to form by crochet. —**cro•chet′er,** *n.*

crock (krok), *n.* an earthenware container. —**crock′er•y,** *n.*

croc•o•dile (krok′ə dīl′), *n.* a narrow-snouted, large reptile found in tropical waters of both hemispheres.

cro•cus (krō′kəs), *n., pl.* **-cus•es.** a small bulbous plant cultivated for its showy flowers.

crois•sant (*Fr.* krwä sän′; *Eng.* krə sänt′), *n., pl.* **-sants** (*Fr.* -sän′; *Eng.* -sänts′). a crescent-shaped roll of rich, flaky pastry.

crone (krōn), *n.* a withered, witchlike old woman.

cro•ny (krō′nē), *n., pl.* **-nies.** a close friend.

crook (krŏŏk), *n.* **1.** a bent or curved implement; hook. **2.** a dishonest person. **3.** a bend or curve. —*v.t., v.i.* **4.** to bend; curve.

crook•ed (krŏŏk′id *for 1–3*; krŏŏkt *for 4*), *adj.* **1.** not straight; curved. **2.** deformed. **3.** dishonest or illegal. **4.** bent. —**crook′ed•ly,** *adv.* —**crook′ed•ness,** *n.*

croon (krōōn), *v.i., v.t.* **1.** to sing or hum in a soft, soothing voice. —*n.* **2.** the act or sound of crooning. —**croon′er,** *n.*

crop (krop), *n., v.,* **cropped, crop•ping.** —*n.* **1.** the cultivated produce of the ground. **2.** the yield of such produce in one season. **3.** the yield of any product in a season. **4.** a group of persons or things. **5.** the handle of a whip. **6.** a short riding whip. **7.** a pouch in the esophagus of many birds, in which food is held for later digestion. **8.** a close cutting of something, as the hair. —*v.t.* **9.** to cut or bite off the top or ends of. **10.** to cut off the ends or a part of: *to crop the ears of a dog.* **11.** to cut short. **12.** to cause to bear a crop. **13. crop up,** to appear unexpectedly.

cro•quet (krō kā′), *n.* a lawn game played by knocking wooden balls through metal wickets with mallets.

cro•quette (krō ket′), *n.* a small, deep-fried cake or ball of minced meat, vegetables, etc.

cro•sier (krō′zhər), *n.* a ceremonial staff carried by a bishop or an abbot.

cross (krôs, kros), *n., v., adj.,* **-er, -est.** —*n.* **1.** a figure consisting of two lines intersecting at right angles. **2.** a structure consisting of an upright and a transverse piece, upon which persons were formerly put to death. **3. the Cross,** the cross upon which Jesus died. **4.** a figure of the Cross as a Christian symbol. **5.** an affliction; misfortune. **6.** a mixing of breeds. **7.** a hybrid; crossbreed. —*v.t.* **8.** to move or extend from one side to the other side of. **9.** to draw a line across. **10.** to intersect. **11.** to place across each other or crosswise: *to cross one's legs.* **12.** to meet and pass. **13.** to crossbreed; hybridize. **14.** to oppose. **15.** to make the sign of the cross upon or over. —*v.i.* **16.** to intersect. **17.** to move or extend from one side or place to another. **18.** to meet and pass. **19.** to crossbreed. **20. cross out off,** to cancel, as by drawing a line through. —*adj.* **21.** angry; ill-humored. **22.** lying crosswise. **23.** contrary; opposite. **24.** crossbred; hybrid. —*Idiom.* **25. cross one's mind,** to occur to one. **26. cross one's path,** to meet. —**cross′ly,** *adv.*

cross′bow′ (-bō′), *n.* a medieval weapon consisting of a bow fixed transversely on a grooved wooden stock.

cross′breed′ *v.,* **-bred, -breed•ing,** *n.* —*v.t., v.i.* **1.** to hybridize. —*n.* **2.** a hybrid.

cross′-coun′try *adj.* **1.** proceeding over fields, through woods, etc., rather than on a road, track, or run. **2.** from one end of the country to the other.

cross′-exam′ine *v.t.,* **-ined, -in•ing.** to examine (a witness called by the opposing side), esp. in order to check or discredit his or her testimony. —**cross′-examina′tion,** *n.*

cross′-eye′ *n.* a condition in which one or both eyes turn inward. —**cross′-eyed′,** *adj.*

cross′ ref′erence *n.* a reference from one part of a book, index, etc., to another part. —**cross′-refer′,** *v.,* **-ferred, -fer•ring.**

cross′roads′ *n.* **1.** intersection. **2.** decisive point.

cross′ sec′tion *n.* **1.** a section made by a plane

cutting something transversely. **2.** a pictorial representation of such a section. **3.** a representative sample of a whole. —**cross′-sec′tional,** *adj.*

cross′walk′ *n.* a lane for pedestrians crossing a street.

cross′word′ puz′zle *n.* a puzzle in which words corresponding to numbered clues are fitted into a pattern of horizontal and vertical squares.

crotch (kroch), *n.* **1.** a place where something divides or forks, as the human body between the legs. **2.** the part of trousers, underpants, etc., where the two legs join.

crotch•et (kroch′it), *n.* an odd fancy or whimsical notion. —**crotch′et•y,** *adj.*

crotch′et•y *adj.* grouchy or cantankerous.

crouch (krouch), *v.i.* **1.** to stoop low with the knees bent. **2.** to cringe. —*n.* **3.** the act of crouching.

croup (krōōp), *n.* any condition of the larynx or trachea characterized by a hoarse cough and difficult breathing.

crou•pi•er (krōō′pē ər, -pē ā′), *n.* an attendant who collects and pays the money at a gaming table.

crou•ton (krōō′ton, krōō ton′), *n.* a small cube of toasted bread, used in salads, soups, etc.

crow¹ (krō), *n.* **1.** a large bird with lustrous black plumage. —*Idiom.* **2. as the crow flies,** in a straight line. **3. eat crow,** to admit a mistake.

crow² (krō), *v.,* **crowed** or, for 1, (*esp. Brit.*), **crew; crowed; crow•ing;** *n.* —*v.i.* **1.** to utter the cry of a rooster. **2.** to boast or brag. **3.** to utter a cry of pleasure. —*n.* **4.** the cry of a rooster. **5.** a cry of pleasure.

crow′bar′ *n.* a flattened steel bar used as a lever.

crowd (kroud), *n.* **1.** a large number of persons or things gathered together. **2.** any group of persons having something in common: *the theater crowd.* —*v.i.* **3.** to gather in large numbers. **4.** to press forward. —*v.t.* **5.** to cram. **6.** to push or shove. —**crowd′ed,** *adj.*

crown (kroun), *n.* **1.** a headgear worn by a monarch as a symbol of sovereignty. **2.** the power of a sovereign. **3.** (*often cap.*) the sovereign. **4.** a wreath worn on the head as a mark of victory. **5.** an award for an achievement. **6.** the highest part or state of anything. **7. a.** the part of a tooth that is covered by enamel. **b.** an artificial substitute for this. **8.** a former British silver coin, equal to five shillings. —*v.t.* **9.** to invest with regal power. **10.** to place a crown on. **11.** to honor. **12.** to be at the highest part of. **13.** to bring to a successful conclusion.

crow's′-foot′ *n., pl.* **-feet.** a tiny wrinkle at the outer corner of the eye.

CRT 1. cathode-ray tube. **2.** a computer monitor that includes a cathode-ray tube.

cru•cial (krōō′shəl), *adj.* of vital or decisive importance. —**cru′cial•ly,** *adv.*

cru•ci•ble (krōō′sə bəl), *n.* **1.** a container used for heating substances to high temperatures. **2.** a severe trial.

cru•ci•fix (krōō′sə fiks), *n.* a cross with the figure of Jesus crucified upon it.

cru′ci•fix′ion (-fik′shən), *n.* **1.** the act of crucifying. **2.** (*cap.*) the death of Jesus upon the Cross.

cru′ci•fy′ *v.t.,* **-fied, -fy•ing. 1.** to put to death by nailing or binding the hands and feet to a cross. **2.** to persecute or torment.

crude (krōōd), *adj.,* **crud•er, crud•est,** *n.* —*adj.* **1.** in a raw or unrefined state. **2.** lacking finish, polish, etc.; rough. **3.** lacking culture, refinement, etc.; vulgar. —*n.* **4.** petroleum before refining. —**crude′ly,** *adv.* —**crude′ness,** *n.*

cru•di•tés (krōō′di tā′), *n.pl.* raw vegetables cut up and served with a dip.

cru•el (krōō′əl), *adj.,* **-er, -est.** willfully causing pain or distress to others. —**cru′el•ly,** *adv.* —**cru′el•ty,** *n., pl.* **-ties.**

cru•et (krōō′it), *n.* a glass bottle to hold vinegar, oil, etc., for the table.

cruise (krōōz), *v.,* **cruised, cruis•ing,** *n.* —*v.i.* **1.** to sail about on a pleasure trip. **2.** to fly, drive, etc., at a constant speed that permits maximum operating efficiency. **3.** to travel or go about slowly, as in search of something. —*v.t.* **4.** to cruise in. —*n.* **5.** a pleasure voyage on a ship.

cruis′er *n.* **1.** one that cruises. **2.** a fast warship of medium tonnage. **3.** SQUAD CAR. **4.** a pleasure boat having a cabin for living aboard.

crumb (krum), *n.* **1.** a small, broken-off particle of bread, cake, etc. **2.** a fragment of anything; bit. **3.** *Slang.* a contemptible person. —*v.t.* **4.** (in cooking) to prepare with crumbs. —**crumb′y,** *adj.,* **-i•er, -i•est.**

crum•ble (krum′bəl), *v.,* **-bled, -bling.** —*v.i.* **1.** to break into small fragments. **2.** to disintegrate gradually. —*v.t.* **3.** to break into crumbs. —**crum′bly,** *adj.,* **-bli•er, -bli•est.**

crum•my (krum′ē), *adj.,* **-mi•er, -mi•est.** *Informal.* **1.** run-down; shabby. **2.** cheap; worthless.

crum•ple (krum′pəl), *v.,* **-pled, -pling.** —*v.t.* **1.** to crush into irregular folds or wrinkles. —*v.i.* **2.** to contract into wrinkles. **3.** to collapse.

crunch (krunch), *v.t.* **1.** to chew, grind, etc., with a sharp crushing noise. **2.** to manipulate (numbers or data), esp. by computer. —*v.i.* **3.** to chew with a crushing noise. —*n.* **4.** an act or sound of crunching. **5.** a shortage or reduction: *the energy crunch.* **6.** a critical situation. —**crunch′y,** *adj.,* **-i•er, -i•est.**

cru•sade (kroo sād′), *n., v.,* **-sad•ed, -sad•ing.** —*n.* **1.** (*often cap.*) any of the Christian military expeditions of the 11th–13th centuries to recover the Holy Land from the Muslims. **2.** any vigorous movement on behalf of a cause. —*v.i.* **3.** to go on or engage in a crusade. —**cru•sad′er,** *n.*

crush (krush), *v.t.* **1.** to press with a force that destroys or deforms. **2.** to pound into small particles. **3.** to force out by squeezing. **4.** to suppress utterly. —*v.i.* **5.** to become crushed. —*n.* **6.** the act of crushing or state of being crushed. **7.** a great crowd. **8.** *Informal.* a usu. short-lived infatuation. —**crush′er,** *n.*

crust (krust), *n.* **1.** the hard outer surface of bread. **2.** the baked shell of a pie. **3.** any hard external covering. **4.** the outer layer of the earth. —*v.t., v.i.* **5.** to cover or become covered with a crust. —**crust′al,** *adj.* —**crust′y,** *adj.,* **-i•er, -i•est.**

crus•ta•cean (kru stā′shən), *n.* any chiefly aquatic arthropod typically having the body covered with a hard shell, including lobsters, shrimps, etc.

crutch (kruch), *n.* **1.** a support to assist a lame person in walking, usu. with a crosspiece fitting under the armpit. **2.** any support or prop.

crux (kruks), *n.* **1.** the central or pivotal point. **2.** a perplexing difficulty.

cry (krī), *v.,* **cried, cry•ing,** *n., pl.* **cries.** —*v.i.* **1.** to utter sounds of grief or suffering. **2.** to shed tears; weep. **3.** to shout. **4.** (of an animal) to utter a characteristic call. —*v.t.* **5.** to utter loudly. **6.** to announce publicly: *to cry one's wares.* —*n.* **7.** a shout, scream, or wail. **8.** a fit of weeping. **9.** the call of an animal. **10.** an entreaty; appeal. —*Idiom.* **11.** a **far cry,** altogether different.

cry•o•gen•ics (krī′ə jen′iks), *n.* the study of extremely low temperatures. —**cry′o•gen′ic,** *adj.*

crypt (kript), *n.* a subterranean vault, esp. one used as a burial place. [< L < Gk *kryptē* hidden place]

cryp•tic (krip′tik), *adj.* **1.** mysterious; puzzling. **2.** secret; occult. —**cryp′ti•cal•ly,** *adv.*

crys•tal (kris′tl), *n.* **1.** a clear, transparent mineral or glass resembling ice. **2.** the transparent form of crystallized quartz. **3.** a solid enclosed by symmetrically arranged plane surfaces, intersecting at definite angles. **4.** a fine-quality, brilliant glass. **5.** glassware, as goblets, made of such glass. **6.** the clear cover over the face of a watch. —*adj.* **7.** composed of crystal. **8.** clear or transparent. —**crys′tal•line** (-in, -īn′, -ēn′), *adj.*

crys•tal•lize′ *v.i., v.t.,* **-lized, -liz•ing. 1.** to form or cause to form into crystals. **2.** to assume or cause to assume a definite form. —**crys′tal•li•za′tion,** *n.*

C′-sec′tion *n. Informal.* CESAREAN.

CST Central Standard Time.

CT Connecticut.

Ct. 1. Connecticut. **2.** Count.

ct. 1. carat. **2.** cent. **3.** court.

Cu *Chem. Symbol.* copper. [< L *cuprum*]

cu or **cu.,** cubic.

cub (kub), *n.* **1.** the young of certain animals, esp. the bear, wolf, lion, and whale. **2.** a young and inexperienced person.

Cu•ba (kyoo′bə), *n.* an island republic in the Caribbean, S of Florida. —**Cu′ban,** *adj., n.*

cub•by•hole (kub′ē hōl′), *n.* a small, snug compartment.

cube (kyoob), *n., v.,* **cubed, cub•ing.** —*n.* **1.** a solid bounded by six equal squares. **2.** a solid or hollow object having or approximating this form: *a sugar cube.* **3.** *Math.* the third power of a quantity, expressed as $a^3 = a \times a \times a.$ —*v.t.* **4.** to make into a cube. **5.** to raise (a quantity or number) to the third power. —**cu′bic,** *adj.*

cu′bi•cle *n.* a small partitioned space or compartment.

cub′ism *n.* (*sometimes cap.*) a style of painting and sculpture marked by the reduction of natural forms to their geometrical equivalents. —**cub′ist,** *n., adj.*

cub′ scout′ *n.* (*sometimes caps.*) a member of the junior division (ages 8–10) of the Boy Scouts.

cuck•old (kuk′əld), *n.* **1.** the husband of an unfaithful wife. —*v.t.* **2.** to make a cuckold of. —**cuck′old•ry,** *n.*

cuck•oo (koo′koo, kook′oo), *n., pl.* **-oos. 1.** a slim, stout-billed, long-tailed bird. **2.** *Informal.* a crazy or foolish person. —*adj.* **3.** *Informal.* crazy; foolish.

cu•cum•ber (kyoo′kum bər), *n.* the edible, greenskinned, cylindrical fruit of a plant of the gourd family.

cud (kud), *n.* the coarse food regurgitated by a ruminant from its first stomach for further chewing.

cud•dle (kud′l), *v.,* **-dled, -dling,** *n.* —*v.t.* **1.** to hug tenderly. —*v.i.* **2.** to lie close and snug. —*n.* **3.** a hug. —**cud′dly,** *adj.,* **-dli•er, -dli•est.**

cudg•el (kuj′əl), *n., v.,* **-eled, -el•ing,** or (*esp. Brit.*) **-elled, -el•ling.** —*n.* **1.** a short, thick stick used as a weapon. —*v.t.* **2.** to strike with a cudgel.

cue¹ (kyoo), *n., v.,* **cued, cu•ing.** —*n.* **1.** anything said or done, on or off stage, that is followed by a specific line or action. **2.** anything that elicits action; stimulus. **3.** a hint; intimation. —*v.t.* **4.** to give a cue to.

cue² (kyoo), *n.* a long, tapering rod used to strike the ball in pool, billiards, etc.

cuff¹ (kuf), *n.* **1.** a fold or band at the bottom of a sleeve. **2.** the turned-up fold at the bottom of a trouser leg. —*Idiom.* **3. off the cuff,** *Informal.* impromptu. **4. on the cuff,** *Slang.* on credit.

cuff² (kuf), *v.t.* **1.** to strike with the open hand. —*n.* **2.** a blow or slap.

cui•sine (kwi zēn′), *n.* **1.** a style of cooking. **2.** the food prepared, as by a restaurant.

cu•li•nar•y (kyoo′lə ner′ē, kul′ə-), *adj.* of cooking or the kitchen.

cull (kul), *v.t.* **1.** to choose; select and gather. **2.** to gather the choice elements from. —*n.* **3.** something picked out and put aside as inferior.

cul•mi•nate (kul′mə nāt′), *v.i.,* **-nat•ed, -nat•ing. 1.** to reach the highest point or climactic stage. —**cul′mi•na′tion,** *n.*

cul•pa•ble (kul′pə bəl), *adj.* deserving blame or censure. —**cul′pa•bil′i•ty,** *n.*

cul•prit (kul′prit), *n.* a person guilty of an offense or fault.

cult (kult), *n.* **1.** a particular system of religious worship. **2.** a group devoted to a person, fad, etc. **3. a.** a religion considered to be false or extremist. **b.** the members of such a religion. —*adj.* **4.** of a cult. **5.** attracting a small group of devotees: *a cult movie.* —**cult′ist,** *n.*

cul•ti•vate (kul′tə vāt′), *v.t.,* **-vat•ed, -vat•ing. 1.** to work on (land) in order to raise crops. **2.** to promote the growth of (a plant or crop). **3.** to develop or improve by education or training. **4.** to seek to promote or foster. —**cul′ti•va•ble** (-və bəl), **cul′ti•vat′a•ble,** *adj.* —**cul′ti•va′tion,** *n.* —**cul′ti•va′tor,** *n.*

cul′ti•vat′ed *adj.* educated; refined; cultured.

cul•ture (kul′chər), *n., v.,* **-tured, -tur•ing.** —*n.* **1.** artistic and intellectual pursuits and products. **2.**

general

development or improvement of the mind, morals, etc. **3.** the ways of living built up by a human group and transmitted to succeeding generations. **4.** a particular form or stage of civilization. **5. a.** the cultivation of microorganisms or tissues, as for scientific study. **b.** the product of such cultivation. **6.** cultivation of the soil. **7.** the raising of plants or animals. —*v.t.* **8.** to cultivate. **9.** to grow (microorganisms, tissues, etc.) in a nutrient medium. —**cul′tur•al,** *adj.* —**cul′tur•al•ly,** *adv.*

cul′ture shock′ *n.* the bewilderment and distress experienced by an individual who is exposed to a new culture.

cul•vert (kul′vərt), *n.* a drain or conduit under a road, sidewalk, etc.

cum′ber•some (-səm), *adj.* **1.** burdensome. **2.** unwieldy.

cu•mu•la•tive (kyoō′myə lə tiv, -lā′tiv), *adj.* increasing by successive additions. —**cu′mu•la•tive•ly,** *adv.*

cu•mu•lus (kyoō′myə ləs), *n., pl.* **-li** (-lī′). a cloud with dense individual elements in the form of puffs, with flat bases.

cu•ne•i•form (kyoō nē′ə fôrm′), *adj.* **1.** composed of slim triangular elements, as the writing of the ancient Babylonians and others. —*n.* **2.** cuneiform writing.

cun•ning (kun′ing), *n.* **1.** craftiness; guile. **2.** adeptness; dexterity. —*adj.* **3.** showing ingenuity. **4.** crafty; sly. **5.** charmingly cute. —**cun′ning•ly,** *adv.*

cup (kup), *n., v.,* **cupped, cup•ping.** —*n.* **1.** a small, open container for beverages, usu. with a handle. **2.** the quantity in a cup. **3.** a unit of capacity equal to 8 fluid ounces (237 milliliters). **4.** a cuplike object, part, etc. —*v.t.* **5.** to form into a cuplike shape: *to cup one's hands.*

cup•board (kub′ərd), *n.* a closet with shelves for dishes, cups, food, etc.

Cu•pid (kyoō′pid), *n.* the Roman god of carnal love, commonly represented as a winged, naked infant boy with a bow and arrows.

cu•pid′i•ty *n.* eager or excessive desire, esp. for wealth.

cu•po•la (kyoō′pə lə), *n., pl.* **-las.** a light structure on a dome or roof.

cur (kûr), *n.* **1.** a mongrel dog. **2.** a mean, cowardly person.

cu•rate (kyoōr′it), *n.* a cleric assisting a rector or vicar. —**cu′ra•cy** (-ə sē), *n., pl.* **-cies.**

cu•ra•tor (kyoō rā′tər, kyoōr′ā-), *n.* one in charge of a museum, art collection, etc. —**cu′ra•to′ri•al** (-ə tôr′ē əl), *adj.*

curb (kûrb), *n.* **1.** an edging, esp. of concrete, for a sidewalk. **2.** a restraint; check. **3.** a bit to which a chain is hooked for control of a horse. —*v.t.* **4.** to control; restrain. **5.** to put a curb on (a horse).

curd (kûrd), *n.* a substance obtained from milk by coagulation and used as food or made into cheese.

cur•dle (kûr′dl), *v.t., v.i.,* **-dled, -dling.** to change into curd; coagulate.

cure (kyoōr), *n., v.,* **cured, cur•ing.** —*n.* **1.** a means of healing; remedy. **2.** a method of remedial treatment. **3.** restoration to health. —*v.t.* **4.** to restore to health. **5.** to relieve or rid of (an illness, bad habit, etc.). **6.** to preserve (meat, fish, etc.), as by smoking or salting. **7.** to process (rubber, tobacco, etc.), as by fermentation or aging. —**cur′a•ble,** *adj.* —**cur′er,** *n.*

cur•few (kûr′fyoō), *n.* **1.** an order establishing a time in the evening after which no unauthorized persons may be outdoors. **2.** a parental regulation requiring a child to be home at a stated time.

cu•ri•o (kyoōr′ē ō′), *n., pl.* **-os.** any article, object of art, etc., valued as a curiosity.

cu•ri•os•i•ty (kyoōr′ē os′i tē), *n., pl.* **-ties. 1.** the desire to know about anything. **2.** a rare or novel thing.

cu′ri•ous *adj.* **1.** eager to know. **2.** prying; meddlesome. **3.** odd or strange. —**cu′ri•ous•ly,** *adv.*

curl (kûrl), *v.t.* **1.** to form into ringlets, as the hair. **2.** to coil. —*v.i.* **3.** to grow in or form ringlets. **4.** to coil or curve. —*n.* **5.** a ringlet of hair. **6.** anything of a spiral or curved shape. —**curl′er,** *n.* —**curl′y,** *adj.,* **-i•er, -i•est.**

cur•lew (kûr′loō), *n.* a large shorebird with a long, slender bill that curves down.

curl•i•cue (kûr′li kyoō′), *n.* an ornamental curl or twist.

cur•mudg•eon (kər muj′ən), *n.* a bad-tempered, difficult person.

cur•rant (kûr′ənt, kur′-), *n.* **1.** a small seedless raisin. **2.** the small, round, sour berry of certain shrubs of the saxifrage family. **3.** the shrub itself.

cur•ren•cy (kûr′ən sē, kur′-), *n., pl.* **-cies. 1.** any form of money that is in circulation in a country. **2.** general acceptance; prevalence.

cur•rent (kûr′ənt, kur′-), *adj.* **1.** belonging to the time actually passing; present: *the current month.* **2.** generally accepted; prevalent. **3.** widely circulating or circulated. —*n.* **4.** a flowing, as of a river. **5.** a portion of a large body of water or air moving in a certain direction. **6.** the movement or flow of electric charge. **7.** a general tendency. —**cur′rent•ly,** *adv.*

cur•ric•u•lum (kə rik′yə ləm), *n., pl.* **-la** (-lə), **-lums.** the aggregate of courses of study in a school, college, etc. —**cur•ric′u•lar,** *adj.*

cur•ry[1] (kûr′ē, kur′ē), *n., pl.* **-ries,** *v.,* **-ried, -ry•ing.** —*n.* **1.** a dish of meat, fish, or vegetables flavored with curry powder. **2.** CURRY POWDER. —*v.t.* **3.** to flavor (food) with curry powder.

cur•ry[2] (kûr′ē, kur′ē), *v.t.,* **-ried, -ry•ing. 1.** to rub and clean (a horse) with a currycomb. **2.** to dress (tanned hides) by soaking, beating, etc. —*Idiom.* **3. curry favor,** to seek to advance oneself through flattery or fawning.

cur′ry•comb′ *n.* **1.** a comb for currying horses. —*v.t.* **2.** to rub or clean with a currycomb.

cur′ry pow′der *n.* a pungent mixture of ground turmeric, cumin, and other spices.

curse (kûrs), *n., v.,* **cursed** or **curst, curs•ing.** —*n.* **1.** the expression of a wish that misfortune, evil, etc., befall someone. **2.** a profane or obscene word. **3.** an evil or misfortune that has been invoked upon one. —*v.t.* **4.** to invoke evil upon. **5.** to swear at. **6.** to afflict with evil. —*v.i.* **7.** to swear profanely.

cur•sive (kûr′siv), *adj.* (of handwriting) in flowing strokes with the letters joined together.

cur•sor (kûr′sər), *n.* a movable symbol used to indicate where data may be input on a computer screen.

cur•so•ry (kûr′sə rē), *adj.* hasty and superficial. —**cur′so•ri•ly,** *adv.*

curt (kûrt), *adj.,* **-er, -est.** rudely brief in speech or abrupt in manner. —**curt′ly,** *adv.* —**curt′ness,** *n.*

cur•tail (kər tāl′), *v.t.* to cut short; reduce. —**cur•tail′ment,** *n.*

cur•tain (kûr′tn), *n.* **1.** a hanging piece of fabric used to shut out the light from a window, adorn a room, etc. **2.** a movable drapery that conceals the stage from the audience. —*v.t.* **3.** to provide, conceal, etc., with or as if with a curtain.

curt•sy (kûrt′sē), *n., pl.* **-sies,** *v.,* **-sied, -sy•ing.** —*n.* **1.** a respectful bow made by women, consisting of bending the knees and lowering the body. —*v.i.* **2.** to make a curtsy.

cur′va•ture (-və chər, -choōr′), *n.* **1.** a curved condition, often abnormal. **2.** the degree of curving of a line or surface.

curve (kûrv), *n., v.,* **curved, curv•ing.** —*n.* **1.** a continuously bending line, without angles. **2.** a curving movement. **3.** any curved form. —*v.i., v.t.* **4.** to bend or move in a curve. —**curv′y,** *adj.,* **-i•er, -i•est.**

cush•ion (koōsh′ən), *n.* **1.** a soft pad or pillow on which to sit, lie, or lean. **2.** anything similar in form or function. **3.** something to absorb shocks. —*v.t.* **4.** to furnish with a cushion. **5.** to lessen or soften the effects of.

cush′y *adj.,* **-i•er, -i•est.** *Informal.* **1.** easy and profitable: *a cushy job.* **2.** soft and comfortable.

cusp (kusp), *n.* a point or pointed end, as on the crown of a tooth.

cus•pid (kus′pid), *n.* any of the four canine teeth in humans.

cuss (kus), *v.t., v.i. Informal.* to curse.

cus•tard (kus′tərd), *n.* a boiled or baked dish made with eggs, milk, and sugar.

cus•to•di•an (ku stō′dē ən), *n.* **1.** a person who has custody; guardian. **2.** the caretaker of a property.

cus•to•dy (kus′tə dē), *n., pl.* **-dies. 1.** guardianship and care. **2.** imprisonment or legal restraint. —**cus•to•di•al** (ku stō′dē əl), *adj.*

cus•tom (kus′təm), *n.* **1.** a habitual practice. **2.** habits or usages collectively; convention. **3. customs,** duties imposed by law on imported or exported goods. **4.** regular patronage of a shop, restaurant, etc. —*adj.* **5.** made specially for individual customers. **6.** dealing in things so made, or doing work to order.

cus•tom•ar•y (kus′tə mer′ē), *adj.* according to custom; usual; habitual. —**cus′tom•ar/i•ly,** *adv.*

cus′tom•er *n.* a person who purchases goods or services from another.

cus′tom•ize′ *v.t.* **-ized, -iz•ing.** to make, alter, or build according to individual specifications. —**cus′tom•i•za′tion,** *n.*

cut (kut), *v.,* **cut, cut•ting,** *adj., n.* —*v.t.* **1.** to penetrate with or as if with a sharp-edged instrument. **2.** to divide with a sharp-edged instrument. **3.** to hew or saw down. **4.** to trim by clipping, paring, etc. **5.** to reap; harvest. **6.** to abridge. **7.** to reduce or curtail: *to cut prices.* **8.** to dilute: *to cut whiskey.* **9.** *Informal.* to cease. **10.** to grow (a tooth) through the gum. **11.** to make by cutting, as a garment. **12.** to refuse to recognize socially. **13.** to strike sharply. **14.** to absent oneself from: *to cut classes.* **15.** to wound the feelings of. **16.** to divide (a pack of cards) at random. —*v.i.* **17.** to penetrate or divide something, as with a sharp-edged instrument. **18.** to admit of being cut. **19.** to move or cross. **20.** to make a sharp change in direction. **21. cut back,** to curtail or discontinue. **22. ~ down,** to lessen or curtail. **23. ~ in, a.** to thrust oneself, a vehicle, etc., abruptly between others. **b.** to interrupt. **c.** to interrupt a dancing couple in order to dance with one of them. **24. ~ off, a.** to shut off or stop. **b.** to disinherit. **c.** to sever; separate. **25. ~ out, a.** to delete or excise. **b.** to stop. **26. ~ up, a.** to cut into pieces. **b.** *Informal.* to play pranks. —*adj.* **27.** divided or detached by cutting. **28.** fashioned by cutting. —*n.* **29.** the result of cutting, as an incision. **30.** the act of cutting. **31.** a piece cut off. **32.** a share, esp. of earnings. **33.** a reduction, as in price. **34.** the fashion in which anything is cut. **35.** a passage or course straight across. **36.** an act, speech, etc., that wounds the feelings. **37.** an engraved plate or block used for printing. **38.** a printed picture or illustration. **39.** an absence, as from a class. **40.** an individual song or musical piece on a record. —*Idiom.* **41. a cut above,** somewhat superior to. **42. cut out for,** fitted for; capable of.

cu•ta•ne•ous (kyŏŏ tā′nē əs), *adj.* of or affecting the skin.

cut′back′ *n.* a reduction in rate, quantity, etc.

cute (kyŏŏt), *adj.,* **cut•er, cut•est. 1.** attractive or pretty in a dainty way. **2.** clever; shrewd. —**cute′ly,** *adv.* —**cute′ness,** *n.*

cu•ti•cle (kyŏŏ′ti kəl), *n.* **1.** the hardened skin that surrounds a fingernail or toenail. **2.** the epidermis.

cut•lass (kut′ləs), *n.* a short, heavy, slightly curved sword.

cut•ler•y (kut′lə rē), *n.* cutting instruments collectively, esp. utensils for serving and eating food.

cut•let (kut′lit), *n.* **1.** a slice of meat, esp. of veal, for broiling or frying. **2.** a flat croquette of minced food, as chicken or fish.

cut′off′ *n.* **1.** something that cuts off. **2.** a point serving as the limit beyond which something is no longer effective, applicable, or possible. **3.** a road that leaves another and provides a shortcut. **4. cutoffs,** shorts made by cutting the legs off a pair of trousers, esp. jeans.

cut′-rate′ *adj.* offered or selling at reduced prices.

cut′ter *n.* **1.** a person who cuts, as one who cuts fabric for garments. **2.** a single-masted sailing ship.

cut′throat′ *n.* **1.** a murderer. —*adj.* **2.** murderous. **3.** ruthless: *cutthroat competition.*

cut•tle•fish (kut′l fish′), *n., pl.* **-fish, -fish•es.** a marine mollusk having ten arms with suckers and a hard internal shell **(cut′tle•bone′).**

cy•a•nide (sī′ə nīd′, -nid), *n.* a highly poisonous compound containing sodium or potassium.

cyber- a combining form representing COMPUTER (*cybernetics, cyberspace*) and by extension meaning "very modern" (*cyberfashion*).

cy•ber•net•ics (sī′bər net′iks), *n.* the study of organic control and communication systems, and mechanical or electronic systems analogous to them, as robots. —**cy′ber•net′ic,** *adj.*

cy•ber•space (sī′bər spās′), *n.* **1.** the realm of electronic communication. **2.** VIRTUAL REALITY.

cy•cle (sī′kəl), *n., v.,* **-cled, -cling.** —*n.* **1.** any complete round or recurring series. **2.** a recurring period of time, esp. one in which certain events repeat themselves in the same order and intervals. **3.** a bicycle, motorcycle, etc. **4.** a group of poems, stories, etc., about a central theme or figure. —*v.i.* **5.** to travel by bicycle, motorcycle, etc. **6.** to move in cycles. —**cy•clic** (sī′klik, sik′lik), **cy′cli•cal,** *adj.*

cy•clone (sī′klōn), *n.* **1.** an atmospheric wind-and-pressure system characterized by low pressure at its center and by circular wind motion. **2.** (not in technical use) a tornado. [< Gk *kyklôn* revolving] —**cy•clon′ic** (-klon′ik), *adj.*

cy•clo•pe•di•a or **-pae•di•a** (sī′klə pē′dē ə), *n., pl.* **-as.** an encyclopedia.

cy•clo•tron (sī′klə tron′), *n.* an accelerator in which particles move in spiral paths in a constant magnetic field.

cyg•net (sig′nit), *n.* a young swan.

cyl•in•der (sil′in dər), *n.* **1.** a surface or solid bounded by two parallel planes and generated by a line tracing a closed curve perpendicular to the planes. **2.** any cylinderlike object or part. **3.** the rotating part of a revolver. —**cy•lin′dri•cal,** *adj.*

cym•bal (sim′bəl), *n.* a percussion instrument consisting of a concave metal plate that produces a sharp, ringing sound when struck. —**cym′bal•ist,** *n.*

cyn•ic (sin′ik), *n.* one who believes that only selfishness motivates human actions. —**cyn′i•cal,** *adj.* —**cyn′i•cal•ly,** *adv.* —**cyn•i•cism** (sin′ə siz′əm), *n.*

cy•no•sure (sī′nə shŏŏr′, sin′ə-), *n.* one that strongly attracts attention.

cy•press (sī′prəs), *n.* **1.** an evergreen tree with dark green, scalelike, overlapping leaves. **2.** its wood.

Cy•prus (sī′prəs), *n.* an island republic in the Mediterranean, S of Turkey. —**Cyp•ri•ot** (sip′rē ət), *n., adj.*

cyst (sist), *n.* an abnormal saclike growth of the body in which matter is retained. —**cys′tic,** *adj.*

cys′tic fibro′sis *n.* a hereditary disease of the exocrine glands characterized by breathing difficulties, infection, and fibrosis.

cy•to•plasm (sī′tə plaz′əm), *n.* the cell substance between the cell membrane and the nucleus. —**cy′to•plas′mic,** *adj.*

czar (zär), *n.* **1.** (*often cap.*) the former emperor of Russia. **2.** any person exercising great authority or power. [< Russ *tsar′* ≪ L *Caesar* Caesar]

cza•ri•na (zä rē′nə), *n., pl.* **-nas.** the wife of a czar.

Czech (chek), *n.* **1.** a native or inhabitant of the Czech Republic. **2.** the Slavic language of the Czechs. —*adj.* **3.** of the Czechs, their homeland, or their language.

Czech′ Repub′lic *n.* a republic in central Europe; formerly part of Czechoslovakia.

D, d (dē), *n., pl.* **Ds** or **D's, ds** or **d's.** the fourth letter of the English alphabet, a consonant.

'd 1. contraction of *had, would,* or *did: He'd already left; I'd like that; Where'd you go?* **2.** contraction of *-ed: She OK'd the plan.*

D Dutch.

D *Symbol.* **1.** the fourth in order or in a series. **2.** a grade or mark indicating poor quality. **3.** (*sometimes l.c.*) the Roman numeral for 500. **4.** *Chem.* deuterium.

D. 1. December. **2.** Democrat. **3.** Doctor. **4.** dose. **5.** Dutch.

d. 1. date. **2.** deceased. **3.** degree. **4.** delete. **5.** *Chiefly Brit.* penny; pence. [< L *denārius*] **6.** deputy. **7.** diameter. **8.** dose. **9.** drachma.

D.A. or **DA, 1.** delayed action. **2.** District Attorney. **3.** doesn't answer.

dab (dab), *v.,* **dabbed, dab•bing,** *n.* —*v.t., v.i.* **1.** to pat or tap gently. **2.** to apply by light strokes, as paint or plaster. —*n.* **3.** a quick or light pat. **4.** a small lump or quantity: *a dab of powder.*

dab•ble (dab′əl), *v.i.,* **-bled, -bling. 1.** to play in or as if in water, esp. with the hands. **2.** to work at anything in a superficial manner: *to dabble in literature.* —**dab′bler,** *n.*

dachs•hund (däks′hŏont′, -hŏond′), *n.* one of a German breed of dogs with very short legs and a long body and ears. [< G, = *Dachs* badger + *Hund* dog]

Da•cron (dā′kron, dak′ron), *Trademark.* a brand of polyester fiber.

dad (dad), *n. Informal.* father.

dad•dy (dad′ē), *n., pl.* **-dies.** *Informal.* father; dad.

dad′dy-long′legs′ or **dad′dy long′legs′,** *n., pl.* **-legs.** a spiderlike arachnid with a compact body and long, slender legs.

daf•fo•dil (daf′ə dil), *n.* a plant having solitary, usu. yellow flowers with a trumpetlike corona.

daft (daft, däft), *adj.,* **-er, -est. 1.** foolish. **2.** crazy; mad.

dag•ger (dag′ər), *n.* **1.** a short, swordlike weapon with a pointed blade and a handle, used for stabbing. **2.** a printer's mark (†) used esp. for references.

dahl•ia (dal′yə, däl′-), *n., pl.* **-ias.** a composite plant with tuberous roots and showy flowers. [after Anders *Dahl* (d. 1789), Swedish botanist]

dai•ly (dā′lē), *adj., n., pl.* **-lies,** *adv.* —*adj.* **1.** of, done, occurring, or issued each day or each weekday. **2.** computed by the day: *a daily quota.* —*n.* **3.** a daily newspaper. —*adv.* **4.** every day.

dain•ty (dān′tē), *adj.,* **-ti•er, -ti•est,** *n., pl.* **-ties.** —*adj.* **1.** of delicate beauty or form. **2.** pleasing to the taste. **3.** of delicate taste; particular; fastidious: *a dainty eater.* **4.** overly particular; finicky. —*n.* **5.** a delicacy. —**dain′ti•ly,** *adv.* —**dain′ti•ness,** *n.*

dair•y (dâr′ē), *n., pl.* **-ies. 1.** a place where milk and cream are kept and butter and cheese are made. **2.** a farm that produces milk. **3.** a store that sells milk and milk products.

da•is (dā′is), *n.* a raised platform, as for seats of honor.

dai•sy (dā′zē), *n., pl.* **-sies.** a composite plant having flowers with a yellow disk and white rays.

Da•ko•ta (da kō′tə), *n., pl.* **-ta, -tas** for 1. **1.** a member of an American Indian people originally of Minnesota and the N Great Plains. **2.** the Siouan language of the Dakota. —**Da•ko′tan,** *adj., n.*

dale (dāl), *n.* a valley, esp. a broad valley.

dal•ly (dal′ē), *v.i.,* **-lied, -ly•ing. 1.** to waste time; loiter; delay. **2.** to act playfully, esp. in a flirtatious way. **3.** to play mockingly; trifle. —**dal′li•ance,** *n.* —**dal′li•er,** *n.*

Dal•ma•tian (dal mā′shən), *n.* a shorthaired dog having a white coat marked with black or brown spots.

dam¹ (dam), *n., v.,* **dammed, dam•ming.** —*n.* **1.** a barrier to obstruct the flow of water, as one built across a stream. —*v.t.* **2.** to furnish with a dam. **3.** to stop up; block up.

dam² (dam), *n.* a female parent of a four-footed domestic animal.

dam•age (dam′ij), *n., v.,* **-aged, -ag•ing.** —*n.* **1.** injury or harm that reduces value, usefulness, etc. **2. damages,** the estimated money equivalent for loss or injury sustained. —*v.t.* **3.** to cause damage to. —**dam′age•a•ble,** *adj.*

dam•ask (dam′əsk), *n.* **1.** an elaborately patterned, usu. reversible fabric woven on a Jacquard loom. **2.** an ancient type of hard steel with a pattern of wavy lines. **3.** a deep pink color.

dame (dām), *n.* **1.** (*cap.*) (in Britain) an official title of honor for a woman, equivalent to that of Sir. **2.** *Slang* (*sometimes disparaging*). a woman; female.

damn (dam), *v.t.* **1.** to declare to be bad, unfit, invalid, etc. **2.** to ruin. **3.** to condemn to hell. **4.** to curse, using the word "damn." —*interj.* **5.** an expression of anger, annoyance, disgust, etc. —*n.* **6.** the utterance of "damn" in swearing. **7.** something of negligible value: *not worth a damn.* —*adj.* **8.** DAMNED (defs. 2, 3). —*adv.* **9.** DAMNED (def. 4).

damned (damd), *adj., superl.* **damned•est, damnd•est,** *adv.* —*adj.* **1.** condemned, esp. to eternal punishment. **2.** detestable; loathsome. **3.** absolute; utter: *a damned nuisance.* —*adv.* **4.** very: *a damned good singer.*

damp (damp), *adj.,* **-er, -est,** *n., v.* —*adj.* **1.** slightly wet; moist. **2.** unenthusiastic: *a damp reception.* —*n.* **3.** moisture; humidity. —*v.t.* **4.** to make damp; moisten. **5.** to check or retard; deaden; dampen. **6.** to stifle or suffocate; extinguish: *to damp a furnace.* —**damp′ness,** *n.*

damp′er *n.* **1.** one that damps or depresses: *The news put a damper on the party.* **2.** a movable plate for regulating the draft in a stove, furnace, etc. **3.** a device in stringed keyboard instruments to deaden the vibration of the strings.

dam•sel (dam′zəl), *n.* a maiden, orig. one of gentle or noble birth.

dam•son (dam′zən, -sən), *n.* a small, dark blue or purple plum.

dance (dans, däns), *v.,* **danced, danc•ing,** *n.* —*v.i.* **1.** to move the feet and body rhythmically, esp. to music. **2.** to leap, skip, etc., as from excitement. **3.** to bob up and down. —*v.t.* **4.** to perform (a dance). **5.** to cause to dance. —*n.* **6.** a pattern of rhythmical bodily motions, usu. to music. **7.** the art of dancing. **8.** a social gathering for dancing. **9.** a piece of music suited to dancing. —**danc′er,** *n.*

dan•de•li•on (dan′dl ī′ən), *n.* a weedy composite plant with edible, toothed leaves and golden-yellow flowers. [< MF *dent de lion* tooth of a lion, in allusion to the toothed leaves]

dan•der (dan′dər), *n. Informal.* anger or temper.

dan•dle (dan′dl), *v.t.,* **-dled, -dling.** to move (a child) lightly up and down on one's knee or in one's arms.

dan•druff (dan′drəf), *n.* a seborrheic scurf that forms on the scalp and comes off in scales.

dan•dy (dan′dē), *n., pl.* **-dies,** *adj.,* **-di•er, -di•est.** —*n.* **1.** a man excessively concerned about his clothes and appearance; fop. **2.** something or someone of exceptional quality. —*adj.* **3.** foppish. **4.** fine; first-rate. —**dan′di•fy,** *v.t.,* **-fied, -fy•ing.**

Dane (dān), *n.* a native or inhabitant of Denmark.

dan•ger (dān′jər), *n.* **1.** liability to harm or injury; risk; peril. **2.** an instance or cause of peril; menace. —**dan′ger•ous,** *adj.* —**dan′ger•ous•ly,** *adv.*

dan•gle (dang′gəl), *v.,* **-gled, -gling.** —*v.i.* **1.** to hang loosely, esp. with a swaying motion. **2.** to follow a person, as if seeking favor or attention. —*v.t.* **3.** to cause to dangle. **4.** to offer as an inducement.

Dan•ish (dā′nish), *adj.* **1.** of Denmark, the Danes, or their language. —*n.* **2.** the Germanic language of the Danes. **3.** (*sometimes l.c.*) Also called **Dan′ish pas′try.** a rich, yeast-leavened pastry filled with cheese or fruit.

dank (dangk), *adj.*, **-er, -est.** unpleasantly moist or humid. —**dank′ly,** *adv.* —**dank′ness,** *n.*

dap•per (dap′ər), *adj.* **1.** neat, trim, or smart in dress or demeanor. **2.** small and nimble.

dap•ple (dap′əl), *n.*, *adj.*, *v.*, **-pled, -pling.** —*n.* **1.** a spot or mottled marking. **2.** an animal with a mottled skin or coat. —*adj.* **3.** marked with spots. —*v.t.*, *v.i.* **4.** to mark or become marked with dapples.

dare (dâr), *v.*, **dared, daring,** *n.* —*v.i.* **1.** to have the necessary courage for something. —*v.t.* **2.** to have the boldness to try. **3.** to face courageously. **4.** to challenge (a person) to do something. —*auxiliary v.* **5.** to have the necessary courage to: *How dare you speak to me like that?* —*n.* **6.** an act of daring; challenge. —*Idiom.* **7. I daresay** (or **dare say**), I assume: *I daresay it's too late now.* —**dar′er,** *n.*

dare′dev′il *n.* **1.** a recklessly daring person. —*adj.* **2.** recklessly daring.

dar′ing *n.* **1.** adventurous courage. —*adj.* **2.** courageous or fearless. —**dar′ing•ly,** *adv.*

dark (därk), *adj.*, **-er, -est,** *n.* —*adj.* **1.** having little or no light. **2.** admitting or reflecting little light: *dark colors.* **3.** approaching black in hue. **4.** not pale or fair; swarthy. **5.** gloomy; dismal. **6.** evil; wicked. **7.** unenlightened. **8.** hard to understand; obscure. —*n.* **9.** the absence of light. **10.** night; nightfall. —*Idiom.* **11. in the dark,** in ignorance; uninformed. —**dark′en,** *v.t.*, *v.i.* —**dark′ly,** *adj.* —**dark′ness,** *n.*

Dark′ Ag′es *n.* the Middle Ages, esp. from about A.D. 476 to about 1000.

dark′ horse′ *n.* a little-known competitor or candidate that wins unexpectedly.

dark′room′ *n.* a room in which photographic materials are handled and from which certain rays of light are excluded.

dar•ling (där′ling), *n.* **1.** a person very dear to another. **2.** a favorite: *the darling of café society.* —*adj.* **3.** very dear; cherished. **4.** charming.

darn¹ (därn), *v.t.* **1.** to mend, esp. by interweaving stitches across a hole. —*n.* **2.** a darned place, as in a garment. —**darn′er,** *n.*

darn² (därn), *v.t.*, *interj.*, *n.*, *adj.*, *adv.* DAMN.

dart (därt), *n.* **1.** a small, slender missile usu. feathered at one end. **2. darts,** (*used with a sing. v.*) a game in which darts are thrown at a target. **3.** a sudden swift movement. **4.** a tapered seam of fabric. —*v.i.* **5.** to move swiftly; dash. —*v.t.* **6.** to thrust or move suddenly or rapidly.

dash (dash), *v.t.* **1.** to strike or smash violently, esp. so as to break to pieces. **2.** to throw violently or suddenly. **3.** to splash, often violently. **4.** to apply roughly, as by splashing. **5.** to ruin or frustrate. —*v.i.* **6.** to strike violently. **7.** to rush. **8. dash off, a.** to hurry away; leave. **b.** to write or do hastily. —*n.* **9.** a small quantity added: *a dash of salt.* **10.** a hasty or sudden movement. **11.** a punctuation mark (—) used to note a break, pause, or hesitation. **12.** the splashing of liquid against something. **13.** spirited action. **14.** a short race. **15.** a signal of longer duration than a dot, used in groups of dots, dashes, and spaces to represent letters in Morse code. **16.** a hasty stroke, esp. of a pen.

dash′board′ *n.* a panel with gauges and controls in front of the driver in an automobile.

dash′ing *adj.* **1.** energetic and spirited. **2.** elegant and gallant.

das•tard (das′tərd), *n.* a mean, sneaking coward. —**das′tard•ly,** *adj.*

da•ta (dā′tə, dat′ə), *n.* **1.** pl. of DATUM. **2.** (*used with a pl. v.*) facts, statistics, or items of information. **3.** (*used with a sing. v.*) a collection of facts; information.

da′ta•base′ or **da′ta base′,** *n.* **1.** a collection of data, esp. one in electronic form that can be accessed and manipulated by computer software. **2.** a fund of information on one or more subjects, accessible by computer.

da′ta proc′essing *n.* the rapid, automated processing of information, esp. by computers. —**da′ta proc′essor,** *n.*

date¹ (dāt), *n.*, *v.*, **dat•ed, dat•ing.** —*n.* **1.** a particular month, day, and year at which some event happened or will happen. **2.** the day of the month. **3.** an inscription on a writing, coin, etc., that shows the time of writing, casting, etc. **4.** the time or period to which any event or thing belongs. **5.** an appointment, esp. a social engagement arranged beforehand. **6.** a person with whom one has such an appointment. **7.** an engagement or booking. —*v.i.* **8.** to have a date. **9.** to belong to a particular period: *This church dates from 1830.* **10.** to go out socially on dates. —*v.t.* **11.** to mark or furnish with a date. **12.** to ascertain the date of. **13.** to show the age of; show to be old-fashioned. **14.** to go out on a date with. —*Idiom.* **15. to date,** up to the present time. —**dat′er,** *n.*

date² (dāt), *n.* the oblong, fleshy fruit of a tropical palm tree.

dat′ed *adj.* **1.** having or showing a date. **2.** out-of-date; outmoded.

da•tive (dā′tiv), *adj.* **1.** designating a grammatical case that indicates the indirect object of a verb or the object of certain prepositions. —*n.* **2.** the dative case.

da•tum (dā′təm, dat′əm), *n.*, *pl.* **da•ta. 1.** a single piece of information, as a fact or statistic; an item of data. **2.** any proposition from which conclusions may be drawn.

daub (dôb), *v.t.*, *v.i.* **1.** to cover or coat with soft, adhesive matter, as plaster or mud. **2.** to paint unskillfully. —*n.* **3.** something daubed on. **4.** a crude, inartistic painting. —**daub′er,** *n.*

daugh•ter (dô′tər), *n.* **1.** a girl or woman in relation to her parents. **2.** any female descendant.

daugh′ter-in-law′ *n.*, *pl.* **daugh•ters-in-law.** the wife of one's son.

daunt (dônt, dänt), *v.t.* **1.** to overcome with fear; intimidate. **2.** to dishearten. —**daunt′ing•ly,** *adv.*

daunt′less *adj.* not to be daunted or intimidated; fearless.

dav•en•port (dav′ən pôrt′), *n.* a large sofa, often one convertible into a bed.

daw•dle (dôd′l), *v.i.*, *v.t.*, **-dled, -dling.** to waste (time) by trifling; idle: *We dawdled away the whole morning.* —**daw′dler,** *n.*

dawn (dôn), *n.* **1.** the first appearance of daylight in the morning; daybreak; sunrise. **2.** the beginning of anything; advent. —*v.i.* **3.** to begin to grow light in the morning. **4.** to begin to open or develop. **5.** to begin to be perceived.

day (dā), *n.* **1.** the interval of light between two successive nights. **2.** the period of 24 hours during which the earth makes one rotation on its axis. **3.** the portion of a day allotted to work. **4.** Often, **days.** a particular era: *in olden days.* **5.** a period of existence, power, or influence: *His day will come.* **6.** the contest or battle at hand: *to win the day.* —*Idiom.* **7. call it a day,** to stop working for the rest of the day. **8. day in, day out,** every day without fail.

day′break′ *n.* the first appearance of daylight in the morning; dawn.

day′ care′ *n.* supervised daytime care for preschool children or the elderly, usu. at a center outside the home. —**day′-care′,** *adj.*

day′dream′ *n.* **1.** a visionary fancy indulged in while awake; reverie. **2.** a fanciful notion or plan. —*v.i.* **3.** to indulge in daydreams. —**day′dream′er,** *n.*

day′light′ *n.* **1.** the period of light during a day. **2.** public knowledge; openness. **3.** daybreak; dawn. **4. daylights,** wits; sanity: *scared the daylights out of me.*

day′light-sav′ing (or **day′light-sav′ings**)

time/, *n.* time one hour later than standard time, usu. used in the summer.

day/time/ *n.* the time between sunrise and sunset.

day/-to-day/ *adj.* **1.** occurring each day; daily. **2.** routine; normal.

daze (dāz), *v.,* **dazed, daz•ing,** *n.* —*v.t.* **1.** to stun with a blow, shock, etc. **2.** to overwhelm; dazzle. —*n.* **3.** a dazed condition.

daz•zle (daz/əl), *v.,* **-zled, -zling,** *n.* —*v.t., v.i.* **1.** to overpower or be overpowered by intense light. **2.** to bewilder or excite admiration by brilliance, splendor, etc. —*n.* **3.** the act of dazzling. —**daz/zler,** *n.*

dba doing business as.

dbl 1. decibel. **2.** double.

DC or **D.C.,** District of Columbia.

D.D. Doctor of Divinity. [< L *Divinitatis Doctor*]

D.D.S. 1. Doctor of Dental Science. **2.** Doctor of Dental Surgery.

DDT a toxic compound, formerly widely used as an insecticide.

de- a prefix meaning: away or off (*depart*); down or lower (*degrade*); completely (*despoil*); reverse (*de-activate*); remove (*decaffeinate*).

DE Delaware.

dea•con (dē/kən), *n.* **1.** a member of the clergy ranking just below a priest. **2.** an appointed or elected officer having variously defined duties. —**dea/con•ness,** *n. fem.*

de•ac•ti•vate (dē ak/tə vāt/), *v.t.,* **-vat•ed, -vat•ing. 1.** to make inactive: *to deactivate a chemical.* **2.** to demobilize (a military unit).

dead (ded), *adj.,* **-er, -est,** *n., adv.* —*adj.* **1.** no longer living. **2.** not endowed with life; inanimate. **3.** resembling death; deathlike: *a dead faint.* **4.** bereft of feeling; numb. **5.** extinguished: *a dead cigarette.* **6.** obsolete; no longer in general use. **7.** inoperative: *a dead battery.* **8.** utterly tired; exhausted. **9.** dull or inactive. **10.** complete; absolute: *dead silence.* **11.** exact; precise: *the dead center.* **12.** without bounce: *a dead ball.* —*n.* **13.** the period of greatest darkness, coldness, etc.: *the dead of night.* **14. the dead,** dead persons collectively. —*adv.* **15.** absolutely; completely. **16.** directly; straight.

dead/beat/ *n.* **1.** a person who avoids paying debts. **2.** a sponger.

dead/en *v.t.* **1.** to make less sensitive, intense, or effective. **2.** to make dull or lifeless. **3.** to sound-proof.

dead/ end/ *n.* **1.** a street, corridor, etc., that has no exit. **2.** a position with no hope of progress. —**dead/-end/,** *adj.*

dead/ heat/ *n.* a race in which two or more competitors finish in a tie.

dead/line/ *n.* the time by which something must be finished, submitted, accomplished, etc.

dead/lock/ *n.* **1.** a state, as in negotiations, in which progress halts; stalemate. —*v.t., v.i.* **2.** to bring or come to a deadlock.

dead/ly *adj.,* **-li•er, -li•est,** *adv.* —*adj.* **1.** causing or tending to cause death. **2.** aiming to kill or destroy; implacable: *a deadly enemy.* **3.** like death; deathly. **4.** excruciatingly boring. **5.** excessive; inordinate. **6.** extremely accurate. —*adv.* **7.** extremely; completely. —**dead/li•ness,** *n.*

dead/pan/ *adj.* marked by a fixed air of seriousness or detachment; expressionless.

dead/wood/ *n.* useless or extraneous persons or things.

deaf (def), *adj.,* **-er, -est. 1.** partially or wholly deprived of the sense of hearing. **2.** refusing to heed or be persuaded; unyielding. —**deaf/en,** *v.t.* —**deaf/ness,** *n.*

deaf/-mute/ *n. Often Offensive.* a person who is unable to hear and speak.

deal (dēl), *v.,* **dealt, deal•ing,** *n.* —*v.i.* **1.** to be occupied or concerned: *Botany deals with the study of plants.* **2.** to take action with respect to a thing or person. **3.** to conduct oneself. **4.** to trade or do business: *to deal in used cars.* —*v.t.* **5.** to apportion or distribute. **6.** to deliver; administer: *to deal a blow.* **7.** *Slang.* to buy and sell (drugs) illegally. —*n.* **8.** a business transaction. **9.** a bargain or arrangement. **10.** a secret or underhand agreement.

11. *Informal.* treatment received: *a raw deal.* **12.** an indefinite quantity: *a great deal of money.* **13. a.** the distribution of cards to the players in a game. **b.** the turn of a player to deal. —**deal/er,** *n.*

deal/ing *n.* Usu. **-ings.** interactions or transactions with others: *business dealings.*

dean (dēn), *n.* **1. a.** the head of a faculty in a university or college. **b.** an official in a university or college in charge of discipline, counseling, or admissions. **2.** the head of the chapter of a cathedral. **3.** the senior member of a group.

dear (dēr), *adj.,* **-er, -est,** *n., interj.* —*adj.* **1.** beloved; loved. **2.** (used in the salutation of a letter): *Dear Sir or Madam.* **3.** precious; cherished: *our dearest possessions.* **4.** earnest: *no dearer wish.* **5.** expensive. —*n.* **6.** a kind or generous person. **7.** a beloved one. —*interj.* **8.** an exclamation of surprise, distress, etc. —**dear/ly,** *adv.* —**dear/ness,** *n.*

dearth (dûrth), *n.* a scarcity or lack.

death (deth), *n.* **1.** the act of dying or state of being dead. **2.** extinction; destruction. **3.** a cause of death. —*Idiom.* **4. at death's door,** gravely ill. **5. to death,** to an intolerable degree: *bored to death.* —**death/like/,** *adj.* —**death/ly,** *adj., adv.*

death/bed/ *n.* **1.** the bed on which a person dies. **2.** the last hours before death.

death/less *adj.* not subject to death; immortal.

de•ba•cle (də bä/kəl, -bak/əl, dā-), *n.* **1.** a disaster or fiasco. **2.** a general rout or dispersal of troops.

de•bar (di bär/), *v.t.,* **-barred, -bar•ring. 1.** to shut out or exclude. **2.** to hinder or prevent; prohibit. —**de•bar/ment,** *n.*

de•bark (di bärk/), *v.i., v.t.* to disembark. —**de•bar•ka•tion** (dē/bär kā/shən), *n.*

de•base (di bās/), *v.t.,* **-based, -bas•ing.** to reduce in quality, value, or dignity. —**de•base/ment,** *n.*

de•bate (di bāt/), *n., v.,* **-bat•ed, -bat•ing.** —*n.* **1.** a discussion involving opposing viewpoints. **2.** a formal contest in which the affirmative and negative sides of a proposition are advocated by opposing speakers. —*v.i., v.t.* **3.** to discuss (a matter or issue) by giving opposing viewpoints. **4.** to participate in a formal debate with (a speaker) or on (an issue). —**de•bat/a•ble,** *adj.* —**de•bat/er,** *n.*

de•bauch (di bôch/), *v.t.* to corrupt by sensuality, intemperance, etc.; seduce. —*n.* **2.** an orgy. —**deb•au•chee** (deb/ô chē/, -shē/), *n., pl.* **-chees.** —**de•bauch/er•y,** *n., pl.* **-ies.**

de•bil•i•tate (di bil/i tāt/), *v.t.,* **-tat•ed, -tat•ing.** to make weak; enfeeble. —**de•bil/i•ta/tion,** *n.*

de•bil/i•ty *n., pl.* **-ties. 1.** a weakened or enfeebled state. **2.** a handicap or disability.

deb•it (deb/it), *n.* **1.** the record kept of another's indebtedness. **2.** a recorded item of debt. —*v.t.* **3.** to charge (a person or account) with a debt. **4.** to enter as a debit in an account.

de•bo•nair (deb/ə nâr/), *adj.* **1.** suave; worldly. **2.** jaunty; carefree. —**deb/o•nair/ly,** *adv.*

de•brief (dē brēf/), *v.t.* **1.** to interrogate (a soldier, astronaut, etc.) to gather information about a completed mission. **2.** to caution against revealing classified information after leaving a position.

de•bris or **dé•bris** (də brē/, dā/brē), *n.* **1.** the remains of anything destroyed or broken. **2.** accumulated loose fragments of rock.

debt (det), *n.* **1.** something that is owed, as money or a favor. **2.** an obligation to pay or render something. **3.** the condition of owing something. —**deb/tor,** *n.*

de•bug (dē bug/), *v.t.,* **-bugged, -bug•ging. 1.** to detect and remove defects or errors from: *to debug a computer program.* **2.** to remove electronic bugs from (a room or building).

de•bunk (di bungk/), *v.t.* to expose as being false or exaggerated.

de•but or **dé•but** (dā byōō/, di-, dā/byōō), *n.* **1.** a first public appearance, as of a performer or new product. **2.** a formal introduction of a young woman into society. —*v.i.* **3.** to make a debut. —*v.t.* **4.** to introduce to the public.

deb•u•tante or **déb•u•tante** (deb/yŏŏ tänt/), *n.* a young woman making a debut into society.

Dec or **Dec.,** December.

dec•ade (dek′ād) *n.* a period of ten years.

dec•a•dence (dek′ə dəns, di kād′ns) *n.* **1.** the act or process of falling into decay. **2.** moral degeneration. —**dec′a•dent,** *adj.*, *n.*

de•caf′fein•at′ed (dē kaf′ə nā′təd) *adj.* having the caffeine removed.

dec′a•he′dron (dek′ə hē′drən) *n.*, *pl.* **-drons, -dra** (-drə). a solid figure having 10 faces.

de•cal (dē′kal, di kal′) *n.* a picture or design on specially prepared paper for transfer to wood, metal, glass, etc.

Dec•a•logue or **-log** (dek′ə lôg′, -log′), *n.* (*often l.c.*) TEN COMMANDMENTS.

de•camp (di kamp′) *v.i.* **1.** to pack up and leave a camping ground. **2.** to depart hastily and often secretly. —**de•camp′ment,** *n.*

de•cant (di kant′) *v.t.* to pour liquor gently so as not to disturb the sediment.

de•cant′er *n.* an ornamental glass bottle for wine, brandy, or the like.

de•cap•i•tate (di kap′i tāt′), *v.t.*, **-tat•ed, -tat• ing.** to cut off the head of. —**de•cap′i•ta′tion,** *n.*

de•cath•lon (di kath′lon) *n.* an athletic contest in which a contestant competes in ten different track-and-field events.

de•cay (di kā′), *v.i.* **1.** to become decomposed; rot. **2.** to decline in health, prosperity, etc.; deteriorate. **3.** (of an atomic nucleus) to undergo radioactive decay. —*v.t.* **4.** to cause to decay. —*n.* **5.** decomposition; rot. **6.** a gradual decline. **7.** a radioactive process in which an atomic nucleus undergoes spontaneous transformation into one or more different nuclei.

de•cease (di sēs′), *n.*, *v.*, **-ceased, -ceas•ing.** —*n.* **1.** death. —*v.i.* **2.** to die. —**de•ceased′,** *adj.*, *n.*

de•ceit (di sēt′), *n.* **1.** the act or practice of deceiving. **2.** a stratagem intended to deceive. **3.** the quality of being deceitful; duplicity. —**de•ceit′ful,** *adj.*

de•ceive (di sēv′), *v.t.*, *v.i.*, **-ceived, -ceiv•ing.** to mislead by a false appearance or statement; trick. —**de•ceiv′er,** *n.* —**de•ceiv′ing•ly,** *adv.*

De•cem•ber (di sem′bər), *n.* the 12th month of the year, containing 31 days.

de•cen•cy (dē′sən sē), *n.*, *pl.* **-cies. 1.** the state or quality of being decent. **2.** courtesy; propriety.

de•cent (dē′sənt), *adj.* **1.** conforming to the recognized standard of propriety, as in behavior or speech. **2.** respectable; worthy. **3.** adequate; passable. **4.** kind; obliging. —**de′cent•ly,** *adv.*

de•cen•tral•ize (dē sen′trə līz′), *v.t.*, **-ized, -iz• ing. 1.** to distribute powers or functions of (a central authority) throughout local or regional divisions, branches, etc. **2.** to disperse (something) from an area of concentration. —**de•cen′tral•i•za′ tion,** *n.*

de•cep•tion (di sep′shən), *n.* **1.** the act of deceiving or state of being deceived. **2.** a trick; ruse. —**de• cep′tive,** *adj.*

dec•i•bel (des′ə bel′, -bəl), *n.* a unit used to express differences in power, esp. of sounds or voltages.

de•cide (di sīd′), *v.*, **-cid•ed, -cid•ing.** —*v.t.* **1.** to solve or conclude (a dispute) by awarding victory to one side. **2.** to make up one's mind about; resolve. —*v.i.* **3.** to come to a decision. —**de•cid′a•ble,** *adj.*

de•cid′ed *adj.* **1.** unquestionable; certain. **2.** resolute; determined. —**de•cid′ed•ly,** *adv.*

de•cid•u•ous (di sij′ōō əs), *adj.* **1.** shedding the leaves annually, as certain trees. **2.** falling off at a particular season or stage of growth, as leaves or horns.

dec•i•mal (des′ə məl), *adj.* **1.** pertaining to tenths or to the number 10. **2.** proceeding by tens: *a decimal system.* —*n.* **3.** DECIMAL FRACTION.

dec′imal frac′tion *n.* a fraction whose denominator is some power of 10, usu. indicated by a dot (**dec′imal point′**) written before the numerator: 0.4 = ⁴/₁₀.

dec•i•mate (des′ə māt′), *v.t.*, **-mat•ed, -mat•ing. 1.** to destroy a great number or proportion of. **2.** (esp. in ancient Rome) to select by lot and kill every tenth person of. —**dec′i•ma′tion,** *n.*

de•ci•pher (di sī′fər), *v.t.* **1.** to make out (a ju-

meaning of (something difficult). **2.** to decode, as something written in cipher. —**de•ci′pher•a•ble,** *adj.*

de•ci•sion (di sizh′ən), *n.* **1.** the act of deciding. **2.** the act of making up one's mind. **3.** something that is decided; resolution. **4.** a judgment, as one pronounced by a court. **5.** firmness; determination. **6.** the final score in any sport or contest.

de•ci′sive (-sī′siv), *adj.* **1.** having the power to decide. **2.** displaying firmness; resolute. **3.** unquestionable; definite: *a decisive lead.* —**de•ci′sive•ly,** *adv.* —**de•ci′sive•ness,** *n.*

deck (dek), *n.* **1.** a floor of a ship. **2.** a porch or other platform suggesting the deck of a ship. **3.** a pack of playing cards. —*v.t.* **4.** to clothe or array in something dressy or festive (often fol. by *out*). **5.** *Informal.* to knock down.

de•claim (di klām′), *v.t.*, *v.i.* to speak or utter loudly and rhetorically. —**de•claim′er,** *n.* —**de• clam′a•to′ry** (-klam′ə tôr′ē), *adj.*

dec′la•ma′tion (dek′lə mā′shən) *n.* speech or writing for oratorical effect.

de•clare′ (-klâr′), *v.t.*, **-clared, -clar•ing. 1.** to make known publicly; announce officially. **2.** to state emphatically. **3.** to reveal; indicate. **4.** to make due statement of, as income for taxation. **5.** to bid (a trump suit or no-trump) in bridge. —**dec•la•ra• tion** (dek′lə rā′shən), *n.* —**de•clar′er,** *n.*

de•clen•sion (di klen′shən), *n.* **1.** the inflection of nouns, pronouns, and adjectives. **2.** a bending, sloping, or moving downward. **3.** deterioration; decline.

de•cline (di klīn′), *v.*, **-clined, -clin•ing,** *n.* —*v.t.* **1.** to refuse with courtesy. **2.** to cause to slope or incline downward. **3.** to inflect (a noun, pronoun, or adjective). —*v.i.* **4.** to express courteous refusal. **5.** to deteriorate or weaken. **6.** to fall or drop. **7.** to slope downward. **8.** to draw toward the close, as the day. —*n.* **9.** a downward slope. **10.** a downward movement, as of prices. **11.** a deterioration, as in strength or power. —**dec′li•na′tion** (dek′lə-nā′shən), *n.*

de•code (dē kōd′), *v.t.*, **-cod•ed, -cod•ing.** to translate (data or a message) from a code into the original language or form.

de′com•mis′sion *v.t.* to retire (a ship, airplane, etc.) from active service.

de′com•pose′ *v.t.*, *v.i.*, **-posed, -pos•ing. 1.** to separate into constituent parts or elements; disintegrate. **2.** to rot; putrefy. —**de′com•po•si′tion** (-kom pə zish′ən), *n.*

de•con•ges•tant (dē′kən jes′tənt), *adj.* **1.** relieving mucus congestion of the upper respiratory tract. —*n.* **2.** a decongestant agent.

de′con•tam′i•nate′ (-nāt′), *v.t.*, **-nat•ed, -nat• ing.** to make safe by removing or neutralizing harmful contaminants. —**de′con•tam′i•na′tion,** *n.*

dé•cor or **de•cor** (dā kôr′, di-), *n.* style of decoration, as of a room.

dec•o•rate (dek′ə rāt′), *v.t.*, **-rat•ed, -rat•ing. 1.** to furnish or adorn with something ornamental or becoming. **2.** to design the interior of (a room or building). **3.** to confer a medal or honor on. —**dec′o•ra′ tion,** *n.* —**dec′o•ra′tive,** *adj.* —**dec′o•ra′tor,** *n.*

dec′o•rous *adj.* showing respect for social customs and manners. —**dec′o•rous•ly,** *adv.*

de•co•rum (di kôr′əm), *n.* **1.** propriety of conduct, manners, or appearance. **2.** (*pl.* **-rums.** of the customs and observances of polite society.

de•coy (*n.* dē′koi, di koi′; *v.* di koi′, dē′koi), *n.* **1.** a person who lures another, as into danger or a trap. **2.** anything used as a lure. **3.** an artificial or trained bird or other animal used to entice game into a trap or within gunshot. —*v.t.* **4.** to lure by or as if by a decoy. [< D *de kooi* the cage]

de•crease (*v.* di krēs′; *n.* dē′krēs, di krēs′), *v.*, **-creased, -creas•ing.** —*v.i.*, *v.t.* **1.** to lessen, as in extent, quantity, or power; diminish. —*n.* **2.** the act or process of decreasing. **3.** the amount by which a thing is lessened.

de•cree (di krē′), *n.*, *v.*, **-creed, -cree•ing.** —*n.* **1.** a formal order usu. having the force of law. **2.** a judicial decision. —*v.t.*, *v.i.* **3.** to ordain or decide by or as if by decree.

de•crep•it (di krep′it), *adj.* **1.** weakened by old age. **2.** worn out by long use. —**de•crep′i•tude′,** *n.*

de•cre•scen•do (dē′kri shen′dō, dā′-), *adj., adv. Music.* gradually decreasing in loudness.

de•crim•i•nal•ize (dē krim′ə nl īz′), *v.t.*, -ized, -iz•ing. to eliminate criminal penalties for. —**de•crim′i•nal•i•za′tion,** *n.*

de•cry (di krī′), *v.t.*, -cried, -cry•ing. to disparage openly; denounce.

ded•i•cate (ded′i kāt′), *v.t.*, -cat•ed, -cat•ing. **1.** to consecrate to a sacred purpose. **2.** to devote to some purpose or person. **3.** to offer (a book, piece of music, etc.) to someone, as on a prefatory inscription. **4.** to set apart for a specific purpose. —**ded′i•ca′tion,** *n.*

de•duce (di dōōs′), *v.t.*, -duced, -duc•ing. **1.** to derive as a conclusion from something known or assumed; infer. **2.** to trace the course of. —**de•duc′i•ble,** *adj.*

de•duct (di dukt′), *v.t.* to take away from a total. —**de•duct′i•ble,** *adj.*

de•duc′tion *n.* **1.** the act of deducting; subtraction. **2.** something deducted. **3.** the act or process of deducing. **4.** something deduced. **5. a.** a process of reasoning from the general to the particular. **b.** a conclusion reached by this process. —**de•duc′tive,** *adj.*

deed (dēd), *n.* **1.** something that is done. **2.** an exploit or achievement. **3.** a document executed under seal and delivered to effect a conveyance, esp. of real estate. —*v.t.* **4.** to convey by deed.

dee•jay (dē′jā′), *n.* DISC JOCKEY.

deem (dēm), *v.t.* to hold as an opinion; think.

deep (dēp), *adj.* and *adv.*, -er, -est, *n.* —*adj.* **1.** extending far down from the top or surface. **2.** extending far in or back from the front. **3.** extending far in width; broad. **4.** having a specified depth: *10 feet deep.* **5.** immersed or involved: *deep in thought.* **6.** difficult to understand. **7.** intense; profound: *deep sorrow.* **8.** dark and vivid: *a deep red.* **9.** low in pitch, as a voice. **10.** mysterious; obscure: *deep, dark secrets.* —*adv.* **11.** to or at a considerable or specified depth. **12.** far on in time: *to look deep into the future.* —*n.* **13.** the deep part of the ocean. **14.** the part of greatest intensity, as of winter. **15. the deep,** *Literary.* the sea or ocean. —**deep′en,** *v.t., v.i.* —**deep′ly,** *adv.* —**deep′ness,** *n.*

deep′-freeze′ *v.t.*, -freezed or -froze, -freezed or -fro•zen, -freez•ing. to freeze (food) rapidly so that it can be stored at freezing temperatures.

deep′-fry′ *v.t.*, -fried, -fry•ing. to fry in oil sufficient to cover the food. —**deep′-fry′er,** *n.*

deep′-seat′ed *adj.* firmly implanted or established.

deep′ space′ *n.* space beyond the solar system.

deer (dēr), *n., pl.* **deer,** (*occasionally*) **deers.** any of a family of hoofed, ruminant mammals, the males usu. growing and shedding antlers.

de•face (di fās′), *v.t.*, -faced, -fac•ing. to mar the appearance of; disfigure. —**de•face′ment,** *n.*

de fac•to (dē fak′tō, dā), *adv.* **1.** in fact; in reality. —*adj.* **2.** actually existing, esp. without lawful authority: *de facto segregation.*

de•fame (di fām′), *v.t.*, -famed, -fam•ing. to attack the good name or reputation of; slander or libel. —**def•a•ma•tion** (def′ə mā′shən), *n.* —**de•fam′a•to′ry** (-fam′ə tôr′ē), *adj.*

de•fault (di fôlt′), *n.* **1.** failure to act or appear, esp. in meeting financial or legal obligations. —*v.t.* **2.** to lose by default. —*v.i.* **3.** to fail to fulfill an obligation.

de•feat (di fēt′), *v.t.* **1.** to overcome in a contest; vanquish. **2.** to frustrate; thwart. —*n.* **3.** the act of defeating or state of being defeated. —**de•feat′er,** *n.*

de•feat′ist *n.* one who accepts defeat too easily. —**de•feat′ism,** *n.*

def•e•cate (def′i kāt′), *v.i.*, -cat•ed, -cat•ing. to void excrement from the bowels through the anus. —**def′e•ca′tion,** *n.*

de•fect (*n.* dē′fekt, di fekt′; *v.* di fekt′), *n.* **1.** a fault or shortcoming; imperfection. **2.** lack of some-

thing essential; deficiency. —*v.i.* **3.** to desert a cause, country, etc.

de•fec′tion *n.* desertion of a cause, country, etc. —**de•fec′tor,** *n.*

de•fec′tive *adj.* faulty or imperfect.

de•fend (di fend′), *v.t.* **1.** to guard against attack or injury. **2.** to maintain by argument; uphold. **3.** to contest (a legal charge or claim). **4.** to serve as attorney for (a defendant). **5.** to attempt to retain (a championship title) in competition. —**de•fend′er,** *n.*

de•fend′ant *n.* one against whom a legal action or suit is brought in a court.

de•fense (di fens′; *esp. for 5,* dē′fens), *n.* **1.** resistance against attack. **2.** something that defends. **3.** the defending of a cause or the like by speech, argument, etc. **4. a.** the defendant's answer to the plaintiff's charge or claim. **b.** a defendant together with counsel. **5. a.** the tactics used to defend oneself or one's goal in a game. **b.** the team defending itself. —**de•fense′less,** *adj.* —**de•fen′si•ble,** *adj.*

de•fen′sive *adj.* **1.** serving or done for the purpose of defense. **2.** sensitive to the threat of criticism. —*n.* **3.** a position or attitude of defense.

de•fer[1] (di fûr′), *v.*, -ferred, -fer•ring. —*v.t.* **1.** to postpone; delay. **2.** to exempt temporarily from induction into military service. —*v.i.* **3.** to put off action; delay. —**de•fer′ment,** *n.*

de•fer[2] (di fûr′), *v.i.*, -ferred, -fer•ring. to yield respectfully in judgment or opinion.

def•er•ence (def′ər əns), *n.* **1.** respectful yielding to the opinion, will, etc., of another. **2.** respectful regard. —**def′er•en′tial,** *adj.*

de•fi•ance (di fī′əns), *n.* **1.** a bold resistance to authority or force. **2.** open disregard; contempt. —**de•fi′ant,** *adj.* —**de•fi′ant•ly,** *adv.*

de•fi•cien•cy (di fish′ən sē) *n., pl.* -cies. lack. —**de•fi′cient,** *adj.*

def•i•cit (def′ə sit), *n.* **1.** the amount by which a sum of money falls short of the required amount. **2.** a loss, as in the operation of a business. **3.** a deficiency or handicap.

de•file[1] (di fīl′), *v.t.*, -filed, -fil•ing. **1.** to make foul, dirty, or unclean. **2.** to violate the chastity of. **3.** to desecrate. **4.** to sully, as a person's reputation. —**de•file′ment,** *n.* —**de•fil′er,** *n.*

de•file[2] (di fīl′, dē′fīl), *n.* a narrow passage, esp. between mountains.

de•fine (di fīn′), *v.t.*, -fined, -fin•ing. **1.** to state the meaning of (a word, phrase, etc.). **2.** to explain or identify the qualities of. **3.** to specify. **4.** to make clear the outline or form of. —**de•fin′er,** *n.*

def•i•nite (def′ə nit), *adj.* **1.** clearly defined or determined; precise. **2.** having fixed limits. **3.** positive; certain. —**def′i•nite•ly,** *adv.* —**def′i•nite•ness,** *n.*

def•i•ni′tion *n.* **1.** the act of making definite, distinct, or clear. **2.** the formal statement of the meaning of a word, phrase, etc. **3.** the condition of being definite. **4.** sharpness of the image formed by an optical system.

de•fin•i•tive (di fin′i tiv), *adj.* **1.** most reliable or complete: *a definitive edition.* **2.** serving to define or specify definitely. **3.** decisive or conclusive: *a definitive answer.* —**de•fin′i•tive•ly,** *adv.*

de•flate (di flāt′), *v.*, -flat•ed, -flat•ing. —*v.t.* **1.** to release the air or gas from. **2.** to reduce in importance or size: *The rebuff deflated his ego.* **3.** to reduce (currency, prices, etc.) from an inflated condition. —*v.i.* **4.** to become deflated.

de•fla′tion *n.* **1.** the act of deflating or state of being deflated. **2.** a fall in the general price level or a contraction of credit and available money.

de•flect (di flekt′), *v.t., v.i.* to bend; turn from a course. —**de•flec′tion,** *n.* —**de•flec′tive,** *adj.* —**de•flec′tor,** *n.*

de•fo′li•ate′ *v.t., v.i.*, -at•ed, -at•ing. **1.** to strip of leaves. **2.** to destroy (an area of jungle, forest, etc.), as to deprive an enemy of concealment. —**de•fo′li•ant,** *n.* —**de•fo′li•a′tion,** *n.* —**de•fo′li•a′tor,** *n.*

de•for•est (dē fôr′ist, -for′-), *v.t.* to clear of forests or trees. —**de•for′est•a′tion,** *n.*

de•form (di fôrm′), *v.t.* **1.** to mar the natural form or shape of; disfigure. **2.** to mar the beauty of;

spoil. —**de′for•ma′tion,** *n.* —**de•formed′,** *adj.*
—**de•form′i•ty,** *n., pl.* **-ties.**

de•fraud (di frôd′), *v.t.,* to deprive of a right, money, or property by fraud. —**de•fraud′er,** *n.*

de•fray (di frā′), *v.t.* to pay all or part of: *to defray the costs.* —**de•fray′al,** *n.*

de•frost (di frôst′, -frost′), *v.t.* **1.** to remove the frost or ice from. **2.** to thaw (frozen food). —*v.i.* **3.** to become free of frost. **4.** to thaw. —**de•frost′er,** *n.*

deft (deft), *adj.,* **-er, -est.** skillful; nimble; facile. —**deft′ly,** *adv.* —**deft′ness,** *n.*

de•funct (di fungkt′), *adj.* **1.** no longer in effect or use. **2.** no longer in existence; dead; extinct.

de•fuse (dē fyōōz′), *v.t.,* **-fused, -fus•ing. 1.** to remove the fuse from (a bomb, mine, etc.). **2.** to make less dangerous or tense.

de•fy (di fī′), *v.t.,* **-fied, -fy•ing. 1.** to resist boldly or openly. **2.** to offer effective resistance to. **3.** to challenge (a person) to do something deemed impossible.

de•gen•er•ate (*v.* di jen′ə rāt′; *adj., n.* -ər it), *v.,* **-at•ed, -at•ing,** *adj.* —*v.i.* **1.** to decline in physical, mental, or moral qualities; deteriorate. —*adj.* **2.** having declined in physical or moral qualities; deteriorated; degraded. —*n.* **3.** a person who has declined, esp. in morals. **4.** a sexual deviate. —**de•gen′er•a•cy** (-ər ə sē), *n.* —**de•gen′er•a′tion,** *n.* —**de•gen′er•a•tive** (-ər ə tiv, -ə rā′tiv), *adj.*

de•grade (di grād′ *or, for 3,* dē-), *v.,* **-grad•ed, -grad•ing.** —*v.t.* **1.** to lower in dignity or estimation. **2.** to lower in character or quality; debase. **3.** to reduce to a lower rank, degree, etc. —**deg•ra•da′tion** (deg′ri dā′shən), *n.*

de•gree (di grē′), *n.* **1.** any of a series of steps or stages, as in a process. **2.** a stage in a scale of intensity or amount. **3.** extent, measure, scope, or the like. **4.** an academic title conferred by universities and colleges upon the completion of studies. **5.** a unit of measure for temperature. **6.** *Math.* the 360th part of a complete angle or turn. **7.** the distinctive classification of a crime according to its gravity. **8.** one of the parallel formations of adjectives and adverbs used to express differences in quality, quantity, or intensity. **9.** the sum of the exponents of the variables in an algebraic term. **10.** a tone, step, or note of a musical scale.

de•hu•man•ize (dē hyōō′mə nīz′; *often* -yōō′-), *v.t.,* **-ized, -iz•ing.** to deprive of human qualities; divest of individuality. —**de•hu′man•i•za′tion,** *n.*

de′hu•mid′i•fi•er *n.* any device for removing moisture from air. —**de′hu•mid′i•fy,** *v.t.,* **-fied, -fy•ing.**

de•hy′drate *v.,* **-drat•ed, -drat•ing.** —*v.t.* **1.** to remove water from; dry. —*v.i.* **2.** to lose fluids or water. —**de′hy•dra′tion,** *n.*

de•i•fy (dē′ə fī′), *v.t.,* **-fied, -fy•ing. 1.** to make a god of. **2.** to exalt as an object of worship. —**de′i•fi•ca′tion,** *n.*

deign (dān), *v.t., v.i.* to condescend (to do or grant).

de•in′sti•tu′tion•al•ize′ *v.,* **-ized, -izing.** to release (a mental patient, disabled person, etc.) from institutionalized care and treat or support with community resources.

de•ism (dē′iz əm), *n.* belief in the existence of a God on the evidence of reason and nature, with rejection of supernatural revelation. —**de′ist,** *n.* —**de•is′tic,** *adj.*

de•i•ty (dē′i tē), *n., pl.* **-ties. 1.** a god or goddess. **2.** divine character or nature; divinity. **3. the Deity,** God.

dé•jà vu (dā′zhä vōō′), *n.* the illusion of having previously experienced something actually being encountered for the first time. [< F: lit., already seen]

de•ject•ed (di jek′tid), *adj.* depressed in spirits; disheartened. —**de•jec′tion,** *n.*

de ju•re (di jōōr′ē, dā jōōr′ā), *adv., adj.* by right or according to law.

Del. Delaware.

de•lay (di lā′), *v.t.* **1.** to put off to a later time; postpone. **2.** to impede or retard. —*v.i.* **3.** to put off action; linger. —*n.* **4.** the act of delaying. **5.** an instance of being delayed. —**de•lay′er,** *n.*

de•lec•ta•ble (di lek′tə bəl), *adj.* **1.** delightful; highly pleasing. **2.** delicious.

del•e•gate (*n.* del′i git, -gāt′; *v.* -gāt′), *n., v.,* **-gat•ed, -gat•ing.** —*n.* **1.** a person designated to act for or represent another or others. **2.** a member of the lower house of the legislatures of Virginia, West Virginia, and Maryland. —*v.t.* **3.** to send or appoint as a delegate. **4.** to commit (powers, functions, etc.) to another as agent. —**del′e•ga′tion,** *n.*

de•lete (di lēt′), *v.t.,* **-let•ed, -let•ing.** to strike out or remove (something written or printed); erase. —**de•le′tion,** *n.*

del•e•te•ri•ous (del′i tēr′ē əs), *adj.* injurious to health; harmful.

del•i (del′ē), *n., pl.* **-is** (-ēz). delicatessen.

de•lib•er•ate (*adj.* di lib′ər it; *v.* -ə rāt′), *adj., v.,* **-at•ed, -at•ing.** —*adj.* **1.** studied or intentional. **2.** careful or slow in deciding. **3.** slow and even; unhurried. —*v.t.* **4.** to weigh in the mind; consider. —*v.i.* **5.** to consult or confer formally. —**de•lib′er•ate•ly,** *adv.* —**de•lib′e•ra′tion,** *n.*

del•i•ca•cy (del′i kə sē), *n., pl.* **-cies. 1.** the quality or state of being delicate. **2.** something delightful or pleasing, esp. a choice food.

del′i•cate (-kit), *adj.* **1.** fine in texture, quality, construction, etc. **2.** fragile; easily damaged. **3.** frail or sickly. **4.** fine or precise in action or execution. **5.** requiring or showing great care, caution, or tact. **6.** keenly sensitive. —**del′i•cate•ly,** *adv.* —**del′i•cate•ness,** *n.*

del•i•ca•tes•sen (del′i kə tes′ən), *n.* **1.** a store selling prepared foods, as cooked meats, cheese, and salads. **2.** the products sold in a delicatessen.

de•li•cious (di lish′əs), *adj.* **1.** highly pleasing to taste or smell. **2.** very pleasing; delightful. —**de•li′cious•ly,** *adv.* —**de•li′cious•ness,** *n.*

de•light (di līt′), *n.* **1.** a high degree of pleasure or enjoyment; joy; rapture. **2.** something that gives great pleasure. —*v.t.* **3.** to give delight to. —*v.i.* **4.** to have or take great pleasure. —**de•light′ed,** *adj.* —**de•light′ful,** *adj.*

de•lim•it (di lim′it), *v.t.* to fix or mark the limits or boundaries of. —**de•lim′i•ta′tion,** *n.*

de•lin•e•ate (di lin′ē āt′), *v.t.,* **-at•ed, -at•ing. 1.** to trace the outline of. **2.** to portray or describe in words. —**de•lin′e•a′tion,** *n.*

de•lin•quent (di ling′kwənt), *adj.* **1.** failing in or neglectful of a duty or obligation; guilty of a misdeed or offense. **2.** past due: *a delinquent account.* —*n.* **3.** a person who is delinquent, esp. a juvenile delinquent. —**de•lin′quen•cy,** *n., pl.* **-cies.** —**de•lin′quent•ly,** *adv.*

de•lir•i•um (di lēr′ē əm), *n., pl.* **-i•ums, -i•a** (-ē ə). **1.** a temporary disturbance of consciousness characterized by restlessness, excitement, and delusions or hallucinations. **2.** a state of violent excitement or emotion. —**de•lir′i•ous,** *adj.*

de•liv•er (di liv′ər), *v.t.* **1.** to carry and turn over (letters, goods, etc.) to the intended recipient. **2.** to hand over; surrender. **3.** to utter or pronounce: *to deliver a speech.* **4.** to strike or throw: *to deliver a blow.* **5.** to set free or liberate. **6.** to assist at the birth of. —*v.i.* **7.** to give birth. **8.** to do or carry out something. —**de•liv′er•ance,** *n.* —**de•liv′er•er,** *n.* —**de•liv′er•y,** *n.*

dell (del), *n.* a small, usu. wooded valley.

del•phin•i•um (del fin′ē əm), *n., pl.* **-i•ums, -i•a** (-ē ə). a plant whose tall branching stalks bear colorful spurred flowers.

del•ta (del′tə), *n., pl.* **-tas. 1.** the fourth letter of the Greek alphabet (Δ, δ). **2.** a nearly flat plain of alluvial, often triangular deposit between diverging branches of the mouth of a river.

de•lude (di lōōd′), *v.t.,* **-lud•ed, -lud•ing.** to mislead or deceive.

del•uge (del′yōōj), *n., v.,* **-uged, -ug•ing.** —*n.* **1.** a great flood; inundation. **2.** a drenching rain; downpour. **3.** anything that overwhelms like a flood. —*v.t.* **4.** to flood; inundate. **5.** to overwhelm.

de•lu•sion (di lōō′zhən), *n.* **1.** the act of deluding or state of being deluded. **2.** a false belief or opinion, esp. one that is irrational or psychotic. —**de•lu′sion•al,** *adj.*

de•luxe (də luks′, -lŏŏks′), *adj.* of special elegance or sumptuousness.

delve (delv), *v.i.,* **delved, delv•ing.** to investigate or search carefully for information.

Dem. 1. Democrat. **2.** Democratic.

dem•a•gogue or **-gog** (dem′ə gog′, -gôg′), *n.* an orator or political leader who gains power by arousing people's emotions and prejudices. —**dem′a•gogu′er•y, dem′a•go′gy** (-gō′jē, -goj′ē), *n.*

de•mand (di mand′, -mänd′), *v.t.* **1.** to ask for with authority; claim as a right. **2.** to ask for peremptorily or urgently. **3.** to call for or require. —*v.i.* **4.** to make a demand; inquire; ask. —*n.* **5.** the act of demanding. **6.** something demanded. **7.** an urgent or pressing requirement. **8. a.** the desire and means to purchase goods. **b.** the amount of goods purchased at a specific price. **9.** the state of being sought for purchase or use: *an article in great demand.* —*Idiom.* **10. on demand,** upon presentation or request for payment.

de•mar•cate (di mär′kāt, dē′mär kāt′), *v.t.,* **-cat•ed, -cat•ing.** to determine or mark off the boundaries of. —**de′mar•ca′tion,** *n.*

de•mean[1] (di mēn′), *v.t.* to lower in dignity or standing; debase.

de•mean[2] (di mēn′), *v.t.* to conduct or behave (oneself) in a specified manner.

de•mean′or *n.* conduct; behavior; deportment. Also, *esp. Brit.,* **de•mean′our.**

de•ment•ed (di men′tid), *adj.* **1.** crazy; insane; mad. **2.** affected with dementia.

de•men′tia (-shə, -shē ə), *n.* severely impaired memory and reasoning ability, associated with damaged brain tissue.

de•mer•it (di mer′it), *n.* a mark against a person for misconduct or deficiency.

demi- a combining form meaning half or lesser (*demigod*).

dem•i•god (dem′ē god′), *n.* **1.** a lesser or minor god. **2.** a deified mortal.

de•mil•i•ta•rize (dē mil′i tə rīz′), *v.t.,* **-rized, -riz•ing. 1.** to deprive of military character; place under civil control. **2.** to forbid military use of. —**de•mil′i•ta•ri•za′tion,** *n.*

de•mise (di mīz′), *n., v.,* **-mised, -mis•ing.** —*n.* **1.** death or decease. **2.** a conveyance or transfer of an estate. —*v.t.* **3.** to transfer (an estate) by bequest or lease.

dem•i•tasse (dem′i tas′, -täs′), *n.* **1.** a small cup for serving black coffee after dinner. **2.** the coffee served.

dem•o (dem′ō), *n., pl.* **-os.** a phonograph or tape recording distributed to demonstrate the merits of a new song or performer.

de•mo•bi•lize (dē mō′bə līz′), *v.t.,* **-lized, -liz•ing.** to disband (troops). —**de•mo′bi•li•za′tion,** *n.*

de•moc•ra•cy (di mok′rə sē), *n., pl.* **-cies. 1.** government in which supreme power is exercised directly by the people or by their elected agents. **2.** a state having such government. **3.** a state of society characterized by formal equality of rights and privileges.

dem•o•crat (dem′ə krat′), *n.* **1.** an advocate of democracy. **2.** (*cap.*) a member of the Democratic Party.

dem′o•crat′ic *adj.* **1.** pertaining to or of the nature of democracy. **2.** advocating democracy. **3.** (*cap.*) of the Democratic Party. —**dem′o•crat′i•cal•ly,** *adv.*

Dem′ocrat′ic Par′ty *n.* one of the two major political parties in the U.S., dating from 1828.

dem′o•graph′ic (dem′ə graf′ik) *adj.* of statistics on population. —**dem′o•graph′i•cal•ly,** *adv.* —**dem′o•graph′ics,** *n.pl.* —**de•mog′ra•phy** (di-mog′rə fē), *n.*

de•mol•ish (di mol′ish), *v.t.* to destroy or ruin; tear down. —**dem•o•li•tion** (dem′ə lish′ən, dē′-mə-), *n.*

de•mon (dē′mən), *n.* **1.** an evil spirit; fiend. **2.** a wicked or cruel person. **3.** one with great energy.

de•mon′ic (di mon′ik) *adj.* **1.** inspired as if by a demon or indwelling spirit. **2.** of, pertaining to, or like a demon.

de•mon•stra•ble (di mon′strə bəl), *adj.* capable of being demonstrated or proved. —**de•mon′stra•bly,** *adv.*

dem•on•strate (dem′ən strāt′), *v.,* **-strat•ed, -strat•ing.** —*v.t.* **1.** to describe, explain, or illustrate by examples, experiments, etc. **2.** to make evident by reasoning; prove. **3.** to display openly. **4.** to exhibit the use of (a product). —*v.i.* **5.** to make a public exhibition of group feelings, as by parades or meetings. —**dem′on•stra′tion,** *n.* —**dem′on•stra′-tor,** *n.*

de•mon•stra•tive (də mon′strə tiv), *adj.* **1.** given to open expression of one's feelings. **2.** explanatory or illustrative. **3.** serving to prove; conclusive. **4.** singling out the thing referred to: *a demonstrative pronoun.* —*n.* **5.** a demonstrative word, as *this* or *there.*

de•mor•al•ize (di môr′ə līz′, -mor′-), *v.t.,* **-ized, -iz•ing. 1.** to destroy the morale of. **2.** to throw into confusion; bewilder. **3.** to corrupt the morals of. —**de•mor′al•i•za′tion,** *n.*

de•mote (di mōt′), *v.t.,* **-mot•ed, -mot•ing.** to reduce to a lower grade or rank. —**de•mo′tion,** *n.*

de•mur (di mûr′), *v.i.,* **-murred, -mur•ring.** to make objection, esp. on the grounds of scruples. —**de•mur′ral,** *n.*

de•mure (di myŏŏr′), *adj.,* **-mur•er, -mur•est. 1.** shy and modest. **2.** affectedly or coyly decorous. —**de•mure′ly,** *adv.*

den (den), *n.* **1.** the lair of a wild animal, esp. a predatory mammal. **2.** a room in a home designed to provide a comfortable place for conversation, reading, etc. **3.** a cave used for shelter or concealment. **4.** a squalid abode.

de•na•ture (dē nā′chər), *v.t.,* **-tured, -tur•ing. 1.** to deprive (something) of its natural character. **2.** to render (any of various alcohols) undrinkable.

de•ni•al (di nī′əl), *n.* **1.** an assertion that an allegation is false. **2.** refusal to believe a doctrine, theory, or the like. **3.** the refusal to satisfy a claim, request, etc. **4.** disavowal or repudiation. **5.** SELF-DENIAL.

den•i•grate (den′i grāt′), *v.t.,* **-grat•ed, -grat•ing.** to speak damagingly of; defame or disparage. —**den′i•gra′tion,** *n.*

den•im (den′əm), *n.* **1.** a coarse twill fabric of cotton or other fibers, used esp. for jeans. **2.** denims, (*used with a pl. v.*) clothes of denim. [< F: short for *serge de Nîmes* serge of Nîmes (city in France)]

den•i•zen (den′ə zən), *n.* **1.** an inhabitant; resident. **2.** a person who frequents a place.

Den•mark (den′märk), *n.* a kingdom in N Europe.

de•nom•i•nate (di nom′ə nāt′), *v.t.,* **-nat•ed, -nat•ing.** to give a name to; denote; designate.

de•nom′i•na′tion *n.* **1.** a particular religious body. **2.** one of the grades or degrees in a series of values: *bills of small denomination.* **3.** a class or kind of persons or things distinguished by a specific name. —**de•nom′i•na′tion•al,** *adj.*

de•nom′i•na′tor *n.* **1.** the term of a fraction, usu. written under or after the line, that indicates the number of equal parts into which the unit is divided. **2.** something held in common.

de•note (di nōt′), *v.t.,* **-not•ed, -not•ing. 1.** to be a mark or sign of; indicate. **2.** to be a name or designation for; mean. —**de•no•ta•tion** (dē′nō tā′-shən), *n.* —**de′no•ta′tive,** *adj.*

de•noue•ment or **dé•noue•ment** (dā′nōō-mäN′), *n.* the final resolution of a plot, as of a drama or novel.

de•nounce (di nouns′), *v.t.,* **-nounced, -nounc•ing. 1.** to condemn or censure openly or publicly. **2.** to make a formal accusation against, as to the police. —**de•nounce′ment,** *n.*

dense (dens), *adj.,* **dens•er, dens•est. 1.** having its parts crowded together; compact. **2.** slow-witted; dull. **3.** opaque; not clear. **4.** difficult to understand. —**dense′ly,** *adv.* —**dense′ness,** *n.* —**den′si•ty,** *n.*

dent (dent), *n.* **1.** a small depression in a surface, as from a blow. **2.** a slight effect. **3.** slight progress: *I haven't made a dent in this pile of work.* —*v.t.* **4.** to make a dent in or on. —*v.i.* **5.** to become dented.

den·tal (den′tl), *adj.* of or for the teeth or dentistry.

den′tal floss′ *n.* thread used to dislodge food particles from between the teeth.

den′ti·frice (-tə fris), *n.* a preparation for cleaning the teeth.

den′tin (-tn, -tin) also **-tine** (-tēn), *n.* the hard, calcareous tissue that forms the major portion of a tooth.

den′tist (-tist), *n.* a person whose profession is the prevention and treatment of diseases of the teeth, gums, and oral cavity. —**den′tist·ry,** *n.*

den′ture (-chər, -chŏŏr), *n.* an artificial replacement of one or more teeth.

de·nude (di nōōd′, -nyōōd′), *v.t.,* **-nud·ed, -nud·ing.** to strip bare.

de·nun·ci·a·tion (di nun′sē ā′shən, -shē-), *n.* an act or instance of denouncing.

de·ny (di nī′), *v.t.,* **-nied, -ny·ing. 1.** to declare that (a statement) is not true. **2.** to refuse to agree to. **3.** to withhold the possession, use, or enjoyment of. **4.** to refuse to grant a request of. **5.** to disavow; repudiate.

de·o·dor·ant (dē ō′dər ənt), *n.* **1.** a substance for inhibiting or masking odors. —*adj.* **2.** capable of destroying odors.

de·o′dor·ize′ *v.t.,* **-ized, -iz·ing.** to rid of odor. —de·o′dor·i·za′tion, *n.* —de·o′dor·iz′er, *n.*

de·part (di pärt′), *v.i.* **1.** to go away; leave. **2.** to diverge or deviate. **3.** to die. —*v.t.* **4.** to go away from; leave. —**de·par′ture,** *n.*

de·part·ment (di pärt′mənt), *n.* **1.** a distinct part or division, as of a government or business. **2.** a sphere of activity or knowledge. —**de·part·men·tal** (di pärt men′tl, dē′pärt-), *adj.*

de·pend (di pend′), *v.i.* **1.** to rely; place trust: *You may depend on our tact.* **2.** to be contingent: *Our plans depend on the weather.* **3.** to rely for aid or support. —**de·pend′ence,** *n.* —**de·pend′ent,** *adj., n.*

de·pend′a·ble *adj.* worthy of trust; reliable. —**de·pend′a·bil′i·ty,** *n.*

de·pict (di pikt′), *v.t.* **1.** to represent by drawing; portray. **2.** to characterize in words; describe. —**de·pic′tion,** *n.*

de·pil·a·to·ry (di pil′ə tôr′ē), *adj., n., pl.* **-ries.** —*adj.* **1.** capable of removing hair. —*n.* **2.** a depilatory agent.

de·plete (di plēt′), *v.t.,* **-plet·ed, -plet·ing.** to decrease seriously or exhaust the supply of. —**de·ple′tion,** *n.*

de·plore′ *v.t.,* **-plored, -plor·ing. 1.** to regret deeply. **2.** to disapprove of; censure. —**de·plor′a·ble,** *adj.*

de·ploy (di ploi′), *v.t.* to spread out (troops, weapons, etc.) strategically. —**de·ploy′ment,** *n.*

de·po·lit·i·cize (dē′pə lit′ə sīz′), *v.t.,* **-cized, -ciz·ing.** to remove from the arena or influence of politics.

de·pop·u·late (dē pop′yə lāt′), *v.t.,* **-lat·ed, -lat·ing.** to remove or reduce the population of.

de·port (di pôrt′), *v.t.* **1.** to expel from a country; banish. **2.** to behave (oneself).

de′por·ta′tion (dē′pôr tā′shən) *n.* the lawful expulsion of an undesired person from a state.

de·port′ment *n.* conduct; behavior.

de·pose (di pōz′), *v.t.,* **-posed, -pos·ing. 1.** to remove from office or position, esp. high office. **2.** to testify under oath. —**dep·o·si·tion** (dep′ə zish′ən), *n.*

de·pos·it (di poz′it), *v.t.* **1.** to place for safekeeping in a bank account. **2.** to put or set down. **3.** to throw down or precipitate. **4.** to give as security or in part payment. —*v.i.* **5.** to become deposited. —*n.* **6.** money placed in a bank account. **7.** anything given as security or in part payment. **8.** something precipitated or thrown down, as by a natural process. —**de·pos′i·tor,** *n.*

de·pos·i·to·ry (di poz′i tôr′ē), *n., pl.* **-ries.** a place where something is deposited for safekeeping.

de·pot (dē′pō; *Mil. or Brit.* dep′ō), *n.* **1.** a railroad or bus station. **2. a.** a warehouse. **b.** a place where military supplies are stored.

de·prave (di prāv′), *v.t.,* **-praved, -prav·ing.** to make morally bad; corrupt. —**de·praved′,** *adj.* —**de·prav′i·ty** (-prav′i tē), *n., pl.* **-ties.**

dep·re·cate (dep′ri kāt′), *v.t.,* **-cat·ed, -cat·ing. 1.** to express earnest disapproval of. **2.** to belittle. —**dep′re·ca′tion,** *n.* —**dep′re·ca·to·ry** (-kə tôr′ē), *adj.*

de·pre·ci·ate (di prē′shē āt′), *v.,* **-at·ed, -at·ing.** —*v.t.* **1.** to lessen the value or price of. **2.** to belittle. —*v.i.* **3.** to decline in value. —**de·pre′ci·a′tion,** *n.*

dep·re·da·tion (dep′ri dā′shən), *n.* the act of preying upon or plundering.

de·press (di pres′), *v.t.* **1.** to make sad; dispirit. **2.** to lower in force or activity; weaken. **3.** to lower in amount or value. —**de·pressed′,** *adj.*

de·pres′sion *n.* **1.** the act of depressing or state of being depressed. **2.** an area lower than the surrounding surface. **3.** sadness or gloom. **4.** emotional dejection and withdrawal greater than that warranted by any objective reason. **5.** a period during which business activity and employment decline severely.

de·prive (di prīv′), *v.t.,* **-prived, -priv·ing. 1.** to divest of something possessed; strip. **2.** to keep from possessing. —**dep·ri·va·tion** (dep′rə vā′shən), *n.*

dept. 1. department. **2.** deputy.

depth (depth), *n.* **1.** a dimension taken through an object, usu. downward or inward. **2.** the quality of being deep. **3.** intensity, as of silence. **4.** Often, **depths.** a deep or inner part or place. **5.** Usu., **depths.** a low intellectual or moral condition. —*Idiom.* **6. in depth,** thoroughly.

dep·u·ta·tion (dep′yə tā′shən), *n.* **1.** the act of appointing a deputy. **2.** the person or body so appointed.

dep·u·ty (dep′yə tē), *n., pl.* **-ties. 1.** a person authorized to act as a substitute for another or others. **2.** an assistant to a public official. **3.** a person representing a constituency in certain legislative bodies. —**dep′u·tize′,** *v.t.* **-tized, -tiz·ing.**

de·rail (dē rāl′), *v.t.* **1.** to cause to run off the rails of a track. **2.** to deflect from a purpose or direction. —*v.i.* **3.** to become derailed. —**de·rail′ment,** *n.*

de·range (di rānj′), *v.t.,* **-ranged, -rang·ing. 1.** to disturb the condition, action, or function of. **2.** to make insane. —**de·range′ment,** *n.*

Der·by (dûr′bē; *Brit.* där′-), *n., pl.* **-bies. 1.** any of several annual horse races, esp. the one at Epsom Downs, England, and the Kentucky Derby. **2.** (*l.c.*) a race or contest, usu. one open to all. **3.** (*l.c.*) a man's stiff felt hat with rounded crown.

de·reg·u·late (dē reg′yə lāt′), *v.t.,* **-lat·ed, -lat·ing.** to remove governing regulations from. —**de·reg′u·la′tion,** *n.*

der·e·lict (der′ə likt), *adj.* **1.** deserted or abandoned. **2.** neglectful of duty; delinquent. —*n.* **3.** a person who has no home or means of support. **4.** a ship abandoned in open water. **5.** any abandoned possession.

der′e·lic′tion *n.* **1.** deliberate neglect. **2.** the act of abandoning something. **3.** the state of being abandoned.

de·ride (di rīd′), *v.t.,* **-rid·ed, -rid·ing.** to laugh at in scorn or contempt; mock. —**de·ri′sion** (-rish′ən), *n.* —**de·ri′sive** (-rī′siv), *adj.* —**de·ri′sive·ly,** *adv.*

de·rive (di rīv′), *v.,* **-rived, -riv·ing.** —*v.t.* **1.** to receive or obtain from a source. **2.** to trace from a source. **3.** to reach or obtain by reasoning. —*v.i.* **4.** to be derived. —**der·i·va·tion** (der′ə vā′shən), *n.* —**de·riv·a·tive** (di riv′ə tiv), *n., adj.*

der·ma·ti·tis (dûr′mə tī′tis), *n.* inflammation of the skin.

der′ma·tol′o·gy (-tol′ə jē), *n.* the branch of medicine dealing with the skin and its diseases. —**der′ma·to·log′i·cal** (-tl oj′i kəl), *adj.* —**der′ma·tol′o·gist,** *n.*

der·o·gate (der′ə gāt′), *v.,* **-gat·ed, -gat·ing.** —*v.i.* **1.** to detract, as from authority or estimation. —*v.t.* **2.** to disparage or belittle. —**der′o·ga′tion,** *n.*

de·rog·a·to·ry (di rog′ə tôr′ē), *adj.* belittling; disparaging.

der•rick (der′ik), *n.* **1.** a boom for lifting heavy cargo. **2.** the towerlike framework over an oil well or the like.

der•ri•ère (der′ē âr′), *n.* the buttocks.

de•scend (di send′), *v.i.* **1.** to pass from a higher to a lower point or place; move down. **2.** to slope or lead downward. **3.** to be inherited or transmitted. **4.** to attack or approach as if attacking. —*v.t.* **5.** to move downward upon or along. —**de•scent′**, *n.*

de•scend′ant *n.* **1.** a person or animal descended from a specific ancestor. **2.** something deriving from an earlier form.

de•scribe (di skrīb′), *v.t.*, **-scribed, -scrib•ing. 1.** to depict in words. **2.** to pronounce or name. **3.** to draw the outline of. —**de•scrib′a•ble**, *adj.*

de•scrip′tion (-skrip′shən), *n.* **1.** a statement or account that describes. **2.** the act or method of describing. **3.** sort; variety. —**de•scrip′tive**, *adj.*

de•scry (di skrī′), *v.t.*, **-scried, -scry•ing. 1.** to see by looking carefully; discern. **2.** to discover; detect.

des•e•crate (des′i krāt′), *v.t.*, **-crat•ed, -crat•ing.** to treat with sacrilege; profane. —**des′e•cra′tion,** *n.*

de•seg•re•gate (dē seg′ri gāt′), *v.t., v.i.*, **-gat•ed, -gat•ing.** to eliminate racial segregation in (schools, etc.). —**de•seg′re•ga′tion,** *n.*

de•sen•si•tize (dē sen′si tīz′), *v.t.*, **-tized, -tiz•ing.** to make less sensitive. —**de•sen′si•ti•za′tion,** *n.*

des•ert[1] (dez′ərt), *n.* **1.** an arid, often sandy region capable of supporting only a few life forms. **2.** any lifeless or dull place.

de•sert[2] (di zûrt′), *v.t., v.i.* **1.** to leave (a person, place, etc.) without intending to return. **2.** (of military personnel) to leave (duty, service, etc.) without permission and with no intention of returning. —**de•sert′er,** *n.* —**de•ser′tion,** *n.*

de•sert[3] (di zûrt′), *n.* Often, **-serts.** reward or punishment that is deserved.

de•serve (di zûrv′), *v.t., v.i.*, **-served, -serv•ing.** to merit or be worthy of (reward, punishment, aid, etc.). —**de•serv′ed•ly,** *adv.*

des•ic•cate (des′i kāt′), *v.t., v.i.*, **-cat•ed, -cat•ing.** to dry thoroughly; dry up. —**des′ic•ca′tion,** *n.*

de•sid•er•a•tum (di sid′ə rā′təm, -rä′-, -zid′-), *n.*, *pl.* **-ta** (-tə). something wanted or needed.

de•sign (di zīn′), *v.t.* **1.** to prepare the preliminary sketches or plans for: *to design a new bridge.* **2.** to plan and fashion skillfully. **3.** to intend for a definite purpose. **4.** to form in the mind. —*v.i.* **5.** to make sketches or plans. **6.** to plan an object, work of art, etc. —*n.* **7.** an outline, sketch, or scheme. **8.** the organization of elements in a work of art or other object. **9.** an ornamental pattern or motif. **10.** a plan or project. **11.** a plot or intrigue. **12.** intention; purpose; end. —**de•sign′er,** *n.*

des•ig•nate (*v.* dez′ig nāt′; *adj.* -nit, -nāt′), *v.*, **-nat•ed, -nat•ing,** *adj.* —*v.t.* **1.** to mark or point out; specify. **2.** to name; entitle. **3.** to select, as for a duty or office. —*adj.* **4.** selected for an office, position, etc., but not yet installed. —**des′ig•na′tion,** *n.*

des′ignated driv′er *n.* a person who abstains from alcoholic beverages at a gathering in order to be fit to drive companions home safely.

de•sign′ing *adj.* scheming; crafty.

de•sir•a•ble (di zīʳr′ə bəl), *adj.* **1.** pleasing; attractive. **2.** arousing desire. **3.** advisable. —**de•sir′a•bil′i•ty,** *n.* —**de•sir′a•bly,** *adv.*

de•sire′ (di zīʳr′, -sired, -sir•ing, —*v.t.* **1.** to wish or long for; crave. **2.** to ask for; request. —*n.* **3.** a longing or craving. **4.** an expressed wish; request. **5.** something desired. **6.** sexual urge.

de•sist (di zist′, -sist′), *v.i.* to cease, as from an action; stop.

desk (desk), *n.* **1.** an article of furniture having a writing surface. **2.** a specialized section of a large organization: *the copy desk.* —*adj.* **3.** suitable for or done at a desk.

desk′top pub′lishing *n.* the design and production of publications using a microcomputer.

des•o•late (*adj.* des′ə lit; *v.* -lāt′), *adj., v.*, **-lat•ed, -lat•ing.** —*adj.* **1.** barren or laid waste. **2.** without inhabitants; deserted. **3.** feeling friendless or hopeless; forlorn. **4.** dismal; gloomy. —*v.t.* **5.** to make

desolate. —**des′o•late•ly,** *adv.* —**des′o•late•ness,** *n.* —**des′o•la′tion** (-lā′shən), *n.*

de•spair (di spâr′), *n.* **1.** loss of hope; hopelessness. **2.** a source of hopelessness. —*v.i.* **3.** to give up hope.

des•per•a•do (des′pə rä′dō, -rä′-), *n.*, *pl.* **-does, -dos.** a reckless criminal or outlaw.

des•per•ate (des′pər it), *adj.* **1.** reckless or dangerous because of despair or urgency. **2.** having an urgent need, desire, etc. **3.** leaving little or no hope. **4.** extreme or excessive. —**des′per•ate•ly,** *adv.* —**des′per•a′tion,** *n.*

des•pi•ca•ble (des′pi kə bəl, di spik′ə-), *adj.* deserving to be despised. —**des′pi•ca•bly,** *adv.*

de•spise (di spīz′), *v.t.*, **-spised, -spis•ing. 1.** to regard with contempt; scorn. **2.** to hate.

de•spite (di spīt′), *prep.* in spite of; notwithstanding.

de•spoil (di spoil′), *v.t.* to strip of possessions; rob; plunder. —**de•spoil′ment,** *n.*

de•spond′ent (di spon′dənt) *adj.* in low spirits; dejected. —**de•spond′en•cy** *n.*

des•pot (des′pət, -pot), *n.* **1.** a ruler with absolute power. **2.** any tyrant or oppressor. —**des•pot•ic** (di spot′ik), *adj.* —**des′pot•ism,** *n.*

des•sert (di zûrt′), *n.* a usu. sweet food, as cake or pudding, served as the final course of a meal. [< F, der. of *desservir* to clear the table]

des•ti•na•tion (des′tə nā′shən), *n.* **1.** the place to which a person or thing travels or is sent. **2.** the purpose for which something is destined.

des′tine (-tin), *v.t.*, **-tined, -tin•ing. 1.** to set apart for a particular purpose. **2.** to determine or ordain beforehand.

des′ti•ny *n.*, *pl.* **-nies. 1.** fate; lot or fortune. **2.** the predetermined course of events.

des•ti•tute (des′ti tōōt′, -tyōōt′), *adj.* **1.** without any means of subsistence. **2.** deprived or lacking: *destitute of feeling.* —**des′ti•tu′tion,** *n.*

de•stroy (di stroi′), *v.t.* **1.** to injure beyond repair; demolish. **2.** to put an end to. **3.** to kill. **4.** to make ineffective or useless.

de•stroy′er *n.* **1.** a person or thing that destroys. **2.** a fast, small warship.

de•struct (di strukt′), *v.i.* to be destroyed automatically.

de•struc′tion *n.* **1.** the act of destroying or state of being destroyed. **2.** a cause or means of destroying. —**de•struc′tive,** *adj.* —**de•struc′tive•ly,** *adv.* —**de•struc′tive•ness,** *n.*

des•ul•to•ry (des′əl tôr′ē), *adj.* **1.** lacking in consistency or order; disconnected. **2.** digressing; random. —**des′ul•to′ri•ly,** *adv.*

de•tach (di tach′), *v.t.* **1.** to unfasten and separate. **2.** to send (a regiment, ship, etc.) on a special mission. —**de•tach′a•ble,** *adj.*

de•tached′ *adj.* **1.** not attached; separated. **2.** impartial or objective. **3.** not involved; aloof.

de•tach′ment *n.* **1.** the act of detaching or state of being detached. **2.** aloofness; disinterest. **3.** freedom from partiality. **4.** a body of troops or ships on a special mission.

de•tail (di tāl′, dē′tāl), *n.* **1.** an individual part; particular. **2.** particulars collectively. **3.** attention to a subject in individual parts. **4. a.** an assignment, as of military personnel, for a special task. **b.** the party so selected: *the kitchen detail.* —*v.t.* **5.** to relate with all particulars. **6.** to assign for some particular duty. —*Idiom.* **7. in detail,** item by item.

de•tain (di tān′), *v.t.* **1.** to keep from proceeding; delay. **2.** to keep under restraint. —**de•tain′ment,** *n.*

de•tect (di tekt′), *v.t.* to discover or notice the existence or presence of. —**de•tect′a•ble,** *adj.* —**de•tec′tion,** *n.* —**de•tec′tor,** *n.*

de•tec′tive *n.* a police officer or private investigator who investigates crimes, obtains evidence, etc.

dé•tente (dā tänt′, -tänt′), *n.* a relaxing of tension, esp. between nations. [< F]

de•ten•tion (di ten′shən), *n.* **1.** the act of detaining or state of being detained. **2.** maintenance of a person in custody. **3.** the keeping of a student after school hours as a punishment.

de·ter (di tûr′), *v.t.*, **-terred, -ter·ring.** to discourage from acting or proceeding, as through fear.

de·ter·gent (di tûr′jənt), *n.* a synthetic water-soluble cleaning agent that acts like soap.

de·te·ri·o·rate (di tēr′ē ə rāt′), *v.t., v.i.,* **-rat·ed, -rat·ing.** to make or become worse in character, quality, etc. —**de·ter/i·o·ra/tion,** *n.*

de·ter′mi·na/tion (-nā′shən), *n.* **1.** the act of coming to a decision. **2.** the decision reached. **3.** firmness of purpose. **4.** the act of ascertaining or fixing something.

de·ter/mine (-min), *v.,* **-mined, -min·ing. —v.t. 1.** to settle or resolve (a dispute, question, etc.) conclusively. **2.** to conclude or ascertain, as after observation. **3.** to fix the position of. **4.** to cause or control. **5.** to decide upon. —*v.i.* **6.** to decide. —**de·ter/mi·na·ble,** *adj.*

de·ter/mined *adj.* **1.** resolute; unwavering. **2.** decided; settled.

de·ter·rence (di tûr′əns), *n.* the act of deterring, esp. of deterring a nuclear attack by the capability for retaliation. —**de·ter/rent,** *adj., n.*

de·test (di test′), *v.t.* to hate; dislike intensely. —**de·test/a·ble,** *adj.* —**de·tes·ta/tion** (dē′te stā′shən), *n.*

de·throne (dē thrōn′), *v.t.,* **-throned, -thron·ing.** to remove from a throne or position of authority; depose.

det·o·nate (det′n āt′), *v.i., v.t.,* **-nat·ed, -nat·ing.** to explode with sudden violence. —**det/o·na/tion,** *n.* —**det/o·na/tor,** *n.*

de·tour (dē′tŏŏr, di tŏŏr′), *n.* **1.** a roundabout course, esp. one used temporarily when a route is closed. —*v.i., v.t.* **2.** to make or cause to make a detour.

de·tox (*n.* dē′toks; *v.* dē toks′), *n., v.,* **-toxed, -tox·ing.** *Informal.* —*n.* **1.** detoxification. —*v.t.* **2.** to detoxify.

de·tox/i·fy *v.t.,* **-fied, -fy·ing.** to rid of poison or the effects of alcohol or drug use. —**de·tox/i·fi·ca/tion,** *n.*

de·tract (di trakt′), *v.i.* **1.** to take away a part, as from value or reputation (usu. fol. by *from*). —*v.t.* **2.** to divert. —**de·trac/tion,** *n.* —**de·trac/tor,** *n.*

det·ri·ment (de′trə mənt), *n.* **1.** loss, damage, or disadvantage. **2.** a cause of loss or damage. —**det/ri·men/tal,** *adj.*

de·tri·tus (di trī′təs), *n.* **1.** rock particles worn away from a mass. **2.** any disintegrated material; debris.

deuce (dŏŏs, dyŏŏs), *n.* **1.** a card or die with two pips. **2.** a tie score, as in tennis, after which a player must score two successive points to win.

de·val/u·ate′ (dē val′yŏŏ āt′) *v.,* **-ated, -ating.** reduce in value; depreciate. —**de·val/u·a/tion,** *n.*

dev·as·tate (dev′ə stāt′), *v.t.,* **-tat·ed, -tat·ing. 1.** to lay waste; render desolate. **2.** to overwhelm, as with shock. —**dev/as·ta/tion,** *n.*

de·vel·op (di vel′əp), *v.t.* **1.** to bring to a more advanced, effective, or usable state. **2.** to cause to grow or expand. **3.** to bring into being or activity. **4.** to generate or acquire, as by natural processes. **5.** to elaborate in detail. **6.** to treat (an exposed film) with chemicals so as to make the image visible. —*v.i.* **7.** to become more advanced, mature, etc. **8.** to come gradually into existence or operation. **9.** to be disclosed: *The plot develops slowly.* —**de·vel/op·er,** *n.* —**de·vel/op·ment,** *n.* —**de·vel/op·men/tal,** *adj.* —**de·vel/op·men/tal·ly,** *adv.*

de·vi·ant (dē′vē ənt), *adj.* **1.** deviating from an accepted norm, esp. of behavior. —*n.* **2.** a deviant person or thing. —**de/vi·ance,** *n.*

de/vi·ate′ (*v.* -āt′; *n.* -it), *v.,* **-at·ed, -at·ing,** *n.* —*v.i.* **1.** to turn aside or differ, as from a course, standard, or topic. —*n.* **2.** a deviant, esp. a person whose sexual behavior departs from the norm. —**de/vi·a/tion,** *n.*

de·vice (di vīs′), *n.* **1.** a thing made for a particular purpose, esp. a mechanical or electronic contrivance. **2.** a plan, scheme, or procedure. **3.** a design used as a badge, emblem, trademark, etc. —*Idiom.* **4. leave to one's own devices,** to allow to act according to one's inclination.

dev·il (dev′əl), *n., v.,* **-iled, -il·ing** or (*esp. Brit.*) **-illed, -il·ling. —n. 1. a.** (*sometimes cap.*) the supreme spirit of evil; Satan. **b.** a subordinate evil spirit. **2.** a wicked, cruel person. **3.** a clever or mischievous person. **4.** a person: *the lucky devil.* —*v.t.* **5.** to annoy; harass. **6.** to prepare with hot seasonings: *deviled eggs.* [< L *diábolos* Satan, lit., slanderer] —**dev/il·ish,** *adj.* —**dev/il·ish·ly,** *adv.* —**dev/il·try,** *n.*

dev/il-may-care/ *adj.* reckless; careless.

dev/il's ad/vocate *n.* a person who advocates an opposing view for the sake of argument.

dev/il's food/ cake/ *n.* a rich, dark chocolate cake.

de·vi·ous (dē′vē əs), *adj.* **1.** departing from the most direct way; roundabout. **2.** not straightforward or sincere. —**de/vi·ous·ly,** *adv.* —**de/vi·ous·ness,** *n.*

de·vise (di vīz′), *v.,* **-vised, -vis·ing,** *n.* —*v.t.* **1.** to contrive or create: *to devise a method.* **2.** to bequeath (property) by will. —*v.i.* **3.** to form a plan. —*n.* **4.** a bequest of real property.

de·vi·tal·ize (dē vīt′l īz′), *v.t.,* **-ized, -iz·ing.** to deprive of vitality.

de·void (di void′), *adj.* totally lacking; destitute: *devoid of humor.*

de·volve (di volv′), *v.t., v.i.,* **-volved, -volv·ing.** to pass or be passed on from one to another, as a responsibility.

de·vote (di vōt′), *v.t.,* **-vot·ed, -vot·ing. 1.** to give up or apply to a particular pursuit, purpose, cause, etc.: *to devote one's time to study.* **2.** to dedicate solemnly; consecrate.

de·vot/ed *adj.* zealous in loyalty or affection. —**de·vot/ed·ly,** *adv.*

dev·o·tee (dev′ə tē′, -tā′), *n., pl.* **-tees.** a person who is greatly devoted to something; enthusiast.

de·vo·tion (di vō′shən), *n.* **1.** earnest attachment to a cause, person, etc. **2.** profound dedication, esp. to religion. **3.** the act of devoting. **4.** Often, **-tions.** religious observances; special prayers. —**de·vo/tion·al,** *adj.*

de·vour (di vour′), *v.t.* **1.** to eat up hungrily. **2.** to consume destructively; demolish. **3.** to take in greedily with the senses or intellect.

de·vout (di vout′), *adj.,* **-er, -est. 1.** devoted to divine worship; pious. **2.** expressing piety. **3.** earnest; fervent. —**de·vout/ly,** *adv.*

dew (dŏŏ, dyŏŏ), *n.* **1.** moisture condensed from the atmosphere, esp. at night, and deposited in small drops on a cool surface. **2.** something compared to dew, as in purity. —**dew/y,** *adj.,* **-i·er, -i·est.**

dex·ter·i·ty (dek ster′i tē), *n.* skill or adroitness in using the hands, body, or mind. —**dex/ter·ous** (-strəs, -stər əs), *adj.*

dex·trose (dek′strōs), *n.* a form of glucose occurring in fruits and in animal tissues.

di·a·be·tes (dī′ə bē′tis, -tēz), *n.* any of several disorders characterized by high levels of glucose in the blood and urine. —**di/a·bet/ic** (-bet′ik), *adj., n.*

di·a·bol·ic (dī′ə bol′ik) also **-i·cal,** *adj.* devilish; fiendish. —**di/a·bol/i·cal·ly,** *adv.*

di·a·crit·ic (dī′ə krit′ik), *n.* **1.** Also called **diacrit/ical mark/.** a mark, as a circumflex, added to a letter to give it a particular phonetic value. —*adj.* Also, **di/a·crit/i·cal. 2.** serving to distinguish.

di·a·dem (dī′ə dem′), *n.* a crown or headband worn as symbol of royalty.

di·ag·nose (dī′əg nōs′, -nōz′), *v.,* **-nosed, -nos·ing.** —*v.t.* **1.** to make a diagnosis (of).

di/ag·no/sis (-nō′sis), *n., pl.* **-ses** (-sēz). **1. a.** the process of determining by medical examination the nature of a diseased condition. **b.** the decision reached. **2.** an analysis of the cause or nature of any problem. —**di/ag·nos/tic** (-nos′tik), *adj.* —**di/ag·nos·ti/cian** (-no stish′ən), *n.*

di·ag·o·nal (dī ag′ə nl), *adj.* **1.** connecting two nonadjacent corners of a polygon or polyhedron: *a diagonal line.* **2.** having an oblique direction. **3.** having oblique lines or markings. —*n.* **4.** a diagonal line or plane. —**di·ag/o·nal·ly,** *adv.*

di·a·gram (dī′ə gram′), *n., v.,* **-gramed** or

general

-grammed, -gram•ing or **-gram•ming. —***n.* **1.** a drawing, chart, or plan that outlines and explains something. —*v.t.* **2.** to make a diagram of.

di•al (dī′əl, dīl), *n.*, *v.*, **-aled, -al•ing** or (*esp. Brit.*) **-alled, -al•ling. —***n.* **1.** a marked plate or disk for indicating time, direction, or amount. **2.** a knob or plate on a radio or television for tuning in stations. **3.** a rotatable disk on a telephone, used in making calls. —*v.t.* **4.** to indicate or measure on or as if on a dial. **5.** to make a telephone call to. —*v.i.* **6.** to use a dial. —**di′al•er,** *n.*

di•a•lect (dī′ə lekt′), *n.* a variety of a language used by a group of speakers set off from others geographically or socially. —**di′a•lec′tal,** *adj.*

di′a•lec′tic *adj.* Also, **di′a•lec′ti•cal. —***n.* **1.** pertaining to or of the nature of logical argumentation. —*n.* **2.** Often, **-tics.** the art or practice of debate or conversation by which the truth of a theory or opinion is arrived at logically.

di•a•logue or **-log** (dī′ə lôg′, -log′), *n.* **1.** conversation between two or more persons. **2.** the conversation between characters in a novel, drama, etc. **3.** an exchange of ideas or opinions.

di•al•y•sis (dī al′ə sis), *n.*, *pl.* **-ses** (-sēz′). **1.** the separation of soluble substances from colloids in a solution by diffusion through a membrane. **2.** (in kidney disease) this process used to remove waste products from the blood.

di•am•e•ter (dī am′i tər), *n.* **1.** a straight line passing through the center of a circle or sphere and meeting the circumference or surface at each end. **2.** the length of such a line. **3.** the width of a circular or cylindrical object.

di•a•met•ri•cal (-ə me′tri kəl) also **-met′ric,** *adj.* directly opposite: *diametrical opinions.* —**di′a•met′ri•cal•ly,** *adv.*

dia•mond (dī′mənd, dī′ə-), *n.* **1.** an extremely hard form of crystallized carbon. **2.** a piece of this substance, valued as a precious gem or used in a cutting tool. **3.** an equilateral figure having two acute and two obtuse angles. **4.** any of a suit of playing cards bearing diamond-shaped figures. **5.** the infield or the entire playing field in baseball. —*adj.* **6.** made of or like diamonds. **7.** indicating the 60th or 75th year, as a wedding anniversary.

dia′mond•back′ *n.* a large venomous rattlesnake with diamond-shaped markings on the back.

dia•per (dī′pər, dī′ə pər), *n.* **1.** a piece of cloth or other absorbent material worn as underpants by a baby not yet toilet-trained. —*v.t.* **2.** to put a diaper on.

di•aph•a•nous (dī af′ə nəs), *adj.* very sheer and light; nearly transparent.

di•a•phragm (dī′ə fram′), *n.* **1.** the muscular wall separating the chest and abdominal cavities. **2.** a disk that vibrates when receiving or producing sound waves, as in a telephone. **3.** a contraceptive device that fits over the uterine cervix. **4.** a plate used to control the amount of light entering an optical instrument.

di•ar•rhe•a or **-rhoe•a** (dī′ə rē′ə), *n.* an intestinal disorder characterized by frequent and fluid bowel movements.

di•a•ry (dī′ə rē), *n.*, *pl.* **-ries. 1.** a daily written record of one's experiences and feelings. **2.** a book for noting daily appointments. —**di′a•rist,** *n.*

di•a•tribe (dī′ə trīb′), *n.* a bitter, abusive denunciation or criticism.

dib•ble (dib′əl), *n.* a pointed implement for making holes in soil, as for planting seedlings and bulbs.

dice (dīs), *n.pl., sing.* **die,** *v.*, **diced, dic•ing. —***n.* **1.** small cubes, marked on each side with one to six spots, used in games or gambling. **2.** a game played with dice. —*v.t.* **3.** to cut into small cubes. —*v.i.* **4.** to play at dice.

dic′ey (dī′sē) *adj.* **-ier, -iest.** risky; uncertain.

di•chot•o•my (dī kot′ə mē), *n.*, *pl.* **-mies. 1.** division into halves or pairs. **2.** division into two opposed or contradictory groups. —**di•chot′o•mous,** *adj.*

dick•er (dik′ər), *v.i.* to bargain; haggle.

di•cot•y•le•don (dī kot′l ēd′n, dī′kot l-), *n.* a flowering plant having two embryonic seed leaves. —**di•cot′y•le′don•ous,** *adj.*

Dic•ta•phone (dik′tə fōn′), *Trademark.* a brand name for a machine that records and plays back dictated speech.

dic•tate (*v.* dik′tāt, dik tāt′; *n.* dik′tāt), *v.*, **-tat•ed, -tat•ing,** *n.* —*v.t.* **1.** to say or read aloud (something) for a person to transcribe or for a machine to record. **2.** to command authoritatively. —*n.* **3.** an authoritative order or command. —**dic•ta′tion,** *n.*

dic′ta•tor *n.* a ruler or tyrant exercising absolute power. —**dic′ta•to′ri•al** (-tə tôr′ē əl), *adj.* —**dic•ta′tor•ship′,** *n.*

dic•tion (dik′shən), *n.* **1.** style of speaking or writing as dependent upon choice of words. **2.** enunciation or delivery.

dic•tion•ar•y (dik′shə ner′ē), *n.*, *pl.* **-ar•ies. 1.** a book containing a selection of the words of a language, usu. arranged alphabetically, with information about their meanings, pronunciations, etc. **2.** a book giving information on particular subjects or on a particular class of words, usu. arranged alphabetically: *a biographical dictionary.* **3.** a list of words used by a word-processing program to check spellings in text.

dic•tum (dik′təm), *n.*, *pl.* **-ta** (-tə), **-tums. 1.** an authoritative pronouncement. **2.** a saying; maxim.

di•dac•tic (dī dak′tik), *adj.* **1.** intended for instruction. **2.** moralizing or preaching.

did′n't (did′nt) contraction of **did not.**

die[1] (dī), *v.i.*, **died, dy•ing. 1.** to cease to live. **2.** to cease to exist. **3.** to lose force, strength, or activity. **4.** to cease to function. **5.** to suffer: *I'm dying of boredom!* **6.** to desire keenly: *I'm dying for coffee.* **7. die off,** to die one after another until the number is greatly reduced. **8. ~ out,** to cease to exist. —*Idiom.* **9. die hard,** to give way or cease to exist only slowly or after a bitter struggle: *Childhood beliefs die hard.* **10. to die for,** stunning; remarkable: *That dress is to die for.*

die[2] (dī), *n.*, *pl.* **dies** for 1, 2; **dice** for 3. **1.** a device for cutting or forming material in a press or a stamping machine. **2.** an engraved stamp for impressing a design upon some softer material, as in coining money. **3.** *sing.* of DICE.

die′-hard′ or **die′hard′,** *n.* a person who vigorously resists change.

di•er•e•sis (dī er′ə sis), *n.*, *pl.* **-ses** (-sēz′). a sign (¨) placed over the second of two adjacent vowels to indicate that it is to be pronounced separately.

die•sel (dē′zəl, -səl), *n.* a vehicle powered by a diesel engine. [after R. *Diesel* (1858–1913), German automotive engineer]

die′sel en′gine *n.* an internal-combustion engine in which fuel oil is ignited by heat produced by air compression.

di•et[1] (dī′it), *n.* **1.** food and drink considered in terms of composition and effects on health. **2.** a particular selection of food, as for losing weight. **3.** anything habitually partaken of. —*v.i., v.t.* **4.** to go or put on a diet. —**di′e•tar•y** (-i ter′ē), *adj.* —**di′et•er,** *n.*

di•et[2] (dī′it), *n.* the legislative body of certain countries.

di•e•tet•ic (-i tet′ik), *adj.* **1.** pertaining to diet. **2.** suitable for special diets, as those requiring a restricted caloric intake. —*n.* **3. dietetics,** the science concerned with nutrition and food preparation.

di•e•ti′tian or **-cian** (dī′i tish′ən), *n.* a person who is an expert in nutrition or dietetics.

dif•fer (dif′ər), *v.i.* **1.** to be unlike or dissimilar. **2.** to disagree in opinion.

dif•fer•ence (dif′ər əns, dif′rəns), *n.* **1.** the state, relation, or degree of being different. **2.** an instance of dissimilarity. **3.** a change from a previous state. **4.** a distinguishing characteristic. **5.** a disagreement or dispute. **6.** the amount by which one quantity is greater or less than another.

dif′fer•ent *adj.* **1.** not alike in character or quality; dissimilar. **2.** not identical; distinct. **3.** various; several. **4.** not ordinary. —**dif′fer•ent•ly,** *adv.*

dif′fer•en′ti•ate′ (-shē āt′), *v.*, **-at•ed, -at•ing.**

—*v.t.* **1.** to form or mark differently from other such things; distinguish. **2.** to perceive the difference in or between. —*v.i.* **3.** to become unlike or dissimilar; become distinct. **4.** to make a distinction. —**dif′fer·en′ti·a′tion,** *n.* —**dif′fer·en′ti·a′tor,** *n.*

dif·fi·cult (dif′i kult′, -kəlt), *adj.* **1.** requiring special effort or skill; hard. **2.** hard to understand or solve. **3.** hard to deal with or satisfy. **4.** fraught with hardship. —**dif′fi·cult′ly,** *adv.*

dif′fi·cul′ty *n.,* *pl.* **-ties. 1.** the fact or condition of being difficult. **2.** an embarrassing situation, esp. of financial affairs. **3.** a trouble or struggle. **4.** a disagreement or dispute. **5.** an impediment; obstacle.

dif·fi·dent (dif′i dənt), *adj.* lacking confidence in oneself; timid; shy. —**dif′fi·dence,** *n.*

dif·frac·tion (di frak′shən), *n.* a modulation of waves, as of sound or light, in response to an obstacle in their path.

dif·fuse (*v.* di fyōoz′; *adj.* -fyōos′), *v.,* **-fused, -fus·ing,** *adj.* —*v.t., v.i.* **1.** to pour out and spread. **2.** to scatter widely or thinly. —*adj.* **3.** discursive or wordy. **4.** widely spread or scattered. —**dif·fuse′ly** (-fyōos′lē), *adv.* —**dif·fuse′ness,** *n.* —**dif·fu′sion,** *n.* —**dif·fu′sive** (-siv), *adj.*

dig¹ (dig), *v.,* **dug, dig·ging,** *n.* —*v.i.* **1.** to break up, turn over, or remove earth, sand, etc. **2.** to make one's way by removing or turning over material. —*v.t.* **3.** to break up, turn over, or loosen (earth, sand, etc.). **4.** to form or excavate by removing material. **5.** to unearth or obtain by digging. **6.** to find or discover by effort or search. **7. dig in, a.** to maintain one's opinion or position. **b.** *Informal.* to start eating. —*n.* **8.** a thrust; poke. **9.** a sarcastic remark. **10.** an archaeological excavation. **11. digs,** *Informal.* living quarters. —**dig′ger,** *n.*

dig² (dig), *v.,* **dug, dig·ging.** *Slang.* —*v.t.* **1.** to understand. **2.** to take notice of. **3.** to like.

di·gest (*v.* di jest′, dī-; *n.* dī′jest), *v.t.* **1.** to convert (food) in the alimentary canal into a form that can be assimilated by the body. **2.** to assimilate mentally. **3.** to abridge or summarize. —*v.i.* **4.** to undergo digestion. —*n.* **5.** a collection or compendium, esp. when classified or condensed. —**di·gest′i·ble,** *adj.* —**di·ges′tion,** *n.* —**di·ges′tive,** *adj.*

dig·it (dij′it), *n.* **1.** any of the Arabic numerals of 1 through 9 and 0. **2.** a finger or toe.

dig′it·al (-i tl), *adj.* **1.** of or resembling a digit or finger. **2.** of or using data in the form of numerical digits. **3.** displaying the time by numerical digits rather than by hands on a dial: *a digital clock.* **4.** readable and manipulable by computer. —**dig′it·al·ly,** *adv.*

dig′i·tize′ (-tīz′) *v.,* **-tized, -tizing.** to convert (data) to digital form.

dig·ni·fied (dig′nə fīd′), *adj.* characterized by dignity of aspect or manner.

dig′ni·fy′ *v.t.,* **-fied, -fy·ing.** to confer honor or dignity upon.

dig′ni·tar′y (-ter′ē), *n., pl.* **-tar·ies.** a person who holds a high rank or office.

dig′ni·ty *n., pl.* **-ties. 1.** bearing, conduct, or manner indicative of self-respect, formality, or gravity. **2.** nobility or elevation of character; worthiness. **3.** elevated rank, office, station, etc.

di·gress (di gres′, dī-), *v.i.* to wander away from the main topic or argument in speaking or writing. —**di·gres′sion,** *n.* —**di·gres′sive,** *adj.*

dike¹ (dīk), *n.* an embankment for controlling or holding back the waters of the sea or a river.

dike² (dīk), *n.* DYKE². —**dike′y,** *adj.*

di·lap·i·dat·ed (di lap′i dā′tid), *adj.* fallen into partial ruin or decay. —**di·lap′i·da′tion,** *n.*

di·late (dī lāt′), *v.,* **-lat·ed, -lat·ing.** —*v.t.* **1.** to make wider or larger. —*v.i.* **2.** to speak or write at length (often fol. by *on* or *upon*). —**di·la′tion,** *n.*

dil·a·to·ry (dil′ə tôr′ē), *adj.* **1.** tending to delay or procrastinate. **2.** intended to cause delay.

di·lem·ma (di lem′ə), *n., pl.* **-mas. 1.** a situation requiring a choice between equally undesirable alternatives. **2.** any perplexing problem.

dil·et·tante (dil′i tänt′, dil′i tänt′, -tän′tä, -tan′tē), *n., pl.* **-tantes, -tan·ti** (-tän′tē). a person who takes

up an art, activity, or subject for amusement, esp. in a superficial way; dabbler. —**dil′et·tant′ism,** *n.*

dil·i·gent (dil′i jənt), *adj.* **1.** constant and earnest in effort and application. **2.** done painstakingly. —**dil′i·gence,** *n.* —**dil′i·gent·ly,** *adv.*

dill (dil), *n.* a plant of the parsley family, having aromatic seeds and leaves used as a flavoring.

dil·ly·dal·ly (dil′ē dal′ē), *v.i.,* **-lied, -ly·ing.** to waste time, esp. by indecision.

di·lute (di lōot′, dī-), *v.,* **-lut·ed, -lut·ing,** *adj.* —*v.t.* **1.** to make (a liquid) thinner or weaker by the addition of water or the like. **2.** to reduce the strength of by admixture. —*adj.* **3.** reduced in strength; weak. —**di·lu′tion,** *n.*

dim (dim), *adj.,* **dim·mer, dim·mest,** *v.,* **dimmed, dim·ming.** —*adj.* **1.** not bright; obscure from insufficient light. **2.** indistinct or faint. **3.** not clear to the mind; vague. **4.** dull in luster. **5.** not seeing clearly. **6.** unlikely to occur. **7.** stupid; dim-witted. —*v.t., v.i.* **8.** to make or become dim or dimmer. —*Idiom.* **9. take a dim view of,** to regard with disapproval or skepticism. —**dim′ly,** *adv.* —**dim′ness,** *n.*

dim. 1. dimension. **2.** diminish. **3.** diminuendo. **4.** diminutive.

dime (dīm), *n.* a coin of the U.S. and Canada worth 10 cents.

di·men·sion (di men′shən, dī-), *n.* **1.** a property of space; extension in a given direction. **2.** Usu. **-sions.** a measurement in length, width, and thickness. **b.** scope; extent. —**di·men′sion·al,** *adj.*

di·min·ish (di min′ish), *v.t., v.i.* to make or become smaller, less, or less important. —**dim·i·nu·tion** (dim′ə nōo′shən, -nyōō′-), *n.*

di·min·u·en·do (di min′yōo en′dō), *adj., adv. Music.* gradually reducing in force or loudness.

di·min·u·tive (di min′yə tiv), *adj.* **1.** much smaller than the average or usual; tiny. **2.** denoting smallness, familiarity, affection, or triviality, as the suffix *-let* in *droplet.* —*n.* **3.** a diminutive word or element.

dim·i·ty (dim′i tē), *n., pl.* **-ties.** a thin cotton fabric woven with a stripe or check of heavier yarn.

dim·ple (dim′pəl), *n., v.,* **-pled, -pling.** —*n.* **1.** a small natural hollow on the surface of the human body, esp. one formed in the cheek when smiling. —*v.t., v.i.* **2.** to mark with or show a dimple. —**dim′ply,** *adj.*

dim′wit′ *n. Slang.* a stupid person. —**dim′wit′- ted,** *adj.*

din (din), *n., v.,* **dinned, din·ning.** —*n.* **1.** a loud, confused noise. —*v.t.* **2.** to assail with a din. **3.** to utter with noisy repetition.

dine (dīn), *v.,* **dined, din·ing,** —*v.i.* **1.** to have dinner. **2.** to eat any meal. —*v.t.* **3.** to entertain at or provide with dinner.

din′er *n.* **1.** a person who dines. **2.** a railroad dining car. **3.** a restaurant shaped like such a car.

di·nette′ (-net′), *n.* a space or alcove serving as a dining area.

din·ghy (ding′gē), *n., pl.* **-ghies.** any small boat, esp. a lifeboat. [< Hindi *ḍiṅgī,* dim. of *ḍiṅgā* boat]

din·gy (din′jē), *adj.,* **-gi·er, -gi·est. 1.** of a dark, dull, or dirty color. **2.** shabby; dismal. —**din′gi·ness,** *n.*

din·ner (din′ər), *n.* **1.** the main meal of the day. **2.** a formal meal in honor of some person or occasion.

di·no·saur (dī′nə sôr′), *n.* any of various extinct, prehistoric reptiles, some of which were huge. [< NL < Gk *deino-* terrible + *sauros* lizard]

dint (dint), *n.* **1.** force; power: *by dint of hard work.* **2.** a dent.

di·o·cese (dī′ə sis, -sēz′, -sēs′), *n.* a district under the jurisdiction of a bishop. —**di·oc′e·san** (-os′ə-sən), *adj.*

di·o·ram·a (dī′ə ram′ə, -rä′mə), *n., pl.* **-ram·as.** a scene in miniature reproduced in three dimensions against a painted background.

di·ox·ide (dī ok′sīd, -sid) *n.* oxide with two atoms of oxygen.

di·ox·in (dī ok′sin), *n.* a hydrocarbon that is a toxic by-product of pesticide manufacture.

dip (dip), *v.,* **dipped, dip·ping.** —*v.t.* **1.** to plunge briefly into a liquid. **2.** to take up by bailing or ladling. **3.** to lower and raise: *to dip a flag in salute.* —*v.i.* **4.** to plunge into a liquid and emerge quickly. **5.** to reach into a container so as to remove something. **6.** to withdraw something in small amounts: *to dip into savings.* **7.** to sink or drop suddenly. **8.** to incline downward. **9.** to look into a subject or book casually or superficially. —*n.* **10.** the act of dipping. **11.** something taken up by dipping. **12.** a substance into which something is dipped. **13.** a creamy mixture of foods for scooping with a cracker, potato chip, etc. **14.** a drop or decline. **15.** a downward slope or course. **16.** a brief swim.

diph•the•ri•a (dif thēr′ē ə, dip-), *n.* an infectious disease marked by high fever and breathing difficulty.

diph•thong (dif′thông, -thong, dip′-), *n.* a gliding speech sound varying continuously in phonetic quality but considered to be a single sound as *oi* in *boil.*

di•plo•ma (di plō′mə), *n.*, *pl.* **-mas.** a document given by an educational institution conferring a degree or certifying the successful completion of a course of study.

di•plo•ma•cy (di plō′mə sē), *n.* **1.** the conduct by government officials of negotiations and other relations between nations. **2.** tactful dealing with others. —**dip•lo•mat** (dip′lə mat′), *n.*

dip′lo•mat′ic *adj.* **1.** of or engaged in diplomacy. **2.** tactful or suave. —**dip′lo•mat′i•cal•ly,** *adv.*

dip•so•ma•ni•a (dip′sə mā′nē ə, -sō-), *n.* an irresistible, typically periodic craving for alcoholic drink. —**dip′so•ma′ni•ac′,** *n.*

dire (dīⁱr), *adj.*, **dir•er, dir•est. 1.** causing or involving great fear or suffering. **2.** indicating trouble or disaster. **3.** urgent; desperate. —**dire′ly,** *adv.*

di•rect (di rekt′, dī-), *v.t.* **1.** to manage or guide by advice, instruction, etc. **2.** to command or order. **3.** to serve as director of (a play, motion picture, etc.). **4.** to show (a person) the way. **5.** to aim or send toward a place or object: *to direct one's aim.* **6.** to address (words, a speech, etc.) to a person or persons. **7.** to address (a letter, package, etc.). —*v.i.* **8.** to give guidance or orders. **9.** to serve as a director. —*adj.* **10.** proceeding in a straight line. **11.** proceeding in an unbroken line of descent. **12.** without intermediary agents, conditions, etc. **13.** straightforward; frank. **14.** absolute; exact: *the direct opposite.* **15.** consisting of the exact words of a speaker: *a direct quote.* —*adv.* **16.** in a direct manner. —**di•rect′ly,** *adv.* —**di•rect′ness,** *n.*

direct′ cur′rent *n.* an electric current flowing continuously in one direction.

di•rec′tion *n.* **1.** an act or instance of directing. **2.** the line along which anything lies, faces, moves, etc., with reference to the point or region toward which it is directed. **3.** a tendency or inclination. **4.** Usu., **-tions.** instruction or guidance for making, using, etc. **5.** an order; command. **6.** management; supervision. —**di•rec′tion•al,** *adj.*

di•rec′tive *adj.* **1.** serving to direct; directing. —*n.* **2.** an authoritative instruction or direction; specific order.

di•rec′tor *n.* **1.** one that directs. **2.** one of a group of persons chosen to govern the affairs of a company. **3.** the person who guides the performers in a play, motion picture, etc.

di•rec′to•ry *n.*, *pl.* **-ries. 1.** an alphabetical listing of the names and addresses of persons in an area, organization, etc. **2. a.** a division in a hierarchical structure that organizes the storage of computer files on a disk. **b.** a listing of such files.

dirge (dûrj), *n.* a song or poem in commemoration of the dead.

dir•i•gi•ble (dir′i jə bəl, di rij′ə-), *n.* AIRSHIP.

dirk (dûrk), *n.* a dagger, esp. of the Scottish Highlands.

dirt (dûrt), *n.* **1.** any foul or filthy substance, as mud or grime. **2.** earth or soil. **3.** moral filth; vileness. **4.** obscene language. **5.** gossip, esp. of a malicious nature.

dirt′y *adj.*, **-i•er, -i•est,** *v.*, **-ied, -y•ing.** —*adj.* **1.**

soiled or soiling with dirt. **2.** vile; contemptible. **3.** obscene; lewd. **4.** undesirable or unpleasant: *dirty work.* **5.** not fair; dishonest. **6.** hostile or resentful: *a dirty look.* **7.** (of the weather) stormy. —*v.t.*, *v.i.* **8.** to make or become dirty. —**dirt′i•ness,** *n.*

dis (dis), *v.*, **dissed, dis•sing,** *n. Slang.* —*v.t.* **1.** to show disrespect for. **2.** to disparage. —*n.* **3.** disparagement or criticism.

dis- a prefix meaning: reversal (*disconnect*); negation or lack (*distrust*); removal or separation (*disbar*).

dis•a•ble (dis ā′bəl), *v.t.*, **-bled, -bling. 1.** to make unable or unfit; incapacitate. **2.** to disqualify legally. —**dis•a•bil′i•ty** (dis′ə bil′i tē), *n.*

dis•a′bled *adj.* handicapped; incapacitated.

dis•a•buse′ (-byōōz′), *v.t.*, **-bused, -bus•ing.** to free from deception or error.

dis•ad•van′tage *n.* **1.** an unfavorable circumstance or condition; handicap. **2.** injury to reputation, credit, etc.; loss. —**dis•ad′van•ta′geous,** *adj.*

dis′ad•van′taged *adj.* lacking economic and social opportunity.

dis•af•fect′ *v.t.* to make discontented or disloyal. —**dis′af•fec′tion,** *n.*

dis•a•gree′ *v.i.* **1.** to fail to agree; differ. **2.** to differ in opinion. **3.** to quarrel. **4.** to cause physical discomfort or ill effect. —**dis′a•gree′ment,** *n.*

dis•a•gree′a•ble *adj.* **1.** contrary to one's taste or liking; offensive. **2.** unpleasant; surly; grouchy. —**dis′a•gree′a•bly,** *adv.*

dis•al•low′ *v.t.* to refuse to allow; reject.

dis•ap•pear′ *v.i.* **1.** to cease to be seen. **2.** to cease to exist or be known. —**dis′ap•pear′ance,** *n.*

dis•ap•point′ *v.t.* to fail to fulfill the expectations or wishes of. —**dis′ap•point′ment,** *n.*

dis•ap•pro•ba′tion *n.* disapproval; condemnation.

dis•ap•prove′ *v.*, **-proved, -prov•ing.** —*v.t.* **1.** to censure or condemn in opinion. **2.** to withhold approval from. —*v.i.* **3.** to have an unfavorable opinion (usu. fol. by *of*). —**dis′ap•prov′al,** *n.* —**dis′ap•prov′ing•ly,** *adv.*

dis•arm′ *v.t.* **1.** to deprive of weapons. **2.** to deprive of the means to attack or defend. **3.** to relieve of hostility; win over. —*v.i.* **4.** (of a country) to reduce armaments or armed forces. —**dis•ar′ma•ment,** *n.*

dis′ar•range′ *v.t.*, **-ranged, -rang•ing.** to disturb the arrangement of; unsettle. —**dis′ar•range′ment,** *n.*

dis′ar•ray′ *v.*, **-rayed, -ray•ing,** *n.* —*v.t.* **1.** to throw into disorder. —*n.* **2.** disorder; confusion.

dis•as•so′ci•ate′ (-āt′), *v.t.*, **-at•ed, -at•ing.** to dissociate.

dis•as′ter (di zas′tər, -zä′stər), *n.* a calamitous event, esp. one occurring suddenly and causing great damage. —**dis•as′trous,** *adj.* —**dis•as′trous•ly,** *adv.*

dis•a•vow′ (dis′ə vou′), *v.t.* to disclaim knowledge of, connection with, or responsibility for; disown. —**dis′a•vow′al,** *n.*

dis•band′ *v.t.*, *v.i.* to break up or dissolve (an organization).

dis•bar′ *v.t.*, **-barred, -bar•ring.** to expel from the legal profession. —**dis•bar′ment,** *n.*

dis′be•lieve′ *v.t.*, *v.i.*, **-lieved, -liev•ing.** to refuse to believe. —**dis′be•lief′,** *n.*

dis•burse (dis bûrs′), *v.t.*, **-bursed, -burs•ing.** to pay out, esp. for expenses. —**dis•burse′ment,** *n.*

disc (disk), *n.* **1.** a phonograph record. **2.** DISK.

dis•card (*v.* di skärd′; *n.* dis′kärd), *v.t.* **1.** to cast aside or dispose of; get rid of. **2.** to throw out (a playing card) from one's hand. —*v.i.* **3.** to discard a playing card. —*n.* **4.** the act of discarding. **5.** a person or thing discarded.

dis•cern (di sûrn′, -zûrn′), *v.t.*, *v.i.* **1.** to perceive by the sight or the intellect. **2.** to distinguish mentally. —**dis•cern′i•ble,** *adj.* —**dis•cern′ing,** *adj.* —**dis•cern′ment,** *n.*

dis•charge (*v.* dis chärj′; *n.* dis′chärj, dis chärj′), *v.*, **-charged, -charg•ing,** *n.* —*v.t.* **1.** to remove the contents of. **2.** to remove or send forth. **3.** to shoot (a firearm or missile). **4.** to pour forth; emit. **5.** to relieve of obligation or responsibility. **6.** to fulfill the requirements of (a duty, function, etc.). **7.** to dismiss from office or employment. **8.** to release or allow to go. **9.** to pay (a debt). **10.** to rid (a battery, capacitor, etc.) of an electric charge. —*v.i.* **11.** to get rid of a burden or load. **12.** to pour forth. **13.** to go off, as a firearm. —*n.* **14.** the act of discharging a ship, load, etc. **15.** the act of shooting a weapon. **16.** an ejection or emission. **17.** fulfillment of an obligation. **18.** a release or dismissal, as from employment. **19.** the removal of an electric charge, as by the conversion of chemical energy to electrical energy.

dis•ci•ple (di sī′pəl), *n.* **1.** any professed follower of Christ in His lifetime, esp. one of the 12 apostles. **2.** a pupil or an adherent of another; follower.

dis•ci•pline (-plin), *n., v.,* **-plined, -plin•ing.** —*n.* **1.** training to act in accordance with rules. **2.** a regimen that develops or improves a skill. **3.** punishment inflicted by way of correction and training. **4.** behavior in accord with rules of conduct. **5.** a branch of instruction or learning. **6.** a system of rules. —*v.t.* **7.** to train by instruction and exercise. **8.** to bring under control. **9.** to punish. —**dis′ci•pli•nar′y,** *adj.*

disc′ jock′ey *n.* a person who plays and comments on popular recorded music on a radio program.

dis•claim (dis klām′), *v.t.* **1.** to deny or repudiate interest in or connection with; disavow; disown. **2.** to renounce a claim or right to. —**dis•claim′er,** *n.*

dis•close (di sklōz′), *v.t.,* **-closed, -clos•ing.** to make known; reveal. —**dis•clo′sure** (-klō′zhər), *n.*

dis•co (dis′kō), *n., pl.* **-cos. 1.** a discotheque. **2.** a style of popular music for dancing, having a heavy, rhythmic beat.

dis•col•or (dis kul′ər), *v.t., v.i.* to change color; fade; stain. —**dis•col′or•a′tion,** *n.*

dis•com•bob•u•late (dis′kəm bob′yə lāt′), *v.t.,* **-lat•ed, -lat•ing.** to confuse or disconcert. —**dis′•com•bob•u•la′tion,** *n.*

dis•com•fit (dis kum′fit), *v.t.* **1.** to confuse and deject. **2.** to frustrate; thwart. —**dis•com′fi•ture** (-fi chər), *n.*

dis•com•fort (dis kum′fərt), *n.* **1.** an absence of comfort or ease; mild pain. **2.** anything that is disturbing to comfort. —*v.t.* **3.** to make uncomfortable or uneasy.

dis′com•pose′ *v.t.,* **-posed, -pos•ing. 1.** to upset the order of. **2.** to disturb the composure of.

dis•con•cert (dis′kən sûrt′), *v.t.* to disturb the self-possession of; perturb.

dis•con•nect′ *v.t.* **1.** to sever or interrupt the connection of or between. **2.** to withdraw into one's private world. —**dis′con•nec′tion,** *n.*

dis•con•so•late (dis kon′sə lit), *adj.* **1.** without consolation or solace. **2.** cheerless or gloomy. —**dis•con′so•late•ly,** *adv.*

dis′con•tent′ (-kən tent′), *adj.* **1.** not content; discontented. —*n.* **2.** Also, **dis′con•tent′ment.** lack of contentment. —*v.t.* **3.** to make discontent.

dis′con•tent′ed *adj.* dissatisfied; restlessly unhappy.

dis′con•tin′ue *v.,* **-tin•ued, -tin•u•ing.** —*v.t.* **1.** to put an end to; stop. **2.** to cease using, taking, etc. —*v.i.* **3.** to come to an end; cease. —**dis′con•tin′u•ance, dis′con•tin′u•a′tion,** *n.* —**dis′con•tin′u•ous,** *adj.*

dis•cord (dis′kôrd), *n.* **1.** lack of concord or harmony. **2.** difference of opinion. **3.** an inharmonious combination of musical sounds. **4.** any confused or harsh noise. —**dis•cord′ance,** *n.* —**dis•cord′ant,** *adj.*

dis•co•theque or **-thèque** (dis′kə tek′, dis′kə tek′), *n.* a nightclub for dancing to live or recorded music.

dis•count (*v.* dis′kount, dis kount′; *n.* dis′kount), *v.t.* **1.** to deduct an amount from (a bill, charge, etc.). **2.** to sell at a reduced price. **3.** to buy, sell, or lend money on (commercial paper) after deducting interest. **4.** to allow for exaggeration in (a statement, opinion, etc.). **5.** to disregard or minimize. —*n.* **6.** an act or instance of discounting. **7.** an

amount deducted from the usual or list price. **8.** a deduction of interest in advance upon a loan of money. —**dis′count•er,** *n.*

dis•coun′te•nance *v.t.,* **-nanced, -nanc•ing. 1.** to disconcert or embarrass regularly. **2.** to show disapproval of.

dis•cour•age (di skûr′ij, -skur′-), *v.t.,* **-aged, -ag•ing. 1.** to deprive of courage or confidence; dishearten. **2.** to dissuade. **3.** to obstruct or hinder. —**dis•cour′age•ment,** *n.* —**dis•cour′ag•ing•ly,** *adv.*

dis•course (*n.* dis′kôrs; *v.* dis kôrs′), *n., v.,* **-coursed, -cours•ing.** —*n.* **1.** communication by words; talk; conversation. **2.** a formal discussion of a subject in speech or writing. —*v.i.* **3.** to talk or converse. **4.** to treat a subject formally in speech or writing.

dis•cour′te•sy *n., pl.* **-sies. 1.** lack of courtesy; rudeness. **2.** an impolite act. —**dis•cour′te•ous,** *adj.*

dis•cov•er (di skuv′ər), *v.t.* **1.** to gain sight or knowledge of for the first time. **2.** to notice or realize. —**dis•cov′er•er,** *n.* —**dis•cov′er•y,** *n., pl.* **-er•ies.**

dis•cred′it *v.t.* **1.** to injure the reputation of; defame. **2.** to show to be unreliable. **3.** to disbelieve. —*n.* **4.** loss or lack of belief or confidence. **5.** disgrace; disrepute. —**dis•cred′it•a•ble,** *adj.*

dis•creet (di skrēt′), *adj.* judicious in one's conduct or speech; prudent. —**dis•creet′ly,** *adv.*

dis•crep•an•cy (di skrep′ən sē), *n., pl.* **-cies. 1.** lack of agreement; difference; inconsistency. **2.** an instance of this. —**dis•crep′ant,** *adj.*

dis•crete (di skrēt′), *adj.* **1.** apart or detached from others; distinct. **2.** consisting of distinct parts.

dis•cre•tion (di skresh′ən), *n.* **1.** the power to decide or act according to one's own judgment. **2.** the quality of being discreet; prudence. —**dis•cre′tion•ar′y,** *adj.*

dis•crim•i•nate (di skrim′ə nāt′), *v.i.,* **-nat•ed, -nat•ing. 1.** to make a distinction on the basis of a prejudice; show partiality. **2.** to note a difference; distinguish accurately. —**dis•crim′i•nat′ing,** *adj.* —**dis•crim′i•na′tion,** *n.* —**dis•crim′i•na•tor′y** (-nə tôr′ē), *adj.*

dis•cur•sive (di skûr′siv), *adj.* passing aimlessly from one subject to another; digressive.

dis•cus (dis′kəs), *n.* a circular disk, usu. wooden with a metal rim, for throwing in athletic competition.

dis•cuss (dis kus′), *v.t.* to consider or examine by argument, comment, etc.; debate. —**dis•cus′sion,** *n.*

dis•dain (dis dān′, di stān′), *v.t.* **1.** to look upon or treat with contempt; scorn. **2.** to think unworthy of notice, response, etc. —*n.* **3.** contempt; scorn. —**dis•dain′ful,** *adj.*

dis•ease (di zēz′), *n.* a disordered or abnormal condition of an organ or other part of an organism; illness. —**dis•eased′,** *adj.*

dis•em•bark (dis′em bärk′), *v.t., v.i.* to leave or unload a ship or airplane. —**dis•em′bar•ka′tion,** *n.*

dis′em•bod′y *v.t.,* **-ied, -y•ing.** to divest of a body or bodily existence. —**dis′em•bod′i•ment,** *n.*

dis′en•chant′ *v.t.* to free from enchantment, illusion, credulity, etc.; disillusion. —**dis′en•chant′ment,** *n.*

dis′en•gage′ *v.,* **-gaged, -gag•ing.** —*v.t.* **1.** to release from attachment or connection. **2.** to free from an engagement, obligation, etc. —*v.i.* **3.** to become disengaged. —**dis′en•gage′ment,** *n.*

dis•fa′vor *n.* **1.** unfavorable regard; displeasure; dislike. **2.** the state of being regarded unfavorably.

dis•fig′ure *v.t.,* **-ured, -ur•ing.** to mar the appearance of; deface. —**dis•fig′ure•ment,** *n.*

dis•fran′chise or **dis′en•fran′chise,** *v.t.,* **-chised, -chis•ing.** to deprive of a right or privilege, esp. the right to vote. —**dis•fran′chise•ment,** *n.*

dis•gorge (dis gôrj′), *v.t.,* **-gorged, -gorg•ing. 1.** to throw up; vomit forth. **2.** to discharge or eject forcefully.

dis•grace (dis grās′), *n., v.,* **-graced, -grac•ing.** —*n.* **1.** loss of respect, honor, or esteem. **2.** a person, act, or thing that causes shame or reproach.

—*v.t.* **3.** to bring or reflect shame or reproach upon. —**dis•grace′ful,** *adj.* —**dis•grace′ful•ly,** *adv.*

dis•grun•tle (dis grun′tl), *v.t.,* **-tled, -tling.** to put into a state of sulky dissatisfaction.

dis•guise (dis gīz′, di skīz′), *v.,* **-guised, -guis•ing,** *n.* —*v.t.* **1.** to conceal identity or mislead, as with deceptive garb. **2.** to conceal the truth or actual character of; misrepresent. —*n.* **3.** something that disguises identity, character, or quality; a deceptive covering. **4.** the state of being disguised.

dis•gust (dis gust′, di skust′), *v.t.* **1.** to cause loathing or nausea in. **2.** to offend the good taste, moral sense, etc., of. —*n.* **3.** a strong loathing; repugnance. —**dis•gust′ed,** *adj.* —**dis•gust′ing,** *adj.*

dish (dish), *n.* **1.** an open, shallow container used esp. for holding food. **2.** a particular article or preparation of food. **3.** the quantity held by a dish. **4.** something like a dish in form or use. **5.** Also called **dish′ anten′na.** a dish-shaped reflector, used esp. for receiving satellite and microwave signals. —*v.t.* **6.** to put into or serve in a dish. —*Idiom.* **7. dish out,** *Informal.* to deal out; distribute. [< L *discus* dish]

dis•ha•bille (dis′ə bēl′, -bē′), *n.* the state of being carelessly or partially dressed.

dis•heart′en *v.t.* to depress the hope, courage, or spirits of; discourage.

di•shev•el (di shev′əl), *v.t.,* **-eled, -el•ing** or (*esp. Brit.*) **-elled, -el•ling.** to let down, as hair, or let hang in loose disorder, as clothing. —**di•shev′el•ment,** *n.*

dis•hon′est *adj.* **1.** not honest; untrustworthy. **2.** disposed to lie or cheat; fraudulent. —**dis•hon′est•ly,** *adv.* —**dis•hon′es•ty,** *n.*

dis•hon′or *n.* **1.** lack or loss of honor; disgrace. **2.** a cause of shame or disgrace. —*v.t.* **3.** to deprive of honor; disgrace. **4.** to refuse to pay (a check, draft, etc.). —**dis•hon′or•a•ble,** *adj.*

dish′wash′er *n.* **1.** a person who washes dishes. **2.** a machine for washing dishes.

dis/il•lu′sion *v.t.* to free from or deprive of illusion, idealism, etc.; disenchant. —**dis/il•lu′sion•ment,** *n.*

dis/in•cline′ *v.t.,* **-clined, -clin•ing.** to make averse or unwilling.

dis/in•fect′ *v.t.* to cleanse in order to destroy disease germs. —**dis/in•fect′ant,** *n., adj.*

dis/in•for•ma′tion *n.* false information released by a government to mislead rivals.

dis/in•gen′u•ous *adj.,* lacking in candor or sincerity; insincere.

dis/in•her′it *v.t.* to deprive of an inheritance or heritage.

dis/in•te•grate′ *v.i., v.t.,* **-grat•ed, -grat•ing. 1.** to separate into parts; break up. **2.** (of a nucleus) to decay. —**dis/in•te•gra′tion,** *n.*

dis/in•ter′ *v.t.,* **-terred, -ter•ring.** to take out of the place of interment; unearth. —**dis/in•ter′ment,** *n.*

dis/in•ter′est *n.* indifference; apathy.

dis/in•ter•est′ed *adj.* **1.** unbiased by personal interest. **2.** not interested; indifferent.

dis•joint′ed *adj.* **1.** separated at joints. **2.** incoherent.

disk (disk), *n.* **1.** any thin, flat, circular plate, object, or surface. **2.** DISC (def. 1). **3.** any of several types of media for storing electronic data consisting of thin round plates of plastic or metal. **4.** a roundish, flat anatomical structure or part.

disk•ette (di sket′), *n.* FLOPPY DISK.

disk jockey DISC JOCKEY.

dis•like′ *v.,* **-liked, -lik•ing,** *n.* —*v.t.* **1.** to regard with displeasure or aversion. —*n.* **2.** a feeling of aversion; antipathy.

dis•lo•cate′ (dis′lō kāt′, dis lō′kāt), *v.t.,* **-cat•ed, -cat•ing. 1.** to put out of place or order; disrupt. **2.** to put out of joint, as a limb. —**dis/lo•ca′tion,** *n.*

dis•lodge′ *v.t.,* **-lodged, -lodg•ing.** to force out of a place or position.

dis•loy′al *adj.* not loyal; faithless. —**dis•loy′al•ty,** *n., pl.* **-ties.**

dis•mal (diz′məl), *adj.* **1.** causing gloom or dejection; dreary. **2.** very bad; poor. —**dis′mal•ly,** *adv.*

dis•man•tle (dis man′tl), *v.t.,* **-tled, -tling. 1.** to

deprive or strip of furniture, equipment, etc. **2.** to take apart. —**dis•man′tle•ment,** *n.*

dis•may (dis mā′), *v.t.* **1.** to break down the courage of completely; daunt. —*n.* **2.** sudden or complete loss of courage; consternation.

dis•mem′ber (dis mem′bər), *v.t.* **1.** to deprive of limbs. **2.** to divide into parts. —**dis•mem′ber•ment,** *n.*

dis•miss (dis mis′), *v.t.* **1.** to direct or allow to leave. **2.** to discharge from office or service. **3.** to put aside from consideration; reject. **4.** to remove from a court's consideration. —**dis•miss′al,** *n.*

dis•mount′ *v.i.* **1.** to alight, as from a horse. —*v.t.* **2.** to throw down, as from a horse. **3.** to take (a mechanism) apart. **4.** to remove (a thing) from its mounting.

dis/o•be′di•ent *adj.* neglecting or refusing to obey. —**dis/o•be′di•ence,** *n.* —**dis/o•bey′,** *v.t., v.i.*

dis•or′der *n.* **1.** lack of order; confusion. **2.** a public disturbance. **3.** a physical or mental disturbance; illness. —*v.t.* **4.** to destroy the order of. **5.** to upset the physical or mental functions of. —**dis•or′der•ly,** *adv.*

dis•or′gan•ize′ *v.t.,* **-ized, -iz•ing.** to destroy the systematic arrangement of; throw into confusion. —**dis•or′gan•i•za′tion,** *n.*

dis/o•ri•ent′ *v.t.* **1.** to cause to lose one's way. **2.** to confuse mentally. —**dis/o•ri•en•ta′tion,** *n.*

dis•own′ *v.t.* to refuse to acknowledge as belonging to oneself; repudiate.

dis•par•age (di spar′ij), *v.t.,* **-aged, -ag•ing. 1.** to speak of or treat slightingly. **2.** to bring reproach or discredit upon. —**dis•par′age•ment,** *n.* —**dis•par′ag•ing,** *adj.*

dis•pa•rate (dis′pər it, di spar′-), *adj.* distinct in kind; dissimilar. —**dis•par′i•ty,** *n., pl.* **-ties.**

dis•pas′sion•ate *adj.* devoid of personal feeling or bias; impartial; calm. —**dis•pas′sion•ate•ly,** *adv.*

dis•patch (di spach′), *v.t.* **1.** to send off with speed, as a messenger or telegram. **2.** to put to death. **3.** to dispose of (a matter) promptly. —*n.* **4.** the sending off of a messenger, letter, etc. **5.** a putting to death; execution. **6.** speedy action. **7.** a message sent with speed. **8.** a news story transmitted to a newspaper by a reporter. —**dis•patch′er,** *n.*

dis•pel′ (di spel′), *v.t.,* **-pelled, -pel•ling. 1.** to drive off in various directions; disperse. **2.** to cause to vanish.

dis•pen•sa•ry (di spen′sə rē), *n., pl.* **-ries.** a place where medicines and emergency medical treatment are available.

dis•pen•sa′tion (dis′pən sā′shən, -pen-), *n.* **1.** an act or instance of dispensing. **2.** something dispensed. **3.** a system of administration. **4.** an official exemption from a law or obligation. **5.** the divine ordering of the affairs of the world.

dis•pense (di spens′), *v.t.,* **-pensed, -pens•ing. 1.** to deal out; distribute. **2.** to administer. **3.** to make up and distribute (medicine). **4. dispense with, a.** to do without. **b.** to do away with. —**dis•pens′er,** *n.*

dis•perse (di spûrs′), *v.,* **-persed, -pers•ing.** —*v.t.* **1.** to send off in various directions; scatter. **2.** to spread widely; disseminate. **3.** to dispel; cause to vanish. —*v.i.* **4.** to become scattered. —**dis•per′sal,** *n.,* **dis•per′sion** (-zhən, -shən), *n.*

dis•pir′it•ed *adj.* deprived of spirit or hope; discouraged.

dis•place′ *v.t.,* **-placed, -plac•ing. 1.** to compel (a person) to leave home, country, etc. **2.** to put out of the usual or proper place. **3.** to take the place of; supplant. **4.** to remove from a position or office. —**dis•place′ment,** *n.*

dis•play (di splā′), *v.t.* **1.** to show or exhibit; make visible. —*n.* **2.** an act or instance of displaying. **3. a.** a visual representation of the output of an electronic device. **b.** the portion of the device, as a screen, that shows this representation.

dis•please′ *v.t., v.i.,* **-pleased, -pleas•ing.** to cause displeasure; annoy or offend.

dis•pos•al (di spō′zəl), *n.* **1.** arrangement, as of troops. **2.** a getting rid of something. **3.** a transferring, as by gift or sale; bestowal. **4.** power to dispose of a thing; control: *left at my disposal.*

dis•pose *v.t.,* **-posed, -pos•ing. 1.** to give a tendency to; incline. **2.** to put in a particular place or order; arrange. **3.** dispose of, **a.** to settle. **b.** to get rid of. **c.** to give away or sell. —**dis•pos′a•ble,** *adj., n.*

dis•po•si•tion (dis′pə zish′ən), *n.* **1.** one's mental outlook; characteristic attitude. **2.** inclination or tendency. **3.** arrangement or placing. **4.** final settlement of a matter. **5.** bestowal, as by gift or sale. **6.** power to settle or control.

dis•pos•sess′ *v.t.* to put (a person) out of possession, esp. of real property. —**dis′pos•ses′sion,** *n.*

dis•pro•por′tion *n.* lack of proportion. —**dis′pro•por′tion•ate,** *adj.*

dis•prove′ *v.t.,* **-proved, -prov•ing.** to prove to be false. —**dis•prov′a•ble,** *adj.*

dis•pute′ (di spyōōt′), *v.,* **-put•ed, -put•ing,** *n.* —*v.i.* **1.** to engage in argument or debate. **2.** to argue vehemently; quarrel. —*v.t.* **3.** to argue or debate about. **4.** to argue against. **5.** to quarrel or fight about. —*n.* **6.** a controversy or difference of opinion. **7.** a quarrel. —**dis•put′a•ble,** *adj.* —**dis•pu′tant** (-pyōōt′nt), *n., adj.* —**dis•pu•ta•tion** (dis′pyōō tā′shən), *n.*

dis•qual′i•fy′ *v.t.,* **-fied, -fy•ing. 1.** to deprive of qualification or fitness. **2.** to declare ineligible or unqualified. —**dis•qual′i•fi•ca′tion,** *n.*

dis•qui′et *n.* **1.** lack of calm or peace. —*v.t.* **2.** to deprive of calm or peace.

dis•re•gard′ *v.t.* **1.** to pay no attention to; ignore. **2.** to treat without due respect or attentiveness. —*n.* **3.** lack of attention; neglect. **4.** lack of due respect or regard. —**dis′re•gard′ful,** *adj.*

dis•re•pair′ *n.* the condition of needing repair.

dis•rep′u•ta•ble *adj.* **1.** having a bad reputation. **2.** shabby or shoddy.

dis•re•pute′ *n.* bad repute; disfavor.

dis•re•spect′ *n.* **1.** lack of respect; rudeness. —*v.t.* **2.** to treat with rudeness; insult. —**dis′re•spect′ful,** *adj.*

dis•robe′ *v.t., v.i.,* **-robed, -rob•ing.** to undress.

dis•rupt′ (dis rupt′), *v.t.* **1.** to cause disorder in. **2.** to disturb or interrupt. **3.** to break apart. —**dis•rup′tion,** *n.* —**dis•rup′tive,** *adj.*

dis•sat′is•fy′ *v.t.,* **-fied, -fy•ing.** to fail to satisfy; disappoint. —**dis′sat•is•fac′tion,** *n.* —**dis•sat′is•fied′,** *adj.*

dis•sect′ (di sekt′, dī-), *v.t.* **1.** to cut apart (an animal body, plant, etc.) to examine the structure. **2.** to examine part by part; analyze. —**dis•sec′tion,** *n.*

dis•sem•ble (di sem′bəl), *v.t., v.i.,* **-bled, -bling.** to conceal by pretense, as one's motives or thoughts. —**dis•sem′blance,** *n.* —**dis•sem′bler,** *n.*

dis•sem•i•nate (di sem′ə nāt′), *v.t.,* **-nat•ed, -nat•ing.** to scatter or spread widely. —**dis•sem′i•na′tion,** *n.*

dis•sen•sion (di sen′shən), *n.* strong disagreement; discord.

dis•sent′ (di sent′), *v.i.* **1.** to differ in sentiment or opinion (often fol. by *from*). **2.** to reject the doctrines or authority of an established church. —*n.* **3.** difference of opinion. **4.** refusal to conform to an established church. —**dis•sent′er,** *n.*

dis•ser•ta•tion (dis′ər tā′shən), *n.* a formal discourse or thesis, esp. one written by a candidate for a doctorate.

dis•serv′ice *n.* harm or injury.

dis•si•dent (dis′i dənt), *n.* **1.** a person who dissents, esp. from established opinions. —*adj.* **2.** dissenting, as in opinion or attitude. —**dis′si•dence,** *n.*

dis•sim′i•lar *adj.* not similar; unlike. —**dis•sim′i•lar′i•ty,** *n., pl.* **-ties.**

dis•sim•u•late (di sim′yə lāt′), *v.t., v.i.,* **-lat•ed, -lat•ing.** to dissemble. —**dis•sim′u•la′tion,** *n.* —**dis•sim′u•la′tor,** *n.*

dis•si•pate (dis′ə pāt′), *v.,* **-pat•ed, -pat•ing.** —*v.t.* **1.** to scatter; dispel. **2.** to spend or use wastefully or extravagantly. —*v.i.* **3.** to become scattered. **4.** to indulge in dissolute behavior. —**dis′si•pa′tion,** *n.*

dis•so•ci•ate (di sō′shē āt′, -sē-), *v.t., v.i.,* **-at•ed,**

-at•ing. to break the association of; disconnect. —**dis•so′ci•a′tion,** *n.*

dis•so•lute (dis′ə lōōt′), *adj.* indifferent to moral restraints; given to improper conduct. —**dis′so•lute′ly,** *adv.* —**dis′so•lute′ness,** *n.*

dis•so•lu′tion *n.* **1.** the act or process of dissolving into parts or elements. **2.** the resulting state. **3.** the breaking of a bond. **4.** the breaking up of an assembly or organization. **5.** death; decease. **6.** disintegration or termination.

dis•solve′ (di zolv′), *v.,* **-solved, -solv•ing.** —*v.t.* **1.** to make a solution of, as by mixing with a liquid. **2.** to melt; liquefy. **3.** to break (a tie, union, etc.). **4.** to dismiss or terminate (an assembly or organization). **5.** to separate into parts or elements. —*v.i.* **6.** to become dissolved. **7.** to disappear gradually; fade away. **8.** to break down emotionally.

dis•so•nance (dis′ə nəns), *n.* **1.** inharmonious sound; discord. **2.** lack of harmony or agreement. —**dis′so•nant,** *adj.*

dis•suade (di swād′), *v.t.,* **-suad•ed, -suad•ing.** to deter by advice or persuasion.

dis•taff (dis′taf, -täf′), *n.* **1.** a staff for holding wool, flax, etc., from which the thread is drawn in spinning. —*adj.* **2.** of or pertaining to women.

dis•tance (dis′təns), *n., v.,* **-tanced, -tanc•ing.** —*n.* **1.** the extent of space between two things, points, etc. **2.** the state or fact of being apart in space or time. **3.** remoteness in aspect. **4.** a distant region. **5.** reserve; coolness. —*v.t.* **6.** to leave behind at a distance, as at a race. **7.** to place at a distance.

dis′tant *adj.* **1.** far off or apart in space or time; remote. **2.** remote or far apart in any respect: *a distant relative.* **3.** reserved or aloof. **4.** arriving from or going to a distance. —**dis′tant•ly,** *adv.*

dis•taste′ *n.* dislike; disinclination. —**dis•taste′ful,** *adj.*

dis•tem′per *n.* an infectious viral disease chiefly of young dogs, characterized by fever, convulsions, and vomiting. **2.** a deranged condition of mind or body.

dis•tend′ (di stend′), *v.t., v.i.* to stretch out or swell. —**dis•ten′tion,** *n.*

dis•till′ (di stil′), *v.t., v.i.* **1.** to subject to or undergo distillation. **2.** to give forth or fall in drops. —**dis•till′er,** *n.*

dis′til•la′tion *n.* **1.** the process of heating, evaporating, and subsequently condensing a liquid. **2.** the purification of a substance or the separation of one substance from another by such a process.

dis•till′er•y *n., pl.* **-ies.** a place for the distilling of liquors.

dis•tinct (di stingkt′), *adj.* **1.** not identical; separate. **2.** different in nature or quality; dissimilar. **3.** clear or plain; unmistakable. **4.** exceptional or notable. —**dis•tinct′ly,** *adv.*

dis•tinc′tion *n.* **1.** a distinguishing as different. **2.** the recognizing of differences; discrimination. **3.** a distinguishing quality or characteristic. **4.** a special honor. **5.** marked superiority.

dis•tinc′tive *adj.* **1.** serving to distinguish; characteristic. **2.** having a special quality; notable. —**dis•tinc′tive•ly,** *adv.* —**dis•tinc′tive•ness,** *n.*

dis•tin•guish (di sting′gwish), *v.t.* **1.** to mark off as different. **2.** to recognize as distinct. **3.** to perceive clearly; discern. **4.** to make prominent or eminent. **5.** to divide into classes; classify. —*v.i.* **6.** to indicate or show a difference. —**dis•tin′guish•a•ble,** *adj.*

dis•tin′guished *adj.* **1.** characterized by distinction or excellence. **2.** dignified or elegant.

dis•tort′ (di stôrt′), *v.t.* **1.** to twist out of shape. **2.** to give a false meaning to; misrepresent. **3.** to reproduce or amplify (an electronic signal) inaccurately. —**dis•tor′tion,** *n.*

dis•tract′ (di strakt′), *v.t.* **1.** to divert, as the mind or attention. **2.** to disturb or trouble greatly. —**dis•tract′ed,** *adj.* —**dis•tract′ing,** *adj.* —**dis•trac′tion,** *n.*

dis•traught (di strôt′), *adj.* **1.** bewildered; deeply agitated. **2.** mentally deranged; crazed.

dis•tress (di stres′), *n.* **1.** acute anxiety, pain, or sorrow. **2.** anything that causes anxiety, pain, or sorrow. **3.** a state of extreme necessity, misfortune, or danger. —*v.t.* **4.** to afflict with pain, anxiety, or sorrow; trouble. —**dis•tress′ful,** *adj.*

dis•trib•ute (di strib′yŏŏt), *v.t.,* **-ut•ed, -ut•ing. 1.** to divide and give out in shares; allot. **2.** to spread over a space; scatter. **3.** to sell and deliver (merchandise). **4.** to divide into classes. —**dis′tri•bu′-tion,** *n.*

dis•trib′u•tor *n.* **1.** one that distributes. **2.** a firm, esp. a wholesaler, that distributes merchandise. **3.** a device in a multicylinder engine that distributes the igniting voltage to the spark plugs.

dis•trict (dis′trikt), *n.* **1.** a division of territory marked off for administrative or other purposes. **2.** a region or locality.

dis′trict attor′ney *n.* an attorney for the government within a specified district.

dis•trust′ *v.t.* **1.** to regard with suspicion; have no trust in. —*n.* **2.** lack of trust; suspicion. —**dis•trust′ful,** *adj.*

dis•turb (di stûrb′), *v.t.* **1.** to interrupt the quiet, rest, or peace of. **2.** to interfere with; interrupt. **3.** to put out of order; disarrange. **4.** to perplex; trouble. —**dis•turb′ance,** *n.*

dis•use (*n.* dis yŏŏs′; *v.* -yŏŏz′), *n., v.,* **-used, -us•ing.** —*n.* **1.** discontinuance of use or practice. —*v.t.* **2.** to cease to use.

ditch (dich), *n.* **1.** a long, narrow channel in the ground, as for irrigation. —*v.t.* **2.** to dig a ditch in. **3.** to crash-land on water and abandon (an aircraft). **4.** *Slang.* to get rid of.

dith•er (diŧẖ′ər), *n.* **1.** a trembling; vibration. **2.** flustered excitement or fear. —*v.i.* **3.** to act irresolutely; vacillate.

dit•to (dit′ō), *n., pl.* **-tos. 1.** the aforesaid; the above or the same (used in accounts, lists, etc., to avoid repetition). **2.** DITTO MARK. [< It < L *dictus* said]

dit′to mark′ *n.* Often, **ditto marks.** two small marks (″) used as a sign for *ditto.*

dit•ty (dit′ē), *n., pl.* **-ties.** a short, simple song.

di•u•ret•ic (dī′ə ret′ik), *adj.* **1.** increasing the volume of the urine excreted. —*n.* **2.** a diuretic medicine or agent.

di•ur•nal (dī ûr′nl), *adj.* **1.** occurring each day; daily. **2.** of, belonging to, or active in the daytime. —**di•ur′nal•ly,** *adv.*

div. 1. dividend. **2.** division. **3.** divorced.

di•va (dē′və, -vä), *n., pl.* **-vas, -ve** (-ve). PRIMA DONNA (def. 1).

di•van (di van′, -vän′), *n.* a sofa or couch, usu. without arms or back.

dive (dīv), *v.,* **dived** or **dove, dived, div•ing,** *n.* —*v.i.* **1.** to plunge into water, esp. headfirst. **2.** to submerge, as a submarine. **3.** to plunge, fall, or descend through the air. **4.** to dart or dash. **5.** to plunge into a subject, activity, etc. —*v.t.* **6.** to cause to plunge, submerge, or descend. —*n.* **7.** an act or instance of diving. **8.** the steep descent of an airplane at a speed far exceeding that in level flight. **9.** a sudden decline, as in stock prices. **10.** *Informal.* a disreputable bar or nightclub. —**div′er,** *n.*

di•verge (di vûrj′, dī-), *v.i.,* **-verged, -verg•ing. 1.** to move or extend in different directions from a common point; branch off. **2.** to differ in opinion, form, etc. **3.** to deviate, as from a path or plan. —**di•ver′gence,** *n.* —**di•ver′gent,** *adj.*

di•vers (dī′vərz), *adj.* various; sundry.

di•verse (di vûrs′, dī-), *adj.* **1.** of a different kind; unlike. **2.** of various kinds; varied. —**di•verse′ly,** *adv.*

di•ver′si•fy *v.,* **-fied, -fy•ing.** —*v.t.* **1.** to make diverse; vary. **2.** to distribute (investments) among different types of securities. —*v.i.* **3.** to become diversified. —**di•ver′si•fi•ca′tion,** *n.*

di•ver•sion (di vûr′zhən dī-), *n.* **1.** the act of diverting or turning aside. **2.** a distraction; pastime. —**di•ver′sion•ar•y** (-zhə ner′ē), *adj.*

di•ver′si•ty *n., pl.* **-ties. 1.** the state or fact of being diverse; difference or variety. **2.** a point of difference.

di•vert (di vûrt′, dī-), *v.t.* **1.** to turn aside, as from

a path or course. **2.** to distract. **3.** to entertain or amuse.

di•vest (di vest′, dī-), *v.t.* **1.** to strip of clothing, ornament, etc. **2.** to deprive, esp. of property or rights. **3.** to rid or free.

di•vide (di vīd′), *v.,* **-vid•ed, -vid•ing,** *n.* —*v.t.* **1.** to separate into parts, sections, etc. **2.** to sever or cut off. **3.** to deal out in parts; apportion. **4.** to separate in opinion or feeling. **5.** to classify. **6.** to separate into equal parts by the process of mathematical division. —*v.i.* **7.** to become divided. **8.** to share with others. **9.** to diverge; branch; fork. **10.** to perform mathematical division. —*n.* **11.** a division. **12.** a ridge dividing two adjacent drainage basins. —**di•vid′a•ble,** *adj.* —**di•vid′er,** *n.*

div•i•dend (div′i dend′), *n.* **1.** a number to be divided by a divisor. **2. a.** a sum paid to shareholders out of company earnings. **b.** a single share of such a sum. **3.** a bonus.

di•vine (di vīn′), *adj.,* **-vin•er, -vin•est,** *n., v.,* **-vined, -vin•ing.** —*adj.* **1.** of, like, or from God or a god. **2.** devoted to God or a god; sacred. **3.** extremely good. —*n.* **4.** a theologian. **5.** a cleric. —*v.t.* **6.** to declare by divination; prophesy. **7.** to discover (water, metal, etc.) by means of a divining rod. **8.** to perceive by intuition; conjecture. —*v.i.* **9.** to practice divination. **10.** to conjecture. [< L *dīvīnus*] —**di•vine′ly,** *adv.* —**di•vin′er,** *n.*

divin′ing rod′ *n.* a forked stick supposedly useful in locating underground water or metal deposits.

di•vin′i•ty (-vin′i tē), *n., pl.* **-ties. 1.** the quality of being divine. **2.** a divine being. **3. the Divinity,** God. **4.** theology.

di•vis•i•ble (di viz′ə bəl), *adj.* capable of being divided, esp. of being evenly divided without a remainder.

di•vi′sion (-vizh′ən), *n.* **1.** the act of dividing or state of being divided. **2.** the arithmetic operation of finding how many times one number is contained in another. **3.** something that divides or separates. **4.** one of the parts into which a thing is divided. **5.** disagreement; dissension. **6.** a major administrative and tactical unit of the army or navy. —**di•vi′sion•al,** *adj.*

di•vi′sive (-vī′siv), *adj.* creating dissension or discord. —**di•vi′sive•ly,** *adv.* —**di•vi′sive•ness,** *n.*

di•vi′sor (-zər), *n.* a number by which another number, the dividend, is divided.

di•vorce (di vôrs′), *n., v.* **-vorced, -vorc•ing.** —*n.* **1.** legal or formal dissolution of a marriage. **2.** total separation. —*v.t.* **3.** to separate by divorce. **4.** to free oneself from (one's spouse) by divorce. **5.** to separate. —*v.i.* **6.** to get a divorce.

di•vor•cée′ or **-cee′** (-vôr sā′, -sē′), *n., pl.* **-cées** or **-cees.** a divorced woman.

div•ot (div′ət), *n.* a piece of turf gouged out with a golf club in making a stroke.

di•vulge (di vulj′, dī-), *v.t.,* **-vulged, -vulg•ing.** to disclose or reveal (something secret).

Dix•ie (dik′sē), *n.* the southern states of the U.S., esp. those that were part of the Confederacy.

Dix′ie•land′ *n.* a style of jazz marked by accented four-four rhythm and improvisation.

diz•zy (diz′ē), *adj.,* **-zi•er, -zi•est. 1.** having a sensation of whirling and a tendency to fall. **2.** bewildered; confused. **3.** causing giddiness or confusion. **4.** *Informal.* foolish; silly. —**diz′zi•ly,** *adv.* —**diz′zi•ness,** *n.*

D.J. 1. Also, **DJ** (dē′jā′). disc jockey. **2.** Doctor of Law. [< L *Doctor Jūris*]

Dji•bou•ti (ji bōō′tē), *n.* a republic in E Africa.

DNA deoxyribonucleic acid: a nucleic acid molecule that is the main constituent of the chromosome and that carries the genes along its strands.

do (dōō; *unstressed* dŏŏ, də), *v.,* **did, done, do•ing,** *n., pl.* **dos, do′s.** —*v.t.* **1.** to perform (an act, duty, role, etc.). **2.** to execute (a piece or amount of work). **3.** to accomplish; finish. **4.** to put forth; exert: *Do your best.* **5.** to be the cause of (good, harm, etc.). **6.** to render, give, or pay: *to do justice.* **7.** to deal with as the case may require: *to do the wash.* **8.** to travel; traverse. **9.** to suffice for. **10.** to travel at the rate of (a specified speed). **11.** to serve (a term of time) in prison. **12.** to create or bring into being. **13.** to study or work at. **14.** to decorate. —*v.i.* **15.** to act or conduct oneself. **16.** to proceed: *to do wisely.* **17.** to get along. **18.** to be in a specified state of health. **19.** to be enough. **20.** to finish or be finished. **21.** to happen; take place. —*auxiliary v.* **22.** (used to avoid repetition of a verb): *I think as you do.* **23.** (used in interrogative and negative constructions): *Do you like music? I don't care.* **24.** (used to lend emphasis): *Do visit us!* **25.** do away with, **a.** to abolish. **b.** to kill. **26.** ~ in, **a.** to kill. **b.** to exhaust. **27.** ~ out of, *Informal.* to swindle; cheat. **28.** ~ up, to wrap up, fasten, or tie. **29.** ~ with, to benefit from; use. **30.** ~ without, to forgo. —*n.* **31.** *Informal.* a hairdo. **32.** a festive gathering; party. —*Idiom.* **33.** dos and don'ts, customs, rules, or regulations. —**do′a•ble,** *adj.*

DOA dead on arrival.

doc•ile (dos′əl), *adj.* readily trained or handled; submissive. —**do•cil•i•ty** (do sil′i tē), *n.*

dock[1] (dok), *n.* **1.** a landing pier or wharf. **2.** a waterway between two piers for receiving a ship while in port. **3.** such a waterway together with the surrounding piers. **4.** a platform for loading trucks, freight cars, etc. —*v.t.* **5.** to bring (a ship) into a dock. **6.** to join (an orbiting space vehicle) with another spacecraft. —*v.i.* **7.** to come into a dock. **8.** (of two space vehicles) to join together.

dock[2] (dok), *v.t.* **1.** to cut off the end of: *to dock a tail.* **2.** to deduct from (wages).

dock[3] (dok), *n.* the place in a courtroom where a prisoner is placed during trial.

dock[4] (dok), *n.* any of various weedy plants of the buckwheat family.

dock•et (dok′it), *n.* **1.** a list of cases scheduled to be heard in a court. **2.** any list of business to be transacted. —*v.t.* **3.** to enter in a docket.

doc•tor (dok′tər), *n.* **1.** a person licensed to practice medicine, as a physician, dentist, or veterinarian. **2.** a person who has been awarded a doctor's degree. —*v.t.* **3.** to give medical treatment to. **4.** to restore; repair. **5.** to tamper with. —*v.i.* **6.** to practice medicine. [< L: teacher < *docēre* to teach] —**doc′tor•al,** *adj.*

doc′tor•ate (-it), *n.* DOCTOR'S DEGREE.

doc′tor's degree′ *n.* any of several degrees of the highest rank awarded by universities, as the Ph.D.

doc′trine (-trin), *n.* **1.** a particular principle, position, or policy taught or advocated, as of a religion or government. **2.** a body of teachings. —**doc′tri•nal,** *adj.*

doc•u•dra•ma (dok′yə drä′mə, -dram′ə), *n., pl.* **-mas.** a fictionalized television drama depicting actual events. [*docu(mentary)* + *drama*]

doc•u•ment (*n.* dok′yə mənt; *v.* -ment′), *n.* **1.** a written or printed paper furnishing information or evidence, as a passport. **2.** a computer data file. —*v.t.* **3.** to furnish with or support by documents. —**doc′u•men•ta′tion,** *n.*

doc′u•men′ta•ry *adj., n., pl.* **-ries.** —*adj.* **1.** pertaining to, consisting of, or derived from documents. **2.** depicting an actual event, life story, etc., without fictional elements. —*n.* **3.** a documentary film, television program, etc.

dod•der (dod′ər), *v.i.* to shake; tremble; totter. —**dod′der•ing,** *adj.*

dodge (doj), *v.,* **dodged, dodg•ing,** *n.* —*v.t.* **1.** to avoid by a sudden shift of position or by strategy; evade. —*v.i.* **2.** to move suddenly, as to avoid a blow. **3.** to use evasive methods. —*n.* **4.** a quick, evasive movement. **5.** a clever scheme or trick. —**dodg′er,** *n.*

do•do (dō′dō), *n., pl.* **-dos, -does. 1.** a large, extinct, flightless bird. **2.** *Slang.* a dull-witted person.

doe (dō), *n., pl.* **does, doe.** the female of the deer, antelope, rabbit, etc.

does (duz), *v.* 3rd pers. sing. pres. indic. of DO[1].

does•n't (duz′ənt), contraction of *does not.*

doff (dof, dôf), *v.t.* **1.** to take off, as clothing. **2.** to tip (the hat), as in greeting. **3.** to get rid of.

dog (dôg, dog), *n., v.,* **dogged, dog•ging.** —*n.* **1.** a domesticated carnivore bred in many varieties. **2.**

any animal belonging to the same family, including wolves and foxes. **3.** a despicable person. **4.** a fellow: *a lucky dog.* **5.** *Slang.* something of poor quality. **6.** *Slang.* an unattractive person. **7.** a mechanical device for holding something. —*v.t.* **8.** to follow or track like a dog; hound. —*Idiom.* **9.** go to the dogs, to deteriorate.

dog′-ear′ *n.* **1.** a folded corner of a book page. —*v.t.* **2.** to fold down the corner of (a page). —**dog′-eared′,** *adj.*

dog•ged (dô′gid, dog′id), *adj.* persistent; stubbornly tenacious. —**dog′ged•ly,** *adv.*

dog′house′ *n.* **1.** a shelter for a dog. —*Idiom.* **2.** in the doghouse, in disfavor.

dog•ma (dôg′mə, dog′-), *n., pl.* **-mas. 1.** a system of principles or tenets, as of a church. **2.** a specific tenet authoritatively put forth.

dog•mat′ic (-mat′ik) *adj.* **1.** of the nature of a dogma. **2.** arrogantly asserting opinions or beliefs. —**dog•mat′i•cal•ly,** *adv.*

dog′ma•tism *n.* dogmatic assertion in matters of opinions. —**dog′ma•tist,** *n.*

dog′wood′ *n.* a tree or shrub with pink or white blossoms.

doi•ly (doi′lē), *n., pl.* **-lies.** any small, ornamental mat, esp. one of embroidery or lace. [after a 17th-century London draper]

dol•drums (dōl′drəmz, dol′-), *n.pl.* **1.** a state of inactivity or stagnation. **2.** a dull, depressed mood. **3. the doldrums,** a belt of calms near the equator.

dole (dōl), *n., v.,* **doled, dol•ing.** —*n.* **1.** an allotment of money or food given by a charity or government to the needy. —*v.t.* **2.** to distribute in charity. **3.** to give out in small quantities.

dole′ful *adj.* sorrowful; mournful. —**dole′ful•ly,** *adv.*

doll (dol), *n.* **1.** a child's toy representing a baby or other human being, esp. an attractive one. **2.** *Slang.* **a.** a woman. **b.** a generous or helpful person. —*v.* **3. doll up,** to dress in fancy clothing, elaborate makeup, etc.

dol•lar (dol′ər), *n.* **1.** the basic monetary unit of the U.S., equal to 100 cents. **2.** the monetary unit of various other countries, as Canada and Australia. **3.** a coin or bill equivalent to one dollar.

dol•lop (dol′əp), *n.* **1.** a lump or blob of some substance. **2.** a small amount.

dol•ly (dol′ē), *n., pl.* **dol•lies. 1.** *Informal.* a doll. **2.** a low truck or cart with small wheels for moving heavy loads. **3.** a mobile platform for moving a movie or television camera about a set.

do•lor•ous (dō′lər əs, dol′ər-), *adj.* full of or causing pain or sorrow. —**do′lor•ous•ly,** *adv.*

dol•phin (dol′fin, dôl′-), *n.* **1.** a marine mammal resembling a small whale, having a beaklike snout. **2.** either of two large, slender fishes of warm and temperate seas.

dolt (dōlt), *n.* a blockhead; dunce. —**dolt′ish,** *adj.*

do•main (dō mān′), *n.* **1.** a field of action, thought, influence, etc. **2.** the territory governed by a single ruler or government.

dome (dōm), *n.* **1.** a hemispheric vault, ceiling, or roof of a room or building. **2.** any covering thought to resemble a dome.

do•mes•tic (də mes′tik), *adj.* **1.** of the home, family, or household affairs. **2.** devoted to home life. **3.** tame; domesticated. **4.** of one's own or a particular country: *domestic trade.* **5.** produced in one's own country. —*n.* **6.** a household servant. —**do•mes′ti•cal•ly,** *adv.* —**do•mes•tic•i•ty** (dō′me stis′i tē), *n., pl.* **-ties.**

do•mes′ti•cate′ (-kāt′), *v.t.,* **-cat•ed, -cat•ing. 1.** to tame, breed, or cultivate for human use. **2.** to accustom to household life. —**do•mes′ti•ca′tion,** *n.*

domes′tic part′ner *n.* either member of an unmarried, cohabiting, and esp. homosexual couple that seeks benefits usu. available only to spouses.

dom•i•cile (dom′ə sīl′, -səl, dō′mə-), *n., v.,* **-ciled, -cil•ing.** —*n.* **1.** a house or home. **2.** a permanent legal residence. —*v.t.* **3.** to establish in a domicile.

dom•i•nant (dom′ə nənt), *adj.* **1.** ruling or controlling; exerting chief authority or influence. **2.** noting or pertaining to one of a pair of hereditary traits that masks the other when both are present in an organism. —**dom′i•nance,** *n.* —**dom′i•nant•ly,** *adv.*

dom′i•nate′ (-nāt′), *v.,* -**nat•ed,** -**nat•ing.** —*v.t.* **1.** to rule over; control. **2.** to tower above. **3.** to be the major factor or influence in. —*v.i.* **4.** to exercise power or control; predominate. **5.** to occupy a commanding position. —**dom′i•na′tion,** *n.*

dom•i•neer (dom′ə nēr′), *v.i., v.t.* to rule arbitrarily or despotically; dominate. —**dom′i•neer′ing,** *adj.*

Dom•i•ni•ca (dom′ə nē′kə, də min′i kə), *n.* an island republic in the E West Indies. —**Dom′i•ni′can,** *adj., n.*

Do•min′i•can Repub′lic (də min′i kən), *n.* a republic in the West Indies on the E part of Hispaniola. —**Do•min′i•can,** *adj., n.*

do•min•ion (də min′yən), *n.* **1.** sovereign authority. **2.** the act or fact of ruling. **3.** a domain or realm. **4.** (*often cap.*) a former title for a self-governing country belonging to the Commonwealth of Nations.

dom•i•no (dom′ə nō′), *n., pl.* -**noes.** **1.** a small, flat block marked with pips or dots. **2.** dominoes, a game played with dominoes.

don¹ (don; *Sp., It.* dôn), *n.* **1.** (*cap.*) Mr. or Sir: a Spanish title of respect. **2.** a Spanish lord or gentleman. **3.** a fellow or tutor at an English university. **4.** the head of a Mafia family.

don² (don), *v.t.,* **donned, don•ning.** to put on or dress in.

do•nate (dō′nāt, dō nāt′), *v.t., v.i.,* -**nat•ed,** -**nat• ing.** to contribute or give. —**do•na′tion,** *n.*

don•key (dong′kē, dông′-, dung′-), *n., pl.* -**keys. 1.** a domesticated ass. **2.** a stupid, silly, or obstinate person.

do•nor (dō′nər), *n.* **1.** one who donates. **2.** a provider of blood, an organ, or other biological tissue for transfusion or transplantation.

doo•dle (dōōd′l), *v.,* -**dled,** -**dling,** *n.* —*v.i., v.t.,* **1.** to draw or scribble idly. —*n.* **2.** a figure produced by doodling. —**doo′dler,** *n.*

doom (dōōm), *n.* **1.** fate or destiny, esp. adverse fate. **2.** ruin or death. **3.** an unfavorable judgment or sentence. —*v.t.* **4.** to destine to an adverse fate. **5.** to sentence; condemn.

dooms′day′ *n.* the day of the Last Judgment.

door (dôr), *n.* **1.** a movable barrier for opening and closing an entrance, cabinet, etc. **2.** a doorway. **3.** any means of access.

door′way′ *n.* **1.** the entryway to a building, room, etc. **2.** any means of access.

door′yard′ *n.* a yard near the front door of a house.

dope (dōp), *n., v.,* **doped, dop•ing.** —*n.* **1.** any thick liquid substance used to prepare a surface or coat a fabric. **2.** *Slang.* any narcotic or illicit drug. **3.** *Slang.* information; news. **4.** *Informal.* a stupid person. —*v.t.* **5.** *Slang.* to affect or treat with dope; drug. **6. dope out,** *Slang.* to figure out.

dop′ey or **dop′y,** *adj.,* -**i•er, i•est.** *Informal.* **1.** stupid; inane. **2.** sluggish or befuddled, as from the use of drugs.

dor•mant (dôr′mənt), *adj.* **1.** temporarily inactive, as in sleep; resting; torpid. **2.** undeveloped; latent. —**dor′man•cy,** *n.*

dor•mer (dôr′mər), *n.* **1.** Also called **dor′mer win′dow.** a vertical window in a projection built out from a sloping roof. **2.** the entire structure.

dor•mi•to•ry (dôr′mi tôr′ē), *n., pl.* -**ries. 1.** a building, as at a college, containing rooms and facilities for residents. **2.** a room serving as communal sleeping quarters.

dor•mouse (dôr′mous′), *n., pl.* -**mice.** a small, bushy-tailed Old World rodent.

dor•sal (dôr′səl), *adj.* of or situated at the back.

do•ry (dôr′ē), *n., pl.* -**ries.** a small, flat-bottomed boat with a high bow and flaring sides.

DOS (dôs, dos), *n.* a disk operating system for microcomputers.

dose (dōs), *n., v.,* **dosed, dos•ing.** —*n.* **1.** a quantity of medicine prescribed to be taken at one time. **2.** an intense and often disagreeable experience. **3.**

the amount of radiation administered to or absorbed by living tissue. —*v.t.* **4.** to give a dose of medicine to. **5.** to administer in doses. —**dos′age,** *n.*

dos•si•er (dos′ē ā′, dô′sē ā′), *n.* a file of documents containing detailed information about a person or topic.

dot (dot), *n., v.,* **dot•ted, dot•ting.** —*n.* **1.** a small, roundish mark made with or as if with a pen. **2.** a small spot; speck. **3.** a signal of shorter duration than a dash, used to represent letters, as in Morse code. **4.** a period, esp. as used when pronouncing an Internet address. —*v.t.* **5.** to mark or cover with or as if with a dot or dots. —*Idiom.* **6. on the dot,** exactly at the time specified.

do′tard (dō′tərd) *n.* senile person.

dote (dōt), *v.i.,* **dot•ed, dot•ing. 1.** to bestow excessive fondness or love. **2.** to be weak-minded or foolish, esp. from old age. —**dot•age** (dō′tij), *n.* —**dot′er,** *n.*

dou•ble (dub′əl), *adj., n., v.,* -**bled, -bling,** *adv.* —*adj.* **1.** twice as large, as strong, as many, etc. **2.** composed of two like parts. **3.** suitable for two persons. **4.** twofold; dual. **5.** marked by duplicity. **6.** folded in two. **7.** (of flowers) having more than the normal number of petals. —*n.* **8.** something that is twice the usual size, quantity, strength, etc. **9.** a duplicate or counterpart. **10.** a fold or plait. **11.** an actor's substitute or understudy. **12.** a hit in baseball that enables the batter to reach second base. **13. doubles,** a game between two pairs of players, as in tennis. **14.** (in bridge) a doubling of an opponent's bid. —*v.t.* **15.** to make double or twice as great. **16.** to fold or bend with one part over another. **17.** to clench: *to double one's fists.* **18.** to repeat or duplicate. **19.** (in bridge) to challenge (an opponent's bid) by increasing the value of tricks won or lost. —*v.i.* **20.** to become double. **21.** to reverse direction sharply (often fol. by *back*). **22.** to serve in two capacities. **23.** to hit a double in baseball. **24. double up, a.** to share quarters. **b.** to bend over, as from pain. —*adv.* **25.** twofold. **26.** in pairs. —*Idiom.* **27. on the double,** without delay.

dou′ble bass′ (bās), *n.* the largest and lowest-pitched instrument of the violin family.

dou′ble-cross′ *v.t.* to betray or swindle. —**dou′-ble-cross′er,** *n.*

dou•ble en•ten•dre (dub′əl än tän′drə, -tänd′; *Fr.* dōō blän tän′dʀ³), *n., pl.* -**ten•dres** (-tän′drəz, -tändz′; *Fr.* -tän′dʀ³). a word or expression with two meanings, esp. when one meaning is risqué.

dou′ble-head′er *n.* two games played on the same day in immediate succession.

dou′ble play′ *n.* a baseball play in which two players are put out.

dou′ble-reed′ *adj.* of or designating a wind instrument producing sounds through two reeds beating together, as the oboe.

dou′ble stand′ard *n.* a moral code permitting men greater freedom than women, esp. in sexual conduct.

dou′ble take′ *n.* a delayed response, as to a person not recognized or a situation not grasped immediately.

dou′ble-talk′ *n.* **1.** speech using nonsense syllables along with real words. **2.** evasive or ambiguous language.

doubt (dout), *v.t.* **1.** to be uncertain and undecided about. **2.** to distrust. —*v.i.* **3.** to be uncertain. —*n.* **4.** a feeling of uncertainty and indecision. **5.** distrust or suspicion. **6.** a situation causing uncertainty. —*Idiom.* **7. beyond** or **without doubt,** with certainty. **8. no doubt, a.** probably. **b.** certainly. —**doubt′er,** *n.*

doubt′ful *adj.* **1.** of uncertain outcome. **2.** admitting of or causing doubt. **3.** unsettled in opinion or belief. —**doubt′ful•ly,** *adv.*

doubt′less *adv.* **1.** certainly. **2.** probably.

douche (dōōsh), *n., v.,* **douched, douch•ing.** —*n.* **1.** a jet of water, sometimes with a cleansing agent, applied to a body part or cavity. **2.** an instrument, as a syringe, for administering a douche. —*v.t., v.i.* **3.** to apply a douche (to).

dough to drag

dough (dō), *n.* **1.** flour or meal combined with water, milk, etc., in a pliable mass for baking into bread, pastry, etc. **2.** *Slang.* money. —**dough′y** *adj.*, **-i•er, -i•est.**

dough•nut (dō′nət, -nut′), *n.* a small, usu. ring-shaped cake of sweetened dough fried in deep fat.

dour (dŏŏr, dou^ər, dou′ər), *adj.* **1.** sullen; gloomy. **2.** severe; stern. —**dour′ness,** *n.*

douse (dous), *v.t.,* **doused, dous•ing. 1.** to plunge into water or the like; drench. **2.** to throw water or other liquid on. **3.** to extinguish.

dove¹ (duv), *n.* **1.** any bird of the pigeon family. **2.** a symbol of peace. **3.** a person who advocates peace.

dove² (dōv), *v.* a pt. of DIVE.

dove′cote′ *n.* structure for tame pigeons. Also, **dove′cot′.**

dove•tail′ *n.* **1.** a tapered tenon; pin. **2.** a joint formed of one or more such tenons fitting tightly within corresponding mortises. —*v.t., v.i.* **3.** to join together by means of a dovetail. **4.** to fit together compactly or harmoniously.

dow•a•ger (dou′ə jər), *n.* **1.** a woman who holds some title or property from her deceased husband. **2.** an elderly woman of stately dignity.

dow•dy (dou′dē), *adj.,* **-di•er, -di•est.** not neat or stylish in dress. —**dow′di•ness,** *n.*

dow•el (dou′əl), *n., v.,* **-eled, -el•ing** or (*esp. Brit.*) **-elled, -el•ling.** —*n.* **1.** a pin, usu. round, fitting into holes in two adjacent pieces to prevent their slipping or to align them. —*v.t.* **2.** to pin with dowels.

dow•er (dou′ər), *n.* **1.** the portion of a deceased husband's real property allowed to his widow for life. **2.** DOWRY. —*v.t.* **3.** to provide with a dower.

down¹ (doun), *adv.* **1.** toward or into a lower position or level. **2.** on or to the ground, floor, or bottom. **3.** to or in a sitting or lying position. **4.** to or toward the south. **5.** to a lower value or rate. **6.** to a lesser pitch or volume. **7.** in or to a calmer state. **8.** from an earlier to a later time. **9.** from a greater to a lesser strength, amount, etc. **10.** earnestly: *to get down to work.* **11.** on paper: *Write this down.* **12.** thoroughly; completely. **13.** in cash at the time of purchase: *$50 down.* **14.** into a condition of ill health. **15.** in or into a lower status or condition. —*prep.* **16.** in a descending or more remote direction on or along. —*adj.* **17.** directed downward. **18.** being at a low position or on the ground or bottom. **19.** downcast; depressed. **20.** ailing or bedridden. **21.** behind an opponent in points, games, etc. **22.** having lost the amount indicated: *to be down $10.* **23.** finished or taken care of: *five down and one to go.* **24.** not working: *The computer is down again.* —*n.* **25.** a downward movement; descent. **26.** a turn for the worse; reverse. **27.** *Football.* one of a series of plays during which a team must advance the ball. —*v.t.* **28.** to knock, throw, or bring down. **29.** to drink down, esp. quickly. —*Idiom.* **30. down and out,** destitute. **31. down on,** hostile to. **32. down with,** to do away with (used imperatively).

down² (doun), *n.* **1.** the soft plumage of birds. **2.** the fine, soft hair on certain leaves and fruit. —**down′y,** *adj.,* **-i•er, -i•est.**

down³ (doun), *n.* Often, **downs.** open, rolling country usu. covered with grass.

down′cast′ *adj.* **1.** directed downward, as the eyes. **2.** dejected; depressed.

down′er *n. Informal.* **1.** a depressing experience or person. **2.** a depressant or sedative drug.

down′fall′ *n.* **1.** overthrow; ruin. **2.** something causing this. **3.** a sudden fall of rain or snow.

down′grade′ *v.,* **-grad•ed, -grad•ing.** —*v.t.* **1.** to reduce in rank, income, importance, etc. —*n.* **2.** a downward slope.

down′heart′ed *adj.* dejected; depressed.

down′hill′ (*adv.* -hil′; *adj.* -hil′), *adv.* **1.** down the slope of a hill. **2.** into a worse condition. —*adj.* **3.** going downward. **4.** free of obstacles; easy.

down′play′ *v.t.* to represent as unimportant, insignificant, etc.; minimize.

down′pour′ *n.* a heavy, drenching rain.

down′right′ *adv.* **1.** completely; thoroughly. —*adj.* **2.** thorough; absolute. **3.** frank; straightforward.

down′scale′ *adj.* characteristic of or suitable for people at the lower end of a social or economic scale.

down′size′ *v.t.,* **-sized, -siz•ing. 1.** to design or make a smaller version of. **2.** to reduce in size or number; cut back.

down′stage′ (*adv.* -stāj′; *adj.* -stāj′), *adv., adj.* at or toward the front of the stage.

down′stairs′ (*adv.* -stârz′; *adj.* -stârz′), *adv.* **1.** down the stairs. **2.** to or on a lower floor. —*adj.* **3.** pertaining to or situated on a lower floor. —*n.* **4.** the lower floor or floors of a building.

down′stream′ *adv., adj.* in the direction of the current of a stream.

Down′ (or **Down′s′**) **syn′drome,** *n.* a genetic disorder characterized by mental retardation, a wide, flattened skull, and slanting eyes. [after J. L. H. *Down* (1828–96), British physician]

down′-to-earth′ *adj.* practical and realistic.

down′town′ *adv., adj.* **1.** to, toward, or in the main business section of a city. —*n.* **2.** the main business section of a city.

down′trod′den *adj.* tyrannized; oppressed.

down′turn′ *n.* a downward trend; decline.

down′ward *adv.* **1.** Also, **down′wards.** from a higher to a lower level or condition. **2.** from a past time. —*adj.* **3.** moving to a lower level or condition.

down′y *adj.,* **-i•er, -i•est.** of or like soft feathers.

dow•ry (dou′rē) *n., pl.* **-ries.** the money, goods, etc., that a wife brings to her husband at marriage.

dowse¹ (dous), *v.t.,* **dowsed, dows•ing.** DOUSE.

dowse² (douz), *v.i.,* **dowsed, dows•ing.** to search for underground sources of water, metal, etc., using a divining rod. —**dows′er,** *n.*

doz. dozen.

doze (dōz), *v.,* **dozed, doz•ing,** *n.* —*v.i.* **1.** to sleep lightly and briefly; nap. —*n.* **2.** a nap.

doz•en (duz′ən), *n., pl.* **-ens, -en.** a group of 12. —**doz′enth,** *adj.*

Dr. 1. Doctor. **2.** Drive.

drab (drab), *adj.,* **drab•ber, drab•best,** *n.* —*adj.* **1.** lacking in brightness, spirit, etc.; dull. **2.** of the color drab. —*n.* **3.** a brownish gray. —**drab′ness,** *n.*

draft (draft, dräft), *n.* **1.** a drawing, sketch, or design. **2.** a preliminary form of any writing. **3.** a current of air in any enclosed space. **4.** a device for regulating the current of air in a fireplace, stove, etc. **5.** the act of pulling loads. **6.** something drawn or pulled. **7.** the force required to pull a load. **8.** the selection of persons for military service, an athletic team, etc. **9.** the persons so selected. **10.** a written order for payment of money. **11.** beer or ale drawn from a cask. **12.** the act of drinking or inhaling. **13.** a drink or dose. **14.** the depth to which a ship is immersed when bearing a given load. —*v.t.* **15.** to sketch. **16.** to compose. **17.** to select by draft, as for military service. —*adj.* **18.** used for drawing loads: *a draft horse.* **19.** drawn from a cask. **20.** being a preliminary outline or sketch. —*Idiom.* **21. on draft,** available from a cask: *beer on draft.* —**draft′er,** *n.*

draft•ee (draf tē′, dräf-), *n.* a person who is drafted for military service.

drafts′man *n., pl.* **-men. 1.** a person employed in making mechanical drawings. **2.** an artist skilled in drawing. —**drafts′man•ship′,** *n.*

draft′y *adj.,* **-i•er, -i•est.** characterized by or admitting drafts of air. —**draft′i•ness,** *n.*

drag (drag), *v.,* **dragged, drag•ging,** *n.* —*v.t.* **1.** to draw or pull slowly and with effort; haul. **2.** to search with a drag or grapnel. **3.** to introduce or insert, as an irrelevant matter. **4.** to protract tediously (often fol. by *out*). **5.** to pull (a graphical image or portion of text) from one place to another on a computer screen, esp. by using a mouse. —*v.i.* **6.** to be drawn or hauled along. **7.** to trail on the ground. **8.** to move slowly and with great effort. **9.** to proceed or pass tediously. **10.** to lag behind. **11.** to puff: *to drag on a cigarette.* —*n.* **12.** any device for searching the bottom of a body of water to recover objects. **13.** a heavy harrow. **14.** *Slang.* a bore. **15.** the force exerted on an aerodynamic body that reduces forward motion. **16.** the act of dragging. **17.** something that retards progress. **18.** a puff on a cigarette, pipe, etc. **19.** *Slang.* clothing characteristically worn by the opposite sex. **20.** a city street: *the main drag.*

drag′net′ *n.* **1.** a net drawn along the bottom of a stream to catch fish. **2.** an interlinked system for finding or catching someone, as a criminal.

drag•on (drag′ən), *n.* a mythical monster generally represented as a huge, winged reptile spouting fire.

drag′on•fly′ *n., pl.* **-flies.** an insect with a long, narrow body and four wings.

dra•goon (drə gōōn′), *n.* **1.** a heavily armed mounted soldier common in European armies from c1600 to World War I. —*v.t.* **2.** to pressure or coerce.

drag′ race′ *n.* a race between two or more automobiles accelerating from a standstill.

drain (drān), *v.t.* **1.** to draw off (a liquid) gradually. **2.** to empty by drawing off liquid. **3.** to exhaust or use up gradually. —*v.i.* **4.** to flow off or empty gradually. —*n.* **5.** a pipe, conduit, etc., by which a liquid drains. **6.** the act of draining. **7.** continuous outflow or depletion. —*Idiom.* **8. down the drain,** lost or wasted. —**drain•age** (drā′nij), *n.* —**drain′er,** *n.*

drake (drāk), *n.* a male duck.

dram (dram), *n.* **1. a.** a unit of apothecaries' weight equal to 60 grains, or ⅛ ounce (3.89 grams). **b.** ¹⁄₁₆ ounce avoirdupois weight (27.34 grains; 1.77 grams). **2.** a small drink of liquor.

dra•ma (drä′mə, dram′ə), *n., pl.* **-mas. 1.** a composition presenting a story in dialogue to be performed by actors; a play. **2.** the art of writing and producing plays. **3.** a series of vivid, exciting, or suspenseful events. **4.** the quality of being vivid or striking. —**dra•mat•ic** (drə mat′ik), *adj.* —**dramat′i•cal•ly,** *adv.*

dra•mat•ics (drə mat′iks), *n.* **1.** (*used with a sing. v.*) the art of producing or acting dramas. **2.** (*used with a pl. v.*) overly emotional or insincere behavior.

dram•a•tist (dram′ə tist, drä′mə-), *n.* a writer of dramas; playwright.

dram′a•tize′ *v.t.,* **-tized, -tiz•ing. 1.** to put into a form suitable for acting. **2.** to express or represent strikingly or vividly. —**dram′a•ti•za′tion,** *n.*

drape (drāp), *v.,* **draped, drap•ing,** *n.* —*v.t.* **1.** to cover or hang with fabric, esp. in graceful folds. **2.** to adjust (fabric, clothes, etc.) into loose folds. **3.** to arrange, hang, or let fall carelessly. —*n.* **4.** a long, heavy curtain, esp. one of a pair. **5.** manner or style of hanging. —**drap′er•y,** *n., pl.* **-ies.**

dras•tic (dras′tik), *adj.* **1.** acting with force; violent. **2.** severe or harsh. —**dras′ti•cal•ly,** *adv.*

draught (draft, dräft), *n., v.t., adj.* Chiefly Brit. DRAFT.

draw (drô), *v.,* **drew, drawn, draw•ing,** *n.* —*v.t.* **1.** to cause to move in a particular direction by or as if by pulling. **2.** to pull down or over, as to cover, or to pull up or aside, as to uncover: *Please draw the curtain. He drew the blanket over him.* **3.** to bring, take, or pull out, as from a receptacle or source. **4.** to attract. **5.** to sketch or depict with lines or words. **6.** to frame or formulate. **7.** to inhale or suck in. **8.** to deduce; infer: *to draw a conclusion.* **9.** to receive: *to draw a salary.* **10.** to withdraw (funds) from an account. **11.** to write (a check or draft). **12.** to produce; bring in: *to draw interest.* **13.** to choose or have assigned to one at random. **14.** to wrinkle or shrink by contraction. **15.** (of a ship) to need (a specific depth of water) to float. —*v.i.* **16.** to exert a pulling or attracting force. **17.** to move or pass, esp. continuously: *The day draws near.* **18.** to take out a sword, pistol, etc., for action. **19.** to hold a lottery: *to draw for prizes.* **20.** to sketch or to trace figures. **21.** to shrink or contract. **22.** to produce or permit a draft, as a pipe or flue. **23. draw on,** to utilize or make use of, esp. as a source: *to draw on the imagination.* **24. ~ out, a.** to pull out. **b.** to prolong. **c.** to persuade or

speak. **25. ~ up, a.** to draft, esp. a legal or formal document. **b.** to put into order. **c.** to stop. —*n.* **26.** the act or result of drawing. **27.** something that attracts. **28.** something drawn. **29.** a contest that ends in a tie.

draw′back′ *n.* a disadvantageous feature.

draw′bridge′ *n.* a bridge that may be raised or moved aside to prevent access or permit passage of ships.

draw•er (drôr *for 1, 2;* drô′ər *for 3*), *n.* **1.** a sliding, lidless box, as in a desk or bureau. **2. drawers,** (*used with a pl. v.*) an undergarment with legs that covers the lower half of the body. **3.** one that draws.

draw′ing *n.* **1.** the act of a person or thing that draws. **2.** the art of making a graphic representation with lines, as with a pencil or crayon. **3.** a picture or design thus produced. **4.** the drawing of lots; lottery.

drawl (drôl), *v.t., v.i.* **1.** to speak in a slow manner, usu. prolonging the vowels. —*n.* **2.** an act or utterance of a person who drawls.

drawn (drôn), *v.* **1.** pp. of DRAW. —*adj.* **2.** tense; haggard. **3.** eviscerated, as a fowl.

dray (drā), *n.* a low, strong cart without fixed sides, for carrying heavy loads.

dread (dred), *v.t.* **1.** to fear greatly. **2.** to be very reluctant to do, meet, or experience. —*n.* **3.** terror or apprehension. —*adj.* **4.** greatly feared. **5.** held in awe.

dread′ful *adj.* **1.** causing dread or terror; terrible. **2.** extremely bad or unpleasant.

dread′ful•ly *adv.* **1.** in a dreadful way. **2.** *Informal.* very; extremely.

dread′locks′ *n.pl.* a hairstyle of many long, rope-like locks.

dream (drēm), *n., v.,* **dreamed** or **dreamt, dream•ing.** —*n.* **1.** a succession of images or thoughts passing through the mind during sleep. **2.** a daydream or reverie. **3.** a goal; aim. **4.** a wild or vain fancy. **5.** something of unreal beauty or excellence. —*v.i.* **6.** to have a dream. **7.** to daydream. **8.** to conceive of something remotely (usu. fol. by *of*). —*v.t.* **9.** to see or imagine in a dream. **10.** to imagine as possible; conceive. **11.** to pass (time) in dreaming (often fol. by *away*). **12. dream up,** to conceive or devise. —**dream′er,** *n.* —**dream′like′,** *adj.*

drear•y (drēr′ē), *adj.,* **-i•er, -i•est. 1.** gloomy; dismal. **2.** dull; boring. —**drear′i•ly,** *adv.*

dredge¹ (drej), *n., v.,* **dredged, dredg•ing.** —*n.* **1.** any of various machines for scooping up mud or earth, as from a river bottom. —*v.t.* **2.** clear out or remove with a dredge. —*v.i.* **3.** to use a dredge. **4. dredge up,** to discover and reveal.

dredge² (drej), *v.t.,* **dredged, dredg•ing.** to coat (food) with a powdery substance, as flour.

dregs (dregz), *n.pl.* **1.** the sediment of liquids; grounds. **2.** the least valuable part of anything.

drench (drench), *v.t.* **1.** to wet thoroughly; soak. **2.** to cover completely; bathe.

dress (dres), *n.* **1.** an outer garment for women, consisting of bodice and skirt in one piece. **2.** clothing; apparel. —*adj.* **3.** of or for dresses. **4.** of or for a formal occasion. —*v.t.* **5.** to put clothing upon; clothe. **6.** to decorate; adorn. **7.** to comb out and do up (hair). **8.** to prepare for cooking, as by removing feathers. **9.** to prepare for use; finish: *to dress leather.* **10.** to apply medication or a dressing to (a wound). **11.** to bring (troops) into line. —*v.i.* **12.** to put on one's clothes. **13.** to put on or wear formal clothes. **14.** to come into line, as troops. **15. dress down, a.** to reprimand; scold. **b.** to dress informally or less formally. **16. ~ up, a.** to put on one's best or fanciest clothing. **b.** to dress in costume.

dres•sage (drə säzh′, dre-), *n.* the art of training a horse in obedience and in precision of movement.

dress′ cir′cle *n.* a semicircular division of seats in a theater, usu. the first gallery.

dress′er¹, *n.* **1.** someone or something that dresses. **2.** a person employed to dress others. **3.** a person who dresses in a particular manner.

dress′er², *n.* a chest of drawers; bureau.

dress′ing *n.* **1.** the act of a person or thing that dresses. **2.** a sauce, esp. for salad. **3.** stuffing for a fowl. **4.** material to dress a wound.

dress′ rehears′al *n.* a final rehearsal, as of a play, with scenery and costumes.

dress′y *adj.*, **-i•er**, **-i•est. 1.** appropriate to formal occasions. **2.** fancy or stylish. —**dress′i•ness**, *n.*

drib•ble (drib′əl), *v.*, **-bled**, **-bling**, *n.* —*v.i.*, *v.t.* **1.** to fall or let fall in drops. **2.** to drool. **3.** to advance (a ball or puck) by bouncing it or giving it short kicks or pushes. —*n.* **4.** a trickle or drop. **5.** a small quantity. **6.** the act of dribbling a ball or puck. —**drib′bler**, *n.*

dri•er (drī′ər), *n.* **1.** any additive that speeds the drying of paints, printing inks, etc. **2.** DRYER. (def. 1).

drift (drift), *n.* **1.** an act or instance of being carried along by currents of water or air. **2.** a gradual deviation from a set course. **3.** a course or tendency: *a drift toward conservatism.* **4.** a meaning; intent: *the drift of a statement.* **5.** something heaped up by wind, as a snowdrift. —*v.i.* **6.** to be carried along, as by currents. **7.** to wander aimlessly. **8.** to be driven into heaps. —*v.t.* **9.** to cause to drift.

drift′er *n.* a person who moves frequently from one place, job, etc., to another, as a hobo.

drill¹ (dril), *n.* **1.** a shaftlike tool for making holes in firm materials, esp. by rotation. **2.** training in formal marching or other precise military movements. **3.** any strict, methodical training or exercise: *a spelling drill.* —*v.t.*, *v.i.* **4.** to pierce or bore with a drill. **5.** to perform or make perform training drills. —**drill′er**, *n.*

drill² (dril), *n.* **1.** a small furrow made in the soil in which to sow seeds. **2.** a machine for sowing in rows and for covering the seeds when sown.

drill³ (dril), *n.* a strong, twilled cotton fabric.

drill′ press′ *n.* a drilling machine having a single vertical spindle.

drink (dringk), *v.*, **drank**, **drunk** or, often, **drank**, **drink•ing**, *n.* —*v.i.* **1.** to take water or other liquid into the mouth and swallow it. **2.** to consume alcoholic drinks, esp. to excess. **3.** to propose or take part in a toast. —*v.t.* **4.** to take (a liquid) into the mouth and swallow. **5.** to absorb (a liquid). **6.** to take in through the senses, esp. with eagerness: *to drink in the beauty of a scene.* **7.** to swallow the contents of (a cup, glass, etc.). —*n.* **8.** any liquid for drinking; beverage. **9.** liquor; alcohol. **10.** indulgence in alcohol. **11.** a swallow or draft of liquid. —**drink′a•ble**, *adj.* —**drink′er**, *n.*

drip (drip), *v.*, **dripped**, **drip•ping**, *n.* —*v.i.* **1.** to let drops fall; shed drops. **2.** to fall in drops, as a liquid. —*v.t.* **3.** to let fall in drops. —*n.* **4.** the act of dripping. **5.** liquid that drips. **6.** *Slang.* a boring or colorless person.

drive (drīv), *v.*, **drove**, **driv•en**, **driv•ing**, *n.* —*v.t.* **1.** to send, expel, or otherwise force to move. **2.** to force in or down; make penetrate. **3.** to cause and guide the movement of (a vehicle, an animal, etc.). **4.** to convey in a vehicle. **5.** to force to work or act. **6.** to urge; compel. **7.** to carry vigorously through: *to drive a hard bargain.* **8.** to hit (a ball, puck, etc.) with force. —*v.i.* **9.** to cause and guide the movement of a vehicle or animal. **10.** to travel in a vehicle. **11.** to hit a ball or puck with force. **12.** to strive vigorously toward a goal. **13.** to be impelled. **14. drive at**, to intend to convey. **15. ~ in**, *Baseball.* to cause (a run) to be scored or (a runner) to score. —*n.* **16.** the act of driving. **17.** a trip in a vehicle. **18.** an impelling along, as of game or cattle, in a particular direction. **19.** an inner urge or instinctive need. **20.** a vigorous effort toward a goal. **21.** a strong military offensive. **22.** energy and initiative. **23.** a road for vehicles, esp. a scenic highway. **24.** a driving mechanism, as of an automobile. —**driv′er**, *n.*

drive′-by′ *adj.*, *n.*, *pl.* **-bys.** —*adj.* **1.** occurring while driving past a person: *a drive-by shooting.* **2.** casual; superficial; offhand: *a drive-by news analysis.* **3.** involving a brief stay in a hospital, clinic,

etc.: *a drive-by mastectomy.* —*n.* **4.** a drive-by shooting.

drive′-in′ *n.* a facility or business, as a movie theater or restaurant, designed to accommodate patrons in automobiles.

driv•el (driv′əl), *n.*, *v.*, **-eled**, **-el•ing** or (*esp. Brit.*) **-elled**, **-el•ling.** —*n.* **1.** silly or meaningless talk; nonsense. —*v.i.*, *v.t.* **2.** to let (saliva) flow from the mouth. **3.** to talk childishly or idiotically.

drive′way′ *n.* a private road leading from a street to a house, garage, etc.

driz•zle (driz′əl), *v.*, **-zled**, **-zling**, *n.* —*v.i.*, *v.t.* **1.** to rain in fine drops; sprinkle. —*n.* **2.** a very light rain. —**driz′zly**, *adj.*

droll (drōl), *adj.*, **-er**, **-est.** amusing in an odd way.

drom•e•dar•y (drom′i der′ē, drum′-), *n.*, *pl.* **-ies.** the single-humped camel of Arabia and N Africa. [< LL *dromedārius* (*camēlus*) running (camel)]

drone¹ (drōn), *n.* **1.** the male of the honeybee and other bees that is stingless and makes no honey. **2.** an aircraft or ship operated by remote control. **3.** a parasitic loafer.

drone² (drōn), *v.*, **droned**, **dron•ing**, *n.* —*v.i.* **1.** to make a continued, low, monotonous sound; hum. **2.** to speak or proceed in a montonous manner. —*v.t.* **3.** to say in a dull, monotonous tone. —*n.* **4.** a low, monotonous sound.

drool (drŏŏl), *v.i.* **1.** to water at the mouth, as in anticipation of food; salivate. **2.** to talk foolishly. —*n.* **3.** saliva running down from one's mouth.

droop (drŏŏp), *v.i.* **1.** to sink, bend, or hang down, as from exhaustion. **2.** to fall into a weakened or disspirited state. —*v.t.* **3.** to let sink or drop. —*n.* **4.** a drooping. —**droop′y**, *adj.*, **-i•er**, **-i•est.** —**droop′i•ness**, *n.*

drop (drop), *n.*, *v.*, **dropped**, **drop•ping.** —*n.* **1.** a small quantity of liquid that falls in a more or less spherical mass. **2.** a small quantity of liquid. **3.** a minute quantity of anything. **4.** Usu., **drops.** liquid medicine given in drops. **5.** an act or instance of falling or dropping. **6.** the distance to which anything drops. **7.** a decline in amount, degree, value, etc. **8.** a spherical piece of candy. **9.** a depository where items are left: *a mail drop.* **10.** something resembling a drop, as an ornament. **11.** a dropping of persons or supplies by parachute. —*v.i.* **12.** to fall in drops. **13.** to fall vertically. **14.** to sink to the ground, as if inanimate. **15.** to fall lower or backward in position, degree, value, etc. **16.** to come to an end: *He let the matter drop.* **17.** to pass without effort into some condition or activity. **18.** to make an unexpected visit: *A neighbor dropped in last night.* **19.** to vanish; to drop from sight. —*v.t.* **20.** to let fall in drops. **21.** to let or cause to fall. **22.** to cause or allow to sink to a lower position. **23.** to reduce in value, quality, etc. **24.** to utter casually. **25.** to send: *Drop me a note.* **26.** to set down or unload. **27.** to omit; leave out. **28.** to abandon; forget. **29.** to remove or dismiss. **30.** (of animals) to give birth to. **31. drop off**, **a.** to fall asleep. **b.** to decline. **32. ~ out**, to withdraw, as from school or a race.

drop′ kick′ *n.* a kick made by dropping a football to the ground and kicking it as it starts to bounce up. —**drop′-kick′**, *v.t.*, *v.i.* —**drop′-kick′er**, *n.*

drop′out′ *n.* a person who withdraws, esp. a student who leaves school before graduation.

drop′per *n.* a small tube with a squeezable bulb at one end for drawing in a liquid and expelling it in drops.

dross (drôs, dros), *n.* **1.** a waste product taken off molten metal during smelting. **2.** waste matter; refuse.

drought (drout), *n.* an extended period of dry weather, esp. one injurious to crops.

drove¹ (drōv), *v.* pt. of DRIVE.

drove² (drōv), *n.* **1.** a number of oxen, sheep, or swine driven in a group. **2.** Usu., **droves.** a large crowd of people, esp. in motion.

drown (droun), *v.i.* **1.** to die of suffocation under water or other liquid. —*v.t.* **2.** to kill by suffocation in water or other liquid. **3.** to flood. **4.** to render inaudible, as by a louder sound (often fol. by *out*).

drow′sy *adj.*, **-si•er, -si•est. 1.** being half asleep. **2.** inducing sleepiness. —**drow′si•ness,** *n.*

drub (drub), *v.t.*, **drubbed, drub•bing. 1.** to beat, as with a stick. **2.** to defeat decisively, as in a game. —**drub′ber,** *n.*

drudge (druj), *n.*, *v.*, **drudged, drudg•ing.** —*n.* **1.** a person who does menial, dull, or hard work. —*v.i.* **2.** to perform such work. —**drudg′er•y,** *n.*, *pl.* **-ies.**

drug (drug), *n.*, *v.*, **drugged, drug•ging.** —*n.* **1.** a chemical substance used in medicines or as a medicine. **2.** any nonfood substance that, when taken, affects functions of the body or mind. **3.** a narcotic. —*v.t.* **4.** to stupefy or poison with a drug. **5.** to mix (food or drink) with a drug, esp. a stupefying or poisonous drug.

drug′gist *n.* **1.** PHARMACIST. **2.** the owner or operator of a drugstore.

drug′store′ *n.* the place of business of a pharmacist, usu. also selling toiletries, cosmetics, stationery, etc.

dru•id (drōō′id), *n.* (*often cap.*) a member of a pre-Christian religious order among the ancient Celts.

drum (drum), *n.*, *v.*, **drummed, drum•ming.** —*n.* **1.** a percussion instrument consisting of a hollow, cylindrical body covered at one or both ends with a tightly stretched membrane, which is struck to produce a sound. **2.** the sound produced by a drum. **3.** the eardrum. **4.** any cylindrical object, esp. a large, metal receptacle for storing liquids. —*v.i.* **5.** to beat a drum. **6.** to tap one's fingers rhythmically. —*v.t.* **7.** to perform by beating a drum. **8.** to drive or force by persistent repetition: *My parents drummed that idea into my head.* **9. drum out,** to expel in disgrace. **10. ~ up,** to obtain or create (trade, interest, etc.) through vigorous effort.

drum′ ma′jor *n.* the leader of a marching band.

drum′ majorette′ *n.* MAJORETTE.

drum′stick′ *n.* **1.** a stick for beating a drum. **2.** the meaty leg of a cooked fowl.

drunk (drungk), *adj.* **1.** having one's faculties impaired by an excess of alcoholic drink. **2.** overcome or dominated by a strong feeling. —*n.* **3. a.** a person who is drunk. **b.** DRUNKARD. **4.** a drinking spree. —*v.* **5.** pp. of DRINK.

drunk•ard (drung′kərd), *n.* a person who is habitually or frequently drunk.

dry (drī), *adj.*, **dri•er, dri•est,** *v.*, **dried, dry•ing,** *n.*, *pl.* **drys, dries.** —*adj.* **1.** free from moisture or excess moisture; not wet. **2.** characterized by little or no rain. **3.** characterized by a deficiency of natural moisture. **4.** not under or on water. **5.** drained, depleted, or empty of liquid. **6.** not yielding milk. **7.** thirsty. **8.** of nonliquid substances or commodities. **9.** (esp. of wines) not sweet. **10.** not allowing the manufacture and sale of alcoholic beverages. **11.** sober. **12.** dull; uninteresting. **13.** expressed in a straight-faced, matter-of-fact way: *dry humor.* **14.** unproductive: *dry years.* —*v.t.*, *v.i.* **15.** to make or become dry. —*n.* **16.** a prohibitionist. —**dry′ly,** **dri′ly,** *adv.* —**dry′ness,** *n.*

dry•ad (drī′əd, -ad), *n.* (*often cap.*) a nymph of the woods.

dry′ clean′ing *n.* the cleaning of garments, fabrics, draperies, etc., with chemicals rather than with water. —**dry′-clean′,** *v.t.* —**dry′ clean′er,** *n.*

dry′er *n.* **1.** a machine or apparatus for removing moisture, as by heat. **2.** DRIER. (def. 1).

dry′ ice′ *n.* the solid form of carbon dioxide, used chiefly as a refrigerant.

dry′ run′ *n.* a rehearsal or trial.

DST or **D.S.T.,** daylight-saving time.

du•al (dōō′əl, dyōō′-), *adj.* **1.** of or noting two. **2.** composed or consisting of two together; twofold; double. —**du•al′i•ty,** *n.*

dub¹ (dub), *v.t.*, **dubbed, dub•bing. 1.** to invest with a name, epithet, nickname, or title. **2.** to smooth by striking or rubbing, as leather. —**dub′ber,** *n.*

dub² (dub), *v.t.*, **dubbed, dub•bing. 1.** to furnish (a film or tape) with a new sound track, as one in another language. **2.** to add (music, speech, etc.) to a film or tape recording. —**dub′ber,** *n.*

du′bi•ous (-bē əs), *adj.* **1.** marked by or occasioning doubt. **2.** of doubtful quality or propriety; questionable. **3.** inclined to doubt; hesitant. —**du′bi•ous•ly,** *adv.*

du•cal (dōō′kəl, dyōō′-), *adj.* of a duke or dukedom.

duch•ess (duch′is), *n.* **1.** the wife or widow of a duke. **2.** a woman who rules a duchy.

duch•y (duch′ē), *n.*, *pl.* **-ies.** the territory ruled by a duke or duchess.

duck¹ (duk), *n.*, *pl.* **ducks, duck. 1.** any of numerous web-footed swimming birds characterized by a broad, flat bill. **2.** the flesh of this bird, eaten as food.

duck² (duk), *v.i.*, *v.t.* **1.** to lower or bend (the head or body) suddenly. **2.** to evade (a blow, unpleasant task, etc.). **3.** to plunge momentarily under water.

duck³ (duk), *n.* **1.** a heavy cotton fabric for tents, clothing, etc. **2. ducks,** (*used with a pl. v.*) trousers made of this.

duck′bill′ *n.* PLATYPUS. Also called **duck′bill plat′-ypus.**

duct (dukt), *n.* **1.** any tube, canal, pipe, or conduit by which a liquid, air, or other substance is conveyed. **2.** a single enclosed runway for electrical conductors or cables. —**duct′less,** *adj.*

duc•tile (duk′tl, -til), *adj.* **1.** capable of being hammered thin or drawn out into wire, as certain metals. **2.** capable of being molded or shaped; malleable. —**duc•til′i•ty,** *n.*

duct′ tape′ (duk, dukt), *n.* a strongly adhesive silver-gray cloth tape, used in plumbing, household repairs, etc.

dud (dud), *n.* **1.** a failure. **2.** a shell or missile that fails to explode after being fired.

dude (dōōd, dyōōd), *n.* **1.** a dandy or fop. **2.** *Slang.* a fellow. **3.** an urban Easterner who vacations on a ranch.

dudg•eon (duj′ən), *n.* anger: *We left in high dudgeon.*

due (dōō, dyōō), *adj.* **1.** owing or owed: *This bill is due.* **2.** owing as a right. **3.** proper; fitting. **4.** adequate; sufficient. **5.** expected or scheduled. —*n.* **6.** something owed or naturally belonging to someone. **7.** Usu., **dues.** a regular fee, as for membership. —*adv.* **8.** directly or exactly: *due east.* —*Idiom.* **9. due to, a.** attributable or ascribable to. **b.** because of. **10. pay one's dues,** to earn something, as a privilege, esp. by having worked hard.

du•el (dōō′əl, dyōō′-), *n.*, *v.*, **-eled, -el•ing** or (*esp. Brit.*) **-elled, -el•ling.** —*n.* **1.** a prearranged combat between two persons, fought with deadly weapons, esp. to settle a private quarrel. **2.** any contest between two parties. —*v.t.*, *v.i.* **3.** to fight in a duel. —**du′el•er, du′el•ist,** *n.*

du•et (dōō et′, dyōō-), *n.* **1.** a musical composition for two voices or instruments. **2.** the performers of a duet.

duf′fel bag′ (duf′əl), *n.* a large, cylindrical canvas bag for carrying clothing and other belongings.

duff•er (duf′ər), *n.* **1.** *Informal.* a plodding, incompetent person. **2.** a person inept at a specific sport, as golf.

dug′out′ *n.* **1.** a boat made by hollowing out a log. **2.** a roofed structure in which baseball players sit when not on the field. **3.** a rough shelter dug in the ground, esp. one used by soldiers.

duke (dōōk, dyōōk), *n.* **1.** (in Continental Europe) the male ruler of a duchy. **2.** a nobleman ranking immediately below a prince. **3. dukes,** *Slang.* fists or hands. [< OF *duc* < L *dux* leader; *dukes* "fists" perh. of distinct origin] —**duke′dom,** *n.*

dul•ci•mer (dul′sə mər), *n.* a musical instrument with metal strings that are struck with light hammers, plucked, or strummed.

dull (dul), *adj.*, **-er, -est. 1.** not sharp; blunt. **2.** causing boredom; tedious. **3.** not spirited; listless. **4.** not bright or clear; dim: *a dull day.* **5.** lacking richness or intensity of color. **6.** not brisk; sluggish. **7.** somewhat stupid. **8.** not intense or acute: *a dull pain.* —*v.t.*, *v.i.* **9.** to make or become dull. —**dull′ness,** *n.* —**dul′ly,** *adv.*

du•ly (do͞o′lē, dyo͞o′-), *adv.* **1.** in a due manner; properly. **2.** in due season; punctually.

dumb (dum), *adj.* **1.** silly or stupid. **2.** lacking the power of speech: *a dumb animal.* **3.** not speaking; silent. **4.** lacking electronic processing power of its own: *a dumb computer terminal.* —*v.i.* **5. dumb down,** to reduce the intellectual or developmental level of. —**dumb′ness,** *n.*

dumb′bell′ *n.* **1.** a weight for exercising, consisting of two heavy balls or disks connected by a graspable bar. **2.** *Slang.* a stupid person.

dumb•found (dum found′, dum′found′), *v.t.* to make speechless with amazement; astonish.

dumb′wait′er *n.* a small elevator used for moving food, garbage, etc.

dum′my *n., pl.* -mies, *adj.* —*n.* **1.** an imitation or copy of something. **2.** a figure, made in the form of a person, as for displaying clothes in store windows. **3.** *Informal.* a stupid person. **4.** one put forward to act for others while ostensibly acting for oneself. **5.** (in bridge) the declarer's partner, whose hand is exposed and played by the declarer. —*adj.* **6.** counterfeit; sham; fictitious.

dump (dump), *v.t.* **1.** to drop or let fall in a heap or mass. **2.** to unload or empty out. **3.** to rid oneself of suddenly and irresponsibly; discard or dismiss. **4.** to put (goods or securities) on the market in large quantities and at an unusually low price. **5.** to output (computer data), esp. to diagnose a failure. **6. dump on,** to criticize harshly; abuse. —*n.* **7.** a place where garbage, refuse, etc., is deposited. **8.** a collection of ammunition, military stores, etc. **9.** *Informal.* a dilapidated, dirty place.

dump′ling (-ling), *n.* **1.** a small mass of steamed or boiled dough served in soups or stews. **2.** a wrapping of dough enclosing fruit or a savory filling.

dump′y *adj.,* -i•er, -i•est. short and stout; squat. —**dump′i•ness,** *n.*

dun¹ (dun), *v.,* **dunned, dun•ning,** *n.* —*v.t.* **1.** to make repeated demands upon, esp. for the payment of a debt. —*n.* **2.** a demand for payment.

dun² (dun), *adj.* dull grayish brown.

dunce (duns), *n.* a dull-witted or ignorant person; dolt.

dune (do͞on, dyo͞on), *n.* a sand hill or sand ridge formed by the wind.

dung (dung), *n.* excrement, esp. of animals; manure.

dun•ga•ree (dung′gə rē′), *n.* **1. dungarees,** work clothes, overalls, or trousers of blue denim. **2.** blue denim.

dun•geon (dun′jən), *n.* a strong, dark prison or cell, usu. underground.

dunk (dungk), *v.t.* **1.** to dip (a doughnut, cake, etc.) into coffee, milk, or the like, before eating. **2.** to submerge briefly in a liquid. **3.** to thrust (a basketball) downward through the basket. —*v.i.* **4.** to submerge oneself in water.

du•o (do͞o′ō, dyo͞o′ō), *n., pl.* **du•os. 1.** DUET. **2.** a couple or pair.

du•o•de•num (do͞o′ə dē′nəm, dyo͞o′-; do͞o od′n-əm, dyo͞o-), *n., pl.* -o•de•na (-ə dē′nə; -od′n ə), -o•de•nums. the first portion of the small intestine, from the stomach to the jejunum. —**du′o•de′nal,** *adj.*

dupe (do͞op, dyo͞op), *n., v.,* **duped, dup•ing.** —*n.* **1.** a person who is easily deceived or fooled. —*v.t.* **2.** to make a dupe of; deceive; delude. —**dup′er,** *n.*

du•plex (do͞o′pleks, dyo͞o′-), *n.* **1.** an apartment with rooms on two floors. **2.** a house for two families. —*adj.* **3.** double; twofold.

du•pli•cate (*n., adj.* do͞o′pli kit, dyo͞o′-; *v.* -kāt′), *n., v.,* -cat•ed, -cat•ing, *adj.* —*n.* **1.** an exact copy. **2.** anything corresponding in all respects to something else. —*v.t.* **3.** to make an exact copy of. **4.** to do again; repeat. —*adj.* **5.** exactly like or corresponding to something else. **6.** consisting of two identical or corresponding parts; double. —**du′pli•ca′tion,** *n.*

du•plic•i•ty (do͞o plis′i tē, dyo͞o-), *n., pl.* -ties. deceitfulness in speech or conduct.

du•ra•ble (do͝or′ə bəl, dyo͝or′-), *adj.* **1.** highly re-

sistant to wear, decay, etc. **2.** lasting; enduring. —**du′ra•bil′i•ty,** *n.*

du•ra•tion (do͝o rā′shən, dyo͞o-), *n.* **1.** the length of time something continues or exists. **2.** continuance in time.

du•ress (do͞o res′, dyo͝o-, do͝or′is, dyo͝or′-), *n.* **1.** compulsion by threat or force; coercion. **2.** forcible restraint, esp. imprisonment.

dur•ing (do͝or′ing, dyo͝or′-), *prep.* **1.** throughout the duration. **2.** at some point in the course of.

du•rum (do͝or′əm, dyo͝or′-), *n.* a wheat, the grain of which yields flour used in making pasta.

dusk (dusk), *n.* **1.** the period of partial darkness between day and night. **2.** partial darkness; gloom. —**dusk′y,** *adj.,* -i•er, -i•est.

dust (dust), *n.* **1.** earth or other matter in fine, dry particles. **2.** the ground; earth. **3.** the disintegrated remains of the dead. **4.** anything worthless. —*v.t.* **5.** to wipe the dust from. **6.** to sprinkle with a powder or dust. —*v.i.* **7.** to wipe dust from furniture, woodwork, etc. —*Idiom.* **8. bite the dust,** to die; be killed. —**dust′y,** *adj.,* -i•er, -i•est.

Dutch (duch), *adj.* **1.** of the Netherlands, its inhabitants, or their language. —*n.* **2.** (*used with a pl. v.*) the people of the Netherlands. **3.** the Germanic language of the Netherlands and N and W Belgium. —*Idiom.* **4. go Dutch,** to pay one's own expenses, as on a date. —**Dutch′man,** *n., pl.* -men.

Dutch′ un′cle *n.* a person, often a mentor, who criticizes with unsparing frankness.

du′ti•a•ble *adj.* subject to customs duty.

du′ti•ful *adj.* **1.** performing the duties expected or required of one. **2.** proceeding from a sense of duty. —**du′ti•ful•ly,** *adv.*

du′ty *n., pl.* -ties. **1.** something that one is expected or required to do by moral or legal obligation. **2.** moral or legal obligation. **3.** action required by one's position or occupation. **4.** the respectful and obedient conduct due a parent, elder, or superior. **5.** an assigned military task or service. **6.** tax imposed on the import or export of goods. —*Idiom.* **7. off duty,** not at one's work. **8. on duty,** at one's work.

dwarf (dwôrf), *n., pl.* **dwarfs, dwarves** (dwôrvz), *adj., v.* —*n.* **1.** a person, animal, or plant of abnormally small size. **2.** (in folklore) a small man having magical powers. —*adj.* **3.** of unusually small size. —*v.t.* **4.** to cause to seem small by comparison. **5.** to prevent the growth of; stunt. —**dwarf′ish,** *adj.* —**dwarf′ism,** *n.*

dwell (dwel), *v.i.,* **dwelt** or **dwelled, dwell•ing, 1.** to live or stay as a resident; reside. **2. dwell on** or **upon,** to think, speak, or write about at length. —**dwell′er,** *n.*

dwell′ing *n.* a place of residence; abode.

dwin•dle (dwin′dl), *v.i., v.t.,* -dled, -dling. to make or become smaller and smaller; diminish.

dye (dī), *n., v.,* **dyed, dye•ing.** —*n.* **1.** a substance used to color cloth, paper, hair, etc. **2.** color or hue produced by dyeing. —*v.t.* **3.** to color with a dye. —**dye′ing,** *n.* —**dye′er,** *n.*

dyed′-in-the-wool′ *adj.* through and through; complete.

dyke¹ (dīk), *n.* DIKE¹.

dyke² (dīk), *n. Slang* (*often disparaging and offensive*). a female homosexual; lesbian. —**dyke′y,** *adj.*

dy•nam•ic (dī nam′ik), *adj.* **1.** forceful; energetic. **2.** of or pertaining to force or energy related to motion. —**dy•nam′i•cal•ly,** *adv.* —**dy•na•mism** (dī′nə miz′əm), *n.*

dy•na•mite (dī′nə mīt′), *n., v.,* -mit•ed, -mit•ing, *adj.* —*n.* **1.** a high explosive, orig. consisting of nitroglycerin mixed with an absorbent substance. —*v.t.* **2.** to blow up with dynamite. —*adj.* **3.** *Informal.* wonderful or exciting.

dy′na•mo′ (-mō′), *n., pl.* -mos. **1.** an electric generator, esp. for direct current. **2.** an energetic, forceful person.

dy•nas•ty (dī′nə stē), *n., pl.* -ties. a succession of rulers from the same family, stock, or group. —**dy•nas′tic** (-nas′tik), *adj.*

dys- a combining form meaning ill or bad (*dysfunction*).

dys•en•ter•y (dis′ən ter′ē), *n.* any infectious disease of the large intestines marked by hemorrhagic diarrhea.

dys•func•tion (dis fungk′shən), *n.* impairment of function or malfunctioning, as of an organ of the body.

dys•lex•i•a (dis lek′sē ə), *n.* an impairment of the ability to read. —**dys•lex′ic,** *adj., n.*

dys•pep•sia (dis pep′shə, -sē ə) *n.* indigestion. —**dys•pep′tic,** *adj.*

dz. dozen.

a b c d E f g h i j k l m n o p q r s t u v w x y z

E, e (ē), *n., pl.* **Es** or **E's, es** or **e's.** the fifth letter of the English alphabet, a vowel.

E **1.** east. **2.** eastern. **3.** English. **4.** excellent.

E *Symbol.* **1.** the fifth in order or in a series. **2.** a grade or mark indicating unacceptable academic work. **3.** the third note of the ascending C major scale. **4.** *Physics.* energy.

E. **1.** Earth. **2.** east. **3.** eastern. **4.** English.

e. **1.** *Football.* end. **2.** *Baseball.* error.

ea. each.

each (ēch), *adj.* **1.** every one of two or more considered individually. —*pron.* **2.** every one individually. —*adv.* **3.** to, from, or for each; apiece.

ea•ger (ē′gər), *adj.* characterized by or full of keen or enthusiastic desire or interest. —**ea′ger•ly,** *adv.* —**ea′ger•ness,** *n.*

ea•gle (ē′gəl), *n.* **1.** a robust, broad-winged bird of prey with a massive bill and talons. **2.** a former gold coin of the U.S., equal to ten dollars. **3.** a golf score of two below par for a single hole.

ea′gle-eyed′ *adj.* having unusually sharp eyesight.

ear[1] (ēr), *n.* **1.** the organ of hearing and equilibrium in vertebrates. **2.** the external part of the ear. **3.** the sense of hearing. **4.** attention; heed. **5.** a part that resembles an ear in position or form. —*Idiom.* **6. be all ears,** to listen intently. **7. by ear,** without reference to musical notation. **8. go in one ear and out the other,** to be heard but without understanding or effect. **9. play it by ear,** to improvise.

ear[2] (ēr), *n.* the spike of a cereal plant, as corn, containing the seed grains.

ear′drum′ *n.* TYMPANIC MEMBRANE.

earl (ûrl), *n.* a British nobleman of a rank below marquis and above viscount. —**earl′dom,** *n.*

ear′lobe′ or **ear′ lobe′,** *n.* the soft, pendulous lower part of the external ear.

ear•ly (ûr′lē), *adv.* and *adj.,* **-li•er, -li•est.** —*adv.* **1.** in or during the first part, as of a period of time or series of events. **2.** before the usual or appointed time. **3.** far back in time. —*adj.* **4.** occurring early. **5.** occurring in the near future: *I look forward to an early reply.* —*Idiom.* **6. early on,** not long after the beginning. —**ear′li•ness,** *n.*

ear′mark′ *n.* **1.** an identifying or distinguishing mark or characteristic. —*v.t.* **2.** to set aside for a specific purpose, use, or recipient. **3.** to mark with an earmark.

ear′muffs′ *n.pl.* warm connected coverings for the ears.

earn (ûrn), *v.t.* **1.** to gain in return for one's labor or service. **2.** to merit; deserve. **3.** to produce as return or profit. —**earn′er,** *n.*

ear•nest[1] (ûr′nist), *adj.* **1.** serious in intention, purpose, or effort. **2.** showing depth and sincerity of feeling. **3.** important; grave. —*n.* **4.** full seriousness, as of intention: *said in earnest.* —**ear′nest•ly,** *adv.* —**ear′nest•ness,** *n.*

ear•nest[2] (ûr′nist), *n.* **1.** something given or done as a pledge. **2.** money given by a buyer to a seller to bind a contract.

earn′ings *n.pl.* money earned; wages or profits.

ear′phone′ *n.* a sound receiver, as of a radio or telephone, that fits in or over the ear.

ear•ring (ēr′ring′, ēr′ing), *n.* **1.** an ornament worn on the earlobe. **2.** a similar ornament decorating another part of the body.

ear′shot′ *n.* the range within which sound can be heard.

ear′split′ting *adj.* extremely loud or shrill.

earth (ûrth), *n.* **1.** (*often cap.*) the planet third in order from the sun. **2.** the earth as the habitation of humans. **3.** the surface of the earth; ground. **4.** soil and dirt. —**earth′ward,** *adv., adj.*

earth′en *adj.* **1.** composed of earth. **2.** made of baked clay. —**earth′en•ware′,** *n.*

earth′ly *adj.,* **-li•er, -li•est. 1.** of the earth, esp. as opposed to heaven. **2.** possible or conceivable: *no earthly reason for it.* —**earth′li•ness,** *n.*

earth′quake′ *n.* a series of vibrations in the earth's crust.

earth′work′ *n.* a military construction formed chiefly of earth for protection against enemy fire.

earth′worm′ *n.* a segmented worm that burrows in soil.

earth′y *adj.,* **-i•er, -i•est. 1.** of, like, or consisting of earth or soil. **2.** realistic; practical. **3.** coarse or unrefined. —**earth′i•ness,** *n.*

ease (ēz), *n., v.,* **eased, eas•ing.** —*n.* **1.** freedom from pain, concern, or anxiety. **2.** freedom from difficulty or great effort. **3.** freedom from stiffness, constraint, or formality. —*v.t.* **4.** to free from anxiety or care. **5.** to mitigate, lighten, or lessen. **6.** to make less difficult. —*v.i.* **7.** to become less painful, severe, or difficult.

ea•sel (ē′zəl), *n.* a stand or frame for supporting or displaying an artist's canvas, a blackboard, or a picture.

east (ēst), *n.* **1.** the cardinal point of the compass 90° to the right of north. **2.** the direction in which east lies. **3.** (*usu. cap.*) a region in the east. **4. the East, a.** the Orient. **b.** the eastern part of the U.S. —*adj.* **5.** lying toward or situated in the east. **6.** coming from the east. —*adv.* **7.** to, toward, or in the east.

Eas•ter (ē′stər), *n.* an annual Christian festival in commemoration of the resurrection of Jesus Christ.

east′ern *adj.* **1.** of, toward, or in the east. **2.** coming from the east. **3.** (*usu. cap.*) of the East. **4.** (*cap.*) of the Christian churches originating in countries of the eastern part of the Roman Empire. —**east′ern•er,** *n.*

East′ern Hem′isphere *n.* the part of the globe east of the Atlantic, including Asia, Africa, Australia, and Europe.

eas•y (ē′zē), *adj.* and *adv.,* **-i•er, -i•est.** —*adj.* **1.** not difficult. **2.** free from pain, worry, or care. **3.** easygoing; relaxed. **4.** not harsh or strict; lenient. **5.** not forced or hurried; moderate. **6.** not steep; gradual. —*adv.* **7.** in an easy manner; easily. —*Idiom.* **8. take it easy, a.** to relax. **b.** to proceed at an unhurried pace. —**eas′i•ly,** *adv.* —**eas′i•ness,** *n.*

eas′y•go′ing *adj.* relaxed and rather casual.

eat (ēt), *v.,* **ate** (āt; *esp. Brit.* et), **eat•en** (ēt′n), **eat•ing.** —*v.t.* **1.** to take into the mouth and swallow for nourishment. **2.** to wear away; corrode. **3.** to use up, esp. wastefully; consume: *Unexpected expenses ate up their savings.* **4.** to cause anxiety or irritation in: *What's eating you?* —*v.i.* **5.** to consume food; have a meal. **6.** to make a way, as by gnawing or corrosion: *Acid ate through the linoleum.* —*n.* **7. eats,** *Informal.* food. —**eat′a•ble,** *adj., n.*

eat′er•y *n., pl.* **-ies.** *Informal.* a restaurant.

eaves (ēvz), *n.pl.* the overhanging lower edge of a roof.

eaves′drop′ *v.i.,* **-dropped, -drop•ping.** to listen

secretly to a private conversation. —**eaves′drop′-per,** *n.*

ebb (eb), *n.* **1.** the flowing back of the tide as the water returns to the sea. **2.** a point or state of decline. —*v.i.* **3.** to flow back or away. **4.** to decline or decay.

eb•on•y (eb′ə nē), *n., pl.* **-ies,** *adj.* —*n.* **1.** a hard, heavy, dark wood from various tropical trees of Africa and Asia. —*adj.* **2.** made of ebony. **3.** of a deep, lustrous black.

eBook or **ebook** (ē′book′), *n.* a portable electronic device used to download and read books or magazines that are in digital form.

e•bul•lient (i bul′yənt, i bool′-), *adj.* **1.** marked by enthusiasm, excitement, or vivacity. **2.** bubbling up; boiling. —**e•bul′lience,** *n.* —**e•bul′lient•ly,** *adv.*

ec•cen•tric (ik sen′trik, ek-), *adj.* **1.** unconventional, as in behavior; odd. **2.** not having the same center. **3.** not situated in the center. **4.** having the axis away from the center. **5.** deviating from a circular form. —*n.* **6.** an eccentric person. **7.** a disk with an off-center axis of revolution that converts rotary motion to reciprocating motion. —**ec•cen′tri•cal•ly,** *adv.* —**ec•cen•tric•i•ty** (ek′sen tris′i tē, -sən-), *n., pl.* **-ties.**

ec•cle•si•as•tic (i klē′zē as′tik), *n.* **1.** a member of the clergy. —*adj.* **2.** ecclesiastical.

ec•cle′si•as′ti•cal *adj.* of a church or the clergy.

ech•e•lon (esh′ə lon′), *n.* **1.** a level of command, authority, or rank. **2.** a steplike formation of troops, airplanes, etc.

ech•o (ek′ō), *n., pl.* **-oes,** *v.,* **-oed, -o•ing.** —*n.* **1.** a repetition of sound produced by the reflection of sound waves from a surface. **2.** a sound so produced. **3.** a repetition or imitation of the ideas or words of another. —*v.i.* **4.** to resound with an echo. **5.** to be repeated by or as if by an echo. —*v.t.* **6.** to emit an echo of. **7.** to repeat in imitation. —**e•cho′ic,** *adj.*

ec•lec•tic (i klek′tik), *adj.* selecting or made up of elements from various sources. —**ec•lec′ti•cal•ly,** *adv.* —**ec•lec′ti•cism,** *n.*

e•clipse (i klips′), *n., v.,* **e•clipsed, e•clips•ing.** —*n.* **1.** the partial or complete interception of the light of one heavenly body by another. **2.** a reduction or loss of splendor, status, or reputation. —*v.t.* **3.** to cause to undergo eclipse.

e•clip•tic (i klip′tik), *n.* the great circle formed by the intersection of the plane of the earth's orbit with the celestial sphere.

eco- a combining form meaning ecology, environment, or natural habitat (*ecocide*).

ec•o•cide (ek′ə sīd′, ē′kə-), *n.* the destruction of large areas of the natural environment, as by dumping harmful chemicals. —**ec′o•ci′dal,** *adj.*

e•col•o•gy (i kol′ə jē), *n.* **1.** the branch of biology dealing with the interactions between organisms and their environment. **2.** the set of relationships existing between organisms and their environment. —**ec•o•log•i•cal** (ek′ə loj′i kəl, ē′kə-), **ec′o•log′ic,** *adj.* —**e•col′o•gist,** *n.*

ec•o•nom•i•cal (ek′ə nom′i kəl, ē′kə-), *adj.* **1.** avoiding waste or extravagance; thrifty. **2.** pertaining to economics. —**ec′o•nom′i•cal•ly,** *adv.*

ec′o•nom′ics *n.* **1.** (*used with a sing. v.*) the science of the production, distribution, and consumption of goods and services. **2.** (*used with a pl. v.*) financial considerations. —**e•con•o•mist** (i kon′ə mist), *n.*

e•con•o•mize (i kon′ə mīz′), *v.i.,* **-mized, -miz•ing.** to avoid waste or extravagance; be thrifty. —**e•con′o•miz′er,** *n.*

e•con′o•my *n., pl.* **-mies,** *adj.* —*n.* **1.** thrifty management of money and materials. **2.** an act or instance of economy. **3.** the management of the resources of an area, as a nation. **4.** an organized system. **5.** the efficient or sparing use of something: *economy of motion.* —*adj.* **6.** intended to save money: *an economy car.*

ec•o•sys•tem (ek′ō sis′təm, ē′kō-), *n.* a system formed by the interaction of a community of organisms with its environment.

ec•ru or **éc•ru** (ek′roo, ā′kroo), *n., adj.* BEIGE.

ec•sta•sy (ek′stə sē), *n., pl.* **-sies. 1.** rapturous delight. **2.** an overpowering emotion; a state of sudden, intense feeling. **3.** the frenzy of poetic inspiration. —**ec•stat′ic** (-stat′ik), *adj.* —**ec•stat′i•cal•ly,** *adv.*

Ec•ua•dor (ek′wə dôr′), *n.* a republic in NW South America. —**Ec′ua•do′ran, Ec′ua•do′re•an, Ec′ua•do′ri•an,** *adj., n.*

ec•u•men•i•cal (ek′yŏŏ men′i kəl; *esp. Brit.* ē′kyŏŏ-) also **-men′ic,** *adj.* **1.** universal; worldwide. **2.** pertaining to, promoting, or fostering Christian unity throughout the world. —**ec′u•me•nism** (-mə niz′əm), **ec′u•men′i•cism** (-men′ə-siz′əm), *n.*

ec•ze•ma (ek′sə mə, eg′zə-, ig zē′-), *n.* a skin inflammation accompanied by itching and scaling.

E•dam (ē′dəm, ē′dam), *n.* a mild yellow cheese produced in a round shape.

ed•dy (ed′ē), *n., pl.* **-dies,** *v.,* **-died, -dy•ing.** —*n.* **1.** a current of water or air running counter to the main current. **2.** a whirlpool. —*v.t., v.i.* **3.** to whirl in eddies.

e•del•weiss (ād′l vīs′, -wīs′), *n.* a small, flowering Alpine plant with white woolly leaves.

e•de•ma (i dē′mə), *n., pl.* **-mas, -ma•ta** (-mə tə). abnormal accumulation of fluid in the tissue spaces, cavities, or joint capsules of the body.

E•den (ēd′n), *n.* **1.** *Bible.* the place where Adam and Eve first lived. **2.** a delightful region; paradise.

edge (ej), *n., v.,* **edged, edg•ing.** —*n.* **1.** the line at which something ends. **2.** a brink or verge: *the edge of disaster.* **3.** the thin, sharp side of a cutting blade. **4.** a quality of sharpness or keenness. **5.** an advantage. —*v.t.* **6.** to provide with an edge or border. **7.** to sharpen. **8.** to make (one's way) gradually. —*v.i.* **9.** to move gradually or cautiously. —*Idiom.* **10. on edge, a.** tense; nervous. **b.** impatient. —**edg′er,** *n.*

edg′y *adj.,* **-i•er, -i•est. 1.** nervous or anxious; tense. **2.** sharp-edged. —**edg′i•ness,** *n.*

ed•i•ble (ed′ə bəl), *adj.* **1.** fit to be eaten. —*n.* **2.** Usu., **-bles.** something edible; food. —**ed′i•bil′i•ty,** **ed′i•ble•ness,** *n.*

e•dict (ē′dikt), *n.* a decree issued by an authority, as a sovereign.

ed•i•fice (ed′ə fis), *n.* a building, esp. a large or imposing one.

ed′i•fy′ *v.t.,* **-fied, -fy•ing.** to instruct and improve, esp. morally; enlighten. —**ed′i•fi•ca′tion,** *n.* —**ed′i•fi′er,** *n.*

ed•it (ed′it), *v.t.* **1.** to supervise the preparation of (a publication). **2.** to prepare (a manuscript) for publication. **3.** to revise or correct, as a manuscript. **4.** to delete; eliminate (often fol. by *out*): *to edit out all references to his family.* **5.** to prepare (film or tape) by deleting, arranging, and splicing. **6.** to modify (computer data or text). —**ed′i•tor,** *n.*

edit. 1. edited. **2.** edition. **3.** editor.

e•di•tion (i dish′ən), *n.* **1.** the format in which a literary work is published. **2.** the whole number of impressions or copies, as of a book, printed at one time. **3.** a version of something.

ed•i•to•ri•al (ed′i tôr′ē əl), *n.* **1.** an article or statement, as in a newspaper or on a broadcast, presenting the opinion of the publishers, editors, or owners. —*adj.* **2.** of an editor or editing. **3.** of, resembling, or being an editorial. —**ed′i•to′ri•al•ly,** *adv.*

EDP electronic data processing.

ed′u•cate′ (-kāt′), *v.t.,* **-cat•ed, -cat•ing. 1.** to develop the faculties and powers of (a person) by schooling; teach. **2.** to provide with training, knowledge, or information. —**ed′u•ca′tion,** *n.* —**ed′u•ca′tor,** *n.*

EEG electroencephalogram.

eel (ēl), *n., pl.* **eels, eel.** any of numerous elongated, snakelike marine or freshwater fishes.

e′er (âr), *adv. Chiefly Literary.* ever.

-eer a suffix denoting a person who produces, handles, or is associated with something (*auctioneer*).

ee•rie or **-ry** (ēr′ē), *adj.,* **-ri•er, -ri•est.** uncanny, so as to inspire superstitious fear; strange and mysterious. —**ee′ri•ly,** *adv.* —**ee′ri•ness,** *n.*

ef·face (i fās′), v.t., **-faced, -fac·ing. 1.** to do away with by or as if by rubbing out. **2.** to make (oneself) inconspicuous. —**ef·face′ment,** n. —**ef·fac′er,** n.

ef·fect (i fekt′), n. **1.** something produced by a cause; result. **2.** power to produce results; force. **3.** operation or execution. **4.** a mental or emotional impression. **5.** general meaning or purpose; intent. **6. effects,** personal property. —v.t. **7.** to bring about; accomplish or produce. —*Idiom.* **8. in effect, a.** virtually; implicitly. **b.** essentially; basically. **c.** operating or functioning; in force. **9. take effect, a.** to begin to function. **b.** to produce a result.

ef·fec′tive adj. **1.** producing the intended or expected effect. **2.** in operation or in force. **3.** producing a deep or vivid impression; striking. —**ef·fec′tive·ly,** adv. —**ef·fec′tive·ness,** n.

ef·fec′tu·al (-chōō əl), adj. producing or capable of producing an intended effect.

ef·fem·i·nate (i fem′ə nit), adj. (of a man or boy) having traits, as softness or delicacy, traditionally considered feminine. —**ef·fem′i·na·cy** (-nə sē), n.

ef·fer·vesce (ef′ər ves′), v.i., **-vesced, -vesc·ing. 1.** to give off bubbles of gas, as a carbonated liquid does. **2.** to show enthusiasm or liveliness. —**ef′fer·ves′cence,** n. —**ef′fer·ves′cent,** adj.

ef·fete (i fēt′), adj. **1.** degenerate; decadent. **2.** exhausted of energy; worn out. —**ef·fete′ness,** n.

ef·fi·ca·cious (ef′i kā′shəs), adj. capable of having the desired result or effect; effective. —**ef′fi·ca′cious·ly,** adv. —**ef′fi·ca·cy** (-kə sē), n.

ef·fi·cient (i fish′ənt), adj. performing or functioning effectively with the least waste of time, effort, or resources. —**ef·fi′cient·ly,** adv.

ef·fi·gy (ef′i jē), n., pl. **-gies.** an image, esp. a crude representation of someone disliked.

ef′flu·ent (ef′lōō ənt) n. something that flows out.

ef·fort (ef′ərt), n. **1.** exertion of physical or mental power. **2.** an earnest or strenuous attempt. **3.** something achieved by exertion or hard work. —**ef′fort·less,** adj. —**ef′fort·less·ly,** adv.

ef·fron·ter·y (i frun′tə rē), n., pl. **-ies. 1.** shameless or impudent boldness; audacity. **2.** an act or instance of this.

ef·fu·sion (i fyōō′zhən) n. **1.** the act or result of pouring forth. **2.** an unrestrained expression, as of feelings. —**ef·fu′sive** (-siv), adj. —**ef·fu′sive·ly,** adv. —**ef·fu′sive·ness,** n.

e.g. for example. [< L *exemplī grātiā*]

e·gal·i·tar·i·an (i gal′i târ′ē ən), adj. **1.** asserting, resulting from, or characterized by belief in the equality of all people. —n. **2.** one who adheres to egalitarian beliefs. —**e·gal′i·tar′i·an·ism,** n.

egg¹ (eg), n. **1.** the roundish reproductive body produced by the female of certain animals, as birds and most reptiles. **2.** an egg produced by a domestic bird, esp. the hen. **3.** the female gamete; ovum. **4.** *Informal.* a person: *He's a good egg.*

egg² (eg), v.t. to incite or urge: *Playmates egged him on.*

egg′head′ n. *Informal.* an intellectual.

egg′nog′ (-nog′), n. a drink made of eggs, milk or cream, sugar, and usu. rum.

egg′plant′ n. **1.** a plant cultivated for its edible, dark-purple fruit, used as a vegetable. **2.** the fruit.

e·go (ē′gō), n., pl. **e·gos. 1.** the self of a person. **2.** *Psychoanalysis.* the component of the psyche that experiences and reacts to the outside world. **3.** egotism; conceit.

e′go·cen′tric (-sen′trik), adj. **1.** regarding the self as the center of all things. **2.** selfish. —**e′go·cen·tric′i·ty** (-tris′i tē), n.

e′go·ism n. **1.** the view in ethics that morality ultimately rests on self-interest. **2.** egotism or conceit. —**e′go·ist,** n. —**e′go·is′tic, e′go·is′ti·cal,** adj.

e·go·tism (ē′gə tiz′əm), n. **1.** excessive reference to oneself. **2.** self-centeredness. —**e′go·tist,** n. —**e′go·tis′tic, e′go·tis′ti·cal, e′go·tis′ti·cal·ly,** adv.

e·gre·gious (i grē′jəs, -jē əs), adj. extraordinarily bad; flagrant; glaring. —**e·gre′gious·ly,** adv.

e·gress (ē′gres), n. a means or place of going out; exit.

e·gret (ē′grit, eg′rit), n. any of several usu. white herons having long, graceful plumes during the breeding season.

E·gypt (ē′jipt), n. a country in NE Africa, on the Mediterranean Sea.

E·gyp·tian (i jip′shən), n. **1.** a native or inhabitant of Egypt. **2.** the extinct language of Egypt under the Pharaohs. —adj. **3.** of Egypt, its people, or their language.

eh (ā, e), *interj.* an exclamation of surprise or doubt.

ei′der duck′ (ī′dər), n. a large diving duck of northern seas.

eight (āt), n. **1.** a cardinal number, seven plus one. **2.** a symbol for this number, as 8 or VIII. —adj. **3.** amounting to eight in number. —**eighth,** adj., n.

eight·een (ā′tēn′), n. **1.** a cardinal number, ten plus eight. **2.** a symbol for this number, as 18 or XVIII. —adj. **3.** amounting to 18 in number. —**eight′eenth′,** adj., n.

eight′y n., pl. **-ies,** adj. —n. **1.** a cardinal number, ten times eight. **2.** a symbol for this number, as 80 or LXXX. —adj. **3.** amounting to 80 in number. —**eight′i·eth,** adj., n.

ei·ther (ē′thər, ī′thər), adj. **1.** one or the other of two: *Read either newspaper.* **2.** the one or the other: *There are trees on either side.* —pron. **3.** one or the other: *Either will do.* —conj. **4.** (used with or to indicate a choice): *Either call or write.* —adv. **5.** as well; likewise: *If you don't go, I won't either.*

e·jac·u·late (i jak′yə lāt′), v.t., v.i., **-lat·ed, -lat·ing. 1.** to eject (semen). **2.** to utter suddenly and briefly; exclaim. —**e·jac′u·la′tion,** n. —**e·jac′u·la·to′ry** (-lə tôr′ē), adj.

e·ject (i jekt′), v.t. to drive, force, or throw out. —**e·jec′tion,** n.

eke (ēk), v.t., **eked, ek·ing.** to obtain, maintain, or supplement with great effort: *eked out her income with odd jobs.*

EKG 1. electrocardiogram. **2.** electrocardiograph.

e·lab·o·rate (adj. i lab′ər it; v. -ə rāt′), adj., v., **-rat·ed, -rat·ing.** —adj. **1.** worked out in great detail; painstaking. **2.** ornate, showy, or gaudy. —v.t. **3.** to work out in minute detail. —v.i. **4.** to add details or information; expand: *Elaborate on your idea.* —**e·lab′o·rate·ly,** adv. —**e·lab′o·rate·ness,** n. —**e·lab′o·ra′tion,** n.

e·lapse (i laps′), v.i., **e·lapsed, e·laps·ing.** (of time) to slip or pass by.

e·las·tic (i las′tik), adj. **1.** capable of returning to an original length or shape after being stretched. **2.** flexible; adaptable. **3.** bouncy or springy. **4.** resilient, esp. after a setback; buoyant. —n. **5.** elastic fabric or material. **6.** RUBBER BAND. —**e·las·tic·i·ty** (i las tis′i tē, ē′las-), n. —**e·las′ti·cize′** (-tə sīz′), v.t., **-cized, -ciz·ing.**

e·late (i lāt′), v.t., **e·lat·ed, e·lat·ing.** to make extremely happy; overjoy. —**e·la′tion,** n.

el·bow (el′bō), n. **1.** the joint of the human arm between the upper arm and forearm. **2.** something bent like an elbow. —v.t. **3.** to push aside with or as if with the elbow. **4.** to make (one's way) by elbowing.

el′bow grease′ n. hard work.

el′bow·room′ n. space in which to move or work freely.

eld·er¹ (el′dər), adj. a compar. of **old** with **eldest** as superl. **1.** older. **2.** of higher rank; senior. **3.** of former times; earlier. —n. **4.** an older person. **5.** an older, influential member of a community. **6.** a lay member who is a governing officer of a church.

eld·er² (el′dər), n. a shrub or tree of the honeysuckle family, bearing red, black, or yellow berries.

eld′er·ly adj. **1.** approaching old age. **2.** of persons in later life.

eld·est (el′dist), adj. a superl. of **old** with **elder** as compar. of greatest age; oldest.

e·lect (i lekt′), v.t. **1.** to select by vote, as for an office. **2.** to pick out; choose. —adj. **3.** elected to office but not yet inducted: *the governor-elect.* **4.** se-

lect or choice. [< L *ēlēctus* chosen] —**e•lect′a•ble,** *adj.* —**e•lec′tion,** *n.*

e•lec′tion•eer′ *v.i.* to work for the success of a particular candidate or party in an election.

e•lec′tor (-tər), *n.* **1.** a qualified voter. **2.** a member of the electoral college. —**e•lec′tor•al,** *adj.*

elec′toral col′lege *n.* a body of electors chosen to elect the president and vice-president of the U.S.

e•lec′tor•ate (-it), *n.* a body of persons entitled to vote.

e•lec•tric (i lek′trik) also **-tri•cal.** *adj.* **1.** pertaining to, derived from, produced by, or operated by electricity. **2.** thrilling; exciting. —**e•lec′tri•cal•ly,** *adv.*

e•lec•tri•cian (i lek trish′ən, ē′lek-), *n.* a person who installs, operates, or repairs electric devices or wiring.

e•lec•tric′i•ty (-tris′i tē) *n.* **1.** a fundamental property of matter caused by the motion of electrons, protons, or positrons and manifesting itself as attraction, repulsion, luminous and heating effects, etc. **2.** electric current or power.

e•lec•tro•car•di•o•gram (i lek′trō kär′dē ə-gram′), *n.* the graphic record produced by an electrocardiograph.

e•lec′tro•car′di•o•graph′ *n.* a device that records variations in the electric potential that triggers the heartbeat. —**e•lec′tro•car′di•og′ra•phy,** *n.*

e•lec•tro•cute (i lek′trə kyōōt′), *v.t.,* **-cut•ed, -cut•ing. 1.** to kill by electricity. **2.** to execute (a criminal) by electricity. —**e•lec′tro•cu′tion,** *n.*

e•lec•trode (i lek′trōd), *n.* a conductor through which an electric current enters or leaves a nonmetallic portion of a circuit.

e•lec•tro•en•ceph•a•lo•gram (i lek′trō en sef′ə-lə gram′), *n.* the graphic record produced by an electroencephalograph.

e•lec′tro•en•ceph′a•lo•graph′ *n.* an instrument for measuring and recording the electric activity of the brain. —**e•lec′tro•en•ceph′a•lo•graph′-ic,** *adj.* —**e•lec′tro•en•ceph′a•log′ra•phy,** *n.*

e•lec•trol•o•gist (i lek trol′ə jist), *n.* a person trained in the use of electrolysis for removing moles, warts, or unwanted hair.

e•lec•trol′y•sis (-ə sis), *n.* **1.** the passage of an electric current through an electrolyte with subsequent migration of ions to the electrodes. **2.** the destruction of hair roots by an electric current.

e•lec′tro•lyte (-trə līt′), *n.* a substance that dissociates into ions when melted or dissolved and thus forms a conductor of electricity. —**e•lec′tro•lyt′ic** (-lit′ik), *adj.*

e•lec•tro•mag′net (i lek′trō-), *n.* a device consisting of an iron or steel core that is magnetized by electric current in a coil that surrounds it. —**e•lec′-tro•mag•net′ic,** *adj.*

elec′tromagnet′ic wave′ *n.* a wave propagated at the speed of light by the periodic variations of electric and magnetic fields.

e•lec•tron (i lek′tron), *n.* an elementary particle that is a fundamental constituent of matter, has a negative charge, and exists outside the nucleus of an atom.

e•lec•tron•ic (i lek tron′ik, ē′lek-), *adj.* **1.** of electronics or devices and systems developed through electronics. **2.** of electrons. —**e•lec•tron′i•cal•ly,** *adv.*

electron′ic mail′ *n.* E-MAIL.

e•lec•tron′ics *n.* the science dealing with the development of devices and systems involving the flow of electrons in a vacuum, in gaseous media, and in semiconductors.

el•e•gant (el′i gənt), *adj.* **1.** splendid or luxurious, as in design. **2.** polished and graceful, as in form or movement. **3.** of superior quality; exceptional. —**el′e•gance,** *n.* —**el′e•gant•ly,** *adv.*

el•e•gi•ac (el′i jī′ək, i lē′jē ak′) also **-gi′a•cal,** *adj.* **1.** of or resembling an elegy. **2.** expressing sorrow; mournful.

el•e•gy (el′i jē), *n., pl.* **-gies.** a mournful, melancholy, or plaintive poem, esp. a lament for the dead. —**el′e•gize′,** *v.t., v.i.,* **-gized, -giz•ing.**

el•e•ment (el′ə mənt), *n.* **1.** a component or con-

stituent of a whole. **2.** a substance that cannot be separated into simpler substances by chemical means. **3.** a natural environment. **4. elements, a.** atmospheric forces; weather. **b.** the rudimentary principles, as of an art. **5.** *Math.* a member of a set.

el′e•men′ta•ry (-men′tə rē, -trē), *adj.* **1.** rudimentary, basic, or irreducible. **2.** of an elementary school.

elemen′tary school′ *n.* a school giving instructions in rudimentary subjects in six to eight grades.

el•e•phant (el′ə fənt), *n., pl.* **-phants, -phant.** either of two very large mammals with a long prehensile trunk and large tusks.

el•e•phan•tine (el′ə fan′tēn, -tīn, -tin) *adj.* **1.** of massive size; huge. **2.** ponderous; clumsy.

el•e•vate (el′ə vāt′), *v.t.,* **-vat•ed, -vat•ing. 1.** to raise to a higher place or position. **2.** to raise to a higher status or rank. **3.** to elate.

el′e•va′tion *n.* **1.** the act of elevating or state of being elevated. **2.** the height to which something is elevated. **3.** altitude above sea or ground level. **4.** an elevated place.

el′e•va′tor *n.* **1.** a moving platform or cage for carrying passengers or freight from one level to another. **2.** a building for the storage and discharge of grain. **3.** a hinged horizontal surface on an aircraft wing used to control inclination.

e•lev•en (i lev′ən), *n.* **1.** a cardinal number, ten plus one. **2.** a symbol for this number, as 11 or XI. —*adj.* **3.** amounting to 11 in number. —**e•lev′enth,** *adj., n.*

elf (elf), *n., pl.* **elves** (elvz). a diminutive, mischievous being in folklore. —**elf′in,** *adj.*

e•lic•it (i lis′it), *v.t.* to draw or bring out or forth; evoke. —**e•lic′i•ta′tion,** *n.* —**e•lic′i•tor,** *n.*

e•lide (i līd′), *v.t.,* **e•lid•ed, e•lid•ing. 1.** to omit (a vowel, consonant, or syllable) in pronunciation. **2.** to pass over; ignore. —**e•li•sion** (i lizh′ən), *n.*

el•i•gi•ble (el′i jə bəl), *adj.* **1.** being a proper or worthy choice. **2.** qualified, as to be elected to office. —**el′i•gi•bil′i•ty,** *n.*

e•lim•i•nate (i lim′ə nāt′), *v.t.,* **-nat•ed, -nat•ing. 1.** to get rid of; remove. **2.** to leave out; omit. **3.** to void or excrete from the body. [< L *ēlīminātus* turned out of doors] —**e•lim′i•na′tion,** *n.*

e•lite or **é•lite** (i lēt′, ā lēt′), *n.* **1.** (*often with a pl. v.*) the choice, best, or most powerful members of a group, class, etc. **2.** a typewriter type with 12 characters to the inch.

e•lit′ism *n.* practice of or belief in rule by an elite. —**e•lit′ist,** *n., adj.*

e•lix•ir (i lik′sər), *n.* **1.** a sweetened solution of alcohol and water used as a medicinal medium. **2.** a preparation formerly believed capable of prolonging life indefinitely. **3.** PANACEA.

elk (elk), *n., pl.* **elks, elk. 1.** a large North American deer. **2.** the moose.

el•lipse (i lips′), *n.* a closed plane curve shaped like an oval.

el•lip•sis (i lip′sis), *n., pl.* **-ses** (-sēz). **1.** the omission from a grammatical construction of a word or phrase understandable from the context. **2.** a mark or series of marks (...) used to indicate an omission.

el•lip′ti•cal (-ti kəl) also **-tic,** *adj.* **1.** of or having the form of an ellipse. **2.** of or marked by ellipsis.

elm (elm), *n.* **1.** a shade tree characterized by gradually spreading branches. **2.** the wood of an elm.

el•o•cu•tion (el′ə kyōō′shən), *n.* the study and practice of public speaking. —**el′o•cu′tion•ar′y** (-shə ner′ē), *adj.* —**el′o•cu′tion•ist,** *n.*

e•lope (i lōp′), *v.i.,* **e•loped, e•lop•ing.** to run off secretly, esp. in order to be married. —**e•lope′-ment,** *n.*

el•o•quent (el′ə kwənt), *adj.* **1.** skilled in or marked by fluent, forceful expression. **2.** forcefully expressive. —**el′o•quence,** *n.* —**el′o•quent•ly,** *adv.*

El Sal•va•dor (el sal′və dôr′), *n.* a republic in NW Central America.

else (els), *adj.* **1.** other; different: *What else could I have done?* **2.** additional: *Who else was there?*

—*adv.* **3.** if not: *Watch your step, or else you'll slip.* **4.** otherwise: *How else could I have acted?*

else•where′ *adv.* in or to another place.

e•lu•ci•date (i lōō′si dāt′), *v.t. v.i.*, **-dat•ed**, **-dat•ing.** to make clear, esp. by explaining. —**e•lu′ci•da′tion**, *n.* —**e•lu′ci•da′tor**, *n.*

e•lude (i lōōd′), *v.t.*, **e•lud•ed**, **e•lud•ing. 1.** to escape detection or capture by; evade. **2.** to escape the comprehension of. —**e•lud′er**, *n.*

em (em), *n.* the square of any size of type used as the unit of measurement for printed matter.

e•ma•ci•ate (i mā′shē āt′), *v.t.*, **-at•ed**, **-at•ing.** to make abnormally thin. —**e•ma′ci•a′tion**, *n.*

e-mail or **email** or **E-mail** (ē′māl′), *n.* **1.** a system for sending messages via telecommunications links between computers. **2.** a message sent by e-mail: *Send me an e-mail on the idea.* —*v.t.* **3.** to send a message to by e-mail.

e•a•nate (em′ə nāt′), *v.i.*, **-nat•ed**, **-nat•ing.** to flow out or issue forth. —**em′a•na′tion**, *n.*

e•man•ci•pate (i man′sə pāt′), *v.t.*, **-pat•ed**, **-pat•ing. 1.** to free from restraint. **2.** to free (a slave) from bondage. —**e•man′ci•pa′tion**, *n.* —**e•man′ci•pa′tor**, *n.*

e•mas•cu•late (i mas′kyə lāt′), *v.t.*, **-lat•ed**, **-lat•ing. 1.** to castrate. **2.** to deprive of strength or vigor; weaken. —**e•mas′cu•la′tion**, *n.* —**e•mas′cu•la′tor**, *n.*

em•balm (em bäm′), *v.t.* to treat (a dead body) so as to preserve it, as with chemicals. —**em•balm′er**, *n.*

em•bank′ment *n.* a bank or mound, as of earth or stone, raised to hold back water, carry a roadway, etc.

em•bar•go (em bär′gō), *n., pl.* **-goes**, *v.*, **-goed**, **-go•ing.** —*n.* **1.** a restriction on commerce, esp. a government order prohibiting the movement of merchant ships into or out of its ports. —*v.t.* **2.** to impose an embargo on. [< Sp, der. of *embargar* to hinder, embarrass]

em•bark (em bärk′), *v.i.* **1.** to board a ship or aircraft. **2.** to start on an enterprise. —*v.t.* **3.** to board (passengers) onto a ship or aircraft. —**em′bar•ka′tion**, *n.*

em•bar•rass (em bar′əs), *v.t.* **1.** to make ashamed or self-conscious; disconcert. **2.** to impede; hinder. **3.** to burden with debt. —**em•bar′rass•ing•ly**, *adv.* —**em•bar′rass•ment**, *n.*

em•bas•sy (em′bə sē), *n., pl.* **-sies. 1.** the official headquarters of an ambassador. **2.** the function or office of an ambassador. **3.** a mission headed by an ambassador.

em•bat′tled *adj.* prepared for, engaged in, or beset by conflict.

em•bed′ *v.t., v.i.*, **-bed•ded**, **-bed•ding.** to fix or be fixed into a surrounding mass.

em•bel•lish (em bel′ish), *v.t.* **1.** to beautify with ornamentation; adorn. **2.** to enhance with elaborative additions. —**em•bel′lish•ment**, *n.*

em•ber (em′bər), *n.* **1.** a small live piece of coal or wood, as in a dying fire. **2. embers,** the smoldering remains of a fire.

em•bez•zle (em bez′əl), *v.t.*, **-zled**, **-zling.** to appropriate fraudulently to one's own use, as money entrusted to one's care. —**em•bez′zle•ment**, *n.* —**em•bez′zler**, *n.*

em•bit′ter *v.t.* **1.** to cause to feel bitterness. **2.** to make bitter in taste.

em•bla•zon (em blā′zən), *v.t.* **1.** to adorn with heraldic devices or emblems. **2.** to decorate brilliantly. **3.** to extol. —**em•bla′zon•ment**, *n.*

em•blem (em′bləm), *n.* **1.** an object symbolizing something else; symbol. **2.** a figure or design that identifies something. —**em′blem•at′ic**, *adj.*

em•bod′y *v.t.*, **-ied**, **-y•ing. 1.** to give concrete form to; personify or exemplify. **2.** to provide with a body; incarnate. **3.** to collect into a body; organize. —**em•bod′i•ment**, *n.*

em•bo•lism (em′bə liz′əm), *n.* the occlusion of a blood vessel, as by a gas bubble or fat globule.

em•boss (em bôs′, -bos′), *v.t.* **1.** to raise (designs) in relief. **2.** to decorate (a surface) with raised ornament. —**em•boss′er**, *n.*

em•brace (em brās′), *v.*, **-braced**, **-brac•ing**, *n.*

—*v.t.* **1.** to clasp in the arms; hug. **2.** to accept or adopt willingly. **3.** to include or contain. —*v.i.* **4.** to join in an embrace. —*n.* **5.** an encircling hug with the arms. —**em•brace′a•ble**, *adj.*

em•broi•der (em broi′dər), *v.t., v.i.* **1.** to decorate with or do embroidery. **2.** to embellish, as with fictitious details. —**em•broi′der•er**, *n.*

em•broi′der•y (-də rē, -drē), *n., pl.* **-ies. 1.** the art of ornamental needlework. **2.** embroidered work or ornamentation. **3.** elaboration, as in telling a story.

em•broil′ *v.t.* **1.** to involve in conflict. **2.** to throw into confusion. —**em•broil′ment**, *n.*

em•bry•o (em′brē ō′), *n., pl.* **-os. 1.** an organism in the earliest stages of development, as in the womb. **2.** a beginning or rudimentary stage. —**em′bry•on′ic** (-on′ik), *adj.*

em•cee (em′sē′), *n., pl.* **-cees**, *v.*, **-ceed**, **-cee•ing.** —*n.* **1.** a master of ceremonies. —*v.i., v.t.* **2.** to serve or direct as master of ceremonies.

e•mend (i mend′), *v.t.* to change (a text), esp. by correcting; edit. —**e•men•da•tion** (ē′mən dā′shən), *n.*

em•er•ald (em′ər əld), *n.* **1.** a green beryl that is valued as a gem. —*adj.* **2.** of a clear, deep green.

e•merge (i mûrj′), *v.i.*, **e•merged**, **e•merg•ing. 1.** to come forth into view. **2.** to rise from or as if from water. **3.** to come into existence. —**e•mer′gence**, *n.* —**e•mer′gent**, *adj.*

e•mer•gen•cy (i mûr′jən sē), *n., pl.* **-cies.** a sudden, urgent, usu. unexpected occurrence requiring immediate action.

em•er•y (em′ə rē), *n.* a mineral used for grinding and polishing.

e•met•ic (i met′ik), *adj.* **1.** causing vomiting. —*n.* **2.** an emetic medicine or agent.

em•i•nence (em′ə nəns), *n.* **1.** high station, rank, or repute. **2.** a high place; hill or height. **3.** (*cap.*) a title of honor applied to cardinals.

em•is•sar•y (em′ə ser′ē), *n., pl.* **-ies.** a representative sent on a mission, esp. a secret mission.

e•mit (i mit′), *v.t.*, **e•mit•ted**, **e•mit•ting. 1.** to send forth; discharge: *a bonfire emitting heat.* **2.** to utter; voice. **3.** to issue formally, as paper money. —**e•mis•sion** (i mish′ən), *n.* —**e•mit′ter**, *n.*

e•mol•li•ent (i mol′yənt), *adj.* **1.** softening or soothing: *an emollient lotion for the skin.* —*n.* **2.** an emollient substance.

e•mol•u•ment (i mol′yə mənt), *n.* compensation, as fees, from employment; recompense.

e•mote (i mōt′), *v.i.*, **e•mot•ed**, **e•mot•ing.** to show emotion in or as if in acting. —**e•mot′er**, *n.*

e•mo•tion (i mō′shən), *n.* **1.** a strong feeling, as joy, sorrow, hate, or love. **2.** strong agitation or excitement. —**e•mo′tion•al**, *adj.* —**e•mo′tion•al•ism**, *n.* —**e•mo′tion•al•ly**, *adv.*

em′pa•thy (-thē), *n.* identification with or vicarious experiencing of the feelings or thoughts of another. —**em′pa•thet′ic** (-thet′ik), *adj.*

em•per•or (em′pər ər), *n.* the male ruler of an empire. —**em′press** (-pris), *n.*

em•pha•sis (em′fə sis), *n., pl.* **-ses** (-sēz′). **1.** special stress or importance: *an emphasis on reliability.* **2.** stress given to particular words or syllables. —**em•phat′ic** (-fat′ik), *adj.* —**em•phat′i•cal•ly**, *adv.* —**em′pha•size′**, *v.t.*, **-sized**, **-siz•ing.**

em•phy•se•ma (em′fə sē′mə, -zē′-), *n.* a chronic lung disease characterized by abnormal enlargement and loss of elasticity of the air spaces.

em•pire (em′pīr′), *n.* **1.** a group of nations, states, or peoples ruled over by a powerful sovereign, esp. an emperor or empress. **2.** sovereignty; dominion. **3.** a powerful enterprise controlled by one person or group: *a shipping empire.* [< AF, OF < L *imperium*]

em•pir•i•cal (em pir′i kəl), *adj.* derived from or depending upon experience or observation alone. —**em•pir′i•cal•ly**, *adv.*

em•ploy (em ploi′), *v.t.* **1.** to engage the services of; hire. **2.** to make use of. **3.** to devote (time, energies, etc.) to a particular activity. —*n.* **4.** employment; service. —**em•ploy′a•ble**, *adj.* —**em•ploy′-**

ee, *n., pl.* **-ees.** —**em•ploy′er,** *n.* —**em•ploy′-ment,** *n.*

em•po•ri•um (em pôr′ē əm), *n., pl.* **-po•ri•ums, -po•ri•a** (-pôr′ē ə). a retail store selling a great variety of articles.

em•pow′er *v.t.* **1.** to give power or authority to. **2.** to enable. —**em•pow′er•ment,** *n.*

emp•ty (emp′tē), *adj.,* **-ti•er, -ti•est,** *v.,* **-tied, -ty-ing,** *n., pl.* **-ties.** —*adj.* **1.** containing nothing. **2.** not occupied; vacant. **3.** lacking force, effect, or significance. —*v.t., v.i.* **4.** to make or become empty. **5.** to discharge: *The river empties into the sea.* —*n.* **6.** an empty container. —**emp′ti•ly,** *adv.* —**emp′ti-ness,** *n.*

emp′ty nest′ syn′drome *n.* a depressed state felt by some parents after their children have grown up and left home.

EMT emergency medical technician.

e•mu (ē′myōō), *n., pl.* **e•mus.** a large, flightless bird of Australia that resembles the ostrich.

EMU or **emu,** electromagnetic unit.

em•u•late (em′yə lāt′), *v.t.,* **-lat•ed, -lat•ing.** to imitate in an effort to equal or surpass. —**em′u•la′-tion,** *n.* —**em′u•la′tive,** *adj.* —**em′u•la′tor,** *n.*

e•mul•si•fy (i mul′sə fī′), *v.t., v.i.,* **-fied, -fy•ing.** to make into or form an emulsion. —**e•mul′si•fi-ca′tion,** *n.* —**e•mul′si•fi′er,** *n.*

e•mul′sion (-shən), *n.* **1.** a colloidal suspension of one liquid in another. **2.** a photosensitive coating on photographic film.

en (en), *n.* a space that is half the width of an em.

en- a prefix meaning: to put into or on (*enthrone*); to cover or surround with (*encircle*); to make or cause to be (*enlarge*).

-en¹, a suffix meaning: to make or become (*harden*); to cause or come to have (*strengthen*).

-en², a suffix meaning made of or resembling (*woolen*).

en•a•ble (en ā′bəl), *v.t.,* **-bled, -bling. 1.** to make able; authorize or empower. **2.** to make possible or easy. —**en•a′bler,** *n.*

en•act′ *v.t.* **1.** to make into law. **2.** to represent in or as if in a play. —**en•act′ment,** *n.*

e•nam•el (i nam′əl), *n., v.,* **-eled, -el•ing** or (*esp. Brit.*) **-elled, -el•ling.** —*n.* **1.** an ornamental or protective glassy substance, usu. opaque, applied by fusion to the surface of metal, pottery, etc. **2.** a paint that dries to a hard, glossy finish. **3.** the hard, glossy covering of the crown of a tooth. —*v.t.* **4.** to inlay or overlay with enamel. —**e•nam′el•er,** *n.*

en•am•or (i nam′ər), *v.t.* to fill or inflame with love: *He was enamored of the princess.* Also, *esp. Brit.,* **en•am′our.**

en•camp′ *v.t., v.i.* to lodge or settle in a camp. —**en•camp′ment,** *n.*

en•cap•su•late (en kap′sə lāt′, -syōō-), *v.t.,* **-lat•ed, -lat•ing. 1.** to place in or as if in a capsule. **2.** to summarize or condense. —**en•cap′su•la′tion,** *n.*

en•case′ *v.t.,* **-cased, -cas•ing.** to enclose in or as if in a case.

en•ceph•a•li•tis (en sef′ə lī′tis), *n.* inflammation of the brain. —**en•ceph′a•lit′ic** (-lit′ik), *adj.*

en•chant (en chant′, -chänt′), *v.t.* **1.** to place under a spell; bewitch. **2.** to delight utterly; captivate. —**en•chant′er,** *n.* —**en•chant′ing•ly,** *adv.* —**en•chant′ment,** *n.*

en•chi•la•da (en′chə lä′də, -lad′ə), *n., pl.* **-das.** a tortilla rolled around a filling, as of meat or cheese, served usu. with a chili-flavored sauce.

en•cir′cle *v.t.,* **-cled, -cling. 1.** to form a circle around. **2.** to make a circuit of. —**en•cir′cle•ment,** *n.*

encl. 1. enclosed. **2.** enclosure.

en•clave (en′klāv, än′-), *n.* a country or a portion of a country surrounded by foreign territory.

en•close (en klōz′), *v.t.,* **-closed, -clos•ing. 1.** to shut or hem in on all sides. **2.** to surround, as with a fence. **3.** to insert in the same envelope or package with something else. —**en•clo′sure,** *n.*

en•code′ *v.t.,* **-cod•ed, -cod•ing.** to convert (a message, etc.) into code. —**en•cod′er,** *n.*

en•co•mi•um (en kō′mē əm), *n., pl.* **-mi•ums,**

-mi•a (-mē ə). a usu. formal expression of high praise.

en•com•pass (en kum′pəs), *v.t.* **1.** to encircle; surround. **2.** to enclose; envelop. **3.** to include comprehensively.

en•core (äng′kôr, än′-), *n., v.,* **-cored, -cor•ing.** —*n.* **1.** a demand by an audience for a repetition, as of a song. **2.** a performance in response to an encore. —*v.t.* **3.** to call for an encore from (a performer).

en•coun•ter (en koun′tər), *v.t.* **1.** to come upon or meet, esp. unexpectedly. **2.** to meet in conflict. —*n.* **3.** a meeting, esp. when casual or unexpected. **4.** a meeting between people or groups in conflict; battle.

en•cour•age (en kûr′ij, -kur′-), *v.t.,* **-aged, -ag-ing. 1.** to inspire with courage or confidence. **2.** to stimulate, as by approval. **3.** to promote; foster. —**en•cour′age•ment,** *n.* —**en•cour′ag•ing•ly,** *adv.*

en•croach (en krōch′), *v.i.* to trespass upon the property, domain, or rights of another, esp. gradually or stealthily. —**en•croach′ment,** *n.*

en•cum•ber (en kum′bər), *v.t.* **1.** to impede or hinder. **2.** to weigh down; burden. —**en•cum′-brance,** *n.*

en•cyc•li•cal (en sik′li kəl, -sī′kli-), *n.* a letter from the pope to all the bishops of the church.

en•cy•clo•pe•di•a or **-pae•di•a** (en sī′klə pē′-dē ə), *n., pl.* **-as.** a book or set of books covering all branches of knowledge or all aspects of one subject. [< NL < Gk *enkýklios paideía* circular (i.e., well-rounded) education] —**en•cy′clo•pe′dic,** *adj.*

end (end), *n.* **1.** the last part; extremity. **2.** a point that indicates the full extent or limit of something. **3.** a part or place at an extremity. **4.** termination, as of life; conclusion. **5.** final status or condition. **6.** an intention or aim. **7.** an outcome or result. **8.** destruction or ruin. **9.** a remnant or fragment. **10.** a share or part. **11.** either of the linemen in football stationed farthest from the center. —*v.t., v.i.* **12.** to bring or come to an end. **13.** to form the end (of). **14.** to kill or die. —*Idiom.* **15. make (both) ends meet,** to live within one's means. **16. no end,** very much.

en•dan•ger *v.t.* **1.** to expose to danger; imperil. **2.** to threaten with extinction. —**en•dan′ger•ment,** *n.*

en•dear′ *v.t.* to make dear or beloved. —**en•dear′-ing•ly,** *adv.*

en•deav•or (en dev′ər), *v.i.* **1.** to make an earnest effort; strive. —*n.* **2.** an earnest effort; attempt. Also, *esp. Brit.,* **en•deav′our.**

en•dem•ic (en dem′ik), *adj.* belonging exclusively or confined to a particular place or people.

end′ing *n.* **1.** a concluding part. **2.** an inflection at the end of a word, esp. a suffix.

en•dive (en′dīv, än dēv′), *n.* **1.** a plant with curly-edged leaves used in salads. **2.** a plant with a narrow head of whitish, edible leaves.

en•do•crine (en′də krin, -krīn′), *adj.* **1.** secreting internally into the blood or lymph. **2.** of or being a gland, as the thyroid, that secretes hormones directly into the blood or lymph.

en•dorse (en dôrs′), *v.t.,* **-dorsed, -dors•ing. 1.** to express approval or support of, esp. publicly. **2.** to designate oneself as payee of (a check) by signing, usu. on the reverse side. **3.** to sign one's name on (a check or commercial document). —**en•dorse′-ment,** *n.* —**en•dors′er,** *n.*

en•dow (en dou′), *v.t.* **1.** to provide with a permanent fund or source of income: *to endow a college.* **2.** to furnish with a talent, faculty, or quality; equip. —**en•dow′er,** *n.* —**en•dow′ment,** *n.*

en•dure′ (-dŏŏr′, -dyŏŏr′), *v.,* **-dured, -dur•ing.** —*v.t.* **1.** to sustain without impairment or yielding; undergo. **2.** to bear patiently; tolerate. —*v.i.* **3.** to continue to exist; last. **4.** to suffer without yielding. —**en•dur′ance,** *n.*

en•e•ma (en′ə mə), *n., pl.* **-mas. 1.** the injection of a fluid into the rectum. **2.** the fluid injected.

en•e•my (en′ə mē), *n., pl.* **-mies. 1.** a person who hates or fosters harmful designs against another. **2.**

an opposing military force. **3.** something harmful or prejudicial.

en•er•gize (en′ər jīz′), *v.t.*, **-gized, -giz•ing.** to give energy to. —**en′er•giz′er,** *n.*

en′er•gy (-jē), *n., pl.* **-gies. 1.** the capacity for vigorous activity. **2.** Often **-gies.** an exertion of energy; effort. **3.** forcefulness of expression. **4.** *Physics.* the capacity to do work. **5.** a source of usable power, as fossil fuel. —**en′er•get′ic** (-jet′ik), *adj.* —**en′er•get′i•cal•ly,** *adv.*

en•er•vate (en′ər vāt′), *v.t.,* **-vat•ed, -vat•ing.** to deprive of force or strength; weaken. —**en′er•va′-tion,** *n.* —**en′er•va′tor,** *n.*

en•fee′ble *v.t.,* **-bled, -bling.** to make feeble; weaken. —**en•fee′ble•ment,** *n.*

en•fold′ *v.t.* **1.** to wrap up; envelop. **2.** to hug or clasp; embrace.

en•fran′chise *v.t.,* **-chised, -chis•ing. 1.** to admit to citizenship, esp. to the right of voting. **2.** to set free, as from slavery; liberate. —**en•fran′chise•ment,** *n.*

en•gage (en gāj′), *v.,* **-gaged, -gag•ing.** —*v.t.* **1.** to occupy the attention or efforts of; involve. **2.** to employ; hire. **3.** to attract and hold fast: *The book engaged my attention.* **4.** to bind by a pledge or promise, esp. by a pledge to marry. **5.** to enter into conflict with. **6.** to cause (gears) to become interlocked. —*v.i.* **7.** to be or become involved: *to engage in politics.* **8.** to assume an obligation. **9.** to enter into conflict. **10.** to interlock. —**en•gage′-ment,** *n.* —**en•gag′er,** *n.*

en•gag′ing *adj.* winning; attractive. —**en•gag′-ing•ly,** *adv.*

en•gen•der (en jen′dər), *v.t.* **1.** to give rise to; cause. **2.** to beget; procreate.

en•gine (en′jən), *n.* **1.** a machine for converting energy into force and motion. **2.** a railroad locomotive. **3.** a mechanical contrivance.

en•gi•neer (en′jə nēr′), *n.* **1.** a person trained in engineering. **2.** a person who operates an engine or locomotive. **3.** a member of the military specially trained in engineering. —*v.t.* **4.** to plan, construct, or manage as an engineer. **5.** to arrange, manage, or carry through with subtle and often devious skill.

en′gi•neer′ing *n.* **1.** the practical application of science and mathematics, as in the design of structures, roads, and systems. **2.** the work or profession of an engineer.

Eng•land (ing′glənd; *often* -lənd), *n.* a division of the United Kingdom, in S Great Britain.

Eng•lish (ing′glish; *often* -lish), *n.* **1.** the Germanic language of England, the U.S., and regions formerly under British or U.S. dominion. **2.** (*used with a pl. v.*) the inhabitants of England. —*adj.* **3.** of or characteristic of England, its inhabitants, or their language.

en•gorge (en gôrj′), *v.t., v.i.,* **-gorged, -gorg•ing. 1.** to swallow greedily; gorge. **2.** to fill or congest, esp. with blood. —**en•gorge′ment,** *n.*

en•grave (en grāv′), *v.t.,* **-graved, -grav•ing. 1. a.** to cut or etch (letters or designs) into a surface. **b.** to print from such a surface. **2.** to mark or ornament with incised letters or designs. —**en•grav′er,** *n.* —**en•grav′ing,** *n.*

en•gross (en grōs′), *v.t.* **1.** to occupy completely; absorb. **2.** to write or copy in a clear, large script. —**en•gross′ing,** *adj.* —**en•gross′ment,** *n.*

en•gulf′ *v.t.* **1.** to swallow up in or as if in a gulf. **2.** to overwhelm or envelop completely.

en•hance (en hans′, -häns′), *v.t.,* **-hanced, -hanc•ing. 1.** to raise to a higher degree; intensify. **2.** to increase the value, attractiveness, or quality of; improve. —**en•hance′ment,** *n.*

e•nig•ma (ə nig′mə), *n., pl.* **-mas. 1.** a puzzling or inexplicable person, occurrence, or situation. **2.** a riddle. —**en•ig•mat•ic** (en′ig mat′ik), *adj.*

en•join (en join′), *v.t.* **1.** to direct or order; command. **2.** to prohibit or restrain by or as if by injunction. —**en•join′der,** *n.*

en•joy (en joi′), *v.t.* **1.** to take pleasure in. **2.** to have the use or benefit of. —**en•joy′a•ble,** *adj.* —**en•joy′er,** *n.* —**en•joy′ment,** *n.*

en•large′ *v.,* **-larged, -larg•ing.** —*v.t.* **1.** to make

larger. —*v.i.* **2.** to grow larger. **3.** to speak or write at length; expatiate. —**en•large′a•ble,** *adj.* —**en•large′ment,** *n.* —**en•larg′er,** *n.*

en•light′en *v.t.* **1.** to give intellectual or spiritual understanding to. **2.** to free of ignorance, false beliefs, or prejudice. —**en•light′en•ment,** *n.*

en•list′ *v.i., v.t.* **1.** to enroll or engage for military service. **2.** to enter into or secure for a cause or enterprise. —**en•list•ee′,** *n., pl.* **-ees.** —**en•list′ment,** *n.*

en•liv′en *v.t.* to make vigorous, active, or lively; animate.

en masse (än mas′, än), *adv.* in a mass; all together. [< F]

en•mesh′ *v.t.* to catch in or as if in the meshes of a net; entangle. —**en•mesh′ment,** *n.*

en•mi•ty (en′mi tē), *n., pl.* **-ties.** a feeling of bitter hatred; ill will.

en•nui (än wē′), *n.* a feeling of utter weariness and discontent; boredom.

e•nor•mi•ty (i nôr′mi tē), *n., pl.* **-ties. 1.** outrageous or heinous character. **2.** an outrageous or heinous act or offense. **3.** greatness of size or scope.

e•nor′mous *adj.* greatly exceeding the common size, extent, amount, or degree; huge. —**e•nor′-mous•ly,** *adv.* —**e•nor′mous•ness,** *n.*

e•nough (i nuf′), *adj.* **1.** sufficient for a purpose, want, or need. —*pron.* **2.** an adequate quantity or number. —*adv.* **3.** sufficiently. **4.** fully or quite. **5.** tolerably or passably.

en•quire (en kwī′r′), *v.i., v.t.,* **-quired, -quir•ing.** INQUIRE. —**en•quir′er,** *n.* —**en•quir•y** (en kwī′r′ē, en′kwə rē), *n., pl.* **-ies.**

en•rage′ *v.t.,* **-raged, -rag•ing.** to put into a rage; infuriate.

en•rap′ture *v.t.,* **-tured, -tur•ing.** to move to rapture; delight.

en•rich′ *v.t.* **1.** to make rich or richer. **2.** to add value or significance to. **3.** to adorn or decorate. **4.** to improve in quality, productivity, or nutritive value. —**en•rich′ment,** *n.*

en•roll or **-rol** (en rōl′), *v.,* **-rolled, -roll•ing** or **-rol•ling.** —*v.t.* **1.** to record in a roll or register. **2.** to enlist (oneself). —*v.i.* **3.** to enroll oneself or become enrolled. —**en•roll′ment,** *n.*

en route (än rōōt′, en, än), *adv.* on or along the way. [< F]

en•sconce (en skons′), *v.t.,* **-sconced, -sconc•ing.** to settle securely or snugly.

en•sem•ble (än säm′bəl, -sämb′, än-), *n.* **1.** all the parts of a thing taken together; set; whole. **2.** an entire outfit with all the parts in harmony. **3.** a group, as of singers or dancers, performing together.

en•shrine (en shrīn′), *v.t.,* **-shrined, -shrin•ing. 1.** to enclose in or as if in a shrine. **2.** to cherish as sacred. —**en•shrine′ment,** *n.*

en•shroud′ *v.t.* to shroud; conceal.

en•sign (en′sən; *for 1,2 also* -sīn), *n.* **1.** a flag or banner, as on a naval vessel. **2.** a badge of office or authority. **3.** the lowest commissioned officer in the U.S. Navy or Coast Guard.

en•slave′ *v.t.,* **-slaved, -slav•ing.** to make a slave of. —**en•slave′ment,** *n.*

en•snare′ *v.t.,* **-snared, -snar•ing.** to capture in or as if in a snare; entrap. —**en•snare′ment,** *n.*

en•sue (en sōō′), *v.i.,* **-sued, -su•ing.** to follow in order or as a consequence.

en•sure (en shōōr′, -shûr′), *v.t.,* **-sured, -sur•ing. 1.** to secure or guarantee. **2.** to make sure or certain. —**en•sur′er,** *n.*

en•tail (en tāl′), *v.t.* **1.** to cause or involve by necessity or as a consequence. **2.** to limit the passage of (real property) to a specified line or category of heirs. —**en•tail′ment,** *n.*

en•tan•gle *v.t.,* **-gled, -gling. 1.** to make tangled. **2.** to involve in difficulties, complications, or confusion. —**en•tan′gle•ment,** *n.*

en•tente (än tänt′), *n.* **1.** an international agreement to follow a common policy. **2.** an alliance of parties to an entente.

en•ter (en′tər), *v.t.* **1.** to come or go in or into. **2.** to become a member of; join. **3.** to begin; start. **4.** to become involved in; take part in. **5.** *Law.* **a.** to make a formal record of (a fact). **b.** to occupy or take possession of (lands). **6.** to put forward, submit, or register, esp. formally: *to enter an objection.* —*v.i.* **7.** to come or go in. **8.** to be admitted, as into a school. **9.** to make a beginning. **10. enter into, a.** to participate in; engage in. **b.** to form a part or ingredient of.

en•ter•i•tis (en'tə rī'tis), *n.* inflammation of the intestines.

en•ter•prise (en'tər prīz'), *n.* **1.** a project undertaken, esp. one requiring originality, boldness, or energy. **2.** adventurous spirit or ingenuity. **3.** a business firm.

en'ter•pris'ing *adj.* characterized by imagination, energy, and initiative.

en•ter•tain (en'tər tān'), *v.t.* **1.** to divert; amuse. **2.** to show hospitality to. **3.** to admit into or hold in the mind. —*v.i.* **4.** to show hospitality to guests. —**en'ter•tain'er,** *n.* —**en'ter•tain'ing,** *adj.* —**en'ter•tain'ment,** *n.*

en•thrall (en thrôl'), *v.t.* **1.** to captivate; spellbind. **2.** to enslave; subjugate.

en•throne' *v.t.,* **-throned, -thron•ing. 1.** to place on or as if on a throne. **2.** to exalt. —**en•throne'ment,** *n.*

en•thuse (en thōōz'), *v.,* **-thused, -thus•ing.** —*v.i.* **1.** to show enthusiasm. —*v.t.* **2.** to cause to become enthusiastic.

en•thu'si•asm (-thōō'zē az'əm), *n.* **1.** lively, absorbing interest or involvement. **2.** something inspiring enthusiasm. —**en•thu'si•ast',** *n.* —**en•thu'si•as'tic,** *adj.* —**en•thu'si•as'ti•cal•ly,** *adv.*

en•tice (en tīs'), *v.t.,* **-ticed, -tic•ing.** to lead on by exciting hope or desire; allure. —**en•tice'ment,** *n.* —**en•tic'ing•ly,** *adv.*

en•tire (en tīᵊr'), *adj.* having all parts or elements; whole or complete. —**en•tire'ly,** *adv.*

en•ti'tle *v.t.,* **-tled, -tling. 1.** to give a right or claim to. **2.** to call by a title or name. —**en•ti'tle•ment,** *n.*

en•ti•ty (en'ti tē), *n., pl.* **-ties. 1.** something that has a real existence; thing. **2.** being or existence.

en•tomb' *v.t.* to place in or as if in a tomb; bury. —**en•tomb'ment,** *n.*

en•to•mol•o•gy (en'tə mol'ə jē), *n.* the branch of zoology dealing with insects. —**en'to•mo•log'i•cal** (-mə loj'i kəl), *adj.* —**en'to•mol'o•gist,** *n.*

en•tou•rage (än'tōō räzh'), *n.* a group of attendants or associates.

en•trails (en'trālz, -trəlz), *n.pl.* inner organs, esp. intestines.

en•trance¹ (en'trəns), *n.* **1.** the act of entering. **2.** a point or place of entering. **3.** the right, privilege, or permission to enter.

en•trance² (en trans', -träns'), *v.t.,* **-tranced, -tranc•ing.** to fill with delight; enrapture. —**en•trance'ment,** *n.* —**en•tranc'ing•ly,** *adv.*

en•trant (en'trənt), *n.* a person who enters a competition or contest.

en•trap' *v.t.,* **-trapped, -trap•ping.** to catch in or as if in a trap; ensnare. —**en•trap'ment,** *n.*

en•treat (en trēt'), *v.t., v.i.* to ask earnestly; implore. —**en•treat'ing•ly,** *adv.* —**en•treat'y,** *n., pl.* **-ies.**

en•trée or **-tree** (än'trā), *n., pl.* **-trées** or **-trees. 1.** the main course of a meal. **2.** the privilege of entering; access.

en•trench (en trench'), *v.t.* **1.** to establish firmly or solidly. **2.** to surround with trenches. —**en•trench'ment,** *n.*

en•tre•pre•neur (än'trə prə nûr'), *n.* a person who organizes and manages an enterprise, esp. a business, usu. with considerable risk. —**en'tre•pre•neur'i•al,** *adj.*

en•tro•py (en'trə pē), *n.* **1.** a measure of the energy that is not available for work in a thermodynamic process. **2.** a hypothetical tendency for the universe to attain a state of maximum homogeneity. **3.** a tendency toward disorder in any system.

en•trust' *v.t.* **1.** to give to as a trust or responsibility. **2.** to give to another for protection, care, or handling.

en•try (en'trē), *n., pl.* **-tries. 1.** the act of entering. **2.** a place of entrance, as a vestibule. **3.** permission

or right to enter. **4. a.** the act of entering something, as in a book. **b.** the item entered. **5.** an entrant in a contest or competition.

en•twine' *v.t., v.i.,* **-twined, -twin•ing.** to twine around or together.

e•nu•mer•ate (i nōō'mə rāt', i nyōō'-), *v.t.,* **-at•ed, -at•ing. 1.** to name one by one; list. **2.** to count. —**e•nu'mer•a•ble,** *adj.* —**e•nu'mer•a'tion,** *n.*

e•nun•ci•ate (i nun'sē āt'), *v.t., v.i.,* **-at•ed, -at•ing. 1.** to pronounce (words), esp. in an articulate manner. **2.** to state definitely; proclaim. —**e•nun'ci•a'tion,** *n.*

en•vel•op (en vel'əp), *v.t.* **1.** to wrap up in or as if in a covering. **2.** to surround entirely. —**en•vel'op•er,** *n.* —**en•vel'op•ment,** *n.*

en•ve•lope (en'və lōp', än'-), *n.* **1.** a flat paper container, as for a letter. **2.** a wrapper or surrounding cover. **3.** the gasbag of a balloon.

en•vi•ron•ment (en vī'rən mənt, -vī'ərn-), *n.* **1.** surroundings; milieu. **2.** the external factors and forces surrounding and affecting an organism, person, or population. —**en•vi'ron•men'tal,** *adj.* —**en•vi'ron•men'tal•ly,** *adv.*

en•vi•ron•men•tal•ist *n.* a person who advocates or works for the protection and preservation of natural resources. —**en•vi'ron•men'tal•ism,** *n.*

en•vi•rons *n.pl.* the surrounding districts, as of a city; outskirts.

en•vis•age (en viz'ij), *v.t.,* **-aged, -ag•ing.** to visualize; envision.

en•vi•sion *v.t.* to picture mentally.

en•voy (en'voi, än'-), *n.* **1.** a diplomatic representative. **2.** an accredited messenger or representative.

en•vy (en'vē), *n., pl.* **-vies,** *v.,* **-vied, -vy•ing.** —*n.* **1.** discontent and resentment over or desire for another's advantages, possessions, or attainments. **2.** an object of envy. —*v.t.* **3.** to regard with envy. —**en'vy•ing•ly,** *adv.*

en•zyme (en'zīm), *n.* any of various proteins originating from living cells and capable of producing certain chemical changes in organic substances by catalytic action, as in digestion. —**en'zy•mat'ic,** *adj.*

e•on (ē'ən, ē'on), *n.* an indefinitely long period of time; age.

EPA Environmental Protection Agency.

ep•au•let or **-lette** (ep'ə let', -lit, ep'ə let'), *n.* an ornamental shoulder piece, esp. on a uniform. [< F *épaulette* = *épaule* shoulder + *-ette*]

e•phem•er•al (i fem'ər əl), *adj.* lasting a very short time; transitory.

ep•ic (ep'ik), *adj.* **1.** of or resembling a long poem in which the great achievements of a hero are narrated in elevated style. **2.** impressively great; heroic. —*n.* **3.** an epic poem. **4.** a novel, film, etc., suggesting an epic.

ep•i•cen•ter (ep'ə sen'tər), *n.* a point directly above the true center of an earthquake from which the shock waves apparently radiate.

ep•i•cure (ep'i kyŏŏr'), *n.* a person with refined taste, esp. in food and wine; connoisseur. —**ep'i•cu•re'an,** *adj., n.*

ep•i•dem•ic (ep'i dem'ik), *adj.* **1.** affecting many individuals at the same time. **2.** prevalent; widespread. —*n.* **3.** an epidemic disease. **4.** a rapid spread or increase. —**ep'i•dem'i•cal•ly,** *adv.*

ep•i•der•mis (ep'i dûr'mis), *n.* the outermost layer of the skin. —**ep'i•der'mal, ep'i•der'mic,** *adj.*

ep•i•glot•tis *n.* a flap of cartilage that helps close the opening to the windpipe during swallowing.

ep•i•gram (ep'i gram'), *n.* a terse, witty saying or poem. —**ep'i•gram•mat'ic** (-grə mat'ik), *adj.*

ep•i•lep•sy (ep'ə lep'sē), *n.* a nervous disorder usu. characterized by convulsions, often with loss of consciousness. —**ep'i•lep'tic** (-lep'tik), *adj., n.*

ep•i•logue or **-log** (ep'ə lôg', -log'), *n.* **1.** a concluding part added to a literary work. **2.** a speech delivered by an actor at the conclusion of a play.

e•piph•a•ny (i pif'ə nē), *n., pl.* **-nies. 1.** an appearance or manifestation, esp. of a deity. **2.** (*cap.*) a Christian festival, observed on Jan. 6, commemorating the manifestation of Christ to the gentiles in the persons of the Magi. **3.** a sudden, intuitive realization.

e•pis•co•pal (i pis′kə pəl), *adj.* **1.** of or governed by a bishop or bishops. **2.** (*cap.*) of or designating the Anglican Church or Protestant Episcopal Church.

ep•i•sode (ep′ə sōd′, -zōd′), *n.* **1.** an incident in the course of a series of events. **2.** an incident or scene within a narrative. —**ep′i•sod′ic** (-sod′ik), *adj.*

e•pis•tle (i pis′əl), *n.* **1.** a letter. **2.** (*usu. cap.*) one of the apostolic letters in the New Testament. —**e•pis′to•lar′y** (-tl er′ē), *adj.*

ep•i•taph (ep′i taf′, -täf′), *n.* a commemorative inscription, esp. on a tomb.

ep•i•thet (ep′ə thet′), *n.* **1.** a characterizing word or phrase. **2.** an abusive or contemptuous word, phrase, or expression.

e•pit•o•me (i pit′ə mē), *n., pl.* **-mes. 1.** one that is typical of a whole class; embodiment. **2.** a summary; abstract.

e plu•ri•bus u•num (e ploo͞o′ri boos′ ōo′noom; *Eng.* ē′ ploor′ə bəs yōo′nəm) *Latin.* out of many, one (motto of the U.S.).

ep•och (ep′ək; *esp. Brit.* ē′pok), *n.* **1.** a period of time marked by distinctive features, noteworthy events, or changed conditions. **2.** a memorable event, date, or state of affairs. **3.** any of several divisions of a geologic period. —**ep′och•al,** *adj.*

ep•ox•y (i pok′sē), *n., pl.* **-ies.** any of a class of resins derived by polymerization, used chiefly in adhesives, coatings, and castings.

Ep′som salts′ (ep′səm), *n.pl.* hydrated magnesium sulfate, used esp. as a cathartic. [after their presence in the mineral water at *Epsom*, England]

eq•ua•ble (ek′wə bəl, ē′kwə-), *adj.* **1.** free from change or variation; uniform. **2.** not easily annoyed or disturbed; calm. —**eq′ua•bil′i•ty,** *n.* —**eq′ua•bly,** *adv.*

e•qual (ē′kwəl), *adj., n., v.,* **e•qualed, e•qual•ing** or (*esp. Brit.*) **e•qualled, e•qual•ling.** —*adj.* **1.** being the same as another in quantity, degree, value, number, or quality. **2.** evenly proportioned or balanced. **3.** uniform in operation or effect: *equal laws.* **4.** having adequate powers, ability, or means: *equal to the task.* **5.** impartial or equitable. —*n.* **6.** a person or thing that is equal. —*v.t.* **7.** to be or become equal to; match. **8.** to do something equal to. —**e•qual•i•ty** (i kwol′i tē), *n., pl.* **-ties.** —**e′qual•ize′,** *v.t.,* **-ized, -iz•ing.** —**e′qual•ly,** *adv.*

E′qual Rights′ Amend′ment *n.* a proposed amendment to the U.S. Constitution prohibiting discrimination on the basis of sex.

e′qual (or **e′quals**) **sign′,** *n.* the symbol (=) used to indicate that the terms it separates are equal.

e•qua•nim•i•ty (ē′kwə nim′i tē, ek′wə-), *n.* composure, esp. under strain; evenness.

e•quate (i kwāt′), *v.t.,* **e•quat•ed, e•quat•ing.** to regard, treat, or represent as equivalent or comparable. —**e•quat′a•ble,** *adj.*

e•qua•tion (i kwā′zhən, -shən), *n.* **1.** the act of equating or state of being equated. **2.** an expression or a proposition, often algebraic, asserting the equality of two quantities.

e•qua′tor (-tər), *n.* the great circle of the earth that is equidistant from the North Pole and South Pole. —**e•qua•to•ri•al** (ē′kwə tôr′ē əl, ek′wə-), *adj.*

E′quato′rial Guin′ea *n.* a republic in W equatorial Africa.

e•ques•tri•an (i kwes′trē ən), *adj.* **1.** of horseback riding or horseback riders. **2.** representing a person mounted on a horse. —*n.* **3.** a person who rides horses. —**e•ques′tri•an•ism,** *n.*

e•qui•dis•tant (ē′kwi dis′tənt, ek′wi-), *adj.* equally distant.

e′qui•lat′er•al (-lat′ər əl), *adj.* having all the sides equal.

e′qui•lib′ri•um (-lib′rē əm), *n., pl.* **-ri•ums, -ri•a** (-rē ə). a state of balance between opposing forces, powers, or influences.

e•quine (ē′kwīn, ek′wīn), *adj.* **1.** of or resembling a horse. —*n.* **2.** a horse.

e•qui•nox (ē′kwə noks′, ek′wə-), *n.* one of the times when the sun crosses the equator, making night and day of approximately equal length all over the earth and occurring about March 21 and Sept. 22. —**e′qui•noc′tial** (-nok′shəl), *adj.*

e•quip (i kwip′), *v.t.,* **e•quipped, e•quip•ping.** to provide with what is needed; fit out. —**e•quip′ment,** *n.*

eq•ui•ta•ble (ek′wi tə bəl), *adj.* fair and impartial; just. —**eq′ui•ta•bly,** *adv.*

eq′ui•ty *n., pl.* **-ties. 1.** the quality of being fair or impartial; fairness. **2.** (in England and the U.S.) a system of jurisprudence serving to supplement the common law. **3.** the value of a property or business beyond any amounts owed on it.

e•quiv•a•lent (i kwiv′ə lənt), *adj.* **1.** equal in value, measure, force, effect, or significance. —*n.* **2.** something equivalent. —**e•quiv′a•lence, e•quiv′a•len•cy,** *n., pl.* **-ces, -cies.** —**e•quiv′a•lent•ly,** *adv.*

e•quiv•o•cal (i kwiv′ə kəl), *adj.* **1.** deliberately ambiguous. **2.** uncertain or doubtful. **3.** questionable or dubious. —**e•quiv′o•cal•ly,** *adv.* —**e•quiv′o•cal•ness,** *n.*

e•quiv•o•cate′ (-kāt′), *v.i.,* **-cat•ed, -cat•ing.** to use ambiguous or evasive expressions. —**e•quiv′o•ca′tion,** *n.* —**e•quiv′o•ca′tor,** *n.*

ER emergency room.

Er *Chem. Symbol.* erbium.

-er[1], a suffix meaning: a person who is occupied with or works at something (*roofer*); a native or resident of a place (*southerner*); a person or thing associated with a particular characteristic or circumstance (*teenager*); one that performs or is used in performing an action (*fertilizer*).

-er[2], a suffix forming the comparative degree of adjectives (*smaller*) and adverbs (*faster*).

e•ra (ēr′ə, er′ə), *n., pl.* **e•ras. 1.** a period of time marked by a distinctive character. **2.** a system of chronologic notation reckoned from a given date. **3.** a major division of geologic time composed of a number of periods.

ERA 1. Also, **era** *Baseball.* earned run average. **2.** Equal Rights Amendment.

e•rad•i•cate (i rad′i kāt′), *v.t.,* **-cat•ed, -cat•ing.** to remove or destroy utterly; extirpate. —**e•rad′i•ca•ble,** *adj.* —**e•rad′i•ca′tion,** *n.*

e•rase (i rās′), *v.t.,* **e•rased, e•ras•ing. 1.** to rub or scrape out (written characters, recorded material, etc.); efface. **2.** to eliminate completely; obliterate. —**e•ras′a•ble,** *adj.* —**e•ras′er,** *n.* —**e•ra′sure** (-shər), *n.*

er•bi•um (ûr′bē əm), *n.* a rare-earth element having pink salts. *Symbol:* Er; *at. wt.:* 167.26; *at. no.:* 68.

ere (âr), *prep., conj.* before.

e•rect (i rekt′), *adj.* **1.** upright in position or posture. —*v.t.* **2.** to build; construct. **3.** to raise and set in an upright position. **4.** to set up; establish. —**e•rect′ly,** *adv.* —**e•rect′ness,** *n.* —**e•rec′tor,** *n.*

e•rec′tion (-shən), *n.* **1.** something erected. **2.** a distended and rigid state of an organ or part containing erectile tissue, esp. the penis.

erg (ûrg), *n.* the centimeter-gram-second unit of work or energy.

er•go (ûr′gō, er′gō), *conj., adv.* therefore. [< L]

er•go•nom•ics (ûr′gə nom′iks), *n.* an applied science that coordinates the design of devices and systems with the requirements of workers. —**er′go•nom′ic,** *adj.* —**er′go•nom′i•cal•ly,** *adv.*

Er•i•tre•a (er′i trē′ə), *n.* a republic in NE Africa. —**Er′i•tre′an,** *adj., n.*

er•mine (ûr′min), *n., pl.* **-mines, -mine. 1.** a weasel having a white coat with a black-tipped tail in the winter. **2.** the white winter fur of the ermine.

e•rode (i rōd′), *v.,* **e•rod•ed, e•rod•ing.** —*v.t.* **1.** to eat into or wear away, esp. slowly or gradually. —*v.i.* **2.** to become eroded. —**e•rod′i•ble,** *adj.*

e•rog•e•nous (i roj′ə nəs), *adj.* sensitive to sexual stimulation.

e•rot•ic (i rot′ik), *adj.* **1.** of or dealing with sexual love. **2.** arousing or satisfying sexual desire. [< Gk *erōtikós* pertaining to Eros] —**e•rot′i•cal•ly,** *adv.* —**e•rot′i•cism** (-ə siz′əm), *n.*

e•rot′i•ca (-i kə), *n.* (*used with a sing. or pl. v.*) erotic literature or art.

err (ûr, er), *v.i.* **1.** to be mistaken or incorrect. **2.** to go astray morally; sin.

er•rand (er′ənd), *n.* **1.** a short trip to accomplish a specific purpose, often for someone else. **2.** the purpose of an errand.

er•rant (er′ənt), *adj.* **1.** deviating from the regular or proper course. **2.** traveling, esp. in quest of adventure. **3.** moving in an aimless manner.

er•rat•ic (i rat′ik), *adj.* **1.** inconsistent or changeable; unpredictable. **2.** peculiar; eccentric. **3.** not fixed; wandering. —**er•rat′i•cal•ly,** *adv.*

er•ra•tum (i rä′təm, i rā′-, i rat′əm), *n., pl.* **-ta** (-tə). an error in writing or printing.

er•ro•ne•ous (ə rō′nē əs, e rō′-), *adj.* containing an error; incorrect. —**er•ro′ne•ous•ly,** *adv.*

er•ror (er′ər), *n.* **1.** a deviation from accuracy or correctness; mistake. **2.** belief in something untrue. **3.** the condition of believing what is not true. **4.** wrongdoing; sin. **5.** a defensive misplay in baseball.

er•satz (er′zäts, -säts), *adj.* serving as a substitute; synthetic or artificial.

erst′while′ (ûrst′-), *adj.* **1.** former. —*adv.* **2.** Archaic. formerly.

ERT estrogen replacement therapy.

er•u•dite (er′yŏŏ dīt′, er′ŏŏ-), *adj.* having much knowledge; learned. —**er′u•dite′ly,** *adv.* —**er′u•di′tion,** *n.*

e•rupt (i rupt′), *v.i.* **1.** to burst forth. **2.** (of a volcano, geyser, etc.) to eject matter. **3.** to break out of a pent-up state. **4.** to break out in a skin rash. —*v.t.* **5.** to cause to burst forth. —**e•rup′tion,** *n.* —**e•rup′tive,** *adj.*

es•ca•late (es′kə lāt′), *v.i., v.t.,* **-lat•ed, -lat•ing.** to increase in intensity, magnitude, number, amount, or scope. —**es′ca•la′tion,** *n.*

es′ca•la′tor *n.* a continuously moving stairway on an endless loop.

es•cal•lop (e skol′əp, e skal′-), *v.t.* **1.** to bake (food) in a sauce, often with breadcrumbs on top. —*n.* **2.** SCALLOP.

es•ca•pade (es′kə pād′, es′kə pād′), *n.* a reckless adventure or wild prank.

es•cape (i skāp′), *v.,* **-caped, -cap•ing,** *n., adj.* —*v.i.* **1.** to get away, as from confinement. **2.** to avoid a threatened evil. **3.** to issue from a confining enclosure, as a gas. —*v.t.* **4.** to get away from. **5.** to succeed in avoiding. **6.** to elude (one's memory or notice). **7.** to slip from or be expressed by inadvertently: *A sigh escaped her lips.* —*n.* **8.** an act or instance of escaping. **9.** a means of escape. **10.** avoidance of reality. **11.** leakage, as of gas. —*adj.* **12.** for or providing an escape.

es•cape•ment (i skāp′mənt), *n.* the portion of a watch or clock that measures beats and controls the speed of wheels in gear.

es•cap′ism *n.* the avoidance of reality by absorption of the mind in entertainment or fantasy. —**es•cap′ist,** *adj., n.*

es•ca•role (es′kə rōl′), *n.* a broad-leaved endive used in salads.

es•carp•ment (i skärp′mənt), *n.* a long, steep clifflike ridge of land or rock.

es•chew (es chōō′), *v.t.* to keep away from; avoid.

es•cort (*n.* es′kôrt; *v.* i skôrt′), *n.* **1.** a person or group accompanying another for protection or courtesy. **2.** a protective guard, as a body of warships. **3.** a man who accompanies a woman in public. —*v.t.* **4.** to accompany as an escort.

es•cutch•eon (i skuch′ən), *n.* a shield or shieldlike surface on which a coat of arms is depicted.

Es•ki•mo (es′kə mō′), *n., pl.* **-mo, -mos** for 1. **1.** a member of a people living in regions from Greenland through Canada and Alaska to NE Siberia. **2.** the languages spoken by the Eskimos.

ESL English as a second language.

e•soph•a•gus (i sof′ə gəs, ē sof′-), *n., pl.* **-gi** (-jī′, -gī′). a muscular tube for the passage of food from the pharynx to the stomach. —**e•soph•a•ge•al** (i sof′ə jē′əl, ē′sə faj′ē əl), *adj.*

es•o•ter•ic (es′ə ter′ik), *adj.* **1.** understood by or meant for only a select few. **2.** private; secret. —**es′o•ter′i•cal•ly,** *adv.*

ESP extrasensory perception.

esp. especially.

es•pa•drille (es′pə dril′), *n.* a flat shoe with a cloth upper and a rope sole.

es•pe•cial (i spesh′əl), *adj.* special; particular. —**es•pe′cial•ly,** *adv.*

Es•pe•ran•to (es′pə rän′tō, -ran′-), *n.* an artificial language based on words common to the major European languages.

es•pi•o•nage (es′pē ə näzh′, -nij), *n.* the act or practice of spying.

es•pla•nade (es′plə näd′, -nād′), *n.* an open level space, esp. one serving for public walks.

es•pouse (i spouz′, i spous′), *v.t.,* **-poused, -pous•ing.** **1.** to adopt or embrace, as a cause; support. **2.** to marry. —**es•pous′al,** *n.*

es•pres•so (e spres′ō), *n., pl.* **-sos.** a strong coffee prepared by forcing hot water through finely ground coffee beans.

es•prit de corps (e sprē′ də kôr′), *n.* a sense of unity and common purpose among the members of a group. [< F]

es•py (i spī′), *v.t.,* **-pied, -py•ing.** to catch sight of.

es•quire (es′kwīr′), *n.* **1.** (*cap.*) a title of respect, in the U.S. chiefly applied to lawyers. **2.** SQUIRE (def. 2). **3.** a man of the English gentry ranking below a knight. **4.** *Archaic.* SQUIRE (def. 1).

es•say (*n.* es′ā or, for 2, e sā′; *v.* e sā′), *n.* **1.** a short literary composition on a particular theme or subject. **2.** an effort; attempt. —*v.t.* **3.** to try; attempt. —**es•say′er,** *n.* —**es′say•ist,** *n.*

es•sence (es′əns), *n.* **1.** the basic, real, and invariable nature of a thing; substance. **2.** a concentrate of a substance. **3.** a perfume; scent. **4.** the true nature or constitution of something.

es•sen•tial (ə sen′shəl), *adj.* **1.** absolutely necessary; indispensable. **2.** of or constituting an essence. —*n.* **3.** something basic, indispensable, or necessary. —**es•sen′tial•ly,** *adv.*

EST Eastern Standard Time.

-est a suffix forming the superlative degree of adjectives (*warmest*) and adverbs (*fastest*).

est. **1.** established. **2.** estimate. **3.** estimated.

es•tab•lish (i stab′lish), *v.t.* **1.** to bring into being; found. **2.** to install or settle, as in a position or business. **3.** to prove. **4.** to cause to be accepted or recognized. **5.** to enact or ordain on a permanent basis, as a law.

es•tab′lish•ment *n.* **1.** the act of establishing or state of being established. **2. the Establishment,** the existing power structure in a society. **3.** a place of residence or business including personnel, equipment, and property. **4.** a permanent civil or military force or organization.

es•tate (i stāt′), *n.* **1.** a piece of landed property, esp. one of large extent. **2. a.** a person's property or possessions. **b.** the property of a deceased person. **3.** a period or condition of life. **4.** a major political or social group or class.

es•teem (i stēm′), *v.t.* **1.** to regard with respect or admiration. **2.** to consider as being; regard. —*n.* **3.** respect or admiration.

es•ter (es′tər), *n.* a chemical compound produced by the reaction between an acid and an alcohol.

es′thete *n.* aesthete.

es•ti•ma•ble (es′tə mə bəl), *adj.* worthy of esteem.

es′ti•mate′ (*v.* -māt′; *n.* -mit, -māt′), *v.,* **-mat•ed, -mat•ing,** *n.* —*v.t.* **1.** to form an approximate judgment regarding the worth, amount, size, etc., of. **2.** to form an opinion of; judge. —*v.i.* **3.** to make an estimate. —*n.* **4.** an approximate judgment or calculation. **5.** a judgment or opinion. **6.** a statement of the approximate charge for doing work. —**es′ti•ma′tor,** *n.* —**es′ti•ma′tion,** *n.*

Es•to•ni•a (e stō′nē ə), *n.* a republic in N Europe, on the Baltic: formerly part of the USSR. —**Es•to′ni•an,** *adj., n.*

es•trange (i strānj′), *v.t.,* **-tranged, -trang•ing.** to alienate the feelings or affections of; make unfriendly or hostile. —**es•trange′ment**, *n.*

es•tro•gen (es′tra jan), *n.* any of several female sex hormones capable of inducing sexual receptiveness and producing secondary female sex characteristics.

es•tu•ar•y (es′chōō er′ē), *n., pl.* **-ies.** the part of the lower course of a river at which the river's current meets the sea's tide.

e•ta (ā′ta, ē′ta), *n., pl.* **-tas.** the seventh letter of the Greek alphabet (H, η).

et al. (et al′, äl′, and others. [< L *et aliī*]

et cet•er•a (et set′ar a, se′tra), *adv.* and others, esp. of the same sort. [< L]

etch (ech), *v.t.* **1.** to engrave furrows in, esp. with an acid. **2.** to produce (a design, image, etc.) by etching. **3.** to outline sharply; delineate. —**etch′er**, *n.* —**etch′ing**, *n.*

e•ter•nal (i tûr′nl), *adj.* **1.** without beginning or end; lasting forever. **2.** perpetual; ceaseless. **3.** not subject to change; immutable. —**e•ter′nal•ness**, *n.* —**e•ter′nal•ly**, *adv.*

e•ter′ni•ty (-ni tē), *n., pl.* **-ties. 1.** infinite time. **2.** eternal existence. **3.** the timeless state after death. **4.** a seemingly endless period of time.

eth•ane (eth′ān), *n.* a colorless, odorless, flammable gas present in natural gas and crude petroleum, used chiefly as a fuel.

e•ther (ē′thar), *n.* **1.** a colorless, highly volatile, flammable liquid used as a solvent and formerly as an anesthetic. **2.** the upper regions of space; the heavens. **3.** a substance formerly supposed to occupy all space.

e•the•re•al (i thēr′ē al), *adj.* **1.** light or airy. **2.** extremely delicate or refined. **3.** heavenly; celestial. —**e•the′re•al•ly**, *adv.*

eth•ics (eth′iks), *n.* **1.** (*used with a sing. or pl. v.*) a system of moral principles. **2.** (*used with a sing. v.*) the branch of philosophy dealing with right and wrong and the morality of motives and ends.

E•thi•o•pi•a (ē′thē ō′pē a), *n.* a republic in E Africa. —**E′thi•o′pi•an**, *adj., n.*

eth•nic (eth′nik), *adj.* **1.** of or pertaining to a people, esp. a group sharing a common and distinctive culture. —*n.* **2.** a member of an ethnic group or minority. —**eth′ni•cal•ly**, *adv.*

eth•nic′i•ty (-nis′i tē), *n.* ethnic traits or association.

eth•nol•o•gy (eth nol′a jē), *n.* **1.** a branch of anthropology that analyzes and compares cultures. **2.** a branch of anthropology dealing with racial origins, distribution, and characteristics. —**eth′no•log′i•cal** (-na loj′i kal), **eth′no•log′ic**, *adj.* —**eth•nol′o•gist**, *n.*

e•thol•o•gy (ē thol′a jē, i thol′-), *n.* the scientific study of animal behavior. —**e•tho•log′i•cal** (ē′tha loj′i kal, eth′a-), *adj.* —**e•thol′o•gist**, *n.*

e•thos (ē′thos, eth′ōs), *n.* the distinguishing character, spirit, or disposition of a person or group.

eth•yl (eth′al), *n.* an antiknock fluid used in gasoline for more even combustion.

et•i•quette (et′i kit, -ket′), *n.* conventional requirements for proper social or professional behavior.

et seq. and the following. [< L *et sequēns*]

et•y•mol•o•gy (et′a mol′a jē), *n., pl.* **-gies. 1.** the history of a word or word element. **2.** an account of the origin and development of a word or word element. **3.** the study of historical linguistic change. —**et′y•mo•log′i•cal** (-ma loj′i kal), *adj.* —**et′y•mol′o•gist**, *n.*

eu- a combining form meaning good (*eugenics*).

Eu *Chem. Symbol.* europium.

eu•ca•lyp•tus (yōō′ka lip′tas), *n., pl.* **-ti** (-tī), **-tus•es.** a tree of the myrtle family, having aromatic evergreen leaves.

Eu•cha•rist (yōō′ka rist), *n.* **1.** the sacrament of Holy Communion. **2.** the consecrated bread and wine used in this sacrament, esp. the bread. —**Eu′cha•ris′tic**, *adj.*

eu•gen•ics (yōō jen′iks), *n.* a science concerned with improving the genetic traits of a breed or species, esp. the human species. —**eu•gen′ic**, *adj.* —**eu•gen′i•cist** (-a sist), *n.*

eu•lo•gy (yōō′la jē), *n., pl.* **-gies. 1.** a speech in praise of a person or thing, esp. a funeral oration. **2.** high praise. —**eu′lo•gis′tic**, *adj.*

eu•nuch (yōō′nak), *n.* a castrated man.

eu•phe•mism (yōō′fa miz′am), *n.* **1.** the substitution of a mild or indirect expression for one thought to be offensive or harsh. **2.** the expression substituted. —**eu′phe•mis′tic**, *adj.* —**eu′phe•mis′ti•cal•ly**, *adv.*

eu•pho•ny (yōō′fa nē), *n., pl.* **-nies.** agreeableness of sound, esp. a pleasing combination of words.

eu•pho•ri•a (yōō fôr′ē a), *n.* a strong feeling of happiness, confidence, or well-being. —**eu•phor′ic** (-fôr′ik, -for′-), *adj.*

Eur•a•sia (yōō rā′zha), *n.* Europe and Asia considered together as one continent. —**Eur•a′sian**, *adj., n.*

eu•re•ka (yōō rē′ka, ya-), *interj.* an exclamation of triumph at a discovery. [< Gk *heúrēka* I have found (it)]

eu•ro (yōōr′ō, yûr′-), *n., pl.* **-ros.** the official common currency of most W European countries.

Eu•rope (yōōr′ap, yûr′-), *n.* a continent in the W part of Eurasia, separated from Asia by the Ural Mountains. —**Eu′ro•pe′an** (-a pē′an), *adj., n.*

Europe′an plan′ *n.* a system of paying a fixed hotel rate that covers lodging only.

eu•ro•pi•um (yōō rō′pē am, ya-), *n.* a rare-earth metallic element. *Symbol:* Eu; *at. wt.:* 151.96; *at. no.:* 63.

Eu•sta′chian tube′ (yōō stā′shan, -stā′kē an), *n.* (*often l.c.*) a canal between the middle ear and the pharynx. [after B. *Eustachio* (1524?–74), Italian anatomist]

eu•tha•na•sia (yōō′tha nā′zha), *n.* painless killing of a person or animal suffering from an incurable disease.

e•vac•u•ate (i vak′yōō āt′), *v.,* **-at•ed, -at•ing.** —*v.t.* **1.** to make empty. **2.** to remove (persons or things) from (a place or area), esp. for safety. **3.** to discharge from the bowels. —*v.i.* **4.** to leave a place; withdraw. —**e•vac′u•a′tion**, *n.*

e•vade (i vād′), *v.t., v.i.,* **e•vad•ed, e•vad•ing.** to escape or avoid, esp. by cleverness or trickery. —**e•vad′er**, *n.* —**e•va′sion**, *n.*

e•val•u•ate (i val′yōō āt′), *v.t.,* **-at•ed, -at•ing.** to determine the value, quality, or significance of. —**e•val′u•a′tion**, *n.* —**e•val′u•a′tor**, *n.*

ev•a•nes•cent (ev′a nes′ant), *adj.* fading away; vanishing. —**ev′a•nes′cence**, *n.*

e•van•gel•i•cal (ē′van jel′i kal, ev′an-), *adj.* **1.** of or in keeping with the Gospels. **2.** of or belonging to the Christian churches that emphasize the authority of the Scriptures. **3.** marked by fervor or zeal. —**e′van•gel′i•cal•ism**, *n.* —**e′van•gel′i•cal•ly**, *adv.*

e•van•ge•list (i van′ja list), *n.* **1.** a preacher of the Christian gospel, esp. a revivalist. **2.** (*cap.*) one of the writers of the four Gospels. —**e•van′ge•lis′tic**, *adj.*

e•vap•o•rate (i vap′a rāt′), *v.,* **-rat•ed, -rat•ing.** —*v.i.* **1.** to change into or pass off in vapor. **2.** to disappear; vanish; fade. —*v.t.* **3.** to convert into vapor. **4.** to extract moisture or liquid from, as by heat. —**e•vap′o•ra′tion**, *n.*

eve (ēv), *n.* **1.** (*sometimes cap.*) the evening or day before an event, esp. a holiday. **2.** the period preceding an event. **3.** evening.

e•ven (ē′van), *adj.* **1.** level; flat. **2.** without irregularities; smooth. **3.** on the same plane or line. **4.** free from variations; uniform. **5.** equal in measure or quantity. **6.** divisible by two. **7.** leaving no balance of debt on either side. **8.** exact. **9.** calm; placid. —*adv.* **10.** still; yet: *even more suitable.* **11.** (used to suggest an extreme case or an unlikely instance): *Even the slightest noise disturbs him.* **12.** exactly; just: *Even as help was coming, the troops surrendered.* **13.** fully; quite: *was moved even to tears.* **14.** indeed: *He is willing, even eager, to do it.* —*v.t., v.i.* **15.** to make or become even. —**e′ven•ly**, *adv.* —**e′ven•ness**, *n.*

e/ven·hand/ed *adj.* impartial; equitable. —**e/ven·hand/ed·ly,** *adv.* —**e/ven·hand/ed·ness,** *n.*

eve·ning (ēv/ning), *n.* the latter part of the day and early part of the night.

eve/ning star/ *n.* a bright planet, esp. Venus, seen in the western sky at or soon after sunset.

e·vent (i vent/), *n.* **1.** an occurrence, esp. one of some importance. **2.** a possible occurrence. **3.** a single sports contest within a scheduled program.

e·ven·tu·al (i ven/chōō əl), *adj.* happening at an indefinite future time. —**e·ven/tu·al·ly,** *adv.*

e·ven/tu·al/i·ty *n., pl.* **-ties.** a possible event, occurrence, or circumstance.

ev·er (ev/ər), *adv.* **1.** at any time. **2.** at all times; always. **3.** in any possible case.

ev/er·glade/ *n.* a tract of low, swampy land.

ev/er·green/ *adj.* **1.** having green leaves throughout the year. —*n.* **2.** an evergreen plant.

ev/er·last/ing *adj.* **1.** lasting forever; eternal. —*n.* **2.** eternity.

eve·ry (ev/rē), *adj.* **1.** being one of a group taken collectively; each. **2.** all possible: *every prospect of success.* —*Idiom.* **3.** every other, every second; each alternate: *every other day.*

e·vict (i vikt/), *v.t.* to expel (a tenant) from property by legal process. —**e·vic/tion,** *n.*

ev·i·dence (ev/i dəns), *n., v.,* **-denced, -denc·ing.** —*n.* **1.** something that constitutes proof. **2.** an indication or sign. **3.** data presented in court to substantiate claims or allegations. —*v.t.* **4.** to show clearly; manifest.

ev·i·dent *adj.* clear to the sight or understanding. —**ev/i·dent·ly,** *adv.*

e·vil (ē/vəl), *adj.* **1.** morally wrong or bad; wicked. **2.** harmful; injurious. **3.** unfortunate; disastrous. —*n.* **4.** evil quality, intention, or conduct; wickedness or sin. **5.** injury or harm. **6.** something causing injury or harm. —**e/vil·do/er,** *n.* —**e/vil·ly,** *adv.*

e/vil eye/ *n.* a look thought capable of inflicting injury or harm.

e·vince (i vins/), *v.t.,* **e·vinced, e·vinc·ing.** to make evident; manifest.

e·vis·cer·ate (i vis/ə rāt/), *v.t.,* **-at·ed, -at·ing.** **1.** to remove the entrails of; disembowel. **2.** to deprive of vital or essential parts. —**e·vis/cer·a/tion,** *n.*

e·voke (i vōk/), *v.t.,* **e·voked, e·vok·ing.** **1.** to call up (memories, feelings, etc.). **2.** to draw forth; elicit: *The comment evoked loud protests.* —**ev·o·ca·tion** (ev/ə kā/shən, ē/vō-), *n.* —**e·voc·a·tive** (i vok/ə tiv, i vō/kə-), *adj.*

ev·o·lu·tion (ev/ə lōō/shən; *esp. Brit.* ē/və-), *n.* **1.** a process of formation or growth; development. **2. a.** change in the gene pool of a population from generation to generation by such processes as mutation and natural selection. **b.** the theory that all existing organisms developed from earlier forms by natural selection. **3.** a pattern formed by a series of movements. —**ev/o·lu/tion·ar/y,** *adv.* —**ev/o·lu/tion·ism,** *n.* —**ev/o·lu/tion·ist,** *n., adj.*

e·volve (i volv/), *v.t., v.i.,* **e·volved, e·volv·ing.** to develop gradually by or as if by a process of evolution. —**e·volve/ment,** *n.*

ewe (yōō; *Dial.* yō), *n.* a female sheep.

ew·er (yōō/ər), *n.* a pitcher or jug with a wide spout.

ex¹ (eks), *prep.* not including; without: *ex dividend.*

ex² (eks), *n. Informal.* a former spouse.

ex- a prefix meaning: out of or from (*export*); utterly or thoroughly (*exacerbate*); former (*ex-governor*).

Ex. Exodus.

ex. **1.** example. **2.** except. **3.** exception. **4.** exchange.

ex·ac·er·bate (ig zas/ər bāt/, ek sas/-), *v.t.,* **-bat·ed, -bat·ing.** to increase the severity, bitterness, or violence of; aggravate. —**ex·ac/er·ba/tion,** *n.*

ex·act (ig zakt/), *adj.* **1.** strictly accurate, correct, or precise. —*v.t.* **2.** to call for, demand, or require. **3.** to force the payment, yielding, or performance of. —**ex·ac/tion,** *n.* —**ex·act/ly,** *adv.* —**ex·act/ness,** *n.*

ex·act/ing *adj.* **1.** severe in making demands or setting requirements. **2.** requiring close application and attention. —**ex·act/ing·ly,** *adv.*

ex·ag·ger·ate (ig zaj/ə rāt/), *v.t., v.i.,* **-at·ed, -at·ing.** to magnify beyond the limits of truth; overstate or overemphasize. —**ex·ag/ger·at/ed·ly,** *adv.* —**ex·ag/ger·a/tion,** *n.* —**ex·ag/ger·a/tor,** *n.*

ex·alt (ig zôlt/), *v.t.* **1.** to raise in rank, power, etc.; elevate. **2.** to praise; extol. —**ex/al·ta/tion,** *n.*

ex·am (ig zam/), *n. Informal.* an examination.

ex·am/ine (-in), *v.t.,* **-ined, -in·ing.** **1.** to inspect or scrutinize carefully. **2.** to test the knowledge or qualifications of (a pupil, witness, etc.), as by questions. —**ex·am/i·na/tion,** *n.* —**ex·am/in·er,** *n.*

ex·am·ple (ig zam/pəl, -zäm/-), *n.* **1.** one of a number of things taken to show the character of the whole. **2.** a pattern or model to be imitated or avoided. **3.** an instance illustrating a rule or method.

ex·as·per·ate (ig zas/pə rāt/), *v.t.,* **-at·ed, -at·ing.** to irritate or provoke to a high degree. —**ex·as/per·a/tion,** *n.*

ex·ceed (ik sēd/), *v.t.* **1.** to go beyond the bounds or limits of. **2.** to be superior to; surpass.

ex·ceed/ing·ly *adv.* to an unusual degree; extremely.

ex·cel (ik sel/), *v.i., v.t.,* **-celled, -cel·ling.** to be superior (to); surpass (others).

Ex·cel·len·cy (ek/sə lən sē), *n., pl.* **-cies.** a title of honor given to certain high officials, as bishops and archbishops.

ex/cel·lent *adj.* remarkably good; first-rate. —**ex/cel·lence,** *n.* —**ex/cel·lent·ly,** *adv.*

ex·cept¹ (ik sept/), *prep.* **1.** with the exclusion of; but. —*conj.* **2.** with the exception that; only.

ex·cept² (ik sept/), *v.t.* **1.** to leave out; exclude. —*v.i.* **2.** to object.

ex·cep/tion *n.* **1.** the act of excepting or fact of being excepted. **2.** something excluded from a general rule or class. **3.** an objection. —*Idiom.* **4. take exception, a.** to object. **b.** to take offense.

ex·cep/tion·a·ble *adj.* liable to exception.

ex·cep/tion·al *adj.* **1.** being an exception; unusual, esp. superior. **2.** needing special schooling, as because of a mental handicap. —**ex·cep/tion·al·ly,** *adv.*

ex·cerpt (*n.* ek/sûrpt; *v.* ik sûrpt/, ek/sûrpt), *n.* **1.** a passage or quotation taken or selected, as from a book. —*v.t.* **2.** to take or select (an excerpt) from.

ex·cess (ik ses/, ek/ses), *n.* **1.** the amount or degree by which one thing exceeds another. **2.** a superabundance or surplus. **3.** immoderate indulgence, as in eating. —*adj.* **4.** being more than what is necessary, usual, or specified; extra.

ex·ces/sive *adj.* exceeding the usual, necessary, or proper limit or degree. —**ex·ces/sive·ly,** *adv.*

ex·change (iks chānj/), *v.,* **-changed, -chang·ing,** *n.* —*v.t.* **1.** to give up (something) for an equivalent or substitute; trade. **2.** to give and receive reciprocally; interchange. —*n.* **3.** an act or instance of exchanging. **4.** something exchanged. **5.** a place where commodities, securities, or services are exchanged. **6.** a central office or station: *a telephone exchange.* **7.** the reciprocal transfer of equivalent sums of money, esp. in the currencies of two different countries. —**ex·change/a·ble,** *adj.*

ex·cheq·uer (eks/chek ər, iks chek/ər), *n.* **1.** a treasury, as of a nation. **2.** (*often cap.*) the British governmental department in charge of the public revenues. **3.** *Informal.* financial resources; funds.

ex·cise¹ (ek/sīz, -sīs), *n.* a tax on the manufacture, sale, or consumption of certain commodities, as liquor or tobacco, within a country.

ex·cise² (ik sīz/), *v.t.,* **-cised, -cis·ing.** to remove by cutting out or off. —**ex·ci/sion** (-sizh/ən), *n.*

ex·cite (ik sīt/), *v.t.,* **-cit·ed, -cit·ing.** **1.** to stir up the emotions or feelings of; arouse. **2.** to arouse (emotions or feelings); awaken. **3.** to stir to action; stimulate. —**ex·cit/a·ble,** *adj.* —**ex·ci·ta·tion** (ek/sī tā/shən), *n.* —**ex·cit/ed·ly,** *adv.* —**ex·cit/er,** *n.* —**ex·cit/ing,** *adj.*

ex·claim (ik sklām/), *v.i., v.t.* to cry out or say suddenly and vehemently, as in surprise. —**ex·cla-**

general

ma•tion (ek′sklə mā′shən), *n.* —**ex•clam•a•to•ry** (ik sklam′ə tôr′ē), *adj.*

ex•clude (ik sklōōd′), *v.t.,* -**clud•ed,** -**clud•ing. 1.** to prevent the entrance of. **2.** to shut out, as from consideration. **3.** to expel; eject. —**ex•clu′sion** (-zhən), *n.*

ex•clu•sive (ik sklōō′siv, -ziv), *adj.* **1.** excluding others, as from a part or share. **2.** expensive or fashionable. **3.** single or sole. **4.** resistant to the admission of outsiders, as to membership, association, or intimacy. **5.** not divided; entire: *paid exclusive attention to business.* —**ex•clu′sive•ly,** *adv.* —**ex•clu′sive•ness, ex•clu•siv•i•ty** (eks′klōō siv′i tē), *n.*

ex•com•mu•ni•cate (eks′kə myōō′ni kāt′), *v.t.,* -**cat•ed,** -**cat•ing.** to cut off from communion or membership, esp. from the sacraments of a church. —**ex′com•mu′ni•ca′tion,** *n.*

ex•co•ri•ate (ik skôr′ē āt′), *v.t.,* -**at•ed,** -**at•ing. 1.** to denounce or berate severely. **2.** to strip off or remove the skin of. —**ex•co′ri•a′tion,** *n.*

ex•cre•ment (ek′skrə mənt), *n.* waste matter, esp. feces, discharged from the body. —**ex′cre•men′tal** (-men′tl), *adj.*

ex•cres•cence (ik skres′əns), *n.* an abnormal outgrowth or addition. —**ex•cres′cent,** *adj.*

ex•crete (ik skrēt′), *v.t.,* -**cret•ed,** -**cret•ing.** to separate and eliminate (waste) from the body. —**ex•cre′tion,** *n.* —**ex•cre•to•ry** (ek′skri tôr′ē), *adj.*

ex•cru•ci•at•ing (ik skrōō′shē ā′ting), *adj.* **1.** causing intense suffering. **2.** intense or extreme. —**ex•cru′ci•at′ing•ly,** *adv.*

ex•cul•pate (ek′skul pāt′, ik skul′pāt), *v.t.,* -**pat•ed,** -**pat•ing.** to clear from a charge of guilt or fault; free from blame. —**ex′cul•pa′tion,** *n.*

ex•cur•sion (ik skûr′zhən), *n.* **1.** a short trip; outing. **2.** a trip, as on a train, at a reduced rate. **3.** a deviation or digression. —**ex•cur′sion•ist,** *n.*

ex•cuse (*v.* ik skyōōz′; *n.* -skyōōs′), *v.,* -**cused, -cus•ing,** *n.* —*v.t.* **1.** to pardon or forgive. **2.** to offer or serve as an apology for. **3.** to release from an obligation or duty. **4.** to allow to leave. —*n.* **5.** an explanation offered as a reason for being excused. **6.** a reason for excusing or being excused. **7.** an inferior specimen: *a poor excuse for a poem.* —**ex•cus′a•ble** (-skyōō′zə-), *adj.*

ex•e•crate (ek′si krāt′), *v.t.,* -**crat•ed,** -**crat•ing. 1.** to detest utterly as being evil or abhorrent. **2.** to denounce. —**ex′e•cra′tion,** *n.*

ex•e•cute (ek′si kyōōt′), *v.t.,* -**cut•ed,** -**cut•ing. 1.** to carry out; accomplish. **2.** to perform or do. **3.** to put to death according to law. **4.** to produce in accordance with a plan or design. **5.** to give validity to (a legal instrument) by fulfilling requirements. **6.** to run (a computer program) or process (a command). —**ex′e•cu′tion,** *n.*

ex•ec•u•tive (ig zek′yə tiv), *n.* **1.** a person or group having administrative or managerial authority in an organization. **2.** the executive branch of a government. —*adj.* **3.** of or suited for carrying out plans, duties, or policies. **4.** of or charged with the administration of laws or public affairs.

ex•ec′u•tor (-tər), *n.* a person named in a will to carry out its provisions.

ex•em•plar (ig zem′plər, -plär), *n.* **1.** a model or pattern to be copied or imitated. **2.** a typical example or instance.

ex•em′pla•ry (-plə rē), *adj.* **1.** worthy of imitation; commendable. **2.** serving as a model or pattern.

ex•em′pli•fy′ (-plə fī′), *v.t.,* -**fied, -fy•ing. 1.** to illustrate by example. **2.** to serve as an example of; typify. —**ex•em′pli•fi•ca′tion,** *n.*

ex•empt (ig zempt′), *v.t.* **1.** to free from an obligation or liability to which others are subject. —*adj.* **2.** released from or not subject to an obligation or liability. —**ex•emp′tion,** *n.*

ex•er•cise (ek′sər sīz′), *n., v.,* -**cised, -cis•ing.** —*n.* **1.** bodily or mental exertion, esp. for the sake of training. **2.** something done for practice or training. **3.** a putting into action, use, or effect: *the exercise of caution.* **4.** Often, -**cises.** a traditional ceremony: *graduation exercises.* —*v.t.* **5.** to put through exercises. **6.** to put into action or use. **7.** to make

uneasy; worry or annoy. —*v.i.* **8.** to take bodily exercise. —**ex′er•cis′er,** *n.*

ex•ert (ig zûrt′), *v.t.* **1.** to put forth: *to exert strength.* **2.** to put in force or operation: *exerted pressure on his father.* **3.** to put (oneself) into vigorous action or effort. —**ex•er′tion,** *n.*

ex•hale (eks hāl′), *v.i., v.t.,* -**haled, -hal•ing. 1.** to breathe out. **2.** to pass or give off as vapor. —**ex′ha•la′tion** (-hə lā′shən), *n.*

ex•haust (ig zôst′), *v.t.* **1.** to drain of strength or energy; wear out. **2.** to use up completely; consume. **3.** to treat or study (a subject) thoroughly. **4.** to draw out or drain off completely. —*n.* **5. a.** the escape of steam or gases from an engine. **b.** the steam or gases ejected. **6.** the parts of an engine through which exhaust is ejected. —**ex•haust′i•ble,** *adj.* —**ex•haus′tion,** *n.*

ex•haus′tive *adj.* exhausting a subject; comprehensive.

ex•hib•it (ig zib′it), *v.t.* **1.** to offer or expose to view; display. **2.** to submit (a document, object, etc.) as evidence in a court. —*v.i.* **3.** to present something, as art, to public view. —*n.* **4.** an act or instance of exhibiting. **5.** something exhibited. **6.** a document or object exhibited as evidence. —**ex•hi•bi•tion** (ek′sə bish′ən), *n.* —**ex•hib′i•tor,** *n.*

ex′hi•bi′tion•ism *n.* a tendency to call attention to oneself, esp. by exhibiting the genitals. —**ex′hi•bi′tion•ist,** *n., adj.*

ex•hil•a•rate (ig zil′ə rāt′), *v.t.,* -**rat•ed, -rat•ing. 1.** to enliven; invigorate. **2.** to make cheerful. —**ex•hil′a•ra′tion,** *n.*

ex•hort (ig zôrt′), *v.t., v.i.* to urge, advise, or caution earnestly; admonish urgently. —**ex•hor•ta•tion** (eg′zôr tā′shən, ek′sôr-), *n.*

ex•hume (ig zōōm′, -zyōōm′, eks hyōōm′), *v.t.,* -**humed, -hum•ing. 1.** to remove from the earth; disinter. **2.** to revive or restore. —**ex•hu•ma•tion** (eks′hyōō mā′shən), *n.*

ex•i•gen•cy (ek′si jən sē), *n., pl.* -**cies. 1.** a state of urgency. **2.** Usu., -**cies.** something needed, demanded, or required in a specific circumstance. **3.** an emergency. —**ex′i•gent,** *adj.*

ex•ile (eg′zīl, ek′sīl), *n., v.,* -**iled, -il•ing.** —*n.* **1. a.** expulsion from one's native land; banishment. **b.** the fact or state of such expulsion. **2.** a person banished or separated from his or her native land. —*v.t.* **3.** to expel (a person) from his or her country; banish.

ex•ist (ig zist′), *v.i.* **1.** to have being; be. **2.** to have life; live. **3.** to continue to be or live. —**ex•ist′ence,** *n.* —**ex•ist′ent,** *adj.*

ex•is•ten•tial (eg′zi sten′shəl, ek′si-), *adj.* **1.** of existence. **2.** of existentialism. —**ex′is•ten′tial•ly,** *adv.*

ex′is•ten′tial•ism *n.* a philosophy that stresses self-determination and responsibility for one's actions. —**ex′is•ten′tial•ist,** *n., adj.*

ex•it (eg′zit, ek′sit), *n.* **1.** a way or passage out. **2.** a going out or away. **3.** a departure of an actor from the stage. —*v.i., v.t.* **4.** to leave. [< L *exitus* act or means of going out]

exo- a combining form meaning outside or outer (*exosphere*).

ex•o•crine (ek′sə krin, -krīn′), *adj.* **1.** of an exocrine gland or its secretion. —*n.* **2.** EXOCRINE GLAND.

ex′ocrine gland′ *n.* a gland, as a salivary gland, that secretes externally through a duct.

ex•o•dus (ek′sə dəs), *n.* **1.** a mass departure or emigration. **2.** (*cap.*) the departure of the Israelites from Egypt under Moses. **3.** (*cap.*) the second book of the Old Testament.

ex of•fi•ci•o (eks′ ə fish′ē ō′), *adv., adj.* by virtue of office or official position. [< L]

ex•on•er•ate (ig zon′ə rāt′), *v.t.,* -**at•ed, -at•ing.** to clear from accusation, guilt, or blame. —**ex•on′er•a′tion,** *n.* —**ex•on′er•a′tor,** *n.*

ex•or•bi•tant (ig zôr′bi tənt), *adj.* exceeding the bounds of custom, propriety, or reason. —**ex•or′bi•tance,** *n.* —**ex•or′bi•tant•ly,** *adv.*

ex•or•cise (ek′sôr sīz′, -sər-), *v.t.,* -**cised, -cis•ing. 1.** to seek to expel (an evil spirit) by religious or solemn ceremonies. **2.** to free of evil spirits. —**ex′-or•cism** (-siz′əm), n. —**ex′or•cist,** n.

ex•o•sphere (ek′sō sfēr′), n. the highest region of the atmosphere.

ex•ot•ic (ig zot′ik), adj. **1.** not native; foreign. **2.** strikingly unusual or strange, as in appearance. —**ex•ot′i•cal•ly,** adv.

ex•pand (ik spand′), v.t., v.i. **1.** to increase in extent, size, scope, or volume. **2.** to stretch out; spread. **3.** to express (something) in fuller form or in greater detail. —**ex•pand′a•ble, ex•pand′i•ble,** adj. —**ex•pan′sion,** n.

ex•panse (ik spans′), n. a broad, unbroken space or area.

ex•pan′sive (-siv), adj. **1.** wide; extensive. **2.** cordial and open. **3.** tending to expand. **4.** causing expansion. —**ex•pan′sive•ly,** adv. —**ex•pan′sive•ness,** n.

ex•pa•ti•ate (ik spā′shē āt′), v.i., -at•ed, -at•ing. to elaborate in discourse or writing. —**ex•pa′ti•a′tion,** n.

ex•pa•tri•ate (v. eks pā′trē āt′; esp. Brit. -pa′trē-; n. -it, -āt′), v., -at•ed, -at•ing, n. —v.t., v.i. **1.** to send into or become an exile. —n. **2.** an expatriated person. —**ex•pa′tri•a′tion,** n.

ex•pect (ik spekt′), v.t. **1.** to anticipate the occurrence or coming of. **2.** to consider as due or justified. **3.** Informal. to suppose; surmise. —**Idiom. 4.** be expecting, to be pregnant. —**ex•pect′an•cy,** n. —**ex•pect′ant,** adj. —**ex•pec•ta′tion** (ek′spek tā′shən), n.

ex•pec′to•rate′ (-rāt′), v.i., v.t., -rat•ed, -rat•ing. to spit. —**ex•pec′to•ra′tion,** n.

ex•pe•di•ent (ik spē′dē ənt), adj. **1.** fit or suitable for a purpose. **2.** governed or marked by self-interest. —n. **3.** a handy means to an end. —**ex•pe′di•en•cy,** n. —**ex•pe′di•ent•ly,** adv.

ex•pe•dite (ek′spi dīt′), v.t., -dit•ed, -dit•ing. **1.** to speed up the progress of. **2.** to perform promptly. —**ex′pe•dit′er, ex′pe•di′tor,** n.

ex•pe•di•tion (ek′spi dish′ən), n. **1. a.** a journey made for a specific purpose. **b.** the group engaged in such an activity. **2.** promptness. —**ex′pe•di′tion•ar′y,** adj.

ex′pe•di′tious adj. characterized by promptness. —**ex′pe•di′tious•ly,** adv. —**ex′pe•di′tious•ness,** n.

ex•pel (ik spel′), v.t., -pelled, -pel•ling. to drive or force out or away; eject.

ex•pend (ik spend′), v.t. **1.** to use up. **2.** to pay out; spend. —**ex•pend′er,** n.

ex•pend′a•ble adj. **1.** capable of being expended. **2.** consumed in use. **3.** capable of being sacrificed in case of need.

ex•pense (ik spens′), n. **1.** cost; charge. **2.** a cause of spending. **3.** expenses, charges incurred in connection with business. —**Idiom. 4.** at the expense of, at the sacrifice or to the detriment of.

ex•pen′sive adj. entailing great expense; costly. —**ex•pen′sive•ly,** adv.

ex•pe•ri•ence (ik spēr′ē əns), n., v., -enced, -enc•ing. —n. **1.** something personally lived through or encountered. **2.** the observing, encountering, or undergoing of events as they occur in the course of time. **3.** knowledge or practical wisdom gained from this process. —v.t. **4.** to have experience of.

ex•pe′ri•enced adj. wise or skillful through experience.

ex•per•i•ment (n. ik sper′ə mənt; v. -ment′), n., v. **1.** a test for the purpose of discovering something unknown or of testing a principle, supposition, or theory. —v.i. **2.** to conduct an experiment. —**ex•per′i•men′tal,** adj. —**ex•per′i•men′tal•ly,** adv. —**ex•per′i•men•ta′tion,** n. —**ex•per′i•ment′er,** n.

ex•pert (ek′spûrt; adj. also ik spûrt′), n. **1.** a person with special skill or knowledge in a particular field. —adj. **2.** possessing or showing special skill or knowledge. —**ex•pert′ly,** adv. —**ex•pert′ness,** n.

ex•per•tise (ek′spər tēz′), n. expert skill or knowledge.

ex•pi•ate′ (ek′spē āt′), v.t., -at•ed, -at•ing. to make amends for. —**ex′pi•a′tion,** n. —**ex′pi•a′tor,** n. —**ex′pi•a•to′ry** (-ə tôr′ē), adj.

ex•pire (ik spīr′), v.i., -pired, -pir•ing. **1.** to come

to an end. **2.** to die. **3.** to breathe out. —**ex•pi•ra•tion** (ek′spə rā′shən), n.

ex•plain (ik splān′), v.t. **1.** to make clear or intelligible. **2.** to make known the cause of or reason for. —v.i. **3.** to give an explanation. —**ex•plain′a•ble,** adj. —**ex•plain′er,** n.

ex•pla•na•tion (ek′splə nā′shən), n. **1.** the act or process of explaining. **2.** something that explains. —**ex•plan′a•to′ry,** adj.

ex•ple•tive (ek′spli tiv), n. an often profane exclamation.

ex′pli•cate′ (-kāt′), v.t., -cat•ed, -cat•ing. to explain in detail. —**ex′pli•ca′tion,** n. —**ex′pli•ca′tor,** n.

ex•plic•it (ik splis′it), adj. fully and clearly expressed. —**ex•plic′it•ly,** adv. —**ex•plic′it•ness,** n.

ex•plode (ik splōd′), v., -plod•ed, -plod•ing. —v.i. **1.** to burst suddenly, noisily, and violently, as from rapid chemical change or from internal pressure. **2.** to burst forth energetically; erupt. —v.t. **3.** to cause to explode. **4.** to discredit; disprove. —**ex•plod′er,** n. —**ex•plo′sion,** n. —**ex•plo′sive,** adj., n.

ex•ploit¹ (ek′sploit, ik sploit′), n. a striking or notable deed; feat.

ex•ploit² (ik sploit′), v.t. **1.** to utilize, esp. for profit. **2.** to take advantage of. **3.** to use selfishly for one's own ends. —**ex•ploi•ta•tion** (ek′sploi tā′shən), n. —**ex•ploit′a•tive, ex•ploit′er,** n.

ex•plore (ik splôr′), v., -plored, -plor•ing. —v.t. **1.** to range over (an area) for the purpose of discovery. **2.** to look into closely; investigate or examine. —v.i. **3.** to engage in exploring. —**ex•plo•ra•tion** (ek′splə rā′shən), n. —**ex•plor′a•to′ry,** adj. —**ex•plor′er,** n.

ex•po•nent (ik spō′nənt or, esp. for 3, ek′spō-nənt), n. **1.** a person or thing that expounds or interprets. **2.** a representative, advocate, or symbol. **3.** Math. a symbol placed above and after another to denote the power to which the latter is to be raised. —**ex•po•nen′tial** (ek′spə nen′shəl), adj. —**ex′po•nen′tial•ly,** adv.

ex•port (v. ik spôrt′, ek′spôrt; n. ek′spôrt), v.t. **1.** to ship or transmit abroad. **2.** to save (electronic documents, data, etc.) in a format usable by another application program. —n. **3.** the act of exporting. **4.** something exported. —**ex′por•ta′tion,** n. —**ex•port′er,** n.

ex•pose (ik spōz′), v.t., -posed, -pos•ing. **1.** to lay open, as to danger. **2.** to uncover; bare. **3.** to present to view; exhibit. **4.** to make known; reveal. **5.** to subject to an influence or action. —**ex•po′sure,** n.

ex•po•sé (ek′spō zā′), n., pl. -sés. a public revelation of something discreditable.

ex•po•si•tion (ek′spə zish′ən), n. **1.** a large-scale public exhibition. **2.** the act of expounding or explaining. **3.** a statement of explanation; explanatory treatise.

ex•pos•i•to•ry (ik spoz′i tôr′ē), adj. serving to expound or explain.

ex post fac•to (eks′ pōst′ fak′tō), adj. made or done after the fact; retroactive. [< L: from a thing done afterward]

ex•pos•tu•late (ik spos′chə lāt′), v.i., -lat•ed, -lat•ing. to reason earnestly with someone by way of warning or rebuke. —**ex•pos′tu•la′tion,** n.

ex•pound (ik spound′), v.t. **1.** to set forth in detail; state. **2.** to explain; interpret. —v.i. **3.** to make a detailed statement. —**ex•pound′er,** n.

ex•press (ik spres′), v.t. **1.** to put into words. **2.** to show; reveal. **3.** to represent by a symbol. **4.** to send by express. **5.** to squeeze out. —adj. **6.** clearly stated; explicit. **7.** specific; particular: an express purpose. **8.** moving fast, esp. with few or no stops: an express train. —n. **9.** an express vehicle. **10.** a system for the rapid delivery of freight, parcels, and mail. —adv. **11.** by express. —**ex•press′i•ble,** adj. —**ex•pres′sion,** n. —**ex•pres′sive,** adj. —**ex•press′ly,** adv.

ex•press′way′ n. a divided highway for high-speed traffic, having few if any intersections.

ex•pro•pri•ate (eks prō′prē āt′), v.t., -at•ed, -at•ing. **1.** to take possession of, esp. for public use. **2.**

to dispossess (a person) of ownership. —**ex•pro′-pri•a′tion,** *n.* —**ex•pro′pri•a′tor,** *n.*

ex•pul•sion (ik spul′shən), *n.* **1.** the act of expelling. **2.** the state of being expelled.

ex•punge (ik spunj′), *v.t.,* **-punged, -pung•ing.** to strike or blot out; obliterate or erase.

ex•pur•gate (ek′spər gāt′), *v.t.,* **-gat•ed, -gat•ing.** to amend by removing words or passages deemed objectionable. —**ex′pur•ga′tion,** *n.*

ex•quis•ite (ik skwiz′it, ek′skwi zit), *adj.* **1.** of special beauty, charm, delicacy, or excellence. **2.** intense; acute. **3.** keenly sensitive or responsive. **4.** of particular refinement. —**ex•quis′ite•ly,** *adv.* —**ex•quis′ite•ness,** *n.*

ex•tant (ek′stənt, ik stant′), *adj.* still existing; not destroyed or lost.

ex•tem•po•ra•ne•ous (ik stem′pə rā′nē əs), *adj.* done, spoken, or performed without preparation; impromptu: *an extemporaneous speech.* —**ex•tem′po•ra′ne•ous•ly,** *adv.* —**ex•tem′po•ra′ne•ous•ness,** ex•tem′po•ra•ne′i•ty (-rə nē′i tē), *n.*

ex•tend (ik stend′), *v.t.* **1.** to stretch or draw out or outward. **2.** to hold out; offer. **3.** to make longer; prolong. **4.** to enlarge, as in scope. **5.** to exert (oneself) to an unusual degree. —*v.i.* **6.** to stretch out; reach. —**ex•tend′er,** *n.* —**ex•tend′i•ble, ex•tend′a•ble, ex•ten′si•ble,** *adj.* —**ex•ten′sion,** *n.*

extend′ed fam′ily *n.* a kinship group consisting of a married couple, their children, and close relatives.

ex•ten′sive (-siv), *adj.* of great extent; broad or thorough. —**ex•ten′sive•ly,** *adv.* —**ex•ten′sive•ness,** *n.*

ex•tent (ik stent′), *n.* **1.** the space or degree to which a thing extends. **2.** something having extension.

ex•ten•u•ate (ik sten′yōō āt′), *v.t.,* **-at•ed, -at•ing.** to make seem less serious, esp. by offering excuses. —**ex•ten′u•a′tion,** *n.*

ex•te•ri•or (ik stēr′ē ər), *adj.* **1.** being on the outer side or the outside. **2.** intended or suitable for outdoor use. —*n.* **3.** an exterior surface or part.

ex•ter•nal (ik stûr′nl), *adj.* **1.** pertaining to or being on the outside or outer part. **2.** acting or coming from without. **3.** pertaining merely to outward appearance; superficial. **4.** pertaining to foreign countries. —*n.* **5. externals,** external features. —**ex•ter′nal•ly,** *adv.*

ex•tinct (ik stingkt′), *adj.* **1.** no longer in existence. **2.** no longer in use. **3.** no longer burning; extinguished. **4.** no longer active. —**ex•tinc′tion,** *n.*

ex•tin•guish (ik sting′gwish), *v.t.* **1.** to cause to stop burning; put out. **2.** to bring to an end; wipe out. —**ex•tin′guish•a•ble,** *adj.* —**ex•tin′guish•er,** *n.*

ex•tir•pate (ek′stər pāt′), *v.t.,* **-pat•ed, -pat•ing. 1.** to destroy totally. **2.** to pull up by or as if by the roots. —**ex′tir•pa′tion,** *n.*

ex•tol or **-toll** (ik stōl′, -stol′), *v.t.,* **-tolled, -tol•ling.** to praise highly; laud. —**ex•tol′ler,** *n.*

ex•tort (ik stôrt′), *v.t.* to obtain (money, information, etc.) by force, intimidation, or abuse of authority. —**ex•tor′tion,** *n.* —**ex•tor′tion•ist,** *n.*

ex•tor•tion•ate (ik stôr′shə nit), *adj.* excessive; exorbitant.

ex•tra (ek′strə), *adj., n., pl.* **-tras,** *adv.* —*adj.* **1.** being more or better than what is usual, expected, or necessary; additional or superior. —*n.* **2.** an additional feature. **3.** an additional expense or charge. **4.** a special edition of a newspaper. **5.** an additional worker, esp. a performer hired to appear in the background action of a film. —*adv.* **6.** in excess of what is usual.

extra- a prefix meaning outside or beyond (*extrasensory*).

ex•tract (*v.* ik strakt′; *n.* ek′strakt), *v.t.* **1.** to pull or draw out, usu. with effort. **2.** to take or copy out (an excerpt), as from a book. **3.** to separate or obtain by pressure, distillation, or treatment with solvents. —*n.* **4.** something extracted. **5.** an excerpt. **6.** a concentrate, as of a food, plant, or drug: *vanilla extract.* —**ex•trac′tion,** *n.* —**ex•trac′tor,** *n.*

ex•tra•cur•ric•u•lar (ek′strə kə rik′yə lər), *adj.* outside a regular curriculum.

ex•tra•dite (ek′strə dīt′), *v.t.,* **-dit•ed, -dit•ing.** to surrender (an alleged fugitive or criminal) to another jurisdiction. —**ex′tra•di′tion** (-dish′ən), *n.*

ex′tra•le′gal *adj.* beyond the authority of law.

ex′tra•mu′ral (-myŏŏr′əl), *adj.* involving representatives of more than one school.

ex•tra•ne•ous (ik strā′nē əs), *adj.* **1.** coming from without. **2.** not essential or pertinent. —**ex•tra′ne•ous•ly,** *adv.*

ex•traor•di•nar•y (ik strôr′dn er′ē, ek′strə ôr′-), *adj.* being beyond what is usual; exceptional or remarkable. —**ex•traor′di•nar′i•ly,** *adv.*

ex•trap•o•late (ik strap′ə lāt′), *v.t., v.i.,* **-lat•ed, -lat•ing.** to infer (an unknown) from something that is known. —**ex•trap′o•la′tion,** *n.* —**ex•trap′o•la′tor,** *n.*

ex•tra•sen•so•ry (ek′strə sen′sə rē), *adj.* outside one's normal sense perception.

ex′tra•ter•res′tri•al *adj.* **1.** existing or originating outside the limits of the earth. —*n.* **2.** an extraterrestrial being.

ex•trav•a•gant (ik strav′ə gənt), *adj.* **1.** spending much more than is necessary or wise. **2.** exceeding the bounds of reason or moderation; excessive. —**ex•trav′a•gance,** *n.* —**ex•trav′a•gant•ly,** *adv.*

ex•trav•a•gan•za (-gan′zə), *n., pl.* **-zas.** a lavish or opulent production or entertainment.

ex•treme (ik strēm′), *adj.,* **-trem•er, -trem•est,** *n.* —*adj.* **1.** going well beyond the ordinary or average. **2.** farthest from the center. **3.** utmost. **4.** immoderate; radical. **5.** last; final. **6.** (esp. of a sport) very dangerous or difficult. —*n.* **7.** one of two things as different from each other as possible. **8.** an extreme degree, act, measure, or condition. **9.** *Math.* the first or the last term, as of a proportion. —**ex•treme′ly,** *adv.* —**ex•treme′ness,** *n.*

ex•trem′ism *n.* a tendency to go to extremes, esp. in politics. —**ex•trem′ist,** *n., adj.*

ex•trem•i•ty (ik strem′i tē), *n., pl.* **-ties. 1.** the extreme or terminal point or part. **2.** a limb of the body, esp. a hand or foot. **3.** a condition of extreme need or danger. **4.** an utmost degree. **5.** a drastic measure or effort.

ex•tri•cate (ek′stri kāt′), *v.t.,* **-cat•ed, -cat•ing.** to free from entanglement; disengage. —**ex′tri•ca•ble,** *adj.* —**ex′tri•ca′tion,** *n.*

ex•trin•sic (ik strin′sik, -zik), *adj.* **1.** not essential or inherent; extraneous. **2.** being or coming from without; external. —**ex•trin′si•cal•ly,** *adv.*

ex•tro•vert (ek′strə vûrt′), *n.* an outgoing person who is concerned more with the physical and social environment than with the self. —**ex′tro•ver′sion** (-vûr′zhən), *n.* —**ex′tro•vert′ed,** *adj.*

ex•trude (ik strōōd′), *v.t.,* **-trud•ed, -trud•ing. 1.** to force or press out. **2.** to shape (metal, plastic, etc.) by forcing through a die. —**ex•tru′sion** (-zhən), *n.* —**ex•tru′sive** (-siv), *adj.*

ex•u•ber•ant (ig zōō′bər ənt), *adj.* **1.** uninhibitedly enthusiastic. **2.** profuse, as in growth; abundant. —**ex•u′ber•ance,** *n.* —**ex•u′ber•ant•ly,** *adv.*

ex•ude (ig zōōd′, ik sōōd′), *v.i., v.t.,* **-ud•ed, -ud•ing. 1.** to ooze or cause to ooze out. **2.** to project abundantly; radiate. —**ex•u•da•tion** (eks′yōō dā′shən), *n.*

ex•ult (ig zult′), *v.i.* to show or feel triumphant joy. —**ex•ult′ant,** *adj.* —**ex•ul•ta•tion** (eg′zul tā′shən, ek′sul-), *n.* —**ex•ult′ing•ly,** *adv.*

eye (ī), *n., v.,* **eyed, ey•ing** or **eye•ing.** —*n.* **1.** the organ of sight, in vertebrates one of a pair of spherical bodies in an orbit of the skull. **2.** sight; vision. **3.** appreciative or discriminating visual perception. **4.** a look, glance, or gaze. **5.** an attentive look; observation. **6.** judgment; opinion: *in the eyes of the law.* **7.** something suggesting an eye, as the bud of a potato or the hole in a needle. —*v.t.* **8.** to look at; view. —*Idiom.* **9. have an eye for,** to be discerning about. **10. keep one's eyes open,** to be alert or observant. **11. see eye to eye,** to agree. —**eyed,** *adj.* —**eye′less,** *adj.* —**ey′er,** *n.*

eye′ball′ *n.* **1.** the globe of the eye. —*v.t.* **2.** *Informal.* to examine closely.

eye′brow′ *n.* **1.** the bony arch or ridge forming

the upper part of the orbit of the eye. **2.** the fringe of hair growing on the eyebrow.

eye•ful (ī′fŏol), *n., pl.* **-fuls. 1.** a thorough view. **2.** *Informal.* a very good-looking person.

eye′glass′es *n.pl.* a pair of corrective lenses in a frame.

eye′lash′ *n.* one of the short hairs growing on the edge of an eyelid.

eye•let (ī′lit), *n.* **1.** a small hole for the passage of a cord or lace or for decoration. **2.** a metal ring for lining a small hole.

eye•lid′ *n.* the movable lid of skin that covers and uncovers the eyeball.

eye′lin′er *n.* a cosmetic applied in a line along the eyelids to accentuate the eyes.

eye′o′pen•er *n.* an experience or disclosure that provides sudden enlightenment. —**eye′o′pen•ing,** *adj.*

eye′sore′ *n.* something unpleasant to look at.

eye′tooth′ *n., pl.* **-teeth.** a canine tooth of the upper jaw.

eye′wash′ *n.* **1.** a soothing solution for the eye. **2.** nonsense; bunk.

eye′wit′ness *n.* a person who has actually seen an act or occurrence and can give a firsthand account of it.

ey•rie or **-ry** (âr′ē, ēr′ē), *n., pl.* **-ries.** AERIE.

F

a b c d e **F** g h i j k l m n o p q r s t u v w x y z

F, f (ef), *n., pl.* **Fs** or **F's, fs** or **f's.** the sixth letter of the English alphabet, a consonant.

F 1. female. **2.** franc. **3.** French.

F *Symbol.* **1.** the sixth in order or in a series. **2.** a grade indicating academic work of the lowest quality. **3.** the fourth note of the C major scale. **4.** Fahrenheit. **5.** *Chem.* fluorine. **6.** *Physics.* **a.** force. **b.** frequency.

f *Symbol.* focal length.

F. 1. Fahrenheit. **2.** February. **3.** franc. **4.** France. **5.** French. **6.** Friday.

f. 1. feet. **2.** female. **3.** feminine. **4.** folio. **5.** following. **6.** foot. **7.** franc.

FAA Federal Aviation Administration.

fa•ble (fā′bəl), *n.* **1.** a short tale used to teach a moral, often with animals as characters. **2.** a story not founded on fact. **3.** a lie; falsehood.

fab•ric (fab′rik), *n.* **1.** a cloth made by weaving, knitting, or felting fibers. **2.** framework; structure.

fab′ri•cate′ (-ri kāt′), *v.t.,* **-cat•ed, -cat•ing. 1.** to construct, esp. by assembling parts or sections; make. **2.** to invent; make up. —**fab′ri•ca′tion,** *n.* —**fab′ri•ca′tor,** *n.*

fab•u•lous (fab′yə ləs), *adj.* **1.** almost impossible to believe; incredible. **2.** exceptionally good; marvelous. **3.** told about or known through fables. —**fab′u•lous•ly,** *adv.*

fa•cade or **-çade** (fə säd′, fa-), *n.* **1.** the front of a building, esp. an imposing or decorative one. **2.** a superficial appearance; illusion.

face (fās), *n., v.,* **faced, fac•ing.** —*n.* **1.** the front part of the head. **2.** a look or expression on the face. **3.** a grimace: *to make a face.* **4.** impudence; boldness. **5.** outward appearance. **6.** good reputation; prestige: *to lose face.* **7.** the surface of something: *the face of the earth.* **8.** the side upon which the use of a thing depends: *the face of a watch.* **9.** the most important or most frequently seen side; front. —*v.t.* **10.** to look toward. **11.** to have the front toward. **12.** to confront directly, courageously, or impudently. **13.** to cover with a different material in front. **14.** to finish the edge of (a garment) with facing. —*v.i.* **15.** to turn or be turned: *She faced toward the sea.* **16.** to be placed with the front in a certain direction: *The barn faces south.* **17. face up to, a.** to admit. **b.** to meet courageously. —*Idiom.* **18. face to face, a.** opposite one another; facing. **b.** confronting one another. **19. in the face of,** in the presence of. **20. to one's face,** in one's very presence. —**faced,** *adj.* —**fa′cial** (fā′shəl), *adj., n.*

face′less *adj.* lacking distinction or identity.

face′-lift′ or **face/lift′,** *n.* **1.** plastic surgery to eliminate facial sagging and wrinkles. **2.** a renovation, as of a building.

face′-sav′ing *adj.* serving to save one's prestige or dignity.

fac•et (fas′it), *n., v.,* **-et•ed, -et•ing** or (*esp. Brit.*) **-et•ted, -et•ting.** —*n.* **1.** one of the small polished plane surfaces of a cut gem. **2.** an aspect; phase. —*v.t.* **3.** to cut facets on.

fa•ce•tious (fə sē′shəs), *adj.* **1.** not meant to be taken seriously or literally. **2.** amusing; humorous. —**fa•ce′tious•ly,** *adv.* —**fa•ce′tious•ness,** *n.*

face val•ue (fās′ val′yŏo *for 1;* fās′ val′yŏo *for 2),* *n.* **1.** the value printed on the face of a stock, bond, etc. **2.** apparent value.

fac•ile (fas′il; *esp. Brit.* -īl), *adj.* **1.** easily accomplished or achieved. **2.** working or moving easily; fluent; effortless. **3.** superficial; shallow.

fa•cil•i•tate (fə sil′i tāt′), *v.t.,* **-tat•ed, -tat•ing.** to make easier; help forward. —**fa•cil′i•ta′tion,** *n.* —**fa•cil′i•ta′tor,** *n.*

fa•cil•i•ty (fə sil′i tē), *n., pl.* **-ties. 1.** something designed, built, or installed for a specific purpose: *a research facility.* **2.** Usu., **-ties.** something that permits the easier performance of an action or process. **3.** ease due to skill, aptitude, or practice. **4.** the quality of being easily performed.

fac•ing (fā′sing), *n.* **1.** a covering in front, as an outer layer of stone on a brick wall. **2.** a lining applied along an edge of a garment.

fac•sim•i•le (fak sim′ə lē), *n., pl.* **-les,** *v.,* **-led, -le•ing.** —*n.* **1.** an exact copy, as of a book. **2.** FAX. —*v.t.* **3.** to make a facsimile of. [< L *fac* make + *simile* similar]

fact (fakt), *n.* **1.** reality; actuality. **2.** something known to exist or to have happened. **3.** something known to be true. **4.** something said to be true. —*Idiom.* **5. after the fact,** done, made, or formulated after something has occurred. **6. in fact,** in truth; indeed. —**fac′tu•al,** *adj.*

fac•tion (fak′shən), *n.* **1.** a group or clique within a larger group. **2.** party strife and intrigue. —**fac′tion•al,** *adj.* —**fac′tion•al•ism,** *n.*

fac′tious *adj.* **1.** given to faction. **2.** of or caused by faction. —**fac′tious•ness,** *n.*

fac•tor (fak′tər), *n.* **1.** one of the elements contributing to a particular result. **2.** *Math.* one of two or more quantities that when multiplied together produce a given product. **3.** a person who transacts business for another. **4.** a gene. —*v.t.* **5.** to express (a mathematical quantity) as a product of two or more factors.

fac•to•ry (fak′tə rē, -trē), *n., pl.* **-ries.** a building or group of buildings with facilities for the manufacture of goods.

fac•ul•ty (fak′əl tē), *n., pl.* **-ties. 1.** an ability for a particular kind of action. **2.** one of the powers of the mind, as speech. **3.** an inherent capability of the body. **4. a.** the teaching and administrative staff of a school. **b.** one of the departments of learning in a university.

fad (fad), *n.* a temporary fashion, esp. one followed enthusiastically by a group. —**fad′dish,** *adj.* —**fad′dist,** *n.*

fade (fād), *v.,* **fad•ed, fad•ing,** *n.* —*v.i.* **1.** to lose brightness or vividness of color. **2.** to become dim, as light. **3.** to lose freshness, vigor, strength, or health. **4.** to disappear gradually; die out. —*v.t.* **5.** to cause to fade. —*n.* **6.** an act or instance of fading. **7.** a hairstyle in which the hair is closely cropped at the sides and shaped into an upright block at the top.

fag[1] (fag), *n., v.,* **fagged, fag•ging.** —*n.* **1.** *Slang.* a cigarette. **2.** a drudge. —*v.t.* **3.** to tire by labor: exhaust. —*v.i.* **4.** *Chiefly Brit.* to work hard.

fag[2] (fag), *n. Slang (offensive).* a male homosexual.

fag•ot (fag′ət), *n.* a bundle of sticks, twigs, or branches bound together and used esp. as fuel.

Fahr•en•heit (far′ən hīt′), *adj.* pertaining to or being a temperature scale in which 32° represents the freezing point of water and 212° the boiling point. [after G. D. *Fahrenheit* (1686-1736), German physicist]

fail (fāl), *v.i.* **1.** to fall short of success. **2.** to receive less than a passing academic grade. **3.** to be or become deficient; fall short. **4.** to become weak. **5.** to stop functioning. **6.** to dwindle or die away. **7.** to become bankrupt. —*v.t.* **8.** to be unsuccessful in the performance of. **9.** to prove of no use or help to: *His friends failed him.* **10.** to receive less than a passing grade or mark in. **11.** to give less than a passing grade to. —**Idiom.** **12. without fail,** with certainty. —**fail′ure,** *n.*

fail′ing *n.* **1.** a defect or fault; shortcoming. —*prep.* **2.** in the absence of.

faille (fīl, fāl), *n.* a ribbed fabric, esp. of silk or rayon.

fail′-safe′ *adj.* **1.** of or being a feature that ensures safety should a system fail to operate properly. **2.** guaranteed to work; totally reliable.

faint (fānt), *adj.,* **-er, -est,** *v., n.* —*adj.* **1.** lacking brightness, vividness, or clarity. **2.** lacking strength; feeble. **3.** feeling weak or dizzy and about to lose consciousness. **4.** lacking courage; cowardly. —*v.i.* **5.** to lose consciousness. —*n.* **6.** a temporary loss of consciousness. —**faint′ly,** *adv.* —**faint′ness,** *n.*

faint′heart′ed *adj.* lacking courage.

fair[1] (fâr), *adj.* and *adv.,* **-er, -est.** —*adj.* **1.** free from bias, dishonesty, or injustice. **2.** proper under the rules: *a fair fight.* **3.** moderately large: *a fair income.* **4.** moderately good: *fair health.* **5.** bright, sunny, and cloudless. **6.** not dark: *fair skin.* **7.** pleasing in appearance; attractive. **8.** likely; promising. **9.** free from blemish or imperfection. **10.** easy to read. —*adv.* **11.** in a fair manner. —**fair′ly,** *adv.* —**fair′ness,** *n.*

fair[2] (fâr), *n.* **1.** a usu. competitive exhibition, as of farm products or livestock. **2.** a periodic gathering of buyers and sellers in an appointed place. **3.** an exhibition and sale of articles to raise money, as for charity.

fair′ shake′ *n.* a just and equal opportunity or treatment.

fair•y (fâr′ē), *n., pl.* **-ies. 1.** an imaginary being having a diminutive human form and possessing magical powers. **2.** *Slang (offensive).* a male homosexual.

fair′y tale′ *n.* **1.** a story, usu. for children, about magical creatures. **2.** an improbable story.

faith (fāth), *n.* **1.** confidence or trust in a person or thing. **2.** belief in God. **3.** a system of religious belief. **4.** loyalty or fidelity.

faith′ful *adj.* **1.** steady in allegiance or affection; loyal. **2.** reliable or believable. **3.** true to fact, a standard, or an original. **4.** thorough in the performance of duty. —**faith′ful•ly,** *adv.* —**faith′ful•ness,** *n.*

fake (fāk), *v.,* **faked, fak•ing,** *n., adj.* —*v.t.* **1.** to create or treat so as to mislead or defraud others. **2.** to pretend; simulate. **3.** to imitate convincingly; counterfeit. —*v.i.* **4.** to fake something; pretend. —*n.* **5.** a counterfeit; sham. **6.** one who fakes. —*adj.* **7.** counterfeit; sham. —**fak′er,** *n.*

fa•kir (fə kēr′, fā′kər), *n.* a Muslim or Hindu ascetic or mendicant considered to be a wonder-worker.

fa•la•fel (fə lä′fəl), *n.* a fried ball of ground chickpeas.

fal•con (fôl′kən, fal′-, fô′kən), *n.* any of various birds of prey that are capable of swift flight. —**fal′con•ry,** *n.*

fall (fôl), *v.,* **fell, fall•en, fall•ing,** *n.* —*v.i.* **1.** to drop under the force of gravity. **2.** to come down

suddenly to a lower position, esp. from a standing or erect position. **3.** to decline, as in level, degree, or value. **4.** to hang down. **5.** to become directed downward: *His eyes fell.* **6.** to become lower in pitch or volume. **7.** to succumb to temptation or sin. **8.** to lose status, dignity, or position. **9.** to succumb to attack: *The city fell to the enemy.* **10.** to be overthrown, as a government. **11.** to drop down wounded or dead. **12.** to pass into a physical or emotional condition: *to fall in love.* **13.** to come as if by dropping: *Night fell.* **14.** to come by lot or chance: *The chore fell to me.* **15.** to occur at a certain time: *Christmas fell on a Monday.* **16.** to have its proper place: *The accent falls on the last syllable.* **17.** to come by right. **18.** to look disappointed: *The child's face fell.* **19.** to slope or extend downward. **20. fall back,** to recede; retreat. **21. ~ back on,** to have recourse to; rely on. **22. ~ for,** *Informal.* **a.** to be deceived by. **b.** to fall in love with. **23. ~ on** or **upon,** to assault. **24. ~ out,** to quarrel; disagree. **25. ~ through,** to fail to be accomplished. **26. ~ to, a.** to begin. **b.** to begin to eat. —*n.* **27.** an act or instance of falling. **28.** something that has fallen. **29.** autumn. **30.** the distance through which something falls: *a long fall to the ground.* **31.** Usu., **falls.** a cataract or waterfall. **32.** downward slope or declivity. **33.** a falling from an erect position, as to the ground. **34.** a succumbing to temptation or sin. **35.** surrender or capture, as of a city. **36.** a hairpiece of long hair that hangs freely.

fal•la•cy (fal′ə sē), *n., pl.* **-cies. 1.** a misleading or false notion; misconception. **2.** a logically unsound argument. **3.** erroneous reasoning.

fall′ guy′ *n. Slang.* **1.** an easy victim. **2.** a scapegoat.

fal•li•ble (fal′ə bəl), *adj.* **1.** liable to be mistaken. **2.** liable to be erroneous. —**fal′li•bil′i•ty, fal′li•ble•ness,** *n.* —**fal′li•bly,** *adv.*

fall′ing-out′ *n., pl.* **fall•ings-out, fall•ing-outs.** a quarrel or estrangement.

fal•lo′pi•an (or **Fal•lo′pi•an**) **tube**′ (fə lō′pē-ən), *n.* either of a pair of long slender ducts in the female abdomen that transport ova from the ovary to the uterus. [< G. *Fallopio* (1523–62), Italian anatomist]

fall′out′ *n.* **1. a.** the settling to the ground of airborne radioactive particles that result from a nuclear explosion. **b.** the particles themselves. **2.** an incidental effect, outcome, or product.

fal•low (fal′ō), *adj.* **1.** (of land) plowed and left unseeded for a season or more; uncultivated. **2.** not in use; inactive.

fal′low deer′ *n.* a Eurasian deer with a yellowish coat that has spots in the summer.

false (fôls), *adj.,* **fals•er, fals•est,** *adv.* —*adj.* **1.** not true or correct. **2.** uttering what is untrue; lying. **3.** not faithful or loyal. **4.** tending to deceive or mislead. **5.** not genuine; counterfeit. **6.** based on mistaken ideas: *false pride.* **7.** inaccurate in pitch. —*adv.* **8.** dishonestly; treacherously. —**false′hood,** *n.* —**false′ly,** *adv.* —**false′ness,** *n.*

fal•set•to (fôl set′ō), *n., pl.* **-tos. 1.** an artificially high-pitched voice, esp. in a man. **2.** a person who sings with a falsetto.

fal•ter (fôl′tər), *v.i.* **1.** to hesitate or waver in action or intent. **2.** to speak hesitatingly. **3.** to move unsteadily; stumble. —*n.* **4.** the act of faltering. **5.** a faltering sound. —**fal′ter•ing•ly,** *adv.*

fame (fām), *n.* widespread reputation, esp. of a favorable character; renown. —**famed,** *adj.*

fa•mil•iar (fə mil′yər), *adj.* **1.** commonly or generally known or seen. **2.** thoroughly conversant; well-acquainted. **3.** informal; unceremonious. **4.** intimate or personal. **5.** unduly intimate; too personal. —*n.* **6.** a familiar friend or associate. —**fa•mil′i•ar′i•ty,** *n., pl.* **-ties.** —**fa•mil′iar•ize′,** *v.t.,* **-ized, -iz•ing.** —**fa•mil′iar•ly,** *adv.*

fam•i•ly (fam′ə lē, fam′lē), *n., pl.* **-lies. 1.** parents and their children considered as a group. **2.** a group of persons descended from a common progenitor. **3.** a group of persons who form a household, esp. under one head. **4.** a group of related things or individuals. **5.** a major subdivision of an order or suborder in the classification of plants or animals.

fam′i·ly tree′ *n.* a genealogical chart of a family.

fam·ine (fam′in), *n.* **1.** extreme and general scarcity of food. **2.** a general scarcity; dearth.

fam′ish *v.t., v.i.* to suffer or cause to suffer extreme hunger.

fa·mous (fā′məs), *adj.* **1.** renowned; celebrated. **2.** first-rate; excellent. **3.** notorious.

fa′mous·ly *adv.* in a splendid manner; very well.

fan¹ (fan), *n., v.,* **fanned, fan·ning.** —*n.* **1.** a device, as a triangular hand implement or an electric machine with blades, for producing a current of air. **2.** something resembling a fan. —*v.t.* **3.** to move (the air) with or as if with a fan. **4.** to cause air to blow upon. **5.** to stir to activity; incite: *to fan emotions.* **6.** to spread out like a fan. **7.** (of a baseball pitcher) to strike out (a batter). —*v.i.* **8.** to spread like a fan. [OE *fann* < L *vannus* winnowing basket]

fan² (fan), *n.* an enthusiastic devotee or follower, as of a sport. [short for *fanatic*]

fa·nat·ic (fə nat′ik), *n.* **1.** a person with an extreme enthusiasm or zeal, as in religion; zealot. —*adj.* Also, **fa·nat′i·cal. 2.** of or like a fanatic. —**fa·nat′i·cism** (-ə siz′əm), *n.*

fan·ci·er (fan′sē ər), *n.* a person having an interest in something, esp. in breeding a particular animal or plant.

fan·ci·ful (-si fəl), *adj.* **1.** whimsical in appearance. **2.** imaginary or unreal. **3.** imaginative or inventive.

fan·cy *n., pl.* **-cies,** *adj.,* **-ci·er, -ci·est,** *v.,* **-cied, -cy·ing.** —*n.* **1.** imagination, esp. as exercised capriciously. **2.** a mental image or conception; notion. **3.** a caprice; whim. **4.** a preference, inclination, or liking. —*adj.* **5.** of exceptional quality. **6.** ornamental or decorative. **7.** depending on imagination or caprice. **8.** much too costly. —*v.t.* **9.** to picture to oneself; imagine. **10.** to believe without being absolutely certain. **11.** to have a liking for. —**fan′ci·ly,** *adv.* —**fan′ci·ness,** *n.*

fan′cy-free′ *adj.* free from emotional ties or influences, esp. from love.

fan′cy·work′ *n.* ornamental needlework.

fan·fare (fan′fâr), *n.* **1.** a flourish played, esp. on a trumpet. **2.** an ostentatious display.

fang (fang), *n.* **1.** one of the long, sharp teeth of a venomous snake by which poison is injected. **2.** a long, sharp, projecting tooth, esp. a canine tooth. —**fanged,** *adj.*

fan′ny *n., pl.* **-nies.** *Informal.* the buttocks.

fan·ta·sia (fan tā′zhə), *n., pl.* **-sias.** a dramatic, somewhat fanciful musical work, as for the piano.

fan′ta·size′ (-tə sīz′), *v.,* **-sized, -siz·ing.** —*v.i.* **1.** to conceive fanciful or extravagant notions. —*v.t.* **2.** to create in one's fancy or daydreams. —**fan′ta·siz′er,** *n.*

fan·tas′tic (-tas′tik) also **-ti·cal,** *adj.* **1.** conceived or seemingly conceived by an unrestrained imagination; bizarre or grotesque. **2.** fanciful or capricious. **3.** imaginary or groundless; irrational. **4.** extremely great or good. —**fan·tas′ti·cal·ly,** *adv.*

fan′ta·sy (-tə sē, -zē), *n., pl.* **-sies. 1.** imagination, esp. when unrestrained. **2.** a daydream or illusion. **3.** fiction based on highly imaginative characters and premises. **4.** a fantasia.

far (fär), *adv., adj.,* **far·ther** or **fur·ther, far·thest** or **fur·thest.** —*adv.* **1.** at or to a great distance or remote point. **2.** at or to a remote or advanced time. **3.** at or to a definite point or degree. **4.** much: *I need far more time.* —*adj.* **5.** being at a great distance. **6.** more distant of two: *the far corner.* —*Idiom.* **7. by far,** by a great deal; very much. **8. far and away,** without doubt; decidedly. **9. far and wide,** over great distances; everywhere. **10. so far, a.** up to now. **b.** up to a certain point or extent.

far′a·way′ (fär′-), *adj.* **1.** distant; remote. **2.** dreamy; preoccupied.

farce (färs), *n.* **1.** a comedy based on unlikely situations and exaggerated effects. **2.** humor of the type displayed in a farce. **3.** a foolish or meaningless show; sham or mockery. —**far′ci·cal,** *adj.*

fare (fâr), *n., v.,* **fared, far·ing.** —*n.* **1.** the price of conveying a passenger, as in a bus. **2.** a paying passenger. **3.** food; diet. **4.** something offered to the public, as for entertainment. —*v.i.* **5.** to get on; manage: *to fare well.*

Far′ East′ *n.* the countries of E Asia, including China, Japan, Korea, and sometimes adjacent areas.

fare·well′ *interj.* **1.** good-bye. —*n.* **2.** an expression of good wishes at parting. **3.** leave-taking; departure. —*adj.* **4.** parting; final: *a farewell performance.*

far′-fetched′ or **far′fetched′,** *adj.* not naturally pertinent; improbable.

far′-flung′ *adj.* **1.** extending over a great distance. **2.** widely distributed.

fa·ri·na (fə rē′nə), *n.* flour or meal made from cereal grains and cooked as cereal or used in puddings.

farm (färm), *n.* **1.** a tract of land on which crops and often livestock are raised. —*v.t.* **2.** to cultivate (land). —*v.i.* **3.** to cultivate the soil; operate a farm. **4. farm out,** to assign or subcontract (work) to another. —**farm′a·ble,** *adj.* —**farm′er,** *n.* —**farm′ing,** *n.*

far·o (fâr′ō), *n.* a gambling game in which players bet on cards.

far′-off′ *adj.* distant; remote.

far′-out′ *adj. Slang.* **1.** unconventional; offbeat. **2.** radical; extreme.

far′-reach′ing *adj.* extending far in influence or effect.

far·row (far′ō), *n.* **1.** a litter of pigs. —*v.i.* **2.** to produce a farrow.

far′sight′ed (-sī′tid, -sī′-), *adj.* **1.** seeing distant objects more clearly than near ones. **2.** wise, as in foreseeing future developments.. —**far′sight′ed·ness,** *n.*

far·ther (fär′thər), *adv., compar. of* **far. 1.** at or to a greater distance or more advanced point. **2.** at or to a greater degree or extent. —*adj., compar. of* **far. 3.** more distant or remote. **4.** additional.

far′thest (-thist), *adj., superl. of* **far. 1.** most distant or remote. **2.** most extended; longest. —*adv., superl. of* **far. 3.** at or to the greatest distance or most advanced point. **4.** at or to the greatest degree or extent.

fas·ci·nate (fas′ə nāt′), *v.t.,* **-nat·ed, -nat·ing. 1.** to attract and hold, as by a unique power or a special quality; spellbind. **2.** to arouse the interest or curiosity of. —**fas′ci·na′tion,** *n.*

fas·cism (fash′iz əm), *n.* (*sometimes cap.*) **1.** a totalitarian governmental system led by a dictator and emphasizing aggressive nationalism, militarism, and often racism. **2.** the philosophy, principles, or methods of fascism. [< It *fascismo* = *fasc(io)* bundle, political group + *-ismo* -ISM] —**fas′cist,** *n., adj.* —**fa·scis·tic** (fə shis′tik), *adj.*

fash·ion (fash′ən), *n.* **1.** a prevailing custom or style, as of dress. **2.** conventional usage or conformity to it. **3.** manner; way. **4.** the make or form of something; shape. —*v.t.* **5.** to give shape or form to; make. **6.** to adjust; adapt. —*Idiom.* **7. after a fashion,** to some minimal extent. —**fash′ion·er,** *n.*

fash′ion·a·ble *adj.* **1.** observant of or conforming to fashion; stylish. **2.** of or characteristic of the world of fashion. —**fash′ion·a·bly,** *adv.*

fast¹ (fast, fäst), *adj. and adv.,* **-er, -est.** —*adj.* **1.** acting or moving with speed. **2.** done in comparatively little time. **3.** (of a timepiece) ahead of the correct time. **4.** characterized by unrestrained conduct. **5.** resistant: *acid-fast.* **6.** firmly fixed, held, or tied. **7.** securely closed, as a shutter. **8.** loyal: *fast friends.* **9.** permanent or unchangeable: *a fast color.* **10.** deep and sound, as sleep. **11.** *Photog.* **a.** (of a lens) able to transmit a large amount of light in a short time. **b.** (of a film) requiring a relatively short exposure to attain a given density. —*adv.* **12.** quickly, swiftly, or rapidly. **13.** tightly; firmly: *to hold fast.* **14.** soundly: *fast asleep.* **15.** in a rash way; recklessly.

fast² (fast, fäst), *v.i.* **1.** to abstain from all food. **2.** to eat only sparingly or of certain kinds of food. —*n.* **3.** the act of fasting. **4.** a period of fasting.

fas·ten (fas′ən, fä′sən), *v.t.* **1.** to attach firmly or securely. **2.** to fix securely to something else;

connect. **3.** to direct (the eyes, thoughts, etc.) intently. —*v.i.* **4.** to become fastened. —**fas′ten•er,** *n.*

fast′-food′ *adj.* specializing in foods, as hamburgers, that can be prepared and served rapidly: *fast-food restaurants.*

fas•tid•i•ous (fa stid′ē əs, fə-), *adj.* **1.** hard to please. **2.** requiring or characterized by excessive care or delicacy. —**fas•tid′i•ous•ly,** *adv.* —**fas•tid′i•ous•ness,** *n.*

fast′ness *n.* a stronghold.

fat (fat), *n., adj.,* **fat•ter, fat•test.** —*n.* **1.** any of several oily substances that are the chief component of animal adipose tissue and many plant seeds. **2.** animal tissue containing much fat. **3.** obesity; corpulence. **4.** the richest or best part. **5.** an overabundance; excess. —*adj.* **6.** having too much fat; obese. **7.** plump; well-fed. **8.** profitable. **9.** profitable; lucrative. **10.** broad or thick. —*Idiom.* **11. fat chance,** a very slight chance. —**fat′ness,** *n.* —**fat′ty,** *adj.,* **-ti•er, -ti•est.**

fa•tal (fāt′l), *adj.* **1.** causing or capable of causing death. **2.** causing misfortune or ruin; calamitous. **3.** decisively important; fateful. —**fa′tal•ly,** *adv.*

fa′tal•ism *n.* the doctrine that all events are subject to fate or inevitable predetermination. —**fa′tal•ist,** *n.* —**fa′tal•is′tic,** *adj.*

fa•tal•i•ty (fā tal′i tē, fə-), *n., pl.* **-ties. 1.** a death caused by a disaster. **2.** the quality of being deadly; deadliness. **3.** predetermined liability to disaster or misfortune.

fate (fāt), *n.* **1.** something that unavoidably befalls a person; fortune. **2.** the ultimate agency by which the order of things is presumably prescribed; destiny. **3.** the ultimate outcome. **4.** death or ruin. **5. Fates,** the three goddesses of destiny in Greek and Roman myth.

fat′ed *adj.* subject to or guided by fate; destined.

fate′ful *adj.* **1.** having momentous significance; decisively important. **2.** fatal, deadly, or disastrous. **3.** controlled by destiny. **4.** prophetic; ominous. —**fate′ful•ly,** *adv.* —**fate′ful•ness,** *n.*

fa•ther (fä′thər), *n.* **1.** a male who begets or rears offspring; male parent. **2.** a male ancestor; forefather. **3.** a person who has invented or created something; originator. **4.** one of the leading men in a city, town, etc. **5.** a priest or a title for a priest. **6.** (*cap.*) God. —*v.t.* **7.** to beget. **8.** to be the creator, founder, or author of. **9.** to act as a father toward. —**fa′ther•hood′,** *n.* —**fa′ther•less,** *adj.* —**fa′ther•ly,** *adj.*

fa′ther-in-law′ *n., pl.* **fa•thers-in-law.** the father of one's husband or wife.

fa′ther•land′ *n.* **1.** one's native country. **2.** the land of one's ancestors.

fath•om (fath′əm), *n., pl.* **-oms, -om,** *v.* —*n.* **1.** a nautical unit of length equal to 6 feet (1.8 m). —*v.t.* **2.** to measure the depth of by means of a sounding line. **3.** to penetrate deeply; understand. —**fath′om•a•ble,** *adj.* —**fath′om•less,** *adj.*

fa•tigue (fə tēg′), *n., v.,* **-tigued, -ti•guing.** —*n.* **1.** weariness from bodily or mental exertion. **2.** the weakening or breakdown of material subjected to repeated stress: *metal fatigue.* **3.** nonmilitary labor by military personnel. **4. fatigues,** military clothing worn for fatigue or field duty. —*v.t., v.i.* **5.** to weary with bodily or mental exertion.

fat′ten *v.t., v.i.* to make or become fat.

fat′ty ac′id *n.* any of a class of organic acids found in animal and vegetable fats.

fat•u•ous (fach′ōō əs), *adj.* complacently foolish or inane; silly. —**fa•tu•i•ty** (fə tōō′i tē, -tyōō′-), *n., pl.* **-ties.** —**fat′u•ous•ly,** *adv.* —**fat′u•ous•ness,** *n.*

fau•cet (fô′sit), *n.* a device for controlling the flow of liquid, as from a pipe, by opening or closing an orifice; tap.

fault (fôlt), *n.* **1.** a defect or imperfection; flaw. **2.** responsibility for failure or a wrongful act. **3.** an error or mistake. **4.** an error in serving the ball in tennis. **5.** a fracture in a body of rock. —*v.i.* **6.** to commit a fault. **7.** *Geol.* to undergo a fault. —*v.t.* **8.** to accuse of a fault; criticize or blame. —*Idiom.* **9. at fault,** open to censure; blameworthy. **10. find**

fault, to complain or be critical. **11. to a fault,** to an extreme degree. —**fault′less,** *adj.*

faun (fôn), *n.* an ancient Roman deity of the countryside, part human and part goat.

fau•na (fô′nə), *n., pl.* **-nas, -nae** (-nē). the animals or animal life of a given region or period.

faux pas (fō pä′), *n., pl.* **faux pas** (fō päz′). a slip or blunder, esp. in manners or conduct. [< F]

fa•vor (fā′vər), *n.* **1.** a kind act. **2.** friendly regard; goodwill. **3.** popularity. **4.** preferential treatment; partiality. **5.** a gift bestowed as a token of regard or love. **6.** a small gift distributed to guests at a party. **7.** Usu., **-vors.** sexual intimacy. —*v.t.* **8.** to regard with favor. **9.** to treat with partiality; prefer. **10.** to show favor to; oblige. **11.** to be favorable to; facilitate. **12.** to treat or use gently: *to favor a sore wrist.* **13.** to bear a physical resemblance to. —*Idiom.* **14. in favor of,** **a.** in support of. **b.** to the advantage of. Also, *esp. Brit.,* **fa′vour.** —**fa′vor•a•ble,** *adj.*

fa′vor•ite (-it), *n.* **1.** a person or thing regarded with special preference or approval. **2.** a competitor or contestant considered likely to win. —*adj.* **3.** being a favorite.

fa′vor•it•ism *n.* the undue favoring of one person or group over others.

fawn¹ (fôn), *n.* **1.** a young deer, esp. an unweaned one. **2.** a light yellowish brown color.

fawn² (fôn), *v.i.* **1.** to seek notice or favor by servile behavior; toady. **2.** (esp. of a dog) to behave affectionately. —**fawn′er,** *n.* —**fawn′ing•ly,** *adv.*

fax (faks), *n.* **a.** a method or device for transmitting graphic matter, as documents or photographs, by telephone or radio for exact reproduction elsewhere. **b.** an exact copy or reproduction so transmitted. —*v.t.* **2.** to transmit by fax.

faze (fāz), *v.t.,* **fazed, faz•ing.** to cause to be disconcerted; daunt; fluster.

FBI Federal Bureau of Investigation.

FCC Federal Communications Commission.

FDA Food and Drug Administration.

FDIC Federal Deposit Insurance Corporation.

fear (fēr), *n.* **1.** a distressing emotion aroused by impending danger, evil, or pain. **2.** a specific instance of or propensity for fear. **3.** concern or anxiety; solicitude. **4.** reverential awe, esp. toward God. —*v.t.* **5.** to regard with fear. **6.** to be worried or afraid. **7.** to have reverential awe of. —*v.i.* **8.** to be afraid. —**fear′ful,** *adj.* —**fear′ful•ly,** *adv.* —**fear′ful•ness,** *n.* —**fear′less,** *adj.* —**fear′less•ly,** *adv.* —**fear′less•ness,** *n.*

fea•si•ble (fē′zə bəl), *adj.* **1.** capable of being done, effected, or accomplished. **2.** probable; likely. **3.** suitable. —**fea′si•bil′i•ty,** *n.* —**fea′si•bly,** *adv.*

feast (fēst), *n.* **1.** a rich or abundant meal. **2.** a sumptuous meal for many guests. **3.** a periodic religious festival. —*v.i.* **4.** to partake of a feast. **5.** to dwell with delight, as on a picture. —*v.t.* **6.** to entertain with a feast. —**feast′er,** *n.*

feat (fēt), *n.* a noteworthy or extraordinary act or achievement.

feath•er (feth′ər), *n.* **1.** one of the horny epidermal structures that form the principal covering of birds. **2.** kind; character: *two boys of the same feather.* **3.** condition, esp. of spirits: *to be in fine feather.* —*v.t.* **4.** to provide (an arrow) with feathers. **5.** to clothe or cover with or as if with feathers. —*Idiom.* **6. a feather in one's cap,** a praiseworthy achievement; honor. —**feath′er•y,** *adj.*

fea•ture (fē′chər), *n., v.,* **-tured, -tur•ing.** —*n.* **1.** a prominent or conspicuous characteristic. **2.** something offered as a special attraction. **3.** the main motion picture in a program. **4.** a part of the face, as the nose. **5. features,** the face; countenance. **6.** the form or appearance of the face. **7.** a prominent story or article in a newspaper or magazine. —*v.t.* **8.** to give prominence to. **9.** to be a feature or distinctive mark of. **10.** to delineate the features of; depict. —*v.i.* **11.** to play a major part.

Feb or **Feb.,** February.

Feb•ru•ar•y (feb′rōō er′ē, feb′yōō-), *n., pl.* **-ies.** the second month of the year, ordinarily containing 28 days but containing 29 days in leap years.

fe·ces (fē′sēz), *n.pl.* waste matter discharged from the intestines; excrement. —**fe′cal** (-kəl), *adj.*

feck·less (fek′lis), *adj.* **1.** ineffective; incompetent. **2.** irresponsible and lazy. —**feck′less·ly,** *adv.*

fe·cund (fē′kund, -kənd, fek′und, -ənd), *adj.* **1.** prolific or fruitful. **2.** very productive or creative. —**fe·cun·di·ty** (fi kun′di tē), *n.*

fed (fed), *v.* **1.** pt. and pp. of FEED. —*Idiom.* **2. fed up,** impatient, disgusted, or bored.

fed. **1.** federal. **2.** federation. **3.** federation.

fed·er·al (fed′ər əl), *adj.* **1.** pertaining to or of the nature of a union of states under a central government distinct from the individual governments of the separate states. **2.** (*sometimes cap.*) of or involving such a government, esp. the U.S. government. [< L *foeder-,* s. of *foedus* league + -AL¹] —**fed′er·al·ly,** *adv.*

fed·er·ate (fed′ə rāt′), *v.t., v.i.* **-at·ed, -at·ing.** to unite in a federal political entity. —**fed′er·a′tion,** *n.*

fe·do·ra (fi dôr′ə), *n., pl.* **-ras.** a soft felt hat with a curved brim.

fee (fē), *n., pl.* **fees. 1.** a sum charged, as for professional services. **2.** *Law.* **a.** a heritable estate in land. **b.** an estate in land held of a feudal lord in return for services performed; fief.

fee·ble (fē′bəl), *adj.,* **-bler, -blest. 1.** weak, as from age or sickness; frail. **2.** lacking in substance, force, or effectiveness: *feeble arguments.* —**fee′ble·ness,** *n.* —**fee′bly,** *adv.*

feed (fēd), *v.,* **fed, feed·ing,** *n.* —*v.t.* **1.** to give food to. **2.** to serve as food for. **3.** to provide as food. **4.** to satisfy or gratify. **5.** to supply for growth, maintenance, development, or operation. —*v.i.* **6.** (esp. of animals) to take food; eat. —*n.* **7.** food, esp. for farm animals. **8.** a meal, esp. a lavish one. **9.** material or an amount of material for feeding a device or machine. **10.** a feeding mechanism. —**feed′er,** *n.*

feed′back′ *n.* **1.** the return of part of the output of a circuit, system, or device to the input. **2.** a reaction or response, as to an activity.

feel (fēl), *v.,* **felt, feel·ing,** *n.* —*v.t.* **1.** to perceive by direct physical contact. **2.** to examine by touch. **3.** to have a physical sensation of. **4.** to find (one's way) by touching or cautious moves. **5.** to be or become conscious of. **6.** to be emotionally affected by. **7.** to experience. **8.** to think; believe. —*v.i.* **9.** to have perception by touch. **10.** to search with the hands or fingers; grope. **11.** to perceive a state of mind or a condition of body: *to feel happy.* **12.** to have a sensation of being: *to feel warm.* **13.** to feel sympathy or compassion. —*n.* **14.** a quality of something that is perceived by touching. **15.** the sense of touch: *soft to the feel.* **16.** native ability or acquired sensitivity: *to have a feel for teaching.* —*Idiom.* **17. feel like,** to be favorably disposed toward. —**feel′ing,** *n., adj.*

feel′er *n.* **1.** a proposal, remark, or suggestion designed to elicit the opinions or reactions of others. **2.** an organ of touch, as an antenna.

feign (fān), *v.t.* **1.** to put on an appearance of: *to feign sickness.* —*v.i.* **2.** to make believe; pretend. —**feign′er,** *n.*

feint (fānt), *n.* **1.** a deceptive attack or blow aimed at one place or point to distract from the real target. —*v.i., v.t.* **2.** to make or deceive with a feint.

feist·y (fī′stē), *adj.,* **-i·er, i·est. 1.** full of animation or energy; spirited. **2.** ill-tempered; pugnacious. —**feist′i·ly,** *adv.* —**feist′i·ness,** *n.*

feld·spar (feld′spär′, fel′-), *n.* any of a group of crystalline minerals, principally silicates of aluminum with potassium, sodium, and calcium.

fe·lic·i·tate (fə lis′i tāt′), *v.,* **-tated, -tating.** to congratulate.

fe·lic·i·tous (-təs), *adj.* **1.** well-suited for an occasion; apt. **2.** having a special ability for felicitous expression. **3.** enjoyable; pleasant. —**fe·lic′i·tous·ly,** *adv.*

fe·lic′i·ty *n., pl.* **-ties. 1.** the state of being happy, esp. to a high degree; bliss. **2.** a source of happiness. **3. a.** a faculty or capacity for skill or grace: *felicity of expression.* **b.** an instance or display of this.

fe·line (fē′līn), *adj.* **1.** of the cat family. **2.** sly, stealthy, or treacherous. —*n.* **3.** an animal of the cat family; cat.

fell¹ (fel), *v.* pt. of FALL.

fell² (fel), *v.t.* **1.** to knock, strike, shoot, or cut down. **2.** (in sewing) to finish (a seam) by sewing the edge down flat.

fell³ (fel), *adj.* **1.** fierce; cruel. **2.** destructive; deadly.

fel·low (fel′ō), *n.* **1.** a man or boy. **2.** a comrade; associate. **3.** a person of the same rank or class; peer. **4.** one of a pair; mate. **5.** a graduate student who receives a stipend. **6.** a member of a learned society. —*adj.* **7.** united by the same occupation, interests, or circumstances.

fel·on¹ (fel′ən), *n.* a person who has committed a felony.

fel·on² (fel′ən), *n.* a painful inflammation of the tissues of a finger or toe, usu. near the nail.

fel·o·ny *n., pl.* **-nies.** an offense, as murder or burglary, of graver character than a misdemeanor. —**fe·lo·ni·ous** (fə lō′nē əs), *adj.*

felt¹ (felt), *v.* pt. and pp. of FEEL.

felt² (felt), *n.* **1.** a nonwoven fabric of wool, fur, or hair, matted together by heat, moisture, and great pressure. **2.** a matted fabric or material that resembles felt. —*v.t.* **3.** to make into felt.

fem. 1. female. **2.** feminine.

fe·male (fē′māl), *n.* **1.** a person of the sex that conceives and bears young. **2.** an organism of the sex or sexual phase that produces egg cells. **3.** a plant having pistils. —*adj.* **4.** of or being a female. **5.** of or characteristic of a girl or woman; feminine. **6.** having a recessed part into which a corresponding projecting part fits: *a female plug.* —**fe′male·ness,** *n.*

fem·i·nine (fem′ə nin), *adj.* **1.** of or characteristic of women or girls. **2.** of or belonging to the female sex. **3.** of or being the grammatical gender that has among its members most nouns referring to females. —*n.* **4.** the feminine gender. **5.** a word or form in the feminine gender. —**fem′i·nine·ly,** *adv.* —**fem′i·nin′i·ty,** *n.*

fem′i·nism *n.* **1.** a doctrine advocating social, political, and economic rights for women equal to those of men. **2.** a movement for the attainment of the goals of feminism. —**fem′i·nist,** *n., adj.*

fe·mur (fē′mər), *n., pl.* **fe·murs, fem·o·ra** (fem′ər ə). the long bone extending from the pelvis to the knee; thighbone. —**fem′o·ral,** *adj.*

fen (fen), *n.* low, boggy land; marsh.

fence (fens), *n., v.,* **fenced, fenc·ing.** —*n.* **1.** a barrier, usu. of posts and wire or wood, used to prevent entrance or mark a boundary. **2. a.** a person who receives and disposes of stolen goods. **b.** the place of business of such a person. —*v.t.* **3.** to enclose or separate with or as if with a fence. **4.** to keep in or out with a fence. **5.** to sell (stolen goods) to a fence. —*v.i.* **6.** to practice the sport of fencing with a foil or saber. **7.** to try to avoid giving direct answers; hedge. —*Idiom.* **8. on the fence,** uncommitted; undecided. —**fenc′er,** *n.*

fend (fend), *v.t.* **1.** to ward off: *to fend off blows.* —*v.i.* **2.** to try to manage; shift: *to fend for oneself.*

fend′er *n.* **1.** a part mounted over the wheels of a vehicle such as an automobile or bicycle to protect it, as from splashes. **2.** a low metal guard before an open fireplace.

fen·nel (fen′l), *n.* **1.** a plant of the parsley family with aromatic feathery leaves. **2.** the aromatic seeds of the fennel, used in cooking.

fe·ral (fēr′əl, fer′-), *adj.* **1.** existing in a wild state; not domesticated or cultivated. **2.** having reverted to the wild state. **3.** ferocious; savage.

fer·ment (n. fûr′ment; v. fər ment′), *n.* **1.** a living organism, as yeast, that causes fermentation. **2.** agitation or excitement; commotion: *political ferment.* —*v.i., v.t.* **3.** to undergo or cause to undergo fermentation. **4.** to be or cause to be agitated or excited.

fer′men·ta′tion *n.* **1.** a chemical change brought about by a ferment, as the conversion of grape sugar into ethyl alcohol by yeast enzymes. **2.** agitation; excitement.

fern (fûrn), *n.* a nonflowering vascular plant having fronds and reproducing by spores.

fe•ro•cious (fə rō′shəs), *adj.* **1.** savagely fierce or cruel; brutal. **2.** extreme or intense. —**fe•ro′cious•ly,** *adv.* —**fe•roc′i•ty** (-ros′i tē), **fe•ro′cious•ness,** *n.*

fer•ret (fer′it), *n.* **1.** a domesticated variety of the polecat used esp. in Europe for driving small mammals from their burrows. **2.** a North American prairie weasel with a black mask and black feet. —*v.t.* **3.** to drive out by or as if by using a ferret. **4.** to hunt with ferrets. **5.** to search out and bring to light.

Fer′ris wheel′ (fer′is), *n.* an amusement ride consisting of a large upright wheel rotating on a fixed stand and having seats suspended freely from its rim. [after G. W. G. *Ferris* (1859–96), U.S. engineer]

fer•rous (fer′əs), *adj.* of or containing iron, esp. in the bivalent state.

fer•ry (fer′ē), *n.,* pl. **-ries,** *v.,* **-ried, -ry•ing.** —*n.* **1.** a service for transporting persons or things across a river, bay, etc. **2.** a boat used for ferrying; ferryboat. **3.** a service for flying airplanes over a particular route. —*v.t.* **4.** to carry or convey over a fixed route in a boat or plane. **5.** to fly (an airplane) over a particular route, esp. for delivery. —*v.i.* **6.** to go in a ferry.

fer•tile (fûr′tl; *esp. Brit.* -tīl), *adj.* **1.** producing or capable of producing abundantly; productive: *fertile soil; a fertile imagination.* **2.** bearing or capable of bearing offspring. **3.** capable of developing, as a seed or egg. —**fer•til•i•ty** (fər til′i tē), *n.*

fer′ti•lize′ *v.t.,* **-lized, -liz•ing. 1. a.** to render (a female gamete) capable of development through union with a male gamete. **b.** to impregnate (an animal or plant). **2.** to make fertile. —**fer′ti•li•za′tion,** *n.* —**fer′ti•liz′er,** *n.*

fer•vent (fûr′vənt), *adj.* **1.** having or showing warmth or intensity of feeling; ardent. **2.** hot; glowing. —**fer′ven•cy,** *n.* —**fer′vent•ly,** *adv.*

fer′vid (-vid), *adj.* **1.** heated or vehement, as in spirit; impassioned. **2.** very hot; fiery. —**fer′vid•ly,** *adv.*

fes•ter (fes′tər), *v.i.* **1.** to form pus; suppurate. **2.** to rankle, as resentment or bitterness.

fes•ti•val (fes′tə vəl), *n.* **1.** a time of celebration marked by special ceremonies. **2.** a period or program of festive activities, cultural events, or entertainment.

fes′tive *adj.* **1.** of or suitable for a feast or festival. **2.** joyous; merry. —**fes′tive•ly,** *adv.* —**fes′tive•ness,** *n.*

fes•tiv′i•ty *n.,* pl. **-ties. 1.** a festive celebration. **2.** **festivities,** festive events or activities. **3.** festive character or quality.

fes•toon (fe stoon′), *n.* **1.** a string or chain, as of foliage, suspended in a curve between two points. **2.** a decorative representation of a festoon, as on pottery. —*v.t.* **3.** to adorn with or as if with festoons. **4.** to form into festoons.

fet•a (fet′ə), *n.* a white, brine-cured Greek cheese usu. made from sheep's or goat's milk.

fetch (fech), *v.t.* **1.** to go and return with. **2.** to cause to come. **3.** to sell for. **4.** to take (a breath). **5.** to utter (a sigh, groan, etc.). **6.** to deliver (a stroke or blow). —**fetch′er,** *n.*

fetch′ing *adj.* charming; captivating. —**fetch′ing•ly,** *adv.*

fete (fāt, fet), *n.,* pl. **fetes** or **fêtes,** *v.,* **fet•ed** or **fêt•ed, fet•ing** or **fêt•ing.** —*n.* **1.** a festive celebration or entertainment. **2.** a religious feast or festival. —*v.t.* **3.** to entertain at or honor with a fete.

fet•id (fet′id, fē′tid), *adj.* having an offensive odor; noisome. —**fet′id•ness,** *n.*

fet•ish (fet′ish, fē′tish), *n.* **1.** an object regarded as having magical power; talisman. **2.** something eliciting unquestioning reverence or devotion. **3.** an object used for achieving sexual excitement or fulfillment. —**fet′ish•ism,** *n.* —**fet′ish•ist,** *n.* —**fet′ish•is′tic,** *adj.*

fet•lock (fet′lok′), *n.* **1.** a projection on the leg of a horse behind the hoof, bearing a tuft of hair. **2.** the tuft of hair itself.

fet•ter (fet′ər), *n.* **1.** a chain or shackle placed on the feet. **2.** Usu., **-ters.** something that confines or restrains. —*v.t.* **3.** to put fetters on. **4.** to confine; restrain.

fet•tle (fet′l), *n.* state; condition: *in fine fettle.*

fe•tus (fē′təs), *n.,* pl. **-tus•es.** the young of an animal in the womb or egg, esp. in the later stages of development. —**fe′tal,** *adj.*

feud (fyood), *n.* **1.** a state of bitter hostility, esp. between families or clans, lasting for years or generations. —*v.i.* **2.** to engage in a feud.

feu•dal (fyood′l), *adj.* of or characteristic of feudalism.

feu′dal•ism *n.* a system of social and economic organization in medieval Europe based on the holding of lands in fief and on the resulting relations between lord and vassal. —**feu′dal•is′tic,** *adj.*

fe•ver (fē′vər), *n.* **1.** an abnormally high body temperature. **2.** a disease, as scarlet fever, in which high temperature is a prominent symptom. **3.** intense nervous excitement. —**fe′ver•ish,** *adj.* —**fe′ver•ish•ly,** *adv.*

few (fyoo), *adj.,* **-er, -est,** *n., pron.* —*adj.* **1.** not many but more than one. —*n.* **2.** (*used with a pl. v.*) a small number. **3.** a special limited number: *the privileged few.* —*pron.* **4.** (*used with a pl. v.*) a small number of persons or things.

fey (fā), *adj.* **1.** whimsical; strange. **2.** supernatural; enchanted. **3.** appearing to be under a spell. **4.** *Chiefly Scot.* doomed.

fez (fez), *n.,* pl. **fez•zes.** a red, cone-shaped felt hat with a tassel, worn by men, esp. in Egypt. [< Turkish, after *Fez,* city in Morocco where originally made]

ff 1. folios. **2.** (and the) following (pages, verses, etc.).

FG field goal(s).

fi•an•cé (fē′än sā′, fē än′sā), *n.,* pl. **-cés.** a man engaged to be married.

fi•an•cée (fē′än sā′, fē än′sā), *n.,* pl. **-cées.** a woman engaged to be married.

fi•as•co (fē as′kō), *n.,* pl. **-cos, -coes.** a complete and ignominious failure.

fi•at (fē′ät, -at; fī′ət, -at), *n.* an authoritative decree, sanction, or order. [< L: let it be done]

fib (fib), *n., v.,* **fibbed, fib•bing.** —*n.* **1.** a minor or trivial lie. —*v.i.* **2.** to tell a fib. —**fib′ber,** *n.*

fi•ber (fī′bər), *n.* **1.** a fine threadlike piece, as of cotton or asbestos. **2.** a slender filament. **3.** matter or material composed of filaments. **4.** essential character, quality, or strength. **5.** plant matter, as cellulose, that is bulky and stimulates peristalsis. Also, *esp. Brit.,* **fi′bre.** —**fi′brous** (-brəs), *adj.*

fi′ber•glass′ *n.* a material consisting of fine filaments of glass, used for textiles, insulation, boat hulls, etc.

fi′ber op′tics *n.* the technology of sending light and images, as around bends and corners, through transparent glass or plastic fibers. —**fi′ber-op′tic,** *adj.*

fi•bril•la•tion (fī′brə lā′shən, fib′rə-), *n.* chaotic contractions across the atrium of the heart, causing fast and irregular ventricular activity. —**fi′bril•late′,** *v.i., v.t.,* **-lat•ed, -lat•ing.**

fib•u•la (fib′yə lə), *n.,* pl. **-lae** (-lē′), **-las.** the outer and thinner of the two bones extending from the knee to the ankle. —**fib′u•lar,** *adj.*

FICA (fī′kə, fē′-), Federal Insurance Contributions Act.

fiche (fēsh), *n.* MICROFICHE.

fick•le (fik′əl), *adj.* not stable or constant; changeable. —**fick′le•ness,** *n.*

fic•tion (fik′shən), *n.* **1. a.** the class of literature comprising works of imaginative narration, esp. in prose form. **b.** works of this class, as novels. **2.** something invented or imagined, esp. a made-up story. —**fic′tion•al,** *adj.*

fic•ti′tious (-tish′əs), *adj.* **1.** created or assumed for the sake of concealment; false. **2.** of or consisting of fiction; created by the imagination. —**fic•ti′tious•ly,** *adv.*

fid•dle (fid′l), *n., v.,* **-dled, -dling.** —*n.* **1.** a violin. —*v.i.* **2.** to play the fiddle. **3.** to make nervous movements with the hands. **4.** to touch something, as to adjust it. **5.** to waste time; trifle. —**fid′dler,** *n.*

fid′dle•sticks′ *interj.* an exclamation of impatience, dismissal, etc.

fi•del•i•ty (fi del′i tē, fī-), *n., pl.* **-ties. 1.** loyalty; faithfulness. **2.** adherence to fact or detail. **3.** accuracy; exactness. **4.** the degree of accuracy with which sound or images are recorded or reproduced.

fidg•et (fij′it), *v.i.* **1.** to move about restlessly, nervously, or impatiently. —*n.* **2.** Often, **fidgets.** the condition of being restless, nervous, or impatient. —**fid′get•er,** *n.* —**fidg′et•y,** *adj.*

fi•du•ci•ar•y (fi dōō′shē er′ē, -dyōō′-), *n., pl.* **-ies,** *adj.* —*n.* **1.** *Law.* a person who holds something in trust for the benefit of another. —*adj.* **2.** *Law.* of or being a fiduciary. **3.** of, based on, or in the nature of trust or confidence.

fief (fēf), *n.* an estate in land held of a feudal lord.

field (fēld), *n.* **1.** a piece of open or cleared land, esp. one suitable for pasture or tillage. **2.** an area devoted to sports; playing field. **3.** a sphere of activity or interest. **4.** a job or research location away from regular work or study facilities. **5. a.** a battleground. **b.** a battle. **6.** an expanse of something: *a field of ice.* **7.** a region characterized by a particular feature or natural resource: *an oil field.* **8.** the background of a flag, shield, or coin. **9.** all the competitors in a contest. **10.** a region of space in which a force acts, as that around a magnet or a charged particle. —*v.t.* **11. a.** (in baseball and cricket) to catch or pick up (the ball) in play. **b.** to place (a player or team) in the field to play. **12.** to answer skillfully: *to field questions.* —*Idiom.* **13. play the field,** *Informal.* to date a number of different persons. —**field′er,** *n.*

field′ day′ *n.* **1.** a day devoted to outdoor sports or athletic contests. **2.** an occasion or opportunity for unrestricted activity or enjoyment.

field′ hock′ey *n.* a field game in which two teams use curved sticks to try to drive a ball into a netted goal.

fiend (fēnd), *n.* **1.** an evil spirit; demon. **2.** a diabolically cruel or wicked person. **3.** *Informal.* a person who is addicted to a habit or practice: *an opium fiend.* **4.** *Informal.* a person who is excessively interested in an activity; fan. —**fiend′ish,** *adj.* —**fiend′ish•ly,** *adv.* —**fiend′ish•ness,** *n.*

fierce (fērs), *adj.,* **fierc•er, fierc•est. 1.** menacingly wild and savage. **2.** violent in force or intensity. **3.** furiously eager or intense: *fierce competition.* **4.** *Informal.* extremely bad or severe. [< OF < L *ferus* wild] —**fierce′ly,** *adv.* —**fierce′ness,** *n.*

fier•y (fī∘r′ē, fī′ə rē), *adj.,* **-i•er, -i•est. 1.** consisting of or characterized by fire. **2.** intensely hot. **3.** like or suggestive of fire: *a fiery red.* **4.** intensely ardent or passionate. **5.** easily angered or provoked. **6.** inflamed, as a sore. —**fier′i•ness,** *n.*

fi•es•ta (fē es′tə), *n., pl.* **-tas.** a festival or festive celebration. [< Sp < L *fēsta* feast]

fife (fīf), *n.* a small high-pitched transverse flute. —**fif′er,** *n.*

fif•teen (fif′tēn′), *n.* **1.** a cardinal number, ten plus five. **2.** a symbol for this number, as 15 or XV. —*adj.* **3.** amounting to 15 in number. —**fif′teenth′,** *adj., n.*

fifth (fifth), *adj.* **1.** next after the fourth; being the ordinal number for five. **2.** being one of five equal parts. —*n.* **3.** a fifth part. **4.** the fifth member of a series. **5.** a fifth part of a gallon of liquor or spirits; ⅘ of a quart (about 750 milliliters). —*adv.* **6.** in the fifth place. —**fifth′ly,** *adv.*

fifth′ col′umn *n.* a group of people within a country who act traitorously out of secret sympathy with an enemy.

fifth′ wheel′ *n.* a superfluous or unwanted person or thing.

fif•ty (fif′tē), *n., pl.* **-ties,** *adj.* —*n.* **1.** a cardinal number, ten times five. **2.** a symbol for this num-

ber, as 50 or L. —*adj.* **3.** amounting to 50 in number. —**fif′ti•eth,** *adj., n.*

fig (fig), *n.* **1.** a tree or shrub of the mulberry family that bears a pear-shaped edible fruit. **2.** its fruit. **3.** a contemptibly trifling amount.

fig. 1. figurative. **2.** figuratively. **3.** figure.

fight (fīt), *n., v.,* **fought, fight•ing.** —*n.* **1.** a battle. **2.** a contest or struggle. **3.** an angry argument or disagreement. **4.** a boxing bout. **5.** ability, will, or inclination to combat, strive, or resist. —*v.i.* **6.** to engage in battle or single combat. **7.** to contend vigorously; strive. —*v.t.* **8.** to contend with in or as if in battle or combat. **9.** to carry on; wage. **10.** to make (one's way) by fighting or striving. —**fight′-er,** *n.*

fig•ment (fig′mənt), *n.* a product of mental invention.

fig′ur•a•tive (-yər ə tiv), *adj.* **1.** of the nature of or involving a figure of speech, esp. a metaphor; metaphorical. **2.** characterized by figures of speech. **3.** representing by a figure or emblem; emblematic. —**fig′ur•a•tive•ly,** *adv.*

fig•ure (fig′yər; *esp. Brit.* fig′ər), *n., v.,* **-ured, -ur•ing.** —*n.* **1.** a numerical symbol; numeral. **2.** an amount or value expressed in numbers. **3. figures,** arithmetic. **4.** a written symbol other than a letter. **5.** the form or shape of something; outline. **6.** the bodily form or frame. **7.** a personage, esp. one of distinction. **8.** the appearance or impression made by a person. **9.** a figure of speech. **10.** a pattern, as in cloth. **11.** a movement or series of movements, as in dancing or skating. —*v.t.* **12.** to compute or calculate. **13.** to adorn with a design or pattern. **14.** to picture or depict. **15.** *Informal.* to conclude, reason, or think. —*v.i.* **16.** to compute or work with numerical figures. **17.** to be or appear, esp. conspicuously. **18.** *Informal.* (of a situation, act, request, etc.) to be logical, expected, or reasonable. **19. figure on, a.** to count on. **b.** to plan on. **20. ~ out,** to come to understand; solve.

fig′ure•head′ *n.* **1.** a person who is titular head, as of a group, but has no real authority. **2.** a carved figure on the bow of a sailing ship.

fig′ure of speech′ *n.* an expression, as in metaphor, in which words are used in a nonliteral sense.

fig′ur•ine′ (-yə rēn′), *n.* a small ornamental figure, as of pottery or glass.

Fi•ji (fē′jē), *n.* a republic consisting of an archipelago (**Fi′ji Is′lands**) in the S Pacific.

fil•a•ment (fil′ə mənt), *n.* **1.** a very fine thread or threadlike structure. **2.** a threadlike conductor in a light bulb that is heated to incandescence. —**fil′a•men′tous** (-men′təs), *adj.*

fil•bert (fil′bərt), *n.* **1.** the thick-shelled edible nut of a European hazel. **2.** a tree or shrub bearing filberts. [< AF, alluding to St. *Philibert,* near whose feast day these nuts ripen]

filch (filch), *v.t.* to steal (something, esp. something of small value). —**filch′er,** *n.*

file¹ (fīl), *n., v.,* **filed, fil•ing.** —*n.* **1.** a container, as a folder or cabinet, in which papers are arranged in order. **2.** a collection of papers arranged in order. **3.** a collection of related computer data or program records stored by name. **4.** a line of persons or things one behind another. —*v.t.* **5.** to place in a file. **6.** to arrange in order for storage or reference. **7.** to transmit (a news story), as by wire. **8.** to submit or register: *to file a petition.* —*v.i.* **9.** to march in a line. **10.** to make application: *to file for divorce.* —*Idiom.* **11. on file,** filed for easy retrieval. —**fil′er,** *n.*

file² (fīl), *n., v.,* **filed, fil•ing.** —*n.* **1.** a metal tool having rough surfaces for reducing or smoothing metal, wood, etc. —*v.t.* **2.** to reduce, smooth, or remove with or as if with a file.

fil•i•al (fil′ē əl), *adj.* of or befitting a son or daughter.

fil•i•bus•ter (fil′ə bus′tər), *n.* **1.** the use of obstructive tactics, as exceptionally long speeches, to prevent or delay the adoption of a legislative measure. —*v.i., v.t.* **2.** to impede (legislation) by obstructive tactics. —**fil′i•bus′ter•er,** *n.*

fil•i•gree (fil′ə grē′), *n., adj., v.,* **-greed, -gree•**

ing. —*n.* **1.** delicate ornamental work, as of fine silver or gold wire. —*adj.* **2.** composed of or resembling filigree. —*v.t.* **3.** to adorn with or form into filigree.

Fil•i•pi•no (fil′ə pē′nō), *n., pl.* **-nos.** a native or inhabitant of the Philippines.

fill (fil), *v.t.* **1.** to put as much as can be held into. **2.** to occupy to full capacity. **3.** to feed fully; satiate. **4.** to pervade completely. **5.** to furnish (a vacancy or office) with an occupant. **6.** to occupy and perform the duties of (a position or post). **7.** to supply the requirements or contents of: *got her prescription filled.* **8.** to meet satisfactorily: *to fill a need.* **9.** to stop up; plug: *to fill a cavity.* —*v.i.* **10.** to become full. **11. fill in, a.** to supply (missing information). **b.** to complete by adding detail. **c.** to act as a substitute. **12. fill out, a.** to complete (a document or form) by supplying required information. **b.** to become rounder and fuller, as the human figure. —*n.* **13.** a full supply: *to eat one's fill.* **14.** material such as earth or stones for building up the level of an area of ground. —**fill′er,** *n.*

fil•let (fil′it; *usually* fi lā′ *for 1, 3*), *n., v.,* **fil•let•ed** (fil′i tid) *or, for 1, 3* **fil•leted** (fi lād′), **fi•let•ing.** —*n.* **1.** a boneless cut or slice of meat or fish. **2.** a narrow strip, as of ribbon or fabric. —*v.t.* **3.** to cut (meat or fish) into a fillet. **4.** to bind or adorn with or as if with a fillet.

fil•lip (fil′əp), *v.t.* **1.** to strike with the nail of a finger snapped from the end of the thumb. —*n.* **2.** an act or instance of filliping. **3.** something that tends to rouse or stimulate.

fil•ly (fil′ē), *n., pl.* **-lies.** a young female horse.

film (film), *n.* **1.** a thin layer or coating. **2.** a thin skin or membrane. **3.** a thin sheet or strip coated with a light-sensitive emulsion for taking photographs or motion pictures. **4.** MOTION PICTURE. —*v.t.* **5.** to cover with a film. **6. a.** to photograph with a motion-picture camera. **b.** to make a motion picture of. —*v.i.* **7.** to become covered by a film.

film′strip′ *n.* a strip of film with a series of transparencies for still projection.

film′y (fil′mē), *adj.,* **-i•er, -i•est. 1.** thin and light like film; gauzy. **2.** covered with a film. —**film/i•ness,** *n.*

fil•ter (fil′tər), *n.* **1.** a substance, as cloth or charcoal, through which liquid or gas is passed to remove suspended impurities. **2.** a device containing a substance for filtering. **3.** a lens screen on a camera that controls the rendering of color or diminishes the intensity of light. **4.** an electronic device that passes certain frequencies and blocks others. —*v.t., v.i.* **5.** to remove by a filter. **6.** to pass through or as if through a filter. —**fil′ter•a•ble, fil′tra•ble,** *adj.* —**fil′ter•er,** *n.*

filth (filth), *n.* **1.** disgusting dirt or refuse; foul matter. **2.** moral impurity or corruption. **3.** vulgar or obscene language or thought. —**filth′y,** *adj.,* **-i•er, -i•est.** —**filth′i•ness,** *n.*

fin (fin), *n.* **1.** a membranous winglike or paddlelike organ on the body of an aquatic animal, as a fish, used for propulsion, steering, or balancing. **2.** a part, as of a mechanism, resembling a fin. **3.** Usu., **fins.** FLIPPER (def. 2). —**finned,** *adj.*

fi•na•gle (fi nā′gəl), *v.i., v.t.,* **-gled, -gling.** to practice or obtain by guile, trickery, or manipulation. —**fi•na′gler,** *n.*

fi•nal (fīn′l), *adj.* **1.** pertaining to or coming at the end; last. **2.** ultimate. **3.** conclusive or decisive. —*n.* **4.** the last and decisive game, match, or round in a series, as in sports. **5.** the last examination in a course of study. —**fi•nal′i•ty,** *n.* —**fi′nal•ly,** *adv.*

fi•na•le (fi nal′ē, -nä′lē), *n., pl.* **-les.** the concluding part of something, esp. of a musical composition.

fi•nance (fi nans′, fī′nans), *n., v.,* **-nanced, -nanc•ing.** —*n.* **1.** the management of funds, esp. those affecting the public. **2. finances,** monetary resources, as of an individual or a government. —*v.t.* **3.** to supply with money or capital. **4.** to obtain money or credit for. —**fi•nan′cial,** *adj.* —**fi•nan′cial•ly,** *adv.*

fin•an•cier (fin′ən sēr′, fī′nən-), *n.* a person

skilled or engaged in managing large financial operations.

finch (finch), *n.* any of various small songbirds with a short bill adapted for eating seeds.

find (fīnd), *v.,* **found, find•ing,** *n.* —*v.t.* **1.** to come upon by chance. **2.** to locate, attain, or obtain by search or effort. **3.** to recover (something lost). **4.** to gain or regain the use of: *to find one's tongue.* **5.** to ascertain by study or calculation. **6.** to feel; perceive. **7.** to determine after judicial inquiry. —*v.i.* **8.** to determine an issue after judicial inquiry: *The jury found for the plaintiff.* **9. find out,** to uncover and expose the true nature or identity of. —*n.* **10.** the act of finding. **11.** something found, esp. a valuable discovery. —**find′er,** *n.*

fine[1] (fīn), *adj.,* **fin•er, fin•est,** *adv.* —*adj.* **1.** of superior quality; excellent. **2.** consisting of minute particles: *fine sand.* **3.** very thin; slender: *fine thread.* **4.** sharp, as a tool. **5.** delicate, as in texture. **6.** highly skilled; accomplished. **7.** polished; refined: *fine manners.* **8.** delicate; subtle: *a fine distinction.* **9.** (of a precious metal or its alloy) free from impurities. —*adv.* **10.** very well; excellently. —**fine′ly,** *adv.* —**fine′ness,** *n.*

fine[2] (fīn), *n., v.,* **fined, fin•ing.** —*n.* **1.** a sum of money imposed as a penalty for an offense or dereliction. —*v.t.* **2.** to subject to or punish by a fine.

fine′ art′ *n.* art, as painting, created primarily for aesthetic purposes and valued for such.

fin′er•y *n., pl.* **-ies.** fine or showy clothing and ornaments.

fi•nesse (fi nes′), *n.* **1.** delicacy or subtlety of performance or skill. **2.** skill and adroitness in handling a situation.

fin•ger (fing′gər), *n.* **1.** one of the jointed terminal members of the hand, esp. one other than the thumb. **2.** something like a finger in form or use. —*v.t.* **3.** to touch with the fingers; handle. **4.** to play on (a musical instrument) with the fingers. —*Idiom.* **5. keep one's fingers crossed,** to hope fervently for something. **6. put one's finger on, a.** to remember precisely. **b.** to locate exactly. **7. wrap around one's finger,** to exert complete control over, esp. through cajolery. —**fin′ger•tip′,** *n.*

fin′ger•print′ *n.* **1.** an impression of the markings of the inner surface of the fingertip, esp. when made for purposes of identification. —*v.t.* **2.** to take or record the fingerprints of.

fin•ick•y (fin′i kē) also **-i•cal** (-i kəl), *adj.* excessively particular or fastidious.

fin•is (fin′is, fē nē′, fī′nis), *n.* the end; conclusion.

fin•ish (fin′ish), *v.t.* **1.** to bring to an end. **2.** to come to the end of. **3.** to use completely. **4.** to destroy or kill. **5.** to complete and perfect in detail. **6.** to put a surface coating on (wood, metal, etc.). —*v.i.* **7.** to come to an end. —*n.* **8.** the final part or last stage; end or conclusion. **9.** educational or social polish. **10.** the surface coating or texture, as of wood. **11.** something that finishes, completes, or perfects a thing. —**fin′ish•er,** *n.*

fi•nite (fī′nīt), *adj.* **1.** having bounds or limits. **2. a.** (of a set of mathematical elements) capable of being completely counted. **b.** not infinite or infinitesimal. —**fi′nite•ly,** *adv.*

Fin•land (fin′lənd), *n.* a republic in N Europe, on the Baltic.

Finn (fin), *n.* a native or inhabitant of Finland.

Finn or **Finn.,** Finland.

Finn•ish (fin′ish), *n.* **1.** the language of Finland. —*adj.* **2.** of Finland, the Finns, or Finnish.

fiord (fyôrd, fē ôrd′), *n.* FJORD.

fir (fûr), *n.* **1.** an evergreen tree of the pine family with flat needles and erect cones. **2.** the wood of a fir.

fire (fī″r), *n., v.,* **fired, fir•ing.** —*n.* **1.** the light, heat, and flame given off by something burning. **2.** a burning mass of material, as in a furnace. **3.** a destructive burning, as of a building. **4.** brilliance, as of a gem. **5.** burning passion. **6.** the discharge of firearms: *enemy fire.* —*v.t.* **7.** to set on fire. **8.** to supply with fuel. **9.** to bake in a kiln. **10.** to fill with excitement or enthusiasm. **11.** to discharge; shoot: *to fire an arrow.* **12.** to dismiss from a job.

—*v.i.* **13.** to take fire. **14.** to become excited or enthusiastic. **15.** to discharge a gun or hurl a projectile. —*Idiom.* **16. under fire, a.** under attack, esp. by military forces. **b.** under censure or criticism. —**fir′er,** *n.*

fire′arm′ *n.* a weapon, as a pistol, from which a projectile is fired by gunpowder.

fire′bomb′ *n.* **1.** an explosive device with incendiary effects. —*v.t.* **2.** to attack with firebombs.

fire′crack′er *n.* a paper cylinder having an explosive and a fuse and set off to make a noise.

fire′fight′er *n.* a person who fights destructive fires. —**fire′fight′ing,** *n., adj.*

fire′fly′ *n., pl.* **-flies.** a nocturnal beetle with a light-producing organ at the rear of the abdomen.

fire′man (-mən*′*), *n., pl.* **-men. 1.** a firefighter. **2.** a person employed to tend fires; stoker.

fire′place′ *n.* **1.** the part of a chimney that opens into a room and in which fuel is burned. **2.** an open structure for keeping a fire, as at a campsite.

fire′plug′ *n.* HYDRANT.

fire′proof′ *adj.* **1.** resistant to destruction by fire. —*v.t.* **2.** to make fireproof.

fire′side′ *n.* **1.** the space around a fire or hearth. **2.** home or family life.

fire′trap′ *n.* a building likely to burn and difficult to escape from.

fire′wood′ *n.* wood suitable for fuel.

fire′works′ *n.pl.* devices ignited for display of light.

firm¹ (fûrm), *adj.,* **-er, -est,** *v.* —*adj.* **1.** not soft or yielding when pressed. **2.** securely fixed in place. **3.** not shaking or trembling. **4.** not subject to change or fluctuation. **5.** indicating determination. —*v.t., v.i.* **6.** to make or become firm. —**firm′ly,** *adv.* —**firm′ness,** *n.*

firm² (fûrm), *n.* a commercial company; business.

fir•ma•ment (fûr′mə mənt), *n.* the arch or vault of heaven; sky.

first (fûrst), *adj.* **1.** being before all others; used as the ordinal number of *one.* —*adv.* **2.** before all others. **3.** for the first time. **4.** in preference to something else; rather: *I'd die first.* —*n.* **5.** the person or thing that is first, as in time, order, or rank. **6.** the beginning. **7.** low gear in an automotive vehicle. **8.** the winning position or rank in a competition.

first′ aid′ *n.* emergency treatment given before regular medical services can be obtained. —**first′-aid′,** *adj.*

first′ class′ *n.* **1.** the best or highest class or grade. **2.** the most expensive class of travel accommodation. **3.** the class of mail consisting of matter sealed against inspection. —**first′-class′,** *adj., adv.*

first′hand′ or **first′-hand′,** *adj., adv.* from the first or original source.

first′ lieuten′ant *n.* a military officer ranking next above second lieutenant.

first′ mate′ *n.* the officer of a merchant ship ranking next below the captain.

first′-rate′ *adj.* **1.** of the highest quality, rank, rate, or class. —*adv.* **2.** very well.

fis•cal (fis′kəl), *adj.* **1.** of a public treasury or public revenues. **2.** of financial matters. —**fis′cal•ly,** *adv.*

fish (fish), *n., pl.* **fish, fish•es,** *v.* —*n.* **1.** any of various cold-blooded aquatic vertebrates having gills, fins, and typically scales. **2.** the flesh of a fish used as food. —*v.t.* **3.** to try to catch fish in. **4.** to draw as if fishing: *He fished a coin out of his pocket.* —*v.i.* **5.** to attempt to catch fish. **6.** to search carefully: *to fish through papers.* **7.** to seek to obtain something indirectly: *fishing for a compliment.* —**fish′er•man,** *n., pl.* **-men.** —**fish′er•y,** *n., pl.* **-er•ies.**

fish′y *adj.,* **-i•er, -i•est. 1.** like a fish, esp. in smell or taste. **2.** of questionable character; dubious: *a fishy excuse.* —**fish′i•ly,** *adv.* —**fish′i•ness,** *n.*

fis•sion (fish′ən), *n.* **1.** the act of cleaving into parts. **2.** the splitting of the nucleus of an atom into nuclei of lighter atoms, accompanied by the release of energy. —**fis′sion•a•ble,** *adj.*

fis•sure (fish′ər), *n.* a narrow opening, division, or groove.

fist (fist), *n.* **1.** the hand closed tightly with the fingers doubled into the palm. **2.** INDEX (def. 4).

fist′ful (-fŏŏl), *n., pl.* **-fuls.** a handful.

fist′i•cuffs′ (-i kufs′) *n.pl.* a fight with the fists.

fit¹ (fit), *adj.,* **fit•ter, fit•test,** *v.,* **fit•ted** or **fit, fit•ting,** *n.* —*adj.* **1.** adapted or suited; appropriate. **2.** proper or becoming. **3.** prepared or ready. **4.** in good physical condition; healthy. —*v.t.* **5.** to be adapted to or suitable for. **6.** to be proper or becoming for. **7.** to be of the right size or shape for. **8.** to make conform; adjust. **9.** to make qualified or competent. **10.** to make ready; prepare. **11.** to provide; equip. —*v.i.* **12.** to be suitable or proper. **13.** to be of the right size or shape. —*n.* **14.** the manner in which a thing fits. **15.** something that fits. —**fit′ly,** *adv.* —**fit′ness,** *n.* —**fit′ter,** *n.*

fit² (fit), *n.* **1.** a sudden acute attack, as of a disease or of convulsions. **2.** a sudden onset, as of emotion. —*Idiom.* **3. by fits and starts,** at irregular intervals.

fit′ful *adj.* spasmodic; irregular. —**fit′ful•ly,** *adv.* —**fit′ful•ness,** *n.*

fit′ting *adj.* **1.** suitable or appropriate. —*n.* **2.** an act or instance of trying on clothes that are being made or altered. **3.** an item provided as standard equipment. —**fit′ting•ly,** *adv.*

five (fīv), *n.* **1.** a cardinal number, four plus one. **2.** a symbol for this number, as 5 or V. —*adj.* **3.** amounting to five in number.

fix (fiks), *v.t.* **1.** to repair; mend. **2.** to put in order; adjust. **3.** to make fast, firm, or stable. **4.** to settle definitely: *to fix a price.* **5.** to direct or hold steadily: *eyes fixed on the page.* **6.** to put into permanent form. **7.** to put or place; assign: *tried to fix the blame on me.* **8.** to arrange or influence the outcome of, esp. dishonestly: *to fix a game.* **9.** to get (a meal) ready. **10.** to get even with. **11.** to castrate or spay (an animal, esp. a pet). **12.** to make (a photographic image) permanent. —*v.i.* **13.** to become fixed. **14. fix up, a.** to provide with an introduction to someone for a date. **b.** to repair. **c.** to refurbish. —*n.* **15.** a difficult situation; predicament. **16.** a charted position of a ship or aircraft. **17.** *Slang.* an injection of a narcotic, esp. heroin. **18.** *Slang.* an underhand or illegal arrangement. —**fix′a•ble,** *adj.* —**fix′er,** *n.*

fix•a•tion (fik sā′shən), *n.* a strong preoccupation, as with one subject or person; obsession. —**fix′ate,** *v.t., v.i.,* **-at•ed, -at•ing.**

fixed *adj.* **1.** firmly attached or placed; stationary. **2.** stable or permanent, as color. **3.** steadily directed; intent: *a fixed stare.* **4.** not fluctuating or varying: *a fixed income.* —**fix•ed•ly** (fik′sid lē, fikst′lē), *adv.*

fix′ings *n.pl. Informal.* appropriate accompaniments; trimmings.

fix′ture (-chər), *n.* **1.** something securely and usu. permanently attached: *a light fixture.* **2.** a person or thing long established in the same place or position.

fizz (fiz), *v.i.* **1.** to make a hissing or sputtering sound; effervesce. —*n.* **2.** a fizzing sound. **3.** an effervescent drink. —**fiz′zy,** *adj.,* **-zi•er, -zi•est.**

fiz•zle (fiz′əl), *v.,* **-zled, -zling,** *n.* —*v.i.* **1.** to fizz. **2.** to fail or expire feebly, esp. after a good start. —*n.* **3.** a failure; fiasco.

fjord (fyôrd, fē ôrd′), *n.* a long narrow arm of the sea bordered by steep cliffs.

FL Florida.

fl. 1. floor. **2.** florin. **3.** (he or she) flourished. [< L *floruit*] **4.** fluid.

Fla. Florida.

flab (flab), *n.* loose, excessive flesh.

flab•ber•gast (flab′ər gast′), *v.t.* to overcome with surprise and bewilderment; astound.

flab•by (flab′ē), *adj.,* **-bi•er, -bi•est. 1.** lacking firmness; flaccid. **2.** lacking determination; weakminded. —**flab′bi•ly,** *adv.* —**flab′bi•ness,** *n.*

flac•cid (flak′sid, flas′id), *adj.* not firm; soft and limp.

flag¹ (flag), *n., v.,* **flagged, flag•ging.** —*n.* **1.** a piece of cloth of distinctive color and design that is used as a symbol, as of a nation, or as a signal. **2.** something, as a tag on a file card, used to attract attention. —*v.t.* **3.** to place a flag over or on. **4.** to signal or warn with or as if with a flag. **—flag′ger,** *n.*

flag² (flag), *n.* any of various plants with long, sword-shaped leaves.

flag³ (flag), *v.i.,* **flagged, flag•ging. 1.** to fall off in vigor, energy, activity, or interest. **2.** to hang limply; droop.

flag⁴ (flag), *n.* FLAGSTONE.

flag•el•late (flaj′ə lāt′), *v.t.,* **-lat•ed, -lat•ing.** to punish by whipping; scourge. **—flag′el•la′tion,** *n.* **—flag′el•la′tor,** *n.*

flag•on (flag′ən), *n.* a container for liquids, esp. one with a handle, a spout, and a cover.

fla•grant (flā′grənt), *adj.* shockingly noticeable or evident; glaring. **—fla′gran•cy, fla′grance,** *n.* **—fla′grant•ly,** *adv.*

flag′ship′ *n.* **1.** a ship carrying the commander of a fleet or squadron. **2.** the most important one of a group.

flag′stone′ *n.* a flat stone slab used esp. for paving.

flail (flāl), *n.* **1.** an instrument for threshing grain. —*v.t., v.i.* **2.** to beat or swing with or as if with a flail.

flair (flâr), *n.* **1.** natural talent or aptitude. **2.** smartness of style or manner.

flak (flak), *n.* **1.** antiaircraft fire. **2.** critical or hostile reaction.

flake (flāk), *n., v.,* **flaked, flak•ing.** —*n.* **1.** a small, flat, thin piece detached from a larger piece or surface. **2.** a small piece or mass, as of snow. —*v.i.* **3.** to peel off, fall in, or form into flakes. —*v.t.* **4.** to remove in flakes.

flak′y *adj.,* **-ier, -iest. 1.** of or like flakes. **2.** lying or coming off in flakes. **3.** *Slang.* eccentric; odd. **—flak′i•ness,** *n.*

flam•bé (fläm bā′), *adj.* served in flaming liquor.

flam•boy•ant (flam boi′ənt), *adj.* **1.** strikingly bold or brilliant. **2.** florid; ornate. **—flam•boy′-ance, flam•boy′an•cy,** *n.* **—flam•boy′ant•ly,** *adv.*

flame (flām), *n., v.,* **flamed, flam•ing.** —*n.* **1.** burning gas or vapor, as from ignited wood. **2.** Often, **flames.** blazing combustion. **3.** a flamelike condition. **4.** brilliant light. **5.** intense ardor or passion. **6.** a sweetheart. **7.** an act or instance of angry criticism or disparagement, esp. on a computer network. —*v.i.* **8.** to burn with or burst into flames. **9.** to glow like flame. **10.** to behave in an offensive manner, esp. on a computer network.

fla•men•co (flä meng′kō, flə-), *n., pl.* **-cos.** a dance style of the Spanish Gypsies marked by stamping of the feet. [< Sp: pertaining to the Gypsies]

fla•min•go (flə ming′gō), *n., pl.* **-gos, -goes.** a wading bird with pinkish to scarlet plumage and very long legs.

flam•ma•ble (flam′ə bəl), *adj.* easily set on fire. **—flam′ma•bil′i•ty,** *n.*

flange (flanj), *n.* a projecting rim, as on a pipe, to give strength or support or to enable attachment of objects.

flank (flangk), *n.* **1.** a side, esp. the side of an animal or a person between the ribs and hip. **2.** the right or left side of a military formation. —*v.t.* **3.** to stand or be placed at the flank of. **4.** to defend at the flank. **5.** to menace or attack the flank of. **6.** to pass around the flank of.

flan•nel (flan′l), *n.* **1.** a warm, soft, napped fabric of wool or cotton. **2. flannels,** trousers or underwear made of flannel.

flap (flap), *v.,* **flapped, flap•ping,** *n.* —*v.i., v.t.* **1.** to swing or cause to swing loosely, esp. with noise. **2.** to move up and down, as wings. **3.** to strike with something broad and flexible. —*n.* **4.** something flat and broad attached at one side only and hanging loose. **5.** a flapping motion or sound. **6.** *Informal.* a state of nervous excitement. **—flap′per,** *n.*

flare (flâr), *v.,* **flared, flar•ing,** *n.* —*v.i.* **1.** to blaze or burn with a sudden unsteady flame. **2.** to burst out in sudden, fierce emotion. **3.** to spread gradually outward, as the bottom of a wide skirt. —*n.* **4.**

a flaring or swaying flame or light. **5. a.** a blaze of fire or light used as a signal or for illumination. **b.** a device producing such a blaze. **6.** a sudden burst, as of anger. **7.** outward curvature.

flare′up′ *n.* a sudden outburst or outbreak.

flash (flash), *n.* **1.** a brief, sudden burst of light. **2.** a sudden, brief outburst, as of wit. **3.** a brief moment; instant. **4.** a flashlight. **5.** ostentatious display. **6.** a brief preliminary news dispatch. **7.** a sudden thought or insight. —*v.i.* **8.** to break forth into sudden flame or light. **9.** to gleam; sparkle. **10.** to appear suddenly: *The answer flashed into his mind.* **11.** to move like a flash. —*v.t.* **12.** to emit (fire or light) in sudden flashes. **13.** to cause to flash. **14.** to communicate instantaneously, as by radio. **15.** to make an ostentatious display of. **16.** to display briefly: *to flash an ID card.* —*adj.* **17.** sudden and brief: *a flash fire.* **—flash′er,** *n.*

flash′back′ *n.* **1.** an earlier event inserted into the chronological structure of a literary or dramatic work. **2.** an abnormally vivid, often recurrent recollection of a disturbing past event.

flash′bulb′ *n.* a glass bulb filled with metal wire or foil that when electrically ignited illuminates a photographic subject momentarily.

flash′light′ *n.* a portable electric lamp powered by dry batteries.

flash′y *adj.,* **-i•er, -i•est. 1.** briefly and superficially brilliant. **2.** ostentatious and tasteless; gaudy. **—flash′i•ly,** *adv.* **—flash′i•ness,** *n.*

flask (flask, fläsk), *n.* a flat metal or glass bottle, esp. for carrying in the pocket: *a flask of brandy.*

flat¹ (flat), *adj.,* **flat•ter, flat•test,** *n., v.,* **flat•ted, flat•ting,** *adv.* —*adj.* **1.** horizontally level. **2.** level, even, or smooth in surface. **3.** lying at full length; prone. **4.** not deep or thick. **5.** spread out, as an unrolled map. **6.** deflated: *a flat tire.* **7.** absolute; downright: *a flat denial.* **8.** unvarying; fixed: *a flat rate.* **9.** lacking vitality or animation. **10.** lacking flavor, piquancy, or effervescence. **11.** pointless, as a joke. **12.** not shiny or glossy; matte. **13. a.** (of a tone) lowered a half step in pitch. **b.** below an intended pitch. —*n.* **14.** something flat. **15.** a flat surface, side, or part. **16.** flat or level ground: *salt flats.* **17. a.** a symbol which indicates that the pitch of a note is lowered one half step. **b.** a tone one half step below another. **18.** a deflated automobile tire. —*v.t., v.i.* **19.** to make or become flat. —*adv.* **20.** in a flat position or manner. **21.** completely; utterly: *flat broke.* **22.** exactly; precisely: *in two minutes flat.* **23.** below the true pitch: *sang flat.* —*Idiom.* **24. flat out,** *Informal.* **a.** directly or openly. **b.** at full speed or with maximum effort. **—flat′ly,** *adv.* **—flat′ness,** *n.*

flat² (flat), *n.* a residential apartment.

flat′bed′ *n.* a truck with a body in the form of an open platform.

flat′car′ *n.* a railroad car without sides or top.

flat′fish′ *n., pl.* **-fish, -fish•es.** any of various fishes, including the flounders and soles, that have a greatly flattened body with both eyes on the upper side.

flat′foot′ *n., pl.* **-feet** for 1b, **-foots** for 2. **1. a.** a condition in which the arch of the foot is flattened. **b.** Usu., **-feet.** feet with flattened arches. **2.** *Slang.* a police officer. **—flat′foot′ed,** *adj.*

flat′-out′ *adj. Informal.* **1.** using full speed or all of one's resources. **2.** downright; thoroughgoing.

flat′ter *v.t.* **1.** to praise or compliment insincerely, effusively, or excessively. **2.** to represent or show favorably: *The portrait flatters her.* **3.** to feel satisfaction with (oneself), often mistakenly: *He flattered himself that the speech had gone well.* **—flat′ter•er,** *n.* **—flat′ter•ing•ly,** *adv.* **—flat′ter•y,** *n.*

flat•u•lent (flach′ə lənt), *adj.* **1.** having an accumulation of gas in the intestinal tract. **2.** inflated and empty; pompous. **—flat′u•lence,** *n.*

fla•tus (flā′təs), *n.* intestinal gas.

flat′ware′ *n.* **1.** table utensils, as knives, forks, and spoons. **2.** flat tableware, as plates and saucers.

flaunt (flônt), *v.t.* **1.** to display ostentatiously; parade. **2.** to flout. **—flaunt′er,** *n.* **—flaunt′ing•ly,** *adv.*

fla•vor (flā′vər), *n.* **1.** the distinctive taste of something. **2.** a flavoring. **3.** the characteristic quality of a thing. —*v.t.* **4.** to give flavor to. Also, *esp. Brit.*, **fla′vour.** —**fla′vor•ful,** *adj.* —**fla′vor•less,** *adj.* —**fla′vor•some,** *adj.*

fla′vor•ing *n.* a substance used to give a particular flavor to food or drink.

flaw (flô), *n.* **1.** a feature that mars the perfection of something; defect, weakness, or blemish. —*v.t.* **2.** to produce a flaw in. —**flaw′less,** *adj.* —**flaw′less•ly,** *adv.* —**flaw′less•ness,** *n.*

flax (flaks), *n.* **1.** a plant with blue flowers that is cultivated for its fiber, used for making linen yarn, and for its seeds, which yield linseed oil. **2.** the fiber of this plant.

flay (flā), *v.t.*, **flayed, flay•ing. 1.** to strip off the skin of. **2.** to criticize with scathing severity. —**flay′er,** *n.*

flea (flē), *n.* a small, bloodsucking, leaping insect parasitic upon mammals and birds.

flea′ mar′ket *n.* a market, often outdoors, where used articles, curios, and antiques are sold.

fleck (flek), *n.* **1.** a small bit; speck. **2.** a small patch, as of color; spot. —*v.t.* **3.** to mark with flecks.

fledg•ling (flej′ling), *n.* **1.** a young bird that has recently acquired flight feathers. **2.** an inexperienced person. Also, *esp. Brit.*, **fledge′ling.**

flee (flē), *v.*, **fled, flee•ing.** —*v.i.* **1.** to run away, as from danger. **2.** to pass swiftly; fly. —*v.t.* **3.** to run away from.

fleece (flēs), *n.*, *v.*, **fleeced, fleec•ing.** —*n.* **1.** the coat of wool that covers a sheep. **2.** a warm fabric with a thick pile. —*v.t.* **3.** to cheat or swindle. **4.** to remove the fleece of (a sheep). —**fleec′er,** *n.* —**fleec′y,** *adj.*, **-i•er, -i•est.**

fleet¹ (flēt), *n.* **1.** the largest organization of warships under the command of a single officer. **2.** a large group of ships, airplanes, trucks, etc., under the same management or ownership.

fleet² (flēt), *adj.*, **-er, -est,** *v.* —*adj.* **1.** swift; rapid. —*v.i.* **2.** to move swiftly; fly. —**fleet′ly,** *adv.* —**fleet′ness,** *n.*

fleet′ing *adj.* passing swiftly. —**fleet′ing•ly,** *adv.* —**fleet′ing•ness,** *n.*

flesh (flesh), *n.* **1.** the soft substance of an animal's body, esp. muscular tissue. **2.** muscular and fatty tissue. **3.** meat, usu. excluding fish and fowl. **4.** the body as distinguished from the spirit or soul. **5.** HUMANKIND. **6.** living creatures in general. **7.** a person's family or relatives. **8.** the soft, pulpy portion of a fruit or vegetable. —*v.t.* **9.** to give dimension or substance to: *The playwright fleshed out the characters.* —*Idiom.* **10. in the flesh,** present before one's eyes; in person. —**flesh′y,** *adj.*, **-i•er, -i•est.**

flesh′pot′ *n.* a place of luxurious and unrestrained pleasure.

flex (fleks), *v.t.*, *v.i.* **1.** to bend. **2.** to tighten (a muscle) by contraction.

flex•i•ble *adj.* **1.** capable of being bent or flexed. **2.** susceptible of modification or change; adaptable. **3.** willing or disposed to yield; tractable. —**flex′i•bil′i•ty,** *n.* —**flex′i•bly,** *adv.*

flick¹ (flik), *n.* **1.** a sudden light blow or tap. **2.** the sound made by a flick. **3.** a light and rapid movement. —*v.t.* **4.** to strike, remove, propel, or operate with a flick. —*v.i.* **5.** to move rapidly or jerkily.

flick² (flik), *n. Slang.* a motion picture.

flick′er¹, *v.i.* **1.** to burn unsteadily. **2.** to flutter. —*n.* **3.** an unsteady flame or light. **4.** a flickering movement. **5.** a brief flurry: *a flicker of interest.*

flick′er², *n.* any of several North American woodpeckers with yellow or red underwings.

fli•er (flī′ər), *n.* **1.** a person, animal, or thing that flies. **2.** a pilot. **3.** something that moves with great speed. **4.** a small handbill; circular. **5.** *Informal.* a risky or speculative venture.

flight¹ (flīt), *n.* **1.** the act, process, or power of flying. **2.** the distance covered or the course taken in a flight. **3.** a trip by or in an airplane. **4.** a number of beings or things flying together. **5.** swift movement, transition, or progression. **6.** a transcending of the ordinary bounds of the mind: *a flight of fancy.* **7.** a series of steps between one floor and the next.

flight² (flīt), *n.* an act or instance of fleeing.

flight′less *adj.* incapable of flying.

flight′y *adj.*, **-i•er, -i•est. 1.** frivolous and irresponsible. **2.** unstable; volatile. —**flight′i•ness,** *n.*

flim•sy (flim′zē), *adj.*, **-si•er, -si•est. 1.** without material strength or solidity. **2.** not effective or convincing; implausible. —**flim′si•ly,** *adv.* —**flim′si•ness,** *n.*

flinch (flinch), *v.i.* **1.** to draw back, as from pain or danger; shrink. **2.** to shrink or tense under pain; wince.

fling (fling), *v.*, **flung, fling•ing,** *n.* —*v.t.* **1.** to throw with force, violence, or abandon. **2.** to put or send suddenly or without preparation. **3.** to involve (oneself) vigorously in an undertaking. **4.** to throw aside or away. —*v.i.* **5.** to move with haste or violence. —*n.* **6.** an act or instance of flinging. **7.** a short period of unrestrained indulgence of one's desires. **8.** an attempt. **9.** a lively Scottish dance. —**fling′er,** *n.*

flint (flint), *n.* **1.** a hard stone that is a form of silica. **2.** a piece of flint, esp. as used for striking fire. —**flint′y,** *adj.*, **-i•er, -i•est.**

flip (flip), *v.*, **flipped, flip•ping,** *n.*, *adj.*, **flip•per, flip•pest.** —*v.t.* **1.** to turn over by or as if by tossing. **2.** to move or activate with a sudden stroke or jerk. **3.** to resell, esp. quickly, or refinance. **4.** to read or look at rapidly or perfunctorily. **5.** *Slang.* **a.** to react with excitement. **b.** to become insane. —*n.* **6.** an act or instance of flipping. —*adj.* **7.** flippant; pert. —*Idiom.* **8. flip one's lid,** *Slang.* to lose control of one's temper.

flip′-flop′ *n.* **1.** a sudden or unexpected reversal, as of opinion. **2.** a backward somersault. **3.** the sound or motion of something flapping.

flip•pant (flip′ənt), *adj.* frivolously disrespectful, shallow, or lacking in seriousness. —**flip′pan•cy,** *n.* —**flip′pant•ly,** *adv.*

flip•per (flip′ər), *n.* **1.** a broad, flat limb, as of a seal, specially adapted for swimming. **2.** a paddlelike device, usu. of rubber, worn on the foot as an aid in swimming.

flirt (flûrt), *v.i.* **1.** to act amorously without serious intentions. **2.** to trifle or toy, as with an idea. **3.** to move jerkily. —*n.* **4.** a person given to flirting. **5.** a sudden jerk. —**flir•ta′tion,** *n.* —**flir•ta′tious,** *adj.* —**flir•ta′tious•ly,** *adv.*

flit (flit), *v.i.*, **flit•ted, flit•ting.** to fly, move, or pass swiftly, lightly, or irregularly from one place or condition to another.

float (flōt), *v.i.* **1.** to rest on the surface of a liquid. **2.** to move gently on or as if on the surface of a liquid; drift along: *a balloon floating through the air.* **3.** to move lightly and gracefully. **4.** to wander aimlessly. —*v.t.* **5.** to cause to float. **6.** to issue (stocks, bonds, etc.) in order to raise money. —*n.* **7.** something that floats, as a raft. **8.** a hollow ball that through its buoyancy automatically regulates the level of a liquid. **9.** a cork supporting a baited fishing line in the water. **10.** a vehicle bearing a display in a parade. **11.** a drink with ice cream floating in it. —**float′er,** *n.*

flock¹ (flok), *n.* **1.** a group of animals, as sheep or birds, that live, travel, or feed together. **2.** a large group, as of people. **3.** the congregation of a church. —*v.i.* **4.** to gather or go in a flock.

flock² (flok), *n.* finely powdered fiber, as of wool, used for producing a velvetlike pattern on wallpaper or cloth or for coating metal.

floe (flō), *n.* a sheet of floating ice.

flog (flog, flôg), *v.t.*, **flogged, flog•ging.** to beat with a whip or stick. —**flog′ger,** *n.*

flood (flud), *n.* **1.** a great overflow of water, esp. over land not usu. submerged. **2.** a great outpouring: *a flood of tears.* **3. the Flood,** *Bible.* the great deluge that occurred in the time of Noah. —*v.t.* **4.** to cover with or as if with a flood. **5.** to overwhelm with an abundance or excess. —*v.i.* **6.** to become flooded.

flood′light′ *n.*, *v.*, **-light•ed** or **-lit, -light•ing.** —*n.* **1.** an artificial light that provides uniform illumination over a large area. —*v.t.* **2.** to illuminate with a floodlight.

floor (flôr), *n.* **1.** the surface of a room on which one walks. **2.** a story of a building. **3.** the lower or bottom surface: *the ocean floor.* **4. a.** the part of a legislative chamber where members sit and from which they speak. **b.** the right to speak from the floor. **5.** a minimum level. —*v.t.* **6.** to cover or furnish with a floor. **7.** to knock down. **8.** to overwhelm; shock. **9.** to confound; nonplus.

floor′ing *n.* **1.** a floor. **2.** material for floors.

flop (flop), *v.*, **flopped, flop•ping,** *n.* —*v.i.* **1.** to move around, drop, or fall in a heavy, clumsy, or negligent manner. **2.** to be a complete failure. —*v.t.* **3.** to drop or move loosely or clumsily. —*n.* **4.** an act or sound of flopping. **5.** a complete failure.

flop′py *adj.*, **-pi•er, -pi•est,** *n.*, *pl.* **-pies.** —*adj.* **1.** tending to flop. —*n.* **2.** FLOPPY DISK. —**flop′pi•ly,** *adv.* —**flop′pi•ness,** *n.*

flop′py disk′ *n.* a thin, usu. flexible plastic disk coated with magnetic material for storing computer data and programs.

flo•ra (flôr′ə), *n.*, *pl.* **flo•ras, flo•rae** (flôr′ē). the plants or plant life of a particular region or period.

flo′ral *adj.* of or consisting of flowers.

flor•id (flôr′id, flor′-), *adj.* **1.** reddish in color; rosy. **2.** excessively ornate; flowery.

flo•rist (flôr′ist, flor′-), *n.* a retailer of flowers and ornamental plants.

floss (flôs, flos), *n.* **1. a.** short, untwisted silk filaments. **b.** embroidery thread of silk or fine cotton. **2.** silky, filamentous matter, as the silk of corn. **5.** DENTAL FLOSS. —*v.i.* **4.** to use dental floss. —*v.t.* **5.** to clean (the teeth) with dental floss.

flo•til•la (flō til′ə), *n.*, *pl.* **-las. 1.** a group of small ships. **2.** a large group moving together.

flot•sam (flot′səm), *n.* wreckage of a ship and its cargo found floating on the water.

flounce[1] (flouns), *v.*, **flounced, flounc•ing,** *n.* —*v.i.* **1.** to go with exaggerated, impatient, or impetuous movements. **2.** to throw the body about; flounder. —*n.* **3.** an act or instance of flouncing.

flounce[2] (flouns), *n.* a strip of gathered or pleated material attached along one edge, as to the bottom of a skirt.

floun•der[1] (floun′dər), *v.i.* **1.** to struggle to gain one's balance or to move. **2.** to act or speak clumsily, helplessly, or falteringly.

floun•der[2] (floun′dər), *n.*, *pl.* **-ders, -der.** any of various flatfishes valued as food.

flour (flou⁀r, flou′ər), *n.* **1.** the finely ground meal of grain, esp. wheat. **2.** a fine, soft powder resembling flour. —*v.t.* **3.** to sprinkle or coat with flour. —**flour′y,** *adj.*

flour•ish (flûr′ish, flur′-), *v.i.* **1.** to be in a vigorous state; thrive. **2.** to be at the height of development. **3.** to be successful; prosper. —*v.t.* **4.** to brandish dramatically. —*n.* **5.** a dramatic gesture or display. **6.** a decoration or embellishment, esp. in writing. **7.** an elaborate musical passage; fanfare. —**flour′ish•er,** *n.*

flout (flout), *v.t.*, *v.i.* to treat with or show disdain or scorn; scoff (at). —**flout′er,** *n.*

flow (flō), *v.i.* **1.** to move in a stream. **2.** to circulate, as blood. **3.** to stream forth. **4.** to issue from a source. **5.** to proceed smoothly or easily. **6.** to hang loosely and gracefully. **7.** to abound. **8.** to rise and advance, as the tide. —*v.t.* **9.** to cause or permit to flow. —*n.* **10.** the act of flowing. **11.** movement in or as if in a stream. **12.** the rate or volume of flow. **13.** something that flows. **14.** an overflow; flood. **15.** the rise of the tide. **16.** a transference of energy.

flow′ chart′ *n.* a graphic representation of the successive steps in a procedure or system.

flow•er (flou′ər), *n.* **1.** the blossom of a plant. **2.** the part of a seed plant comprising the reproductive organs. **3.** a plant cultivated for its blossom. **4.** a state of efflorescence or bloom. **5.** the finest or most flourishing period. **6.** the best or finest member, product, or example. —*v.i.* **7.** to produce flowers; blossom. **8.** to develop fully; mature. —**flow′ered,** *adj.* —**flow′er•y,** *adj.*, **-er•i•er, -er•i•est.**

flow′er•pot′ *n.* a container in which to grow plants.

flu (flōō), *n.* influenza.

flub (flub), *v.t.*, *v.i.*, **flubbed, flub•bing.** to botch or bungle.

fluc•tu•ate (fluk′chōō āt′), *v.i.*, **-at•ed, -at•ing.** to shift back and forth; vary irregularly. —**fluc′tu•a′-tion,** *n.*

flue (flōō), *n.* a passage or duct for smoke, air, or gas.

flu•ent (flōō′ənt), *adj.* **1.** spoken with ease: *fluent French.* **2.** able to speak smoothly or readily. **3.** flowing or capable of flowing; fluid. —**flu′en•cy,** *n.* —**flu′ent•ly,** *adv.*

fluff (fluf), *n.* **1.** light, downy particles, as of cotton. **2.** a soft, light, downy mass. **3.** something light or frivolous. **4.** a mistake, esp. an actor's memory lapse. —*v.t.*, *v.i.* **5.** to make or become fluffy. **6.** to make a mistake (in). —**fluff′y,** *adj.*, **-i•er, -i•est.**

flu•id (flōō′id), *n.* **1.** a substance, as a liquid or gas, that is capable of flowing and changes its shape when acted upon by a force. —*adj.* **2.** flowing or capable of flowing. **3.** not fixed or rigid: *Our plans are fluid.* **4.** convertible into cash: *fluid assets.* —**flu•id′i•ty,** *n.* —**flu′id•ly,** *adv.*

fluke[1] (flōōk), *n.* **1.** the part of an anchor that catches in the ground. **2.** a barbed head, as of a spear. **3.** either half of the tail of a whale.

fluke[2] (flōōk), *n.* a stroke of good luck. —**fluk′y,** *adj.*, **-i•er, -i•est.**

fluke[3] (flōōk), *n.* **1.** any of several American flounders. **2.** TREMATODE.

flume (flōōm), *n.* **1.** a deep, narrow gorge containing a stream or torrent. **2.** an artificial channel or trough for conducting water.

flunk (flungk), *v.i.*, *v.t.* to fail, esp. in a course or examination.

flun•ky or **-key** (flung′kē), *n.*, *pl.* **-kies** or **-keys. 1.** a liveried male servant. **2.** one who does menial work. **3.** a servile follower.

fluo•res•cence (flōō res′əns, flô-, flō-), *n.* **1.** the emission of radiation, esp. of visible light, by a substance during exposure to external radiation, as light or x-rays. **2.** the radiation so produced. —**fluo•res′cent,** *adj.*

fluores′cent lamp′ *n.* a tubular electric lamp in which light is produced by the fluorescence of phosphors coating the inside of the tube.

fluor•i•da•tion (flōōr′ə dā′shən, flôr′-) *n.* the addition of fluorides to drinking water to reduce tooth decay.

fluor′ide (-īd), *n.* a compound containing fluorine.

fluor′ine (-ēn), *n.* the most reactive nonmetallic element, a pale yellow, corrosive, toxic gas. *Symbol:* F; *at. wt.:* 18.9984; *at. no.:* 9.

flur•ry (flûr′ē, flur′ē), *n.*, *pl.* **-ries,** *v.*, **-ried, -ry•ing.** —*n.* **1.** a light, brief shower of snow. **2.** sudden commotion, excitement, or bustle. **3.** a sudden gust of wind. —*v.t.* **4.** to make confused or agitated. —*v.i.* **5.** to move in a confused or agitated manner. [b. of *flutter* and *hurry*]

flush[1] (flush), *n.* **1.** a rosy glow; blush. **2.** a rushing flow, as of water. **3.** a sudden rise, esp. of emotion. **4.** glowing freshness or vigor. **5.** a sensation of heat. —*v.t.* **6.** to cause to blush. **7.** to wash out by a sudden rush of water. **8.** to excite; inflame. —*v.i.* **9.** to blush. **10.** to flow and spread suddenly with a rush.

flush[2] (flush), *adj.* **1.** even or level with an adjoining surface. **2.** in direct contact; immediately adjacent. **3.** well supplied, esp. with money. **4.** ruddy or reddish in color. **5.** full of vigor. **6.** full to overflowing. **7.** even with the right or left margin of a type page. —*adv.* **8.** so as to be on the same level or plane or in direct contact. —*v.t.* **9.** to make flush.

flush[3] (flush), *v.t.* to cause to start up or fly off suddenly: *to flush a woodcock.*

flush[4] (flush), *n.* a hand of cards all of one suit.

flus•ter (flus′tər), *v.t.* to put into a state of nervous or agitated confusion.

flute (flōōt), *n.* **1.** a wind instrument with a high range, consisting of a tube with a series of

fingerholes or keys. **2.** a groove, as on the shaft of a column. —**flut′ed,** adj. —**flut′ing,** n.

flut•ist or **flau•tist** (flô′tist, flou′), n. a flute player.

flut•ter (flut′ər), v.i. **1.** to wave or flap about. **2.** to flap the wings rapidly. **3.** to move with quick, irregular motions. **4.** to beat rapidly, as the heart. **5.** to be tremulous or agitated. —v.t. **6.** to cause to flutter. —n. **7.** a fluttering movement. **8.** a state of nervous excitement or mental agitation. **9.** a stir; flurry. —**flut′ter•y,** adj.

flux (fluks), n. **1.** a flowing or flow. **2.** continuous change. **3.** a substance used to prevent oxidation of fused metal, as in soldering. **4.** an abnormal discharge of liquid matter from the bowels. —v.t. **5.** to make fluid; melt. **6.** to fuse with flux.

fly¹ (flī), v., **flew** or, for 8, **flied, flown, fly•ing,** n., pl. **flies.** —v.i. **1.** to move through the air using wings. **2.** to be carried through the air. **3.** to float or flutter in the air. **4.** to travel in or operate an aircraft or spacecraft. **5.** to move suddenly and quickly. **6.** to flee; escape. **7.** to pass swiftly. **8.** to bat a fly ball in baseball. —v.t. **9.** to cause to float or move through the air. **10.** to operate (an aircraft or spacecraft). **11.** to operate an aircraft over. **12.** to transport by air. **13.** to escape from. —n. **14.** a fold of material that conceals fasteners in a garment opening. **15.** a flap forming the door of a tent. **16.** an act of flying; flight. **17.** FLY BALL. **18. flies,** the space above the stage of a theater. —**Idiom.** **19. on the fly, a.** while in the air. **b.** without pausing. —**fly′a•ble,** adj.

fly² (flī), n., pl. **flies. 1.** any of numerous two-winged insects, esp. the common housefly. **2.** a fishhook dressed to resemble an insect.

fly′ ball′ n. a baseball batted high into the air.

fly′blown′ adj. tainted or contaminated; spoiled.

fly′-by-night′ adj. **1.** not reliable or stable, esp. in business. **2.** not lasting; transitory.

fly′ing sau′cer n. any of various disk-shaped objects reportedly seen flying at high speeds and altitudes.

fly′leaf′ n., pl. **-leaves.** a blank leaf in the front or the back of a book.

fly′wheel′ n. a heavy wheel that rotates on a shaft and regulates the speed of the shaft and connected machinery.

foal (fōl), n. **1.** the nursing young of a mammal of the horse family. —v.i. **2.** to give birth to a foal.

foam (fōm), n. **1.** a collection of minute bubbles formed on the surface of a liquid. **2.** a thick, frothy substance, as shaving cream. **3.** a lightweight material, as foam rubber, in which gas bubbles are dispersed in a solid. —v.i. **4.** to form or gather foam; froth. —**foam′y,** adj. **-i•er, -i•est.**

foam′ rub′ber n. spongy rubber used esp. for mattresses and cushions.

fob¹ (fob), n. **1.** a short chain or ribbon attached to a pocket watch. **2.** an ornament on a fob.

fob² (fob), v.t., **fobbed, fob•bing. fob off,** to dispose of (something inferior) by deception or trickery; palm off.

fob or **FOB,** free on board.

fo′cal length′ n. the distance from the center of a lens or mirror to the focus.

fo•cus (fō′kəs), n., pl. **-cus•es, -ci** (-sī, -kī), v., **-cused, -cus•ing** or (esp. Brit.) **-cussed, -cus•sing.** —n. **1.** a central point, as of attraction, attention, or activity. **2.** a point at which rays of light, heat, etc., meet after being refracted or reflected. **3. a.** FOCAL LENGTH. **b.** the adjustment of an optical device necessary to produce a clear image: in focus; out of focus. —v.t. **4.** to bring to a focus or into focus. **5.** to concentrate. —v.i. **6.** to become focused. —**fo′cal,** adj.

fod•der (fod′ər), n. coarse food for livestock.

foe (fō), n. **1.** an enemy. **2.** an opponent, as in a contest.

fog (fog, fôg), n., v., **fogged, fog•ging.** —n. **1.** a cloudlike mass or layer of minute water droplets near the surface of the earth, appreciably reducing visibility. **2.** a state of mental confusion. —v.t., v.i.

3. to envelop or become enveloped with or as if with fog. —**fog′gy,** adj., **-gi•er, -gi•est.**

fo•gy or **-gey** (fō′gē), n., pl. **-gies** or **-geys.** an old-fashioned or conservative person. —**fo′gy•ish,** adj.

foi•ble (foi′bəl), n. a minor weakness or failing of character.

foil¹ (foil), v.t. to prevent the success of; frustrate or thwart.

foil² (foil), n. **1.** metal in the form of very thin sheets: aluminum foil. **2.** a person or thing that makes another seem better by contrast.

foil³ (foil), n. a flexible four-sided fencing sword with a blunt point.

foist (foist), v.t. to impose fraudulently; palm off.

fold¹ (fōld), v.t. **1.** to bend (cloth, paper, etc.) over upon itself. **2.** to make compact by folding: She folded up the map. **3.** to bring together and intertwine or cross. **4.** to bring (wings) close to the body, as a bird. **5.** to enclose, wrap, or envelop. **6.** to embrace. **7.** to blend (a cooking ingredient) into a mixture by turning one part over another. —v.i. **8.** to be folded. **9.** to fail, esp. to go out of business. —n. **10.** a part, as a pleat, that is folded. **11.** a line, crease, or hollow made by folding. —**fold′a•ble,** adj.

fold² (fōld), n. **1.** an enclosure for sheep. **2.** a flock of sheep. **3.** a group sharing common beliefs or values.

-fold a combining form meaning: having a specified number of parts (a fourfold plan); multiplied the number of times specified (to increase tenfold).

fold′er n. **1.** a folded sheet of light cardboard used to hold papers. **2.** a printed sheet, as a circular, folded into a number of pagelike sections.

fo•li•age (fō′lē ij), n. leaves, as of a tree or plant.

fo′lic ac′id (fō′lik, fol′ik), n. a vitamin of the vitamin B complex, used in treating anemia.

fo•li•o (fō′lē ō′), n., pl. **-os. 1. a.** a sheet of paper folded once to make two leaves, or four pages, of a book. **b.** a book having pages of the largest size, formerly made from such a sheet. **2.** a page number in a book.

folk (fōk), n. **1.** Usu., **folks.** (used with a pl. v.) people in general. **2.** Often, **folks.** (used with a pl. v.) people of a specified class or group: poor folks. **3.** (used with a pl. v.) a group of people as the carriers of a society's customs and traditions. **4. folks,** Informal. the members of one's family; relatives. —adj. **5.** of or originating among the common people: folk music.

folk′lore′ n. the traditional beliefs, legends, and customs of a people. —**folk′lor′ic,** adj. —**folk′lor′-ist,** n. —**folk′lor•is′tic,** adj.

folk′ song′ n. **1.** a song originating among the common people and marked by simple melody and stanzaic, narrative verse. **2.** a song of similar character written by a known composer. —**folk′ sing′-er,** n.

folk′sy adj., **-si•er, -si•est. 1.** friendly; sociable. **2.** informal; unceremonious. —**folk′si•ness,** n.

fol•li•cle (fol′i kəl), n. Anatomy. a small cavity, sac, or gland.

fol•low (fol′ō), v.t. **1.** to come after in sequence or order; succeed. **2.** to go or come after. **3.** to act in accordance with; obey. **4.** to result from. **5.** to go in pursuit of. **6.** to engage in as a pursuit. **7.** to keep up with and understand. —v.i. **8.** to come next after something else in sequence or order. **9.** to occur as a consequence. **10. follow through,** to continue a motion, stroke, activity, or undertaking to its completion.

fol′low•er n. **1.** one that follows. **2.** a disciple or adherent. **3.** an attendant, servant, or retainer.

fol′low•ing n. **1.** a body of followers, adherents, admirers, or patrons. —adj. **2.** next in order or time; ensuing. **3.** that is now to follow.

fol′low-through′ n. **1.** the last part of a motion, as after a ball has been struck. **2.** the act of continuing a plan, program, etc., to completion.

fol•ly (fol′ē), n., pl. **-lies. 1.** lack of understanding or sense. **2.** a foolish action, practice, or idea. **3.** a costly and foolish undertaking.

fo•ment (fō ment′), *v.t.* to foster; instigate: *to fo-
ment trouble.* —**fo′men•ta′tion,** *n.* —**fo•ment′er,**
n.

fond (fond), *adj.,* **-er, -est. 1.** having a liking or affection: *fond of animals.* **2.** loving; affectionate. **3.**
excessively tender; doting. **4.** cherished: *fond hopes.*
—**fond′ly,** *adv.* —**fond′ness,** *n.*

fon•dant (fon′dənt), *n.* **1.** a thick, creamy sugar
paste. **2.** a candy made of fondant.

fon•dle (fon′dl), *v.t.,* **-dled, -dling.** to handle or
touch lovingly; caress. —**fon′dler,** *n.*

fon•due (fon dōō′, -dyōō′), *n.* a dish consisting of
melted cheese, often with brandy, served hot with
pieces of bread for dipping.

font¹ (font), *n.* **1.** a receptacle for holy water, esp.
that used in baptism. **2.** a productive source.

font² (font), *n. Print.* a complete set of type of one
style and size.

food (fōōd), *n.* **1.** a substance that is taken into the
body to sustain life, provide energy, and promote
growth. **2.** solid nourishment as distinguished from
liquids. **3.** a particular kind of nourishment: *dog
food.* **4.** something serving for consumption or use:
food for thought.

food′ proc′essor *n.* an electric appliance with interchangeable blades that can chop, shred, or otherwise process food at high speed.

fool (fōōl), *n.* **1.** a silly or stupid person. **2.** a court
jester. **3.** a person who has been tricked into appearing foolish. —*v.t.* **4.** to trick or deceive. —*v.i.* **5.**
to act like a fool. **6.** to jest; joke. **7. fool around, a.**
to putter aimlessly. **b.** to trifle or flirt. **c.** to engage
casually in sexual activity. **8. ~ with,** to play with
idly. [< OF < L *follis* bellows, bag]

fool′har′dy *adj.,* **-di•er, -di•est.** recklessly bold;
rash. —**fool′har′di•ly,** *adv.* —**fool′har′di•ness,** *n.*

fool′proof′ *adj.* **1.** involving no risk or harm even
when tampered with. **2.** never-failing: *a foolproof
method.*

foot (fōōt), *n., pl.* **feet,** *v.* —*n.* **1.** the terminal part
of the leg on which the body stands. **2.** a part similar to a foot in position or function. **3.** a unit of
length equal to 12 inches or 30.48 centimeters. **4.**
the part, as of a stocking or sock, covering the foot.
5. the lowest part, as of a hill; bottom. **6.** the part
of something opposite the top or head. **7.** a group
of syllables constituting a metrical unit of verse.
—*v.i.* **8.** to go on foot; walk. **9.** to move the feet
rhythmically, esp. in dance. —*v.t.* **10.** to pay or settle: *to foot the bill.* —*Idiom.* **11. on foot,** by walking or running. **12. under foot,** in the way.

foot′ball′ *n.* **1.** a game in which two opposing
teams of 11 players each defend goals at opposite
ends of a field. **2.** the ball used in football. **3.**
Chiefly Brit. **a.** RUGBY. **b.** SOCCER.

foot′hill′ *n.* a low hill at the base of a mountain.

foot′hold′ *n.* **1.** a support for the feet. **2.** a firm
basis for further progress.

foot′ing *n.* **1.** a basis; foundation. **2.** a place or
support for the foot; foothold. **3.** a firm placing of
the feet; stability. **4.** mutual standing; status. **5. a.**
the act of adding up a column of figures. **b.** the total of such a column.

foot′less *adj.* **1.** lacking feet. **2.** having no basis;
unsubstantial. **3.** awkward or inefficient.

foot′lights′ *n.pl.* **1.** the lights at the front of a
stage floor. **2.** the acting profession.

foot′lock′er *n.* a small trunk kept at the foot of a
bed.

foot′loose′ *adj.* free to go or travel about.

foot′man *n., pl.* **-men.** a household servant who
ranks below a butler.

foot′note′ *n.* **1.** an explanatory note, comment, or
reference at the bottom of a page. **2.** a minor or
tangential comment or event.

foot′-pound′ *n.* a unit of energy equal to the energy expended in raising one pound a distance of
one foot.

foot′print′ *n.* a mark left by the foot, as in earth.

foot′step′ *n.* **1. a.** the setting down of a foot. **b.**
the sound so produced. **2.** the distance covered by
a footstep. **3.** FOOTPRINT.

foot′stool′ *n.* a low stool upon which to rest the
feet.

fop (fop), *n.* a man excessively concerned with his
clothes; dandy. —**fop′per•y,** *n.* —**fop′pish,** *adj.*
—**fop′pish•ness,** *n.*

for (fôr; *unstressed* fər), *prep.* **1.** with the purpose
of: *He runs for exercise.* **2.** intended to benefit or be
used by: *equipment for the baseball team; medicine
for the aged.* **3.** in order to obtain: *to work for a salary.* **4.** in return for: *three for a dollar.* **5.** appropriate or adapted to: *clothes for travel.* **6.** with respect
to: *pressed for time.* **7.** during the continuance of:
for two years. **8.** in favor of: *rooted for the home
team.* **9.** instead of: *a substitute for butter.* **10.** on
behalf of: *to act for a client.* **11.** in exchange for:
blow for blow. **12.** in honor of: *to give a dinner for
a friend.* **13.** with the purpose of reaching: *to start
for home.* **14.** in consideration of: *tall for his age.*
15. as being: *knew it for a fact.* **16.** because of: *to
shout for joy.* **17.** in spite of: *They're decent people
for all their faults.* **18.** to the extent of: *to walk for a
mile.* **19.** (used to introduce a subject in an infinitive phrase): *It's time for me to go.* —*conj.* **20.** because.

for•age (fôr′ij, for′-), *n., v.,* **-aged, -ag•ing.** —*n.* **1.**
food for horses or cattle; fodder. **2.** the seeking or
obtaining of forage. —*v.i.* **3.** to wander or go in
search of provisions. **4.** to search about; rummage.
—*v.t.* **5.** to collect forage from. **6.** to obtain by foraging. —**for′ag•er,** *n.*

for•ay (fôr′ā, for′ā), *n., v.,* **-ayed, -ay•ing.** —*n.* **1.**
a quick raid, usu. for spoils. **2.** a venture or attempt. —*v.i.* **3.** to make a raid.

for•bear¹ (fôr bâr′), *v.,* **-bore, -borne, -bear•ing.**
—*v.t.* **1.** to refrain from. —*v.i.* **2.** to be patient or self-
controlled. —**for•bear′ance,** *n.* —**for•bear′er,** *n.*

for•bear² (fôr′bâr′), *n.* FOREBEAR.

for•bid (fər bid′, fôr-), *v.t.,* **-bade** or **-bad** or **-bid,**
-bid•den or **-bid, -bid•ding. 1.** to command (a person) not to do something. **2.** to prohibit (something); bar. **3.** to make impossible; prevent.

for•bid′ding *adj.* **1.** grim; threatening. **2.** daunt-
ing; discouraging. —**for•bid′ding•ly,** *adv.*

force (fôrs), *n., v.,* **forced, forc•ing.** —*n.* **1.** physical
power or strength. **2.** physical coercion; violence. **3.**
vigor; energy. **4.** power to influence, convince, or persuade. **5.** Often, **forces.** military or fighting strength,
esp. of a nation. **6.** a body of persons combined for
joint action: *a sales force.* **7.** *Physics.* an influence on
a body or system producing or tending to produce a
change in movement or shape. —*v.t.* **8.** to compel to
do something. **9.** to drive or propel against resistance.
10. to bring about or effect by force. **11.** to bring about
of necessity. **12.** to obtain by or as if by force. **13.** to
break open: *forced the lock.* **14.** to cause (plants,
fruits, etc.) to grow or mature at an increased rate by
artificial means. —*Idiom.* **15. in force, a.** in operation; effective. **b.** in large numbers. —**forc′er,** *n.*

for•ceps (fôr′səps, -seps), *n., pl.* **-ceps.** an instrument resembling pincers for seizing and holding objects firmly, as in surgical operations.

for•ci•ble (fôr′sə bəl), *adj.* **1.** done or effected by
force. **2.** having or showing force; powerful. —**for′-
ci•bly,** *adv.*

ford (fôrd), *n.* **1.** a place where a body of water
can be crossed by wading. —*v.t.* **2.** to cross at a
ford. —**ford′a•ble,** *adj.*

fore¹ (fôr), *adj.* **1.** situated in front. **2.** first in place,
time, order, or rank. —*adv.* **3.** at or toward the bow
of a ship. **4.** forward. —*n.* **5.** the front.

fore² (fôr), *interj.* a cry of warning on a golf course
to persons in danger of being struck by a ball.

fore- a prefix meaning: before (*forewarn*); front
(*forehead*); preceding (*forefather*); superior (*foreman*).

fore′-and-aft′ *adj. Naut.* located along or parallel
to a line from the stem to the stern.

fore′arm′¹, *n.* the part of the arm between the elbow and the wrist.

fore•arm′², *v.t.,* to arm beforehand; prepare.

fore′bear′ *n.* an ancestor; forefather.

fore•bode′ *v.t.,* **-bod•ed, -bod•ing. 1.** to foretell;

portend. **2.** to have a presentiment of. —**fore•bod′-ing,** n.

fore′cast′ (-kast′, -käst′), v., **-cast** or **-cast•ed, -cast•ing,** n. —v.t. **1.** to predict (a future condition or occurrence). **2.** to serve as a prediction of; foreshadow. —n. **3.** a prediction, esp. of weather conditions. —**fore′cast′er,** n.

fore•cas•tle (fōk′səl, fôr′kas′əl, -kä′səl) n. **1.** a superstructure at or immediately aft of the bow of a ship. **2.** sailors' quarters located in the forward part of a ship.

fore•close′ (-klōz′), v., **-closed, -closing.** —v.t. **1.** to deprive (a mortgagor) of the right to redeem a property, esp. after a default in mortgage payments. **2.** to shut out; exclude. —v.i. **3.** to foreclose a mortgage.

fore′fa′ther n. an ancestor; progenitor.

fore′fin′ger n. the finger next to the thumb.

fore′front′ n. **1.** the foremost part or place. **2.** the leading position; vanguard.

fore•go′ing adj. previous; preceding.

fore′gone′ conclu′sion n. an inevitable conclusion or result.

fore′ground′ n. **1.** the portion of a scene nearest to the viewer. **2.** a prominent position.

fore′hand′ adj. **1.** of or being a stroke, as in tennis, made with the palm of the hand facing the direction of movement. —n. **2.** a forehand stroke.

fore•head (fôr′id, for′-; fôr′hed′, for′-), n. the part of the face above the eyebrows.

for•eign (fôr′in, for′-), adj. **1.** of or from another country or nation. **2.** of contact or dealings with other countries. **3.** external to one's own country or nation. **4.** not belonging to the place or body where found. **5.** not related or connected; irrelevant.

fore′man or **-wom′an** or **-per′son,** n., pl. **-men** or **-wom•en** or **-per•sons. 1.** a person in charge of a department or group of workers. **2.** the chairperson of a jury.

fore′most′ adj., adv. first in place, rank, or importance.

fore′noon′ n. the period of day before noon.

fo•ren•sic (fə ren′sik), adj. of, suited to, or used in courts of law or in public debate. —**fo•ren′si•cal•ly,** adv.

fore′play′ n. sexual stimulation leading to intercourse.

fore′run′ner n. **1.** a predecessor or ancestor. **2.** an indication of something to follow; portent or harbinger.

fore•see′ v.t., **-saw, -seen, -see•ing.** to see or know in advance. —**fore•see′a•ble,** adj. —**fore•se′er,** n.

fore•shad′ow v.t. to show or indicate beforehand. —**fore•shad′ow•er,** n.

fore′skin′ n. the prepuce.

for•est (fôr′ist, for′-), n. **1.** a large tract of land covered with trees and underbrush. —v.t. **2.** to supply or cover with trees. —**for′est•ed,** adj.

fore•stall′ v.t. **1.** to prevent, hinder, or thwart by action in advance. **2.** to deal with or realize beforehand; anticipate. —**fore•stall′ment,** n.

for•est•a•tion (fôr′ə stā′shən, for′-), n. the planting of forests.

for′est rang′er n. an officer who supervises the care and preservation of forests, esp. public forests.

fore•tell′ v.t., **-told, -tell•ing.** to tell of beforehand. —**fore•tell′er,** n.

fore′thought′ n. **1.** thoughtful advance provision. **2.** previous consideration or planning.

for•ev•er (fôr ev′ər, fər-), adv. **1.** without ever ending; eternally. **2.** without stopping; continually.

fore•warn′ v.t. to warn in advance.

fore′word′ n. an introductory statement in a published work, as a book.

for•feit (fôr′fit), n. **1.** a fine or penalty. **2.** the act of forfeiting. **3.** something to which the right is lost, as for commission of a crime. —v.t. **4.** to lose as a forfeit.

for•gath′er v.i. to gather together; convene.

for•get (fər get′), v., **-got, -got•ten** or **-got, -get•ting.** —v.t. **1.** to be unable to recall. **2.** to omit or neglect unintentionally. **3.** to fail to think of. —v.i.

4. to cease or fail to think of something. —**Idiom. 5. forget oneself,** to say or do something improper. —**for•get′ta•ble,** adj.

forget′-me-not′ n. a small plant with light blue flowers.

for•give (fər giv′), v., **-gave, -giv•en, -giv•ing.** —v.t. **1.** to grant pardon for or to. **2.** to cancel (a debt or payment). **3.** to cease to feel resentment against. —v.i. **4.** to grant pardon. —**for•giv′a•ble,** adj. —**for•give′ness,** n. —**for•giv′er,** n.

for•go (fôr gō′), v.t., **-went, -gone, -go•ing.** to abstain or refrain from; give up. —**for•go′er,** n.

fork (fôrk), n. **1.** an instrument with two or more prongs for holding, digging, or lifting, esp. an implement for handling food. **2.** something resembling a fork. **3. a.** a division into branches. **b.** the point at which something branches. **c.** one of the branches. —v.t. **4.** to pierce, raise, pitch, dig, or carry with a fork. —v.i. **5.** to divide into branches. **6.** Informal. **fork over,** to deliver; pay; hand over. —**fork′ful** (-fŏol), n., pl. **-fuls.**

fork′lift′ n. a vehicle with two power-operated prongs at the front for lifting and moving heavy loads.

for•lorn (fôr lôrn′), adj. **1.** miserable; wretched. **2.** forsaken; desolate. **3.** hopeless; despairing. —**for•lorn′ly,** adv.

form (fôrm), n. **1.** shape as distinguished from color or material; configuration. **2.** a body, esp. of a human being. **3.** a model of the human body used for fitting or displaying clothing. **4.** a mold. **5.** the mode in which something appears or exists: water in the form of ice. **6.** a manner or style of arranging and coordinating parts, as in musical composition. **7.** the formal structure of a work of art. **8.** a kind, type, or variety. **9.** a prescribed or customary order or method of doing something. **10.** a set order of words, as in a legal document. **11.** a document with blank spaces to be filled in with particulars. **12.** procedure according to a set order or method. **13.** conformity to the usages of society; manners. **14.** a manner or method of performing. **15.** physical condition or fitness, as for performing. **16.** a particular shape of a word that occurs in more than one shape. **17.** a grade in a British secondary school or in certain U.S. private schools. —v.t. **18.** to construct or frame. **19.** to make or produce. **20.** to serve to make up; constitute. **21.** to arrange; organize. **22.** to frame (ideas, opinions, etc.) in the mind. **23.** to develop (habits, friendships, etc.). **24.** to give a particular form or shape to. **25.** to mold or develop by discipline or instruction. —v.i. **26.** to take form. **27.** to take a particular form or arrangement. —**form′less,** adj. —**form′less•ness,** n.

-form a combining form meaning having the form of (cruciform).

for•mal (fôr′məl), adj. **1.** being in accordance with accepted custom; conventional. **2.** marked by form or ceremony. **3. a.** designed for wear or use at ceremonial events. **b.** requiring formal dress. **4.** prim; decorous. **5.** made or done in accordance with procedures that ensure validity. **6.** being such merely in name; nominal. —n. **7.** a social occasion, as a dance, that requires formal attire. —**for′mal•ly,** adv.

form•al•de•hyde (fôr mal′də hīd′, fər-), n. a toxic gas used chiefly as a disinfectant and preservative.

for•mal′i•ty (-mal′i tē), n., pl. **-ties. 1.** the condition or quality of being formal. **2.** strict adherence to established rules and procedures. **3.** a formal act or observance.

for•mat (fôr′mat), n., v., **-mat•ted, -mat•ting.** —n. **1.** the general appearance or style of a book, magazine, or newspaper. **2.** the organization and plan of something. **3.** the arrangement of data for computer input or output. —v.t. **4.** to plan or provide a format for. **5.** to produce in a specified format.

for•ma•tion (fôr mā′shən), n. **1.** the act or process of forming. **2.** the manner in which something is formed. **3.** an arrangement or disposition, as of troops or airplanes. **4.** something formed.

form•a•tive (fôr′mə tiv), adj. **1.** giving or capable

of giving form or shape. **2.** pertaining to formation or development.

for•mer (fôr′mər), *adj.* **1.** preceding in time; earlier. **2.** being the first mentioned of two. **3.** having previously been.

for•mi•da•ble (fôr′mi də bəl *or, sometimes,* fərmid′ə-), *adj.* **1.** causing fear, awe, or apprehension. **2.** of discouraging difficulty; intimidating. —**for′mi•da•bly,** *adv.*

form′ let′ter *n.* a standardized letter that can be sent to any number of persons.

for•mu•la (fôr′mya lə), *n., pl.* **-las, -lae** (-lē′). **1.** a set form of words, as for prescribed use on a ceremonial occasion. **2.** a conventional method or approach. **3.** a mathematical rule or principle, frequently expressed in algebraic symbols. **4.** an expression of the constituents of a chemical compound by symbols and figures. **5.** a recipe or prescription. **6.** a special nutritive mixture, esp. of milk or milk substitute, for feeding a baby. —**for′mu•la′ic** (-lā′ik), *adj.*

for′mu•late′ *v.t.,* **-lat•ed, -lat•ing. 1.** to express in precise form. **2.** to devise or develop. **3.** to express in a formula. —**for′mu•la′tion,** *n.* —**for′mu•la′tor,** *n.*

for•ni•cate (fôr′ni kāt′) *v.i.,* **-cat•ed, -cat•ing.** to have illicit sexual relations. —**for′ni•ca′tion,** *n.* —**for′ni•ca′tor,** *n.*

for•sake (fôr sāk′), *v.t.,* **-sook** (-sŏŏk′), **-sak•en, -sak•ing. 1.** to quit or leave entirely; abandon. **2.** to give up; renounce.

for•swear′ *v.,* **-swore, -sworn, -swearing.** —*v.t.* **1.** to renounce under oath. **2.** to deny vehemently or under oath. —*v.i.* **3.** to commit perjury.

for•syth•i•a (fôr sith′ē ə, fər-), *n., pl.* **-as.** a shrub bearing yellow flowers that blossom in early spring. [after W. *Forsyth* (1737–1804), English horticulturist]

fort (fôrt), *n.* **1.** a fortified location occupied by troops. **2.** a permanent army post.

forte[1] (fôrt, fôr′tā), *n.* an area in which a person excels; specialty.

for•te[2] (fôr′tā), *Music.* —*adj.* **1.** loud. —*adv.* **2.** loudly.

forth (fôrth), *adv.* **1.** onward, outward, or forward: *to go forth.* **2.** out into view: *Love shines forth in her eyes.*

forth′com′ing *adj.* **1.** coming or about to come; approaching. **2.** ready or available.

forth′right′ *adj.* going straight to the point; direct; outspoken: *a forthright answer.* —**forth′right′ly,** *adv.* —**forth′right′ness,** *n.*

forth′with′ *adv.* immediately.

for•ti•fi•ca•tion (fôr′tə fi kā′shən) *n.* a defensive military construction.

for•ti•fy (fôr′tə fī′), *v.t.,* **-fied, -fy•ing. 1.** to increase the defenses of. **2.** to impart strength or vigor to. **3.** to increase the effectiveness of, as by additional ingredients. **4.** to strengthen mentally or morally. —**for′ti•fi•ca′tion,** *n.* —**for′ti•fi′er,** *n.*

for•tis•si•mo (fôr tis′ə mō′), *Music.* —*adj.* **1.** very loud. —*adv.* **2.** very loudly.

for•ti•tude (fôr′ti tŏŏd′, -tyŏŏd′), *n.* strength in facing adversity, danger, or temptation courageously.

fort′night′ *n.* two weeks. —**fort′night′ly,** *adj., adv.*

FORTRAN (fôr′tran) *n.* a computer programming language used esp. for solving problems in science and engineering.

for•tress (fôr′tris), *n.* a fort or group of forts.

for•tu•i•tous (fôr tŏŏ′i təs, -tyŏŏ′-), *adj.* **1.** happening or produced by chance; accidental. **2.** lucky. —**for•tu′i•tous•ly,** *adv.*

for•tu•nate (fôr′chə nit), *adj.* **1.** having good fortune; lucky. **2.** bringing or indicating good fortune. —**for′tu•nate•ly,** *adv.*

for′tune *n.* **1.** wealth; riches. **2.** chance; luck. **3. fortunes,** varied occurrences that happen or are to happen to a person in life. **4.** fate; destiny. [< OF < L *fortūna* chance, luck]

for′tune-tell′er *n.* a person who claims the ability to predict the future. —**for′tune-tell′ing,** *n.*

for•ty (fôr′tē), *n., pl.* **-ties,** *adj.* —*n.* **1.** a cardinal number, ten times four. **2.** a symbol for this number, as 40 or XL. —*adj.* **3.** amounting to 40 in number. —**for′ti•eth,** *adj., n.*

fo•rum (fôr′əm), *n.* **1.** the marketplace or public square of an ancient Roman city. **2.** a court; tribunal. **3.** a meeting place or medium for discussion of matters of public interest.

for•ward (fôr′wərd), *adv.* Also, **for′wards. 1.** toward or to what is in front. **2.** into view or consideration; forth. —*adj.* **3.** directed toward a point in advance. **4.** well-advanced. **5.** ready; eager. **6.** presumptuous; bold. **7.** situated in the front. **8.** of or for the future. **9.** radical or extreme. —*n.* **10.** a player stationed in front of others on a team, as in hockey. —*v.t.* **11.** to send onward, esp. to a new address. **12.** to promote; advance. —**for′ward•er,** *n.* —**for′ward•ly,** *adv.* —**for′ward•ness,** *n.*

fos•sil (fos′əl), *n.* **1.** the preserved remains or imprint of a living organism, usu. of a former geologic age. **2.** an outdated or old-fashioned person or thing. —*adj.* **3.** like or being a fossil. **4.** formed from the remains of prehistoric life, as oil: *a fossil fuel.*

fos•ter (fô′stər, fos′tər), *v.t.* **1.** to promote the growth or development of. **2.** to bring up; rear. —*adj.* **3.** giving or receiving parental care though not kin by blood or related legally: *a foster parent.*

foul (foul), *adj.* **1.** grossly offensive to the senses. **2.** very dirty; filthy. **3.** clogged or obstructed with dirt. **4.** stormy; inclement. **5.** morally offensive. **6.** profane; obscene. **7.** contrary to the rules, as in a sport. **8. a.** indicating the limits of a baseball field: *foul lines.* **b.** hit outside the foul line: *a foul ball.* **9.** obstructed; entangled. —*adv.* **10.** in a foul manner. —*n.* **11.** a collision; entanglement. **12.** a violation of the rules of a sport or game. **13.** a foul ball. —*v.t.* **14.** to make foul. **15.** to clog; obstruct. **16.** to collide with. **17.** to cause to become entangled. **18.** to dishonor; disgrace. **19.** to hit (a pitched ball) foul. —*v.i.* **20.** to become foul. **21.** to commit a foul in a sport or game. **22.** to hit a foul ball. **23. foul up,** to bungle or confuse. —**foul′ly,** *adv.* —**foul′ness,** *n.*

foul′-up′ *n.* a condition of disorder brought on by inefficiency or stupidity.

found[1] (found), *v.* pt. and pp. of FIND.

found[2] (found), *v.t.* **1.** to establish on a firm basis or for enduring existence. **2.** to provide a firm basis for; ground. —**found′er,** *n.*

found[3] (found), *v.t.* to melt and pour (metal) into a mold. —**found′er,** *n.*

foun•da′tion *n.* **1.** basis; groundwork. **2.** the base on which a structure rests. **3.** the act of founding. **4.** the state of being founded. **5. a.** an institution financed by a donation or legacy. **b.** an endowment for such an institution. **6.** a corset or girdle.

foun•der (foun′dər), *v.i.* **1.** to fill with water and sink. **2.** to fail utterly. **3.** to stumble or go lame, as a horse.

found′ling *n.* an abandoned infant without a known parent.

found′ry (foun′drē), *n., pl.* **-ries.** an establishment for producing castings in molten metal.

foun•tain (foun′tn), *n.* **1.** a spring of water from the earth. **2.** a source; origin. **3.** a mechanically created jet or stream of water. **4.** a reservoir for a liquid to be supplied continuously.

foun′tain-head′ *n.* a source.

four (fôr), *n.* **1.** a cardinal number, three plus one. **2.** a symbol for this number, as 4 or IV. —*adj.* **3.** amounting to four in number. —**fourth,** *adj., n.*

four′-flush′ *v.i.* to bluff. —**four′flush′er,** *n.*

four′score′ *adj.* four times twenty; eighty.

four′some (-səm) *n.* **1.** a company or set of four. **2.** a golf match between two pairs of players.

four′square′ *adj.* **1.** square in shape. **2.** firm; forthright. —*adv.* **3.** firmly; forthrightly.

four′teen′ *n.* **1.** a cardinal number, ten plus four. **2.** a symbol for this number, as 14 or XIV. —*adj.* **3.** amounting to 14 in number. —**four′teenth′,** *adj., n.*

fowl (foul), *n., pl.* **fowls, fowl,** *v.* —*n.* **1.** a domestic hen or rooster. **2.** a bird such as a turkey or pheasant. **3.** the meat of a domestic fowl. —*v.i.* **4.** to hunt wildfowl.

fox (foks), *n., pl.* **fox•es, fox,** *v.* —*n.* **1.** a small carnivore of the dog family with a sharply pointed muzzle and a long bushy tail. **2.** the fur of the fox. **3.** a cunning or crafty person. —*v.t.* **4.** to deceive or trick.

fox′glove′ *n.* a plant with purple flowers on a tall spike and leaves that yield digitalis.

fox′hole′ *n.* a pit used as a shelter in a battle zone.

fox′ trot′ *n.* a ballroom dance in duple meter. —**fox′-trot′,** *v.i.,* **-trot•ted, -trot•ting.**

fox′y *adj.,* **-i•er, -i•est.** slyly clever; cunning.

foy•er (foi′ər, foi′ā), *n.* **1.** a lobby, esp. of a theater. **2.** an entrance hall.

FPO 1. field post office. **2.** fleet post office.

Fr *Chem. Symbol.* francium.

Fr. 1. Father. **2.** France. **3.** French. **4.** Friar. **5.** Friday.

fr 1. fragment. **2.** *pl.* **fr, frs** franc. **3.** from.

fra•cas (frā′kəs, frak′əs), *n.* a disorderly disturbance.

frac•tion (frak′shən), *n.* **1. a.** a number usu. expressed in the form *a/b.* **b.** a ratio of algebraic quantities similarly expressed. **2.** a part of a whole; portion. **3.** a fragment. —**frac′tion•al,** *adj.*

frac•tious (frak′shəs), *adj.* **1.** rebellious; unruly. **2.** readily angered or annoyed. —**frac′tious•ly,** *adv.*

frac•ture (frak′chər), *n., v.,* **-tured, -tur•ing.** —*n.* **1.** the breaking of something, esp. a bone. **2.** a break; split. —*v.t., v.i.* **3.** to break; crack.

frag•ile (fraj′əl; *Brit.* -īl), *adj.* **1.** easily broken or damaged. **2.** lacking in substance; flimsy. —**fra•gil•i•ty** (frə jil′i tē), **frag′ile•ness,** *n.*

frag•ment (*n.* frag′mənt; *v.* frag′ment), *n.* **1. a** part broken off or detached. **2.** an unfinished or incomplete part. —*v.i., v.t.* **3.** to break into fragments. —**frag′men•tar′y,** *adj.* —**frag′men•ta′tion,** *n.*

fra′grance (frā′grəns) *n.* a pleasant smell. —**fra′grant,** *adj.*

frail (frāl), *adj.,* **-er, -est. 1.** not physically strong; delicate. **2.** easily broken; fragile. —**frail′ly,** *adv.*

frame (frām), *n., v.,* **framed, fram•ing.** —*n.* **1.** a decorative border, as for a picture. **2.** a rigid supporting structure formed of joined parts, as in a building. **3.** the size and build of the human body. **4.** an enclosing structure or case: *a window frame.* **5.** form, constitution, or structure. **6.** a particular state: *an unhappy frame of mind.* **7.** one of the successive pictures on a strip of film. —*v.t.* **8.** to construct; shape. **9.** to devise; compose. **10.** to cause (an innocent person) to seem guilty. **11.** to provide with or put into a frame. —**fram′er,** *n.*

frame′-up′ *n.* a fraudulent incrimination of an innocent person.

franc (frangk), *n.* **1.** the basic monetary unit of France, Belgium, and Luxembourg, which has a fixed value relative to the euro. **2.** the basic monetary unit of Switzerland, Guinea, Madagascar, Rwanda, Burundi, and Djibouti.

France (frans, fräns), *n.* a republic in W Europe.

fran•chise (fran′chīz), *n., v.,* **-chised, -chis•ing.** —*n.* **1.** a privilege conferred on an individual or group by a government. **2.** the right or license granted by a company to an individual or group to market its products or services. **3.** the right to vote. —*v.t.* **4.** to grant a franchise to. —**fran′chise•ment** (-chīz mənt, -chiz-), *n.*

fran•ci•um (fran′sē əm), *n.* a radioactive element of the alkali metal group. *Symbol:* Fr; *at. no.:* 87.

frank[1] (frangk), *adj.,* **-er, -est,** *n., v.* —*adj.* **1.** direct and unreserved in expression. —*n.* **2.** a stamp, printed marking, or signature on a piece of mail indicating that it can be sent postage free. —*v.t.* **3.** to mark (mail) with a frank. —**frank′ly,** *adv.* —**frank′ness,** *n.*

frank[2] (frangk), *n.* a frankfurter.

frank•furt•er (frangk′fər tər), *n.* a smoked sausage usu. of beef or beef and pork.

frank•in•cense (frang′kin sens′), *n.* an aromatic gum resin used chiefly as incense.

fran•tic (fran′tik), *adj.* desperate or wild with emotion; frenzied. —**fran′ti•cal•ly,** *adv.*

fra•ter•nal (frə tûr′nl), *adj.* **1.** of or befitting a brother. **2.** of or being a society of men associated in brotherly union. —**fra•ter′nal•ism,** *n.* —**fra•ter′nal•ly,** *adv.*

fra•ter′ni•ty *n., pl.* **-ties. 1.** a social organization of male college students. **2.** a group of persons with common purposes or interests: *the medical fraternity.* **3.** the quality or state of being brotherly; brotherhood.

frat•er•nize (frat′ər nīz′), *v.i.,* **-nized, -niz•ing. 1.** to associate in a friendly way. **2.** to associate cordially with members of a hostile group. —**frat′er•ni•za′tion,** *n.* —**frat′er•niz′er,** *n.*

frat•ri•cide (fra′tri sīd′, frā′-), *n.* **1.** the act of killing one's brother. **2.** a person who kills his or her brother. —**frat′ri•cid′al,** *adj.*

fraud (frôd), *n.* **1.** deceit or trickery. **2.** a particular instance of deceit or trickery: *mail fraud.* **3.** a deceitful person; impostor. —**fraud′u•lent,** *adj.*

fraught (frôt), *adj.* filled or accompanied: *an undertaking fraught with danger.*

fray[1] (frā), *n.* **1.** a fight; skirmish. **2.** a noisy quarrel.

fray[2] (frā), *v.,* **frayed, fray•ing.** —*v.t.* **1.** to wear (material) into loose threads at the edge. **2.** to wear out by rubbing. **3.** to cause strain on. —*v.i.* **4.** to become frayed.

fraz•zle (fraz′əl), *v.,* **-zled, -zling,** *n.* —*v.t., v.i.* **1.** to make or become physically or mentally fatigued. **2.** to wear to threads; fray. —*n.* **3.** a state of physical or mental fatigue.

freak (frēk), *n.* **1.** an abnormal, unusual, or strange person, animal, or thing. **2.** a sudden and apparently causeless notion or turn of events. **3.** *Slang.* **a.** a habitual drug user. **b.** a devoted fan; enthusiast. —*v.t., v.i.* **4.** to make or become frightened, nervous, or excited. **5. freak out,** *Slang.* **a.** to hallucinate under the influence of a drug. **b.** to lose or cause to lose emotional control. —**freak′ish,** *adj.* —**freak′y,** *adj.,* **-i•er, -i•est.**

freck•le (frek′əl), *n., v.,* **-led, -ling.** —*n.* **1.** a small brownish spot on the skin. —*v.t., v.i.* **2.** to cover or become covered with freckles. —**freck′ly,** *adj.,* **-li•er, -li•est.**

free (frē), *adj.,* **fre•er, fre•est,** *adv., v.,* **freed, free•ing.** —*adj.* **1.** enjoying personal liberty. **2.** possessing civil and political liberties. **3.** exempt from external restriction. **4.** able to do something at will. **5.** clear of obstructions or obstacles. **6.** not occupied or in use. **7.** unaffected by something; exempt or released. **8.** provided without a charge. **9.** not attached or tied; loose. **10.** lacking self-restraint. **11.** generous or lavish, as in giving. **12.** not literal: *a free translation.* —*adv.* **13.** in a free manner. **14.** at no cost or charge. —*v.t.* **15.** to set at liberty. **16.** to relieve or rid. **17.** to disengage; clear. —**free′ly,** *adv.*

free′boot′er *n.* a pirate; buccaneer.

free′-for-all′ *n.* a fight or contest open to everyone and usu. without rules.

free′lance′ or **free′-lance′** (-lans′, -läns′), *n., v.,* **-lanced, -lanc•ing,** *adj., adv.* —*n.* **1.** Also, **free′lanc′er.** a person who sells services without working on a regular basis for any single employer. —*v.i.* **2.** to work as a freelance. —*adj.* **3.** of or being a freelance. —*adv.* **4.** as a freelance.

free′load′ *v.i. Informal.* to take advantage of the generosity of others for free food, lodging, etc. —**free′load′er,** *n.*

Free′ma′son *n.* a member of a secret fraternal association for mutual assistance and the promotion of brotherly love. —**Free′ma′son•ry,** *n.*

free′ rad′ical *n.* a molecule capable of multiplying rapidly and harming the immune system.

free′think′er *n.* a person who forms opinions on the basis of reason alone, esp. in religious matters. —**free′think′ing,** *adj., n.*

free′way′ *n.* an express highway with no intersections.

freeze (frēz), *v.,* **froze, fro•zen, freez•ing,** *n.* —*v.i.* **1.** to become hardened into ice. **2.** to become hard or stiffened because of loss of heat. **3.** to suffer the effects of intense cold. **4.** to be at the degree of cold at which water freezes. **5.** to lose warmth of feeling. **6.** to become immobilized, as through fear. **7.** to become obstructed by the formation of ice: *The water pipes froze.* **8.** to die or be injured because of frost or cold. **9.** to become unfriendly or aloof. **10.** to become temporarily inoperable; cease to function (often fol. by *up*): *My keyboard froze.* —*v.t.* **11.** to harden into ice. **12.** to form ice on the surface of. **13.** to harden or stiffen by cold. **14.** to subject to freezing temperature, as in a freezer. **15.** to cause to suffer the effects of intense cold. **16.** to kill or damage by frost or cold. **17.** to obstruct or clog by the formation of ice. **18.** to fix (rents, prices, or wages) at a particular level. **19.** to prevent (assets) from being liquidated or collected. **20.** to act toward in an unfriendly or aloof manner. —*n.* **21.** an act or instance of freezing. **22.** the state of being frozen. **23.** a period of very cold weather. —**freez′a•ble,** *adj.*

freez′er *n.* **1.** a compartment, cabinet, or room for freezing and storing food. **2.** a machine containing a refrigerant for making ice cream or sherbet.

freight (frāt), *n.* **1.** goods or cargo transported for pay. **2. a.** transportation of goods provided by common carriers. **b.** the charges for such transportation. **3.** a train that carries freight. —*v.t.* **4.** to load with goods for transportation. **5.** to transport by freight.

freight′er *n.* a ship or aircraft used mainly for carrying freight.

French (french), *n.* **1.** the Romance language of France. **2.** (*used with a pl. v.*) the natives or inhabitants of France. —*adj.* **3.** of or characteristic of France, its inhabitants, or their language. —**French′man,** *n., pl.* **-men.** —**French′wom′an,** *n., pl.* **-wom′en.**

French′ dress′ing *n.* **1.** a salad dressing made of oil, vinegar, and seasonings. **2.** a creamy, orange-colored salad dressing.

French′ (or **french′**) **fries′,** *n.pl.* strips of potato that have been deep-fried.

French′ horn′ *n.* a brass wind instrument with a long coiled tube and a flaring bell.

fre•net•ic (frə net′ik), *adj.* frantic; frenzied. —**fre•net′i•cal•ly,** *adv.*

fren•zy (fren′zē), *n., pl.* **-zies. 1.** extreme agitation or wild excitement. **2.** a spell of mental derangement. **3.** agitated activity. —**fren′zied,** *adj.*

fre•quen•cy (frē′kwən sē), *n., pl.* **-cies. 1.** the state or fact of being frequent. **2.** rate of occurrence. **3.** *Physics.* the number of cycles or completed alternations per unit time of a wave or oscillation.

fre•quent (*adj.* frē′kwənt; *v.* fri kwent′, frē′kwənt), *adj.* **1.** happening at short intervals. **2.** constant, habitual, or regular. —*v.t.* **3.** to visit often or habitually. —**fre•quent′er,** *n.* —**fre′quent•ly,** *adv.*

fres•co (fres′kō), *n., pl.* **-coes, -cos. 1.** the art of painting on a moist plaster surface. **2.** a picture or design so painted.

fresh (fresh), *adj.,* **-er, -est,** *adv.* —*adj.* **1.** newly made or obtained. **2.** recently arrived. **3.** not previously known; new or novel. **4.** additional or further. **5.** not salty, as water. **6.** not stale or spoiled. **7.** not preserved by canning, pickling, etc. **8.** not fatigued; vigorous. **9.** not faded. **10.** pure, cool, or refreshing, as air. **11.** (of wind) brisk. **12.** inexperienced: *fresh recruits.* **13.** *Informal.* impertinent; impudent. —*adv.* **14.** newly; recently. —**fresh′ly,** *adv.* —**fresh′ness,** *n.*

fresh•et (fresh′it), *n.* a flooding of a stream caused by heavy rains or the rapid melting of snow and ice.

fresh′man *n., pl.* **-men. 1.** a student in the first year at a high school or college. **2.** a novice; beginner.

fresh′wa′ter *adj.* **1.** of or living in water that is not salty. **2.** accustomed only to fresh water.

fret¹ (fret), *v.,* **fret•ted, fret•ting,** *n.* —*v.i., v.t.* **1.** to feel or cause to feel worry, annoyance, or discontent. **2.** to wear or cause to be worn away; corrode. **3.** to agitate or become agitated, as water. **4.** to

form by wearing away. —*n.* **5.** an irritated state of mind; vexation. **6.** erosion or corrosion. **7.** a worn or eroded place.

fret² (fret), *n.* an angular design of intersecting bands within a border.

fret³ (fret), *n.* a ridge of wood or metal set across the fingerboard of a stringed instrument, as a guitar.

Freud′i•an (froi′dē ən) *adj.* **1.** relating to the psychoanalytic theories of Sigmund Freud. —*n.* **2.** a person who follows Freud's theories.

Fri. Friday.

fri•a•ble (frī′ə bəl), *adj.* easily crumbled or reduced to powder.

fri•ar (frī′ər), *n.* a member of a Roman Catholic religious order, esp. a mendicant order. [< OF < L *frāter* brother]

fric•as•see (frik′ə sē′), *n., pl.* **-sees,** *v.,* **-seed, -see•ing.** —*n.* **1.** pieces of meat, esp. chicken, stewed in a sauce. —*v.t.* **2.** to prepare as a fricassee.

fric•tion (frik′shən), *n.* **1.** surface resistance to relative motion, as of a body sliding or rolling. **2.** the rubbing of one surface against another. **3.** dissension or conflict, as between persons or nations. —**fric′tion•al,** *adj.*

Fri•day (frī′dā, -dē), *n.* the sixth day of the week, following Thursday.

friend (frend), *n.* **1.** a person attached to another by affection or regard. **2.** a patron; supporter. **3.** a person who is not hostile. **4.** (*cap.*) a member of the Society of Friends; Quaker. —*Idiom.* **5.** **make friends with,** to become a friend to. —**friend′less,** *adj.* —**friend′ly,** *adj.,* **-li•er, -li•est.**

frieze (frēz), *n.* a decorative, often carved band, as around the top of a wall.

frig•ate (frig′it), *n.* **1.** a fast ship of the late 18th and early 19th centuries. **2.** a modern warship larger than a destroyer.

fright (frīt), *n.* **1.** sudden and extreme fear. **2.** a shocking or grotesque person or thing. —**fright′en,** *v.t., v.i.*

fright′ful *adj.* **1.** causing fright; alarming. **2.** horrible or shocking. **3.** *Informal.* unpleasant; disagreeable. **4.** *Informal.* very great; extreme.

fright′ful•ly *adv. Informal.* very.

frig•id (frij′id), *adj.* **1.** very cold in temperature. **2.** lacking warmth of feeling. **3.** (of a woman) sexually unresponsive. —**fri•gid′i•ty,** *n.* —**frig′id•ly,** *adv.*

frill (fril), *n.* **1.** a trimming, as a strip of lace, gathered at one edge. **2.** something superfluous; luxury. —**frill′i•ness,** *n.* —**frill′y,** *adj.,* **-i•er, -i•est.**

fringe (frinj), *n., v.,* **fringed, fring•ing.** —*n.* **1.** a decorative border of short threads, cords, or loops. **2.** something resembling a fringe; border. **3.** an outer edge; margin; periphery. **4.** something peripheral or marginal to something else. —*v.t.* **5.** to furnish with or as if with a fringe. **6.** to serve as a fringe for.

frip•per•y (frip′ə rē), *n., pl.* **-ies. 1.** finery in dress, esp. when gaudy. **2.** empty display; ostentation.

frisk (frisk), *v.i.* **1.** to dance, leap, skip, or gambol; frolic. —*v.t.* **2.** to search (a person), as for concealed weapons, by feeling the person's clothing.

frisk′y *adj.,* **-i•er, -i•est.** lively and playful. —**frisk′i•ly,** *adv.* —**frisk′i•ness,** *n.*

frit•ter¹ (frit′ər), *v.t.* **1.** to squander or disperse piecemeal. **2.** to break into small pieces.

frit•ter² (frit′ər), *n.* a small cake of fried batter, usu. containing corn, fruit, or meat.

friv•o•lous (friv′ə ləs), *adj.* **1.** characterized by lack of seriousness or sense. **2.** not worthy of serious notice; trivial. —**fri•vol•i•ty** (fri vol′i tē), *n., pl.* **-ties.** —**friv′o•lous•ly,** *adv.*

frizz (friz), *v.i., v.t.* **1.** to form into small crisp curls. —*n.* **2.** something frizzed, as hair. —**frizz′y,** *adj.,* **-i•er, -i•est.**

fro (frō), *adv.* from; back (used esp. in the phrase *to and fro*).

frock (frok), *n.* **1.** a dress worn by a girl or woman. **2.** a smock worn by peasants and workers. **3.** a coarse outer garment worn by monks.

frog[1] (frog, frôg), *n.* **1.** a tailless amphibian with smooth, moist skin and long hind legs used for leaping. **2.** a slight hoarseness.

frog[2] (frog, frôg), *n.* an ornamental fastening for the front of a garment, consisting of a button and a loop.

frol•ic (frol'ik), *n., v.,* **-icked, -ick•ing.** —*n.* **1.** merriment; gaiety. **2.** playful behavior or action. —*v.i.* **3.** to play in a frisky manner; romp. **4.** to engage in merrymaking. —**frol'ick•er,** *n.* —**frol'ic•some,** *adj.*

from (frum, from; *unstressed* frəm), *prep.* **1.** (used to specify a starting point in space): *ran away from home.* **2.** (used to specify a starting point in an expression of limits): *works from 9 to 5.* **3.** (used to express removal or separation): *30 minutes from now.* **4.** (used to express discrimination or distinction): *differs from her father.* **5.** (used to indicate source, origin, agent, or cause): *came from the Midwest.*

frond (frond), *n.* an often large, finely divided leaf, esp. of a fern palm.

front (frunt), *n.* **1.** the forward part or surface. **2.** the part or side of something that faces or is directed forward. **3.** a place or position directly before something else. **4.** a place where combat operations are carried on. **5.** an area of activity or competition. **6.** land facing a road, river, etc. **7.** a person or thing that serves as a cover or disguise for an activity, esp. a disreputable one. **8.** bearing; demeanor: *a calm front.* **9. a.** the forehead. **b.** the entire face. **10.** a zone of transition between two dissimilar air masses. —*adj.* **11.** of or situated in or at the front. —*v.t., v.i.* **12.** to face. **13.** to serve as a front (for). —*Idiom.* **14. in front of, a.** ahead of. **b.** in the presence of. **15. up front,** *Informal.* **a.** before anything else. **b.** frank; open. —**fron'tal,** *adj.*

front•age (frun'tij), *n.* **1.** the front of a building or lot. **2.** the lineal extent of a frontage. **3.** FRONT (def. 6).

front' burn'er *n.* a condition of top priority.

fron•tier (frun tēr'), *n.* **1.** the part of a country that borders another country. **2.** land that forms the farthest extent of a country's settled regions. **3.** Often, **-tiers.** the limit of knowledge or achievement. —**fron•tiers'man,** *n., pl.* **-men.**

fron•tis•piece (frun'tis pēs', fron'-), *n.* an illustrated leaf preceding the title page of a book.

front'-run'ner or **front'run'ner,** *n.* a person who leads in a competition.

frost (frôst, frost), *n.* **1.** a degree of cold sufficient to cause water to freeze. **2.** a covering of minute ice crystals formed from the atmosphere on cold surfaces. —*v.t.* **3.** to cover with frost. **4.** to give a frostlike surface to (glass, metal, etc.). **5.** to put frosting on: *to frost a cake.* —**frost'y,** *adj.,* **-i•er, -i•est.** —**frost'i•ness,** *n.*

frost'bite' *n., v.,* **-bit, -bit•ten, -bit•ing.** —*n.* **1.** injury to a part of the body from excessive exposure to extreme cold. —*v.t.* **2.** to injure by extreme cold.

frost'ing *n.* **1.** a sweet, creamy mixture for coating baked goods; icing. **2.** a dull or lusterless finish, as on metal or glass.

froth (frôth, froth), *n.* **1.** an aggregation of bubbles, as on an agitated liquid; foam. **2.** a foam of saliva. **3.** something unsubstantial or trivial. —*v.t., v.i.* **4.** to cover with or give out froth. —**froth'y,** *adj.,* **-i•er, -i•est.**

fro•ward (frō'wərd, frō'ərd), *adj.* willfully contrary. —**fro'ward•ness,** *n.*

frown (froun), *v.i.* **1.** to contract the brow, as in displeasure; scowl. **2.** to view with disapproval: *They frown on gambling.* —*n.* **3.** a frowning look; scowl. —**frown'er,** *n.* —**frown'ing•ly,** *adv.*

frowz•y (frou'zē), *adj.,* **-i•er, -i•est.** dirty and untidy; slovenly. —**frowz'i•ly,** *adv.* —**frowz'i•ness,** *n.*

fruc•ti•fy (fruk'tə fī', frŏŏk'-, frōōk'-), *v.,* **-fied, -fy•ing.** —*v.i.* **1.** to bear fruit. —*v.t.* **2.** to make fruitful or productive.

fruc'tose (-tōs), *n.* an extremely sweet sugar occurring in honey and many fruits.

fru•gal (frōō'gəl), *adj.* **1.** not wasteful; economical. **2.** marked by economy; sparse. —**fru•gal'i•ty,** *n., pl.* **-ties.** —**fru'gal•ly,** *adv.*

fruit (frōōt), *n., pl.* **fruits, fruit,** *v.* —*n.* **1.** the edible part of a plant developed from a flower, as a peach or banana. **2.** the developed ovary of a seed plant with its contents and accessory parts, as a nut or tomato. **3.** a product, result, or effect. —*v.i., v.t.* **4.** to bear or cause to bear fruit.

fruit'ful *adj.* **1.** producing good results; productive. **2.** abounding in fruit. —**fruit'ful•ly,** *adv.* —**fruit'ful•ness,** *n.*

fru•i•tion (frōō ish'ən), *n.* **1.** attainment of something desired; realization. **2.** enjoyment, as of something attained. **3.** the state of bearing fruit.

fruit'less *adj.* **1.** not producing results or success. **2.** bearing no fruit; barren. —**fruit'less•ly,** *adv.* —**fruit'less•ness,** *n.*

frump (frump), *n.* a dowdy, drab, and unattractive woman. —**frump'y,** *adj.,* **-i•er, -i•est.**

frus•trate (frus'trāt), *v.t.,* **-trat•ed, -trat•ing. 1.** to defeat (plans, efforts, etc.); block. **2.** to cause feelings of disappointment in; thwart. —**frus'trat•ing•ly,** *adv.* —**frus•tra'tion,** *n.*

fry[1] (frī), *v.,* **fried, fry•ing,** *n., pl.* **fries.** —*v.t.* **1.** to cook in fat or oil, usu. over direct heat. —*v.i.* **2.** to undergo frying. —*n.* **3.** a dish of fried food. **4.** a party or gathering at which fried food is served. [< OF < L *frīgere* to roast] —**fry'a•ble,** *adj.* —**fry'er,** *n.*

fry[2] (frī), *n., pl.* **fry. 1.** the young of fish. **2.** individuals, esp. children: *games for the small fry.* [ME: seed, descendant]

ft. 1. feet. **2.** foot. **3.** fort.

FTC Federal Trade Commission.

fuch•sia (fyōō'shə), *n., pl.* **-sias. 1.** a shrubby plant with pink to purplish drooping flowers. **2.** a bright purplish red color.

fudge[1] (fuj), *n.* a soft candy made of sugar, butter, milk, and flavoring.

fudge[2] (fuj), *n.* nonsense or foolishness.

fudge[3] (fuj), *v.,* **fudged, fudg•ing.** —*v.i.* **1.** to behave in a dishonest way; cheat or welsh. **2.** to avoid coming to grips with something. —*v.t.* **3.** to evade; dodge. **4.** to falsify; fake.

fu•el (fyōō'əl), *n., v.,* **-eled, -el•ing** or (*esp. Brit.*) **-elled, -el•ling.** —*n.* **1.** combustible matter, as coal, wood, or oil, used to create heat or power, or as an energy source for a nuclear reactor. **2.** something that sustains or stimulates. —*v.t., v.i.* **3.** to supply with or obtain fuel.

fu•gi•tive (fyōō'ji tiv), *n.* **1.** a person who flees, as from prosecution. —*adj.* **2.** having taken flight or run away. **3.** passing quickly; fleeting.

ful•crum (fŏŏl'krəm, ful'-), *n., pl.* **-crums, -cra** (-krə). the support or point of rest on which a lever turns.

ful•fill or **-fil** (fŏŏl fil'), *v.t.,* **-filled, -fill•ing** or **-fil•ling. 1.** to bring to realization. **2.** to carry out; perform. **3.** to satisfy (requirements, obligations, etc.). **4.** to bring to an end. —**ful•fill'er,** *n.* —**ful•fill'ment,** *n.*

full[1] (fŏŏl), *adj.,* **-er, -est,** *adv., n.* —*adj.* **1.** filled to capacity. **2.** complete in all respects. **3.** of maximum size, amount, extent, or degree: *full pay.* **4.** having ample room; roomy: *a full skirt.* **5.** having an abundance; well supplied: *a cabinet full of medicine.* **6.** rounded in form: *a full figure.* **7.** engrossed; occupied: *full of her own anxieties.* **8.** of the highest rank: *a full professor.* **9.** ample and rich in sound. —*adv.* **10.** exactly or directly: *struck him full in the face.* **11.** very: *knew full well what I meant.* —*n.* **12.** the fullest state, amount, or degree. —**full'ness,** *n.*

full[2] (fŏŏl), *v.t.* to shrink and thicken (woolen cloth). —**full'er,** *n.*

full'back' *n.* (in football) a running back who lines up behind the quarterback.

full'-bod'ied *adj.* of full strength, flavor, or richness.

full'-fledged' (-flejd'), *adj.* **1.** of full rank or standing. **2.** fully developed.

full'-scale' *adj.* **1.** having the exact size or proportions of an original. **2.** using all possible means; complete.

ful•mi•nate (ful'mə nāt'), *v.i.,* **-nat•ed, -nat•ing. 1.** to explode with a loud noise. **2.** to issue violent denunciation or strong condemnation. —**ful′mi•na′tion,** *n.* —**ful′mi•na′tor,** *n.*

ful•some (fŏŏl′səm, ful′-), *adj.* offensive to good taste, esp. as being excessive or insincere; sickening. —**ful′some•ly,** *adv.* —**ful′some•ness,** *n.*

fum•ble (fum′bəl), *v.,* **-bled, -bling,** *n.* —*v.i.* **1.** to grope clumsily. **2.** to fail to hold a baseball or football after having touched or carried it. **3.** to do or handle something clumsily or ineffectively. —*v.t.* **4.** to handle clumsily; botch. **5.** to fail to hold (a ball). —*n.* **6.** the act of fumbling. **7.** a fumbled ball. —**fum′bler,** *n.* —**fum′bling•ly,** *adv.*

fume (fyŏŏm), *n., v.,* **fumed, fum•ing.** —*n.* **1.** a smokelike or vaporous exhalation, esp. of an irritating nature. —*v.t.* **2.** to treat with or expose to fumes. —*v.i.* **3.** to show irritation or anger. **4.** to emit fumes. —**fum′y,** *adj.,* **-i•er, -i•est.**

fu′mi•gate′ *v.t.,* **-gat•ed, -gat•ing.** to expose to fumes, as in killing vermin. —**fu′mi•ga′tion,** *n.* —**fu′mi•ga′tor,** *n.*

fun (fun), *n.* **1.** something that provides mirth or amusement. **2.** enjoyment or playfulness. —*adj.* **3.** *Informal.* providing fun; enjoyable: *a fun thing to do.* —**Idiom. 4. make fun of,** to ridicule; deride.

func•tion (fungk′shən), *n.* **1.** the kind of action or activity proper to a person or thing. **2.** the purpose for which something is designed or exists. **3.** a ceremonious public or social gathering or occasion. **4.** a factor related to or dependent upon other factors. **5.** *Math.* a relation between two sets in which one element of the second set is assigned to each element of the first set. —*v.i.* **6.** to work; operate. **7.** to perform a function; serve.

func′tion•ar′y (-shə ner′ē), *n., pl.* **-ies.** a person who functions in a specified capacity, esp. a government official.

fund (fund), *n.* **1.** a sum of money set aside for a specific purpose. **2.** a supply; stock. **3. funds,** money immediately available. **4.** an organization created to manage money contributed or invested. —*v.t.* **5.** to provide funds for. **6.** to provide a fund to pay the interest or principal of (a debt).

fun•da•men•tal (fun′də men′tl), *adj.* **1.** of or being a foundation or basis; basic. **2.** of great importance; essential. **3.** being an original or primary source. —*n.* **4.** something fundamental, as a principle or rule. —**fun′da•men′tal•ly,** *adv.*

fun′da•men′tal•ist *n.* a believer in the literal interpretation of a religious text, as the Bible.

fu•ner•al (fyŏŏ′nər əl), *n.* the ceremonies for a dead person prior to burial or cremation.

fu′neral direc′tor *n.* a person who supervises or arranges funerals.

fu′neral home′ *n.* an establishment where the dead are prepared for burial or cremation and where funeral services are often held.

fu•ne′re•al (-nēr′ē əl), *adj.* of or suitable for a funeral. **2.** gloomy; dismal. —**fu•ne′re•al•ly,** *adv.*

fun•gus (fung′gəs), *n., pl.* **fun•gi** (fun′jī, fung′gī), **fun•gus•es.** any of a number of organisms, including mushrooms, molds, and mildews, that live by decomposing and absorbing the organic material in which they grow. —**fun′gal, fun′gous,** *adj.*

funk (fungk), *n.* **1.** a state of cowering fear. **2.** a dejected mood; depression.

funk′y *adj.,* **-i•er, -i•est. 1.** having an earthy, blues-based character: *funky jazz.* **2.** *Slang.* offbeat or unconventional. —**funk′i•ness,** *n.*

fun•nel (fun′l), *n., v.,* **-neled, -nel•ing** or (*esp.* *Brit.*) **-nelled, -nel•ling.** —*n.* **1.** a cone-shaped utensil with a tube for channeling a substance through a small opening. **2.** a smokestack, esp. of a steamship. **3.** a flue or shaft. —*v.t., v.i.* **4.** to pass through or as if through a funnel.

fun•ny (fun′ē), *adj.,* **-ni•er, -ni•est,** *n., pl.* **-nies.** —*adj.* **1.** provoking laughter; comical. **2.** warranting suspicion; underhanded. **3.** strange; peculiar. —*n.* **4. funnies, a.** comic strips. **b.** the section of a newspaper reserved for comic strips. —**fun′ni•ly,** *adv.* —**fun′ni•ness,** *n.*

fun′ny bone′ *n.* the part of the elbow where a blow to the nerve causes a tingling sensation.

fur (fûr), *n.* **1.** the soft, thick, hairy coat of a mam-

mal. **2.** the processed pelt of an animal, as a mink, used esp. for garments. **3.** a garment made of fur. **4.** a coating resembling fur. —**furred,** *adj.* —**fur′ry,** *adj.,* **-ri•er, -ri•est.**

fur•bish (fûr′bish), *v.t.* to restore to good condition; renovate.

fu•ri•ous (fyŏŏr′ē əs), *adj.* **1.** full of fury or rage. **2.** violent, as a storm. **3.** very intense: *furious activity.* —**fu′ri•ous•ly,** *adv.*

furl (fûrl), *v.t.* **1.** to gather into a roll and bind securely, as a flag against its staff. —*v.i.* **2.** to become furled.

fur•long (fûr′lông, -long), *n.* a unit of distance equal to 220 yards (201 m) or ⅛ of a mile (0.2 km).

fur•lough (fûr′lō), *n.* **1.** a leave of absence, esp. one granted to a person in the military. —*v.t.* **2.** to grant a furlough to.

fur•nace (fûr′nis), *n.* a structure or apparatus in which heat is generated, as for heating houses.

fur•nish (fûr′nish), *v.t.* **1.** to supply with what is necessary, esp. with furniture. **2.** to provide; give. **fur′nish•ings** *n.pl.* **1.** articles, esp. furniture, for a room. **2.** articles or accessories of dress.

fur•ni•ture (-chər), *n.* movable articles, as tables or chairs, required for use or ornament in a room.

fu•ror (fyŏŏr′ôr, -ər), *n.* **1.** a general outburst of excitement; uproar. **2.** a fad or craze. **3.** fury; rage. Also, *esp. Brit.,* **fu′rore** (for defs. 1, 2).

fur•ri•er (fûr′ē ər), *n.* a fur dealer or fur dresser.

fur•row (fûr′ō, fur′ō), *n.* **1.** a narrow groove made in the ground, esp. by a plow. **2.** a narrow groovelike depression, as a wrinkle. —*v.t.* **3.** to make furrows in. —*v.i.* **4.** to become furrowed.

fur•ther (fûr′thər), *adv., adj., compar. of* **far,** *v.* —*adv.* **1.** at or to a greater distance; farther. **2.** to a greater extent. **3.** in addition; moreover. —*adj.* **4.** more distant or remote; farther. **5.** more extended. **6.** additional; more. —*v.t.* **7.** to help forward; advance. —**fur′ther•ance,** *n.*

fur′ther•more′ *adv.* in addition; moreover.

fur′ther•most′ *adj.* most distant.

fur•thest (fûr′thist), *adj., adv., superl. of* **far.** FARTHEST.

fur•tive (fûr′tiv), *adj.* **1.** taken, done, or used by stealth; surreptitious. **2.** sly; shifty. —**fur′tive•ly,** *adv.* —**fur′tive•ness,** *n.*

fu•ry (fyŏŏr′ē), *n., pl.* **-ries. 1.** unrestrained or violent anger; rage. **2.** a fit of such anger. **3.** violence; fierceness.

fuse¹ (fyŏŏz), *n.* **1.** a tube or cord filled or saturated with combustible matter for igniting an explosive. **2.** a mechanical or electronic device for detonating an explosive charge.

fuse² (fyŏŏz), *n., v.,* **fused, fus•ing.** —*n.* **1.** a safety device containing a conductor that melts when excess current runs through an electric circuit, breaking the circuit. —*v.t., v.i.* **2.** to blend or unite by or as if by melting together. **3.** to melt. —**fu′si•ble,** *adj.*

fu•se•lage (fyŏŏ′sə läzh′, -lij, -zə-), *n.* the central structure of an airplane, containing passenger and cargo compartments.

fu•sil•lade (fyŏŏ′sə läd′, -lād′, -zə-), *n.* a simultaneous or continuous discharge of firearms.

fuss (fus), *n.* **1.** needless or useless bustle. **2.** a quarrel or dispute. **3.** a complaint, esp. about something unimportant. —*v.i.* **4.** to make a fuss. **5.** to complain, esp. about something unimportant. —**fuss′y,** *adj.,* **-i•er, -i•est.**

fus•ty (fus′tē), *adj.,* **-ti•er, -ti•est. 1.** moldy; musty. **2.** old-fashioned or out-of-date. —**fus′ti•ness,** *n.*

fu•ton (fŏŏ′ton), *n.* a thin, quiltlike mattress placed on a floor for sleeping or used as seating.

fu•ture (fyŏŏ′chər), *n.* **1.** time that is to come hereafter. **2.** something that will happen in the future. **3.** a condition, esp. of success or failure, to come. **4. a.** the future tense. **b.** a verb form in the future tense. **5.** Usu., **-tures.** commodities bought and sold speculatively for future delivery. —*adj.* **6.** being or coming hereafter. **7.** of or being a verb tense that refers to events or states in time to come. **—fu′tur•is′tic,** *adj.*

fuzz[1] (fuz), *n.* loose, light, fibrous, or fluffy matter; down.

fuzz[2] (fuz), *n. Slang.* the police.

fuzz′y *adj.,* **-i•er, -i•est. 1.** resembling or covered with fuzz. **2.** indistinct; blurred. **—fuzz′i•ly,** *adv.* **—fuzz′i•ness,** *n.*

FYI for your information.

abcdef G hijklmnopqrstuvwxyz

G, g (jē), *n., pl.* **Gs** or **G's, gs** or **g's.** the seventh letter of the English alphabet, a consonant.

G 1. general: a motion-picture rating advising that the film is suitable for all age groups. **2.** German.

G *Symbol.* **1.** the seventh in order or in a series. **2.** the fifth note of the C major scale.

g 1. good. **2.** gram. **3.** gravity.

g *Symbol.* acceleration of gravity.

GA 1. Gamblers Anonymous. **2.** general of the army. **3.** Georgia.

Ga *Chem. Symbol.* gallium.

Ga. Georgia.

gab (gab), *v.,* **gabbed, gab•bing,** *n. Informal.* **—v.i. 1.** to talk idly; chatter. **—n. 2.** idle talk. **—gab′ber,** *n.*

gab•ar•dine (gab′ər dēn′), *n.* a firm, woven fabric of worsted, cotton, or other fiber, with a twill weave.

gab•ble (gab′əl), *v.,* **-bled, -bling,** *n.* **—v.i., v.t. 1.** to speak or utter rapidly and unintelligibly. **—n. 2.** rapid, unintelligible talk.

ga•ble (gā′bəl), *n.* the portion of the front or side of a building enclosed by or masking the end of a pitched roof. **—ga′bled,** *adj.*

Ga•bon (gᴀ bôn′), *n.* a republic in W equatorial Africa. **—Gab•o•nese** (gab′ə nēz′, -nēs′, gä′bə-), *adj., n., pl.* **-nese.**

gad (gad), *v.i.,* **gad•ded, gad•ding.** to move aimlessly or restlessly about.

gad′a•bout′ *n.* a person who moves about aimlessly or restlessly, esp. from one social activity to another.

gad′fly′ *n., pl.* **-flies. 1.** any of various flies that bite or annoy livestock. **2.** a person who persistently annoys or stirs up others.

gadg•et (gaj′it), *n.* a usu. small mechanical or electronic contrivance or device. **—gad′get•ry,** *n.*

gaff[1] (gaf), *n.* **1.** an iron hook with a handle for landing large fish. **2.** a spar that supports the head of a fore-and-aft sail.

gaff[2] (gaf), *n. Informal.* harsh treatment, criticism, or ridicule (used esp. in the phrase *stand the gaff*).

gaffe (gaf), *n.* a social blunder.

gaf′fer *n.* **1.** the chief electrician on a motion-picture or television production. **2.** *Informal.* an old man.

gag[1] (gag), *v.,* **gagged, gag•ging,** *n.* **—v.t. 1.** to stop up the mouth of (a person) by putting something in it, thus preventing speech, shouts, etc. **2.** to restrain from free speech. **3.** to cause to retch or choke. **—v.i. 4.** to retch or choke. **—n. 5.** something put into a person's mouth to prevent speech, shouting, etc. **6.** any suppression of free speech. **7.** a surgical instrument for holding the jaws open.

gag[2] (gag), *n., v.,* **gagged, gag•ging.** *Informal.* **—n. 1.** a joke. **2.** any contrived piece of wordplay or horseplay. **—v.i 3.** to tell jokes.

gage[1] (gāj), *n.* something, as a glove, thrown down by a medieval knight in token of a challenge to combat.

gage[2] (gāj), *v.t.,* **gaged, gag•ing,** *n.* (chiefly in technical use) GAUGE.

gag•gle (gag′əl), *n.* **1.** a flock of geese when not flying. **2.** any disorderly group or gathering.

gai•e•ty (gā′i tē), *n., pl.* **-ties. 1.** the quality or state of being gay or cheerful; merriment. **2.** merrymaking or festivity. **3.** showiness; finery.

gai•ly (gā′lē), *adv.* **1.** merrily; cheerfully. **2.** brightly; showily.

gain (gān), *v.t.* **1.** to get (something desired), esp. as a result of one's efforts. **2.** to acquire as an increase or addition: *to gain speed.* **3.** to obtain as a profit or advantage. **4.** to win. **5.** to reach by effort. **—v.i. 6.** to improve: *to gain in health.* **7.** to get nearer, as in pursuit: *Our horse gained on the favorite.* **—n. 8.** profit or advantage. **9.** an increase or advance. **10. gains,** profits or winnings.

gain•say (gān′sā′, gān sā′), *v.t.,* **-said, -say•ing. 1.** to deny; contradict. **2.** to speak or act against. **—gain′say′er,** *n.*

gait (gāt), *n.* **1.** a manner of walking, stepping, or running. **2.** any of the manners in which a horse moves, as a trot, canter, or gallop.

gal (gal), *n. Informal.* a girl.

gal. gallon.

ga•la (gā′lə, gal′ə; *esp. Brit.* gä′lə), *adj., n., pl.* **-las. —adj. 1.** festive; showy. **—n. 2.** a festive occasion or celebration.

gal•ax•y (gal′ək sē), *n., pl.* **-ax•ies. 1. a.** a large system of stars held together by mutual gravitation. **b.** (*usu. cap.*) MILKY WAY. **2.** any large and brilliant assemblage of persons or things. [≪ Gk *galaxías (kýklos)* the Milky (Way)] **—ga•lac•tic** (gə lak′tik), *adj.*

gale (gāl), *n.* **1.** a very strong wind. **2.** a noisy outburst: *a gale of laughter.*

gall[1] (gôl), *n.* **1.** impudence; effrontery. **2.** BILE (def. 1). **3.** something bitter or severe. **4.** bitterness of spirit; rancor.

gall[2] (gôl), *v.t.* **1.** to make sore by rubbing. **2.** to vex or irritate. **—n. 3.** a sore on the skin, esp. of a horse, due to rubbing. **4.** something vexing or irritating. **—gall′ing,** *adj.*

gall[3] (gôl), *n.* any abnormal swelling on a plant, as from insects.

gal•lant (gal′ənt; *for 2, 5 also* gə lant′, -länt′), *adj.* **1.** brave, spirited, or noble-minded. **2.** polite and attentive to women; chivalrous. **3.** stately; grand. **4.** showy or stylish. **—n. 5.** a man exceptionally attentive to women. **6.** a stylish and dashing man. **—gal′lant•ly,** *adv.*

gall′blad′der (gôl′-), *n.* a membranous sac attached to the liver, in which bile is stored and concentrated.

gal•le•on (gal′ē ən, gal′yən), *n.* a large sailing ship of the 15th to 17th centuries.

gal•ler•y (gal′ə rē), *n., pl.* **-ies. 1.** a balcony in a theater, church, or other public building. **2.** the uppermost or highest of such balconies in a theater, usu. containing the cheapest seats. **3.** the occupants of these seats. **4.** a group of spectators, as at a legislative session. **5.** a room or building devoted to the exhibition of works of art. **6.** a long covered area used as a walk or corridor. **7.** a long porch; veranda. **8.** a large room or building used for photography, target practice, etc.

gal•ley (gal′ē), *n., pl.* **-leys. 1. a.** the kitchen area of a ship, plane, or camper. **b.** any small narrow kitchen. **2.** a seagoing ship propelled mainly by oars, used in ancient and medieval times. **3. a.** a tray for holding type that has been set. **b.** Also called **gal′ley proof′.** a proof printed from type in such a tray.

gal•li•um (gal′ē əm), *n.* a rare steel-gray metallic element used in high-temperature thermometers. *Symbol:* Ga; *at. wt.:* 69.72; *at. no.:* 31.

gal•li•vant (gal′ə vant′), *v.i.* to wander about, seeking pleasure or diversion.

gal•lon (gal′ən), *n.* a unit of capacity equal to four quarts or 231 cubic inches (3.7853 liters).

gal•lop (gal′əp), *n.* **1.** a fast gait of a horse or other quadruped in which all four feet are off the ground at once. —*v.i., v.t.* **2.** to move or cause to move at a gallop.

gal•lows (gal′ōz, -əz), *n., pl.* **-lows, -lows•es.** a frame consisting of two upright timbers with a crossbeam from which condemned persons are hanged.

gall′stone′ *n.* an abnormal stony mass in the gallbladder or the bile passages.

ga•lore (gə lôr′), *adv.* in abundance; in plentiful amounts: *food and drink galore.*

ga•losh•es (gə losh′iz) *n.pl.* overshoes.

gal′va•nize′ *v.t.* **-nized, -niz•ing. 1.** to stimulate by an electric current. **2.** to stimulate or startle into sudden activity. **3.** to coat (iron or steel) with zinc.

Gam•bi•a (gam′bē ə), *n.* **the,** a republic in W Africa. —**Gam′bi•an,** *n., adj.*

gam•bit (gam′bit), *n.* **1.** a chess opening to obtain some advantage by sacrificing a pawn or piece. **2.** any maneuver used to gain an advantage.

gam•ble (gam′bəl), *v.,* **-bled, -bling,** *n.* —*v.i.* **1.** to play at a game of chance for money or other stakes. **2.** to stake or risk something of value on the outcome of something involving chance. —*v.t.* **3.** to lose by betting. **4.** to wager or risk (something of value). —*n.* **5.** any matter or thing involving risk. —**gam′bler,** *n.*

gam•bol (gam′bəl), *v.,* **-boled, -bol•ing** or (*esp.* Brit.) **-bolled, -bol•ling,** *n.* —*v.i.* **1.** to skip about in play; frolic. —*n.* **2.** a skipping or frisking about.

game[1] (gām), *n., adj.,* **gam•er, gam•est,** *v.,* **gamed, gam•ing.** —*n.* **1.** an amusement or pastime. **2.** the equipment used in playing certain games. **3.** a competitive activity involving skill, chance, or endurance played according to rules. **4.** a single occasion of such an activity. **5.** the number of points required to win. **6.** a particular manner or style of playing. **7.** *Informal.* a business or profession. **8.** a trick or strategy. **9.** wild animals, including birds and fishes, hunted for food or sport. **10.** any object of attack, abuse, etc.: *to be fair game for practical jokers.* —*adj.* **11.** of or noting hunted animals or their flesh. **12.** having a fighting spirit; plucky. **13.** having the required spirit or will. —*v.i.* **14.** to play games of chance for stakes. —**game′ly,** *adv.* —**game′ness,** *n.*

game[2] (gām), *adj.* lame: *a game leg.*

game′ plan′ *n.* a carefully planned strategy or course of action.

gam•ete (gam′ēt, gə mēt′), *n.* a mature sexual reproductive cell that unites with another cell to form a new organism.

gam•ut (gam′ət), *n.* **1.** the entire scale or range. **2.** the whole series of recognized musical notes.

gam•y (gā′mē), *adj.,* **-i•er, -i•est. 1.** having the tangy flavor of game, esp. game kept uncooked until slightly tainted. **2.** plucky. **3.** risqué. —**gam′i•ness,** *n.*

gan•der (gan′dər), *n.* **1.** the male of the goose. **2.** *Slang.* a look; glance.

gang (gang), *n.* **1.** a group of people associated or working together. **2.** a group of persons associated for some criminal or other antisocial purpose. —*v.t., v.i.* **3.** to form into a gang. **4. gang up on,** to attack as a group.

gan•gling (gang′gling) also **-gly** (-glē) *adj.* awkwardly tall and spindly.

gan•gli•on (gang′glē ən), *n., pl.* **-gli•a** (-glē ə) **-gli•ons.** a concentrated mass of interconnected nerve cells.

gang•plank (gang′plangk′), *n.* a movable bridgelike structure for use by persons boarding or leaving a ship.

gan•grene (gang′grēn, gang grēn′), *n.* necrosis of soft tissue due to obstructed circulation. —**gan′gre•nous** (-grə nəs), *adj.*

gang′ster *n.* a member of a gang of criminals.

gang•way (*n.* gang′wā′; *interj.* gang′wā′), *n.* **1.** a passageway. **2. a.** an opening in the railing or bulwark of a ship. **b.** GANGPLANK. —*interj.* **3.** clear the way!

gan•try (gan′trē), *n., pl.* **-tries. 1.** a spanning framework, as a bridgelike portion of certain cranes. **2.** a frame consisting of scaffolds on various levels used to erect rockets.

gaol (jāl), *n., v.t. Brit.* JAIL. —**gaol′er,** *n.*

gap (gap), *n.* **1.** a break or opening, as in a fence or wall. **2.** an empty space or interval. **3.** a wide divergence or difference; disparity. **4.** a deep ravine or mountain pass.

gape (gāp, gap), *v.,* **gaped, gap•ing,** *n.* —*v.i.* **1.** to stare with open mouth, as in wonder. **2.** to open the mouth wide involuntarily, as the result of sleepiness. **3.** to open as a gap. —*n.* **4.** a wide opening or gap. **5.** an act or instance of gaping.

ga•rage (gə räzh′, -räj′; *esp. Brit.* gar′ij, -äzh), *n., v.,* **-raged, -rag•ing.** —*n.* **1.** a structure for parking or storing motor vehicles. **2.** a commercial establishment for repairing and servicing motor vehicles. —*v.t.* **3.** to put or keep in a garage.

garb (gärb), *n.* **1.** a fashion or mode of dress, esp. of a distinctive, uniform kind. **2.** outward appearance or form. —*v.t.* **3.** to dress; clothe.

gar•bage (gär′bij), *n.* **1.** discarded matter, esp. kitchen refuse. **2.** anything worthless, inferior, or vile.

gar•ble (gär′bəl), *v.t.,* **-bled, -bling.** to distort or confuse (a report, message, etc.) so as to be misleading or unintelligible.

gar•den (gär′dn), *n.* **1.** a plot of ground where flowers, vegetables, fruits, or herbs are cultivated. **2.** a planted area used for public recreation. **3.** a fertile and delightful spot. —*adj.* **4.** of, for, or produced in a garden. —*v.i.* **5.** to tend a garden. [< OF *jardin* < Gmc] —**gar′den•er,** *n.*

gar•de•nia (gär dē′nyə, -nē ə), *n., pl.* **-nias. 1.** an evergreen tree or shrub with shiny leaves and fragrant white flowers. **2.** its flower.

gar′den-vari′ety *adj.* common or ordinary; unexceptional.

gar•gan•tu•an (gär gan′chōō ən), *adj.* gigantic.

gar•gle (gär′gəl), *v.,* **-gled, -gling.** —*v.t., v.i.* **1.** to rinse (the throat) with a liquid kept in motion by a stream of air from the lungs. —*n.* **2.** a liquid used for gargling.

gar•goyle (gär′goil), *n.* a grotesquely carved figure of a human or animal, often functioning as a waterspout, projecting from a building.

gar•ish (gâr′ish, gar′-), *adj.* crudely or tastelessly colorful, showy, or elaborate. —**gar′ish•ly,** *adv.* —**gar′ish•ness,** *n.*

gar•land (gär′lənd), *n.* **1.** a wreath or festoon of flowers, leaves, or other material. —*v.t.* **2.** to deck with garlands.

gar•lic (gär′lik), *n.* a hardy plant of the amaryllis family, having a strongly pungent bulb that is used in cooking. —**gar′lick•y,** *adj.*

gar•ment (gär′mənt), *n.* any article of clothing.

gar•ner (gär′nər), *v.t.* **1.** to gather and store. **2.** to get or acquire.

gar•net (gär′nit), *n.* any of a group of deep red, brownish, or green vitreous minerals: several varieties are used as gems.

gar•nish (gär′nish), *v.t.* **1.** to provide with something ornamental. **2.** to provide (a food) with something that adds flavor, decorative color, etc. **3.** GARNISHEE. —*n.* **4.** something used to garnish a food.

gar•nish•ee (gär′ni shē′), *v.t.,* **-eed, -ee•ing.** *Law.* to attach (money or property) by garnishment.

gar′nish•ment *n.* *Law.* a warning served on a third party to hold wages, property, etc., belonging to a debtor pending settlement in court.

gar•ret (gar′it), *n.* an attic, usu. a small, cramped one.

gar•ri•son (gar′ə sən), *n.* **1.** a body of troops stationed in a fortified place. **2.** any military post, esp. a permanent one. —*v.t.* **3.** to station (troops) in a fort, post, etc.

gar•rote (gə rot′, -rōt′), *n., v.,* **-rot•ed, -rot•ing** or **-rot•ted, -rot•ting.** —*n.* **1.** a method of capital punishment of Spanish origin in which a person is strangled by an iron collar. **2.** strangulation, esp. in the course of a robbery. **3.** a cord or wire with attached handles, used to strangle a victim. —*v.t.* **4.** to strangle or throttle, as by a garrote. —**gar•rot′er,** *n.*

gar•ru•lous (gar′ləs, gar′yə-), *adj.* **1.** excessively talkative in a rambling manner. **2.** wordy or diffuse. —**gar•ru•li•ty** (gə rōō′li tē), **gar′ru•lous•ness,** *n.* —**gar′ru•lous•ly,** *adv.*

gar′ter (gär′tər), *n.* a device for holding up a stocking or sock.

gar′ter snake′ *n.* a harmless, striped snake common in North and Central America.

gas (gas), *n., pl.* **gas•es,** *v.,* **gassed, gas•sing. —*n.*** **1.** a fluid substance with the ability to expand indefinitely. **2.** any such fluid or mixture of fluids used as a fuel, anesthetic, asphyxiating agent, etc. **3. a.** gasoline. **b.** the accelerator of an automotive vehicle. **4.** FLATUS. —*v.t.* **5.** to overcome, poison, or asphyxiate with gas. **6.** to treat with gas. —**gas′e•ous** (gas′ē əs, gash′əs), *adj.*

gash (gash), *n.* **1.** a long, deep wound or cut. —*v.t.* **2.** to make a gash in.

gas•ket (gas′kit), *n.* a rubber, metal, or rope ring for packing a piston or placing around a joint to make it watertight.

gas•o•line (gas′ə lēn′, gas′ə lēn′), *n.* a volatile, flammable liquid mixture of hydrocarbons obtained from petroleum, used chiefly as fuel for internal-combustion engines.

gasp (gasp, gäsp), *n.* **1.** a sudden, short intake of breath. **2.** a short, convulsive utterance. —*v.i.* **3.** to struggle for breath with the mouth open; breathe convulsively. —*v.t.* **4.** to utter with gasps.

gas•tric (gas′trik), *adj.* pertaining to the stomach.

gas•tro•nom•i•cal (gas′trə nom′i kəl) *adj.* of good eating. —**gas•tron′o•my** (ga stron′ə mē) *n.*

gate (gāt), *n.* **1.** a movable barrier closing an opening in a fence, wall, etc. **2.** any movable barrier, as at a tollbooth. **3.** any means of access or entrance. **4.** a sliding barrier for regulating the passage of water or steam. **5.** the total number of persons who pay for admission to a sports event, performance, etc. **6. the gate,** rejection.

gate′way′ *n.* **1.** an entrance or passage that may be closed by a gate. **2.** any means of entrance.

gath•er (gath′ər), *v.t.* **1.** to bring together into one group or place. **2.** to pick or harvest. **3.** to scoop up: *She gathered the child in her arms.* **4.** to increase gradually: *The car gathered speed.* **5.** to assemble or collect for an effort: *to gather one's strength.* **6.** to conclude from observation. **7.** to wrap or draw around, as a garment. **8.** to draw (cloth) into fine folds by means of stitches. —*v.i.* **9.** to come together or assemble. **10.** to increase. —*n.* **11.** Often, **-ers.** a fold or pucker. —**gath′er•er,** *n.* —**gath′er•ing,** *n.*

gauche (gōsh), *adj.* lacking social grace; tactless. —**gauche′ly,** *adv.*

gaud•y (gô′dē), *adj.,* **-i•er, -i•est.** showy in a tasteless way. —**gaud′i•ly,** *adv.* —**gaud′i•ness,** *n.*

gauge (gāj), *v.,* **gauged, gaug•ing,** *n.* —*v.t.* **1.** to determine the exact dimensions, capacity, quantity, or force of. **2.** to appraise or judge. —*n.* **3.** a standard of measure or measurement. **4.** any device for measuring or testing something. **5.** a means of estimating or judging. **6.** the internal diameter of a shotgun barrel. **7.** the distance between the two rails in a track. **8.** the thickness or diameter of various thin objects, as wire.

gaunt (gônt), *adj.,* **-er, -est. 1.** extremely thin and bony; haggard. **2.** bleak, desolate, or grim. —**gaunt′ness,** *n.*

gaunt•let¹ (gônt′lit, gänt′-), *n.* **1.** a mailed glove worn with a suit of armor to protect the hand. **2.** a glove with an extended cuff. —*Idiom.* **3. throw down the gauntlet,** to challenge someone to fight.

gaunt•let² (gônt′lit, gänt′-), *n.* **1.** a former military punishment in which the offender ran between two rows of men who struck at him as he passed. —*Idiom.* **2. run the gauntlet,** to suffer severe criticism or tribulation.

gauze (gôz), *n.* a thin, transparent fabric in a loose weave, used esp. for surgical dressings. —**gauz′y,** *adj.,* **-i•er, -i•est.**

gav•el (gav′əl), *n.* a small mallet used, as by a judge, to signal for attention or order.

gawk (gôk), *v.i.* to stare stupidly.

gawk′y *adj.,* **-i•er, -i•est.** awkward or ungainly. —**gawk′i•ly,** *adv.* —**gawk′i•ness,** *n.*

gay (gā), *adj.,* **-er, -est,** *n.* —*adj.* **1.** having or showing a lively mood; merry. **2.** bright or showy: *gay colors.* **3.** homosexual. —*n.* **4.** a homosexual person, esp. a male.

gaze (gāz), *v.,* **gazed, gaz•ing,** *n.* —*v.i.* **1.** to look steadily and intently. —*n.* **2.** a steady or intent look. —**gaz′er,** *n.*

ga•ze•bo (gə zā′bō, -zē′-), *n., pl.* **-bos, -boes.** a structure, as a pavilion, built on a site that provides an attractive view.

ga•zelle (gə zel′), *n., pl.* **-zelles, -zelle.** any of various small graceful antelopes of Africa and Asia.

ga•zette (gə zet′), *n., v.,* **-zet•ted, -zet•ting.** —*n.* **1.** a newspaper (now used chiefly in names). **2.** *Brit.* a government journal listing appointments, promotions, etc. —*v.t.* **3.** *Brit.* to announce or list in a gazette.

gaz•et•teer (gaz′i tēr′), *n.* a geographical dictionary.

gaz•pa•cho (gäz pä′chō) *n.* a Spanish chilled vegetable soup.

gear (gēr), *n.* **1. a.** a part, esp. a wheel, having teeth that mesh with teeth in another part to transmit or receive force and motion. **b.** an assembly of such parts. **2.** implements, tools, or apparatus: *fishing gear.* **3.** portable items of personal property, including clothing. —*v.t.* **4.** to provide with or connect by gears. **5.** to put in gear. **6.** to adjust or regulate so as to match or conform to something: *to gear output to seasonal demands.* **7. gear up,** to get ready; prepare. —*Idiom.* **8. in gear, a.** in the state in which gears are engaged. **b.** in proper working order. **9. out of gear,** in the state in which gears are disengaged.

gear′shift′ *n.* a lever used for engaging and disengaging the gears in a power-transmission system, esp. in a motor vehicle.

geck′o (gek′ō) *n., pl.* **-os** or **-oes.** a small tropical lizard.

GED general equivalency diploma.

gee (jē), *interj.* an exclamation of surprise, disappointment, etc.

gee•zer (gē′zər), *n. Slang.* an odd or eccentric man.

Gei′ger count′er, *n.* an instrument for detecting ionizing radiations, used chiefly to measure radioactivity.

gei•sha (gā′shə, gē′-), *n., pl.* **-shas, -sha.** a Japanese woman trained as a professional singer, dancer, and companion for men.

gel (jel), *n., v.,* **gelled, gel•ling.** —*n.* **1.** a semirigid colloidal dispersion of a solid with a liquid or gas, as a jelly or glue. —*v.i.* **2.** to form or become a gel.

gel•a•tin or **-tine** (jel′ə tn), *n.* a glutinous substance obtained by boiling animal bones, ligaments, etc., or a similar vegetable substance, used in making jellies, glues, and the like. [< F *gélatine* < ML *gelātīna* < L *gelātus* frozen] —**ge•lat•i•nous** (jə-lat′n əs), *adj.*

geld′ing *n.* a castrated horse.

gel•id (jel′id), *adj.* very cold; icy.

gem (jem), *n.* **1.** a mineral, pearl, or other natural substance fine enough for use in jewelry. **2.** something prized because of its beauty or worth.

-gen a suffix meaning something that produces (*carcinogen*).

Gen. 1. General. **2.** Genesis.

gen•darme (zhän′därm; *Fr.* zhän DARM′), *n.* a police officer, esp. in France.

gen•der (jen′dər), *n.* **1.** a set of grammatical categories applied to nouns, as masculine, feminine, or neuter, often correlated in part with sex or animateness. **2.** sex: *the feminine gender.*

gene (jēn), *n.* the basic physical unit of heredity, carried on a chromosome and transmitted from parent to offspring.

ge•ne•al•o•gy (jē′nē ol′ə jē, -al′-, jen′ē-), *n., pl.* **-gies. 1.** a record or account of the ancestry of a person, family, etc. **2.** the study of family ancestries. **3.** descent from an ancestor or progenitor. —**ge′ne•a•log′i•cal** (-ə loj′i kəl), *adj.* —**ge′ne•al′o•gist,** *n.*

gen•er•al (jen′ər əl), *adj.* **1.** of or affecting all persons or things belonging to a group or category. **2.** of or true of such persons or things in the main. **3.** not limited to one class, field, etc.: *the general public.* **4.** dealing with broad, universal, or important aspects: *general guidelines.* **5.** not specific or definite: *a general idea.* **6.** having superior rank: *the general manager.* —*n.* **7.** an officer ranking below a general of the army or general of the air force. **8.** an officer holding the highest rank in the U.S. Marine Corps. —*Idiom.* **9.** in general, **a.** as a whole. **b.** as a rule. —**gen′er•al•ly,** *adv.*

gen′er•al′i•ty *n., pl.* **-ties. 1.** an indefinite or undetailed statement. **2.** a general principle or rule. **3.** the greater part or majority. **4.** the state or quality of being general.

gen′er•al•ize′ *v.,* **-ized, -iz•ing.** —*v.t.* **1.** to infer (a general principle) from particular facts or instances. **2.** to form a general opinion or conclusion from. **3.** to give a general character to. **4.** to bring into general use or knowledge. —*v.i.* **5.** to form general principles, opinions, etc. **6.** to think or speak in generalities. —**gen′er•al•i•za′tion,** *n.*

gen′eral prac′ti′tioner *n.* a medical practitioner whose practice is not limited to any specific branch of medicine.

gen•er•ate (jen′ə rāt′), *v.t.,* **-at•ed, -at•ing. 1.** to bring into existence. **2.** to reproduce; procreate. —**gen′er•a′tive,** *adj.*

gen•er•a′tion *n.* **1.** the entire body of individuals born and living at about the same time. **2.** the average period between the birth of parents and the birth of their offspring. **3.** a single step in natural descent, as of human beings. **4.** a stage of technological development or production distinct from but based upon another stage. **5.** the act or process of generating. —**gen′er•a′tion•al,** *adj.*

Generation X (eks), *n.* the generation born in the U.S. after 1965. Also called **Gen X** (jen′ eks′). [after *Generation X,* a novel by Douglas Coupland] —**Generation X′er,** *n.*

gen′er•a′tor *n.* **1.** a machine that converts mechanical energy into electrical energy, as a dynamo. **2.** one that generates.

ge•ner•ic (jə ner′ik), *adj.* **1.** of or applicable to all the members of a genus, class, group, or kind. **2.** of or constituting a genus. **3.** applicable or referring to both men and women: *a generic pronoun.* **4.** not protected by trademark registration. —*n.* **5.** a generic term. **6.** any product that can be sold without a brand name. —**ge•ner′i•cal•ly,** *adv.*

gen•er•ous (jen′ər əs), *adj.* **1.** liberal in giving or sharing. **2.** free from meanness or pettiness; magnanimous. **3.** large; abundant; ample. —**gen′er•os′i•ty** (-ə ros′i tē), *n.* —**gen′er•ous•ly,** *adv.*

gen•e•sis (jen′ə sis), *n., pl.* **-ses** (-sēz′). an origin or beginning.

Gen•e•sis (jen′ə sis), *n.* the first book of the Old Testament.

ge•net•ics (jə net′iks), *n.* the branch of biology that deals with heredity and with the genetic contribution to similarities and differences among related organisms. —**ge•net′ic,** *adj.* —**ge•net′i•cal•ly,** *adv.* —**ge•net′i•cist** (-ə sist), *n.*

gen., genl. general.

gen•ial (jēn′yəl, jē′nē əl), *adj.* **1.** pleasantly cheerful; cordial. **2.** pleasantly warm; comfortably mild: *a genial climate.* —**ge′ni•al′i•ty** (-al′i tē), *n.* —**gen′ial•ly,** *adv.*

ge•nie (jē′nē), *n., pl.* **-nies.** JINN. a spirit, often appearing in human form, that when summoned by a person carries out the wishes of the summoner.

gen•i•ta•li•a (jen′i tā′lē ə, -tāl′yə), *n.pl.* the organs of reproduction.

gen′i•tals *n.pl.* GENITALIA.

gen•i•tive (jen′i tiv), *adj.* **1.** of or noting a grammatical case typically indicating possession, origin, or other close association. —*n.* **2.** the genitive case.

gen•ius (jēn′yəs), *n., pl.* **-ius•es. 1.** an exceptional natural capacity of intellect. **2.** a person having such capacity. **3.** natural ability or talent. **4.** distinctive character or spirit, as of a nation or period.

gen•o•cide (jen′ə sīd′), *n.* the deliberate and systematic extermination of a national, racial, political, or cultural group.

gen•re (zhän′rə; *Fr.* zhän′ʀᵃ), *n., pl.* **-res. 1.** a class or category of artistic endeavor having a particular form, content, or technique. **2.** painting in which scenes of everyday life form the subject matter.

gen•teel (jen tēl′), *adj.* **1.** belonging or suited to polite society. **2.** well-bred or refined. **3.** affectedly or pretentiously polite or delicate.

gen•tian (jen′shən), *n.* any of numerous plants having usu. blue but sometimes yellow, white, or red flowers.

gen•tile (jen′tīl), (*often cap.*) —*adj.* **1.** of or characteristic of any people not Jewish. —*n.* **2.** a person who is not Jewish, esp. a Christian.

gen•tle (jen′tl), *adj.,* **-tler, -tlest. 1.** kindly; amiable. **2.** not severe, rough, or violent: *a gentle tap.* **3.** moderate: *gentle heat.* **4.** not steep. **5.** of or characteristic of good birth. **6.** easily handled or managed. **7.** soft or low. **8.** polite or refined. —**gen′tle•ness,** *n.* —**gen′tly,** *adv.*

gen′tle•man *n., pl.* **-men. 1.** a man of good family or social position. **2.** (used as a polite term) a man. **3. gentlemen,** (used as a form of address): *Gentlemen, please follow me.* **4.** a civilized, educated, or well-mannered man. —**gen′tle•man•ly,** *adj.*

gen•tri•fi•ca•tion (jen′trə fi kā′shən) *n.* the replacement of an existing population by others with more wealth or status. —**gen′tri•fy,** *v.t.,* **-fied, -fy•ing.**

gen′try *n.* **1.** wellborn and well-bred people. **2.** (in England) the class below the nobility.

gen•u•flect (jen′yŏŏ flekt′), *v.i.* to bend or touch one knee to the floor in reverence or worship. —**gen′u•flec′tion,** *n.*

gen•u•ine (jen′yŏŏ in or, *sometimes,* -īn′), *adj.* **1.** possessing the claimed character, quality, or origin; real. **2.** free from pretense, affectation, or hypocrisy: *genuine admiration.* —**gen′u•ine•ly,** *adv.* —**gen′u•ine•ness,** *n.*

ge•nus (jē′nəs), *n., pl.* **gen•e•ra** (jen′ər ə), **ge•nus•es. 1.** the major subdivision of a biological family or subfamily, usu. consisting of more than one species. **2.** a kind; sort; class.

Gen X or **GenX** (jen′ eks′), *n.* Generation X.

geo- a combining form meaning the earth or ground (*geography*).

ge•ode (jē′ōd), *n.* a hollow nodular stone often lined with crystals.

ge′o•des′ic dome′ (jē′ə des′ik, -dē′sik), *n.* a dome consisting of a framework of straight members that form a grid of polygonal faces.

ge•og•ra•phy (jē og′rə fē), *n., pl.* **-phies. 1.** the science dealing with the earth's surface features and the climate, vegetation, population, etc., of its countries and other divisions. **2.** the topographical features of a region. —**ge•og′ra•pher,** *n.* —**ge′o•graph′i•cal** (-ə graf′i kəl), **ge′o•graph′ic,** *adj.* —**ge′o•graph′i•cal•ly,** *adv.*

ge•ol•o•gy (jē ol′ə jē), *n., pl.* **-gies. 1.** the science that deals with the earth's physical history and changes, its rocks, etc. **2.** these features and processes occurring in a given region on the earth or another celestial body. —**ge′o•log′ic** (-ə loj′ik), **ge′o•log′i•cal,** *adj.* —**ge′o•log′i•cal•ly,** *adv.* —**ge•ol′o•gist,** *n.*

ge•o•mag•net•ic (jē′ō mag net′ik), *adj.* of or characteristic of terrestrial magnetism. —**ge′o•mag′net•ism** (-ni tiz′əm), *n.*

ge•om•e•try (jē om′i trē), *n.* the branch of mathematics that deals with the deduction of the properties, measurement, and relationships of points, lines, angles, and figures in space. —**ge′o•met′ric** (-ə me′trik), **ge′o•met′ri•cal,** *adj.* —**ge′o•met′ri•cal•ly,** *adv.*

ge•o•phys•ics (jē′ō fiz′iks), *n.* the branch of geology that deals with the physics of the earth and its atmosphere, including oceanography, seismology, etc. —**ge•o•phys′i•cal**, *adj.*

ge′o•pol′i•tics *n.* the study of the influence of physical geography on the politics, national power, or foreign policy of a state. —**ge′o•po•lit′i•cal** (-pə lit′i kəl), *adj.*

Geor•gia (jôr′jə), *n.* Also called **Geor′gian Repub′lic.** a republic in the Caucasus, bordering on the Black Sea: formerly a part of the USSR. —**Geor′gian**, *adj.*, *n.*

ge•o•sta•tion•ar•y (jē′ō stā′shə ner′ē), *adj.* designating a satellite traveling at the same speed as the earth does so as to remain in the same spot over the earth.

ge′o•ther′mal also **-mic**, *adj.* of the internal heat of the earth.

ge•ra•ni•um (ji rā′nē əm), *n.* a common garden plant cultivated for its red, white, or pink flowers.

ger•bil (jûr′bəl), *n.* a small burrowing rodent with long hind legs.

ger•i•at•rics (jer′ē a′triks, jēr′-), *n.* the branch of medicine dealing with the diseases, debilities, and care of aged persons. —**ger′i•at′ric**, *adj.*

germ (jûrm), *n.* **1.** a microorganism, esp. when disease-producing. **2.** a bud or seed. **3.** the rudiment of a living organism. **4.** a source of development; origin. [< MF < L *germen* shoot, seed, sprout]

Ger•man (jûr′mən), *n.* **1.** a native or inhabitant of Germany. **2.** the Germanic language of Germany, Austria, and most of Switzerland. —*adj.* **3.** of Germany, its inhabitants, or their language.

ger•mane (jər mān′), *adj.* closely or significantly related.

Ger•man•ic (-man′ik), *n.* **1.** a family of languages, a branch of the Indo-European family, that includes English, Dutch, German, the Scandinavian languages, and Gothic. —*adj.* **2.** of Germanic or its speakers.

Ger′man mea′sles *n.* RUBELLA.

Ger′man shep′herd *n.* one of a breed of large dogs with a thick, usu. gray or black-and-tan coat.

Ger•ma•ny *n.* a republic in central Europe: formerly divided into East Germany and West Germany; reunited in 1990.

ger•mi•cide′ (jûr′mə sīd′), *n.* an agent for killing germs or microorganisms. —**ger′mi•cid′al**, *adj.*

ger•mi•nate′ *v.i., v.t.,* **-nat•ed, -nat•ing.** to begin or cause to grow or develop; sprout. —**ger′mi•na′tion,** *n.*

ger•on•tol•o•gy (jer′ən tol′ə jē, jēr′-), *n.* the study of aging and the problems and care of aged people. —**ge•ron•to•log•i•cal** (jə ron′tl oj′i kəl), *adj.* —**ger′on•tol′o•gist,** *n.*

ger•ry•man•der (jer′i man′dər, ger′-), *v.t.* to divide (a state, county, etc.) into election districts so as to give one political party an unfair advantage.

ger•und (jer′ənd), *n.* the -*ing* form of an English verb when functioning as a noun.

ges•ta•tion (je stā′shən), *n.* the process, state, or period of carrying young in the womb. —**ges′tate,** *v.t., v.i.,* **-tat•ed, -tat•ing.** —**ges•ta′tion•al,** *adj.*

ges•tic•u•late (je stik′yə lāt′), *v.i.,* **-lat•ed, -lat•ing.** to make or use gestures, esp. in an animated manner. —**ges•tic′u•la′tion,** *n.*

ges•ture (jes′chər), *n., v.,* **-tured, -tur•ing.** —*n.* **1.** a movement or position of the hand, arm, body, head, or face that is expressive of an idea, emotion, etc. **2.** any action or communication intended for effect or as a formality. —*v.i.* **3.** to make or use a gesture or gestures. —**ges′tur•al,** *adj.*

get (get), *v.,* **got, got** or **got•ten, get•ting,** *n.* —*v.t.* **1.** to come to have possession, use, or enjoyment of; obtain; receive. **2.** to go after (something); fetch: *She got the trunk from the attic.* **3.** to cause or cause to become, to move, etc., as specified: *She got her hair cut.* **4.** to communicate with over a distance: *You can get me by phone.* **5.** to hear clearly: *I didn't get your name.* **6.** to understand: *I get your meaning.* **7.** to capture; seize. **8.** to receive as a punishment: *to get a year in jail.* **9.** to persuade: *Get him to go with us.* **10.** to prepare: *to get dinner.* **11.** (esp. of animals) to beget. **12.** to affect emotionally: *Her tears got me.* **13.** to hit. **14.** to take

vengeance on. **15.** to catch or be afflicted with: *to get malaria.* **16.** to puzzle or annoy: *Their silly remarks get me.* —*v.i.* **17.** to come to or reach a specified place: *What time do we get there?* **18.** to become: *to get ready.* **19.** to succeed in coming, going, etc.: *I don't get into town very often.* **20.** to leave immediately: *He told us to get.* **21.** to start or enter upon the action of: *to get moving.* **22. get about, a.** to move about. **b.** to become known. **c.** to be socially active. **23. ~ across,** to make or become clearly understood. **24. ~ ahead,** to be successful. **25. ~ along, a.** to go away. **b.** to get on. **26. ~ around, a.** to circumvent. **b.** to ingratiate oneself with. **c.** to get about. **27. ~ at, a.** to reach. **b.** to hint at or imply. **c.** to discover; determine: *to get at the root of a problem.* **28. ~ away, a.** to escape. **b.** to start out. **29. ~ away with,** to do without detection or punishment. **30. ~ back, a.** to return. **b.** to recover. **31. ~ by,** to survive or manage minimally. **32. ~ down,** to concentrate; attend: *to get down to work.* **33. ~ in, a.** to enter. **b.** to arrive. **c.** to enter into close association: *He got in with the wrong crowd.* **34. ~ off, a.** to dismount from or leave. **b.** to escape or help to escape punishment. **35. ~ on, a.** to proceed; advance. **b.** to have sufficient means to manage or survive. **c.** to be on good terms. **36. ~ out, a.** to leave. **b.** to become publicly known. **c.** to produce or complete. **37. ~ over,** to recover from. **38. ~ through, a.** to complete. **b.** to make oneself understood. **c.** to bear or survive. **39. ~ to, a.** to contact. **b.** to affect. **40. ~ together, a.** to gather. **b.** to congregate; meet. **c.** to come to an accord. **41. ~ up, a.** to rise, as from bed. **b.** to prepare or organize. —*n.* **42.** the offspring, esp. of a male animal. —*Idiom.* **43. get it, a.** to be punished. **b.** to understand something. **44. has** or **have got, a.** to possess: *Have you got the tickets?* **b.** must: *He's got to get to a doctor.* **c.** to suffer from: *Have you got a cold?*

get′a•way′ *n.* **1.** an escape. **2.** the start of a race. **3.** a place where one escapes for relaxation, a vacation, etc.

get′-up′ *n. Informal.* costume; outfit.

gey•ser (gī′zər, -sər), *n.* a hot spring that intermittently sends up jets of water and steam into the air.

Gha•na (gä′nə, gan′ə), *n.* a republic in W Africa. —**Gha′na•ian, Gha′ni•an,** *n., adj.*

ghast•ly (gast′lē, gäst′-), *adj.,* **-li•er, -li•est. 1.** shockingly frightful or dreadful; horrible. **2.** resembling a ghost, esp. in being very pale. —**ghast′li•ness,** *n.*

gher•kin (gûr′kin), *n.* the small immature fruit of a variety of cucumber, used in pickling.

ghet•to (get′ō), *n., pl.* **-tos, -toes. 1.** a section of a city inhabited predominantly by members of a minority group. **2.** (formerly, in certain European cities) a section in which all Jews were required to live. **3.** a situation or environment to which a group has been relegated or in or which a group has segregated itself.

ghost (gōst), *n.* **1.** the disembodied spirit of a dead person imagined as wandering among or haunting the living. **2.** a mere shadow or semblance. **3.** a remote possibility: *not a ghost of a chance.* **4.** a secondary image, as on a television screen. —*v.t., v.i.* **5.** to ghostwrite. —**ghost′ly,** *adj.,* **-li•er, -li•est.**

ghost′writ′er *n.* a person who writes a speech, book, etc., for another who is presumed to be the author. —**ghost′write′,** *v.t., v.i.,* **-wrote, -writ•ten, -writ•ing.**

ghoul (gōōl), *n.* an evil demon believed to rob graves, prey on corpses, etc. —**ghoul′ish,** *adj.*

GI (jē′ī′), *n., pl.* **GIs** or **GI's,** *adj.* —*n.* **1.** a member or former member of the U.S. armed forces, esp. an enlisted soldier. —*adj.* **2.** rigidly adhering to military regulations and practices. **3.** of a standardized style or type issued or required by the U.S. armed forces: *a GI haircut.*

gi•ant (jī′ənt), *n.* **1.** (in folklore) a being with human form but superhuman size and strength. **2.** a person or thing of usually great size, achievement, etc. —*adj.* **3.** unusually large; huge.

gib•ber (jib′ər, gib′-), *v.i.* to speak inarticulately or foolishly.

gib•bet (jib′it), *n.*, *v.*, **-bet•ed, -bet•ing.** —*n.* **1.** a structure from which the bodies of executed criminals were hung for public display. **2.** a gallows. —*v.t.* **3.** to hang on a gibbet. **4.** to hold up to public scorn.

gib•bon (gib′ən), *n.* a small, slender arboreal ape of S Asia.

gibe (jīb), *v.*, **gibed, gib•ing,** *n.* —*v.i.*, *v.t.* **1.** to mock; jeer. —*n.* **2.** a taunting or sarcastic remark.

gib′lets (jib′lits) *n.pl.* the heart, liver, and gizzard of a fowl.

gid•dy (gid′ē), *adj.*, **-di•er, -di•est. 1.** affected with or causing dizziness. **2.** frivolous and lighthearted. —**gid′di•ly,** *adv.* —**gid′di•ness,** *n.*

gift (gift), *n.* **1.** something given voluntarily without payment in return. **2.** the act of giving. **3.** a special ability; talent. —*v.t.* **4.** to present with a gift.

gift′ed *adj.* **1.** having a special ability; talented. **2.** having exceptionally high intelligence.

gig[1] (gig), *n.* **1.** a light, two-wheeled one-horse carriage. **2.** a light ship's boat.

gig[2] (gig), *n.* a spearlike device for fishing.

gig[3] (gig), *n. Slang.* a single professional engagement, as of jazz or rock musicians.

gi•gan•tic (jī gan′tik, ji-), *adj.* **1.** very large. **2.** of, like, or befitting a giant. —**gi•gan′ti•cal•ly,** *adv.*

gig•gle (gig′əl), *v.*, **-gled, -gling,** *n.* —*v.i.* **1.** to laugh in a silly, undignified way, esp. with short, repeated gasps. —*n.* **2.** a silly, spasmodic laugh. —**gig′gler,** *n.* —**gig′gly,** *adj.*

GIGO (gī′gō), *n.* the axiom that faulty data fed into a computer will result in distorted information. [*g(arbage) i(n) g(arbage) o(ut)*]

gig•o•lo (jig′ə lō′), *n.*, *pl.* **-los.** a man living off the earnings or gifts of a woman.

Gi′la mon′ster (hē′lə), *n.* a large, venomous lizard of the SW United States and NW Mexico.

gild (gild), *v.t.*, **gild•ed** or **gilt, gild•ing. 1.** to coat with gold, gold leaf, or a gold-colored substance. **2.** to give a bright, pleasing, or specious aspect to. —**gild′er,** *n.* —**gild′ing,** *n.*

gill[1] (gil), *n.* the respiratory organ of aquatic animals, as fish, that breathe oxygen dissolved in water.

gill[2] (jil), *n.* a unit of liquid measure equal to ¼ of a pint (118.2937 ml).

gilt (gilt), *v.* **1.** a pt. and pp. of GILD. —*n.* **2.** the gold or other material applied in gilding. —*adj.* **3.** coated with gilt.

gilt′-edged′ or **-edge′,** *adj.* of the highest quality.

gim•let (gim′lit), *n.* a small tool for boring holes, consisting of a shaft with a pointed screw at one end.

gim•mick (gim′ik), *n.* **1.** an ingenious or novel device or stratagem used to draw attention. **2.** a concealed disadvantage. **3.** a hidden mechanical device, as one used by a magician. —**gim′mick•ry,** *n.*, *pl.* **-ries.** —**gim′mick•y,** *adj.*

gimp′y (gim′pē) *adj.*, **gimpier, gimpiest.** *Slang.* limping or lame.

gin[1] (jin), *n.* an alcoholic liquor distilled with juniper berries.

gin[2] (jin), *n.*, *v.*, **ginned, gin•ning.** —*n.* **1.** COTTON GIN. **2.** a trap or snare for game. —*v.t.* **3.** to clear (cotton) of seeds with a cotton gin.

gin[3] (jin), *n.* a variety of rummy for two players. Also called **gin′ rum′my.**

gin•ger (jin′jər), *n.* **1.** a reedlike plant with a pungent, spicy rhizome used in cookery and medicine. **2.** the rhizome itself. **3.** piquancy; animation. —**gin′ger•y,** *adj.*

gin′ger ale′ *n.* a carbonated soft drink flavored with ginger extract.

gin′ger•bread′ *n.* **1.** a cake flavored with ginger and molasses. **2.** elaborate or gaudy architectural ornamentation.

gin′ger•ly *adv.* **1.** with great care or caution. —*adj.* **2.** cautious or wary.

gin′ger•snap′ *n.* a crisp cookie flavored with ginger and molasses.

ging•ham (ging′əm), *n.* a yarn-dyed, plain-weave cotton fabric, usu. striped or checked. [< D *gingang* < Malay *gəŋ gaŋ* striped]

gin•gi•vi•tis (jin′jə vī′tis), *n.* inflammation of the gums.

gink•go or **ging•ko** (ging′kō, jing′-), *n.*, *pl.* **-goes** or **-koes.** a shade tree native to China, with fanshaped leaves.

gin•seng (jin′seng), *n.* **1.** a perennial plant with an aromatic root used medicinally. **2.** the root itself.

gi•raffe (jə raf′; *esp. Brit.* -räf′), *n.* a tall, longnecked, spotted ruminant of Africa. [< F < It < dial. Ar *zirāfah*]

gird (gûrd), *v.t.*, **gird•ed** or **girt, gird•ing. 1.** to encircle or bind with a belt or band. **2.** to surround. **3.** to prepare (oneself) for action. **4.** to equip or invest, as with power or strength.

gird′er *n.* a large beam, as of steel or timber, for supporting masonry, joists, etc.

gir′dle *n.*, *v.*, **-dled, -dling.** —*n.* **1.** a woman's undergarment for supporting the abdomen, hips, and buttocks. **2.** a belt or sash worn about the waist. **3.** anything that encircles or confines. —*v.t.* **4.** to encircle with or as if with a belt.

girl (gûrl), *n.* **1.** a female child. **2.** a young, immature woman, esp. an unmarried one. **3.** *Sometimes Disparaging.* a grown woman. **4.** a girlfriend; sweetheart. **5.** *Often Disparaging.* a female servant or employee. —**girl′hood′,** *n.* —**girl′ish,** *adj.*

girl′friend′ *n.* **1.** a frequent or favorite female companion; sweetheart. **2.** a female friend.

girl′ scout′ *n.* (*sometimes caps.*) a member of an organization of girls (**Girl′ Scouts′**) that promotes character development, health, etc.

girth (gûrth), *n.* **1.** the measure around a body or object; circumference. **2.** a band that passes underneath a horse or other animal to hold a saddle in place.

gis•mo (giz′mō), *n.*, *pl.* **-mos.** *Informal.* a gadget.

gist (jist), *n.* the main or essential point of a matter.

give (giv), *v.*, **gave, giv•en, giv•ing,** *n.* —*v.t.* **1.** to present voluntarily and without expecting compensation. **2.** to hand to someone. **3.** to place in someone's care. **4.** to grant (permission, opportunity, etc.) to someone. **5.** to transmit or communicate. **6.** to pay or deliver in exchange. **7.** to furnish or proffer: *to give evidence.* **8.** to provide as an entertainment: *to give a party.* **9.** to administer: *to give medicine.* **10.** to put forth or utter: *to give a cry.* **11.** to produce or yield: *to give good results.* **12.** to make, do, or perform: *to give a concert.* **13.** to sacrifice: *to give one's life for a cause.* **14.** to assign or allot, as a name. **15.** to attribute or ascribe. **16.** to cause or occasion: *Strawberries give me a rash.* **17.** to devote: *to give one's attention to a problem.* **18.** to inflict as a punishment. **19.** to concede, as a point in an argument. —*v.i.* **20.** to make a gift. **21.** to yield under force, pressure, etc. **22.** to be warm and open in relationships. **23. give away, a.** to give as a present. **b.** to present (the bride) to the bridegroom. **c.** to disclose or betray. **24. ~ back,** to return or restore. **25. ~ in, a.** to acknowledge defeat. **b.** to hand in. **26. ~ off,** to put forth; emit. **27. ~ out, a.** to send out; emit. **b.** to make public. **c.** to distribute; issue. **d.** to become exhausted or used up. **28. ~ up, a.** to abandon hope. **b.** to desist from. **c.** to surrender. —*n.* **29.** the quality or state of being resilient. —*Idiom.* **30. give it to,** *Informal.* to reprimand or punish. **31. give or take,** plus or minus a specified amount; more or less. —**giv′er,** *n.*

give′a•way′ *n.* **1.** something given away, esp. as a premium. **2.** an unintentional betrayal or disclosure. **3.** a radio or television program on which prizes are awarded to contestants.

giv′en *v.* **1.** pp. of GIVE. —*adj.* **2.** stated or specified: *a given time.* **3.** inclined; disposed: *given to making snide remarks.* **4.** bestowed; conferred. **5.** granted or assumed. —*n.* **6.** something assumed or accepted as a fact.

giz•zard (giz′ərd), *n.* the muscular lower stomach of many birds and reptiles that grinds partially digested food.

gla•cial (glā′shəl), *adj.* **1.** of or pertaining to glaciers or ice sheets. **2.** bitterly cold. **3.** happening or moving extremely slowly.

gla′cier *n.* an extended mass of ice formed from snow falling and accumulating over the years and moving very slowly.

glad¹ (glad), *adj.*, **glad•der, glad•dest. 1.** feeling joy or pleasure. **2.** showing or causing joy or pleasure. **3.** very willing. —**glad′ly,** *adv.* —**glad′ness,** *n.*

glad² (glad), *n.* GLADIOLUS.

glade (glād), *n.* an open space in a forest.

glad•i•a•tor (glad′ē ā′tər), *n.* **1.** (in ancient Rome) an armed man compelled to fight to the death in an arena for the entertainment of spectators. **2.** someone who engages in a fight or controversy. —**glad′-i•a•to/ri•al** (-ə tôr′ē əl), *adj.*

glad•i•o•lus (glad′ē ō′ləs), *n., pl.* **-li** (-lī), **-lus.** a plant of the iris family with sword-shaped leaves and spikes of flowers. [< L: small sword]

glam•or•ize (glam′ə rīz′), *v.t.,* **-ized, -iz•ing.** to make glamorous. —**glam′or•i•za/tion,** *n.*

glam′our or **-or** (glam′ər), *n.* **1.** alluring charm, fascination, and attractiveness. **2.** magic or enchantment. —**glam′or•ous, glam′our•ous,** *adj.*

glance (glans, gläns), *v.,* **glanced, glanc•ing.** *n.* —*v.i.* **1.** to look quickly or briefly. **2.** to gleam or flash. **3.** to strike a surface obliquely and bounce off at an angle. —*n.* **4.** a quick or brief look. **5.** a gleam or flash. **6.** a deflected movement or course.

gland (gland), *n.* any organ or group of cells specialized for producing secretions. —**glan•du•lar** (glan′jə lər), *adj.*

glans (glanz), *n., pl.* **glan•des** (glan′dēz). the head of the penis or of the clitoris.

glare (glâr), *n., v.,* **glared, glar•ing.** —*n.* **1.** a very harsh, dazzling light. **2.** a fiercely piercing stare. **3.** dazzling or showy appearance. —*v.i.* **4.** to shine with a very harsh, dazzling light. **5.** to stare with a fiercely piercing look. —*v.t.* **6.** to express with a glare.

glar′ing *adj.* **1.** dazzlingly bright. **2.** very conspicuous or obvious. **3.** staring fiercely. **4.** excessively or tastelessly showy. —**glar′ing•ly,** *adv.*

glass (glas, gläs), *n.* **1.** a hard, brittle, more or less transparent substance usu. produced by fusing silicates containing soda and lime, used for windows, bottles, etc. **2.** something made of glass, as a drinking container. **3. glasses,** a device to compensate for defective vision or to protect the eyes from light, dust, etc. **4.** GLASSWARE. **5.** an amount contained by a drinking glass. —*adj.* **6.** made of or fitted with glass. —*v.t.* **7.** to fit or enclose with glass.

glass′ ceil′ing *n.* an upper limit to professional advancement, esp. as imposed on women and other minorities, that is not readily perceived or acknowledged.

glass•ware′ *n.* articles of glass, esp. drinking glasses.

glass′y *adj.,* **-i•er, -i•est. 1.** resembling glass, as in transparency. **2.** expressionless; dull: *glassy eyes.*

glau•co•ma (glô kō′mə, glou-), *n.* a condition of elevated fluid pressure within the eyeball, causing progressive loss of vision.

glaze (glāz), *v.,* **glazed, glaz•ing.** —*v.t.* **1.** to fit with glass, as a window. **2.** to cover (a ceramic or the like) with a smooth, glossy surface or coating. **3.** to coat (a food) with sugar syrup. —*v.i.* **4.** to become glazed or glassy. —*n.* **5.** a smooth, glossy surface or coating. **6.** the substance for producing such a coating.

gla•zier (glā′zhər), *n.* a person who fits windows with glass.

gleam (glēm), *n.* **1.** a flash or beam of light. **2.** a subdued or reflected light. **3.** a brief or slight manifestation. —*v.i.* **4.** to send forth a gleam. **5.** to appear suddenly and clearly.

glean (glēn), *v.t., v.i.* **1.** to gather (grain) after the reapers. **2.** to collect (facts or information) little by little or slowly. —**glean′er,** *n.*

glee (glē), *n.* open delight or pleasure. —**glee′ful,** *adj.*

glen (glen), *n.* a small, narrow, secluded valley.

glib (glib), *adj.,* **glib•ber, glib•best.** readily fluent, often thoughtlessly or insincerely so. —**glib′ly,** *adv.* —**glib′ness,** *n.*

glide (glīd), *v.,* **glid•ed, glid•ing.** *n.* —*v.i.* **1.** to move smoothly and effortlessly along. **2.** to fly downward at an easy angle, with little or no engine power. —*v.t.* **3.** to cause to glide. —*n.* **4.** a gliding movement, as in dancing. **5. a.** a transitional sound heard during the articulation linking two contiguous speech sounds. **b.** a semivowel. **6.** the act of gliding.

glid′er *n.* **1.** a motorless aircraft launched by towing or catapult. **2.** one that glides. **3.** a couchlike porch swing suspended from a steel framework.

glim•mer (glim′ər), *n.* **1.** a faint or unsteady light. **2.** a dim or faint perception; inkling. —*v.i.* **3.** to shine faintly or unsteadily. **4.** to appear faintly or dimly. —**glim′mer•ing,** *n.*

glimpse (glimps), *n., v.,* **glimpsed, glimps•ing.** —*n.* **1.** a very brief, passing look. **2.** a vague idea; inkling. —*v.t.* **3.** to catch a glimpse of. —*v.i.* **4.** to look briefly.

glint (glint), *n.* **1.** a tiny, quick flash of light. **2.** a brief or slight manifestation or occurrence; trace. —*v.i.* **3.** to shine with a glint.

glis•ten (glis′ən), *v.i.* **1.** to reflect a sparkling light or a faint intermittent glow. —*n.* **2.** a glistening; sparkle.

glitch (glich), *n. Informal.* a defect, error, or malfunction, as in a machine or plan.

glit•ter (glit′ər), *v.i.* **1.** to reflect light with a brilliant, sparkling luster. **2.** to make a brilliant show. —*n.* **3.** a sparkling light or luster. **4.** showy splendor. **5.** small glittering ornaments. —**glit′ter•y,** *adj.*

glitz•y (glit′sē), *adj.,* **-i•er, -i•est.** *Informal.* pretentiously or tastelessly showy; flashy.

gloam•ing (glō′ming), *n.* twilight; dusk.

gloat (glōt), *v.i.* to indulge in malicious or excessive satisfaction.

glob (glob), *n.* **1.** a drop of a liquid. **2.** a rounded lump or mass.

glob•al (glō′bəl), *adj.* **1.** of or involving the whole world; universal. **2.** of or involving a whole; general. —**glob′al•ly,** *adv.*

glo′bal warm′ing *n.* an increase in the earth's average atmospheric temperature that causes changes in climate.

globe (glōb), *n.* **1.** the planet Earth. **2.** a sphere on which a map of the earth is depicted. **3.** anything more or less spherical.

globe′trot′ter *n.* one who travels regularly all over the world.

glob•ule (glob′yōol), *n.* a small spherical body.

gloom (glōom), *n.* **1.** total or partial darkness. **2.** a state of melancholy or depression. —**gloom′y,** *adj.,* **-i•er, -i•est.** —**gloom′i•ly,** *adv.*

glop (glop), *n. Informal.* **1.** any gooey or gelatinous substance, esp. unappetizing food. **2.** sentimentality. —**glop′py,** *adj.,* **-pi•er, -pi•est.**

glo•ri•fy (glôr′ə fī′), *v.t.,* **-fied, -fy•ing. 1.** to treat as more splendid or excellent than would normally be considered. **2.** to honor, extol, or worship. **3.** to give glory to. —**glor/i•fi•ca/tion,** *n.*

glo′ry *n., pl.* **-ries,** *v.,* **-ried, -ry•ing.** —*n.* **1.** very great praise, honor, or distinction. **2.** a source of praise or honor. **3.** adoring praise given in worship. **4.** resplendent beauty or magnificence. **5.** a state of absolute happiness: *to be in one's glory.* **6.** the splendor and bliss of heaven. —*v.i.* **7.** to exult with triumph. —**glo′ri•ous,** *adj.*

gloss¹ (glos, glôs), *n.* **1.** a superficial luster or shine. **2.** a deceptively good appearance. —*v.t.* **3.** to put a gloss upon. **4. gloss over,** to give a deceptively good appearance to: *to gloss over flaws.* —**gloss′y,** *adj.,* **-i•er, -i•est.**

gloss² (glos, glôs), *n.* **1.** a marginal or interlinear explanation or translation. —*v.t.* **2.** to insert glosses on; annotate. **3.** to give a misleading interpretation of.

glos•sa•ry (glos′ə rē, glô′sə-), *n., pl.* **-ries.** a list of difficult or specialized terms with accompanying definitions.

glot•tis (glot′is), *n.* the opening at the upper part of the larynx, between the vocal cords. —**glot′tal,** *adj.*

general

glove (gluv), *n.*, *v.*, **gloved, glov•ing.** —*n.* **1.** a covering for the hand made with a separate sheath for each finger. **2.** any of various leather-padded coverings for the hand used in baseball, boxing, etc. —*v.t.* **3.** to cover with a glove.

glow (glō), *n.* **1.** a light emitted by or as if by a heated substance. **2.** brightness of color, esp. ruddiness. **3.** a sensation of bodily heat. **4.** warmth of emotion or passion. —*v.i.* **5.** to emit light and heat without flame. **6.** to shine like something intensely heated. **7.** to exhibit a bright, usu. ruddy color. **8.** to show emotion or elation: *to glow with pride.* —**glow′ing,** *adj.*

glow•er (glou′ər), *v.i.* **1.** to stare with sullen dislike or anger. —*n.* **2.** a look of sullen dislike or anger.

glow•worm (glō′wûrm′), *n.* the larva or wingless female of a beetle that emits a greenish light.

glu•cose (glōō′kōs), *n.* **1.** a simple sugar occurring in fruits and honey. **2.** a syrup obtained by the incomplete hydrolysis of starch.

glue (glōō), *n.*, *v.*, **glued, glu•ing.** —*n.* **1.** a protein gelatin obtained by boiling animal substances in water, used as an adhesive. **2.** any of various similar preparations. —*v.t.* **3.** to join or attach firmly with or as if with glue. —**glue′y,** *adj.*, **glu•i•er, glu•i•est.**

glum (glum), *adj.*, **glum•mer, glum•mest.** sullenly or silently gloomy. —**glum′ly,** *adv.* —**glum′ness,** *n.*

glut (glut), *v.*, **glut•ted, glut•ting.** —*v.t.* **1.** to feed or fill to satiety or to excess. **2.** to flood (the market) with a particular item or service so that supply greatly exceeds demand. —*n.* **3.** an excessive supply or amount.

glu•ten (glōōt′n), *n.* a grayish, sticky component of wheat flour and other grain flours. [< L *glūten* glue] —**glu′ten•ous,** *adj.*

glu′ti•nous *adj.* viscid; sticky. —**glu′ti•nous•ly,** *adv.*

glut•ton (glut′n), *n.* **1.** a person who eats and drinks excessively. **2.** a person with a great desire or capacity for something. —**glut′ton•ous,** *adj.* —**glut′ton•ous•ly,** *adv.* —**glut′ton•y,** *n.*

glyc•er•in (glis′ər in) also **-er•ine** (-ər in, -ə rēn′), *n.* GLYCEROL.

glyc′er•ol′ (-ə rôl′, -rol′), *n.* a colorless liquid made from fats, used as a sweetener, in skin emollients, etc.

gnarl (närl), *n.* **1.** a knotty protuberance on a tree. —*v.t.* **2.** to twist into a knotted form. —**gnarled,** *adj.*

gnash (nash), *v.t.*, *v.i.* to grind (the teeth) together, esp. in rage or pain.

gnat (nat), *n.* any of certain small flies, most of which bite or suck.

gnaw (nô), *v.*, **gnawed, gnawed** or **gnawn, gnaw•ing.** —*v.t.* **1.** to bite on persistently. **2.** to wear away or corrode. **3.** to torment by constant annoyance. —*v.i.* **4.** to bite persistently. **5.** to cause corrosion. **6.** to cause an effect resembling corrosion: *Her mistake gnawed at her conscience.*

gnome (nōm), *n.* any of a group of dwarflike beings believed to inhabit the interior of the earth. —**gnom′ish,** *adj.*

GNP gross national product.

gnu (nōō, nyōō), *n.*, *pl.* **gnus, gnu.** a stocky, oxlike African antelope.

go (gō), *v.*, **went, gone, go•ing,** *n.*, *pl.* **goes,** *adj.* —*v.i.* **1.** to move or proceed, esp. to or from something. **2.** to leave a place. **3.** to function or operate: *The engine is going.* **4.** to become as specified: *to go mad.* **5.** to continue in a certain state: *to go barefoot.* **6.** to act so as to come into a certain state: *to go to sleep.* **7.** to be known: *to go by a false name.* **8.** to reach or extend: *This door goes outside.* **9.** (of time) to elapse. **10.** to be applied to a particular purpose. **11.** to be sold. **12.** to be considered usually: *He's tall, as jockeys go.* **13.** to conduce or tend. **14.** to result; turn out. **15.** to have a place: *The book goes here.* **16.** (of colors, styles, etc.) to harmonize. **17.** to be consumed, discarded, etc. **18.** to develop or proceed. **19.** to make a certain sound. **20.** to be phrased or composed. **21.** to resort: *to go to court.* **22.** to die. **23.** to fail or give way. **24.** to begin: *Go when you hear the bell.* **25.** to be able to be divided: *Three goes fifteen five times.* **26.** to contribute to an end result. **27.** to have as one's goal; intend: *I am going to be a doctor.* **28.** to be approved or accepted: *Anything goes.* **29.** to be authoritative: *What I say goes!* **30.** to subject oneself: *Don't go to any trouble.* **31.** (used as an intensifier): *He had to go ask for a loan.* —*v.t.* **32.** to proceed along. **33.** to share in to the extent of: *to go halves.* **34.** *Informal.* to bet or bid. **35.** to assume the obligation of: *His father went bail for him.* **36.** *Informal.* to say. **37. go after,** to attempt to obtain. **38. ~ around, a.** to be sufficient for all. **b.** to pass or circulate. **39. ~ at, a.** to assault; attack. **b.** to begin vigorously. **40. ~ for, a.** to try for. **b.** to assault. **c.** to favor. **41. ~ in for,** to adopt as one's particular interest. **42. ~ into, a.** to discuss or investigate. **b.** to undertake as one's study or work. **43. ~ off, a.** to explode. **b.** to happen. **c.** to leave. **44. ~ on, a.** to happen. **b.** to continue. **c.** to talk effusively. **45. ~ out, a.** to cease to function. **b.** to participate in social activities. **46. ~ over, a.** to review. **b.** to be effective or successful. **c.** to examine. **47. ~ through, a.** to bear. **b.** to examine carefully. **c.** to use up. **48. ~ through with,** to bring to completion. **49. ~ under,** to fail or founder. —*n.* **50.** the act of going. **51.** energy or spirit. **52.** a try or attempt. **53.** a success. **54.** *Informal.* approval or permission. —*adj.* **55.** functioning properly; ready: *All systems are go.* —*Idiom.* **56. go together, a.** to be harmonious. **b.** to date steadily. **57. let go, a.** to free. **b.** to cease to employ. **58. let oneself go,** to free oneself of inhibitions. **59. no go,** *Informal.* **a.** futile. **b.** canceled. **60. on the go,** very busy. **61. to go,** (of food) for consumption off the premises where sold.

goad (gōd), *n.* **1.** a pointed stick for driving cattle, oxen, etc. **2.** anything that pricks or urges on. —*v.t.* **3.** to drive with or as if with a goad.

goal (gōl), *n.* **1.** the result toward which effort is directed. **2.** the terminal point in a race. **3.** a place into which players of various games try to propel a ball or puck to score. **4.** the score made.

goal′keep′er *n.* (in hockey, soccer, etc.) a player whose chief duty is to prevent the ball or puck from crossing the goal. —**goal′keep′ing,** *n.*

goat (gōt), *n.* **1.** an agile, hollow-horned ruminant closely related to the sheep. **2.** a lecherous man.

goat•ee (gō tē′), *n.*, *pl.* **-ees.** a man's beard trimmed to a tuft on the chin.

gob¹ (gob), *n.* **1.** a mass or lump. **2. gobs,** *Informal.* a large quantity.

gob² (gob), *n. Slang.* a sailor, esp. a seaman in the U.S. Navy.

gob•ble¹ (gob′əl), *v.t.*, *v.i.*, **-bled, -bling. 1.** to eat hastily or hungrily. **2.** to seize eagerly.

gob•ble² (gob′əl), *v.*, **-bled, -bling,** *n.* —*v.i.* **1.** to make the throaty cry of a male turkey. —*n.* **2.** the cry itself.

gob′ble•de•gook′ (-dē gōōk′) *n.* nonsense.

gob•bler (gob′lər), *n.* a male turkey.

go′-between′ *n.* a person who acts as an intermediary between parties.

gob•let (gob′lit), *n.* a drinking glass with a foot and stem.

gob•lin (gob′lin), *n.* a grotesque, mischievous sprite or elf.

God (god), *n.* **1.** the creator and ruler of the universe. **2.** (*l.c.*) one of several immortal powers, esp. a male deity, presiding over some portion of worldly affairs. **3.** (*l.c.*) any deified person or object. —*interj.* **4.** an exclamation of disappointment, disbelief, frustration, or the like. —**god′dess,** *n.* —**god′like′,** *adj.*

god′ly *adj.*, **-li•er, -li•est. 1.** devout; pious. **2.** coming from God; divine. —**god′li•ness,** *n.*

god′par′ent *n.* a sponsor of a child at baptism. —**god′child′,** *n.* —**god′daugh′ter,** *n.* —**god′fath′er,** *n.* —**god′moth′er,** *n.* —**god′son′,** *n.*

god′send′ *n.* an unexpected thing or event that is particularly welcome and timely, as if sent by God.

goes (gōz) third pers. sing. pres. indic. of **go.**

go•fer (gō′fər), *n. Slang.* an employee whose chief duty is running errands.

gog•gle (gog′əl), *n., v.,* **-gled, -gling.** —*n.* **1.** **goggles,** large spectacles worn to protect the eyes from strong wind, flying objects, etc. **2.** a bulging or wide-open look of the eyes; stare. —*v.i.* **3.** to stare with bulging or wide-open eyes.

goi•ter (goi′tər), *n.* an enlargement of the thyroid gland on the front and sides of the neck. Also, *esp. Brit.,* **goi′tre.**

gold (gōld), *n.* **1.** a precious, yellow, metallic element that is highly malleable and not subject to oxidation. *Symbol:* Au; *at. wt.:* 196.967; *at. no.:* 79. **2.** money; riches. **3.** a bright yellow color. —**gold′en,** *adj.*

gold′brick′ *Slang.* —*n.* **1.** Also, **gold′brick′er.** a person, esp. a soldier, who loafs on the job. —*v.i.* **2.** to shirk work.

gold′en•rod′ *n.* a North American plant with small, yellow flower heads on wandlike stalks.

gold′finch′ *n.* a New World finch, the male of which has yellow body plumage in the summer.

gold′fish′ *n.* **-fish, -fish•es.** a small, yellow or orange fish of the carp family, often kept in aquariums and pools.

golf (golf, gôlf; *Brit.* also gof), *n.* **1.** a game in which clubs are used to hit a small ball into a series of 9 or 18 holes. —*v.i.* **2.** to play golf. —**golf′er,** *n.*

go•nad (gō′nad, gon′ad), *n.* any organ or gland in which gametes are produced; an ovary or testis. —**go•nad′al,** *adj.*

gon•do•la (gon′dl ə *or, esp. for 1,* gon dō′lə), *n., pl.* **-las.** **1.** a long, narrow boat used on the canals in Venice, Italy. **2.** a passenger compartment suspended beneath a balloon or airship. **3.** a cabin suspended from a cable, used esp. to transport skiers. **4.** an open railroad freight car with low sides.

gon′er *n. Informal.* one that is dead, lost, or past recovery.

gong (gông, gong), *n.* a large bronze disk that produces a vibrant, hollow tone when struck.

gon•or•rhe•a (gon′ə rē′ə), *n.* a contagious, purulent inflammation of the urethra or the vagina. Also, *esp. Brit.,* **gon′or•rhoe′a.** —**gon′or•rhe′al,** *adj.*

goo (gōō), *n., pl.* **goos.** *Informal.* **1.** a thick or sticky substance. **2.** maudlin sentimentality. —**goo′ey,** *adj.,* **goo•i•er, goo•i•est.**

good (gōōd), *adj.,* **bet•ter, best,** *n., interj., adv.* —*adj.* **1.** morally excellent; virtuous. **2.** satisfactory or superior in quality, quantity, or degree. **3.** proper, suitable, or right. **4.** well-behaved. **5.** kind or friendly. **6.** honorable or worthy. **7.** not counterfeit. **8.** sound or valid: *good judgment.* **9.** beneficial. **10.** healthy: *good teeth.* **11.** not spoiled or tainted. **12.** favorable: *good news.* **13.** agreeable; pleasant. **14.** attractive: *a good figure.* **15.** competent or skillful. **16.** full: *a good day's journey away.* **17.** fairly large; ample. —*n.* **18.** profit or advantage. **19.** kindness. **20.** moral righteousness; virtue. **21. goods, a.** personal property. **b.** merchandise. **22. the good,** good things or persons collectively. —*interj.* **23.** an exclamation of approval or satisfaction. —*adv.* **24.** *Informal.* well. —**Idiom. 25. for good,** finally and permanently. **26. good and,** very: *good and hot.* **27. good for, a.** certain to repay (money owed). **b.** worth. **c.** serviceable or useful for.

good′-bye′ or **-by′,** *interj., n., pl.* **-byes** or **-bys.** farewell.

Good′ Fri′day *n.* the Friday before Easter, commemorating the Crucifixion.

good′ly *adj.,* **-li•er, -li•est. 1.** of substantial size or amount. **2.** of good appearance.

good′ Sa•mar′i•tan (sə mar′i tn), *n.* a person who voluntarily gives help to those in distress or need.

good′will′ or **good′ will′,** *n.* **1.** friendly disposition. **2.** cheerful consent. **3.** an intangible, salable asset arising from the reputation of a business and its relations with its customers.

good′y *n., pl.* **-ies,** *interj.* —*n.* **1.** something pleasing to eat, as candy. —*interj.* **2.** a childish exclamation of delight.

goof (gōōf), *Informal.* —*v.i.* **1.** to make an error,

misjudgment, etc. **2.** to waste time; evade work: *We goofed off all morning.* —*v.t.* **3.** to make a mess of. —*n.* **4.** a foolish or stupid person. **5.** a mistake or blunder. —**goof′y,** *adj.,* **-i•er, -i•est.**

goon (gōōn), *n. Slang.* **1.** a hired hoodlum. **2.** a stupid, foolish, or awkward person.

goose (gōōs), *n., pl.* **geese. 1.** any of numerous web-footed swimming birds, most of which are larger and have a longer neck than the ducks. **2.** the female of this bird. **3.** the flesh of a goose, used as food. **4.** a silly or foolish person. —**Idiom. 5. cook someone's goose,** *Informal.* to ruin someone's chances.

goose′ber′ry (gōōs′-, gōōz′-), *n., pl.* **-ries. 1.** a small, sour, sometimes prickly fruit. **2.** the shrub it grows on.

goose′ flesh′ *n.* a bristling of the hair on the skin, as from cold or fear. Also called **goose′ pim′-ples, goose′ bumps′.**

GOP or **G.O.P.,** Grand Old Party (an epithet of the Republican Party).

go•pher (gō′fər), *n.* any of various New World burrowing rodents with external cheek pouches.

gore[1] (gôr), *n.* **1.** blood that is shed, esp. when clotted. **2.** bloodshed; violence.

gore[2] (gôr), *v.t.,* **gored, gor•ing.** to pierce with or as if with a horn or tusk.

gore[3] (gôr), *n.* a triangular piece of material inserted in a garment, sail, etc.

gorge (gôrj), *n., v.,* **gorged, gorg•ing.** —*n.* **1.** a narrow ravine with steep, rocky walls. **2.** something that is swallowed. **3.** an obstructing mass: *an ice gorge.* **4.** the throat; gullet. **5.** strong disgust or anger. —*v.t., v.i.* **6.** to stuff (oneself) with food.

gor•geous (gôr′jəs), *adj.* **1.** splendid or magnificent. **2.** very attractive or beautiful. —**gor′-geous•ly,** *adv.*

go•ril•la (gə ril′ə), *n., pl.* **-las.** the largest anthropoid ape, native to equatorial Africa.

gos•ling (goz′ling), *n.* a young goose.

gos•pel (gos′pəl), *n.* **1.** the teachings of Jesus and the apostles. **2.** (*usu. cap.*) any of the first four books of the New Testament. **3.** Also called **gos′pel truth′.** something absolutely or unquestionably true. **4.** impassioned rhythmic spiritual music, influential in the development of rhythm and blues.

gos•sa•mer (gos′ə mər), *n.* **1.** a fine, filmy cobweb. **2.** something extremely light, flimsy, or delicate. —*adj.* **3.** thin and light.

gos•sip (gos′əp), *n., v.,* **-siped** or **-sipped, -sip•ing** or **-sip•ping.** —*n.* **1.** idle talk or rumor, esp. about the private affairs of others. **2.** a person given to such talk. —*v.i.* **3.** to relate or spread gossip. —**gos′sip•y,** *adj.*

Goth (goth), *n.* a member of a Germanic people who, from the 3rd to 5th centuries, invaded parts of the Roman Empire.

Goth′ic *adj.* **1.** noting a style of architecture of W Europe from the 12th to 16th centuries, marked by pointed arches, rich ornamentation, etc. **2.** of the Goths or their language. **3.** (*often l.c.*) noting a style of literature marked by a gloomy setting and mysterious or sinister events. —*n.* **4.** Gothic architecture. **5.** the extinct Germanic language of the Goths.

Gou•da (gou′də, gōō′-), *n.* a yellowish Dutch cheese, usu. coated with red wax.

gouge (gouj), *n., v.,* **gouged, goug•ing.** —*n.* **1.** a chisel with a partly cylindrical blade. **2.** a groove or hole made by or as if by a gouge. **3.** an act of extortion; swindle. —*v.t.* **4.** to scoop out with or as if with a gouge. **5.** to swindle or overcharge. —**goug′er,** *n.*

gou•lash (gōō′läsh, -lash), *n.* a stew of beef or veal and vegetables, seasoned with paprika. [< Hungarian *gulyás,* short for *gulyáshús* herdsman's meat]

gourd (gôrd, gōōrd), *n.* **1.** the hard-shelled fruit of a vine related to the squash, melon, etc. **2.** a plant bearing such a fruit. **3.** a dried gourd shell used as a bottle, dipper, etc.

gour•mand (gōōr mänd′, gōōr′mənd), *n.* one who is fond of good eating, often to excess. [< OF *gourmant* a glutton]

gour•met (gŏŏr mā′, gŏŏr′mā), n. a connoisseur of fine food and drink.

gout (gout), n. a painful inflammation, esp. of the big toe, characterized by an excess of uric acid in the blood. —**gout•y,** adj., **-i•er, -i•est.**

gov. **1.** government. **2.** governor.

gov•ern (guv′ərn), v.t. **1.** to rule by right of authority. **2.** to exercise a directing influence over. **3.** to hold in check; control. **4.** to serve as a law for. —v.i. **5.** to exercise the function of government. —**gov′ern•a•ble,** adj. —**gov′ern•ance** (-ər nəns), n.

gov•ern•ess n. a woman employed in a private household to take charge of a child's upbringing and education.

gov′ern•ment (-ərn mənt, -ər mənt), n. **1.** the political direction and control exercised over communities, societies, and states. **2.** the form or system of rule by which a state, community, etc., is governed. **3.** a governing body of persons. **4.** direction; control; rule. —**gov′ern•men′tal** (-men′tl), adj.

gov′er•nor (-ər nər, -ə nər), n. **1.** the executive head of a state in the U.S. **2.** the head of an institution, society, etc. **3.** a ruler appointed to govern a province, town, or the like. **4.** a device for maintaining uniform speed in an engine. —**gov′er•nor•ship′,** n.

govt. government.

gown (goun), n. **1.** a woman's formal dress, esp. a full-length one. **2.** a nightgown or robe. **3.** a loose, flowing outer garment worn by judges, members of the clergy, etc.

G.P. General Practitioner.

grab (grab), v., **grabbed, grab•bing,** n. —v.t. **1.** to seize suddenly, eagerly, or roughly. **2.** to seize forcibly or unscrupulously. **3.** to obtain and consume quickly: Let's grab a sandwich. **4.** Informal. to impress or affect. —n. **5.** the act of grabbing. —**grab′ber,** n.

grace (grās), n., v., **graced, grac•ing.** —n. **1.** elegance or beauty of form, manner, or motion. **2.** a pleasing or attractive quality. **3.** favor or goodwill. **4.** mercy; clemency. **5.** favor shown in granting a delay. **6.** the favor and love of God. **7.** a short prayer before or after a meal. **8.** (cap.) a title for a duke, duchess, or archbishop. —v.t. **9.** to lend or add grace to. **10.** to favor or honor. —Idiom. **11. in someone's good** (or **bad) graces,** regarded with favor (or disfavor) by someone. —**grace′ful,** adj. —**grace′ful•ly,** adv. —**grace′ful•ness,** n. —**grace′less,** adj. —**grace′less•ly,** adv. —**grace′less•ness,** n.

gra•cious (grā′shəs), adj. **1.** pleasantly kind or courteous. **2.** characterized by good taste, comfort, or luxury. —**gra′cious•ly,** adv. —**gra′cious•ness,** n.

grack•le (grak′əl), n. any of several long-tailed North American blackbirds with iridescent black plumage.

gra•da•tion (grā dā′shən), n. **1.** a change taking place through a series of stages or by degrees. **2.** a stage or degree in such a series. **3.** the act of grading.

grade (grād), n., v., **grad•ed, grad•ing.** —n. **1.** a degree in a scale, as of rank or quality. **2.** a class of persons or things; category. **3.** a step or stage in a course or process. **4.** any of the divisions corresponding to a year's work in school. **5.** a letter or number indicating the quality of a student's work. **6. a.** a slope of a road, railroad, etc. **b.** the degree of such slope. —v.t. **7.** to arrange in a series of grades. **8.** to assign a grade to (a student's work). **9.** to reduce the inclination of: to grade a road. —Idiom. **10. make the grade,** to succeed.

grade′ cross′ing n. an intersection of a railroad track and another track, a road, etc., at the same level.

grade′ school′ n. ELEMENTARY SCHOOL.

grad•u•al (graj′ōō əl), adj. changing, moving, etc., by degrees or little by little. —**grad′u•al•ly,** adv.

grad′u•ate (n., adj. -it, -āt′; v. -āt′), n., adj., v., **-at•ed, -at•ing.** —n. **1.** a person who has received an academic degree or diploma. —adj. **2.** of or involved in academic study beyond the bachelor's degree. **3.** having an academic degree or diploma. —v.i. **4.** to receive an academic degree or diploma: to graduate from college. —v.t. **5.** to grant an academic degree or diploma to. **6.** to receive a degree or diploma from. **7.** to arrange in grades or gradations. **8.** to divide into or mark by degrees or other divisions.

graf•fi′ti (grə fē′tē) n.pl., sing. **graf•fi•to** (-tō). markings written on public walls, etc.

graft¹ (graft, gräft), n. **1. a.** a bud or shoot of a plant inserted into another plant in which it continues to grow. **b.** the plant resulting from this. **2.** a portion of living tissue transplanted to another part of the body or from one individual to another. —v.t., v.i. **3.** to insert (a graft). **4.** to transplant (a portion of living tissue) as a graft. —**graft′er,** n.

graft² (graft, gräft), n. **1.** the acquisition of money or advantage by dishonest means, esp. through political influence. **2.** the gain or advantage acquired. —v.t., v.i. **3.** to obtain by graft. —**graft′er,** n.

gra•ham (grā′əm, gram), adj. made of wholewheat flour. [after S. Graham (1794–1851), U.S. dietary reformer]

Grail (grāl), n. (in medieval legend) the cup or chalice supposedly used at the Last Supper.

grain (grān), n. **1.** a small, hard seed of a food plant, esp. a cereal plant such as wheat or rye. **2.** the gathered seed of such plants. **3.** such plants collectively. **4.** any small, hard particle, as of sand. **5.** the smallest unit of weight in the U.S. and British systems. **6.** a tiny amount. **7.** the arrangement or direction of fibers in wood, meat, etc. **8.** texture: sugar of fine grain. **9.** temperament or natural character. —**grained,** adj. —**grain′y,** adj., **-i•er, -i•est.**

gram (gram), n. a metric unit of mass or weight equal to 15.432 grains, or $1/1000$ of a kilogram. Also, esp. Brit., **gramme.**

-gram a combining form meaning something written or drawn (diagram).

gram•mar (gram′ər), n. **1.** the study of the way the sentences of a language are constructed, esp. the study of morphology and syntax. **2.** a set of rules accounting for the features or constructions of a given language. **3.** knowledge or usage of the preferred forms in speaking or writing. —**gram•mar•i•an** (grə mâr′ē ən), n. —**gram•mat′i•cal** (-mat′i-kəl), adj. —**gram•mat′i•cal•ly,** adv.

gra•na•ry (grā′nə rē, gran′ə-), n., pl. **-ries.** a storehouse or repository for grain.

grand (grand), adj., **grand•er, grand•est,** n., pl. **grands** for 8, **grand** for 9. —adj. **1.** impressive in size, appearance, or effect. **2.** stately; dignified. **3.** highly ambitious. **4.** high in rank or official dignity. **5.** of great importance or pretension. **6.** complete; comprehensive: a grand total. **7.** first-rate; splendid. —n. **8.** GRAND PIANO. **9.** Informal. a thousand dollars. —**grand′ly,** adv. —**grand′ness,** n.

grand- a combining form meaning one generation more remote (grandmother).

grand•child (gran′chīld′), n., pl. **-chil•dren.** a child of one's son or daughter. —**grand′daugh′ter,** n. —**grand′son′,** n.

gran•dee (gran dē′), n., pl. **-dees.** a man of high social rank, esp. a Spanish or Portuguese nobleman.

gran•deur (gran′jər, -jŏŏr), n. the quality or state of being grand.

gran•dil•o•quence (gran dil′ə kwəns), n. speech that is lofty in tone and often bombastic. —**gran•dil′o•quent,** adj.

gran•di•ose (gran′dē ōs′), adj. **1.** affectedly grand; pompous. **2.** grand in an imposing way.

grand′ ju′ry n. a jury designated to determine if a law has been violated and whether the evidence warrants prosecution.

grand′par′ent n. a parent of a son or daughter who is a parent. —**grand′fa′ther,** n. —**grand′moth′er,** n.

grand′ pian′o n. a piano having the frame supported horizontally on three legs.

grand′ slam′ n. **1.** the winning of or bid for all thirteen tricks of a deal in bridge. **2.** a home run with three runners on base.

grand′stand′ (gran′-, grand′-), n. **1.** a main seating area, as of a stadium or racetrack. —v.i. **2.** to conduct oneself or perform showily to impress on-lookers.

grange (grānj), *n.* **1.** a farm with its nearby build-ings. **2.** (*cap.*) a U.S. farmers' organization, or one of its local branches.

gran•ite (gran'it), *n.* a coarse-grained igneous rock composed chiefly of feldspar and quartz. —**gra•nit•ic** (grə nit'ik), *adj.*

gra•no•la (grə nō'lə), *n., pl.* **-las.** a breakfast food of rolled oats, nuts, dried fruit, brown sugar, etc. [orig. a trademark]

grant (grant, gränt), *v.t.* **1.** to confer, esp. by a for-mal act. **2.** to give; accord: *to grant permission.* **3.** to agree to. **4.** to accept for the sake of argument. **5.** to transfer (property), esp. by deed. —*n.* **6.** something granted, as a right, a sum of money, or a tract of land. **7.** the act of granting. —*Idiom.* **8. take for granted, a.** to assume without question. **b.** to fail to appreciate. —**grant'er, gran'tor,** *n.*

grants'man•ship *n.* skill in securing grants, as for research.

gran•u•late' *v.t., v.i.,* **-lat•ed, -lat•ing.** to form into granules or grains. —**gran'u•la'tion,** *n.*

gran'ule (-yōōl), *n.* **1.** a little grain. **2.** a small par-ticle.

grape (grāp), *n.* **1.** an edible, smooth-skinned fruit that grows in clusters on a vine. **2.** GRAPEVINE (def. 1). **3.** a dark purplish red color.

grape'fruit' *n.* a large, roundish, yellow-skinned, edible citrus fruit.

grape'vine' *n.* **1.** a vine that bears grapes. **2.** a person-to-person method of spreading gossip or in-formation.

graph (graf, gräf), *n.* **1.** a diagram representing a system of connections or interrelations among things, as by a number of dots or lines. —*v.t.* **2.** to represent by a graph.

-graph a combining form meaning: something writ-ten or drawn (*autograph*); an instrument that writes or records (*seismograph*).

graph'ic *adj.* Also, **graph'i•cal. 1.** giving a clear and effective picture; vivid. **2.** of or using diagrams or graphs. **3.** of or expressed by writing. **4.** of the graphic arts. —*n.* **5.** a product of the graphic arts, as a print. **6.** a graphic representation, as a picture or map. **7.** a computer-generated image. —**graph'i•cal•ly,** *adv.*

graph'ic arts', *n.pl.* **1.** the arts, as engraving or li-thography, by which copies of a design are printed from a plate, block, or the like. **2.** the arts of draw-ing, painting, and printmaking.

graph'ics *n.* **1.** (*used with a sing. v.*) the art of drawing, esp. in architecture, engineering, etc. **2.** (*used with a pl. v.*) GRAPHIC ARTS (def. 1). **3.** (*used with a sing. v.*) **a.** pictorial computer output pro-duced, through the use of software, on a display screen or printer. **b.** the technique used to produce such output.

graph'ite (-īt), *n.* a soft carbon used for pencil leads, as a lubricant, etc.

graph•ol•o•gy (gra fol'ə jē), *n.* the study of hand-writing, esp. to find clues to the writer's character. —**graph•ol'o•gist,** *n.*

grap•nel (grap'nl), *n.* **1.** a device consisting of one or more hooks for grasping or holding. **2.** a small anchor with three or more flukes.

grap•ple (grap'əl), *v.,* **-pled, -pling,** *n.* —*v.i.* **1.** to use a grapnel. **2.** to seize another in a firm grip, as in wrestling. **3.** to cope or struggle: *to grapple with a problem.* —*v.t.* **4.** to seize or hold. —*n.* **5.** GRAPNEL (def. 1). **6.** a seizing or gripping. **7.** a hand-to-hand fight.

grasp (grasp, gräsp), *v.t.* **1.** to seize and hold with or as if with the hand. **2.** to seize upon. **3.** to com-prehend; understand. —*v.i.* **4.** to make a motion of seizing. —*n.* **5.** the act of grasping. **6.** a hold or grip. **7.** one's power to seize; reach. **8.** mastery or comprehension. —**grasp'a•ble,** *adj.*

grasp'ing *adj.* greedy; avaricious.

grass (gras, gräs), *n.* **1.** any of various plants that have jointed stems and bladelike leaves. **2.** such plants collectively. **3.** grass-covered ground. **4.** *Slang.* MARIJUANA. —**grass'y,** *adj.,* **-i•er, -i•est.**

grass'hop'per *n.* any of numerous insects having the hind legs adapted for leaping.

grass'land' *n.* open grass-covered land; prairie.

grass' roots' (*used with a sing. or pl. v.*) **1.** or-dinary citizens, as contrasted with the leadership or elite. **2.** the people inhabiting rural areas, esp. as a political group. —**grass'-roots',** *adj.*

grass' wid'ow *n.* a woman who is separated or divorced from her husband.

grate¹ (grāt), *n.* **1.** a frame of metal bars for hold-ing burning fuel, as in a fireplace. **2.** Also, **grat'ing.** a framework of parallel or crossed bars used as a partition, guard, or cover.

grate² (grāt), *v.,* **grat•ed, grat•ing.** —*v.i.* **1.** to have an irritating effect. **2.** to make a sound of rough scraping. —*v.t.* **3.** to reduce to small particles by rubbing against a rough surface. **4.** to rub to-gether with a harsh sound. **5.** to irritate; annoy. —**grat'er,** *n.* —**grat'ing•ly,** *adv.*

grate'ful *adj.* **1.** warmly or deeply appreciative; thankful. **2.** expressing gratitude. —**grate'ful•ly,** *adv.* —**grate'ful•ness,** *n.*

grat•i•fy (grat'ə fī'), *v.t.,* **-fied, -fy•ing. 1.** to give pleasure to. **2.** to satisfy, humor, or indulge. —**grat'i•fi•ca'tion,** *n.*

grat•is (grat'is, grā'tis), *adv., adj.* without charge or payment.

grat•i•tude (grat'i tōōd', -tyōōd'), *n.* the quality or feeling of being grateful or thankful.

gra•tu•i•tous (grə tōō'i təs, -tyōō'-), *adj.* **1.** given, done, or obtained without charge. **2.** being without apparent reason or justification.

gra•tu'i•ty *n., pl.* **-ties.** a gift of money for service rendered; tip.

grave¹ (grāv), *n.* **1.** an excavation made in the earth to bury a dead body. **2.** any place of inter-ment.

grave² (grāv), *adj.,* **grav•er, grav•est. 1.** sedate or solemn. **2.** weighty; momentous. **3.** serious; critical. —**grave'ly,** *adv.* —**grave'ness,** *n.*

grave³ (grāv), *v.t.,* **graved, grav•en** or **graved, grav•ing. 1.** to carve or engrave. **2.** to impress deeply.

grav•el (grav'əl), *n.* small stones and pebbles or a mixture of these with sand.

grav'el•ly *adj.* **1.** made up of or like gravel. **2.** harsh-sounding.

grave'yard shift' *n.* a work shift usu. beginning about midnight.

grav•i•ta'tion *n.* **1.** the force of attraction be-tween any two masses. **2.** a movement toward something or someone. —**grav'i•ta'tion•al,** *adj.*

grav'i•ty *n., pl.* **-ties. 1.** the force of attraction by which terrestrial bodies tend to fall toward the cen-ter of the earth. **2.** gravitation in general. **3.** heavi-ness or weight. **4.** serious or critical nature.

gra•vy (grā'vē), *n., pl.* **-vies. 1.** the fat and juices of cooked meat, often used to make a sauce. **2.** *Slang.* profit or money easily or unexpectedly ob-tained.

gray (grā), *adj.,* **gray•er, gray•est,** *n., v.,* **grayed, gray•ing.** —*adj.* **1.** of a color between white and black. **2.** dismal or gloomy. **3.** having gray hair. **4.** indeterminate in character. —*n.* **5.** something gray. —*v.t., v.i.* **6.** to make or become gray. —**gray'ish,** *adj.* —**gray'ness,** *n.*

gray' mat'ter *n.* **1.** a reddish gray nerve tissue of the brain and spinal cord. **2.** *Informal.* brains or in-tellect.

graze¹ (grāz), *v.,* **grazed, graz•ing.** —*v.i.* **1.** to feed on growing grass and herbage. **a.** *Informal.* **a.** to eat snacks in place of regular meals. **b.** to eat small portions of a variety of foods at one meal. —*v.t.* **3.** to put (livestock) out to graze. —**graz'er,** *n.*

graze² (grāz), *v.t., v.i.,* **grazed, graz•ing.** to touch, rub, or scrape (something) lightly in passing.

grease (*n.* grēs; *v.* grēs, grēz), *n., v.,* **greased, greas•ing.** —*n.* **1.** the melted fat of animals. **2.** fatty or oily matter in general. —*v.t.* **3.** to put grease on.

great (grāt), *adj.,* **-er, -est,** *adv., n.* —*adj.* **1.** compar-atively large in size or dimensions. **2.** large in num-ber. **3.** considerable in degree, intensity, etc. **4.** first-

general

rate; excellent. **5.** highly significant or consequential. **6.** distinguished; famous. **7.** of extraordinary ability or achievement. **8.** of marked duration. **9.** skillful; expert: *She's great at golf.* **10.** being of one generation more remote from the relative specified: *a great-grandson.* —*adv.* **11.** *Informal.* very well. —*n.* **12.** a person who has achieved importance or distinction. —**great′ly,** *adv.* —**great′ness,** *n.*

Great′ Dane′ *n.* a large and powerful shorthaired dog.

grebe (grēb), *n.* a diving bird with a rudimentary tail and lobed toes.

Greece (grēs), *n.* a republic in S Europe.

greed (grēd), *n.* excessive or rapacious desire, esp. for wealth. —**greed′y,** *adj.,* -i•er, -i•est.

Greek (grēk), *n.* **1.** a native or inhabitant of Greece. **2.** the Indo-European language of the Greeks. —*adj.* **3.** of Greece, the Greeks, or their language. **4.** of the Greek Orthodox Church.

Greek′ Or′thodox Church′ *n.* the branch of the Orthodox Church constituting the national church of Greece.

green (grēn), *adj.,* -er, -est, *n., v.* —*adj.* **1.** of the color of growing foliage, between yellow and blue in the spectrum. **2.** covered with foliage. **3.** made of green vegetables. **4.** not fully developed or matured. **5.** unseasoned: *green lumber.* **6.** immature or inexperienced. **7.** sickly or pale. —*n.* **8.** a color intermediate between yellow and blue. **9. greens,** the edible leaves and stems of certain plants, as spinach or lettuce. **10.** grassy land. **11.** the area of closely cropped grass surrounding each hole on a golf course. —*v.i., v.t* **12.** to become or make green. —**green′ish,** *adj.* —**green′ness,** *n.*

green′back′ *n.* a U.S. legal-tender note, printed in green on the back.

green′belt′ *n.* an area of woods, parks, or open land surrounding a community.

green′er•y *n.* foliage or vegetation.

green′gro′cer *n.* a retailer of fresh vegetables and fruit.

green′horn′ *n.* **1.** an inexperienced person. **2.** a naive or gullible person.

green′house′ *n.* a glass building with controlled temperature, used for cultivating plants.

green′house effect′ *n.* heating of the atmosphere resulting from the absorption by certain gases of solar radiation.

Green′land (-lǝnd, -land′), *n.* a self-governing Danish island NE of North America: the largest island in the world. —**Green′land•er,** *n.*

green′room′ *n.* a lounge in a theater, television studio, etc., for use by performers.

green′ thumb′ *n.* an exceptional skill for growing plants.

greet (grēt), *v.t.* **1.** to address with some form of salutation. **2.** to receive: *to greet a proposal with boos.* **3.** to manifest itself to: *Music greeted our ears.*

gre•gar•i•ous (gri gâr′ē ǝs), *adj.* **1.** fond of the company of others. **2.** living in flocks or herds. —**gre•gar′i•ous•ly,** *adv.* —**gre•gar′i•ous•ness,** *n.*

grem•lin (grem′lin), *n.* an imaginary, mischievous being humorously alleged to cause disruptions in any activity.

Gre•na•da (gri nā′dǝ), *n.* an island country in the E West Indies. —**Gre•na′di•an** (-dē ǝn), *adj., n.*

gre•nade (gri nād′), *n.* a small shell containing an explosive, usu. thrown by hand.

gren•a•dier (gren′ǝ dēr′), *n.* **1.** a member of a British infantry regiment. **2.** (formerly) a soldier who threw grenades.

grey (grā), *adj., n., v.t., v.i.,* greyed, grey•ing. GRAY.

grey′hound′ *n.* a tall, slender shorthaired dog noted for its keen sight and swiftness.

grid (grid), *n.* **1.** a grating of crossed bars. **2.** a network of horizontal and perpendicular lines for locating points on a map, chart, etc. **3.** a system of electrical distribution serving a large area. **4.** a metallic framework in a storage battery for conducting the electric current. **5.** an electrode in a vacuum tube for controlling the flow of electrons.

grid•dle (grid′l), *n.* a flat pan for cooking pancakes, bacon, etc., over direct heat.

grid′i′ron *n.* **1.** a football field. **2.** a utensil consisting of parallel metal bars on which to broil food.

grid′lock′ *n.* **1.** a complete stoppage of all vehicular movement due to traffic blocking key intersections. —*v.t., v.i.* **2.** to cause or undergo a gridlock.

grief (grēf), *n.* **1.** keen mental suffering over affliction or loss. **2.** a cause of keen distress or sorrow.

griev•ance (grē′vǝns), *n.* **1.** a wrong considered as grounds for complaint. **2.** a complaint against an unjust act.

grieve (grēv), *v.i., v.t.,* grieved, griev•ing. to feel or cause to feel grief. —**griev′er,** *n.*

griev′ous *adj.* **1.** causing or expressing grief. **2.** very serious; severe. **3.** burdensome or oppressive. —**griev′ous•ly,** *adv.*

grif•fin (grif′in), *n.* a fabled monster with the head and wings of an eagle and the body of a lion.

grill[1] (gril), *n.* **1.** an apparatus topped by a grated metal framework for cooking food over direct heat. **2.** GRIDIRON (def. 2). **3.** a flat metal surface for broiling food. **4.** a dish of grilled food. **5.** a restaurant serving grilled food. —*v.t.* **6.** to broil on a grill. **7.** to subject to severe and persistent questioning.

grill[2] (gril), *n.* GRILLE.

grille (gril), *n.* a grating or openwork barrier, as for a gate.

grim (grim), *adj.,* grim•mer, grim•mest. **1.** stern and unyielding. **2.** of a sinister or ghastly character. **3.** having a harsh or forbidding air. —**grim′ly,** *adv.* —**grim′ness,** *n.*

grim•ace (grim′ǝs, gri mās′), *n., v.,* -aced, -ac•ing. —*n.* **1.** a facial expression that indicates disapproval, pain, etc. —*v.i.* **2.** to make grimaces.

grime (grīm), *n.* dirt or soot adhering to or embedded in a surface. —**grim′y,** *adj.,* -i•er, -i•est.

grin (grin), *v.,* grinned, grin•ning, *n.* —*v.i.* **1.** to smile broadly, as in amusement. **2.** to draw back the lips so as to show the teeth, as a snarling dog. —*n.* **3.** the act or expression of grinning.

grind (grīnd), *v.,* ground, grind•ing, *n.* —*v.t.* **1.** to wear, smooth, or sharpen by abrasion or friction. **2.** to reduce to fine particles. **3.** to oppress or crush. **4.** to rub together harshly or gratingly, as the teeth. **5.** to operate by turning a crank. **6. grind out,** to produce in a routine or mechanical way. —*n.* **7.** the act or sound of grinding. **8.** a grade of particle fineness. **9.** laborious, usu. uninteresting work. **10.** *Informal.* an excessively diligent student.

grip (grip), *n., v.,* gripped, grip•ping. —*n.* **1.** the act of grasping firmly. **2.** the power of grasping. **3.** mastery or control. **4.** mental or intellectual hold. **5.** a device that seizes and holds. **6.** a handle or hilt. **7.** *Older Use.* a small traveling bag. —*v.t.* **8.** to grasp firmly. **9.** to hold the attention of: *to grip the imagination.* —*v.i.* **10.** to take firm hold. —**Idiom.** **11. come to grips with,** to face and cope with. —**grip′per,** *n.*

gripe (grīp), *v.,* griped, grip•ing, *n.* —*v.i.* **1.** *Informal.* to complain naggingly or constantly. —*v.t.* **2.** to produce pain in the bowels of. **3.** to annoy or irritate. **4.** *Informal.* a nagging complaint. **5.** Usu., **gripes.** a pain in the bowels. —**grip′er,** *n.*

grippe (grip), *n. Older Use.* INFLUENZA.

gris•ly (griz′lē), *adj.,* -li•er, -li•est. causing a shudder or feeling of horror; gruesome.

grist (grist), *n.* **1.** grain to be ground. **2.** ground grain.

gris•tle (gris′ǝl), *n.* cartilage, esp. in meat. —**gris′tly,** *adj.,* -tli•er, -tli•est.

grit (grit), *n., v.,* grit•ted, grit•ting. —*n.* **1.** hard, abrasive particles, as of sand or gravel. **2.** firmness of character. —*v.t.* **3.** to clamp or grind (the teeth) together, as to show determination. —**grit′ty,** *adj.,* -ti•er, -ti•est.

grits (grits), *n.* (*used with a pl. v.*) coarsely ground hominy.

griz′zly *adj.,* -zli•er, -zli•est, *n., pl.* -zlies. —*adj.* **1.** somewhat gray. **2.** gray-haired. —*n.* **3.** GRIZZLY BEAR.

griz′zly bear′ *n.* a large North American brown bear with coarse, gray-tipped fur.

groan (grōn), *n.* **1.** a low, mournful sound uttered

in pain, grief, disapproval, etc. **2.** a creaking sound due to overburdening. —*v.i.*, *v.t.* **3.** to utter (with) a groan.

gro•cer (grō′sər), *n.* the owner or operator of a store that sells general food supplies and articles of household use. [< OF *gross(i)er* wholesale merchant]

gro′cer•y *n.*, *pl.* **-cer•ies. 1.** a grocer's store. **2.** Usu., **-ceries.** the goods sold by a grocer.

grog (grog), *n.* **1.** a mixture of rum and water, sometimes served hot. **2.** any alcoholic drink.

grog′gy *adj.*, **-gi•er, -gi•est.** staggering or dazed, as from exhaustion or blows. —**grog′gi•ly**, *adv.* —**grog′gi•ness**, *n.*

groin (groin), *n.* **1.** the fold where the thigh joins the abdomen. **2.** the general region of this fold. **3.** *Architecture.* the curved edge formed by the intersection of two vaults.

grom•met (grom′it, grum′-), *n.* **1.** a reinforcing metal eyelet, as in cloth. **2.** a ring of rope or wire used to secure sails, oars, etc.

groom (grōom, grŏŏm), *n.* **1.** BRIDEGROOM. **2.** a man or boy in charge of horses or a stable. —*v.t.* **3.** to make neat or tidy. **4.** to clean and brush (a horse, dog, etc.). **5.** to prepare or train for a position. —**groom′er**, *n.*

grooms′man *n.*, *pl.* **-men.** an attendant of a bridegroom.

groove (grōov), *n.*, *v.*, **grooved, groov•ing.** —*n.* **1.** a long, narrow cut in a surface. **2.** a track or channel of a phonograph record. **3.** a fixed routine. **4.** *Slang.* an enjoyable time or experience. —*v.t.* **5.** to cut a groove in. —*v.i.* **6.** *Slang.* **a.** to take great pleasure. **b.** to interact well.

grope (grōp), *v.*, **groped, grop•ing**, *n.* —*v.i.* **1.** to feel about with the hands. **2.** to search uncertainly. —*v.t.* **3.** to seek (one's way) by groping. —**grop′er**, *n.*

gros•beak (grōs′bēk′), *n.* a finch with a thick, conical bill.

gross (grōs), *adj.*, **gross•er, gross•est**, *n.*, *pl.* **gross** for 6, **gross•es** for 7, *v.* —*adj.* **1.** without deductions: *gross earnings.* **2.** flagrant and extreme. **3.** indelicate, coarse, or vulgar. **4.** very fat or large. **5.** broad or general. —*n.* **6.** twelve dozen. **7.** total income, profits, etc., before deductions. —*v.t.* **8.** to earn as a total before deductions, as of taxes or expenses. —**gross′ly**, *adv.* —**gross′ness**, *n.*

gross′ na′tional prod′uct *n.* the total monetary value of all goods and services produced in a country during one year.

gro•tesque (grō tesk′), *adj.* odd or unnatural in shape, appearance, or character; fantastically ugly or absurd. —**gro•tesque′ly**, *adv.*

grot•to (grot′ō), *n.*, *pl.* **-toes, -tos. 1.** a cave or cavern. **2.** an artificial cavernlike recess or structure.

grouch (grouch), *n.* **1.** a sulky or complaining person. **2.** a sulky mood. —*v.i.* **3.** to be sulky or morose. —**grouch′y**, *adj.*, **-i•er, -i•est.**

ground[1] (ground), *n.* **1.** the solid surface of the earth. **2.** earth or soil. **3.** Often, **grounds.** a tract of land: *picnic grounds.* **4.** Usu., **grounds.** the basis on which a belief or action rests. **5.** a subject for discussion. **6.** the background, as in a painting. **7. grounds,** dregs or sediment. **8. grounds,** the gardens, lawn, etc., surrounding and belonging to a building. **9.** a conducting connection between an electric circuit or equipment and the earth or some other conducting body. —*adj.* **10.** of, on, at, or near the ground. —*v.t.* **11.** to lay on the ground. **12.** to place on a foundation. **13.** to instruct in first principles. **14.** to establish a ground for (an electric circuit, device, etc.). **15.** to cause (a ship) to run aground. **16.** to restrict (an aircraft or pilot) to the ground. **17.** *Informal.* to restrict the activities, esp. the social activities, of. —*v.i.* **18.** to come to or strike the ground. **19. ground out,** *Baseball.* to be put out at first base after hitting a ground ball. —*Idiom.* **20. from the ground up, a.** gradually from the most elementary level to the highest level. **b.** extensively; thoroughly. **21. gain** (or **lose**) **ground, a.** to advance (or fail to advance). **b.** to

gain (or lose) approval or acceptance. **22. give ground,** to retreat. **23. hold** or **stand one's ground,** to maintain one's position. **24. off the ground,** into action or well under way: *The play never got off the ground.*

ground[2] (ground), *v.* pt. and pp. of GRIND.

ground′ ball′ *n.* a batted baseball that rolls or bounces along the ground. Also called **ground′er.**

ground′hog′ *n.* WOODCHUCK.

ground′less *adj.* without rational basis.

ground rule *n.* Usu., **ground rules.** a basic rule of conduct in a situation.

ground′swell′ *n.* **1.** a broad, deep swell or rolling of the sea. **2.** a surge of feelings, esp. among the general public.

ground′work′ *n.* the foundation or basis of a project.

group (grōop), *n.* **1.** a number of persons, animals, or things gathered, classed, or acting together. —*v.t.*, *v.i.* **2.** to form into a group or groups.

group′er *n.*, *pl.* **-ers, -er.** any of various large warm-water sea basses.

group′ie *n.*, *pl.* **-ies. 1.** a young female fan of rock musicians, who may follow them on tour. **2.** an ardent fan of any celebrity.

grouse[1] (grous), *n.*, *pl.* **grous•es, grouse.** a game bird related to the pheasant, with a short bill and feathered legs.

grouse[2] (grous), *v.*, **groused, grous•ing**, *n. Informal.* —*v.i.* **1.** to grumble; complain. —*n.* **2.** a complaint. —**grous′er**, *n.*

grout (grout), *n.* **1.** a thin, coarse mortar used to fill crevices, as between tiles. —*v.t.* **2.** to fill or consolidate with grout.

grove (grōv), *n.* a small wood or orchard.

grov•el (grov′əl, gruv′-), *v.i.*, **-eled, -el•ing** or (*esp. Brit.*) **-elled, -el•ling. 1.** to humble oneself; act in an abject manner. **2.** to lie or crawl with the face downward, as in abject humility or fear. —**grov′el•er**, *esp. Brit.*, **grov′el•ler**, *n.*

grow (grō), *v.*, **grew, grown, grow•ing.** —*v.i.* **1.** to increase in size by a natural process of development. **2.** to arise or issue as a natural development. **3.** to increase gradually in size, amount, etc. **4.** to become united by or as if by growth. **5.** to become by degrees: *to grow old.* —*v.t.* **6.** to cause or allow to grow. **7. grow on,** to become gradually more liked or accepted by. **8. ~ up,** to be fully grown; attain maturity. —**grow′er**, *n.*

growl (groul), *v.i.* **1.** to utter a deep guttural sound of anger or hostility. **2.** to complain angrily. —*v.t.* **3.** to express by growling. —*n.* **4.** the act or sound of growling. —**growl′er**, *n.*

grown′-up′ (grōn′-), *adj.* **1.** having reached maturity; adult. **2.** of or suitable for adults.

grown′up′ (grōn′-), *n.* an adult.

growth (grōth), *n.* **1.** the act or process of growing. **2.** a size or stage of development: *to reach one's full growth.* **3.** something that has grown: *a growth of weeds.* **4.** an abnormal mass of tissue, as a tumor. —*adj.* **5.** of or noting a stock, industry, etc., that grows in value or earnings at a rate higher than average.

grub (grub), *n.*, *v.*, **grubbed, grub•bing.** —*n.* **1.** a thick-bodied, sluggish larva, esp. of the beetle. **2.** *Slang.* food. —*v.t.* **3.** to clear of roots, stumps, etc. **4.** to uproot. **5.** *Slang.* to scrounge. —*v.i.* **6.** to search by digging. **7.** to lead a laborious life. —**grub′ber**, *n.*

grub′by *adj.*, **-bi•er, -bi•est.** dirty; slovenly. —**grub′bi•ness**, *n.*

grudge (gruj), *n.*, *v.*, **grudged, grudg•ing.** —*n.* **1.** a feeling of ill will or resentment. —*v.t.* **2.** to give or permit with reluctance. **3.** to resent the good fortune of (another). —**grudg′ing•ly**, *adv.*

gru•el (grōō′əl), *n.* a thin cooked cereal.

gru•el•ing (grōō′ə ling, grōō′ling), *adj.* exhausting; arduously severe.

grue•some (grōō′səm), *adj.* causing horror and repugnance: *a gruesome murder.* —**grue′some•ly**, *adv.* —**grue′some•ness**, *n.*

gruff (gruf), *adj.*, **-er, -est. 1.** low and harsh. **2.** brusque or surly. —**gruff′ly**, *adv.* —**gruff′ness**, *n.*

grum•ble (grum′bəl), v., **-bled, -bling.** n. —v.i. **1.** to mutter in discontent. **2.** to growl. **3.** to rumble. —v.t. **4.** to utter by grumbling. —n. **5.** an expression of discontent; complaint. —**grum′bler,** n.

grump•y (grum′pē), adj., **-i•er, -i•est.** discontentedly or sullenly irritable. —**grump′i•ness,** n.

grun•gy (grun′jē), adj., **-gi•er, -gi•est.** Slang. dirty or run-down.

grunt (grunt), v.i., v.t. **1.** to utter (with) the deep, guttural sound characteristic of a hog. —n. **2.** a sound of grunting.

gryph′on (grif′ən) n. GRIFFIN.

gua•no (gwä′nō), n. a manure composed chiefly of the excrement of sea birds, valued as a fertilizer.

guar. guarantee(d).

guar•an•tee (gar′ən tē′), n., pl. **-tees,** v., **-teed, -tee•ing.** —n. **1.** an assurance, esp. one in writing, that something is of specified quality, content, etc., or will perform satisfactorily for a given time. **2.** GUARANTY (defs. 1, 2). **3.** something that assures a particular outcome or condition. **4.** GUARANTOR. —v.t. **5.** to make or give a guarantee for. **6.** to promise or make certain.

guar′an•tor′ (-tôr′, -tər), n. a person, group, etc., that guarantees.

guar′an•ty n., pl. **-ties,** v., **-tied, -ty•ing.** —n. **1.** a formal assurance given as security that another's debt or obligation will be fulfilled. **2.** something taken or given as security. **3.** the act of giving security. **4.** GUARANTOR. —v.t. **5.** to guarantee.

guard (gärd), v.t. **1.** to keep safe from harm or danger. **2.** to keep under close watch or control. **3.** (in sports) to try to impede the movement or progress of (an opponent). —v.i. **4.** to take precautions. **5.** to keep watch. —n. **6.** one that guards. **7.** a close watch, as over a prisoner. **8.** a device or attachment that prevents injury, loss, etc. **9.** a posture of defense or readiness, as in boxing. **10.** a football or basketball player who guards an opponent. —**guard′er,** n.

guard′ed adj. **1.** cautious; prudent: *a guarded comment.* **2.** protected or restrained. —**guard′ed•ly,** adv.

guard′i•an n. **1.** a person who guards, protects, or preserves. **2.** a person legally entrusted with the care of another's person or property, as that of a minor. —**guard′i•an•ship′,** n.

Gua•te•ma•la (gwä′tə mä′lə), n. a republic in N Central America. —**Gua′te•ma′lan,** adj., n.

gua•va (gwä′və), n., pl. **-vas. 1.** a tropical tree of the myrtle family. **2.** its large yellow fruit.

gu•ber•na•to•ri•al (gōō′bər nə tôr′ē əl, gyōō′-), adj. of a state governor or the office of state governor.

guer•ril•la or **gue•ril•la** (gə ril′ə), n., pl. **-las.** a member of a band of irregular soldiers that harasses the enemy, as by surprise raids. [< Sp: band of guerrillas, dim. of *guerra* war]

guess (ges), v.t., v.i. **1.** to risk a judgment or opinion about (something) without sufficient evidence. **2.** to figure out or judge correctly. **3.** to think or suppose. —n. **4.** an opinion reached by guessing. **5.** the act of guessing. —**guess′er,** n.

guess′work′ n. **1.** an act of guessing. **2.** conclusions from guesses.

guest (gest), n. **1.** a person who spends time at another's home in a social activity. **2.** a person who patronizes a hotel, restaurant, etc. **3.** a person invited to appear in a program or performance. —adj. **4.** of or for guests. **5.** appearing as a guest.

guf•faw (gu fô′, gə-), n. **1.** a loud, unrestrained burst of laughter. —v.i. **2.** to laugh loudly and boisterously.

guid•ance (gīd′ns), n. **1.** the act or function of guiding. **2.** advice or counseling, esp. for students.

guide (gīd), v., **guid•ed, guid•ing.** n. —v.t. **1.** to show the way to; lead. **2.** to direct the movement or course of. **3.** to lead or direct in any course or action. —n. **4.** a person who guides, esp. one hired to conduct tours. **5.** a mark, tab, or sign that guides. **6.** a guidebook. **7.** a device that directs motion or action: *a sewing-machine guide.* —**guid′er,** n.

guide′book′ n. a book of directions, advice, and information, as for tourists.

guid′ed mis′sile n. a missile steered during its flight by radio signals, clockwork controls, etc.

guide′line′ n. any guide or indication of a future course of action.

guild (gild), n. **1.** an organization of persons with related interests, goals, etc. **2.** a medieval association of merchants or artisans.

guile (gīl), n. insidious cunning or duplicity in attaining a goal. —**guile′ful,** adj. —**guile′less,** adj.

guil•lo•tine (gil′ə tēn′, gē′ə-; esp. for v. gil′ə tēn′, gē′ə-), n., v., **-tined, -tin•ing.** —n. **1.** a device for beheading a person, consisting of a heavy blade that drops between two posts. —v.t. **2.** to behead by the guillotine. [< F, after J. I. *Guillotin* (1738–1814), French physician who urged its use as a humane method of execution]

guilt (gilt), n. **1.** the fact or state of being guilty. **2.** a feeling of responsibility or remorse for some real or imagined offense, crime, wrong, etc. —**guilt′less,** adj.

guilt′y adj., **-i•er, -i•est. 1.** having committed an offense, crime, violation, or wrong. **2.** connected with or involving guilt. **3.** having or showing guilt.

Guin•ea (gin′ē), n., pl. **-eas** for 2. **1.** a republic on the W coast of Africa. **2.** (l.c.) a former gold coin of Great Britain, worth 21 shillings. —**Guin′e•an,** n., adj.

Guin′ea-Bissau′ n. a republic on the W coast of Africa.

guin′ea fowl′ n. an African game bird with spotted gray plumage.

guin′ea pig′ n. **1.** a tailless rodent raised as a pet and for use in laboratories. **2.** the subject of any test or experiment.

guise (gīz), n. **1.** general external appearance. **2.** assumed appearance or mere semblance.

gui•tar (gi tär′), n. a musical instrument with typically six strings plucked with the fingers or a plectrum. [< Sp *guitarra* ≪ Gk *kithára* lyre-like musical instrument] —**gui•tar′ist,** n.

gulch (gulch), n. a deep, narrow ravine, esp. one marking the course of a stream.

gulf (gulf), n. **1.** a portion of an ocean or sea partly enclosed by land. **2.** a chasm or abyss. **3.** any wide gap or divergence.

gull¹ (gul), n. a long-winged aquatic bird, typically white with gray or black wings and back.

gull² (gul), v.t. **1.** to deceive, trick, or cheat. —n. **2.** a person who is easily deceived or cheated.

gul•let (gul′it), n. **1.** the esophagus. **2.** the throat or pharynx.

gul•li•ble (gul′ə bəl), adj. easily deceived or cheated. —**gul′li•bil′i•ty,** n.

gul•ly (gul′ē), n., pl. **-lies.** a small valley or ravine formed by running water, esp. rainwater.

gulp (gulp), v.i. **1.** to gasp, as if taking large drafts of a liquid. —v.t. **2.** to swallow eagerly or hastily, or in large amounts. **3.** to choke back as if by swallowing. —n. **4.** the act of gulping. **5.** a mouthful. —**gulp′er,** n.

gum¹ (gum), n., v., **gummed, gum•ming.** —n. **1.** any of various sticky substances exuded from plants, hardening on exposure to air, and soluble in or forming a viscid mass with water. **2.** any of various similar substances, as resin. **3.** a flavored preparation for chewing; chewing gum. —v.t. **4.** to smear, stick together, or clog with gum. —v.i. **5.** to become clogged with or as if with gum. **6. gum up,** Slang. to spoil or ruin. —**gum′my,** adj., **-mi•er, -mi•est.**

gum² (gum), n., v., **gummed, gum•ming.** —n. **1.** Often, **gums.** the firm, fleshy tissue enveloping the bases of the teeth. —v.t. **2.** to chew with toothless gums.

gum′ ar′abic n. a gum obtained from acacia trees, used chiefly as an emulsifier or adhesive.

gum•bo (gum′bō), n., pl. **-bos.** a soup of chicken or seafood, thickened with okra.

gum′drop′ n. a small candy made of sweetened and flavored gum arabic, gelatin, or the like.

gump•tion (gump/shən), *n.* **1.** initiative; resourcefulness. **2.** courage or spunk.

gum/shoe/ *n., pl.* **-shoes. 1.** *Slang.* a detective. **2.** a rubber overshoe.

gun (gun), *n., v.,* **gunned, gun•ning.** —*n.* **1.** a weapon consisting of a metal tube from which projectiles are shot by the force of an explosive. **2.** any portable firearm. **3.** a long-barreled cannon. **4.** any device for shooting or ejecting something under pressure, as paint. —*v.t.* **5.** to shoot with a gun. **6.** to cause (an engine) to increase in speed very quickly by increasing the supply of fuel. —*v.i.* **7.** to shoot or hunt with a gun. **8. gun for,** to try earnestly to obtain. —*Idiom.* **9. stick to one's guns,** to maintain one's position in the face of opposition. **10. under the gun,** under pressure, as to meet a deadline. —**gun/ner,** *n.*

gun/fire/ *n.* the firing of guns.

gung-ho (gung/hō/), *adj. Informal.* wholeheartedly enthusiastic and loyal.

gunk (gungk), *n. Slang.* any sticky or greasy matter.

gun/man *n., pl.* **-men.** a person armed with a gun, esp. a criminal.

gun•ny (gun/ē), *n., pl.* **-nies.** a strong coarse material made commonly from jute.

gun/pow/der *n.* an explosive mixture, as of potassium nitrate, sulfur, and charcoal, used in guns and for blasting.

gun/shot/ *n.* **1.** the shooting of a gun. **2.** a bullet or other shot fired from a gun.

gun/smith/ *n.* a person who makes or repairs firearms.

gun•wale (gun/l), *n.* the upper edge of the side or bulwark of a vessel.

gup•py (gup/ē), *n., pl.* **-pies.** a small freshwater fish often kept in aquariums.

gur•gle (gûr/gəl), *v.,* **-gled, -gling,** *n.* —*v.i.* **1.** to flow in a broken, irregular, noisy current. **2.** to make a sound as of water doing this. —*n.* **3.** the act or noise of gurgling.

gur•ney (gûr/nē), *n., pl.* **-neys.** a wheeled table or stretcher for transporting patients.

gu•ru (gōōr/ōō, gŏŏ rōō/), *n., pl.* **-rus. 1.** (in Hinduism) one's personal religious or spiritual instructor. **2.** any person who counsels or advises; mentor. **3.** a leader in a particular field. [< Hindi *gurū* < Skt *guru* venerable]

gush (gush), *v.i.* **1.** to flow out or issue copiously or forcibly. **2.** to talk effusively. —*v.t.* **3.** to cause to gush. —*n.* **4.** a sudden copious outflow. —**gush•y,** *adj.,* **-i•er, -i•est.**

gush/er *n.* **1.** one that gushes. **2.** a flowing oil well, usu. of large capacity.

gus•set (gus/it), *n.* a triangular piece of material inserted into a shirt, shoe, etc., to improve the fit or for reinforcement.

gus•sy (gus/ē), *v.t., v.i.,* **-sied, -sy•ing.** *Informal.* to dress up or decorate in a showy manner: *all gussied up for the celebration.*

gust (gust), *n.* **1.** a sudden strong blast of wind. **2.**

an outburst of emotion. —*v.i.* **3.** to blow in gusts. —**gust/y,** *adj.,* **-i•er, -i•est.**

gus•ta•to•ry (gus/tə tôr/ē), *adj.* of taste or tasting.

gus•to (gus/tō), *n.* hearty enjoyment or enthusiasm.

gut (gut), *n., v.,* **gut•ted, gut•ting,** *adj.* —*n.* **1.** the alimentary canal, esp. the intestine. **2. guts, a.** the bowels or entrails. **b.** courage and fortitude. **3.** intestinal tissue or fiber. **4.** CATGUT. —*v.t.* **5.** to take out the entrails of. **6.** to destroy the interior of. —*adj.* **7. a.** basic or essential. **b.** based on instincts or emotions: *a gut reaction.* —**gut/less,** *adj.*

guts/y *adj.,* **-i•er, -i•est. 1.** daring or courageous. **2.** robust or lusty.

gut•ter (gut/ər), *n.* **1.** a channel for leading off water, as at the side of a road or along the eaves of a roof. —*v.i.* **2.** to flow in streams.

gut•tur•al (gut/ər əl), *adj.* **1.** of the throat. **2.** harsh; throaty. **3.** pronounced in the throat.

guy¹ (gī), *n.* **1.** a man or boy. **2. guys,** people.

guy² (gī), *n.* **1.** a rope, cable, or appliance used to guide and steady an object. —*v.t.* **2.** to guide or steady with a guy.

Guy•a•na (gī an/ə, -ä/nə), *n.* a republic on the NE coast of South America. —**Guy/a•nese/** (-ə nēz/, -nēs/), *n., pl.* **-nese,** *adj.*

guz•zle (guz/əl), *v.i., v.t.,* **-zled, -zling.** to drink, or sometimes eat, greedily or excessively. —**guz/zler,** *n.*

gym•na/si•um (-nä/zē əm), *n., pl.* **-si•ums, -si•a** (-zē ə, -zhə). a building or room equipped for indoor sports, exercise, or physical education.

gym•nas/tics (-nas/tiks), *n.* **1.** (*used with a pl. v.*) physical exercises that develop and demonstrate strength, balance, and agility. **2.** (*used with a sing. v.*) the practice, art, or competitive sport of such exercises. —**gym/nast** (-nast, -nəst), *n.* —**gym•nas/tic,** *adj.*

gy•ne•col•o•gy (gī/ni kol/ə jē, jin/i-), *n.* the branch of medicine that deals with the health maintenance and diseases of women, esp. of the reproductive organs. —**gy/ne•co•log/ic** (-kə loj/ik), **gy/ne•co•log/i•cal,** *adj.* —**gy/ne•col/o•gist,** *n.*

gyp (jip), *v.,* **gypped, gyp•ping,** *n. Informal.* —*v.t., v.i.* **1.** to swindle or cheat. —*n.* **2.** a swindle or fraud. **3.** Also, **gyp/per, gyp/ster** (-stər). a swindler.

gyp•sum (jip/səm), *n.* a common soft mineral used to make plaster of Paris and as a fertilizer.

Gyp•sy (jip/sē), *n., pl.* **-sies. 1.** a member of a traditionally itinerant people, orig. of N India, now residing mostly in permanent communities in many countries. **2.** the language of the Gypsies; Romany. **3.** (*l.c.*) a person who resembles the stereotype of a Gypsy, as in an itinerant way of life.

gy•rate (jī/rāt, jī rāt/), *v.i.,* **-rat•ed, -rat•ing.** to move in a circle or spiral. —**gy•ra/tion,** *n.*

gy•ro•scope (jī/rə skōp/), *n.* a rotating wheel so mounted that its axis can turn freely in all directions, used to maintain equilibrium and to determine direction.

abcdefg H ijklmnopqrstuvwxyz

H, h (āch), *n., pl.* **Hs** or **H's, hs** or **h's.** the eighth letter of the English alphabet, a consonant.

H 1. *Slang.* heroin. **2.** high.

H *Chem. Symbol.* hydrogen.

h. or **H., 1.** height. **2.** high. **3.** *Baseball.* hit. **4.** hour. **5.** hundred. **6.** husband.

ha (hä), *interj.* an exclamation of surprise, suspicion, triumph, etc.

ha•be•as cor•pus (hā/bē əs kôr/pəs), *n.* a writ requiring a person to be brought before a court to determine whether the person has been detained legally. [< L: lit., have the body (first words of writ)]

hab/er•dash/er•y (hab/ər dash/ə rē) *n., pl.* **-eries.** a shop selling men's items. —**hab/er•dash/er,** *n.*

hab•it (hab/it), *n.* **1.** a pattern of behavior acquired as a result of frequent repetition. **2.** customary practice or use. **3.** addiction, esp. to narcotics. **4.** the garb of a particular profession, religious order, etc. —**ha•bit/u•al** (hə bich/ōō əl), *adj.* —**ha•bit/u•al•ly,** *adv.*

hab•it•a•ble (hab/i tə bəl), *adj.* capable of being inhabited. —**hab/it•a•bil/i•ty,** *n.*

hab/i•tat/ (-tat/), *n.* **1.** the natural environment of a plant or animal. **2.** the place where a person is usu. found.

hab/i•ta/tion *n.* **1.** a dwelling; abode. **2.** the act of inhabiting.

ha•bit/u•ate/ (-āt/), *v.t.*, **-at•ed, -at•ing.** to accustom, as to a particular situation. **—ha•bit/u•a/tion,** *n.*

ha•bit•u•é (hə bich/ōō ā/), *n., pl.* **-és.** a habitual visitor to a place. [< F]

hack¹ (hak), *v.t.* **1.** to cut or chop with crude, often heavy strokes. **2.** *Slang.* to deal or cope with. **—v.i. 3.** to make rough cuts or notches. **4.** to cough harshly and dryly. **—n. 5.** a cut or notch. **6.** a tool for hacking. **7.** a rasping, dry cough.

hack² (hak), *n.* **1.** a professional, esp. a writer, who does routine work primarily for money. **2.** a horse for hire. **3.** an old or worn-out horse. **4.** a carriage for hire; hackney. **5.** a taxicab. **6.** to drive a taxi. **7.** to work as a hack. **—adj. 8.** hired as a hack. **9.** trite; banal.

hack/er *n. Slang.* **1.** a computer enthusiast who is especially proficient. **2.** a computer user who attempts to gain unauthorized access to computer systems.

hack/les (hak/əlz) *n.pl.* **1.** hair that can bristle on the back of an animal's neck. **2.** anger.

hack/ney (-nē), *n., pl.* **-neys. 1.** a carriage for hire. **2.** a horse used for ordinary riding or driving.

hack/neyed *adj.* made commonplace or trite.

hack/saw/ or **hack/ saw/,** *n.* a saw for cutting metal, consisting of a fine-toothed blade fixed in a frame.

had•dock (had/ək), *n., pl.* **-docks, -dock.** a fish of the cod family, of the N Atlantic.

Ha•des (hā/dēz), *n.* **1.** (in Greek myth) the underworld inhabited by the dead. **2.** (*often l.c.*) hell.

haft (haft, häft), *n.* a handle, esp. of a knife, sword, or dagger.

hag (hag), *n.* **1.** an ugly old woman, esp. a malicious one. **2.** a witch. **—hag/gish,** *adj.*

hag•gard (hag/ərd), *adj.* appearing gaunt, wasted, or exhausted. **—hag/gard•ly,** *adv.* **—hag/gard•ness,** *n.*

hag•gle (hag/əl), *v.,* **-gled, -gling. —v.i. 1.** to bargain in a petty, quibbling manner. **—n. 2.** the act of haggling. **—hag/gler,** *n.*

hail¹ (hāl), *v.t.* **1.** to salute or greet. **2.** to acclaim. **3.** to call or signal to. **—v.i. 4.** to call out. **5. hail from,** to come or be from. **—n. 6.** a call or greeting. **—interj. 7.** an exclamation of greeting or acclamation.

hail² (hāl), *n.* **1.** precipitation in the form of irregular pellets of ice. **2.** a shower of anything. **—v.i. 3.** to pour down or fall like hail. **—v.t. 4.** to pour down as or like hail.

hair (hâr), *n.* **1.** any of the numerous fine filaments growing from the skin of mammals. **2.** an aggregate of such filaments. **3.** any fine, filamentous outgrowth. **4.** a very small amount, degree, etc. **—Idiom. 5. get in someone's hair,** to annoy someone. **6. split hairs,** to make tiny, petty distinctions. **—haired,** *adj.* **—hair/less,** *adj.* **—hair/like/,** *adj.*

hair/breadth/ or **hairs/breadth/,** *n.* **1.** a very small space or distance. **—adj. 2.** extremely narrow or close.

hair/cut/ *n.* **1.** the act of cutting the hair. **2.** the style in which the hair is cut and worn.

hair/do/ (-dōō/), *n., pl.* **-dos.** the style in which hair is cut and arranged; coiffure.

hair/piece/ *n.* a toupee or wig.

hair/pin/ *n.* **1.** a slender U-shaped pin used to fasten up the hair. **—adj. 2.** sharply curved back, as in a U shape: *a hairpin turn.*

hair/-rais/ing *adj.* terrifying or horrifying.

hair/spray/ *n.* liquid spray for holding the hair in place.

hair/style/ *n.* a way of cutting or arranging hair; hairdo. **—hair/styl/ist,** *n.*

hair/-trig/ger *adj.* easily activated or set off.

Hai•ti (hā/tē), *n.* a republic in the West Indies occupying the W part of the island of Hispaniola. **—Hai/tian** (-shən, -tē ən), *adj., n.*

hake (hāk), *n., pl.* **hakes, hake.** any of various codlike marine food fishes.

hal•cy•on (hal/sē ən), *adj.* peaceful; happy; carefree.

hale¹ (hāl), *adj.,* **hal•er, hal•est.** healthy; robust.

hale² (hāl), *v.t.,* **haled, hal•ing.** to compel (someone) to go.

half (haf, häf), *n., pl.* **halves** (havz, hävz), *adj., adv. —n.* **1.** one of two equal parts of something. **2.** either of two equal periods of play in a game. **3.** one of a pair. **—adj. 4.** being a half. **5.** partial or incomplete. **—adv. 6.** in or to the extent of a half. **7.** in part; incompletely.

half/back/ *n. Football.* one of two backs who typically line up on each side of the fullback.

half/-baked/ *adj.* **1.** insufficiently cooked. **2.** insufficiently planned or prepared. **3.** foolish.

half/-breed/ *n. Offensive.* the offspring of parents of different races.

half/ broth/er *n.* a male sibling related through one parent only.

half/-cocked/ *adj.* ill-considered or ill-prepared.

half/heart/ed *adj.* having or showing little enthusiasm: *a halfhearted attempt to work.* **—half/heart/edly,** *adv.* **—half/heart/ed•ness,** *n.*

half/ sis/ter *n.* a female sibling related through one parent only.

half/-truth/ *n.* a statement that is only partly true, esp. one intended to deceive.

half/way/ (-wā/, -wā/), *adv.* **1.** to the midpoint. **2.** partially or almost. **—adj. 3.** midway. **4.** partial or inadequate. **—Idiom. 5. meet halfway,** to compromise with.

half/way house/ *n.* a residence for persons released from a hospital, prison, or other institution that eases their return to society.

half/-wit/ *n.* a feeble-minded or foolish person. **—half/-wit/ted,** *adj.*

hal•i•but (hal/ə bət, hol/-), *n., pl.* **-buts, -but.** any of various large, edible flounders.

hal•i•to•sis (hal/i tō/sis), *n.* a condition of having offensive-smelling breath.

hall (hôl), *n.* **1.** a corridor in a building. **2.** the large entrance room of a house or building. **3.** a large room or building for public gatherings. **4.** a building at a college or university. **5.** the main house of a large estate.

hal•le•lu•jah or **-iah** (hal/ə lōō/yə), *interj.* **1.** Praise ye the Lord! **2.** an exclamation of joy, praise, or gratitude.

hall/mark/ *n.* **1.** any mark or indication of genuineness, quality, etc. **2.** any distinguishing characteristic.

hal•low (hal/ō), *v.t.* to make or honor as holy. **—hal/low•er,** *n.*

Hal•low•een or **-e'en** (hal/ə wēn/, -ō ēn/, hol/-), *n.* the evening of October 31; the eve of All Saints' Day. [*(All)hallow(s)* + *e(v)en* evening]

hal•lu•ci•na/tion *n.* **1.** a sensory experience, as of images or sounds, that does not exist outside the mind. **2.** an illusion or delusion. **—hal•lu/ci•nate/,** *v.i., v.t.,* **-nat•ed, -nat•ing. —hal•lu/ci•na•to/ry** (-nə tôr/ē), *adj.*

hal•lu/ci•no•gen (-nə jən), *n.* a substance that produces hallucinations. **—hal•lu/ci•no•gen/ic** (-jen/ik), *adj.*

hall/way/ *n.* **1.** a corridor, as in a building. **2.** an entrance hall.

ha•lo (hā/lō), *n., pl.* **-los, -loes. 1.** a symbolic circle of radiant light around the head in pictures of holy personages. **2.** a bright circle or arc centered on the sun or moon.

hal•o•gen (hal/ə jən, -jen/, hā/lə-), *n.* any of the nonmetallic elements, fluorine, chlorine, iodine, bromine, and astatine.

halt¹ (hôlt), *v.i.* **1.** to stop or cause to stop. **—n. 2.** a stop or pause.

halt² (hôlt), *v.i.* **1.** to falter or hesitate. **—adj. 2.** lame.

hal•ter (hôl/tər), *n.* **1.** a rope or strap for leading or restraining horses or cattle. **2.** a hangman's noose. **3.** a woman's top, tied behind the neck and across the back. **—v.t. 4.** to put a halter on; restrain as by a halter.

halve (hav, häv), *v.t.,* **halved, halv•ing. 1.** to divide into two equal parts. **2.** to share equally. **3.** to reduce to half.

ham¹ (ham), *n.* **1.** a cut of meat from a hog's hind quarter, between hip and hock. **2.** that part of a hog's hind leg. **3.** the part of the human leg behind the knee. **4.** Often, **hams.** the back of the thigh, or the thigh and the buttock together.

ham² (ham), *n., v.,* **hammed, ham•ming.** —*n.* **1.** a performer who overacts. **2.** an operator of an amateur radio station. —*v.i., v.t.* **3.** to overact. —**ham/my,** *adj.,* **-mi•er, -mi•est.**

ham•burg•er (ham/bûr/gər), *n.* **1.** a patty of ground beef. **2.** a sandwich consisting of such a patty and a bun.

ham•let (ham/lit), *n.* a small village.

ham•mer (ham/ər), *n.* **1.** a tool consisting of a solid head set crosswise on a handle, used for driving nails, beating metals, etc. **2.** something resembling this in form, action, or use. **3.** the part of a firearm that strikes the firing pin and causes the discharge. —*v.t.* **4.** to beat with a hammer, esp. repeatedly. **5.** to shape, drive, or work, as with a hammer. —**ham/mer•er,** *n.*

ham•mock (ham/ək), *n.* a bed of canvas, cord, or the like that hangs between two supports.

ham•per¹ (ham/pər), *v.t.* to hold back; hinder; impede. —**ham/per•er,** *n.*

ham•per² (ham/pər), *n.* a large covered basket: *a picnic hamper.*

ham•ster (ham/stər), *n.* a short-tailed, burrowing rodent with large cheek pouches.

ham/string/ *n., v.,* **-strung, -string•ing.** —*n.* **1.** any of the tendons behind the knee. —*v.t.* **2.** to disable by cutting a hamstring. **3.** to make powerless, ineffective, etc.

hand (hand), *n.* **1.** the terminal, prehensile part of the arm in humans and other primates. **2.** anything resembling a hand in shape or function, as a pointer. **3.** a manual worker or crew member. **4.** a person skilled or experienced at some job. **5.** skill or workmanship. **6.** Often, **hands.** possession or power; control or care: *in fate's hands.* **7.** means; agency. **8.** assistance; aid: *to lend a hand.* **9.** side; direction: *the left hand of the road.* **10.** handwriting. **11.** a round of applause. **12.** a promise of marriage. **13.** a linear measure equal to 4 inches (10.2 centimeters). **14.** *Cards.* **a.** the cards held by each player at one time. **b.** a single round of a game. —*v.t.* **15.** to deliver or pass with or as if with the hand. **16.** to help, guide, etc., with the hand. **17.** to give or provide with. **18. hand down,** to deliver or transmit. **19. ~ out,** to distribute. —*adj.* **20.** of, belonging to, using, or operated by the hand. —*Idiom.* **21.** at **hand,** near. **22. hand in hand,** close together. **23. hand it to,** to give credit to. **24. hand over fist,** speedily and abundantly. **25. hands down,** effortlessly; easily. **26. on hand,** available or present. **27. on the one hand,** from one perspective. **28. on the other hand,** from the opposing perspective.

hand/bag/ *n.* a bag, usu. with a handle or strap, used by women to carry money, cosmetics, etc.

hand/ball/ *n.* a game in which players strike a small ball against a wall with the hand.

hand/bill/ *n.* a small printed notice or announcement, usu. for distribution by hand.

hand/book/ *n.* a concise guide or reference book; manual.

hand/cuff/ *n.* **1.** a metal ring that can be locked around a prisoner's wrist, usu. one of a pair connected by a chain. —*v.t.* **2.** to put handcuffs on. **3.** to restrain or thwart.

hand/ful (-fool), *n., pl.* **-fuls. 1.** the quantity or amount that the hand can hold. **2.** a small amount or quantity. **3.** *Informal.* a person or thing that is hard to manage or control.

hand/gun/ *n.* any firearm that can be held and fired with one hand.

hand•i•cap (han/dē kap/), *n., v.,* **-capped, -cap•ping.** —*n.* **1.** a contest in which disadvantages or advantages of weight, distance, etc., are given to competitors to equalize their chances of winning. **2.** the disadvantage or advantage itself. **3.** any disadvantage. **4.** a physical or mental disability. —*v.t.* **5.** to place at a disadvantage. **6.** to assign handicaps to. **7.** to predict the winner of (a contest, esp. a horse race). —**hand/i•cap/per,** *n.*

hand/i•craft/ *n.* **1.** manual skill. **2.** an art, craft, or trade requiring manual skill. **3.** the articles made by handicraft.

hand/i•work/ *n.* **1.** work done by hand. **2.** the work of a particular person.

hand•ker•chief (hang/kər chif, -chēf/), *n.* a small piece of fabric used for wiping the nose, eyes, etc.

han•dle (han/dl), *n., v.,* **-dled, -dling.** —*n.* **1.** a part of a tool, vessel, etc., by which it is grasped or held by the hand. —*v.t.* **2.** to touch, pick up, carry, or feel with the hands. **3.** to manage or deal with. **4.** to train or control. **5.** to deal or trade in. —*v.i.* **6.** to perform in a particular way when operated: *The jet was handling poorly.* —**han/dler,** *n.*

hand/made/ *adj.* made by hand, rather than by machine.

hand/out/ *n.* **1.** food, clothing, etc., given to a needy person. **2.** a press release. **3.** a flyer or other printed material distributed to a group. **4.** anything given away for nothing.

hand/shake/ *n.* a gripping and shaking of each other's hand in greeting, agreement, etc.

hands/-off/ *adj.* characterized by nonintervention or noninterference.

hand•some (han/səm), *adj.,* **-som•er, -som•est. 1.** attractive and well-proportioned, esp. in an imposing or manly way; good-looking. **2.** considerable or ample. **3.** gracious; generous. —**hand/some•ly,** *adv.* —**hand/some•ness,** *n.*

hands/-on/ *adj.* characterized by or involving active personal participation.

hand/spring/ *n.* an acrobatic movement in which a person starts from a standing position and turns the body in a complete circle, landing first on the hands and then on the feet.

hand/-to-mouth/ *adj.* providing barely enough to survive: *a hand-to-mouth existence.*

hand/writ/ing *n.* **1.** writing done by hand with a pen or pencil. **2.** a style or manner of such writing. —**hand/writ/ten** (-rit/n), *adj.*

hand/y *adj.,* **-i•er, -i•est. 1.** within easy reach; accessible. **2.** easily used. **3.** skillful with the hands; dexterous. —**hand/i•ly,** *adv.* —**hand/i•ness,** *n.*

hand/y•man/ *n., pl.* **-men.** a person hired to do small maintenance or repair jobs.

hang (hang), *v.,* **hung** or (*esp. for 3, 11*) **hanged, hang•ing,** *n.* —*v.t.* **1.** to fasten or attach (a thing) so that it is supported from above or near its own top. **2.** to attach or suspend so as to allow free movement. **3.** to execute by suspending from a gallows or the like. **4.** to decorate with something suspended. **5.** to attach (wallpaper, pictures, etc.) to a wall. **6.** to let (one's head) droop. **7.** to bring (a jury) to a deadlock. —*v.i.* **8.** to be suspended; dangle. **9.** to swing freely. **10.** to incline downward, jut out, or lean over. **11.** to suffer death by hanging. **12.** to be contingent: *Our future hangs on their decision.* **13.** to fall or drape, as a garment. **14.** *Informal.* to hang out. **15. hang around,** *Informal.* **a.** to spend time in a certain place. **b.** to loiter. **16. ~ back,** to hesitate. **17. ~ in (there),** *Informal.* to persevere or endure. **18. ~ on, a.** to cling tightly. **b.** to persevere or endure. **c.** to persist. **d.** to keep a telephone line open. **19. ~ out,** *Informal.* to spend one's time habitually. **20. ~ up, a.** to suspend, as on a hook. **b.** to stop or delay. **c.** to end a telephone call by breaking the connection. —*n.* **21.** the way in which a thing hangs. **22.** *Informal.* the precise manner of doing, using, etc., something. **23.** *Informal.* meaning or significance: *to get the hang of a subject.* —*Idiom.* **24. hang loose,** *Slang.* to remain relaxed or calm. **25. hang tough,** *Informal.* to be unyielding or inflexible.

hang•ar (hang/ər), *n.* a structure for housing aircraft. [< F: shed, shelter]

hang/dog/ *adj.* abject or shamefaced.

hang glider *n.* a kitelike glider for soaring through the air from hilltops, etc. (**hang/ glid/ing**).

hang/nail/ *n.* a small piece of partly detached skin at the side or base of the fingernail.

hang′o′ver *n.* **1.** the disagreeable physical aftereffects of drunkenness. **2.** something remaining from a former period or state.

hang′-up′ *n. Slang.* a psychological preoccupation or problem.

hank (hangk), *n.* **1.** SKEIN. **2.** a coil or loop: *a hank of hair.*

han•ker (hang′kər), *v.i.* to have a restless or incessant longing. —**han′ker•ing,** *n.*

han•ky-pan•ky (hang′kē pang′kē), *n. Informal.* **1.** mischief; deceit. **2.** illicit sexual relations.

han•som (han′səm), *n.* a two-wheeled, covered vehicle drawn by one horse, with the driver mounted on an elevated seat behind. Also called **han′som cab′.** [after J. A. *Hansom* (1803–82), English architect who designed it]

Ha•nuk•kah (hä′nə kə, KHä′-), *n.* an eight-day Jewish festival commemorating the rededication of the Temple in Jerusalem.

hap•haz•ard (hap haz′ərd), *adj.* characterized by lack of order or planning; random. —**hap•haz′ard•ly,** *adv.*

hap′less *adj.* luckless; unfortunate.

hap•pen (hap′ən), *v.i.* **1.** to take place; come to pass; occur. **2.** to come to pass by chance. **3.** to have the fortune or occasion: *I happened to see him.* **4.** to meet or discover by chance. **5.** to be, come, go, etc., casually or by chance.

hap′pen•stance′ (-stans′), *n.* a chance happening or event.

hap•py (hap′ē), *adj.,* **-pi•er, -pi•est. 1.** delighted or pleased. **2.** characterized by or indicative of pleasure or joy. **3.** favored by fortune. **4.** apt or felicitous. —**hap′pi•ly,** *adv.* —**hap′pi•ness,** *n.*

ha•rangue (hə rang′), *n., v.,* **-rangued, -rangu•ing.** —*n.* **1.** a long, passionate, and pompous speech. —*v.t.* **2.** to address in a harangue. —*v.i.* **3.** to deliver a harangue.

ha•rass (hə ras′, har′əs), *v.t.* **1.** to disturb persistently. **2.** to trouble by repeated attacks. —**ha•rass′er,** *n.* —**ha•rass′ment,** *n.*

har•bin•ger (här′bin jər), *n.* one that heralds the approach of someone or something.

har•bor (här′bər), *n.* **1.** a sheltered part of a body of water along the shore deep enough for anchoring a ship. **2.** any place of shelter or refuge. —*v.t.* **3.** to give shelter to. **4.** to conceal. **5.** to hold in the mind: *to harbor suspicion.* —*v.i.* **6.** to take shelter. Also, *esp. Brit.,* **harbour.** —**har′bor•er,** *n.*

hard (härd), *adj.* and *adv.,* **-er, -est.** —*adj.* **1.** solid and firm to the touch. **2.** firmly formed; tight. **3.** difficult to do, deal with, understand, etc. **4.** involving a great deal of effort, energy, or persistence. **5.** energetic or persistent. **6.** violent or severe: *a hard fall.* **7.** bad or unbearable: *hard luck.* **8.** oppressive; harsh. **9.** undeniable: *hard facts.* **10.** factual: *hard information.* **11.** unfriendly; resentful: *hard feelings.* **12.** stern or searching: *a hard look.* **13.** (of water) containing mineral salts that interfere with the action of soap. **14.** in currency as distinguished from checks or promissory notes. **15.** (of paper money) readily convertible into foreign currency. **16.** (of alcoholic beverages) containing much alcohol. **17.** (of a drug) addictive. —*adv.* **18.** with great exertion, vigor, or violence. **19.** earnestly or critically. **20.** harshly or severely. **21.** so as to be solid or firm: *frozen hard.* **22.** with force: *hit hard.* —*Idiom.* **23. hard by,** near. **24. hard up,** *Informal.* urgently in need of money. —**hard′ness,** *n.*

hard′-bit′ten *adj.* tough; stubborn.

hard′-boiled′ *adj.* **1.** (of an egg) boiled long enough for the yolk and white to solidify. **2.** unsentimental; tough.

hard′ ci′der *n.* fermented cider.

hard′-core′ *adj.* **1.** absolute and uncompromising. **2.** (of pornography) explicit. **3.** persistent or chronic: *hard-core unemployment.*

hard′ hat′ *n.* **1.** a protective helmet worn by construction workers, miners, etc. **2.** a construction worker.

hard′head′ed *adj.* **1.** practical; shrewd. **2.** obstinate; willful. —**hard′head′ed•ly,** *adv.* —**hard′head•ed•ness,** *n.*

hard′heart′ed *adj.* unfeeling; pitiless. —**hard′heart′ed•ly,** *adv.* —**hard′heart′ed•ness,** *n.*

hard′-line′ or **hard′line′,** *adj.* adhering rigidly to a set of principles or demands, as in politics. —**hard′-lin′er,** *n.*

hard′ly *adv.* **1.** barely or scarcely. **2.** with little likelihood: *He will hardly come now.*

hard′-nosed′ *adj. Informal.* practical and shrewd.

hard′ship *n.* **1.** a condition that is difficult to endure, as poverty or illness. **2.** an instance or cause of this.

hard′tack′ *n.* a hard, saltless biscuit, formerly much used aboard ships.

hard′ware′ *n.* **1.** metalware, as tools, locks, or cutlery. **2.** the mechanical and electronic devices composing a computer system.

hard′wood′ *n.* **1.** the hard, compact wood or timber of various trees, as the oak or cherry. —*adj.* **2.** made of hardwood.

har•dy (här′dē), *adj.,* **-di•er, -di•est. 1.** sturdy; strong. **2.** bold or daring; courageous. —**har′di•ly,** *adv.* —**har′di•ness,** *n.*

hare (hâr), *n., pl.* **hares, hare.** a mammal closely related to but usu. larger than the rabbit.

hare′brained′ *adj.* giddy; reckless.

hare′lip′ *n. Sometimes Offensive.* CLEFT LIP. —**hare′lipped′,** *adj.*

har•em (hâr′əm, har′-), *n.* **1.** the part of a Muslim house reserved for the residence of women. **2.** the women in a Muslim household. [< Ar *ḥarīm* harem, lit., forbidden]

hark (härk), *v.i.* **1.** to listen attentively. **2. hark back,** to recollect a previous event or topic.

har•le•quin (här′lə kwin, -kin), *n.* **1.** (*often cap.*) a character in comic theater and pantomime, usu. masked, dressed in multicolored, diamond-patterned tights. **2.** a buffoon.

har•lot (här′lət), *n.* a prostitute. —**har′lot•ry,** *n.*

harm (härm), *n.* **1.** injury or damage. —*v.t.* **2.** to cause harm to. —**harm′ful,** *adj.* —**harm′ful•ly,** *adv.* —**harm′less,** *adj.* —**harm′less•ly,** *adv.*

har•mon•i•ca (-i kə), *n., pl.* **-cas.** a wind instrument played by exhaling and inhaling air through a set of metal reeds.

har′mo•ny *n., pl.* **-nies. 1.** agreement; accord. **2.** a consistent or pleasing arrangement of parts. **3.** the simultaneous combination of tones, esp. when blended into chords pleasing to the ear. [< OF < L *harmonia* < Gk: joint, agreement, harmony] —**har•mo′ni•ous,** *adj.*

har•ness (här′nis), *n.* **1.** the combination of straps, bands, and other parts forming the working gear of a draft animal. —*v.t.* **2.** to put a harness on. **3.** to gain control over for a particular end: *to harness water power.*

harp (härp), *n.* **1.** a musical instrument having strings stretched across a triangular frame, played by plucking with the fingers. —*v.i.* **2.** to play on a harp. **3. harp on** or **upon,** to repeat interminably and tediously. —**harp′ist,** *n.*

har•poon (här pōōn′), *n.* **1.** a barbed, spearlike missile attached to a rope, used to spear whales and large fish. —*v.t.* **2.** to strike with a harpoon. —**har•poon′er,** *n.*

harp•si•chord (härp′si kôrd′), *n.* a keyboard instrument, precursor of the piano, in which the strings are plucked by leather or quill points connected with the keys. —**harp′si•chord′ist,** *n.*

har•ri•dan (har′i dn), *n.* a scolding, vicious woman.

har•ri•er (har′ē ər), *n.* **1.** one of a breed of medium-sized hunting hounds. **2.** a cross-country runner.

har•row (har′ō), *n.* **1.** an agricultural implement with spikelike teeth or upright disks, for breaking up plowed land. —*v.t.* **2.** to draw a harrow over. **3.** to disturb painfully. —**har′row•ing,** *adj.*

har•ry (har′ē), *v.t.,* **-ried, -ry•ing. 1.** to harass; torment. **2.** to ravage, as in war.

harsh (härsh), *adj.* **1.** ungentle in action or effect. **2.** grim; cruel. **3.** unpleasant to the senses. —**harsh′ly,** *adv.* —**harsh′ness,** *n.*

har•vest (här′vist), *n.* **1.** the gathering of crops. **2.**

the season when ripened crops are gathered. **3.** a crop or yield of one growing season. **4.** the result of any act, process, etc. —*v.t., v.i.* **5.** to gather or reap. —**har/vest•er,** *n.*

has (haz; *unstressed* həz, əz), *v.* a 3rd pers. sing. pres. indic. of HAVE.

has/-been/ *n.* a person or thing that is no longer effective, successful, etc.

hash[1] (hash), *n.* **1.** diced cooked meat and potatoes or other vegetables browned together. **2.** a mess or muddle. —*v.t.* **3.** to discuss or review thoroughly: *to hash over a proposal.* [< F *hacher* to cut up]

hash[2] (hash), *n. Slang.* hashish.

hash•ish (hash/ēsh, hä shēsh/), *n.* a narcotic and intoxicant made from Indian hemp.

has•n't (haz/ənt), contraction of *has not.*

hasp (hasp), *n.* a clasp for a door, lid, etc., esp. one passing over a staple and fastened by a pin or padlock.

has•sle (has/əl), *n., v.,* **-sled, -sling.** *Informal.* —*n.* **1.** a disorderly dispute. **2.** a troublesome situation. —*v.i.* **3.** to quarrel. **4.** to be put to inconvenience, exertion, etc. —*v.t.* **5.** to bother or harass.

has•sock (has/ək), *n.* a thick, firm cushion used as a footstool.

haste (hāst), *n.* **1.** swiftness of motion; speed. **2.** unnecessarily quick or rash action. —*Idiom.* **3. make haste,** to hurry.

has•ten (hā/sən), *v.i.* **1.** to move or act with haste. —*v.t.* **2.** to cause to hasten.

hat (hat), *n.* **1.** a shaped covering for the head, usu. with a crown and brim. —*Idiom.* **2. pass the hat,** to ask for contributions of money. **3. talk through one's hat,** to make absurd statements. **4. throw one's hat into the ring,** to declare one's candidacy for political office. **5. under one's hat,** confidential.

hatch[1] (hach), *v.t.* **1.** to bring forth (young) from the egg. **2.** to cause young to emerge from (the egg), as by incubating. **3.** to devise; plot. —*v.i.* **4.** to be hatched.

hatch[2] (hach), *n.* **1.** an opening in the deck of a ship or in the floor or roof of a building, used as a passageway. **2.** the cover over such an opening.

hatch[3] (hach), *v.t.* to mark with closely set parallel lines, as for shading. —**hatch/ing,** *n.*

hatch•et (hach/it), *n.* a small, short-handled ax.

hatch/et job/ *n.* a maliciously destructive critique.

hatch/way/ *n.* HATCH[2] (def. 1).

hate (hāt), *v.,* **hat•ed, hat•ing,** *n.* —*v.t.* **1.** to dislike intensely; detest. **2.** to be unwilling; dislike: *I hate to accept it.* —*v.i.* **3.** to feel hatred. —*n.* **4.** intense dislike or hostility. **5.** the object of hatred. —**hat/er,** *n.*

hate/ful *adj.* arousing or deserving hate. —**hate/-ful•ly,** *adv.* —**hate/ful•ness,** *n.*

haugh•ty (hô/tē), *adj.,* **-ti•er, -ti•est.** disdainfully proud; snobbish; arrogant. —**haugh/ti•ly,** *adv.* —**haugh/ti•ness,** *n.*

haul (hôl), *v.t., v.i.* **1.** to pull with force. **2.** to transport; carry. **3. haul off,** *Informal.* to draw back the arm in order to strike. —*n.* **4.** an act or instance of hauling. **5.** the load hauled. **6.** the distance over which anything is hauled. —*Idiom.* **7. long** (or **short**) **haul,** a relatively great (or small) period of time. —**haul/er,** *n.*

haunch (hônch, hänch), *n.* **1.** the hip or the fleshy part of the body about the hip. **2.** the leg and loin of an animal, used for food.

haunt (hônt, hänt), *v.t.* **1.** to visit habitually or appear to frequently as a spirit or ghost. **2.** to recur persistently to the consciousness of. **3.** to visit frequently. —*n.* **4.** a place frequently visited. —**haunt/ed,** *adj.* —**haunt/er,** *n.*

haunt/ing *adj.* remaining in the consciousness; not quickly forgotten. —**haunt/ing•ly,** *adv.*

haute cou•ture (ōt/ kōō tōōr/), *n.* high fashion.

haute cui•sine (ōt/ kwi zēn/), *n.* gourmet cooking; food preparation as an art.

have (hav; *unstressed* həv, əv; *for 14 usually* haf), *v. and auxiliary v.,* **had, hav•ing,** *n.* —*v.t.* **1.** to possess; own; hold. **2.** to get or take: *Have a part in a play.* **3.** to experience: *Have a good time.* **4.** to hold in mind, sight, etc.: *to have doubts.* **5.** to cause

to or cause to be: *Have him come at five.* **6.** to engage in: *to have a talk.* **7.** to eat or drink. **8.** to permit; allow. **9.** to assert or maintain: *Rumor has it that she's moving.* **10.** to give birth to. **11.** to hold an advantage over: *He has you there.* **12.** to outwit; cheat: *We were had by a con artist.* —*auxiliary verb.* **13.** (used with a past participle to form perfect tenses): *She has gone.* **14.** (used with an infinitive to express obligation or compulsion): *I have to leave now.* —*n.* **15.** Usu., **haves.** a wealthy individual or group. —*Idiom.* **16. have had it,** to be tired and disgusted. **17. have it in for,** to wish harm to. **18. have it out,** to reach an understanding through fighting or discussion.

ha•ven (hā/vən), *n.* **1.** a harbor; port. **2.** any place of shelter and safety.

have/-not/ *n.* Usu., **-nots.** an individual or group that is without wealth.

have•n't (hav/ənt), contraction of *have not.*

hav•er•sack (hav/ər sak/), *n.* a single-strapped shoulder bag for carrying supplies.

hav•oc (hav/ək), *n.* **1.** great destruction or devastation. —*Idiom.* **2. play havoc with,** to destroy; ruin.

haw[1] (hô), *v.i.* to hesitate while speaking (usu. in the phrase *to hem and haw*).

haw[2] (hô), *n.* **1.** the fruit of the hawthorn. **2.** the hawthorn.

Haw. Hawaii.

hawk[1] (hôk), *n.* **1.** any of various birds of prey, having a hooked beak, broad wings, and curved talons. **2.** a person who advocates war. —**hawk/-ish,** *adj.*

hawk[2] (hôk), *v.t.* to offer for sale by calling aloud in public. —**hawk/er,** *n.*

hawk[3] (hôk), *v.i.* **1.** to make an effort to raise phlegm from the throat. —*v.t.* **2.** to raise by hawking.

hawk/er *n.* a peddler.

haw•thorn (hô/thôrn/), *n.* any of various small trees of the rose family, with stiff thorns and bright-colored fruit.

hay (hā), *n.* **1.** herbage, as grass or clover, dried for use as forage. —*v.i.* **2.** to cut grass, clover, etc., for use as forage.

hay/ fe/ver *n.* inflammation of the mucous membranes of the eyes and respiratory tract, caused by pollen of certain plants.

hay/wire/ *adj.* out of control; disordered; crazy.

haz•ard (haz/ərd), *n.* **1.** something causing danger, risk, etc. **2.** an obstacle on a golf course. —*v.t.* **3.** to venture or risk. —**haz/ard•ous,** *adj.* —**haz/ard•ous•ly,** *adv.*

haze[1] (hāz), *n., v.,* **hazed, haz•ing.** —*n.* **1.** an aggregation in the atmosphere of very fine, widely dispersed particles, giving the air a blurred appearance. **2.** vagueness, as of the mind. —*v.t., v.i.* **3.** to make or become hazy.

haze[2] (hāz), *v.t.,* **hazed, haz•ing.** to subject (freshmen, newcomers, etc.) to abusive or humiliating tricks and ridicule. —**haz/er,** *n.*

ha•zel (hā/zəl), *n.* **1.** a small tree or shrub of the birch family, with toothed ovate leaves and edible nuts. **2.** a light golden- or greenish-brown color.

ha•zy (hā/zē), *adj.,* **-zi•er, -zi•est. 1.** misty. **2.** vague.

H/-bomb/ *n.* HYDROGEN BOMB.

hdqrs. headquarters.

HDTV high-definition television.

he (hē; *unstressed* ē), *pron., n., pl.* **hes.** —*pron.* **1.** the male person or animal last mentioned. **2.** anyone: *He who hesitates is lost.* —*n.* **3.** any male person or animal.

He *Chem. Symbol.* helium.

head (hed), *n.* **1.** the upper part of the body, containing the skull with mouth, eyes, ears, nose, and brain. **2.** the mind; brain. **3.** a position of leadership or honor. **4.** a leader or chief. **5.** the uppermost part of anything: *the head of a pin.* **6.** the foremost or forward part of anything: *at the head of a procession.* **7.** one of a number, herd, or group: *a dinner at $50 a head.* **8.** a culmination; crisis or climax. **9.** froth at the top of a liquid. **10.** any dense flower cluster or compact part of a plant, as that composed of leaves in the cabbage. **11.** the obverse of a coin. **12.** the source of a river or stream. **13.** HEADLINE. **14.** the stretched membrane covering the end of a drum. **15.** any of the parts of a tape recorder that record, play back, or erase magnetic signals. —*adj.* **16.** first in rank or position. **17.** of or for the head. **18.** situated at the top or front. **19.** moving or coming from the front: *head tide.* —*v.t.* **20.** to lead; precede. **21.** to be the chief of. **22.** to direct the course of. —*v.i.* **23.** to go in a certain direction: *to head east.* **24. head off,** to intercept. —*Idiom.* **25. come to a head, a.** to suppurate, as a boil. **b.** to reach a crisis; culminate. **26. go to one's head, a.** to exhilarate or intoxicate. **b.** to fill one with conceit. **27. head over heels,** intensely; completely. **28. keep** (or **lose**) **one's head,** to keep (or lose) one's poise. **29. on one's head,** as one's responsibility or fault. **30. over one's head,** beyond one's comprehension. **31. turn someone's head,** to make someone conceited. —**head′less,** *adj.*

head′ache′ *n.* **1.** a pain located in the head. **2.** an annoying person, situation, etc.

head′dress′ *n.* a covering or decoration for the head.

head′first′ *adv.* **1.** with the head in front. **2.** rashly; precipitately.

head′ing *n.* **1.** something that serves as a head, top, or front. **2.** a title or caption of a page, chapter, etc. **3.** the direction toward which a traveler or vehicle is moving.

head′light′ *n.* a light with a reflector on the front of a motor vehicle.

head′line′ *n., v.,* **-lined, -lin·ing.** —*n.* **1.** a heading in a newspaper for any written material. —*v.t.* **2.** to furnish with a headline. **3.** to be the star of (a show, nightclub act, etc.). —*v.i.* **4.** to be the star of an entertainment. —**head′lin′er,** *n.*

head′long′ *adv.* **1.** headfirst. **2.** hastily. **3.** rashly. —*adj.* **4.** hasty. **5.** done with the head foremost. **6.** rash; impetuous.

head′-on′ *adj., adv.* with the front or head foremost.

head′phone′ *n.* Usu. **-phones.** a headset for use with a stereo system.

head′quar′ters *n., pl.* **-ters.** (*used with a sing. or pl. v.*) a center of operations from which orders are issued.

head′stone′ *n.* a stone marker at the head of a grave.

head′strong′ *adj.* willful; stubborn.

head·wait·er (hed′wātər), *n.* a person in charge of the waiters, busboys, etc., in a restaurant.

head′way′ *n.* **1.** forward movement. **2.** progress.

head′y *adj.,* **-i·er, -i·est. 1.** intoxicating: *heady perfume.* **2.** rashly impetuous.

heal (hēl), *v.t.* **1.** to restore to health or soundness. **2.** to repair or reconcile. —*v.i.* **3.** to effect a cure. **4.** to become well or sound. —**heal′er,** *n.*

health (helth), *n.* **1.** the general condition of the body or mind: *in poor health.* **2.** soundness of body or mind; freedom from disease or ailment. **3.** a wish for a person's health and happiness, as a toast. **4.** vigor; vitality: *economic health.* —**health′y,** *adj.* **-i·er, -i·est.**

heap (hēp), *n.* **1.** a group of things lying one on another. **2.** *Informal.* a great quantity or number. —*v.t.* **3.** to put in a heap; pile. **4.** to give in great quantity. **5.** to fill abundantly. —*v.i.* **6.** to become heaped.

hear (hēr), *v.,* **heard** (hûrd), **hear·ing.** —*v.t.* **1.** to perceive by the ear. **2.** to be informed of. **3.** to listen to. **4.** to consider officially, as a judge: *to hear a case.* —*v.i.* **5.** to be capable of perceiving sound by the ear. **6.** to receive information. **7.** to listen with favor or assent: *I will not hear of your going.* —**hear′er,** *n.* —**hear′ing,** *n.*

hear′say′ *n.* unverified information acquired from another.

hearse (hûrs), *n.* a vehicle for conveying a dead person to the place of burial.

heart (härt), *n.* **1.** a muscular organ in vertebrates

that receives blood from the veins and pumps it through the arteries to oxygenate the blood. **2.** the center of the personality, esp. with reference to emotion. **3.** capacity for sympathy; affection. **4.** spirit or courage. **5.** the central part of anything: *in the heart of Paris.* **6.** the essential part; core. **7.** a conventional figure shaped like the heart. **8.** any of a suit of playing cards bearing heart-shaped figures. —*Idiom.* **9. after one's own heart,** in accord with one's preference. **10. at heart,** fundamentally; basically. **11. by heart,** entirely from memory. **12. set one's heart on,** to wish for intensely. **13. take to heart, a.** to consider seriously. **b.** to grieve over.

heart′ache′ *n.* sorrow; grief.

heart′ attack′ *n.* any sudden insufficiency of oxygen supply to the heart that results in heart muscle damage.

heart′break′ *n.* great sorrow or anguish. —**heart′break′ing,** *adj.* —**heart′bro′ken,** *adj.*

heart′burn′ *n.* a burning sensation in the stomach and esophagus, sometimes associated with the backflow of an acid fluid.

heart′en *v.t.* to give courage or confidence to.

heart′felt′ *adj.* deeply felt.

hearth (härth), *n.* **1.** the floor of a fireplace, usu. of stone or brick. **2.** the fireside. **3.** home and family life.

heart′rend′ing *adj.* causing or expressing intense grief or anguish. —**heart′rend′ing·ly,** *adv.*

heart′sick′ *adj.* extremely depressed or unhappy. —**heart′sick′ness,** *n.*

heart′-to-heart′ *adj.* frank; sincere and intimate.

heart′y *adj.,* **-i·er, -i·est 1.** warm-hearted; cordial. **2.** genuine; sincere: *hearty dislike.* **3.** exuberant; unrestrained: *hearty laughter.* **4.** vigorous: *hale and hearty.* **5.** abundant or nourishing: *a hearty meal.* —**hear′ti·ly,** *adv.* —**heart′i·ness,** *n.*

heat (hēt), *n.* **1.** the condition or quality of being hot. **2.** degree of hotness. **3.** the sensation of hotness. **4.** energy that causes a rise in temperature, expansion, or other physical change. **5.** hot weather or climate. **6.** intensity of feeling. **7.** maximum intensity in an activity or condition: *the heat of battle.* **8.** *Slang.* coercive pressure: *to put the heat on someone.* **9.** a single division of a race or other contest. **10.** the period of sexual receptiveness in animals, esp. females. —*v.t., v.i.* **11.** to make or become hot or warm. **12.** to make or become excited emotionally.

heat′ed *adj.* excited or angry; impassioned. —**heat′ed·ly,** *adv.*

heath (hēth), *n.* **1.** a tract of open and uncultivated land. **2.** any of various shrubs common on such land.

hea·then (hē′thən), *n., pl.* **-thens, -then,** *adj.* —*n.* **1.** an unconverted individual of a people that do not acknowledge the God of the Bible or Koran. **2.** an irreligious or uncivilized person. —*adj.* **3.** pagan. **4.** irreligious or uncivilized. —**hea′then·ish,** *adj.*

heat′stroke′ *n.* a condition of headache, fever, etc., caused by exposure to excessive heat.

heave (hēv), *v.,* **heaved** or (*esp. Naut.*) **hove; heav·ing;** *n.* —*v.t.* **1.** to lift with effort. **2.** to lift and throw with effort. **3.** to utter laboriously. **4.** to haul or pull on (a rope, cable, etc.). —*v.i.* **5.** to rise and fall rhythmically. **6.** to breathe with effort; pant. **7.** to vomit; retch. **8.** to swell or bulge. **9.** to pull or haul on a rope, cable, etc. **10.** *Naut.* to move in a certain direction or into a certain position: *The ship hove into sight.* **11. heave to,** *Naut.* to come to a halt. —*n.* **12.** an act or effort of heaving. —**heav′er,** *n.*

heav·en (hev′ən), *n.* **1.** the abode of God, the angels, and the spirits of the righteous after death. **2.** (*cap.*) God. **3.** Usu. **-ens.** the sky or firmament. **4.** a place or state of supreme happiness. —**heav′en·ly,** *adj.* —**heav′en·ward,** *adv., adj.*

heav·y (hev′ē), *adj.,* **-i·er, -i·est,** *n., pl.* **-ies,** *adv.* —*adj.* **1.** of great weight. **2.** of great amount or size: *a heavy vote.* **3.** of great force or intensity: *heavy fighting.* **4.** of more than the usual or average weight. **5.** of high specific gravity: *a heavy metal.* **6.** grave; serious. **7.** deep or intense: *a heavy slumber.*

8. designating the more powerful types of weapons: *heavy artillery.* **9.** burdensome; oppressive. **10.** being as indicated to an unusual degree: *a heavy drinker.* **11.** broad, thick, or coarse: *heavy lines.* **12.** depressed; sad: *a heavy heart.* **13.** ponderous or clumsy. **14.** overcast or cloudy. **15.** not easily digested. **16.** producing or refining basic materials, as steel or coal: *heavy industry.* —*n.* **17.** a theatrical character or role that is unsympathetic or villainous. **18.** *Slang.* a very important person. —*adv.* **19.** in a heavy manner. —*Idiom.* **20. heavy with child,** in a state of advanced pregnancy. —**heav′i•ly,** *adv.* —**heav′i•ness,** *n.*

heav′y-du′ty *adj.* made to withstand great strain or use.

heav′y-hand′ed *adj.* **1.** clumsy; graceless. **2.** oppressive; harsh.

heav′y-heart′ed *adj.* sorrowful; melancholy.

heav′y•set′ *adj.* stocky; stout.

He•brew (hē′brōō), *n.* **1.** a member of any of a group of Semitic peoples who claimed descent from Abraham, Isaac, and Jacob. **2.** the Semitic language of the ancient Hebrews, revived as a vernacular in the 20th century. —*adj.* **3.** of the Hebrews or their language.

heck•le (hek′əl), *v.t.,* **-led, -ling.** to harass (a public speaker or performer) with impertinent questions or gibes. —**heck′ler,** *n.*

hec•tare (hek′târ), *n.* a unit of surface or land measure equal to 10,000 square meters (2.471 acres).

hec•tic (hek′tik), *adj.* **1.** characterized by confusion, excitement, or hurried activity. **2.** feverish or flushed. —**hec′ti•cal•ly,** *adv.*

hec•tor (hek′tər), *v.t.* **1.** to harass by bullying, nagging, etc. —*v.i.* **2.** to be a bully.

hedge (hej), *n., v.,* **hedged, hedg•ing.** —*n.* **1.** a dense row of bushes or small trees forming a fence or boundary. **2.** any barrier or boundary. **3.** an act or means of hedging. —*v.t.* **4.** to surround or obstruct with or as if with a hedge. **5.** to mitigate a possible loss by counterbalancing (one's bets, investments, etc.). —*v.i.* **6.** to avoid commitment. —**hedg′er,** *n.*

hedge′hog′ *n.* **1.** an Old World insect-eating mammal with spiny hairs on the back and sides. **2.** the American porcupine.

he′don•ist (hēd′n ist) *n.* a person living for pleasure.

heed (hēd), *v.t., v.i.* **1.** to give careful attention (to). —*n.* **2.** careful attention (usu. with *give* or *take*). —**heed′ful,** *adj.* —**heed′less,** *adj.* —**heed′less•ly,** *adv.* —**heed′less•ness,** *n.*

heel¹ (hēl), *n.* **1.** the back part of the foot, below the ankle. **2.** the part of a stocking, shoe, etc., covering this part. **3.** a solid raised base attached to the back of the sole of a shoe. **4.** something resembling a heel in position or shape. —*v.t.* **5.** to furnish with heels. **6.** to follow closely. —*v.i.* **7.** (of a dog) to follow at one's heels on command. —*Idiom.* **8. down at (the) heel(s),** dressed shabbily. **9. kick up one's heels,** to have a lively time. **10. on** or **upon the heels of,** closely following.

heel² (hēl), *v.i., v.t.* to lean or cause to lean to one side, as a ship.

heel³ (hēl), *n.* a dishonorable or irresponsible person.

heft (heft), *n.* **1.** weight; heaviness. **2.** significance; importance. —*v.t.* **3.** to test the weight of by lifting.

heft′y *adj.,* **-i•er, -i•est. 1.** heavy; weighty. **2.** big and strong; powerful; muscular. **3.** notably large or substantial. —**heft′i•ness,** *n.*

he•gem•o•ny (hi jem′ə nē, hej′ə mō′-), *n., pl.* **-nies.** leadership or domination, esp. of one nation over others.

heif•er (hef′ər), *n.* a young cow that has not produced a calf.

height (hīt), *n.* **1.** extent or distance upward. **2.** the distance between the lowest and highest points of a person standing upright. **3.** great altitude or elevation. **4.** Often, **heights.** a high place; hill or mountain. **5.** the highest or most intense point: *the height of pleasure.*

height′en *v.t., v.i.* **1.** to make or become higher. **2.** to increase in degree or amount.

Heim′lich maneu′ver (hīm′lik), *n.* a procedure to aid a choking victim by applying sudden pressure to the victim's upper abdomen to force an object from the windpipe.

hei•nous (hā′nəs), *adj.* utterly reprehensible or evil. —**hei′nous•ly,** *adv.* —**hei′nous•ness,** *n.*

heir (âr), *n.* a person who inherits or has a right to inherit the property, title, etc., of another. —**heir′ess,** *n.*

heir′loom′ *n.* a family possession handed down from generation to generation.

heist (hīst), *n. Slang.* **1.** a robbery. —*v.t.* **2.** to rob.

hel•i•cop•ter (hel′i kop′tər, hē′li-), *n.* **1.** an aircraft that is lifted and sustained in the air horizontally by rotating blades turning on vertical axes. —*v.i., v.t.* **2.** to fly in a helicopter. [< F *hélicoptère* < Gk *hélix* spiral + *pterón* wing]

he•li•um (hē′lē əm), *n.* an inert, gaseous element present in natural gas, used in balloons and dirigibles. *Symbol:* He; *at. wt.:* 4.0026; *at. no.:* 2. [< NL < Gk *hḗlios* the sun]

he•lix (hē′liks), *n., pl.* **hel•i•ces** (hel′ə sēz′), **he•lix•es.** a spiral. —**hel•i•cal** (hel′i kəl, hē′li-), *adj.*

hell (hel), *n.* **1.** the place or state of punishment of the wicked after death. **2.** any place, state, or cause of torment or misery. —*interj.* **3.** an exclamation of irritation, surprise, etc. —*Idiom.* **4. give someone hell,** *Informal.* to reprimand severely. **5. raise hell,** *Informal.* to create an uproar. —**hell′ish,** *adj.*

he'll (hēl; *unstressed* ēl, hil, il), contraction of *he will.*

Hel•len•ic (he len′ik, -lē′nik), *adj.* **1.** of the ancient Greeks or their language, culture, thought, etc. **2.** GREEK (def. 1). —**Hel•len•ism** (hel′ə niz′əm), *n.* —**Hel′len•ist,** *n.*

hel•lo (he lō′, hə-, hel′ō) *interj.* **1.** an exclamation of greeting. **2.** an exclamation used derisively to question the comprehension, intelligence, or sense of the person being addressed.

helm (helm), *n.* **1.** a wheel or tiller by which a ship is steered. **2.** the place or post of control.

hel•met (hel′mit), *n.* any of various forms of protective, rigid head covering worn by soldiers, football players, etc.

help (help), *v.t.* **1.** to provide what is necessary to accomplish a task or satisfy a need. **2.** to rescue. **3.** to facilitate or promote. **4.** to be useful to. **5.** to refrain from: *I can't help teasing him.* **6.** to prevent: *The disagreement could not be helped.* **7.** to remedy. **8.** to serve or wait on (a customer). —*v.i.* **9.** to give aid; be of service. **10. help out,** to assist, as during a time of need. —*n.* **11.** the act of helping. **12.** one that helps. **13.** a hired helper or helpers. **14.** relief or remedy. —*Idiom.* **15. cannot** or **can't help but,** to be unable to refrain from or avoid; be obliged to: *Still, you can't help but admire her.* **16. help oneself to, a.** to serve oneself with. **b.** to take without asking permission. —**help′er,** *n.*

help′ing *n.* a portion of food served to a person at one time.

help′less *adj.* **1.** unable to help oneself. **2.** without aid or protection. **3.** deprived of strength or power. —**help′less•ly,** *adv.* —**help′less•ness,** *n.*

help′mate′ *n.* a companion and helper, esp. a spouse.

hel•ter-skel•ter (hel′tər skel′tər), *adv.* **1.** in headlong and disorderly haste. **2.** in a haphazard manner. —*adj.* **3.** disorderly.

hem¹ (hem), *v.,* **hemmed, hem•ming,** *n.* —*v.t.* **1.** to fold back and sew down the edge of (cloth, a garment, etc.). **2.** to enclose or confine: *hemmed in by enemies.* —*n.* **3.** an edge made by hemming. —**hem′mer,** *n.*

hem² (hem), *interj., n., v.,* **hemmed, hem•ming.** —*interj., n.* **1.** a sound resembling a clearing of the throat, used esp. to attract attention. —*v.i.* **2.** to make this sound. —*Idiom.* **3. hem and haw,** to hesitate while speaking so as to avoid giving a direct answer.

hem•i•sphere (hem′i sfēr′), *n.* **1.** (*often cap.*) half of the terrestrial globe or celestial sphere, esp. one of the halves into which the earth is divided: *Eastern Hemisphere.* **2.** a half or a sphere. —**hem′i·spher′ic** (-sfer′ik), **hem′i·spher′i·cal,** *adj.*

hem·lock (hem′lok′), *n.* **1.** a poisonous plant of the parsley family. **2.** a poisonous drink made from this plant. **3.** any of several tall coniferous trees of the pine family. **4.** the wood of a hemlock tree.

he·mo·glo·bin (hē′mə glō′bin, hem′ə-), *n.* a compound in red blood cells that transports oxygen from the lungs to the tissues.

he·mo·phil·i·a (hē′mə fil′ē ə), *n.* a genetic disorder, chiefly in males, characterized by prolonged or excessive bleeding. —**he′mo·phil′i·ac′** (-ak′), *n.*

hem·or·rhage (hem′ər ij), *n., v.,* -**rhaged, -rhag·ing.** —*n.* **1.** a profuse discharge of blood. —*v.i.* **2.** to bleed profusely. —**hem′or·rhag′ic** (-ə raj′ik), *adj.*

hem·or·rhoid (hem′ə roid′), *n.* Usu. -**rhoids.** a usu. painful varicose vein in the region of the anal sphincter.

hemp (hemp), *n.* **1.** a tall, coarse Asian plant. **2.** its tough fiber, used for making rope, coarse fabric, etc. **3.** an intoxicating drug, as marijuana or hashish, prepared from the hemp plant. —**hemp′en,** *adj.*

hen (hen), *n.* **1.** the female of the domestic fowl. **2.** the female of any bird.

hence (hens), *adv.* **1.** as an inference from this fact; therefore. **2.** from this time: *a month hence.* **3.** from this source or origin. **4.** from this place; away.

hence·forth (hens′fôrth′, hens′fôrth′), *adv.* from now on.

hench·man (hench′mən), *n., pl.* -**men.** **1.** an unscrupulous and ruthless subordinate. **2.** a political supporter, esp. one motivated by the hope of personal gain.

hen·na (hen′ə), *n., pl.* -**nas,** *v.,* -**naed, -na·ing.** —*n.* **1.** an Asian shrub or small tree. **2.** a hair dye made from its leaves. **3.** a reddish brown color. —*v.t.* **4.** to tint or dye with henna.

hen′pecked′ *adj.* nagged or controlled by one's wife.

hep·a·ti·tis (hep′ə tī′tis), *n.* inflammation of the liver.

her (hûr; *unstressed* hər, ər), *pron.* **1.** the objective case of SHE, used as a direct or indirect object. **2.** a form of the possessive case of SHE, used as an attributive adjective.

her·ald (her′əld), *n.* **1.** a royal or official messenger. **2.** a forerunner; harbinger. **3.** one that proclaims or announces. —*v.t.* **4.** to announce; proclaim. **5.** to usher in.

her·ald·ry (her′əl drē), *n.* **1.** the art of devising and describing coats of arms, tracing genealogies, etc. **2.** ceremonial splendor; pageantry. —**he·ral′dic** (he ral′dik, hə-), *adj.*

herb (ûrb; *esp. Brit.* hûrb), *n.* **1.** a flowering plant whose stem above ground does not become woody. **2.** such a plant valued for its medicinal properties, flavor, or scent. —**her·ba·ceous** (hûr bā′shəs, ûr-), *adj.* —**herb·al** (ûr′bəl, hûr′-), *adj.*

herb·i·cide (hûr′bə sīd′, ûr′-), *n.* a substance or preparation for killing plants, esp. weeds. —**her′bi·cid′al,** *adj.*

her·biv·o·rous (hûr biv′ər əs, ûr-), *adj.* feeding on plants.

her·cu·le·an (hûr′kyə lē′ən, hûr kyōō′lē-), *adj.* **1.** requiring extraordinary strength or exertion. **2.** of enormous strength, courage, or size.

herd (hûrd), *n.* **1.** a number of animals feeding, traveling, or kept together. **2.** a crowd; mob. —*v.i., v.t.* **3.** to move or assemble as a herd. —**herd′er,** *n.*

here (hēr), *adv.* **1.** in or at this place: *Put the pen here.* **2.** to or toward this place: *Come here.* **3.** at this point: *Here the speaker paused.* **4.** in the present life or existence. —*n.* **5.** this place or point: *It's a long way from here.* —**Idiom. 6.** neither here nor there, without relevance.

here′a·bout′ or -**a·bouts′,** *adv.* in this neighborhood.

here·af′ter *adv.* **1.** in the future; from now on. **2.** in the life or world to come. —*n.* **3.** a life after death. **4.** the future.

here·by′ *adv.* by means of this.

he·red·i·tar·y (hə red′i ter′ē), *adj.* **1.** passing, or capable of passing, genetically from parent to offspring. **2.** existing by reason of feelings or opinions held by predecessors: *a hereditary enemy.* **3.** holding title, rights, etc., by inheritance.

he·red′i·ty *n.* **1.** the passing on of characters or traits from parents to offspring through genes. **2.** the genetic characters so transmitted.

here·in′ *adv.* **1.** in or into this place. **2.** in view of this.

her·e·sy (her′ə sē), *n., pl.* -**sies. 1.** religious opinion at variance with the orthodox doctrine. **2.** any belief at variance with established beliefs, customs, etc. —**her′e·tic,** *n.* —**he·ret′i·cal,** *adj.*

here′to·fore′ *adv.* before this time; until now.

here·with′ *adv.* **1.** along with this. **2.** by means of this.

her·it·a·ble (her′i tə bəl), *adj.* capable of being inherited.

her·it·age (her′i tij), *n.* **1.** something that comes or belongs to one by reason of birth: *a heritage of democracy.* **2.** property, esp. land, that is passed on by inheritance.

her·maph·ro·dite (hûr maf′rə dīt′), *n.* an animal or plant in which reproductive organs of both sexes are present. —**her·maph′ro·dit′ic** (-dit′ik), *adj.*

her·met·ic (hûr met′ik) also -**i·cal,** *adj.* made airtight by fusion or sealing. —**her·met′i·cal·ly,** *adv.*

her·mit (hûr′mit), *n.* a person living in seclusion; recluse.

her′mit·age (-mi tij), *n.* **1.** the habitation of a hermit. **2.** any secluded place of residence.

her·ni·a (hûr′nē ə), *n., pl.* -**ni·as, -ni·ae** (-nē ē′). the protrusion of an organ or tissue through an opening in its surrounding walls. —**her′ni·al,** *adj.*

he·ro (hēr′ō), *n., pl.* -**roes;** for 4 also -**ros. 1.** a man who has performed brave deeds. **2.** any person admired for noble qualities or special achievements. **3.** the principal male character in a story, play, etc. **4.** HERO SANDWICH. —**her′oine** (her′ ō in), *n.* —**he·ro′ic** (hi rō′ik), *adj.*

her·o·in (her′ō in), *n.* a white crystalline powder, derived from morphine, that is narcotic and addictive.

her·on (her′ən), *n.* any of various long-legged, long-necked wading birds, usu. having a spearlike bill.

he′ro sand′wich *n.* a large sandwich consisting of a small loaf of bread filled with various meats, cheese, etc.

her·pes (hûr′pēz), *n.* any of several viral diseases characterized by eruption of blisters on the skin or mucous membranes.

her·ring (her′ing), *n., pl.* -**rings, -ring.** an important food fish of the N Atlantic.

her′ring·bone′ *n.* **1.** a pattern consisting of adjoining vertical rows of slanting lines, any two contiguous lines forming a V or inverted V. **2.** a fabric with this pattern.

hers (hûrz), *pron.* **1.** a form of the possessive case of SHE, used as a predicate adjective: *The red umbrella is hers.* **2.** that or those belonging to her: *Hers are the red ones.*

her·self′ *pron.* **1.** the reflexive form of HER: *She supports herself.* **2.** an intensive form of SHE: *She herself wrote the letter.* **3.** her normal self: *After some rest, she will be herself again.*

hertz (hûrts), *n., pl.* **hertz, hertz·es.** a unit of frequency equal to one cycle per second.

hes·i·tate′ (-tāt′), *v.i.,* -**tat·ed, -tat·ing. 1.** to wait to act because of fear, indecision, or disinclination. **2.** to be unwilling; have reservations. **3.** to pause. **4.** to falter in speaking. —**hes′i·tat′ing·ly,** *adv.* —**hes′i·ta′tion,** *n.*

het·er·o·dox (het′ər ə doks′), *adj.* not in accordance with established doctrines, esp. in theology. —**het′er·o·dox′y,** *n., pl.* -**ies.**

het′er·o·ge′ne·ous (-jē′nē əs), *adj.* **1.** different in kind. **2.** composed of parts of different kinds. —**het′er·o·ge′ne·ous·ness,** *n.* —**het′er·o·ge′ne·ous·ly,** *adv.*

het′er·o·sex′u·al *adj.* **1.** of or having sexual desire for persons of the opposite sex. **2.** pertaining to the opposite sex or to both sexes. —*n.* **3.** a heterosexual person. —**het′er•o•sex′u•al′i•ty,** *n.*

hew (hyōō; *often* yōō), *v.*, **hewed, hewed** or **hewn, hew•ing.** —*v.t.* **1.** to strike forcibly with a cutting instrument. **2.** to make or shape with or as if with cutting blows. —*v.i.* **3.** to conform: *to hew to the party line.* —**hew′er,** *n.*

hex (heks), *v.t.* **1.** to practice witchcraft on. **2.** to bring bad luck to. —*n.* **3.** a spell; charm; jinx.

hex•a•gon (hek′sə gon′, -gən), *n.* a polygon having six angles and six sides. —**hex•ag′o•nal** (-sag′ə nl), *adj.*

hey•day (hā′dā′), *n.* the period of greatest vigor, success, etc.; prime.

hgt. height.

hgwy. highway.

hi (hī), *interj. Informal.* an exclamation of greeting.

HI Hawaii.

hi•a•tus (hī ā′təs), *n., pl.* **-tus•es, -tus.** a break or interruption in the continuity of a work, series, action, etc.

hi•ba•chi (hi bä′chē), *n., pl.* **-chis.** a small charcoal brazier covered with a grill. [< Japn: fire pot]

hi•ber•nate (hī′bər nāt′), *v.i.,* **-nat•ed, -nat•ing.** to spend the winter in a dormant condition, as certain animals. —**hi′ber•na′tion,** *n.* —**hi′ber•na′tor,** *n.*

hi•bis•cus (hī bis′kəs, hi-), *n., pl.* **-cus•es.** a woody plant of the mallow family, with large, showy flowers.

hic•cup or **-cough** (hik′up, -əp), *n., v.,* **-cuped** or **-cupped** or **-coughed, -cup•ing** or **-cup•ping** or **-cough•ing.** —*n.* **1.** a quick inhalation that follows a spasm of the diaphragm and is checked by closure of the glottis, producing a short, sharp sound. **2.** Usu., **-cups.** the condition of having such spasms. —*v.i.* **3.** to make the sound of a hiccup.

hick (hik), *n.* an unsophisticated, provincial person.

hick•o•ry (hik′ə rē), *n., pl.* **-ries.** **1.** a North American tree of the walnut family, bearing edible nuts. **2.** the wood of this tree.

hide¹ (hīd), *v.,* **hid, hid•den** or **hid, hid•ing.** —*v.t.* **1.** to conceal from sight. **2.** to obstruct the view of. **3.** to keep secret. —*v.i.* **4.** to conceal oneself. **5.** to lie concealed. —**hid′er,** *n.*

hide² (hīd), *n.* the raw or dressed pelt or skin of a large animal.

hide′a•way′ *n.* a place to which a person can retreat.

hide′bound′ *adj.* narrow and rigid in opinion.

hid•e•ous (hid′ē əs), *adj.* **1.** horrible or frightful to the senses. **2.** shocking to the moral sense. —**hid′e•ous•ly,** *adv.* —**hid′e•ous•ness,** *n.*

hide′out′ *n.* a safe place for hiding, esp. from the law.

hi•er•ar•chy (hī′ə rär′kē), *n., pl.* **-chies.** **1.** any system of persons or things ranked one above another. **2.** government by ecclesiastical rulers. —**hi′er•ar′chi•cal, hi′er•ar′chic,** *adj.* —**hi′er•ar′chi•cal•ly,** *adv.*

hi•er•o•glyph•ic (hī′ər ə glif′ik, hī′rə-), *adj.* **1.** of or designating a pictographic script, as that of the ancient Egyptians, in which many of the symbols are conventionalized pictures of the things represented. —*n.* **2.** a hieroglyphic symbol. **3. hieroglyphics,** symbols that are difficult to decipher.

hi-fi (hī′fī′), *n., pl.* **-fis.** **1.** high fidelity. **2.** a phonograph, radio, etc., possessing high fidelity.

high (hī), *adj. and adv.,* **-er, -est,** *n.* —*adj.* **1.** lofty; tall. **2.** having a specified height. **3.** situated above the ground or some base. **4.** greater than usual or normal in degree, force, etc.: *high speed.* **5.** expensive; costly. **6.** exalted, as in rank or station. **7.** elevated in pitch: *high notes.* **8.** extending to or performed from an elevation: *a high dive.* **9.** important; grave: *high crimes.* **10.** elated: *high spirits.* **11.** luxurious: *high living.* **12.** under the influence of alcohol or narcotics. **13.** advanced to the utmost extent: *high tide.* **14.** haughty or arrogant. —*adv.* **15.** at or to a high point, place, or level. **16.** luxuriously; extravagantly. —*n.* **17.** an automotive transmission gear producing the highest speed. **18.** an atmos-

pheric pressure system characterized by high pressure at its center. **19.** a high point, place, or level. **20.** a euphoric state induced by or as if by alcohol or narcotics. —*Idiom.* **21. high and low,** everywhere. **22. high on,** enthusiastic about. **23. on high, a.** above. **b.** in heaven. —**high′ly,** *adv.*

high′ball′ *n.* a drink of whiskey mixed with club soda or ginger ale.

high′brow′ *n.* **1.** a person who has or affects superior intellectual or cultural interests and tastes. —*adj.* **2.** of or characteristic of a highbrow.

high′ fidel′ity *n.* sound reproduction over the full range of audible frequencies with little distortion of the original signal.

high′-flown′ *adj.* **1.** extravagant in aims, pretensions, etc. **2.** pretentiously lofty.

high′ fre′quency *n.* the range of frequencies in the radio spectrum between 3 and 30 megahertz.

high′-hand′ed *adj.* overbearing and arbitrary; presumptuous. —**high′-hand′ed•ly,** *adv.* —**high′-hand′ed•ness,** *n.*

High′lands *n.* **the,** a mountainous region in N Scotland. —**high′land•er,** *n.*

high′light′ *v.t.* **1.** to make prominent. **2.** to create highlights in. —*n.* **3.** an important or conspicuous event, scene, etc. **4.** an area of contrasting lightness or brightness. —**high′light′er,** *n.*

high′-mind′ed *adj.* having or showing exalted principles or feelings; noble. —**high′-mind′ed•ly,** *adv.* —**high′-mind′ed•ness,** *n.*

high′ness (-nis), *n.* **1.** the quality or state of being high. **2.** (*cap.*) a title given to members of a royal family (usu. prec. by *His, Your,* etc.).

high′-pres′sure *adj., v.,* **-sured, -sur•ing.** —*adj.* **1.** involving a pressure above the normal. **2.** involving a high degree of stress. **3.** persistent; aggressive. —*v.t.* **4.** to use aggressively forceful tactics on.

high′-rise′ *adj.* **1.** (of a building) having a comparatively large number of stories. —*n.* **2.** a high-rise building.

high′road′ *n.* **1.** *Chiefly Brit.* HIGHWAY. **2.** an easy or certain course.

high′ school′ *n.* a school consisting of grades 9 or 10 through 12.

high sea *n. Usu.,* **high seas.** open ocean, esp. beyond territorial waters.

high′-spir′ited *adj.* **1.** characterized by energetic enthusiasm. **2.** boldly courageous.

high′-strung′ *adj.* being highly sensitive or nervous.

high′-tech′ *n.* **1.** high technology. **2.** a style of interior design using industrial and commercial fixtures, materials, etc. —*adj.* **3.** of or suggesting high-tech.

high′ technol′ogy *n.* technology that uses highly sophisticated equipment and advanced engineering techniques.

high′-ten′sion *adj.* subjected to or operating under relatively high voltage: *high-tension wire.*

high′way′ *n.* **1.** a main road, esp. one between towns or cities. **2.** any public road.

high′way′man *n., pl.* **-men.** a holdup man who robbed travelers along a public road.

hi•jack (hī′jak′), *v.t.* **1.** to seize (an airplane or other vehicle in transit) by threat or force. **2.** to steal (cargo) from a vehicle in transit. —**hi′jack′er,** *n.*

hike (hīk), *v.,* **hiked, hik•ing,** *n.* —*v.i.* **1.** to walk a great distance, esp. through rural areas. —*v.t.* **2.** to move or raise with a jerk: *to hike up one's socks.* **3.** to increase, often sharply: *to hike the price of milk.* —*n.* **4.** a long walk. **5.** a sharp increase. —**hik′er,** *n.*

hi•lar•i•ous (hi lâr′ē əs, -lar′-, hī-), *adj.* **1.** very funny. **2.** boisterously merry. —**hi•lar′i•ous•ly,** *adv.* —**hi•lar′i•ty,** *n.*

hill (hil), *n.* **1.** a natural elevation of the earth's surface, smaller than a mountain. **2.** an artificial heap, pile, or mound. —**hill′y,** *adj.,* **-i•er, -i•est.**

hill′bil′ly (-bil′ē), *n., pl.* **-lies.** *Informal.* a person from a backwoods area. [*hill* + *Billy,* familiar form of William]

hill•ock (hil′ək), *n.* a small hill.

hilt (hilt), *n.* the handle of a sword, dagger, or tool.

him (him), *pron.* the objective case of HE, used as a direct or indirect object.

him•self (him self'; *medially often* im-), *pron.* **1.** the reflexive form of HIM: *He cut himself.* **2.** an intensive form of HE: *He himself told me.* **3.** his normal self: *He is himself again.*

hind¹ (hīnd), *adj.* situated in the rear; posterior.

hind² (hīnd), *n., pl.* **hinds, hind.** the female of the European red deer.

Hind. **1.** Hindu. **2.** Hindustan.

hin•der¹ (hin'dər), *v.t.* **1.** to cause delay or difficulty in; hamper; impede. **2.** to prevent from doing or happening. **—hin'der•er,** *n.*

hind•er² (hīn'dər), *adj.* situated at the rear; posterior.

hind'most' (hīnd'-), *adj.* nearest the rear.

hind'sight' *n.* recognition of the nature or requirements of a situation or event after its occurrence.

Hin•du (hin'dōō), *n., pl.* **-dus,** *adj.* **—n. 1.** an adherent of Hinduism. **—adj. 2.** of Hindus or Hinduism.

Hin'du•ism *n.* the dominant religion of India.

Hin'du•stan' (-stän'), *n.* **1.** a region of N India. **2.** the predominantly Hindu areas of India.

hinge (hinj), *n., v.,* **hinged, hing•ing. —n. 1.** a jointed device on which a door, lid, etc., moves. **2.** a natural anatomical joint, as that of the knee. **—v.i. 3.** to be contingent: *Everything hinges on her decision.* **—v.t. 4.** to attach by or as if by a hinge.

hint (hint), *n.* **1.** an indirect, covert, or helpful suggestion. **2.** a very slight amount. **—v.t., v.i. 3.** to give a hint (of). **—hint'er,** *n.*

hin•ter•land (hin'tər land'), *n.* **1.** the remote area of a country. **2.** the land lying behind a coastal region.

hip¹ (hip), *n.* the projecting part on each side of the body surrounding the hip joint.

hip² (hip), *n.* the fleshy fruit of a rose.

hip³ (hip), *adj.,* **hip•per, hip•pest.** *Slang.* **1.** familiar with the latest ideas, styles, etc. **—Idiom.** **2.** **hip to,** knowledgeable about.

hip'-hop' *n. Slang.* the popular subculture of usu. black urban youth, esp. as characterized by rap music.

hip•pie (hip'ē), *n., pl.* **-pies.** a young person of the 1960s who rejected established social values and wore long hair and unconventional clothes.

hip•po (hip'ō), *n., pl.* **-pos.** a hippopotamus.

hip•po•drome (hip'ə drōm'), *n.* an arena for equestrian and other spectacles.

hip•po•pot•a•mus (hip'ə pot'ə məs), *n., pl.* **-mus•es, -mi** (-mī'). a large African mammal with a thick body and short legs, living in and alongside rivers. [< L < Gk *hippopótamos* river horse]

hire (hīªr), *v.,* **hired, hir•ing,** *n.* **—v.t. 1.** to engage the services of (a person) for a fee. **2.** to engage the temporary use of (a thing) at a set price. **—n. 3.** the act of hiring or condition of being hired. **4.** the price or compensation paid in hiring.

hire'ling (-ling), *n.* a person who works only for pay, esp. in a menial or boring job.

hir•sute (hûr'sōōt, hûr sōōt'), *adj.* hairy; shaggy. **—hir'sute•ness,** *n.*

his (hiz; *unstressed* iz), *pron.* **1.** the possessive form of HE, used as an attributive or predicate adjective. **2.** that or those belonging to him: *His is the blue one.*

His•pan•ic (hi span'ik), *adj.* **1.** of Spain or Spanish-speaking countries. **2.** of Hispanics. **—n. 3.** a U.S. citizen or resident of Spanish or Latin-American descent.

hiss (his), *v.i.* **1.** to make a sound like that of the letter *s* when prolonged. **2.** to express disapproval by making this sound. **—v.t. 3.** to express disapproval of by hissing. **—n. 4.** a hissing sound.

his•ta•mine (his'tə mēn', -min), *n.* an organic compound released from human tissues during allergic reactions.

his•tor•ic (-stôr'ik, -stor'-), *adj.* **1.** well-known or important in history. **2.** HISTORICAL.

his•tor'i•cal *adj.* **1.** of or concerned with history. **2.** based on history or documented material from the past. **3.** HISTORIC. **—his•tor'i•cal•ly,** *adv.*

his•to•ry (his'tə rē, -trē), *n., pl.* **-ries. 1.** the branch of knowledge dealing with past events. **2.** a systematic narrative of past events as relating to a particular people, country, etc. **3.** the record of past events. **4.** a past notable for its important events: *a ship with a history.*

his'tri•on'ics *n.* (*used with a sing. or pl. v.*) **1.** overly dramatic behavior or speech. **2.** dramatic representation.

hit (hit), *v.,* **hit, hit•ting,** *n.* **—v.t. 1.** to deal a blow to. **2.** to come against with an impact. **3.** to reach with a missile, weapon, etc. **4.** *Baseball.* to make (a base hit). **5.** to drive or propel by a stroke: *to hit a ball.* **6.** to have a marked effect on: *to be hit hard by inflation.* **7.** to reach (a specified level or amount): *Prices hit a new high.* **8.** to come upon: *to hit the right answer.* **9.** *Informal.* to begin to travel on: *Let's hit the road.* **—v.i. 10.** to strike; deal a blow. **11.** to come into collision. **12.** to come or light: *to hit on a new method.* **—n. 13.** a collision. **14.** a stroke that reaches an object; blow. **15.** BASE HIT. **16.** a success. **17.** *Slang.* a dose of a narcotic drug. **18.** *Slang.* a murder. **19. a.** an instance of successfully locating an item of data in the memory bank of a computer. **b.** an instance of accessing a Web site. **—Idiom. 20. hit it off,** to get along. **—hit'ter,** *n.*

hitch¹ (hich), *v.t.* **1.** to fasten or harness by means of a hook, rope, etc. **2.** to raise with jerks: *to hitch up one's trousers.* **3.** *Slang.* to unite in marriage. **—v.i. 4.** to become fastened. **5.** to move jerkily. **—n. 6.** any of various knots or loops made to attach a rope to something. **7.** a period of military service. **8.** an unexpected difficulty, delay, etc. **9.** a jerk or pull. **10.** a fastening; catch.

hitch² (hich), *n. Informal.* hitchhike. **—hitch'er,** *n.*

hitch'hike' *v.i.,* **-hiked, -hik•ing.** to travel by soliciting rides from passing vehicles. **—hitch'hik'er,** *n.*

hith•er (hith'ər), *adv.* **1.** to or toward this place. **—adj. 2.** being on this side.

hith'er•to' *adv.* until now.

HIV *n.* a retrovirus that invades and inactivates T cells and is a cause of AIDS. [*h(uman) i(mmunodeficiency) v(irus)*]

hive (hīv), *n., v.,* **hived, hiv•ing. —n. 1.** a shelter for a colony of honeybees. **2.** the bees inhabiting a hive. **3.** a place swarming with busy occupants. **4.** a swarming multitude. **—v.t. 5.** to gather into a hive. **—v.i. 6.** (of bees) to enter a hive.

hives (hīvz), *n.* (*used with a sing. or pl. v.*) a transient eruption of large, itchy swellings on the skin.

HMO *pl.* **HMOs, HMO's.** health maintenance organization: a prepaid health plan in which subscribers receive comprehensive health services from member physicians, usually in a central facility.

HMS or **H.M.S.,** Her (or His) Majesty's Ship.

hoa'gie or **-gy** (hō'gē) *n.* HERO SANDWICH.

hoard (hôrd), *n.* **1.** a supply that is hidden or carefully guarded for future use. **—v.t., v.i. 2.** to accumulate a hoard (of). **—hoard'er,** *n.*

hoar•frost (hôr'frôst', -frost'), *n.* FROST (def. 2).

hoarse (hôrs), *adj.,* **hoars•er, hoars•est. 1.** having a low and harsh vocal tone; husky. **2.** having a raucous voice. **—hoarse'ly,** *adv.* **—hoarse'ness,** *n.*

hoar•y (hôr'ē), *adj.,* **-i•er, -i•est. 1.** gray or white with age. **2.** ancient or venerable. **—hoar'i•ness,** *n.*

hoax (hōks), *n.* **1.** something intended to deceive or defraud. **—v.t. 2.** to deceive by a hoax. **—hoax'er,** *n.*

hob•ble (hob'əl), *v.,* **-bled, -bling,** *n.* **—v.i. 1.** to walk lamely. **—v.t. 2.** to cause to limp. **3.** to fasten together the legs of (a horse, mule, etc.) by a short rope to prevent free motion. **4.** to impede. **—n. 5.** a limp. **6.** a rope, strap, etc., used to hobble an animal. **—hob'bler,** *n.*

hob•by (hob'ē), *n., pl.* **-bies. 1.** an activity pursued for pleasure, not as an occupation. **2.** a child's hobbyhorse. **—hob'by•ist,** *n.*

hob'by•horse' *n.* **1.** a stick with a horse's head, or a rocking horse, ridden by children. **2.** a pet idea or project.

hob'gob'lin *n.* **1.** something causing superstitious fear. **2.** a mischievous goblin.

hob′nob′ (-nob′), *v.i.*, **-nobbed, -nob•bing.** to associate on very friendly terms.

ho•bo (hō′bō), *n., pl.* **-bos, -boes. 1.** a tramp or vagrant. **2.** a migratory worker.

hock[1] (hok), *n.* the joint in the hind leg of a horse, cow, etc., corresponding to the ankle in humans.

hock[2] (hok), *v.t.* **1.** to pawn. —*n.* **2.** the state of being held as security. **3.** the condition of owing.

hock•ey (hok′ē), *n.* **1.** ICE HOCKEY. **2.** FIELD HOCKEY.

hock′shop′ *n.* PAWNSHOP.

ho•cus-po•cus (hō′kəs pō′kəs), *n.* **1.** meaningless words used in conjuring. **2.** a sleight of hand. **3.** mysterious talk for covering up a deception. [pseudo-Latin rhyming formula used by magicians]

hod (hod), *n.* **1.** a portable trough for carrying bricks, mortar, etc., on the shoulder. **2.** a coal scuttle.

hodge•podge (hoj′poj′), *n.* a heterogeneous mixture; jumble.

hoe (hō), *n., v.,* **hoed, hoe•ing.** —*n.* **1.** a long-handled implement with a thin, flat blade set transversely, used in breaking up the soil and in weeding. —*v.t., v.i.* **2.** to scrape or weed with a hoe. —**ho′er,** *n.*

hog (hôg, hog), *n., v.,* **hogged, hog•ging.** —*n.* **1.** any swine, esp. a domesticated adult swine raised for market. **2.** a selfish, gluttonous, or filthy person. —*v.t.* **3.** to take more than one's share of. —*Idiom.* **4.** go (the) whole hog, to do something thoroughly. **5. live high off (**or **on) the hog,** to live prosperously. —**hog′ger,** *n.* —**hog′gish,** *adj.* —**hog′gish•ly,** *adv.*

hogs′head′ *n.* **1.** a large cask holding from 63 to 140 gallons (238 to 530 liters). **2.** a liquid measure, esp. one equivalent to 63 gallons (238 liters).

hog′wash′ *n.* **1.** refuse given to hogs; swill. **2.** nonsense; bunk.

hog′-wild′ *adj.* wildly enthusiastic.

hoi pol•loi (hoi′ pə loi′), *n.* the common people; the masses. [< Gk: the many]

hoist (hoist), *v.t.* **1.** to raise or lift, esp. by some mechanical appliance. —*n.* **2.** an apparatus for hoisting, as a crane. **3.** the act of hoisting; a lift.

hok′ey *adj.* **hok•i•er, hok•i•est. 1.** cloyingly sentimental; mawkish. **2.** contrived in an obvious way.

hold[1] (hōld), *v.,* **held, hold•ing,** *n.* —*v.t.* **1.** to have in the hand; grasp. **2.** to bear or support. **3.** to keep in a specified state or relation: *He held them spellbound.* **4.** to conduct: *to hold a meeting.* **5.** to restrain. **6.** to possess or occupy: *to hold office.* **7.** to contain. **8.** to make accountable: *held her to her word.* **9.** to keep in the mind. **10.** to regard; consider: *They held him responsible.* **11.** to keep forcibly: *to hold the fort.* **12.** to decide legally. —*v.i.* **13.** to remain in a specified state or relation: *Hold still.* **14.** to maintain a grasp: *The clamp held.* **15.** to agree; sympathize: *She doesn't hold with new ideas.* **16.** to remain faithful: *to hold to one's purpose.* **17.** to remain valid: *The rule still holds.* **18. hold forth,** to speak at great length. **19. ~ out, a.** to offer. **b.** to last. **c.** to refuse to yield. **d.** *Informal.* to withhold something expected. **20. ~ over, a.** to keep for future consideration. **b.** to keep beyond the arranged period. **21. ~ up, a.** to support. **b.** to delay. **c.** to persevere. **d.** to display. **e.** to rob at gunpoint. —*n.* **22.** a grasp; grip. **23.** something to grasp, esp. for support. **24.** something that holds something else. **25.** a controlling force. **26.** a prison cell. —**hold′er,** *n.*

hold[2] (hōld), *n.* **1.** the cargo space in the hull of a vessel. **2.** the cargo compartment of an aircraft.

hold′ing *n.* **1.** a section of land leased, esp. for agricultural purposes. **2.** Often, **-ings.** legally owned property, as securities.

hold′out′ *n.* one who refuses to take part, give in, etc.

hold′up′ *n.* **1.** a robbery at gunpoint. **2.** a delay.

hole (hōl), *n.* **1.** an opening through something; gap. **2.** a hollow place in a solid mass; cavity. **3.** the burrow of an animal. **4.** a cramped or shabby place. **5.** an embarrassing predicament. **6.** a fault; flaw: *serious holes in your reasoning.* **7.** *Golf.* **a.** the cup in a green into which the ball is to be played.

b. a part of a course leading to it. —*v.t., v.i.* **8.** to make a hole (in). **9. hole up, a.** to hibernate, as in a cave. **b.** to hide from or as if from pursuers. —*Idiom.* **10. in the hole,** in debt.

hol•i•day (hol′i dā′), *n.* **1.** a day on which ordinary business is suspended in commemoration of some event or person. **2.** a religious festival; holy day. **3.** Sometimes, **-days.** *Chiefly Brit.* a vacation. —*adj.* **4.** festive; joyous.

ho′li•ness *n.* **1.** the quality or state of being holy. **2.** (*cap.*) a title of the pope (usu. prec. by *His* or *Your*).

ho•lis•tic (hō lis′tik), *adj.* **1.** pertaining to the theory that whole entities are more than the sum of their parts. **2.** of or using therapies that consider one's total physical and psychological state in the treatment of disease.

hol•low (hol′ō), *adj.,* **-er, -est,** *n., v.* —*adj.* **1.** having a space inside; empty. **2.** having a concavity. **3.** sunken: *hollow cheeks.* **4.** not resonant: *a hollow voice.* **5.** meaningless: *a hollow victory.* **6.** insincere: *hollow compliments.* —*n.* **7.** a hole; cavity. **8.** a valley. —*v.t., v.i.* **9.** to make or become hollow. —**hol′low•ness,** *n.*

hol•ly (hol′ē), *n., pl.* **-lies.** a tree or shrub with glossy leaves and red berries.

hol′ly•hock′ (-hok′, -hôk′), *n.* a tall Asian plant with a long cluster of showy, colored flowers.

hol•o•caust (hol′ə kôst′, hō′lə-), *n.* **1.** a great devastation, esp. by fire. **2. the Holocaust,** the systematic mass slaughter of European Jews by the Nazis.

hol•o•gram (hol′ə gram′, hō′lə-), *n.* a three-dimensional picture produced by recording the patterns of interference formed by a split laser beam on photographic film.

ho•log•ra•phy (hə log′rə fē), *n.* the technique of making holograms.

hol•ster (hōl′stər), *n.* a case for a firearm, attached to a belt, shoulder sling, etc.

ho•ly (hō′lē), *adj.,* **-li•er, -li•est. 1.** recognized as sacred by religious use or authority: *holy ground.* **2.** spiritually pure: *a holy love.* **3.** venerated as sacred: *a holy relic.*

Ho′ly Commun′ion *n.* a Christian sacrament in which the Last Supper of Jesus is commemorated with consecrated bread and wine.

Ho′ly Ghost′ *n.* HOLY SPIRIT.

Ho′ly Spir′it *n.* the third person of the Trinity.

hom•age (hom′ij, om′-), *n.* respect, honor, or reverence given or shown: *to pay homage to one's forebears.*

home (hōm), *n., adj., adv., v.,* **homed, hom•ing.** —*n.* **1.** a house or other place of residence. **2.** the place in which one's domestic affections are centered. **3.** an institution for people with special needs: *a nursing home.* **4.** the place or region where something is native or most common. **5.** a person's native place or country. **6.** headquarters. —*adj.* **7.** of one's home. **8.** principal: *the home office.* —*adv.* **9.** to, toward, or at home. **10.** deep; to the heart: *The truth struck home.* **11.** to the point aimed at: *He drove the nail home.* —*v.i.* **12.** to go or return home. **13.** to proceed toward a specified point: *The missile homed in on the target.* —*Idiom.* **14. at home, a.** in one's home. **b.** at ease. —**home′less,** *adj.*

home′ly *adj.,* **-li•er, -li•est. 1.** unattractive; plain. **2.** simple; unpretentious. —**home′li•ness,** *n.*

home′mak′er *n.* a person who manages a household.

ho•me•op•a•thy (hō′mē op′ə thē), *n.* a method of treating disease by minute doses of drugs that in a healthy person would produce symptoms similar to those of the disease. —**ho′me•o•path′ic** (-ə path′ik), *adj.*

home′ plate′ *n.* the base in baseball at which the batter stands and which a runner must reach safely to score a run.

home′sick′ *adj.* longing for home while away from it. —**home′sick′ness,** *n.*

home′spun′ *adj.* **1.** spun at home. **2.** made of homespun cloth. **3.** plain; simple. —*n.* **4.** a plain-weave cloth made of homespun yarn. **5.** any cloth of similar appearance.

home′stead′ (-sted, -stid), *n.* a family dwelling with its land and buildings.

home′stretch′ *n.* **1.** the straight part of a racetrack from the last turn to the finish line. **2.** the final phase of any endeavor.

hom′ey *adj.*, **hom•i•er, hom•i•est.** comfortably informal and inviting; cozy. —**hom′ey•ness,** *n.*

hom•i•cide (hom′ə sīd′, hō′mə-), *n.* **1.** the killing of one human being by another. **2.** a person who kills another. —**hom′i•cid′al,** *adj.*

hom•i•ly (hom′ə lē), *n.*, *pl.* **-lies. 1.** a sermon. **2.** an admonitory or moralizing discourse. —**hom′i•let′ic** (-let′ik), *adj.*

hom•i•ny (hom′ə nē), *n.* hulled corn from which the bran and germ have been removed.

homo- a combining form meaning same or identical (*homogeneous*).

ho•mo•ge•ne•ous (hō′mə jē′nē əs), *adj.* **1.** composed of parts all of the same kind. **2.** of the same kind or nature. —**ho′mo•ge•ne′i•ty** (-jə nē′i tē), *n.* —**ho′mo•ge′ne•ous•ly,** *adv.*

ho•mog•e•nize (hə moj′ə nīz′, hō-), *v.t.*, **-nized, -niz•ing. 1.** to make homogeneous. **2.** to emulsify the fat globules in (milk), causing them to be distributed throughout. —**ho•mog′e•ni•za′tion,** *n.*

hom•o•graph (hom′ə graf′, -gräf′, hō′mə-), *n.* a word of the same written form as another but of different meaning and origin, whether pronounced the same way or not.

hom•o•nym (hom′ə nim), *n.* **1.** HOMOPHONE. **2.** a word the same as another in sound and spelling but different in meaning. **3.** HOMOGRAPH.

ho•mo•pho•bi•a (hō′mə fō′bē ə), *n.* unreasoning fear or hatred of homosexuals and homosexuality.

hom•o•phone (hom′ə fōn′, hō′mə-), *n.* a word pronounced the same as another but differing in meaning, whether spelled the same way or not.

Ho•mo sa•pi•ens (hō′mō sā′pē ənz), *n.* the species of bipedal primates to which modern humans belong.

ho•mo•sex•u•al (hō′mə sek′shoo̅ əl), *adj.* **1.** of or showing sexual desire toward another person of the same sex. —*n.* **2.** a homosexual person. —**ho′mo•sex′u•al′i•ty,** *n.*

Hon. 1. Honorable. **2.** Honorary.

hon′cho (hon′chō) *n.*, *pl.* **-chos.** *Slang.* a leader or important person.

Hon•du•ras (hon door′əs, -dyoor′-), *n.* a republic in NE Central America. —**Hon•du′ran,** *adj.*, *n.*

hone (hōn), *n.*, *v.*, **honed, hon•ing.** —*n.* **1.** a whetstone for sharpening tools. —*v.t.* **2.** to sharpen on or as if on a hone. —**hon′er,** *n.*

hon•est (on′ist), *adj.* **1.** honorable in principles, intentions, and actions. **2.** gained fairly: *to earn an honest living.* **3.** sincere; frank: *an honest face.* **4.** truthful. —**hon′est•ly,** *adv.* —**hon′es•ty,** *n.*

hon•ey (hun′ē), *n.*, *pl.* **-eys. 1.** a sweet, viscid fluid produced by bees from the nectar collected from flowers. **2.** something sweet or delightful. **3.** *Informal.* sweetheart; darling. —**hon′eyed,** *adj.*

hon′ey•comb′ *n.* **1.** a structure of hexagonal wax cells, formed by bees to store honey, pollen, and their eggs. **2.** anything resembling such a structure. —*adj.* **3.** having the appearance of a honeycomb. —*v.t.* **4.** to cause to be full of holes.

hon′ey•dew′ mel′on *n.* a winter melon with a pale greenish rind and light green flesh.

hon′ey•moon′ *n.* **1.** a vacation taken by a newly married couple. **2.** any new relationship characterized by an initial period of harmony. —*v.i.* **3.** to spend one's honeymoon. —**hon′ey•moon′er,** *n.*

hon′ey•suck′le *n.* an upright or climbing shrub cultivated for its fragrant flowers.

honk (hongk, hôngk), *n.* **1.** the cry of a goose. **2.** any similar sound, as of an automobile horn. —*v.i., v.t.* **3.** to make or cause to make a honk. —**honk′er,** *n.*

hon•or (on′ər), *n.* **1.** honesty or integrity in one's beliefs and actions. **2.** a source of credit or distinction. **3.** high respect. **4.** a token of respect: *the place of honor at the table.* **5.** high public esteem;

glory. **6.** a privilege: *I have the honor of introducing this evening's speaker.* **7.** (*cap.*) a title of respect, as for judges (prec. by *His, Her, or Your*). **8.** chastity. —*v.t.* **9.** to hold in high respect. **10.** to treat with honor. **11.** to confer distinction upon. **12.** to accept or pay (a credit card, check, etc.). —*Idiom.* **13. do the honors,** to act as host. Also, *esp. Brit.,* **hon′our.** —**hon′or•ee′,** *n.*, *pl.* **-ees.** —**hon′or•er,** *n.*

hon′or•a•ble *adj.* **1.** characterized by principles of honor; upright. **2.** worthy of honor. **3.** bringing honor. —**hon′or•a•bly,** *adv.*

hon′or•ar′y (-rer′ē), *adj.* **1.** given for honor only: *an honorary degree.* **2.** holding a position conferred for honor only, without the usual emoluments. —**hon′or•ar′i•ly** (-râr′ə lē), *adv.*

hood¹ (hood), *n.* **1.** a flexible covering for the head and neck, usu. attached to a coat. **2.** something resembling this. **3.** the part of an automobile body covering the engine. —**hood′ed,** *adj.*

hood² (hood, hood), *n. Slang.* a hoodlum.

-hood a suffix meaning: state or condition (*childhood*); character or nature (*likelihood*); a body of persons of a particular class (*priesthood*).

hood•lum (hood′ləm, hood′-), *n.* **1.** a thug or gangster. **2.** a young street ruffian.

hood•wink (hood′wingk′), *v.t.* to deceive or trick.

hoof (hoof, hoof), *n.*, *pl.* **hoofs** or **hooves,** *v.* —*n.* **1.** the horny covering protecting the ends of the digits or encasing the foot in certain animals, as the horse. **2.** the entire foot of a horse, donkey, etc. —*v.t.* **3.** *Slang.* to walk: *Let's hoof it.* —**hoofed,** *adj.*

hook (hook), *n.* **1.** a curved or angular piece of metal, etc., for catching, pulling, or suspending something. **2.** a fishhook. **3.** something having a sharp curve, bend, or angle at one end. **4.** the path described by a ball that curves in a direction opposite to the throwing hand. **5.** (in boxing) a short circular punch delivered with the elbow bent. —*v.t.* **6.** to seize, fasten, or catch hold of with or as if with a hook. **7.** *Slang.* to steal. —*v.i.* **8.** to become hooked. **9.** to curve or bend like a hook. **10. hook up,** to connect, as components of a machine. —*Idiom.* **11. by hook or by crook,** by any means whatsoever. **12. off the hook,** released from some difficulty.

hook′er *n. Slang.* a prostitute.

hook′up′ *n.* an assembly and connection of parts or apparatus into a circuit, network, machine, or system.

hoo•li•gan (hoo′li gən), *n.* a hoodlum.

hoop (hoop, hoop), *n.* **1.** a rigid circular band, as of metal or wood, used esp. for holding together the staves of a barrel. **2.** a circular or ringlike object, part, or figure. —*v.t.* **3.** to fasten with or as if with a hoop.

hoop•la (hoop′lä), *n. Informal.* **1.** commotion. **2.** sensational publicity.

hoo•ray (hoo rā′), *interj.*, *v.i.*, *n.* HURRAH.

hoot (hoot), *v.i.* **1.** to shout in derision. **2.** to utter the cry characteristic of an owl. —*v.t.* **3.** to assail by hooting. —*n.* **4.** the cry of an owl. **5.** a shout of derision. —**hoot′er,** *n.*

hop¹ (hop), *v.*, **hopped, hop•ping,** *n.* —*v.i.* **1.** to make a short, bouncing leap. **2.** to leap on one foot. **3.** to make a short, quick trip. —*v.t.* **4.** to jump over. **5.** to board (a vehicle). —*n.* **6.** a short leap, esp. on one foot. **7.** a short trip, esp. by air. **8.** *Informal.* a dance.

hop² (hop), *n.*, *v.*, **hopped, hop•ping.** —*n.* **1.** a twining plant of the hemp family. **2. hops,** its dried ripe cones, used in brewing, medicine, etc. —*v.* **hop up,** *Slang.* **3.** to excite. **4.** to add to the power of.

hope (hōp), *n.*, *v.*, **hoped, hop•ing.** —*n.* **1.** the feeling that what is wanted can be had or that events will turn out well. **2.** a person or thing in which expectations are centered. **3.** something hoped for. —*v.t.* **4.** to look forward to with desire and reasonable confidence. **5.** to believe or trust: *I hope you will be happy.* —*v.i.* **6.** to have hope. —**hope′ful,** *adj.* —**hope′ful•ly,** *adv.* —**hope′ful•ness,** *n.* —**hope′less,** *adj.* —**hope′less•ly,** *adv.* —**hope′less•ness,** *n.*

Ho•pi (hō′pē), *n.*, *pl.* **-pi, -pis.** a member of an American Indian people of NE Arizona.

hop•per (hop′ər), *n.* **1.** one that hops. **2.** any jumping insect. **3.** a bin in which loose material, as grain, is stored temporarily.

horde (hôrd), *n.*, *v.*, **hord•ed, hord•ing. —***n.* **1.** a large multitude; crowd. **—***v.i.* **2.** to gather in a horde.

ho•ri•zon (hə rī′zən), *n.* **1.** the line that forms the apparent boundary between earth and sky. **2.** Usu. **-zons.** the scope of a person's interest, education, understanding, etc. [< L < Gk *horízōn* (*kýklos*) bounding (circle)]

hor•i•zon•tal (hôr′ə zon′tl, hor′-), *adj.* **1.** at right angles to the vertical; parallel to level ground. **2.** flat or level. **3.** near, on, or parallel to the horizon. **—hor′i•zon′tal•ly,** *adv.*

hor•mone (hôr′mōn), *n.* an internally secreted compound formed in endocrine glands that affects the functions of specifically receptive organs or tissues when transported to them. **—hor•mo′nal,** *adj.*

horn (hôrn), *n.* **1.** one of the hard, usu. paired growths on the head of certain mammals, as goats. **2.** the substance of which horns are composed. **3.** any projection resembling an animal horn. **4.** a brass wind instrument, esp. a French horn. **5.** an instrument for sounding a warning: *an automobile horn.* **—***v.* **6. horn in,** *Informal.* to thrust oneself forward obtrusively. **—***adj.* **7.** made of horn. **—horned,** *adj.* **—horn′less,** *adj.* **—horn′y,** *adj.*, **-i•er, -i•est.**

hor•net (hôr′nit), *n.* a large, stinging social wasp.

horn′pipe′ *n.* a lively jiglike dance, traditionally a favorite of sailors.

hor•o•scope (hôr′ə skōp′, hor′-), *n.* a diagram of the position of planets and the signs of the zodiac, as at the moment of a person's birth, used to predict events in a person's life.

hor•ren•dous (hə ren′dəs), *adj.* dreadful; horrible. **—hor•ren′dous•ly,** *adv.*

hor•ri•ble (hôr′ə bəl, hor′-), *adj.* **1.** causing horror. **2.** extremely unpleasant. **—hor′ri•ble•ness,** *n.* **—hor′ri•bly,** *adv.*

hor′rid (-id), *adj.* **1.** such as to cause horror. **2.** extremely disagreeable. **—hor′rid•ly,** *adv.* **—hor′rid•ness,** *n.*

hor•ror (hôr′ər, hor′-), *n.* **1.** an overwhelming and painful feeling caused by something shocking or terrifying. **2.** anything that causes such a feeling. **3.** a strong aversion. **—hor′ri•fy′,** *v.t.* **-fied, -fy•ing.**

hors d'oeuvre (ôr dûrv′), *n.*, *pl.* **hors d'oeuvre** (ôr dûrv′), **hors d'oeuvres** (ôr dûrvz′, dûrv′). a small portion of food served as an appetizer or as a snack with cocktails. [< F]

horse (hôrs), *n.*, *pl.* **hors•es, horse,** *v.,* **horsed, hors•ing,** *adj.* **—***n.* **1.** a large, solid-hoofed mammal, domesticated for pulling loads and for riding. **2.** a frame with legs on which something is mounted or supported. **—***v.t.* **3.** to provide with a horse. **4.** to set on horseback. **5. horse around,** *Informal.* to fool around. **—***adj.* **6.** of or for a horse. **—***Idiom.* **7. hold one's horses,** *Informal.* to be patient.

horse′hair′ *n.* **1.** hair from the mane or tail of a horse. **2.** a sturdy glossy fabric woven of this hair.

horse′play′ *n.* rough or boisterous play.

horse′pow′er *n.* a unit for computing the power of an engine, equivalent to 550 foot-pounds per second, or 745.7 watts.

horse′rad′ish *n.* **1.** a cultivated plant of the mustard family. **2.** the pungent root of this plant, grated and used as a condiment.

horse′ sense′ *n.* COMMON SENSE.

horse′shoe′ *n.* **1.** a U-shaped metal plate nailed to a horse's hoof to protect it. **2.** something U-shaped. **3. horseshoes,** a game in which horseshoes are tossed at an iron stake to encircle it.

hors′y *adj.*, **-i•er, -i•est. 1.** of or characteristic of a horse. **2.** dealing with or interested in horses or sports involving them.

hor•ti•cul•ture (hôr′ti kul′chər), *n.* the science or art of cultivating flowers, fruits, vegetables, or ornamental plants. **—hor′ti•cul′tur•al,** *adj.* **—hor′ti•cul′tur•ist,** *n.*

ho•san•na (hō zan′ə), *interj.* an exclamation in praise of God.

hose (hōz), *n.*, *pl.* **hos•es** for 1, **hose** for 2, *v.,* **hosed, hos•ing. —***n.* **1.** a flexible tube for conveying a liquid, as water, to a desired point. **2.** (*used with a pl. v.*) stockings or socks. **—***v.t.* **3.** to water, wash, or spray with a hose.

ho•sier•y (hō′zhə rē), *n.* stockings or socks.

hos•pice (hos′pis), *n.* **1.** a shelter for pilgrims, strangers, etc., esp. one kept by a religious order. **2.** a facility for supportive care of the terminally ill.

hos•pi•ta•ble (hos′pi tə bəl, ho spit′ə-), *adj.* **1.** treating guests or strangers warmly and generously. **2.** favorably receptive or open: *hospitable to new ideas.* **—hos′pi•ta•bly,** *adv.*

hos•pi•tal (hos′pi tl), *n.* an institution in which sick or injured persons are given medical or surgical treatment.

hos′pi•tal′i•ty *n.*, *pl.* **-ties.** the friendly treatment of guests or strangers; an act or show of welcome.

host¹ (hōst), *n.* **1.** a person who receives or entertains guests. **2.** an emcee or moderator for a television or radio program. **3.** a living animal or plant from which a parasite obtains nutrition. **—***v.i., v.t.* **4.** to act as host (to).

host² (hōst), *n.* **1.** a multitude or great number. **2.** an army.

Host (hōst), *n.* the bread or wafer consecrated in the celebration of the Eucharist.

hos•tage (hos′tij), *n.* a person given or held as security for the fulfillment of certain conditions or terms.

hos•tel (hos′tl), *n.* an inexpensive, supervised lodging place for young travelers. [< OF < L *hospitāle* guesthouse]

hos•tile (hos′tl; *esp. Brit.* -tīl), *adj.* **1.** of or characteristic of an enemy. **2.** opposed in feeling, action, or character; antagonistic. **—hos′tile•ly,** *adv.* **—hos•til′i•ty,** *n.*, *pl.* **-ties.**

hot (hot), *adj.*, **hot•ter, hot•test. 1.** having a high temperature. **2.** hot or causing a sensation of great bodily heat. **3.** peppery or pungent: *hot mustard.* **4.** showing intense or violent feeling: *a hot temper.* **5.** *Slang.* **a.** lustful. **b.** sexy. **6.** violent or intense: *a hot battle.* **7.** new; fresh: *hot off the press.* **8.** following closely: *hot on the trail.* **9.** *Informal.* very good: *not so hot.* **10.** *Informal.* currently popular. **11.** *Slang.* stolen recently. **12.** *Informal.* performing exceedingly well or rapidly. **13.** actively conducting an electric current: *a hot wire.* **—hot′ly,** *adv.* **—hot′ness,** *n.*

hot′bed′ *n.* **1.** a glass-covered bed of earth heated by electric cables or fermenting manure, for growing plants out of season. **2.** an environment favoring rapid growth, esp. of something unwanted.

hot′-blood′ed *adj.* **1.** excitable; impetuous. **2.** ardent; passionate.

hot′ cake′ *n.* **1.** a pancake. **—***Idiom.* **2. sell like hot cakes,** to be disposed of very quickly.

hot′ dog′ *n.* a frankfurter, esp. one served in a split roll.

hot′-dog′ *v.i.,* **-dogged, -dog•ging.** *Slang.* to perform intricate maneuvers in surfing or skiing.

ho•tel (hō tel′), *n.* a commercial establishment offering lodging to travelers and often having public restaurants, meeting rooms, etc. [< F *hôtel,* OF *hostel* HOSTEL]

hot′ flash′ *n.* a sudden, temporary sensation of heat experienced by some women during menopause.

hot′head′ *n.* an impetuous or short-tempered person. **—hot′head′ed,** *adj.* **—hot′head′ed•ly,** *adv.* **—hot′head′ed•ness,** *n.*

hot′house′ *n.* an artificially heated greenhouse for tender plants.

hot′ line′ *n.* **1.** a direct telecommunications link for immediate communication between heads of state in a crisis. **2.** a telephone number providing direct access to a company, agency, etc., as for information or counseling.

hot′ plate′ *n.* a portable electrical appliance for cooking.

hot′ pota′to *n. Informal.* a situation or issue that is unpleasant or risky to deal with.

hot′ rod′ *n.* an automobile specially built or altered for fast acceleration and increased speed. —**hot′ rod′der,** *n.*

hot′shot′ *n. Slang.* an impressively skillful and often vain person.

hot′ tub′ *n.* a wooden tub, usu. big enough for several persons, filled with hot water.

hot′ wa′ter *n. Informal.* trouble; a predicament.

hound (hound), *n.* **1.** any of several breeds of dogs that pursue game either by sight or scent. **2.** any dog. **3.** an addict or devotee. —*v.t.* **4.** to hunt or track with hounds. **5.** to annoy or persecute relentlessly. —**hound′er,** *n.*

hour (ou³r, ou′ər), *n.* **1.** a period of time equal to ¹⁄₂₄ of a day, equivalent to 60 minutes. **2.** any specific time of day: *What is the hour?* **3.** a customary or usual time: *dinner hour.* **4. hours,** time spent at a workplace or in working. **5.** one unit of academic credit.

hour′glass′ *n.* an instrument for measuring time by the draining of sand or mercury from a top to a bottom glass bulb.

house (*n.* hous; *v.* houz), *n., pl.* **hous•es** (hou′ziz), *v.,* **housed, hous•ing.** —*n.* **1.** a building in which people live. **2.** a household. **3.** (*often cap.*) a family, including ancestors and descendants. **4.** a building for any purpose: *a house of worship.* **5. a.** a theater or the like. **b.** the audience of a theater or the like. **6.** (*often cap.*) a legislative body. **7.** (*often cap.*) a commercial establishment: *a publishing house.* —*v.t.* **8.** to provide shelter or lodging for. **9.** to provide with a place to work or study. **10.** to store; hold: *This casing houses the batteries.* —*Idiom.* **11. keep house,** to maintain a home. **12. on the house,** as a gift from the management. —**house′ful,** *n., pl.* **-fuls.**

house′break′er *n.* a person who breaks into and enters a house with felonious intent. —**house′break′ing,** *n.*

house′bro′ken *adj.* trained to excrete outdoors or to behave appropriately indoors.

house′fly′ *n., pl.* **-flies.** a medium-sized fly, common around human habitations.

house′hold′ *n.* **1.** the people of a house collectively. **2.** a home and its related affairs.

house′hold′er *n.* **1.** a person who owns a house. **2.** the head of a household.

house′hus′band *n.* a married man who stays at home to manage the household.

house′keep′er *n.* a person, often hired, who does or directs the domestic work in a home. —**house′keep′ing,** *n.*

house′plant′ *n.* an ornamental plant that is grown indoors.

house′warm′ing *n.* a party to celebrate a person's or family's move to a new home.

house′wife′ *n., pl.* **-wives.** a married woman who manages her own household as her principal occupation.

house′work′ *n.* the work of cleaning, cooking, etc., done in housekeeping.

hous•ing (hou′zing), *n.* **1.** any lodging or dwelling place. **2.** houses collectively. **3.** the providing of houses or shelter. **4.** anything that covers or protects; casing.

hov•el (huv′əl, hov′-), *n.* a small, mean dwelling.

hov•er (huv′ər, hov′-), *v.i.* **1.** to hang fluttering or suspended in the air. **2.** to wait near at hand. **3.** to waver: *to hover between life and death.*

Hov′er•craft′ *n. Trademark.* a vehicle that can skim over water on a cushion of air.

how (hou), *adv.* **1.** in what way or manner? **2.** to what extent, degree, etc.?: *How difficult was the test?* **3.** in what state or condition? **4.** for what reason?: *How can you talk such nonsense?* **5.** with what meaning?: *How is one to interpret this?* **6.** what?: *How do you mean?* **7.** (used as an intensifier): *How nice!* —*conj.* **8.** the manner or way in which: *I knew how to solve the problem.* **9.** how-

ever: *You can dress how you please.* —*Idiom.* **10. how about,** what is your response to?

how•ev′er *adv.* **1.** nevertheless; yet. **2.** to whatever extent or degree. —*conj.* **3.** in whatever manner or state.

how•itz•er (hou′it sər), *n.* a short-barreled cannon for firing shells at an elevated angle.

howl (houl), *v.i.* **1.** to utter the loud, prolonged, mournful cry of a wolf, dog, etc. **2.** to utter a similar cry, as in pain. **3.** to utter a loud laugh. —*v.t.* **4.** to utter with howls. **5.** to drive or force by howls. —*n.* **6.** the cry of a dog, wolf, etc. **7.** any similar cry or sound. **8.** something that causes a laugh. —**howl′er,** *n.*

how′so•ev′er *adv.* **1.** to whatsoever extent or degree. **2.** in whatsoever manner.

hoy•den (hoid′n), *n.* a boisterous, bold girl; tomboy. —**hoy′den•ish,** *adj.*

HP or **hp,** horsepower.

HQ or **hq,** headquarters.

hr. hour.

H.R. House of Representatives.

H.S. High School.

ht. height.

hub (hub), *n.* **1.** the central part of a wheel, propeller, fan, etc. **2.** a center of activity.

hub•bub (hub′ub), *n.* tumult; uproar.

hu•bris (hyōō′bris, hōō′-), *n.* excessive pride or self-confidence.

huck•le•ber•ry (huk′əl ber′ē), *n., pl.* **-ries. 1.** the dark blue, edible berry of various shrubs of the heath family. **2.** a shrub bearing such fruit.

huck•ster (huk′stər), *n.* **1.** an aggressive seller or promoter. **2.** a peddler, esp. of fruits and vegetables.

HUD (hud), *n.* Department of Housing and Urban Development.

hud•dle (hud′l), *v.,* **-dled, -dling,** *n.* —*v.i., v.t.* **1.** to crowd together closely. **2.** to draw (oneself) together. —*n.* **3.** a closely gathered group or heap. **4.** a close gathering of football players to hear instructions for the next play. **5.** a conference or consultation, esp. a private one.

hue (hyōō), *n.* **1.** a gradation or variety of a color; tint. **2.** color. —**hued,** *adj.*

huff (huf), *n.* **1.** a mood of sulking anger. —*v.i.* **2.** to puff or blow; breathe heavily. —**huff′y,** *adj.,* **-i•er, -i•est.**

hug (hug), *v.,* **hugged, hug•ging,** *n.* —*v.t.* **1.** to clasp tightly in the arms, esp. with affection. **2.** to cling firmly or fondly to: *to hug an opinion.* **3.** to keep close to: *to hug the shore.* —*n.* **4.** a tight clasp with the arms.

huge (hyōōj; *often* yōōj), *adj.,* **hug•er, hug•est.** extraordinarily large; gigantic; enormous. —**huge′ly,** *adv.* —**huge′ness,** *n.*

hu•la (hōō′lə), *n., pl.* **-las.** a Hawaiian native dance with intricate arm movements.

hulk (hulk), *n.* **1.** the body of an old or dismantled ship. **2.** a bulky or unwieldy person or thing.

hulk′ing *adj.* heavy and clumsy.

hull¹ (hul), *n.* **1.** the husk, shell, or outer covering of a seed or fruit. **2.** any covering or envelope. —*v.t.* **3.** to remove the hull of. —**hull′er,** *n.*

hull² (hul), *n.* the hollow, lowermost portion of a ship.

hul•la•ba•loo (hul′ə bə lōō′), *n., pl.* **-loos.** a clamorous noise or disturbance.

hum (hum), *v.,* **hummed, hum•ming,** *n.* —*v.i.* **1.** to make a low, continuous droning sound. **2.** to sing with closed lips, without articulating words. **3.** to be in a state of busy activity. —*v.t.* **4.** to utter by humming. —*n.* **5.** the act or sound of humming. —**hum′mer,** *n.*

hu•man (hyōō′mən; *often* yōō′-), *adj.* **1.** of, characteristic of, or having the nature of people. —*n.* **2.** Also called **hu′man be′ing.** a person. —**hu′man•ness,** *n.*

hu•mane′ (-mān′), *adj.* **1.** characterized by compassion and sympathy for others. **2.** of humanistic studies. —**hu•mane′ly,** *adv.* —**hu•mane′ness,** *n.*

hu′man•ism *n.* **1.** any system of thought in which

human interests, values, and dignity predominate. **2.** (*sometimes cap.*) the study of the cultures of ancient Rome and Greece as pursued by Renaissance scholars. —**hu′man•ist,** *n., adj.* —**hu′man•is′tic,** *adj.*

hu•man′i•tar′i•an (-man′i târ′ē ən), *adj.* **1.** having concern for the welfare of people. —*n.* **2.** a person engaged in promoting human welfare. —**hu•man′i•tar′i•an•ism,** *n.*

hu•man′i•ty *n., pl.* **-ties. 1.** the human race. **2.** the quality or condition of being human or humane. **3. the humanities,** literature, philosophy, art, etc., as distinguished from the sciences.

hu′man•ize′ (-mə nīz′), *v.t., v.i.,* **-ized, -iz•ing.** to make or become human or humane. —**hu′man•i•za′tion,** *n.* —**hu′man•iz′er,** *n.*

hu′man•kind′ *n.* the human race; humanity.

hu′man•ly *adv.* **1.** in the manner of human beings. **2.** within the limits of human capability.

hum•ble (hum′bəl, um′-), *adj.,* **-bler, -blest,** *v.,* **-bled, -bling.** —*adj.* **1.** not proud or arrogant. **2.** low in status, condition, etc. **3.** respectful: *in my humble opinion.* —*v.t.* **4.** to lower in status or condition. **5.** to lower the pride of. —**hum′ble•ness,** *n.* —**hum′bly,** *adv.*

hum•bug (hum′bug′), *n.* **1.** something intended to deceive. **2.** an impostor. —*v.t.* **3.** to deceive; trick. —*interj.* **4.** nonsense!

hum•drum (hum′drum′), *adj.* boring; dull.

hu•mid (hyōō′mid; *often* yōō′-), *adj.* noticeably moist.

hu′mi•dor′ (-mi dôr′), *n.* a container to keep tobacco moist.

hu•mil•i•ate (hyōō mil′ē āt′; *often* yōō-), *v.t.,* **-at•ed, -at•ing.** to cause (a person) a painful loss of pride or self-respect. —**hu•mil′i•at′ing•ly,** *adv.* —**hu•mil′i•a′tion,** *n.*

hu•mil′i•ty *n.* the quality or state of being humble.

hum′ming•bird′ *n.* a tiny, colorful bird with narrow wings that beat very rapidly.

hum•mock (hum′ək), *n.* a knoll or hillock.

hu•mon•gous (hyōō mung′gəs, -mong′-; *often* yōō-), *Slang.* extraordinarily large. [expressive coinage, perh. reflecting *huge* and *monstrous,* with stress pattern of *tremendous*]

hu•mor (hyōō′mər; *often* yōō′-), *n.* **1.** a comic quality causing amusement. **2.** the faculty of perceiving and expressing what is amusing or comical. **3.** comical writing, talk, or actions. **4.** a mood or frame of mind. **5.** a whim. **6.** any animal or plant fluid, as bile. —*v.t.* **7.** to comply with the humor or mood of. Also, *esp. Brit.,* **hu′mour.** —**hu′mor•ist,** *n.* —**hu′mor•less,** *adj.*

hump (hump), *n.* **1.** a rounded protuberance, esp. on the back, as of a camel. **2.** a low, rounded rise of ground. —*v.t.* **3.** to raise (the back) in a hump. —*Idiom.* **4. over the hump,** past the greatest difficulties. —**humped,** *adj.*

hump′back′ *n.* **1.** a back that is humped. **2.** HUNCHBACK. **3.** a large whale with long, narrow flippers. —**hump′backed′,** *adj.*

hu•mus (hyōō′məs; *often* yōō′-), *n.* the dark organic material in soils, produced by the decomposition of vegetable or animal matter.

hunch (hunch), *v.t.* **1.** to thrust out or up in a hump; arch. —*v.i.* **2.** to thrust oneself forward jerkily. —*n.* **3.** a premonition or suspicion.

hunch′back′ *n.* a person whose back is humped because of abnormal spinal curvature. —**hunch′-backed′,** *adj.*

hun•dred (hun′drid), *n., pl.* **-dreds, -dred,** *adj.* —*n.* **1.** a cardinal number, ten times ten. **2.** a symbol for this number, as 100 or C. **3. hundreds,** a number between 100 and 999. —*adj.* **4.** amounting to 100 in number. —**hun′dredth,** *adj., n.*

Hun•gar•i•an (hung gâr′ē ən), *n.* **1.** a native or inhabitant of Hungary. **2.** the language of Hungary. —*adj.* **3.** of Hungary, its people, or their language.

Hun•ga•ry (hung′gə rē), *n.* a republic in central Europe.

hun•ger (hung′gər), *n.* **1.** a compelling need or desire for food. **2.** discomfort caused by the need of

food. **3.** any strong desire or craving. —*v.i.* **4.** to feel hunger. **5.** to have a strong desire. —**hun′gry,** *adj.,* **-gri•er, -gri•est.** —**hun′gri•ly,** *adv.*

hunk (hungk), *n.* **1.** a large piece or lump. **2.** *Slang.* a handsome man with a well-developed physique.

hun•ker (hung′kər), *v.i.* **1.** to squat on one's heels. —*n.* **2. hunkers,** the haunches.

hunt (hunt), *v.t.* **1.** to chase or search for (game) to catch or kill. **2.** to pursue (a person) in order to capture. **3.** to scour (an area) in pursuit of game. **4.** to search for; seek. —*v.i.* **5.** to capture or kill wild animals for food or sport. **6.** to make a search. —*n.* **7.** the act of hunting game. **8.** a search or pursuit. **9.** a group of hunters. —**hunt′er,** *n.* —**hunt′ress,** *n.*

hur•dle (hûr′dl), *n., v.,* **-dled, -dling.** —*n.* **1.** a fencelike barrier over which runners or horses must leap in certain races. **2.** a difficulty to be overcome. —*v.t.* **3.** to leap over. **4.** to master (a difficulty). —**hur′dler,** *n.*

hurl (hûrl), *v.t.* **1.** to throw with great force. **2.** to throw down. **3.** to utter with vehemence. —**hurl′er,** *n.*

hurl•y-burl•y (hûr′lē bûr′lē), *n.* noisy disorder and confusion.

hur•rah (hə rä′, -rô′) also **-ray** (-rā′), *interj.* **1.** an exclamation of joy, exultation, encouragement, etc. —*v.i.* **2.** to shout "hurrah." **3.** an exclamation of "hurrah."

hur•ri•cane (hûr′i kān′, hur′-), *n.* a violent, tropical, cyclonic storm, esp. of the W North Atlantic. [< Sp *huracán* < Taino (West Indian language)]

hur•ry (hûr′ē, hur′ē), *v.,* **-ried, -ry•ing,** *n., pl.* **-ries.** —*v.i.* **1.** to move or act with haste. —*v.t.* **2.** to cause to move or act with speed. **3.** to hasten; urge forward. **4.** to impel or perform with undue haste; rush. —*n.* **5.** a state of urgency or eagerness. **6.** hurried movement or action. —**hur′ried•ly,** *adv.*

hurt (hûrt), *v.,* **hurt, hurt•ing,** *n., adj.* —*v.t.* **1.** to cause injury to or pain. **2.** to affect adversely; harm. **3.** to offend. —*v.i.* **4.** to feel or suffer pain. **5.** to cause pain, damage, or distress. —*n.* **6.** something that hurts, as a wound. **7.** injury, damage, or harm. —*adj.* **8.** injured or damaged. —**hurt′ful,** *adj.*

hur•tle (hûr′tl), *v.i., v.t.,* **-tled, -tling.** to move or fling with great speed or force.

hus•band (huz′bənd), *n.* **1.** a married man. —*v.t.* **2.** to manage with economy.

hus′band•ry *n.* **1.** the cultivation of crops and the raising of livestock. **2.** careful or thrifty management.

hush (hush), *interj.* **1.** a command to be silent or quiet. —*v.i.* **2.** to become silent or quiet. —*v.t.* **3.** to make silent. **4.** to suppress mention of. **5.** to calm or quiet. —*n.* **6.** silence or quiet.

husk (husk), *n.* **1.** the dry external covering of certain fruits or seeds, esp. of an ear of corn. **2.** the outer part of anything, esp. when dry or worthless. —*v.t.* **3.** to remove the husk from. —**husk′er,** *n.*

husk•y¹ *adj.,* **-i•er, -i•est. 1.** big and strong. **2.** (of the voice) somewhat hoarse. —**husk′i•ly,** *adv.* —**husk′i•ness,** *n.*

husk•y² *n., pl.* **-ies.** (*sometimes cap.*) a sturdy dog of arctic regions, used for pulling sleds.

hus•sy (hus′ē, huz′ē), *n., pl.* **-sies. 1.** a disreputable woman. **2.** a mischievous or impudent girl.

hus•tle (hus′əl), *v.,* **-tled, -tling,** *n.* —*v.i.* **1.** to proceed or work rapidly or energetically. **2.** to push or force one's way. **3.** to be aggressive or unethical in making money. —*v.t.* **4.** to force roughly or hurriedly. **5.** to urge or speed up. **6.** to obtain or sell by aggressive and often illicit means. **7.** to jostle or push roughly. —*n.* **8.** energetic activity. **9.** the act of hustling.

hus′tler *n. Slang.* **1.** a person eager for success. **2.** a swindler. **3.** a prostitute.

hut (hut), *n.* a small or humble dwelling of simple construction.

hutch (huch), *n.* **1.** a pen or coop for small animals. **2.** a chestlike cabinet with open shelves above. **3.** a small cottage.

hwy. highway.

hy•a•cinth (hī′ə sinth), *n.* a plant of the lily family, with a cylindrical cluster of colorful flowers.

hy•brid (hī′brid), *n.* **1.** the offspring of two animals or plants of different breeds, varieties, or species. **2.** anything derived from unlike sources or composed of disparate elements. —*adj.* **3.** of or characteristic of a hybrid. —**hy′brid•ism,** *n.*

hy′brid•ize′ *v.i., v.t.,* **-ized, -iz•ing.** to produce or cause to produce hybrids. —**hy′brid•i•za′tion,** *n.*

hy•dran•gea (hī drān′jə), *n., pl.* **-geas.** a shrub with large flower clusters of white, pink, or blue.

hy•drant (hī′drənt), *n.* an upright pipe with an outlet for drawing water from a water main.

hy•drau•lic (hī drô′lik, -drol′ik), *adj.* **1.** operated by water or other liquid under pressure. **2.** of hydraulics. —**hy•drau′li•cal•ly,** *adv.*

hy•drau′lics *n.* the science that deals with the laws governing water or other liquids in motion and their applications in engineering.

hydro-¹, a combining form meaning water (*hydroplane*).

hydro-², a combining form representing HYDROGEN (*hydrocarbon*).

hy•dro•car•bon (hī′drə kär′bən), *n.* any of a class of compounds containing only hydrogen and carbon, as methane.

hy′dro•e•lec′tric *adj.* pertaining to the generation and distribution of electricity derived from the energy of falling water. —**hy′dro•e•lec•tric′i•ty,** *n.*

hy•dro•foil (hī′drə foil′), *n.* **1.** a winglike structure that lifts the hull of a moving boat out of water when traveling at high speed. **2.** a boat with hydrofoils.

hy•dro•gen (hī′drə jən), *n.* a colorless, odorless, flammable gas, the lightest of the elements. *Symbol:* H; *at. wt.:* 1.00797; *at. no.:* 1. —**hy•drog′e•nous** (-droj′ə nəs), *adj.*

hy•dro•gen•ate (hī′drə jə nāt′, hī droj′ə-), *v.t.,* **-at•ed, -at•ing.** to combine with or treat with hydrogen. —**hy′dro•gen•a′tion,** *n.*

hy′drogen bomb′ *n.* a bomb, more powerful than an atomic bomb, that derives its explosive energy from the thermonuclear fusion reaction of hydrogen isotopes.

hy′drogen perox′ide *n.* a colorless liquid used as an antiseptic and a bleaching agent.

hy•drol′y•sis (-ə sis), *n., pl.* **-ses** (-sēz′). decomposition in which a compound is split into other compounds by reacting with water.

hy•dro•pho•bi•a (hī′drə fō′bē ə), *n.* **1.** an abnormal dread of water. **2.** RABIES. [< LL < Gk: horror of water]

hy′dro•plane′ *n.* **1.** a seaplane. **2.** a light, high-powered speedboat designed to plane along the surface of the water.

hy′dro•ther′a•py *n.* the use of water in the treatment of disease or injury.

hy•e•na (hī ē′nə), *n., pl.* **-nas.** a large carnivore of Africa and S Asia, feeding chiefly on carrion.

hy•giene (hī′jēn), *n.* **1.** the application of scientific knowledge to the preservation of health. **2.** a condition or practice conducive to health, as cleanliness. —**hy′gi•en′ic** (-jē en′ik, -jen′-, -jē′nik), *adj.* —**hy′gi•en′i•cal•ly,** *adv.* —**hy′gien•ist** (-jē′nist, -jen′ist), *n.*

hy•grom•e•ter (hī grom′i tər), *n.* any instrument for measuring the water-vapor content of the atmosphere. —**hy•grom′e•try,** *n.*

hy•men (hī′mən), *n.* a fold of mucous membrane partly closing the external orifice of the vagina in a virgin.

hymn (him), *n.* a song in praise of God, a nation, etc.

hym•nal (him′nl), *n.* a book of hymns. Also called **hymn′book′.**

hype (hīp), *v.,* **hyped, hyp•ing,** *n. Informal.* —*v.t.* **1.** to stimulate or agitate. **2.** to create interest in by flamboyant methods. —*n.* **3.** intensive or exaggerated promotion. **4.** a flamboyant or questionable claim or method used in advertising.

hy•per (hī′pər), *adj. Informal.* very excitable or nervous.

hyper- a prefix meaning over, above, or excessive (*hypersensitive*).

hy•per•ac•tive (hī′pər ak′tiv), *adj.* **1.** unusually active. **2.** (of children) displaying excessive physical activity. —**hy′per•ac•tiv′i•ty,** *n.*

hy•per•bo•le (hī pûr′bə lē), *n., pl.* **-les.** obvious and intentional exaggeration not intended to be taken literally. —**hy′per•bol′ic** (-pər bol′ik), *adj.*

hy′per•crit′i•cal (hī′pər-) *adj.* excessively critical.

hy•per•gly•ce•mi•a (hī′pər glī sē′mē ə), *n.* an abnormally high level of glucose in the blood. —**hy′per•gly•ce′mic,** *adj.*

hy′per•ten′sion *n.* high blood pressure. —**hy′per•ten′sive,** *adj., n.*

hy′per•text′ *n.* data, as text, graphics, or sound, stored in a computer so that a user can move nonsequentially through a link from one object or document to another.

hy•per•ven′ti•la′tion *n.* prolonged rapid or deep breathing, resulting in excessive oxygen levels in the blood. —**hy′per•ven′ti•late′,** *v.i.,* **-lat•ed, -lat•ing.**

hy•phen (hī′fən), *n.* a short line (-) used to connect the parts of a compound word or the parts of a word divided for any purpose. [< L < Gk: together] —**hy′phen•ate′,** *v.t.,* **-at•ed, -at•ing.**

hyp•no•sis (hip nō′sis), *n., pl.* **-ses** (-sēz). an artificially induced trance, characterized by heightened susceptibility to suggestion. —**hyp′no•tize′,** *v.t.,* **-tized, -tiz•ing.**

hy•po (hī′pō), *n., pl.* **-pos.** a hypodermic syringe or injection.

hypo- a prefix meaning: under or beneath (*hypodermic*); lacking or insufficient (*hypothyroidism*).

hy′po•al′ler•gen′ic *adj.* designed to minimize the likelihood of an allergic response.

hy•po•chon•dri•a (hī′pə kon′drē ə), *n.* an excessive preoccupation with one's health, usu. focusing on some particular symptom. —**hy′po•chon′-dri•ac′,** *n., adj.*

hy•poc•ri•sy (hi pok′rə sē), *n., pl.* **-sies.** the professing of publicly approved qualities, beliefs, or feelings that one does not really possess.

hyp•o•crite (hip′ə krit), *n.* a person who practices hypocrisy. —**hyp′o•crit′i•cal,** *adj.* —**hyp′o•crit′i•cal•ly,** *adv.*

hy•po•der•mic (hī′pə dûr′mik), *adj.* **1.** introduced or injected under the skin. —*n.* **2.** a hypodermic injection. **3.** a hypodermic syringe or needle.

hy•po•gly•ce•mi•a (hī′pō glī sē′mē ə), *n.* an abnormally low level of glucose in the blood. —**hy′po•gly•ce′mic,** *adj.*

hy•pot•e•nuse (hī pot′n ōōs′, -yōōs′), *n.* the side of a right triangle opposite the right angle.

hy•po•ther•mi•a (hī′pə thûr′mē ə), *n.* subnormal body temperature.

hy•poth•e•sis (hī poth′ə sis, hi-), *n., pl.* **-ses** (-sēz′). a provisional theory or assumption set forth to explain some class of phenomena. —**hy′po•thet′i•cal,** *adj.*

hys•ter•ec•to•my (his′tə rek′tə mē), *n., pl.* **-mies.** surgical excision of the uterus.

hys•te•ri•a (hi ster′ē ə, -stēr′-), *n., pl.* **-as.** **1.** a neurosis characterized by violent emotional outbreaks, sensory disturbances, etc. **2.** an uncontrollable emotional outburst, as from fear. —**hys•ter′i•cal,** *adj.* —**hys•ter′i•cal•ly,** *adv.*

hys•ter′ics (-ster′iks) *n.pl.* a fit of hysteria.

Hz hertz.

I, i (ī), *n., pl.* **Is** or **I's, is** or **i's.** the ninth letter of the English alphabet, a vowel.

I (ī), *pron.* the nominative singular pronoun used by a speaker or writer in referring to himself or herself.

I interstate: *I-95.*

I *Symbol.* **1.** the ninth in order or in a series. **2.** (*sometimes l.c.*) the Roman numeral for 1. **3.** *Chem.* iodine.

IA or **Ia.,** Iowa.

i•amb (ī′am, ī′amb), *n.* a prosodic foot of two syllables, an unstressed followed by a stressed one. —**i•am′bic,** *adj.*

i•bex (ī′beks), *n., pl.* **i•bex•es, ib•i•ces** (ib′ə sēz′, ī′bə-), **i•bex.** a wild goat of Eurasia and N Africa, with long, backward-curving horns.

ibid. (ib′id), ibidem.

i•bi•dem (ib′i dəm, i bī′dəm), *adv.* in the same book, chapter, page, etc., previously cited. [< L]

i•bis (ī′bis), *n., pl.* **i•bis•es, i•bis.** a large wading bird of warm regions.

i•bu•pro•fen (ī′byōō prō′fən), *n.* an anti-inflammatory drug, used esp. for reducing local pain and swelling.

ICC Interstate Commerce Commission.

ice (īs), *n., v.,* **iced, ic•ing.** —*n.* **1.** the solid form of water, produced by freezing. **2.** a frozen dessert made of sweetened water and fruit juice. **3.** *Slang.* diamonds. —*v.t.* **4.** to change into ice; freeze. **5.** to cool with ice. **6.** to cover with icing. —*v.i.* **7.** to change to ice. **8.** to become coated with ice: *The windshield has iced up.* —*Idiom.* **9. break the ice,** to overcome reserve or formality. **10. on thin ice,** in a precarious situation. —**iced,** *adj.* —**i′cy,** *adj.,* **i•ci•er, i•ci•est.**

Ice. **1.** Iceland. **2.** Icelandic.

ice′berg (-bûrg), *n.* a large floating mass of ice detached from a glacier and carried out to sea.

ice′box′ *n.* **1.** an insulated cabinet packed with ice, used for cooling food and beverages. **2.** a refrigerator.

ice′ cream′ *n.* a frozen dessert made with cream or milk, sweeteners, and flavoring.

ice′ hock′ey *n.* a game played on ice between two teams, the object being to shoot a puck into the opponents' cage.

Ice′land *n.* an island republic in the N Atlantic between Greenland and Scandinavia. —**Ice′land′er,** *n.*

Ice•lan′dic (-lan′dik), *adj.* **1.** of Iceland, its inhabitants, or their language. —*n.* **2.** the Germanic language of Iceland.

ice′ skate′ *n.* a shoe or boot fitted with a metal blade, used for skating on ice. —**ice′-skate′,** *v.i.,* **-skat•ed, -skat•ing.** —**ice′ skat′er,** *n.*

ich•thy•ol•o•gy (ik′thē ol′ə jē), *n.* the branch of zoology dealing with fishes. —**ich′thy•ol′o•gist,** *n.*

i•ci•cle (ī′si kəl), *n.* a hanging piece of ice formed by the freezing of dripping water.

ic′ing *n.* a mixture, as of sugar, liquid, butter, and flavoring, used to coat cakes, cookies, etc.

i•con (ī′kon), *n.* **1.** a picture, image, or other representation. **2.** (in the Eastern Church) a sacred image of Christ, a saint, etc. **3.** a small graphic image on a computer screen representing a file or a command.

i•con′o•clast′ (-ə klast′), *n.* a person who attacks cherished beliefs or traditional institutions. —**i•con′o•clas′tic,** *adj.*

ICU intensive care unit.

id (id), *n. Psychoanalysis.* the part of the psyche that is the source of unconscious and instinctive impulses.

ID (ī′dē′), *n., pl.* **IDs, ID′s.** a document, card, or other means of identification.

ID or **Id.,** Idaho.

I′d (īd), contraction of *I would* or *I had.*

I.D. **1.** identification. **2.** identity. **3.** Intelligence Department.

i•de•a (ī dē′ə, ī dēə′), *n.* **1.** a conception existing in the mind as a result of mental activity. **2.** an opinion or belief. **3.** a. plan. **4.** a purpose or guiding principle.

i•de•al (ī dē′əl, ī dēl′), *n.* **1.** a conception of something in its perfection. **2.** a standard of perfection. **3.** a person or thing regarded as conforming to such a standard. **4.** an ultimate aim. —*adj.* **5.** conforming to an ideal. **6.** regarded as perfect. **7.** existing only in the imagination. —**i•de′al•ize′,** *v.t.,* **-ized, -iz•ing.**

i•de′al•ism *n.* **1.** the pursuit of one's ideals. **2.** the practice of idealizing. —**i•de′al•ist,** *n.* —**i•de′al•is′tic,** *adj.* —**i•de′al•is′ti•cal•ly,** *adv.*

i•den•ti•cal (ī den′ti kal, i den′-), *adj.* **1.** similar or alike in every way. **2.** the very same. —**i•den′ti•cal•ly,** *adv.*

i•den′ti•fy′ *v.t.,* **-fied, -fy•ing. 1.** to verify the identity of. **2.** to regard as identical. **3.** to associate closely. —**i•den′ti•fi′a•ble,** *adj.*

i•den′ti•ty (-tē), *n., pl.* **-ties. 1.** the state or fact of remaining the same. **2.** the condition of being oneself or itself and not another. **3.** the state or fact of being the same one as described. **4.** the sense of self.

i•de•ol•o•gy (ī′dē ol′ə jē, id′ē-), *n., pl.* **-gies. 1.** the body of doctrine or thought that guides an individual, social movement, institution, or group. **2.** such a body of doctrine or thought forming a political or social program. —**i′de•o•log′i•cal,** *adj.*

id•i•om (id′ē əm), *n.* **1.** an expression whose meaning is not predictable from the usual meanings of its elements. **2.** a language, dialect, or style of speaking peculiar to a people, occupational group, etc. **3.** the manner of expression characteristic of a given language. —**id′i•o•mat′ic,** *adj.* —**id′i•o•mat′i•cal•ly,** *adv.*

id•i•o•syn•cra•sy (id′ē ə sing′krə sē, -sin′-), *n., pl.* **-sies.** a habit or mannerism peculiar to an individual. —**id′i•o•syn•crat′ic** (-ō sin krat′ik, -sing-), *adj.*

id•i•ot (id′ē ət), *n.* **1.** an utterly stupid or foolish person. **2.** (in a former classification of mental retardation) a person having a mental age of less than three years. —**id′i•ot′ic** (-ot′ik), *adj.* —**id′i•ot′i•cal•ly,** *adv.*

i•dle (īd′l), *adj.,* **i•dler, i•dlest,** *v.,* **i•dled, i•dling.** —*adj.* **1.** not working or active. **2.** not filled with activity: *idle hours.* **3.** lazy. **4.** of no real worth: *idle talk.* **5.** having no basis or reason: *idle fears.* —*v.i.* **6.** to pass time doing nothing. **7.** to move aimlessly. **8.** (of a machine, engine, or mechanism) to operate at a low speed. —*v.t.* **9.** to pass (time) doing nothing: *to idle away the afternoon.* **10.** to cause to be idle. —**i′dle•ness,** *n.* —**i′dler,** *n.* —**i′dly,** *adv.*

i•dol (īd′l), *n.* **1.** an image representing a deity and worshiped as such. **2.** a person or thing devotedly admired.

i•dol•a•try (ī dol′ə trē), *n., pl.* **-tries. 1.** the religious worship of idols. **2.** excessive admiration or devotion. —**i•dol′a•ter,** *n.* —**i•dol′a•trous,** *adj.*

i•dyll or **i•dyl** (īd′l), *n.* **1.** a poem or prose composition that describes pastoral scenes or events or any charmingly simple episode. **2.** an episode or scene of charming simplicity. —**i•dyl′lic** (ī dil′ik), *adj.*

IE or **I.E.,** Indo-European.

i.e. that is. [< L *id est*]

if (if), *conj.* **1.** in case that; granting or supposing that; on condition that: *I'll go if you do.* **2.** even though: *an enthusiastic if small audience.* **3.** whether: *She asked if I knew Spanish.*

if'fy adj., **-fi•er, -fi•est.** *Informal.* full of unresolved points or questions. **—if/fi•ness,** n.

ig•loo (ig'lōō), n., pl. **-loos.** an Eskimo dwelling usu. built of blocks of hard snow and shaped like a dome.

ig•ne•ous (ig'nē əs), adj. **1.** produced under intense heat, as rocks of volcanic origin. **2.** of or characteristic of fire.

ig•nite (ig nīt'), v., **-nit•ed, -nit•ing. —v.t. 1.** to set on fire. **—v.i. 2.** to catch fire. **—ig•nit/a•ble, ig•nit/i•ble,** adj. **—ig•ni/tion,** (-nish/ən), n.

ig•no•ble (ig nō'bəl), adj. of low character. **—ig/-no•bil/i•ty, ig•no/ble•ness,** n. **—ig•no/bly,** adv.

ig•no•min•i•ous (ig'nə min'ē əs), adj. **1.** marked by disgrace or dishonor. **2.** bearing or deserving contempt. **—ig/no•min/i•ous•ly,** adv. **—ig/no•min/y,** n.

ig•no•ra•mus (ig'nə rā'məs, -ram'əs), n., pl. **-mus•es.** an extremely ignorant person.

ig•no•rant (ig'nər ənt), adj. **1.** lacking in knowledge, education, or training. **2.** uninformed; unaware. **3.** showing lack of knowledge. **—ig/no•rance,** n. **—ig/no•rant•ly,** adv.

ig•nore (ig nôr'), v.t., **-nored, -nor•ing.** to refrain from noticing or recognizing.

i•gua•na (i gwä'nə), n., pl. **-nas.** a large lizard of tropical America.

IL Illinois.

il-[1], var. of IN-[1] before l.

il-[2], var. of IN-[2] before l.

ilk (ilk), n. family, class, or kind.

ill (il), adj., **worse, worst,** n., adv. **—adj. 1.** of unsound physical or mental health. **2.** objectionable; faulty. **3.** hostile; unkindly: *ill feeling.* **4.** evil; wicked: *of ill repute.* **5.** unfavorable; adverse. **—n. 6.** trouble; misfortune. **7.** evil. **8.** sickness. **—adv. 9.** unsatisfactorily; poorly: *It ill befits a man to betray old friends.* **10.** badly. **11.** with difficulty; scarcely: *an expense we can ill afford.* **—Idiom. 12.** ill at ease, uncomfortable; uneasy.

I'll (īl), contraction of *I will.*

Ill. Illinois.

ill'-bred' adj. unmannerly; rude.

il•le•gal (i lē'gəl), adj. **1.** forbidden by law. **2.** contrary to official rules or regulations. **—il/le•gal/i•ty,** n. **—il•le/gal•ly,** adv.

il•leg•i•ble adj. impossible or hard to read. **—il•leg/i•bil/i•ty,** n. **—il•leg/i•bly,** adv.

il/le•git/i•mate (-mit), adj. **1.** born out of wedlock. **2.** not sanctioned by law or custom. **—il/le•git/i•ma•cy** (-mə sē), n. **—il/le•git/i•mate•ly,** adv.

ill'-fat'ed adj. **1.** destined to an unhappy fate. **2.** bringing bad fortune.

il•lib/er•al adj. narrow-minded; bigoted.

il•lic/it adj. not legally permitted. **—il•lic/it•ly,** adv. **—il•lic/it•ness,** n.

il•lim•it•a•ble (i lim'i tə bəl), adj. not limitable; boundless.

il•lit/er•ate (-it), adj. **1.** unable to read and write. **2.** having little education. **3.** showing lack of culture. **—n. 4.** an illiterate person. **—il•lit/er•a•cy** n.

ill'-man'nered adj. having bad manners.

ill/ness n. **1.** the state of being ill. **2.** a particular ailment; sickness.

il•log/i•cal adj. not logical; unreasonable.

ill'-starred' adj. unlucky; ill-fated.

ill'-treat' v.t. to treat badly. **—ill'-treat'ment,** n.

il•lu•mi•nate (i lōō'mə nāt'), v.t., **-nat•ed, -nat•ing. 1.** to supply with light. **2.** to clarify. **3.** to enlighten. **4.** to decorate (a manuscript or book) with colors and gold or silver. **—il•lu/mi•na/tion,** n.

illus. **1.** illustrated. **2.** illustration.

ill-use (v. il'yōōz'; n. -yōōs'), v., **-used, -us•ing,** n. **—v.t. 1.** to treat badly or unjustly. **—n. 2.** Also, **ill/-us/age.** bad or unjust treatment.

il•lu•sion (i lōō'zhən), n. **1.** something that deceives by producing a false impression of reality. **2.** a misleading perception of visual stimuli.

il•lus•trate (il'ə strāt', i lus'trāt), v.t., **-trat•ed, -trat•ing. 1.** to furnish with drawings, pictures, or other artwork. **2.** to make intelligible with examples or analogies. **—il/lus•tra/tor,** n.

il•lus/tri•ous adj. distinguished; renowned. **—il•lus/tri•ous•ly,** adv. **—il•lus/tri•ous•ness,** n.

ill' will' n. hostile feeling.

I'm (īm), contraction of *I am.*

im-[1], var. of IN-[1] before b, m, p.

im-[2], var. of IN-[2] before b, m, p.

im•age (im'ij), n., v., **-aged, -ag•ing. —n. 1.** a physical likeness or representation of a person, animal, or thing. **2.** an optical counterpart of an object, as is produced by reflection from a mirror. **3.** a mental representation. **4.** form; semblance: *created in God's image.* **5.** counterpart; copy: *That child is the image of his mother.* **6.** a general or public perception, as of a company. **7.** type; embodiment: *He was the image of frustration.* **8.** a figure of speech. **—v.t. 9.** to picture in the mind. **10.** to reflect the likeness of.

im/age•ry n., pl. **-ries. 1.** mental images collectively. **2.** figurative description or illustration.

im•ag•ine (i maj'in), v.t., v.i., **-ined, -in•ing. 1.** to form a mental image of (something not actually present to the senses). **2.** to believe. **3.** to suppose or guess. **—im•ag/i•na/tion,** n.

i•mam/ (i mäm'), n. a Muslim religious leader.

im•bal•ance (im bal'əns), n. the state or condition of lacking balance.

im•be•cile (im'bə sil), n. **1.** (in a former classification of mental retardation) a person having a mental age of seven or eight years. **2.** a stupid person. **—im/be•cil/ic,** adj.

im•bibe (im bīb'), v., **-bibed, -bib•ing. —v.t. 1.** to consume (liquids) by drinking. **2.** to receive into the mind. **—v.i. 3.** to drink, esp. alcoholic beverages. **—im•bib/er,** n.

im•bro•glio (im brōl'yō), n., pl. **-glios. 1.** a complicated misunderstanding or disagreement. **2.** an intricate and perplexing state of affairs.

im•bue (im byōō'), v.t., **-bued, -bu•ing. 1.** to permeate or inspire profoundly: *imbued with patriotism.* **2.** to saturate with moisture or color.

im•i•tate (im'i tāt'), v.t., **-tat•ed, -tat•ing. 1.** to follow as a model or example. **2.** to mimic; impersonate. **3.** to reproduce closely. **4.** to assume the appearance of. **—im/i•ta/tion,** n. **—im/i•ta/tor,** n.

im•mac•u•late (i mak'yə lit), adj. **1.** free from spot or stain. **2.** free from moral blemish. **3.** free from errors. **—im•mac/u•late•ly,** adv. **—im•mac/-u•late•ness,** n.

im•ma•nent (im'ə nənt), adj. **1.** remaining within; inherent. **2.** (of the Deity) indwelling the universe, time, etc. **—im/ma•nence, im/ma•nen•cy,** n. **—im/ma•nent•ly,** adv.

im•ma•te•ri•al (im'ə tēr'ē əl), adj. **1.** not pertinent; unimportant. **2.** incorporeal; spiritual. **—im/-ma•te/ri•al•ly,** adv. **—im/ma•te/ri•al•ness,** n.

im/ma•ture/ adj. **1.** not yet mature or ripe. **2.** emotionally undeveloped; childish. **—im/ma•ture/ly,** adv. **—im/ma•tur/i•ty,** n.

im•meas/ur•a•ble adj. incapable of being measured; limitless. **—im•meas/ur•a•bly,** adv.

im•me/di•ate (-it), adj. **1.** occurring without delay. **2.** following or preceding without a lapse of time. **3.** having no object or space intervening; very close. **4.** of the present time. **5.** without intervening medium or agent. **—im•me/di•ate•ly,** adv.

im•me•mo/ri•al adj. extending back beyond memory, record, or knowledge. **—im/me•mo/ri•al•ly,** adv.

im•mense (i mens'), adj. vast; immeasurable. **—im•mense/ly,** adv. **—im•men/si•ty,** n.

im•merse (i mûrs'), v.t., **-mersed, -mers•ing. 1.** to plunge into or place under a liquid. **2.** to involve deeply; absorb. **3.** to baptize by submerging in the water. **—im•mers/i•ble,** adj. **—im•mer/sion** (-zhən, -shən), n.

im•mi•grant (im'i grənt), n. **1.** a person who immigrates. **2.** an organism found in a new habitat.

im/mi•grate/ (-grāt'), v.i., **-grat•ed, -grat•ing.** to come to a country of which one is not a native, usu. for permanent residence. **—im/mi•gra/tion,** n.

im•mi•nent (im'ə nənt), adj. likely to occur at any moment. **—im/mi•nence,** n. **—im/mi•nent•ly,** adv.

im·mo·bile (i mō′bəl, -bēl) *adj.* **1.** incapable of moving or being moved. **2.** motionless. —**im′mo·bil′i·ty**, *n.* —**im·mo′bi·lize′**, *v.t.*, -**lized, -liz·ing.** —**im·mo/bi·li·za′tion**, *n.*

im·mod′er·ate (-it), *adj.* exceeding just or reasonable limits.

im·mod′est *adj.* **1.** indecent; shameless. **2.** impudent. —**im·mod′est·ly**, *adv.* —**im·mod′es·ty**, *n.*

im·mo·late (im′ə lāt′), *v.t.*, -**lat·ed, -lat·ing.** to kill as a sacrificial victim, as by fire. —**im′mo·la′tion**, *n.*

im·mor′al *adj.* **1.** violating moral principles. **2.** licentious; lascivious. —**im·mor′al·ly**, *adv.*

im·mor′tal *adj.* **1.** not subject to death. **2.** perpetual; everlasting. **3.** remembered through all time. —*n.* **4.** an immortal being. **5.** a person of enduring fame. —**im′mor·tal′i·ty**, *n.* —**im·mor′tal·ly**, *adv.*

im·mov·a·ble (i mōō′və bəl), *adj.* **1.** fixed; stationary. **2.** implacable; unyielding. —**im·mov′a·bil′i·ty**, *n.*

im·mune (i myōōn′), *adj.* **1.** protected from a disease or infection, as by inoculation. **2.** exempt or not susceptible. —**im·mu′ni·ty**, *n.*, *pl.* -**ties.**

immune system *n.* a network of cells and tissues that protects the body from pathogens.

im·mu·nol′o·gy (-nol′ə jē), *n.* the branch of science dealing with immunity, as to a disease. —**im′mu·no·log′ic** (-nl oj′ik), **im′mu·no·log′i·cal**, *adj.* —**im′mu·nol′o·gist**, *n.*

im·mure (i myōōr′), *v.t.*, -**mured, -mur·ing.** to enclose within or as if within walls.

im·mu·ta·ble *adj.* not mutable; unchangeable. —**im·mu·ta·bil′i·ty**, *n.* —**im·mu′ta·bly**, *adv.*

imp (imp), *n.* **1.** a small devil or demon. **2.** a mischievous child.

imp. **1.** imperative. **2.** imperfect. **3.** imperial.

im·pact (*n.* im′pakt; *v.* im pakt′), *n.* **1.** the striking of one thing against another. **2.** influence; effect. **3.** a forcible impinging. —*v.t.* **4.** to drive or press firmly into something. **5.** to collide with. **6.** to have an effect on. —*v.i.* **7.** to make contact forcefully. **8.** to have an effect.

im·pact′ed *adj.* (of a tooth) so confined in its socket as to be incapable of normal eruption.

im·pair (im pâr′), *v.t.* to make worse; weaken; damage. —**im·pair′ment**, *n.*

im·pale (im pāl′), *v.t.*, -**paled, -pal·ing.** to pierce or fix with something pointed. —**im·pale′ment**, *n.* —**im·pal′er**, *n.*

im·pal′pa·ble *adj.* **1.** incapable of being perceived by the sense of touch. **2.** difficult for the mind to grasp readily. —**im·pal′pa·bly**, *adv.*

im·pan′el *v.t.*, -**eled, -el·ing** or (*esp. Brit.*) -**elled, -el·ling.** **1.** to enter on a panel for jury duty. **2.** to select (a jury) from a panel.

im·part (im pärt′), *v.t.* **1.** to make known. **2.** to give; bestow.

im·par′tial *adj.* not partial or biased. —**im·par′ti·al′i·ty** (-shē al′i tē), *n.* —**im·par′tial·ly**, *adv.*

im·pass′a·ble *adj.* not allowing passage.

im·passe (im′pas, im pas′), *n.* **1.** a position or situation from which there is no escape. **2.** a road or way that has no outlet.

im·pas′sioned *adj.* filled with intense feeling or passion.

im·pas′sive *adj.* showing or feeling no emotion. —**im·pas′sive·ly**, *adv.* —**im′pas·siv′i·ty**, *n.*

im·pa′tience *n.* **1.** intolerance of anything that thwarts, delays, or hinders. **2.** eager desire for relief or change. —**im·pa′tient**, *adj.*

im·peach (im pēch′), *v.t.* **1.** to accuse (a public official) of misconduct in office by bringing charges before an appropriate tribunal. **2.** to challenge the credibility of. —**im·peach′a·ble**, *adj.* —**im·peach′er**, *n.* —**im·peach′ment**, *n.*

im·pec·ca·ble (im pek′ə bəl), *adj.* **1.** faultless; flawless. **2.** not liable to sin. —**im·pec′ca·bil′i·ty**, *n.* —**im·pec′ca·bly**, *adv.*

im·pe·cu·ni·ous (im′pi kyōō′nē əs), *adj.* having little or no money. —**im′pe·cu′ni·ous·ly**, *adv.* —**im′pe·cu′ni·ous·ness**, *n.*

im·pede (im pēd′), *v.t.*, -**ped·ed, -ped·ing.** to

slow in movement or progress by means of obstacles or hindrances. —**im·ped′er**, *n.*

im·ped′i·ment (-ped′ə mənt), *n.* **1.** an obstruction; hindrance. **2.** any physical defect that impedes normal or easy speech.

im·pel (im pel′), *v.t.*, -**pelled, -pel·ling.** **1.** to drive or urge forward. **2.** to impart motion to. —**im·pel′ler**, *n.*

im·pend (im pend′), *v.i.* **1.** to be about to happen. **2.** to threaten; menace.

im·pen′e·tra·ble *adj.* **1.** incapable of being penetrated, pierced, or entered. **2.** incapable of being understood. —**im·pen′e·tra·bil′i·ty**, *n.* —**im·pen′e·tra·bly**, *adv.*

im·per′a·tive (im per′ə tiv), *adj.* **1.** absolutely necessary or required. **2.** expressing a command. **3.** of or noting a grammatical mood that is used in commands, exhortations, etc. —*n.* **4.** something imperative. **5.** the imperative mood. —**im·per′a·tive·ly**, *adv.*

im·per′cep′ti·ble *adj.* **1.** very slight, gradual, or subtle. **2.** not perceived by or affecting the senses. —**im′per·cep′ti·bil′i·ty**, *n.* —**im′per·cep′ti·bly**, *adv.*

im·per′fect *adj.* **1.** of or characterized by defects or weaknesses. **2.** lacking completeness. **3.** of or noting a verb tense typically indicating a habitual, repeated, or continuing action or state in the past. —*n.* **4.** the imperfect tense. —**im·per′fect·ly**, *adv.* —**im·per′fect·ness**, *n.*

im·pe·ri·al[1] (im pēr′ē əl), *adj.* **1.** of or characteristic of an empire, emperor, or empress. **2.** characterizing the rule or authority of a sovereign state over its dependencies. **3.** regal; imperious. **4.** of superior size or quality. —**im·pe′ri·al·ly**, *adv.* —**im·pe′ri·al·ness**, *n.*

im·pe·ri·al[2] (im pēr′ē əl), *n.* a small, pointed beard beneath the lower lip.

im·pe′ri·al·ism *n.* the policy of extending the rule or authority of a nation over foreign countries, or of acquiring colonies and dependencies. —**im·pe′ri·al·ist**, *n.*, *adj.* —**im·pe′ri·al·is′tic**, *adj.*

im·per′il *v.t.*, -**iled, -il·ing** or (*esp. Brit.*) -**illed, -il·ling.** to put in peril. —**im·per′il·ment**, *n.*

im·pe·ri·ous (im pēr′ē əs), *adj.* **1.** domineering in a haughty manner. **2.** urgent; imperative. —**im·pe′ri·ous·ly**, *adv.* —**im·pe′ri·ous·ness**, *n.*

im·per′ish·a·ble *adj.* not perishable; enduring. —**im·per′ish·a·bly**, *adv.*

im·per′me·a·ble *adj.* **1.** not permeable or passable. **2.** not permitting the passage of a fluid. —**im·per′me·a·bil′i·ty**, *n.* —**im·per′me·a·bly**, *adv.*

im·per′son·al *adj.* **1.** lacking reference to a particular person. **2.** devoid of human character or traits. **3.** (of a verb) having only third person singular forms, usu. with the pronoun *it* as the subject. —**im·per′son·al·ly**, *adv.*

im·per·son·ate (im pûr′sə nāt′), *v.t.*, -**at·ed, -at·ing.** to assume the character or appearance of. —**im·per′son·a′tion**, *n.* —**im·per′son·a′tor**, *n.*

im·per′ti·nence *n.* **1.** rude presumption. **2.** irrelevance. —**im·per′ti·nent**, *adj.*

im·per·turb·a·ble *adj.* incapable of being upset or agitated. —**im′per·turb·a·bil′i·ty**, *n.* —**im′per·turb′a·bly**, *adv.*

im·per·vi·ous (im pûr′vē əs), *adj.* **1.** not permitting penetration or passage. **2.** incapable of being influenced or affected. —**im·per′vi·ous·ly**, *adv.*

im·pe·ti·go (im′pi tī′gō), *n.* a contagious skin infection characterized by pustules.

im·pet·u·ous (im pech′ōō əs), *adj.* **1.** of or characterized by sudden or rash action or emotion. **2.** moving with great force. —**im·pet′u·os′i·ty** (-os′i tē), *n.* —**im·pet′u·ous·ly**, *adv.*

im·pe·tus (im′pi təs), *n.*, *pl.* -**tus·es.** **1.** a driving force; impulse. **2.** the momentum of a moving body.

im·pi·e·ty *n.*, *pl.* -**ties.** **1.** the quality or state of being impious. **2.** an impious act.

im·pinge (im pinj′), *v.i.*, -**pinged, -ping·ing.** **1.** to encroach; infringe. **2.** to strike; collide. **3.** to make an impression. —**im·pinge′ment**, *n.*

im·pi·ous (im′pē əs, im pī′-), *adj.* **1.** not pious; irreligious. **2.** disrespectful. —**im′pi·ous·ly,** *adv.*

im·plac·a·ble (im plak′ə bəl, -plā′kə-), *adj.* not to be appeased, mollified, or pacified. —**im·plac′a·bil′i·ty,** *n.* —**im·plac′a·bly,** *adv.*

im·plant (*v.* im plant′, -plänt′; *n.* im′plant′, -plänt′), *v.t.* **1.** to establish firmly in the mind. **2.** to plant securely. **3.** to insert or graft (a tissue, organ, or inert substance) into the body. —*n.* **4.** a device or material used for repairing or replacing part of the body. —**im·plant′a·ble,** *adj.*

im·plau·si·ble *adj.* not plausible; causing disbelief. —**im·plau′si·bil′i·ty,** *n.* —**im·plau′si·bly,** *adv.*

im·ple·ment (*n.* im′plə mənt; *v. also* -ment′), *n.* **1.** an instrument, tool, or utensil for accomplishing work. —*v.t.* **2.** to put into effect according to a plan or procedure. —**im′ple·men·ta′tion,** *n.*

im·pli·cate (im′pli kāt′), *v.t.,* **-cat·ed, -cat·ing. 1.** to show to be involved, usu. in an incriminating manner. **2.** to imply.

im′pli·ca′tion *n.* **1.** something implied or suggested. **2.** the act of implying or state of being implied. **3.** the act of implicating or state of being implicated.

im·plic·it (im plis′it), *adj.* **1.** not expressly stated; implied. **2.** unquestioning; absolute. **3.** potentially contained. —**im·plic′it·ly,** *adv.* —**im·plic′it·ness,** *n.*

im·plode (im plōd′), *v.i., v.t.,* **-plod·ed, -plod·ing.** to burst inward. —**im·plo′sion** (-plo′zhən), *n.* —**im·plo′sive** (-siv), *adj.*

im·plore (im plôr′), *v.t.,* **-plored, -plor·ing. 1.** to beg urgently or piteously. **2.** to beg urgently or piteously for. —**im·plor′ing·ly,** *adv.*

im·ply (im plī′), *v.t.,* **-plied, -ply·ing. 1.** to indicate or suggest without being explicitly stated. **2.** to involve as a necessary circumstance.

im′po·lite′ *adj.* not polite. —**im′po·lite′ly,** *adv.*

im·pol′i·tic *adj.* not politic or expedient. —**im·pol′i·tic·ly,** *adv.*

im·pon′der·a·ble *adj.* **1.** not susceptible to precise measurement or evaluation. —*n.* **2.** something imponderable.

im·port (*v.* im pôrt′; *n.* im′pôrt), *v.t.* **1.** to bring in from a foreign country or other source, esp. for resale. **2.** to mean or signify. **3.** to bring (electronic documents, data, etc.) into one application program from another. —*n.* **4.** something imported. **5.** consequence; importance. **6.** meaning; implication. —**im·port′a·ble,** *adj.* —**im′por·ta′tion,** *n.* —**im·port′er,** *n.*

im·por·tant (im pôr′tnt), *adj.* **1.** of much significance or consequence. **2.** of considerable authority or distinction. —**im·por′tance,** *n.* —**im·por′tant·ly,** *adv.*

im·por·tune (im′pôr tōōn′, -tyōōn′, im pôr′chən), *v.t., v.i.,* **-tuned, -tun·ing.** to urge or entreat with excessive persistence. —**im′por·tun′i·ty,** *n., pl.* **-ties.**

im·pose (im pōz′), *v.t.,* **-posed, -pos·ing. 1.** to apply or establish by or as if by authority: *to impose taxes.* **2.** to thrust intrusively upon others. **3.** **im·pose on,** to take unfair advantage of. —**im·pos′er,** *n.* —**im′po·si′tion** (-pə zish′ən), *n.*

im·pos′ing *adj.* impressive because of great size, stately appearance, etc. —**im·pos′ing·ly,** *adv.*

im·pos′si·ble *adj.* **1.** incapable of being or happening. **2.** unable to be performed or effected. **3.** difficult beyond reason or propriety. **4.** utterly impracticable. **5.** hopelessly unsuitable or objectionable. —**im·pos′si·bil′i·ty,** *n., pl.* **-ties.** —**im·pos′si·bly,** *adv.*

im·post (im′pōst), *n.* a tax; duty.

im·pos·tor or **-post·er** (im pos′tər), *n.* a person who practices deception under an assumed identity or name.

im′po·tence (im′pə təns) *n.* **1.** lack of power. **2.** lack of sexual powers. —**im′po·tent,** *adj.*

im·pound′ *v.t.* **1.** to shut up in or as if in a pound. **2.** to seize and retain in custody of the law.

im·pov·er·ish (im pov′ər ish, -pov′rish), *v.t.* to

reduce to poverty. **2.** to exhaust the strength or vitality of. —**im·pov′er·ish·ment,** *n.*

im·prac′ti·ca·ble *adj.* incapable of being put into practice or use.

im·prac′ti·cal *adj.* **1.** not practical or useful. **2.** incapable of dealing sensibly with practical matters. **3.** impracticable. —**im·prac′ti·cal′i·ty,** *n.*

im′pre·ca′tion (-pri kā′shən) *n.* a curse. —**im′pre·cate,** *v.t.* **-cat·ed, -cat·ing.**

im′pre·cise′ *adj.* vague; inexact. —**im′pre·cise′ly,** *adv.* —**im′pre·ci′sion, im′pre·cise′ness,** *n.*

im·preg·na·ble (im preg′nə bəl), *adj.* **1.** strong enough to resist or withstand attack. **2.** irrefutable, as an argument. —**im·preg′na·bil′i·ty,** *n.* —**im·preg′na·bly,** *adv.*

im·preg′nate (-nāt), *v.t.,* **-nat·ed, -nat·ing. 1.** to make pregnant. **2.** to permeate or imbue. —**im′preg·na′tion,** *n.* —**im·preg′na·tor,** *n.*

im·pre·sa·ri·o (im′prə sär′ē ō′, -sâr′-), *n., pl.* **-os.** one who organizes or manages public entertainments or operas.

im·press[1] (*v.* im pres′; *n.* im′pres), *v.t.* **1.** to affect deeply or strongly; influence. **2.** to establish firmly in the mind. **3.** to produce (a mark) by pressure. **4.** to apply with pressure so as to leave a mark. —*n.* **5.** the act of impressing. **6.** a mark made by pressure. —**im·press′er,** *n.*

im·press[2] (im pres′), *v.t.* **1.** to press or force into public service, esp. into the navy. **2.** to take for public use.

im·pres′sion *n.* **1.** a strong effect produced on the intellect, feelings, or senses. **2.** the effect produced by an agency or influence. **3.** a somewhat vague awareness, notion, etc. **4.** a mark produced by pressure. **5.** a caricatured imitation of a famous person by an entertainer.

im·pres′sion·a·ble *adj.* readily impressed.

im·pres′sion·ism *n.* (*often cap.*) a style of 19th-century painting characterized by short brush strokes of bright colors to represent the effect of light on objects. —**im·pres′sion·ist,** *n., adj.* —**im·pres′sion·is′tic,** *adj.*

im·pri·ma·tur (im′pri mä′tər, -mā′-), *n.* **1.** permission to print or publish a book, pamphlet, etc., granted by the Roman Catholic Church. **2.** sanction; approval.

im·print (*n.* im′print; *v.* im print′), *n.* **1.** a mark or indentation impressed on something. **2.** any impressed effect. **3.** the designation under which a publisher issues a given list of titles. —*v.t.* **4.** to mark by or as if by pressure. **5.** to produce (a mark) by pressure. **6.** to fix firmly on the mind. —**im·print′er,** *n.*

im·pris′on *v.t.* to confine in or as if in a prison. —**im·pris′on·ment,** *n.*

im·prob′a·ble *adj.* unlikely to be true or to happen. —**im·prob′a·bil′i·ty,** *n.* —**im·prob′a·bly,** *adv.*

im·promp·tu (im promp′tōō, -tyōō), *adj., adv.* without previous preparation.

im·prop′er *adj.* **1.** not strictly suitable, applicable, or correct. **2.** not in accordance with propriety or regulations. —**im·prop′er·ly,** *adv.* —**im·prop′er·ness,** *n.*

im·prove (im prōōv′), *v.,* **-proved, -prov·ing.** —*v.t.* **1.** to bring into a more desirable or excellent condition; make better. **2.** to make (land) more useful or valuable, as by cultivation. —*v.i.* **3.** to increase in quality or value; become better. —**im·prov′a·ble,** *adj.* —**im·prove′ment,** *n.*

im·prov′i·dent *adj.* neglecting to provide for future needs. —**im·prov′i·dence,** *n.* —**im·prov′i·dent·ly,** *adv.*

im·pro·vise (im′prə vīz′), *v.t., v.i.,* **-vised, -vis·ing. 1.** to perform, deliver, or compose without previous preparation. **2.** to make or provide from whatever materials are available. —**im′pro·vi·sa′tion** (-prov′ə zā′shən), *n.* —**im′pro·vi′sa′tion·al,** *adj.* —**im′pro·vis′er, im′pro·vi′sor,** *n.*

im·pru′dent *adj.* not prudent; lacking discretion; rash. —**im·pru′dence,** *n.*

im·pu·dent (im′pyə dənt), *adj.* characterized by

offensive boldness or disrespect. —**im′pu•dence,** *n.* —**im′pu•dent•ly,** *adv.*

im•pugn (im pyōōn′), *v.t.* to challenge as false; cast doubt upon. —**im•pugn′er,** *n.*

im•pulse (im′puls), *n.* **1.** the influence of a particular feeling or mental state. **2.** sudden inclination prompting to action. **3.** an impelling force; impetus. **4.** the motion caused by such an impetus. **5.** a sudden flow of electric current in one direction.

im•pu•ni•ty (im pyōō′ni tē), *n.* exemption from punishment or detrimental effects.

im•pure′ *adj.* **1.** not pure; mixed with extraneous matter, esp. of an inferior nature. **2.** not morally pure; unchaste. —**im•pure′ly,** *adv.* —**im•pur′i•ty,** *n., pl.* **-ties.**

im•pute (im pyōōt′), *v.t.,* **-put•ed, -put•ing.** to attribute or ascribe (esp. something discreditable) to someone or something. —**im′pu•ta′tion** (-pyōō tā′shən), *n.*

in (in), *prep.* **1.** (used to indicate inclusion within space or a place): *walking in the park.* **2.** (used to indicate inclusion within something immaterial): *in politics.* **3.** (used to indicate occurrence during a period of time): *in ancient times.* **4.** (used to indicate qualification, as of condition or manner): *spoken in a whisper.* **5.** (used to indicate means): *written in French.* **6.** into: *Let's go in the house.* **7.** (used to indicate purpose): *a party in honor of the winner.* —*adv.* **8.** in or into some place, position, etc. **9.** on the inside. **10.** in one's house or office. —*adj.* **11.** inner; internal. **12.** fashionable; stylish. **13.** comprehensible only to a special group. **14.** being in power. —*n.* **15.** Usu., **ins.** persons in power. **16.** pull or influence. —*Idiom.* **17. in for,** certain to undergo (a disagreeable experience). **18. in that,** because; inasmuch as.

IN Indiana.

In *Chem. Symbol.* indium.

in-¹, a prefix meaning in, into, within, or toward (*incarcerate*).

in-², a prefix meaning not or lack of (*inexperience*).

-in a combining form meaning any organized protest or social activity (*sing-in*).

in. inch.

in ab•sen•tia (in ab sen′shə, -shē ə), *adv. Latin.* in absence.

in•ac•ti•vate (in ak′tə vāt′), *v.t.,* **-vat•ed, -vat•ing.** to make inactive. —**in•ac′ti•va′tion,** *n.*

in•ad•vert•ent (in′əd vûr′tnt), *adj.* **1.** unintentional. **2.** not attentive; heedless. —**in′ad•vert′ence,** *n.* —**in′ad•vert′ent•ly,** *adv.*

in•al′ien•a•ble *adj.* not transferable or capable of being taken away: *inalienable rights.* —**in•al′ien•a•bil′i•ty,** *n.* —**in•al′ien•a•bly,** *adv.*

in•am•o•ra•ta (in am′ə rä′tə, in′am-), *n., pl.* **-tas.** a woman who loves or is loved.

in•ane (i nān′), *adj.* **1.** lacking sense, significance, or ideas. **2.** empty; void. —**in•an•i•ty** (i nan′i tē), *n., pl.* **-ties.**

in•an′i•mate (-mit), *adj.* **1.** not animate; lifeless. **2.** not animated; dull. —**in•an′i•mate•ly,** *adv.* —**in•an′i•mate•ness,** *n.*

in′ar•tic′u•late (-lit), *adj.* **1.** lacking the ability to express oneself in clear and effective speech. **2.** unable to use articulate speech. **3.** not uttered with intelligible modulations. **4.** not fully expressed or expressible. —**in′ar•tic′u•late•ly,** *adv.* —**in′ar•tic′u•late•ness,** *n.*

in′as•much′ as′ *conj.* **1.** seeing that; since. **2.** to such a degree as.

in•at•ten′tion *n.* **1.** lack of attention. **2.** an act of neglect. —**in′at•ten′tive,** *adj.*

in•au′gu•rate (-rāt′), *v.t.,* **-rat•ed, -rat•ing. 1.** to begin formally. **2.** to induct into office with formal ceremonies. **3.** to introduce into public use by some formal ceremony. —**in•au′gu•ra′tion,** *n.*

in′board′ *adj., adv.* **1.** located inside a hull or aircraft. **2.** located nearer the center, as of an airplane.

in′born′ *adj.* present at birth; innate.

in′bound′ *adj.* inward bound.

in′breed′ *v.t.* to produce by the repeated breeding of closely related individuals. —**in′breed′ing,** *n.*

inc. 1. incomplete. **2.** incorporated. **3.** increase.

In•ca (ing′kə), *n., pl.* **-cas.** a member of any of the groups of South American Indian peoples dominant in Peru prior to the Spanish conquest.

in•cal′cu•la•ble *adj.* **1.** unable to be calculated. **2.** very numerous or great. **3.** uncertain; unpredictable. —**in•cal′cu•la•bly,** *adv.*

in′can•des′cence (in′kən des′əns) *n.* the glow of intense heat. —**in′can•des′cent,** *adj.*

in•can•ta•tion (in′kan tā′shən), *n.* **1.** the chanting or uttering of words purporting to have magical power. **2.** the formula employed.

in•ca′pa•ble *adj.* **1.** not having the necessary ability, qualification, or strength. **2.** utterly incompetent. —**in•ca′pa•bil′i•ty,** *n.* —**in•ca′pa•bly,** *adv.*

in•ca•pac•i•tate (in′kə pas′i tāt′), *v.t.,* **-tat•ed, -tat•ing. 1.** to deprive of ability, qualification, or strength. **2.** to deprive of legal power.

in′ca•pac′i•ty *n.* **1.** lack of capacity or ability. **2.** lack of legal power to act.

in•car•cer•ate (in kär′sə rāt′), *v.t.,* **-at•ed, -at•ing.** to imprison. —**in•car′cer•a′tion,** *n.*

in•car•nate (*adj.* in kär′nit, -nāt; *v.* -nāt), *adj., v.,* **-nat•ed, -nat•ing.** —*adj.* **1.** given a bodily, esp. a human, form. **2.** personified; typified. —*v.t.* **3.** to give a bodily form to. **4.** to be the embodiment of. —**in′car•na′tion,** *n.*

in•cen•di•ar•y (in sen′dē er′ē), *adj., n., pl.* **-ar•ies.** —*adj.* **1.** used or adapted for setting property on fire. **2.** of arson. **3.** tending to arouse strife, sedition, etc. —*n.* **4.** a person who commits arson. **5.** a device that burns with an intense heat. **6.** a person who stirs up strife.

in•cense¹ (in′sens), *n.* **1.** an aromatic substance producing a sweet odor when burned. **2.** the perfume or smoke arising from incense.

in•cense² (in sens′), *v.t.,* **-censed, -cens•ing.** to arouse the wrath of.

in•cen•tive (in sen′tiv), *n.* something that incites to action or greater effort.

in•cep•tion (in sep′shən), *n.* beginning; commencement.

in•ces•sant (in ses′ənt), *adj.* continuing without interruption. —**in•ces′sant•ly,** *adv.*

in•cest (in′sest), *n.* sexual relations between persons so closely related that they are forbidden by law or religion to marry. —**in•ces′tu•ous** (-ses′chōō əs), *adj.*

inch (inch), *n.* **1.** a unit of length, ¹/₁₂ of a foot, equivalent to 2.54 centimeters. —*v.t., v.i.* **2.** to move by small degrees. —*Idiom.* **3. every inch,** in every respect. **4. within an inch of,** close to.

in•cho•ate (in kō′it), *adj.* **1.** not yet fully developed. **2.** just begun; incipient.

inch′worm′ *n.* a moth larva that moves in a looping motion.

in•ci•dence (in′si dəns), *n.* the rate or range of occurrence or influence.

in′ci•dent *n.* **1.** an occurrence or event. **2.** a seemingly minor occurrence that can lead to serious consequences. —*adj.* **3.** likely to happen. **4.** falling or striking on something, as light rays.

in•cin•er•ate (in sin′ə rāt′), *v.t., v.i.,* **-at•ed, -at•ing.** to burn to ashes. —**in•cin′er•a′tion,** *n.*

in•cip•i•ent (in sip′ē ənt), *adj.* beginning to exist or appear. —**in•cip′i•ence,** *n.* —**in•cip′i•ent•ly,** *adv.*

in•cise (in sīz′), *v.t.,* **-cised, -cis•ing. 1.** to cut marks or figures upon. **2.** to engrave.

in•ci•sive (-sī′siv), *adj.* **1.** penetrating; cutting. **2.** mentally sharp; keen. —**in•ci′sive•ly,** *adv.* —**in•ci′sive•ness,** *n.*

in•ci•sor (in sī′zər), *n.* any of the four anterior teeth in each jaw, used for cutting.

in•cite (in sīt′), *v.t.,* **-cit•ed, -cit•ing.** to stimulate to action; urge on. —**in•cite′ment,** *n.* —**in•cit′er,** *n.*

in′ci•vil′i•ty *n., pl.* **-ties. 1.** the quality or state of being uncivil. **2.** an uncivil act.

incl. including.

in•clem′ent *adj.* **1.** severe; stormy. **2.** not kind or merciful. —**in•clem′en•cy,** *n.*

in•cline (*v.* in klīn′; *n.* in′klīn, in klīn′), *v.,* **-clined, -clin•ing,** *n.* —*v.i.* **1.** to deviate from the vertical or horizontal. **2.** to have a mental tendency or preference. **3.** to tend in character or in course of action. **4.** to lean; bend. —*v.t.* **5.** to persuade; dispose. **6.** to cause to lean or bend in a particular direction. —*n.* **7.** a sloping surface. —**in′cli•na′tion** (-klə nā′shən), *n.*

in•clude (in klōōd′), *v.t.* -clud•ed, -clud•ing. **1.** to contain or encompass as part of a whole. **2.** to put in or consider as part of a group or category. —**in•clu′sion** (-klōō′zhən), *n.*

in•cog•ni•to (in′kog nē′tō, in kog′ni tō′), *adv.*, *adj.* with one's identity hidden or unknown.

in′co•her′ent *adj.* lacking logical or meaningful connection. —**in′co•her′ence,** *n.* —**in′co•her′ent•ly,** *adv.*

in′com•bus′ti•ble *adj.* incapable of being burned.

in•come (in′kum), *n.* the monetary payment received for goods or services, or from other sources, such as rents or investments.

in′com′ing *adj.* coming in: *the incoming class.*

in′com•men′su•rate *adj.* not commensurate; disproportionate; inadequate. —**in′com•men′su•rate•ly,** *adv.*

in•com•mu•ni•ca•do (in′kə myōō′ni kä′dō), *adv.*, *adj.* without means of communication with others.

in′com′pa•ra•ble *adj.* **1.** fine beyond comparison. **2.** not fit for comparison.

in′com•pat′i•ble *adj.* **1.** unable to exist together in harmony. **2.** incongruous; discordant. —**in′com•pat′i•bil′i•ty,** *n.* —**in′com•pat′i•bly,** *adv.*

in′com•pe′tent *adj.* **1.** lacking qualification or ability. **2.** not legally qualified. —*n.* **3.** an incompetent person. —**in′com•pe′tence,** *n.* —**in′com•pe′tent•ly,** *adv.*

in′com•plete′ *adj.* lacking some part or parts. **2.** not finished. —**in′com•plete′ly,** *adv.* —**in′com•plete′ness,** *n.*

in•con′gru•ous *adj.* **1.** out of keeping or place. **2.** not harmonious in character. —**in′con•gru′i•ty,** *n.*, *pl.* **-ties.** —**in•con′gru•ous•ly,** *adv.*

in′con•se•quen′tial *adj.* having little or no consequence or importance. —**in′con•se•quen′tial•ly,** *adv.*

in′con•sid′er•ate *adj.* **1.** lacking regard for the rights or feelings of others. **2.** thoughtless; heedless. —**in′con•sid′er•ate•ly,** *adv.* —**in′con•sid′er•ate•ness, in′con•sid′er•a′tion,** *n.*

in′con•sol′a•ble *adj.* not consolable.

in′con•spic′u•ous *adj.* not conspicuous or noticeable. —**in′con•spic′u•ous•ly,** *adv.* —**in′con•spic′u•ous•ness,** *n.*

in•con′stant *adj.* not constant; changeable. —**in•con′stan•cy,** *n.* —**in•con′stant•ly,** *adv.*

in′con•test′a•ble *adj.* not open to dispute. —**in′con•test′a•bil′i•ty,** *n.* —**in′con•test′a•bly,** *adv.*

in•con′ti•nent *adj.* **1.** unable to restrain natural discharges of urine or feces. **2.** lacking in moderation or control. —**in•con′ti•nence,** *n.*

in′con•tro•vert′i•ble *adj.* not open to question.

in′con•ven′ience *n.*, *v.*, -ienced, -ienc•ing. —*n.* **1.** the quality or state of being inconvenient. **2.** an inconvenient circumstance or thing. —*v.t.* **3.** to put to trouble.

in′con•ven′ient *adj.* **1.** not accessible or at hand. **2.** inopportune. **3.** not suiting one's needs or purposes. —**in′con•ven′ient•ly,** *adv.*

in•cor′po•rate′ (-pə rāt′), *v.*, -rat•ed, -rat•ing. —*v.t.* **1.** to form into a corporation. **2.** to introduce as an integral part. **3.** to include as a part. **4.** to combine into one body. —*v.i.* **5.** to form a corporation. **6.** to combine so as to form one body. —**in•cor′po•ra′tion,** *n.*

in′cor•po′re•al *adj.* not corporeal or material.

in′cor•rect′ *adj.* **1.** not correct as to fact. **2.** improper; inappropriate. —**in′cor•rect′ly,** *adv.*

in•cor•ri•gi•ble (in kôr′i jə bəl, -kor′-), *adj.* bad beyond reform; uncontrollable: *an incorrigible liar.* —**in•cor′ri•gi•bil′i•ty,** *n.* —**in•cor′ri•gi•bly,** *adv.*

in′cor•rupt′i•ble *adj.* **1.** not corruptible; honest. **2.** not susceptible to decay. —**in′cor•rupt′i•bil′i•ty,** *n.*

in•crease (*v.* in krēs′; *n.* in′krēs), *v.*, -creased, -creas•ing, *n.* —*v.t.*, *v.i.* **1.** to make or become greater, as in number, size, or quality. —*n.* **2.** the act or process of increasing. **3.** an amount by which something is increased. —**in•creas′ing•ly,** *adv.*

in•cred′i•ble *adj.* so extraordinary as to seem impossible or unbelievable. —**in•cred′i•bil′i•ty,** *n.* —**in•cred′i•bly,** *adv.*

in•cred′u•lous *adj.* **1.** disinclined or indisposed to believe. **2.** indicating disbelief. —**in′cre•du′li•ty,** *n.*

in•cre•ment (in′krə mənt, ing′-), *n.* **1.** something added or gained. **2.** an amount by which something increases. —**in′cre•men′tal** (-men′tl), *adj.*

in•crim•i•nate (in krim′ə nāt′), *v.t.* -nat•ed, -nat•ing. to accuse of or indicate involvement in a crime or fault. —**in•crim′i•na′tion,** *n.* —**in•crim′i•na•to•ry** (-nə tôr′ē), *adj.*

in•cu•bate (in′kyə bāt′, ing′-), *v.t.*, *v.i.*, -bat•ed, -bat•ing. **1.** to sit on (eggs) for the purpose of hatching. **2.** to hatch (eggs), as by sitting on them or by artificial heat. **3.** to maintain under favorable conditions promoting development, as premature infants. **4.** to develop as if by hatching. —**in′cu•ba′tion,** *n.*

in′cu•ba′tor *n.* **1.** an apparatus for hatching eggs. **2.** an apparatus in which premature infants are cared for in controlled conditions. **3.** an apparatus in which microorganisms are cultivated at a constant temperature.

in•cul•cate (in kul′kāt, in′kul kāt′), *v.t.*, -cat•ed, -cat•ing. to implant by repeated statement or admonition. —**in′cul•ca′tion,** *n.*

in•cum•bent (in kum′bənt), *adj.* **1.** currently holding an indicated office: *the incumbent president.* **2.** obligatory: *a duty incumbent upon me.* —*n.* **3.** the holder of an office.

in•cur (in kûr′), *v.t.*, -curred, -cur•ring. **1.** to come into or acquire: *to incur debts.* **2.** to bring upon oneself: *incurred our displeasure.*

in•cur′a•ble *adj.* incapable of being cured or remedied. —**in•cur′a•bly,** *adv.*

in•cur•sion (in kûr′zhən, -shən), *n.* a hostile entrance into or invasion of a place or territory.

Ind. 1. India. **2.** Indiana.

ind. 1. independent. **2.** index. **3.** indicative. **4.** industry.

in•debt′ed *adj.* **1.** obligated to repay money. **2.** obligated for favors or kindness received. —**in•debt′ed•ness,** *n.*

in•de′cent *adj.* **1.** offensive to good taste or propriety. **2.** unbecoming; unseemly. —**in•de′cen•cy,** *n.* —**in•de′cent•ly,** *adv.*

in′de•ci′pher•a•ble *adj.* incapable of being deciphered; illegible.

in′de•ci′sion *n.* inability to decide.

in′de•ci′sive *adj.* **1.** characterized by indecision. **2.** not decisive or conclusive. —**in′de•ci′sive•ly,** *adv.* —**in′de•ci′sive•ness,** *n.*

in•dec′o•rous *adj.* unseemly; unbecoming.

in•deed (in dēd′), *adv.* **1.** in fact; truly. —*interj.* **2.** an exclamation of surprise or skepticism.

in′de•fat′i•ga•ble (in′di fat′i gə bəl), *adj.* incapable of being tired out. —**in′de•fat′i•ga•bly,** *adv.*

in′de•fen′si•ble *adj.* **1.** not justifiable; inexcusable. **2.** incapable of being defended, as against attack. —**in′de•fen′si•bly,** *adv.*

in′de•fin′a•ble *adj.* not readily identified, described, or analyzed.

in•def′i•nite *adj.* **1.** having no fixed limit. **2.** not clearly defined or determined. **3.** uncertain; vague. —**in•def′i•nite•ly,** *adv.*

in•del•i•ble (in del′ə bəl), *adj.* **1.** making marks that cannot be removed. **2.** incapable of being removed or erased. —**in•del′i•bly,** *adv.*

in•del′i•cate *adj.* **1.** offensive to propriety or decency. **2.** lacking sensitivity; tactless. —**in•del′i•ca•cy,** *n.*, *pl.* **-cies.** —**in•del′i•cate•ly,** *adv.*

in•dem•ni•fy (in dem′nə fī′), *v.t.*, -fied, -fy•ing. **1.** to compensate for damage or loss sustained. **2.** to secure against anticipated loss. —**in•dem′ni•fi•ca′tion,** *n.* —**in•dem′ni•ty,** *n.*

in•dent¹ (in dent′), *v.t.* **1.** to form notches in the edge of. **2.** to set in from the margin: *Indent the first line of a paragraph.* —*v.i.* **3.** to form an indentation. **4.** to space in from the margin. —**in′·den·ta′tion,** n.

in·dent² (in dent′), v.t., to form a dent in.

in·den·ture (in den′chər), n., v., **-tured, -tur·ing.** —n. **1.** a contract, esp. one by which an apprentice is bound to service. —v.t. **2.** to bind by indenture.

in·de·pend′ent adj. **1.** not influenced or controlled by others. **2.** not depending upon something else. **3.** not relying on another for aid or support. **4.** not subject to another's authority or jurisdiction. **5.** free from political party commitments. **6.** capable of standing syntactically as a complete sentence: an independent clause. —n. **7.** an independent person, esp. a voter not committed to a party. —**in′de·pend′ence,** n. —**in′de·pend′ent·ly,** adv.

in′-depth′ adj. intensive; thorough.

in′de·scrib′a·ble adj. not describable; too extraordinary for description. —**in′de·scrib′a·bly,** adv.

in′de·struct′i·ble adj. incapable of being destroyed. —**in′de·struct′i·bil′i·ty,** n. —**in′de·struct′i·bly,** adv.

in′de·ter′mi·nate (-nit), adj. **1.** not precisely fixed or determined; vague. **2.** not settled in advance. —**in′de·ter′mi·na·cy** (-nə sē), n. —**in′de·ter′mi·nate·ly,** adv.

in·dex (in′deks), n., pl. **-dex·es, -di·ces** (-də sēz′), v. —n. **1.** (in a printed work) an alphabetical list of names, places, and topics with the page numbers on which they are mentioned. **2.** a sign or indication: an index of character. **3.** a pointer, as on a dial. **4.** a printed sign, a hand with extended index finger, used to point out a note or paragraph. **5.** a number or formula expressing a property or ratio: index of growth. **6.** INDEX NUMBER. —v.t. **7.** to provide with an index. **8.** to enter in an index. —**in′dex·er,** n.

in′dex num′ber n. a quantity whose variation over a period of time measures the change in some phenomenon.

In·di·a (in′dē ə), n. a republic in S Asia.

In′di·an n. **1.** AMERICAN INDIAN. **2.** any of the indigenous languages of the American Indians. **3.** a native or inhabitant of the Republic of India. —adj. **4.** of the American Indians or their languages. **5.** of India or S Asia.

In′dian sum′mer n. a period of mild, dry weather in late fall or early winter.

in·di·cate (in′di kāt′), v.t., **-cat·ed, -cat·ing. 1.** to be a sign of. **2.** to point out or point to. **3.** to express minimally. —**in′di·ca′tion,** n.

in·dict (in dīt′), v.t. to charge with a crime or accuse of wrongdoing. —**in·dict′a·ble,** adj. —**in·dict′ment,** n.

in·dif′fer·ent adj. **1.** without interest or concern. **2.** having no bias or preference. **3.** not particularly good. **4.** immaterial or unimportant. —**in·dif′fer·ence,** n. —**in·dif′fer·ent·ly,** adv.

in·dig·e·nous (in dij′ə nəs), adj. originating in and characteristic of a particular region or country.

in·di·gent (in′di jənt), adj. **1.** lacking the necessities of life because of poverty. —n. **2.** an indigent person. —**in′di·gence,** n. —**in′di·gent·ly,** adv.

in′di·gest′i·ble adj. not easily digested.

in′di·ges′tion n. **1.** a feeling of discomfort after eating, as of heartburn. **2.** inadequate or abnormal digestion.

in·dig·na·tion (in′dig nā′shən), n. strong displeasure at something considered unjust, offensive, insulting, or base.

in·dig′ni·ty n., pl. **-ties.** an injury to a person's dignity; slighting or contemptuous treatment.

in·di·go (in′di gō′), n., pl. **-gos, -goes. 1.** a blue dye obtained from plants or manufactured synthetically. **2.** a deep violet blue.

in′di·rect′ adj. **1.** deviating from a straight line, as a path. **2.** not resulting immediately, as consequences. **3.** not direct in action or procedure. **4.** devious. —**in′di·rect′ly,** adv. —**in′di·rect′ness,** n.

in′dis·creet′ adj. lacking prudence, good judgment, or circumspection. —**in′dis·creet′ly,** adv.

in′dis·cre′tion n. **1.** lack of discretion. **2.** an indiscreet act, remark, etc.

in·dis·crim·i·nate (in′di skrim′ə nit), adj. **1.** not discriminating; lacking in care, judgment, selectivity, etc. **2.** thrown together; jumbled. —**in′dis·crim′i·nate·ly,** adv.

in′dis·pen′sa·ble adj. absolutely necessary, essential, or requisite. —**in′dis·pen′sa·bil′i·ty,** n. —**in′dis·pen′sa·bly,** adv.

in′dis·posed′ adj. **1.** sick or ill, esp. mildly. **2.** disinclined or unwilling. —**in′dis·po·si′tion,** n.

in′dis·put′a·ble adj. not disputable or deniable. —**in′dis·put′a·bly,** adv.

in·dis·sol·u·ble (in′di sol′yə bəl), adj. incapable of being dissolved, decomposed, undone, or destroyed.

in′dis·tinct′ adj. **1.** not clearly marked or defined. **2.** not clearly distinguishable or perceptible. —**in′dis·tinct′ly,** adv.

in·di·um (in′dē əm), n. a rare metallic element that is soft, white, and malleable. Symbol: In; at. wt.: 114.82; at. no.: 49.

in·di·vid·u·al (in′də vij′ōō əl), n. **1.** a single human being, as distinguished from a group. **2.** a person. **3.** a distinct, indivisible entity. —adj. **4.** single; separate. **5.** intended for one person only. **6.** of or characteristic of a particular person or thing. **7.** distinguished by special characteristics. —**in′di·vid′u·al·ly,** adv.

in′di·vid′u·al·ist n. a person who is dependent only on himself or herself.

in·doc·tri·nate (in dok′trə nāt′), v.t., **-nat·ed, -nat·ing.** to instruct in a doctrine or ideology, esp. dogmatically. —**in·doc′tri·na′tion,** n.

In·do-Eu·ro·pe·an (in′dō yŏŏr′ə pē′ən), n. **1.** a family of languages spoken or formerly spoken in Europe and SW, central, and S Asia. **2.** a member of any of the peoples speaking an Indo-European language. —adj. **3.** of or belonging to Indo-European.

in·do·lent (in′dl ənt), adj. lazy; slothful. —**in′do·lence,** n.

in·dom·i·ta·ble (in dom′i tə bəl), adj. incapable of being subdued or overcome. —**in·dom′i·ta·bly,** adv.

In·do·ne·sia (in′də nē′zhə), n. **Republic of,** a republic in the Malay Archipelago, consisting of Sumatra, Java, most of Borneo, and many small islands. —**In′do·ne′sian,** n., adj.

in′door′ adj. located, used, or existing inside a building.

in·du·bi·ta·ble (in dōō′bi tə bəl, -dyōō′-), adj. not to be doubted. —**in·du′bi·ta·bly,** adv.

in·duce (in dōōs′, -dyōōs′), v.t., **-duced, -duc·ing. 1.** to lead or move by persuasion. **2.** to bring about: It induces sleep. **3.** to produce (magnetism or electric current) by induction. **4.** to infer by logical induction. —**in·duc′er,** n.

in·duct (in dukt′), v.t. **1.** to install in an office, esp. formally. **2.** to take (a draftee) into military service. **3.** to bring in as a member.

in·duc′tion n. **1.** the act of inducing. **2.** formal installation in an office. **3. a.** any form of reasoning in which a general conclusion is reached from particular cases. **b.** a conclusion reached by this process. **4.** the process by which a body having electric or magnetic properties produces magnetism, an electric charge, or an electromotive force in a neighboring body without contact. —**in·duc′tive,** adj.

in·dulge (in dulj′), v., **-dulged, -dulg·ing.** —v.t. **1.** to yield to or gratify (desires, feelings, etc.). **2.** to yield to the wishes or whims of (oneself or another). —v.i. **3.** to yield to an inclination or desire.

in·dus·tri·al·ist (in dus′trē ə list), n. a person who owns or manages an industrial enterprise.

in·dus′tri·al·ize′ v., **-ized, -iz·ing.** —v.t. **1.** to introduce industry into on a large scale. —v.i. **2.** to become industrial. —**in·dus′tri·al·i·za′tion,** n.

in·dus′tri·ous adj. working energetically and devotedly; hard-working. —**in·dus′tri·ous·ly,** adv. —**in·dus′tri·ous·ness,** n.

in·dus·try (in′də strē), n., pl. **-tries. 1.** the aggregate of manufacturing or technically productive enterprises. **2.** any general business activity: the *tourist industry.* **3.** energetic, devoted activity at any task. —**in•dus'tri•al,** *adj.*

in•e•bri•ate (*v.* in ē'brē āt', i nē'-; *n.* -it), *v.,* -at•ed, -at•ing, *n.* —*v.t.* **1.** to make drunk. —*n.* **2.** a drunkard. —**in•e'bri•a'tion,** *n.*

in•ef•fa•ble (in ef'ə bəl), *adj.* **1.** incapable of being expressed in words. **2.** not to be spoken. —**in•ef'fa•bly,** *adv.*

in'ef•fec'tive *adj.* **1.** not producing results. **2.** inefficient or incompetent. —**in'ef•fec'tive•ly,** *adv.*

in'ef•fec'tu•al *adj.* **1.** producing no satisfactory or decisive effect. **2.** unavailing; futile.

in'ef•fi'cient *adj.* unable to achieve the desired result with reasonable economy of means. —**in'ef•fi'cien•cy,** *n., pl.* -cies. —**in'ef•fi'cient•ly,** *adv.*

in•ept (in ept', i nept'), *adj.* **1.** lacking skill or aptitude; incompetent. **2.** inappropriate; unsuitable. **3.** absurd or foolish. —**in•ept'i•tude',** *n.* —**in•ept'ly,** *adv.* —**in•ept'ness,** *n.*

in'e•qual'i•ty *n., pl.* -ties. **1.** the condition of being unequal. **2.** injustice; partiality. **3.** unevenness, as of surface. **4.** a mathematical statement that two quantities are unequal.

in•ert (in ûrt', i nûrt'), *adj.* **1.** having no inherent power of action, motion, or resistance. **2.** *Chem.* having little or no ability to react. **3.** sluggish by habit or nature. —**in•ert'ly,** *adv.* —**in•ert'ness,** *n.*

in•es•cap•a•ble (in'ə skā'pə bəl), *adj.* incapable of being escaped or avoided. —**in'es•cap'a•bly,** *adv.*

in•es'ti•ma•ble *adj.* **1.** incapable of being estimated or assessed. **2.** too precious to be estimated or appreciated. —**in•es'ti•ma•bly,** *adv.*

in•ev•i•ta•ble (in ev'i tə bəl), *adj.* unable to be avoided or escaped. —**in•ev'i•ta•bil'i•ty,** *n.* —**in•ev'i•ta•bly,** *adv.*

in'ex•haust'i•ble *adj.* **1.** incapable of being depleted. **2.** untiring; tireless. —**in'ex•haust'i•bly,** *adv.*

in•ex•o•ra•ble (in ek'sər ə bəl), *adj.* **1.** unyielding; unalterable. **2.** not to be persuaded or moved by entreaties. —**in•ex'o•ra•bly,** *adv.*

in'ex•pert (in eks'pûrt, in'ik spûrt'), *adj.* not expert; unskilled.

in•ex'pli•ca•ble *adj.* incapable of being explained. —**in•ex'pli•ca•bly,** *adv.*

in'ex•press'i•ble *adj.* incapable of being uttered or described in words.

in•ex'tri•ca•ble *adj.* **1.** from which one cannot extricate oneself. **2.** incapable of being disentangled or loosed. **3.** hopelessly intricate or perplexing. —**in•ex'tri•ca•bly,** *adv.*

in•fal'li•ble *adj.* **1.** unfailing; sure. **2.** exempt from liability to error. —**in•fal'li•bil'i•ty,** *n.* —**in•fal'li•bly,** *adv.*

in•fa•mous (in'fə məs), *adj.* **1.** having an extremely bad reputation. **2.** causing an evil reputation.

in•fa•my *n., pl.* -mies. **1.** extremely bad reputation as the result of a shameful or outrageous act. **2.** infamous character or conduct. **3.** an infamous act.

in•fan•cy (in'fən sē), *n., pl.* -cies. **1.** very early childhood. **2.** the earliest stage of anything.

in•fant (in'fənt), *n.* **1.** a child during the earliest period of its life. —*adj.* **2.** of infants or infancy. **3.** being in the earliest stage.

in•fan•try (in'fən trē), *n., pl.* -tries. a branch of an army composed of soldiers who fight on foot. —**in'fan•try•man,** *n., pl.* -men.

in'farct' (in' färkt, in färkt'), *n.* an area of dead or dying tissue, as in the heart. Also called **in•farc'tion.**

in•fat•u•ate (in fach'o͞o āt'), *v.t.,* -at•ed, -at•ing. to inspire or possess with a foolish or unreasoning admiration or love. —**in•fat'u•a'tion,** *n.*

in•fect (in fekt'), *v.t.* **1.** to contaminate with disease-producing germs. **2.** to affect with disease. **3.** to affect, esp. adversely, with a feeling, belief, etc. **4.** to affect with a computer virus. —**in•fec'tion,** *n.*

in•fec'tious *adj.* **1.** communicable by infection. **2.** causing or communicating infection. **3.** tending to spread quickly: *infectious laughter.* —**in•fec'tious•ly,** *adv.* —**in•fec'tious•ness,** *n.*

in'fe•lic'i•tous *adj.* inapt or inappropriate. —**in'fe•lic'i•ty,** *n., pl.* -ties.

in•fer (in fûr'), *v.t.,* -ferred, -fer•ring. **1.** to conclude by reasoning from premises or evidence. **2.** to guess; surmise. —**in'fer•ence** (-fər əns), *n.* —**in'fer•en'tial** (-fa ren'shal), *adj.*

in•fe•ri•or (in fēr'ē ər), *adj.* **1.** lower in rank or importance. **2.** lower in quality or value. **3.** lower in place or position. **4.** poor in quality. —*n.* **5.** an inferior person. —**in•fe'ri•or'i•ty** (-ôr'i tē, -or'-), *n.*

in•fer•nal (in fûr'nl), *adj.* **1.** hellish; diabolical. **2.** of hell or the underworld.

in•fer'no (-nō), *n., pl.* -nos. **1.** hell. **2.** a place that resembles hell.

in•fer'tile *adj.* not fertile; unproductive; sterile; barren. —**in'fer•til'i•ty,** *n.*

in•fest (in fest'), *v.t.* to overrun in a troublesome manner, as vermin do. —**in'fes•ta'tion,** *n.*

in•fi•del (in'fi dl, -del'), *n.* **1.** a person who does not accept a particular religion, esp. Christianity or Islam. **2.** a person who has no religious faith.

in'fi•del'i•ty *n., pl.* -ties. **1.** marital unfaithfulness. **2.** disloyalty.

in'field' *n.* **1.** the area of a baseball field bounded by the base lines. **2.** the players (in'field'ers) positioned there.

in'fight'ing *n.* **1.** fighting at close range. **2.** fighting between rivals or people closely associated. —**in'fight'er,** *n.*

in•fil•trate (in fil'trāt, in'fil trāt'), *v.t., v.i.,* -trat•ed, -trat•ing. **1.** to move into (an organization, enemy area, etc.) surreptitiously and with hostile intent. **2.** to filter into or through (a substance). —**in'fil•tra'tion,** *n.* —**in'fil•tra'tor,** *n.*

in•fi•nite (in'fə nit), *adj.* **1.** immeasurably great. **2.** unbounded or unlimited. **3.** *Math.* not finite. —*n.* **4.** something infinite. —**in'fi•nite•ly,** *adv.*

in•fin•i•tes•i•mal (in'fin i tes'ə məl), *adj.* **1.** immeasurably or exceedingly small. —*n.* **2.** *Math.* a variable having zero as a limit. —**in'fin•i•tes'i•mal•ly,** *adv.*

in•fin•i•tive (in fin'i tiv), *n.* a verb form not inflected for person, number, or tense, and in English usu. preceded by *to.* —**in'fin•i•ti'val** (-tī'vəl), *adj.*

in•firm (in fûrm'), *adj.* **1.** feeble in body or health. **2.** not firm, solid, or strong. —**in•firm'i•ty,** *n., pl.* -ties.

in•fir'ma•ry (-fûr'mə rē), *n., pl.* -ries. a place for the care of the infirm, sick, or injured.

in•flame' *v.t., v.i.,* -flamed, -flam•ing. **1.** to kindle or excite (passions, desires, etc.). **2.** to affect or become affected with inflammation. **3.** to set aflame or afire. —**in•flam'ma•to'ry** (-flam'ə tôr'ē, -tōr'ē), *adj.*

in•flam•ma•tion (in'flə mā'shən), *n.* redness, swelling, and fever in a local area of the body in reaction to an infection or an injury.

in•flate (in flāt'), *v.,* -flat•ed, -flat•ing. —*v.t.* **1.** to expand or distend with or as if with air or gas. **2.** to puff up with pride, satisfaction, etc. **3.** to increase unduly, as prices. —*v.i.* **4.** to become inflated. —**in•flat'a•ble,** *adj.*

in•fla'tion *n.* **1.** a steady rise in the level of prices related to an increased volume of money and credit and resulting in a loss of value of currency. **2.** the act of inflating or state of being inflated. —**in•fla'tion•ar'y** (-shə ner'ē), *adj.*

in•flect (in flekt'), *v.t.* **1.** to modulate (the voice). **2.** to change the form of (a word) by inflection.

in•flec'tion *n.* **1.** modulation of the voice. **2.** the change in the form of a word to express grammatical or syntactic relations, as of case or number.

in•flex'i•ble *adj.* **1.** incapable of or resistant to being bent. **2.** of an unyielding temper, purpose, etc. **3.** not permitting change or variation. —**in•flex'i•bil'i•ty,** *n.* —**in•flex'i•bly,** *adv.*

in•flict (in flikt'), *v.t.* **1.** to impose (anything unwelcome). **2.** to deal or deliver, as a blow. —**in•flic'tion,** *n.* —**in•flic'tive,** *adj.*

in•flu•ence (in'flo͞o əns), *n., v.,* -enced, -enc•ing. —*n.* **1.** the power to produce effects on others by intangible or indirect means. **2.** a person or thing that exerts influence. **3.** the power to persuade or

obtain advantages resulting from one's status, wealth, etc. —*v.t.* **4.** to exercise influence on. **5.** to move or impel (a person) to some action. —**in′flu•en′tial** (-en′shəl), *adj.*

in•flu•en•za (in′floo en′zə), *n.* an acute, contagious viral disease characterized by respiratory symptoms, fever, muscular aches, etc.

in′flux′ *n.* a flowing or coming in.

in•fo•mer•cial (in′fō mûr′shəl), *n.* a program-length television commercial cast in a standard format, as a documentary.

in•form (in fôrm′), *v.t.* **1.** to give knowledge of a fact or circumstance to. —*v.i.* **2.** to give information. **3.** to furnish incriminating evidence about someone. —**in•form′er,** *n.*

in•for′mal *adj.* **1.** without formality or ceremony. **2.** not according to the prescribed or customary manner. **3.** suitable to or characteristic of casual or familiar speech or writing. —**in′for•mal′i•ty,** *n., pl.* **-ties.** —**in•for′mal•ly,** *adv.*

in′for•ma′tion (-fər mā′shən), *n.* **1.** knowledge communicated or received concerning a particular fact. **2.** knowledge gained through study, research, etc. **3.** computer data at any stage of processing. —**in′for•ma′tion•al,** *adj.*

information superhighway *n.* the large-scale communications network linking computers, television sets, etc.

in′fo•tain′ment (in′fō tān′mənt) *n.* broadcasting or publishing that treats factual matter in an entertaining way, as by dramatizing real events.

in•frac′tion (in frak′shən), *n.* a breach; violation.

in′fra•red′ (in′frə-), *n.* the part of the invisible spectrum contiguous to the red end of the visible spectrum.

in′fra•struc′ture *n.* **1.** the basic framework of a system or organization. **2.** fundamental facilities, as transportation and communication systems.

in•fre′quent *adj.* **1.** happening or occurring at long intervals or rarely. **2.** not constant, habitual, or regular. —**in•fre′quen•cy, in•fre′quence,** *n.* —**in•fre′quent•ly,** *adv.*

in•fringe (in frinj′), *v.,* **-fringed, -fring•ing.** —*v.t.* **1.** to commit a breach or infraction of. —*v.i.* **2.** to encroach or trespass: *to infringe on someone's privacy.* —**in•fringe′ment,** *n.*

in•fu•ri•ate (in fyoor′ē āt′), *v.t.,* **-at•ed, -at•ing.** to make furious. —**in•fu′ri•at′ing•ly,** *adv.*

in•fuse (in fyooz′), *v.t.,* **-fused, -fus•ing. 1.** to introduce, as if by pouring. **2.** to imbue or inspire. **3.** to steep or soak (leaves, bark, etc.) to extract the soluble properties. —**in•fus′er,** *n.* —**in•fu′sion** (-fyoo′zhən), *n.*

in•gen•ious (in jēn′yəs), *adj.* **1.** characterized by cleverness or originality. **2.** cleverly inventive; resourceful. —**in•gen′ious•ly,** *adv.* —**in•gen′ious•ness,** *n.*

in•gé•nue or **-ge•nue** (an′zhə noō′), *n.* **1.** the role of an artless, innocent young woman, esp. as represented on the stage. **2.** an actress who plays such a role.

in•gen•u•ous (in jen′yoō əs), *adj.* **1.** free from deceit or disguise; open. **2.** artless; innocent. —**in•gen′u•ous•ly,** *adv.* —**in•gen′u•ous•ness,** *n.*

in•gest (in jest′), *v.t.* to take into the body, as food or liquid. —**in•ges′tion,** *n.*

in•glo′ri•ous *adj.* **1.** shameful; disgraceful. **2.** not famous or honored. —**in•glo′ri•ous•ly,** *adv.*

in•got (ing′gət), *n.* a mass of metal cast in a form for shaping, remelting, or refining.

in•grained′ *adj.* firmly fixed; deep-rooted; inveterate: *ingrained superstition.*

in•grate (in′grāt), *n.* an ungrateful person.

in•gra•ti•ate (in grā′shē āt′), *v.t.,* **-at•ed, -at•ing.** to establish (oneself) in the favor of others. —**in•gra′ti•a′tion,** *n.*

in•grat′i•tude′ *n.* the state of being ungrateful.

in•gre•di•ent (in grē′dē ənt), *n.* **1.** something that enters as an element into a mixture. **2.** a constituent element of anything.

in•gress (in′gres), *n.* the act of going in or entering.

in•hab•it (in hab′it), *v.t.* to live or dwell in. —**in•hab′it•a•ble,** *adj.* —**in•hab′it•ant,** *n.*

in•ha•la•tor (in′hə lā′tər), *n.* **1.** an apparatus to help one inhale anesthetics, medicinal vapors, etc. **2.** RESPIRATOR (def. 1).

in•hale (in hāl′), *v.t., v.i.,* **-haled, -hal•ing.** to draw in (air, smoke, etc.) by breathing. —**in′ha•la′tion** (-hə lā′shən), *n.*

in•hal′er *n.* **1.** INHALATOR. **2.** a person who inhales.

in•here (in hēr′), *v.i.,* **-hered, -her•ing.** to be an inseparable part or element. —**in•her′ent** (-hēr′ənt, -her′-), *adj.*

in•her•it (in her′it), *v.t., v.i.* **1.** to receive (property, a title, etc.) by succession or will, as an heir. **2.** to receive from predecessors. **3.** to receive (a genetic character) by heredity. —**in•her′it•ance,** *n.*

in•hib•it (in hib′it), *v.t.* to restrain, hinder, arrest, or check (an action, impulse, etc.). —**in′hi•bi′tion,** *n.*

in-house (*adj.* in′hous′; *adv.* -hous′), *adj., adv.* within or utilizing an organization's own staff or resources.

in•hu′man *adj.* **1.** lacking sympathy, pity, warmth, or compassion. **2.** not human.

in′hu•mane′ *adj.* lacking humanity, kindness, compassion, etc. —**in′hu•mane′ly,** *adv.*

in•im•i•cal (i nim′i kəl), *adj.* **1.** adverse in tendency or effect. **2.** unfriendly; hostile. —**in•im′i•cal•ly,** *adv.*

in•im•i•ta•ble (i nim′i tə bəl), *adj.* incapable of being imitated or copied. —**in•im′i•ta•bly,** *adv.*

in•iq•ui•ty (i nik′wi tē), *n., pl.* **-ties. 1.** gross injustice or wickedness. **2.** a wicked act; sin. —**in•iq′ui•tous,** *adj.*

in•i•tial (i nish′əl), *adj., n., v.,* **-tialed, -tial•ing** (*esp. Brit.*) **-tialled, -tial•ling.** —*adj.* **1.** of or occurring at the beginning. —*n.* **2.** an initial letter, as of a word. **3.** the first letter of a proper name. —*v.t.* **4.** to mark or sign with initials. —**in•i′tial•ly,** *adv.*

in•i•ti•ate (*v.* i nish′ē āt′; *n.* -it, -āt′), *v.,* **-at•ed, -at•ing,** *n.* —*v.t.* **1.** to begin, set going, or originate. **2.** to introduce into the knowledge of some art or subject. **3.** to admit into the membership of an organization or group. —*n.* **4.** a person who has been initiated. —**in•i′ti•a′tion,** *n.* —**in•i′ti•a′tor,** *n.*

in•i•ti•a•tive (i nish′ē ə tiv, i nish′ə-), *n.* **1.** an introductory act or step. **2.** readiness and ability in initiating action. **3.** one's personal, responsible decision. **4.** a procedure by which a specified number of voters may propose legislation.

in•ject (in jekt′), *v.t.* **1.** to force (a fluid) into a passage, cavity, or tissue. **2.** to introduce or interject (a remark, suggestion, etc.), as into conversation. —**in•jec′tion,** *n.* —**in•jec′tor,** *n.*

in•junc•tion (in jungk′shən), *n.* **1.** a judicial order requiring a person or persons to do or refrain from doing a particular act. **2.** an act or instance of enjoining. **3.** a command; order.

in•jure (in′jər), *v.t.,* **-jured, -jur•ing. 1.** to do or cause harm of any kind to. **2.** to treat unjustly or unfairly. —**in•ju′ri•ous** (-jŏŏr′ē əs), *adj.* —**in′ju•ry,** *n., pl.* **-ries.**

in•jus′tice *n.* **1.** the quality or fact of being unjust. **2.** an unjust act.

ink (ingk), *n.* **1.** a colored fluid used for writing or printing. —*v.t.* **2.** to mark, stain, or smear with ink.

ink•ling (ingk′ling), *n.* **1.** a slight suggestion. **2.** a vague idea.

in•land (*adj.* in′lənd; *adv., n.* -land′, -lənd), *adj.* **1.** of or situated in the interior part of a country or region. —*adv.* **2.** in or toward the interior of a country. —*n.* **3.** the interior part of a country.

in′-law′ *n.* a relative by marriage.

in•lay (*v.* in′lā′, in′lā′; *n.* in′lā′), *v.,* **-laid, -lay•ing,** *n.* —*v.t.* **1.** to insert (pieces of wood, ivory, etc.) in the surface of an object. **2.** to decorate with such pieces. —*n.* **3.** inlaid work. **4.** a filling of metal, porcelain, etc., that is cemented into a tooth cavity.

in•let *n.* **1.** an indentation of a shoreline, usu. long and narrow. **2.** a narrow passage between islands.

in′-line′ skate′ *n.* a roller skate with four hard-rubber wheels in a straight line resembling the blade of an ice skate. —**in′-line skat′ing,** *n.*

in′mate′ *n.* a person confined in a prison, hospital, etc.

in me•mo•ri•am (in mə môr′ē əm), *prep.* in memory (of).

in′most′ *adj.* **1.** situated farthest within. **2.** most intimate.

inn (in), *n.* **1.** a small establishment that provides lodging and food for the public, esp. travelers. **2.** a tavern.

in•nards (in′ərdz), *n.pl.* **1.** the internal parts of the body. **2.** the internal parts, structure, etc., of something.

in•nate (i nāt′, in′āt), *adj.* **1.** existing in one from birth. **2.** inherent in the character of something. —**in•nate′ly,** *adv.* —**in•nate′ness,** *n.*

in•ner (in′ər), *adj.* **1.** situated within or farther within. **2.** more intimate or private. **3.** mental; spiritual: *the inner life.*

in′ner cit′y *n.* a central part of a city, densely populated, and often deteriorating.

in′ner-direct′ed *adj.* guided by one's own set of values rather than by external pressures.

in•ning (in′ing), *n.* **1.** *Baseball.* a division of a game during which each team has an opportunity to score. **2. innings,** (*used with a sing. v.*) *Cricket.* a unit of play in which each team has a turn at bat.

in′no•cence (in′ə səns) *n.* **1.** freedom from guilt. **2.** lack of worldly knowledge. —**in′no•cent,** *adj., n.*

in•noc•u•ous (i nok′yōō əs), *adj.* **1.** not harmful or injurious. **2.** not likely to irritate or offend. —**in•noc′u•ous•ly,** *adv.* —**in•noc′u•ous•ness,** *n.*

in•no•vate (in′ə vāt′), *v.i., v.t.* **-vat•ed, -vat•ing.** to introduce (something new). —**in′no•va′tion,** *n.* —**in′no•va′tive,** *adj.* —**in′no•va′tor,** *n.*

in•nu•en•do (in′yōō en′dō), *n., pl.* **-dos, -does.** an indirect intimation about a person or thing, esp. of a disparaging nature.

in•nu•mer•a•ble (i nōō′mər ə bəl, i nyōō′-), *adj.* too numerous to be counted.

in•oc•u•late (i nok′yə lāt′), *v.t.* **-lat•ed, -lat•ing.** to inject a vaccine, microorganism, etc., into (a person, animal, or plant) to protect against or study a disease. —**in•oc′u•la′tion,** *n.*

in′of•fen′sive *adj.* **1.** causing no harm, trouble, or annoyance. **2.** not objectionable. —**in′of•fen′sive•ly,** *adv.*

in•op′er•a•tive *adj.* **1.** not in operation. **2.** without effect.

in•or•di•nate (in ôr′dn it), *adj.* **1.** exceeding proper limits. **2.** not regulated or regular. —**in•or′di•nate•ly,** *adv.*

in′or•gan′ic *adj.* **1.** not having the structure or organization characteristic of living bodies. **2.** noting or pertaining to chemical compounds that are not hydrocarbons or their derivatives.

in′pa′tient *n.* a patient who stays in a hospital while receiving medical care or treatment.

in′put′ *n., v.,* **-put•ted** or **-put, -put•ting.** —*n.* **1.** something that is put in. **2.** the power or energy supplied to a machine. **3.** data entered into a computer for processing. **4.** contribution of ideas, opinions, etc. —*v.t.* **5.** to enter (data) into a computer for processing.

in′quest′ *n.* a judicial inquiry, usu. before a jury, esp. one made by a coroner.

in•quire (in kwī^ər′), *v.,* **-quired, -quir•ing.** —*v.i.* **1.** to seek information by questioning. **2.** to investigate: *They inquired into the incident.* —*v.t.* **3.** to seek to learn by asking. —**in•quir′er,** *n.* —**in•quir′y** (in kwī^ər′ē, in′kwə rē), *n., pl.* **-ries.**

in•qui•si•tion (in′kwə zish′ən, ing′-), *n.* **1.** an official investigation, esp. one of a political or religious nature. **2.** any harsh or prolonged questioning. **3.** (*cap.*) *Roman Catholic Church.* a former special tribunal, engaged chiefly in combating and punishing heresy. —**in•quis′i•tor** (-kwiz′i tər), *n.*

in•quis′i•tive (-kwiz′i tiv), *adj.* **1.** given to inquiry or research. **2.** unduly curious. —**in•quis′i•tive•ness,** *n.*

in′road′ *n.* **1.** a damaging or serious encroachment: *inroads on our savings.* **2.** a hostile raid.

ins. **1.** inches. **2.** insurance.

in•sane (in sān′), *adj.* **1.** (*not in technical use*) mentally unsound or deranged. **2.** of or for persons who are mentally deranged. **3.** utterly senseless. —**in•sane′ly,** *adv.* —**in•san′i•ty** (-san′i tē), *n.*

in•sa•tia•ble (in sā′shə bəl, -shē ə-), *adj.* incapable of being satisfied.

in•scribe (in skrīb′), *v.t.* **-scribed, -scrib•ing. 1.** to address or dedicate (a book, photograph, etc.) to someone. **2.** to mark (a surface) with words, characters, etc., esp. in a durable way. **3.** to write, print, or engrave (words, characters, etc.). **4.** to enroll, as on an official list. **5.** *Geom.* to draw (one figure) within another figure so as to touch at as many points as possible. —**in•scrib′er,** *n.* —**in•scrip′tion** (-skrip′shən), *n.*

in•scru•ta•ble (in skrōō′tə bəl), *adj.* **1.** incapable of being investigated or scrutinized. **2.** not easily understood; mysterious. —**in•scru′ta•bil′i•ty, in•scru′ta•ble•ness,** *n.* —**in•scru′ta•bly,** *adv.*

in•sect (in′sekt), *n.* any of a large class of small, air-breathing arthropods having the body divided into three parts and having three pairs of legs and usu. two pairs of wings.

in•sec′ti•cide′ (-sek′tə sīd′), *n.* a substance or preparation used for killing insects.

in′se•cure′ *adj.* **1.** subject to fears, doubts, etc. **2.** exposed or liable to risk or danger. **3.** not firmly or reliably placed or fastened. —**in′se•cure′ly,** *adv.* —**in′se•cu′ri•ty,** *n., pl.* **-ties.**

in•sem•i•nate (in sem′ə nāt′), *v.t.* **-nat•ed, -nat•ing.** to inject semen into (the female reproductive tract). —**in•sem′i•na′tion,** *n.*

in•sen′si•ble *adj.* **1.** incapable of feeling or perceiving. **2.** unaware; unconscious. **3.** not perceptible by the senses. —**in•sen′si•bil′i•ty,** *n.* —**in•sen′si•bly,** *adv.*

in•sen′si•tive *adj.* **1.** not emotionally sensitive or sympathetic. **2.** not physically sensitive. —**in•sen′si•tive•ly,** *adv.* —**in•sen′si•tiv′i•ty,** *n.*

in•sep′a•ra•ble *adj.* incapable of being separated, parted, or disjoined. —**in•sep′a•ra•bil′i•ty,** *n.* —**in•sep′a•ra•bly,** *adv.*

in•sert (*v.* in sûrt′; *n.* in′sûrt), *v.t.* **1.** to put or place in. **2.** to introduce into the body of something. —*n.* **3.** something inserted or to be inserted. —**in•ser′tion,** *n.*

in′shore′ *adj.* **1.** situated or carried on close to the shore. —*adv.* **2.** toward the shore.

in•side (in′sīd′, in′sīd′), *prep.* **1.** on the inner side or part of. **2.** prior to. —*adv.* **3.** in or into the inner part. **4.** indoors. —*n.* **5.** the inner part. **6.** the inner side or surface. **7. insides,** *Informal.* the stomach and intestines. **8.** a position of power, prestige, etc. **9.** inward nature, thoughts, or feelings. —*adj.* **10.** interior; internal. **11.** private; confidential. —*Idiom.* **12. inside of,** within the space or period of. **13. inside out, a.** with the inner side turned out. **b.** thoroughly; completely.

in•sid′er *n.* **1.** a member of a certain organization, society, etc. **2.** a person who has influence, esp. one privy to confidential information.

in•sid•i•ous (in sid′ē əs), *adj.* **1.** stealthily treacherous or deceitful. **2.** operating or proceeding inconspicuously but with grave effect.

in′sight′ *n.* the act or power of apprehending the true nature of a thing, esp. through intuitive understanding. —**in•sight′ful,** *adj.*

in•sig•ni•a (in sig′nē ə), *n., pl.* **-ni•a** or **-ni•as.** **1.** a badge or mark of office or honor. **2.** a distinguishing mark or sign of anything. Sometimes, **in•sig′ne** (-nē).

in′sin•cere′ *adj.* not honest in the expression of actual feeling. —**in′sin•cere′ly,** *adv.* —**in′sin•cer′i•ty,** *n.*

in•sin•u•ate (in sin′yōō āt′), *v.t.* **-at•ed, -at•ing. 1.** to suggest or hint slyly. **2.** to instill or infuse subtly or artfully, as into the mind. **3.** to bring or introduce into a position by indirect or artful methods. —**in•sin′u•a′tion,** *n.* —**in•sin′u•a′tive** (-ā′tiv, -ə-tiv), *adj.*

in•sip•id (in sip′id), *adj.* **1.** without distinctive or interesting qualities. **2.** without sufficient taste or flavor.

in•sist (in sist′), *v.i.* **1.** to be emphatic, firm, or resolute: *to insist on accuracy.* —*v.t.* **2.** to assert or demand firmly or persistently. —**in•sist′ing•ly,** *adv.*

in′so•far′ *adv.* to such an extent: *insofar as I am able.*

in′sole′ *n.* **1.** the inner sole of a shoe or boot. **2.** a removable sole put inside a shoe for comfort.

in•so•lent (in′sə lənt), *adj.* boldly rude or disrespectful. —**in′so•lence,** *n.* —**in′so•lent•ly,** *adv.*

in•sol′u•ble *adj.* **1.** incapable of being dissolved. **2.** incapable of being solved. —**in•sol′u•bil′i•ty,** *n.*

in•sol′vent *adj.* unable to satisfy creditors or discharge liabilities. —**in•sol′ven•cy,** *n.*

in•som•ni•a (in som′nē ə), *n.* difficulty in falling or staying asleep, esp. when chronic. —**in•som′ni•ac′,** *n.,* *adj.*

in′so•much′ *adv.* **1.** to such a degree (usu. fol. by *that*). **2.** inasmuch (usu. fol. by *as*).

in•sou•ci•ant (in sōō′sē ənt), *adj.* free from concern or anxiety. —**in•sou′ci•ance,** *n.*

in•spect (in spekt′), *v.t.* **1.** to look carefully at or over. **2.** to view or examine formally or officially. —**in•spec′tion,** *n.* —**in•spec′tor,** *n.*

in•spire (in spī²r′), *v.,* **-spired, -spir•ing.** —*v.t.* **1.** to fill with an animating or exalting influence. **2.** to arouse or generate (a feeling, thought, etc.). **3.** to affect with a feeling, thought, etc. **4.** to guide or control by divine influence. —*v.i.* **5.** to give an inspiring influence. **6.** to inhale. —**in′spi•ra′tion,** *n.*

Inst. **1.** Institute. **2.** Institution.

in′sta•bil′i•ty *n.* lack of stability or steadiness.

in•stall or **-stal** (in stôl′), *v.t.,* **-stalled, -stall•ing** or **-stal•ling.** **1.** to put in place or connect for service or use. **2.** to establish in a place. **3.** to induct into an office with formalities. —**in′stal•la′tion** (-stə lā′shən), *n.* —**in•stall′er,** *n.*

in•stall′ment¹ or **in•stal′ment,** *n.* **1.** any of several parts into which a debt is divided for payment at specified intervals. **2.** a single portion of something issued in parts at successive times.

in•stall′ment² or **in•stal′ment,** *n.* the act of installing or fact of being installed; installation.

install′ment plan′ *n.* a system for paying for an item in installments.

in•stance (in′stəns), *n.,* *v.,* **-stanced, -stanc•ing.** —*n.* **1.** a case or occurrence of something. **2.** an example put forth in proof or illustration. **3.** the institution and prosecution of a legal case. —*v.t.* **4.** to cite as an instance.

in′stant *n.* **1.** a very short time; moment. **2.** a particular moment. —*adj.* **3.** immediate. **4.** pressing or urgent. **5.** processed so as to require minimal time to prepare: *instant coffee.* —**in′stant•ly,** *adv.*

in′stan•ta′ne•ous (-stən tā′nē əs), *adj.* occurring, done, or completed in an instant. —**in′stan•ta′ne•ous•ly,** *adv.*

in•stead (in sted′), *adv.* **1.** as a substitute or replacement. **2.** as a preferred or accepted alternative. —*Idiom.* **3.** instead of, in place of.

in′step′ *n.* the arched upper surface of the human foot between the toes and the ankle.

in•sti•gate (in′sti gāt′), *v.t.,* **-gat•ed, -gat•ing.** **1.** to cause by incitement. **2.** to provoke to some action or course. —**in′sti•ga′tion,** *n.* —**in′sti•ga′tor,** *n.*

in•still or **-stil** (in stil′), *v.t.,* **-stilled, -still•ing** or **-stil•ling.** **1.** to infuse slowly, as into the mind. **2.** to put in drop by drop.

in•stinct (in′stingkt), *n.* **1.** an inborn pattern of activity or tendency to action common to a given biological species. **2.** a natural inclination or aptitude. **3.** natural intuitive power. —**in•stinc′tive, in•stinc′tu•al** (-stingk′chōō əl), *adj.*

in•sti•tute (in′sti tōōt′, -tyōōt′), *v.,* **-tut•ed, -tut•ing,** *n.* —*v.t.* **1.** to set up; establish. **2.** to initiate; start. —*n.* **3.** a society for the promotion of the arts, scientific research, etc. **4. a.** a college for instruction in technical subjects. **b.** a unit within a university for advanced instruction and research. —**in′sti•tut′er, in′sti•tu′tor,** *n.*

in′sti•tu′tion *n.* **1.** an organization devoted to the promotion of a cause or program, esp. one of a public character. **2.** the building occupied by such an organization. **3.** a place for the care or confine-

ment of people, as mental patients. **4.** any established law, custom, etc. **5.** any familiar person, thing, or practice. —**in′sti•tu′tion•al,** *adj.*

in•struct (in strukt′), *v.t.* **1.** to furnish with knowledge, esp. by a systematic method. **2.** to direct; command. —**in•struc′tion,** *n.* —**in•struc′tor,** *n.*

in•stru•ment (in′strə mənt), *n.* **1.** a mechanical tool or implement, esp. one used for precision work. **2.** a device for producing musical sounds. **3.** a means by which something is done; agency. **4.** a mechanical or electronic device for monitoring or controlling, esp. one used in navigation. **5.** a formal legal document, as a bond. —*adj.* **6.** relying only on the observation of instruments for navigation: *instrument flying.* —*v.t.* **7.** to equip with instruments. —**in′stru•men′tal** (-men′tl), *adj.*

in′sub•or′di•nate (-dn it), *adj.* not submitting to authority. —**in′sub•or′di•na′tion,** *n.*

in•suf•fer•a•ble (in suf′ər ə bəl), *adj.* not to be endured; intolerable. —**in•suf′fer•a•bly,** *adv.*

in•su•lar (in′sə lər, ins′yə-), *adj.* **1.** of an island or islands. **2.** detached; isolated. **3.** narrow-minded or illiberal. —**in′su•lar′i•ty,** *n.*

in′su•late′ (-lāt′), *v.t.,* **-lat•ed, -lat•ing.** **1.** to cover with a material that prevents or reduces the passage or transfer of heat, electricity, or sound. **2.** to place in an isolated situation. —**in′su•la′tion,** *n.* —**in′su•la′tor,** *n.*

in•su•lin (in′sə lin, ins′yə-), *n.* **1.** a hormone, secreted by the pancreas, that regulates the metabolism of glucose and other nutrients. **2.** a commercial preparation of this substance, used for treating diabetes.

in•sult (*v.* in sult′; *n.* in′sult), *v.t.* **1.** to treat insolently or with contemptuous rudeness. —*n.* **2.** an insolent or contemptuously rude action or remark.

in•su•per•a•ble (in sōō′pər ə bəl), *adj.* incapable of being overcome or surmounted.

in•sur•ance (in shōōr′əns, -shûr′-), *n.* **1.** the act or business of insuring property, life, etc., against loss or harm, in return for payment. **2.** coverage by contract in which one party agrees to indemnify another for a specified loss. **3.** the contract itself. **4.** the amount for which anything is insured. **5.** any means of guaranteeing against loss or harm.

in•sure′ *v.t.,* **-sured, -sur•ing.** **1.** to issue or obtain insurance on or for. **2.** to ensure. —**in•sur′a•ble,** *adj.*

in•sur•gent (in sûr′jənt), *n.* **1.** a person who takes part in forcible opposition to an established government or authority. **2.** a member of a group, esp. a political party, who revolts against the leadership. —*adj.* **3.** rebellious. —**in•sur′gence,** *n.* —**in•sur′gen•cy,** *n.,* *pl.* **-cies.**

in•sur•rec•tion (in′sə rek′shən), *n.* the act of rising in arms or open rebellion against an established government or authority. —**in′sur•rec′tion•ist,** *n.*

int. **1.** interest. **2.** interior. **3.** interjection. **4.** internal. **5.** international. **6.** intransitive.

in•tact (in takt′), *adj.* remaining uninjured, sound, or whole.

in′take′ *n.* **1.** the place at which a fluid is taken into a channel, pipe, etc. **2.** the act of taking in. **3.** a quantity taken in.

in•tan•gi•ble *adj.* **1.** incapable of being perceived by touch. **2.** not definite or clear to the mind. —*n.* **3.** something intangible, esp. an intangible asset, as goodwill. —**in•tan′gi•bil′i•ty,** *n.*

in•te•ger (in′ti jər), *n.* one of the positive or negative numbers 1, 2, 3, etc., or zero.

in•te•gral (in′ti grəl, in teg′rəl), *adj.* **1.** necessary to completeness; constituent. **2.** composed of parts that together constitute a whole. **3.** complete; whole.

in•te•grate (in′ti grāt′), *v.,* **-grat•ed, -grat•ing.** —*v.t.* **1.** to bring together into a unified or interrelated whole. **2.** to combine to produce a whole or a larger unit. **3.** to make (a school, neighborhood, etc.) available to all racial and other ethnic groups. —*v.i.* **4.** to become integrated. —**in′te•gra′tion,** *n.* —**in′te•gra′tive,** *adj.*

in•teg•ri•ty (in teg′ri tē), *n.* **1.** uncompromising adherence to moral and ethical principles. **2.** the state of being whole or entire. **3.** a sound or unimpaired condition.

in•teg•u•ment (in teg′yə mənt), *n.* a natural covering, as a skin or shell.

in•tel•lect (in′tl ekt′), *n.* **1.** the faculty of the mind by which one knows or understands. **2.** a particular mind or intelligence, esp. of a high order. **3.** a highly intelligent person.

in•tel•lec•tu•al *adj.* **1.** appealing to or engaging the intellect. **2.** developed by or relying on the intellect. **3.** showing mental capacity to a high degree. —*n.* **4.** a person who values or pursues intellectual interests. —**in′tel•lec′tu•al•ly,** *adv.*

in•tel•li•gence (in tel′i jəns), *n.* **1.** capacity for learning, reasoning, and understanding. **2.** manifestation of a high mental capacity. **3.** information received or imparted. **4. a.** secret information, esp. about an enemy. **b.** an organization engaged in gathering such information.

in•tel′li•gent *adj.* having good understanding or a high mental capacity. —**in•tel′li•gent•ly,** *adv.*

in•tel′li•gi•ble (-jə bəl), *adj.* capable of being understood. —**in•tel′li•gi•bil′i•ty,** *n.* —**in•tel′li•gi•bly,** *adv.*

in•tem′per•ate *adj.* **1.** given to immoderate indulgence in alcoholic beverages. **2.** immoderate in indulgence of appetite or passion. —**in•tem′per•ance,** *n.*

in•tend (in tend′), *v.t.* **1.** to have in mind as something to be done or brought about. **2.** to design for a particular purpose or use. **3.** to mean or signify.

in•tend′ed *n. Informal.* the person one plans to marry.

in•tense (in tens′), *adj.* **1.** existing in a high or extreme degree. **2.** acute or vehement, as emotions. **3.** strenuous or earnest. **4.** having or showing great seriousness or strong feeling. —**in•tense′ly,** *adv.* —**in•tens′i•ty,** *n.*

in•ten′sive *adj.* **1.** of or characterized by intensity. **2.** (of a grammatical form or construction) indicating increased emphasis or force. —*n.* **3.** an intensive form or construction. —**in•ten′sive•ly,** *adv.* —**in•ten′sive•ness,** *n.*

in•tent¹ (in tent′), *n.* **1.** something intended. **2.** the act of intending. **3.** meaning or significance. —*Idiom.* **4. to** or **for all intents and purposes,** practically speaking.

in•tent² (in tent′), *adj.* **1.** firmly fixed or directed. **2.** having the attention sharply focused. **3.** determined or resolved: *intent on revenge.* —**in•tent′ly,** *adv.* —**in•tent′ness,** *n.*

in•ten′tion *n.* **1.** the act of determining upon some action or result. **2.** the end or object intended. **3. intentions,** purpose or attitude toward the effect of one's actions.

in•ter (in tûr′), *v.t.,* **-terred, -ter•ring.** to place (a dead body) in a grave or tomb.

inter- a prefix meaning: between or among (*interdepartmental*); mutual or reciprocally (*interdependent*).

inter. **1.** intermediate. **2.** interrogation. **3.** interrogative.

in•ter•act (in′tər akt′), *v.i.* to act upon one another. —**in′ter•ac′tion,** *n.* —**in′ter•ac′tive,** *adj.*

in′ter•breed′ *v.t., v.i.,* **-bred, -breed•ing.** to crossbreed (a plant or animal).

in′ter•cede′ (-sēd′), *v.i.,* **-ced•ed, -ced•ing. 1.** to plead in behalf of one in trouble. **2.** to mediate. —**in′ter•ces′sion,** *n.*

in′ter•cept′ (-sept′), *v.t.* **1.** to stop or interrupt the course, progress, or transmission of. **2.** *Math.* to mark off or include, as between two points or lines. —**in′ter•cep′tion,** *n.* —**in′ter•cep′tor,** *n.*

in′ter•change (*v.* in′tər chānj′; *n.* in′tər chānj′), *v.,* **-changed, -chang•ing,** *n.* —*v.t.* **1.** to put each in the place of the other. **2.** to give and receive reciprocally; exchange. —*n.* **3.** an act or instance of interchanging. **4.** a multilevel highway intersection allowing vehicles to move without crossing the streams of traffic. —**in′ter•change′a•ble,** *adj.*

in′ter•con′ti•nen′tal *adj.* **1.** between or among continents. **2.** capable of traveling between continents.

in′ter•course′ *n.* **1.** dealings or communication between individuals, countries, etc. **2.** sexual relations or a sexual coupling, esp. coitus.

in′ter•de•nom′i•na′tion•al *adj.* between or involving different religious denominations.

in′ter•de•pend′ent *adj.* mutually dependent. —**in′ter•de•pend′ence,** *n.*

in•ter•dict (*n.* in′tər dikt′; *v.* in′tər dikt′), *n.* **1.** any prohibitory act or decree. —*v.t.* **2.** to prohibit officially. **3.** to impede the flow or use of by steady bombardment. —**in′ter•dic′tion,** *n.*

in•ter•est (in′tər ist, -trist), *n.* **1.** a feeling of having one's attention or curiosity engaged by something. **2.** something that arouses such feelings. **3.** the power to excite such feelings. **4.** a business, cause, etc., in which a person has a share or concern. **5.** a legal share or right, as in a business. **6.** Often, **-ests.** a group involved in an enterprise, industry, etc. **7.** benefit; advantage. **8.** self-interest. **9. a.** a sum charged for borrowing money. **b.** the rate for such charge. —*v.t.* **10.** to excite the attention or curiosity of. **11.** to involve. —*Idiom.* **12. in the interest(s) of,** on behalf of. —**in′ter•est•ed,** *adj.*

in′terest group *n.* a group of people acting together because of a common interest, concern, or purpose.

in′ter•est•ing (-tər ə sting, -trə sting, -tə res′ting), *adj.* engaging the attention or curiosity.

in•ter•face (*n.* in′tər fās′; *v. also* in′tər fās′), *n., v.,* **-faced, -fac•ing.** —*n.* **1.** a surface regarded as the common boundary of two bodies or spaces. **2.** a common boundary between systems, equipment, concepts, or people. **3.** computer hardware or software designed to communicate information, as between a computer and a user. —*v.t., v.i.* **4.** to bring into or be in an interface.

in′ter•fere′ (-fēr′), *v.i.,* **-fered, -fer•ing. 1.** to come into opposition so as to hinder or obstruct action. **2.** to meddle. **3.** (in sports) to obstruct the action of an opposing player in an illegal way. —**in′ter•fer′ence,** *n.*

in•ter•im (in′tər əm), *n.* **1.** an intervening time. —*adj.* **2.** for an interim; temporary.

in•te•ri•or (in tēr′ē ər), *adj.* **1.** situated within. **2.** situated well inland from a coast. —*n.* **3.** the internal or inner part. **4.** a representation of the inside of a room or building. **5.** the inland parts of a region, country, etc. **6.** the domestic affairs of a country.

in′ter•ject′ (-jekt′), *v.t.* to insert, often abruptly, between other things.

in′ter•jec′tion *n.* **1.** the act of interjecting. **2.** something interjected, as a remark. **3.** a word or expression typically used in grammatical isolation to express emotion.

in′ter•lace′ *v.i, v.t.,* **-laced, -lac•ing.** to unite by or as if by weaving together; intertwine.

in′ter•lock′ *v.i., v.t.* to lock, join, or fit together closely.

in′ter•loc′u•tor (-lok′yə tər) *n.* a participant in a conversation.

in′ter•loc•u•to•ry (in′tər lok′yə tôr′ē), *adj. Law.* (of a decision, decree, etc.) not finally decisive.

in′ter•lop′er (-lō′pər) *n.* an intruder.

in′ter•lude′ *n.* **1.** an intervening episode, period, or space. **2.** an entertainment between the acts of a play. **3.** an instrumental piece of music played between the parts of a song, church service, etc.

in′ter•mar′ry *v.i.,* **-ried, -ry•ing. 1.** to become connected by marriage, as two families. **2.** to marry within one's family. **3.** to marry outside one's religion, ethnic group, etc. —**in′ter•mar′riage,** *n.*

in′ter•me′di•ar′y (-mē′dē er′ē), *n., pl.* **-ar•ies,** *adj.* —*n.* **1.** an intermediate agent or agency. —*adj.* **2.** being between; intermediate. **3.** acting as an intermediary between persons or parties.

in′ter•me′di•ate (-it), *adj.* **1.** being or acting between two points, stages, etc. —*n.* **2.** something intermediate, as a form or class.

in•ter•ment (in tûr′mənt), *n.* the act or ceremony of interring.

in•ter•mi•na•ble (in tûr′mə nə bəl), *adj.* having no apparent limit or end. —**in•ter′mi•na•bly,** *adv.*

in′ter•mis′sion (-mish′ən), *n.* an interval between periods of action or activity, as between the acts of a play.

in′ter•mit′tent (-mit′nt), *adj.* alternately ceasing and beginning again.

in•tern′[1] (in tûrn′), *v.t.* to confine within prescribed limits, as prisoners of war. **—in•tern′ment,** *n.*

in•tern′[2] (in′tûrn), *n.* **1.** a recent medical school graduate serving under supervision in a hospital. **2.** someone working as a trainee to gain practical experience in an occupation. **—v.i. 3.** to serve as an intern. **—in′tern•ship′,** *n.*

in•ter•nal (in tûr′nl), *adj.* **1.** of or on the inside or inner part. **2.** inherent or intrinsic. **3.** of the domestic affairs of a country. **4.** to be taken inside the body, esp. orally. **—in•ter′nal•ize′,** *v.t.,* **-ized, -iz•ing. —in•ter′nal•ly,** *adv.*

inter′nal-combus′tion en′gine *n.* an engine in which the process of combustion takes place within the cylinder or cylinders.

inter′nal med′icine *n.* the branch of medicine dealing with the diagnosis and nonsurgical treatment of diseases.

in′ter•na′tion•al *adj.* **1.** between or among nations. **2.** of two or more nations or their citizens. **3.** pertaining to the relations between nations. **4.** having members or activities in several nations. **—in′ter•na′tion•al•ize′,** *v.t., v.i.,* **-ized, -iz•ing. —in′ter•na′tion•al•ly,** *adv.*

in′ter•na′tion•al•ism *n.* **1.** the principle of cooperation among nations. **2.** international character, relations, or control.

in•ter•ne′cine (-nē′sēn, -sīn, -nes′ēn, -nes′īn), *adj.* **1.** involving conflict or struggle within a group. **2.** mutually destructive.

In•ter•net (in′tər net′), *n.* a large computer network linking smaller computer networks worldwide (usu. prec. by *the*).

in•tern•ist (in′tûr nist, in tûr′nist), *n.* a physician specializing in internal medicine.

in′ter•per′son•al *adj.* between persons.

in′ter•plan′e•tar′y *adj.* between planets.

in′ter•play′ *n.* reciprocal relationship, action, or influence.

in•ter•po•late (in tûr′pə lāt′), *v.t.,* **-lat•ed, -lat•ing. 1.** to introduce (something extraneous) between other things or parts. **2.** to alter (a text) by the insertion of new matter, esp. without authorization. **—in•ter′po•la′tion,** *n.*

in′ter•pose′ *v.t., v.i.,* **-posed, -pos•ing. 1.** to place or come between (other things). **2.** to put in (a remark, question, etc.) in the midst of a conversation or discourse. **3.** to bring (influence, action, etc.) to bear between parties. **—in′ter•po•si′tion** (-pə zish′ən), *n.*

in•ter•pret (in tûr′prit), *v.t.* **1.** to give the meaning of. **2.** to understand in a particular way. **3.** to translate orally. **4.** to perform (a song, role in a play, etc.) according to one's own understanding or sensitivity. **—v.i. 5.** to translate orally. **6.** to explain. **—in•ter′pret•er,** *n.*

in′ter•ra′cial *adj.* of or involving members of different races.

in′ter•re•lat′ed *adj.* closely associated.

in•ter•ro•gate (in ter′ə gāt′), *v.t., v.i.,* **-gat•ed, -gat•ing.** to ask questions of (a person), esp. formally and thoroughly: *to interrogate a suspect.* **—in•ter′ro•ga′tion,** *n.* **—in•ter′ro•ga′tor,** *n.*

in•ter•rupt (in′tə rupt′), *v.t.* **1.** to break the continuity or uniformity of (a process, activity, etc.). **2.** to stop (a person) in the midst of something, esp. by an interjected remark. **—v.i. 3.** to interfere with action or speech. **—in′ter•rup′tion,** *n.*

in′ter•scho•las′tic *adj.* existing or occurring between schools.

in′ter•sect′ (-sekt′), *v.t.* **1.** to cut or divide by passing through or across. **—v.i. 2.** to cross, as lines or wires.

in′ter•sec′tion *n.* **1.** a place where two or more roads meet. **2.** the act or fact of intersecting.

in′ter•sperse′ (-spûrs′), *v.t.,* **-spersed, -spers•ing. 1.** to scatter here and there. **2.** to diversify with something scattered.

in′ter•state′ *adj.* connecting or involving different states, esp. of the U.S.

in′ter•stel′lar *adj.* situated or occurring between the stars.

in•ter•stice (in tûr′stis), *n., pl.* **-stic•es** (-stə sēz′, -stə siz). a small or narrow space between things or parts.

in′ter•twine′ *v.t., v.i.,* **-twined, -twin•ing.** to unite by twining together.

in′ter•ur′ban *adj.* between cities.

in•ter•val (in′tər vəl), *n.* **1.** an intervening period of time. **2.** a space between things, points, etc. **3.** the difference in pitch between two tones. **—Idiom. 4. at intervals, a.** now and then. **b.** here and there.

in′ter•vene′ (-vēn′), *v.i.,* **-vened, -ven•ing. 1.** to come between disputing people, groups, etc. **2.** to occur between other events or periods. **3.** to occur incidentally so as to modify. **4.** to interfere with force or a threat of force. **—in′ter•ven′tion** (-ven′-shən), *n.*

in′ter•view′ *n.* **1.** a formal meeting in which a person questions or evaluates another. **2. a.** a conversation in which a writer or reporter obtains information from a person. **b.** the report of such a conversation. **—v.t. 3.** to have an interview with. **—in′ter•view•ee′,** *n., pl.* **-ees. —in′ter•view′er,** *n.*

in•tes•tate (in tes′tāt, -tit), *adj.* **1.** not having made a will: *to die intestate.* **2.** not disposed of by will. **—in•tes′ta•cy** (-tə sē), *n.*

in•tes•tine (in tes′tin), *n.* Usu. **-tines.** the lower part of the alimentary canal, extending from the pylorus to the anus and consisting of a narrow, longer part **(small intestine)** and a broad, shorter part **(large intestine). —in•tes′ti•nal,** *adj.*

in•ti•mate′[1] (in′tə mit), *adj.* **1.** associated in close personal relations. **2.** characterized by warm friendship. **3.** private; closely personal. **4.** characterized by privacy; cozy. **5.** inmost or deep within. **—n. 6.** an intimate friend. **—in′ti•ma•cy** (-mə sē), *n., pl.* **-cies. —in′ti•mate•ly,** *adv.*

in•ti•mate′[2] (in′tə māt′), *v.t.,* **-mat•ed, -mat•ing.** to make known indirectly. **—in′ti•ma′tion,** *n.*

in•tim•i•date (in tim′i dāt′), *v.t.,* **-dat•ed, -dat•ing. 1.** to make timid or fearful. **2.** to force into or deter from some action by inducing fear. **—in•tim′i•da′tion,** *n.*

in•to (in′tōō; *unstressed* -tōō, -tə), *prep.* **1.** to the inside of: *We walked into the room.* **2.** toward or in the direction of: *going into town.* **3.** to a point of contact with: *backed into a parked car.* **4.** to the state or form assumed or brought about: *lapsed into disrepair.* **5.** to the occupation, action, circumstance, or acceptance of: *coerced into complying.* **6.** (used to indicate a continuing extent in time or space): *lasted into the night.* **7.** *Informal.* interested or absorbed in: *She's into yoga.*

in•tol′er•a•ble *adj.* **1.** unbearable; insufferable. **2.** excessive. **—in•tol′er•a•bly,** *adv.*

in•tol′er•ant *adj.* **1.** not tolerating beliefs, manners, etc., different from one's own, as in religious matters. **2.** unable or unwilling to tolerate or endure: *intolerant of heat.* **—in•tol′er•ance,** *n.*

in•tone′ *v.t.,* **-toned, -ton•ing. 1.** to utter with a particular tone or voice modulation. **2.** to recite or chant in monotone. **—in•ton′er,** *n.*

in•tox•i•cate (in tok′si kāt′), *v.t.,* **-cat•ed, -cat•ing. 1.** to excite or stupefy with liquor. **2.** to elate; exhilarate. **—in•tox′i•cant** (-kənt), *n.* **—in•tox′i•ca′tion,** *n.*

in•trac′ta•ble *adj.* not docile or manageable. **—in•trac′ta•bil′i•ty,** *n.*

in•tra•mu•ral (in′trə myōōr′əl), *adj.* **1.** involving students at the same school: *intramural sports.* **2.** within the walls or confines, as of an institution.

in•tran•si•gent (in tran′si jənt), *adj.* refusing to agree or compromise. **—in•tran′si•gence,** *n.*

in•tran′si•tive *adj.* of or being a verb that indicates a complete action without being accompanied by a direct object. **—in•tran′si•tive•ly,** *adv.*

in′tra•u′ter•ine device *n.* any of various devices for insertion into the uterus as a contraceptive.

in•tra•ve•nous *adj.* within or into a vein. —**in′-tra•ve′nous•ly,** *adv.*

in•trep•id (in trep′id), *adj.* fearless; dauntless. —**in•trep′id•ly,** *adv.*

in•tri•cate (in′tri kit), *adj.* **1.** having many interrelated parts or facets. **2.** hard to understand, work, or make. —**in′tri•ca•cy** (-kə sē), *n., pl.* **-cies.** —**in′-tri•cate•ly,** *adv.*

in•trigue (*v.* in trēg′; *n.* also in′trēg), *v.,* **-trigued, -tri•guing,** *n.* —*v.t.* **1.** to arouse the curiosity or interest of. —*v.i.* **2.** to plot craftily or underhandedly. —*n.* **3.** a crafty or underhanded plot. **4.** the act of plotting. **5.** a secret love affair. —**in•tri′guing•ly,** *adv.*

in•trin•sic (in trin′sik, -zik), *adj.* belonging to a thing by its very nature. —**in•trin′si•cal•ly,** *adv.*

in•tro•duce (in′trə dōōs′, -dyōōs′), *v.t.,* **-duced, -duc•ing. 1.** to present (a person) to another so as to make acquainted. **2.** to present (a person, product, etc.) to a group or to the public for the first time. **3.** to bring to first knowledge or experience of something: *He introduced me to skiing.* **4.** to bring into notice or use. **5.** to begin; preface. **6.** to insert. —**in′tro•duc′tion** (-duk′shən), *n.* —**in′tro•duc′to•ry** (-ta rē), *adj.*

in•tro•spec•tion (in′trə spek′shən), *n.* observation or examination of one's own emotional state and mental processes. —**in′tro•spec′tive,** *adj.*

in′tro•vert′ (-vûrt′), *n.* a shy person concerned primarily with inner thoughts and feelings. —**in′-tro•ver′sion** (-vûr′zhən), *n.* —**in′tro•vert′ed,** *adj.*

in•trude (in trōōd′), *v.,* **-trud•ed, -trud•ing.** —*v.t.* **1.** to thrust in. —*v.i.* **2.** to come in without permission or welcome. —**in•trud′er,** *n.* —**in•tru′sion** (-trōō′zhən), *n.* —**in•tru′sive** (-siv), *adj.* —**in•tru′-sive•ly,** *adv.*

in•tu•i•tion (in′tōō ish′ən, -tyōō-), *n.* **1.** direct perception of truth, fact, etc., independent of any reasoning process. **2.** a keen and quick insight. —**in•tu′i•tive** (-i tiv), *adj.* —**in•tu′i•tive•ly,** *adv.*

in•un•date (in′ən dāt′, -un-), *v.t.,* **-dat•ed, -dat•ing. 1.** to cover with a flood. **2.** to overwhelm with abundance. —**in′un•da′tion,** *n.*

in•ure (in yōōr′, i nōōr′), *v.t.,* **-ured, -ur•ing.** to toughen or accustom by use or exposure.

in•vade (in vād′), *v.t.,* **-vad•ed, -vad•ing. 1.** to enter forcefully as an enemy. **2.** to enter and affect injuriously. **3.** to intrude upon. —**in•vad′er,** *n.*

in•va•lid¹ (in′və lid), *n.* **1.** an infirm or sickly person. —*adj.* **2.** unable to care for oneself due to infirmity or disability. **3.** of or for invalids. —*v.t.* **4.** to make an invalid.

in•val•id² (in val′id), *adj.* **1.** without force or foundation. **2.** deficient in substance or cogency. **3.** without legal force, as a contract. —**in′va•lid′i•ty,** *n.*

in•val′i•date′ (-dāt′), *v.t.,* **-dat•ed, -dat•ing. 1.** to make invalid. **2.** to deprive of legal force. —**in•val′-i•da′tion,** *n.*

in•val′u•a•ble *adj.* beyond calculable value. —**in•val′u•a•bly,** *adv.*

in•vec•tive (in vek′tiv), *n.* vehement denunciation, censure, or abuse.

in•veigh (in vā′), *v.i.* to protest strongly or attack vehemently with words.

in•vei•gle (in vā′gəl, -vē′-), *v.t.,* **-gled, -gling. 1.** to entice or lure by artful talk. **2.** to obtain by such talk. —**in•vei′gler,** *n.*

in•vent (in vent′), *v.t.* **1.** to originate as a product of one's own ingenuity or contrivance. **2.** to make up or fabricate: *to invent excuses.* —**in•ven′tion,** *n.* —**in•ven′tor,** *n.*

in•ven•to•ry (in′vən tôr′ē), *n., pl.* **-ries,** *v.,* **-ried, -ry•ing.** —*n.* **1.** a complete list of stock on hand, raw materials, etc., made by a business. **2.** the items listed. **3.** the act of making such a list. —*v.t.* **4.** to make an inventory of.

in•verse (in vûrs′, in′vûrs), *adj.* **1.** reversed in position, direction, or tendency. —*n.* **2.** something inverse; the opposite. —**in•verse′ly,** *adv.*

in•vert′ (-vûrt′), *v.t.* **1.** to turn upside down. **2.** to reverse in position, direction, or relationship. **3.** to turn inside out.

in•ver′te•brate *adj.* **1.** without a backbone or spinal column. —*n.* **2.** an invertebrate animal.

in•vest (in vest′), *v.t.* **1.** to put (money) to use in something offering profitable returns. **2.** to use or devote (time, talent, etc.), as to achieve something. **3.** to furnish with power, authority, etc. **4.** to install in office. **5.** to cover, adorn, or envelop. —*v.i.* **6.** to invest money. —**in•vest′ment,** *n.* —**in•ves′tor,** *n.*

in•ves•ti•gate (in ves′ti gāt′), *v.t., v.i.,* **-gat•ed, -gat•ing.** to search or inquire (into) systematically. —**in•ves′ti•ga′tion,** *n.* —**in•ves′ti•ga′tive,** *adj.* —**in•ves′ti•ga′tor,** *n.*

in•vet•er•ate (in vet′ər it), *adj.* **1.** confirmed in a habit, feeling, or the like. **2.** firmly established by long continuance. —**in•vet′er•a•cy** (-ə sē), *n.*

in•vid•i•ous (in vid′ē əs), *adj.* **1.** calculated to create ill will. **2.** offensively or unfairly discriminating. —**in•vid′i•ous•ly,** *adv.* —**in•vid′i•ous•ness,** *n.*

in•vig•or•ate (in vig′ə rāt′), *v.t.,* **-at•ed, -at•ing.** to fill with life and energy. —**in•vig′or•a′tion,** *n.*

in•vin′ci•ble *adj.* incapable of being conquered, defeated, or subdued. —**in•vin′ci•bil′i•ty,** *n.*

in•vi′o•la•ble *adj.* **1.** secure from destruction, infringement, or desecration. **2.** incapable of being violated; unassailable. —**in•vi′o•la•bil′i•ty,** *n.*

in•vi′o•late (-lit, -lāt′), *adj.* free from violation, injury, or desecration.

in•vis′i•ble *adj.* **1.** not perceptible by the eye. **2.** out of sight. **3.** not perceptible or discernible by the mind. —**in•vis′i•bil′i•ty,** *n.* —**in•vis′i•bly,** *adv.*

in•vite′ (-vīt′), *v.t.,* **-vit•ed, -vit•ing. 1.** to request the presence or participation of. **2.** to request politely or formally. **3.** to act so as to bring on or make probable. **4.** to attract or entice. —**in′vi•tee′,** *n., pl.* **-tees.**

in•vit′ing *adj.* attractive, alluring, or tempting.

in vi•tro (in vē′trō) *adj.* (of a biological entity or process) developed or maintained in a controlled, nonliving environment, as a laboratory vessel.

in•vo•ca•tion (in′və kā′shən), *n.* **1.** the act of invoking a deity, spirit, etc. **2.** a prayer at the beginning of a public or religious ceremony.

in•voice (in′vois), *n., v.,* **-voiced, -voic•ing.** —*n.* **1.** an itemized list of goods sold or services provided, containing prices, terms, etc. —*v.t.* **2.** to present an invoice to or for.

in•voke (in vōk′), *v.t.,* **-voked, -vok•ing. 1.** to call for with earnest desire. **2.** to call on (a deity, Muse, etc.), as in prayer. **3.** to declare to be binding or in effect: *to invoke the law.* **4.** to petition for help or aid. **5.** to call forth or upon (a spirit) by incantation. **6.** to cause or bring about.

in•vol′un•tar′y *adj.* **1.** independent of one's will. **2.** unintentional; unconscious. **3.** functioning without volition: *involuntary muscles.* —**in•vol′un•tar′-i•ly,** *adv.*

in•volve (in volv′), *v.t.,* **-volved, -volv•ing. 1.** to include as a necessary circumstance, condition, or consequence. **2.** to include within itself or its scope. **3.** to make intricate. **4.** to bring into a troublesome matter. **5.** to absorb fully; preoccupy. —**in•volved′,** *adj.* —**in•volve′ment,** *n.*

in•ward (in′wərd), *adv.* Also, **in′wards. 1.** toward the inside, as of a place. **2.** toward the mind or soul. —*adj.* **3.** directed toward the inside. **4.** situated within. **5.** mental or spiritual.

in′-your′-face′ *adj. Informal.* involving confrontation; defiant; provocative.

Io. Iowa.

I/O *Computers.* input/output.

i•o•dine (ī′ə dīn′, -din; *in Chem. also* -dēn′), *n.* a nonmetallic halogen element occurring as a grayish-black crystalline solid, used in medicine and dyes. *Symbol:* I; *at. wt.:* 126.904; *at. no.:* 53.

i•on (ī′ən, ī′on), *n.* an electrically charged atom or atom group. —**i•on′ic,** *adj.*

-ion a suffix meaning: action or process (*inspection*); result of action (*creation*); state or condition (*depression*).

i•on•ize (ī′ə nīz′), *v.,* **-ized, -iz•ing.** —*v.t.* **1.** to separate or change into ions. **2.** to produce ions in. —*v.i.* **3.** to become ionized. —**i′on•i•za′tion,** *n.* —**i′on•iz′er,** *n.*

general

i·on·o·sphere (ī on′ə sfēr′), *n.* the outermost region of the earth's atmosphere, consisting of several ionized layers. —**i·on·o·spher′ic** (-sfer′ik), *adj.*

i·o·ta (ī ō′tə), *n., pl.* **-tas.** **1.** a very small quantity. **2.** the ninth letter of the Greek alphabet (I, ι).

IOU *n., pl.* **IOUs, IOU's.** a written acknowledgment of a debt.

ip·so fac·to (ip′sō fak′tō), *adv.* by the fact itself. [< L]

IQ or **I.Q.,** intelligence quotient.

IRA or **I.R.A., 1.** individual retirement account: a personal savings plan that offers tax advantages to set aside money for retirement. **2.** Irish Republican Army.

I·ran (i ran′, i rän′, ī ran′), *n.* a republic in SW Asia. Formerly, **Persia.** —**I·ra·ni·an** (i rā′nē ən), *adj., n.*

I·raq (i rak′, i räk′), *n.* a republic in SW Asia, W of Iran. —**I·ra·qi** (i rak′ē, i rä′kē), *adj., n., pl.* **-qis.**

i·ras·ci·ble (i ras′ə bəl), *adj.* **1.** easily provoked to anger. **2.** produced by anger. —**i·ras′ci·bil′i·ty,** *n.*

ire (īr), *n.* intense anger. —**ire′ful,** *adj.* —**ire′ful·ly,** *adv.*

Ire. Ireland.

Ire·land (īr′lənd), *n.* **1.** an island of the British Isles, W of Great Britain, comprising Northern Ireland and the Republic of Ireland. **2. Republic of, a** republic occupying most of the island of Ireland.

ir·i·des′cence (ir′i des′əns) *n.* a play of rainbow-like colors. —**ir′i·des′cent,** *adj.*

i·ris (ī′ris), *n., pl.* **i·ris·es;** *esp.* for 1 **ir·i·des** (ir′i-dēz′, ī′ri-). **1.** the circular diaphragm forming the colored portion of the eye. **2.** a plant having flowers with three upright petals and three drooping, petal-like sepals.

I·rish (ī′rish), *n.* **1.** (*used with a pl. v.*) the natives or inhabitants of Ireland. **2.** the Celtic language of Ireland. —*adj.* **3.** of Ireland, its inhabitants, or their language.

irk (ûrk), *v.t.* to irritate, annoy, or exasperate.

i·ron (ī′ərn), *n.* **1.** a ductile, malleable, silver-white metallic element, used for making tools, machinery, etc. *Symbol:* Fe; *at. wt.:* 55.847; *at. no.:* 26. **2.** something hard, strong, or unyielding: *hearts of iron.* **3.** something made of iron. **4.** an appliance with a flat metal bottom, used to press clothes and linens. **5.** any of a series of iron-headed golf clubs. **6. irons,** shackles or fetters. —*adj.* **7.** made of iron. **8.** resembling iron. —*v.t., v.i.* **9.** to press with a heated iron. **10. iron out,** to clear away (difficulties).

i′ron·clad′ *adj.* **1.** covered or cased with iron plates, as a ship. **2.** very rigid or exacting: *an iron-clad contract.*

i′ron cur′tain *n.* a barrier to the exchange of information and ideas, esp. such a barrier between the Soviet bloc and other countries after World War II.

i·ro·ny (ī′rə nē, ī′ər-), *n., pl.* **-nies. 1.** the use of words to convey a meaning that is the opposite of its literal meaning. **2.** an outcome of events contrary to what was, or might have been, expected.

Ir·o·quois (ir′ə kwoi′, -kwoiz′), *n., pl.* **-quois.** a member of a confederacy of American Indian peoples formerly centered in New York. —**Ir′o·quoi′an,** *n., adj.*

ir·ra·di·ate (i rā′dē āt′), *v.t.,* **-at·ed, -at·ing. 1.** to shed rays of light upon. **2.** to illumine intellectually. **3.** to radiate. **4.** to expose to radiation, as for medical treatment. —**ir·ra′di·a′tion,** *n.*

ir·ra′tion·al *adj.* **1.** lacking the faculty of reason. **2.** lacking sound judgment. **3.** not governed by reason. **4.** (of a number) not capable of being expressed exactly as a ratio of two integers. —**ir·ra′tion·al′i·ty,** *n.* —**ir·ra′tion·al·ly,** *adv.*

ir·rec′on·cil′a·ble *adj.* **1.** incapable of being brought into harmony or adjustment. **2.** incapable of being made to acquiesce or compromise.

ir′re·deem′a·ble *adj.* **1.** incapable of being bought back or paid off. **2.** beyond redemption or reform. **3.** (of paper money) not convertible into gold or silver.

ir′re·duc′i·ble (ir′i dōō′sə bəl, -dyōō′-) *adj.* that cannot be reduced.

ir·ref′u·ta·ble *adj.* incapable of being refuted.

ir·reg′u·lar *adj.* **1.** lacking symmetry, even shape, etc. **2.** not conforming to established rules, methods, etc. **3.** not conforming to the prevalent pattern of formation, inflection, etc., in a language. —*n.* **4.** a combatant not of a regular military force, as a guerrilla. —**ir·reg′u·lar′i·ty,** *n., pl.* **-ties.**

ir·rel′e·vant *adj.* not relevant or pertinent. —**ir·rel′e·vance,** *n.*

ir·re·li′gious *adj.* **1.** not practicing a religion and feeling no religious impulses. **2.** showing a lack of religion. **3.** showing hostility to religion.

ir·rep·a·ra·ble (i rep′ər ə bəl), *adj.* incapable of being rectified, remedied, or made good. —**ir·rep′a·ra·bly,** *adv.*

ir·re·press·i·ble (ir′i pres′ə bəl), *adj.* incapable of being repressed or restrained. —**ir′re·press′i·bly,** *adv.*

ir·re·proach·a·ble (ir′i prō′chə bəl), *adj.* free from blame.

ir·re·sist·i·ble (ir′i zis′tə bəl), *adj.* **1.** incapable of being resisted or withstood. **2.** enticing; tempting. —**ir′re·sist′i·bly,** *adv.*

ir·res′o·lute′ *adj.* doubtful; infirm of purpose. —**ir·res′o·lute′ly,** *adv.* —**ir·res′o·lu′tion,** *n.*

ir′re·spec′tive *adj.* without regard to: *Irrespective of the weather, I should go.*

ir′re·spon′si·ble *adj.* characterized by a lack of a sense of responsibility. **2.** not capable of responsibility. —**ir′re·spon′si·bil′i·ty,** *n.* —**ir′re·spon′si·bly,** *adv.*

ir·re·triev·a·ble (ir′i trē′və bəl), *adj.* incapable of being retrieved or recovered.

ir·rev′er·ent (i rev′ər ənt) *adj.* lacking respect. —**ir·rev′er·ence,** *n.*

ir·rev·o·ca·ble (i rev′ə kə bəl), *adj.* not to be revoked or recalled. —**ir·rev′o·ca·bly,** *adv.*

ir·ri·gate (ir′i gāt′), *v.t.* **-gat·ed, -gat·ing. 1.** to supply (land) with water by artificial means, as by diverting streams. **2.** to wash (an orifice, wound, etc.) with liquid. —**ir′ri·ga·ble,** *adj.* —**ir′ri·ga′tion,** *n.*

ir·ri·ta·ble (ir′i tə bəl), *adj.* **1.** easily irritated or annoyed. **2.** abnormally sensitive to stimulation. —**ir′ri·ta·bil′i·ty,** *n.* —**ir′ri·ta·bly,** *adv.*

ir′ri·tate′ (-tāt′), *v.t.,* **-tat·ed, -tat·ing. 1.** to excite to impatience or anger. **2.** to make sore, red, or swollen. —**ir′ri·ta′tion,** *n.*

IRS Internal Revenue Service.

is (iz), *v.* 3rd pers. sing. pres. indic. of BE.

is. 1. island. **2.** isle.

Is·lam (is läm′, is′ləm, iz′-), *n.* **1.** the religion of the Muslims, as set forth in the Koran. **2.** the whole body of Muslim believers and countries. —**Is·lam′ic,** *adj.*

is·land (ī′lənd), *n.* **1.** a tract of land completely surrounded by water and not large enough to be called a continent. **2.** something resembling an island, esp. in being isolated.

isle (īl), *n.* **1.** a small island. **2.** any island.

is·let (ī′lit), *n.* a very small island.

ism (iz′əm), *n.* a distinctive doctrine, theory, or system.

-ism a suffix meaning: action or practice (*baptism*); state or condition (*barbarism*); doctrine or principle (*Marxism*); distinctive feature or usage (*witticism*).

i·so·bar (ī′sə bär′), *n.* a line on a map that connects points at which the barometric pressure is the same. —**i′so·bar′ic** (-bar′-), *adj.* —**i′so·bar′ism** (-bär′-), *n.*

i·so·late (ī′sə lāt′), *v.t.,* **-lat·ed, -lat·ing.** to detach or separate so as to be alone. —**i′so·la′tion,** *n.*

i′so·la′tion·ist *n.* a person opposed to participation in world affairs.

i′so·met′rics *n.pl.* exercises in which one body part is tensed against another. —**i′so·met′ric,** *adj.*

i·sos·ce·les (ī sos′ə lēz′), *adj.* (of a straight-sided plane figure) having two sides equal.

i·so·tope (ī′sə tōp′), *n.* one of two or more forms of a chemical element having the same atomic number but different atomic weights. —**i′so·top′ic** (-top′ik), *adj.*

Is·ra·el (iz′rē əl, -rā-), *n.* a republic in SW Asia, on the Mediterranean.

Is•rae′li (-rä′lē), *n., pl.* **-lis, -li,** *adj.* —*n.* **1.** a native or inhabitant of modern Israel. —*adj.* **2.** of modern Israel or its inhabitants.

Is′ra•el•ite′ (-rē ə līt′, -rä-), *n.* a member of the Hebrew people who inhabited ancient Israel.

is•sue (ish′ōō; *esp. Brit.* is′yōō), *n., v.,* **-sued, -su•ing.** —*n.* **1.** the act of sending out or putting forth. **2.** one thing or a series of things printed, published, or distributed at one time. **3.** a matter in dispute, the resolution of which is of special or public importance. **4.** something proceeding from any source, as a consequence. **5.** offspring; progeny. **6.** an outlet or exit. **7.** a discharge of blood, pus, or the like. —*v.t.* **8.** to mint, print, or publish for sale or distribution. **9.** to distribute (food, clothing, etc.). **10.** to send out; discharge. —*v.i.* **11.** to go, pass, or flow out. **12.** to be printed or published. **13.** to arise as a result. —*Idiom.* **14.** **at issue,** being disputed. **15.** **take issue,** to disagree.

isth•mus (is′məs), *n., pl.* **-mus•es, -mi** (-mī). a narrow strip of land, bordered on both sides by water, connecting two larger bodies of land. —**isth′mi•an** (-mē ən), *adj.*

it (it), *pron., nom.* **it,** *poss.* **its,** *obj.* **it,** *pl. nom.* **they,** *poss.* **their** or **theirs,** *obj.* **them,** *n.* —*pron.* **1.** (used to represent an inanimate thing understood, previously mentioned, or present in the context). **2.** (used to represent a person or animal whose gender is unknown). **3.** (used to represent a group of persons). **4.** (used to represent a concept or abstract idea). **5.** (used as the impersonal subject of the verb *to be*): *It is six o'clock.* **6.** (used in referring to an implied action, condition, or situation). **7.** (used as an anticipatory subject or object): *It is necessary that you do your duty.* —*n.* **8.** (in children's games) the player who is to perform some task, as the one who must catch the others in tag.

It. or **Ital., 1.** Italian. **2.** Italy.

ital. italic.

I•tal•ian (i tal′yən), *n.* **1.** a native or inhabitant of Italy. **2.** the Romance language of Italy. —*adj.* **3.** of Italy, its people, or their language.

i•tal•ic (i tal′ik, ī tal′-), *adj.* **1.** designating a printing type in which the letters slope to the right, used esp. for emphasis. —*n.* **2.** Often, **-ics.** italic type.

It•a•ly (it′l ē), *n.* a republic in S Europe.

itch (ich), *v.i.* **1.** to feel a tingling irritation of the skin that causes a desire to scratch the part affected. **2.** to have a desire to do or get something. —*n.* **3.** the sensation of itching. **4.** a restless longing. —**itch′y,** *adj.,* **-i•er, -i•est.** —**itch′i•ness,** *n.*

i•tem (ī′təm), *n.* **1.** a separate article or particular. **2.** a piece of information or news.

i′tem•ize′ *v.t.,* **-ized, -iz•ing.** to state or present by items. —**i′tem•i•za′tion,** *n.*

i•tin•er•ant (ī tin′ər ənt, i tin′-), *adj.* **1.** traveling from place to place, esp. on a circuit: *an itinerant preacher.* —*n.* **2.** an itinerant person.

i•tin′er•ar′y (-ə rer′ē), *n., pl.* **-ar•ies. 1.** a detailed plan for a journey. **2.** a line of travel. **3.** an account of a journey.

its (its), *pron.* the possessive form of IT (used as an attributive adjective): *The book has lost its jacket.*

it's (its), **1.** contraction of *it is.* **2.** contraction of *it has.*

it•self′ *pron.* **1.** a reflexive form of IT: *The battery recharges itself.* **2.** (used as an intensive of IT or a noun): *The land itself was not for sale.* **3.** its normal self: *The injured cat was never quite itself again.*

IV (ī′vē′), *n., pl.* **IVs, IV's.** an apparatus for intravenous delivery of medicines, nutrients, etc.

I've (īv), contraction of *I have.*

-ive a suffix meaning: tending to (*destructive*); of the nature of (*festive*).

i•vo•ry (ī′və rē, ī′vrē), *n., pl.* **-ries,** *adj.* —*n.* **1.** the hard white substance composing the main part of the tusks of the elephant, walrus, etc. **2.** any substance resembling ivory. **3. ivories,** *Slang.* **a.** the keys of a piano. **b.** dice. **4.** a creamy or yellowish white. —*adj.* **5.** made of ivory. **6.** of the color ivory.

I′vory Coast′ *n.* a republic in W Africa. Also called **Côte d'Ivoire.**

i′vory tow′er *n.* **1.** a place remote from worldly affairs. **2.** an attitude of aloofness from worldly affairs.

i•vy (ī′vē), *n., pl.* **i•vies. 1.** a climbing vine with smooth, shiny evergreen leaves. **2.** any of various other climbing plants. —**i′vied,** *adj.*

a b c d e f g h i **J** k l m n o p q r s t u v w x y z

J, j (jā), *n., pl.* **Js** or **J's, js** or **j's.** the tenth letter of the English alphabet, a consonant.

jab (jab), *v.,* **jabbed, jab•bing,** *n.* —*v.t., v.i.* **1.** to poke sharply, as with a point. **2.** to punch, esp. with a short, quick blow. —*n.* **3.** a sharp, quick thrust. **4.** a short, quick punch.

jab•ber (jab′ər), *v.i., v.t.* **1.** to speak rapidly, indistinctly, or nonsensically. —*n.* **2.** gibberish. —**jab′ber•er,** *n.*

jack (jak), *n.* **1.** any of various devices for lifting heavy objects short heights: *an automobile jack.* **2.** a playing card bearing the picture of a soldier or servant. **3.** a connecting device in an electrical circuit designed for the insertion of a plug: *a telephone jack.* **4.** one of a set of small, six-pointed metal objects used in a game (**jacks**). **5.** a small national flag flown at the bow of a ship. —*v.t.* **6.** to lift with a jack. **7.** to increase or raise: *to jack up prices.*

jack•al (jak′əl), *n.* any of several wild dogs of Asia and Africa.

jack′ass′ *n.* **1.** a male donkey. **2.** a foolish or stupid person.

jack•et (jak′it), *n.* **1.** a short coat, usu. opening down the front. **2.** a protective outer covering: *a book jacket.* —**jack′et•ed,** *adj.*

Jack′ Frost′ *n.* frost or freezing cold personified.

jack′ham′mer *n.* a portable drill operated by compressed air and used to drill rock, concrete, etc.

jack′-in-the-box′ *n., pl.* **-box•es.** a toy consisting of a box from which a figure springs up when the lid is opened.

jack′knife′ *n.,* **-knives,** *v.,* **-knifed, -knif•ing.** —*n.* **1.** a large pocketknife. **2.** a dive during which the diver bends to touch the toes and then straightens out. —*v.i.* **3.** to bend over from the middle. **4.** (of a trailer truck) to have the cab and trailer swivel until they form a V. —*v.t.* **5.** to cause to jackknife.

jack′pot′ *n.* the cumulative stakes in a contest, lottery, or the like.

jack′ rab′bit *n.* a large hare of W North America, having long hind legs and long ears.

Ja•cuz•zi (jə kōō′zē), *pl.* **-zis.** *Trademark.* a brand name for a device for a whirlpool bath and related products.

jade¹ (jād), *n.* either of two minerals, jadeite or nephrite, sometimes green, used for carvings, jewelry, etc.

jade² (jād), *n., v.,* **jad•ed, jad•ing.** —*n.* **1.** a broken-down, worthless horse. **2.** a disreputable woman. —*v.t., v.i.* **3.** to make or become dull or weary, as from overwork. —**jad′ed•ly,** *adv.* —**jad′ed•ness,** *n.*

jad′ed weary.

jag¹ (jag), *n.* a sharp projection on an edge or surface.

jag² (jag), *n.* a spree; binge: *a crying jag.*

jag•ged (jag′id), *adj.* having ragged notches or points. —**jag′ged•ly,** *adv.* —**jag′ged•ness,** *n.*

jag•uar (jag′wär), *n.* a large, powerful cat of tropical America.

jai a•lai (hī′ lī′, hī′ ə lī′), *n.* a game resembling handball, played on a three-walled court with wicker, basketlike rackets.

jail (jāl), *n.* **1.** a prison, esp. one for persons awaiting trial or convicted of minor offenses. —*v.t.* **2.** to confine in a jail. —**jail′er,** *n.*

ja•la•pe•ño (hä′lə pän′yō), *n., pl.* **-ños.** a hot pepper used esp. in Mexican cooking.

ja•lop•y (jə lop′ē), *n., pl.* **-lop•ies.** an old, decrepit automobile.

jam¹ (jam), *v.,* **jammed, jam•ming,** —*v.t.* **1.** to squeeze into a confined space. **2.** to crush by squeezing. **3.** to fill tightly; cram. **4.** to push violently against something: *He jammed his foot on the brake.* **5.** to block up by crowding. **6.** to make unworkable by causing parts to become stuck or blocked. **7.** to interfere with (radio signals or the like) by sending out other signals of approximately the same frequency. —*v.i.* **8.** to become stuck, wedged, etc. **9.** to press or push, as into a confined space. **10.** to become unworkable, as through the jamming of a part. **11.** to participate in a jam session. —*n.* **12.** the act of jamming or state of being jammed. **13.** *Informal.* a difficult situation.

jam² (jam), *n.* a preserve of slightly crushed fruit boiled with sugar.

Jam. Jamaica.

Ja•mai•ca (jə mā′kə), *n.* an island republic in the West Indies, S of Cuba. —**Ja•mai′can,** *n., adj.*

jamb (jam), *n.* either of the vertical sides of a doorway or other opening.

jam•bo•ree (jam′bə rē′), *n., pl.* **-rees. 1.** any noisy merrymaking. **2.** a large gathering of the Boy Scouts or Girl Scouts.

Jan or **Jan.,** January.

jan•gle (jang′gəl), *v.,* **-gled, -gling,** *n.* —*v.i.* **1.** to produce a harsh, usu. metallic sound. —*v.t.* **2.** to cause to jangle. **3.** to cause to become irritated. —*n.* **4.** a harsh, usu. metallic sound. —**jan′gler,** *n.*

jan•i•tor (jan′i tər), *n.* a person employed to clean the public areas of a building and do minor repairs. —**jan′i•to′ri•al** (-tôr′ē əl), *adj.*

Jan•u•ar•y (jan′yōō er′ē), *n., pl.* **-ar•ies.** the first month of the year, containing 31 days.

Ja•pan (jə pan′), *n.* a constitutional monarchy on a chain of islands off the E coast of Asia.

Jap•a•nese (jap′ə nēz′, -nēs′), *n., pl.* **-nese,** *adj.* —*n.* **1.** a native or inhabitant of Japan. **2.** the language of Japan. —*adj.* **3.** of Japan, its people, or their language.

jar¹ (jär), *n.* a broad-mouthed container, usu. of glass or earthenware.

jar² (jär), *v.,* **jarred, jar•ring,** —*v.t.* **1.** to have a sudden and unpleasant effect on. **2.** to cause to vibrate or shake. —*v.i.* **3.** to have a harshly unpleasant effect, as on the nerves. **4.** to produce a harsh, grating sound. **5.** to vibrate or shake. —*n.* **6.** a jolt or shake. **7.** an unpleasant effect; shock. **8.** a harsh or discordant sound.

jar•gon (jär′gən, -gon), *n.* **1.** the vocabulary peculiar to a particular profession or group. **2.** unintelligible language.

jas•mine (jaz′min, jas′-), *n.* any of numerous shrubs or vines with fragrant flowers.

jas•per (jas′pər), *n.* an opaque variety of quartz, usu. red or brown.

jaun•dice (jôn′dis, jän′-), *n.* yellow discoloration of the skin, whites of the eyes, etc., due to an increase of bile pigments in the blood.

jaun′diced *adj.* **1.** affected with jaundice. **2.** distorted or prejudiced, as by envy or resentment.

jaunt (jônt, jänt), *n.* **1.** a short journey, esp. for pleasure. —*v.i.* **2.** to make such a journey.

jaun•ty (jôn′tē, jän′-), *adj.,* **-ti•er, -ti•est. 1.** easy and sprightly in manner or bearing. **2.** smartly trim, as clothing. —**jaun′ti•ly,** *adv.* —**jaun′ti•ness,** *n.*

jave•lin (jav′lin, jav′ə-), *n.* a light spear, usu. thrown by hand.

jaw (jô), *n.* **1.** either of two tooth-bearing bones that form the framework of the vertebrate mouth. **2.** one of two or more parts, as of a machine, that

grasp or hold something. —*v.i.* **3.** *Slang.* to chat; gossip. —**jawed,** *adj.* —**jaw′less,** *adj.*

jaw′bone′ *n., v.,* **-boned, -bon•ing.** —*n.* **1.** any bone of a jaw, esp. a mandible. —*v.t.* **2.** to influence by persuasion, esp. by public appeal.

jay (jā), *n.* any of various noisy songbirds, often having blue or gray plumage.

jay′walk′ *v.i.* to cross a street at a place other than a regular crossing. —**jay′walk′er,** *n.*

jazz (jaz), *n.* **1.** music originating in New Orleans, marked by propulsive rhythms, ensemble playing, and improvisation. **2.** *Slang.* insincere or pretentious talk. —*v.t.* **3.** jazz up, *Slang.* **a.** to enliven. **b.** to embellish.

jazz′y *adj.,* **-i•er, -i•est. 1.** of or suggestive of jazz music. **2.** *Slang.* fancy or flashy.

J.D. 1. Doctor of Jurisprudence; Doctor of Law. [< NL *Jūris Doctor*] **2.** Doctor of Laws. [< NL *Jūrum Doctor*] **3.** Justice Department.

jeal•ous (jel′əs), *adj.* **1.** resentful and envious, as of someone's success. **2.** inclined to suspicions of rivalry, unfaithfulness, etc. **3.** watchful in guarding something: *She is jealous of her independence.* —**jeal′ous•ly,** *adv.* —**jeal′ous•y,** *n., pl.* **-ies.**

jeans (jēnz) *n.pl.* cotton trousers.

Jeep (jēp), *Trademark.* a small, rugged utility vehicle with four-wheel drive.

jeer (jēr), *v.i., v.t.* **1.** to speak or shout derisively (at). —*n.* **2.** a jeering utterance. —**jeer′ing•ly,** *adv.*

Je•ho•vah (ji hō′və), *n.* a name of God in the Old Testament.

je•june (ji jōōn′), *adj.* **1.** lacking interest or significance; insipid. **2.** lacking maturity; childish.

jell (jel), *v.i., v.t.* **1.** to become or cause to become jellylike in consistency. **2.** to become or cause to become clear or definite.

jel•ly (jel′ē), *n., pl.* **-lies,** *v.,* **-lied, -ly•ing.** —*n.* **1.** a sweet spread of fruit juice boiled with sugar and sometimes pectin. **2.** any substance having such consistency. —*v.i., v.t.* **3.** JELL (def. 1).

jel′ly•bean′ *n.* a small, bean-shaped, chewy candy.

jel′ly•fish′ *n., pl.* **-fish, -fish•es. 1.** a stinging, jellylike marine animal with trailing tentacles. **2.** an indecisive or weak person.

jel′ly roll′ *n.* a thin layer of sponge cake spread with jelly and rolled up.

jen′ny (jen′ē) *n., pl.* **-nies.** a female donkey, wren, etc.

jeop•ard•ize (jep′ər dīz′), *v.t.,* **-ized, -iz•ing.** to put in jeopardy.

jeop′ard•y (-dē), *n.* exposure to loss, harm, death, or injury.

jerk (jûrk), *n.* **1.** a quick, sharp pull, thrust, or the like. **2.** a sudden involuntary muscle contraction, as of a reflex. **3.** *Slang.* a contemptibly naive or stupid person. —*v.t.* **4.** to pull, thrust, etc., with a jerk. —*v.i.* **5.** to move spasmodically.

jer•kin (jûr′kin), *n.* a close-fitting jacket or short coat, usu. sleeveless.

jerk′wa′ter *adj.* insignificant and out-of-the-way.

jer′ry-built′ (jer′ē-), *adj.* **1.** built cheaply and flimsily. **2.** developed haphazardly.

jer•sey (jûr′zē), *n., pl.* **-seys. 1.** a machine-made fabric, characteristically soft and elastic. **2.** a close-fitting knitted sweater or shirt. **3.** (*cap.*) one of a breed of dairy cattle, raised orig. on Jersey, one of the Channel Islands.

jest (jest), *n.* **1.** a joke or witty remark. **2.** a taunt; jeer. **3.** sport or fun. **4.** the object of laughter. —*v.i.* **5.** to joke or banter. **6.** to gibe or scoff.

Je•sus (jē′zəs, -zəz), *n.* born 4? B.C., crucified A.D. 29?, the source of the Christian religion. Also called **Je′sus Christ′.**

jet¹ (jet), *n., v.,* **jet•ted, jet•ting,** *adj.* —*n.* **1.** a stream of liquid or gas shooting forth from a nozzle, orifice, etc. **2.** a spout or nozzle for emitting liquid or gas. **3.** Also called **jet′ plane′.** an airplane moved by jet propulsion. —*v.t., v.i.* **4.** to travel or transport by jet plane. **5.** to shoot (something) forth in a stream. —*adj.* **6.** of or powered by jet propulsion.

jet² (jet), *n.* **1.** a hard black coal, polished and used in jewelry. **2.** a deep black. —*adj.* **3.** of the color jet.

jet′ lag′ *n.* a temporary disruption of the body's biological rhythms after high-speed air travel through several time zones.

jet′lin·er *n.* a jet plane carrying passengers.

jet′ propul′sion *n.* the propulsion of a body by its reaction to a force ejecting a gas or a liquid from it. —**jet′-propelled′,** *adj.*

jet·sam (jet′səm), *n.* goods cast overboard to lighten a ship in an emergency.

jet·ti·son (jet′ə sən, -zən), *v.t.* **1.** to cast (cargo) overboard. **2.** to discard.

jet·ty (jet′ē), *n., pl.* **-ties. 1.** a structure projecting into a body of water to protect a harbor, deflect the current, etc. **2.** a wharf or landing pier.

Jew (jōō), *n.* **1.** a member of a people who trace their descent from the Israelites of the Bible. **2.** a person whose religion is Judaism.

jew·el (jōō′əl), *n., v.,* **-eled, -el·ing** or (*esp. Brit.*) **-elled, -el·ling.** —*n.* **1.** a precious stone; gem. **2.** a valuable piece of jewelry. **3.** a person or thing that is treasured. **4.** a bearing made of natural or synthetic precious stone, used in timepieces. —*v.t.* **5.** to adorn with jewels.

jib (jib), *n.* a triangular sail set forward of a mast.

jibe¹ (jīb), *v.i.,* **jibed, jib·ing. 1.** to shift from one side to the other, as a fore-and-aft sail. **2.** to alter course so that a fore-and-aft sail shifts in this manner.

jibe² (jīb), *v.i., v.t.,* **jibed, jib·ing,** *n.* GIBE.

jibe³ (jīb), *v.i., v.t.,* **jibed, jib·ing,** to be in harmony or accord.

jif·fy (jif′ē), *n., pl.* **-fies.** *Informal.* a very short time.

jig¹ (jig), *n.* a plate, box, or open frame for holding work and for guiding a machine tool to the work.

jig² (jig), *n., v.,* **jigged, jig·ging.** —*n.* **1.** a lively dance, usu. in triple meter. —*v.t., v.i.* **2.** to dance (a jig). —*Idiom.* **3. in jig time,** rapidly.

jig′ger *n.* **1.** a measure of 1½ oz. (45 ml) used in cocktail recipes. **2.** a small whiskey glass holding this amount.

jig′gle *v.,* **-gled, -gling,** *n.* —*v.t., v.i.* **1.** to move up and down or to and fro with short, quick jerks. —*n.* **2.** a jiggling movement. —**jig′gly,** *adj.,* **-gli·er, -gli·est.**

jig′saw′ *n.* a saw with a narrow, vertically mounted blade, for cutting curves, complex patterns, etc.

jig′saw puz′zle *n.* a set of irregularly cut pieces of pasteboard or the like that form a picture when fitted together.

jilt (jilt), *v.t.* to reject or cast aside (a lover or sweetheart). —**jilt′er,** *n.*

Jim′ Crow′ (jim), *n.* (*sometimes l.c.*) a practice or policy of segregating or discriminating against blacks. —**Jim′-Crow′,** *adj.*

jim·my (jim′ē), *n., pl.* **-mies,** *v.,* **-mied, -my·ing.** —*n.* **1.** a short crowbar. —*v.t.* **2.** to force open with or as if with a jimmy.

jim·son·weed (jim′sən wēd′), *n.* a coarse weed with poisonous leaves and tubular flowers.

jin·gle (jing′gəl), *v.,* **-gled, -gling,** *n.* —*v.i., v.t.* **1.** to make or cause to make clinking or tinkling sounds. —*n.* **2.** a jingling sound. **3.** a short verse or song with a catchy succession of repetitious sounds.

jin·go·ism (jing′gō iz′əm), *n.* chauvinism marked by the advocacy of an aggressive foreign policy. —**jin′go·ist,** *n.* —**jin′go·is′tic,** *adj.*

jinn (jin) also **jin·ni** (ji nē′, jin′ē), *n., pl.* **jinns** also **jin·nis.** (in Islamic myth) a spirit capable of influencing humankind for good or evil.

jin·rik·i·sha or **-rik·sha** (jin rik′shô, -shä), *n., pl.* **-shas.** a two-wheeled passenger vehicle pulled by one person, formerly used in Japan and China.

jinx (jingks), *n.* **1.** one thought to bring bad luck. —*v.t.* **2.** to bring bad luck to.

jit·ters *n.pl.* a feeling of fright or uneasiness (usu. prec. by *the*). —**jit′ter·y,** *adj.*

jive (jīv), *n., v.,* **jived, jiv·ing.** —*n.* **1.** swing music or early jazz. **2.** *Slang.* deceptive or meaningless talk. —*v.t., v.i.* **3.** *Slang.* to fool or kid (someone).

job (job), *n., v.,* **jobbed, job·bing.** —*n.* **1.** a piece of work done as part of one's occupation or for a price. **2.** a post of employment. **3.** any task or project. **4.** the material or item being worked upon. —*v.i.* **5.** to work at jobs or odd pieces of work. **6.** to do business as a jobber. —*v.t.* **7.** to assign (work) in separate portions, as to different contractors. —**job′hold′er,** *n.* —**job′less,** *adj.* —**job′less·ness,** *n.*

job′ ac′tion *n.* a work slowdown or other protest by employees to win specified demands.

job′ber *n.* **1.** a wholesale merchant, esp. one selling to retailers. **2.** a person who does piecework.

job′ lot′ *n.* a large assortment of goods sold as a single unit.

jock (jok), *n.* **1.** a jockstrap. **2.** *Informal.* an athlete. **3.** *Informal.* an enthusiast: *a computer jock.*

jock·ey (jok′ē), *n., pl.* **-eys,** *v.,* **-eyed, -ey·ing.** —*n.* **1.** a person who rides horses professionally in races. —*v.t.* **2.** to ride (a horse) as a jockey. **3.** to move by skillful maneuvering. —*v.i.* **4.** to aim at an advantage by skillful maneuvering.

jock′strap′ *n.* an elasticized belt with a pouch for the genitals, worn by men while participating in athletics.

jo·cose (jō kōs′, jə-), *adj.* given to or characterized by joking. —**jo·cose′ly,** *adv.* —**jo·cos′i·ty** (-kos′i-tē), *n.* —**jo·cose′ness,** *n.*

joc·u·lar (jok′yə lər), *adj.* given to or characterized by joking or jesting. —**joc′u·lar′i·ty,** *n.* —**joc′u·lar·ly,** *adv.*

jodh·purs (jod′pərz), *n.pl.* riding breeches cut very full over the hips and tightfitting below the knees.

jog¹ (jog), *v.,* **jogged, jog·ging,** *n.* —*v.t.* **1.** to move or shake with a push or jerk. **2.** to stir into activity or alertness: *to jog one's memory.* —*v.i.* **3.** to run at a slow, steady pace, esp. as an exercise. —*n.* **4.** a slight push; nudge. **5.** an act or instance of jogging. —**jog′ger,** *n.*

jog² (jog), *n., v.,* **jogged, jog·ging.** —*n.* **1.** an irregularity of line or surface. **2.** a bend or turn. —*v.i.* **3.** to bend or turn.

joie de vi·vre (zhwʌd° vē′vʀ°), *n. French.* a delight in being alive.

join (join), *v.t., v.i.* **1.** to put together or in contact. **2.** to come into contact or union (with). **3.** to become a member of (a club, society, etc.). **4.** to participate with (someone) in some act or activity.

join′er *n.* **1.** a carpenter, esp. one who constructs doors and other permanent woodwork. **2.** a person given to joining organizations. —**join′er·y,** *n.*

joint (joint), *n.* **1.** the place at which two things are joined. **2.** the place of union between two bones or elements of a skeleton. **3.** a large piece of meat, usu. with a bone. **4.** *Slang.* a marijuana cigarette. **5.** *Slang.* a cheap or disreputable place of public entertainment. —*adj.* **6.** shared by or common to two or more. **7.** sharing or acting in common: *joint authorship.* —*v.t.* **8.** to unite by a joint. **9.** to provide with joints. **10.** to cut (meat) at the joints. —*Idiom.* **11. out of joint, a.** dislocated, as a bone. **b.** disordered. —**joint′ly,** *adv.*

joist (joist), *n.* one of a number of small parallel beams that support a floor or ceiling.

joke (jōk), *n., v.,* **joked, jok·ing.** —*n.* **1.** a short humorous anecdote with a punch line. **2.** anything said or done to cause amusement. **3.** an object of laughter or ridicule. **4.** a trifling matter: *The loss was no joke.* —*v.i.* **5.** to make or tell jokes. **6.** to say something in fun rather than in earnest. —**jok′er,** *n.* —**jok′ing·ly,** *adv.*

jol·ly (jol′ē), *adj.,* **-li·er, -li·est,** *v.,* **-lied, -ly·ing.** —*adj.* **1.** in good spirits; merry. **2.** cheerfully festive. —*v.t.* **3.** to try to keep (a person) in good humor (usu. fol. by *along*). **4.** to tease, esp. good-naturedly. —**jol′li·ly,** *adv.* —**jol′li·ness,** *n.*

jolt (jōlt), *v.t.* **1.** to shake up roughly. **2.** to shock or startle. —*v.i.* **3.** to move with sharp jerks. —*n.* **4.** a jolting movement or blow. **5.** a psychological shock.

jon·quil (jong′kwil, jon′-), *n.* a narcissus with yellow or white flowers.

Jor•dan (jôr′dn), *n.* a kingdom in SW Asia, E of Israel. —**Jor•da′ni•an** (-dā′nē ən), *n., adj.*

josh (josh), *v.t., v.i.* to tease in a bantering way. —**josh′er,** *n.*

jos•tle (jos′əl), *v.,* **-tled, -tling,** *n.* —*v.t.,* **1.** to bump or shove roughly or rudely, as in a crowd. —*n.* **2.** the act of jostling.

jot (jot), *v.,* **jot•ted, jot•ting,** *n.* —*v.t.* **1.** to write down quickly or briefly (usu. fol. by *down*). —*n.* **2.** a little bit. —**jot′ter,** *n.*

jounce (jouns), *v.,* **jounced, jounc•ing,** *n.* —*v.t., v.i.* **1.** to move joltingly. —*n.* **2.** a jouncing movement. —**jounc′y,** *adj.*

jour•nal (jûr′nl), *n.* **1.** a daily record of occurrences or observations. **2.** a newspaper, esp. a daily one. **3.** a professional or academic periodical. **4.** a record of proceedings, as of a legislative body. **5.** (in bookkeeping) a book into which all transactions are entered before being posted into the ledger. **6.** the portion of a shaft or axle contained by a bearing.

jour′nal•ese′ (-ēz′, -ēs′), *n.* a style of writing regarded as typical of newspapers and magazines.

jour′nal•ism *n.* the occupation of gathering, writing, editing, and publishing or broadcasting news. —**jour′nal•ist,** *n.* —**jour′nal•is′tic,** *adj.*

jour•ney (jûr′nē), *n., pl.* **-neys,** *v.,* **-neyed, -ney•ing.** —*n.* **1.** a traveling from one place to another, usu. taking a long time. —*v.i.* **2.** to make a journey. —**jour′ney•er,** *n.*

jour′ney•man *n., pl.* **-men.** **1.** a person who has served an apprenticeship at a trade. **2.** a competent but routine worker or performer.

joust (joust, just), *n.* **1.** a combat between two mounted knights armed with lances. —*v.i.* **2.** to engage in a joust. —**joust′er,** *n.*

jo•vi•al (jō′vē əl), *adj.* characterized by hearty, joyous humor. —**jo′vi•al′i•ty,** *n.* —**jo′vi•al•ly,** *adv.*

jowl¹ (joul), *n.* **1.** a jaw, esp. the lower jaw. **2.** the meat of the cheek of a hog.

jowl² (joul), *n.* a fold of flesh hanging from the jaw, as of a fat person. —**jowl′y,** *adj.,* **-i•er, -i•est.**

joy (joi), *n.* **1.** a feeling of great delight or happiness; elation. **2.** a cause of keen pleasure or delight. —**joy′ful,** *adj.* —**joy′less,** *adj.*

joy′ride′ *n.* a pleasure ride in an automobile, esp. when the vehicle is driven recklessly. —**joy′rid′er,** *n.*

joy′stick′ *n.* **1.** *Informal.* the control stick of an airplane or other vehicle. **2.** a lever used to control the movement of a cursor or other graphic element, as in a video game.

JP Justice of the Peace.

Jr. or **jr.,** junior.

ju•bi•lant (jōō′bə lənt), *adj.* showing great joy or triumph; exultant. —**ju′bi•lant•ly,** *adv.*

ju•bi•lee (jōō′bə lē′), *n., pl.* **-lees.** **1.** the celebration of any of certain anniversaries, as the 25th, 50th, or 75th. **2.** any season or occasion of rejoicing. **3.** rejoicing or jubilation.

Ju′da•ism (-dē iz′əm, -də-), *n.* the monotheistic religion of the Jews.

judge (juj), *n., v.,* **judged, judg•ing.** —*n.* **1.** a public officer authorized to hear and decide cases in a court of law. **2.** a person appointed to decide in a competition or contest. **3.** a person qualified to pass critical judgment. —*v.t.* **4.** to pass legal judgment on. **5.** to form a judgment or opinion concerning. **6.** to decide or settle authoritatively. **7.** to think or hold as an opinion. **8.** to act as a judge in. —*v.i.* **9.** to act as a judge. **10.** to form an opinion. —**judge′ship,** *n.*

judg′ment *n.* **1.** the act of judging. **2.** the ability to judge objectively or wisely. **3.** an opinion formed. **4. a.** a judicial decision. **b.** the certificate embodying such a decision. **5.** (*cap.*) LAST JUDGMENT. Also, *esp. Brit.,* **judge′ment.**

judg•men′tal *adj.* tending to make judgments, esp. moral judgments.

ju•di•cial (jōō dish′əl), *adj.* **1.** pertaining to courts of law or to judges. **2.** proper to the character of a judge. **3.** decreed, sanctioned, or enforced by a court. —**ju•di′cial•ly,** *adv.*

ju•di′ci•ar′y (-dish′ē er′ē, -dish′ə rē), *n., pl.* **-ar•ies,** *adj.* —*n.* **1.** the judicial branch of government. **2.** the system of courts in a country. **3.** judges collectively. —*adj.* **4.** pertaining to the judicial branch or system or to judges.

ju•di′cious *adj.* having, exercising, or characterized by good judgment. —**ju•di′cious•ly,** *adv.* —**ju•di′cious•ness,** *n.*

ju•do (jōō′dō), *n.* a martial art based on jujitsu but banning dangerous throws and blows.

jug (jug), *n.* **1.** a container for liquid, having a handle and a narrow neck. **2.** *Slang.* a jail; prison.

jug•ger•naut (jug′ər nôt′, -not′), *n.* any large, overpowering, destructive force or object.

jug•gle (jug′əl), *v.,* **-gled, -gling.** —*v.t.* **1.** to keep (several objects, as balls) in the air simultaneously by tossing and catching. **2.** to manipulate in order to deceive: *to juggle the accounts.* **3.** to handle the requirements of (two or more activities) simultaneously: *to juggle the obligations of work and school.* —*v.i.* **4.** to juggle objects. —**jug′gler,** *n.* —**jug′gler•y,** *n.*

jug•u•lar (jug′yə lər), *adj.* **1.** of the throat or neck. —*n.* **2.** any of several veins of the neck that convey blood from the head to the neck.

juice (jōōs), *n., v.,* **juiced, juic•ing.** —*n.* **1.** the natural fluid in a plant, esp. a fruit. **2.** the natural fluids of an animal body: *gastric juices.* **3.** strength or vitality. **4.** *Slang.* **a.** electricity. **b.** gasoline or fuel oil. **5.** *Slang.* alcoholic liquor. —*v.t.* **6.** to extract juice from.

juic′er *n.* **1.** an appliance for extracting juice from fruits and vegetables. **2.** *Slang.* a heavy drinker of alcohol.

ju•jit•su (jōō jit′sōō) also **-jut′su** (-jut′sōō, -jōōt′-), *n.* a Japanese method of defending oneself without weapons by using the strength and weight of one's adversary to disable him or her.

ju•jube (jōō′jōōb, jōō′jōō bē′), *n.* a chewy fruit-flavored lozenge.

juke•box (jōōk′boks′), *n.* a coin-operated phonograph having records selected by push button.

Jul or **Jul.,** July.

ju•li•enne (jōō′lē en′), *adj.* (of vegetables) cut into thin strips.

Ju•ly (jōō lī′, jə-), *n., pl.* **-lies.** the seventh month of the year, containing 31 days.

jum•ble (jum′bəl), *v.,* **-bled, -bling,** *n.* —*v.t., v.i.* **1.** to mix or be mixed in a confused mass. —*n.* **2.** a mixed or disordered mass.

jum•bo (jum′bō), *n., pl.* **-bos,** *adj.* —*n.* **1.** a very large person, animal, or thing. —*adj.* **2.** very large.

jump (jump), *v.i.* **1.** to spring from the ground or other support by a sudden muscular effort. **2.** to move or jerk suddenly, as from shock. **3.** *Informal.* to be full of activity. **4.** to rise suddenly: *Prices jumped.* **5.** to proceed abruptly: *to jump to a conclusion.* **6.** to take eagerly; seize: *We jumped at the offer.* —*v.t.* **7.** to leap or spring over. **8.** to cause to leap. **9.** to skip or bypass. **10.** to move or start before (a signal); anticipate. **11.** to increase suddenly. **12.** to attack without warning, as from ambush. **13.** to flee from: *to jump town.* —*n.* **14.** an act or instance of jumping. **15.** a sudden rise in amount, price, etc. **16.** an abrupt transition. **17.** a sudden start, as from nervous excitement. —*Idiom.* **18. get** or **have the jump on,** to have an initial advantage over.

jump′er¹, *n.* **1.** one that jumps. **2.** a short wire used to make a temporary electrical connection. **3.** either of a pair of electric cables for starting the engine of a vehicle whose battery is dead.

jump′er², *n.* **1.** a sleeveless dress worn over a blouse. **2.** a loose jacket.

jump′-start′ *n.* **1.** the starting of an internal-combustion engine by means of jumpers. —*v.t.* **2.** to give a jump-start to. **3.** to enliven or revive: *to jump-start a sluggish economy.*

jump′suit′ *n.* **1.** a one-piece suit worn by parachutists. **2.** a garment fashioned after it.

jump′y *adj.,* **-i•er, -i•est.** **1.** nervous or apprehensive; jittery. **2.** characterized by sudden jerks. —**jump′i•ness,** *n.*

Jun or **Jun.,** June.
junc•tion (jungk′shən), *n.* **1.** the act of joining or state of being joined. **2.** a place where things meet or cross.
junc′ture (-chər), *n.* **1.** a point of time, esp. one made critical by circumstances. **2.** a crisis. **3.** the point at which two bodies are joined.
June (jōōn), *n.* the sixth month of the year, containing 30 days.
jun•gle (jung′gəl), *n.* **1.** wild land overgrown with dense vegetation, esp. in the tropics. **2.** a place of violence, struggle, or ruthless competition.
jun•ior (jōōn′yər), *adj.* **1.** younger (designating a son named after his father; often written as *Jr.* following the name). **2.** of more recent election, appointment, or admission. **3.** of lower rank. **4.** of juniors in school. —*n.* **5.** a person who is younger or of lower rank than another. **6.** a student in the next to the last year at a high school or college.
jun′ior col′lege *n.* a school offering courses only through the first two years of college.
jun′ior high′ school′ *n.* a secondary school usu. consisting of grades seven through nine.
ju•ni•per (jōō′nə pər), *n.* an evergreen shrub or tree with berrylike cones that yield an oil used to flavor gin.
junk¹ (jungk), *n.* **1.** old or discarded material or objects. **2.** something regarded as worthless. —*v.t.* **3.** to discard as junk. —**junk′y,** *adj.,* **-i•er, -i•est.**
junk² (jungk), *n.* a seagoing ship used primarily in Chinese waters, having a flat bottom.
junk³ (jungk), *n. Slang.* narcotics, esp. heroin.
junk′er *n. Informal.* a car in bad enough repair to be scrapped.
Jun•ker (yŏŏng′kər), *n.* a member of a politically conservative class of Prussian landowners.
jun•ket (jung′kit), *n.* **1.** a custardlike dessert of flavored milk curdled with rennet. **2.** a pleasure excursion. **3.** a trip by a government official at public expense, ostensibly to obtain information. —*v.i.* **4.** to go on a junket. —**jun′ke•teer′** (-ki tēr′), **jun′ket•er,** *n.*
junk′ food′ *n.* food that is high in calories but of little nutritional value.
junk′ie *n. Informal.* **1.** a drug addict, esp. one addicted to heroin. **2.** a person with a craving or enthusiasm for something: *a chocolate junkie.*
junk′ mail′ *n.* unsolicited commercial material, as advertisements, mailed in bulk.
jun•ta (hŏŏn′tə, jun′-, hun′-), *n., pl.* **-tas.** a small group ruling a country, esp. immediately after a coup d′état.
Ju•pi•ter (jōō′pi tər), *n.* **1.** the supreme deity of the ancient Romans, associated with the sky and rain. **2.** the largest planet in the solar system, fifth in order from the sun.

ju•ris•dic•tion (jŏŏr′is dik′shən), *n.* **1.** the right, power, or authority to administer justice. **2.** power; authority; control. **3.** the territory over which authority is exercised. —**ju′ris•dic′tion•al,** *adj.*
ju′ris•pru′dence *n.* **1.** the science or philosophy of law. **2.** a system of laws. **3.** a branch of law.
ju′rist *n.* a person versed in the law, as a judge.
ju•ror (jŏŏr′ər, -ôr), *n.* a member of a jury.
ju′ry *n., pl.* **-ries.** **1.** a group of persons selected and sworn to examine the evidence in a case and render a verdict to a court. **2.** a group of persons chosen to adjudge prizes, awards, etc. —*Idiom.* **3. the jury is still out,** a decision or opinion is yet to be rendered: *The jury is still out on his job performance.*
just (just), *adv.* **1.** within a brief preceding time: *The sun just came out.* **2.** precisely: *That's just what I mean.* **3.** barely: *just in time.* **4.** merely: *just a child.* **5.** at this moment: *The movie is just ending.* **6.** simply: *We'll just have to wait and see.* —*adj.* **7.** guided by reason and fairness. **8.** proper: *a just reply.* **9.** lawful: *a just claim.* **10.** true; correct: *a just analysis.* **11.** deserved: *a just punishment.* **12.** proper or right: *just proportions.* **13.** righteous. —**just′ly,** *adv.* —**just′ness,** *n.*
jus•tice (jus′tis), *n.* **1.** the quality of being just; moral rightness. **2.** rightfulness or lawfulness, as of a claim. **3.** the administering of deserved punishment or reward. **4.** the administration of what is just according to law. **5.** a judge or magistrate. —*Idiom.* **6. do justice to, a.** to act fairly toward. **b.** to appreciate properly.
jus′tice of the peace′ *n.* a local public officer having authority to try minor cases, solemnize marriages, etc.
jus′ti•fy′ *v.t.,* **-fied, -fy•ing.** **1.** to show to be just, right, or reasonable. **2.** to uphold as warranted: *Don't try to justify his rudeness.* **3.** to absolve of guilt. —**jus′ti•fi′a•ble,** *adj.* —**jus′ti•fi•a•bly,** *adv.* —**jus′ti•fi•ca′tion,** *n.*
jut (jut), *v.,* **jut•ted, jut•ting,** *n.* —*v.i., v.t.* **1.** to project; protrude. —*n.* **2.** something that juts out.
jute (jōōt), *n.* **1.** a strong fiber used for making burlap, cordage, etc., obtained from two East Indian plants. **2.** either of these plants.
ju•ve•nile (jōō′və nl, -nīl′), *adj.* **1.** characteristic of or suitable for young people. **2.** young. **3.** immature; childish. —*n.* **4.** a young person. **5.** an actor or actress who plays youthful roles. **6.** a book for children.
ju′venile delin′quency *n.* illegal or antisocial behavior by a minor. —**ju′venile delin′quent,** *n.*
jux•ta•pose (juk′stə pōz′, juk′stə pōz′), *v.t.,* **-posed, -pos•ing.** to place close together or side by side, as for contrast. —**jux′ta•po•si′tion** (-pə zish′ən), *n.*

a b c d e f g h i j **K** l m n o p q r s t u v w x y z

K, k (kā), *n., pl.* **Ks** or **K's, ks** or **k's.** the 11th letter of the English alphabet, a consonant.
K 1. *Computers.* **a.** the number 1024 or 2^{10}. **b.** kilobyte. **2.** the number 1000: *a $50K salary.* **3.** kindergarten.
K *Symbol.* **1.** *Chem.* potassium. [< NL *kalium*] **2.** Kelvin. **3.** strikeout.
k. or **k, 1.** karat. **2.** kilogram.
ka•bu•ki (kə bōō′kē, kä′bōō kē′), *n.* a popular drama of Japan characterized by stylized acting and the performance of all roles by male actors. [< Japn: song-and-dance art]
kai•ser (kī′zər), *n.* a German emperor: the title used from 1871 to 1918.
kale (kāl), *n.* an edible cabbagelike plant with wrinkled leaves.
ka•lei•do•scope (kə lī′də skōp′), *n.* **1.** a tubular optical toy in which bits of colored glass are re-

flected by mirrors to display changing patterns. **2.** a continually shifting pattern, scene, etc. —**ka•lei′do•scop′ic** (-skop′ik), *adj.*
kan•ga•roo (kang′gə rōō′), *n., pl.* **-roos.** a herbivorous leaping marsupial of Australia and adjacent islands, with short forelimbs and powerful hind legs.
kan′garoo court′ *n.* a self-appointed tribunal that disregards existing principles of law or human rights.
Kans. Kansas.
ka•o•lin or **-line** (kā′ə lin), *n.* a fine white clay used in making porcelain.
ka•pok (kā′pok), *n.* the silky down that covers the seeds of a tropical tree, used for stuffing pillows, life jackets, etc.
ka•put (kä pŏŏt′, -pōōt′, kə-), *adj. Slang.* ruined or broken.
ka•ra•o•ke (kar′ē ō′kē), *n.* the act of singing along

general

to a music video, esp. one from which the original vocals have been eliminated. [< Japn, = *kara* empty + *oke* orchestra]

kar•at (kar′ət), *n.* a unit for measuring the fineness of gold, pure gold being 24 karats fine.

ka•ra•te (kə rä′tē), *n.* a Japanese method of self-defense using fast, hard blows with the hands, elbows, knees, or feet. [< Japn, = *kara* empty + *te* hand(s)]

kar•ma (kär′mə), *n.* (in Hinduism and Buddhism) action seen as bringing upon oneself inevitable results, either in this life or in a reincarnation.

Kas. Kansas.

ka•ty•did (kā′tē did), *n.* any of several large, usu. green, American grasshoppers.

kay•ak (kī′ak), *n.* **1.** an Eskimo canoe with a skin cover on a light framework. **2.** a small boat resembling this, used in sports.

Ka•zakh•stan (kä′zäk stän′), *n.* a republic in central Asia, NE of the Caspian Sea: formerly a part of the USSR.

ka•zoo (kə zōō′), *n., pl.* **-zoos.** a tubular musical toy with a membrane that vibrates with a buzz when one hums into it.

KB kilobyte.

K.C. Kansas City.

ke•bab or **-bob** (kə bob′), *n.* small pieces of meat, marinated and broiled on a skewer.

keel (kēl), *n.* **1.** a central structural member in the bottom of a ship's hull, extending from the stem to the stern. —*v.* **2. keel over, a.** to capsize. **b.** to fall or cause to fall over without warning. —*Idiom.* **3. on an even keel,** in a stable or calm state.

keen[1] (kēn), *adj.,* **-er, -est. 1.** finely sharpened: *a keen razor.* **2.** sharp or piercing: *a keen wind.* **3.** highly sensitive or perceptive: *keen ears.* **4.** shrewdly intelligent: *a keen observer.* **5.** intense: *keen desire.* **6.** eager: *keen to go swimming.* —**keen′ly,** *adv.* —**keen′ness,** *n.*

keen[2] (kēn), *n.* **1.** a wailing lament for the dead. —*v.t., v.i.* **2.** to wail in lamentation for (the dead).

keep (kēp), *v.,* **kept, keep•ing,** *n.* —*v.t.* **1.** to retain in one's possession. **2.** to hold in a given place: *to keep mints in a dish.* **3.** to cause to continue in a given position, state, etc.: *to keep a light burning.* **4.** to maintain in good condition: *to keep meat by freezing it.* **5.** to detain. **6.** to maintain in one's service or for one's use: *to keep a chauffeur.* **7.** to take care of or support. **8.** to refrain from disclosing: *to keep a secret.* **9.** to restrain or prevent: *to keep a pipe from leaking.* **10.** to record regularly: *to keep attendance figures.* **11.** to obey or fulfill (a law, promise, etc.). **12.** to observe with formalities: *to keep the Sabbath.* **13.** to protect: *He kept her from harm.* —*v.i.* **14.** to continue in a specified position, state, etc.: *to keep cool.* **15.** to continue or go on: *Keep trying.* **16.** to stay in good condition. **17.** to refrain: *Try to keep from smiling.* **18. keep up, a.** to perform as swiftly or successfully as others. **b.** to continue. **c.** to maintain in good condition. **d.** to stay informed. —*n.* **19.** subsistence; support. **20.** the innermost and strongest structure of a medieval castle. —*Idiom.* **21. for keeps,** permanently. **22. keep to oneself, a.** to remain aloof from others. **b.** to hold as secret. —**keep′er,** *n.*

keep′ing *n.* agreement or conformity: *actions in keeping with one's words.*

keep′sake′ *n.* anything kept, or given to be kept, as a token of friendship.

keg (keg), *n.* **1.** a small cask. **2.** a unit of weight equal to 100 pounds (45 kg), used for nails.

kelp (kelp), *n.* any large, brown, cold-water seaweed.

Kel•vin (kel′vin), *adj.* of or noting an absolute scale of temperature in which 0° equals -273.16° Celsius. [after 1st Baron *Kelvin* (1824–1907), English physicist]

ken (ken), *n., v.,* **kenned, ken•ning.** —*n.* **1.** knowledge or understanding. —*v.t., v.i.* **2.** *Chiefly Scot.* to know; understand.

Ken. Kentucky.

ken•nel (ken′l), *n., v.,* **-neled, -nel•ing** or (*esp. Brit.*) **-nelled, -nel•ling.** —*n.* **1.** a shelter for a dog

or cat. **2.** Often, **-nels.** an establishment where dogs or cats are bred, trained, or boarded. —*v.t.* **3.** to put or keep in a kennel.

Ken•ya (ken′yə, kēn′-), *n.* a republic in E Africa. —**Ken′yan,** *adj., n.*

ker•chief (kûr′chif, -chēf), *n.* **1.** a woman's square scarf worn as a covering for the head or neck. **2.** HANDKERCHIEF.

ker•nel (kûr′nl), *n.* **1.** the softer, usu. edible part of a nut or fruit pit. **2.** the body of a seed within its husk. **3.** the central or most important part of anything.

ker•o•sene (ker′ə sēn′), *n.* a white oily liquid obtained by distilling petroleum, used as a fuel and cleaning solvent.

kes•trel (kes′trəl), *n.* any of various small falcons that hover as they hunt.

ketch•up (kech′əp, kach′-), *n.* a condiment consisting of puréed tomatoes, onions, vinegar, sugar, and spices. [< Malay *kəchap* fish sauce, perh. < dial. Chin.]

ket•tle (ket′l), *n.* a metal container in which to boil liquids or cook foods.

ket′tle•drum′ *n.* a drum consisting of a hollow hemisphere of brass, copper, or fiberglass over which is stretched a skin.

key[1] (kē), *n., pl.* **keys,** *adj., v.,* **keyed, key•ing.** —*n.* **1.** a metal instrument inserted into a lock to move its bolt. **2.** any device resembling or functioning like a key. **3.** something that affords a means to achieve something else: *the key to happiness.* **4.** something that serves to clarify, solve, etc., as a list of answers to a test. **5.** one of a set of levers or buttons pressed by the fingers in operating a typewriter, computer, piano, etc. **6.** the principal tonality of a musical composition: *a symphony in the key of C minor.* **7.** degree of intensity, as of feeling. —*adj.* **8.** chief; major; essential. —*v.t.* **9.** to adjust (actions, speech, etc.) to a particular state or activity. **10.** to regulate the pitch of. **11.** to provide with a key. **12.** to keyboard: *to key in data.* **13. key up,** to increase tension in.

key[2] (kē), *n., pl.* **keys.** a reef or low island.

key′board′ *n.* **1.** the row or set of keys on a piano, computer, etc. **2.** a musical instrument with a pianolike keyboard. —*v.t., v.i.* **3.** to enter (data) into a computer by means of a keyboard. —**key′board′er,** *n.*

key′note′ *n., v.,* **-not•ed, -not•ing.** —*n.* **1.** the note on which a key or system of tones is founded; tonic. **2.** the basic idea, principle, or theme. —*v.t.* **3.** to deliver a keynote address at. —**key′not′er,** *n.*

key′note address′ *n.* a speech, as at a political convention, that presents important issues, policies, etc.

key′stone′ *n.* **1.** the wedge-shaped piece at the summit of an arch. **2.** something on which associated things depend.

kg kilogram.

khak•i (kak′ē, kä′kē), *n., pl.* **-is. 1.** a dull yellowish brown. **2.** a stout, twilled fabric of this color. **3.** Usu., **khakis.** a uniform or trousers made of khaki. —*adj.* **4.** made of khaki. [< Urdu < Pers *khākī* dusty]

khan (kän, kan), *n.* **1.** a title of rulers of the empire founded by Genghis Khan, and of the states that succeeded his empire. **2.** a title of respect used in numerous Asian countries.

kHz kilohertz.

KIA killed in action.

kib•butz (ki bŏŏts′, -bŏŏts′), *n., pl.* **-but•zim** (-bŏŏt sēm′). a collective, usu. agricultural settlement in Israel. [< ModHeb *qibbūṣ* lit., gathering]

kib•itz•er (kib′it sər), *n. Informal.* **1.** a spectator at a card game who gives unsolicited advice. **2.** a giver of unsolicited advice; busybody. —**kib′itz,** *v.i.*

kick (kik), *v.t.* **1.** to strike with the foot. **2.** to drive or force by or as if by kicks. **3.** *Football.* to score (a field goal) by kicking the ball. **4.** *Slang.* to give up (a habit). —*v.i.* **5.** to make a rapid, forceful thrust with the foot. **6.** to object or complain. **7.** (of a firearm) to recoil. **8. kick in,** to contribute as one's share. **9. ~ over,** (of an internal-combustion engine) to begin ignition. —*n.* **10.** the act of kicking. **11.** an objection or complaint. **12.** *Slang.* **a.** pleasurable excitement or stimulation. **b.** a strong but temporary interest: *Photography is her latest kick.* **13.** a recoil of a gun. —**kick′er,** *n.*

kick′back′ *n.* a portion of an income given to someone as payment for having made the income possible.

kick′off′ *n.* **1.** a kick that puts the ball into play in football or soccer. **2.** the start of something.

kick′stand′ *n.* a pivoting bar for holding a bicycle or motorcycle upright when not in use.

kid¹ (kid), *n.* **1.** *Informal.* a child. **2.** a young goat. **3.** leather made from the skin of a young goat.

kid² (kid), *v.t., v.i.,* **kid•ded, kid•ding.** *Informal.* **1.** to tease. **2.** to deceive as a joke. —**kid′der,** *n.*

kid•nap (kid′nap), *v.t.,* **-napped** or **-naped, -nap•ping** or **-nap•ing.** to carry off (a person) by force or fraud, esp. for ransom. —**kid′nap•per, kid′nap•er,** *n.*

kid•ney (kid′nē), *n., pl.* **-neys. 1.** one of a pair of organs that filter waste from the blood and excrete uric acid or urea. **2.** an animal's kidney used as food. **3.** temperament. **4.** kind; sort.

kid′ney bean′ *n.* **1.** a bean plant cultivated in many varieties for its edible seeds. **2.** its mature seed.

kid′ney stone′ *n.* a mineral concretion formed abnormally in the kidney.

kill (kil), *v.t.* **1.** to cause the death of; slay. **2.** to destroy; extinguish. **3.** to spend (time) unprofitably. **4.** *Informal.* to cause discomfort to. **5.** to cancel publication of. **6.** to defeat or veto (a legislative bill, etc.). **7.** to turn off: *to kill an engine.* —*n.* **8.** the act of killing, esp. game. **9.** an animal or animals killed. —**kill′er,** *n.*

kill′er whale′ *n.* a large, predatory, black-and-white dolphin.

kill′ing *n.* **1.** the act of a person or thing that kills. **2.** a quick, large profit. —*adj.* **3.** fatal. **4.** exhausting.

kill′-joy′ *n.* a person who spoils the pleasure of others.

kiln (kil, kiln), *n.* a furnace or oven for burning, baking, or drying something, esp. one for firing pottery.

ki•lo (kē′lō, kil′ō), *n., pl.* **-los. 1.** a kilogram. **2.** a kilometer.

kilo- a combining form meaning thousand (*kilowatt*).

kil•o•byte (kil′ə bīt′), *n. Computers.* **1.** 1024 bytes. **2.** (loosely) 1000 bytes.

kil′o•gram′ *n.* the basic unit of mass in the metric system, equal to 1000 grams.

kil′o•hertz′ *n., pl.* **-hertz, -hertz•es.** a unit of frequency equal to 1000 cycles per second.

kil′o•li′ter (-lē′-), *n.* 1000 liters.

kil•o•me•ter (ki lom′i tər, kil′ə mē′-), *n.* a unit of length equal to 1000 meters.

kil′o•watt′ *n.* a unit of power equal to 1000 watts.

kilt (kilt), *n.* **1.** a pleated, knee-length tartan skirt worn by Scotsmen in the Highlands. **2.** a woman's skirt modeled on this.

ki•mo•no (ka mō′na, -nō), *n., pl.* **-nos. 1.** a loose, wide-sleeved Japanese robe, fastened with a broad sash. **2.** a woman's dressing gown.

kin (kin), *n.* all of a person's relatives.

-kin a suffix meaning little or diminutive (*lambkin*).

kind¹ (kīnd), *adj.,* **-er, -est.** gentle; considerate; benevolent.

kind² (kīnd), *n.* **1.** a class or group of animals, people, objects, etc., classified on the basis of common traits. **2.** nature or character. **3.** variety; sort. —*Idiom.* **4. in kind, a.** in the same way. **b.** in goods or services rather than money. **5. kind of,** *Informal.* somewhat.

kin•der•gar•ten (kin′dər gär′tn, -dn), *n.* a class or school for young children, usu. five-year-olds. —**kin′der•gart′ner, kin′der•gar′ten•er** (-gärt′nər, -gärd′-), *n.* [< G]

kind′heart′ed *adj.* having or showing kindness. —**kind′heart′ed•ly,** *adv.* —**kind′heart′ed•ness,** *n.*

kin•dle (kin′dl), *v.,* **-dled, -dling.** —*v.t.* **1.** to set fire to or ignite. **2.** to excite or arouse. —*v.i.* **3.** to begin to burn. **4.** to become aroused or animated.

kin′dling *n.* material that can be readily ignited, used in starting a fire.

kind′ly *adj.,* **-li•er, -li•est,** *adv.* —*adj.* **1.** kind or sympathetic. **2.** pleasant or beneficial. —*adv.* **3.** in a kind manner. **4.** cordially: *We thank you kindly.* **5.** obligingly; please: *Kindly close the door.* **6.** with liking; favorably: *to take kindly to an idea.* —**kind′li•ness,** *n.*

kin•dred (kin′drid), *n.* **1.** a person's relatives collectively; kin. —*adj.* **2.** related or similar.

ki•net•ic (ki net′ik, kī-), *adj.* of or caused by motion.

king (king), *n.* **1.** a male sovereign or monarch. **2.** a person or thing preeminent in its class. **3.** a playing card bearing a picture of a king. **4.** the chief chess piece of each color. —*adj.* **5.** large. **6.** preeminent. —**king′ly,** *adj.* —**king′ship,** *n.*

king′dom (-dəm), *n.* **1.** a state having a king or queen as its head. **2.** anything constituting an independent realm: *the kingdom of thought.* **3.** one of the three broad divisions of natural objects: *the animal, vegetable, and mineral kingdoms.*

king′fish′er *n.* a fish- or insect-eating bird with a long, stout bill.

king′-size′ or **-sized′,** *adj.* larger or longer than the usual size.

kink (kingk), *n.* **1.** a twist or curl, as in a thread or hair. **2.** a muscular stiffness or soreness, as in the neck. **3.** a flaw likely to hinder the operation of something. **4.** a mental twist; eccentricity. —*v.i., v.t.* **5.** to form or cause to form a kink or kinks. —**kink′y,** *adj.,* **-i•er, -i•est.**

kin′ship *n.* **1.** family relationship. **2.** affinity; likeness.

ki•osk (kē′osk, kē osk′), *n.* a small, open structure used as a newsstand, refreshment stand, etc. [< F *kiosque* stand in a public park ≪ Turkish *köşk* < Pers *küshk* palace, villa]

kip•per (kip′ər), *v.t.* **1.** to cure (herring or salmon) by salting and drying or smoking. —*n.* **2.** a kippered fish.

kis•met (kiz′mit, -met, kis′-), *n.* fate; destiny.

kiss (kis), *v.t., v.i.* **1.** to touch with the lips or join lips, as in affection, greeting, etc. **2.** to touch gently or lightly. —*n.* **3.** an act or instance of kissing. **4.** a slight touch. **5.** a chocolate candy. —**kiss′a•ble,** *adj.*

kit (kit), *n.* **1.** a set of tools or materials for a specific purpose: *a first-aid kit.* **2.** a container for these. **3.** a set of materials or parts from which something can be assembled. —*Idiom.* **4. the whole kit and caboodle,** all the persons or things concerned.

kitch•en (kich′ən), *n.* a room or place equipped for cooking or preparing food.

kite (kīt), *n.* **1.** a light frame covered with some thin material, to be flown in the wind at the end of a string. **2.** any of various slim, graceful hawks with long, pointed wings.

kith and kin (kith), *n.* friends and relations.

kitsch (kich), *n.* something of tawdry design or content created to appeal to undiscriminating taste. —**kitsch′y,** *adj.*

kit•ten (kit′n), *n.* a young cat. —**kit′ten•ish,** *adj.*

kit′ty-cor′nered or **-cor′ner,** *adj., adv.* CATER-CORNERED.

ki•wi (kē′wē), *n., pl.* **-wis. 1.** any of several flightless birds of New Zealand. **2.** a brown, egg-sized berry with an edible, green pulp.

KKK Ku Klux Klan.

Klee′nex (klē′neks) *Trademark.* a soft paper tissue.

klep•to•ma•ni•a (klep′tə mā′nē ə), *n.* a compulsion to steal having no relation to need or the value of the object. —**klep′to•ma′ni•ac′,** *n., adj.*

klutz (kluts), *n. Slang.* a clumsy or stupid person. —**klutz′y,** *adj.,* **-i•er, -i•est.** —**klutz′i•ness,** *n.*

km kilometer.

knack (nak), *n.* **1.** a special skill or talent. **2.** a clever way of doing something.

knack•wurst (näk′wûrst, -wŏŏrst), *n.* a short, thick, highly seasoned sausage.

knap•sack (nap′sak′), *n.* a fabric or leather bag for carrying clothes or other supplies on the back.

knave (nāv), *n.* **1.** an unprincipled or dishonest person. **2.** (in cards) the jack. —**knav′er•y,** *n.* —**knav′ish,** *adj.*

knead (nēd), *v.t.* **1.** to work (dough, clay, etc.) into a uniform mixture by pressing and stretching. **2.** to manipulate by similar movements, as the body in a massage.

knee (nē), *n., v.,* **kneed, knee•ing.** —*n.* **1.** the joint of the human leg that allows for movement between the femur and tibia. **2.** something resembling a bent knee. —*v.t.* **3.** to strike or touch with the knee.

knee′cap′ *n., v.,* **-capped, -cap•ping.** —*n.* **1.** the patella. —*v.t.* **2.** to cripple (a person) by shooting in the knee.

knee′-jerk′ *adj. Informal.* reacting in an automatic, habitual manner.

kneel (nēl), *v.i.,* **knelt** or **kneeled, kneel•ing.** to go down or rest on the knees or a knee.

knell (nel), *n.* **1.** the sound made by a bell rung slowly, as at a funeral. **2.** a sound or sign announcing someone's death or the end of something. —*v.i.* **3.** (of a bell) to ring slowly. **4.** to give forth a mournful or ominous sound. —*v.t.* **5.** to proclaim or summon by a knell.

knick•ers (nik′ərz), *n.* (*used with a pl. v.*) loose-fitting short trousers gathered in at the knees.

knick•knack (nik′nak′), *n.* an ornamental trinket.

knife (nīf), *n., pl.* **knives** (nīvz), *v.,* **knifed, knif•ing.** —*n.* **1.** a cutting instrument having a sharp-edged blade fitted with a handle. **2.** any blade for cutting, as in a machine. —*v.t.* **3.** to cut or stab with a knife. **4.** to undermine in an underhanded way. —*Idiom.* **5. under the knife,** undergoing surgery.

knight (nīt), *n.* **1.** (in the Middle Ages) a man raised to honorable military rank and bound to chivalrous conduct. **2.** a man honored by a sovereign with a nonhereditary rank and dignity. **3.** a chess piece shaped like a horse's head. —*v.t.* **4.** to make (a man) a knight. —**knight′hood,** *n.* —**knight′ly,** *adj.*

knit (nit), *v.,* **knit•ted** or **knit, knit•ting.** —*v.t.* **1.** to make (a garment, fabric, etc.) by interlocking loops of yarn with needles. **2.** to join or grow together closely and firmly. **3.** to contract into wrinkles, as the brow. —*n.* **4.** a fabric or garment produced by knitting. —**knit′ter,** *n.*

knob (nob), *n.* **1.** a rounded projecting part forming a handle, as on a door, or a control device, as on a radio. **2.** a rounded lump or protuberance on the surface of something.

knock (nok), *v.i.* **1.** to strike a sounding blow. **2.** to strike in collision: *to knock into a table.* **3.** to make a pounding noise: *The engine is knocking.* —*v.t.* **4.** to give a sounding blow to. **5.** to make or drive by striking: *to knock a hole in the wall.* **6.** to strike (a thing) against something else. **7.** *Informal.* to criticize. **8. knock around** or **about,** to wander. **9. ~ down, a.** to cause to fall by striking. **b.** to dismantle. **c.** to lower (a price). **d.** to sell at auction. **10. ~ off, a.** to cease. **b.** *Informal.* to do or produce quickly or with ease. **c.** *Slang.* to murder. **d.** to deduct. **11. ~ out, a.** to defeat by a knockout. **b.** to make unconscious. **c.** to make exhausted. **d.** to damage or destroy. —*n.* **12.** the act or sound of knocking. **13.** a blow or thump. **14.** *Informal.* an adverse criticism. **15.** a pounding noise in an engine.

knock′-knee′ *n.* inward curvature of the legs at the knees. —**knock′-kneed′,** *adj.*

knock′out′ *n.* **1.** the act of knocking out or state of being knocked out. **2.** (in boxing) a blow that knocks an opponent to the canvas and immobilizes him for a certain time. **3.** *Informal.* a person or thing overwhelmingly attractive or successful.

knoll (nōl), *n.* a small, rounded hill or mound.

knot (not), *n., v.,* **knot•ted, knot•ting.** —*n.* **1.** an interlacing of a cord, rope, etc., drawn tight into a

knob. **2.** an ornamental bow of ribbon. **3.** a cluster of persons or things. **4.** the hard, cross-grained mass of wood where a branch joins a tree trunk. **5.** a part of this mass showing in a piece of lumber. **6.** a complicated problem. **7.** a unit of speed equal to one nautical mile, or about 1.15 statute miles per hour. **8.** a bond or tie: *the knot of matrimony.* —*v.t.* **9.** to form a knot in. —*v.i.* **10.** to become tied or tangled in a knot. **11.** to form knots. —**knot′ty,** *adj.*

know (nō), *v.,* **knew, known, know•ing.** —*v.t.* **1.** to perceive or understand as fact or truth. **2.** to have fixed in the mind or memory. **3.** to be aware of. **4.** to be acquainted or familiar with. **5.** to understand from experience or practice: *to know how to make bread.* **6.** to be able to distinguish or recognize: *to know right from wrong.* —*v.i.* **7.** to have knowledge, as of fact or truth. **8.** to be aware, as of some occurrence. —*Idiom.* **9. in the know,** privy to information. —**know′a•ble,** *adj.*

know′-how′ *n.* knowledge of how to do something.

know′ing *adj.* **1.** revealing knowledge of private information: *a knowing glance.* **2.** having knowledge or information. **3.** intentional; deliberate. —**know′ing•ly,** *adv.*

knowl•edge (nol′ij), *n.* **1.** familiarity, understanding, or information gained by study or experience. **2.** the fact or state of knowing. **3.** something that is or may be known. **4.** the body of truths or facts accumulated in the course of time. **5.** the sum of what is known.

knowl′edge•a•ble (-i jə bəl), *adj.* possessing or exhibiting knowledge.

knuck•le (nuk′əl), *n., v.,* **-led, -ling.** —*n.* **1.** a joint of a finger, esp. one of the joints at the roots of the fingers. —*v.t.* **2.** to rub or press with the knuckles. **3. knuckle down,** to apply oneself earnestly. **4. ~ under,** to submit; yield.

knuck′le•head′ *n. Informal.* a stupid, inept person.

KO (*n.* kā′ō′, kā′ō′; *v.* kā′ō′), *n., pl.* **KOs** or **KO's,** *v.,* **KO'd, KO′•ing.** —*n.* **1.** a knockout in boxing. —*v.t.* **2.** to knock out in boxing.

ko•a•la (kō ä′lə), *n., pl.* **-las.** a gray, tree-dwelling Australian marsupial.

kohl•ra•bi (kōl rä′bē, -rab′ē), *n., pl.* **-bies.** a cultivated cabbage with an edible bulblike stem.

koi (koi) *n., pl.* **kois, koi.** a colorful carp.

ko•la (kō′lə), *n., pl.* **-las. 1.** a tropical African tree grown for its brown seeds (**ko′la nuts′**) whose extract is used in soft drinks. **2.** COLA.

kook (kŏŏk), *n. Slang.* an eccentric, strange, or crazy person. —**kook′y,** *adj.,* **-i•er, -i•est.** —**kook′-i•ness,** *n.*

Ko•ran (kə rän′, -ran′, kô-), *n.* the sacred text of Islam. [< Ar *qur'ān* book, reading]

Ko•re•a (kə rē′ə), *n.* **1. Democratic People's Republic of,** official name of NORTH KOREA. **2. Republic of,** official name of SOUTH KOREA.

Ko•re•an (kə rē′ən), *n.* **1.** a native or inhabitant of Korea. **2.** the language of this people. —*adj.* **3.** of Korea, the Koreans, or their language.

ko•sher (kō′shər), *adj.* **1. a.** fit to be eaten or used according to Jewish dietary laws. **b.** adhering to these laws. **2.** *Informal.* proper; legitimate.

kow•tow (kou′tou′, -tou′, kō′-), *v.i.,* **-towed, -tow•ing. 1.** to act in a fawning or servile manner. **2.** to touch the forehead to the ground while kneeling, as an act of worship, respect, etc. [< Chin *kòutóu* lit., knock (one's) head]

kryp•ton (krip′ton), *n.* an inert gaseous element, present in very small amounts in the atmosphere. *Symbol:* Kr; *at. wt.:* 83.80; *at. no.:* 36.

KS Kansas.

ku•dos (kŏŏ′dōz, -dōs, -dos, kyŏŏ′-), *n.* honor; glory; acclaim.

Ku Klux Klan (kŏŏ′ kluks′ klan′), *n.* **1.** a secret, chiefly antiblack, terrorist organization in the southern U.S., active after the Civil War. **2.** a secret organization founded in 1915 and directed against blacks, Catholics, Jews, and other groups.

kum•quat (kum′kwot), *n.* a small, orange-colored citrus fruit with a sweet rind and acid pulp.

kung fu (kung′ fōō′, kŏŏng′), *n.* a Chinese martial art based on the use of fluid movements of the arms and legs. [< Chin *gōngfú* lit., skill]

Ku•wait (kŏŏ wāt′), *n.* a sovereign monarchy in NE Arabia. —**Ku•wai′ti** (-wā′tē) *n., pl.* **-tis,** *adj.*

kvetch (kvech), *Slang.* —*v.* **1.** to complain chronically. —*n.* **2.** a person who kvetches.

kW or **kw,** kilowatt.

KY or **Ky.,** Kentucky.

Kyr•gyz•stan (kēr′gi stan′, -stän′), *n.* a republic in central Asia: formerly a part of the USSR.

L

a b c d e f g h i j k L m n o p q r s t u v w x y z

L, l (el), *n., pl.* **Ls** or **L's, ls** or **l's. 1.** the 12th letter of the English alphabet, a consonant. **2.** something shaped like an L.

L or **L., 1.** lake. **2.** large. **3.** Latin. **4.** left. **5.** length. **6.** *Brit.* pound. [< L *lībra*] **7.** long.

L *Symbol.* the Roman numeral for 50.

l. or **l, 1.** left. **2.** length. **3.** *pl.* **ll.** line. **4.** liter.

LA or **La.,** Louisiana.

La *Chem. Symbol.* lanthanum.

L.A. 1. Latin America. **2.** Los Angeles.

lab (lab), *n.* laboratory.

la•bel (lā′bəl), *n., v.,* **-beled, -bel•ing** or (*esp. Brit.*) **-belled, -bel•ling.** —*n.* **1.** a slip of paper or other material attached to something to indicate its manufacturer, nature, destination, etc. **2.** a short word or phrase descriptive of a person, group, etc. —*v.t.* **3.** to affix a label to. **4.** to designate or describe by or on a label.

la•bi•um (lā′bē əm), *n., pl.* **-bi•a** (-bē ə). **1.** a lip or liplike part. **2.** any of the folds of skin bordering the vulva.

la•bor (lā′bər), *n.* **1.** productive activity, esp. for economic gain. **2.** the body of persons engaged in such activity, esp. those working for wages. **3.** physical or mental work; toil. **4.** a job or task. **5.** the uterine contractions of childbirth. —*v.i.* **6.** to perform labor. **7.** to strive, as toward a goal. **8.** to move slowly and with effort. **9.** to function at a disadvantage: *to labor under a misapprehension.* **10.** to undergo childbirth. —*v.t.* **11.** to develop in excessive detail: *Don't labor the point.* Also, *esp. Brit.,* **la′bour.** —**la′bor•er,** *n.*

lab•o•ra•to•ry (lab′rə tôr′ē, lab′ər ə-), *n., pl.* **-ries.** a place equipped to conduct scientific experiments, tests, etc.

la′bored *adj.* done with difficulty; strained; forced: *labored breathing.*

la•bo•ri•ous (lə bôr′ē əs), *adj.* **1.** requiring much work or exertion. **2.** industrious. —**la•bo′ri•ous•ly,** *adv.*

la′bor un′ion *n.* an organization of workers for mutual aid and protection, esp. by collective bargaining.

la•bur•num (lə bûr′nəm), *n.* a poisonous tree or shrub with drooping clusters of yellow flowers.

lab•y•rinth (lab′ə rinth), *n.* an intricate combination of paths or passages in which it is difficult to find one's way. —**lab′y•rin′thine** (-rin′thin, -thīn), *adj.*

lace (lās), *n., v.,* **laced, lac•ing.** —*n.* **1.** a netlike ornamental fabric made of threads. **2.** a string for holding or drawing together opposite edges. —*v.t.* **3.** to fasten by means of a lace. **4.** to interlace; intertwine. **5.** to add a small amount of alcoholic liquor to (a beverage). **6.** to beat; thrash. —*v.i.* **7.** to attack physically or verbally (usu. fol. by *into*). —**lac′y,** *adj.,* **-i•er, -i•est.**

lac•er•ate (las′ə rāt′), *v.t.,* **-at•ed, -at•ing.** to tear roughly. —**lac′er•a′tion,** *n.*

lach•ry•mal (lak′rə məl), *adj.* **1.** of or characterized by tears. **2.** LACRIMAL.

lach′ry•mose′ (-mōs′), *adj.* **1.** tending to cause tears; mournful. **2.** given to shedding tears readily.

lack (lak), *n.* **1.** deficiency or absence of something needed or desirable. **2.** something missing or wanted. —*v.t., v.i.* **3.** to be wanting or deficient (in).

lack•a•dai•si•cal (lak′ə dā′zi kəl), *adj.* being

without vigor or spirit; listless. —**lack′a•dai′si•cal•ly,** *adv.*

lack•ey (lak′ē), *n., pl.* **-eys. 1.** a servile follower. **2.** a liveried manservant.

lack′lus′ter *adj.* lacking brilliance or vitality.

la•con•ic (lə kon′ik), *adj.* using few words; terse. —**la•con′i•cal•ly,** *adv.*

lac•quer (lak′ər), *n.* **1.** a protective coating consisting of a resin, cellulose ester, or both, dissolved in a volatile solvent. **2.** any of various resinous varnishes, esp. one obtained from a Japanese tree. —*v.t.* **3.** to coat with lacquer.

lac•ri•mal (lak′rə məl), *adj.* of or situated near the glands that secrete tears.

la•crosse (lə krôs′, -kros′), *n.* a game played by two teams using a small ball and long-handled sticks with netted pockets. [< CanF: lit., the crook]

lac•tate (lak′tāt), *v.i.,* **-tat•ed, -tat•ing.** to secrete milk. —**lac•ta′tion,** *n.*

lac′tose (-tōs), *n.* a sweet crystalline substance present in milk, used in infant foods, confections, etc.

la•cu•na (lə kyōō′nə), *n., pl.* **-nae** (-nē) **-nas.** a gap or missing part, as in a manuscript.

lad (lad), *n.* a boy or youth.

lad•der (lad′ər), *n.* **1.** a structure for climbing, consisting of two sidepieces between which a series of rungs are set. **2.** a graded series of stages or levels.

lad•en (lād′n), *adj.* burdened.

lad•ing (lā′ding), *n.* a load; cargo.

la•dle (lād′l), *n., v.,* **-dled, -dling.** —*n.* **1.** a long-handled utensil with a cup-shaped bowl for dipping or conveying liquids. —*v.t.* **2.** to dip or convey with a ladle.

la•dy (lā′dē), *n., pl.* **-dies. 1.** a woman who is refined, polite, and well-spoken. **2.** a woman of high social position or economic class. **3.** any woman. **4.** (*cap.*) a British title for the wives or daughters of certain nobles.

la′dy•bug′ *n.* any of numerous small, round, often brightly colored and spotted beetles.

la′dy•fin′ger *n.* a small finger-shaped sponge cake.

la′dy's-slip′per or **la′dy-slip′per,** *n.* an orchid having a slipper-shaped flower lip.

lag (lag), *v.,* **lagged, lag•ging,** *n.* —*v.i.* **1.** to fail to maintain a desired pace or speed. **2.** to decrease gradually; flag. —*n.* **3.** a lagging or falling behind. **4.** an interval of time.

la•ger (lä′gər, lô′-), *n.* a light beer aged from six weeks to six months.

lag•gard (lag′ərd), *n.* **1.** one that lags. —*adj.* **2.** moving or responding slowly. —**lag′gard•ly,** *adj., adv.*

la•gniappe (lan yap′, lan′yap), *n.* **1.** a small gift given with a purchase to a customer. **2.** a gratuity.

la•goon (lə gōōn′), *n.* **1.** an area of shallow water separated from the sea by low sand dunes. **2.** any pondlike body of water, esp. one connected with a larger body of water.

laid′-back′ (lād-), *adj. Informal.* relaxed; easygoing.

lair (lâr), *n.* a den or retreat, esp. of a wild animal.

lais•sez faire (les′ā fâr′), *n.* the theory that government should intervene as little as possible in the direction of economic affairs. [< F: lit., allow to act]

la•i•ty (lā′i tē), *n.* **1.** the body of religious worshipers, as distinguished from the clergy. **2.** the people outside of a particular profession.

lake (lāk), *n.* **1.** an inland body of water of considerable size. **2.** a pool of any liquid, as oil.

La•ko•ta (lə kō′tə) *n., pl.* **-tas** or **-ta.** a member of a Plains Indian people.

lam (lam), *n., v.,* **lammed, lam•ming.** *Slang.* —*n.* **1.** a hasty escape; flight. —*v.i.* **2.** to escape; flee. —*Idiom.* **3. on the lam,** hiding or in flight from the police.

la•ma (lä′mə), *n., pl.* **-mas.** a Tibetan or Mongolian Buddhist monk.

La•maze′ meth′od (lə mäz′), *n.* a method by which an expectant mother is prepared for childbirth by education, breathing exercises, etc.

lamb (lam), *n.* **1.** a young sheep. **2.** the meat of a young sheep. **3.** a person who is gentle, meek, or innocent.

lam•baste (lam bāst′, -bast′), *v.t.,* **-bast•ed, -bast•ing.** *Informal.* **1.** to beat severely. **2.** to reprimand harshly.

lam•bent (lam′bənt), *adj.* **1.** moving lightly over a surface: *lambent tongues of flame.* **2.** dealing lightly and gracefully with a subject: *lambent wit.* **3.** softly bright or radiant. —**lam′ben•cy,** *n.* —**lam′bent•ly,** *adv.*

lame (lām), *adj.,* **lam•er, lam•est,** *v.,* **lamed, lam•ing.** —*adj.* **1.** crippled or physically disabled, esp. in the foot or leg. **2.** stiff and sore. **3.** weak; inadequate: *lame excuses.* —*v.t.* **4.** to make lame or defective. —**lame′ly,** *adv.* —**lame′ness,** *n.*

la•mé (la mā′, lä-), *n., pl.* **-més.** an ornamental fabric interwoven with metallic threads.

lame′ duck′ *n.* an elected official who is completing a term after the election of a successor.

la•ment (lə ment′), *v.t., v.i.* **1.** to express grief or regret (for or over). —*n.* **2.** a vocal expression of grief. **3.** an elegy; dirge. —**la•ment′a•ble,** *adj.* —**lam•en•ta•tion** (lam′ən tā′shən), *n.*

lam•i•na (lam′ə nə), *n., pl.* **-nae** (-nē′), **-nas.** a thin plate, scale, or layer. —**lam′i•nar,** *adj.*

lam•i•nate (*v.* lam′ə nāt′; *adj.* -nāt′, -nit), *v.,* **-nat•ed, -nat•ing,** *adj.* —*v.t.* **1.** to construct from layers of material bonded together. **2.** to cover with laminae. —*adj.* **3.** Also, **lam′i•nat′ed.** composed of or having laminae. —**lam/i•na′tion,** *n.*

lamp (lamp), *n.* **1.** a device furnishing artificial light, as by electricity or gas. **2.** a device furnishing heat, ultraviolet, or other radiation.

lam•poon (lam pōōn′), *n.* **1.** a broad, often harsh satire directed against an individual or institution. —*v.t.* **2.** to ridicule in a lampoon.

lam•prey (lam′prē), *n., pl.* **-preys.** an eellike jawless fish with a round, sucking mouth.

lance (lans, läns), *n., v.,* **lanced, lanc•ing.** —*n.* **1.** a long wooden spear with a metal head. **2.** LANCER. **3.** LANCET. —*v.t.* **4.** to open with a lancet. **5.** to pierce with a lance.

lanc′er *n.* a cavalry soldier armed with a lance.

lan•cet (lan′sit, län′-), *n.* a sharp-pointed surgical instrument, usu. with two edges.

land (land), *n.* **1.** any part of the earth's surface not covered by water. **2.** an area of ground: *arable land.* **3.** any part of the earth's surface that can be owned as property. **4.** a region or country. —*v.t.* **5.** to bring to or set on land. **6.** to bring to a particular place or condition: *His behavior will land him in jail.* **7.** *Informal.* to secure or gain: *to land a job.* —*v.i.* **8.** to come to land or shore. **9.** to go or come ashore from a ship. **10.** to alight upon a surface. **11.** to come to rest or arrive in a particular place or condition.

lan′dau (lan′dô, -dou) *n.* a carriage with a folding top.

land′ed *adj.* **1.** owning land: *landed gentry.* **2.** consisting of land: *landed property.*

land′fall′ *n.* **1.** an approach to or sighting of land. **2.** the land sighted or reached.

land′fill′ *n.* **1.** a low area of land that is built up from deposits of solid refuse in layers covered by soil. **2.** the solid refuse itself.

land′ing *n.* **1.** the act of one that lands. **2.** a place

where persons or goods are landed. **3.** the level floor between flights of stairs.

land′locked′ *adj.* **1.** shut in completely, or almost completely, by land: *a landlocked bay.* **2.** having no direct access to the sea: *any landlocked country.* **3.** living in waters shut off from the sea, as some fish.

land′lord′ *n.* **1.** a person or organization that owns and leases land, buildings, apartments, etc. **2.** a person who runs an inn.

land′lub′ber (-lub′ər), *n.* an unseasoned sailor; someone unfamiliar with the sea.

land′mark′ *n.* **1.** a prominent object on land that serves as a guide. **2.** a building or site of historical or cultural importance. **3.** a significant or historic event, achievement, etc.

land′mass′ *n.* a large area of land having a distinct identity, as a continent.

land′scape′ (-skāp′), *n., v.,* **-scaped, -scap•ing.** —*n.* **1.** an expanse of natural scenery that can be seen from a single viewpoint. **2.** a picture representing such scenery. —*v.t.* **3.** to improve the appearance of (an area of land), as by planting shrubs. —**land′scap′er,** *n.*

land′slide′ *n.* **1.** the sliding of a mass of soil or rock from a steep slope. **2.** the mass itself. **3.** an overwhelming victory, esp. in an election.

lane (lān), *n.* **1.** a narrow way or passage, as between houses. **2.** any well-defined path, route, or channel.

lan•guage (lang′gwij), *n.* **1.** a body of words and systems for their use common to a people of the same community or nation. **2.** communication using a system of vocal sounds or written symbols in conventional ways. **3.** any system of symbols, sounds, or gestures used for communication. **4.** the vocabulary used by a particular group. **5.** a set of symbols and syntactic rules by means of which a computer can be given directions. [< AF < L *lingua* language, tongue]

lan•guid (lang′gwid), *adj.* **1.** lacking in vigor or vitality. **2.** lacking in spirit or interest. **3.** drooping from weakness or fatigue.

lan•guish (-gwish), *v.i.* **1.** to be or become weak; droop. **2.** to suffer neglect or hardship: *to languish in prison.* **3.** to pine; long. **4.** to assume an expression of sentimental melancholy.

lank (langk), *adj.,* **-er, -est. 1.** (of hair) straight and limp. **2.** lean; thin.

lan•o•lin (lan′l in), *n.* a fatty substance extracted from wool, used in ointments, cosmetics, etc.

lan•tern (lan′tərn), *n.* a portable, transparent case for enclosing and protecting a light.

lan′tern jaw′ *n.* a long, thin jaw. —**lan′tern-jawed′,** *adj.*

lan•tha•num (lan′thə nəm), *n.* a rare-earth metallic element allied to aluminum. *Symbol:* La; *at. wt.:* 138.91; *at. no.:* 57.

lan•yard (lan′yərd), *n.* a short rope used on ships to secure riggings.

La•os (lä′ōs), *n.* a country in SE Asia. —**La•o•tian** (lā ō′shən), *n., adj.*

lap¹ (lap), *n.* **1.** the front part of the human body from the waist to the knees when in a sitting position. **2.** the part of the clothing that covers this. **3.** a place or situation of rest or nurture: *the lap of luxury.* **4.** an area of care, charge, or control: *They dropped the problem right in my lap.* **5.** a part of a garment that extends over another.

lap² (lap), *v.,* **lapped, lap•ping.** —*v.t.* **1.** to fold over or around something. **2.** to enwrap in something. **3.** to lay (something) partly over something underneath. **4.** to overlap. **5.** to get a lap ahead of (a competitor) in racing. —*v.i.* **6.** to fold or wind around something. **7.** to extend beyond a limit. —*n.* **8.** the act of lapping. **9.** a complete circuit of a course in racing. **10.** an overlapping part.

lap³ (lap), *v.,* **lapped, lap•ping,** *n.* —*v.t., v.i.* **1.** (of water) to wash against (something) with a light, splashing sound. **2.** to take in (liquid) with the tongue. **3. lap up,** to receive enthusiastically. —*n.* **4.** the act or sound of lapping.

la•pel (lə pel′), *n.* the front part of a garment that

is folded back and forms a continuous piece with the collar.

lap•i•dar•y (lap′i der′ē), *n.*, *pl.* **-dar•ies.** a worker who cuts, polishes, and engraves precious stones.

lap•in (lap′in), *n.* rabbit fur, esp. when trimmed and dyed.

lap•is laz•u•li (lap′is laz′ŏŏ lē, -lī′, laz′yŏŏ-), *n.*, *pl.* **-lis.** 1. a deep blue semiprecious gemstone. 2. a sky-blue color; azure.

lapse (laps), *n.*, *v.*, **lapsed, laps•ing.** —*n.* 1. a slip or error, often of a trivial sort. 2. an interval of time. 3. a moral fall. 4. a decline to a lower condition or degree. 5. the termination of a right or privilege, as through neglect to exercise it. —*v.i.* 6. to fall or deviate from a previous standard. 7. to come to an end: *We let our subscription lapse.* 8. to fall, slip, or sink: *to lapse into silence.* 9. to fall spiritually. 10. to pass away, as time. 11. to become void.

lap′top′ *n.* a portable, usu. battery-powered microcomputer small enough to rest on the lap.

lar•ce•ny (lär′sə nē), *n.*, *pl.* **-nies.** the wrongful taking of the personal goods of another; theft. —**lar′ce•nist,** *n.* —**lar′ce•nous,** *adj.*

larch (lärch), *n.* 1. a deciduous conifer yielding a tough, durable wood. 2. its wood.

lard (lärd), *n.* 1. the rendered fat of hogs. —*v.t.* 2. to insert strips of fat in (lean meat) before cooking. 3. to supplement or enrich: *a literary work larded with mythological allusions.*

lar•der (lär′dər), *n.* 1. a room or place where food is kept; pantry. 2. a supply of food.

large (lärj), *adj.*, **larg•er, larg•est.** 1. of more than average size, quantity, degree, etc. 2. on a great scale. 3. of great scope or range. —*Idiom.* 4. **at large, a.** not incarcerated. **b.** as a whole; in general. **c.** Also **at-large.** representing the whole of a political division rather than one part of it. —**large′-ness,** *n.*

large′ly *adv.* 1. to a great extent; generally. 2. in great quantity.

large′-scale′ *adj.* 1. very extensive. 2. made to a large scale.

lar•gess or **-gesse** (lär jes′, lär′jis), *n.* 1. a generous giving of gifts. 2. the gift or gifts so given.

lar•go (lär′gō), *adj.*, *adv.* *Music.* in a slow, dignified style.

lar•i•at (lar′ē ət), *n.* 1. a lasso. 2. a rope used to picket grazing animals.

lark¹ (lärk), *n.* any of numerous, chiefly Old World songbirds, esp. the skylark.

lark² (lärk), *n.* 1. a merry, carefree adventure. —*v.i.* 2. to have fun; frolic.

lark′spur′ *n.* any of several plants characterized by the spur-shaped formation of the calyx and petals.

lar•va (lär′və), *n.*, *pl.* **-vae** (-vē). 1. the immature, wingless, feeding stage of an insect that undergoes complete metamorphosis. 2. any animal in an analogous immature form. —**lar′val,** *adj.*

lar•yn•gi•tis (lar′ən jī′tis), *n.* inflammation of the larynx, often with accompanying loss of voice.

lar•ynx (lar′ingks), *n.*, *pl.* **la•ryn•ges** (lə rin′jēz), **lar•ynx•es.** a muscular structure at the upper part of the trachea, in which the vocal cords are located. —**la•ryn•ge•al** (lə rin′jē əl, lar′ən jē′əl), *adj.*

la•sa•gna (lə zän′yə, lä-), *n.* a baked dish of wide strips of pasta layered with cheese, tomato sauce, and usu. meat.

las•civ•i•ous (lə siv′ē əs), *adj.* 1. inclined to or expressive of lustfulness; lewd. 2. arousing sexual desire. —**las•civ′i•ous•ness,** *n.*

la•ser (lā′zər), *n.* a device that produces a narrow beam of intense light by exciting atoms and causing them to radiate their energy in phase. [*l(ight) a(m-plification by) s(timulated) e(mission of) r(radia-tion)*]

lash¹ (lash), *n.* 1. the flexible extremity of a whip. 2. a swift stroke or blow, as with a whip. 3. an eyelash. —*v.t.* 4. to strike or beat, as with a whip. 5. to attack severely with words. 6. to dash or switch suddenly and swiftly. —*v.i.* 7. to strike vigorously. 8. to attack with harsh words: *to lash out at injustice.*

lash² (lash), *v.t.* to bind or fasten with a rope, cord, etc.

lass (las), *n.* a girl or young woman.

las•si•tude (las′i tŏŏd′, -tyŏŏd′), *n.* weariness of body or mind, as from strain.

las•so (las′ō, la sŏŏ′), *n.*, *pl.* **-sos, -soes,** *v.,* **-soed, -so•ing.** —*n.* 1. a long rope with a running noose at one end, used for roping horses, cattle, etc. —*v.t.* 2. to catch with or as if with a lasso.

last¹ (last, läst), *adj.* 1. occurring after all others, as in time or place. 2. most recent: *last week.* 3. being the only remaining: *my last dollar.* 4. conclusive; definitive. 5. least likely or probable: *the last person we'd want to represent us.* —*adv.* 6. after all others. 7. on the most recent occasion. 8. in the end. —*n.* 9. a person or thing that is last. —*Idiom.* 10. **at (long) last,** after considerable delay. —**last′ly,** *adv.*

last² (last, läst), *v.i.* 1. to continue in time, force, etc. 2. to be enough: *Will the food last?* 3. to remain in usable condition.

last³ (last, läst), *n.* a foot-shaped form on which shoes are shaped or repaired.

last′ing *adj.* continuing or enduring a long time. —**last′ing•ly,** *adv.*

Last′ Judg′ment *n.* God's final judgment of all people at the end of the world.

Last′ Sup′per *n.* the supper of Jesus and His disciples on the eve of His Crucifixion.

Lat. Latin.

lat. latitude.

latch (lach), *n.* 1. a device for holding a door, gate, etc., closed. —*v.t.*, *v.i.* 2. to close or fasten with a latch. 3. **latch onto, a.** to obtain. **b.** to attach oneself to.

late (lāt), *adj.* and *adv.,* **lat•er, lat•est.** —*adj.* 1. occurring or coming after the usual or proper time. 2. at the end of the day or well into the night: *a late hour.* 3. recent: *a late bulletin.* 4. recently deceased: *the late Mr. Phipps.* —*adv.* 5. after the usual or proper time. 6. at or to an advanced time. 7. recently but no longer. —*Idiom.* 8. **of late,** lately. —**late′ness,** *n.*

late′ly *adv.* recently; not long since.

la•tent (lāt′nt), *adj.* present but not visible, actualized, or active. —**la′ten•cy,** *n.*

lat•er•al (lat′ər əl), *adj.* of, at, from, or to a side. —**lat′er•al•ly,** *adv.*

la•tex (lā′teks), *n.*, *pl.* **lat•i•ces** (lat′ə sēz′), **la•tex•es.** 1. a milky liquid in certain plants, as milkweeds. 2. an emulsion in water of particles of synthetic rubber or plastic, used in paints.

lath (lath, läth), *n.*, *pl.* **laths** (la͟thz, lathz, lä͟thz, läths). 1. a thin, narrow strip of wood, used as a backing for plaster or stucco. 2. any building material used for a similar purpose.

lathe (lā͟th), *n.*, *v.,* **lathed, lath•ing.** —*n.* 1. a machine for use in working a piece of wood, metal, etc., by rotating it against a tool that shapes it. —*v.t.* 2. to cut or shape on a lathe.

lath•er (la͟th′ər), *n.* 1. foam made by a soap stirred or rubbed in water. 2. foam formed in profuse sweating, as on a horse. 3. *Informal.* a state of excitement. —*v.i.*, *v.t.* 4. to form or cover with lather. —**lath′er•y,** *adj.*

Lat•in (lat′n), *n.* 1. the language of ancient Rome. 2. a member of any of the Latin peoples. 3. a native or inhabitant of ancient Rome. —*adj.* 4. pertaining to those peoples speaking languages descended from Latin. 5. of ancient Rome or its inhabitants.

Lat′in Amer′ica *n.* the part of the American continents south of the United States in which Romance languages are spoken. —**Lat′in-Amer′ican,** *adj.* —**Lat′in Amer′ican,** *n.*

La•ti•no (lə tē′nō, la-), *n.*, *pl.* **-nos.** HISPANIC.

lat•i•tude (lat′i tŏŏd′, -tyŏŏd′), *n.* 1. **a.** the angular distance north or south from the equator of a point on the earth's surface, expressed in degrees. **b.** a region as marked by this distance. 2. freedom from narrow restrictions. —**lat′i•tu′di•nal** (-tŏŏd′n-l, -tyŏŏd′-), *adj.*

la•trine (lə trēn′), *n.* a communal toilet, esp. in a military installation.

lat•ter (lat′ər), *adj.* **1.** being the second mentioned of two. **2.** more advanced in time. **3.** near to the end. —**lat′ter•ly,** *adv.*

lat•tice (lat′is), *n.* a structure of crossed wooden or metal strips usu. arranged to form a diagonal pattern of open spaces. —**lat′ticed,** *adj.*

Lat•vi•a (lat′vē ə, lät′-), *n.* a republic in N Europe, on the Baltic: formerly a part of the USSR. —**Lat′vi•an,** *adj., n.*

laud (lôd), *v.t.* to praise highly.

laugh (laf, läf), *v.i.* **1.** to express mirth, derision, etc., with inarticulate sounds and facial or bodily movements. —*v.t.* **2.** to drive, bring, etc., by or with laughter: *They laughed him out of town.* **3.** **laugh at, a.** to ridicule. **b.** to find amusing. —*n.* **4.** the act or sound of laughing. **5.** one that provokes laughter. —**laugh′ing•ly,** *adv.*

laugh′a•ble *adj.* such as to cause laughter. —**laugh′a•bly,** *adv.*

laugh′ing•stock′ *n.* an object of ridicule.

laugh′ter (-tər), *n.* the action or sound of laughing.

launch¹ (lônch, länch), *v.t.* **1.** to float (a newly constructed ship). **2.** to send forth forcefully: *to launch a spacecraft.* **3.** to set going; start: *to launch a new product.* **4.** *Computers.* to start (an application program). —*v.i.* **5.** to plunge boldly into action, speech, etc. **6.** to start out or forth. —*n.* **7.** the act of launching. —**launch′er,** *n.*

launch² (lônch, länch), *n.* a heavy, open or half-decked boat.

launch′ (or **launch′ing**) **pad′,** *n.* the platform on which a rocket, missile, etc., is launched.

laun•der (lôn′dər, län′-), *v.t., v.i.* **1.** to wash or wash and iron (clothes or linens). **2.** *Informal.* to disguise the source of (illegal money), as by transmitting it through a foreign bank. —**laun′der•er,** *n.* —**laun′dress** (-dris), *n.*

laun′der•ette′ (-də ret′), *n.* a self-service laundry having coin-operated washers and driers.

Laun′dro•mat′ (-drə mat′), *Trademark.* a type of launderette.

laun′dry *n., pl.* **-dries. 1.** articles of clothing, linens, etc., that have been or are to be washed. **2.** a place where articles are laundered. —**laun′dry•man′** or **-wom′an,** *n., pl.* **-men** or **-wom•en.**

lau•re•ate (lôr′ē it, lor′-), *n.* **1.** a person who has been honored in a particular field: *a poet laureate.* —*adj.* **2.** crowned with laurel as a mark of honor.

lau•rel (lôr′əl, lor′-), *n.* **1.** a small European evergreen tree with dark, glossy leaves. **2.** any of various similar trees or shrubs. **3.** the foliage of the laurel as an emblem of victory or distinction. **4.** a wreath of laurel foliage. **5.** Usu., **-rels.** honor won, as for achievement in a field or activity.

la•va (lä′və, lav′ə), *n., pl.* **-vas. 1.** the molten rock that issues from a volcano. **2.** the rock formed when this solidifies. [< It: avalanche ≪ L *lābēs* a sliding down]

lav•a•to•ry (lav′ə tôr′ē), *n., pl.* **-ries.** a room fitted with washbowls and toilets.

lave (lāv), *v.t., v.i.* **laved, lav•ing.** to wash; bathe.

lav•en•der (lav′ən dər), *n.* **1.** a pale bluish purple. **2.** an Old World plant with spikes of pale purple flowers. **3.** its dried flowers placed among linen, clothes, etc., for scent.

lav•ish (lav′ish), *adj.* **1.** bestowed or occurring in abundance. **2.** using or giving in great amounts. —*v.t.* **3.** to expend or give in great amounts. —**lav′ish•ly,** *adv.*

law (lô), *n.* **1.** a rule or system of rules established by a government or other authority and applicable to a people. **2.** the condition of society brought about by observance of such rules: *maintaining law and order.* **3.** the field of knowledge concerned with these rules; jurisprudence. **4.** the profession that deals with law and legal procedure. **5.** any rule or injunction that must be obeyed. **6.** (in philosophy, science, etc.) a statement of a relation or sequence of phenomena invariable under the same conditions. **7.** a commandment or a revelation from God. —**law′less,** *adj.*

law′ful *adj.* **1.** allowed by law. **2.** sanctioned or recognized by law. —**law′ful•ly,** *adv.* —**law′ful•ness,** *n.*

lawn¹ (lôn), *n.* a stretch of grass-covered land, esp. one closely mowed, as near a house.

lawn² (lôn), *n.* a sheer linen or cotton fabric.

lawn′ bowl′ing *n.* a game played on a bowling green by rolling a ball toward a stationary ball.

law′suit′ *n.* a case brought before a court.

law•yer (lô′yər, loi′ər), *n.* a person who represents clients in court or advises them in legal matters.

lax (laks), *adj.,* **-er, -est. 1.** not strict or severe; careless or negligent. **2.** loose or slack. —**lax′i•ty,** **lax′ness,** *n.* —**lax′ly,** *adv.*

lax•a•tive (lak′sə tiv), *n.* **1.** an agent for relieving constipation. —*adj.* **2.** of or constituting a laxative.

lay¹ (lā), *v.,* **laid, lay•ing,** —*v.t.* **1.** to place in a horizontal position. **2.** to strike or throw to the ground. **3.** to put or place. **4.** to place in proper position: *to lay bricks.* **5.** to present for notice or consideration: *I laid my case before the commission.* **6.** to bring forward, as a claim. **7.** to attribute or ascribe: *to lay blame.* **8.** to bring forth and deposit (an egg). **9.** to devise, as a plan. **10.** to wager; stake. **11.** to quiet or allay. **12. lay aside,** to save for use at a later time. **13. ~ away,** to reserve for later use. **14. ~ off, a.** to dismiss (an employee), esp. temporarily. **b.** *Informal.* to cease or quit. **15. ~ open, a.** to cut open. **b.** to expose. **16. ~ out, a.** to spread out in order; arrange. **b.** to ready (a corpse) for burial. **c.** *Informal.* to spend or contribute (money). **17. ~ over,** to make a stopover. **18. ~ up, a.** to put away for future use. **b.** to confine to bed. —*n.* **19.** the way or position in which a thing is laid or lies: *the lay of the land.*

lay² (lā), *v.* pt. of LIE².

lay³ (lā), *adj.* **1.** of or involving the laity. **2.** not belonging to or connected with a profession.

lay⁴ (lā), *n.* **1.** a short narrative or other poem. **2.** a song.

lay′a•way plan′ (lā′ə wā′), *n.* a method of purchasing by which an item is reserved by the store until the customer has completed payments.

lay′er *n.* **1.** a thickness of some material laid on or spread over a surface. **2.** one that lays, as a hen.

lay•ette (-et′), *n.* an outfit of clothing, bedding, etc., for a newborn baby.

lay′off′ *n.* the act of dismissing employees.

lay′out′ *n.* **1.** an arrangement or plan. **2.** a plan or sketch for an advertisement or other printed matter.

laze (lāz), *v.i., v.t.,* **lazed, laz•ing.** to pass (time) lazily.

la•zy (lā′zē), *adj.,* **-zi•er, -zi•est. 1.** averse to work or activity; indolent. **2.** slow-moving; sluggish. —**la′zi•ly,** *adv.* —**la′zi•ness,** *n.*

lb. *pl.* **lbs., lb.** pound. [< L *lībra*]

l.c. lowercase.

lea (lē, lā), *n.* a meadow.

leach (lēch), *v.t.* **1.** to dissolve out soluble constituents from (ashes, soil, etc.) by percolation. **2.** to cause (a liquid) to percolate through something. —*v.i.* **3.** to undergo the action of percolating water. —**leach′er,** *n.*

lead¹ (lēd), *v.,* **led, lead•ing,** *n.* —*v.t.* **1.** to go before or with to show the way. **2.** to conduct by holding and guiding: *to lead a horse by a rope.* **3.** to influence or induce. **4.** to live: *to lead a full life.* **5.** to be in control or command of; direct. **6.** to be or go at the head of: *The mayor will lead the parade.* **7.** to have the advantage over. —*v.i.* **8.** to act as a guide. **9.** to afford passage to a place: *That path leads to the house.* **10.** to be or go first. **11.** to result in: *The incident led to her resignation.* **12.** to make the first play in a card game. **13. lead off,** to begin. **14. ~ on,** to mislead. —*n.* **15.** the position in advance of others. **16.** the extent of such advance. **17.** one that leads. **18.** a tip or clue. **19.** the principal part in a play. **20.** the right of playing first in a card game. —*idiom.* **21. lead up to,** to prepare the way for. —**lead′er,** *n.* —**lead′er•ship′,** *n.*

lead² (led), *n.* **1.** a heavy, comparatively soft, malleable, bluish-gray metal. *Symbol:* Pb; *at. wt.:* 207.19; *at. no.:* 82. **2.** a plummet of lead for taking soundings. **3.** bullets collectively. **4.** a small stick of graphite, as used in pencils. **5.** a thin strip of metal used for increasing the space between lines of type. —*v.t.* **6.** to cover, weight, or treat with lead.

lead′ing ques′tion, *n.* a question so worded as to suggest the proper or desired answer.

lead′ time′ (lēd), *n.* the period of time between the initial phase of a process and the emergence of results.

leaf (lēf), *n.*, *pl.* **leaves** (lēvz), *v.* —*n.* **1.** one of the expanded, usu. green organs borne by the stem of a plant. **2.** a sheet of paper, one side of each sheet constituting a page. **3.** a thin sheet of metal. **4.** a hinged or detachable flat part, as of a tabletop. —*v.i.* **5.** to put forth leaves. **6.** to turn pages quickly (usu. fol. by *through*). —**leaf′less,** *adj.* —**leaf′y,** *adj.*, **-i•er, -i•est.**

leaf′let (-lit), *n.* **1.** a small flat or folded sheet of printed matter. **2.** a small leaf.

league¹ (lēg), *n.*, *v.*, **leagued, lea•guing.** —*n.* **1.** an association of persons, states, etc., for the promotion of common interests or for mutual assistance. **2.** a group of athletic teams organized to compete chiefly among themselves. —*v.t.*, *v.i.* **3.** to unite in a league.

league² (lēg), *n.* a unit of distance, roughly 3 miles (4.8 kilometers).

leak (lēk), *n.* **1.** an unintended hole, crack, etc., through which fluid or light enters or escapes. **2.** any means of unintended entrance or escape. **3.** a disclosure of secret information. —*v.i.* **4.** to let a fluid or light enter or escape through a leak. **5.** to pass in or out in this manner. **6.** to become known unintentionally: *The news leaked out.* —*v.t.* **7.** to let (fluid or light) enter or escape. **8.** to allow to become known. —**leak′y,** *adj.*, **-i•er, -i•est.**

lean¹ (lēn), *v.*, **leaned** or (*esp. Brit.*) **leant** (lent), **lean•ing.** —*v.i.* **1.** to incline or bend from a vertical position. **2.** to incline in feeling, opinion, etc. **3.** to rest or lie for support: *to lean against a wall.* **4.** to depend or rely. —*v.t.* **5.** to cause to lean.

lean² (lēn), *adj.*, **-er, -est. 1.** without much flesh or fat. **2.** lacking in richness, quantity, etc.: *lean years.* **3.** spare; economical. —**lean′ness,** *n.*

lean′-to′ *n.*, *pl.* **-tos. 1.** a roof of a single pitch with the higher end abutting a wall. **2.** a structure with such a roof.

leap (lēp), *v.*, **leaped** or **leapt** (lept, lēpt), **leap•ing.** *n.* —*v.i.* **1.** to spring from one point to another; jump. **2.** to move or act quickly or suddenly: *to leap at an opportunity.* —*v.t.* **3.** to jump over. **4.** to cause to leap. —*n.* **5.** a spring or jump. **6.** the distance covered in a leap. **7.** an abrupt transition. —**leap′er,** *n.*

leap′frog′ *n.*, *v.*, **-frogged, -frog•ging.** —*n.* **1.** a game in which players take turns leaping over another player bent over from the waist. —*v.t.*, *v.i.* **2.** to jump over (a person or thing) in or as if in leapfrog.

leap′ year′ *n.* a year occurring every four years that contains 366 days, with February 29 as an additional day.

learn (lûrn), *v.*, **learned** (lûrnd) or **learnt** (lûrnt), **learn•ing.** —*v.t.* **1.** to acquire knowledge of or skill in by study, instruction, or experience. **2.** to become informed of. **3.** to memorize. —*v.i.* **4.** to acquire knowledge or skill. **5.** to become informed: *to learn of an accident.* —**learn′er,** *n.*

learn•ed (lûr′nid), *adj.* having much knowledge; scholarly; erudite.

learn′ing dis•a•bil′i•ty *n.* any of several conditions characterized by difficulty in reading, writing, etc., and associated with impairment of the central nervous system. —**learn′ing-disa′bled,** *adj.*

lease (lēs), *n.*, *v.*, **leased, leas•ing.** —*n.* **1.** a contract renting property to another for a specified period in consideration of rent. —*v.t.* **2.** to grant or hold by lease. —**leas′er,** *n.*

leash (lēsh), *n.* **1.** a chain, strap, etc., for controlling a dog or other animal. —*v.t.* **2.** to secure or control by or as if by a leash.

least (lēst), *adj.*, *a superl.* of **little** *with* **less** or **lesser** *as compar.* **1.** smallest in size, amount, degree, etc. **2.** lowest in consideration or importance.

—*n.* **3.** the least amount, quantity, degree, etc. —*adv., superl.* of **little** *with* **less** *as compar.* **4.** to the smallest extent, amount, or degree. —*Idiom.* **5. at least, a.** at the lowest estimate. **b.** in any case. **6. not in the least,** not at all.

leath•er (le*th*′ər), *n.* **1.** the skin of an animal with the hair removed, prepared for use by tanning or a similar process. —*adj.* **2.** of or made of leather. —**leath′er•y,** *adj.*

leath′er•neck′ *n. Informal.* a U.S. marine.

leave¹ (lēv), *v.*, **left, leav•ing.** —*v.t.* **1.** to go away from, as a place. **2.** to depart from permanently; quit. **3.** to let remain behind: *The bear left tracks.* **4.** to let stay or be as specified: *to leave a motor running.* **5.** to let remain in a position to do something without interference: *We left him to his work.* **6.** to give up or abandon. **7.** to give for use after one's death. —*v.i.* **8.** to go away or depart. **9. leave off,** to stop; cease. **10. ~ out,** to omit. —**leav′er,** *n.*

leave² (lēv), *n.* **1.** permission to do something. **2.** permission to be absent, as from military duty. **3.** the time this permission lasts. —*Idiom.* **4. take one's leave,** to depart. **5. take leave of,** to part or separate from.

leav•en (lev′ən), *n.* **1.** a substance, as yeast, that causes fermentation and expansion of dough. **2.** an element that produces an altering or transforming influence. —*v.t.* **3.** to make (dough) rise with a leaven. **4.** to permeate with an altering or transforming element.

Leb•a•non (leb′ə nən, -non′), *n.* a republic at the E end of the Mediterranean. —**Leb′a•nese′** (-nēz′, -nēs′), *adj.*, *n.*, *pl.* **-nese.**

lech′er•ous (lech′ər əs) *adj.* lustful. —**lech′er•y,** *n.* —**lech′er,** *n.*

lec•tern (lek′tərn), *n.* a stand with a slanted top, used to hold a book, speech, etc., for a standing speaker.

lec•ture (lek′chər), *n.*, *v.*, **-tured, -tur•ing.** —*n.* **1.** a discourse delivered before an audience or class, esp. for instruction. **2.** a long, tedious reprimand. —*v.i.* **3.** to give a lecture. —*v.t.* **4.** to deliver a lecture to. **5.** to reprimand at length. —**lec′tur•er,** *n.*

ledge (lej), *n.* **1.** a narrow, horizontal, shelflike projection on a wall or cliff. **2.** a reef or ridge of rocks in the sea.

ledg•er (lej′ər), *n.* an account book in which business transactions are recorded in final form.

lee (lē), *n.*, *pl.* **lees. 1.** protective shelter. **2.** the side that is sheltered from the wind. **3.** *Chiefly Naut.* the region toward which the wind blows. —*adj.* **4.** of or on the lee. —**lee′ward,** *adj.*, *adv.*, *n.*

leech (lēch), *n.* **1.** a bloodsucking annelid worm, once used for bloodletting. **2.** a person who clings to another for personal gain. —*v.i.* **3.** to hang on to a person in the manner of a leech.

leek (lēk), *n.* a plant related to the onion, used in cookery.

leer (lēr), *v.i.* **1.** to look with a sideways glance suggestive of lascivious interest or malicious intention. —*n.* **2.** a lascivious or sly look.

leer′y (lēr′ē), *adj.*, **-i•er, -i•est.** wary; suspicious. —**leer′i•ness,** *n.*

lee•way (lē′wā′), *n.* **1.** extra time, space, etc., within which to act. **2.** a degree of freedom of action or thought. **3.** the drift of a ship leeward from its heading.

left¹ (left), *adj.* **1.** of, on, or near the side of a person or thing that is toward the west when the subject is facing north. **2.** (*often cap.*) of or belonging to the political Left. —*n.* **3.** the left side. **4.** a turn toward the left. **5. the Left,** those individuals or groups advocating liberal reform or revolutionary change in the established order. —*adv.* **6.** toward the left.

left² (left), *v.* pt. and pp. of LEAVE.¹

leg (leg), *n.* **1.** either of the two lower limbs of a biped, or any of the paired limbs of an animal, that support and move the body. **2.** something resembling a leg in use, position, or appearance. **3.** the part of a garment that covers the leg. **4.** one of the distinct sections of any course: *the last leg of a trip.* —**leg′less,** *adj.*

leg•a•cy (leg′ə sē), *n., pl.* **-cies. 1.** a gift of money or property left to someone in a will. **2.** anything handed down from the past, as from an ancestor.

le•gal (lē′gəl), *adj.* **1.** permitted by law. **2.** of or established by law. **3.** of or characteristic of lawyers. —**le•gal′i•ty,** *n., pl.* **-ties.** —**le′gal•ly,** *adv.*

le′gal•ese′ (-gə lēz′, -lēs′), *n.* language containing an excessive amount of legal terminology or jargon.

le•ga•tion (li gā′shən), *n.* **1.** a diplomatic minister and staff in a foreign mission. **2.** the official headquarters of a diplomatic minister.

le•ga•to (lə gä′tō), *adj., adv. Music.* smooth and connected; without breaks between tones.

leg•end (lej′ənd), *n.* **1.** an unverifiable story or collection of stories handed down by tradition and popularly accepted as historical. **2.** an inscription on a monument, coin, etc. **3.** a table on a map, chart, or illustration explaining the symbols used. **4.** an admirable person about whom stories are told. —**leg′en•dar′y** (-ən der′ē), *adj.*

leg•er•de•main (lej′ər də mān′), *n.* **1.** sleight of hand. **2.** trickery; deception.

leg′ging *n.* **1.** a covering for the leg, usu. from ankle to knee. **2. leggings, a.** close-fitting knit pants. **b.** the pants of a two-piece snowsuit.

leg•i•ble (lej′ə bəl), *adj.* capable of being read with ease, as writing. —**leg′i•bil′i•ty,** *n.* —**leg′i•bly,** *adv.*

le•gion (lē′jən), *n.* **1.** the largest unit of the ancient Roman army. **2.** a great number of persons or things. —*adj.* **3.** very great in number: *His followers were legion.* —**le′gion•ar′y** (-jə ner′ē), *adj., n., pl.* **-ar•ies.** —**le′gion•naire′** (-nâr′), *n.*

leg•is•late (lej′is lāt′), *v.,* **-lat•ed, -lat•ing.** —*v.i.* **1.** to make or enact laws. —*v.t.* **2.** to create or control by legislation: *attempts to legislate morality.* —**leg′is•la′tor,** *n.*

leg′is•la′ture (-chər), *n.* a body of persons empowered to make, change, or repeal laws.

le•git•i•mate (*adj.* li jit′ə mit; *v.* -māt′), *adj., v.,* **-mat•ed, -mat•ing.** —*adj.* **1.** according to law. **2.** in accordance with established rules, standards, etc. **3.** born of legally married parents. **4.** valid; logical: *a legitimate conclusion.* **5.** justified: *a legitimate complaint.* **6.** of stage plays, as distinguished from burlesque, vaudeville, etc. —*v.t.* **7.** to make lawful or legal. **8.** to sanction or authorize. —**le•git′i•ma•cy** (-mə sē), *n.* —**le•git′i•mate•ly,** *adv.*

le•git′i•mize′ *v.t.,* **-mized, -miz•ing.** LEGITIMATE. —**le•git′i•mi•za′tion,** *n.*

leg•ume (leg′yōōm, li gyōōm′), *n.* **1.** any of a large family of plants having pods that split open when dry, comprising beans, peas, etc. **2.** the pod or seed of such a plant. —**le•gu′mi•nous,** *adj.*

lei (lā, lā′ē), *n., pl.* **leis.** (in Hawaii) a wreath of flowers worn around the neck.

lei•sure (lē′zhər, lezh′ər), *n.* **1.** freedom from the demands of work or duty. **2.** free or unoccupied time. —*adj.* **3.** free or unoccupied. **4.** having leisure.

lei′sure•ly *adj.* **1.** acting or done without haste. —*adv.* **2.** in a leisurely manner.

leit•mo•tif (līt′mō tēf′), *n.* a theme associated throughout a music drama with a particular person, situation, or idea.

lem•ming (lem′ing), *n.* any of various small, mainly arctic rodents, noted for periodic mass migrations.

lem•on (lem′ən), *n.* **1.** the yellowish, acid fruit of a subtropical citrus tree. **2.** the tree itself. **3.** *Informal.* a person or thing that is defective or unsatisfactory. —**lem′on•y,** *adj.*

lem′on•ade′ (-ə nād′), *n.* a beverage of lemon juice, sweetener, and water.

le•mur (lē′mər), *n.* a small, arboreal primate with large eyes and a foxlike face.

lend (lend), *v.,* **lent, lend•ing.** —*v.t.* **1.** to grant the use of (something) on condition that it will be returned. **2.** to give (money) temporarily, usu. at interest. **3.** to adapt: *The building lends itself to remodeling.* **4.** to give or impart. —*v.i.* **5.** to make a loan. —**lend′er,** *n.*

length (lengkth, length, lenth), *n.* **1.** the longest extent of anything as measured from end to end. **2.** extent in time or space. **3.** a piece of a certain extent: *a length of rope.* **4.** a large extent or expanse of something. —*Idiom.* **5. at length, a.** finally. **b.** fully; in detail. —**length′en,** *v.t., v.i.* —**length′wise′,** *adv.*

le•ni•ent (lē′nē ənt, lēn′yənt), *adj.* agreeably tolerant; not strict or severe. —**le′ni•en•cy,** *n.* —**le′ni•ent•ly,** *adv.*

lens (lenz), *n., pl.* **lens•es. 1.** a curved piece of transparent substance, usu. glass, used in optical devices for changing the convergence of light rays, as for magnification or correcting vision defects. **2.** some analogous device, as for affecting sound waves, electromagnetic radiation, etc. **3.** a transparent body in the eye that focuses light on the retina.

lent (lent), *v.* pt. and pp. of LEND.

Lent (lent), *n.* (in the Christian religion) a season of fasting and penitence, before Easter. —**Lent′en,** **lent′en,** *adj.*

len•til (len′til, -tl), *n.* **1.** a legume having flattened seeds used as food. **2.** the seed itself.

le•o•nine (lē′ə nīn′), *adj.* of or resembling a lion.

leop•ard (lep′ərd), *n.* a large, powerful Asian or African cat, usu. tawny with black spots.

le•o•tard (lē′ə tärd′), *n.* a skintight one-piece garment for the torso, worn by acrobats, dancers, etc.

lep•er (lep′ər), *n.* a person who has leprosy.

lep•re•chaun (lep′rə kôn′, -kon′), *n.* a sprite of Irish folklore, often represented as a little old man.

lep•ro•sy (lep′rə sē), *n.* a mildly infectious disease marked by ulcerations, destruction of tissue, loss of sensation, etc. —**lep′rous,** *adj.*

les•bi•an (lez′bē ən), *n.* a female homosexual. —**les′bi•an•ism,** *n.*

lese maj•es•ty or **lèse maj•es•té** (lēz′ maj′əs-tē), *n.* **1.** an offense against the dignity of a ruler. **2.** an attack on any revered custom, institution, etc.

le•sion (lē′zhən), *n.* any localized area of diseased or injured tissue or of abnormal structural change.

Le•so•tho (lə sōō′tō, -sō′tō), *n.* a monarchy in S Africa.

less (les), *adv., a compar. of* **little** *with* **least** *as superl.* **1.** to a smaller extent, amount, or degree. —*adj., a compar. of* **little** *with* **least** *as superl.* **2.** smaller in size, amount, or degree. **3.** lower in consideration, rank, etc.: *no less a person than the mayor.* **4.** fewer. —*n.* **5.** a smaller amount or quantity. —*prep.* **6.** minus. —*Idiom.* **7. less and less,** to a decreasing extent or degree.

-less a suffix meaning: without (*childless*); not able to (*sleepless*); not able to be (*useless*).

les•see (le sē′), *n., pl.* **-sees.** a person to whom a lease is granted.

less′en *v.t., v.i.* to make or become less.

less′er *adj., a compar. of* **little** *with* **least** *as superl.* smaller, as in size, value, or importance.

les•son (les′ən), *n.* **1.** a section into which a course of study is divided. **2.** a chapter, exercise, etc., assigned to a student for study. **3.** something learned or studied. **4.** an instructive example. **5.** a reproof or punishment. **6.** a portion of Scripture read at a divine service.

les•sor (les′ôr, le sôr′), *n.* a person who grants a lease.

lest (lest), *conj.* for fear that.

let¹ (let), *v.,* **let, let•ting.** —*v.t.* **1.** to allow or permit. **2.** to cause to; make: *to let her know the truth.* **3.** (used as an auxiliary expressive of a request, warning, etc.): *Let me see.* **4.** to rent or lease. —*v.i.* **5.** to be rented or leased. **6. let down, a.** to disappoint or betray. **b.** to lower. **7. ~ off, a.** to release explosively. **b.** to release without punishment. **8. ~ on, a.** to reveal, as information. **b.** to pretend. **9. ~ out, a.** to release, as from confinement. **b.** to alter (a garment) so as to make larger. **10. ~ up, a.** to abate. **b.** to cease. —*Idiom.* **11. let be,** to refrain from interfering with.

let² (let), *n.* **1.** (in tennis, badminton, etc.) any shot or action that must be replayed. **2.** *Chiefly Law.* an obstacle: *to act without let or hindrance.*

-let a suffix meaning: small (*booklet*); an article worn on (*anklet*).

let′down′ *n.* **1.** a disappointment. **2.** a decrease in volume, force, energy, etc.

le•thal (lē′thəl), *adj.* deadly; fatal. —**le′thal•ly,** *adv.*

leth•ar•gy (leth′ər jē), *n.* the quality or state of being drowsy; apathetic or sluggish inactivity. —**le•thar•gic** (lə thär′jik), *adj.* —**le•thar′gi•cal•ly,** *adv.*

let•ter (let′ər), *n.* **1.** a written communication usu. transmitted by mail. **2.** a character that is part of an alphabet. **3.** literal meaning: *the letter of the law.* **4. letters, a.** literature in general. **b.** learning; knowledge, esp. of literature. —*v.t.* **5.** to mark with letters. —**let′ter•er,** *n.*

let′tered *adj.* **1.** educated or learned. **2.** literate. **3.** marked with letters.

let′ter•head′ *n.* **1.** a printed heading on stationery giving a name and address. **2.** a sheet of paper bearing a letterhead.

let′ter-per′fect *adj.* precise in every detail.

let•tuce (let′is), *n.* a cultivated plant with succulent leaves used for salads.

let′up′ *n.* cessation; pause; relief.

leu•ke•mi•a (lōō kē′mē ə), *n.* any of several cancers of the bone marrow characterized by an abnormal increase of white blood cells. —**leu•ke′mic,** *adj.*

leu•ko•cyte (lōō′kə sīt′), *n.* WHITE BLOOD CELL.

lev•ee (lev′ē), *n., pl.* **-ees. 1.** an embankment designed to prevent the flooding of a river. **2.** a landing place for ships; quay.

lev•el (lev′əl), *adj., n., v.,* **-eled, -el•ing** or (*esp. Brit.*) **-elled, -el•ling.** —*adj.* **1.** having a flat or even surface. **2.** being parallel to the horizon. **3.** equal, as in height or status. **4.** steady or uniform: *a level voice.* **5.** sensible; rational: *a level head.* —*n.* **6.** the horizontal line or plane in which anything is situated, with regard to its elevation: *a shelf at eye level.* **7.** elevation; height: *The water rose to a level of 30 feet.* **8.** a position in a graded scale of values: *an average level of skill.* **9.** a horizontal surface: *the upper level of the bridge.* **10.** a surveying instrument used for establishing a horizontal. —*v.t.* **11.** to make level or even. **12.** to bring to the level of the ground: *to level trees.* **13.** *Informal.* to knock down (a person). **14.** to make equal, as in status. **15.** to aim (a weapon, criticism, etc.) at a mark. **16. level with,** to be frank with. —*v.i.* **17.** to bring persons or things to a common level. —**lev′el•er, lev′el•ler,** *n.*

lev′el•head′ed *adj.* having common sense and sound judgment. —**lev′el•head′ed•ness,** *n.*

lev•er (lev′ər, lē′vər), *n.* **1.** a rigid bar that pivots about one point and is used to move an object at a second point by a force applied at a third. **2.** a means to an end.

lev′er•age (-ij), *n.* **1.** the mechanical advantage gained by using a lever. **2.** power to act effectively or to influence people.

le•vi•a•than (li vī′ə thən), *n.* **1.** (*often cap.*) *Bible.* a sea monster. **2.** something of immense size or power. [< LL « Heb *liwyāthān*]

lev•i•tate (lev′i tāt′), *v.i., v.t.,* **-tat•ed, -tat•ing.** to rise or cause to rise in the air, esp. in apparent defiance of gravity. —**lev′i•ta′tion,** *n.*

lev•i•ty (lev′i tē), *n.* lightness of mind, character, or behavior.

lev•y (lev′ē), *n., pl.* **-ies,** *v.,* **-ied, -y•ing.** —*n.* **1.** an imposing or collecting, as of a tax, by authority or force. **2.** the amount collected. **3.** the conscription of troops. **4.** the troops conscripted. —*v.t.* **5.** to impose (a tax, fine, etc.). **6.** to conscript (troops). **7.** to wage (war). —**lev′i•er,** *n.*

lewd (lōōd), *adj.,* **-er, -est. 1.** inclined to or inciting to lust or lechery. **2.** obscene or indecent. —**lewd′ly,** *adv.* —**lewd′ness,** *n.*

lex•i•cog•ra•phy (lek′si kog′rə fē), *n.* the writing, editing, or compiling of dictionaries. —**lex′i•cog′ra•pher,** *n.* —**lex′i•co•graph′ic** (-kə graf′ik), **lex′i•co•graph′i•cal,** *adj.*

lex′i•con′ (-kon′, -kən), *n.* **1.** a dictionary, esp. of Greek, Latin, or Hebrew. **2.** the vocabulary of a particular language, field, etc. —**lex′i•cal,** *adj.*

lg. 1. large. **2.** long.

li•a•bil•i•ty (lī′ə bil′i tē), *n., pl.* **-ties. 1. liabilities,** debts or monetary obligations. **2.** something disadvantageous. **3.** the state or quality of being liable.

li′a•ble *adj.* **1.** legally responsible. **2.** subject or susceptible. **3.** likely or apt.

li•ai•son (lē ā′zən, -zon), *n.* **1.** the contact maintained between military or organizational units. **2.** a person who maintains such a contact. **3.** an illicit sexual relationship.

li•ar (lī′ər), *n.* a person who tells lies.

li•bel (lī′bəl), *n., v.,* **-beled, -bel•ing** or (*esp. Brit.*) **-belled, -bel•ling.** —*n.* **1. a.** defamation by written or printed matter, rather than by spoken words. **b.** the crime of publishing such matter. —*v.t.* **2.** to publish a libel against. —**li′bel•er, li′bel•ler,** *n.* —**li′bel•ous, li′bel•lous,** *adj.*

lib•er•al (lib′ər əl, lib′rəl), *adj.* **1.** favoring progress or reform. **2.** free from prejudice; tolerant. **3.** characterized by generosity. **4.** ample or abundant. **5.** not strict or literal. **6.** of the liberal arts. —*n.* **7.** a person of liberal principles or views. —**lib′er•al•ism,** *n.* —**lib′er•al•ly,** *adv.*

lib′eral arts′ *n.pl.* college courses comprising the arts, humanities, natural sciences, and social sciences.

lib•er•ate′ (-ə rāt′), *v.t.,* **-at•ed, -at•ing. 1.** to set free, as from bondage or foreign control. **2.** to free (a group or individual) from social or economic constraints. **3.** to set free from combination, as a gas. —**lib′er•a′tion,** *n.* —**lib′er•a′tor,** *n.*

Li•be•ri•a (lī bēr′ē ə), *n.* a republic in W Africa. —**Li•be′ri•an,** *adj., n.*

lib•er•tar•i•an (lib′ər târ′ē ən), *n.* a person who advocates liberty, esp. with regard to thought or conduct.

lib′er•tine′ (-tēn′, -tin), *n.* **1.** a person who is morally or sexually unrestrained. —*adj.* **2.** dissolute; licentious.

lib′er•ty *n., pl.* **-ties. 1.** freedom from arbitrary or despotic government. **2.** freedom from external or foreign rule. **3.** freedom from captivity, confinement, etc. **4.** permission granted to a sailor to go ashore. **5.** impertinent freedom in action or speech: *to take liberties.* —*Idiom.* **6. at liberty, a.** free from captivity. **b.** free to do or be specified.

li•bi•do (li bē′dō), *n., pl.* **-dos.** *Psychoanalysis.* all of the instinctual energies and desires derived from the id. **2.** sexual drive. —**li•bid′i•nal** (-bid′n l), *adj.* —**li•bid′i•nous,** *adj.*

li•brar•y (lī′brer′ē, -brə rē, -brē), *n., pl.* **-ies. 1.** a place containing books, films, etc., arranged and cataloged in a fixed way. **2.** any collection of books, or the space containing them.

li•bret•to (li bret′ō), *n., pl.* **-bret•tos, -bret•ti** (-bret′ē). **1.** the text of an opera or similar work. **2.** a book containing such a text. —**li•bret′tist,** *n.*

Lib•y•a (lib′ē ə), *n.* a republic in N Africa. —**Lib′y•an,** *adj., n.*

li•cense (lī′səns), *n., v.,* **-censed, -cens•ing.** —*n.* **1.** formal permission from a constituted authority to do something, as to carry on some business. **2.** a certificate of such permission. **3.** deviation from rule, fact, etc., as for the sake of literary effect: *poetic license.* —*v.t.* **4.** to issue or grant a license to or for.

li′cen•see′ (-sən sē′), *n., pl.* **-sees.** a person to whom a license is granted.

li•cen′tious (-sen′shəs), *adj.* sexually unrestrained; lascivious. —**li•cen′tious•ly,** *adv.* —**li•cen′tious•ness,** *n.*

li•chen (lī′kən), *n.* an organism composed of a fungus in union with an alga, commonly forming patches on rocks and trees.

lic•it (lis′it), *adj.* legal; lawful. —**lic′it•ly,** *adv.*

lick (lik), *v.t.* **1.** to pass the tongue over the surface of. **2.** (of waves, flames, etc.) to pass lightly over. **3.** *Informal.* **a.** to hit or beat. **b.** to defeat. —*n.* **4.** a stroke of the tongue over something. **5.** SALT LICK. **6.** *Informal.* **a.** a blow. **b.** a brief, brisk burst of activity. **c.** a small amount. —*Idiom.* **7. lick and a promise,** a perfunctory performance of a chore.

lick′e•ty-split′ (lik′i tē), *adv. Informal.* at great speed.

lick′ing *n. Informal.* **1.** a beating or thrashing. **2.** a defeat or setback.

lic•o•rice (lik′ər ish, -ə ris), *n.* **1.** the sweet-tasting, dried root of a Eurasian plant, or an extract made from it. **2.** a candy flavored with licorice root.

lid (lid), *n.* **1.** a movable cover, as for a jar. **2.** an eyelid. **3.** a restraint or curb, as on prices or news. —**lid′ded,** *adj.*

lie¹ (lī), *n., v.,* **lied, ly•ing.** —*n.* **1.** a false statement made with deliberate intent to deceive. —*v.i.* **2.** to tell a lie. —*v.t.* **3.** to bring about or affect by lying.

lie² (lī), *v.,* **lay, lain, ly•ing,** *n.* —*v.i.* **1.** to be in or assume a horizontal or recumbent position. **2.** to rest on a surface in a horizontal position. **3.** to remain in a state of inactivity, restraint, etc.: *to lie in ambush.* **4.** to be situated: *land lying along the coast.* **5.** to be found; exist: *The fault lies here.* —*n.* **6.** the manner, position, or direction in which something lies.

Liech•ten•stein (lik′tən stīn′, likн′-), *n.* a small principality in central Europe between Austria and Switzerland.

lie′ detec′tor *n.* a polygraph used to determine the truth or falsity of a person's answers under questioning.

lien (lēn, lē′ən), *n.* the legal right to hold another's property, esp. to satisfy a debt.

lieu (lōo), *n.* **1.** place; stead. —*Idiom.* **2. in lieu of,** instead of.

lieu•ten•ant (lōo ten′ənt; *in Brit. use, except in the navy,* lef ten′ənt), *n.* **1. a.** FIRST LIEUTENANT. **b.** SECOND LIEUTENANT. **2.** a naval officer ranking above a lieutenant junior grade. **3.** a person who acts in the place of a superior. —**lieu•ten′an•cy,** *n.*

life (līf), *n., pl.* **lives** (līvz). —*n.* **1.** the condition that distinguishes organisms from inorganic objects and dead organisms, being manifested by metabolism, growth, reproduction, etc. **2.** the animate existence or period of animate existence of an individual. **3.** the period of existence or activity of something inanimate. **4.** a living being. **5.** living things collectively: *insect life.* **6.** a particular aspect of existence: *enjoyed an active physical life.* **7.** the sum of experiences and actions that constitute a person's existence. **8.** a biography. **9.** animation; liveliness. **10.** a manner of living. —**life′less,** *adj.* —**life′like′,** *adj.* —**life′time′,** *n.*

life′blood′ *n.* **1.** the blood, considered as essential to life. **2.** a vital or animating element.

life′boat′ *n.* a ship's boat designed to rescue persons from a sinking ship.

life′guard′ *n.* an expert swimmer employed, as at a beach, to protect bathers from drowning.

life′ preserv′er *n.* a buoyant device for keeping a person afloat.

lif′er *n. Informal.* a person serving a term of life imprisonment.

life′sav′er *n.* **1.** one who rescues another from danger of death. **2.** one that saves a person, as from a difficult situation. —**life′sav′ing,** *adj., n.*

life′-size′ or **-sized′,** *adj.* of the natural size of an object, person, etc.

life′style′ or **life′ style′,** *n.* the typical way of living of an individual or group.

life′-sup•port′ *adj.* of equipment or techniques that sustain or substitute for essential body functions.

life′work′ *n.* the complete or principal work of a lifetime.

lift (lift), *v.t.* **1.** to bring up to a higher position. **2.** to raise or direct upward: *to lift one's head.* **3.** to rescind or stop, as a curfew or blockade. **4.** to raise in rank, condition, etc. **5.** *Informal.* to steal. **6.** to pay off (a debt). —*v.i.* **7.** to go up. **8.** to strain upward in raising something. —*n.* **9.** the act of lifting. **10.** the distance that anything is raised. **11.** a lifting force. **12.** the quantity lifted. **13.** a ride, esp. one given to a pedestrian. **14.** a feeling of exaltation. **15.** a device for lifting. **16.** *Brit.* ELEVATOR (def. 1). **17.** the component of the aerodynamic forces exerted on an airfoil perpendicular to the forward motion and opposing gravity.

lift′off′ *n.* **1.** the vertical ascent by a spacecraft or aircraft. **2.** the instant of this.

lig•a•ment (lig′ə mənt), *n.* a band of strong tissue that connects bones or holds organs in place.

lig•a•ture (lig′ə chər, -chŏŏr′), *n.* **1.** the act of binding or tying up. **2.** a tie or bond. **3.** a character or type combining two or more letters, as *fl.* **4.** a thread or wire for surgical constriction of blood vessels.

light¹ (līt), *n., adj.,* **light•er, light•est,** *v.,* **light•ed** or **lit, light•ing.** —*n.* **1.** something that makes things visible or affords illumination. **2. a.** electromagnetic radiation to which the organs of sight react. **b.** ultraviolet or infrared radiation. **3.** an illuminating source, as the sun or a lamp. **4.** radiance or illumination. **5.** daybreak or dawn. **6.** a means of igniting, as a spark. **7.** the aspect in which a thing is regarded: *saw things in a new light.* **8.** mental or spiritual enlightenment. **9.** a window or a windowpane. —*adj.* **10.** having light or illumination. **11.** pale. —*v.t.* **12.** to set burning, as a fire. **13.** to turn on (an electric light). **14.** to give light to. **15.** to brighten. —*v.i.* **16.** to become kindled. **17.** to ignite a cigar, cigarette, or pipe (usu. fol. by *up*). **18.** to become illuminated. **19.** to brighten. —*Idiom.* **20. in (the) light of,** considering. **21. see the light, a.** to come into existence or prominence. **b.** to understand something at last. —**light′ness,** *n.*

light² (līt), *adj.* and *adv.,* **-er, -est.** —*adj.* **1.** of little weight. **2.** of little weight in proportion to bulk. **3.** of less than the usual weight, force, intensity, etc. **4.** not difficult or burdensome. **5.** not profound or serious. **6.** of little importance. **7.** easily digested: *light food.* **8.** (esp. of beer and wine) having fewer calories than the standard product. **9.** airy or buoyant in movement. **10.** cheerful; carefree: *a light heart.* **11.** dizzy. **12.** using small-scale machinery primarily for the production of consumer goods: *light industry.* —*adv.* **13.** without much baggage: *to travel light.* —**light′ly,** *adv.* —**light′ness,** *n.*

light³ (līt), *v.i.,* **light•ed** or **lit, light•ing. 1.** to come to rest; land. **2.** to come by chance: *to light on a clue.* **3. light into,** to attack physically or verbally.

light′en¹, *v.t.* to make or become lighter or less dark; brighten. —**light′en•er,** *n.*

light′en², *v.t., v.i.* **1.** to make or become lighter in weight. **2.** to make or become less burdensome. **3.** to make or become less gloomy.

light′er¹, *n.* a device used in lighting cigarettes, cigars, or pipes.

light′er², *n.* a large barge used to load or unload ships or to transport goods short distances.

light′-fin′gered *adj.* skillful at or given to pilfering.

light′head′ed *adj.* **1.** giddy or dizzy. **2.** having a frivolous disposition.

light′heart′ed *adj.* carefree; cheerful. —**light′-heart′ed•ly,** *adv.* —**light′heart′ed•ness,** *n.*

light′house′ *n.* a tower displaying a light for the guidance of mariners.

light′ning (-ning), *n.* **1.** a luminous electric spark discharge in the atmosphere. —*adj.* **2.** of or resembling lightning, esp. in regard to speed.

light′ning bug′ *n.* FIREFLY.

light′ning rod′ *n.* a metal rod installed to divert lightning away from a structure by providing a direct path to the ground.

light′-year′ *n.* the distance traversed by light in one year, about 5.88 trillion mi. (9.46 trillion km).

lig•ne•ous (lig′nē əs), *adj.* of the nature of or resembling wood.

lig′nite (lig′nīt) *n.* a kind of coal.

like¹ (līk), *adj.* **1.** of the same form, appearance, kind, etc. —*prep.* **2.** similarly to: *She works like a beaver.* **3.** resembling: *Your necklace is like mine.* **4.** characteristic of: *It would be like him to be late.* **5.** indicative of: *It looks like rain.* **6.** disposed or inclined to: *to feel like going to bed.* —*adv.* **7.** *Informal.* likely or probably: *like as not.* —*conj.* **8.** as: *It happened like you said it would.* **9.** as if: *He acted like he was afraid.* **10.** *Informal.* (used esp. after forms of *be* to introduce reported speech or thought): *She's like, "I don't believe it," and I'm* *like,* "No, it's true!" —*n.* **11.** a counterpart, match, or equal: *No one has seen her like in a long time.* **12. the like,** something of a similar nature: *They grow oranges, lemons, and the like.* —*Idiom.* **13. something like,** approximately the same as. **14. the like** or **likes of,** the equal of.

like² (līk), *v.,* **liked, lik•ing,** *n.* —*v.t.* **1.** to find agreeable or congenial to one's taste. **2.** to regard with favor. **3.** to wish or want. —*v.i.* **4.** to feel inclined: *Stay if you like.* —*n.* **5.** Usu., **likes.** the things a person likes.

-like a suffix meaning like or characteristic of (*childlike*).

like′ly *adj.,* **-li•er, -li•est,** *adv.* —*adj.* **1.** probably destined: *something not likely to happen.* **2.** seeming like truth or fact: *a likely story.* **3.** apparently suitable: *a likely place to live.* —*adv.* **4.** probably: *We will most likely stay home.*

lik′en *v.t.* to represent as similar or like.

like′ness *n.* **1.** a portrait or copy. **2.** the state or fact of being similar. **3.** the semblance of something; guise.

like′wise′ *adv.* **1.** in addition. **2.** in like manner; similarly.

li•lac (lī′lək, -läk, -lak), *n.* **1.** a shrub with large clusters of fragrant purple or white flowers. **2.** pale reddish purple.

Lil•li•pu•tian (lil′i pyōō′shən), *adj.* **1.** extremely small. **2.** petty; trivial.

lilt (lilt), *n.* **1.** a rhythmic swing or cadence. **2.** a light, cheerful song or tune. —**lilt′ing,** *adj.*

lil•y (lil′ē), *n., pl.* **lil•ies,** *adj.* —*n.* **1.** any of various scaly-bulbed plants with funnel-shaped or bell-shaped flowers. **2.** the flower of such a plant. **3.** any similar plant, as the water lily. —*adj.* **4.** white as a lily.

lil′y-liv′ered *adj.* cowardly.

lil′y of the val′ley *n., pl.* **lilies of the valley.** a plant with an elongated cluster of bell-shaped, fragrant white flowers.

li′ma bean′ (lī′mə), *n.* **1.** a bean with a broad, flat, edible seed. **2.** the seed.

limb (lim), *n.* **1.** one of the paired bodily appendages of animals, as a leg, arm, or wing. **2.** a main branch of a tree. —*Idiom.* **3. out on a limb,** in a risky situation. —**limb′less,** *adj.*

lim•ber (lim′bər), *adj.* **1.** characterized by ease in bending the body; supple. **2.** bending readily; flexible. —*v.t., v.i.* **3.** to make or become limber: *to limber up before the game.* —**lim′ber•ness,** *n.*

lim•bo¹ (lim′bō), *n., pl.* **-bos.** **1.** (*often cap.*) *Theology.* a region for the souls of unbaptized infants and of the righteous who died before the coming of Christ. **2.** a place or state of oblivion. **3.** an intermediate state or place. [< ML *in limbō* on hell's border (L: on the edge)]

lim•bo² (lim′bō), *n., pl.* **-bos.** a West Indian dance done by bending backward to pass under a successively lowered horizontal bar. [cf. Jamaican E *limba* limber]

lime¹ (līm), *n., v.,* **limed, lim•ing.** —*n.* **1.** a white or grayish white solid, calcium oxide, used in mortars, plasters, and cements and as a fertilizer. —*v.t.* **2.** to treat or cover with lime. —**lim′y,** *adj.*

lime² (līm), *n.* the small, greenish yellow, acid fruit of a citrus tree. **2.** the tree itself.

lime′light′ *n.* **1.** a position at the center of public attention. **2.** (formerly) a spotlight unit for the stage, using a flame of mixed gases directed at a cylinder of lime.

lim•er•ick (lim′ər ik), *n.* a humorous, often nonsensical poem of five lines. [alluding to *Limerick,* county and city in Ireland]

lime′stone′ *n.* a sedimentary rock consisting predominantly of calcium carbonate.

lim•it (lim′it), *n.* **1.** the final or furthest boundary or point as to extent, amount, continuance, etc. **2. limits,** the premises enclosed within boundaries. —*v.t.* **3.** to restrict by establishing limits. **4.** to confine within limits. —**lim′i•ta′tion,** *n.* —**lim′it•er,** *n.* —**lim′it•less,** *adj.*

lim′it•ed *adj.* **1.** confined within limits. **2.** (of

trains, buses, etc.) making only a limited number of stops en route.

lim•o (lim′ō), *n., pl.* **lim•os.** *Informal.* a limousine.

lim•ou•sine (lim′ə zēn′, lim′ə zēn′), *n.* **1.** a large, luxurious automobile, esp. one driven by a chauffeur. **2.** a small bus for transporting passengers to and from an airport, train station, etc.

limp¹ (limp), *v.i.* **1.** to walk with a labored movement, as when lame. **2.** to progress with difficulty. —*n.* **3.** a lame movement or gait.

limp² (limp), *adj.,* **-er, -est.** **1.** lacking stiffness or rigidity. **2.** lacking force or energy. —**limp′ly,** *adv.* —**limp′ness,** *n.*

lim•pet (lim′pit), *n.* a small cone-shaped marine animal, usu. adhering to rocks.

lim•pid (lim′pid), *adj.* clear or transparent, as water. —**lim•pid′i•ty, lim′pid•ness,** *n.* —**lim′pid•ly,** *adv.*

linch•pin (linch′pin′), *n.* a pin inserted through the end of an axle to keep the wheel on.

lin•den (lin′dən), *n.* any of various trees with fragrant yellowish white flowers and heart-shaped leaves.

line¹ (līn), *n., v.,* **lined, lin•ing.** —*n.* **1.** a long, thin mark made with a pen, tool, etc., on a surface. **2.** the trace of a moving point. **3.** a number of persons or things arranged along an imaginary line. **4.** a wrinkle on the face or neck. **5.** an indication of demarcation; boundary. **6.** a unit in the metrical structure of a poem. **7.** Usu., **lines.** the words of an actor's part. **8.** a short written message. **9.** a transportation company or system, or one of its routes. **10.** a course of movement or progress: *the line of march.* **11.** a course of action, thought, etc.: *a conservative line.* **12.** a piece of information: *I've got a line on a good used car.* **13.** a series of persons descended from a common ancestor: *a line of kings.* **14.** a person's occupation or business. **15.** *Informal.* a mode of conversation intended to impress. **16.** outline or contour. **17.** a telephone connection. **18.** a stock of goods of the same general class. **19.** *Mil.* **a.** a series of fortifications. **b.** a formation of troops or ships drawn up for battle. **20.** a string, cord, wire, etc. **21.** a pipe or hose: *a steam line.* **22.** the football players stationed on the line of scrimmage. —*v.i.* **23.** to take a position in a line: *to line up for play.* —*v.t.* **24.** to bring into a line. **25.** to mark with lines. **26.** to form a line along. —*Idiom.* **27. draw the line,** to impose a limit. **28. hold the line,** to maintain the status quo. **29. into line,** into conformity or alignment. **30. on line,** actively linked to a computer.

line² (līn), *v.t.,* **lined, lin•ing,** to cover the inner side or surface of.

lin•e•age (lin′ē ij), *n.* **1.** lineal descent from an ancestor. **2.** family or stock.

lin′e•al (-əl), *adj.* **1.** being in a direct line: *a lineal descendant.* **2.** of or transmitted by lineal descent. **3.** LINEAR.

lin′e•a•ment (-ə mənt), *n.* Often, **-ments.** a distinguishing feature or detail, esp. of the face.

lin′e•ar (-ər), *adj.* **1.** of, consisting of, or using lines. **2.** involving measurement in one dimension only. **3.** narrow and elongated. —**lin′e•ar•ly,** *adv.*

line′ drive′ *n.* a batted baseball that travels low, fast, and straight.

line′man *n., pl.* **-men.** **1.** a person who installs or repairs telephone, telegraph, or other wires. **2.** one of the football players in the defensive line.

lin•en (lin′ən), *n.* **1.** fabric woven from flax yarns. **2.** Often, **-ens.** bedding, tablecloths, etc., made of linen or a substitute, as cotton.

lin•er¹ (lī′nər), *n.* **1.** a ship or airplane operated by a transportation company. **2.** EYELINER.

lin•er² (lī′nər), *n.* **1.** something serving as a lining. **2.** a person who fits or provides linings.

line′up′ *n.* **1.** an arrangement of persons or things in a line, as to allow identification. **2.** a list of the participating players in a game.

lin•ger (ling′gər), *v.i.* **1.** to remain in a place longer than is usual or expected. **2.** to dwell in thought or enjoyment. **3.** to be tardy in action. —**lin′ger•er,** *n.* —**lin′ger•ing•ly,** *adv.*

lin·ge·rie (län′zhə rā′, -jə-, lan′zhə rē′), *n.* women's undergarments.

lin·go (ling′gō), *n., pl.* **-goes. 1.** the jargon of a particular field, group, etc. **2.** language, esp. if strange or foreign.

lin·gui·ni (ling gwē′nē) *n.pl.* pasta in a slender flat form.

lin·guist (ling′gwist), *n.* **1.** a specialist in linguistics. **2.** a person skilled in several languages.

lin·guis′tics *n.* the study of language. —**lin·guis′-tic,** *adj.*

lin·i·ment (lin′ə mənt), *n.* a liquid preparation for rubbing on the skin, as to relieve soreness.

lin·ing (lī′ning), *n.* something used to line the inner side of something, as a garment.

link (lingk), *n.* **1.** one of the separate pieces forming a chain. **2.** a bond or tie. **3.** any of a number of connected sausages. **4.** *Computers.* an object, as text or graphics, linked through hypertext to a document, another object, etc. —*v.t., v.i.* **5.** to join by or as if by links; unite.

links *n.pl.* a golf course.

link′up′ *n.* **1.** a contact established, as between military units. **2.** something serving as a linking element or system.

lin·net (lin′it), *n.* a small Old World finch.

li·no·le·um (li nō′lē əm), *n.* a hard, washable floor covering. [< L *līn(um)* flax, linen + *oleum* oil]

lin·seed (lin′sēd′), *n.* the seed of flax.

lin′sey-wool′sey (lin′zē wŏŏl′zē) *n.* a fabric of linen and wool.

lint (lint), *n.* **1.** minute shreds or ravelings of yarn. **2.** staple cotton fiber used to make yarn. —**lint′y,** *adj.,* **-i·er, -i·est.**

lin·tel (lin′tl), *n.* a horizontal piece supporting the weight above an opening, as a door.

li·on (lī′ən), *n.* **1.** a large, usu. tawny-yellow cat of Africa and S Asia. **2.** a person of great strength or courage. **3.** a prominent or influential person.

li′on·heart′ed *adj.* exceptionally courageous.

li′on·ize′ *v.t.,* **-ized, -iz·ing.** to treat (a person) as a celebrity.

lip (lip), *n.* **1.** either of the two fleshy folds forming the margins of the mouth. **2.** an edge or rim, as of a pitcher or canyon. **3.** *Slang.* impudent talk. **4.** a liplike anatomical part; labium. —*Idiom.* **5.** keep a stiff upper lip, to face misfortune bravely. —**lipped,** *adj.*

lip·o·suc·tion (lip′ə suk′shən, lī′pə-), *n.* the surgical withdrawal of excess fat from local areas under the skin.

lip′read′ing *n.* a method, as used by a deaf person, of understanding spoken words by interpreting the speaker's lip movements. —**lip′read′,** *v.t., v.i.,* **-read** (-red′), **-read·ing.** —**lip′read′er,** *n.*

lip′ serv′ice *n.* an insincere profession of friendship, admiration, etc.

lip′stick′ *n.* a crayonlike cosmetic for coloring the lips.

liq·ue·fy (lik′wə fī′), *v.t., v.i.,* **-fied, -fy·ing.** to make or become liquid. —**liq′ue·fac′tion** (-fak′-shən), *n.*

li·queur (li kûr′, -kyŏŏr′), *n.* a strong, sweet, and highly flavored alcoholic liquor.

liq·uid (lik′wid), *adj.* **1.** composed of freely moving molecules that do not separate; neither gaseous nor solid. **2.** of or consisting of liquids. **3.** flowing like water. **4.** clear or bright: *liquid eyes.* **5.** (of sounds or movements) smooth; flowing freely. **6.** readily convertible into cash: *liquid assets.* —*n.* **7.** a liquid substance. —**liq·uid′i·ty,** *n.*

liq′ui·date′ (-wi dāt′), *v.t.,* **-dat·ed, -dat·ing. 1.** to settle or pay (a debt). **2.** to dissolve (a business or estate) by apportioning the assets to offset the liabilities. **3.** to convert (assets) into cash. **4.** to get rid of, esp. by killing. —**liq′ui·da′tion,** *n.* —**liq′ui·da′tor,** *n.*

liq·uor (lik′ər), *n.* **1.** a distilled beverage, as brandy or whiskey. **2.** any liquid substance.

li·ra (lēr′ə), *n., pl.* **li·re** (lēr′ā), **li·ras. 1.** the basic monetary unit of Italy, which has a fixed value relative to the euro. **2.** the basic monetary unit of Turkey and Malta.

lisle (līl), *n.* a fine, hard-twisted cotton thread, used esp. for hosiery.

lisp (lisp), *n.* **1.** a speech defect consisting in pronouncing *s* and *z* like the *th*-sounds of *thin* and *this,* respectively. **2.** the act or sound of lisping. —*v.t., v.i.* **3.** to speak with a lisp. **4.** to speak imperfectly, esp. in a childish manner. —**lisp′er,** *n.*

lis·some or **-som** (lis′əm), *adj.* **1.** lithe; supple. **2.** agile or nimble.

list¹ (list), *n.* **1.** a series of items written together in a meaningful sequence. —*v.t.* **2.** to set down or enter in a list.

list² (list), *n.* **1.** a leaning to one side, as of a ship. —*v.i., v.t.* **2.** to incline or cause to incline to one side.

lis·ten (lis′ən), *v.i.* **1.** to give attention for the purpose of hearing. **2.** to heed; obey. —**lis′ten·er,** *n.*

list′less (-lis), *adj.* having little interest in anything; languid. —**list′less·ly,** *adv.* —**list′less·ness,** *n.*

list′ price′ *n.* the price at which a product is usu. sold to the public.

lit¹ (lit), *v.* a pt. and pp. of LIGHT¹.

lit² (lit), *v.* a pt. and pp. of LIGHT³.

lit. 1. literally. **2.** literature.

lit·a·ny (lit′n ē), *n., pl.* **-nies. 1.** a prayer consisting of a series of invocations with responses. **2.** a prolonged or tedious account: *a litany of complaints.*

li·ter (lē′tər), *n.* a metric unit of liquid capacity equivalent to 1.0567 liquid quarts.

lit·er·al (lit′ər əl), *adj.* **1.** in accordance with the strict meaning of a word or text. **2.** following the words of the original very closely: *a literal translation.* **3.** true to fact: *a literal description.* **4.** tending to construe words in an unimaginative way. —**lit′er·al·ly,** *adv.* —**lit′er·al·ness,** *n.*

lit′er·al-mind′ed *adj.* interpreting without imagination.

lit·er·ar·y (lit′ə rer′ē), *adj.* **1.** of or characteristic of literature. **2.** versed in literature; well-read.

lit′er·ate (-ər it), *adj.* **1.** able to read and write. **2.** educated. **3.** having knowledge or skill: *computer-literate.* —*n.* **4.** a literate person. —**lit′er·ate·ly,** *adv.*

lit·e·ra·ti (lit′ə rä′tē, -rā′-), *n.pl.* persons of scholarly or literary attainments.

lit·er·a·ture (lit′ər ə chər, -chŏŏr′, li′trə-), *n.* **1.** writing in prose or verse regarded as having permanent worth through its intrinsic excellence. **2.** the entire body of writings of a specific language, period, etc. **3.** the writings dealing with a particular subject. **4.** any kind of printed material.

lithe (līth), *adj.,* **lith·er, lith·est.** bending readily; supple.

lith·i·um (lith′ē əm), *n.* a soft, silver-white metallic element. *Symbol:* Li; *at. wt.:* 6.939; *at. no.:* 3.

lith·o·graph (lith′ə graf′, -gräf′), *n.* **1.** a print produced by lithography. —*v.t.* **2.** to produce by lithography. —**li·thog·ra·pher** (li thog′rə fər), *n.*

li·thog·ra·phy (li thog′rə fē), *n.* a printing technique by which an image is fixed on a stone or metal plate with a combination of ink-absorbent and ink-repellent vehicles. —**lith·o·graph·ic** (lith′ə-graf′ik), *adj.*

Lith·u·a·ni·a (lith′ŏŏ ā′nē ə), *n.* a republic in N Europe, on the Baltic: formerly a part of the USSR. —**Lith′u·a′ni·an,** *n., adj.*

lit·i·gant (lit′i gənt), *n.* a person engaged in a lawsuit.

lit′i·gate′ (-gāt′), *v.,* **-gat·ed, -gat·ing.** —*v.t.* **1.** to make the subject of a lawsuit. —*v.i.* **2.** to carry on a lawsuit. —**lit′i·ga′tion,** *n.* —**lit′i·ga′tor,** *n.*

lit·mus (lit′məs), *n.* a coloring matter obtained from lichens that turns blue in alkaline solution and red in acid solution.

lit′mus pa′per *n.* a strip of paper impregnated with litmus, used as a chemical indicator.

litmus test *n.* the use of a single issue or factor as a basis for judgment.

Litt. D. Doctor of Letters; Doctor of Literature. [< L *Lit(t)erārum Doctor*]

lit•ter (lit′ər), *n.* **1.** scattered objects, rubbish, etc. **2.** a number of young brought forth by an animal at one birth. **3.** a stretcher for transporting a sick or wounded person. **4.** a vehicle carried by people or animals, consisting of a couch suspended between shafts. **5.** straw, hay, etc., used as bedding for animals. **6.** any of various absorbent materials used for lining a box **(lit′ter box′)** in which a cat can eliminate waste. —*v.t.* **7.** to strew (a place) with litter. **8.** to scatter (objects) in disorder. —**lit′ter•er,** *n.*

lit′ter•bug′ *n.* a person who litters public places with trash.

lit•tle (lit′l), *adj.,* **lit•tler** or **less** or **less•er, lit•tlest** or **least,** *adv.,* **less, least,** *n.* —*adj.* **1.** small in size, amount, degree, scale, etc. **2.** short in duration. **3.** minor; unimportant. **4.** mean or narrow: *a little mind.* —*adv.* **5.** not at all: *He little knows what awaits him.* **6.** slightly. **7.** seldom; infrequently. —*n.* **8.** a small amount, quantity, or degree. —*Idiom.* **9. little by little,** gradually. —**lit′tle•ness,** *n.*

lit•to•ral (lit′ər əl), *adj.* of the shore of a lake, sea, or ocean.

lit•ur•gy (lit′ər jē), *n., pl.* **-gies.** a form of public worship; ritual. —**li•tur•gi•cal** (li tûr′ji kəl), *adj.* —**lit′ur•gist,** *n.*

liv•a•ble or **live•a•ble** (liv′ə bəl), *adj.* **1.** suitable for living in. **2.** worth living. —**liv′a•bil′i•ty,** *n.*

live[1] (liv), *v.,* **lived** (livd), **liv•ing.** —*v.i.* **1.** to be alive. **2.** to remain alive. **3.** to continue in existence, operation, memory, etc. **4.** to maintain one's existence; subsist: *to live on one's income.* **5.** to reside. **6.** to pass life in a specified manner. —*v.t.* **7.** to pass or spend: *to live a life of ease.* **8.** to exhibit in one's life: *to live one's philosophy.* **9. live down,** to live so as to allow (a mistake, disgrace, etc.) to be forgotten or forgiven. **10. ~ up to,** to behave so as to satisfy (an ideal or standard).

live[2] (līv), *adj.* **1.** being alive; living. **2.** of or during the life of a living being. **3.** full of life, energy, or activity. **4.** burning or glowing: *live coals.* **5.** being in play, as a football. **6.** unexploded: *live ammunition.* **7.** broadcast while happening or being performed. **8.** of current interest: *live issues.* **9.** electrically connected or charged: *a live wire.*

live•li•hood (līv′lē hŏŏd′), *n.* a means of supporting one's existence, esp. financially.

live′long′ (liv′-), *adj.* entire, esp. when tediously long: *to fret the livelong day.*

live•ly (līv′lē), *adj.,* **-li•er, -li•est. 1.** full of life or energy; vigorous. **2.** animated; sprightly. **3.** stirring or exciting. **4.** strong or keen. **5.** rebounding quickly: *a lively tennis ball.* —**live′li•ness,** *n.*

liv•er (liv′ər), *n.* **1.** a glandular organ in vertebrates, functioning in the secretion of bile and in metabolic processes. **2.** this organ of an animal used as food.

liv′er•wurst′ (-wûrst′), *n.* a cooked sausage containing a large percentage of liver.

liv•er•y (liv′ə rē, liv′rē), *n., pl.* **-er•ies. 1.** a uniform worn by servants. **2.** the care and feeding of horses for pay. **3.** a stable where horses and vehicles are kept for hire. **4.** a company that rents out automobiles, boats, etc. —**liv′er•ied,** *adj.*

live•stock (līv′stok′), *n.* the animals raised on a farm or ranch.

live′ wire′ (līv), *n. Informal.* an energetic, keenly alert person.

liv•id (liv′id), *adj.* **1.** having a discolored, bluish appearance caused by a bruise. **2.** furiously angry. **3.** deathly pale. —**liv′id•ly,** *adv.*

liv•ing (liv′ing), *adj.* **1.** being alive. **2.** in actual existence or use: *living languages.* **3.** of or suitable for life: *living conditions.* **4.** of living persons: *within living memory.* **5.** lifelike; true to life. **6.** sufficient for living: *a living wage.* —*n.* **7.** the act or condition of one that lives. **8.** livelihood. **9.** a particular manner of life. **10. the living,** living persons collectively.

liv′ing room′ *n.* a room in a home used for leisure activities, entertaining guests, etc.

liv′ing will′ *n.* a document stipulating that no ex-

traordinary measures be used to prolong the signer's life during a terminal illness.

liz•ard (liz′ərd), *n.* any of various scaly reptiles typically having a long body, long tail, and four legs.

lla•ma (lä′mə, yä′-), *n., pl.* **-mas.** a South American ruminant related to the camel.

LL.B. Bachelor of Laws. [< L *Lēgum Baccalaureus*]

LL.D. Doctor of Laws. [< L *Lēgum Doctor*]

load (lōd), *n.* **1.** a quantity carried or supported at one time. **2.** the normal maximum amount of something carried by a vehicle, ship, etc. **3.** the amount of work assigned to a person, team, machine, etc. **4.** something that weighs down like a burden. **5. loads,** *Informal.* a great quantity or number. **6.** a commission charged to buyers of mutual-fund shares. —*v.t.* **7.** to put a load on or in. **8.** to supply abundantly. **9.** to weigh down or burden. **10.** to insert ammunition into (a firearm). **11.** to place film, tape, etc., into (a camera or other device). **12.** to bring (a program or data) into a computer's RAM, as from a disk. —**load′er,** *n.*

loaf[1] (lōf), *n., pl.* **loaves. 1.** a portion of bread baked in an oblong mass. **2.** a shaped or molded mass of food, as of ground meat.

loaf[2] (lōf), *v.i.* **1.** to idle away time. **2.** to lounge lazily and idly. —**loaf′er,** *n.*

loam (lōm), *n.* a rich soil containing sand, silt, and clay. —**loam′y,** *adj.*

loan (lōn), *n.* **1.** the act of lending. **2.** something lent, esp. a sum of money lent at interest. —*v.t., v.i.* **3.** to lend. —**loan′er,** *n.*

loan′ shark′ *n. Informal.* a person who lends money at excessively high rates of interest; usurer. —**loan′shark′ing,** *n.*

loan′word′ *n.* a word in one language that has been borrowed from another language.

loath (lōth, lōth), *adj.* unwilling; reluctant.

loathe (lōth), *v.t.,* **loathed, loath•ing.** to feel intense aversion or dislike for; abhor.

lob (lob), *v.,* **lobbed, lob•bing,** *n.* —*v.t., v.i.* **1.** to hit (a ball) in a high arc. —*n.* **2.** a lobbed ball. —**lob′ber,** *n.*

lob•by (lob′ē), *n., pl.* **-bies,** *v.,* **-bied, -by•ing.** —*n.* **1.** an entrance hall, as in a public building. **2.** a group of persons who try to influence legislators to vote in favor of a special interest. —*v.i.* **3.** to try to influence legislation. —*v.t.* **4.** to try to influence the votes of (legislators). **5.** to urge the passage of (legislation) by lobbying. —**lob′by•ist,** *n.*

lobe (lōb), *n.* **1.** a roundish projection or division, as of an organ or a leaf. **2. EARLOBE.** —**lo•bar** (lō′-bər, -bär), *adj.*

lo•bot•o•my (lə bot′ə mē, lō-), *n., pl.* **-mies.** a surgical incision into or across a lobe of the brain to treat a mental disorder. —**lo•bot′o•mize′** (-mīz′), *v.t.,* **-mized, -miz•ing.**

lob•ster (lob′stər), *n., pl.* **-sters, -ster.** an edible marine crustacean with large pincers.

lo•cal (lō′kəl), *adj.* **1.** of, characteristic of, or restricted to a particular place. **2.** stopping at most or all stations: *a local train.* **3.** of or affecting a particular part of the body. —*n.* **4.** a local train, bus, etc. **5.** a local branch of a union, fraternity, etc. —**lo′cal•ly,** *adv.*

lo•cale (lō kal′, -käl′), *n.* a locality, esp. with reference to events or circumstances connected with it.

lo•cal/i•ty *n., pl.* **-ties.** a specific place or area; location.

lo′cal•ize′ (-kə līz′), *v.t.,* **-ized, -iz•ing.** to confine or restrict to a particular place. —**lo′cal•i•za′tion,** *n.*

lo•cate (lō′kāt, lō kāt′), *v.,* **-cat•ed, -cat•ing.** —*v.t.* **1.** to discover the place of. **2.** to establish in a position or place. **3.** to assign a particular place to. —*v.i.* **4.** to become settled. —**lo′ca•tor,** *n.*

lo•ca′tion *n.* **1.** a place, position, or situation. **2.** a site outside a movie studio used for filming: *shot on location.*

loc. cit. (lok′ sit′), in the place cited. [< L *locō citātō*]

lock[1] (lok), *n.* **1.** a device for fastening or securing a door, lid, etc. **2.** (in a firearm) the mechanism that explodes the charge. **3.** a chamber in a canal, dam, etc., with gates for raising or lowering ships by admitting or releasing water. —*v.t.* **4.** to fasten or secure with a lock. **5.** to shut in by or as if by means of a lock. **6.** to make fast or immovable. **7.** to interlink: *to lock arms.* —*v.i.* **8.** to become locked. **9.** to become fastened, fixed, or interlocked.

lock² (lok), *n.* **1.** a curl of hair. **2. locks,** the hair of the head. **3.** a tuft of wool, cotton, etc.

lock′er *n.* **1.** a chest, compartment, etc., that can be locked. **2.** a large compartment for keeping frozen foods.

lock′et (-it), *n.* a small case for a keepsake, usu. worn on a necklace.

lock′jaw′ *n.* tetanus in which the jaws become firmly locked together.

lock′out′ *n.* the temporary closing of a business during a labor dispute until employees accept the employer's terms.

lock′smith′ *n.* a person who makes or repairs locks and keys.

lock′step′ *n.* **1.** a way of marching in very close file. **2.** a rigidly inflexible pattern or process.

lock′up′ *n.* a jail.

lo•co (lō′kō), *adj. Slang.* insane; crazy.

lo•co•mo•tion (lō′kə mō′shən), *n.* the act or power of moving from place to place.

lo•co•mo′tive *n.* **1.** a self-propelled vehicular engine for pulling a railroad train. —*adj.* **2.** of locomotion.

lo•co•weed′ (lō′kō-), *n.* any of various plants of the southwestern U.S. and Mexico, causing a disease in livestock.

lo•cust (lō′kəst), *n.* **1.** a grasshopper commonly migrating in swarms that strip the vegetation from large areas. **2.** any of various cicadas, as the seventeen-year locust. **3.** a North American tree with clusters of fragrant white flowers.

lo•cu•tion (lō kyōō′shən), *n.* **1.** a word, phrase, or expression. **2.** a style of speech or verbal expression.

lode (lōd), *n.* a veinlike deposit of ore.

lode′star′ *n.* a star that shows the way, esp. Polaris.

lode′stone′ *n.* a variety of magnetite that possesses magnetic polarity.

lodge (loj), *n., v.,* **lodged, lodg•ing.** —*n.* **1.** a makeshift or rough shelter. **2.** a temporary residence, as in the hunting season. **3.** a resort hotel or motel. **4.** the meeting place of a branch of certain fraternal organizations. —*v.i.* **5.** to live in a place temporarily. **6.** to live in rented quarters. **7.** to be fixed in a place or position: *The bullet lodged in the wall.* —*v.t.* **8.** to furnish with living quarters, esp. temporarily. **9.** to bring into a particular place or position. **10.** to vest (power, authority, etc.). **11.** to put (a complaint, etc.) before a court or other authority.

lodg′ing *n.* **1.** a temporary place to stay. **2. lodgings,** a room or rooms rented for residence in another's house.

loft (lôft, loft), *n.* **1.** a room or space under a sloping roof; attic. **2.** a gallery in a church, hall, etc.: *a choir loft.* **3.** an upper story of a warehouse usu. not partitioned into rooms. **4.** Also called **loft′ bed′.** a platform built over a living area and used for sleeping. —*v.t.* **5.** to hit or throw aloft.

loft′y *adj.,* **-i•er, -i•est. 1.** extending high in the air. **2.** exalted in rank, dignity, or character. **3.** elevated in style, tone, or sentiment. **4.** haughty. —**loft′i•ness,** *n.*

log¹ (lôg, log), *n., v.,* **logged, log•ging.** —*n.* **1.** a portion of the trunk or of a large limb of a felled tree. **2.** a detailed record, esp. of the trip of a ship or aircraft. **3.** a device for determining the speed of a ship. —*v.t.* **4.** to cut (trees) into logs. **5.** to enter in a log. **6.** to travel for (a certain distance or a certain amount of time). —*v.i.* **7.** to cut down trees and get out logs for timber. **8. log in** or **on,** to gain access to a computer system by keying in identifying information. **9. ~ off** or **out,** to end a session on a computer system. —**log′ger,** *n.*

log² (lôg, log), *n.* LOGARITHM.

-log var. of -LOGUE.

lo•gan•ber•ry (lō′gən ber′ē), *n., pl.* **-ries. 1.** a dark red, tart berry of a hybrid blackberry bush. **2.** the plant itself.

log•a•rithm (lô′gə riŧħ′əm, log′ə-), *n.* the exponent of the power to which a base number must be raised to equal a given number. —**log′a•rith′mic,** *adj.*

loge (lōzh), *n.* (in a theater) a box or the front section of the lowest balcony.

log•ger•head (lô′gər hed′, log′ər-), *n.* **1.** a stupid person. —*Idiom.* **2. at loggerheads,** in conflict.

log•ic (loj′ik), *n.* **1.** the science that investigates the principles governing correct inference. **2.** a particular method of reasoning. **3.** reason or sound judgment. **4.** any connection between facts that seems reasonable. **5.** the arrangement of circuitry in a computer. —**lo•gi•cian** (lō jish′ən), *n.*

lo•gis•tics (lō jis′tiks, lə-), *n.* (*used with a sing. or pl. v.*) **1.** the military science dealing with the procurement of equipment, movement of personnel, etc. **2.** the planning and implementation of the details of any operation. —**lo•gis′tic, lo•gis′ti•cal,** *adj.* —**lo•gis′ti•cal•ly,** *adv.*

log′jam′ *n.* **1.** a pileup of logs, as in a river, causing a blockage. **2.** a blockage or impasse.

lo•go (lō′gō), *n., pl.* **-gos.** a representation or symbol of a company name, trademark, etc. Also called **lo′go•type′.**

log′roll′ing *n.* the exchange of support or favors, esp. by legislators for mutual political gain.

-logue a combining form meaning a specified kind of spoken or written discourse (*monologue*).

lo•gy (lō′gē), *adj.,* **-gi•er, -gi•est.** lacking vitality; sluggish. —**lo′gi•ness,** *n.*

-logy a combining form meaning: the science or study of (*theology*); speaking or expression (*tautology*).

loin (loin), *n.* **1.** Usu. **loins.** the part of the body between the ribs and hipbone. **2.** a cut of meat from this region. **3. loins,** the hips and groin regarded as the seat of physical strength and generative power.

loin′cloth′ *n.* a cloth worn around the loins or hips.

loi•ter (loi′tər), *v.i.* **1.** to linger aimlessly in or about a place. **2.** to move in a slow, idle manner. **3.** to dawdle. —**loi′ter•er,** *n.*

loll (lol), *v.i.* **1.** to recline in a relaxed or lazy manner. **2.** to hang loosely; droop. —*v.t.* **3.** to allow to droop.

lol•li•pop (lol′ē pop′), *n.* a piece of hard candy attached to the end of a stick.

lone (lōn), *adj.* **1.** being alone; solitary. **2.** standing apart; isolated. **3.** sole; only.

lone•ly (lōn′lē), *adj.,* **-li•er, -li•est. 1.** affected with or causing a depressing feeling of being alone. **2.** lone; solitary. —**lone′li•ness,** *n.*

lon′er *n.* a person who is or prefers to be alone.

lone′some (-səm), *adj.* **1.** depressed because of the lack of companionship. **2.** attended with or causing such a feeling. **3.** remote or isolated. —**lone′some•ness,** *n.*

long¹ (lông, long), *adj. and adv.,* **long•er** (lông′gər, long′-), **long•est** (lông′gist, long′-), *n.* —*adj.* **1.** having considerable extent in space or duration in time. **2.** totaling a number of specified units: *eight miles long.* **3.** containing many items or units. **4.** taking a long time; slow. **5.** broad; considering all aspects: *to take a long view.* **6.** having an ample supply: *long on brains.* —*adv.* **7.** for a great extent of time. **8.** for or throughout a specified period of time: *How long did he stay?* **9.** at a distant point in time: *long before.* —*n.* **10.** a comparatively long time: *They haven't been gone for long.* —*Idiom.* **11. as long as, a.** provided that. **b.** seeing that; since. **c.** during the time that; while. **12. before long,** soon.

long² (lông, long), *v.i.* to have a strong desire; yearn.

long. longitude.

lon•gev•i•ty (lon jev′i tē, lôn-), *n.* **1.** long life. **2.** length of life.

long′hand′ *n.* writing in which words are written out in full by hand.

lon•gi•tude (lon′ji tōōd′, -tyōōd′), *n.* angular distance east or west from the prime meridian at some particular place to the prime meridian at Greenwich, England.

lon′gi•tu′di•nal (-tōōd′n l, -tyōōd′-), *adj.* **1.** of longitude or length. **2.** lengthwise. —**lon′gi•tu′di•nal•ly,** *adv.*

long′ jump′ *n.* a jump for distance from a running start.

long′-lived′ (-līvd′, -livd′), *adj.* having a long life or duration.

long′-range′ *adj.* **1.** considering or extending into the future. **2.** designed to cover or operate over a long distance.

long′shore′man *n.*, *pl.* **-men.** a person employed on the wharves of a port, as in loading and unloading ships.

long′ shot′ *n.* **1.** a horse, team, etc., that has little chance of winning. **2.** an undertaking that offers much but has little chance for success.

long′-term′ *adj.* covering or involving a relatively long period of time.

long′-wind′ed *adj.* **1.** talking or writing at tedious length. **2.** (of speech or writing) continued to a tedious length. —**long′-wind′ed•ness,** *n.*

look (lŏŏk), *v.i.* **1.** to turn one's eyes toward something in order to see. **2.** to use one's sight in searching, examining, etc. **3.** to appear to the eye: *to look pale.* **4.** to appear to the mind: *It looks promising.* **5.** to face or afford a view: *The room looks out on the garden.* —*v.t.* **6.** to give (someone) a look. **7.** to have an appearance appropriate to: *to look one's age.* **8. look after,** to take care of. **9. ~ down on** or **upon,** to regard with contempt. **10. ~ for, a.** to seek. **b.** to anticipate. **11. ~ forward to,** to anticipate with pleasure. **12. ~ in (on),** to visit briefly. **13. ~ into,** to investigate. **14. ~ out,** to be careful. **15. ~ over,** to examine. **16. ~ to, a.** to pay attention to. **b.** to depend on. **17. ~ up,** to search for, as in a reference book. **18. ~ up to,** to admire. —*n.* **19.** the act of looking. **20.** the way in which a person or thing appears; aspect. **21. looks, a.** general appearance. **b.** personal appearance.

look′ing glass′ *n.* a mirror.

look′out′ *n.* **1.** the act of keeping watch. **2.** a person keeping a watch. **3.** a place from which a watch is kept.

loom¹ (lōōm), *n.* **1.** an apparatus for weaving fabrics. —*v.t.* **2.** to weave on a loom.

loom² (lōōm), *v.i.* **1.** to come into view in indistinct and enlarged form. **2.** to assume form as an impending event.

loon¹ (lōōn), *n.* a large, ducklike diving bird of the Northern Hemisphere.

loon² (lōōn), *n.* a crazy or simple-minded person.

loon′y *adj.*, **-i•er, -i•est.** *Informal.* **1.** lunatic; insane. **2.** extremely foolish.

loop (lōōp), *n.* **1.** a portion of a cord, ribbon, etc., folded or doubled upon itself so as to leave an opening between the parts. **2.** anything shaped like a loop. **3.** INTRAUTERINE DEVICE. —*v.t.* **4.** to form into a loop. **5.** to make a loop in. —*v.i.* **6.** to make or form a loop.

loop′hole′ *n.* **1.** a narrow opening in a wall for looking or shooting through. **2.** a means of escape or evasion.

loose (lōōs), *adj.*, **loos•er, loos•est,** *adv.*, *v.*, **loosed, loos•ing.** —*adj.* **1.** not firmly fastened or attached: *a loose tooth.* **2.** free from confinement or restraint. **3.** not firm or taut: *loose skin.* **4.** relaxed or limber: *a loose, open stride.* **5.** not compact: *a loose weave.* **6.** not strict or exact: *a loose translation.* **7.** lacking in restraint: *a loose tongue.* **8.** sexually promiscuous. —*adv.* **9.** in a loose manner. —*v.t.* **10.** to let loose; set free. **11.** to unfasten or untie. **12.** to shoot; discharge: *to loose missiles.* **13.** to make less tight. —*v.i.* **14.** to let go a hold. —*Idiom.* **15. on the loose,** free; unconfined. —**loose′ly,** *adv.* —**loose′ness,** *n.*

loot (lōōt), *n.* **1.** plunder taken in war. **2.** anything

taken by dishonesty, force, etc. **3.** *Slang.* money or gifts. —*v.t.*, *v.i.* **4.** to take (as) loot. —**loot′er,** *n.*

lop¹ (lop), *v.t.*, **lopped, lop•ping. 1.** to cut off (branches, twigs, etc.) from a tree or other plant. **2.** to cut off. **3.** to eliminate as unnecessary.

lop² (lop), *v.i.*, **lopped, lop•ping.** to hang loosely; droop.

lope (lōp), *v.*, **loped, lop•ing,** *n.* —*v.i.* **1.** to move or run with a long, easy stride. —*n.* **2.** a long, easy stride.

lop′sid′ed *adj.* heavier, larger, or more developed on one side. —**lop′sid′ed•ly,** *adv.* —**lop′sid′ed•ness,** *n.*

lo•qua•cious (lō kwā′shəs), *adj.* exceedingly talkative. —**lo•qua′cious•ness, lo•quac′i•ty** (-kwas′i-tē), *n.*

lord (lôrd), *n.* **1.** a master or ruler. **2.** the proprietor of a feudal manor. **3.** a titled nobleman or peer. **4.** (*cap.*) God. **5.** (*cap.*) Jesus Christ. —*v.* *Idiom.* **6. lord it (over),** to behave in a domineering manner (toward).

lore (lôr), *n.* the body of knowledge, esp. of a traditional nature, on a particular subject.

lor•ry (lôr′ē, lor′ē), *n.*, *pl.* **-ries.** *Chiefly Brit.* a large motor truck.

lose (lōōz), *v.*, **lost, los•ing.** —*v.t.* **1.** to come to be without through accident, misfortune, etc. **2.** to fail to retain or maintain: *to lose one's balance.* **3.** to have slip from sight or awareness: *We lost him in the crowd.* **4.** to stray from: *to lose one's way.* **5.** to waste: *to lose time in waiting.* **6.** to fail to win. **7.** to cause the loss of: *The delay lost the battle for them.* **8.** to allow (oneself) to become engrossed. —*v.i.* **9.** to suffer loss. —**los′er,** *n.*

loss (lôs), *n.* **1.** the act of losing. **2.** disadvantage or deprivation from loss. **3.** one that is lost. **4.** an amount lost. —*Idiom.* **5. at a loss,** bewildered or uncertain.

lot (lot), *n.* **1.** one of a set of objects, as straws or pebbles, drawn or thrown to decide a question by chance. **2.** the casting or drawing of such objects. **3.** the decision made by such a method. **4.** allotted share; portion. **5.** fate; destiny. **6.** a distinct piece of land. **7.** a distinct parcel of merchandise. **8.** a number of things or persons. **9.** kind; sort: *He's a bad lot.* **10.** Often, **lots.** *Informal.* a great many or a great deal: *a lot of books.*

Lo•thar•i•o (lō thâr′ē ō′), *n.*, *pl.* **-os.** (*often l.c.*) a man who obsessively seduces women.

lo•tion (lō′shən), *n.* a liquid preparation applied to the skin, as for cleansing or soothing.

lot•ter•y (lot′ə rē), *n.*, *pl.* **-ter•ies. 1.** a gambling game in which a large number of tickets are sold and a drawing is held for prizes. **2.** a drawing of lots.

lot•to (lot′ō), *n.*, *pl.* **-tos. 1.** a game in which a leader randomly draws numbers and players cover the corresponding numbers on cards, the winner being the first to cover a row. **2.** a lottery in which players choose numbers that are matched against those of the official drawing.

lo•tus (lō′təs), *n.*, *pl.* **-tus•es. 1.** (in Greek legend) a plant whose fruit induced a state of contented forgetfulness. **2.** any of several water lilies.

loud (loud), *adj.* and *adv.*, **-er, -est.** —*adj.* **1.** having exceptional volume or intensity. **2.** making strongly audible sounds. **3.** clamorous; noisy. **4.** emphatic; insistent. **5.** garish; ostentatious. **6.** vulgar; coarse. —*adv.* **7.** in a loud manner. —**loud′ly,** *adv.* —**loud′ness,** *n.*

loud′mouth′ *n.* a person given to loud or indiscreet talk. —**loud′mouthed′,** *adj.*

loud′speak′er *n.* any of various devices that convert amplified electronic signals into audible sound.

lounge (lounj), *v.*, **lounged, loung•ing,** *n.* —*v.i.* **1.** to pass time indolently. **2.** to recline indolently. —*n.* **3.** a backless sofa having a headrest at one end. **4.** a public room for waiting, socializing, etc.

louse (*n.* lous; *v. also* louz), *n.*, *pl.* **lice** (līs) for 1, 2, **lous•es** for 3, *v.*, **loused, lous•ing.** —*n.* **1.** any of various small, wingless insects that are parasitic on humans and other animals. **2.** APHID. **3.** *Slang.* a contemptible person. —*v.* **4. louse up,** *Slang.* to spoil; botch.

lous•y (lou′zē), *adj.,* **-i•er, -i•est. 1.** infested with lice. **2.** *Informal.* **a.** mean; contemptible. **b.** wretchedly bad; miserable. —*Idiom.* **3. lousy with,** *Slang.* well supplied with. —**lous′i•ness,** *n.*

lout (lout), *n.* a clumsy, boorish person. —**lout′-ish,** *adj.*

lou•ver (lōō′vər), *n.* **1.** a window or opening having a series of slanting, overlapping slats, adjustable for admitting light and air while shutting out rain. **2.** one of these slats. —**lou′vered,** *adj.*

love (luv), *n., v.,* **loved, lov•ing.** —*n.* **1.** a profoundly tender, passionate affection for another person. **2.** an intense personal attachment or affection. **3.** a person toward whom love is felt. **4.** a strong enthusiasm or liking. **5.** a score of zero in tennis. —*v.t., v.i.* **6.** to have love or affection (for). —*Idiom.* **7. in love (with),** feeling love (for). **8. make love, a.** to have sexual relations. **b.** to embrace and kiss. —**lov′a•ble, love′a•ble,** *adj.* —**love′less,** *adj.*

love′lorn′ *adj.* being without love or a lover.

love•ly (luv′lē), *adj.,* **-li•er, -li•est. 1.** charmingly or gracefully beautiful. **2.** very pleasing; delightful. —**love′li•ness,** *n.*

lov′er *n.* **1.** a person who is in love with another. **2.** a person who has a sexual relationship with another. **3.** a devotee: *a lover of music.*

love′sick′ *adj.* languishing with love.

lov′ing cup′ *n.* a large drinking cup with two handles, often given as a prize.

low¹ (lō), *adj.* and *adv.,* **-er, -est,** *n.* —*adj.* **1.** not far above the ground or floor. **2.** of small extent upward. **3.** lying below the general level: *low ground.* **4.** of less than normal height or depth: *The river is low.* **5.** ranked near the bottom on a scale of measurement: *a low income bracket.* **6.** depressed or dejected. **7.** of small number, degree, force, etc. **8.** not loud. **9.** deep in pitch. **10.** humble: *of low birth.* **11.** of inferior quality: *a low grade of fabric.* **12.** base; disreputable. **13.** coarse; vulgar. —*adv.* **14.** in or to a low position, degree, level, etc. —*n.* **15.** a low point, place, or level. **16.** a transmission gear producing the lowest speed and maximum power. **17.** an atmospheric low-pressure system. —*Idiom.* **18. lay low,** to overpower or kill. **19. lie low,** to hide oneself. —**low′ness,** *n.*

low² (lō), *v.i.* **1.** to utter the deep sound characteristic of cattle; moo. —*n.* **2.** the act or sound of lowing.

low′brow′ *n.* a person with little interest in matters of intellect or culture.

low-cal (lō′kal′, -kal′), *adj.* containing fewer calories than usual or standard: *a low-cal diet.*

low•down (*n.* lō′doun′; *adj.* -doun′), *n.* **1.** the real and unadorned facts. —*adj.* **2.** contemptible; mean.

low•er¹ (lō′ər), *v.t.* **1.** to cause to descend. **2.** to make lower in height or level. **3.** to reduce in amount, degree, etc. **4.** to bring down in rank or estimation. —*v.i.* **5.** to become lower. —*adj.* **6.** comparative of LOW¹. —**low′er•most,** *adj.*

low•er² (lou′ər, lou°r), *v.i.* **1.** to be dark and threatening. **2.** to scowl; glower. —**low′er•ing•ly,** *adv.*

low′er•case′ (lō′ər), *adj.* **1.** (of an alphabetical letter) of a form often different from and smaller than its corresponding capital letter. —*n.* **2.** a lowercase letter.

low′ fre′quency *n.* a radio frequency between 30 and 300 kilohertz.

low′-key′ *adj.* restrained; understated.

low′life′ *n., pl.* **-lifes.** a disreputable or degenerate person.

low′ly *adj.,* **-li•er, -li•est,** *adv.* —*adj.* **1.** having a low status or rank. **2.** humble; meek. —*adv.* **3.** in a low position, manner, or degree. —**low′li•ness,** *n.*

low′-mind′ed *adj.* having or showing coarse or vulgar taste or interests.

low′ pro′file *n.* a deliberately inconspicuous manner.

lox¹ (loks), *n.* brine-cured salmon.

lox² or **LOX** (loks), *n.* liquid oxygen, used in liquid rocket propellants.

loy•al (loi′əl), *adj.* **1.** faithful to one's allegiance, as to a government or friends. **2.** faithful to one's oath or obligations. **3.** characterized by faithfulness. —**loy′al•ly,** *adv.* —**loy′al•ty,** *n., pl.* **-ties.**

loz•enge (loz′inj), *n.* **1.** a small flavored tablet, often medicated. **2.** a diamond-shaped heraldic charge.

LPN licensed practical nurse.

LSD (el′es′dē′), *n.* lysergic acid diethylamide: a powerful psychedelic drug.

Lt. lieutenant.

Ltd. or **ltd.,** limited.

lub•ber (lub′ər), *n.* **1.** a big, clumsy, stupid person. **2.** an awkward or unskilled sailor. —**lub′ber•ly,** *adj., adv.*

lu•bri•cant (lōō′bri kənt), *n.* **1.** a substance, as oil or grease, for lessening friction, esp. in the working parts of a mechanism. —*adj.* **2.** capable of lubricating.

lu′bri•cate′ (-kāt′), *v.,* **-cat•ed, -cat•ing.** —*v.t.* **1.** to apply a lubricant to in order to diminish friction; make slippery. —*v.i.* **2.** to act as a lubricant. —**lu′-bri•ca′tion,** *n.* —**lu′bri•ca′tor,** *n.*

lu•cid (lōō′sid), *adj.* **1.** easily understood. **2.** rational; sane. **3.** luminous. **4.** clear; transparent. —**lu•cid′i•ty,** *n.* —**lu′cid•ly,** *adv.*

Lu•cite (lōō′sīt), *Trademark.* a transparent plastic.

luck (luk), *n.* **1.** the force that seems to operate for good or ill in a person's life. **2.** good fortune. —*v.* **3. luck out,** *Informal.* to have an occasion of good luck. —**luck′less,** *adj.*

luck′y *adj.,* **-i•er, -i•est. 1.** having good luck. **2.** happening fortunately. **3.** believed to bring good luck. —**luck′i•ly,** *adv.* —**luck′i•ness,** *n.*

lu•cra•tive (lōō′krə tiv), *adj.* profitable; moneymaking. —**lu′cra•tive•ly,** *adv.* —**lu′cra•tive•ness,** *n.*

lu•cre (lōō′kər), *n.* monetary reward or gain.

lu•di•crous (lōō′di krəs), *adj.* causing or deserving laughter because of absurdity; ridiculous. —**lu′di•crous•ly,** *adv.* —**lu′di•crous•ness,** *n.*

lug¹ (lug), *v.t., v.i.,* **lugged, lug•ging.** to pull or carry with effort.

lug² (lug), *n.* **1.** a projecting piece by which anything is held or supported. **2.** *Slang.* an awkward, clumsy fellow.

luge (lōōzh), *n., v.,* **luged, lug•ing.** —*n.* **1.** a one- or two-person sled for coasting or racing down a chute, used esp. in Europe. —*v.i.* **2.** to go or race on a luge. —**lug′er,** *n.*

lug′gage (-ij), *n.* suitcases, trunks, etc.; baggage.

lug′ nut′ *n.* a large nut, esp. for attaching a wheel to an automobile.

lu•gu•bri•ous (lōō gōō′brē əs, -gyōō′-), *adj.* mournful or gloomy, esp. exaggeratedly so. —**lu•gu′bri•ous•ly,** *adv.* —**lu•gu′bri•ous•ness,** *n.*

luke•warm (lōōk′wôrm′), *adj.* **1.** moderately warm. **2.** having little ardor or enthusiasm. —**luke′-warm′ly,** *adv.*

lull (lul), *v.t.* **1.** to put to sleep or rest by soothing means. **2.** to give a false sense of safety. —*v.i.* **3.** to quiet down; subside. —*n.* **4.** a temporary calm.

lull′a•by′ (-ə bī′), *n., pl.* **-bies.** a song used to lull a child to sleep.

lum•ba•go (lum bā′gō), *n.* pain in the lower back.

lum•bar (lum′bər, -bär), *adj.* of the loin or loins.

lum•ber¹ (lum′bər), *n.* **1.** timber sawed into planks, boards, etc. —*v.i.* **2.** to cut timber and prepare it for market. —**lum′ber•er,** *n.* —**lum′ber•man,** *n., pl.* **-men.**

lum•ber² (lum′bər), *v.i.* to move clumsily or heavily.

lum′ber•jack′ *n.* a person who works at lumbering.

lum′ber•yard′ *n.* a yard where lumber is stored for sale.

lu•mi•nar•y (lōō′mə ner′ē), *n., pl.* **-nar•ies. 1.** a celestial body that gives light, as the sun or moon. **2.** a person who has attained eminence in a field.

lu′min•es′cent (-nes′ənt) *adj.* luminous at relatively low temperatures. —**lu′min•es′cence,** *n.*

lu′mi•nous *adj.* **1.** radiating or reflecting light. **2.** clear; readily intelligible. —**lu′mi•nos′i•ty** (-nos′-i tē), *n.*

lum•mox (lum′əks), *n. Informal.* a clumsy, stupid person.

lump[1] (lump), *n.* **1.** a piece or mass of no particular shape. **2.** a protuberance or swelling. **3. lumps,** *Informal.* harsh criticism, punishment, or defeat. —*adj.* **4.** in the form of a lump or lumps. **5.** made up of a number of items taken together: *a lump sum.* —*v.t.* **6.** to unite into one collection or mass. **7.** to deal with, consider, etc., in a lump or mass. —*v.i.* **8.** to form a lump or lumps. —**lump′y,** *adj.,* **-i•er, -i•est.** —**lump′i•ness,** *n.*

lump[2] (lump), *v.t. Informal.* to put up with: *If you don't like it, you can lump it.*

lu•na•cy (lŌŌ′nə sē), *n.* **1.** insanity. **2.** extreme foolishness.

lu′nar (-nər), *adj.* of the moon.

lu′na•tic (-tik), *n.* **1.** an insane person. —*adj.* **2.** insane; crazy. **3.** recklessly foolish. **4.** for the insane. [< OF *lunatique* < LL *lūnāticus* moonstruck]

lunch (lunch), *n.* **1.** a light midday meal between breakfast and dinner. —*v.i.* **2.** to eat lunch. —*Idiom.* **3. out to lunch,** *Slang.* inattentive or unaware.

lunch′eon•ette′ (-chə net′), *n.* a small restaurant where light meals are served.

lung (lung), *n.* either of the two saclike respiratory organs in the thorax of humans and other air-breathing vertebrates.

lunge (lunj), *n., v.,* **lunged, lung•ing.** —*n.* **1.** a sudden forward thrust, as with a sword. **2.** any sudden forward movement. —*v.i., v.t.* **3.** to move or cause to move with a lunge.

lu•pine[1] (lŌŌ′pin), *n.* a leguminous plant with tall, dense clusters of blue, pink, or white flowers.

lu•pine[2] (lŌŌ′pīn), *adj.* of or resembling the wolf.

lu•pus (lŌŌ′pəs), *n.* any of several diseases characterized by skin eruptions or inflammation.

lurch[1] (lûrch), *n.* **1.** a sudden tip or roll to one side, as of a ship or a staggering person. —*v.i.* **2.** (of a ship) to roll or pitch suddenly. **3.** to stagger or sway.

lurch[2] (lûrch), *n.* an uncomfortable or difficult situation: *Our supervisor resigned and left us in the lurch.*

lure (lŌŌr), *n., v.,* **lured, lur•ing.** —*n.* **1.** anything that entices or allures. **2.** an artificial bait used in fishing or trapping. —*v.t.* **3.** to attract, entice, or tempt.

lu•rid (lŌŌr′id), *adj.* **1.** gruesome; revolting. **2.** wildly sensational; shocking. **3.** shining with an unnatural, fiery glow. —**lu′rid•ly,** *adv.* —**lu′rid•ness,** *n.*

lurk (lûrk), *v.i.* **1.** to lie hidden, as in ambush. **2.** to go furtively.

lus•cious (lush′əs), *adj.* **1.** highly pleasing to the taste or smell. **2.** richly satisfying to the senses or the mind. —**lus′cious•ly,** *adv.* —**lus′cious•ness,** *n.*

lush[1] (lush), *adj.,* **-er, -est. 1.** characterized by luxuriant vegetation. **2.** characterized by abundance, opulence, etc. —**lush′ness,** *n.*

lush[2] (lush), *n. Slang.* a drunkard.

lust (lust), *n.* **1.** intense sexual desire or appetite. **2.** an overwhelming desire: *a lust for power.* **3.** ardent enthusiasm: *a lust for life.* —*v.i.* **4.** to have a strong desire. —**lust′ful,** *adj.* —**lust′ful•ness,** *n.*

lus•ter (lus′tər), *n.* **1.** the state or quality of shining by reflecting light; sheen or gloss. **2.** radiant or luminous brightness. **3.** radiance of beauty, excellence, distinction, or glory. Also, *esp. Brit.,* **lus′tre.** —**lus′ter•less,** *adj.* —**lus′trous,** *adj.*

lust′y *adj.,* **-i•er, -i•est.** full of healthy vigor. —**lust′i•ly,** *adv.* —**lust′i•ness,** *n.*

lute (lŌŌt), *n.* a stringed instrument having a long, fretted neck and a hollow, pear-shaped body. —**lu•te•nist, lu•ta•nist** (lŌŌt′n ist), *n.*

Lu′ther•an (lŌŌ′thər ən), *adj.* **1.** of the Protestant denomination following the doctrines by Luther. —*n.* **2.** a member of the Lutheran Church. —**Lu′-ther•an•ism,** *n.*

Lux•em•bourg or **-burg** (luk′səm bûrg′), *n.* a grand duchy in W Europe.

lux•u•ri•ant (lug zhŌŌr′ē ənt, luk shŌŌr′-), *adj.* **1.** abundant in growth, as vegetation. **2.** producing abundantly, as soil. **3.** florid, as ornamentation. —**lux•u′ri•ance,** *n.* —**lux•u′ri•ant•ly,** *adv.*

lux•u′ri•ate′ (-āt′), *v.i.,* **-at•ed, -at•ing. 1.** to indulge in luxury. **2.** to grow abundantly. **3.** to take great delight. —**lux•u′ri•a′tion,** *n.*

lux•u•ry (luk′shə rē, lug′zhə-), *n., pl.* **-ries,** *adj.* —*n.* **1.** an object, service, etc., conducive to physical comfort or sumptuous living. **2.** indulgence in the pleasures afforded by such things. —*adj.* **3.** of or providing luxury. —**lux•u′ri•ous,** *adj.*

ly•ce•um (lī sē′əm), *n.* **1.** an institution for popular education, providing lectures, concerts, etc. **2.** a building for such activities.

lye (lī), *n.* a white, powerful alkaline substance used for washing and in making soap.

ly′ing-in′ *n., pl.* **ly•ings-in, ly•ing-ins,** *adj.* —*n.* **1.** the confinement of a woman giving birth. —*adj.* **2.** of or for childbirth.

lymph (limf), *n.* a yellowish fluid containing lymphocytes and fats that surrounds body cells and carries away their wastes.

lym′pho•cyte′ (-fə sīt′), *n.* a type of white blood cell important in the production of antibodies.

lynch (linch), *v.t.* to put to death, esp. by hanging, by mob action and without legal authority. [shortening of *lynch law,* after the self-instituted tribunals presided over by William *Lynch* (1742–1820) of Virginia] —**lynch′er,** *n.*

lynx (lingks), *n., pl.* **lynx•es, lynx.** a wildcat having long limbs and a short tail.

lyre (lī²r), *n.* a small harplike musical instrument of ancient Greece.

lyr•ic (lir′ik), *adj.* Also, **lyr′i•cal. 1.** (of a poem) having the form of a song expressing the writer's feelings. **2.** expressing strong, spontaneous feeling: *lyric writing.* **3.** having a voice of light volume and modest range: *a lyric soprano.* —*n.* **4.** a lyric poem. **5.** Usu. **-ics.** the words of a song. —**lyr′i•cal•ly,** *adv.* —**lyr′i•cism** (-ə siz′əm), *n.*

abcdefghijkl **M** nopqrstuvwxyz

M, m (em), *n., pl.* **Ms** or **M's, ms** or **m's.** the 13th letter of the English alphabet, a consonant.

M 1. major. **2.** Medieval. **3.** medium. **4.** Middle.

M *Symbol.* the Roman numeral for 1000.

m 1. *Physics.* mass. **2.** medieval. **3.** medium. **4.** meter. **5.** middle. **6.** minor.

M. 1. majesty. **2.** meridian. **3.** noon. [< L *merīdiēs*] **4.** Monday. **5.** *pl.* **MM.** monsieur.

m. 1. male. **2.** married. **3.** masculine. **4.** *Physics.* mass. **5.** medium. **6.** noon. **7.** meter. **8.** mile. **9.** minute. **10.** month.

ma (mä), *n., pl.* **mas.** mother.

MA Massachusetts.

M.A. Master of Arts. [< L *Magister Artium*]

ma′am (mam, mäm; *unstressed* məm), *n.* (*often cap.*) MADAM (def. 1).

ma•ca•bre (mə kä′brə, -käb′), *adj.* gruesome in character; ghastly.

mac•ad•am (mə kad′əm), *n.* **1.** a road or pavement of compacted broken stone, often with asphalt or tar. **2.** broken stone used for macadam. —**mac•ad′am•ize′,** *v.t.,* **-ized, -iz•ing.**

mac·a·ro·ni (mak′ə rō′nē), *n.* small tubular pasta made of wheat flour.

mac·a·roon (mak′ə rōōn′), *n.* a cookie made of beaten egg whites, sugar, and almond paste or coconut.

ma·caw (mə kô′), *n.* a large, long-tailed parrot of the New World tropics.

mace¹ (mās), *n.* **1.** a clublike armor-breaking weapon used chiefly in the Middle Ages. **2.** a ceremonial staff symbolic of office.

mace² (mās), *n.* a spice made from the inner husk of the nutmeg.

Mace (mās), *v.*, **Maced, Mac·ing. 1.** *Trademark.* a chemical spray that causes severe eye and skin irritation. —*v.t.* **2.** (*sometimes l.c.*) to spray with Mace.

Mac·e·do·ni·a (mas′i dō′nē ə), *n.* a republic in SE Europe: formerly part of Yugoslavia. —**Mac′e·do′ni·an,** *n.*

mac·er·ate (mas′ə rāt′), *v.t.*, **-at·ed, -at·ing. 1.** to soften or separate into parts by steeping in a liquid. **2.** to cause to waste away. —**mac′er·a′tion,** *n.*

ma·chet·e (mə shet′ē, -chet′ē), *n., pl.* **-es.** a heavy swordlike knife used esp. as a cutting implement.

Mach·i·a·vel·li·an (mak′ē ə vel′ē ən), *adj.* characterized by unscrupulous cunning, deception, or expediency. [after N. *Machiavelli* (1469–1527), Italian political philosopher]

mach·i·na·tion (mak′ə nā′shən), *n.* Usu. **-tions.** a crafty scheme or maneuver.

ma·chine (mə shēn′), *n., v.,* **-chined, -chin·ing.** —*n.* **1.** an apparatus consisting of interrelated parts with separate functions, used in the performance of some kind of work. **2.** a device, as a pulley, that transmits or modifies force or motion. **3.** an automobile or airplane. **4.** an electric, mechanical, or electronic device, as a vending machine. **5.** a group of persons that controls a political party. —*v.t.* **6.** to make, prepare, or finish with a machine.

machine′ gun′ *n.* a firearm capable of shooting a continuous stream of bullets. —**ma·chine′-gun′,** *v.t.,* **-gunned, -gun·ning.**

ma·chin·er·y *n., pl.* **-ies. 1.** machines collectively. **2.** the parts of a machine. **3.** a system by which action is maintained or a result is obtained.

ma·chin·ist *n.* a person who makes, repairs, or operates machinery.

ma·chis·mo (mä chēz′mō), *n.* an exaggerated sense of manliness.

Mach′ (or **mach′**) **num′ber** (mäk), *n.* the ratio of the speed of an object to the speed of sound in the surrounding atmosphere.

ma·cho (mä′chō), *adj., n., pl.* **-chos.** —*adj.* **1.** characterized by machismo. —*n.* **2.** MACHISMO. **3.** an assertively virile or domineering male.

mack·er·el (mak′ər əl), *n., pl.* **-els, -el.** a food fish of the N Atlantic.

mack·i·naw (mak′ə nô′), *n.* a short, double-breasted coat of heavy, usu. plaid wool.

mack·in·tosh or **mac·in·tosh** (mak′in tosh′), *n. Chiefly Brit.* RAINCOAT.

mac·ra·mé (mak′rə mā′), *n.* a lacelike webbing made of knotted cord or yarn.

macro- a combining form meaning large (*macrocosm*).

mac′ro·bi·ot′ic (mak′rō bi ot′ik) *adj.* of or giving long life.

mac·ro·cosm (mak′rə koz′əm), *n.* the universe considered as a whole.

ma·cron (mā′kron, mak′ron), *n.* a horizontal line used over a vowel to show that it is long, as (ā) in *fate* (fāt).

mad (mad), *adj.,* **mad·der, mad·dest. 1.** very angry; enraged. **2.** mentally disturbed; deranged. **3.** affected with rabies. **4.** extremely foolish; imprudent. **5.** impetuous: frantic. **6.** brimming with enthusiasm. **7.** wildly frivolous; hilarious. —**mad′ly,** *adv.* —**mad′ness,** *n.*

Mad·a·gas·car (mad′ə gas′kər), *n.* an island republic in the Indian Ocean, off the SE coast of Africa. —**Mad′a·gas′can,** *n., adj.*

mad·am (mad′əm), *n., pl.* **mes·dames** (mā dam′, -däm′) for 1; **mad·ams** for 2. **1.** (*often cap.*) a re-

spectful term of address to a woman. **2.** a woman in charge of a brothel. [< OF, orig. *ma dame* my lady]

mad′cap′ *adj.* **1.** recklessly impulsive; rash. —*n.* **2.** a madcap person.

made (mād), *v.* pt. and pp. of MAKE.

mad·e·moi·selle (mad′ə mə zel′, mad′mwə-, mam zel′), *n., pl.* **mad·e·moi·selles, mes·de·moi·selles** (mā′də mə zel′, -zelz′, mād′mwə-). (*often cap.*) a French title equivalent to Miss.

mad′man′ or **-wom′an,** *n., pl.* **-men** or **-wom·en.** an insane person.

Ma·don·na (mə don′ə), *n., pl.* **-nas. 1.** the Virgin Mary. **2.** a picture or statue representing the Virgin Mary. [< It: my lady]

mad·ras (mad′rəs, mə dras′, -dräs′), *n.* a light cotton fabric, esp. one in multicolored plaid or stripes.

mad·ri·gal (mad′ri gəl), *n.* an unaccompanied polyphonic vocal composition, esp. of the 16th and 17th centuries.

mael·strom (māl′strəm), *n.* **1.** a powerful whirlpool. **2.** a tumultuous state of affairs.

maes·tro (mī′strō), *n., pl.* **-tros. 1.** an eminent composer, teacher, or conductor of music. **2.** a master of an art.

Ma·fi·a (mä′fē ə, maf′ē ə), *n.* a secret organization allegedly engaged in criminal activities internationally. [< dial. It (Sicily): courage, boldness]

Ma·fi·o·so (mä′fē ō′sō), *n., pl.* **-si** (-sē), **-sos.** (*often cap.*) a member of the Mafia.

mag·a·zine (mag′ə zēn′), *n.* **1.** a periodical publication typically containing essays, stories, and poems. **2.** a room for keeping explosives, as gunpowder. **3.** a military depot for arms or provisions. **4.** a receptacle on a gun for holding cartridges. **5.** a compartment in a camera for holding film.

ma·gen·ta (mə jen′tə), *n., pl.* **-tas.** a purplish red.

mag·got (mag′ət), *n.* the soft-bodied, legless larva of certain flies. —**mag′got·y,** *adj.*

Ma·gi (mā′jī), *n.pl., sing.* **-gus** (-gəs). (*sometimes l.c.*) the three wise men who paid homage to the infant Jesus.

mag·ic (maj′ik), *n.* **1.** the art of producing illusions, esp. by sleight of hand. **2.** the use of techniques such as incantation to exert alleged control over the supernatural or the forces of nature. **3.** an extraordinary influence or power. —*adj.* **4.** done by or employed in magic. **5.** mysteriously enchanting. —**mag′i·cal,** *adj.* —**mag′i·cal·ly,** *adv.*

mag·is·te·ri·al (maj′ə stēr′ē əl), *adj.* **1.** of or befitting a master or a magistrate. **2.** imperious; domineering. —**mag′is·te′ri·al·ly,** *adv.*

mag′is·trate′ (-strāt′, -strit), *n.* **1.** a civil officer charged with the administration of the law. **2.** a minor judicial officer, as a justice of the peace.

mag·ma (mag′mə), *n.* molten material beneath or within the earth's crust, from which igneous rock is formed.

mag·nan·i·mous (mag nan′ə məs), *adj.* **1.** generous in forgiving. **2.** showing noble sensibility; high-minded. —**mag′na·nim′i·ty** (-nə nim′i tē), *n.* —**mag·nan′i·mous·ly,** *adv.*

mag′nate (-nāt, -nit), *n.* a person of great influence, importance, or standing.

mag·ne·sia (mag nē′zhə), *n.* a white tasteless substance used as an antacid and laxative.

mag·ne′si·um (-zē əm, -zhəm, -shē əm), *n.* a ductile, silver-white metallic element that burns with a dazzling light. *Symbol:* Mg; *at. wt.:* 24.312; *at. no.:* 12.

mag·net (mag′nit), *n.* **1.** a body that possesses the property of attracting certain substances, as iron. **2.** LODESTONE. **3.** a person or thing that attracts.

mag·net′ic (-net′ik), *adj.* **1.** of a magnet or magnetism. **2.** having the properties of a magnet. **3.** capable of being magnetized. **4.** pertaining to the earth's magnetic field. **5.** exerting a strong attractive power or charm. —**mag·net′i·cal·ly,** *adv.*

magnet′ic field′ *n.* a region of space near a magnet, electric current, or moving charged particle in which a magnetic force acts.

magnet′ic res′o·nance im′aging *n.* a process

of producing images of the body by means of a strong magnetic field and low-energy radio waves.

mag′net•ism *n.* **1.** the properties of attraction possessed by magnets. **2.** the agency producing magnetic phenomena. **3.** strong attractive power. —**mag′net•ize′,** *v.t.,* -**ized,** -**iz•ing.**

mag′net•ite′ (-ni tīt′), *n.* a common black iron oxide, an important iron ore.

mag•ne′to (-nē′tō) *n., pl.* -**tos.** a small electric generator in which permanent magnets provide the magnetic field.

mag•nif′i•cent (mag nif′ə sənt), *adj.* **1.** splendid or impressive, esp. in appearance; superb. **2.** noble; sublime. —**mag•nif′i•cence,** *n.* —**mag•nif′i•cent•ly,** *adv.*

mag•ni•fy (mag′nə fī′), *v.t.,* -**fied,** -**fy•ing.** **1.** to increase the apparent or actual size of; enlarge. **2.** to exaggerate; overstate. **3.** to intensify; heighten. **4.** to praise. —**mag′ni•fi•ca′tion,** *n.* —**mag′ni•fi′er,** *n.*

mag′ni•tude′ (-ni tōōd′, -tyōōd′), *n.* **1.** size; extent. **2.** great importance or consequence. **3.** greatness of size or amount. **4.** the brightness of a celestial body as expressed on a logarithmic scale.

mag•no′lia (mag nōl′yə, -nō′lē ə), *n., pl.* -**lias.** a shrub or tree bearing large, usu. fragrant flowers.

mag′num o′pus (mag′nəm), *n.* a great work, esp. the chief work of a writer, composer, or artist.

mag•pie (mag′pī′), *n.* a noisy, black-and-white bird of the jay family.

ma•ha•ra•jah or -**ja** (mä′hə rä′jə, -zhə), *n., pl.* -**jahs** or -**jas.** a former ruling prince in India.

ma•hat•ma (mə hät′mə, -hat′-), *n., pl.* -**mas.** (*sometimes cap.*) a person, esp. in India, who is held in the highest esteem for wisdom and saintliness.

mah-jongg or **mah•jong** (mä′jông′, -jong′, -zhông′, -zhong′), *n.* a game of Chinese origin played with dominolike tiles.

ma•hog•a•ny (mə hog′ə nē), *n., pl.* -**nies.** **1.** any of several tropical American trees yielding hard, reddish brown wood used for making furniture. **2.** the wood of a mahogany.

Ma•hom•et (mə hom′it), *n.* MUHAMMAD.

maid (mād), *n.* **1.** a female servant. **2.** a girl or young unmarried woman.

maid′en *n.* **1.** MAID (def. 2). —*adj.* **2.** of or befitting a maiden. **3. a.** unmarried. **b.** virgin. **4.** first: *a maiden flight.* —**maid′en•hood′,** *n.* —**maid′en•ly,** *adj.*

maid′en•hair′ *n.* a fern with slender stalks and finely divided fronds.

mail¹ (māl), *n.* **1.** matter, as letters, sent or delivered by a postal service. **2.** a single collection or delivery of mail. **3.** Also, **mails.** a system, usu. operated by a government, for sending or delivering mail. —*v.t.* **4.** to send by mail. —**mail′er,** *n.*

mail² (māl), *n.* flexible armor of metal rings or plates. —**mailed,** *adj.*

mail′ car′rier *n.* a person employed to deliver mail.

maim (mām), *v.t.* **1.** to deprive of the use of a part of the body, esp. by wounding. **2.** to impair; disfigure.

main (mān), *adj.* **1.** chief, as in importance; principal. **2.** syntactically independent. **3.** sheer; utmost: *by main strength.* —*n.* **4.** a principal distributing pipe or duct in a utility system. **5.** physical strength or force: *might and main.* **6.** the chief part or point. **7.** the open ocean. —**main′ly,** *adv.*

main′frame′ *n.* a large computer, often the hub of a system serving many users.

main′land′ (-land′, -lənd), *n.* the principal land of a continent, country, or region.

main′mast′ (-mast′, -mäst′; *Naut.* -məst), *n.* the principal mast of a sailing ship.

main′stay′ *n.* **1.** a chief support. **2.** the stay that secures the mainmast forward.

main′stream′ *n.* **1.** the principal or dominant course, tendency, or trend. —*adj.* **2.** of or characteristic of a mainstream. —*v.t.* **3.** to place in regular school classes: *to mainstream disabled children.*

main•tain (mān tān′), *v.t.* **1.** to keep in existence or continuance. **2.** to keep in due condition, opera-

tion, or force. **3.** to affirm; assert. **4.** to support or defend. **5.** to provide for the upkeep of. —**main•tain′a•ble,** *adj.* —**main′te•nance** (-tə nəns), *n.*

mai•tre d'hô•tel (mā′trə dō tel′; *Fr.* me tʀ³ dō-tel′), *n., pl.* **maî•tres d'hôtel** (mā′traz; *Fr.* me tʀ³). **1.** a headwaiter. **2.** a steward or butler.

maize (māz), *n.* CORN¹ (def. 1).

maj•es•ty (maj′ə stē), *n., pl.* -**ties.** **1.** regal, lofty, or stately dignity. **2.** supreme greatness or authority. **3.** (*usu. cap.*) a title of a sovereign. —**ma•jes′tic** (mə jes′tik), *adj.* —**ma•jes′ti•cal•ly,** *adv.*

ma•jol•i•ca (mə jol′i kə, mə yol′-), *n.* Italian earthenware with an opaque glaze of tin oxide.

ma•jor (mā′jər), *n.* **1.** a commissioned military officer ranking next above a captain. **2. a.** a field of study in which a student specializes. **b.** a student specializing in such a field. —*adj.* **3.** greater in size, extent, or amount. **4.** marked by risk; serious: *a major operation.* **5.** *Music.* of, based on, or being a scale with half steps between the third and fourth and seventh and eighth degrees. —*v.i.* **6.** to follow an academic major.

ma′jor-do′mo (-dō′mō), *n., pl.* -**mos.** **1.** a man in charge of a great household, as that of a sovereign. **2.** a steward; butler.

ma′jor•ette′ (-jə ret′), *n.* a girl or woman who twirls a baton with or leads a marching band.

ma′jor gen′eral *n.* a military officer ranking next above a brigadier general.

ma•jor•i•ty (mə jôr′i tē, -jor′-), *n., pl.* -**ties. 1. a.** a number larger than half of a total. **b.** the amount by which this greater number surpasses the remainder. **2.** the state or time of being of full legal age. **3.** the military rank of a major.

make (māk), *v.,* **made, mak•ing,** *n.* —*v.t.* **1.** to create by shaping, changing, or combining material: *to make a dress.* **2.** to cause to exist or happen: *made trouble.* **3.** to cause to become: *to make someone happy.* **4.** to appoint; name. **5.** to put in proper condition, as for use; prepare: *Make your bed.* **6.** to force; compel: *made them do it.* **7.** to produce, earn, or win: *made many friends.* **8.** to draw up; draft: *to make a will.* **9.** to establish; enact: *to make laws.* **10.** to develop into; become: *You'll make a good lawyer.* **11.** to form in the mind: *to make a decision.* **12.** to interpret or judge: *What do you make of that remark?* **13.** to amount to: *Two plus two makes four.* **14.** to constitute: *a table made of wood.* **15.** to assure the success of: *The book made her reputation.* **16.** to deliver; utter: *to make a speech.* **17.** to reach; attain: *didn't make the station in time.* —*v.i.* **18.** to cause someone or something to be as specified: *to make sure.* **19.** to act in a certain way: *to make merry.* **20. make away with,** to carry off; steal. **21. ~ for, a.** to move toward. **b.** to promote or result in: *Calm makes for fewer arguments.* **22. ~ out, a.** to write out. **b.** to perceive the meaning of. **c.** to see with effort; discern. **d.** to suggest or impute: *made me out to be a liar.* **e.** to manage; fare: *How are you making out in school?* **23. ~ over,** to remodel; alter. **24. ~ up, a.** to concoct; invent. **b.** to compensate. **c.** to settle; decide: *Make up your mind.* **d.** to become reconciled. **e.** to apply cosmetics. —*n.* **25.** the style or manner in which something is made. **26.** brand: *a foreign make of car.* —*Idiom.* **27. make believe,** to pretend; imagine. **28. make do,** to manage with whatever is available. **29. make it,** to achieve success.

make′-believe′ *n.* **1.** pretense, esp. of an innocent or playful kind. —*adj.* **2.** pretended; imaginary.

make′shift′ *n.* **1.** a temporary expedient or substitute. —*adj.* **2.** being or serving as a makeshift.

make′up′ or **make′-up′,** *n.* **1.** cosmetics, esp. for the face. **2.** the total ensemble of items, as cosmetics and costumes, used by a theatrical performer. **3.** the manner of being put together; composition. **4.** physical or mental constitution.

mal- a combining form meaning bad, wrongful, or ill (*malfunction*).

mal•a•chite (mal′ə kīt′), *n.* a green mineral that is an ore of copper, used for making ornamental articles.

mal•ad•just•ed (mal′ə jus′tid), adj. badly adjusted, as to one's social circumstances. —**mal′ad•just′ment,** n.

mal•a•droit (mal′ə droit′), adj. lacking in adroitness; awkward. —**mal′a•droit′ly,** adv.

mal•a•dy (mal′ə dē), n., pl. **-dies.** a disorder or disease of the body.

ma•laise (ma lāz′, -lez′, mə-), n. a vague feeling of discomfort or unease.

mal•a•mute (mal′ə myōōt′), n. one of an Alaskan breed of large dogs, raised orig. for pulling sleds.

mal•a•prop•ism (mal′ə prop iz′əm), n. a usu. ludicrous confusion of words that are similar in sound.

ma•lar•i•a (mə lâr′ē ə), n. a mosquito-borne disease characterized by recurring chills, fever, and sweating. [< It, contr. of *mala aria* bad air] —**ma•lar′i•al,** adj.

ma•lar•key (mə lär′kē), n. Informal. nonsensical speech or writing.

Ma•la•wi (mə lä′wē), n. a republic in SE Africa. —**Ma•la′wi•an,** adj., n.

Ma•lay•sia (mə lā′zhə), n. a constitutional monarchy in SE Asia. —**Ma•lay′sian,** adj., n.

mal•con•tent (mal′kən tent′), adj. 1. not satisfied with current conditions. —n. 2. a malcontent person.

mal de mer (mʌl də meʀ′), n. seasickness.

Mal•dives (môl′dēvz, mal′dīvz), n. a republic in a group of islands in the Indian Ocean, SW of Sri Lanka. —**Mal•div′i•an** (-div′ē ən), adj., n.

male (māl), n. 1. an individual or organism of the sex or sexual phase that normally produces a sperm cell or male gamete. —adj. 2. of or being a male. 3. of or characteristic of a boy or man; masculine. 4. made to fit into a corresponding open or recessed part: *a male plug.* —**male′ness,** n.

mal•e•dic•tion (mal′i dik′shən), n. a curse; imprecation.

mal•e•fac•tor (mal′ə fak′tər), n. 1. a person who violates the law; criminal. 2. an evildoer. —**mal′e•fac′tion,** n.

ma•lev•o•lent (mə lev′ə lənt), adj. 1. wishing evil or harm to others; malicious. 2. producing evil or harm; injurious. —**ma•lev′o•lence,** n.

mal•fea•sance (mal fē′zəns), n. misconduct or wrongdoing, esp. by a public official.

mal•formed′ adj. badly formed. —**mal′for•ma′tion,** n.

Ma•li (mä′lē), n. a republic in W Africa. —**Ma′li•an,** n., adj.

mal•ice (mal′is), n. 1. a desire to inflict harm or suffering on another. 2. Law. malevolence, deliberate lying, or recklessness in the commission of a wrong. —**ma•li•cious** (mə lish′əs), adj. —**ma•li′cious•ly,** adv.

ma•lign (mə līn′), v.t. 1. to speak harmful untruths about. —adj. 2. evil in effect. 3. evil in disposition.

ma•lig•nant (mə lig′nənt), adj. 1. inclined to cause harm, suffering, or distress. 2. dangerous or harmful in influence or effect. 3. tending to produce death, as a tumor. —**ma•lig′nan•cy,** n., pl. **-cies.** —**ma•lig′ni•ty** (-ni tē), n.

ma•lin•ger (mə ling′gər), v.i. to pretend illness, esp. in order to shirk duty or work. —**ma•lin′ger•er,** n.

mall (môl), n. 1. a large retail shopping complex. 2. an urban street lined with shops and closed to motor vehicles. 3. a large shaded public walk or promenade. 4. a strip of land separating two roadways.

mal•lard (mal′ərd), n., pl. **-lards, -lard.** a common wild duck from which domestic ducks are descended.

mal•le•a•ble (mal′ē ə bəl), adj. 1. capable of being extended or shaped by hammering or pressure from rollers. 2. adaptable; tractable. —**mal′le•a•bil′i•ty,** n.

mal•let (mal′it), n. 1. a hammerlike tool with an enlarged head for driving another tool or striking a surface without causing damage. 2. a wooden implement used to strike a ball, as in croquet.

mal•low (mal′ō), n. any of various plants with lobed leaves and purple, pink, or white flowers.

mal′nu•tri′tion n. inadequate or unbalanced nutrition.

mal•o′dor•ous adj. having a foul odor.

mal•prac′tice n. dereliction of professional duty, as by a physician or lawyer, esp. when injury or loss follows.

malt (môlt), n. 1. germinated grain used esp. in brewing and distilling. 2. an alcoholic beverage, as beer, fermented from malt. —**malt′y,** adj., **-i•er, -i•est.**

Mal•ta (môl′tə), n. an island republic in the Mediterranean, south of Sicily. —**Mal•tese′** (-tēz′, -tēs′), n., pl. **-tese,** adj.

mal•treat (mal trēt′), v.t. to treat badly or roughly. —**mal•treat′ment,** n.

ma•ma or **mam•ma** (mä′mə, mə mä′), n., pl. **-mas.** MOTHER. [nursery word, with parallels in other European languages]

mam•mal (mam′əl), n. a warm-blooded vertebrate of the class that nourishes its young with milk from maternal mammary glands. —**mam•ma•li•an** (mə mā′lē ən, -māl′yən), n., adj.

mam•ma•ry (mam′ə rē), adj. of or pertaining to a gland in the female breast that secretes milk.

mam′mo•gram (mam′ə gram′), n. an x-ray photograph obtained by mammography.

mam•mog•ra•phy (ma mog′rə fē), n. x-ray photography of a breast, esp. for detection of tumors.

mam•mon (mam′ən), n. riches or material wealth, esp. as an influence for evil or immorality.

mam•moth (mam′əth), n. 1. an extinct Pleistocene elephant with hairy skin. —adj. 2. very large; enormous.

mam′my (mam′ē) n., pl. **-mies.** Informal. mother.

man (man), n., pl. **men,** v., **manned, man•ning.** —n. 1. an adult male person. 2. the human race; humankind. 3. a human being; person. 4. a husband. 5. a male having qualities considered appropriately masculine. 6. a male servant or attendant. 7. a playing piece used in certain games, as chess. —v.t. 8. to supply with people, as for service. 9. to take one's place at, as to defend or operate.

Man (man), n. **Isle of,** an island of the British Isles, in the Irish Sea.

Man. Manitoba.

man•a•cle (man′ə kəl), n., v., **-cled, -cling.** —n. 1. a shackle for the hand. —v.t. 2. to handcuff; fetter. 3. to hamper; restrain.

man•age (man′ij), v., **-aged, -ag•ing.** —v.t. 1. to succeed in accomplishing. 2. to take or be in charge or control of. 3. to dominate or influence, esp. by tact. —v.i. 4. to be in charge or control of an undertaking. 5. to get along; function. —**man′age•a•ble,** adj.

man′age•ment n. 1. the act or process of managing. 2. executive ability. 3. the persons managing an enterprise.

ma•ña•na (mä nyä′nä), n., adv. Spanish. tomorrow.

man•a•tee (man′ə tē′), n., pl. **-tees.** a plant-eating aquatic mammal of Caribbean and W African waters.

man•da•rin (man′də rin), n. 1. a member of any of the nine ranks of public officials in the Chinese Empire. 2. (cap.) the principal dialect of Chinese. 3. a small, loose-skinned citrus fruit.

man•date (man′dāt), n. 1. an authorization to act given by an electorate to a representative. 2. an authoritative order or command. 3. a commission given by the League of Nations to a member nation to administer a former Turkish territory or German colony.

man•da•to•ry (man′də tôr′ē), adj. 1. of, containing, or being a command. 2. having received a mandate, as a nation.

man•di•ble (man′də bəl), n. 1. the bone comprising the lower jaw of vertebrates. 2. the lower part of a bird's bill. —**man•dib′u•lar** (-dib′yə lər), adj.

man•do•lin (man′dl in, man′dl in′), n. a stringed musical instrument with a pear-shaped body and a fretted neck.

man•drake (man′drāk, -drik), *n.* a narcotic plant with a fleshy, forked root somewhat resembling a human form.

mane (mān), *n.* the long hair around or at the back of the neck of some animals, as the horse or lion. —**maned,** *adj.*

ma•neu•ver (mə nōō′vər), *n.* **1.** a planned movement of troops, warships, etc. **2. maneuvers,** a series of tactical military exercises. **3.** a physical movement or procedure, esp. when carried out skillfully. **4.** a clever or crafty tactic; ploy. —*v.i., v.t.* **5.** to perform or cause to perform a maneuver. **6.** to position, manipulate, or steer skillfully or adroitly. [< F ≪ L, = *manū operārī* to work with the hands] —**ma•neu′ver•a•ble,** *adj.* —**ma•neu′ver•a•bil′i•ty,** *n.*

man′ Fri′day *n., pl.* **men Friday.** a reliable male assistant.

man′ful *adj.* having or showing boldness, courage, or strength. —**man′ful•ly,** *adv.*

man•ga•nese (mang′gə nēs′, -nēz′), *n.* a hard, brittle, grayish white metallic element, used chiefly in strengthening steel. *Symbol:* Mn; *at. wt.:* 54.938; *at. no.:* 25.

mange (mānj), *n.* a skin disease, esp. of animals, characterized by hair loss and scabby eruptions. —**mang′y,** *adj.,* -**i•er, -i•est.**

man•ger (mān′jər), *n.* a trough from which livestock eat.

man•gle¹ (mang′gəl), *v.t.,* -**gled, -gling. 1.** to injure, disfigure, or mutilate by cutting, slashing, or crushing. **2.** to spoil; ruin.

man•gle² (mang′gəl), *n.* a machine for pressing laundry by passing it between heated rollers.

man•go (mang′gō), *n., pl.* -**goes, -gos. 1.** the oblong sweet fruit of a tropical tree of the cashew family. **2.** a tree bearing mangoes.

man•grove (mang′grōv, man′-), *n.* a tropical tree growing in marshes or tidal shores, noted for its interlacing above-ground roots.

man•han•dle (man′han′dl), *v.t.,* -**dled, -dling. 1.** to handle roughly. **2.** to move by human strength alone.

Man•hat•tan (man hat′n, mən-), *n.* a borough of New York City. 1,427,533.

man′hole′ *n.* a hole giving access to a sewer, drain, or conduit.

man′hood *n.* **1.** the state or time of being a man. **2.** traditional manly qualities. **3.** men collectively.

man′-hour′ *n.* a unit of measurement based on an ideal amount of work accomplished by one person in an hour.

man′hunt′ *n.* an intensive search for a person, esp. a criminal or fugitive.

ma•ni•a (mā′nē ə), *n., pl.* -**as. 1.** an excessive enthusiasm; craze. **2.** a pathological state characterized by euphoria, excessive activity, and impaired judgment.

ma′ni•ac′ *n.* **1.** an insane person; lunatic. —*adj.* **2.** insane; mad. —**ma•ni•a•cal** (mə nī′ə kəl), *adj.*

man•ic (man′ik), *adj.* pertaining to or affected by mania.

man′ic-depres′sive *adj.* **1.** suffering from a mental disorder marked by periods of mania alternating with depression. —*n.* **2.** a manic-depressive person.

man•i•cure (man′i kyŏōr′), *n., v.,* -**cured, -cur•ing.** —*n.* **1.** a cosmetic treatment of the hands or fingernails. —*v.t.* **2.** to apply manicure treatment to. **3.** to trim or cut meticulously. —**man′i•cur′ist,** *n.*

man•i•fest (man′ə fest′), *adj.* **1.** readily perceived; evident. —*v.t.* **2.** to make evident; show. —*n.* **3.** a list of cargo or passengers. —**man′i•fes•ta′tion,** *n.* —**man′i•fest′ly,** *adv.*

man′i•fes′to (-fes′tō), *n., pl.* -**tos, -toes.** a public declaration of intentions, opinions, or purposes.

man•i•fold (man′ə fōld′), *adj.* **1.** of many kinds; varied. **2.** having numerous different parts, features, or forms. —*n.* **3.** a pipe with several openings for funneling the flow of liquids or gases. —*v.t.* **4.** to make many copies of.

man•i•kin (man′i kin), *n.* **1.** a little man; dwarf. **2.** MANNEQUIN.

Ma•nil′a (or **ma•nil′a**) **pa′per,** (mə nil′ə), *n.* strong, light brown or buff paper.

man′ in the street′ *n.* an ordinary person.

ma•nip•u•late (mə nip′yə lāt′), *v.t.,* -**lat•ed, -lat•ing. 1.** to manage or influence skillfully and often unfairly. **2.** to handle or use, esp. with skill. **3.** to examine or treat by skillful use of the hands. —**ma•nip′u•la′tion,** *n.* —**ma•nip′u•la′tive,** *adj.* —**ma•nip′u•la′tor,** *n.*

man•kind (man′kīnd′ *for 1;* man′kīnd′ *for 2*), *n.* **1.** human beings collectively. **2.** men as distinguished from women.

man′ly *adj.,* -**li•er, -li•est,** *adv.* —*adj.* **1.** having qualities traditionally ascribed to men; virile. **2.** suitable for males. —*adv.* **3.** in a manly manner. —**man′li•ness,** *n.*

man•na (man′ə), *n.* **1.** *Bible.* the food miraculously supplied to the Israelites in the wilderness. **2.** a sudden or unexpected source of help or gratification.

man•ne•quin (man′i kin), *n.* **1.** a three-dimensional model of the human form, as that used for fitting clothes. **2.** a person employed to model clothing.

man•ner (man′ər), *n.* **1.** a way of doing, being done, or happening. **2. manners, a.** the prevailing customs of a people, class, or period. **b.** ways of behaving with reference to polite standards. **3.** customary way of doing or making. **4.** kind; sort. **5.** characteristic style in art or literature.

man′ner•ism *n.* **1.** a habitual or characteristic manner of doing something. **2.** excessive or affected adherence to a particular manner.

man′ner•ly *adj.* showing good manners; courteous.

man•nish (man′ish), *adj.* being typical or suggestive of a man rather than a woman. —**man′nish•ly,** *adv.* —**man′nish•ness,** *n.*

man′-of-war′ *n., pl.* **men-of-war. 1.** WARSHIP. **2.** PORTUGUESE MAN-OF-WAR.

man•or (man′ər), *n.* **1.** a feudal estate. **2.** (in England) the landed estate of a lord. **3.** the main house on an estate. —**ma•no•ri•al** (mə nôr′ē əl), *adj.*

man′pow′er *n.* power in terms of people available or required for work or military service.

man•qué (mäng kā′, män-), *adj.* unsuccessful; unfulfilled: *a poet manqué.* [< F]

man•sard (man′särd), *n.* a roof having four sides, each with two slopes, the lower slope being steeper than the upper.

manse (mans), *n.* the house occupied by a minister or parson.

man′serv′ant *n., pl.* **men•serv•ants.** a male servant.

man•sion (man′shən), *n.* a very large or stately residence.

man′slaugh′ter *n.* the unlawful killing of a human being without malice.

man•tel (man′tl), *n.* **1.** a decorative construction framing the opening of a fireplace. **2.** a shelf above a fireplace.

man•til•la (man til′ə, -tē′ə), *n., pl.* -**las.** a woman's silk or lace scarf worn over the head and shoulders, esp. in Spain or Latin America.

man•tis (man′tis), *n., pl.* -**tis•es, -tes** (-tēz). any of several insects typically holding the forelegs upraised as if in prayer.

man•tle (man′tl), *n., v.,* -**tled, -tling.** —*n.* **1.** a long, loose, sleeveless cloak. **2.** something that covers or conceals. **3.** the portion of the earth between the crust and the core. **4.** an incombustible hood that gives off a brilliant light when placed around a flame. **5.** MANTEL. —*v.t.* **6.** to cover with or as if with a mantle. —*v.i.* **7.** to flush; blush.

man•tra (man′trə, män′-), *n., pl.* -**tras.** (in Hinduism and Buddhism) a sacred word or formula repeated as an incantation.

man•u•al (man′yŏō əl), *adj.* **1.** operated by hand. **2.** involving or requiring human effort; physical. **3.** of the hands. —*n.* **4.** a small book, esp. one giving information or instructions. **5.** the prescribed drill in handling a rifle. **6.** a keyboard, esp. of a pipe organ. —**man′u•al•ly,** *adv.*

man•u•fac•ture (man′yə fak′chər), *v.*, **-tured,** **-tur•ing,** *n.* —*v.t.* **1.** to make by hand or machinery, esp. on a large scale. **2.** to make up; invent: *to manufacture an excuse.* —*n.* **3.** the making of goods or wares by hand or machinery, esp. on a large scale. **4.** something manufactured. —**man′u•fac′-tur•er,** *n.*

man•u•mit (man′yə mit′), *v.t.*, **-mit•ted, -mit•ting.** to release from slavery. —**man′u•mis′sion,** *n.*

ma•nure (mə nŏŏr′, -nyŏŏr′), *n.*, *v.*, **-nured, -nur•ing.** —*n.* **1.** a substance, esp. animal excrement, used for fertilizing the soil. —*v.t.* **2.** to fertilize (land) with manure.

man•u•script (man′yə skript′), *n.* **1.** a written, typewritten, or computer-produced text. **2.** writing as distinguished from print.

man•y (men′ē), *adj.*, **more, most,** *n.*, *pron.* —*adj.* **1.** constituting or forming a large number. —*n.* **2.** a large number. —*pron.* **3.** many persons or things.

Mao•ism (mou′iz əm), *n.* the theories and policies of Chinese Communist leader Mao Zedong. —**Mao′-ist,** *n.*, *adj.*

map (map), *n.*, *v.*, **mapped, map•ping.** —*n.* **1.** a representation, usu. on a flat surface, of all or a part of the earth or the heavens. —*v.t.* **2.** to represent on a map. **3.** to sketch or plan: *mapped out a financial strategy.* —**map′mak′er,** *n.* —**map′per,** *n.*

ma•ple (mā′pəl), *n.* **1.** any of numerous trees or shrubs grown for shade or ornament, for timber, or for sap. **2.** the wood of a maple.

mar (mär), *v.t.*, **marred, mar•ring.** to damage the attractiveness or appeal of; impair.

Mar or **Mar.,** March.

ma•rac•a (mə rä′kə, -rak′ə), *n.*, *pl.* **-rac•as.** a gourd-shaped rattle filled with seeds or pebbles and used as a rhythm instrument.

mar′a•schi′no cher′ry (mar′ə skē′nō, -shē′-, mar′-), *n.* a cherry preserved in cherry cordial **(maraschino)** or an imitation of it.

mar•a•thon (mar′ə thon′, -thən), *n.* **1.** a foot race of 26 mi. 385 yd. (42 km 195 m). **2.** a long-distance race. **3.** a contest or event requiring great endurance. —**mar′a•thon′er,** *n.*

ma•raud (mə rôd′), *v.i.*, *v.t.* to rove in quest of plunder; raid. —**ma•raud′er,** *n.*

mar•ble (mär′bəl), *n.*, *adj.*, *v.*, **-bled, -bling.** —*n.* **1.** a limestone that takes a high polish and is used esp. in sculpture and architecture. **2.** something resembling marble, as in hardness. **3. a.** a small ball, as of agate, for use in games. **b. marbles,** any of various children's games played with marbles. —*adj.* **4.** consisting of or resembling marble. —*v.t.* **5.** to color or stain in imitation of marble, as book edges. —**mar′bly,** *adj.*

mar•bling (mär′bling), *n.* the intermixture of fat with lean in a cut of meat.

march¹ (märch), *v.i.* **1.** to walk with regular, measured steps, as soldiers in military formation. **2.** to proceed in a deliberate manner. **3.** to advance. —*v.t.* **4.** to cause to march. —*n.* **5.** the act or course of marching. **6.** the distance covered in marching. **7.** advance; progress. **8.** a piece of music with a rhythm suited to accompany marching. —**march′er,** *n.*

march² (märch), *n.* a border district; frontier.

March *n.* the third month of the year, containing 31 days.

mar•chion•ess (mär′shə nis, -nes′), *n.* **1.** the wife or widow of a marquess. **2.** a woman holding a rank equal to that of a marquess.

Mar•di Gras (mär′dē grä′, grä′), *n.* the day before Lent, often celebrated as a day of carnival.

mare¹ (mâr), *n.* a female equine animal, esp. a horse.

ma•re² (mär′ā, mär′ē), *n.*, *pl.* **ma•ri•a** (mär′ē ə, mâr′-). any of several large, dark plains on the moon and Mars.

mare's′-nest′ *n.* **1.** a discovery that proves to be a delusion or hoax. **2.** a confused or disordered situation.

mar•ga•rine (mär′jər in), *n.* a butterlike product made of vegetable oils emulsified usu. with water or milk.

mar•gin (mär′jin), *n.* **1.** the space around the printed or written matter on a page. **2.** a border; edge. **3.** an amount beyond what is necessary. **4.** an amount or degree of difference.

mar′gin•al *adj.* **1.** of or at a margin. **2.** barely acceptable. —**mar′gin•al•ly,** *adv.*

mar•gue•rite (mär′gə rēt′), *n.* any of several daisylike chrysanthemums.

mar•i•gold (mar′i gōld′), *n.* a plant with golden or orange flowers and strong-scented foliage.

ma•ri•jua•na *or* **-hua•na** (mar′ə wä′nə), *n.* **1.** the dried leaves and flowers of the hemp plant used esp. in cigarette form as an intoxicant. **2.** HEMP (def. 1).

ma•rim•ba (mə rim′bə), *n.*, *pl.* **-bas.** a kind of xylophone, often with resonators beneath the bars to reinforce the sound. [< Pg < a Bantu language]

ma•ri•na (mə rē′nə), *n.*, *pl.* **-nas.** a boat basin offering dockage and services for small craft.

mar•i•nade (mar′ə nād′), *n.* a pungent liquid mixture in which food is steeped before cooking.

mar′i•nate′ *v.t.*, **-nat•ed, -nat•ing.** to steep (food) in a marinade. —**mar′i•na′tion,** *n.*

ma•rine (mə rēn′), *adj.* **1.** of the sea. **2.** of navigation or shipping. **3.** of the marines. —*n.* **4.** (*sometimes cap.*) a member of the U.S. Marine Corps. **5.** a soldier serving both on shipboard and on land. **6.** seagoing ships.

Marine′ Corps′ *n.* a branch of the U.S. armed forces trained for sea-launched assaults on land targets.

mar•i•ner (mar′ə nər), *n.* a sailor.

mar•i•on•ette (mar′ē ə net′), *n.* a puppet manipulated by strings attached to its jointed limbs.

mar•i•tal (mar′i tl), *adj.* of marriage. —**mar′i•tal•ly,** *adv.*

mar•i•time (mar′i tīm′), *adj.* **1.** of navigation or shipping on the sea. **2.** of or bordering on the sea.

mar•jo•ram (mär′jər əm), *n.* an aromatic herb of the mint family with leaves used as a seasoning.

mark¹ (märk), *n.* **1.** a visible impression on a surface, as scratch. **2.** a symbol used in writing or printing: *a punctuation mark.* **3.** a token or indication; sign. **4.** a lasting effect; imprint. **5.** a distinctive or characteristic trait. **6.** a device or symbol serving to identify or indicate origin or ownership. **7.** TRADEMARK. **8.** a symbol used in rating a student's achievement; grade. **9.** an object or sign serving to indicate position. **10.** a recognized or required standard. **11.** a target; goal. **12.** distinction; note. **13.** an object of derision or abuse. **14.** the starting line in a race. —*v.t.* **15.** to be a distinguishing feature of. **16.** to put a mark or marks on. **17.** to rate or grade. **18.** to designate by or as if by marks. **19.** to make manifest. **20.** to give heed to: *Mark my words.* **21. mark down,** to reduce the price of. **22. ~ up,** to raise the price of. —*Idiom.* **23. make one's mark,** to achieve success. **24. mark time, a.** to function in an unproductive way. **b.** to move the feet alternately as if marching but without advancing. —**mark′er,** *n.*

mark² (märk), *n.* the basic monetary unit of Germany, which has a fixed value relative to the euro.

Mark (märk), *n.* **1.** an early Christian disciple, believed to be the author of the second Gospel. **2.** the second Gospel.

mark′down′ *n.* **1.** a reduction in price. **2.** the amount by which a price is reduced.

marked *adj.* striking; conspicuous. —**mark′ed•ly,** *adv.*

mar•ket (mär′kit), *n.* **1.** a place where buyers and sellers convene for trade. **2.** a store for the sale of food. **3.** a meeting of people for buying and selling. **4.** demand for a commodity. **5.** a particular group of potential buyers. **6.** a region in which goods and services are bought or used. —*v.i.* **7.** to buy provisions for the home. —*v.t.* **8.** to offer for sale. **9.** to sell. —**mar′ket•a•ble,** *adj.* —**mar′ket•er,** *n.*

mar′ket•place′ *n.* **1.** an open area in a town where a market is held. **2.** the world of business, trade, and economics.

marks′man *n.*, *pl.* **-men.** a person skilled in shooting at a target. —**marks′man•ship′,** *n.*

mark'up' *n.* **1.** an increase in price. **2.** the difference between cost and selling price. **3.** a set of instructions on a manuscript or tags in an electronic document to determine type styles, page makeup, etc.

mar•lin (mär'lin), *n., pl.* **-lins, -lin.** a large saltwater game fish with a spearlike upper jaw.

mar•ma•lade (mär'mə lād'), *n.* a jellylike preserve containing pieces of citrus fruit and rind.

mar•mo•set (mär'mə zet', -set'), *n.* a squirrel-sized South and Central American monkey.

mar•mot (mär'mət), *n.* a stocky burrowing rodent, as the woodchuck.

ma•roon¹ (mə rōōn'), *n.* a dark brownish red.

ma•roon² (mə rōōn'), *v.t.* **1.** to put ashore and abandon on a desolate island or coast. **2.** to isolate without aid or resources.

mar•quee (mär kē'), *n., pl.* **-quees. 1.** a projecting structure over an entrance, as to a theater. **2.** a large tent, as for an outdoor reception.

mar•quess (mär'kwis), *n.* **1.** a British nobleman ranking below a duke and above an earl. **2.** MARQUIS.

mar•que•try (mär'ki trē), *n.* inlaid work forming a picture or pattern, esp. in furniture.

mar•quis (mär'kwis, mär kē'), *n.* a European nobleman ranking below a duke and above a count.

mar•riage (mar'ij), *n.* **1.** the state, condition, or relationship of being married. **2.** the ceremony that formalizes marriage. **3.** an intimate association or union. —**mar'riage•a•ble,** *adj.*

mar•row (mar'ō), *n.* the soft, fatty, vascular tissue in the cavities of bones.

mar•ry (mar'ē), *v.,* **-ried, -ry•ing.** —*v.t.* **1.** to take as a husband or wife. **2.** to join in wedlock. **3.** to join or unite intimately. —*v.i.* **4.** to take a husband or wife.

Mars (märz), *n.* **1.** the ancient Roman god of war. **2.** the planet fourth in order from the sun.

marsh (märsh), *n.* a tract of waterlogged soil. —**marsh'y,** *adj.,* **-i•er, -i•est.**

mar•shal (mär'shəl), *n., v.,* **-shaled, -shal•ing** or (*esp. Brit.*) **-shalled, -shal•ling.** —*n.* **1.** an officer of a U.S. judicial district with duties similar to those of a sheriff. **2.** the chief of a police or fire department. **3.** an official who leads special ceremonies, as a parade. **4.** an army officer of the highest rank, as in France. —*v.t.* **5.** to arrange in proper or effective order. **6.** to usher or lead ceremoniously.

marsh' gas' *n.* a gaseous decomposition product of organic matter, consisting primarily of methane.

marsh'mal'low (-mel'ō, -mal'ō), *n.* a spongy confection made from gelatin, sugar, corn syrup, and flavoring.

marsh' mar'igold *n.* a yellow-flowered plant of the buttercup family.

mar•su•pi•al (mär sōō'pē əl), *n.* a mammal, as an opossum or kangaroo, bearing immature young that complete their development in a pouch on the mother's abdomen. [< NL *marsupiālis* pertaining to a pouch]

mart (märt), *n.* a trading center; market.

mar•ten (mär'tn), *n., pl.* **-tens, -ten. 1.** a carnivore of the weasel family with soft, glossy fur. **2.** the fur of a marten.

mar•tial (mär'shəl), *adj.* **1.** inclined to war. **2.** of or suitable for war or the armed forces. **3.** characteristic of or befitting a warrior.

mar'tial art' *n.* any of the traditional forms of East Asian self-defense or combat, as karate or judo.

mar'tial law' *n.* law imposed, as in occupied territory, by military forces.

mar•tin (mär'tn), *n.* any of various small swallows.

mar•ti•net (mär'tn et'), *n.* a strict disciplinarian.

mar•ti•ni (mär tē'nē), *n., pl.* **-nis.** a cocktail made with gin or vodka and dry vermouth.

mar•tyr (mär'tər), *n.* **1.** a person who willingly suffers death rather than renounce his or her religion. **2.** a person who suffers on behalf of a cause. **3.** a person who undergoes severe suffering. —*v.t.* **4.** to make a martyr of. **5.** to torment; torture. —**mar'tyr•dom,** *n.*

mar•vel (mär'vəl), *n., v.,* **-veled, -vel•ing** or (*esp. Brit.*) **-velled, -vel•ling.** —*n.* **1.** something that arouses wonder, admiration, or astonishment. **2.** a feeling of wonder. —*v.t.* **3.** to wonder at. —*v.i.* **4.** to be filled with wonder.

Marx•ism (märk'siz əm), *n.* the doctrine of a classless society developed by Karl Marx; communism. —**Marx'ist,** *n., adj.*

mar•zi•pan (mär'zə pan'), *n.* a confection of almond paste and sugar.

mas•car•a (ma skar'ə), *n., pl.* **-as.** a cosmetic for darkening the eyelashes.

mas•cot (mas'kot, -kət), *n.* an animal, person, or thing thought to bring good luck.

mas•cu•line (mas'kyə lin), *adj.* **1.** of or characteristic of a man. **2.** having qualities traditionally ascribed to men; manly. **3.** of or being the grammatical gender that has among its members most nouns referring to males. **4.** (of a woman) mannish. —*n.* **5.** the masculine gender. **6.** a word or form in the masculine gender. —**mas'cu•lin'i•ty,** *n.*

ma•ser (mā'zər), *n.* a device for producing or amplifying electromagnetic waves.

mash (mash), *v.t.* **1.** to reduce to a soft pulpy mass. **2.** to crush. —*n.* **3.** a soft pulpy mass. **4.** a mixture of boiled grain, bran, or meal, fed to livestock. **5.** crushed malt or meal mixed with hot water to form wort, used in making beer. —**mash'er,** *n.*

MASH (mash), *n.* mobile army surgical hospital.

mask (mask, mäsk), *n.* **1.** a covering for the face, worn esp. for concealment or protection. **2.** something that disguises or conceals. **3.** a likeness of a face cast in a mold. **4.** a molded or carved covering for the face of an actor in Greek drama. **5.** the face or head of an animal, as a fox. —*v.t.* **6.** to disguise, cover, conceal, or shield with or as if with a mask. —**masked,** *adj.* —**mask'er,** *n.*

mas•och•ism (mas'ə kiz'əm, maz'-), *n.* **1.** a disorder in which sexual gratification is derived from pain or degradation. **2.** the tendency to find pleasure in suffering. [after L. von Sacher-*Masoch* (1836-95), Austrian novelist] —**mas'och•ist,** *n.* —**mas'och•is'tic,** *adj.* —**mas'och•is'ti•cal•ly,** *adv.*

ma•son (mā'sən), *n.* **1.** a person whose trade is building with firm units, as stones or bricks. **2.** (*cap.*) FREEMASON.

mas•quer•ade (mas'kə rād'), *n., v.,* **-ad•ed, -ad•ing.** —*n.* **1. a.** a festive gathering of people wearing masks and costumes. **b.** a costume worn at such a gathering. **2.** false show; pretense. —*v.i.* **3.** to represent oneself falsely. **4.** to take part in a masquerade. —**mas'quer•ad'er,** *n.*

mass¹ (mas), *n.* **1.** a body of coherent matter, usu. of indefinite shape. **2.** aggregate; whole. **3.** a considerable number or quantity. **4.** bulk; massiveness. **5.** the greater part. **6.** *Physics.* the quantity of matter as determined from its weight or from Newton's second law of motion. **7. the masses,** the ordinary or common people as a whole. —*adj.* **8.** of or affecting the masses. **9.** done on a large scale: *mass destruction.* —*v.i., v.t.* **10.** to form or assemble in a mass.

mass² (mas), *n.* (*often cap.*) the liturgy or celebration of the Eucharist.

Mass. Massachusetts.

mas•sa•cre (mas'ə kər), *n., v.,* **-cred, -cring.** —*n.* **1.** the wanton killing of a large number of human beings. **2.** a general slaughter. —*v.t.* **3.** to kill in a massacre; slaughter.

mas•sage (mə säzh', -säj'), *n., v.,* **-saged, -sag•ing.** —*n.* **1.** manipulation of the body, esp. by rubbing or kneading, to stimulate circulation or relieve tension. —*v.t.* **2.** to treat by massage.

mas•sive (mas'iv), *adj.* **1.** consisting of or forming a large mass. **2.** imposingly large or prominent. **3.** large in scale, amount, or degree. —**mas'sive•ly,** *adv.* —**mas'sive•ness,** *n.*

mass' me'dia *n.pl.* the means of communication, as television and newspapers, that reach great numbers of people.

mass' noun' *n.* a noun, as *water* or *happiness,* that refers to an indefinitely divisible substance or an abstract notion.

mass′-produce′ *v.t.*, **-duced, -duc·ing.** to produce (goods) in large quantities, esp. by machine. —**mass′ produc′tion,** *n.*

mast (mast, mäst), *n.* **1.** a spar rising above the upper portions of a ship to hold sails, spars, and rigging. **2.** an upright pole.

mas·tec·to·my (ma stek′tə mē), *n., pl.* **-mies.** surgical removal of a breast.

mas·ter (mas′tər, mä′stər), *n.* **1.** a person with the ability or power to control. **2.** a person highly skilled in an art, craft, etc. **3.** a male teacher. **4.** a person who commands a merchant ship. **5.** a person with a master's degree. **6.** a boy or young man (used as a term of address). **7.** an original, as of a document, from which copies can be made. —*adj.* **8.** of or being a master. —*v.t.* **9.** to make oneself an expert in. **10.** to conquer; overcome.

mas·ter·ful *adj.* **1.** having or showing the qualities of a master. **2.** dominating; imperious. —**mas′ter·ful·ly,** *adv.*

mas′ter·ly *adj.* befitting a master.

mas·ter·mind′ *v.t.* **1.** to plan and direct skillfully. —*n.* **2.** a person who originates or oversees a project.

mas′ter of cer′emonies *n.* a person who conducts events, as at a formal occasion or entertainment.

mas′ter·piece′ *n.* **1.** a person's greatest piece of work, as in an art. **2.** a fine example of skill or excellence.

mas′ter's degree′ *n.* an academic degree awarded to a student who has completed at least one year of graduate study.

mas′ter ser′geant *n.* a noncommissioned officer ranking in the U.S. Army above a sergeant first class, in the Air Force above a technical sergeant, and in the Marine Corps above a gunnery sergeant.

mas′ter·stroke′ *n.* an extremely skillful action.

mas·ter·y *n., pl.* **-ies. 1.** command; grasp. **2.** superiority; dominance. **3.** expert skill or knowledge.

mas·ti·cate (mas′ti kāt′), *v.t., v.i.,* **-cat·ed, -cat·ing.** to chew. —**mas′ti·ca′tion,** *n.*

mas·tiff (mas′tif, mä′stif), *n.* a large, powerful shorthaired dog.

mas·to·don (mas′tə don′), *n.* any of numerous extinct elephantlike mammals.

mas·toid (mas′toid), *n.* a bony prominence on the base of the skull behind the ear.

mas·tur·ba·tion (mas′tər bā′shən), *n.* stimulation of the genitals, esp. to orgasm. —**mas′tur·bate′,** *v.i., v.t.,* **-bat·ed, -bat·ing.**

mat[1] (mat), *n., v.,* **mat·ted, mat·ting.** —*n.* **1.** a piece of fabric, as of plaited fiber, used esp. as a floor covering. **2.** a floor pad used to protect wrestlers and gymnasts. **3.** a thick tangled mass, as of hair or weeds. —*v.t., v.i* **4.** to form into a mat.

mat[2] (mat), *n., v.,* **mat·ted, mat·ting.** —*n.* **1.** material serving as a border for a picture. —*v.t.* **2.** to provide with a mat.

mat[3] (mat), *adj., n.* MATTE.

mat·a·dor (mat′ə dôr′), *n.* the bullfighter who traditionally kills the bull.

match[1] (mach), *n.* **1.** a slender piece of flammable material tipped with a chemical substance that ignites by friction.

match[2] (mach), *n.* **1.** a person or thing that equals or resembles another. **2.** a corresponding or suitably associated pair. **3.** a game or contest with two or more contestants or teams. **4.** a person considered as a marriage partner: *a good match.* **5.** a marriage. —*v.t.* **6.** to equal. **7.** to be the match or counterpart of. **8.** to cause to correspond. **9.** to fit together. **10.** to place in opposition or conflict. **11.** to unite in marriage. —*v.i.* **12.** to be equal or suitable. **13.** to correspond.

match′less *adj.* having no equal.

match′mak′er *n.* a person who arranges marriages.

mate (māt), *n., v.,* **mat·ed, mat·ing.** —*n.* **1.** a husband or wife. **2.** one of a pair of mated animals. **3.** one of a pair. **4.** an associate or companion. **5.** FIRST MATE. —*v.t., v.i.* **6.** to join as mates. **7.** to bring or come together for breeding.

ma·té or **-te** (mä′tā, mat′ā, mä tā′), *n., pl.* **-tés** or **-tes.** a tealike South American beverage.

ma·te·ri·al (mə tēr′ē əl), *n.* **1.** the substance of which something is made or composed. **2.** something that can be further developed. **3.** a constituent element. **4.** a textile. **5.** Often, **-als.** apparatus needed to make or do something: *writing materials.* —*adj.* **6.** of or consisting of matter: *the material world.* **7.** physical rather than spiritual or intellectual: *material comforts.* **8.** of substantial import; significant. **9.** pertinent; essential. —**ma·te′ri·al·ly,** *adv.*

ma·te′ri·al·ism *n.* **1.** preoccupation with material as opposed to spiritual or intellectual values. **2.** the philosophical theory that regards matter as constituting the universe, and all phenomena, including those of mind, as due to material agencies. —**ma·te′ri·a·list,** *n., adj.* —**ma·te′ri·al·is′tic,** *adj.*

ma·te′ri·al·ize′ *v.,* **-ized, -iz·ing.** —*v.i.* **1.** to come into actual existence. **2.** to appear, esp. unexpectedly. **3.** to assume material form. —*v.t.* **4.** to give material form to. —**ma·te′ri·al·i·za′tion,** *n.*

ma·té·ri·el or **-te·ri·el** (mə tēr′ē el′), *n.* the aggregate of equipment and supplies used by an organization, as the military.

ma·ter·ni·ty (mə tûr′ni tē), *n.* **1.** the state of being a mother; motherhood. —*adj.* **2.** applicable immediately before, during, and just after childbirth: *maternity leave.* **3.** designed for wear by pregnant women.

math·e·mat·ics (math′ə mat′iks), *n.* the systematic treatment of magnitude, relationships between figures and forms, and relations between quantities expressed symbolically. —**math′e·mat′i·cal,** *adj.* —**math′e·mat′i·cal·ly,** *adv.* —**math′e·ma·ti′cian** (-mə tish′ən), *n.*

mat·i·née or **-nee** (mat′n ā′), *n., pl.* **-nées** or **nees.** a dramatic or musical performance held in the afternoon. [< F: morning]

mat·ins (mat′nz), *n.* **1.** (*often cap.*) (*used with a sing. or pl. v.*) prayers read at midnight or daybreak. **2.** the service of morning prayer in Anglican churches.

ma·tri·arch (mā′trē ärk′), *n.* the female head of a family or tribe. —**ma′tri·ar′chal,** *adj.* —**ma′tri·ar′chy,** *n., pl.* **-chies.**

mat·ri·cide (ma′tri sīd′, mā′-), *n.* **1.** the act of killing one's mother. **2.** a person who kills his or her mother. —**mat′ri·cid′al,** *adj.*

ma·tric·u·late (mə trik′yə lāt′), *v.t., v.i.,* **-lat·ed, -lat·ing.** to enroll as a student in a college or university. —**ma·tric′u·la′tion,** *n.*

mat·ri·mo·ny (ma′trə mō′nē), *n., pl.* **-nies. 1.** the state of being married. **2.** the ceremony of marriage. —**mat′ri·mo′ni·al,** *adj.*

ma·trix (mā′triks, ma′-), *n., pl.* **-tri·ces** (-tri sēz′), **-trix·es.** **1.** a place or point within which something else originates. **2.** a mold for casting typefaces.

ma·tron (mā′trən), *n.* **1.** a married woman, esp. one who is mature and dignified. **2.** a woman officer, as in a prison for women. —**ma′tron·ly,** *adj.*

matte or **matt** (mat), *adj.* **1.** having a dull or lusterless surface. —*n.* **2.** a dull surface or finish.

mat·ter (mat′ər), *n.* **1.** the substance of which a physical object consists or is composed. **2.** something that occupies space. **3.** a situation, subject, or affair. **4.** an approximate amount or extent: *a matter of 10 miles.* **5.** something written or printed. **6.** things sent by mail. **7.** a substance, esp. pus, discharged by a living body. —*v.i.* **8.** to be of importance; signify. —*Idiom.* **9. as a matter of fact,** in reality; actually. **10. no matter,** regardless of. **11. to be the matter,** to be amiss or awry: *What's the matter with you?*

mat′ter-of-fact′ *adj.* adhering strictly to fact. —**mat′ter-of-fact′ly,** *adv.* —**mat′ter-of-fact′ness,** *n.*

mat′ting *n.* **1.** material for mats. **2.** mats collectively.

mat·tock (mat′ək), *n.* a digging tool shaped like a pickax.

mat·tress (ma′tris), *n.* a cloth case filled with

straw, cotton, foam rubber, etc., used as or on a bed.

ma•ture (mə tŏŏr′, -tyŏŏr′, -chŏŏr′, -chûr′), *adj.*, **-tur•er, -tur•est,** *v.,* **-tured, -tur•ing.** —*adj.* **1.** fully developed. **2.** complete in natural growth or development. **3.** fully aged: *mature wine.* **4.** payable; due: *a mature bond.* —*v.t.,* *v.i.* **5.** to make or become mature. —**mat•u•ra•tion** (mach′ə rā′shən), *n.* —**ma•ture′ly,** *adv.* —**ma•tu′ri•ty,** *n.*

mat•zo (mät′sə), *n.,* *pl.* **-zos** (-səz), **-zoth, -zot** (-sōt, -sōs). unleavened bread eaten by Jews during Passover.

maud•lin (môd′lin), *adj.* embarrassingly sentimental.

maul (môl), *n.* **1.** a heavy hammer used esp. for driving stakes or wedges. —*v.t.* **2.** to handle roughly. **3.** to injure by rough treatment. —**maul′er,** *n.*

maun•der (môn′dər), *v.i.* **1.** to talk ramblingly or unintelligibly. **2.** to wander.

Mau•ri•ta•ni•a (môr′i tā′nē ə), *n.* a republic in NW Africa. —**Mau′ri•ta′ni•an,** *adj.,* *n.*

Mau•ri•tius (mô rish′əs), *n.* an island republic in the Indian Ocean, E of Madagascar. —**Mau•ri′tian,** *adj.,* *n.*

mau•so•le•um (mô′sə lē′əm, -zə-), *n.,* *pl.* **-le•ums, -le•a** (-lē′ə). a large and stately tomb.

mauve (mōv, môv), *n.* a pale bluish purple.

ma•ven or **-vin** (mā′vən), *n.* an expert; connoisseur. [< Yiddish < Heb]

mav•er•ick (mav′ər ik), *n.* **1.** an unbranded animal. **2.** a person who thinks and acts independently of others.

maw (mô), *n.* the mouth, throat, or stomach, esp. of a voracious carnivore.

mawk•ish (mô′kish), *adj.* sentimental; maudlin. —**mawk′ish•ly,** *adv.*

max•i (mak′sē), *n.,* *pl.* **-is.** an ankle-length coat or skirt.

max•im (mak′sim), *n.* a pithy saying; aphorism.

max•i•mum (mak′sə məm), *n.,* *pl.* **-mums, -ma** (-mə), *adj.* —*n.* **1.** the highest amount, value, or degree. **2.** an upper limit allowed by law or regulation. —*adj.* **3.** of or being a maximum.

may (mā), *auxiliary v., pres.* **may;** *past* **might;** *imperative, infinitive, and participles lacking.* **1.** (used to express possibility): *It may rain.* **2.** (used to express opportunity or permission): *You may enter.* **3.** (used to express contingency, concession, or purpose): *I may be old, but I'm energetic.* **4.** (used to express wish or prayer): *Long may you live!*

May (mā), *n.* the fifth month of the year, having 31 days.

may•be *adv.* perhaps; possibly.

May′ Day′ *n.* the first day of May, variously celebrated with festivities and observances.

may′flow′er *n.* any of various plants, as the arbutus, that blossom in May.

may′fly′ *n.,* *pl.* **-flies.** an insect with large transparent forewings that lives only briefly as an adult.

may•hem (mā′hem, -əm), *n.* the crime of willfully crippling or mutilating another.

may•on•naise (mā′ə nāz′), *n.* a thick dressing of egg yolks, vinegar or lemon juice, oil, and seasonings.

may•or (mā′ər), *n.* the chief executive official of a municipality. —**may′or•al,** *adj.* —**may′or•al•ty,** *n., pl.* **-ties.**

maze (māz), *n.* **1.** a confusing network of paths or passages; labyrinth. **2.** an intricate system that daunts or perplexes.

MD 1. Maryland. **2.** Doctor of Medicine. [< NL *Medicīnae Doctor*] **3.** Middle Dutch.

Md *Chem. Symbol.* mendelevium.

Md. Maryland.

me (mē), *pron.* the objective case of I.

ME 1. Maine. **2.** Middle English.

Me. Maine.

mead¹ (mēd), *n.* an alcoholic drink of fermented honey and water.

mead² (mēd), *n. Archaic.* a meadow.

mead•ow (med′ō), *n.* a tract of low vegetation dominated by grasses.

mead′ow•lark′ *n.* a North American songbird with a brown-streaked back and a yellow breast.

mea•ger (mē′gər), *adj.* **1.** deficient in quantity or quality; scanty. **2.** lean; thin. Also, *esp. Brit.,* **mea′gre.** —**mea′ger•ly,** *adv.* —**mea′ger•ness,** *n.*

meal¹ (mēl), *n.* **1.** the food served and eaten at one time. **2.** the time or an occasion for eating a meal.

meal² (mēl), *n.* **1.** coarse powder ground from the edible seeds of a grain. **2.** a ground or powdery substance. —**meal′y,** *adj.,* **-i•er, -i•est.**

meal′y-mouthed′ *adj.* avoiding the use of plain or honest language.

mean¹ (mēn), *v.,* **meant** (ment), **mean•ing.** —*v.t.* **1.** to have in mind as a purpose; intend. **2.** to intend to express or indicate: *What do you mean by "perfect"?* **3.** to have as a signification; denote. **4.** to bring as a result. **5.** to have the value or importance of: *Money means everything to them.* —*v.i.* **6.** to have specified intentions: *We meant well.*

mean² (mēn), *adj.,* **-er, -est. 1.** uncharitable; malicious. **2.** small-minded; ignoble. **3.** stingy; miserly. **4.** inferior in quality or character. **5.** bad-tempered. **6.** excellent; topnotch: *plays a mean game of tennis.* —**mean′ly,** *adv.* —**mean′ness,** *n.*

mean³ (mēn), *n.* **1. means,** (*used with a sing. or pl. v.*) an agency or method used to attain an end. **2. means,** resources, esp. money; wealth. **3.** something midway between two extremes. **4.** an average, esp. the arithmetic mean. —*adj.* **5.** occupying a middle position or intermediate place. —*Idiom.* **6. by all means,** certainly. **7. by means of,** by the agency of; through. **8. by no means,** not at all.

me•an•der (mē an′dər), *v.i.* **1.** to proceed by a winding course. **2.** to wander aimlessly. —*n.* **3.** a winding path or course.

mean′ing *n.* **1.** what is intended to be expressed or indicated; import. **2.** the end, purpose, or significance of something. —**mean′ing•ful,** *adj.* —**mean′ing•less,** *adj.*

mean′time′ *n.* **1.** the intervening time. —*adv.* **2.** MEANWHILE.

mean′while′ *n.* **1.** MEANTIME. —*adv.* **2.** in the intervening time.

mea•sles (mē′zəlz), *n.* (*used with a sing. or pl. v.*) an acute infectious disease characterized by small red spots, fever, and coldlike symptoms.

mea•sly (mē′zlē), *adj.,* **-sli•er, -sli•est.** contemptibly small: *a measly salary.*

meas•ure (mezh′ər), *n.,* *v.,* **-ured, -ur•ing.** —*n.* **1.** a unit of measurement. **2.** a system of measurement. **3.** an instrument for measuring. **4.** the extent, dimensions, quantity, or capacity of something ascertained esp. by comparison with a standard. **5.** the act or process of measuring; measurement. **6.** a standard of comparison; criterion. **7.** a moderate amount. **8.** reasonable bounds or limits: *spending without measure.* **9.** a legislative bill or enactment. **10.** Usu., **-ures.** means to an end. **11.** rhythmical movement or structure, as in poetry. **12.** the music between two bar lines; bar. —*v.t.* **13.** to ascertain the extent, dimensions, quantity, or capacity of. **14.** to mark off by way of measurement. **15.** to judge or appraise by comparison. **16.** to serve as the measure of. —*v.i.* **17.** to take measurements. **18.** to be of a specified measure. **19. measure up, a.** to attain equality. **b.** to have the right qualifications. —*Idiom.* **20. for good measure,** as an extra. —**meas′ur•a•ble,** *adj.* —**meas′ur•a•bly,** *adv.*

meas′ured *adj.* careful, deliberate.

meas′ure•ment *n.* **1.** the act or process of measuring. **2.** an extent, dimension, or capacity ascertained by measuring.

meat (mēt), *n.* **1.** the flesh of animals used for food. **2.** the edible part of something, as a nut. **3.** the essential point or part. **4.** solid food: *meat and drink.* —**meat′y,** *adj.,* **-i•er, -i•est.**

Mec•ca (mek′ə), *n.,* *pl.* **-cas. 1.** a city in W Saudi Arabia: birthplace of Muhammad; spiritual center of Islam. 550,000. **2.** (*often l.c.*) a place that attracts many people.

me•chan•ic (mə kan′ik), *n.* **1.** a person who repairs machinery. **2.** a worker skilled in the use of tools and equipment.

me·chan′i·cal *adj.* **1.** of machinery or tools. **2.** operated, caused, or produced by machinery. **3.** lacking spontaneity; routine. **4.** of the science of mechanics. —**me··chan′i·cal·ly,** *adv.*

me··chan′ics *n.* **1.** (*used with a sing. v.*) the branch of physics that deals with the action of forces on bodies and with motion. **2.** (*used with a sing. v.*) the theoretical and practical application of mechanics, as to machinery. **3.** (*used with a pl. v.*) the technical aspect of something: *knew little about the mechanics of managing an orchestra.*

mech··an·ism (mek′ə niz′əm), *n.* **1.** a system of parts performing a function. **2.** an agency or means by which a purpose is accomplished. **3.** a mechanical appliance; machine. **4.** the structure or arrangement of parts of a device, as a machine. —**mech′a·nis′tic** (-nis′tik), *adj.*

mech′a·nize *v.t.,* **-nized, -niz·ing. 1.** to make mechanical. **2.** to introduce machinery into, esp. in order to replace manual labor. **3.** to equip with armored vehicles, as tanks. —**mech′a·ni·za′tion,** *n.*

med·al (med′l), *n.* **1.** a flat piece of metal issued as a token of commemoration or as an award, as for merit. **2.** a piece of metal bearing a religious image.

med′al·ist *n.* **1.** a person who has been awarded a medal. **2.** a designer, engraver, or maker of medals. Also, *esp. Brit.,* **med′al·list.**

me··dal·lion (mə dal′yən), *n.* **1.** a large medal. **2.** something, as an ornament, resembling a medal.

med·dle (med′l), *v.i.,* **-dled, -dling.** to involve oneself in a matter without right or invitation; interfere. —**med′dler,** *n.* —**med′dle·some,** *adj.*

me··di·a (mē′dē ə), *n.* **1.** a pl. of MEDIUM. **2.** (*usu. with a pl. v.*) the means of communication, as radio, television, and newspapers, with wide reach and influence.

me··di·an (mē′dē ən), *adj.* **1.** pertaining to a plane that divides something into two equal parts. **2.** situated in the middle. —*n.* **3.** the middle number in a sequence, or the average of the middle two numbers when the sequence has an even number of numbers. **4.** a straight line from a vertex of a triangle to the midpoint of the opposite side. **5.** Also called **me′dian strip′.** a strip in the middle of a highway that separates opposing lanes of traffic.

me··di·ate (*v.* mē′dē āt′; *adj.* -it), *v.,* **-at·ed, -at·ing,** *adj.* **-it. 1.** to settle (a dispute) as an intermediary. —*v.i.* **2.** to act as an intermediary. —*adj.* **3.** involving an intermediate agency; not direct. —**me′di·a′tion,** *n.* —**me′di·a′tor,** *n.*

med·ic (med′ik), *n.* **1.** a member of the medical corps trained to give first aid in battle. **2.** a doctor or intern.

Med·i·caid (med′i kād′), *n.* (*sometimes l.c.*) a federal and state program of medical insurance for persons with very low incomes.

med′i·cal *adj.* of the science or practice of medicine. —**med′i·cal·ly,** *adv.*

me··dic·a·ment (mə dik′ə mənt, med′i kə-), *n.* a healing substance; medicine.

Med·i·care (med′i kâr′), *n.* (*sometimes l.c.*) a U.S. government program of medical insurance for aged or disabled persons.

med′i·cate′ *v.t.,* **-cat·ed, -cat·ing.** to treat with medicine. —**med′i·ca′tion,** *n.*

me··dic·i·nal (mə dis′ə nl), *adj.* of or having the properties of a medicine. —**me·dic′i·nal·ly,** *adv.*

med··i·cine (med′ə sin), *n.* **1.** a substance used in treating disease or illness. **2.** the art or science of preserving health and treating disease.

med′i·cine man′ *n.* a person believed to possess magical powers, esp. among North American Indians.

me··di·e·val or **-ae·val** (mē′dē ē′vəl, mid ē′-), *adj.* of, like, or characteristic of the Middle Ages. —**me′di·e′val·ist,** *n.*

me′di·e·val·ism *n.* a characteristic of the Middle Ages.

me′di·e′val·ist *n.* an expert in medieval history, art, etc.

me··di·o·cre (mē′dē ō′kər), *adj.* of only ordinary or moderate quality; barely adequate. —**me′di·oc′-ri·ty** (-ok′ri tē), *n.*

med·i·tate (med′i tāt′), *v.,* **-tat·ed, -tat·ing.** —*v.i.* **1.** to engage in contemplation; reflect. —*v.t.* **2.** to plan; intend. —**med′i·ta′tion,** *n.* —**med′i·ta′-tive,** *adj.*

Med·i·ter·ra·ne·an (med′i tə rā′nē ən), *n.* **1.** Also called **Med′iterra′nean Sea′.** a sea surrounded by Africa, Europe, and Asia. —*adj.* **2.** of the Mediterranean Sea and its islands and countries.

me··di·um (mē′dē əm), *n.,* pl. **-di·a** (-dē ə) except for 7, **-di·ums,** *adj.* —*n.* **1.** a middle state or condition. **2.** something intermediate. **3.** an intervening or surrounding substance, as air. **4.** surrounding conditions or influences; environment. **5.** a means or instrument by which something is conveyed or accomplished. **6.** a means or channel of communication, information, or entertainment, as television. **7.** a person through whom the spirits of the dead are alleged to be able to contact the living. **8.** the material or technique with which an artist works. —*adj.* **9.** halfway between extremes in degree, quantity, position, or quality.

med·ley (med′lē), *n.,* pl. **-leys. 1.** a heterogeneous mixture; jumble. **2.** a piece of music combining passages from various sources.

meek (mēk), *adj.,* **-er, -est. 1.** humbly patient or docile. **2.** overly submissive or compliant. —**meek′ly,** *adv.* —**meek′ness,** *n.*

meer·schaum (mēr′shəm, -shôm), *n.* **1.** a white, claylike mineral used esp. for pipes. **2.** a tobacco pipe made of meerschaum. [< G, = *Meer* sea + *Schaum* foam]

meet[1] (mēt), *v.,* **met, meet·ing,** *n.* —*v.t.* **1.** to come upon; encounter. **2.** to be introduced to. **3.** to be present at the arrival of. **4.** to come to the apprehension of: *A strange sight met my eyes.* **5.** to come into physical contact with. **6.** to oppose; fight. **7.** to deal effectively with: *met the challenge.* **8.** to comply with: *to meet a deadline.* —*v.i.* **9.** to come together. **10.** to assemble for action or conference. **11.** to come into contact or form a junction. **12. meet with,** to encounter; experience. —*n.* **13.** an assembly, esp. for sports competition.

meet[2] (mēt), *adj.* suitable; fitting.

meet′ing *n.* **1.** the act of coming together. **2.** an assembly of persons. **3.** a place or point of contact.

mega- a combining form meaning: large or great (*megalopolis*); 1,000,000 times a given unit of measure (*megaton*).

meg′a·hertz′ *n.,* pl. **-hertz, -hertz·es.** a unit of frequency equal to one million cycles per second.

meg·a·lo·ma·ni·a (meg′ə lō mā′nē ə), *n.* a highly exaggerated or delusional concept of one's own importance. —**meg′a·lo·ma′ni·ac′,** *n.*

meg′a·phone′ *n.* a cone-shaped device for amplifying the voice.

meg′a·ton′ *n.* an explosive force equal to that of one million tons of TNT.

mel·a·mine (mel′ə mēn′), *n.* a crystalline solid used esp. in manufacturing resins.

mel·an·cho·li·a (mel′ən kō′lē ə), *n.* a severe form of depression characterized typically by weight loss and insomnia.

mel′an·chol·y (-kol′ē), *n.,* pl. **-ies. 1.** a gloomy state of mind; dejection. —*adj.* **2.** affected with melancholy; depressed. **3.** causing melancholy.

mé··lange (mā länzh′, -länj′), *n.* a mixture; medley.

mel·a·nin (mel′ə nin), *n.* a pigment that accounts for the dark color of skin, hair, fur, scales, and feathers.

mel′a·no′ma (-nō′mə), *n.,* pl. **-mas, -ma·ta** (-mə·tə). a darkly pigmented malignant skin tumor.

meld (meld), *v.t., v.i.* **1.** to announce and display (a combination of playing cards) for a score. —*n.* **2.** a combination of cards to be melded.

me··lee or **mê·lée** (mā′lā), *n.,* pl. **-lees** or **lées. 1.** a confused hand-to-hand fight. **2.** a state of tumultuous confusion.

mel·io·rate (mēl′yə rāt′), *v.t., v.i.,* **-rat·ed, -rat·ing.** AMELIORATE. —**mel′io·ra′tion,** *n.* —**mel′io·ra′-tive** (-yə rā′tiv, -yər ə tiv), *adj.*

mel•lif•lu•ous (mə lif′lo͞o əs), *adj.* sweetly or smoothly flowing. —**mel•lif′lu•ous•ly,** *adv.*
mel•low (mel′ō), *adj.,* **-er, -est,** *v.* —*adj.* **1.** sweet and full-flavored from ripeness, as fruit. **2.** soft and rich, as sound or colors. **3.** made gentle by age or maturity. **4.** pleasantly intoxicated. **5.** free from tension or discord. —*v.t., v.i.* **6.** to make or become mellow.
me•lo′de•on (mə lō′dē ən) *n.* a reed organ.
me•lo•di•ous (mə lō′dē əs), *adj.* **1.** of or characterized by melody. **2.** sweet-sounding; musical. —**me•lo′di•ous•ly,** *adv.* —**me•lo′di•ous•ness,** *n.*
mel•o•dra•ma (mel′ə drä′mə, -dram′ə), *n., pl.* **-mas.** a dramatic form that exaggerates emotion and emphasizes plot or action at the expense of characterization. —**mel′o•dra•mat′ic,** *adj.*
mel•o•dy (mel′ə dē), *n., pl.* **-dies. 1.** musical sounds in agreeable succession. **2.** a rhythmical succession of musical tones. —**me•lod•ic** (mə-lod′ik), *adj.* —**me•lod′i•cal•ly,** *adv.*
mel•on (mel′ən), *n.* the fruit of any of various plants of the gourd family, as the muskmelon or watermelon.
melt (melt), *v.i., v.t.* **1.** to change to a liquid state by heat. **2.** to dissolve. **3.** to diminish to nothing; dissipate. **4.** to pass or cause to pass gradually; blend. **5.** to soften in feeling.
melt′down′ *n.* the melting of a nuclear-reactor core due to inadequate cooling of the fuel elements.
melt′ing pot′ *n.* a locality in which a blending of races, peoples, or cultures takes place.
mem•ber (mem′bər), *n.* **1.** an individual belonging to or forming part of a group. **2.** a part of an animal or plant body. **3.** a constituent part of a structural or composite whole. —**mem′ber•ship′,** *n.*
mem•brane (mem′brān), *n.* a thin, pliable sheet or layer of animal or vegetable tissue. —**mem′bra•nous** (-brə nəs), *adj.*
me•men•to (mə men′tō), *n., pl.* **-tos, -toes.** something that serves as a reminder or warning.
mem•oir (mem′wär, -wôr), *n.* **1.** a record of events based on the writer's personal observation. **2.** Usu., **-oirs. a.** an autobiography. **b.** the published proceedings of a learned society.
mem′o•ra•bil′i•a (-ər ə bil′ē ə, -bil′yə), *n.pl.* **1.** mementos; souvenirs. **2.** matters or events worth remembering.
mem′o•ra•ble *adj.* worth remembering; notable. —**mem′o•ra•bly,** *adv.*
mem•o•ran•dum (mem′ə ran′dəm), *n., pl.* **-dums, -da** (-də). **1.** a short note written as a reminder. **2.** a written message, esp. one circulated within a company.
me•mo•ri•al (mə môr′ē əl), *n.* **1.** something, as a monument, designed to preserve the memory of a person or event. **2.** a statement of facts presented to a governing body, often with a petition. —*adj.* **3.** serving to keep a memory alive. —**me•mo′ri•al•ize′,** *v.t.,* **-ized, -iz•ing.**
mem•o•rize (mem′ə rīz′), *v.t., v.i.,* **-rized, -riz•ing.** to commit to memory. —**mem′o•ri•za′tion,** *n.*
mem′o•ry *n., pl.* **-ries. 1.** the faculty or process of retaining or recalling past experiences. **2.** the act or fact of remembering. **3.** the length of time over which recollection extends. **4.** the state or fact of being remembered. **5.** a person or thing remembered. **6.** commemorative remembrance. **7. a.** the capacity of a computer to store information subject to recall. **b.** the components of the computer in which such information is stored.
men•ace (men′is), *n., v.,* **-aced, -ac•ing.** —*n.* **1.** something that threatens. **2.** an annoying person. —*v.t., v.i.* **3.** to threaten or be threatening. —**men′ac•ing•ly,** *adv.*
me•nag•er•ie (mə naj′ə rē, -nazh′-), *n., pl.* **-ies.** a collection of wild or unusual animals, esp. for exhibition.
mend (mend), *v.t.* **1.** to make whole, sound, or usable by repairing. **2.** to set right; correct. —*v.i.* **3.** to progress toward recovery; heal. —*n.* **4.** the act of mending. **5.** a mended place. —***Idiom.*** **6. on the mend,** improving, esp. in health. —**mend′er,** *n.*
men•da•cious (men dā′shəs), *adj.* telling lies, esp. habitually; untruthful. —**men•da′cious•ly,** *adv.* —**men•dac′i•ty** (-das′i tē), *n.*
men•de•le•vi•um (men′dl ē′vē əm), *n.* a synthetic, radioactive metallic element. *Symbol:* Md, Mv; *at. no.:* 101.
men•di•cant (men′di kənt), *adj.* **1.** asking for or living on alms; begging. —*n.* **2.** a beggar. **3.** a mendicant friar. —**men′di•can•cy,** *n.*
me•ni•al (mē′nē əl), *adj.* **1.** servile; degrading. **2.** of or suitable for servants. —*n.* **3.** a domestic servant. —**me′ni•al•ly,** *adv.*
me•nin•ges (mi nin′jēz), *n.pl., sing.* **me•ninx** (mē′ningks). the three membranes covering the brain and spinal cord. —**me•nin′ge•al** (-jē əl), *adj.*
men•in•gi•tis (men′in jī′tis), *n.* inflammation of the meninges.
men•o•pause (men′ə pôz′), *n.* the period of natural cessation of menstruation. —**men′o•pau′sal,** *adj.*
me•nor•ah (mə nôr′ə), *n.* a candelabrum used during the Jewish festival of Hanukkah.
men•stru•a•tion (men′stro͞o ā′shən, -strā′-), *n.* the discharge of blood and tissue debris from the uterus, occurring approximately monthly in non-pregnant female primates. —**men′stru•al,** *adj.* —**men′stru•ate′,** *v.i.,* **-at•ed, -at•ing.**
men•sur•a•ble (men′shər ə bəl, -sər ə bəl) *adj.* measurable.
mens′wear′ *n.* clothing for men.
men•tal (men′tl), *adj.* **1.** of, performed by, or existing in the mind. **2.** of or affected by a disorder of the mind. **3.** for persons with a psychiatric disorder. —**men•tal•ly,** *adv.*
men•tal′i•ty *n., pl.* **-ties. 1.** mental capacity or endowment. **2.** mental inclination; outlook.
men•thol (men′thôl, -thol), *n.* a colorless alcohol obtained from peppermint oil. —**men′tho•lat′ed** (-thə lā′tid), *adj.*
men•tion (men′shən), *v.t.* **1.** to refer briefly to. **2.** to cite formally for merit or achievement. —*n.* **3.** a brief reference. **4.** a formal citation for merit or achievement. —**men′tion•a•ble,** *adj.*
men•tor (men′tôr, -tər), *n.* a wise and trusted counselor or teacher.
men•u (men′yo͞o, mā′nyo͞o), *n., pl.* **-us. 1.** a list of the dishes that can or will be served at a meal. **2.** the dishes served. **3.** a list of options available to a user, as displayed on a computer screen.
me•ow (mē ou′, myou), *n.* **1.** the characteristic sound a cat makes. —*v.i.* **2.** to make a meow.
mer•can•tile (mûr′kən tēl′, -tīl′, -til), *adj.* of or pertaining to merchants or trade.
mer′ce•nar′y (-sə ner′ē), *adj., n., pl.* **-nar•ies.** —*adj.* **1.** working or acting merely for money or material reward. —*n.* **2.** a professional soldier hired to serve in a foreign army.
mer•chan•dise (*n.* mûr′chən dīz′, -dīs′; *v.* -dīz′), *n., v.,* **-dised, -dis•ing.** —*n.* **1.** goods bought and sold; commodities. —*v.i.* **2.** to carry on trade. —*v.t.* **3.** to buy and sell. **4.** to promote the sale of. —**mer′chan•dis′er,** *n.*
mer′chant (-chənt), *n.* **1.** a person whose business is buying and selling goods for profit. **2.** a storekeeper; retailer.
mer′chant marine′ *n.* **1.** the ships of a nation that are engaged in commerce. **2.** the officers and crews of such ships.
mer•cu•ri•al (mər kyo͝or′ē əl), *adj.* **1.** changeable and erratic. **2.** of, containing, or caused by the metal mercury.
mer•cu•ry (mûr′kyə rē), *n., pl.* **-ries. 1.** a heavy, silver-white metallic element used in barometers, thermometers, and pharmaceuticals. *Symbol:* Hg; *at. wt.:* 200.59; *at. no.:* 80. **2.** (*cap.*) the Roman god of commerce and science and messenger to the other gods. **3.** (*cap.*) the planet nearest the sun and the smallest in the solar system.
mer•cy (mûr′sē), *n., pl.* **-cies. 1.** compassion shown toward an offender or an enemy. **2.** the disposition to be compassionate or forbearing. **3.** a cause for gratitude; blessing: *It was a mercy they weren't hurt.* —**mer′ci•ful,** *adj.* —**mer′ci•ful•ly,** *adv.* —**mer′ci•less,** *adj.* —**mer′ci•less•ly,** *adv.*

mere (mēr), *adj., superl.* **mer•est.** being nothing more nor better than what is specified: *a mere child.* —**mere′ly,** *adv.*

merge (mûrj), *v.i., v.t.,* **merged, merg•ing. 1.** to combine, coalesce, or unite into a single entity. **2.** to lose or cause to lose identity by gradual blending.

me•rid•i•an (mə rid′ē ən), *n.* **1. a.** a great circle of the earth passing through the poles and any given point on the earth's surface. **b.** the half of such a circle included between the poles. **2.** the greatest or highest point or period.

me•ringue (mə rang′), *n.* egg whites stiffly beaten with sugar and browned in the oven, often used as topping, as for pies.

me•ri•no (mə rē′nō), *n., pl.* **-nos. 1.** (*often cap.*) one of a breed of sheep valued for their fine wool. **2.** wool from a merino. **3.** a yarn or fabric made from this wool.

mer•it (mer′it), *n.* **1.** claim to respect and praise; worth. **2.** a commendable quality. **3. merits,** the inherent rights and wrongs of a matter, as a legal case. **4.** Often, **-its.** the fact of deserving; desert. —*v.t.* **5.** to be worthy of; deserve. —**mer′i•to/ri•ous** (-i tôr′ē əs), *adj.*

mer•maid (mûr′mād′), *n.* (in folklore) a marine creature with the head and torso of a woman and the tail of a fish.

mer•ry (mer′ē), *adj.,* **-ri•er, -ri•est. 1.** full of cheer or gaiety; joyous. **2.** characterized by festive conviviality. —**mer′ri•ly,** *adv.* —**mer′ri•ness,** *n.*

mer′ry-go-round′ *n.* **1.** a revolving circular platform with seats often formed like animals on which people ride, as at an amusement park. **2.** a busy round, as of activities.

mer′ry•mak/ing *n.* **1.** indulgence in gaiety or conviviality. **2.** a merry party; festivity; revel. —**mer′ry•mak/er,** *n.*

me•sa (mā′sə), *n., pl.* **-sas.** a land formation with steep walls and a relatively flat top.

mesh (mesh), *n.* **1.** a knit, woven, or knotted fabric of open texture. **2.** an interwoven or intertwined structure; network. **3. a.** one of the open spaces between the cords or wires of a net. **b. meshes,** the cords or wires that bind such spaces. **4.** something that catches or holds fast. **5.** the engagement of gear teeth. —*v.t.* **6.** to entangle or become entangled in or as if in a net. **7.** to engage or become engaged, as gear teeth. **8.** to match; coordinate.

mes•mer•ize (mez′mə rīz′, mes′-), *v.t.,* **-ized, -iz•ing. 1.** to hypnotize. **2.** to spellbind; fascinate. [after F. A. Mesmer (1733–1815), Austrian physician] —**mes′mer•ism,** *n.* —**mes′mer•iz/er,** *n.*

Mes•o•zo•ic (mez′ə zō′ik, mes′-), *adj.* noting or pertaining to a geologic era occurring between 230 and 65 million years ago, characterized by flowering plants and dinosaurs.

mes•quite (me skēt′, mes′kēt), *n.* a spiny tree or shrub of W North America bearing beanlike pods.

mess (mes), *n.* **1.** a dirty, untidy, unpleasant, or confused condition. **2.** a dirty or untidy accumulation; jumble. **3. a.** a group regularly taking meals together. **b.** the meal taken. **4.** a quantity of food. —*v.t.* **5.** to make dirty or untidy. **6.** to make a muddle of; bungle. —*v.i.* **7.** to eat in company, esp. as a member of a mess. **8. mess around, a.** to waste time. **b.** to involve oneself; associate. —**mess/y,** *adj.,* **-i•er, -i•est.** —**mess/i•ly,** *adv.* —**mess/i•ness,** *n.*

mes•sage (mes′ij), *n.* **1.** a written or spoken communication delivered esp. by an intermediary. **2.** the main point, moral, or meaning, as of a speech.

mes•sen•ger (mes′ən jər), *n.* **1.** a person who conveys messages or parcels. —*v.t.* **2.** to send by messenger.

Mes•si•ah (mi sī′ə), *n.* **1.** the promised and expected deliverer of the Jews. **2.** Jesus Christ. —**Mes•si•an•ic** (mes′ē ən′ik), *adj.*

mes•ti•zo (me stē′zō), *n., pl.* **-zos, -zoes.** a person of racially mixed ancestry, esp. of mixed American Indian and European ancestry.

meta- a prefix meaning: after (*metaphysics*); beyond (*metalinguistics*); behind (*metacarpus*); change (*metamorphosis*).

me•tab•o•lism (mə tab′ə liz′əm), *n.* the sum of the processes in an organism by which its substance is produced, maintained, and destroyed and by which energy is made available. —**met•a•bol•ic** (met′ə bol′ik), *adj.* —**me•tab′o•lize′,** *v.t., v.i.,* **-lized, -liz•ing.**

met•al (met′l), *n.* **1.** any of a class of elementary substances, as gold, that are typically characterized by opacity, ductility, conductivity, and luster. **2.** an alloy of metals, as brass. **3.** METTLE. —**me•tal•lic** (mə tal′ik), *adj.*

met•al•lur•gy (met′l ûr′jē), *n.* the technology or science of metals. —**met/al•lur′gic, met/al•lur/gi•cal,** *adj.* —**met/al•lur/gist,** *n.*

met•a•mor•phism (met′ə môr′fiz əm), *n.* a change in the constitution of a body by natural means, as pressure and heat. —**met/a•mor/phic,** *adj.*

met/a•mor/phose (-fōz, -fōs), *v.t, v.i.,* **-phosed, -phos•ing.** to subject to or undergo metamorphosis or metamorphism.

met/a•mor/pho•sis (-fə sis), *n., pl.* **-ses** (-sēz′). **1.** a change in form from one stage to the next in the life of an organism, as from pupa to butterfly. **2.** a change of form, structure, or substance, as by magic. **3.** a remarkable change, as in appearance. [< L < Gk: transformation]

met•a•phor (met′ə fôr′, -fər), *n.* the application of a word or phrase to an object or concept it does not literally denote in order to suggest comparison, as in "A mighty fortress is our God." —**met/a•phor/i•cal** (-fôr′i kəl, -for′-), *adj.* —**met/a•phor/i•cal•ly,** *adv.*

met•a•phys•ics (met′ə fiz′iks), *n.* **1.** the branch of philosophy that treats of the ultimate nature of existence, reality, and experience. **2.** philosophy, esp. in its more abstruse branches.

me•tas•ta•sis (mə tas′tə sis), *n., pl.* **-ses** (-sēz′). the spread of disease-producing organisms or malignant cells from one to another part of the body.

me•tas/ta•size/ (-sīz′), *v.i.,* **-sized, -siz•ing. 1.** to spread by or as if by metastasis: *Street gangs have metastasized in our city.* **2.** to transform, esp. into a dangerous form: *Truth metastasized into lurid fantasy.*

mete (mēt), *v.t.,* **met•ed, met•ing.** to distribute by measure; dole: *to mete out punishment.*

me•te•or (mē′tē ər, -ôr′), *n.* **1.** a meteoroid that has entered the earth's atmosphere. **2.** a transient fiery streak in the sky produced by passage of a meteor.

me/te•or/ic (-ôr′ik, -or′-), *adj.* **1.** of meteors. **2.** resembling a meteor in transient brilliance: *a meteoric rise in politics.*

me/te•or•ite/ (-ə rīt′), *n.* the remains of a meteoroid that has reached the earth.

me/te•or•oid/ (-ə roid′), *n.* any of the small bodies of rock and metal traveling through space.

me/te•or•ol/o•gy (-ə rol′ə jē), *n.* the science dealing with the atmosphere, weather, and climate. —**me/te•or•ol/o•gist,** *n.*

me•ter¹ (mē′tər), *n.* the basic unit of length in the metric system, equivalent to 39.37 inches.

me•ter² (mē′tər), *n.* the rhythmic element in music and poetry.

me•ter³ (mē′tər), *n.* **1.** an instrument for measuring and recording something, as amount or time. —*v.t.* **2.** to measure by means of a meter. **3.** to process (mail) by means of a postage meter.

-meter a combining form meaning measuring instrument (*barometer*).

meth•a•done (meth′ə dōn′) also **-don′** (-don′), *n.* a synthetic narcotic used in the treatment of heroin addiction.

meth•ane (meth′ān), *n.* a colorless, odorless, flammable gas that is the main constituent of marsh gas and is obtained commercially from natural gas.

meth•a•nol (meth′ə nôl′, -nol′), *n.* METHYL ALCOHOL.

meth•od (meth′əd), *n.* **1.** a procedure, technique, or planned way of doing something. **2.** orderly or systematic arrangement. —**me•thod•i•cal** (mə-thod′i kəl), *adj.* —**me•thod/i•cal•ly,** *adv.*

meth′od·ol′o·gy (-ə dol′ə jē), *n., pl.* **-gies.** a set or system of methods, principles, and rules, as in the sciences. **—meth′od·o·log′i·cal** (-dl oj′i kəl), *adj.* **—meth′od·ol′o·gist,** *n.*

meth′yl al′cohol (meth′əl), *n.* a colorless, poisonous liquid used chiefly as a solvent, fuel, and antifreeze.

me·tic·u·lous (mə tik′yə ləs), *adj.* taking or showing extreme care about minute details. **—me·tic′u·lous·ly,** *adv.* **—me·tic′u·lous·ness,** *n.*

mé·tier or **me·tier** (mā′tyā), *n.* a field of activity in which one has special ability.

met·ric[1] (me′trik), *adj.* pertaining to the meter or to the metric system.

met·ric[2] (me′trik), *adj.* METRICAL.

met′ri·cal *adj.* **1.** pertaining to or composed in rhythmic meter. **2.** pertaining to measurement. **—met′ri·cal·ly,** *adv.*

met·ro·nome (me′trə nōm′), *n.* an instrument that makes repeated clicks for marking rhythm, esp. in practicing music.

me·trop·o·lis (mi trop′ə lis), *n.* a large, busy city, esp. the chief city of a country or region. [< L < Gk: mother state or city] **—met′ro·pol′i·tan** (me′trə pol′i tn), *adj.*

met·tle (met′l), *n.* **1.** courage and fortitude. **2.** disposition or temperament.

met′tle·some (-səm), *adj.* spirited; courageous.

mew[1] (myoō), *n.* **1.** the high-pitched cry of a cat. **—v.i. 2.** to emit a mew.

mew[2] (myoō), *n.* **1. mews,** (*usu. with a sing. v.*) **a.** stables and usu. servants' quarters built around a courtyard. **b.** a street with apartments converted from stables. **—v.t. 2.** *Archaic.* to shut up; confine.

Mex·i·co (mek′si kō′), *n.* a republic in S North America. **—Mex′i·can,** *n., adj.*

mez·za·nine (mez′ə nēn′, mez′ə nēn′), *n.* **1.** the lowest balcony or forward part of such a balcony in a theater. **2.** a low-ceilinged story between two stories of greater height in a building. [< F < It *mezzanino,* dim. of *mezzano* middle < L *mediānus* median]

mez′zo-sopran′o (met′sō-, med′zō-), *n., pl.* **-pran·os.** a voice, voice part, or singer intermediate in range between soprano and contralto.

M.F.A. Master of Fine Arts.

MI Michigan.

mi. mile.

mi·as·ma (mī az′mə, mē-), *n., pl.* **-mas, -ma·ta** (-mə tə). **1.** a noxious exhalation from putrescent organic matter. **2.** a dangerous or corruptive influence or atmosphere.

mi·ca (mī′kə), *n., pl.* **-cas.** one of a group of minerals that separate readily into thin, often transparent sheets.

Mich. Michigan.

micro- a combining form meaning: very small (*microfilm*); microscopic (*microorganism*); one millionth (*micron*).

mi·crobe (mī′krōb), *n.* a microorganism, esp. a disease-causing bacterium.

mi′cro·brew′er·y *n., pl.* **-er·ies.** a relatively small brewery usu. concentrating on exotic or high quality beer.

mi′cro·chip′ *n.* CHIP (def. 5).

mi′cro·com·put′er *n.* a compact computer with less capability than a minicomputer.

mi·cro·cosm (mī′krə koz′əm), *n.* **1.** a world in miniature. **2.** something regarded as a microcosm.

mi′cro·fiche′ (-fēsh′), *n., pl.* **-fiche, -fich·es.** a flat sheet of microfilmed printed or graphic matter.

mi′cro·film′ *n.* **1.** a film bearing a miniature photographic copy of printed or graphic matter. **—v.t. 2.** to make a microfilm of.

mi·crom·e·ter (mī krom′i tər), *n.* a device for measuring minute distances, used esp. with a telescope or microscope.

mi·cron (mī′kron), *n., pl.* **-crons, -cra** (-krə). the millionth part of a meter.

Mi·cro·ne·sia (mī′krə nē′zhə), *n.* **1.** the small Pacific islands N of the equator and E of the Philippines. **2. Federated States of,** a group of islands in the W Pacific: a self-governing area associated with the U.S. **—Mi′cro·ne′sian,** *adj., n.*

mi·cro·or′gan·ism (mī′krō-), *n.* an organism, as a bacterium, too small to be viewed by the unaided eye.

mi·cro·phone (mī′krə fōn′), *n.* an instrument for transforming sound waves into changes in electric currents, used in recording or transmitting sound.

mi·cro·proc·es·sor (mī′krō pros′es ər, -ə sər; *esp. Brit.* -prō′ses ər, -sə sər), *n.* an integrated computer circuit that performs all the functions of a CPU.

mi·cro·scope (mī′krə skōp′), *n.* an optical instrument for magnifying objects too small to be seen by the unaided eye. **—mi·cros′co·py** (-kros′kə pē), *n.*

mi′cro·scop′ic (-skop′ik) also **-i·cal,** *adj.* **1.** too small to be visible without the use of a microscope. **2.** of or requiring the use of a microscope. **—mi′cro·scop′i·cal·ly,** *adv.*

mi′cro·sur·ger·y (mī′krō sûr′jə rē), *n.* surgery performed under magnification with very small specialized instruments.

mi′cro·wave′ *n., v.,* **-waved, -wav·ing. —n. 1.** an electromagnetic wave with wavelengths from 1 mm to 30 cm. **2.** MICROWAVE OVEN. **—v.t. 3.** to cook or heat in a microwave oven. **—mi′cro·wav′a·ble,** *adj.*

mi′crowave ov′en *n.* an oven that uses microwaves to generate heat within the food.

mid[1] (mid), *adj.* being at or near the middle.

mid[2] or **′mid** (mid), *prep.* AMID.

mid′day′ (-dā′, -dā′), *n.* the middle of the day; noon.

mid·dle (mid′l), *adj.* **1.** equally distant from the extremes; central. **2.** intermediate or intervening. **3.** (*cap.*) intermediate between linguistic periods classified as Old and New or Modern: *Middle English.* **—n. 4.** a middle point, part, or position. **5.** the human waist.

Mid′dle Ag′es *n.* the time in European history from the late 5th century to about 1500.

mid′dle class′ *n.* a class of people intermediate between the upper and the lower class. **—mid′dle-class′,** *adj.*

mid′dle ear′ *n.* the middle portion of the ear consisting of the eardrum and an air-filled chamber lined with mucous membrane.

Mid′dle East′ *n.* the area from Libya east to Afghanistan. **—Mid′dle East′ern,** *adj.*

Mid′dle Eng′lish *n.* the English language of the period c1150–c1475.

mid′dle·man′ *n., pl.* **-men.** an intermediary, esp. one person who buys goods from the producer and resells them to the retailer or consumer.

mid′dle-of-the-road′ *adj.* following or favoring a position between extremes, esp. in politics; moderate.

mid′dle school′ *n.* a school encompassing grades five or six through eight.

mid′dling *adj.* **1.** medium, moderate, or average in size, quantity, or quality. **2.** not first-rate; mediocre.

midge (mij), *n.* a minute insect somewhat resembling a mosquito.

midg·et (mij′it), *n.* **1.** a very small person. **2.** something, as an animal, that is very small for its kind.

mid·land (-lənd), *n.* the middle or interior part of a country.

mid′night′ *n.* **1.** twelve o'clock at night. **—adj. 2.** of or resembling midnight.

mid′point′ *n.* a point at or near the middle.

mid′riff (-rif), *n.* **1.** DIAPHRAGM (def. 1). **2.** the middle portion of the human body, between the chest and the waist.

mid′ship·man *n., pl.* **-men.** a student in training for commission as an officer in the U.S. Navy or Marine Corps.

midst[1] (midst), *n.* **1.** a position among other persons, things, or parts. **2.** the state of being surrounded or involved: *in the midst of work.* **3.** the middle or central point or part.

midst[2] (midst), *prep.* among; amidst.

mid′sum′mer (-sum′ər, -sum′-), *n.* **1.** the middle of summer. **2.** the summer solstice, around June 21.

mid′term′ *n.* **1.** the halfway point of a school term. **2.** an examination given at midterm.

mid•way (*adv.*, *adj.* mid′wā′; *n.* -wā′), *adv.*, *adj.* **1.** in the middle of the way or distance. —*n.* **2.** a way, as at a carnival, along which amusements and concessions are located.

mid′wife′ *n.*, *pl.* **-wives.** a person who assists women in childbirth. —**mid•wife′ry** (-wif′ə rē), *n.*

mid′win′ter (-win′tər, -win′-), *n.* **1.** the middle of winter. **2.** the winter solstice, around December 22.

mien (mēn), *n.* bearing or demeanor, esp. as showing character or feeling.

miff (mif), *v.t.* to put into an irritable mood, esp. by offending.

miffed (mift), *adj.* irritated; offended.

might¹ (mīt), *auxiliary v.*, *pres. sing. and pl.* **might**; *past* **might.** **1.** pt. of MAY. **2.** (used to express possibility): *I might stay home.* **3.** (used to express obligation): *They might at least have tried.* **4.** (used to express contingency, concession, or purpose): *difficult as it might be.* **5.** (used in polite requests for permission): *Might I speak to you now?*

might² (mīt), *n.* **1.** physical strength. **2.** power or strength; force.

might′y *adj.*, **-i•er, -i•est,** *adv.* —*adj.* **1.** having or showing power or strength. **2.** of great size; huge. **3.** great, as in importance; exceptional. —*adv.* **4.** *Informal.* very; extremely. —**might′i•ly,** *adv.* —**might′i•ness,** *n.*

mi•graine (mī′grān), *n.* a severe, recurrent headache often accompanied by nausea.

mi•grate (mī′grāt), *v.i.*, **-grat•ed, -grat•ing. 1.** to move from one country, region, or place to another. **2.** to pass periodically from one region or climate to another, as certain birds. —**mi•gra′tion,** *n.* —**mi′gra•to′ry** (-grə tôr′ē), *adj.*

mi•ka•do (mi kä′dō), *n.*, *pl.* **-dos.** an emperor of Japan.

mike (mīk), *n.* a microphone.

mil (mil), *n.* a unit of length equal to 0.001 of an inch (0.0254 mm).

mild (mīld), *adj.*, **-er, -est. 1.** gentle in feeling, behavior, or manner. **2.** not cold, severe, or extreme; temperate. **3.** gentle in force or effect; moderate. —**mild′ly,** *adv.* —**mild′ness,** *n.*

mil•dew (mil′dōō′, -dyōō′), *n.* **1.** a cottony, usu. whitish coating caused by a fungus and appearing on plants and materials such as fabrics and leather. —*v.t.*, *v.i.* **2.** to affect or become affected with mildew.

mile (mīl), *n.* **1.** a unit of distance equal to 5280 feet, or 1760 yards (1.609 kilometers). **2.** NAUTICAL MILE.

mile•age (mī′lij), *n.* **1.** the aggregate number of miles traveled in a given time. **2.** the average number of miles a vehicle can travel on a specified quantity of fuel. **3.** an allowance for traveling expenses at a fixed rate per mile.

mile′post′ *n.* a post showing the distance in miles to or from a place.

mile′stone′ *n.* **1.** a stone functioning as a milepost. **2.** a significant event or point in development.

mi•lieu (mil yōō′, mēl-; *Fr.* mē lyœ′), *n.*, *pl.* **mi•lieus** (mil yōō′z′, mēl-), **mi•lieux** (*Fr.* mē lyœ′). surroundings; environment.

mil•i•tant (mil′i tənt), *adj.* **1.** vigorously active, often combative, esp. in support of a cause. **2.** engaged in warfare. —*n.* **3.** a militant person. —**mil′i•tan•cy,** *n.* —**mil′i•tant•ly,** *adv.*

mil′i•ta•rism (-tə riz′əm), *n.* **1.** strong military spirit. **2.** the principle or policy of maintaining a large military establishment. —**mil′i•ta•rist,** *n.* —**mil′i•ta•ris′tic,** *adj.*

mil′i•ta•rize′ *v.t.*, **-rized, -riz•ing. 1.** to equip with armed forces and military supplies. **2.** to imbue with militarism. —**mil′i•ta•ri•za′tion,** *n.*

mil′i•tar′y (-ter′ē), *adj.*, *n.*, *pl.* **-tar•y.** —*adj.* **1.** of or for the army, the armed forces, soldiers, or war. **2.** performed by soldiers. —*n.* **3.** the armed forces of a nation. **4.** military personnel. —**mil′i•tar′i•ly,** *adv.*

mil′itary police′ *n.* soldiers who perform police duties within the army.

mil•i•tate (-tāt′), *v.i.*, **-tat•ed, -tat•ing.** to have a substantial effect; weigh heavily.

mi•li•tia (mi lish′ə), *n.* a body of citizens enrolled for military service but called out only in emergencies. —**mi•li′tia•man,** *n.*, *pl.* **-men.**

milk (milk), *n.* **1.** a white liquid secreted by the mammary glands of female mammals and serving to nourish their young. **2.** a liquid resembling milk, as the liquid within a coconut. —*v.t.* **3.** to draw milk from the udder or breast of. **4.** to draw out as if by milking; extract. —**milk′y,** *adj.*, **-i•er, -i•est.** —**milk′i•ness,** *n.*

milk′man′ *n.*, *pl.* **-men.** a person who sells or delivers milk.

milk′shake′ *n.* a beverage of cold milk, flavoring, and often ice cream, blended in a mixer.

milk′weed′ *n.* a plant with milky juice and pods filled with silky tufted seeds.

Milk′y Way′ *n.* the galaxy containing the solar system, visible as a luminous band stretching across the night sky and composed of approximately a trillion stars.

mill¹ (mil), *n.* **1.** a factory, as one for the manufacture of paper or steel. **2.** a building equipped with machinery for grinding grain into meal or flour. **3.** a device for grinding, crushing, or pulverizing: *a coffee mill.* **4.** any of various machines that modify the shape or size of a piece of work by rotating tools or the work. —*v.t.* **5.** to grind, work, treat, or shape in or with a mill. —*v.i.* **6.** to move around aimlessly or confusedly.

mill² (mil), *n.* a money of account equal to .001 of a U.S. dollar.

mil•len•ni•um (mi len′ē əm), *n.*, *pl.* **-ni•ums, -ni•a** (-nē ə). **1.** a period of 1000 years. **2.** *Bible.* the period of 1000 years during which Christ is to reign on earth. **3.** a period of general happiness. **4.** a thousandth anniversary. —**mil•len′ni•al,** *adj.*

mil′let (-it), *n.* **1.** any of various cereal grasses cultivated as food and fodder. **2.** the grain of a millet.

milli- a combining form meaning: thousand (*millipede*); thousandth (*millimeter*).

mil•liard (mil′yərd, -yärd), *n. Brit.* one billion.

mil•li•gram (mil′i gram′), *n.* a unit of mass or weight equal to ¹/₁₀₀₀ of a gram.

mil′li•li′ter *n.* a unit of capacity equal to ¹/₁₀₀₀ of a liter.

mil′li•me′ter *n.* a unit of length equal to ¹/₁₀₀₀ of a meter.

mil•li•ner (mil′ə nər), *n.* a person who creates or sells hats for women.

mil′li•ner′y (-ner′ē, -nə rē), *n.* **1.** women's hats and related articles. **2.** the business or trade of a milliner.

mil•lion (mil′yən), *n.*, *pl.* **-lions, -lion. 1.** a cardinal number, 1000 times 1000. **2.** a symbol for this number, as 1,000,000. **3.** a very great number or amount. —**mil′lionth,** *adj.*, *n.*

mil•lion•aire or **mil•lion•naire** (mil′yə nâr′), *n.* a person whose wealth amounts to a million or more, as in pounds or dollars.

mill′race′ *n.* a channel for the current of water driving a mill wheel.

mill′stone′ *n.* **1.** either of a pair of circular stones between which grain is ground, as in a mill. **2.** a heavy burden.

mill′stream′ *n.* the stream in a millrace.

mime (mīm, mēm), *n.*, *v.*, **mimed, mim•ing. 1.** the art or technique of character portrayal or narration by gestures and body movements. **2.** an actor who specializes in mime. **3.** MIMIC (def. 3). —*v.t.* **4.** to mimic. **5.** to act out in mime. —*v.i.* **6.** to engage in mime.

mim•e•o•graph (mim′ē ə graf′, -gräf′), *n.* **1.** a machine for making copies from a stencil on an inkfed drum. —*v.t.* **2.** to duplicate by means of a mimeograph.

mim•ic (mim′ik), *v.*, **-icked, -ick•ing,** *n.* —*v.t.* **1.** to imitate, as in action or speech, often playfully or derisively. **2.** to resemble closely. —*n.* **3.** a person or thing that mimics, esp. a performer who mimics others. —**mim′ick•er,** n. —**mim′ic•ry,** n.

mi•mo•sa (mi mō′sə, -zə), n., pl. **-sas.** a plant, shrub, or tree of warm regions that bears small flowers in globular heads.

min•a•ret (min′ə ret′), n. a lofty, slender tower attached to a mosque.

mince (mins), v., **minced, minc•ing.** —v.t. **1.** to cut or chop into small pieces. **2.** to moderate (words) esp. for the sake of decorum. —v.i. **3.** to move with short, affectedly dainty steps. —**minc′ing,** adj.

mince′meat′ n. a diced mixture, as of apples, raisins, and sometimes meat, for filling a pie.

mind (mīnd), n. **1.** the part or process in a conscious being that reasons, thinks, feels, wills, perceives, and judges. **2.** intellectual power; intelligence. **3.** sound mental condition; sanity: *lost his mind.* **4.** opinion, view, or sentiments: *Don't change your mind again.* **5.** inclination, intention, or desire: *He was of a mind to listen.* **6.** recollection; memory. **7.** attention; thoughts: *He can't keep his mind on his studies.* —v.t. **8.** to pay attention to. **9.** to heed or obey. **10.** to attend to. **11.** to look after; tend. **12.** to be careful or wary about. **13.** to care about. **14.** to object to: *I don't mind the interruption.* —v.i. **15.** to pay attention. **16.** to obey. **17.** to be careful or wary. **18.** to care or object.

mind′-blow′ing adj. **1.** overwhelming; astounding. **2.** producing a hallucinogenic effect.

mind′ful adj. attentive; aware. —**mind′ful•ly,** adv. —**mind′ful•ness,** n.

mind′less adj. **1.** showing, using, or requiring no intelligence or thought. **2.** not mindful; heedless. —**mind′less•ly,** adv. —**mind′less•ness,** n.

mine[1] (mīn), pron. **1.** a form of the possessive case of I: *The yellow sweater is mine.* **2.** that or those belonging to me: *Mine is on the left.*

mine[2] (mīn), n., v., **mined, min•ing.** —n. **1.** an excavation made in the earth for extracting mineral substances, as ore. **2.** a natural deposit of mineral substances. **3.** an abundant source: *a mine of information.* **4.** an explosive device for blowing up enemy shipping, personnel, or vehicles. **5.** a passage dug under an enemy position. —v.i. **6.** to dig a mine. **7.** to extract a mineral substance from a mine. —v.t. **8.** to dig in (earth) to extract a mineral substance. **9.** to extract from a mine. **10.** to place military mines under or in. **11.** to undermine. —**min′er,** n.

min•er•al (min′ər əl), n. **1.** a natural inorganic substance, as quartz, of definite chemical composition and usu. of definite crystal structure. **2.** an ore. **3.** a substance that is neither animal nor vegetable. —adj. **4.** of or containing minerals.

min′er•al′o•gy (-ə rol′ə jē, -ral′ə-), n. the science or study of minerals. —**min′er•al•o•gist,** n.

min′eral wa′ter n. water containing dissolved mineral salts or gases.

min•e•stro•ne (min′ə strō′nē), n., pl. **-nes.** a thick vegetable soup.

mine′sweep′er n. a ship used to remove or destroy explosive mines.

min•gle (ming′gəl), v., **-gled, -gling.** —v.i. **1.** to become mixed, blended, or united. **2.** to mix in company. —v.t. **3.** to put together in a mixture; blend.

min•i (min′ē), n., pl. **-is. 1.** MINISKIRT. **2.** something small of its kind.

mini- a combining form meaning: smaller than others of its kind (*minibike*); very short (*miniskirt*).

min•i•a•ture (min′ē ə chər, min′ə-), n. **1.** a representation of something on a small or reduced scale. **2.** something small of its class or kind. **3.** a very small painting, as on ivory. —adj. **4.** represented or being on a small or reduced scale: *a miniature poodle.* —**min′i•a•tur•ist,** n.

min′i•a•tur•ize′ v.t., **-ized, -iz•ing.** to make in greatly reduced size. —**min′i•a•tur•i•za′tion,** n.

min′i•bus′ n. a small bus typically used for short distances.

min′i•com•put′er n. a computer with processing and storage capabilities smaller than those of a

mainframe but larger than those of a microcomputer.

min•im (min′əm), n. the smallest unit of liquid measure, $1/60$ of a fluid dram.

min•i•mal (min′ə məl), adj. **1.** of or constituting a minimum. **2.** of minimalism. —**min′i•mal•ly,** adv.

min′i•mal•ism n. a style or method, as in art or music, that is spare, simple, and often repetitious. —**min′i•mal•ist,** n.

min′i•mize′ (-mīz′), v.t., **-mized, -miz•ing. 1.** to reduce to the minimum. **2.** to represent as being of minimum value or importance, often in a disparaging way. —**min′i•miz′er,** n.

min′i•mum (-məm), n., pl. **-mums, -ma** (-mə), adj. —n. **1.** the least amount possible or allowable. **2.** the lowest amount, value, or degree attained or recorded. —adj. **3.** of or being a minimum.

min•ion (min′yən), n. **1.** a servile follower. **2.** a minor official. **3.** a favored person.

min′i•skirt′ n. a skirt ending several inches above the knee.

min•is•ter (min′ə stər), n. **1.** a member of the clergy, esp. the Protestant clergy. **2.** a high officer of state, esp. one who heads an administrative department. **3.** a diplomatic representative, usu. ranking below an ambassador. **4.** an agent for another. —v.i. **5.** to perform the functions of a religious minister. **6.** to give service, care, or aid. —**min′is•te′ri•al** (-stēr′ē əl), adj. —**min′is•trant** (-strənt), adj., n. —**min′is•tra′tion,** n.

min•is•try n., pl. **-tries. 1.** the service, functions, or profession of a minister. **2.** the body of ministers of religion; clergy. **3.** the body of ministers of state. **4.** an administrative department headed by a minister of state. **5.** ministration; service.

min•i•van (min′ē van′), n. a small passenger van.

mink (mingk), n., pl. **minks, mink. 1.** a semiaquatic weasel of North America and Eurasia. **2.** the soft, lustrous fur of the mink.

Minn. Minnesota.

min•now (min′ō), n., pl. **-nows,** (*Rare*) **-now.** a small freshwater fish often used as bait.

mi•nor (mī′nər), adj. **1.** lesser, as in size, extent, amount, or importance. **2.** under full legal age. **3.** *Music.* of, based on, or being a scale with half steps between the second and third and fifth and sixth degrees. —n. **4.** a person under full legal age. **5.** an academic subject pursued secondarily to a major. —v.i. **6.** to choose or study as an academic minor.

mi•nor•i•ty (mi nôr′i tē, -nor′-, mī-), n., pl. **-ties. 1.** a number, part, or amount forming less than half of a whole. **2.** a group differing, esp. in race, religion, or ethnic background, from the majority of a population. **3.** the state or period of being under full legal age.

min•strel (min′strəl), n. **1.** an often itinerant medieval poet, singer, and musician. **2.** a performer in a minstrel show. —**min′strel•sy,** n.

mint[1] (mint), n. **1.** an aromatic herb with leaves used as flavoring. **2.** a mint-flavored candy. —**mint′y,** adj., **-i•er, -i•est.**

mint[2] (mint), n. **1.** a place where coins are produced, esp. under government authority. **2.** a vast amount, esp. of money. —adj. **3.** being in pristine condition as if newly made: *a book in mint condition.* —v.t. **4.** to make coins by stamping metal. —**mint′er,** n.

min•u•et (min′yŏŏ et′), n. a slow, stately dance in triple meter.

mi•nus (mī′nəs), prep. **1.** less by the subtraction of: *Ten minus six is four.* **2.** lacking or without: *a book minus a page.* —adj. **3.** involving subtraction. **4.** algebraically negative: *a minus quantity.* **5.** less than; just below: *got C minus on the test.* —n. **6.** MINUS SIGN. **7.** a minus quantity. **8.** a deficiency or loss.

mi•nus•cule (min′ə skyōōl′, mi nus′kyōōl), adj. very small.

mi′nus sign′ n. a symbol (−) denoting subtraction or a negative quantity.

min•ute[1] (min′it), n. **1.** the sixtieth part ($1/60$) of an hour. **2.** a short space of time. **3.** an exact point in time. **4. minutes,** the official record of the proceedings at a meeting. **5.** *Geom.* the sixtieth part of a degree of angular measure.

mi•nute² (mī nōōt′, -nyōōt′, mi-), *adj.*, **-nut•er, -nut•est. 1.** extremely small. **2.** of minor importance. **3.** attentive to small details. **—mi•nute′ly,** *adv.* **—mi•nute′ness,** *n.*

mi•nu•ti•ae (mi nōō′shē ē′) *n.pl.* trifling matters.

minx (mingks), *n.* a pert or flirtatious girl.

mir•a•cle (mir′ə kəl), *n.* **1.** an extraordinary occurrence that is ascribed to a divine or supernatural cause, esp. to God. **2.** a superb example; marvel. **—mi•rac•u•lous** (mi rak′yə ləs), *adj.* **—mi•rac′u•lous•ly,** *adv.*

mi•rage (mi räzh′), *n.* **1.** an optical phenomenon by which reflected images of distant objects are seen, often distorted. **2.** something illusory.

mire (mīᵉr), *n., v.,* **mired, mir•ing. —***n.* **1.** an area of wet, swampy ground. **2.** deep mud. **—***v.i., v.t.* **3.** to sink or stick in or as if in mire. **—mir′y,** *adj.*

mir•ror (mir′ər), *n.* **1.** a reflecting surface, usu. of glass with a silvery backing. **2.** something that gives a faithful representation. **—***v.t.* **3.** to reflect in or as if in a mirror.

mirth (mûrth), *n.* gaiety or jollity, esp. when accompanied by laughter. **—mirth′ful,** *adj.* **—mirth′less,** *adj.*

mis- a prefix meaning: wrong (*misconduct*); wrongly (*misjudge*); lack of (*mistrust*).

mis•ad•ven•ture (mis′əd ven′chər), *n.* a misfortune; mishap.

mis•al•li•ance *n.* an incompatible association, esp. in marriage.

mis•an•thrope (mis′ən thrōp′, miz′-) also **mis•an′thro•pist** (-an′thrə pist), *n.* a hater of humankind. **—mis•an•throp•ic** (-throp′ik), *adj.* **—mis•an′thro•py** (-an′thrə pē), *n.*

mis•ap•pre•hend′ (mis′-), *v.t.* MISUNDERSTAND. **—mis•ap•pre•hen′sion** (-hen′shən), *n.*

mis•ap•pro′pri•ate (-āt′), *v.t.,* **-at•ed, -at•ing.** to appropriate wrongfully or dishonestly. **—mis′ap•pro′pri•a′tion,** *n.*

mis•be•got•ten (mis′bi got′n), *adj.* unlawfully or irregularly begotten; illegitimate.

mis•be•have′ *v.t.,* **-haved, -hav•ing.** to behave badly or improperly. **—mis′be•hav′ior,** *n.*

misc. 1. miscellaneous. **2.** miscellany.

mis•call′ *v.t.* to call by a wrong name.

mis•car•ry (mis kar′ē; *for 1 also* mis′kar′ē), *v.i.,* **-ried, -ry•ing. 1.** to give birth to a fetus before it is viable. **2.** to be unsuccessful. **3.** to go astray. **—mis•car′riage** (-kar′ij), *n.*

mis•cast′ *v.t.* to cast in an unsuitable role.

mis•cel•la•ne•ous (mis′ə lā′nē əs), *adj.* consisting of members or elements of different kinds. **—mis′cel•la′ny** (-ə lā′nē), *n.*

mis•chance′ *n.* **1.** a mishap. **2.** bad luck.

mis•chief (mis′chif), *n.* **1.** conduct or activity that causes annoyance. **2.** harm or trouble. **3.** an injury caused by a person or thing. **4.** a source of harm or annoyance.

mis′con•ceive′ *v.t., v.i.,* **-ceived, -ceiv•ing.** to interpret wrongly; misunderstand. **—mis′con•cep′tion,** *n.*

mis•con•duct (-kon′dukt) *n.* **1.** improper behavior. **2.** unlawful conduct, as by a public official.

mis•con•strue (mis′kən strōō′), *v.t.,* **-strued, -stru•ing.** to misunderstand the meaning of; misinterpret.

mis•cre•ant (mis′krē ənt), *adj.* **1.** depraved; villainous. **—***n.* **2.** a vicious or depraved person.

mis•deed′ *n.* an immoral deed.

mis′de•mean′or *n.* **1.** a criminal offense less serious than a felony. **2.** a misdeed.

mise-en-scène (mē zän sen′), *n., pl.* **-scènes** (-sens′, -sen′). **1.** the placement of actors, scenery, and properties on a stage. **2.** a stage setting. **3.** surroundings; environment.

mi•ser (mī′zər), *n.* a person who hoards money. **—mi′ser•ly,** *adj.* **—mi′ser•li•ness,** *n.*

mis•er•a•ble (miz′ər ə bəl), *adj.* **1.** wretchedly unhappy. **2.** of wretched character or quality; contemptible. **3.** causing misery. **4.** worthy of pity. **—mis′er•a•bly,** *adv.*

mis′er•y *n., pl.* **-er•ies. 1.** suffering caused by privation or poverty. **2.** great emotional distress. **3.** a source of distress.

mis•fea•sance (mis fē′zəns), *n.* the wrongful and injurious exercise of lawful authority.

mis•fire (*v.* mis fīᵉr′; *n.* mis′fīᵉr′), *v.,* **-fired, -fir•ing,** *n.* **—***v.i.* **1.** to fail to fire, explode, or ignite. **2.** to fail to achieve a desired result or effect. **—***n.* **3.** an act or instance of misfiring.

mis•fit (mis fit′, mis′fit′ *for 1;* mis′fit′ *for 2*), *n.* **1.** something, as a garment, that fits badly. **2.** a person who is unable to adjust to a situation.

mis•for′tune *n.* **1.** bad luck. **2.** an instance of bad luck.

mis•giv′ing *n.* Often, **-ings.** a feeling of doubt, distrust, or apprehension.

mis•guid′ed *adj.* mistaken; ill-informed.

mis•han′dle *v.t.,* **-dled, -dling. 1.** to handle roughly. **2.** to manage badly.

mis•hap (mis′hap, mis hap′), *n.* an unfortunate accident.

mish•mash (mish′mäsh′, -mash′), *n.* a confused mess; hodgepodge.

mis′in•form′ *v.t.* to give false or misleading information to. **—mis′in•for•ma′tion,** *n.*

mis′in•ter′pret *v.t., v.i.* to interpret, explain, or understand incorrectly. **—mis′in•ter′pre•ta′tion,** *n.*

mis•judge′ *v.t., v.i.,* **-judged, -judg•ing.** to judge or estimate wrongly or unjustly. **—mis•judg′ment,** *n.*

mis•lay′ *v.t.,* **-laid, -lay•ing.** to lose temporarily; misplace.

mis•lead′ (-lēd′), *v.t.,* **-led, -lead•ing. 1.** to lead in the wrong direction. **2.** to lead into error, as of conduct. **—mis•lead′ing,** *adj.*

mis•man′age *v.t., v.i.,* **-aged, -ag•ing.** to manage incompetently or dishonestly. **—mis•man′age•ment,** *n.*

mis•match (mis mach′; *for 2 also* mis′mach′), *v.t.* **1.** to match badly or unsuitably. **—***n.* **2.** a bad or unsuitable match.

mis•no•mer (mis nō′mər), *n.* an incorrect name or designation.

mi•sog•a•my (mi sog′ə mē, mī-), *n.* hatred of marriage. **—mi•sog′a•mist,** *n.*

mi•sog•y•ny (mi sog′ə nē, mī-), *n.* hatred of or hostility toward women. **—mi•sog′y•nist,** *n.* **—mi•sog′y•nous,** *adj.*

mis•place′ *v.t.,* **-placed, -plac•ing. 1.** to put in a wrong place. **2.** to mislay. **3.** to place unsuitably or unwisely.

mis•print (*n.* mis′print′, mis print′; *v.* mis print′), *n.* **1.** a mistake in printing. **—***v.t.* **2.** to print incorrectly.

mis′pro•nounce′ *v.t., v.i.,* **-nounced, -nounc•ing.** to pronounce incorrectly. **—mis′pro•nun′ci•a′tion,** *n.*

mis•quote′ *v.,* **-quot•ed, -quot•ing,** *n.* **—***v.t., v.i.* **1.** to quote incorrectly. **—***n.* **2.** Also, **mis′quo•ta′tion.** an incorrect quotation.

mis•read′ (-rēd′), *v.t., v.i.,* **-read** (-red′), **-read•ing. 1.** to read wrongly. **2.** to misinterpret.

mis′rep•re•sent′ *v.t.* to represent incorrectly, improperly, or falsely. **—mis′rep•re•sen•ta′tion,** *n.*

mis•rule′ *n., v.,* **-ruled, -rul•ing. 1.** bad or unwise rule. **2.** disorder. **—***v.t.* **3.** to rule badly.

miss¹ (mis), *v.t.* **1.** to fail to hit, encounter, meet, or catch. **2.** to fail to take advantage of. **3.** to fail to be present at or for. **4.** to notice or regret the absence or loss of. **5.** to escape or avoid: *just missed being caught.* **6.** to fail to understand. **7.** to leave out; omit. **—***v.i.* **8.** to fail to hit something. **9.** to be unsuccessful; fail. **10.** to misfire. **—***n.* **11.** a failure, esp. a failure to hit something. **12.** MISFIRE.

miss² (mis), *n.* **1.** (*cap.*) a title of respect prefixed to the name of an unmarried woman. **2.** a young unmarried woman. [short for *mistress*]

Miss. Mississippi.

mis•sal (mis′əl), *n.* a book containing the prayers and rites of the Roman Catholic mass over the course of the year.

mis•shap•en (mis shā′pən, mish-), *adj.* deformed.

mis•sile (mis′əl; *esp. Brit.* -īl), *n.* **1.** an object or weapon that is thrown, shot, or propelled at a target. **2.** GUIDED MISSILE. **3.** BALLISTIC MISSILE.

mis•sion (mish/ən), *n.* **1.** a group of persons sent by a government to a foreign country, as to conduct negotiations. **2.** a task to be performed. **3.** a permanent diplomatic establishment abroad. **4.** a group of missionaries sent out by a church. **5.** the place of work of religious missionaries.

mis/sion•ar/y (-ə ner/ē), *n., pl.* **-ar•ies,** *adj.* **—n. 1.** a person sent by a church into an area to carry on religious or humanitarian work. **—adj. 2.** of religious missions or missionaries.

mis•sive (mis/iv), *n.* a written message; letter.

mis•spell/ *v.t., v.i.,* **-spelled** or **-spelt, -spell•ing.** to spell incorrectly. **—mis•spell/ing,** *n.*

mis•spend/ *v.t.,* **-spent, -spend•ing.** to squander; waste.

mis•state/ *v.t.,* **-stat•ed, -stat•ing.** to state wrongly or misleadingly. **—mis•state/ment,** *n.*

mis•step/ *n.* **1.** a wrong step. **2.** an error, as in conduct.

mist (mist), *n.* **1.** a foglike mass of minute globules of water suspended in or falling from the atmosphere. **2.** something that dims, obscures, or blurs. **—v.t., v.i. 3.** to make or become like or covered with mist. **—mist/y,** *adj.,* **-i•er, -i•est.**

mis•take (mi stāk/), *n., v.,* **-took, -tak•en, -tak•ing. —n. 1.** an error in action, opinion, or judgment. **2.** a misunderstanding or misconception. **—v.t. 3.** to regard, identify, understand, or interpret wrongly. **—mis•tak/a•ble,** *adj.* **—mis•tak/en,** *adj.*

mis•ter (mis/tər), *n.* **1.** (*cap.*) a title of respect prefixed to a man's name or position (usu. written *Mr.*). **2.** (used by itself as an informal term of address to a man).

mis•tle•toe (mis/əl tō/), *n.* a parasitic plant that bears white berries, used in Christmas decorations.

mis•treat/ *v.t.* to treat badly or abusively. **—mis•treat/ment,** *n.*

mis•tress (mis/tris), *n.* **1.** a woman who has authority, as over a household or institution. **2.** a woman who has a continuing extramarital sexual relationship with a man. **3.** something regarded as feminine that has supremacy: *Great Britain, mistress of the seas.* **4.** (*cap.*) a former term of address corresponding to Mrs., Miss, or Ms.

mis•tri/al *n.* a trial terminated without conclusion, esp. because of a prejudicial error in the proceedings.

mis•trust/ *n.* **1.** lack of trust or confidence. **—v.t. 2.** to regard with mistrust. **—mis•trust/ful,** *adj.*

mis/un•der•stand/ *v.t., v.i.,* **-stood, -stand•ing.** to understand or interpret incorrectly.

mis•use (*n.* mis yōōs/; *v.* -yōōz/), *n., v.,* **-used, -us•ing. —n. 1.** wrong or improper use. **—v.t. 2.** to use incorrectly or improperly. **3.** to treat badly; mistreat.

mite¹ (mīt), *n.* any of numerous tiny arachnids that are often parasitic on animals and plants.

mite² (mīt), *n.* **1.** a very small sum of money. **2.** a very small creature, person, or thing.

mi•ter (mī/tər), *n.* **1.** a headdress worn by a bishop or abbot. **2.** Also called **mi/ter joint/.** a joint formed by two pieces of wood whose beveled edges fit together at an angle. **—v.t. 3.** to join with a miter joint. Also, *esp. Brit.,* **mi/tre.**

mit•i•gate (mit/i gāt/), *v.t., v.i.,* **-gat•ed, -gat•ing.** to make or become less severe, intense, or painful. **—mit/i•ga/tion,** *n.*

mi•to•sis (mī tō/sis), *n.* the method of cell division in which chromosomes separate into two parts, one part of each chromosome being retained in each of the two new daughter cells. **—mi•tot/ic** (-tot/ik), *adj.*

mitt (mit), *n.* **1.** a thickly padded glove used by baseball catchers. **2.** *Slang.* a hand. **3.** a woman's glove that leaves the lower ends of the fingers bare.

mit/ten *n.* a hand covering enclosing the four fingers together and the thumb separately.

mix (miks), *v.t.* **1.** to combine into one mass. **2.** to combine or unite. **3.** to form or make by combining ingredients. **4.** to crossbreed. **—v.i. 5.** to associate or mingle, as in company. **6. mix up, a.** to confuse

completely. **b.** to involve or entangle. **—n. 7.** the result of mixing. **8.** a commercial mixture of dry food or drink ingredients. **—mix/a•ble,** *adj.* **—mix/er,** *n.*

mixed/ num/ber *n.* a number consisting of a whole number and a fraction or decimal, as 4½ or 4.5.

mix/ture (-chər), *n.* **1.** a product of mixing. **2.** the act of mixing or state of being mixed.

mix/-up/ *n.* a state of confusion.

ml milliliter.

mm millimeter.

MM. Messieurs.

MN Minnesota.

Mn *Chem. Symbol.* manganese.

mne•mon•ic (ni mon/ik), *adj.* **1.** assisting or intended to assist the memory. **—n. 2.** a mnemonic device, as a verse. **3.** a short form, as a symbol, used as a computer code or function.

MO 1. Missouri. **2.** modus operandi.

Mo *Chem. Symbol.* molybdenum.

Mo. 1. Missouri. **2.** Monday.

mo. *pl.* **mos.** month.

M.O. or **m.o., 1.** mail order. **2.** modus operandi. **3.** money order.

moan (mōn), *n.* **1.** a prolonged, low sound of pain or suffering. **—v.i., v.t. 2.** to make or utter with a moan. **3.** to complain or lament.

moat (mōt), *n.* a deep, wide trench, usu. filled with water, surrounding a fortress or castle.

mob (mob), *n., v.,* **mobbed, mob•bing. —n. 1.** a disorderly, riotous, or lawless crowd. **2.** the common people; masses. **3.** *Informal.* a criminal gang. **—v.t. 4.** to crowd around and harass or attack. **5.** to fill with people; crowd.

mo•bile (mō/bəl, -bēl for 1–4; -bēl for 5), *adj.* **1.** capable of moving or being moved. **2.** utilizing a motor vehicle for ready movement: *a mobile library.* **3.** changing easily, as in expression or mood. **4.** permitting relatively free movement from one social class or level to another. **—n. 5.** an abstract sculpture with delicately balanced units that move independently, as when stirred by a breeze. **—mo•bil/i•ty** (-bil/i tē), *n.*

mo•bi•lize (mō/bə līz/), *v.t., v.i.,* **-lized, -liz•ing.** to assemble and organize for action or use, esp. for war. **—mo/bi•li•za/tion,** *n.* **—mo/bi•liz/er,** *n.*

mob•ster (mob/stər), *n.* a member of a criminal mob.

moc•ca•sin (mok/ə sin, -zən), *n.* **1.** a heelless shoe made of soft leather. **2.** a hard-soled shoe resembling a moccasin. **3.** COTTONMOUTH.

mo•cha (mō/kə), *n.* **1.** a choice variety of coffee orig. grown in Arabia. **2.** a flavoring obtained by blending coffee with chocolate.

mock (mok), *v.t.* **1.** to treat with ridicule or contempt. **2.** to mimic or imitate, esp. derisively. **3.** to challenge; defy. **—v.i. 4.** to scoff; jeer. **—adj. 5.** feigned: *a mock battle.* **—mock/er,** *n.* **—mock/er•y,** *n., pl.* **-er•ies. —mock/ing•ly,** *adv.*

mock/ing•bird/ *n.* any of several New World songbirds that mimic the calls of other birds.

mock/-up/ or **mock/up/,** *n.* a model, often fullsize, for study, testing, or teaching.

mode¹ (mōd), *n.* **1.** a manner of acting or doing; method. **2.** a particular type or form of something. **—mod/al,** *adj.* **—mo•dal/i•ty,** *n., pl.* **-ties.**

mode² (mōd), *n.* fashion or style, as in manners or dress.

mod•el (mod/l), *n., adj., v.,* **-eled, -el•ing** or (*esp. Brit.*) **-elled, -el•ling. —n. 1.** a standard or example for imitation or comparison. **2.** a representation, usu. in miniature. **3.** an image, as in clay, to be reproduced in more durable material. **4.** a person whose occupation is posing for artists or photographers. **5.** a person employed to wear and display clothing. **6.** a style or design of a particular product. **—adj. 7.** serving as or worthy to serve as a model. **8.** being a miniature version of something: *a model ship.* **—v.t. 9.** to form or plan according to a model. **10.** to make a miniature model of. **11.** to display, esp. by wearing: *to model dresses.* **—v.i. 12.** to be employed as a model. **—mod/el•er,** *n.*

mo•dem (mō′dəm, -dem), *n.* **1.** an electronic device that makes possible the transmission of data to or from a computer via telephone or other communication lines. —*v.t.* **2.** to send (information, data, or the like) via a modem. [*mo(dulator)- dem(odulator)*]

mod•er•ate (*adj., n.* mod′ər it; *v.* -ə rāt′), *adj., n., v.,* **-at•ed, -at•ing.** —*adj.* **1.** not extreme, excessive, or intense. **2.** average in quantity, extent, or amount. **3.** mediocre or fair. **4.** calm or mild, as of the weather. —*n.* **5.** a person who holds moderate opinions, as in politics. —*v.t., v.i.* **6.** to make or become moderate. **7.** to preside over or act as moderator. —**mod′er•ate•ly,** *adv.* —**mod′er•a′tion,** *n.*

mod′er•a′tor *n.* a person who presides over a meeting, discussion, or debate.

mod•ern (mod′ərn), *adj.* **1.** of or characteristic of present and recent time; contemporary. —*n.* **2.** a person of modern times. **3.** a person with modern views and tastes. —**mo•der′ni•ty,** *n.* —**mod′-ern•ly,** *adv.* —**mod′ern•ness,** *n.*

Mod′ern Eng′lish *n.* the English language since c1475.

mod•ern•ism *n.* **1.** modern character, tendencies, or values. **2.** a modern usage or characteristic. **3.** estrangement or divergence from the past in the arts or literature occurring esp. in the 20th century. —**mod′ern•ist,** *n., adj.* —**mod′ern•is′tic,** *adj.*

mod•est (mod′ist), *adj.* **1.** having or showing a moderate estimate of oneself. **2.** free from ostentation; unpretentious. **3.** having or showing regard for the decencies of behavior, speech, and dress. **4.** limited in amount, size, or extent. —**mod′est•ly,** *adv.* —**mod′es•ty,** *n.*

mod•i•cum (mod′i kəm), *n.* a moderate or small amount.

mod•i•fy (mod′ə fī′), *v.t.,* **-fied, -fy•ing. 1.** to change somewhat; alter partially. **2.** (of a word, phrase, or clause) to limit or particularize the meaning of. **3.** to reduce in degree or extent. —**mod′i•fi•ca′tion,** *n.* —**mod′i•fi′er,** *n.*

mod•ish (mō′dish), *adj.* fashionable; stylish. —**mod′ish•ness,** *n.*

mo•diste (mō dēst′) *n.* a maker of women's attire.

mod•u•late (moj′ə lāt′), *v.,* **-lat•ed, -lat•ing.** —*v.t.* **1.** to regulate by or adjust to a proper measure or proportion. **2.** to cause the amplitude, frequency, phase, or intensity of (a carrier wave) to vary. —*v.i.* **3.** to move harmonically from one musical key to a related one. —**mod′u•la′tion,** *n.* —**mod′u•la′tor,** *n.*

mod•ule (moj′ōol) *n.* **1.** a component, frequently interchangeable with others, for assembly into an integrated system. **2.** a self-contained segment of a spacecraft, designed for a particular task. —**mod′u•lar,** *adj.*

mo•dus op•e•ran•di (mō′dəs op′ə ran′dē, -dī), *n., pl.* **mo•di op•er•an•di** (mō′dē, -dī). a method of working or operating. [< L]

mo•gul¹ (mō′gəl), *n.* a bump on a ski slope.

mo•gul² (mō′gəl), *n.* a powerful or influential person.

mo•hair (mō′hâr′), *n.* **1.** the hair of the Angora goat. **2.** a fabric made from mohair.

Mo•ham′med•an•ism (mŏŏ ham′i dn iz′əm, mō-) *n.* Islam. —**Mo•ham′med•an,** *n., adj.*

moi•ré (mwä rā′, mô-), *n., pl.* **-rés.** a fabric, as of silk, with a watery or wavelike appearance.

moist (moist), *adj.,* **-er, -est.** slightly wet; damp. —**moist′ly,** *adv.* —**moist′ness,** *n.*

mois′ture (-chər), *n.* condensed or diffused liquid, esp. water.

mois′tur•ize′ *v.t.,* **-ized, -iz•ing.** to add moisture to. —**mois′tur•iz′er,** *n.*

mo•lar (mō′lər), *n.* **1.** a tooth with a broad biting surface adapted for grinding. —*adj.* **2.** of the molar teeth.

mo•las•ses (mə las′iz), *n.* a thick syrup produced during the refining of sugar.

mold¹ (mōld), *n.* **1.** a hollow form for shaping something in a molten or plastic state. **2.** something formed in or on a mold. **3.** a frame on which something is formed or made. **4.** shape; form. **5.** distinc-tive nature, character, or type. —*v.t.* **6.** to shape or form in or as if in a mold. —**mold′a•ble,** *adj.* —**mold′er,** *n.*

mold² (mōld), *n.* **1.** an often downy or furry growth of minute fungi on vegetable or animal matter. **2.** a fungus that produces mold. —*v.i.* **3.** to become covered with mold. —**mold′y,** *adj.* **-i•er, -i•est.**

mold³ (mōld), *n.* loose, crumbly earth rich in organic matter.

mold′er *v.i.* to turn to dust by natural decay; crumble.

mold′ing *n.* **1.** the act or process of shaping in a mold. **2.** something molded. **3.** an ornamental strip of contoured material, esp. wood.

Mol•do•va (mōl dō′və), *n.* a republic in SE Europe, NE of Romania: formerly a part of the USSR. —**Mol•do′van,** *adj., n.*

mole¹ (mōl), *n.* **1.** a small burrowing mammal with velvety fur and very small eyes. **2.** a spy who is part of and works from within the ranks of an enemy governmental staff or intelligence agency.

mole² (mōl), *n.* a small, usu. dark-colored, slightly elevated blemish on the human skin.

mole³ (mōl), *n.* a massive stone structure set up in the sea as a breakwater, pier, or jetty.

mol•e•cule (mol′ə kyōōl′), *n.* the smallest physical unit of an element or compound, consisting of one or more like atoms in an element and two or more different atoms in a compound. —**mo•lec•u•lar** (mə lek′yə lər), *adj.*

mole′hill′ *n.* a small mound of earth dug up by a mole.

mole′skin′ *n.* **1.** the fur of the mole. **2.** a strong, heavy cotton fabric with a suedelike finish.

mo•lest (mə lest′), *v.t.* **1.** to bother or annoy. **2.** to make indecent sexual advances to. —**mo•les•ta•tion** (mō′le stā′shən, mol′e-), *n.* —**mo•lest′er,** *n.*

moll (mol), *n. Slang.* a female companion of a criminal.

mol•li•fy (mol′ə fī′), *v.t.,* **-fied, -fy•ing. 1.** to soften in feeling or temper. **2.** to mitigate; reduce. —**mol′li•fi•ca′tion,** *n.*

mol•lusk (mol′əsk), *n.* any of a large group of invertebrates with a soft body usu. protected by a shell, and including snails, squids, and octopuses.

mol•ly•cod•dle (mol′ē kod′l), *v.,* **-dled, -dling.** —*v.t.* **1.** to coddle; pamper. —*n.* **2.** a coddled man or boy. —**mol′ly•cod′dler,** *n.*

molt (mōlt), *v.i.* **1.** to cast or shed an outer layer or covering, as feathers or skin, in the process of renewal or growth. —*n.* **2.** the act or process of molting. —**molt′er,** *n.*

mol′ten *adj.* liquefied or fused by heat.

mo•lyb•de•num (mə lib′də nəm), *n.* a silverwhite metallic element used as an alloy. *Symbol:* Mo; *at. wt.:* 95.94; *at. no.:* 42.

mom (mom), *n. Informal.* mother.

mo•ment (mō′mənt), *n.* **1.** a very short period of time; instant. **2.** a particular time, esp. the present. **3.** importance or consequence. **4.** a time of success, excellence, or satisfaction.

mo′men•tar′y *adj.* **1.** lasting but a moment. **2.** likely to occur at any moment. —**mo′men•tar′i•ly,** *adv.*

mo•men′tous (-men′təs), *adj.* of great importance or consequence. —**mo•men′tous•ly,** *adv.* —**mo•men′tous•ness,** *n.*

mo•men′tum (-təm), *n., pl.* **-ta** (-tə), **-tums. 1.** force or speed of movement; impetus. **2.** the product of the mass of a body and its velocity.

mom•my (mom′ē), *n., pl.* **-mies.** *Informal.* mother.

Mon. **1.** Monday. **2.** Monsignor.

Mon•a•co (mon′ə kō′, mə nä′kō), *n.* a principality on the Mediterranean coast, bordering SE France.

mon•arch (mon′ərk, -ärk), *n.* **1.** a hereditary sovereign, as a king or emperor. **2.** one holding a dominant position. **3.** a large, deep orange butterfly with black and white markings. [< LL < Gk *monárchēs* sole ruler] —**mo•nar•chi•cal** (mə när′ki-kəl), **mo•nar′chic,** *adj.*

mon′ar•chy *n., pl.* **-chies. 1.** government by a monarch. **2.** a state ruled by a monarch.

mon•as•ter•y (mon′ə ster′ē), *n.*, *pl.* **-ter•ies.** a residence for a community of persons, esp. monks, under religious vows.

Mon•day (mun′dā, -dē), *n.* the second day of the week.

mon•e•tar•y (mon′i ter′ē, mun′-), *adj.* **1.** of the coinage or currency of a country. **2.** of money; pecuniary. —**mon′e•tar′i•ly** (-târ′ə lē), *adv.*

mon•ey (mun′ē), *n.*, *pl.* **mon•eys, mon•ies. 1.** a circulating medium of exchange, including coins and paper money. **2.** money or property as a measure of wealth.

mon′eyed *adj.* **1.** having much money; wealthy. **2.** of the wealthy.

mon′ey or′der *n.* an order for the payment of money, as one issued by one bank or post office and payable at another.

mon•ger (mung′gər, mong′-), *n.* **1.** a person involved with something in a petty or contemptible way: *a gossipmonger.* **2.** *Chiefly Brit.* a dealer or trader: *fishmongers.*

Mon•go•li•a (mong gō′lē ə, mon-), *n.* a region in Asia including Inner Mongolia in China and the Mongolian People's Republic.

mon•gol•ism (mong′gə liz′əm, mon′-), *n.* (*sometimes cap.*) DOWN SYNDROME.

Mon•gol•oid (mong′gə loid′, mon′-), *adj.* **1.** of, designating, or characteristic of one of the traditional racial divisions of humankind, marked by yellowish complexion, straight black hair, and high cheekbones, and including the Mongols, Chinese, Japanese, etc. **2.** (*often l.c.*) of or affected with Down syndrome. —*n.* **3.** a member of the Mongoloid race. **4.** (*often l.c.*) a person affected with Down syndrome.

mon•goose (mong′gōōs′, mon′-), *n.*, *pl.* **-goos•es.** a ferretlike carnivore of India that is noted for its ability to kill cobras.

mon•grel (mung′grəl, mong′-), *n.* an animal or plant, esp. a dog, resulting from an uncontrolled or accidental crossing of breeds or varieties.

mon•i•ker or **mon•ick•er** (mon′i kər), *n. Slang.* a name or nickname.

mon•i•tor (mon′i tər), *n.* **1.** a student appointed to assist a teacher. **2.** a device for observing, detecting, or recording the operation of a machine or system. **3.** *Radio and Television.* a receiver for monitoring transmissions. **4.** a component with a display screen for viewing computer data. —*v.t.* **5.** to check the quality of (transmitted signals) on a receiving set. **6.** to observe, record, or detect with instruments. **7.** to watch closely; keep track of.

monk (mungk), *n.* a man who is a member of a religious order and usu. lives in a monastery.

mon•key (mung′kē), *n.*, *pl.* **-keys,** *v.*, **-keyed, -key•ing.** —*n.* **1.** a primate mammal, excluding humans, characterized by a flattened face and usu. a long tail. —*v.i.* **2.** *Informal.* to trifle idly; fool.

mon′key busi′ness *n.* mischievous or improper behavior.

mon′key wrench′ *n.* a wrench with an adjustable jaw.

mon•o¹ (mon′ō), *n.* MONONUCLEOSIS.

mon•o² (mon′ō), *adj.* MONOPHONIC.

mono- a combining form meaning one, single, or lone (*monochromatic*).

mon•o•chrome (mon′ə krōm′), *adj.* being or made in shades of a single color. —**mon′o•chro•mat′ic,** *adj.*

mon•o•cle (mon′ə kəl), *n.* an eyeglass for one eye. —**mon′o•cled,** *adj.*

mon•o•cot•y•le•don (mon′ə kot′l ēd′n), *n.* a plant characterized by an embryo containing a single seed leaf. —**mon′o•cot′y•le′don•ous,** *adj.*

mo•noc•u•lar (mə nok′yə lər), *adj.* **1.** having one eye. **2.** of or for the use of only one eye.

mo•nog•a•my (mə nog′ə mē), *n.* the practice or condition of having only one spouse at a time. —**mo•nog′a•mist,** *n.* —**mo•nog′a•mous,** *adj.* —**mo•nog′a•mous•ly,** *adv.*

mon•o•gram (mon′ə gram′), *n.*, *v.*, **-grammed, -gram•ming.** —*n.* **1.** a design consisting of the combined initials of a name. —*v.t.* **2.** to decorate with a monogram.

mon′o•graph′ *n.* a learned treatise on a particular subject.

mon′o•lith (-lith), *n.* **1.** a single block of stone, esp. one formed into an obelisk or column. **2.** something having a uniform, massive, or inflexible quality or character. —**mon′o•lith′ic,** *adj.*

mon′o•logue′ or **-log′** (-lôg′, -log′), *n.* **1. a.** a dramatic or comic piece delivered by a single performer. **b.** SOLILOQUY (def. 1). **2.** a prolonged talk or discourse by a single speaker. —**mon•o•log•ist** (mon′ə lô′gist, -log′ist, mə nol′ə jist), **mon•o•logu•ist** (mon′ə lô′gist, -log′ist), *n.*

mon′o•ma′ni•a *n.* an obsessive zeal for or interest in a single thing. —**mon′o•ma′ni•ac′,** *n.*

mon′o•nu′cle•o′sis (-nōō′klē ō′sis, -nyōō′-), *n.* an infectious disease characterized by fever, swelling of lymph nodes, and an abnormally large number of certain leukocytes in the blood.

mon′o•phon′ic (-fon′ik), *adj.* of or noting a system of sound recording and reproduction using only a single channel.

mon′o•plane′ *n.* an airplane with one wing on each side.

mo•nop•o•ly (mə nop′ə lē), *n.*, *pl.* **-lies. 1.** exclusive control, as of a commodity or service. **2.** a commodity or service controlled by one individual or group. **3.** an individual or group that has a monopoly. —**mo•nop′o•list,** *n.* —**mo•nop′o•lis′tic,** *adj.* —**mo•nop′o•lize′,** *v.t.,* **-lized, -liz•ing.** —**mo•nop′o•li•za′tion,** *n.*

mon•o•rail (mon′ə rāl′), *n.* a single rail functioning as a track for wheeled vehicles.

mon•o•so•di•um glu•ta•mate (mon′ə sō′dē əm glōō′tə māt′), *n.* a white crystalline powder used to intensify the flavor of foods.

mon′o•syl′la•ble *n.* a word of one syllable. —**mon′o•syl•lab′ic,** *adj.*

mon′o•the•ism *n.* the doctrine or belief that there is only one God. —**mon′o•the′ist,** *n.,* *adj.* —**mon′o•the•is′tic,** *adj.*

mon′o•tone′ *n.* a vocal utterance or series of speech sounds in one unvaried tone.

mo•not′o•ny (mə not′n ē) *n.* wearisome uniformity. —**mo•not′o•nous,** *adj.*

mon•sieur (mə syœ′), *n.,* *pl.* **mes•sieurs** (mesyœ′). a French title corresponding to *Mr.* or *sir.*

mon•si•gnor (mon sē′nyər, mon′sē nyôr′, môn′-), *n.,* *pl.* **mon•si•gnors,** **mon•si•gno•ri** (môn′sē nyôr′ē). a title conferred on certain Roman Catholic prelates.

mon•soon (mon sōōn′), *n.* **1.** a seasonal wind of the Indian Ocean and S Asia. **2.** the season during which the SW monsoon blows. —**mon•soon′al,** *adj.*

mon•ster (mon′stər), *n.* **1.** a grossly anomalous or markedly malformed animal or plant. **2.** an imaginary creature of strange appearance. **3.** a wicked or cruel person. **4.** a huge animal or thing. —**mon•stros′i•ty** (-stros′i tē), *n.,* *pl.* **-ties.** —**mon′strous,** *adj.* —**mon′strous•ly,** *adv.*

Mont. Montana.

mon•tage (mon täzh′; *Fr.* môN tazh′), *n.,* *pl.* **-tag•es** (-tä′zhiz; *Fr.* -tazh′). **1.** the combining of pictorial or other artistic elements from different sources in a single composition. **2.** *Motion Pictures, Television.* juxtaposition or partial superimposition of several shots to form a single image.

month (munth), *n.* **1.** any of the 12 parts into which the calendar year is divided. **2.** a period of four weeks or 30 days.

month′ly *adj., n., pl.* **-lies,** *adv.* —*adj.* **1.** done, happening, or appearing once a month. **2.** computed or payable by the month. —*n.* **3.** a monthly periodical. —*adv.* **4.** once a month.

mon•u•ment (mon′yə mənt), *n.* **1.** something, as a pillar, erected in memory of a person or event. **2.** something, as a building, surviving from a past age and preserved for its historical or archaeological importance.

mon′u•men′tal *adj.* **1.** of or serving as a monument. **2.** exceptionally great: *monumental egotism.*

3. of enduring significance. —**mon′u•men′tal•ly,** *adv.*

moo (mōō), *n., pl.* **moos,** *v.,* **mooed, moo•ing.** —*n.* **1.** the deep, low sound characteristic of a cow. —*v.i.* **2.** to utter a moo.

mooch (mōōch), *v.t., v.i. Slang.* to scrounge; cadge. —**mooch′er,** *n.*

mood¹ (mōōd), *n.* **1.** a person's emotional state or outlook. **2.** a prevailing emotional tone or general attitude.

mood² (mōōd), *n.* a set of categories of the verb serving to indicate whether the verb expresses a fact, possibility, wish, or command.

mood′y *adj.,* **-i•er, -i•est. 1.** given to moods, esp. gloomy or sullen moods. **2.** gloomy; sullen. —**mood′i•ly,** *adv.* —**mood′i•ness,** *n.*

moon (mōōn), *n.* **1.** the earth's natural satellite. **2.** a planetary satellite. **3.** something shaped like an orb or a crescent. —*v.i.* **4.** to act abstractedly or dreamily.

moon′light′ *n.* **1.** the light of the moon. —*v.i.* **2.** to work at an additional job after one's regular one. —**moon′light′er,** *n.* —**moon′lit′** (-lit′), *adj.*

moon′shine′ *n.* **1.** *Informal.* smuggled or illicitly distilled liquor. **2.** empty or foolish talk. **3.** MOON-LIGHT.

moon′stone′ *n.* an opalescent, pearly blue variety of feldspar used as a gem.

moor¹ (mōōr), *n.* a tract of open, peaty wasteland, often overgrown with heath.

moor² (mōōr), *v.t., v.i.* to secure or be secured in place, as by cables and anchors or by lines.

Moor (mōōr), *n.* a member of a North African people who conquered Spain in the 8th century. —**Moor′ish,** *adj.*

moor′ing *n.* **1. moorings,** a place where a ship, boat, or aircraft may be moored. **2.** Usu., **moorings.** a source of stability or security.

moose (mōōs), *n., pl.* **moose.** a large deer of the Northern Hemisphere.

moot (mōōt), *adj.* **1.** open to discussion or debate. **2.** of little or no practical value or meaning; purely academic.

mop (mop), *n., v.,* **mopped, mop•ping.** —*n.* **1.** a device consisting of absorbent material, as a sponge, fastened to a handle and used esp. for washing floors. **2.** a thick mass of hair. —*v.t.* **3.** to clean or remove with or as if with a mop. **4. mop up,** to complete or finish.

mope (mōp), *v.i.,* **moped, mop•ing.** to be sunk in dejection or apathy; brood. —**mop′er,** *n.* —**mop′ey, mop′y,** *adj.,* **-i•er, -i•est.** —**mop′ish,** *adj.*

mo•ped (mō′ped′), *n.* a motorized bicycle with pedals. [≪ Sw (*trampcykel med*) *mo(tor och) ped-(aler)* pedal cycle with engine and pedals]

mop•pet (mop′it), *n.* a young child.

mor•al (môr′əl, mor′-), *adj.* **1.** of or concerned with the principles of right and wrong conduct. **2.** conforming to principles of right conduct. **3.** capable of recognizing and conforming to the rules of right conduct. **4.** acting on the mind, feelings, will, or character: *moral support.* **5.** based on strong probability: *a moral certainty.* —*n.* **6.** a moral teaching or practical lesson, as in a fable. **7. morals,** principles or habits with respect to right or wrong conduct. —**mor′al•ly,** *adv.*

mo•rale (mə ral′), *n.* emotional or mental condition, as of cheerfulness, with respect to work or a duty.

mo•ral•i•ty (mə ral′i tē, mô-), *n., pl.* **-ties. 1.** conformity to the rules of right conduct. **2.** moral quality or conduct. **3.** a doctrine of morals.

mor•al•ize (môr′ə līz′, mor′-), *v.i.,* **-ized, -iz•ing.** to reflect on or discuss moral matters, esp. in a self-righteous or tiresome way. —**mor′al•i•za′tion,** *n.* —**mor′al•iz′er,** *n.*

mo•rass (mə ras′), *n.* **1.** a marsh or bog. **2.** something from which it is difficult to free oneself.

mor•a•to•ri•um (môr′ə tôr′ē əm, mor′-), *n., pl.* **-to•ri•a** (-tôr′ē ə), **-to•ri•ums.** a suspension of activity.

mo•ray (môr′ā, mô rā′), *n., pl.* **-rays.** a tropical eel lacking pectoral fins.

mor•bid (môr′bid), *adj.* **1.** suggesting an unhealthy mental attitude; unwholesomely gloomy. **2.** gruesome; grisly. **3.** of or characteristic of disease. —**mor′bid•ly,** *adv.* —**mor•bid′i•ty, mor′bid•ness,** *n.*

mor•dant (môr′dnt), *adj.* **1.** sharply caustic; biting. **2.** burning; corrosive. —**mor′dan•cy,** *n.*

more (môr), *adj., compar. of* **much** or **many** *with* **most** *as superl.* **1.** in greater quantity, amount, or number. **2.** additional or further. —*n.* **3.** an additional amount. **4.** a greater quantity, amount, or degree. —*pron.* **5.** (*used with a pl. v.*) a greater number of persons or things. —*adv., compar. of* **much** *with* **most** *as superl.* **6.** in or to a greater extent or degree: *more interesting; more slowly.* **7.** in addition; further.

mo•rel (mə rel′), *n.* an edible mushroom with a deeply furrowed cap.

more•o′ver *adv.* in addition; besides.

mo•res (môr′āz, -ēz), *n.pl.* the fundamental moral views of a social group.

morgue (môrg), *n.* **1.** a place in which dead bodies are kept pending identification or burial. **2.** a reference file, as of clippings, esp. in a newspaper office.

mor•i•bund (môr′ə bund′, mor′-), *adj.* dying.

Mor•mon•ism (môr′mən iz′əm) *n.* a religion founded in the U.S. in 1830. —**Mor′mon,** *n., adj.*

morn (môrn), *n.* morning.

morn′ing *n.* **1.** the first part of the day, from dawn or from midnight to noon. **2.** an early period; beginning.

morn′ing glo′ry *n.* a twining plant with funnel-shaped flowers that often open only in the morning.

morn′ing sick′ness *n.* nausea occurring in the early part of the day during the first months of pregnancy.

Mo•roc•co (mə rok′ō), *n.* **1.** a kingdom in NW Africa. **2.** (*l.c.*) a pebble-grained leather made from goatskin. —**Mo•roc′can,** *n., adj.*

mo•ron (môr′on), *n.* **1.** a stupid person. **2.** (in a former classification of mental retardation) a person having an intelligence quotient of 50 to 69. —**mo•ron′ic** (mə ron′ik), *adj.* —**mo•ron′i•cal•ly,** *adv.*

mo•rose (mə rōs′), *adj.* **1.** gloomily or sullenly ill-humored. **2.** gloomy or sullen. —**mo•rose′ly,** *adv.* —**mo•rose′ness,** *n.*

mor•pheme (môr′fēm), *n.* a minimal grammatical unit that cannot be divided into smaller meaningful parts. —**mor•phe′mic,** *adj.*

mor•phine (môr′fēn), *n.* an addictive narcotic obtained from opium, used as a pain reliever or sedative.

mor•phol•o•gy (môr fol′ə jē), *n.* **1.** the branch of biology that deals with the form and structure of organisms. **2.** the study of patterns of word formation in a language. —**mor′pho•log′i•cal,** *adj.*

Morse′ code′ (môrs), *n.* either of two systems of dots and dashes, short and long sounds, or flashes of light used to represent letters, numerals, etc.: used esp. in telegraphy. [after S. F. B. *Morse* (1791–1872), U.S. inventor]

mor•sel (môr′səl), *n.* **1.** a small piece or amount, esp. of food; bit. **2.** an appetizing dish; treat.

mor•tal (môr′tl), *adj.* **1.** subject to death. **2.** of human beings. **3.** implacable; relentless: *a mortal enemy.* **4.** severe; grievous: *mortal fear.* **5.** causing death; fatal: *a mortal wound.* **6.** involving spiritual death: *a mortal sin.* —*n.* **7.** a human being. —**mor′tal•ly,** *adv.*

mor•tal•i•ty (môr tal′i tē), *n., pl.* **-ties. 1.** the state or condition of being subject to death. **2.** the relative frequency of deaths in a population.

mor•tar¹ (môr′tər), *n.* **1.** a bowl-shaped receptacle in which substances can be pounded or ground with a pestle. **2.** a short-barreled cannon for throwing shells at high angles.

mor•tar² (môr′tər), *n.* a mixture, esp. of lime or cement with sand and water, used as a bonding agent, as between bricks.

mor′tar•board′ *n.* **1.** a board, usu. square, used

by masons to hold mortar. **2.** an academic cap with a square, flat top and a tassel.

mort•gage (môr′gij), *n., v.,* **-gaged, -gag•ing.** —*n.* **1.** a conveyance of an interest in property as security for the repayment of a loan. **2.** the deed by which a mortgage is effected. —*v.t.* **3.** to convey or place (property) under a mortgage. **4.** to place under an obligation; pledge. —**mort′ga•gee′** (-gə jē′), *n., pl.* **-gees.** —**mort′ga•gor, mort′gag•er,** *n.*

mor•ti•cian (môr tish′ən), *n.* FUNERAL DIRECTOR.

mor•ti•fy (môr′tə fī′), *v.t.,* **-fied, -fy•ing. 1.** to humiliate or shame. **2.** to subjugate (the body, passions, etc.) by abstinence, ascetic discipline, or self-inflicted suffering. —**mor′ti•fi•ca′tion,** *n.*

mor•tise (môr′tis), *n.* a notch, hole, or slot made in a piece of wood to receive a tenon.

mor•tu•ar•y (môr′chŏŏ er′ē), *n., pl.* **-ar•ies.** FUNERAL HOME.

mo•sa•ic (mō zā′ik), *n.* **1.** a picture or decoration made of small, usu. colored inlaid pieces, as of stone or glass. **2.** the process of producing a mosaic. **3.** something resembling a mosaic.

Mo•ses (mō′ziz, -zis), *n.* a Hebrew prophet and lawgiver. —**Mo•sa′ic** (-zā′ik), *adj.*

mo•sey (mō′zē), *v.i.,* **-seyed, -sey•ing.** *Informal.* to stroll in a leisurely way.

Mos•lem (moz′ləm, mos′-), *adj., n., pl.* **-lems, -lem.** MUSLIM.

mosque (mosk, môsk), *n.* a Muslim place of public worship.

mos•qui•to (mə skē′tō), *n., pl.* **-toes, -tos.** an insect, the female of which sucks the blood of animals and humans.

moss (môs, mos), *n.* a tiny, leafy-stemmed plant that grows in tufts or mats, esp. on moist ground, tree trunks, and rocks. —**moss′y,** *adj.,* **-i•er, -i•est.**

moss′back′ *n. Informal.* a person holding very antiquated notions.

most (mōst), *adj., superl. of* **much** *or* **many** *with* **more** *as compar.* **1.** greatest, as in number: *the most votes.* **2.** the majority of: *most people.* —*n.* **3.** the greatest amount or degree: *the most we can do.* —*pron.* **4.** (*used with a sing. or pl. v.*) the greatest part; majority: *Most were pleased with the decision.* —*adv., superl. of* **much** *with* **more** *as compar.* **5.** in or to the greatest extent or degree: *most wisely.* **6.** very: *most puzzling.*

most′ly *adv.* for the most part; in the main.

mote (mōt), *n.* a small particle or speck, esp. of dust.

mo•tel (mō tel′), *n.* a hotel for motorists, typically with rooms adjacent to an outside parking area.

moth (môth, moth), *n., pl.* **moths** (môthz, mothz, môths, moths). any of numerous insects related to but distinguished from the butterflies by their feathery antennae and nocturnal habits.

moth′ball′ *n.* **1.** a small ball, as of camphor, placed in storage areas to repel moths from clothing. **2. in mothballs, a.** in storage. **b.** in a state of disuse.

moth•er (muth′ər), *n.* **1.** a female who bears or rears offspring; female parent. **2.** a woman in authority. **3.** something that gives rise to something else; source. —*adj.* **4.** of, characteristic of, or being a mother. —*v.t.* **5.** to give birth, origin, or rise to. **6.** to care for or protect like a mother. —**moth′er•hood′,** *n.* —**moth′er•less,** *adj.*

moth′er-in-law′ *n., pl.* **mothers-in-law.** the mother of one's husband or wife.

moth′er•land′ *n.* **1.** one's native land. **2.** the land of one's ancestors.

moth′er-of-pearl′ *n.* a hard, iridescent substance that forms the inner layer of certain mollusk shells.

mo•tif (mō tēf′), *n.* a recurring subject, theme, or idea, esp. in a literary, artistic, or musical work.

mo•tile (mōt′l, mō′til), *adj. Biol.* capable of moving spontaneously. —**mo•til′i•ty,** *n.*

mo•tion (mō′shən), *n.* **1.** the action or process of moving. **2.** an expressive bodily movement; gesture. **3.** a formal proposal, esp. one made to a deliberative assembly. **4. in motion,** in active operation; moving. —*v.t., v.i.* **5.** to direct by or make a meaningful motion. —**mo′tion•less,** *adj.*

mo′tion pic′ture *n.* **1.** a sequence of photographic images projected onto a screen in such rapid succession as to give the illusion of natural movement. **2.** a story, incident, etc., presented in this form.

mo•ti•vate (mō′tə vāt′), *v.t.,* **-vat•ed, -vat•ing.** to provide with a motive; spur. —**mo′ti•va′tion,** *n.* —**mo′ti•va′tion•al,** *adj.* —**mo′ti•va′tor,** *n.*

mo•tive (-tiv), *n.* **1.** something that causes a person to act; incentive. **2.** MOTIF. —*adj.* **3.** of or causing motion. **4.** prompting to action.

mot•ley (mot′lē), *adj.,* **-li•er, -li•est. 1.** exhibiting diversity of elements; heterogeneous. **2.** being of different colors combined; variegated.

mo•to•cross (mō′tō krôs′, -kros′), *n.* a motorcycle race over a course of very rough terrain.

mo•tor (mō′tər), *n.* **1.** a comparatively small engine, esp. an internal-combustion engine, as in an automobile. **2.** something that imparts motion. **3.** a machine that converts electrical energy into mechanical energy. —*adj.* **4.** equipped with or operated by a motor. **5.** of, by, or for motor vehicles or motorists. **6.** causing or producing motion. **7.** of or involving muscular movement. —*v.i.* **8.** to ride in an automobile.

mo′tor•bike′ *n.* a small, lightweight motorcycle.

mo′tor•boat′ *n.* a boat propelled by an inboard or outboard motor.

mo′tor•cade′ (-kād′), *n.* a procession or parade of motor vehicles.

mo′tor•car′ *n.* AUTOMOBILE.

mo′tor•cy′cle *n.* a two-wheeled motor vehicle. —**mo′tor•cy′clist,** *n.*

mo′tor•ist *n.* a person who drives or travels in an automobile.

mo′tor•ize′ *v.t.,* **-ized, -iz•ing. 1.** to furnish with a motor. **2.** to supply with motor vehicles.

mot•tle (mot′l), *v.t.,* **-tled, -tling.** to mark with blotches of a different color; spot.

mot•to (mot′ō), *n., pl.* **-toes, -tos. 1.** a pithy expression of a guiding principle. **2.** a sentence, phrase, or word inscribed on something to express its spirit or purpose. [< It < LL *muttum* sound, utterance]

moue (mŏŏ), *n., pl.* **moues** (mŏŏ). a pouting grimace.

mould (mōld), *n., v.t., v.i. Chiefly Brit.* MOLD.

mould′er *v.i. Chiefly Brit.* MOLDER.

moult (mōlt), *v.i., n. Chiefly Brit.* MOLT.

mound (mound), *n.* **1.** a natural elevation of earth; knoll. **2.** an artificial elevation of earth; embankment. **3.** the slightly raised ground on which a baseball pitcher stands.

mount[1] (mount), *v.t.* **1.** to go up; ascend. **2.** to get up on (a platform, a horse, etc.). **3.** to place at an elevation. **4.** to organize and launch (an attack, campaign, etc.). **5.** to put into position for use. **6.** to fix on or in a support, backing, or setting: *to mount a photograph.* **7.** to prepare for exhibition or study as a specimen. —*v.i.* **8.** to increase in amount or intensity. **9.** to rise; ascend. **10.** to get up on something, as a platform. —*n.* **11.** a horse or other animal for riding. **12.** a support, backing, or setting on or in which something is mounted. —**mount′a•ble,** *adj.* —**mount′er,** *n.*

mount[2] (mount), *n.* a mountain.

moun•tain (moun′tn), *n.* **1.** a natural elevation of land higher than a hill. **2.** a huge amount. —**moun′tain•ous,** *adj.*

moun′tain bike′ *n.* a sturdy bicycle designed for off-road use.

moun′tain•eer′ *n.* **1.** an inhabitant of a mountainous district. **2.** a climber of mountains, esp. for sport. —*v.i.* **3.** to climb mountains.

moun′tain li′on *n.* COUGAR.

moun•te•bank (moun′tə bangk′), *n.* a charlatan.

mourn (môrn), *v.i., v.t.* to feel or express sorrow or grief (for). —**mourn′er,** *n.* —**mourn′ful,** *adj.*

mouse (*n.* mous; *v. also* mouz), *n., pl.* **mice,** *v.,* **moused, mous•ing.** —*n.* **1.** any of numerous small rodents with small ears and a long, thin tail. **2.** a quiet, timid person. **3.** a palm-sized device used to select items on a computer display screen and to control the cursor. —*v.i.* **4.** to hunt for or catch mice.

mousse (mōōs), *n.* **1.** a sweetened dessert made with whipped cream, egg whites, and gelatin and chilled in a mold. **2.** a foamy preparation used to style the hair.

mous•tache (mus′tash, mə stash′), *n.* MUSTACHE.

mous•y or **-ey** (mou′sē, -zē), *adj.,* **-i•er, -i•est.** resembling a mouse, as in being drab and colorless or meek and timid. —**mous′i•ness,** *n.*

mouth (*n.* mouth; *v.* mouœͤ), *n., pl.* **mouths** (mouœͤhz), *v.* **1.** the opening through which an animal takes in food. **2.** something, as an opening, resembling a mouth: *the mouth of a cave.* —*v.t.* **3.** to utter in a sonorous or pompous manner. **4.** to form (a word, sound, etc.) silently or indistinctly with the mouth. —*Idiom.* **5. down in** or **at the mouth,** dejected.

mouth′ or′gan *n.* HARMONICA.

mouth′piece′ *n.* **1.** a part, as of a musical instrument, applied to or held in the mouth. **2.** one that voices the opinions of others.

mouth′wash′ *n.* a solution, often containing an antiseptic or astringent, for cleaning the mouth.

mouth′-wa′tering *adj.* appetizing, as in appearance or aroma.

mou•ton (mōō′ton), *n.* sheepskin processed to resemble seal or beaver.

move (mōōv), *v.,* **moved, mov•ing,** *n.* —*v.i.* **1.** to pass from one place or position to another. **2.** to change one's place of residence or business. **3.** to advance or progress. **4.** to be active. **5.** to take action; proceed. **6.** to make a formal request, application, or proposal. —*v.t.* **7.** to cause to go from one place or position to another. **8.** to set or keep in motion. **9.** to prompt or impel to take action. **10.** to arouse the feelings of. **11.** to evacuate (the bowels). **12.** to propose formally, as for consideration by a deliberative assembly. **13. move in,** to begin to occupy a residence or workplace. —*n.* **14.** an act or instance of moving. **15.** an action toward an objective. **16.** (in chess, checkers, etc.) a player's right or turn to make a play. —*Idiom.* **17. on the move, a.** busy; active. **b.** moving from place to place. **c.** making progress; advancing. —**mov′er,** *n.*

move′ment *n.* **1.** the act, process, or result of moving. **2.** a shift in the position of troops or ships. **3.** a series of actions directed toward a particular end. **4.** a course, tendency, or trend. **5.** a group of people or organizations working toward or favoring a common goal. **6.** an evacuation of the bowels. **7.** the working parts of a mechanism, as a watch. **8.** *Music.* a principal division or section of a composition, as a sonata or symphony.

mov•ie (mōō′vē), *n.* **1.** MOTION PICTURE. **2. movies, a.** the motion-picture industry. **b.** the showing of a motion picture.

mow¹ (mō), *v.t.,* **mowed, mowed** or **mown, mow•ing. 1.** to cut down (grass, grain, etc.) with a scythe or a machine. **2.** to cut grass, grain, etc., from. **3. mow down, a.** to destroy or kill in great numbers. **b.** to overwhelm. —**mow′er,** *n.*

mow² (mou), *n.* the place in a barn where hay or grain is stored.

Mo•zam•bique (mō′zam bēk′, -zəm-), *n.* a republic in SE Africa. —**Mo′zam•bi′can,** *n., adj.*

moz•za•rel•la (mot′sə rel′lə, mōt′-), *n., pl.* **-las.** a mild, white, semisoft cheese.

MP 1. Member of Parliament. **2.** Military Police.

mp melting point.

mph miles per hour.

Mr. (mis′tər), *n., pl.* **Messrs.** (mes′ərz). mister: a title of respect prefixed to a man's name or position. [abbr. of *mister*]

MRI magnetic resonance imaging.

Mrs. (mis′iz, miz′iz), *pl.* **Mmes.** (mā däm′, -dam′). a title of respect prefixed to the name of a married woman.

MS 1. Also, **ms, ms.** manuscript. **2.** Mississippi. **3.** multiple sclerosis.

Ms. (miz), *pl.* **Mses.** (miz′əz). a title of respect prefixed to a woman's name: unlike *Miss* or *Mrs.*, it does not indicate marital status. [b. of *Miss* and *Mrs.*]

M.S. Master of Science.

MSG monosodium glutamate.

MT 1. Montana. **2.** Mountain time.

Mt. or **mt.,** **1.** mount. **2.** mountain.

much (much), *adj.,* **more, most,** *n., pron., adv.,* **more, most.** —*adj.* **1.** great in quantity, measure, or degree: *too much cake.* —*n., pron.* **2.** a great quantity, measure, or degree: *not much to do.* **3.** a great, important, or notable thing or matter: *not much to look at.* —*adv.* **4.** to a great extent or degree: *much earlier.* **5.** nearly or about: *much like the others.*

mu•ci•lage (myōō′sə lij), *n.* a sticky, usu. liquid preparation used as an adhesive. —**mu′ci•lag′i•nous** (-laj′ə nəs), *adj.*

muck (muk), *n.* **1.** moist dung; manure. **2.** a highly organic dark or black soil. **3.** mire; mud. **4.** filth; dirt. —**muck′y,** *adj.,* **-i•er, -i•est.**

muck′rake′ *v.i.,* **-raked, -rak•ing.** to search for and expose real or alleged corruption, esp. in politics. —**muck′rak′er,** *n.*

mu•cous (myōō′kəs), *adj.* **1.** of, consisting of, or resembling mucus. **2.** containing or secreting mucus.

mu′cous mem′brane *n.* a mucus-secreting membrane lining all bodily passages that are open to the air.

mu′cus (-kəs), *n.* a viscous protective and lubricating solution secreted by mucous membranes.

mud (mud), *n.* wet, soft earth; mire.

mud•dle (mud′l), *v.,* **-dled, -dling,** *n.* —*v.t.* **1.** to mess up; bungle. **2.** to confuse mentally with or as if with liquor; stupefy. —*v.i.* **3.** to think or act in a confused manner. —*n.* **4.** a confused mental state. **5.** a confused state of affairs; mess.

mud′dle•head′ed *adj.* confused in one's thinking.

mud′sling′ing *n.* efforts to discredit an opponent by malicious or scandalous attacks. —**mud′sling′er,** *n.*

mu•ez•zin (myōō ez′in, mōō-), *n.* a crier who calls Muslims to prayer.

muff (muf), *n.* **1.** a thick tubular case for warming the hands. **2.** a bungled action or performance. —*v.t., v.i.* **3.** to handle or act clumsily.

muf•fin (muf′in), *n.* a small quick bread baked in a cuplike mold.

muf•fle (muf′əl), *v.t.,* **-fled, -fling. 1.** to wrap with something to deaden sound. **2.** to wrap or envelop, esp. for warmth or protection. **3.** to suppress; stifle.

muf′fler *n.* **1.** a scarf worn around the neck for warmth. **2.** a device for deadening sound.

muf•ti (muf′tē), *n.* civilian clothes.

mug (mug), *n., v.,* **mugged, mug•ging.** —*n.* **1.** a cylindrical drinking cup with a handle. **2.** *Slang.* **a.** the face. **b.** a thug; ruffian. —*v.t.* **3.** to assault usu. with intent to rob. **4.** to photograph (a suspect or criminal). —*v.i.* **5.** to make exaggerated faces; grimace. —**mug′ger,** *n.*

mug′gy *adj.,* **-gi•er, -gi•est.** oppressively damp and close. —**mug′gi•ness,** *n.*

mug′ shot′ *n.* a photograph of the face of a criminal suspect.

Mu•ham•mad (mōō ham′əd, -hä′məd), *n.* A.D. 570–632, Arab prophet: founder of Islam.

mu•lat•to (mə lat′ō, -lä′tō), *n., pl.* **-toes. 1.** the offspring of one white and one black parent. **2.** a person of mixed Negro and Caucasian ancestry.

mul•ber•ry (mul′ber′ē, -bə rē), *n., pl.* **-ries. 1.** a tree bearing edible, dark-purple, berrylike fruit. **2.** the fruit of the mulberry.

mulch (mulch), *n.* **1.** a covering, as of straw or compost, spread on the ground around plants, esp. to prevent evaporation or erosion and enrich the soil. —*v.t.* **2.** to cover with mulch.

mulct (mulkt), *v.t.* **1.** to defraud; swindle. **2.** to punish by a fine. —*n.* **3.** a fine.

mule¹ (myōōl), *n.* **1.** the offspring of a female horse and a male donkey. **2.** a stubborn person.

mule² (myōōl), *n.* a backless lounging slipper.

mul′ish *adj.* unyieldingly stubborn; obstinate.

mull[1] (mul), *v.t.* to think about carefully; ponder: *mulled over the advice.*

mull[2] (mul), *v.t.* to heat, sweeten, and spice (ale or wine).

mul•let (mul′it), *n., pl.* **-lets, -let.** an edible marine or freshwater fish with spiny fins.

mul•li•gan (mul′i gən), *n.* a stew of meat and vegetables.

mul•li•ga•taw•ny (mul′i gə tô′nē), *n.* a curry-flavored soup made usu. with chicken stock.

mul•lion (mul′yən), *n.* a vertical member separating the lights of a window.

multi- a combining form meaning: many (*multiform*); many times (*multimillionaire*); more than two (*multinational*).

mul•ti•cul•tur•al•ism (mul′tē kul′chər ə liz′əm, mul′tī-), *n.* the existence, recognition, or preservation of different cultures or cultural identities within a unified society. **—mul′ti•cul′tur•al,** *adj.*

mul•ti•far•i•ous (mul′tə fâr′ē əs), *adj.* having many different parts, elements, or forms; varied. **—mul′ti•far′i•ous•ly,** *adv.* **—mul′ti•far′i•ous•ness,** *n.*

mul′ti•me′di•a (mul′tē-, mul′tī-), *n.* (*used with a sing. v.*) **1.** the combined use of several media, as music and video in computer applications, or radio and newspapers. **—adj. 2.** of or involving the use of several media.

mul′ti•na′tion•al *n.* **1.** a large corporation with operations and subsidiaries in several nations. **—adj. 2.** of or involving several nations or multinationals.

mul•ti•ple (mul′tə pəl), *adj.* **1.** consisting of, having, or involving several or many; manifold. **—n. 2.** a number that contains another number an integral number of times without a remainder.

mul′tiple sclero′sis *n.* a disease marked by destruction of small areas of the brain and spinal cord, leading to neural and muscular impairments.

mul′ti•pli•ca′tion (-pli kā′shən), *n.* **1.** the act or process of multiplying. **2.** the addition of a number to itself as often as is indicated by another number, as in 5 × 10.

mul′ti•plic′i•ty (-plis′i tē), *n., pl.* **-ties.** a large number or variety.

mul•ti•ply′ *v.t., v.i.,* **-plied, -ply•ing. 1.** to increase in number or quantity. **2.** to perform the process of multiplication (on).

mul•ti•tude (mul′ti tōōd′, -tyōōd′), *n.* a great number.

mul′ti•tu′di•nous *adj.* **1.** numerous. **2.** having many parts.

mum[1] (mum), *adj.* silent: *kept mum.*

mum[2] (mum), *n.* CHRYSANTHEMUM.

mum•ble (mum′bəl), *v.,* **-bled, -bling,** *n.* **—v.i., v.t. 1.** to speak softly and indistinctly. **—n. 2.** a soft, indistinct utterance. **—mum′bler,** *n.*

mum•ble•ty•peg (mum′bəl tē peg′) also **mum′-ble-the-peg′** (-ᴛᵺə-), *n.* a game in which a pocketknife is flipped so that its blade sticks into the ground.

mum•bo jum•bo (mum′bō jum′bō), *n.* **1.** meaningless incantation or ritual. **2.** senseless or confusing language.

mum•mer (mum′ər), *n.* **1.** a person who wears a mask or fantastic costume while merrymaking, as at Christmas. **2.** an actor, esp. a pantomimist. **—mum′mer•y,** *n., pl.* **-ies.**

mum•my (mum′ē), *n., pl.* **-mies.** a dead body preserved by or as if by the ancient Egyptian embalming process.

mumps (mumps), *n.* (*used with a sing. v.*) an infectious viral disease characterized by inflammatory swelling of the salivary glands.

munch (munch), *v.t., v.i.* to chew steadily and often audibly.

mun•dane (mun dān′, mun′dān), *adj.* **1.** of this world. **2.** common; ordinary. **—mun•dane′ly,** *adv.*

mu•nic•i•pal (myōō nis′ə pəl), *adj.* of a municipality or its local government. **—mu•nic′i•pal•ly,** *adv.*

mu•nic′i•pal′i•ty (-pal′i tē), *n., pl.* **-ties.** a city,

town, village, or borough with corporate status and usu. its own local government.

mu•nif•i•cent (myōō nif′ə sənt), *adj.* characterized by great generosity. **—mu•nif′i•cence,** *n.*

mu•ni•tions (myōō nish′ənz), *n.pl.* materials, esp. weapons and ammunition, used in war.

mu•ral (myōŏr′əl), *n.* **1.** a picture painted directly on a wall. **—adj. 2.** of or like a wall. **—mu′ral•ist,** *n.*

mur•der (mûr′dər), *n.* **1.** the unlawful killing of a person, esp. when deliberate or premeditated. **2.** *Informal.* something very difficult, dangerous, or unpleasant. **—v.t. 3.** to kill by an act constituting murder. **4.** to spoil or mar through incompetence: *The singer murdered the aria.* **5.** *Informal.* to defeat thoroughly. **—mur′der•er,** *n.* **—mur′der•ess,** *n.*

murk (mûrk), *n.* darkness; gloom.

murk′y *adj.,* **-i•er, -i•est. 1.** dark; gloomy. **2.** vague; unclear. **—murk′i•ly,** *adv.* **—murk′i•ness,** *n.*

mur•mur (mûr′mər), *n.* **1.** a low and indistinct continuous sound. **2.** a mumbled or private expression of discontent. **3.** an abnormal sound heard within the body, esp. in the heart valves. **—v.i., v.t. 4.** to make or express in a murmur. **—mur′mur•er,** *n.* **—mur′mur•ous,** *adj.*

mus′ca•dine (mus′kə din, -dīn′), *n.* an American grape.

mus•cat (mus′kət, -kat), *n.* a variety of grape with a pronounced sweet aroma and flavor, used esp. for making wine.

mus•ca•tel (mus′kə tel′), *n.* a sweet wine made from muscat grapes.

mus•cle (mus′əl), *n., v.,* **-cled, -cling. —n. 1.** bodily tissue composed of elongated cells that contract to produce movement. **2.** bodily strength; brawn. **3.** power or force, esp. of a coercive nature. **—v.i. 4.** *Informal.* to make one's way by force. **—mus′cu•lar** (-kyə lər), *adj.*

mus′cle•bound′ *adj.* having enlarged and inelastic muscles, as from excessive exercise.

mus′cular dys′tro•phy (dis′trə fē), *n.* a hereditary disease characterized by gradual wasting of the muscles.

muse (myōōz), *v.,* **mused, mus•ing. —v.i. 1.** to meditate quietly; reflect. **—v.t. 2.** to say or think meditatively. **—mus′er,** *n.*

Muse *n.* **1.** one of the nine Greek goddesses who presided over the arts. **2.** (*l.c.*) the inspiration that motivates a poet, artist, or thinker.

mu•se•um (myōō zē′əm), *n.* a building or place where objects of permanent value, as works of art, are kept and displayed.

mush[1] (mush *or,* esp. *for* 2, 3, mŏŏsh), *n.* **1.** meal, esp. cornmeal, boiled in water or milk. **2.** a thick, soft mass. **3.** mawkish sentimentality. **—mush′y,** *adj.,* **-i•er, -i•est. —mush′i•ness,** *n.*

mush[2] (mush), *v.i.* to go or travel, esp. over snow with a dog team and sled.

mush•room (mush′rōōm, -rŏŏm), *n.* **1.** any of various fleshy fungi, including toadstools, puffballs, and morels. **—v.i. 2.** to spread, grow, or develop quickly.

mu•sic (myōō′zik), *n.* **1.** the art of ordering sounds into cohesive and structured forms. **2.** sounds organized to have melody, rhythm, harmony, and dynamics. **3.** the score of a musical composition. **4.** musical quality.

mu′si•cal *adj.* **1.** of or producing music. **2.** melodious; harmonious. **3.** fond of or skilled in music. **—n. 4.** a play or motion picture in which the plot is developed by songs and dances. **—mu′si•cal′i•ty,** *n.* **—mu′si•cal•ly,** *adv.*

mu′si•col′o•gy (-zi kol′ə jē), *n.* the scholarly or scientific study of music. **—mu′si•col′o•gist,** *n.*

mu′sic vid′eo *n.* a videotape featuring a dramatized rendition of a popular song.

musk (musk), *n.* a pungent glandular secretion of an Asiatic deer: used in perfumery. **—musk′y,** *adj.,* **-i•er, -i•est. —musk′i•ness,** *n.*

mus•ket (mus′kit), *n.* a heavy, large-caliber smoothbore gun: predecessor of the modern rifle. **—mus′ket•eer′,** *n.*

musk′mel′on *n.* a round or oblong melon with sweet, edible flesh.

musk′ox′ or **musk′ ox′,** *n., pl.* **-ox•en.** a large, shaggy, oxlike mammal of arctic regions of North America.

musk′rat′ *n., pl.* **-rats, -rat. 1.** a large, aquatic North American rodent with glossy dark-brown fur. **2.** the fur of a muskrat.

Mus•lim (muz′lim, mooz′-, moos′-), *adj., n., pl.* **-lims, -lim.** —*adj.* **1.** of the religion, law, or civilization of Islam. —*n.* **2.** an adherent of Islam.

mus•lin (muz′lin) *n.* a plain-weave cotton fabric used esp. for sheets.

muss (mus), *v.t.* **1.** to put into disorder. —*n.* **2.** a state of disorder; untidiness. —**muss′y,** *adj.,* **-i•er, -i•est.**

mus•sel (mus′əl), *n.* any of various bivalve mollusks, esp. an edible marine bivalve.

must (must), *auxiliary v.* **1.** (used to express obligation, compulsion, or necessity): *The rules must be obeyed.* **2.** (used to express strong probability or reasonable expectation): *He must be at least 70.* **3.** (used to express inevitability): *Human beings must die.* —*n.* **4.** something necessary or required: *Getting enough sleep is a must.*

mus•tache (mus′tash, mə stash′), *n.* the hair growing on the upper lip. —**mus′tached,** *adj.*

mus•tang (mus′tang), *n.* a small, hardy horse of the American plains. [< Sp *mestengo* stray or ownerless beast]

mus•tard (mus′tərd), *n.* **1.** any of various acrid or pungent plants with yellow flowers. **2.** a pungent powder or paste prepared from the seed of the mustard plant and used as a condiment.

mus′tard gas′ *n.* an oily liquid used in warfare for its irritating, blinding, and poisonous properties.

mus•ter (mus′tər), *v.t.* **1.** to bring together, as for inspection. **2.** to summon up; gather. —*v.i.* **3.** to come together; assemble. **4. muster out,** to discharge from military service. —*n.* **5.** an assembling, as for formal inspection. **6.** an assemblage, as of troops. —*Idiom.* **7. pass muster,** to be found acceptable.

mus•ty (mus′tē), *adj.,* **-ti•er, -ti•est. 1.** having an odor or flavor suggestive of mold, as old buildings. **2.** outdated; antiquated. —**mus′ti•ness,** *n.*

mu•ta•ble (myoo′tə bəl), *adj.* **1.** liable or subject to change or alteration. **2.** given to changing; inconstant. —**mu′ta•bil′i•ty,** *n.* —**mu′ta•bly,** *adv.*

mu•tant (myoot′nt), *n.* **1.** an organism resulting from mutation. —*adj.* **2.** undergoing or resulting from mutation.

mu•tate (myoo′tāt), *v.i., v.t.,* **-tat•ed, -tat•ing.** to undergo or cause to undergo mutation. —**mu′ta•tive** (-tə tiv), *adj.*

mu•ta′tion *n.* **1.** *Biol.* **a.** a sudden change in a heritable characteristic. **b.** an individual or species characterized by such a change. **2.** a change or alteration, as in form. —**mu•ta′tion•al,** *adj.*

mute (myoot), *adj., n., v.,* **mut•ed, mut•ing.** —*adj.* **1.** not speaking; silent. **2.** incapable of speech. —*n.* **3.** a person incapable of speech. **4.** a mechanical device for muffling the tone of a musical instrument. —*v.t.* **5.** to deaden or muffle the sound of. —**mute′ly,** *adv.* —**mute′ness,** *n.*

mu•ti•late (myoot′l āt′), *v.t.,* **-lat•ed, -lat•ing. 1.** to injure or disfigure by irreparably damaging parts. **2.** to deprive (a person or animal) of an essential part, as a limb. —**mu′ti•la′tion,** *n.* —**mu′ti•la′tor,** *n.*

mu•ti•ny (myoot′n ē), *n., pl.* **-nies,** *v.,* **-nied, -ny• ing.** —*n.* **1.** rebellion against constituted authority, esp. by sailors or soldiers against their officers. —*v.i.* **2.** to commit mutiny. —**mu′ti•neer′,** *n.* —**mu′ti•nous,** *adj.*

mutt (mut), *n. Slang.* a mongrel dog.

mut•ter (mut′ər), *v.i., v.t.* **1.** to speak or utter indistinctly or in a barely audible tone. **2.** to grumble. —*n.* **3.** the act or utterance of a person who mutters.

mut•ton (mut′n), *n.* the flesh of a mature sheep.

mut′ton•chops′ *n.pl.* side whiskers that are narrow at the temples and broad and trimmed short at the jawline.

mu•tu•al (myoo′choo əl), *adj.* **1.** exchanged in equal measure; reciprocal: *mutual respect.* **2.** having the same relation toward each other: *mutual enemies.* **3.** held in common; shared: *mutual interests.* —**mu′tu•al′i•ty,** *n.* —**mu′tu•al•ly,** *adv.*

mu′tual fund′ *n.* an investment company that invests its pooled money in a diversified list of securities.

muz•zle (muz′əl), *n., v.,* **-zled, -zling.** —*n.* **1.** the projecting part of an animal's head, including jaws, mouth, and nose. **2.** the open end of the barrel of a gun. **3.** a device placed over an animal's muzzle to prevent the animal from biting or eating. —*v.t.* **4.** to put a muzzle on (an animal). **5.** to restrain from speech or expression.

my (mī), *pron.* **1.** a form of the possessive case of I used as an attributive adjective. —*interj.* **2.** an exclamation of mild surprise or dismay.

My•an•mar (mī än′mär), *n.* a republic in SE Asia. Formerly, **Burma.**

my•col•o•gy (mī kol′ə jē), *n.* the branch of biology dealing with fungi. —**my•col′o•gist,** *n.*

my•na or **-nah** (mī′nə), *n., pl.* **-nas** or **-nahs.** any of various Asian birds of the starling family, esp. those with the ability to mimic human speech.

my•o•pi•a (mī ō′pē ə), *n.* **1.** a condition of the eye in which objects are seen distinctly only at short distances. **2.** lack of foresight. —**my•op′ic** (-op′ik, -ō′pik), *adj.*

myr•i•ad (mir′ē əd), *n.* **1.** an indefinitely great number. —*adj.* **2.** consisting of a myriad; innumerable.

myrrh (mûr), *n.* an aromatic gum resin obtained from plants and used chiefly in making incense and perfumes.

myr•tle (mûr′tl), *n.* **1.** a plant of S Europe with evergreen leaves, fragrant white flowers, and aromatic berries. **2.** any of certain unrelated plants, as the periwinkle.

my•self′ *pron.* **1.** the reflexive form of ME: *I cut myself.* **2.** (used as an intensive of I or ME): *I myself don't like it.* **3.** my normal self: *I wasn't myself when I said that.*

mys•ter•y (mis′tə rē), *n., pl.* **-ter•ies. 1.** something unexplained or inexplicable. **2.** a person or thing having qualities that arouse curiosity or speculation. **3.** a fictional work that involves the solving of a puzzle, esp. a crime. **4.** the quality of being obscure or enigmatic. **5.** a truth unknowable except by divine revelation. —**mys•te′ri•ous** (mi stēr′ē-əs), *adj.*

mys•tic (mis′tik), *adj.* **1.** of or characterized by esoteric or otherworldly practices or content. **2.** of occult character or significance. **3.** of mystics or mysticism. —*n.* **4.** a person who claims insight into mysteries transcending ordinary human knowledge. —**mys′ti•cal,** *adj.*

mys′ti•cism (-tə siz′əm), *n.* the doctrine of an immediate spiritual intuition of truths, or of a direct, intimate union of the soul with God through contemplation or spiritual ecstasy.

mys′ti•fy′ *v.t., -fied, -fy•ing.* **1.** to perplex or bewilder. **2.** to make mysterious. —**mys′ti•fi•ca′tion,** *n.*

mys•tique (mi stēk′), *n.* **1.** a framework of attitudes and beliefs constructed around a person or object. **2.** an aura of mystery or mystical power surrounding a particular occupation or pursuit.

myth (mith), *n.* **1.** a traditional or legendary story, esp. one that involves gods and heroes and explains a cultural practice or natural phenomenon. **2.** a fictitious person, story, etc. **3.** an unproven or false belief. —**myth′i•cal,** *adj.*

my•thol•o•gy (mi thol′ə jē), *n., pl.* **-gies. 1.** a body of myths, as that of a particular people. **2.** the study of myths. —**myth•o•log•i•cal** (mith′ə loj′i-kəl), *adj.* —**my•thol′o•gist,** *n.*

N, n (en), *n.*, *pl.* **Ns** or **N's, ns** or **n's.** the 14th letter of the English alphabet, a consonant.

N 1. north. **2.** northern.

N *Chem. Symbol.* nitrogen.

N. 1. Navy. **2.** north. **3.** northern. **4.** November.

n. 1. name. **2.** neuter. **3.** new. **4.** nominative. **5.** noon. **6.** north. **7.** northern. **8.** noun. **9.** number.

nab (nab), *v.t.*, **nabbed, nab•bing.** *Informal.* **1.** to arrest or capture. **2.** to snatch or seize.

na•bob (nā′bob), *n.* any very wealthy, influential, or powerful person.

na•cre (nā′kər), *n.* MOTHER-OF-PEARL. —**na′cre•ous** (-krē əs), *adj.*

na•dir (nā′dər, -dēr), *n.* **1.** the point on the celestial sphere directly beneath a given position or observer and diametrically opposite the zenith. **2.** the lowest point.

nag[1] (nag), *v.*, **nagged, nag•ging,** *n.* —*v.t.* **1.** to annoy by persistent faultfinding, complaints, etc. **2.** to be a constant source of unease to. —*v.i.* **3.** to find fault or complain persistently. —*n.* **4.** a person who nags. —**nag′ger,** *n.*

nag[2] (nag), *n.* an old or worthless horse.

nai•ad (nā′ad, -əd, nī′-), *n.*, *pl.* **-ads, -a•des** (-ə dēz). (in Greek myth) a nymph presiding over a river or spring.

nail (nāl), *n.* **1.** a piece of metal with a pointed tip and flattened head, hammered into wood as a fastener. **2.** a thin, horny plate growing on the upper side of the end of a finger or toe. —*v.t.* **3.** to fasten with a nail. **4.** *Informal.* to catch or seize. **5.** *Informal.* to accomplish perfectly.

na•ive or **-ïve** (nä ēv′), *adj.* **1.** having unaffected simplicity of nature. **2.** lacking in experience, judgment, or information. [< F < L *nātīvus* native] —**na•ive′ly,** *adv.*

na•ive•té or **-ïve•té** (nä ēv tā′, -ēv′tā, -ē′və-), *n.* **1.** the quality or state of being naive. **2.** a naive action, remark, etc. [< F]

na•ked (nā′kid), *adj.* **1.** being without clothing; nude. **2.** without covering: *a naked sword.* **3.** (of the eye, sight, etc.) unassisted by an optical instrument. **4.** plain; unadorned: *the naked truth.* —**na′ked•ly,** *adv.* —**na′ked•ness,** *n.*

name (nām), *n.*, *v.*, **named, nam•ing,** *adj.* —*n.* **1.** a word or phrase by which a person or thing is designated. **2.** mere designation rather than fact: *a king in name only.* **3.** an abusive epithet. **4.** reputation or fame. —*v.t.* **5.** to give a name to. **6.** to identify by name. **7.** to designate or nominate for office. **8.** to specify: *Name your price.* —*adj.* **9.** well-known. —**Idiom. 10. in the name of, a.** with appeal to. **b.** by the authority of. —**name′a•ble,** *adj.*

name′less *adj.* **1.** having no name. **2.** not referred to by name. **3.** incapable of being described.

name′ly *adv.* that is to say; specifically.

name′sake′ *n.* **1.** a person named after another. **2.** a person having the same name as another.

nan•ny (nan′ē), *n.*, *pl.* **-nies.** a person employed to take care of a young child in the home.

nan′ny goat′ *n.* a female goat.

nan•o•sec•ond (nan′ə sek′ənd, nā′nə-), *n.* one billionth of a second.

nap[1] (nap), *v.*, **napped, nap•ping,** *n.* —*v.i.* **1.** to sleep for a short time. **2.** to be off one's guard: *The question caught him napping.* —*n.* **3.** a brief period of sleep. —**nap′per,** *n.*

nap[2] (nap), *n.* the short fuzzy ends of fibers on the surface of cloth. —**nap′less,** *adj.* —**napped,** *adj.*

na•palm (nā′päm), *n.* **1.** a highly incendiary jelly-like substance used in firebombs, flamethrowers, etc. —*v.t.* **2.** to bomb or attack with napalm.

nape (nāp, nap), *n.* the back of the neck.

naph•tha (naf′thə, nap′-), *n.* a colorless, explosive liquid distilled from oil, used as a solvent and a fuel. —**naph′thous,** *adj.*

nap•kin (nap′kin), *n.* a small piece of cloth or paper used to wipe the lips and fingers and to protect the clothes while eating.

na•po•le•on (nə pō′lē ən, -pōl′yən), *n.* a pastry made of thin layers of puff paste and custard or cream filling.

nar•cis•sism (när′sə siz′em), *n.* inordinate fascination with oneself; excessive self-love. —**nar′cis•sist,** *n.* —**nar′cis•sis′tic,** *adj.*

nar•cis•sus (när sis′əs), *n.*, *pl.* **-cis•sus, -cis•sus•es, -cis•si** (-sis′ē, -sis′ī). any of various bulbous plants with showy yellow or white flowers and a cup-shaped corona.

nar•co•sis (när kō′sis), *n.* a state of drowsiness or stupor.

nar•cot′ic (-kot′ik), *n.* **1.** any addictive substance that blunts the senses and can cause confusion, stupor, coma, and death. —*adj.* **2.** pertaining to narcotics or their use.

nar•rate (nar′āt, na rāt′), *v.t.*, *v.i.*, **-rat•ed, -rat•ing. 1.** to tell or relate (a story, event, etc.). **2.** to add a spoken commentary to (a film or television program). —**nar•ra′tion,** *n.* —**nar′ra•tor,** *n.*

nar′ra•tive (-ə tiv), *n.* **1.** a story or account, whether true or fictitious. **2.** the art or process of narrating. —*adj.* **3.** of a narrative or narration.

nar•row (nar′ō), *adj.*, **-er, -est,** *v.*, *n.* —*adj.* **1.** of little breadth or width. **2.** limited in range or scope. **3.** lacking breadth of view or sympathy. **4.** barely adequate or successful: *a narrow escape.* —*v.i.*, *v.t.* **5.** to become or make narrower in width or scope. —*n.* **6. narrows,** a narrow part of a body of water. —**nar′row•ly,** *adv.* —**nar′row•ness,** *n.*

nar′row-mind′ed *adj.* having a closed mind; prejudiced. —**nar′row-mind′ed•ness,** *n.*

nar•whal (när′wəl), *n.* a small arctic whale, the male of which has a long, twisted tusk.

NASA (nas′ə), *n.* National Aeronautics and Space Administration.

na•sal (nā′zəl), *adj.* **1.** of the nose. **2.** (of a speech sound) pronounced with the voice issuing through the nose. —**na•sal′i•ty,** *n.* —**na′sal•ly,** *adv.*

nas•cent (nas′ent, nā′sənt), *adj.* beginning to exist or develop. —**nas′cence,** *n.*

nas•tur•tium (nə stûr′shəm, na-), *n.* a garden plant with shield-shaped leaves and bright, irregular flowers.

nas•ty (nas′tē), *adj.*, **-ti•er, -ti•est. 1.** filthy. **2.** indecent or obscene. **3.** highly unpleasant. **4.** vicious or spiteful. —**nas′ti•ly,** *adv.* —**nas′ti•ness,** *n.*

na•tal (nāt′l), *adj.* of a person's birth.

na•tion (nā′shən), *n.* **1.** a body of people associated with a particular territory and possessing its own government. **2.** an American Indian people or tribe. —**na′tion•hood′,** *n.*

na•tion•al (nash′ə nl), *adj.* **1.** of or belonging to a nation. **2.** peculiar or common to a nation. —*n.* **3.** a citizen or subject of a particular nation. —**na′tion•al•ly,** *adv.*

na′tion•al•ism *n.* **1.** devotion to one's nation; patriotism. **2.** the desire for national advancement or independence. —**na′tion•al•ist,** *adj.*, *n.* —**na′tion•al•is′tic,** *adj.*

na′tion•al′i•ty *n.*, *pl.* **-ties. 1.** the status of belonging to a particular nation by birth or naturalization. **2.** a nation or people.

na′tion•al•ize′ *v.t.*, **-ized, -iz•ing. 1.** to bring under the ownership or control of a nation, as an industry or land. **2.** to make national in extent or scope. —**na′tion•al•i•za′tion,** *n.*

na′tion•wide′ *adj.* extending throughout the nation.

na•tive (nā′tiv), *adj.* **1.** being the place of origin of a person or thing. **2.** belonging to a person by birth or to a thing by nature. **3.** belonging to the original inhabitants of a region. **4.** born in a particular place. **5.** originating naturally in a particular region. —*n.* **6.** one of the people indigenous to a place. **7.** a person born in a particular place. **8.** an indigenous animal or plant. [< MF < L *nātīvus* inborn, natural]

Na′tive Amer′ican *n.* AMERICAN INDIAN.

na•tiv•i•ty (nə tiv′i tē, nā-), *n., pl.* **-ties. 1.** birth. **2.** (*cap.*) the birth of Christ.

NATO (nā′tō), *n.* North Atlantic Treaty Organization.

nat•ty (nat′ē), *adj.,* **-ti•er, -ti•est.** neatly or trimly smart. —**nat′ti•ly,** *adv.*

nat•u•ral (nach′ər əl), *adj.* **1.** existing in or formed by nature. **2.** of or pertaining to nature. **3.** inborn; innate. **4.** free from affectation. **5.** to be expected: *a natural result.* **6.** true to or closely imitating nature. **7.** *Music.* neither sharp nor flat. —*n.* **8.** a person or thing that is likely to be successful. **9.** a symbol placed before a note, canceling the effect of a previous sharp or flat. —**nat′u•ral•ness,** *n.*

nat′ural child′birth *n.* childbirth involving little or no use of drugs or anesthetics.

nat′ural gas′ *n.* a mixture of gaseous hydrocarbons that accumulates in porous sedimentary rocks, used as a fuel.

nat′ural his′tory *n.* the study of organisms and natural objects.

nat•u•ral•ism (-ər ə liz′əm), *n.* an artistic or literary style that represents objects and events as they occur in nature or real life. —**nat′u•ral•is′tic,** *adj.*

nat•u•ral•ist *n.* **1.** a person who studies natural history. **2.** an adherent of naturalism.

nat•u•ral•ize′ *v.t.,* **-ized, -iz•ing.** to confer citizenship upon (an alien). —**nat′u•ral•i•za′tion,** *n.*

nat′ural re′source *n.* a source of wealth occurring in nature, as a forest or water.

nat′ural selec′tion *n.* the process by which forms of life having traits that better enable them to adapt to environmental pressures will survive and reproduce in greater numbers than others of their kind.

na•ture (nā′chər), *n.* **1.** the natural world as it exists without human beings. **2.** the universe, with all its phenomena. **3.** the inherent character of a person, animal, or thing. **4.** kind or sort. **5.** the primitive condition of humankind.

naught (nôt), *n.* **1.** nothing. **2.** a cipher (0); zero.

naugh•ty (nô′tē), *adj.,* **-ti•er, -ti•est. 1.** disobedient; mischievous. **2.** improper or indecent. —**naugh′ti•ly,** *adv.* —**naugh′ti•ness,** *n.*

nau•se•a (nô′zē ə, -zhə, -sē ə, -shə), *n.* **1.** sickness at the stomach, accompanied by an involuntary impulse to vomit. **2.** extreme disgust.

nau•ti•cal (nô′ti kəl, not′i-), *adj.* of sailors, ships, or navigation. —**nau′ti•cal•ly,** *adv.*

nau′tical mile′ *n.* a unit of distance at sea or in the air equal to 1.852 kilometers.

nau•ti•lus (nôt′l əs, not′-), *n., pl.* **nau•ti•lus•es, nau•ti•li** (nôt′l ī′, not′-). a deep-sea mollusk having a spiral, chambered shell.

Nav•a•jo or **-ho** (nav′ə hō′, nä′və-), *n., pl.* **-jo, -jos, -joes** or **-ho, -hos, -hoes.** a member of an American Indian people of the U.S. Southwest.

na•val (nā′vəl), *adj.* of, for, or possessing a navy.

nave (nāv), *n.* the principal area of a church, from the main entrance to the chancel.

na•vel (nā′vəl), *n.* the depression in the surface of the abdomen where the umbilical cord was connected with the fetus.

nav•i•gate (nav′i gāt′), *v.t., v.i.,* **-gat•ed, -gat•ing. 1.** to move on or through (water, air, or land) in a ship or aircraft. **2.** to direct or manage (a ship or aircraft) on its course. **3.** to walk or find one's way (in or across). —**nav′i•ga′tion,** *n.* —**nav′i•ga′tor,** *n.*

na•vy (nā′vē), *n., pl.* **-vies. 1.** the warships belonging to a country. **2.** (*often cap.*) the complete body of such warships, together with their personnel, equipment, etc. **3.** NAVY BLUE.

na′vy blue′ *n.* a dark blue.

nay (nā), *adv.* **1.** and not only so but: *many good, nay, noble qualities.* —*n.* **2.** a denial or refusal. **3.** a negative vote or voter.

Na•zi (nät′sē, nat′-), *n., pl.* **-zis.** a member of the fascist political party which controlled Germany from 1933 to 1945 under Adolf Hitler. —**Na′zism** (-siz əm), **Na′zi•ism,** *n.*

NB or **N.B., 1.** New Brunswick. **2.** nota bene.

Nb *Chem. Symbol.* niobium.

NC or **N.C., 1.** network computer. **2.** no charge. **3.** North Carolina.

NC-17 (en′sē′sev′ən tēn′), *Trademark.* no children under 17: a motion-picture rating advising that persons under 17 will not be admitted.

ND or **N.D.,** North Dakota.

Nd *Chem. Symbol.* neodymium.

N.Dak. North Dakota.

NE 1. Nebraska. **2.** northeast. **3.** northeastern.

Ne *Chem. Symbol.* neon.

neap tide (nēp), *n.* a tide having the lowest high point.

near (nēr), *adv.* and *adj.,* **-er, -est,** *prep., v.* —*adv.* **1.** at a short distance in space or time. **2.** close in relation. **3.** almost. —*adj.* **4.** close in distance or time. **5.** closely related or connected. **6.** intimate or familiar. **7.** narrow or close: *a near escape.* —*prep.* **8.** close to. —*v.t., v.i.* **9.** to come near (to). —**near′ness,** *n.*

near′by′ *adj., adv.* close at hand.

near′ly *adv.* almost.

near′sight′ed (-sī′tid, -sī′-), *adj.* seeing distinctly at a short distance only; myopic. —**near′sight′ed•ness,** *n.*

neat (nēt), *adj.,* **-er, -est. 1.** orderly and clean. **2.** trim and graceful. **3.** skillful; adroit. **4.** *Slang.* great; wonderful. **5.** undiluted. —**neat′ly,** *adv.* —**neat′ness,** *n.*

Neb. Nebraska.

Nebr. Nebraska.

neb•u•la (neb′yə lə), *n., pl.* **-lae** (-lē′, -lī′), **-las.** a cloud of interstellar gas and dust. —**neb′u•lar,** *adj.*

neb′u•lous (-ləs), *adj.* **1.** hazy or vague. **2.** of or resembling a nebula or nebulae.

nec•es•sar•i•ly (nes′ə sâr′ə lē, -ser′-), *adv.* **1.** by or of necessity. **2.** as a necessary result.

nec•es•sar•y (nes′ə ser′ē), *adj., n., pl.* **-sar•ies.** —*adj.* **1.** essential; indispensable. **2.** unavoidable. **3.** acting or proceeding from compulsion or obligation. —*n.* **4.** something necessary.

ne•ces•si•tate (nə ses′i tāt′), *v.t.,* **-tat•ed, -tat•ing. 1.** to make necessary or unavoidable. **2.** to compel or oblige.

ne•ces′si•ty *n., pl.* **-ties. 1.** something necessary or indispensable. **2.** an imperative requirement or need. **3.** the state or fact of being necessary. **4.** a compulsion to do something. **5.** poverty. —*Idiom.* **6. of necessity,** inevitably; unavoidably.

neck (nek), *n.* **1.** the part of the body that connects the head and the trunk. **2.** the part of a garment closest to the neck. **3.** a slender part that resembles a neck, as on a bottle or vase. **4.** a narrow strip of land. —*v.i.* **5.** *Informal.* to embrace, kiss, and caress amorously. —*Idiom.* **6. neck and neck,** just even or very close.

neck•er•chief (nek′ər chif, -chēf′), *n.* a cloth or scarf worn around the neck.

neck′lace (-lis), *n.* a piece of jewelry worn around the neck, as a string of pearls or beads.

neck′tie′ *n.* a band of decorative fabric worn around the neck and tied in front with a knot or bow.

nec•ro•man•cy (nek′rə man′sē), *n.* **1.** a method of divination through invocation of the dead. **2.** black magic; sorcery. —**nec′ro•man′cer,** *n.*

ne•cro•sis (nə krō′sis), *n.* death of a portion of animal or plant tissue. —**ne•crot′ic** (-krot′ik), *adj.*

nec•tar (nek′tər), *n.* **1.** the saccharine secretion of a plant, which attracts the insects or birds that pollinate the flower. **2.** (in Greek myth) the life-giving drink of the gods. **3.** any delicious drink.

nec•tar•ine (nek′tə rēn′, nek′tə rēn′), *n.* a variety of peach having a smooth skin.

nee or **née** (nā), *adj.* born (used to introduce the

maiden name of a married woman): *Mrs. Jones, nee Berg.*

need (nēd), *n.* **1.** a requirement or obligation. **2.** a lack of something wanted or deemed necessary. **3.** urgent want, as of something requisite. **4.** a situation or time of difficulty. **5.** destitution; poverty. —*v.t.* **6.** to have need of. —*v.i.* **7.** to be in need. —*auxiliary v.* **8.** (used to express obligation or necessity, esp. in interrogative or negative statements): *Need I say more?* —*Idiom.* **9. if need be,** should the necessity arise.

nee•dle (nēd′l), *n.*, *v.*, **-dled, -dling.** —*n.* **1.** a small, slender, steel implement with a point at one end and a hole for thread at the other, used in sewing. **2.** any of various larger implements for making stitches, as in knitting. **3.** a hypodermic needle. **4.** the pointer on a dial or compass. **5.** a slender, pointed device used to transmit vibrations from the groove of a phonographic record. **6.** a needle-shaped leaf, as of a pine. —*v.t.* **7.** *Informal.* **a.** to prod or goad. **b.** to tease.

nee•dle•point′ *n.* **1.** embroidery on canvas. —*adj.* **2.** noting a lace in which a needle works out the design on paper.

nee•dle•work′ *n.* the art or product of working with a needle, esp. in embroidery or needlepoint.

needs (nēdz), *adv.* of necessity (usu. prec. or fol. by *must*): *It needs must be.*

need′y *adj.*, **-i•er, -i•est.** extremely poor; destitute. —**need′i•ness,** *n.*

ne′er′-do-well′ (nâr′-), *n.* an idle, worthless person.

ne•far•i•ous (ni fâr′ē əs), *adj.* extremely wicked or villainous: *a nefarious plot.* —**ne•far′i•ous•ly,** *adv.* —**ne•far′i•ous•ness,** *n.*

ne•gate (ni gāt′, neg′āt), *v.t.*, **-gat•ed, -gat•ing. 1.** to deny the existence or truth of (something). **2.** to nullify or invalidate (something).

neg•a•tive (neg′ə tiv), *adj.*, *n.*, *v.*, **-tived, -tiv•ing.** —*adj.* **1.** expressing negation or denial. **2.** expressing refusal or resistance. **3.** lacking positive attributes. **4.** lacking in constructiveness or helpfulness. **5.** *Math.* expressing a quantity less than zero. **6.** *Photog.* noting an image in which the light and dark tones are reversed. **7.** of or pertaining to the electric charge of a body that has an excess of electrons. **8.** *Med.* failing to show a positive result in a diagnostic test. —*n.* **9.** a negative answer, word, etc. **10.** a negative quality or characteristic. **11.** *Photog.* a negative image, as on a film. —*v.t.* **12.** to deny; contradict. **13.** to veto. —*Idiom.* **14. in the negative,** in the form of a negative response. —**neg′a•tive•ly,** *adv.* —**neg′a•tive•ness, neg′a•tiv′i•ty,** *n.*

ne•glect (ni glekt′), *v.t.* **1.** to pay too little attention to; disregard. **2.** to be remiss in the care of. **3.** to fail to carry out or perform. —*n.* **4.** an act or instance of neglecting. **5.** the fact or state of being neglected. —**ne•glect′ful,** *adj.* —**ne•glect′ful•ly,** *adv.*

neg•li•gee (neg′li zhā′, neg′li zhā′), *n.*, *pl.* **-gees.** a woman's dressing gown of sheer, soft fabric.

neg•li•gent (neg′li jənt), *adj.* **1.** guilty of or characterized by neglect. **2.** careless and indifferent. —**neg′li•gence,** *n.* —**neg′li•gent•ly,** *adv.*

neg′li•gi•ble (-jə bəl), *adj.* so small or unimportant as to be safely disregarded.

ne•go•ti•a•ble (ni gō′shē ə bəl, -shə bəl), *adj.* **1.** capable of being negotiated. **2.** (esp. of securities) transferable by delivery. —**ne•go′ti•a•bil′i•ty,** *n.*

ne•go′ti•ate′ (-shē āt′), *v.*, **-at•ed, -at•ing.** —*v.i.* **1.** to deal or bargain with another or others. —*v.t.* **2.** to arrange for by discussion and settlement of terms. **3.** to move through in a satisfactory manner: *to negotiate a sharp curve.* **4.** to transfer (a draft, promissory note, etc.) to a new owner by delivery. —**ne•go′ti•a′tion,** *n.* —**ne•go′ti•a′tor,** *n.*

Ne•gro (nē′grō), *adj.*, *n.*, *pl.* **-groes.** —*adj.* **1.** of, designating, or characteristic of one of the traditional racial divisions of humankind, marked by brown to black skin and including esp. the indigenous peoples of sub-Saharan Africa. —*n.* **2.** a member of the Negro race. [< Sp and Pg *negro* black < L]

neigh (nā), *n.* **1.** the high-pitched, snorting sound of a horse. —*v.i.* **2.** to utter such a sound.

neigh•bor (nā′bər), *n.* **1.** a person who lives near another. **2.** a person or thing that is near another. **3.** one's fellow human being. —*v.t.*, *v.i.* **4.** to live or be situated nearby. Also, *esp. Brit.,* **neigh′bour.** —**neigh′bor•ing,** *adj.*

neigh′bor•hood′ *n.* **1.** a district or locality, often with reference to its character. **2.** a number of persons living in a particular locality. —*Idiom.* **3. in the neighborhood of,** approximately; about.

nei•ther (nē′thər, nī′-), *conj.* **1.** not either: *Neither John nor Betty is at home.* **2.** nor: *Bob can't go; neither can I.* —*adj.* **3.** not either: *neither path.* —*pron.* **4.** not either: *Neither is to be trusted.*

nem•e•sis (nem′ə sis), *n.*, *pl.* **-ses** (-sēz′). **1.** a source of harm or failure. **2.** an unconquerable opponent. **3.** an agent or act of retribution.

neo- a combining form meaning new, recent, or revived (*neoclassic*).

ne•o•dym•i•um (nē′ō dim′ē əm), *n.* a rare-earth element occurring with cerium and other rare-earth metals. *Symbol:* Nd; *at. wt.:* 144.24; *at. no.:* 60.

Ne•o•lith•ic (nē′ə lith′ik), *adj.* noting or pertaining to the last phase of the Stone Age.

ne•ol•o•gism (nē ol′ə jiz′əm), *n.* a new word or phrase or an existing word used in a new sense.

ne•on (nē′on), *n.* an inert gaseous element occurring in small amounts in the earth's atmosphere, used chiefly in a type of electrical lamp. *Symbol:* Ne; *at. wt.:* 20.183; *at. no.:* 10.

ne•o•nate (nē′ə nāt′), *n.* a newborn child. —**ne′o•na′tal,** *adj.*

ne′o•phyte′ (-fīt′), *n.* **1.** a beginner or novice. **2.** a new convert to a belief.

ne′o•plasm (-plaz′əm), *n.* a new growth of abnormal tissue; tumor. —**ne′o•plas′tic** (-plas′tik), *adj.*

Ne•pal (nə pôl′, -päl′), *n.* a constitutional monarchy in the Himalayas. —**Nep•a•lese** (nep′ə lēz′, -lēs′), *n.*, *pl.* **-lese,** *adj.*

neph•ew (nef′yōo; *esp. Brit.* nev′yōo), *n.* **1.** a son of one's brother or sister. **2.** a son of one's spouse's brother or sister.

ne•phri•tis (nə frī′tis), *n.* inflammation of the kidneys. —**ne•phrit′ic** (-frit′ik), *adj.*

ne plus ul•tra (nē′ plus′ ul′trə, nā′), *n.* the highest point or stage. [< L: not further beyond]

nep•o•tism (nep′ə tiz′əm), *n.* favoritism based on family relationship. —**nep′o•tist,** *n.*

Nep•tune (nep′tōōn, -tyōōn), *n.* **1.** the Roman god of the sea. **2.** the planet eighth in order from the sun.

nerd (nûrd), *n. Slang.* a dull, ineffectual, or unattractive person.

nerve (nûrv), *n.*, *v.*, **nerved, nerv•ing.** —*n.* **1.** one or more bundles of fibers that convey impulses between the brain or spinal cord and other parts of the body. **2.** courage. **3.** boldness; impudence. **4.** nerves, nervousness. —*v.t.* **5.** to give courage to someone. —*Idiom.* **6. get on someone's nerves,** to irritate someone.

nerve′ gas′ *n.* any of several poison gases that interfere with nerve conduction and respiration.

nerv′ous *adj.* **1.** uneasy; fearful; timid. **2.** highly excitable or agitated. **3.** of or affecting the nerves: *nervous tension.* —**nerv′ous•ly,** *adv.* —**nerv′ous•ness,** *n.*

nerv′y *adj.*, **-i•er, -i•est. 1.** brashly presumptuous. **2.** showing courage.

nest (nest), *n.* **1.** a structure of twigs, grasses, and mud prepared by a bird for incubating eggs and rearing young. **2.** any structure used for depositing eggs or raising young. **3.** a snug retreat or refuge. **4.** a set of items that fit one within another: *a nest of tables.* **5.** a place where something bad flourishes: *a nest of thieves.* —*v.i., v.t.* **6.** to build or settle in a nest. **7.** to fit one within another.

nest′ egg′ *n.* money saved and held for emergencies, retirement, etc.

nes•tle (nes′əl), *v.*, **-tled, -tling.** —*v.i.* **1.** to lie close and snug. **2.** to be located in a sheltered spot. —*v.t.* **3.** to settle snugly. **4.** to press affectionately.

net¹ (net), *n.*, *v.*, **net•ted, net•ting.** —*n.* **1.** a fabric with a uniform open mesh. **2.** a contrivance of such fabric, for catching fish or other animals. **3.** a piece of meshed fabric used to divide a court, as in tennis. **4.** anything serving to catch or ensnare. **5.** a computer or telecommunications network. **6. the Net,** the Internet. —*v.t.* **7.** to catch or ensnare.

net² (net), *adj., n., v.,* **net•ted, net•ting.** —*adj.* **1.** remaining after deductions, as for expenses. —*n.* **2.** net income, profit, etc. —*v.t.* **3.** to gain as clear profit.

neth•er (neth′ər), *adj.* lying beneath; lower or under.

Neth•er•lands (neth′ər ləndz), *n.* **the,** a kingdom in W Europe. —**Neth′er•land′er** (-lan′dər, -lən-), *n.*

net′tle *n., v.,* **-tled, -tling.** —*n.* **1.** a plant covered with stinging hairs. —*v.t.* **2.** to irritate or annoy.

net′tle•some *adj.* **1.** causing irritation or annoyance. **2.** easily provoked or annoyed.

net′work′ *n.* **1.** any combination of intersecting filaments, lines, etc. **2.** a group of broadcasting stations linked together so that the same program can be carried by all. **3.** any system of interconnected elements. **4.** a computer or telecommunications system linked to permit exchange of information. —*v.i.* **5.** to engage in networking. —*v.t.* **6.** to place in or connect to a network. **7.** to organize into a network.

net′work′ing *n.* **1.** the informal sharing of information among individuals linked by a common interest. **2.** the design, establishment, or utilization of a computer network.

neu•ral (noor′əl, nyoor′-), *adj.* of a nerve or the nervous system. —**neu′ral•ly,** *adv.*

neu•ral•gia (noo ral′jə, nyoo-), *n.* sharp and paroxysmal pain along a nerve. —**neu•ral′gic,** *adj.*

neu•ri•tis (-rī′tis), *n.* inflammation of a nerve.

neu•rol′o•gy (-rol′ə jē), *n.* the branch of medicine dealing with the nervous system. —**neu•ro•log•i•cal** (noor′ə loj′i kəl), *adj.* —**neu•rol′o•gist,** *n.*

neu•ron (noor′on, nyoor′-), *n.* a cell that is the functional unit of the nervous system, consisting of the cell body and its processes. —**neu•ron•al** (noor′ə nl, nyoor′-, noo rōn′l, nyoo-), *adj.*

neu•ro•sis (noo rō′sis, nyoo-), *n., pl.* **-ses** (-sēz). a disorder in which anxiety, obsessional thoughts, compulsive acts, etc., dominate the personality. —**neu•rot′ic** (-rot′ik), *adj., n.* —**neu•rot′i•cal•ly,** *adv.*

neu•ro•sur•ger•y (noor′ō sûr′jə rē, nyoor′-), *n.* surgery of the brain or other nerve tissue. —**neu′ro•sur′geon** (-jən), *n.*

neu′ro•trans•mit•ter *n.* any of several chemical substances that transmit nerve impulses across a synapse.

neu•ter (noo′tər, nyoo′-), *adj.* **1.** of or being a grammatical gender that refers to things classed as neither masculine nor feminine. **2.** having no organs of reproduction; asexual. **3.** *Zool.* having imperfectly developed sexual organs, as worker bees. —*v.t.* **4.** to spay or castrate (a dog, cat, etc.).

neu•tral (noo′trəl, nyoo′-), *adj.* **1.** not taking the part of either side in a dispute or war. **2.** of no particular kind, characteristics, etc.: *a neutral personality.* **3.** (of a color) **a.** without hue. **b.** matching well with most other colors. —*n.* **4.** a neutral person or nation. **5.** the position of gears when not engaged. **6.** a neutral color. —**neu′tral•ly,** *adv.*

neu•tron (noo′tron, nyoo′-), *n.* an elementary particle having no charge and a mass slightly greater than that of a proton.

Nev. Nevada.

nev•er (nev′ər), *adv.* **1.** not ever; at no time. **2.** absolutely not: *This will never do.*

nev′er•the•less′ *adv.* however; in spite of that.

new (noo, nyoo), *adj.,* **-er, -est,** *adv.* —*adj.* **1.** of recent origin, production, purchase, etc. **2.** of a kind now existing for the first time. **3.** having but lately become known. **4.** unfamiliar or strange. **5.** having but lately come to a place, position, status, etc.: *a new minister.* **6.** unaccustomed. **7.** further; additional. **8.** fresh or unused. **9.** other than the former or the old. **10.** (*cap.*) (of a language) in its latest

known period. —*adv.* **11.** recently or freshly.

new•el (noo′əl, nyoo′-), *n.* **1.** Also called **new′el post′.** the post supporting the handrail at the top or bottom of a flight of stairs. **2.** a central pillar from which the steps of a winding stair radiate.

New′ Eng′land an area in the NE United States, including Connecticut, Maine, Massachusetts, New Hampshire, Rhode Island, and Vermont. —**New′ Eng′land•er,** *n.*

new′fan′gled (-fang′gəld, -fang′-), *adj.* of a new kind or fashion.

new′ly *adv.* **1.** recently; lately. **2.** anew or afresh.

new′ly•wed′ *n.* a person who has recently married.

news (nooz, nyooz), *n.* **1.** a report of a recent event. **2.** a report on recent events in a newspaper or on radio or television. **3.** such reports taken collectively.

news′cast′ *n.* a broadcast of news on radio or television. —**news′cast′er,** *n.*

news′let′ter *n.* an informational report issued periodically by an organization to employees, contributors, etc.

news′man′ or **-wom′an,** *n., pl.* **-men** or **-wom•en.** a person employed to gather and report news.

news′pa′per (nooz′-, nyooz′-, noos′-, nyoos′-), *n.* a publication, usu. issued daily or weekly, containing news, comment, features, and advertising.

news′print′ *n.* a low-grade paper used chiefly for newspapers.

news′reel′ *n.* a short motion picture presenting current or recent events.

news′stand′ *n.* a stall or stand at which newspapers and periodicals are sold.

news′wor′thy *adj.* of sufficient interest to warrant press coverage. —**news′wor′thi•ness,** *n.*

newt (noot, nyoot), *n.* any of several brilliantly colored, semiaquatic salamanders.

New′ Tes′tament *n.* the portion of the Christian Bible recording the experience and teachings of Christ and His disciples.

new•ton (noot′n, nyoot′n), *n.* a unit of force, equal to the force that produces an acceleration of one meter per second per second on a mass of one kilogram.

new′ wave′ *n.* (*often caps.*) a movement, esp. in French filmmaking of the 1950s, that breaks with traditional values, techniques, etc.

New′ World′ *n.* WESTERN HEMISPHERE.

new year *n.* **1.** (*cap.*) the first day of the year. **2.** the year approaching.

New′ Zea′land (zē′lənd), *n.* a country in the S Pacific, SE of Australia, consisting of two large islands. 3,587,275. —**New′ Zea′land•er,** *n.*

next (nekst), *adj.* **1.** immediately following in time, order, etc. **2.** nearest in place or position. —*adv.* **3.** in the nearest place, time, order, etc. **4.** on the first occasion to follow.

next′-door′ *adj.* situated in the next house, apartment, etc.

nex•us (nek′səs), *n., pl.* **nex•us.** a means of connection; tie; link.

NH or **N.H.,** New Hampshire.

ni•a•cin (nī′ə sin), *n.* NICOTINIC ACID.

nib (nib), *n.* **1.** the writing end of a pen. **2.** any pointed end.

nib′ble *v.,* **-bled, -bling,** *n.* —*v.t., v.i.* **1.** to eat small bits of (something). **2.** to bite gently. —*n.* **3.** a small or gentle bite. —**nib′bler,** *n.*

Nic•a•ra•gua (nik′ə rä′gwə), *n.* a republic in Central America. —**Nic′a•ra′guan,** *n., adj.*

nice (nīs), *adj.,* **nic•er, nic•est. 1.** pleasing; agreeable. **2.** amiable; pleasant; kind. **3.** requiring or displaying great skill, tact, or precision. **4.** fine or subtle: *a nice distinction.* **5.** refined in manners, language, etc. [< OF: silly, simple < L *nescius* ignorant] —**nice′ly,** *adv.* —**nice′ness,** *n.*

ni•ce•ty (nī′si tē), *n., pl.* **-ties. 1.** a delicate or fine point. **2.** exactness, as in workmanship. **3.** Usu. **-ties.** refined or fine things or manners.

niche (nich), *n.* **1.** a recess in a wall, as for a decorative object. **2.** a suitable place or position. **3.** the position of a particular population in an ecological community.

nick (nik), *n.* **1.** a small notch, groove, etc., cut into a surface. —*v.t.* **2.** to injure slightly. **3.** to make a nick in. —*Idiom.* **4. in the nick of time,** at the last possible moment.

nick•el (nik′əl), *n.* **1.** a hard, silvery white metallic element, used in alloys and in electroplating. *Symbol:* Ni; *at. wt.:* 58.71; *at. no.:* 28. **2.** a copper and nickel coin of the U.S., equal to five cents.

nick′name′ *n., v.,* **-named, -nam•ing.** —*n.* **1.** a name substituted for the proper name of a person, place, etc. **2.** a familiar form of a proper name, as *Jim* for *James.* —*v.t.* **3.** to give a nickname to.

nic•o•tine (nik′ə tēn′), *n.* a highly toxic liquid alkaloid found in tobacco.

nic′o•tin′ic ac′id (nik′ə tin′ik, -tē′nik, nik′ə-), *n.* a crystalline acid that is a component of the vitamin B complex.

niece (nēs), *n.* **1.** a daughter of one's brother or sister. **2.** a daughter of one's spouse's brother or sister.

nif•ty (nif′tē) *adj.,* **-ti•er, -ti•est.** *Informal.* **1.** fine; excellent. **2.** stylish or smart.

Ni•ger (nī′jər, nē zhâr′), *n.* a republic in NW Africa. —**Ni•ge•ri•en** (nī jēr′ē en′), *adj., n.*

Ni•ge•ri•a (nī jēr′ē ə), *n.* a republic in W Africa. —**Ni•ge′ri•an,** *n., adj.*

nig•gard•ly (nig′ərd lē) *adj.* stingy.

nig•gling (nig′ling), *adj.* **1.** petty; trivial. **2.** demanding too much care, time, etc. —**nig′gler,** *n.*

nigh (nī), *adv., adj.,* **-er, -est,** *prep.* near.

night (nīt), *n.* **1.** the period of darkness between sunset and sunrise. **2.** a condition or time of ignorance, misfortune, etc.

night′cap′ *n.* **1.** an alcoholic drink taken at the end of the day. **2.** a cap worn in bed.

night′club′ *n.* an establishment open at night, offering food, drink, and entertainment.

night′ crawl′er *n.* an earthworm.

night′fall′ *n.* the coming of night; dusk.

night′gown′ *n.* a loose gown, worn in bed by women or children.

night′hawk′ *n.* any of several long-winged, nightflying birds related to the whippoorwill.

night•in•gale (nīt′n gāl′, nī′ting-), *n.* any of several small Old World birds noted for the melodious song of the male, often heard at night.

night′ly *adj.* **1.** occurring each night or at night. **2.** of or characteristic of night. —*adv.* **3.** on every night. **4.** at or by night.

night′mare′ (-mâr′), *n.* **1.** a terrifying dream. **2.** a thought or experience suggestive of a nightmare. —**night′mar′ish,** *adj.*

night′ owl′ *n.* a person who often stays up late at night.

night′shade′ *n.* **1.** any of various plants related to the potato and tomato and bearing black or red berries, some species of which are poisonous. **2.** BELLADONNA (def. 1).

night′shirt′ *n.* a loose shirtlike garment for wearing in bed.

night′ stick′ *n.* a billy carried by police officers.

ni•hil•ism (nī′ə liz′əm, nē′-), *n.* **1.** total rejection of established laws and institutions. **2.** the belief that all existence is senseless and that there is no possibility of an objective basis for truth. —**ni′hil•ist,** *n., adj.* —**ni′hil•is′tic,** *adj.*

nil (nil), *n.* nothing; zero.

nim•ble (nim′bəl), *adj.,* **-bler, -blest. 1.** quick and light in movement; agile. **2.** quick to understand, devise, etc. —**nim′ble•ness,** *n.* —**nim′bly,** *adv.*

nim•bus (nim′bəs), *n., pl.* **-bi** (-bī), **-bus•es. 1.** HALO (def. 1). **2.** a rain cloud.

Nim•rod (nim′rod), *n. Bible.* a great hunter.

nin•com•poop (nin′kəm pōōp′, ning′-), *n.* a fool or simpleton.

nine (nīn), *n.* **1.** a cardinal number, eight plus one. **2.** a symbol for this number, as 9 or IX. —*adj.* **3.** amounting to nine. —**ninth,** *adj., n.*

nine′pins′ *n.* tenpins played without the head pin.

nine′teen′ *n.* **1.** a cardinal number, ten plus nine.

2. a symbol for this number, as 19 or XIX. —*adj.* **3.** amounting to 19. —**nine′teenth′,** *adj., n.*

nine′ty *n., pl.* **-ties,** *adj.* —*n.* **1.** a cardinal number, ten times nine. **2.** a symbol for this number, as 90 or XC. —*adj.* **3.** amounting to 90. —**nine′ti•eth,** *adj., n.*

nin•ny (nin′ē), *n., pl.* **-nies.** a fool or simpleton.

ni•o•bi•um (nī ō′bē əm), *n.* a steel-gray metallic element, used chiefly in alloy steels. *Symbol:* Nb; *at. no.:* 41; *at. wt.:* 92.906.

nip[1] (nip), *v.,* **nipped, nip•ping,** *n.* —*v.t.* **1.** to pinch; bite. **2.** to sever by pinching, biting, or snipping. **3.** to check in growth or development. **4.** to affect painfully, as cold does. —*n.* **5.** the act of nipping. **6.** a biting quality, as of frosty air. **7.** sharp cold. **8.** a small quantity of anything. —*Idiom.* **9. nip and tuck,** closely contested.

nip[2] (nip), *v.,* **nipped, nip•ping,** *n.* **1.** a small drink of alcoholic liquor; sip. —*v.i.* **2.** to drink alcoholic liquor in small sips.

nip′ple *n.* **1.** a protuberance of the breast where, in the female, the milk ducts discharge. **2.** something resembling it, as the mouthpiece of a nursing bottle.

nip′py *adj.,* **-pi•er, -pi•est. 1.** chilly; cold. **2.** sharp; pungent.

nir•va•na (nir vä′nə, -van′ə, nər-), *n.* **1.** (*often cap.*) (in Buddhism) release from the cycle of reincarnations as a result of the extinction of individual passion, hatred, and delusion. **2.** a state of freedom from pain and worry.

nit (nit), *n.* **1.** the egg of a parasitic insect, esp. of a louse. **2.** the young of such an insect.

ni•ter (nī′tər), *n.* **1.** POTASSIUM NITRATE. **2.** SODIUM NITRATE. Also, *esp. Brit.,* **ni′tre.**

nit′pick′ *v.i.* to be critical of inconsequential details. —**nit′pick′er,** *n.*

ni•trate (*n.* nī′trāt, -trit; *v.* -trāt), *n., v.,* **-trat•ed, -trat•ing.** —*n.* **1.** a salt or ester of nitric acid. —*v.t.* **2.** to treat with nitric acid or a nitrate.

ni′tric ac′id (nī′trik), *n.* a caustic liquid used in the manufacture of explosives, fertilizers, etc.

ni•tro•gen (nī′trə jən), *n.* a colorless, odorless, gaseous element that constitutes about four-fifths of the volume of the atmosphere. *Symbol:* N; *at. wt.:* 14.0067; *at. no.:* 7. —**ni•trog′e•nous** (-troj′ə nəs), *adj.*

ni•tro•glyc•er•in (nī′trə glis′ər in) also **-er•ine** (-ər in, -ə ren′), *n.* a highly explosive oily liquid used in explosives and as a vasodilator.

ni•trous (nī′trəs) *adj.* **1.** of niter. **2.** Also, **ni′tric.** containing nitrogen.

nit′ty-grit′ty (nit′ē-), *n., pl.* **-grit•ties.** the crux of a matter.

nit′wit′ *n.* a slow-witted or foolish person.

nix (niks), *n.* **1.** nothing. —*adv.* **2.** no. —*v.t.* **3.** to veto.

NJ or **N.J.,** New Jersey.

NM or **N.M.,** New Mexico.

N. Mex. New Mexico.

no[1] (nō), *adv., n., pl.* **noes, nos.** —*adv.* **1.** (a negative expressing dissent, denial, or refusal.) **2.** not at all: *He is no better.* —*n.* **3.** a denial or refusal. **4.** a negative vote or voter.

no[2] (nō), *adj.* **1.** not any. **2.** far from being: *He is no genius.*

No *Chem. Symbol.* nobelium.

no. or **No.,** **1.** north. **2.** northern. **3.** number. [< L *numero*]

no•bel•i•um (nō bel′ē əm, -bē′lē-), *n.* a synthetic radioactive element. *Symbol:* No; *at. no.:* 102.

no•bil•i•ty (nō bil′i tē), *n., pl.* **-ties. 1.** the noble class in a country. **2.** the state or quality of being noble. **3.** noble birth or rank.

no•ble (nō′bəl), *adj.,* **-bler, -blest,** *n.* —*adj.* **1.** of or belonging to a hereditary class distinguished by high birth, rank, or status. **2.** of an exalted moral character. **3.** imposing in appearance. **4.** of an admirably high quality. —*n.* **5.** a person of noble birth or rank. —**no′ble•ness,** *n.* —**no′bly,** *adv.*

no•blesse o•blige (nō bles′ ō blēzh′), *n.* the moral obligation of the rich or highborn to display honorable and generous conduct.

no·bod·y (nō′bod′ē, -bud′ē, -bə dē), *pron., n., pl.* **-bod·ies.** —*pron.* **1.** no person. —*n.* **2.** a person of no importance or influence.

no′-brain′er *n. Informal.* something requiring little thought or effort.

noc·tur·nal (nok tûr′nl), *adj.* **1.** of or occurring in the night. **2.** active at night. —**noc·tur′nal·ly,** *adv.*

noc′turne (-tûrn), *n.* a dramatic, brooding piano composition.

nod (nod), *v.,* **nod·ded, nod·ding,** *n.* —*v.i.* **1.** to make a slight, quick inclination of the head, as in assent. **2.** to let the head fall slightly forward when sleepy. —*v.t.* **3.** to bend (the head) in a short, quick downward movement, as of assent. **4.** to express by such a movement. —*n.* **5.** a short, quick inclination of the head.

node (nōd), *n.* **1.** a protuberance or swelling. **2.** a part of a stem that bears a leaf or branch. —**nod′al,** *adj.*

nod·ule (noj′ōol), *n.* **1.** a small node. **2.** a small, rounded mass or lump. —**nod′u·lar,** *adj.*

No·el (nō el′), *n.* CHRISTMAS.

no′-fault′ *adj.* **1.** of or being a form of automobile insurance entitling a policyholder to collect basic compensation without determination of liability. **2.** holding neither party responsible: *a no-fault divorce.*

nog·gin (nog′ən), *n.* **1.** a small mug. **2.** *Informal.* a person's head.

noise (noiz), *n., v.,* **noised, nois·ing.** —*n.* **1.** sound, esp. of a loud or harsh kind. **2.** loud shouting or clamor. —*v.t.* **3.** to spread, as a report or rumor. [< OF < L *nausea* seasickness] —**noise′less,** *adj.* —**noise′less·ly,** *adv.* —**nois′y,** *adj.,* **-i·er, -i·est.** —**nois′i·ly,** *adv.* —**nois′i·ness,** *n.*

noi·some (noi′səm), *adj.* **1.** offensive, as an odor. **2.** harmful or injurious to health.

no·mad (nō′mad), *n.* **1.** a member of a people that has no permanent abode but moves about in search of pasturage or food. **2.** any wanderer. —**no·mad′ic,** *adj.*

no′ man′s′ land′ *n.* an area between warring armies that no one controls.

nom de plume (nom′ də plōōm′), *n., pl.* **noms de plume.** PEN NAME.

no·men·cla·ture (nō′mən klā′chər), *n.* a system of terms, as those of a particular science or art.

nom·i·nal (nom′ə nl), *adj.* **1.** being such in name only. **2.** trifling in comparison with the actual value: *a nominal fee.* **3.** of or constituting a name or names. —**nom′i·nal·ly,** *adv.*

nom′i·nate′ (-nāt′), *v.t.,* **-nat·ed, -nat·ing.** to name as a candidate for an office or honor. —**nom′i·na′tion,** *n.* —**nom′i·na′tor,** *n.*

nom′i·na·tive (-nə tiv), *adj.* **1.** noting the grammatical case typically indicating the subject of a finite verb. —*n.* **2.** the nominative case. **3.** a word in the nominative case.

nom′i·nee′ *n., pl.* **-nees.** a person nominated, as for an office.

non- a prefix meaning not (*nonaligned*).

non·age (non′ij, nō′nij), *n.* **1.** the period of legal minority. **2.** any period of immaturity.

non·a·ge·nar·i·an (non′ə jə nâr′ē ən, nō′nə-), *adj.* **1.** of the age of 90 years, or between 90 and 100 years old. —*n.* **2.** a nonagenarian person.

non·cha·lant (non′shə länt′), *adj.* coolly unconcerned. —**non′cha·lance′,** *n.* —**non′cha·lant′ly,** *adv.*

non·com·bat·ant (non′kəm bat′nt, non kom′bə tnt), *n.* **1.** a member of a military force who is not a fighter, as a chaplain. **2.** a civilian in wartime.

non′com·mis′sioned *adj. Mil.* not commissioned.

non′com·mit′tal *adj.* having or giving no particular view, feeling, etc. —**non′com·mit′tal·ly,** *adv.*

non com·pos men·tis (non′ kom′pəs men′tis), *adj. Law.* not of sound mind. [< L]

non′con·duc′tor *n.* a substance that does not readily conduct heat, sound, or electricity.

non′con·form′ist *n.* **1.** one who refuses to conform, as to established customs. **2.** (*often cap.*) a Protestant in England who is not a member of the Church of England. —**non′con·form′i·ty,** *n.*

non·de·script (non′di skript′), *adj.* **1.** undistinguished or dull. **2.** of no recognized or specific type or kind.

none (nun), *pron.* **1.** no one; not one. **2.** not any. **3.** no part; nothing: *I'll have none of that.* **4.** (used with a pl. v.) not any persons or things: *None were left when I came.* —*adv.* **5.** not at all: *We saw the ceremony none too well.*

non·en·ti·ty (non en′ti tē), *n., pl.* **-ties.** a person or thing of no importance.

none′the·less′ *adv.* nevertheless.

non·met′al *n.* an element not having the character of a metal, as carbon or nitrogen.

no′-no′ *n. Informal.* a forbidden thing.

non·pa·reil (non′pə rel′), *adj.* **1.** having no equal; peerless. —*n.* **2.** a person or thing having no equal.

non·par′ti·san *adj.* **1.** not partisan. **2.** not affiliated with any of the established political parties.

non·plus (non plus′, non′plus), *v.t.,* **-plussed** or **-plused, -plus·sing** or **-plus·ing.** to render utterly perplexed.

non·prof′it *adj.* not established for the purpose of making a profit.

non′rep·re·sen·ta′tion·al *adj.* not resembling any object in nature: *a nonrepresentational painting.*

non′sec·tar′i·an *adj.* not affiliated with a specific religious denomination.

non·sense (non′sens, -səns), *n.* **1.** meaningless or absurd words or actions. **2.** anything trifling or of little use. —**non·sen′si·cal,** *adj.* —**non·sen′si·cal·ly,** *adv.*

non se·qui·tur (non sek′wi tər, -tōōr′), *n.* **1.** a conclusion that does not follow from the premises. **2.** a comment that is unrelated to a preceding one. [< L: it does not follow]

non′stand′ard *adj.* not conforming in pronunciation, grammar, etc., to the usage considered acceptable by educated native speakers.

non′stop′ *adj.* **1.** being without a single stop en route. **2.** happening without a pause: *nonstop meetings.*

non′sup·port′ *n.* failure to provide financial support for a dependent.

non·un′ion *adj.* **1.** not belonging to a labor union. **2.** not recognizing labor unions. **3.** not produced by union workers.

non·vi′o·lence *n.* the policy of refraining from the use of violence, as in protesting injustice. —**non·vi′o·lent,** *adj.*

noo·dle¹ (nōōd′l), *n.* a dried strip of egg dough that is boiled and served in soups, casseroles, etc.

noo·dle² (nōōd′l), *n. Slang.* the head.

nook (nōōk), *n.* **1.** a corner, as in a room. **2.** any remote or sheltered spot.

noon (nōōn), *n.* twelve o'clock in the daytime.

no′ one′ *pron.* no person.

noose (nōōs), *n.* a loop with a running knot, as in a lasso, that tightens as the rope is pulled.

nor (nôr; *unstressed* nər), *conj.* **1.** (used in negative phrases, esp. after *neither,* to introduce the following member or members of a series): *Neither he nor I will go.* **2.** (used to continue the force of a preceding negative phrase): *I never saw him again, nor did I care.*

Nor·dic (nôr′dik), *adj.* having the physical features associated with the peoples of northern Europe, typically tall stature, blond hair, and blue eyes.

norm (nôrm), *n.* **1.** a standard, model, or pattern. **2.** the general level or average.

nor·mal (nôr′məl), *adj.* **1.** conforming to the standard or the common type; usual. **2.** average in any psychological trait, as intelligence or personality. **3.** free from any mental disorder. —*n.* **4.** the average or mean. **5.** the standard or common type. —**nor′mal·cy, nor·mal′i·ty,** *n.* —**nor′mal·ize′,** *v.t., v.i.,* **-ized, -iz·ing.** —**nor′mal·ly,** *adv.*

nor′mal school′ *n.* a school for training teachers.

nor·ma·tive (nôr′mə tiv), *adj.* of or tending to establish a norm.

Norse (nôrs), *adj.* **1.** of medieval Scandinavia, its inhabitants, or their speech. —*n.* **2.** the inhabitants of medieval Scandinavia.

general

north (nôrth), *n.* **1.** a cardinal point of the compass, lying to the left of a person facing the rising sun. **2.** the direction in which north lies. **3.** (*usu. cap.*) a region situated in this direction. **4. the North,** the northern area of the United States, esp. the states that fought to preserve the Union in the Civil War. —*adj.* **5.** lying toward or situated in the north. **6.** coming from the north. —*adv.* **7.** to, toward, or in the north.

north′east′ *n.* **1.** a point on the compass midway between north and east. **2.** a region in this direction. **3. the Northeast,** the northeastern part of the United States. —*adj.* **4.** in, toward, or facing the northeast. **5.** coming from the northeast. —*adv.* **6.** toward or from the northeast. —**north′east′er•ly,** *adj., adv.* —**north′east′ern,** *adj.*

north•ern (nôr′thərn), *adj.* **1.** toward or in the north. **2.** from the north. **3.** (*often cap.*) of the North, esp. the northern U.S.

north′ern•er *n.* (*often cap.*) a native or inhabitant of the north.

North′ern Hem′isphere *n.* the half of the earth between the North Pole and the equator.

North′ Kore′a *n.* a country in E Asia. —**North′ Kore′an,** *n., adj.*

North′ Star′ *n.* POLARIS.

north′west′ *n.* **1.** a point on the compass midway between north and west. **2.** a region in this direction. **3. the Northwest,** the northwestern part of the United States. —*adj.* **4.** in, toward, or facing the northwest. **5.** coming from the northwest. —*adv.* **6.** toward or from the northwest. —**north′west′er•ly,** *adj., adv.* —**north′west′ern,** *adj.*

Nor•way (nôr′wā), *n.* a kingdom in N Europe.

nose (nōz), *n., v.,* **nosed, nos•ing.** —*n.* **1.** the part of the face that contains the nostrils and organs of smell and that functions as a passage for air in respiration. **2.** the sense of smell. **3.** anything resembling a nose. **4.** a faculty of detecting: *a nose for news.* —*v.t.* **5.** to perceive by or as if by smell. **6.** to move or push forward with or as if with the nose. **7.** to nuzzle. —*v.i.* **8.** to move or push forward. **9.** to meddle or pry. **10. nose out, a.** to defeat by a narrow margin. **b.** to discover by prying. —*Idiom.* **11. on the nose,** precisely; exactly.

nose′ cone′ *n.* the cone-shaped forward section of a rocket or guided missile.

nose′dive′ *n., v.,* **-dived** or **-dove, -dived, -div•ing.** —*n.* Also, **nose′ dive′. 1.** a plunge of an aircraft with the forward part pointing downward. **2.** a sudden drop or decline. —*v.i.* Also, **nose′-dive′. 3.** to go into a nosedive.

nose′gay′ *n.* a small bunch of flowers.

nosh (nosh), *Informal.* —*v.i., v.t.* **1.** to snack (on). —*n.* **2.** a snack. [< Yiddish *nashn*] —**nosh′er,** *n.*

no′-show′ *n.* a person who neither uses nor cancels a reservation.

nos•tal•gia (no stal′jə), *n.* a sentimental longing for something in the past. —**nos•tal′gic,** *adj.*

nos•tril (nos′trəl), *n.* either of the two external openings of the nose.

nos•trum (nos′trəm), *n.* **1.** a quack medicine. **2.** a pet remedy, esp. for social ills.

nos•y (nō′zē), *adj.,* **-i•er, -i•est.** unduly curious; prying. —**nos′i•ly,** *adv.* —**nos′i•ness,** *n.*

not (not), *adv.* **1.** (used to express negation, denial, refusal, prohibition, etc.): *It's not far from here.* **2.** *Slang.* (used jocularly to indicate that a previous statement is untrue): *That's a lovely dress. Not!*

no•ta be•ne (nō′tə ben′ē), *Latin.* note well.

no•ta•ble (nō′tə bəl), *adj.* **1.** worthy of notice. **2.** prominent; distinguished. —*n.* **3.** a prominent or distinguished person. —**no′ta•bly,** *adv.*

no•ta•rize (nō′tə rīz′), *v.t.,* **-rized, -riz•ing.** to certify (a contract or other document) through a notary public. —**no′ta•ri•za′tion,** *n.*

no′ta•ry (-tə rē) *n., pl.* **-ries.** an official authorized to verify documents. Also called **no′tary pub′lic.**

no•ta•tion (nō tā′shən), *n.* **1.** a system of graphic symbols for a specialized use: *musical notation.* **2.** the process of writing down by means of such a system. **3.** a short note.

notch (noch), *n.* **1.** a V-shaped cut or indentation.

2. a narrow pass between mountains. **3.** a step; degree. —*v.t.* **4.** to make a notch in.

note (nōt), *n., v.,* **not•ed, not•ing.** —*n.* **1.** a brief written record, as to assist the memory. **2.** a short, informal letter. **3. notes,** a written summary or outline of something heard, read, etc. **4.** an annotation of a text. **5.** distinction or importance. **6.** notice or observation. **7.** a distinctive quality, mood, etc. **8.** *Music.* a symbol used to represent a tone, its position and form indicating the pitch and duration of the tone. **9.** a written promise to pay a specified sum of money at a fixed time. —*v.t.* **10.** to write down. **11.** to make particular mention of. **12.** to annotate. **13.** to observe carefully.

note′book′ *n.* **1.** a book with blank pages on which to write notes. **2.** a small, lightweight laptop computer.

not′ed *adj.* well-known; renowned.

note′wor′thy *adj.* worthy of notice or attention.

noth•ing (nuth′ing), *pron.* **1.** no thing; not anything. **2.** no part or trace: *The house showed nothing of its former splendor.* **3.** something of no importance or value: *Money is nothing to him.* —*n.* **4.** a person or thing of no importance. **5.** nonexistence; nothingness. **6.** a zero; naught. —*adv.* **7.** not at all. —*Idiom.* **8. for nothing, a.** free of charge. **b.** for no reason. **c.** futilely.

noth′ing•ness *n.* **1.** lack of being. **2.** unconsciousness or death. **3.** absence of meaning or worth.

no•tice (nō′tis), *n., v.,* **-ticed, -tic•ing.** —*n.* **1.** information or warning. **2.** a written statement conveying information or warning to the public. **3.** a formal notification of one's intention to terminate an agreement. **4.** observation or attention. **5.** a brief review of a book, play, etc. —*v.t.* **6.** to become aware of or observe. **7.** to mention or refer to. —**no′tice•a•ble,** *adj.*

no•ti•fy (nō′ti fī′), *v.t.,* **-fied, -fy•ing.** to inform; give notice to. —**no′ti•fi•ca′tion,** *n.* —**no′ti•fi′er,** *n.*

no•tion (nō′shən), *n.* **1.** a general or vague idea. **2.** an opinion or belief. **3.** a whim. **4. notions,** small articles, as buttons or thread, displayed for sale. —**no′tion•al,** *adj.*

no•to•ri•ous (nō tôr′ē əs, nə-), *adj.* widely and unfavorably known. —**no′to•ri′e•ty** (-tə rī′i tē), *n.* —**no•to′ri•ous•ly,** *adv.*

not′with•stand′ing *prep.* **1.** in spite of. —*adv.* **2.** nevertheless. —*conj.* **3.** although.

nou•gat (nōō′gət), *n.* a candy containing nuts and sometimes fruit.

nought (nôt), *n., adj., adv.* NAUGHT.

noun (noun), *n.* a word that refers to a person, place, thing, state, or quality.

nour•ish (nûr′ish, nur′-), *v.t.* **1.** to sustain with food or nutriment. **2.** to strengthen or promote. —**nour′ish•ing,** *adj.* —**nour′ish•ment,** *n.*

nou•veau riche (nōō′vō rēsh′), *n., pl.* **nou•veaux riches** (nōō′vō rēsh′). a person who is newly rich, esp. when ostentatious or uncultivated. [< F]

nou•velle′ cuisine′ (nōō vel′), *n.* a style of cooking that emphasizes the use of fresh ingredients, light sauces, and the artful presentation of food. [< F]

Nov or **Nov.,** November.

no•va (nō′və), *n., pl.* **-vas, -vae** (-vē). a star that suddenly becomes thousands of times brighter and then gradually fades.

nov•el[1] (nov′əl), *n.* a fictitious prose narrative of considerable length. —**nov′el•ist,** *n.* —**nov′el•is′tic,** *adj.* —**nov′el•ize′,** *v.t.,* **-ized, -iz•ing.** —**nov′el•i•za′tion,** *n.*

nov•el[2] (nov′əl), *adj.* of a new kind.

nov′el•ty (-tē), *n., pl.* **-ties. 1.** the state or quality of being novel. **2.** a novel occurrence, experience, etc. **3.** a small decorative or amusing article.

No•vem•ber (nō vem′bər), *n.* the 11th month of the year, containing 30 days.

no•ve•na (nō vē′nə, nə-), *n., pl.* **-nae** (-nē) **-nas.** a Roman Catholic devotion occurring on nine consecutive days.

nov•ice (nov′is), *n.* **1.** a person who is new to a situation or position; beginner. **2.** a person admitted into a religious order for a probation period before taking vows.

no•vi•ti•ate (nō vish′ē it, -āt′), *n.* the state or period of being a novice.

No•vo•caine (nō′və kān′), *Trademark.* a brand of procaine, a local anesthetic.

now (nou), *adv.* **1.** at the present time. **2.** immediately. **3.** at the time being referred to: *The case was now ready for the jury.* **4.** in the very recent past. **5.** under the present circumstances: *I see now what you meant.* **6.** (used to introduce a statement, question, command, etc.): *Now, may I ask you something?* —*conj.* **7.** since. —*n.* **8.** the present time. —*adj.* **9.** current; fashionable.

NOW (nou), National Organization for Women.

now′a•days′ (-ə dāz′), *adv.* at the present time.

no′where′ *adv.* **1.** not anywhere. —*n.* **2.** a state or place of nonexistence. —*Idiom.* **3. nowhere near,** not nearly.

nox•ious (nok′shəs), *adj.* **1.** harmful to health. **2.** morally harmful.

noz•zle (noz′əl), *n.* a spout serving as an outlet, as of a hose.

nth (enth), *adj.* **1.** being the last in a series of infinitely decreasing or increasing values, amounts, etc. **2.** utmost: *to the nth degree.*

nu•ance (nōō′äns, nyōō′-), *n.* a subtle distinction, as in color, expression, or meaning. —**nu′anced,** *adj.*

nub (nub), *n.* **1.** the point or gist of something. **2.** a knob or lump. —**nub′by,** *adj.,* **-bi•er, -bi•est.**

nu•bile (nōō′bil, -bīl, nyōō′-), *adj.* **1.** (of a young woman) marriageable. **2.** (of a young woman) sexually attractive.

nu•cle•ar (nōō′klē ər, nyōō′-; *by metathesis* -kyə-lər), *adj.* **1.** of or involving atomic weapons. **2.** operated or powered by atomic energy. **3.** having atomic weapons. **4.** of or forming a nucleus.

nu′clear en′ergy *n.* energy released by reactions within atomic nuclei, as in nuclear fission or fusion.

nu′clear fam′ily *n.* a social unit composed of father, mother, and children.

nu′clear phys′ics *n.* the branch of physics that deals with atomic nuclei.

nu′clear win′ter *n.* the worldwide devastation, darkness, and cold that conceivably could result from a nuclear war.

nu•cle•on (nōō′klē on′, nyōō′-), *n.* a proton or neutron, esp. when considered as a component of a nucleus.

nu′cle•us (-klē əs), *n., pl.* **-cle•i** (-klē ī′), **-cle•us•es. 1.** a central part about which other parts are grouped; core. **2.** a specialized, usu. spherical mass of protoplasm found in most living cells, containing most of the genetic material. **3.** the positively charged mass within an atom, composed of neutrons and protons.

nude (nōōd, nyōōd), *adj.,* **nud•er, nud•est,** *n.* —*adj.* **1.** unclothed, as a person or the body. —*n.* **2.** an unclothed human figure, esp. in a work of art. **3.** the condition of being unclothed: *to sleep in the nude.* —**nu′di•ty,** *n.*

nudge (nuj), *v.,* **nudged, nudg•ing,** *n.* —*v.t.* **1.** to push gently with the elbow, esp. to get someone's attention. —*n.* **2.** a gentle push with the elbow.

nud•ism (nōō′diz əm, nyōō′-), *n.* the practice of going nude. —**nud′ist,** *n., adj.*

nug•get (nug′it), *n.* **1.** a lump, esp. of native gold. **2.** anything small but of great value.

nui•sance (nōō′səns, nyōō′-), *n.* **1.** an annoying person, thing, etc. **2.** *Law.* harm, injury, or disturbance.

nuke (nōōk, nyōōk), *n., v.,* **nuked, nuk•ing.** *Informal.* —*n.* **1.** a nuclear weapon. —*v.t.* **2.** to attack with nuclear weapons.

null (nul), *adj.* **1.** without value or significance. **2.** amounting to nothing. —*Idiom.* **3. null and void,** not valid. —**nul′li•ty,** *n., pl.* **-ties.**

nul′li•fy′ *v.t.,* **-fied, -fy•ing. 1.** to render or declare legally void. **2.** to deprive of value or effectiveness. [< LL *nūllificāre* to despise] —**nul′li•fi•ca′tion,** *n.*

numb (num), *adj.,* **-er, -est,** *v.* —*adj.* **1.** deprived of

sensation, as by anesthesia. —*v.t.* **2.** to make numb. —**numb′ly,** *adv.* —**numb′ness,** *n.*

num•ber (num′bər), *n.* **1.** a mathematical unit used to express an amount, quantity, etc. **2.** a numeral. **3.** the total of a collection of persons or things. **4.** a numeral or numerals assigned to an object, person, etc., for identification or classification. **5.** an imprecise but considerable quantity. **6. numbers, a.** many. **b.** numerical superiority. **c.** arithmetic. **7.** a distinct performance within a show, as a song. **8.** a category of inflection or other variation in the form of a word that indicates whether the word has one or more than one referent. —*v.t.* **9.** to mark with numbers. **10.** to amount to in number. **11.** to include in a number: *I number myself among his friends.* **12.** to count; enumerate. **13.** to fix the number of. —*v.i.* **14.** to be numbered. —*Idiom.* **15. without number,** of countless number; vast.

num′ber•less *adj.* innumerable; countless.

nu•mer•al (nōō′mər əl, nyōō′-), *n.* **1.** a word, letter, or figure representing a number. —*adj.* **2.** of or noting a number or numbers.

nu′mer•ate′ (*v.* -mə rāt′; *adj.* -mər it), *v.,* **-at•ed, -at•ing,** *adj.* —*v.t.* **1.** ENUMERATE (def. 2). —*adj.* **2.** able to use or understand numerical techniques of mathematics. —**nu′mer•a•cy,** *n.*

nu′mer•a′tor *n.* the term of a fraction written above or before the line.

nu•mer•i•cal (nōō mer′i kəl, nyōō-) also **-ic,** *adj.* **1.** of numbers. **2.** expressed in numbers. —**nu•mer′i•cal•ly,** *adv.*

nu•mer•ol•o•gy (nōō′mə rol′ə jē, nyōō′-), *n.* the study of numbers, as one's year of birth, to determine their supernatural meaning. —**nu′mer•ol′o•gist,** *n.*

nu′mer•ous *adj.* **1.** very many. **2.** comprising a great number of units or individuals.

nu•mis•mat•ics (nōō′miz mat′iks, -mis-, nyōō′-), *n.* the study or collecting of money, medals, etc. —**nu′mis•mat′ic,** *adj.* —**nu•mis′ma•tist** (-mə tist), *n.*

num•skull or **numb•skull** (num′skul′), *n.* a dullwitted or stupid person.

nun (nun), *n.* a woman bound to a religious order, esp. by vows of poverty, chastity, and obedience.

nun•ner•y *n., pl.* **-ner•ies.** a convent for nuns.

nup•tial (nup′shəl, -chəl), *adj.* **1.** of marriage or a wedding. —*n.* **2.** Usu. **-tials.** a wedding or marriage.

nurse (nûrs), *n., v.,* **nursed, nurs•ing.** —*n.* **1.** a person trained in the care of the sick or infirm. **2.** a woman who has the general care of a child. **3.** WET NURSE. —*v.t.* **4.** to minister to in sickness, infirmity, etc. **5.** to try to cure (an ailment) by taking care of oneself. **6.** to suckle (an infant). **7.** to use slowly or carefully: *to nurse a drink.* **8.** to promote the growth and development of. —*v.i.* **9.** to suckle a child. **10.** (of a child) to suckle. **11.** to tend the sick or infirm. —**nurs′er,** *n.*

nurs′er•y *n., pl.* **-er•ies. 1.** a room set apart for young children. **2.** a nursery school or day nursery. **3.** a place where young trees or other plants are raised.

nurs′ery school′ *n.* a prekindergarten school for children.

nur•ture (nûr′chər), *v.,* **-tured, -tur•ing,** *n.* —*v.t.* **1.** to feed and protect. **2.** to support and encourage. **3.** to bring up; train; educate. —*n.* **4.** upbringing; training; education. **5.** development. **6.** something that nourishes. —**nur′tur•er,** *n.*

nut (nut), *n.* **1.** a dry fruit consisting of an edible kernel enclosed in a woody shell. **2.** the kernel itself. **3.** a hard, one-seeded fruit, as the acorn. **4.** a metal block perforated with a threaded hole so that it can be screwed onto a bolt. **5.** *Slang.* a devotee or zealot. **6.** *Slang.* an insane or eccentric person.

nut′hatch′ *n.* a small, sharp-beaked songbird that seeks food along tree trunks.

nut′meg (-meg), *n.* the hard, aromatic seed of an East Indian tree, used as a spice.

nu•tri•ent (nōō′trē ənt, nyōō′-), *adj.* **1.** providing nourishment or nutriment. —*n.* **2.** a nutrient substance.

nu′tri•ment (-trə mənt), *n.* something that nourishes, as food.

nu•tri′tion (-trish′ən), *n.* **1.** the study of dietary requirements for proper health and development. **2.** the process by which organisms take in and utilize food. **3.** food; nutriment. —**nu•tri′tion•al**, *adj.* —**nu•tri′tion•al•ly**, *adv.* —**nu•tri′tion•ist**, *n.* —**nu•tri′tious, nu′tri•tive** (-tri tiv), *adj.*

nuts (nuts), *Slang.* —*interj.* **1.** an exclamation of disgust, defiance, etc. —*adj.* **2.** insane; crazy. —*Idiom.* **3. be nuts about, a.** to love deeply. **b.** to be wildly enthusiastic about.

nut′ty *adj.*, **-ti•er, -ti•est. 1.** abounding in or producing nuts. **2.** nutlike in flavor. **3.** *Slang.* crazy. —**nut′ti•ness,** *n.*

nuz•zle (nuz′əl), *v.t., v.i.*, **-zled, -zling. 1.** to touch or rub with the nose, snout, etc. **2.** to cuddle or snuggle. —**nuz′zler,** *n.*

NV Nevada.

NW or **N.W., 1.** northwest. **2.** northwestern.

NY or **N.Y.,** New York.

ny•lon (nī′lon), *n.* **1.** a strong, elastic synthetic material used for yarn, fabrics, and bristles. **2. nylons,** stockings made of nylon. [coined by the du Pont Chemical Co.]

nymph (nimf), *n.* **1.** any of a class of female deities in mythology, inhabiting waters or forests. **2.** a beautiful young woman. **3.** the young of an insect that undergoes incomplete metamorphosis.

nym•pho•ma•ni•a (nim′fə mā′nē ə), *n.* abnormal, uncontrollable sexual desire in a female. —**nym′pho•ma′ni•ac′,** *n., adj.*

O

a b c d e f g h i j k l m n **O** p q r s t u v w x y z

O, o (ō), *n., pl.* **Os** or **O′s, os** or **o′s** or **oes.** the 15th letter of the English alphabet, a vowel.

O (ō), *interj.* **1.** (used in direct address, esp. in solemn or poetic language): *Hear, O Israel!* **2.** ОН.

O *Symbol.* **1.** the Arabic numeral; zero. **2.** a major blood group. **3.** *Chem.* oxygen.

oaf (ōf), *n.* a stupid or clumsy person. —**oaf′ish,** *adj.* —**oaf′ish•ly,** *adv.* —**oaf′ish•ness,** *n.*

oak (ōk), *n.* **1.** a tree of the beech family, bearing the acorn as fruit. **2.** the wood of the oak. —**oak′en,** *adj.*

oar (ôr), *n.* **1.** a long shaft with a broad blade at one end, used for rowing or steering a boat. —*Idiom.* **2. rest on one′s oars,** to cease to make further effort. —**oars′man,** *n., pl.* **-men.**

oar′lock′ *n.* a U-shaped device providing a pivot for an oar in rowing.

o•a•sis (ō ā′sis), *n., pl.* **-ses** (-sēz). a fertile area in a desert region, usu. having a spring or well.

oat (ōt), *n.* **1.** a cereal grass cultivated for its edible grain. **2.** Usu., **oats.** the grain of this plant. —**oat′en,** *adj.*

oath (ōth), *n., pl.* **oaths** (ō<u>th</u>z, ōths). **1.** a solemn appeal to a deity to witness one′s determination to speak the truth or keep a promise. **2.** a blasphemous use of the name of God. **3.** any profane expression or utterance.

oat′meal′ *n.* **1.** meal made from oats. **2.** a cooked breakfast food made from this.

ob•du•rate (ob′dŏŏ rit, -dyŏŏ-), *adj.* **1.** stubborn and unyielding. **2.** stubbornly resistant to moral influence; impenitent. —**ob′du•ra•cy** (-rə sē), **ob′du•rate•ness,** *n.* —**ob′du•rate•ly,** *adv.*

o•be•di•ent (ō bē′dē ənt), *adj.* complying with or submissive to authority. —**o•be′di•ence,** *n.* —**o•be′di•ent•ly,** *adv.*

o•bei•sance (ō bā′səns, ō bē′-), *n.* **1.** a bodily movement, as a bow, expressing respect or deferential courtesy. **2.** deference; homage. —**o•bei′sant,** *adj.*

ob•e•lisk (ob′ə lisk), *n.* a four-sided shaft of stone that tapers to a pyramidal apex.

o•bese (ō bēs′), *adj.* very fat. —**o•be′si•ty,** *n.*

o•bey (ō bā′), *v.t.* **1.** to comply with the commands of. **2.** to comply with: *to obey orders.* **3.** to submit or conform to. —*v.i.* **4.** to be obedient.

ob•fus•cate (ob′fə skāt′, ob fus′kāt), *v.t.*, **-cat•ed, -cat•ing. 1.** to confuse. **2.** to darken. —**ob′fus•ca′tion,** *n.*

ob•i•ter dic•tum (ob′i tər dik′təm), *n., pl.* **obiter dic•ta** (dik′tə). an incidental remark or opinion.

o•bit•u•ar•y (ō bich′ŏŏ er′ē), *n., pl.* **-ar•ies.** a notice of the death of a person, often with a biographical sketch.

obj. 1. object. **2.** objective.

ob•ject (*n.* ob′jikt, -jekt; *v.* əb jekt′), *n.* **1.** anything that is visible or tangible. **2.** a thing or person to which thought or action is directed. **3.** a goal; objective. **4.** a noun, noun phrase, or pronoun representing the goal or recipient of the action of a verb or the goal of a preposition. **5.** *Computers.* any item that can be individually selected or manipulated, as a picture or piece of text. —*v.i.* **6.** to offer a reason in opposition. **7.** to express or feel disapproval or dislike. —*v.t.* **8.** to state or cite in opposition. —**ob•jec′tor,** *n.*

ob•jec•tion (əb jek′shən), *n.* **1.** a reason or argument offered in opposition. **2.** the act of objecting. **3.** a feeling of disapproval, dislike, or disagreement. —**ob•jec′tion•a•ble,** *adj.*

ob•jec′tive *n.* **1.** a purpose; goal. **2.** the lens, as in a telescope, that first receives the rays from an observed object and forms its image. —*adj.* **3.** not influenced by personal feelings; unbiased. **4.** existing without regard to thought, imagination, etc.; real. **5.** of or being a grammatical case that indicates the object of a transitive verb or preposition. —**ob•jec′tive•ly,** *adv.* —**ob•jec•tiv′i•ty** (ob′jik tiv′i tē, -jek-), **ob•jec′tive•ness,** *n.*

ob′ject les′son *n.* a practical or concrete illustration of a principle.

ob•jet d′art (ob′zhā där′), *n., pl.* **ob•jets d′art** (ob′zhā där′). an object of artistic worth or interest.

ob•late (ob′lāt, o blāt′), *adj.* flattened at the poles, as a spheroid.

ob•la•tion (o blā′shən), *n.* an offering made to a deity.

ob•li•gate (ob′li gāt′), *v.t.*, **-gat•ed, -gat•ing.** to bind or oblige morally or legally. —**ob′li•ga′tion,** *n.*

o•blig•a•to•ry (ə blig′ə tôr′ē, ob′li gə-), *adj.* **1.** required as a matter of obligation; mandatory. **2.** incumbent or compulsory.

o•blige (ə blīj′), *v.t.*, **o•bliged, o•blig•ing. 1.** to bind morally or legally. **2.** to place under a debt of gratitude for a favor. **3.** to do a favor for: *He obliged us with a song.*

o•blig′ing *adj.* willing to help.

o•blique (ə blēk′, ō blēk′), *adj.* **1.** neither perpendicular nor parallel to a given line or surface; slanting. **2.** indirectly stated or expressed. —**o•blique′ly,** *adv.* —**o•bliq•ui•ty** (ə blik′wi tē, ō blik′-), **o•blique′ness,** *n.*

ob•lit•er•ate (ə blit′ə rāt′), *v.t.*, **-at•ed, -at•ing. 1.** to remove or destroy all traces of. **2.** to blot out. —**ob•lit′er•a′tion,** *n.*

ob•liv•i•on (ə bliv′ē ən), *n.* **1.** the state of being completely forgotten. **2.** the state of forgetting completely.

ob•long (ob′lông′, -long′), *adj.* **1.** in the form of a rectangle one of whose dimensions is greater than the other. —*n.* **2.** an oblong figure.

ob•lo•quy (ob′lə kwē), *n., pl.* **-quies. 1.** censure or blame. **2.** discredit or disgrace.

ob•nox•ious (əb nok′shəs), *adj.* highly objectionable or offensive.

o•boe (ō′bō), *n.* a woodwind instrument having a slender conical body and a double-reed mouthpiece.

[< It < F *hautbois* = *haut* high + *bois* wood] —o′bo•ist, *n.*

obs. obsolete.

ob•scene (əb sēn′), *adj.* **1.** offensive to morality or decency; indecent; lewd. **2.** abominable; disgusting. —ob•scen′i•ty (-sen′i-, -sē′ni-), *n., pl.* **-ties.**

ob•scu•rant•ism (əb skyōōr′ən tiz′əm), *n.* **1.** opposition to the increase and spread of knowledge. **2.** deliberate evasion of clarity. —ob•scu′rant•ist, *n., adj.*

ob•scure (əb skyōōr′), *adj.,* -scur•er, -scur•est, *v.,* -scured, -scur•ing. —*adj.* **1.** not clear to the understanding; ambiguous or vague. **2.** not readily seen, heard, etc. **3.** not easily noticed; inconspicuous. **4.** not famous; unknown. **5.** dark; dim. —*v.t.* **6.** to make obscure. —ob•scure′ly, *adv.* —ob•scur′i•ty, *n.*

ob•se•qui•ous (əb sē′kwē əs), *adj.* servilely complaisant or deferential; fawning.

ob•se•quy (ob′si kwē), *n., pl.* **-quies.** Usu., **obse-quies.** a funeral rite or ceremony.

ob•serv•ance (əb zûr′vəns), *n.* **1.** the act of observing a law, custom, etc. **2.** a keeping or celebration of a holiday or ritual.

ob•serv′ant *adj.* **1.** quick to perceive; alert. **2.** regarding attentively. **3.** careful in the observing of a law, religious ritual, etc.

ob•serv′a•to′ry (-və tôr′ē), *n., pl.* **-ries.** a place used for making observations of astronomical or other natural phenomena.

ob•serve′ *v.t.,* -served, -serv•ing. **1.** to see or notice. **2.** to regard with attention. **3.** to watch or note for a scientific or other special purpose. **4.** to remark. **5.** to obey or conform to: *to observe laws.* **6.** to celebrate, as a holiday, in an appropriate way. —ob•serv′a•ble, *adj.* —ob′ser•va′tion, *n.* —ob•serv′er, *n.*

ob•sess (əb ses′), *v.t.* **1.** to excessively preoccupy the thoughts or feelings of. —*v.i.* **2.** to think about something unceasingly. —ob•sess′ive, *adj.* —ob•sess′ive•ly, *adv.*

ob•so•les•cent (ob′sə les′ənt), *adj.* becoming obsolete. —ob′so•les′cence, *n.*

ob′so•lete′ (-lēt′), *adj.* **1.** no longer in general use. **2.** out-of-date.

ob•sta•cle (ob′stə kəl), *n.* something that obstructs or hinders progress.

ob•stet•rics (əb stet′riks), *n.* the branch of medicine concerned with pregnancy and childbirth. —ob•stet′ric, ob•stet′ri•cal, *adj.* —ob•ste•tri•cian (ob′-sti trish′ən), *n.*

ob•sti•nate (ob′stə nit), *adj.* **1.** stubbornly adhering to a purpose, opinion, etc. **2.** not easily treated, as a disease. —ob′sti•na•cy (-nə sē), *n.* —ob′sti•nate•ly, *adv.*

ob•strep•er•ous (əb strep′ər əs), *adj.* resisting control in a noisy and difficult manner; unruly. —ob•strep′er•ous•ly, *adv.*

ob•struct (əb strukt′), *v.t.* **1.** to block with an obstacle. **2.** to hinder the passage, progress, etc., of. **3.** to block from sight. —ob•struc′tion, *n.* —ob•struc′tive, *adj.*

ob•struc′tion•ism (-shə niz′əm) *n.* the deliberate obstruction of progress. —ob•struc′tion•ist, *n., adj.*

ob•tain (əb tān′), *v.t.* **1.** to get, as through effort or request. —*v.i.* **2.** to be prevalent or customary: *the morals that obtained in Rome.* —ob•tain′a•ble, *adj.*

ob•trude (əb trōōd′), *v.,* -trud•ed, -trud•ing. —*v.t.* **1.** to thrust forward without warrant or invitation. **2.** to push out. —*v.i.* **3.** to thrust oneself unduly; intrude. —ob•tru′sion (-trōō′zhən), *n.* —ob•tru′sive, *adj.* —ob•tru′sive•ness, *n.*

ob•tuse (əb tōōs′, -tyōōs′), *adj.* **1.** not quick in perception, feeling, or intellect. **2.** not sharp or pointed; blunt.

ob•verse (*n.* ob′vûrs; *adj.* ob vûrs′, ob′vûrs), *n.* **1.** the side, as of a coin, that bears the principal design. **2.** a counterpart. —*adj.* **3.** facing the observer. **4.** corresponding to something else as a counterpart.

ob•vi•ate (ob′vē āt′), *v.t.,* -at•ed, -at•ing. to anticipate and prevent by effective measures. —ob′vi•a′tion, *n.*

ob•vi•ous (ob′vē əs), *adj.* **1.** easily seen or understood. **2.** lacking in subtlety. —ob′vi•ous•ly, *adv.*

oc•a•ri•na (ok′ə rē′nə), *n., pl.* **-nas.** a simple musical wind instrument with a mouthpiece and finger holes.

oc•ca•sion (ə kā′zhən), *n.* **1.** a particular time, esp. as marked by certain occurrences. **2.** a special or important time, event, etc. **3.** a convenient or favorable time. **4.** the immediate or incidental cause or reason. —*v.t.* **5.** to cause; bring about. —*Idiom.* **6. on occasion,** once in a while. —oc•ca′sion•al, *adj.* —oc•ca′sion•al•ly, *adv.*

Oc•ci•dent (ok′si dənt), *n.* **1. the Occident, a.** the West; the countries of Europe and America. **b.** WESTERN HEMISPHERE. **2.** (*l.c.*) the west. —Oc′ci•den′tal, oc′ci•den′tal, *adj., n.*

oc•cult (ə kult′, ok′ult), *adj.* **1.** pertaining to any system claiming knowledge of supernatural agencies. **2.** beyond ordinary knowledge. **3.** secret; disclosed only to the initiated. **4.** hidden from view.

oc•cu•pa•tion (ok′yə pā′shən), *n.* **1.** a person's usual or principal work in earning a living. **2.** any activity in which a person is engaged. **3.** the seizure and control of an area by military forces. —oc′cu•pa′tion•al, *adj.*

occupa′tional ther′apy *n.* therapy that utilizes useful activities to facilitate psychological or physical rehabilitation.

oc′cu•py′ *v.t.,* -pied, -py•ing. **1.** to take or fill up (time, space, etc.). **2.** to be a resident of; dwell in. **3.** to employ or engage; busy. **4.** to take possession and control of (a place), as by military invasion. **5.** to hold (a position, office, etc.). —oc′cu•pant, *n.*

oc•cur (ə kûr′), *v.i.,* -curred, -cur•ring. **1.** to happen; take place. **2.** to be found; appear. **3.** to come to mind. —oc•cur′ence, *n.*

o•cean (ō′shən), *n.* **1.** the body of salt water that covers almost three-fourths of the earth's surface. **2.** any of the geographical divisions of this body: the Atlantic, Pacific, Indian, Arctic, and Antarctic oceans. **3.** a vast quantity. —o•ce•an•ic (ō′shē-an′ik), *adj.*

o•cea•nog•ra•phy (ō′shə nog′rə fē, ō′shē ə-), *n.* the branch of physical geography dealing with the ocean and marine life. —o′cea•nog′ra•pher, *n.* —o′cea•no•graph′ic (-nə graf′ik), *adj.*

oc•e•lot (os′ə lot′, ō′sə-), *n.* a spotted wildcat, ranging from Texas through South America.

o•cher or **o•chre** (ō′kər), *n.* a mixture of hydrated oxide of iron with various earthy materials, ranging in color from yellow to orange and red, and used as a pigment.

o′clock (ə klok′), *adv.* of, by, or according to the clock.

Oct or **Oct.,** October.

oc•ta•gon (ok′tə gon′, -gən), *n.* a polygon having eight angles and eight sides. —oc•tag′o•nal (-tag′-ə nl), *adj.*

oc•tane (ok′tān), *n.* any of 18 isomeric saturated hydrocarbons.

oc′tane num′ber *n.* a designation of antiknock quality of gasoline.

oc•tave (ok′tiv, -tāv), *n.* **1. a.** a tone on the eighth degree from a given musical tone. **b.** the interval encompassed by such tones. **c.** a series of tones extending through this interval. **2.** a series or group of eight.

oc•tet or **-tette** (ok tet′), *n.* **1.** a company of eight singers or musicians. **2.** a musical composition for an octet.

Oc•to•ber (ok tō′bər), *n.* the tenth month of the year, containing 31 days.

oc•to•ge•nar•i•an (ok′tə jə nâr′ē ən), *n.* **1.** a person between 80 and 90 years old. —*adj.* **2.** between 80 and 90 years old.

oc•to•pus (ok′tə pəs), *n., pl.* **-pus•es, -pi** (-pī′). a marine mollusk having a soft, oval body and eight sucker-bearing arms. [< NL < Gk *oktōpous* eight-footed]

oc•u•lar (ok′yə lər), *adj.* **1.** of or for the eyes. **2.** performed or perceived by eyesight.

oc′u•list (-list), *n.* an ophthalmologist.

OD (ō′dē′), *n., pl.* **ODs** or **OD's,** *v.,* **OD'd** or **ODed,**

OD'•ing. *Slang.* —*n.* **1.** an overdose of a drug, esp. a fatal one. —*v.i.* **2.** to take a drug overdose.

O.D. Doctor of Optometry.

odd (od), *adj.,* **-er, -est. 1.** differing in nature from what is usual or expected. **2.** peculiar or eccentric. **3.** leaving a remainder of 1 when divided by 2. **4.** more or less: *sixty-odd dollars.* **5.** being part of a pair or set of which the rest is lacking: *an odd glove.* **6.** remaining after all others are grouped. **7.** not regular or full-time: *odd jobs.* —**odd'ly,** *adv.*

odd'ball' *n. Informal.* a peculiar person or thing.

odd'i•ty *n., pl.* **-ties. 1.** an odd person, thing, or event. **2.** the quality of being odd.

odds (odz), *n.* (*usu. with a pl. v.*) **1.** the probability that something is so or is more likely to occur than something else. **2.** this probability, expressed as a ratio: *The odds are two-to-one that it will rain today.* **3.** an equalizing allowance, as that given the weaker player in a contest. **4.** an advantage favoring one of two contestants. —*Idiom.* **5. at odds,** in disagreement.

odds' and ends' *n.pl.* **1.** miscellaneous items, matters, etc. **2.** remnants; scraps.

odds'-on' *adj.* being the one most likely to achieve something: *the odds-on favorite.*

ode (ōd), *n.* a lyric poem expressing exalted or enthusiastic emotion.

o•di•ous (ō'dē əs), *adj.* **1.** deserving or causing hatred. **2.** highly offensive; disgusting.

o'di•um (-əm), *n.* **1.** intense hatred. **2.** the reproach, discredit, etc., attaching to some discreditable action.

o•dor (ō'dər), *n.* **1.** the property of a substance that activates the sense of smell. **2.** a smell or scent. **3.** a quality suggestive of something: *an odor of suspicion.* **4.** repute: *in bad odor.* Also, *esp. Brit.,* **odour.** —**o'dor•ous,** *adj.*

o•dor•if•er•ous (ō'də rif'ər əs), *adj.* yielding an odor, esp. an unpleasant one.

od•ys•sey (od'ə sē), *n., pl.* **-seys.** (*l.c.*) any long, adventurous journey.

oed•i•pal (ed'ə pal, ē'də-), *adj.* (*often cap.*) of or resulting from the Oedipus complex.

Oed'i•pus com'plex (ed'ə pas, ē'də-), *n.* libidinous feelings toward the parent of the opposite sex, esp. toward the mother.

o'er (ôr), *prep., adv.* OVER.

oeu•vre (Fr. œ'vRə), *n., pl.* **oeu•vres** (Fr. œ'vRə). the works of a writer, painter, etc., taken as a whole.

of (uv, ov; *unstressed* əv *or, esp. before consonants,* ə), *prep.* **1.** from or away from: *within a mile of the house.* **2.** by or coming from: *the songs of Gershwin.* **3.** owing to or because of: *the king of Spain.* **4.** containing or consisting of: *a book of poems.* **5.** ruling or possessing: *the king of Spain.* **6.** possessed or ruled by: *property of the church.* **7.** (used to indicate inclusion in a whole): *one of us.* **8.** (used to indicate the object of action following a noun, verb, or adjective): *the ringing of bells.* **9.** having particular attributes: *a woman of courage.* **10.** so as to be left without: *robbed of one's money.* **11.** before; until: *ten minutes of one.* **12.** on the part of: *It was nice of you to come.* **13.** set aside for: *a minute of prayer.* **14.** about: *There is talk of peace.* **15.** named: *the city of London.* **16.** belonging to: *the sleeve of a dress.*

off (ôf, of), *adv.* **1.** so as to be no longer attached: *The button came off.* **2.** so as to be no longer covering: *Pull the wrapping off.* **3.** so as to be away or on one's way: *to start off early.* **4.** from a charge or price: *Take 10 percent off.* **5.** at a distance in space or future time: *Summer is only a week off.* **6.** out of operation: *Turn the lights off.* **7.** in absence from work, service, etc.: *to get two days off.* —*prep.* **8.** so as no longer to be supported by, resting on, etc.: *Wipe the dirt off your shoes.* **9.** deviating from: *to be off course.* **10.** below the usual level or standard: *20 percent off the marked price.* **11.** disengaged or resting from: *to be off duty.* **12.** abstaining from: *He's off gambling.* **13.** located apart from: *a village off the main road.* **14.** by means of: *living off his parents.* —*adj.* **15.** in error. **16.** less than sane: *a little*

off, but harmless. **17.** no longer in effect: *The agreement is off.* **18.** in a specified state, circumstance, etc.: *to be badly off for money.* **19.** free from work or duty: *one's off hours.* **20.** of less than the ordinary activity: *an off-season in the tourist trade.* **21.** unlikely: *on the off chance she's at home.* **22.** starting on one's way: *I'm off to Europe.* —*v.t.* **23.** *Slang.* to kill. —*Idiom.* **24. off and on,** intermittently. **25. off of,** off: *Take your feet off of the table!*

of•fal (ô'fəl, of'əl), *n.* **1.** the viscera or inedible remains of a butchered animal. **2.** refuse or rubbish.

off'beat' (*adj.* -bēt'; *n.* -bēt'), *adj.* **1.** unconventional. —*n.* **2.** an unaccented beat of a measure in music.

off'-col'or *adj.* **1.** not having the usual color. **2.** of doubtful propriety or taste.

of•fend (ə fend'), *v.t.* **1.** to irritate, annoy, or anger; insult. **2.** to affect (the sense, taste, etc.) disagreeably. —*v.i.* **3.** to cause resentful displeasure. **4.** to err in conduct.

of•fend'er *n.* **1.** a person who offends. **2.** a criminal.

of•fense (ə fens' *or, for 6, 7,* ô'fens, of'ens), *n.* **1.** a breaking of a social or moral rule. **2.** a transgression of the law; misdemeanor. **3.** something that offends. **4.** the act of offending. **5.** a feeling of resentful displeasure: *to give offense.* **6.** aggression or assault. **7.** the side that is attacking or attempting to score in a game. Also, *esp. Brit.,* **of•fence'.**

of•fen•sive (ə fen'siv *or, for 4,* ô'fen-, of'en-), *adj.* **1.** causing resentful displeasure. **2.** unpleasant or disagreeable to the senses. **3.** repugnant to the moral sense, good taste, etc. **4.** pertaining to offense or attack. —*n.* **5.** the position or attitude of aggression or attack. **6.** an aggressive movement or attack.

of•fer (ô'fər, of'ər), *v.t.* **1.** to present for acceptance or rejection. **2.** to propose for consideration. **3.** to present as an act of worship. **4.** to present for sale. **5.** to tender or bid as a price. **6.** to put forth; exert: *to offer resistance.* —*v.i.* **7.** to present itself; occur. —*n.* **8.** the act of offering. **9.** something offered. —**of'fer•ing,** *n.*

of•fer•to•ry (-tôr'ē), *n., pl.* **-ries. 1.** (*sometimes cap.*) the offering to God of the unconsecrated elements in a Eucharistic service. **2. a.** the verses or music accompanying the offerings made at a religious service. **b.** that part of a service at which offerings are made.

off'hand' *adv.* **1.** without previous thought or preparation. —*adj.* **2.** casual or curt. **3.** done or made offhand. —**off'hand'ed•ness,** *n.*

of•fice (ô'fis, of'is), *n.* **1.** a place where business is conducted. **2.** the staff that works in a place of business. **3.** a position of duty, trust, or authority: *the office of president.* **4.** position as an official: *to seek office.* **5.** the duty or function of a person or agency. **6.** Often, **-fices.** something done or said for or to another: *the good offices of a friend.* **7. a.** the prescribed form for a church service or for devotional use. **b.** the services so prescribed.

of'fice•hold'er *n.* a public official.

of•fi•cer *n.* **1.** a person holding a commission in the armed services. **2.** a member of a police department. **3.** a person holding a position of authority in some organization.

of•fi•cial (ə fish'əl), *n.* **1.** a person holding an office or charged with certain duties. —*adj.* **2.** of an office or position of authority. **3.** appointed or authorized by a government or organization. **4.** public and formal. —**of•fi'cial•dom,** *n.* —**of•fi'cial•ism,** *n.* —**of•fi'cial•ly,** *adv.*

of•fi•ci•ant (ə fish'ē ənt), *n.* a person who officiates at a religious service.

of•fi•ci•ate (-āt'), *v.i.,* **-at•ed, -at•ing. 1.** to perform the duties or function of some office or position. **2.** to perform the office of a cleric, as at a divine service.

of•fi•cious *adj.* objectionably aggressive in offering unwanted help or advice.

off•ing (ô'fing, of'ing), *n.* **1.** the distant part of the sea seen from the shore. —*Idiom.* **2. in the off-ing, a.** at a distance but within sight. **b.** in the projected future.

off′-key′ *adj.* out of tune.

off′-lim′its *adj.* forbidden to be patronized, used, etc., by certain persons.

off′-put′ting *adj.* provoking uneasiness, dislike, annoyance, etc.

off•set (*n.* ôf′set′, of′-; *v.* ôf′set′, of′-), *n.*, *v.*, **-set, -set•ting.** —*n.* **1.** something that compensates for something else. **2.** a process in which a lithographic plate is used to make an inked impression on a rubber blanket that transfers it to the paper being printed. —*v.t.* **3.** to compensate for. **4.** to print by the process of offset lithography.

off′shoot′ *n.* **1.** a branch from a main stem, as of a plant. **2.** anything conceived of as or proceeding from a main stock.

off′shore′ *adv.* **1.** off or away from the shore. **2.** at a distance from the shore. **3.** in a foreign country. —*adj.* **4.** moving or tending away from the shore. **5.** located or operating at some distance from the shore. **6.** registered or located in a foreign country.

off′spring′ *n.*, *pl.* **-spring, -springs.** children or young of a particular parent or progenitor.

off′stage′ *adv.*, *adj.* away from the view of the audience.

off′-the-cuff′ *adj.* with little or no preparation; impromptu.

off′-the-rec′ord *adj.* not to be published or quoted.

off′-the-wall′ *adj. Informal.* markedly unconventional; bizarre.

off′ year′ *n.* **1.** a year without a major, esp. presidential, election. **2.** a year marked by reduced or inferior production or activity.

oft (ôft, oft), *adv.* OFTEN.

of•ten (ô′fən, of′ən; ôf′tən, of′-), *adv.* many times; frequently.

o•gle (ō′gəl), *v.*, **o•gled, o•gling.** —*v.t.*, *v.i.* **1.** to look (at) amorously or flirtatiously. —*n.* **2.** an amorous or flirtatious look.

o•gre (ō′gər), *n.* **1.** a monster in fairy tales who feeds on human flesh. **2.** a monstrously ugly or cruel person.

oh (ō), *interj.*, *n.*, *pl.* **ohs, oh′s.** —*interj.* **1.** an exclamation of surprise, pain, sympathy, etc. —*n.* **2.** the exclamation "oh."

OH Ohio.

ohm (ōm), *n.* a unit of electrical resistance.

oil (oil), *n.* **1.** any of various unctuous, viscous, combustible substances that are not soluble in water. **2.** petroleum. **3. a.** OIL COLOR. **b.** OIL PAINTING. —*v.t.* **4.** to smear, lubricate, or supply with oil. —*adj.* **5.** of or resembling oil. —**oil′y** *adj.*, **-i•er, -i•est.**

oil′cloth′ *n.* a cotton fabric made waterproof by treatment with oil.

oil′ col′or *n.* a paint made by grinding a pigment in oil.

oil′ paint′ing *n.* **1.** the art of painting with oil colors. **2.** a painting in oil colors.

oil′skin′ *n.* **1.** a cotton fabric made waterproof by treatment with oil. **2.** Often, **-skins.** a garment made of this, as a raincoat.

oint•ment (oint′mənt), *n.* a soft, unctuous preparation, often medicated, for application to the skin.

OK Oklahoma.

OK or **O.K.** or **o•kay** (ō′kā′, ō′kā′, ō′kā′), *adj.*, *adv.*, *n.*, *pl.* **OKs, OK′s** or **O.K.′s** or **o•kays,** *v.*, **OK′d** or **O.K.′ed** or **o•kayed, OK′•ing** or **O.K.′•ing** or **o•kay•ing.** —*adj.*, *adv.* **1.** all right or all correct. **2.** correct or acceptable. —*n.* **3.** an approval, agreement, or endorsement. —*v.t.* **4.** to endorse or indicate approval of. [initials of *oll korrect,* facetious spelling of *all correct*]

Okla. Oklahoma.

o•kra (ō′krə), *n.*, *pl.* **o•kras. 1.** a shrub bearing sticky pods. **2.** the pods, used in soups, stews, etc.

old (ōld), *adj.*, **old•er, old•est** or **eld•er, eld•est,** *n.* —*adj.* **1.** having lived or existed for a long time. **2.** of the latter part of life or existence. **3.** having lived

or existed for a specified time: *a six-month-old company.* **4.** deteriorated through age or use: *old clothes.* **5.** of long standing: *an old friend.* **6.** former: *an old classmate.* **7.** of an earlier period: *old maps.* **8.** ancient: *old civilizations.* **9.** (*cap.*) (of a language) in its oldest known period: *Old English.* **10.** experienced: *an old sailor.* —*n.* **11. the old,** old persons collectively. **12.** time long past: *days of old.*

Old′ Eng′lish *n.* the English language before c1150.

old′-fash′ioned *adj.* reflecting or favoring the styles, customs, or methods of the past.

Old′ Guard′ *n.* (*sometimes l.c.*) the conservative members of any group.

old′ hand′ *n.* a person with long experience in a subject, area, etc.

old′ hat′ *adj.* old-fashioned; dated.

old′ school′ *n.* supporters of established custom or of conservatism.

old′ster *n. Informal.* an elderly person.

Old′ Tes′tament *n.* the complete Bible of the Jews, being the first of the two main divisions of the Christian Bible.

old′-tim′er *n.* a person whose residence, membership, etc., dates from long ago.

Old′ World′ *n.* **1.** Europe, Asia, and Africa. **2.** EASTERN HEMISPHERE.

old′-world′ *adj.* old-fashioned; traditional.

o•le•ag•i•nous (ō′lē aj′ə nəs), *adj.* **1.** having the nature or qualities of oil. **2.** unctuous; fawning.

o•le•an•der (ō′lē an′dər), *n.* a poisonous evergreen shrub with clusters of pink, red, or white flowers.

o′le•o•mar′ga•rine (ō′lē ō-), *n. Older Use.* MARGARINE.

ol•fac•to•ry (ol fak′tə rē, ōl-), *adj.* of the sense of smell. —**ol•fac′tion,** *n.*

ol•i•gar•chy (ol′i gär′kē), *n.*, *pl.* **-chies. 1.** a form of government in which power is vested in a few persons. **2.** a state so ruled. **3.** the persons so ruling. —**ol′i•garch′,** *n.* —**ol′i•gar′chic,** *adj.*

ol•ive (ol′iv), *n.* **1.** an evergreen tree of Mediterranean and other warm regions. **2.** the small, oval fruit of this tree, eaten as a relish and used as a source of oil. **3.** the dull yellow-green of the unripe fruit.

O•man (ō män′), *n.* an independent sultanate in SE Arabia. —**O•ma•ni** (ō mä′nē), *n.*, *adj.*

om•buds•man (om′bədz mən, ôm′-, om bŏŏdz′-, ôm-), *n.*, *pl.* **-men. 1.** a public official who investigates complaints by citizens against government agencies or officials. **2.** a person who investigates and resolves complaints. [< Sw: legal representative]

o•me•ga (ō mē′gə, ō meg′ə), *n.*, *pl.* **-gas.** the 24th and last letter of the Greek alphabet (Ω, ω).

om•e•let or **-lette** (om′lit, om′ə-), *n.* a dish of beaten eggs cooked and served folded, often around a filling.

o•men (ō′mən), *n.* any event believed to portend something good or evil.

om•i•nous (om′ə nəs), *adj.* portending evil or harm.

o•mit (ō mit′), *v.t.*, **o•mit•ted, o•mit•ting. 1.** to leave out; fail to include. **2.** to fail (to do, make, use, etc.). —**o•mis′sion,** *n.*

omni- a combining form meaning all (*omnipotent*).

om•ni•bus (om′nə bus′, -bəs), *n.*, *pl.* **-bus•es, bus•ses,** *adj.* —*n.* **1.** BUS (def. 1). —*adj.* **2.** dealing with numerous items at once.

om•nip•o•tent (om nip′ə tənt), *adj.* **1.** having unlimited authority or power. —*n.* **2. the Omnipotent,** GOD. —**om•nip′o•tence,** *n.*

om•ni•pres•ent (om′nə prez′ənt), *adj.* present everywhere at the same time. —**om′ni•pres′ence,** *n.*

om•nis•cient (om nish′ənt), *adj.* **1.** having complete knowledge, awareness, or understanding. —*n.* **2. the Omniscient,** GOD. —**om•nis′cience,** *n.*

om•niv•o•rous (om niv′ər əs), *adj.* **1.** eating all kinds of foods, esp. both animals and plants. **2.** taking in everything, as with the mind: *an omnivorous reader.* —**om′ni•vore** (-nə vôr′), *n.*

on (on, ôn), *prep.* **1.** so as to be attached to,

supported by, or suspended from: *a package on a table.* **2.** so as to be in contact with. **3.** connected or associated with: *to serve on a jury.* **4.** having as a place, location, etc.: *a scar on the face.* **5.** in proximity to: *a house on the lake.* **6.** in the direction of: *to sail on a southerly course.* **7.** by the agency or means of: *drunk on wine.* **8.** about: *a book on birds.* **9.** in a condition or process of: *on strike.* **10.** engaged in or occupied with: *I'm on the second chapter.* **11.** having as a source or agent: *to depend on friends for support.* **12.** having as a basis or ground: *on my word of honor.* **13.** at the time or occasion of: *on Sunday.* **14.** paid for by: *Dinner is on me.* **15.** regularly taking or addicted to: *on drugs.* —*adv.* **16.** in, into, or onto a position of being supported or attached: *Sew the buttons on.* **17.** toward a place, point, activity, or object: *to look on while others work.* **18.** forward, onward, or along: *further on.* **19.** with continuous activity: *to work on.* **20.** into or in operation: *Turn the gas on.* —*adj.* **21.** operating or in use: *Is the radio on?* —*Idiom.* **22.** **on and off,** intermittently. **23. on and on,** at great length.

ON Ontario.

once (wuns), *adv.* **1.** formerly: *a once powerful nation.* **2.** a single time: *I go once a week.* —*n.* **3.** a single occasion: *Once is enough.* —*conj.* **4.** as soon as: *Once you're finished, you can leave.* —*Idiom.* **5. at once, a.** simultaneously. **b.** immediately. **6. once and for all,** decisively; finally. **7. once in a while,** occasionally.

once′-o′ver *n.* a quick look.

on•col′o•gy (on kol′ə jē), *n.* the branch of medical science dealing with tumors. —**on•col′o•gist,** *n.*

on′com′ing *adj.* approaching; nearing.

one (wun), *adj.* **1.** being a single unit or individual. **2.** of the same kind, nature, or condition: *of one mind.* **3.** a certain: *One John Smith was chosen.* **4.** being a unique individual or item: *the one person I can trust.* —*n.* **5.** the first and lowest whole number, being a cardinal number. **6.** a symbol of this, as 1 or I. **7.** a single person or thing. —*pron.* **8.** a person or thing of a number or kind: *one of the Elizabethan poets.* **9.** any person or thing indefinitely: *as good as one could desire.* **10.** something or someone of the kind just mentioned: *The portraits are good ones.* —*Idiom.* **11. at one,** united in thought or feeling. **12. one by one,** singly and successively.

one′ness *n.* **1.** the quality of being one. **2.** unity of thought, feeling, etc.

on•er•ous (on′ər əs, ō′nər-), *adj.* burdensome or oppressive.

one•self (wun self′, wunz-), *pron.* **1.** a person's self (used as a reflexive or emphatic form of ONE). —*Idiom.* **2. be oneself, a.** to be in one's normal state. **b.** to be unpretentious. **3. by oneself,** alone.

one′-sid′ed *adj.* **1.** considering but one side of a matter or question; partial or unfair. **2.** unequal: *a one-sided fight.* —**one′-sid′ed•ness,** *n.*

one′-time′ *adj.* **1.** former. **2.** occurring, done, etc., only once.

one′-track′ *adj.* unable to cope with more than one idea, subject, etc., at a time: *a one-track mind.*

one′-way′ *adj.* moving or allowing movement in one direction only.

on′go′ing *adj.* continuing without interruption.

on•ion (un′yən), *n.* **1.** a plant with an edible, pungent bulb. **2.** this bulb.

on′-line′ or **on′line′,** *adj.* **1.** operating under the direct control of, or connected to, a main computer. **2.** connected by computer to one or more other computers or networks, as through a commercial database service or the Internet. **3.** using a computer. —*adv.* **4.** with or through a computer, esp. over a network.

on′look′er *n.* a spectator.

on•ly (ōn′lē), *adv.* **1.** solely; exclusively. **2.** no more than; merely; just: *only on weekends.* **3.** as recently as: *only yesterday.* **4.** in the final outcome: *That will only make matters worse.* —*adj.* **5.** being the single one of the kind; lone; sole. —*conj.* **6.** but:

I would have gone, only you objected. —*Idiom.* **7. only too,** very; extremely.

on•o•mat•o•poe•ia (on′ə mat′ə pē′ə, -mä′tə-), *n.* the formation of a word, as *boom,* by imitation of a sound. —**on′o•mat′o•poe′ic, on′o•mat′o•po•et′ic** (-pō et′ik), *adj.*

on′rush′ *n.* a strong forward rush, flow, etc. —**on′rush′ing,** *adj.*

on′set′ *n.* **1.** a beginning or start. **2.** an assault or attack.

on•slaught (on′slôt, ôn′-), *n.* a vigorous assault.

on′to *prep.* **1.** to a position on. **2.** *Informal.* aware of the true nature of: *I'm onto your tricks.*

on•tol•o•gy (on tol′ə jē), *n.* the branch of metaphysics studying existence or being.

o•nus (ō′nəs), *n., pl.* **o•nus•es. 1.** an annoying or unfair burden. **2.** blame; responsibility.

on′ward (-wərd), *adv.* **1.** Also, **on′wards.** toward a point ahead; forward. —*adj.* **2.** directed or moving onward.

on•yx (on′iks, ō′niks), *n.* a variety of chalcedony having parallel bands of alternating colors.

oo•dles (ōōd′lz), *n.pl. Informal.* a large quantity.

ooze[1] (ōōz), *v.,* **oozed, ooz•ing,** *n.* —*v.i.* **1.** to flow or exude slowly, as through holes. —*v.t.* **2.** to exude (moisture, air, etc.) slowly. —*n.* **3.** something that oozes.

ooze[2] (ōōz), *n.* **1.** mud composed chiefly of the shells of one-celled organisms, found on the ocean bottom. **2.** soft mud or slime.

o•pal (ō′pəl), *n.* **1.** a mineral found in many varieties and colors. **2.** a gemstone made of this, esp. of an iridescent variety.

o•pal•es•cent (ō′pə les′ənt), *adj.* exhibiting a play of colors like that of the opal. —**o′pal•es′cence,** *n.*

o•paque (ō pāk′), *adj.* **1.** not allowing light to pass through. **2.** dark; dull. **3.** hard to understand. —**o•pac•i•ty** (ō pas′i tē), *n.* —**o•paque′ly,** *adv.*

op. cit. (op′ sit′), (in the work cited. [< L *opere citātō*]

OPEC (ō′pek), *n.* Organization of Petroleum Exporting Countries.

Op′-Ed′ *n.* a newspaper page or section devoted to signed articles, letters, etc. [*op(posite)-ed(itorial page)*]

o•pen (ō′pən), *adj.* **1.** not closed, covered, or barred. **2.** having large or numerous spaces or intervals: *open ranks of soldiers.* **3.** relatively unoccupied by buildings, trees, etc.: *open country.* **4.** extended or unfolded: *an open newspaper.* **5.** without restrictions as to who may participate: *an open session.* **6.** accessible or available: *Which job is open?* **7.** ready to carry on normal business: *The new store is now open.* **8.** exposed to general view or knowledge: *open disregard of the rules.* **9.** candid or frank. **10.** generous. **11.** liable or subject: *open to question.* **12.** undecided: *an open question.* **13.** without legal or moral regulations: *an open town.* —*v.t., v.i.* **14.** to make or become open. **15.** to make or become accessible or available. **16.** to begin, start, or commence. **17.** to expand or spread out. **18.** to make or become less compact or closely spaced. **19.** to reveal or become revealed. **20.** to make or become receptive to knowledge, sympathy, etc. —**o′pen•er,** *n.* —**o′pen•ly,** *adv.*

o′pen-and-shut′ *adj.* easily decided.

o′pen-end′ed *adj.* **1.** unrestricted. **2.** having no fixed answer: *an open-ended question.*

o′pen•hand′ed *adj.* generous; liberal.

o′pen•ing *n.* **1.** an unobstructed or unoccupied space or place. **2.** a hole in solid matter. **3.** the act of beginning; start. **4.** the initial stage of anything. **5.** an employment vacancy. **6.** an opportunity; chance.

o′pen-mind′ed *adj.* **1.** having a mind receptive to new ideas. **2.** unprejudiced; impartial.

op•er•a[1] (op′ər ə, op′rə), *n.* a dramatic work in which the parts are sung to orchestral accompaniment. —**op′er•at′ic,** *adj.*

o•pe•ra[2] (ō′pər ə, op′ər ə), *n.* a pl. of OPUS.

op•er•a•ble (op′ər ə bəl), *adj.* **1.** treatable by a surgical operation. **2.** capable of being put into use or practice.

op′era glass′es *n.pl.* small, low-power binoculars.

op•er•ate′ (-ə rāt′), *v.*, **-at•ed, -at•ing. —v.i. 1.** to work or function, as a machine does. **2.** to exert force or influence. **3.** to perform a surgical procedure. —*v.t.* **4.** to manage or use (a machine, device, etc.). **5.** to put or keep in operation.

op′erating sys′tem *n.* the software that directs a computer's operations, as by controlling and scheduling the execution of other programs.

op′er•a′tion *n.* **1.** the act, process, or manner of operating. **2.** the state of being operative: *a rule no longer in operation.* **3.** the exertion of force or influence. **4.** a process of a practical or mechanical nature. **5.** a surgical procedure aimed at restoring or improving the health of a patient.

op′er•a′tion•al *adj.* **1.** concerning operations. **2.** in operation.

op′er•a•tive (-ər ə tiv, -ə rā′tiv), *n.* **1.** a person engaged or skilled in some branch of work. **2.** a secret agent; spy. —*adj.* **3.** exerting force or influence. **4.** being in operation. **5.** significant; key.

op•er•et•ta (op′ə ret′ə), *n., pl.* **-tas.** a short opera of a light and amusing character.

oph•thal•mol•o•gy (of′thəl mol′ə jē, -thə-, -thal-, op′-), *n.* the branch of medicine dealing with the eye. —**oph′thal•mol′o•gist,** *n.*

o•pi•ate (ō′pē it, -āt′), *n.* **1.** a drug containing opium or its derivatives. **2.** anything that soothes the feelings.

o•pine (ō pīn′), *v.t., v.i.,* **o•pined, o•pin•ing.** to express or hold (an opinion).

o•pin•ion (ə pin′yən), *n.* **1.** a belief based on grounds insufficient to produce certainty. **2.** a personal attitude or appraisal. **3.** the formal expression of a professional judgment. **4.** a favorable estimate; esteem.

o•pin′ion•at′ed (-yə nā′tid), *adj.* obstinate regarding the merit of one's own opinions.

o•pi•um (ō′pē əm), *n.* a narcotic prepared from the condensed juice of a certain poppy.

o•pos•sum (ə pos′əm, pos′əm), *n., pl.* **-sums, -sum.** a marsupial of the eastern U.S., noted for feigning death when in danger.

op•po•nent (ə pō′nənt), *n.* a person who is on an opposing side; adversary.

op•por•tune (op′ər tōon′, -tyōon′), *adj.* **1.** suitable; apt. **2.** occurring at an appropriate time.

op′por•tun′ism *n.* the practice of adapting actions, decisions, etc., to expediency without regard to moral principles or consequences. —**op′por•tun′ist,** *n.*

op′por•tu′ni•ty *n., pl.* **-ties. 1.** an appropriate or favorable time or occasion. **2.** a condition favorable for attainment of a goal. **3.** a good chance, as for success.

op•pose (ə pōz′), *v.t.,* **-posed, -pos•ing. 1.** to resist; combat. **2.** to be hostile or averse to. **3.** to set (something) opposite something else. —**op•po•si′tion** (op′ə zish′ən), *n.*

op•po•site (op′ə zit, -sit), *adj.* **1.** situated in corresponding positions across an intervening line, space, etc. **2.** radically different; opposed. —*n.* **3.** a person or thing that is opposite or contrary. —*prep.* **4.** across from.

op•press (ə pres′), *v.t.* **1.** to exercise harsh authority or power over. **2.** to lie heavily on; weigh down. —**op•pres′sive,** *adj.* —**op•pres′sor,** *n.*

op•pro•bri•um (ə prō′brē əm), *n.* **1.** the disgrace incurred by shameful conduct. **2.** the cause of such disgrace. —**op•pro′bri•ous,** *adj.*

opt (opt), *v.i.* to make a choice: *They opted for compromise.*

op•tic (op′tik), *adj.* of the eye or sight.

op′ti•cal *adj.* **1.** of or applying optics. **2.** of the eye or sight. **3.** constructed to assist sight. —**op′ti•cal•ly,** *adv.*

op′tical disc′ *n.* a disk on which digital data, as text or music, is stored and read by a laser.

op′tical scan′ner *n.* a device capable of scanning printed text or illustrations and converting the information into digital form.

op•ti•cian (op tish′ən), *n.* a person who makes or sells eyeglasses, contact lenses, and other optical goods.

op′tics *n.* the branch of physical science that deals with light and vision.

op•ti•mal (op′tə məl), *adj.* optimum. —**op′ti•mal•ly,** *adv.*

op•ti•mism (op′tə miz′əm), *n.* **1.** a tendency to look on the more favorable side of events or conditions. **2.** the belief that good will ultimately triumph over evil. —**op′ti•mist,** *n.* —**op′ti•mis′tic,** *adj.*

op′ti•mum (-məm), *n., pl.* **-ma** (-mə), **-mums,** *adj.* —*n.* **1.** the most favorable point, degree, or amount of something for obtaining a given result. —*adj.* **2.** Also, **op′ti•mal.** most favorable; best.

op•tion (op′shən), *n.* **1.** the power or right of choosing. **2.** something that may be chosen; choice. **3.** the act of choosing. **4.** part of a legal agreement giving one the right to buy property, use services, etc., within a specified time. —**op′tion•al,** *adj.*

op•tom•e•try (op tom′i trē), *n.* the profession of examining the eyes for defects of vision in order to prescribe corrective lenses. —**op•tom′e•trist,** *n.*

op•u•lent (op′yə lənt), *adj.* **1.** wealthy or rich. **2.** richly supplied; plentiful. —**op′u•lence,** *n.*

o•pus (ō′pəs), *n., pl.* **o•pus•es, o•pe•ra** (ō′pər ə, op′ər ə), a musical or literary work or composition.

or (ôr; *unstressed* ər), *conj.* **1.** (used to connect words denoting alternatives): *to be or not to be.* **2.** (used to connect alternative terms for the same thing): *the tympanic membrane, or eardrum.* **3.** (used in correlation): *Either we go now or wait till tomorrow.*

OR 1. operating room. **2.** Oregon.

-or¹, a suffix meaning condition or quality (*pallor*).

-or², a suffix meaning a person or thing that does something (*orator*).

or•a•cle (ôr′ə kəl, or′-), *n.* **1.** (in the ancient world) **a.** a shrine at which inquiries were made of a deity. **b.** the priest who answered the inquiry. **c.** the response of the deity. **2.** a person who delivers authoritative or wise pronouncements. —**o•rac•u•lar** (ô rak′yə lər), *adj.*

o•ral (ôr′əl), *adj.* **1.** uttered by the mouth; spoken. **2.** of or using speech. **3.** of or involving the mouth. —**o′ral•ly,** *adv.*

or•ange (ôr′inj, or′-), *n.* **1.** any of various reddish yellow, edible citrus fruits. **2.** a tree bearing such fruit. **3.** a color between yellow and red.

or′ange•ade′ (-ād′), *n.* a beverage of orange juice, sweetener, and water.

o•rang•u•tan (ô rang′ōō tan′, ə rang′-), *n.* a large, mostly arboreal, long-armed anthropoid ape of Borneo and Sumatra.

o•ra•tion (ô rā′shən, ō rā′-), *n.* a formal public speech, esp. for a special occasion.

or•a•tor (ôr′ə tər, or′-), *n.* a public speaker of great eloquence.

or•a•to•ri•o (ôr′ə tôr′ē ō′, or′-), *n., pl.* **-os.** a musical work for voices and orchestra, usu. based on a religious theme.

or′a•to′ry *n.* **1.** eloquence in public speaking. **2.** the art of public speaking. —**or′a•tor′i•cal** (-tôr′i-kəl, -tor′-), *adj.*

orb (ôrb), *n.* a sphere or globe. —**or•bic•u•lar** (ôr-bik′yə lər), *adj.*

or•bit (ôr′bit), *n.* **1.** the curved path, usu. elliptical, described by a planet, satellite, etc., around a celestial body. **2.** a sphere of influence, as of a nation. —*v.t., v.i.* **3.** to travel in or send into an orbit. —**or′-bit•al,** *adj.*

or•chard (ôr′chərd), *n.* **1.** land devoted to the cultivation of fruit or nut trees. **2.** a group of such trees.

or•ches•tra (ôr′kə strə, -kes trə), *n., pl.* **-tras. 1.** a group of performers who play various musical instruments together. **2.** (in a theater) **a.** the space reserved for the musicians, usu. the front part of the main floor. **b.** the front section of seats on the main floor. —**or•ches′tral,** *adj.*

or•ches•trate (ôr′kə strāt′), *v.t.,* **-trat•ed, -trat•ing. 1.** to compose or arrange (music) for an orchestra. **2.** to arrange the elements of to achieve a goal or effect. —**or′ches•tra′tion,** *n.*

general

or•chid (ôr′kid), *n.* **1.** any of various chiefly tropical plants having showy flowers with three petals, the lowest of which is enlarged. **2.** the flower of an orchid. **3.** a bluish to reddish purple.
or•dain (ôr dān′), *v.t.* **1.** to invest with ministerial or priestly functions. **2.** to decree; give orders for. —*v.i.* **3.** to command. —**or•dain′ment,** *n.*
or•deal (ôr dēl′, ôr′dēl), *n.* any extremely severe or trying experience.
or•der (ôr′dər), *n.* **1.** an authoritative instruction; command. **2.** a succession or sequence: *alphabetical order.* **3.** a methodical or harmonious arrangement. **4.** state or condition generally: *in working order.* **5.** conformity or obedience to established authority: *to maintain law and order.* **6.** customary mode of procedure. **7.** a direction or commission to make or provide something. **8.** goods purchased or sold. **9.** a class, kind, or sort: *talents of a high order.* **10.** a major subdivision of a class in the classification of organisms, consisting of one or more families. **11.** a body or society of persons living under the same religious, moral, or social regulations. **12. orders,** the rank of an ordained Christian minister. —*v.t., v.i.* **13.** to give an order (to). **14.** to place an order (for). **15.** to put (things) in order. —*Idiom.* **16. in order, a.** appropriate. **b.** properly arranged. **c.** correct according to the rules. **17. in order to,** with the purpose of. **18. in short order,** rapidly. **19. out of order, a.** not in correct arrangement. **b.** inappropriate. **c.** not operating properly. **d.** incorrect according to the rules. **20. to order,** according to the purchaser's requirements.
or′der•ly *adj., n., pl.* **-lies,** *adv.* —*adj.* **1.** arranged in a tidy manner. **2.** observant of law, rule, or discipline. —*n.* **3.** a hospital attendant. **4.** an enlisted soldier assigned to perform various chores for an officer. —*adv.* **5.** methodically. **6.** according to established order. —**or′der•li•ness,** *n.*
or•di•nal (ôr′dn əl), *adj.* **1.** of or showing order in a series. —*n.* **2.** an ordinal number.
or•di•nance (ôr′dn əns), *n.* a public regulation, esp. a municipal one.
or•di•nar•y (ôr′dn er′ē), *adj.* **1.** commonplace; unexceptional. **2.** customary; usual; normal. —*Idiom.* **3. out of the ordinary,** unusual. —**or′di•nar′i•ness,** *n.*
or•di•na•tion (ôr′dn ā′shən), *n.* **1.** the act of ordaining as a priest, minister, etc. **2.** the fact or state of being ordained.
ord•nance (ôrd′nəns), *n.* **1.** artillery. **2.** military weapons with their equipment, ammunition, etc.
or•dure (ôr′jər, -dyŏor), *n.* dung; excrement.
ore (ôr), *n.* a mineral or rock that is the source of a valuable metal or nonmetallic substance.
Ore. Oregon.
o•reg•a•no (ə reg′ə nō′), *n., pl.* **-nos.** an aromatic herb with leaves used as seasoning.
or•gan (ôr′gən), *n.* **1.** a musical instrument having sets of pipes actuated by keyboard and sounded by compressed air. **2.** a grouping of animal or plant tissues into a distinct structure that performs a specialized task. **3.** a periodical representing a special group. **4.** a means of action.
or•gan•dy (ôr′gən dē), *n., pl.* **-dies.** a fine, thin cotton fabric with a crisp finish.
or•gan•ic (ôr gan′ik), *adj.* **1.** of or noting a class of chemical compounds containing carbon. **2.** of, characteristic of, or derived from living organisms. **3.** raised or grown without synthetic fertilizers, pesticides, or drugs. **4.** of the organs of an animal or plant. **5.** organized; systematic. **6.** fundamental; inherent. —**or•gan′i•cal•ly,** *adv.*
or′gan•ism (-gə niz′əm), *n.* any individual life form.
or′gan•ize′ *v.,* **-ized, -iz•ing.** —*v.t.* **1.** to form as or into a whole, esp. for united action. **2.** to systematize; order. **3.** to give organic structure or character to. **4.** to enlist the employees of (a business) into a labor union. —*v.i.* **5.** to become organized. —**or′gan•i•za′tion,** *n.* —**or′gan•iz′er,** *n.*
or•gan•za (ôr gan′zə), *n., pl.* **-zas.** a sheer fabric of rayon, nylon, or silk with a crisp finish.
or•gasm (ôr′gaz əm), *n.* the sensation experienced

at the peak of sexual excitation; climax. —**or•gas′-mic, or•gas′tic** (-gas′tik), *adj.*
or•gy (ôr′jē), *n., pl.* **-gies. 1.** a party characterized by sexual promiscuity. **2.** any unbridled indulgence of passions. —**or′gi•as′tic** (-as′tik), *adj.*
o•ri•el (ôr′ē əl), *n.* a bay window projecting out from a wall, supported by brackets.
o•ri•ent (*n.* ôr′ē ənt, -ē ent′; *v.* ôr′ē ent′), *n.* **1. the Orient,** the countries of Asia, esp. East Asia. **2.** the east. —*v.t.* **3.** to familiarize with new surroundings or circumstances. **4.** to place in a position with reference to the points of the compass. —**o′ri•en•ta′tion,** *n.*
o′ri•en•teer′ing (-tēr′ing) *n.* the sport of navigating unknown terrain.
or•i•fice (ôr′ə fis, or′-), *n.* a mouthlike opening or hole.
o•ri•ga•mi (ôr′i gä′mē), *n.* the Japanese art of folding paper into decorative or representational forms. [< Japn: folding paper]
or•i•gin (ôr′i jin, or′-), *n.* **1.** the source from which anything arises or is derived. **2.** the beginning of something. **3.** ancestry; parentage.
o•rig•i•nal (ə rij′ə nl), *adj.* **1.** of or belonging to the beginning of something. **2.** inventive; novel. **3.** undertaken or presented for the first time. **4.** being that from which a copy, translation, etc., is made. —*n.* **5.** a primary type from which varieties are derived. **6.** an original work, document, etc. —**o•rig′i•nal′i•ty,** *n.* —**o•rig′i•nal•ly,** *adv.*
o•rig′i•nate′ *v.,* **-nat•ed, -nat•ing.** —*v.i.* **1.** to take or have origin; arise. —*v.t.* **2.** to give origin or rise to; initiate. —**o•rig′i•na′tion,** *n.* —**o•rig′i•na′-tor,** *n.*
o•ri•ole (ôr′ē ōl′), *n.* any of various songbirds, the males of which are usu. black and orange or yellow.
or′i•son (ôr′i zən) *n.* a prayer.
Or•lon (ôr′lon), *Trademark.* a brand of acrylic textile fiber.
or•mo•lu (ôr′mə lōō′), *n., pl.* **-lus.** an alloy of copper and zinc used to imitate gold.
or•na•ment (*n.* ôr′nə mənt; *v.* -ment′, -mənt), *n.* **1.** an object or feature that embellishes; decoration. **2.** a person or thing that adds to the credit or glory of a society, era, etc. —*v.t.* **3.** to embellish; decorate. —**or′na•men′tal,** *adj.* —**or′na•men•ta′tion,** *n.*
or•nate (ôr nāt′), *adj.* elaborately adorned, often excessively so. —**or•nate′ly,** *adv.* —**or•nate′ness,** *n.*
or•ner•y (ôr′nə rē), *adj.,* **-i•er, -i•est. 1.** disagreeable in disposition. **2.** stubborn. —**or′ner•i•ness,** *n.*
or•ni•thol•o•gy (ôr′nə thol′ə jē), *n.* the branch of zoology that deals with birds. —**or′ni•thol′o•gist,** *n.*
o•ro•tund (ôr′ə tund′), *adj.* **1.** (of the voice or speech) strong, full, and clear. **2.** (of speech or writing) pompous or bombastic. —**o′ro•tun′di•ty,** *n.*
or•phan (ôr′fən), *n.* **1.** a child who has lost both parents through death. —*adj.* **2.** bereft of parents. **3.** of or for orphans. —*v.t.* **4.** to cause to become an orphan.
or′phan•age (-fə nij), *n.* an institution for the housing and care of orphans.
or•tho•don•tics (ôr′thə don′tiks) also **-don′tia** (-don′shə), *n.* a branch of dentistry dealing with the prevention and correction of irregular teeth. —**or′tho•don′tic,** *adj.* —**or′tho•don′tist,** *n.*
or•tho•dox (ôr′thə doks′), *adj.* **1.** conforming to the approved form of any doctrine, philosophy, etc. **2.** conforming to generally approved beliefs, attitudes, etc. **3.** *(cap.)* of the Eastern Church, esp. the Greek Orthodox Church. [< LL *orthodoxus* < Gk *orthódoxos* = *ortho-* straight, right, correct + *dóxa* belief, opinion] —**or′tho•dox′y,** *n., pl.* **-ies.**
or•thog•ra•phy (ôr thog′rə fē), *n., pl.* **-phies. 1.** the art of spelling according to accepted usage. **2.** language study concerned with spelling. —**or′tho•graph′ic** (-thə graf′ik), *adj.*
or•tho•pe•dics (ôr′thə pē′diks), *n.* the medical specialty concerned with correction of deformities or disorders of the skeletal system. —**or′tho•pe′-dic,** *adj.* —**or′tho•pe′dist,** *n.*
os•cil•late (os′ə lāt′), *v.i.,* **-lat•ed, -lat•ing. 1.** to swing to and fro. **2.** to waver or vacillate. **3.** *Phys-*

ics. to vary between maximum and minimum values, as of a cycle. —**os′cil•la′tion**, n. —**os′cil•la′tor**, n.

os•cil•lo•scope (ə sil′ə skōp′), n. a device that uses a cathode-ray tube to display on a screen periodic changes in an electric quantity.

os•cu•late (os′kyə lāt′), v.t., v.i., **-lat•ed, -lat•ing.** to kiss. —**os′cu•la′tion**, n.

o•sier (ō′zhər), n. **1.** any of various willows with tough, flexible twigs used for wickerwork. **2.** a twig from such a willow.

os•mo•sis (oz mō′sis, os-), n. **1.** the tendency of a fluid to pass through a membrane into a solution where the solvent concentration is higher, thus equalizing the concentrations of materials on either side. **2.** a subtle or gradual absorption: *to learn by osmosis.* —**os•mot′ic** (-mot′ik), adj.

os•prey (os′prē, -prā), n., pl. **-preys.** a large bird of prey that feeds on fish.

os•se•ous (os′ē əs) adj. of, like, or containing bone.

os′si•fy′ (-ə fī′), v.t., v.i., **-fied, -fy•ing. 1.** to convert into or become bone. **2.** to make or become rigid in habits, opinions, etc. —**os′si•fi•ca′tion**, n.

os•ten•si•ble (o sten′sə bəl), adj. outwardly appearing as such. —**os•ten′si•bly,** adv.

os•ten•ta•tion (os′ten tā′shən, -tən-), n. pretentious display. —**os′ten•ta′tious,** adj.

os•te•o•ar•thri•tis (os′tē ō är thrī′tis), n. arthritis marked by chronic breakdown of cartilage in the joints.

os•te•op•a•thy (os′tē op′ə thē), n. a system of medical practice emphasizing the manipulation of muscles and bones to relieve certain disorders. —**os′te•o•path′** (-ə path′), n.

os•te•o•po•ro•sis (os′tē ō pa rō′sis), n. a disorder in which the bones become increasingly porous, brittle, and subject to fracture.

os•tra•cize (os′trə sīz′), v.t., **-cized, -ciz•ing.** to exclude, by general consent, from society, privileges, etc. —**os′tra•cism,** n.

os•trich (ô′strich, os′trich), n. a two-toed, swift-footed, flightless bird, orig. of Africa and SW Asia.

oth•er (uŧħ′ər), adj. **1.** additional or further: *one other person.* **2.** different from the one mentioned: *in some other city.* **3.** different in nature or kind: *I would not have him other than he is.* **4.** being the remaining one or ones of a number: *the other men.* **5.** not long past: *the other night.* —pron. **6.** Usu., **-ers.** other persons or things. **7.** some person or thing else. —adv. **8.** otherwise: *We can't collect the rent other than by suing.*

oth′er•wise′ adv. **1.** under other circumstances. **2.** in another manner. **3.** in other respects. —adj. **4.** of a different kind.

oth′er•world′ly adj. concerned with the world of imagination or the world to come.

ot•ter (ot′ər), n., pl. **-ters, -ter. 1.** any of several aquatic, furbearing mammals with webbed feet. **2.** the fur of an otter.

ot•to•man (ot′ə mən), n., pl. **-mans. 1.** a cushioned footstool. **2.** a cushioned seat or sofa without back or arms.

ought (ôt), auxiliary verb. **1.** (used to express duty or moral obligation): *Every citizen ought to help.* **2.** (used to express justice or moral rightness): *He ought to be punished.* **3.** (used to express propriety or appropriateness): *We ought to bring her flowers.* **4.** (used to express probability): *That ought to be our train now.*

ounce (ouns), n. **1.** a unit of weight equal to ¹⁄₁₆ of a pound (28.349 grams) avoirdupois. **2.** a unit of weight equal to ¹⁄₁₂ of a pound (31.103 grams) troy. **3.** a fluid ounce.

our (ou²r, ou′ər; unstressed är), pron. a form of the possessive case of WE used as an attributive adjective: *Our team won.*

ours pron. **1.** a form of the possessive case of WE used as a predicate adjective: *Which house is ours?* **2.** that or those belonging to us: *Ours are the pink ones.*

our•selves′ pron.pl. **1.** the reflexive form of WE: *We deceived ourselves.* **2.** an intensive form of WE:

We ourselves decided. **3.** our normal selves: *We were ourselves again after a nap.*

oust (oust), v.t. to expel from a place or position occupied.

oust′er n. expulsion from a place or position occupied.

out (out), adv. **1.** not in the usual place, position, etc. **2.** in or into the outdoors. **3.** to the end or conclusion: *Please hear me out.* **4.** to a state of depletion, nonexistence, or extinction: *a practice on the way out.* **5.** in or into neglect, disuse, etc.: *That style has gone out.* **6.** in or into public notice: *The truth is out.* **7.** so as to project or extend: *to stretch out.* **8.** from a specified source or material: *made out of scraps.* **9.** aloud or loudly: *to cry out.* **10.** thoroughly; completely: *tired out.* **11.** in or into activity, existence, or manifestation: *A riot broke out.* **12.** from a number, stock, or store: *to pick out.* **13.** not at one's home or place of work. **14.** not in effective operation, use, etc. **15.** not fashionable. **16.** *Baseball.* not succeeding in getting on base. **17.** beyond fixed or usual limits. **18.** having a financial loss: *I'm out ten dollars.* **19.** inaccurate: *calculations out by $27.* **20.** external; outer. —prep. **21.** out from or through: *She ran out the door.* **22.** out along or on: *Let's drive out the old parkway.* —n. **23.** a means of escape, as from responsibility. **24.** Usu., **outs.** those persons or groups lacking status, power, etc. **25.** *Baseball.* an instance of putting out a batter or base runner. —v.i. **26.** to become known: *The truth will out.* —**Idiom. 27. on the outs,** quarreling; at odds. **28. out for,** determined to acquire, achieve, etc. **29. out of, a.** not within. **b.** beyond the reach of: *out of hearing.* **c.** not in a condition of: *out of danger.* **d.** without or lacking. **e.** from within or among. **f.** because of: *out of loyalty.*

out- a prefix meaning: outward or external (*outburst*); outside or at a distance from (*outpost*); to surpass (*outbid*).

out′age (ou′tij), n. an interruption or failure in the supply of power, esp. electricity.

out′-and-out′ adj. complete; absolute.

out′back′ n. the back country or remote settlements, esp. in Australia.

out′board′ adj. located on the exterior of a hull or aircraft.

out′break′ n. a sudden occurrence; eruption.

out′build′ing n. a detached building subordinate to a main building.

out′burst′ n. a sudden and violent release or outpouring.

out′cast′ n. **1.** a person who is rejected, as from society. —adj. **2.** cast out or rejected.

out′class′ v.t. to surpass in excellence.

out′come′ n. a final product or end result.

out′crop′ n. **1.** an emergence of a rock stratum or mineral vein at the surface of the earth. **2.** the exposed portion of such a stratum or vein.

out′cry′ n., pl. **-cries. 1.** a strong and public expression of protest. **2.** a loud cry or shout.

out′dat′ed adj. outmoded.

out′dis′tance v.t., **-tanced, -tanc•ing.** to leave behind, as in running.

out′do′ v.t., **-did, -done, -do•ing.** to surpass in execution or performance.

out′door′ adj. located, occurring, or belonging outdoors.

out′doors′ adv. **1.** in the open air. —n. **2.** the world outside of or away from buildings; open air.

out′er adj. **1.** situated on or toward the outside. **2.** situated farther out.

out′er•most′ adj. farthest out.

out′er space′ n. **1.** space beyond the earth's atmosphere. **2.** space beyond the solar system.

out′field′ n. **1.** the part of a baseball field beyond the diamond. **2.** the players (**out′field′ers**) positioned there.

out′fit′ n., v., **-fit•ted, -fit•ting.** —n. **1.** the gear for a particular task or role. **2.** a set of harmonious garments worn together. **3.** a group or team of people, as a business firm or military unit. —v.t. **4.** to furnish with an outfit. —**out′fit′ter,** n.

out′go′ *n.*, *pl.* **-goes.** money paid out.

out′go′ing (-gō′ing *or*, *for 3*, -gō′-), *adj.* **1.** departing. **2.** retiring from a position or office. **3.** friendly; sociable.

out′grow′ *v.t.*, **-grew, -grown, -grow•ing. 1.** to grow too large for. **2.** to discard or lose in the course of development. **3.** to surpass in growing.

out′growth′ *n.* an additional, supplementary result.

out′house′ *n.* an outbuilding serving as a toilet.

out′ing *n.* **1.** a pleasure trip, picnic, etc. **2.** the exposure of a secret homosexual, esp. a prominent figure.

out•land′ish (-lan′dish) *adj.* grotesquely strange or odd.

out′last′ *v.t.* to endure or last longer than.

out′law′ *n.* **1.** a habitual criminal. —*v.t.* **2.** to make illegal.

out•lay (*n.* out′lā′; *v.* out′lā′), *n.*, *v.*, **-laid, -lay•ing.** —*n.* **1.** an expending, as of money. **2.** an amount expended. —*v.t.* **3.** to expend.

out′let′ (-let, -lit), *n.* **1.** an opening by which anything is let out. **2.** a point on a wiring system at which current may be taken to supply electric devices. **3.** a means of expression: *an outlet for sorrow.* **4.** a store selling the goods of a particular manufacturer.

out′line′ *n.*, *v.*, **-lined, -lin•ing.** —*n.* **1.** the line by which a figure or object is bounded. **2.** a drawing restricted to line without shading. **3.** a general report, indicating only the main features. —*v.t.* **4.** to draw in outline. **5.** to indicate the main features of.

out′live′ *v.t.*, **-lived, -liv•ing.** to live or last longer than.

out′look′ *n.* **1.** the view from a place. **2.** mental attitude; point of view. **3.** prospect for the future.

out′ly′ing *adj.* lying at a distance from the main body; remote.

out′mod′ed (-mō′did), *adj.* **1.** no longer fashionable. **2.** obsolete.

out′num′ber *v.t.* to exceed in number.

out′-of-bod′y *adj.* of or characterized by the sensation that the mind or soul has left the body and is acting on its own.

out′-of-date′ *adj.* outmoded.

out′-of-doors′ *adj.* **1.** OUTDOOR. —*n.* **2.** OUTDOORS.

out′-of-the-way′ *adj.* **1.** remote; isolated. **2.** unusual.

out′pa′tient *n.* a person who receives treatment at a hospital but is not hospitalized.

out′place′ment *n.* assistance in finding a new job, provided by a company for an employee who is being let go.

out′post′ *n.* **1.** a station established at a distance from an army to protect it from surprise attack. **2.** the body of troops stationed there. **3.** a post in a foreign environment.

out′put′ *n.*, *v.*, **-put•ted** or **-put, -put•ting.** —*n.* **1.** the quantity of something produced in a specified period. **2.** the material produced. **3.** the current, voltage, or power produced by an electrical or electronic device. **4. a.** any information made available by computer. **b.** the process of transferring such information from computer memory to or by means of an output device. —*v.t.* **5.** to transfer (computer output). **6.** to produce; yield.

out′rage (-rāj), *n.*, *v.*, **-raged, -rag•ing.** —*n.* **1.** an act of wanton violence. **2.** anything that strongly offends the feelings. **3.** great anger. —*v.t.* **4.** to subject to grievous violence. **5.** to anger or offend.

out•ra′geous (-rā′jəs), *adj.* **1.** of or involving gross injury or wrong. **2.** grossly offensive to the sense of right or decency. **3.** passing reasonable bounds: *an outrageous price.* —**out•ra′geous•ly,** *adv.*

ou•tré (ōō trā′), *adj.* unconventional; bizarre.

out•reach (*v.* out′rēch′; *n.*, *adj.* out′rēch′), *v.*, **-reached, -reach•ing,** *n.*, *adj.* —*v.t.* **1.** to reach beyond; exceed. —*v.i.* **2.** to reach out. —*n.* **3.** an act or instance of reaching out. —*adj.* **4.** concerned with extending community services: *outreach programs in education.*

out′right′ (*adj.* -rīt′; *adv.* -rīt′, -rīt′), *adj.* **1.** complete; total. **2.** downright; unqualified. —*adv.* **3.** entirely. **4.** openly. **5.** at once.

out′run′ *v.t.*, **-ran, -run, -run•ning. 1.** to run faster or farther than. **2.** to exceed; surpass.

out′sell′ *v.t.*, **-sold, -sell•ing.** to exceed in number of sales.

out′set′ *n.* beginning; start.

out′shine′ *v.t.*, **-shone** or **-shined, -shin•ing. 1.** to shine more brightly than. **2.** to surpass in excellence, achievement, etc.

out•side (*n.* out′sīd′, -sīd′; *adj.* out′sīd′, out′-; *adv.* out′sīd′; *prep.* out′sīd′, out′sīd′), *n.* **1.** the outer side, surface, or part; exterior. **2.** the external appearance. **3.** the space beyond an enclosure or boundary. —*adj.* **4.** of, situated on, or coming from the outside. **5.** not belonging to a specified group: *outside influences.* **6.** extremely unlikely: *an outside chance.* **7.** extreme or maximum: *an outside estimate.* —*adv.* **8.** on or to the outside. —*prep.* **9.** on the outside of. **10.** beyond the confines of. —*Idiom.* **11.** outside of, other than.

out′sid′er *n.* a person who is not part of a particular group.

out′skirts′ *n.pl.* outlying districts.

out′smart′ *v.t.* to outwit.

out′spo′ken *adj.* **1.** expressed with frankness. **2.** unreserved in speech.

out′spread′ *v.t.*, *v.i.*, **-spread, -spread•ing.** to spread out; extend.

out′stand′ing *adj.* **1.** prominent; conspicuous. **2.** excellent; distinguished. **3.** remaining unpaid, unresolved, etc.: *outstanding debts.* **4.** projecting.

out′strip′ *v.t.*, **-stripped, -strip•ping. 1.** to surpass or exceed. **2.** to get ahead of in a race.

out′take′ *n.* a segment of film or a part of a recording edited out of the final version.

out′ward (-ward), *adj.* **1.** proceeding or directed toward the outside or exterior. **2.** pertaining to surface qualities only; superficial. **3.** of or situated on the outside. —*adv.* **4.** Also, **out′wards.** toward the outside. —**out′ward•ly,** *adv.*

out′weigh′ *v.t.* **1.** to exceed in value or importance. **2.** to exceed in weight.

out′wit′ *v.t.*, **-wit•ted, -wit•ting.** to get the better of by cleverness.

o•va (ō′və), *n.* pl. of OVUM.

o•val (ō′vəl), *adj.* **1.** egg-shaped. **2.** ellipsoidal or elliptical. —*n.* **3.** something oval in shape.

o•va•ry (ō′və rē), *n.*, *pl.* **-ries. 1.** the female reproductive gland, in which the ova develop. **2.** the enlarged lower part of the pistil in flowering plants enclosing the new seeds. —**o•var•i•an** (ō vâr′ē ən), *adj.*

o•vate (ō′vāt), *adj.* egg-shaped.

o•va•tion (ō vā′shən), *n.* an enthusiastic public acclamation, marked by loud, prolonged applause.

ov•en (uv′ən), *n.* a chamber, as in a stove, for baking, roasting, etc.

o•ver (ō′vər), *prep.* **1.** above in place or position. **2.** above and to the other side of: *to leap over a wall.* **3.** above in authority, rank, etc. **4.** so as to cover: *Throw a sheet over the bed.* **5.** throughout: *to travel over Europe.* **6.** on or to the other side of: *to go over a bridge.* **7.** in excess of. **8.** in preference to. **9.** throughout the duration of: *over the years.* **10.** concerning: *to quarrel over a matter.* —*adv.* **11.** so as to cover or affect the whole surface: *to paint the room over.* **12.** through a region or area: *known the world over.* **13.** from one side to another or across an intervening space: *to sail over.* **14.** across or beyond an edge or rim: *The soup boiled over.* **15.** from beginning to end: *Think it over.* **16.** from one person to another: *He made the property over to his brother.* **17.** from one opinion or belief to another: *won them over.* **18.** on the other side, as of a sea or any space: *over in Japan.* **19.** from an upright position: *to knock over a glass.* **20.** to a reversed position: *The dog rolled over.* **21.** once more: *Do the work over.* **22.** in repetition or succession: *20 times over.* **23.** in excess or addition. —*adj.* **24.** upper; higher up. **25.** surplus; extra. **26.** too great. **27.** ended; past: *when the war was over.*

over- a prefix meaning: too or too much (*overact*);

over or above (*overflow*); higher in authority or rank (*overlord*).

o′ver•a•chieve′ *v.i.*, **-chieved, -chiev•ing. 1.** to perform academically above the potential indicated by tests of one's ability. **2.** to perform better than is expected. —**o′ver•a•chiev′er,** *n.*

o′ver•act′ *v.t., v.i.* to perform (a role) in an exaggerated manner.

o•ver•age¹ (ō′vər āj′), *adj.* beyond the acceptable, desired, or usual age.

o•ver•age² (ō′vər ij), *n.* an excess supply of merchandise.

o•ver•all (*adv.* ō′vər ôl′; *adj., n.* ō′vər ôl′), *adv., adj.* **1.** from one end to the other. **2.** including everything. —*n.* **3.** overalls, (*used with a pl. v.*) loose, sturdy trousers, usu. having a bib with attached shoulder straps.

o′ver•awe′ *v.t.*, **-awed, -aw•ing.** to restrain or subdue by inspiring awe.

o′ver•bear′ing *adj.* domineering; arrogant.

o′ver•bite′ *n.* occlusion in which the upper incisor teeth overlap the lower ones.

o′ver•blown′ *adj.* **1.** overdone or excessive. **2.** pretentious.

o′ver•board′ *adv.* **1.** over the side of a ship into the water. —*Idiom.* **2. go overboard,** to go to extremes.

o′ver•cast′ (-kast′, -käst′, -kast′, -käst′), *adj.* covered with clouds: *an overcast sky.*

o•ver•charge (*v.* ō′vər chärj′; *n.* ō′vər chärj′), *v.*, **-charged, -charg•ing,** *n.* —*v.t., v.i.* **1.** to charge too high a price. **2.** to load too full. —*n.* **3.** a charge in excess of a just price. **4.** an excessive load.

o′ver•coat′ *n.* a coat worn over the ordinary indoor clothing.

o′ver•come′ *v.*, **-came, -come, -com•ing.** —*v.t.* **1.** to get the better of in a conflict. **2.** to prevail over (opposition, temptations, etc.). **3.** to overpower or overwhelm in body or mind. —*v.i.* **4.** to win.

o′ver•do′ *v.*, **-did, -done, -do•ing.** —*v.t.* **1.** to do to excess. **2.** to exaggerate. **3.** to overcook. —*v.i.* **4.** to do too much; go to extremes.

o•ver•dose (*n.* ō′vər dōs′; *v.* ō′vər dōs′, ō′vər dōs′), *n., v.*, **-dosed, -dos•ing.** —*n.* **1.** an excessive dose of a drug. —*v.i.* **2.** to take an excessive dose. —*v.t.* **3.** to give an excessive dose to.

o′ver•draft′ *n.* **1.** the act of overdrawing a checking account. **2.** an overdrawn check. **3.** the amount overdrawn.

o′ver•draw′ *v.t.*, **-drew, -drawn, -draw•ing.** to draw upon (an account) in excess of the balance.

o′ver•drive′ *n.* a mechanism that reduces the power required to maintain a speed by lowering the gear ratio.

o′ver•due′ *adj.* past due, as a bill remaining unpaid.

o•ver•flow (*v.* ō′vər flō′; *n.* ō′vər flō′), *v.i.* **1.** to flow or run over, as water. **2.** to be supplied with in great measure. —*v.t.* **3.** to flow over; flood. **4.** to flow over the edge or brim of. —*n.* **5.** an overflowing. **6.** a superabundance. **7.** an outlet for excess liquid.

o•ver•grow *v.*, **-grew, -grown, -grow•ing.** —*v.t.* **1.** to cover with growth. —*v.i.* **2.** to grow too fast or too large. —**o′ver•grown′,** *adj.* —**o′ver•growth′,** *n.*

o′ver•hand′ *adj., adv.* with the hand and part or all of the arm raised over the shoulder.

o•ver•hang (*v.* ō′vər hang′; *n.* ō′vər hang′), *v.*, **-hung, -hang•ing,** *n.* —*v.t.* **1.** to hang or project over (something). —*n.* **2.** something that extends or juts out over.

o•ver•haul (*v.* ō′vər hôl′, ō′vər hôl′; *n.* ō′vər hôl′), *v.t.* **1.** to restore to working condition. **2.** to examine thoroughly and revise or refurbish. **3.** to gain on or catch up with. —*n.* **4.** a general examination and repair.

o′ver•head′ (*adv.* -hed′; *adj., n.* -hed′), *adv.* **1.** above one's head; up in the sky. —*adj.* **2.** situated or operating above or over the head. —*n.* **3.** the general, fixed costs of running a business, as rent and lighting.

o′ver•hear′ *v.t.*, **-heard, -hear•ing.** to hear (speech or a speaker) without the speaker's intention or knowledge.

o′ver•joyed′ (-joid′) *adj.* very happy.

o′ver•kill′ *n.* **1.** the capacity of a nation to destroy by nuclear weapons more of an enemy than would be necessary for a victory. **2.** an excess of what is required or suitable.

o′ver•land′ (-land′, -lənd), *adv., adj.* by, over, or across land.

o•ver•lap (*v.* ō′vər lap′; *n.* ō′vər lap′), *v.*, **-lapped, -lap•ping,** *n.* —*v.t., v.i.* **1.** to extend over and cover a part (of). **2.** to coincide in part (with). —*n.* **3.** the extent or state of overlapping. **4.** an overlapping part.

o′ver•lay′ *v.t.*, **-laid, -lay•ing. 1.** to lay or place (one thing) over or upon another. **2.** to finish with a superimposed decorative layer.

o′ver•lie′ *v.t.*, **-lay, -lain, -ly•ing.** to lie over or on.

o′ver•look′ *v.t.* **1.** to fail to notice. **2.** to disregard indulgently. **3.** to excuse; pardon. **4.** to look over, as from a higher position. **5.** to supervise.

o′ver•ly *adv.* excessively; too.

o′ver•night′ (*adv.* -nīt′; *adj.* -nīt′), *adv.* **1.** for or during the night. **2.** very quickly; suddenly. —*adj.* **3.** done or continuing during the night. **4.** for one night. **5.** sudden: *an overnight sensation.*

o′ver•pass′ *n.* a road, walkway, or bridge providing access over another route.

o′ver•play′ *v.t.* **1.** to exaggerate (one's role, an emotion, etc.). —*Idiom.* **2. overplay one's hand,** to overestimate the strength of one's position.

o′ver•pow′er *v.t.* **1.** to overcome by superior force. **2.** to affect or impress excessively.

o′ver•reach′ *v.t.* **1.** to reach or extend over or beyond. **2.** to defeat (oneself) by excessive eagerness.

o′ver•ride′ *v.t.*, **-rode, -rid•den, -rid•ing. 1.** to prevail over; overrule. **2.** to set aside or nullify. **3.** to ride over or across.

o′ver•rule′ *v.t.*, **-ruled, -rul•ing. 1.** to rule against; reject. **2.** to prevail over.

o•ver•run (*v.* ō′vər run′; *n.* ō′vər run′), *v.*, **-ran, -run, -run•ning,** *n.* —*v.t.* **1.** to swarm over in great numbers. **2.** to defeat decisively and occupy the position of. **3.** to exceed, as a budget. **4.** to overflow. —*n.* **5.** an act or instance of overrunning. **6.** an amount in excess of that needed or ordered.

o•ver•seas (*adv.* ō′vər sēz′; *adj.* ō′vər sēz′), *adv.* **1.** over, across, or beyond the sea. —*adj.* **2.** across or over the sea. **3.** of, from, or located in places across the sea; foreign.

o′ver•see′ *v.t.*, **-saw, -seen, -see•ing.** to supervise; manage. —**o′ver•se′er,** *n.*

o′ver•shad′ow *v.t.* **1.** to exceed in importance. **2.** to cast a shadow over.

o′ver•shoe′ *n.* a shoe or boot worn over another for protection in wet or cold weather.

o′ver•shoot′ *v.t.*, **-shot, -shoot•ing. 1.** to shoot or go over or beyond so as to miss. **2.** to pass or go beyond.

o′ver•sight′ *n.* **1.** a careless omission or error. **2.** the act of overseeing; supervision.

o′ver•sleep′ *v.i.*, **-slept, -sleep•ing.** to sleep beyond the intended time of waking.

o′ver•state′ *v.t.*, **-stat•ed, -stat•ing.** to state too strongly; exaggerate.

o′ver•stay′ *v.t.*, **-stayed, -stay•ing.** to stay beyond the time or duration of.

o′ver•step′ *v.t.*, **-stepped, -step•ping.** to go beyond; exceed.

o•vert (ō vûrt′, ō′vûrt), *adj.* open to view or knowledge; not concealed. —**o•vert′ly,** *adv.*

o′ver•take′ *v.t.*, **-took, -tak•en, -tak•ing. 1.** to catch up with or pass. **2.** to befall suddenly.

o′ver-the-count′er *adj.* **1.** not listed on or transacted through an organized securities exchange. **2.** sold legally without a prescription.

o•ver•throw (*v.* ō′vər thrō′; *n.* ō′vər thrō′), *v.*, **-threw, -thrown, -throw•ing,** *n.* —*v.t.* **1.** to depose, as from power. **2.** to overturn; topple. **3.** to throw past or over. —*n.* **4.** an act or instance of overthrowing or being overthrown.

o′ver•time′ *n.* **1.** working time before or after one's regular working hours. **2.** pay for such time.

—*adv.* **3.** during overtime. —*adj.* **4.** of or for overtime.

o'ver•tone' *n.* **1.** an acoustical frequency higher than and simultaneous with the fundamental in a complex musical tone. **2.** an additional, usu. implicit meaning or quality.

o•ver•ture (ō′vər chər, -chŏŏr′), *n.* **1.** an initiating move in a negotiation, relationship, etc. **2.** an orchestral prelude to a musical work, as an opera.

o'ver•turn' *v.t.* **1.** to cause to turn over on the side, face, or back. **2.** to destroy the power of. —*v.i.* **3.** to turn over; capsize.

o'ver•view' *n.* a general outline of a subject or situation.

o•ver•ween•ing (ō′vər wē′ning), *adj.* **1.** presumptuously conceited, overconfident, or proud. **2.** excessive.

o'ver•whelm' (-hwelm′, -welm′), *v.t.* **1.** to overpower in mind or feeling. **2.** to overpower with superior force. **3.** to bury beneath a mass of something.

o•ver•wrought (ō′vər rôt′, ō′vər-), *adj.* **1.** extremely excited or agitated. **2.** excessively complex or ornate.

o•vi•duct (ō′vi dukt′), *n.* a tube through which ova are transported from the ovary to the uterus.

o•void (ō′void), *adj.* **1.** egg-shaped. —*n.* **2.** an ovoid body.

ov•u•late (ov′yə lāt′, ō′vyə-), *v.i.* **-lat•ed, -lat•ing.** to produce and discharge eggs from an ovary. —*ov′u•la′tion, n.*

ov•ule (ov′yōōl, ō′vyōōl), *n.* **1.** the structure in seed plants that develops into a seed after fertilization. **2.** a small egg. —*ov•u•lar* (ov′yə lər, ō′vyə-), *adj.*

o•vum (ō′vəm), *n., pl.* **o•va** (ō′və). a female reproductive cell.

owe (ō), *v.t.,* **owed, ow•ing. 1.** to be under obligation to pay or render. **2.** to be in debt to. **3.** to be indebted for: *to owe one's fame to good fortune.*

owl (oul), *n.* a nocturnal bird of prey with large eyes. —*owl′ish, adj.*

own (ōn), *adj.* **1.** of or belonging to oneself or itself: *his own money.* —*pron.* **2.** something that belongs to oneself. —*v.t.* **3.** to have as one's own. **4.** to acknowledge or admit. —*v.i.* **5.** to confess: *He owned to being uncertain.* —*Idiom.* **6. on one's own, a.** through one's own efforts. **b.** living independently. —*own′er, n.* —*own′er•ship′, n.*

ox (oks), *n., pl.* **ox•en.** any bovine animal, esp. a castrated adult bull used as a draft animal.

ox′blood′ *n.* a deep, dull red color.

ox•ford (oks′fərd), *n.* **1.** a low shoe laced over the instep. **2.** a cotton or synthetic fabric with a plain or basket weave.

ox•i•dant (ok′si dənt), *n.* a chemical agent that oxidizes.

ox•ide (ok′sīd, -sid), *n.* a compound containing oxygen and another element or radical. —*ox•id′ic* (-sid′ik), *adj.*

ox•i•dize (ok′si dīz′), *v.,* **-dized, -diz•ing.** —*v.t.* **1.** to combine chemically with oxygen. —*v.i.* **2.** to become oxidized. —*ox′i•diz′er, n.*

ox•y•a•cet•y•lene (ok′sē ə set′l ēn′, -in), *n.* a mixture of oxygen and acetylene, used in a blowtorch.

ox•y•gen (ok′si jən), *n.* a colorless, odorless, gaseous element constituting about one-fifth of the volume of the atmosphere. *Symbol:* O; *at. wt.:* 15.9994; *at. no.:* 8. —*ox′y•gen′ic* (-jen′ik), *ox•yg′e•nous* (-sij′ə nəs), *adj.*

ox′y•gen•ate′ (-jə nāt′), *v.t.,* **-at•ed, -at•ing.** to treat, combine, or enrich with oxygen. —*ox′y•gen•a′tion, n.*

ox•y•mo•ron (ok′si môr′on), *n., pl.* **-mo•ra** (-môr′ə). a figure of speech that uses seeming contradictions, as "cruel kindness."

oys•ter (oi′stər), *n.* any of several edible, marine, bivalve mollusks having an irregularly shaped shell.

oz. ounce.

o•zone (ō′zōn, ō zōn′), *n.* a form of oxygen produced when an electric spark passes through air: used for bleaching, sterilizing, etc.

o′zone hole′ *n.* any part of the ozone layer that has become depleted by atmospheric pollution, resulting in excess ultraviolet radiation passing through the atmosphere.

o′zone lay′er *n.* the layer of the upper atmosphere where most atmospheric ozone is concentrated, serving to absorb much solar ultraviolet radiation.

a b c d e f g h i j k l m n o **P** q r s t u v w x y z

P, p (pē), *n., pl.* **Ps** or **P's, ps** or **p's.** the 16th letter of the English alphabet, a consonant.

P *Chem. Symbol.* phosphorus.

p. 1. page. **2.** participle. **3.** past. **4.** per. **5.** pint.

pa (pä, pô), *n., pl.* **pas.** *Informal.* father.

PA 1. Parents' Association. **2.** Pennsylvania. **3.** public-address system.

Pa *Chem. Symbol.* protactinium.

Pa. Pennsylvania.

PAC (pak), *n., pl.* **PACs, PAC's.** political action committee.

pace¹ (pās), *n., v.,* **paced, pac•ing.** —*n.* **1.** a rate of movement in stepping or walking. **2.** a rate of activity, progress, etc. **3.** a single step. **4.** the distance covered in a step. **5.** a manner of stepping; gait. **6.** a gait of a horse in which the feet on the same side are lifted and put down together. —*v.t.* **7.** to set the pace for, as in racing. **8.** to traverse with slow, regular steps. **9.** to measure by paces. **10.** to train to a certain pace. —*v.i.* **11.** to take slow, regular steps. **12.** (of a horse) to go at a pace. —*Idiom.* **13. put through one's paces,** to cause to demonstrate a set of skills.

pa•ce² (pā′sē, pä′chā), *prep.* with all due respect to.

pace′mak′er *n.* **1.** an electronic device implanted beneath the skin to provide a normal heartbeat. **2.** PACESETTER.

pace′set′ter *n.* a person or group that serves as a model to be imitated or followed.

pach•y•derm (pak′i dûrm′), *n.* any large, thick-skinned, hoofed mammal, as the elephant or rhinoceros.

pa•cif•ic (pə sif′ik), *adj.* **1.** tending to make or preserve peace. **2.** calm; tranquil.

pac•i•fi•er (pas′ə fī′ər), *n.* **1.** one that pacifies. **2.** a device, often shaped like a nipple, for a baby to suck on.

pac′i•fism (-fiz′əm), *n.* opposition to war or violence as a method of settling disputes. —*pac′i•fist, n., adj.*

pac′i•fy′ *v.t.,* **-fied, -fy•ing. 1.** to bring or restore to a state of peace or tranquillity. **2.** to reduce to a submissive state. —*pac′i•fi•ca′tion, n.*

pack¹ (pak), *n.* **1.** a group of things wrapped or tied together for easy handling or carrying. **2.** a definite quantity of merchandise together with its wrapping: *a pack of cigarettes.* **3.** a group of people or things: *a pack of lies.* **4.** a group of animals of the same kind: *a pack of wolves.* —*v.t.* **5.** to make into a pack. **6.** to fill compactly with anything: *to pack a trunk.* **7.** to put into a case, trunk, etc., as for traveling. **8.** to press or crowd together within: *The crowd packed the room.* **9.** to make airtight or watertight by stuffing. **10.** to carry: *to pack a gun.* **11.** *Informal.* to be able to deliver: *to pack a mean punch.* —*v.i.* **12.** to pack goods in compact form, as for shipping. **13.** to place clothes in luggage preparatory to traveling. **14.** to crowd together. **15.** to become compacted: *Wet snow packs readily.* **16. pack off,** to send away with dispatch: *packed the kids off to camp.* —*adj.* **17.** used in carrying a load: *pack animals.*

pack² (pak), *v.t.* to choose (cards, persons, etc.) so as to serve one's own purposes: *to pack a jury.*

pack'age (-ij), *n., v.,* **-aged, -ag•ing.** —*n.* **1.** a bundle of something that is packed and wrapped or boxed; parcel. **2.** a container in which something is packed. **3.** a group of related elements offered as a single unit: *a tax package.* —*v.t.* **4.** to make or put into a package.

pack'et (-it), *n.* **1.** a small package. **2.** a small ship that carries mail, passengers, and goods regularly on a fixed route.

pack' rat' *n.* **1.** a North and Central American rat noted for carrying off shiny articles to its nest. **2.** *Informal.* a person who saves useless small items.

pact (pakt), *n.* an agreement or compact.

pad¹ (pad), *n., v.,* **pad•ded, pad•ding.** —*n.* **1.** a cushionlike mass of soft material used for comfort, protection, or stuffing. **2.** a number of sheets of paper glued together at one edge to form a tablet. **3.** any of the cushionlike parts on the feet of vertebrates. **4.** the large floating leaf of a water lily. **5.** *Slang.* one's living quarters. —*v.t.* **6.** to furnish or stuff with a pad or padding. **7.** to expand unnecessarily or dishonestly: *to pad an expense account.*

pad² (pad), *n., v.,* **pad•ded, pad•ding.** —*n.* **1.** a dull, muffled sound, as of footsteps on the ground. —*v.i.* **2.** to walk with a dull, muffled sound.

pad'ding *n.* **1.** material used to pad something. **2.** something added unnecessarily or dishonestly.

pad•dle¹ (pad'l), *n., v.,* **-dled, -dling.** —*n.* **1.** a short, flat-bladed oar for propelling a canoe or small boat. **2.** a similar implement used for mixing, stirring, or beating. **3.** a short-handled racket, as that used in table tennis. **4.** a blade of a paddle wheel. —*v.i., v.t.* **5.** to propel (a canoe or the like) with a paddle. **6.** to stir or beat with a paddle.

pad•dle² (pad'l), *v.i.,* **-dled, -dling.** to move the feet or hands playfully in shallow water.

pad•dock (pad'ək), *n.* **1.** a small, enclosed field near a stable for pasturing or exercising animals. **2.** the enclosure in which horses are saddled and mounted before a race.

pad•dy (pad'ē), *n., pl.* **-dies.** a rice field.

pad'dy wag'on *n.* an enclosed van used by the police to transport prisoners.

pad'lock' *n.* **1.** a detachable lock with a sliding shackle that can be passed through a link, ring, etc. —*v.t.* **2.** to fasten with or as if with a padlock.

pa•dre (pä'drā, -drē), *n., pl.* **-dres.** a clergyman, esp. a priest. [< Sp, Pg, It: father < L *pater*]

pae•an (pē'ən), *n.* a song of praise, joy, or triumph.

pa•gan (pā'gən), *n.* **1.** one of a people observing a polytheistic religion, as the ancient Romans. **2.** a person who is not a Christian, Jew, or Muslim; heathen. **3.** an irreligious person. —*adj.* **4.** of pagans or their religion. —**pa'gan•ism,** *n.*

page¹ (pāj), *n., v.,* **paged, pag•ing.** —*n.* **1.** one side of a leaf of something printed or written, as a book. **2.** the entire leaf. **3.** a block of computer memory up to 4,096 bytes long. —*v.t.* **4.** to number the pages of. —*v.i.* **5.** to turn pages (usu. fol. by *through*).

page² (pāj), *n., v.,* **paged, pag•ing.** —*n.* **1.** a boy servant or attendant. **2.** an employee who carries messages, runs errands, etc., as in a hotel. —*v.t.* **3.** to summon (a person) in a public place by calling out his or her name.

pag•eant (paj'ənt), *n.* **1.** a costumed procession or parade forming part of public festivities. **2.** a public spectacle illustrative of the history of a place, institution, etc. **3.** a show or exhibition: *a beauty pageant.* —**pag'eant•ry,** *n., pl.* **-ries.**

pag•er (pā'jər), *n.* BEEPER.

pag•i•nate (paj'ə nāt'), *v.t.,* **-nated, -nating.** to number the pages of (a book, etc.). —**pag'i•na'tion,** *n.*

pa•go•da (pə gō'də), *n., pl.* **-das.** a temple of the

Far East, usu. a tower having an upward-curving roof over each story.

pail (pāl), *n.* a cylindrical container with a handle; bucket.

pain (pān), *n.* **1.** physical suffering typically from injury or illness. **2.** severe mental or emotional distress. **3. pains,** diligent care: *Take pains with your work.* —*v.t.* **4.** to cause pain to. —*Idiom.* **5. on** or **under pain of,** subject to the penalty of. —**pain'ful,** *adj.* —**pain'less,** *adj.*

pain'kill•er *n.* something that relieves pain, esp. an analgesic. —**pain'kill'ing,** *adj.*

pains•tak•ing (pānz/tā'king, pān/stā'-), *adj.* expending or showing diligent care; careful. —**pains'tak'ing•ly,** *adv.*

paint (pānt), *n.* **1.** a mixture of solid coloring matter and a liquid, applied as a protective or decorative coating to various surfaces or to an artist's canvas. **2.** the dried surface pigment. —*v.t.* **3.** to coat, cover, or decorate with paint. **4.** to produce (a picture or design) in paint. **5.** to represent in paint. **6.** to describe vividly in words. —*v.i.* **7.** to engage in painting as an art. —**paint'er,** *n.*

paint'ing *n.* **1.** a picture or design executed in paints. **2.** the act, art, or work of a person who paints.

pair (pâr), *n., pl.* **pairs, pair,** *v.* —*n.* **1.** two corresponding things that are matched for use together: *a pair of gloves.* **2.** something having two pieces joined together: *a pair of scissors.* **3.** two individual persons or things that are in some way associated: *a pair of horses.* —*v.t., v.i.* **4.** to form (into) a pair. **5.** (of animals) to mate or cause to mate.

pais•ley (pāz/lē), *adj.* (*often cap.*) having a pattern of colorful, minutely detailed, usu. curving figures.

pa•ja•mas (pə jä'məz, -jam'əz), *n.* (*used with a pl. v.*) nightclothes consisting of loose-fitting trousers and a jacket.

Pak•i•stan (pak'ə stan', pä'kə stän'), *n.* a republic in S Asia, between India and Afghanistan. —**Pak'i•stan'i,** *n., pl.* **-stan•is, -stan•i,** *adj.*

pal (pal), *n. Informal.* a close friend.

pal•ace (pal'is), *n.* **1.** the official residence of a sovereign or other exalted personage. **2.** a large and stately building.

pal•at•a•ble (pal'ə tə bəl), *adj.* **1.** acceptable to the palate or taste. **2.** acceptable to the mind or feelings.

pal•ate (pal'it), *n.* **1.** the roof of the mouth in mammals. **2.** the sense of taste. —**pal'a•tal** (-ə tl), *adj.*

pa•la•tial (pə lā'shəl), *adj.* **1.** of or resembling a palace. **2.** suitable for a palace; magnificent.

pal•a•tine (pal'ə tīn', -tin), *adj.* **1.** having royal privileges. **2.** of a palatine or palatinate. —*n.* **3.** a vassal exercising royal privileges in a province. **4.** a high official of an imperial court.

pa•lav•er (pə lav'ər, -lä'vər), *n.* **1.** profuse and idle talk. —*v.i.* **2.** to talk profusely and idly. [< Pg *palavra* word, speech]

pale¹ (pāl), *adj.,* **pal•er, pal•est,** *v.,* **paled, pal•ing.** —*adj.* **1.** lacking intensity of color. **2.** approaching white or gray: *pale yellow.* —*v.t., v.i.* **3.** to make or become pale. —**pale'ness,** *n.*

pale² (pāl), *n.* **1.** a stake or picket, as of a fence. **2.** limits; bounds: *outside the pale of my jurisdiction.*

Pa•le•o•lith•ic (pā'lē ə lith'ik), *adj.* noting or pertaining to the early phase of the Stone Age.

pa•le•on•tol•o•gy (-ən tol'ə jē), *n.* the science of the forms of life existing in former geologic periods, as represented by their fossils. —**pa'le•on•tol'o•gist,** *n.*

Pa'le•o•zo'ic (-ə zō'ik), *adj.* noting or pertaining to a geologic era occurring between 570 million and 230 million years ago, when fish, insects, and reptiles first appeared.

pal•ette (pal'it), *n.* **1.** a thin board used by painters for holding and mixing colors. **2.** the set of colors on such a board.

pal•i•mo•ny (pal'ə mō'nē), *n.* a form of alimony awarded to one member of an unmarried couple who separated after a period of living together.

pal•imp•sest (pal'imp sest'), *n.* a parchment or

the like from which writing has been partially or completely erased to make room for another text.

pal•in•drome (pal′in drōm′), *n.* a word, verse, etc., reading the same backward as forward, as *madam.*

pal•ing (pā′ling), *n.* **1.** a fence of pales. **2.** pales collectively.

pal•i•sade (pal′ə sād′), *n.* **1.** a fence of pales or stakes, as for defense. **2. palisades,** a line of cliffs.

pall¹ (pôl), *n.* **1.** something that covers with darkness or gloom. **2.** a cloth for spreading over a coffin.

pall² (pôl), *v.i.* **1.** to have a wearying effect. **2.** to become satiated or cloyed with something.

pall′bear′er *n.* one of several persons who carry or attend the coffin at a funeral.

pal•let¹ (pal′it), *n.* **1.** a bed or mattress of straw. **2.** a small or makeshift bed.

pal•let² (pal′it), *n.* a low, portable platform on which goods are placed for storage or moving.

pal•li•ate (pal′ē āt′), *v.t.,* **-at•ed, -at•ing. 1.** to relieve without curing. **2.** to try to mitigate the gravity of (an offense) by excuses, apologies, etc.

pal′li•a′tive (-ā′tiv, -ə tiv) *n.* a drug that relieves symptoms but does not cure disease.

pal•lid (pal′id), *adj.* **1.** faint or deficient in color. **2.** lacking in vitality or interest.

pal•lor (pal′ər), *n.* extreme paleness, as from fear or ill health.

palm¹ (päm), *n.* **1.** the inner surface of the hand between the wrist and the fingers. —*v.t.* **2.** to conceal in the palm, as in sleight of hand. **3.** to pick up stealthily. **4. palm off,** to foist upon someone, as by fraud.

palm² (päm), *n.* **1.** any of numerous tropical plants, most of which are tall, unbranched trees with a crown of large leaves. **2.** a leaf of such a tree, formerly carried to signify victory.

pal•met•to (pal met′ō, päl-, pä-), *n., pl.* **-tos, -toes.** any of various palms with fan-shaped leaves.

palm•is•try (pä′mə strē), *n.* the practice of reading fortunes and character from the lines on the palm of a person's hand.

palm′y *adj.,* **-i•er, -i•est. 1.** prosperous or flourishing. **2.** abounding in palms.

pal•o•mi•no (pal′ə mē′nō), *n., pl.* **-nos.** a horse with a golden coat and a white mane and tail.

pal•pa•ble (pal′pə bəl), *adj.* **1.** readily or plainly seen or perceived; obvious. **2.** capable of being touched or felt; tangible. —**pal′pa•bly,** *adv.*

pal•pate (pal′pāt), *v.t.,* **-pat•ed, -pat•ing.** to examine by touch, esp. for the purpose of diagnosing disease or illness. —**pal•pa′tion,** *n.*

pal•pi•tate (pal′pi tāt′), *v.i.,* **-tat•ed, -tat•ing. 1.** to pulsate, as the heart, with unusual rapidity. **2.** to quiver; throb. —**pal′pi•ta′tion,** *n.*

pal•sy (pôl′zē), *n., pl.* **-sies.** any of several conditions characterized by paralysis or tremors. —**pal′sied,** *adj.*

pal•try (pôl′trē), *adj.,* **-tri•er, -tri•est. 1.** ridiculously small. **2.** utterly worthless.

pam•pas (pam′pəz; *attributively* -pəs), *n.pl., sing.* **-pa.** the vast grassy plains of S South America, esp. in Argentina.

pam•per (pam′pər), *v.t.* to treat with excessive indulgence, kindness, or care.

pam•phlet (pam′flit), *n.* a short unbound publication, often on a contemporary or controversial subject. —**pam′phlet•eer′** (-fli tēr′), *n.*

pan¹ (pan), *n., v.,* **panned, pan•ning.** —*n.* **1.** a broad, shallow container used for cooking, washing, etc. **2.** any similar receptacle or part, as the scales of a balance. —*v.t.* **3.** *Informal.* to criticize harshly, as in a review. **4.** to wash (gravel, sand, etc.) in a pan to separate gold. —*v.i.* **5.** to wash gravel, sand, etc., in a pan in seeking gold. **6. pan out,** *Informal.* to have an outcome, esp. a successful one.

pan² (pan), *v.,* **panned, pan•ning,** *n.* —*v.i., v.t.* **1.** to swivel (a television or motion-picture camera) horizontally to keep a moving subject in view or record a panorama. —*n.* **2.** the act of panning a camera.

pan- a combining form meaning: all (*pantheism*);

the union of all branches of a group (*Pan-American*).

pan•a•ce•a (pan′ə sē′ə), *n., pl.* **-as. 1.** a remedy for all ills. **2.** a solution for all difficulties.

pa•nache (pə nash′, -näsh′), *n.* **1.** a grand or flamboyant manner; flair. **2.** a plume, esp. on a helmet.

Pan•a•ma (pan′ə mä′, -mô′), *n.* a republic in S Central America. —**Pan′a•ma′ni•an** (-mä′nē ən), *adj., n.*

pan′cake′ *n.* a thin, flat cake of batter fried on a griddle or in a frying pan.

pan•cre•as (pan′krē əs, pang′-), *n.* a large gland that secretes digestive enzymes into the intestine and insulin into the bloodstream. —**pan′cre•at′ic** (-at′ik), *adj.*

pan•da (pan′də), *n., pl.* **-das. 1.** a white-and-black bearlike mammal, now restricted to central China. **2.** a reddish brown, raccoonlike mammal of the Himalayas and adjacent regions.

pan•dem•ic (pan dem′ik), *adj.* (of a disease) epidemic over a large area.

pan•de•mo•ni•um (pan′də mō′nē əm), *n.* wild uproar or disorder; tumult or chaos.

pan•der (pan′dər), *n.* **1.** a procurer; pimp. **2.** a person who caters to or profits from the weaknesses or vices of others. —*v.i.* **3.** to cater basely. —**pan′der•er,** *n.*

pane (pān), *n.* one of the divisions of a window or the like, consisting of a single plate of glass in a frame.

pan•e•gyr•ic (pan′i jir′ik, -jī′rik), *n.* **1.** a lofty oration or writing in praise of a person or thing. **2.** elaborate praise.

pan•el (pan′l), *n., v.,* **-eled, -el•ing** or (*esp. Brit.*) **-elled, -el•ling.** —*n.* **1.** a distinct section of a wall, wainscot, door, etc. **2.** a group of persons gathered to conduct a public discussion, judge a contest, etc. **3.** a list of persons summoned for service as jurors. **4.** a surface on a machine on which controls and dials are mounted. **5.** a strip of material set vertically in a dress, skirt, etc. —*v.t.* **6.** to arrange in or furnish with panels. —**pan′el•ing,** *n.*

pan′el•ist *n.* a member of a panel convened for public discussion, judging, etc.

pang (pang), *n.* **1.** a sudden feeling of mental or emotional distress. **2.** a sudden sharp physical pain.

pan′han′dle¹, *n.* a long, narrow, projecting strip of a larger territory.

pan′han′dle², *v.i., v.t.,* **-dled, -dling.** *Informal.* to accost (passers-by) on the street and beg (from). —**pan′han′dler,** *n.*

pan•ic (pan′ik), *n., v.,* **-icked, -ick•ing.** —*n.* **1.** a sudden, overwhelming fear that can spread quickly. **2.** *Informal.* someone or something considered hilariously funny. —*v.t.* **3.** to affect with panic. **4.** *Informal.* to keep (an audience or the like) highly amused. —*v.i.* **5.** to be stricken with panic. —**pan′ick•y, pan′ic-strick′en,** *adj.*

pan•nier (pan′yər, -ē ər), *n.* **1.** a large basket for carrying goods, provisions, etc. **2.** one of a pair of baskets to be slung across the back of a pack animal.

pan•o•ply (pan′ə plē), *n., pl.* **-plies. 1.** a wide-ranging and impressive array or display. **2.** a complete suit of armor.

pan•o•ram•a (pan′ə ram′ə, -rä′mə), *n., pl.* **-as. 1.** a wide, unobstructed view of an extensive area. **2.** a continuously changing scene or unfolding of events: *the panorama of Chinese history.* —**pan′o•ram′ic,** *adj.*

pan•sy (pan′zē), *n., pl.* **-sies.** a violet with richly and variously colored flowers.

pant (pant), *v.i.* **1.** to breathe hard and quickly, as after exertion. **2.** to long eagerly; yearn. —*v.t.* **3.** to breathe or utter gaspingly. —*n.* **4.** a short, quick, labored breath; gasp.

pan•ta•loons (pan′tl ōōnz′), *n.* (*used with a pl. v.*) a man's close-fitting trousers, worn esp. in the 19th century.

pan•the•ism (pan′thē iz′əm), *n.* any religious belief or philosophical doctrine that identifies God with the universe. —**pan′the•ist,** *n.* —**pan′the•is′tic,** *adj.*

pan•the•on (pan′thē on′), *n.* **1.** a public building containing tombs or memorials of the illustrious dead of a nation. **2.** the realm of the heroes of any group, movement, etc. **3.** a temple dedicated to all the gods.

pan•ther (pan′thər), *n., pl.* **-thers, -ther.** **1.** the cougar. **2.** any leopard in the black color phase.

pant•ies (pan′tēz), *n.* (*used with a pl. v.*) short underpants for women and children.

pan•to•mime (pan′tə mīm′), *n., v.,* **-mimed, -mim•ing.** —*n.* **1.** an entertainment in which the performers express themselves by gesture alone. **2.** significant gesture without speech. —*v.t., v.i.* **3.** to express (oneself) in pantomime. —**pan′to•mim′ic** (-mim′ik), *adj.* —**pan′to•mim′ist** (-mī′mist), *n.*

pan•try (pan′trē), *n., pl.* **-tries.** a room or closet, usu. near a kitchen, in which food, dishes, etc., are kept.

pants (pants), *n.* (*used with a pl. v.*) **1.** TROUSERS. **2.** PANTIES.

pant′y•hose′ *n.* (*used with a pl. v.*) a one-piece woman's garment combining panties and stockings.

pant′y•waist′ *n. Informal.* an effeminate man; sissy.

pan′zer (pan′zər) *adj.* **1.** armored. —*n.* **2.** tank or armored vehicle.

pap (pap), *n.* **1.** soft food for infants or invalids. **2.** ideas, writings, etc., lacking substance or real value.

pa•pa (pä′pə, pə pä′), *n., pl.* **-pas.** FATHER.

pa•pa•cy (pā′pə sē), *n., pl.* **-cies.** **1.** the office or jurisdiction of the pope. **2.** the system of Roman Catholic government. **3.** the period during which a pope is in office. —**pa′pal,** *adj.*

pa•pa•ya (pə pä′yə), *n., pl.* **-yas.** **1.** a small tropical American tree bearing a yellow, melonlike fruit. **2.** the fruit itself.

pa•per (pā′pər), *n.* **1.** a substance made from wood pulp or other fibrous material, usu. in thin sheets, used for writing, wrapping, etc. **2.** a piece or sheet of this. **3.** a newspaper or journal. **4.** a scholarly essay, article, or dissertation. **5.** a written piece of schoolwork, as a report. **6.** a document verifying identity, status, etc. **7.** WALLPAPER. —*v.t.* **8.** to cover with paper, esp. wallpaper. —*adj.* **9.** made of paper. **10.** like paper, as in being thin.

pa′per•back′ *n.* a book bound in a flexible paper cover.

pa′per ti′ger *n.* a person, nation, etc., that has the appearance of power but is actually weak and ineffectual.

pa′per•weight′ *n.* a small, heavy object placed on papers to keep them from scattering.

pa′per•work′ *n.* written or clerical work forming an incidental but necessary part of some work or job.

pa•pier-mâ•ché (pā′pər mə shā′, pä pyä′-), *n.* moistened paper pulp mixed with glue, molded when moist to form various articles and becoming hard when dry. [< F: lit., chewed paper]

pa•pist (pā′pist), *n., adj. Usu. Disparaging.* Roman Catholic. —**pa′pism,** *n.*

pa•poose (pa pōōs′, pə-), *n.* a North American Indian baby.

pap•ri•ka (pa prē′kə, pə-, pä-, pap′ri kə), *n.* a red, powdery condiment derived from dried, ripe sweet peppers.

Pap′ test′ (pap), *n.* a test for cancer of the cervix. [after G. *Papanicolaou* (1883–1962), U.S. cytologist]

Pap′u•a New′ Guin′ea (pap′yōō ə, pä′pōō ä), *n.* a country comprising the E part of the island of New Guinea and nearby islands.

pa•py•rus (pə pī′rəs), *n., pl.* **-ri** (-rī, -rē), **-py•rus•es.** **1.** a tall, aquatic plant, native to the Nile valley. **2.** a writing material made from the pith of this plant, used by ancient peoples.

par (pär), *n.* **1.** an equality in value or standing. **2.** an average or normal amount, degree, etc. **3.** the number of golf strokes set as a standard for one hole or a complete course. **4. a.** the value of the monetary unit of one country in terms of that of another. **b.** the face value of a note, stock, or bond. —*adj.* **5.** average or normal.

par. 1. paragraph. **2.** parish.

para- a prefix meaning: beside (*paradigm*); beyond (*parapsychology*); auxiliary (*paralegal*).

par•a•ble (par′ə bəl), *n.* a short allegorical story designed to teach some truth or moral lesson.

pa•rab•o•la (pə rab′ə lə), *n., pl.* **-las.** a plane curve formed by the intersection of a right circular cone with a plane parallel to a generator of the cone. —**par•a•bol•ic** (par′ə bol′ik), *adj.*

par•a•chute (par′ə shōōt′), *n., v.,* **-chut•ed, -chut•ing.** —*n.* **1.** a folding, umbrellalike device for allowing a person, object, etc., to descend slowly from a height, esp. from an aircraft. —*v.t., v.i.* **2.** to drop by parachute. —**par′a•chut′ist,** *n.*

pa•rade (pə rād′), *n., v.,* **-rad•ed, -rad•ing.** —*n.* **1.** a public procession held in honor of an event, person, etc. **2.** a military ceremony involving the formation and marching of troops. **3.** an ostentatious display. —*v.t.* **4.** to walk up and down on. **5.** to display ostentatiously. —*v.i.* **6.** to march in a procession. **7.** to promenade in a public place.

par•a•digm (par′ə dīm′, -dim), *n.* **1.** a set of all the inflected forms of a word based on a single stem or root. **2.** an example serving as a model. —**par′a•dig•mat′ic** (-dig mat′ik), *adj.*

par•a•dise (par′ə dīs′, -dīz′), *n.* **1.** heaven. **2.** (*often cap.*) EDEN (def. 1). **3.** a place or state of supreme happiness. —**par′a•di•sa′i•cal** (-di sā′i kəl, -zā′-, -dī-), *adj.*

par•a•dox (par′ə doks′), *n.* **1.** a seemingly contradictory statement that expresses a possible truth. **2.** a self-contradictory and false proposition. **3.** a person or situation exhibiting an apparently contradictory nature. —**par′a•dox′i•cal,** *adj.*

par•af•fin (par′ə fin), *n.* a waxy, solid substance, used in candles and sealing materials.

par•a•gon (par′ə gon′, -gən), *n.* a model of excellence.

par′a•graph′ *n.* **1.** a distinct portion of written matter, beginning on a new line that is usu. indented. —*v.t.* **2.** to divide into paragraphs.

Par•a•guay (par′ə gwī′, -gwā′), *n.* a republic in central South America. —**Par′a•guay′an,** *n., adj.*

par•a•keet (par′ə kēt′), *n.* any of various small to medium-sized parrots with a long, graduated tail.

par′a•le′gal *n.* an attorney's assistant trained to perform certain legal tasks but not licensed to practice law.

par•al•lax (par′ə laks′), *n.* the apparent displacement of an observed object due to a change in the position of the observer.

par•al•lel (par′ə lel′, -ləl), *adj., n., v.,* **-leled, -lel•ing** or (*esp. Brit.*) **-lelled, -lel•ling.** —*adj.* **1.** extending in the same direction, equidistant at all points, and never converging or diverging. **2.** having the same direction, nature, etc.; similar or corresponding. —*n.* **3.** a parallel line or plane. **4.** anything parallel or similar to something else. **5.** any of the imaginary lines on the earth's surface, parallel to the equator, that mark the latitude. **6.** a comparison made between things. —*v.t.* **7.** to provide a parallel for; match. **8.** to be in a parallel course to. **9.** to form a parallel to; equal. **10.** to compare. [< L *parallēlus* < Gk *parállēlos* side by side] —**par′al•lel•ism,** *n.*

par′al•lel′o•gram′ (-lel′ə gram′), *n.* a quadrilateral having both pairs of opposite sides parallel to each other.

pa•ral•y•sis (pə ral′ə sis), *n., pl.* **-ses** (-sēz′). **1.** a loss or impairment of movement or sensation in a body part. **2.** a state of helpless stoppage or inability to act. —**par•a•lyt•ic** (par′ə lit′ik), *adj., n.* —**par•a•lyze** (par′ə līz′), *v.t.,* **-lyzed, -lyz•ing.**

par′a•med′ic *n.* a person trained to assist a physician or to give medical treatment in the absence of a physician.

pa•ram•e•ter (pə ram′i tər), *n.* **1.** a constant or variable term in a mathematical function that determines the specific form of the function but not its general nature. **2.** Usu., **-ters.** limits or boundaries; guidelines. **3.** a determining characteristic. —**par•a•met′ric** (par′ə me′trik), *adj.*

par•a•mil•i•tar•y (par′ə mil′i ter′ē), *adj.* of or

noting an organization operating in place of or as a supplement to a regular military force.

par•a•mount (par′ə mount′), adj. chief in importance, rank, etc.

par•a•mour (par′ə mŏŏr′), n. **1.** an illicit lover. **2.** any lover.

par•a•noi•a (par′ə noi′ə), n. **1.** a mental disorder characterized by delusions ascribing hostile intentions to others. **2.** baseless or excessive distrust of others. —**par′a•noid′**, adj., n.

par•a•pet (par′ə pit, -pet′), n. **1.** a wall or elevation in a fortification. **2.** any low protective wall or barrier at the edge of a balcony, roof, etc.

par′a•pher•na′lia (-fər näl′yə, -fə näl′-), n. (used with sing. or pl. v.) **1.** equipment, apparatus, etc., used in a particular activity. **2.** personal belongings.

par′a•phrase n., v., **-phrased, -phras•ing.** —n. **1.** a restatement of a passage giving the meaning in another form, as for clearness. —v.t., v.i. **2.** to render in or make a paraphrase.

par′a•ple′gi•a (-plē′jē ə, -jə), n. paralysis of both lower limbs. —**par′a•ple′gic** (-plē′jik, -plej′ik), adj., n.

par′a•pro•fes′sion•al n. a person trained to assist a doctor, lawyer, or other professional.

par′a•psy•chol′o•gy n. the branch of psychology that studies psychic phenomena, as clairvoyance. —**par′a•psy•chol′o•gist,** n.

par•a•site (par′ə sīt′), n. **1.** an organism that lives on or within a plant or animal of another species, from which it obtains nutrients. **2.** one who receives support or advantage from another without giving any return. —**par′a•sit′ic** (-sit′ik), adj.

par•a•sol (par′ə sôl′, -sol′), n. a lightweight umbrella used as a sunshade.

par•a•thy′roid gland′ (par′ə thī′roid), n. any of several small paired glands that lie near the thyroid gland and secrete a hormone that helps regulate the blood levels of calcium and phosphate.

par′a•troops′ n. force of soldiers who reach battle by parachuting from planes.

par•boil (pär′boil′), v.t. to boil partially or for a short time.

par•cel (pär′səl), n., v., **-celed, -cel•ing** or (esp. Brit.) **-celled, -cel•ling.** —n. **1.** an object or objects wrapped to form a small bundle; package. **2.** a distinct, continuous tract of land. —v.t. **3.** to divide into or distribute in portions (usu. fol. by out).

parch (pärch), v.t. **1.** to make extremely dry, as heat, sun, and wind do. **2.** to make thirsty. —v.i. **3.** to suffer from heat or thirst.

parch•ment (pärch′mənt), n. **1.** the skin of sheep, goats, etc., prepared for writing on. **2.** a manuscript on such material. **3.** a stiff off-white paper treated to resemble this material.

par•don (pär′dn), n. **1.** a legal release from the penalty of an offense. **2.** forgiveness of an offense or discourtesy. —v.t. **3.** to excuse or make courteous allowance for. **4.** to release from liability for an offense. **5.** to remit the penalty of (an offense). —**par′don•a•ble,** adj.

pare (pâr), v.t., **pared, par•ing. 1.** to cut off the outer coating, layer, etc., of. **2.** to reduce gradually.

par•ent (pâr′ənt, par′-), n. **1.** a father or mother. **2.** a source, origin, or cause. **3.** any organism that produces another. —adj. **4.** of or noting an enterprise that owns controlling interests in a subsidiary. —v.t. **5.** to be or act as parent of. —**pa•ren′tal** (pə ren′tl), adj. —**par′ent•hood′,** n.

par′ent•age (-ən tij) n. derivation or descent from parents or ancestors.

pa•ren•the•sis (pə ren′thə sis), n., pl. **-ses** (-sēz′). **1.** either or both of a pair of signs ( ) used to mark off an interjected explanatory or qualifying remark. **2.** a qualifying or explanatory word, phrase, or clause that interrupts a syntactic construction without otherwise affecting it. —**par•en•thet•ic** (par′ən-thet′ik), **par′en•thet′i•cal,** adj.

par ex•cel•lence (pär ek′sə läns′), adj. being an example of excellence; superior. [< F]

par•fait (pär fā′), n. **1.** a dessert of layered ice cream, fruit, syrup, and whipped cream. **2.** a frozen dessert of flavored whipped cream or custard.

pa•ri•ah (pə rī′ə), n. OUTCAST.

par•i•mu•tu•el (par′i myŏŏ′chŏŏ əl), n. a form of betting on horse races in which the winners divide the total amount bet in proportion to their wagers.

par•ish (par′ish), n. **1.** an ecclesiastical district having its own church and cleric. **2.** a local church with its field of activity. **3.** (in Louisiana) a county. —**pa•rish•ion•er** (pə rish′ə nər), n.

par•i•ty (par′i tē), n., pl. **-ties. 1.** equality, as in amount, status, or character. **2.** equivalent value at a fixed ratio between different currencies. **3.** a system of regulating prices of farm commodities to provide farmers with the same purchasing power they had in a selected base period.

park (pärk), n. **1.** a public area of land, usu. in a natural state, having facilities for recreation. **2.** an enclosed area or a stadium used for sports. **3.** a setting in an automatic transmission in which the transmission is in neutral and the brake is engaged. —v.t. **4.** to put or leave (a vehicle) in a place temporarily.

par•ka (pär′kə), n., pl. **-kas.** a hooded jacket made of materials that protect against very cold temperatures.

Par′kin•son's disease′ (pär′kin sənz), n. a neurologic disease characterized by tremors, esp. of the fingers and hands, muscle rigidity, and a shuffling gait. [after J. Parkinson (1755–1824), English physician]

park′way′ n. a broad thoroughfare with a dividing strip or side strips planted with grass, trees, etc.

par•lance (pär′ləns), n. a way or manner of speaking; vernacular: legal parlance.

par•lay (pär′lā, -lē), v., **-layed, -lay•ing,** n., pl. **-lays.** —v.t. **1.** to bet (an original amount and its winnings) on a subsequent contest. **2.** to use (assets) to achieve a relatively great gain: to parlay a modest inheritance into a fortune. —n. **3.** a bet parlayed.

par•ley (pär′lē), n., pl. **-leys,** v., **-leyed, -ley•ing.** —n. **1.** a discussion; conference. **2.** a conference between enemies under a truce. —v.i. **3.** to hold a parley.

par•lia•ment (pär′lə mənt), n. **1.** (cap.) the national legislature in various countries, esp. Great Britain. **2.** an assembly on public or national affairs.

par′lia•men•tar′i•an (-men târ′ē ən, -mən-), n. an expert in parliamentary rules and procedures.

par′lia•men′ta•ry (-men′tə rē) adj. **1.** of, by, or having a parliament. **2.** in accordance with rules of debate.

par•lor (pär′lər), n. **1.** a room in a home for receiving visitors; living room. **2.** a shop or business establishment: an ice-cream parlor.

Par•me•san (pär′mə zän′, -zan′, -zən), n. (sometimes l.c.) a hard, dry Italian cheese.

par•mi•gia•na (pär′mə zhä′nə, -zhän′), adj. cooked with Parmesan cheese.

pa•ro•chi•al (pə rō′kē əl), adj. **1.** of a parish. **2.** of very limited or narrow scope; provincial. —**pa•ro′chi•al•ism,** n.

paro′chial school′ n. a primary or secondary school maintained by a religious organization.

par•o•dy (par′ə dē), n., pl. **-dies,** v., **-died, -dy•ing.** —n. **1.** a humorous or satirical imitation of a serious piece of literature or music. —v.t. **2.** to imitate (a composition, author, etc.) for purposes of ridicule or satire.

pa•role (pə rōl′), n., v., **-roled, -rol•ing.** —n. **1.** the conditional release of a person from prison prior to the end of the sentence imposed. —v.t. **2.** to place or release on parole. [< MF, short for parole d'honneur word of honor] —**pa•rol•ee′** (-rō lē′), n., pl. **-ees.**

par•ox•ysm (par′ək siz′əm), n. **1.** any sudden, violent outburst, as of emotion. **2.** a severe attack of a disease, usu. recurring periodically. —**par′ox•ys′mal,** adj.

par•quet (pär kā′), n., v., **-queted** (-kād′), **-quet•ing** (-kā′ing). —n. **1.** a floor made of parquetry. **2.**

the part of the main floor of a theater for spectators. —*v.t.* **3.** to construct (a floor) of parquetry.

par•ri•cide (par′ə sīd′), *n.* **1.** the killing of one's father, mother, or other close relative. **2.** a person who commits such an act. —**par′ri•cid′al,** *adj.*

par•rot (par′ət), *n.* **1.** any of numerous brilliantly colored birds of warmer regions, some of which can mimic speech. **2.** a person who mindlessly repeats the words of another. —*v.t.* **3.** to repeat without thought or understanding.

par•ry (par′ē), *v.,* **-ried, -ry•ing,** *n., pl.* **-ries.** —*v.t.* **1.** to ward off (a sword blow, weapon, etc.). **2.** to turn aside; dodge. —*n.* **3.** an act or instance of parrying.

parse (pärs), *v.,* **parsed, pars•ing.** —*v.t.* **1.** to analyze (a sentence) grammatically, identifying parts of speech, syntactic relations, etc. —*v.i.* **2.** to admit of being parsed.

par•si•mo•ny (pär′sə mō′nē), *n.* excessive economy or frugality; stinginess. —**par′si•mo′ni•ous,** *adj.*

pars•ley (pär′slē), *n.* an herb with either curled leaf clusters or flat compound leaves.

pars•nip (pär′snip), *n.* **1.** a plant with a large, white, edible root. **2.** its root.

par•son (pär′sən), *n.* a member of the Protestant clergy.

par′son•age (-sə nij), *n.* the residence provided by a parish for its parson.

part (pärt), *n.* **1.** a portion or division of a whole that is separate or distinct. **2.** an essential or integral quality. **3.** an allotted portion; share. **4.** Usu., **parts,** a region or district. **5.** either of the opposing sides in a contest, contract, etc. **6.** the dividing line formed in separating the hair when combing it. **7.** a constituent piece of a machine or tool. **8.** the score for one of the instruments or voices in concerted music. **9.** participation or concern in something; role. **10.** a role given to an actor or actress. —*v.t.* **11.** to divide into parts. **12.** to comb (the hair) away from a dividing line. **13.** to put or keep apart; separate. —*v.i.* **14.** to be or become divided into parts. **15.** to go apart from one another, as persons. **16.** to break apart. **17.** to depart. **18. part with,** to relinquish. —*adj.* **19.** partial. —*adv.* **20.** partly. —*Idiom.* **21. for one's part,** as far as concerns one. **22. in part,** in some measure or degree. **23. take part,** to participate.

par•take (pär tāk′), *v.i.,* **-took, -tak•en, -tak•ing.** **1.** to participate: *to partake in a celebration.* **2.** to receive, take, or have a portion: *to partake of a meal.*

par•terre (pär târ′), *n.* **1.** the rear part of theater seats under the balcony. **2.** an arrangement of ornamental flower beds separated by walks.

par•the•no•gen•e•sis (pär′thə nō jen′ə sis), *n.* development of an egg without fertilization.

par•tial (pär′shəl), *adj.* **1.** incomplete. **2.** favoring one person, group, etc., over another. —*Idiom.* **3. partial to,** especially fond of. —**par′ti•al′i•ty** (-shē-al′i tē), *n., pl.* **-ties.** —**par′tial•ly,** *adv.*

par•tic•i•pate (pär tis′ə pāt′), *v.i.,* **-pat•ed, -pat•ing.** to take part or have a share, as with others. —**par•tic′i•pant,** *n.* —**par•tic′i•pa′tion,** *n.* —**par•tic′i•pa•to′ry** (-pə tôr′ē), *adj.*

par•ti•ci•ple (pär′tə sip′əl, -sə pəl), *n.* a verbal form that can function as an adjective or be used with an auxiliary to form certain tenses. —**par′ti•cip′i•al** (-sip′ē əl), *adj.*

par•ti•cle (pär′ti kəl), *n.* **1.** a minute portion, piece, or amount. **2.** one of the extremely small constituents of matter, as an atom or proton. **3.** a small word having functional or relational rather than lexical use, as *to* used in forming the infinitive.

par•tic•u•lar (pər tik′yə lər, pə tik′-), *adj.* **1.** pertaining to a single or specific person, thing, etc. **2.** considered separately from others; specific. **3.** special; unusual. **4.** exacting; fussy. —*n.* **5.** an individual or distinct part, as an item of a list. —*Idiom.* **6. in particular,** particularly; especially. —**par•tic′u•lar′i•ty,** *n., pl.* **-ties.**

par•tic′u•lar•ize′ *v.,* **-ized, -iz•ing.** —*v.t.* **1.** to

state or treat in detail. —*v.i.* **2.** to give details; be specific.

par•tic′u•lar•ly *adv.* **1.** especially. **2.** specifically. **3.** in detail.

par•tic•u•late (pər tik′yə lit, -lāt′, pär-), *adj.* of or composed of distinct particles.

part′ing *n.* **1.** a division; separation. **2.** departure; leave-taking. —*adj.* **3.** given, taken, or done at parting: *a parting glance.* **4.** departing.

par•ti•san (pär′tə zən, -san), *n.* **1.** an adherent or supporter of a person, cause, etc. **2.** a member of a guerrilla band fighting an occupying army. —*adj.* **3.** of or characteristic of partisans. —**par′ti•san•ship′,** *n.*

par•ti•tion (pär tish′ən, pər-), *n.* **1.** a division into portions. **2.** something that separates or divides. —*v.t.* **3.** to divide into portions. **4.** to divide or separate by a partition. —**par•ti′tioned,** *adj.*

part′ly *adv.* partially.

part•ner (pärt′nər), *n.* **1.** a person who is associated with another in some endeavor; associate. **2.** a spouse or lover. **3.** either of two people who dance together. **4.** a player on the same team as another. —**part′ner•ship′,** *n.*

par•tridge (pär′trij), *n., pl.* **-tridg•es, -tridge. 1.** any of various birds of the pheasant family. **2.** any game bird resembling the partridge, as the bobwhite.

part′-song′ *n.* a song with parts for several voices, esp. one sung without accompaniment.

part′-time′ (*adj.* -tīm′; *adv.* -tīm′), *adj.* **1.** involving, working, or studying less than the usual or full time. —*adv.* **2.** on a part-time basis.

par•tu•ri•tion (pär′tŏŏ rish′ən, -tyŏŏ-), *n.* childbirth.

par•ty (pär′tē), *n., pl.* **-ties,** *v.,* **-tied, -ty•ing.** —*n.* **1.** a social gathering for conversation, entertainment, etc. **2.** a group gathered for some special purpose: *a search party.* **3.** a political group organized for gaining governmental control. **4.** a person or group that participates in some action, plan, etc.: *He was a party to the merger deal.* **5.** one of the litigants in a legal proceeding. **6.** a specific individual. —*v.i.* **7.** to go to or give parties.

par•ty line (pär′tē līn′ *for 1;* līn′ *for 2*), *n.* **1.** the guiding policy, tenets, or practices of a political party. **2.** a telephone line connecting the telephones of a number of subscribers.

par•ve•nu (pär′və nŏŏ′, -nyŏŏ′), *n., pl.* **-nus.** a person who has newly acquired wealth or influence but not the social acceptance associated with it.

pass (pas, päs), *v.t.* **1.** to move past. **2.** to cause or allow to go through a barrier, obstacle, etc. **3.** to go across or over. **4.** to undergo successfully: *to pass a test.* **5.** to go beyond; surpass. **6.** to cause to go or move onward. **7.** to allow to elapse: *How did you pass the time?* **8.** to circulate or transmit: *to pass rumors.* **9.** to approve, esp. by vote. **10.** to obtain the approval of: *The bill passed the Senate.* **11.** to express; pronounce: *to pass judgment.* **12.** to transfer (a ball or puck) to a teammate. —*v.i.* **13.** to go or move onward. **14.** to elapse. **15.** to come to an end. **16.** to die (often fol. by *away* or *on*). **17.** to take place. **18.** to go by or move past. **19.** to be transferred, as by inheritance. **20.** to go or get through a barrier, test, etc., successfully. **21.** to go unchallenged: *I let the insult pass.* **22.** to pronounce judgment. **23.** to obtain the approval of a committee or the like. **24.** to make a pass, as in football. **25.** *Cards.* to forgo one's opportunity to bid. **26. pass off, a.** to present or sell by deceit. **27. ~ out, a.** to faint. **b.** to give out. **28. ~ over,** to disregard; ignore. **29. ~ up,** to refuse or neglect to take advantage of. —*n.* **30.** the act of passing. **31.** a road or other means of passage, as through an obstructed region. **32.** a permission to go, come, or enter. **33.** permission given a soldier to be absent briefly from a station. **34.** a free ticket or permit. **35.** a particular stage or state of affairs. **36.** a single movement or effort: *We made a pass at the enemy airfield.* **37.** an action or remark intended to be sexually inviting. **38.** the transfer of a ball or puck from one teammate to another. —*Idiom.* **39. bring to pass,** to cause to happen. **40. come to pass,** to happen.

pass′a•ble *adj.* **1.** capable of being passed, penetrated, or crossed. **2.** marginally acceptable; adequate. —**pass′a•bly,** *adv.*

pas•sage (pas′ij), *n.* **1.** a portion of a written work or musical composition. **2.** an act or instance of passing from one place, condition, etc., to another. **3.** the right or freedom to pass. **4.** the route or course by which a person or thing passes or travels. **5.** the enactment into law of a legislative measure.

pas•sé (pa sā′), *adj.* **1.** old-fashioned; out-of-date. **2.** past one's prime.

pas•sen•ger (pas′ən jər), *n.* a person traveling in an automobile, train, etc. who is not the operator.

pass•er•by (pas′ər bī′, -bī′, päs′ər-), *n.*, *pl.* **pass•ers•by.** a person passing by.

pass′ing *adj.* **1.** going past; elapsing. **2.** brief: *a passing fancy.* **3.** superficial: *a passing mention.* **4.** satisfactory: *a passing grade.* —*n.* **5.** the act of a person or thing that passes. **6.** death. —*Idiom.* **7. in passing,** incidentally.

pas•sion (pash′ən), *n.* **1.** any compelling emotion. **2.** strong amorous feeling. **3.** strong sexual desire. **4.** a strong fondness or enthusiasm. **5.** the object of one's passion. **6.** violent anger; wrath. **7.** (*often cap.*) the sufferings of Christ on the cross or subsequent to the Last Supper. —**pas′sion•less,** *adj.*

pas•sion•ate (-ə nit), *adj.* **1.** having or compelled by intense emotion. **2.** ardently sensual. **3.** intense or vehement, as emotions. **4.** easily moved to anger. —**pas′sion•ate•ly,** *adv.*

pas•sive (pas′iv), *adj.* **1.** acted upon by some external force, agency, etc. **2.** submitting without resistance. **3.** noting a voice, verb form, or construction having a subject represented as undergoing the action expressed by the verb. —**pas′sive•ly,** *adv.* —**pas•siv′i•ty,** *n.*

pas′sive resist′ance *n.* opposition to a government or to specific laws by the use of noncooperation or other nonviolent methods.

pas′sive smok′ing *n.* the inhaling of the cigarette, cigar, or pipe smoke of others.

pass′key′ *n.* **1.** a key that will open a number of different locks. **2.** SKELETON KEY.

Pass•o•ver (pas′ō′vər, päs′-), *n.* a Jewish festival that commemorates the Exodus of the Israelites from Egypt.

pass′port′ *n.* a governmental document issued to a citizen, authenticating the bearer's identity and right to travel to other countries.

pass′word′ *n.* a secret word used by authorized persons to gain access, information, etc.

past (past, päst), *adj.* **1.** gone by or elapsed in time. **2.** of a previous time; bygone. **3.** gone by just before the present time. **4.** previous; earlier. **5.** designating a verb tense referring to events or states in times gone by. —*n.* **6.** the time gone by. **7.** the history of a person, nation, etc. **8.** an earlier period of a person's life that is characterized by questionable conduct. —*adv.* **9.** so as to pass by or beyond. —*prep.* **10.** beyond in space, time, amount, scope, etc.

pas•ta (pä′stə), *n.*, *pl.* **-tas.** a food preparation of thin, unleavened dough, processed into a variety of forms, as spaghetti or ravioli.

paste (pāst), *n.*, *v.*, **past•ed, past•ing.** —*n.* **1.** a mixture of flour and water, often with starch, used as an adhesive. **2.** any soft, smooth material or preparation. **3.** dough, esp. when prepared with shortening. **4.** a brilliant, heavy glass used for making artificial gems. —*v.t.* **5.** to fasten or stick with paste or the like. **6.** *Slang.* to hit (a person) hard.

paste′board′ *n.* a stiff board made of sheets of paper pasted or layers of paper pulp pressed together.

pas•tel (pa stel′), *n.* **1.** a paste made of ground pigment. **2.** a crayon made from such paste. **3.** a drawing made with such crayons. **4.** a color having a soft, subdued shade.

pas•teur•ize (pas′chə rīz′, pas′tə-), *v.t.*, **-ized, -iz•ing.** to expose (a food) to a high temperature to destroy harmful or undesirable microorganisms. —**pas′teur•i•za′tion,** *n.*

pas•tiche (pa stēsh′, pä-), *n.* a literary, musical, or artistic piece consisting of motifs or techniques from borrowed sources.

pas•tille′ (pa stēl′), *n.* a flavored or medicated lozenge.

pas•time (pas′tīm′, päs′-), *n.* something, as a hobby, that makes time pass agreeably.

past′ mas′ter *n.* one who is thoroughly skilled in a profession or art; expert.

pas•tor (pas′tər, pä′stər), *n.* a minister or priest in charge of a church. —**pas′tor•ate** (-it), *n.*

pas′to•ral *adj.* **1.** having the simplicity, serenity, etc., attributed to rural areas. **2.** rural; rustic. **3.** of shepherds. **4.** of a pastor or the duties of a pastor.

pas′to•rale′ (-räl′) *n.* dreamy musical composition.

pas•tra•mi (pə strä′mē), *n.* a brisket of beef cured in seasonings and smoked before cooking. [< Yiddish < Romanian *pastramă* pressed, cured meat]

pas•try (pā′strē), *n.*, *pl.* **-tries.** **1.** a sweet baked food, esp. one made with a crust of dough. **2.** PASTE (def. 3).

pas•ture (pas′chər, päs′-), *n.*, *v.*, **-tured, -tur•ing.** —*n.* **1.** ground suitable for the grazing of livestock. **2.** grass or other plants for feeding livestock. **3.** to put out (livestock) to graze on pasture. —*v.t.* **3.** to put out (livestock) to graze on pasture.

past•y (pā′stē), *adj.*, **-i•er, -i•est.** of or like paste, as in texture or color.

pat¹ (pat), *v.*, **pat•ted, pat•ting,** *n.* —*v.t.* **1.** to strike lightly or tap gently, as with the hand or a small object. —*n.* **2.** a light stroke or gentle tap. **3.** the sound of a light stroke. **4.** a small piece, usu. flat and square: *a pat of butter.* —*Idiom.* **5. pat on the back,** praise, congratulations, or encouragement.

pat² (pat), *adj.* **1.** exactly to the point. **2.** excessively glib. **3.** mastered perfectly: *to have something pat.* —*Idiom.* **4. stand pat,** to cling firmly to one's decision, beliefs, etc.

pat. **1.** patent. **2.** patented.

patch (pach), *n.* **1.** a small piece of material used to mend a tear, cover a hole, etc. **2.** a piece of material used to cover an injured part. **3.** a small piece or area: *a patch of ice.* **4.** a small plot of land: *a cabbage patch.* —*v.t.* **5.** to mend or cover with a patch. **6.** to repair in a hasty way (usu. fol. by *up*). **7.** to settle or smooth over: *to patch up a quarrel.*

patch′ test′ *n.* a test for allergy in which a patch impregnated with an allergen is applied to the skin.

patch′work′ *n.* **1.** something made up of incongruous pieces or parts. **2.** sewn work made of pieces of material in various colors or shapes.

patch′y *adj.*, **-i•er, -i•est.** **1.** made up of patches. **2.** irregular in quality, distribution, etc.: *patchy fog.*

pate (pāt), *n.* the crown of the head.

pâ•té (pä tā′, pa-), *n.*, *pl.* **-tés.** a paste of puréed or chopped meat, liver, etc.

pa•tel•la (pə tel′ə), *n.*, *pl.* **-tel•las, -tel•lae** (-tel′ē). the flat, movable bone at the front of the knee; kneecap.

pat•ent (pat′nt; *for 6* pāt′-), *n.* **1.** the exclusive right granted to an inventor to manufacture or sell an invention for a specified number of years. **2.** an invention or process protected by this right. **3.** an official document conferring such a right. —*adj.* **4.** protected by a patent. **5.** dealing with patents. **6.** evident; obvious. —*v.t.* **7.** to obtain a patent on.

pat′ent leath′er (pat′nt, pat′n), *n.* a hard, glossy, smooth leather used esp. for shoes and accessories.

pat′ent med′icine *n.* a nonprescription drug that is protected by the trademark of a company.

pa•ter•nal (pə tûr′nl), *adj.* **1.** of, characteristic of, or befitting a father. **2.** related on the father's side. **3.** inherited from a father. —**pa•ter′nal•ly,** *adv.*

pa•ter′nal•ism *n.* the practice of managing individuals, businesses, etc., in the manner of a father dealing with his children. —**pa•ter′nal•is′tic,** *adj.*

pa•ter′ni•ty (-ni tē) *n.* **1.** the state of being a father. **2.** derivation or descent from a father.

pa′ter•nos′ter (pā′tər nos′tər) *n.* the prayer

given by Jesus to His disciples, beginning with the words *Our Father.*

path (path, päth), *n., pl.* **paths** (pathz, päthz, paths, päths). **1.** a way formed by the feet of persons or animals. **2.** a narrow walk or way: *a bicycle path.* **3.** a route along which something moves. **4.** a course of action, conduct, or procedure.

pa•thet•ic (pə thet′ik), *adj.* evoking pity, either sympathetically or contemptibly. —**pa•thet′i•cal•ly,** *adv.*

path•o•gen (path′ə jən, -jen′), *n.* any disease-producing agent, esp. a microorganism. —**path′o•gen′ic** (-jen′ik), *adj.*

pa•thol•o•gy (pə thol′ə jē), *n., pl.* **-gies. 1.** the science of the origin, nature, and course of diseases. **2.** any deviation from a healthy or normal condition. —**path•o•log•i•cal** (path′ə loj′i kəl), *adj.* —**pa•thol′o•gist,** *n.*

pa•thos (pā′thos, -thōs), *n.* the quality or power of evoking pity or compassion.

pa•tience (pā′shəns), *n.* the quality or capacity of being patient.

pa′tient *n.* **1.** a person who is under medical care. —*adj.* **2.** tolerating delay, provocation, annoyance, etc., without complaint or anger. **3.** persevering or diligent. —**pa′tient•ly,** *adv.*

pat•i•na (pat′n ə, pə tē′nə), *n., pl.* **-nas.** a green film produced by oxidation on the surface of old bronze.

pat•i•o (pat′ē ō′, pä′tē ō′), *n., pl.* **-os. 1.** a paved area adjoining a house and used for outdoor lounging, dining, etc. **2.** a courtyard enclosed by low buildings or walls.

pa•tri•arch (pā′trē ärk′), *n.* **1.** the male head of a family or tribal line. **2.** any of the three great progenitors of the Israelites: Abraham, Isaac, and Jacob. **3.** the head of any of the Eastern Orthodox sees of Alexandria, Antioch, Constantinople, or Jerusalem. **4.** a venerable old man. —**pa′tri•ar′chal,** *adj.*

pa′tri•arch′y *n., pl.* **-arch•ies. 1.** a form of social organization in which the father is the head of the family, clan, or tribe and descent is reckoned in the male line. **2.** an institution or organization in which power is held by males.

pa•tri•cian (pə trish′ən), *n.* a person of noble or high rank; aristocrat.

pat•ri•cide (pa′trə sīd′), *n.* **1.** the act of killing one's father. **2.** a person who commits such an act.

pat•ri•mo•ny (pa′trə mō′nē), *n., pl.* **-nies.** an estate inherited from one's father or ancestors. —**pat′ri•mo′ni•al,** *adj.*

pa•tri•ot (pā′trē ət, -ot′; *esp. Brit.* pa′trē ət), *n.* a person who loves, supports, and defends his or her country. [< MF < LL < Gk *patriōtēs* fellow-countryman] —**pa′tri•ot′ic,** *adj.* —**pa′tri•ot′i•cal•ly,** *adv.* —**pa′tri•ot•ism,** *n.*

pa•trol (pə trōl′), *v.,* **-trolled, -trol•ling,** *n.* —*v.t., v.i.* **1.** to pass regularly through or along (a specified area or route) in order to maintain order and security. —*n.* **2.** a person or group that patrols. **3.** the act of patrolling.

pa•trol′man or **-wom•an,** *n., pl.* **-men** or **-wom•en.** a police officer who patrols a specific route or area.

pa•tron (pā′trən), *n.* **1.** a person who is a customer, client, etc., esp. a regular one. **2.** a person who supports an artist, charity, etc., with money or efforts. **3.** PATRON SAINT.

pa•tron•age (pā′trə nij, pa′-), *n.* **1.** the business provided to a store or the like by customers, clients, etc. **2. a.** the power of public officials to make appointments to government jobs or grant other favors. **b.** the jobs or favors so distributed. **3.** the support of a patron, as toward an artist.

pa′tron•ize′ *v.t.,* **-ized, -iz•ing. 1.** to give (a store, restaurant, etc.) one's patronage. **2.** to behave in a condescending manner toward. **3.** to act as a patron toward; support.

pa′tron saint′ *n.* a saint regarded as the special guardian of a person, group, etc.

pat•sy (pat′sē), *n., pl.* **-sies.** *Slang.* **1.** a person

who is easily swindled or manipulated. **2.** a person upon whom the blame for something falls.

pat•ter[1] (pat′ər), *v.i.* **1.** to make a rapid succession of light taps. —*n.* **2.** a rapid succession of light tapping sounds. **3.** the act of pattering.

pat•ter[2] (pat′ər), *n.* **1.** glib and rapid talk used to attract attention, entertain, etc. —*v.i., v.t.* **2.** to speak glibly or rapidly.

pat•tern (pat′ərn), *n.* **1.** a decorative design composed of elements in a regular arrangement. **2.** a combination of qualities, acts, etc., forming a characteristic arrangement: *behavior patterns.* **3.** a model considered for or deserving of imitation. **4.** anything designed to serve as a model for something to be made. —*v.t.* **5.** to make or fashion after a pattern.

pat•ty (pat′ē), *n., pl.* **-ties. 1.** a thin, round piece of ground or minced food, as of meat. **2.** a little pie.

pau•ci•ty (pô′si tē), *n.* **1.** smallness of quantity; scarcity. **2.** smallness or insufficiency of number.

paunch (pônch, pänch), *n.* a large and protruding belly; potbelly. —**paunch′y,** *adj.,* **-i•er, -i•est.**

pau•per (pô′pər), *n.* a very poor person. —**pau′per•ism,** *n.*

pause (pôz), *n., v.,* **paused, paus•ing.** —*n.* **1.** a temporary stop or rest. **2.** a break in speaking or writing to emphasize or clarify meaning. —*v.i.* **3.** to make a pause.

pave (pāv), *v.t.,* **paved, pav•ing. 1.** to cover or lay (a road, walk, etc.) with concrete, stones, or asphalt. —*Idiom.* **2. pave the way for,** to prepare the way for. —**pave′ment,** *n.*

pa•vil•ion (pə vil′yən), *n.* **1.** a light, usu. open building, used for concerts, exhibits, etc. **2.** any of a number of separate or attached buildings forming a hospital or the like. **3.** a large, elaborate tent.

paw (pô), *n.* **1.** the foot of an animal that has claws. **2.** *Informal.* the human hand. —*v.t., v.i.* **3.** to strike or scrape with the paws. **4.** to handle clumsily, rudely, or with unwelcome familiarity.

pawn[1] (pôn), *v.t.* **1.** to deposit as security, as for money borrowed. **2.** to stake; risk. —*n.* **3.** the state of being pawned. **4.** something pawned. —**pawn′shop′,** *n.*

pawn[2] (pôn), *n.* **1.** a chess piece of the lowest value. **2.** someone used to further another's purposes.

pawn′bro′ker *n.* a person whose business is lending money at interest on personal property deposited until redeemed.

paw•paw (pô′pô′, pə pô′), *n.* **1.** a tree of the eastern U.S. with large, oblong leaves and purplish flowers. **2.** the fleshy, edible fruit of this tree. **3.** PAPAYA.

pay (pā), *v.,* **paid, pay•ing,** *n., adj.* —*v.t.* **1.** to settle (a debt or obligation). **2.** to give over (money) in exchange for something. **3.** to transfer money to (a person or organization) for work done or services rendered. **4.** to be profitable to. **5.** to give (attention, a compliment, etc.), as if due or fitting. **6.** to make (a call, visit, etc.). —*v.i.* **7.** to transfer money, goods, etc., as in making a purchase or settling a debt. **8.** to be worthwhile: *It pays to be courteous.* **9. pay back, a.** to repay. **b.** to retaliate against. **10.** ~ **off, a.** to pay everything that is due. **b.** to pay (a debt) in full. **c.** *Informal.* to bribe. **d.** to result in success. **11.** ~ **up,** to pay fully. —*n.* **12.** wages, salary, or a stipend. —*adj.* **13.** requiring payment for service or use: *a pay phone.* —**pay′a•ble,** *adj.* —**pay•ee′,** *n., pl.* **-ees.** —**pay′er,** *n.*

pay′ dirt′ *n.* **1.** soil, gravel, or ore that can be mined profitably. **2.** *Informal.* any source of wealth.

pay′load′ *n.* **1.** the part of a cargo producing revenue. **2.** the bomb load, warhead, cargo, or passengers of an aircraft, missile, etc.

pay′mas′ter *n.* a person in charge of paying out wages or salaries.

pay′ment (-mənt), *n.* **1.** something paid. **2.** the act of paying. **3.** reward or punishment.

pay′off′ *n.* **1.** the payment of a salary, debt, etc. **2.** the outcome of a series of events; climax. **3.** a settlement or reckoning, as in retribution or reward. **4.** *Informal.* BRIBE.

pay•o•la (pā ō′lə), *n.* secret payment in return for the promotion of a product, service, etc., through the abuse of one's position.
pay′roll′ *n.* **1.** a list of employees to be paid, with the amount due to each. **2.** the sum total of these amounts.
PC **1.** Peace Corps. **2.** *pl.* **PCs** or **PC's.** personal computer. **3.** politically correct.
p/e price-earnings ratio.
pea (pē), *n., pl.* **peas. 1.** the round edible seed of a widely cultivated plant of the legume family. **2.** the plant itself.
peace (pēs), *n.* **1.** freedom from war. **2.** a state of harmony between people or groups. **3.** freedom from civil commotion. **4.** a state of tranquillity or serenity. **5.** (*often cap.*) an agreement that ends a war. —*Idiom.* **6.** hold or keep one's peace, to keep silent. —**peace′a•ble,** *adj.* —**peace′ful,** *adj.* —**peace′ful•ly,** *adv.*
peace′mak′er *n.* a person, group, or nation that attempts to make peace.
peace′time′ *n.* a period of freedom from war.
peach (pēch), *n.* **1.** a round, pink-to-yellow, fuzzy-skinned fruit. **2.** the tree bearing this fruit. **3.** *Informal.* a person or thing that is especially attractive.
pea′cock′ *n., pl.* **-cocks, -cock.** the male peafowl, having long, iridescent tail feathers that can be spread in a fan.
pea′fowl′ *n.* a large Asiatic bird of the pheasant family.
pea′hen′ *n.* the female peafowl.
pea′ jack′et *n.* a short, double-breasted coat of navy-blue wool, worn originally by seamen.
peak (pēk), *n.* **1.** the pointed top of a mountain or ridge. **2.** a mountain with a pointed summit. **3.** the pointed top of anything. **4.** the highest or most important point or level. —*v.i.* **5.** to attain a peak of activity, popularity, etc. —*adj.* **6.** attaining or being at the highest or maximum level, point, etc.
peak•ed (pē′kid), *adj.* pale and drawn.
peal (pēl), *n.* **1.** a loud, prolonged ringing of bells. **2.** a set of bells tuned to one another. **3.** any loud, sustained sound, as of thunder. —*v.t., v.i.* **4.** to sound or sound forth in a peal.
pea′nut′ (-nut′, -nət), *n.* **1.** the pod or the enclosed edible seed of a plant of the legume family. **2.** the plant itself. **3. peanuts,** *Informal.* a very small amount of money.
pear (pâr), *n.* **1.** an edible fruit, usu. rounded but elongated and growing smaller toward the stem. **2.** the tree bearing this fruit.
pearl (pûrl), *n.* **1.** a smooth, rounded bead formed within the shells of oysters and other mollusks, valued as a gem. **2.** something similar in form or luster. **3.** something precious or choice. **4.** a very pale bluish gray. **5.** MOTHER-OF-PEARL. —**pearl′y,** *adj.,* **-i•er, -i•est.**
peas•ant (pez′ənt), *n.* **1.** a small farmer or farm laborer, as in Europe, Asia, or Latin America. **2.** a boorish, uneducated person. —**peas′ant•ry,** *n.*
peat (pēt), *n.* partially decayed vegetable matter found in bogs, cut and then dried for use as fuel. —**peat′y,** *adj.*
peb•ble (peb′əl), *n.* a small, rounded stone, esp. one worn by the action of water. —**peb′bly,** *adj.*
pe•can (pi kän′, -kan′, pē′kan), *n.* **1.** a hickory tree of the southern U.S. and Mexico, cultivated for its edible nuts. **2.** a nut of this tree.
pec•ca•dil•lo (pek′ə dil′ō), *n., pl.* **-loes, -los.** a slight sin or offense.
pec•ca•ry (pek′ə rē), *n., pl.* **-ries.** a piglike New World mammal having a dark gray coat with a white collar.
peck¹ (pek), *n.* a dry measure of 8 quarts; the fourth part of a bushel.
peck² (pek), *v.t.* **1.** to strike with the beak or with some pointed instrument. **2.** to make (a hole) by doing this. **3.** to take (food) bit by bit. —*v.i.* **4.** to make strokes with the beak or a pointed instrument. **5. peck at, a.** to nibble indifferently at (food). **b.** to nag or carp at. —*n.* **6.** a quick stroke. **7.** a quick kiss.

peck′ing or′der *n.* a hierarchy of status or authority in a social or business group.
pec•tin (pek′tin), *n.* a carbohydrate present in ripe fruits: used in jellies for its thickening and emulsifying properties.
pec•to•ral (pek′tər əl), *adj.* of, in, or on the chest or breast.
pe•cu•liar (pi kyōōl′yər), *adj.* **1.** strange; odd. **2.** distinctive in nature or character from others. **3.** belonging exclusively to some person, group, or thing. —**pe•cu′li•ar′i•ty** (-kyōō′lē ar′i tē), *n., pl.* **-ties.** —**pe•cu′liar•ly,** *adv.*
pe•cu•ni•ar•y (pi kyōō′nē er′ē), *adj.* of or consisting of money.
ped•a•gogue (ped′ə gog′, -gôg′), *n.* **1.** a teacher. **2.** a person who is pedantic and dogmatic. —**ped′a•gog′ic** (-goj′ik, -gō′jik), **ped′a•gog′i•cal,** *adj.* —**ped′a•go′gy** (-gō′jē, -goj′ē), *n., pl.* **-gies.**
ped•al (ped′l), *n., v.,* **-aled, -al•ing** or (*esp. Brit.*) **-alled, -al•ling.** —*n.* **1.** a foot-operated lever used to control power to various mechanisms. —*v.i.* **2.** to work or use pedals, as in riding a bicycle. —*v.t.* **3.** to work the pedals of.
ped•ant (ped′nt), *n.* **1.** a person who makes an excessive display of learning. **2.** a person who overemphasizes rules or minor details. —**pe•dan•tic** (pə dan′tik), *adj.* —**ped′ant•ry,** *n., pl.* **-ries.**
ped•dle (ped′l), *v.t., v.i.,* **-dled, -dling.** to carry (small articles) from place to place for sale. —**ped′dler,** *n.*
ped•er•as•ty (ped′ə ras′tē, pē′də-), *n.* sexual relations between a man and a boy. —**ped′er•ast′,** *n.*
ped•es•tal (ped′ə stl), *n.* an architectural support for a column, statue, etc.
pe•des•tri•an (pə des′trē ən), *n.* **1.** a person who travels on foot. —*adj.* **2.** going or performed on foot. **3.** of or intended for walking.
pe•di•at•rics (pē′dē a′triks), *n.* the branch of medicine concerned with the development, care, and diseases of children. —**pe′di•at′ric,** *adj.* —**pe′di•a•tri′cian** (-ə trish′ən), *n.*
ped•i•cure (ped′i kyōōr′), *n.* professional care of the feet, as the trimming of toenails. —**ped′i•cur′ist,** *n.*
ped•i•gree (ped′i grē′), *n., pl.* **-grees. 1.** an ancestral line; lineage. **2.** a genealogical record, esp. of a purebred animal. —**ped′i•greed′,** *adj.*
ped•i•ment (ped′ə mənt), *n.* (in classical architecture) a low triangular gable surmounting a colonnade, an end wall, etc.
pe•dom•e•ter (pə dom′i tər), *n.* an instrument that measures the distance walked.
peek (pēk), *v.i.* **1.** to look quickly or furtively. —*n.* **2.** a quick or furtive look.
peel (pēl), *v.t.* **1.** to strip (something) of its skin, rind, etc. **2.** to strip away from something. —*v.i.* **3.** (of skin, paint, etc.) to come off in pieces. **4.** to lose the skin, paint, etc. —*n.* **5.** the skin or rind of a fruit or vegetable.
peep¹ (pēp), *v.i.* **1.** to look through a small opening or from a concealed location. **2.** to come partially into view. —*n.* **3.** a quick or furtive look.
peep² (pēp), *n.* **1.** a short, shrill cry, as of a young bird. —*v.i.* **2.** to utter a short, shrill cry.
peer¹ (pēr), *n.* **1.** a person who is the equal of another in abilities, social status, etc. **2.** a member of the nobility in Great Britain. —**peer′age,** *n.*
peer² (pēr), *v.i.* **1.** to look searchingly, as in the effort to discern clearly. **2.** to appear slightly; peep out.
peer′age (-ij) *n.* **1.** the body of peers of a country. **2.** the rank or dignity of a peer.
peer′less *adj.* having no equal.
peeve (pēv), *v.,* **peeved, peev•ing,** *n.* —*v.t.* **1.** to make peevish. —*n.* **2.** a source of annoyance or irritation. **3.** a peevish mood.
pee•vish (pē′vish), *adj.* cross, querulous, or fretful. —**pee′vish•ly,** *adv.*
pee•wee (pē′wē′), *n., pl.* **-wees.** *Informal.* a person or thing that is unusually small.
peg (peg), *n., v.,* **pegged, peg•ging.** —*n.* **1.** a pin driven or fitted into something as a fastening, support, stopper, or marker. **2.** a notch or degree. **3.**

Informal. a hard throw, esp. in baseball. —*v.t.* **4.** to fasten or mark with pegs. **5.** to keep (a price) at a set level. **6.** *Informal.* to throw (a ball) forcefully. **7.** *Informal.* to identify or classify. —*v.i.* **8.** to work persistently: *pegging away at homework.*

peg′ leg′ *n.* **1.** an artificial leg, esp. a wooden one. **2.** a person with an artificial leg.

peign·oir (pān wär′, pen-), *n.* a woman's loose dressing gown.

pe·jo·ra·tive (pi jôr′ə tiv, -jor′-), *adj.* **1.** having a disparaging effect or force. —*n.* **2.** a pejorative form or word.

Pe·king·ese or **-kin·ese** (pē′kə nēz′, -nēs′) *n., pl.* **-ese.** one of a Chinese breed of small, long-haired dogs having a flat, wrinkled muzzle.

pel·i·can (pel′i kən), *n.* a large, web-footed, fish-eating bird with an expandable throat pouch.

pel·la·gra (pə lag′rə, -lā′grə, -lä′-), *n.* a disease caused by a deficiency of niacin in the diet, characterized by skin changes, nerve dysfunction, and mental symptoms.

pel·let (pel′it), *n.* **1.** a small, rounded body, as of food or medicine. **2.** one of a charge of small shot, as for a shotgun.

pell-mell (pel′mel′), *adv.* **1.** in a recklessly hurried manner. **2.** in a disordered mass. —*adj.* **3.** disorderly or confused. **4.** overhasty or precipitate.

pel·lu·cid (pə loo′sid), *adj.* **1.** allowing the maximum passage of light, as glass. **2.** clear in meaning.

pelt[1] (pelt), *v.t.* **1.** to attack with or as if with repeated blows or missiles. —*v.i.* **2.** to beat or pound unrelentingly.

pelt[2] (pelt), *n.* the untanned skin of an animal.

pel·vis (pel′vis), *n., pl.* **-vis·es, -ves** (-vēz). **1.** the basinlike cavity in the lower trunk of the body. **2.** the bones forming this cavity. [< L: basin] —**pel′vic,** *adj.*

pen[1] (pen), *n., v.,* **penned, pen·ning.** —*n.* **1.** any of various instruments for writing or drawing with ink. **2.** the pen as a symbol of authorship. —*v.t.* **3.** to write or draw with a pen.

pen[2] (pen), *n., v.,* **penned, pen·ning.** —*n.* **1.** a small enclosure for domestic animals. —*v.t.* **2.** to confine in or as if in a pen.

pen[3] (pen), *n. Slang.* PENITENTIARY (def. 1).

Pen. or **pen.,** peninsula.

pe·nal (pēn′l), *adj.* **1.** of or involving punishment. **2.** prescribing punishment. —**pe′nal·ize,** *v.t.,* -ized, -iz·ing.

pen·al·ty (pen′l tē), *n., pl.* **-ties. 1.** a punishment for a violation of law or rule. **2.** something forfeited, as a sum of money.

pen′ance (-əns), *n.* a punishment undergone as penitence for sin.

pence (pens), *n. Brit.* a pl. of PENNY.

pen·chant (pen′chənt), *n.* a strong taste or liking for something.

pen·cil (pen′səl), *n., v.,* -ciled, -cil·ing or (*esp. Brit.*) -cilled, -cil·ling. —*n.* **1.** a slender tube of wood, metal, etc., containing a core of graphite or crayon, used for writing or drawing. —*v.t.* **2.** to write, draw, or mark with a pencil.

pend (pend) *v.i.* to remain undecided or unsettled.

pend·ant (pen′dənt), *n.* a hanging ornament, as a jewel suspended from a necklace.

pend·ent (pen′dənt), *adj.* **1.** hanging or suspended. **2.** overhanging; jutting. **3.** (esp. of a lawsuit) pending.

pend′ing *prep.* **1.** while awaiting. **2.** during: *pending the trial.* —*adj.* **3.** awaiting decision or settlement. **4.** about to happen.

pen·du·lous (pen′jə ləs, pen′dyə-), *adj.* hanging down loosely.

pen·du·lum (-ləm), *n.* a body so suspended from a fixed point as to move to and fro by the action of gravity and acquired momentum.

pen·e·trate (pen′i trāt′), *v.t., v.i.,* -trat·ed, -trat·ing. **1.** to pierce or pass into or through (something). **2.** to permeate. **3.** to comprehend. **4.** to affect deeply. —**pen′e·tra·ble,** *adj.* —**pen′e·tra′tion,** *n.*

pen′e·trat′ing *adj.* **1.** able to penetrate; piercing; sharp. **2.** acute; discerning.

pen·guin (peng′gwin, pen′-), *n.* a flightless aquatic bird of the Southern Hemisphere, having webbed feet and flippers.

pen·i·cil·lin (pen′ə sil′in), *n.* any of several antibiotics widely used to prevent and treat bacterial infection and other diseases.

pen·in·su·la (pə nin′sə lə, -nins′yə lə), *n., pl.* **-las.** an area of land almost completely surrounded by water. [< L *paeninsula* = *paene* almost + *insula* island] —**pen·in′su·lar,** *adj.*

pe·nis (pē′nis), *n., pl.* **-nis·es, -nes** (-nēz). the male organ of copulation and urination. —**pe·nile** (pēn′l, pē′nīl), *adj.*

pen·i·tent (pen′i tənt), *adj.* **1.** feeling sorrow for sin or wrongdoing and disposed to atonement. —*n.* **2.** a penitent person. —**pen′i·tence,** *n.* —**pen′i·ten′tial** (-ten′shəl), *adj.* —**pen′i·tent·ly,** *adv.*

pen·i·ten·tia·ry (-ten′shə rē), *n., pl.* **-ries,** *adj.* —*n.* **1.** a state or federal prison for serious offenders. —*adj.* **2.** punishable by imprisonment in a penitentiary.

pen′knife′ *n., pl.* **-knives.** a small pocketknife.

pen′light′ *n.* a flashlight similar in size and shape to a fountain pen.

pen′man *n., pl.* **-men. 1.** a scribe; copyist. **2.** a writer or author.

pen′man·ship′ *n.* **1.** the art of handwriting. **2.** a person's style of handwriting.

pen′ name′ *n.* a writer's pseudonym.

pen·nant (pen′ənt), *n.* **1.** a long, tapering flag. **2.** a flag serving as an emblem of championship, esp. in baseball.

pen·ni·less (pen′i lis), *adj.* totally without money.

pen·ny (pen′ē), *n., pl.* **pen·nies** for 1, **pence** for 2, 3. **1.** a monetary unit of the U.S. or Canada, equal to ¹/₁₀₀ of a dollar. **2.** a monetary unit of the United Kingdom, equal to ¹/₁₀₀ of a pound. **3.** a monetary unit equal to ¹/₁₂ of the former British shilling.

pen′ny pinch′er *n.* a stingy person. —**pen′ny-pinch′ing,** *n., adj.*

pen′ny·weight′ *n.* (in troy weight) a unit of 24 grains or ¹/₂₀ of an ounce (1.555 grams).

pen′ pal′ *n.* a person with whom one keeps up an exchange of letters.

pen·sion (pen′shən), *n.* **1.** a fixed amount, other than wages, paid regularly to a person for past services, injury sustained, etc. —*v.t.* **2.** to grant or pay a pension to. —**pen′sion·er,** *n.*

pen·sive (pen′siv), *adj.* dreamily or wistfully thoughtful. —**pen′sive·ly,** *adv.*

pent (pent) *adj.* shut in; confined: *pent emotions.*

penta- a combining form meaning five (*pentagon*).

pen·ta·gon (pen′tə gon′), *n.* **1.** a polygon having five angles and five sides. **2. the Pentagon,** the U.S. Department of Defense; the U.S. military establishment. —**pen·tag′o·nal** (-tag′ə nl), *adj.*

pen′ta·gram′ (-gram′), *n.* a five-pointed, star-shaped figure, used as an occult symbol.

pen·tam·e·ter (pen tam′i tər), *n.* a line of verse consisting of five metrical feet.

Pen·ta·teuch (pen′tə took′, -tyook′), *n.* the first five books of the Old Testament.

pen·tath·lon (pen tath′lən, -lon), *n.* an athletic contest comprising five different track and field events.

Pen·te·cost (pen′ti kôst′, -kost′), *n.* a Christian festival celebrated on the seventh Sunday after Easter, commemorating the descent of the Holy Ghost upon the apostles. [< OE < LL < Gk *pentēkostē (hēmera)* fiftieth (day)]

Pen′te·cos′tal *adj.* **1.** of Pentecost. **2.** noting or pertaining to various fundamentalist Christian groups that emphasize inspiration by the Holy Spirit.

pent·house (pent′hous′), *n.* **1.** an apartment on the roof of a building. **2.** any specially designed apartment on the top floor of a building.

pent′-up′ *adj.* not vented or expressed.

pe·nul·ti·mate (pi nul′tə mit), *adj.* next to the last.

pe·num·bra (pə num′brə) *n., pl.* **-brae** (-brē), **-bras.** partial shadow outside complete shadow of celestial body in eclipse. —**pe·num′bral,** *adj.*

pe•nu•ri•ous (pə nŏŏr′ē əs, -nyŏŏr′-), *adj.* **1.** extremely stingy. **2.** extremely poor. —**pe•nu′ri•ous•ly,** *adv.* —**pe•nu′ri•ous•ness,** *n.*

pen•u•ry (pen′yə rē), *n.* extreme poverty.

pe•on (pē′ən, pē′on), *n.* **1.** (in Spanish America) a farm worker or unskilled laborer. **2.** (formerly, esp. in Mexico) a person held in servitude to work off debts. **3.** any person of low social status. —**pe′on•age** (-ə nij), *n.*

pe•o•ny (pē′ə nē), *n., pl.* **-nies.** a plant with large showy flowers.

peo•ple (pē′pəl), *n., pl.* **-ples** for 2, *v.,* **-pled, -pling.** —*n.* **1.** persons indefinitely or collectively. **2.** the body of persons who constitute a group by virtue of a common culture, religion, or the like. **3.** the persons of any particular group or number: *educated people.* **4.** the ordinary persons; populace. **5.** a person's family or relatives. —*v.t.* **6.** to populate.

pep (pep), *n., v.,* **pepped, pep•ping.** —*n.* **1.** lively spirits or energy. —*v.* **2. pep up,** to make or become spirited or vigorous. —**pep′py,** *adj.,* **-pi•er, -pi•est.**

pep•per (pep′ər), *n.* **1. a.** the pungent dried berries of a tropical climbing shrub, used as a condiment. **b.** the shrub itself. **2. a.** the usu. green or red fruit of any of several plants, ranging from mild to pungent in flavor. **b.** any of these plants. —*v.t.* **3.** to season or sprinkle with or as if with pepper. **4.** to pelt with missiles. —**pep′per•y,** *adj.*

pep′per•corn′ *n.* the dried berry of the pepper plant.

pep′per mill′ *n.* a hand-held device for grinding peppercorns.

pep′per•mint′ (-mint′, -mənt), *n.* **1.** an aromatic herb of the mint family, having lance-shaped leaves. **2.** its oil, used as a flavoring. **3.** a confection flavored with peppermint.

pep•per•o•ni (pep′ə rō′nē), *n., pl.* **-nis.** a highly seasoned, hard sausage.

pep•sin (pep′sin), *n.* an enzyme, produced in the stomach, that promotes the digestion of proteins.

pep•tic (pep′tik), *adj.* **1.** of or promoting digestion. **2.** of or due to the action of pepsin.

per (pûr; *unstressed* pər), *prep.* **1.** for or in each: *$10 per yard.* **2.** according to: *per your instructions.* **3.** by means of: *Send it per messenger.*

Per. **1.** Persia. **2.** Persian.

per•am•bu•late (pər am′byə lāt′), *v.,* **-lat•ed, -lat•ing.** —*v.t.* **1.** to walk through, about, or over. —*v.i.* **2.** to stroll.

per•am′bu•la′tor *n.* a conveyance for pushing a baby about, resembling a basket set on four wheels.

per an•num (pər an′əm), *adv.* yearly.

per•cale (pər kāl′), *n.* a smooth, plain-weave cotton cloth, used esp. for bedsheets.

per cap•i•ta (pər kap′i tə), *adj., adv.* by or for each person.

per•ceive (pər sēv′), *v.t.,* **-ceived, -ceiv•ing. 1.** to become aware of by means of the senses. **2.** to recognize or understand. —**per•ceiv′a•ble,** *adj.*

per•cent (pər sent′), *n.* **1.** one one-hundredth part; ¹/₁₀₀. **2.** PERCENTAGE (defs. 1, 3). —*adj.* **3.** figured or expressed on the basis of a rate or proportion per hundred. [short for ML *per centum* by the hundred]

per•cent′age (-sen′tij), *n.* **1.** a rate or proportion per hundred. **2.** an allowance, commission, or rate of interest calculated by percent. **3.** a proportion in general. **4.** profit; advantage.

per•cen•tile (-tīl, -til), *n.* one of the values of a statistical variable that divides the distribution of the variable into 100 groups having equal frequencies.

per•cep•ti•ble (pər sep′tə bəl), *adj.* capable of being perceived. —**per•cep′ti•bly,** *adv.*

per•cep′tion *n.* **1.** the act or faculty of perceiving. **2.** intuitive recognition or appreciation; insight. **3.** the result or product of perceiving.

per•cep′tive *adj.* **1.** having or showing keenness of perception. **2.** of perception. —**per•cep′tive•ly,** *adv.* —**per•cep′tive•ness,** *n.*

per•cep′tu•al (-chŏŏ əl), *adj.* of or involving perception.

perch¹ (pûrch), *n.* **1.** a horizontal pole or rod serving as a roost for birds. **2.** an elevated position, resting place, or the like. —*v.i., v.t.* **3.** to rest or set on or as if on a perch.

perch² (pûrch), *n., pl.* **perch•es, perch. 1.** a small freshwater fish with a spiny anterior dorsal fin. **2.** any of various related or similar fishes.

per•chance (pər chans′, -chäns′), *adv.* **1.** perhaps. **2.** *Archaic.* by chance.

per•co•late (pûr′kə lāt′), *v.,* **-lat•ed, -lat•ing.** —*v.t.* **1.** to cause (a liquid) to pass through a porous body; filter. **2.** to brew (coffee) in a percolator. —*v.i.* **3.** to pass through a porous substance; filter. —**per′co•la′tion,** *n.*

per′co•la′tor *n.* a coffeepot in which boiling water is forced up a hollow stem and filters down through ground coffee.

per•cus•sion (pər kush′ən), *n.* **1.** the striking of one body against another with some sharpness. **2.** the percussion instruments of an orchestra. **3.** a sharp blow for detonating a small metallic cap **(percus′sion cap′)** containing explosive powder in a firearm.

per di•em (pər dē′əm, dī′əm), *adv.* **1.** by the day. —*n.* **2.** a daily allowance for living expenses, as while traveling on business. [< L]

per•di•tion (pər dish′ən), *n.* **1.** a state of final spiritual ruin. **2.** hell.

per•e•gri•nate (per′i grə nāt′), *v.,* **-nat•ed, -nat•ing.** —*v.i.* **1.** to travel or journey, esp. on foot. —*v.t.* **2.** to travel over or through. —**per′e•gri•na′tion,** *n.*

per′e•grine fal′con (per′i grin, -grēn′), *n.* a cosmopolitan falcon that feeds on birds taken in flight.

per•emp•to•ry (pə remp′tə rē), *adj.* **1.** leaving no opportunity for denial or refusal. **2.** imperious or dictatorial. **3.** *Law.* decisive or final.

per•en•ni•al (pə ren′ē əl), *adj.* **1.** lasting for an indefinitely long time. **2.** (of plants) living more than two years. **3.** continuing throughout the entire year, as a stream. **4.** continuing; recurrent. —*n.* **5.** a perennial plant. —**per•en′ni•al•ly,** *adv.*

per•fect (*adj., n.* pûr′fikt; *v.* pər fekt′), *adj.* **1.** conforming absolutely to an ideal type: *a perfect gentleman.* **2.** excellent or complete beyond improvement. **3.** without flaws. **4.** accurate in every detail. **5.** thorough; utter: *perfect strangers.* **6.** designating a verb tense that indicates an action or state brought to a close prior to some temporal point of reference. —*v.t.* **7.** to make perfect. —*n.* **8.** the perfect tense. **9.** a verb form in the perfect tense. —**per′fect•ly,** *adv.*

per•fec′tion *n.* **1.** the state or quality of being perfect. **2.** the highest degree of excellence. **3.** a perfect embodiment of something. **4.** the act or fact of perfecting.

per•fec′tion•ism *n.* a personal standard that demands perfection. —**per•fec′tion•ist,** *n., adj.*

per•fi•dy (pûr′fi dē), *n., pl.* **-dies.** deliberate breach of faith or trust; treachery. —**per•fid•i•ous** (pər fid′ē əs), *adj.*

per•fo•rate (pûr′fə rāt′), *v.,* **-rat•ed, -rat•ing.** —*v.t.* **1.** to make a hole or holes through, as by boring or punching. **2.** to pierce with a row of small holes to facilitate separation. —*v.i.* **3.** to penetrate. —**per′fo•ra′tion,** *n.*

per•force (pər fôrs′), *adv.* of necessity; necessarily.

per•form (pər fôrm′), *v.t.* **1.** to carry out; do. **2.** to carry into effect; fulfill: *to perform a contract.* **3.** to present (a play, musical work, etc.) before an audience. —*v.i.* **4.** to execute or do something. **5.** to give a performance. —**per•form′er,** *n.*

per•for′mance (-fôr′məns), *n.* **1.** an entertainment presented before an audience. **2.** the act of performing. **3.** the execution of work, feats, etc. **4.** a particular action, deed, etc.

perform′ing arts′ *n.pl.* arts or skills that require public performance, as acting and singing.

per•fume (*n.* pûr′fyŏŏm, pər fyŏŏm′; *v.* pər-fyŏŏm′, pûr′fyŏŏm), *n., v.,* **-fumed, -fum•ing.** —*n.* **1.** a substance that imparts an agreeable smell, esp. a fluid containing fragrant oils extracted from flowers. **2.** an agreeable scent. —*v.t.* **3.** to fill with perfume or a pleasant fragrance. —**per•fum′er•y,** *n., pl.* **-ies.**

per•func•to•ry (pər fungk′tə rē), *adj.* **1.** performed merely as a routine duty. **2.** lacking interest or enthusiasm. —**per•func′to•ri•ly,** *adv.*

per•haps (pər haps′), *adv.* maybe; possibly.

peri- a prefix meaning: about or around (*periscope*); enclosing or surrounding (*peritoneum*); near (*perigee*).

per•i•car•di•um (per′i kär′dē əm), *n., pl.* **-di•a** (-dē ə). the membranous sac enclosing the heart.

per•il (per′əl), *n., v.,* **-iled, -il•ing** or (*esp. Brit.*) **-illed, -il•ling.** —*n.* **1.** grave risk; jeopardy. **2.** something that may cause injury, loss, or destruction. —*v.t.* **3.** to expose to peril. —**per′il•ous,** *adj.*

pe•rim•e•ter (pə rim′i tər), *n.* **1.** the outer boundary of a two-dimensional figure. **2.** the length of such a boundary.

per•i•ne•um (per′ə nē′əm), *n., pl.* **-ne•a** (-nē′ə). the area in front of the anus extending to the genitals. —**per′i•ne′al,** *adj.*

pe•ri•od (pēr′ē əd), *n.* **1.** an interval of time marked by particular qualities, conditions, or events: *a period of illness.* **2.** any of the parts of equal length into which something, as a sports contest, is divided. **3.** the time during which something runs its course. **4.** the character (.) used to mark the end of a declarative sentence or indicate an abbreviation. **5.** an occurrence of menstruation. **6.** the basic unit of geologic time, comprising two or more epochs and included with other periods in an era.

pe′ri•od′ic (-od′ik), *adj.* **1.** occurring at regular intervals. **2.** recurring irregularly; intermittent. —**pe′ri•od′i•cal•ly,** *adv.* —**pe′ri•o•dic′i•ty** (-ə dis′i tē), *n.*

pe′ri•od′i•cal *n.* **1.** a publication, as a magazine, that is issued under the same title at regular intervals. —*adj.* **2.** of such publications. **3.** published at regular intervals. **4.** PERIODIC.

pe′ri•od′ic ta′ble *n.* a table in which the chemical elements, arranged according to their atomic numbers, are shown in related groups.

per•i•pa•tet•ic (per′ə pə tet′ik), *adj.* walking or traveling about; itinerant.

pe•riph•er•al (pə rif′ər əl), *adj.* **1.** of, on, or constituting the periphery. **2.** comparatively superficial or unessential. —*n.* **3.** an external hardware device, as a printer, connected to a computer's CPU.

pe•riph′er•y *n., pl.* **-ies. 1.** the boundary of any surface or area. **2.** the external surface of a body. **3.** a surrounding region or area.

pe•riph•ra•sis (pə rif′rə sis), *n., pl.* **-ses** (-sēz′). the use of a verbose or roundabout form of expression. —**per•i•phras′tic** (per′ə fras′tik), *adj.*

per•i•scope (per′ə skōp′), *n.* an optical instrument for viewing objects in an obstructed field of vision, used esp. in submarines.

per•ish (per′ish), *v.i.* **1.** to die as a result of violence, privation, etc. **2.** to suffer destruction or ruin.

per′ish•a•ble *adj.* **1.** subject to decay or destruction. —*n.* **2.** Usu., **-bles.** something perishable, esp. food.

per•i•stal•sis (per′ə stôl′sis, -stal′-), *n., pl.* **-ses** (-sēz). waves of muscle contractions and relaxations that move matter along certain tubelike organs, as food along the alimentary canal. —**per′i•stal′tic** (-tik), *adj.*

per•i•to•ne•um (per′i tn ē′əm), *n., pl.* **-to•ne•ums, -to•ne•a** (-tn ē′ə). the serous membrane lining the abdominal cavity. —**per′i•to•ne′al,** *adj.*

per′i•to•ni′tis (-ī′tis), *n.* inflammation of the peritoneum.

per•i•win•kle¹ (per′i wing′kəl), *n.* a small edible sea snail.

per•i•win•kle² (per′i wing′kəl), *n.* any of various plants with glossy evergreen foliage and blue-violet flowers.

per•jure (pûr′jər), *v.t.,* **-jured, -jur•ing.** to make (oneself) guilty of perjury. —**per′jur•er,** *n.*

per′ju•ry *n., pl.* **-ries.** the willful giving of false testimony under oath.

perk¹ (pûrk), *v.i.* **1.** to become lively, vigorous, etc., again (usu. fol. by *up*). —*v.t.* **2.** to enhance or

enliven (often fol. by *up*). **3.** to raise smartly or briskly: *The dog perked up his ears.*

perk² (pûrk), *v.t., v.i.* to percolate.

perk³ (pûrk), *n.* perquisite.

perk′y *adj.,* **-i•er, -i•est.** jaunty, cheerful. —**perk′i•ness,** *n.*

per•ma•frost (pûr′mə frôst′, -frost′), *n.* (in arctic or subarctic regions) permanently frozen subsoil.

per•ma•nent (pûr′mə nənt), *adj.* **1.** existing perpetually. **2.** intended to serve, function, etc., for a long, indefinite period. —*n.* **3.** a wave or curl set into the hair by the application of chemicals or heat and lasting for a number of months. —**per′ma•nence,** *n.* —**per′ma•nent•ly,** *adv.*

per•me•a•ble (pûr′mē ə bəl), *adj.* capable of being permeated. —**per′me•a•bil′i•ty,** *n.*

per′me•ate′ (-āt′), *v.t., v.i.,* **-at•ed, -at•ing. 1.** to penetrate through the pores or interstices (of). **2.** to be or become diffused through; spread throughout.

per•mis•si•ble (pər mis′ə bəl), *adj.* capable of being permitted; allowable.

per•mis′sion (-mish′ən), *n.* authorization to do something; formal consent.

per•mis′sive *adj.* **1.** tolerant of something that others might disapprove or forbid. **2.** granting or expressing permission. —**per•mis′sive•ly,** *adv.* —**per•mis′sive•ness,** *n.*

per•mit (*v.* pər mit′; *n.* pûr′mit, pər mit′), *v.,* **-mit•ted, -mit•ting,** *n.* —*v.t.* **1.** to allow to do something. **2.** to allow to be done or occur. —*v.i.* **3.** to afford opportunity: *when time permits.* —*n.* **4.** an authoritative certificate of permission; license.

per•mu•ta•tion (pûr′myōō tā′shən), *n.* **1.** alteration or transformation. **2.** *Math.* **a.** the act of changing the order of set elements arranged in a particular way, as *abc* into *acb.* **b.** any of the resulting arrangements.

per•ni•cious (pər nish′əs), *adj.* causing insidious harm or ruin.

per•ox•ide (pə rok′sīd), *n., v.,* **-id•ed, -id•ing.** —*n.* **1. a.** hydrogen peroxide. **b.** an oxide in which two oxygen atoms are bonded to each other. —*v.t.* **2.** to bleach with peroxide.

per•pen•dic•u•lar (pûr′pən dik′yə lər), *adj.* **1.** vertical; straight up and down. **2.** meeting a given line or surface at right angles. —*n.* **3.** a perpendicular line, plane, or position.

per•pe•trate (pûr′pi trāt′), *v.t.,* **-trat•ed, -trat•ing.** to carry out; commit. —**per′pe•tra′tion,** *n.* —**per′pe•tra′tor,** *n.*

per•pet•u•al (pər pech′ōō əl), *adj.* **1.** continuing forever. **2.** lasting an indefinitely long time. **3.** continuing without interruption. —**per•pet′u•al•ly,** *adv.*

per•pet′u•ate′ (-āt′), *v.t.,* **-at•ed, -at•ing.** to make perpetual; preserve from extinction or oblivion. —**per•pet′u•a′tion,** *n.*

per•pe•tu•i•ty (pûr′pi tōō′i tē, -tyōō′-), *n., pl.* **-ties. 1.** the state or character of being perpetual. **2.** endless duration or existence.

per•plex (pər pleks′), *v.t.* to cause to be puzzled or bewildered. —**per•plex′ing,** *adj.* —**per•plex′i•ty,** *n., pl.* **-ties.**

per•qui•site (pûr′kwə zit), *n.* a payment, benefit, or privilege over and above regular income or salary.

per se (pûr sā′, sē′, pər), *adv.* by, of, for, or in itself; intrinsically.

per•se•cute (pûr′si kyōōt′), *v.t.,* **-cut•ed, -cut•ing.** to subject to harassing or cruel treatment, as because of religion, race, or beliefs. —**per′se•cu′tion,** *n.* —**per′se•cu′tor,** *n.*

per•se•vere (pûr′sə vēr′), *v.i.,* **-vered, -ver•ing.** to persist in pursuing something in spite of obstacles or opposition. —**per′se•ver′ance,** *n.*

per•sim•mon (pər sim′ən), *n.* **1.** any of several trees bearing a plumlike, orange, edible fruit. **2.** the fruit itself.

per•sist (pər sist′, -zist′), *v.i.* **1.** to continue steadily in some purpose or course of action in spite of opposition. **2.** to endure tenaciously: *The legend of King Arthur still persists.* **3.** to be insistent in a request, question, etc. —**per•sist′ence,** *n.* —**per•sist′ent,** *adj.*

per•snick•et•y (pər snik′i tē), *adj. Informal.* **1.** excessively particular; fussy. **2.** requiring painstaking care.

per•son (pûr′sən), *n.* **1.** a human being. **2.** the individual personality of a human being. **3.** the body of a living human being. **4.** a human being or other entity, as a corporation, recognized by law as having rights and duties. **5.** a grammatical category applied esp. to pronouns and verbs, used to distinguish between the speaker, the person addressed, and the people or things spoken about. —*Idiom.* **6. in person,** in one's own bodily presence.

-person a combining form of PERSON, replacing such paired, sex-specific forms as -MAN and -WOMAN: *salesperson.*

per′son•a•ble *adj.* having an agreeable personality.

per′son•age (-nij), *n.* a person of distinction or importance.

per′son•al (-nl), *adj.* **1.** of or concerning a particular person: *a personal opinion.* **2.** referring to a particular person, esp. in an offensive manner: *personal remarks.* **3.** done, carried out, etc., in person. **4.** of the body, clothing, or appearance. **5.** of or indicating grammatical person. **6.** *Law.* pertaining to property consisting of movable articles. —*n.* **7. a.** a brief, private message to a particular person, placed in a newspaper or magazine. **b.** a notice placed by a person seeking companionship, marriage, etc.

per′sonal comput′er *n.* a microcomputer designed for individual use, as for word processing.

per′sonal effects′ *n.pl.* privately owned articles consisting chiefly of items for intimate use, as clothing.

per′son•al′i•ty *n., pl.* **-ties. 1.** the visible aspect of one's character as it impresses others. **2.** the sum total of the distinctive characteristics of an individual. **3.** pleasingly distinctive qualities in a person. **4.** a prominent person.

per′son•al•ize′ *v.t.* **-ized, -iz•ing. 1.** to have marked with one's initials or name. **2.** to make personal.

per′son•al•ly *adv.* **1.** in person. **2.** as if directed at oneself: *Don't take this personally.* **3.** as regards oneself: *Personally, I don't care.* **4.** as a person: *I like her personally.*

per•so′na non gra′ta (pər sō′nə non grä′tə), *adj.* not being personally acceptable or welcome.

per•son•i•fy (pər son′ə fī′), *v.t.,* **-fied, -fy•ing. 1.** to attribute a human character to (an idea or thing). **2.** to be an embodiment of; typify. —**per•son′i•fi•ca′tion,** *n.*

per•son•nel (pûr′sə nel′), *n.* **1.** the body of persons employed in an organization. **2.** an organizational department supervising matters of personnel.

per•spec•tive (pər spek′tiv), *n.* **1.** a technique of depicting spatial relationships on a flat surface. **2.** the manner in which objects appear to the eye in respect to their relative positions and distance. **3.** the ability to see all the relevant data in a meaningful relationship. **4.** a mental view or prospect.

per•spi•ca•cious (pûr′spi kā′shəs), *adj.* having keen mental perception and understanding. —**per′spi•ca′cious•ly,** *adv.* —**per′spi•cac′i•ty** (-kas′i tē), *n.*

per•spire (pər spīr′), *v.i.,* **-spired, -spir•ing.** to secrete a salty, watery fluid from the sweat glands; sweat. —**per•spi•ra•tion** (pûr′spə rā′shən), *n.*

per•suade (pər swād′), *v.t.,* **-suad•ed, -suad•ing. 1.** to prevail on (a person) to do something, as by advising or urging. **2.** to induce to believe; convince. —**per•suad′er,** *n.*

per•sua′sion (-zhən), *n.* **1.** the act of persuading or state of being persuaded. **2.** power to persuade. **3.** a deep conviction. **4.** a system of religious belief.

per•sua′sive (-siv, -ziv), *adj.* able to persuade. —**per•sua′sive•ly,** *adv.*

pert (pûrt), *adj.,* **-er, -est. 1.** impertinent; saucy. **2.** jaunty and stylish. **3.** lively; sprightly. —**pert′ly,** *adv.*

per•tain (pər tān′), *v.i.* **1.** to have reference or re-

lation. **2.** to belong or be connected as a part, attribute, etc. **3.** to be appropriate.

per′ti•nent (-tn ənt), *adj.* pertaining directly to the matter at hand; relevant. —**per′ti•nence,** *n.* —**per′ti•nent•ly,** *adv.*

per•turb (pər tûrb′), *v.t.* to disturb or disquiet greatly in mind; agitate. —**per•turb′a•ble,** *adj.* —**per•tur•ba•tion** (pûr′tər bā′shən), *n.*

Pe•ru (pə rōō′), *n.* a republic in W South America. —**Pe•ru′vi•an** (-vē ən), *adj., n.*

pe•ruke (pə rōōk′), *n.* a man's wig of the 17th and 18th centuries.

pe•ruse (pə rōōz′), *v.t.,* **-rused, -rus•ing. 1.** to read through thoroughly or carefully. **2.** to read in an often desultory way. —**pe•rus′al,** *n.*

per•vade (pər vād′), *v.t.,* **-vad•ed, -vad•ing.** to become spread throughout all parts of. —**per•va′sive** (-siv), *adj.*

per•verse (pər vûrs′), *adj.* **1.** willfully determined not to do what is expected or desired. **2.** wayward or cantankerous. **3.** turned away from what is right, good, or proper. —**per•verse′ly,** *adv.* —**per•ver′si•ty,** *n., pl.* **-ties.**

per•ver′sion (-zhən, -shən), *n.* **1.** the act of perverting or state of being perverted. **2.** any of various sexual practices that are regarded as abnormal.

per•vert (*v.* pər vûrt′; *n.* pûr′vərt), *v.t.* **1.** to lead astray morally. **2.** to turn to an improper use. **3.** to misinterpret, esp. deliberately; distort. **4.** to debase. —*n.* **5.** a person who practices a sexual perversion. —**per•vert′ed,** *adj.*

pe•se•ta (pə sā′tə), *n., pl.* **-tas.** the basic monetary unit of Spain, which has a fixed value relative to the euro.

pes•ky (pes′kē), *adj.,* **-ki•er, -ki•est.** annoying; troublesome. —**pesk′i•ly,** *adv.*

pe•so (pā′sō), *n., pl.* **-sos.** the basic monetary unit of Argentina, Chile, Colombia, Cuba, the Dominican Republic, Guinea-Bissau, Mexico, the Philippines, and Uruguay.

pes•si•mism (pes′ə miz′əm), *n.* **1.** the tendency to see only what is gloomy or to anticipate the worst. **2.** the belief that the evil in the world outweighs any goodness. —**pes′si•mist,** *n.* —**pes′si•mis′tic,** *adj.* —**pes′si•mis′ti•cal•ly,** *adv.*

pest (pest), *n.* a troublesome or destructive person, animal, or thing.

pes•ter (pes′tər), *v.t.* to bother persistently with petty annoyances.

pes•ti•cide (pes′tə sīd′), *n.* a chemical for destroying plant, fungal, or animal pests.

pes•tif•er•ous (pe stif′ər əs), *adj.* **1.** bearing disease. **2.** pernicious; dangerous. **3.** troublesome; annoying.

pes•ti•lence (pes′tl əns), *n.* **1.** a deadly epidemic disease. **2.** something regarded as harmful. —**pes′ti•lent,** *adj.*

pes•tle (pes′əl, pes′tl), *n.* a tool for pounding or grinding substances in a mortar.

pes•to (pes′tō), *n., pl.* **-tos.** a pasta sauce of basil ground together with pine nuts, garlic, olive oil, and cheese.

pet¹ (pet), *n., adj., v.,* **pet•ted, pet•ting.** —*n.* **1.** any domesticated animal kept as a companion. **2.** a person or thing especially cherished: *teacher's pet.* —*adj.* **3.** kept or treated as a pet. **4.** favorite; preferred: *a pet theory.* **5.** showing affection: *pet names.* —*v.t.* **6.** to treat as a pet. **7.** to caress amorously. —*v.i.* **8.** to engage in amorous caressing.

pet² (pet), *n.* a fit of sulking.

pet•al (pet′l), *n.* one of the segments of the corolla of a flower.

pe•tard (pi tärd′), *n.* **1.** an explosive device formerly used to blow in a door, gate, etc. —*Idiom.* **2. hoist by** or **with one's own petard,** caught by the very device one had contrived to hurt another.

pe•ter (pē′tər), *v.i.* **peter out,** to diminish gradually and stop or disappear.

pet′it (pet′ē) *adj. Law.* small; petty; minor.

pe•tite (pə tēt′), *adj.* (of a woman) short and having a trim figure.

pe•ti•tion (pə tish′ən), *n.* **1.** a formal request signed by those endorsing it and addressed to a person or persons in authority. **2.** a respectful or humble request. **3.** something that is sought by request or entreaty. —*v.t.* **4.** to address a petition to (a sovereign, legislature, etc.). **5.** to ask by petition for (something). —*v.i.* **6.** to present a petition. —**pe•ti'tion•er**, *n.*

pet•ri•fy (pe'trə fī'), *v.t.,* **-fied, -fy•ing. 1.** to convert into stone or a stony substance. **2.** to benumb with strong emotion, as fear. **3.** to harden; deaden. —**pet'ri•fac'tion** (-fak'shən), *n.*

pet•ro•chem•i•cal (pe'trō kem'i kəl), *n.* a chemical substance obtained from petroleum or natural gas, as gasoline.

pe•tro•le•um (pə trō'lē əm), *n.* an oily naturally occurring liquid that is a form of bitumen or a mixture of various hydrocarbons: used as fuel or separated by distillation into gasoline, paraffin, etc.

pe•trol•o•gy (pi trol'ə jē), *n.* the scientific study of rocks. —**pe•trol'o•gist**, *n.*

pet•ti•coat (pet'ē kōt'), *n.* an underskirt, often trimmed and ruffled.

pet•tish (pet'ish), *adj.* petulant; peevish.

pet•ty (pet'ē), *adj.,* **-ti•er, -ti•est. 1.** of little or no importance. **2.** of lesser importance or merit; minor. **3.** having or showing narrow ideas, interests, etc. **4.** showing meanness of spirit. —**pet'ti•ness**, *n.*

pet'ty cash' *n.* a cash fund for paying minor expenses, as in an office.

pet'ty ju'ry, *n.* a jury, usu. of 12 persons, impaneled to render a verdict in a civil or criminal proceeding.

pet'ty of'ficer *n.* a noncommissioned officer in the navy or coast guard.

pet•u•lant (pech'ə lant), *adj.* showing sudden irritation, esp. over some trifling annoyance. —**pet'u•lance**, *n.*

pe•tu•nia (pi tōō'nyə, -nē ə, -tyōō'-), *n., pl.* **-nias.** a garden plant with funnel-shaped flowers of various colors.

pew (pyōō), *n.* one of a number of fixed benches with backs in a church.

pe•wee (pē'wē), *n., pl.* **-wees.** any of several New World flycatchers.

pew•ter (pyōō'tər), *n.* **1.** any of various alloys in which tin is the chief constituent. **2.** articles made of pewter.

pf. (of stock) preferred.

PG parental guidance: a motion-picture rating indicating that some material may be unsuitable for children.

PG-13 (pē'jē'thûr'tēn'), a motion-picture rating indicating that some material may be unsuitable for children under 13.

pg. page.

pH the symbol used to describe the acidity or alkalinity of a chemical solution on a scale of 0 (more acidic) to 14 (more alkaline).

pha•lanx (fā'langks, fal'angks), *n., pl.* **pha•lanx•es** for 1, 2, **pha•lan•ges** (fə lan'jēz) for 3. **1.** (in ancient Greece) a group of heavily armed infantry formed in close ranks and files. **2.** a compact body of persons, animals, or things. **3.** a bone of a finger or toe.

phal•lus (fal'əs), *n., pl.* **phal•li** (fal'ī), **phal•lus•es. 1.** a representation of the penis as a symbol of male generative powers. **2.** PENIS. —**phal'lic**, *adj.*

phan•tasm (fan'taz əm), *n.* **1.** a creation of the imagination; fantasy. **2.** an illusory likeness of something.

phan•tas'ma•go'ri•a (-mə gôr'ē ə), *n., pl.* **-ri•as.** a shifting series of phantasms or deceptive appearances, as in a dream.

phan•tom (-təm), *n.* **1.** an apparition or specter. **2.** an illusion without material substance. —*adj.* **3.** illusory. **4.** nonexistent; fictitious.

Phar•aoh (fâr'ō, far'ō), *n.* a title of an ancient Egyptian king.

Phar•i•see (far'ə sē'), *n., pl.* **-sees. 1.** a member of an ancient Jewish sect that emphasized liberal interpretation of the Bible and strict adherence to oral laws and traditions. **2.** (*l.c.*) a self-righteous or hypocritical person. —**Phar'i•sa'ic** (-sā'ik), **Phar'i•sa'i•cal**, *adj.*

phar•ma•ceu•ti•cal (fär'mə sōō'ti kəl), *adj.* **1.** of pharmacy or pharmacists. —*n.* **2.** a pharmaceutical preparation.

phar'ma•cist (-sist), *n.* a person licensed to prepare and dispense drugs and medicines.

phar•ma•col•o•gy (-kol'ə jē), *n.* the science dealing with the preparation, uses, and effects of drugs. —**phar•ma•col'o•gist**, *n.*

phar'ma•co•poe'ia (-kə pē'ə), *n., pl.* **-ias. 1.** a book containing a list of drugs, their formulas, and other related information. **2.** a stock of drugs.

phar'ma•cy (-sē), *n., pl.* **-cies. 1.** DRUGSTORE. **2.** the art and science of preparing and dispensing drugs and medicines. —**phar'ma•cist**, *n.*

phar•ynx (far'ingks), *n., pl.* **pha•ryn•ges** (fə rin'-jēz), **phar•ynx•es.** the portion of the alimentary canal that connects the mouth and nasal passages with the larynx. —**pha•ryn•ge•al** (fə rin'jē əl), *adj.* —**phar'yn•gi'tis**, *n.*

phase (fāz), *n., v.,* **phased, phas•ing.** —*n.* **1.** any of the major aspects in which a thing of varying modes or conditions manifests itself. **2.** a stage in a process of change or development. **3.** a side, aspect, or point of view. **4.** the particular appearance presented by the moon or a planet at a given time. —*v.* **5. phase in**, to put into use gradually. **6. ~ out**, to bring to an end gradually.

phase'out' *n.* a phasing out; planned discontinuation or expiration.

Ph.D. Doctor of Philosophy. [< NL *Philosophiae Doctor*]

pheas•ant (fez'ənt), *n.* any of numerous large, long-tailed game birds.

phe•no•bar•bi•tal (fē'nō bär'bi tôl', -tal', -nə-), *n.* a white, crystalline powder used as a sedative and hypnotic.

phe•nol (fē'nôl, -nol), *n.* a white, crystalline, poisonous substance used as a disinfectant, as an antiseptic, and in organic synthesis.

phe•nom•e•non (fi nom'ə non', -nən), *n., pl.* **-na** (-nə) or, esp. for 3, **-nons. 1.** a fact, occurrence, or circumstance observed or observable. **2.** something remarkable or extraordinary. **3.** a remarkable or exceptional person. —**phe•nom'e•nal**, *adj.*

pher•o•mone (fer'ə mōn'), *n.* any chemical substance released by an animal that influences the physiology or behavior of other members of the species.

phi•al (fī'əl), *n.* VIAL.

phil- a prefix meaning loving, having affinity for (*philanthropy*).

phi•lan•der•er (fi lan'dər ər) *n.* a man who has many love affairs. —**phi•lan'der**, *v.i.*

phi•lan•thro•py (fi lan'thrə pē), *n., pl.* **-pies. 1.** altruistic concern for human beings manifested by donations to institutions advancing human welfare. **2.** a philanthropic act or donation. **3.** a philanthropic institution. —**phil•an•throp•ic** (fil'ən-throp'ik), *adj.* —**phi•lan'thro•pist**, *n.*

phi•lat•e•ly (fi lat'l ē), *n.* the collection and study of postage stamps and related material. —**phil•a•tel•ic** (fil'ə tel'ik), *adj.* —**phi•lat'e•list**, *n.*

phil•har•mon•ic (fil'här mon'ik), *n.* (*often cap.*) a symphony orchestra.

Phil•ip•pines (fil'ə pēnz'), *n.pl.* a republic comprising an archipelago of 7083 islands (**Phil'ippine Is'lands**) in the Pacific, SE of China. —**Phil'ip•pine'**, *adj.*

phil•is•tine (fil'ə stēn', -stīn', fi lis'tin, -tēn), *n.* **1.** (*sometimes cap.*) a person lacking in or smugly indifferent to culture, aesthetic refinement, etc. **2.** (*cap.*) a member of a people who controlled SW Palestine from c1200 to 604 B.C.

phil•o•den•dron (fil'ə den'drən), *n., pl.* **-drons, -dra.** a tropical American climbing plant, grown as a houseplant.

phi•lol•o•gy (fi lol'ə jē), *n.* **1.** the study and analysis of literary works and other written records. **2.** (esp. in older use) linguistics, esp. historical and comparative linguistics. —**phil•o•log•i•cal** (fil'ə-loj'i kəl), *adj.* —**phi•lol'o•gist**, *n.*

phi•los•o•pher (fi los'ə fər), *n.* **1.** a student of or expert in philosophy. **2.** a person who regulates his or her life by the light of philosophy or reason. **3.** a person who is calm or rational under trying circumstances.

phi•los′o•phy *n., pl.* **-phies. 1.** the rational investigation of the truths and principles of being, knowledge, or conduct. **2.** a system of philosophical doctrine. **3.** the study of the basic concepts of a particular branch of knowledge: *the philosophy of science.* **4.** a system of principles for guidance in practical affairs: *a philosophy of life.* **5.** a calm or rational attitude. **—phil′o•soph′ic, phil•o•soph•i•cal** (fil′ə sof′i kəl), *adj.*

phle•bi•tis (flə bī′tis), *n.* inflammation of a vein.

phle•bot′o•my (-bot′ə mē) *n., pl.* **-mies.** the practice of opening a vein to draw blood as a therapeutic or diagnostic measure. **—phle•bot′o•mize,** *v.t.,* **-ized, -iz•ing.**

phlegm (flem), *n.* **1.** thick mucus secreted in the respiratory passages and discharged through the mouth, as during a cold. **2.** sluggishness or apathy.

phleg•mat•ic (fleg mat′ik), *adj.* having a calm or apathetic temperament.

phlo•em (flō′em), *n.* the complex vascular tissue through which dissolved food passes to all parts of a plant.

phlox (floks), *n., pl.* **phlox, phlox•es.** a North American plant, certain species of which are cultivated for their showy flowers.

pho•bi•a (fō′bē ə), *n., pl.* **-as.** a persistent, irrational fear of a specific object, activity, or situation. **—pho′bic,** *adj., n.*

-phobia a combining form meaning fear, dread, or aversion (*xenophobia*).

phoe•be (fē′bē), *n., pl.* **-bes.** any of several New World flycatchers.

phoe•nix (fē′niks), *n.* a fabulous bird that after a life of five centuries burns itself to death and rises from the ashes.

phone (fōn), *n., v.t., v.i.,* **phoned, phon•ing.** telephone.

pho•neme (fō′nēm), *n.* any of the minimal units of speech sound in a language that can distinguish one word from another. **—pho•ne′mic** (fə-, fō-), *adj.*

pho•net•ics (fə net′iks, fō-), *n.* the study of speech sounds and their production, classification, and transcription. **—pho•net′ic,** *adj.*

phon•ics (fon′iks), *n.* a method of teaching reading and spelling based upon the phonetic interpretation of ordinary spelling.

phono- a combining form meaning sound or voice (*phonology*).

pho•no•graph (fō′nə graf′, -gräf′), *n.* any sound-reproducing machine using records in the form of grooved disks. **—pho′no•graph′ic,** *adj.*

pho•nol•o•gy (fə nol′ə jē, fō-), *n., pl.* **-gies. 1.** the system of speech sounds of a language. **2.** the study of sound changes in a language. **—pho•no•log•i•cal** (fōn′l oj′i kəl), *adj.*

pho•ny or **-ney** (fō′nē), *adj.,* **-ni•er, -ni•est,** *n., pl.* **-nies** or **-neys.** *—adj.* **1.** not real or genuine; fake. **2.** false or deceiving. *—n.* **3.** something that is phony. **4.** an insincere or affected person. **—pho′ni•ness,** *n.*

phos′gene (fos′jēn) *n.* poisonous gas, COCl, used as a chemical-warfare compound.

phos′phate (fos′fāt) *n.* **1.** (loosely) a salt or ester of phosphoric acid. **2.** a fertilizer containing compounds of phosphorus. **3.** a carbonated drink of water and fruit syrup.

phos•phor (fos′fər, -fôr), *n.* a substance that exhibits luminescence when struck by light of certain wavelengths.

phos′pho•res′cent (-fə res′ənt) *adj.* luminous. **—phos′pho•res′cence,** *n.*

phos′pho•rus (-fər əs), *n., pl.* **-pho•ri** (-fə rī′). a nonmetallic element used, in combined form, in matches and fertilizers. *Symbol:* P; *at. wt.:* 30.974; *at. no.:* 15. **—phos•phor′ic** (-fôr′ik), **phos′pho•rous,** *adj.*

photo- a combining form meaning: light (*photograph*); photograph or photographic (*photoengraving*).

pho•to•cop•y (fō′tə kop′ē), *n., pl.* **-ies,** *v.,* **-ied, -y•ing.** *—n.* **1.** a photographic reproduction of a document or the like. *—v.t.* **2.** to make a photocopy of. **—pho′to•cop′i•er,** *n.*

pho•to•e•lec•tric (fō′tō i lek′trik), *adj.* pertaining to electronic effects produced by light.

pho′to•en•grav′ing *n.* a photographic process of preparing printing plates for letterpress printing.

pho′to fin′ish *n.* a finish of a race so close as to require scrutiny of a photograph to determine the winner.

pho•to•gen•ic (fō′tə jen′ik), *adj.* forming an appealing subject for photography or looking attractive in a photograph.

pho′to•graph′ *n.* **1.** a picture produced by photography. *—v.t.* **2.** to take a photograph of. *—v.i.* **3.** to be photographed.

pho•tog•ra•phy (fə tog′rə fē), *n.* the process or art of producing images of objects on sensitized surfaces by the chemical action of light. **—pho•tog′ra•pher,** *n.* **—pho•to•graph•ic** (fō′tə graf′ik), *adj.* **—pho′to•graph′i•cal•ly,** *adv.*

pho•ton (fō′ton), *n.* a quantum of electromagnetic radiation.

pho•to•sen•si•tive (fō′tə sen′si tiv), *adj.* sensitive to light or similar radiation.

Pho•to•stat (fō′tə stat′), *n., v.,* **-stat•ed** or **-stat•ted, -stat•ing** or **-stat•ting. 1.** *Trademark.* a camera for making facsimile copies of documents, drawings, etc., in the form of paper negatives. *—n.* **2.** (*often l.c.*) a copy so made. *—v.t.* **3.** (*l.c.*) to copy with this camera.

pho′to•syn′the•sis *n.* the production of carbohydrates from carbon dioxide and water, using sunlight as the source of energy and with the aid of chlorophyll.

phrase (frāz), *n., v.,* **phrased, phras•ing.** *—n.* **1.** a sequence of two or more grammatically related words that does not contain a subject and predicate. **2.** a brief utterance or remark. **3.** a division of a musical composition, commonly a passage of four or eight measures. *—v.t.* **4.** to express in a particular way. **5.** to express in words. **—phras′al,** *adj.*

phra•se•ol•o•gy (frā′zē ol′ə jē), *n.* style of verbal expression; characteristic language.

phre•nol•o•gy (fri nol′ə jē, fre-), *n.* a system of character analysis based upon the configurations of the skull.

phy•log•e•ny (fī loj′ə nē), *n.* the development or evolution of a particular group of organisms. **—phy•log′e•nist,** *n.*

phy•lum (fī′ləm), *n., pl.* **-la** (-lə). the primary subdivision of a taxonomic kingdom, grouping together all classes of organisms that have the same body plan.

phys•ic (fiz′ik), *n.* a medicine that purges.

phys′i•cal *adj.* **1.** of the body. **2.** of that which is material: *the physical universe.* **3.** of or noting the properties of matter and energy other than those peculiar to living matter. *—n.* **4.** an examination of one's body by a physician to determine one's state of health. **—phys′i•cal•ly,** *adv.*

phys′ical anthropol′ogy *n.* the branch of anthropology dealing with the evolutionary changes in human body structure and the classification of modern races.

phys′ical sci′ence *n.* any of the natural sciences dealing with inanimate matter or energy, as physics or chemistry.

phys′ical ther′apy *n.* the treatment of physical disability or pain by physical techniques, as exercise or massage. **—phys′ical ther′apist,** *n.*

phy•si•cian (fi zish′ən), *n.* a doctor of medicine.

phys•ics (fiz′iks), *n.* the science that deals with matter, energy, motion, and force. **—phys′i•cist** (-ə sist), *n.*

phys•i•og•no•my (fiz′ē og′nə mē, -on′ə-), *n., pl.* **-mies.** the face, esp. when considered as an index to character.

phys′i•og′ra•phy (-og′rə fē), *n.* the branch of geography concerned with natural features and phenomena of the earth's surface.

phys′i•ol′o•gy (-ol′ə jē), *n.* the branch of biology

dealing with the functions and activities of living organisms and their parts. —**phys′i•o•log′i•cal** (-ə loj′i kal), *adj.* —**phys′i•ol′o•gist,** *n.*

phys′i•o•ther′a•py (fiz′ē ō-), *n.* PHYSICAL THERAPY. —**phys′i•o•ther′a•pist,** *n.*

phy•sique (fi zēk′), *n.* bodily structure and appearance.

pi (pī), *n., pl.* **pis. 1.** the 16th letter of the Greek alphabet (Π, π). **2. a.** the letter π, used as the symbol for the ratio of the circumference of a circle to its diameter. **b.** the ratio itself: 3.14159 + .

pi•a•nis•si•mo (pē′ə nis′ə mō′, pyä-), *Music.* —*adj.* **1.** very soft. —*adv.* **2.** very softly.

pi•an•o¹ (pē an′ō, pyan′ō), *n., pl.* **-os.** a musical instrument in which felt-covered hammers, operated from a keyboard, strike metal strings. —**pi•an•ist** (pē an′ist, pyan′-, pē′ə nist), *n.*

pi•a•no² (pē ä′nō, pyä′-), *Music.* —*adj.* **1.** soft. —*adv.* **2.** softly.

pi•az•za (pē az′ə, *or, for 1,* -ät′sə), *n., pl.* **-zas. 1.** an open public square, esp. in Italy. **2.** *Chiefly New Eng. and Southern U.S.* a large porch.

pi•ca (pī′kə), *n., pl.* **-cas.** a 12-point type, widely used for typewriters, having 10 characters to the inch.

pic•a•resque (pik′ə resk′), *adj.* of or noting a form of prose fiction that humorously describes the adventures of a roguish hero.

pic•a•yune (pik′ē yōōn′, pik′ə-), *adj.* **1.** of little value or account. **2.** petty, carping, or prejudiced.

pic•ca•lil•li (pik′ə lil′ē), *n., pl.* **-lis.** a relish of chopped vegetables, mustard, vinegar, and hot spices.

pic•co•lo (pik′ə lō′), *n., pl.* **-los.** a small flute sounding an octave higher than the ordinary flute. [< It: lit., small]

pick¹ (pik), *v.t.* **1.** to choose or select. **2.** to provoke: *to pick a fight.* **3.** to steal the contents of: *to pick a pocket.* **4.** to open (a lock) with a device other than the key. **5.** to pierce, dig into, or break up with a pointed instrument. **6.** to use a pointed instrument or the fingers on to remove adhering matter: *to pick one's teeth.* **7.** to prepare by removing feathers: *to pick a fowl.* **8.** to detach piece by piece with the fingers: *to pick meat from the bones.* **9.** to pluck one by one: *to pick flowers.* **10.** to separate or pull to pieces: *to pick fibers.* **11.** to pluck (the strings of a musical instrument). —*v.i.* **12.** to use a pointed instrument on something. **13.** to select carefully or fastidiously. **14. pick at,** to eat sparingly. **15. ~ off, a.** to remove by plucking off. **b.** to single out and shoot. **16. ~ on,** to criticize, tease, or harass. **17. ~ out,** to select. **18. ~ up, a.** to lift or take up. **b.** to obtain or learn casually. **c.** to take on as a passenger. **d.** to accelerate. **e.** to improve. **f.** to become acquainted with casually, often in hope of a sexual relationship. —*n.* **19.** the act of choosing. **20.** a person or thing selected. **21.** the choicest part or example.

pick² (pik), *n.* **1.** a heavy tool with a curved metal head pointed at one or both ends, mounted on a handle, and used for breaking up soil, rock, etc. **2.** any of various other pointed tools for picking: *an ice pick.* **3.** a small piece of metal, plastic, etc., for picking the strings of a musical instrument.

pick•er•el (pik′ər əl), *n., pl.* **-els, -el.** any of several small pikes.

pick•et (pik′it), *n.* **1.** a stake driven into the ground for use in a fence or to fasten down a tent. **2.** a person stationed by a striking union outside a factory, store, etc., to dissuade workers or customers from entering. **3.** a person engaged in any similar demonstration. **4.** a soldier or soldiers posted to warn against an enemy advance. —*v.t.* **5.** to enclose within a picket fence. **6.** to tether to a picket. **7.** to place pickets at (a factory, embassy, etc.). **8.** to guard with pickets. —*v.i.* **9.** to stand or march as a picket. —**pick′et•er,** *n.*

pick′et line′ *n.* a line of strikers or other pickets.

pick•le (pik′əl), *n., v.,* **-led, -ling.** —*n.* **1.** a vegetable, esp. a cucumber, that has been preserved and flavored in brine, vinegar, or the like. **2.** a brine or marinade. **3.** a troublesome situation; predicament.

—*v.t.* **4.** to preserve or steep in brine or other liquid.

pick′pock′et *n.* a person who steals from people's pockets, purses, etc., as in a crowd.

pick′up′ *n.* **1.** an improvement, as in health or business. **2.** a casual acquaintance, as one offering hope of a sexual encounter. **3.** acceleration, or the capacity for acceleration. **4.** a small truck with a low-sided open body. **5.** a device in a phonograph that translates the movement of the stylus into a changing electrical voltage.

pick′y *adj.* **-i•er, -i•est.** extremely fussy or finicky.

pic•nic (pik′nik), *n., v.,* **-nicked, -nick•ing.** —*n.* **1.** an excursion in which the participants eat a meal in the open air. —*v.i.* **2.** to go on a picnic. —**pic′nick•er,** *n.*

pi•cot (pē′kō), *n.* one of a number of small decorative loops along the edge of lace, ribbon, etc.

pic•to•ri•al (pik tôr′ē əl), *adj.* **1.** of or expressed in pictures. **2.** having the visual appeal or imagery of a picture. —**pic•to′ri•al•ly,** *adv.*

pic•ture (pik′chər), *n., v.,* **-tured, -tur•ing.** —*n.* **1.** a visual representation of a person, object, or scene, as a painting or photograph. **2.** a graphic or vivid description. **3.** MOTION PICTURE (def. 2). **4.** the perfect likeness of someone else: *She is the picture of her father.* **5.** a concrete embodiment of some quality or condition: *the picture of health.* **6.** a situation or set of circumstances: *the economic picture.* **7.** the image on a television or motion-picture screen. —*v.t.* **8.** to represent pictorially. **9.** to form a mental picture of. **10.** to describe graphically.

pic′tur•esque′ (-chə resk′), *adj.* visually charming, as if resembling a painting.

pid′dling *adj.* trifling; negligible.

pidg•in (pij′ən), *n.* an auxiliary language that has developed from the need of speakers of two different languages to communicate and is primarily a simplified form of one of the languages.

pidg′in Eng′lish *n.* English trade jargon used in other countries.

pie (pī), *n.* **1.** a pastry crust filled with fruit, meat, etc., and baked, often with a top crust. —*Idiom.* **2. easy as pie,** extremely easy.

pie•bald (pī′bôld′), *adj.* **1.** having patches of two colors. —*n.* **2.** a piebald animal.

piece (pēs), *n., v.,* **pieced, piec•ing.** —*n.* **1.** a quantity of some material forming a separate entity. **2.** a portion or quantity of a whole: *a piece of pie.* **3.** an artistic work, as a painting or musical composition. **4.** an example, specimen, or instance of something. —*v.t.* **5.** to mend by adding a piece or pieces. **6.** to make by or as if by joining pieces. —*Idiom.* **7. go to pieces, a.** to break into fragments. **b.** to lose control of oneself.

pièce de ré•sis•tance (pyes də RĀ zē stäns′), *n., pl.* **pièces de ré•sis•tance** (pyes də RĀ zē stäns′), *French.* **1.** the principal dish of a meal. **2.** the principal item of a series.

piece′ goods′ *n.pl.* goods, esp. fabrics, sold at retail by linear measure.

piece′meal′ *adv.* **1.** one piece at a time. —*adj.* **2.** done piecemeal.

piece′work′ *n.* work done and paid for by the piece.

pie′ chart′ *n.* a data display in which sectors of a circle correspond in area to the relative size of the quantities represented.

pied (pīd), *adj.* having patches of two or more colors.

pied-à-terre (pyā′də târ′, -dä-), *n., pl.* **pieds-à-terre** (pyā′də târ′, -dä-). an apartment for part-time use. [< F: lit., foot on ground]

pie′-eyed′ *adj. Slang.* intoxicated.

pier (pēr), *n.* **1.** a structure built on posts over water, used as a landing place for ships, an entertainment area, etc. **2.** (in a bridge or the like) a support for the ends of adjacent spans. **3.** a pillar or post on which a gate or door is hung. **4.** a support of masonry or steel for sustaining vertical pressure.

pierce (pērs), *v.,* **pierced, pierc•ing.** —*v.t.* **1.** to penetrate (something), as a pointed object does. **2.** to make a hole in. **3.** to force a way into or through. **4.** to penetrate with the eye or mind. **5.** to sound sharply through (the air, stillness, etc.), as a cry. —*v.i.* **6.** to force a way into or through something.

pi•e•ty (pī′i tē), *n.*, *pl.* **-ties. 1.** reverence for God or devout fulfillment of religious obligations. **2.** dutiful respect for parents, homeland, etc. **3.** a pious act, belief, etc.

pif•fle (pif′əl), *n. Informal.* nonsense, as idle talk. —**pif′fling,** *adj.*

pig (pig), *n.*, *v.*, **pigged, pig•ging.** —*n.* **1.** any swine, esp. a young domesticated hog weighing less than 120 lb. (54 kg). **2.** a person who is gluttonous or slovenly. **3.** an oblong mass of metal run while still molten into a mold. —*v.* **4. pig out,** *Slang.* to overindulge in eating. —**pig′gish,** *adj.*

pi•geon (pij′ən), *n.* **1.** any of numerous birds having a plump body and small head. **2.** *Slang.* a person who is easily fooled or cheated.

pi′geon•hole′ *n.*, *v.*, **-holed, -hol•ing.** —*n.* **1.** one of a series of small, open compartments, as in a desk, for filing papers, letters, etc. —*v.t.* **2.** to assign to a definite place in an orderly system. **3.** to put aside for the present. **4.** to place in a pigeonhole.

pi′geon-toed′ *adj.* having the toes or feet turned inward.

pig′gy•back′ *adv.* **1.** on the back or shoulders. —*adj.* **2.** astride the back or shoulders. **3.** attached to or allied with something else: *a piggyback clause.* **4.** noting or pertaining to the carrying of truck trailers on flatcars.

pig′head′ed *adj.* stupidly obstinate.

pig′ i′ron *n.* iron cast into pigs for conversion into steel, cast iron, etc.

pig′let *n.* baby pig.

pig•ment (pig′mənt), *n.* **1.** a coloring matter or substance. **2.** a biological substance that produces color in the tissues of organisms. —**pig′men•tar′y,** *adj.*

pig′men•ta′tion *n.* coloration with or deposition of pigment.

pig′my (-mē) *n.*, *pl.* **-mies.** PYGMY.

pig′pen′ *n.* **1.** a pen for keeping pigs. **2.** a filthy or flagrantly untidy place.

pig′tail′ *n.* a braid of hair hanging down the back of the head.

pike¹ (pīk), *n.*, *pl.* **pikes, pike.** a large, slender, freshwater fish with a long, flat snout.

pike² (pīk), *n.* a shafted weapon with a pointed head, formerly used by infantry.

pike³ (pīk), *n.* a turnpike.

pik′er *n.* a person who does anything in a contemptibly small or cheap way.

pi•laf (pē′läf, pi läf′), *n.* a Middle Eastern dish of rice cooked in bouillon.

pi•las•ter (pi las′tər), *n.* a shallow rectangular feature projecting from a wall, usu. imitating the form of a column.

pil•chard (pil′chərd), *n.* a marine fish, related to the herring but smaller and rounder.

pile¹ (pīl), *n.*, *v.*, **piled, pil•ing.** —*n.* **1.** an assemblage of things lying one upon the other. **2.** a large amount of anything. **3.** a pyre. **4.** a large building or group of buildings. —*v.t.* **5.** to lay or dispose in a pile. **6.** to accumulate (often fol. by *up*). **7.** to cover or load with a pile. —*v.i.* **8.** to accumulate (usu. fol. by *up*). **9.** to move as a group in a confused, disorderly cluster: *They piled off the train.*

pile² (pīl), *n.* a long beam of wood, steel, etc., hammered vertically into soil to form part of a foundation or retaining wall.

pile³ (pīl), *n.* a soft surface on cloth, rugs, etc., formed by upright yarns that have been cut straight across or left standing in loops. —**piled,** *adj.*

pile⁴ (pīl), *n.* Usu., **piles.** HEMORRHOID.

pil•fer (pil′fər), *v.i.*, *v.t.* to steal, esp. in small quantities. —**pil′fer•age** (-ij), *n.* —**pil′fer•er,** *n.*

pil•grim (pil′grim, -grəm), *n.* **1.** a person who journeys to some sacred place as an act of religious devotion. **2.** a traveler or wanderer. **3.** (*cap.*) one of the band of Puritans who founded the colony of Plymouth, Mass., in 1620.

pil′grim•age (-grə mij), *n.* **1.** a journey of a pilgrim. **2.** any long journey.

pill (pil), *n.* **1.** a small tablet or capsule of medicine. **2.** *Slang.* a tiresomely disagreeable person. **3. the pill,** (*sometimes cap.*) an oral contraceptive.

pil•lage (pil′ij), *v.*, **-laged, -lag•ing,** *n.* —*v.t.*, *v.i.* **1.** to strip of money or goods by violence, as in war. —*n.* **2.** the act of plundering. **3.** booty or spoil.

pil•lar (pil′ər), *n.* **1.** an upright, slender structure used as a building support or as a monument. **2.** a person who is a chief supporter of a state, institution, etc.

pill′box′ *n.* **1.** a small box for holding pills. **2.** a small, boxlike fortification for machine guns or antitank weapons.

pil•lo•ry (pil′ə rē), *n.*, *pl.* **-ries,** *v.*, **-ried, -ry•ing.** —*n.* **1.** a wooden framework with holes for securing the head and hands, formerly used to expose an offender to public derision. —*v.t.* **2.** to set in the pillory. **3.** to expose to public derision.

pil•low (pil′ō), *n.* **1.** a cloth case filled with soft material, used to cushion the head during sleep. **2.** a similar cushion used for decoration, as on a sofa. —*v.t.* **3.** to rest on or as if on a pillow. **4.** to serve as a pillow for. —**pil′low•case′,** *n.*

pi•lot (pī′lət), *n.* **1.** a person qualified to operate an aircraft. **2.** a person qualified to steer ships into or out of a harbor. **3.** a person who steers a ship. **4.** a guide or leader. **5.** a television program serving to introduce a possible new series. —*v.t.* **6.** to act as pilot on, in, or over. **7.** to lead or guide. —*adj.* **8.** serving as a trial undertaking prior to full-scale operation or use.

pi′lot light′ *n.* a small flame burning continuously, as in a gas stove, to relight the main burners.

pi•men•to (pi men′tō), *n.*, *pl.* **-tos.** the red, mild-flavored fruit of a sweet pepper.

pi•mien′to (-myen′tō, -men′-), *n.*, *pl.* **-tos.** PIMENTO.

pimp (pimp), *n.* **1.** a person who solicits customers for a prostitute. —*v.i.* **2.** to act as a pimp.

pim•ple (pim′pəl), *n.* a small, usu. inflammatory swelling of the skin. —**pim′ply,** *adj.*, **-pli•er, -pli•est.**

pin (pin), *n.*, *v.*, **pinned, pin•ning.** —*n.* **1.** a small, slender, often pointed piece of metal, wood, etc., used as a fastener or support. **2.** a short, slender piece of wire with a point at one end, used for fastening things together. **3.** an ornament or badge consisting essentially or partly of a penetrating wire. **4.** one of the rounded wooden clubs set up as the target in bowling. —*v.t.* **5.** to fasten with or as if with a pin. **6.** to hold fast in a spot or position. **7. pin down,** to force (someone) to deal with a situation or come to a decision. —*Idiom.* **8. pin something on someone,** *Informal.* to ascribe the blame for something to a person.

PIN (pin), *n.* an identification number assigned to an individual to gain access to a computer system via an ATM or other device.

pin•a•fore (pin′ə fôr′), *n.* a sleeveless, apronlike garment worn over a dress or with a blouse.

pin′ball′ *n.* a game in which a spring-driven ball is shot to the top of a sloping board and rolls down against pins and through holes that record one's score.

pince-nez (pans′nā′, pins′-), *n.*, *pl.* **pince-nez.** a pair of glasses held on the face by a spring that grips the nose.

pin•cers (pin′sərz), *n.* (*usu. with a pl. v.*) **1.** a gripping tool consisting of a pair of jaws and a pair of handles. **2.** a grasping organ, as the claw of a lobster.

pinch (pinch), *v.t.* **1.** to squeeze between the finger and thumb, the jaws of an instrument, etc. **2.** to squeeze painfully, as a tight shoe does. **3.** to make unnaturally constricted: *a face pinched with fear.* **4.** to affect with sharp discomfort or distress, as hunger does. **5.** *Slang.* **a.** to steal. **b.** to arrest. —*v.i.* **6.** to squeeze painfully. **7.** to economize unduly. —*n.* **8.** the act of pinching. **9.** an amount taken up between the finger and thumb. **10.** sharp or painful stress. **11.** an emergency. —*Idiom.* **12. pinch pennies,** to be frugal with expenditures.

pinch′-hit′ *v.i.,* **-hit, -hit•ting. 1.** to substitute at bat for a teammate in baseball. **2.** to substitute for someone in an emergency. —**pinch′ hit′ter,** *n.*

pine¹ (pīn), *n.* **1.** an evergreen tree with needlelike leaves and woody cones enclosing winged seeds. **2.** the wood of a pine.

pine² (pīn), *v.i.,* **pined, pin•ing. 1.** to yearn deeply. **2.** to fail in health or vitality from grief, regret, etc.

pine′ap′ple *n.* **1.** the edible, juicy fruit of a tropical plant having spiny-edged leaves. **2.** the plant itself.

pin′feath′er *n.* an undeveloped feather just coming through the skin.

ping (ping), *v.i.* **1.** to produce a sharp sound like that of a bullet striking metal. —*n.* **2.** a pinging sound.

ping-pong (ping′pong′, -pông′), *v.t., v.i.* to move back and forth.

Ping′-Pong′ *Trademark.* TABLE TENNIS.

pin′head′ *n.* **1.** the head of a pin. **2.** a stupid person.

pin•ion¹ (pin′yən), *n.* a gear with a small number of teeth that engages a rack or larger gear.

pin•ion² (pin′yən), *n.* **1.** the terminal segment of a bird's wing. **2.** the wing of a bird. —*v.t.* **3.** to cut off the pinion of (a wing) or bind (the wings), as to prevent a bird from flying. **4.** to bind (a person's arms or hands) so they cannot be used.

pink¹ (pingk), *n., adj.,* **-er, -est.** —*n.* **1.** a pale reddish purple. **2.** any of several garden plants with pink, white, or red flowers resembling carnations. **3.** the highest form or degree: *in the pink of condition.* **4.** *Slang (disparaging).* a person with mildly left-wing political opinions. —*adj.* **5.** of the color pink. **6.** *Slang (disparaging).* mildly left-wing.

pink² (pingk), *v.t.* **1.** to pierce with a rapier or the like. **2.** to cut (fabric) at the edge with a notched pattern.

pink′eye′ *n.* a contagious, epidemic form of acute conjunctivitis.

pink′ing shears′ *n.* (*used with a pl. v.*) shears with notched blades, for simultaneously cutting and pinking fabric.

pin′ mon′ey *n.* any small sum set aside for minor expenditures.

pin•na•cle (pin′ə kəl), *n.* **1.** the highest or culminating point, as of success. **2.** any pointed, towering formation, as of rock. **3.** a relatively small upright structure, commonly terminating in a pyramid or cone.

pin•nate (pin′āt, -it), *adj.* (of a leaf) having leaflets on each side of a common stalk.

pi•noch•le (pē′nuk əl, -nok-), *n.* a card game played with a 48-card deck.

pin′point′ *v.t.* to locate or describe exactly.

pin′stripe′ *n.* a very thin stripe in fabrics. —**pin′-striped′,** *adj.*

pint (pīnt), *n.* a liquid and dry measure of capacity, equal to one half of a quart, approximately 35 cubic inches (0.6 liter).

pin•to (pin′tō, pēn′-), *adj., n., pl.* **-tos.** —*adj.* **1.** marked with spots of white and other colors. —*n.* **2.** a pinto horse.

pinto bean *n.* a bean with pinkish mottled seeds.

pin′up′ *n.* **1.** a large photograph of a sexually attractive person, suitable for pinning on a wall. **2.** a person in such a photograph. —*adj.* **3.** of, suitable for, or appearing in a pinup.

pin′wheel′ *n.* **1.** a toy consisting of a wheel with vanes attached to a stick, designed to revolve when blown. **2.** a firework that makes a wheel of sparks.

pin•yin (pin′yin′), *n.* (*sometimes cap.*) a system for transliterating Chinese into the Latin alphabet.

pi•o•neer (pī′ə nēr′), *n.* **1.** a person who is among those who first enter or settle a region. **2.** one who is among the earliest in any field of inquiry, enterprise, etc. —*v.i.* **3.** to act as a pioneer. —*v.t.* **4.** to be a pioneer of or in. [< MF < OF *peonier* foot soldier]

pi•ous (pī′əs), *adj.* **1.** having or showing reverence for God or an earnest wish to fulfill religious obliga-

tions. **2.** characterized by a hypocritical concern with virtue or religious devotion. —**pi′ous•ly,** *adv.*

pip¹ (pip), *n.* one of the spots on dice, playing cards, or dominoes.

pip² (pip), *n.* a small seed of a fleshy fruit, as an orange.

pipe (pīp), *n., v.,* **piped, pip•ing.** —*n.* **1.** a hollow cylinder, as of metal, used to convey water, gas, etc. **2.** a tube with a small bowl at one end, used for smoking tobacco, opium, etc. **3. a.** a musical wind instrument, as a flute, constructed of a single tube. **b.** one of the tubes from which the tones of an organ are produced. **c. pipes,** BAGPIPE. **4.** a tubular organ or passage. —*v.i.* **5.** to play on a pipe. **6.** to utter a shrill sound like that of a pipe. —*v.t.* **7.** to convey by or as if by pipes. **8.** to play (music) on a pipe. **9.** to utter in a shrill tone. **10. pipe down,** *Slang.* to stop talking; be quiet. **11. pipe up,** to make oneself heard, esp. as to assert oneself.

pipe′ dream′ *n.* an unrealistic hope or plan.

pipe′line′ *n.* **1.** a linked series of pipes used to transport crude oil, water, etc., over great distances. **2.** a route along which supplies pass. **3.** a channel of information.

pip′ing *n.* **1.** pipes collectively. **2.** a shrill sound. **3.** the music of pipes. **4.** a narrow band of ornamental material used for trimming the edges of clothing, upholstery, etc. —*Idiom.* **5. piping hot,** (of food or drink) very hot.

pip•pin (pip′in), *n.* any of numerous varieties of apple.

pip•squeak (pip′skwēk′), *n. Informal.* a small or unimportant person.

pi•quant (pē′kənt, -känt), *adj.* **1.** agreeably pungent in taste. **2.** interestingly provocative. —**pi′-quan•cy,** *n.*

pique (pēk), *v.,* **piqued, piqu•ing,** *n.* —*v.t.* **1.** to affect with sharp irritation and resentment. **2.** to excite or arouse. —*n.* **3.** a feeling of irritation or resentment.

pi•qué or **-que** (pi kā′, pē-), *n., pl.* **-qués** or **-ques.** a fabric of cotton, rayon, or silk, woven with lengthwise cords or with an overall design.

pi•ra•cy (pī′rə sē), *n., pl.* **-cies. 1.** robbery or illegal violence at sea. **2.** the unauthorized reproduction or use of copyrighted material, a patented invention, etc.

pi•ra•nha (pi rän′yə, -ran′-, -rä′nə, -ran′ə), *n., pl.* **-nhas, -nha.** any of several small, predatory South American freshwater fishes with sharp interlocking teeth: dangerous when swimming in schools.

pi•rate (pī′rət), *n., v.,* **-rat•ed, -rat•ing.** —*n.* **1.** a person who practices piracy. —*v.t.* **2.** to take by piracy. **3.** to use or reproduce (a book, invention, etc.) without authorization or legal right.

pir•ou•ette (pir′ŏŏ et′), *n., v.,* **-et•ted, -et•ting.** —*n.* **1.** a whirling about on one foot or on the points of the toes, as in ballet dancing. —*v.i.* **2.** to perform a pirouette.

pis•tach•i•o (pi stash′ē ō′, -stä′shē ō′), *n., pl.* **-os. 1.** Also, **pistach′io nut′.** the nut of a Eurasian tree containing an edible, greenish kernel. **2.** the tree itself.

pis•til (pis′tl), *n.* the seed-bearing organ of a flower. —**pis′til•late** (-it, -āt′), *adj.*

pis•tol (pis′tl), *n.* a short firearm held and fired with one hand.

pis′tol-whip′ *v.t.,* **-whipped, -whip•ping.** to beat with a pistol.

pis•ton (pis′tən), *n.* a disk or cylinder moving within a longer cylinder and exerting pressure on, or receiving pressure from, a fluid or gas.

pit¹ (pit), *n., v.,* **pit•ted, pit•ting.** —*n.* **1.** a deep hole in the ground. **2.** a trap; pitfall. **3. the pits,** *Slang.* a very unpleasant place, condition, etc. **4.** a hollow or indentation in a surface, as of the body. **5.** POCKMARK. **6.** an enclosure for staging fights, esp. between dogs or cocks. **7.** ORCHESTRA (def. 2a). **8.** an area at a racing track for servicing and refueling the cars. —*v.t.* **9.** to mark or indent with pits. **10.** to set in opposition or combat. —*v.i.* **11.** to become marked with pits.

pit² (pit), *n., v.,* **pit•ted, pit•ting.** —*n.* **1.** the stone of a fruit, as of a cherry. —*v.t.* **2.** to remove the pit from.

pi•ta (pē′tä, -tə), *n.*, *pl.* **-tas.** a round, flat Middle Eastern bread having a pocket that can be filled to make a sandwich. Also called **pi′ta bread′.**

pitch[1] (pich), *v.t.* **1.** to set up (a tent, camp, etc.). **2.** to put or set in a fixed place. **3.** to throw or toss. **4.** *Baseball.* **a.** to throw (the ball) to the batter. **b.** to serve as pitcher of (a game). **5.** to set at a certain point, degree, etc. —*v.i.* **6.** to fall forward or headlong. **7.** *Baseball.* **a.** to throw the ball to the batter. **b.** to serve as pitcher. **8.** to slope downward; dip. **9.** to plunge with alternate fall and rise of bow and stern. **10.** **pitch in,** *Informal.* to contribute to a common cause. —*n.* **11.** relative point or degree: *a high pitch of excitement.* **12.** the degree of slope. **13.** the degree of height or depth of a tone or of sound. **14.** the act or manner of pitching. **15.** a throw or toss. **16.** *Informal.* a sales talk.

pitch[2] (pich), *n.* **1.** any of various dark, viscous substances for caulking and paving, distilled from coal tar or wood tar.

pitch′-black′ *adj.* extremely black.

pitch′-dark′ *adj.* extremely dark.

pitched *adj.* fought with all available troops.

pitch′er[1] *n.* a container, usu. with a handle and spout or lip, for holding and pouring liquids.

pitch′er[2] *n. Baseball.* the player who throws the ball to the batter.

pitch′fork′ *n.* a large, long-handled fork for lifting and pitching hay, stalks of grain, etc.

pitch′ pipe′ *n.* a small pipe producing one or more pitches when blown into.

pit•e•ous (pit′ē əs), *adj.* evoking or deserving pity; pathetic.

pit′fall′ *n.* **1.** a lightly covered and unnoticeable pit for trapping people or animals. **2.** any danger for the unwary.

pith (pith), *n.* **1.** the soft, spongy central tissue in the stems of dicotyledonous plants. **2.** the important or essential part.

pith′y *adj.,* **-i•er, -i•est. 1.** brief, forceful, and meaningful in expression. **2.** of, like, or abounding in pith. —**pith′i•ly,** *adv.*

pit′i•a•ble (pit′ē ə bəl) *adj.* **1.** deserving pity. **2.** contemptible. —**pit′i•a•bly,** *adv.*

pit•i•ful (pit′i fəl), *adj.* **1.** evoking or deserving pity. **2.** arousing contempt by smallness, poor quality, etc. —**pit′i•ful•ly,** *adv.*

pit′i•less *adj.* feeling or showing no pity; merciless. —**pit′i•less•ly,** *adv.*

pit•tance (pit′ns), *n.* **1.** a small amount or share. **2.** a small allowance of money.

pi•tu′i•tary gland′ (pi too′i ter′ē, -tyoo′-), *n.* the master endocrine gland, attached to the base of the brain, affecting all hormonal functions of the body.

pit•y (pit′ē), *n., pl.* **-ies,** *v.,* **-ied, -y•ing.** —*n.* **1.** sympathetic sorrow evoked by the suffering of another. **2.** a cause or reason for pity, sorrow, or regret. —*v.t., v.i.* **3.** to feel pity (for).

piv•ot (piv′ət), *n.* **1.** a pin or short shaft on which something turns or around which something rotates. **2.** a person or thing on which something depends. **3.** a whirling around on one foot. —*v.i.* **4.** to turn on or as if on a pivot. —*v.t.* **5.** to provide with a pivot. —**piv′ot•al,** *adj.*

pix•el (pik′səl, -sel), *n.* the smallest element of an image that can be individually processed in a video display system.

pix•ie (pik′sē), *n.* a mischievous fairy or sprite.

pi•zazz or **piz•zazz** (pə zaz′), *n. Informal.* **1.** energy; vigor. **2.** dash; flair.

piz•za (pēt′sə), *n., pl.* **-zas.** a baked, open-faced pie consisting of a thin layer of dough topped with tomato sauce, cheese, etc.

piz′ze•ri′a (-rē′ə), *n., pl.* **-as.** a place where pizzas are made and sold.

piz•zi•ca•to (pit′si kä′tō), *adj. Music.* played by plucking the strings with the finger, as on a violin.

pkg. package.

pkwy. parkway.

pl. 1. place. **2.** plural.

P/L profit and loss.

plac′a•ble (plak′ə bəl, plā′kə-) *adj.* forgiving.

plac•ard (plak′ärd, -ərd), *n.* **1.** a sign or notice, as one posted in a public place. —*v.t.* **2.** to display placards on or in.

pla•cate (plā′kāt, plak′āt), *v.t.,* **-cat•ed, -cat•ing.** to appease or pacify. —**pla•ca′tion,** *n.*

place (plās), *n., v.,* **placed, plac•ing.** —*n.* **1.** a particular portion of space, as that occupied by a person or thing. **2.** any part of a body or surface. **3.** a space or seat for a person, as in a theater. **4.** position or situation. **5.** a proper or appropriate location, position, or time. **6.** a post or office. **7.** a function or duty. **8.** a region or area of habitation. **9.** a short street or court. **10.** a building, location, etc., set aside for a specific purpose. **11.** a residence or dwelling. **12.** lieu; substitution: *Use milk in place of cream.* **13.** a step or point in order of proceeding: *in the first place.* **14.** the position of the competitor who comes in second in a horse race. —*v.t.* **15.** to put in a particular position, situation, or condition. **16.** to put in a suitable place for some purpose: *to place an ad.* **17.** to appoint to a post or office. **18.** to find employment or living quarters for. **19.** to assign a certain position or rank to. **20.** to identify: *to place a face.* **21.** to make (a bet, phone call, etc.). —*v.i.* **22.** to finish second in a horse race. **23.** to earn a specified standing, as in a competition.

pla•ce•bo (plə sē′bō), *n., pl.* **-bos, -boes.** a substance having no pharmacological effect but given to placate a patient or as a control in testing a drug.

place′ment *n.* **1.** the act of placing or state of being placed. **2.** location; arrangement.

pla•cen•ta (plə sen′tə), *n., pl.* **-tas, -tae** (-tē). the organ in the lining of the uterus that provides for the nourishment of the fetus. —**pla•cen′tal,** *adj.*

plac•id (plas′id), *adj.* pleasantly calm or peaceful. —**pla•cid•i•ty** (plə sid′i tē), *n.* —**plac′id•ly,** *adv.*

plack•et (plak′it), *n.* a slit at the neck, waist, or wrist of a garment for ease in putting it on or taking it off.

pla•gia•rize (plā′jə rīz′), *v.t., v.i.,* **-rized, -riz•ing.** to take and use (ideas, passages, etc.) from (another's work), representing them as one's own. —**pla′gia•rism,** *n.* —**pla′gia•rist,** *n.*

plague (plāg), *n., v.,* **plagued, pla•guing.** —*n.* **1.** an epidemic disease that causes high mortality. **2.** any widespread affliction or calamity. —*v.t.* **3.** to torment in any manner. **4.** to smite with a plague.

plaid (plad), *n.* **1.** any fabric woven of differently colored yarns in a cross-barred pattern. **2.** a pattern of this kind.

plain (plān), *adj.,* **-er, -est,** *adv., n.* —*adj.* **1.** clear or distinct to the eye or ear. **2.** easily understood. **3.** sheer; utter: *plain stupidity.* **4.** free from ambiguity or evasion: *the plain truth.* **5.** without pretensions; ordinary: *plain people.* **6.** not beautiful: *a plain face.* **7.** without intricacies. **8.** with little or no decoration. —*adv.* **9.** clearly and simply. —*n.* **10.** an area of land with relatively minor differences in elevation. —**plain′ly,** *adv.* —**plain′ness,** *n.*

plain′clothes′man *n., pl.* **-men.** a police officer who wears ordinary civilian clothes while on duty.

plain′song′ *n.* the ancient traditional unisonal music of the Christian Church.

plaint (plānt), *n.* **1.** a complaint. **2.** a lament.

plain•tiff (plān′tif), *n.* one who brings a suit in a court.

plain•tive (plān′tiv), *adj.* expressing sorrow or melancholy; mournful. —**plain′tive•ly,** *adv.*

plait (plāt, plat), *n.* **1.** a braid, esp. of hair or straw. **2.** a pleat. —*v.t.* **3.** to braid. **4.** to pleat.

plan (plan), *n., v.,* **planned, plan•ning.** —*n.* **1.** a scheme or method of acting, proceeding, etc., developed in advance. **2.** a drawing made to scale to represent a horizontal section of a structure or machine. **3.** an outline, diagram, or sketch. —*v.t.* **4.** to formulate a plan for. **5.** to draw a plan of, as a building. **6.** to have in mind as an intention. —*v.i.* **7.** to make plans. —**plan′ner,** *n.*

plane[1] (plān), *n.* **1.** a flat or level surface. **2.** *Geom.* a surface generated by a straight line moving at a constant velocity with respect to a fixed point. **3.** a level of dignity, character, etc.: *a high moral plane.*

4. an airplane or hydroplane. —*adj.* **5.** flat or level. **6.** of planes or plane figures. —**pla•nar** (plā′nər), *adj.*

plane² (plān), *n.*, *v.*, **planed, plan•ing.** —*n.* **1.** a woodworking instrument for paring, truing, or smoothing. —*v.t.* **2.** to smooth or dress with a plane.

plan•et (plan′it), *n.* **1.** any of the nine large heavenly bodies revolving about the sun. **2.** a similar body revolving about a star other than the sun. —**plan′e•tar′y** (-i ter′ē), *adj.*

plan′e•tar′i•um (-i târ′ē əm), *n.*, *pl.* **-i•ums, -i•a** (-ē ə). **1.** a model representing the planetary system. **2.** a device that simulates the heavens by use of moving projectors. **3.** the building or room housing such a device.

plane′ tree′ *n.* any of several large, spreading shade trees, esp. the North American sycamore.

plan•gent (plan′jənt), *adj.* resounding loudly, esp. with a plaintive sound.

plank (plangk), *n.* **1.** a long, flat piece of timber, thicker than a board. **2.** one of the principles or objectives in the platform of a political party. —*v.t.* **3.** to lay or cover with planks. **4.** to bake or broil and serve (steak, fish, etc.) on a board. **5.** PLUNK (def. 2).

plank•ton (plangk′tən), *n.* the passively floating organisms in a body of water, primarily comprising microscopic algae and protozoa.

plant (plant, plänt), *n.* **1.** a multicellular organism that produces food from sunlight and inorganic matter by photosynthesis and has rigid cell walls containing cellulose. **2.** an herb or other small vegetable growth, in contrast with a tree or shrub. **3.** the buildings, equipment, etc., necessary to carry on any industrial business. —*v.t.* **4.** to put in the ground for growth. **5.** to establish or implant (ideas, principles, etc.). **6.** to place or set firmly. **7.** to place or station covertly or for purposes of deception: *to plant a spy.*

plan•tain¹ (plan′tin, -tn), *n.* **1.** a tropical plant resembling the banana. **2.** its fruit.

plan•tain² (plan′tin, -tn), *n.* a weed with large, spreading basal leaves and long spikes of small flowers.

plan•ta•tion (plan tā′shən), *n.* **1.** a large estate, esp. in a tropical country, on which crops are cultivated, usu. by resident laborers. **2.** a group of planted trees.

plant′er *n.* **1.** an implement for planting seeds. **2.** the owner or manager of a plantation. **3.** a container for growing ornamental plants.

plaque (plak), *n.* **1.** a thin, flat plate or tablet of metal, porcelain, etc., intended for ornament, as on a wall. **2.** an inscribed commemorative tablet, as on a monument. **3.** a soft, sticky film formed on tooth surfaces.

plas•ma (plaz′mə), *n.* **1.** the fluid part of blood or lymph. **2.** a highly ionized gas containing an approximately equal number of positive ions and electrons.

plas•ter (plas′tər, plä′stər), *n.* **1.** a composition, as of lime, sand, and water, applied in a pasty form to walls, ceilings, etc., and allowed to harden and dry. **2.** PLASTER OF PARIS. **3.** a preparation spread on cloth and applied to the body for some healing purpose. —*v.t.* **4.** to cover or fill with plaster. **5.** to lay flat (often fol. by *down*). **6.** to apply a plaster to (the body). **7.** to overspread with something, esp. excessively: *to plaster a wall with posters.* —**plas′ter•er,** *n.*

plas′ter•board′ *n.* a material used for insulating or covering walls, consisting of paper-covered sheets of gypsum and felt.

plas′ter of Par′is *n.* calcined gypsum in white, powdery form, used in making plasters and casts.

plas′tic *n.* **1.** any of a group of synthetic or natural organic materials that may be shaped when soft and then hardened. **2.** a credit card, or credit cards collectively. —*adj.* **3.** made of plastic. **4.** capable of being molded. **5.** having the power to mold or shape material. [< L *plasticus* that may be molded < Gk *plastikós*] —**plas•tic′i•ty** (-tis′i tē), *n.*

plas′tic sur′gery *n.* the branch of surgery dealing with the repair, replacement, or reshaping of mal-

formed, injured, or lost parts of the body. —**plas′tic sur′geon,** *n.*

plate (plāt), *n.*, *v.*, **plat•ed, plat•ing.** —*n.* **1.** a shallow dish from which food is eaten. **2.** the contents of such a dish. **3.** household dishes, utensils, etc., of or plated with gold or silver. **4.** a thin, flat sheet of metal. **5.** a sheet of metal, plastic, etc., on which a picture or text has been engraved, used as a printing surface. **6.** a printed impression from such a surface. **7.** the part of a denture that conforms to the mouth and contains the teeth. **8. the plate,** HOME PLATE. **9.** a sheet of glass or metal coated with a sensitized emulsion, used for taking a photograph. —*v.t.* **10.** to coat (metal) with a thin film of gold, silver, etc. **11.** to cover or overlay with metal plates for protection. —**plat′ed,** *adj.*

pla•teau (pla tō′), *n.*, *pl.* **-teaus.** **1.** a level land area considerably raised above adjoining land. **2.** a period of little growth or decline.

plate′ glass′ *n.* smooth, polished glass used in large windows, mirrors, etc.

plat•en (plat′n), *n.* **1.** a flat plate in a printing press for pressing the paper against an inked surface. **2.** the roller of a typewriter or computer printer.

plat•form (plat′fôrm), *n.* **1.** a raised flooring or other horizontal surface for use as a stage. **2.** the raised area between or alongside the tracks of a railroad station. **3.** a set of principles on which a political party or other group takes a public stand. **4.** the underlying hardware or software for a computer system.

plat•i•num (plat′n əm), *n.* a heavy, grayish white metallic element, resistant to most chemicals: used for making scientific apparatus and in jewelry. *Symbol:* Pt; *at. wt.:* 195.09; *at. no.:* 78.

plat•i•tude (plat′i tōōd′, -tyōōd′), *n.* a dull or trite remark. —**plat′i•tu′di•nous** (-n əs), *adj.*

pla•ton•ic (plə ton′ik), *adj.* free from sensual desire; purely spiritual: *a platonic relationship.*

pla•toon (plə tōōn′), *n.* **1.** a military unit consisting of two or more squads and a headquarters. —*v.t.* **2.** *Sports.* to use (a player) at a position in a game alternately with another player.

plat•ter (plat′ər), *n.* a large, shallow dish for holding and serving food.

plat•y•pus (plat′i pəs, -pōōs′), *n.*, *pl.* **-pus•es, -pi** (-pī′), **-pus.** an aquatic, egg-laying mammal of Australia and Tasmania, having webbed feet and a ducklike bill.

plau•dit (plô′dit), *n.* Usu., **-dits.** **1.** an enthusiastic expression of approval. **2.** a round of applause.

plau•si•ble (plô′zə bəl), *adj.* credible; believable. —**plau′si•bil′i•ty,** *n.* —**plau′si•bly,** *adv.*

play (plā), *n.*, *v.*, **played, play•ing.** —*n.* **1.** a dramatic composition or performance; drama. **2.** activity engaged in for recreation. **3.** fun or jest, as opposed to earnest. **4.** the action or conduct of a game. **5.** one's turn to play. **6.** action of a specified kind: *fair play.* **7.** action or operation: *the play of fancy.* **8.** brisk, light, or changing movement: *the play of a water fountain.* **9.** freedom for movement or activity. **10.** attention; coverage. —*v.t.* **11.** to portray; enact: *to play Macbeth.* **12.** to act the part of in real life: *to play the fool.* **13.** to engage in (a game, pastime, etc.). **14.** to contend against in a game. **15.** to employ in a game: *to play a high card.* **16.** to use as if in playing a game: *He played his brothers against each other.* **17.** to bet on. **18.** to imitate, as for recreation: *to play house.* **19.** to perform on (a musical instrument). **20.** to perform (music) on an instrument. **21.** to cause to produce sound or pictures: *played the VCR.* **22.** to perform or do in sport: *to play tricks.* —*v.i.* **23.** to occupy oneself in amusement or recreation. **24.** to do something that is not to be taken seriously. **25.** to toy; trifle. **26.** to take part in a game. **27.** to conduct oneself in a specified way: *to play fair.* **28.** to act on or as if on the stage. **29.** to perform on a musical instrument. **30.** to give forth sound. **31.** to be performed or shown. **32.** to move about lightly or quickly: *A smile played about her lips.* **33. play down,** to treat as of little importance. **34. ~ out,** to use up; exhaust. **35. ~ up,** to emphasize. **36. ~ up to,** to try to please; flatter.

play′back′ n. **1.** the act of reproducing a sound or video recording. **2.** the apparatus used in producing playbacks.

play′bill′ n. a program or announcement of a play.

play′boy′ or **-girl′,** n. a person who pursues a life of pleasure without responsibility or attachments.

play′er n. **1.** a person who takes part in some game or sport. **2.** a stage actor. **3.** a musician. **4.** a sound– or image–reproducing machine: *a videodisc player.*

play′ful (-fəl), adj. **1.** full of play or fun. **2.** pleasantly humorous or jesting. —**play′ful•ly,** adv. —**play′ful•ness,** n.

play′ground′ n. an area used by children for outdoor recreation.

play′house′ n. **1.** THEATER (def. 1). **2.** a small house for children to play in.

play′mate′ n. a companion, esp. of a child, in play or recreation.

play′-off′ n. **1.** an extra game, inning, etc., played to settle a tie. **2.** a series of games played to decide a championship.

play′ on words′ n. a pun.

play′pen′ n. a small, portable enclosure in which a baby can play.

play′thing′ n. a toy.

play′wright′ (-rīt′), n. a writer of plays.

pla•za (plä′zə, plaz′ə), n., pl. **-zas. 1.** a public square or open space in a city or town. **2.** a shopping center. **3.** an area along an expressway where public facilities are available.

plea (plē), n., pl. **pleas. 1.** an appeal or entreaty. **2.** something that is alleged, urged, or pleaded in defense or justification. **3.** an excuse; pretext. **4.** a defendant's answer to a charge.

plea′ bar′gain n. an agreement in which a criminal defendant pleads guilty to a lesser charge. —**plea′-bar′gain,** v.i.

plead (plēd), v., **plead•ed** or **pled; plead•ing.** —v.i. **1.** to entreat earnestly; beg. **2.** to put forward a plea in a law court. —v.t. **3.** to offer as an excuse: *to plead ignorance.* **4. a.** to argue (a case) before a court. **b.** to make a plea of: *to plead guilty.* —**plead′er,** n.

pleas•ant (plez′ənt), adj. **1.** giving pleasure; agreeable or enjoyable. **2.** having a pleasing manner, appearance, etc. —**pleas′ant•ly,** adv.

pleas′ant•ry n., pl. **-ries. 1.** a humorous action or remark. **2.** a courteous remark used to facilitate conversation.

please (plēz), adv., v., **pleased, pleas•ing.** —adv. **1.** (used in polite requests) be so kind as to: *Please come here.* —v.t. **2.** to give pleasure to. **3.** to be the pleasure of: *May it please your Majesty.* —v.i. **4.** to like or wish: *Do as you please.* **5.** to give pleasure or satisfaction.

pleas•ur•a•ble (plezh′ər ə bəl), adj. enjoyable; agreeable; pleasant. —**pleas′ur•a•bly,** adv.

pleas′ure n. **1.** enjoyment or satisfaction; gratification. **2.** a source of enjoyment or delight. **3.** one's will or desire.

pleat (plēt), n. **1.** a fold of even width made by doubling cloth or the like upon itself. —v.t. **2.** to arrange in pleats.

ple•be•ian (pli bē′ən), adj. **1.** of the common people. **2.** common or vulgar. —n. **3.** a member of the common people.

pleb•i•scite (pleb′ə sīt′, -sit), n. a direct vote of the qualified voters of a state on some public question.

pledge (plej), n., v., **pledged, pledg•ing.** —n. **1.** a solemn promise or agreement. **2.** something delivered as security, as for the fulfillment of a promise. **3.** the state of being given or held as security. **4.** a person accepted for membership in a club, fraternity, etc., but not yet formally approved. —v.t. **5.** to bind by a pledge. **6.** to promise solemnly. **7.** to give as a pledge.

Pleis•to•cene (plī′stə sēn′), adj. noting or pertaining to the geologic epoch forming the earlier half of

the Quaternary Period, characterized by the advent of modern humans.

ple•na•ry (plē′nə rē, plen′ə-), adj. **1.** full; complete: *plenary powers.* **2.** attended by all qualified members.

plen•i•po•ten•ti•ar•y (plen′ə pə ten′shē er′ē, -shə rē), n., pl. **-ar•ies.** —n. **1.** a person, esp. a diplomatic agent, invested with full authority to transact business. —adj. **2.** invested with full power or authority.

plen•i•tude (plen′i tōōd′, -tyōōd′), n. **1.** fullness; abundance. **2.** the state of being full or complete.

plen′ty n., pl. **-ties,** adv. —n. **1.** a full or abundant supply or amount. **2.** the state or quality of being plentiful. —adv. **3.** *Informal.* fully; quite.

pleth•o•ra (pleth′ər ə), n. an overabundance; excess.

pleu•ra (plŏŏr′ə), n., pl. **pleu•rae** (plŏŏr′ē). one of a pair of membranes that cover the lungs and line the chest wall.

pleu′ri•sy (-ə sē), n. inflammation of the pleura.

Plex•i•glas (plek′si glas′, -gläs′), *Trademark.* a lightweight, transparent plastic material, used for signs, windows, etc.

pli•a•ble (plī′ə bəl), adj. **1.** easily bent; flexible. **2.** easily influenced or persuaded. **3.** adaptable. —**pli′a•bil′i•ty,** n.

pli′ant (-ənt), adj. **1.** bending readily; pliable. **2.** adapting readily to different situations. —**pli′an•cy,** n.

pli•ers (plī′ərz), n. (*used with a sing. or pl. v.*) small pincers for bending wire, holding small objects, etc.

plight[1] (plīt), n. a distressing condition or situation.

plight[2] (plīt), v.t. to give in pledge, as one's word, or to pledge, as one's honor.

PLO Palestine Liberation Organization.

plod (plod), v.i., **plod•ded, plod•ding. 1.** to walk heavily or move laboriously. **2.** to work with steady and monotonous perseverance. —**plod′der,** n.

plop (plop), v., **plopped, plop•ping.** —v.t., v.i. **1.** to drop with a sound like that of an object striking water without a splash. **2.** to drop with direct impact: *to plop into a chair.* —n. **3.** a plopping sound or fall.

plot (plot), n., v., **plot•ted, plot•ting.** —n. **1.** a secret plan, usu. evil or unlawful. **2.** the main story of a literary or dramatic work. **3.** a small piece of ground. —v.t. **4.** to plan secretly or conspiratorially. **5.** to mark on a map or chart, as the course of a ship. —v.i. **6.** to plan secretly; conspire. —**plot′ter,** n.

plov•er (pluv′ər, plō′vər), n. any of various shorebirds with a compact body and pigeonlike head.

plow (plou), n. **1.** an agricultural implement used for cutting and turning up soil. **2.** any of various implements resembling this, as a snowplow. —v.t. **3.** to turn up (soil) with a plow. **4.** to make with or as if with a plow: *to plow furrows.* —v.i. **5.** to work with a plow. **6.** to move forcefully: *to plow through a crowd.* **7.** to proceed laboriously: *to plow through a pile of reports.* Also, *esp. Brit.,* **plough.** —**plow′-man,** n., pl. **-men.**

plow′share′ n. the cutting part of a plow.

ploy (ploi), n. a stratagem to gain the advantage.

pluck (pluk), v.t. **1.** to pull off or out from the place of growth, as flowers. **2.** to grasp or grab. **3.** to remove feathers or hair from by pulling: *to pluck a chicken.* **4.** to sound (the strings of an instrument) by pulling at them. —v.i. **5.** to pull or tug sharply. —n. **6.** the act of plucking. **7.** courage.

pluck′y adj., **-i•er, -i•est.** courageous; brave. —**pluck′i•ness,** n.

plug (plug), n., v., **plugged, plug•ging.** —n. **1.** a piece of wood or other material used to stop up a hole. **2.** an attachment at the end of an electrical cord that allows its insertion into an outlet. **3.** a cake of pressed tobacco. **4.** the favorable mention of a product, performer, etc., as in a television interview. **5.** an artificial fishing lure. —v.t. **6.** to stop with or as if with a plug. **7.** to mention (a product or the like) favorably. **8.** *Slang.* to shoot or kill with a bullet. —v.i. **9.** to work with stubborn persistence. **10. plug in,** to connect to an electrical power source: *Plug in the toaster.*

plum (plum), *n.* **1.** a round fruit with a smooth skin and an oblong stone. **2.** the tree that bears this fruit. **3.** a raisin, as in a cake. **4.** a deep purple. **5.** an excellent or desirable thing.

plum•age (plōō′mij), *n.* the entire feathery covering of a bird.

plumb (plum), *n.* **1.** a small mass of lead suspended by a line **(plumb′ line′)** and used to measure the depth of water or to ascertain a vertical line. —*adj.* **2.** true according to a plumb line; perpendicular. —*adv.* **3.** in a perpendicular or vertical direction. **4.** exactly or precisely. **5.** completely or absolutely. —*v.t.* **6.** to test or adjust by a plumb line. **7.** to examine closely in order to understand. [< L *plumbum* lead]

plumb′er *n.* a person who installs and repairs piping, fixtures, etc., of a water or drainage system.

plumb′ing *n.* **1.** the system of pipes and other apparatus of a water or drainage system. **2.** the work of a plumber.

plume (plōōm), *n., v.,* **plumed, plum•ing.** —*n.* **1.** a large or conspicuous feather. **2.** any plumelike part or formation. —*v.t.* **3.** to adorn with plumes. **4.** to preen. —**plumed,** *adj.*

plum•met (plum′it), *n.* **1.** the weight attached to a plumb line. —*v.i.* **2.** to fall straight down; plunge.

plump[1] (plump), *adj.,* **-er, -est.** well filled out or rounded in form; fleshy. —**plump′ness,** *n.*

plump[2] (plump), *v.i., v.t.* **1.** to drop heavily or suddenly. **2. plump for,** to support enthusiastically. —*n.* **3.** a heavy or sudden fall. **4.** the sound of such a fall. —*adv.* **5.** heavily or suddenly. **6.** straight down.

plun•der (plun′dər), *v.t.* **1.** to rob of goods by force, as in war. **2.** to rob or fleece. —*v.i.* **3.** to take plunder. —*n.* **4.** plundering or pillage. **5.** that which is taken in plundering.

plunge (plunj), *v.,* **plunged, plung•ing,** *n.* —*v.t.* **1.** to cast or thrust forcibly or suddenly into something. —*v.i.* **2.** to fall or cast oneself into water, from a great height, etc. **3.** to rush or dash with haste. **4.** to bet or speculate recklessly. **5.** to descend abruptly. —*n.* **6.** the act of plunging. —*Idiom.* **7. take the plunge,** to enter upon a course of action, esp. after hesitation.

plung′er *n.* **1.** a pistonlike part moving within the cylinder of a pump or hydraulic device. **2.** a device consisting of a handle with a rubber suction cup at one end, used to free clogged drains.

plunk (plungk), *v.t.* **1.** PLUCK (def. 4). **2.** to throw, drop, etc., heavily or suddenly. —*v.i.* **3.** to give forth a twanging sound. **4.** to drop heavily or suddenly. —*n.* **5.** the act or sound of plunking. —**plunk′er,** *n.*

plu•ral (plŏŏr′əl), *adj.* **1.** of or involving more than one. **2.** of or belonging to the grammatical category of number indicating that a word has more than one referent. —*n.* **3.** the plural number. **4.** a word or other form in the plural. —**plu′ral•ize,** *v.t., v.i.* **-ized, iz•ing.**

plu′ral•ism *n.* a condition in which minority groups participate fully in the dominant society, yet maintain their cultural differences. —**plu′ral•is′tic,** *adj.*

plu•ral•i•ty (plŏŏ ral′i tē), *n., pl.* **-ties. 1.** (in an election involving three or more candidates) the excess of votes received by the leading candidate over those received by the next candidate. **2.** a majority. **3.** the state or fact of being plural or numerous.

plus (plus), *prep.* **1.** increased by: *Ten plus two is twelve.* **2.** in addition to. —*adj.* **3.** involving or noting addition. **4.** positive: *on the plus side.* **5.** more or greater than: *A plus for effort.* **6.** and more: *She has personality plus.* —*n.* **7.** a plus quantity. **8.** Also called **plus′ sign′.** the symbol (+) indicating addition or a positive quantity. **9.** something additional. **10.** an advantage or gain.

plush (plush), *n., adj.,* **-er, -est.** —*n.* **1.** a fabric resembling velvet but having a deeper pile. —*adj.* **2.** luxurious.

Plu•to (plōō′tō), *n.* the planet ninth in order from the sun.

plu′to•crat′ (plōō′tə krat′) *n.* **1.** a wealthy person. **2.** a member of wealthy governing class. —**plu•toc′ra•cy** (-tok′rə sē) *n., pl.* **-cies.** —**plu′to•crat′ic,** *adj.*

plu•to•ni•um (plōō tō′nē əm), *n.* a radioactive metallic element with a fissile isotope of mass number 239 that can be produced from nonfissile uranium 238. *Symbol:* Pu; *at. no.:* 94.

plu•vi•al (plōō′vē əl), *adj.* **1.** of rain. **2.** formed by the action of rain.

ply[1] (plī), *v.,* **plied, ply•ing.** —*v.t.* **1.** to work with diligently: *to ply the needle.* **2.** to carry on busily or steadily: *to ply a trade.* **3.** to assail persistently. **4.** to offer something pressingly to: *to ply a person with drink.* **5.** to pass over or along (a river, stream, etc.) steadily or regularly. —*v.i.* **6.** to travel regularly between certain places, as a boat. **7.** to perform one's work busily or steadily.

ply[2] (plī), *n., pl.* **plies. 1.** a thickness or layer. **2.** a strand of yarn or rope.

ply′wood′ *n.* a building material consisting of wood veneers glued over each other.

Pm *Chem. Symbol.* promethium.

p.m. or **P.M., 1.** after noon. **2.** the period between noon and midnight. [< L *post merīdiem*]

PMS premenstrual syndrome: the physical and emotional changes that may be experienced in the several days before menstruation.

pneu•mat•ic (nōō mat′ik, nyōō-), *adj.* **1.** of air, gases, or wind. **2.** filled with or operated by compressed air, as a tire. —**pneu•mat′i•cal•ly,** *adv.*

pneu•mo•nia (nōō mōn′yə, nyōō-), *n.* **1.** inflammation of the lungs with congestion. **2.** an acute infection of the lungs.

poach[1] (pōch), *v.i., v.t.* **1.** to trespass on (private property) in order to hunt or fish. **2.** to take (game or fish) illegally. —**poach′er,** *n.*

poach[2] (pōch), *v.t.* to cook (eggs, fish, etc.) in a hot liquid just below the boiling point.

pock•et (pok′it), *n.* **1.** a small pouch attached to a garment, used for carrying small articles. **2.** financial resources. **3.** any pouchlike receptacle or cavity. **4.** an isolated group, area, or element: *pockets of resistance.* —*adj.* **5.** small enough for carrying in the pocket. **6.** relatively small: *a pocket war.* —*v.t.* **7.** to put into one's pocket. **8.** to take as one's own, often dishonestly. **9.** to conceal or suppress: *to pocket one's pride.* **10.** to enclose; confine. —**pock′et•ful′,** *n., pl.* **-fuls.**

pock′et•book′ *n.* **1.** a woman's purse or handbag. **2.** financial resources.

pock′et•knife′ *n., pl.* **-knives.** a small knife with one or more blades that fold into the handle.

pock′mark′ *n.* a scar left by a pustule of smallpox, chickenpox, etc.

pod (pod), *n.* an elongated seed vessel, as that of the pea or bean.

po•di•a•try (pə dī′ə trē, pō-), *n.* the diagnosis and treatment of foot disorders. —**po•di′a•trist,** *n.*

po•di•um (pō′dē əm), *n., pl.* **-di•ums, -di•a** (-dē ə). **1.** a small platform, as for an orchestra conductor. **2.** LECTERN.

po•em (pō′əm), *n.* a composition in verse, esp. one characterized by the use of heightened language and rhythm.

po•e•sy (-ə sē, -zē), *n., pl.* **-sies.** poetry.

po′et (-it), *n.* one who writes poetry.

po•et′ic (-et′ik), *adj.* Also, **po•et′i•cal. 1.** possessing the qualities of poetry. **2.** of or characteristic of a poet or poetry. —**po•et′i•cal•ly,** *adv.*

poet′ic jus′tice *n.* a particularly fitting distribution of rewards and punishments.

poet′ic li′cense *n.* liberty, esp. as taken by a poet or other writer, in deviating from conventional form, fact, etc., to produce a desired effect.

po′et•ry (-i trē), *n.* **1.** poems collectively. **2.** the art of writing poems. **3.** poetic qualities however manifested.

po•grom (pə grum′, -grom′, pō-), *n.* an organized massacre, esp. of Jews. [< Russ *pogróm* destruction]

poign·ant (poin′yənt), *adj.* **1.** keenly distressing to the feelings. **2.** affecting the emotions. **3.** pungent to the smell. —**poign′an·cy,** *n.* —**poign′ant·ly,** *adv.*

poin·set·ti·a (poin set′ē ə, -set′ə), *n., pl.* -**as.** a plant, native to Mexico and Central America, having scarlet, pink, or white petallike bracts.

point (point), *n.* **1.** a sharp or tapering end. **2.** a projecting part of anything. **3.** something that has position but not extension, as the intersection of two lines. **4.** a dot used in writing, esp. a period. **5.** any of 32 horizontal directions on a compass. **6.** a degree or stage. **7.** a particular instant of time. **8.** a place or locality. **9.** the main idea or purpose. **10.** a strikingly effective fact, idea, etc. **11.** an individual element or item. **12.** a distinguishing mark or quality. **13.** a unit in counting, measuring, or scoring a game. **14.** a unit of price quotation, as one dollar in stock transactions. **15.** *Print.* a unit of type measurement equal to $1/72$ inch. —*v.t.* **16.** to direct (the finger, a weapon, etc.); aim. **17.** to direct attention to; indicate: *to point out advantages.* **18.** to furnish with a point; sharpen. **19.** to give added force to: *to point up the need for caution.* —*v.i.* **20.** to indicate position or direction or call attention, as with the finger. **21.** to be directed; tend: *Conditions point to inflation.* —*Idiom.* **22.** beside the point, irrelevant. **23.** to the point, relevant. —**point′y,** *adj.,* -**i·er, -i·est.**

point′-blank′ *adj.* **1.** aimed or fired straight at the mark, esp. from close range. **2.** straightforward or explicit. —*adv.* **3.** with a direct aim. **4.** bluntly; frankly.

point′ed *adj.* **1.** having a point. **2.** sharp or piercing: *pointed wit.* **3.** aimed at a particular person: *a pointed remark.* **4.** marked; emphasized. —**point′ed·ly,** *adv.*

point′er *n.* **1.** a long, tapering stick used in pointing things out, as on a blackboard. **2.** the hand on a watch dial, scale, etc. **3.** a large, shorthaired hunting dog. **4.** a piece of advice.

poin·til·lism (pwan′tl iz′əm), *n.* (*sometimes cap.*) a technique in painting of using dots of pure color that are optically mixed into the resulting hue by the viewer. —**poin′til·list,** *n., adj.*

point′less *adj.* **1.** without relevance or force; meaningless. **2.** without a point. —**point′less·ly,** *adv.* —**point′less·ness,** *n.*

poise (poiz), *n., v.,* **poised, pois·ing.** —*n.* **1.** a state of balance or equilibrium. **2.** a dignified, self-confident manner or bearing. **3.** the way of being poised or carried. —*v.t., v.i.* **4.** to balance or be balanced.

poi·son (poi′zən), *n.* **1.** a substance that has an inherent tendency to destroy life or impair health. —*v.t.* **2.** to kill or injure with or as if with poison. **3.** to put poison into or upon. **4.** to ruin or corrupt. —**poi′son·ous,** *adj.*

poi′son i′vy *n.* **1.** a vine or shrub with trifoliate leaves and whitish berries: may cause dermatitis when touched. **2.** the rash caused by poison ivy.

poke (pōk), *v.,* **poked, pok·ing,** *n.* —*v.t.* **1.** to prod or push, as with something pointed. **2.** to make by or as if by poking. **3.** to thrust or push: *She poked her head out of the window.* —*v.i.* **4.** to make a thrusting movement, as with the finger. **5.** to thrust oneself obtrusively. **6.** to search curiously; pry. **7.** to proceed in a slow or aimless way. —*n.* **8.** a thrust or push. —*Idiom.* **9.** poke fun at, to ridicule.

pok·er[1] (pō′kər), *n.* a metal rod for stirring a fire.

pok·er[2] (pō′kər), *n.* a card game in which the players bet on the value of their hands.

pok′er-faced′ *adj.* showing no emotion or intention.

pok′y or -**ey,** *adj.,* -**i·er, -i·est. 1.** slow; dawdling. **2.** (of a place) small and cramped.

Po·land (pō′lənd), *n.* a republic in E central Europe.

po·lar (pō′lər), *adj.* **1.** of or near the North or South Pole. **2.** of the poles of a magnet, sphere, etc.

po′lar bear′ *n.* a large white bear of arctic regions.

Po·lar·is (pō lâr′is, -lar′-, pə-), *n.* the bright star close to the north pole of the heavens.

po′lar·i·za′tion (-lər ə zā′shən), *n.* **1.** a sharp division of a group into opposing factions. **2.** a state, or the production of a state, in which rays of light or similar radiation exhibit different properties in different directions. —**po′lar·ize′,** *v.t., v.i.* -**ized, -iz·ing.**

pole[1] (pōl), *n., v.,* **poled, pol·ing.** —*n.* **1.** a long, cylindrical, slender piece of wood, metal, etc. —*v.t., v.i.* **2.** to push or propel (a boat, raft, etc.) with a pole.

pole[2] (pōl), *n.* **1.** each of the extremities of the axis of the earth or of any spherical body. **2.** one of two opposite principles or tendencies. **3.** either of the two regions of an electric battery, magnet, etc., that exhibits electrical or magnetic polarity.

Pole (pōl), *n.* a native or inhabitant of Poland.

pole′cat′ *n., pl.* -**cats,** -**cat. 1.** a European weasel that ejects a fetid fluid when attacked or disturbed. **2.** any of various North American skunks.

po·lem·ic (pə lem′ik, pō-), *n.* **1.** a controversial argument, as one against some opinion, doctrine, etc. —*adj.* **2.** Also, **po·lem′i·cal.** of a polemic.

po·lem′ics *n.* the art or practice of disputation. —**po·lem′i·cist** (-ə sist), *n.*

pole′ vault′ *n.* a field event in which a vault over a crossbar is performed with the aid of a long pole. —**pole′-vault′,** *v.i.* —**pole′-vault′er,** *n.*

po·lice (pə lēs′), *n., v.,* -**liced, -lic·ing.** —*n.* **1.** an organized civil force for maintaining order, preventing and detecting crime, and enforcing the laws. **2.** (*used with a pl. v.*) members of such a force. **3.** people who seek to regulate a specified activity, practice, etc.: *the language police.* —*v.t.* **4.** to regulate or keep in order with or as if with police. **5.** to clean and keep clean (a military camp, post, etc.). —**po·lice′man,** *n., pl.* -**men.** —**po·lice′wom′an,** *n. fem.,* -**wom·en.**

pol·i·cy[1] (pol′ə sē), *n., pl.* -**cies. 1.** a course of action adopted and pursued by a government, corporation, etc. **2.** prudence or practical wisdom.

pol·i·cy[2] (pol′ə sē), *n., pl.* -**cies.** a document embodying a contract of insurance.

po·li·o·my·e·li·tis (pō′lē ō mī′ə lī′tis), *n.* an infectious viral disease of the spinal cord, sometimes resulting in paralysis. Also called **po′li·o′.**

pol·ish (pol′ish), *v.t.* **1.** to make smooth and glossy, esp. by rubbing. **2.** to make refined or elegant. —*v.i.* **3.** to become smooth and glossy through polishing. **4.** polish off, to finish or dispose of quickly. —*n.* **5.** a substance used to give smoothness or gloss. **6.** smoothness and gloss of surface. **7.** refinement; elegance.

Po·lish (pō′lish), *n.* **1.** the Slavic language of Poland. —*adj.* **2.** of Poland, its inhabitants, or their language.

po·lite (pə līt′), *adj.,* -**lit·er, -lit·est. 1.** showing good manners; courteous. **2.** refined or cultured: *polite society.* —**po·lite′ly,** *adv.* —**po·lite′ness,** *n.*

pol·i·tic (pol′i tik), *adj.* **1.** shrewd or prudent in practical matters. **2.** expedient: *a politic reply.*

po·lit·i·cal (pə lit′i kal), *adj.* of or concerned with government or politics. —**po·lit′i·cal·ly,** *adv.*

polit′ically correct′ *adj.* marked by a typically progressive orthodoxy on issues involving gender, race, sexual affinity, etc. —**polit′ical correct′ness,** *n.*

polit′ical sci′ence *n.* a social science dealing with political institutions and with the principles and conduct of government.

pol·i·ti·cian (pol′i tish′ən), *n.* a person who is active in politics, esp. as a career.

po·lit·i·cize (pə lit′ə sīz′), *v.t.,* -**cized, -ciz·ing.** to give a political character or bias to.

pol·i·tick·ing (pol′i tik′ing), *n.* political activity, esp. campaigning.

pol·i·tics (pol′i tiks), *n.* (*used with a sing. or pl. v.*) **1.** the science or art of government. **2.** political affairs. **3.** political methods. **4.** political opinions. **5.** the use of strategy or intrigue in obtaining power or status.

pol·ka (pōl′kə, pō′kə), *n., pl.* -**kas. 1.** a lively

couple dance of Bohemian origin. **2.** a piece of music for such a dance. [« Czech: lit., Polish woman]

pol′ka dot′ (pō′kə), *n.* a round spot repeated to form a pattern, esp. on a fabric.

poll (pōl), *n.* **1.** a sampling or collection of opinions on a subject, as in a public survey. **2.** the act of voting in an election. **3.** Usu., **polls.** the place where votes are cast. **4.** the number of votes cast. **5.** a list of individuals, as for purposes of taxing or voting. **6.** the head. —*v.t.* **7.** to take a sampling of the opinions of. **8.** to receive at the polls, as votes. **9.** to register the votes of. **10.** to cast at the polls, as a vote. **11.** to cut short or cut off the hair or wool of (an animal) or the horns of (cattle). —**poll′er,** *n.*

pol•len (pol′ən), *n.* the fertilizing element of flowering plants, consisting of fine, powdery, yellowish grains.

pol•li•wog or **-ly•wog** (pol′ē wog′), *n.* TADPOLE.

poll•ster (pōl′stər), *n.* a person whose occupation is the taking of public-opinion polls.

pol•lute (pə lōōt′), *v.t.* **-lut•ed, -lut•ing.** to make foul or unclean, esp. with harmful chemical or waste products; contaminate. —**pol•lu′tant,** *n.* —**pol•lut′er,** *n.* —**pol•lu′tion,** *n.*

po•lo (pō′lō), *n.* a game played on horseback between two teams, who score points by driving a ball into the opponents' goal with a long-handled mallet.

pol•ter•geist (pōl′tər gīst′), *n.* a spirit supposed to manifest its presence by noises, knockings, etc.

pol•troon (pol trōōn′), *n.* a wretched coward; craven.

poly- a combining form meaning much or many (*polygamy*).

pol′y•an′dry (pol′ē an′drē) *n.* the practice or condition of having more than one husband at a time.

pol′y•es•ter (pol′ē es′tər), *n.* a polymer used to make resins, plastics, and textile fibers.

pol′y•eth′yl•ene′ *n.* a plastic polymer used chiefly for containers, electrical insulation, and packaging.

po•lyg•a•my (pə lig′ə mē), *n.* the practice or condition of having more than one spouse, esp. a wife, at one time. —**po•lyg′a•mist,** *n.* —**po•lyg′a•mous,** *adj.*

pol′y•glot (pol′ē glot′), *adj.* **1.** able to speak, write, or read several languages. **2.** written in several languages. —*n.* **3.** a polyglot person. **4.** a book containing the same text in several languages.

pol′y•gon (pol′ē gon′), *n.* a closed plane figure having three or more, usu. straight, sides. —**po•lyg•o•nal** (pə lig′ə nl), *adj.*

pol′y•graph (pol′i graf′, -gräf′), *n.* **1.** an instrument for recording tracings of variations in certain body activities. **2.** LIE DETECTOR.

pol′y•he•dron (pol′ē hē′drən), *n., pl.* **-drons, -dra** (-drə). a solid figure having many faces. —**pol′y•he′dral,** *adj.*

pol′y•math (pol′ē math′), *n.* a person of great learning in several fields.

pol′y•mer (pol′ə mər), *n.* a compound of high molecular weight derived by the addition of many smaller molecules or by the condensation of many smaller molecules with the elimination of water, alcohol, or the like. —**po•lym•er•i•za•tion** (pə lim′ər ə zā′shən, pol′ə mər-), *n.*

pol′y•no•mi•al (pol′ə nō′mē əl), *n.* an algebraic expression consisting of the sum of two or more terms.

pol′y•yp (pol′ip), *n.* a projecting growth from a mucous surface, as of the nose.

po•lyph•o•ny (pə lif′ə nē), *n.* a musical style in which two or more melodic lines are in equitable juxtaposition. —**pol•y•phon•ic** (pol′ē fon′ik), *adj.*

pol′y•sty•rene (pol′ē stī′rēn, -stēr′ēn), *n.* a clear plastic or stiff foam, used in molded objects and as an insulator.

pol′y•tech•nic (pol′ē tek′nik), *adj.* of or offering instruction in a variety of industrial arts, applied sciences, or technical subjects.

pol′y•the′ism *n.* the doctrine of or belief in more than one god. —**pol′y•the′ist,** *n., adj.* —**pol′y•the•is′tic,** *adj.*

pol′y•un•sat′u•rat′ed *adj.* of or noting a class of fats of animal or vegetable origin, associated with a low cholesterol content.

po•made (po mād′, -mäd′, pō-), *n.* a scented ointment, as for the hair.

pome•gran•ate (pom′gran′it, pom′i-, pum′-), *n.* **1.** a round fruit with a leathery red rind, tart red pulp, and many seeds. **2.** the tree that bears this fruit.

pom•mel (pum′əl, pom′-), *n., v.,* **-meled, -mel•ing** or (*esp. Brit.*) **-melled, -mel•ling.** —*n.* **1.** a knob, as on the hilt of a sword. **2.** the protuberant part at the front and top of a saddle. —*v.t.* **3.** PUMMEL.

pomp (pomp), *n.* **1.** stately or splendid display. **2.** ostentatious display.

pom•pa•dour (pom′pə dôr′, -dōōr′), *n.* an arrangement of hair in which it is brushed up high from or raised over the forehead.

pom•pom (pom′pom′) also **-pon** (-pon′), *n.* an ornamental tuft, as of feathers or wool, used esp. on clothing.

pomp•ous (pom′pəs), *adj.* **1.** characterized by an ostentatious display of importance. **2.** ostentatiously lofty or high-flown. **3.** characterized by stately splendor. —**pom•pos′i•ty** (-pos′i tē), *n.* —**pomp′ous•ly,** *adv.*

pon•cho (pon′chō), *n., pl.* **-chos.** a blanketlike cloak with a center opening for the head, esp. a waterproof one worn as a raincoat.

pond (pond), *n.* a body of water smaller than a lake.

pon•der (pon′dər), *v.i., v.t.* to consider (something) carefully and thoroughly. —**pon′der•er,** *n.*

pon•der•ous (pon′dər əs), *adj.* **1.** heavy; massive. **2.** awkward or unwieldy. **3.** dull and labored. —**pon′der•ous•ly,** *adv.*

pon•iard (pon′yard), *n.* a small, slender dagger.

pon•tiff (pon′tif), *n.* **1.** the pope. **2.** any high or chief priest. —**pon•tif′i•cal,** *adj.*

pon•tif•i•cate (*v.* pon tif′i kāt′; *n.* -kit, -kāt′), *v.,* **-cat•ed, -cat•ing.** —*v.i.* **1.** to speak in a pompous or dogmatic manner. **2.** to discharge the duties of a pontiff. —*n.* **3.** the office or term of office of a pontiff.

pon•toon (pon tōōn′), *n.* **1.** a boat or other float used as one of the supports for a temporary bridge. **2.** a float for a derrick, landing stage, etc. **3.** a seaplane float.

po•ny (pō′nē), *n., pl.* **-nies. 1.** a small horse of any of several breeds. **2.** *Informal.* a literal translation of a text, used illicitly as an aid in schoolwork. **3.** a small glass holding about one ounce (30 ml) of liqueur.

po′ny•tail′ *n.* a hairstyle in which the hair is gathered and fastened at the back of the head, so as to hang freely there.

poo•dle (pōōd′l), *n.* one of a breed of dogs with long, thick, frizzy or curly hair.

pool¹ (pōōl), *n.* **1.** a small pond. **2.** any small collection of liquid on a surface: *a pool of blood.* **3.** a large artificial basin filled with water for swimming.

pool² (pōōl), *n.* **1.** any of various games played on a table (**pool′ ta′ble**) with a cue ball and 15 other balls that are driven into pockets. **2.** the total amount staked by a combination of bettors. **3.** a combination of resources, funds, etc., for common advantage. **4.** a facility or service shared by a group of people: *a car pool.* —*v.t., v.i.* **5.** to combine in a common fund.

poop¹ (pōōp), *n.* **1.** a superstructure at the stern of a ship. **2.** a weather deck on top of a poop.

poop² (pōōp), *v.t. Informal.* to cause to become exhausted.

poop³ (pōōp), *n. Slang.* a candid factual report; low-down.

poor (pōōr), *adj.,* **-er, -est,** *n.* —*adj.* **1.** having little or no money or other means of support. **2.** characterized by poverty. **3.** lacking in resources, ability, etc. **4.** wretched; unfortunate. —*n.* **5. the poor,** poor persons collectively. —**poor′ly,** *adv.*

poor′-mouth′ *v.i. Informal.* to plead or complain about poverty, usu. as an excuse.

pop¹ (pop), *v.,* **popped, pop•ping,** *n.* —*v.i.* **1.** to make or burst open with a sudden, explosive sound. **2.** to come or go quickly or suddenly. **3.** (of eyes) to protrude from the sockets. —*v.t.* **4.** to cause to pop. **5.** to put or thrust quickly: *Pop the muffins into the oven.* **6. pop up,** to hit a pop fly. —*n.* **7.** a short, quick, explosive sound. **8.** a carbonated, flavored, and sweetened soft drink.

pop² (pop), *adj.* **1.** of popular songs. **2.** of pop art. **3.** reflecting or aimed at the tastes of the general public: *pop culture.* —*n.* **4.** popular music.

pop. 1. popular. **2.** population.

pop′corn′ *n.* **1.** a variety of corn whose kernels burst open and puff out when heated. **2.** such corn when popped.

pope (pōp), *n.* (*often cap.*) the bishop of Rome as head of the Roman Catholic Church.

pop•in•jay (pop′in jā′), *n.* a vain, shallow person.

pop•lar (pop′lər), *n.* **1.** any of several rapidly growing softwood trees of the willow family. **2.** the wood of any such tree.

pop•lin (pop′lin), *n.* a finely corded fabric of cotton, rayon, silk, or wool.

pop′o′ver *n.* a puffy, hollow muffin.

pop•py (pop′ē), *n., pl.* **-pies.** any of various plants with showy, usu. red flowers.

pop′py•cock′ *n.* nonsense; foolishness.

pop•u•lace (pop′yə ləs), *n.* **1.** (in a community or nation) the common people. **2.** the inhabitants of a place.

pop′u•lar (-lər), *adj.* **1.** approved or favored by people in general: *a popular preacher.* **2.** of or representing the people as a whole: *popular government.* **3.** prevailing among the people generally: *a popular superstition.* **4.** appealing to the public at large: *popular music.* —**pop′u•lar′i•ty** (-lar′i tē), *n.* —**pop′u•lar•ize′,** *v.t.,* **-ized, -iz•ing.** —**pop′u•lar•ly,** *adv.*

pop′u•late′ (-lāt′), *v.t.,* **-lat•ed, -lat•ing. 1.** to inhabit. **2.** to furnish with inhabitants.

pop′u•la′tion *n.* **1.** the total number of persons inhabiting a country, city, etc. **2.** the number of inhabitants of a particular class or group in a place: *the working-class population.* **3.** the things or individuals subject to a statistical study. **4.** the act or process of populating.

pop′u•lism *n.* a political philosophy or movement that promotes the interests of the common people. —**pop′u•list,** *n., adj.*

pop′u•lous *adj.* **1.** heavily populated: *a populous area.* **2.** crowded with people. —**pop′u•lous•ness,** *n.*

por•ce•lain (pôr′sə lin, pôrs′lin), *n.* a strong, vitreous, translucent ceramic material.

porch (pôrch), *n.* **1.** a covered approach or vestibule to a doorway. **2.** an open or enclosed room attached to the outside of a house.

por•cu•pine (pôr′kyə pīn′), *n.* a large rodent with stiff, sharp, erectile quills.

pore¹ (pôr), *v.i.,* **pored, por•ing. 1.** to read or study with steady attention: *to pore over old manuscripts.* **2.** to ponder.

pore² (pôr), *n.* a minute opening, as in the skin or a leaf, for perspiration, absorption, etc.

pork (pôrk), *n.* the flesh of a hog or pig used as food. [< OF < L *porcus* hog]

por•nog•ra•phy (pôr nog′rə fē), *n.* writings, photographs, etc., intended to arouse sexual desire. —**por•nog′ra•pher,** *n.* —**por′no•graph′ic** (-nə-graf′ik), *adj.*

po•rous (pôr′əs), *adj.* **1.** permeable by water, air, etc. **2.** full of pores. —**po•ros•i•ty** (pô ros′i tē, pə-), *n.*

por•poise (pôr′pəs), *n., pl.* **-pois•es, -poise.** any of certain toothed aquatic mammals having a blunt, rounded snout.

por•ridge (pôr′ij, por′-), *n.* a thick cereal made of oatmeal boiled in water or milk.

por•rin•ger (pôr′in jər, por′-), *n.* a low dish or cup, often with a handle, for soup, porridge, etc.

port¹ (pôrt), *n.* **1.** a city, town, or other place where ships load or unload. **2.** a harbor.

port² (pôrt), *n.* **1.** the left-hand side of a ship or aircraft, facing forward. —*adj.* **2.** of or located on this side.

port³ (pôrt), *n.* a very sweet, dark red wine.

port⁴ (pôrt), *n.* **1.** an opening in a ship for admitting air and light or for taking on cargo. **2.** an aperture in a cylinder, as in machinery, for the passage of steam, air, etc.

port⁵ (pôrt), *v.t.* to carry (a rifle or other weapon) diagonally in front of the body, with the muzzle pointing upward to the left.

port′a•ble *adj.* **1.** capable of being carried. **2.** easily carried by hand. —*n.* **3.** something portable. —**port′a•bil′i•ty,** *n.*

por•tage (pôr′tij, pôr täzh′), *n., v.,* **-taged, -tag•ing.** —*n.* **1.** the carrying of boats, supplies, etc., overland from one navigable water to another. **2.** the route over which this is done. —*v.i., v.t.* **3.** to carry (boats, supplies, etc.) over a portage.

por′tal (-tl), *n.* a door, gate, or entrance, esp. one of imposing appearance.

port•cul•lis (pôrt kul′is), *n.* a strong iron grating at the gateway of a castle that can be let down to prevent passage.

por•tend (pôr tend′), *v.t.* **1.** to indicate in advance, as an omen does. **2.** to signify; mean.

por′tent (-tent), *n.* **1.** an indication or omen of something momentous about to happen. **2.** threatening or disquieting significance. —**por•ten′tous,** *adj.*

por•ter¹ (pôr′tər), *n.* **1.** a person hired to carry baggage, as at a railroad station. **2.** an attendant in a railroad parlor car or sleeping car.

por•ter² (pôr′tər), *n.* a doorkeeper.

por′ter•house′ *n.* a choice cut of beef between the prime ribs and the sirloin.

port•fo•li•o (pôrt fō′lē ō′), *n., pl.* **-os. 1.** a flat, portable case for carrying loose papers, drawings, etc. **2.** a collection of drawings, photographs, etc., representative of a person's work. **3.** the securities held by an investor. **4.** the office or post of a minister of state.

port′hole′ *n.* a small, round window in the side of a ship.

por•ti•co (pôr′ti kō′), *n., pl.* **-coes, -cos.** a porchlike structure consisting of a roof supported by columns.

por•tion (pôr′shən), *n.* **1.** a part of a whole; segment. **2.** the part of a whole allotted to a person or group; share. **3.** a person's fate or lot. **4.** a dowry. —*v.t.* **5.** to divide into portions. **6.** to furnish with a portion.

port′ly *adj.,* **-li•er, -li•est.** rather heavy or fat. —**port′li•ness,** *n.*

port•man•teau (pôrt man′tō), *n., pl.* **-teaus, -teaux** (-tōz, -tō). *Chiefly Brit.* a leather trunk that opens into two halves.

por•trait (pôr′trit, -trāt), *n.* **1.** a painting or photograph of a person, esp. of the face. **2.** a verbal description. —**por′trai•ture,** *n.*

por′trait•ist *n.* a person who makes portraits.

por•tray (pôr trā′), *v.t.,* **-trayed, -tray•ing. 1.** to make a likeness of by drawing, painting, etc. **2.** to depict in words. **3.** to represent dramatically, as on the stage. —**por•tray′al,** *n.*

Por•tu•gal (pôr′chə gəl), *n.* a republic in SW Europe.

Por′tu•guese′ (-gēz′, -gēs′), *n., pl.* **-guese,** *adj.* —*n.* **1.** a native or inhabitant of Portugal. **2.** a Romance language spoken in Portugal, Brazil, the Azores, and Madeira. —*adj.* **3.** of Portugal, its people, or their language.

Por′tuguese man′-of-war′ *n.* a large colonial marine animal having a buoyant sac from which dangle poisonous stinging tentacles.

pose (pōz), *v.,* **posed, pos•ing,** *n.* —*v.i.* **1.** to assume or hold a physical position or attitude, as for an artistic purpose. **2.** to pretend to be what one is not: *to pose as a police officer.* **3.** to behave in an affected manner. —*v.t.* **4.** to place in a particular position, as for a picture. **5.** to state or put forward:

That poses a problem. —*n.* **6.** a bodily attitude or posture, esp. one assumed for an artistic purpose. **7.** a mental posture that is assumed for effect. —**pos′er,** *n.*

po•seur (pō zûr′), *n.* a person who affects a character, manner, etc., to impress others.

posh (posh), *adj.* stylishly elegant; luxurious.

pos•it (poz′it), *v.t.* to lay down or assume as a fact or principle; postulate.

po•si•tion (pə zish′ən), *n.* **1.** the location or place of a person or thing at a given moment. **2.** the proper or usual place: *out of position.* **3.** situation or condition with relation to circumstances: *The question put me in an awkward position.* **4.** status or standing; rank. **5.** a post of employment; job. **6.** the manner of being placed, disposed, or arranged. **7.** attitude or opinion. —*v.t.* **8.** to put in a particular position.

pos•i•tive (poz′i tiv), *adj.* **1.** confident in opinion or assertion; sure. **2.** showing approval or agreement. **3.** affirmative: *a positive answer.* **4.** constructive: *a positive attitude.* **5.** explicitly stated, stipulated, etc.: *a positive denial.* **6.** certain: *positive proof.* **7.** overconfident or dogmatic. **8.** possessing an actual force, existence, etc. **9.** proceeding in a direction assumed as beneficial, auspicious, etc.: *a positive trend.* **10. a.** noting or pertaining to the electricity in a body or substance that is deficient in electrons. **b.** indicating a point in a circuit that has a higher potential than that of another point. **11.** (of a diagnostic test) indicating the presence of the disease, condition, etc., tested for. **12.** noting a numerical quantity greater than zero. **13.** designating the initial degree of grammatical comparison, used with reference to the base form of an adjective or adverb, as *good* or *smoothly.* **14.** of or noting a photographic print showing the brightness values as they are in the subject. —*n.* **15.** something positive. **16. a.** the positive degree in grammatical comparison. **b.** the positive form of an adjective or adverb. **17.** a positive photographic image. —**pos′i•tive•ly,** *adv.*

pos•i•tron (poz′i tron′), *n.* an elementary particle with the same mass as an electron but a positive charge.

pos•se (pos′ē), *n.* a body of persons given legal authority to assist a peace officer, esp. in an emergency.

pos•sess (pə zes′), *v.t.* **1.** to have as property; own. **2.** to have as a faculty, quality, or the like. **3.** to have a powerful influence on; control or dominate: *possessed by an idea.* —**pos•ses′sor,** *n.*

pos•sessed′ *adj.* controlled or moved by a strong feeling, madness, or a supernatural power.

pos•ses′sion *n.* **1.** the act of possessing or state of being possessed. **2.** a thing possessed or owned. **3. possessions,** property or wealth. **4.** a territorial dominion of a state.

pos•ses′sive *adj.* **1.** desiring to dominate or be the only influence on someone. **2.** of possession or ownership. **3.** (of a word, construction, or grammatical case) indicating possession, ownership, origin, etc., as *Jane's* in *Jane's coat.* —*n.* **4.** the possessive case. **5.** a possessive form or construction. —**pos•ses′sive•ly,** *adv.* —**pos•ses′sive•ness,** *n.*

pos•si•ble (pos′ə bəl), *adj.* **1.** that may or can exist, happen, be done, etc. **2.** capable of being true: *It is possible that she has gone.* —**pos′si•bil′i•ty,** *n., pl.* **-ties.** —**pos′si•bly,** *adv.*

pos•sum (pos′əm), *n., pl.* **-sums, -sum. 1.** OPOSSUM. —*Idiom.* **2. play possum,** to feign sleep or death.

post¹ (pōst), *n.* **1.** a piece of timber or metal set upright as a support, a point of attachment, etc. **2.** the point where a race begins or ends. —*v.t.* **3.** to affix (a notice) to a post, wall, etc. **4.** to bring to public notice, as by a poster: *to post a reward.* **5.** to publish the name of in a list. **6.** to put up signs on (property) forbidding trespass.

post² (pōst), *n.* **1.** a position of duty, employment, or trust: *a diplomatic post.* **2.** a military station with permanent buildings. **3.** the body of troops occupying a military station. —*v.t.* **4.** to station at a post. **5.** to provide, as bail.

post³ (pōst), *n.* **1.** *Chiefly Brit.* **a.** a single delivery of mail. **b.** the mail itself. —*v.t.* **2.** to supply with up-to-date information: *Keep me posted on your activities.* **3.** *Chiefly Brit.* to send by mail. **4.** *Bookkeeping.* to transfer (an entry or item) from a journal to a ledger. **5.** to travel with speed; hasten.

post- a prefix meaning: subsequent to or after (*postdate*); at the rear of or behind (*postnasal*).

post•age (pō′stij), *n.* the charge for the conveyance of matter sent by mail.

post•al (pōs′tl), *adj.* **1.** of or pertaining to the post office or mail service. —*Idiom.* **2. go postal,** *Slang.* to lose control or go crazy.

post•bel′lum (-bel′əm) *adj.* after war, esp. U.S. Civil War.

post′card′ *n.* **1.** a small card usu. having a picture on one side and space for a stamp, address, and message on the other. **2.** a card sold by the post office with a stamplike motif and value printed on it.

post•date (pōst dāt′, pōst′-), *v.t.,* **-dat•ed, -dat•ing. 1.** to date (a check, invoice, etc.) with a date later than the current or actual date. **2.** to follow in time.

post′er *n.* a placard or bill for posting in a public place, as for advertising.

pos•te•ri•or (po stēr′ē ər, pō-), *adj.* **1.** situated behind or at the rear of. **2.** coming after in order or in time. —*n.* **3.** the buttocks.

pos•ter•i•ty (po stēr′i tē), *n.* **1.** future generations collectively. **2.** all the descendants of one person.

post•grad•u•ate (pōst graj′ō̄o it, -āt′), *adj.* **1.** of or consisting of postgraduates. —*n.* **2.** a student who is taking advanced work after graduation.

post′haste′ *adv.* with the greatest possible speed.

post•hu•mous (pos′chə məs, -chō̄o-), *adj.* **1.** occurring after one's death. **2.** published after the death of the author. **3.** born after the death of the father. —**post′hu•mous•ly,** *adv.*

post′man *n., pl.* **-men.** MAIL CARRIER.

post′mark′ *n.* **1.** an official mark stamped on mail passed through a postal system, showing the place and date of sending. —*v.t.* **2.** to stamp with a postmark.

post′mas′ter *n.* the official in charge of a post office.

post′ me•rid′i•em (mə rid′ē əm, -em′), *adj.* See P.M.

post′mis′tress *n.* a woman in charge of a post office.

post•mod′ern *adj.* (*sometimes cap.*) pertaining to any of various movements in the arts or literature developing in the late 20th century in reaction to modernism.

post•mor′tem (-môr′təm), *adj.* **1.** of or occurring in the time following death. **2.** pertaining to examination of the body after death. —*n.* **3.** a postmortem examination; autopsy. **4.** an evaluation after the end or fact of something.

post•na′tal *adj.* subsequent to childbirth.

post′ of′fice *n.* **1.** an office of a government postal system at which mail is handled, stamps are sold, and other services rendered. **2.** (*often caps.*) the department of a government in charge of the mail.

post′paid′ *adj., adv.* with the postage prepaid.

post•par′tum (-pär′təm), *adj.* following childbirth.

post•pone (pōst pōn′, pōs-), *v.t.,* **-poned, -pon•ing.** to put off to a later time. —**post•pone′ment,** *n.*

post′script′ (pōst′skript′, pōs′-), *n.* a note added to a letter that has already been signed.

pos•tu•late (*v.* pos′chə lāt′; *n.* -lit, -lāt′), *v.,* **-lat•ed, -lat•ing,** *n.* —*v.t.* **1.** to assume the existence or truth of as a basis for reasoning or arguing. **2.** to assume without proof; take for granted. —*n.* **3.** something postulated. **4.** a necessary condition; prerequisite. —**pos′tu•la′tion,** *n.*

pos•ture (pos′chər), *n., v.,* **-tured, -tur•ing.** —*n.* **1.** the position or carriage of the body. **2.** an affected or unnatural attitude. **3.** a policy or stance, as that adopted by a government. —*v.i.* **4.** to act in an affected or artificial manner.

post′war′ *adj.* following a war.

po•sy (pō′zē), *n., pl.* **-sies.** a flower, nosegay, or bouquet.

pot¹ (pot), *n., v.,* **pot•ted, pot•ting.** —*n.* **1.** a container of earthenware, metal, etc., usu. round and deep, used for cooking, serving, etc. **2.** such a container with its contents. **3.** FLOWERPOT. **4.** all the money bet at a single time. —*v.t.* **5.** to put into a pot. **6.** to cook or preserve in a pot. —*Idiom.* **7. go to pot,** to become ruined.

pot² (pot), *n. Slang.* MARIJUANA.

po•ta•ble (pō′tə bəl), *adj.* **1.** fit for drinking. —*n.* **2.** Usu., **-bles.** drinkable liquids.

pot•ash (pot′ash′), *n.* a potassium compound obtained from wood ashes, used in making soap, glass, etc.

po•tas•si•um (pə tas′ē əm), *n.* a silvery white metallic element whose compounds are used in industry and medicine. *Symbol:* K; *at. wt.:* 39.102; *at. no.:* 19.

potas′sium ni′trate *n.* a crystalline compound used in gunpowders, fertilizers, and preservatives.

po•ta•to (pə tā′tō, -tə), *n., pl.* **-toes. 1.** the edible tuber of a cultivated plant of the nightshade family. **2.** the plant itself.

pot′bel′ly *n., pl.* **-lies.** a protuberant belly. —**pot′-bel′lied,** *adj.*

pot′boil′er *n.* a mediocre work of literature or art produced merely for financial gain.

po•tent (pōt′nt), *adj.* **1.** powerful; mighty. **2.** cogent; persuasive. **3.** producing powerful physical or chemical effects. **4.** (of a male) capable of sexual intercourse. —**po′ten•cy,** *n., pl.* **-cies.**

po′ten•tate′ (-tāt′), *n.* a person who possesses great power, as a monarch.

po•ten•tial (pə ten′shəl), *adj.* **1.** possible, as opposed to actual. **2.** capable of being or becoming. —*n.* **3.** something potential; possibility. **4.** a latent excellence or ability that may or may not be developed. **5.** the relative electrification of a point or body with respect to some other electrification, as that of the earth. —**po•ten′ti•al•i•ty** (-shē al′i tē), *n., pl.* **-ties.** —**po•ten′tial•ly,** *adv.*

poth•er (poth′ər), *n.* **1.** commotion; uproar. —*v.t., v.i.* **2.** to worry; bother.

pot′hole′ *n.* a hole formed in pavement.

po•tion (pō′shən), *n.* a drink, esp. one having or reputed to have medicinal, poisonous, or magical powers.

pot′luck′ *n.* **1.** a meal that happens to be available without special preparation. **2.** Also called **pot′luck sup′per.** a meal to which participants bring food to be shared.

pot•pour•ri (pō′pŏŏ rē′), *n., pl.* **-ris. 1.** a fragrant mixture of dried flower petals and spices. **2.** any miscellaneous grouping.

pot′shot′ *n.* **1.** a shot at an animal or person within easy range. **2.** a casual or aimless shot. **3.** a random or incidental criticism.

pot′ted *adj.* **1.** transplanted into or grown in a pot. **2.** *Slang.* drunk.

pot′ter *n.* a person who makes pottery.

pot′ter•y *n., pl.* **-ies. 1.** ceramic ware, esp. earthenware and stoneware. **2.** the art or business of a potter. **3.** a place where earthen vessels are made.

pouch (pouch), *n.* **1.** a small bag or similar receptacle: *a tobacco pouch.* **2.** a bag for carrying mail. **3.** a baglike anatomical structure, as the receptacle for the young of marsupials. —*v.t.* **4.** to put into a pouch. —*v.i.* **5.** to form a pouch or pouchlike cavity.

poul•tice (pōl′tis), *n., v.,* **-ticed, -tic•ing.** —*n.* **1.** a soft, moist mass of cloth, meal, herbs, etc., applied as a medicament to the body. —*v.t.* **2.** to apply a poultice to.

poul•try (pōl′trē), *n.* domesticated fowl valued for their meat and eggs, as chickens and turkeys.

pounce (pouns), *v.,* **pounced, pounc•ing,** *n.* —*v.i.* **1.** to swoop down or spring suddenly. **2.** to seize eagerly or suddenly. —*n.* **3.** a sudden swoop or spring.

pound¹ (pound), *v.t.* **1.** to strike repeatedly with great force, as with the fist. **2.** to crush into a powder or paste by beating repeatedly. —*v.i.* **3.** to strike heavy blows repeatedly. **4.** to throb violently, as the heart. **5.** to walk or go with heavy steps.

pound² (pound), *n., pl.* **pounds, pound. 1. a.** an avoirdupois unit of weight equal to 7000 grains, divided into 16 ounces (0.453 kg). **b.** a troy unit of weight equal to 5760 grains, divided into 12 ounces (0.373 kg). **2.** Also called **pound′ ster′ling.** the basic monetary unit of the United Kingdom, formerly equal to 20 shillings or 240 pence: equal to 100 new pence after decimalization in 1971. **3.** the basic monetary unit of Cyprus, Egypt, Ireland, Lebanon, and Syria.

pound³ (pound), *n.* an enclosure maintained by public authorities for confining stray or homeless animals.

pound′ cake′ *n.* a rich cake made with flour, butter, sugar, and eggs.

pour (pôr), *v.t.* **1.** to send (a liquid, fluid, etc.) flowing, as from one container to another. **2.** to emit, propel, or utter continuously or rapidly. —*v.i.* **3.** to move or proceed in great quantity or number. **4.** to flow forth or along; stream. **5.** to rain heavily.

pout (pout), *v.i.* **1.** to thrust out the lips, esp. in displeasure or sullenness. **2.** to look or be sullen. —*n.* **3.** the act of pouting. **4.** a fit of sullenness: *to be in a pout.*

pov•er•ty (pov′ər tē), *n.* **1.** the state or condition of being poor. **2.** deficiency of necessary or desirable ingredients, qualities, etc. **3.** scantiness; insufficiency.

POW *pl.* **POWs, POW's.** prisoner of war.

pow•der (pou′dər), *n.* **1.** matter reduced to a state of fine, loose particles by grinding, disintegration, etc. **2.** a preparation in this form, as face powder. **3.** loose, fresh snow that is not granular, wet, or packed. —*v.t.* **4.** to reduce to powder; pulverize. **5.** to sprinkle or cover with powder. —**pow′der•y,** *adj.*

pow′der keg′ *n.* **1.** a barrellike container for gunpowder. **2.** a dangerously explosive situation.

pow•er (pou′ər), *n.* **1.** ability to do or act. **2.** strength; might; force. **3.** the possession of control over others; authority. **4.** legal ability or authority. **5.** a person or thing that possesses authority or influence. **6.** a nation having international authority or influence. **7.** mechanical or physical energy: *hydroelectric power.* **8.** *Math.* the product obtained by multiplying a quantity by itself one or more times. **9.** the magnifying capacity of a microscope, telescope, etc. —*v.t.* **10.** to supply with electricity or other means of power. —*adj.* **11.** operated by a motor or electricity. **12.** operated by a procedure in which manual effort is supplemented or replaced by hydraulic, mechanical, or electric means: *power brakes.* **13.** conducting electricity. **14.** *Informal.* involving or characteristic of those having power or authority: *a power breakfast.*

pow′er•ful (-fəl), *adj.* having or exerting great power, strength, authority, influence, etc. —**pow′er•ful•ly,** *adv.*

pow′er•house′ *n.* **1.** a building where electricity is generated. **2.** a person or group with great energy or potential for success.

pow′er•less *adj.* **1.** unable to produce an effect; ineffective. **2.** lacking power to act; helpless. —**pow′er•less•ly,** *adv.*

pow′er of attor′ney *n.* written legal authorization for another person to act in one's place.

pow•wow (pou′wou′), *n.* **1.** a council or conference of or with North American Indians. **2.** *Informal.* any conference.

pox (poks), *n.* **1.** a disease characterized by multiple skin pustules, as smallpox. **2.** syphilis.

pp. **1.** pages. **2.** past participle.

P.P.S. or **p.p.s.,** an additional postscript.

PR or **P.R., 1.** public relations. **2.** Puerto Rico.

Pr *Chem. Symbol.* praseodymium.

prac•ti•ca•ble (prak′ti kə bəl), *adj.* **1.** capable of being put into practice. **2.** capable of being used. —**prac′ti•ca•bil′i•ty,** *n.* —**prac′ti•ca•bly,** *adv.*

prac′ti•cal *adj.* **1.** of, involving, or resulting from practice or action. **2.** adapted or suited for actual use: *practical instructions.* **3.** inclined toward or fitted for action or useful activities. **4.** engaged or experienced in actual practice or work: *a practical politician.* **5.** matter-of-fact; prosaic. **6.** being such in practice or effect: *a practical certainty.* —**prac'ti•cal•i•ty,** *n., pl.* **-ties.**

prac•ti•cal•ly *adv.* **1.** in a practical manner. **2.** from a practical point of view. **3.** almost; nearly.

prac•tice (-tis), *n., v.,* **-ticed, -tic•ing.** —*n.* **1.** habitual or customary course of action or way of doing something. **2.** repeated performance or exercise in order to acquire skill. **3.** skill so gained. **4.** the action of doing something: *to put a scheme into practice.* **5.** the exercise or pursuit of a profession. —*v.t.* **6.** to perform or do habitually or usually. **7.** to pursue as a profession. **8.** to perform or exercise repeatedly in order to acquire skill. —*v.i.* **9.** to do something repeatedly in order to acquire skill. Also, *Brit.,* **prac'tise** (for defs. 6–9).

prac•ti'tion•er (-tish'ə nər), *n.* a person engaged in the practice of a profession or occupation.

prag•mat•ic (prag mat'ik), *adj.* **1.** concerned with practical considerations or consequences. **2.** of philosophical pragmatism. —**prag•mat'i•cal•ly,** *adv.*

prag'ma•tism (-mə tiz'əm), *n.* **1.** emphasis on practical results or concerns. **2.** a philosophical system stressing practical consequences as constituting the essential criterion in determining truth or value. —**prag'ma•tist,** *n., adj.*

prai•rie (prâr'ē), *n., pl.* **-ries.** an extensive, grassy, level or rolling tract of land.

prai'rie dog' *n.* a burrowing squirrel of W North American and N Mexican plains and prairies.

praise (prāz), *n., v.,* **praised, prais•ing.** —*n.* **1.** an expression of approval or admiration. **2.** the offering of grateful homage as an act of worship. —*v.t.* **3.** to express approval or admiration of. **4.** to offer grateful homage to (God or a deity).

praise'wor'thy *adj.* deserving of praise. —**praise'wor'thi•ness,** *n.*

pra•line (prā'lēn, prä'-), *n.* a confection made of nuts and sugar cooked until caramelized.

prance (prans, präns), *v.,* **pranced, pranc•ing.** *n.* —*v.i.* **1.** to move in a lively or spirited manner; caper. **2.** to move in a proud or insolent manner. **3.** (esp. of a horse) to spring from the hind legs, or move by springing. —*n.* **4.** the act of prancing.

prank (prangk), *n.* a playful, sometimes malicious, trick. —**prank'ster,** *n.*

prate (prāt), *v.i., v.t.,* **prat•ed, prat•ing.** to talk excessively and pointlessly.

prat•fall (prat'fôl'), *n.* a fall on the buttocks, often regarded as comical or humiliating.

prat•tle (prat'l), *v.,* **-tled, -tling,** *n.* —*v.i., v.t.* **1.** to talk in a childish or simple-minded way. —*n.* **2.** chatter; babble.

prawn (prôn), *n.* any of various shrimplike crustaceans, some of which are used as food.

pray (prā), *v.,* **prayed, pray•ing.** —*v.t.* **1.** to offer devout petition, praise, thanks, etc., to (God or an object of worship). **2.** to make earnest petition to (a person). —*v.i.* **3.** to engage in prayer. **4.** to make entreaty to a person or for a thing.

prayer (prâr), *n.* **1.** a devout petition to or spiritual communion with God or an object of worship. **2.** the act of praying. **3.** a formula of words used in praying. **4. prayers,** a religious observance consisting mainly of prayer. **5.** something prayed for. **6.** a petition; entreaty. **7.** a negligible hope or chance.

pre- a prefix meaning: before or earlier than (*precursor*); in front or ahead of (*preface*); above or surpassing (*preeminent*).

preach (prēch), *v.t.* **1.** to deliver (a sermon). **2.** to advocate (moral principles, conduct, etc.) as right or advisable. —*v.i.* **3.** to deliver a sermon. **4.** to give advice in an insistent, tedious, or moralizing way. —**preach'er,** *n.* —**preach'y,** *adj.,* **-i•er, -i•est.**

pre•am•ble (prē'am'bəl, prē am'-), *n.* an introductory statement, as of a statute or constitution, stating the intent of what follows.

pre•can'cer•ous *adj.* showing pathological changes that may be preliminary to malignancy.

pre•car•i•ous (pri kâr'ē əs), *adj.* **1.** dependent on circumstances beyond one's control; uncertain. **2.**

dangerous because insecure or unsteady. —**pre•car'i•ous•ly,** *adv.*

pre•cau•tion (pri kô'shən), *n.* a measure taken in advance to avert possible harm. —**pre•cau'tion•ar'y,** *adj.*

pre•cede (pri sēd'), *v.t., v.i.,* **-ced•ed, -ced•ing.** to go or come before, as in place, rank, importance, or time.

prec•e•dence (pres'i dəns, pri sēd'ns), *n.* the act, fact, or right of preceding.

prec•e•dent (*n.* pres'i dənt; *adj.* pri sēd'nt, pres'i-dənt), *n.* **1.** an act, decision, or case that may serve as an example, guide, or justification for subsequent ones. **2.** established practice; custom. —*adj.* **3.** preceding; prior.

pre•cept (prē'sept), *n.* an injunction as to moral conduct; maxim.

pre•cep•tor (pri sep'tər, prē'sep-), *n.* a teacher; tutor.

pre•cinct (prē'singkt), *n.* **1.** a district, as of a city, marked out for administrative purposes or for police protection. **2.** the police station in such a district. **3.** one of a fixed number of voting districts of a city, town, etc. **4. precincts,** environs. **5.** a bounded space within which a building or place is situated.

pre•ci•os•i•ty (presh'ē os'i tē), *n., pl.* **-ties.** fastidious or carefully affected refinement.

pre•cious (presh'əs), *adj.* **1.** of high price or great value. **2.** dear; beloved. **3.** affectedly or excessively refined. —**pre'cious•ly,** *adv.*

prec•i•pice (pres'ə pis), *n.* a cliff with a vertical or overhanging face.

pre•cip'i•tate' (*v.* -tāt'; *adj., n.* -tit, -tāt'), *v.,* **-tat•ed, -tat•ing,** *adj., n.* —*v.t.* **1.** to hasten the occurrence of. **2.** to fling or hurl down. **3.** to separate (a substance) in solid form from a solution. —*v.i.* **4.** to condense from vapor and fall to the earth's surface as rain, snow, etc. **5.** to separate from a solution as a precipitate. —*adj.* **6.** overhasty; rash. **7.** exceedingly sudden or abrupt. —*n.* **8.** a substance precipitated from a solution. —**pre•cip'i•tate•ly,** *adv.*

pre•cip'i•ta'tion *n.* **1. a.** falling products of condensation in the atmosphere, as rain or snow. **b.** the amount of rain, snow, etc., that has fallen at a given place within a given period. **2.** the act of precipitating. **3.** the precipitating of a substance from a solution. **4.** sudden or rash haste.

pre•cip'i•tous *adj.* **1.** extremely steep. **2.** PRECIPITATE.

pré•cis (prā sē', prā'sē), *n., pl.* **-cis** (-sēz', -sēz). a concise summary.

pre•cise (pri sīs'), *adj.* **1.** definitely or strictly stated, defined, or fixed. **2.** exact in measuring, recording, etc. **3.** excessively or rigidly particular. —**pre•cise'ly,** *adv.* —**pre•cise'ness,** *n.*

pre•ci'sion (-sizh'ən), *n.* **1.** the state or quality of being precise. —*adj.* **2.** of or characterized by precision: *precision instruments.*

pre•clude (pri klood'), *v.t.,* **-clud•ed, -clud•ing. 1.** to make impossible. **2.** to exclude or debar. —**pre•clu'sion** (-kloo'zhən), *n.*

pre•co•cious (pri kō'shəs), *adj.* unusually advanced in mental development or talent. —**pre•coc'i•ty** (-kos'i tē), *n.*

pre•cog•ni•tion (prē'kog nish'ən), *n.* knowledge of a future event through extrasensory means. —**pre•cog'ni•tive** (-kog'ni tiv), *adj.*

pre'•Co•lum'bi•an *adj.* of the period before the arrival of Columbus in the Americas.

pre'con•ceive' *v.t.,* **-ceived, -ceiv•ing.** to form (an idea or opinion) beforehand. —**pre'con•cep'-tion,** *n.*

pre'con•di'tion *n.* **1.** something that is necessary to a subsequent result. —*v.t.* **2.** to subject to a special treatment in preparation for a subsequent experience, process, etc.

pre•cur•sor (pri kûr'sər, prē'kûr-), *n.* **1.** a person or thing that precedes, as in a job or method; forerunner. **2.** a harbinger. —**pre•cur'so•ry,** *adj.*

pred•a•to•ry (pred'ə tôr'ē), *adj.* **1.** preying upon other organisms for food. **2.** characterized by plunder, robbery, or exploitation. —**pred'a•tor,** *n.*

pred•e•ces•sor (pred′ə ses′ər), *n.* a person who precedes another in an office, position, etc.

pre•des•ti•na•tion (pri des′tə nā′shən, prē′des-), *n.* **1.** fate; destiny. **2.** the foreordination by God of whatever comes to pass, esp. the salvation and damnation of souls. **—pre•des′tine** (-tin), *v.t.*, **-tined, -tin•ing.**

pre•de•ter•mine (prē′di tûr′min), *v.t.*, **-mined, -min•ing. 1.** to decide in advance. **2.** to ordain in advance; predestine. **—pre′de•ter′mi•na′tion,** *n.*

pre•dic•a•ment (pri dik′ə mənt), *n.* an unpleasantly difficult or perplexing situation.

pred•i•cate (*v.* pred′i kāt′; *adj., n.* -kit), *v.*, **-cat•ed, -cat•ing,** *adj., n.* **—v.t. 1.** to declare or assert as an assumed quality or attribute. **2.** to found or derive (a statement, action, etc.); base: *to predicate one's behavior on faith in humanity.* **—adj. 3.** belonging to the predicate of a sentence. **—n. 4.** a syntactic unit that expresses the action performed by or the state attributed to the subject. **—pred′i•ca′tive** (-kā′tiv, -kə-), *adj.*

pre•dict (pri dikt′), *v.t., v.i.* to tell (what will happen) in advance; foretell. **—pre•dict′a•ble,** *adj.* **—pre•dic′tion,** *n.* **—pre•dic′tor,** *n.*

pre•di•lec•tion (pred′l ek′shən, prēd′-), *n.* a partiality; preference.

pre•dis•pose (prē′di spōz′), *v.t.*, **-posed, -pos•ing. 1.** to make susceptible or liable. **2.** to dispose beforehand; incline. **—pre•dis′po•si′tion,** *n.*

pre•dom•i•nate (pri dom′ə nāt′), *v.i.*, **-nat•ed, -nat•ing. 1.** to have numerical superiority or advantage. **2.** to have or exert controlling power. **—pre•dom′i•nance** (-nəns), *n.* **—pre•dom′i•nant** (-nənt), *adj.* **—pre•dom′i•nant•ly,** *adv.*

pre•em•i•nent (prē em′ə nənt), *adj.* eminent above or before others. **—pre•em′i•nence,** *n.* **—pre•em′i•nent•ly,** *adv.*

pre•empt (prē empt′), *v.t.* **1.** to occupy (land) in order to establish a prior right to buy. **2.** to acquire or appropriate before someone else can. **3.** to take the place of; supplant: *A news report preempted the game show.* **—pre•emp′tion,** *n.* **—pre•emp′tive,** *adj.*

preen (prēn), *v.t.* **1.** to trim or dress (feathers, fur, etc.) with the beak or tongue. **2.** to dress (oneself) carefully or smartly; primp. **3.** to pride (oneself) on something.

pre•fab (prē′fab′), *Informal.* **—adj. 1.** prefabricated. **—n. 2.** something prefabricated, as a building.

pre•fab′ri•cate′ *v.t.*, **-cat•ed, -cat•ing.** to manufacture in standardized sections ready for quick assembly, as a house. **—pre′fab•ri•ca′tion,** *n.*

pref•ace (pref′is), *n., v.*, **-aced, -ac•ing. —n. 1.** an introductory statement, as of a book or speech. **—v.t. 2.** to provide with or introduce by a preface. **—pref′a•to′ry** (-ə tôr′ē), *adj.*

pre•fect (prē′fekt), *n.* a chief magistrate or administrative official. **—pre′fec•ture** (-fek chər), *n.*

pre•fer (pri fûr′), *v.t.*, **-ferred, -fer•ring. 1.** to like better. **2.** to promote or advance, as in rank or office. **—Idiom. 3. prefer charges,** to make an accusation of misconduct, wrongdoing, etc., against another.

pref•er•a•ble (pref′ər ə bəl), *adj.* more desirable. **—pref′er•a•bly,** *adv.*

pref•er•ence (pref′ər əns), *n.* **1.** the act of preferring or state of being preferred. **2.** something preferred. **3.** an advantage given to one person or country over others. **—pref′er•en′tial** (-ə ren′shəl), *adj.*

pre•fer•ment (pri fûr′mənt), *n.* advancement or promotion, esp. in the church.

pre•fig•ure (prē fig′yər), *v.t.*, **-ured, -ur•ing.** to foreshadow.

pre•fix (*n.* prē′fiks; *v. also pre* fiks′), *n., v.*, **-fixed, -fix•ing. —n. 1.** an affix placed before a word or stem. **—v.t. 2.** to put before or in front. **3.** to add as a prefix.

preg•nant (preg′nənt), *adj.* **1.** having a child or other offspring developing in the body. **2.** fraught or abounding (usu. fol. by *with*). **3.** fertile; rich. **4.** full of meaning. **—preg′nan•cy,** *n., pl.* **-cies.**

pre•hen•sile (pri hen′sil, -sīl), *adj.* adapted for taking hold of something: *a prehensile tail.*

pre•his•tor•ic (prē′hi stôr′ik, -stor′-, prē′i-), *adj.* of the time prior to recorded history.

pre•judge′ *v.t.*, **-judged, -judg•ing.** to judge prematurely or without sufficient investigation. **—pre•judg′ment,** *n.*

prej•u•dice (prej′ə dis), *n., v.*, **-diced, -dic•ing. —n. 1.** an opinion, esp. an unfavorable one, formed beforehand or without knowledge or thought. **2.** unreasonable, hostile attitudes regarding a racial, religious, or national group. **3.** damage or injury. **—v.t. 4.** to affect with a prejudice. **—prej′u•di′cial** (-dish′əl), *adj.*

prel•ate (prel′it), *n.* an ecclesiastic of high rank, as a bishop.

pre•lim•i•nar•y (pri lim′ə ner′ē), *adj., n., pl.* **-ies. —adj. 1.** leading up to the main part or business. **—n. 2.** something preliminary, as an introductory or preparatory step.

prel•ude (prel′yōōd, prā′lōōd), *n.* **1.** a preliminary to an action, work, etc., of broader scope and higher importance. **2.** *Music.* **a.** a short, independent instrumental composition. **b.** a piece that is introductory to another piece.

pre•mar•i•tal (prē mar′i tl), *adj.* preceding marriage.

pre•ma•ture (prē′mə chŏŏr′, -tŏŏr′, -tyŏŏr′), *adj.* **1.** occurring, coming, or done too soon. **2.** born before gestation is complete. **—pre′ma•ture′ly,** *adv.*

pre•med•i•tate (pri med′i tāt′), *v.t., v.i.*, **-tat•ed, -tat•ing.** to consider or plan beforehand. **—pre•med′i•ta′tion,** *n.*

pre•mier (pri mēr′, -myēr′), *n.* **1.** the head of the cabinet in France and certain other countries; prime minister. **—adj. 2.** first in rank; chief.

pre•miere (pri mēr′, -myâr′), *n., v.*, **-miered, -mier•ing. —n. 1.** a first public performance of a play, opera, etc. **—v.t., v.i. 2.** to present or perform publicly for the first time. [< F: lit., first]

prem•ise (prem′is), *n., v.*, **-ised, -is•ing. —n. 1.** a proposition supporting or helping to support a conclusion or argument. **2. premises,** a tract of land including its buildings. **—v.t. 3.** to state or assume as a premise.

pre•mi•um (prē′mē əm), *n.* **1.** a bonus given as an inducement, as to purchase products. **2.** a sum additional to the usual price, wages, etc. **3.** the amount usu. paid in installments by a policyholder for coverage under a contract. **4.** great value or esteem: *She puts a premium on loyalty.*

pre•mo•lar (prē mō′lər), *n.* **1.** any of eight teeth located in pairs on each side of the upper and lower jaws in front of the molars. **—adj. 2.** of the premolars.

pre•mo•ni•tion (prem′ə nish′ən, prē′mə-), *n.* an intuitive anticipation of a future event; presentiment. **—pre•mon•i•to•ry** (pri mon′i tôr′ē), *adj.*

pre•na•tal (prē nāt′l), *adj.* previous to birth or to giving birth.

pre•oc•cu•py′ *v.t.*, **-pied, -py•ing. 1.** to engross to the exclusion of other things. **2.** to occupy beforehand or before others. **—pre•oc′cu•pa′tion,** *n.* **—pre•oc′cu•pied′,** *adj.*

pre•or•dain′ *v.t.* to ordain or decree beforehand.

prep (prep), *adj., v.*, **prepped, prep•ping. —adj. 1.** preparatory: *a prep school.* **—v.t. 2.** to prepare (a person), as for a surgical procedure. **—v.i. 3.** to prepare; get ready.

prep. 1. preparatory. **2.** preposition.

prep•a•ra•tion (prep′ə rā′shən), *n.* **1.** a plan, measure, etc., by which one prepares for something. **2.** the act of preparing or state of being prepared. **3.** something prepared or manufactured: *a preparation for burns.*

pre•par•a•to•ry (pri par′ə tôr′ē, -pâr′-, prep′-ər ə-), *adj.* **1.** serving to prepare. **2.** introductory.

prepar′atory school′ *n.* a private secondary school providing a college-preparatory education.

pre•pare (pri pâr′), *v.*, **-pared, -par•ing. —v.t. 1.** to put in readiness. **2.** to put together, as a meal. **3.** to provide with what is necessary. **—v.i. 4.** to put things or oneself in readiness.

pre•par′ed•ness (-pâr′id nis, -pârd′nis), *n.* the state of being prepared or ready, esp. for war.

pre•pay (prē pā′), *v.t.,* **-paid, -pay•ing.** to pay beforehand or before due. —**pre•pay′ment,** *n.*

pre•pon′der•ant (pri pon′dər ənt) *adj.* superior in force or numbers; predominant. —**pre•pon′der•ance,** *n.*

prep•o•si•tion (prep′ə zish′ən), *n.* a word used before a noun, pronoun, or other substantive to form a phrase. —**prep′o•si′tion•al,** *adj.*

pre′pos•sess′ing *adj.* impressing favorably.

pre•pos•ter•ous (pri pos′tər əs), *adj.* completely senseless or foolish.

prep•py or **-pie** (prep′ē), *n., pl.* **-pies,** *adj.,* **-pi•er, -pi•est.** —*n.* **1.** a student or graduate of a preparatory school. —*adj.* **2.** of or characteristic of a preppy.

pre•puce (prē′pyōōs), *n.* the fold of skin that covers the head of the penis.

pre•quel (prē′kwəl), *n.* a sequel to a film, play, etc., that prefigures the original.

pre•req•ui•site (pri rek′wə zit, prē-), *adj.* **1.** required beforehand. —*n.* **2.** something prerequisite.

pre•rog•a•tive (pri rog′ə tiv, pə rog′-), *n.* an exclusive right or privilege, exercised by virtue of rank, office, etc.

pres. 1. present. **2.** president.

pres•age (pres′ij; *v. also* pri sāj′), *v.,* **-aged, -ag•ing,** *n.* —*v.t.* **1.** to portend; foreshadow. **2.** to forecast; predict. —*n.* **3.** presentiment; foreboding. **4.** something that portends a future event; omen.

pres•by•o•pi•a (prez′bē ō′pē ə, pres′-), *n.* farsightedness, usu. associated with aging.

pres•by•ter (prez′bi tər, pres′-), *n.* **1.** (in hierarchical churches) a priest. **2.** an elder in a Presbyterian church.

Pres•by•te•ri•an (prez′bi tēr′ē ən, pres′-), *adj.* **1.** designating various churches governed by presbyters and professing modified forms of Calvinism. —*n.* **2.** a member of a Presbyterian church.

pres′by•ter′y *n., pl.* **-teries.** body of church elders and (in Presbyterian churches) ministers.

pre•school (*adj.* prē′skōōl′; *n.* prē′skōōl′), *adj.* **1.** of or for a child between infancy and kindergarten age. —*n.* **2.** a school or nursery for preschool children. —**pre′school′er,** *n.*

pre•science (presh′əns, -ē əns, prē′shəns, -shē əns), *n.* knowledge of things before they exist or happen. —**pre′scient,** *adj.*

pre•scribe (pri skrīb′), *v.t.,* **-scribed, -scrib•ing. 1.** to lay down as a rule or course of action to be followed. **2.** to order the use of (a medicine, remedy, etc.). —**pre•scrip•tive** (pri skrip′tiv), *adj.*

pre•scrip•tion (pri skrip′shən), *n.* **1. a.** a written direction by a physician for the preparation and use of a medicine. **b.** the medicine prescribed. **2.** the act of prescribing. **3.** something prescribed.

pres•ence (prez′əns), *n.* **1.** the state or fact of being present. **2.** immediate vicinity. **3.** personal appearance or bearing, esp. of a dignified or imposing kind.

pres′ence of mind′ *n.* the ability to think clearly and act appropriately, as during a crisis.

pres•ent¹ (prez′ənt), *adj.* **1.** existing or occurring now. **2.** designating a verb tense used to refer to an action or state occurring or existing at the moment of speaking or to a habitual event. **3.** being in a specified or understood place: *to be present at the wedding.* **4.** being actually under consideration: *the present topic.* —*n.* **5.** the present time. **6. a.** the present tense. **b.** a verb form in the present tense. —*Idiom.* **7. for the present,** for now; temporarily.

pre•sent² (*v.* pri zent′; *n.* prez′ənt), *v.t.* **1.** to furnish with a gift or the like, esp. by formal act. **2.** to offer or give in a formal way: *to present one's credentials.* **3.** to introduce (a person) to another, esp. in a formal manner. **4.** to bring before the public: *to present a play.* **5.** to offer for consideration: *to present a plan.* —*n.* **pres•ent 6.** a gift.

pre•sent•a•ble (pri zen′tə bəl), *adj.* **1.** capable of being presented. **2.** fit to be seen.

pres•en•ta•tion (prez′ən tā′shən, prē′zen-), *n.* **1.** the act of presenting or state of being presented. **2.**

an exhibition or performance, as of a play. **3.** a demonstration, lecture, or welcoming speech.

pre•sen•ti•ment (pri zen′tə mənt), *n.* a feeling that something is about to happen, esp. something evil.

pres•ent•ly (prez′ənt lē), *adv.* **1.** in a little while; soon. **2.** at the present time: *He is presently on sabbatical leave.*

pres•er•va•tion•ist (prez′ər vā′shə nist), *n.* one who advocates preservation, esp. of wildlife, natural areas, or historical places.

pre•serve (pri zûrv′), *v.,* **-served, -serv•ing,** *n.* —*v.t.* **1.** to keep alive or in existence: *to preserve our liberties.* **2.** to keep safe from harm or injury. **3.** to keep up; maintain. **4.** to prepare (any perishable substance) so as to resist decomposition or fermentation. **5.** to prepare (fruit, vegetables, etc.) by pickling, canning, etc. —*n.* **6.** Usu. **-serves.** fruit, vegetables, etc., prepared by cooking with sugar. **7.** a place set apart for protection of game or fish. —**pres•er•va•tion** (prez′ər vā′shən), *n.* —**pre•serv•a•tive,** *n., adj.*

pre•side (pri zīd′), *v.i.,* **-sid•ed, -sid•ing. 1.** to have charge of an assembly, meeting, etc. **2.** to exercise management or control.

pres•i•dent (prez′i dənt), *n.* **1.** (*often cap.*) the chief of state of a modern republic, as the United States. **2.** the chief officer of a university, corporation, etc. —**pres•i•den•cy,** *n., pl.* **-cies.** —**pres′i•den′tial** (-den′shəl), *adj.*

press¹ (pres), *v.t.* **1.** to act upon with steadily applied weight or force. **2.** to compress or squeeze. **3.** to hold closely, as in an embrace. **4.** to make smooth by ironing. **5.** to extract juice or contents from by pressure. **6.** to trouble or oppress, as by lack of something. **7.** to beset; harass. **8.** to urge insistently. **9.** to propound forcefully. **10.** to urge onward. —*v.i.* **11.** to exert weight or force. **12.** to bear heavily, as upon the mind. **13.** to push forward with force or haste. **14.** to crowd; throng. —*n.* **15.** a machine for printing on paper or the like from type, plates, etc. **16.** printed publications collectively, esp. newspapers and periodicals. **17.** their editorial employees. **18.** the consensus of critical commentary. **19.** an establishment for printing books, magazines, etc. **20.** any of various devices for exerting pressure, stamping, or crushing. **21.** a crowding together. **22.** the smooth effect caused by ironing. **23.** urgency, as of business. **24.** a large upright cupboard for holding clothes, linens, etc.

press² (pres), *v.t.* to force into service, esp. naval or military service.

press′ a′gent *n.* a person employed to promote a client by obtaining favorable publicity.

press′ con′ference *n.* an interview with reporters held by a government official or prominent person.

press′ing *adj.* demanding immediate attention.

press′ release′ *n.* a statement or news story distributed to the press by a public relations firm, governmental agency, etc.

pres•sure (presh′ər), *n., v.,* **-sured, -sur•ing.** —*n.* **1.** the exertion of force upon a surface by an object, fluid, etc., in contact with it. **2.** *Physics.* force per unit area. **3.** harassment; stress. **4.** a constraining or compelling force or influence. **5.** urgency, as of business: *He works well under pressure.* —*v.t.* **6.** to put pressure on.

pres′sure cook′er *n.* a cooking pot with an airtight lid for cooking food quickly by steam maintained under pressure.

pres′sure group′ *n.* an interest group that attempts to influence legislation.

pres′sur•ize′ *v.t.,* **-ized, -iz•ing.** to produce or maintain normal air pressure in (an airplane, spacesuit, etc.) at high altitudes. —**pres′sur•i•za′tion,** *n.*

pres•ti•dig•i•ta•tion (pres′ti dij′i tā′shən), *n.* sleight of hand.

pres•tige (pre stēzh′, -stēj′), *n.* reputation or influence arising from success, achievement, rank, etc. —**pres•tig′ious** (-stij′əs), *adj.*

pres•to (pres′tō), *adv.* **1.** quickly or immediately. **2.** *Music.* at a rapid tempo. —*adj.* **3.** quick or rapid.

4. *Music.* executed at a rapid tempo. [< It: quick, quickly < L *praestō* ready, at hand]

pre•sume (pri zōōm′), *v.*, **-sumed, -sum•ing.** —*v.t.* **1.** to take for granted, assume, or suppose. **2.** to undertake (to do something) without right or permission. —*v.i.* **3.** to go too far in acting unwarrantably; take liberties. —**pre•sum′a•ble,** *adj.* —**pre•sum′a•bly,** *adv.*

pre•sump′tion (-zump′shən), *n.* **1.** the act of presuming. **2.** something presumed; assumption. **3.** a reason for presuming. **4.** unwarrantable or impertinent boldness. —**pre•sump′tive,** *adj.*

pre•sump′tu•ous (-chōō əs), *adj.* unwarrantedly or impertinently bold.

pre•sup•pose (prē′sə pōz′), *v.t.*, **-posed, -pos•ing. 1.** to suppose or assume beforehand. **2.** to require as an antecedent condition. —**pre′sup•po•si′tion** (-sup ə zish′ən), *n.*

pre•teen′ *n.* a child between the ages of 10 and 13.

pre•tend (pri tend′), *v.t.* **1.** to feign: *to pretend illness.* **2.** to make believe: *The children pretended they were cowboys.* **3.** to presume; venture. **4.** to claim or profess falsely: *He pretended not to know.* —*v.i.* **5.** to make believe, as in play. **6.** to lay claim: *to pretend to the throne.* —**pre•tend′er,** *n.*

pre•tense (pri tens′, prē′tens), *n.* **1.** a false show of something: *a pretense of friendship.* **2.** a pretending or feigning. **3.** a false claim or justification; pretext. **4.** a claim; pretension.

pre•ten•sion (pri ten′shən), *n.* **1.** a claim to something. **2.** Often, **-sions.** an unwarranted or false claim, as to merit, importance, or wealth.

pre•ten′tious *adj.* **1.** characterized by the assumption of dignity, importance, artistic distinction, etc. **2.** making an exaggerated outward show; ostentatious. —**pre•ten′tious•ly,** *adv.* —**pre•ten′-tious•ness,** *n.*

pret•er•it or **-ite** (pret′ər it), *n.* **1.** a verb tense referring to a past or completed action or state. **2.** a verb form in this tense. —*adj.* **3.** expressing a past action or state.

pre•ter•nat•u•ral (prē′tər nach′ər əl), *adj.* **1.** being outside the ordinary course of nature; exceptional or abnormal. **2.** supernatural.

pre•text (prē′tekst), *n.* something put forward to conceal a true purpose.

pret•ty (prit′ē), *adj.*, **-ti•er, -ti•est,** *adv.*, *v.*, **-tied, -ty•ing.** —*adj.* **1.** attractive in a delicate or graceful way. **2.** fine; grand (often used ironically): *a pretty mess!* **3.** *Informal.* fairly great: *a pretty sum.* —*adv.* **4.** moderately: *a pretty good time.* —*v.t.* **5.** to make pretty: *to pretty up a room.* —**pret′ti•ly,** *adv.* —**pret′ti•ness,** *n.*

pret•zel (pret′səl), *n.* a crisp, dry biscuit, typically in the form of a knot or stick, salted on the outside.

pre•vail (pri vāl′), *v.i.* **1.** to be widespread or current. **2.** to occur as the most important or frequent element. **3.** to prove superior in power or influence: *to prevail over one's enemies.* **4.** to succeed. **5.** to use persuasion successfully: *Can you prevail on him to go?*

pre•vail′ing *adj.* **1.** most frequent or common. **2.** having superior power or influence.

prev•a•lent (prev′ə lənt), *adj.* **1.** widespread. **2.** dominant. —**prev′a•lence,** *n.*

pre•var•i•cate (pri var′i kāt′), *v.i.*, **-cat•ed, -cat•ing.** to speak falsely or misleadingly; equivocate; lie. —**pre•var′i•ca′tion,** *n.* —**pre•var′i•ca′tor,** *n.*

pre•vent (pri vent′), *v.t.* **1.** to keep from occurring. **2.** to stop from doing something. —**pre•vent′a•ble, pre•vent′i•ble,** *adj.* —**pre•ven′tion,** *n.* —**pre•ven′tive,** *adj.*

pre•view (prē′vyōō′), *n.* **1.** an earlier or advance view. **2.** an advance showing of a motion picture, play, etc., before its public opening. **3.** a showing of brief scenes from a motion picture for purposes of advertisement. —*v.t.* **4.** to view or show beforehand or in advance.

pre•vi•ous (prē′vē əs), *adj.* **1.** coming or occurring before something else; prior. —*Idiom.* **2.** previous to, before. —**pre′vi•ous•ly,** *adv.*

prey (prā), *n.*, *v.*, **preyed, prey•ing.** —*n.* **1.** an animal hunted or seized for food by a carnivorous ani-

mal. **2.** any victim. **3.** the action or habit of preying: *a beast of prey.* —*v.i.* (usu. fol. by *on* or *upon*) **4.** to seize and devour prey. **5.** to make attacks for plunder. **6.** to exert a harmful and often obsessive influence: *The problem preyed upon his mind.* **7.** to victimize others.

price (prīs), *n.*, *v.*, **priced, pric•ing.** —*n.* **1.** the amount of money for which anything is bought or sold. **2.** that which must be given, done, or undergone to obtain something. —*v.t.* **3.** to fix the price of. **4.** to find out the price of.

price′less *adj.* having a value beyond all price; invaluable.

pric′ey *adj.*, **-i•er, -i•est.** *Informal.* expensive or unduly expensive.

prick (prik), *n.* **1.** a puncture made by a needle, thorn, or the like. **2.** a sharp pain or feeling of discomfort; twinge. —*v.t.* **3.** to pierce with a sharp point. **4.** to affect with sharp pain. **5.** to cause sharp mental pain to. **6.** to cause to point upward: *The dog pricked up its ears.*

prick′le *n.*, *v.*, **-led, -ling.** —*n.* **1.** a small, sharp projection, as on a plant. **2.** a pricking sensation. —*v.t.* **3.** to cause a pricking or tingling sensation in. —*v.i.* **4.** to tingle. —**prick′ly,** *adj.*, **-li•er, -li•est.**

prick′ly heat′ *n.* a skin eruption accompanied by an itching sensation, due to an inflammation of the sweat glands.

pride (prīd), *n.*, *v.*, **prid•ed, prid•ing.** —*n.* **1.** self-respect; self-esteem. **2.** gratification arising from association with something laudable. **3.** conceit; arrogance. **4.** something that causes one to be proud. **5.** a group of lions. —*v.t.* **6.** to indulge (oneself) in a feeling of pride: *He prides himself on his good memory.* —**pride′ful,** *adj.*

priest (prēst), *n.* **1.** (in certain Christian, esp. Catholic, churches) a member of the clergy ranking below a bishop. **2.** a person whose office it is to perform religious rites. —**priest′hood,** *n.* —**priest′ly,** *adj.*

priest•ess (prē′stis), *n.* a woman who officiates in sacred rites.

prig (prig), *n.* a person self-righteously concerned with the rigid observance of proprieties. —**prig′-gish,** *adj.*

prim (prim), *adj.*, **-mer, -mest.** formally precise or proper; prissy. —**prim′ly,** *adv.* —**prim′ness,** *n.*

pri•ma•cy (prī′mə sē), *n.*, *pl.* **-cies. 1.** the state of being first in order, rank, importance, etc. **2.** the office or rank of an ecclesiastical primate.

pri•ma don•na (prē′mə don′ə, prim′ə), *n.*, *pl.* **prima don•nas. 1.** a principal female singer in an opera. **2.** a vain, temperamental person.

pri•ma fa•ci•e (prī′mə fā′shē ē′, fā′shē), *adj.* sufficient to establish a fact unless rebutted: *prima facie evidence.*

pri•mal (prī′məl), *adj.* **1.** first; original. **2.** of first importance.

pri•ma•ri•ly (prī mâr′ə lē, -mer′-), *adv.* **1.** essentially; chiefly. **2.** at first; originally.

pri•ma•ry (prī′mer ē, -mə rē), *adj.*, *n.*, *pl.* **-ries.** —*adj.* **1.** first in importance; chief. **2.** first in order or time. **3.** being of the most basic order of its kind: *a primary classification.* **4.** immediate or direct: *primary perceptions.* —*n.* **5.** something first in order or importance. **6.** a preliminary election in which voters of each party nominate candidates for office, party officers, etc.

pri•mate (prī′māt *or, esp. for 1,* -mit), *n.* **1.** an archbishop or bishop ranking first among the bishops of a province or country. **2.** any of an important order of mammals including humans, the apes, monkeys, and lemurs.

prime (prīm), *adj.*, *n.*, *v.*, **primed, prim•ing.** —*adj.* **1.** of the first rank or importance. **2.** of the greatest value or best quality. **3.** first in order of time or development. **4.** basic; fundamental. **5.** (of any two or more numbers) having no common divisor except unity. —*n.* **6.** the most flourishing stage or state. **7.** the choicest part of anything. **8.** the earliest stage of any period. —*v.t.* **9.** to prepare; make ready. **10.** to supply (a firearm) with powder. **11.** to pour liquid into (a pump) to expel air and prepare for action.

12. to cover (a surface) with an undercoat of paint or the like. **13.** to supply with needed information, facts, etc.

prime′ merid′ian *n.* the meridian running through Greenwich, England, from which longitude east and west is reckoned.

prime′ min′ister *n.* the head of government and of the cabinet in parliamentary systems.

prim•er¹ (prim′ər; *esp. Brit.* prī′mər), *n.* **1.** an elementary book for teaching children to read. **2.** any book of elementary principles.

prim•er² (prī′mər), *n.* **1.** one that primes. **2.** an explosive cap, cylinder, etc., used to ignite a charge of powder. **3.** a first coat of paint, size, etc.

prime′ rate′ *n.* the minimum interest rate charged by a commercial bank on business loans to large, best-rated customers.

prime′ time′ *n.* the hours, generally between 7 and 11 P.M., considered to have the largest television audience.

pri•me•val (prī mē′vəl), *adj.* of the first ages of the world; primordial.

prim•i•tive (prim′i tiv), *adj.* **1.** being the first or earliest of the kind: *primitive forms of life.* **2.** characteristic of early ages or of an early state of human development. **3.** simple or crude: *primitive equipment.* —*n.* **4.** someone or something primitive.

pri•mo•gen•i•ture (prī′mə jen′i chər, -chŏŏr′), *n.* **1.** the state of being the firstborn of the same parents. **2.** inheritance by the eldest son.

pri•mor•di•al (prī môr′dē əl), *adj.* existing at or from the very beginning.

primp (primp), *v.t., v.i.* to dress or groom (oneself) with care.

prim•rose (prim′rōz′), *n.* any of several plants with showy, five-lobed flowers in a variety of colors.

prince (prins), *n.* **1.** a nonreigning male member of a royal family, esp. a son of the sovereign. **2.** the ruler of a small or subordinate state. **3.** a person who is preeminent in any class or group.

prince′ly *adj.,* **-li•er, -li•est. 1.** lavish; magnificent. **2.** of a prince. —**prince′li•ness,** *n.*

prin•cess (prin′sis, -ses), *n.* **1.** a nonreigning female member of a royal family, esp. a daughter of the sovereign. **2.** the consort of a prince.

prin•ci•pal (prin′sə pəl), *adj.* **1.** first in rank, importance, value, etc. —*n.* **2.** a chief or head. **3.** the head of a school. **4.** a chief actor or performer. **5.** a person who authorizes another to act for him or her. **6.** a capital sum, as distinguished from interest or profit. —**prin′ci•pal•ly,** *adv.*

prin•ci•pal•i•ty (-pal′i tē), *n., pl.* **-ties.** a state ruled by a prince.

prin•ci•ple (prin′sə pəl), *n.* **1.** a rule of conduct. **2.** a fundamental law, axiom, or doctrine. **3.** a guiding sense of the requirements of right conduct: *a man of principle.* **4.** a law exemplified in natural phenomena, the operation of a machine, etc.: *the principle of capillary attraction.* **5.** a method of formation, operation, or procedure: *a family organized on the patriarchal principle.* —**prin′ci•pled,** *adj.*

print (print), *v.t., v.i.* **1.** to produce (a text, picture, etc.) by applying inked type or plates to paper or other material. **2.** to publish in printed form. **3.** to write in letters like those used in print. **4.** *Photog.* to produce a positive picture from (a negative). **5.** **print out,** *Computers.* to produce (data) in printed form. —*n.* **6.** printed lettering. **7.** printed material. **8.** an indentation, mark, etc., made by the pressure of one thing on another. **9.** a cloth displaying a stamped design or pattern. **10.** a photograph, esp. a positive made from a negative. —*Idiom.* **11.** in (or **out of**) **print,** (of a book or the like) still (or no longer) available from the publisher. —**print′a•ble,** *adj.*

print′out′ *n.* computer output produced by a printer.

pri•or¹ (prī′ər), *adj.* **1.** preceding in time or order. **2.** preceding in importance or privilege. —*Idiom.* **3.** prior to, preceding.

pri•or² (prī′ər), *n.* an officer in a religious house. —**pri′or•ess,** *n. fem.* —**pri′o•ry,** *n., pl.* **-ries.**

pri•or•i•tize (prī ôr′i tīz′, -or′-), *v.t.,* **-tized, -tiz•ing.** to arrange or do in order of priority.

pri•or•i•ty *n., pl.* **-ties. 1.** the state or quality of being earlier in time or occurrence. **2.** the right to take precedence in obtaining something. **3.** the right to precede others in rank, privilege, etc. **4.** something given special or prior attention.

prism (priz′əm), *n.* **1.** a transparent solid body used for dispersing light into a spectrum or for reflecting rays of light. **2.** a solid having bases or ends that are parallel, congruent polygons and sides that are parallelograms. —**pris•mat′ic** (-mat′ik), *adj.*

pris•on (priz′ən), *n.* a building for the confinement of persons convicted of crimes or awaiting trial.

pris′on•er *n.* a person confined in prison or kept in custody.

pris•sy (pris′ē), *adj.,* **-si•er, -si•est.** excessively or affectedly proper.

pris•tine (pris′tēn, pri stēn′), *adj.* **1.** uncorrupted or unsullied. **2.** of the earliest period or state.

pri•va•cy (prī′və sē; *Brit. also* priv′ə-), *n., pl.* **-cies. 1.** the state of being private. **2.** freedom from the intrusion of others in one's private life. **3.** secrecy.

pri•vate (prī′vit), *adj.* **1.** of or belonging to some particular person or persons. **2.** confined to or intended for only one person. **3.** not of an official or public character: *to return to private life.* **4.** personal; secret. **5.** not open to the general public. **6.** preferring privacy; retiring. **7.** not maintained under public funds: *a private school.* —*n.* **8.** a soldier of one of the three lowest enlisted ranks. **9. privates,** the external genital organs. —*Idiom.* **10. in private,** not publicly. —**pri′vate•ly,** *adv.*

pri•va•teer (prī′və tēr′), *n.* **1.** a privately owned ship commissioned to fight or harass enemy ships. **2.** the captain or a crew member of such a ship.

pri′vate eye′ *n. Informal.* a private detective.

pri•va•tion (prī vā′shən), *n.* lack of the usual comforts or necessaries of life.

priv•et (priv′it), *n.* an evergreen shrub commonly grown as a hedge.

priv•i•lege (priv′ə lij, priv′lij), *n., v.,* **-leged, -leg•ing.** —*n.* **1.** a right, immunity, or benefit enjoyed by a particular person or group. —*v.t.* **2.** to grant a privilege to.

priv•y (priv′ē), *adj.,* **-i•er, -i•est,** *n., pl.* **-ies.** —*adj.* **1.** having knowledge of something private or secret: *Many people were privy to the plot.* —*n.* **2.** OUTHOUSE.

priv′y coun′cil *n.* a board or select body of personal advisers, as of a sovereign.

prize¹ (prīz), *n.* **1.** a reward for victory or superiority, as in a contest or competition. **2.** anything striven for or worth striving for. —*adj.* **3.** having won a prize. **4.** worthy of a prize. **5.** awarded as a prize.

prize² (prīz), *v.t.,* **prized, priz•ing.** to value or esteem highly.

pro¹ (prō), *adv., n., pl.* **pros.** —*adv.* **1.** in favor of a proposition, opinion, etc. —*n.* **2.** a person who upholds the affirmative in a debate. **3.** an argument or vote in favor of something.

pro² (prō), *adj., n., pl.* **pros.** professional.

pro-¹, a prefix meaning: favoring or supporting (*pro-choice*); forth or forward (*proceed*); in place of (*pronoun*).

pro-², a prefix meaning: before or beforehand (*prognosis*); in front of (*proscenium*).

prob′a•ble *adj.* **1.** likely to occur or prove true. **2.** having more evidence for than against, but not proven conclusively. —**prob′a•bil′i•ty,** *n., pl.* **-ties.** —**prob′a•bly,** *adv.*

pro•bate (prō′bāt), *n., adj., v.,* **-bat•ed, -bat•ing.** —*n.* **1.** the official proving of a will as authentic or valid. —*adj.* **2.** of or involving probate. —*v.t.* **3.** to establish the authenticity or validity of (a will).

pro•ba•tion *n.* **1.** the testing of a person's conduct, character, etc. **2.** the period of such testing. **3.** the conditional release of an offender under supervision. —**pro•ba′tion•al, pro•ba′tion•ar′y,** *adj.* —**pro•ba′tion•er,** *n.*

probe (prōb), *v.,* **probed, prob•ing,** *n.* —*v.t.* **1.** to search into thoroughly. **2.** to examine or explore with a probe. —*v.i.* **3.** to examine or explore something with or as if with a probe. —*n.* **4.** a slender surgical instrument for exploring a wound, sinus, etc. **5.** an investigation of suspected illegal activity. **6.** a spacecraft designed to explore the solar system and transmit data back to earth.

pro•bi•ty (prō′bi tē, prob′i-), *n.* integrity and uprightness. [< L *probitās*]

prob•lem (prob′ləm), *n.* **1.** any question or matter involving doubt, uncertainty, or difficulty. **2.** a question proposed for solution or discussion. **3.** a source of difficulty or trouble. —**prob′le•mat′ic,** *adj.*

pro•bos•cis (prō bos′is, -kis), *n.* **1.** the trunk of an elephant. **2.** any long flexible snout.

pro•ce•dure (prə sē′jər), *n.* the act or manner of proceeding in any action. —**pro•ce′dur•al,** *adj.*

pro•ceed (*v.* prə sēd′; *n.* prō′sēd), *v.i.* **1.** to go forward or onward, esp. after stopping. **2.** to carry on any action. **3.** to initiate a legal action (often fol. by *against*). **4.** to come forth; issue (often fol. by *from*). —*n.* **5. proceeds,** the amount or profit derived from a sale or other transaction.

pro•ceed•ing (prə sē′ding), *n.* **1.** a particular action or course of action. **2. proceedings, a.** a record of the business discussed at a meeting, as of an academic society. **b.** legal action. **3.** the act of a person or thing that proceeds.

proc•ess (pros′es; *esp. Brit.* prō′ses), *n., pl.* **proc•ess•es** (pros′es iz, -ə siz, -ə sēz′; *esp. Brit.* prō′ses-, prō′sə-), *v.* —*n.* **1.** a systematic series of actions directed to some end: *a process for homogenizing milk.* **2.** a continuous action or series of changes taking place in a definite manner: *the process of decay.* **3.** the summons by which a defendant is brought to court. **4.** *Anatomy.* a natural outgrowth or projection. **5.** the action of going forward or on. —*v.t.* **6.** to treat or prepare by some particular process, as in manufacturing. **7.** to handle (persons, papers, etc.) according to a routine procedure.

pro•ces•sion (prə sesh′ən), *n.* **1.** the act of proceeding in an orderly succession or a ceremonious manner. **2.** a line of persons, vehicles, etc., moving in such a manner.

pro•ces′sion•al *n.* a piece of music suitable for accompanying a procession.

pro-choice (prō chois′), *adj.* supporting the right to legalized abortion.

pro•claim (prō klām′, prə-), *v.t.* to announce officially or formally. —**proc•la•ma•tion** (prok′lə mā′shən), *n.*

pro•cliv•i•ty (prō kliv′i tē), *n., pl.* **-ties.** a natural or habitual inclination or tendency.

pro•cras•ti•nate (prō kras′tə nāt′, prə-), *v.i., v.t.,* **-nat•ed, -nat•ing.** to defer or delay (action). —**pro•cras′ti•na′tion,** *n.*

pro•cre•ate (prō′krē āt′), *v.t., v.i.,* **-at•ed, -at•ing.** to beget or generate (offspring). —**pro′cre•a′tion,** *n.* —**pro′cre•a′tive,** *adj.*

proc•tor (prok′tər), *n.* **1.** a person who keeps watch over students at examinations. —*v.t., v.i.* **2.** to supervise or monitor.

pro•cure (prō kyŏŏr′, prə-), *v.t.,* **-cured, -cur•ing. 1.** to obtain by effort. **2.** to obtain (a person) for the purpose of prostitution. —**pro•cur′a•ble,** *adj.* —**pro•cure′ment,** *n.* —**pro•cur′er,** *n.*

prod (prod), *v.,* **prod•ded, prod•ding,** *n.* —*v.t.* **1.** to jab with or as if with something pointed. **2.** to nag; goad. —*n.* **3.** a poke or jab. **4.** any pointed instrument used as a goad.

prod•i•gal (prod′i gəl), *adj.* **1.** wastefully or recklessly extravagant. **2.** lavishly abundant. —*n.* **3.** one who is wastefully extravagant. —**prod′i•gal′i•ty** (-gal′i tē), *n., pl.* **-ties.**

pro•di•gious (prə dij′əs), *adj.* **1.** extraordinary in size, amount, etc. **2.** arousing admiration or amazement. —**pro•di′gious•ly,** *adv.*

prod•i•gy (prod′i jē), *n., pl.* **-gies.** a person, esp. a child, having extraordinary talent or ability.

pro•duce (*v.* prə dōōs′, -dyōōs′; *n.* prod′ōōs, -yōōs, prō′dōōs, -dyōōs), *v.,* **-duced, -duc•ing,** *n.* —*v.t.* **1.** to bring about; give rise to **2.** to bring into exist-

ence by intellectual or creative ability. **3.** to make or manufacture. **4.** to bear or yield. **5.** to present; exhibit: *to produce one's credentials.* **6.** to bring (a play, motion picture, etc.) before the public. —*v.i.* **7.** to yield products, offspring, etc. —*n.* **prod•uce 8.** agricultural products collectively, esp. vegetables and fruits. —**pro•duc′er,** *n.*

prod•uct (prod′əkt, -ukt), *n.* **1.** a thing produced, as by labor. **2.** a person or thing seen as resulting from a process, as a historical one. **3.** *Math.* the result obtained by multiplying two or more quantities together.

pro•duc•tion (prə duk′shən), *n.* **1.** the act of producing. **2.** something produced; product. **3.** the total amount produced. —**pro•duc′tive,** *adj.* —**pro•duc′tive•ly,** *adv.* —**pro•duc′tive•ness,** *n.*

pro′duc•tiv′i•ty (prō′duk tiv′i tē), *n.* **1.** the quality of being productive. **2.** the rate at which things are produced.

pro•fane (prə fān′, prō-), *adj., v.,* **-faned, -fan•ing.** —*adj.* **1.** showing irreverence toward God or sacred things. **2.** not devoted to holy purposes; secular. —*v.t.* **3.** to misuse (anything sacred); defile. —**prof•a•na•tion** (prof′ə nā′shən), *n.*

pro•fan•i•ty (-fan′i tē), *n., pl.* **-ties. 1.** the quality of being profane. **2.** irreverent or blasphemous speech.

pro•fess (prə fes′), *v.t.* **1.** to lay claim to, often insincerely; pretend to. **2.** to declare openly; affirm. **3.** to affirm one's faith in (a religion, God, etc.). —**pro•fessed′,** *adj.*

pro•fes•sion (prə fesh′ən) *n.* **1.** an occupation requiring extensive education, as law. **2.** the body of persons engaged in such an occupation. **3.** the act of professing.

pro•fes•sion•al *adj.* **1.** following an occupation as a means of livelihood. **2.** of or engaged in a profession. **3.** following as a business something usu. regarded as a pastime: *a professional golfer.* —*n.* **4.** a member of a profession. **5.** a person who earns a living in a sport or other occupation frequently engaged in by amateurs. **6.** an expert. —**pro•fes′sion•al•ly,** *adv.*

pro•fes′sor *n.* a college or university teacher, esp. one of the highest rank. —**pro•fes•so•ri•al** (prō′fə sôr′ē əl), *adj.*

prof•fer (prof′ər), *v.t.* to offer.

pro•fi•cient (prə fish′ənt), *adj.* fully competent in any endeavor; skilled. —**pro•fi′cien•cy** (-sē), *n.* —**pro•fi′cient•ly,** *adv.*

pro•file (prō′fīl), *n.* **1.** the outline of the human face viewed from one side. **2.** a picture or representation of this. **3.** an outline of an object. **4.** an informal biographical sketch.

prof•it (prof′it), *n.* **1.** the monetary surplus left after all expenses of a business transaction or venture have been met. **2.** advantage; benefit; gain. —*v.i., v.t.* **3.** to gain or cause to gain a profit. —**prof′it•a•ble,** *adj.* —**prof′it•a•bly,** *adv.*

prof′it•eer′ *n.* **1.** a person who makes excessive profits on the sale of scarce or rationed goods. —*v.i.* **2.** to act as a profiteer.

prof•li•gate (prof′li git, -gāt′), *adj.* **1.** utterly and shamelessly immoral. **2.** recklessly prodigal. —*n.* **3.** a profligate person. —**prof′li•ga•cy** (-gə sē), *n.*

pro for•ma (prō fôr′mə), *adj.* done as a matter of form or for the sake of form.

pro•found (prə found′), *adj.,* **-er, -est. 1.** showing deep insight or understanding. **2.** originating in the depths of one's being: *profound grief.* **3.** complete and pervasive: *a profound silence.* **4.** extending far beneath the surface: *the profound depths of the ocean.* —**pro•found′ly,** *adv.* —**pro•fun′di•ty** (-fun′di tē), *n., pl.* **-ties.**

pro•fuse (-fyōōs′), *adj.* **1.** extravagantly generous. **2.** made or done freely and abundantly. —**pro•fuse′ly,** *adv.* —**pro•fu′sion** (-fyōō′zhən), *n.*

pro•gen•i•tor (prō jen′i tər), *n.* **1.** a biologically related ancestor. **2.** a precursor.

prog•e•ny (proj′ə nē), *n., pl.* **-nies.** offspring collectively.

pro•ges•ter•one (prō jes′tə rōn′), *n.* a female

hormone, produced in the ovary or prepared synthetically.

prog•no•sis (prog nō′sis), *n., pl.* **-ses** (-sēz). a forecast, esp. of the probable course and outcome of a disease. —**prog•nos′tic** (-nos′tik), *adj.*

prog•nos′ti•cate′ (-nos′ti kāt′), *v.t.,* **-cat•ed,** **-cat•ing.** to forecast or prophesy from present signs or indications; foretell. —**prog•nos′ti•ca′tion,** *n.* —**prog•nos′ti•ca′tor,** *n.*

pro•gram (prō′gram, -grəm), *n., v.,* **-grammed** or **-gramed, -gram•ming** or **-gram•ing.** —*n.* **1.** a plan of action to accomplish a specified end. **2.** a schedule to be followed. **3.** a radio or television production. **4.** a list of pieces, performers, etc., in an entertainment. **5.** a sequence of instructions enabling a computer to perform a task. —*v.t.* **6.** to schedule as part of a program. **7.** to provide a program for. **8.** to insert (instructions) into a machine or apparatus. Also, *esp. Brit.,* **pro′gramme.** —**pro′gram•ma•ble,** *adj.* —**pro′gram•mat′ic** (-grə mat′ik), *adj.* —**pro′gram•mer,** *n.*

prog•ress (*n.* prog′res, -rəs; *esp. Brit.* prō′gres; *v.* prə gres′), *n.* **1.** advancement toward a goal or to a higher stage. **2.** continuous improvement. **3.** forward or onward movement. —*v.i.* **pro•gress 4.** to go forward or onward in space or time. **5.** to grow or develop.

pro•gres•sion (prə gresh′ən), *n.* **1.** the act of progressing; advance. **2.** a succession or series. **3.** *Math.* a succession of quantities in which there is a constant relation between each member and the one succeeding it.

pro•gres′sive *adj.* **1.** advocating progress or reform, esp. in political and social matters. **2.** noting or characterized by progress. **3.** advancing step by step. **4.** of or designating a verb form that indicates a continuing action or state. —*n.* **5.** a person who favors progress or reform. —**pro•gres′sive•ly,** *adv.*

pro•hib•it (prō hib′it), *v.t.* **1.** to forbid by authority or law. **2.** to prevent; hinder. —**pro•hib′i•tive, pro•hib′i•to′ry** (-i tôr′ē), *adj.*

pro•hi•bi•tion (prō′ə bish′ən), *n.* **1.** the act of prohibiting. **2.** the legal prohibiting of the manufacture, sale, and transportation of alcoholic beverages. —**pro′hi•bi′tion•ist,** *n.*

pro•hib′i•tive (-hib′ə tiv) *adj.* **1.** serving to prohibit something. **2.** sufficing to prevent the use, purchase, etc., of something.

proj•ect (*n.* proj′ekt, -ikt; *esp. Brit.* prō′jekt; *v.* prə jekt′), *n.* **1.** a plan or scheme. **2.** a large or important undertaking. —*v.t.* **pro•ject 3.** to propose or plan. **4.** to throw or impel forward or outward. **5.** to cast onto a surface or into space, as a shadow. **6.** to cause to jut out or protrude. —*v.i.* **pro•ject 7.** to jut out; protrude. —**pro•jec′tion,** *n.*

pro•jec•tile (prə jek′til, -tīl), *n.* **1.** an object fired from a gun, as a bullet. **2.** a body projected or impelled forward.

pro•jec′tion•ist *n.* an operator of a motion-picture or slide projector.

pro•jec′tor *n.* an apparatus for throwing an image onto a screen.

pro•le•tar•i•at (prō′li târ′ē ət), *n.* the working class, esp. industrial wage earners. —**pro′le•tar′i•an,** *adj., n.*

pro-life′ *adj.* opposed to legalized abortion.

pro•lif•er•ate (prə lif′ə rāt′), *v.i., v.t.,* **-at•ed, -at•ing.** to increase in number or spread rapidly. —**pro•lif′er•a′tion,** *n.*

pro•lif′ic *adj.* **1.** producing offspring, fruit, etc., abundantly. **2.** highly productive. —**pro•lif′i•cal•ly,** *adv.*

pro•lix (prō liks′, prō′liks), *adj.* tediously long and wordy.

pro•logue (prō′lôg, -log), *n.* **1.** an introductory part of a discourse, poem, or novel. **2.** anything that serves as an introduction.

pro•long (prə lông′, -long′), *v.t.* to extend the duration or spatial extent of. —**pro•lon•ga•tion** (prō′lông gā′shən), *n.*

prom (prom), *n.* a formal dance held by a high school or college class. [short for *promenade*]

prom•e•nade (prom′ə nād′, -näd′), *n., v.,*

-nad•ed, -nad•ing. —*n.* **1.** a leisurely walk in a public place. **2.** an area used for such walking. **3.** a march of guests opening a formal ball. —*v.i., v.t.* **4.** to take a promenade (through or about).

prom•i•nent (prom′ə nənt), *adj.* **1.** conspicuous. **2.** projecting. **3.** well-known; eminent. —**prom′i•nence,** *n.* —**prom′i•nent•ly,** *adv.*

pro•mis•cu•ous (prə mis′kyōō əs), *adj.* **1.** characterized by or having numerous sexual partners on a casual basis. **2.** consisting of a disordered mixture of various elements. —**prom•is•cu•i•ty** (prom′is-kyōō′i tē), *n.* —**pro•mis′cu•ous•ly,** *adv.*

prom•ise (prom′is), *n., v.,* **-ised, -is•ing.** —*n.* **1.** a declaration that something will or will not be done, given, etc. **2.** indication of future excellence or achievement. **3.** something promised. —*v.t., v.i.* **4.** to make a promise of (something). **5.** to afford ground for expecting.

prom•is•so•ry (prom′ə sôr′ē), *adj.* containing or implying a promise.

prom•on•to•ry (prom′ən tôr′ē), *n., pl.* **-ries.** a high point of land projecting into water; headland.

pro•mote (prə mōt′), *v.t.,* **-mot•ed, -mot•ing. 1.** to encourage to exist or flourish: *to promote peace.* **2.** to advance in rank, position, etc. **3.** to encourage the sales, acceptance, or recognition of, esp. through advertising. —**pro•mot′er,** *n.* —**pro•mo′tion,** *n.* —**pro•mo′tion•al,** *adj.*

prompt (prompt), *adj.,* **-er, -est,** *v.* —*adj.* **1.** done, performed, delivered, etc., without delay. **2.** quick to act or respond. **3.** punctual. —*v.t.* **4.** to induce to action. **5.** to give rise to or inspire. **6.** to give a cue to; remind. —**prompt′er,** *n.* —**prompt′ly,** *adv.* —**prompt′ness,** *n.*

prom•ul•gate (prom′əl gāt′, prō mul′gāt), *v.t.,* **-gat•ed, -gat•ing. 1.** to put into operation by formal proclamation, as a law. **2.** to set forth publicly, as a doctrine. —**prom′ul•ga′tion,** *n.*

prone (prōn), *adj.* **1.** having a natural tendency toward something. **2.** lying facedown.

prong (prông, prong), *n.* **1.** one of the pointed tines of a fork. **2.** any pointed, projecting part, as of an antler. —**pronged,** *adj.*

prong′horn′ *n., pl.* **-horns, -horn.** a fleet, antelopelike ruminant of the plains of W North America.

pro•noun (prō′noun′), *n.* a word used as a substitute for a noun or noun phrase. —**pro•nom′i•nal** (-nom′ə nl), *adj., n.*

pro•nounce (prə nouns′), *v.t.,* **-nounced, -nounc•ing. 1.** to enunciate or articulate (sounds, words, etc.). **2.** to utter or deliver formally or officially. —**pro•nounce′a•ble,** *adj.* —**pro•nun′ci•a′tion** (-nun′sē ā′shən), *n.*

pro•nounced′ *adj.* **1.** clearly apparent. **2.** decided; unequivocal.

pro•nounce′ment *n.* a formal or official statement.

pron•to (pron′tō), *adv.* promptly; quickly.

pro•nun•ci•a′tion (prə nun′sē ā′shən) *n.* production of sounds of speech.

proof (prōōf), *n.* **1.** evidence sufficient to establish a thing as true or believable. **2.** the establishment of a truth or fact. **3.** the strength of an alcoholic liquor with reference to a standard. **4.** *Photog.* a trial print from a negative. **5.** *Print.* a trial impression taken to correct errors and make alterations. —*adj.* **6.** impervious or invulnerable: *proof against attack.* **7.** of standard strength, as an alcoholic liquor.

-proof a combining form meaning: resistant or impervious to (*waterproof*); protected against (*bulletproof*).

proof′read′ (-rēd′), *v.t., v.i.,* **-read** (-red′), **-read•ing.** to read (printers' proofs, copy, etc.) to detect and mark errors to be corrected. —**proof′read′er,** *n.*

prop¹ (prop), *n., v.,* **propped, prop•ping.** —*n.* **1.** a stick or other rigid support. **2.** a person or thing serving as a support or stay. —*v.t.* **3.** to support with or as if with a prop. **4.** to rest (a thing) against a support.

prop² (prop), *n.* PROPERTY (def. 5).

prop³ (prop), *n.* a propeller.

prop•a•gan•da (prop′ə gan′də), *n.* **1.** information

or ideas methodically spread to promote or injure a cause, nation, etc. **2.** the deliberate spreading of such information or ideas. —**prop′a•gan/dist,** n. —**prop/a•gan/dize,** v.t., v.i., **-dized, -diz•ing.**

prop•a•gate (prop′ə gāt′), v., **-gat•ed, -gat•ing.** —v.t. **1.** to cause (an organism) to multiply by natural reproduction. **2.** to reproduce (itself, its kind, etc.), as an organism does. **3.** to transmit (hereditary features or elements) to or through offspring. **4.** to spread (a doctrine, practice, etc.) from person to person; disseminate. —v.i. **5.** to multiply by natural reproduction. —**prop/a•ga/tion,** n.

pro•pane (prō′pān), n. a colorless, flammable gas, used as a fuel and in organic synthesis.

pro•pel (prə pel′), v.t., **-pelled, -pel•ling.** to drive forward or onward. —**pro•pel/lant, pro•pel/lent,** n.

pro•pel/ler n. a device having a revolving hub with radiating blades, for propelling an airplane, ship, etc.

pro•pen•si•ty (prə pen′si tē), n., pl. **-ties.** a natural inclination or tendency.

prop•er (prop′ər), adj. **1.** appropriate to the purpose or circumstances. **2.** correct or decorous. **3.** fitting; right. **4.** belonging exclusively to a person, thing, or group. **5.** noting a particular person, place, or thing: a proper noun. **6.** in the strict sense: Boston proper. —**prop/er•ly,** adv.

prop•er•ty (prop′ər tē), n., pl. **-ties. 1.** that which a person owns. **2.** land or real estate. **3.** ownership; right of possession. **4.** an essential or distinctive attribute or quality of a thing. **5.** a usu. movable item used onstage or in a film set.

proph•e•cy (prof′ə sē), n., pl. **-cies. 1.** the foretelling of what is to come. **2.** something declared by a prophet. **3.** any prediction.

proph′e•sy/ (-sī′), v.t., v.i, **-sied, -sy•ing. 1.** to foretell or predict (future events). **2.** to foretell (something) by divine inspiration. —**proph/e•si/er,** n.

proph′et (-it), n. **1.** a person who speaks by divine inspiration. **2.** a person who foretells the future. —**pro•phet•ic** (prə fet′ik), adj. —**pro•phet/i•cal•ly,** adv.

pro•phy•lax•is (prō′fə lak′sis), n. the prevention of disease, as by protective measures or treatment. —**pro/phy•lac/tic,** adj., n.

pro•pin•qui•ty (prō ping′kwi tē), n. **1.** nearness in time or place. **2.** nearness of relation.

pro•pi•ti•ate (prə pish′ē āt′), v.t. **-at•ed, -at•ing.** to make favorably inclined; appease. —**pro•pit/i•a/tion,** n. —**pro•pi/ti•a•to/ry** (-ə tôr′ē), adj.

pro•pi/tious (-pish′əs), adj. **1.** presenting favorable conditions. **2.** indicative of favor; auspicious. **3.** favorably disposed. —**pro•pi/tious•ly,** adv.

pro•po•nent (prə pō′nənt), n. **1.** a person who puts forward a proposition. **2.** an adherent of a cause or doctrine.

pro•por•tion (prə pôr′shən), n. **1.** comparative relation between things or magnitudes. **2.** **proportions,** dimensions or size. **3.** a portion or part in its relation to the whole. **4.** symmetry or balance. —v.t. **5.** to adjust in proper proportion or relation. **6.** to balance or harmonize the proportions of. —**pro•por/tion•al, pro•por/tion•ate** (-shə nit), adj.

pro•pose (prə pōz′), v., **-posed, -pos•ing.** —v.t. **1.** to offer for consideration, action, etc. **2.** to offer (a toast). **3.** to plan; intend. —v.i. **4.** to make an offer of marriage. —**pro•pos/al,** n.

prop•o•si•tion (prop′ə zish′ən), n. **1.** the act of proposing or a plan proposed. **2.** an offer of terms for a transaction, as in business. **3.** a matter to be dealt with: a tough proposition. **4.** anything stated for discussion. **5.** Math. a formal statement of a truth to be demonstrated or an operation to be performed. **6.** a proposal of sexual relations. —v.t. **7.** to propose sexual relations to.

pro•pound (prə pound′), v.t. to put forward for consideration.

pro•pri•e•tar•y (prə prī′i ter′ē), adj. **1.** of or belonging to a proprietor. **2.** manufactured and sold only by the owner of the patent, trademark, etc.: proprietary medicine.

pro•pri•e•tor (prə prī′i tər), n. the owner of a

business establishment, property, etc. —**pro•pri/e•tor•ship/,** n.

pro•pri/e•ty n., pl. **-ties.** conformity to established standards of proper behavior or manners.

pro•pul•sion (prə pul′shən), n. **1.** the act of propelling or the state of being propelled. **2.** a propelling force, impulse, etc. —**pro•pul/sive** (-siv), adj.

pro•rate (prō rāt′, prō′rāt′), v.t., v.i., **-rat•ed, -rat•ing.** to divide, distribute, or calculate proportionately.

pro•sa•ic (prō zā′ik), adj. commonplace or dull. —**pro•sa/i•cal•ly,** adv.

pro•sce•ni•um (prō sē′nē əm, prə-), n., pl. **-ni•ums, -ni•a** (-nē ə). **1.** Also called **prosce/nium arch/.** the arch that separates a stage from the auditorium. **2.** (formerly) the apron or, esp. in ancient theater, the stage itself.

pro•scribe (prō skrīb′), v.t., **-scribed, -scrib•ing. 1.** to condemn (a thing) as harmful or odious; prohibit. **2.** to outlaw. **3.** to banish or exile. —**pro•scrip/tion** (-skrip′shən), n.

prose (prōz), n. **1.** ordinary language, as distinguished from poetry or verse.

pros•e•cute (pros′i kyōōt′), v.t., **-cut•ed, -cut•ing. 1.** to conduct legal proceedings against. **2.** to carry forward (an undertaking), usu. to completion: to prosecute a war. —**pros/e•cu/tion,** n. —**pros/e•cu/tor,** n.

pros•e•lyt•ize (pros′ə li tīz′), v.t., v.i., **-ized, -iz•ing.** to attempt to convert (someone) to another opinion, religious belief, etc. —**pros/e•lyte/** (-līt′), n. —**pros/e•lyt•iz/er,** n.

pros•pect (pros′pekt), n. **1.** Usu., **-pects. a.** the probability of success, profit, etc. **b.** the outlook for the future. **2.** anticipation; expectation. **3.** a potential customer, candidate, etc. **4.** a view, esp. of scenery. **5.** a mental view or survey. —v.t., v.i. **6.** to search (a region), as for gold. —**pros/pec•tor,** n.

pro•spec•tive (prə spek′tiv), adj. potential or likely.

pro•spec/tus (-təs), n., pl. **-tus•es.** a document describing a proposed business venture, literary work, etc., for evaluation by prospective investors, participants, or buyers.

pros•per (pros′pər), v.i. to be successful or fortunate, esp. financially. —**pros•per•i•ty** (pro sper′i tē), n. —**pros/per•ous,** adj.

pros′tate gland/ (pros′tāt), n. a gland surrounding the urethra of males that secretes a fluid that makes up part of the semen.

pros•the•sis (pros thē′sis), n., pl. **-ses** (-sēz). a device that substitutes for or supplements a missing or defective part of the body. —**pros•thet/ic** (-thet′ik), adj.

pros•ti•tute (pros′ti tōōt′, -tyōōt′), n., v., **-tut•ed, -tut•ing.** —n. **1.** a person who engages in sexual acts for money. —v.t. **2.** to offer (oneself) as a prostitute. **3.** to put (one's talent or ability) to unworthy use. —**pros/ti•tu/tion,** n.

pros•trate (pros′trāt), v., **-trat•ed, -trat•ing,** adj. —v.t. **1.** to cast (oneself) facedown on the ground, as in humility. **2.** to reduce to helplessness, weakness, or exhaustion. —adj. **3.** lying flat on the ground. **4.** lying facedown on the ground. **5.** helpless, weak, or exhausted. —**pros•tra/tion,** n.

pro•tag•o•nist (prō tag′ə nist), n. the leading character of a literary work.

pro•te•an (prō′tē ən, prō tē′-), adj. readily assuming different forms or characters.

pro•tect (prə tekt′), v.t. to defend from attack, loss, etc.; shield. —**pro•tec/tion,** n. —**pro•tec/tive,** adj. —**pro•tec/tor,** n.

pro•tec/tion•ism n. the practice of protecting domestic industries from foreign competition by imposing import duties.

pro•tec/tor•ate (-tar it), n. a weak state or territory that is protected and partly controlled by a stronger state.

pro•té•gé (prō′tə zhā′), n., pl. **-gés.** a person under the patronage or protection of someone interested in his or her career or welfare. —**pro/te•gée/,** n. fem.

pro•tein (prō′tēn, -tē in), n. any of numerous organic molecules constituting a large portion of the mass of every life form, composed of amino acids linked in chains.

pro tem•po•re (prō′ tem′pə rē′, -rä′), *adv.* **1.** temporarily. —*adj.* **2.** temporary.

pro•test (*n.* prō′test; *v.* prə test′, prō′test), *n.* **1.** an expression or declaration of objection, disapproval, or dissent. —*v.i., v.t.* **2.** to make a protest or remonstrance (against). **3.** to make solemn or earnest declaration (of). —**prot•es•ta•tion** (prot′ə stā′shən, prō′te-), *n.* —**pro•test′er,** *n.*

Prot•es•tant (prot′ə stənt), *n.* **1.** (loosely) any Christian not an adherent of a Catholic, Anglican, or Eastern church. **2.** an adherent of one of the Christian churches arising from the Reformation. —**Prot′•es•tant•ism,** *n.*

proto- a combining form meaning: earliest or original (*prototype*); foremost or essential (*protoplasm*).

pro•to•col (prō′tə kôl′, -kol′, -kōl′), *n.* **1.** the customs and regulations dealing with diplomatic formality, precedence, and etiquette. **2.** an original draft from which a document, esp. a treaty, is prepared. **3.** a set of rules governing the format of messages that are exchanged between computers.

pro•ton (prō′ton), *n.* a positively charged elementary particle found in all atomic nuclei.

pro•to•plasm (prō′tə plaz′əm), *n.* the colloidal and liquid substance of which cells are formed. —**pro′to•plas′mic,** *adj.*

pro′to•type′ *n.* the original or model on which something is based; pattern. —**pro′to•typ′i•cal** (-tip′i kəl), *adj.*

pro′to•zo′an (-zō′ən), *n., pl.* **-zo•ans, -zo•a** (-zō′ə). any of various one-celled organisms that usu. obtain nourishment by ingesting food particles rather than by photosynthesis. —**pro′to•zo′ic,** *adj.*

pro•tract (prō trakt′, prə-), *v.t.* to draw out or lengthen, esp. in time. —**pro•trac′tion,** *n.*

pro•trac′tor *n.* (in surveying, mathematics, etc.) an instrument having a graduated arc for plotting or measuring angles.

pro•trude (prō trood′, prə-), *v.i., v.t.,* **-trud•ed, -trud•ing.** to jut out or cause to jut out. —**pro•tru′sion,** *n.* —**pro•tru′sive,** *adj.*

pro•tu′ber•ant (prō too′bər ənt) *adj.* bulging out. —**pro•tu′ber•ance,** *n.*

proud (proud), *adj.,* **-er, -est. 1.** feeling satisfaction over something regarded as creditable to oneself. **2.** having or showing self-esteem. **3.** giving a sense of pride: *a proud moment.* **4.** highly honorable or creditable: *a proud achievement.* **5.** arrogant; haughty. **6.** stately or magnificent: *proud cities.* —**proud′ly,** *adv.*

prove (proov), *v.,* **proved, proved** or **prov•en, prov•ing.** —*v.t.* **1.** to establish the truth, genuineness, or validity of. **2.** to establish the quality or worth of, as by a test. —*v.i.* **3.** to turn out: *The experiment proved to be successful.* **4.** to be found to be: *His story proved false.* —**prov′a•ble,** *adj.*

prov•e•nance (prov′ə nəns, -näns′), *n.* place or source of origin.

prov•en•der (prov′ən dər), *n.* **1.** dry food for livestock. **2.** food.

prov•erb (prov′ərb), *n.* a short popular saying expressing some commonplace truth. —**pro•ver•bi•al** (prə vûr′bē əl), *adj.*

pro•vide (prə vīd′), *v.,* **-vid•ed, -vid•ing.** —*v.t.* **1.** to make available; furnish. **2.** to supply or equip. **3.** to stipulate beforehand. —*v.i.* **4.** to take measures with due foresight. **5.** to supply means of support: *to provide for one's children.* —**pro•vid′er,** *n.*

pro•vid′ed or **-vid′ing,** *conj.* on the condition or understanding (that).

prov′i•dent (-dənt), *adj.* **1.** providing carefully for the future. **2.** frugal; thrifty. —**prov′i•dent•ly,** *adv.*

prov′i•den′tial (-den′shəl), *adj.* **1.** of or resulting from divine providence. **2.** fortunate or lucky. —**prov′i•den′tial•ly,** *adv.*

prov•ince (prov′ins), *n.* **1.** an administrative division or unit of a country. **2. the provinces,** the parts of a country outside of the capital or the largest cities. **3.** a territory, district, or region. **4.** a sphere of activity or authority.

pro•vin•cial (prə vin′shəl), *adj.* **1.** belonging to a particular province. **2.** of the provinces. **3.** unsophisticated; parochial. —**pro•vin′cial•ism,** *n.*

pro•vi•sion (prə vizh′ən), *n.* **1.** the act of providing or supplying. **2.** something provided or supplied. **3.** an arrangement made beforehand. **4.** a legal or formal stipulation; proviso. **5. provisions,** supplies of food.

pro•vi′sion•al *adj.* **1.** temporary. **2.** accepted or adopted tentatively; conditional. —**pro•vi′sion•al•ly,** *adv.*

pro•vi•so (prə vī′zō), *n., pl.* **-sos, -soes. 1.** a clause, as in a contract, by which a condition is introduced. **2.** a stipulation or condition.

pro•voc•a•tive (prə vok′ə tiv), *adj.* serving to provoke; stimulating, exciting, or vexing. —**pro•voc′a•tive•ly,** *adv.*

pro•voke′ (-vōk′), *v.t.,* **-voked, -vok•ing. 1.** to anger or vex. **2.** to stir up or call forth (feelings, desires, or activity). **3.** to incite to action. **4.** to induce or bring about. —**prov•o•ca•tion** (prov′ə kā′shən), *n.*

pro•vost (prō′vōst), *n.* **1.** a person appointed to superintend or preside. **2.** a high-ranking administrative officer of some colleges and universities. [< OE < ML *prōpositus* abbot, lit., (one) placed before < L]

prow (prou), *n.* the forepart of a ship or boat.

prow•ess (prou′is), *n.* **1.** exceptional ability or skill. **2.** exceptional bravery, esp. in battle.

prowl (proul), *v.i., v.t.* **1.** to rove about stealthily, as in search of prey or something to steal. —*n.* **2.** the act of prowling. —**prowl′er,** *n.*

prox•im•i•ty (prok sim′i tē), *n.* nearness in place, time, relation, etc.

prox•y (prok′sē), *n., pl.* **-ies. 1.** the function or power of a person authorized to act for another. **2.** the person so authorized.

prude (prood), *n.* one who is excessively proper or modest, esp. in matters involving sex. —**prud′er•y,** *n.* —**prud′ish,** *adj.*

pru•dent (prood′nt), *adj.* **1.** wise or judicious in practical affairs. **2.** cautious. **3.** careful in providing for the future. —**pru′dence,** *n.* —**pru•den•tial** (proo den′shəl), *adj.* —**pru′dent•ly,** *adv.*

prune¹ (proon), *n.* any plum when dried.

prune² (proon), *v.t.,* **pruned, prun•ing. 1.** to cut off undesired twigs, branches, or roots from. **2.** to remove (anything undesirable). —**prun′er,** *n.*

pru•ri•ent (proor′ē ənt), *adj.* **1.** having lascivious or lustful desires. **2.** causing lasciviousness or lust. —**pru′ri•ence,** *n.*

Prus•sia (prush′ə), *n.* a former German Kingdom and state in N Europe. —**Prus′sian,** *adj., n.*

pry¹ (prī), *v.i.,* **pried, pry•ing. 1.** to inquire impertinently into something. **2.** to look closely or curiously.

pry² (prī), *v.,* **pried, pry•ing,** *n., pl.* **pries.** —*v.t.* **1.** to move, raise, or open by leverage. **2.** to obtain with difficulty. —*n.* **3.** a tool, as a crowbar, for raising, moving, or opening something by leverage. **4.** the leverage exerted.

P.S. 1. Also, **p.s.** postscript. **2.** Public School.

psalm (säm), *n.* **1.** a sacred song or hymn. **2.** (*cap.*) any of the songs, hymns, or prayers contained in the Book of Psalms. —**psalm′ist,** *n.*

pseu•do (soo′dō), *adj.* false or spurious.

pseudo- a combining form meaning false or pretended (*pseudonym*).

pseu•do•nym (sood′n im), *n.* a fictitious name used by an author to conceal his or her identity. —**pseu•don•y•mous** (soo don′ə məs), *adj.*

pso•ri•a•sis (sə rī′ə sis), *n.* a chronic, inflammatory skin disease characterized by scaly patches.

psych (sīk), *v.t. Informal.* **1.** to intimidate or frighten psychologically (often fol. by *out*). **2.** to prepare psychologically: *psyched herself up for the test.*

psych. psychology.

psy•che (sī′kē), *n.* **1.** the human soul, spirit, or mind. **2.** the mental structure of a person, esp. as a motive force.

psy•che•del•ic (sī′ki del′ik), *adj.* **1.** of or noting a mental state of intensified sensory perception. **2.** of or noting any drug that produces this state.

psy•chi•a•try (sĭ kīⁱ∕ə trē, sī-), *n.* the branch of medicine concerned with the study, diagnosis, and treatment of mental disorders. **—psy•chi•at•ric** (sīⁱ∕kē a∕trik), *adj.* **—psy•chi∕a•trist,** *n.*

psy•chic (sīⁱ∕kik), *adj.* Also, **psyⁱ∕chi•cal. 1.** of the human soul or mind. **2.** outside of natural or scientific knowledge. **3.** sensitive to influences of a nonphysical or supernatural nature. **—n. 4.** a person who is sensitive to psychic influences. **—psyⁱ∕chi•cal•ly,** *adv.*

psycho- a combining form meaning: the mind (*psychology*); mental processes or disorders (*psychotherapy*).

psyⁱ∕cho•ac∕tive *adj.* significantly affecting mood or mental state, as a drug.

psyⁱ∕cho•a•nal∕y•sis *n.* a professional technique for investigating unconscious mental processes and treating mental illness. **—psyⁱ∕cho•an∕a•lyst** (-an∕l-ist), *n.* **—psyⁱ∕cho•an∕a•lyze∕,** *v.t.,* **-lyzed, -lyz•ing.**

psy•cho•gen•ic (sīⁱ∕kə jen∕ik), *adj.* having origin in the mind or in a mental condition or process.

psy•chol•o•gy (sĭ kolⁱ∕ə jē), *n., pl.* **-gies. 1.** the science of the mind or of mental states and processes. **2.** the science of human and animal behavior. **—psyⁱ∕cho•log∕i•cal** (-kə lojⁱ∕i kəl), *adj.* **—psy•chol∕o•gist,** *n.*

psy•cho•neu•ro•sis (sīⁱ∕kō nŏŏ rō∕sis, -nyŏŏ-), *n., pl.* **-ses** (-sēz). NEUROSIS.

psy•cho•path (sīⁱ∕kə path∕), *n.* a person having a character disorder distinguished by amoral or antisocial behavior. **—psyⁱ∕cho•path∕ic,** *adj.* **—psy•chop∕a•thy** (-kopⁱ∕ə thē), *n., pl.* **-thies.**

psy•cho•sis (sĭ kō∕sis), *n., pl.* **-ses** (-sēz). a severe mental disorder characterized by symptoms, as delusions or hallucinations, that indicate impaired contact with reality. **—psy•chot∕ic** (-kot∕ik), *adj., n.*

psyⁱ∕cho•so•mat∕ic (-sə mat∕ik), *adj.* of or noting a physical disorder caused or influenced by emotional factors.

psyⁱ∕cho•ther∕a•py *n., pl.* **-pies.** the treatment of psychological disorders or maladjustments by a professional technique, as psychoanalysis. **—psyⁱ∕cho•ther∕a•pist,** *n.*

psyⁱ∕cho•tro∕pic (-trō∕pik), *adj.* affecting mental activity, behavior, or perception, as a mood-altering drug.

Pt *Chem. Symbol.* platinum.

pt. 1. part. **2.** pint. **3.** point. **4.** preterit.

ptar•mi•gan (tär∕mi gən), *n., pl.* **-gans, -gan.** any of several grouses of mountainous and cold northern regions.

pter•o•dac•tyl (ter∕ə dak∕til), *n.* an extinct flying reptile with membranous wings supported by one elongated finger on each hand.

pto•maine (tō∕mān), *n.* any of a class of nitrogenous substances produced by bacteria during putrefaction of protein, formerly thought to cause food poisoning.

pub (pub), *n.* a bar or tavern.

pu•ber•ty (pyŏŏ∕bər tē), *n.* the period of life during which an individual becomes capable of sexual reproduction. **—pu∕ber•tal,** *adj.*

pu•bes•cent (-bes∕ənt), *adj.* arriving or arrived at puberty. **—pu•bes∕cence,** *n.*

pu∕bic *adj.* of or situated near the genitalia.

pub•lic (pub∕lik), *adj.* **1.** of or affecting a population or community as a whole: *a public nuisance.* **2.** done, acting, etc., for the community: *public prosecution.* **3.** open to all persons: *a public meeting.* **4.** maintained by or for a community: *a public library.* **5.** generally known. **6.** devoted to the welfare or well-being of the community: *public spirit.* **—n. 7.** the people constituting a community, state, etc. **8.** a group of people with a common interest, aim, etc.: *the book-buying public.* **—Idiom. 9. in public,** not in private; openly. **—pub∕lic•ly,** *adv.*

pub∕li•ca∕tion *n.* **1.** the act of publishing a book, piece of music, etc. **2.** something published, esp. a periodical.

pub∕lic defend∕er *n.* a lawyer appointed to represent indigents in criminal cases at public expense.

pub∕lic domain∕ *n.* the legal status of material never or no longer protected by a copyright or patent.

pub•lic•i•ty (pu blis∕i tē), *n.* **1.** extensive mention in the news or other media. **2.** public notice so gained. **3.** the process or business of securing public notice. **4.** information, articles, etc., issued to secure public notice.

pub∕li•cize∕ *v.t.,* **-cized, -ciz•ing.** to give publicity to. **—pub∕li•cist,** *n.*

pub∕lic rela∕tions *n.pl.* the actions of a corporation, organization, etc., in promoting goodwill with the public.

pub∕lic util∕ity *n.* a business enterprise, as a gas company, performing an essential public service and regulated by the government.

pub•lish (pub∕lish), *v.t.* **1.** to issue (printed or otherwise reproduced textual or graphic material) for sale. **2.** to make publicly or generally known. **—v.i. 3.** to issue newspapers, books, etc. **4.** to have one's work published. **—pub∕lish•er,** *n.*

puck (puk), *n.* a black rubber disk that is hit into the goal in ice hockey.

puck•er (puk∕ər), *v.t., v.i.* **1.** to draw or gather into wrinkles or irregular folds. **—n. 2.** an irregular fold; wrinkle.

puck•ish (puk∕ish), *adj.* mischievous.

pud•ding (pŏŏd∕ing), *n.* a soft, thickened dessert, typically made with milk, sugar, flour, and flavoring.

pud•dle (pud∕l), *n.* a small pool of water, as of rainwater on the ground.

pudg•y (puj∕ē), *adj.,* **-i•er, -i•est.** short and fat or thick. **—pudg∕i•ness,** *n.*

pu•er•ile (pyŏŏ∕ər il, -ə rīl∕, pyŏŏr∕il, -īl), *adj.* immature; silly. **—pu∕er•ile•ly,** *adv.* **—pu∕er•il∕i•ty,** *n.*

Puer•to Ri•co (pwer∕tə rē∕kō, pwer∕tō, pôr∕tə), *n.* an island in the central West Indies: a commonwealth associated with the U.S. 3,196,520. *Cap.:* San Juan. *Abbr:* PR, P.R. **—Puer∕to Ri∕can,** *n., adj.*

puff (puf), *n.* **1.** a short, quick blast or emission of air, smoke, etc. **2.** an act of inhaling and exhaling, as on a cigarette. **3.** a light pastry filled with whipped cream, custard, etc. **4.** an exaggerated commendation of a book, performance, etc. **5.** a ball or pad of soft material. **—v.i. 6.** to blow with puffs. **7.** to breathe quick and hard. **8.** to take puffs in smoking. **9.** to become inflated or distended (usu. fol. by *up*). **—v.t. 10.** to send forth in puffs. **11.** to smoke (a cigar, cigarette, etc.). **12.** to inflate or make fluffy. **13.** to inflate with pride or vanity (often fol. by *up*). **—puff∕i•ness,** *n.* **—puff∕y,** *adj.,* **-i•er, -i•est.**

puf•fin (puf∕in), *n.* any of several sea birds with a short neck and a colorful, triangular bill.

pug (pug), *n.* one of a breed of small, squarely built dogs with a deeply wrinkled face.

pu•gi•lism (pyŏŏ∕jə liz∕əm), *n.* the practice of fighting with the fists; boxing. **—pu∕gi•list,** *n.* **—pu∕gi•lis∕tic,** *adj.*

pug•na•cious (pug nā∕shəs), *adj.* inclined to quarrel or fight readily. **—pug•na∕cious•ly,** *adv.* **—pug•nac∕i•ty** (-nas∕i tē), *n.*

pug∕ nose∕ *n.* a short, broad, somewhat turned-up nose. **—pug∕-nosed∕,** *adj.*

puke (pyōōk), *v.,* **puked, puk•ing,** *n. Slang.* **—v.i., v.t. 1.** to vomit. **—n. 2.** vomit.

pul•chri•tude (pul∕kri tōōd∕, -tyōōd∕), *n.* beauty; comeliness.

pule (pyōōl), *v.i.,* **puled, pul•ing.** to cry in a thin voice; whine.

pull (pōōl), *v.t.* **1.** to use force to cause (something) to move toward or after oneself or itself. **2.** to rip; tear. **3.** to dislodge or extract, as a tooth. **4.** to draw out (a weapon). **5.** to perform; carry out: *They pulled a spectacular coup.* **6.** to strain (a muscle). **—v.i. 7.** to exert a drawing, tugging, or hauling force. **8.** to become or come as specified, by being pulled. **9.** to move or go: *The train pulled away from the station.* **10. pull for,** to support actively. **11. ~ off,** *Informal.* to perform successfully. **12. ~ out, a.** to depart. **b.** to abandon abruptly. **13. ~ through,** to come safely through (a crisis, illness, etc.). **14.** ~ **up, a.** to bring or come to a halt. **b.** to bring or draw closer. —*n.* **15.** the act of pulling. **16.** force used in pulling. **17.** influence, as with persons able to grant favors. **18.** a part or thing to be pulled, as a handle. **19.** the ability to attract; drawing power. —*Idiom.* **20. pull oneself together,** to regain command of one's emotions.

pul•let (pŏŏl'it), *n.* a hen less than one year old.

pul•ley (pŏŏl'ē), *n., pl.* **-leys.** a wheel for supporting, guiding, or transmitting force to or from a moving rope or cable that rides in a groove in its edge.

Pull•man (pŏŏl'mən), *pl.* **-mans.** *Trademark.* a railroad sleeping car or parlor car. [after G. M. *Pullman* (1831–97), U.S. inventor]

pull′out′ *n.* **1.** a withdrawal, as of troops or funds. **2.** a section of a newspaper or magazine that can be pulled out.

pull′o′ver *adj.* **1.** designed to be put on by being drawn over the head. —*n.* **2.** a pullover garment, esp. a sweater.

pul•mo•nar•y (pul'mə ner′ē, pŏŏl'-), *adj.* of or affecting the lungs.

pulp (pulp), *n.* **1.** the soft, juicy, edible part of a fruit. **2.** the pith of a plant stem. **3.** the inner substance of the tooth, containing blood vessels and nerves. **4.** a soft, moist mass, as of linen or wood, used in making paper. **5.** a magazine or book printed on low-quality paper, usu. containing lurid material. —**pulp′y,** *adj.,* **-i•er, -i•est.**

pul•pit (pŏŏl'pit, pul'-), *n.* **1.** a raised structure in a church, from which the sermon is delivered or the service is conducted. **2. the pulpit,** the clerical profession; ministry.

pul•sar (pul'sär), *n.* any of several hundred known celestial objects that emit regular pulses of radiation, esp. radio waves.

pul•sate (pul'sāt), *v.i.,* **-sat•ed, -sat•ing. 1.** to expand and contract rhythmically. **2.** to vibrate; quiver. —**pul•sa′tion,** *n.*

pulse (puls), *n., v.,* **pulsed, puls•ing.** —*n.* **1.** the regular throbbing of the arteries, caused by the successive contractions of the heart. **2.** a stroke or vibration, or a rhythmic series of these. **3.** a momentary, sudden fluctuation in an electrical quantity. —*v.i.* **4.** to beat or throb.

pul•ver•ize (pul'və rīz′), *v.t., v.i.,* **-ized, -iz•ing.** to reduce or become reduced to dust or powder, as by pounding. —**pul′ver•i•za′tion,** *n.*

pu•ma (pyŏŏ'mə, pŏŏ'-), *n., pl.* **-mas.** COUGAR.

pum•ice (pum′is), *n.* a porous or spongy form of volcanic glass, used as an abrasive.

pum•mel (pum′əl), *v.t.,* **-meled, -mel•ing** or (*esp. Brit.*) **-melled, -mel•ling.** to beat or thrash with or as if with the fists.

pump¹ (pump), *n.* **1.** an apparatus or machine for driving or compressing fluids or gases, as by means of a piston. —*v.t.* **2.** to drive with a pump. **3.** to force or inject as a pump does. **4.** to remove the liquid from by means of a pump. **5.** to operate or move by an up-and-down action. **6.** to question persistently so as to elicit information. **7. pump up, a.** to inflate with a pump: *to pump up a tire.* **b.** to infuse with enthusiasm. —*Idiom.* **8. pump iron,** to lift weights as an exercise.

pump² (pump), *n.* a woman's lightweight, low-cut shoe without fastenings.

pum•per•nick•el (pum′pər nik′əl), *n.* a coarse, dark, slightly sour rye bread.

pump•kin (pump′kin *or, commonly,* pung′kin), *n.* a large, edible, orange-yellow fruit borne by a coarse vine.

pun (pun), *n., v.,* **punned, pun•ning.** —*n.* **1.** the humorous use of a word or phrase so as to suggest its different meanings or the use of words that are nearly alike in sound but different in meaning. —*v.i.* **2.** to make puns. —**pun′ster,** *n.*

punch¹ (punch), *n.* **1.** a thrusting blow with the fist. **2.** forcefulness or effectiveness. —*v.t.* **3.** to hit with the fist. **4.** to drive (cattle). **5.** to prod, as with a stick. **6.** to strike or hit in operating: *to punch an elevator button.* **7. punch in** (or **out**), to record one's time of arrival (or departure) by punching a time clock.

punch² (punch), *n.* **1.** a tool or machine for perforating materials, driving nails, etc. —*v.t.* **2.** to perforate, drive, etc., with a punch. **3.** to make (a hole) with a punch.

punch³ (punch), *n.* **1.** a beverage of wine or spirits mixed with fruit juice, soda, etc. **2.** a beverage of two or more fruit juices, sugar, and water.

punch′-drunk′ *adj.* **1.** (of a boxer) showing symptoms of cerebral injury, as unsteadiness, caused by repeated blows to the head. **2.** befuddled; dazed.

punch′ line′ *n.* the climactic phrase or sentence in a joke that produces the desired effect.

punch′y *adj.,* **-i•er, -i•est. 1.** punch-drunk. **2.** vigorously effective; forceful.

punc•til•i•ous (pungk til′ē əs), *adj.* strict or exact in the observance of the formalities of conduct. —**punc•til′i•ous•ly,** *adv.* —**punc•til′i•ous•ness,** *n.*

punc•tu•al (pungk′chŏŏ əl), *adj.* arriving or happening at the time appointed; prompt. —**punc′tu•al′i•ty,** *n.* —**punc′tu•al•ly,** *adv.*

punc′tu•ate′ (-āt′), *v.t.,* **-at•ed, -at•ing. 1.** to mark or divide (something written) with punctuation marks. **2.** to interrupt at intervals. **3.** to give emphasis or force to.

punc′tu•a′tion *n.* the use of certain conventional marks (**punctua′tion marks′**) in writing or printing in order to separate elements and make the meaning clear.

punc•ture (pungk′chər), *n., v.,* **-tured, -tur•ing.** —*n.* **1.** the act of piercing with a pointed object. **2.** a hole so made. —*v.t., v.i.* **3.** to pierce or be pierced, as with something sharp.

pun•dit (pun′dit), *n.* a learned person; an expert or authority.

pun•gent (pun′jənt), *adj.* **1.** sharply affecting the organs of taste or smell; biting. **2.** incisive; forceful and sharp. —**pun′gen•cy,** *n.* —**pun′gent•ly,** *adv.*

pun•ish (pun′ish), *v.t.* **1.** to subject to pain, loss, etc., as a penalty for some offense or fault. **2.** to inflict such a penalty for (an offense or fault). **3.** to treat harshly. —**pun′ish•a•ble,** *adj.* —**pun′ish•ment,** *n.*

pu•ni•tive (pyŏŏ′ni tiv), *adj.* concerned with or inflicting punishment. —**pu′ni•tive•ly,** *adv.*

punk¹ (pungk), *n.* **1.** any prepared substance that will smolder and can be used to light fireworks, fuses, etc. **2.** dry, decayed wood that can be used as tinder.

punk² (pungk), *n.* **1.** *Slang.* **a.** something or someone worthless or unimportant. **b.** a young ruffian; hoodlum. **2.** PUNK ROCK. **3.** a style characterized by bizarre clothing, hairstyles, etc., and the defiance of social norms. —*adj.* **4.** *Informal.* poor in quality. **5.** of punk rock or the punk style.

punk′ rock′ *n.* rock music marked by loud, insistent music and aggressive, often abusive lyrics. —**punk′ rock′er,** *n.*

punt¹ (punt), *n.* **1.** a kick, as in football, executed by dropping the ball and kicking it before it touches the ground. —*v.t., v.i.* **2.** to kick (a dropped ball) before it touches the ground. —**punt′er,** *n.*

punt² (punt), *n.* **1.** a small, flat-bottomed boat propelled by a pole. —*v.t., v.i.* **2.** to propel (a punt) by a pole.

punt³ (pŏŏnt, punt), *n., pl.* **punt.** the basic monetary unit of the Republic of Ireland.

pu•ny (pyŏŏ′nē), *adj.,* **-ni•er, -ni•est. 1.** of less than normal size and strength. **2.** unimportant; insignificant. —**pu′ni•ness,** *n.*

pup (pup), *n.* **1.** a young dog. **2.** the young of certain other animals, as the seal.

pu•pa (pyŏŏ′pə), *n., pl.* **-pae** (-pē), **-pas.** an insect in the transformation stage between the larva and the adult. —**pu′pal,** *adj.*

pu•pil¹ (pyŏŏ′pəl), *n.* a person, usu. young, who is learning under the supervision of a teacher.

pu•pil² (pyŏŏ′pəl), *n.* the expanding and contracting opening in the iris of the eye.

pup•pet (pup′it), *n.* **1.** a small figure of a person or animal, manipulated by the hand or by rods, wires, etc. **2.** a person or group whose actions are controlled by another. —**pup′pet•ry,** *n.*

pup·pet·eer' *n.* a person who manipulates puppets.

pup·py (pup'ē), *n.*, *pl.* **-pies.** a young dog.

pur·chase (pûr'chəs), *v.*, **-chased, -chas·ing,** *n.* —*v.t.* **1.** to acquire by the payment of money; buy. —*n.* **2.** acquisition by the payment of money. **3.** something purchased. **4.** an effective hold for applying power in moving or raising a heavy object; leverage. —**pur'chas·a·ble,** *adj.* —**pur'chas·er,** *n.*

pure (pyŏŏr), *adj.*, **pur·er, pur·est. 1.** free from adulterating or extraneous matter. **2.** absolute; utter. **3.** being that and nothing else: *a pure accident.* **4.** clear; spotless. **5.** abstract or theoretical: *pure science.* **6.** untainted with evil or guilt. **7.** physically chaste; virgin. —**pure'ly,** *adv.* —**pure'ness,** *n.*

pure·bred (*adj.* pyŏŏr'bred'; *n.* pyŏŏr'bred'), *adj.* **1.** of an individual whose ancestors derive over many generations from a recognized breed. —*n.* **2.** a purebred animal.

pu·rée (pyŏŏ rā', -rē'), *n.*, *pl.* **-rées,** *v.* **-réed, -rée·ing.** —*n.* **1.** a thick liquid prepared from cooked food passed through a sieve or broken down in a blender. **2.** a soup made of puréed ingredients. —*v.t.* **3.** to make a purée of. [< F < *purer* to strain, lit., make pure]

pur·ga·to·ry (pûr'gə tôr'ē), *n.*, *pl.* **-ries. 1.** (esp. in Roman Catholic belief) a place or state following death in which penitent souls are purified and thereby are made ready for heaven. **2.** any condition or place of temporary punishment or expiation. —**pur'ga·to'ri·al,** *adj.*

purge (pûrj), *v.*, **purged, purg·ing,** *n.* —*v.t.* **1.** to rid of impurities. **2.** to clear of imputed guilt. **3.** to clear (the stomach or intestines) by inducing vomiting or evacuation. **4.** to eliminate (undesirable members) from a government, political organization, etc. —*n.* **5.** the act or process of purging. **6.** something that purges, as a purgative medicine. —**pur·ga·tive** (pûr'gə tiv), *adj.*, *n.* —**purg'er,** *n.*

pu·ri·fy (pyŏŏr'ə fī'), *v.*, **-fied, -fy·ing.** —*v.t.* **1.** to make pure. **2.** to free from guilt or evil. —*v.i.* **3.** to become pure. —**pu/ri·fi·ca/tion,** *n.* —**pu/ri·fi/er,** *n.*

Pu·rim (pŏŏr'im), *n.* a Jewish festival commemorating the deliverance of the Jews in Persia from destruction.

pur·ism (pyŏŏr'iz əm), *n.* strict observance of or insistence on purity or correctness in language, style, etc. —**pur'ist,** *n.*

Pu·ri·tan (pyŏŏr'i tn), *n.* **1.** a member of a group of Protestants that arose in the 16th century within the Church of England, demanding the simplification of doctrine and worship. **2.** (*l.c.*) a person who is excessively strict in moral or religious matters. —**pur/i·tan/i·cal,** *adj.* —**Pur/i·tan·ism, pur/i·tan·ism,** *n.*

pu·ri·ty (pyŏŏr'i tē), *n.* the condition or quality of being pure.

purl¹ (pûrl), *n.* **1.** a basic stitch in knitting, the reverse of the knit. —*v.i.*, *v.t.* **2.** to knit with a purl stitch.

purl² (pûrl), *v.i.* **1.** to flow with rippling motion. **2.** to flow with a murmuring sound. —*n.* **3.** the action or sound of purling.

pur·lieu (pûr'lŏŏ, pûrl'yŏŏ), *n.*, *pl.* **-lieus. 1. purlieus,** environs or neighborhood. **2.** an outlying district of a city.

pur·loin (pər loin', pûr'loin), *v.t.*, *v.i.* to take dishonestly; steal. —**pur·loin'er,** *n.*

pur·ple (pûr'pəl), *n.*, *adj.*, **-pler, -plest.** —*n.* **1.** any color having components of both red and blue, esp. one deep in tone. **2.** cloth or clothing of this hue, esp. as formerly worn distinctively by royalty. —*adj.* **3.** of the color purple. **4.** imperial or regal. **5.** full of exaggerated literary devices and effects. **6.** profane or shocking, as language. —**pur'plish,** *adj.*

pur·port (*v.* pər pôrt'; *n.* pûr'pôrt), *v.t.* **1.** to profess or claim. **2.** to convey; express or imply. —*n.* **3.** the meaning or sense. **4.** a purpose or intention. —**pur'port·ed,** *adj.* —**pur'port·ed·ly,** *adv.*

pur·pose (pûr'pəs), *n.*, *v.*, **-posed, -pos·ing.** —*n.* **1.** the reason for which something exists or is done, made, etc. **2.** an intended or desired result. **3.** determination; resoluteness. —*v.t.*, *v.i.* **4.** to intend;

design; resolve. —*Idiom.* **5. on purpose,** intentionally. —**pur'pose·ful,** *adj.* —**pur'pose·less,** *adj.*

purr (pûr), *n.* **1.** the low, continuous, vibrating sound a cat makes. **2.** any similar sound. —*v.i.* **3.** to utter such a sound. **4.** to speak in a murmuring tone. —*v.t.* **5.** to express in or as if in a purr.

purse (pûrs), *n.*, *v.*, **pursed, purs·ing.** —*n.* **1.** a woman's handbag. **2.** a small bag or case for carrying money. **3.** a sum of money offered as a prize or collected as a gift. **4.** financial resources. —*v.t.* **5.** to pucker.

purs'er *n.* an officer in charge of the accounts and documents of a ship.

pur·su·ant *adj.* **1.** pursuing. —*Idiom.* **2. pursuant to,** in accordance with.

pur·sue (pər sŏŏ'), *v.t.*, **-sued, -su·ing. 1.** to follow in order to overtake, capture, etc. **2.** to strive to attain or accomplish. **3.** to follow or carry out. **4.** to carry on or engage in: *to pursue one's studies.* —**pur·su'er,** *n.*

pur·suit' (-sŏŏt'), *n.* **1.** the act of pursuing. **2.** an occupation or regular pastime.

pur·vey (pər vā'), *v.t.*, **-veyed, -vey·ing.** to supply (esp. food), usu. as a business. —**pur·vey'or,** *n.*

pus (pus), *n.* a yellow-white, viscid substance produced by suppuration and found in abscesses, sores, etc.

push (pŏŏsh), *v.t.* **1.** to press against (a thing) with force in order to move it. **2.** to make (one's way) by pushing. **3.** to urge to some action or course. **4.** to press (an action, proposal, etc.) insistently. **5.** to press the use, sale, etc., of. **6.** *Slang.* to peddle (illicit drugs). —*v.i.* **7.** to exert a thrusting force upon something. **8.** to proceed by force or effort. **9.** to put forth persistent efforts. —*n.* **10.** the act of pushing. **11.** a vigorous effort. **12.** a vigorous advance or military attack. **13.** *Informal.* persevering energy; enterprise.

push'o·ver *n.* **1.** anything done easily. **2.** a person who is easily persuaded or influenced.

push'y *adj.*, **-i·er, -i·est.** obnoxiously self-assertive. —**push/i·ness,** *n.*

pu·sil·lan·i·mous (pyŏŏ'sə lan'ə məs), *adj.* lacking courage or resolve; cowardly. —**pu/sil·la·nim/i·ty** (-lə nim'i tē), *n.*

puss·y (pŏŏs'ē), *n.*, *pl.* **-ies.** a cat, esp. a kitten.

puss'y·foot' *v.i.* **1.** to move in a stealthy or cautious manner. **2.** to act timidly or irresolutely.

puss'y wil'low *n.* a small willow with silky catkins.

pus·tule (pus'chŏŏl), *n.* a small elevation of the skin containing pus.

put (pŏŏt), *v.*, **put, put·ting.** —*v.t.* **1.** to move (anything) into a specific location or position. **2.** to bring into some condition, relation, etc. **3.** to set to a task or action. **4.** to assign or attribute: *to put the blame on others.* **5.** to estimate (distance, time, etc.). **6.** to bet or wager. **7.** to express or state: *put it honestly.* **8.** to apply (knowledge, skill, etc.) to a purpose. **9.** to submit for answer, consideration, etc. **10.** to impose (a tax, charge, etc.). **11.** to throw or cast: *to put the shot.* —*v.i.* **12.** to go or proceed: *to put out to sea.* **13. put across,** to cause to be understood or received favorably. **14. ~ aside** or **by,** to store up; reserve. **15. ~ down, a.** to write down. **b.** to suppress. **c.** to humiliate or embarrass. **d.** to pay as a deposit. **16. ~ in for,** to apply for or request. **17. ~ off, a.** to postpone. **b.** to get rid of by evasion. **18. ~ on, a.** to clothe oneself in. **b.** to stage, as a show. **c.** *Informal.* to deceive (someone) as a joke. **19. ~ out, a.** to extinguish, as a fire. **b.** to subject to inconvenience. **c.** *Baseball.* to prevent from reaching base or scoring. **20. ~ through, a.** to bring about; effect. **b.** to cause to suffer or endure. **21. ~ up, a.** to construct. **b.** to can or preserve (food). **c.** to set (the hair). **d.** to provide (money). **e.** to lodge. **f.** to offer, esp. for public sale. **22. ~ up with,** to endure; tolerate. —*Idiom.* **23. stay put,** to remain in the same position.

pu·ta·tive (pyŏŏ'tə tiv), *adj.* commonly regarded as such.

put'-down' *n. Informal.* a disparaging or snubbing remark.

pu·tre·fy (pyōō′trə fī′), *v.t., v.i.,* **-fied, -fy·ing.** to make or become putrid; rot. —**pu′tre·fac′tion** (-fak′shən), *n.*

pu·tres′cent (-tres′ənt), *adj.* becoming putrid. —**pu·tres′cence,** *n.*

pu′trid (-trid), *adj.* (of organic material) in a state of foul decay or decomposition.

putsch (pōōch), *n.* a sudden political revolt or uprising.

putt (put), *v.t., v.i.* **1.** to strike (a golf ball) gently so as to make it roll into the hole. —*n.* **2.** a stroke made in putting.

put·ter¹ (put′ər), *v.i.* to occupy oneself in a leisurely or ineffective manner. —**put′ter·er,** *n.*

putt·er² (put′ər), *n.* a golf club used in putting.

put·ty (put′ē), *n., pl.* **-ties,** *v.,* **-tied, -ty·ing.** —*n.* **1.** a compound of whiting and linseed oil used to secure windowpanes, patch woodwork, etc. —*v.t.* **2.** to secure, cover, etc., with putty.

puz·zle (puz′əl), *n., v.,* **-zled, -zling.** —*n.* **1.** a toy, game, or problem designed to amuse by presenting difficulties to be solved. **2.** a puzzling question, matter, or person. —*v.t.* **3.** to mystify; baffle. —*v.i.* **4.** to ponder over some perplexing problem. **5. puzzle out,** to solve by careful study or effort. —**puz′zle·ment,** *n.* —**puz′zler,** *n.*

Pvt. Private.

PX *pl.* **PXs.** post exchange.

Pyg·my (pig′mē), *n., pl.* **-mies,** *adj.* —*n.* **1.** a member of any of several small-statured peoples of Africa and SE Asia. **2.** (*l.c.*) a small person or thing. —*adj.* **3.** of the Pygmies. **4.** (*l.c.*) of very small size.

py·lon (pī′lon), *n.* **1.** a tower for guiding aviators. **2.** a monumental gateway, as to an ancient Egyptian temple. **3.** a steel tower used as a support. [< Gk: gateway]

pyr·a·mid (pir′ə mid), *n.* **1.** a massive masonry structure having four sloping sides meeting at an apex, as a tomb of ancient Egypt. **2.** any object or arrangement of objects shaped like a pyramid. **3.** a solid having a polygonal base and triangular sides that meet in a point. —*v.i., v.t.* **4.** to arrange or build in the form of a pyramid. **5.** to increase gradually. —**py·ram′i·dal** (-ram′i dl), *adj.*

pyre (pī³r), *n.* a pile of wood for burning a dead body.

py·rite (pī′rīt), *n.* a brass-yellow mineral containing sulfur and iron.

pyro- a combining form meaning fire or heat (*pyromania*).

py·ro·ma·ni·a (pī′rə mā′nē ə), *n.* a compulsion to set things on fire. —**py′ro·ma′ni·ac,** *n.*

py′ro·tech′nics (-tek′niks), *n.pl.* **1.** a display of fireworks. **2.** a brilliant or sensational display, as of musicianship. —**py′ro·tech′nic,** *adj.*

py·thon (pī′thon, -thən), *n.* any of several Old World snakes that crush their prey to death in their coils.

a b c d e f g h i j k l m n o p **Q** r s t u v w x y z

Q, q (kyōō), *n., pl.* **Qs** or **Q's, qs** or **q's.** the 17th letter of the English alphabet, a consonant.

q. **1.** farthing. **2.** quart. **3.** query. **4.** question. **5.** quintal. **6.** quire.

Qa·tar (kä′tär, kə tär′), *n.* an independent emirate on the Persian Gulf. —**Qa·tar′i,** *adj., n.*

Q.E.D. which was to be shown or demonstrated. [< L *quod erat dēmōnstrandum*]

qt. **1.** quantity. **2.** *pl.* **qt., qts.** quart.

q.t. or **Q.T.,** *Informal.* **1.** quiet. —*Idiom.* **2. on the q.t.,** stealthily.

qty. quantity.

quack¹ (kwak), *n.* **1.** the harsh, throaty cry of a duck. —*v.i.* **2.** to utter a quack.

quack² (kwak), *n.* **1.** a fraudulent pretender to medical skill. **2.** a charlatan. —*adj.* **3.** being or befitting a quack. —**quack′er·y,** *n., pl.* **-ies.**

quad¹ (kwod), *n.* a quadrangle.

quad² (kwod), *n.* a quadruplet.

quad′ran·gle (-rang′gəl), *n.* **1.** a plane figure having four angles and four sides. **2.** a square or court surrounded by buildings, as on a college campus. —**quad·ran′gu·lar** (-gyə lər), *adj.*

quad′rant (-rənt), *n.* **1.** a quarter of a circle; an arc of 90°. **2.** one of the four parts into which a plane, as the face of a heavenly body, is divided by two perpendicular lines. **3.** an instrument used, as in astronomy, for measuring altitudes.

quad′ra·phon′ic (-rə fon′ik), *adj.* of the recording, reproduction, or transmission of sound by means of four channels.

quad·ri·lat·er·al (kwod′rə lat′ər əl), *adj.* **1.** having four sides. —*n.* **2.** *Geom.* a polygon with four sides.

quad·rille (kwo dril′, kwə-), *n.* a square dance for four couples.

quad·ri·ple·gi·a (kwod′rə plē′jē ə, -jə), *n.* paralysis of the entire body below the neck. —**quad′ri·ple′gic,** *n., adj.*

quad·ru·ped (kwod′rōō ped′), *n.* an animal, esp. a mammal, that has four feet.

quad·ru·ple (kwo drōō′pəl, -drup′əl, kwod′rōō-pəl), *adj., n., v.,* **-pled, -pling.** —*adj.* **1.** consisting of four parts. **2.** four times as great. —*n.* **3.** a number or amount four times as great as another. —*v.t., v.i.* **4.** to make or become four times as great.

quad·ru·plet (kwo drup′lit, -drōō′plit), *n.* **1.** a group or combination of four. **2.** one of four children or offspring born of one pregnancy.

quad·ru·pli·cate (*n., adj.* kwo drōō′pli kit; *v.* -kāt′), *n., adj., v.,* **-cat·ed, -cat·ing.** —*n.* **1.** one of four copies or identical items. —*adj.* **2.** consisting of four identical parts. **3.** noting a fourth item or copy. —*v.t.* **4.** to produce in quadruplicate. **5.** to make four times as great. —**quad·ru′pli·ca′tion,** *n.*

quaff (kwof, kwaf), *v.i., v.t.* **1.** to drink copiously and with hearty enjoyment. —*n.* **2.** a beverage quaffed.

quag·mire (kwag′mī³r′, kwog′-), *n.* **1.** miry or boggy ground whose surface yields under the tread. **2.** a difficult situation.

qua·hog or **-haug** (kwô′hôg, -hog, kō′-), *n.* a thick-shelled, edible clam of North American Atlantic coasts.

quail¹ (kwāl), *n., pl.* **quails, quail. 1.** any of various small, plump New World birds of the pheasant family. **2.** any of various Old World birds similar to the quail.

quail² (kwāl), *v.i.* to shrink in fear.

quaint (kwānt), *adj.,* **-er, -est. 1.** having an old-fashioned charm. **2.** peculiar or unusual in an interesting or amusing way; oddly picturesque. —**quaint′ly,** *adv.* —**quaint′ness,** *n.*

quake (kwāk), *v.,* **quaked, quak·ing,** *n.* —*v.i.* **1.** to quiver, as from cold or fear. **2.** to tremble, as from shock or instability. —*n.* **3.** an earthquake. **4.** the act of quaking.

Quak·er (kwā′kər), *n.* a member of the Society of Friends. —**Quak′er·ism,** *n.*

qual·i·fi·ca·tion (kwol′ə fi kā′shən), *n.* **1.** a quality or accomplishment that fits a person for a function, office, or position. **2.** the act of qualifying or state of being qualified. **3.** modification, limitation, or restriction.

qual′i·fy′ *v.,* **-fied, -fy·ing.** —*v.t.* **1.** to provide with proper or necessary skills, knowledge, or credentials. **2.** to make less general; modify or limit. **3.** to make less violent or severe; moderate. **4.** *Gram.* MODIFY (def. 2). —*v.i.* **5.** to be fit or competent, as for a position. **6.** to demonstrate the required ability in a preliminary contest. —**qual′i·fied′,** *adj.*

qual′i•ty *n.*, *pl.* **-ties**, *adj.* —*n.* **1.** an essential characteristic, property, or attribute. **2.** character or nature belonging to or distinguishing a thing. **3.** degree of excellence or fineness. **4.** superiority; excellence. **5.** a personality or character trait. —*adj.* **6.** of or having superior quality.

qual′ity time′ *n.* time devoted exclusively to nurturing a cherished person or activity.

qualm (kwäm, kwôm), *n.* **1.** a pang of conscience; compunction. **2.** a sudden feeling of apprehension; misgiving. **3.** a sudden onset of illness, esp. of nausea.

quan•da•ry (kwon′də rē, -drē), *n.*, *pl.* **-ries.** a state of perplexity or uncertainty.

quan•ti•fy (kwon′tə fī′), *v.t.*, **-fied**, **-fy•ing.** to determine, indicate, or express the quantity of.

quan′ti•ty *n.*, *pl.* **-ties. 1.** an indefinite or aggregate amount. **2.** an exact or specified amount or measure. **3.** a considerable or great amount.

quan′tum (-təm), *n.*, *pl.* **-ta** (-tə), *adj.* —*n.* **1.** quantity or amount. **2.** *Physics.* a very small, indivisible quantity of energy. —*adj.* **3.** sudden and significant: *a quantum increase in productivity.*

quar•an•tine (kwôr′ən tēn′, kwor′-), *n.*, *v.*, **-tined**, **-tin•ing.** —*n.* **1.** strict isolation imposed to prevent the spread of disease. **2.** a period of detention imposed upon ships, people, animals, or plants suspected of carrying a contagious disease. **3.** a place where quarantine is imposed. —*v.t.* **4.** to subject to quarantine.

quark (kwôrk, kwärk), *n.* any of a group of subatomic particles having a fractional electric charge and thought to form the basis of all matter. [coined by U.S. physicist M. Gell-Mann, who associated it with a word in Joyce's *Finnegans Wake*]

quar•rel (kwôr′əl, kwor′-), *n.*, *v.*, **-reled**, **-rel•ing** or (*esp. Brit.*) **-relled**, **-rel•ling.** —*n.* **1.** an angry dispute or altercation. **2.** a cause of dispute, complaint, or hostile feeling. —*v.i.* **3.** to disagree angrily. **4.** to make a complaint. —**quar′rel•some**, *adj.*

quar•ry¹ (kwôr′ē, kwor′ē), *n.*, *pl.* **-ries**, *v.*, **-ried**, **-ry•ing.** —*n.* **1.** a usu. open excavation or pit from which building stone or slate is obtained. —*v.t.* **2.** to obtain from or as if from a quarry.

quar•ry² (kwôr′ē, kwor′ē), *n.*, *pl.* **-ries. 1.** an animal or bird hunted or pursued. **2.** an object of search, pursuit, or attack.

quart (kwôrt), *n.* **1.** a unit of liquid measure equal to one fourth of a gallon, or 57.749 cubic inches (0.946 liter). **2.** a unit of dry measure equal to one eighth of a peck, or 67.201 cubic inches (1.101 liters).

quar•ter (kwôr′tər), *n.* **1.** one of four equal or equivalent parts. **2. a.** one fourth of a U.S. or Canadian dollar, equivalent to 25 cents. **b.** a coin of this value. **3.** one fourth of an hour; 15 minutes. **4.** one fourth of a calendar or fiscal year. **5.** one of the four equal periods of play in certain games, as basketball. **6.** a district of a city or town. **7.** Usu., **-ters.** housing accommodations. **8.** Often, **-ters.** an unspecified source. **9.** mercy or indulgence: *gave no quarter.* —*v.t.* **10.** to divide into four equal or equivalent parts. **11.** to furnish with lodging. —*adj.* **12.** being one of four equal or equivalent parts.

quar′ter•back′ *n.* **1.** a back in football who directs the offense of the team. —*v.t.* **2.** to direct the offense of (a team). **3.** to lead; direct.

quar′ter•ly *adj.*, *n.*, *pl.* **-lies**, *adv.* —*adj.* **1.** occurring, done, paid, or issued at the end of every quarter of a year. —*n.* **2.** a periodical issued every three months. —*adv.* **3.** once each quarter of a year.

quar′ter•mas′ter *n.* **1.** a military officer charged with providing quarters, clothing, and food for troops. **2.** a petty officer in charge of a ship's helm and navigating apparatus.

quar•tet or **-tette** (kwôr tet′), *n.* **1.** a group of four singers or players. **2.** a musical composition for a quartet. **3.** a group of four.

quar•to (kwôr′tō), *n.*, *pl.* **-tos. 1.** a book size of about 9½ × 12 in. (24 × 30 cm), determined by folding printed sheets twice to form four leaves or eight pages. **2.** a book of this size.

quartz (kwôrts), *n.* a common mineral that is a form of silica and is the chief component of sand.

qua•sar (kwā′zär, -zər), *n.* any of numerous starlike celestial objects that may be the most distant and brightest objects in the universe.

quash (kwosh), *v.t.* **1.** to put down or suppress completely; quell. **2.** to set aside (a law, indictment, etc.).

qua•si (kwā′zī, -sī, kwä′sē, -zē), *adj.* resembling; seeming to be: *a quasi liberal.*

quasi- a combining form meaning in part or somewhat (*quasi-scientific*).

Quat•er•nar•y (kwot′ər ner′ē, kwə tûr′nə rē), *adj.* noting or pertaining to the present geologic period forming the latter part of the Cenozoic Era.

quat•rain (kwo′trān), *n.* a stanza or poem of four lines.

qua•ver (kwā′vər), *v.i.* **1.** to shake tremulously. **2.** to sound, speak, or sing tremulously. —*n.* **3.** a quivering or trembling. **4.** a quavering tone or utterance. —**qua′ver•y**, *adj.*

quay (kē, kā, kwā), *n.* a landing place, esp. one of solid masonry; wharf.

quea•sy (kwē′zē), *adj.*, **-si•er**, **-si•est. 1.** feeling or causing nausea. **2.** uneasy; uncomfortable. —**quea′si•ness**, *n.*

queen (kwēn), *n.* **1.** a female sovereign or monarch. **2.** the wife or consort of a king. **3.** a woman preeminent in a particular respect. **4.** a playing card bearing a picture of a queen. **5.** the most powerful chess piece. **6.** a fertile female ant, bee, termite, or wasp. —**queen′ly**, *adj.*, **-li•er**, **-li•est.**

queer (kwēr), *adj.*, **-er**, **-est**, *v.*, *n.* —*adj.* **1.** strange or odd from a conventional viewpoint; eccentric. **2.** questionable in nature or character; suspicious. **3.** *Slang* (*offensive*). homosexual. **4.** *Slang.* bad, worthless, or counterfeit. —*v.t.* **5.** to spoil; ruin. —*n.* **6.** *Slang* (*offensive*). a homosexual, esp. a male. —**queer′ly**, *adv.*

quell (kwel), *v.t.* **1.** to suppress; crush. **2.** to quiet; allay.

quench (kwench), *v.t.* **1.** to satisfy (thirst, desires, etc.); allay. **2.** to put out (fire, flames, etc.); extinguish. **3.** to cool suddenly by plunging into a liquid, as in tempering steel. **4.** to overcome; quell.

quer•u•lous (kwer′ə ləs, kwer′yə-), *adj.* **1.** full of complaints; petulant. **2.** characterized by complaint; peevish. —**quer′u•lous•ly**, *adv.*

que•ry (kwēr′ē), *n.*, *pl.* **-ries**, *v.*, **-ried**, **-ry•ing.** —*n.* **1.** a question. **2.** QUESTION MARK. —*v.t.* **3.** to question.

quest (kwest), *n.* **1.** a search. **2.** an adventurous expedition, as by knights in medieval romances.

ques•tion (kwes′chən), *n.* **1.** a sentence in interrogative form intended to elicit a reply. **2.** a matter for discussion, dispute, or investigation. **3.** a matter of some difficulty; problem. **4.** a proposal to be voted on, as in a meeting. —*v.t.* **5.** to ask questions of; interrogate. **6.** to make a question of; doubt. **7.** to challenge; dispute. —*v.i.* **8.** to ask questions. —*Idiom.* **9.** out of the question, not to be considered; impossible. —**ques′tion•er**, *n.*

ques′tion•a•ble *adj.* **1.** of doubtful propriety, honesty, or morality. **2.** open to question; uncertain.

ques′tion mark′ *n.* a punctuation mark (?) indicating a question.

ques′tion•naire′ (-chə nâr′), *n.* a list of questions submitted to obtain information.

queue (kyōō), *n.*, *v.*, **queued**, **queu•ing.** —*n.* **1.** a braid of hair worn hanging down behind. **2.** a line, esp. of people. **3.** a sequence of items waiting for electronic action in a computer system. —*v.i.*, *v.t.* **4.** to form in or arrange in a queue.

quib•ble (kwib′əl), *n.*, *v.*, **-bled**, **-bling.** —*n.* **1.** a petty or carping criticism. **2.** an evasion of a point at issue. —*v.i.* **3.** to bicker, carp, or cavil. **4.** to use evasive language; equivocate. —**quib′bler**, *n.*

quiche (kēsh), *n.* a pie containing unsweetened custard baked with other ingredients, as cheese.

quick (kwik), *adj.* and *adv.*, **-er**, **-est**, *n.* —*adj.* **1.** done, proceeding, or occurring with promptness; rapid. **2.** finished or completed in a short time. **3.**

moving or able to move with speed. **4.** easily provoked or excited. **5.** keenly responsive; acute. **6.** acting with rapidity. **7.** prompt or swift in doing, perceiving, or understanding. —*n.* **8.** living persons: *the quick and the dead.* **9.** tender, sensitive flesh, esp. under the nails. **10.** the vital or most important part. —*adv.* **11.** in a quick manner. —**quick′ly,** *adv.* —**quick′ness,** *n.*

quick′en *v.t.* **1.** to make more rapid; accelerate. **2.** to give or restore vigor to; stimulate. —*v.i.* **3.** to become more rapid. **4.** to come to life; revive. **5.** to begin to manifest signs of life.

quick′ie *n.* something produced, done, or enjoyed in only a short time.

quick′lime′ *n.* LIME¹ (def. 1).

quick′sand′ *n.* a deep bed of loose sand saturated with water that yields under weight and into which objects tend to sink.

quick′sil′ver *n.* MERCURY (def. 1).

quid¹ (kwid), *n.* a portion of something, esp. tobacco, for chewing.

quid² (kwid), *n., pl.* **quid.** *Brit. Informal.* one pound sterling.

quid pro quo (kwid′ prō kwō′), *n., pl.* **quid pro quos, quids pro quo.** something given or taken for something else. [< L: lit., something for something]

qui•es•cent (kwē es′ənt, kwī-), *adj.* being at rest; quiet. —**qui•es′cence,** *n.*

qui•et¹ (kwī′it), *adj.,* **-er, -est,** *v.* —*adj.* **1.** making little or no noise or sound; silent. **2.** free from noise. **3.** free from disturbance or tumult; tranquil. **4.** mild; gentle. **5.** not showy or obtrusive. —*v.t., v.i.* **6.** to make or become quiet. —**qui′et•ly,** *adv.* —**qui′et•ness,** *n.*

qui•et² (kwī′it), *n.* **1.** freedom from noise. **2.** freedom from disturbance or tumult.

quill (kwil), *n.* **1.** one of the large wing or tail feathers of a bird. **2.** the hard, hollow, tubular part of a feather. **3.** a feather, as of a goose, used as a pen for writing. **4.** one of the hollow spines on a porcupine or hedgehog.

quilt (kwilt), *n.* **1.** a padded bed coverlet made of two layers of fabric. —*v.t.* **2.** to stitch together (two pieces of cloth and a soft interlining). **3.** to pad or line like a quilt. —*v.i.* **4.** to make quilts. —**quilt′ed,** *adj.*

quince (kwins), *n.* **1.** a small tree bearing hard, yellowish fruit used esp. for making preserves. **2.** the fruit of a quince.

qui•nine (kwī′nīn), *n.* a white crystalline alkaloid used chiefly for treating malaria.

quint (kwint), *n.* a quintuplet.

quin•tes•sence (kwin tes′əns), *n.* **1.** the pure and concentrated essence of a substance. **2.** the most perfect embodiment of something. —**quin′tes•sen′-tial** (-tə sen′shəl), *adj.*

quin•tet or **-tette** (kwin tet′), *n.* **1.** a set or group of five. **2.** a group of five singers or players. **3.** a musical composition for a quintet.

quin•tu•plet (kwin tup′lit, -tōō′plit, -tyōō′-), *n.* **1.** a group or combination of five. **2.** five children or offspring born of one pregnancy.

quip (kwip), *n., v.,* **quipped, quip•ping.** —*n.* **1.** a clever or witty remark. —*v.i.* **2.** to utter a quip. —**quip′ster** (-stər), *n.*

quire (kwīʳr), *n.* a set of 24 uniform sheets of paper.

quirk (kwûrk), *n.* **1.** a peculiarity of action, behavior, or personality. **2.** a sudden twist or turn. —**quirk′y,** *adj.,* **-i•er, i•est.** —**quirk′i•ness,** *n.*

quis•ling (kwiz′ling), *n.* a person who betrays his or her country by aiding an invading enemy. [after V. *Quisling* (1887–1945), pro-Nazi Norwegian leader]

quit (kwit), *v.,* **quit** or **quit•ted, quit•ting.** —*v.t.* **1.** to stop, cease, or discontinue. **2.** to depart from; leave. **3.** to let go; relinquish. **4.** to conduct (oneself). —*v.i.* **5.** to cease from doing something. **6.** to give up or resign one's job or position. **7.** to acknowledge defeat.

quit′claim′ *n.* a transfer of one's interest in a property, esp. without a warranty of title.

quite (kwīt), *adv.* **1.** completely, wholly, or entirely. **2.** actually, really, or truly. **3.** to a considerable extent or degree.

quits (kwits), *adj.* **1.** being on equal terms, as by retaliation. —*Idiom.* **2. call it quits,** to end an activity or relationship.

quit•tance (kwit′ns), *n.* **1.** recompense or requital. **2.** discharge from a debt or obligation.

quiv•er¹ (kwiv′ər), *v.t., v.i.* **1.** to shake with a slight but rapid motion. —*n.* **2.** the act of quivering. —**quiv′er•y,** *adj.*

quiv•er² (kwiv′ər), *n.* a case for arrows.

quix•ot•ic (kwik sot′ik), *adj.* extravagantly chivalrous or romantic but impractical. [after Don *Quixote,* hero of Cervantes' novel of the same name]

quiz (kwiz), *n., pl.* **quiz•zes,** *v.,* **quizzed, quiz•zing.** —*n.* **1.** an informal test or examination. —*v.t.* **2.** to examine or test (a student or class) informally by questions. —**quiz′zer,** *n.*

quiz′zi•cal *adj.* **1.** odd or comical. **2.** questioning or puzzled. —**quiz′zi•cal•ly,** *adv.*

quoin (koin, kwoin), *n.* **1.** an external solid angle, as of a wall. **2.** a stone forming a quoin; cornerstone. **3.** a wedge of wood or metal for locking type in a chase.

quoit (kwoit, koit), *n.* **1. quoits,** (*used with a sing. v.*) a game in which rope or metal rings are thrown at an upright peg. **2.** a ring used in quoits.

quon•dam (kwon′dəm, -dam), *adj.* former; onetime. [< L]

quo•rum (kwôr′əm), *n.* the number of members of a group required to be present to transact business.

quo•ta (kwō′tə), *n., pl.* **-tas.** **1.** a proportional part of a total; share. **2.** the number or percentage of persons of a specified kind admitted to a college, country, etc.

quo•ta•tion (kwō tā′shən), *n.* **1.** the act of quoting. **2.** the words quoted. **3.** the quoted or current price of a commodity or security.

quota′tion mark′ *n.* one of a pair of punctuation marks used to enclose a quotation, usu. shown as (") at the beginning and (") at the end.

quote *v.,* **quot•ed, quot•ing,** *n.* —*v.t.* **1.** to repeat (a passage, phrase, etc.), as from a book or speech. **2.** to repeat words from (a book, author, etc.). **3.** to state the price of (a stock, bond, etc.). **4.** to state (a price). —*n.* **5.** something quoted. **6.** QUOTATION MARK. —**quot′a•ble,** *adj.*

quo•tid•i•an (kwō tid′ē ən), *adj.* **1.** daily. **2.** ordinary; everyday.

quo•tient (kwō′shənt), *n.* the result obtained by dividing one quantity by another.

R, r (är), *n., pl.* **Rs** or **R's, rs** or **r's.** the 18th letter of the English alphabet, a consonant.
R 1. *Chem.* radical. **2.** *Math.* ratio. **3.** restricted: a motion-picture rating advising that children under 17 will not be admitted unless accompanied by an adult. **4.** right. **5.** roentgen. **6.** *Baseball.* run.
R *Symbol.* **1.** registered trademark: written as superscript ® following a name. **2.** *Elect.* resistance.
r 1. radius. **2.** roentgen.
R. 1. radius. **2.** railroad. **3.** railway. **4.** Republican. **5.** right. **6.** river. **7.** road.
r. 1. railroad. **2.** railway. **3.** range. **4.** right. **5.** river. **6.** road. **7.** rod.
rab•bi (rab′ī), *n., pl.* **-bis. 1.** the ordained chief religious official of a synagogue. **2.** a Jewish scholar or teacher. **—rab•bin′ic, rab•bin•i•cal** (rə bin′i-kəl), *adj.*
rab•bin•ate (rab′ə nit, -nāt′), *n.* **1.** the office of a rabbi. **2.** rabbis collectively.
rab•bit (rab′it), *n., pl.* **-bits, -bit.** any of several large-eared hopping mammals resembling but usu. smaller than the hares.
rab•ble (rab′əl), *n.* **1.** a disorderly crowd; mob. **2.** the common people.
rab′ble-rous′er (-rou′zər), *n.* a person who stirs up the passions or prejudices of the public; demagogue.
rab•id (rab′id), *adj.* **1.** irrationally extreme. **2.** furious or raging; violent. **3.** affected with rabies. **—rab′id•ly,** *adv.*
ra•bies (rā′bēz), *n.* an infectious, usu. fatal viral disease transmitted by the bite of an infected animal.
rac•coon (ra kōōn′), *n., pl.* **-coons, -coon. 1.** a North American nocturnal carnivore with a masklike black stripe across the eyes and a ringed tail. **2.** the fur of the raccoon.
race¹ (rās), *n., v.,* **raced, rac•ing. —n. 1.** a contest of speed. **2.** a competition, esp. to achieve superiority. **3.** onward movement or course. **4. a.** a strong current of water. **b.** the channel of such a current. **—v.i. 5.** to run a race. **6.** to run, move, or go swiftly. **—v.t. 7.** to run a race against. **8.** to enter in a race. **9.** to cause to run or go at high speed. **—rac′er,** *n.*
race² (rās), *n.* **1.** a group of people related by common descent. **2.** a classification of human beings based on physical characteristics or genetic markers. **3.** a people united by common history, language, etc. **4.** any group of people, animals, or plants having common characteristics. **—ra′cial** (rā′shəl), *adj.*
rac•ism (rā′siz əm), *n.* **1.** a belief that one's own race is superior. **2.** a policy or practice based on racism. **—rac′ist,** *n., adj.*
rack¹ (rak), *n.* **1.** a framework, as of bars, on which articles are placed or arranged. **2.** a bar with teeth that engage with the teeth of a pinion. **3.** an instrument of torture on which a victim was stretched. **4.** a cause or state of intense suffering. **—v.t. 5.** to distress acutely. **6.** to strain, as if in mental effort. **7.** to torture on a rack.
rack² (rak), *n.* wreckage or destruction: *to go to rack and ruin.*
rack•et¹ (rak′it), *n.* **1.** loud noise; din. **2.** an organized illegal activity. **3.** a dishonest scheme, business, or activity.
rack•et² or **rac•quet** (rak′it), *n.* a light bat with netting stretched in an oval frame, used in tennis, badminton, etc.
rack′et•eer′ *n.* a person engaged in an organized illegal activity, as extortion. **—rack′et•eer′ing,** *n.*
rac•on•teur (rak′on tûr′, -tōōr′, -ən-), *n.* a person skilled in telling anecdotes.
ra•coon′ (ra kōōn′) *n.* raccoon.

rac′quet•ball′ *n.* a game similar to handball that is played with rackets on a four-walled court.
rac•y (rā′sē), *adj.,* **-i•er, -i•est. 1.** slightly improper; risqué. **2.** lively; spirited. **3.** piquant; pungent. **4.** having an agreeably peculiar taste, as fruit. **—rac′i•ly,** *adv.* **—rac′i•ness,** *n.*
ra•dar (rā′där), *n.* a device for determining the presence and location of an object by measuring the direction and timing of radio waves. [*ra(dio) d(etecting) a(nd) r(anging)*]
ra•di•al (rā′dē əl), *adj.* **1.** arranged or having parts arranged like radii or rays. **2.** of a radius or a ray. **—ra′di•al•ly,** *adv.*
ra•di•ant (-ənt), *adj.* **1.** emitting rays of light. **2.** bright with joy, hope, or happiness. **3.** *Physics.* emitted or propagated by radiation. **—ra′di•ance,** *n.* **—ra′di•ant•ly,** *adv.*
ra•di•ate (-āt′), *v.,* **-at•ed, -at•ing. —v.i. 1.** to extend, spread, or move from a center like rays or radii. **2.** to emit rays, as of light or heat. **—v.t. 3.** to emit in or as if in rays.
ra•di•a′tion *n.* **1.** the process in which energy is emitted as particles or waves, transmitted, and absorbed. **2.** the act or process of radiating. **3.** something radiated.
ra•di•a′tor *n.* **1.** a heating device, as a series of pipes through which steam or hot water passes. **2.** a device for cooling circulating water, as in an automobile engine.
rad•i•cal (rad′i kəl), *adj.* **1.** of or going to a root or origin; fundamental. **2.** thoroughgoing or extreme. **3.** favoring drastic political, economic, or social reforms. **—n. 4.** a person who advocates drastic reforms. **5.** *Math.* **a.** a quantity expressed as a root of another quantity. **b.** the symbol √ or ⌐ indicating extraction of a root of the quantity that follows it. **6.** *Chem.* a group of atoms that act together as a single unit. **—rad′i•cal•ism,** *n.* **—rad′i•cal•ly,** *adv.*
ra•di•o (rā′dē ō′), *n., pl.* **-os,** *adj., v.,* **-oed, -o•ing. —n. 1.** a telecommunication system employing electromagnetic waves to transmit speech or other sound over long distances without wires. **2.** an apparatus for receiving or transmitting radio broadcasts. **—adj. 3.** of, used in, or sent by radio. **—v.t. 4.** to transmit by radio. **5.** to send a message to by radio.
radio- a combining form meaning: radiant energy (*radiometer*); radio waves (*radiotelephone*); emission of rays as a result of the breakup of atomic nuclei (*radioactivity*).
ra′di•o•ac•tiv′i•ty *n.* the property of certain elements of spontaneously emitting radiation as a result of changes in the nuclei of atoms of the element. **—ra′di•o•ac′tive,** *adj.*
ra′di•ol′o•gy (-ol′ə jē), *n.* the use of radiation, as x-rays, and various imaging techniques for medical diagnosis and treatment. **—ra′di•ol′o•gist,** *n.*
rad•ish (rad′ish), *n.* **1.** the crisp, pungent, edible root of a plant of the mustard family. **2.** the plant itself.
ra•di•um (rā′dē əm), *n.* a highly radioactive metallic element whose decay yields radon gas and alpha rays. *Symbol:* Ra; *at. wt.:* 226; *at. no.:* 88.
ra•di•us (rā′dē əs), *n., pl.* **-di•i** (-dē ī′), **-di•us•es. 1.** a straight line extending from the center of a circle or sphere to the circumference or surface. **2.** a circular area whose extent is determined by the length of its radius. **3.** the bone of the forearm on the thumb side. [< L: staff, spoke]
ra•don (rā′don), *n.* a chemically inert radioactive gaseous element produced by the decay of radium. *Symbol:* Rn; *at. no.:* 86; *at. wt.:* 222.
RAF Royal Air Force.
raf•fi•a (raf′ē ə), *n., pl.* **-as.** a fiber obtained from

the leaves of a palm and used esp. for making mats and baskets.

raff·ish (raf′ish), *adj.* **1.** jaunty; rakish. **2.** gaudily vulgar or cheap; tawdry. —**raff′ish·ly,** *adv.* —**raff′-ish·ness,** *n.*

raf·fle (raf′əl), *n., v.,* **-fled, -fling.** —*n.* **1.** a form of lottery in which a number of persons buy chances to win a prize. —*v.t.* **2.** to dispose of by a raffle.

raft¹ (raft, räft), *n.* **1.** a floating platform made of buoyant materials. **2.** a collection of logs or planks fastened together for floating on water. —*v.t.* **3.** to transport or travel by raft. —*v.i.* **4.** to go or travel on a raft.

raft² (raft, räft), *n. Informal.* a great quantity or number.

raf·ter (raf′tər, räf′-), *n.* a usu. sloping timber for supporting a roof.

rag¹ (rag), *n.* a worthless piece of cloth, esp. one that is torn or worn. —**rag·ged** (rag′id), *adj.*

rag² (rag), *v.t.,* **ragged, rag·ging.** *Informal.* **1.** to scold. **2.** to tease.

rag³ (rag), *n.* a musical composition in ragtime.

ra·ga (rä′gə), *n., pl.* **-gas.** one of the traditional melodic formulas of Hindu music.

rag·a·muf·fin (rag′ə muf′in), *n.* a ragged, dirty person, esp. a child.

rage (rāj), *n., v.,* **raged, rag·ing.** —*n.* **1.** violent anger; fury. **2.** a fit of violent anger. **3.** an object of current popularity; fad. —*v.i.* **4.** to show or feel violent anger. **5.** to move or act with violent force or intensity. —**rag′ing·ly,** *adv.*

ra·gout (ra gōō′), *n.* a highly seasoned stew of meat or fish.

rag′time′ *n.* **1.** rhythm marked by an accompaniment in strict two-four time and a syncopated melody. **2.** music in ragtime rhythm.

rag′weed′ *n.* a plant with ragged leaves whose pollen is the chief cause of hay fever.

raid (rād), *n.* **1.** a sudden assault or attack. —*v.t., v.i.* **2.** to make a raid (on). —**raid′er,** *n.*

rail¹ (rāl), *n.* **1.** a horizontal bar fixed to upright posts and forming a support, barrier, fence, or railing. **2.** one of a pair of steel bars forming the running surfaces for the wheels of railroad cars. **3.** railroad: *traveled by rail.* —*v.t.* **4.** to furnish or enclose with a rail or railing.

rail² (rāl), *v.i.* to utter bitter complaints.

rail³ (rāl), *n.* any of numerous short-winged marsh birds.

rail′ing *n.* **1.** a fencelike barrier of horizontal rails. **2.** rails collectively.

rail′ler·y *n., pl.* **-ies.** good-humored ridicule; banter.

rail′road′ *n.* **1.** a permanent road laid with rails forming a track on which locomotives and cars are run. **2.** an entire system of railroads together with its property and equipment. —*v.t.* **3.** to transport by railroad. **4.** to push (a law or bill) too hastily through a legislature. **5.** to convict hastily and unfairly. —*v.i.* **6.** to work on a railroad.

rail′way′ *n., pl.* **-ways.** **1.** a railroad. **2.** a line of rails forming a road for wheeled equipment.

rai·ment (rā′mənt), *n.* clothing; apparel.

rain (rān), *n.* **1.** water condensed from atmospheric vapor that falls to earth in drops. **2.** a heavy and continuous descent: *a rain of blows.* —*v.i.* **3.** (of rain) to fall. **4.** to fall like rain. —*v.t.* **5.** to send down. **6.** to offer or bestow in great quantity. **7. rain out,** to cancel or postpone because of rain. —**rain′y,** *adj.,* **-i·er, -i·est.**

rain′bow′ (-bō′), *n.* an arc of prismatic colors appearing opposite the sun and caused by the refraction and reflection of the sun's rays in raindrops.

rain′ check′ *n.* **1.** postponement of an invitation. **2.** a ticket for future admission to an event that has been postponed or interrupted by rain.

rain′coat′ *n.* a waterproof or water-repellent coat.

rain′fall′ *n.* **1.** a fall of rain. **2.** the amount of water falling within a given time and area.

rain′ for′est *n.* a tropical forest, usu. of tall, broad-leaved evergreens, in an area of high annual rainfall.

rain′mak′er *n.* one who induces or tries to induce rainfall by artificial means. —**rain′mak′ing,** *n.*

raise (rāz), *v.,* **raised, rais·ing,** *n.* —*v.t.* **1.** to move to a higher position; lift. **2.** to set upright. **3.** to increase in amount, degree, intensity, pitch, or force. **4.** to grow or breed: *to raise corn.* **5.** to bring up; rear. **6.** to present for consideration; put forward. **7.** to build; erect: *to raise a house.* **8.** to give rise to; provoke. **9.** to give vigor to; animate: *raised our spirits.* **10.** to advance in rank or position. **11.** to assemble or collect: *to raise money.* **12.** to cause (dough or bread) to rise. —*n.* **13.** an increase in amount, as of wages.

rai·sin (rā′zin), *n.* a dried sweet grape.

rai·son d'ê·tre (rā′zōn de′trə, rez′ōN), *n., pl.* **rai·sons d'ê·tre** (rā′zōnz, rez′ōN). reason or justification for existence. [< F]

ra·jah or **-ja** (rä′jə), *n., pl.* **-jahs** or **-jas.** a prince in India.

rake¹ (rāk), *n., v.,* **raked, rak·ing.** —*n.* **1.** an agricultural implement with a long handle and row of teeth or tines, as for gathering hay. —*v.t.* **2.** to gather, smooth, or remove with or as if with a rake. **3.** to gather or collect in abundance: *raked in money.* **4.** to fire guns along the length of (a body of troops, a ship, etc.). —*v.i.* **5.** to use a rake.

rake² (rāk), *n.* a dissolute and licentious man.

rake³ (rāk), *v.,* **raked, rak·ing,** *n.* —*v.i., v.t.* **1.** to incline from the vertical or horizontal. —*n.* **2.** inclination away from the vertical or horizontal.

rake′-off′ *n.* a share or amount taken or received, esp. illicitly.

rak·ish¹ (rā′kish), *adj.* like a dissolute rake. —**rak′-ish·ly,** *adv.*

rak·ish² (rā′kish), *adj.* **1.** jaunty; dashing. **2.** (of a ship) having an appearance suggesting speed.

ral·ly¹ (ral′ē), *v.,* **-lied, -ly·ing,** *n., pl.* **-lies.** —*v.t., v.i.* **1.** to bring or come together for common action or effort. **2.** to bring or come into order. **3.** to revive or recover, as from illness. —*n.* **4.** a renewal or recovery, as of strength or activity. **5.** a mass meeting to support a common cause. **6.** a sharp rise in stock prices or trading after a declining market. **7.** a long-distance automobile race, esp. for sports cars.

ral·ly² (ral′ē), *v.t.,* **-lied, -ly·ing.** to ridicule in a good-natured way.

ram (ram), *n., v.,* **rammed, ram·ming.** —*n.* **1.** a male sheep. **2.** any of various devices for battering, crushing, or forcing something. —*v.t.* **3.** to drive or force by heavy blows. **4.** to strike against with great force. **5.** to cram; stuff.

RAM (ram), *n.* random-access memory: volatile computer memory for creating, loading, and running programs and manipulating and temporarily storing data.

ram·ble (ram′bəl), *v.,* **-bled, -bling,** *n.* —*v.i.* **1.** to wander around in a leisurely, aimless manner. **2.** to grow or spread in a random fashion, as a vine. **3.** to talk or write in a discursive, aimless manner. —*n.* **4.** a leisurely walk without a definite route.

ram′bler *n.* **1.** one that rambles. **2.** a climbing rose with clusters of small flowers.

ram·bunc·tious (ram bungk′shəs), *adj.* difficult to control or handle; wildly boisterous. —**ram·bunc′tious·ness,** *n.*

ram·i·fi·ca′tion (ram′ə fi kā′shən), *n.* a related or derived development; consequence.

ram·i·fy (ram′ə fī′), *v.t., v.i.,* **-fied, -fy·ing.** to divide or spread out into branches or branchlike parts.

ramp (ramp), *n.* **1.** a sloping surface connecting two levels. **2.** a movable staircase for entering or leaving an airplane.

ram·page (ram′pāj; *v. also* ram pāj′), *n., v.,* **-paged, -pag·ing.** —*n.* **1.** an eruption of violently uncontrolled, reckless, or destructive behavior. —*v.i.* **2.** to rush or act furiously or violently.

ramp·ant (ram′pənt), *adj.* **1.** prevailing or unchecked; widespread. **2.** growing luxuriantly, as weeds. —**ramp′ant·ly,** *adv.*

ram·part (ram′pärt, -pərt), *n.* a mound, as of earth, raised as a fortification.

ram′rod′ *n.* **1.** a rod for ramming down the charge of a muzzleloading firearm. **2.** a rod for cleaning the barrel of a firearm.

ram′shack′le *adj.* loosely made or held together; rickety.

ranch (ranch), *n.* **1.** an establishment for raising livestock under range conditions. **2.** a farm that raises a single crop or animal. —*v.i.* **3.** to manage or work on a ranch. —**ranch′er,** *n.*

ran•cid (ran′sid), *adj.* having a rank, unpleasant smell or taste.

ran•cor (rang′kər), *n.* bitter resentment or ill will; malice. Also, *esp. Brit.,* **ran′cour.** —**ran′cor•ous,** *adj.*

rand (rand), *n., pl.* **rand.** the basic monetary unit of South Africa.

ran•dom (ran′dəm), *adj.* **1.** occurring or done without definite aim, reason, or pattern. —*Idiom.* **2. at random,** in a random manner. —**ran′dom•ly,** *adv.*

rand•y (ran′dē), *adj.,* **-i•er, -i•est.** sexually aroused; lustful.

range (rānj), *n., v.,* **ranged, rang•ing.** —*n.* **1.** the limits between which variation is possible. **2.** extent; scope: *one's range of vision.* **3.** the distance of a target from a weapon. **4.** an area with targets for shooting practice. **5.** an area for flight-testing missiles. **6.** a rank, class, or order. **7.** a row, line, or series, as of persons or things. **8.** the act of moving around over an area or region. **9.** an open region where livestock can roam or graze. **10.** the region over which a population or species is distributed. **11.** a chain of mountains. **12.** a large stove with burners and an oven. —*v.t.* **13.** to arrange in rows or lines, esp. in an orderly way. **14.** to place in a particular class. **15.** to pass over or through (an area or region), as in exploring. —*v.i.* **16.** to vary within specified limits. **17.** to roam or wander. **18.** to extend in a certain direction.

rang′er *n.* **1.** FOREST RANGER. **2.** one of a body of armed guards who patrol a region. **3.** (*often cap.*) a soldier trained for making surprise raids.

rang•y (rān′jē), *adj.,* **-i•er, -i•est.** slender and long-limbed.

rank¹ (rangk), *n.* **1.** a social or official position or standing. **2.** high position or station. **3.** relative position or standing: *a writer of the first rank.* **4.** a row or series. **5. ranks,** enlisted soldiers as a group. **6.** an orderly arrangement; array. **7.** a line of soldiers standing abreast. —*v.t.* **8.** to arrange in ranks or in regular formation. **9.** to assign to a particular position or class. **10.** to outrank. —*v.i.* **11.** to hold a certain rank or position. **12.** to be the senior in rank.

rank² (rangk), *adj.,* **-er, -est. 1.** growing with excessive luxuriance. **2.** having an offensive smell. **3.** utter; absolute: *a rank amateur.*

rank′ and file′ *n.* **1.** the members of an organization, apart from its leaders or officers. **2.** the enlisted soldiers of an army.

rank′ing *adj.* **1.** senior in rank or position. **2.** highly regarded; renowned.

ran•kle (rang′kəl), *v.i., v.t.,* **-kled, -kling.** to cause keen irritation or bitter resentment (in).

ran•sack (ran′sak), *v.t.* **1.** to search thoroughly or vigorously through. **2.** to search through for plunder; pillage.

ran•som (ran′səm), *n.* **1.** the redemption for a price of a prisoner or captive. **2.** the price paid or demanded. —*v.t.* **3.** to redeem, as from detention, by paying a demanded price.

rant (rant), *v.i.* **1.** to talk in a wild or vehement way; rave. —*n.* **2.** wild or vehement talk. —**rant′er,** *n.*

rap (rap), *v.,* **rapped, rap•ping,** *n.* —*v.t.* **1.** to strike with a quick, smart blow. **2.** to utter sharply or vigorously. **3.** *Slang.* to criticize severely. —*v.i.* **4.** to knock smartly or vigorously. **5.** *Slang.* to talk; chat. —*n.* **6.** a quick, smart blow. **7.** *Slang.* blame or punishment. **8.** *Slang.* a criminal charge. **9.** *Slang.* talk; conversation. **10.** a kind of popular music marked by the rhythmical intoning of rhymed verses to an insistent beat. —**rap′per,** *n.*

ra•pa•cious (rə pā′shəs), *adj.* **1.** extremely greedy. **2.** subsisting on living prey; predatory. —**ra•pac′i•ty** (-pas′i tē), *n.*

rape (rāp), *n., v.,* **raped, rap•ing.** —*n.* **1.** the unlawful act of forcing a person, esp. a female, to have sexual intercourse. **2.** an act of plunder or despoliation. —*v.i., v.t.* **3.** to commit rape (on). —**rap′ist,** *n.*

rap•id (rap′id), *adj.,* **-er, -est,** *n.* —*adj.* **1.** characterized by speed; swift. —*n.* **2.** Usu., **rapids.** a part of a river where the current runs very swiftly. —**ra•pid•i•ty** (rə pid′i tē), *n.* —**rap′id•ly,** *adv.*

ra•pi•er (rā′pē ər), *n.* a sword with a double-edged blade.

rap•ine (rap′in, -īn), *n.* the violent seizure and carrying off of another's property.

rap•port (ra pôr′, rə-), *n.* a relation, esp. a harmonious or sympathetic one.

rap•proche•ment (rap′rōsh män′), *n.* an establishment or renewal of harmonious relations.

rap′ sheet′ *n. Slang.* a record of a person's arrests and convictions.

rapt (rapt), *adj.* **1.** deeply engrossed; absorbed. **2.** transported with emotion.

rap•ture (rap′chər), *n.* **1.** ecstatic joy or delight. **2.** religious or spiritual ecstasy. **3.** *Archaic.* the act of carrying off. —**rap′tur•ous,** *adj.*

rare¹ (râr), *adj.,* **rar•er, rar•est. 1.** occurring or found infrequently; uncommon. **2.** having component parts loosely compacted; thin: *rare gases.* **3.** unusually great; extraordinary. —**rare′ly,** *adv.* —**rar′i•ty,** *n., pl.* **-ties.**

rare² (râr), *adj.,* **rar•er, rar•est.** (of meat) cooked just slightly.

rare•bit (râr′bit), *n.* melted cheese, often mixed with ale or beer, served over toast.

rare′-earth′ el′ement *n.* any of a group of related metallic elements of atomic numbers 57 through 71.

rar•e•fy (râr′ə fī′), *v.t., v.i.,* **-fied, -fy•ing.** to make or become rare or less dense; thin.

rar′ing *adj.* very eager or anxious: *raring to go.*

ras•cal (ras′kəl), *n.* **1.** a dishonest or unscrupulous person. **2.** a mischievous person or animal. —**ras′cal•ly,** *adj.*

rash¹ (rash), *adj.,* **-er, -est.** marked by or resulting from reckless or ill-considered haste. —**rash′ly,** *adv.* —**rash′ness,** *n.*

rash² (rash), *n.* **1.** a skin eruption. **2.** multiple occurrences; outbreak: *a rash of robberies.*

rash′er *n.* **1.** a thin slice of bacon or ham for frying or broiling. **2.** a serving of three or four slices, esp. of bacon.

rasp (rasp, räsp), *v.t.* **1.** to scrape with or as if with a rough instrument. **2.** to grate upon or irritate. —*v.i.* **3.** to speak with a grating sound. —*n.* **4.** a rasping sound. **5.** a coarse file with separate conical teeth. —**rasp′y,** *adj.,* **-i•er, -i•est.**

rasp•ber•ry (raz′ber′ē, -bə rē, räz′-), *n., pl.* **-ries. 1.** the small, juicy red, black, or pale yellow fruit of a prickly shrub of the rose family. **2.** a shrub bearing raspberries. **3.** a vulgar noise made with the lips and tongue to express contempt.

rat (rat), *n., v.,* **rat•ted, rat•ting.** —*n.* **1.** any of several long-tailed rodents resembling but larger than the mouse. **2.** *Slang.* **a.** a person who betrays associates. **b.** an informer. **3.** *Slang.* a person who frequents a specified place: *mall rat.* —*v.i.* **4.** *Slang.* to inform on one's associates; squeal. **5.** to hunt or catch rats.

ratch•et (rach′it), *n.* **1.** a toothed bar or wheel with which a pivoted bar engages. **2.** a mechanism consisting of a ratchet with a pivoted bar.

rate¹ (rāt), *n., v.,* **rat•ed, rat•ing.** —*n.* **1.** a price, charge, or payment fixed with reference to a scale or standard. **2.** a certain amount of one thing, as speed, considered in relation to a unit of another, as time. **3.** degree of speed or progress. **4.** position in a class; rank. —*v.t.* **5.** to estimate the value or worth of. **6.** to esteem, consider, or regard. **7.** to deserve; merit. **8.** to place in a rank or class. —*v.i.* **9.** to have value or standing. —*Idiom.* **10. at any rate, a.** in any event. **b.** at least.

rate² (rāt), *v.t., v.i.,* **rat•ed, rat•ing.** to scold vehemently.

rath•er (rath′ər, rä′thər), *adv.* **1.** to some extent. **2.** more properly or justly. **3.** sooner: *to die rather than yield.* **4.** more truly. **5.** on the contrary.

raths•kel•ler (rät′skel′ər, rat′-, rath′-), *n.* a restaurant or bar usu. below street level.

rat•i•fy (rat′ə fī′), *v.t.,* **-fied, -fy•ing.** to confirm by expressing approval or formal sanction. —**rat′i•fi•ca′tion,** *n.*

ra′tio (rā′shō, -shē ō′), *n., pl.* **-tios. 1.** the relation between two similar magnitudes with respect to the number of times the first contains the second. **2.** proportional relation; rate. [< L *ratiō* reckoning, proportion]

ra′ti•oc′i•na′tion (rash′ē os′ə nā′shən) *n.* logical reasoning.

ra•tion (rash′ən, rā′shən), *n.* **1.** a fixed allowance of food, esp. for one day. **2.** an allotted amount. —*v.t.* **3.** to distribute as or provide with rations. **4.** to restrict consumption of.

ra′tion•al *adj.* **1.** based on, agreeable to, or exercising reason. **2.** sane; lucid. **3.** *Math.* capable of being expressed exactly by a ratio of two integers: *a rational number.* —**ra′tion•al′i•ty,** *n., pl.* **-ties.** —**ra′tion•al•ly,** *adv.*

ra′tion•ale′ (-nal′), *n.* **1.** a fundamental reason. **2.** a statement of reasons or principles.

ra′tion•al•ism *n.* the principle or habit of accepting reason as the sole authority in matters of opinion, belief, or conduct. —**ra′tion•al•ist,** *n.*

ra′tion•al•ize′ *v.,* **-ized, -iz•ing.** —*v.t.* **1.** to ascribe (one's actions) to plausible but spurious causes. **2.** to cause to conform to reason. —*v.i.* **3.** to invent plausible but spurious explanations. —**ra′tion•al•i•za′tion,** *n.*

rat′ race′ *n.* an exhausting and usu. competitive routine activity.

rat•tan (ra tan′, rə-), *n.* any of various Asian climbing palms with tough stems used esp. for wickerwork and canes.

rat•tle (rat′l), *v.,* **-tled, -tling,** *n.* —*v.i.* **1.** to make a rapid succession of short, sharp sounds. **2.** to move noisily. **3.** to chatter. —*v.t.* **4.** to cause to make a rattling noise. **5.** to utter or perform in a rapid or lively manner. **6.** to disconcert; confuse. —*n.* **7.** a rapid succession of short, sharp sounds. **8.** a baby's toy that rattles when shaken. **9.** the series of horny rings at the end of a rattlesnake's tail.

rat′tle•snake′ *n.* any of several New World pit vipers with a rattle at the end of the tail.

rat′ty *adj.,* **-ti•er, -ti•est. 1.** full of rats. **2.** of or characteristic of rats. **3.** wretched; shabby.

rau•cous (rô′kəs), *adj.* **1.** harsh; strident. **2.** rowdy; disorderly. —**rau′cous•ly,** *adv.*

raun•chy (rôn′chē, rän′-), *adj.,* **-chi•er, -chi•est. 1.** vulgar; smutty. **2.** dirty; grubby. —**raun′chi•ly,** *adv.*

rav•age (rav′ij), *v.,* **-aged, -ag•ing.** —*v.t., v.i.* **1.** to do ruinous damage (to); devastate. —*n.* **2.** ruinous damage. —**rav′ag•er,** *n.*

rave (rāv), *v.,* **raved, rav•ing,** *n.* —*v.i.* **1.** to talk irrationally, as in delirium. **2.** to talk or write with extravagant enthusiasm. —*n.* **3.** the act of raving. **4.** an extravagantly approving appraisal.

rav•el (rav′əl), *v.,* **-eled, -el•ing** or (*esp. Brit.*) **-elled, -el•ling,** *n.* —*v.t.* **1.** to disentangle the threads or fibers of; unravel. **2.** to make clear; unravel. **3.** to entangle; confuse. —*v.i.* **4.** to become unwound; fray. —*n.* **5.** a tangle.

ra•ven (rā′vən), *n.* **1.** a large black bird, related to the crow, having a loud, harsh call. —*adj.* **2.** lustrous black: *raven hair.*

rav•en•ing (rav′ə ning), *adj.* greedy for prey.

rav′en•ous (rav′-) *adj.* **1.** extremely hungry. **2.** predatory. **3.** intensely eager. —**rav′en•ous•ly,** *adv.*

ra•vine (rə vēn′), *n.* a narrow, steep-sided valley.

ra•vi•o•li (rav′ē ō′lē), *n.* (*used with a sing. or pl. v.*) small pockets of pasta filled esp. with cheese or meat.

rav•ish (rav′ish), *v.t.* **1.** to transport with strong emotion, esp. joy. **2.** to rape. **3.** to seize and carry off by force.

rav′ish•ing *adj.* extremely beautiful or attractive.

raw (rô), *adj.,* **-er, -est. 1.** not cooked. **2.** not processed, finished, or refined: *raw cotton.* **3.** unnaturally or painfully exposed: *raw flesh.* **4.** indelicate; crude: *raw jokes.* **5.** inexperienced; untrained: *a raw recruit.* **6.** brutally harsh or unfair: *a raw deal.* **7.** damp and chilly: *a raw day.* —*Idiom.* **8.** in the raw, **a.** in the natural or unrefined state. **b.** nude; naked.

raw′boned′ *adj.* lean and bony.

raw′hide′ *n.* **1.** the untanned skin of cattle. **2.** a rope or whip made of rawhide.

ray¹ (rā), *n.* **1.** a narrow beam of light or other radiation. **2.** a slight manifestation: *a ray of hope.* **3.** one of the lines or streams in which light appears to radiate from a luminous body. **4.** one of a system of straight lines emanating from a point. **5.** a stream of radioactive particles. **6.** a radiating body part, as the arm of a starfish.

ray² (rā), *n.* a fish with a flattened body and greatly enlarged pectoral fins.

ray•on (rā′on), *n.* **1.** a textile filament made esp. from cellulose treated with caustic soda. **2.** a fabric or yarn of rayon.

raze (rāz), *v.t.,* **razed, raz•ing.** to level to the ground; tear down.

ra•zor (rā′zər), *n.* a sharp-edged instrument used esp. for shaving.

R.C. Roman Catholic.

rd rod.

Rd. Road.

rd. 1. road. **2.** round.

RD Rural Delivery.

Re *Chem. Symbol.* rhenium.

re- a prefix meaning: back or backward (*repay*); again or anew (*recapture*).

reach (rēch), *v.t.* **1.** to get to; arrive at. **2.** to succeed in touching or seizing. **3.** to hold out; stretch. **4.** to extend as far as. **5.** to establish communication with. **6.** to amount to. —*v.i.* **7.** to make a stretch with or as if with the hand. **8.** to extend, as in operation or effect. —*n.* **9.** an act or instance of reaching. **10.** the extent or distance of reaching. **11.** range, as of effective action. **12.** a continuous extent, as of land.

re•act (rē akt′), *v.i.* **1.** to act in response to an agent, influence, or stimulus. **2.** to act reciprocally. **3.** to act in a reverse manner, esp. to return to a prior condition. **4.** to act in opposition. **5.** to undergo a chemical reaction.

re•ac′tant *n.* a substance that undergoes a change in a chemical reaction.

re•ac′tion *n.* **1.** a reverse movement or tendency. **2.** a movement toward extreme political conservatism. **3.** action in response to an agent, influence, or stimulus. **4.** a chemical change. **5.** a change in the nucleus of an atom. —**re•ac′tion•ar′y,** *adj., n., pl.* **-ies.**

re•ac′tor *n.* **1.** one that reacts. **2.** an apparatus in which a nuclear-fission chain reaction is sustained and controlled.

read¹ (rēd), *v.,* **read** (red), **read•ing** (rē′ding), *n.* —*v.t.* **1.** to look at and understand the meaning of (something written or printed). **2.** to utter aloud (something written or printed). **3.** to recognize and understand the meaning of: *to read an x-ray.* **4.** to foretell or predict. **5.** to register, as a thermometer. **6.** to learn or interpret by or as if by reading: *to read a person's thoughts.* **7.** to obtain (data or programs) from an external storage medium and place in a computer's memory. **8.** to study (a subject). —*v.i.* **9.** to read written or printed matter. **10.** to learn about something by reading. **11.** to be capable of being interpreted when read: *a rule that reads two different ways.* **12.** something read: *Her new novel is a good read.* —*Idiom.* **13.** read between the lines, to understand from implications only. —**read′a•ble,** *adj.* —**read′er,** *n.*

read² (red), *adj.* knowledgeable from reading: *a well-read person.*

read•er•ship (rē′dər ship′), *n.* the people who read a particular publication.

read•ing (rē′ding), *n.* **1.** the action of a person

who reads. **2.** matter read or for reading. **3.** the form of a given passage in a particular text. **4.** a public recitation of a text. **5.** an interpretation, as of a musical composition. **6.** the indication of a graduated instrument, as a gauge.

read′-on′ly (rēd), *adj.* noting or pertaining to computer files or memory that can be read but cannot normally be changed.

read•y (red′ē), *adj.,* **-i•er, -i•est,** *v.,* **-ied, -y•ing.** —*adj.* **1.** prepared for action or use. **2.** not hesitant; willing. **3.** prompt, as in comprehending. **4.** showing skill or dexterity: *a ready wit.* **5.** inclined; disposed. **6.** likely at any moment. **7.** immediately available for use: *ready cash.* —*v.t.* **8.** to make ready; prepare. —**read′i•ly,** *adv.* —**read′i•ness,** *n.*

read′y-made′ *adj.* made in advance for sale to any purchaser.

re•a•gent (rē ā′jənt), *n. Chem.* a substance that because of the reactions it causes is used in analysis and synthesis.

re•al (rē′əl, rēl), *adj.* **1.** true rather than ostensible. **2.** actual rather than imaginary, ideal, or fictitious. **3.** not artificial; genuine. **4.** *Law.* of immovable or permanent things, as land or buildings. —*n.* **5.** *Informal.* very or extremely. —*Idiom.* **6. for real, a.** in reality; actually. **b.** genuine; sincere. —**re′al•ness,** *n.*

re′al estate′ *n.* property, esp. in land and buildings.

re′al•ism *n.* **1.** the tendency to see things as they really are. **2.** the representation of things as they really are in art or literature. —**re′al•ist,** *n.* —**re′al•is′tic,** *adj.* —**re′al•is′ti•cal•ly,** *adv.*

re•al•i•ty (rē al′i tē), *n., pl.* **-ties. 1.** the state or quality of being real. **2.** a real thing or fact. **3.** real things, facts, or events as a whole. —*Idiom.* **4. in reality,** in fact; actually.

re′al•ize′ *v.t.,* **-ized, -iz•ing. 1.** to grasp or understand clearly. **2.** to give reality to (a hope, plan, etc.); fulfill. **3.** to gain; obtain: *realized a profit.* **4.** to bring as proceeds, as from a sale. —**re′al•iz′a•ble,** *adj.* —**re′al•i•za′tion,** *n.*

re′al•ly *adv.* **1.** actually. **2.** genuinely; truly. **3.** indeed.

realm (relm), *n.* **1.** a royal domain; kingdom. **2.** a sphere, domain, or province.

ream (rēm), *n.* **1.** a standard quantity of paper consisting of 480, 500, or 516 sheets. **2.** Usu., **reams.** a large quantity.

reap (rēp), *v.t.* **1.** to cut (wheat, rye, etc.) with a sickle, reaper, etc. **2.** to gather or take (a crop, harvest, etc.). **3.** to get as a return, recompense, or result.

rear¹ (rēr), *n.* **1.** the back of something. **2.** a space or position at the back of something. **3.** the buttocks; rump. **4.** the hindmost portion, as of an army. —*adj.* **5.** situated at the rear.

rear² (rēr), *v.t.* **1.** to take care of up to maturity. **2.** to breed and raise (livestock). **3.** to raise by building; erect. **4.** to raise to an upright position. —*v.i.* **5.** to rise on the hind legs, as a horse. **6.** to rise high.

rear′ ad′miral *n.* a commissioned officer in the U.S. Navy or Coast Guard ranking above a captain.

rear′most′ *adj.* farthest in the rear.

rear′ward (-wərd), *adv.* **1.** Also, **rear′wards.** toward or in the rear. —*adj.* **2.** located in or directed toward the rear.

rea•son (rē′zən), *n.* **1.** a basis or cause for a belief, action, fact, or event. **2.** a statement presented in justification or explanation. **3.** the mental power concerned with forming conclusions or inferences. **4.** sound judgment; good sense. **5.** soundness of mind. —*v.i.* **6.** to use the power of reason; think. **7.** to argue in a logical manner. —*v.t.* **8.** to think through logically. **9.** to conclude or infer. —*Idiom.* **10. within reason,** in accord with reason; justifiable. —**reas′on•ing,** *n.*

rea•son•a•ble (rē′zə nə bəl, rēz′nə-), *adj.* **1.** in accord with reason; logical. **2.** not excessive; moderate. **3.** not expensive. **4.** endowed with reason; rational. —**rea′son•a•bly,** *adv.*

re•as•sure (rē′ə shoŏr′, -shûr′), *v.t.,* **-sured, -sur•**

ing. 1. to restore to assurance or confidence. **2.** to assure again. —**re′as•sur′ance,** *n.*

re•bate (rē′bāt; *v.* also ri bāt′), *n., v.,* **-bat•ed, -bat•ing.** —*n.* **1.** a return of part of an original payment, as for merchandise. —*v.t.* **2.** to allow a rebate of or on.

reb•el (*n., adj.* reb′əl; *v.* ri bel′), *n., adj., v.,* **-belled, -bel•ling.** —*n.* **1.** a person who rises in arms against a government or ruler. **2.** a person who resists authority, control, or tradition. —*adj.* **3.** rebellious; defiant. **4.** of rebels. —*v.i.* **re•bel 5.** to act as a rebel. **6.** to show or feel utter repugnance. —**re•bel′lion,** *n.* —**re•bel′lious,** *adj.* —**re•bel′lious•ly,** *adv.*

re•bound (*v.* ri bound′, rē′bound′; *n.* rē′bound′, ri bound′), *v.i.* **1.** to spring back from force of impact. **2.** to recover, as from ill health. —*n.* **3.** the act of rebounding. —*Idiom.* **4. on the rebound,** after being rejected by another: *to marry on the rebound.*

re•buff (*n.* ri buf′, rē′buf; *v.* ri buf′), *n.* **1.** a blunt or abrupt rejection or refusal. **2.** a check to action or progress. —*v.t.* **3.** to give a rebuff to.

re•buke (ri byook′), *v.,* **-buked, -buk•ing,** *n.* —*v.t.* **1.** to express sharp, stern disapproval to; reprove. —*n.* **2.** a sharp reproof; reprimand. —**re•buk′ing•ly,** *adv.*

re•bus (rē′bəs), *n., pl.* **-bus•es.** a representation of a word or phrase by means of pictures.

re•but (ri but′), *v.t.,* **-but•ted, -but•ting.** to refute by evidence or argument. —**re•but′tal,** *n.*

re•cal•ci•trant (ri kal′si trant), *adj.* **1.** resisting authority or control; refractory. **2.** hard to deal with, manage, or operate. —**re•cal′ci•trance,** *n.*

re•call (*v.* ri kôl′; *n.* ri kôl′, rē′kôl *for 4, 5;* rē′kôl *for 6, 7*), *v.t.* **1.** to recollect; remember. **2.** to call or order back. **3.** to revoke or withdraw. —*n.* **4.** the act of recalling. **5.** recollection; remembrance. **6.** the removal of or right to remove a public official from office by popular vote. **7.** a summons by a manufacturer for the return of a defective product.

re•cant (ri kant′), *v.t., v.i.* to withdraw (a statement, opinion, etc.), esp. formally.

re•cap (rē′kap′), *n., v.,* **-capped, -cap•ping.** —*n.* **1.** a recapitulation. —*v.t., v.i.* **2.** to recapitulate.

re′ca•pit′u•late′ *v.t., v.i.,* **-lat•ed, -lat•ing.** to sum up; summarize. —**re′ca•pit′u•la′tion,** *n.*

re•cap′ture *v.,* **-tured, -tur•ing,** *n.* —*v.t.* **1.** to capture again; retake. **2.** to experience anew. —*n.* **3.** recovery or retaking by capture.

recd. or **rec′d.,** received.

re•cede (ri sēd′), *v.i.,* **-ced•ed, -ced•ing. 1.** to move back or away. **2.** to become or seem to become more distant. **3.** to slope backward.

re•ceipt (ri sēt′), *n.* **1.** a written acknowledgment of having received money or goods. **2. receipts,** an amount or quantity received. **3.** the act of receiving. **4.** a recipe. —*v.t.* **5.** to acknowledge the receipt of. **6.** to give a receipt for.

re•ceive (ri sēv′), *v.,* **-ceived, -ceiv•ing.** —*v.t.* **1.** to take (something offered, given, or sent); get. **2.** to hold, bear, or contain. **3.** to take into the mind. **4.** to meet with; experience. **5.** to welcome or accept as a guest, member, etc. **6.** to accept as true, valid, or approved. —*v.i.* **7.** to welcome visitors.

re•ceiv′er *n.* **1.** one that receives. **2.** an apparatus that receives electrical signals and makes them visible or audible. **3.** a person appointed by a court to take charge of a business or property in bankruptcy or litigation. **4.** *Football.* a player on the offensive team who is eligible to catch a forward pass.

re•cent (rē′sənt), *adj.* **1.** lately happening, done, or made. **2.** of or belonging to a time not long past. **3.** (*cap.*) *Geol.* noting or pertaining to the present geological epoch. —**re′cent•ly,** *adv.*

re•cep•ta•cle (ri sep′tə kəl), *n.* **1.** a container or holder. **2.** a contact device with a socket installed at an electrical outlet.

re•cep•tion (ri sep′shən), *n.* **1.** the act of receiving or the state of being received. **2.** a manner of being received. **3.** a function or occasion when persons are formally received. **4.** the fidelity of a radio or television broadcast.

re•cep'tion•ist *n.* a person employed to receive callers in an office.

re•cep'tive *adj.* **1.** able or quick to receive. **2.** willing or inclined to receive.

re•cep'tor *n.* a sensory nerve ending or sense organ that is sensitive to stimuli.

re•cess (ri ses′, rē′ses), *n.* **1. a.** a temporary cessation of work or activity; break. **b.** a period of such cessation. **2.** an indentation, as in a coastline. **3.** recesses, a secluded or inner area or part. —*v.t.* **4.** to place in a recess. **5.** to make a recess in. —*v.i.* **6.** to take a recess.

re•ces•sion (ri sesh′ən), *n.* **1.** a period of economic decline. **2.** the act of receding. **3.** a withdrawing procession, as at the end of a religious service. —**re•ces′sion•ar′y,** *adj.*

re•ces'sive *adj.* **1.** tending to recede; receding. **2.** noting or pertaining to one of a pair of hereditary traits that is masked by the other when both are present in an organism.

re•cher•ché (rə shâr′shā, rə shâr shā′), *adj.* **1.** very rare or choice. **2.** affectedly refined.

re•cid•i•vism (ri sid′ə viz′əm), *n.* repeated or habitual relapse, as into crime. —**re•cid′i•vist,** *n.,* *adj.*

rec•i•pe (res′ə pē), *n.,* *pl.* **-pes. 1.** a set of instructions for preparing food or drink. **2.** a method for attaining a desired end.

re•cip•i•ent (ri sip′ē ənt), *n.* one that receives.

re•cip•ro•cal (ri sip′rə kəl), *adj.* **1.** given or felt by each toward the other; mutual. **2.** given or felt in return. **3.** inversely related; opposite. —*n.* **4.** one that is reciprocal to another. **5.** *Math.* the ratio of unity to a given quantity or expression. —**re•cip′ro•cal•ly,** *adv.*

re•cip′ro•cate′ (-kāt′), *v.t.,* *v.i.,* **-cat•ed, -cat•ing. 1.** to give or feel in return. **2.** to give and receive reciprocally; interchange. **3.** to move alternately backward and forward. —**re•cip′ro•ca′tion,** *n.*

rec•i•proc•i•ty (res′ə pros′i tē), *n.,* *pl.* **-ties. 1.** a reciprocal state or relation. **2.** a trade policy between countries by which corresponding advantages or privileges are granted by each country.

re•cit•al (ri sīt′l), *n.* **1.** a musical or dance performance, esp. by one artist. **2.** a public demonstration of progress by dance or music students. **3.** an act or instance of reciting, esp. from memory. **4.** a detailed statement or account. —**re•cit′al•ist,** *n.*

rec•i•ta•tive (res′i tə tēv′), *n.* a style of vocal music intermediate between speaking and singing.

re•cite (ri sīt′), *v.t.,* *v.i.,* **-cit•ed, -cit•ing. 1.** to repeat (something) exactly, esp. from memory and before an audience. **2.** to narrate (something) in detail. **3.** to answer a teacher's questions on (a lesson). —**rec•i•ta•tion** (res′i tā′shən), *n.*

reck•less (rek′lis), *adj.* heedless of danger or consequences; rash; careless. —**reck′less•ly,** *adv.* —**reck′less•ness,** *n.*

reck•on (rek′ən), *v.t.* **1.** to compute or calculate. **2.** to regard as; deem. **3.** *Chiefly Dial.* to think or suppose. —*v.i.* **4.** to make a computation. **5.** to depend or rely. **6. reckon with,** to consider.

reck′on•ing *n.* **1.** count; computation. **2.** a settlement of accounts.

re•claim (ri klām′), *v.t.* **1.** to bring (land) into a condition for cultivation or other use. **2.** to recover (substances) in a pure or usable form from refuse or waste. **3.** to bring back to a more wholesome way of life; reform. —**rec•la•ma•tion** (rek′lə mā′shən), *n.*

re•cline (ri klīn′), *v.i.,* *v.t.,* **-clined, -clin•ing.** to lean or cause to lean back; lie or lay.

re•clin′er *n.* an easy chair with an adjustable back and footrest.

re•cluse (rek′lōōs, ri klōōs′), *n.* a person who lives in seclusion or apart from society. —**re•clu′sive,** *adj.*

re•cog•ni•zance (ri kog′nə zəns, -kon′ə-), *n.* an obligation of record that binds a person to do something, as to appear for trial.

rec•og•nize (rek′əg nīz′), *v.t.,* **-nized, -niz•ing. 1.** to identify as previously seen or known. **2.** to identify from knowledge of appearance or characteristics: *to recognize a swindler.* **3.** to perceive or acknowledge as existing, true, or valid. **4.** to acknowledge as being entitled to speak. **5.** to acknowledge as entitled to treatment as a political unit. **6.** to show appreciation of. —**rec′og•ni′tion** (-nish′ən), *n.* —**rec′og•niz′a•ble,** *adj.*

re•coil (*v.* ri koil′; *n.* rē′koil′, ri koil′), *v.i.* **1.** to shrink back, as in horror or disgust. **2.** to spring or fly back, as a firearm when discharged. —*n.* **3.** an act or instance of recoiling.

rec•ol•lect (rek′ə lekt′), *v.t.,* *v.i.* to remember; recall. —**rec′ol•lec′tion,** *n.*

rec•om•mend (rek′ə mend′), *v.t.* **1.** to present as worthy of confidence, acceptance, or use. **2.** to urge or suggest as appropriate or beneficial. **3.** to make desirable or attractive. —**rec′om•men•da′tion,** *n.*

rec•om•pense (rek′əm pens′), *v.,* **-pensed, -pens•ing,** *n.* —*v.t.* **1.** to make payment to, as for work done. **2.** to make restitution for; compensate. —*n.* **3.** a repayment, requital, or reward. **4.** compensation; reparation.

rec•on•cile (rek′ən sīl′), *v.t.,* **-ciled, -cil•ing. 1.** to cause to accept something not desired. **2.** to cause to become friendly again. **3.** to settle (a quarrel, dispute, etc.). **4.** to make compatible or consistent: *reconciled her bank statement.* —**rec′on•cil′i•a′tion** (-sil′ē ā′shən), *n.*

rec•on•dite (rek′ən dīt′), *adj.* **1.** very profound, difficult, or abstruse. **2.** known by relatively few; esoteric.

re•con•nais•sance (ri kon′ə səns, -zəns), *n.* a general survey of a region, esp. in order to gain information for military purposes.

re•con•noi•ter (rē′kə noi′tər, rek′ə-), *v.t.,* *v.i.* to make a reconnaissance of.

re•cord (*v.* ri kôrd′; *n.,* *adj.* rek′ərd), *v.t.* **1.** to set down, esp. in writing, for the purpose of preserving. **2.** to register or indicate. **3.** to register (sound or images) on a disk or tape for reproduction. —*n.* **rec′ord 4.** an account of facts or events preserved esp. in writing. **5.** information or knowledge about a person's achievements or performance. **6.** something, as a disk, on which sound or images have been recorded. **7.** standing with respect to contests won, lost, and tied. **8.** the best performance of its kind to date. —*adj.* **rec′ord 9.** surpassing all others. —*Idiom.* **10. off the record,** not for publication. **11. on record,** having stated one's position publicly. —**re•cord′ing,** *n.*

re•cord′er *n.* **1.** a person who records, esp. as an official duty. **2.** a recording apparatus or device. **3.** a flute with a mouthpiece like a whistle and eight finger holes.

re-count (*v.* rē kount′; *n.* rē′kount′, rē kount′), *v.t.* **1.** to count again. —*n.* **2.** a second or additional count.

re•count (ri kount′), *v.t.* to tell in detail; relate.

re•coup (ri kōōp′), *v.t.* **1.** to get back the equivalent of. **2.** to regain; recover.

re•course (rē′kôrs, ri kôrs′), *n.* **1.** a resorting to a person or thing for help or protection. **2.** a source of help or protection.

re•cov•er (ri kuv′ər), *v.t.* **1.** to get back; regain. **2.** to make up for. **3.** to regain the strength, composure, or balance of (oneself). **4.** to regain (a substance) in usable form; reclaim. —*v.i.* **5.** to regain health, strength, composure, or balance. **6.** to obtain a favorable judgment in a lawsuit. —**re•cov′er•a•ble,** *adj.* —**re•cov′er•y,** *n.,* *pl.* **-ies.**

re-cre•ate (rē′krē āt′), *v.t.,* **-at•ed, -at•ing.** to create anew.

rec•re•a•tion (rek′rē ā′shən), *n.* **1.** mental or physical refreshment after work, as by means of a pastime. **2.** a means of enjoyable relaxation. —**rec′re•a′tion•al,** *adj.*

re•crim•i•nate (ri krim′ə nāt′), *v.t.,* **-nat•ed, -nat•ing.** to bring a countercharge against (an accuser). —**re•crim′i•na′tion,** *n.*

re•cruit (ri krōōt′), *n.* **1.** a new member, esp. a newly enlisted or drafted member of the armed forces. —*v.t.* **2.** to enlist for military service. **3.** to supply (an armed force) with new members. **4.** to seek to hire, enroll, or enlist: *to recruit executives.*

—*v.i.* **5.** to enlist new members. —**re•cruit′er,** *n.* —**re•cruit′ment,** *n.*

rec•tan•gle (rek′tang′gəl), *n.* a parallelogram with four right angles. —**rec′tan′gu•lar** (-tang′gyə lər), *adj.*

rec•ti•fy (rek′tə fī′), *v.t.,* **-fied, -fy•ing. 1.** to set right; correct. **2.** to change (alternating current) into direct current. —**rec′ti•fi′a•ble,** *adj.* —**rec′ti•fi•ca′tion,** *n.*

rec•ti•lin•e•ar (rek′tl in′ē ər), *adj.* **1.** forming or moving in a straight line. **2.** characterized by straight lines.

rec•ti•tude (rek′ti tōōd′, -tyōōd′), *n.* **1.** moral virtue; righteousness. **2.** correctness.

rec•tor (rek′tər), *n.* **1.** a member of the clergy in charge of a parish. **2.** the head of certain universities, colleges, or schools.

rec′to•ry *n.,* *pl.* **-ries.** a rector's house; parsonage.

rec•tum (rek′təm), *n.,* *pl.* **-tums, -ta** (-tə). the terminal section of the large intestine, ending in the anus. —**rec′tal,** *adj.*

re•cum•bent (ri kum′bənt), *adj.* lying down. —**re•cum′ben•cy,** *n.*

re•cu•per•ate (ri kōō′pə rāt′, -kyōō′-), *v.,* **-at•ed, -at•ing.** —*v.i.* **1.** to regain health or strength. —*v.t.* **2.** to get back; recover. —**re•cu′per•a′tion,** *n.* —**re•cu′per•a′tive,** *adj.*

re•cur (ri kûr′), *v.i.,* **-curred, -cur•ring. 1.** to occur again, as an event. **2.** to return to the mind. —**re•cur′rence,** *n.* —**re•cur′rent,** *adj.*

re•cy•cle (rē sī′kəl), *v.t.,* **-cled, -cling. 1.** to treat or process (used or waste materials) so as to make suitable for reuse. **2.** to use again with minimal alteration. **3.** to cause to pass through a cycle again. —**re•cy′cla•ble,** *adj., n.*

red (red), *n., adj.,* **red•der, red•dest.** —*n.* **1.** any of various colors resembling the color of blood. **2.** (*often cap.*) a radical leftist in politics, esp. a communist. —*adj.* **3.** of the color red. **4.** (*often cap.*) radically left politically, esp. communist. —**Idiom. 5. in the red,** being in debt. —**red′den,** *v.t., v.i.* —**red′dish,** *adj.*

red′ blood′ cell′ *n.* any of the blood cells that contain hemoglobin and carry oxygen to the cells and tissues.

red′cap′ *n.* a baggage porter, as at a railroad station.

re•deem (ri dēm′), *v.t.* **1.** to pay off, as a mortgage. **2.** to recover (something pawned or mortgaged) by payment. **3.** to exchange (bonds, coupons, etc.) for money or goods. **4.** to fulfill (a pledge, promise, etc.). **5.** to make up for. **6.** to set free or save, as a sinner. —**re•deem′a•ble,** *adj.* —**re•deem′er,** *n.* —**re•demp′tion** (-demp′shən), *n.*

red′-hand′ed *adj., adv.* in the very act of wrongdoing. —**red′-hand′ed•ly,** *adv.*

red′head′ *n.* a person with red hair. —**red′head′ed,** *adj.*

red′ her′ring *n.* something intended to divert attention from the real problem or matter at hand.

red′-hot′ *adj.* **1.** red with heat. **2.** violent; furious. **3.** very fresh or new.

red′-let′ter *adj.* of special importance; memorable.

red′lin′ing *n.* a discriminatory practice in which mortgages or insurance are withheld in areas considered to be deteriorating. [as if such areas had been outlined in red on a map]

red•o•lent (red′l ənt), *adj.* **1.** having a pleasant odor. **2.** having a particular odor: *redolent of garlic.* **3.** suggestive; reminiscent. —**red′o•lence,** *n.*

re•doubt (ri dout′), *n.* an earthwork inside or outside a larger fortification.

re•doubt′a•ble *adj.* **1.** evoking fear; formidable. **2.** commanding respect.

re•dound (ri dound′), *v.i.* **1.** to have a good or bad effect. **2.** to result or accrue.

re•dress (*n.* rē′dres, ri dres′; *v.* ri dres′), *n.* **1.** the setting right of what is wrong. **2.** relief from wrong. **3.** compensation for wrong. —*v.t.* **4.** to set right; remedy. **5.** to compensate.

red′ tape′ *n.* bureaucratic routine that delays or prevents action.

re•duce (ri dōōs′, -dyōōs′), *v.,* **-duced, -duc•ing.** —*v.t.* **1.** to bring down, as to a smaller size or amount. **2.** to lower, as in degree or intensity. **3.** to demote to a lower rank or authority. **4.** to treat analytically. **5.** to act destructively upon. **6.** to bring to a certain state. **7.** to change the denomination or form but not the value of (a fraction, polynomial, etc.). —*v.i.* **8.** to become reduced. **9.** to lose weight, as by dieting. —**re•duc′i•ble,** *adj.* —**re•duc′tion** (-duk′shən), *n.* —**re•duc′tive** (-duk′tiv), *adj.*

re•dun•dant (ri dun′dənt), *adj.* **1.** characterized by unnecessary repetition; wordy. **2.** exceeding what is usual or necessary. —**re•dun′dan•cy,** *n., pl.* **-cies.**

red′wood′ *n.* **1.** a coniferous tree native to California and noted for its great height. **2.** its brownish red timber.

reed (rēd), *n.* **1. a.** the straight stalk of any of various tall marsh grasses. **b.** any of the plants themselves. **2. a.** a flexible piece of cane, wood, metal, or plastic attached to the mouth of various wind instruments and set into vibration to produce a tone. **b.** a wind instrument played with a reed. —**reed′y,** *adj.,* **-i•er, -i•est.**

reef[1] (rēf), *n.* a ridge of rocks, sand, or coral at or near the surface of the water.

reef[2] (rēf), *n.* **1.** a part of a sail that is rolled and tied down to reduce the area exposed to the wind. —*v.t.* **2.** to shorten (a sail) by tying in one or more reefs.

reef′er (rē′fər), *n. Slang.* a marijuana cigarette.

reek (rēk), *v.i.* **1.** to smell strongly and unpleasantly. **2.** to be strongly pervaded with something unpleasant. —*v.t.* **3.** to give off; emit. —*n.* **4.** a strong, unpleasant smell.

reel[1] (rēl), *n.* **1.** a device, as a cylinder, that turns on an axis and is used to wind up or let out wire, rope, or film. **2.** a quantity of something wound on a reel. —*v.t.* **3.** to wind on a reel. **4.** to pull by winding a line on a reel: *to reel in a fish.* **5. reel off,** to say or write fluently and quickly.

reel[2] (rēl), *v.i.* **1.** to sway or fall back from or as if from a blow. **2.** to sway in standing or walking. **3.** to whirl. **4.** to have a sensation of whirling. —*n.* **5.** a reeling movement.

reel[3] (rēl), *n.* a lively Scottish dance.

re•en•try (rē en′trē), *n., pl.* **-tries. 1.** a second entry. **2.** the return into the earth's atmosphere of a satellite, spacecraft, or rocket.

ref (ref), *n., v.t., v.i.,* **reffed, ref•fing.** REFEREE.

re•fec•to•ry (ri fek′tə rē), *n., pl.* **-ries.** a dining hall, esp. in a monastery.

re•fer (ri fûr′), *v.,* **-ferred, -fer•ring.** —*v.t.* **1.** to direct to a person or place, as for information or aid. **2.** to direct the attention of. **3.** to submit for decision, consideration, etc. —*v.i.* **4.** to direct attention. **5.** to have recourse, as for information. **6.** to make reference or allusion. —**re•fer′ral,** *n.*

ref•er•ee (ref′ə rē′), *n., pl.* **-ees,** *v.,* **-eed, -ee•ing.** —*n.* **1.** a person to whom something is referred for decision or settlement. **2.** a judge in certain games and sports; umpire. —*v.t., v.i.* **3.** to preside over or act as referee.

ref•er•ence (ref′ər əns), *n.* **1.** the act of referring. **2.** mention or allusion. **3.** a direction of the attention, as in a book, to another book or passage. **4.** use or recourse for purposes of information. **5.** a source of facts or information. **6. a.** a person to whom one can refer for testimony as to another's character or abilities. **b.** a statement regarding a person's character or abilities. **7.** regard or relation: *without reference to age.*

ref•er•en•dum (ref′ə ren′dəm), *n., pl.* **-dums, -da** (-də). **1.** the practice of referring legislative measures to the vote of the electorate for approval or rejection. **2.** a vote on a measure thus referred.

re•fill (*v.* rē fil′; *n.* rē′fil′), *v.t., v.i.* **1.** to fill again. —*n.* **2.** a material or supply to replace something used up. —**re•fill′a•ble,** *adj.*

re•fine (ri fīn′), *v.t., v.i.,* **-fined, -fin•ing. 1.** to bring or come to a pure state; purify. **2.** to make or become more elegant or polished. —**re•fined′,** *adj.* —**re•fin′er,** *n.*

re•fine′ment *n.* **1.** fineness or elegance of feeling, taste, or manners. **2.** the act of refining or state of being refined. **3.** the quality or state of being refined. **4.** a subtle distinction. **5.** an improvement.

re•fin′er•y *n., pl.* **-ies.** an establishment for refining something, as sugar or petroleum.

re•flect (ri flekt′), *v.t.* **1.** to cast back (light, sound, etc.) from a surface. **2.** to give back an image of. **3.** to cast or bring (credit, discredit, etc.). —*v.i.* **4.** to be cast back, as light. **5.** to ponder or meditate. **6.** to bring reproach or discredit. **7.** to give a particular aspect or impression. —**re•flec′tive,** *adj.* —**re•flec′tor,** *n.*

re•flec′tion *n.* **1.** the act of reflecting or state of being reflected. **2.** something reflected. **3.** careful thought or consideration. **4.** an unfavorable remark or observation; reproach.

re•flex (rē′fleks), *adj.* **1.** of or caused by an involuntary response to a stimulus. **2.** bent or turned back. —*n.* **3.** movement caused by a reflex response.

re•flex•ive (ri flek′siv), *adj.* **1. a.** (of a verb) taking a subject and object with identical referents, as *cut* in I *cut myself.* **b.** (of a pronoun) used as an object with the same referent as the subject of a verb, as *myself* in I *cut myself.* —*n.* **2.** a reflexive verb or pronoun. —**re•flex′ive•ly,** *adv.*

re•for•est (rē fôr′ist, -for′-), *v.t., v.i.* to replant trees on (land denuded by cutting, fire, etc.). —**re′for•est•a′tion,** *n.*

re-form (rē fôrm′), *v.t., v.i.* to form again.

re-form (ri fôrm′), *n.* **1.** the improvement of what is wrong, corrupt, or unsatisfactory. **2.** improvement, as of conduct or belief. —*v.t.* **3.** to change to a better state or form. **4.** to cause to abandon wrong or evil ways of life or conduct. —*v.i.* **5.** to abandon evil conduct or error. —**re•form′er,** *n.*

ref•or•ma•tion (ref′ər mā′shən), *n.* **1.** the act of reforming or state of being reformed. **2.** (*cap.*) the 16th-century movement that resulted in the establishment of the Protestant churches.

re•form•a•to•ry (ri fôr′mə tôr′ē), *adj., n., pl.* **-ries.** —*adj.* **1.** serving or designed to reform. —*n.* **2.** Also called **reform′ school′.** a penal institution for reforming young offenders, esp. minors.

re•fract (ri frakt′), *v.t.* to subject to refraction.

re•frac′tion *n.* the change of direction of a ray, as of light, in passing obliquely from one medium into another in which its wave velocity is different. —**re•frac′tive,** *adj.*

re•frac′to•ry *adj.* **1.** difficult to manage; stubbornly disobedient. **2.** difficult to fuse, reduce, or work, as an ore.

re•frain[1] (ri frān′), *v.i.* to keep oneself from doing or saying something.

re•frain[2] (ri frān′), *n.* a phrase or verse recurring at intervals in a song or poem.

re•fresh (ri fresh′), *v.t.* **1.** to provide new vigor and energy to, as by rest. **2.** to stimulate (the memory). **3.** to freshen, as in appearance. —*v.i.* **4.** to become fresh again; revive. —**re•fresh′ing,** *adj.*

re•fresh′ment *n.* **1.** something that refreshes. **2.** refreshments, food and drink, esp. for a light meal. **3.** the act of refreshing or state of being refreshed.

re•frig•er•ate (ri frij′ə rāt′), *v.t.,* **-at•ed, -at•ing.** to make or keep cold or cool, esp. for preservation. —**re•frig′er•ant,** *adj., n.* —**re•frig′er•a′tion,** *n.*

re•frig′er•a′tor *n.* a cabinet or room in which food and drink are kept cool by refrigeration.

ref•uge (ref′yōōj), *n.* **1.** shelter from danger or trouble. **2.** a place of shelter or safety.

ref•u•gee (ref′yōō jē′, ref′yōō jē′), *n., pl.* **-gees.** a person who flees for refuge, as in time of political upheaval or war.

re•ful•gent (ri ful′jənt), *adj.* shining brightly; radiant. —**re•ful′gence,** *n.*

re•fund (*v.* ri fund′, rē′fund; *n.* rē′fund), *v.t.* **1.** to give back or restore (esp. money); repay. —*n.* **2.** the act of refunding. **3.** an amount refunded. —**re•fund′a•ble,** *adj.*

re•fur•bish (rē fûr′bish), *v.t.* to furbish again; renovate. —**re•fur′bish•ment,** *n.*

re•fuse[1] (ri fyōōz′), *v.,* **-fused, -fus•ing.** —*v.t.* **1.** to

decline to accept, give, do, or comply. —*v.i.* **2.** to decline acceptance, consent, or compliance. —**re•fus′al,** *n.*

ref•use[2] (ref′yōōs), *n.* something discarded as worthless or useless; rubbish.

re•fute (ri fyōōt′), *v.t.,* **-fut•ed, -fut•ing.** to prove to be false or erroneous. —**ref•u•ta•tion** (ref′yōō-tā′shən), *n.*

re•gain (rē gān′), *v.t.* **1.** to get again; recover. **2.** to succeed in reaching again.

re•gal (rē′gəl), *adj.* **1.** of, befitting, or resembling a king or queen. **2.** stately; splendid. —**re′gal•ly,** *adv.*

re•gale (ri gāl′), *v.t.,* **-galed, -gal•ing.** **1.** to entertain agreeably; divert. **2.** to entertain with choice food or drink.

re•ga•lia (ri gāl′yə), *n.pl.* **1.** the ensigns or emblems of royalty, as the crown and scepter. **2.** the decorations, insignia, or ceremonial clothes of an office or order. **3.** fancy clothing; finery.

re•gard (ri gärd′), *v.t.* **1.** to look at or think of in a particular way; consider. **2.** to have or show respect for. **3.** to think highly of; esteem. **4.** to relate to; concern. —*n.* **5.** reference; relation. **6.** an aspect, point, or particular. **7.** thought or attention. **8.** respect or esteem. **9. regards,** sentiments of esteem or affection. —*Idiom.* **10. as regards,** concerning; about.

re•gard′ing *prep.* with regard to; concerning.

re•gard′less *adj.* **1.** heedless; unmindful. —*adv.* **2.** despite everything; anyway. —*Idiom.* **3. regardless of,** in spite of.

re•gat•ta (ri gat′ə, -gä′tə), *n., pl.* **-tas.** **1.** a boat race, as of yachts. **2.** an organized series of such races.

re•gen•er•ate (*v.* ri jen′ə rāt′; *adj.* -ər it), *v.,* **-at•ed, -at•ing,** *adj.* —*v.t.* **1.** to effect a complete moral or spiritual reform in. **2.** to make over, esp. in a better form. **3.** to bring into existence again. **4.** to restore (a body part) by the growth of new tissue. —*v.i.* **5.** to be formed again. **6.** to become spiritually renewed. —*adj.* **7.** made over; reconstituted. **8.** born again spiritually. —**re•gen′er•a′tion,** *n.* —**re•gen′er•a′tive,** *adj.*

re•gent (rē′jənt), *n.* **1.** a person who rules a kingdom during the minority, absence, or disability of the sovereign. **2.** a member of a governing board, as of a state educational system. —**re′gen•cy,** *n., pl.* **-cies.**

reg•gae (reg′ā), *n.* a style of Jamaican music blending blues, calypso, and rock.

reg•i•cide (rej′ə sīd′), *n.* **1.** the killing of a king. **2.** a person who kills a king.

re•gime or **ré•gime** (rə zhēm′, rā-), *n.* **1.** a mode or system of government. **2.** a government in power. **3.** REGIMEN (def. 1).

reg•i•men (rej′ə mən), *n.* **1.** a regulated course, as of diet or exercise, to preserve or restore health. **2.** government or rule. [< L: rule]

reg•i•ment (*n.* rej′ə mənt; *v.* -ment′), *n.* **1.** a military unit of ground forces consisting of two or more battalions. —*v.t.* **2.** to subject to strict discipline. **3.** to organize, usu. for the purpose of rigid or complete control. —**reg′i•men′tal,** *adj.* —**reg′i•men•ta′tion,** *n.*

re•gion (rē′jən), *n.* **1.** an often extensive, continuous part of a surface, space, or body; area. **2.** a part of the body: *the abdominal region.* —**re′gion•al,** *adj.* —**re′gion•al•ly,** *adv.*

re′gion•al•ism *n.* a feature, as a speech form, that is peculiar to or characteristic of a geographical region.

reg•is•ter (rej′ə stər), *n.* **1. a.** a book in which records, as of events, are kept. **b.** a list or record of such items. **2.** a mechanical device by which certain data are automatically recorded. **3.** CASH REGISTER. **4.** the range of a voice or an instrument. **5.** a device for controlling the flow of warmed or cooled air through an opening. —*v.t.* **6.** to enter in a register. **7.** to cause (mail) to be recorded at a post office as a safeguard against loss. **8.** to enroll (a student, voter, etc.). **9.** to indicate on or as if on a scale. **10.** to show (an emotion). —*v.i.* **11.** to enter one's name in a register. **12.** to show: *A smile registered on her face.* **13.** to make an impression. —**reg′is•trant,** *n.*

reg′is•trar (-strär′), *n.* a person who keeps records, as at a school or college.

reg′is•tra′tion *n.* **1.** the act of registering. **2.** the group or number registered. **3.** a certificate attesting to the fact that someone or something has been registered.

reg′is•try *n., pl.* **-tries. 1.** registration. **2.** an office of registration. **3.** an official record; register. **4.** the state of being registered.

re•gress (*v.* ri gres′; *n.* rē′gres), *v.i.* **1.** to move backward. **2.** to revert to an earlier or less advanced state or form. —*n.* **3.** the act of regressing. —**re•gres′sive,** *adj.*

re•gres•sion (ri gresh′ən), *n.* **1.** the act of regressing. **2.** *Psychoanalysis.* reversion to an earlier, less adaptive emotional state or behavior pattern.

re•gret (ri gret′), *v.,* **-gret•ted, -gret•ting,** *n.* —*v.t.* **1.** to feel sorrow or remorse for. **2.** to think of with a sense of loss. —*n.* **3.** a sense of loss. **4.** a feeling of sorrow or remorse, as for a fault. **5. regrets,** a polite, usu. formal refusal of an invitation. —**re•gret′ful,** *adj.* —**re•gret′ta•ble,** *adj.*

re•group (rē grōōp′), *v.t., v.i.* to form into a new or restructured group.

reg•u•lar (reg′yə lər), *adj.* **1.** usual; customary. **2.** evenly or uniformly arranged. **3.** characterized by fixed principle or procedure. **4.** recurring at fixed intervals. **5.** adhering to a rule or procedure; methodical. **6.** habitual or long-standing: *a regular user.* **7.** legitimate or proper: *a regular doctor.* **8.** *Informal.* **a.** decent; nice: *a regular guy.* **b.** absolute; thoroughgoing: *a regular rascal.* **9.** conforming to the most prevalent pattern of formation or inflection in a language: *a regular verb.* **10.** *Math.* having all sides and angles equal. **11.** of or belonging to the standing army of a state. **12.** belonging to a religious or monastic order. —*n.* **13.** a long-standing or habitual customer or client. **14.** a professional soldier. **15.** a faithful party member. **16.** an athlete who plays in most games, usu. from the start. —**reg′u•lar′i•ty,** *n.* —**reg′u•lar•ize′,** *v.t.,* **-ized, -iz•ing.** —**reg′u•lar•ly,** *adv.*

reg′u•late′ (-lāt′), *v.t.,* **-lat•ed, -lat•ing. 1.** to control or direct by a rule, principle, or method. **2.** to adjust in accordance with a standard or requirement. **3.** to adjust so as to ensure accuracy of operation. **4.** to put in good order. —**reg′u•la•to′ry** (-lə tôr′ē), *adj.*

reg′u•la′tion *n.* **1.** a law or rule, esp. to regulate conduct. **2.** the act of regulating or state of being regulated. —*adj.* **3.** prescribed by or conforming to regulation.

re•gur•gi•tate (ri gûr′ji tāt′), *v.i., v.t.,* **-tat•ed, -tat•ing. 1.** to rush or cause to rush back. **2.** to vomit. —**re•gur′gi•ta′tion,** *n.*

re•ha•bil•i•tate (rē′hə bil′i tāt′, rē′ə-), *v.t.,* **-tat•ed, -tat•ing. 1.** to restore to a condition of good health, ability to work, etc. **2.** to restore to good condition, operation, or management. **3.** to restore to former rank, rights, or privileges. —**re′ha•bil′i•ta′tion,** *n.* —**re′ha•bil′i•ta′tive,** *adj.*

re•hash (*v.* rē hash′; *n.* rē′hash′), *v.t.* **1.** to rework or reuse in a new form without significant change. —*n.* **2.** the act of rehashing. **3.** something rehashed.

re•hearse′ *v.t., v.i.,* **-hearsed, -hears•ing. 1.** to practice (a play, musical piece, etc.) before public presentation. **2.** to train by rehearsal. **3.** to relate the facts or particulars (of). —**re•hears′al,** *n.*

reign (rān), *n.* **1.** the period during which a sovereign occupies a throne. **2.** royal rule or authority. —*v.i.* **3.** to exercise sovereign power or authority; rule. **4.** to be prevalent; prevail.

re•im•burse (rē′im bûrs′), *v.t.,* **-bursed, -burs•ing.** to pay back; repay. —**re′im•burse′ment,** *n.*

rein (rān), *n.* **1.** Often, **reins.** a leather strap fastened to a bridle and used by a rider or driver to control an animal, esp. a horse. **2.** a means of curbing or controlling. —*v.t.* **3.** to check or guide with or as if with reins. —*Idiom.* **4. give (free) rein to,** to give complete freedom to.

re•in•car•na•tion (rē′in kär nā′shən), *n.* rebirth of the soul in a new body.

rein•deer (rān′dēr′), *n., pl.* **-deer,** (*occasionally*) **-deers.** a large deer of arctic regions.

re•in•force (rē′in fôrs′), *v.t.,* **-forced, -forc•ing. 1.** to strengthen with added support or material. **2.** to strengthen (a military force) with additional personnel or equipment. —**re′in•force′ment,** *n.*

re•in•state (rē′in stāt′), *v.t.,* **-stat•ed, -stat•ing.** to put back into a former position or state. —**re′in•state′ment,** *n.*

re•it•er•ate (rē it′ə rāt′), *v.t.,* **-at•ed, -at•ing.** to say or do again or repeatedly. —**re•it′er•a′tion,** *n.* —**re•it′er•a′tive** (-ə rā′tiv, -ər ə tiv), *adj.*

re•ject (*v.* ri jekt′; *n.* rē′jekt), *v.t.* **1.** to refuse to have, take, or use. **2.** to refuse to grant; deny. **3.** to refuse to accept or admit; rebuff. **4.** to discard as useless or unsatisfactory. —*n.* **5.** one that is rejected. —**re•jec′tion,** *n.*

re•joice (ri jois′), *v.i., v.t.,* **-joiced, -joic•ing.** to feel or cause to feel joy; delight. —**re•joic′ing,** *n.*

re•join¹ (rē join′), *v.t., v.i.* to join together again; reunite.

re•join² (ri join′), *v.t.* to say in response; answer.

re•join′der (-dər), *n.* an answer to a reply; response.

re•ju•ve•nate (ri jōō′və nāt′), *v.t.,* **-nat•ed, -nat•ing.** to restore to youthful vigor or appearance; make young again. —**re•ju′ve•na′tion,** *n.*

re•lapse (*v.* ri laps′; *n. also* rē′laps), *v.,* **-lapsed, -laps•ing.** —*v.i.* **1.** to fall back into a former state, esp. into illness after apparent recovery. —*n.* **2.** an act or instance of relapsing.

re•late (ri lāt′), *v.,* **-lat•ed, -lat•ing.** —*v.t.* **1.** to give an account of; tell. **2.** to connect in thought or meaning. —*v.i.* **3.** to have reference or relation. **4.** to establish a sympathetic relationship.

re•lat′ed *adj.* **1.** associated; connected. **2.** allied by kinship, marriage, or common origin. —**re•lat′ed•ness,** *n.*

re•la′tion *n.* **1.** a significant association; connection. **2. relations, a.** connections or dealings, as between countries. **b.** sexual intercourse. **3.** connection by blood or marriage; kinship. **4.** a relative. **5.** the act of narrating. **6.** regard; reference. —**re•la′tion•al,** *adj.* —**re•la′tion•ship,** *n.*

rel•a•tive (rel′ə tiv), *n.* **1.** a person related to another by blood or marriage. **2.** something related to something else. **3.** a relative pronoun, adjective, or adverb. —*adj.* **4.** considered or existing only in relation to something else; comparative. **5.** having relation or connection. **6.** having reference; relevant. **7.** introducing a subordinate clause and referring to an antecedent. —**rel′a•tive•ly,** *adv.*

rel′ative humid′ity *n.* the amount of water vapor in the air expressed as a percentage of the maximum amount that the air could hold at the same temperature.

rel•a•tiv•i•ty (rel′ə tiv′i tē), *n.* **1.** the state or fact of being relative. **2.** *Physics.* Einstein's two-part theory that mass and energy are equivalent, that space and time are relative concepts, and that gravitational and inertial forces are equivalent.

re•lax (ri laks′), *v.t., v.i.* **1.** to make or become less tense, rigid, or firm. **2.** to make or become less strict or severe. **3.** to relieve or find relief from inhibition, worry, or tension. —**re•lax•a•tion** (rē′lak-sā′shən), *n.*

re•lay (rē′lā; *v. also* ri lā′), *n., pl.* **-lays,** *v.,* **-layed, -lay•ing.** —*n.* **1.** a crew or team, as of persons or animals, relieving one another or taking turns. **2.** a race between teams in which each contestant runs part of the distance. **3.** an electrical device that responds to a change of current or voltage in one circuit by making or breaking a connection in another. —*v.t.* **4.** to carry or convey by or as if by relays. **5.** to provide with fresh relays.

re•lease (ri lēs′), *v.,* **-leased, -leas•ing.** —*v.t.* **1.** to free from confinement, obligation, pain, or restraint. **2.** to allow to be known, issued, done, or seen. **3.** to surrender (a legal right, claim, etc.). —*n.* **4.** a releasing, as from confinement or restraint. **5.** a device that holds and releases a mechanism, as a catch. **6.** permission to publish, use, or sell something. **7. a.** the releasing of something to the public. **b.** a film, record, etc., that is released. **8.** a document by which one surrenders a legal right.

rel•e•gate (rel′i gāt′), *v.t.,* **-gat•ed, -gat•ing. 1.** to send or consign to an inferior position, place, or condition. **2.** to turn over (a matter, task, etc.) to someone. **3.** to assign to a particular class or kind. **4.** to send into exile.

re•lent (ri lent′), *v.i.* to become more mild, compassionate, or forgiving.

re•lent′less *adj.* unyieldingly severe, strict, or harsh.

rel•e•vant (rel′ə vənt), *adj.* bearing upon the matter at hand; pertinent. —**rel′e•vance, rel′e•van•cy,** *n.*

re•li•a•ble (ri lī′ə bəl), *adj.* capable of being relied on; dependable. —**re•li′a•bil′i•ty,** *n.* —**re•li′a•bly,** *adv.*

re•li′ance (-əns), *n.* **1.** dependence. **2.** confidence. **3.** something or someone relied on. —**re•li′ant,** *adj.*

rel•ic (rel′ik), *n.* **1.** something surviving from the past. **2.** a surviving trace; vestige. **3. relics,** remaining parts or fragments. **4.** a souvenir; memento. **5.** an object associated with a saint and venerated as sacred.

re•lief¹ (ri lēf′), *n.* **1.** alleviation of or deliverance from pain or distress. **2.** help, as money or food, given to those in poverty or need. **3.** something affording a pleasing change, as from monotony. **4. a.** release from a post or duty, as by a replacement. **b.** the person or persons acting as replacement. **5.** the rescue of a besieged town, fort, etc.

re•lief² (ri lēf′), *n.* **1.** prominence or distinctness due to contrast. **2.** projection of a figure from its background, as in sculpture. **3.** differences in elevation and slope in a land surface.

re•lieve (ri lēv′), *v.t.,* **-lieved, -liev•ing. 1.** to ease or free from (pain, distress, etc.). **2.** to give aid to. **3.** to free from a burden, wrong, or oppression. **4.** to make less tedious or unpleasant. **5.** to release (a person on duty) by being or providing a replacement. **6.** to release from an obligation or position: *He was relieved of his post.*

re•li•gion (ri lij′ən), *n.* **1.** a set of beliefs concerning the nature and purpose of the universe, esp. when considered as the creation of a superhuman agency. **2.** an institutionalized system of religious beliefs and worship: *the Christian religion.* **3.** something a person believes in devotedly.

re•li′gious *adj., n., pl.* **-gious.** —*adj.* **1.** of or concerned with religion. **2.** pious; devout. **3.** scrupulously faithful; conscientious. —*n.* **4.** a member of a religious order. —**re•li′gious•ly,** *adv.*

re•lin•quish (ri ling′kwish), *v.t.* **1.** to give up (a possession, right, etc.); surrender. **2.** to put aside or desist from. **3.** to let go of; release.

rel•i•quar•y (rel′i kwer′ē), *n., pl.* **-ies.** a receptacle for religious relics.

rel•ish (rel′ish), *n.* **1.** enjoyment of the taste of something. **2.** pleasurable appreciation; liking. **3.** something savory, as pickles, added to a meal. **4.** flavor, esp. when appetizing. —*v.t.* **5.** to take pleasure in; enjoy. **6.** to like the taste of.

re•live (rē liv′), *v.t.,* **-lived, -liv•ing. 1.** to experience again. **2.** to live (one's life) again.

re•lo′cate *v.t., v.i.,* **-cat•ed, -cat•ing.** to move to a different location. —**re′lo•ca′tion,** *n.*

re•luc•tant (ri luk′tənt), *adj.* **1.** not willing; disinclined. **2.** marked by unwillingness. —**re•luc′tance,** *n.* —**re•luc′tant•ly,** *adv.*

re•ly (ri lī′), *v.i.,* **-lied, -ly•ing.** to depend confidently.

REM (rem), *n.* quick, darting movement of the eyes during sleep, esp. during dreams. [*r(apid) e(ye) m(ovement)*]

re•main (ri mān′), *v.i.* **1.** to continue to be as specified. **2.** to stay behind or in the same place. **3.** to be left after the removal or destruction of all else. **4.** to be left to be done, told, etc. —*n.* **5.** Usu., **remains.** something that remains or is left over. **6. remains,** a dead body; corpse.

re•main′der (-dər), *n.* **1.** something that remains

or is left. **2.** *Math.* **a.** the quantity that remains after subtraction. **b.** the portion of the dividend that is not evenly divisible by the divisor. **3.** a book discounted by its publisher when sales have practically ceased.

re•mand (ri mand′, -mänd′), *v.t.* to send back, esp. to return to custody, as to await further proceedings.

re•mark (ri märk′), *v.t.* **1.** to say as a comment or observation. **2.** to note; observe. —*v.i.* **3.** to make a comment or observation. —*n.* **4.** notice, comment, or mention. **5.** a casual or brief expression of thought or opinion.

re•mark′a•ble *adj.* notably unusual; noteworthy. —**re•mark′a•bly,** *adv.*

rem•e•dy (rem′i dē), *n., pl.* **-dies,** *v.,* **-died, -dy•ing.** —*n.* **1.** something, as a medicine, that cures or relieves a bodily disorder. **2.** something that corrects or removes an evil or error. —*v.t.* **3.** to cure or relieve. **4.** to put right; rectify. —**re•me•di•al** (ri mē′dē əl), *adj.*

re•mem•ber (ri mem′bər), *v.t.* **1.** to recall to the mind. **2.** to retain in the mind. **3.** to bear in mind as deserving a gift or reward. **4.** to mention (a person) to another as sending greetings. —*v.i.* **5.** to have or use the faculty of memory.

re•mem′brance (-brəns), *n.* **1.** a recollection; memory. **2.** the act of remembering or state of being remembered. **3.** the ability to remember. **4.** length of time over which memory extends. **5.** something that serves as a reminder. **6.** a gift given as a token of friendship.

re•mind (ri mīnd′), *v.t.* to cause to remember. —**re•mind′er,** *n.*

rem•i•nisce (rem′ə nis′), *v.i.,* **-nisced, -nisc•ing.** to recall or talk about past experiences. —**rem′i•nis′cence,** *n.* —**rem′i•nis′cent,** *adj.*

re•miss (ri mis′), *adj.* **1.** negligent or careless in performing a duty or task. **2.** characterized by negligence or carelessness. —**re•miss′ness,** *n.*

re•mis•sion (ri mish′ən), *n.* **1.** the act of remitting. **2.** forgiveness, as of sins. **3. a.** a subsidence of manifestations of a disease. **b.** a period of such a subsidence.

re•mit (ri mit′), *v.t.,* **-mit•ted, -mit•ting. 1.** to send (money), usu. in payment. **2.** to refrain from inflicting, enforcing, or exacting. **3.** to forgive (a sin, offense, etc.). **4.** to slacken; abate. —**re•mit′tance,** *n.*

rem•nant (rem′nənt), *n.* **1.** a remaining, usu. small part or number. **2.** a small unsold or unused piece of fabric. **3.** a trace; vestige.

re•mod•el (rē mod′l), *v.t.,* **-eled, -el•ing** or (*esp. Brit.*) **-elled, -el•ling.** to alter in structure or form; make over.

re•mon•strate (ri mon′strāt), *v.t., v.i.,* **-strat•ed, -strat•ing.** to reason or plead in protest, objection, or complaint.

re•morse (ri môrs′), *n.* deep and painful regret for wrongdoing. —**re•morse′ful,** *adj.* —**re•morse′less,** *adj.*

re•mote (ri mōt′), *adj.,* **-mot•er, -mot•est.** —*adj.* **1.** far away; distant. **2.** distant in time or relationship. **3.** slight or faint: *a remote chance.* **4.** reserved and distant in manner. —*n.* **5.** REMOTE CONTROL (def. 2). —**re•mote′ly,** *adv.*

remote′ control′ *n.* **1.** control of an apparatus from a distance, as by radio signals. **2.** a device used to control a machine or apparatus from a distance. —**remote′-control′,** *adj.*

re•move (ri mōōv′), *v.,* **-moved, -mov•ing,** *n.* —*v.t.* **1.** to move from one place or position to another. **2.** to take off; shed. **3.** to dismiss from a position; discharge. **4.** to do away with; eliminate. —*n.* **5.** the act of removing. **6.** a distance by which one person or thing is separated from another. **7.** a degree of difference. —**re•mov′a•ble,** *adj.* —**re•mov′al,** *n.*

re•mu•ner•ate (ri myōō′nə rāt′), *v.t.,* **-at•ed, -at•ing.** to pay for work, services, or trouble. —**re•mu′ner•a′tion,** *n.* —**re•mu′ner•a′tive,** *adj.*

Ren•ais•sance (ren′ə säns′, -zäns′), *n.* **1.** the great revival of art, literature, and learning in

Europe from the 14th to the 17th centuries. **2.** (*l.c.*) renewal; rebirth. [< F, MF: rebirth]

re•nal (rēn′l), *adj.* of or near the kidneys.

rend (rend), *v.t.*, **rent, rend•ing. 1.** to tear apart with force or violence. **2.** to distress with painful feelings.

ren•der (ren′dər), *v.t.* **1.** to cause to be or become; make. **2.** to do; perform. **3.** to furnish; provide. **4.** to present, as for payment; submit. **5.** to translate. **6.** to depict, as in painting. **7.** to give in return. **8.** to melt down: *to render fat.*

ren•dez•vous (rän′də vōō′, -dā-), *n.*, *pl.* **-vous** (-vōōz′), *v.*, **-voused** (-vōōd′), **-vous•ing** (-vōō′ing). —*n.* **1. a.** an agreement to meet at a certain time and place. **b.** the meeting itself. **2.** a place designated for a meeting, esp. of ships. **3.** a meeting of spacecraft in outer space. **4.** a popular gathering place. —*v.t., v.i.* **5.** to assemble at an agreed time and place. [< MF *rendez-vous* betake yourselves]

ren•di•tion (ren dish′ən), *n.* **1.** the act of rendering. **2.** a translation. **3.** an interpretation, as of a role.

ren•e•gade (ren′i gād′), *n.* a person who deserts a party, cause, or religion for another.

re•nege (ri nig′, -neg′), *v.i.*, **-neged, -neg•ing. 1.** to go back on one's word. **2.** to play a card that is not of the suit led when one can follow suit.

re•new (ri nōō′, -nyōō′), *v.t.* **1.** to begin or take up again; resume. **2.** to make effective for an additional period. **3.** to restore, revive, or replenish. **4.** to make, say, or do again. —**re•new′al,** *n.*

ren•net (ren′it), *n.* **1.** the lining membrane of the stomach of a young animal, esp. a calf. **2.** an extract of the rennet membrane used esp. in making cheese.

re•nounce (ri nouns′), *v.t.*, **-nounced, -nounc•ing. 1.** to give up, esp. by formal declaration. **2.** to repudiate; disown. —**re•nun•ci•a•tion** (ri nun′sē ā′shən), *n.*

ren•o•vate (ren′ə vāt′), *v.t.*, **-vat•ed, -vat•ing.** to restore to good condition. —**ren′o•va′tion,** *n.*

re•nown (ri noun′), *n.* widespread and high repute; fame. —**re•nowned′,** *adj.*

rent¹ (rent), *n.* **1.** a payment made periodically in return for the use of another's land or property. —*v.t.* **2.** to grant the possession and use of in return for rent. **3.** to take and hold in return for rent. —*v.i.* **4.** to be leased or let for rent. —*Idiom.* **5. for rent,** available to be rented.

rent² (rent), *n.* **1.** an opening made by rending. **2.** a breach of relations; schism.

rent³ (rent), *v.* pt. and pp. of REND.

rent′al *n.* **1.** an amount received or paid as rent. **2.** the act of renting. **3.** property offered or occupied for rent. —*adj.* **4.** of or available for rent.

rep (rep), *n.* a horizontally ribbed fabric.

Rep. 1. Representative. **2.** Republic. **3.** Republican.

re•pair¹ (ri pâr′), *v.t.* **1.** to restore to sound condition; mend. **2.** to restore or renew. **3.** to make up for; remedy. —*n.* **4.** an act, instance, or result of repairing. **5.** condition with respect to soundness and usability.

re•pair² (ri pâr′), *v.i.* to betake oneself; go: *They repaired to the living room.*

rep•a•ra•tion (rep′ə rā′shən), *n.* **1.** the making of amends for wrong or injury. **2.** Usu., **-tions.** compensation payable by a defeated nation for damages or loss caused during war.

rep•ar•tee (rep′ər tē′, -tā′, -är-), *n.*, *pl.* **-tees. 1.** a quick, witty reply. **2.** conversation full of such replies.

re•past (ri past′, -päst′), *n.* **1.** food and drink for a meal. **2.** a meal.

re•pa•tri•ate (rē pā′trē āt′), *v.t., v.i.*, **-at•ed, -at•ing.** to send or go back to the country of birth or citizenship. —**re•pa′tri•a′tion,** *n.*

re•pay (ri pā′), *v.t.*, **-paid, -pay•ing. 1.** to pay back; refund. **2.** to make return for or to. —**re•pay′ment,** *n.*

re•peal (ri pēl′), *v.t.* **1.** to revoke or annul formally or officially. —*n.* **2.** the act of repealing.

re•peat (ri pēt′), *v.t.* **1.** to say or do again. **2.** to say in reproducing the words or inflections of an-

other. **3.** to tell (something heard) to another. —*v.i.* **4.** to say or do something again. —*n.* **5.** the act of repeating. **6.** something repeated, as a rerun on television.

re•peat′ed *adj.* said or done again and again. —**re•peat′ed•ly,** *adv.*

re•pel (ri pel′), *v.t.*, **-pelled, -pel•ling. 1.** to drive or force back or away. **2.** to fail to mix with. **3.** to resist the absorption of: *This coat repels rain.* **4.** to cause distaste or aversion in. —**re•pel′lent,** *adj., n.*

re•pent (ri pent′), *v.i., v.t.* **1.** to feel contrite (for); regret. **2.** to be penitent (for) and determine to change for the better. —**re•pent′ance,** *n.* —**re•pent′ant,** *adj.*

re•per•cus•sion (rē′pər kush′ən), *n.* **1.** an effect or result of a previous action or event. **2.** a rebounding or recoil after impact. **3.** reverberation; echo.

rep•er•toire (rep′ər twär′, -twôr′, rep′ə-), *n.* **1.** all the works that a performing company or artist is prepared to present. **2.** the skills, techniques, and devices used or required in a field or occupation.

rep•e•ti•tion (rep′i tish′ən), *n.* **1.** the act of repeating. **2.** something repeated. —**rep′e•ti′tious,** *adj.* —**re•pet•i•tive** (ri pet′i tiv), *adj.*

re•pine (ri pīn′), *v.i.*, **-pined, -pin•ing. 1.** to fret or complain. **2.** to yearn for something.

re•place (ri plās′), *v.t.*, **-placed, -plac•ing. 1.** to assume the function of; substitute for. **2.** to provide a substitute or equivalent for. **3.** to restore to the proper place. —**re•place′a•ble,** *adj.* —**re•place′ment,** *n.*

re•play (*v.* rē plā′; *n.* rē′plā′), *v.t.*, **-played, -play•ing,** *n.*, *pl.* **-plays.** —*v.t.* **1.** to play (a record, tape, etc.) again. —*n.* **2.** an act or instance of replaying. **3.** something replayed.

re•plen•ish (ri plen′ish), *v.t.* **1.** to make full or complete again. **2.** to supply again or anew. —**re•plen′ish•ment,** *n.*

re•plete (ri plēt′), *adj.* **1.** abundantly supplied. **2.** stuffed with food. —**re•ple′tion,** *n.*

rep•li•ca (rep′li kə), *n.*, *pl.* **-cas. 1.** a close copy, as of a work of art. **2.** a reproduction.

rep•li•cate (rep′li kāt′), *v.t.*, **-cat•ed, -cat•ing.** to repeat, duplicate, or reproduce. —**rep•li•ca′tion,** *n.*

re•ply (ri plī′), *v.*, **-plied, -ply•ing,** *n.*, *pl.* **-plies.** —*v.i., v.t.* to give or return as an answer; respond. —*n.* **2.** an answer; response.

re•port (ri pôrt′), *n.* **1.** a usu. detailed account, as of an event. **2.** rumor or gossip. **3.** a loud noise, as from an explosion. **4.** repute; reputation. —*v.t.* **5.** to carry and repeat (an answer or message). **6.** to give an account or statement of. **7.** (of a committee) to return (a bill) to a legislative body with findings. **8.** to make a charge against (a person), as to a superior. **9.** to make known the presence, absence, or condition of. **10.** to relate; tell. —*v.i.* **11.** to make a report. **12.** to work as a reporter. **13.** to present oneself as ordered: *to report for duty.* —**re•port′ed•ly,** *adv.*

re•port′er *n.* **1.** a person who reports. **2.** a person employed to gather and report news, as for a newspaper.

re•pose¹ (ri pōz′), *n.*, *v.*, **-posed, -pos•ing.** —*n.* **1.** the state of being at rest. **2.** tranquillity; calm. **3.** absence of movement or animation. —*v.i.* **4.** to lie at rest. **5.** to lie dead. —*v.t.* **6.** to lay to rest.

re•pose² (ri pōz′), *v.t.*, **-posed, -pos•ing.** to put (confidence, trust, etc.) in a person or thing.

re•pos•i•to•ry (ri poz′i tôr′ē), *n.*, *pl.* **-tor•ies. 1.** a place where things are deposited, stored, or offered for sale. **2.** a person to whom something is entrusted or confided.

re•pos•sess (rē′pə zes′), *v.t.* to take possession of again, esp. for nonpayment of money that is due.

rep′re•hen′si•ble (-hen′sə bəl), *adj.* deserving rebuke or censure; blameworthy. —**rep′re•hen′si•bly,** *adv.*

rep•re•sent (rep′ri zent′), *v.t.* **1.** to serve to stand for; denote or symbolize. **2.** to act or speak for, esp. as an elected representative. **3.** to portray; depict. **4.** to set forth with a view to influencing opinion. **5.**

to impersonate, as in acting. **6.** to serve as an example of. —**rep′re•sen•ta′tion,** *n.*

rep′re•sent′a•tive (-tə tiv), *n.* **1.** a person who represents another or others. **2.** a person who represents a constituency in a legislative body, esp. in the U.S. House of Representatives. **3.** a typical example. —*adj.* **4.** serving to represent. **5.** made up of representatives. **6.** of or founded on representation of the people in government. **7.** exemplifying a group or kind.

re•press (ri pres′), *v.t.* **1.** to check or inhibit. **2.** to keep down; suppress. **3.** to suppress (memories, emotions, etc.) unconsciously. —**re•pres′sion,** *n.* —**re•pres′sive,** *adj.*

re•prieve (ri prēv′), *v.,* -**prieved, -priev•ing.** —*v.t.* **1.** to delay the punishment of. **2.** to relieve temporarily. —*n.* **3.** the act of reprieving or state of being reprieved.

rep•ri•mand (rep′rə mand′, -mänd′; *v. also* rep′rə-mand′, -mänd′), *n.* **1.** a severe rebuke, esp. an official one. —*v.t.* **2.** to rebuke severely, esp. officially.

re•pris•al (ri prī′zəl), *n.* retaliation against another by the infliction of equal or greater injuries.

re•proach (ri prōch′), *v.t.* **1.** to express disapproval of; censure. —*n.* **2.** blame or censure. **3.** an expression of blame or censure. —**re•proach′ful,** *adj.*

rep•ro•bate (rep′rə bāt′), *n.* **1.** a depraved or wicked person. —*adj.* **2.** depraved; wicked. —**rep′ro•ba′tion,** *n.*

re•pro•duce (rē′prə dōōs′, -dyōōs′), *v.,* -**duced, -duc•ing.** —*v.t.* **1.** to make a copy of; duplicate. **2.** to produce again or anew. **3.** to produce by a process of generation or propagation. —*v.i.* **4.** to bear offspring. —**re′pro•duc′i•ble,** *adj.* —**re′pro•duc′-tion,** *n.* —**re′pro•duc′tive,** *adj.*

re•proof (ri prōōf′), *n.* an act or expression of reproving.

re•prove (ri prōōv′), *v.t.,* -**proved, -prov•ing.** **1.** to criticize or correct, esp. gently. **2.** to express disapproval of; censure. —**re•prov′ing•ly,** *adv.*

rep•tile (rep′til, -tīl), *n.* an air-breathing vertebrate, as a snake, lizard, or turtle, characterized by a bony skeleton and a covering of dry scales or horny plates. —**rep•til′i•an** (-til′ē ən), *adj.*

re•pub•lic (ri pub′lik), *n.* **1.** a state in which the supreme power rests in the citizens entitled to vote and is exercised by their chosen representatives. **2. a.** a state in which the head of government is not a monarch but is usu. a president. **b.** the form of government of such a state. [< F < L *rēs pūblica* public affairs, the state]

re•pub•li•can *adj.* **1.** of or of the nature of a republic. **2.** favoring a republic. **3.** (*cap.*) of or belonging to the Republican Party. —*n.* **4.** one who favors a republican form of government. **5.** (*cap.*) a member of the Republican Party. —**re•pub′li•can•ism,** *n.*

re•pu•di•ate (ri pyōō′dē āt′), *v.t.,* -**at•ed, -at•ing.** **1.** to reject as having no authority or binding force. **2.** to refuse to accept; disown. **3.** to refuse to acknowledge and pay (a debt). —**re•pu′di•a′tion,** *n.*

re•pug•nant (ri pug′nənt), *adj.* **1.** objectionable or offensive. **2.** not consistent or compatible. —**re•pug′nance,** *n.*

re•pulse (ri puls′), *v.,* -**pulsed, -puls•ing,** *n.* —*v.t.* **1.** to drive back; repel. **2.** to repel with rudeness or denial. **3.** to cause repulsion in; disgust. —*n.* **4.** the act of repelling. **5.** a refusal or rejection. **6.** the fact of being repelled. —**re•pul′sion,** *n.*

re•pul•sive *adj.* **1.** causing repugnance or aversion. **2.** tending or serving to repulse. —**re•pul′-sive•ly,** *adv.* —**re•pul′sive•ness,** *n.*

rep•u•ta•ble (rep′yə tə bəl), *adj.* held in good repute; respectable.

rep′u•ta′tion, *n.* **1.** the estimation in which a person or thing is generally held. **2.** favorable repute.

re•pute (ri pyōōt′), *n., v.,* -**put•ed, -put•ing.** —*n.* **1.** reputation. —*v.t.* **2.** to consider; believe: *He was reputed to be a millionaire.*

re•quest (ri kwest′), *n.* **1.** an act or instance of asking for something. **2.** something asked for. —*v.t.* **3.** to ask for. **4.** to ask (someone) to do something.

req•ui•em (rek′wē əm, rē′kwē-, rā′-), *n.* **1.** (*often cap.*) **a.** a mass for the dead. **b.** a celebration of this mass. **2.** a musical service or hymn for the repose of the dead.

re•quire (ri kwī^ər′), *v.t.,* -**quired, -quir•ing.** **1.** to have need of. **2.** to order to do something. **3.** to call for as necessary or indispensable; demand. **4.** to place under an obligation. —**re•quire′ment,** *n.*

req•ui•site (rek′wə zit), *adj.* **1.** required. —*n.* **2.** something required.

req′ui•si′tion (-zish′ən), *n.* **1.** a formal or official written request for something, as supplies. **2.** the state of being in or required for use. —*v.t.* **3.** to demand or take, as for military purposes.

re•quite (ri kwīt′), *v.t.,* -**quit•ed, -quit•ing.** **1.** to make repayment for (service, benefits, etc.). **2.** to retaliate for; avenge. **3.** to give or do in return. —**re•quit′al,** *n.*

re•run (rē′run′), *n.* **1.** the showing of a motion picture or television program after its initial run. **2.** the motion picture or television program shown.

re•scind (ri sind′), *v.t.* to revoke, annul, or repeal.

res•cue (res′kyōō), *v.,* -**cued, -cu•ing,** *n.* —*v.t.* **1.** to free from confinement or danger. —*n.* **2.** the act of rescuing.

re•search (ri sûrch′, rē′sûrch), *n.* **1.** diligent and systematic inquiry into a subject in order to discover facts or revise theories. **2.** a particular instance or piece of research. —*v.i., v.t.* **3.** to investigate carefully. —**re•search′er,** *n.*

re•sem•ble (ri zem′bəl), *v.t.,* -**bled, -bling.** to be like or similar to. —**re•sem′blance,** *n.*

re•sent (ri zent′), *v.t.* to feel or show displeasure or indignation at. —**re•sent′ful,** *adj.* —**re•sent′ment,** *n.*

res•er•va•tion (rez′ər vā′shən), *n.* **1.** the act of reserving. **2.** an exception or qualification. **3.** a tract of public land set apart for a special purpose. **4.** a prior arrangement to secure accommodations, as at a restaurant.

re•serve (ri zûrv′), *v.,* -**served, -serv•ing,** *n., adj.* —*v.t.* **1.** to keep back, esp. for future use; save. **2.** to retain or secure by prior arrangement. **3.** to set apart for oneself. —*n.* **4.** cash or assets held aside to meet unexpected demands. **5.** something kept for future use or need; stock. **6.** a resource not normally called upon but available if needed. **7.** RESERVATION (def. 3). **8.** the act of reserving. **9. a.** a military force held in readiness. **b. reserves,** the enrolled but not regular components of the U.S. Army. **10.** formality and self-restraint. —*adj.* **11.** kept in reserve. —*Idiom.* **12. in reserve,** put aside for future need; reserved.

re•served′ *adj.* **1.** kept, held, or set apart for future use. **2.** formal and self-restrained. —**re•serv′-ed•ly,** *adv.*

re•serv′ist *n.* a member of a military reserve.

res•er•voir (rez′ər vwär′, -vwôr′, rez′ə-), *n.* **1.** a place where water is collected and stored for future use. **2.** a receptacle for holding a fluid. **3.** a large supply or stock.

re•side (ri zīd′), *v.i.,* -**sid•ed, -sid•ing.** **1.** to live in as one's home; dwell. **2.** to be present or inherent. **3.** to be vested, as powers.

res•i•dence (rez′i dəns), *n.* **1.** the place, esp. the house, in which a person resides; home. **2.** the act or fact of residing. **3.** the time during which a person resides in a place.

res′i•den•cy *n., pl.* -**cies.** **1.** RESIDENCE (def. 2). **2.** the position or tenure of a medical resident.

res′i•dent *n.* **1.** one who resides in a place. **2.** a physician receiving specialized training at a hospital. —*adj.* **3.** residing; dwelling. **4.** living or staying at a place in discharge of duty. —**res′i•den′tial** (-den′shəl), *adj.*

res•i•due (rez′i dōō′, -dyōō′), *n.* something that remains after a part is removed, disposed of, or used; remainder. —**re•sid•u•al** (ri zij′ōō əl), *adj.*

re•sign (ri zīn′), *v.i., v.t.* **1.** to give up (an office or position), esp. formally. **2.** to relinquish (a right, claim, etc.). **3.** to submit (oneself, one's mind, etc.) without resistance.

res•ig•na•tion (rez′ig nā′shən), *n.* **1.** the act of

resigning. **2.** a formal statement or document that one has resigned. **3.** an accepting, unresisting attitude or state; submission.

re•signed (ri zīnd′), *adj.* submissive or acquiescent.

re•sil•ient (ri zil′yənt), *adj.* **1.** capable of springing back to an original form and size after compression, bending, or stretching; elastic. **2.** recovering readily, as from adversity or illness; buoyant. —**re•sil′ience,** *n.*

res•in (rez′in), *n.* a substance obtained from certain plants or made artificially, used in making varnishes and plastics.

re•sist (ri zist′), *v.t.* **1.** to strive against; oppose. **2.** to withstand the action or effect of. **3.** to refrain or abstain from, esp. with difficulty. —*v.i.* **4.** to act or make efforts in opposition.

re•sist′ance *n.* **1.** the act or power of resisting. **2.** the tendency of a conductor to oppose the flow of electric current. —**re•sist′ant,** *adj.*

re•sis′tor *n.* a device designed to introduce resistance into an electric circuit.

res•o•lute (rez′ə lōōt′), *adj.* determined; resolved. —**res′o•lute•ly,** *adv.*

res′o•lu′tion *n.* **1.** a formal expression of opinion or intention by a group, as a legislature. **2.** the act or process of resolving. **3.** the state or quality of being resolute; determination. **4.** a solution, as of a problem. **5.** the degree of sharpness of a computer-generated image as measured by the number of dots per linear inch in a printout or the number of pixels across and down on a screen.

re•solve (ri zolv′), *v.,* **-solved, -solv•ing,** *n.* —*v.t.* **1.** to come to a firm decision about; determine. **2.** to separate into constituent parts. **3.** to state in a formal resolution. **4.** to settle or solve (a question, controversy, etc.). **5.** to dispel (doubts, fears, etc.). —*v.i.* **6.** to make up one's mind. **7** to break up into constituent parts. —*n.* **8.** a resolution or decision. **9.** firmness of purpose; determination.

res•o•nant (rez′ə nənt), *adj.* **1.** continuing to resound. **2.** deep and full in sound. **3.** producing resonance. —**res′o•nance,** *n.*

res′o•nate′ (-nāt′), *v.i.,* **-nat•ed, -nat•ing. 1.** to resound. **2.** to produce or exhibit resonance.

re•sort (ri zôrt′), *v.i.* **1.** to turn for help, solution, etc.; have recourse: *resorted to violence.* **2.** to go frequently or customarily. —*n.* **3.** a place with facilities for vacationers. **4.** recourse. **5.** a person or thing resorted to.

re•sound (ri zound′), *v.i.* **1.** to ring with sound; reverberate. **2.** to sound loudly. —**re•sound′ing,** *adj.* —**re•sound′ing•ly,** *adv.*

re•source (rē′sôrs, ri sôrs′), *n.* **1.** a source of supply, support, or aid, esp. one that can be readily drawn upon when needed. **2. resources,** a country's means of producing wealth. **3.** Usu., **resources.** money or property; assets. **4.** capability in dealing with a situation or in meeting difficulties.

re•source′ful *adj.* able to deal skillfully with difficulties, etc.

re•spect (ri spekt′), *n.* **1.** a particular; detail. **2.** relation; reference: *inquiries with respect to a route.* **3.** esteem; admiration. **4.** proper courtesy. **5.** the condition of being esteemed. **6. respects,** a formal expression of esteem or deference. —*v.t.* **7.** to hold in esteem. **8.** to refrain from intruding upon: *to respect a person's privacy.* **9.** to have reference to; concern. —**re•spect′ful,** *adj.* —**re•spect′ful•ly,** *adv.*

re•spect′a•ble *adj.* **1.** worthy of respect. **2.** good enough to be seen or used. **3.** of moderate excellence. **4.** appreciable in size, number, or amount. —**re•spect′a•bil′i•ty,** *n.* —**re•spect′a•bly,** *adv.*

re•spect′ing *prep.* regarding; concerning.

re•spec′tive *adj.* pertaining individually to each of a number; particular.

res•pi•ra•tion (res′pə rā′shən), *n.* the act or process of respiring; breathing. —**res′pi•ra•to′ry** (-rə tôr′ē), *adj.*

res′pi•ra′tor *n.* **1.** an apparatus to produce artificial respiration. **2.** a device worn over the nose and mouth to prevent inhalation of harmful substances.

res•pite (res′pit), *n.* **1.** an interval of relief. **2.** a temporary suspension; stay.

re•splend•ent (ri splen′dənt), *adj.* shining brilliantly. —**re•splend′ence,** *n.*

re•spond (ri spond′), *v.i., v.t.* **1.** to answer; reply. **2.** to react, esp. favorably.

re•spond′ent *n.* **1.** a person who responds. **2.** a defendant, esp. in divorce proceedings.

re•sponse′ (-spons′), *n.* **1.** an answer; reply. **2.** a reaction to a stimulus.

re•spon′si•bil•i•ty *n., pl.* **-ties. 1.** the state or fact of being responsible. **2.** a person or thing for which one is responsible.

re•spon′si•ble *adj.* **1.** accountable, as for something within one's power. **2.** involving duties or obligations. **3.** being the source or cause of something. **4.** having the capacity to make moral decisions. **5.** able to discharge obligations or pay debts. **6.** reliable or dependable. —**re•spon′si•bly,** *adv.*

re•spon′sive *adj.* responding readily and sympathetically. —**re•spon′sive•ly,** *adv.* —**re•spon′sive•ness,** *n.*

rest[1] (rest), *n.* **1.** the quiet or repose of sleep. **2.** ease or inactivity after exertion or labor. **3.** relief or freedom, esp. from trouble. **4.** a period of rest. **5.** cessation or absence of motion. **6.** *Music.* **a.** an interval of silence between notes. **b.** a sign indicating it. **7.** a shelter or lodging. **8.** a supporting piece or device. —*v.i.* **9.** to refresh oneself, as by lying down. **10.** to cease from motion or activity. **11.** to lie, sit, lean, or be set. **12.** to be based or founded. **13.** to be found: *The blame rests with them.* **14.** to be fixed on something. —*v.t.* **15.** to give rest to. **16.** to lay or place for rest or support. **17.** to direct or cast. —**rest′ful,** *adj.* —**rest′ful•ly,** *adv.*

rest[2] (rest), *n.* **1.** a part that is left; remainder. **2.** the others: *All the rest are going.* —*v.i.* **3.** to continue to be: *Rest assured that all is well.*

res•tau•rant (res′tər ənt, -tə ränt′), *n.* an establishment where meals are served to customers.

res′tau•ra•teur′ (-ə tûr′), *n.* the owner or manager of a restaurant.

res•ti•tu•tion (res′ti tōō′shən, -tyōō′-), *n.* **1.** compensation for loss, damage, or injury. **2.** the restoration of something, as property, to the rightful owner.

res•tive (res′tiv), *adj.* **1.** restless; uneasy. **2.** stubborn; balky. —**res′tive•ly,** *adv.* —**res′tive•ness,** *n.*

rest′less *adj.* **1.** marked by inability to remain at rest. **2.** unquiet; uneasy. **3.** perpetually agitated or in motion. **4.** without rest or restful sleep. —**rest′less•ly,** *adv.* —**rest′less•ness,** *n.*

re•store (ri stôr′), *v.t.,* **-stored, -stor•ing. 1.** to bring back into existence or use. **2.** to bring back to an original or a former, more desirable condition. **3.** to put back in a former place or rank. **4.** to give back. —**res•to•ra•tion** (res′tə rā′shən), *n.* —**re•stor′a•tive** (-ə tiv), *adj.*

re•strain (ri strān′), *v.t.* **1.** to hold back; check or control. **2.** to deprive of liberty. **3.** to limit or hamper. —**re•strained′,** *adj.*

re•straint′ (-strānt′), *n.* **1.** a restraining action or influence. **2.** a means of restraining. **3.** a restraining device. **4.** the act of restraining or state of being restrained. **5.** caution or reserve, as in feelings.

re•strict (ri strikt′), *v.t.* to keep within limits, as of choice. —**re•strict′ed,** *adj.* —**re•stric′tion,** *n.* —**re•stric′tive,** *adj.*

rest′ room′ *n.* a room in a public building having washbowls and toilets.

re•sult (ri zult′), *v.i.* **1.** to arise or proceed as a consequence. **2.** to end in a particular manner. —*n.* **3.** something that results. **4.** Often, **-sults.** a desirable outcome. **5.** *Math.* a quantity or expression obtained by calculation. —**re•sult′ant,** *adj., n.*

re•sume (ri zōōm′), *v.,* **-sumed, -sum•ing.** —*v.t.* **1.** to begin again after interruption. **2.** to take, occupy, or assume again. —*v.i.* **3.** to continue after interruption. —**re•sump′tion** (-zump′shən), *n.*

ré•su•mé or **re•su•me** or **re•su•mé** (rez′ŏŏ mā′, rez′ŏŏ mā′), *n.* **1.** SUMMARY. **2.** an account of one's education, employment, etc., submitted to a potential employer.

re•sur•gent (ri sûr′jənt), *adj.* rising or tending to rise again. —**re•sur′gence,** *n.*

res•ur•rect (rez′ə rekt′), *v.t.* **1.** to raise from the dead. **2.** to bring back, as into use or practice.

res′ur•rec′tion *n.* **1.** a rising again, as from disuse; revival. **2.** (*cap.*) the rising of Christ after His death and burial. **3.** (*cap.*) the rising of the dead on Judgment Day.

re•sus•ci•tate (ri sus′i tāt′), *v.t.,* **-tat•ed, -tat•ing.** to revive, esp. from apparent death. —**re•sus′ci•ta′-tion,** *n.* —**re•sus′ci•ta′tor,** *n.*

re•tail (rē′tāl), *n.* **1.** the sale of goods to ultimate consumers, usu. in small quantities. —*adj.* **2.** connected with or engaged in sale at retail. —*adv.* **3.** at a retail price. —*v.t., v.i.* **4.** to sell or be sold at retail.

re•tain (ri tān′), *v.t.* **1.** to keep possession of. **2.** to continue to use, practice, or hold. **3.** to keep in mind. **4.** to hold in place or position. **5.** to hire, esp. by payment of a retainer. —**re•tain′a•ble,** *adj.*

re•tain′er[1], *n.* **1.** one that retains. **2.** a servant or attendant.

re•tain′er[2], *n.* a fee paid to secure services, as of a lawyer.

re•take (*v.* rē tāk′; *n.* rē′tāk′), *v.,* **-took, -tak•en, -tak•ing.** —*v.t.* **1.** to take again. **2.** to photograph or film again. —*n.* **3.** a picture or scene photographed or filmed again.

re•tal•i•ate (ri tal′ē āt′), *v.i.,* **-at•ed, -at•ing.** to return like for like, esp. evil for evil. —**re•tal′i•a′-tion,** *n.* —**re•tal′i•a•to′ry** (-ə tôr′ē), *adj.*

re•tard (ri tärd′), *v.t.* to delay the progress of. —**re′tar•da′tion,** *n.*

re•tard′ed *adj.* characterized by slowness or limitation in intellectual or emotional development.

retch (rech), *v.i.* to make efforts to vomit.

re•ten•tion (ri ten′shən), *n.* **1.** the act of retaining or state of being retained. **2.** the power to retain, esp. in the mind. —**re•ten′tive,** *adj.*

ret•i•cent (ret′ə sənt), *adj.* disposed to be silent or not to speak freely. —**ret′i•cence,** *n.*

ret•i•na (ret′n ə), *n., pl.* **-nas, -i•nae** (-n ē′). the innermost coat of the posterior part of the eyeball that receives the image produced by the lens. —**ret′i•nal,** *adj.*

ret•i•nue (ret′n ōō′, -yōō′), *n.* a body of retainers attending an important personage.

re•tire (ri tī*ə*r′), *v.,* **-tired, -tir•ing.** —*v.i.* **1.** to withdraw to a place of privacy, shelter, or seclusion. **2.** to go to bed. **3.** to give up an office, occupation, or career, usu. because of age. **4.** to retreat, as from battle. —*v.t.* **5.** to withdraw (bonds, bills, etc.) from circulation. **6.** to withdraw (troops, ships, etc.), as from battle. **7.** to remove from an office or active service. **8.** *Sports.* to put out (a batter, side, etc.). —**re•tire′ment,** *n.*

Re•tired′ *adj.* **1.** withdrawn from an office, occupation, or career. **2.** due or given a retired person. **3.** secluded or sequestered.

re•tir′ee′ *n., pl.* **-ees.** a person who has retired from working.

re•tir′ing *adj.* reserved; shy.

re•tort[1] (ri tôrt′), *v.t.* **1.** to reply to, esp. sharply. **2.** to return (an accusation, epithet, etc.) upon the person uttering it. —*v.i.* **3.** to reply, esp. sharply. —*n.* **4.** a sharp, incisive, or witty reply. **5.** the act of retorting.

re•tort[2] (ri tôrt′), *n.* a glass bulb with a long neck bent downward, used for distilling or decomposing substances by heat.

re•touch (rē tuch′), *v.t.* to improve, as with new touches, details, or corrections; touch up.

re•trace (ri trās′), *v.t.,* **-traced, -trac•ing.** **1.** to trace backward. **2.** to go back over.

re•tract[1] (ri trakt′), *v.t.* to draw back or in, as claws or fangs. —**re•tract′a•ble,** *adj.*

re•tract[2] (ri trakt′), *v.t.* to withdraw (a statement, promise, etc.); recant. —**re•trac′tion,** *n.*

re•tread (*v.* rē tred′; *n.* rē′tred′), *v.t.* **1.** to put a new tread on (a worn pneumatic tire casing). —*n.* **2.** a retreaded tire.

re•treat (ri trēt′), *n.* **1.** the forced or strategic withdrawal of a military force. **2.** the act of withdraw-

ing, as into privacy. **3.** a place of refuge, seclusion, or privacy. **4.** a period of withdrawal, as for religious meditation. **5. a.** a military flag-lowering ceremony held at sunset. **b.** the bugle call for this. —*v.i.* **6.** to make a retreat. **7.** to slope backward.

re•trench (ri trench′), *v.t., v.i.* to reduce (expenses); economize. —**re•trench′ment,** *n.*

ret•ri•bu•tion (re′trə byōō′shən), *n.* requital according to merits or deserts, esp. for evil. —**re•trib•u•tive** (ri trib′yə tiv), *adj.*

re•trieve (ri trēv′), *v.,* **-trieved, -triev•ing,** *n.* —*v.t.* **1.** to recover or regain. **2.** to make amends for; make good. **3.** (of hunting dogs) to fetch (killed or wounded game). **4.** to locate and read (data) from computer storage. —*v.i.* **5.** to retrieve game. —*n.* **6.** the act of retrieving. —**re•triev′al,** *n.*

ret•ro•ac•tive (re′trō ak′tiv), *adj.* effective as of a past date.

ret′ro•fit′ *v.t.,* **-fit•ted** or **-fit, -fit•ting.** to furnish (an automobile, airplane, etc.) with parts or equipment made available only after manufacture.

ret•ro•grade (re′trə grād′), *adj., v.,* **-grad•ed, -grad•ing.** —*adj.* **1.** moving backward. **2.** *Chiefly Biol.* exhibiting degeneration or deterioration. —*v.i.* **3.** to move backward. **4.** *Chiefly Biol.* to degenerate.

ret•ro•gress (re′trə gres′, re′trə gres′), *v.i.* to go backward, esp. into an earlier and usu. worse condition. —**ret′ro•gres′sion,** *n.* —**ret′ro•gres′sive,** *adj.*

ret•ro•spect (re′trə spekt′), *n.* contemplation of the past. —**ret′ro•spec′tive,** *adj., n.*

re•turn (ri tûrn′), *v.i.* **1.** to go or come back. **2.** to reply or retort. —*v.t.* **3.** to put, bring, take, give, or send back. **4.** to do or give in reciprocation, recompense, or requital. **5.** to yield (a profit, revenue, etc.). **6.** to report officially. **7.** to reelect, as to a legislative body. —*n.* **8.** the act of returning or fact of being returned. **9.** something returned. **10.** a recurrence. **11.** reciprocation, repayment, or requital. **12.** response or reply. **13.** Often, **-turns.** a yield or profit. **14.** a formal report of income and taxes due. **15.** Usu., **-turns.** a report on a count of votes or candidates elected. —*adj.* **16.** of or being a return. **17.** sent, given, or done in return. —**re•turn′a•ble,** *adj.*

re•turn•ee (ri tûr nē′, -tûr′nē), *n., pl.* **-ees.** a person who has returned, as from overseas military duty.

re•un•ion (rē yōōn′yən), *n.* **1.** the act of uniting again or state of being united again. **2.** a gathering of relatives, friends, or associates after separation.

rev (rev), *n., v.,* **revved, rev•ving.** —*n.* **1.** a revolution of a rotating part in an engine. —*v.t.* **2.** to accelerate sharply the speed of (an internal-combustion engine). [short for *revolution*]

Rev. **1.** Revelation; Revelations. **2.** Reverend.

re•vamp (rē vamp′), *v.t.* to renovate, revise, or restructure; redo.

re•veal (ri vēl′), *v.t.* **1.** to make known; disclose. **2.** to lay open to view; display.

rev•eil•le (rev′ə lē), *n.* a bugle call in the early morning to awaken military personnel.

rev•el (rev′al), *v.,* **-eled, -el•ing** or (*esp. Brit.*) **-elled, -el•ling,** *n.* —*v.i.* **1.** to take great pleasure; delight. **2.** to make merry. —*n.* **3.** boisterous merrymaking. —**rev′el•er;** *esp. Brit.,* **rev′el•ler,** *n.* —**rev′el•ry,** *n., pl.* **-ries.**

rev•e•la•tion (rev′ə lā′shən), *n.* **1.** the act of revealing. **2.** something revealed, esp. a striking or surprising disclosure. **3.** (*cap.*) Usu., **-tions.** the last book in the New Testament.

re•venge (ri venj′), *v.,* **-venged, -veng•ing,** *n.* —*v.t.* **1.** to inflict pain or harm in return for; avenge. —*n.* **2.** the act of revenging. **3.** something done in vengeance. **4.** the desire to revenge. —**re•venge′ful,** *adj.*

rev•e•nue (rev′ən yōō′, -ə nōō′), *n.* **1.** the income of a government from taxation and other sources. **2.** the return or yield from investments; income.

re•ver•ber•ate (ri vûr′bə rāt′), *v.i., v.t.,* **-at•ed, -at•ing.** **1.** to reecho or resound. **2.** to rebound or recoil. —**re•ver′ber•a′tion,** *n.*

re•vere (ri vēr′), *v.t.*, **-vered, -ver•ing.** to regard with respect tinged with awe; venerate.

rev•er•ence (rev′ər əns), *n., v.*, **-enced, -enc•ing.** —*n.* **1.** deep respect tinged with awe; veneration. **2.** a manifestation or gesture indicative of reverence. —*v.t.* **3.** to regard or treat with reverence. —**rev′er•ent, rev′er•en′tial** (-ə ren′shəl), *adj.*

rev•er•end *adj.* **1.** (*cap.*) (used as a title of respect prefixed to the name of a member of the clergy). **2.** worthy of being revered. —*n.* **3.** a member of the clergy.

rev•er•ie (rev′ə rē), *n., pl.* **-ies.** **1.** a state of dreamy meditation. **2.** a daydream.

re•verse (ri vûrs′), *adj., n., v.,* **-versed, -vers•ing.** —*adj.* **1.** opposite or contrary in position, direction, order, or character. **2.** with the back or rear part toward the observer. **3.** producing backward movement: *reverse gear.* —*n.* **4.** the opposite or contrary of something. **5.** the back or rear of something, as of a coin. **6.** an adverse change of fortune. **7.** a reversing mechanism. —*v.t.* **8.** to turn in an opposite position, direction, or order. **9.** to turn inside out or upside down. **10.** to cause (a mechanism) to run in a reverse direction. **11.** to revoke or annul (a decree, judgment, etc.). —*v.i.* **12.** to shift into reverse gear. **13.** to turn or move in the opposite or contrary direction. —**re•ver′sal,** *n.* —**re•vers′i•ble,** *adj.*

re•vert′ (-vûrt′), *v.i.* **1.** to return to a former habit, practice, belief, or condition. **2.** to return to a former owner or that person's heirs. **3.** to return to an ancestral type or characteristic. —**re•ver′sion** (-vûr′zhən), *n.*

re•view (ri vyoo′), *n.* **1.** a critical report, as on a book or play. **2.** the process of going over a subject again in study or recitation. **3.** a general survey, esp. in words. **4.** an inspection, esp. a formal military inspection. **5.** a periodical containing articles on current affairs, books, etc. **6.** a judicial reexamination, as by a higher court. —*v.t.* **7.** to go over (lessons, studies, etc.) in review. **8.** to inspect, esp. formally. **9.** to survey mentally. **10.** to evaluate in a critical review. **11.** to look back upon. **12.** to reexamine judicially. —**re•view′er,** *n.*

re•vile (ri vīl′), *v.t., v.i.,* **-viled, -vil•ing.** to speak (of) abusively.

re•vise (ri vīz′), *v.,* **-vised, -vis•ing,** *n.* —*v.t.* **1.** to amend or alter. **2.** to correct or improve (something written or printed). —*n.* **3.** a revised form of something. —**re•vi′sion** (-vizh′ən), *n.*

re•vi•sion•ism (ri vizh′ə niz′əm), *n.* advocacy of revision, esp. of some authoritative or generally accepted doctrine, theory, or practice. —**re•vi′sion•ist,** *n., adj.*

re•vi•tal•ize (rē vīt′l īz′), *v.t.,* **-ized, -iz•ing.** to give new life, vitality, or vigor to.

re•viv•al (ri vī′vəl), *n.* **1.** a new presentation of an old play or motion picture. **2.** an evangelistic service to effect a religious awakening. **3.** the act of reviving or state of being revived. —**re•viv′al•ist,** *n.*

re•vive′ *v.,* **-vived, -viv•ing.** —*v.t.* **1.** to restore to life, consciousness, or vigor. **2.** to present (an old play or motion picture) again. **3.** to bring back into use, acceptance, or currency. **4.** to renew in the mind. —*v.i.* **5.** to return to life, consciousness, or vigor.

re•viv′i•fy′ *v.t.,* **-fied, -fy•ing.** to give new life to.

re•voke (ri vōk′), *v.t.,* **-voked, -vok•ing.** to take back or withdraw; annul or cancel. —**rev•o•ca•ble** (rev′ə kə bəl), *adj.*

re•volt (ri vōlt′), *v.i.* **1.** to break away from or rise against constituted authority; rebel. **2.** to turn away in disgust or abhorrence. —*v.t.* **3.** to affect with disgust or abhorrence. —*n.* **4.** an uprising; rebellion. —**re•volt′ing,** *adj.*

rev•o•lu•tion (rev′ə loo′shən), *n.* **1.** the overthrow and replacement of an established government or political system by the people governed. **2.** a sudden, complete, or radical change. **3.** rotation on or as if on an axis. **4.** the orbiting of one heavenly body around another. **5.** a single cycle in a rotation or orbit. —**rev′o•lu′tion•ar′y,** *adj., n., pl.* **-ies.**

rev′o•lu′tion•ize′ *v.t.,* **-ized, -iz•ing.** to effect a radical change in.

re•volve (ri volv′), *v.,* **-volved, -volv•ing.** —*v.i.* **1.** to move in a circular course or orbit. **2.** to rotate. **3.** to occur in cycles; recur. —*v.t.* **4.** to cause to revolve. **5.** to turn over in the mind; consider.

re•volv′er *n.* a handgun with a revolving chambered cylinder for holding cartridges.

re•vue (ri vyoo′), *n.* a theatrical show featuring skits, dances, and songs.

re•vul•sion (ri vul′shən), *n.* **1.** a strong feeling of repugnance or distaste. **2.** a sudden and violent change of feeling or response.

re•ward (ri wôrd′), *n.* **1.** a sum of money offered, as for the recovery of lost property. **2.** something given or received in return for service, merit, etc. —*v.t.* **3.** to give a reward to or for.

re•ward′ing *adj.* affording satisfaction; gratifying.

re•word (rē wûrd′), *v.t.* to put into other words.

re•write′ *v.t.,* **-wrote, -writ•ten, -writ•ing. 1.** to write in a different form; revise. **2.** to write again. **3.** to write (news submitted by a reporter) for inclusion in a newspaper.

RFD rural free delivery.

rhap•so•dize (rap′sə dīz′), *v.i.,* **-dized, -diz•ing.** to talk with extravagant enthusiasm.

rhap′so•dy (-sə dē), *n., pl.* **-dies. 1.** a musical composition irregular in form and suggestive of improvisation. **2.** an ecstatic expression of feeling or enthusiasm. —**rhap•sod′ic** (-sod′ik), *adj.*

rhe•o•stat (rē′ə stat′), *n.* an adjustable resistor that controls the electric current in a circuit.

rhet•o•ric (ret′ər ik), *n.* **1.** the art of effectively using language in speech or writing. **2.** the use of exaggerated language; bombast.

rhetor′ical ques′tion *n.* a question asked for effect, not to elicit a reply.

rheu•ma•tism (roo′mə tiz′əm), *n.* any of several disorders characterized by pain and stiffness in the joints or muscles. —**rheu•mat′ic** (-mat′ik), *adj., n.*

Rh factor (är′āch′), *n.* an antigen present in blood cells that may induce a severe reaction in an individual lacking the antigen. [so called because first found in the blood of *rhesus* monkeys]

rhine•stone (rīn′stōn′), *n.* an artificial gemstone of brilliant glass or paste, esp. one cut in imitation of a diamond.

rhi•noc•er•os (rī nos′ər əs), *n., pl.* **-os•es, -os.** a large, thick-skinned mammal of Africa and Asia, with one or two upright horns on the snout.

rhi•zome (rī′zōm), *n.* a rootlike stem that usu. produces roots below and sends up shoots from the upper surface.

rho•do•den•dron (rō′də den′drən), *n.* an evergreen shrub or tree with showy pink, purple, or white flowers.

rhom•boid (rom′boid), *n.* an oblique-angled parallelogram with only the opposite sides equal.

rhom′bus (-bəs), *n., pl.* **-bus•es, -bi** (-bī). an equilateral parallelogram with oblique angles.

rhu•barb (roo′bärb), *n.* **1.** a plant with edible leafstalks often used in making pies. **2.** *Slang.* a quarrel or squabble.

rhyme (rīm), *n., v.,* **rhymed, rhym•ing.** —*n.* **1.** identity in terminal sounds of words or lines of verse. **2.** a word agreeing with another in terminal sound. **3.** verse or poetry having correspondence in the terminal sounds of the lines. —*v.t.* **4.** to turn into rhyme. **5.** to use as a rhyme. —*v.i.* **6.** to make rhymes. **7.** to form a rhyme.

rhythm (rith′əm), *n.* **1.** movement or procedure with uniform or patterned recurrence of an element. **2.** the pattern of pulses in music resulting from the occurrence of strong and weak melodic and harmonic beats. **3.** the pattern of recurrent strong and weak accents and long and short syllables in speech. —**rhyth′mic** (-mik), **rhyth′mi•cal,** *adj.*

RI or **R.I.,** Rhode Island.

rib¹ (rib), *n., v.,* **ribbed, rib•bing.** —*n.* **1.** one of a series of curved bones that are attached to the spine, occur in pairs, and form the thoracic wall. **2.** something resembling a rib: *the ribs of an umbrella.* **3.** a ridge in cloth, esp. in knitted fabrics. —*v.t.* **4.**

to furnish or strengthen with ribs. **5.** to mark with riblike ridges or markings.

rib² (rib), *v.t.*, **ribbed, rib•bing.** to make fun of; tease. —**rib′ber,** *n.*

rib•ald (rib′əld; *spelling pron.* rī′bəld), *adj.* vulgar or indecent, as in language; coarse. —**rib′ald•ry,** *n.*

rib•bon (rib′ən), *n.* **1.** a woven strip or band of fine material used esp. for ornament. **2. ribbons,** torn or ragged strips; shreds: *torn to ribbons.* **3.** a band of inked material, as that used in a typewriter.

ri•bo•fla•vin (rī′bō flā′-, -bə-), *n.* a vitamin B complex factor essential for growth and abundant in milk, meat, eggs, and leafy vegetables.

rice (rīs), *n., v.,* **riced, ric•ing.** —*n.* **1.** the edible starchy seeds or grain of a grass cultivated in warm climates. —*v.t.* **2.** to reduce to a form resembling rice: *to rice potatoes.* —**ric′er,** *n.*

rich (rich), *adj.,* **-er, -est,** *n.* —*adj.* **1.** abundantly supplied with resources, means, or funds; wealthy. **2.** abounding: *rich in beauty.* **3.** of great value or worth; costly. **4.** abounding in sugar or fat. **5.** (of color) deep or vivid. **6.** full and mellow in tone. **7.** producing or yielding abundantly. **8.** abundant; plentiful. —*n.* **9. the rich,** rich persons collectively.

rich′es *n.pl.* abundant and valuable possessions.

Rich′ter scale′ (rik′tər), *n.* a logarithmic scale for indicating the intensity of an earthquake. [after C. F. *Richter* (1900–85), U.S. seismologist]

rick (rik), *n.* a large stack of hay, straw, etc., in a field.

rick•ets (rik′its), *n.* a childhood disease in which the bones soften from an inadequate intake of vitamin D.

rick•et•y (rik′i tē), *adj.,* **-i•er, -i•est. 1.** likely to fall or collapse; shaky. **2.** affected with rickets.

rick•shaw (rik′shô, -shä), *n.* JINRIKISHA.

ric•o•chet (rik′ə shā′), *n., v.,* **-cheted** (-shād′), **-chet•ing** (-shā′ing). —*n.* **1.** the rebound of an object after it hits a glancing blow against a surface. —*v.i.* **2.** to move with or as if with ricochets.

ri•cot•ta (ri kot′ə, -kô′tə), *n., pl.* **-tas.** a soft Italian cheese that resembles cottage cheese.

rid (rid), *v.t.,* **rid** or **rid•ded, rid•ding. 1.** to free of something objectionable. —*Idiom.* **2. be** or **get rid of,** to be or become free of.

rid•dle¹ (rid′l), *n.* **1.** a question requiring ingenuity to be answered. **2.** a puzzling thing or person.

rid•dle² (rid′l), *v.t.,* **-dled, -dling.** to pierce with or as if with many holes.

ride (rīd), *v.,* **rode, rid•den, rid•ing,** *n.* —*v.i.* **1.** to be carried on the back of an animal or in a vehicle. **2.** to move along as if by vehicle. **3.** to continue without interruption or interference. **4.** to turn or rest on something. **5.** to float or seem to float. **6.** to lie at anchor. —*v.t.* **7.** to sit on and manage (a horse, bicycle, etc.) so as to be carried along. **8.** to be carried along on: *The ship rode the waves.* **9.** to ride over, along, or through (a road, region, etc.). **10.** to ridicule or harass. **11.** to control or dominate: *a man ridden by fear.* —*n.* **12.** a journey on a horse, camel, etc., or in a vehicle. **13.** a vehicle or device, as a roller coaster, on which people ride for amusement.

rid′er *n.* **1.** a person who rides. **2.** an additional, usu. unrelated clause attached to a legislative bill. **3.** an addition or amendment to a document.

ridge (rij), *n., v.,* **ridged, ridg•ing.** —*n.* **1.** a long, narrow elevation of land. **2.** a long, narrow upper edge, as of a wave; crest. **3.** a raised, narrow strip, as on cloth. **4.** the horizontal line in which the tops of the rafters of a roof meet. —*v.t.,* *v.i.* **5.** to provide with or form ridges. —**ridg′y,** *adj.,* **-i•er, -i•est.**

rid•i•cule (rid′i kyōōl′), *n., v.,* **-culed, -cul•ing.** —*n.* **1.** speech or action intended to cause contemptuous laughter; derision. —*v.t.* **2.** to make fun of.

ri•dic•u•lous (ri dik′yə ləs), *adj.* causing or worthy of ridicule; laughable. —**ri•dic′u•lous•ly,** *adv.*

rife (rīf), *adj.* **1.** of common or frequent occurrence; prevalent. **2.** abundant; abounding.

riff (rif), *n.* **1.** a constantly repeated melodic phrase in jazz or rock music. —*v.i.* **2.** to perform a riff.

riff•raff (rif′raf′), *n.* the lowest classes; rabble.

ri•fle¹ (rī′fal), *n., v.,* **-fled, -fling.** —*n.* **1.** a shoulder firearm with a rifled bore. —*v.t.* **2.** to cut spiral grooves within (a gun barrel, pipe, etc.).

ri•fle² (rī′fal), *v.t.,* **-fled, -fling.** to ransack and rob.

rift (rift), *n.* **1.** a fissure; cleft. **2.** a break in friendly relations. **3.** Geol. a fault. —*v.t.,* *v.i.* **4.** to burst open; split.

rig (rig), *v.,* **rigged, rig•ging,** *n.* —*v.t.* **1.** to fit (a ship, mast, etc.) with rigging. **2.** to furnish with equipment or clothing. **3.** to assemble or install. **4.** to manipulate fraudulently. —*n.* **5.** the arrangement of masts, spars, and sails on a ship. **6.** apparatus; equipment. **7.** a tractor-trailer. **8.** a carriage with its horse. **9.** costume; clothing.

rig′ging *n.* **1.** the ropes, chains, and tackle used to support and work the masts, sails, etc., of a ship. **2.** lifting or hauling tackle.

right (rīt), *adj.* **1.** in accordance with what is good, proper, or just. **2.** in conformity with fact or reason; correct. **3.** appropriate; suitable; desirable. **4.** of or located on the side of a person or thing that is turned toward the east when the subject is facing north. **5.** sound; sane. **6.** principal, front, or upper: *right side up.* **7.** (*often cap.*) of or belonging to the political Right. —*n.* **8.** something to which a person is entitled, as by just claim or legal guarantee. **9.** that which is morally, legally, or ethically proper. **10.** the right side. **11.** a right-hand turn. **12. the Right,** those individuals or groups holding conservative or reactionary political views. —*adv.* **13.** in a straight or direct line. **14.** quite; completely. **15.** immediately; promptly. **16.** exactly; precisely. **17.** correctly or accurately. **18.** righteously; properly. **19.** on or to the right. **20.** (*often cap.*) very (used in certain titles): *the right reverend.* —*v.t.* **21.** to put in an upright position. **22.** to bring into conformity with fact. **23.** to redress. —*Idiom.* **24. right away** or **off,** without hesitation; immediately. **25. right on,** *Slang.* exactly right. —**right′ly,** *adv.*

right′ an′gle *n.* an angle of 90°.

right•eous (rī′chəs), *adj.* **1.** acting in an upright, moral way. **2.** morally right or justifiable: *righteous indignation.* —**right′eous•ly,** *adv.* —**right′eous•ness,** *n.*

right′ful *adj.* **1.** having or held by a valid or just claim; legitimate. **2.** equitable or just. —**right′ful•ly,** *adv.*

right′-hand′ed *adj.* **1.** using the right hand or arm more easily than the left. **2.** adapted to or performed by the right hand. —*adv.* **3.** with the right hand.

right′ of way′ or **right′-of-way′,** *n., pl.* **rights of way, right of ways** or **rights-of-way, right-of-ways. 1.** the right of a vehicle to proceed ahead of another. **2.** a right of passage over another's land. **3.** land acquired by a railroad for tracks. **4.** land covered by a public road.

right′-to-life′ *adj.* pertaining to or advocating laws making abortion illegal.

right′ wing′ *n.* the conservative or reactionary element in a political party or organization. —**right′-wing′,** *adj.* —**right′-wing′er,** *n.*

rig•id (rij′id), *adj.* **1.** not pliant; stiff. **2.** firmly fixed or set. **3.** strict; severe. —**ri•gid′i•ty,** *n.* —**rig′id•ly,** *adv.*

rig•ma•role (rig′mə rōl′) *n.* **1.** a complicated procedure. **2.** confused or meaningless talk.

rig•or (rig′ər), *n.* **1.** the quality of being strict; inflexibility. **2.** harshness, as of attitude; severity. **3.** hardship; austerity. **4.** scrupulous accuracy; precision. Also, *esp. Brit.,* **rig′our.** —**rig′or•ous,** *adj.* —**rig′or•ous•ly,** *adv.*

rig•or mor•tis (rig′ər môr′tis), *n.* the stiffening of the body after death.

rile (rīl), *v.t.,* **riled, ril•ing. 1.** to irritate; vex. **2.** to make turbulent; roil.

rill (ril), *n.* a small rivulet or brook.

rim (rim), *n., v.,* **rimmed, rim•ming.** —*n.* **1.** the outer, often curved edge of something. **2.** the outer circle of a wheel. —*v.t.* **3.** to furnish with a rim.

rime¹ (rīm), *n.* FROST (def. 2). —**rim′y,** *adj.,* **-i•er, -i•est.**

rime² (rīm), *n., v.t., v.i.,* **rimed, rim•ing.** RHYME.

rind (rīnd), *n.* a thick and firm outer coat or covering: *watermelon rind.*

ring[1] (ring), *n.* **1.** a circular band, as of gold, worn on the finger esp. as an ornament. **2.** something shaped like a ring. **3.** a circular line, mark, or course. **4.** a number of persons or things situated in a circle. **5.** an enclosed area, often circular, for a sports contest or exhibition: *a circus ring.* **6.** the sport of boxing. **7.** a group of persons cooperating for unethical or illegal purposes. —*v.t.* **8.** to surround with a ring. **9.** to form into a ring. —*Idiom.* **10. run rings around,** to surpass; outdo.

ring[2] (ring), *v.,* **rang, rung, ring•ing,** *n.* —*v.i.* **1.** to give forth a clear resonant sound. **2.** to cause a bell to sound, esp. as a signal. **3.** to resound; reecho. **4.** (of the ears) to have the sensation of a continued ringing sound. **5.** to seem to be; appear: *a story that rings true.* —*v.t.* **6.** to cause to ring. **7.** to announce by or as if by the sound of a bell. **8.** to telephone. **9. ring up,** to register (the amount of a sale) on a cash register. —*n.* **10.** a ringing sound. **11.** a sound like that of a ringing bell: *the ring of laughter.* **12.** a telephone call. **13.** an act or instance of ringing a bell. **14.** a characteristic sound or quality: *the ring of truth.* —*Idiom.* **15. ring a bell,** to evoke a memory.

ring′er[1], *n.* a quoit or horseshoe thrown so as to encircle the peg.

ring′er[2], *n.* **1.** one that rings or makes a ringing noise. **2.** a person that closely resembles another. **3.** a racehorse or athlete entered in a competition under false representation.

ring′lead′er *n.* a person who leads others, esp. in unlawful activities.

ring′let (-lit), *n.* a curled lock of hair.

ring′mas′ter *n.* a person in charge of the performances in a circus ring.

ring′worm′ *n.* a contagious skin disease caused by a fungus and characterized by ring-shaped patches.

rink (ringk), *n.* **1.** a smooth expanse of ice for ice-skating. **2.** a smooth floor, usu. of wood, for roller-skating.

rinse (rins), *v.,* **rinsed, rins•ing,** *n.* —*v.t.* **1.** to wash lightly, as by dipping in water. **2.** to drench in clean water as a final stage in washing. **3.** to remove (soap, dirt, etc.) by rinsing. —*n.* **4.** an act or instance of rinsing. **5.** the water used for rinsing. **6.** a preparation used, esp. after washing, to tint or condition the hair.

ri•ot (rī′ət), *n.* **1.** a noisy, violent public disorder. **2.** disturbance of the public peace. **3.** a profuse outpouring or display. **4.** something or someone hilariously funny. —*v.i.* **5.** to take part in a riot. —**ri′ot•er,** *n.* —**ri′ot•ous,** *adj.*

rip (rip), *v.,* **ripped, rip•ping,** *n.* —*v.t.* **1.** to cut or tear apart roughly. **2.** to tear away or off in a rough manner. **3.** to saw (wood) in the direction of the grain. —*v.i.* **4.** to become torn apart. **5.** to move with great speed. **6. rip into,** to attack physically or verbally. **7. ~ off,** *Slang.* **a.** to steal. **b.** to steal from or exploit. —*n.* **8.** a tear made by ripping.

R.I.P. may he, she, or they rest in peace. [< L *requiēsca(n)t in pāce*]

rip′ cord′ *n.* a cord that when pulled opens a parachute.

ripe (rīp), *adj.,* **rip•er, rip•est. 1.** completely matured and developed: *ripe grain; a ripe peach.* **2.** sufficiently aged for use, as cheese. **3.** ready, as for action or use. **4.** ready enough; auspicious: *The time is ripe for a new policy.* —**ripe′ly,** *adv.* —**rip′en,** *v.t., v.i.* —**ripe′ness,** *n.*

rip′-off′ *n. Slang.* **1.** a theft or exploitation. **2.** a copy; imitation.

ri•poste (ri pōst′), *n.* **1.** a quick, sharp reply or reaction. **2.** *Fencing.* a quick thrust given after parrying a lunge.

rip•ple (rip′əl), *v.,* **-pled, -pling,** *n.* —*v.i.* **1.** (of a liquid surface) to form small waves. **2.** (of sound) to move with a rising and falling tone or inflection. —*v.t.* **3.** to form small waves on. —*n.* **4.** a small wave. **5.** a sound as of water rippling: *a ripple of laughter.*

rip′-roar′ing *adj.* boisterously wild and exciting; riotous.

rip′saw′ *n.* a saw for cutting wood with the grain.

rip′tide′ *n.* a tide that opposes other tides, causing a violent disturbance in the sea.

rise (rīz), *v.,* **rose, ris•en** (riz′ən), **ris•ing,** *n.* —*v.i.* **1.** to get up from a lying, sitting, or kneeling posture. **2.** to get up from bed. **3.** to revolt or rebel. **4.** to come into existence. **5.** to move from a lower to a higher position; ascend. **6.** to ascend above the horizon, as the sun. **7.** to extend or slope upward. **8.** to attain a higher level, as of importance. **9.** to prove oneself equal to a demand or emergency: *rose to the occasion.* **10.** to increase, as in amount or intensity. **11.** to puff up, as dough. **12.** to return from the dead. —*n.* **13.** an act or instance of rising. **14.** an increase or elevation, as in amount. **15.** origin or beginning. **16.** extension upward. **17.** upward slope, as of ground. **18.** a piece of rising ground.

risk (risk), *n.* **1.** exposure to the chance of injury or loss; danger. —*v.t.* **2.** to expose to the chance of injury or loss; hazard. **3.** to take the chance of. —**risk′y,** *adj.,* **-i•er, -i•est.**

ris•qué (ri skā′), *adj.* daringly close to indelicacy or impropriety.

rite (rīt), *n.* a formal ceremony or act prescribed or customary in religious use.

rite′ of pas′sage *n.* an act or event marking a passage from one stage of life to another.

rit•u•al (rich′ōō əl), *n.* **1.** an established procedure for a religious rite. **2.** a practice or pattern of behavior regularly performed in a set manner. —*adj.* **3.** of, being, or practiced as a ritual. —**rit′u•al•is′tic,** *adj.* —**rit′u•al•ly,** *adv.*

ri•val (rī′vəl), *n., adj., v.,* **-valed, -val•ing** or (*esp. Brit.*) **-valled, -val•ling.** —*n.* **1.** a person who competes with or tries to outdo another. **2.** a person or thing that equals another. —*adj.* **3.** competing. —*v.t.* **4.** to prove to be a worthy rival of. **5.** to equal (another); match. **6.** to compete with. —**ri′val•ry,** *n., pl.* **-ries.**

riv•er (riv′ər), *n.* a fairly large natural stream of water.

riv•et (riv′it), *n., v.,* **-et•ed, -et•ing** or (*esp. Brit.*) **-et•ted, -et•ting.** —*n.* **1.** a metal pin for passing through holes in two or more pieces to hold them together, usu. made with a head at one end. —*v.t.* **2.** to fasten with a rivet. **3.** to hold (the eye, attention, etc.) firmly. —**riv′et•er,** *n.*

riv•u•let (riv′yə lit), *n.* a small stream.

Rn *Chem. Symbol.* radon.

RN or **R.N.,** registered nurse.

roach (rōch), *n.* **1.** a cockroach. **2.** *Slang.* the butt of a marijuana cigarette.

road (rōd), *n.* **1.** an open way for passage or travel, as by motor vehicle. **2.** a way or course. **3.** Often, **roads.** a sheltered place where ships may ride or anchor. —*Idiom.* **4. down the road,** at some future time. **5. on the road,** traveling or touring.

road′block′ *n.* **1.** an obstruction placed across a road for halting or hindering traffic. **2.** an obstruction to progress.

road′run′ner *n.* a large terrestrial cuckoo of the western U.S.

roam (rōm), *v.i., v.t.* to walk or travel (over or through) without purpose or direction; wander. —**roam′er,** *n.*

roan (rōn), *adj.* **1.** (chiefly of horses) of the color sorrel, chestnut, or bay sprinkled with gray or white. —*n.* **2.** an animal with a roan coat.

roar (rôr), *v.i.* **1.** to utter a loud, deep, extended sound. **2.** to laugh loudly. **3.** to make a loud din, as thunder. —*v.t.* **4.** to utter or express in a roar. —*n.* **5.** a roaring sound.

roast (rōst), *v.t.* **1.** to cook (food) by dry heat, as in an oven. **2.** to parch (coffee beans, chestnuts, etc.) by exposure to heat. **3.** to heat excessively. **4.** to criticize severely. —*v.i.* **5.** to roast food. **6.** to undergo the process of becoming roasted. —*n.* **7.** a piece of meat for roasting. **8.** something roasted. **9.** an outdoor get-together at which food is roasted. —*adj.* **10.** roasted: *roast beef.* —**roast′er,** *n.*

rob (rob), *v.,* **robbed, rob•bing.** —*v.t.* **1.** to steal from. **2.** to deprive of something unjustly or injuriously. —*v.i.* **3.** to commit robbery. —**rob′ber,** *n.* —**rob′ber•y,** *n., pl.* **-ies.**

robe (rōb), *n., v.,* **robed, rob•ing.** —*n.* **1.** a long, loose or flowing outer garment, esp. one worn as ceremonial dress. **2.** a bathrobe or dressing gown. **3.** a piece of fur or fabric used as a blanket or wrap. —*v.t., v.i.* **4.** to clothe with or put on a robe.

rob•in (rob′in), *n.* **1.** a large North American thrush with a chestnut-red breast. **2.** any of several small Old World birds with a reddish breast.

ro•bot (rō′bət, -bot), *n.* **1.** a machine that resembles a human and does mechanical, routine tasks on command. **2.** a person who acts and responds in a mechanical, routine manner. **3.** an automatic machine or device. [coined by Karel Čapek (1890–1938), Czech playwright, in his play *R.U.R.*, from Czech *robota* labor] —**ro•bot′ic,** *adj.*

ro•bot′ics *n.* the technology connected with using computer-controlled robots.

ro•bust (rō bust′, rō′bust), *adj.* **1.** strong and healthy; vigorous. **2.** rich and full-bodied: *a robust flavor.*

rock¹ (rok), *n.* **1. a.** a large mass of stone. **b.** a piece of stone. **2.** mineral matter assembled in masses in nature. **3.** something resembling a rock, as in firmness or support. **4.** *Slang.* a diamond. —**Idiom. 5. on the rocks, a.** *Informal.* ruined or destroyed. **b.** (of an alcoholic beverage) served over ice cubes. —**rock′y,** *adj.,* **-i•er, -i•est.**

rock² (rok), *v.i., v.t.* **1.** to move to and fro or from side to side. **2.** to shake or disturb violently. —*n.* **3.** a rocking movement. **4.** popular music derived from blues and folk music and marked by an accented beat.

rock′ bot′tom *n.* the very lowest level.

rock′er (rok′ər), *n.* **1.** one of the curved pieces on which a cradle or a rocking chair rocks. **2.** Also called **rock′ing chair′.** a chair mounted on rockers. —**Idiom. 3. off one's rocker,** *Slang.* insane; crazy.

rock•et (rok′it), *n.* **1.** any of various tubelike devices containing combustibles that on being ignited propel the tube through the air. **2.** a space capsule or vehicle put into orbit by a rocket. **3.** an engine with its own solid or liquid fuel and oxidizer. —*v.i., v.t.* **4.** to move like or by a rocket.

rock′et•ry *n.* the science of rocket design, development, and flight.

rock′ salt′ *n.* common salt occurring in rocklike masses.

ro•co•co (rə kō′kō, rō′kə kō′), *n.* **1.** an artistic style marked by studied elegance and delicate ornamentation. —*adj.* **2.** of or characteristic of rococo. **3.** ornate or florid.

rod (rod), *n.* **1.** a straight bar or stick. **2. a.** a stick for measuring. **b.** a unit of linear measure, 5½ yards (5.03 m). **3.** a stick used as an instrument of punishment. **4.** punishment. **5.** a staff or scepter carried as a symbol of office or authority. **6.** FISHING ROD. **7.** *Slang.* a pistol or revolver.

ro•dent (rōd′nt), *adj.* **1.** of or being a gnawing or nibbling mammal characterized by four continually growing incisors. —*n.* **2.** a rodent mammal, as a mouse.

ro•de•o (rō′dē ō′, rō dā′ō), *n., pl.* **-os. 1.** a public exhibition of cowboy skills. **2.** a roundup of cattle.

roe¹ (rō), *n.* the eggs of a fish.

roe² (rō), *n., pl.* **roes, roe.** a small, agile Eurasian deer with three-pointed antlers.

rog•er (roj′ər), *interj.* **1.** *Informal.* all right; OK. **2.** message received and understood (a response to radio communications).

rogue (rōg), *n.* **1.** a dishonest person; scoundrel. **2.** a playfully mischievous person. —**ro′guer•y,** *n.* —**ro′guish,** *adj.*

roil (roil), *v.t.* **1.** to make (a fluid) cloudy by stirring up sediment. **2.** to disturb or disquiet; irritate.

role or **rôle** (rōl), *n.* **1.** a part or character played by an actor or singer. **2.** the proper or customary function of a person or thing.

role′ mod′el *n.* a person whose behavior is imitated by others.

roll (rōl), *v.i.* **1.** to move along a surface by turning

over and over. **2.** to move on wheels. **3.** to advance with an undulating motion, as waves. **4.** to extend in undulations, as land. **5.** to elapse, as time. **6.** to move as in a cycle, as seasons. **7.** to make a deep, prolonged sound, as thunder. **8.** (of the eyes) to rotate. **9.** (of a ship) to rock from side to side in open water. **10.** to walk with a swinging gait. —*v.t.* **11.** to cause to move along a surface by turning over and over. **12.** to move along on wheels. **13.** to utter or give forth with a full, continuous sound. **14.** to trill: *He rolls his r's.* **15.** to cause to turn over. **16.** to rotate, as the eyes. **17.** to cause to rock from side to side. **18.** to wrap around an axis or around itself; wind. **19.** to wrap or envelop, as in a covering. **20.** to spread out or flatten, as with a rolling pin. **21.** to throw (dice). **22. roll back,** to reduce (prices, wages, etc.) to a former level. **23. ~ over,** to reinvest (funds). —*n.* **24.** something, as a piece of parchment, that is rolled up. **25.** a register or list, as of members. **26.** something rolled up in a cylindrical form. **27.** a rounded mass: *rolls of fat.* **28.** a small cake of bread sometimes folded over before baking. **29.** an act or instance of rolling. **30.** a deep, prolonged sound, as of thunder. **31.** a rolling motion or gait.

roll′back′ *n.* a return to a lower level, as of prices.

roll′ call′ *n.* the calling of a list of names for checking attendance.

Roll′er•blade′ *v.,* **-blad•ed, -blad•ing. 1.** *Trademark.* a brand of in-line skates. —*v.i.* **2.** (*often l.c.*) to skate on in-line skates.

roll′er coast′er *n.* a small railroad, esp. in an amusement park, that moves along a high, sharply winding trestle with steep inclines.

roll′er skate′ *n.* a skate with wheels for use on a surface such as a sidewalk. —**roll′er-skate′,** *v.i.,* **-skat•ed, -skat•ing.**

rol′lick•ing (rol′i king) *adj.* carefree and joyous.

roll′o′ver *n.* the reinvestment of funds.

roll′-top desk′ *n.* a desk with a flexible sliding cover for the working surface.

ro•ly-po•ly (rō′lē pō′lē, -pō′lē), *adj.* short and plumply round.

ROM (rom), *n.* read-only memory: nonmodifiable computer memory containing programmed instructions to the system.

Rom. 1. Roman. **2.** Also, **Rom** Romance. **3.** Romania. **4.** Romanian.

ro•maine (rō mān′, rə-), *n.* a variety of lettuce with a cylindrical head of long, loose leaves.

Ro•man (rō′mən), *adj.* **1.** of or typical of ancient or modern Rome or its inhabitants. **2.** (*usu. l.c.*) of or noting the upright style of printing types most commonly used. **3.** of the Roman Catholic Church. —*n.* **4.** a native, inhabitant, or citizen of ancient or modern Rome. **5.** (*usu. l.c.*) roman type or lettering.

Ro′man can′dle *n.* a firework consisting of a tube that sends out sparks and balls of fire.

Ro′man Cath′olic Church′ *n.* the Christian church of which the pope is the supreme head.

ro•mance (*n., adj.* rō mans′, rō′mans; *v.* rō-mans′), *n., v.,* **-manced, -manc•ing.** —*n.* **1.** a story depicting heroic or marvelous deeds, pageantry, and romantic exploits. **2.** a medieval narrative treating of heroic, fantastic, or supernatural events. **3.** a romantic spirit, sentiment, or quality. **4.** a love affair. —*v.i.* **5.** to indulge in fanciful stories or daydreams. —*v.t.* **6.** to court romantically. —*adj.* **7.** (*cap.*) of or noting the languages descended from Latin, including French, Spanish, Portuguese, Italian, and Romanian.

Ro•ma•ni•a (rō mā′nē ə), *n.* a republic in SE Europe. —**Ro•ma′ni•an,** *n., adj.*

Roman numerals *n.pl.* system of numbers using letters as symbols: I = 1, V = 5, X = 10, L = 50, C = 100, D = 500, M = 1,000.

ro•man•tic (rō man′tik), *adj.* **1.** of or marked by romance. **2.** impractical or unrealistic. **3.** imbued with idealism; utopian. **4.** preoccupied with love or by the idealizing of love. **5.** passionate; fervent. **6.** (*often cap.*) of or characteristic of a style of literature and art that subordinates form to content and emphasizes imagination and emotion. —*n.* **7.** a romantic person. —**ro•man′ti•cal•ly,** *adv.*

ro•man′ti•cism (-tə siz′əm), *n.* (*often cap.*) the Romantic style in literature and art.

ro•man′ti•cize′ *v.,* **-cized, -ciz•ing.** —*v.t.* **1.** to invest with a romantic character. —*v.i.* **2.** to hold romantic notions.

romp (romp), *v.i.* **1.** to play in a lively or boisterous manner; frolic. **2.** to win easily. —*n.* **3.** a lively or boisterous frolic. **4.** an easy victory.

romp′ers *n.pl.* a one-piece children's garment combining a shirt and short, bloomerlike pants.

rood (rō̄d), *n.* **1.** a crucifix, esp. a large one. **2.** a unit of land measure equal to 40 square rods or ¹⁄₄ acre.

roof (rōōf, rŏŏf), *n.* **1.** the external upper covering of a building. **2.** something like a roof in form or function. —*v.t.* **3.** to provide with a roof. —**roof′er,** *n.*

rook¹ (rŏŏk), *n.* **1.** a black, bare-faced Eurasian crow. —*v.t.* **2.** to cheat or swindle.

rook² (rŏŏk), *n.* a chess piece that may move any number of unobstructed squares horizontally or vertically.

rook′ie *n., pl.* **-ies. 1.** an inexperienced recruit. **2.** a novice; beginner.

room (rōōm, rŏŏm), *n.* **1.** an enclosed or partitioned portion of space within a building. **2. rooms,** lodgings or quarters. **3.** the persons present in a room. **4.** an extent of space occupied by or available for something. **5.** opportunity or scope: *room for improvement.* —*v.i.* **6.** to occupy rooms; lodge. —**room′er,** *n.* —**room′mate′,** *n.* —**room′y,** *adj.,* **-i•er, -i•est.**

roost (rōōst), *n.* **1.** a perch upon which birds or fowl rest at night. —*v.i.* **2.** to sit or rest on or as if on a roost.

roost′er *n.* the male of the domestic fowl.

root¹ (rōōt, rŏŏt), *n.* **1.** a plant part that grows downward into the soil, anchoring the plant and absorbing nutriment and moisture. **2.** any underground plant part, as a rhizome. **3.** the embedded portion of a hair, tooth, nail, etc. **4.** a fundamental or essential part. **5.** a source or origin. **6.** a quantity that when multiplied by itself a certain number of times produces a given quantity. **7.** a morpheme that underlies an inflectional or derivational paradigm, as *dance,* the root in *danced* and *dancer.* —*v.i.* **8.** to become fixed or established. —*v.t.* **9.** to fix by or as if by roots. **10.** to pull, tear, or dig up by the roots. **11.** to remove completely; extirpate. —**root′less,** *adj.*

root² (rōōt, rŏŏt), *v.i.* **1.** to turn up the soil with the snout. **2.** to poke, pry, or search. —*v.t.* **3.** to turn over with the snout.

root³ (rōōt *or, sometimes,* rŏŏt), *v.i.* **1.** to encourage a team or contestant by cheering enthusiastically. **2.** to lend moral support. —**root′er,** *n.*

root′ beer′ *n.* a carbonated beverage flavored with extracts of roots, barks, and herbs.

root′ canal′ *n.* the root portion of the pulp cavity of a tooth.

rope (rōp), *n., v.,* **roped, rop•ing.** —*n.* **1.** a strong line or cord of twisted or braided strands, as of hemp. **2. ropes,** the operations of a business or the details of an undertaking: *to learn the ropes.* **3.** a hangman's noose. **4.** material or objects twisted or strung together in the form of a cord. —*v.t.* **5.** to tie, bind, or fasten with a rope. **6.** to enclose or mark with a rope. **7.** to catch with a lasso. **8. rope in,** to lure, esp. by trickery.

Roque•fort (rōk′fərt), *Trademark.* a strong-flavored cheese veined with mold, made from sheep's milk.

ro•sa•ry (rō′zə rē), *n., pl.* **-ries. 1.** a series of prayers recited by Roman Catholics as a private devotion. **2.** a string of beads used in counting these prayers. [< ML *rosārium* rose garden]

rose (rōz), *n.* **1.** any of various prickly-stemmed shrubs with showy, often fragrant flowers. **2.** the flower of a rose. **3.** a pinkish red, purplish pink, or light crimson. **4.** an ornament shaped like a rose. —*adj.* **5.** of the color rose.

ro•sé (rō zā′), *n.* a pink wine.

rose•mar•y (rōz′mâr′ē, -mə rē), *n., pl.* **-ies.** an aromatic evergreen shrub of the mint family, with leaves used as a seasoning and in perfumes.

ro•sette (rō zet′), *n.* **1.** a rose-shaped ornament or badge, esp. of ribbon. **2.** an architectural ornament resembling a rose.

ros•ter (ros′tər), *n.* a list of persons or groups, as of military personnel.

ros•trum (ros′trəm), *n., pl.* **-trums, -tra** (-trə). a platform or stage for public speaking.

ros•y (rō′zē), *adj.,* **-i•er, i•est. 1.** pink or pinkish red; roseate. **2.** bright or promising: *a rosy future.* —**ros′i•ly,** *adv.*

rot (rot), *v.,* **rot•ted, rot•ting,** *n.* —*v.i., v.t.* **1.** to undergo or cause to undergo decomposition; decay. —*n.* **2.** the process of rotting. **3.** the state of being rotten. **4.** rotting or rotten matter. **5.** an animal or plant disease caused by a fungal or bacterial infection and characterized by decay.

ro•tate (rō′tāt), *v.i., v.t.,* **-tat•ed, -tat•ing. 1.** to turn around on or as if on an axis; revolve. **2.** to proceed or cause to proceed in a fixed routine of succession. —**ro•ta′tion,** *n.*

ROTC (är′ō tē sē′, rot′sē), Reserve Officers Training Corps.

rote (rōt), *n.* **1.** a fixed, habitual, or mechanical course of procedure. —*Idiom.* **2. by rote,** from memory, without thought of the meaning.

ro•tis•ser•ie (rō tis′ə rē), *n., pl.* **-ies.** a cooking unit with a spit for barbecuing.

ro•tor (rō′tər), *n.* **1.** a rotating member of a mechanical or electrical device. **2.** a system of rotating airfoils, as the horizontal ones of a helicopter.

ro•to•till•er (rō′tə til′ər), *n.* a motorized device with spinning blades for tilling soil.

rot•ten (rot′n), *adj.,* **-er, -est. 1.** having rotted. **2.** foul-smelling; putrid. **3.** morally offensive; corrupt. **4.** wretchedly bad; miserable. —**rot′ten•ness,** *n.*

ro•tund (rō tund′), *adj.* **1.** rounded. **2.** plump. **3.** full-toned; sonorous.

ro•tun•da (rō tun′də), *n., pl.* **-das. 1.** a round building, esp. one with a dome. **2.** a large circular hall or room.

rou•é (rōō ā′, rōō′ā), *n., pl.* **-és.** a licentious man; rake. [< F]

rouge (rōōzh), *n., v.,* **rouged, roug•ing.** —*n.* **1.** a red cosmetic for coloring the cheeks or lips. **2.** a reddish powder used for polishing metal, glass, and gems. —*v.t., v.i.* **3.** to use rouge (on).

rough (ruf), *adj.,* **rough•er, rough•est,** *n., adv., v.,* **roughed, rough•ing.** —*adj.* **1.** having a coarse or uneven surface. **2.** shaggy or coarse. **3.** characterized by violence. **4.** characterized by turbulence. **5.** tempestuous. **6.** lacking in gentleness, care, or consideration. **7.** unmannerly; rude. **8.** difficult or unpleasant: *had a rough time of it.* **9.** lacking culture or refinement. **10.** not elaborated, perfected, or corrected; unpolished. **11.** approximate or tentative: *a rough guess.* —*n.* **12.** something rough, esp. rough ground. **13.** a part bordering a golf fairway on which the grass is not trimmed. —*adv.* **14.** in a rough manner. —*v.t.* **15.** to roughen. **16.** to subject to physical violence. **17.** to make or do roughly in haste. —*Idiom.* **18. rough it,** to live without customary comforts or conveniences. —**rough′ly,** *adv.* —**rough′ness,** *n.*

rough′age (-ij), *n.* FIBER (def. 5).

rough′en *v.t., v.i.* to make or become rough or rougher.

rou•lette (rōō let′), *n.* **1.** a game of chance in which a small ball is spun on a wheel. **2.** a small wheel, esp. one with sharp teeth for making rows of marks or perforations.

round (round), *adj.,* **-er, -est,** *n., adv., prep., v.* —*adj.* **1.** circular in form. **2.** curved like part of a circle. **3.** cylindrical. **4.** spherical or globular. **5.** consisting of full, curved lines or shapes, as handwriting. **6.** full or complete: *a round dozen.* **7.** expressed by a whole number with no fraction. **8.** considerable in amount; ample. **9.** brought to completeness or perfection. **10.** full and sonorous, as sound. **11.** plain or candid; outspoken. —*n.* **12.** any round shape or object. **13.** a completed course of time or series of events or operations. **14.** a complete course, series, or succession: *a round of talks.* **15.** Often, **rounds.** a habitual or definite circuit. **16.** a single outburst, as of applause. **17.** a single discharge of shot by each of a number of guns. **18.** ammunition for a single shot. **19.** a single serving of drink to everyone present. **20.** movement in a circle. **21.** a cut of beef below the rump and above the leg. **22.** a short musical canon in which the voices enter at equally spaced intervals of time. **23.** one of a series of periods, as in a boxing match. —*adv.* **24.** throughout. **25.** Also, **'round.** around. —*prep.* **26.** throughout. **27.** around. —*v.t.* **28.** to make round. **29.** to pass or travel around. **30.** to express as a round number. **31.** to encircle or surround. —*v.i.* **32.** to become round. **33.** to make a turn or circuit. **34.** to turn around as if on an axis. **35.** **round up,** to bring together; assemble. —*Idiom.* **36.** **in the round, a.** (of a theater) having a stage completely surrounded by seats. **b.** (of sculpture) freestanding. —**round'ness,** *n.*

round'a•bout' *adj.* circuitous or indirect, as a statement.

round'house' *n.* a building for the servicing and repair of locomotives.

round'ly *adv.* **1.** in a round manner. **2.** vigorously. **3.** outspokenly or unsparingly. **4.** completely or fully.

round' trip' *n.* a trip to a given place and back again. —**round'-trip',** *adj.*

round'up' *n.* **1.** the driving together of cattle, as for branding or shipping to market. **2.** a gathering together of scattered items or people. **3.** a summary, as of news.

rouse (rouz), *v.t., v.i.,* **roused, rous•ing. 1.** to bring or come out of a state of sleep, unconsciousness, or inactivity. **2.** to stir or be stirred up.

roust•a•bout (roust'ə bout'), *n.* an unskilled laborer, as at a circus or in an oil field.

rout¹ (rout), *n.* **1.** a disorderly flight. **2.** an overwhelming defeat. —*v.t.* **3.** to disperse in disorderly flight. **4.** to defeat decisively.

rout² (rout), *v.t.* **1.** to find or get by searching or rummaging. **2.** to force or drive out. **3.** to make a hollow in; furrow.

route (ro͞ot, rout), *n., v.,* **rout•ed, rout•ing.** —*n.* **1.** a way for passage or travel. **2.** a regular line of passage or travel. **3.** a specific itinerary or regular round of stops. —*v.t.* **4.** to fix the route of. **5.** to send by a particular route. [< OF < L *rupta (via)* broken (i.e., freshly made) (way)]

rou•tine (ro͞o tēn'), *n.* **1.** a customary or regular course of procedure. **2.** habitual, unvarying, or unimaginative procedure. **3.** a set of instructions directing a computer to perform a specific task. —*adj.* **4.** of, adhering to, or being routine. **5.** dull or uninteresting; commonplace. —**rou•tine'ly,** *adv.*

rove (rōv), *v.i., v.t.,* **roved, rov•ing.** to wander (over or through) aimlessly or at random. —**rov'er,** *n.*

row¹ (rō), *n.* **1.** a number of persons or things arranged in a line. **2.** a line of adjacent seats facing the same way, as in a theater. **3.** a street formed by two continuous lines of buildings.

row² (rō), *v.t., v.i.* **1.** to propel (a boat) with oars. **2.** to convey in a rowboat. —*n.* **3.** an act or period of rowing. **4.** an excursion in a rowboat. —**row'boat',** *n.*

row³ (rou), *n.* **1.** a noisy dispute or quarrel. —*v.i.* **2.** to quarrel noisily.

row•dy (rou'dē), *adj.,* **-di•er, -di•est,** *n., pl.* **-dies.** —*adj.* **1.** rough and disorderly. —*n.* **2.** a rough, disorderly person. —**row'di•ness,** *n.*

roy•al (roi'əl), *adj.* **1.** of a king or queen. **2.** appropriate to or befitting a sovereign; magnificent. —**roy'al•ly,** *adv.*

roy•al•ist *n.* a supporter of a monarch or royal government.

roy•al•ty *n., pl.* **-ties. 1.** royal persons collectively. **2.** royal status, dignity, or power. **3.** compensation paid to the owner of a right, as a patent, for the use of it. **4.** an agreed portion of the income from a work paid to its author or composer.

rpm revolutions per minute.

RR, 1. railroad. **2.** rural route.

RSVP or **R.S.V.P.,** please reply. [< F *r(épondez) s('il) v(ous) p(laît)*]

rub (rub), *v.,* **rubbed, rub•bing,** *n.* —*v.t.* **1.** to subject to pressure and friction, as in polishing. **2.** to move, spread, or apply with pressure and friction. **3.** to move (two things) with pressure and friction over each other. **4.** to make sore from friction. **5.** to remove or erase by pressure and friction. —*v.i.* **6.** to rub something. **7.** to move with pressure against something. **8. rub down,** to massage. **9. ~ out, a.** to obliterate; erase. **b.** *Slang.* to murder. —*n.* **10.** an act or instance of rubbing. **11.** something annoying or irritating. **12.** an annoying experience or circumstance. **13.** an obstacle or difficulty. —*Idiom.* **14. rub the wrong way,** to irritate; annoy.

rub•ber¹ (rub'ər), *n.* **1.** a highly elastic solid substance obtained from the milky juice of various tropical trees and plants. **2.** a similar substance made synthetically. **3.** an eraser of rubber. **4.** a low overshoe or rubber. **5.** one that rubs. **6.** *Slang.* a condom. —*adj.* **7.** made of or coated with rubber. —**rub'ber•y,** *adj.*

rub•ber² (rub'ər), *n.* **1.** a series or round, as in bridge, played until one side has won two out of three games. **2.** a deciding contest when a competition is tied.

rub'ber band' *n.* a band of rubber used esp. for holding things together.

rub'ber cement' *n.* a liquid adhesive consisting of unvulcanized rubber dispersed in benzene or gasoline.

rub'ber•neck' *Informal.* —*v.i.* **1.** to look about or stare with curiosity. —*n.* **2.** a curious onlooker. **3.** a sightseer or tourist.

rub'ber stamp' *n.* **1.** a stamp with a rubber printing surface used for imprinting names, standard messages, etc. **2.** a person or group that gives approval automatically or routinely. **3.** such approval.

rub•bish (rub'ish), *n.* **1.** worthless material; trash. **2.** nonsense, as in writing.

rub•ble (rub'əl), *n.* broken bits and pieces, as of something demolished.

rub'down' *n.* a massage.

ru•bel•la (ro͞o bel'ə), *n.* a usu. mild viral infection that may cause fetal damage if contracted during pregnancy.

ru•ble (ro͞o'bəl), *n.* the basic monetary unit of Russia, the Soviet Union, and its successor states.

ru•bric (ro͞o'brik), *n.* **1.** a title or heading, as in a manuscript, esp. when written or printed in red. **2.** a direction for the conduct of divine service. **3.** a class or category.

ru•by (ro͞o'bē), *n., pl.* **-bies,** *adj.* —*n.* **1.** a red variety of the mineral corundum used as a gem. **2.** a deep red. —*adj.* **3.** ruby-colored.

ruck•sack (ruk'sak', ro͞ok'-), *n.* a type of knapsack.

ruck•us (ruk'əs), *n.* a noisy commotion; uproar.

rud•der (rud'ər), *n.* a vertical blade or flap that can be turned to steer a boat or an airplane.

rud•dy (rud'ē), *adj.,* **-di•er, -di•est. 1.** having a fresh, healthy red color. **2.** red or reddish.

rude (ro͞od), *adj.,* **rud•er, rud•est. 1.** discourteous; impolite. **2.** lacking culture or refinement. **3.** crude in behavior; uncouth. **4.** not gentle; harsh. **5.** roughly built or made. —**rude'ly,** *adv.* —**rude'ness,** *n.*

ru•di•ment (ro͞o'də mənt), *n.* **1.** Usu., **-ments. a.** the elements or first principles of a subject. **b.** an undeveloped or imperfect form of something. **2.** an incompletely developed part. —**ru'di•men'ta•ry** (-men'tə rē), *adj.*

rue¹ (ro͞o), *v.i., v.t.,* **rued, ru•ing.** to feel sorrow or remorse (for). —**rue'ful,** *adj.*

rue² (ro͞o), *n.* a strongly scented plant with yellow flowers and leaves formerly used in medicine.

ruff (ruf), *n.* **1.** a gathered or pleated collar worn in the 16th and 17th centuries. **2.** a collarlike growth of hairs or feathers on the neck of an animal.

ruf•fi•an (ruf'ē ən, ruf'yən), *n.* a tough, lawless person.

ruf•fle (ruf'əl), *v.,* **-fled, -fling,** *n.* —*v.t.* **1.** to destroy the evenness of. **2.** to erect (the feathers), as a bird in anger. **3.** to vex or irritate. **4.** to turn (pages) rapidly. **5.** to draw up (cloth, lace, etc.) into gathers or pleats. —*v.i.* **6.** to become ruffled. —*n.* **7.** a strip of fabric gathered along one edge and used as a trimming. **8.** vexation; irritation.

rug (rug), *n.* **1.** a piece of thick fabric for covering part of a floor. **2.** *Chiefly Brit.* a lap robe.

Rug•by (rug′bē), *n.* (*sometimes l.c.*) a form of football characterized by continuous action and prohibition against the use of substitute players.

rug•ged (rug′id), *adj.* **1.** having a rough or jagged surface. **2.** (of a face) wrinkled or furrowed. **3.** rough, harsh, or severe. **4.** capable of enduring; strong. **5.** requiring great endurance, determination, or stamina. **6.** tempestuous; stormy. —**rug′ged•ly,** *adv.*

ru•in (rōō′in), *n.* **1. ruins,** the remains of something destroyed or decaying. **2.** downfall, decay, or destruction. **3.** complete loss, as of means or position. **4.** something that causes destruction; blight. **5.** the act of causing destruction. —*v.t.* **6.** to reduce to ruin. **7.** to bankrupt. **8.** to injure (a thing) irretrievably. —*v.i.* **9.** to come to ruin. —**ru′in•a′tion,** *n.* —**ru′in•ous,** *adj.*

rule (rōōl), *n., v.,* **ruled, rul•ing.** —*n.* **1.** a principle or regulation governing conduct. **2.** the customary or normal circumstance, occurrence, or practice. **3.** control, government, or dominion. **4.** RULER (def. 2). —*v.t., v.i.* **5.** to exercise dominating power, authority, or influence (over); govern. **6.** to decide judicially or authoritatively. **7.** to mark with lines, esp. with the aid of a ruler. **8.** to be superior or preeminent (in). **9. rule out,** to eliminate from consideration. —**rul′ing,** *n., adj.*

rul′er *n.* **1.** a person who rules; sovereign. **2.** a strip of material, as wood, that has a straight edge and is used for drawing lines and measuring.

rum (rum), *n.* an alcoholic liquor distilled from a fermented sugarcane product, esp. molasses.

rum•ba (rum′bə, rōōm′-, rōōm′-), *n., pl.* **-bas** (-bəz), *v.,* **-baed** (-bəd), **-ba•ing** (-bə ing). —*n.* **1.** a dance of Cuban origin. —*v.i.* **2.** to dance the rumba. [< AmerSp]

rum•ble (rum′bəl), *v.,* **-bled, -bling,** *n.* —*v.i.* **1.** to make a deep, somewhat muffled, continuous sound, as thunder. **2.** to move or travel with a rumbling sound. —*n.* **3.** a rumbling sound. **4.** *Slang.* a street fight between rival teenage gangs.

ru•mi•nant (rōō′mə nant), *n.* **1.** an even-toed hoofed mammal, as a cow or camel, characterized by cud-chewing. —*adj.* **2.** chewing the cud. **3.** contemplative; meditative. —**ru′mi•nant•ly,** *adv.*

ru′mi•nate′ (-nāt′), *v.i., v.t.,* **-nat•ed, -nat•ing. 1.** to chew (the cud). **2.** to meditate (on); ponder.

rum•mage (rum′ij), *v.,* **-maged, -mag•ing,** *n.* —*v.i., v.t.* **1.** to search thoroughly (through), esp. by moving around or turning over contents. —*n.* **2.** odds and ends. **3.** a rummaging search.

rum•my (rum′ē), *n., pl.* **-mies.** any of various card games in which the object is to match cards into sets and sequences.

ru•mor (rōō′mər), *n.* **1.** a story or statement in general circulation without confirmation or certainty as to facts. **2.** gossip; hearsay. —*v.t.* **3.** to report or circulate by rumor. Also, *esp. Brit.,* **ru′mour.**

rump (rump), *n.* **1.** the fleshy hind part of an animal's body. **2.** a cut of beef from the rump. **3.** the lower back part of the human trunk; the buttocks. **4.** a remnant.

rum•pus (rum′pəs), *n.* a noisy or violent disturbance; commotion.

run (run), *v.,* **ran, run, run•ning,** *n.* —*v.i.* **1.** to go quickly by moving the legs more rapidly than at a walk. **2.** to move or pass quickly. **3.** to depart quickly; flee. **4.** to make a quick trip or visit. **5.** to move freely and without restraint. **6.** to take part in a race or contest. **7.** to be a candidate for election. **8.** (of fish) to migrate, as for spawning. **9.** to go regularly; ply. **10.** to unravel, as a fabric. **11.** to flow in or as if in a stream. **12.** to include a specific range of variations: *Your work runs from fair to bad.* **13.** to spread on being applied, as a liquid. **14.** to undergo a spreading of colors: *materials that run*

when washed. **15.** to operate or function. **16.** to encounter a certain condition: *to run into difficulties.* **17.** to amount; total. **18.** to be stated or worded. **19.** to continue or extend. **20.** to appear, as in print or on a stage. **21.** to spread or circulate. **22.** to recur persistently: *Musical ability runs in my family.* **23.** to tend to have or be a specified size, quality, etc. —*v.t.* **24.** to move along (a surface, path, etc.). **25.** to perform or compete in by or as if by running. **26.** to convey or transport. **27.** to cause to move or pass quickly. **28.** to get past or through: *to run a blockade.* **29.** to smuggle. **30.** to operate or drive. **31.** to print or publish. **32.** to sponsor as a candidate for election. **33.** to manage or conduct. **34.** to process (the instructions in a program) by computer. **35.** to expose oneself to (danger, a risk, etc.). **36.** to cause (a liquid) to flow. **37.** to bring into a certain condition. **38.** to drive or force. **39.** to extend in a particular direction: *to run a cable under the road.* **40.** to cost. **41. run across,** to meet or find accidentally. **42.** ~ **along,** a. to go away; leave. **43.** ~ **down,** a. to strike and knock down, esp. with a vehicle. **b.** to chase after and seize. **c.** to cease operation. **d.** to speak disparagingly of. **44.** ~ **in,** a. to pay a casual visit. **b.** to arrest. **45.** ~ **off,** a. to create quickly and easily. **b.** to print or duplicate. **46.** ~ **on,** a. to continue without interruption. **b.** to add at the end of a text. **47.** ~ **out,** to become used up. **48.** ~ **out of,** to use up a supply of. **49.** ~ **over,** a. to hit and drive over with a vehicle. **b.** to repeat; review. **50.** ~ **through,** a. to pierce as with a sword. **b.** to consume or squander. **c.** to practice or rehearse. **51.** ~ **up,** a. to sew rapidly. **b.** to amass; incur. —*n.* **52.** an act or instance of running. **53.** a fleeing; flight. **54.** a running pace. **55.** a distance covered, as in running. **56.** a quick trip. **57.** a routine or regular trip. **58. a.** a period of continuous operation of a machine. **b.** the amount of something produced in such a period. **59.** a ravel, as in a stocking. **60.** trend or tendency: *the normal run of events.* **61.** freedom to move around in or use something: *has the run of the house.* **62.** a continuous series, course, or extent. **63.** an extensive and continued demand: *a run on umbrellas.* **64.** a series of sudden and urgent demands for payment, as on a bank. **65.** a small stream; brook. **66.** the typical or ordinary kind. **67.** an inclined course, as on a slope: *a bobsled run.* **68.** an enclosure for domestic animals: *a sheep run.* **69.** large numbers of migrating fish. **70.** *Baseball.* a score made by running around all the bases. —*Idiom.* **71. in the long run,** in the course of long experience. **72. on the run, a.** scurrying about. **b.** while rushing to get somewhere.

run′a•round′ *n.* an indecisive or evasive response.

run′a•way′ *n.* **1.** one that runs away. **2.** the act of running away. —*adj.* **3.** having run away; fugitive. **4.** (of a contest) easily won. **5.** unchecked; rampant.

run′-down′ *adj.* **1.** fatigued; exhausted. **2.** in poor health. **3.** in dilapidated condition. **4.** (of a clock, watch, etc.) unwound.

run′down′ *n.* a short summary.

rung (rung), *n.* **1.** one of the usu. rounded crosspieces forming the steps of a ladder. **2.** a rounded piece fixed horizontally between the legs of a chair. **3.** a spoke of a wheel.

run′-in′ *n.* a quarrel; argument.

run′ner *n.* **1.** one that runs, esp. as a racer. **2.** a messenger. **3.** *Baseball.* a player on base or trying to reach a base. **4.** either of the long strips of metal or wood on which a sled or sleigh slides. **5.** the blade of an ice skate. **6.** a long, narrow rug. **7.** a guiding or supporting strip for a drawer or sliding door. **8. a.** a slender, trailing stem that sends out roots at the nodes, as in the strawberry. **b.** a plant that spreads by such stems.

run′ner-up′ *n., pl.* **run•ners-up.** the competitor, player, or team finishing in second place.

run′off′ *n.* a final contest held to break a tie or eliminate semifinalists.

run′-of-the-mill′ *adj.* merely average; mediocre.

runt (runt), *n.* **1.** a small animal, esp. the smallest of a litter. **2.** a small and contemptible person.

run•way *n.* **1.** a way along which something runs. **2.** a strip on which planes land and take off. **3.** a narrow ramp extending from a stage into an aisle, as in a theater.

rup•ture (rup′chər), *n., v.,* **-tured, -tur•ing.** —*n.* **1.** the act of breaking or bursting. **2.** the state of being broken or burst. **3.** hernia, esp. abdominal hernia. —*v.i., v.t.* **4.** to suffer or cause to suffer a rupture.

ru•ral (rŏŏr′əl), *adj.* of or characteristic of the country, country life, or country people; rustic.

ruse (rōōz), *n.* a trick, stratagem, or artifice.

rush[1] (rush), *v.i., v.t.* **1.** to move or cause to move, act, or progress with speed, impetuosity, or violence. **2.** to carry with haste. **3.** to attack suddenly and violently; charge. —*n.* **4.** rapid, impetuous, or violent forward movement. **5.** hurried activity. **6.** a hurried state. **7.** an eager rushing of numbers of persons to a region: *the California gold rush.* —*adj.* **8.** requiring or done in haste.

rush[2] (rush), *n.* a grasslike marsh plant with pithy or hollow stems used esp. for making chair bottoms and baskets.

rusk (rusk), *n.* a slice of sweet raised bread dried and baked again.

rus•set (rus′it), *n.* **1.** a yellowish or reddish brown. **2.** a winter apple with a rough brownish skin. —*adj.* **3.** of the color russet.

Rus•sia (rush′ə), *n.* **1.** RUSSIAN FEDERATION. **2.** Also called **Rus′sian Em′pire,** a former empire in E Europe and N Asia: overthrown by the Russian Revolution 1917. **3.** UNION OF SOVIET SOCIALIST REPUBLICS.

Rus′sian *n.* **1. a.** a native or inhabitant of Russia or the Russian Federation. **b.** the Slavic language of Russia or the Russian Federation. —*adj.* **2.** of Russia, its inhabitants, or their language.

Rus′sian Federa′tion *n.* a republic extending from E Europe to N Asia: formerly a part of the USSR. Also called **Russia, Rus′sian Repub′lic.**

rust (rust), *n.* **1.** the red or orange coating that forms on the surface of iron exposed to air and moisture. **2.** a plant disease characterized by reddish, brownish, or black pustules. **3.** a reddish brown. —*v.i., v.t.* **4.** to form rust (on). **5.** to deteriorate, as through inaction or disuse. —*rust′y, adj.,* **-i•er, -i•est.**

rus•tic (rus′tik), *adj.* **1.** of or appropriate for the country; rural. **2.** simple or unsophisticated. **3.** uncouth, rude, or boorish. —*n.* **4.** a country person.

rus′ti•cate′ (-ti kāt′), *v.i., v.t.,* **-cat•ed, -cat•ing. 1.** to go or send to the country. **2.** to make or become rustic.

rus•tle (rus′əl), *v.,* **-tled, -tling,** *n.* —*v.i., v.t.* **1.** to make or cause to make the slight, soft sounds of gentle rubbing, as of leaves. **2.** to move, proceed, or work energetically. **3.** to steal (livestock, esp. cattle). **4. rustle up,** *Informal.* to find or gather by search. —*n.* **5.** a rustling sound. —**rus′tler,** *n.*

rut[1] (rut), *n., v.,* **rut•ted, rut•ting.** —*n.* **1.** a furrow or track in the ground, esp. one made by the passage of vehicles. **2.** a fixed, usu. dull way of proceeding. —*v.t.* **3.** to make a rut in; furrow.

rut[2] (rut), *n.* the periodically recurring sexual excitement of the male of animals such as the deer.

ru•ta•ba•ga (rōō′tə bā′gə), *n., pl.* **-gas.** a turnip with a yellow- or white-fleshed edible tuber.

ruth•less (rōōth′lis), *adj.* without pity or compassion; merciless. —**ruth′less•ly,** *adv.* —**ruth′less•ness,** *n.*

RV 1. recreational vehicle. **2.** Revised Version (of the Bible).

Rwan•da (rōō än′də), *n.* a republic in central Africa. —**Rwan′dan,** *adj., n.*

Rx prescription.

rye (rī), *n.* **1.** a widely cultivated cereal grass raised for its seeds and grain. **2.** a whiskey distilled from a mash containing rye grain.

a b c d e f g h i j k l m n o p q r **S** t u v w x y z

S, s (es), *n., pl.* **Ss** or **S′s, ss** or **s′s. 1.** the 19th letter of the English alphabet, a consonant. **2.** something shaped like an S.

S 1. satisfactory. **2.** sentence. **3.** signature. **4.** small. **5.** soft. **6.** Also, **s** south. **7.** southern.

S *Chem. Symbol.* sulfur.

′s[1], an ending used to form the possessive of most singular nouns and of plural nouns not ending in *s: man's; women's.*

′s[2], **1.** contraction of *is: She's here.* **2.** contraction of *has: He's been there.* **3.** contraction of *does: What's he look like?*

′s[3], contraction of *us: Let's go.*

-s[1], an ending marking the third person sing. present indicative of verbs: *walks.*

-s[2], an ending marking nouns as plural: *weeks.*

S. 1. Sabbath. **2.** Saint. **3.** Saturday. **4.** Sea. **5.** Senate. **6.** September. **7.** south. **8.** southern. **9.** Sunday.

s. 1. school. **2.** section. **3.** series. **4.** shilling. **5.** singular. **6.** small. **7.** son. **8.** south. **9.** southern.

Sab•bath (sab′əth), *n.* **1.** the seventh day of the week, Saturday, as the day of rest and religious observance among Jews and some Christians. **2.** the first day of the week, Sunday, observed by most Christians as a day of rest and worship.

sab•bat•i•cal (sə bat′i kəl), *adj.* **1.** (*cap.*) of or appropriate to the Sabbath. **2.** pertaining to a sabbatical year. —*n.* **3.** a year, usually every seventh, of release from normal teaching duties granted to a professor, as for research.

sa•ber (sā′bər), *n.* a one-edged sword, usu. slightly curved, used esp. by cavalry. Also, *esp. Brit.,* **sa′bre.**

sa•ble (sā′bəl), *n., pl.* **-bles, -ble. 1.** a dark-colored Eurasian marten valued for its fur. **2.** the fur of the sable.

sab•o•tage (sab′ə täzh′), *n., v.,* **-taged, -tag•ing.** —*n.* **1.** deliberate damage of equipment or interference with production, as by disgruntled employees. **2.** destruction or obstruction intended to undermine a national military effort. **3.** undermining of a cause. —*v.t.* **4.** to injure or attack by sabotage.

sab′o•teur′ (-tûr′), *n.* a person who commits sabotage.

sac (sak), *n.* a baglike structure in an animal, plant, or fungus.

sac•cha•rin (sak′ər in), *n.* a synthetic powder used as a noncaloric sugar substitute.

sac′cha•rine (-ər in, -ə rēn′), *adj.* **1.** of, resembling, or containing sugar. **2.** cloyingly sweet or sentimental.

sa•chet (sa shā′), *n.* a small bag containing scented powder or fragrant flower parts.

sack[1] (sak), *n.* **1.** a large bag of strong, coarsely woven material. **2.** a bag. **3.** *Slang.* dismissal from a job. **4.** a loose-fitting coat or jacket. —*v.t.* **5.** to put into a sack. **6.** *Slang.* to dismiss from a job. —**sack′ful,** *n., pl.* **-fuls.**

sack[2] (sak), *v.t.* **1.** to loot (a place) after capture; plunder. —*n.* **2.** the plundering of a captured place. —**sack′er,** *n.*

sack′cloth′ *n.* **1.** coarsely woven material, as of hemp or jute, used chiefly for sacks. **2.** a coarse cloth worn to show repentance or grief.

sac•ra•ment (sak′rə mənt), *n.* **1.** a rite, as baptism, considered to have been established by Christ as a channel for grace. **2.** (*often cap.*) the Eucharist. —**sac′ra•men′tal** (-men′tl), *adj.*

sa•cred (sā′krid), *adj.* **1.** devoted or dedicated to a deity or to a religious purpose. **2.** meriting veneration or religious respect. **3.** of or connected with religion. **4.** dedicated to some person, purpose, or object. **5.** regarded with reverence.

sac•ri•fice (sak′rə fīs′), *n., v.,* **-ficed, -fic•ing.** —*n.* **1.** the offering of something to a deity, as in propitiation. **2.** something so offered. **3.** the surrender or destruction of something valued for the sake of something else. **4.** a loss incurred in selling something below its value. —*v.t., v.i.* **5.** to make a sacrifice (of). **6.** to surrender for the sake of something else. —**sac′ri•fi′cial** (-fish′əl), *adj.*

sac•ri•lege (sac′rə lij), *n.* violation or profanation of something sacred. —**sac′ri•le′gious** (-lij′əs, -lē′jəs), *adj.*

sac•ris•tan (sak′ri stən), *n.* an official in charge of a sacristy.

sac′ris•ty (-ri stē), *n., pl.* **-ties.** a room in a church in which sacred vessels and vestments are kept.

sac•ro•il•i•ac (sak′rō il′ē ak′, sā′krō-), *n.* the joint where the sacrum and the broad upper portion of each hipbone meet.

sac•ro•sanct (sak′rō sangkt′), *adj.* sacred; inviolable.

sac•rum (sak′rəm, sā′krəm), *n., pl.* **sac•ra** (sak′rə, sā′krə). a bone forming the posterior wall of the pelvis.

sad (sad), *adj.,* **sad•der, sad•dest. 1.** affected by unhappiness or grief. **2.** expressive of, characterized by, or causing sorrow. **3.** deplorably bad; sorry: *a sad attempt.* —**sad′den,** *v.t., v.i.* —**sad′ly,** *adv.* —**sad′ness,** *n.*

sad•dle (sad′l), *n., v.,* **-dled, -dling.** —*n.* **1.** a seat for a rider, as on the back of a horse or other animal. **2.** a cut of meat, as lamb, comprising both loins. —*v.t.* **3.** to put a saddle on. **4.** to load or charge, as with a burden.

sad′dle•bag′ *n.* a pouch laid over the back of a horse behind the saddle or mounted over the rear wheel of a bicycle or motorcycle.

sa•dism (sā′diz əm, sad′iz-), *n.* **1.** a disorder in which sexual gratification is derived by causing pain or degradation to others. **2.** pleasure in being cruel. [after D. A. F. de *Sade* (1740–1814), Fr. novelist] —**sa′dist,** *n., adj.* —**sa•dis•tic** (sə dis′tik), *adj.*

sa•do•mas•o•chism (sā′dō mas′ə kiz′əm) *n.* sexual or other enjoyment gained through causing or experiencing pain. —**sa′do•mas′o•chist′,** *n.*

sa•fa•ri (sə fär′ē), *n., pl.* **-ris. 1.** an expedition for hunting, esp. in East Africa. **2.** a long expedition.

safe (sāf), *adj.,* **saf•er, saf•est,** *n.* —*adj.* **1.** offering security from harm or danger. **2.** free from injury or risk. **3.** dependable; trustworthy. —*n.* **4.** a steel or iron box or repository for valuable items. —**safe• keep′ing,** *n.* —**safe′ly,** *adv.*

safe′-con′duct *n.* a document authorizing safe passage through a region, esp. in time of war.

safe′-de•pos′it *adj.* providing safekeeping for valuables.

safe′guard′ *n.* **1.** something that serves as a protection or defense. —*v.t.* **2.** to guard; protect.

safe′ sex′ *n.* sexual activity in which precautions are taken to prevent diseases transmitted by sexual contact.

safe′ty *n., pl.* **-ties. 1.** the state of being safe. **2.** a device to prevent injury. **3. a.** a football play in which a player on the offensive team downs the ball in his own end zone. **b.** a defensive player farthest behind the line of scrimmage.

safe′ty glass′ *n.* shatter-resistant glass consisting of two sheets of glass with a layer of plastic between them.

safe′ty pin′ *n.* a pin bent back on itself to form a spring, with a guard to cover the point.

safe′ty ra′zor *n.* a razor with a blade guard to prevent serious cuts.

saf•flow•er (saf′lou′ər), *n.* a thistlelike plant with orange-red flower heads and seeds from which a cooking oil is extracted.

saf•fron (saf′rən), *n.* **1.** a crocus bearing showy purple flowers. **2.** an orange-colored condiment consisting of dried saffron stigmas used to color and flavor foods.

sag (sag), *v.,* **sagged, sag•ging,** *n.* —*v.i.* **1.** to sink downward by or as if by weight or pressure. **2.** to wane in vigor or intensity. **3.** to decline in value. —*n.* **4.** a place where something sags.

sa•ga (sä′gə), *n., pl.* **-gas. 1.** a medieval Scandinavian narrative of historical or legendary events. **2.** a narrative of heroic exploits.

sa•ga•cious (sə gā′shəs), *adj.* having acute mental discernment and keen practical sense; shrewd. —**sa•gac′i•ty** (-gas′i tē), *n.*

sage¹ (sāj), *n., adj.,* **sag•er, sag•est.** —*n.* **1.** a profoundly wise person. —*adj.* **2.** wise, judicious, or prudent.

sage² (sāj), *n.* **1.** a plant or shrub of the mint family with aromatic grayish green leaves used in cooking. **2.** sagebrush.

sage′brush′ *n.* any of several sagelike, bushy plants common on the dry plains of the western U.S.

sa•go (sā′gō), *n., pl.* **-gos.** a starch derived from the pith of a tropical Asian palm.

sa′hib (sä′ib), *n.* (in colonial India) a term of respect for a European.

said (sed), *v.* pt. and pp. of SAY.

sail (sāl), *n.* **1.** a piece of fabric, as canvas, that catches the wind to propel a boat or ship. **2.** something similar to a sail. **3.** a trip in a sailing craft. —*v.i.* **4.** to travel on water in a sailing craft. **5.** to manage a sailboat. **6.** to begin a journey by water. **7.** to move along in a stately, effortless way. —*v.t.* **8.** to sail upon, over, or through. **9.** to navigate (a boat or ship). —**sail′or,** *n.*

sail′cloth′ *n.* any of various fabrics, as of cotton, for boat sails or tents.

sail′fish′ *n., pl.* **-fish, -fish•es.** a large marlinlike fish with a long, high dorsal fin.

saint (sānt), *n.* **1.** a person formally recognized by the Christian Church, esp. by canonization, as being exceptionally holy. **2.** a person of great virtue or benevolence. —**saint′hood′,** *n.* —**saint′ly,** *adj.,* **-li•er, -li•est.**

sake¹ (sāk), *n.* **1.** benefit or well-being: *for the sake of all students.* **2.** purpose; end: *art for art's sake.*

sa•ke² (sä′kē), *n.* a mildly alcoholic Japanese beverage made from fermented rice.

sa•laam (sə läm′), *n.* **1.** a salutation used esp. in Islamic countries. **2.** a very low bow with the palm of the right hand on the forehead.

sa•la•cious (sə lā′shəs), *adj.* grossly indecent; lewd.

sal•ad (sal′əd), *n.* **1.** a usu. cold dish of vegetables or fruit, served with a dressing. **2.** a mixture of chopped food and mayonnaise: *egg salad.*

sal•a•man•der (sal′ə man′dər), *n.* a tailed amphibian with soft, moist, scaleless skin.

sa•la•mi (sə lä′mē), *n., pl.* **-mis.** a spicy, garlic-flavored sausage.

sal•a•ry (sal′ə rē), *n., pl.* **-ries.** fixed compensation paid periodically for work or services. —**sal′a• ried′,** *adj.*

sale (sāl), *n.* **1.** the act of selling. **2.** a special offering of goods at reduced prices. **3.** transfer of property for money or credit. **4.** opportunity to sell; demand. **5.** an auction. —**sales′man,** *n., pl.* **-men.** —**sales′peo′ple,** *n. pl.* —**sales′per′son,** *n.* —**sales′room,** *n.* —**sales′wom′an,** *n.fem., pl.* **-wom•en.**

sales′man•ship′ *n.* the skill or technique of selling a product or idea.

sa•li•ent (sā′lē ənt, sāl′yənt), *adj.* **1.** prominent or conspicuous. **2.** projecting or pointing outward. —*n.* **3.** a salient angle or part. —**sa′li•ence,** *n.*

sa•line (sā′lēn, -līn), *adj.* **1.** of, containing, or tasting of salt; salty. —*n.* **2.** a saline solution.

sa•li•va (sə lī′və), *n.* a viscid, watery secretion that moistens the mouth and starts the digestion of starches. —**sal•i•var•y** (sal′ə ver′ē), *adj.* —**sal•i• vate** (sal′ə vāt′), *v.i.,* **-vat•ed, -vat•ing.** —**sal•i•va• tion** (sal′ə vā′shən), *n.*

sal•low (sal′ō), *adj.,* **-er, -est.** of a sickly yellowish color.

sal•ly (sal′ē), *n., pl.* **-lies,** *v.,* **-lied, -ly•ing.** —*n.* **1.** a sortie of troops from a besieged place against an enemy. **2.** an excursion. **3.** a witty remark; quip. —*v.i.* **4.** to make a sally.

salm•on (sam′ən), *n., pl.* **-ons, -on** for 1. **1.** a marine and freshwater food fish with pink flesh. **2.** a light yellowish pink.

sal•mo•nel•la (sal′mə nel′ə), *n., pl.* **-nel•lae** (-nel′ē), **-nel•las.** any of several rod-shaped bacteria that enter the digestive tract in contaminated food, causing food poisoning.

sa•lon (sə lon′; *Fr.* SA LÔN′), *n.* **1.** a drawing room in a large house. **2.** an assembly of leaders, as in the arts, esp. as a regular event. **3.** a specialized shop catering to fashionable clients.

sa•loon (sə lōōn′), *n.* **1.** a place where alcoholic drinks are sold and consumed. **2.** a large public room, as on a passenger ship.

sal•sa (säl′sə, -sä), *n., pl.* **-sas. 1.** Latin American music with elements of jazz, rock, and soul. **2.** a sauce, esp. a hot sauce containing chilies. [< AmerSp: sauce]

salt (sôlt), *n.* **1.** a crystalline compound of sodium and chlorine, sodium chloride, used for seasoning food and as a preservative. **2.** a chemical compound formed by neutralization of an acid by a base. **3.** a sailor. —*v.t.* **4.** to season, cure, sprinkle, or preserve with salt. **5. salt away,** to save for future use. —*adj.* **6.** containing or tasting of salt. **7.** cured or preserved with salt. —*Idiom.* **8. take with a grain of salt,** to be skeptical about. —**salt′y,** *adj.,* **-i•er, -i•est.**

SALT (sôlt), *n.* Strategic Arms Limitation Talks (or Treaty).

salt′cel′lar *n.* a shaker or dish for salt.

sal•tine (sôl tēn′), *n.* a crisp, salted cracker.

salt′ lick′ *n.* a place to which animals go to lick naturally occurring salt deposits.

salt′ of the earth′ *n.* an individual or group considered to embody the noblest human qualities.

salt′pe′ter or **-pe′tre** (-pē′tər), *n.* potassium nitrate, a crystalline powder used in gun powders, fertilizers, and preservatives.

sa•lu•bri•ous (sə lōō′brē əs), *adj.* favorable to health.

sal•u•tar•y (sal′yə ter′ē), *adj.* promoting health; healthful.

sal′u•ta′tion *n.* **1.** something uttered, written, or done by way of greeting, welcome, or recognition. **2.** a word or phrase serving as the prefatory greeting in a letter or speech.

sa•lute (sə lōōt′), *n., v.,* **-lut•ed, -lut•ing.** —*n.* **1.** a formal gesture of respect, as raising the hand to the head or firing cannon. **2.** a greeting or welcome. —*v.t., v.i.* **3.** to give a salute (to).

sal•vage (sal′vij), *n., v.,* **-vaged, -vag•ing.** —*n.* **1.** the saving of a ship or its cargo. **2. a.** the saving of property from destruction. **b.** the property saved. **3.** compensation given to those who save a ship or its cargo. —*v.t.* **4.** to save from peril, as shipwreck. —**sal′vage•a•ble,** *adj.*

sal•va′tion (-vā′shən), *n.* **1.** the act of saving or state of being saved, as from harm or loss. **2.** a means of being saved. **3.** *Theology.* deliverance from the power and penalty of sin.

salve (sav, säv), *n., v.,* **salved, salv•ing.** —*n.* **1.** a medicinal ointment for treating wounds, burns, and sores. —*v.t.* **2.** to soothe with or as if with salve; ease.

sal•ver (sal′vər), *n.* a tray, esp. one for serving food or drinks.

sal•vo (sal′vō), *n., pl.* **-vos, -voes.** a simultaneous or successive discharge of guns.

sam•ba (sam′bə, säm′-), *n., pl.* **-bas,** *v.,* **-baed, -ba•ing.** —*n.* **1.** a Brazilian dance of African origin. —*v.i.* **2.** to dance the samba.

same (sām), *adj.* **1.** identical with what has just been mentioned. **2.** agreeing, as in kind; corresponding. **3.** unchanged, as in character or condition. —*pron.* **4.** the same person, thing, or kind of thing. **5. the same,** in the same manner. —**same′ness,** *n.*

Sa•mo•a (sə mō′ə), *n.* a group of islands in the S Pacific: divided into American Samoa and Western Samoa. —**Sa•mo′an,** *adj., n.*

sam•ple (sam′pəl, säm′-), *n., adj., v.,* **-pled, -pling.** —*n.* **1.** a part of or selection from something that shows the quality, style, or nature of the whole. **2.** a sound of short duration, as a drumbeat, digitally stored in a synthesizer for playback. —*adj.* **3.** serving as a specimen. —*v.t.* **4.** to take a sample of.

sam′pler *n.* a piece of cloth embroidered with various stitches to show a beginner's skill.

sam•u•rai (sam′ŏŏ rī′), *n., pl.* **-rai.** (in feudal Japan) a member of the hereditary warrior class.

san•a•to•ri•um (san′ə tôr′ē əm), *n., pl.* **-to•ri•ums, -to•ri•a** (-tôr′ē ə). **1.** a hospital for the treatment of chronic diseases, as tuberculosis. **2.** SANITARIUM.

sanc•ti•fy (sangk′tə fī′), *v.t.,* **-fied, -fy•ing. 1.** to make holy; consecrate. **2.** to purify or free from sin. —**sanc′ti•fi•ca′tion,** *n.*

sanc•ti•mo•ni•ous (sangk′tə mō′nē əs), *adj.* hypocritically religious or virtuous.

sanc•tion (sangk′shən), *n.* **1.** authoritative permission or approval. **2.** a provision of a law requiring a penalty for disobedience. **3.** action by a state or states to force another state to comply with an obligation. —*v.t.* **4.** to authorize, approve, or allow. **5.** to ratify or confirm.

sanc•ti•ty (sangk′ti tē), *n., pl.* **-ties. 1.** holiness, saintliness, or godliness. **2.** sacred or hallowed character.

sanc′tu•ar′y (-chōō er′ē), *n., pl.* **-ar•ies. 1.** a sacred or holy place, as the chancel of a church. **2.** a place of refuge.

sanc′tum (-təm), *n., pl.* **-tums, -ta** (-tə). **1.** a sacred place. **2.** an inviolably private place or retreat.

sand (sand), *n.* **1.** small, loose grains of rock debris. —*v.t.* **2.** to smooth or polish with an abrasive, esp. sandpaper. **3.** to sprinkle or fill with sand. —**sand′y,** *adj.,* **-i•er, -i•est.**

san•dal (san′dl), *n.* **1.** a shoe consisting of a sole fastened to the foot by thongs or straps. **2.** a low shoe or slipper.

san′dal•wood′ *n.* the fragrant reddish yellow heartwood of an Indian tree used for incense and ornamental carving.

sand′bag′ *n.* a bag filled with sand that is used in fortification, as ballast, or as a weapon.

sand′bank′ *n.* a large mass of sand, as on a shoal.

sand′ bar′ *n.* a bar of sand formed in a river or sea by the action of tides or currents.

sand′blast′ *n.* **1.** a blast of air or steam laden with sand, used to clean, grind, cut, or decorate hard surfaces. —*v.t.* **2.** to clean, decorate, etc., with a sandblast.

sand′box′ *n.* a box or receptacle holding sand for children to play in.

sand′ dol′lar *n.* any of various flat, disklike sea animals that live on sandy ocean bottoms.

sand′lot′ *n.* **1.** a vacant lot used by youngsters for games or sports. —*adj.* **2.** of or played in a sandlot.

sand′man′ *n., pl.* **-men.** a being of folklore who puts sand in the eyes of children to make them sleepy.

sand′pa′per *n.* **1.** strong paper coated with a layer of abrasive, esp. sand, used for smoothing or polishing. —*v.t.* **2.** to smooth or polish with sandpaper.

sand′pi′per (-pī′pər), *n.* a plump, thin-billed shorebird.

sand′stone′ *n.* a sedimentary rock consisting of sand cemented together by various substances, as by silica.

sand′storm′ *n.* a windstorm that blows along clouds of sand.

sand•wich (sand′wich, san′-), *n.* **1.** two or more slices of bread with a filling, as of meat, between them. **2.** something that resembles a sandwich. —*v.t.* **3.** to insert or squeeze between two other things. [after John Montagu, fourth Earl of *Sandwich* (1718–1792)]

sane (sān), *adj.,* **san•er, san•est. 1.** free from mental derangement. **2.** reasonable; sensible. —**sane′ly,** *adv.*

sang-froid (*Fr.* sän frwA′), *n.* coolness of mind; composure. [< F: lit., cold blood]

san•gri•a or **-gri•a** (sang grē′ə, san-), *n.* an iced drink typically of red wine, sugar, sliced fruit and fruit juice, soda water, and spices.

san•gui•nar•y (sang′gwə ner′ē), *adj.* **1.** characterized by bloodshed; bloody. **2.** eager to shed blood; bloodthirsty.

san′guine (-gwin), *adj.* **1.** cheerfully optimistic, hopeful, or confident. **2.** reddish; ruddy.

san′i•tar′i•um (san′i târ′ē əm), *n., pl.* **-i•ums, -i•a** (-ē ə). a health resort.

san′i•tar′y (-ter′ē), *adj.* **1.** of health or the conditions affecting health. **2.** free from dirt and bacteria.

san′itary nap′kin *n.* a disposable pad worn by women to absorb menstrual flow.

san′i•ta′tion *n.* **1.** the application of sanitary measures for the protection of public health. **2.** the disposal of sewage and solid waste.

san′i•tize′ *v.t.,* **-tized, -tiz•ing. 1.** to free from dirt and bacteria. **2.** to make less offensive by eliminating unwholesome or objectionable elements.

san′i•ty *n.* the state of being sane.

San′ Ma•ri′no (mə rē′nō), *n.* a small republic in E Italy.

San•skrit (san′skrit), *n.* an ancient language retained in India in a classical form as a language of literature and Hinduism.

Sāo′ To•mé′ and Prín′cipe or **Sao′ To•me′ and Prin′cipe** (soun′ tŏŏ mä′), *n.* a republic in W Africa, comprising two islands (**Sāo Tomé** and **Prín′cipe).**

sap¹ (sap), *n.* **1.** a fluid containing mineral salts and sugar that circulates through the tissues of a plant. **2.** energy; vitality. **3.** a fool; dupe.

sap² (sap), *v.t.,* **sapped, sap•ping. 1.** to dig below (an enemy fortification). **2.** to weaken or destroy insidiously.

sa•pi•ent (sā′pē ənt), *adj.* having or showing great wisdom. —**sa′pi•ence,** *n.*

sap•ling (sap′ling), *n.* a young tree.

sap•phire (saf′ī°r), *n.* **1.** a blue gem variety of the mineral corundum. **2.** a deep blue.

sar•casm (sär′kaz əm), *n.* **1.** harsh or bitter derision or irony. **2.** a sneering or cutting remark. —**sar•cas′tic** (-kas′tik), *adj.*

sar•co•ma (sär kō′mə), *n., pl.* **-mas, -ma•ta** (-mə tə). a malignant tumor resembling embryonic connective tissue.

sar•coph•a•gus (sär kof′ə gəs), *n., pl.* **-gi** (-jī′, -gī′), **-gus•es.** a stone coffin.

sar•dine (sär dēn′), *n., pl.* **-dines, -dine.** a fish of the herring family, often canned in oil.

sar•don•ic (sär don′ik), *adj.* scornfully derisive or mocking; cynical. —**sar•don′i•cal•ly,** *adv.*

sa•ri (sär′ē), *n., pl.* **-ris.** a woman's garment, worn esp. in India, consisting of a long cloth wrapped around the body.

sa•rong (sə rông′, -rong′), *n.* a loose-fitting skirtlike garment worn by both sexes in the Malay Archipelago and some Pacific islands.

sar•sa•pa•ril•la (sas′pə ril′ə, sär′sə pə-, sär′spə-), *n., pl.* **-las. 1.** the root of a tropical American vine used medicinally and as a flavoring. **2.** a soft drink, as root beer, flavored with extract of sarsaparilla.

sar•to•ri•al (sär tôr′ē əl), *adj.* **1.** of tailors or their trade. **2.** of clothing or style of dress.

SASE self-addressed stamped envelope.

sash¹ (sash), *n.* a long band worn over one shoulder or around the waist.

sash² (sash), *n.* a framework, as in a window, in which panes of glass are set.

sass (sas), *Informal.* —*n.* **1.** impudent back talk. —*v.t.* **2.** to answer back in an impudent manner. —**sas′sy,** *adj.,* **-si•er, -si•est.**

sas•sa•fras (sas′ə fras′), *n.* **1.** an E North American tree of the laurel family. **2.** the aromatic bark of the sassafras root, used esp. as a flavoring agent.

Sa•tan (sāt′n), *n.* the devil. —**sa•tan•ic** (sə tan′ik), *adj.*

satch•el (sach′əl), *n.* a small bag, sometimes with a shoulder strap.

sate (sāt), *v.t.,* **sat•ed, sat•ing. 1.** to satisfy fully. **2.** to supply or indulge to excess; surfeit.

sat•el•lite (sat′l īt′), *n.* **1.** a natural body that revolves around a planet. **2.** a device designed to orbit a celestial body, as the earth. **3.** a country under the domination or influence of another. **4.** an often obsequious attendant or follower.

satellite dish *n.* a dish-shaped reflector, used esp. for receiving satellite and microwave signals.

sa•ti•ate (sā′shē āt′), *v.t.,* **-at•ed, -at•ing. 1.** to supply to excess; surfeit. **2.** to satisfy to the full. —**sa′ti•a′tion,** *n.*

sat•in (sat′n), *n.* a fabric with a glossy finish and a soft, slippery texture. —**sat′in•y,** *adj.*

sat•ire (sat′ī°r), *n.* **1.** the use of irony, sarcasm, or ridicule in exposing vice or folly. **2.** a literary composition or genre marked by satire. —**sa•tir′ic, sa•tir•i•cal** (sə tir′i kəl), *adj.* —**sat′i•rist** (-ər ist), *n.*

sat•i•rize (sat′ə rīz′), *v.t.,* **-rized, -riz•ing.** to attack or ridicule with satire.

sat•is•fac•to•ry (sat′is fak′tə rē), *adj.* serving to satisfy; adequate. —**sat′is•fac′to•ri•ly,** *adv.*

sat′is•fy′ (-fī′), *v.t.,* **-fied, -fy•ing. 1.** to fulfill the desires, needs, or demands of; content. **2.** to fulfill the requirements or conditions of. **3.** to overcome the doubts of; convince. **4.** to discharge (an obligation) fully. **5.** to make reparation to or for. **6.** to pay (a creditor). —**sat′is•fac′tion,** *n.*

sat•u•rate (sach′ə rāt′), *v.t.,* **-rat•ed, -rat•ing. 1.** to load, fill, treat, or charge to the utmost. **2.** to soak, impregnate, or imbue thoroughly. —**sat′u•ra′tion,** *n.*

Sat•ur•day (sat′ər dā′, -dē), *n.* the seventh day of the week.

Sat•urn (sat′ərn), *n.* the planet sixth in order from the sun and second largest in the solar system.

sat•ur•nine (sat′ər nīn′), *adj.* gloomy or morose in temperament; sullen.

sa•tyr (sā′tər, sat′ər), *n.* **1.** a lascivious ancient Greek woodland deity, part human and part horse or goat. **2.** a lascivious man.

sauce (sôs), *n., v.,* **sauced, sauc•ing.** —*n.* **1.** a liquid or semiliquid preparation, as gravy, eaten as an accompaniment to food. **2.** stewed fruit. **3.** *Informal.* impertinence. —*v.t.* **4.** to dress or prepare with a sauce. **5.** *Informal.* to speak impertinently to; sass.

sauce′pan′ *n.* a cooking pan with a handle.

sau•cer (sô′sər), *n.* a round, shallow dish for holding a cup.

sau•cy (sô′sē), *adj.,* **-ci•er, -ci•est. 1.** impertinent; insolent. **2.** pert; jaunty. —**sau′ci•ly,** *adv.*

Sau′di Ara′bia (sou′dē, sô′-, sä ōō′-), a kingdom occupying most of Arabia. —**Sau′di,** *n., pl.* **-dis,** *adj.*

sau•er•kraut (souʳr′krout′, souʳ′ər-), *n.* finely cut salted and fermented cabbage. [< G: sour greens]

sau•na (sô′nə, sou′-), *n., pl.* **-nas. 1.** a bath that uses dry heat to induce perspiration. **2.** a bath in which steam is produced by pouring water on heated stones. [< Finnish]

saun•ter (sôn′tər, sän′-), *v.i.* **1.** to stroll. —*n.* **2.** a stroll.

sau•sage (sô′sij; *esp. Brit.* sos′ij), *n.* finely chopped, seasoned meat, usu. stuffed into a casing.

sau•té (sō tā′, sô-), *v.t.,* **-téed (-tād′), -té•ing** (-tā′ing). to fry in a small amount of fat.

sau•terne′ (sō tûrn′) *n.* a semisweet white wine of California.

sav•age (sav′ij), *adj.* **1.** wild; untamed. **2.** uncivilized; barbarous. **3.** fierce, brutal, or cruel. —*n.* **4.** an uncivilized person. **5.** a fierce, brutal, or cruel person. —**sav′age•ly,** *adv.* —**sav′age•ry,** *n., pl.* **-ries.**

sa•van•na or **-nah** (sə van′ə), *n., pl.* **-nas** or **-nahs.** a grassy plain with scattered tree growth.

sa•vant (sa vänt′, sav′ənt; *Fr.* sa vän′), *n., pl.* **-vants** (sa vänts′, sav′ənts; *Fr.* sa vän′). a person of profound learning.

save¹ (sāv), *v.,* **saved, sav•ing.** —*v.t.* **1.** to rescue from danger, harm, or loss. **2.** to keep safe, intact, or unhurt. **3.** to prevent the spending, consumption, loss, or waste of. **4.** to set aside in reserve; lay by. **5.** to deliver from sin. **6.** to copy (computer data) onto a hard or floppy disk, a tape, etc. —*v.i.* **7.** to set aside money. **8.** to be economical in expenditure.

save² (sāv), *prep.* **1.** with the exception of; except; but. —*conj.* **2.** except; but.

sav′ing *n.* **1.** a reduction in expenditure or outlay. **2. savings,** sums of money set aside. —*prep.* **3.** with the exception of. —*conj.* **4.** except.

sav•ior or **-iour** (sāv′yər), *n.* **1.** a person who saves. **2.** (*cap.*) Jesus Christ.

sa•voir-faire (sav′wär fâr′; *Fr.* sA vwAR feR′), *n.* knowledge of just what to do in any situation.

sa•vor (sā′vər), *n.* **1.** a particular taste or odor. **2.** distinctive quality or property. —*v.i.* **3.** to have a particular savor. —*v.t.* **4.** to taste with relish. Also, *esp. Brit.,* **sa′vour.**

sa′vor•y *adj., n., pl.* **-ories.** —*adj.* **1.** pleasing in taste or smell. —*n.* **2.** an aromatic herb of the mint family, having leaves used in cooking.

sav•vy (sav′ē), *n., adj.,* **-vi•er, -vi•est,** *v.,* **-vied, -vy•ing.** —*n.* **1.** practical understanding: *political savvy.* —*adj.* **2.** shrewd and well-informed; canny. —*v.t., v.i.* **3.** to know; understand.

saw¹ (sô), *n., v.,* **sawed, sawed** or **sawn, saw•ing.** —*n.* **1.** a cutting tool consisting of a thin serrated metal blade. —*v.t., v.i.* **2.** to cut or divide with or as if with a saw. —**saw′mill′,** *n.*

saw² (sô), *n.* a familiar saying; proverb.

saw′buck′ *n.* **1.** a sawhorse. **2.** *Slang.* a ten-dollar bill.

saw′dust′ *n.* fine particles of wood produced in sawing.

saw′horse′ *n.* a movable frame or trestle for supporting wood while it is being sawed.

sax (saks), *n.* a saxophone.

Sax•on (sak′sən), *n.* **1.** a member of a Germanic people, groups of whom invaded Britain in the 5th–6th centuries. —*adj.* **2.** of the Saxons.

sax•o•phone (sak′sə fōn′), *n.* a wind instrument with a conical tube, keys or valves, and a reed mouthpiece. —**sax′o•phon′ist,** *n.*

say (sā), *v.,* **said, say•ing,** *n.* —*v.t.* **1.** to pronounce; speak. **2.** to express in words; state. **3.** to state as an opinion or judgment. **4.** to recite or repeat. **5.** to report or allege. **6.** to indicate or show: *What does your watch say?* —*n.* **7.** what a person says or has to say. **8.** the right or opportunity to state an opinion or exercise influence. —*Idiom.* **9. that is to say,** in other words.

say′ing *n.* something said, esp. a proverb or maxim.

say′-so′ *n., pl.* **say-sos. 1.** the right of final authority. **2.** an authoritative statement.

SC or **S.C.,** South Carolina.

Sc *Chem. Symbol.* scandium.

s.c. *Print.* small capitals.

scab (skab), *n., v.,* **scabbed, scab•bing.** —*n.* **1.** an incrustation that forms over a healing sore or wound. **2.** a worker who refuses to join a labor union or takes a striking worker's place on the job. —*v.i.* **3.** to become covered with a scab. **4.** to act or work as a scab. —**scab′by,** *adj.* **-bi•er, -bi•est.**

scab′bard (skab′ərd), *n.* a sheath for a sword, bayonet, or dagger.

sca•bies (skā′bēz, -bē ēz′), *n.* a form of mange caused by a mite that burrows into the skin.

scad (skad), *n.* Usu. **scads.** a great number or quantity.

scaf•fold (skaf′əld, -ōld), *n.* **1.** a raised platform for holding workers and materials, as during the erection of a building. **2.** an elevated platform on which a criminal is executed.

scal•a•wag (skal′ə wag′), *n.* a scamp; rascal.

scald (skôld), *v.t.* **1.** to burn with or as if with hot liquid or steam. **2.** to heat to a temperature just short of the boiling point. —*n.* **3.** a burn caused by scalding.

scale¹ (skāl), *n., v.,* **scaled, scal•ing.** —*n.* **1.** one of the thin flat plates forming the covering of certain animals, as snakes or fishes. **2.** a thin flake, as one that peels off from the skin. **3.** a thin coating, as of rust. —*v.t.* **4.** to remove the scales from. —*v.i.* **5.** to come off in scales. —**scal′y,** *adj.,* **-i•er, -i•est.**

scale² (skāl), *n.* **1.** Often, **scales.** a balance or other device for weighing. **2.** either of the pans or dishes of a balance.

scale³ (skāl), *n., v.,* **scaled, scal•ing.** —*n.* **1.** a progression or series of steps or degrees. **2.** a series of marks laid down at regular intervals along a line, used for measuring. **3.** a measuring instrument with such markings. **4.** the proportion that a representation bears to what it represents. **5.** a graduated line, as on a map, representing proportionate size. **6.** relative size or extent. **7.** a succession of musical tones ascending or descending at fixed intervals. —*v.t.* **8.** to climb by or as if by a ladder. **9.** to make according to a scale. **10.** to adjust to a standard or measure.

scal•lion (skal′yən), *n.* an onion that does not form a large bulb.

scal•lop (skol′əp, skal′-), *n.* **1.** a bivalve mollusk with a fluted shell. **2.** the fleshy muscle of a scallop, used as food. **3.** the shell of a scallop. **4.** any of a series of curved projections cut along an edge, as of fabric. —*v.t.* **5.** to finish (an edge) with scallops. **6.** to escallop.

scalp (skalp), *n.* **1.** the skin of the top and back of the head, usu. covered with hair. —*v.t.* **2.** to cut or tear the scalp from. **3.** to resell at inflated prices: *to scalp tickets.* —**scalp′er,** *n.*

scal•pel (skal′pəl), *n.* a small, usu. straight knife used in surgery.

scam (skam), *n., v.,* **scammed, scam•ming.** —*n.* **1.** a fraudulent scheme; swindle. —*v.t.* **2.** to cheat; defraud.

scamp (skamp), *n.* **1.** an unscrupulous person; rascal. **2.** a playful or mischievous young person.

scamp′er *v.i.* **1.** to run hastily or playfully. —*n.* **2.** an act or instance of scampering.

scam•pi (skam′pē, skäm′-), *n., pl.* **-pi. 1.** a large shrimp. **2.** a dish of scampi cooked esp. in butter and garlic. [< It, pl. of *scampo* a type of shrimp]

scan (skan), *v.,* **scanned, scan•ning,** *n.* —*v.t.* **1.** to examine minutely. **2.** to glance at hastily. **3.** to observe repeatedly or sweepingly. **4.** to analyze (verse) for metrical structure. **5.** to read (data) for use by a computer, esp. using an optical scanner. **6.** to traverse with a radar beam. —*v.i.* **7.** (of verse) to conform to the rules of meter. —*n.* **8.** an act or instance of scanning.

Scan. or **Scand.,** **1.** Scandinavia. **2.** Scandinavian.

scan•dal (skan′dl), *n.* **1.** a disgraceful or discreditable action or circumstance. **2.** damage to reputation; disgrace. **3.** malicious gossip. —**scan′dal•mon′ger,** *n.* —**scan′dal•ous,** *adj.*

scan′dal•ize′ *v.t.,* **-ized, -iz•ing.** to shock by being immoral or disgraceful.

scan′ner *n.* **1.** a person or thing that scans. **2.** a device that monitors selected radio frequencies and reproduces any signal detected. **3.** a device that optically scans bar codes, etc., and identifies data.

scan•sion (skan′shən), *n.* the metrical analysis of verse.

scant (skant), *adj.,* **-er, -est. 1.** barely sufficient. **2.** amounting to a bit less than indicated. **3.** having an inadequate or limited supply. —**scant′ly,** *adv.* —**scant′ness,** *n.*

scant′y *adj.,* **-i•er, -i•est.** insufficient, as in amount. —**scant′i•ly,** *adv.*

scape•goat (skāp′gōt′), *n.* **1.** a person or group made to bear the blame for others. —*v.t.* **2.** to make a scapegoat of.

scar (skär), *n., v.,* **scarred, scar•ring,** *n.* —*n.* **1.** a mark left by a healed wound. **2.** a trace or lasting aftereffect of damage. —*v.t., v.i.* **3.** to mark with or form a scar.

scar•ab (skar′əb), *n.* **1.** a large beetle with a dark shell. **2.** a representation of a scarab.

scarce (skârs), *adj.,* **scarc•er, scarc•est. 1.** insufficient to satisfy a need or demand. **2.** rarely encountered. —**scarc′i•ty, scarce′ness,** *n.*

scarce′ly *adv.* **1.** not quite; barely. **2.** definitely not. **3.** probably not.

scare (skâr), *v.,* **scared, scar•ing,** *n.* —*v.t., v.i.* **1.** to frighten or become frightened, esp. suddenly. **2.**

scare up, to find or get despite difficulties. —*n.* **3.** a sudden fright. **4.** a condition of alarm.

scare′crow′ *n.* an object, usu. a figure of a person, set up to frighten birds away from crops.

scarf (skärf), *n.*, *pl.* **scarfs, scarves** (skärvz). **1.** a long, sometimes broad strip of cloth worn about the neck, shoulders, or head. **2.** a long ornamental cloth, as for a bureau.

scar•i•fy (skar′ə fī′), *v.t.*, **-fied, -fy•ing. 1.** to make scratches or superficial cuts in. **2.** to wound with severe criticism.

scar•let (skär′lit), *n.* a bright red.

scar′let fe′ver *n.* a contagious disease characterized by fever and a red rash.

scar•y (skâr′ē), *adj.*, **-i•er, -i•est. 1.** causing fright. **2.** easily frightened. —**scar′i•ly,** *adv.* —**scar′i•ness,** *n.*

scat (skat), *v.i.*, **scat•ted, scat•ting.** to go off hastily.

scath•ing (skā′t̠hing), *adj.* bitterly severe. —**scath′ing•ly,** *adv.*

scat′o•log′i•cal (skat′l oj′i kəl) *adj.* concerned with excrement or obscenity.

scat•ter (skat′ər), *v.t.* **1.** to throw loosely about. **2.** to cause to disperse. —*v.i.* **3.** to separate and disperse.

scat′ter•brain′ *n.* a person incapable of serious, connected thought. —**scat′ter•brained′,** *adj.*

scav•enge (skav′inj), *v.*, **-enged, -eng•ing.** —*v.t.* **1.** to take or gather (something usable) from discarded material. —*v.i.* **2.** to act as a scavenger.

scav′en•ger *n.* **1.** an animal that feeds on dead organic matter. **2.** a person who searches through refuse for useful material.

sce•nar•i•o (si nâr′ē ō′, -när′-), *n.*, *pl.* **-os. 1.** an outline of the plot of a dramatic work. **2.** the outline of a motion picture or television program. **3.** an imagined sequence of events.

scene (sēn), *n.* **1.** the place where an action or event occurs. **2.** a view or picture. **3.** an incident or situation. **4.** an embarrassing display of emotion, esp. in public. **5.** a division of a play, film, etc., representing a single episode. **6.** the setting of a story or drama. **7.** SCENERY (def. 2). **8.** a sphere of activity or interest. —**sce′nic,** *adj.*

scen•er•y (sē′nə rē), *n.* **1.** all the features that give character to a landscape. **2.** the hangings, draperies, and structures used on a stage to represent the scene of action.

scent (sent), *n.* **1.** a distinctive odor, esp. when agreeable. **2.** an odor left in passing, by means of which an animal can be tracked. **3.** a perfume. **4.** the sense of smell. —*v.t.* **5.** to perceive by or as if by the sense of smell. **6.** to fill with an odor; perfume. —**scent′ed,** *adj.*

scep•ter (sep′tər), *n.* a rod or wand held as an emblem of regal or imperial power. Also, *esp. Brit.,* **scep′tre.**

scep•tic (skep′tik), *n.*, *adj.* SKEPTIC.

sched•ule (skej′ōōl, -ōōl; *Brit.* shed′yōōl, shej′ōōl), *n.*, *v.*, **-uled, -ul•ing.** —*n.* **1.** a plan of procedure listing the sequence of events and the time allotted for each. **2.** a series of things to be done; agenda. **3.** a timetable. **4.** a statement of details. —*v.t.* **5.** to make a schedule of. **6.** to enter in a schedule. **7.** to plan for a certain date.

scheme (skēm), *n.*, *v.*, **schemed, schem•ing.** —*n.* **1.** a plan or program of action. **2.** an underhand plot; intrigue. **3.** a system of correlated things or parts. —*v.t.*, *v.i.* **4.** to devise a scheme (for); plan or plot. —**sche•mat′ic,** *adj.* —**schem′ing,** *adj.*

scher•zo (skert′sō), *n.*, *pl.* **scher•zos, scher•zi** (skert′sē). a playful musical movement.

schil•ling (shil′ing), *n.* the basic monetary unit of Austria, which has a fixed value relative to the euro.

schism (siz′əm, skiz′-), *n.* **1.** division or disunion, esp. into mutually opposed parties. **2.** a division within or separation from a religious body. —**schis•mat′ic** (-mat′ik), *adj.*

schiz•oid (skit′soid), *adj.* **1.** of or noting a personality disorder marked by passivity, indifference, etc. **2.** of schizophrenia. —*n.* **3.** a schizoid person.

schiz•o•phre•ni•a (skit′sə frē′nē ə), *n.* a severe mental disorder typically marked by disorganized behavior, delusions, and hallucinations. —**schiz′o•phren′ic** (-fren′ik), *adj.*, *n.*

schle•miel (shlə mēl′), *n. Slang.* an awkward and unlucky person for whom things never turn out right. [< Yiddish *shlemil*]

schlep (shlep), *v.*, **schlepped, schlep•ping,** *n. Slang.* —*v.t.*, *v.i.* **1.** to carry or move with great effort. —*n.* **2.** a slow or awkward person. **3.** a tedious journey. [< Yiddish *shlepn* to pull, drag]

schlock (shlok), *n. Slang.* something of cheap or inferior quality. [< Yiddish *shlak* apoplectic stroke, evil, nuisance] —**schlock′y,** *adj.*

schmaltz (shmälts, shmôlts), *n. Informal.* exaggerated sentimentalism, as in music. [< Yiddish *shmalts* fat, grease] —**schmaltz′y,** *adj.*, **-i•er, -i•est.**

schnapps or **schnaps** (shnäps, shnaps), *n.* a strong alcoholic liquor.

schol•ar (skol′ər), *n.* **1.** a learned or erudite person. **2.** a student; pupil. —**schol′ar•ly,** *adj.*

schol′ar•ship′ *n.* **1.** the qualities, knowledge, or attainments of a scholar. **2.** money given to enable a student to pursue his or her studies.

scho•las•tic (skə las′tik), *adj.* of schools, scholars, or education.

school¹ (skōōl), *n.* **1.** an institution for teaching. **2.** the activity of teaching or of learning, esp. at a school. **3.** the body of persons belonging to a school. **4.** a place, as a building, housing a school. **5.** a group of persons having common attitudes or beliefs. —*v.t.* **6.** to educate in or as if in a school. —**school′teach′er,** *n.*

school² (skōōl), *n.* a large number of marine animals, as fish, feeding or migrating together.

schoon•er (skōō′nər), *n.* **1.** a sailing ship with fore-and-aft sails. **2.** a very tall glass, as for beer.

schwa (shwä), *n.* **1.** the neutral vowel sound typical of unstressed syllables in English, as the *a* in *alone.* **2.** the symbol ə used to represent the schwa.

sci•at•i•ca (sī at′i kə), *n.* pain in the lower back and along the back of the thigh. —**sci•at′ic,** *adj.*

sci•ence (sī′əns), *n.* **1.** a branch of knowledge or study dealing with a body of facts systematically arranged and showing the operation of general laws. **2.** systematic knowledge of the physical or material world gained through observation and experimentation. —**sci′en•tif′ic** (-ən tif′ik), *adj.* —**sci′en•tif′i•cal•ly,** *adv.* —**sci′en•tist** (-tist), *n.*

sci′ence fic′tion *n.* a form of fiction that draws imaginatively on scientific knowledge and speculation.

sci-fi (sī′fī′), *n.*, *adj. Informal.* science fiction.

scim•i•tar (sim′i tər), *n.* a curved, single-edged sword.

scin•til•la (sin til′ə), *n.*, *pl.* **-las.** a minute particle; trace.

scin′til•late′ (-tl āt′), *v.i.*, **-lat•ed, -lat•ing. 1.** to emit sparks; flash. **2.** to be animated; sparkle. —**scin′til•la′tion,** *n.*

sci•on (sī′ən), *n.* **1.** a descendant, esp. of an illustrious family. **2.** a plant shoot or twig, esp. one cut for grafting.

scis•sors (siz′ərz), *n.* (*used with a sing. or pl. v.*) a cutting instrument consisting of two blades so pivoted together that their sharp edges work one against the other.

scle•ro•sis (skli rō′sis), *n.*, *pl.* **-ses** (-sēz). a hardening of a body tissue or part, as of an artery. —**scle•rot′ic** (-rot′ik), *adj.*

scoff (skôf, skof), *v.i.* **1.** to express derision, mockery, or scorn. —*n.* **2.** an expression of derision, mockery, or scorn.

scoff′law′ *n.* a person who flouts the law.

scold (skōld), *v.t.* **1.** to find fault with angrily. —*v.i.* **2.** to find fault angrily; rebuke. —*n.* **3.** a person who is constantly scolding.

sconce (skons), *n.* a wall bracket for candles or electric lights.

scone (skōn, skon), *n.* a biscuitlike quick bread baked on a griddle.

scoop (skōōp), *n.* **1.** a small shovel for taking up flour, sugar, etc. **2.** a utensil for dishing out balls of ice cream or other soft food. **3.** the bucket of a dredge or steam shovel. **4.** the quantity held in a scoop. **5.** the act of scooping. **6.** a news item revealed in one information medium before all others. —*v.t.* **7.** to take out or form with or as if with a scoop. **8.** to make a hollow in. **9.** to reveal a news item before (one's competitors).

scoot (skōot), *v.i.* to go swiftly or hastily.

scoot•er *n.* **1.** a child's two-wheeled vehicle steered by a handlebar and propelled by pushing one foot against the ground. **2.** a motor vehicle similar to but larger and heavier than a scooter.

scope (skōp), *n.* **1.** extent or range of view, outlook, or understanding. **2.** opportunity or freedom for movement or activity. **3.** extent in space.

-scope a combining form meaning instrument for viewing (*telescope*).

scorch (skôrch), *v.t.* **1.** to burn slightly so as to affect color or taste. **2.** to parch or shrivel with heat. —*v.i.* **3.** to become scorched. —*n.* **4.** a superficial burn.

score (skôr), *n., pl.* **scores; score** for 6; *v.,* **scored, scor•ing.** —*n.* **1.** a record of points made by competitors, as in a game. **2.** performance on an examination or test expressed by a symbol. **3.** a notch, scratch, or mark, esp. for keeping a record. **4.** an account showing indebtedness. **5.** an amount due. **6.** a group or set of 20. **7.** **scores,** a great many. **8.** a reason, ground, or cause. **9.** *Informal.* the basic facts of a situation. **10. a.** a musical composition with all the vocal and instrumental parts written or printed on staves. **b.** the music for a movie, play, or television show. **11.** *Slang.* success, as in purchasing illicit drugs. —*v.t.* **12.** to make, gain, or earn in or as if in a game. **13.** to evaluate and assign a score to. **14.** *Music.* to compose a score for. **15.** to make notches, cuts, marks, or lines in, into, or on. **16.** to record the score of. —*v.i.* **17.** to make, gain, or earn points, as in a game. **18.** to keep score, as of a game. **19.** to achieve success. —**scor'er,** *n.*

scorn (skôrn), *n.* **1.** open or unqualified contempt; disdain. —*v.t.* **2.** to treat or regard with scorn; disdain. —**scorn'ful,** *adj.*

scor•pi•on (skôr'pē ən), *n.* an arachnid with a long, upcurved tail ending in a venomous stinger.

Scot (skot), *n.* a native or inhabitant of Scotland.

Scot. 1. Scotland. **2.** Scottish.

scotch (skoch), *v.t.* to put an end to; crush: *to scotch a rumor.*

Scotch (skoch), *adj.* **1.** of Scottish origin; characteristic of Scotland or the Scottish people: *Scotch plaid.* **2.** *Sometimes Offensive.* —*n.* **3.** (*used with a pl. v.*) *Sometimes Offensive.* the inhabitants of Scotland. *n.* (*often l.c.*) Also called **Scotch' whis'-ky.** a whiskey distilled in Scotland from malted barley.

scot'-free' (skot'-), *adj.* free from harm, punishment, or obligation.

Scot'land *n.* a division of the United Kingdom in the N part of Great Britain.

Scots (skots), *n.* **1.** the dialect of English spoken in Scotland. —*adj.* **2.** SCOTTISH.

Scots'man *n., pl.* **-men.** a native or inhabitant of Scotland.

Scot•tish (skot'ish), *adj.* **1.** of Scotland or its inhabitants. —*n.* **2.** (*used with a pl. v.*) the inhabitants of Scotland. **3.** SCOTS.

scoun•drel (skoun'drəl), *n.* an unprincipled, dishonorable person; villain.

scour[1] (skouᵉr), *v.t., v.i.* **1.** to cleanse or polish by rubbing, as with an abrasive. **2.** to remove by rubbing. **3.** to clear or dig out by or as if by the force of water.

scour[2] (skouᵉr), *v.t.* **1.** to range over, as in search. **2.** to pass quickly over or along.

scourge (skûrj), *n., v.,* **scourged, scourg•ing.** —*n.* **1.** a whip or lash. **2.** a cause of affliction or calamity. —*v.t.* **3.** to whip or lash. **4.** to punish or chastise severely.

scout (skout), *n.* **1.** a person, ship, or airplane employed in reconnoitering. **2.** a person sent out to obtain information. **3.** a person employed to dis-

cover new talent. **4.** (*sometimes cap.*) a Boy Scout or Girl Scout. —*v.t., v.i.* **5.** to reconnoiter as a scout. **6.** to search (for). **7.** to find by searching.

scowl (skoul), *v.i.* **1.** to draw down or contract the brows in a sullen, displeased, or angry manner. —*n.* **2.** a scowling expression.

scrab•ble (skrab'əl), *v.i., v.t.,* **-bled, -bling. 1.** to scratch, scrape, or dig frantically. **2.** to scramble. **3.** to scrawl; scribble. —**scrab'bler,** *n.*

scrag (skrag) *n.* a scrawny creature.

scrag•gly (skrag'lē), *adj.,* **-gli•er, -gli•est. 1.** irregular; uneven. **2.** shaggy; unkempt.

scram (skram), *v.i.,* **scrammed, scram•ming.** *Informal.* to go away quickly.

scram•ble (skram'bəl), *v.,* **-bled, -bling,** *n.* —*v.i.* **1.** to climb or move quickly, esp. on the hands and knees. **2.** to compete or struggle for possession or gain. —*v.t.* **3.** to mix together confusedly. **4.** to cook (eggs) while stirring together whites and yolks. **5.** to make (a radio, telephonic, or television signal) unintelligible to interceptors. —*n.* **6.** a quick climb or progression. **7.** a disorderly struggle, as for possession or gain.

scrap[1] (skrap), *n., v.,* **scrapped, scrap•ping.** —*n.* **1.** a small piece; fragment. **2. scraps,** bits of food, esp. of leftover food. **3.** discarded or leftover material, esp. metal that can be reworked. —*v.t.* **4.** to make into scrap. **5.** to discard as useless.

scrap[2] (skrap), *n., v.,* **scrapped, scrap•ping.** *Informal.* —*n.* **1.** a fight or quarrel. —*v.i.* **2.** to engage in a scrap. —**scrap'py,** *adj.,* **-pi•er, -pi•est.**

scrap'book' *n.* an album in which keepsakes, as clippings, can be pasted or mounted.

scrape (skrāp), *v.,* **scraped, scrap•ing,** *n.* —*v.t.* **1.** to draw something rough or sharp over (a surface), as to smooth it. **2.** to remove by scraping. **3.** to injure or mar by brushing against something rough or sharp. **4.** to collect laboriously or with difficulty. —*v.i.* **5.** to rub against something gratingly. **6.** to produce a grating sound. **7.** to get by with difficulty. **8.** to be very frugal; economize. —*n.* **9.** an act or instance of scraping. **10.** a grating sound. **11.** a scraped place. **12.** a distressing situation. —**scrap'er,** *n.*

scrap'ple (skrap'əl) *n.* sausagelike food of pork, corn meal, and seasonings.

scratch (skrach), *v.t.* **1.** to mar or mark the surface of with something sharp, as the fingernails. **2.** to rub or scrape slightly to relieve itching. **3.** to strike out or cancel by or as if by drawing a line through. **4.** to withdraw (an entry) from a race. —*v.i.* **5.** to use nails or claws, as for tearing or digging. **6.** to relieve itching by rubbing, esp. with the nails. —*n.* **7.** an injury or mark caused by scratching. **8.** the act or sound of scratching. —*adj.* **9.** used for hasty writing or figuring: *scratch paper.* **10.** gathered hastily and indiscriminately: *a scratch crew.* —**Idiom. 11. from scratch,** from the very beginning or from nothing. **12. up to scratch,** meeting a standard; satisfactory. —**scratch'y,** *adj.,* **-i•er, -i•est.**

scrawl (skrôl), *v.t., v.i.* **1.** to write awkwardly, carelessly, or illegibly. —*n.* **2.** awkward, careless, or illegible handwriting.

scrawn•y (skrô'nē), *adj.,* **-i•er, -i•est.** excessively thin; skinny. —**scrawn'i•ness,** *n.*

scream (skrēm), *v.i.* **1.** to utter a loud, sharp, piercing cry. **2.** to emit a shrill, piercing sound. —*v.t.* **3.** to utter with or as if with a scream. —*n.* **4.** a loud, sharp, piercing cry or sound. **5.** *Informal.* someone or something that is hilariously funny.

screech (skrēch), *v.t., v.i.* **1.** to utter with or make a harsh, shrill cry or sound. —*n.* **2.** a harsh, shrill cry or sound. —**screech•y,** *adj.,* **-i•er, -i•est.**

screen (skrēn), *n.* **1.** a movable or fixed device that provides protection or concealment or serves as a partition. **2.** a surface on which motion pictures or slides can be projected. **3. a.** motion pictures collectively. **b.** the motion-picture industry. **4.** the part of a television or computer on which a picture or information is displayed. **5.** something that shelters, protects, or conceals. **6.** a frame holding a mesh of wire, used in a window or doorway to exclude insects. **7.** a sieve used to separate smaller from larger particles. —*v.t.* **8.** to shelter, protect, or conceal with or as if with a screen. **9.** to provide with a screen. **10.** to sift, sort, or separate by or as if by passing through a screen. **11.** to project (a motion picture, slide, etc.) on a screen.

screen′play′ *n.* the outline or full script of a motion picture.

screw (skrōō), *n.* **1.** a metal fastener with a spirally threaded shank and slotted head that is driven into wood or the like by rotating. **2.** something having a spiral form. **3.** PROPELLER. —*v.t.* **4.** to fasten or attach with a screw. **5.** to attach, detach, or adjust by a twisting motion. **6.** to contort as if by twisting; distort. —*v.i.* **7.** to become attached, detached, or adjusted by being twisted. **8. screw around,** *Slang.* to waste time. **9. ~ up,** *Slang.* to make a mess of; botch. —*Idiom.* **10. put the screws on,** to use coercion on.

screw′ball′ *n.* **1.** *Slang.* an eccentric or wildly whimsical person. **2.** a pitched baseball that veers toward the side from which it was thrown.

screw′driv′er *n.* **1.** a hand tool for tightening or loosening a screw. **2.** a mixed drink of vodka and orange juice.

screw′y *adj.,* **-i•er, -i•est.** *Slang.* **1.** crazy; nutty. **2.** absurd; odd.

scrib•ble (skrib′əl), *v.,* **-bled, -bling,** *n.* —*v.t., v.i.* **1.** to write or draw hastily or carelessly. —*n.* **2.** hasty, careless, or illegible drawing or writing.

scribe (skrīb), *n.* **1.** a professional copyist of manuscripts. **2.** a writer, esp. a journalist. —**scrib′al,** *adj.*

scrim•mage (skrim′ij), *n., v.,* **-maged, -mag•ing.** *Football.* —*n.* **1. a.** the action from the snap of the ball to the end of a play. **b.** a practice session or informal game. —*v.i.* **2.** to engage in a scrimmage.

scrimp (skrimp), *v.i., v.t.* to be sparing (of) or frugal (with).

scrip (skrip), *n.* **1.** paper currency issued for temporary use. **2.** a certificate representing a fraction of a share of stock.

script (skript), *n.* **1.** handwriting. **2.** the written text of a play, motion picture, or radio or television program.

Scrip•ture (skrip′chər), *n.* **1.** Often, **-tures.** the sacred writings of the Old or New Testament or both together. **2.** (*often l.c.*) a sacred or religious writing or book. —**scrip′tur•al,** *adj.*

scrive•ner (skriv′nər), *n.* a scribe.

scrod (skrod), *n.* a young Atlantic codfish or haddock.

scrof•u•la (skrof′yə lə), *n.* tuberculosis of the lymphatic glands, esp. of the neck. —**scrof′u•lous,** *adj.*

scroll (skrōl), *n.* **1.** a roll of parchment, paper, or other material, esp. one with writing on it. **2.** a spiral or coiled ornament resembling a partly unrolled scroll. —*v.i.* **3.** to move a cursor smoothly, vertically or sideways, gradually causing new data to replace what was previously on a computer screen.

scro•tum (skrō′təm), *n., pl.* **-ta** (-tə), **-tums.** the pouch of skin that contains the testes. —**scro′tal,** *adj.*

scrounge (skrounj), *v.,* **scrounged, scroung•ing.** —*v.t.* **1.** to take with no intention of repaying. **2.** to get by or as if by foraging. —*v.i.* **3.** to look around for what is needed. —**scroung′er,** *n.*

scrub¹ (skrub), *v.,* **scrubbed, scrub•bing,** *n.* —*v.t.* **1.** to rub hard in washing. **2.** to remove by scrubbing. **3.** *Informal.* to cancel; eliminate. —*v.i.* **4.** to cleanse something by hard rubbing. —*n.* **5.** an act or instance of scrubbing.

scrub² (skrub), *n.* **1.** low trees or shrubs collectively. **2.** an area covered with scrub. **3.** a domestic animal of inferior breeding. **4.** something undersized or inferior. **5.** *Sports.* a player not on the first-string team. —**scrub′by,** *adj.,* **-bi•er, -bi•est.**

scruff (skruf), *n.* the back of the neck; nape.

scruff•y (skruf′ē), *adj.,* **-i•er, -i•est.** untidy; shabby.

scrump•tious (skrump′shəs), *adj.* extremely pleasing, esp. to the taste.

scru•ple (skrōō′pəl), *n., v.,* **-pled, -pling.** —*n.* **1.** a moral or ethical consideration that inhibits action.

2. a unit of apothecaries' weight equal to 20 grains. —*v.i.* **3.** to hesitate because of scruples.

scru•pu•lous (skrōō′pyə ləs), *adj.* **1.** having scruples; principled. **2.** rigorously precise; exact.

scru•ti•nize (skrōōt′n īz′), *v.t.,* **-nized, -niz•ing.** to examine minutely. —**scru′ti•ny,** *n., pl.* **-nies.**

scu•ba (skōō′bə), *n., pl.* **-bas.** a portable breathing device for free-swimming divers. [*s(elf)-c(ontained) u(nderwater) b(reathing) a(pparatus)*]

scud (skud), *v.,* **scud•ded, scud•ding,** *n.* —*v.i.* **1.** to run or move quickly. —*n.* **2.** clouds, spray, or mist driven by the wind.

scuff (skuf), *v.t., v.i.* **1.** to mar or become marred by scraping or hard use. **2.** to scrape (the feet) over or back and forth over something. —*n.* **3.** a flat-heeled slipper open at the back. **4.** a mar or scratch caused by scuffing.

scuf•fle *v.,* **-fled, -fling,** *n.* —*v.i.* **1.** to struggle or fight in a rough, confused manner. **2.** to walk with a shuffle. —*n.* **3.** a rough, confused struggle or fight. **4.** a shuffle.

scull (skul), *n.* **1.** an oar mounted on the stern of a boat and moved from side to side to propel the boat. **2.** either of a pair of oars for one rower. **3.** a light, narrow racing boat. —*v.t., v.i.* **4.** to propel (a boat) by means of sculls.

scul•ler•y (skul′ə rē), *n., pl.* **-ler•ies.** a room off a kitchen where cooking utensils are cleaned and stored.

scul′lion (-yən), *n.* a kitchen servant.

sculp•ture (skulp′chər), *n., v.,* **-tured, -tur•ing.** —*n.* **1.** the art of carving, modeling, or welding works of art in three dimensions. **2.** works of sculpture collectively. **3.** an individual work of sculpture. —*v.t.* **4.** to carve, model, or weld (a piece of sculpture). **5.** to represent in sculpture. —*v.i.* **6.** to work as a sculptor. —**sculp′tor,** *n.*

scum (skum), *n.* **1.** a film of foul matter that forms on the surface of a liquid. **2.** waste material; refuse. **3.** low, worthless persons; dregs.

scup•per (skup′ər), *n.* an opening at the edge of a ship's deck that allows accumulated water to drain away.

scurf (skûrf), *n.* **1.** loose scales of skin. **2.** scaly matter on a surface.

scur•ril•ous (skûr′ə ləs, skur′-), *adj.* grossly or obscenely abusive.

scur•ry (skûr′ē, skur′ē), *v.i.,* **-ried, -ry•ing.** to move in haste.

scur•vy (skûr′vē), *n., adj.,* **-vi•er, -vi•est.** —*n.* **1.** a disease caused by a lack of vitamin C and marked by swollen and bleeding gums and livid spots on the skin. —*adj.* **2.** contemptible; despicable.

scut•tle¹ (skut′l), *n.* a deep bucket for carrying coal.

scut•tle² (skut′l), *v.i.,* **-tled, -tling.** to run with short, quick steps.

scut•tle³ (skut′l), *n., v.,* **-tled, -tling.** —*n.* **1.** a small hatch with a cover in the deck, side, or bottom of a ship. —*v.t.* **2.** to sink (a ship) deliberately by making openings in the bottom.

scut•tle•butt (skut′l but′), *n. Informal.* rumor; gossip.

scythe (sīth), *n., v.,* **scythed, scyth•ing.** —*n.* **1.** a tool with a long, curving blade for cutting grass or grain by hand. —*v.t.* **2.** to cut or mow with a scythe.

SD or **S.D., 1.** South Dakota. **2.** special delivery.

S. Dak. South Dakota.

SE 1. southeast. **2.** southeastern. **3.** Standard English.

Se *Chem. Symbol.* selenium.

sea (sē), *n.* **1.** the salt waters that cover much of the earth's surface. **2.** an ocean. **3.** water turbulence, as caused by the wind. **4.** a large wave. **5.** a great or overwhelming quantity: *a sea of faces.* —*Idiom.* **6. at sea,** perplexed; uncertain.

sea′ anem′one *n.* a solitary marine polyp with flowerlike tentacles.

sea bass (bas) *n.* a marine food fish.

sea′bed′ *n.* the ocean floor.

sea′board′ *n.* a region bordering a seacoast.

sea′coast′ *n.* land immediately adjacent to the sea.

sea′far′ing *adj.* traveling by or working at sea. —**sea′far′er,** *n.*

sea′food′ *n.* edible marine fish or shellfish.

sea′go′ing *adj.* designed or fit for going to sea.

sea′ gull′ *n.* a gull, esp. one of the marine species.

sea′ horse′ *n.* a fish with an elongated snout and a head bent at right angles to the body.

seal¹ (sēl), *n.* **1.** an emblem or symbol used as evidence of authenticity. **2. a.** a device, as a stamp, engraved with a seal for impressing wax or clay. **b.** the impression obtained. **3.** an authenticating mark on a legal document. **4.** an adhesive used to close or fasten an envelope, door, etc. **5.** anything that closes or fastens securely, as a rubber gasket. **6.** a stamplike label: *an Easter seal.* **7.** anything that serves as assurance or confirmation. —*v.t.* **8.** to affix a seal to. **9.** to assure or confirm with or as if with a seal. **10.** to fasten or close by or as if by a seal. **11.** to decide irrevocably: *His fate was sealed.* —**seal′ant,** *n.*

seal² (sēl), *n., pl.* **seals, seal,** *v.* —*n.* **1.** any of numerous marine carnivores with limbs like flippers. **2.** the skin or fur of a seal. —*v.i.* **3.** to hunt, kill, or capture seals.

sea′ legs′ *n.pl.* the ability to adjust one's balance to the motion of a ship.

sea′ lev′el *n.* the position of the sea's surface at mean level between high and low tide.

sea′ li′on *n.* a large eared seal of the N Pacific.

seam (sēm), *n.* **1.** the line formed by sewing together pieces, as of cloth. **2.** a line formed by abutting edges. **3.** a wrinkle or scar. **4.** *Geol.* a thin stratum, as of coal. —*v.t.* **5.** to join together in a seam. **6.** to mark with lines, as wrinkles. —**seam′less,** *adj.*

sea′man *n., pl.* **-men. 1.** a person who assists in the handling of a ship; sailor. **2.** an enlisted person in the U.S. Navy ranking below petty officer. —**sea′man•ship′,** *n.*

seam•stress (sēm′stris), *n.* a woman whose occupation is sewing.

seam′y *adj.,* **-i•er, -i•est.** sordid; disagreeable: *the seamy side of life.*

sé•ance (sā′äns), *n.* a meeting in which a spiritualist attempts to communicate with the spirits of the dead.

sea′plane′ *n.* an airplane with floats for water takeoffs and landings.

sea′port′ *n.* a port or harbor for seagoing ships.

sear (sēr), *v.t.* **1.** to burn or char the surface of. **2.** to mark with a branding iron. **3.** to dry up or wither.

search (sûrch), *v.t.* **1.** to look through carefully in order to find something. **2.** to examine carefully; scrutinize or probe. **3.** to uncover or find by examination or exploration. **4.** to command software to find specified characters or codes in (an electronic file). —*v.i.* **5.** to conduct a search. —*n.* **6.** an act or instance of searching. —**search′er,** *n.* —**search′ing,** *adj.*

search′light′ *n.* **1.** a device for projecting a powerful beam of light. **2.** a beam of light so projected.

sea′shell′ *n.* the shell of a marine mollusk.

sea′shore′ *n.* land along the sea.

sea′sick′ness *n.* nausea induced by the motion of a ship or boat at sea. —**sea′sick′,** *adj.*

sea•son (sē′zən), *n.* **1.** one of the four periods of the year: spring, summer, autumn, and winter. **2.** a period of the year marked by a particular condition, activity, or event: *the baseball season.* —*v.t.* **3.** to flavor (food) by adding seasoning. **4.** to add piquancy to; enhance. **5.** to make fit by experience. **6.** to prepare for use, as by drying. —*v.i.* **7.** to become seasoned.

sea′son•a•ble *adj.* **1.** suitable to the season. **2.** timely.

sea′son•al *adj.* of, dependent on, or affected by the season. —**sea′son•al•ly,** *adv.*

sea′son•ing *n.* something, as a spice, for enhancing the flavor of food.

seat (sēt), *n.* **1.** something, as a chair, for a person

to sit on. **2.** the part of something on which a person sits. **3.** the buttocks. **4.** a place in which something is established: *a seat of learning.* **5.** a place in which administrative power is centered: *the seat of government.* **6.** a right to sit as a member, as in a legislative body. —*v.t.* **7.** to place in or on a seat. **8.** to accommodate with seats.

seat′ belt′ *n.* straps designed to keep a passenger secure in the seat of a vehicle.

seat′ing *n.* **1.** arrangement of seats. **2.** material for seats.

sea′ ur′chin *n.* a small, round sea animal with a spiny shell.

sea′way′ *n.* a waterway giving oceangoing ships access to a landlocked port.

sea′weed′ *n.* **1.** any of numerous marine algae. **2.** any of various marine plants.

sea′wor′thy *adj.,* **-thi•er, -thi•est.** (of a ship) fit for a voyage at sea.

se•ba•ceous (si bā′shəs), *adj.* of, resembling, or secreting a fatty substance.

seb•or•rhe•a (seb′ə rē′ə), *n.* abnormally heavy discharge from the sebaceous glands. —**seb′or•rhe′ic,** *adj.*

se•cede (si sēd′), *v.i.,* **-ced•ed, -ced•ing.** to withdraw formally from an alliance, federation, or association. —**se•ces′sion** (-sesh′ən), *n.*

se•clude (si klōōd′), *v.t.,* **-clud•ed, -clud•ing. 1.** to remove from contact with others; isolate. **2.** to shut off; keep apart. —**se•clu′sion,** *n.*

sec•ond¹ (sek′ənd), *adj.* **1.** being the ordinal number for two. **2.** next after the first, as in place, time, value, or rank. **3.** alternate: *every second week.* **4.** other; another: *a second Shakespeare.* **5.** of or being the gear transmission ratio at which drive shaft speed is greater than that of low gear. —*n.* **6.** a second part. **7.** the second member of a series. **8.** a person who aids or supports another, as in boxing. **9.** second gear. **10. seconds,** an additional helping of food. **11.** Usu., **seconds.** goods of inferior quality. —*v.t.* **12.** to assist or support. **13.** to express formal support of (a motion, proposal, etc.) before further discussion or voting. —*adv.* **14.** in the second place. —**sec′ond•ly,** *adv.*

sec•ond² (sek′ənd), *n.* **1.** the sixtieth part of a minute of time. **2.** a moment or instant. **3.** the sixtieth part of a minute of angular measure.

sec′ond•ar′y (-an der′ē), *adj.* **1.** second in order, rank, or time. **2.** not primary or original. **3.** of minor or lesser importance.

sec′ond-guess′ *v.t.* **1.** to use hindsight in criticizing or correcting. **2.** to outguess.

sec′ond•hand′ *adj.* **1.** not directly known or experienced. **2.** previously used or owned. **3.** dealing in used goods. —*adv.* **4.** after another user or owner. **5.** indirectly.

sec′ond lieuten′ant *n.* an officer in the U.S. Army, Air Force, or Marines of the lowest commissioned rank.

sec′ond na′ture *n.* a deeply ingrained habit or tendency.

sec′ond-rate′ *adj.* of lesser or minor quality or importance.

sec′ond string′ *n.* the squad of players available to replace or relieve those who start a game.

sec′ond wind′ (wind), *n.* energy for a renewed effort.

se•cret (sē′krit), *adj.* **1.** done, made, or carried out without the knowledge of others. **2.** kept from general knowledge. **3.** hidden from sight; concealed. **4.** close-mouthed; secretive. —*n.* **5.** something that is secret, hidden, or concealed. **6.** a mystery. **7.** a reason or explanation not readily apparent. —**se′cre•cy** (-krə sē), *n., pl.* **-cies.** —**se′cret•ly,** *adv.*

sec•re•tar•i•at (sek′ri târ′ē ət), *n.* **1.** the office or the officials entrusted with overseeing administrative duties for a governmental department. **2.** a group or department of secretaries.

sec′re•tar′y (-ter′ē), *n., pl.* **-ies. 1.** a person in charge of records and correspondence for an organization. **2.** a person employed to do clerical work, as typing. **3.** (*often cap.*) an officer of state who heads a governmental department. **4.** a writing desk. —**sec′re•tar′i•al** (-târ′ē əl), *adj.*

se•crete[1] (si krēt′), *v.t.*, **-cret•ed, -cret•ing.** to discharge, generate, or release by secretion.

se•crete[2] (si krēt′), *v.t.*, **-cret•ed, -cret•ing.** to place out of sight; hide.

se•cre′tion *n.* (in a cell or gland) the process or product of separating, elaborating, and releasing a substance that fulfills a function within the organism or undergoes excretion.

se•cre•tive (sē′kri tiv, si krē′-), *adj.* having or showing a disposition to secrecy. —**se′cre•tive•ly,** *adv.* —**se′cre•tive•ness,** *n.*

sect (sekt), *n.* **1.** a religious denomination. **2.** a religious group deviating from a generally accepted tradition. **3.** a group united by a specific doctrine or under a particular leader. —**sec•tar′i•an,** *adj., n.*

sec•tion (sek′shən), *n.* **1.** a distinct subdivision, as of a community. **2.** a distinct part, as of a newspaper. **3.** a part that is cut off or separated. **4.** an act or instance of cutting apart. **5.** a representation of an object as it would appear if cut by a plane, showing its internal structure. —*v.t.* **6.** to cut or divide into sections.

sec•tor (sek′tər), *n.* **1.** a plane figure bounded by two radii and the included arc of a circle. **2.** an area that a particular military unit is assigned to defend. **3.** a distinct part.

sec•u•lar (sek′yə lər), *adj.* **1.** of worldly or nonreligious things or subjects; temporal. **2.** not relating to or concerned with religion. **3.** not bound by monastic vows. —**sec′u•lar•ism,** *n.* —**sec′u•lar•ize,** *v.t.,* **-ized, -iz•ing.**

se•cure (si kyŏŏr′), *adj.,* **-cur•er, -cur•est,** *v.,* **-cured, -cur•ing.** —*adj.* **1.** free from danger or harm; safe. **2.** not liable to fail or yield; firm. **3.** free from care or anxiety. **4.** certain; assured. —*v.t.* **5.** to get hold of; obtain. **6.** to keep from danger or harm; make safe. **7.** to make certain of; ensure. **8.** to make fast. **9.** to assure payment of (a debt) by pledging property. —**se•cure′ly,** *adv.*

se•cu′ri•ty (-kyŏŏr′i tē), *n., pl.* **-ties. 1.** freedom from danger or risk; safety. **2.** freedom from care, anxiety, or doubt. **3.** something that protects, shelters, or makes safe. **4.** precautions taken against crime, sabotage, escape, or attack. **5.** something given as surety for the fulfillment of an obligation. **6. securities,** stocks or bonds.

secu′rity blan′ket *n.* something, as an object, that gives a feeling of security.

se•dan (si dan′), *n.* **1.** an enclosed automobile with two or four doors and seats for four or more persons. **2.** an enclosed chair carried on poles by two persons.

se•date (si dāt′), *adj., v.,* **-dat•ed, -dat•ing.** —*adj.* **1.** calm, dignified, and composed. —*v.t.* **2.** to treat with a sedative. —**se•date′ly,** *adv.* —**se•da′tion,** *n.*

sed•a•tive (sed′ə tiv), *adj.* **1.** tending to calm or to lessen irritability or excitement. —*n.* **2.** a sedative drug.

sed•en•tar•y (sed′n ter′ē), *adj.* characterized by or requiring much sitting.

sedge (sej), *n.* a grasslike plant that grows in wet places.

sed•i•ment (sed′ə mənt), *n.* **1.** the matter that settles to the bottom of a liquid. **2.** *Geol.* matter deposited by water, air, or ice. —**sed′i•men′ta•ry** (-men′-tə rē), *adj.*

se•di•tion (si dish′ən), *n.* incitement of discontent or rebellion against a government. —**se•di′tious,** *adj.*

se•duce (si dŏŏs′, -dyŏŏs′), *v.t.,* **-duced, -duc•ing. 1.** to lead astray, as from duty. **2.** to induce to have sexual intercourse. —**se•duc′er,** *n.* —**se•duc′tion** (-duk′shən), *n.* —**se•duc′tive,** *adj.*

see[1] (sē), *v.,* **saw, seen, see•ing.** —*v.t.* **1.** to perceive with the eyes; look at. **2.** to perceive mentally; understand. **3.** to have a mental image of; visualize. **4.** to be cognizant of; recognize. **5.** to find out; ascertain. **6.** to have experience of. **7.** to make sure: *See that the door is locked.* **8.** to meet and converse with. **9.** to visit. **10.** to escort or accompany: *He saw her home.* —*v.i.* **11.** to have the

power of sight. **12.** to have insight; understand. **13. see after,** to attend to; take care of. **14. ~ through, a.** to ascertain the true nature of. **b.** to remain with until completion.

see[2] (sē), *n.* the authority, office, or jurisdiction of a bishop.

seed (sēd), *n., pl.* **seeds, seed,** *v.* —*n.* **1.** a fertilized, matured plant ovule containing an embryo or rudimentary plant. **2.** a propagative part of a plant, as a tuber or a bulb. **3.** the germ or source of something. **4.** offspring; progeny. —*v.t.* **5.** to sow with seed. **6.** to remove the seeds from. **7.** to rank (players or teams) so that the most superior competitors will not meet in early rounds. —*v.i.* **8.** to produce or shed seed. —*Idiom.* **9. go** or **run to seed, a.** to pass to the stage of yielding seed. **b.** to deteriorate, as in appearance. —**seed′less,** *adj.*

seed•ling (-ling), *n.* **1.** a plant or tree grown from a seed. **2.** any young plant.

seed′ mon′ey *n.* capital for the initial stages of an enterprise.

seed′y *adj.,* **-i•er, -i•est. 1.** containing or bearing seeds. **2.** poorly kept; run-down. **3.** shabbily dressed.

see′ing *conj.* inasmuch as; considering.

seek (sēk), *v.t.,* **sought, seek•ing. 1.** to try to find, discover, or obtain. **2.** to try; attempt. —**seek′er,** *n.*

seem (sēm), *v.i.* **1.** to appear to be. **2.** to appear to one's own senses or judgment. **3.** to appear to be true or probable.

seem′ing *adj.* apparent; ostensible. —**seem′-ing•ly,** *adv.*

seem′ly *adj.,* **-li•er, -li•est.** fitting or proper; appropriate.

seep (sēp), *v.i.* to pass, flow, or ooze gradually, as through a porous substance. —**seep′age,** *n.*

seer (sēr), *n.* a person who prophesies future events; prophet.

seer•suck•er (sēr′suk′ər), *n.* a cotton or cottonlike fabric, usu. striped and having a crinkled texture.

see•saw (sē′sô′), *n.* **1.** a balanced plank on which two children alternately ride up and down while seated at opposite ends. **2.** an alternating up-and-down or back-and-forth movement or procedure. —*v.i., v.t.* **3.** to move on or as if on a seesaw.

seethe (sēth), *v.i.,* **seethed, seeth•ing. 1.** to surge or foam as if boiling. **2.** to be in a state of agitation or excitement.

see′-through′ *adj.* transparent.

seg•ment (*n.* seg′mənt; *v.* seg′ment, seg ment′), *n.* **1.** one of the parts into which something is divided; section. **2.** *Geom.* a part cut off from a figure, esp. a circle or sphere, by a line or plane. —*v.t., v.i.* **3.** to separate or divide into segments. —**seg′men•tar′y** (-mən ter′ē), *adj.* —**seg′men•ta′-tion,** *n.*

seg•re•gate (seg′ri gāt′), *v.t.,* **-gat•ed, -gat•ing. 1.** to set apart from others; isolate. **2.** to require the separation of (a specific racial, religious, or other group) from the body of society. —**seg′re•ga′tion,** *n.* —**seg′re•ga′tion•ist,** *n.*

se•gue (sā′gwā, seg′wā), *v.i.,* **-gued, -gue•ing,** *n.* —*v.i.* **1.** to continue at once with the next section (used as a musical direction). **2.** to make a smooth transition, as from one topic to another. —*n.* **3.** a smooth, uninterrupted transition from one thing or part to another.

seis•mic (sīz′mik, sīs′-), *adj.* of, resembling, or caused by an earthquake. —**seis′mi•cal•ly,** *adv.*

seis′mo•graph (-mə graf′, -grāf′), *n.* an instrument for measuring and recording the vibrations of earthquakes. —**seis•mog′ra•phy,** *n.*

seis•mol′o•gy (-mol′ə jē), *n.* the science of earthquakes and their phenomena. —**seis′mo•log′ic** (-mə loj′ik), **seis′mo•log′i•cal,** *adj.* —**seis•mol′o•gist,** *n.*

seize (sēz), *v.t.,* **seized, seiz•ing. 1.** to take hold of suddenly or forcibly. **2.** to grasp mentally; understand. **3.** to take complete control of; possess. **4.** to take legal possession of. **5.** to capture or arrest. **6.** to take prompt advantage of.

sei•zure (sē′zhər), *n.* **1.** an act or instance of seizing. **2.** a sudden attack, as of epilepsy.

sel•dom (sel′dəm), *adv.* on only a few occasions; rarely.

se•lect (si lekt′), *v.t., v.i.* **1.** to choose in preference to others. —*adj.* **2.** chosen in preference to others; choice. **3.** careful in choosing. **4.** carefully chosen.

se•lec′tion *n.* **1.** an act or instance of selecting or the state of being selected. **2.** something selected. **3.** a process that results in some members of a population having greater success in perpetuating their genetic traits. —**se•lec′tive,** *adj.*

se•lect′man *n., pl.* **-men.** (in most New England states) one of a board of officers chosen to manage town affairs.

self (self), *n.* and *pron., pl.* **selves,** *adj.* —*n.* **1.** a person or thing referred to with respect to complete individuality. **2.** a person's nature or character. **3.** personal interest. —*pron.* **4.** myself, himself, etc. —*adj.* **5.** being the same throughout.

self- a combining form meaning: of the self (*self-image*); by oneself or itself (*self-defense*); to, with, toward, for, on, or in oneself or itself (*self-centered*); independent (*self-determination*); automatic (*self-winding*).

self′-addressed′ *adj.* addressed for return to the sender.

self′-asser′tion *n.* an expression of one's own importance, opinions, etc. —**self′-asser′tive,** *adj.*

self′-assur′ance *n.* confidence in oneself; self-confidence. —**self′-assured′,** *adj.*

self′-cen′tered *adj.* engrossed in oneself; selfish.

self′-con′fidence *n.* faith in one's own judgment, ability, etc. —**self′-con′fident,** *adj.*

self′-con′scious *adj.* excessively aware of being observed by others; embarrassed or uneasy.

self′-contained′ *adj.* **1.** containing within itself all that is necessary. **2.** reserved in behavior. **3.** having or showing self-control.

self′-control′ *n.* restraint of one's actions or feelings. —**self′-controlled′,** *adj.*

self′-defense′ *n.* **1.** the act of defending oneself or one's own interests or property. **2.** a plea that the use of force was necessary in defending one's own person.

self′-deni′al *n.* the sacrifice or restraint of one's own desires.

self′-determina′tion *n.* **1.** freedom to act as one chooses without consulting others. **2.** freedom of a people to determine the way in which they shall be governed.

self′-effac′ing *adj.* keeping oneself in the background, as in humility.

self′-ev′ident *adj.* evident in itself without proof or demonstration.

self′-im′age *n.* the conception one has of oneself.

self′-impor′tant *adj.* having or showing an exaggerated opinion of one's own importance.

self′-in′terest *n.* **1.** regard for one's own interest or advantage, esp. with disregard for others. **2.** personal interest or advantage.

self•ish (sel′fish), *adj.* **1.** caring chiefly for oneself or one's own interests, regardless of others. **2.** characterized by concern only for oneself. —**self′ish•ly,** *adv.* —**self′ish•ness,** *n.*

self′less *adj.* having little concern for oneself; unselfish.

self′-made′ *adj.* having succeeded in life unaided: *a self-made man.*

self′-pos•sessed′ *adj.* calm; poised.

self′-preserva′tion *n.* the instinctive desire to preserve one's own life and safety.

self′-respect′ *n.* proper respect for the dignity of one's character. —**self′-respect′ing,** *adj.*

self′-restraint′ *n.* self-control.

self′-right′eous *adj.* confident of one's own righteousness; smugly moralistic.

self•same (self′sām′, -sām′), *adj.* being the very same; identical.

self′-sat′isfied *adj.* feeling or showing a usu. smug satisfaction with oneself or one's achievements.

self′-seek′ing *n.* **1.** the selfish seeking of one's own interests or ends. —*adj.* **2.** given to or characterized by self-seeking.

self′-serv′ice *adj.* **1.** of or being a commercial establishment, as a restaurant, in which customers serve themselves. **2.** designed to be used without the aid of an attendant.

self′-serv′ing *adj.* serving to further one's own selfish interests.

self′-styled′ *adj.* called or considered by oneself.

self′-suffi′cient *adj.* able to supply one's own needs without external assistance.

sell (sel), *v.,* **sold, sell•ing,** *n.* —*v.t.* **1.** to transfer (goods or property) or render (services) in exchange for money. **2.** to offer for sale; deal in. **3.** to promote or effect the sale, acceptance, or approval of. —*v.i.* **4.** to engage in selling. **5.** to be offered for sale. **6.** to be in demand by buyers. **7. sell out, a.** to dispose of entirely by selling. **b.** to betray. —*n.* **8.** an act or method of selling. —**sell′er,** *n.*

sel•vage or **-vedge** (sel′vij), *n.* the edge of woven fabric finished to prevent raveling. —**sel′vaged,** *adj.*

se•man•tics (si man′tiks), *n.* **1.** the study of meaning in language, including historical changes in meaning and form. **2.** the branch of semiotics dealing with the relationship between signs or symbols and what they denote. —**se•man′tic,** *adj.* —**se•man′ti•cist** (-tə sist), *n.*

sem•a•phore (sem′ə fôr′), *n., v.,* **-phored, -phor•ing.** —*n.* **1.** an apparatus for visual signaling, as by a light whose position may be changed. **2.** a system of signaling by a flag held in each hand. —*v.t., v.i.* **3.** to signal by or as if by semaphore.

sem•blance (sem′bləns), *n.* **1.** outward appearance. **2.** assumed or unreal appearance. **3.** a likeness; image.

se•men (sē′mən), *n.* a fluid produced in the male reproductive organs, containing sperm.

se•mes•ter (si mes′tər), *n.* an academic session constituting half of the academic year.

sem•i (sem′ē, sem′ī), *n., pl.* **-is. 1.** a semitrailer. **2.** a semifinal contest or round.

semi- a combining form meaning: half (*semicircle*); partially or somewhat (*semiconductor*).

sem•i•cir•cle (sem′i sûr′kəl), *n.* half of a circle. —**sem′i•cir′cu•lar,** *adj.*

sem•i•co′lon *n.* a punctuation mark (;) used to indicate a more distinct separation than is indicated by a comma.

sem•i•con•duc′tor (sem′ē-, sem′ī-), *n.* a substance, as silicon, with electrical conductivity intermediate between that of an insulator and a conductor.

sem•i•fi′nal *adj.* **1.** being the next to last round in an elimination tournament. —*n.* **2.** a semifinal round or bout. —**sem′i•fi′nal•ist,** *n.*

sem•i•nal (sem′ə nl), *adj.* **1.** of or consisting of semen. **2.** influencing future development; original and creative.

sem•i•nar (sem′ə när′), *n.* **1.** a group of advanced students undertaking original research under a faculty member. **2.** a course of study for advanced students.

sem•i•nar•y (sem′ə ner′ē), *n., pl.* **-nar•ies. 1.** a school that prepares students for the priesthood, ministry, or rabbinate. **2.** a secondary school for young women. —**sem′i•nar′i•an,** *n.*

Sem•i•nole (sem′ə nōl′), *n., pl.* **-nole, -noles.** a member of an American Indian people of Florida and Oklahoma.

sem•i•pre′cious *adj.* having commercial value as a gem but not classified as precious.

Se•mit•ic (sə mit′ik), *n.* **1.** a branch of the Afroasiatic language family that includes Hebrew and Arabic. —*adj.* **2.** of the Semitic languages or their speakers.

sem•i•tone′ *n.* a musical pitch halfway between two whole tones.

sem•i•vow•el (sem′i vou′əl), *n.* a speech sound of vowel quality used as a consonant, as (w) in *wet* or (y) in *yet.*

sem•o•li•na (sem′ə lē′nə) *n.* ground durum.

sen•ate (sen′it), *n.* **1.** (*sometimes cap.*) the upper house of a national or state legislature, as in the U.S. and Canada. **2.** the supreme council of state of ancient Rome. **3.** a governing body, as at some universities. —**sen′a•tor** (-ə tər), *n.*

send (send), *v.t.,* **sent, send•ing. 1.** to cause or enable to go. **2.** to cause to be conveyed to a destination. **3.** to propel or drive. **4.** to emit or utter. **5.** *Slang.* to delight; excite. **6. send for,** to summon. —**send′er,** *n.*

send′-off′ *n.* **1.** a demonstration of good wishes, as for a person beginning a new venture. **2.** a start; impetus.

Sen•e•gal (sen′i gôl′, -gäl′), *n.* a republic in W Africa. —**Sen′e•ga•lese′** (-gə lēz′, -lēs′), *adj., n., pl.* **-lese.**

se•nile (sē′nīl, sen′īl), *adj.* **1.** showing a deterioration in mental functioning as a result of old age. **2.** of or resulting from old age. —**se•nil•i•ty** (si nil′i tē), *n.*

sen•ior (sēn′yər), *adj.* **1.** older or elder (written as *Sr.* following the name of a father with the same name as his son). **2.** of higher rank or longer service. **3.** of or for seniors. —*n.* **4.** a person who is older than another. **5.** a person of higher rank or longer service than another. **6.** a student in the final year at a high school or college.

sen′ior cit′izen *n.* an older person, esp. one who is retired.

sen•ior•i•ty (sēn yôr′i tē, -yor′-), *n., pl.* **-ties. 1.** the state of being senior. **2.** precedence conferred by length of service.

se•ñor (sān yôr′), *n., pl.* **se•ñors, se•ño•res** (sān-yôr′ās). a Spanish term of address for a man, equivalent to *sir* or *Mr.*

se•ño•ri•ta (sān′yə rē′tə), *n., pl.* **-tas.** a Spanish term of address for a girl or unmarried woman, equivalent to *miss.*

sen•sa′tion (sen sā′shən), *n.* **1.** perception of stimuli through the senses. **2.** a mental process or physical feeling from stimulation of a sense organ. **3.** the faculty of perceiving stimuli. **4.** a general feeling: *a sensation of anxiety.* **5. a.** widespread excitement or interest. **b.** a cause of such feeling.

sen•sa′tion•al *adj.* **1.** producing a startling or scandalous effect. **2.** extraordinarily good. **3.** of the senses or sensation. —**sen•sa′tion•al•ly,** *adv.*

sen•sa′tion•al•ism *n.* the use of sensational subject matter or style.

sense (sens), *n., v.,* **sensed, sens•ing.** —*n.* **1.** one of the faculties, sight, hearing, smell, taste, or touch, by which humans and animals perceive stimuli. **2.** a feeling or perception based on one of the senses: *a sense of cold.* **3.** a special capacity for perception, estimation, or appreciation: *a sense of humor.* **4.** Often, **senses.** sound judgment; practical intelligence. **5.** an often vague perception or impression. **6.** meaning, as of a word or phrase. —*v.t.* **7.** to perceive by or as if by the senses. **8.** to detect (physical phenomena) mechanically, electrically, or photoelectrically.

sen•si•bil•i•ty (sen′sə bil′i tē), *n., pl.* **-ties. 1.** capacity for feeling. **2.** mental responsiveness. **3.** Often, **-ties.** capacity for intellectual and aesthetic discrimination.

sen′si•ble *adj.* **1.** having, using, or showing good sense. **2.** cognizant; aware. **3.** capable of being perceived by the senses or the mind. **4.** capable of feeling or perceiving. —**sen′si•bly,** *adv.*

sen′si•tive *adj.* **1.** endowed with sensation. **2.** readily or excessively affected by external influences. **3.** responsive to the feelings of others. **4.** easily hurt or offended. —**sen′si•tive•ly,** *adv.* —**sen′si•tiv′i•ty,** *n.*

sen′si•tize′ (-tīz′), *v.t., v.i.,* **-tized, -tiz•ing.** to make or become more sensitive.

sen•sor (sen′sôr, -sər), *n.* a device sensitive to light, temperature, or radiation level that transmits a signal to a measuring or control instrument.

sen′so•ry (-sə rē), *adj.* of the senses or sensation.

sen•su•al (sen′shoō əl), *adj.* **1.** arousing the senses. **2.** preoccupied with gratification of the senses, esp. the sexual appetite. **3.** sensory. —**sen′su•al′i•ty,** *n.* —**sen′su•al•ly,** *adv.*

sen′su•ous *adj.* **1.** of, perceived by, or affecting

the senses. **2.** readily affected through the senses. —**sen′su•ous•ly,** *adv.*

sen•tence (sen′tns), *n., v.,* **-tenced, -tenc•ing.** —*n.* **1.** a structurally independent grammatical unit that typically consists of a subject and predicate and expresses a statement, question, request, command, or exclamation. **2.** a judicial decision, esp. one decreeing punishment to be inflicted. —*v.t.* **3.** to pronounce sentence upon. [< OF < L *sententia* opinion, decision]

sen•ten′tious (sen ten′shəs), *adj.* **1.** given to or abounding in pithy aphorisms. **2.** given to excessive moralizing.

sen′tient (sen′shənt), *adj.* capable of perceiving through the senses. —**sen′tience,** *n.*

sen•ti•ment (sen′tə mənt), *n.* **1.** an attitude, feeling, or opinion. **2.** refined or tender emotion. **3.** a thought influenced by or based on emotion.

sen′ti•men′tal (-men′tl), *adj.* **1.** expressive of or appealing to the tender emotions. **2.** nostalgic. **3.** weakly emotional; mawkish. —**sen′ti•men′tal•ism,** *n.* —**sen′ti•men•tal′i•ty,** *n.* —**sen′ti•men′tal•ly,** *adv.*

sen•ti•nel (sen′tn l, -tə nl), *n.* one that stands watch; sentry.

sen•try (sen′trē), *n., pl.* **-tries.** a guard, esp., a soldier.

se•pal (sē′pəl), *n.* one of the individual leaves of a flower calyx.

sep•a•rate (*v.* sep′ə rāt′; *adj., n.* -ər it), *v.,* **-rat•ed, -rat•ing,** *adj., n.* —*v.t.* **1.** to put or keep apart by or as if by a barrier; divide or disconnect. **2.** to extract: *to separate metal from ore.* —*v.i.* **3.** to withdraw from an association; part. **4.** to come apart. **5.** to go in different directions. —*adj.* **6.** not connected or joined; distinct. **7.** existing or maintained independently. **8.** not shared; individual: *separate checks.* —*n.* **9.** Usu., **-rates.** women's garments designed to be worn with other garments in various combinations. —**sep′a•ra•ble,** *adj.* —**sep′a•rate•ly,** *adv.* —**sep′a•ra′tion,** *n.*

sep′a•ra•tist (-ər ə tist, -ə rā′-), *n.* an advocate of separation, as from a church. —**sep′a•ra•tism,** *n.*

sep′a•ra′tor *n.* a person or thing that separates, esp. a device for separating cream from milk.

se•pi•a (sē′pē ə), *n., pl.* **-as. 1.** a brown pigment. **2.** a dark brown.

sep•sis (sep′sis), *n.* invasion of the body by pathogenic microorganisms or their toxins. —**sep′tic,** *adj.*

Sept. September.

Sep•tem•ber (sep tem′bər), *n.* the ninth month of the year, containing 30 days.

sep•tet (sep tet′), *n.* **1.** a group of seven, esp. a group of seven musicians. **2.** a musical composition for a septet.

sep•ti•ce•mi•a (sep′tə sē′mē ə), *n.* the presence of pathogenic bacteria in the bloodstream.

sep′tic tank′ *n.* a tank in which sewage is decomposed by bacteria.

sep•tu•a•ge•nar•i•an (sep′chōō ə jə nâr′ē ən, -tōō-, -tyōō-), *n.* a person between 70 and 80 years of age.

Sep•tu•a•gint (sep′chōō ə jint′, -tōō-, -tyōō-), *n.* the oldest Greek version of the Old Testament.

sep•ul•cher (sep′əl kər), *n.* **1.** a burial place; tomb. —*v.t.* **2.** to place in a sepulcher. —**se•pul•chral** (sə pul′krəl), *adj.*

seq. 1. sequel. **2.** the following (one). [< L *sequēns*]

se•quel (sē′kwəl), *n.* **1.** a literary or filmic work that continues the narrative of a preceding work. **2.** a subsequent development. **3.** a result; consequence.

se′quence (-kwəns), *n.* **1.** the following of one thing after another. **2.** order of succession. **3.** a continuous connected series. **4.** a series of related scenes or shots that make up one episode of a film narrative. —**se•quen•tial** (si kwen′shəl), *adj.*

se•ques•ter (si kwes′tər), *v.t.* **1.** to remove or withdraw into solitude or retirement. **2.** to set apart; separate.

se•quin (sē'kwin), *n.* a small shiny disk used for ornamentation, as on clothing.

se•quoi•a (si kwoi'ə), *n., pl.* **-as.** either of two extremely large coniferous trees of California.

se•ra•glio (si ral'yō, -räl'-), *n., pl.* **-glios. 1.** a harem. **2.** a sultan's palace.

ser•aph (ser'əf), *n., pl.* **-aphs, -a•phim** (-ə fim). a member of the highest order of angels. —**se•raph•ic** (si raf'ik), *adj.*

sere (sēr), *adj.* dry; withered.

ser•e•nade (ser'ə nād'), *n., v.,* **-nad•ed, -nad•ing.** —*n.* **1.** music performed in the open air at night, as by a lover to his lady. —*v.t., v.i.* **2.** to entertain with or perform a serenade.

ser•en•dip•i•ty (ser'ən dip'i tē), *n.* an aptitude for making desirable discoveries by accident. —**ser'en•dip'i•tous,** *adj.*

se•rene (sə rēn'), *adj.* **1.** peaceful; tranquil. **2.** clear; fair: *serene weather.* —**se•ren'i•ty** (-ren'i tē), *n.*

serf (sûrf), *n.* a person in feudal servitude, attached to a lord's land and transferred with it from one owner to another. [< MF < L *servus* slave] —**serf'dom,** *n.*

serge (sûrj), *n.* a twill-weave fabric with a characteristic diagonal wale.

ser•geant (sär'jənt), *n.* **1.** a noncommissioned officer in the U.S. Army and Marine Corps ranking above a corporal. **2.** a noncommissioned officer in the U.S. Air Force ranking above airman first class. **3.** a police officer ranking below a captain or lieutenant.

se•ri•al (sēr'ē əl), *n.* **1.** something that appears in installments at regular intervals. —*adj.* **2.** of or being a serial. **3.** of, arranged in, or occurring in a series.

se•ries (sēr'ēz), *n., pl.* **-ries.** a number of related or similar objects, events, etc., arranged or occurring in order or succession.

ser•if (ser'if), *n.* a smaller line used to finish off a main stroke of a letter.

ser•i•graph (ser'i graf', -gräf'), *n.* a silkscreen print.

se•ri•ous (sēr'ē əs), *adj.* **1.** of, requiring, or characterized by deep thought. **2.** grave or somber. **3.** not trifling; earnest. **4.** weighty, important, or significant. **5.** giving cause for apprehension; critical or threatening. —**se'ri•ous•ly,** *adv.* —**se'ri•ous•ness,** *n.*

ser•mon (sûr'mən), *n.* **1.** a religious discourse, usu. delivered by a cleric during services. **2.** a long, tedious speech, esp. on a moral issue.

ser•pent (sûr'pənt), *n.* a snake.

ser'pen•tine' (-pən tēn', -tīn'), *adj.* **1.** of or resembling a serpent, as in form or movement. **2.** having a winding course, as a road; sinuous.

ser'rat•ed (ser'ā tid) *adj.* toothed; notched. Also, **ser'rate** (ser'it).

se•rum (sēr'əm), *n., pl.* **se•rums, se•ra** (sēr'ə). **1.** the clear, pale yellow liquid that separates from the clot in the coagulation of blood. **2.** a watery animal fluid.

serv•ant (sûr'vənt), *n.* a person employed by another, esp. to perform domestic duties.

serve (sûrv), *v.,* served, serv•ing, *n.* —*v.i.* **1.** to act as a servant. **2.** to distribute food or drink. **3.** to give assistance; help. **4.** to go through a term of service. **5.** to have definite use. **6.** to answer a purpose. **7.** (in tennis, badminton, etc.) to put the ball or shuttlecock in play. —*v.t.* **8.** to work for as a servant. **9.** to be of service to; help. **10.** to go through (a term of service, imprisonment, etc.). **11.** to render homage or obedience to (God, a sovereign, etc.). **12.** to answer the requirements of. **13.** to wait upon at table. **14.** to distribute (food or drink) to another. **15.** to offer (a person) food or drink. **16.** to provide with a supply of something. **17.** (in tennis, badminton, etc.) to put (the ball or shuttlecock) in play. **18.** to make legal delivery of (a process or writ). —*n.* **19.** the act, manner, or right of serving, as in tennis.

serv•ice (sûr'vis), *n., v.,* **-iced, -ic•ing.** —*n.* **1.** an act of helpful activity. **2.** the supplying or supplier of a utility, as electricity, that meets a public need. **3.** the providing or a provider of maintenance or re-

pair. **4.** the performance of duties or the duties performed. **5. a.** a department of public employment. **b.** the personnel in it. **6.** the work of a servant. **7. a.** the armed forces. **b.** a branch of the armed forces. **8.** a meeting, ritual, or form for religious worship. **9.** a set of dishes or utensils. **10.** (in tennis, badminton, etc.) the act or manner of serving the ball or shuttlecock. —*v.t.* **11.** to maintain, repair, or restore. **12.** to supply with services.

serv'ice•a•ble *adj.* **1.** being of service; useful. **2.** wearing well; durable.

ser•vile (sûr'vil, -vīl), *adj.* **1.** slavishly submissive. **2.** of or suitable for slaves. —**ser•vil'i•ty,** *n.*

ser•vi•tor (sûr'vi tər), *n.* a servant or attendant.

ser•vi•tude (-tōōd', -tyōōd'), *n.* slavery; bondage.

ses•a•me (ses'ə mē), *n.* **1.** a tropical plant whose edible seeds yield an oil. **2.** the seeds of the sesame.

ses•sion (sesh'ən), *n.* **1. a.** a meeting, as of a court or legislature, for the transaction of business. **b.** a series of such meetings. **2.** a period of instruction at a school or college. **3.** a meeting or period of time for a particular activity.

set (set), *v.,* **set, set•ting,** *n., adj.* —*v.t.* **1.** to put in a particular place, position, or posture. **2.** to cause to pass into a certain condition. **3.** to fix definitely; establish. **4.** to place or plant firmly. **5.** to establish for others to follow: *Try to set a good example.* **6.** to arrange or prepare for use: *Please set the table.* **7.** to style (the hair), as by using rollers. **8.** to adjust (a clock or watch) to accord with a standard. **9.** to fix (a gem) in a setting. **10.** to cause to sit; seat. **11.** to put (a broken or dislocated bone) back in position. **12.** to fit (words) to music. **13.** to spread (a sail) to catch the wind. **14.** to arrange (type) for printing. —*v.i.* **15.** to sink below the horizon: *The sun has set.* **16.** to decline; wane. **17.** to become firm, solid, or permanent, as dye. **18.** to sit on eggs, as a hen. **19.** to have a certain direction, as a wind. **20. set about,** to begin. **21. ~ aside, a.** to put to one side; reserve. **b.** to discard or annul. **22. ~ back, a.** to hinder; impede. **b.** *Informal.* to cost. **23. ~ forth, a.** to state or describe. **b.** to begin a journey. **24. ~ off, a.** to cause to explode. **b.** to begin; start. **c.** to intensify by contrast. **25. ~ on** or **upon,** to attack or cause to attack. **26. ~ out, a.** to begin a journey. **b.** to undertake; attempt. **27. ~ up, a.** to put upright; raise. **b.** to inaugurate or establish. —*n.* **28.** the act of setting or state of being set. **29.** a collection of articles for use together. **30.** a group of similar things. **31.** a group of persons associated esp. by common interests. **32.** fixed direction, bent, or inclination. **33.** an apparatus for receiving radio or television programs. **34.** a construction representing the site of the action in a play or film. **35.** *Tennis.* a unit of a match consisting of six or more games. **36.** *Math.* a collection of objects or elements classed together. —*adj.* **37.** fixed or prescribed beforehand. **38.** customary: *set phrases.* **39.** fixed; rigid. **40.** resolved or determined. **41.** prepared; ready.

set'back' *n.* a check to progress; a reverse or defeat.

set•tee (se tē'), *n., pl.* **-tees.** a long seat with a back and usu. arms.

set•ter (set'ər), *n.* a long-haired hunting dog with feathering on the tail.

set'ting *n.* **1.** the act of one that sets. **2.** the position of something, as a thermostat, that has been set. **3.** surroundings or scenery. **4.** a mounting, as for a jewel. **5.** the locale and period of a story, play, etc.

set•tle (set'l), *v.,* **-tled, -tling.** —*v.t.* **1.** to put in order. **2.** to pay (a bill, debt, etc.). **3.** to cause to take up residence. **4.** to furnish with inhabitants. **5.** to quiet or calm. **6.** to determine or decide; resolve: *to settle a dispute.* **7.** to establish in a permanent position or on a permanent basis. —*v.i.* **8.** to come to an agreement, arrangement, or decision. **9.** to take up residence. **10.** to come to rest. **11.** to become fixed, as in a particular place. **12.** to sink gradually. **13.** to become clear by the sinking of suspended particles, as a liquid. **14.** to become firm or compact by sinking, as the ground. —**set'tle•ment,** *n.* —**set'tler,** *n.*

set′-to′ (-tōō′), *n., pl.* **-tos.** a usu. brief, sharp fight or argument.

set′•up′ *n.* **1.** organization; arrangement. **2.** glass, ice, mixer, etc., for patrons who provide their own liquor. **3.** an undertaking or contest deliberately made easy.

sev•en (sev′ən), *n.* **1.** a cardinal number, 6 plus 1. **2.** a symbol for this number, as 7 or VII. —*adj.* **3.** amounting to seven in number. —**sev′enth, *adj., n.***

sev′en•teen′ *n.* **1.** a cardinal number, 10 plus 7. **2.** a symbol for this number, as 17 or XVII. —*adj.* **3.** amounting to 17 in number. —**sev′en•teenth′, *adj., n.***

sev′enth heav′en *n.* a state of intense happiness; bliss.

sev′en•ty *n., pl.* **-ties,** *adj.* —*n.* **1.** a cardinal number, 10 times 7. **2.** a symbol for this number, as 70 or LXX. —*adj.* **3.** amounting to 70 in number. —**sev′en•ti•eth,** *adj., n.*

sev•er (sev′ər), *v.t., v.i.* to separate, divide, or break off. —**sev′er•ance,** *n.*

sev•er•al (sev′ər əl, sev′rəl), *adj.* **1.** being more than two but fewer than many. **2.** respective; individual: *They went their several ways.* —*n.* **3.** several persons or things.

se•vere (sə vēr′), *adj.,* **-ver•er, -ver•est. 1.** causing distress; harsh. **2.** serious or stern, as in manner. **3.** austere, as in style; plain. **4.** extreme, intense, or violent. **5.** difficult or rigorous. **6.** rigidly exact; demanding. —**se•vere′ly,** *adv.* —**se•ver′i•ty** (-ver′i-tē), *n.*

sew (sō), *v.,* **sewed, sewn** or **sewed, sew•ing.** —*v.t.* **1.** to make, repair, join, or attach by stitches. —*v.i.* **2.** to work with a needle and thread or with a sewing machine. **3. sew up,** *Informal.* to get, accomplish, or control successfully or completely. —**sew′er** (sō′ər), *n.*

sew•age (sōō′ij), *n.* waste matter that passes through sewers.

sew•er (sōō′ər), *n.* an artificial conduit, usu. underground, for carrying off waste water and refuse.

sex (seks), *n.* **1.** either the female or the male division of a species, esp. as differentiated by reproductive function. **2.** the structural and functional differences by which the female and male are distinguished. **3.** SEXUAL INTERCOURSE. —**sex•u•al** (sek′shōō əl), *adj.* —**sex′u•al/i•ty,** *n.*

sex- a combining form meaning six (*sextet*).

sex•a•ge•nar•i•an (sek′sə jə nâr′ē ən), *adj.* **1.** of the age of 60 years or between 60 and 70 years old. —*n.* **2.** a sexagenarian person.

sex′ chro′mosome *n.* a chromosome that determines the sex of an individual.

sex′ism *n.* discrimination, esp. against women, based on sex. —**sex′ist,** *adj., n.*

sex•tant (sek′stənt), *n.* an instrument used to determine latitude and longitude at sea by measuring angular distances, esp. of sun, moon, and stars.

sex•tet (seks tet′), *n.* **1.** a group of six. **2. a.** a group of six musicians. **b.** a musical composition for six voices or instruments.

sex•ton (sek′stən), *n.* an official who maintains church property.

sex′ual harass′ment *n.* unwelcome sexual advances, esp. by an employer or superior.

sex′ual in′tercourse *n.* genital contact or coupling between individuals, esp. involving penetration of the penis into the vagina.

sex′ually transmit′ted disease′ *n.* any disease characteristically transmitted by sexual contact, as gonorrhea.

sex′y *adj.,* **-i•er, -i•est.** sexually interesting or exciting; erotic.

Sey•chelles (sā shel′, -shelz′), *n.* (*used with a pl. v.*) a republic comprising a group of islands in the Indian Ocean, NE of Madagascar.

Sgt. Sergeant.

shab•by (shab′ē), *adj.,* **-bi•er, -bi•est. 1.** showing signs of long or hard use; worn or run-down. **2.** wearing worn clothes. **3.** mean; contemptible. —**shab′bi•ly,** *adv.*

shack (shak), *n.* a rough cabin; shanty.

shack•le (shak′əl), *n., v.,* **-led, -ling.** —*n.* **1.** a

metal fastening for securing the wrist or ankle; fetter. **2.** a fastening or coupling device. **3.** Often, **-les.** something that serves to inhibit thought or action. —*v.t.* **4.** to confine, restrain, or inhibit by or as if by shackles.

shad (shad), *n., pl.* **shad.** an edible marine fish that spawns in rivers upstream from the sea.

shade (shād), *n., v.,* **shad•ed, shad•ing.** —*n.* **1.** comparative darkness caused by the screening of rays of light. **2.** a place or area sheltered from light, esp. sunlight. **3.** something used to reduce or shut out light or heat: *a window shade.* **4. shades,** *Informal.* sunglasses. **5.** comparative obscurity. **6.** a ghost; specter. **7.** the degree of darkness of a color. **8.** a slight amount or degree. —*v.t.* **9.** to dim or darken. **10.** to screen or protect from light, heat, or view. **11.** to introduce degrees of darkness into (a drawing or painting). —*v.i.* **12.** to change by degrees.

shad•ow (shad′ō), *n.* **1.** a dark figure or image cast on a surface by a body intercepting light. **2.** comparative darkness. **3.** a slight suggestion; trace. **4.** a specter or ghost. **5.** the dark part of a picture. **6.** a cause or period of gloom or unhappiness. —*v.t.* **7.** to cover with shadow; shade. **8.** to follow and watch (a person) secretly. **9.** to represent faintly or prophetically. —**shad′ow•y,** *adj.,* **-i•er, -i•est.**

shad′ow•box′ *v.i.* to go through the motions of boxing without an opponent, as in training.

shad′y *adj.,* **-i•er, -i•est.** abounding in or giving shade.

shaft (shaft, shäft), *n.* **1.** the long, slender body of a weapon, as a lance. **2.** a ray or beam. **3.** the handle of a tool or implement. **4.** a rotating rod that transmits motion. **5.** a monument in the form of a column or obelisk. **6.** either of the parallel bars between which a draft animal is hitched. **7.** a vertical enclosed space, as in a building: *an elevator shaft.* **8.** a vertical or sloping underground passageway, as in a mine. **9.** *Slang.* harsh or unfair treatment. —*v.t.* **10.** *Slang.* to treat in a harsh or unfair manner.

shag¹ (shag), *n.* **1.** a rough, matted mass, as of hair or wool. **2.** a long, thick pile or nap. —**shag′gy,** *adj.,* **-gi•er, -gi•est.** —**shag′gi•ness,** *n.*

shag² (shag), *v.t.,* **shagged, shag•ging.** to retrieve and throw back (a fly ball) in batting practice.

shah (shä, shô), *n.* (*often cap.*) (formerly, in Iran) king; sovereign.

shake (shāk), *v.,* **shook, shak•en, shak•ing.** —*v.i., v.t.* **1.** to move up and down or back and forth with short, quick movements. **2.** to tremble or cause to tremble. **3.** to clasp (another's hand), as in greeting. **4.** to brandish, esp. menacingly. **5.** to come or force off or out by short, quick movements. **6.** to agitate or disturb profoundly. **7.** to weaken. **8. shake down, a.** to cause to descend by shaking. **b.** to extort money from. **c.** to search for concealed weapons. —*n.* **9.** an act or instance of shaking. **10. shakes,** (*used with a sing. v.*) a state or spell of trembling, as from fever or cold. **11.** MILK SHAKE. **12.** treatment; deal: *a fair shake.* —*Idiom.* **13. no great shakes,** not exceptional; ordinary. —**shaker,** *n.*

shake′down′ *n.* **1.** extortion, as by blackmail. **2.** a thorough search. **3.** a test cruise or flight for familiarizing the crew with a craft's operation and remedying problems.

shake′-up′ *n.* a thorough change of administration in an organization.

shak′y *adj.,* **-i•er, -i•est. 1.** tending to shake. **2.** liable to break down or give way; insecure or wavering.

shale (shāl), *n.* a rock of laminated structure formed from clay.

shall (shal; *unstressed* shəl), *auxiliary v., pres.* **shall;** *past* **should. 1.** plan to or intend to: *I shall go later.* **2.** will have to or is determined to: *You shall do it.* **3.** (in laws, directives, etc.) is or are obliged to; must: *Council meetings shall be public.* **4.** (used interrogatively): *Shall we go?*

shal·lot (shal/ət, shə lot/), *n.* an onionlike plant with an edible bulb used in cooking.

shal·low (shal/ō), *adj.*, **-er, -est,** *n.* —*adj.* **1.** of little depth. **2.** lacking depth of intellect or emotion; superficial. —*n.* **3.** Usu., **-lows.** (*used with a sing. or pl. v.*) a shallow part of a body of water.

sham (sham), *n.*, *adj.*, *v.*, **shammed, sham·ming.** —*n.* **1.** a spurious imitation. **2.** a person who gives a false impression. **3.** a decorative cover, esp. for a pillow. —*adj.* **4.** not real; pretended. —*v.t.*, *v.i.* **5.** to make a false show (of); pretend.

sham·ble (sham/bəl), *v.*, **-bled, -bling,** *n.* —*v.i.* **1.** to walk awkwardly with a shuffle. —*n.* **2.** a shambling gait.

shame (shām), *n.*, *v.*, **shamed, sham·ing.** —*n.* **1.** the painful feeling of having done something dishonorable or improper. **2.** disgrace; ignominy. **3.** a cause for regret or disappointment. —*v.t.* **4.** to cause to feel shame. **5.** to motivate through shame. **6.** to cause to suffer disgrace. —*Idiom.* **7. put to shame,** to outdo; surpass. —**shame/ful,** *adj.*

shame/faced/ *adj.* **1.** feeling or showing shame. **2.** modest or bashful.

sham·poo (sham pōō/), *n.*, *pl.* **-poos,** *v.*, **-pooed, -poo·ing.** —*n.* **1.** a special cleansing preparation that produces suds. **2.** the act of washing or cleansing with shampoo. —*v.t.* **3.** to wash (the hair), esp. with shampoo. **4.** to clean (rugs, upholstery, etc.) with shampoo.

sham·rock (sham/rok), *n.* any of several plants with a three-part leaf, esp. a small clover that is the national emblem of Ireland.

shang·hai (shang/hī, shang hī/), *v.t.*, **-haied, -hai·ing.** to coerce (a sailor) to join the crew of a ship.

shank (shangk), *n.* **1. a.** the part of the human leg between the knee and ankle. **b.** a corresponding part in other vertebrates. **2.** a cut of meat from the leg. **3.** a straight, shaftlike part of an implement or tool that connects two more important or complex parts. **4.** *Informal.* the early part of a period of time.

shan·tung (shan/tung/), *n.* a plain-weave silk with an irregular or uneven texture.

shan·ty (shan/tē), *n.*, *pl.* **-ties.** a crudely built hut, cabin, or house.

shape (shāp), *n.*, *v.*, **shaped, shap·ing.** —*n.* **1.** the outline or form of the external surface of something. **2.** something seen in outline, as in silhouette. **3.** an imaginary form; phantom. **4.** organized form or orderly arrangement. **5.** condition or state of repair. **6.** the figure or physique of a person. —*v.t.* **7.** to give definite shape to. **8.** to adjust; adapt. **9.** to direct (one's course, future, etc.). **10. shape up,** to improve or develop. —*Idiom.* **11. take shape,** to assume a fixed or more complete form. —**shape/less,** *adj.*

shape/ly *adj.*, **-li·er, -li·est.** having a pleasing shape. —**shape/li·ness,** *n.*

share¹ (shâr), *n.*, *v.*, **shared, shar·ing.** —*n.* **1.** a portion allotted to one person. **2.** one of the equal parts into which the capital stock of a corporation is divided. —*v.t.* **3.** to divide and distribute in shares; apportion. **4.** to use, participate in, or receive jointly. —*v.i.* **5.** to have a share.

share² (shâr), *n.* a plowshare.

share/crop/per *n.* a tenant farmer who pays as rent a share of the crop.

share/hold/er *n.* one that owns shares of stock, as in a corporation.

shark¹ (shärk), *n.* any of various predatory fishes with a rough scaleless skin.

shark² (shärk), *n.* **1.** a person who preys greedily on others. **2.** *Informal.* one with unusual ability in a particular field.

sharp (shärp), *adj.*, **-er, -est,** *v.*, *adv.*, *n.* —*adj.* **1.** having a thin cutting edge or a fine point. **2.** not blunt or rounded. **3.** involving an abrupt change in direction or course. **4.** clearly defined; distinct. **5.** pungent or biting in taste. **6.** piercing or shrill in sound. **7.** keenly cold, as weather. **8.** felt acutely; intense. **9.** merciless, caustic, or harsh. **10.** alert or vigilant. **11.** mentally acute. **12.** shrewd, often to the point of dishonesty. **13.** *Music.* **a.** raised a half

step in pitch. **b.** above the correct pitch. **14.** *Informal.* very stylish. —*v.t.*, *v.i.* **15.** *Music.* to make or become sharp. —*adv.* **16.** keenly or acutely. **17.** abruptly or suddenly. **18.** punctually. **19.** *Music.* above the correct pitch. —*n.* **20.** SHARPER. **21.** *Music.* a symbol indicating a tone one half step above a given tone. —**sharp/ly,** *adv.* —**sharp/ness,** *n.*

sharp/shoot/er *n.* a person skilled in shooting, esp. with a rifle.

shat·ter (shat/ər), *v.t.*, *v.i.* to break or burst into pieces or fragments.

shat/ter·proof/ *adj.* made to resist shattering.

shave (shāv), *v.*, **shaved, shaved** or (*esp. in combination*) **shav·en, shav·ing,** *n.* —*v.t.* **1.** to remove hair or a beard with a razor. —*v.t.* **2.** to remove hair from (the face, legs, etc.) close to the skin. **3.** to cut off (hair, esp. the beard) close to the skin. **4.** to cut or scrape away the surface of. **5.** to reduce to shavings. **6.** to come very near to; graze. —*n.* **7.** the act, process, or result of shaving.

shav/ings *n.pl.* thin slices of wood.

shawl (shôl), *n.* a piece of fabric worn, esp. by women, around the shoulders or head.

Shaw·nee (shô nē/), *n.*, *pl.* **-nee, -nees.** a member of an American Indian people probably orig. of the upper Ohio River valley.

she (shē), *pron.*, *n.*, *pl.* **shes.** —*pron.* **1.** the female person or animal last mentioned. **2.** something considered to be feminine. —*n.* **3.** a female person or animal.

sheaf (shēf), *n.*, *pl.* **sheaves.** **1.** a bundle of cut stalks of a cereal plant. **2.** a bundle, cluster, or collection, as of papers.

shear (shēr), *v.*, **sheared, sheared** or **shorn, shear·ing,** *n.* —*v.t.* **1.** to cut (something). **2.** to remove or deprive by or as if by cutting. **3.** to clip the hair, fleece, or wool from. —*n.* **4. shears,** (*used with a pl. v.*) **a.** large scissors. **b.** any of various cutting implements resembling scissors. **5.** the act or process of shearing. **6.** the tendency of a force applied to a solid body to cause deformation or rupture along a plane parallel to the force.

sheath (shēth), *n.*, *pl.* **sheaths** (shēthz). **1.** a case for a blade, as of a dagger. **2.** a closely enveloping part or structure, as in an animal. **3.** a close-fitting dress.

sheathe (shēth), *v.t.*, **sheathed, sheath·ing.** **1.** to put into a sheath. **2.** to cover or provide with a protective layer or sheathing.

she·bang (shə bang/), *n.* *Informal.* an organization, contrivance, or affair: *threw the whole shebang away.*

shed¹ (shed), *n.* a slight or rude structure built for shelter or storage.

shed² (shed), *v.*, **shed, shed·ding.** —*v.t.* **1.** to pour forth; let fall. **2.** to give forth (light, influence, etc.). **3.** to resist being penetrated by: *cloth that sheds water.* **4.** to cast off (leaves, skin, etc.) by a natural process. —*v.i.* **5.** to cast off a natural covering.

she'd (shēd), **1.** contraction of *she had.* **2.** contraction of *she would.*

sheen (shēn), *n.* luster; brightness.

sheep (shēp), *n.*, *pl.* **sheep. 1.** a ruminant mammal related to the goat and bred for wool and meat. **2.** a meek or easily led person.

sheep/ dog/ *n.* a dog trained to herd and guard sheep.

sheep/fold/ *n.* an enclosure for sheep.

sheep/ish *adj.* **1.** embarrassed or shamefaced. **2.** like a sheep, as in meekness.

sheer¹ (shēr), *adj.*, **-er, -est,** *adv.* —*adj.* **1.** transparent and thin; diaphanous. **2.** unqualified; utter: *sheer nonsense.* **3.** almost vertical; very steep. —*adv.* **4.** completely; quite. **5.** very steeply.

sheer² (shēr), *v.i.*, *v.t.* to turn from a course; swerve.

sheet¹ (shēt), *n.* **1.** a large rectangular piece of fabric, as cotton, used as an article of bedding. **2.** a broad, thin layer or covering: *a sheet of ice.* **3.** a relatively thin, usu. rectangular piece, as of glass or metal. **4.** a rectangular piece of paper.

sheet² (shēt), *n.* a rope or wire used to secure or adjust a ship's sail.

sheik or **sheikh** (shēk, shāk), *n.* (in Arab countries) the patriarch of a tribe or family; chief: also used as a term of polite address.

shek•el (shek'əl), *n.* **1.** the basic monetary unit of Israel. **2.** a coin of the ancient Hebrews. **3. shekels,** *Slang.* money; cash.

shelf (shelf), *n., pl.* **shelves** (shelvz). **1.** a slab, as of wood or metal, fixed horizontally to a wall to hold objects. **2.** something resembling a shelf, as a rock ledge or a sandbank. **—Idiom. 3. on the shelf,** inactive or useless.

shelf′ life′ *n.* the period during which a stored commodity remains suitable for use.

shell (shel), *n.* **1.** a hard outer covering of an animal, as a clam or turtle. **2.** the hard outer covering of a seed, fruit, nut, or egg. **3.** a hollow projectile filled with an explosive charge. **4.** a metallic cartridge used in small arms. **5.** an unfilled pastry crust. **6.** a light, long, and narrow racing boat for rowing. **7.** a computer program with an interface designed to simplify use of the operating system. **—v.t. 8.** to remove the shell of. **9.** to fire shells at, on, or among; bombard. **10. shell out,** *Informal.* to pay (money).

she'll (shēl; *unstressed* shil), contraction of *she will.*

shel•lac or **-lack** (shə lak'), *n., v.,* **-lacked, -lacking. —n. 1.** a purified lac used for making varnish. **2.** a varnish made by dissolving shellac in alcohol. **—v.t. 3.** to coat or treat with shellac. **4.** *Slang.* to defeat; trounce.

shell′fish′ *n., pl.* **-fish, -fish•es.** an aquatic animal having a shell, as a clam or lobster.

shell′ shock′ *n.* COMBAT FATIGUE. **—shell′-shocked′,** *adj.*

shel•ter (shel'tər), *n.* **1.** something that affords cover or protection; refuge. **2.** the protection or refuge afforded by a shelter. **—v.t. 3.** to provide with a shelter. **—v.i. 4.** to take shelter.

shelve (shelv), *v.t.,* **shelved, shelv•ing. 1.** to place on a shelf. **2.** to put off or aside. **3.** to remove from active use or service. **4.** to furnish with shelves.

she•nan′i•gans (shə nan′i gənz) *n.pl. Informal.* **1.** mischief; prankishness. **2.** deceit; trickery.

shep•herd (shep'ərd), *n.* **1.** a person who herds and tends sheep. **—v.t. 2.** to tend as or like a shepherd.

sher•bet (shûr'bit), *n.* a frozen, fruit-flavored ice with milk, egg white, or gelatin added.

sher•iff (sher'if), *n.* a county law-enforcement officer.

sher•ry (sher'ē), *n., pl.* **-ries.** a fortified, amber-colored wine. [< Sp *(vino de) Xeres* (wine of) Jerez, a city in Spain]

shib•bo•leth (shib'ə lith, -leth'), *n.* **1.** a peculiarity of pronunciation or usage that distinguishes a particular group. **2.** a slogan; catchword.

shield (shēld), *n.* **1.** a broad piece of armor carried on the arm or in the hand. **2.** a person or thing that guards, protects, or defends. **3.** something shaped like a shield. **—v.t. 4.** to protect or conceal with or as if with a shield.

shift (shift), *v.t.* **1.** to move from one place, position, or direction to another. **2.** to replace by another; exchange. **3.** to change (gears) from one ratio to another in a motor vehicle. **—v.i. 4.** to move from one place, position, or direction to another. **5.** to manage to get along. **6.** to change gears in a motor vehicle. **—n. 7.** a change or transfer from one place, position, or direction to another. **8. a.** a person's scheduled period of work. **b.** a group scheduled to work together during such a period. **9.** a gearshift. **10.** a straight, loose-fitting dress. **11.** an ingenious device for getting something done; expedient. **12.** an evasion or trick.

shift′less *adj.* lacking incentive, ambition, or aspiration; lazy.

shift′y *adj.,* **-i•er, -i•est.** evasive or crafty.

shill (shil), *n.* a person who poses as a customer in order to decoy others into participating, as at a gambling house.

shil•le•lagh (shə lā′lē, -lə), *n.* a cudgel.

shil•ling (shil′ing), *n.* **1.** a coin and former monetary unit of the United Kingdom, the 20th part of a pound, equal to 12 pence. **2.** the basic monetary unit of Kenya, Somalia, Tanzania, and Uganda.

shil•ly-shal•ly (shil′ē shal′ē), *v.i.,* **-shal•lied, -shal•ly•ing. 1.** to show indecision or hesitation; vacillate. **2.** to waste time.

shim•mer (shim′ər), *v.i.* **1.** to shine with or reflect a soft, tremulous light. **—n. 2.** a soft, tremulous light. **—shim′mer•y,** *adj.*

shin (shin), *n., v.,* **shinned, shin•ning. —n. 1.** the front part of the leg from the knee to the ankle. **—v.t., v.i. 2.** to climb (a pole, tree, etc.) by gripping with the legs after pulling oneself up with the hands.

shin′bone′ *n.* the tibia.

shin•dig (shin′dig′), *n. Informal.* an elaborate and usu. large party.

shine (shīn), *v.,* **shone** or, esp. for 6, **shined; shin•ing;** *n.* **—v.i. 1.** to give forth or glow with light. **2.** to glisten or sparkle. **3.** to be outstanding; excel. **—v.t. 4.** to cause to shine. **5.** to direct the light of (a lamp, mirror, etc.). **6.** to polish (shoes, silverware, etc.). **—n. 7.** radiance or brightness. **8.** a polish given to shoes. **9.** fair weather: *rain or shine.* **—Idiom. 10. take a shine to,** to develop a liking for.

shin′er *n. Informal.* discoloration of the skin around the eye, resulting from a blow, bruise, etc.; black eye.

shin•gle¹ (shing′gəl), *n., v.,* **-gled, -gling. —n. 1.** a thin piece of wood, asbestos, etc., laid in overlapping rows to cover the roofs or outside walls of buildings. **2.** a small signboard. **—v.t. 3.** to cover with shingles.

shin•gle² (shing′gəl), *n.* **1.** waterworn pebbles lying loose esp. on a beach. **2.** a beach or riverbank covered with shingle.

shin′ splints′ *n. (used with a pl. v.)* a painful condition of the front lower leg associated with strenuous activity.

Shin•to (shin′tō), *n.* the native religion of Japan, primarily a system of nature and ancestor worship. Also, **Shin′to•ism.** [< Japn: the way of the gods]

ship (ship), *n., v.,* **shipped, ship•ping. —n. 1.** a vessel, esp. a large oceangoing one, for navigating in water. **2.** the crew and passengers of a ship. **3.** an airship, airplane, or spacecraft. **—v.t. 4.** to transport by ship, rail, truck, or plane. **5.** to take in (water) over the side of a ship. **6.** to put in place for use on a ship or boat: *Ship the oars.* **7.** to send away. **—v.i. 8.** to go on board ship. **—ship′board′,** *n.* **—ship′mate′,** *n.* **—ship′ment,** *n.*

-ship a suffix meaning: state or quality (*friendship*); office or position (*governorship*); rank or title (*lordship*); skill or art (*horsemanship*); all people involved (*ridership*).

ship′shape′ *adj.* in good order; trim or tidy.

ship′wreck′ *n.* **1.** the destruction of a ship. **2.** the remains of a wrecked ship. **3.** ruin or destruction. **—v.i., v.t. 4.** to suffer or cause to suffer shipwreck.

ship′wright′ *n.* carpenter in ship repair or construction.

ship′yard′ *n.* a place where ships are built or repaired.

shire (shīⁱr), *n.* one of the counties of Great Britain.

shirk (shûrk), *v.t., v.i.* to evade (work, duty, etc.). **—shirk′er,** *n.*

shirr (shûr), *v.t.* **1.** to draw up or gather (fabric) on parallel threads. **2.** to bake (eggs), esp. in individual dishes. **—n. 3.** Also, **shirr′ing.** an ornamental gathering of fabric.

shirt (shûrt), *n.* **1.** a garment for the upper part of the body, usu. having a collar and a front opening. **2.** an undershirt. **—Idiom. 3. keep one's shirt on,** *Informal.* to remain calm.

shirt′tail′ *n.* the part of a shirt below the waistline.

shirt′waist′ *n.* a tailored blouse for women.

shish ke•bab (shish′ kə bob′), *n.* cubes of meat, as lamb, broiled on a skewer.

shiv•er¹ (shiv′ər), *v.i.* **1.** to shake or tremble, as with cold or excitement. **—n. 2.** a tremble or quiver. **—shiv′er•y,** *adj.*

shiv•er² (shiv′ər), v.t., v.i. to break or split into fragments.

shoal¹ (shōl), n. **1.** a shallow place in a body of water. **2.** a sandbank or sand bar.

shoal² (shōl), n. **1.** a large number or group. **2.** a school of fish.

shock¹ (shok), n. **1.** a sudden or violent disturbance of the emotions or sensibilities. **2.** a sudden and violent blow or impact. **3.** gravely diminished blood circulation caused by severe trauma and characterized by pallor and weak pulse. **4.** the effect produced by the passage of an electric current through the body. **5.** a shock absorber. —v.t. **6.** to affect with intense surprise, horror, or outrage. **7.** to give an electric shock to.

shock² (shok), n. a thick, bushy mass, as of hair.

shock′ absorb′er n. a device for damping sudden and rapid motion, as the recoil of a spring-mounted object from shock.

shock′ ther′apy n. the use of a drug or electricity to induce convulsions for symptomatic relief in certain mental disorders.

shod•dy (shod′ē), adj., **-di•er, -di•est,** n., pl. **-dies.** —adj. **1.** of inferior quality or workmanship. **2.** shabby. —n. **3. a.** fiber made of reclaimed wool. **b.** a low-grade fabric made from this. **4.** inferior products or merchandise. —**shod′di•ly,** adv.

shoe (shoo), n., v., **shod** or **shoed, shoe•ing.** —n. **1.** an external covering for the human foot. **2.** a horseshoe. **3.** the outer casing of an automobile tire. —v.t. **4.** to provide with a shoe or shoes.

shoe′horn′ n. a curved device used to make a shoe slip on more easily.

shoe′lace′ n. a string or lace for fastening a shoe.

shoe′mak′er n. a person who makes or mends shoes.

shoe′string′ n. **1.** SHOELACE. **2.** a very small amount of money.

shoe′tree′ n. a foot-shaped device placed inside a shoe to preserve its shape.

sho•gun (shō′gən, -gun), n. one of the chief military commanders of Japan from the 8th to 12th centuries.

shoo (shoo), interj., v., **shooed, shoo•ing.** —interj. **1.** (used to scare or drive away chickens, birds, etc.). —v.t. **2.** to drive away by shouting "shoo."

shoo′-in′ n. a candidate, competitor, etc., regarded as certain to win.

shoot (shoot), v., **shot, shoot•ing,** n. —v.t. **1.** to hit, wound, or kill with a missile, as a bullet. **2.** to send forth (a missile) from a weapon. **3.** to discharge (a weapon). **4.** to send forth rapidly or suddenly. **5.** to direct toward a target or goal. **6.** to pass rapidly through, over, or down: *to shoot the rapids.* **7.** to emit (a ray, as of light). **8.** to variegate with streaks or flecks of another color. **9.** to thrust forward. **10.** to take a picture of; photograph. —v.i. **11.** to send forth a missile, as from a bow. **12.** to hunt with a gun for sport. **13.** to move or pass suddenly or swiftly. **14.** to put forth buds or shoots. **15.** to project; jut. **16.** to dart through the body, as pain. **17. shoot for** or **at,** to attempt to obtain or accomplish. **18. ~ up, a.** to grow rapidly or suddenly. **b.** *Slang.* to inject a narcotic drug intravenously. —n. **19.** a shooting expedition or contest. **20.** new or young growth from a plant. —**shoot′er,** n.

shoot′ing star′ n. METEOR (def. 1).

shop (shop), n., v., **shopped, shop•ping.** —n. **1.** a retail store, esp. a small one. **2.** a workshop. **3.** a factory, office, or business. —v.i. **4.** to visit stores for the purpose of purchasing or examining goods. —*Idiom.* **5. talk shop,** to talk about a shared trade, profession, or business. —**shop′per,** n.

shop′lift′er n. a person who steals goods from a retail store.

shop′talk′ n. conversation about one's work or occupation.

shore¹ (shôr), n. the land along the edge of a sea, lake, or river.

shore² (shôr), n., v., **shored, shor•ing.** —n. **1.** a supporting post or beam; prop. —v.t. **2.** to support with or as if with a shore; prop.

shorn (shôrn), v. a pp. of SHEAR.

short (shôrt), adj., **-er, -est,** adv., n., v. —adj. **1.** having little length or height. **2.** brief in duration. **3.** concise, as writing. **4.** rudely brief; abrupt. **5.** not sufficient; scanty. **6.** not reaching a mark, target, or standard. **7.** made with a large amount of shortening; crisp and flaky. **8.** noting a sale of securities or commodities that the seller does not possess, depending for profit on a decline in prices. —adv. **9.** abruptly or suddenly. **10.** briefly; curtly. **11.** on the near side of an intended or particular point. —n. **12.** something that is short. **13. shorts, a.** short trousers. **b.** undershorts. **14.** SHORT CIRCUIT. **15.** a short film, as one shown with a feature-length film. —v.i., v.t. **16.** to form a short circuit (in). —*Idiom.* **17. in short,** in brief. —**short′en,** v.t., v.i.

short•age (shôr′tij), n. a deficiency in quantity.

short′bread′ n. a rich, short butter cookie.

short′cake′ n. a rich biscuit or cake topped with fruit and whipped cream.

short′change′ v.t., **-changed, -chang•ing. 1.** to give less than the correct change to. **2.** to cheat; defraud.

short′ cir′cuit n. a condition of relatively low resistance between two points of differing potential in an electric circuit, usu. resulting in a flow of excess current. —**short′-cir′cuit,** v.t., v.i.

short′com′ing n. a defect or deficiency, as in conduct.

short′cut′ n. **1.** a shorter way to get somewhere. **2.** a quicker method of accomplishing something.

short•en•ing (shôrt′ning, shôr′tn ing), n. a fat, as butter, used to make pastry or bread crisp and flaky.

short′hand′ n. a method of rapid handwriting using simple strokes, abbreviations, or symbols to designate letters, words, or phrases.

short′-hand′ed adj. not having the necessary number of workers.

short′-lived′ (līvd, livd), adj. living or lasting only a little while.

short′ly adv. **1.** in a short time; soon. **2.** briefly; concisely.

short′ shrift′ n. little attention or consideration.

short′sight′ed adj. **1.** nearsighted. **2.** lacking in foresight.

short′stop′ n. Baseball. the player or position of the player covering the area between second and third base.

short′-tem′pered adj. having a quick, hasty temper; irascible.

short′wave′ n. a radio wave corresponding to frequencies of over 1600 kilohertz that is used for long-distance reception or transmission.

Sho•sho•ne or **-ni** (shō shō′nē), n., pl. **-ne, -nes** or **-ni, -nis.** a member of an American Indian people or group living mainly in Nevada, Utah, Idaho, and Wyoming.

shot¹ (shot), n., pl. **shots** or, for 4, 5, **shot. 1.** the discharge of a weapon, as a firearm. **2.** an act or instance of shooting. **3.** reach or range. **4.** small balls or pellets of lead for a shotgun. **5. a.** a projectile for discharge from a firearm. **b.** such projectiles collectively. **6.** a marksman. **7.** a heavy metal ball used in the shot put. **8.** a stroke or throw in certain games. **9.** an attempt or try. **10.** a hypodermic injection. **11.** a small quantity of undiluted liquor. **12.** a photograph, esp. a snapshot. **13.** Motion Pictures, Television. a single unit of action photographed without interruption by one camera.

shot² (shot), v. **1.** pt. and pp. of SHOOT. —adj. **2.** in hopelessly bad condition.

shot′gun′ n. a smoothbore gun for firing small shot.

shot′ put′ n. a field event in which a heavy metal ball is thrown for distance. —**shot′-put′ter,** n.

should (shood), auxiliary v. **1.** pt. of SHALL. **2.** (used to indicate duty, propriety, or expediency): *You should not do that.* **3.** (used to express condition): *Were he to arrive, I should be pleased.*

shoul•der (shōl′dər), n. **1.** the part of the human body, from the base of the neck to the upper arm, where the arm joins the trunk. **2.** a corresponding part in animals. **3.** a shoulderlike part or projection. **4.** a border alongside a roadway. —*v.t.* **5.** to push or carry with or as if with the shoulder. **6.** to assume as a responsibility.

shout (shout), *v.i., v.t.* **1.** to call or cry out loudly. —*n.* **2.** a loud call or cry.

shove (shuv), *v.*, **shoved, shov•ing**, *n.* —*v.t., v.i.* **1.** to push roughly or rudely. **2.** shove off, to go away; depart. —*n.* **3.** an act or instance of shoving.

shov•el (shuv′əl), *n., v.*, **-eled, -el•ing** or (*esp. Brit.*) **-elled, -el•ling.** —*n.* **1.** an implement consisting of a scoop attached to a long handle, used for lifting or throwing loose matter. —*v.t.* **2.** to take up and throw with a shovel. **3.** to dig, move, or clear with or as if with a shovel. —*v.i.* **4.** to use a shovel.

show (shō), *v.*, **showed, shown** or **showed, show• ing**, *n.* —*v.t.* **1.** to cause or allow to be seen; display. **2.** to point out; indicate. **3.** to guide; escort. **4.** to make known; explain. **5.** to reveal; demonstrate. **6.** to offer; grant: *to show mercy.* —*v.i.* **7.** to be or become visible. **8.** to finish third, as in a horse race. **9. show off, a.** to display to advantage. **b.** to present with pride. **c.** to seek attention by ostentatious behavior. **10. ~ up, a.** to come to a place; arrive. **b.** to make (another) seem inferior by comparison. —*n.* **11.** a theatrical production or performance. **12.** a radio or television program. **13.** a public exhibition. **14.** ostentatious and often false display. **15.** third place, as in a horse race. **16.** appearance; impression.

show′case′ *n., v.*, **-cased, -cas•ing.** —*n.* **1.** a glass case for displaying and protecting articles. **2.** a setting or vehicle for displaying something on a trial basis. —*v.t.* **3.** to exhibit to best advantage.

show′down′ *n.* a conclusive confrontation or settlement of a matter.

show•er (shou′ər), *n.* **1.** a brief fall of rain, hail, or snow. **2.** a bath in which water is sprayed on the body. **3.** something resembling a shower. **4.** a party at which presents are given to the honoree. —*v.t.* **5.** to give or give to in abundance. —*v.i.* **6.** to rain in a shower. **7.** to bathe in a shower.

show′-off′ *n.* a person given to showing off.

show′piece′ *n.* something worthy of being exhibited as a fine example of its kind.

show′place′ *n.* a place, as a mansion, notable for its beauty or historical interest.

show′y *adj.*, **-i•er, -i•est.** **1.** making an imposing display. **2.** ostentatious; gaudy.

shrap•nel (shrap′nl), *n.* **1.** fragments from a shell, mine, or bomb. **2.** a hollow projectile containing bullets and a bursting charge that explodes in the air. [after its inventor, H. *Shrapnel* (1761–1842), English army officer]

shred (shred), *n., v.*, **shred•ded** or **shred, shred• ding.** —*n.* **1.** a piece cut or torn off, esp. in a narrow strip. **2.** a bit; scrap. —*v.t., v.i.* **3.** to cut, tear, or fragment into shreds. —**shred′der,** *n.*

shrew¹ (shrōō), *n.* a scolding woman; nag. —**shrew′ish,** *adj.*

shrew² (shrōō), *n.* a small, mouselike mammal with a long, sharp snout.

shrewd (shrōōd), *adj.*, **-er, -est.** **1.** clever or sharp in practical matters. **2.** marked by cleverness, perceptiveness, etc. —**shrewd′ly,** *adv.*

shriek (shrēk), *n.* **1.** a loud, sharp, shrill cry. —*v.i., v.t.* **2.** to utter or utter with a shriek.

shrill (shril), *adj.*, **-er, -est**, *v.* —*adj.* **1.** high-pitched and piercing. —*v.t., v.i.* **2.** to cry shrilly.

shrimp (shrimp), *n., pl.* **shrimps** or, for 1, **shrimp.** **1.** any of various small, chiefly marine, often edible crustaceans. **2.** a small or insignificant person.

shrine (shrīn), *n.* **1.** a place consecrated to a saint or deity. **2.** the tomb of a saint. **3.** a place or object hallowed by its history or associations. **4.** a receptacle for sacred relics.

shrink (shringk), *v.*, **shrank** or, often, **shrunk; shrunk** or **shrunk•en; shrink•ing;** *n.* —*v.i.* **1.** to contract in size. **2.** to become reduced, esp. in value. **3.** to draw back; recoil. —*v.t.* **4.** to cause to shrink. —*n.* **5.** *Slang.* a psychiatrist.

shrink•age (shring′kij), *n.* **1.** the process of shrinking. **2.** the amount or degree of shrinking.

shrink′ing vi′olet *n.* a shy or modest person.

shrink′-wrap′ *v.*, **-wrapped, -wrap•ping**, *n.* —*v.t.* **1.** to wrap and seal in a plastic film that when exposed to heat shrinks tightly around the thing it covers. —*n.* **2.** the plastic used to shrink-wrap something.

shrive (shrīv), *v.t.*, **shrove** or **shrived, shriv•en** or **shrived, shriv•ing.** **1.** to impose penance on. **2.** to grant absolution to.

shriv•el (shriv′əl), *v.t., v.i.*, **-eled, -el•ing** or (*esp. Brit.*) **-elled, -el•ling.** to shrink and wrinkle, as from dryness.

shroud (shroud), *n.* **1.** a cloth in which a corpse is wrapped for burial. **2.** something that covers, conceals, or protects. **3.** any of the ropes that converge from a ship's masthead to keep the mast from swaying. —*v.t.* **4.** to hide from view; cover.

shrub (shrub), *n.* a woody plant smaller than a tree, usu. having multiple permanent stems. —**shrub′ber•y,** *n., pl.* **-ies.**

shrug (shrug), *v.*, **shrugged, shrug•ging**, *n.* —*v.t., v.i.* **1.** to raise and contract (the shoulders), as to express ignorance or indifference. **2. shrug off, a.** to disregard; minimize. **b.** to rid oneself of. —*n.* **3.** the act of shrugging.

shtick (shtik), *n. Slang.* a show-business routine or bit. [< Yiddish *shtik* pranks, whims, lit., piece]

shuck (shuk), *n.* **1.** a husk, as of corn, or shell, as of an oyster. —*v.t.* **2.** to remove the shucks from. **3.** to peel off; remove.

shud•der (shud′ər), *v.i.* **1.** to tremble convulsively, as from horror. —*n.* **2.** a convulsive trembling.

shuf•fle (shuf′əl), *v.*, **-fled, -fling**, *n.* —*v.i.* **1.** to walk or dance without lifting the feet. **2.** to intermix playing cards. —*v.t.* **3.** to move (the feet) along the ground or floor without lifting. **4.** to move this way and that or from one place to another. **5.** to rearrange in random order: *to shuffle playing cards.* —*n.* **6.** an act or instance of shuffling.

shuf′fle•board′ *n.* a game in which disks are pushed with cues toward scoring sections marked on a floor or deck.

shun (shun), *v.t.*, **shunned, shun•ning.** to take pains to keep away from; avoid.

shunt (shunt), *v.t., v.i.* **1.** to turn aside or out of the way. **2.** to switch (railroad rolling stock) from one track to another. —*n.* **3.** the act of shunting. **4.** a railroad switch.

shut (shut), *v.*, **shut, shut•ting.** —*v.t.* **1.** to move into a closed position. **2.** to close the doors of. **3.** to close by bringing together the parts of. **4.** to confine; enclose. **5.** to cause to suspend operations: *The factory was shut down for two weeks.* —*v.i.* **6.** to become shut. **7. shut off, a.** to stop the passage of. **b.** to isolate; separate. **8. ~ out, a.** to keep from scoring. **b.** to prevent (an opponent) from scoring. **9. ~ up,** to stop or cause to stop talking.

shut′out′ *n.* a game in which one side does not score.

shut′ter *n.* **1.** a solid or louvered movable cover for a window or door. **2.** a mechanical device for opening and closing the aperture of a camera lens to expose the film. —*v.t.* **3.** to close or provide with shutters.

shut•tle (shut′l), *n., v.*, **-tled, -tling.** —*n.* **1.** a device in a loom for passing the filling thread back and forth through the warp. **2.** a public conveyance, as a train, that travels back and forth at regular intervals over a short route. **3.** (*often cap.*) SPACE SHUTTLE. —*v.i., v.t.* **4.** to move or cause to move to and fro.

shut′tle•cock′ *n.* the conical feathered cork device used in badminton.

shy¹ (shī), *adj.*, **shy•er** or **shi•er, shy•est** or **shi• est**, *v.*, **shied, shy•ing.** —*adj.* **1.** bashful; retiring. **2.** easily frightened; timid. **3.** distrustful; wary. **4.** deficient; lacking. —*v.i.* **5.** to start back or aside in alarm. **6.** to draw back; recoil. —**shy′ly,** *adv.* —**shy′ness,** *n.*

shy² (shī), *v.t., v.i.*, **shied, shy•ing.** to throw with a swift, sudden movement.

shy•ster (shī′stər), *n.* a lawyer who uses unprofessional or questionable methods.

Si′amese twins′ *n.pl.* twins who are congenitally joined together.

sib•i•lant (sib′ə lənt), *adj.* **1.** of, producing, or being a hissing sound. —*n.* **2.** a sibilant speech sound, as (s).

sib•ling (sib′ling), *n.* a brother or sister.

sib•yl (sib′əl), *n.* a female prophet. —**sib′yl•line** (-ə lēn′, -līn′), *adj.*

sic (sik), *v.t.,* **sicked, sick•ing.** to incite (a dog) to attack.

sic (sēk; *Eng.* sik), *adv. Latin.* so; thus: used within brackets to indicate that a wording has been quoted exactly though it may appear incorrect.

sick (sik), *adj.,* **-er, -est. 1.** not healthy; ill. **2.** affected with nausea. **3.** deeply affected, as with sorrow. **4.** mentally or emotionally unsound. **5.** gruesome; sadistic. **6.** of or for use during sickness: *sick benefits.* **7.** disgusted; chagrined. —**sick′en,** *v.t., v.i.* —**sick′ness,** *n.*

sick•le (sik′əl), *n.* a curved, hooklike blade mounted in a short handle, for cutting grain or grass.

sick′ly *adj.,* **-li•er, -li•est. 1.** not well; ailing. **2.** of or arising from ill health. **3.** nauseating. **4.** maudlin; mawkish. **5.** faint or feeble.

side (sīd), *n., adj., v.,* **sid•ed, sid•ing.** —*n.* **1.** one of the surfaces forming the outside of something. **2.** either of the two surfaces of a thin flat object, as a door. **3.** either of the two lateral parts or areas of a thing. **4.** the right or left half of the body. **5.** an aspect; phase. **6.** region, direction, or position with reference to a central point. **7.** one of two or more contesting teams or groups. **8.** the position or course of a person or group opposing another. **9.** line of descent through either parent. **10.** the space immediately adjacent: *Stand at my side.* —*adj.* **11.** at or on one side. **12.** from or toward one side. **13.** subordinate; incidental: *a side issue.* —*v.i.* **14. side with** (or **against**), to support (or oppose), as in a dispute. —*Idiom.* **15. side by side,** next to one another. **16. take sides,** to support one party in a dispute.

side′bar′ *n.* a short news feature alongside and highlighting a longer story.

side′board′ *n.* a piece of furniture, as in a dining room, for holding articles of table service.

side′burns′ *n.pl.* projections of the hairline forming a border in front of each ear.

side′ effect′ *n.* an often adverse secondary effect, as of a drug.

side′kick′ *n.* **1.** a close friend. **2.** a confederate or assistant.

side′light′ *n.* an item of incidental information.

side′line′ *n.* **1.** a business or activity pursued in addition to one's primary business. **2.** an additional line or goods. **3.** either of the two lines defining the side boundaries of an athletic field or court.

side′long′ *adj.* **1.** directed to one side. —*adv.* **2.** toward the side; obliquely.

side′sad′dle *n.* **1.** a saddle for women on which the rider sits with both feet on the same side of the horse. —*adv.* **2.** on a sidesaddle.

side′show′ *n.* **1.** a minor show in connection with a principal one, as at a circus. **2.** a subordinate event or spectacle.

side′split′ting *adj.* **1.** convulsively uproarious. **2.** extremely funny.

side′step′ *v.i., v.t.,* **-stepped, -step•ping. 1.** to step to one side (of). **2.** to dodge by or as if by stepping aside.

side′swipe′ *v.,* **-swiped, -swip•ing,** *n.* —*v.t.* **1.** to strike with a glancing blow in passing. —*n.* **2.** a glancing blow in passing.

side′track′ *v.t., v.i.* **1.** to move from a main railroad track to a siding. **2.** to move or distract from a main subject or course. —*n.* **3.** a railroad siding.

side′walk′ *n.* a usu. paved walk at the side of a roadway.

side′ward (-wərd) *adj.* toward one side. —**side′ward, side′wards,** *adv.*

side′ways′ *adv.* **1.** with one side forward. **2.** to-

ward or from one side. —*adj.* **3.** moving, facing, or directed toward one side. Also, **side′wise′.**

sid′ing *n.* **1.** a short railroad track opening onto a main track. **2.** any of several varieties of weatherproof facing for frame buildings.

si•dle (sīd′l), *v.i.,* **-dled, -dling.** to move sideways, esp. in a furtive manner.

SIDS sudden infant death syndrome.

siege (sēj), *n.* **1.** the surrounding and attacking of a fortified place to compel its surrender. **2.** a series of besetting illnesses or troubles. **3.** a prolonged period of trouble.

si•en′na (sē en′ə) *n.* yellowish- or reddish-brown pigment.

si•er•ra (sē er′ə), *n., pl.* **-ras.** a chain of hills or mountains whose peaks suggest the teeth of a saw. [< Sp: lit., saw < L]

Si•er′ra Le•o′ne (lē ō′nē, lē ōn′), *n.* a republic in W Africa.

si•es•ta (sē es′tə), *n., pl.* **-tas.** a midday or afternoon rest or nap.

sieve (siv), *n.* a utensil with a meshed or perforated surface for sifting or straining.

sift (sift), *v.t.* **1.** to pass through a sieve. **2.** to scatter by means of a sieve. **3.** to separate by or as if by a sieve. **4.** to examine closely. —*v.i.* **5.** to pass or fall as if through a sieve.

sigh (sī), *v.i.* **1.** to let out the breath audibly, as from sorrow or weariness. **2.** to yearn or long; pine. —*n.* **3.** the act or sound of sighing.

sight (sīt), *n.* **1.** the power, faculty, or act of seeing. **2.** one's range of vision. **3.** a view; glimpse. **4.** something seen or worth seeing. **5.** one that is unusual, shocking, or distressing to see. **6.** a viewing device, as on a firearm, for aiding the eye in aiming. —*v.t.* **7.** to see or observe. **8.** to aim by a sight. —*Idiom.* **9. on sight,** immediately upon seeing. **10. out of sight, a.** *Informal.* exceedingly high. **b.** *Slang.* fantastic; marvelous. **11. sight unseen,** without previous examination. —**sight′less,** *adj.*

sight′ed *adj.* having functional vision; not blind.

sight′-read′ (rēd), *v.t., v.i.,* **-read** (red), **-read•ing.** to read or perform without previous practice, rehearsal, or study. —**sight′-read′er,** *n.*

sight′see′ing *n.* **1.** the act of visiting and seeing places and things of interest. —*adj.* **2.** participating in or used for sightseeing. —**sight′se′er,** *n.*

sign (sīn), *n.* **1.** a token; indication. **2.** a conventional mark, figure, or symbol used instead of the word or words it represents. **3.** a motion or gesture used to convey information. **4.** an inscribed board, placard, or plate bearing a warning, advertisement, etc. **5.** a trace; vestige. **6.** an omen; portent. **7.** one of the 12 divisions of the zodiac. —*v.t.* **8.** to affix a signature to. **9.** to write as a signature. **10.** to engage by written agreement. **11.** to communicate by means of a sign. —*v.i.* **12.** to write one's signature. **13. sign in** (or **out**), to record one's arrival (or departure) by signing a register. **14. ~ off,** to cease radio or television broadcasting. **15. ~ up,** to enlist, as in an organization. —**sign′er,** *n.*

sig•nal (sig′nl), *n., adj., v.,* **-naled, -nal•ing** (*esp. Brit.*) **-nalled, -nal•ling.** —*n.* **1.** something, as a gesture, that serves to indicate, warn, direct, or command. **2.** something agreed upon as the indication for concerted action. **3.** an electrical quantity or effect, as current or voltage, that can be varied to convey information. —*adj.* **4.** serving as a signal. **5.** notable; outstanding. —*v.t., v.i.* **6.** to make a signal (to). **7.** to communicate by a signal. —**sig′nal•er,** *n.*

sig′nal•ly *adv.* conspicuously; notably.

sig•na•to•ry (sig′nə tôr′ē), *n., pl.* **-ries.** one of the signers of a document.

sig•na•ture (sig′nə chər), *n.* **1.** a person's name as signed personally. **2.** *Music.* a sign or set of signs following a clef to indicate the key or the meter of a piece.

sig•net (sig′nit), *n.* a small seal, as on a finger ring.

sig•nif•i•cance (sig nif′i kəns), *n.* **1.** importance; consequence. **2.** meaning; import. **3.** the quality of being significant. —**sig•nif′i•cant,** *adj.*

signif′icant oth′er *n.* **1.** a person, as a parent,

who has great influence on one's behavior and self-esteem. **2.** a spouse or cohabiting lover.

sig′ni•fy′ *v.*, **-fied, -fy•ing.** —*v.t.* **1.** to make known by or as if by a sign. **2.** to mean; denote. —*v.i.* **3.** to be of importance. —**sig′ni•fi•ca′tion,** *n.*

Sikh (sēk), *n.* a member of a monotheistic religion of India that refuses to recognize the Hindu caste system. —**Sikh′ism,** *n.*

si•lage (sī′lij), *n.* fodder preserved through fermentation in a silo.

si•lence (sī′ləns), *n.*, *v.*, **-lenced, -lenc•ing. 1.** absence of sound or noise. **2.** the state of being silent. **3.** absence or omission of mention. **4.** secrecy. —*v.t.* **5.** to put or bring to silence; still. **6.** to put (doubts, fears, etc.) to rest.

si′lenc•er *n.* a device for deadening the report of a firearm.

sil•hou•ette (sil′ōō et′), *n.*, *v.*, **-et•ted, -et•ting.** —*n.* **1.** a representation of the outline of an object, as a person's profile, filled in with black or another color. **2.** the outline of something. —*v.t.* **3.** to show in or as if in a silhouette.

sil•i•ca (sil′i kə), *n.*, *pl.* **-cas.** the dioxide form of silicon occurring esp. as quartz sand, flint, and agate.

sil′i•cate (-kit, -kāt′), *n.* a mineral, as quartz, consisting of silicon and oxygen with a metal.

sil′i•con (-kən, -kon′), *n.* a nonmetallic element occurring in a combined state in minerals and rocks and constituting more than one fourth of the earth's crust. *Symbol:* Si; *at. wt.:* 28.086; *at. no.:* 14.

sil′i•cone′ (-kōn′), *n.* any of a number of polymers containing alternate silicon and oxygen atoms, very resistant to heat and water: used in adhesives, lubricants, etc.

sil′i•co′sis (-kō′sis), *n.* a lung disease caused by the inhaling of silica particles.

silk (silk), *n.* **1.** the soft, lustrous fiber obtained from the cocoon of the silkworm. **2.** thread or cloth made from silk. **3.** a fiber or filament resembling silk. —**silk′en,** *adj.* —**silk′y,** *adj.*, **-i•er, -i•est.**

silk′worm′ *n.* any of several moth caterpillars that spin a silken cocoon.

sill (sil), *n.* a horizontal member forming the bottom of a window or door.

sil•ly (sil′ē), *adj.*, **-li•er, -li•est. 1.** lacking good sense; stupid or foolish. **2.** absurd; ridiculous. **3.** stunned; dazed: *knocked me silly.* —**sil′li•ness,** *n.*

si•lo (sī′lō), *n.*, *pl.* **-los. 1.** a pit or cylindrical structure in which fodder or forage is kept. **2.** an underground installation that houses a ballistic missile.

silt (silt), *n.* **1.** earthy matter or fine sand carried by water and deposited as sediment. —*v.t.*, *v.i.* **2.** to fill or choke up with silt. —**silt′y,** *adj.*

sil•ver (sil′vər), *n.* **1.** a white, ductile metallic element used for making coins, table utensils, etc. *Symbol:* Ag; *at. wt.:* 107.870; *at. no.:* 47. **2.** coins made of silver. **3.** silverware. **4.** a lustrous grayish white. —*adj.* **5.** made of or plated with silver. **6.** of the color silver. **7.** eloquent; persuasive. —*v.t.* **8.** to coat with or as if with silver. —**sil′ver•y,** *adj.*

sil′ver•fish′ *n.* a wingless, silvery-gray insect that feeds on starch, damaging books, wallpaper, etc.

sil′ver lin′ing *n.* a prospect of hope or comfort.

sil′ver ni′trate *n.* a corrosive, poisonous powder used in photographic emulsions and as an antiseptic and astringent.

sil′ver-tongued′ *adj.* persuasive; eloquent.

sil′ver•ware′ *n.* articles, esp. eating utensils, made of silver, silver-plated metals, or stainless steel.

sim•i•an (sim′ē ən), *adj.* **1.** of or characteristic of an ape or monkey. —*n.* **2.** an ape or monkey.

sim•i•lar (sim′ə lər), *adj.* characterized by likeness or resemblance. —**sim′i•lar′i•ty,** *n.*, *pl.* **-ties.** —**sim′i•lar•ly,** *adv.*

sim•i•le (sim′ə lē), *n.*, *pl.* **-les.** a figure of speech in which two distinct things are compared by using "like" or "as," as in "a mouth like a rosebud." [< L: image, likeness]

si•mil•i•tude (si mil′i tōōd′, -tyōōd′), *n.* likeness; resemblance.

sim•mer (sim′ər), *v.i.* **1.** to cook just at or below

the boiling point. **2.** to be in a state of barely contained agitation. —*v.t.* **3.** to keep just at or below the boiling point. **4. simmer down,** to become calm or quiet. —*n.* **5.** the state or process of simmering.

si•mo•ny (sī′mə nē, sim′ə-), *n.* the buying or selling of ecclesiastical preferments or benefices.

sim•pa•ti•co (sim pä′ti kō′, -pat′i-), *adj.* congenial or like-minded.

sim•per (sim′pər), *v.i.* **1.** to smile in a silly, self-conscious way. —*n.* **2.** a silly, self-conscious smile.

sim•ple (sim′pəl), *adj.*, **-pler, -plest. 1.** not difficult; easy. **2.** not elaborate, complicated, or ornate; plain. **3.** not affected; unassuming. **4.** mere; bare: *the simple truth.* **5.** humble or lowly. **6.** lacking intelligence or sense. **7.** naive; artless. **8.** *Chem.* composed of only one substance or element. **9.** *Bot.* not divided. **10.** *Zool.* not compound. —**sim•plic′i•ty** (-plis′i tē), *n.*

sim′ple in′terest *n.* interest payable only on the principal.

sim′ple-mind′ed *adj.* **1.** lacking in complexity or subtlety; artless or unsophisticated. **2.** mentally deficient.

sim′ple•ton (-tən), *n.* a foolish person.

sim′pli•fy′ (-plə fī′), *v.t.*, **-fied, -fy•ing.** to make simple or simpler. —**sim′pli•fi•ca′tion,** *n.*

sim•plis′tic (-plis′tik), *adj.* characterized by excessive simplification.

sim′ply *adv.* **1.** in a simple manner. **2.** merely; only. **3.** absolutely; really.

sim•u•late (sim′yə lāt′), *v.t.*, **-lat•ed, -lat•ing. 1.** to create a model of. **2.** to make a pretense of; feign. **3.** to create the appearance or characteristics of: *simulated leather.* —**sim′u•la′tion,** *n.*

si•mul•cast (sī′məl kast′, -käst′), *n.*, *v.*, **-cast, -cast•ed, -cast•ing.** —*n.* **1.** a program broadcast simultaneously on radio and television. —*v.t., v.i.* **2.** to broadcast (in) a simulcast.

si•mul•ta•ne•ous (sī′məl tā′nē əs), *adj.* existing, occurring, or operating at the same time. —**si′mul•ta′ne•ous•ly,** *adv.*

sin (sin), *n.*, *v.*, **sinned, sin•ning.** —*n.* **1.** a transgression of divine law. **2.** a willful violation of a moral principle. **3.** a serious fault or offense. —*v.i.* **4.** to commit a sin. —**sin′ful,** *adj.* —**sin′ful•ly,** *adv.* —**sin′ner,** *n.*

since (sins), *adv.* **1.** from then until now. **2.** after a particular past time; subsequently. **3.** before now; ago: *long since.* —*prep.* **4.** continuously from. **5.** between a past time and the present. —*conj.* **6.** in the period following the time when. **7.** inasmuch as; because.

sin•cere (sin sēr′), *adj.*, **-cer•er, -cer•est. 1.** free of deceit or hypocrisy. **2.** genuine; real. —**sin•cere′ly,** *adv.* —**sin•cer′i•ty** (-ser′i tē), *n.*

si•ne•cure (sī′ni kyōōr′, sin′i-), *n.* an office or position that pays well but requires little or no work.

si•ne di•e (sī′nē dī′ē, sin′ā dē′ā), *adv.* without fixing a day for future action. [< L: without (a fixed) day]

si•ne qua non (sin′ā kwä nōn′, non′, kwā), *n.* an indispensable condition or element. [< LL: without which not]

sin•ew (sin′yōō), *n.* **1.** a tendon. **2.** strength; power. —**sin′ew•y,** *adj.*

sing (sing), *v.*, **sang** or, often, **sung; sung; sing•ing.** —*v.i.* **1.** to use the voice to produce musical sounds. **2.** to make a whistling, ringing, or whizzing sound. **3.** to produce a melodious sound: *nightingales singing.* **4.** *Slang.* to confess or act as an informer. —*v.t.* **5.** to utter with musical modulations of the voice. **6.** to proclaim enthusiastically: *sang his praises.* **7.** to chant or intone: *to sing mass.* —**sing′er,** *n.*

sing. singular.

Sin•ga•pore (sing′gə pôr′, sing′ə-), *n.* an island republic in the South China Sea, off the S tip of the Malay Peninsula. —**Sin′ga•po′re•an,** *n., adj.*

singe (sinj), *v.*, **singed, singe•ing,** *n.* —*v.t.* **1.** to burn superficially or slightly; scorch. **2.** to remove hair, bristles, feathers, or down from by subjecting to flame. —*n.* **3.** a superficial burn. **4.** the act of singeing.

sin•gle (sing′gəl), *adj., v.,* **-gled, -gling,** *n.* —*adj.* **1.** one only; sole. **2.** intended or suitable for one person only. **3.** not married. **4.** consisting of only one part, element, or member. **5.** separate, particular, or distinct; individual. —*v.t.* **6.** to pick or choose (one) from others. —*v.i.* **7.** to hit a single in baseball. —*n.* **8.** a single person or thing; individual. **9.** an accommodation or ticket for one person only. **10.** an unmarried person. **11.** a one-dollar bill. **12.** (in baseball) a hit that enables a batter to reach first base. **13. singles,** (*used with a sing. v.*) a match, as in tennis, with one player on each side.

sin′gle file′ *n.* a line of persons or things one behind the other.

sin′gle-hand′ed *adj.* **1.** accomplished by one person alone. **2.** by one's own effort; unaided. —*adv.* **3.** by one person alone; without aid.

sin′gle-mind′ed *adj.* having or showing a single aim or purpose.

sin′gly *adv.* **1.** separately. **2.** one at a time. **3.** single-handed.

sing′song′ *n.* a monotonous, rhythmical rising and falling in pitch of the voice when speaking.

sin•gu•lar (sing′gyə lər), *adj.* **1.** extraordinary; remarkable. **2.** strange; odd. **3.** unique. **4.** of or belonging to the grammatical category denoting one person, place, thing, or instance. —*n.* **5.** the singular number. **6.** a form in the singular. —**sin′gu•lar′i•ty,** *n.* —**sin′gu•lar•ly,** *adv.*

sin•is•ter (sin′ə stər), *adj.* **1.** threatening or portending evil; ominous. **2.** evil or malevolent; wicked.

sink (singk), *v.,* **sank** or, often, **sunk; sunk** or **sunk•en; sink•ing;** *n.* —*v.i.* **1.** to fall, drop, or descend gradually to a lower level, position, or state. **2.** to fail in physical strength or health. **3.** to decrease in amount, extent, or intensity. **4.** to become lower in volume or pitch. **5.** to slope downward; dip. —*v.t.* **6.** to cause to sink. **7.** to cause to penetrate. **8.** to dig or excavate (a shaft, well, etc.). **9.** to invest, esp. with the hope of profit. **10. sink in,** to enter or permeate the mind. —*n.* **11.** a basin connected with a water supply and drainage system. **12.** SINKHOLE (def. 2). **13.** a drain or sewer. **14.** a cesspool.

sink′hole′ *n.* **1.** a hole in soluble rock through which surface water drains into an underground passage. **2.** a depressed area in which waste or drainage collects.

sin•u•ous (sin′yoo əs), *adj.* having many curves or turns; winding.

si•nus (sī′nəs), *n.* **1.** a bodily cavity or passage, as a channel for venous blood. **2.** one of the hollow cavities in the skull connecting with the nasal cavities.

Sioux (soo), *n., pl.* **Sioux** (soo, sooz). DAKOTA (defs. 3, 4).

sip (sip), *v.,* **sipped, sip•ping,** *n.* —*v.t., v.i.* **1.** to drink a little at a time. —*n.* **2.** an act or instance of sipping. **3.** a quantity taken by sipping.

si•phon (sī′fən), *n.* **1.** a U-shaped pipe that uses atmospheric pressure to draw liquid from one container, place, or level to another. —*v.t., v.i.* **2.** to draw or pass through or as if through a siphon.

sir (sûr), *n.* **1.** a respectful or formal term of address for a man, used without the name. **2.** (*cap.*) the distinctive title of a knight or baronet.

sire (sī°r), *n., v.,* **sired, sir•ing.** —*n.* **1.** the male parent of a quadruped. **2.** a respectful term of address for a male sovereign. **3.** *Archaic.* a father or forefather. —*v.t.* **4.** to beget; procreate.

si•ren (sī′rən), *n.* **1.** any of several beings in Greek legend, part woman and part bird, whose seductive singing lured mariners to destruction. **2.** a seductively beautiful woman. **3.** an acoustical device that produces a loud piercing sound and is used esp. as a warning signal.

sir•loin (sûr′loin), *n.* the portion of the loin of beef in front of the rump.

si•sal (sī′səl, sis′əl), *n.* a fiber yielded by an agave and used esp. for making rope or rugs.

sis•sy (sis′ē), *n., pl.* **-sies. 1.** an effeminate boy or man. **2.** a timid person. —**sis′si•fied′** (-ə fīd′), *adj.*

sis•ter (sis′tər), *n.* **1.** a female having both parents in common with another offspring. **2.** HALF SISTER. **3.** STEPSISTER. **4.** a woman connected, as by race, to another. **5.** a female member of a religious order. —*adj.* **6.** being in close relationship with another: *our sister cities.* —**sis′ter•hood′,** *n.* —**sis′ter•ly,** *adj.*

sis′ter-in-law′ *n., pl.* **sis•ters-in-law. 1.** the sister of one's spouse. **2.** the wife of one's brother. **3.** the wife of the brother of one's spouse.

sit (sit), *v.,* **sat, sat, sit•ting.** —*v.i.* **1.** to rest with the body supported by the buttocks. **2.** to be located or situated. **3.** to pose, as for an artist. **4.** to remain quiet or inactive. **5.** (of a bird) to cover eggs for hatching. **6.** to occupy an official seat, as a legislator. **7.** to be convened or in session. **8.** to babysit. **9.** to have a particular effect. —*v.t.* **10.** to cause to sit. **11.** to keep one's seat on (an animal, esp. a horse). **12. sit in on,** to be a spectator, observer, or visitor at. **13. ~ out,** to fail to participate in. **14. ~ up, a.** to be awake and active after one's usual sleep time. **b.** to become interested; take notice.

si•tar (si tär′), *n.* an Indian lute with a pear-shaped body and a long, fretted neck. —**si•tar′ist,** *n.*

sit′-down′ *n.* a strike in which workers occupy their place of employment and refuse to work.

site (sīt), *n.* position or location, as of a town or building.

sit′-in′ *n.* an organized protest in which demonstrators occupy and refuse to leave a public place.

sit′ting duck′ *n.* a helpless or easy target or victim.

sit•u•ate (sich′oo āt′), *v.t.,* **-at•ed, -at•ing.** to put in or on a particular site or place; locate.

sit•u•a′tion *n.* **1.** location or position. **2.** state of affairs; circumstances. **3.** a position of employment; job.

six (siks), *n.* **1.** a cardinal number, five plus one. **2.** a symbol for this number, as 6 or VI. —*adj.* **3.** amounting to six in number. —**sixth,** *adj., n.*

six′teen′ *n.* **1.** a cardinal number, ten plus six. **2.** a symbol for this number, as 16 or XVI. —*adj.* **3.** amounting to 16 in number. —**six′teenth′,** *adj., n.*

sixth′ sense′ *n.* the power of intuition.

six′ty *n., pl.* **-ties,** *adj.* —*n.* **1.** a cardinal number, ten times six. **2.** a symbol for this number, as 60 or LX. —*adj.* **3.** amounting to 60 in number. —**six′ti•eth,** *adj., n.*

siz•a•ble or **size•a•ble** (sī′zə bəl), *adj.* of considerable size; fairly large.

size¹ (sīz), *n., v.,* **sized, siz•ing.** —*n.* **1.** spatial dimensions, proportions, magnitude, or extent. **2.** one of a series of graduated measures for articles of manufacture or trade. —*v.t.* **3.** to separate or sort according to size. **4. size up,** to form an estimate of; judge.

size² (sīz), *n., v.,* **sized, siz•ing.** —*n.* **1.** a gelatinous or glutinous substance used for filling pores in surfaces, as of cloth or paper. —*v.t.* **2.** to coat or treat with size.

siz•zle (siz′əl), *v.,* **-zled, -zling,** *n.* —*v.i.* **1.** to make a hissing sound, as in frying. **2.** to be very angry. —*n.* **3.** a sizzling sound.

skate¹ (skāt), *n., v.,* **skat•ed, skat•ing.** —*n.* **1.** ICE SKATE. **2.** ROLLER SKATE. —*v.i.* **3.** to glide or move on or as if on skates. —**skat′er,** *n.*

skate² (skāt), *n., pl.* **skates, skate.** a ray with winglike pectoral fins.

skate′board′ *n.* **1.** a board mounted on roller-skate wheels. —*v.i.* **2.** to ride a skateboard.

ske•dad•dle (ski dad′l), *v.i.,* **-dled, -dling.** *Informal.* to run away hurriedly; flee.

skein (skān), *n.* a loose coil of thread or yarn.

skel•e•ton (skel′i tn), *n.* **1.** the bones of a vertebrate that form the body's internal framework. **2.** a supporting framework, as of a building. **3.** an outline, as of a literary work. [< Gk: mummy] —**skel′e•tal,** *adj.*

skel′eton key′ *n.* a key that opens various simple locks.

skep•tic (skep′tik), *n.* **1.** a person who questions the validity or truth of religion or religious tenets. **2.**

a person with a doubting attitude. **3.** one who maintains that real knowledge is impossible. —skep′ti•cal, *adj.* —skep′ti•cism (-siz′əm), *n.*

sketch (skech), *n.* **1.** a simply or hastily executed drawing. **2.** a rough plan or draft, as of a book. **3.** a short piece of writing, often descriptive. **4. a.** a short comic routine. **b.** a brief dramatic scene. —*v.i., v.t.* **5.** to make a sketch (of).

sketch′y *adj.*, **-ier, -iest.** vague; approximate. —sketch′i•ly, *adv.*

skew (skyōō), *v.i., v.t.* **1.** to turn aside; swerve or slant. —*n.* **2.** a slanting movement, direction, or position.

skew′er *n.* **1.** a long pin for holding together pieces of meat while they cook. —*v.t.* **2.** to fasten with or as if with a skewer.

ski (skē), *n.*, *pl.* **skis, ski,** *v.*, **skied, ski•ing.** —*n.* **1.** one of a pair of long, slender runners used in gliding over snow. **2.** WATER SKI. —*v.i.* **3.** to travel on skis. —*v.t.* **4.** to travel on skis over. —ski′er, *n.*

skid (skid), *n.*, *v.*, **skid•ded, skid•ding.** —*n.* **1.** a plank, bar, or platform on which something can be slid, rolled along, or stored. **2.** a plank on or by which a load is supported. **3.** a device for preventing a wheel from rotating. **4.** an unexpected or uncontrollable sideways slide on a surface. —*v.i.* **5.** to slide without rotating, as a wheel. **6.** to slip or slide, esp. sideways; lose traction.

skid′ row′ (rō), *n.* a run-down urban area frequented by alcoholics and vagrants.

skiff (skif), *n.* a small, light sailboat or rowboat.

skill (skil), *n.* **1.** the ability to do something well. **2.** expertness or dexterity in performance. **3.** a craft, trade, or job, esp. one requiring manual dexterity. —skilled, *adj.* —skill′ful, *adj.* —skill′ful•ly, *adv.*

skil•let (skil′it), *n.* a frying pan.

skim (skim), *v.*, **skimmed, skim•ming.** —*v.t.* **1. a.** to remove (floating matter) from the surface of a liquid. **b.** to clear (liquid) thus: *to skim milk.* **2.** to move lightly over or along. **3.** to read superficially or hastily. —*v.i.* **4.** to move lightly over, along, or near a surface. **5.** to read something superficially or hastily.

skim′ milk′ *n.* milk with the cream removed.

skimp (skimp), *v.i., v.t.* to scrimp.

skimp′y *adj.*, **-i•er, -i•est.** lacking in size or fullness; scanty.

skin (skin), *n.*, *v.*, **skinned, skin•ning.** —*n.* **1.** the external covering of an animal body. **2.** a pelt or hide. **3.** an outer covering, casing, or layer, as the rind of fruit. —*v.t.* **4.** to strip or deprive of skin. **5.** to scrape a small piece of skin from (a part of the body).

skin′ div′ing *n.* underwater swimming with a face mask and flippers and sometimes with scuba. —skin′ div′er, *n.*

skin′flint′ *n.* a stingy person; miser.

skin′ny *adj.*, **-ni•er, -ni•est.** very lean or thin.

skin′ny-dip′ *v.*, **-dipped, -dip•ping,** *n. Informal.* —*v.i.* **1.** to swim in the nude. —*n.* **2.** a swim in the nude.

skip (skip), *v.*, **skipped, skip•ping,** *n.* —*v.i.* **1.** to bound along with alternate hops on each foot. **2.** to pass from one point to another, disregarding what intervenes. **3.** to leave hastily and secretly. **4.** to ricochet or bounce. —*v.t.* **5.** to jump lightly over. **6.** to pass over without taking notice or action. **7.** to be advanced beyond (a grade or class) in school. **8.** to go away from hastily and secretly: *They skipped town.* —*n.* **9.** a skipping movement or gait.

skip′per *n.* the master or captain of a ship.

skir•mish (skûr′mish), *n.* **1.** a fight between small bodies of troops. **2.** a minor conflict or encounter. —*v.i.* **3.** to engage in a skirmish.

skirt (skûrt), *n.* **1.** the part of a dress or coat that extends downward from the waist. **2.** a woman's one-piece garment extending downward from the waist. —*v.t.* **3.** to lie or pass along the border of. **4.** to avoid. —*v.i.* **5.** to move or lie along the border of something.

skit (skit), *n.* a short, usu. comical theatrical scene or act.

skit′tish *adj.* **1.** apt to start or shy: *a skittish horse.* **2.** frisky; lively. **3.** fickle; uncertain.

skiv•vy (skiv′ē), *n.*, *pl.* **-vies. 1.** a man's cotton T-shirt. **2. skivvies,** men's underwear consisting of a T-shirt and shorts.

skul•dug•ger•y or **skull•dug•ger•y** (skul dug′ə-rē), *n.* dishonorable or deceitful behavior.

skulk (skulk), *v.i.* **1.** to lie or keep in hiding, as for some evil reason. **2.** to move stealthily; slink.

skull (skul), *n.* the bony or cartilaginous framework of the vertebrate head, enclosing the brain.

skull′cap′ *n.* a small, brimless, close-fitting cap.

skunk (skungk), *n.*, *pl.* **skunks, skunk,** *v.* —*n.* **1.** a bushy-tailed New World mammal with black and white fur that sprays a fetid defensive fluid. **2.** a thoroughly contemptible person. —*v.t.* **3.** *Slang.* to defeat thoroughly in a game.

sky (skī), *n.*, *pl.* **skies. 1.** the upper atmosphere of the earth. **2.** the celestial heaven.

sky′cap′ *n.* a porter at an airport.

sky′div′ing *n.* the sport of jumping from an airplane and descending in free fall for a considerable distance before opening a parachute.

sky′jack′ *v.t.* to hijack (an airliner).

sky′light′ *n.* a glass-fitted opening in a roof or ceiling.

sky′line′ *n.* **1.** the apparent horizon. **2.** an outline, esp. of buildings, seen against the sky.

sky′rock′et *n.* **1.** a rocket firework that explodes high in the air, usu. in brilliant and colorful sparks. —*v.i., v.t.* **2.** to rise or cause to rise rapidly or suddenly.

sky′scrap′er *n.* a tall building of many stories.

sky′writ′ing *n.* writing in the sky formed by smoke released from an airplane.

slab (slab), *n.* a broad, flat, somewhat thick piece.

slack (slak), *adj.*, **-er, -est,** *n.*, *v.* —*adj.* **1.** not tight or taut; loose. **2.** negligent; careless. **3.** slow, sluggish, or indolent. **4.** not active or busy. —*n.* **5.** a slack condition or part. **6.** a period of decreased activity. —*v.t., v.i.* **7.** to slacken. —slack′ly, *adv.* —slack′ness, *n.*

slack′en *v.t., v.i.* **1.** to make or become less active, intense, etc. **2.** to make or become looser.

slack′er *n.* a person who evades work or military service.

slacks (slaks), *n.* (*used with a pl. v.*) trousers for informal or casual wear.

slag (slag), *n.* the fused and vitrified matter separated during the reduction of a metal from its ore.

slake (slāk), *v.t.*, **slaked, slak•ing. 1.** to allay (thirst, desire, etc.) by satisfying; quench. **2.** to cause disintegration of (lime) by treatment with water.

sla•lom (slä′ləm, -lōm), *n.* a downhill ski race over a winding and zigzag course.

slam¹ (slam), *v.*, **slammed, slam•ming,** *n.* —*v.t., v.i.* **1.** to shut with force and noise. **2.** to strike, throw, or move with violence or noisy force. —*n.* **3.** the act or sound of slamming.

slam² (slam), *n.* the winning of all or all but one of the tricks in a deal of cards.

slam′mer *n. Slang.* a prison.

slan•der (slan′dər), *n.* **1.** a malicious, false, and defamatory statement or report. —*v.t.* **2.** to utter slander against; defame. —slan′der•ous, *adj.*

slang (slang), *n.* very informal vocabulary that is characteristically more metaphorical, playful, vivid, and ephemeral than ordinary language. —slang′y, *adj.*, **-i•er, -i•est.**

slant (slant, slänt), *v.i.* **1.** to turn at an angle away from a given level or line; slope. —*v.t.* **2.** to cause to slant. **3.** to present in a way that favors a particular viewpoint or appeals to a particular group. —*n.* **4.** a slanting direction, line, or surface. **5.** a particular viewpoint, opinion, or attitude. —slant′wise′, *adj.*, *adv.*

slap (slap), *n.*, *v.*, **slapped, slap•ping.** —*n.* **1.** a sharp blow, esp. with the open hand. **2.** a sharp or sarcastic rebuke or comment. —*v.t.* **3.** to strike sharply, esp. with the open hand. **4.** to put, place, or cast forcibly.

slap′dash′ *adj.* hasty and careless; offhand.

slap/hap/py *adj.*, **-pi•er, -pi•est. 1.** severely befuddled. **2.** agreeably giddy or foolish.

slap/stick/ *n.* boisterous comedy characterized by broad farce and horseplay.

slash (slash), *v.t.* **1.** to cut with a violent sweeping stroke, as of a knife. **2.** to reduce sharply. **3.** to make slits in (a garment). —*n.* **4.** a violent sweeping stroke. **5.** a cut or mark made with a slash. **6.** VIRGULE.

slat (slat), *n.* a long, narrow strip, as of wood or metal.

slate (slāt), *n.*, *v.*, **slat•ed, slat•ing.** —*n.* **1.** a fine-grained rock that tends to split along parallel cleavage planes. **2.** a thin piece or plate of slate used esp. for roofing or as a writing surface. **3.** a list of candidates for nomination or election. —*v.t.* **4.** to cover with slate. **5.** to set down for nomination or appointment.

slat•tern (slat/ərn), *n.* a slovenly, untidy woman. —**slat/tern•ly,** *adj.*

slaugh•ter (slô/tər), *n.* **1.** the killing of animals for food. **2.** brutal or violent killing, esp. of great numbers of people. —*v.t.* **3.** to butcher (animals) for food. **4.** to kill brutally or in great numbers. —**slaugh/ter•house/,** *n.*

slave (slāv), *n.*, *v.*, **slaved, slav•ing.** —*n.* **1.** a person who is the property of and wholly subject to another. **2.** a person entirely under the domination of an influence or person. —*v.i.* **3.** to work like a slave; drudge. —**slav/er•y,** *n.*

slav•er (slav/ər, slā/vər, slä/-), *v.i.* to slobber; drool.

Slav•ic (slä/vik, slav/ik), *n.* **1.** a branch of the Indo-European language family that includes Polish, Czech, and Russian. —*adj.* **2.** of the Slavs or their languages.

slav•ish (slā/vish), *adj.* **1.** of or resembling a slave. **2.** deliberately imitative. —**slav/ish•ly,** *adv.*

slaw (slô), *n.* coleslaw.

slay (slā), *v.t.*, **slew, slain, slay•ing.** to kill by violence. —**slay/er,** *n.*

slea•zy (slē/zē), *adj.*, **-zi•er, -zi•est. 1.** contemptibly low or disreputable. **2.** squalid; tawdry. **3.** thin and limp in texture.

sled (sled), *n.*, *v.*, **sled•ded, sled•ding.** —*n.* **1.** a platform on runners, used by children for sliding over snow or ice. **2.** a sledge. —*v.i.*, *v.t.* **3.** to ride on or convey by sled.

sledge[1] (slej), *n.* a heavy vehicle on runners for conveying people or loads over snow or ice.

sledge[2] (slej), *n.* SLEDGEHAMMER.

sledge/ham/mer *n.* a large, heavy hammer wielded with both hands.

sleek (slēk), *adj.*, **-er, -est. 1.** smooth and glossy, as hair. **2.** well-fed or well-groomed. **3.** finely contoured; streamlined. —*v.t.* **4.** to make sleek. —**sleek/ly,** *adv.*

sleep (slēp), *v.*, **slept, sleep•ing,** *n.* —*v.i.* **1.** to take the rest afforded by the natural suspension of consciousness; cease being awake. **2.** to be dormant, quiescent, or inactive. **3. sleep away,** to pass (time) in sleep. **4. sleep off,** to get rid of (a headache, hangover, etc.) by sleeping. —*n.* **5.** the state of one that sleeps. **6.** a state, as dormancy, resembling sleep. —**sleep/less,** *adj.* —**sleep/y,** *adj.*, **-i•er, -i•est.**

sleep/er *n.* **1.** one that sleeps. SLEEPING CAR. **3.** an unexpected success.

sleep/ing bag/ *n.* a warmly lined bag in which a person can sleep, esp. outdoors.

sleep/ing car/ *n.* a railroad car equipped with sleeping accommodations.

sleet (slēt), *n.* **1.** precipitation created by the freezing of rain as it falls. —*v.i.* **2.** to send down or fall as sleet.

sleeve (slēv), *n.* **1.** the part of a garment that covers the arm. **2.** a tubular piece fitting over another part. —*Idiom.* **3. up one's sleeve,** kept hidden for future use. —**sleeve/less,** *adj.*

sleigh (slā), *n.* a horse-drawn vehicle on runners, used for conveying people over snow or ice.

sleight/ of hand/ *n.* **1.** skill in feats or tricks requiring manual dexterity. **2.** any such feat or trick.

slen•der (slen/dər), *adj.*, **-der•er, -der•est. 1.** narrow or small in circumference in proportion to height or length. **2.** thin, esp. gracefully slim. **3.** not adequate; meager.

sleuth (slooth), *n.* a detective.

slew[1] (sloo), *v.* pt. of SLAY.

slew[2] (sloo), *n.* Informal. a large number or quantity.

slice (slīs), *n.*, *v.*, **sliced, slic•ing.** —*n.* **1.** a thin, flat piece cut from something. **2.** a part or portion. **3.** the path described by a ball, as a golf ball, that curves toward the side from which it was struck. —*v.t.* **4.** to cut into slices. **5.** to cut off or remove a slice from. **6.** to hit (a ball) so as to result in a slice. —**slic/er,** *n.*

slick[1] (slik), *adj.*, **-er, -est,** *n.* —*adj.* **1.** smooth and slippery. **2.** shrewdly adroit; sly. **3.** ingenious; clever. **4.** having surface appeal but shallow or glib. —*n.* **5.** a smooth or slippery place or spot. —**slick/ly,** *adv.* —**slick/ness,** *n.*

slick[2] (slik), *v.t.* **1.** to make sleek or smooth. **2.** Informal. to make smart or spruce.

slick/er *n.* **1.** a loose oilskin raincoat. **2.** Informal. a swindler.

slide (slīd), *v.*, **slid** (slid), **slid•ing,** *n.* —*v.i.* **1.** to move along in continuous contact with a smooth or slippery surface. **2.** to slip or skid. **3.** to glide or pass smoothly. —*v.t.* **4.** to cause to slide. **5.** to hand or pass along quietly or furtively. —*n.* **6.** an act or instance of sliding. **7.** a smooth surface for sliding on. **8.** a part that functions by sliding. **9.** a mass of matter, as earth, sliding down. **10.** a transparency, as a frame of positive film, mounted for projection on a screen. **11.** a plate of glass on which objects are placed for microscopic examination.

slid/ing scale/ *n.* a scale, as of wages or prices, that varies with such conditions as the cost of living or the ability of individuals to pay.

slight (slīt), *adj.*, **-er, -est,** *v.*, *n.* —*adj.* **1.** small in amount or degree. **2.** of little importance or influence. **3.** slender or slim. **4.** frail; delicate. —*v.t.* **5.** to treat as unimportant. **6.** to treat with indifference; snub. **7.** to do negligently. —*n.* **8.** an instance of slighting; indifference or discourtesy.

slight/ly *adv.* barely; partly.

slim (slim), *adj.*, **slim•mer, slim•mest,** *v.*, **slimmed, slim•ming.** —*adj.* **1.** slender, as in form. **2.** meager; scanty. —*v.t.*, *v.i.* **3.** to make or become slim. —**slim/ness,** *n.*

slime (slīm), *n.* **1.** thin, glutinous mud. **2.** a ropy or viscous liquid substance, esp. of a foul kind. —**slim/y,** *adj.*, **-i•er, -i•est.**

sling (sling), *n.*, *v.*, **slung, sling•ing.** —*n.* **1.** a strap with a string at each end that is whirled around to hurl a missile, esp. a stone. **2.** a strap or band forming a loop by which something is suspended, supported, or carried. —*v.t.* **3.** to throw or hurl; fling. **4.** to place in or move by a sling.

sling/shot/ *n.* a Y-shaped stick with an elastic strip between the prongs for shooting small missiles.

slink (slingk), *v.i.*, **slunk, slink•ing. 1.** to move or go in a furtive, abject manner. **2.** to walk in a sinuous, provocative way. —**slink/y,** *adj.*, **-i•er, -i•est.**

slip[1] (slip), *v.*, **slipped, slip•ping,** *n.* —*v.i.* **1.** to move smoothly or easily. **2.** to slide suddenly and accidentally. **3.** to pass without having been done or used. **4.** to elapse quickly or imperceptibly. **5.** to move or go quietly or unobtrusively. **6.** to make a mistake. **7.** to decline; deteriorate. —*v.t.* **8.** to cause to move with a smooth or sliding motion. **9.** to put, pass, or insert quickly or stealthily. **10.** to put on or take off (a garment). **11.** to pass from or escape (the memory, attention, etc.). —*n.* **12.** an act or instance of slipping. **13.** a sudden, accidental slide. **14.** a mistake or blunder. **15.** a woman's undergarment worn under the outer dress. **16.** a pillowcase. **17.** a space for a ship between two wharves or in a dock.

slip[2] (slip), *n.* **1.** a piece suitable for propagation cut from a plant. **2.** a long, narrow strip, as of paper.

slip′cov′er *n.* an easily removable cover, esp. of cloth, for a piece of furniture.

slip′knot′ or **slip′ knot′,** *n.* a knot that slips easily along the cord or line around which it is made.

slipped′ disk′ *n.* an abnormal protrusion of a spinal disk between vertebrae.

slip′per *n.* a light, low-cut shoe into which the foot slips easily.

slip•per•y (slip′ə rē), *adj.,* **-i•er, -i•est. 1.** tending or liable to cause slipping or sliding. **2.** likely to slip away or escape. **3.** not trustworthy; shifty or tricky.

slip′shod′ *adj.* careless, untidy, or slovenly.

slip′-up′ *n.* a mistake, blunder, or oversight.

slit (slit), *v.,* **slit, slit•ting,** *n.* —*v.t.* **1.** to make a long cut or opening in. **2.** to cut into strips. —*n.* **3.** a straight, narrow cut or opening.

slith•er (sli*t͟h*′ər), *v.i.* to move, walk, or slide like a snake.

sliv•er (sliv′ər), *n.* **1.** a small, slender, often sharp piece, as of glass; splinter. —*v.t., v.i.* **2.** to cut or split into slivers.

slob (slob), *n.* a slovenly or boorish person.

slob•ber (slob′ər), *v.i.* **1.** to let saliva dribble from the mouth; drool. —*n.* **2.** saliva dribbling from the mouth.

sloe (slō), *n.* the small, sour, blackish fruit of the blackthorn.

sloe′-eyed′ *adj.* **1.** having very dark eyes. **2.** having slanted eyes.

slog (slog), *v.i.,* **slogged, slog•ging. 1.** to walk heavily; plod. **2.** to work long and hard; toil.

slo•gan (slō′gən), *n.* a distinctive phrase identified with a group, cause, or product; motto or catchword. [< Scottish Gaelic *sluagh-ghairm* army cry]

sloop (slōōp), *n.* a single-masted, fore-and-aft-rigged sailing boat.

slop (slop), *v.,* **slopped, slop•ping,** *n.* —*v.t., v.i.* **1.** to spill or splash (liquid). —*n.* **2.** kitchen waste used as feed for swine. **3.** unappetizing food or drink. **4.** liquid mud. **5.** spilled liquid.

slope (slōp), *v.,* **sloped, slop•ing,** *n.* —*v.i., v.t.* **1.** to incline or cause to incline; slant. —*n.* **2.** ground that has a natural incline. **3. a.** inclination or slant, esp. downward or upward. **b.** amount or degree of slant.

slop′py *adj.,* **-pi•er, -pi•est. 1.** muddy, slushy, or very wet. **2.** untidy; slovenly. **3.** careless; slipshod. **4.** overly emotional; gushy. —**slop′pi•ly,** *adv.* —**slop′pi•ness,** *n.*

slosh (slosh), *v.i.* **1.** to splash or move through water, mud, or slush. **2.** (of a liquid) to move about actively within a container.

slot (slot), *n., v.,* **slot•ted, slot•ting.** —*n.* **1.** a long, narrow opening, esp. one for receiving something, as a letter. **2.** a place or position, as in a sequence or series. —*v.t.* **3.** to make a slot in. **4.** to place or fit into a slot.

sloth (slôth; *esp. for 2* slōth), *n.* **1.** indolence; laziness. **2.** a slow-moving, arboreal tropical American mammal that usually hangs upside down. —**sloth′-ful,** *adj.*

slot′ machine′ *n.* a gambling or vending machine operated by inserting coins into a slot.

slouch (slouch), *v.i.* **1.** to sit, stand, or walk with an awkward, drooping posture. —*n.* **2.** an awkward, drooping posture, carriage, or gait. **3.** a lazy, inept person. —**slouch′er,** *n.* —**slouch′y,** *adj.,* **-i•er, -i•est.**

slough¹ (slou), *n.* **1.** an area of soft, muddy ground. **2.** a swamp or swamplike region. **3.** a condition of despair.

slough² (sluf), *n.* **1.** something, as the outer layer of a snake's skin, that is shed or cast off. —*v.t.* **2.** to cast off as or like a slough; shed.

Slo•va•ki•a (slō vä′kē ə, -vak′ē ə), *n.* a republic in central Europe: formerly part of Czechoslovakia. Also called **Slo′vak Repub′lic.** —**Slo′vak,** *n.* —**Slo•va′ki•an,** *adj., n.*

Slo•ve•ni•a (slō vē′nē ə), *n.* a republic in SE Europe: formerly part of Yugoslavia. —**Slo•ve′ni•an,** **Slo•vene,** *adj., n.*

slov•en•ly (sluv′ən lē), *adj.,* **-li•er, -li•est. 1.** untidy or unclean. **2.** slipshod; negligent. —**slov′en•li•ness,** *n.*

slow (slō), *adj.* and *adv.,* **-er, -est,** *v.* —*adj.* **1.** moving or proceeding with little or less than usual speed. **2.** characterized by lack of speed. **3.** taking or requiring a longer time than usual. **4.** mentally dull. **5.** not busy; slack. **6.** running at less than the proper rate of speed, as a clock. **7.** tedious. —*adv.* **8.** in a slow manner. —*v.t., v.i.* **9.** to make or become slow or slower. —**slow′ly,** *adv.* —**slow′ness,** *n.*

slow′ burn′ *n. Informal.* a gradual building up of anger.

slow′down′ *n.* a slowing down, as in progress, action, or pace.

slow′ mo′tion *n.* the process or technique of projecting or replaying a motion-picture or television sequence so that the action appears to be slowed down. —**slow′-mo′tion,** *adj.*

slow′poke′ *n. Informal.* a person who moves, works, or acts very slowly.

slow′-wit′ted *adj.* slow in comprehension; dull.

sludge (sluj), *n.* **1.** mud, mire, or ooze; slush. **2.** a mudlike deposit, esp. sediment produced during the treatment of sewage.

slue (slōō), *v.i., v.t.,* **slued, slu•ing.** to turn or swing around.

slug¹ (slug), *n.* **1.** a snaillike terrestrial crawling mollusk having no shell. **2.** a metal disk used as a coin or token. **3.** a piece of metal, esp. lead, for firing from a gun. **4.** a shot of liquor.

slug² (slug), *v.,* **slugged, slug•ging,** *n.* —*v.t.* **1.** to strike hard, esp. with the fist. —*n.* **2.** a hard blow or hit, esp. with the fist. —**slug′ger,** *n.*

slug•gard (slug′ərd), *n.* a habitually inactive or lazy person.

slug′gish *adj.* **1.** lazy; indolent. **2.** slow to function, act, flow, or respond. **3.** slack, as sales. —**slug′gish•ly,** *adv.*

sluice (slōōs), *n., v.,* **sluiced, sluic•ing.** —*n.* **1.** an artificial channel for water with a gate (**sluice′ gate′**) for regulating the flow. **2.** a channel, esp. one carrying off surplus water. **3.** a long, sloping trough, as for washing ores. —*v.t.* **4.** to let out (water) by opening a sluice. **5.** to flush or cleanse with a rush of water.

slum (slum), *n., v.,* **slummed, slum•ming.** —*n.* **1.** a run-down part of a city, usu. thickly populated by poor people. —*v.i.* **2.** to visit slums, esp. out of curiosity.

slum•ber (slum′bər), *v.i.* **1.** to sleep, esp. lightly. **2.** to be in a state of inactivity, quiescence, or calm. —*n.* **3.** sleep, esp. light sleep. **4.** a state of inactivity, quiescence, or calm.

slum′lord′ *n.* a landlord who charges exorbitant rents in slum buildings.

slump (slump), *v.i.* **1.** to fall or drop heavily. **2.** to slouch. **3.** to decline markedly. —*n.* **4.** an act or instance of slumping.

slur¹ (slûr), *v.,* **slurred, slur•ring,** *n.* —*v.t.* **1.** to pronounce (a syllable, word, etc.) indistinctly. **2.** to pass over without due mention or consideration. **3.** to sing or play (two or more tones of different pitch) without a break. —*n.* **4.** a slurred utterance or sound. **5.** a curved mark indicating that two or more tones of different pitch are to be slurred.

slur² (slûr), *n.* a disparaging remark; slight.

slurp (slûrp), *v.t., v.i.* **1.** to eat or drink with loud sucking noises. —*n.* **2.** a slurping sound.

slush (slush), *n.* **1.** partly melted snow. **2.** liquid mud; mire. **3.** silly, sentimental talk or writing. —**slush′y,** *adj.,* **-i•er, -i•est.**

slush′ fund′ *n.* money used for illicit or corrupt political purposes.

slut (slut), *n.* **1.** a slovenly woman. **2.** a sexually immoral woman. —**slut′tish,** *adj.*

sly (slī), *adj.,* **sly•er** or **sli•er, sly•est** or **sli•est,** *n.* —*adj.* **1.** cunning or wily. **2.** stealthy; surreptitious. **3.** mischievous or roguish. —*n.* **Idiom. 4. on the sly,** secretly. —**sly′ly,** *adv.*

smack¹ (smak), *n.* **1.** a slight or distinctive taste or flavor. **2.** a trace or suggestion. —*v.i.* **3.** to have a smack.

smack² (smak), *v.t.* **1.** to strike or kiss with a loud sound. **2.** to close and open (the lips) with a sharp sound. —*n.* **3.** a loud blow or kiss. **4.** a smacking of the lips. —*adv.* **5.** suddenly and violently. **6.** directly; straight.

small (smôl), *adj.* and *adv.*, **-er**, **-est**, *n.* —*adj.* **1.** not big; little. **2.** not great, as in amount or extent. **3.** carrying on an activity on a limited scale: *a small business.* **4.** of minor importance. **5.** humble or modest. **6.** mean-spirited; petty. **7.** very young: *a small boy.* —*adv.* **8.** in a small manner. **9.** into small pieces. —*n.* **10.** a small or narrow part, as of the back. —**small′ish,** *adj.* —**small′ness,** *n.*

small′ fry′ *n.pl.* **1.** young children. **2.** unimportant persons.

small′-mind′ed *adj.* selfish, petty, or narrow-minded.

small′pox′ *n.* an acute, highly contagious viral disease characterized by fever and pustular eruptions.

small′-scale′ *adj.* **1.** of limited extent or scope. **2.** (of a map, model, etc.) being a relatively small version of an original.

small′ talk′ *n.* light conversation.

small′-time′ *adj.* of little or no importance or influence.

smarm′y (smär′mē), *adj.*, **-ier**, **-iest.** excessively flattering, servile, etc.

smart (smärt), *v.*, *adj.*, **-er**, **-est**, *n.* —*v.i.* **1.** to cause or feel a sharp, stinging pain. **2.** to suffer from wounded feelings, shame, or distress. —*adj.* **3.** having or showing quick intelligence. **4.** clever or witty. **5.** neat or trim in appearance. **6.** elegant or fashionable. **7.** brisk or vigorous. **8.** sharp or keen. **9.** equipped with electronic control devices, as a missile. **10.** containing built-in electronic processing power: *a smart terminal.* —*n.* **11.** a sharp, stinging pain, as from a wound. **12. smarts,** *Informal.* intelligence.

smart′ al′eck (or **al′ec**) (al′ik), *n. Informal.* an obnoxiously conceited person.

smart′ bomb′ *n.* an air-to-surface missile guided to its target by television or a laser beam.

smart′en *v.t.* **1.** to improve in appearance (usu. followed by *up*). **2. smarten up, a.** to groom oneself. **b.** to become more aware, shrewd, or clever.

smash (smash), *v.t.*, *v.i.* **1.** to break into pieces with violence. **2.** to destroy or be destroyed completely. **3.** to hit, dash, collide, or strike with force. —*n.* **4.** the act or sound of smashing. **5.** a blow, hit, or slap. **6.** a destructive collision; crash. **7.** a state of collapse or ruin, esp. financial failure. **8.** *Informal.* a great success; hit. **9.** (in racket sports) a powerful, downward overhand stroke. —**smash′er,** *n.*

smat•ter•ing (smat′ər ing), *n.* slight or superficial knowledge.

smear (smēr), *v.t.* **1.** to spread or apply (an oily, viscous, or dirty substance). **2.** to spread or stain with an oily, viscous, or dirty substance. **3.** to defame or slander. **4.** to smudge or blur. —*n.* **5.** a stain or spot made by smearing. **6.** defamation or slander.

smell (smel), *v.*, **smelled** or **smelt**, **smell•ing,** *n.* —*v.t.* **1.** to perceive the odor of through the nose. **2.** to perceive, detect, or discover by shrewdness. —*v.i.* **3.** to give off or have an odor. —*n.* **4.** the faculty of smelling. **5.** odor; scent. **6.** an act or instance of smelling. —**smell′y,** *adj.*, **-i•er, -i•est.**

smelt¹ (smelt), *v.t.* **1.** to fuse or melt (ore) in order to separate the metal contained. **2.** to refine (metal) by smelting.

smelt² (smelt), *n.*, *pl.* **smelts, smelt.** a small, silvery food fish of cold northern waters.

smelt³ (smelt), *v.* a pt. and pp. of SMELL.

smid•gen or **-gin** or **-geon** (smij′ən), *n.* a very small amount.

smile (smīl), *v.*, **smiled, smil•ing,** *n.* —*v.i.* **1.** to assume a facial expression indicating pleasure, amusement, derision, or scorn. **2.** to regard with or show favor. —*v.t.* **3.** to express by a smile. —*n.* **4.** an act or instance of smiling. **5.** a smiling facial expression.

smirch (smûrch), *v.t.* **1.** to discolor or soil with or as if with soot. **2.** to disgrace; discredit. —*n.* **3.** a dirty mark or smear. **4.** a stain, as on reputation.

smirk (smûrk), *v.i.* **1.** to smile in an affected, smug, or offensively familiar way. —*n.* **2.** the facial expression of one who smirks.

smite (smīt), *v.t.*, **smote, smit•ten** (smit′n) or **smote, smit•ing. 1.** to hit hard with or as if with the hand. **2.** to injure or slay by striking hard. **3.** to affect strongly and suddenly.

smith (smith), *n.* **1.** a worker in metal. **2.** BLACK-SMITH.

smith•er•eens (smith′ə rēnz′), *n.pl.* small pieces; bits.

smith•y (smith′ē, smith′ē), *n.*, *pl.* **-ies.** the workshop of a smith, esp. a blacksmith.

smit′ten (smit′n), *adj.* very much in love.

smock (smok), *n.* **1.** a loose overgarment worn esp. to protect the clothing while working. —*v.t.* **2.** to gather (fabric) into a honeycomb pattern with diamond-shaped recesses.

smog (smog, smôg), *n.* atmospheric pollutants, esp. smoke, combined with fog. [*sm(oke)* + *(f)og*] —**smog′gy,** *adj.*, **-gi•er, -gi•est.**

smoke (smōk), *n.*, *v.*, **smoked, smok•ing.** —*n.* **1.** the visible vapor and gases given off by a burning substance. **2.** something, as mist, resembling smoke. **3.** the act of smoking something. —*v.i.* **5.** to give off smoke. **6.** to inhale and puff out tobacco smoke. —*v.t.* **7.** to inhale and puff out the smoke of: *He smoked a cigar.* **8.** to cure (meat, fish, etc.) by exposure to smoke. **9. smoke out, a.** to drive out by means of smoke. **b.** to expose to public view or knowledge. —**smoke′less,** *adj.* —**smok′er,** *n.* —**smok′y,** *adj.*, **-i•er, -i•est.**

smoke′ detec′tor *n.* an alarm activated by the presence of smoke.

smoke′house′ *n.* a building or place in which meat or fish is cured with smoke.

smoke′ screen′ *n.* **1.** a mass of dense smoke for concealing an area, ship, or plane from an enemy. **2.** something intended to conceal or deceive.

smoke′stack′ *n.* a pipe for escape of smoke or combustion gases, as on a locomotive.

smol•der or **smoul•der** (smōl′dər), *v.i.* **1.** to burn without flame. **2.** to exist in a suppressed state. **3.** to show repressed feelings, as of anger.

smooch (smōōch), *Informal.* —*v.i.* **1.** to kiss. —*n.* **2.** a kiss.

smooth (smōōth), *adj.*, **-er**, **-est,** *adv.*, *v.* —*adj.* **1.** having an even surface; not rough. **2.** of uniform consistency; free from lumps. **3.** allowing or marked by an even, uninterrupted movement or flow. **4.** free from hindrances or difficulties. **5.** elegant or polished. **6.** ingratiatingly polite; suave. **7.** bland or mellow. —*adv.* **8.** in a smooth manner. —*v.t.* **9.** to make smooth of surface. **10.** to free from hindrances or difficulties. **11.** to refine or polish. **12.** to calm or soothe. —**smooth′ly,** *adv.* —**smooth′ness,** *n.*

smooth′bore′ *adj.* (of gun) not rifled.

smör•gas•bord or **smör•gås•bord** (smôr′gəs-bôrd′; *often* shmôr′-), *n.* a buffet meal consisting of a number of hot and cold dishes. [< Sw: sandwich table]

smoth•er (smuth′ər), *v.t.* **1.** to stifle or suffocate. **2.** to cover closely or thickly; envelop. **3.** to suppress or repress. —*v.i.* **4.** to be stifled or suffocated.

smudge (smuj), *n.*, *v.*, **smudged, smudg•ing.** —*n.* **1.** a dirty mark or smear. **2.** stifling smoke. —*v.t.*, *v.i.* **3.** to make or become dirty with streaks or smears. —**smudg′y,** *adj.*, **-i•er, -i•est.**

smug (smug), *adj.*, **smug•ger, smug•gest.** full of self-satisfaction; complacent. —**smug′ly,** *adv.*

smug•gle (smug′əl), *v.*, **-gled, -gling.** —*v.t.* **1.** to import or export secretly, in violation of the law, esp. without paying legal duty. **2.** to bring, take, or put secretly. —*v.i.* **3.** to engage in smuggling. —**smug′gler,** *n.*

smut (smut), *n.* **1.** sooty matter. **2.** a black or dirty mark; smudge. **3.** indecent language or writing; obscenity. **4.** a fungous disease of plants, characterized by black, powdery masses. —**smut′ty,** *adj.*, **-ti•er, -ti•est.**

general

snack (snak), *n.* **1.** a light meal, esp. one eaten between regular meals. —*v.i.* **2.** to eat a snack.

snag (snag), *n.*, *v.*, **snagged, snag•ging.** —*n.* **1.** a tree or part of a tree held fast in the bottom of a body of water. **2.** a sharp or rough projection. **3.** a tear, pull, or run in a fabric. **4.** an obstacle or impediment. —*v.t.* **5.** to run, catch up, or damage on a snag. **6.** to obstruct or impede. **7.** to grab; seize.

snail (snāl), *n.* a slow-moving mollusk with a spirally coiled shell and a muscular foot.

snake (snāk), *n.*, *v.*, **snaked, snak•ing.** —*n.* **1.** a limbless, scaly, elongate reptile. **2.** a treacherous person. —*v.i.* **3.** to move, twist, or wind like a snake. —*v.t.* **4.** to wind or make (one's course, way, etc.) like a snake. —**snake′like′**, *adj.* —**snak′y**, *adj.*, **-i•er, -i•est.**

snap (snap), *v.*, **snapped, snap•ping**, *n.*, *adj.*, *adv.* —*v.i.*, *v.t.* **1.** to make or cause to make a sudden, sharp, cracking sound. **2.** to move, shut, or catch with a sharp sound, as a door. **3.** to break suddenly with a sharp, cracking sound. **4.** to move or cause to move with quick or abrupt motions. **5.** to grasp or seize with or as if with a quick bite. **6.** to speak or say quickly and sharply. **7.** to flash, as the eyes. **8.** to take a snapshot (of). **9.** *Football.* to put (the ball) into play. —*n.* **10.** a quick, sudden action or movement. **11.** a short, sharp sound. **12.** a fastener that snaps when it closes. **13.** *Informal.* vigor or energy. **14.** a brittle cookie. **15.** a short spell of cold weather. **16.** *Informal.* an easy task, duty, etc. **17.** *Football.* the act of snapping the ball. —*adj.* **18.** made, done, or taken suddenly or offhand: *a snap judgment.* **19.** easy: *a snap course.* —*adv.* **20.** in a brisk, sudden manner.

snap′drag′on *n.* a plant cultivated for its spikes of showy, two-lipped flowers.

snap′pish *adj.* cross or irritable.

snap′py *adj.* **-pier, -piest.** *Informal.* **1.** quick. **2.** smart; stylish.

snap′shot′ *n.* an informal photograph, esp. one taken with a hand-held camera.

snare[1] (snâr), *n.*, *v.*, **snared, snar•ing.** —*n.* **1.** a device, often consisting of a noose, for capturing small game. **2.** something that entraps or entangles. —*v.t.* **3.** to catch with or as if with a snare.

snare[2] (snâr), *n.* a gut or metal string stretched across the skin of a drum.

snarl[1] (snärl), *v.i.* **1.** to growl angrily or viciously, esp. with bared teeth. **2.** to speak in an angry or nasty manner. —*n.* **3.** an act or sound of snarling. —**snarl′ing•ly**, *adv.*

snarl[2] (snärl), *n.* **1.** a tangle, as of thread. **2.** a complicated or confused condition. —*v.i.*, *v.t.* **3.** to become or cause to become tangled or confused. —**snarl′y**, *adj.*

snatch (snach), *v.i.* **1.** to make a sudden effort to seize something. —*v.t.* **2.** to seize by a sudden or hasty grasp. —*n.* **3.** an act or instance of snatching. **4.** a bit, scrap, or fragment. **5.** a brief spell, as of activity. —**snatch′er**, *n.*

sneak (snēk), *v.*, **sneaked** or **snuck, sneak•ing**, *n.*, *adj.* —*v.i.*, *v.t.* **1.** to go, act, move, or take in a stealthy or furtive manner. —*n.* **2.** a sneaking or underhand person. **3.** a sneaking act or move. —*adj.* **4.** stealthy; furtive. —**sneak′y**, *adj.*, **-i•er, -i•est.**

sneak′er *n.* a sports shoe of fabric, esp. canvas, with a flat rubber or synthetic sole.

sneak′ pre′view *n.* a preview of a motion picture, often shown in addition to an announced film.

sneer (snēr), *v.i.* **1.** to smile, laugh, or contort the face in a manner that shows scorn or contempt. —*n.* **2.** a sneering look, expression, or remark.

sneeze (snēz), *v.*, **sneezed, sneez•ing**, *n.* —*v.i.* **1.** to expel the breath suddenly and audibly by involuntary spasmodic action. —*n.* **2.** an act or sound of sneezing.

snick•er (snik′ər), *v.i.* **1.** to laugh in a half-suppressed or disrespectful manner. —*n.* **2.** a snickering laugh.

snide (snīd), *adj.*, **snid•er, snid•est.** derogatory in a nasty, insinuating manner.

sniff (snif), *v.i.*, *v.t.* **1.** to inhale audibly through the nose. **2.** to show disdain or contempt. **3.** to perceive by or as if by sniffing. —*n.* **4.** an act or sound of sniffing. **5.** an amount sniffed.

snif•ter (snif′tər), *n.* a pear-shaped glass for brandy or liqueur.

snip (snip), *v.*, **snipped, snip•ping**, *n.* —*v.t.*, *v.i.* **1.** to cut or remove with small, quick strokes. —*n.* **2.** the act of snipping. **3.** a small piece snipped off. **4.** a small piece; bit. **5.** *Informal.* a small or insignificant person.

snipe (snīp), *n.*, *pl.* **snipes, snipe**, *v.*, **sniped, snip•ing.** —*n.* **1.** any of several long-billed sandpipers inhabiting marshy areas. —*v.i.* **2.** to shoot at individuals, esp. enemy soldiers, from a concealed or distant position. **3.** to make a petulant or snide attack. —**snip′er**, *n.*

snip•pet (snip′it), *n.* a small bit, scrap, or fragment.

snip′py *adj.*, **-pi•er, -pi•est.** sharp or curt, esp. in a contemptuous or haughty way.

snit (snit), *n.* an agitated or irritated state.

snitch[1] (snich), *v.t.* *Informal.* to steal; pilfer.

snitch[2] (snich), *Informal.* —*v.i.* **1.** to turn informer; tattle. —*n.* **2.** an informer.

sniv•el (sniv′əl), *v.i.*, **-eled, -el•ing** or (*esp. Brit.*) **-elled, -el•ling. 1.** to weep or cry with sniffling. **2.** to have a runny nose.

snob (snob), *n.* a person who imitates, cultivates, or slavishly admires social superiors and is condescending to others. —**snob′ber•y, snob′bish•ness,** *n.* —**snob′bish,** *adj.*

snoop (snōōp), *Informal.* —*v.i.* **1.** to prowl or pry in a sneaking way. —*n.* **2.** an act or instance of snooping. **3.** a person who snoops. —**snoop′er**, *n.* —**snoop′y**, *adj.*, **-i•er, -i•est.**

snoot′y *adj.*, **-i•er, -i•est.** *Informal.* snobbish; condescending.

snooze (snōōz), *v.*, **snoozed, snooz•ing**, *n.* —*v.i.* **1.** to sleep for a short time; nap. —*n.* **2.** a short sleep; nap.

snore (snôr), *v.*, **snored, snor•ing**, *n.* —*v.i.* **1.** to breathe during sleep with hoarse or harsh sounds. —*n.* **2.** an act or sound of snoring.

snor•kel (snôr′kəl), *n.* **1.** a tube through which a swimmer can breathe while moving face down at or just below the surface of the water. —*v.i.* **2.** to swim while using a snorkel. [< G]

snort (snôrt), *v.i.* **1.** to force the breath violently and noisily through the nostrils with a loud, harsh sound, as a horse. **2.** to express contempt, indignation, or annoyance by snorting. —*v.t.* **3.** *Slang.* to take (a drug) by inhaling. —*n.* **4.** an act or sound of snorting. **5.** *Slang.* a quick drink of liquor.

snot (snot), *n.* **1.** *Vulgar.* mucus from the nose. **2.** *Informal.* an impudently disagreeable person, esp. a youth. —**snot′ty**, *adj.*, **-ti•er, -ti•est.**

snout (snout), *n.* the part of an animal's head projecting forward and containing the nose and jaws; muzzle.

snow (snō), *n.* **1. a.** precipitation in the form of ice crystals formed directly from water vapor freezing in air. **b.** a layer or fall of snow. **2.** something, as white spots on a television screen, resembling snow. —*v.i.* **3.** to fall as or like snow. —*v.t.* **4.** to let fall as or like snow. **5.** to cover, obstruct, or confine with snow. **6.** *Slang.* to persuade or deceive by insincere talk. —**snow′drift′**, *n.* —**snow′fall′**, *n.* —**snow′flake′**, *n.* —**snow′storm′**, *n.* —**snow′y**, *adj.*, **-i•er, -i•est.**

snow′ball′ *n.* **1.** a ball of snow pressed or rolled together. —*v.i.*, *v.t.* **2.** to increase or cause to increase at an accelerating rate.

snow′board′ *n.* a board for gliding on snow, resembling a wide ski, that one rides in a standing position.

snow′drop′ *n.* an early-blooming plant with drooping white flowers.

snow′man′ *n.*, *pl.* **-men.** a figure of a person made out of packed snow.

snow′mo•bile′ (-mə bēl′), *n.* a motor vehicle with a tread in the rear and skis in the front, for traveling over snow.

snow'shoe' *n.* a racket-shaped contrivance for the foot for walking on deep snow without sinking.

snow'suit' *n.* a child's warmly insulated outer garment for cold weather.

snow' tire' *n.* a tire with a deep tread for increased traction on snow or ice.

snub (snub), *v.,* **snubbed, snub•bing,** *n.* —*v.t.* **1.** to treat with contempt, esp. by ignoring. **2.** to check or stop (a rope or cable that is running out), esp. by means of a rope around a fixed object. —*n.* **3.** an affront, slight, or rebuff.

snuff¹ (snuf), *v.t., v.i.* **1.** to inhale noisily; sniff. **2.** to perceive by or as if by smelling. —*n.* **3.** a sniff. **4.** powdered tobacco inhaled through the nostrils or placed between cheek and gum. —*Idiom.* **5. up to snuff,** *Informal.* up to a certain standard.

snuff² (snuf), *v.t.* **1.** to cut off or remove the charred portion of (a candle). **2. snuff out,** to suppress; crush.

snuf'fle *v.,* **-fled, -fling,** *n.* —*v.i.* **1.** to sniff or snuff. **2.** to draw the breath or mucus through the nostrils audibly or noisily. —*n.* **3.** an act or sound of snuffling.

snug (snug), *adj.,* **snug•ger, snug•gest. 1.** warmly comfortable or cozy. **2.** fitting closely, as a garment. **3.** trim or compactly arranged, as a ship. **4.** concealed; well-hidden. —**snug'ly,** *adv.* —**snug'ness,** *n.*

snug'gle *v.i., v.t.,* **-gled, -gling.** to lie or draw comfortably close; nestle or cuddle.

so (sō), *adv.* **1.** in the manner indicated; thus: *Hold the racket so.* **2.** to the extent or degree indicated: *Don't walk so fast.* **3.** very: *I'm so happy.* **4.** to such a degree or extent: *so far as I know.* **5.** hence; therefore: *She was ill, and so stayed home.* **6.** indeed; truly: *I was so at the party!* **7.** likewise; also: *If he is going, then so am I.* **8.** then; subsequently: *and so to bed.* —*conj.* **9.** in order that: *Study so you won't fail.* **10.** with the result that. —*pron.* **11.** such as has been stated: *If you're leaving, do so now.* **12.** about or near the person or thing in question: *a cup or so of sugar.* —*adj.* **13.** true: *Say it isn't so.*

soak (sōk), *v.i.* **1.** to lie in and become saturated with a liquid. **2.** to pass through or as if through pores or holes. —*v.t.* **3.** to wet thoroughly; saturate. **4.** to take in; absorb. **5.** *Slang.* to overcharge. —*n.* **6.** the act of soaking. **7.** the liquid in which something is soaked. **8.** *Slang.* a heavy drinker.

so'-and-so' *n., pl.* **so-and-sos.** a person or thing not definitely named.

soap (sōp), *n.* **1.** a cleansing substance usu. made by treating a fat with an alkali. **2.** *Informal.* SOAP OPERA. —*v.t.* **3.** to rub or treat with soap. —*Idiom.* **4. no soap,** *Informal.* useless or unacceptable. —**soap'y,** *adj.,* **-i•er, -i•est.**

soap'box' *n.* an improvised platform, as one on a street, on which a speaker stands.

soap' op'era *n.* an often melodramatic radio or television series depicting the interconnected lives of many characters. [so called because soap manufacturers were among the original sponsors of such programs]

soap'stone' *n.* a variety of talc with a soapy feel.

soar (sôr), *v.i.* **1.** to fly or glide high in the air. **2.** to rise or ascend to a higher or more exalted level.

sob (sob), *v.,* **sobbed, sob•bing,** *n.* —*v.i., v.t.* **1.** to weep or utter with a convulsive catching of the breath. —*n.* **2.** an act or sound of sobbing.

so•ber (sō'bər), *adj.,* **-ber•er, -ber•est,** *v.* —*adj.* **1.** not drunk. **2.** habitually temperate, esp. in the use of liquor. **3.** serious or solemn. **4.** free from excess, extravagance, or exaggeration; restrained. —*v.t., v.i.* **5.** to make or become sober. —**so'ber•ly,** *adv.* —**so•bri•e•ty** (sə brī'i tē), *n.*

so•bri•quet (sō'bri kā', -ket'), *n.* a nickname.

so'-called' *adj.* called thus, esp. incorrectly.

soc•cer (sok'ər), *n.* a form of football in which the ball may be kicked or bounced off any part of the body but the arms and hands.

so•cia•ble (sō'shə bəl), *adj.* **1.** inclined to enjoy the company of others; companionable. **2.** characterized by agreeable companionship. —**so'cia•bil'i•ty,** *n.* —**so'cia•bly,** *adv.*

so•cial (sō'shəl), *adj.* **1.** of or characterized by friendly relations or companionship. **2.** of or connected with fashionable society. **3.** living or disposed to live with others in a community. **4.** of or based on status in a society. **5.** of the life and welfare of human beings in a community. **6.** living together in colonies, hives, etc., as bees. —*n.* **7.** a social gathering. —**so'cial•ly,** *adv.*

so'cial•ism *n.* a theory or system of social organization in which the means of production and distribution of goods are owned and controlled collectively or by the government. —**so'cial•ist,** *n.* —**so'cial•is'tic,** *adj.*

so'cial•ite' (-shə līt'), *n.* a socially prominent person.

so'cial•ize' *v.,* **-ized, -iz•ing.** —*v.t.* **1.** to make fit for life in society. **2.** to establish or regulate according to the theories of socialism. —*v.i.* **3.** to mingle sociably with others. —**so'cial•i•za'tion,** *n.*

so'cialized med'icine *n.* a system to provide a nation with complete medical care through government subsidization.

so'cial secu'rity *n.* (*often caps.*) a federal program of old age, unemployment, health, disability, and survivors' insurance.

so'cial work' *n.* services or activities designed to improve social conditions among poor, sick, or troubled persons. —**so'cial work'er,** *n.*

so•ci•e•ty (sə sī'i tē), *n., pl.* **-ties.** —*n.* **1.** a group of persons associated together by religion, culture, or shared interests or purposes. **2.** a body of individuals living as members of a community. **3.** human beings collectively. **4.** companionship; company. **5.** the social class comprising wealthy or fashionable persons. —**so•ci'e•tal,** *adj.*

Soci'ety of Friends' *n.* a Christian sect founded in England that is opposed to oath-taking and war.

so'ci•o•ec•o•nom'ic (sō'sē ō-, sō'shē ō-), *adj.* of or involving a combination of social and economic factors.

so•ci•ol•o•gy (sō'sē ol'ə jē, sō'shē-), *n.* the study of the origin, development, organization, and functioning of human society. —**so'ci•o•log'i•cal** (-ə loj'i kəl), *adj.* —**so'ci•ol'o•gist,** *n.*

sock¹ (sok), *n., pl.* **socks** or sometimes **sox.** a short stocking reaching to the calf or just above the ankle.

sock² (sok), *v.t.* **1.** to strike or hit hard. **2. sock away,** to put into savings or reserve. —*n.* **3.** a hard blow.

sock•et (sok'it), *n.* a hollow or concave part or piece that holds a complementary part.

sod (sod), *n., v.,* **sod•ded, sod•ding.** —*n.* **1.** the surface of the ground when covered with grass. **2.** a section of sod. —*v.t.* **3.** to cover with sod.

so•da (sō'də), *n., pl.* **-das. 1.** any of several compounds containing sodium. **2.** SODA WATER. **3.** a drink made with soda water, flavored syrup, and often ice cream. **4.** a carbonated, flavored, and sweetened soft drink.

so'da crack'er *n.* a crisp cracker made with a yeast dough containing baking soda.

so'da foun'tain *n.* a counter, as in a drugstore, at which sodas, ice cream, etc., are served.

so'da wa'ter *n.* water charged with carbon dioxide.

sod•den (sod'n), *adj.* **1.** saturated with liquid or moisture. **2.** soggy, as poorly cooked food. **3.** torpid or listless. —**sod'den•ly,** *adv.* —**sod'den•ness,** *n.*

so•di•um (sō'dē əm), *n.* a soft, silver-white, chemically active metallic element that occurs naturally only in combination. *Symbol:* Na; *at. wt.:* 22.9898; *at. no.:* 11.

so'dium bicar'bonate *n.* a white water-soluble powder used esp. as an antacid and in baking.

so'dium chlo'ride *n.* SALT (def. 1).

so'dium ni'trate *n.* a crystalline, water-soluble compound that occurs naturally and is used in fertilizers and explosives.

sod•om•y (sod'ə mē), *n.* **1.** anal or oral copulation with a member of the same sex or the opposite sex. **2.** sexual relations between a person and an animal. —**sod'om•ite'** (-mīt'), *n.*

so•fa (sō′fə), *n., pl.* **-fas.** an upholstered couch with a back and arms.

soft (sôft, soft), *adj.* and *adv.,* **-er, -est.** —*adj.* **1.** yielding readily to touch or pressure. **2.** relatively deficient in hardness, as metal. **3.** not rough in texture; smooth. **4.** not harsh or unpleasant to the senses. **5.** gentle or mild: *soft breezes.* **6.** SOFT-HEARTED. **7.** not strong or robust. **8.** not demanding; easy: *a soft job.* **9.** (of water) relatively free from mineral salts that interfere with the action of soap. **10.** (of the landing of a space vehicle) executed with deceleration. **11.** foolish or stupid: *soft in the head.* —*adv.* **12.** in a soft manner. —**soft•en** (sô′fən, sof′ən), *v.t., v.i.* —**soft′ly,** *adv.* —**soft′ness,** *n.*

soft′ball′ *n.* **1.** a form of baseball played with a larger and softer ball. **2.** the ball itself.

soft′-boiled′ *adj.* (of an egg) boiled only until the yolk is partially set.

soft′-core′ *adj.* sexually provocative without being explicit.

soft′ drink′ *n.* a nonalcoholic and often carbonated beverage.

soft′-heart′ed *adj.* very sympathetic or responsive.

soft′-ped′al *v.t.,* **-aled, -al•ing** or (*esp. Brit.*) **-alled, -al•ling.** to make less obvious, important, or objectionable.

soft′ sell′ *n.* a quietly persuasive method of selling.

soft′ soap′ *n.* persuasive talk; flattery.

soft′ware′ *n.* programs for directing the operation of a computer or for processing electronic data.

sog•gy (sog′ē), *adj.,* **-gi•er, -gi•est. 1.** thoroughly wet. **2.** damp and heavy, as poorly baked bread.

soi•gné or **-gnée** (swän yā′; *Fr.* swA nyā′), *adj.* **1.** elegantly designed or done. **2.** well-groomed.

soil[1] (soil), *n.* **1.** the portion of the earth's surface consisting of disintegrated rock and humus. **2.** ground; earth. **3.** a country, land, or region.

soil[2] (soil), *v.t.* **1.** to make dirty. **2.** to sully, as with disgrace. —*v.i.* **3.** to become soiled. —*n.* **4.** a spot or stain. **5.** foul matter, esp. sewage or excrement.

soi•ree or **-rée** (swä rā′), *n., pl.* **-rees, -rées.** an evening party.

so•journ (*n.* sō′jûrn; *v. also* sō jûrn′), *n.* **1.** a temporary stay: *a week's sojourn in Paris.* —*v.i.* **2.** to stay temporarily. —**so′journ•er,** *n.*

sol•ace (sol′is), *n., v.,* **-aced, -ac•ing.** —*n.* **1.** comfort in sorrow or misfortune. **2.** a source of solace. —*v.t.* **3.** to comfort; console.

so•lar (sō′lər), *adj.* **1.** of, determined by, or proceeding from the sun. **2.** utilizing, operated by, or depending on solar energy.

so′lar cell′ *n.* a photovoltaic cell that converts sunlight directly into electricity.

so•lar•i•um (sə lâr′ē əm, sō-), *n., pl.* **-i•ums, -i•a** (-lâr′ē ə). a glass-enclosed room exposed to the sun's rays.

so′lar plex′us *n.* **1.** a network of nerves in the upper abdomen behind the stomach. **2.** a point on the stomach wall just below the sternum.

so′lar sys′tem *n.* the sun with all the celestial bodies that revolve around it.

sol•der (sod′ər), *n.* **1.** an alloy fused and applied to the joint between metal objects to unite them. —*v.t., v.i.* **2.** to join with or as if with solder.

sol•dier (sōl′jər), *n.* **1.** a person, esp. an enlisted person, engaged in military service. **2.** a person dedicated to a cause. —*v.i.* **3.** to act or serve as a soldier. **4.** to idle while pretending to work.

sole[1] (sōl), *adj.* being the only one. —**sole′ly,** *adv.*

sole[2] (sōl), *n., v.,* **soled, sol•ing.** —*n.* **1.** the undersurface of a foot. **2.** the undersurface of a shoe. —*v.t.* **3.** to furnish with a sole.

sole[3] (sōl), *n., pl.* **sole, soles.** any of various chiefly marine flatfishes used for food.

sol•emn (sol′əm), *adj.* **1.** grave; mirthless. **2.** serious; earnest. **3.** formal or ceremonious in character. **4.** marked by or observed with religious rites. —**so•lem•ni•ty** (sə lem′ni tē), *n.* —**sol′emn•ly,** *adv.*

sol′em•nize′ (-nīz′), *v.t.,* **-nized, -niz•ing. 1.** to observe with ceremony or formality. **2.** to perform the ceremony of (marriage).

so•lic•it (sə lis′it), *v.t.* **1.** to try to obtain by earnest plea. **2.** to entreat; petition. **3.** to lure; entice. —*v.i.* **4.** to solicit something desired, as orders or trade. —**so•lic′i•ta′tion,** *n.*

so•lic′i•tor (-i tər), *n.* **1.** a person who solicits. **2.** a legal officer of a city, town, or state. **3.** (in England and Wales) a lawyer who advises clients and prepares cases for barristers.

so•lic′i•tous *adj.* **1.** anxious or concerned. **2.** anxiously desirous. —**so•lic′i•tous•ly,** *adv.* —**so•lic′i•tous•ness,** *n.* —**so•lic′i•tude,** *n.*

sol•id (sol′id), *adj.* **1.** not hollow. **2.** having or involving three dimensions. **3.** having no openings or breaks. **4.** firm or compact: *solid ground.* **5.** not liquid or gaseous. **6.** serious in character: *solid scholarship.* **7.** consisting entirely of one substance or material: *solid gold.* **8.** real; genuine: *solid comfort.* **9.** sound or reliable: *a solid citizen.* **10.** written without a hyphen, as a compound word. **11.** unanimous: *a solid majority.* —*n.* **12.** a body or object having three dimensions. **13.** a solid substance. —**so•lid′i•fy,** *v.t., v.i.,* **-fied, -fy•ing.** —**so•lid•i•ty** (sə lid′i tē), *n.*

sol′i•dar′i•ty (-i dar′i tē), *n.* unanimity of attitude or purpose among members of a group.

sol′id•ly *adv.* **1.** so as to be solid. **2.** wholeheartedly; fully.

so•lil•o•quy (sə lil′ə kwē), *n., pl.* **-quies. 1.** a speech in a drama in which a character reveals inner thoughts as if alone. **2.** the act of talking to oneself. —**so•lil′o•quize′** (-kwīz′), *v.i., v.t.,* **-quized, -quiz•ing.**

sol•i•taire (sol′i târ′), *n.* **1.** a card game for one person. **2.** a precious stone, esp. a diamond, set by itself.

sol•i•tar•y (sol′i ter′ē), *adj.* **1.** lacking or avoiding the society of others. **2.** marked by or done in the absence of companions. **3.** being the only one; sole. **4.** secluded; remote.

sol′i•tude′ (-tōōd′, -tyōōd′), *n.* **1.** the state of being alone; seclusion. **2.** a lonely, unfrequented place.

so•lo (sō′lō), *n., pl.* **-los** or, for 1, **-li** (-lē), *adj., adv., v.,* **-loed, -lo•ing.** —*n.* **1.** a musical composition for one performer with or without accompaniment. **2.** a performance by one person. —*adj.* **3.** of or being a solo. —*adv.* **4.** on one's own; alone. —*v.i.* **5.** to perform a solo. [< It < L *sōlus* alone] —**so′lo•ist,** *n.*

Sol′o•mon Is′lands (sol′ə mən), *n.pl.* a country on an archipelago in the W Pacific Ocean, E of New Guinea. —**Sol′omon Is′lander,** *n.*

sol•stice (sol′stis, sōl′-), *n.* either of the two times a year, about June 21 and about Dec. 22, when the sun is at its greatest distance from the celestial equator.

sol•u•ble (sol′yə bəl), *adj.* **1.** capable of being dissolved. **2.** capable of being solved. —**sol′u•bil′i•ty,** *n.*

so•lu•tion (sə lōō′shən), *n.* **1.** the act or process of solving a problem. **2.** an answer to a problem. **3. a.** the process by which a gas, liquid, or solid is dispersed homogeneously in a gas, liquid, or solid without chemical change. **b.** the mixture thus formed.

solve (solv), *v.t.,* **solved, solv•ing.** to find the answer for or solution to.

sol•vent (sol′vənt), *adj.* **1.** able to pay all just debts. **2.** having the power of dissolving. —*n.* **3.** a substance that dissolves another to form a solution. —**sol′ven•cy,** *n.*

So•ma•li•a (sō mä′lē ə), *n.* a republic on the E coast of Africa. —**So•ma′li•an,** *adj., n.*

som•ber (som′bər), *adj.* **1.** gloomily dark. **2.** downcast; glum. **3.** extremely serious; grave. Also, *esp. Brit.,* **som′bre.** —**som′ber•ly,** *adv.*

som•bre•ro (som brâr′ō), *n., pl.* **-ros.** a broad-brimmed straw or felt hat worn esp. in Mexico and the southwestern U.S.

some (sum; *unstressed* səm), *adj.* **1.** being an undetermined or unspecified one: *Some salesman called.* **2.** unspecified in number, amount, or degree: *Have some popcorn.* **3.** *Informal.* remarkable of its type:

That was some storm. —*pron.* **4.** an unspecified number or amount: *Some of the books are damaged.* —*adv.* **5.** approximately; about: *Some 300 were present.* **6.** to some degree or extent: *I like baseball some.*

-some¹, a suffix meaning: like (*burdensome*); tending to: (*quarrelsome*).

-some², a suffix meaning a group of a certain number (*threesome*).

some•bod•y (sum′bod′ē, -bud′ē, -bə dē), *pron.*, *n.*, *pl.* **-ies.** —*pron.* **1.** some person. —*n.* **2.** a person of importance.

some′day′ *adv.* at an indefinite future time.

some′how′ *adv.* in a way not specified, apparent, or known.

some′one′ (-wun′, -wən), *pron.* some person; somebody.

some′place′ *adv.* somewhere.

som•er•sault (sum′ər sôlt′), *n.* **1.** an acrobatic movement in which the body rolls end over end, making a complete revolution. —*v.i.* **2.** to perform a somersault.

some′thing′ *pron.* **1.** an undetermined or unspecified thing. **2.** (used in combination to indicate an additional amount, as of years, that is unknown or forgotten): *fortysomething.* —*adv.* **3.** to some extent; somewhat: *The bird looked something like a hawk.*

some′time′ *adv.* **1.** at an indefinite or indeterminate time. **2.** at an indefinite future time. —*adj.* **3.** having been formerly. **4.** being so only at times or in some ways.

some′times′ *adv.* on some occasions; now and then.

some′what′ *adv.* **1.** to some extent or degree. —*pron.* **2.** some part, portion, or degree.

some′where′ *adv.* **1.** in, at, or to an unspecified or unknown place. **2.** in the neighborhood of; approximately: *somewhere around 60 years old.*

som•nam•bu•lism (som nam′byə liz′əm, səm-), *n.* the act or state of walking while asleep. —**som• nam′bu•list,** *n.*

som•no•lent (som′nə lənt), *adj.* **1.** sleepy; drowsy. **2.** tending to cause sleep. —**som′no• lence,** *n.*

son (sun), *n.* **1.** a male child or person in relation to his parents. **2.** a male descendant. **3. the Son,** Jesus Christ.

so•nar (sō′när), *n.* a method or apparatus for detecting and locating objects submerged in water by means of the sound waves they reflect or produce. [*so(und) na(vigation) r(anging)*]

so•na•ta (sə nä′tə), *n.*, *pl.* **-tas.** an instrumental composition typically in three or four movements in contrasting forms and keys.

song (sông, song), *n.* **1.** an often short metrical composition for singing. **2.** poetry. **3.** the art or act of singing. **4.** a patterned, sometimes elaborate vocal signal produced by an animal, as a bird. —*Idiom.* **5. for a song,** at a very low price.

son•ic (son′ik), *adj.* of or pertaining to sound or the speed of sound.

son′ic boom′ *n.* a loud noise caused by an aircraft moving at supersonic speed.

son′-in-law′ *n.*, *pl.* **sons-in-law.** the husband of one's daughter.

son•net (son′it), *n.* a poem of 14 lines, usu. with each line composed of five feet of two syllables each, an unstressed followed by a stressed one, with rhymes arranged in a fixed scheme.

so•no•rous (sə nôr′əs, son′ər əs), *adj.* **1.** resonant or resonating with sound. **2.** rich and full in sound. **3.** high-flown; grandiloquent. —**so•nor′i•ty** (-nôr′i tē, -nor′-), *n.*, *pl.* **-ties.**

soon (soon), *adv.*, **-er, -est. 1.** before long. **2.** promptly; quickly. **3.** readily or willingly.

soot (soot, soot), *n.* a powdery black carbonaceous substance produced during incomplete combustion, as of coal. —**soot′y,** *adj.,* **-i•er, -i•est.**

soothe (sooth), *v.t.,* **soothed, sooth•ing. 1.** to offer reassurance or comfort to. **2.** to make less severe; allay. —**sooth′ing,** *adj.* —**sooth′ing•ly,** *adv.*

sooth•say•er (sooth′sā′ər), *n.* a person who foretells events.

sop (sop), *n.*, *v.*, **sopped, sop•ping.** —*n.* **1.** something offered to conciliate, pacify, or bribe. —*v.t.* **2.** to dip or soak in liquid. **3.** to drench. **4.** to take up by absorption.

SOP Standard Operating Procedure; Standing Operating Procedure.

so•phis•ti•cat•ed (sə fis′ti kā′tid), *adj.* **1.** not naive; worldly-wise. **2.** appealing to cultivated tastes. **3.** complex; intricate. —**so•phis′ti•cate** (-kit), *n.* —**so•phis′ti•ca′tion,** *n.*

soph•ist•ry (sof′ə strē), *n.*, *pl.* **-ries.** subtle, plausible, but fallacious reasoning or argumentation.

soph•o•more (sof′ə môr′), *n.* a student in the second year at a high school or college. [earlier *sophumer,* perh. = *sophum* sophism + -ER¹]

soph′o•mor′ic (-môr′ik, -mor′-), *adj.* **1.** of or like a sophomore. **2.** intellectually pretentious but immature and ill-informed.

sop•o•rif•ic (sop′ə rif′ik, sō′pə-), *adj.* **1. a.** causing or tending to cause sleep. **b.** sleepy; drowsy. —*n.* **2.** something soporific, as a drug.

sop•py (sop′ē), *adj.,* **-pi•er, -pi•est. 1.** very wet; drenched. **2.** sentimental; mawkish.

so•pran•o (sə pran′ō, -prä′nō), *n.*, *pl.* **-os. 1. a.** the highest singing voice in women and boys. **b.** a singer with such a voice. **2.** a part for a soprano.

sor•bet (sôr bā′, sôr′bit), *n.* a fruit or vegetable ice, often served between courses.

sor•cer•er (sôr′sər ər) *n.* magician; wizard. —**sor′cer•ess,** *n. fem.*

sor•cer•y (sôr′sə rē), *n.*, *pl.* **-ies.** the exercise of supernatural powers granted by evil spirits.

sor•did (sôr′did), *adj.* **1.** morally base; vile. **2.** filthy; squalid.

sore (sôr), *adj.,* **sor•er, sor•est,** *n.* —*adj.* **1.** physically painful or sensitive. **2.** suffering physical or mental pain. **3.** causing distress, sorrow, misery, or hardship. **4.** annoyed; irritated. —*n.* **5.** a sore spot on the body. **6.** a source of grief or distress. —**sore′ly,** *adv.* —**sore′ness,** *n.*

sore′head′ *n. Informal.* a disgruntled or vindictive person.

sor•ghum (sôr′gəm), *n.* **1.** a cereal grass with a tall stem bearing grain. **2.** syrup made from sorghum.

so•ror•i•ty (sə rôr′i tē, -ror′-), *n.*, *pl.* **-ties.** a society or club of women, esp. in a college.

sor•rel¹ (sôr′əl, sor′-), *n.* **1.** a light reddish brown. **2.** a horse of this color.

sor•rel² (sôr′əl, sor′-), *n.* any of several plants with edible acid leaves.

sor•row (sor′ō, sôr′ō), *n.* **1.** distress, as that caused by loss; grief. **2.** a cause or occasion of grief. **3.** the expression of grief. —*v.i.* **4.** to feel or express sorrow. —**sor′row•ful,** *adj.*

sor•ry (sor′ē, sôr′ē), *adj.,* **-ri•er, -ri•est. 1.** feeling regret, compunction, or sorrow. **2.** regrettable or deplorable; unfortunate. **3.** wretched, poor, or useless. —**sor′ri•ly,** *adv.* —**sor′ri•ness,** *n.*

sort (sôrt), *n.* **1.** a particular kind, class, or group; category. **2.** character, quality, or nature. **3.** manner, fashion, or way. —*v.t.* **4.** to arrange according to kind or class. **5.** to place (computerized data) in order numerically or alphabetically. —*Idiom.* **6. out of sorts, a.** irritable or depressed. **b.** indisposed; ill. **7. sort of,** *Informal.* somewhat; rather. —**sort′er,** *n.*

sor•tie (sôr′tē), *n.*, *v.*, **-tied, -tie•ing.** —*n.* **1.** an attack of troops from a besieged place on the enemy. **2.** a combat mission or raid by an airplane. —*v.i.* **3.** to go on a sortie.

SOS (es′ō′es′), *n.*, *pl.* **SOSs, SOS's. 1.** a radiotelegraphic distress signal, used esp. by ships. **2.** a call for help.

so′-so′ *adj.* **1.** neither very good nor very bad; mediocre. —*adv.* **2.** in a passable manner.

sot (sot), *n.* a drunkard.

sot•to vo•ce (sot′ō vō′chē), *adv.* in a low voice; softly. [< It: lit., under (the) voice]

souf•flé (soo flā′), *n.*, *pl.* **-flés.** a light, puffed-up baked dish made fluffy with stiffly beaten egg whites.

sough (sou, suf), *v.i.* **1.** to make a rushing,

rustling, or murmuring sound. —*n.* **2.** a soughing sound.

sought (sôt), *v.* pt. and pp. of SEEK.

soul (sōl), *n.* **1.** the spiritual part of a human being that is believed to survive death. **2.** the seat of human feelings. **3.** a person: *a brave soul.* **4.** an essential or central element or part. **5.** the embodiment of a quality: *He was the very soul of tact.* **6.** shared ethnic awareness and pride among black Americans. **7.** deeply felt emotion, as conveyed by a performer. —*adj.* **8.** of or typical of black Americans or their culture: *soul food.*

soul′ful *adj.* expressive of deep feeling. —**soul′-ful•ly,** *adv.* —**soul′ful•ness,** *n.*

sound[1] (sound), *n.* **1.** the sensation produced by stimulation of the organs of hearing. **2.** vibrations transmitted through an elastic medium, esp. air, that can be perceived by the ear. **3.** something heard, as noise or a musical tone. **4.** the distance within which something can be heard. —*v.i.* **5.** to make a sound. **6.** to convey a certain impression; seem: *The report sounds true.* —*v.t.* **7.** to cause to sound. **8.** to announce or order by a sound. **9.** to pronounce clearly.

sound[2] (sound), *adj.*, **-er, -est,** *adv.* —*adj.* **1.** free from injury, damage, defect, or disease. **2.** strong, secure, or reliable. **3.** competent or sensible. **4.** having a logical basis. **5.** uninterrupted and untroubled: *sound sleep.* **6.** thorough or severe. **7.** having no legal defect: *a sound title.* —*adv.* **8.** deeply: *sound asleep.* —**sound′ly,** *adv.*

sound[3] (sound), *v.t.* **1.** to measure the depth of (water), esp. with a weighted line. **2.** to seek to ascertain the views of, esp. by subtle or indirect inquiries. —**sound′ing,** *n.*

sound[4] (sound), *n.* **1.** a relatively narrow passage of water between larger bodies of water or between the mainland and an island. **2.** an inlet or arm of the sea.

sound′ bar′rier *n.* an abrupt increase in drag experienced by an aircraft approaching the speed of sound.

sound′ bite′ *n.* a brief, striking statement excerpted from an audiotape or videotape for insertion in a broadcast news story.

sound′ing board′ *n.* **1.** a thin board placed in a musical instrument to enhance resonance. **2.** a person whose reactions reveal the acceptability of an idea or plan.

sound′proof *adj.* **1.** impervious to sound. —*v.t.* **2.** to make soundproof. —**sound′proof•ing,** *n.*

sound′track′ *n.* the band on a strip of motion-picture film on which sound is recorded.

soup (sōōp), *n.* **1.** a liquid food made by simmering vegetables, seasonings, and often meat or fish. —*v.* **2. soup up,** *Slang.* to increase the power or speed of.

soup′y *adj.*, **-i•er, -i•est. 1.** resembling soup in consistency. **2.** very thick; dense. **3.** overly sentimental.

sour (sou^ər), *adj.*, **-er, -est,** *v.* —*adj.* **1.** acid in taste, as vinegar or lemon juice; tart. **2.** spoiled or fermented. **3.** distasteful or disagreeable. —*v.t., v.i.* **4.** to make or become sour. —**sour′ly,** *adv.* —**sour′ness,** *n.*

source (sôrs), *n.* **1.** any thing or place from which something comes or is obtained. **2.** the beginning of a stream or river. **3.** a book, person, or document that supplies information.

sour′ grapes′ *n.* pretended disdain for something unattainable.

souse (sous), *v.*, **soused, sous•ing,** *n.* —*v.t., v.i.* **1.** to plunge into liquid. **2.** to steep in brine; pickle. **3.** to make or become wet all over. —*n.* **4.** the act of sousing. **5.** something, as pigs' feet, steeped in pickle. **6.** a liquid for pickling. **7.** *Slang.* a drunkard.

south (south), *n.* **1.** a cardinal point of the compass lying directly opposite north. **2.** the direction in which south lies. **3.** (*usu. cap.*) a region situated in this direction. **4. the South, a.** the area south of Pennsylvania and the Ohio River and east of the Mississippi. **b.** the Confederacy. —*adj.* **5.** lying toward or situated in the south. **6.** coming from the

south. —*adv.* **7.** to, toward, or in the south. —**south•er•ly** (su<u>th</u>′ər lē), *adj., adv.* —**south•ern** (su<u>th</u>′ərn), *adj.* —**south′ern•er,** *n.* —**south′ward** (-wərd), *adj., adv.*

South′ Af′rica *n.* **Republic of,** a country in S Africa. —**South′ Af′rican,** *adj., n.*

south′east′ *n.* **1.** the point or direction midway between south and east. **2.** a region in this direction. **3. the Southeast,** the southeast region of the United States. —*adj.* **4.** in, toward, or facing the southeast. **5.** coming from the southeast. —*adv.* **6.** toward or from the southeast. —**south′east′er•ly,** *adj., adv.* —**south′east′ern,** *adj.*

South′ Kore′a *n.* a country in E Asia. Official name, **Republic of Korea.** —**South′ Kore′an,** *n., adj.*

south′paw′ *n. Informal.* a left-handed person, esp. a left-handed baseball pitcher.

south′west′ *n.* **1.** the point or direction midway between south and west. **2.** a region in this direction. **3. the Southwest,** the southwest region of the United States. —*adj.* **4.** in, toward, or facing the southwest. **5.** coming from the southwest. —*adv.* **6.** toward or from the southwest. —**south′west′er•ly,** *adj., adv.* —**south′west′ern,** *adj.*

sou•ve•nir (sōō′və nēr′), *n.* an article kept as a reminder, as of a place visited; memento.

sov•er•eign (sov′rin, -ər in), *n.* **1.** a supreme ruler, as a monarch. **2.** a former British gold coin equal to one pound sterling. —*adj.* **3.** supreme in rank, power, or authority. **4.** having independence; autonomous: *a sovereign state.* **5.** surpassing all others in quality.

So•vi•et (sō′vē et′, -it), *n.* **1.** Usu., **Soviets.** the governing officials and citizens of the former Soviet Union. **2.** (*l.c.*) an elected governmental council in the former Soviet Union. —*adj.* **3.** of the Soviet Union or the Soviets. [< Russ *sovét* council, advice]

So′viet Un′ion *n.* UNION OF SOVIET SOCIALIST REPUBLICS.

sow[1] (sō), *v.*, **sowed, sown** or **sowed, sow•ing.** —*v.t.* **1.** to scatter (seed) for growth. **2.** to scatter seed over (land, earth, etc.). **3.** to implant or introduce; disseminate. —*v.i.* **4.** to sow seed. —**sow′er,** *n.*

sow[2] (sou), *n.* an adult female swine.

soy′bean′ *n.* **1.** a plant of the legume family grown chiefly for forage and its edible seed. **2.** the seed of the soybean.

soy sauce *n.* a salty sauce made from soybeans.

spa (spä), *n.*, *pl.* **spas. 1.** a mineral spring. **2.** a luxurious resort, esp. one with a spa.

space (spās), *n.*, *v.*, **spaced, spac•ing.** —*n.* **1.** the unlimited three-dimensional expanse in which all material objects are located. **2.** a portion or extent of space. **3.** OUTER SPACE. **4.** an available or allocated place: *a parking space.* **5.** an extent, period, or interval of time. **6.** a blank area, as in a text. **7.** freedom, as to express oneself or fulfill one's needs. —*v.t.* **8.** to divide into or separate by spaces.

space′craft′ *n.*, *pl.* **-crafts, -craft.** a vehicle designed to operate beyond the earth's atmosphere or orbit the earth.

spaced′-out′ *adj. Slang.* dazed by or as if by narcotic drugs.

space′ heat′er *n.* a device for heating a limited area.

space′ship′ *n.* a spacecraft.

space′ shut′tle *n.* a reusable spacecraft for shuttling passengers and cargo into orbit and back.

space′ sta′tion *n.* a manned spacecraft or satellite orbiting the earth and serving as a base for research.

spa•cious (spā′shəs), *adj.* containing much space; roomy.

spade[1] (spād), *n.*, *v.*, **spad•ed, spad•ing.** —*n.* **1.** a digging tool with a long handle and a flat blade. —*v.t.* **2.** to dig or cut with a spade. —**spade′ful,** *n.*, *pl.* **-fuls.**

spade[2] (spād), *n.* **1.** a black figure shaped like an inverted heart with a short stem, used on playing cards. **2.** a card of the suit bearing spades.

spa•ghet•ti (spə get′ē), *n.* pasta in the form of long strings.

Spain (spān), *n.* a kingdom in SW Europe. —**Span•iard**, *n.*

span[1] (span), *n., v.,* **spanned, span•ning.** —*n.* **1.** the full extent or reach of something. **2.** a short period of time. **3.** the distance or space between two supports, as of a bridge. **4.** the distance, about 9 inches, between the tips of the thumb and the little finger of a fully extended hand. —*v.t.* **5.** to extend or reach across. **6.** to measure by the span of the hand.

span[2] (span), *n.* a pair of animals, as horses, driven together.

Span. Spanish.

span•dex (span′deks), *n.* an elastic synthetic fiber used esp. in garments.

span•gle (spang′gəl), *n., v.,* **-gled, -gling.** —*n.* **1.** a small, thin piece of glittering metal used esp. for decorating garments. —*v.t.* **2.** to decorate with or as if with spangles.

span•iel (span′yəl), *n.* any of several dogs usu. having drooping ears and a long, silky coat.

Span•ish (span′ish), *n.* **1.** the Romance language of Spain, Mexico, and most of Central and South America. **2.** (*used with a pl. v.*) the inhabitants of Spain. —*adj.* **3.** of Spain, its inhabitants, or their language.

Span′ish fly′ *n.* **1.** a preparation of powdered green European beetles once used as an aphrodisiac. **2.** this beetle.

spank (spangk), *v.t.* **1.** to strike on the buttocks with the open hand. —*n.* **2.** a blow given in spanking.

spank′ing *adj.* **1.** quick and vigorous; brisk: *a spanking breeze.* —*adv.* **2.** extremely; very: *spanking clean.*

spar[1] (spär), *n.* a stout pole, as a mast or yard, for supporting sails.

spar[2] (spär), *v.i.,* **sparred, spar•ring. 1.** to box with light blows, esp. as a part of training. **2.** to engage in a dispute.

spare (spâr), *v.,* **spared, spar•ing,** *adj.,* **spar•er, spar•est,** *n.* —*v.t.* **1.** to refrain from harming, punishing, or killing. **2.** to save, as from discomfort. **3.** to refrain from using; do without. **4.** to use or give frugally: *Don't spare the whipped cream!* —*adj.* **5.** kept in reserve: *a spare part.* **6.** exceeding present needs; extra: *spare time.* **7.** restricted; meager. **8.** lean or thin. —*n.* **9.** a spare thing or part, esp. a spare tire. **10.** the knocking down of all the bowling pins with two bowls. —**spare′ly,** *adv.*

spare′ribs′ *n.pl.* a cut of meat from the ribs, esp. of pork, with some meat adhering to the bones.

spark (spärk), *n.* **1.** an ignited or glowing particle, as one thrown off by burning wood or produced by friction. **2.** the light produced by a sudden discharge of electricity. **3.** something that activates or stimulates. **4.** a small amount or trace. —*v.i.* **5.** to emit sparks. —*v.t.* **6.** to kindle, animate, or stimulate.

spar′kle *v.,* **-kled, -kling,** *n.* —*v.i.* **1.** to give off or shine with flashes of light; glitter. **2.** to be brilliant or vivacious. **3.** to effervesce, as wine. —*n.* **4.** brilliance or vivacity. **5.** a little spark. **6.** effervescence.

spark′ plug′ *n.* a device that ignites the fuel mixture in an internal-combustion engine.

spar•row (spar′ō), *n.* any of numerous small, typically gray-brown New World songbirds.

sparse (spärs), *adj.,* **spars•er, spars•est.** thinly scattered or distributed; not dense. —**sparse′ly,** *adv.* —**sparse′ness, spar′si•ty,** *n.*

spar•tan (spär′tn), *adj.* sternly disciplined and austere.

spasm (spaz′əm), *n.* **1.** a sudden involuntary muscular contraction. **2.** a sudden burst of energy, activity, or feeling.

spas•mod•ic (spaz mod′ik), *adj.* **1.** of or characterized by spasms. **2.** fitful or intermittent. —**spas•mod′i•cal•ly,** *adv.*

spas•tic (spas′tik), *adj.* **1.** of, characterized by, or afflicted with muscular spasms. —*n.* **2.** a person afflicted with spasms.

spat[1] (spat), *n., v.,* **spat•ted, spat•ting.** —*n.* **1.** a petty quarrel. —*v.i.* **2.** to engage in a spat.

spat[2] (spat), *n.* a short gaiter worn over the instep.

spat[3] (spat), *n.* the spawn of a shellfish, as an oyster.

spate (spāt), *n.* a sudden outpouring.

spa•tial (spā′shəl), *adj.* of, existing in, or occurring in space. —**spa′tial•ly,** *adv.*

spat•ter (spat′ər), *v.t., v.i.* **1.** to scatter or spout in drops. **2.** to splash in or as if in a shower. —*n.* **3.** an act or sound of spattering. **4.** a splash or spot spattered.

spat•u•la (spach′ə lə), *n., pl.* **-las.** an implement with a flexible blade used for blending or spreading substances such as food.

spawn (spôn), *n.* **1.** the eggs deposited in water by aquatic creatures, as fishes. **2.** progeny, esp. when numerous. —*v.i., v.t.* **3.** to deposit or produce (spawn). **4.** to bring forth; produce.

spay (spā), *v.t.* to remove the ovaries of (an animal).

speak (spēk), *v.,* **spoke, spo•ken, speak•ing.** —*v.i.* **1.** to utter words; talk. **2.** to communicate one's emotions or thoughts by or as if by speaking. **3.** to deliver an address or speech. —*v.t.* **4.** to utter (words). **5.** to express with or as if with the voice. **6.** to use or be able to use (a language) in oral utterance.

speak′eas′y *n., pl.* **-eas•ies.** a place selling alcoholic beverages illegally.

speak′er *n.* **1.** a person who speaks. **2.** (*usu. cap.*) the presiding officer of a legislative assembly. **3.** LOUDSPEAKER.

spear[1] (spēr), *n.* **1.** a weapon for thrusting or throwing that consists of a long shaft with a sharp-pointed head. **2.** a similar implement for use in fishing. —*v.t.* **3.** to pierce with or as if with a spear.

spear[2] (spēr), *n.* a sprout or shoot of a plant, as a blade of grass.

spear′head′ *n.* **1.** the sharp-pointed head of a spear. **2.** a person or force that leads an undertaking. —*v.t.* **3.** to act as a spearhead for.

spear′mint′ *n.* an aromatic herb of the mint family that is used for flavoring.

spe•cial (spesh′əl), *adj.* **1.** distinct or particular in kind; unique. **2.** intended for a specific function, purpose, or occasion. **3.** not ordinary or usual. **4.** exceptional. **5.** particularly valued. —*n.* **6.** a special person or thing.

spe′cial•ize′ *v.i.,* **-ized, -iz•ing.** to pursue a specialty. —**spe′cial•ist,** *n.* —**spe′cial•i•za′tion,** *n.*

spe′cial•ty *n., pl.* **-ties. 1.** a subject of study, line of work, or activity on which one concentrates. **2.** an article, product, or service of superior quality. **3.** a special point, item, or feature.

spe•cie (spē′shē, -sē), *n.* coined money; coin.

spe•cies (spē′shēz, -sēz), *n., pl.* **-cies. 1.** a distinct sort or kind. **2.** a basic category of biological classification composed of related individuals that are able to breed among themselves.

spe•cif•ic (spi sif′ik), *adj.* **1.** clearly specified; precise or explicit. **2.** peculiar, proper, or limited to someone or something, as a characteristic. **3.** of or being a species. **4.** effective in the prevention or cure of a certain disease. —*n.* **5.** something specific. —**spe•cif′i•cal•ly,** *adv.* —**spec′i•fic′i•ty** (spes′ə fis′i tē), *n.*

spec•i•fi•ca•tion (spes′ə fi kā′shən), *n.* **1.** Usu. **-tions.** a detailed statement, as of requirements for a proposed building. **2.** something specified.

specif′ic grav′ity *n.* the ratio of the density of a substance to the density of a standard substance, water being the standard for liquids and solids.

spec′i•fy′ *v.t.,* **-fied, -fy•ing. 1.** to mention or name explicitly. **2.** to set forth as a specification.

spec•i•men (spes′ə mən), *n.* **1.** a part or an individual taken as exemplifying a whole or group. **2.** a sample, esp. of urine, for examination.

spe•cious (spē′shəs), *adj.* apparently true, right, or attractive but lacking real merit. —**spe′cious•ly,** *adv.*

speck (spek), *n.* **1.** a small spot. **2.** a small amount; bit. —*v.t.* **3.** to mark with specks.

speck′le *n., v.,* **-led, -ling.** —*n.* **1.** a small speck. —*v.t.* **2.** to mark with speckles.

specs (speks), *n.pl. Informal.* **1.** spectacles; eyeglasses. **2.** specifications.

spec•ta•cle (spek′tə kəl), *n.* **1.** something presented to the sight or view. **2.** a public display, esp. on a large scale. **3. spectacles,** eyeglasses.

spec•tac′u•lar (-tak′yə lər), *adj.* **1.** dramatic or impressive. —*n.* **2.** an impressive spectacle. —**spec•tac′u•lar•ly,** *adv.*

spec•ta•tor (spek′tā tər), *n.* a person who looks on or watches; observer.

spec•ter (spek′tər), *n.* a ghost; phantom. Also, *esp. Brit.,* **spec′tre.** —**spec′tral** (-trəl), *adj.*

spec′trum (-trəm), *n., pl.* **-tra** (-trə), **-trums. 1.** a band or series of colors produced by the dispersion of radiant energy, as by a prism. **2.** a broad range or sequence.

spec•u•late (spek′yə lāt′), *v.i.* **-lat•ed, -lat•ing. 1.** to engage in thought, esp. conjectural thought. **2.** to engage in a risky business transaction in the hope of making a large profit. —**spec′u•la′tion,** *n.* —**spec′u•la′tive,** *adj.* —**spec′u•la′tor,** *n.*

speech (spēch), *n.* **1.** the faculty of speaking. **2.** the act or manner of speaking. **3.** something spoken. **4.** an address by a speaker to an audience. **5.** a language or dialect.

speed (spēd), *n., v.,* **sped** or **speed•ed, speed•ing.** —*n.* **1.** rapidity; swiftness. **2.** relative rate of motion or progress. **3.** a gear ratio in a motor vehicle or bicycle. **4.** *Slang.* a stimulating drug, esp. amphetamine. —*v.t.* **5.** to promote the progress of. **6.** to increase the rate of speed of. —*v.i.* **7.** to go or proceed fast. **8.** to drive fast, esp. at an illegal rate of speed. **9.** to go faster; accelerate. —**speed′er,** *n.* —**speed′i•ly,** *adv.* —**speed′y,** *adj.,* **-i•er, -i•est.**

speed•om•e•ter (spē dom′i tər, spi-), *n.* an instrument on an automobile or other vehicle for indicating speed.

speed′well′ *n.* a plant of the figwort family with spikes of small flowers.

spe•le•ol•o•gy (spē′lē ol′ə jē), *n.* the exploration and study of caves. —**spe′le•ol′o•gist,** *n.*

spell¹ (spel), *v.,* **spelled** or **spelt, spell•ing.** —*v.t.* **1.** to name or write the letters of in order. **2.** (of letters) to form (a word, syllable, etc.). **3.** to signify; mean. —*v.i.* **4.** to spell words. **5. spell out,** to make the meaning of unmistakable.

spell² (spel), *n.* **1.** a word or phrase supposed to have magic power. **2.** a state of enchantment. **3.** an irresistible influence; fascination.

spell³ (spel), *n.* **1.** a continuous period of activity: *a spell at the wheel.* **2.** a turn at work. **3.** a bout, fit, or attack: *a coughing spell.* **4.** an indefinite period of time. **5.** a period of weather of a particular kind. —*v.t.* **6.** to take the place of for a time.

spell′bound′ *adj.* held by or as if by a spell; enchanted.

spe•lunk•er (spi lung′kər), *n.* a person who explores caves.

spend (spend), *v.,* **spent, spend•ing.** —*v.t.* **1.** to pay out (money). **2.** to expend (labor, thought, etc.) on an undertaking. **3.** to pass (time). **4.** to use up; exhaust. —*v.i.* **5.** to spend money, energy, resources, or time. —**spend′er,** *n.*

spend′thrift′ *n.* a person who spends extravagantly and wastefully.

sperm (spûrm), *n.* **1.** a spermatozoon. **2.** semen. —**sper•mat•ic** (spûr mat′ik), *adj.*

sper•mat•o•zo•on (spûr mat′ə zō′ən, -on), *n., pl.* **-zo•a** (-zō′ə). a mature male reproductive cell.

sper′mi•cide′ (-mə sīd′), *n.* a sperm-killing agent.

spew (spyo͞o), *v.i., v.t.* **1.** to vomit. **2.** to gush or pour out violently or copiously.

sphere (sfēr), *n.* **1.** a solid geometric figure whose surface is at all points equidistant from the center. **2.** any rounded, globular body. **3.** a heavenly body. **4.** surroundings; environment. **5.** field; domain. [≪ L *sphaera* globe < Gk *sphaîra*] —**spher•i•cal** (sfer′i kəl, sfēr′-), *adj.*

sphe•roid (sfēr′oid), *n.* a solid figure, as an ellipsoid, similar in shape to a sphere. —**sphe•roi′dal,** *adj.*

sphinc•ter (sfingk′tər), *n.* a circular band of muscle that closes a bodily orifice.

sphinx (sfingks), *n., pl.* **sphinx•es, sphin•ges** (sfin′jēz). **1.** an ancient Egyptian figure with a lion's body and a human or animal head. **2.** (*cap.*) (in Greek myth) a winged monster with a woman's head and a lion's body that killed wayfarers unable to answer the riddle it posed. **3.** a mysterious, inscrutable person.

spice (spīs), *n., v.,* **spiced, spic•ing.** —*n.* **1.** an aromatic vegetable substance, as pepper or cinnamon, used to season food. **2.** something that gives zest or piquancy. —*v.t.* **3.** to season with spice. **4.** to give zest to. —**spic′y,** *adj.,* **-i•er, -i•est.** —**spic′i•ness,** *n.*

spick-and-span (spik′ən span′), *adj.* **1.** spotlessly clean. **2.** perfectly new.

spi•der (spī′dər), *n.* **1.** any of numerous arachnids with a body divided into two parts and silk-secreting spinnerets for spinning webs. **2.** a frying pan, orig. one with legs.

spiel (spēl, shpēl), *n. Informal.* a glib and usu. extravagant talk or speech, esp. one used to persuade.

spiff•y (spif′ē), *adj.,* **-i•er, -i•est.** *Informal.* smart; fine.

spig•ot (spig′ət), *n.* **1.** a plug for stopping the vent of a cask. **2.** a faucet.

spike¹ (spīk), *n., v.,* **spiked, spik•ing.** —*n.* **1.** a long thick nail. **2.** a naillike metal projection, as on the sole of a shoe, for improving traction. —*v.t.* **3.** to fasten or secure with spikes. **4.** to pierce with or impale on a spike. **5.** to suppress or thwart: *We spiked the rumor.* **6.** *Informal.* to add alcoholic liquor to (a drink). —**spik′y,** *adj.,* **-i•er, -i•est.**

spike² (spīk), *n.* **1.** an ear of grain. **2.** an elongated flower cluster.

spill (spil), *v.,* **spilled** or **spilt, spill•ing,** *n.* —*v.t.* **1.** to cause or allow to run, flow, or escape from a container, esp. accidentally. **2.** to shed (blood), as in wounding. **3.** to throw off: *spilled by a horse.* —*v.i.* **4.** to run, flow, or escape from or as if from a container. —*n.* **5.** a spilling, as of liquid. **6.** a quantity spilled. **7.** a fall, as from a horse. —**spill′age** (-ij), *n.*

spill′way′ *n.* a passageway through which surplus water escapes, as from a reservoir.

spin (spin), *v.,* **spun, spin•ning,** *n.* —*v.t.* **1.** to make (yarn) by drawing out and twisting fibers. **2.** to form (fibers) into yarn. **3.** to produce (a web, cocoon, etc.) by extruding a viscous filament that hardens in the air. **4.** to cause to rotate rapidly; twirl. **5.** to produce or fabricate slowly and bit by bit: *to spin a tale.* **6.** to draw out; protract. —*v.i.* **7.** to rotate rapidly. **8.** to extrude a viscous filament, as a spider. **9.** to spin yarn or thread. **10.** to move or travel rapidly. **11.** to have a sensation of whirling; reel. **12. spin off,** to create or derive from something already in existence. —*n.* **13.** a spinning motion. **14.** a short ride in a motor vehicle. **15.** *Slang.* a viewpoint or bias, esp. in the media.

spin•ach (spin′ich), *n.* a plant cultivated for its edible green leaves.

spi•nal (spīn′l), *adj.* of or pertaining to the spine or spinal cord.

spi′nal col′umn *n.* the series of vertebrae forming the axis of the skeleton in vertebrates.

spi′nal cord′ *n.* the cord of nerve tissue extending through a canal in the spinal column.

spin′ control′ *n. Slang.* an attempt to give a bias to news coverage, esp. of a political event.

spin•dle (spin′dl), *n.* **1.** a rounded, tapered rod on which fibers are twisted and thread is wound in spinning. **2.** a rod or pin that turns or on which something turns. **3.** something, as a turned piece of wood, that resembles a spindle.

spin′dly *adj.,* **-dli•er, -dli•est.** long, thin, and usu. frail.

spin′ doc′tor *n. Slang.* a press agent skilled at spin control.

spine (spīn), *n.* **1.** SPINAL COLUMN. **2.** a stiff-pointed process on a plant or animal. **3.** the back of a book binding. —**spin′y,** *adj.,* **-i•er, -i•est.**

spine′less *adj.* **1.** having no backbone or spines. **2.** lacking resolution or courage.

spin•et (spin′it), *n.* a small upright piano.

spin′ning wheel′ *n.* a device used for spinning

yarn or thread that consists of a single spindle driven by a large wheel.

spin′-off′ or **spin′off′,** *n.* a by-product or incidental outgrowth of something preexisting.

spin•ster (spin′stər), *n.* an unmarried woman beyond the conventional age for marriage. —**spin′-ster•hood′,** *n.* —**spin′ster•ish,** *adj.*

spi•ral (spī′rəl), *n., adj., v.,* **-raled, -ral•ing** or (*esp. Brit.*) **-ralled, -ral•ling.** —*n.* **1.** a plane curve generated by a point moving around a fixed point while constantly receding from or approaching it. **2.** a single circle of a spiral object. **3.** something resembling a spiral. **4.** a continuously accelerating increase or decrease. —*adj.* **5.** of, shaped like, or being a spiral. —*v.i., v.t.* **6.** to take or cause to take a spiral form or course.

spire (spī°r), *n.* **1.** a tall, acutely pointed roof forming the top of a tower or steeple. **2.** a tall, sharppointed part; tip. —**spir′y,** *adj.*

spi•re•a or **-rae•a** (spī rē′ə), *n., pl.* **-as.** a shrub of the rose family with clusters of small white or pink flowers.

spir•it (spir′it), *n.* **1.** the animating principle of life, esp. of humans. **2.** the incorporeal part of humans, esp. the mind or soul. **3.** a supernatural being: *evil spirits.* **4.** (*cap.*) the Holy Spirit. **5.** Often, **-its.** temper, mood, or disposition. **6.** an individual; person: *a few brave spirits.* **7.** dominant tendency or character: *the spirit of the age.* **8.** vigorous sense of group membership: *college spirit.* **9.** general meaning or intent: *the spirit of the law.* **10.** Often, **-its.** a distilled alcoholic liquor. —*v.t.* **11.** to carry off mysteriously or secretly. —**spir′it•ed,** *adj.* —**spir′it•less,** *adj.*

spir•it•u•al (-chōō əl), *adj.* **1.** of the spirit or the soul. **2.** of sacred matters; religious. **3.** of a church; ecclesiastical. —*n.* **4.** a religious song originating among blacks in the southern U.S. —**spir′it•u•al′i•ty,** *n., pl.* **-ties.** —**spir′it•u•al•ly,** *adv.*

spir•it•u•al•ism *n.* the belief that the spirits of the dead communicate with the living, esp. through a medium. —**spir′it•u•al•ist,** *n.*

spit¹ (spit), *v.,* **spit** or **spat, spit•ting,** *n.* —*v.i.* **1.** to eject saliva from the mouth. —*v.t.* **2.** to eject from the mouth. **3.** to send forth like saliva. —*n.* **4.** saliva, esp. when ejected. **5.** the act of spitting.

spit² (spit), *n., v.,* **spit•ted, spit•ting.** —*n.* **1.** a pointed rod for skewering and holding meat over a fire. **2.** a narrow point of land projecting into the water. —*v.t.* **3.** to pierce with or as if with a spit.

spite (spīt), *n., v.,* **spit•ed, spit•ing.** —*n.* **1.** a malicious, usu. petty desire to harm, annoy, or humiliate another. —*v.t.* **2.** to treat with spite. —*Idiom.* **3. in spite of,** notwithstanding; despite. —**spite′-ful,** *adj.*

spit′fire′ *n.* a person with a fiery temper.

spit′tle *n.* saliva; spit.

spit•toon (spi tōōn′), *n.* a large bowl serving as a receptacle for spit, esp. from chewing tobacco.

splash (splash), *v.t.* **1.** to wet or soil by dashing water, mud, etc., upon. **2.** to dash (water, mud, etc.) about in scattered masses. —*v.i.* **3.** to fall, move, or go with a splash. —*n.* **4.** an act or sound of splashing. **5.** a spot caused by splashing. **6.** a striking show or impression. —**splash′y,** *adj.,* **-i•er, -i•est.**

splash′down′ *n.* the landing of a space vehicle in the ocean.

splat¹ (splat), *n.* a broad piece, as of wood, forming part of a chair back.

splat² (splat), *n.* a sound made by splattering or slapping.

splat′ter *v.t., v.i.* **1.** to spatter. —*n.* **2.** a spatter.

splay (splā), *v.,* **splayed, splay•ing,** *adj.* —*v.t., v.i.* **1.** to spread out. **2.** to slant. —*adj.* **3.** spread or turned outward.

spleen (splēn), *n.* **1.** a vascular organ near the stomach that destroys worn-out red blood cells and stores blood. **2.** ill humor, peevish temper, or spite.

splen•did (splen′did), *adj.* **1.** magnificent or sumptuous. **2.** distinguished or glorious. **3.** very good. **4.** brilliant, as in appearance or color. —**splen′did•ly,** *adv.*

splen′dor (-dər), *n.* **1.** grandeur; magnificence. **2.** great brightness or luster; brilliance. Also, *esp. Brit.,* **splen′dour.**

splice (splīs), *v.,* **spliced, splic•ing,** *n.* —*v.t.* **1.** to unite (two ropes) by the interweaving of strands. **2.** to unite (timbers, spars, etc.) by overlapping and binding their ends. **3.** to unite (film, magnetic tape, etc.) as if by splicing. —*n.* **4.** a union, joint, or junction made by splicing.

splint (splint), *n.* **1.** a piece of rigid material, as wood, used to immobilize a fractured or dislocated bone. **2.** a thin strip of wood interwoven with others, as to make a basket.

splin′ter *n.* **1.** a thin, sharp piece, as of wood or bone, split or broken off from a main body. —*v.t., v.i.* **2.** to split into splinters.

split (split), *v.,* **split, split•ting,** *n.* —*v.t., v.i.* **1.** to divide or separate from end to end or into layers. **2.** to burst or break into parts or pieces. **3.** to divide or separate into different factions. **4.** to divide and share. —*n.* **5.** the act of splitting. **6.** a crack or break caused by splitting. **7.** a breach or rupture, as between persons.

split′-lev′el *adj.* **1.** (of a house) having rooms about a half story above or below adjacent rooms. —*n.* **2.** a split-level house.

split′ pea′ *n.* a dried green pea, split and used esp. for soup.

split′ personal′ity *n.* a mental disorder in which a person acquires several personalities that function independently.

splotch (sploch), *n.* **1.** a large, irregular spot. —*v.t.* **2.** to mark or cover with splotches. —**splotch′y,** *adj.,* **-i•er, -i•est.**

splurge (splûrj), *v.,* **splurged, splurg•ing,** *n.* —*v.i.* **1.** to indulge oneself in a luxury or pleasure. **2.** to show off. —*n.* **3.** an ostentatious display. **4.** a bout of extravagant spending.

splut•ter (splut′ər), *v.i.* **1.** to talk rapidly and confusedly. **2.** to make a sputtering sound. —*v.t.* **3.** to sputter. —*n.* **4.** an act or sound of spluttering.

spoil (spoil), *v.,* **spoiled** or **spoilt, spoil•ing,** *n.* —*v.t.* **1.** to harm severely; ruin. **2.** to impair the quality of. **3.** to impair the character of by coddling. **4.** *Archaic.* to plunder; rob. —*v.i.* **5.** to become unfit for use, as food. —*n.* **6.** Often, **spoils.** booty, loot, or plunder. —*Idiom.* **7. be spoiling for,** *Informal.* to be eager for. —**spoil•age** (spoi′lij), *n.* —**spoil′er,** *n.*

spoil′sport′ *n.* a person whose conduct spoils the pleasure of others.

spoils′ sys′tem *n.* the practice of filling nonelective public offices with supporters of a victorious political party.

spoke (spōk), *n.* **1.** one of the bars or rods radiating from the hub of a wheel and supporting the rim. **2.** a rung of a ladder.

spokes′man or **-wom′an** or **-per′son,** *n., pl.* **-men** or **-wom•en** or **-per•sons.** a person who speaks for another or for a group.

sponge (spunj), *n., v.,* **sponged, spong•ing.** *n.* **1.** an aquatic animal with a porous skeleton. **2.** the absorbent skeleton of a sponge used esp. for cleaning or wiping. **3.** any of various absorbent materials resembling a sponge. —*v.t.* **4.** to wipe, rub, clean, or absorb with or as if with a sponge. **5.** to get by imposing on another's good nature. —*v.i.* **6.** to live at the expense of others. —**spong′er,** *n.* —**spong′y,** *adj.,* **-i•er, -i•est.**

sponge′ cake′ *n.* a light cake containing no shortening.

spon•sor (spon′sər), *n.* **1.** a person who is responsible for a person or thing. **2.** a person or firm that finances a radio or television program by buying time for advertising. **3.** a godparent. —*v.t.* **4.** to act as sponsor for. —**spon′sor•ship′,** *n.*

spon•ta•ne•ous (spon tā′nē əs), *adj.* **1.** coming or resulting from a natural impulse or tendency. **2.** arising from internal forces or causes. —**spon′ta•ne′i•ty** (-tə nē′i tē, -nā′-), *n.* —**spon•ta′ne•ous•ly,** *adv.*

sponta′neous combus′tion *n.* the ignition of a

spoof (spo͞of), *n.* **1.** a lighthearted imitation; parody. **2.** a hoax; prank. —*v.t.*, *v.i.* **3.** to make fun (of) lightly and good-humoredly; kid.

spook (spo͞ok), *n.* **1.** a ghost; specter. **2.** *Informal.* a spy. —*v.t.*, *v.i.* **3.** to frighten or become frightened. —**spook′y**, *adj.*, **-i•er, -i•est.**

spool (spo͞ol), *n.* a cylinder on which something, as thread, is wound.

spoon (spo͞on), *n.* **1.** an eating or cooking utensil consisting of a small, shallow bowl with a handle. **2.** a fishing lure consisting of a spoon-shaped piece of metal. —*v.t.* **3.** to eat with or take up in or as if in a spoon. —*v.i.* **4.** *Informal.* to hug and kiss. —**spoon′ful**, *n.*, *pl.* **-fuls.**

spoon′bill′ *n.* a large wading bird having a long, flat bill with a spoonlike tip.

spoon•er•ism (spo͞o′nə riz′əm), *n.* the inadvertent transposition of usu. initial sounds of words, as in *a blushing crow* for *a crushing blow.* [after W. A. Spooner (1844–1930), English clergyman noted for such slips]

spoon′-feed′ *v.t.*, **-fed, -feed•ing. 1.** to feed with a spoon. **2.** to provide so fully with information that independent thought or action is prevented.

spoor (spo͞or, spôr), *n.* a track or trail, esp. of a wild animal.

spo•rad•ic (spə rad′ik), *adj.* appearing or happening at irregular intervals or in isolated instances. —**spo•rad′i•cal•ly**, *adv.*

spore (spôr), *n.* the asexual reproductive body of a fungus or nonflowering plant.

sport (spôrt), *n.* **1.** an often competitive athletic activity requiring skill or physical prowess. **2.** diversion; recreation. **3.** jest; pleasantry. **4.** mockery; ridicule: *They made sport of his haircut.* **5.** LAUGHINGSTOCK. **6.** a sportsmanlike person. **7.** a debonair person; bon vivant. **8.** an organism that shows a genetic deviation; mutation. —*adj.* Also, **sports.** **9.** of or used in sports. **10.** suitable for informal wear: *sport clothes.* —*v.i.* **11.** to amuse oneself pleasantly. —*v.t.* **12.** to wear or display, esp. with ostentation. —**sports′man**, *n.*, *pl.* **-men.** —**sports′wear**, *n.*

spor′tive *adj.* playful; frolicsome.

sports′ car′ *n.* a low, small, high-powered automobile.

sports′man•ship′ *n.* the ability to win or lose gracefully.

sport′-util′ity ve′hicle *n.* a rugged vehicle with a trucklike chassis and four-wheel drive, designed for occasional off-road use.

sport′y *adj.*, **-i•er, -i•est. 1.** flashy; showy. **2.** like or befitting a sportsman. **3.** designed for or suitable for sport.

spot (spot), *n.*, *v.*, **spot•ted, spot•ting,** *adj.* —*n.* **1.** a discolored mark; stain. **2.** a blemish or flaw. **3.** a small part, as of a surface, differing from the rest. **4.** a place; locality. **5.** a position, esp. an awkward or difficult one. —*v.t.* **6.** to stain or mark with spots. **7.** to notice, recognize, or detect. —*v.i.* **8.** to make a spot; stain. —*adj.* **9.** made, paid, or delivered at once: *a spot sale.* —**spot′less**, *adj.* —**spot′ted**, *adj.*

spot′ check′ *n.* a random sampling or investigation. —**spot′-check′**, *v.t.*, *v.i.*

spot′light′ *n.* **1. a.** an intense light focused on an object, person, or group, as on a stage. **b.** a lamp producing such a light. **2.** conspicuous public attention.

spouse (spous), *n.* a husband or wife. —**spous•al** (spou′zəl), *adj.*

spout (spout), *v.t.*, *v.i.* **1.** to discharge or issue in a stream or jet. **2.** to say or speak volubly or pompously. —*n.* **3.** a pipe or tube through which a liquid spouts. **4.** a jet or stream of liquid.

sprain (sprān), *v.t.* **1.** to wrench and injure (the ligaments around a joint) without fracture or dislocation. —*n.* **2.** the act of spraining or condition of being sprained.

sprat (sprat), *n.*, *pl.* **sprats, sprat.** a herring of the E North Atlantic.

sprawl (sprôl), *v.i.* **1.** to sit or lie with limbs spread out. **2.** to spread out or be distributed irregularly. —*n.* **3.** an act or instance of sprawling.

spray[1] (sprā), *n.*, *v.*, **sprayed, spray•ing.** —*n.* **1.** liquid, as water, blown or falling through the air in minute droplets. **2. a.** a jet of fine particles of liquid, as from an atomizer. **b.** a device for discharging such a jet. —*v.t.*, *v.i.* **3.** to apply in a spray (to). **4.** to scatter or discharge as spray. —**spray′er**, *n.*

spray[2] (sprā), *n.* a branch or arrangement of leaves, flowers, or berries.

spread (spred), *v.*, **spread, spread•ing,** *n.* —*v.t.*, *v.i.* **1.** to stretch or open out, esp. over a flat surface. **2.** to force or move apart. **3.** to distribute or extend over an area. **4.** to apply in a layer or coating. **5.** to set (a table) for a meal. **6.** to become or cause to become widely known. —*n.* **7.** the act or process of spreading. **8.** expanse; extent. **9.** a distance or range between two points. **10.** a cloth covering for a bed. **11.** *Informal.* an abundance of food; feast. **12.** a food for spreading, as peanut butter. **13.** two facing pages, as of a newspaper.

spread′-ea′gle *adj.*, *v.*, **-gled, -gling.** —*adj.* **1.** having or suggesting the form of an eagle with outspread wings. —*v.t.* **2.** to stretch out in a spread-eagle position.

spread′sheet′ *n.* **1.** an outsize ledger sheet used by accountants. **2.** such a sheet simulated electronically by computer software, used esp. for financial planning.

spree (sprē), *n.*, *pl.* **sprees. 1.** a period, spell, or bout of indulgence. **2.** a binge; carousal.

sprig (sprig), *n.* a small shoot, twig, or spray.

spright•ly (sprīt′lē), *adj.*, **-li•er, -li•est.** animated; lively. —**spright′li•ness**, *n.*

spring (spring), *v.*, **sprang** or, often, **sprung; sprung; spring•ing;** *n.* —*v.i.* **1.** to rise, leap, or move suddenly. **2.** to move suddenly with resilience. **3.** to issue or occur suddenly or forcefully. **4.** to come into being; arise. —*v.t.* **5.** to cause to spring. **6.** to cause the sudden operation of: *to spring a trap.* **7.** to cause to work loose, warp, or split. **8.** to develop: *sprang a leak.* **9.** to produce by surprise: *to spring a joke.* **10.** *Slang.* to secure the release of from confinement. —*n.* **11.** the act of springing. **12.** an elastic quality. **13.** an issue of water from the ground. **14.** a source; fountainhead. **15.** an elastic contrivance or body that recovers its shape after being compressed, bent, or stretched. **16.** the season between winter and summer. —**spring′time′**, *n.* —**spring′y**, *adj.*, **-i•er, -i•est.**

spring′board′ *n.* **1.** a flexible board used in diving and gymnastics. **2.** a starting point.

spring′ fe′ver *n.* a listless, lazy, or restless feeling commonly associated with the beginning of spring.

sprin•kle (spring′kəl), *v.*, **-kled, -kling,** —*v.t.*, *v.i.* **1.** to scatter in drops or particles. **2.** to disperse or distribute here and there. **3.** to rain slightly in scattered drops. —*n.* **4.** an act or instance of sprinkling. **5.** a light rain.

sprint (sprint), *v.i.* **1.** to race or move at full speed for a short distance. —*n.* **2.** a short race at full speed. **3.** a burst of speed. —**sprint′er**, *n.*

sprite (sprīt), *n.* an elf, fairy, or goblin.

sprock•et (sprok′it), *n.* **1.** a toothed wheel engaging with a chain. **2.** a tooth on a sprocket.

sprout (sprout), *v.i.* **1.** to begin to grow. **2.** to put forth buds or shoots. —*n.* **3.** a shoot of a plant. **4.** a new growth, as from a seed.

spruce[1] (spro͞os), *n.* **1.** an evergreen coniferous tree with short needle-shaped leaves. **2.** the wood of a spruce.

spruce[2] (spro͞os), *adj.*, **spruc•er, spruc•est,** *v.*, **spruced, spruc•ing.** —*adj.* **1.** trim in appearance; neat. —*v.t.*, *v.i.* **2.** to make or become spruce.

spry (sprī), *adj.*, **spry•er** or **spri•er, spry•est** or **spri•est. 1.** nimbly energetic; agile. —**spry′ly**, *adv.* —**spry′ness**, *n.*

spud (spud), *n.* **1.** *Informal.* a potato. **2.** a spadelike digging instrument.

spume (spyo͞om), *n.* foamy matter on a liquid; froth.

spunk (spungk), *n.* spirit; mettle. —**spunk′y,** *adj.,* **-i•er, -i•est.**

spur (spûr), *n., v.,* **spurred, spur•ring.** —*n.* **1.** a device with a pointed projection that is secured to the heel of a rider's boot and used to urge a horse forward. **2.** something that goads to action. **3.** a stiff, often sharp process or projection, as on the leg of the domestic rooster. **4.** a ridge projecting from a mountain. **5.** a short branch track connecting with a main railroad track. —*v.t.* **6.** to incite or urge on with or as if with spurs. —*Idiom.* **7. on the spur of the moment,** impulsively; suddenly. —**spurred,** *adj.*

spu•ri•ous (spyŏŏr′ē əs), *adj.* not genuine; counterfeit. —**spu′ri•ous•ly,** *adv.*

spurn (spûrn), *v.t.* to reject with disdain; scorn.

spurt (spûrt), *n.* **1.** a sudden, forceful gush, as of liquid. **2.** a sudden brief increase in activity or effort. —*v.i., v.t.* **3.** to gush, expel in, or make a spurt.

sput•ter (sput′ər), *v.i.* **1.** to make explosive, popping sounds. **2.** to eject particles of saliva, food, etc., as when speaking angrily. **3.** to talk explosively or incoherently. —*v.t.* **4.** to utter by sputtering. —*n.* **5.** an act or sound of sputtering.

spu•tum (spyŏŏ′təm), *n., pl.* **-ta** (-tə). expectorated matter, as saliva mixed with mucus.

spy (spī), *n., pl.* **spies,** *v.,* **spied, spy•ing.** —*n.* **1.** a person employed by a government to obtain intelligence about another, usu. hostile country. **2.** a person who keeps secret watch on others. —*v.i.* **3.** to act as a spy. —*v.t.* **4.** to catch sight of; espy.

spy′glass′ *n.* a small telescope.

squab (skwob), *n., pl.* **squabs, squab.** a nestling, unfledged pigeon.

squab•ble (skwob′əl), *v.,* **-bled, -bling,** *n.* —*v.i.* **1.** to engage in a petty quarrel. —*n.* **2.** a petty quarrel.

squad (skwod), *n.* **1.** the smallest military unit. **2.** a small group, as of police officers, engaged in a common task.

squad′ car′ *n.* a police car with a radiotelephone for communicating with headquarters.

squad′ron (-rən), *n.* any of various units of troops, ships, or airplanes.

squal•id (skwol′id, skwô′lid), *adj.* **1.** filthy and repulsive. **2.** degraded; sordid. —**squal′id•ly,** *adv.*

squall¹ (skwôl), *n.* a sudden, violent wind, often with rain, snow, or sleet. —**squal′ly,** *adj.* **-li•er, -li•est.**

squall² (skwôl), *v.i.* **1.** to cry out loudly; scream. —*n.* **2.** an act or sound of squalling.

squal•or (skwol′ər, skwô′lər), *n.* the condition of being squalid.

squan•der (skwon′dər), *v.t.* to spend or use extravagantly or wastefully.

square (skwâr), *n., v.,* **squared, squar•ing,** *adj.,* **squar•er, squar•est,** *adv.* —*n.* **1.** a rectangle with four sides of equal length and four right angles. **2.** something shaped like a square. **3.** an open area formed by intersecting streets. **4.** an instrument for drawing or testing right angles. **5.** the product obtained when a number is multiplied by itself. **6.** *Slang.* a conventional or conservative person. —*v.t.* **7.** to make square in form. **8.** to multiply (a number or quantity) by itself. **9.** to make straight, level, erect, or even. **10.** to adjust harmoniously or satisfactorily. **11.** to pay off; settle. —*v.i.* **12.** to accord; agree. **13. square off,** to assume a fighting stance. —*adj.* **14.** forming a right angle. **15.** having four equal sides and four right angles. **16.** having the form of a square and designated by a unit of linear measurement forming a side of the square: *one square foot.* **17.** solid and substantial. **18.** having all accounts settled. **19.** fair; honest. **20.** *Slang.* conventional or conservative. —*adv.* **21.** in a square shape. **22.** at right angles. **23.** fairly or honestly. —**square′ly,** *adv.*

square′ dance′ *n.* a dance by a set of four couples arranged in a square. —**square′-dance′,** *v.i.,* **-danced, -danc•ing.**

square′-rigged′ *adj.* having square sails as the principal sails.

square′ root′ *n.* a quantity of which a given quantity is the square.

squash¹ (skwosh, skwôsh), *v.t.* **1.** to press into a flat mass or pulp; crush. **2.** to suppress; quash. —*n.* **3.** an act or sound of squashing. **4.** a squashed mass. **5.** a game played on a four-walled court with rackets and a rubber ball.

squash² (skwosh, skwôsh), *n., pl.* **squash•es, squash. 1.** the fruit of any of various plants of the gourd family, used as a vegetable. **2.** a plant that bears squash.

squat (skwot), *v.,* **squat•ted, squat•ting,** *adj.,* **squat•ter, squat•test,** *n.* —*v.i.* **1.** to sit on the haunches or heels. **2.** to occupy another's property without right or title. **3.** to settle on public land in order to acquire title to it. —*adj.* **4.** short and thickset. —*n.* **5.** the act, position, or posture of squatting. —**squat′ter,** *n.*

squaw (skwô), *n. Often Offensive.* an American Indian woman.

squawk (skwôk), *v.i.* **1.** to utter a loud, harsh cry, as a duck. **2.** to complain loudly. —*n.* **3.** a loud, harsh cry. **4.** a loud complaint.

squeak (skwēk), *n.* **1.** a short, shrill or high-pitched sound. **2.** an escape, as from danger. —*v.i., v.t.* **3.** to utter (with) a squeak. **4. squeak by** or **through,** to succeed or survive by a narrow margin. —**squeak′y,** *adj.,* **-i•er, -i•est.**

squeal (skwēl), *n.* **1.** a somewhat prolonged, sharp, shrill cry. —*v.i.* **2.** to utter a squeal. **3.** *Slang.* **a.** to turn informer. **b.** to protest or complain. —*v.t.* **4.** to utter with a squeal. —**squeal′er,** *n.*

squeam•ish (skwē′mish), *adj.* **1.** easily nauseated or disgusted. **2.** excessively particular or scrupulous in moral matters. —**squeam′ish•ness,** *n.*

squee•gee (skwē′jē), *n., pl.* **-gees.** an implement with a rubber edge used esp. for removing water from windows after washing.

squeeze (skwēz), *v.,* **squeezed, squeez•ing,** *n.* —*v.t.* **1.** to press forcibly together; compress. **2.** to extract by applying pressure. **3.** to force, force out, or obtain by pressure. —*v.i.* **4.** to exert pressure. **5.** to force one's way. —*n.* **6.** an act or instance of squeezing. **7.** a troubled financial condition. **8.** a quantity obtained by squeezing.

squelch (skwelch), *v.t.* **1.** to put down or silence, as with a crushing reply. —*n.* **2.** a crushing reply.

squib (skwib), *n.* **1.** a short witty or sarcastic saying or writing. **2.** a firecracker that burns with a hissing noise but does not explode.

squid (skwid), *n., pl.* **squid, squids.** a ten-armed marine animal with a slender, elongated body.

squig•gle (skwig′əl), *n., v.,* **-gled, -gling.** —*n.* **1.** a short, irregular curve or twist, as in writing. —*v.i., v.t.* **2.** to move in or form squiggles. —**squig′gly,** *adj.*

squint (skwint), *v.i.* **1.** to look with the eyes partly closed. **2.** to be cross-eyed. **3.** to look sidewise. —*n.* **4.** an act or instance of squinting. **5.** CROSS-EYE. **6.** a quick glance.

squire (skwi°r), *n., v.,* **squired, squir•ing.** —*n.* **1.** an English country gentleman. **2.** a young man of noble birth who served a knight. **3.** a man who accompanies or escorts a woman. **4.** a local dignitary, as a justice of the peace. —*v.t.* **5.** to attend as a squire; escort.

squirm (skwûrm), *v.i.* **1.** to wriggle or writhe, as in embarrassment or pain. —*n.* **2.** the act of squirming.

squir•rel (skwûr′əl, skwur′-), *n., pl.* **-rels, -rel.** —*n.* **1.** an arboreal, bushy-tailed rodent with thick, soft fur. **2.** its fur.

squirt (skwûrt), *v.i.* **1.** to eject liquid in a thin jet or spurt. —*v.t.* **2.** to cause to squirt. **3.** to wet by squirting. —*n.* **4.** a jet or spurt of liquid. **5.** an amount squirted. **6.** *Informal.* an impudent youngster. **7.** an instrument for squirting.

squish (skwish), *v.t.* **1.** to squash. —*v.i.* **2.** (of water, soft mud, etc.) to make a gushing sound when walked in. —*n.* **3.** a squishing sound.

Sr *Chem. Symbol.* strontium.

Sr. 1. Senior. **2.** Sister. [< L *Soror*]

Sri Lan•ka (srē′ läng′kə, lang′kə, shrē′), *n.* an island republic in the Indian Ocean, S of India. —**Sri′ Lan′·kan,** *adj., n.*

SRO 1. single-room occupancy. **2.** standing room only.

SS 1. social security. **2.** steamship. **3.** supersonic.

SST supersonic transport.

St. 1. Saint. **2.** Strait. **3.** Street.

stab (stab), *v.,* **stabbed, stab·bing,** *n.* —*v.t., v.i.* **1.** to pierce or wound with or as if with a pointed weapon. **2.** to thrust, plunge, or penetrate. —*n.* **3.** a thrust with or as if with a pointed weapon. **4.** an attempt; try. **5.** a wound made by stabbing.

sta·bi·lize (stā′bə līz′), *v.t., v.i.,* **-lized, -liz·ing. 1.** to make or become stable, firm, or steadfast. **2.** to maintain or remain at an unfluctuating level. —**sta′·bi·li·za′tion,** *n.*

sta·ble[1] (stā′bəl), *n., v.,* **-bled, -bling.** —*n.* **1.** a building for the lodging and feeding of animals, esp. horses or cattle. **2.** the group of racehorses belonging to one owner. —*v.t., v.i.* **3.** to put or stay in or as if in a stable.

sta·ble[2] (stā′bəl), *adj.,* **-bler, -blest. 1.** not likely to give way; steady. **2.** firmly established; enduring. **3.** not wavering in purpose; steadfast. **4.** mentally sound. **5.** resistant to physical or chemical change. —**sta·bil·i·ty** (stə bil′i tē), *n.*

stac·ca·to (stə kä′tō), *adj.* **1.** shortened and detached when played or sung: *staccato notes.* **2.** having short breaks between notes.

stack (stak), *n.* **1.** a usu. orderly pile or heap. **2.** a large, usu. conical pile of hay or straw. **3.** Often, **stacks.** a set of shelves for books, as in a library. **4.** SMOKESTACK. **5.** a great quantity. **6.** a linear list, as in a computer, in which the last item stored is the first retrieved. —*v.t.* **7.** to pile or arrange in a stack. **8.** to fix or arrange to force a desired result: *to stack a jury.* **9. stack up,** to measure up; compare.

sta·di·um (stā′dē əm), *n., pl.* **-di·ums, -di·a** (-dē ə). a sports arena, usu. oval or horseshoe-shaped, with tiers of seats for spectators. [< L < Gk *stádion* running track]

staff (staf, stäf), *n., pl.* **staffs** for 1–3; **staves** (stāvz) or **staffs** for 4, 5; *v.* —*n.* **1.** a group of personnel, as of a business establishment. **2.** a group of assistants to a manager, superintendent, or executive. **3.** a body of military officers concerned with administration rather than combat. **4.** a stick or rod used for support, as a weapon, or as a symbol of office or authority. **5.** the set of five horizontal lines on which music is written. —*v.t.* **6.** to provide with a staff. **7.** to serve on the staff of.

staff′er *n.* a member of a staff, as at a newspaper.

stag (stag), *n.* **1.** an adult male deer. —*adj.* **2.** of or for men only: *a stag dinner.* —*adv.* **3.** without a companion or date.

stage (stāj), *n., v.,* **staged, stag·ing.** —*n.* **1.** a phase, degree, or step in a process, development, or series. **2.** a raised platform, esp. one on which actors perform in a theater. **3. the stage,** the theater, esp. acting, as a profession. **4.** the scene of an action. **5.** a stagecoach. **6.** a place of rest on a journey. **7.** a section of a rocket, usu. designed to separate after burnout. —*v.t.* **8.** to represent, produce, or exhibit on or as if on a stage. **9.** to plan, organize, and carry out.

stage′coach′ *n.* a horse-drawn passenger and mail coach that formerly traveled regularly over a fixed route.

stage′hand′ *n.* a worker who deals with properties, lighting, and scenery in a theater.

stage′struck′ or **stage′-struck′,** *adj.* obsessed with the desire to become an actor or actress.

stag·ger (stag′ər), *v.i.* **1.** to walk or move unsteadily; totter. —*v.t.* **2.** to cause to stagger. **3.** to astonish or shock. **4.** to arrange in an alternating or overlapping pattern: *to stagger lunch hours.* —*n.* **5.** a reeling or tottering movement. **6. staggers,** (used with a sing. v.) any of several diseases of livestock characterized by a staggering gait. —**stag′ger·ing,** *adj.*

stag′ger·ing *adj.* tending to overwhelm; amazing.

stag′ing (stā′jing) *n.* a temporary structure used in building; scaffolding.

stag·nant (stag′nənt), *adj.* **1.** not flowing or moving, as water. **2.** stale, as air. **3.** inactive or sluggish. —**stag′nate,** *v.i.* **-nat·ed, -nat·ing.** —**stag·na′tion,** *n.*

staid (stād), *adj.* **1.** decorous, sedate, or solemn. —*v.* **2.** *Archaic.* a pt. and pp. of STAY[1].

stain (stān), *n.* **1.** an often permanent discoloration produced by foreign matter; spot. **2.** a cause of reproach; stigma. **3.** a dye, esp. one for coloring wood. —*v.t.* **4.** to discolor. **5.** to color with a stain; dye. **6.** to bring reproach upon; stigmatize. —*v.i.* **7.** to produce a stain. **8.** to become stained. —**stain′·less,** *adj.*

stain′less steel′ *n.* steel alloyed with chromium to resist rust and corrosion.

stair (stâr), *n.* **1.** one of a flight or series of steps for going from one level to another. **2.** Usu., **stairs.** a flight of steps. —**stair′case′,** *n.* —**stair′way′,** *n.*

stair′well′ *n.* a vertical shaft containing stairs.

stake[1] (stāk), *n., v.,* **staked, stak·ing.** —*n.* **1.** a pointed stick or post driven into the ground as a mark or support. **2. a.** a post to which a person is bound for execution by burning. **b.** death by burning. —*v.t.* **3.** to mark with or as if with stakes. **4.** to support or fasten with a stake. **5. stake out,** to keep under police surveillance.

stake[2] (stāk), *n., v.,* **staked, stak·ing.** —*n.* **1.** something wagered, as in a race. **2.** an investment or share, as in an undertaking. **3.** Often, **stakes.** a prize or reward in a contest. —*v.t.* **4.** to risk; gamble. **5.** to furnish with resources, esp. money. —*Idiom.* **6. at stake,** in danger; at risk.

stake′out′ *n.* surveillance, as of a location, by the police.

sta·lac·tite (stə lak′tīt), *n.* an icicle-shaped mineral deposit hanging from the roof of a cave.

sta·lag·mite (stə lag′mīt), *n.* a mineral deposit resembling an inverted stalactite formed on the floor of a cave.

stale (stāl), *adj.,* **stal·er, stal·est,** *v.,* **staled, stal·ing.** —*adj.* **1.** not fresh; flat, dry, or tasteless. **2.** musty; stagnant. **3.** hackneyed; trite. **4.** lacking interest, initiative, or enthusiasm, as from boredom. —*v.t., v.i.* **5.** to make or become stale.

stale′mate′ (-māt′), *n., v.,* **-mat·ed, -mat·ing.** —*n.* **1.** a situation permitting no further action or progress; deadlock. —*v.t., v.i.* **2.** to subject to or result in a stalemate.

stalk[1] (stôk), *n.* **1.** the stem or main axis of a plant. **2.** a slender supporting part.

stalk[2] (stôk), *v.i.* **1.** to walk with stiff or haughty strides. —*v.t.* **2.** to pursue prey or quarry stealthily. —*n.* **3.** a stiff or haughty stride or gait.

stall[1] (stôl), *n.* **1.** a compartment in a stable for one animal. **2.** a booth or stand in which merchandise is displayed for sale. **3.** an enclosed seat in a church choir or chancel. **4.** a pew. **5.** a small compartment: *a shower stall.* **6.** a condition, caused by a poor fuel supply or overload, in which an engine stops functioning. —*v.t., v.i.* **7.** to put or keep in a stall. **8.** to bring or come to a standstill, esp. unintentionally.

stall[2] (stôl), *v.i., v.t.* **1.** to delay, esp. by evasion or deception. —*n.* **2.** a tactic, as a ruse, used to delay.

stal·lion (stal′yən), *n.* an uncastrated adult male horse.

stal·wart (stôl′wərt), *adj.* **1.** sturdy and robust. **2.** strong and brave. **3.** firm; steadfast. —*n.* **4.** a stalwart person.

sta·men (stā′mən), *n.* the pollen-bearing organ of a flower.

stam·i·na (stam′ə nə), *n.* power to endure; strength.

stam·mer (stam′ər), *v.i., v.t.* **1.** to speak with involuntary pauses and spasmodic repetitions of sounds. —*n.* **2.** a speech defect or utterance marked by stammering.

stamp (stamp), *v.t.* **1.** to strike with a forcible downward thrust of the foot. **2.** to bring (the foot) down forcibly. **3.** to crush, extinguish, etc., by or as if by stamping: *to stamp out crime.* **4.** to impress with a mark or device. **5.** to impress (a design, mark, etc.) on something. **6.** to affix a postage stamp to. —*v.i.* **7.** to bring the foot down forcibly. **8.** to walk with heavy, forcible steps. —*n.* **9.** a gummed printed label officially used as evidence of the payment of postage. **10.** a die or block for impressing or imprinting. **11.** a design made by imprinting. **12.** an official mark or seal indicating validity or payment of a tax or fee. **13.** a distinctive mark or impression.

stam•pede (stam pēd′), *n.*, *v.*, **-ped•ed, -ped•ing.** —*n.* **1.** a sudden, frenzied rush or flight, esp. of a herd of frightened animals. —*v.i., v.t.* **2.** to flee or cause to flee in a stampede. **3.** to act or cause to act in an unreasoning, often frantic rush.

stamp′ing ground′ *n.* a habitual or favorite haunt.

stance (stans), *n.* **1.** the position of the body while standing. **2.** a mental or emotional position.

stanch¹ (stônch, stanch, stänch), *v.t.* **1.** to stop the flow of (a liquid, esp. blood). —*v.i.* **2.** to stop flowing, as blood.

stanch² (stônch, stänch, stanch), *adj.,* **-er, -est.** STAUNCH².

stan•chion (stan′shən), *n.* an upright bar, beam, post, or support.

stand (stand), *v.,* **stood, stand•ing,** *n.* —*v.i.* **1.** to rise to, be in, or remain in an upright position on the feet. **2.** to take an indicated position: *I stood aside.* **3.** to rest in an upright position. **4.** to be located or situated. **5.** to remain unchanged. **6.** to be or remain in a specified state or condition. —*v.t.* **7.** to set upright. **8.** to submit to; undergo. **9.** to endure or withstand. **10. stand by, a.** to abide by; uphold. **b.** to be loyal to. **c.** to wait, esp. in anticipation. **11. ~ for, a.** to represent; symbolize. **b.** to tolerate; allow. **12. ~ out, a.** to project; protrude. **b.** to be conspicuous or prominent. **13. ~ up, a.** to be or remain convincing. **b.** to be durable or serviceable. **c.** to fail to keep an appointment with. —*n.* **14.** the act of standing. **15.** a policy, position, or attitude. **16.** the place occupied by a witness testifying in court. **17.** a raised platform, as for a speaker. **18. stands,** a raised section of seats for spectators. **19.** a framework or rack for supporting or displaying something. **20.** a stall or booth where goods are sold. **21.** a place occupied by vehicles for hire. **22.** a standing growth of trees. **23.** a stop on a tour for a performance.

stand•ard (stan′dərd), *n.* **1.** something accepted as a basis of comparison. **2.** a rule used as a basis for judgment. **3.** the authorized exemplar of a unit of weight or measure. **4.** a flag, as one indicating the presence of a sovereign. **5.** an upright support. —*adj.* **6.** being or meeting a standard. **7.** of recognized excellence or authority: *a standard reference book.* **8.** usual or customary.

stand′ard-bear′er *n.* the leader of a movement, political party, or cause.

stand′ard•ize′ *v.t.,* **-ized, -iz•ing.** to cause to conform with a standard. —**stand′ard•i•za′tion,** *n.*

stand′ard time′ *n.* the civil time officially adopted for a country or region, under a system that divides the world into 24 time zones.

stand′by′ *n., pl.* **-bys. 1.** a person or thing that can be relied on. **2.** one held ready to serve as a substitute.

stand′-in′ *n.* a substitute, as for an actor during the preparation of lighting and cameras.

stand′ing *n.* **1.** rank, status, or position in an occupation or in society. **2.** good reputation. **3.** length of continuance; duration. —*adj.* **4.** erect; upright. **5.** performed in or from an erect position. **6.** not flowing; still. **7.** lasting or permanent.

stand′off′ *n.* a tie or draw, as in a game.

stand′off′ish *adj.* tending to be aloof.

stand′out′ *n.* one that is conspicuously superior to others.

stand′pipe′ *n.* a vertical pipe into which water is pumped to obtain a required pressure.

stand′point′ *n.* the mental attitude from which a person views and judges things.

stand′still′ *n.* a halt; stop.

stand′-up′ *adj.* **1.** erect; upright. **2.** performing a

comic monologue while standing alone before an audience or camera.

stan•za (stan′zə), *n., pl.* **-zas.** a number of lines forming a division of a poem. —**stan•za′ic** (-zā′ik), *adj.*

sta•ple¹ (stā′pəl), *n., v.,* **-pled, -pling.** —*n.* **1.** a short, thin bracket-shaped piece of wire driven through sheets of paper to bind and clinch them. **2.** a U-shaped piece of metal with pointed ends driven into a surface to hold something, as a hook. —*v.t.* **3.** to secure or fasten by a staple. —**sta′pler,** *n.*

sta•ple² (stā′pəl), *n.* **1.** a principal raw material or commodity of a locality. **2.** a basic or necessary item, as of food. **3.** a fiber, as of cotton or rayon, with respect to length and fineness. —*adj.* **4.** regularly and plentifully produced. **5.** basic, chief, or principal.

star (stär), *n., adj., v.,* **starred, star•ring.** —*n.* **1.** a hot, gaseous, self-luminous celestial body, as the sun. **2.** a celestial body that appears as a fixed point of light in the night sky. **3.** Usu., **stars.** a heavenly body regarded as an astrological influence on human affairs. **4.** a conventionalized figure representing a star, usu. having five radiating points. **5. a.** an actor or actress who plays the leading role. **b.** a famous or gifted performer. **6.** an asterisk. —*adj.* **7.** distinguished; preeminent. **8.** of or being a star. —*v.t.* **9.** to decorate with stars. **10.** to feature as a star. **11.** to mark with an asterisk. —*v.i.* **12.** to be brilliant or outstanding. **13.** to perform as a star. —**star′dom,** *n.* —**star′ry,** *adj.,* **-ri•er, -ri•est.**

star′board′ (-bərd, -bôrd′), *n.* **1.** the right-hand side of a ship or aircraft facing forward. —*adj.* **2.** of or located to the starboard.

starch (stärch), *n.* **1.** a white, tasteless, solid carbohydrate found in rice, corn, wheat, potatoes, and many other vegetables. **2.** a commercial preparation of starch used esp. to stiffen fabrics in laundering. —*v.t.* **3.** to stiffen with or as if with starch. —**starch′y,** *adj.,* **-i•er, -i•est.**

stare (stâr), *v.,* **stared, star•ing,** *n.* —*v.i.* **1.** to gaze fixedly and intently, esp. with wide-open eyes. —*v.t.* **2.** to stare at. —*n.* **3.** a staring gaze. —**star′er,** *n.*

star′fish′ *n., pl.* **-fish, -fish•es.** a star-shaped sea animal with five or more radiating arms.

star′gaze′ *v.i.,* **-gazed, -gaz•ing. 1.** to gaze at the stars. **2.** to daydream.

stark (stärk), *adj.,* **-er, -est,** *adv.* —*adj.* **1.** complete; utter: *stark madness.* **2.** grim or desolate. **3.** extremely simple or severe. **4.** blunt; harsh: *stark reality.* —*adv.* **5.** completely; utterly: *stark mad.* —**stark′ly,** *adv.*

star′let (-lit), *n.* a young actress, esp. in motion pictures.

star′light′ *n.* the light emanating from the stars. —**star′lit′,** *adj.*

star′ling (-ling), *n.* a Eurasian songbird with seasonally speckled iridescent black plumage.

star′ry-eyed′ *adj.* overly romantic or idealistic.

start (stärt), *v.i.* **1.** to begin to move, go, or act. **2.** to become active, manifest, or operative. **3.** to give a sudden involuntary jerk or jump, as from shock. —*v.t.* **4.** to set moving, going, or acting. **5.** to establish or found. **6.** to cause to be an entrant in a game or contest. —*n.* **7.** a beginning, as of a journey. **8.** a place from which to begin. **9.** a sudden involuntary movement of the body. **10.** a lead or advance, as over competitors. —**start′er,** *n.*

star′tle (-tl), *v.,* **-tled, -tling.** —*v.t.* **1.** to surprise or alarm suddenly and usu. briefly. —*v.i.* **2.** to become startled. —**star′tling,** *adj.*

starve (stärv), *v.,* **starved, starv•ing.** —*v.i.* **1.** to weaken, waste, or die from lack of food. **2.** to be extremely hungry. **3.** to feel a strong need or desire. —*v.t.* **4.** to cause to starve. **5.** to subdue or force by hunger. —**star•va′tion** (-vā′shən), *n.*

stash (stash), *v.t.* **1.** to put by or away in a secret place. —*n.* **2.** something stashed away. **3.** a hiding place.

stat (stat), *n.* a statistic.

state (stāt), *n., adj., v.,* **stat•ed, stat•ing.** —*n.* **1.** the condition of a person or thing, as with respect to circumstances. **2.** the condition of matter, as with respect to form. **3.** status or position in life. **4.** a particular emotional condition. **5.** an unusually tense or perturbed condition: *in a state over losing his job.* **6. a.** a politically unified people occupying a definite territory. **b.** the territory or government of a state. **7.** one of the political units making up a federal union. —*adj.* **8.** of a state or a government. **9.** marked by or involving ceremony. —*v.t.* **10.** to express in speech or writing. **11.** to fix or settle, as by authority. —**state′hood′,** *n.*

state′craft′ *n.* the art of government and diplomacy.

state′house′ *n.* the building in which a state legislature sits.

state′less *adj.* lacking nationality.

state′ly *adj.,* **-li•er, -li•est. 1.** majestic; imposing. **2.** dignified. —**state′li•ness,** *n.*

state′ment *n.* **1.** something stated; declaration or assertion. **2.** an abstract of a financial account. **3.** the act or manner of stating.

state′ of the art′ *n.* the most sophisticated or advanced stage of a technology, art, or science. —**state′-of-the-art′,** *adj.*

state′room′ *n.* a private room on a ship or train.

states′man or **-wom′an,** *n., pl.* **-men** or **-wom•en.** a highly respected and influential political leader who shows devotion to public service. —**states′man•like′,** *adj.* —**states′man•ship′,** *n.*

stat•ic (stat′ik), *adj.* **1.** of bodies or forces at rest or in equilibrium. **2.** not moving; stationary. **3.** showing little or no change. **4.** pertaining to stationary electrical charges. —*n.* **5. a.** static or atmospheric electricity. **b.** interference, as with radio broadcasts, caused by such electricity. **6.** resistance or hostility, as to one's actions. —**stat′i•cal•ly,** *adv.*

sta•tion (stā′shən), *n.* **1.** the place or position where a person or thing is located. **2.** a regular stopping place, as for trains or buses. **3.** the headquarters of a public service. **4.** social position or standing. **5.** an assigned position, place, or office. **6.** a place from which radio or television broadcasts originate. —*v.t.* **7.** to assign a station to.

sta′tion•ar′y (-shə ner′ē), *adj.* **1.** not moving or movable; fixed. **2.** remaining in the same condition; not changing.

sta′tion•er *n.* a seller of stationery.

sta′tion•er′y (-shə ner′ē), *n.* **1.** writing paper. **2.** writing materials, as pens and ink.

sta′tion wag′on *n.* an automobile with folding or removable seats and space into which cargo can be loaded through a tailgate.

sta•tis•tic (stə tis′tik), *n.* a numerical fact or datum.

sta•tis•tics (stə tis′tiks), *n.* **1.** (*used with a sing. v.*) the science that deals with the analysis and interpretation of numerical data. **2.** (*used with a pl. v.*) a collection of numerical data. —**sta•tis′ti•cal,** *adj.* —**sta•tis′ti•cal•ly,** *adv.* —**stat′•is•ti•cian** (stat′is tish′ən), *n.*

stat•u•ar•y (stach′ōō er′ē), *n., pl.* **-ies.** statues collectively.

stat•ue (stach′ōō), *n.* a carved, molded, cast, or sculpted three-dimensional work of art.

stat′u•esque′ (-esk′), *adj.* like a statue, as in dignity or grace.

stat′u•ette′ (-et′), *n.* a small statue.

stat′ure (-ər), *n.* **1.** height, as of a person. **2.** esteem or status based on qualities or achievements.

sta•tus (stā′təs, stat′əs), *n.* **1.** the position or rank of an individual in relation to others; standing. **2.** high standing; prestige. **3.** state of affairs.

sta′tus quo′ (kwō), *n.* the existing state or condition.

sta′tus sym′bol *n.* a possession that is believed to indicate high social status.

stat•ute (stach′ōōt, -ōōt), *n.* a formal enactment by a legislature; law. —**stat′u•to′ry** (-ōō tôr′ē), *adj.*

stat′ute of limita′tions *n.* a statute defining the period within which legal action may be taken.

staunch¹ (stônch), *v.t., v.i.* STANCH¹.

staunch² (stônch, stänch), *adj.,* **-er, -est. 1.** firm or

steadfast. **2.** strong; substantial. **3.** impervious to water or other liquids. —**staunch′ly,** *adv.*

stave (stāv), *n., v.,* **staved** or **stove, stav•ing.** —*n.* **1.** one of the thin, narrow pieces of wood that form the sides of a vessel, as a barrel. **2.** a stick, rod, or pole. **3.** a verse or stanza of a poem or song. —*v.t.* **4.** to break in the staves of. **5.** to break a hole in. **6.** **stave off,** to keep off or prevent.

stay¹ (stā), *v.,* **stayed, stay•ing,** *n.* —*v.i.* **1.** to remain in a place, condition, or situation; continue. **2.** to live; dwell. **3.** to wait briefly; pause. **4.** to be steadfast; persevere. **5.** to keep up, as with a competitor. **6.** to stop or halt. —*v.t.* **7.** to stop or halt. **8.** to hold back or restrain. **9.** to suspend or delay. **10.** to satisfy temporarily the hunger of. **11.** to remain through or during. —*n.* **12.** a stop, halt, or pause. **13.** a sojourn or temporary residence. **14.** a suspension of a judicial proceeding.

stay² (stā), *n., v.,* **stayed, stay•ing.** —*n.* **1.** something used as a support; prop. **2.** a flat strip, as of steel or whalebone, used esp. for stiffening corsets. **3. stays,** a corset. —*v.t.* **4.** to hold up with or as if with stays; prop.

stay³ (stā), *n., v.,* **stayed, stay•ing.** —*n.* **1.** a strong rope or wire for steadying something, as a mast. —*v.t.* **2.** to secure with stays.

stay′ing pow′er *n.* endurance; stamina.

STD sexually transmitted disease.

std. standard.

stead (sted), *n.* **1.** the function or place of a person or thing as occupied by a substitute. —*Idiom.* **2. stand in good stead,** to prove useful to.

stead′fast′ *adj.* **1.** fixed in place, position, or direction. **2.** firm in purpose, resolution, or faith; unwavering. —**stead′fast′ly,** *adv.*

stead′y *adj.,* **-i•er, -i•est,** *n., pl.* **-ies,** *v.,* **-ied, -y•ing,** *adj.* —*adj.* **1.** firmly placed or fixed. **2.** free from change, variation, or interruption. **3.** constant, regular, or habitual. **4.** free from excitement or agitation; calm. **5.** firm; unfaltering. **6.** steadfast or unwavering. **7.** sober and dependable. —*n.* **8.** a person whom one dates exclusively. **9.** a steady customer. —*v.t., v.i.* **10.** to make or become steady. —*adv.* **11.** in a steady manner. —*Idiom.* **12. go steady,** to date one person exclusively. —**stead′i•ly,** *adv.*

steak (stāk), *n.* a fleshy slice of meat, esp. beef, or of fish. [< ON]

steal (stēl), *v.,* **stole, sto•len, steal•ing,** *n.* —*v.t.* **1.** to take (another's property) without permission or right. **2.** to take or get insidiously or surreptitiously. **3.** *Baseball.* to gain (a base) by running while the ball is being pitched to the batter. —*v.i.* **4.** to commit theft. **5.** to move or pass secretly, imperceptibly, or gradually. —*n.* **6.** the act of stealing. **7.** a bargain.

stealth (stelth), *n.* **1.** secret or surreptitious procedure or action. —*adj.* **2.** (*often cap.*) having or providing the capacity to evade detection by radar: *Stealth planes.* **3.** secret; not openly acknowledged: *stealth issues.* —**stealth′y,** *adj.,* **-i•er, -i•est.**

steam (stēm), *n.* **1.** water in the form of an invisible gas or vapor. **2.** water changed to steam by boiling and used to generate mechanical power and heat. **3.** the mist formed when the gas or vapor from boiling water condenses. **4.** power or energy. —*v.i.* **5.** to emit or pass off in the form of steam. **6.** to become covered with condensed steam. **7.** to move by or as if by the agency of steam. —*v.t.* **8.** to expose to or treat with steam, as in cooking. —*adj.* **9.** employing or operated by steam. —**steam′y,** *adj.,* **-i•er, -i•est.**

steam′er *n.* **1.** a steamship. **2.** a device or container in which something is steamed.

steam′roll′er *n.* **1.** a heavy steam-powered vehicle with a roller used esp. in paving roads. —*v.t.* **2.** to crush, flatten, or overwhelm with or as if with a steamroller.

steam′ shov′el *n.* a steam-powered machine for digging or excavating.

steed (stēd), *n.* a horse, esp. a spirited one.

steel (stēl), *n.* **1.** a hard, strong alloy consisting principally of iron and containing carbon and

steel' adj. **3.** of, made of, or resembling steel. —v.t. **4.** to cause to be unyielding or determined. —**steel'y,** adj., **-i•er, -i•est.**

steel' wool' n. a mass of stringlike steel shavings used esp. for scouring and smoothing.

steep[1] (stēp), adj., **-er, -est. 1.** having an almost vertical slope or gradient. **2.** unduly high; exorbitant. —**steep'ly,** adv. —**steep'ness,** n.

steep[2] (stēp), v.t. **1.** to soak in a liquid, as to extract some constituent. **2.** to saturate: *an incident steeped in mystery.* —v.i. **3.** to lie soaking in a liquid.

stee•ple (stē'pəl), n. **1.** a structure ending in a spire, erected on a tower of a church or public building. **2.** a tower with a steeple.

stee'ple•chase' n. a horse race over a course with artificial obstacles, as ditches.

stee'ple•jack' n. a person who builds or repairs steeples or towers.

steer[1] (stēr), v.t. **1.** to guide the course of (something in motion), as by a rudder. **2.** to pursue (a particular course). **3.** to direct; guide. —v.i. **4.** to steer a vessel or vehicle. **5.** to pursue a course of action. —*Idiom.* **6. steer clear of,** to stay away from; avoid.

steer[2] (stēr), n., pl. **steers, steer.** a castrated male bovine, esp. one raised for beef.

steer'age (-ij), n. **1.** accommodations in a passenger ship for travelers who pay the cheapest fare. **2.** management; direction.

steg•o•saur (steg'ə sôr'), n. a plant-eating dinosaur with bony plates along the back.

stein (stīn), n. an earthenware mug, esp. for beer.

stel•lar (stel'ər), adj. **1.** of or consisting of stars. **2.** of, befitting, or like a star performer; preeminent or outstanding.

stem[1] (stem), n., v., **stemmed, stem•ming.** —n. **1.** the ascending axis of a plant. **2.** the stalk that supports a leaf, flower, or fruit. **3.** something resembling a stem. **4.** the line of descent of a family. **5.** the underlying form of a word to which inflectional endings may be added. —v.i. **6.** to arise or originate.

stem[2] (stem), v.t., **stemmed, stem•ming.** to stop or check by or as if by damming.

stem[3] (stem), n., v., **stemmed, stem•ming.** —n. **1.** the forward part of a ship. —v.t. **2.** to make headway or progress against.

stem'ware' n. glassware with footed stems.

stench (stench), n. an offensive smell.

sten•cil (sten'səl), n., v., **-ciled, -cil•ing** or (*esp. Brit.*) **-cilled, -cil•ling.** —n. **1.** a thin sheet of material into which letters or designs have been cut so that they can be reproduced on another surface when ink or paint is applied over the cutout areas. —v.t. **2.** to mark or make with a stencil.

ste•nog•ra•phy (stə nog'rə fē), n. the art of writing in shorthand. —**ste•nog'ra•pher,** n. —**sten•o•graph•ic** (sten'ə graf'ik), adj.

sten•to•ri•an (sten tôr'ē ən), adj. very loud.

step (step), n., v., **stepped, step•ping.** —n. **1.** a movement made by lifting the foot and setting it down in a new position. **2.** the distance covered by a step. **3.** the sound made by the foot in taking a step. **4.** a footprint. **5.** a manner of walking. **6.** a stage in a process. **7.** rank or degree in a series or scale. **8.** a support for the foot in ascending or descending. **9.** a short distance. —v.i. **10.** to move in steps. **11.** to walk a short distance. **12.** to go briskly. **13.** to come easily and naturally: *to step into a fortune.* **14.** to press with the foot. —v.t. **15.** to measure by steps. **16. step down, a.** to decrease by degrees. **b.** to resign or retire. **17. ~ up, a.** to increase by degrees. **b.** to advance. —*Idiom.* **18.** in (or **out of**) **step,** in (or not in) harmony or agreement.

step- a prefix denoting members of a family related by marriage and not by blood: *stepmother; stepsister.*

step'lad'der n. a ladder with flat steps and hinged supporting frame.

steppe (step), n. a vast treeless plain, esp. in SE Europe and Asia.

ster•e•o (ster'ē ō', stēr'-), n., pl. **-os,** adj. —n. **1.** a stereophonic sound system. **2.** stereophonic reproduction. **3.** a stereoscopic photograph. —adj. **4.** stereophonic. **5.** stereoscopic.

stereo- a combining form meaning three dimensions (*stereoscope*).

ster•e•o•phon•ic (ster'ē ə fon'ik, stēr'-), adj. of or being a system of recording and reproducing sound in which two channels are used instead of one to enhance realism.

ster•e•o•type n., v., **-typed, -typ•ing.** —n. **1.** a printing plate cast from a mold of composed type. **2.** an idea, expression, etc., lacking in originality. **3.** a simplified and standardized conception or image shared by members of a group. —v.t. **4.** to make a stereotype of. —**ster'e•o•typed',** adj. —**ster'e•o•typ'ic** (-tip'ik), **ster'e•o•typ'i•cal,** adj.

ster•ile (ster'il; *esp. Brit.* -īl), adj. **1.** free from microorganisms. **2.** incapable of producing offspring or vegetation. **3.** not productive; fruitless. —**ste•ril•i•ty** (stə ril'i tē), n.

ster'i•lize' v.t., **-lized, -liz•ing.** to make sterile. —**ster'i•li•za'tion,** n. —**ster'i•liz'er,** n.

ster•ling (stûr'ling), adj. **1.** of or noting the currency of Great Britain. **2.** (of silver) having the standard fineness of 0.925. **3.** made of sterling silver. **4.** thoroughly excellent. —n. **5.** British currency. **6.** sterling silver.

stern[1] (stûrn), adj., **-er, -est. 1.** firm, strict, or uncompromising. **2.** hard, harsh, or severe. **3.** unpleasantly serious; rigorous or austere. **4.** grim or forbidding. —**stern'ly,** adv. —**stern'ness,** n.

stern[2] (stûrn), n. the after part of a ship or boat.

ster•num (stûr'nəm), n., pl. **-na** (-nə), **-nums.** the bony plate or series of bones to which the ribs are attached.

ster•oid (stēr'oid, ster'-), n. any of a large group of fat-soluble organic compounds, as the sex hormones.

stet (stet), v., **stet•ted, stet•ting.** —v.i. **1.** let it stand (used as a direction on a printer's proof or manuscript to retain material previously deleted). —v.t. **2.** to mark with the word "stet."

steth•o•scope (steth'ə skōp'), n. an instrument used to detect sounds in the body, esp. in the chest.

ste•ve•dore (stē'vi dôr'), n. one engaged in the loading or unloading of ships.

stew (stōō, styōō), v.t. **1.** to cook by slow boiling. —v.i. **2.** to fret or worry. —n. **3.** a dish, esp. of meat and vegetables, cooked by stewing. **4.** a state of agitation or worry.

stew•ard (stōō'ərd, styōō'-), n. **1.** a person who manages another's property or finances. **2.** a person in charge of running a large estate. **3.** an employee in charge of the table, wine, and servants in a club or restaurant. **4.** an employee on a ship, train, or airplane who serves passengers. —**stew'ard•ship',** n.

stick[1] (stik), n. **1.** a cut or broken-off branch or shoot of a tree or shrub. **2.** a long, slender piece of wood. **3.** a rod, wand, or baton. **4.** a long, slender piece or part: *a stick of celery.* **5. the sticks,** *Informal.* the rural districts.

stick[2] (stik), v., **stuck, stick•ing,** n. —v.t. **1.** to pierce with something pointed. **2.** to thrust (something pointed) into or through. **3.** to fasten in position by or as if by something thrust through. **4.** to impale. **5.** to thrust or poke: *She stuck her head out the window.* **6.** to attach with or as if with glue. **7.** to keep from moving or proceeding. **8.** to puzzle. **9.** *Informal.* to impose something disagreeable upon. —v.i. **10.** to be fastened in position by something pointed. **11.** to remain attached by or as if by adhesion. **12.** to remain firm or faithful. **13.** to persevere or persist. **14.** to become obstructed or jammed. **15.** to be unable to move or proceed. **16.** to be puzzled. **17.** to extend or protrude. **18. stick around,** *Informal.* to wait around; linger. **19. ~ up,** *Informal.* to rob, esp. at gunpoint. **20. ~ up for,** to defend or support. —n. **21.** a thrust with a pointed instrument.

stick'er n. **1.** one that sticks. **2.** an adhesive label.

stick′-in-the-mud′ *n.* someone who avoids new activities, ideas, or attitudes.

stick•ler (stik′lər), *n.* **1.** a person who insists on something unyieldingly. **2.** a puzzling or difficult problem.

stick′pin′ *n.* an ornamental pin, esp. one for holding a necktie in place.

stick′ shift′ *n.* a manual transmission for a motor vehicle.

stick′y *adj.*, **-i•er, -i•est. 1.** having the property of adhering; adhesive. **2.** tending to adhere. **3.** hot and humid. **4.** awkwardly difficult. —**stick′i•ness,** *n.*

stiff (stif), *adj.*, **-er, -est,** *adv.* —*adj.* **1.** difficult to bend or flex. **2.** not moving or working easily. **3.** not supple. **4.** strong; powerful. **5.** rigidly formal in manner. **6.** harsh, as a penalty. **7.** excessive; unusually high: *a stiff price.* **8.** relatively firm in consistency: *a stiff cake batter.* —*adv.* **9.** completely or extremely: *scared stiff.* —**stiff′en,** *v.t., v.i.* —**stiff′ly,** *adv.*

stiff′-necked′ *adj.* haughty and obstinate.

sti•fle (stī′fəl), *v.,* **-fled, -fling.** —*v.t.* **1.** to suppress, curb, or withhold. **2.** to kill by impeding respiration; smother. —*v.i.* **3.** to suffocate. —**sti′fling,** *adj.*

stig•ma (stig′mə), *n., pl.* **stig•ma•ta** (stig′mə tə, stig mä′tə, -mat′ə), **stig•mas. 1.** a mark of reproach or disgrace. **2.** the part of a pistil that receives the pollen. **3. stigmata,** marks resembling the wounds of the crucified body of Christ. —**stig•mat′ic** (-mat′ik), *adj.* —**stig′ma•tize′,** *v.t.,* **-tized, -tiz•ing.**

stile (stīl), *n.* steps for scaling a wall or fence.

sti•let•to (sti let′ō), *n., pl.* **-tos, -toes.** a short dagger with a slender blade.

still¹ (stil), *adj.*, **-er, -est,** *n., adv., conj., v.* —*adj.* **1.** motionless; stationary. **2.** free from sound or noise; quiet. **3.** free from turbulence; calm. **4.** of or being a single photograph. —*n.* **5.** calmness or silence. **6.** a still photograph. —*adv.* **7.** at or up to this or that time. **8.** even; yet. **9.** even then; nevertheless. **10.** without sound or movement; quietly. —*conj.* **11.** and yet; nevertheless. —*v.t., v.i.* **12.** to make or become still. —**still′ness,** *n.*

still² (stil), *n.* **1.** a distilling apparatus. **2.** a distillery.

still′born′ *adj.* dead when born.

still′ life′ *n., pl.* **still lifes.** a picture of inanimate objects.

stilt (stilt), *n.* **1.** one of two poles, each with a foot support, enabling the wearer to walk above the ground. **2.** a post supporting a structure above the surface of land or water.

stilt′ed *adj.* stiffly dignified or formal.

stim•u•lant (stim′yə lənt), *n.* **1.** an agent that temporarily quickens the functional activity of an organ or part. **2.** an alcoholic beverage.

stim′u•late′ (-lāt′), *v.t.,* **-lat•ed, -lat•ing. 1.** to rouse to action or effort; incite. **2.** to excite (a nerve, gland, etc.) to functional activity. —**stim′u•la′tion,** *n.*

stim′u•lus (-ləs), *n., pl.* **-li** (-lī′). something that stimulates.

sting (sting), *v.,* **stung, sting•ing,** *n.* —*v.t.* **1.** to prick painfully with a sharp-pointed, often venom-bearing organ. **2.** to cause to feel a sharp physical or mental pain. **3.** *Slang.* to cheat, esp. to overcharge. —*v.i.* **4.** to use or wound with a sting. **5.** to feel or cause a sharp, smarting pain. —*n.* **6.** the act of stinging. **7.** a wound or pain caused by or as if by stinging. **8.** a sharp-pointed, often venom-bearing organ, as of a bee, capable of inflicting a painful wound. —**sting′er,** *n.*

stin•gy (stin′jē), *adj.*, **-gi•er, -gi•est. 1.** reluctant to give or spend. **2.** meager.

stink (stingk), *v.,* **stank** or, often, **stunk; stunk; stink•ing;** *n.* —*v.i.* **1.** to emit a strong offensive smell. **2.** *Informal.* to be disgustingly inferior. —*n.* **3.** a strong offensive smell. **4.** *Informal.* an unpleasant fuss.

stint (stint), *v.i.* **1.** to be frugal or sparing. —*v.t.* **2.** to limit, often unduly. —*n.* **3.** a period of time spent doing something. **4.** limitation or restriction. **5.** a limited or prescribed amount of work.

sti•pend (stī′pend), *n.* a periodic fixed payment, as a scholarship allowance.

stip•ple (stip′əl), *v.t.,* **-pled, -pling.** to paint, engrave, or draw by means of dots or small strokes.

stip•u•late (stip′yə lāt′), *v.t.,* **-lat•ed, -lat•ing. 1.** to specify in the terms of an agreement. **2.** to require as an essential condition of an agreement. —**stip′u•la′tion,** *n.*

stir¹ (stûr), *v.,* **stirred, stir•ring,** *n.* —*v.t., v.i.* **1.** to agitate (a substance) with a continuous or repeated movement of an implement. **2.** to affect or be moved strongly. **3.** to incite, instigate, or prompt. **4.** to move, esp. in a slight way. **5.** to rouse or be roused, as from inactivity. —*n.* **6.** the act of stirring. **7.** a state of excitement; commotion.

stir² (stûr), *n. Slang.* prison.

stir′-cra′zy *adj. Slang.* restless or frantic from long confinement.

stir′-fry′ *v.t.,* **-fried, -fry•ing.** to fry quickly while stirring constantly in a small amount of oil over high heat.

stir′ring *adj.* **1.** rousing or exciting. **2.** active or lively.

stir•rup (stûr′əp, stir′-), *n.* **1.** a loop or ring suspended from the saddle of a horse to support the rider's foot. **2. a.** a strap of fabric or elastic at the bottom of a pair of pants, worn around and under the foot. **b. stirrups,** (*used with a pl. v.*) close-fitting knit pants with such straps. [bef. 1000; ME; OE *stigrāp* (*stige* ascent + *rāp* ROPE), c. OHG *stegareif*]

stitch (stich), *n.* **1. a.** one complete movement of a threaded needle in sewing. **b.** a loop or portion of thread left after a stitch. **2.** the least bit, as of clothing. **3.** a sudden, sharp pain, esp. in the side. —*v.t.* **4.** to join or mend with stitches. **5.** to ornament with stitches. —*v.i.* **6.** to sew.

St. Kitts-Nevis *n.* a twin-island state in the E West Indies, consisting of St. Kitts and Nevis.

St. Lu•cia (lōō′shə, -sē ə), *n.* an island country in the E West Indies. —**St. Lu′cian,** *n., adj.*

stock (stok), *n.* **1.** a supply of goods kept on hand, as by a merchant or manufacturer. **2.** a quantity accumulated, as for future use. **3.** LIVESTOCK. **4.** a stock company. **5. a.** the shares of a company or corporation. **b.** a certificate showing ownership of one or more shares. **6.** the type from which a group of animals or plants has been derived. **7.** a race, breed, or family, as of animals or plants. **8.** a line of descent. **9.** a wooden supporting structure, as the handle of a whip or the piece to which the barrel of a rifle is attached. **10. stocks,** a framework with holes for the ankles and, sometimes, the wrists, formerly used to expose an offender to public derision. **11.** raw material. **12.** the broth from boiled meat, fish, or poultry. —*adj.* **13.** kept regularly on hand. **14.** common or ordinary; standard. —*v.t.* **15.** to furnish with stock; supply. **16.** to lay up in store, as for future use. —*v.i.* **17.** to lay in a stock of something. —*Idiom.* **18. take** or **put stock in,** to believe; trust. **19. take stock, a.** to make an inventory of stock on hand. **b.** to appraise resources or prospects.

stock•ade (sto kād′), *n.* **1.** a defensive barrier of upright stakes or timbers driven into the ground one beside the other. **2.** an enclosure consisting of stockades. **3.** a military prison.

stock′brok′er *n.* a broker who buys and sells securities for customers.

stock′ com′pany *n.* a theatrical company acting a repertoire of plays, usu. at its own theater.

stock′ exchange′ *n.* **1.** a place where securities are bought and sold. **2.** an association of stockbrokers.

stock′hold′er *n.* an owner of stock in a corporation.

stock′ing *n.* a close-fitting knitted covering for the foot and leg.

stock′ing cap′ *n.* a conical knitted cap with a tassel or pompom.

stock′ mar′ket *n.* **1.** STOCK EXCHANGE (def. 1). **2.** the market for stocks throughout a nation.

stock′pile′ *n., v.,* **-piled, -pil•ing.** —*n.* **1.** a supply of an essential material held in reserve. —*v.t., v.i.* **2.** to store or accumulate in a stockpile.

stock′-still′ *adj.* completely still; motionless.

stock′y *adj.,* **-i•er, -i•est.** sturdy and usu. short; thickset.

stock′yard′ *n.* an enclosure for the temporary housing of livestock.

stodg•y (stoj′ē), *adj.,* **-i•er, -i•est. 1.** dull or uninteresting; boring. **2.** unduly formal and traditional.

sto•gy or **-gie** (stō′gē), *n., pl.* **-gies.** a long, slender, inexpensive cigar.

Sto•ic (stō′ik), *adj.* **1.** of or noting an ancient Greek school of philosophy teaching that people should be free of passion and submit without complaint to unavoidable necessity. **2.** (*l.c.*) stoical. —*n.* **3.** a member of the Stoic school of philosophy. **4.** (*l.c.*) a stoical person. —**Sto′i•cism** (-ə siz′əm), *n.*

sto′i•cal *adj.* **1.** marked by a calm, austere fortitude befitting the Stoics; impassive. **2.** (*cap.*) of the Stoics. —**sto′i•cal•ly,** *adv.*

stoke (stōk), *v.t., v.i.,* **stoked, stok•ing. 1.** to poke, stir up, and feed (a fire). **2.** to tend the fire of (a furnace). —**stok′er,** *n.*

stole[1] (stōl), *v.* pt. of STEAL.

stole[2] (stōl), *n.* **1.** a narrow strip of material worn over the shoulders by some clergymen. **2.** a woman's long shoulder scarf of fur or other material.

stol•id (stol′id), *adj.* not easily moved emotionally; impassive. —**sto•lid•i•ty** (stə lid′i tē), *n.* —**stol′id•ly,** *adv.*

stom•ach (stum′ək), *n.* **1.** the saclike enlargement of the alimentary canal in which food is stored and partially digested. **2.** the belly; abdomen. **3.** appetite for food. **4.** desire; inclination. —*v.t.* **5.** to endure or tolerate; bear.

stomp (stomp), *v.t., v.i.* to tread on or step heavily; trample.

stone (stōn), *n., pl.* **stones** for 1–3, 5, 6, **stone** for 4, *v.,* **stoned, ston•ing.** —*n.* **1.** the hard substance, formed of mineral matter, of which rocks consist. **2.** a small piece of rock. **3.** a gemstone. **4.** a British unit of weight equivalent to 14 pounds (6.4 kg). **5.** a hard seed, as of a date; pit. **6.** a concretion in the body, as in the kidney. —*v.t.* **7.** to pelt or kill by pelting with stones. **8.** to remove stones from (fruit). —**ston′y,** *adj.,* **-i•er, -i•est.**

Stone′ Age′ *n.* the early period of human history characterized by the use of stone implements and weapons.

stoned (stōnd), *adj. Informal.* **1.** drunk. **2.** affected by a drug; high.

stone′wall′ *v.i.* to be evasive or uncooperative; use obstructive tactics.

stooge (stōōj), *n.* **1.** an entertainer who feeds lines to the main comedian. **2.** an underling, assistant, or accomplice.

stool (stōōl), *n.* **1.** a simple armless and backless seat. **2.** a low support on which to kneel or rest the feet. **3.** fecal matter.

stool′ pi′geon *n. Slang.* a decoy or informer, esp. for the police.

stoop[1] (stōōp), *v.i.* **1.** to bend the body forward and downward. **2.** to bow the head and shoulders forward habitually. **3.** to descend from one's level of dignity; condescend. —*n.* **4.** the act of stooping. **5.** a stooping position or posture.

stoop[2] (stōōp), *n.* a small porch at the entrance of a house.

stop (stop), *v.,* **stopped, stop•ping,** *n.* —*v.t.* **1.** to desist from; discontinue. **2.** to cause to cease. **3.** to interrupt or check. **4.** to cut off, intercept, or withhold. **5.** to prevent from proceeding, acting, or operating. **6.** to block (an opening) by closing, filling, or obstructing. —*v.i.* **7.** to come to a halt. **8.** to cease proceeding, acting, or operating. **9.** to halt for a stay or visit. **10. stop by** or **in,** to make a brief visit. **11. ~ over,** to stop briefly in the course of a journey. —*n.* **12.** the act of stopping. **13.** a cessation; end. **14.** a stay or visit. **15.** a place where

trains or other vehicles stop. **16.** a plug; stopper. **17.** an obstacle, impediment, or hindrance. **18. a.** a set of organ pipes producing tones of the same quality. **b.** a knob or handle that controls such a set. **19.** a consonant sound made with complete closure at some part of the vocal tract, usu. followed by sudden release of the interrupted air. **20.** a punctuation mark, esp. a period.

stop′gap′ *n.* something serving as a temporary substitute; makeshift.

stop′o′ver *n.* a stop in the course of a journey.

stop′per *n.* something, as a plug or cork, used to close an opening or hole.

stop′watch′ *n.* a watch with a hand that can be stopped or started at any instant, used for precise timing.

stor•age (stôr′ij), *n.* **1.** the act of storing or state of being stored. **2.** capacity for storing. **3.** MEMORY (def. 7).

store (stôr), *n., v.,* **stored, stor•ing.** —*n.* **1.** a retail establishment where merchandise is sold. **2.** a supply or stock, esp. for future use. **3.** *Chiefly Brit.* a storehouse or warehouse. **4.** a great quantity; abundance. —*v.t.* **5.** to supply or furnish. **6.** to put away for future use. **7.** to deposit, as in a storehouse, for safekeeping. **8.** to put or retain (data) in a computer memory unit. —*Idiom.* **9. in store, a.** in reserve. **b.** about to happen. **10. set store by,** to have regard for; value.

store′front′ *n.* **1.** the side of a store facing a street. **2.** a street-level store that has frontage on a street.

store′house′ *n.* **1.** a building in which things are stored; warehouse. **2.** a source of abundant supplies.

store′keep′er *n.* a person who owns or operates a store.

store′room′ *n.* a room in which supplies or goods are stored.

stork (stôrk), *n., pl.* **storks, stork.** a large wading bird with long legs and a long neck and bill.

storm (stôrm), *n.* **1.** an atmospheric disturbance marked by strong winds and often accompanied by rain, snow, or hail. **2.** a violent military assault. **3.** a violent outburst or outbreak: *a storm of abuse.* —*v.i.* **4.** to blow, rain, snow, or hail heavily. **5.** to be furious; rage. **6.** to rush angrily. —*v.t.* **7.** to attack or assault. —**storm′y,** *adj.,* **-i•er, -i•est.**

sto•ry[1] (stôr′ē), *n., pl.* **-ries. 1.** a written or spoken account of something that has happened. **2.** a fictitious tale shorter than a novel. **3.** the plot of a literary or dramatic work. **4.** a news report. **5.** a lie; fabrication.

sto•ry[2] (stôr′ē), *n., pl.* **-ries.** a complete horizontal section of a building.

stoup (stōōp), *n.* a basin for holy water.

stout (stout), *adj.,* **-er, -est,** *n.* —*adj.* **1.** overweight; fat. **2.** courageous; brave. **3.** firm; resolute. **4.** strong of body; sturdy. **5.** substantial; solid. —*n.* **6.** a dark, sweet ale. —**stout′ly,** *adv.* —**stout′ness,** *n.*

stout′-heart′ed *adj.* brave and resolute.

stove[1] (stōv), *n.* an apparatus that furnishes heat for warmth or cooking and uses fuel or electricity for power.

stove[2] (stōv), *v.* a pt. and pp. of STAVE.

stow (stō), *v.t.* **1.** to put away, esp. in an orderly fashion. **2. stow away, a.** to conceal oneself on a conveyance as a means of getting transportation. **b.** to hide away. —**stow′age** (-ij), *n.*

strad•dle (strad′l), *v.,* **-dled, -dling,** *n.* —*v.i., v.t.* **1.** to stand or sit astride (of). **2.** to favor or appear to favor both sides (of). —*n.* **3.** an act or instance of straddling.

strafe (strāf, sträf), *v.t.,* **strafed, straf•ing.** to attack (ground troops or installations) with fire from low-flying airplanes. [< G propaganda slogan (*Gott*) *strafe* (*England*) (may God) punish (England)] —**straf′er,** *n.*

strag•gle (strag′əl), *v.i.,* **-gled, -gling. 1.** to stray from the road or course. **2.** to wander about or ramble. **3.** to spread at irregular intervals. —**strag′-gler,** *n.*

straight (strāt), *adj.,* **-er, -est,** *adv.,* *n.* —*adj.* **1.**

without a bend, angle, wave, or curve. **2.** direct in character; candid. **3.** honest; upright. **4.** cogent; rational: *straight thinking.* **5.** in the proper order or condition. **6.** continuous; unbroken. **7.** thoroughgoing; complete. **8.** *Informal.* **a.** heterosexual. **b.** traditional; conventional. **9.** not diluted; unmixed: *straight whiskey.* —*adv.* **10.** in a straight manner. —*n.* **11.** the condition of being straight. **12.** a straight form, part, or position. **13.** a sequence of five consecutive cards in poker. —*Idiom.* **14. straight off** or **away,** without delay; immediately. —**straight′en,** *v.t., v.i.* —**straight′ly,** *adv.* —**straight′ness,** *n.*

straight′-arm′ *v.t.* to deflect (an opponent) by pushing away with the arm held straight.

straight′ ar′row *n.* an often righteously conventional person.

straight′a•way′ *n.* a straight stretch, as of a highway.

straight′edge′ *n.* a bar, as of wood or metal, with a straight edge for use in drawing or testing straight lines.

straight′ face′ *n.* a facial expression that conceals one's feelings.

straight′for′ward *adj.* **1.** going or directed straight ahead. **2.** free from deceit; honest. —*adv.* **3.** Also, **straight′for′wards.** straight ahead.

straight′ man′ *n.* an entertainer who acts as a foil for a comedian.

strain[1] (strān), *v.t.* **1.** to draw tight; make taut. **2.** to exert to the utmost. **3.** to injure (a muscle, tendon, etc.) by overexertion. **4.** to stretch beyond the proper limit. **5.** to cause to pass through a strainer. —*v.i.* **6.** to make strenuous efforts. **7.** to filter, percolate, or ooze. —*n.* **8.** great effort in pursuit of a goal. **9.** an injury, as to a muscle, due to overexertion. **10.** deformation of a solid body or structure in response to application of a force. **11.** severe or fatiguing pressure or exertion.

strain[2] (strān), *n.* **1.** the body of descendants of a common ancestor. **2.** a variety of domestic animal or cultivated plant. **3.** ancestry or descent. **4.** hereditary character or tendency. **5.** a streak or trace.

strain[3] (strān), *n.* **1.** a melody; tune. **2.** a pervading style; spirit.

strained *adj.* not natural or spontaneous.

strait (strāt), *n.* **1.** Often, **straits.** (*used with a sing. v.*) a narrow passage of water connecting two large bodies of water. **2.** Usu., **straits.** a position of difficulty, distress, or need. —*adj. Archaic.* **3.** narrow or confined. **4.** strict.

strait′en *v.t.* **1.** to put into difficulties, esp. financial ones. **2. a.** to make narrow. **b.** to confine narrowly.

strait′jack′et *n.* a garment made of strong material and designed to bind the arms of a violent person.

strait′-laced′ *adj.* excessively strict in conduct or morality.

strand[1] (strand), *v.t.* **1.** to drive or run onto a shore. **2.** to leave in a helpless position. —*n.* **3.** land bordering a body of water; shore.

strand[2] (strand), *n.* **1.** one of the fibers or wires plaited or twisted together to form a rope, cable, cord, or string. **2.** a filament, as of hair. **3.** a length of cord or string.

strange (strānj), *adj.,* **strang•er, strang•est. 1.** exciting curiosity or wonder; odd. **2.** estranged; alienated. **3.** unfamiliar; foreign. **4.** unaccustomed; inexperienced. **5.** reserved; aloof. —**strange′ly,** *adv.*

stran•ger (strān′jər), *n.* **1.** a person with whom one is not personally acquainted. **2.** a newcomer. **3.** an outsider. **4.** a person unacquainted with or unaccustomed to something.

stran•gle (strang′gəl), *v.,* **-gled, -gling.** —*v.t.* **1.** to kill by choking; throttle. **2.** to stifle or suppress. —*v.i.* **3.** to become strangled. —**stran′gler,** *n.* —**stran′gu•la′tion,** *n.*

stran′gle•hold′ *n.* **1.** an illegal wrestling hold by which an opponent is choked. **2.** a restrictive force or influence.

stran′gu•late′ (-gyə lāt′), *v.t.,* **-lat•ed, -lat•ing.**

to constrict (a duct, intestine, vessel, etc.) so as to prevent circulation.

strap (strap), *n., v.,* **strapped, strap•ping.** —*n.* **1.** a narrow strip of flexible material, esp. leather, as for fastening or holding things together. —*v.t.* **2.** to secure or fasten with a strap.

strapped *adj.* needy; wanting.

strat•a•gem (strat′ə jəm), *n.* **1.** a scheme or maneuver for surprising or deceiving an enemy. **2.** a trick or ruse.

strat•e•gy (strat′i jē), *n., pl.* **-gies. 1.** the science or art of planning and directing large-scale military movements and operations. **2.** a plan or method for achieving a goal. —**stra•te•gic** (strə tē′jik), *adj.* —**strat′e•gist,** *n.*

strat•i•fy (strat′ə fī′), *v.t., v.i.,* **-fied, -fy•ing.** to form into or become arranged in layers or strata. —**strat′i•fi•ca′tion,** *n.*

strat•o•sphere (strat′ə sfēr′), *n.* the region of the upper atmosphere extending from about 12 to 30 miles (20–50 km) above the earth. —**strat′o•spher′ic** (-sfer′ik), *adj.*

stra•tum (strā′təm, strat′əm), *n., pl.* **stra•ta** (strā′tə, strat′ə), **stra•tums. 1.** a layer of material, often formed one upon another. **2.** a single bed of sedimentary rock. **3.** a social or cultural level.

straw (strô), *n.* **1. a.** a single stalk of grass, esp. of a cereal grass. **b.** a mass of such stalks after drying and threshing. **2.** something of negligible value. **3.** a tube for sucking up a beverage. —*adj.* **4.** of, resembling, or made of straw. **5.** of the color of straw; pale yellow. **6.** of little value; inconsequential.

straw•ber•ry (strô′ber′ē, -bə rē), *n., pl.* **-ries. 1.** the red, juicy fruit of a plant of the rose family. **2.** the plant itself.

straw′ boss′ *n.* an assistant foreman, as in a logging camp.

straw′ vote′ *n.* an unofficial vote taken to determine the general trend of opinion. Also called **straw′ poll′.**

stray (strā), *v.,* **strayed, stray•ing,** *n., adj.* —*v.i.* **1.** to deviate from a direct or proper course. **2.** to wander; roam. **3.** to become distracted. —*n.* **4.** a lost, homeless, or friendless person or animal. —*adj.* **5.** straying or having strayed. **6.** incidental; occasional.

streak (strēk), *n.* **1.** a long, narrow mark or band of color. **2.** a vein; stratum: *streaks of fat in bacon.* **3.** a trace: *a streak of humor.* **4. a.** a spell; run. **b.** an uninterrupted series. **5.** a bolt of lightning. —*v.t.* **6.** to mark with streaks. —*v.i.* **7.** to become streaked. **8.** to run, go, or work rapidly.

stream (strēm), *n.* **1.** a body of water, as a brook, flowing in a channel. **2.** a flow or current, as of fluid. **3.** a continuous succession: *a stream of words.* —*v.i.* **4.** to flow, pass, or issue in or as if in a stream. **5.** to emit a fluid copiously. **6.** to wave, as a flag in the wind. —*v.t.* **7.** to discharge in a stream.

stream′er *n.* **1.** a long narrow flag; pennant. **2.** a long narrow strip, as a ribbon. **3.** a stream of light, as from the aurora borealis. **4.** BANNER (def. 2).

stream′lined′ *adj.* **1.** contoured to offer the least resistance to a current, as of air or water. **2.** designed or organized for maximum efficiency. **3.** modernized. —**stream′line′,** *v.t.,* **-lined, lin•ing.**

street (strēt), *n.* **1.** a usu. paved public road, as in a town or city. **2.** a street together with the sidewalks and adjacent property. **3.** the inhabitants or frequenters of a street.

street′car′ *n.* a public vehicle on rails running regularly along city streets.

street′ smarts′ *n.pl.* shrewd awareness of how to survive in an urban environment. —**street′-smart′,** *adj.*

street′walk′er *n.* a prostitute who solicits on the streets.

street′wise′ *adj.* possessing street smarts.

strength (strengkth, strength, strenth), *n.* **1.** the quality or state of being strong; physical power. **2.** intellectual or moral force. **3.** force in numbers, as of an organization. **4.** effective force or cogency. **5.**

power of resisting strain, force, etc. **6.** degree of potency or concentration. **7.** intensity, as of light. **8.** a strong or valuable attribute. **9.** a source of power; sustenance. ***—Idiom.*** **10. on the strength of,** on the basis of.

strength′en *v.t., v.i.* to make or grow stronger.

stren•u•ous (stren′yo͞o əs), *adj.* **1.** characterized by or calling for vigorous exertion. **2.** intensely active; energetic. **—stren′u•ous•ly,** *adv.*

strep′ throat′ *n.* an acute sore throat caused by streptococci.

strep•to•coc•cus (strep′tə kok′əs), *n., pl.* **-ci** (-sī, -sē). any of several spherical bacteria occurring in pairs or chains, some of which cause serious diseases. **—strep′to•coc′cal,** *adj.*

stress (stres), *n.* **1.** importance or significance. **2.** prominent relative loudness of a speech sound. **3.** physical force, as pressure, exerted on one thing by another. **4.** the action on a body of a system of forces that results in deformation. **5.** a stimulus, as pain, that disturbs the equilibrium. **6.** physical, mental, or emotional tension. **—***v.t.* **7.** to emphasize. **8.** to accent. **9.** to subject to strain or tension. **—stress′ful,** *adj.*

stretch (strech), *v.t.* **1.** to spread out fully. **2.** to extend or cause to extend from one point or place to another. **3.** to draw tight or taut. **4.** to extend or enlarge beyond normal or proper limits. **—***v.i.* **5.** to recline at full length. **6.** to extend one's limbs or body. **7.** to extend over a distance or in time. **8.** to become stretched without breaking. **—***n.* **9.** the act of stretching or state of being stretched. **10.** a continuous length. **11.** the homestretch of a racetrack. **12.** an extent in time. **—***adj.* **13.** capable of being stretched.

stretch′er *n.* **1.** a litter, as of canvas, for carrying a sick or dead person. **2.** one that stretches.

strew (stro͞o), *v.t.,* **strewed, strewn** (stro͞on) or **strewed, strew•ing. 1.** to scatter freely; sprinkle. **2.** to overspread by scattering. **3.** to disseminate.

stri′at•ed (strī′ā tid) *adj.* furrowed; streaked. **—stri•a′tion** (-ā′shən) *n.*

strick•en (strik′ən), *v.* **1.** a pp. of STRIKE. **—***adj.* **2.** wounded by or as if by a missile. **3.** afflicted, as with disease or sorrow.

strict (strikt), *adj.,* **-er, -est. 1.** closely conforming to requirements or principles. **2.** stringent; exacting. **3.** rigorously enforced. **4.** exact; precise. **5.** narrowly limited. **6.** absolute; complete. **—strict′ly,** *adv.*

stric•ture (strik′chər), *n.* **1.** an abnormal contraction of a bodily passage or duct. **2.** limitation; restriction. **3.** an adverse criticism.

stride (strīd), *v.,* **strode, strid•den** (strid′n), **strid•ing,** *n.* **—***v.i., v.t.* **1.** to walk (over or along) with long steps. **2.** to take or pass over in one long step. **—***n.* **3.** a striding manner or gait. **4.** a long step. **5.** the distance covered in a stride. **6.** a step forward, as in development.

stri•dent (strīd′nt), *adj.* harsh and loud in sound; grating. **—stri′den•cy,** *n.* **—stri′dent•ly,** *adv.*

strife (strīf), *n.* **1.** violent or bitter conflict. **2.** a struggle; clash. **3.** competition; rivalry.

strike (strīk), *v.,* **struck; struck** or (*esp. for 14–16*) **strick•en; strik•ing;** *n.* **—***v.t.* **1.** to deal a blow to with or as if with the fist. **2.** to inflict; deliver: *struck a blow.* **3.** to produce by percussion or friction. **4.** to ignite (a match) by friction. **5.** to collide with. **6.** to enter the mind of. **7.** to impress strongly. **8.** to happen upon; find: *struck oil.* **9.** to arrive at; achieve: *to strike a compromise.* **10.** to lower: *to strike a sail.* **11.** to cross out; cancel. **12.** to stamp: *to strike a medal.* **13.** to mark by or as if by chimes: *The clock struck 12.* **14.** to afflict suddenly: *stricken with fever.* **15.** to overwhelm emotionally. **16.** to implant; induce: *struck fear in our hearts.* **17.** to take on; assume: *struck a pose.* **—***v.i.* **18.** to deal a blow. **19.** to make an attack. **20.** to hit or collide. **21.** to come suddenly: *struck on a new method.* **22.** to sound by percussion: *The clock strikes.* **23.** to go on strike against an employer. **24. strike out, a.** to put or be put out by a strikeout in baseball. **b.** to set out; venture forth. **25. ~ up, a.** to begin to play or sing. **b.** to bring into being. **—***n.* **26.** an act or instance of striking. **27.** a group work stoppage to compel changes in working conditions. **28.** a baseball pitch that is swung at and missed or in the strike zone but not swung at. **29.** the knocking down of all the bowling pins with the first bowl. **30.** the discovery of a rich mineral deposit. **31.** an attack, esp. by military aircraft.

strik′ing *adj.* **1.** conspicuously attractive or impressive. **2.** noticeable; conspicuous.

string (string), *n., v.,* **strung, string•ing. —***n.* **1.** a slender cord or thick thread for binding or tying. **2.** a collection of objects threaded on a string: *a string of pearls.* **3.** a series of things arranged in or as if in a line: *a string of questions.* **4. a.** the tightly stretched cord or wire of a musical instrument. **b. strings,** stringed instruments, esp. those played with a bow. **5.** a plant fiber. **6.** Usu., **strings.** conditions or limitations: *no strings attached.* **—***v.t.* **7.** to furnish with a string. **8.** to extend or stretch like a string. **9.** to thread on or as if on a string. **10.** to arrange in a series or succession. **11.** to strip the strings from: *to string beans.* **12.** to make tense. **—string′y,** *adj.,* **-i•er, -i•est.**

string′ bean′ *n.* a bean, as the green bean, whose unripe pods are used as food.

stringed *adj.* fitted with strings: *violins and other stringed instruments.*

strin•gent (strin′jənt), *adj.* rigorously binding or exacting; strict. **—strin′gen•cy,** *n.* **—strin′gent•ly,** *adv.*

string′er *n.* **1.** a long horizontal timber connecting upright posts. **2.** a part-time news reporter.

strip[1] (strip), *v.,* **stripped, strip•ping. —***v.t.* **1.** to deprive of covering or clothing. **2.** to take off; remove. **3.** to take away; divest. **4.** to clear out; empty. **5.** to shear or damage the thread or teeth of: *to strip gears.* **—***v.i.* **6.** to remove one's clothes.

strip[2] (strip), *n.* **1.** a long, narrow piece. **2.** an airstrip.

stripe (strīp), *n., v.,* **striped, strip•ing. —***n.* **1.** a narrow band differing in color, material, or texture from the background. **2.** a strip of braid or fabric worn on a uniform to indicate length of service or rank. **3.** variety; sort. **—***v.t.* **4.** to mark or furnish with stripes.

strip•ling (strip′ling), *n.* a youth.

strip′ mine′ *n.* a mine in an open pit formed by removing the earth and rock covering a mineral deposit. **—strip′-mine′,** *v.t., v.i.,* **-mined, min•ing.**

strip′tease′ *n.* an act, as in a burlesque show, in which a performer removes garments one at a time.

strive (strīv), *v.i.,* **strove** or **strived, striv•en** (striv′ən) or **strived, striv•ing. 1.** to make a strenuous effort. **2.** to contend in opposition; struggle.

strobe (strōb), *n.* **1.** Also called **strobe′ light′.** an electronic flash that produces rapid, brilliant bursts of light. **2.** a device for studying the motion of a body by making it appear to slow down or stop, as by periodic illumination.

stroke[1] (strōk), *n.* **1.** an act or instance of striking. **2.** the sound of striking, as of a bell. **3.** a blockage or hemorrhage of a blood vessel leading to the brain, causing loss of consciousness and often long-term impairment. **4.** a sudden vigorous action or movement. **5.** a single complete movement, esp. one continuously repeated, as in swimming. **6.** a single mark made by a pen, pencil, or brush. **7.** a feat; achievement: *a stroke of genius.* **8.** a sudden or chance happening: *a stroke of luck.*

stroke[2] (strōk), *v.,* **stroked, strok•ing,** *n.* **—***v.t.* **1.** to pass the hand or an instrument over gently, as in caressing. **—***n.* **2.** an act or instance of stroking.

stroll (strōl), *v.i., v.t.* **1.** to walk leisurely (along or through); ramble. **—***n.* **2.** a leisurely walk.

stroll′er *n.* **1.** one who strolls. **2.** a chairlike carriage in which small children are pushed.

strong (strông, strong), *adj.,* **strong•er** (strông′gər, strong′-), **strong•est** (strông′gist, strong′-). **1.** physically powerful; vigorous or robust. **2.** mentally or morally powerful. **3.** powerful in influence, authority, or resources. **4.** of great force, effectiveness, or potency. **5.** able to resist strain, force, or wear.

6. strenuous or energetic; vigorous: *strong efforts.* **7.** not weak; intense or concentrated: *strong tea.* **8.** of a designated number: *an army 20,000 strong.* —**strong′ly,** *adv.*

strong′-arm′ *adj.* **1.** using or involving physical force. —*v.t.* **2.** to use physical force on.

strong′box′ *n.* a strongly made box or chest for valuables or money.

strong′hold′ *n.* a well-fortified place; fortress.

stron•ti•um (stron′shē əm, -shəm, -tē əm), *n.* a metallic chemical element whose compounds are used in fireworks. *Symbol:* Sr; *at. wt.:* 87.62; *at. no.:* 38.

strop (strop), *n., v.,* **stropped, strop•ping.** —*n.* **1.** a strip of flexible material, esp. leather, for sharpening razors. —*v.t.* **2.** to sharpen on or as if on a strop.

struc•ture (struk′chər), *n., v.,* **-tured, -tur•ing.** —*n.* **1.** the manner in which something is constructed. **2.** the manner in which the elements of something are organized or interrelated. **3.** something constructed, as a bridge. **4.** something composed of organized or interrelated elements. —*v.t.* **5.** to give structure to. —**struc′tur•al,** *adj.*

stru•del (strood′l; *Ger.* shtroōd′l), *n.* a pastry consisting of fruit or cheese rolled in a paper-thin sheet of dough and baked. [< G: lit., whirlpool]

strug•gle (strug′əl), *v.,* **-gled, -gling,** *n.* —*v.i.* **1.** to contend vigorously, as with an adversary or problem. **2.** to advance with great effort. —*n.* **3.** an act or instance of struggling. **4.** a war, fight, conflict, or contest.

strum (strum), *v.t., v.i.,* **strummed, strum•ming.** to play on (a stringed instrument) by running the fingers lightly across the strings.

strum•pet (strum′pit), *n.* a prostitute.

strut[1] (strut), *v.,* **strut•ted, strut•ting,** *n.* —*v.i.* **1.** to walk with a vain, pompous bearing. —*n.* **2.** a strutting walk or gait.

strut[2] (strut), *n.* any of various structural members for resisting longitudinal compression.

strych•nine (strik′nin, -nēn, -nīn), *n.* a colorless crystalline poison formerly used as a central nervous system stimulant.

stub (stub), *n., v.,* **stubbed, stub•bing.** —*n.* **1.** a short remaining piece, as of a pencil or cigar. **2.** the short detachable part of a check or receipt kept as a record. **3.** the returned portion of a ticket. **4.** a tree stump. —*v.t.* **5.** to strike (one's toe or foot) accidentally against something. **6.** to put out (a cigarette or cigar) by crushing. —**stub′by,** *adj.,* **-bi•er, -bi•est.**

stub•ble (stub′əl), *n.* **1.** the stumps of grain and other stalks left in the ground when the crop is cut. **2.** a short, rough growth, as of beard. —**stub′bly,** *adj.*

stub•born (stub′ərn), *adj.* **1.** unreasonably or perversely obstinate; unyielding. **2.** fixed, as in purpose; resolute. **3.** difficult to handle, treat, or manage. —**stub′born•ly,** *adv.*

stuc•co (stuk′ō), *n., pl.* **-coes, -cos,** *v.,* **-coed, -co• ing.** —*n.* **1.** a plasterlike finish for exterior walls. —*v.t.* **2.** to cover with stucco.

stuck′-up′ *adj. Informal.* snobbishly conceited.

stud[1] (stud), *n., v.,* **stud•ded, stud•ding.** —*n.* **1.** something, as a knob or nailhead, projecting from a surface. **2.** a buttonlike device on a shank used as an ornament or fastener: *a collar stud.* **3.** one of the slender, upright posts forming the frame of a wall and covered with plasterwork, paneling, etc. —*v.t.* **4.** to set with or as if with studs. **5.** to be scattered over the surface of.

stud[2] (stud), *n.* a male animal, esp. a stallion, kept for breeding.

stu•dent (stood′nt, styood′-), *n.* **1.** a person who studies, esp. at a school or college. **2.** a person who investigates, observes, or examines thoughtfully.

stud•ied (stud′ēd), *adj.* marked by conscious effort; intentional.

stu•di•o (stoo′dē ō′, styoo′-), *n., pl.* **-os.** **1.** the workroom of an artist, as a painter. **2.** a place for instruction in one of the performing arts. **3.** a place equipped for producing radio or television programs, films, or recordings.

stu•di•ous (stoo′dē əs, styoo′-), *adj.* **1.** disposed or

given to diligent study. **2.** giving or showing careful attention. —**stu′di•ous•ly,** *adv.*

stud•y (stud′ē), *n., pl.* **-ies,** *v.,* **-ied, -y•ing.** —*n.* **1.** application of the mind to the acquisition of knowledge. **2.** Often, **-ies.** a student's work at school or college. **3.** a detailed investigation and analysis, as of a subject. **4.** a branch of learning or knowledge. **5.** a room set apart for study, reading, or writing. —*v.i.* **6.** to apply the mind to the acquisition of knowledge. **7.** to think deeply; reflect. —*v.t.* **8.** to apply the mind to acquiring knowledge of (a subject). **9.** to examine or investigate carefully and in detail.

stuff (stuf), *n.* **1.** the material of which something is made. **2.** material to be used in making something. **3.** matter, objects, or items of an unspecified kind. **4.** personal belongings or equipment. **5.** inward character, qualities, or capabilities. **6.** a specialty or special skill: *did his stuff.* **7.** worthless or foolish ideas, talk, or writing. **8.** *Chiefly Brit.* woven material or fabric, esp. wool. —*v.t.* **9.** to fill by packing the contents to. **10.** to thrust or cram into a receptacle or opening. **11.** to fill or cram with food. **12.** to fill with stuffing. **13.** to pack tightly; crowd. **14.** to stop up or plug.

stuffed′ shirt′ *n.* a pompous, self-satisfied, and inflexible person.

stuff′ing *n.* **1.** material used to stuff something. **2.** a filling, as seasoned bread crumbs, used to stuff poultry, vegetables, etc.

stuff′y *adj.,* **-i•er, -i•est. 1.** poorly ventilated; close. **2.** blocked or stopped up: *a stuffy nose.* **3.** dull or tedious. **4.** self-important; pompous.

stul•ti•fy (stul′tə fī′), *v.t.,* **-fied, -fy•ing. 1.** to cause to appear foolish or ridiculous. **2.** to make futile or ineffectual.

stum•ble (stum′bəl), *v.,* **-bled, -bling,** *n.* —*v.i.* **1.** to trip in walking or running. **2.** to walk or go unsteadily. **3.** to make a slip or blunder, esp. a sinful one. **4.** to discover or meet with by chance. —*n.* **5.** the act of stumbling.

stum′bling block′ *n.* an obstacle; hindrance.

stump (stump), *n.* **1.** the lower end of a tree trunk or plant left after the upper part falls or is cut off. **2.** the part of a bodily limb remaining after the rest has been cut off. **3.** a part of a broken or decayed tooth left in the gum. **4.** the figurative place of political speechmaking. —*v.t.* **5.** to baffle or perplex. **6.** to make political campaign speeches to or in. —*v.i.* **7.** to walk heavily or clumsily. **8.** to make political campaign speeches.

stun (stun), *v.t.,* **stunned, stun•ning. 1.** to deprive of consciousness, feeling, or strength by or as if by a blow. **2.** to shock or amaze.

stun′ning *adj.* of striking beauty or excellence.

stunt[1] (stunt), *v.t.* to stop, slow down, or hinder the growth or development of.

stunt[2] (stunt), *n.* **1.** a feat displaying skill, dexterity, or daring. **2.** a feat performed chiefly to attract attention.

stu•pe•fy (stoo′pə fī′, styoo′-), *v.t.,* **-fied, -fy•ing. 1.** to put into a stupor. **2.** to astound; astonish. —**stu′pe•fac′tion** (-fak′shən), *n.*

stu•pen•dous (stoo pen′dəs, styoo-), *adj.* **1.** causing amazement; astounding. **2.** amazingly large or great.

stu•pid (stoo′pid, styoo′-), *adj.,* **-er, -est. 1.** lacking intelligence; dull. **2.** showing or proceeding from a lack of intelligence. **3.** tediously dull. —**stu•pid′- i•ty,** *n., pl.* **-ties.** —**stu′pid•ly,** *adv.*

stu•por (stoo′pər, styoo′-), *n.* **1.** a state marked by suspension or great diminution of sensibility. **2.** mental torpor; apathy.

stur•dy (stûr′dē), *adj.,* **-di•er, -di•est. 1.** strongly built; robust. **2.** firm; determined.

stur•geon (stûr′jən), *n., pl.* **-geons, -geon.** any of several large food fishes valued as a source of caviar.

stut•ter (stut′ər), *v.i., v.t.* **1.** to speak or say with repetitions, blocks or spasms, or prolongations of sounds. —*n.* **2.** an act or instance of stuttering. **3.** a speech defect marked by stuttering.

St. Vin′cent and the Gren′adines (vin′sənt;

gren′ə dēnz′), *n.* a country in the SE West Indies, comprising an island (**St. Vincent**) and the N Grenadines.

sty[1] (stī), *n., pl.* **sties. 1.** a pen or enclosure for swine; pigpen. **2.** a filthy place or abode.

sty[2] or **stye** (stī), *n., pl.* **sties** or **styes.** a swelling of a gland on the edge of the eyelid.

style (stīl), *n., v.,* **styled, styl•ing.** —*n.* **1.** a particular or characteristic manner of acting, speaking, or writing. **2.** the prevailing fashion, as in dress. **3.** a fashionable or luxurious mode of living. **4.** a mode of design, construction, or execution, esp. as characteristic of a person, group, or period. **5.** elegance or flair. **6.** STYLUS (defs. 1, 2). **7.** the rules or customs of spelling, punctuation, and the like, observed by a publisher. —*v.t.* **8.** to designate; name. **9.** to design in accordance with a given or new style.

styl′ish *adj.* conforming to the current style.

styl′ist *n.* a person who cultivates or maintains a distinctive style, esp. in writing. —**sty•lis′tic,** *adj.*

styl′ize *v.t.,* **-ized, -iz•ing.** to cause to conform to a conventionalized style.

sty•lus (stī′ləs), *n., pl.* **-li** (-lī), **-lus•es. 1.** a pointed instrument used by the ancients for writing on wax tablets. **2.** any of various pointed, pen-shaped instruments used esp. in artwork. **3.** a phonograph needle.

sty•mie or **-my** (stī′mē), *v.,* **-mied, -mie•ing** or **-my•ing,** *n., pl.* **-mies.** —*v.t.* **1.** to hinder, block, or thwart. —*n.* **2.** *Golf.* an instance of a ball's lying on a direct line between the cup and the ball of an opponent about to putt.

styp•tic (stip′tik), *adj.* serving to check bleeding.

Sty•ro•foam (stī′rə fōm′), *Trademark.* a lightweight plastic made from polystyrene.

suave (swäv), *adj.,* **suav•er, suav•est.** smoothly agreeable or polite. —**suave′ly,** *adv.* —**suav′i•ty,** *n.*

sub (sub), *n., v.,* **subbed, sub•bing.** —*n.* **1.** a submarine. **2.** a substitute. —*v.i.* **3.** to act as a substitute for another.

sub- a prefix meaning: under, below, or beneath (*subway*); just outside of or near (*subtropical*); less than or not quite (*subcontinent*); secondary or subordinate (*subcommittee*).

sub. 1. subordinated. **2.** subscription. **3.** substitute. **4.** suburb. **5.** suburban. **6.** subway.

sub•a•tom•ic (sub′ə tom′ik), *adj.* **1.** of a process that occurs within an atom. **2.** noting particles, as electrons, contained in an atom.

sub′com•mit•tee *n., pl.* **-tees.** a secondary committee appointed out of a main committee.

sub•con•scious *adj.* **1.** existing or operating in the mind beneath or beyond conscious awareness. —*n.* **2.** subconscious mental processes. —**sub•con′-scious•ly,** *adv.*

sub•con•ti•nent (sub kon′tn ənt, sub′kon′-), *n.* a very large subdivision of a continent.

sub′cul′ture *n.* a group having social, economic, or other traits distinctive enough to distinguish it from others within the same culture or society.

sub′cu•ta′ne•ous *adj.* situated or introduced under the skin.

sub•di•vide (sub′di vīd′, sub′di vīd′), *v.t., v.i.,* **-vid•ed, -vid•ing. 1.** to divide into smaller parts. **2.** to divide (land) into building lots. —**sub′di•vi′sion,** *n.*

sub•due (səb dōō′, -dyōō′), *v.t.,* **-dued, -du•ing. 1.** to conquer and subjugate. **2.** to bring under control. **3.** to reduce the intensity, force, or vividness of.

sub•fam•i•ly (sub fam′ə lē, sub′fam′ə lē), *n., pl.* **-lies. 1.** *Biol.* a category of related genera within a family. **2.** a group of related languages within a family.

sub′head′ also **-head′ing,** *n.* **1.** a heading of a subdivision, as of a chapter. **2.** a subordinate division of a title or heading.

sub•ject (*n., adj.* sub′jikt; *v.* səb jekt′), *n.* **1.** a person or thing forming the basis of thought, discussion, or investigation. **2.** a course of study. **3.** something or someone represented, as in a work of art. **4.** a person owing allegiance to or under the domination of a sovereign or state. **5.** a word or phrase referring to the one performing the action or

being in the state expressed by the predicate. **6.** one that undergoes a treatment or experiment. —*adj.* **7.** being under the domination or control of another. **8.** open or exposed: *subject to ridicule.* **9.** dependent upon something: *subject to your approval.* **10.** liable; prone: *subject to headaches.* —*v.t.* **11.** to bring under domination or control. **12.** to cause to undergo. **13.** to make liable or vulnerable. —**sub•jec′-tion,** *n.*

sub•jec′tive *adj.* **1.** of or belonging to the thinking subject rather than to the object of thought. **2.** of or characteristic of an individual; personal. —**sub′jec•tiv′i•ty,** *n.*

sub•join (səb join′), *v.t.* to add at the end; append.

sub•ju•gate (sub′jə gāt′), *v.t.,* **-gat•ed, -gat•ing. 1.** to bring under complete control; conquer. **2.** to make submissive; enslave. —**sub′ju•ga′tion,** *n.*

sub•junc•tive (səb jungk′tiv), *adj.* **1.** of or being a grammatical mood typically used for subjective, doubtful, hypothetical, or grammatically subordinate statements or questions. —*n.* **2.** the subjunctive mood. **3.** a verb form in the subjunctive mood.

sub•lease (*n.* sub′lēs′; *v.* sub lēs′), *n., v.,* **-leased, -leas•ing.** —*n.* **1.** a lease granted to another by the lessee of a property. —*v.t., v.i.* **2.** to grant, take, or hold a sublease (of).

sub•let (sub let′, sub′let′), *v.t., v.i.,* **-let, -let•ting. 1.** to sublease. **2.** to subcontract.

sub•li•mate (sub′lə māt′), *v.t.,* **-mat•ed, -mat•ing. 1.** to divert the energy of (a sexual or other biological impulse) into more socially acceptable activities. **2.** to sublime. —**sub′li•ma′tion,** *n.*

sub•lime (sə blīm′), *adj., v.,* **-limed, -lim•ing.** —*adj.* **1.** elevated, as in thought; lofty. **2.** inspiring awe or veneration. —*v.t.* **3.** to convert (a solid substance) by heat into a vapor that on cooling condenses again to solid form. —**sub•lim′i•ty** (-blim′i tē), *n.*

sub•lim•i•nal (sub lim′ə nl), *adj.* existing or operating below the threshold of consciousness.

sub′ma•chine′ gun′ *n.* an automatic firearm fired from the shoulder or hip.

sub•ma•rine (sub′mə rēn′, sub′mə rēn′), *n.* **1.** a naval boat that can be submerged and navigated under water. **2.** a hero sandwich. —*adj.* **3.** situated, operating, or living under the surface of the sea.

sub•merge (səb mûrj′), *v.t., v.i.,* **-merged, -merg•ing. 1.** to put or sink below the surface of water. **2.** to cover or be covered with or as if with water. —**sub•mer′gence,** *n.*

sub•merse (səb mûrs′), *v.t.,* **-mersed, -mers•ing.** to submerge. —**sub•mers′i•ble,** *adj.* —**sub•mer′-sion** (-mûr′zhən, -shən), *n.*

sub•mis′sive *adj.* yielding or obeying readily. —**sub•mis′sive•ly,** *adv.*

sub•mit (səb mit′), *v.,* **-mit•ted, -mit•ting.** —*v.t.* **1.** to give over or yield to the power or authority of another. **2.** to present for approval or consideration. **3.** to state as an opinion. —*v.i.* **4.** to yield oneself to the power or authority of another. —**sub•mis′sion,** *n.*

sub•nor•mal (sub nôr′məl), *adj.* being below normal, as in intelligence.

sub•or•di•nate (*adj., n.* sə bôr′dn it; *v.* -dn āt′), *adj., n., v.,* **-nat•ed, -nat•ing.** —*adj.* **1.** belonging to a lower order or rank. **2.** subject to or under the authority of a superior. **3.** of or noting a clause that is syntactically dependent on another clause. —*n.* **4.** a subordinate person or thing. —*v.t.* **5.** to place in a lower order or rank. **6.** to make subservient or dependent. —**sub•or′di•na′tion,** *n.*

sub•orn (sə bôrn′), *v.t.* to induce (a witness) to give false testimony. —**sub•or•na•tion** (sub′ôr nā′-shən), *n.*

sub•plot (sub′plot′), *n.* a secondary plot, as in a novel.

sub•poe•na or **-pe•na** (sə pē′nə, səb-), *n., pl.* **-nas,** *v.,* **-naed, -na•ing.** —*n.* **1.** a writ to summon witnesses or evidence before a court. —*v.t.* **2.** to serve with a subpoena.

sub ro•sa (sub rō′zə), *adv.* secretly; privately. [< L: lit., under the rose]

sub•scribe (səb skrīb′), *v.t., v.i.,* **-scribed, -scrib•ing. 1.** to pay or pledge (money) as a contribution or investment. **2.** to sign one's name to (a document), as in approval. **3.** to obtain a subscription, as to a publication. **4.** to give one's consent (to). **—sub•scrib′er,** *n.*

sub•script (sub′skript), *n.* a letter, number, or symbol written or printed low on a line of text.

sub•scrip•tion (səb skrip′shən), *n.* **1.** a sum of money subscribed. **2.** the right to receive a publication or service or to attend a series of performances for a sum paid.

sub•se•quent (sub′si kwənt), *adj.* following, as in order; succeeding.

sub•ser•vi•ent (səb sûr′vē ənt), *adj.* **1.** subordinate. **2.** servile; obsequious. **—sub•ser′vi•ence,** *n.*

sub•side (səb sīd′), *v.i.* **-sid•ed, -sid•ing. 1.** to sink to a lower level. **2.** to become quiet, less active, or less violent. **3.** to sink to the bottom; settle. **—sub•sid•ence** (səb sīd′ns, sub′si dns), *n.*

sub•sid•i•ar•y (səb sid′ē er′ē), *adj., n., pl.* **-ies.** *—adj.* **1.** serving to assist or supplement. **2.** subordinate or secondary. *—n.* **3.** a subsidiary thing or person. **4.** a company owned and controlled by another company.

sub′si•dy *n., pl.* **-dies.** direct financial aid furnished by a government, as to a private enterprise or another government. **—sub′si•dize′,** *v.t.,* **-dized, -diz•ing.**

sub•sist (səb sist′), *v.i.* **1.** to continue in existence. **2.** to remain alive, as on food.

sub•soil (sub′soil′), *n.* the stratum of earth immediately under the surface soil.

sub•son′ic *adj.* **1.** of or being a speed less than that of sound. **2.** noting or pertaining to a sound wave with a frequency below the range of audible sound.

sub•stance (sub′stəns), *n.* **1.** physical matter or material. **2.** matter of definite chemical composition: *a metallic substance.* **3.** substantial or solid quality. **4.** consistency; body. **5.** the essential part, as of speech; gist. **6.** means or wealth.

sub•stand′ard *adj.* below a standard.

sub•stan•tial (səb stan′shəl), *adj.* **1.** considerable, as in amount; ample. **2.** corporeal or material in nature; real. **3.** firm, stout, or strong. **4.** being such essentially: *stories in substantial agreement.* **5.** wealthy or influential. **6.** of real worth, value, or effect. **—sub•stan′tial•ly,** *adv.*

sub•stan′ti•ate′ (-shē āt′), *v.t.,* **-at•ed, -at•ing.** to establish by proof or competent evidence.

sub•stan•tive (sub′stən tiv), *adj.* **1.** essential. **2.** real or actual. **3.** having practical importance, value, or effect. *—n.* **4.** a noun. **5.** a word or phrase functioning as a noun.

sub•sti•tute (sub′sti tōōt′, -tyōōt′), *n., v.,* **-tut•ed, -tut•ing.** *—n.* **1.** a person or thing acting or serving in place of another. **—v.t. 2.** to put in the place of another. **—v.i. 3.** to act as a substitute. **—sub′sti•tu′tion,** *n.*

sub•struc•ture (sub struk′chər, sub′struk′-), *n.* a structure forming a foundation, as of a building.

sub•sume (səb sōōm′), *v.t.,* **-sumed, -sum•ing.** to consider or include as part of something more comprehensive.

sub•ter•fuge (sub′tər fyōōj′), *n.* an artifice or expedient used to evade, escape, or conceal.

sub′ter•ra′ne•an (-tə rā′nē ən), *adj.* **1.** existing, situated, or operating below the earth's surface. **2.** hidden or secret.

sub′text *n.* the underlying or implicit meaning, as of a literary work.

sub′ti′tle *n., v.,* **-tled, -tling.** *—n.* **1.** a secondary, often explanatory title, as of a literary work. **2.** (in motion pictures and television) a translation of dialogue projected onto the bottom of the screen. **—v.t. 3.** to give a subtitle to.

sub•tle (sut′l), *adj.,* **-tler, -tlest. 1.** difficult to perceive; fine or delicate. **2.** characterized by or requiring mental acuteness. **3.** cunning or crafty. **4.** skillful or clever. **—sub′tle•ty,** *n., pl.* **-ties. —sub′tly,** *adv.*

sub•to•tal (sub′tōt′l, sub tōt′-), *n., v.,* **-taled, -tal•ing** or (*esp. Brit.*) **-talled, -tal•ling.** *—n.* **1.** the total

of a part of a group or series of figures. **—v.t., v.i. 2.** to determine a subtotal (for).

sub•tract (səb trakt′), *v.t., v.i.* to take (one number or quantity) away from another. **—sub•trac′-tion,** *n.*

sub•trop′i•cal *adj.* bordering on the tropics.

sub•urb (sub′ûrb), *n.* **1.** a usu. residential community outside a city or town. **2. the suburbs,** the area composed of such communities. **—sub•ur•ban** (sə bûr′bən), *adj.*

sub•ur′bi•a (-bē ə), *n.* **1.** suburbs or suburbanites collectively. **2.** life in the suburbs.

sub•vert (səb vûrt′), *v.t.* **1.** to overthrow (something established). **2.** to undermine the principles of; corrupt. **—sub•ver′sion** (-vûr′zhən, -shən), *n.* **—sub•ver′sive** (-vûr′siv), *adj.*

sub•way (sub′wā′), *n.* an underground electric railroad, usu. in a large city.

sub•ze′ro *adj.* indicating or recording lower than zero on some scale.

suc•ceed (sək sēd′), *v.i.* **1.** to turn out successfully. **2.** to accomplish what is attempted or intended. **3.** to take over an office, rank, etc. **4.** to come next in order. **—v.t. 5.** to come after; follow.

suc•cess′ (-ses′), *n.* **1.** a favorable outcome, as of endeavors. **2.** the attainment of wealth, position, etc. **3.** someone or something that is successful. **—suc•cess′ful,** *adj.*

suc•ces′sion (-sesh′ən), *n.* **1.** the coming of one person or thing after another. **2.** a number of persons or things following one another. **3. a.** the act or right by which one person succeeds to the position or rank of another. **b.** the order or line of those entitled to succeed one another.

suc•ces′sive *adj.* following in uninterrupted sequence; consecutive. **—suc•ces′sive•ly,** *adv.*

suc•ces′sor *n.* a person who succeeds another, as in an office.

suc•cinct (sək singkt′), *adj.* characterized by brevity; concise.

suc•cor (suk′ər), *n.* **1.** help; aid. **—v.t. 2.** to help; aid.

suc•co•tash (suk′ə tash′), *n.* a cooked dish of lima beans and corn kernels. [< Algonquian]

suc•cu•lent (suk′yə lənt), *adj.* **1.** full of juice; juicy. **2.** (of a plant) having fleshy and juicy tissues. *—n.* **3.** a succulent plant, as a cactus.

suc•cumb (sə kum′), *v.i.* **1.** to give way; yield. **2.** to die.

such (such), *adj.* **1.** of the kind indicated or implied. **2.** like or similar: *tea, coffee, and such commodities.* **3.** of so extreme a kind: *never met such a liar.* **—adv. 4.** to such a degree; so. **—pron. 5.** such a person or thing or such persons or things. **6.** someone or something indicated. **—Idiom. 7. such as,** for example.

suck (suk), *v.t.* **1.** to draw into the mouth by action of the lips and tongue. **2.** to draw (water, air, etc.) by or as if by suction. **3.** to draw liquid from by sucking. **4.** to put into the mouth and draw upon. **—v.i. 5.** to draw something in by sucking. **—n. 6.** an act or instance of sucking.

suck′er *n.* **1.** one that sucks. **2.** *Informal.* a person easily cheated or deceived. **3.** a part or organ adapted for sucking or for clinging by suction. **4.** a thick-lipped freshwater food fish, mainly of North America. **5.** a lollipop. **6.** a shoot rising from an underground stem or root.

suck•le (suk′əl), *v.t., v.i.,* **-led, -ling. 1.** to nurse or suck at the breast or udder. **2.** to bring up; rear.

suck′ling *n.* an unweaned infant or young animal.

su•crose (sōō′krōs), *n.* SUGAR (def. 1).

suc•tion (suk′shən), *n.* **1.** the act or process of sucking. **2.** the force that owing to a pressure differential attracts a fluid or solid to where the pressure is lowest.

Su•dan (sōō dan′), *n.* **Republic of the.** a republic in NE Africa. **—Su•da•nese** (sōōd′n ēz′, -ēs′), *n., adj.*

sud•den (sud′n), *adj.* **1.** happening, coming, or done quickly or unexpectedly. **2.** occurring without transition; abrupt. **3.** impetuous; rash. **—Idiom. 4.**

all of a sudden, without warning; unexpectedly. —**sud′den•ly,** *adv.*

sud′den death′ *n.* an overtime period in which a tied contest is won after one of the contestants scores.

suds (sudz), *n. (used with a sing. or pl. v.)* **1.** soapy water. **2.** foam; lather. —**suds′y,** *adj.,* **-i•er, -i•est.**

sue (sōō), *v.t., v.i.,* **sued, su•ing. 1.** to bring a civil action (against). **2.** to make petition or appeal (to).

suede or **suède** (swād), *n.* **1.** leather finished with a soft, napped surface. **2.** a fabric resembling suede.

su•et (sōō′it), *n.* the hard fatty tissue about the loins and kidneys of cattle and sheep that is the source of tallow.

suf•fer (suf′ər), *v.i., v.t.* **1.** to undergo or feel (pain or distress). **2.** to sustain (injury or loss). **3.** to undergo or experience (an action, process, or condition). **4.** to tolerate or allow. —**suf′fer•er,** *n.*

suf•fer•ance (suf′ər əns), *n.* **1.** passive permission resulting from lack of interference; tolerance. **2.** capacity to endure pain or hardship.

suf•fice (sə fīs′), *v.i., v.t.,* **-ficed, -fic•ing.** to be enough or adequate (for).

suf•fi′cient (-fish′ənt), *adj.* adequate for the purpose; enough. —**suf•fi′cien•cy,** *n.* —**suf•fi′cient•ly,** *adv.*

suf•fix (*n.* suf′iks; *v.* suf′iks, sə fiks′), *n.* **1.** an affix that follows the element to which it is added. —*v.t.* **2.** to add as a suffix.

suf•fo•cate (suf′ə kāt′), *v.,* **-cat•ed, -cat•ing.** —*v.t.* **1.** to kill by depriving of oxygen. **2.** to impede the respiration of. **3.** to smother or stifle; suppress. —*v.i.* **4.** to become suffocated. **5.** to be uncomfortable due to a lack of air. —**suf′fo•ca′tion,** *n.*

suf•frage (suf′rij), *n.* **1.** the right to vote. **2.** a vote. —**suf′fra•gist,** *n.*

suf•fuse (sə fyōōz′), *v.t.,* **-fused, -fus•ing.** to overspread with or as if with liquid or color; pervade.

sug•ar (shŏŏg′ər), *n.* **1.** a sweet crystalline substance obtained esp. from sugarcane and the sugar beet. **2.** a substance of the same class of carbohydrates, as fructose. —*v.t.* **3.** to sprinkle or mix with sugar. **4.** to make agreeable. —*v.i.* **5.** to form sugar or sugar crystals. —**sug′ar•less,** *adj.* —**sug′ar•y,** *adj.*

sug′ar beet′ *n.* a beet with a white root, cultivated for the sugar it yields.

sug′ar•cane′ *n.* a tall grass of warm regions that is the chief source of sugar.

sug′ar•coat′ *v.t.* **1.** to cover with sugar. **2.** to make more pleasant or acceptable.

sug′ar ma′ple *n.* a maple with a sweet sap that is the chief source of maple syrup and maple sugar.

sug′ar•plum′ *n.* a sweetmeat or bonbon.

sug•gest (səg jest′, sə-), *v.t.* **1.** to mention, introduce, or propose for consideration or possible action. **2.** to indicate indirectly; imply. **3.** to call to mind through association or natural connection of ideas.

sug•gest′i•ble *adj.* easily influenced by suggestion. —**sug•gest′i•bil′i•ty,** *n.*

sug•ges′tion *n.* **1.** the act of suggesting. **2.** something suggested. **3.** a slight trace.

sug•ges′tive *adj.* **1.** tending to suggest. **2.** hinting at something improper or indecent.

su•i•cide (sōō′ə sīd′), *n.* **1.** the intentional taking of one's own life. **2.** a person who intentionally takes his or her own life. —**su′i•cid′al,** *adj.*

su•i ge•ne•ris (sōō′ē jen′ər is, sōō′ī), *adj.* being one of a kind; unique. [< L]

suit (sōōt), *n.* **1.** a set of clothing consisting typically of trousers or a skirt and a matching jacket. **2.** an act or instance of suing in a court of law; lawsuit. **3.** one of the four classes into which playing cards are divided. **4.** the courting of a woman. **5.** a petition, as to a person of rank. —*v.t.* **6.** to be appropriate or becoming to. **7.** to satisfy or please. —*v.i.* **8.** to be appropriate or suitable. —**Idiom. 9. follow suit,** to follow the example of another.

suit′a•ble *adj.* appropriate; fitting. —**suit′a•bil′i•ty,** *n.* —**suit′a•bly,** *adv.*

suit′case′ *n.* a usu. rectangular piece of luggage.

suite (swēt; *for 2 often* sōōt), *n.* **1.** a connected series of rooms to be used together. **2.** a set of matching furniture. **3.** a company of attendants; retinue. **4.** a series of instrumental dances in the same or related keys. **5.** a group of computer software programs sold as a unit and designed to work together.

suit•ing (sōō′ting), *n.* fabric for making suits.

suit•or (sōō′tər), *n.* a man who courts a woman.

su•ki•ya•ki (sōō′kē yä′kē, sŏŏk′ē-, skē yä′kē), *n.* slices of meat and vegetables cooked together in soy sauce.

sul•fate (sul′fāt), *n.* a salt or ester of sulfuric acid.

sul′fide (-fīd, -fid), *n.* a compound of sulfur.

sul′fur (-fər), *n.* a yellow nonmetallic element used in making gunpowder and matches, in medicine, and in vulcanizing rubber. *Symbol:* S; *at. wt.:* 32. 064; *at. no.:* 16.

sulfu′ric ac′id *n.* an oily, corrosive liquid used chiefly in the manufacture of fertilizers, chemicals, explosives, and dyestuffs.

sulk (sulk), *v.i.* **1.** to remain silent or aloof in an ill-humored manner. —*n.* **2.** a state or fit of sulking.

sulk′y *adj.,* **-i•er, -i•est,** *n., pl.* **-ies.** —*adj.* **1.** marked by or given to sulking; moody. —*n.* **2.** a light, two-wheeled, one-horse carriage for one person. —**sulk′i•ly,** *adv.*

sul•len (sul′ən), *adj.* **1.** persistently and silently ill-humored or resentful. **2.** gloomy or dismal, as weather. —**sul′len•ly,** *adv.* —**sul′len•ness,** *n.*

sul•ly (sul′ē), *v.t.,* **-lied, -ly•ing.** to soil, stain, or tarnish.

sul•phur (sul′fər), *n. Chiefly Brit.* SULFUR.

sul•tan (sul′tn), *n.* a sovereign of an Islamic country. —**sul′tan•ate′** (-āt′), *n.*

sul•tan′a (-tan′ə, -tä′nə), *n., pl.* **-as. 1.** a small seedless raisin. **2.** a wife, concubine, or female relative of a sultan.

sul•try (sul′trē), *adj.,* **-tri•er, -tri•est. 1.** oppressively hot and humid; sweltering. **2.** characterized by or arousing passion. —**sul′tri•ness,** *n.*

sum (sum), *n., v.,* **summed, sum•ming.** —*n.* **1.** the result obtained by the mathematical process of addition. **2.** an amount, esp. of money. **3.** an arithmetic problem. **4.** the full amount; total. **5.** a summary. —*v.t.* **6.** to get the sum of, as by addition. **7. sum up,** to summarize.

su•mac or **-mach** (sōō′mak, shōō′-), *n.* a shrub or small tree with compound leaves and clusters of red, fleshy fruit.

sum•ma•rize (sum′ə rīz′), *v.t.,* **-rized, -riz•ing.** to make or be a summary of.

sum′ma•ry *n., pl.* **-ries,** *adj.* —*n.* **1.** a usu. brief restatement of the main points or facts. —*adj.* **2.** brief and comprehensive; concise. **3.** prompt and unceremonious.

sum•ma•tion (sə mā′shən), *n.* **1.** the act, process, or result of summing up. **2.** the final arguments of opposing attorneys before a case goes to the jury.

sum•mer (sum′ər), *n.* **1.** the warm season between spring and autumn. —*v.i.* **2.** to spend or pass the summer. —**sum′mer•y,** *adj.*

sum′mer•house′ *n.* an often rustic structure in a garden to provide shade.

sum•mit (sum′it), *n.* **1.** the highest point or part, as of a hill. **2.** the highest state or degree.

sum•mon (sum′ən), *v.t.* **1.** to call for the presence of, as by command. **2.** to notify to appear before a court. **3.** to call together; convene. **4.** to call into action; rouse: *summoned up her courage.* —**sum′mon•er,** *n.*

sum′mons *n., pl.* **-mons•es. 1.** an order to appear before a court or a judicial officer. **2.** an authoritative call to appear at a place for a particular purpose or duty.

su•mo (sōō′mō), *n.* a form of wrestling in Japan in which the contestants are extremely heavy.

sump (sump), *n.* a pit, basin, cesspool, or reservoir in which liquid is collected or into which it drains.

sump•tu•ous (sump′chōō əs), *adj.* **1.** entailing great expense, as from choice materials; costly. **2.** luxurious; lavish.

sun (sun), *n., v.,* **sunned, sun•ning.** —*n.* **1.** *(often cap.)* the star that is the central body of the solar system, around which the planets revolve and from which they receive light and heat. **2.** sunshine. **3.** a self-luminous heavenly body; star. —*v.t., v.i.* **4.** to expose or be exposed to the sun's rays.

Sun. Sunday.

sun′bathe′ *v.*, **-bathed, -bathing.** to expose the body to sunlight.

Sun′belt′ or **Sun′ Belt′,** *n.* the southern and southwestern regions of the U.S.

sun′block′ or **sun′ block′,** *n.* a lotion, cream, etc., containing a substance that provides a high degree of protection against sunburn, often preventing most tanning.

sun′burn′ *n., v.,* **-burned** or **-burnt, -burn·ing.** —*n.* **1.** inflammation of the skin caused by overexposure to sunlight. —*v.i., v.t.* **2.** to suffer or cause to suffer from sunburn.

sun·dae (sun′dā, -dē), *n.* a dish of ice cream topped with syrup, nuts, whipped cream, etc.

Sun·day (sun′dā, -dē), *n.* the first day of the week, observed as the Sabbath by most Christians.

sun·der (sun′dər), *v.t., v.i.* to separate; part.

sun′di′al *n.* an instrument that indicates time by the shadow of a pointer cast by the sun on a dial.

sun′dry (sun′drē), *adj.* various or diverse.

sun′fish′ *n., pl.* **-fish, -fish·es.** a North American freshwater fish with a deep, compressed body.

sun′flow′er *n.* a tall plant with showy, yellow-rayed flower heads and edible seeds that yield an oil.

sun′glass′es *n.pl.* eyeglasses with tinted lenses that protect the eyes from the sun.

sun′light′ *n.* the light of the sun.

sun′lit′ *adj.* lighted by the sun.

sun′ny *adj.,* **-ni·er, -ni·est. 1.** abounding in sunshine. **2.** cheery, cheerful, or joyous. **3.** of or resembling the sun.

sun′rise′ *n.* **1.** the rise of the sun above the horizon in the morning. **2.** the time of sunrise.

sun′roof′ *n.* a section of an automobile roof that can be slid or lifted open.

sun′screen′ *n.* a substance that protects the skin from excessive exposure to the sun's ultraviolet radiation.

sun′set′ *n.* **1.** the setting of the sun below the horizon in the evening. **2.** the time of sunset.

sun′shine′ *n.* **1.** the direct light of the sun. **2.** cheerfulness or happiness. **3.** a source of cheer or happiness. —**sun′shin′y,** *adj.*

sun′spot′ *n.* one of the dark patches that appear periodically on the surface of the sun.

sun′stroke′ *n.* a sudden and sometimes fatal condition caused by overexposure to the sun's rays.

sun′tan′ *n.* a darkening of the skin caused by exposure to sunlight.

sup (sup), *v.i.,* **supped, sup·ping.** to eat supper.

sup- var. of **sub-** before *p.*

su·per (sŏo′pər), *n.* **1.** a superintendent, esp. of an apartment house. **2.** a supernumerary. —*adj.* **3.** extreme or excessive. **4.** very good; first-rate.

super- a prefix meaning: above or over (*superimpose*); exceeding a customary norm (*superconductivity*); larger or more powerful than others of its kind (*superpower*); great or excessive in degree (*supermarket*).

su′per·a·bun′dant *adj.* exceedingly abundant. —**su′per·a·bun′dance,** *n.*

su′per·an′nu·at′ed (-an′yŏo ā′tid), *adj.* **1.** retired because of age or infirmity. **2.** too old for use, work, or service.

su·perb (sŏo pûrb′, sə-), *adj.* **1.** admirably fine; excellent. **2.** sumptuous; rich. **3.** proudly imposing; majestic. —**su·perb′ly,** *adv.*

su′per·charge′ *v.t.,* **-charged, -charg·ing.** to supply air to (an internal-combustion engine) at greater than atmospheric pressure. —**su′per·charg′er,** *n.*

su·per·cil·i·ous (sŏo′pər sil′ē əs), *adj.* haughtily disdainful.

su′per·con·duc·tiv′i·ty *n.* the disappearance of electrical resistance in certain metals at temperatures near absolute zero. —**su′per·con·duc′tor,** *n.*

su′per·e′go *n., pl.* **-gos.** *Psychoanalysis.* the part of the personality representing the conscience.

su′per·fi′cial (-fish′əl), *adj.* **1.** being at, on, or near the surface. **2.** apparent rather than real. **3.** not profound or thorough; shallow. —**su′per·fi′ci·al′i·ty** (-fish′ē al′i tē), *n., pl.* **-ties.** —**su′per·fi′cial·ly,** *adv.*

su·per·flu·ous (sŏo pûr′flŏo əs), *adj.* being more than is sufficient or required. —**su·per·flu·i·ty** (sŏo′pər flŏo′i tē), *n.*

su·per·high·way (sŏo′pər hī′wā, sŏo′pər hī′wā′), *n.* a highway designed for travel at high speeds.

su′per·hu′man *adj.* **1.** above or beyond what is human. **2.** exceeding ordinary human power, achievement, or experience.

su′per·im·pose′ *v.t.,* **-posed, -pos·ing.** to impose or place over, above, or on something else.

su·per·in·tend (sŏo′pər in tend′, sŏo′prin-), *v.t.* to exercise supervision over (an institution, district, etc.). —**su′per·in·tend′ent,** *n.*

su·pe·ri·or (sə pēr′ē ər, sŏo-), *adj.* **1.** higher in station, rank, or degree. **2.** above the average in excellence, merit, or intelligence. **3.** of higher grade or quality. **4.** greater in number or amount. **5.** showing a feeling of being better than others. **6.** not yielding or susceptible. —*n.* **7.** one superior to another. **8.** the head of a monastery or convent. —**su·pe′ri·or′i·ty** (-ôr′i tē, -or′-), *n.*

su·per·la·tive (sə pûr′lə tiv, sŏo-), *adj.* **1.** of the highest kind or order. **2.** of or being the highest degree of comparison of adjectives and adverbs. —*n.* **3.** the utmost degree. **4. a.** the superlative degree. **b.** the superlative form of an adjective or adverb. —**su·per′la·tive·ly,** *adv.*

su′per·man′ *n., pl.* **-men.** a person of extraordinary or superhuman powers.

su′per·mar′ket *n.* a large self-service retail store that sells food and household goods.

su′per·nat′u·ral (sŏo′pər-), *adj.* **1.** being above or beyond what is natural or explainable by natural law. **2.** of or attributed to God or a deity. **3.** of or attributed to ghosts, goblins, or other unearthly beings.

su′per·no′va *n., pl.* **-vas, -vae** (-vē). a nova millions of times brighter than the sun.

su′per·nu′mer·ar′y (-nŏo′mə rer′ē, -nyŏo′-), *adj., n., pl.* **-ies.** —*adj.* **1.** being in excess of the usual or prescribed number; extra. —*n.* **2.** a supernumerary person or thing. **3.** a performer, as in a play or opera, without speaking lines.

su′per·pow′er *n.* a very powerful nation, esp. one with significant interests and influence outside its own region.

su′per·script′ *n.* a letter, number, or symbol written or printed high on a line of text.

su′per·sede′ (-sēd′), *v.t.,* **-sed·ed, -sed·ing. 1.** to replace, as in power or authority. **2.** to set aside as void, useless, or obsolete.

su′per·son′ic *adj.* **1.** greater than the speed of sound. **2.** capable of achieving supersonic speed: *a supersonic plane.* **3.** ULTRASONIC.

su′per·star′ *n.* a very popular and successful performer or athlete.

su′per·sti′tion (-stish′ən), *n.* **1.** an irrational belief in the ominous significance of a particular thing, circumstance, or occurrence. **2.** a custom or act based on superstition. —**su·per·sti′tious,** *adj.*

su′per·store′ *n.* a very large store that stocks a wide variety of merchandise.

su′per·struc′ture *n.* **1.** the part of a building above its foundation or basement. **2.** a structure built on something else, as one above the main deck of a ship.

su′per·vene′ (-vēn′), *v.i.,* **-vened, -ven·ing.** to take place or occur as something additional or extraneous. —**su′per·ven′tion** (-ven′shən), *n.*

su′per·vise′ (-vīz′), *v.t.,* **-vised, -vis·ing.** to watch over and direct (work, workers, etc.); oversee. —**su′per·vi′sion** (-vizh′ən), *n.* —**su′per·vi′sor,** *n.* —**su′per·vi′so·ry,** *adj.*

su′per·wom′an *n., pl.* **-wom·en. 1.** a woman of extraordinary or superhuman powers. **2.** a woman who copes successfully with the simultaneous demands of a career, marriage, and motherhood.

su·pine (*adj.* sōō pīn′; *n.* sōō′pīn), *adj.* **1.** lying on the back, face upward. **2.** inactive, passive, or inert.

sup·per (sup′ər), *n.* the evening meal.

sup·plant (sə plant′, -plänt′), *v.t.* **1.** to take the place of (another), as through force or scheming. **2.** to replace (one thing) by something else.

sup·ple (sup′əl), *adj.*, **-pler, -plest. 1.** bending readily without breaking or splitting; flexible. **2.** limber; lithe. **3.** compliant or yielding. **—sup·ply** (sup′lē), *adv.*

sup·ple·ment (*n.* sup′lə mənt; *v.* -ment′), *n.* **1.** something added to complete a thing or supply a deficiency. **2.** a part added to a book or an extra part of a newspaper. **—***v.t.* **3.** to form or provide a supplement to. **—sup′ple·men′tal, sup′ple·men′·ta·ry,** *adj.*

sup·pli·cate′ (-li kāt′), *v.*, **-cat·ed, -cat·ing. —***v.i.* **1.** to make humble entreaty. **—***v.t.* **2.** to entreat humbly. **3.** to ask for by humble entreaty. **—sup′·pli·ant** (-lē ənt), **sup′pli·cant** (-kənt), *n.*, *adj.* **—sup′pli·ca′tion,** *n.*

sup·ply (sə plī′), *v.*, **-plied, -ply·ing,** *n.*, *pl.* **-plies. —***v.t.* **1.** to furnish with what is lacking or requisite. **2.** to furnish (something wanting or requisite). **3.** to compensate for (a deficiency or loss). **—***n.* **4.** the act of supplying. **5.** a quantity of something on hand or available; stock. **6.** Usu., **-plies.** a stock or store of necessary items, as food. **—sup·pli′er,** *n.*

supply′-side′ *adj.* of or being a hypothesis in economics that reduced taxes will stimulate investment and economic growth.

sup·port (sə pôrt′), *v.t.* **1.** to hold up the weight of (a load, structure, etc.) without giving way. **2.** to provide with the necessities of existence. **3.** to sustain (a person, the spirits, etc.) under affliction. **4.** to uphold or advocate (a cause, principle, etc.). **5.** to corroborate (a statement, opinion, etc.). **6.** to endure; tolerate. **7.** to perform with (a leading actor) in a secondary role. **—***n.* **8.** the act of supporting or state of being supported. **9.** one that supports. **—sup·port′a·ble,** *adj.* **—sup·port′er,** *n.* **—sup·port′ive,** *adj.*

support′ group′ *n.* a group of people who meet regularly to support each other by discussing shared problems.

sup·pose (sə pōz′), *v.*, **-posed, -pos·ing. —***v.t.* **1.** to assume (something), as for the sake of argument. **2.** to think or hold as an opinion. **3.** to require logically. **4.** to expect or require: *She was supposed to meet me here.* **—***v.i.* **5.** to assume something; presume. **—sup·posed′** (-pōzd′, -pō′zid), *adj.* **—sup·pos′ed·ly,** *adv.* **—sup·po·si·tion** (sup′ə zish′ən), *n.*

sup·pos·i·to·ry (sə pozˈi tôr′ē), *n.*, *pl.* **-ries.** a solid mass of medicinal substance that melts upon insertion into the rectum or vagina.

sup·press (sə pres′), *v.t.* **1.** to put an end to by or as if by authority; quell. **2.** to hold back or restrain. **3.** to withhold from disclosure or publication. **4.** to keep (a thought, memory, etc.) out of conscious awareness. **—sup·pres′sant,** *n.* **—sup·pres′sion,** *n.*

sup·pu·rate (sup′yŏŏ rāt′), *v.i.*, **-rat·ed, -rat·ing.** to produce or discharge pus. **—sup′pu·ra′tion,** *n.*

su·pra (sōō′prə), *adv.* above, esp. in a text.

su·prem·a·cist (sə prem′ə sist, sōō-), *n.* a person who advocates the supremacy of a particular group, esp. a racial group.

su·prem′a·cy *n.* **1.** the state of being supreme. **2.** supreme authority or power.

su·preme (sə prēm′, sōō-), *adj.* **1.** highest in rank or authority. **2.** of the highest quality, degree, importance, etc. **3.** last or final. **—su·preme′ly,** *adv.*

sur·charge (*n.* sûr′chärj′; *v.* sûr chärj′, sûr′chärj′), *n.*, *v.*, **-charged, -charg·ing. —***n.* **1.** an additional charge, tax, or cost. **2.** a mark printed over a stamp that alters its face value. **—***v.t.* **3.** to subject to a surcharge. **4.** to print a surcharge on (a stamp).

sure (shŏŏr, shûr), *adj.*, **sur·er, sur·est,** *adv.* **—***adj.* **1.** free from doubt. **2.** confident, as of something expected. **3.** certain beyond question. **4.** reliable or unfailing. **5.** unerring. **6.** admitting of no doubt; positive. **7.** destined; inevitable. **—***adv.* **8.** in a sure manner; certainly. **—Idiom. 9. for sure,** without a doubt; certainly. **10. sure enough,** *Informal.* as

might have been expected. **—sure′ly,** *adv.* **—sure′·ness,** *n.*

sure′fire′ *adj. Informal.* sure to work.

sure′foot′ed *adj.* not likely to stumble, slip, or fall.

sur·e·ty (shŏŏr′i tē, shŏŏr′tē, shûr′-), *n.*, *pl.* **-ties. 1.** security against loss or damage. **2.** a person who has assumed legal responsibility for another. **3.** the state or quality of being sure; certainty.

surf (sûrf), *n.* **1.** the swell of the sea that breaks upon a shore. **—***v.i.* **2.** to ride a surfboard. **3.** to search haphazardly, as for information on the Internet or for an interesting program on TV. **—***v.t.* **4.** to search through (a computer network or TV channels) for information or entertainment.

sur·face (sûr′fis), *n.*, *adj.*, *v.*, **-faced, -fac·ing. —***n.* **1.** the outermost or uppermost layer or area of something. **2.** a face of a body or thing. **3.** outward appearance. **—***adj.* **4.** of or on a surface; external. **5.** apparent rather than real; superficial. **—***v.t.* **6.** to finish the surface of. **—***v.i.* **7.** to rise to or appear on the surface.

surf′board′ *n.* a long, narrow board on which a person rides in surfing.

sur·feit (sûr′fit), *n.* **1.** an excessive amount. **2.** overindulgence, esp. in eating or drinking. **3.** disgust caused by excess or satiety. **—***v.t.* **4.** to supply or feed to excess or satiety.

surge (sûrj), *n.*, *v.*, **surged, surg·ing. —***n.* **1.** a strong, wavelike forward movement. **2.** a sudden strong rush or burst: *a surge of anger.* **3.** a sudden increase of electric current. **—***v.i.* **4.** to move in or as if in a surge. **5.** to increase suddenly.

sur·geon (sûr′jən), *n.* a physician who specializes in surgery.

surge′ protec′tor *n.* a small device to protect a computer, telephone, television set, or the like from damage by high-voltage electrical surges.

sur·ger·y (-jə rē), *n.*, *pl.* **-ger·ies** for 2, 3. **1.** the art or work of treating diseases, injuries, or deformities by operation on the body, usu. with instruments. **2.** treatment performed by a surgeon. **3.** a room for surgical operations. **—sur′gi·cal,** *adj.* **—sur′gi·cal·ly,** *adv.*

Su·ri·na·me (sŏŏr′ə nä′mə) also **Su′ri·nam′** (-näm′, -nam′), *n.* a republic on the NE coast of South America. —**Su′ri·na·mese′** (-nə mēz′, -mēs′), *n.*, *pl.* **-mese,** *adj.*

sur·ly (sûr′lē), *adj.*, **-li·er, -li·est.** sullenly rude or bad-tempered. **—sur′li·ness,** *n.*

sur·mise (sər mīz′; *n. also* sûr′mīz), *v.*, **-mised, -mis·ing,** *n.* **—***v.t.* **1.** to conjecture; guess. **—***n.* **2.** a conjecture; guess.

sur·mount (sər mount′), *v.t.* **1.** to get over or across (barriers, obstacles, etc.). **2.** to prevail over; overcome. **3.** to get to or be on the top of.

sur·name (sûr′nām′), *n.* the name a person has in common with other family members.

sur·pass (sər pas′, -päs′), *v.t.* **1.** to be greater than; exceed. **2.** to be superior to; excel. **3.** to be beyond the range or capacity of; transcend. **—sur·pass′ing,** *adj.*

sur·plice (sûr′plis), *n.* a loose-fitting, broad-sleeved white vestment worn over a cassock.

sur·plus (sûr′plus, -pləs), *n.* **1.** an amount or quantity greater than needed. **—***adj.* **2.** being a surplus.

sur·prise (sər prīz′, sə-), *v.*, **-prised, -pris·ing,** *n.* **—***v.t.* **1.** to strike with a sudden feeling of astonishment. **2.** to come upon suddenly and unexpectedly. **3.** to make an unexpected assault on. **—***n.* **4.** a feeling of sudden astonishment. **5.** something that surprises. **6.** the act of surprising. **—sur·pris′ing,** *adj.* **—sur·pris′ing·ly,** *adv.*

sur·re·al·ism (sə rē′ə liz′əm), *n.* a 20th-century style of art and literature stressing the subconscious significance of imagery or the exploitation of unexpected juxtapositions. **—sur·re′al,** *adj.* **—sur·re′al·ist,** *n.*, *adj.*

sur·ren·der (sə ren′dər), *v.t.* **1.** to yield to the possession or power of another on demand or under duress. **2.** to give (oneself) up, as to an emotion. **3.** to abandon or relinquish. —*v.i.* **4.** to give oneself up. —*n.* **5.** an act or instance of surrendering.

sur•rep•ti•tious (sûr′əp tish′əs), *adj.* obtained, done, or made by stealth; clandestine. —**sur′rep•ti′tious•ly,** *adv.*

sur•ro•gate (sûr′ə gāt′, -git, sur′-), *n.* **1.** a deputy. **2.** a substitute. **3.** a judge in some states having jurisdiction over the probate of wills and the administration of estates.

sur′rogate moth′er *n.* a woman who bears a child for another couple, as by being inseminated with the man's sperm.

sur•round (sə round′), *v.t.* **1.** to enclose on all sides; encircle. **2.** to enclose so as to cut off communication or retreat.

sur•round′ings *n.pl.* circumstances or conditions that surround a person; environment.

sur•tax (sûr′taks′), *n.* an additional or extra tax on something already taxed.

sur•veil•lance (sər vā′ləns), *n.* a watch kept over someone or something, as a suspect.

sur•vey (*v.* sər vā′; *n.* sûr′vā, sər vā′), *v.,* -**veyed,** -**vey•ing,** *n., pl.* -**veys.** —*v.t.* **1.** to view, consider, or study in a comprehensive way. **2.** to view in detail. **3.** to determine the exact dimensions and position of (a tract of land). —*n.* **4.** a comprehensive view. **5.** a detailed examination, as to ascertain condition. **6. a.** the act of surveying land. **b.** a plan or description resulting from this.

sur•vey′ing *n.* the science of making land surveys. —**sur•vey′or,** *n.*

sur•vive (sər vīv′), *v.,* -**vived,** -**viv•ing.** —*v.i.* **1.** to continue to live or exist. —*v.t.* **2.** to continue to live or exist after; outlive. **3.** to live through (adversity, misery, etc.). —**sur•viv′al,** *n.* —**sur•vi′vor,** *n.*

sus•cep•ti•ble (sə sep′tə bəl), *adj.* **1.** admitting or permitting: *susceptible to various interpretations.* **2.** liable or subject to an influence or agency: *susceptible to colds.* **3.** capable of being affected emotionally. —**sus•cep′ti•bil′i•ty,** *n., pl.* -**ties.**

su′shi (sōō′shē) *n.* a Japanese dish of rice cakes with raw fish, vegetables, etc.

sus•pect (*v.* sə spekt′; *n.* sus′pekt; *adj.* sus′pekt, sə spekt′), *v.t.* **1.** to believe to be guilty with little or no proof. **2.** to doubt or mistrust. **3.** to think likely or probable; surmise. —*n.* **4.** a person who is suspected, esp. of a crime. —*adj.* **5.** open to or under suspicion.

sus•pend (sə spend′), *v.t.* **1.** to hang from above so as to allow free movement. **2.** to keep from falling or sinking as if by hanging: *particles suspended in a liquid.* **3.** to defer or postpone. **4.** to make inactive or cause to cease for a time. **5.** to debar temporarily from office, membership, or privilege.

sus•pend′ers *n.pl.* adjustable straps worn over the shoulders to support trousers or a skirt.

sus•pense (sə spens′), *n.* **1.** mental uncertainty accompanied by anxiety or excitement. **2.** a state of mental indecision. —**sus•pense′ful,** *adj.*

sus•pen′sion *n.* **1.** the act of suspending or state of being suspended. **2. a.** a state in which the particles of a substance are mixed with a fluid but are undissolved. **b.** a substance in such a state. **3.** something on or by which something else is suspended. **4.** something suspended.

suspen′sion bridge′ *n.* a bridge with a deck suspended from cables anchored at their extremities.

sus•pi•cion (sə spish′ən), *n.* **1.** the act of suspecting or state of being suspected. **2.** the state of mind of one who suspects. **3.** a slight trace; hint.

sus•pi′cious *adj.* **1.** tending to cause suspicion. **2.** inclined to suspect; distrustful. **3.** feeling or expressing suspicion.

sus•tain (sə stān′), *v.t.* **1.** to bear the weight of; support. **2.** to undergo (injury, loss, etc.) without giving way; endure. **3.** to keep (a person, the spirits, etc.) from giving way. **4.** to keep up or keep going; maintain. **5.** to supply with the necessities of life, as food. **6.** to uphold as valid, just, or correct. **7.** to confirm or corroborate. —**sus•tain′er,** *n.*

sus•te•nance (sus′tə nəns), *n.* **1.** means of sustaining life; nourishment. **2.** means of livelihood. **3.**

the process of sustaining. **4.** the state of being sustained.

su•ture (sōō′chər), *n.* **1. a.** a joining of the edges of a wound by stitching. **b.** one of the stitches employed. **2.** a seam where two parts, as two bones of the skull, join.

SUV *pl.* **SUVs.** sport-utility vehicle.

su′ze•rain•ty (sōō′zə rin tē), *n., pl.* -**ties.** sovereignty of one state over another.

svelte (svelt, sfelt), *adj.,* **svelt•er, svelt•est.** slender, esp. gracefully slender.

SW or **S.W.,** **1.** southwest. **2.** southwestern.

Sw or **Sw.,** **1.** Sweden. **2.** Swedish.

swab (swob), *n., v.,* **swabbed, swab•bing.** —*n.* **1.** a mop used esp. on shipboard, as for cleaning decks. **2.** a wad of absorbent material used esp. for cleaning or for applying medicaments. **3.** *Slang.* a sailor. —*v.t.* **4.** to clean, apply, or take up with or as if with a swab.

swad•dle (swod′l), *v.t.,* -**dled, -dling.** to bind (a newborn infant) with strips of cloth to prevent free movement.

swag[1] (swag), *n., v.,* **swagged, swag•ging.** —*n.* **1.** something, as a valance, fastened at each end and hanging down in the middle. —*v.i., v.t.* **2.** to hang in or adorn with swags.

swag[2] (swag), *n. Slang.* plunder; booty.

swag′ger *v.i.* **1.** to strut about with an insolent air. **2.** to boast noisily; bluster. —*n.* **3.** a swaggering manner or walk.

Swa•hi•li (swä hē′lē), *n.* a Bantu language serving as a lingua franca in E and E central Africa.

swain (swān), *n.* **1.** a male admirer or lover. **2.** a country lad.

swal•low[1] (swol′ō), *v.t.* **1.** to take into the stomach through the throat and esophagus. **2.** to take in so as to envelop. **3.** to accept without question. **4.** to put up with; endure. **5.** to suppress (emotion, pride, etc.). **6.** to take back; retract. —*v.i.* **7.** to perform the act of swallowing. —*n.* **8.** the act of swallowing. **9.** a quantity swallowed at one time.

swal•low[2] (swol′ō), *n.* a long-winged, fork-tailed songbird noted for its swift, graceful flight.

swal′low•tail′ *n.* **1.** a deeply forked tail like that of a swallow. **2.** any of several butterflies with elongated hind wings.

swa•mi (swä′mē), *n., pl.* -**mis.** a Hindu religious teacher. [< Skt, *pl.* of *svāmin* master]

swamp (swomp), *n.* **1.** a tract of wet, spongy land. —*v.t.* **2.** to flood or drench, esp. with water. **3.** to sink or fill (a boat) with water. **4.** to overwhelm, esp. with an excess of something. —**swamp′y,** *adj.*

swan (swon), *n.* a large aquatic bird with a long, slender neck and usu. pure-white plumage.

swank (swangk), *n., adj.,* -**er, -est.** —*n.* **1.** dashing smartness, as in dress; style. **2.** pretentiousness. —*adj.* **3.** stylish or elegant. **4.** pretentiously stylish. —**swank′y,** *adj.,* -**i•er, -i•est.**

swan′ song′ *n.* a final act or farewell appearance.

swap (swop), *v.,* **swapped, swap•ping,** *n.* —*v.t., v.i.* **1.** to trade or barter. —*n.* **2.** a trade or exchange.

swarm (swôrm), *n.* **1.** a body of honeybees that emigrate, accompanied by a queen, to start a new colony. **2.** a body of bees in a hive. **3.** a great number of things or persons, esp. moving together. —*v.i.* **4.** to fly off in a swarm, as bees. **5.** to move about or congregate in great numbers. **6.** (of a place) to abound or teem.

swarth•y (swôr′thē, -thē), *adj.,* -**i•er, -i•est.** dark or darkish in skin color or complexion.

swash′buck′ler *n.* a swaggering swordsman, soldier, or adventurer. —**swash′buck′ling,** *adj., n.*

swas•ti•ka (swos′ti ka), *n., pl.* -**kas.** **1.** a symbolic or ornamental figure consisting of a cross with arms of equal length, each arm having a continuation at right angles. **2.** a swastika as the emblem of the Nazi Party.

swat (swot), *v.,* **swat•ted, swat•ting,** *n.* —*v.t.* **1.** to hit sharply; slap; smack. —*n.* **2.** a sharp blow; slap; smack. —**swat′ter,** *n.*

SWAT (*as initials or* swot), *n.* a law-enforcement

swatch (swoch), *n.* a sample, as of cloth.

swath (swoth, swôth), *n.* **1. a.** the space covered by the stroke of a scythe or the cut of a mowing machine. **b.** the piece or strip so cut. **2.** a long strip, belt, or line.

swathe[1] (swoth, swāth), *v.*, **swathed, swath•ing,** *n.* —*v.t.* **1.** to wrap, bind, or swaddle with bands of material. **2.** to bandage. —*n.* **3.** a wrapping or bandage.

swathe[2] (swoth, swāth), *n.* SWATH.

sway (swā), *v.*, **swayed, sway•ing,** *n.* —*v.i.* **1.** to move or swing to and fro. **2.** to move or incline to one side. **3.** to vacillate, as in opinion; waver. —*v.t.* **4.** to cause to sway. **5.** to influence (the mind, emotions, etc., or a person). **6.** to rule or govern. —*n.* **7.** a swaying movement. **8.** dominating power or influence. **9.** rule; dominion.

sway'back' *n.* an excessive downward curvature of the back, esp. of horses. —**sway'backed',** *adj.*

Swa•zi•land (swä'zē land'), *n.* a kingdom in SE Africa.

swear (swâr), *v.*, **swore, sworn, swear•ing.** —*v.i.* **1.** to make a solemn declaration by a sacred being or object. **2.** to bind oneself by oath; vow. **3.** to use profane language. —*v.t.* **4.** to declare by swearing by a sacred being or object. **5.** to testify or state on oath. **6.** to bind by an oath. **7. swear by,** to have great confidence in. **8. ~ in,** to admit to office by administering an oath. **9. ~ off,** to promise to give up.

sweat (swet), *v.*, **sweat** or **sweat•ed, sweat•ing,** *n.* —*v.i.* **1.** to perspire, esp. freely. **2.** to exude moisture. **3.** to gather moisture from the surrounding air by condensation. **4.** *Informal.* to work hard. —*v.t.* **5.** to excrete (moisture) through the pores of the skin. **6.** to exude in drops. **7.** to cause to perspire. **8.** to force to work too hard. **9. sweat out,** *Informal.* to await anxiously the outcome of. —*n.* **10.** perspiration. **11.** *Informal.* a state of anxiety or impatience. **12.** moisture exuded from something or gathered on a surface. **13. sweats,** clothes, as sweatpants, clothes, as worn esp. during exercise. —**sweat'y,** *adj.*, **-i•er, -i•est.**

sweat'er *n.* a knitted jacket or pullover.

sweat' gland' *n.* one of the minute, tubular glands of the skin that secrete sweat.

sweat'pants' *n.* (*used with a pl. v.*) pants of soft, absorbent fabric worn esp. during athletic activity.

sweat'shirt' *n.* a loose, collarless cotton jersey pullover.

sweat'shop' *n.* a shop employing workers at low wages, for long hours, and under poor conditions.

Swe•den (swēd'n), *n.* a kingdom in N Europe.

Swed'ish *adj.* **1.** of Sweden, the Swedes, or their language. —*n.* **2.** the Germanic language of the Swedes.

sweep (swēp), *v.*, **swept, sweep•ing,** *n.* —*v.t.* **1.** to remove, clean, or clear with or as if with a broom or brush. **2.** to drive or carry by a steady force, as the wind. **3.** to pass or draw over a surface with a continuous stroke or movement. **4.** to win all of (a series of contests). —*v.i.* **5.** to sweep a floor, room, etc., with or as if with a broom. **6.** to move swiftly and forcefully. **7.** to move or extend in a wide curve or circuit. —*n.* **8.** the act of sweeping. **9.** a sweeping motion. **10.** a swinging or curving movement or stroke. **11.** a continuous extent or stretch. **12.** a winning of all the games or prizes in a contest. —**sweep'er,** *n.*

sweep'ing *adj.* **1.** of wide range or scope. —*n.* **2.** the act of one that sweeps. **3. sweepings,** matter swept up, as refuse. —**sweep'ing•ly,** *adv.*

sweep'stakes' also **-stake',** *n.* (*used with a sing. or pl. v.*) **1.** a contest, as a race, for which the prize consists of the stakes contributed by the competitors. **2.** a lottery in which each participant contributes a stake and the stakes are awarded to one or several winners.

sweet (swēt), *adj.* **1.** having the taste or flavor of sugar, honey, or the like. **2.** not rancid or stale. **3.** not salted: *sweet butter.* **4.** pleasing to the ear. **5.** fragrant; perfumed. **6.** agreeable in disposition. —*n.*

7. Usu., **sweets.** sweet foods, as candy. **8.** a beloved person. —**sweet'en,** *v.t., v.i.* —**sweet'ly,** *adv.* —**sweet'ness,** *n.*

sweet'bread' *n.* the thymus or pancreas of a young animal, esp. a calf, used as food.

sweet'bri'er or **-bri'ar,** *n.* a Eurasian rose with a tall prickly stem and pink flowers.

sweet'en•er *n.* a substance, esp. a substitute for sugar, to sweeten food or drink.

sweet'heart' *n.* a beloved person; lover.

sweet'meat' *n.* a candy.

sweet' pea' *n.* a climbing plant with sweet-scented flowers.

sweet' pep'per *n.* **1.** a pepper bearing a mild-flavored, bell-shaped fruit. **2.** its fruit.

sweet' pota'to *n.* **1.** a Central American trailing vine widely grown for its sweet, edible, tuberous root. **2.** its root.

sweet'-talk' *v.t., v.i.* to use cajoling words (on); flatter.

sweet' tooth' *n.* a liking or craving for sweets.

sweet' wil'liam (wil'yəm) *n.*, a low plant with dense flower clusters.

swell (swel), *v.*, **swelled, swol•len** or **swelled, swell•ing,** *n., adj.* —*v.i., v.t.* **1.** to grow or cause to grow in bulk, as by absorption of fluid. **2.** to enlarge excessively or abnormally; protrude. **3.** to bulge out, as a sail. **4.** to increase in amount, degree, intensity, or force. **5.** to puff up or become puffed up with pride. —*n.* **6.** inflation or distention. **7.** a protuberant part. **8.** a long and unbroken wave. **9.** an increase in amount, degree, intensity, or force. **10.** a gradual increase in loudness of sound. **11.** *Informal.* a fashionably dressed person. —*adj. Informal.* **12.** stylish; elegant. **13.** first-rate; fine.

swel•ter (swel'tər), *v.i.* to suffer from oppressive heat.

swel'ter•ing *adj.* suffering from or marked by oppressive heat.

swerve (swûrv), *v.*, **swerved, swerv•ing,** *n.* —*v.i., v.t.* **1.** to turn or cause to turn aside abruptly from a straight or direct course. —*n.* **2.** the act of swerving.

swift (swift), *adj.*, **-er, -est,** *adv., n.* —*adj.* **1.** moving with great speed. **2.** coming, happening, or performed quickly. **3.** quick to act or respond. —*adv.* **4.** in a swift manner. —*n.* **5.** a long-winged, swallowlike bird noted for its rapid flight. —**swift'ly,** *adv.*

swig (swig), *n., v.*, **swigged, swig•ging.** *Informal.* —*n.* **1.** a swallow of liquid, esp. liquor. —*v.t., v.i.* **2.** to drink heartily or greedily.

swill (swil), *n.* **1.** liquid or partly liquid food for animals. **2.** kitchen refuse; garbage. —*v.i., v.t.* **3.** to drink greedily or excessively.

swim (swim), *v.*, **swam, swum, swim•ming,** *n.* —*v.i.* **1.** to move in water by using bodily parts, as limbs or fins. **2.** to float on a liquid. **3.** to move or glide smoothly. **4.** to be flooded: *eyes swimming with tears.* **5.** to be dizzy or giddy. —*v.t.* **6.** to move along in or cross by swimming. —*n.* **7.** an act, instance, or period of swimming. —*Idiom.* **8. in the swim,** alert to or engaged in what is current. —**swim'mer,** *n.*

swim'ming hole' *n.* a place, as in a stream, with water deep enough for swimming.

swim'suit' *n.* BATHING SUIT.

swin•dle (swin'dl), *v.*, **-dled, -dling,** *n.* —*v.t., v.i.* **1.** to cheat out of assets, as money; defraud. —*n.* **2.** an act or instance of swindling; fraud. —**swin'dler,** *n.*

swine (swīn), *n., pl.* **swine. 1.** any of a family of hoofed mammals with a disklike snout and a thick hide, esp. the domestic hog. **2.** a coarse, gross, or contemptible person. —**swin'ish,** *adj.*

swing (swing), *v.*, **swung, swing•ing,** *n., adj.* —*v.t.* **1.** to cause to move to and fro. **2.** to cause to move on a fixed point or axis. **3.** to cause to move in a circle or curve. **4.** to suspend so as to hang freely. **5.** *Informal.* to manage as desired: *They swung the deal.* —*v.i.* **6.** to sway to and fro. **7.** to turn on a fixed point or axis. **8.** to move in a circle or curve. **9.** to move with a free, swaying motion.

general

10. to hang freely, as a hammock. **11.** to hit at someone or something with or as if with the hand. **12.** *Slang.* **a.** to be lively, fashionable, or trendy. **b.** to engage uninhibitedly in sexual activities. —*n.* **13.** the act or manner of swinging. **14.** the amount or extent of a swing. **15.** freedom of action. **16.** active operation; progression: *got into the swing of things.* **17.** a seat suspended from above on which a person may sit and swing for recreation. **18.** a style of jazz often played by a large dance band and marked by a smooth beat and flowing phrasing. —*adj.* **19.** capable of determining an outcome: *the swing vote.*

swing′er *n.* **1.** one that swings. **2.** *Slang.* a lively, fashionable, or trendy person. **3.** *Slang.* a person who indulges in promiscuous sex.

swing′ shift′ *n.* a work shift in industry from midafternoon until midnight.

swipe (swīp), *n., v.,* **swiped, swip•ing.** —*n.* **1.** a strong, sweeping blow. —*v.t.* **2.** to strike with a swipe. **3.** to slide (a magnetic card) quickly through an electronic device that reads data. **4.** *Informal.* to steal.

swirl (swûrl), *v.i., v.t.* **1.** to move or cause to move with a whirling motion; spin. —*n.* **2.** a swirling movement. **3.** a twist, as of hair.

swish (swish), *v.i., v.t.* **1.** to move with or make a sibilant sound. **2.** to rustle, as silk. —*n.* **3.** a swishing movement or sound.

Swiss (swis), *n., pl.* **Swiss,** *adj.* —*n.* **1.** a native or inhabitant of Switzerland. **2.** Swiss cheese. —*adj.* **3.** of Switzerland or its inhabitants.

Swiss′ cheese′ *n.* a firm, pale yellow cheese with many holes.

switch (swich), *n.* **1.** a slender, flexible shoot, rod, or twig. **2.** the act of whipping with or as if with a switch. **3.** a bunch of real or synthetic hair used to supplement one's own hair. **4.** a device for diverting an electric current or for making or breaking a circuit. **5.** a mechanism for diverting moving trains or rolling stock from one track to another. **6.** a shift or change. —*v.t.* **7.** to whip with or as if with a switch. **8.** to move (a cane, tail, etc.) with a swift, lashing stroke. **9.** to change or exchange. **10.** to connect, disconnect, or redirect by operating a switch. **11.** to divert (a train, car, etc.) from one set of tracks to another. —*v.i.* **12.** to change, as direction; shift. **13.** to make an exchange. **14.** to move back and forth briskly; lash. —**switch′er,** *n.*

switch′back′ *n.* a zigzag highway or railroad track arrangement for climbing a steep grade.

switch′blade′ *n.* a pocketknife with a blade held and released by a spring.

switch′board′ *n.* a unit on which are mounted switches and devices for completing telephone circuits manually.

Switz•er•land (swit′sər lənd), *n.* a republic in central Europe.

swiv•el (swiv′əl), *n., v.,* **-eled, -el•ing** or (*esp. Brit.*) **-elled, -el•ling.** —*n.* **1.** a fastening device that allows the thing fastened to rotate freely on it. —*v.t., v.i.* **2.** to turn or pivot on or as if on a swivel.

swiz′zle stick′ (swiz′əl), *n.* a small wand for stirring mixed drinks.

swol•len (swō′lən), *v.* a pp. of SWELL.

swoon (swōōn), *v.i.* **1.** to lose consciousness; faint. —*n.* **2.** a faint.

swoop (swōōp), *v.i.* **1.** to sweep down through the air, as a bird upon prey. —*n.* **2.** an act or instance of swooping.

sword (sôrd), *n.* **1.** a weapon with a long, sharp-edged blade affixed to a hilt. **2.** the sword as a symbol of military power. **3.** military force or aggression. —*Idiom.* **4.** **at swords' points,** mutually ready to fight.

sword′fish′ *n., pl.* **-fish, -fish•es.** a large marine food fish with an upper jaw elongated into a blade-like structure.

syb•a•rite (sib′ə rīt′), *n.* a person devoted to luxury and pleasure. —**syb′a•rit′ic** (-rit′ik), *adj.*

syc•a•more (sik′ə môr′), *n.* **1.** a North American plane tree with lobed leaves and globular seed heads. **2.** a European and Asian maple tree.

syc•o•phant (sik′ə fənt, -fant′, sī′kə-), *n.* a self-

seeking, servile flatterer. —**syc′o•phan•cy,** *n.* —**syc′o•phan′tic,** *adj.*

syl•lab•i•cate (si lab′i kāt′), *v.t.,* **-cat•ed, -cat•ing.** to form or divide into syllables; syllabify. —**syl•lab′i•ca′tion,** *n.*

syl•lab′i•fy′ (-fī′), *v.t.,* **-fied, -fy•ing.** to form or divide into syllables. —**syl•lab′i•fi•ca′tion,** *n.*

syl•la•ble (sil′ə bəl), *n.* **1.** an uninterrupted segment of speech consisting of a single pulse of breath and forming a word or part of a word. **2.** one or more letters representing a syllable. —**syl•lab′ic,** *adj.*

syl•la•bus (sil′ə bəs), *n., pl.* **-bus•es, -bi** (-bī′). an outline or other brief statement, as of a course of study.

syl•lo•gism (sil′ə jiz′əm), *n.* an argument of a form containing two premises leading to a conclusion.

sylph (silf), *n.* **1.** a slender, graceful woman or girl. **2.** an imaginary being supposed to inhabit the air.

syl•van (sil′vən), *adj.* **1.** of or inhabiting the woods. **2.** consisting of or abounding in woods or trees.

sym•bi•o•sis (sim′bē ō′sis, -bī-), *n., pl.* **-ses** (-sēz). the living together of two dissimilar organisms, as in parasitism. —**sym′bi•ot′ic** (-ot′ik), *adj.*

sym•bol (sim′bəl), *n.* **1.** a material object used to represent something, often something immaterial. **2.** a letter, figure, or other conventional mark designating an object, quantity, operation, or function, as in mathematics. —**sym•bol′ic** (-bol′ik), *adj.* —**sym•bol′i•cal•ly,** *adv.* —**sym′bol•ize′,** *v.t.,* **-ized, -iz•ing.**

sym′bol•ism *n.* **1.** the practice of representing things by symbols. **2.** symbolic meaning or character.

sym•me•try (sim′i trē), *n., pl.* **-tries. 1.** correspondence in size, form, and arrangement of parts on opposite sides of a plane, line, or point. **2. a.** excellence of proportion. **b.** beauty characterized by excellence of proportion. —**sym•met′ri•cal** (si me′tri kəl), *adj.*

sym′pa•thize′ *v.i.,* **-thized, -thiz•ing. 1.** to share in a feeling. **2.** to feel or express a compassionate sympathy. —**sym′pa•thiz′er,** *n.*

sym′pa•thy *n., pl.* **-thies. 1.** agreement in feeling, as between persons. **2.** harmony of taste, opinion, or disposition. **3.** the ability to share the feelings of another, esp. in sorrow or trouble. **4.** an expression of compassion or commiseration. **5.** favorable or approving accord. —**sym′pa•thet′ic** (-thet′ik), *adj.*

sym•pho•ny (sim′fə nē), *n., pl.* **-nies. 1.** an extended sonatalike musical composition for large orchestra. **2.** Also called **sym′phony or′chestra.** a large orchestra that plays symphonies. **3.** harmony of sounds. —**sym•phon′ic** (-fon′ik), *adj.*

sym•po•si•um (sim pō′zē əm), *n., pl.* **-si•ums, -si•a** (-zē ə). **1.** a meeting or conference at which several speakers discuss a topic. **2.** a collection of opinions or articles on a given topic.

symp•tom (simp′təm), *n.* **1.** a sign or indication. **2.** a phenomenon that arises from and accompanies a disease or disorder and serves as an indication of it. —**symp′to•mat′ic,** *adj.*

syn•a•gogue or **-gog** (sin′ə gog′, -gôg′), *n.* **1.** a Jewish house of worship. **2.** a congregation of Jews.

sync or **synch** (singk), *n., v.,* **synced** or **synched, sync•ing** or **synch•ing.** —*n.* **1.** synchronization. **2.** harmonious relationship. —*v.t., v.i.* **3.** to synchronize.

syn•chro•nize (sing′krə nīz′), *v.,* **-nized, -niz•ing.** —*v.t.* **1.** to cause to indicate the same time. **2.** to cause to move, operate, or work at the same rate and exactly together. —*v.i.* **3.** to occur at the same time. —**syn′chro•ni•za′tion,** *n.* —**syn′chro•nous,** *adj.*

syn•co•pate (sing′kə pāt′, sin′-), *v.t.,* **-pat•ed, -pat•ing.** to shift (a musical accent) to a beat that is normally unaccented. —**syn′co•pa′tion,** *n.*

syn•di•cate (*n.* sin′di kit; *v.* -kāt′), *n., v.,* **-cat•ed, -cat•ing.** —*n.* **1.** a group of individuals or organizations combined to undertake a specific transaction. **2.** an agency that sells material for simultaneous

publication in a number of newspapers or periodicals. —*v.t.* **3.** to combine into a syndicate. **4.** to publish through a syndicate. —*v.i.* **5.** to combine to form a syndicate. —**syn′di•ca′tion,** *n.*

syn•drome (sin′drōm, -drəm), *n.* a group of symptoms that together are characteristic of a specific disorder or disease.

syn•er•gism (sin′ər jiz′əm), *n.* the joint action of agents, as drugs, that when taken together increase each other's effectiveness. —**syn′er•gis′tic,** *adj.*

syn•od (sin′əd), *n.* an assembly of church delegates, esp. ecclesiastics.

syn•o•nym (sin′ə nim), *n.* a word having the same or nearly the same meaning as another in the language. —**syn•on•y•mous** (si non′ə məs), *adj.*

syn•op•sis (si nop′sis), *n.*, *pl.* **-ses** (-sēz). a brief or condensed statement; summary.

syn•tax (sin′taks), *n.* the patterns of formation of sentences and phrases from words and the rules for the formation of grammatical sentences in a language. —**syn•tac′tic** (-tak′tik), *adj.*

syn•the•sis (sin′thə sis), *n.*, *pl.* **-ses** (-sēz′). the combining of elements into a single or unified entity. —**syn′the•size′** (-sīz′), *v.t.*, *v.i.*, **-sized, -siz•ing.**

syn′the•siz′er *n.* an electronic, usu. computerized device for creating or modifying the sounds of musical instruments.

syn•thet•ic (sin thet′ik), *adj.* **1.** of or involving synthesis. **2.** produced by artificial, esp. chemical, means. **3.** not real or genuine. —*n.* **4.** something made by a synthetic process.

syph•i•lis (sif′ə lis), *n.* an infectious, usu. venereal disease. —**syph′i•lit′ic,** *adj.*, *n.*

Syr•i•a (sēr′ē ə), *n.* a republic in SW Asia at the E end of the Mediterranean. —**Syr′i•an,** *n.*, *adj.*

sy•ringe (sə rinj′, sir′inj), *n.*, *v.*, **-ringed, -ring•ing.** —*n.* **1.** a tube with a piston or rubber bulb for drawing in or ejecting fluid. —*v.t.* **2.** to cleanse, wash, or inject by means of a syringe.

syr•up (sir′əp, sûr′-), *n.* a thick, sweet liquid, as of water and sugar or molasses boiled together. —**syr′up•y,** *adj.*

sys•tem (sis′təm), *n.* **1.** an assemblage or combination of things or parts forming a complex or unitary whole. **2.** an ordered assemblage of facts, principles, or doctrines in a particular field. **3.** a method or plan of procedure or classification; scheme. **4. a.** a group of bodily organs or related tissues concerned with the same function. **b.** the body considered as a functioning unit. **5.** a working combination of computer hardware, software, and data communications devices. —**sys′tem•at′ic** (-tə mat′ik), *adj.*

sys′tem•a•tize′ (-tə mə tīz′), *v.t.*, **-tized, -tiz•ing.** to arrange in or according to a system.

sys•tem•ic (si stem′ik), *adj.* of, affecting, or circulating through the entire body. —**sys•tem′i•cal•ly,** *adv.*

sys′tem (or **sys′tems**) **pro′gram,** *n.* a program, as an operating system, compiler, or utility program, that controls some aspect of the operation of a computer. Compare APPLICATION PROGRAM.

sys′tems anal′ysis the methodical study of the data-processing needs of a business or project. —**sys′tems an′alyst,** *n.*

sys•to•le (sis′tə lē′), *n.* the rhythmic contraction of the heart during which the blood in the chambers is forced onward. —**sys•tol′ic** (si stol′ik), *adj.*

a b c d e f g h i j k l m n o p q r s T u v w x y z

T, t (tē), *n.*, *pl.* **Ts** or **T's,** **ts** or **t's. 1.** the 20th letter of the English alphabet, a consonant. —*Idiom.* **2. to a T,** exactly; perfectly.

't a shortened form of *it,* as in *'twas.*

T. 1. tablespoon. **2.** Tuesday.

t. 1. teaspoon. **2.** temperature. **3.** tense. **4.** ton. **5.** transitive.

tab (tab), *n.* **1.** a small flap, loop, etc., used for pulling or hanging. **2.** a small projection from a paper or folder, used as a filing aid. **3.** *Informal.* a bill; check. —*Idiom.* **4. keep tabs on,** to maintain a watch over.

Ta•bas′co (tə bas′kō) *n.* *Trademark.* a pungent condiment sauce.

tab•by (tab′ē), *n.*, *pl.* **-bies. 1.** a cat with a striped or brindled coat. **2.** a domestic cat, esp. a female one.

tab•er•nac•le (tab′ər nak′əl), *n.* **1.** a large place of worship. **2.** (*often cap.*) *Bible.* the portable place of worship used by the Israelites during their wandering in the wilderness. **3.** an ornamental receptacle for the reserved Eucharist.

ta•ble (tā′bəl), *n.*, *v.*, **-bled, -bling.** —*n.* **1.** an article of furniture consisting of a flat top supported on one or more legs. **2.** such a piece of furniture used for meals. **3.** the food served at a table. **4.** the people at a table. **5.** a flat surface. **6.** a concise list or guide: *a table of contents.* **7.** a compact, orderly arrangement of words, numbers, etc., usu. in columns. —*v.t.* **8.** to lay aside (a bill, motion, etc.) for future discussion. —*Idiom.* **9. turn the tables,** to reverse a situation.

tab•leau (ta blō′, tab′lō), *n.*, *pl.* **tab•leaux** (ta-blōz′, tab′lōz), **tab•leaus.** a representation of a picture, scene, etc., by persons suitably costumed and posed.

ta′ble•cloth′ *n.* a cloth for covering a table, esp. during a meal.

ta•ble d'hôte (tä′bəl dōt′, tab′əl), *n.*, *pl.* **ta•bles d'hôte** (tä′bəlz, tab′əlz). a restaurant meal of pre-selected courses served at a fixed time and price. [< F: lit., the host's table]

ta′ble•land′ *n.* PLATEAU (def. 1).

ta′ble•spoon′ *n.* **1.** a large spoon used in serving food. **2.** a cooking measure equal to ½ fluid ounce (14.8 ml). —**ta′ble•spoon•ful′,** *n.*, *pl.* **-fuls.**

tab•let (tab′lit), *n.* **1.** a small, flattish piece of some solid, as a drug. **2.** a number of sheets of writing paper glued together at the edge. **3.** a flat slab bearing an inscription or carving.

ta′ble ten′nis *n.* a game resembling tennis, played on a table with paddles and a lightweight hollow ball.

ta′ble•ware′ *n.* the dishes, utensils, etc., used at the table.

tab•loid (tab′loid), *n.* a newspaper with small pages, usu. heavily illustrated and concentrating on sensational news.

ta•boo (tə bōō′, ta-), *adj.*, *n.*, *pl.* **-boos,** *v.*, **-booed, -boo•ing.** —*adj.* **1.** proscribed by society as improper or unacceptable. **2.** set apart as sacred; forbidden for general use. —*n.* **3.** a ban based on social convention. **4.** the practice of setting things apart as sacred or forbidden for general use. —*v.t.* **5.** to put under a taboo.

tab•u•lar (tab′yə lər), *adj.* **1.** of or arranged in a table. **2.** flat like a table.

tab′u•late′ (-lāt′), *v.t.*, **-lat•ed, -lat•ing.** to put in a tabular form. —**tab′u•la′tion,** *n.*

ta•chom•e•ter (ta kom′i tər, tə-), *n.* an instrument for measuring the speed of rotation.

tach•y•car•di•a (tak′i kär′dē ə), *n.* excessively rapid heartbeat.

tac•it (tas′it), *adj.* **1.** understood without being openly expressed. **2.** unspoken. —**tac′it•ly,** *adv.*

tac•i•turn (tas′i tûrn′), *adj.* inclined to silence; uncommunicative. —**tac′i•tur′ni•ty,** *n.*

tack (tak), *n.* **1.** a short, sharp-pointed nail with a broad, flat head. **2.** a course of action. **3. a.** the direction of a sailing ship with reference to the wind direction. **b.** one movement in the zigzag course of a ship proceeding to windward. **4.** a long, temporary stitch used in fastening seams. —*v.t.* **5.** to fasten with tacks. **6.** to attach as something supplementary. **7.** to change the course of (a sailing ship) to the opposite tack. —*v.i.* **8.** (of a sailing ship) to change course. —**tack′er,** *n.*

tack•le (tak′əl), *n., v.,* **-led, -ling.** —*n.* **1.** equipment, esp. for fishing. **2.** any system of leverage using pulleys to hoist, lower, and shift objects. **3.** Football. **a.** the act of tackling. **b.** either of the linemen stationed between a guard and an end. —*v.t.* **4.** to undertake to handle, solve, etc. **5.** Football. to seize and throw down (a ballcarrier). —**tack′ler,** *n.*

tack′y¹, *adj.,* **-i•er, -i•est.** sticky to the touch. —**tack′i•ness,** *n.*

tack′y², *adj.,* **-i•er, -i•est.** **1.** in poor taste; vulgar. **2.** of poor quality; shoddy. —**tack′i•ness,** *n.*

ta•co (tä′kō), *n., pl.* **-cos.** a fried tortilla folded over and filled with chopped meat, cheese, lettuce, etc.

tact (takt), *n.* skill in dealing with difficult or delicate situations. —**tact′ful,** *adj.* —**tact′less,** *adj.*

tac′tics *n.* the science of deploying military forces and maneuvering them in battle. —**tac′ti•cal,** *adj.* —**tac•ti′cian** (-tish′ən), *n.*

tac•tile (tak′til, -tīl), *adj.* of or affecting the sense of touch.

tad (tad), *n. Informal.* **1.** a small child. **2.** a small amount or degree.

tad•pole (tad′pōl), *n.* the aquatic larva of frogs and toads.

taf•fe•ta (taf′i tə), *n., pl* **-tas.** a smooth, crisp, lustrous fabric, as of silk or rayon.

taf•fy (taf′ē), *n., pl.* **-fies.** a chewy candy made of sugar or molasses boiled down.

tag¹ (tag), *n., v.,* **tagged, tag•ging.** —*n.* **1.** a piece of paper, plastic, etc., attached to something as a marker or label. **2.** any small hanging part. **3.** a hard tip at the end of a shoelace or cord. **4.** a symbol or other label indicating the beginning or end of a unit of information in an electronic document. **5.** a descriptive epithet. —*v.t.* **6.** to furnish with a tag. **7.** to follow closely. —*v.i.* **8.** to follow closely: *to tag along behind someone.* —**tag′ger,** *n.*

tag² (tag), *n., v.,* **tagged, tag•ging.** —*n.* **1.** a children's game in which one player chases the others in an effort to touch one of them, who then becomes the pursuer. —*v.t.* **2.** to touch in or as if in the game of tag.

t'ai chi ch'uan (tī′ jē′ chwän′, chē′), *n.* a Chinese system of meditative exercises, characterized by slow and stylized movements. Also called **tai′ chi′.**

tail (tāl), *n.* **1.** the hindmost part of an animal, esp. that forming a distinct, flexible appendage. **2.** something resembling this in shape or position. **3.** the reverse of a coin. **4. tails,** men's full-dress attire. **5.** a person who keeps a close surveillance of another. **6.** the bottom or end part of something. —*adj.* **7.** coming from behind: *a tail breeze.* **8.** being in the rear. —*v.t.* **9.** to follow in order to observe. —*v.i.* **10.** to follow close behind.

tail′gate′ *n., v.,* **-gat•ed, -gat•ing.** —*n.* **1.** a board or gate at the back of a vehicle that can be removed or let down, as for unloading. —*v.i., v.t.* **2.** to drive hazardously close to the rear of (another vehicle).

tail′light′ *n.* a light, usu. red, at the rear of a vehicle.

tai•lor (tā′lər), *n.* **1.** a person whose occupation is the making, mending, or altering of clothes. —*v.t.* **2.** to make by tailor's work. **3.** to fashion or adapt to a particular taste, need, etc. —*v.i.* **4.** to do the work of a tailor.

tail′pipe′ *n.* an exhaust pipe at the rear of a motor vehicle.

tail′spin′ *n.* **1.** the descent of an aircraft, nosedown, in a helical path. **2.** a sudden collapse into failure or confusion.

tail′wind′ (-wind′) *n.* wind from directly behind.

taint (tānt), *n.* **1.** a trace of something bad or offensive. **2.** a trace of infection or contamination. —*v.t.* **3.** to affect with something bad or offensive. **4.** to corrupt or contaminate.

Tai•wan (tī′wän′), *n.* an island off the SE coast of China. Also called **Republic of China.** —**Tai′wan• ese′** (-wä nēz′, -nēs′), *adj., n., pl.* **-ese.**

Ta•jik•i•stan (tə jik′ə stan′, -stän′, -jē′kə-), *n.* a republic in central Asia, N of Afghanistan: formerly a part of the USSR.

take (tāk), *v.,* **took, tak•en, tak•ing,** *n.* —*v.t.* **1.** to get into one's possession. **2.** to hold or grasp. **3.** to seize or capture. **4.** to choose or select. **5.** to receive and accept. **6.** to receive into some relation: *to take a wife.* **7.** to react to: *She took his death hard.* **8.** to derive: *The book takes its title from Dante.* **9.** to receive into the body: *to take a pill.* **10.** to undergo or endure. **11.** to carry off or remove. **12.** to subtract. **13.** to carry with one. **14.** to lead. **15.** to escort. **16.** to affect with or as if with a disease: *taken with a fit of laughter.* **17.** to absorb: *The cloth will not take a dye.* **18.** to require: *That takes courage.* **19.** to employ: *to take measures.* **20.** to use as transportation: *to take a bus to work.* **21.** to occupy: *Take a seat.* **22.** to consume: *It took ten minutes.* **23.** to avail oneself of: *I took the opportunity to leave.* **24.** to do, perform, etc.: *to take a walk.* **25.** to make (a reproduction or photograph). **26.** to write down: *to take notes.* **27.** to study: *to take ballet.* **28.** to deal with. **29.** to assume the obligation of: *to take an oath.* **30.** to experience or feel: *to take pride.* **31.** to understand. **32.** to regard or consider. **33.** *Informal.* to cheat or swindle. **34.** to be used with (a certain grammatical form, case, etc.). —*v.i.* **35.** to catch or engage, as a lock. **36.** to begin to grow, as a plant. **37.** to win favor or acceptance. **38.** to have the intended effect: *The vaccination took.* **39.** to make one's way. **40.** to become: *to take sick.* **41. take after,** to resemble. **42. ~ back, a.** to retract. **b.** to regain. **43. ~ down, a.** to write down. **44. ~ in, a.** to make (a garment) smaller. **b.** to comprehend. **c.** to deceive; cheat. **45. ~ off, a.** to remove. **b.** to leave the ground, as an airplane. **c.** to depart. **d.** to achieve sudden, marked growth, success, etc. **46. ~ on, a.** to hire. **b.** to undertake; assume. **47. ~ over,** to assume management or possession of. —*n.* **48.** the act of taking. **49.** something taken. **50.** *Informal.* money taken in. **51.** a movie or television scene photographed without interruption. **52.** a recording of a musical performance.

take′off′ *n.* **1.** the leaving of the ground, as in beginning an airplane flight. **2.** a humorous imitation; parody.

take′out′ *adj.* intended to be taken from a restaurant and consumed elsewhere: *takeout meals.*

take′o•ver *n.* **1.** the act of seizing authority or control. **2.** the acquisition of a corporation through the purchase or exchange of stock.

talc (talk), *n.* a soft green-to-gray mineral.

tal′cum pow′der (tal′kəm), *n.* a powder for the skin made of purified talc.

tale (tāl), *n.* **1.** a narrative of some real or imaginary incident. **2.** a falsehood; lie. **3.** a malicious rumor.

tal•ent (tal′ənt), *n.* **1.** a special, often creative natural ability. **2.** a person or persons with special ability. **3.** any of various ancient units of weight or money. —**tal′ent•ed,** *adj.*

tal•is•man (tal′is mən, -iz-), *n., pl.* **-mans.** an object engraved with figures supposed to possess occult powers, worn as a charm.

talk (tôk), *v.i.* **1.** to exchange ideas or information by speaking. **2.** to consult or confer. **3.** to chatter. **4.** to deliver a speech or lecture. **5.** to give confidential or incriminating information. **6.** to communicate by means other than speech, as by signs. —*v.t.* **7.** to express in words. **8.** to use in speaking: *to talk French.* **9.** to discuss: *to talk politics.* **10.** to drive or influence by talk: *He talked me into going.* **11. talk back,** to reply disrespectfully. **12. ~ down,** to speak condescendingly. **13. ~ up,** to promote enthusiastically. —*n.* **14.** the act of talking. **15.** an informal speech or lecture. **16.** a conference: *peace talks.* **17.** rumor; gossip. **18.** dialect or lingo. —**talk′a•tive,** *adj.* —**talk′er,** *n.*

talk′ing-to′ *n.* a scolding.

tall (tôl), *adj.,* **-er, -est,** *adv.* —*adj.* **1.** having a relatively great height. **2.** having height as specified: *a* *man six feet tall.* **3.** exaggerated: *a tall tale.* —*adv.* **4.** in a proud, erect manner: *to stand tall.*

tal•low (tal′ō), *n.* the hard, rendered fat of sheep and cattle, used to make candles and soap.

tal•ly (tal′ē), *n.*, *pl.* **-lies**, *v.*, **-lied**, **-ly•ing**. —*n.* **1.** an account; reckoning. **2.** a stick with notches cut to indicate the amount of a debt or payment. **3.** anything on which a score or account is kept. —*v.t.* **4.** to mark on a tally; record. **5.** to count; reckon. —*v.i.* **6.** to correspond; agree. **7.** to score a point.

tal•ly•ho (tal′ē hō′), *interj.* a hunter's cry on sighting the fox.

Tal•mud (täl′mood, tal′mǝd), *n.* a collection of ancient Jewish law and tradition. [< Heb: lit., instruction] —**Tal•mud′ic**, *adj.*

tal•on (tal′ǝn), *n.* a claw, esp. of a bird of prey.

tam (tam), *n.* a tam-o′-shanter.

ta•ma•le (tǝ mä′lē), *n.*, *pl.* **-les**. minced meat packed in cornmeal dough, wrapped in corn husks, and steamed.

tam•a•rack (tam′ǝ rak′), *n.* **1.** a North American larch. **2.** its wood.

tam•a•rind (tam′ǝ rind), *n.* **1.** the pod of a tropical tree, containing seeds in a juicy acid pulp. **2.** the tree itself.

tam•bou•rine (tam′bǝ rēn′), *n.* a small drum with metal jingles attached, played by striking and shaking.

tame (tām), *adj.*, **tam•er**, **tam•est**, *v.*, **tamed**, **tam•ing**. —*adj.* **1.** changed from the wild or savage state; domesticated. **2.** docile or submissive. **3.** spiritless; dull. —*v.t.* **4.** to make tame; domesticate. **5.** to deprive of courage or zest. —**tame′ly**, *adv.* —**tam′er**, *n.*

tam-o′-shan•ter (tam′ǝ shan′tǝr), *n.* a cap of Scottish origin, having a round, flat top with a pompom.

tamp (tamp), *v.t.* to pack in tightly by light strokes.

tam•per (tam′pǝr), *v.i.* **1.** to meddle: *to tamper with a lock.* **2.** to alter improperly: *to tamper with a passport.* **3.** to engage in underhand dealings: *to tamper with a jury.*

tam•pon (tam′pon), *n.* a plug of cotton or the like for insertion into a wound or body cavity for absorbing blood.

tan (tan), *v.*, **tanned**, **tan•ning**, *n.*, *adj.*, **tan•ner**, **tan•nest**. —*v.t.* **1.** to convert (a hide) into leather. **2.** to brown by exposure to the sun. **3.** to thrash; spank. —*v.i.* **4.** to become tanned. —*n.* **5.** a brown color imparted to the skin by the sun. **6.** a yellowish brown. —*adj.* **7.** yellowish brown. —**tan′ner** *n.* —**tan′ner•y** *n.*, *pl.* **-ies**.

tan•dem (tan′dǝm), *adv.* **1.** one following or behind the other. —*n.* **2.** a bicycle for two persons, one behind the other. **3.** a two-wheeled carriage drawn by horses harnessed tandem.

tang (tang), *n.* **1.** a strong taste, flavor, or odor. **2.** a projection from an object, as a knife, serving as attachment for a handle.

tan•ge•lo (tan′jǝ lō′), *n.*, *pl.* **-los**. a fruit that is a cross between a grapefruit and a tangerine.

tan•gent (tan′jǝnt), *n.* **1.** a line or plane that touches but does not intersect a curve or surface. —*adj.* **2.** in physical contact; touching. **3.** touching at a single point or along a line. —**Idiom.** **4. off on a tangent**, changing suddenly from one course of action or thought to another. —**tan•gen′tial** (-jen′shǝl), *adj.*

tan•ge•rine (tan′jǝ rēn′), *n.* any of several varieties of mandarin, cultivated widely, esp. in the U.S.

tan•gi•ble (tan′jǝ bǝl), *adj.* **1.** capable of being touched. **2.** real or actual. **3.** (of an asset) having physical existence and capable of being appraised. —*n.* **4.** something tangible, esp. a tangible asset. —**tan′gi•bil′i•ty**, *n.* —**tan′gi•bly**, *adv.*

tan•gle (tang′gǝl), *v.*, **-gled**, **-gling**, *n.* —*v.t.* **1.** to bring together into a confused mass of strands. **2.** to catch in or as if in a snare. —*v.i.* **3.** to become tangled. **4.** to come into conflict. —*n.* **5.** a tangled condition or situation. **6.** a tangled mass.

tan•go (tang′gō), *n.*, *pl.* **-gos**, *v.*, **-goed**, **-go•ing**. —*n.* **1.** a dramatic ballroom dance of Latin-

American origin. **2.** music for this dance. —*v.i.* **3.** to dance the tango. [< AmSp]

tank (tangk), *n.* **1.** a large container for holding a liquid or gas. **2.** an armored combat vehicle, moving on treads and armed with a cannon. —**tank′ful**, *n.*, *pl.* **-fuls**.

tan•kard (tang′kǝrd), *n.* a large drinking cup with a handle and hinged cover.

tank′er *n.* a ship, airplane, or truck designed for bulk shipment of liquids or gases.

tank′ top′ *n.* a sleeveless pullover shirt with shoulder straps.

tan•nin (tan′in), *n.* any of a group of astringent vegetable compounds, as the compound that gives the tanning properties to oak bark. Also called **tan′nic ac′id**.

tan•ta•lize (tan′tl īz′), *v.t.*, **-lized**, **-liz•ing**. to torment with the sight or prospect of something desired but out of reach. —**tan′ta•li•za′tion**, *n.* —**tan′ta•liz′er**, *n.*

tan•ta•mount (tan′tǝ mount′), *adj.* equivalent, as in value or effect.

tan•trum (tan′trǝm), *n.* a sudden burst of ill temper.

Tan•za•ni•a (tan′zǝ nē′ǝ), *n.* a republic in E Africa. —**Tan′za•ni′an**, *n.*, *adj.*

tap[1] (tap), *v.*, **tapped**, **tap•ping**, *n.* —*v.t.* **1.** to strike or touch lightly. **2.** to make, put, etc., by tapping: *to tap a nail into a wall.* —*v.i.* **3.** to strike lightly. —*n.* **4.** a light but audible blow. **5.** the sound made by this. **6.** a piece of metal attached to the toe or heel of a shoe. —**tap′per**, *n.*

tap[2] (tap), *n.*, *v.*, **tapped**, **tap•ping**. —*n.* **1.** a cylindrical stopper for closing an opening, as in a cask. **2.** a faucet. **3.** a connection made at an intermediate point on an electrical circuit. **4.** an act or instance of wiretapping. **5.** the surgical withdrawal of fluid: *a spinal tap.* **6.** a tool for cutting screw threads inside a hole. —*v.t.* **7.** to draw liquid from (a container). **8.** to draw off (liquid). **9.** to draw upon: *to tap resources.* **10.** to wiretap. **11.** to furnish with a tap. **12.** to cut a screw thread inside (a hole).

tap′ dance′ *n.* a dance in which the rhythm is made audible by taps on the dancer's shoes. —**tap′-dance′**, *v.i.*, **-danced**, **-danc•ing**. —**tap′-danc′er**, *n.*

tape (tāp), *n.*, *v.*, **taped**, **tap•ing**. —*n.* **1.** a long, narrow strip of fabric, paper, metal, etc. **2.** a strip of material with an adhesive surface, used for sealing, binding, etc. **3.** a magnetic tape. —*v.t.* **4.** to tie up, bind, or attach with tape. **5.** to record on magnetic tape.

tape′ deck′ *n.* a component of an audio system for playing tapes.

tape′ meas′ure *n.* a tape marked with subdivisions of the foot or meter and used for measuring.

ta•per (tā′pǝr), *v.t.*, *v.i.* **1.** to make or become smaller or thinner toward one end. **2. taper off**, to decrease gradually. —*n.* **3.** gradual diminution of width or thickness. **4.** a slender candle.

tape′ record′er *n.* an electrical device for recording or playing back sound recorded on magnetic tape. —**tape′-record′**, *v.t.* —**tape′ record′ing**, *n.*

tap•es•try (tap′ǝ strē), *n.*, *pl.* **-tries**. a heavy, decorative, woven fabric used esp. for wall hangings.

tape′worm′ *n.* a long, flat worm that is parasitic in the digestive system of vertebrates.

tap•i•o•ca (tap′ē ō′kǝ), *n.* a cassava preparation used in puddings and as a thickener.

ta•pir (tā′pǝr, tǝ pēr′), *n.*, *pl.* **-pirs**, **-pir**. a stout, hoofed mammal of tropical America and SE Asia.

tap′room′ *n.* a barroom.

tap′root′ *n.* a main root descending downward and giving off small lateral roots.

tar (tär), *n.*, *v.*, **tarred**, **tar•ring**. —*n.* **1.** a dark, sticky product obtained by the destructive distillation of certain organic substances, as coal or wood. **2.** smoke solids or components: *cigarette tar.* —*v.t.* **3.** to smear or cover with tar.

tar′an•tel′la (tar′ǝn tel′ǝ) *n.* rapid, whirling southern Italian dance.

ta•ran•tu•la (tǝ ran′chǝ lǝ), *n.*, *pl.* **-las**, **-lae** (-lē′).

a large, hairy spider with a painful but not highly venomous bite.

tar•dy (tär′dē), *adj.*, **-di•er, -di•est. 1.** late; not on time. **2.** moving or acting slowly. —**tar′di•ly,** *adv.* —**tar′di•ness,** *n.*

tare[1] (târ), *n.* **1.** any of various vetches. **2.** *Bible.* a noxious weed.

tare[2] (târ), *n.* the weight of the wrapping or receptacle that must be subtracted to give the weight of the goods inside.

tar•get (tär′git), *n.* **1.** an object, usu. marked with concentric circles, to be aimed at in shooting practice or contests. **2.** anything fired at. **3.** a goal or aim. **4.** an object of abuse, scorn, etc. —*v.t.* **5.** to make a target of.

tar•iff (tar′if), *n.* **1.** a schedule of duties imposed by a government on imports or exports. **2.** a duty or rate of duty in such a schedule. **3.** any table of charges or fares.

tar•nish (tär′nish), *v.t.* **1.** to dull the luster of (a metallic surface). **2.** to sully or disgrace. —*v.i.* **3.** to become tarnished. —*n.* **4.** a dull coating caused by tarnishing.

ta•ro (tär′ō, târ′ō, tar′ō), *n., pl.* **-ros.** a stemless tropical plant cultivated for its edible tuber. [< Polynesian]

ta•rot (tar′ō, ta rō′), *n.* any of a set of 22 playing cards used for fortune-telling.

tar•pau•lin (tär pô′lin, tär′pə lin), *n.* a sheet of waterproofed material used as a protective covering.

tar•ra•gon (tar′ə gon′, -gən), *n.* an Old World plant with aromatic leaves used for seasoning.

tar•ry (tar′ē), *v.i.* **-ried, -ry•ing. 1.** to stay in a place. **2.** to delay in acting, starting, etc.

tart[1] (tärt), *adj.,* **-er, -est. 1.** sharp to the taste. **2.** sharp in character or expression. —**tart′ly,** *adv.*

tart[2] (tärt), *n.* **1.** a small pie without a top crust, filled with fruit or custard. **2.** a prostitute.

tar•tan (tär′tn), *n.* a woolen cloth woven with stripes crossing at right angles, worn chiefly by the Scottish Highlanders.

tar•tar (tär′tər), *n.* **1.** a hard, yellowish deposit on the teeth. **2.** a sediment that collects in wine casks, consisting chiefly of cream of tartar. —**tar•tar′ic** (-tar′ik, -tär′-), *adj.*

tar′tar sauce′ *n.* a mayonnaise sauce containing chopped pickles, onions, etc.

task (task, täsk), *n.* **1.** any piece of work. **2.** a matter of considerable difficulty. —*v.t.* **3.** to put a strain on. —*Idiom.* **4. take to task,** to reprimand; censure.

task′ force′ *n.* a group, esp. of military units, for carrying out a specific task or operation.

task′mas′ter *n.* a person who assigns tasks, esp. burdensome ones, to others.

tas•sel (tas′əl), *n.* **1.** a pendent ornament consisting of threads or cords hanging from a roundish knob. **2.** something resembling this, as at the top of a cornstalk.

taste (tāst), *v.,* **tast•ed, tast•ing,** *n.* —*v.t.* **1.** to test the flavor of by taking some into the mouth. **2.** to eat or drink a little of. **3.** to perceive the flavor of. **4.** to experience slightly. —*v.i.* **5.** to have a particular flavor. —*n.* **6.** the sense by which the flavor of things is perceived when brought into contact with the tongue. **7.** the quality so perceived; flavor. **8.** the act of tasting. **9.** a small quantity tasted. **10.** a partiality for something: *a taste for music.* **11.** a sense of what is proper, harmonious, or beautiful. **12.** a slight experience of something. —**taste′ful,** *adj.* —**taste′less,** *adj.*

taste′ bud′ *n.* one of numerous small bodies, chiefly in the tongue, that are the organs for the sense of taste.

tast′y *adj.,* **-i•er, -i•est.** good-tasting; savory. —**tast′i•ness,** *n.*

tat•ter (tat′ər), *n.* **1.** a torn, loosely hanging piece, as of a garment. **2. tatters,** torn or ragged clothing. —*v.t., v.i.* **3.** to make or become ragged.

tat•tle (tat′l), *v.,* **-tled, -tling.** —*v.i.* **1.** to tell something secret about another. **2.** to chatter or gossip. —*v.t.* **3.** to disclose by gossiping. —**tat′tler, tat′tle•tale′,** *n.*

tat•too[1] (ta tōō′), *n., pl.* **-toos. 1.** a bugle call or other signal ordering soldiers to their quarters. **2.** a knocking or strong pulsation.

tat•too[2] (ta tōō′), *n., pl.* **-toos,** *v.,* **-tooed, -too•ing.** —*n.* **1.** an indelible design made on the skin by puncturing it and inserting pigments. —*v.t.* **2.** to mark with tattoos. **3.** to put (tattoos) on the skin. —**tat•too′er, tat•too′ist,** *n.*

taunt (tônt, tänt), *v.t.* **1.** to reproach in a sarcastic or insulting manner. —*n.* **2.** a scornful or sarcastic remark.

taupe (tōp), *n.* a dark brownish gray.

taut (tôt), *adj.,* **-er, -est. 1.** tightly drawn, as a rope. **2.** emotionally tense. **3.** tidy or neat, as a ship. —**taut′ly,** *adv.* —**taut′ness,** *n.*

tau•tol•o•gy (tô tol′ə jē), *n., pl.* **-gies. 1.** needless repetition of an idea in different words. **2.** an instance of such repetition. —**tau•to•log•i•cal** (tôt′l-oj′i kəl), *adj.*

tav•ern (tav′ərn), *n.* a place where liquors are sold to be consumed on the premises. [< OF < L *taberna* hut, inn, shop]

taw•dry (tô′drē), *adj.,* **-dri•er, -dri•est.** showy and cheap; gaudy; tasteless.

taw•ny (tô′nē), *adj.,* **-ni•er, -ni•est.** of a yellowish brown color.

tax (taks), *n.* **1.** a sum of money levied on incomes, property, etc., by a government for its support. **2.** a burdensome charge or demand. —*v.t.* **3.** to impose a tax on. **4.** to burden or strain. **5.** to reprove or accuse. —**tax′a•ble,** *adj.* —**tax•a′tion,** *n.*

tax•i (tak′sē), *n., pl.* **tax•is,** *v.,* **tax•ied, tax•i•ing** or **tax•y•ing.** —*n.* **1.** a taxicab. —*v.i.* **2.** to ride in a taxicab. **3.** (of an airplane) to move on the ground or water, as in preparing for takeoff.

tax′i•cab′ *n.* a public passenger automobile for hire.

tax•i•der•my (tak′si dûr′mē), *n.* the art of preserving, stuffing, and mounting the skins of animals in lifelike form. —**tax′i•der′mist,** *n.*

tax′pay′er *n.* a person who pays a tax. —**tax′-pay′ing,** *adj.*

tax′ shel′ter *n.* any financial arrangement, as an investment, that reduces or eliminates the taxes due. —**tax′-shel′tered,** *adj.*

TB or **T.B.,** tuberculosis.

Tb *Chem. Symbol.* terbium.

tbs. or **tbsp., 1.** tablespoon. **2.** tablespoonful.

T cell *n.* any of several closely related lymphocytes that regulate the immune system's response to infected or malignant cells.

tea (tē), *n.* **1.** the dried leaves of an evergreen Asian shrub. **2.** the shrub itself. **3.** a beverage prepared by infusing tea leaves in boiling water. **4.** any similar beverage prepared from other plants. **5.** a light meal or social gathering in the afternoon at which tea is usu. served. [< dialectal Chinese] —**tea′cup′,** *n.* —**tea′ket′tle,** *n.* —**tea′pot′,** *n.*

teach (tēch), *v.,* **taught, teach•ing.** —*v.t.* **1.** to give instruction in. **2.** to impart knowledge or skill to; give instruction to. **3.** to help to learn, as by example. —*v.i.* **4.** to give instruction.

teach′er *n.* a person who teaches, esp. as a profession.

teak (tēk), *n.* **1.** a large East Indian tree yielding a hard, medium brown wood. **2.** its wood.

teal (tēl), *n., pl.* **teals** or, for 1, **teal. 1.** any of several small freshwater ducks. **2.** a medium to dark greenish blue.

team (tēm), *n.* **1.** a number of persons forming a side in a game or contest. **2.** a number of persons associated in some joint action. **3.** two or more draft animals harnessed together. —*v.i.* **4.** to join in a team. —*adj.* **5.** of or performed by a team. —**team′mate′,** *n.* —**team′work′,** *n.*

team•ster (-stər), *n.* a person who drives a team or a truck for hauling.

tear[1] (tēr), *n.* **1.** a drop of the saline, watery fluid lubricating the eye and sometimes flowing from it, as in crying. —*v.i.* **2.** (of the eyes) to fill up with tears. —*Idiom.* **3. in tears,** weeping. —**tear′ful,** *adj.*

tear[2] (târ), *v.,* **tore, torn, tear•ing,** *n.* —*v.t.* **1.** to pull apart or in pieces by force. **2.** to divide or disrupt. **3.** to produce by tearing. **4.** to injure by or as if by tearing. **5.** to remove by force or effort. —*v.i.* **6.** to become torn. **7.** to move with force, haste, or energy. **8. tear down,** to pull down; demolish. —*n.* **9.** the act of tearing. **10.** a rip or hole. —**tear′-a•ble,** *adj.*

tear′ gas′ (tēr), *n.* a gas that makes the eyes smart and water.

tear•jerk•er (tēr′jûr′kər), *n. Informal.* a sentimental story, play, etc., designed to elicit tears.

tease (tēz), *v.,* **teased, teas•ing,** *n.* —*v.t.* **1.** to irritate with taunts, mockery, pretended offers, etc., often in sport. **2.** to comb or card (wool). **3.** to comb (the hair) toward the scalp so as to give body to a hairdo. —*v.i.* **4.** to tease a person or animal. —*n.* **5.** a person who teases. —**teas′er,** *n.* —**teas′ing•ly,** *adv.*

tea′spoon′ *n.* **1.** a small spoon used to stir tea, eat desserts, etc. **2.** a cooking measure equal to ⅙ fluid ounce (4.9 ml). —**tea′spoon•ful′,** *n., pl.* **-fuls.**

teat (tēt, tit), *n.* the nipple on a breast or udder.

tech•ni•cal (tek′ni kəl), *adj.* **1.** of or characteristic of an art, science, or trade. **2.** of or showing technique. **3.** concerned with the mechanical or industrial arts and the applied sciences. **4.** considered so by a stringent interpretation of the rules. —**tech′ni•cal•ly,** *adv.*

tech•ni•cal•i•ty *n., pl.* **-ties. 1.** a technical point or detail. **2.** technical character.

Tech′ni•col′or *Trademark.* a system of making color motion pictures.

tech•nique′ (-nēk′), *n.* **1.** the manner in which a person employs technical skills. **2.** technical procedures and methods. **3.** any method used to accomplish something.

tech•noc′ra•cy (-nok′rə sē), *n., pl.* **-cies.** government by technological experts. —**tech′no•crat′** (-nə krat′), *n.*

tech•nol′o•gy (-nol′ə jē), *n., pl.* **-gies. 1.** the branch of knowledge that deals with applied science, engineering, etc. **2.** the practical application of knowledge. **3.** the materials, techniques, etc., used for a practical end. —**tech′no•log′i•cal** (-nə loj′i kəl), *adj.* —**tech•nol′o•gist,** *n.*

tech•no-thrill•er (tek′nō thril′ər), *n.* a suspense novel in which the manipulation of sophisticated technology plays a prominent part.

ted′dy bear′ *n.* a stuffed toy bear.

Te De′um (tā dā′əm) hymn of praise and thanksgiving.

te•di•ous (tē′dē əs, tē′jəs), *adj.* long and tiresome. —**te′di•ous•ly,** *adv.* —**te′di•um,** *n.*

tee (tē), *n., v.,* **teed, tee•ing.** —*n. Golf.* **1.** the area from which the first stroke on each hole is played. **2.** a small peg from which the ball is driven. —*v.t.* **3.** to place (a ball) on a tee. **4. tee off, a.** to strike a ball from a tee. **b.** *Slang.* to make angry.

teem (tēm), *v.i.* to abound or swarm.

teen (tēn), *adj.* **1.** teenage. —*n.* **2.** a teenager.

teen′age′ *adj.* of, being, or like people in their teens. —**teen′ag′er,** *n.*

teens *n.pl.* **1.** the numbers 13 through 19. **2.** the ages of 13 to 19 inclusive.

tee•ter (tē′tər), *v.i.* **1.** to move unsteadily. **2.** to waver.

teethe (tēth), *v.i.,* **teethed, teeth•ing.** to grow teeth; cut one's teeth.

tee•to•tal•er (tē tōt′l ər, tē′tōt′-), *n.* a person who abstains totally from intoxicating drink. Also, *esp. Brit.,* **tee•to′tal•ler.**

Tef•lon (tef′lon), **1.** *Trademark.* a polymer with nonsticking properties, used for cookware coatings. —*adj.* **2.** characterized by imperviousness to blame or criticism: *a Teflon politician.*

tel. 1. telegram. **2.** telegraph. **3.** telephone.

tel•e•cast (tel′i kast′, -käst′), *v.,* **-cast** or **-cast•ed, -cast•ing,** *n.* —*v.t., v.i.* **1.** to broadcast by television. —*n.* **2.** a television broadcast.

tel′e•com•mu′ni•ca′tions *n.* the science and technology of transmitting information over great distances in the form of electromagnetic signals.

tel′e•con′fer•ence *n.* a conference of participants in different locations via telecommunications equipment.

tel′e•gen′ic (-jen′ik), *adj.* having physical qualities that televise well.

tel′e•gram′ *n.* a message sent by telegraph.

tel′e•graph′ *n.* **1.** a system or apparatus for transmitting messages over a distance by coded electrical signals sent by wire or radio. —*v.t., v.i.* **2.** to transmit (a message) to (a person) by telegraph. —**te•leg•ra•pher** (tə leg′rə fər), *n.* —**tel′e•graph′ic,** *adj.* —**te•leg•ra•phy** (tə leg′rə fē), *n.*

tel′e•mar′ket•ing *n.* selling or advertising by telephone.

te•lep•a•thy (tə lep′ə thē), *n.* communication between minds by some means other than sensory perception. —**tel•e•path•ic** (tel′ə path′ik), *adj.*

tel•e•phone (tel′ə fōn′), *n., v.,* **-phoned, -phon•ing.** —*n.* **1.** an apparatus or system for transmission of sound to a distant point, esp. by an electric device. —*v.t., v.i.* **2.** to send (a message) to (a person) by telephone. —**tel•e•phon′er,** *n.*

tel•e•pho•to (tel′ə fō′tō), *adj.* noting a lens that produces a large image of a small or distant object.

tel′e•scope′ *n., v.,* **-scoped, -scop•ing.** —*n.* **1.** an optical instrument for making distant objects appear larger and therefore nearer. —*v.t., v.i.* **2.** to force or slide together in the manner of the sliding tubes of a jointed telescope. **3.** to condense or become condensed. —**tel′e•scop′ic** (-skop′ik), *adj.*

tel′e•thon′ (-thon′), *n.* a lengthy television broadcast, usu. to raise money for a charity.

tel•e•van•ge•list (tel′i van′jə list), *n.* an evangelist who regularly conducts religious services on television. —**tel′e•van′ge•lism,** *n.*

tel•e•vise (tel′ə vīz′), *v.t., v.i.,* **-vised, -vis•ing.** to broadcast by television.

tel′e•vi′sion *n.* **1.** the broadcasting of images via radio waves to receivers that project them on a picture tube or screen. **2.** a set for receiving television broadcasts. **3.** the television broadcasting industry.

tel•ex (tel′eks), *n.* **1.** (*sometimes cap.*) a teletypewriter service channeled through a public telecommunications system. **2.** a message transmitted by telex. —*v.t.* **3.** to send by telex. [*tel(etypewriter) ex(change)*]

tell (tel), *v.,* **told, tell•ing.** —*v.t.* **1.** to narrate or relate. **2.** to express in words. **3.** to reveal or divulge. **4.** to discern or recognize: *to tell twins apart.* **5.** to inform: *He told me his name.* **6.** to order or command. —*v.i.* **7.** to give an account. **8.** to produce a marked effect. **9. tell off,** to rebuke severely. **10. ~ on,** to tattle on.

tell′-all′ *adj.* thoroughly revealing; candid.

tell′er *n.* **1.** a person employed in a bank to receive or pay out money. **2.** one that tells; narrator.

tell′ing *adj.* **1.** having force or effect. **2.** revealing. —**tell′ing•ly,** *adv.*

tell′tale′ *adj.* revealing what is not intended to be known.

te•mer•i•ty (tə mer′i tē), *n.* reckless boldness.

temp (temp), *n. Informal.* **1.** a temporary. —*v.i.* **2.** to work as a temporary.

temp. 1. temperature. **2.** temporary.

tem•per (tem′pər), *n.* **1.** a state of mind or feelings. **2.** heat of mind or passion, shown in outbursts of anger. **3.** calm disposition: *lost his temper.* **4.** the degree of hardness and strength imparted to a metal. —*v.t.* **5.** to moderate: *to temper justice with mercy.* **6.** to make suitable by or as if by blending. **7.** to impart hardness and strength to metal by heating and cooling.

tem•per•a (tem′pər ə), *n.* a technique of painting in which an emulsion of water and egg or of eggs and oil is used as a medium.

tem•per•a•ment (tem′pər ə mənt, -prə mənt), *n.* **1.** the combination of mental and emotional traits of a person; nature. **2.** personal nature that is unusually emotional or unpredictable.

tem′per•a•men′tal (-men′tl) *adj.* **1.** moody or sensitive. **2.** pertaining to temperament.

tem•per•ance (tem′pər əns), *n.* **1.** moderation or

self-restraint. **2.** total abstinence from alcoholic liquors.

tem′per•ate (-pər it), *adj.* **1.** showing or characterized by temperance. **2.** moderate in respect to temperature.

Tem′perate Zone′ *n.* the part of the earth between the tropic of Cancer and the Arctic Circle or between the tropic of Capricorn and the Antarctic Circle.

tem′per•a•ture (-pər ə chər, -prə-), *n.* **1.** a measure of the warmth or coldness of an object or substance. **2. a.** the degree of heat in a living body. **b.** a level of such heat above the normal; fever.

tem•pest (tem′pist), *n.* a violent windstorm, esp. one with rain.

tem•pes′tu•ous (-pes′chōō əs), *adj.* tumultuous; stormy. —**tem•pes′tu•ous•ly,** *adv.*

tem•plate (tem′plit), *n.* a pattern, mold, or the like, as a thin plate of metal, serving as a gauge or guide in mechanical work.

tem•ple[1] (tem′pəl), *n.* **1.** a building dedicated to the worship of a deity or deities. **2.** any large or pretentious public building.

tem•ple[2] (tem′pəl), *n.* the region of the face that lies on either side of the forehead.

tem•po (tem′pō), *n., pl.* **-pos, -pi** (-pē). **1.** the rate of speed of a musical passage or work. **2.** any characteristic rate or rhythm: *the tempo of city life.* [< It < L *tempus* time]

tem•po•ral[1] (tem′pər əl), *adj.* **1.** pertaining to time. **2.** pertaining to the present life; worldly. **3.** temporary or transitory. **4.** secular.

tem•po•ral[2] (tem′pər əl), *adj.* of or near the temples of the head.

tem′po•rar′y (-pə rer′ē), *adj., n., pl.* **-rar•ies.** —*adj.* **1.** lasting or serving for a time only; not permanent. —*n.* **2.** a temporary office worker. —**tem′po•rar′i•ly,** *adv.*

tem′po•rize′ *v.i.,* **-rized, -riz•ing.** to be indecisive or evasive to gain time or delay acting.

tempt (tempt), *v.t.* **1.** to entice to do something unwise or wrong. **2.** to appeal strongly to. **3.** to put to the test in a venturesome way: *to tempt fate.* —**temp′ta′tion,** *n.* —**tempt′er,** *n.*

tempt′ress *n.* a woman who tempts.

tem•pu•ra (tem pŏŏr′ə), *n.* a Japanese dish of seafood or vegetables dipped in batter and deep-fried. [< Japn < Pg]

ten (ten), *n.* **1.** a cardinal number, nine plus one. **2.** a symbol for this number, as 10 or X. —*adj.* **3.** amounting to ten in number.

ten•a•ble (ten′ə bəl), *adj.* capable of being held, maintained, or defended. —**ten′a•bil′i•ty,** *n.*

te•na•cious (tə nā′shəs), *adj.* **1.** holding fast: *a tenacious grip.* **2.** highly retentive: *a tenacious memory.* **3.** persistent or stubborn. **4.** holding together; cohesive. —**te•na′cious•ly,** *adv.* —**te•nac′i•ty** (-nas′i tē), *n.*

ten•ant (ten′ənt), *n.* **1.** a person or group that rents and occupies land, a house, etc., from another. **2.** an occupant or inhabitant. —*v.t.* **3.** to occupy as a tenant. —**ten′an•cy,** *n., pl.* **-cies.**

Ten′ Command′ments *n.pl. Bible.* the precepts given by God to Moses on Mount Sinai.

tend[1] (tend), *v.i.* **1.** to be disposed or inclined to do something. **2.** to lead in a particular direction.

tend[2] (tend), *v.t.* **1.** to attend to by work or services, care, etc. **2.** to watch over and care for.

ten•den•cy (ten′dən sē), *n., pl.* **-cies.** a natural disposition to move or act in some direction or toward some point or result.

ten•den′tious (-den′shəs), *adj.* having a tendency to favor a point of view; biased. —**ten•den′tious•ly,** *adv.*

ten•der[1] (ten′dər), *adj.,* **-er, -est. 1.** soft or delicate in substance. **2.** weak or delicate in constitution. **3.** young or immature. **4.** light or gentle. **5.** easily moved to compassion. **6.** affectionate or sentimental. **7.** acutely or painfully sensitive. **8.** requiring tactful handling. —**ten′der•ly,** *adv.* —**ten′der•ness,** *n.*

ten•der[2] (ten′dər), *v.t.* **1.** to present formally for acceptance. —*n.* **2.** an offer of something for ac-

ceptance. **3.** something offered, esp. money, as in payment.

tend•er[3] (ten′dər), *n.* **1.** one who tends someone or something. **2.** a ship that attends other ships, as for supplying provisions. **3.** a railroad car attached to a steam locomotive to carry fuel and water.

ten′der•foot′ *n., pl.* **-foots, -feet. 1.** an inexperienced person. **2.** a newcomer to the ranching and mining regions of the western U.S., unused to hardships.

ten′der-heart′ed *adj.* soft-hearted; sympathetic.

ten′der•ize′ *v.t.,* **-ized, -iz•ing.** to make (meat) tender, as by pounding. —**ten′der•iz′er,** *n.*

ten′der•loin′ *n.* (in beef or pork) the tenderest portion of the loin.

ten•di•ni•tis (ten′də nī′tis), *n.* inflammation of a tendon.

ten•don (ten′dən), *n.* a cord of dense, tough tissue connecting a muscle with a bone or part.

ten•dril (ten′dril), *n.* a threadlike organ of a climbing plant that winds around something else and supports the plant.

ten•e•ment (ten′ə mənt), *n.* a run-down apartment house in a poor section of a city.

ten•et (ten′it), *n.* any principle, doctrine, etc., held as true by members of a group.

Tenn. Tennessee.

ten•nis (ten′is), *n.* a game played on a court by players equipped with rackets, in which a ball is driven back and forth over a net.

ten•on (ten′ən), *n.* a projection on the end of a piece of wood for insertion into a mortise to form a joint.

ten•or (ten′ər), *n.* **1.** general sense; purport; drift. **2.** continuous course or movement. **3. a.** the adult male voice intermediate between the bass and the alto. **b.** a part for such a voice. **c.** a singer with such a voice.

ten′pins′ *n.* a form of bowling, played with ten wooden pins.

tense[1] (tens), *adj.,* **tens•er, tens•est,** *v.,* **tensed, tens•ing.** —*adj.* **1.** stretched tight; taut. **2.** in a state of mental or nervous strain. —*v.t., v.i.* **3.** to make or become tense. —**tense′ly,** *adv.*

tense[2] (tens), *n.* the inflected form of a verb that indicates the time of its action or state.

ten•sile (ten′səl, -sil, -sīl), *adj.* **1.** of or by tension. **2.** capable of being stretched or drawn out.

ten′sion *n.* **1.** the act of stretching or state of being stretched. **2.** mental or emotional strain. **3.** a strained relationship between individuals, nations, etc. **4.** the longitudinal deformation of an elastic body that results in its elongation. **5.** electromotive force; potential.

tent (tent), *n.* **1.** a portable shelter of fabric or skins supported by poles. —*v.t.* **2.** to provide with tents. —*v.i.* **3.** to live in a tent.

ten•ta•cle (ten′tə kəl), *n.* a slender, flexible appendage in some invertebrates, used for touching, grasping, etc.

ten•ta•tive (ten′tə tiv), *adj.* **1.** made or done as a trial, experiment, or attempt. **2.** unsure; hesitant. —**ten′ta•tive•ly,** *adv.*

ten•ter•hook (ten′tər hŏŏk′), *n.* **1.** one of the hooks that hold cloth stretched on a drying framework **(ten′ter). —Idiom. 2. on tenterhooks,** in suspense.

tenth (tenth), *adj.* **1.** next after the ninth; being the ordinal number for ten. **2.** being one of ten equal parts. —*n.* **3.** a tenth part, esp. of one ($1/10$). **4.** the tenth member of a series.

ten•u•ous (ten′yŏō əs), *adj.* **1.** lacking a sound basis; flimsy. **2.** thin or slender in form. **3.** rare or rarefied. —**ten′u•ous•ly,** *adv.*

ten•ure (ten′yər), *n.* **1.** the holding of something, as property or an office. **2.** the period of holding something. **3.** permanent status granted to an employee. —**ten′ured,** *adj.*

te•pee (tē′pē), *n., pl.* **-pees.** a conical tent of animal skins used by Plains Indians.

tep•id (tep′id), *adj.* **1.** moderately warm. **2.** showing little enthusiasm. —**te•pid′i•ty, tep′id•ness,** *n.* —**tep′id•ly,** *adv.*

te•qui•la (tə kē′lə), *n.* a strong liquor from Mexico.

ter′cen•ten′ni•al *n.* a 300th anniversary or its celebration.

term (tûrm), *n.* **1.** a word or group of words designating something, esp. in a particular field. **2.** the time or period through which something lasts. **3.** an appointed time or date, as for payment. **4. terms, a.** conditions or stipulations. **b.** footing or standing: *on friendly terms.* **5.** each of the members of which a mathematical expression, a series of quantities, etc., is composed. —*v.t.* **6.** to apply a term to; designate. —*Idiom.* **7. come to terms,** to reach an agreement.

ter•mi•nal (tûr′mə nl), *adj.* **1.** situated at or forming the end of something. **2.** closing; concluding. **3.** of or lasting for a term or period. **4.** occurring at or causing the end of life. —*n.* **5.** a terminal part of a structure. **6.** a terminus or a major junction within a transportation system. **7.** a device for entering information into a computer or receiving information from it. **8.** the point where current enters or leaves any conducting component in an electric circuit. —**ter′mi•nal•ly,** *adv.*

ter′mi•nate′ (-nāt′), *v.,* **-nat•ed, -nat•ing.** —*v.t.* **1.** to bring to an end. **2.** to occur at or form the conclusion of. **3.** to dismiss from a job. —*v.i.* **4.** to end. **5.** to issue or result. —**ter′mi•na′tion,** *n.*

ter•mi•nol•o•gy (tûr′mə nol′ə jē), *n., pl.* **-gies.** the terms peculiar to a specialized subject.

ter•mi•nus (tûr′mə nəs), *n., pl.* **-ni** (-nī′), **-nus•es. 1.** the end or extremity of anything. **2.** either end of a transportation line.

ter•mite (tûr′mīt), *n.* any of various social insects that can be destructive to wood.

tern (tûrn), *n.* any of various aquatic birds resembling gulls, though typically smaller.

ter•race (ter′əs), *n., v.,* **-raced, -rac•ing.** —*n.* **1.** a raised level of earth with vertical or sloping sides. **2.** an open, often paved area connected to a house; patio. **3.** a porch or balcony. **4.** a row of houses on or near the top of a slope. —*v.t.* **5.** to form into a terrace or terraces.

ter′ra cot′ta (ter′ə kot′ə), *n., pl.* **-tas.** a hard, brownish red fired clay used for pottery, building, etc.

ter′ra fir′ma (fûr′mə), *n.* firm or solid earth. [< L]

ter•rain (tə rān′), *n.* a tract of land considered with reference to its natural features.

ter•ra•pin (ter′ə pin), *n.* any of several edible North American turtles inhabiting fresh or brackish waters.

ter•rar•i•um (tə râr′ē əm), *n., pl.* **-i•ums, -i•a** (-ē ə). an enclosed glass container in which plants or land animals are kept.

ter•raz•zo (tə rä′tsō, -raz′ō), *n., pl.* **-zos.** a mosaic flooring composed of stone chips and cement.

ter•res•tri•al (tə res′trē əl), *adj.* **1.** of or representing the earth. **2.** of land as distinct from water. **3.** growing or living on land. **4.** worldly; mundane.

ter•ri•ble (ter′ə bəl), *adj.* **1.** distressing; severe. **2.** extremely bad; horrible. **3.** exciting terror or great fear. **4.** formidably great: *a terrible responsibility.* —**ter′ri•bly,** *adv.*

ter•ri•er (ter′ē ər), *n.* any of several breeds of usu. small dogs, used orig. to drive game out of its hole.

ter•rif•ic (tə rif′ik), *adj.* **1.** extraordinarily great or intense. **2.** extremely good; wonderful. **3.** causing terror. —**ter•rif′i•cal•ly,** *adv.*

ter•ri•fy (ter′ə fī′), *v.t.,* **-fied, -fy•ing.** to fill with terror or alarm.

ter•ri•to•ry (ter′i tôr′ē), *n., pl.* **-ries. 1.** any large tract of land. **2.** the land and waters under the jurisdiction of a state, sovereign, etc. **3.** a region of a country that does not have the status of a state or province. **4.** a field of action, thought, etc. **5.** an assigned district, as of a sales representative. —**ter′ri•to′ri•al** (-tôr′ē əl), *adj.*

ter•ror (ter′ər), *n.* **1.** intense fear. **2.** a person or thing that causes such fear. **3.** TERRORISM.

ter′ror•ism *n.* the use of violence and threats to intimidate or coerce, esp. for political purposes. —**ter′ror•ist,** *n., adj.*

ter′ror•ize′ *v.t.,* **-ized, -iz•ing. 1.** to fill with terror. **2.** to dominate or coerce by intimidation. —**ter′ror•i•za′tion,** *n.*

ter•ry (ter′ē), *n., pl.* **-ries.** a pile fabric with uncut loops, used for toweling. Also called **ter′ry cloth′.**

terse (tûrs), *adj.,* **ters•er, ters•est. 1.** neatly or effectively concise, as language. **2.** curt; brusque. —**terse′ly,** *adv.* —**terse′ness,** *n.*

ter•ti•ar•y (tûr′shē er′ē), *adj.* **1.** of the third order, rank, etc. **2.** (*cap.*) noting or pertaining to the earlier period of the Cenozoic Era, during which mammals gained ascendancy.

tes•sel•late (tes′ə lāt′), *v.t.,* **-lat•ed, -lat•ing.** to form of small squares in a mosaic pattern.

test (test), *n.* **1.** the means by which the presence, quality, or genuineness of anything is determined. **2.** a set of problems, questions, etc., for evaluating knowledge or skills. **3.** a reaction used to identify or detect the presence of a chemical constituent. —*v.t.* **4.** to subject to a test. —*v.i.* **5.** to undergo or conduct a test. **6.** to perform on a test.

tes•ta•ment (tes′tə mənt), *n.* **1.** a will disposing of one's personal property after death. **2.** (*cap.*) either the New Testament or the Old Testament. **3.** a proof; testimony. —**tes′ta•men′ta•ry** (-men′tə rē, -men′trē), *adj.*

tes•tate (tes′tāt), *adj.* having left a valid will. —**tes′ta′tor,** *n.*

tes•ti•cle (tes′ti kəl), *n.* TESTIS.

tes•ti•fy (tes′tə fī′), *v.,* **-fied, -fy•ing.** —*v.i.* **1.** to serve as evidence. **2.** to give testimony under oath. —*v.t.* **3.** to be evidence of. **4.** to declare under oath.

tes′ti•mo′ni•al (-mō′nē əl), *n.* **1.** a written declaration recommending a person or thing. **2.** something given or done as an expression of admiration or gratitude.

tes′ti•mo′ny *n., pl.* **-nies. 1.** the statement of a witness under oath. **2.** evidence in support of a fact or statement. **3.** open declaration, as of faith.

tes•tis (tes′tis), *n., pl.* **-tes** (-tēz). either of two reproductive glands located in the scrotum.

tes•tos•ter•one (tes tos′tə rōn′), *n.* the sex hormone secreted by the testes.

test′ tube′ *n.* a thin glass tube closed at one end, used in laboratory experimentation.

tes•ty (tes′tē), *adj.,* **-ti•er, -ti•est.** irritably impatient; touchy. —**tes′ti•ly,** *adv.*

tet•a•nus (tet′n əs), *n.* an infectious, sometimes fatal disease characterized by spasms and rigidity of muscles, esp. of the jaw and neck.

tête-à-tête (tāt′ə tāt′, tet′ə tet′), *n., pl.* **tête-à-têtes.** a private conversation between two people. [< F: lit., head to head]

teth•er (teth′ər), *n.* **1.** a rope, chain, etc., by which an animal is fastened to a fixed object. **2.** the utmost extent of one's ability or resources. —*v.t.* **3.** to fasten with or as if with a tether.

tet•ra (te′trə), *n., pl.* **-ras.** a small, brightly colored fish of tropical American waters.

tetra- a combining form meaning four (*tetrahedron*).

tet′ra•he′dron (-hē′drən), *n., pl.* **-drons, -dra** (-drə). a solid contained by four plane faces. —**tet′ra•he′dral,** *adj.*

Tex. Texas.

text (tekst), *n.* **1.** the main body of matter in a written work, as distinguished from notes, appendixes, etc. **2.** the actual words of an author or speaker. **3.** any form in which a writing exists. **4.** any theme or topic. **5.** a textbook. **6.** a passage of Scripture, esp. one chosen as the subject of a sermon. —**tex•tu•al** (teks′chōō əl), *adj.*

text•book (tekst′bŏŏk′), *n.* a book used by students as a standard work for a particular branch of study.

tex•tile (teks′tīl, -til), *n.* **1.** any cloth or goods produced by weaving, knitting, or felting. **2.** a material, as a yarn, suitable for weaving. —*adj.* **3.** of textiles or their production.

tex•ture (teks′chər), *n.* **1.** the physical structure given to a material, object, etc., by the arrangement of its parts. **2.** the structure of the threads, fibers, etc., that make up a textile fabric.

Thai (tī), *n., pl.* **Thais. 1.** a native or inhabitant of Thailand. **2.** the language of Thailand.

Thai′land′ (-land′, -lənd), *n.* a kingdom in SE Asia.

thal•a•mus (thal′ə məs), *n., pl.* **-mi** (-mī′). the part of the brain that transmits and integrates sensory impulses.

tha•lid•o•mide (thə lid′ə mīd′), *n.* a drug formerly used as a sedative, found to cause severe fetal abnormalities.

thal•li•um (thal′ē əm), *n.* a rare metallic element, used in the manufacture of alloys. *Symbol:* Tl; *at. wt.:* 204.37; *at. no.:* 81.

than (*than, then; unstressed* thən, ən), *conj.* **1.** (used after comparative adjectives and adverbs to introduce the second member of a comparison): *She's taller than I am.* **2.** (used after some adverbs and adjectives, as *other,* to denote a difference in kind, place, etc.): *I had no choice other than that.*

thank (thangk), *v.t.* **1.** to express gratitude to. **2.** to hold personally responsible: *We have him to thank for this lawsuit.* —*n.* **3.** thanks, an acknowledgment of a kindness, favor, or the like. —*interj.* **4.** thanks, I thank you. —*Idiom.* **5.** thanks to, because of. **6.** thank you, I thank you. —**thank′ful,** *adj.* —**thank′less,** *adj.*

thanks′giv′ing *n.* **1.** a public celebration in acknowledgment of divine favor. **2.** (*cap.*) a U.S. holiday observed on the fourth Thursday of November.

that (*that; unstressed* thət), *pron.* and *adj., pl.* **those;** *adv.; conj.* —*pron.* **1.** the person or thing pointed out or mentioned before: *That is her mother.* **2.** the one more remote in place, time, or thought: *This is my sister and that's my cousin.* who, whom, or which: *the horse that he bought.* —*adj.* **4.** (used to indicate the person or thing pointed out or mentioned before). **5.** (used to indicate the one more remote in time, place, or thought). **6.** (used to imply contradistinction; opposed to *this*). —*adv.* **7.** to the extent or degree indicated: *Don't take that much.* —*conj.* **8.** (used to introduce a subordinate clause expressing cause, purpose, result, etc.): *I'm sure that you'll like it.* **9.** (used elliptically to introduce an exclamation): *Oh, that I were young again!* —*Idiom.* **10.** at that, a. nevertheless. b. in addition. **11.** that is, to be more accurate.

thatch (thach), *n.* **1.** Also, **thatch′ing.** a material, as straw or rushes, used to cover roofs. **2.** a covering of such a material. —*v.t.* **3.** to cover with or as if with thatch.

thaw (thô), *v.i.* **1.** to pass from a frozen to a liquid state; melt. **2.** to become warm enough to melt ice and snow. **3.** to become less hostile or aloof. —*v.t.* **4.** to cause to thaw. —*n.* **5.** the act of thawing. **6.** weather warm enough to melt ice and snow.

the¹ (*stressed* thē; *unstressed before a consonant* thə, *unstressed before a vowel* thē), *definite article.* **1.** (used to indicate a particular person or thing): *the book you gave me.* **2.** (used to mark a noun as indicating the best-known, most approved, etc.): *the place to ski.* **3.** (used to mark a noun as being used generically): *The dog is a quadruped.* **4.** (used before adjectives that are used substantively): *from the sublime to the ridiculous.*

the² (*before a consonant* thə; *before a vowel* thē), *adv.* **1.** in or by so much: *He looks the better for his nap.* **2.** by how much … by so much: *the more the merrier.*

the•a•ter or **-tre** (thē′ə tər, thē³′-), *n.* **1.** a building or a place for dramatic presentations, motion-picture shows, etc. **2.** a room or hall with tiers of seats. **3.** the theater, dramatic performances as a branch of art. **4.** dramatic works collectively. **5.** a place of action; area of activity.

the•at•ri•cal (-a′tri kəl), *adj.* **1.** of or suitable for the theater. **2.** artificial and exaggerated; histrionic. —**the•at′ri•cal′i•ty,** *n.* —**the•at′ri•cal•ly,** *adv.*

thee (thē), *pron.* the objective case of THOU.

theft (theft), *n.* an act or instance of stealing.

their (thâr; *unstressed* thər), *pron.* a form of the possessive case of THEY used attributively: *their home.*

the•ism (thē′iz əm), *n.* belief in the existence of a god or gods. —**the′ist,** *n., adj.*

them (them; *unstressed* thəm, əm), *pron.* the objective case of THEY.

theme (thēm), *n.* **1.** a topic of discourse, discussion, etc. **2.** the central subject of a work of art. **3.** a short, informal essay. **4.** a principal melodic subject in a musical composition. —**the•mat′ic,** *adj.* —**the•mat′i•cal•ly,** *adv.*

them•selves (them selvz′, them′-), *pron.pl.* **1.** a reflexive form of THEY: *They washed themselves quickly.* **2.** (used as an intensive): *The authors themselves left the theater.* **3.** their normal selves: *After some rest, they were themselves again.*

then (then), *adv.* **1.** at that time: *Prices were lower then.* **2.** soon afterward: *The rain stopped and then started again.* **3.** next in order of time or place: *We ate, then we slept.* **4.** in addition: *I love my job, and then it pays so well.* **5.** as a consequence. —*adj.* **6.** existing or being at the time indicated: *the then prime minister.* —*n.* **7.** that time: *We haven't been back since then.*

thence (thens), *adv.* **1.** from that place. **2.** from that time; thenceforth. **3.** therefore.

thence•forth (thens′fôrth′, thens′fôrth′), *adv.* from that time onward.

the•ol•o•gy (thē ol′ə jē), *n., pl.* **-gies.** the study of God and of God's relations to the universe; the study of religious truth. —**the′o•lo′gian** (-ə lō′jən, -jē ən), *n.* —**the′o•log′i•cal** (-loj′i kəl), *adj.*

the•o•rem (thē′ər əm, thēr′əm), *n.* **1.** *Math.* a proposition or formula containing something to be proved from other propositions or formulas. **2.** *Logic.* a proposition that can be deduced from the premises of a system.

the•o•ret•i•cal (thē′ə ret′i kəl), *adj.* **1.** of or consisting in theory. **2.** existing only in theory. **3.** forming or dealing with theories.

the•o•ry *n., pl.* **-ries. 1.** a group of general propositions used as principles of explanation for a class of phenomena. **2.** an explanation whose status is still conjectural. **3.** the branch of a science or art that deals with its principles rather than its practice. **4.** a guess or conjecture. —**the′o•rist,** *n.* —**the′o•rize,** *v.i.,* **-rized, -riz•ing.**

ther•a•peu•tic (ther′ə pyoo′tik), *adj.* serving to cure, heal, or maintain health. —**ther′a•peu′ti•cal•ly,** *adv.*

ther′a•py *n., pl.* **-pies.** the treatment of disease or disorders, as by some remedial, rehabilitative, or curative process. —**ther′a•pist,** *n.*

there (thâr; *unstressed* thər), *adv.* **1.** in or at that place. **2.** at that point: *He stopped there for applause.* **3.** in that matter: *I agree with you there.* **4.** into or to that place: *We went there last year.* —*pron.* **5.** (used to introduce a sentence or clause in which the verb comes before its subject): *There is no hope.* —*n.* **6.** that place or point: *I come from there, too.* —*interj.* **7.** an exclamation of satisfaction, relief, etc.

there′a•bout′ or **-a•bouts′,** *adv.* **1.** near that place or time. **2.** about that number, amount, etc.

there′af′ter *adv.* after that in time or sequence.

there•by (thâr′bī′, thâr′bī′), *adv.* **1.** by means of that. **2.** in that connection or relation: *Thereby hangs a tale.*

there′fore′ *adv.* as a result.

there′in′ *adv.* **1.** in or into that place. **2.** in that matter, circumstance, etc.

there′of′ *adv.* **1.** of that or it. **2.** from that origin or cause.

there′on′ *adv.* **1.** on that or it. **2.** thereupon.

there′to′ also **there′un•to′,** *adv.* to that place or thing.

there′up•on′ *adv.* **1.** immediately following that. **2.** in consequence of that. **3.** upon that or it.

there′with′ *adv.* **1.** with that. **2.** following upon that.

ther•mal (thûr′məl), *adj.* **1.** of or caused by heat. **2.** designed to promote the retention of body heat. —**ther′mal•ly,** *adv.*

ther•mo•dy•nam•ics (thûr′mō dī nam′iks), *n.* the science concerned with the relations between heat and mechanical energy or work. **—ther′mo•dy•nam′ic,** adj.

ther•mom•e•ter (thər mom′i tər), n. an instrument for measuring temperature, often a glass tube containing a column of mercury that rises and falls with temperature changes.

ther′mo•nu′cle•ar (thûr′mō-), adj. 1. of or involving fusion reactions between nuclei of a light element, as hydrogen, that require temperatures of several million degrees to occur. 2. of or using energy from such reactions.

ther′mo•plas′tic (thûr′mə-), adj. 1. soft and pliable when heated, as some plastics. —n. 2. a plastic of this type.

ther•mos (thûr′məs), n. a vacuum bottle used for keeping liquids hot or cold. Also called **ther′mos bot′tle.**

ther′mo•sphere′ n. the region of the upper atmosphere in which temperature increases continually with altitude.

ther′mo•stat′ (-mə stat′), n. a device that establishes and maintains a desired temperature automatically. **—ther′mo•stat′ic,** adj.

the•sau•rus (thi sôr′əs), n., pl. **-sau•rus•es, -sau•ri** (-sôr′ī). a dictionary of synonyms and antonyms.

these (thēz), pron., adj. pl. of THIS.

the•sis (thē′sis), n., pl. **-ses** (-sēz). 1. a proposition proved or maintained against objections. 2. a formal paper incorporating original research, esp. one presented by a candidate for a degree.

Thes•pi•an (thes′pē ən), (often l.c.) —adj. 1. pertaining to the drama. —n. 2. an actor or actress.

they (thā), pron.pl. 1. nominative plural of HE, SHE, and IT. 2. people in general.

thi•a•mine (thī′ə min, -mēn′) also **-min** (-min), n. a vitamin-B compound, abundant in liver, legumes, and cereal grains.

thick (thik), adj., **-er, -est,** n. —adj. 1. having relatively great extent between two surfaces. 2. measured between opposite surfaces: a board one inch thick. 3. dense: thick fog. 4. not distinctly articulated: thick speech. 5. marked; pronounced: a thick accent. 6. heavy or viscous: thick syrup. 7. close in friendship. 8. stupid. —n. 9. the thickest part. **—thick′en,** v.t., v.i. **—thick′en•er,** n. **—thick′ly,** adv. **—thick′ness,** n.

thick′et n. a dense growth of shrubs or small trees.

thick′set′ adj. 1. heavily or solidly built. 2. set in close arrangement.

thick′-skinned′ adj. 1. having a thick skin. 2. insensitive to criticism.

thief (thēf), n., pl. **thieves.** a person who steals. **—thiev′er•y** (thē′və rē), n.

thigh (thī), n. the part of the lower limb between the hip and the knee.

thigh′bone′ n. FEMUR.

thim•ble (thim′bəl), n. a small cap worn to protect the fingertip when sewing.

thin (thin), adj., thin•ner, thin•nest, adv., v., thinned, thin•ning. —adj. 1. having relatively little extent between two surfaces. 2. having little flesh; lean. 3. widely separated; sparse: thin vegetation. 4. of slight consistency: thin soup. 5. rarefied, as air. 6. flimsy: a thin excuse. 7. lacking volume: a thin voice. 8. lacking body or richness: a thin wine. —adv. 9. in a thin manner. —v.t., v.i. 10. to make or become thin or thinner. **—thin′ly,** adv. **—thin′ness,** n.

thing (thing), n. 1. an inanimate object. 2. a matter or affair. 3. an event or circumstance. 4. an action or deed. 5. a particular; detail. 6. an article of clothing. 7. things, personal possessions. 8. a living being; creature. 9. a thought; observation. 10. a peculiar attitude or feeling: She has a thing about cats. 11. Informal. issue; topic. **—Idiom.** 12. do one's thing, Informal. to pursue a lifestyle that expresses one's self.

think (thingk), v., thought, think•ing. —v.i. 1. to use one's mind rationally. 2. to have a certain thing as the subject of one's thoughts: thinking about school. 3. to call something to mind: to think of a number. 4. to conceive of something. 5. to have

consideration: to think of others. 6. to have a belief or opinion. —v.t. 7. to have or form in the mind. 8. to evaluate for possible action upon: Think the deal over. 9. to regard: He thought me unkind. **—think′er,** n.

think′ tank′ n. a research organization employed to analyze problems and plan future developments.

thin′ner n. a liquid used to dilute paint to a desired consistency.

thin′-skinned′ adj. 1. having a thin skin. 2. sensitive to criticism.

third (thûrd), adj. 1. next after the second; being the ordinal number for three. 2. of or being the third forward gear in an automobile transmission. —n. 3. a third part, esp. of one (¹/₃). 4. the third member of a series. 5. third gear. —adv. 6. in the third place. **—third′ly,** adv.

third′ class′ n. 1. the least costly class of accommodations. 2. the class of mail consisting of merchandise weighing up to 16 ounces, or unsealed printed material.

third′-class′ adj. of the lowest class or quality; inferior.

third′ degree′ n. intensive questioning and rough treatment in order to get a confession.

third′ dimen′sion n. 1. thickness or depth. 2. an aspect that heightens reality.

third party n. 1. a party to a case or quarrel who is incidentally involved. 2. in a two-party political system, a usu. temporary party composed of independents.

third′-rate′ adj. 1. of the third rate or quality. 2. distinctly inferior.

Third′ World′ n. (sometimes l.c.) the underdeveloped or developing nations of Africa, Asia, and Latin America.

thirst (thûrst), n. 1. a sensation of dryness in the mouth and throat caused by need of liquid. 2. eager desire; craving. —v.i. 3. to feel thirst. 4. to have a strong desire. **—thirst′y,** adj., **-i•er, -i•est.** **—thirst′i•ly,** adv.

thir•teen (thûr′tēn′), n. 1. a cardinal number, ten plus three. 2. a symbol for this number, as 13 or XIII. —adj. 3. amounting to 13 in number. **—thir′teenth′,** adj., n.

thir•ty (thûr′tē), n., pl. **-ties,** adj. —n. 1. a cardinal number, ten times three. 2. a symbol for this number, as 30 or XXX. —adj. 3. amounting to 30 in number. **—thir′ti•eth,** adj., n.

this (this), pron. and adj., pl. **these** (thēz); adv. —pron. 1. the person or thing present, near, or just mentioned: This is my coat. 2. the one nearer in place, time, or thought: This is Liza and that is Amy. 3. what is about to follow: Watch this! —adj. 4. (used to indicate the person or thing present, near, or just mentioned). 5. (used to indicate the one nearer in time, place, or thought). 6. (used to imply contradistinction; opposed to that). —adv. 7. to the extent indicated: this far.

this•tle (this′əl), n. a prickly plant usu. having purple flower heads.

thith•er (thith′ər, thith′-), adv. to or toward that place.

tho or **tho′** (thō), conj., adv. a simplified spelling of THOUGH.

thong (thông, thong), n. 1. a narrow strip of leather used for fastening or whipping. 2. a sandal having a strip of leather or the like that passes between the first two toes.

tho•rax (thôr′aks), n., pl. **tho•rax•es, tho•ra•ces** (thôr′ə sēz′). 1. the part of the trunk between the neck and the abdomen. 2. the portion of an insect's body between the head and the abdomen. **—tho•rac•ic** (thô ras′ik), adj.

thorn (thôrn), n. 1. a hard, sharp outgrowth on a plant. 2. a thorny tree or shrub. 3. a source of continual irritation or trouble. **—thorn′y,** adj., **-i•er, -i•est.**

thor•ough (thûr′ō, thur′ō), adj. 1. done without negligence or omissions. 2. complete; utter: thorough enjoyment. 3. extremely attentive to detail. **—thor′ough•ly,** adv.

thor′ough•bred′ (-ō bred′, -ə bred′), adj. 1. of

pure breed or stock. —*n.* **2.** (*cap.*) one of a breed of light racehorses. **3.** a thoroughbred animal.

thor'ough•fare' *n.* a major road or highway.

thor'ough•go'ing *adj.* extremely thorough.

those (t͟hōz), *pron., adj.* pl. of THAT.

thou (t͟hou), *pron. Archaic* (*except in elevated or ecclesiastical prose*). the second person singular in the nominative case.

though (t͟hō), *conj.* **1.** in spite of the fact that. **2.** even if. —*adv.* **3.** however.

thought[1] (thôt), *n.* **1.** the product of mental activity. **2.** an idea or notion. **3.** the act or process of thinking. **4.** the capacity or faculty of thinking. **5.** consideration or attention. **6.** an opinion or belief.

thought[2] (thôt), *v.* pt. and pp. of THINK.

thought'ful *adj.* **1.** showing consideration for others. **2.** showing careful thought. **3.** occupied with thought. —**thought'ful•ly,** *adv.* —**thought'- ful•ness,** *n.*

thought'less *adj.* **1.** lacking in consideration for others. **2.** showing lack of thought; heedless. —**thought'less•ly,** *adv.*

thou•sand (thou'zənd), *n., pl.* **-sands, -sand,** *adj.* —*n.* **1.** a cardinal number, 10 times 100. **2.** a symbol for this number, as 1000 or M. —*adj.* **3.** amounting to 1000 in number. —**thou'sandth,** *adj., n.*

thrall (thrôl), *n.* **1.** a person in bondage; slave. **2.** slavery; bondage.

thrash (thrash), *v.t.* **1.** to beat; flog. **2.** to defeat thoroughly. —*v.i.* **3.** to toss about wildly. **4. thrash out,** to resolve by full discussion.

thread (thred), *n.* **1.** a fine cord of a fibrous material spun out to considerable length, used for sewing. **2.** something having the fineness of a thread. **3.** the helical ridge of a screw. **4.** something that runs through the whole course of a thing. —*v.t.* **5.** to pass a thread through the eye of (a needle). **6.** to make (one's way), as around obstacles. **7.** to form a thread on or in (a bolt, hole, etc.).

thread'bare' *adj.* **1.** having the nap worn off so as to lay bare the threads. **2.** wearing threadbare clothes. **3.** hackneyed; trite.

threat (thret), *n.* **1.** a declaration of an intention to cause harm. **2.** an indication of probable trouble. **3.** one that threatens.

threat'en *v.t., v.i.* **1.** to utter a threat (against). **2.** to be a threat (to). **3.** to give an ominous indication (of).

three (thrē), *n.* **1.** a cardinal number, 2 plus 1. **2.** a symbol for this number, as 3 or III. —*adj.* **3.** amounting to three in number.

three'-dimen'sional *adj.* having or seeming to have depth as well as width and height.

three'fold' *adj.* **1.** having three parts. **2.** three times as great or as much. —*adv.* **3.** in threefold measure.

three' R's' *n.pl.* reading, writing, and arithmetic, regarded as the fundamentals of education.

three'score' *adj.* sixty.

thresh (thresh), *v.t., v.i.* **1.** to separate (grain or seeds) from (a cereal plant or the like), as with a flail or machine. **2.** to beat or thrash. —**thresh'er,** *n.*

thresh•old (thresh'ōld, -hōld), *n.* **1.** the sill of a doorway. **2.** any point of entering or beginning.

thrice (thrīs), *adv.* **1.** three times. **2.** threefold.

thrift (thrift), *n.* economical management; economy; frugality. [< ON] —**thrift'y,** *adj.,* **-i•er, -i•est.** —**thrift'i•ly,** *adv.* —**thrift'i•ness,** *n.*

thrift' shop' *n.* a retail store that sells secondhand goods at reduced prices.

thrill (thril), *v.t.* **1.** to affect with a sudden wave of excitement. —*v.i.* **2.** to experience a wave of excitement. **3.** to move tremulously. —*n.* **4.** a feeling of excitement. **5.** something that produces a thrill.

thrill'er *n.* a suspenseful play or story, esp. a mystery story.

thrive (thrīv), *v.i.,* **thrived** or **throve, thrived** or **thriv•en** (thriv'ən), **thriv•ing. 1.** to prosper; be successful. **2.** to develop vigorously; flourish.

throat (thrōt), *n.* **1.** the first part of the passage from the mouth to the stomach and lungs. **2.** any narrowed part or passage. **3.** the front of the neck.

throat'y *adj.,* **-i•er, -i•est.** (of sound) husky; hoarse.

throb (throb), *v.,* **throbbed, throb•bing,** *n.* —*v.i.* **1.** to beat with increased force or rapidity, as the heart. **2.** to feel emotion. **3.** to vibrate, as a sound. —*n.* **4.** a violent beat or pulsation.

throe (thrō), *n.* **1.** a violent spasm or pang. **2.** **throes,** any violent convulsion or struggle.

throm•bo•sis (throm bō'sis), *n.* coagulation of blood in the blood vessels or heart.

throne (thrōn), *n.* **1.** the seat occupied by a sovereign, bishop, etc., on ceremonial occasions. **2.** the office or dignity of a sovereign. **3.** sovereign power.

throng (thrông, throng), *n.* **1.** a great number of people or things crowded together. —*v.i.* **2.** to assemble in large numbers. —*v.t.* **3.** to fill with a crowd.

throt•tle (throt'l), *n., v.,* **-tled, -tling.** —*n.* **1. a.** the valve that controls the flow of fuel to an engine. **b.** the lever that controls this valve. —*v.t.* **2.** to choke or strangle. **3.** to silence or check. **4.** to control the speed of (an engine) with a throttle.

through (thrō̄o), *prep.* **1.** in one side and out the other side of. **2.** past; beyond. **3.** between or among. **4.** throughout. **5.** done with: *What time are you through work?* **6.** to and including. **7.** by the means of. **8.** by reason of: *He ran away through fear.* —*adv.* **9.** in at one side and out at the other. **10.** all the way: *This train goes through to Boston.* **11.** throughout. **12.** from beginning to end. **13.** to completion: *to see a matter through.* —*adj.* **14.** finished. **15.** extending from one side to the other. **16.** proceeding to a destination, goal, etc., without deviation: *a through flight.* **17.** permitting uninterrupted passage: *a through street.*

through•out' *prep.* **1.** in, to, or during every part of. —*adv.* **2.** in or during every part.

throw (thrō), *v.,* **threw, thrown, throw•ing,** *n.* —*v.t.* **1.** to propel from the hand by a sudden forward motion. **2.** to cast or send forth (words, a glance, etc.). **3.** to put into some place, condition, etc., as if by hurling: *to throw a man into prison.* **4.** to move (a lever or switch) in order to turn on or disconnect. **5.** to lose (a contest) intentionally. **6.** to cause to fall to the ground. **7.** to give or host: *to throw a party.* **8.** to amaze or confuse: *Her dark glasses threw me.* —*v.i.* **9.** to fling or hurl something. **10. throw away. a.** to discard. **b.** to squander. **11. ~ in,** to add as a bonus. **12. ~ off, a.** to free oneself of. **b.** to give off; discharge. **c.** to confuse; fluster. **13. ~ out, a.** to discard or reject. **b.** to eject; expel. **14. ~ together,** to put together hurriedly. **15. ~ up,** to vomit. —*n.* **16.** an act or instance of throwing. **17.** the distance to which something can be thrown. **18.** a lightweight blanket. —**throw'er,** *n.*

throw'a•way' *adj.* **1.** intended to be discarded after use. —*n.* **2.** a handbill or circular distributed free.

throw'back' *n.* **1.** a reversion to an earlier type or state. **2.** an example of this.

thru (thrō̄o), *prep., adv., adj.* an informal spelling of THROUGH.

thrush (thrush), *n.* any of various typically dull-plumaged songbirds.

thrust (thrust), *v.,* **thrust, thrust•ing,** *n.* —*v.t.* **1.** to push forcibly; shove. **2.** to put boldly into some position, situation, etc. —*v.i.* **3.** to make a lunge or stab. **4.** to force one's way. —*n.* **5.** an act or instance of thrusting. **6.** a lunge or stab. **7.** a force exerted by a propeller or propulsive gases to propel a missile, ship, or the like. **8.** the main point; essence. **9.** pressure exerted by a thing against a contiguous one. **10.** a military assault.

thru•way (thrō̄o'wā'), *n.* an expressway providing a direct route between distant areas.

thud (thud), *n., v.,* **thud•ded, thud•ding.** —*n.* **1.** a dull sound, as of a heavy blow. —*v.i.* **2.** to strike or fall with a thud.

thug (thug), *n.* a vicious criminal or ruffian.

thumb (thum), *n.* **1.** the short, thick, inner digit of the hand. —*v.t.* **2.** to soil or wear with the thumbs in handling. **3.** to glance through the pages of. **4.** to

thumb'nail' *n.* **1.** the nail of the thumb. —*adj.* **2.** brief and concise.

thumb'screw' *n.* a screw that may be turned with the thumb and forefinger.

thumb'tack' *n.* a tack with a broad head, designed to be pressed into a surface with the thumb.

thump (thump), *n.* **1.** a blow with a heavy object. **2.** the dull sound made by such a blow. —*v.t.* **3.** to beat with a thump. —*v.i.* **4.** to strike or fall with a thump.

thump'ing *adj.* **1.** exceptional or impressive. **2.** of or like a thump.

thun•der (thun'dər), *n.* **1.** a loud noise produced by the expansion of air heated by a lightning discharge. **2.** any loud, resounding noise. —*v.i.* **3.** to give forth thunder. **4.** to make a noise like thunder. **5.** to speak loudly or vehemently. —*v.t.* **6.** to express loudly or vehemently. —**thun'der•ous,** *adj.*

thun'der•bolt' *n.* a flash of lightning with the accompanying thunder.

thun'der•clap' *n.* a crash of thunder.

thun'der•cloud' *n.* a cloud indicative of thunderstorm conditions.

thun'der•head' *n.* THUNDERCLOUD.

thun'der•storm' *n.* a storm with lightning and thunder.

thun'der•struck' *adj.* astonished or dumbfounded.

Thurs. Thursday.

Thurs•day (thûrz'dā, -dē), *n.* the fifth day of the week, following Wednesday.

thus (thus), *adv.* **1.** in this way. **2.** consequently. **3.** to this extent or degree.

thwack (thwak), *v.t.* **1.** to strike vigorously with something flat. —*n.* **2.** a sharp blow with something flat.

thwart (thwôrt), *v.t.* **1.** to oppose successfully. **2.** to frustrate or baffle (a plan, purpose, etc.).

thy (thī), *pron.* the possessive case of THOU used as an attributive adjective.

thyme (tīm; *spelling pron.* thīm), *n.* an herb with aromatic leaves used for seasoning.

thy•mus (thī'məs), *n.* a gland at the base of the neck that aids in the production of T cells.

thy•roid (thī'roid), *adj.* **1.** of or being an endocrine gland at the base of the neck that secretes hormones to regulate the rates of metabolism and growth. —*n.* **2.** the thyroid gland.

thy•self (thī self'), *pron.* a reflexive and intensive form of THOU.

ti•ar•a (tē ar'ə, -är'ə, -âr'ə), *n., pl.* -ar•as. **1.** a jeweled coronet worn by women. **2.** the pope's crown. [< L < Gk *tiára*]

Ti•bet (ti bet'), *n.* an autonomous region in SW China, on a plateau N of the Himalayas. 2,030,000. —**Ti•bet'an,** *n., adj.*

tib•i•a (tib'ē ə), *n., pl.* -i•ae (-ē ē'), -i•as. the inner of the two bones of the leg, extending from the knee to the ankle. —**tib'i•al,** *adj.*

tic (tik), *n.* a spasmodic, involuntary muscular contraction.

tick¹ (tik), *n.* **1.** a slight, sharp, recurring click, as of a clock. **2.** a mark used to check off items. —*v.i.* **3.** to emit a tick or ticks. —*v.t.* **4.** to mark with a tick.

tick² (tik), *n.* any of numerous bloodsucking arachnids, some of which transmit disease.

tick³ (tik), *n.* the cloth case of a mattress or pillow.

tick'er *n.* **1.** one that ticks. **2.** a telegraphic instrument that prints stock prices and market reports, etc., on tape (**ticker tape**). **3.** *Slang.* the heart.

tick'et (-it), *n.* **1.** a printed slip of paper or cardboard indicating that the holder is entitled to some service: *a train ticket.* **2.** a summons for a traffic or parking violation. **3.** a tag indicating price, content, etc. **4.** a slate of candidates nominated by a party. —*v.t.* **5.** to attach a ticket to. **6.** to give a ticket to.

tick'ing *n.* a strong fabric used to cover mattresses and pillows.

tick'le *v.,* -led, -ling, *n.* —*v.t.* **1.** to stroke lightly so

as to excite a tingling sensation in. **2.** to excite agreeably; gratify. —*v.i.* **3.** to have or produce a tingling sensation. —*n.* **4.** a tickling sensation.

tick'ler file' *n.* a file for reminding the user at appropriate times of matters needing attention.

tick'lish *adj.* **1.** sensitive to tickling. **2.** requiring delicate or tactful handling.

tick-tack-toe or **tic-tac-toe** (tik'tak tō'), *n.* a game for two players, each trying to make a complete row of three X's or three O's on a nine-square grid.

tid'al wave' *n.* **1.** (not in technical use) a tsunami or other large, destructive ocean wave. **2.** any powerful or widespread movement, opinion, etc.

tid•bit (tid'bit'), *n.* a choice bit, as of food.

tid•dly•winks (tid'lē wingks'), *n.* a game in which small disks are snapped with larger disks into a cup.

tide (tīd), *n., v.,* **tid•ed, tid•ing.** —*n.* **1.** the rise and fall of the waters of the ocean, produced by the attraction of the moon and sun and occurring about every 12 hours. **2.** anything that alternately rises and falls. **3.** tendency or drift. **4.** a season or period: *Eastertide.* —*v.* **5. tide over,** to assist in getting over a period of difficulty. —**tid'al,** *adj.*

tide'land' *n.* **1.** land alternately exposed and covered by the tide. **2.** Often, **-lands.** submerged offshore land within the territorial waters of a nation.

ti•dings (tī'dingz), *n.pl.* news; information.

ti•dy (tī'dē), *adj.,* -di•er, -di•est, *v.,* -died, -dy•ing. —*adj.* **1.** neat and orderly. **2.** fairly large; considerable: *a tidy sum.* —*v.t., v.i.* **3.** to make tidy. —**ti'di•ly,** *adv.* —**ti'di•ness,** *n.*

tie (tī), *v.,* **tied, ty•ing,** *n.* —*v.t.* **1.** to fasten with a cord, string, etc. **2.** to fasten by tightening and knotting the strings of. **3.** to fasten together into a knot or bow. **4.** to form (a knot or bow). **5.** to bind or confine. **6.** to make the same score as. —*v.i.* **7.** to make the same score. **8. tie down,** to curtail the activities of. **9. ~ up, a.** to fasten securely by tying. **b.** to stop or impede. **c.** to moor. **d.** to occupy completely. —*n.* **10.** a cord, string, etc., used for tying. **11.** a necktie. **12.** a bond, as of mutual interest. **13.** an equality of scores or votes. **14.** a beam, rod, etc., for keeping two objects from separating. **15.** one of the crossbeams used for supporting and fastening the rails of a railroad track.

tie'-dye'ing *n.* a method of dyeing fabric in which sections are bound so as not to receive the dye, producing a variegated pattern. —**tie'-dyed',** *adj.*

tie'-in' *n.* a link, association, or relationship.

tier (tēr), *n.* one of a series of rows rising one behind or above another.

tie'-up' *n.* a temporary stoppage or slowing of traffic, production, etc.

tiff (tif), *n.* a slight quarrel.

ti•ger (tī'gər), *n.* a large, powerful Asian cat having a tawny coat with black stripes. —**ti•gress,** *n. fem.*

ti'ger lil'y *n.* a lily with flowers of dull-orange color spotted with black.

tight (tīt), *adj.* and *adv.,* -er, -est. —*adj.* **1.** firmly fixed in place. **2.** stretched so as to be tense. **3.** fitting too closely. **4.** difficult to deal with: *a tight situation.* **5.** of such close texture or fit as to be impervious to water, air, etc. **6.** firm; rigid: *tight control.* **7.** packed closely or full. **8.** nearly even: *a tight race.* **9.** stingy. **10.** *Slang.* drunk. **11.** characterized by scarcity: *a tight job market.* —*adv.* **12.** securely. **13.** soundly: *to sleep tight.* —**tight'en,** *v.t., v.i.* —**tight'ly,** *adv.* —**tight'ness,** *n.*

tight'fist'ed *adj.* stingy.

tight'-lipped' *adj.* reluctant to speak.

tight'rope' *n.* a taut rope or wire cable on which acrobats perform.

tights *n.* (*used with a pl. v.*) a skintight garment for the lower part of the body and the legs.

tight'wad' *n.* a stingy person.

ti•gress (tī'gris), *n.* a female tiger.

til•de (til'də), *n., pl.* -des. a diacritic (¯) placed over a letter, as in Spanish, to indicate a nasal sound.

tile (tīl), *n., v.,* **tiled, til•ing.** —*n.* **1.** a thin slab, as of baked clay or linoleum, used for covering roofs, floors, etc. **2.** a pottery tube or pipe used as a drain. —*v.t.* **3.** to cover with tiles. —**til′ing,** *n.*

till¹ (til), *prep., conj.* UNTIL.

till² (til), *v.t., v.i.* to prepare (land) for the raising of crops, as by plowing. —**till′age,** *n.*

till³ (til), *n.* a drawer, box, etc., in which money is kept, as in a shop.

til′ler *n.* a bar or lever for turning the rudder in steering.

tilt (tilt), *v.t.* **1.** to cause to slope. —*v.i.* **2.** to slope or lean. **3.** to charge with a lance or the like. **4.** to engage in a joust or tournament. —*n.* **5.** a slope. **6.** a joust or tournament. —**Idiom. 7. (at) full tilt,** at maximum speed.

tim•ber (tim′bər), *n.* **1.** wood suitable for construction purposes. **2.** growing trees. **3.** a single piece of wood forming part of a structure. —**tim′bered,** *adj.*

tim′ber•line′ *n.* the altitude above sea level at which timber ceases to grow.

timber wolf *n.* a large brindled wolf of forested Canada and the northern United States.

tim•bre (tam′bər, tim′-), *n.* the characteristic quality of a sound, independent of pitch and loudness.

time (tīm), *n., adj., v.,* **timed, tim•ing.** —*n.* **1.** the duration of all existence, past, present, or future. **2.** (*sometimes cap.*) a system of measuring the passage of time: *solar time.* **3.** a limited or particular period or interval: *a long time.* **4.** Often, **times. a.** an age or era. **b.** a period with reference to its conditions: *hard times.* **5.** a period experienced in a particular way: *Have a good time.* **6.** a period of work of an employee, or the pay for it. **7.** *Informal.* a term of enforced duty or imprisonment. **8.** leisure or spare time. **9.** a definite point in time: *What time is it?* **10.** the proper moment for something. **11.** each occasion of a recurring action or event: *We saw it five times.* **12. times,** the number of instances a quantity or factor are taken together: *Two goes into six three times.* **13.** *Music.* **a.** tempo. **b.** meter; rhythm. **14.** rate of marching: *double time.* —*adj.* **15.** of or showing the passage of time. **16.** set to detonate at the desired moment: *a time bomb.* —*v.t.* **17.** to measure the speed, duration, or rate of. **18.** to regulate (a train, clock, etc.) as to time. **19.** to choose the proper moment for. —*Idiom.* **20.** ahead of time, early. **21. at the same time,** nevertheless. **22. at times,** occasionally. **23. for the time being,** temporarily. **24. from time to time,** occasionally. **25. in time, a.** early enough. **b.** eventually. **26. make time,** to move quickly. **27. on time, a.** punctually. **b.** to be paid for in installments. **28. time after time,** again and again. —**tim′er,** *n.*

time′ clock′ *n.* a clock with an attachment that records the times of arrival and departure of employees.

time′-hon′ored *adj.* respected because of long observance.

time′keep′er *n.* an official who times, regulates, and records the duration of a sports contest.

time′less *adj.* **1.** without beginning or end. **2.** restricted to no particular time: *timeless beauty.*

time′ line′ *n.* **1.** a linear representation of events in the order in which they occurred. **2.** a schedule.

time′ly *adj.,* **-li•er, -li•est.** occurring at a suitable time.

time′-out′ *n., pl.* **-outs.** a brief suspension of activity, as in a sports contest.

time′piece′ *n.* a device for measuring and recording time, as a watch.

times *prep.* multiplied by.

time′-shar′ing *n.* **1.** a plan in which several persons share the costs of a vacation home, with each using it at separate, specified times. **2.** a system in which users at different terminals simultaneously use a single computer.

time′ta′ble *n.* a schedule showing arrival and departure times of trains, airplanes, etc.

time′worn′ *adj.* **1.** impaired by time. **2.** trite; hackneyed.

time′ zone′ *n.* one of the 24 divisions of the globe coinciding with meridians at successive hours from the observatory at Greenwich, England.

tim•id (tim′id), *adj.,* **-er, -est.** lacking in self-assurance; shy. —**ti•mid′i•ty,** *n.* —**tim′id•ly,** *adv.*

tim•ing (tī′ming), *n.* the adjustment of the time or speed of an action so as to achieve the best effect.

tim•or•ous (tim′ər əs), *adj.* fearful or timid. —**tim′or•ous•ly,** *adv.*

tim•pa•ni (tim′pə nē), *n.* (*used with a sing. or pl. v.*) a set of kettledrums, esp. as used in an orchestra. —**tim′pa•nist,** *n.*

tin (tin), *n., v.,* **tinned, tin•ning.** —*n.* **1.** a malleable metallic element, used in plating and in making alloys. *Symbol:* Sn; *at. wt.:* 118.69; *at. no.:* 50. **2.** TIN PLATE. **3.** a container made of tin plate. —*v.t.* **4.** to cover or coat with tin.

tinc•ture (tingk′chər), *n., v.,* **-tured, -tur•ing.** —*n.* **1.** a solution of a drug in alcohol. **2.** a trace; tinge. **3.** a dye or pigment. —*v.t.* **4.** to tinge.

tin•der (tin′dər), *n.* any dry, easily ignitable substance.

tin′der•box′ *n.* **1.** a box for holding tinder. **2.** a potential source of violence.

tine (tīn), *n.* a sharp point or prong, as of a fork.

tin′foil′ *n.* tin, or an alloy of tin and lead, in a thin sheet, used as a wrapping.

tinge (tinj), *v.,* **tinged, tinge•ing** or **ting•ing,** *n.* —*v.t.* **1.** to color slightly. **2.** to add a trace of any quality to. —*n.* **3.** a slight trace, as of color.

tin•gle (ting′gəl), *v.,* **-gled, -gling,** *n.* —*v.i.* **1.** to have a slight prickling or stinging sensation. —*n.* **2.** a tingling sensation.

tin•ker (ting′kər), *n.* **1.** a mender of pots and pans. **2.** a clumsy worker. —*v.i.* **3.** to putter or fiddle. **4.** to work clumsily. —**tin′ker•er,** *n.*

tin•kle (ting′kəl), *v.,* **-kled, -kling,** *n.* —*v.i., v.t.* **1.** to make or cause to make light ringing sounds. —*n.* **2.** a tinkling sound.

tin′ plate′ *n.* thin sheet iron or steel coated with tin.

tin•sel (tin′səl), *n.* **1.** thin strips or threads of glittering metal, paper, or plastic, used for decoration. **2.** anything showy but of little value.

tint (tint), *n.* **1.** a shade of a color. **2.** a delicate or pale color. **3.** a hair dye. —*v.t.* **4.** to give a tint to.

tin•tin•nab•u•la•tion (tin′ti nab′yə lā′shən), *n.* **1.** the ringing of bells. **2.** a sound produced by bells. [< L *tintinnābulum* bell]

ti•ny (tī′nē), *adj.,* **-ni•er, -ni•est.** very small. —**ti′ni•ness,** *n.*

tip¹ (tip), *n., v.,* **tipped, tip•ping.** —*n.* **1.** the point or end, esp. of something tapered. **2.** a small piece covering the end of something. —*v.t.* **3.** to furnish with a tip. **4.** to form the top of. **5.** to adorn the tip of.

tip² (tip), *v.,* **tipped, tip•ping,** *n.* —*v.t., v.i.* **1.** to slant or tilt. **2.** to overturn. —*n.* **3.** the act of tipping or state of being tipped.

tip³ (tip), *n., v.,* **tipped, tip•ping.** —*n.* **1.** GRATUITY. **2.** a piece of confidential information. **3.** a useful hint or idea. —*v.t., v.i.* **4.** to give a gratuity (to). **5. tip off,** to supply with confidential information, esp. as a warning.

tip⁴ (tip), *n., v.,* **tipped, tip•ping.** —*n.* **1.** a light blow. —*v.t.* **2.** to strike lightly and smartly.

tip′-off′ *n.* a tip; warning.

tip•ple (tip′əl), *v.i., v.t.,* **-pled, -pling.** to drink (liquor), esp. repeatedly and in small quantities. —**tip′pler,** *n.*

tip′ster (-stər), *n.* a person who sells tips, as for betting.

tip′sy *adj.,* **-si•er, -si•est. 1.** slightly drunk. **2.** unsteady; shaky.

tip′toe′ *n., v.,* **-toed, -toe•ing.** —*n.* **1.** the tip of a toe. —*v.i.* **2.** to go on one's tiptoes, as with stealth. —*Idiom.* **3. on tiptoe, a.** on one's tiptoes. **b.** expectant; eager. **c.** stealthily.

tip′top′ (-top′, -top′), *n.* **1.** the highest point. —*adj.* **2.** at the very top. **3.** of the highest quality. —*adv.* **4.** very well.

ti•rade (tī′rād, tī rād′), *n.* a prolonged outburst of bitter denunciation.

tire¹ (tīr), *v.t., v.i.,* **tired, tir•ing. 1.** to make or become exhausted. **2.** to make or become bored. —**tire′less,** *adj.* —**tire′some,** *adj.*

tire² (tīr), *n.* a ring of rubber or metal placed over

the rim of a wheel to provide traction or resistance to wear.

tired (tīªrd), *adj.* **1.** exhausted; fatigued. **2.** bored. **3.** hackneyed.

tis•sue (tish′ōō), *n.* **1.** a mass of cells and cell products forming one of the structural materials of an organism. **2.** TISSUE PAPER. **3.** any of several kinds of soft, gauzy papers: *toilet tissue.* **4.** an interconnected mass: *a tissue of falsehoods.*

tis′sue pa′per *n.* a very thin, nearly transparent paper used for wrapping or packing.

ti•tan (tīt′n), *n.* a person or thing of great size or power.

ti•ta•ni•um (tī tā′nē əm), *n.* a corrosion-resistant metallic element, used to toughen steel. *Symbol:* Ti; *at. wt.:* 47.90; *at. no.:* 22.

tit for tat (tit′ fər tat′), *n.* an equivalent given in retaliation.

tithe (tīth), *n., v.,* **tithed, tith•ing. —***n.* **1.** the tenth part of goods or income paid to support a church. —*v.t., v.i.* **2.** to give or pay a tithe (of).

ti•tian (tish′ən), *n.* a bright golden brown color.

tit•il•late (tit′l āt′), *v.t.,* **-lat•ed, -lat•ing.** to excite agreeably. —**tit′il•lat′ing•ly,** *adv.* —**tit′il•la′tion,** *n.*

tit′i•vate′ (-ə vāt′) *v.t.,* **-vat•ed, -vat•ing.** make smart or spruce.

ti•tle (tīt′l), *n., v.,* **-tled, -tling. —***n.* **1.** the name of a work, as a book or poem. **2.** a descriptive appellation of rank or office. **3.** a sports championship. **4. a.** legal right to the possession of property, esp. real estate. **b.** the instrument constituting evidence of such right. —*v.t.* **5.** to furnish with a title.

tit•mouse (tit′mous′), *n., pl.* **-mice.** any of various small, stout-billed songbirds.

tit•ter (tit′ər), *v.i.* **1.** to laugh in a half-restrained, self-conscious way. —*n.* **2.** a tittering laugh.

tit•tle (tit′l), *n.* a very small thing; jot.

tit•u•lar (tich′ə lər, tit′yə-), *adj.* **1.** being such in title only. **2.** of or constituting a title.

tiz•zy (tiz′ē), *n., pl.* **-zies.** *Slang.* a nervous, excited, or distracted state.

TN Tennessee.

TNT a flammable substance used as a high explosive. [*t(ri)n(itro)t(oluene)*]

to (tōō; *unstressed* tŏŏ, tə), *prep.* **1.** so as to reach: *Come to the house.* **2.** in the direction of: *from north to south.* **3.** to the extent or limit of: *He grew to six feet.* **4.** before; until: *ten minutes to six.* **5.** (used to express destination or end): *sentenced to jail.* **6.** (used to express a resulting condition): *torn to pieces.* **7.** (used to express the object of inclination or desire): *They drank to her health.* **8.** compared with: *inferior to last year's crop.* **9.** in accordance with: *a room to your liking.* **10.** with respect or relation to: *parallel to the roof.* **11.** contained or included in: *12 to the dozen.* **12.** (used to indicate the indirect object): *Give it to me.* **13.** (used to indicate the infinitive): *To err is human.* —*adv.* **14.** toward a closed position: *Pull the door to.* **15.** toward action or work. **16.** into a state of consciousness: *after he came to.* —*Idiom.* **17. to and fro,** back and forth.

toad (tōd), *n.* any of various mostly terrestrial amphibians related to frogs but having dry, warty skin.

toad′stool′ *n.* a mushroom, esp. a poisonous one.

toad′y *n., pl.* **-ies,** *v.,* **-ied, -y•ing. —***n.* **1.** a fawning flatterer. —*v.i.* **2.** to be a toady.

toast¹ (tōst), *n.* **1.** sliced bread browned by dry heat. —*v.t.* **2.** to brown (bread, cheese, etc.) by heat. **3.** to warm thoroughly. —*v.i.* **4.** to become toasted.

toast² (tōst), *n.* **1.** a few words of welcome, congratulation, etc., said before drinking to a person or event. **2.** a person or event so honored. —*v.t., v.i.* **3.** to propose or drink a toast (to).

toast′er *n.* an appliance for toasting bread.

toast′mas′ter *n.* a person who presides at a dinner, introducing the speakers and proposing toasts.

toast′y *adj.,* **-i•er, -i•est.** cozily warm.

to•bac•co (tə bak′ō), *n., pl.* **-cos, -coes. 1.** a plant whose leaves are prepared for smoking or chewing or as snuff. **2.** any product made from such leaves.

to•bac′co•nist (-bak′ə nist), *n.* a dealer in tobacco.

To•ba•go (tə bā′gō), *n.* an island in the SE West Indies: part of Trinidad and Tobago. —**To•ba•go•ni•an** (tō′bə gō′nē ən), *n.*

to•bog•gan (tə bog′ən), *n.* **1.** a long, narrow, flat-bottomed sled, used in coasting. —*v.i.* **2.** to coast on a toboggan. **3.** to plummet, as prices.

to•day (tə dā′), *n.* **1.** this present day. **2.** this present age. —*adv.* **3.** on this present day. **4.** at the present time.

tod•dle (tod′l), *v.i.,* **-dled, -dling.** to move with short, unsteady steps, as a young child. —**tod′dler,** *n.*

tod•dy (tod′ē), *n., pl.* **-dies.** a drink of liquor, hot water, sugar, and spices.

to-do (tə dōō′), *n., pl.* **-dos.** bustle; fuss.

toe (tō), *n., v.,* **toed, toe•ing. —***n.* **1.** one of the terminal digits of the foot. **2.** the forepart of a shoe or stocking. **3.** a part resembling a toe in shape or position. —*v.t.* **4.** to touch with the toes. —*v.i.* **5.** to stand or walk with the toes in a specified position: *to toe in.* —*Idiom.* **6.** on one's toes, alert. **7. toe the line** or **mark,** to conform strictly to a rule or command. —**toe′nail′,** *n.*

toe′hold′ *n.* **1.** a small niche that supports the toes, as in climbing. **2.** any slight advantage or support.

tof•fee or **-fy** (tô′fē, tof′ē), *n., pl.* **-fees** or **-fies.** a confection made of brown sugar, butter, and vinegar.

to•fu (tō′fōō), *n., pl.* **-fus.** a soft cheeselike food made from curdled soybean milk. [< Japn]

to•ga (tō′gə), *n., pl.* **-gas, -gae** (-jē, -gē). (in ancient Rome) the traditional formal outer garment of freeborn men. —**to′gaed,** *adj.*

to•geth•er (tə geth′ər), *adv.* **1.** into or in one gathering: *Call the people together.* **2.** into or in union, proximity, etc.: *to sew things together.* **3.** considered collectively: *to cost more than all the others together.* **4.** at the same time. **5.** without interruption: *for days together.* **6.** in cooperation: *to undertake a task together.* —*adj.* **7.** *Informal.* emotionally stable.

to•geth′er•ness *n.* warm fellowship, as among family members.

To•go (tō′gō), *n.* a country in W Africa. —**To′go•lese′** (-gə lēz′, -lēs′), *adj., n., pl.* **-lese.**

togs *n.pl. Informal.* clothes.

toil (toil), *n.* **1.** exhausting labor or effort. —*v.i.* **2.** to work very hard. **3.** to move with great effort. —**toil′er,** *n.* —**toil′some,** *adj.*

toi•let (toi′lit), *n.* **1.** a bathroom fixture consisting of a bowl and a water-flushing device, used for defecation and urination. **2.** a bathroom; lavatory. **3.** the act of dressing or grooming oneself. **4.** a person's dress or costume.

toi′let•ry *n., pl.* **-ries.** any article or preparation used in grooming oneself, as deodorant.

toi′let wa′ter *n.* a scented liquid used as a light perfume.

to•kay′ (tō kā′) *n.* **1.** a rich, sweet, aromatic wine from Hungary. **2.** the variety of grape from which it is made.

toke (tōk), *n., v.,* **toked, tok•ing.** *Slang.* —*n.* **1.** a puff on a marijuana cigarette. —*v.t., v.i.* **2.** to puff or smoke (a marijuana cigarette).

to•ken (tō′kən), *n.* **1.** something serving to represent or indicate a feeling, fact, etc.; sign. **2.** a memento; souvenir. **3.** a piece of metal used in place of money, as for bus fares. —*adj.* **4.** serving as a token. **5.** slight; minimal: *token resistance.* —*Idiom.* **6. by the same token,** for similar reasons.

to′ken•ism *n.* the practice of making only a minimal effort to offer equal opportunities to minorities.

tole (tōl), *n.* enameled or lacquered metal, used for trays, boxes, etc.

tol•er•a•ble (tol′ər ə bəl), *adj.* **1.** capable of being tolerated. **2.** fairly good. —**tol′er•a•bly,** *adv.*

tol′er•ance (-əns), *n.* **1.** a fair and permissive attitude toward those whose race, religion, beliefs, etc., differ from one's own. **2.** the capacity to endure something, as pain. **3.** the capacity to resist the action of a drug, poison, etc. **4.** the permissible variation of an object in some characteristic such as hardness or quantity. —**tol′er•ant,** *adj.* —**tol′er•ant•ly,** *adv.*

tol′er•ate′ (-ə rāt′), *v.t.,* **-at•ed, -at•ing. 1.** to allow without hindrance; permit. **2.** to put up with; endure. **3.** to resist the action of (a drug, poison, etc.). —**tol′er•a′tion,** *n.*

toll[1] (tōl), *n.* **1.** a fee exacted for some privilege, as for passage over a bridge. **2.** the extent of loss, damage, etc., resulting from a calamity. **3.** a payment for services, as for a long-distance telephone call.

toll[2] (tōl), *v.t.* **1.** to ring (a large bell) with slow, repeated strokes. **2.** to announce, summon, or dismiss by this means. —*v.i.* **3.** (of a bell) to ring slowly. —*n.* **4.** the sound of tolling a bell.

toll′booth′ *n.* a booth, as at a bridge, where a toll is collected.

tom (tom), *n.* the male of various animals, as the cat or turkey.

tom•a•hawk (tom′ə hôk′), *n.* a light ax used by American Indians as a weapon or tool.

to•ma•to (tə mā′tō, -mä′-), *n., pl.* **-toes. 1.** a large, pulpy berry, red when ripe, eaten as a vegetable. **2.** the plant bearing this berry.

tomb (tōōm), *n.* a grave or burial chamber for a corpse.

tom′boy′ *n.* an energetic, boisterous girl whose behavior is considered boyish. —**tom′boy′ish,** *adj.*

tomb′stone′ *n.* a stone marker on a tomb or grave.

tom′cat′ *n.* a male cat.

Tom Col′lins (kol′inz), *n.* a tall iced drink containing gin, lemon or lime juice, and carbonated water.

tome (tōm), *n.* a very heavy, large, or learned book.

tom•fool•er•y (tom′fōō′lə rē) *n.* foolish or silly behavior.

Tom′my gun′ *n.* a submachine gun.

tom′my•rot′ *n. Slang.* nonsense.

to•mor•row (tə môr′ō, -mor′ō), *n.* **1.** the day following today. **2.** a future period or time. —*adv.* **3.** on the day following today.

tom′-tom′ *n.* a drum of American Indian or Asian origin, usu. played with the hands.

ton (tun), *n.* a unit of weight, equivalent to 2000 pounds (0.907 metric ton) avoirdupois **(short ton)** in the U.S. and 2240 pounds (1.016 metric tons) avoirdupois **(long ton)** in Great Britain.

to•nal•i•ty (tō nal′i tē), *n., pl.* **-ties.** the sum of relations existing between the tones of a scale or musical system.

tone (tōn), *n., v.,* **toned, ton•ing.** —*n.* **1.** any sound considered with reference to its quality, pitch, etc. **2.** quality of sound. **3.** vocal sound. **4.** a musical sound of definite pitch. **b.** a musical interval, as A–B, encompassing two semitones. **5.** a tint or shade of a color. **6.** the normal state of tension or responsiveness of the body's organs or tissues. **7.** a particular style or manner, as of writing. **8.** prevailing character or style: *the liberal tone of the 1960s.* **9.** distinction or elegance. —*v.t.* **10.** to give a certain tone to. **11. tone down,** to soften or moderate. —**ton′al,** *adj.*

tone′-deaf′ *adj.* unable to distinguish differences in musical pitch.

tongs *n.* (*usu. with a pl. v.*) an implement consisting of two movable arms fastened together, used for picking up an object.

tongue (tung), *n.* **1.** a movable organ in the mouth, functioning in tasting, eating, and, in humans, speaking. **2.** the power of speech. **3.** manner or character of speech: *a flattering tongue.* **4.** a language or dialect. **5. tongues,** incomprehensible speech, typically uttered during religious ecstasy. **6.** anything resembling a tongue in shape or function. —*Idiom.* **7. hold one's tongue,** to refrain from speaking.

tongue′-lash′ing *n.* a severe scolding.

tongue′-tied′ *adj.* unable to speak, as from shyness.

tongue′ twist′er *n.* a sequence of words difficult to pronounce rapidly, as "She sells seashells by the seashore."

ton•ic (ton′ik), *n.* **1.** anything that invigorates or strengthens, as a medicine. **2.** carbonated water flavored with quinine, lemon, and lime. **3.** the first degree of a musical scale; keynote. —*adj.* **4.** invigorating physically, mentally, or morally. **5.** pertaining to or based on the keynote.

to•night (tə nīt′), *n.* **1.** this present or coming night. —*adv.* **2.** on this present night.

ton•nage (tun′ij), *n.* **1.** the capacity of a merchant ship, expressed in tons. **2.** ships collectively considered with reference to their carrying capacity.

ton•sil (ton′səl), *n.* a prominent oval mass of lymphoid tissue on each side of the throat.

ton•sil•lec•to•my (-sə lek′tə mē), *n., pl.* **-mies.** the surgical removal of one or both tonsils.

ton•sil•li•tis (-lī′tis), *n.* inflammation of the tonsils.

ton•so•ri•al (ton sôr′ē əl), *adj.* of a barber or barbering.

ton•sure (ton′shər), *n.* **1.** the shaving of the head or of some part of it upon entering the priesthood or a monastic order. **2.** the part of a cleric's head so shaven.

ton•y (tō′nē), *adj.,* **-i•er, -i•est.** stylish; swank.

too (tōō), *adv.* **1.** in addition. **2.** to an excessive degree. **3.** extremely; very: *none too pleased with the results.*

tool (tōōl), *n.* **1.** a hand implement for performing mechanical operations. **2.** the cutting or working part of a drill or similar machine. **3.** anything used for accomplishing a task or purpose. **4.** a person manipulated by another. —*v.t.* **5.** to work or shape with a tool. **6.** to work decoratively with a hand tool. **7. tool up,** to install machinery and tools for a job.

toot (tōōt), *v.i., v.t.* **1.** to sound (a horn or whistle) in quick, short blasts. —*n.* **2.** an act or sound of tooting. —**toot′er,** *n.*

tooth (tōōth), *n., pl.* **teeth. 1.** one of the hard bodies attached in a row to each jaw, used for biting and chewing. **2.** any projection suggesting a tooth, as on a comb. **3. teeth,** effective power to enforce something. —*Idiom.* **4. in the teeth of,** straight into, against, or in defiance of.

tooth′ache′ *n.* a pain in a tooth.

tooth′ and nail′ *adv.* with all one's resources or energy.

tooth′brush′ *n.* a small brush for cleaning the teeth.

tooth′paste′ *n.* a dentifrice in paste form.

tooth′pick′ *n.* a small pointed stick for removing food particles from between the teeth.

tooth′some (-səm), *adj.* **1.** pleasing to the taste. **2.** pleasing or desirable.

tooth•y (tōō′thē, -thē), *adj.,* **-i•er, -i•est.** having or displaying conspicuous teeth.

top[1] (top), *n., adj., v.,* **topped, top•ping.** —*n.* **1.** the highest or uppermost point, part, surface, or end of anything. **2.** a lid or covering of a container. **3.** the highest position or rank. **4.** the highest pitch or degree: *at the top of one's voice.* **5. tops,** the part of a plant that grows above ground. **6.** the crown of the head. —*adj.* **7.** of, situated at, or forming the top. **8.** chief or principal. —*v.t.* **9.** to furnish with a top. **10.** to be at the top of. **11.** to reach the top of. **12.** to exceed in amount, number, etc. **13.** to surpass or outdo. **14.** to remove the top of; prune. —*Idiom.* **15. on top,** successful. **16. on top of, a.** in addition to. **b.** in complete control.

top[2] (top), *n.* a cone-shaped toy with a point on which it is made to spin.

to•paz (tō′paz), *n.* a yellow or brownish mineral used as a gem.

top′ brass′ *n.* high-ranking officers or important officials.

top′coat′ *n.* a lightweight overcoat.

top′flight′ *adj.* excellent; superior.

top′ hat′ *n.* a man's tall hat with a stiff brim, worn on formal occasions.

top/-heav/y adj. having the top disproportionately heavy.

top•ic (top/ik), n. a subject of conversation, discussion, discourse, etc.

top/i•cal adj. dealing with matters of current or local interest.

top/ kick/ n. Mil. Slang. first sergeant.

top/mast/ n. the mast next above a lower mast on a sailing ship.

top/most/ adj. highest; uppermost.

top/notch/ adj. first-rate.

to•pog•ra•phy (tə pog/rə fē), n., pl. **-phies.** 1. the detailed mapping or charting of the physical features of an area. 2. the relief features or surface configuration of an area. —**top•o•graph•ic** (top/ə-graf/ik), adj.

top/per n. 1. one that tops. 2. Slang. top hat. 3. a short coat worn by women.

top/ping n. a sauce or garnish placed on food before serving.

top/ple v., **-pled, -pling.** —v.i. 1. to fall forward, as from being top-heavy. —v.t. 2. to cause to topple. 3. to overthrow.

top/-se/cret adj. of or designating the highest category of security classification.

top/soil/ n. the fertile, upper part of the soil.

top•sy-tur•vy (top/sē tûr/vē), adv., adj. 1. upside down. 2. in confusion or disorder.

tor (tôr) n. hill.

To•rah (tōr/ə, tôr/ə), n. (sometimes l.c.) 1. the Pentateuch. 2. a parchment scroll containing the Pentateuch, used in a synagogue. 3. the body of Jewish religious literature, law, and teaching. [< Heb tōrāh instruction, law]

torch (tôrch), n. 1. a light consisting of a stick ignited at the upper end. 2. a source of illumination or enlightenment. 3. a lamplike device producing a hot flame, as for soldering. 4. Chiefly Brit. FLASHLIGHT. —v.t. 5. to set fire to, esp. maliciously.

torch/bear/er n. 1. a person who carries a torch. 2. a leader in a movement, campaign, etc.

tor•e•a•dor (tôr/ē ə dôr/), n. a bullfighter.

tor•ment (v. tôr ment/, tôr/ment; n. tôr/ment), v.t. 1. to afflict with great bodily or mental suffering. 2. to worry or annoy excessively. —n. 3. a state of great bodily or mental suffering. 4. something that causes suffering. —**tor•men/tor,** n.

tor•na•do (tôr nā/dō), n., pl. **-does, -dos.** a violent windstorm occurring over land, characterized by a funnel-shaped cloud that extends to the ground. [< Sp tronada thunderstorm ≪ L tonāre to thunder]

tor•pe•do (tôr pē/dō), n., pl. **-does.** 1. a self-propelled underwater missile containing explosives. 2. any of various other explosive devices. —v.t. 3. to attack, destroy, etc., with or as if with torpedoes.

tor•pid (tôr/pid), adj. 1. inactive or sluggish. 2. apathetic; lethargic. —**tor•pid/i•ty,** n.

tor/por (-pər) n. 1. sluggish inactivity or inertia. 2. lethargic indifference; apathy.

torque (tôrk), n. something that produces or tends to produce torsion or rotation.

tor•rent (tôr/ənt, tor/-), n. 1. a rushing, violent stream of water. 2. a violent or abundant stream of anything. —**tor•ren•tial** (tô ren/shəl, tə-), adj. —**tor•ren/tial•ly,** adv.

tor•rid (tôr/id, tor/-), adj. 1. subject to parching heat, esp. of the sun. 2. oppressively hot. 3. ardent; passionate.

tor•sion (tôr/shən), n. 1. the act of twisting or state of being twisted. 2. the twisting of an object by two equal and opposite torques. —**tor/sion•al,** adj.

tor•so (tôr/sō), n., pl. **-sos, -si** (-sē). the trunk of the human body.

tort (tôrt), n. Law. a wrongful act resulting in injury, for which the injured party is entitled to compensation.

torte (tôrt; Ger. tôʀ/tə), n., pl. **tortes** (tôrts), Ger. **tor•ten** (tôʀ/tn). a rich cake made with eggs, ground nuts, and little or no flour.

tor•tel•li•ni (tôr/tl ē/nē), n. (used with a sing. or pl. v.) small ring-shaped pieces of pasta filled with meat, cheese, etc.

tor•til•la (tôr tē/ə), n., pl. **-las.** a thin, round, unleavened bread made from cornmeal or flour.

tor•toise (tôr/təs), n. a turtle, esp. a terrestrial one.

tor/toise•shell/ n. the horny brown and yellow outer layer of the shell of certain turtles, used for combs and ornaments.

tor•tu•ous (tôr/chōō əs), adj. 1. full of turns or bends; twisting; winding. 2. deceitfully indirect; devious. —**tor/tu•ous•ly,** adv. —**tor/tu•ous•ness,** n.

tor•ture (tôr/chər), n., v., **-tured, -tur•ing.** —n. 1. the act of inflicting excruciating pain, esp. as a means of punishment or coercion. 2. extreme anguish of body or mind. —v.t. 3. to subject to torture. 4. to twist, as in shape. —**tor/tur•er,** n. —**tor/tur•ous,** adj.

To•ry (tôr/ē), n., pl. **-ries.** 1. a member of the Conservative Party in Great Britain or Canada. 2. (often l.c.) a conservative. 3. a person who supported the British in the American Revolution.

toss (tôs, tos), v., **tossed** or **tost** (tôst, tost), **toss•ing,** n. —v.t. 1. to throw lightly or carelessly. 2. to throw or fling about. 3. to jerk upward suddenly, as the head. —v.i. 4. to move irregularly, as a ship on a rough sea. 5. to move restlessly about, esp. on a bed. 6. to throw a coin into the air to decide something by the way it falls (sometimes fol. by up). —n. 7. an act or instance of tossing.

toss/up/ n. 1. the tossing of a coin to decide something. 2. an even chance.

tot¹ (tot), n. 1. a small child. 2. a small portion, as of liquor.

tot² (tot), v.t., v.i., **tot•ted, tot•ting.** to add; total (often fol. by up).

to•tal (tōt/l), adj., n., v., **-taled, -tal•ing** or (esp. Brit.) **-talled, -tal•ling.** —adj. 1. comprising a whole; entire. 2. complete; utter: a total failure. —n. 3. the total amount. —v.t. 4. to bring to a total. 5. to reach a total of. 6. to demolish beyond repair. —v.i. 7. to amount. —**to•tal/i•ty,** n. —**to/tal•ly,** adv.

to•tal•i•tar•i•an (tō tal/i târ/ē ən), adj. 1. noting or pertaining to a government in which one party exercises dictatorial control. —n. 2. an adherent of totalitarian government. —**to•tal/i•tar/i•an•ism,** n.

tote (tōt), v., **tot•ed, tot•ing,** n. —v.t. 1. to carry or transport. —n. 2. an open handbag or shopping bag.

tote/ bag/ n. an open handbag.

to•tem (tō/təm), n. 1. a natural object or animate being assumed as the emblem of a clan or family. 2. a representation of such an object or being. —**to•tem/ic** (-tem/ik), adj.

to/tem pole/ n. a pole carved and painted with totemic figures by Indians of the NW coast of North America.

tot•ter (tot/ər), v.i. 1. to walk with faltering steps. 2. to sway on the ground, as if about to fall.

tou•can (tōō/kan, -kän), n. a brightly colored bird of the New World tropics, with a very large bill.

touch (tuch), v.t. 1. to put the hand, finger, etc., into contact with, so as to feel. 2. to bring into contact with an object or surface. 3. to come into contact with; be adjacent to. 4. to attain equality with. 5. to color slightly. 6. to affect in some way. 7. to move to tenderness or sympathy. 8. to handle, use, or consume. 9. Slang. to seek or get money from. —v.i. 10. to touch someone or something. 11. to come into or be in contact. 12. **touch down,** (of an aircraft or spacecraft) to land. 13. ~ **up,** to make minor improvements in the appearance of. —n. 14. the act of touching or state of being touched. 15. that sense by which an object is perceived by physical contact. 16. ability; knack. 17. relationship or communication: Let's keep in touch. 18. a slight attack of illness. 19. a slight addition or change in completing any piece of work: finishing touches. 20. the manner of fingering a keyboard instrument. 21. a slight trace. —**touch/a•ble,** adj.

touch/ and go/ n. a precarious state of affairs. —**touch/-and-go/,** adj.

touch/down/ *n.* **1.** the act of scoring six points in football by being in possession of the ball on or behind the opponent's goal line. **2.** the act or moment of landing, as of an aircraft.

tou•ché (tōō shā/), *interj.* (used to acknowledge a touch in fencing or a telling remark or rejoinder.)

touched *adj.* **1.** moved; stirred. **2.** slightly crazy; unbalanced.

touch/ing *adj.* affecting; moving; pathetic.

touch/-me-not/ *n.* yellow-flowered plant whose ripe seed vessels burst open when touched.

touch/stone/ *n.* a test or criterion for the qualities of a thing.

touch/y *adj.*, **-i•er, -i•est. 1.** apt to take offense on slight provocation. **2.** requiring tactfulness in handling. —**touch/i•ness,** *n.*

tough (tuf), *adj.*, **-er, -est,** *n.* —*adj.* **1.** strong and durable. **2.** difficult to chew. **3.** sturdy; hardy. **4.** unyielding; stubborn. **5.** hardened; incorrigible. **6.** difficult to perform, accomplish, or deal with. **7.** vicious; unruly; or rough. —*n.* **8.** a ruffian. —**tough/en,** *v.t., v.i.*

tou•pee (tōō pā/), *n., pl.* **-pees.** a patch of false hair for covering a bald spot.

tour (tŏŏr), *n.* **1.** a long journey including the visiting of a number of places. **2.** a journey from town to town, as by a performer. **3.** a period of duty at one place or in one job. —*v.i., v.t.* **4.** to go on a tour (through).

tour de force (tŏŏr/ də fôrs/), *n., pl.* **tours de force** (tŏŏrz). an exceptional achievement by an artist, author, or the like. [< F: feat of strength or skill]

tour/ism *n.* **1.** the occupation of providing various services to tourists. **2.** the promotion of tourist travel.

tour/ist *n.* a person who makes a tour, esp. for pleasure.

tour•na•ment (tŏŏr/nə mənt, tûr/-), *n.* **1.** a contest in which a number of competitors take part in a series of matches. **2.** a medieval contest in which mounted knights fought with blunted lances for a prize.

tour•ni•quet (tûr/ni kit, tŏŏr/-), *n.* any device for stopping bleeding by compressing a blood vessel, as a bandage tightened by twisting.

tou•sle (tou/zəl, -səl), *v.t.*, **-sled, -sling.** to disorder or dishevel, as hair.

tout (tout), *Informal.* —*v.i.* **1.** to solicit business, votes, etc., importunately. —*v.t.* **2.** to solicit importunately. **3.** to praise extravagantly. **4.** to sell information on (a racehorse).

tow (tō), *v.t.* **1.** to pull or haul (a car, barge, etc.) by a rope or chain. —*n.* **2.** an act or instance of towing. **3.** something towed. —*Idiom.* **4. in tow, a.** being towed. **b.** in one's charge.

to•ward (tôrd, twôrd) also **-wards/,** *prep.* **1.** in the direction of. **2.** for: *saving money toward a house.* **3.** turned to; facing. **4.** shortly before: *toward midnight.* **5.** with respect to.

tow/boat/ *n.* a boat for pushing barges.

tow•el (tou/əl, toul), *n., v.*, **-eled, -el•ing** or (*esp. Brit.*) **-elled, -el•ling.** —*n.* **1.** an absorbent cloth or paper for wiping and drying something wet. —*v.t.* **2.** to wipe or dry with a towel.

tow/el•ing *n.* a fabric used for hand towels or dishtowels. Also, *esp. Brit.,* **tow/el•ling.**

tow•er (tou/ər), *n.* **1.** a structure higher than it is wide, either isolated or forming part of a building. **2.** such a structure used as a stronghold or fortress. **3.** a vertical case designed to house a computer system standing on the floor. —*v.i.* **4.** to reach or stand high.

tow/er•ing *adj.* **1.** very high or tall. **2.** surpassing others. **3.** extreme or intense.

tow•head (tō/hed/), *n.* **1.** a head of very light blond hair. **2.** a person with such hair. —**tow/head/ed,** *adj.*

town (toun), *n.* **1.** a thickly populated area, usu. smaller than a city and larger than a village. **2.** a city or borough. **3.** a township. **4.** the inhabitants of a town. —*Idiom.* **5. go to town,** *Informal.* to

do something with speed and efficiency. **6. on the town,** *Informal.* out to have a good time.

town/ house/ *n.* one of a group of similar houses joined by common side walls.

town/ meet/ing *n.* a meeting of the voters of a town, esp. in New England.

town/ship *n.* a unit of local government, usu. a subdivision of a county.

towns/peo/ple *n.pl.* the inhabitants of a town.

tow•path (tō/path/, -päth/), *n.* a path along the bank of a canal or river, for use in towing boats.

tox•e•mi•a (tok sē/mē ə), *n.* blood poisoning resulting from the presence of toxins in the blood. —**tox•e/mic,** *adj.*

tox•ic (tok/sik), *adj.* **1.** of or caused by a toxin. **2.** poisonous. —**tox•ic•i•ty** (-sis/i tē), *n.*

tox/i•col/o•gy (-si kol/ə jē), *n.* the branch of pharmacology dealing with the effects, antidotes, etc., of poisons. —**tox/i•col/o•gist,** *n.*

tox/ic shock/ syn/drome *n.* a rapidly developing toxemia, occurring esp. in women using high-absorbency tampons.

tox•in (tok/sin), *n.* a poison produced by an animal, plant, or bacterium.

toy (toi), *n., adj., v.,* **toyed, toy•ing.** —*n.* **1.** an object for children to play with. **2.** a thing of little importance. —*adj.* **3.** made for use as a toy. **4.** resembling a toy, esp. in size. —*v.i.* **5.** to play or trifle: *to toy with one's food.*

trace¹ (trās), *n., v.,* **traced, trac•ing.** —*n.* **1.** a surviving mark or sign of the former existence or action of some agent or event. **2.** a barely discernible quantity or quality. —*v.t.* **3.** to follow the track or trail of. **4.** to follow the course or development of. **5.** to ascertain by investigation. **6.** to draw (a line, figure, etc.). **7.** to copy (a drawing) by following its lines on a superimposed transparent sheet. —**trace/a•ble,** *adj.*

trace² (trās), *n.* either of the two straps or chains by which a vehicle is drawn by a harnessed draft animal.

trac/er•y *n., pl.* **-ies.** ornamental work consisting of branching ribs, bars, or the like.

tra•che•a (trā/kē ə), *n., pl.* **-che•ae** (-kē ē/), **-che•as.** a tube extending from the larynx to the bronchi, through which air passes in breathing; windpipe. —**tra/che•al,** *adj.*

tra/che•ot/o•my (-ot/ə mē), *n., pl.* **-mies.** the operation of cutting into the trachea.

track (trak), *n.* **1.** a pair of parallel lines of rails on which a train runs. **2.** a mark or series of marks left by an animal, person, or vehicle in passing. **3.** a path; trail. **4.** a course of action or procedure. **5.** a sequence of events or ideas. **6. a.** a course laid out for running or racing. **b.** sports performed on such a course. **c.** track and field events as a whole. **7.** a band of recorded sound, as on a phonograph record. —*v.t.* **8.** to follow the track of. **9.** to make footprints on or with. **10.** to monitor the path of (an aircraft, hurricane, etc.). —*Idiom.* **11. keep (or lose) track,** to keep (or fail to keep) informed. —**track/er,** *n.* —**track/less,** *adj.*

track/ball/ *n.* a computer input device for controlling the pointer on a display screen by rotating a ball set inside a case.

track/ record/ *n.* a record of achievements or performance.

tract¹ (trakt), *n.* **1.** an expanse or area of land. **2.** a definite region of the body, esp. a system of organs: *the digestive tract.*

tract² (trakt), *n.* a brief pamphlet, usu. on a religious or political topic.

trac•ta•ble (trak/tə bəl), *adj.* **1.** easily managed or controlled. **2.** easily shaped; malleable. —**trac/ta•bil/i•ty,** *n.*

trac•tion (trak/shən), *n.* **1.** the adhesive friction of a body on some surface, as a tire on a road. **2.** the act of drawing or pulling. **3.** the state of being drawn or pulled.

trac•tor (trak/tər), *n.* **1.** a motor-driven vehicle with large, heavy treads, used for pulling machinery. **2.** a truck with a driver's cab but no body, used for hauling a trailer.

trade (trād), *n.*, *v.*, **trad•ed, trad•ing.** —*n.* **1.** the act of buying or selling commodities. **2.** a purchase or sale. **3.** an exchange of items. **4.** an occupation requiring skilled manual or mechanical work. **5.** the customers of a business. —*v.t.* **6.** to buy and sell. **7.** to exchange. —*v.i.* **8.** to carry on trade. **9.** to make an exchange. **10. trade on** or **upon,** to turn to one's advantage. —**trad′er,** *n.*

trade′-in′ *n.* goods given in whole or part payment of a purchase.

trade′mark′ *n.* **1.** any name, symbol, etc., used and usu. officially registered by a manufacturer or merchant to distinguish a product from those of competitors. —*v.t.* **2.** to register the trademark of.

trade′ name′ *n.* **1.** a name used in a trade to designate a commodity, service, etc. **2.** the name under which a firm does business.

trade′-off′ or **trade′off′,** *n.* the exchange of one thing for another, esp. to effect a compromise.

trades′man *n.*, *pl.* **-men. 1.** a craftsman; artisan. **2.** *Chiefly Brit.* a shopkeeper.

trade′ un′ion *n.* LABOR UNION.

trade′ wind′ (wind), *n.* any of the winds blowing mainly from the northeast in the Northern Hemisphere and from the southeast in the Southern Hemisphere.

tra•di•tion (trə dish′ən), *n.* **1.** the handing down of legends, customs, etc., from generation to generation, esp. by word of mouth. **2.** something that is so handed down. **3.** a long-established way of thinking or acting. —**tra•di′tion•al,** *adj.* —**tra•di′tion•al•ist,** *n.* —**tra•di′tion•al•ly,** *adv.*

tra•duce (trə dōōs′, -dyōōs′), *v.t.*, **-duced, -duc•ing.** to slander; defame.

traf•fic (traf′ik), *n.*, *v.*, **-ficked, -fick•ing.** —*n.* **1.** the movement of vehicles, persons, etc., in an area or over a route. **2.** the quantity, intensity, or rate of such movement. **3.** trade; commercial dealings. **4.** communication or dealings between persons or groups. —*v.i.* **5.** to carry on traffic, esp. illegally. —**traf′fick•er,** *n.*

traf′fic cir′cle *n.* a circular roadway at a multiple intersection to facilitate the passage of vehicles from one road to another.

traf′fic light′ *n.* a set of signal lights used to direct traffic at intersections.

tra•ge•di•an (trə jē′dē ən), *n.* an actor who performs tragic roles.

tra•ge′di•enne′ (-en′), *n.* an actress who performs tragic roles.

trag•e•dy (traj′i dē), *n.*, *pl.* **-dies. 1.** an unfortunate or dreadful event or affair. **2.** a drama dealing with a serious or somber theme and ending in disaster. —**trag′ic,** *adj.* —**trag′i•cal•ly,** *adv.*

trail (trāl), *v.t.* **1.** to draw or drag along behind. **2.** to follow the track or scent of. **3.** to follow along behind, as in a race. —*v.i.* **4.** to drag along the ground or some other surface. **5.** to float after something moving, as smoke does. **6.** to gradually become weaker or smaller: *Her voice trailed off into silence.* **7.** to lag behind. **8.** to grow along the ground rather than taking root. —*n.* **9.** a path in overgrown or rough terrain. **10.** the track, scent, etc., left by an animal, person, or thing. **11.** something that trails behind.

trail′blaz′er *n.* **1.** a person who blazes a trail. **2.** a pioneer in any field.

trail′er *n.* **1.** a large vehicle drawn by another vehicle, used esp. in hauling freight. **2.** a vehicle attached to an automobile and used as a mobile home. **3.** one that trails.

train (trān), *n.* **1.** a connected group of railroad cars pulled by a locomotive. **2.** a line of persons, vehicles, etc., traveling together. **3.** something drawn along, as a trailing skirt. **4.** a body of followers; retinue. **5.** a series of events, ideas, etc. —*v.t.* **6.** to form the habits, thoughts, or behavior of by discipline and instruction. **7.** to make proficient by instruction and practice. **8.** to make fit, as for an athletic performance. **9.** to bring (a plant) into a particular shape or position. **10.** to point or direct, as a firearm. —*v.i.* **11.** to be trained. —**train•ee′,** *n.*, *pl.* **-ees.** —**train′er,** *n.* —**train′ing,** *n.*

traipse (trāps), *v.i.*, *v.t.*, **traipsed, traips•ing.** to walk (over) aimlessly or idly.

trait (trāt), *n.* a distinguishing characteristic or quality.

trai•tor (trā′tər), *n.* a person who betrays another, a cause, or any trust. —**trai′tor•ous,** *adj.*

tra•jec•to•ry (trə jek′tə rē), *n.*, *pl.* **-ries.** the curve described by a projectile in its flight.

tram (tram), *n. Brit.* a streetcar.

tram•mel (tram′əl), *n.*, *v.*, **-meled, -mel•ing** or (*esp. Brit.*) **-melled, -mel•ling.** —*n.* **1.** Usu., **-mels.** a hindrance to free action; restraint. —*v.t.* **2.** to hinder or restrain.

tramp (tramp), *v.i.* **1.** to walk with a firm, heavy step. **2.** to travel on foot; hike. —*v.t.* **3.** to step on heavily; trample. **4.** to traverse on foot. —*n.* **5.** a firm, heavy tread. **6.** the sound made by such a tread. **7.** a long, steady walk. **8.** a vagabond; vagrant. **9.** a promiscuous woman. **10.** a freight ship that takes a cargo wherever shippers desire.

tram′ple (-pəl), *v.*, **-pled, -pling.** —*v.i.* **1.** to tread heavily. —*v.t.* **2.** to tread heavily, roughly, or carelessly on.

tram•po•line (tram′pə lēn′, -lin), *n.* a canvas sheet attached by springs to a frame, used in tumbling.

trance (trans, träns), *n.* **1.** a half-conscious and sleeplike state, as that produced by hypnosis. **2.** a dazed condition. **3.** a state of complete mental absorption.

tran•quil (trang′kwil), *adj.* peaceful; calm. [< L *tranquillus*] —**tran•quil′li•ty, tran•quil′i•ty,** *n.* —**tran′quil•ly,** *adv.*

tran′quil•ize′ or **-quil•ize′,** *v.t.*, *v.i.*, **-quil•ized** or **-quil•ized, -quil•iz•ing** or **-quil•iz•ing.** to make or become tranquil.

tran′quil•iz′er or **-quil•liz′er,** *n.* a drug that has a calming or muscle-relaxing effect.

trans- a prefix meaning: across, through, or on the other side (*transatlantic*); changing thoroughly (*transmute*); beyond or surpassing (*transnational*).

trans. 1. transitive. **2.** translated. **3.** translation.

trans•act (tran sakt′, -zakt′), *v.t.* to carry on or conduct (business, negotiations, etc.).

trans•ac′tion *n.* **1.** the act of transacting or fact of being transacted. **2.** something transacted, esp. a business agreement. **3. transactions,** the published record of the proceedings of a learned society.

trans•at•lan•tic (trans′ət lan′tik, tranz′-), *adj.* **1.** crossing the Atlantic. **2.** situated beyond the Atlantic.

trans•ceiv•er (tran sē′vər), *n.* a radio transmitter and receiver combined in one unit.

tran•scend (tran send′), *v.t.* **1.** to go beyond the ordinary limits of. **2.** to surpass; excel. —**tran•scend′ence,** *n.*

tran•scend′ent *adj.* **1.** extraordinary. **2.** superior; supreme.

tran•scen•den•tal (tran′sen den′tl, -sən-), *adj.* **1.** being beyond ordinary experience, thought, or belief; supernatural. **2.** abstract or metaphysical.

trans•con•ti•nen•tal (trans′kon tn en′tl), *adj.* **1.** extending across a continent. **2.** on the other side of a continent.

tran•scribe (tran skrīb′), *v.t.*, **-scribed, -scrib•ing. 1.** to make a written or typed copy of (spoken material). **2.** to represent (speech sounds) in written phonetic symbols. **3.** to make a musical transcription of.

tran′script (-skript), *n.* **1.** a written, typewritten, or printed copy of something transcribed. **2.** an official copy, as of a student's academic record.

tran•scrip′tion *n.* **1.** the act of transcribing. **2.** a transcript; copy. **3.** the arrangement of a musical composition for a medium other than that for which it was written.

trans•duc•er (trans dōō′sər, -dyōō′-, tranz-), *n.* a device, such as a microphone, that converts a signal from one form of energy to another.

tran•sept (tran′sept), *n.* **1.** the part of a church crossing the nave at right angles. **2.** an arm of this.

trans•fer (*v.* trans fûr′, trans′fər; *n.* trans′fər), *v.*, **-ferred, -fer•ring,** *n.* —*v.t.* **1.** to convey or remove from one place or person to another. **2.** *Law.* to make over the possession or control of. **3.** to convey (a drawing) from one surface to another. —*v.i.* **4.** to transfer oneself or be transferred. **5.** to change from one bus, train, etc., to another. —*n.* **6.** the act of transferring or fact of being transferred. **7.** a ticket entitling a passenger to change to another bus, train, etc. **8.** a person who has transferred, as to another college. **9.** *Law.* the conveyance of property to another. —**trans•fer′a•ble,** *adj.* —**trans•fer′al,** *n.* —**trans•fer′ence,** *n.*

trans•fig′ure *v.t.,* **-ured, -ur•ing. 1.** to change in outward appearance. **2.** to change so as to glorify or exalt. —**trans′fig•u•ra′tion,** *n.*

trans•fix′ *v.t.,* **-fixed** or **fixt, fix•ing. 1.** to make motionless, as with awe. **2.** to pierce through with or as if with a pointed weapon.

trans•form′ *v.t.* **1.** to change in form or appearance. **2.** to change in condition, nature, or character. —**trans′for•ma′tion,** *n.*

trans•form′er *n.* **1.** one that transforms. **2.** a device that transfers electrical energy from one circuit to another, usu. with a change in voltage.

trans•fuse′ (-fyōōz′), *v.t.,* **-fused, -fus•ing. 1.** to transfer from one to another; instill. **2.** to diffuse into or through. **3.** to transfer (blood) by injection into a vein or artery. —**trans•fu′sion,** *n.*

trans•gress (trans gres′, tranz-), *v.i.* **1.** to violate a law, moral code, etc. —*v.t.* **2.** to go beyond (a limit or bound). —**trans•gres′sion** (-gresh′ən), *n.* —**trans•gres′sor,** *n.*

tran•sient (tran′shənt, -zhənt, -zē ənt), *adj.* **1.** not permanent; transitory. **2.** lasting or staying only a short time. —*n.* **3.** a transient person, esp. a temporary boarder.

tran•sis•tor (tran zis′tər), *n.* **1.** a compact electronic device that performs the primary functions of a vacuum tube but uses less power. **2.** a radio that uses transistors.

tran•sit (tran′sit, -zit), *n.* **1.** the act or fact of passing across or through. **2.** transportation of persons or goods from one place to another. **3.** a system of urban public transportation. **4.** a surveyor's instrument for measuring angles.

tran•si•tion (tran zish′ən, -sish′-), *n.* passage from one position, state, etc., to another. —**tran•si′tion•al,** *adj.*

tran•si•tive (tran′si tiv, -zi-), *adj.* of or designating a verb that takes a direct object. —**tran′si•tive•ly,** *adv.*

tran•si•to•ry (tran′si tôr′ē, -zi-), *adj.* lasting only a short time; temporary.

trans•late (trans lāt′, tranz-, trans′lāt, tranz′-), *v.t.,* **-lat•ed, -lat•ing. 1.** to turn from one language into another. **2.** to change the form, condition, or nature of. **3.** to explain in simpler terms. —**trans•lat′a•ble,** *adj.* —**trans•la′tion,** *n.* —**trans•la′tor,** *n.*

trans•lit′er•ate′ (-lit′ə rāt′), *v.t.,* **-at•ed, -at•ing.** to change (letters or words) into characters of another alphabet. —**trans•lit′er•a′tion,** *n.*

trans•lu′cent (-lōō′sənt), *adj.* permitting light to pass through but diffusing it so that objects are not clearly visible. —**trans•lu′cence,** *n.*

trans′mi•gra′tion *n.* passage of soul into another body.

trans•mis′sion (-mish′ən), *n.* **1.** the act or process of transmitting. **2.** something transmitted. **3. a.** the transference of force between machines or mechanisms. **b.** a unit of gears for this purpose, as in an automobile. **4.** the broadcasting of radio waves from one location to another.

trans•mit′ (-mit′), *v.t.,* **-mit•ted, -mit•ting. 1.** to send or convey from one person or place to another. **2.** to pass on by heredity. **3.** to cause (light, sound, etc.) to pass through a medium. **4.** to emit (radio or television signals).

trans•mit′ter *n.* **1.** one that transmits. **2.** a device for transmitting signals, as in radio.

trans•mog′ri•fy′ (-mog′rə fī′) *v.t.,* **-fied, -fy.ing.** to change in appearance or form; transform.

trans•mute′ (-myōōt′), *v.t., v.i.,* **-mut•ed, -mut•ing.** to change from one nature, substance, etc., into another. —**trans•mut′a•ble,** *adj.* —**trans′mu•ta′tion,** *n.*

trans•na′tion•al *adj.* going beyond national boundaries or interests.

trans′o•ce•an′ic *adj.* crossing the ocean.

tran•som (tran′səm), *n.* **1.** a crosspiece separating a door or window from a window above it. **2.** a window above such a crosspiece.

trans′pa•cif′ic (trans′-), *adj.* **1.** crossing the Pacific. **2.** situated beyond the Pacific.

trans•par′ent (-pâr′ənt), *adj.* **1.** transmitting rays of light through its substance so that objects beyond can be distinctly seen. **2.** so sheer as to permit light to pass through. **3.** easily recognized or detected. **4.** easily understood; obvious. —**trans•par′en•cy,** *n., pl.* **-cies.**

tran•spire (tran spī′r′), *v.i.,* **-spired, -spir•ing. 1.** to occur; happen. **2.** to give off waste matter, watery vapor, etc., through the surface. **3.** to become known.

trans•plant (*v.* trans plant′, -plänt′; *n.* trans′-plant′, -plänt′), *v.t.* **1.** to remove and plant in another place. **2.** to transfer (an organ or tissue) from one part of the body or from one individual to another. **3.** to bring from one region to another for settlement. —*n.* **4.** the act of transplanting. **5.** something transplanted. —**trans′plan•ta′tion,** *n.*

trans•port (*v.* trans pôrt′; *n.* trans′pôrt), *v.t.* **1.** to carry or convey from one place to another. **2.** to carry away by strong emotion. —*n.* **3.** the act of transporting. **4.** a means of transporting, as a ship. **5.** strong emotion, as of joy. —**trans•port′er,** *n.*

trans′por•ta′tion (-pər tā′shən), *n.* **1.** the act of transporting or state of being transported. **2.** the means of transport. **3.** the business of conveying people, goods, etc.

trans•pose′ (-pōz′), *v.t.,* **-posed, -pos•ing. 1.** to reverse the position or order of. **2.** to put (a musical composition) into a different key. —**trans′po•si′-tion** (-pə zish′ən), *n.*

trans•sex′u•al *n.* **1.** a person who desires to belong to the opposite sex. **2.** a person whose sex has been changed by surgery.

trans•ship′ *v.t., v.i.,* **-shipped, -ship•ping.** to transfer from one ship, truck, freight car, or other conveyance to another. —**trans•ship′ment,** *n.*

trans′sub•stan′ti•a′tion *n.* (in the Eucharist) conversion of whole substance of bread and wine into body and blood of Christ.

trans•verse′ (trans vûrs′, tranz-; trans′vûrs, tranz′-), *adj.* **1.** lying or extending across. —*n.* **2.** something transverse. —**trans•verse′ly,** *adv.*

trans•ves•tite (trans ves′tīt, tranz-), *n.* a person who assumes the dress of the opposite sex, esp. for psychological gratification. —**trans•ves′tism,** *n.*

trap¹ (trap), *n., v.,* **trapped, trap•ping.** —*n.* **1.** a device for catching game or other animals, as one that springs shut suddenly. **2.** any stratagem for catching a person unawares. **3.** a U-shaped section in a pipe for preventing the escape of air or gases. **4.** **traps,** the percussion instruments of a band. —*v.t.* **5.** to catch in or as if in a trap. —*v.i.* **6.** to trap animals for their furs. —**trap′per,** *n.*

trap² (trap), *v.t.,* **trapped, trap•ping.** to furnish with trappings.

tra•peze (tra pēz′, trə-), *n.* a short horizontal bar attached to the ends of two suspended ropes, used in acrobatics.

trap•e•zoid (trap′ə zoid′), *n.* a quadrilateral plane figure with two parallel sides. —**trap′e•zoi′dal,** *adj.*

trap′pings *n.pl.* **1.** ornamental articles of equipment or dress. **2.** conventional outward forms or symbols. **3.** an ornamental covering for a horse.

trap′shoot′ing *n.* the sport of shooting at clay pigeons hurled into the air from a trap.

trash (trash), *n.* **1.** anything worthless or useless. **2.** a disreputable person. **3.** such persons collectively. —*v.t.* **4.** to vandalize. **5.** to criticize as worthless. —**trash′y,** *adj.,* **-i•er, -i•est.**

trau•ma (trou′mə, trô′-), *n., pl.* **-mas, -ma•ta** (-mə tə). **1.** a bodily injury, as from an accident. **2.** psychological shock from experiencing a disastrous event. **3.** any distressing experience. —**trau•mat′ic**

(trə mat′ik, trô-, trou-), *adj.* —**trau′ma•tize′**, *v.t.*, **-tized, -tiz•ing.**

tra•vail (trə vāl′, trav′āl), *n.* **1.** painfully burdensome work. **2.** pain resulting from mental or physical hardship.

trav•el (trav′əl), *v.*, **-eled, -el•ing** or (*esp. Brit.*) **-elled, -el•ling,** *n.* —*v.i.* **1.** to go from one place to another. **2.** to pass or be transmitted, as light. —*v.t.* **3.** to journey or pass through or over. —*n.* **4.** the act of traveling, esp. to distant places. —**trav′el•er, trav′el•ler,** *n.*

tra•verse (*v.* trə vûrs′, trav′ərs; *n., adj.* trav′ərs, trə vûrs′), *v.*, **-versed, -vers•ing,** *n., adj.* —*v.t.* **1.** to pass or move over, along, or through. **2.** to extend across or over. **3.** to move laterally. —*n.* **trav• erse 4.** something that crosses or extends across. —*adj.* **trav•erse 5.** lying or extending across.

trav•es•ty (trav′ə stē), *n., pl.* **-ties,** *v.,* **-tied, -ty• ing.** —*n.* **1.** a grotesque or debased imitation. —*v.t.* **2.** to make a travesty of.

trawl (trôl), *n.* **1.** a strong net dragged along the sea bottom to catch fish. **2.** a buoyed line with many short, baited fishing lines attached. —*v.i., v.t.* **3.** to fish or catch with a trawl. —**trawl•er,** *n.*

tray (trā), *n., pl.* **trays.** a flat, shallow receptacle with raised edges, for carrying or holding articles.

treach•er•ous (trech′ər əs), *adj.* **1.** likely to betray trust. **2.** deceptive or untrustworthy. **3.** dangerous. —**treach′er•ous•ly,** *adv.* —**treach′er•ous•ness,** *n.*

treach′er•y *n., pl.* **-ies.** betrayal of trust or allegiance.

tread (tred), *v.*, **trod, trod•den** or **trod, tread•ing,** *n.* —*v.i.* **1.** to step or walk. **2.** to trample. —*v.t.* **3.** to walk on, in, or along. **4.** to trample underfoot. **5.** to perform by walking or dancing: *to tread a measure.* —*n.* **6.** the act, sound, or manner of treading. **7.** something on which a person or thing treads, stands, or moves. **8.** the pattern raised on the face of a rubber tire.

trea•dle (tred′l), *n.* a lever worked by the foot to impart motion to a machine.

tread′mill′ *n.* **1.** a device worked by treading on moving steps or an endless moving belt. **2.** an exercise machine that allows the user to walk or run in place, usu. on an endless belt. **3.** a monotonous routine.

trea•son (trē′zən), *n.* a violation of allegiance to one's country, esp. by acting to overthrow the government. —**trea′son•a•ble, trea′son•ous,** *adj.*

treas•ure (trezh′ər), *n., v.,* **-ured, -ur•ing.** —*n.* **1.** accumulated wealth, as money or jewels. **2.** any person or thing greatly valued. —*v.t.* **3.** to regard as precious. **4.** to put away, as for future use. [< OF < L *thēsaurus* storehouse, hoard]

treas′ur•er *n.* an officer in charge of the receipt, care, and disbursement of money.

treas′ure-trove′ (-trōv′), *n.* **1.** anything valuable that one finds. **2.** treasure of unknown ownership, found hidden in the earth or elsewhere.

treas′ur•y *n., pl.* **-ies. 1.** a place where the funds of a government, corporation, etc., are kept. **2.** public or private funds or revenue. **3.** (*cap.*) the department of government that has control over the public revenue.

treat (trēt), *v.t.* **1.** to act or behave toward in some specified way. **2.** to consider or regard in a specified way. **3.** to give medical or surgical care to. **4.** to subject to some agent or action to achieve a particular result. **5.** to provide with food, gifts, etc., at one's own expense. **6.** to deal with in speech, writing, art, etc. —*v.i.* **7.** to deal with a subject. —*n.* **8.** entertainment, food, etc., paid for by another. **9.** anything that affords particular pleasure or enjoyment.

trea•tise (trē′tis), *n.* a formal exposition in writing of some subject.

treat′ment *n.* **1.** the act, manner, or process of treating. **2.** medicinal, surgical, or therapeutic care.

trea•ty (trē′tē), *n., pl.* **-ties.** a formal agreement between two or more nations.

tre•ble (treb′əl), *adj., v., n.,* **-bled, -bling.** —*adj.* **1.** threefold; triple. **2. a.** of the highest part in harmonized music. **b.** of the highest pitch or range. —*n.*

3. a. the treble part. **b.** a treble voice or instrument. **4.** a high-pitched voice or sound. —*v.t., v.i.* **5.** to triple.

tree (trē), *n., v.,* **treed, tree•ing.** —*n.* **1.** a plant with a permanently woody trunk and branches. **2.** something resembling a tree in shape: *a clothes tree.* —*v.t.* **3.** to drive up a tree.

tre•foil (trē′foil, tref′oil), *n.* **1.** a plant having leaves with three leaflets, as the clover. **2.** a three-lobed figure or design.

trek (trek), *v.,* **trekked, trek•king,** *n.* —*v.i.* **1.** to travel slowly or with difficulty. —*n.* **2.** a journey involving hardship.

trel•lis (trel′is), *n.* a lattice used as a support for growing vines.

trem•a•tode (trem′ə tōd′, trē′mə-), *n.* any of various parasitic flatworms with external suckers.

trem•ble (trem′bəl), *v.,* **-bled, -bling,** *n.* —*v.i.* **1.** to shake involuntarily, as from fear or cold. **2.** to be troubled with fear. **3.** to quiver or vibrate: *His voice trembled.* —*n.* **4.** the act or state of trembling.

tre•men•dous (tri men′dəs), *adj.* **1.** extraordinarily great in size, amount, or intensity. **2.** extraordinary in excellence. **3.** terrifying. —**tre•men′dous•ly,** *adv.*

trem•o•lo (trem′ə lō′), *n., pl.* **-los.** a vibrating effect produced on certain instruments and in the human voice.

trem•or (trem′ər, trē′mər), *n.* **1.** involuntary shaking of the body. **2.** any vibratory movement, as of the earth.

trem•u•lous (trem′yə ləs), *adj.* **1.** characterized by trembling or quivering. **2.** timid; fearful. —**trem′u• lous•ly,** *adv.* —**trem′u•lous•ness,** *n.*

trench (trench), *n.* **1.** a long, narrow ditch dug by soldiers as a defense against enemy fire or attack. **2.** a deep furrow or ditch.

trench•ant (tren′chənt), *adj.* **1.** incisive or keen: *trenchant wit.* **2.** vigorous; effective. —**trench′• ant•ly,** *adv.*

trench′ coat′ *n.* a belted, double-breasted raincoat with epaulets.

trench′er *n.* a flat piece of wood on which meat is served or carved.

trench′er•man *n., pl.* **-men.** a person with a hearty appetite.

trench′ foot′ *n.* a disease of the feet due to prolonged exposure to cold and moisture.

trench′ mouth′ *n.* an acute ulcerating infection of the gums and throat.

trend (trend), *n.* **1.** the general course or prevailing tendency. **2.** style; vogue.

trend′y *adj.,* **-i•er, -i•est.** of or in the latest trend or style. —**trend′i•ness,** *n.*

trep•i•da•tion (trep′i dā′shən), *n.* fearful anxiety.

tres•pass (tres′pəs, -pas), *n.* **1.** wrongful entry upon the lands of another. **2.** an encroachment or intrusion. **3.** an offense or sin. —*v.i.* **4.** to commit a trespass. —**tres′pass•er,** *n.*

tress (tres), *n.* Usu. **tresses.** long locks of hair, esp. those of a woman.

tres•tle (tres′əl), *n.* **1.** a supporting frame composed of a horizontal bar on two pairs of spreading legs. **2.** one of many transverse frames joined together to support a bridge.

tri- a combining form meaning three (*triangle*).

tri•ad (trī′ad, -əd), *n.* a group of three.

tri•age (trē äzh′), *n.* **1.** the process of sorting victims to determine priority of medical treatment. **2.** the determination of priorities for action in an emergency.

tri•al (trī′əl), *n.* **1.** the hearing and deciding of a case in a court of law. **2.** the act of trying, testing, or putting to the proof. **3.** an attempt or effort. **4.** an affliction or trouble. **5.** an annoying thing or person. —*adj.* **6.** of or used in a trial. **7.** done or made by way of trial or test.

tri•an•gle (trī′ang′gəl), *n.* **1.** a plane figure having three sides and three angles. **2.** any three-cornered or three-sided figure or object. **3.** a situation involving three persons. —**tri•an′gu•lar** (-gyə lər), *adj.*

Tri•as•sic (trī as′ik), *adj.* noting or pertaining to a period of the Mesozoic Era, characterized by the advent of dinosaurs.

tribe (trīb), *n.* **1.** a group of people, esp. an aboriginal people, descended from a common ancestor and sharing customs and traditions. **2.** a group of related plants or animals. —**trib′al,** *adj.*

tribes′man *n., pl.* **-men.** a member of a tribe.

trib•u•la•tion (trib′yə lā′shən), *n.* **1.** severe trial or suffering. **2.** an instance of this.

tri•bu•nal (trī byoōn′l, tri-), *n.* **1.** a court of justice. **2.** a seat of judgment.

trib•une (trib′yoōn, tri byoōn′), *n.* **1.** a person who defends the rights of the people. **2.** (in ancient Rome) an official elected to protect the rights of the plebeians.

trib•u•tar•y (trib′yə ter′ē), *n., pl.* **-ies,** *adj.* —*n.* **1.** a stream that flows into a larger body of water. **2.** a person or nation that pays tribute. —*adj.* **3.** flowing into a larger body of water. **4.** paying tribute.

trib•ute (trib′yoōt), *n.* **1.** a gift, speech, etc., given as an expression of gratitude or esteem. **2.** a sum paid by one state to another in acknowledgment of subjugation or as the price of peace.

trice (trīs), *n.* a very short time: *in a trice.*

tri•cen•ten•ni•al (trī′sen ten′ē əl), *n.* TERCENTENNIAL.

tri•ceps (trī′seps), *n., pl.* **-ceps•es** (-sep siz), **-ceps.** a muscle at the back of the upper arm.

trick (trik), *n.* **1.** a device or stratagem intended to deceive or cheat. **2.** a practical joke; prank. **3.** the knack of doing something skillfully. **4.** a clever feat intended to entertain. **5.** a behavioral peculiarity. **6.** a tour of duty. **7.** the set of cards played and won in one round. —*adj.* **8.** inclined to stiffen or weaken suddenly: *a trick shoulder.* —*v.t.* **9.** to deceive or cheat. —**trick′er•y,** *n., pl.* **-ies.** —**trick′ster** (-stər), *n.*

trick•le (trik′əl), *v.,* **-led, -ling,** *n.* —*v.i.* **1.** to flow in a small, gentle stream. **2.** to move slowly or irregularly: *The guests trickled out of the room.* —*n.* **3.** a trickling flow or stream.

trick′y *adj.,* **-i•er, -i•est. 1.** given to deceitful tricks. **2.** unreliable or uncooperative. **3.** involving intricate or clever maneuvers.

tri•col•or (trī′kul′ər), *n.* a flag with three colors, esp. the flag of France.

tri•cus′pid *adj.* having three cusps or points, as a tooth.

tri•cy•cle (trī′si kəl, -sik′əl), *n.* a child's three-wheeled vehicle propelled by foot pedals.

tri•dent (trīd′nt), *n.* a three-pronged instrument or weapon.

tried (trīd), *v.* **1.** pt. and pp. of TRY. —*adj.* **2.** tested and proved good or trustworthy. **3.** subjected to hardship.

tri•en•ni•al (trī en′ē əl), *adj.* **1.** occurring every three years. **2.** lasting three years. —**tri•en′ni•al•ly,** *adv.*

tri•fle (trī′fəl), *n., v.,* **-fled, -fling.** —*n.* **1.** something of very little value or importance. **2.** a small amount. —*v.i.* **3.** to deal lightly or without due respect. **4.** to play or toy.

tri′fling *adj.* **1.** trivial; insignificant. **2.** frivolous; shallow.

trig•ger (trig′ər), *n.* **1.** a small lever in a firearm that, when pressed by the finger, actuates the mechanism that discharges the weapon. —*v.t.* **2.** to initiate or precipitate (a reaction, process, etc.).

trig•o•nom•e•try (trig′ə nom′i trē), *n.* the branch of mathematics that deals with the relations between the sides and angles of triangles.

trill (tril), *n.* **1.** a rapid alternation of two adjacent musical tones. **2.** a similar quavering sound, as that made by a bird. **3.** a speech sound produced with rapid vibration of the tongue or uvula. —*v.t., v.i.* **4.** to sing, utter, or play with a trill.

tril•lion (tril′yən), *n., pl.* **-lions, -lion.** a cardinal number represented in the U.S. by 1 followed by 12 zeros, and in Great Britain by 1 followed by 18 zeros. —**tril′lionth,** *n., adj.*

tril•o•gy (tril′ə jē), *n., pl.* **-gies.** a group of three plays, novels, etc., that are closely related.

trim (trim), *v.,* **trimmed, trim•ming,** *n., adj.,* **trim•mer, trim•mest.** —*v.t.* **1.** to make neat or orderly by clipping, paring, etc. **2.** to remove by cutting. **3.** to level off (an airplane) in flight. **4. a.** to balance (a ship), as by rearranging the cargo. **b.** to adjust (the sails) to the direction of the wind. **5.** to decorate with ornaments. —*n.* **6.** the condition or fitness of a person or thing for action or use. **7.** material used for decoration or embellishment. **8.** a trimming by cutting, clipping, or the like. —*adj.* **9.** pleasingly neat or smart. **10.** in good condition or order. **11.** slim; lean. —*trim′ly, adv.* —*trim′mer, n.*

tri•ma•ran (trī′mə ran′), *n.* a boat similar to a catamaran but having three hulls.

tri•mes•ter (trī mes′tər, trī′mes-), *n.* **1.** a period of three months. **2.** one of the three terms into which the academic year is sometimes divided.

trim′ming *n.* **1.** anything used to decorate. **2.** Usu., **trimmings.** an accompaniment to a main dish. **3. trimmings,** pieces cut off in trimming. **4.** a beating or defeat.

Trin•i•dad (trin′i dad′), *n.* an island in the SE West Indies. —**Trin′i•da′di•an** (-dā′dē ən, -dad′ē-), *adj., n.*

Trin′idad and Toba′go a republic in the West Indies, comprising the islands of Trinidad and Tobago.

tri•ni•tro•tol•u•ene (trī nī′trō tol′yoō ēn′) *n.* a high explosive, known as TNT.

Trin•i•ty (trin′i tē), *n., pl.* **-ties** for 2. **1.** the union of Father, Son, and Holy Spirit in one Godhead. **2.** (*l.c.*) a group of three.

trin•ket (tring′kit), *n.* **1.** a small ornament of little value. **2.** anything of trivial value.

tri•o (trē′ō), *n., pl.* **-os. 1.** a group of three. **2.** a musical composition for three voices or instruments. **3.** a company of three singers or players.

trip (trip), *n., v.,* **tripped, trip•ping.** —*n.* **1.** a journey or voyage. **2.** a stumble. **3.** an error or blunder. **4.** a light, nimble step. **5.** a device for releasing a spring or lever to stop or reverse a machine. **6.** *Slang.* **a.** an instance of being under the influence of a hallucinogenic drug, esp. LSD. **b.** a stimulating or exciting experience. —*v.i.* **7.** to stumble or cause to stumble. **8.** to make or cause to make an error. **9.** to move or perform with light, nimble steps. **10.** to release or operate suddenly, as a lever. —*trip′per, n.*

tri•par•tite (trī pär′tīt), *adj.* **1.** consisting of three parts. **2.** involving three parties.

tripe (trīp), *n.* **1.** a part of the stomach of a ruminant, as an ox, used as food. **2.** *Slang.* something false or worthless.

tri•ple (trip′əl), *adj., n., v.,* **-pled, -pling.** —*adj.* **1.** consisting of three parts. **2.** three times as great. —*n.* **3.** an amount three times as great as another. **4.** a hit in baseball that enables a batter to reach third base. —*v.t., v.i.* **5.** to make or become triple. —*trip′ly, adv.*

tri•plet (trip′lit), *n.* one of three offspring born at the same time.

trip′li•cate (*n., adj.* -li kit, -kāt′; *v.* -kāt′), *n., v.,* **-cat•ed, -cat•ing,** *adj.* —*n.* **1.** one of three identical items, esp. copies of typewritten material. —*v.t.* **2.** to make three copies of. —*adj.* **3.** consisting of three identical parts. **4.** noting the third copy or item. —*Idiom.* **5. in triplicate,** in three copies.

tri•pod (trī′pod), *n.* a three-legged stand or support, as for a camera.

trip•tych (trip′tik), *n.* a set of three panels side by side, bearing pictures or carvings.

trite (trīt), *adj.,* **trit•er, trit•est.** lacking in freshness because of constant use; hackneyed. [< L *trītus* worn, common]

tri•umph (trī′əmf, -umf), *n.* **1.** victory; success. **2.** exultation over victory or success. —*v.i.* **3.** to gain victory or success. **4.** to rejoice over victory or success. —**tri•um′phal, tri•um′phant,** *adj.* —**tri•um′phant•ly,** *adv.*

tri•um•vir (trī um′vər), *n., pl.* **-virs, -vi•ri** (-və rī′). a member of a triumvirate.

tri•um′vi•rate (-vər it, -və rāt′), *n.* a group of three officials or magistrates jointly exercising authority, as in ancient Rome.

triv•et (triv′it), *n.* **1.** a short-legged plate placed under a hot dish on a table. **2.** a three-legged stand placed over a fire to support cooking vessels.

triv•i•a (triv′ē ə), *n.* (*used with a sing. or pl. v.*) matters or things that are very unimportant.

triv′i•al *adj.* of very little importance. —**triv′i•al′i•ty,** *n., pl.* **-ties.** —**triv′i•al•ly,** *adv.*

tro•chee (trō′kē), *n., pl.* **-chees.** a foot of two syllables, the first stressed and the second unstressed. —**tro•cha′ic** (-kā′ik), *adj.*

trog•lo•dyte (trog′lə dīt′), *n.* **1.** a prehistoric cave dweller. **2.** a hermit.

troi•ka (troi′kə), *n., pl.* **-kas. 1.** a Russian vehicle drawn by a team of three horses abreast. **2.** a ruling group of three. [< Russ]

troll[1] (trōl), *v.t., v.i.* **1.** to sing in a full, rolling voice. **2.** to sing the parts of (a round) in succession. **3.** to fish (in) by trailing a line behind a slow-moving boat.

troll[2] (trōl), *n.* (in Scandinavian folklore) a supernatural being who lives underground or in caves.

trol•ley (trol′ē), *n., pl.* **-leys. 1.** TROLLEY CAR. **2.** a carriage or truck traveling on an overhead track. **3.** a grooved wheel on the end of a pole, used by a streetcar to draw current from an overhead conductor.

trol′ley bus′ *n.* a bus drawing power from overhead wires.

trol′ley car′ *n.* a streetcar propelled electrically by current taken by means of a trolley.

trol•lop (trol′əp), *n.* a promiscuous woman, esp. a prostitute.

trom•bone (trom bōn′, trom′bōn), *n.* a musical wind instrument with a U-shaped metal tube and a slide for varying the tone. —**trom•bon′ist,** *n.*

troop (trōop), *n.* **1.** an assemblage of persons or things. **2.** a cavalry unit about the size of an infantry company. **3. troops,** a body of soldiers. **4.** a unit of Boy Scouts or Girl Scouts. —*v.i.* **5.** to gather or move in great numbers. **6.** to walk, as if in a march.

troop′ship′ *n.* ship for conveyance of military troops; transport.

tro•phy (trō′fē), *n., pl.* **-phies.** anything taken in war, competition, etc., esp. when preserved as a memento.

trop•ic (trop′ik), *n.* **1.** either of two corresponding parallels of latitude, one **(trop′ic of Can′cer)** about 23½° N, the other **(trop′ic of Cap′ricorn)** about 23½° S of the equator. **2. the tropics,** the regions lying between these parallels of latitude. —*adj.* **3.** of the tropics.

trop•i•cal *adj.* **1.** suitable for, characteristic of, or inhabiting the tropics. **2.** very hot and humid.

trop•o•sphere (trop′ə sfēr′, trō′pə-), *n.* the lowest layer of the atmosphere, within which nearly all clouds and weather conditions occur.

trot (trot), *v.,* **trot•ted, trot•ting,** *n.* —*v.i.* **1.** (of a horse or other quadruped) to go at a gait in which the legs move in diagonal pairs. **2.** to hurry. —*v.t.* **3.** to cause to trot. —*n.* **4.** the gait of a quadruped when trotting. **5.** the jogging gait of a human being. —**trot′ter,** *n.*

troth (trôth, trōth), *n. Archaic.* **1.** faithfulness; fidelity. **2.** truth or verity. **3.** one's promise, esp. to marry.

trou•ba•dour (trōo′bə dôr′), *n.* one of a class of lyric poets who lived principally in S France from the 11th to 13th centuries.

trou•ble (trub′əl), *v.,* **-bled, -bling,** *n.* —*v.t.* **1.** to disturb mentally; distress. **2.** to inconvenience. **3.** to cause bodily pain or discomfort to. **4.** to disturb or agitate, as water. —*v.i.* **5.** to put oneself to inconvenience or extra effort. —*n.* **6.** difficulty, annoyance, or disturbance. **7.** a physical disease, ailment, etc. **8.** mental or emotional distress. **9.** inconvenience or extra effort. —**trou′ble•some,** *adj.*

trou′bled *adj.* **1.** emotionally or mentally distressed. **2.** economically or socially distressed.

trou′ble•mak′er *n.* a person who causes trouble.

trou′ble•shoot′er *n.* an expert in discovering and eliminating the cause of trouble, as in mechanical equipment.

trough (trôf, trof), *n.* **1.** a long, narrow, open receptacle, used chiefly to hold water or food for animals. **2.** a gutter under the eaves of a building. **3.** a long depression or hollow, as between waves.

trounce (trouns), *v.t.,* **trounced, trounc•ing. 1.** to beat severely. **2.** to defeat decisively. —**trounc′er,** *n.*

troupe (trōop), *n., v.,* **trouped, troup•ing.** —*n.* **1.** a company of actors or other performers. —*v.i.* **2.** to travel as a member of a troupe. —**troup′er,** *n.*

trou•sers (trou′zərz), *n.* (*used with a pl. v.*) an outer garment for the lower part of the body, having individual leg portions.

trous•seau (trōo′sō, trōo sō′), *n., pl.* **-seaux** (-sōz, -sōz′), **-seaus.** an outfit of clothing, household linen, etc., for a bride.

trout (trout), *n., pl.* **trouts, trout.** any of various freshwater game fishes of the salmon family.

trow•el (trou′əl), *n.* **1.** a tool with a flat blade, used for working mortar, plaster, etc. **2.** a tool with a scooplike blade, used in gardening.

troy (troi), *adj.* expressed or computed in troy weight.

troy′ weight′ *n.* a system of weights in use for precious metals and gems, in which a pound equals 12 ounces, 240 pennyweights, or 5,760 grains.

tru•ant (trōo′ənt), *n.* **1.** a student who stays away from school without permission. **2.** a person who neglects duty. —*adj.* **3.** absent from school without permission. **4.** neglectful of duty. [< OF: beggar < Celtic] —**tru′an•cy,** *n., pl.* **-cies.**

truce (trōos), *n.* **1.** a temporary suspension of hostilities by mutual agreement of the warring parties. **2.** a temporary respite, as from trouble.

truck[1] (truk), *n.* **1.** a large motor vehicle for carrying goods and materials. **2.** a wheeled frame or cart for transporting heavy objects. **3.** a frame with two or more pairs of wheels for supporting one end of a railroad car or locomotive. —*v.t.* **4.** to transport by truck. —*v.i.* **5.** to drive a truck. —**truck′er,** *n.*

truck[2] (truk), *n.* **1.** vegetables raised for the market. **2.** *Informal.* rubbish; trash. **3.** dealings. —*v.t., v.i.* **4.** to exchange; barter.

truck•le (truk′əl), *v.i.,* **-led, -ling.** to submit or yield obsequiously.

truc•u•lent (truk′yə lənt, trōo′kyə-), *adj.* **1.** aggressively hostile. **2.** savagely brutal. —**truc′u•lence,** *n.*

trudge (truj), *v.,* **trudged, trudg•ing,** *n.* —*v.i.* **1.** to walk, esp. laboriously or wearily. —*n.* **2.** a laborious or tiring walk.

true (trōo), *adj.,* **tru•er, tru•est,** *n., adv., v.,* **trued, tru•ing** or **true•ing.** —*adj.* **1.** conforming to reality or fact. **2.** real; genuine. **3.** loyal; faithful. **4.** conforming to a standard, pattern, etc. **5.** legitimate or rightful. **6.** accurately shaped, fitted, etc. —*n.* **7. the true,** something true; truth. —*adv.* **8.** truly. **9.** in conformity with the ancestral type: *to breed true.* —*v.t.* **10.** to adjust, shape, place, etc., accurately.

true′-blue′ *adj.* unwaveringly loyal.

truf•fle (truf′əl), *n.* any of several subterranean, edible fungi.

tru•ism (trōo′iz əm), *n.* a self-evident, obvious truth.

tru•ly (trōo′lē), *adv.* **1.** truthfully or accurately. **2.** really; genuinely. **3.** indeed. **4.** sincerely: *yours truly.*

trump (trump), *n.* **1. a.** any playing card of a suit that for the time outranks the other suits. **b.** Often, **trumps.** (*used with a sing. v.*) the suit itself. —*v.t., v.i.* **2.** to take (a trick) with a trump. **3. trump up,** to devise deceitfully.

trump′er•y *n., pl.* **-ies. 1.** something without use or value. **2.** nonsense; twaddle.

trum•pet (trum′pit), *n.* **1.** a brass wind instrument consisting of a curved tube and a flaring bell. **2.** something resembling a trumpet, esp. in sound. **3.** a sound like that of a trumpet. —*v.i.* **4.** to emit a loud, trumpetlike sound. —*v.t.* **5.** to proclaim loudly or widely. —**trum′pet•er,** *n.*

trun•cate (trung′kāt), *v.t.,* **-cat•ed, -cat•ing.** to shorten by or as if by cutting off a part; cut short.

trun•cheon (trun′chən), *n.* the club carried by a police officer.

trun·dle (trun′dl), *v.i., v.t.,* **-dled, -dling.** to roll along.

trun′dle bed′ *n.* a low bed on casters, usu. pushed under another bed when not in use.

trunk (trungk), *n.* **1.** the main stem of a tree. **2.** a large sturdy box for carrying clothes, personal effects, etc. **3.** a large compartment in an automobile for luggage and storage. **4.** the body of a person or animal excluding the head and appendages. **5.** the long, flexible nasal appendage of the elephant. **6. trunks,** brief shorts worn by men chiefly for athletics.

trunk′ line′ *n.* **1.** a major long-distance transportation line. **2.** a telephone line between two switching devices.

truss (trus), *v.t.* **1.** to tie or bind. **2.** to fasten the legs and wings of (a fowl) before cooking. **3.** to support with a truss. —*n.* **4.** a structural frame designed to support bridges, roofs, etc. **5.** a pad supported by a belt, used for maintaining a hernia in a reduced state.

trust (trust), *n.* **1.** reliance on the integrity, ability, etc., of a person or thing. **2.** confident expectation; hope. **3.** one upon which a person relies. **4.** the responsibility imposed on a person in whom confidence is placed. **5.** charge or custody. **6.** something entrusted to one's care. **7. a.** a fiduciary relationship in which a trustee holds title to property for the beneficiary. **b.** the property so held. **8.** a combination of business firms for the purpose of eliminating competition. —*v.t.* **9.** to have confidence in. **10.** to expect confidently; hope. **11.** to commit with confidence. **12.** to permit to do something without fear. —*v.i.* **13.** to have confidence.

trust·ee′ *n., pl.* **-ees. 1.** a person appointed to administer the affairs of a company, institution, etc. **2.** a person who holds title to property for the benefit of another.

trus·tee′ship *n.* **1.** the office or function of a trustee. **2.** the administrative control of a territory granted to a country by the United Nations. **3.** TRUST TERRITORY.

trust′ fund′ *n.* money, securities, etc., held in trust.

trust′ ter′ritory *n.* a territory placed under the administrative control of a country by the United Nations.

trust′wor′thy *adj.* deserving of trust or confidence. —**trust′wor′thi·ness,** *n.*

trust′y *adj.,* **-i·er, -i·est.** able to be trusted or relied on.

truth (trooth), *n., pl.* **truths** (troothz, trooths). **1.** the true or actual state of a matter. **2.** conformity with fact or reality. **3.** a verified or indisputable fact, proposition, etc. **4.** the state or character of being true. —*Idiom.* **5. in truth,** in reality. —**truth′ful,** *adj.*

try (trī), *v.,* **tried, try·ing,** *n., pl.* **tries.** —*v.t.* **1.** to make an effort to do or accomplish. **2.** to sample, test, or experiment with, as to evaluate. **3.** to examine and determine judicially. **4.** to put to a severe test. **5.** to melt down (fat, blubber, etc.) to obtain the oil. —*v.i.* **6.** to make an effort. **7. try on,** to put on (an article of clothing) to judge its appearance and fit. **8. ~ out, a.** to use experimentally. **b.** to take part in a competitive test, as for a position or role. —*n.* **9.** an attempt or effort.

try′ing *adj.* straining one's patience and goodwill.

try′out′ *n.* a test of fitness, ability, etc.

tryst (trist, trīst), *n.* **1.** a clandestine appointment to meet, esp. one made by lovers. **2.** an appointed meeting or meeting place.

tsar (zär, tsär), *n.* CZAR.

tset′se fly′ (tset′sē, tsē′tsē), *n.* any of several bloodsucking African flies, some of which can transmit sleeping sickness.

T-shirt *n.* a lightweight pullover shirt with short sleeves and a collarless round neckline.

tsp. 1. teaspoon. **2.** teaspoonful.

T square *n.* a T-shaped ruler for drawing parallel lines, right angles, etc.

tsu·na·mi (tsoo nä′mē), *n., pl.* **-mis.** an unusually large sea wave produced by an undersea earthquake or volcanic eruption. [< Japn: tidal wave]

tub (tub), *n.* **1.** a bathtub. **2.** a broad, round, open container, orig. one made of wooden staves.

tu·ba (too′bə, tyoo′-), *n., pl.* **-bas.** a valved brass wind instrument having a low range.

tub·by (tub′ē), *adj.,* **-bi·er, -bi·est.** short and fat.

tube (toob, tyoob), *n.* **1.** a hollow, cylindrical body of metal, glass, etc., used for conveying fluids. **2.** a collapsible cylinder from which a paste may be squeezed. **3.** any hollow, cylindrical vessel or organ: *the bronchial tubes.* **4. the tube,** *Informal.* television. **5.** *Brit.* SUBWAY. —**tub′ing,** *n.* —**tu·bu·lar** (too′byə lər), *adj.*

tu·ber (too′bər, tyoo′-), *n.* a fleshy outgrowth of an underground stem, as the potato. —**tu′ber·ous,** *adj.*

tu·ber·cle (-kəl), *n.* **1.** a small, rounded projection, as on a bone. **2.** a firm, rounded swelling, esp. the lesion of tuberculosis.

tu·ber′cu·lo′sis (-lō′sis), *n.* an infectious disease characterized by tubercles esp. in the lungs. —**tu·ber′cu·lar, tu·ber′cu·lous,** *adj.*

tube′rose′ (toob′-, tyoob′-) *n.* a cultivated plant with white, fragrant, lilylike flowers.

tu′bule (-byool), *n.* a small tube.

tuck (tuk), *v.t.* **1.** to put into a small, close, or concealing place. **2.** to thrust in the edge of (a garment, sheet, etc.) so as to hold in place. **3.** to cover or wrap snugly. **4.** to draw or pull up into folds. **5.** to sew tucks in. —*n.* **6.** a fold sewn into cloth, as to make a tighter fit. **7.** *Informal.* a plastic surgery operation: *a tummy tuck.*

tuck′er *v.t. Informal.* to tire; exhaust.

Tues. Tuesday. Also, **Tue.**

Tues·day (tooz′dā, -dē, tyooz′-), *n.* the third day of the week, following Monday.

tuft (tuft), *n.* **1.** a bunch of hairs, feathers, grass, etc., growing or fastened closely together. **2.** a cluster of cut threads tied together at the base. —*v.t.* **3.** to furnish or decorate with tufts. **4.** to arrange in tufts. —**tuft′ed,** *adj.*

tug (tug), *v.,* **tugged, tug·ging,** *n.* —*v.t.* **1.** to pull at with force or effort. **2.** to move by pulling forcibly. **3.** to tow with a tugboat. —*v.i.* **4.** to pull with force or effort. —*n.* **5.** an act or instance of tugging. **6.** TUGBOAT.

tug′boat′ *n.* a small, powerful boat for towing or pushing ships, barges, etc.

tug′ of war′ *n.* **1.** a contest between two teams pulling on opposite ends of a rope. **2.** a struggle for supremacy.

tu·i·tion (too ish′ən, tyoo-), *n.* the fee for instruction, as at a college.

tu·lip (too′lip, tyoo′-), *n.* **1.** a plant with large, cup-shaped flowers of various colors. **2.** a flower or bulb of such a plant.

tulle (tool), *n.* a thin, fine net of acetate, nylon, rayon, or silk.

tum·ble (tum′bəl), *v.,* **-bled, -bling,** *n.* —*v.i.* **1.** to fall helplessly down, esp. headfirst. **2.** to roll end over end, as in falling. **3.** to decline or collapse suddenly. **4.** to perform gymnastic feats, as somersaults. **5.** to move in a hasty and confused way. —*v.t.* **6.** to cause to tumble. —*n.* **7.** the act of tumbling. **8.** disorder or confusion.

tum′ble-down′ *adj.* dilapidated.

tum′bler *n.* **1.** a person who performs acrobatic feats. **2.** a part of a lock that, when lifted by a key, allows the bolt to move. **3.** a drinking glass without a stem and handle.

tum′ble·weed′ *n.* a plant whose upper parts become detached from the roots and are driven about by the wind.

tum·brel or **-bril** (tum′brəl), *n.* a farmer's cart that can be tilted to discharge its load.

tu·mes·cent (too mes′ənt, tyoo-), *adj.* swelling; tumid. —**tu·mes′cence,** *n.*

tu′mid (-mid), *adj.* **1.** swollen or bulging. **2.** pompous or inflated. —**tu·mid′i·ty,** *n.*

tum·my (tum′ē), *n., pl.* **-mies.** *Informal.* the stomach or abdomen.

tu·mor (too′mər, tyoo′-), *n.* an uncontrolled,

abnormal, circumscribed growth of cells. Also, *esp. Brit.,* **tu′mour.** —**tu′mor•ous,** *adj.*

tu•mult (tōō′mult, -məlt, tyōō′-), *n.* **1.** violent and noisy commotion; uproar. **2.** agitation of mind or feelings. —**tu•mul′tu•ous** (-mul′chōō əs), *adj.*

tun (tun), *n.* a large cask.

tu•na (tōō′nə, tyōō′-), *n., pl.* **-nas, -na. 1.** any of several large marine food and game fishes. **2.** Also called **tu′na fish′.** the flesh of the tuna, used as food.

tun•dra (tun′drə, tōōn′-), *n., pl.* **-dras.** a vast, tree-less plain of arctic regions.

tune (tōōn, tyōōn), *n., v.,* **tuned, tun•ing.** —*n.* **1.** a succession of musical sounds forming a melody. **2.** the state of being in the proper pitch. **3.** accord; agreement. —*v.t.* **4.** to adjust (a musical instrument) to a correct pitch. **5.** to bring into harmony. **6.** to adjust (a motor, mechanism, etc.) for proper functioning. **7.** to adjust (a radio or television) so as to receive a broadcast. **8. tune in,** to adjust a radio or television so as to receive (signals, a station, etc.). —*Idiom.* **9. to the tune of,** in the amount of. —**tun′er,** *n.* —**tune′ful,** *adj.* —**tune′less,** *adj.*

tune′-up′ *n.* an adjustment, as of a motor, to improve working condition.

tung•sten (tung′stən), *n.* a rare metallic element, used in electric-lamp filaments. *Symbol:* W; *at. wt.:* 183.85; *at. no.:* 74.

tu•nic (tōō′nik, tyōō′-), *n.* **1.** a gownlike outer garment worn by the ancient Greeks and Romans. **2.** a woman's straight upper garment, usu. extending to the hips.

tun′ing fork′ *n.* a two-pronged steel instrument producing a tone of constant pitch when struck, used for tuning musical instruments.

Tu•ni•sia (tōō nē′zhə, -nizh′ə, tyōō-), *n.* a republic in N Africa. —**Tu•ni′sian,** *adj., n.*

tun•nel (tun′l), *n., v.,* **-neled, -nel•ing** or (*esp. Brit.*) **-nelled, -nel•ling.** —*n.* **1.** an underground passage. **2.** a passageway, as for trains or automobiles, through or under a mountain or other obstruction. —*v.t., v.i.* **3.** to construct a tunnel (through or under).

tur•ban (tûr′bən), *n.* **1.** a man's headdress worn chiefly by Muslims, consisting of a long cloth wound around the head. **2.** any headdress resembling this.

tur•bid (tûr′bid), *adj.* **1.** unclear or murky because of stirred-up sediment. **2.** thick or dense, as clouds. **3.** confused; muddled.

tur•bine (tûr′bin, -bīn), *n.* any of various machines having a rotor with vanes or blades, driven by the pressure of a moving fluid.

tur′bo•jet′ *n.* **1.** Also called **tur′bojet en′gine.** a jet engine in which air is compressed for combustion by a turbine-driven compressor. **2.** an airplane equipped with such engines.

tur′bo•prop′ (-prop′), *n.* **1.** Also called **tur′bo-propel′ler en′gine.** a turbojet engine with a turbine-driven propeller. **2.** an airplane equipped with such engines.

tur•bot (tûr′bət), *n., pl.* **-bots, -bot.** any of several flatfishes.

tur•bu•lent (tûr′byə lənt), *adj.* **1.** being in a state of agitation. **2.** characterized by disturbance, disorder, etc. —**tur′bu•lence,** *n.*

tu•reen (tōō rēn′, tyōō-), *n.* a large, deep, covered dish for serving soup, stew, etc.

turf (tûrf), *n.* **1.** a layer of matted earth formed by grass and plant roots. **2.** a block of peat. **3. the turf, a.** a track for horse racing. **b.** horse racing. **4. a.** the area over which a street gang asserts its authority. **b.** a familiar area, as of expertise.

tur•gid (tûr′jid), *adj.* **1.** swollen; distended. **2.** pompous; bombastic. —**tur•gid′i•ty,** *n.* —**tur′gid•ly,** *adv.*

tur•key (tûr′kē), *n., pl.* **-keys. 1.** a large North American bird with brownish plumage and a bare head and neck. **2.** the edible flesh of this bird.

Tur′key *n.* a republic in W Asia and SE Europe. —**Turk,** *n.* —**Turk′ish,** *adj., n.*

tur′key vul′ture *n.* a blackish brown New World vulture.

Turk•me•ni•stan (tûrk′me nə stan′, -stän′), *n.* a republic in central Asia: formerly a part of the USSR.

tur•mer•ic (tûr′mər ik), *n.* **1.** the aromatic rhizome of an Asian plant. **2.** a powder prepared from it, used as a condiment or a yellow dye.

tur•moil (tûr′moil), *n.* a state of great confusion or disturbance.

turn (tûrn), *v.t.* **1.** to rotate: *to turn a wheel.* **2.** to move around or partly around: *to turn a key.* **3.** to reverse the position of: *to turn a page.* **4.** to change the position or course of. **5.** to change or convert: *to turn water into ice.* **6.** to cause to become sour or spoiled. **7.** to affect (the stomach) with nausea. **8.** to put to some use or purpose. **9.** to go around: *to turn a corner.* **10.** to reach or pass (a certain age, amount, etc.). **11.** to direct or aim. **12.** to shape on a lathe. **13.** to send; drive. **14.** to cause to be antagonistic toward. **15.** to earn or gain: *to turn a profit.* **16.** to wrench: *He turned his ankle.* —*v.i.* **17.** to rotate. **18.** to move around or partly around. **19.** to hinge or depend. **20.** to direct one's interest, effort, etc. **21.** to change or reverse position or course. **22.** to be affected with nausea. **23.** to change one's loyalties, attitude, etc. **24.** to change or alter, as in appearance. **25.** to become sour or spoiled. **26.** to change color. **27.** to become: *to turn pale.* **28.** to have recourse. **29. turn down, a.** to refuse or reject. **30. ~ in, a.** to hand in. **b.** to go to bed. **31. ~ off, a.** to stop the flow of (water, gas, etc.). **b.** to extinguish (a light). **c.** *Slang.* to alienate. **32. ~ on, a.** to cause to flow. **b.** to switch on (a light). **c.** *Slang.* to arouse the interest of. **d.** to become hostile to. **33. ~ out, a.** to extinguish (a light). **b.** to produce. **c.** to result or end. **34. ~ over,** to transfer; give. **35. ~ up, a.** to uncover; find. **b.** to intensify or increase. **c.** to appear; arrive. —*n.* **36.** a movement of partial or total rotation. **37.** a time for action that comes in due order. **38.** the act of changing course or direction. **39.** the point at which such a change occurs. **40.** a single revolution, as of a wheel. **41.** any change, as in nature or circumstances. **42.** a single twist or coil. **43.** a distinctive form or style of language. **44.** a short walk, ride, etc. **45.** a natural inclination. **46.** a period of work. **47.** an act of service or disservice. **48.** a nervous shock. —*Idiom.* **49. in turn,** in due order. **50. out of turn,** out of proper order.

turn′a•bout′ *n.* a change of opinion, loyalty, etc.

turn′coat′ *n.* a person who changes to the opposite party or faction.

turn′ing point′ *n.* a point at which a decisive change takes place.

tur•nip (tûr′nip), *n.* **1.** the thick, fleshy, edible root of either of two plants of the mustard family. **2.** either of these plants.

turn′off′ *n.* a small road that branches off from a larger one.

turn′out′ *n.* **1.** the gathering of persons who come to an exhibition, party, etc. **2.** a short side passage that enables trains, automobiles, etc., to pass one another.

turn′o•ver *n.* **1.** an act or result of turning over. **2.** the rate at which workers are replaced in a given period. **3.** the amount of business done in a given time. **4.** the rate at which items are sold and restocked. **5.** a baked pastry in which half the dough is turned over the filling and sealed.

turn′pike′ (-pīk′), *n.* a high-speed highway, esp. one maintained by tolls.

turn′stile′ *n.* a gate with revolving arms set in a passageway to control the flow of people.

turn′ta′ble *n.* the rotating disk that spins the record on a phonograph.

tur•pen•tine (tûr′pən tīn′), *n.* a strong-smelling liquid distilled from a substance derived from coniferous trees, used as a paint thinner and solvent.

tur•pi•tude (tûr′pi tōōd′, -tyōōd′), *n.* vile or base character; depravity.

tur•quoise (tûr′koiz, -kwoiz), *n.* **1.** a sky-blue or greenish blue mineral, used as a gem. **2.** a greenish blue.

tur•ret (tûr′it, tur′-), *n.* **1.** a small tower forming part of a larger structure. **2.** a revolving structure in which a gun is mounted, as on an armored vehicle. **3.** a pivoted attachment on a lathe for holding tools.

tur•tle (tûr′tl), *n., pl.* **-tles, -tle.** any of various aquatic and terrestrial reptiles with the trunk enclosed in a bony shell.

tur′tle•dove′ (-duv′), *n.* any of several doves, esp. a small dove noted for its plaintive coo.

tur′tle•neck′ *n.* **1.** a high, close-fitting collar, esp. on pullover sweaters. **2.** a garment with such a collar.

tusk (tusk), *n.* an animal tooth developed to great length, as in the elephant.

tus•sle (tus′əl), *v.,* **-sled, -sling,** *n.* —*v.i.* **1.** to struggle or fight roughly. —*n.* **2.** any vigorous struggle.

tus•sock (tus′ək), *n.* a tuft or clump of growing grass or the like.

tu•te•lage (tōōt′l ij, tyōōt′-), *n.* **1.** the act of teaching or guiding. **2.** instruction or guidance. **3.** the state of being under a guardian or tutor. —**tu′te•lar′y** (-er′ē), *adj.*

tu•tor (tōō′tər, tyōō′-), *n.* **1.** a person employed to instruct another, esp. privately. —*v.t., v.i.* **2.** to act as a tutor (to). —**tu•to′ri•al** (-tôr′ē əl), *adj., n.*

tut•ti-frut•ti (tōō′tē frōō′tē), *n.* a confection, esp. ice cream, flavored with a variety of fruits.

tu•tu (tōō′tōō′), *n., pl.* **-tus.** a short, full skirt worn by ballerinas.

tux (tuks), *n. Informal.* a tuxedo.

tux•e•do (tuk sē′dō), *n., pl.* **-dos.** a man's semiformal suit, traditionally of black or dark blue.

TV television.

twad•dle (twod′l), *n.* silly or tedious talk or writing. —**twad′dler,** *n.*

twain (twān), *adj., n.* two.

twang (twang), *v.i., v.t.* **1.** to make or cause to make a sharp, vibrating sound. **2.** to speak or utter with a nasal tone. —*n.* **3.** a sharp, vibrating sound, as one made by plucking the string of a musical instrument. **4.** a sharp, nasal tone.

tweak (twēk), *v.t.* **1.** to pinch and pull with a jerk and twist. **2.** to make a minor adjustment to: *to tweak a computer program.* —*n.* **3.** the act of tweaking.

tweed (twēd), *n.* **1.** a coarse wool cloth in a variety of weaves and colors. **2. tweeds,** garments made of this cloth. —**tweed′y,** *adj.,* **-i•er, -i•est.**

tweet (twēt), *n.* **1.** a chirping sound, as of a small bird. —*v.i.* **2.** to chirp.

tweez•ers (twē′zərz), *n.* (*used with a sing. or pl. v.*) small pincers for plucking out hairs, extracting splinters, etc.

twelve (twelv), *n.* **1.** a cardinal number, 10 plus 2. **2.** a symbol for this number, as 12 or XII. —*adj.* **3.** amounting to 12 in number. —**twelfth,** *adj., n.*

Twelve′ Step′ or **12-step,** *adj.* of or based on a program for recovery from addiction that provides 12 progressive levels toward attainment.

twen•ty (twen′tē), *n., pl.* **-ties,** *adj.* —*n.* **1.** a cardinal number, 10 times 2. **2.** a symbol for this number, as 20 or XX. —*adj.* **3.** amounting to 20 in number. —**twen′ti•eth,** *adj., n.*

twerp (wûrp), *n. Slang.* an insignificant or despicable person.

twice (twīs), *adv.* **1.** two times. **2.** in twofold quantity or degree.

twid•dle (twid′l), *v.t., v.i.,* **-dled, -dling. 1.** to turn about or play with (something) idly. —*Idiom.* **2. twiddle one's thumbs,** to be idle.

twig (twig), *n.* a small offshoot of a branch or stem.

twi•light (twī′līt′), *n.* **1.** the soft, diffused light from the sky when the sun is below the horizon. **2.** the period during which this light prevails. **3.** a waning period after full development, success, etc. —*adj.* **4.** of or resembling twilight.

twill (twil), *n.* a fabric with a pattern of diagonal, raised lines.

twin (twin), *n.* **1.** either of two offspring brought forth at a birth. **2.** either of two persons or things related to or resembling each other. —*adj.* **3.** born at the same birth. **4.** being one of a pair.

twine (twīn), *n., v.,* **twined, twin•ing.** —*n.* **1.** a strong thread or string composed of two or more strands twisted together. —*v.t.* **2.** to twist together. **3.** to coil or wind. —*v.i.* **4.** to wind around something.

twinge (twinj), *n., v.,* **twinged, twing•ing.** —*n.* **1.** a sudden, sharp pain. **2.** a mental or emotional pang. —*v.t., v.i.* **3.** to affect with or feel a twinge.

twin•kle (twing′kəl), *v.,* **-kled, -kling,** *n.* —*v.i.* **1.** to shine with a flickering gleam of light. **2.** (of the eyes) to be bright with amusement. **3.** to move flutteringly and quickly. —*n.* **4.** a flickering light. **5.** a brightness in the eyes. **6.** an instant; twinkling.

twin′kling *n.* the time required for a wink; an instant.

twirl (twûrl), *v.i., v.t.* **1.** to rotate rapidly; whirl. —*n.* **2.** the act of twirling. **3.** a spiral or coil. —**twirl′er,** *n.*

twist (twist), *v.t.* **1.** to combine (strands or threads) by winding together. **2.** to wind or coil about something. **3.** to wrench; sprain. **4.** to break off by turning forcibly. **5.** to contort. **6.** to distort the meaning of. **7.** to form into a coil by winding, rolling, etc. **8.** to turn by rotating. —*v.i.* **9.** to become twisted. **10.** to writhe or squirm. **11.** to take a spiral form or course. **12.** to turn so as to face in another direction. —*n.* **13.** a curve; bend; turn. **14.** a rotary motion or spin. **15.** anything formed by twisting. **16.** the act or process of twining strands together. **17.** distortion, as of meaning. **18.** a sudden, unanticipated change, as of events. **19.** a novel treatment, method, etc.

twist′er *n.* **1.** a person or thing that twists. **2.** *Informal.* a whirlwind or tornado.

twit (twit), *v.,* **twit•ted, twit•ting,** *n.* —*v.t.* **1.** to taunt with reference to anything embarrassing. —*n.* **2.** the act of twitting.

twitch (twich), *v.t., v.i.* **1.** to pull (at) or move with a quick, jerking movement. —*n.* **2.** a quick, jerky movement of the body or a muscle.

twit•ter (twit′ər), *v.i.* **1.** to utter a succession of small, tremulous sounds, as a bird. **2.** to chatter. **3.** to giggle. **4.** to tremble with excitement. —*n.* **5.** the act of twittering. **6.** a twittering sound. **7.** a state of tremulous excitement.

two (tōō), *n., pl.* **twos,** *adj.* —*n.* **1.** a cardinal number, 1 plus 1. **2.** a symbol for this number, as 2 or II. —*adj.* **3.** amounting to two in number. —*Idiom.* **4. in two,** into two parts.

two′-bit′ *adj. Informal.* inferior or unimportant.

two′ bits′ *n. Informal.* 25 cents.

two′-faced′ *adj.* **1.** having two faces. **2.** deceitful or hypocritical.

two′-fist′ed *adj.* strong and vigorous.

two′fold′ (*adj.* -fōld′; *adv.* -fōld′), *adj.* **1.** having two parts. **2.** twice as great or as much. —*adv.* **3.** in twofold measure.

two′-ply′ *adj.* consisting of two layers, strands, etc.

two′some (-səm), *n.* **1.** two people together; a couple. **2.** a golf match between two persons.

two′-time′ *v.t.,* **-timed, -tim•ing.** *Informal.* to be unfaithful to (a lover or spouse).

two′-way′ *adj.* **1.** allowing movement or communication in two directions. **2.** involving two participants.

twp. township.

TX Texas.

-ty a suffix meaning state or condition (*certainty*).

ty•coon (tī kōōn′), *n.* a businessperson of great wealth and power. [< Japn]

tyke (tīk), *n.* a small child.

tym•pan′ic mem′brane (tim pan′ik), *n.* a membrane in the ear canal between the external ear and the middle ear.

tym•pa•num (tim′pə nəm), *n., pl.* **-nums, -na** (-nə). **1.** MIDDLE EAR. **2.** TYMPANIC MEMBRANE.

type (tīp), *n., v.,* **typed, typ•ing.** —*n.* **1.** a group of things or persons sharing certain characteristics. **2.** a thing or person that is representative of a class or group. **3. a.** a metal block with a raised character on its surface, used in printing. **b.** such blocks collectively. **c.** a printed character or characters. —*v.t.*

4. to write on a typewriter, computer keyboard, or the like. **5.** to classify. —*v.i.* **6.** to write using a typewriter, computer keyboard, or the like. —**typ/ist**, *n.*

type/cast/ *v.t.*, **-cast**, **-cast•ing.** to cast (an actor) repeatedly or exclusively in the same kind of role.

type/script/ *n.* typewritten matter.

type/set/ter *n.* **1.** a person who sets type. **2.** a machine for setting type. —**type/set/**, *v.t.*, **-set**, **-set•ting.**

type/writ/er *n.* a machine for writing in characters similar to printers' types.

ty•phoid (tī/foid), *n.* an infectious disease characterized by fever and intestinal inflammation, spread by food or water contaminated with a bacillus. Also called **ty/phoid fe/ver.**

ty•phoon (tī fōōn/), *n.* a tropical hurricane of the W Pacific and the China seas.

ty•phus (tī/fəs), *n.* an acute infectious disease caused by a microorganism, transmitted by lice and fleas, and characterized by reddish spots on the skin. Also called **ty/phus fe/ver.**

typ•i•cal (tip/i kəl), *adj.* **1.** conforming to or serving as a type. **2.** having the essential characteristics of a particular type.

typ/i•fy/ *v.t.*, **-fied**, **-fy•ing. 1.** to serve as a typical example of. **2.** to serve as a symbol of.

ty•po (tī/pō), *n.*, *pl.* **-pos.** an error in typesetting or typing.

ty•pog•ra•phy (tī pog/rə fē), *n.* **1.** the work of setting and arranging types and of printing from them. **2.** the general appearance of printed matter. —**ty/po•graph/i•cal** (-pə graf/i kəl), **ty/po•graph/ic**, *adj.*

ty•ran•ni•cal (ti ran/i kəl, tī-), *adj.* **1.** unjustly cruel or severe. **2.** of or characteristic of a tyrant. —**ty•ran/ni•cal•ly**, *adv.*

tyr•an•nize (tir/ə nīz/), *v.*, **-nized**, **-niz•ing.** —*v.t.* **1.** to govern tyrannically. —*v.i.* **2.** to exercise absolute power cruelly or oppressively. **3.** to govern as a tyrant.

ty•ran•no•saur (ti ran/ə sôr/, tī-), *n.* a large dinosaur that walked upright on its hind feet.

tyr•an•ny (tir/ə nē), *n.*, *pl.* **-nies. 1.** arbitrary or unrestrained exercise of power. **2.** the government of a tyrant. **3.** oppressive or unjust government. **4.** a tyrannical act.

ty•rant (tī/rənt), *n.* **1.** a ruler or other person in authority who exercises power oppressively or despotically. **2.** an absolute ruler.

ty•ro (tī/rō), *n.*, *pl.* **-ros.** a beginner in learning anything; novice.

tzar (zär, tsär), *n.* CZAR.

---

a b c d e f g h i j k l m n o p q r s t **U** v w x y z

U, u (yōō), *n.*, *pl.* **Us** or **U's**, **us** or **u's. 1.** the 21st letter of the English alphabet, a vowel. **2.** something shaped like a U.

U (yōō), *adj.* characteristic of the upper classes.

U *Chem. Symbol.* uranium.

U. 1. union. **2.** unit. **3.** university. **4.** unsatisfactory.

u•biq•ui•tous (yōō bik/wi təs), *adj.* existing or being everywhere, esp. at the same time.

ud•der (ud/ər), *n.* a baggy mammary gland with more than one teat, as in cows.

UFO (yōō/ef/ō/; *sometimes* yōō/fō), *n.*, *pl.* **UFOs**, **UFO's.** unidentified flying object: any unexplained flying object, esp. one assumed to be from outer space.

U•gan•da (yōō gan/də, ōō gän/-), *n.* a republic in E Africa. —**U•gan/dan**, *adj.*, *n.*

ug•ly (ug/lē), *adj.*, **-li•er**, **-li•est. 1.** very unattractive in appearance. **2.** disagreeable; objectionable. **3.** morally revolting. **4.** threatening or ominous. **5.** hostile; quarrelsome.

U•kraine (yōō krān/), *n.* a republic in SE Europe: formerly a part of the USSR.

u•ku•le•le (yōō/kə lā/lē), *n.*, *pl.* **-les.** a small, guitarlike musical instrument.

ul•cer (ul/sər), *n.* **1.** a sore on the skin or a mucous membrane, often containing pus. **2.** any corrupting condition. —**ul/cer•ate/**, *v.i.*, *v.t.*, **-at•ed**, **-at•ing.** —**ul/cer•ous**, *adj.*

ul•na (ul/nə), *n.*, *pl.* **-nae** (-nē), **-nas.** the bone of the forearm on the side opposite the thumb. —**ul/nar**, *adj.*

ul•te•ri•or (ul tēr/ē ər), *adj.* **1.** intentionally concealed: *an ulterior motive.* **2.** subsequent; future. **3.** lying beyond or outside a specified boundary.

ul•ti•mate (ul/tə mit), *adj.* **1.** furthest or farthest. **2.** decisive; conclusive. **3.** basic; fundamental. **4.** final; total. **5.** unequaled or unsurpassed. —*n.* **6.** the final point or result. **7.** a fundamental fact. —**ul/ti•mate•ly**, *adv.*

ul•ti•ma•tum (-mā/təm, -mä/-), *n.*, *pl.* **-tums**, **-ta** (-tə). a final demand or set of terms, as in a dispute.

ul•tra (ul/trə), *adj.* going beyond what is usual or ordinary; extreme.

ultra- a prefix meaning: beyond or on the far side of (*ultraviolet*); extremely (*ultraconservative*).

ul•tra•con•serv•a•tive (ul/trə kən sûr/və tiv), *adj.* **1.** extremely conservative, esp. in politics. —*n.* **2.** an ultraconservative person.

ul•tra•fiche (ul/trə fēsh/), *n.* a form of microfiche with the images greatly reduced in size, generally by a factor of 100 or more.

ul/tra•high fre/quency *n.* a radio frequency between 300 and 3000 megahertz.

ul/tra•ma•rine/ *adj.* **1.** of a deep blue color. —*n.* **2.** a deep blue pigment or color.

ul/tra•sound/ *n.* **1.** sound with a frequency greater than 20,000 Hz, approximately the upper limit of human hearing. **2.** the application of ultrasonic waves to medical diagnosis and therapy. —**ul/tra•son/ic**, *adj.*

ul/tra•vi/o•let *adj.* **1.** of, producing, or using electromagnetic radiation with wavelengths shorter than visible light but longer than x-rays. —*n.* **2.** ultraviolet radiation.

um•ber (um/bər), *n.* **1.** a brown earth used as a pigment. **2.** a dark dusky or reddish brown.

um•bil•i•cal (um bil/i kəl), *adj.* of, adjacent to, or characteristic of an umbilicus or umbilical cord.

umbil/ical cord/ *n.* a cordlike structure connecting a fetus with the placenta, conveying nourishment and removing wastes.

um•bil/i•cus (-kəs), *n.*, *pl.* **-ci** (-sī/). NAVEL.

um•brage (um/brij), *n.* **1.** offense; displeasure: *took umbrage at his rudeness.* **2.** foliage. **3.** shade or shadows.

um•brel•la (um brel/ə), *n.*, *pl.* **-las. 1.** a fabric cover on a frame mounted on a carrying stick, used for protection against rain or sun. **2.** something that protects. **3.** something that encompasses a number of groups or elements. [< It < L *umbella* sunshade]

um•laut (ōōm/lout), *n.* **1.** (in Germanic languages) assimilation in which a vowel is influenced by a following vowel or semivowel. **2.** a diacritical mark (¨) used over a vowel, esp. in German, to indicate umlaut.

ump (ump), *n.*, *v.t.*, *v.i.* UMPIRE.

um•pire (um/pīᵊr), *n.*, *v.*, **-pired**, **-pir•ing.** —*n.* **1.** a person selected to rule on plays in a sport. **2.** a person selected to settle a dispute. —*v.t.*, *v.i.* **3.** to decide or act as umpire.

ump•teen (ump/tēn/), *adj. Informal.* innumerable; many. —**ump•teenth/**, *adj.*

UN United Nations.

un-¹, a prefix meaning: not (*unable*); the opposite of (*unrest*).

un-², a prefix meaning: reversal of an action (*unbutton*); removal or depriving (*unburden*); completely (*unloose*).

un•a•ble (un ā′bəl), *adj.* lacking the necessary power, skill, or resources.

un′ac•count′a•ble *adj.* **1.** impossible to account for; inexplicable. **2.** not responsible. —**un′ac•count′a•bly,** *adv.*

un′af•fect′ed¹, *adj.* free from affectation.

un′af•fect′ed², *adj.* not altered or influenced.

u•nan•i•mous (yoō nan′ə məs), *adj.* being in or showing complete agreement. —**u•na•nim•i•ty** (yoō′nə nim′i tē), *n.* —**u•nan′i•mous•ly,** *adv.*

un′as•sum′ing *adj.* modest; unpretentious.

un′at•tached′ *adj.* **1.** not attached. **2.** not engaged or married.

un′a•vail′ing *adj.* not effectual; futile.

un′a•void′a•ble *adj.* incapable of being avoided. —**un′a•void′a•bly,** *adv.*

un′a•ware′ *adj.* **1.** not aware or conscious. —*adv.* **2.** UNAWARES.

un′a•wares′ *adv.* **1.** unknowingly or inadvertently. **2.** without warning; unexpectedly.

un•bal′anced *adj.* **1.** lacking balance. **2.** mentally disordered; disturbed.

un•bear′a•ble *adj.* unendurable; intolerable. —**un•bear′a•bly,** *adv.*

un′be•com′ing *adj.* not becoming; unattractive or unseemly.

un′be•liev′a•ble *adj.* **1.** too improbable to be believed. **2.** extraordinarily impressive. —**un′be•liev′a•bly,** *adv.*

un•bend′ *v.t., v.i.,* -bent, -bend•ing. **1.** to straighten from a bent form or position. **2.** to relax.

un•bend′ing *adj.* not bending; inflexible.

un•bid′den *adj.* **1.** not commanded. **2.** not asked or invited.

un•blush′ing *adj.* **1.** showing no remorse; shameless. **2.** not blushing. —**un•blush′ing•ly,** *adv.*

un•born′ *adj.* not yet born.

un•bos′om *v.t.* **1.** to disclose (a confidence, secret, etc.). —*Idiom.* **2.** unbosom oneself, to reveal one's thoughts and feelings.

un•bound′ed *adj.* having no limits or bounds.

un•bowed′ (-boud′), *adj.* **1.** not bowed or bent. **2.** not subjugated.

un•bri′dled *adj.* **1.** not restrained; uninhibited. **2.** not fitted with a bridle.

un•bro′ken *adj.* **1.** not broken; whole. **2.** not interrupted; undisturbed. **3.** not tamed, as a horse.

un•bur′den *v.t.* **1.** to free from a burden. **2.** to relieve (one's mind, conscience, etc.) by or as if by confessing.

un•but′ton *v.t.* to undo the buttons of.

un•called′-for′ *adj.* **1.** not required or wanted. **2.** unwarranted; improper.

un•can′ny *adj.,* -ni•er, -ni•est. **1.** seeming to have a supernatural basis. **2.** strange; mysterious.

un′cer•e•mo′ni•ous *adj.* **1.** abrupt; rude. **2.** without formalities; informal. —**un′cer•e•mo′ni•ous•ly,** *adv.*

un•cer′tain *adj.* **1.** not precisely known or fixed. **2.** not confident. **3.** not clearly determined. **4.** variable; unstable. **5.** not reliable or dependable. —**un•cer′tain•ty,** *n., pl.* -ties.

un•chart′ed *adj.* not shown on a map; unexplored.

un•clad′ *v.* **1.** a pt. and pp. of UNCLOTHE. —*adj.* **2.** not dressed; naked.

un•cle (ung′kəl), *n.* **1.** a brother of one's father or mother. **2.** an aunt's husband.

un•clean′ *adj.* **1.** not clean; dirty. **2.** morally impure. **3.** impure according to Biblical laws, esp. dietary laws.

Un′cle Sam′ (sam), *n.* the government or people of the U.S. personified as a tall man with white whiskers.

un•cloak′ *v.t.* **1.** to remove the cloak from. **2.** to reveal; expose.

un•clothe′ *v.t.* -clothed or -clad, -cloth•ing. **1.** to strip of clothes. **2.** to lay bare; uncover.

un•com′fort•a•ble *adj.* **1.** causing discomfort. **2.** experiencing discomfort. —**un•com′fort•a•bly,** *adv.*

un•com′mon *adj.,* -er, -est. **1.** not common; unusual. **2.** exceptional; outstanding. —**un•com′mon•ly,** *adv.*

un•com•pro•mis′ing *adj.* not accepting or making compromises; unyielding.

un′con•cern′ *n.* **1.** absence of concern; indifference. **2.** freedom from anxiety. —**un′con•cerned′,** *adj.*

un′con•di′tion•al *adj.* not limited by conditions; absolute. —**un′con•di′tion•al•ly,** *adv.*

un′con•scion•a•ble (un kon′shə nə bəl), *adj.* **1.** not restrained by conscience; unscrupulous. **2.** excessive or unreasonable. —**un′con′scion•a•bly,** *adv.*

un•con′scious *adj.* **1.** lacking awareness, sensation, or cognition, esp. temporarily. **2.** not perceived at the level of awareness. **3.** done unintentionally. —*n.* **4. the unconscious,** the part of the psyche that is rarely accessible to awareness but has an influence on behavior. —**un•con′scious•ly,** *adv.* —**un•con′scious•ness,** *n.*

un•cork′ *v.t.* **1.** to draw the cork from. **2.** to release or unleash.

un•couth (un kōōth′), *adj.* **1.** lacking grace; clumsy. **2.** rude or boorish.

un•cov′er *v.t.* **1.** to remove the cover, covering, or hat from. **2.** to lay bare; reveal. —*v.i.* **3.** to take off one's hat in respect.

unc′tion (ungk′shən), *n.* **1.** the act of anointing, esp. as medical treatment or religious rite. **2.** the oil used in anointing. **3.** affected or excessive earnestness.

unc′tu•ous (-chōō əs), *adj.* **1.** characterized by affected earnestness; excessively suave or smug. **2.** oily; greasy. —**unc′tu•ous•ness,** *n.*

un•cut′ *adj.* **1.** not cut. **2.** not shortened; unabridged. **3.** not yet given shape, as a diamond.

un•daunt′ed *adj.* not discouraged or dismayed.

un′de•cid′ed *adj.* **1.** not yet decided. **2.** not having one's mind made up.

un′de•mon′stra•tive *adj.* not given to expression of emotion; reserved.

un′de•ni′a•ble *adj.* **1.** incapable of being denied; incontestable. **2.** indisputably good. —**un′de•ni′a•bly,** *adv.*

un•der (un′dər), *prep.* **1.** beneath and covered by: *under a tree.* **2.** below the surface of: *under the ground.* **3.** in the position of receiving, sustaining, or enduring: *sank under the heavy load.* **4.** within the heading or category of: *books classified under fiction.* **5.** less than, as in degree or amount: *under $10.* **6.** below in rank. **7.** subject to the authority, effect, or guidance of: *worked under the prime minister.* **8.** in accordance with: *under the provisions of the law.* **9.** in the process of: *under construction.* —*adv.* **10.** below or beneath something. **11.** in or into a lower degree, amount, or limit. **12.** in or into a subordinate position or condition. —*adj.* **13.** lower, as in position, degree, or importance.

under- a prefix meaning: place or situation below or beneath (*underbrush*); lower in grade or dignity (*understudy*); of lesser degree, extent, or amount (*underage*).

un′der•a•chieve′ *v.i.,* -a•chieved, -a•chiev•ing. to perform below one's intellectual potential, esp. in school. —**un′der•a•chiev′er,** *n.*

un′der•age′ *adj.* being below the legal or required age.

un′der•bel′ly *n., pl.* -lies. **1.** the lower abdomen. **2.** a vulnerable area.

un′der•brush′ *n.* shrubs, saplings, and low vines growing under large trees.

un′der•car′riage *n.* the supporting framework underneath a vehicle, as an automobile.

un′der•clothes′ or **-cloth′ing,** *n.* (*used with a pl. v.*) UNDERWEAR.

un′der•cov′er *adj.* **1.** clandestine or secret. **2.** engaged in securing confidential information.

un′der•cur′rent *n.* **1.** a hidden tendency or feeling. **2.** a current, as of water, that flows below an upper current or surface.

un′der•cut′ *v.t.,* **-cut, -cut•ting. 1.** to cut under or beneath. **2.** to weaken or destroy the effectiveness of. **3.** to offer goods or services at a lower price or rate than. **4.** to hit (a ball) underhand so as to cause backspin.

un′der•de•vel′oped *adj.* **1.** improperly or insufficiently developed. **2.** (of a nation or area) having relatively low living standards or industrial productivity.

un′der•dog′ *n.* **1.** a person expected to lose in a contest or conflict. **2.** a victim of injustice.

un′der•done′ *adj.* not cooked enough.

un′der•es′ti•mate′ (-māt′), *v.t.,* **-mat•ed, -mat•ing.** to estimate at too low a value.

un′der•ex•pose′ *v.t.,* **-posed, -pos•ing.** to expose (film) to insufficient light or for too short a period.

un′der•gar′ment *n.* an article of underwear.

un′der•go′ *v.t.,* **-went, -gone, -go•ing. 1.** to be subjected to; experience. **2.** to endure or suffer.

un′der•grad′u•ate (-it, -āt′), *n.* a college or university student who has not received a first, esp. a bachelor's, degree.

un′der•ground′ (*adv.* -ground′; *adj.,* -ground′), *adv.* **1.** beneath the surface of the ground. **2.** in secrecy. —*adj.* **3.** existing, situated, or growing underground. **4.** hidden or secret. **5.** published or produced to reflect nonconformist or radical views. —*n.* **6.** the region beneath the surface of the ground. **7.** a secret organization fighting an established government or occupation forces. **8.** *Brit.* a subway.

un′der•growth′ *n.* UNDERBRUSH.

un′der•hand′ *adj.* **1.** secret and crafty. **2.** executed with the hand below the level of the shoulder. —*adv.* **3.** with an underhand motion. **4.** secretly; stealthily.

un′der•hand′ed *adj.* sly; secret.

un′der•line′ *v.t.,* **-lined, -lin•ing. 1.** to draw a line underneath. **2.** to stress or emphasize.

un′der•ling (-ling) *n.* a subordinate.

un•der•mine (un′dər mīn′; *esp. for 1,* un′dər mīn′), *v.t.,* **-mined, -min•ing. 1.** to impair or weaken by imperceptible stages. **2.** to make an excavation under.

un•der•neath (un′dər nēth′, -nēth′), *prep.* **1.** directly beneath; under. **2.** under the control of. —*adv.* **3.** at a lower level or position; below.

un′der•pass′ *n.* a passage running underneath, esp. under a railroad.

un′der•pin′ning *n.* **1.** a system of supports, as beneath a wall. **2.** Often, **-nings.** a foundation or basis.

un′der•priv′i•leged *adj.* denied the normal privileges of a society because of low economic and social status.

un′der•score′ *v.t.,* **-scored, -scor•ing.** UNDERLINE.

un′der•sec′re•tar′y *n., pl.* **-ies.** a government official subordinate to a principal secretary.

un′der•signed′ *n.* **the undersigned,** the person or persons signing a letter or document.

un′der•staffed′ *adj.* having an insufficient number of workers.

un′der•stand′ *v.,* **-stood, -stand•ing.** —*v.t.* **1.** to perceive the meaning of; comprehend. **2.** to have a thorough knowledge of. **3.** to interpret: *She understood his comment to be a criticism.* **4.** to regard as agreed or settled. **5.** to learn or hear. **6.** to infer (something not stated). —*v.i.* **7.** to perceive what is meant. **8.** to accept something tolerantly or sympathetically.

un′der•stand′ing *n.* **1.** comprehension. **2.** personal interpretation. **3.** intellectual ability; intelligence. **4.** a mutual agreement, esp. of a private or tacit kind. —*adj.* **5.** characterized by tolerance or sympathy.

un′der•state′ *v.t.,* **-stat•ed, -stat•ing. 1.** to state less strongly than the facts warrant. **2.** to set forth in restrained terms. —**un′der•state′ment,** *n.*

un′der•stud′y *n., pl.* **-ies,** *v.,* **-ied, -y•ing.** —*n.* **1.** a performer who learns another's role in order to serve as a replacement if necessary. —*v.t., v.i.* **2.** to learn (a role) as an understudy (to).

un•der•take′ *v.t.,* **-took, -tak•en, -tak•ing. 1.** to take upon oneself, as a task. **2.** to obligate oneself. **3.** to warrant or guarantee.

un′der•tak′er *n.* a person who supervises or arranges funerals.

un•der•tak•ing (un′dər tā′king, un′dər tā′-), *n.* **1.** something undertaken. **2.** a pledge or guarantee.

un′der-the-coun′ter *adj.* illegal; unauthorized.

un′der•tone′ *n.* **1.** a low or subdued tone. **2.** an underlying quality or element. **3.** a subdued color.

un′der•tow′ *n.* a strong subsurface current moving in a direction opposite that of the surface current.

un′der•wear′ *n.* clothing worn next to the skin under outer clothes.

un′der•world′ *n.* **1.** the criminal element of human society. **2.** the place where the spirits of the dead reside.

un•der•write (un′dər rīt′, un′dər rīt′), *v.t.,* **-wrote, -writ•ten, -writ•ing. 1.** to agree to finance (an undertaking). **2.** to guarantee the sale of (a security to be offered for public subscription). **3.** to write one's name at the end of (an insurance policy), becoming liable in case of specified losses. —**un′der•writ′er,** *n.*

un•do (un dōō′), *v.t.,* **-did, -done, -do•ing. 1.** to reverse or annul. **2.** to bring to ruin; destroy. **3.** to unfasten, unlatch, or untie.

un•do•ing *n.* **1.** a reversing or annulment. **2.** ruin. **3.** a cause of ruin.

un•doubt′ed *adj.* not doubted or disputed; accepted. —**un•doubt′ed•ly,** *adv.*

un•dress′ *v.t., v.i.* **1.** to remove the clothing (of). —*n.* **2.** informal dress. **3.** the state of being unclothed.

un•due′ *adj.* **1.** unwarranted; excessive. **2.** inappropriate; improper.

un•du•late (un′jə lāt′, un′dyə-, -də-), *v.i., v.t.,* **-lat•ed, -lat•ing. 1.** to move or cause to move with a wavelike motion. **2.** to have or cause to have a wavy form or surface. —**un′du•la′tion,** *n.*

un•du′ly *adv.* **1.** excessively. **2.** inappropriately.

un•dy′ing *adj.* deathless; eternal.

un•earned′ *adj.* **1.** not earned by work or service. **2.** not merited or deserved. **3.** (of income) derived from investments.

un•earth′ *v.t.* **1.** to dig out of the earth. **2.** to bring to light; uncover.

un•earth′ly *adj.* **1.** not of this earth or world. **2.** supernatural; weird. **3.** unreasonable or absurd.

un•eas′y *adj.,* **-i•er, -i•est. 1.** lacking ease of mind; restless or perturbed. **2.** constrained in manner; awkward. **3.** not conducive to ease. —**un•eas′i•ly,** *adv.* —**un•eas′i•ness,** *n.*

un•e′qual *adj.* **1.** not equal, as in rank or ability. **2.** not adequate: *unequal to the task.* **3.** uneven or variable. —**un•e′qual•ly,** *adv.*

un′e•quiv′o•cal *adj.* not ambiguous; clear. —**un′e•quiv′o•cal•ly,** *adv.*

un•err′ing *adj.* not erring; accurate. —**un•err′ing•ly,** *adv.*

un•e′ven *adj.* **1.** not level or flat. **2.** not uniform; varying. **3.** not equitable or fair. **4.** not straight, symmetrical, or parallel. **5.** (of a number) odd. —**un•e′ven•ly,** *adv.*

un′e•vent′ful *adj.* lacking in important or interesting occurrences; routine.

un′ex•cep′tion•al *adj.* not exceptional; ordinary.

un′ex•pect′ed *adj.* not expected; unforeseen. —**un′ex•pect′ed•ly,** *adv.*

un•fail′ing *adj.* **1.** completely dependable. **2.** inexhaustible; endless.

un•fair′ *adj.* not conforming to standards of justice, honesty, or impartiality. —**un•fair′ly,** *adv.* —**un•fair′ness,** *n.*

un•faith′ful *adj.* **1.** not faithful to duty, obligation, or promises; disloyal. **2.** not accurate or reliable; inexact. —**un•faith′ful•ly,** *adv.* —**un•faith′ful•ness,** *n.*

un′fa•mil′iar *adj.* **1.** not acquainted or conversant: *unfamiliar with the city.* **2.** different, unusual, or novel. —**un′fa•mil′i•ar′i•ty,** *n.*

un•feel′ing *adj.* **1.** lacking feeling or sensation. **2.** not sympathetic; hardhearted. —**un•feel′ing•ly,** *adv.*

un•fit′ *adj.* **1.** not suited or suitable. **2.** not competent; unqualified. **3.** not physically fit.

un•flap•pa•ble (un flap′ə bəl), *adj.* not easily upset or confused.

un•fledged (un flejd′), *adj.* **1.** lacking sufficient feathers for flight, as a young bird. **2.** immature or inexperienced.

un•fold′ *v.t.* **1.** to open from a folded state; spread out. **2.** to lay open to view; reveal. **3.** to disclose in words, esp. gradually. —*v.i.* **4.** to become unfolded. **5.** to develop; evolve.

un′for•get′ta•ble *adj.* impossible to forget.

un•for′tu•nate *adj.* **1.** suffering from bad luck. **2.** unfavorable or inauspicious. **3.** regrettable or deplorable. —*n.* **4.** an unfortunate person. —**un•for′-tu•nate•ly,** *adv.*

un•found′ed *adj.* not based on fact or reality; groundless.

un•friend′ly *adj.,* **-li•er, -li•est. 1.** not friendly or kind. **2.** not favorable; inhospitable.

un•frock′ *v.t.* to deprive of ecclesiastical rank, authority, and function.

un•gain•ly (un gān′lē), *adj.,* **-li•er, li•est.** not graceful; awkward.

un•god′ly *adj.,* **-li•er, -li•est. 1.** lacking piety; irreligious. **2.** sinful; wicked. **3.** outrageous; shocking.

un•gra′cious *adj.* **1.** not courteous; ill-mannered. **2.** not pleasant; disagreeable.

un•guard′ed *adj.* **1.** not guarded; unprotected. **2.** open; guileless. **3.** not cautious or discreet.

un•guent (ung′gwənt), *n.* an ointment or salve.

un•hand′ *v.t.* to release from a grasp.

un•hap′py *adj.,* **-pi•er, -pi•est. 1.** sad; wretched. **2.** unfortunate; unlucky. **3.** inappropriate; unsuitable. —**un•hap′pi•ly,** *adv.* —**un•hap′pi•ness,** *n.*

unheard′-of′ *adj.* not previously known; unprecedented.

un•hinge′ *v.t.,* **-hinged, -hing•ing. 1.** to remove from hinges. **2.** to throw into confusion; upset.

un•ho′ly *adj.,* **-li•er, -li•est. 1.** not holy; not sacred. **2.** sinful; wicked. **3.** dreadful; outrageous.

uni- a combining form meaning one (*unicorn*).

u′ni•corn′ *n.* a mythical creature resembling a horse, with a single horn in the center of its forehead.

u•ni•form (yōō′nə fôrm′), *adj.* **1.** identical or consistent with others. **2.** not varying; constant. —*n.* **3.** an identifying outfit worn by the members of a given group. —*v.t.* **4.** to clothe in or furnish with a uniform. —**u′ni•form′i•ty,** *n.* —**u′ni•form′ly,** *adv.*

u•ni•fy (yōō′nə fī′), *v.t., v.i.,* **-fied, -fy•ing.** to make or become a single unit. —**u′ni•fi•ca′tion,** *n.*

u′ni•lat′er•al *adj.* **1.** of, occurring on, or affecting one side only. **2.** undertaken or done by one side or party only; not mutual. —**u′ni•lat′er•al•ly,** *adv.*

un•im•peach•a•ble (un′im pē′chə bəl), *adj.* above suspicion or reproach.

un′in•hib′it•ed *adj.* not inhibited, esp. unrestrained by convention.

un•in′ter•est•ed *adj.* not interested; indifferent.

un•ion (yōōn′yən), *n.* **1.** the act of uniting or state of being united. **2.** something formed by uniting; combination. **3.** a number of persons, states, or nations joined together for a common purpose. **4. the Union,** the United States, esp. during the Civil War. **5.** LABOR UNION. **6.** a device emblematic of union, used in a flag or ensign. **7.** the state of being united in marriage. **8.** a contrivance for connecting parts, as of machinery.

un′ion jack′ *n.* **1.** a national flag consisting of a union. **2.** (*caps.*) the British national flag.

Un′ion of So′viet So′cialist Repub′lics, *n.* a former federal union of 15 constituent republics, in E Europe and N Asia, comprising the larger part of the former Russian Empire: dissolved in December 1991.

u•nique (yōō nēk′), *adj.* **1.** existing as the only one of a kind. **2.** having no equal; unparalleled. **3.** not typical; unusual. —**u•nique′ly,** *adv.* —**u•nique′-ness,** *n.*

u•ni•sex (yōō′nə seks′), *adj.* designed or suitable for both sexes.

u•ni•son (yōō′nə sən, -zən), *n.* **1. a.** identity in pitch. **b.** the performance of musical parts at the same pitch or at the octave. **2.** perfect agreement; accord.

u•nit (yōō′nit), *n.* **1.** a single entity. **2.** one of the individuals, parts, or elements into which a whole may be divided. **3.** a fixed quantity, as of money, used as a standard of measurement. **4.** the least positive integer; one. **5.** a machine, part, or system of machines having a specified purpose: *a heating unit.*

U•ni•tar•i•an (yōō′ni târ′ē ən), *n.* a member of a Christian denomination giving each congregation complete control over its affairs. —**U′ni•tar′i•an•ism,** *n.*

u•nite (yōō nīt′), *v.t., v.i.,* **u•nit•ed, u•nit•ing. 1.** to bring or come together in a single whole or unit. **2.** to join in mutual sympathy or a common goal. —**u•nit′ed,** *adj.*

Unit′ed Ar′ab Em′irates *n.* (*used with a sing. or pl. v.*) an independent federation in E Arabia.

Unit′ed King′dom *n.* a kingdom in NW Europe, consisting of Great Britain and Northern Ireland.

Unit′ed Na′tions *n.* (*used with a sing. v.*) an international organization formed in 1945 to promote peace, security, and cooperation.

Unit′ed States′ *n.* a republic comprising 48 conterminous states, the District of Columbia, and Alaska in North America, and Hawaii in the N Pacific.

u•ni•ty (yōō′ni tē), *n., pl.* **-ties. 1.** the state of being united; oneness. **2.** the state of being combined with others into a whole. **3.** concord, harmony, or agreement. **4.** *Math.* the number one. **5.** (in literature and art) harmony among the parts or elements of a work.

u•ni•ver•sal (yōō′nə vûr′səl), *adj.* **1.** of, characteristic of, or affecting all or the whole. **2.** applicable everywhere or in all cases. **3.** used or understood by all. **4.** present or existing everywhere.

U′niver′sal Prod′uct Code′ *n.* a standardized bar code used esp. in ringing up purchases at the supermarket.

u•ni•verse (yōō′nə vûrs′), *n.* **1.** the totality of objects and phenomena throughout space. **2.** the whole world.

u•ni•ver•si•ty (yōō′nə vûr′si tē), *n., pl.* **-ties.** an institution of higher learning authorized to confer both undergraduate and graduate degrees.

un•kempt (un kempt′), *adj.* **1.** not combed. **2.** disheveled; messy.

un•kind′ *adj.,* **-er, -est.** lacking in kindness or mercy; harsh.

un•known′ *adj.* **1.** not known; unfamiliar. **2.** not discovered, identified, or ascertained. —*n.* **3.** one that is unknown. **4.** a symbol representing an unknown quantity, esp. in algebra.

un•lace′ *v.t.,* **-laced, -lac•ing.** to loosen or undo the lacing of.

un•law′ful *adj.* **1.** not lawful; illegal. **2.** born out of wedlock; illegitimate. —**un•law′ful•ly,** *adv.*

un•lead′ed *adj.* (of gasoline) containing none of the poisonous antiknock agent tetraethyllead.

un•less (un les′, ən-), *conj.* except under the circumstances that.

un•let′tered *adj.* **1.** not educated. **2.** illiterate.

un•like′ *adj.* **1.** not alike; different. —*prep.* **2.** different from. **3.** not characteristic of.

un•like′ly *adj.,* **-li•er, -li•est. 1.** not likely; improbable. **2.** holding little prospect of success. —**un•like′li•hood′,** *n.*

un•load′ *v.t.* **1.** to take the load, charge, or cargo from. **2.** to discharge (cargo, passengers, etc.). **3.** to relieve of something burdensome or oppressive. **4.** to express (feelings, grievances, etc.) freely. **5.** to get rid of by sale in large quantities. —*v.i.* **6.** to unload something.

un•lock′ *v.t.* **1.** to undo the lock of. **2.** to release by or as if by unlocking. **3.** to lay open; disclose.

un•mask′ *v.t.* **1.** to strip a mask from. **2.** to reveal the true character of. —*v.i.* **3.** to take off one's mask.

un•mis•tak′a•ble *adj.* not mistakable; obvious. —**un′mis•tak′a•bly,** *adv.*

un•mit′i•gat′ed *adj.* **1.** not softened or lessened. **2.** unqualified or absolute.

un•mor′al *adj.* lacking or unaffected by a moral sense or moral principles.

un•nat′u•ral *adj.* **1.** contrary to nature. **2.** at variance with human nature. **3.** at variance with what is normal or to be expected. **4.** not genuine or spontaneous. —**un•nat′u•ral•ly,** *adv.*

un•nec′es•sar′y *adj.* not necessary; needless. —**un•nec′es•sar′i•ly,** *adv.*

un•nerve′ *v.t.*, **-nerved, -nerv•ing.** to deprive of courage, strength, or determination.

un•pack′ *v.t.* **1.** to remove the contents from (a box, trunk, etc.). **2.** to remove from a container, suitcase, or package. —*v.i.* **3.** to unpack a container.

un•par′al•leled′ *adj.* without parallel; unequaled. Also, *esp. Brit.,* **un•par′al•lelled′.**

un•plumbed′ *adj.* **1.** not measured with a plumb line. **2.** not understood or explored in depth.

un•pop′u•lar *adj.* not popular; disliked, disapproved, or ignored. —**un′pop•u•lar′i•ty,** *n.*

un•prin′ci•pled *adj.* lacking or not based on moral principles; unscrupulous.

un•print′a•ble *adj.* unfit for print, esp. because of obscenity.

un•rav′el *v.*, **-eled, -el•ing** or (*esp. Brit.*) **-elled, -el•ling.** —*v.t.* **1.** to separate the threads of (a fabric, rope, etc.). **2.** to make plain or clear; solve. —*v.i.* **3.** to become unraveled.

un•rea′son•a•ble *adj.* **1.** not guided by reason or sound judgment. **2.** excessive or immoderate. —**un•rea′son•a•bly,** *adv.*

un′re•con•struct′ed *adj.* stubbornly maintaining positions or beliefs considered out of date.

un′re•mit′ting *adj.* not abating; incessant.

un•rest′ *n.* disturbance or turmoil; agitation.

un•roll′ *v.t.* **1.** to spread out (something rolled). **2.** to display; reveal. —*v.i.* **3.** to become unrolled or spread out.

un•ruf′fled *adj.* **1.** calm; composed. **2.** not ruffled, as a surface.

un•ru•ly (un rōō′lē), *adj.*, **-li•er, -li•est.** difficult to discipline or control; not cooperative.

un•sa′vor•y *adj.* **1.** tasteless or insipid. **2.** unpleasant in taste or smell. **3.** morally objectionable.

un•screw′ *v.t.* **1.** to loosen a screw from. **2.** to unfasten or withdraw by turning.

un•sea′son•a•ble *adj.* **1.** being out of season. **2.** not timely; inopportune.

un•seat′ *v.t.* **1.** to dislodge from a seat, esp. from a saddle. **2.** to remove from political office.

un•seem′ly *adj.*, **-li•er, -li•est. 1.** not in keeping with accepted standards of taste or proper form. **2.** not appropriate.

un•set′tle *v.*, **-tled, -tling.** —*v.t.* **1.** to cause to be unstable; disturb. **2.** to agitate the mind or emotions of. —*v.i.* **3.** to become unsettled.

un•shack′le *v.t.*, **-led, -ling.** to free from or as if from shackles.

un•sight′ly *adj.*, **-li•er, -li•est.** unpleasant to look at; ugly.

un•skilled′ *adj.* **1.** lacking skill. **2.** not demanding skill. **3.** showing a lack of skill.

un•sound′ *adj.*, **-er, -est. 1.** unhealthy, as the body or mind. **2.** not solid or firm, as foundations. **3.** not valid; fallacious. **4.** not strong or secure.

un•spar′ing *adj.* **1.** liberal or profuse. **2.** unmerciful; harsh.

un•speak′a•ble *adj.* **1.** exceeding the power of speech; inexpressible. **2.** inexpressibly bad, evil, or objectionable: *unspeakable crimes.* —**un•speak′a•bly,** *adv.*

un•sta′ble *adj.* **1.** not stable; unsteady. **2.** liable to change or fluctuate. **3.** marked by emotional instability. **4.** not constant; wavering. **5.** of or being a chemical compound that readily decomposes.

un•strung′ *adj.* nervously upset; unnerved.

un•sung′ *adj.* **1.** not sung. **2.** not celebrated in song or verse.

un•tan′gle *v.t.*, **-gled, -gling. 1.** to disentangle; unsnarl. **2.** to clear up; resolve.

un•ten′a•ble (un ten′ə bəl), *adj.* incapable of being defended, as an argument; indefensible.

un•think′a•ble *adj.* not to be considered; inconceivable.

un•tie′ *v.*, **-tied, -ty•ing.** —*v.t.* **1.** to loose or unfasten (something tied). **2.** to free from or as if from restraint. —*v.i.* **3.** to become untied.

un•til (un til′), *conj.* **1.** up to the time that or when. **2.** before: *won't go until next year.* —*prep.* **3.** onward to the time or occurrence of: *worked until 6 P.M.* **4.** before: *didn't go until night.*

un•to (un′tōō; *unstressed* -tə), *prep.* **1.** to. **2.** until.

un•told′ *adj.* **1.** not told or revealed. **2.** not counted; incalculable.

un•touch′a•ble *adj.* **1.** not permitted to be touched. —*n.* **2.** a member of the lowest caste in India.

un•to′ward *adj.* **1.** unfavorable or unfortunate. **2.** not proper; unseemly.

un•true′ *adj.*, **-tru•er, -tru•est. 1.** not true to fact; false. **2.** not faithful; disloyal. **3.** not true to a standard.

un•truth′ *n.* **1.** the state or character of being untrue. **2.** divergence from truth. **3.** something untrue; a falsehood or lie. —**un•truth′ful,** *adj.* —**un•truth′ful•ly,** *adv.*

un•used (un yōōzd′ *for 1, 2;* un yōōst′ *for 3*), *adj.* **1.** not put to use. **2.** never having been used. **3.** not accustomed.

un•u′su•al *adj.* not usual; uncommon. —**un•u′su•al•ly,** *adv.*

un•veil′ *v.t.* **1.** to remove a veil or covering from. **2.** to reveal by or as if by unveiling.

un•well′ *adj.* not well; ailing.

un•wield′y *adj.*, **-i•er, -i•est.** wielded with difficulty; not easily handled or managed.

un•wind (un wīnd′), *v.*, **-wound, -wind•ing.** —*v.t.* **1.** to undo or loosen from a coiled condition. **2.** to disentangle or disengage. —*v.i.* **3.** to become unwound. **4.** to become relaxed.

un•wise′ *adj.*, **-wis•er, -wis•est.** not wise; foolish. —**un•wise′ly,** *adv.*

un•wit′ting *adj.* **1.** not intentional; inadvertent. **2.** not knowing; unaware. —**un•wit′ting•ly,** *adv.*

un•wont′ed *adj.* not customary, habitual, or usual.

un•wor′thy *adj.*, **-thi•er, -thi•est. 1.** lacking worth or excellence. **2.** not proper; inappropriate. **3.** not deserving.

un•wrap′ *v.t.*, **-wrapped, -wrap•ping.** to remove or open the wrapping of.

up (up), *adv.*, *prep.*, *adj.*, *n.*, *v.*, **upped, up•ping.** —*adv.* **1.** to, toward, or in a higher position. **2.** to or in an erect position. **3.** out of bed. **4.** above the horizon. **5.** to or at a higher point. **6.** to or at a higher degree, as of intensity. **7.** to or at a point of equal advance or extent: *caught up in the race.* **8.** into or in activity or operation: *to set up shop.* **9.** into existence, view, or consideration: *The lost papers turned up.* **10.** into or in safekeeping or storage: *to put up preserves.* **11.** to an end; entirely: *to be used up.* **12.** to a halt: *The car pulled up.* **13.** (used with a verb for additional emphasis): *Wake him up.* **14.** at bat in baseball. **15.** in the lead. **16.** each; apiece: *The score was seven up.* —*prep.* **17.** to, toward, or at a higher place on or in: *went up the stairs.* **18.** at or to a farther point on or in: *a store up the street.* **19.** toward the source of: *to float up a stream.* **20.** toward the interior of. —*adj.* **21.** moving or facing upward: *the up elevator.* **22.** informed; aware: *up on current events.* **23.** concluded; ended: *Your time is up.* **24.** going on; happening: *What's up?* **25.** in an erect or raised position. **26.** risen above the horizon. **27.** out of bed. **28.** in a state of agitation or excitement. **29.** higher than formerly: *Prices are up.* **30.** ahead of an opponent: *He's two sets up.* **31.** under consideration: *a candidate up for reelection.* —*n.* **32.** a time of good fortune or prosperity: *the ups and downs in a career.*

33. an upward slope. —*v.t.* **34.** to increase or raise. —*v.i.* **35.** *Informal.* to begin something abruptly: *He upped and ran away.* —*Idiom.* **36. on the up and up,** honest. **37. up against,** faced with. **38. up to,** **a.** as far as. **b.** as many as. **c.** capable of: *Is he up to the job?* **d.** dependent upon: *It's up to you.* **e.** doing: *What is he up to lately?*

up- a combining form meaning up (*upland*).

up′-and-com′ing *adj.* likely to succeed; promising.

up′beat′ *n.* **1.** an unaccented beat in music. —*adj.* **2.** optimistic; happy.

up•braid (up brād′), *v.t.* to criticize or reproach severely.

up′bring′ing *n.* the care and training of children.

UPC Universal Product Code.

up′com′ing *adj.* about to take place or appear.

up′coun′try *adj., adv.* of, toward, or situated in the interior of a region or country.

up•date (up′dāt′; *v. also* up′dāt′), *v.,* **-dat•ed, -dat•ing,** *n.* —*v.t.* **1.** to bring up to date. —*n.* **2.** new or current information used in updating. **3.** an updated version or account.

up•end′ *v.t., v.i.* to set or stand on end.

up′-front′ *adj.* **1.** invested or paid in advance. **2.** honest; candid.

up•grade (*n.* up′grād′; *v.* up grād′, up′grād′), *n., v.,* **-grad•ed, -grad•ing.** —*n.* **1.** an upward incline. **2.** an increase, rise, advance, or improvement. **3.** an enhanced version, improved model, etc. **4.** something that improves or enhances. —*v.t.* **5.** to raise in rank, quality, value, etc.

up•heav•al (up hē′vəl), *n.* **1.** violent change or disturbance. **2.** a thrusting upward, esp. of a part of the earth's crust.

up′hill′ *adv.* **1.** up the slope of a hill or incline. —*adj.* **2.** going upward on a hill. **3.** laboriously fatiguing or difficult.

up•hold′ *v.t.,* **-held, -hold•ing. 1.** to defend, as against opposition. **2.** to keep from sinking. **3.** to lift upward.

up•hol•ster (up hōl′stər, ə pōl′-), *v.t.* to provide (furniture) with coverings, cushions, stuffing, etc. —**up•hol′ster•er,** *n.* —**up•hol′ster•y,** *n., pl.* **-ies.**

up′keep′ *n.* **1.** the maintenance necessary for the proper functioning of a machine, building, etc. **2.** the cost of upkeep.

up•land (up′lənd, -land′), *n.* land elevated above other land.

up•lift (*v.* up lift′; *n.* up′lift′), *v.t.* **1.** to lift up; raise. **2.** to improve socially, intellectually, or morally. —*n.* **3.** the act of lifting up. **4.** social, intellectual, or moral improvement.

up•on (ə pon′, ə pôn′), *prep.* on.

up′per[1], *adj.* **1.** higher, as in place, position, or rank. —*n.* **2.** the part of a shoe or boot above the sole.

up′per[2], *n. Slang.* a stimulant drug, esp. an amphetamine.

up′per•case′ *adj.* **1.** (of an alphabetical character) capital. —*n.* **2.** a capital letter.

up′per hand′ *n.* the controlling position; advantage.

up•pi•ty (up′i tē), *adj. Informal.* haughty, snobbish, or arrogant.

up•right (up′rīt′, up rīt′), *adj.* **1.** erect, as in posture. **2.** raised or directed vertically. **3.** righteous, honest, or just. —*n.* **4.** something standing upright. —*adv.* **5.** in an upright position or direction.

up•ris•ing (up′rī′zing, up rī′-), *n.* an insurrection or revolt.

up′roar′ *n.* a state of violent and noisy disturbance; tumult.

up•roar′i•ous (-ē əs), *adj.* characterized by uproar. **2.** very funny.

up•root′ *v.t.* **1.** to pull out by or as if by the roots. **2.** to displace from a country or way of life.

up′scale′ *adj.* of or for people at the upper end of an economic scale.

up•set (*v., adj.* up set′; *n.* up′set′), *v.,* **-set, -set•ting,** *n., adj.* —*v.t.* **1.** to knock over; overturn. **2.** to disturb emotionally. **3.** to throw into disorder. **4.** to disturb physically. **5.** to defeat (an opponent fa-

vored to win). —*v.i.* **6.** to become overturned. —*n.* **7.** an upsetting or instance of being upset. **8.** an unexpected defeat. **9.** a disturbance or disorder. —*adj.* **10.** overturned. **11.** disturbed or disordered.

up′shot′ *n.* the final outcome; result.

up′side down′ *adv.* **1.** with the upper part undermost. **2.** in or into complete disorder. —**up′side-down′,** *adj.*

up′stage′ *adv., adj., v.,* **-staged, -stag•ing.** —*adv.* **1.** at or toward the back of a stage. —*adj.* **2.** of the back of a stage. —*v.t.* **3.** to draw attention away from (another actor), as by moving upstage. **4.** to outdo professionally or socially.

up′stairs′ *adv.* **1.** up the stairs; to or on an upper floor. **2.** to or at a higher level of authority. —*adj.* **3.** of or situated on an upper floor. —*n.* **4.** (*usu. with a sing. v.*) the part of a building above the ground floor.

up′start′ *n.* **1.** a person who has risen suddenly to wealth, power, or importance, esp. one who is arrogant. —*adj.* **2.** being or like an upstart.

up′tight′ *adj. Informal.* **1.** tense or nervous. **2.** stiffly conventional.

up′-to-date′ *adj.* **1.** in keeping with the times; modern. **2.** extending to the present time; current.

up•ward (up′wərd), *adv.* Also, **up′wards. 1.** toward a higher place, position, or level. —*adj.* **2.** moving or tending upward. —*Idiom.* **3. upward(s) of,** more than. —**up′ward•ly,** *adv.*

u•ra•ni•um (yŏŏ rā′nē əm), *n.* a white, radioactive metallic element used in nuclear weapons and as a nuclear fuel. *Symbol:* U; *at. wt.:* 238.03; *at. no.:* 92.

U•ra•nus (yŏŏr′ə nəs, yŏŏ rā′-), *n.* the planet seventh in order from the sun.

ur•ban (ûr′bən), *adj.* of, characteristic of, or being a city. [< L *urbānus* < *urbs* city]

ur•bane (ûr bān′), *adj.* suave and polished in manner or style; sophisticated. —**ur•ban′i•ty** (-ban′i tē), *n.*

ur•chin (ûr′chin), *n.* a mischievous child.

u•re•a (yŏŏ rē′ə, yŏŏr′ē ə), *n.* a compound occurring in body fluids, esp. urine.

u•re•ter (yŏŏ rē′tər), *n.* a duct that conveys urine from a kidney to the bladder.

u•re•thra (yŏŏ rē′thrə), *n., pl.* **-thrae** (-thrē), **-thras.** a duct that conveys urine and in most male mammals also conveys semen.

urge (ûrj), *v.,* **urged, urg•ing,** *n.* —*v.t.* **1.** to push along; impel. **2.** to incite, as to speed or effort. **3.** to try to induce or persuade. **4.** to insist on or assert earnestly. **5.** to recommend earnestly. —*n.* **6.** the act of urging. **7.** an impelling action, influence, or force.

ur•gent (ûr′jənt), *adj.* **1.** requiring immediate action or attention. **2.** insistent in urging; importunate. —**ur′gen•cy,** *n., pl.* **-cies.** —**ur′gent•ly,** *adv.*

u•ri•nal (yŏŏr′ə nl), *n.* **1.** a wall fixture used by men for urinating. **2.** a receptacle for urine.

u′ri•nar′y (-ner′ē), *adj.* **1.** of urine. **2.** of the organs that secrete and discharge urine.

u′ri•nate′ (-nāt′), *v.i.,* **-nat•ed, -nat•ing.** to discharge urine. —**u′ri•na′tion,** *n.*

u•rine (yŏŏr′in), *n.* the yellowish liquid excreted by the kidneys.

urn (ûrn), *n.* **1.** a vase, esp. one with a pedestal. **2.** a vase for holding the ashes of the cremated dead. **3.** a container with a spigot for serving hot tea or coffee.

u•rol•o•gy (yŏŏ rol′ə jē), *n.* the medical study of the urinary or genitourinary tract. —**u•rol′o•gist,** *n.*

U•ru•guay (yŏŏr′ə gwā′, -gwī′, ŏŏr′-), *n.* a republic in SE South America. —**U′ru•guay′an,** *adj., n.*

us (us), *pron.* the objective case of WE.

US or **U.S.,** United States.

us•age (yŏŏ′sij, -zij), *n.* **1.** a custom, habit, or practice. **2.** the manner in which a language is spoken or written. **3.** a particular expression: *a new usage.* **4.** a way of using; treatment.

use (*v.* yŏŏz *or, for pt. form of* 7, yŏŏst; *n.* yŏŏs), *v.,* **used, us•ing,** —*v.t.* **1.** to put into service; employ. **2.** to consume or expend. **3.** to treat or behave toward. **4.** to take unfair advantage of. **5.** to consume habitually. **6.** to habituate; accustom.

—*v.i.* **7.** to be accustomed, wont, or customarily found: *He used to go every day.* —*n.* **8.** the act of using or state of being used. **9.** a way of using. **10.** the purpose for which something is used. **11.** the power or right of using something: *lost the use of an eye.* **12.** utility; usefulness. **13.** occasion or need to use: *Have you any use for a calendar?* —**use′ful** (yōōs′-), *adj.* —**use′less** (yōōs′-), *adj.* —**us′er,** *n.*

us′er-friend′ly *adj.* easy to operate or understand: *a user-friendly computer.*

ush•er (ush′ər), *n.* **1.** a person who escorts people to seats, as in a theater. **2.** a male attendant of a bridegroom. **3.** an officer whose duty it is to walk before a person of rank. —*v.t.* **4.** to act as an usher to. **5.** to precede or herald.

u•su•al (yōō′zhōō əl), *adj.* **1.** predictable on the basis of previous experience: *her usual skill.* **2.** commonly met with or observed in experience. **3.** commonplace; everyday. —**u′su•al•ly,** *adv.*

u•surp (yōō sûrp′, -zûrp′), *v.t.* **1.** to seize and hold (a position, office, power, etc.) by force or without legal right. **2.** to use without authority or right. —**u•surp′er,** *n.*

u•su•ry (yōō′zhə rē), *n., pl.* **-ries. 1.** the practice of lending money at an exorbitant interest rate. **2.** an exorbitant rate of interest. —**u′su•rer,** *n.* —**u•su′ri•ous** (-zhōōr′ē əs), *adj.*

UT or **Ut.,** Utah.

u•ten•sil (yōō ten′səl), *n.* **1.** an instrument or ves-

sel commonly used esp. in a kitchen. **2.** any useful instrument or tool.

u•ter•us (yōō′tər əs), *n., pl.* **u•ter•i** (yōō′tə rī′), **u•ter•us•es.** a hollow organ of female mammals in which the fertilized egg develops during pregnancy. —**u′ter•ine** (-in), *adj.*

u•til•i•tar•i•an (yōō til′i târ′ē ən), *adj.* **1.** of or characterized by utility. **2.** designed for or concerned with usefulness rather than beauty.

u•til•i•ty *n., pl.* **-ties. 1.** the state or quality of being useful. **2.** a public service, as the providing of electricity or gas. **3.** PUBLIC UTILITY.

u•ti•lize (yōōt′l īz′), *v.t.,* **-lized, -liz•ing.** to put to profitable or practical use. —**u′ti•li•za′tion,** *n.*

ut•most (ut′mōst′), *adj.* **1.** of the greatest or highest degree or quantity. **2.** being at the farthest point or extremity. —*n.* **3.** the greatest degree or amount.

U•to′pi•an (yōō tō′pē ən) *adj.* impossibly perfect.

ut•ter[1] (ut′ər), *v.t.* **1.** to give audible, esp. verbal, expression to. **2.** to give forth (a sound).

ut•ter[2] (ut′ər), *adj.* total; absolute. —**ut′ter•ly,** *adv.*

ut′ter•ly *adv.* completely; absolutely.

u•vu•la (yōō′vyə lə), *n., pl.* **-las, -lae** (-lē′). the fleshy, conical body projecting downward from the soft palate. —**u′vu•lar,** *adj.*

Uz•bek•i•stan (ōōz bek′ə stan′, -stän′, uz-), *n.* a republic in S central Asia: formerly a part of the USSR.

---

a b c d e f g h i j k l m n o p q r s t u V w x y z

V, v (vē), *n., pl.* **Vs** or **V's, vs** or **v's. 1.** the 22nd letter of the English alphabet, a consonant. **2.** something shaped like a V.

V *Symbol.* **1.** the Roman numeral for five. **2.** *Chem.* vanadium.

v. 1. vector. **2.** verb. **3.** verse. **4.** version. **5.** verso. **6.** versus. **7.** see. [< L *vidē*] **8.** vocative. **9.** voice. **10.** volt. **11.** voltage. **12.** volume.

VA 1. Veterans Administration. **2.** Virginia.

Va. Virginia.

va•can•cy (vā′kən sē), *n., pl.* **-cies. 1.** the state of being vacant. **2.** a vacant or unoccupied place, esp. one for rent. **3.** an unoccupied position or office.

va′cant (-kənt), *adj.* **1.** having no contents; empty. **2.** having no occupant. **3.** lacking in thought or intelligence. **4.** not filled, as by an incumbent. **5.** free from work, business, or activity.

va•cate (vā′kāt), *v.t.,* **-cat•ed, -cat•ing. 1.** to cause to be vacant. **2.** to deprive of validity; annul.

va•ca•tion (vā kā′shən, və-), *n.* **1.** a period of rest or freedom from regular work, study, etc. —*v.i.* **2.** to take or have a vacation. —**va•ca′tion•er,** *n.*

vac•ci•nate (vak′sə nāt′), *v.t.,* **-nat•ed, -nat•ing.** to inoculate with a vaccine. —**vac′ci•na′tion,** *n.*

vac•cine (vak sēn′), *n.* **1.** a preparation of weakened or killed bacteria or viruses introduced into the body to prevent a disease by stimulating antibodies against it. **2.** a software program that helps to protect against computer viruses.

vac•il•late (vas′ə lāt′), *v.i.,* **-lat•ed, -lat•ing. 1.** to be indecisive or irresolute. **2.** to sway unsteadily. **3.** to oscillate or fluctuate. —**vac′il•la′tion,** *n.*

va•cu•i•ty (va kyōō′i tē, və-), *n., pl.* **-ties. 1.** the state of being vacuous. **2.** absence of thought or intelligence. **3.** something senseless or stupid. **4.** an empty space. —**vac•u•ous** (vak′yōō əs), *adj.* —**vac′u•ous•ly,** *adv.*

vac•u•um (vak′yōōm, -yōō əm, -yəm), *n., pl.* **-u•ums** for 1-4, **-u•a** (-yōō ə) for 1-3; *v.* —*n.* **1.** a space entirely devoid of matter. **2.** an enclosed space from which matter, esp. air, has been partially removed. **3.** an emptiness; void. **4.** VACUUM CLEANER. —*v.t., v.i.* **5.** to clean with a vacuum cleaner.

vac′uum bot′tle *n.* a bottle or flask with a double wall enclosing a vacuum to retard heat transfer.

vac′uum clean′er *n.* an electrical appliance for cleaning carpets, floors, etc., by suction.

vac′uum-packed′ *adj.* packed, as in a can, with as much air as possible evacuated before sealing.

vac′uum tube′ *n.* an electron tube from which almost all air or gas has been evacuated.

vag•a•bond (vag′ə bond′), *adj.* **1.** wandering without a settled home. **2.** leading an unsettled or carefree life. —*n.* **3.** a usu. homeless person who wanders from place to place. **4.** a tramp; vagrant.

va•gar•y (və gâr′ē, vā′gə rē), *n., pl.* **-ies.** a capricious or erratic action, notion, or course.

va•gi•na (və jī′nə), *n., pl.* **-nas, -nae** (-nē). the passage leading from the uterus to the vulva in female mammals. —**vag•i•nal** (vaj′ə nəl), *adj.*

va•grant (vā′grənt), *n.* **1.** a person who wanders about idly with no permanent home or employment. —*adj.* **2.** wandering from place to place. **3.** of or characteristic of a vagrant. **4.** not fixed or settled in course. —**va′gran•cy,** *n., pl.* **-cies.**

vague (vāg), *adj.,* **va•guer, va•guest. 1.** not clearly stated or expressed. **2.** indefinite or indistinct in nature or character. —**vague′ly,** *adv.* —**vague′ness,** *n.*

vain (vān), *adj.,* **-er, -est. 1.** excessively proud of or concerned about one's own appearance or achievements. **2.** unsuccessful; futile. **3.** without significance or value. —*Idiom.* **4. in vain, a.** without effect or avail. **b.** in an irreverent manner. —**vain′ly,** *adv.*

vain′glo′ry *n.* **1.** excessive and often boastful vanity. **2.** empty pomp or show. —**vain•glo′ri•ous,** *adj.*

val•ance (val′əns, vā′ləns), *n.* **1.** a short curtain across the top of a window. **2.** a drapery hung from an edge, as of a bed.

vale (vāl), *n.* VALLEY.

val•e•dic•to•ri•an (val′i dik tôr′ē ən), *n.* the student in a graduating class who delivers the valedictory.

val′e•dic′to•ry (-tə rē), *n., pl.* **-ries.** a farewell address, esp. one delivered at commencement exercises.

va•lence (vā′ləns) also **-len•cy** (-lən sē), *n.* the relative combining capacity of an atom or group compared with that of the standard hydrogen atom.

val•en•tine (val′ən tīn′), *n.* **1.** an amatory or sentimental card or gift sent on Valentine's Day. **2.** a sweetheart chosen or greeted on this day.

val•et (va lā′, val′it, val′ā), *n.* **1.** a male servant who attends to his employer's personal needs, as by taking care of clothing. **2.** an employee who cares for the clothing of hotel patrons.

val•iant (val′yənt), *adj.* boldly courageous; heroic.

val•id (val′id), *adj.* **1.** well-founded; sound. **2.** legally effective or binding. —**val′i•date′**, *v.t.*, -**dat• ed, -dat•ing.** —**va•lid′i•ty** (və lid′i tē), *n.*

va•lise (və lēs′), *n.* a small piece of hand luggage.

val•ley (val′ē), *n.*, *pl.* **-leys. 1.** an elongated depression between uplands, hills, or mountains. **2.** a region drained by a river system.

val•or (val′ər), *n.* great courage. Also, *esp. Brit.,* **val′our.** —**val′or•ous,** *adj.*

val•u•a•ble (val′yo͞o ə bəl, -yə bəl), *adj.* **1.** having considerable monetary worth. **2.** of considerable use or importance. —*n.* **3.** Usu., **-bles.** personal articles of great value.

val′u•a′tion (-yo͞o ā′shən), *n.* **1.** the act of appraisal. **2.** an estimated value.

val′ue *n.*, *v.*, -**ued,** -**u•ing.** —*n.* **1.** relative or assigned worth or importance. **2.** monetary or material worth. **3.** equivalent worth in money, goods, or services. **4.** a numerical quantity represented by a figure or symbol. **5.** Often, **-ues.** the abstract concepts of what is right or worthwhile. **6.** degree of lightness or darkness in a color. **7.** the relative duration of a musical tone as expressed by a note. —*v.t.* **8.** to calculate the monetary value of. **9.** to consider with respect to worth or importance. **10.** to regard highly. —**val′ue•less,** *adj.*

valve (valv), *n.* **1.** a device for controlling the flow of a fluid. **2.** a movable part that opens or closes the passage in a valve. **3.** a membranous structure that permits the flow of a body fluid in one direction only. **4.** (in musical wind instruments) a device for changing the length of the air column to alter the pitch of a tone. **5.** one of the separable pieces composing a mollusk shell. —**valved,** *adj.*

va•moose (va mo͞os′), *v.i.,* -**moosed, -moos•ing.** *Slang.* to leave hurriedly.

vamp¹ (vamp), *n.* **1.** the portion of a shoe or boot upper that covers the instep and toes. **2.** an introductory musical passage often consisting of a repeated succession of chords. —*v.t.* **3.** to repair with a new vamp. —*v.i.* **4.** to play a musical vamp.

vamp² (vamp), *n.* **1.** a seductive woman who exploits men. —*v.t.*, *v.i.* **2.** to seduce (a man) with feminine charms.

vam•pire (vam′pīⁿr), *n.* **1.** (in folklore) a reanimated corpse that is said to suck the blood of sleeping persons at night. **2.** a person who preys on others.

van¹ (van), *n.* the vanguard.

van² (van), *n.* **1.** a large covered truck for moving goods or animals. **2.** a boxlike vehicle for passengers, camping, etc.

van•dal (van′dl), *n.* a person who willfully destroys or mars property.

Van•dyke′ (van dīk′), *n.* short, pointed beard.

vane (vān), *n.* **1.** WEATHER VANE. **2.** a blade or plate attached radially to a cylinder or shaft that moves or is moved by a fluid.

van′guard′ *n.* **1.** the front part of an advancing army. **2.** the forefront in a movement or field.

va•nil•la (və nil′ə; *often* -nel′ə), *n.*, *pl.* **-las. 1.** a climbing orchid bearing podlike fruit. **2.** Also called **vanil′la bean′.** the fruit of this orchid. **3.** a flavoring extract made from this fruit.

van•ish (van′ish), *v.i.* **1.** to disappear quickly from sight. **2.** to come to an end.

van•i•ty (van′i tē), *n.*, *pl.* **-ties. 1.** excessive pride in oneself or one's appearance. **2.** lack of real value; worthlessness. **3.** something worthless or pointless. **4.** a small case for cosmetics. **5.** a table surmounted by a mirror, used while dressing, applying makeup, etc.

van•quish (vang′kwish, van′-), *v.t.* **1.** to defeat in battle or in a contest. **2.** to overcome: *vanquished all doubt.* —**van′quish•er,** *n.*

van•tage (van′tij, vän′-), *n.* **1.** a position affording a strategic advantage or commanding view. **2.** an advantage or superiority.

Va•nu•a•tu (vä′no͞o ä′to͞o), *n.* a republic consisting of a group of islands in the SW Pacific, W of Fiji. —**Va′nu•a′tu•an,** *adj.*, *n.*

vap•id (vap′id), *adj.* lacking spirit or interest; dull.

va•por (vā′pər), *n.* **1.** visible matter, as fog or smoke, suspended in the air. **2.** a substance in gaseous form that is a liquid or solid under normal conditions. Also, *esp. Brit.,* **va′pour.**

va′por•ize′ *v.t.*, *v.i.*, -**ized, -iz•ing.** to change into vapor. —**va′por•i•za′tion,** *n.* —**va′por•iz′er,** *n.*

var•i•a•ble (vâr′ē ə bəl), *adj.* **1.** apt to vary. **2.** capable of being varied. **3.** inconstant; fickle. —*n.* **4.** something variable. **5. a.** a quantity that may assume any given value or set of values. **b.** a symbol that represents this. —**var′i•a•bil′i•ty,** *n.* —**var′i• a•bly,** *adv.*

var′i•ance (-əns), *n.* **1.** the state of being variable. **2.** degree of difference. **3.** a permit to do something normally regulated by law. —*Idiom.* **4. at variance,** in a state of disagreement.

var′i•ant *adj.* **1.** exhibiting variety or variation. **2.** differing, esp. from something of the same kind. —*n.* **3.** one that varies. **4.** a different spelling, pronunciation, or form of the same word.

var′i•a′tion (-ā′shən), *n.* **1.** an act or instance of varying. **2.** amount or degree of change. **3.** a different form of something. **4.** the transformation of a musical theme with changes in harmony, rhythm, and melody.

var•i•col•ored (vâr′i kul′ərd), *adj.* having various colors.

var•i•cose (var′i kōs′), *adj.* abnormally swollen: *a varicose vein.*

var•i•e•gate (vâr′ē i gāt′, vâr′i-), *v.t.*, -**gat•ed, -gat•ing. 1.** to make varied in appearance, as by adding different colors. **2.** to give variety to. —**var′• i•e•gat′ed,** *adj.*

va•ri•e•ty *n.*, *pl.* **-ties. 1.** the state of being diversified. **2.** difference; discrepancy. **3.** a number of different things, esp. ones in the same category. **4.** a kind or sort. **5.** a category within a species, based on a hereditary difference.

var•i•ous (vâr′ē əs), *adj.* **1.** of different kinds. **2.** different; dissimilar. **3.** several; many. **4.** individual; separate. **5.** having many different qualities. —**var′• i•ous•ly,** *adv.*

var•mint (vär′mənt), *n.* **1.** an undesirable, usu. verminous animal. **2.** an obnoxious person.

var•nish (vär′nish), *n.* **1.** a preparation for coating surfaces, as of wood, consisting of resinous matter dissolved, esp. in oil or alcohol. **2.** a coating of varnish. **3.** superficial polish or show. —*v.t.* **4.** to coat with varnish. **5.** to give a superficially pleasing appearance to.

var•y (vâr′ē), *v.*, **var•ied, var•y•ing.** —*v.t.* **1.** to change, as in form, appearance, or substance. **2.** to give variety to; diversify. —*v.i.* **3.** to show diversity; differ. **4.** to undergo change. **5.** to diverge; deviate.

vas•cu•lar (vas′kyə lər), *adj.* of, composed of, or provided with vessels that convey fluids, as blood or sap.

vase (vās, vāz, väz), *n.* a vessel, as of glass, used to hold flowers or for decoration.

va•sec•to•my (va sek′tə mē, və-), *n.*, *pl.* **-mies.** surgical excision of part or all of the sperm-carrying duct of the testis to effect sterility.

vas•sal (vas′əl), *n.* **1.** (in the feudal system) a person granted the use of land in return for homage and fealty to a lord. **2.** a person subject or subordinate to another.

vast (vast, väst), *adj.*, **-er, -est. 1.** of very great area or extent. **2.** very great in size, quantity, or degree. —**vast′ly,** *adv.* —**vast′ness,** *n.*

vat (vat), *n.* a large container, as a tank, for holding liquids.

VAT value-added tax: a tax based on the value added to a product at each stage of production.

vaude•ville (vôd′vil, vōd′-, vô′də-), *n.* a form of popular entertainment having a program of separate and varied acts. —**vaude•vil′lian,** *n.*, *adj.*

vault¹ (vôlt), *n.* **1.** an arched structure forming a ceiling or roof. **2.** a chamber or passage enclosed by a vault. **3.** a room or compartment for the safekeeping of valuables. **4.** a burial chamber. **5.** something resembling an arched roof. —*v.t.* **6.** to cover with or curve in the form of a vault. —**vault′ed,** *adj.*

vault² (vôlt), *v.i., v.t.* **1.** to leap (over), esp. with the hands supported by a horizontal pole. —*n.* **2.** the act of vaulting.

vault′ing *adj.* **1.** leaping. **2.** excessive; overweening: *vaulting ambition.*

vaunt (vônt, vänt), *v.i.* **1.** to boast (of). —*n.* **2.** a boastful utterance. —**vaunt′ed,** *adj.*

VCR videocassette recorder: an electronic device for recording and playing back videocassettes.

VD venereal disease.

V′-Day′ *n.* a day of military victory.

VDT video display terminal.

veal (vēl), *n.* the flesh of a calf used for food.

vec•tor (vek′tər), *n.* **1.** a quantity possessing both magnitude and direction. **2.** a person or animal that transmits a disease-causing organism.

veep (vēp), *n. Informal.* a vice president.

veer (vēr), *v.i., v.t.* **1.** to change from one course, position, or direction to another. —*n.* **2.** a change of course, position, or direction.

veg•e•ta•ble (vej′tə bəl, vej′i tə-), *n.* **1.** a plant whose fruit, seeds, roots, tubers, bulbs, stems, leaves, or flower parts are used as food. **2.** an edible plant part. **3.** a plant. —*adj.* **4.** of or made from edible vegetables. **5.** of or derived from plants.

veg•e•tar•i•an (vej′i târ′ē ən), *n.* **1.** a person who does not eat meat, fish, or fowl. —*adj.* **2.** of vegetarians. **3.** consisting solely of vegetables. —**veg′e•tar′i•an•ism,** *n.*

veg•e•tate (-tāt′), *v.i.* **-tat•ed, -tat•ing. 1.** to grow as or like a plant. **2.** to lead an inactive and lackluster life. —**veg′e•ta′tive,** *adj.*

veg′e•ta′tion *n.* **1.** all the plants or plant life of a place. **2.** the act or process of vegetating.

ve•he•ment (vē′ə mənt), *adj.* **1.** ardent; impassioned. **2.** marked by great energy or vigor. —**ve′he•mence, ve′he•men•cy,** *n.* —**ve′he•ment•ly,** *adv.*

ve•hi•cle (vē′i kəl), *n.* **1.** a means of carrying or transporting; conveyance. **2.** a means of transmission or communication. **3.** a liquid, as oil, in which a paint pigment is mixed. —**ve•hic•u•lar** (-hik′yə lər), *adj.*

veil (vāl), *n.* **1.** a piece of opaque or transparent material worn over the face, as for concealment. **2.** a part of a headdress, as of a nun or bride. **3.** something that covers or conceals. —*v.t.* **4.** to cover or conceal with or as if with a veil. —**Idiom. 5. take the veil,** to become a nun. —**veiled,** *adj.*

vein (vān), *n.* **1.** one of the branching vessels conveying blood to the heart. **2.** one of the riblike thickenings that form the framework of an insect's wing. **3.** one of the strands of vascular tissue forming the framework of a leaf. **4.** a mineral deposit occupying a fissure in rock. **5.** a streak, as in marble. **6.** an attitude or mood. **7.** a tendency or quality. —*v.t.* **8.** to furnish with veins. **9.** to mark with or as if with veins. —**veined,** *adj.*

Vel•cro (vel′krō), *Trademark.* a fastening tape consisting of opposing pieces of nylon fabric that interlock when pressed together.

veld or **veldt** (velt, felt), *n.* the open country, with grass, bushes, or shrubs, characteristic of parts of S Africa.

vel•lum (vel′əm), *n.* **1.** calfskin, lambskin, or kidskin treated for use as a writing surface. **2.** writing paper resembling vellum.

ve•loc•i•ty (və los′i tē), *n., pl.* **-ties.** rapidity of motion, action, or operation; speed.

ve•lour (və lŏŏr′) also **-lours′,** *n.* a velvetlike fabric used for clothing and upholstery.

vel•vet (vel′vit), *n.* **1.** a fabric, as of silk or nylon, with a thick, soft pile. **2.** something that resembles velvet, as in softness. **3.** the soft covering of a growing antler. —*adj.* **4.** made of velvet. **5.** resembling velvet. —**vel′vet•y,** *adj.*

vel′vet•een′ (-vi tēn′), *n.* a cotton fabric with a short pile resembling velvet.

ve•nal (vēn′l), *adj.* **1.** open to or associated with bribery. **2.** capable of being purchased, as by a bribe. —**ve•nal′i•ty,** *n.*

vend (vend), *v.t., v.i.* to sell, esp. by peddling.

ven•det•ta (ven det′ə), *n., pl.* **-tas.** a prolonged and bitter feud, esp. between families.

vend′ing machine′ *n.* a coin-operated machine for selling small articles, as candy bars.

ve•neer (və nēr′), *n.* **1.** a thin layer of material for facing or inlaying wood. **2.** a superficially good or pleasing appearance. —*v.t.* **3.** to face or inlay with veneer.

ven•er•a•ble (ven′ər ə bəl), *adj.* **1.** worthy of respect or reverence. as because of great age or high office. **2.** hallowed by religious or historic association.

ven′er•ate′ (-ə rāt′), *v.t.,* **-at•ed, -at•ing.** to regard or treat with reverence; revere. —**ven′er•a′tion,** *n.*

ve•ne•re•al (və nēr′ē əl), *adj.* **1.** transmitted through sexual intercourse. **2.** of sexual intercourse.

ve•ne′tian blind′ (və nē′shən), *n.* a window blind with horizontal slats that may be opened, closed, or set at an angle.

Ven•e•zue•la (ven′ə zwā′lə, -zwē′-), *n.* a republic in N South America. —**Ven′e•zue′lan,** *adj., n.*

venge•ance (ven′jəns), *n.* **1.** infliction of injury, harm, or humiliation in return for an injury or offense. —**Idiom. 2. with a vengeance, a.** with violent force. **b.** with excessive energy.

venge′ful *adj.* desiring or seeking vengeance; vindictive.

ve•ni•al (vē′nē əl, vēn′yəl), *adj.* capable of being forgiven.

ven•i•son (ven′ə sən, -zən), *n.* the flesh of a deer used for food.

ven•om (ven′əm), *n.* **1.** the poisonous fluid secreted by some animals, as snakes, and introduced into the victim by biting or stinging. **2.** malice; spite. —**ven′om•ous,** *adj.*

ve•nous (vē′nəs), *adj.* **1.** of, having, or composed of veins. **2.** of or being the oxygen-poor dark red blood carried back to the heart by the veins.

vent¹ (vent), *n.* **1.** an opening serving as an outlet, as for fumes. **2.** a means of exit or escape. **3.** expression; utterance: *giving vent to anger.* —*v.t.* **4.** to give free expression to. **5.** to release or discharge (liquid, smoke, etc.) through a vent. **6.** to provide with a vent.

vent² (vent), *n.* a slit in a garment.

ven•ti•late (ven′tl āt′), *v.t.,* **-lat•ed, -lat•ing. 1.** to provide (a room, mine, etc.) with fresh air. **2.** to submit to open examination and discussion. **3.** to give expression to; vent. **4.** to furnish with a vent. —**ven′ti•la′tion,** *n.* —**ven′ti•la′tor,** *n.*

ven•tral (ven′trəl), *adj.* **1.** of or near the belly; abdominal. **2.** situated on the lower, abdominal plane of an animal's body.

ven•tri•cle (ven′tri kəl), *n.* either of the two lower chambers of the heart that force blood into the arteries. —**ven•tric′u•lar** (-trik′yə lər), *adj.*

ven•tril•o•quism (ven tril′ə kwiz′əm), *n.* the art or practice of speaking so that the voice appears not to come from the speaker but from another source. —**ven•tril′o•quist,** *n.*

ven•ture (ven′chər), *n., v.,* **-tured, -tur•ing.** —*n.* **1.** an undertaking, as a business enterprise, involving risk or uncertainty. **2.** something, as money, risked in a venture. —*v.t.* **3.** to expose to hazard; risk. **4.** to take the risk of. **5.** to undertake to express in spite of possible contradiction or opposition: *won't venture a guess.* —*v.i.* **6.** to undertake or embark upon a venture. —**ven′ture•some, ven′tur•ous,** *adj.*

ven•ue (ven′yōō), *n.* **1.** the place of a crime or cause of action. **2.** the place where a jury is gathered and a case tried. **3.** the scene or locale of an action or event.

Ve•nus (vē′nəs), *n.* the most brilliant planet, second in order from the sun.

Ve′nus's-fly′trap *n.* a bog plant with hinged leaves that snap shut to trap insects.

ve•rac′i•ty (-ras′i tē), *n.* **1.** habitual observance of truth; truthfulness. **2.** conformity to fact; accuracy.

ve•ran•da or **-dah** (və ran′də), *n.*, *pl.* **-das** or **-dahs.** a usu. roofed porch, often extending across the front and sides of a house.

verb (vûrb), *n.* a word that functions as the main element of a predicate and typically expresses action, state, or a relation.

ver•bal (vûr′bəl), *adj.* **1.** of or consisting of words. **2.** spoken rather than written; oral. **3.** concerned with words rather than with the ideas expressed. **4.** of or derived from a verb. —**ver′bal•ly,** *adv.*

ver′bal•ize′ *v.,* **-ized, -iz•ing.** —*v.t.* **1.** to express in or put into words. —*v.i.* **2.** to express something verbally. —**ver′bal•i•za′tion,** *n.*

ver•ba•tim (vər bā′tim), *adv., adj.* word for word. [< ML]

ver•be•na (vər bē′nə), *n.*, *pl.* **-nas.** a plant with showy flower clusters.

ver•bi•age (vûr′bē ij), *n.* **1.** overabundance of words. **2.** manner of expression in words.

ver•bose (vər bōs′), *adj.* expressed in or characterized by the use of many or too many words; wordy. —**ver•bos′i•ty** (-bos′i tē), *n.*

ver•bo•ten (vər bōt′n, fər-), *adj.* forbidden, as by law. [< G]

ver•dant (vûr′dnt), *adj.* **1.** green with vegetation. **2.** of the color green.

ver•dict (vûr′dikt), *n.* **1.** the finding of a jury in a matter submitted to their judgment. **2.** a judgment or decision.

ver•di•gris (vûr′di grēs′, -gris), *n.* a green or bluish patina formed on copper, brass, or bronze surfaces.

ver•dure (vûr′jər), *n.* **1.** the greenness of flourishing vegetation. **2.** green vegetation.

verge¹ (vûrj), *n., v.,* **verged, verg•ing.** —*n.* **1.** the point beyond which something begins or occurs; brink. **2.** an edge, rim, or margin. **3.** a staff carried as an emblem of authority or office. —*v.i.* **4.** to be on the verge; border.

verge² (vûrj), *v.i.,* **verged, verg•ing. 1.** to incline; tend. **2.** to slope or sink.

ver•i•fy (ver′ə fī′), *v.t.,* **-fied, -fy•ing. 1.** to prove the truth of. **2.** to ascertain the truth, authenticity, or correctness of. —**ver′i•fi′a•ble,** *adj.* —**ver′i•fi•ca′tion,** *n.*

ver′i•ly (-lē), *adv. Archaic.* in truth; really.

ver′i•si•mil′i•tude′ (-si mil′i tōōd′, -tyōod′), *n.* the appearance or semblance of truth.

ver′i•ta•ble (-tə bəl), *adj.* being truly so; genuine.

ver′i•ty (-tē), *n.*, *pl.* **-ties. 1.** the state or quality of being true. **2.** something, as a statement, that is true.

ver•mi•cel•li (vûr′mi chel′ē, -sel′ē), *n. (used with a sing. or pl. v.)* pasta in the form of long threads.

ver•mil•ion (vər mil′yən), *n.* **1.** a brilliant scarlet red. **2.** a bright red pigment.

ver•min (vûr′min), *n.*, *pl.* **-min. 1.** small objectionable animals, esp. those, as lice or cockroaches, that are difficult to control. **2.** an obnoxious person. —**ver′min•ous,** *adj.*

ver•mouth (vər mōōth′), *n.* a white wine in which herbs have been steeped.

ver•nac•u•lar (vər nak′yə lər, və nak′-), *n.* **1.** the native speech or language of a country or region. **2.** the distinctive language or vocabulary of a class or profession. **3.** the variety of language in everyday use by ordinary people. —*adj.* **4.** of, using, or in the vernacular.

ver•nal (vûr′nl), *adj.* of or occurring in spring.

ver•sa•tile (vûr′sə tl; *esp. Brit.* -tīl′), *adj.* **1.** capable of turning easily from one thing to another. **2.** having many uses or applications. —**ver′sa•til′i•ty,** *n.*

verse (vûrs), *n.* **1.** one of the lines of a poem. **2.** a particular type of metrical composition. **3.** a poem. **4.** poetry, esp. as involving metrical form. **5.** a stanza. **6.** one of the short divisions of a chapter of the Bible.

versed *adj.* experienced or practiced; skilled.

ver•si•fy (vûr′sə fī′), *v.,* **-fied, -fy•ing.** —*v.t.* **1.** to put into verse. —*v.i.* **2.** to compose verses. —**ver′si•fi•ca′tion,** *n.*

ver•sion (vûr′zhən, -shən), *n.* **1.** an account from a particular standpoint. **2.** a particular form or variant. **3.** a translation, esp. of the Bible.

ver•sus (vûr′səs, -səz), *prep.* **1.** against: *Smith versus Jones.* **2.** as compared to or in contrast with: *democracy versus totalitarianism.* [late ME < L: towards]

ver•te•bra (vûr′tə brə), *n.*, *pl.* **-brae** (-brē′, -brā′), **-bras.** one of the bones or segments of the spinal column. —**ver′te•bral,** *adj.*

ver′te•brate (-brit, -brāt′), *adj.* **1.** having a spinal column. **2.** of or belonging to a subphylum of animals having a spinal column and comprising mammals, birds, reptiles, amphibians, and fishes. —*n.* **3.** a vertebrate animal.

ver•tex (vûr′teks), *n.*, *pl.* **-tex•es, -ti•ces** (-tə sēz′). **1.** the highest point; apex. **2.** *Geom.* **a.** the point farthest from the base. **b.** the intersection of two sides of a plane figure.

ver•ti•cal (vûr′ti kəl), *adj.* **1.** being perpendicular to the plane of the horizon; upright. **2.** of or at the vertex. —*n.* **3.** something vertical, as a line. **4.** a vertical position. —**ver′ti•cal•ly,** *adv.*

ver•tig•i•nous (vər tij′ə nəs), *adj.* **1.** whirling; spinning. **2.** affected with or liable to cause vertigo.

ver•ti•go (vûr′ti gō′), *n.*, *pl.* **ver•ti•goes, ver•tig•i•nes** (vər tij′ə nēz′). a disordered condition in which one feels oneself or one's surroundings whirling about; dizziness.

verve (vûrv), *n.* vivaciousness, energy, or enthusiasm.

ver•y (ver′ē), *adv., adj.,* **-i•er, -i•est.** —*adv.* **1.** to a high degree; extremely. **2.** absolutely; truly: *in the very same place.* —*adj.* **3.** precise; particular: *the very book I wanted.* **4.** mere: *The very thought is distressing.* **5.** sheer; utter: *the very joy of living.* **6.** actual: *caught in the very act.* **7.** (used as an intensive): *the very heart of the matter.*

ves•i•cle (ves′i kəl), *n.* **1.** a small sac, cyst, or cavity. **2.** BLISTER (def. 1).

ves′pers (ves′pərz) *n.* (often cap.) a religious service in the late afternoon or evening.

ves•sel (ves′əl), *n.* **1.** a craft, esp. a fairly large one, for traveling on water. **2.** a hollow utensil used esp. for holding liquids. **3.** a tube or duct, as a vein, containing or conveying a body fluid. **4.** a water-conducting duct within the tissue of vascular plants.

vest (vest), *n.* **1.** a waist-length sleeveless garment for men, usu. worn under a jacket. **2.** a similar garment for women. **3.** *Brit.* an undershirt. —*v.t.* **4.** to clothe, as in ecclesiastical vestments. **5.** to place in the possession or control of. **6.** to endow with something, as powers or rights. —*v.i.* **7.** to become vested.

ves•tal (ves′tl), *adj.* **1.** chaste; pure. —*n.* **2.** a chaste woman.

vest′ed *adj.* held completely, permanently, and inalienably.

vest′ed in′terest *n.* a special interest in a system, arrangement, or institution for personal reasons.

ves•ti•bule (ves′tə byōōl′), *n.* **1.** a passage or hall between the outer door and the interior of a building. **2.** a hollow body part serving as an entrance to another hollow part.

ves•tige (ves′tij), *n.* **1.** a trace of something no longer in existence. **2.** a very small amount. **3.** a degenerate or imperfectly developed biological structure that once performed a useful function. —**ves•tig•i•al** (ve stij′ē əl, -stij′əl), *adj.*

vest′ing *n.* the granting to an employee of the right to pension benefits despite early retirement.

vest′ment *n.* **1.** an official or ceremonial robe. **2.** a garment worn by the clergy and their assistants, esp. during divine service.

vest′-pock′et *adj.* very small; compact.

ves•try (ves′trē), *n.*, *pl.* **-tries. 1.** a room in a church in which the vestments are kept. **2.** a room in a church used for meetings and for Sunday school. **3.** a committee that manages the temporal affairs of an Episcopal church.

vet¹ (vet), *n. Informal.* a veterinarian.

vet² (vet), *n., adj. Informal.* veteran.

vetch (vech), *n.* a climbing plant with pealike flowers, cultivated esp. for forage.

vet•er•an (vet′ər ən), *n.* **1.** a person of long service or experience in an occupation or office. **2.** a person who has served in the armed forces. —*adj.* **3.** of or for veterans.

vet•er•i•nar•i•an (vet′ər ə nâr′ē ən), *n.* a person who practices veterinary medicine.

vet′er•i•nar′y (-ner′ē), *n., pl.* **-nar•ies,** *adj.* —*n.* **1.** a veterinarian. —*adj.* **2.** of or being the medical and surgical treatment of animals, esp. domesticated animals.

ve•to (vē′tō), *n., pl.* **-toes,** *v.,* **-toed, -to•ing.** —*n.* **1.** the power of one branch of a government to cancel the decisions or actions of another, esp. the right of a chief executive to reject bills passed by a legislature. **2.** the exercise of this power. **3.** an emphatic prohibition. —*v.t.* **4.** to reject (a proposed bill) by a veto. **5.** to prohibit emphatically.

vex (veks), *v.t.* **1.** to irritate; annoy. **2.** to trouble; distress. —**vex•a′tion,** *n.*

vi•a (vī′ə, vē′ə), *prep.* by way of.

vi•a•ble (vī′ə bəl), *adj.* **1.** capable of living or growing. **2.** (of a fetus) sufficiently developed to be capable of living outside the uterus. **3.** practicable; workable. —**vi′a•bil′i•ty,** *n.*

vi′a•duct′ *n.* a bridge for carrying a road or railroad, as over a valley.

vi•al (vī′əl, vīl), *n.* a small container, as of glass, for holding liquids.

vi•and (vī′ənd), *n.* an article of food.

vibes¹ (vībz), *n.pl. Slang.* something, esp. an emotional aura, emitted as if by vibration and intuitively perceived; ambiance.

vibes² (vībz), *n.pl.* vibraphone.

vi•brant (vī′brənt), *adj.* **1.** vibrating. **2.** pulsating with vigor and energy. —**vi′bran•cy,** *n.* —**vi′-brant•ly,** *adv.*

vi•bra•phone (vī′brə fōn′), *n.* a percussion instrument that resembles a xylophone but has metal bars and electrically powered resonators. —**vi′bra-phon′ist,** *n.*

vi•brate (vī′brāt), *v.,* **-brat•ed, -brat•ing.** —*v.i.* **1.** to move to and fro or up and down quickly and repeatedly; quiver. **2.** (of sounds) to have a pulsating effect; resonate. **3.** to thrill in emotional response. —*v.t.* **4.** to cause to vibrate. —**vi•bra′tion,** *n.* —**vi′-bra•tor,** *n.*

vi•bra•to (vi brä′tō, vī-), *n., pl.* **-tos.** a pulsating effect produced by rapid but slight alternations in pitch.

vi•bur•num (vī bûr′nəm), *n.* a shrub of the honeysuckle family bearing white flower clusters.

vic•ar (vik′ər), *n.* **1.** a parish priest in the Anglican Church. **2.** an Episcopalian cleric in charge of a chapel. **3.** a Roman Catholic ecclesiastic representing a bishop.

vic′ar•age (-ij), *n.* the residence, benefice, or duties of a vicar.

vi•car•i•ous (vī kâr′ē əs, vi-), *adj.* **1.** performed, received, or suffered in place of another. **2.** taking the place of another. **3.** felt or enjoyed through imagined participation in the experience of another. —**vi•car′i•ous•ly,** *adv.*

vice¹ (vīs), *n.* **1.** an immoral habit or practice. **2.** immoral conduct. **3.** a personal shortcoming; foible.

vice² (vīs), *n.* VISE.

vi•ce³ (vī′sē, -sə, vīs), *prep.* instead of.

vice- a combining form meaning deputy (*vice president*).

vice′-ad′mi•ral (vīs), *n.* a commissioned officer in the U.S. Navy or Coast Guard ranking above a rear admiral.

vice•ge•rent (vīs jēr′ənt), *n.* a deputy to a sovereign or magistrate.

vice′ pres′ident or **vice′-pres′ident** (vīs), *n.* **1.** (*often caps.*) an officer next in rank to a president, serving as president if the president dies, is disa-

bled, or resigns. **2.** a deputy to a president, as in a corporation. —**vice′ pres′idency,** *n.*

vice•roy (vīs′roi), *n.* a person appointed to rule a country or province as the deputy of the sovereign.

vi•ce ver•sa (vī′sə vûr′sə, vīs′, vī′sē), *adv.* in reverse order; conversely. [< L]

vi•chys•soise (vish′ē swäz′, vē′shē-), *n.* a cream soup made of potatoes and leeks, usu. served cold.

vi•cin•i•ty (vi sin′i tē), *n., pl.* **-ties. 1.** the area around a place; neighborhood. **2.** the state or fact of being near; proximity.

vi•cious (vish′əs), *adj.* **1.** addicted to or characterized by vice; evil or depraved. **2.** spiteful; malicious. **3.** unpleasantly severe. **4.** savage; ferocious. —**vi′cious•ly,** *adv.* —**vi′cious•ness,** *n.*

vi•cis•si•tude (vi sis′i tōōd′, -tyōōd′), *n.* **1.** change or variation. **2. vicissitudes,** changing phases or conditions, as of life.

vic•tim (vik′təm), *n.* **1.** a person who suffers from a destructive or injurious action or agency. **2.** a person who is deceived or cheated. **3.** a living creature sacrificed in religious rites. —**vic′tim•ize′,** *v.t.,* **-ized, -iz•ing.**

vic•tor (vik′tər), *n.* a winner in a battle, struggle, or contest.

vic′to•ry (-tə rē), *n., pl.* **-ries. 1.** a success or triumph over an enemy, as in war. **2.** success against any opponent, opposition, or difficulty. —**vic•to′ri•ous** (-tôr′ē əs), *adj.*

vict•ual (vit′l), *n.* **1. victuals,** food supplies; provisions. **2.** food for human consumption.

vid•e•o (vid′ē ō′), *n., pl.* **-os,** *adj.* —*n.* **1.** the visual elements of television. **2.** television. **3.** a videotape. —*adj.* **4.** of television, esp. the visual elements. **5.** of or being the images displayed on a computer screen.

vid′e•o•cas•sette′ *n.* a cassette containing a videotape.

vid′eocassette record′er *n.* See VCR.

vid′e•o•disc′ *n.* an optical disc on which a motion picture or television program is recorded for playback on a television set.

vid′eo game′ *n.* **1.** a game played on a video screen or television set with a microcomputer. **2.** a game played on a microchip-controlled device, as a handheld toy or arcade machine.

vid′e•o•tape′ *n., v.,* **-taped, -tap•ing.** —*n.* **1.** magnetic tape on which a television program can be recorded. —*v.t.* **2.** to record on videotape.

vie (vī), *v.i.,* **vied, vy•ing.** to strive in competition or rivalry; contend.

Vi•et•nam or **Vi•et Nam** (vē et′näm′, -nam′), *n.* a country in SE Asia, divided into two republics **(North Vietnam** and **South Vietnam)** in 1954 and reunified in 1976. —**Vi•et′nam•ese′** (-nä mēz′, -mēs′, -nə-), *adj., n., pl.* **-ese.**

view (vyōō), *n.* **1.** an act or instance of seeing or looking. **2.** range of sight or vision. **3.** a sight, as of a landscape; scene. **4.** a picture of a scene. **5.** a manner of looking at something: *from a practical view.* **6.** a mental survey. **7.** aim, intention, or purpose. **8.** prospect or expectation. **9.** a personal opinion; judgment. —*v.t.* **10.** to see; watch. **11.** to look at carefully; inspect. **12.** to contemplate mentally; consider. —*Idiom.* **13. on view,** on exhibition. —**view′er,** *n.*

view′find′er *n.* a camera part for viewing what will appear in the picture.

view′point′ *n.* a mental attitude; point of view.

vig•il (vij′əl), *n.* **1.** wakefulness maintained during normal sleeping hours. **2.** a watch or period of watchful attention. **3.** the eve of a church festival.

vig′i•lant (-lənt), *adj.* keenly watchful, esp. to detect danger; wary. —**vig′i•lance,** *n.* —**vig′i•lant•ly,** *adv.*

vig•i•lan′te (-lan′tē), *n., pl.* **-tes.** a member of a group of volunteers organized but not legally authorized to dispense summary justice. —**vig′i•lan′-tism,** *n.*

vi•gnette (vin yet′), *n.* **1.** a decorative design used on a page of a book. **2.** a picture shaded off gradually at the edges. **3. a.** a short, graceful literary sketch. **b.** a brief, appealing scene, as in a movie.

vig•or (vig′ər), *n.* **1.** active strength or force; intensity. **2.** healthy physical or mental energy; vitality. Also, *esp. Brit.,* **vig′our.** —**vig′or•ous,** *adj.* —**vig′or•ous•ly,** *adv.*

Vi•king (vī′king), *n.* one of the Scandinavian pirates of the late 8th to 11th centuries.

vile (vīl), *adj.,* **vil•er, vil•est. 1.** wretchedly bad: *vile weather.* **2.** highly offensive; objectionable. **3.** morally debased; depraved. —**vile′ness,** *n.*

vil•i•fy (vil′ə fī′), *v.t.,* **-fied, -fy•ing.** to speak ill of; defame. —**vil′i•fi•ca′tion,** *n.*

vil•la (vil′ə), *n., pl.* **-las.** a country residence, esp. an imposing estate.

vil•lage (vil′ij), *n.* **1.** a small rural community, usu. smaller than a town. **2.** the inhabitants of a village. —**vil′lag•er,** *n.*

vil•lain (vil′ən), *n.* **1.** a cruelly malicious person; scoundrel. **2.** a character, as in a play, with the role of a villain. —**vil′lain•ous,** *adj.* —**vil′lain•y,** *n., pl.* **-ies.**

vil•lein (vil′ən, -ān), *n.* a feudal serf with the rights of a freeman with respect to all persons except his lord.

vim (vim), *n.* lively or energetic spirit; vitality.

vin•ai•grette (vin′ə gret′), *n.* a dressing, esp. for salad, of oil and vinegar usu. flavored with herbs. [< F]

vin•di•cate (vin′di kāt′), *v.t.,* **-cat•ed, -cat•ing. 1.** to clear, as from an accusation. **2.** to afford justification for. **3.** to maintain or defend against opposition. —**vin′di•ca′tion,** *n.* —**vin′di•ca′tor,** *n.*

vin•dic•tive (vin dik′tiv), *adj.* **1.** disposed to revenge. **2.** proceeding from or showing a revengeful spirit. —**vin•dic′tive•ly,** *adv.* —**vin•dic′tive•ness,** *n.*

vine (vīn), *n.* **1.** a plant with a long stem that grows along the ground or climbs a support. **2.** the stem of a vine. **3.** a grape plant.

vin•e•gar (vin′i gər), *n.* a sour liquid obtained by fermentation, as of wine or cider, used as a condiment or preservative. [< OF: sour wine] —**vin′e•gar•y,** *adj.*

vine•yard (vin′yərd), *n.* a plantation of grapevines.

vin•tage (vin′tij), *n.* **1.** the wine or grapes from a particular harvest or crop. **2.** a superior wine from the crop of a good year. **3.** the act or season of gathering grapes or making wine. **4.** the output of a particular time: *a car of 1917 vintage.* —*adj.* **5.** being of a specified vintage. **6.** representing the best of a past time; classic: *vintage movies.* **7.** being the best of a kind: *vintage Shakespeare.*

vint•ner (vint′nər), *n.* a person who makes or sells wine.

vi•nyl (vīn′l), *n.* any of various flexible, tough plastics used esp. in coatings, phonograph records, and flooring.

vi•o•la (vē ō′lə), *n., pl.* **-las.** a stringed instrument of the violin family, slightly larger than the violin and deeper in tone. —**vi•o′list,** *n.*

vi•o•late (vī′ə lāt′), *v.t.,* **-lat•ed, -lat•ing. 1.** to break (a law, promise, etc.). **2.** to break in upon; disturb rudely. **3.** to rape. **4.** to treat disrespectfully; desecrate. —**vi′o•la′tion,** *n.* —**vi′o•la′tor,** *n.*

vi′o•lent *adj.* **1.** acting with or characterized by uncontrolled physical force. **2.** caused by destructive force: *a violent death.* **3.** intense; severe. **4.** immoderately vehement. —**vi′o•lent•ly,** *adv.*

vi•o•let (vī′ə lit), *n.* **1.** a low plant with purple, blue, yellow, or white flowers. **2.** a reddish blue. —*adj.* **3.** of the color violet.

vi•o•lin (vī′ə lin′), *n.* the treble instrument of the family of modern bowed four-stringed instruments. —**vi′o•lin′ist,** *n.*

vi•o•lon•cel•lo (vē′ə lən chel′ō, vī′-), *n., pl.* **-los.** CELLO. —**vi′o•lon•cel′list,** *n.*

VIP (vē′ī′pē′), *Informal.* very important person.

vi•per (vī′pər), *n.* **1.** any of various venomous snakes. **2.** a malignant or treacherous person. —**vi′per•ous,** *adj.*

vi•ra•go (vi rä′gō, -rā′-), *n., pl.* **-goes, -gos.** a loud-voiced, ill-tempered, scolding woman; shrew.

vi•ral (vī′rəl), *adj.* of or caused by a virus.

vir•gin (vûr′jin), *n.* **1.** a person who has never had sexual intercourse. **2. the Virgin,** Mary, the mother of Jesus. —*adj.* **3.** of, being, or characteristic of a virgin. **4.** pure; unsullied. **5.** not previously exploited or used: *a virgin forest.* —**vir′gin•al,** *adj.* —**vir•gin•i•ty** (vər jin′i tē), *n.*

vir•gule (vûr′gyōōl), *n.* an oblique stroke (/) used as a dividing line in dates or fractions (²/₄) or between words to indicate two alternatives (his/her).

vir•ile (vir′əl), *adj.* **1.** having or showing masculine strength or qualities; manly. **2.** vigorous; energetic. **3.** capable of copulating. —**vi•ril•i•ty** (və ril′i tē), *n.*

vi•rol•o•gy (vī rol′ə jē, vi-), *n.* the study of viruses and viral diseases. —**vi•rol′o•gist,** *n.*

vir•tu•al (vûr′chōō əl), *adj.* **1.** being such in force or effect, though not actually or expressly such. **2. a.** temporarily simulated or extended by computer software. **b.** of, by means of, or existing on computers. —**vir′tu•al•ly,** *adv.*

vir′tual real′ity *n.* a realistic simulation of an environment, including three-dimensional graphics, by a computer system using interactive software and hardware.

vir•tue (vûr′chōō), *n.* **1.** conformity to moral and ethical principles. **2.** a particular moral excellence. **3.** chastity. **4.** an admirable quality. **5.** effective force; potency. —*Idiom.* **6. by virtue of,** by reason of.

vir•tu•o•so (vûr′chōō ō′sō), *n., pl.* **-sos, -si** (-sē). a person with special knowledge or skill, esp. one who excels in musical technique or execution. —**vir′tu•os′i•ty** (-os′i tē), *n.*

vir•tu•ous (vûr′chōō əs), *adj.* **1.** conforming to moral and ethical principles. **2.** chaste. —**vir′tu•ous•ly,** *adv.* —**vir′tu•ous•ness,** *n.*

vir•u•lent (vir′yə lənt, vir′ə-), *adj.* **1.** extremely poisonous; noxious. **2.** highly infectious; deadly. **3.** violently hostile. —**vir′u•lence,** *n.*

vi•rus (vī′rəs), *n., pl.* **-rus•es. 1.** an ultramicroscopic infectious agent that replicates only within the cells of living hosts. **2.** a disease caused by a virus. **3.** a corrupting influence. **4.** a segment of self-replicating code planted illegally in a computer program.

vi•sa (vē′zə), *n., pl.* **-sas.** an official endorsement on a passport that permits the bearer to enter a country.

vis•age (viz′ij), *n.* **1.** the face; countenance. **2.** aspect; appearance.

vis-à-vis (vē′zə vē′), *adv., adj.* **1.** face to face. —*prep.* **2.** in relation to; compared with. **3.** opposite. [< F]

vis•cer•a (vis′ər ə), *n.pl., sing.* **vis•cus** (vis′kəs). the internal organs of the body, esp. those in the abdominal cavity.

vis′cer•al *adj.* **1.** of or affecting the viscera. **2.** characterized by or proceeding from instinct rather than intellect.

vis•count (vī′kount′), *n.* a nobleman below an earl or count and above a baron.

vis′count•ess (vī′-), *n.* **1.** the wife of a viscount. **2.** a woman holding in her own right a rank equivalent to that of a viscount.

vis•cous (vis′kəs), *adj.* **1.** thick and sticky in consistency; gluey. **2.** having the property of viscosity.

vise (vīs), *n.* a device, usu. having two jaws closed by means of a screw or lever, used to hold firmly an object being worked on.

vis•i•ble (viz′ə bəl), *adj.* **1.** capable of being seen. **2.** apparent; manifest. —**vis′i•bil′i•ty,** *n.* —**vis′i•bly,** *adv.*

vi•sion (vizh′ən), *n.* **1.** the act or power of seeing. **2.** unusual foresight. **3.** something seen in or as if in a dream or trance. **4.** a vivid imaginative conception. **5.** something of extraordinary beauty.

vi′sion•ar′y (-ə ner′ē), *adj., n., pl.* **-ies.** —*adj.* **1.** given to seeing visions. **2.** seen in a vision. **3.** given to or characterized by fanciful or impractical ideas. —*n.* **4.** a person of unusual foresight. **5.** one who sees visions. **6.** a person given to impractical ideas; dreamer.

vis•it (viz′it), *v.t.* **1.** to go or come to see, as for sightseeing. **2.** to stay with as a guest. **3.** to go to for the purpose of official inspection. **4.** to come upon; afflict. **5.** to access (a Web site). —*v.i.* **6.** to make a visit. **7.** to chat casually. —*n.* **8.** an act or instance of visiting. —**vis′i•tor,** *n.*

vis•it•a′tion (-tā′shən), *n.* **1.** a visit, esp. a formal or official one. **2.** an affliction or punishment, as from God.

vi•sor (vī′zər), *n.* **1.** the projecting front brim of a cap. **2.** a flap mounted on the inside of an automobile to shield the eyes from glare. **3.** the movable front piece on a medieval helmet. —**vi′sor•less,** *adj.*

vis•ta (vis′tə), *n.*, *pl.* **-tas.** **1.** a view, esp. one seen through a long, narrow passage. **2.** a far-reaching mental view.

VISTA (vis′tə), *n.* Volunteers in Service to America.

vis•u•al (vizh′ōō əl), *adj.* **1.** of or used in seeing or sight. **2.** perceptible by the sense of sight; visible. **3.** performed by sight alone: *a visual landing.* **4.** of or involving the use of materials, as pictures, that instruct through the sense of sight. —**vis′u•al•ly,** *adv.*

vis•u•al•ize *v.i.*, *v.t.*, **-ized, -iz•ing.** to form a mental image (of). —**vis′u•al•i•za′tion,** *n.*

vi•tal (vīt′l), *adj.* **1.** of or necessary to life. **2.** energetic, lively, or forceful. **3.** indispensable; essential. **4.** of critical importance. **5.** fatal; deadly. —**vi′tal•ly,** *adv.*

vi•tal′i•ty *n.* **1.** exuberant physical or mental vigor. **2.** capacity for survival or continuation. **3.** power to live or grow.

vi′tal signs′ *n.pl.* essential body functions, comprising pulse rate, body temperature, and respiration.

vi′tal statis′tics *n.pl.* statistics concerning deaths, births, and marriages.

vi•ta•min (vī′tə min), *n.* any of a group of organic substances found in food and essential in small quantities to normal metabolism.

vitamin A *n.* a vitamin found esp. in green and yellow vegetables and egg yolk, essential to growth and the prevention of night blindness.

vitamin B₁ *n.* THIAMINE.

vitamin B₂ *n.* RIBOFLAVIN.

vitamin B₃ *n.* NICOTINIC ACID.

vitamin B₁₂ *n.* a vitamin obtained esp. from liver and fish, used to treat anemia.

vitamin B complex *n.* an important group of water-soluble vitamins containing vitamin B₁, vitamin B₂, etc.

vi•ti•ate (vish′ē āt′), *v.t.*, **-at•ed, -at•ing.** **1.** to impair the quality of. **2.** to make less effective. **3.** to debase; corrupt. **4.** to make legally invalid.

vit•i•cul•ture (vit′i kul′chər, vī′ti-), *n.* the cultivation of grapes or grapevines.

vit•re•ous (vi′trē əs), *adj.* **1.** of or resembling glass. **2.** obtained from or containing glass.

vit′reous hu′mor *n.* the transparent gelatinous substance that fills the eyeball behind the lens.

vit′ri•fy′ *v.t.*, *v.i.*, **-fied, -fy•ing.** to change into glass or a glasslike substance.

vi•trine (vi trēn′), *n.* a glass cabinet esp. for displaying art objects.

vit•ri•ol (vi′trē əl), *n.* **1.** any of various glassy metallic sulfates. **2.** SULFURIC ACID. **3.** something highly caustic in effect. —**vit′ri•ol′ic** (-ol′ik), *adj.*

vi•tu•per•ate (vī tōō′pə rāt′, -tyōō′-, vi-), *v.t.*, **-at•ed, -at•ing.** to censure harshly; revile. —**vi•tu′per•a′tion,** *n.* —**vi•tu′per•a′tive,** *adj.*

vi•va•cious (vi vā′shəs, vī-), *adj.* lively; animated. —**vi•va′cious•ly,** *adv.* —**vi•vac′i•ty** (-vas′i tē), **vi•va′cious•ness,** *n.*

viv•id (viv′id), *adj.* **1.** strikingly bright or intense; brilliant. **2.** having bright or striking colors. **3.** presenting the appearance, freshness, and spirit of life. **4.** clearly perceptible. **5.** forming striking mental images. **6.** full of life; animated. —**viv′id•ly,** *adv.* —**viv′id•ness,** *n.*

viv′i•fy′ *v.t.*, **-fied, -fy•ing.** **1.** to give life to; animate. **2.** to enliven; brighten.

viv•i•sec•tion (viv′ə sek′shən), *n.* the cutting into or dissection of a living body, esp. in order to advance scientific knowledge.

vix•en (vik′sən), *n.* **1.** a female fox. **2.** an ill-tempered or quarrelsome woman.

vi•zier (vi zēr′, viz′yər), *n.* a high governmental official in certain Muslim countries, esp. in the former Ottoman Empire.

vo•cab•u•lar•y (vō kab′yə ler′ē), *n.*, *pl.* **-ies.** **1.** the stock of words used by or known to a particular person or group. **2.** a list of words and phrases, usu. arranged in alphabetical order and defined.

vo•cal (vō′kəl), *adj.* **1.** of or uttered with the voice. **2.** rendered by or composed for singing. **3.** having a voice. **4.** giving forth sound or speech. **5.** inclined to express oneself freely; outspoken. —*n.* **6.** a vocal sound. **7.** a musical piece for a singer; song. —**vo′cal•ly,** *adv.*

vo′cal cords′ *n.pl.* either of two pairs of folds of mucous membrane in the larynx that vibrate to produce sound or voice.

vo′cal•ist (-kə list), *n.* a singer.

vo′cal•ize′ *v.*, **-ized, -iz•ing.** —*v.t.* **1.** to make vocal; articulate. —*v.i.* **2.** to utter sounds with the vocal cords, esp. to sing. —**vo′cal•i•za′tion,** *n.*

vo•ca•tion (vō kā′shən), *n.* **1.** an occupation, business, or profession. **2.** a strong impulse to follow a particular activity or career. **3.** a divine call to a religious life. —**vo•ca′tion•al,** *adj.*

voc•a•tive (vok′ə tiv), *adj.* of or being a grammatical case, as in Latin, used to indicate the one being addressed.

vo•cif•er•ate (vō sif′ə rāt′), *v.i.*, *v.t.*, **-at•ed, -at•ing.** to cry out loudly, noisily, or vehemently.

vo•cif′er•ous *adj.* characterized by or making a loud, noisy, or vehement outcry. —**vo•cif′er•ous•ly,** *adv.*

vod•ka (vod′kə), *n.*, *pl.* **-kas.** a colorless distilled liquor made esp. from rye or wheat mash.

vogue (vōg), *n.* **1.** the prevailing fashion at a particular time. **2.** popular favor; popularity. —**vogu′ish,** *adj.*

voice (vois), *n.*, *v.*, **voiced, voic•ing.** —*n.* **1. a.** sound uttered through the mouth, esp. of human beings. **b.** the faculty of uttering such sound. **2.** a sound resembling vocal utterance. **3.** expression, esp. in words: *gave voice to her disapproval.* **4.** the right to express desires or opinions: *wants a voice in company policy.* **5.** an expressed will or desire: *the voice of the people.* **6.** an agency or medium of expression. **7.** a melodic part in a musical composition. **8.** the audible result produced by vibration of the vocal cords. **9.** a verb form indicating the relation of the subject to the action of the verb. —*v.t.* **10.** to give utterance or expression to. —**voice′less,** *adj.*

voice′ box′ *n.* the larynx.

voice′ mail′ *n.* an electronic communications system that routes voice messages interactively to appropriate recipients.

voice′-o′ver *n.* the voice of an offscreen narrator or announcer, as on television.

void (void), *adj.* **1.** having no legal force or effect. **2.** useless; ineffectual. **3.** devoid; destitute. **4.** lacking contents; empty. —*n.* **5.** an empty space; emptiness. **6.** a state or feeling of loss or privation. —*v.t.* **7.** to invalidate; nullify. **8.** to empty; evacuate.

voile (voil), *n.* a lightweight, semisheer fabric.

vol. volume.

vol•a•tile (vol′ə tl), *adj.* **1.** evaporating rapidly. **2.** tending or threatening to erupt in violence; explosive. **3.** changeable; unstable. **4.** (of computer storage) not retaining data when electrical power is turned off. —**vol′a•til′i•ty** (-til′i tē), *n.* —**vol′a•til•ize′,** *v.i.*, *v.t.*, **-ized, -iz•ing.**

vol•ca•no (vol kā′nō), *n.*, *pl.* **-noes, -nos.** **1.** a vent in the earth's crust through which lava, steam, and ashes are expelled. **2.** a mountain or hill formed from the ash and lava so expelled. —**vol•can′ic** (-kan′ik), *adj.*

vole (vōl), *n.* any of several short-tailed, stocky rodents.

vo•li•tion (vō lish′ən, və-), *n.* the act or power of willing, choosing, or resolving. —**vo•li′tion•al,** *adj.*

vol•ley (vol′ē), *n.*, *pl.* **-leys,** *v.*, **-leyed, -ley•ing.** —*n.* **1.** the simultaneous discharge of a number of missiles or firearms. **2.** the missiles so discharged. **3.** a burst of many things at once or in quick succession. **4.** the return of a ball, as in tennis, before it hits the ground. —*v.t., v.i.* **5.** to discharge or be discharged in a volley. **6.** to return (a ball) before it hits the ground.

vol′ley•ball′ *n.* **1.** a game in which a large ball is volleyed back and forth over a high net. **2.** the ball used in this game.

volt (vōlt), *n.* the unit of potential difference and electromotive force equal to the difference of electric potential between two points of a conductor carrying a constant current of one ampere when the power dissipated between these points is one watt.

volt•age (vōl′tij), *n.* electromotive force or potential difference expressed in volts.

volt′me′ter *n.* an instrument for measuring the voltage between two points.

vol•u•ble (vol′yə bəl), *adj.* characterized by an easy and continuous flow of words; fluent. —**vol′u•bil′i•ty,** *n.*

vol•ume (vol′yōōm, -yəm), *n.* **1.** the amount of space in cubic units that an object or substance occupies. **2.** a quantity, esp. a large quantity. **3.** amount; total. **4.** mass; bulk. **5.** the degree of sound intensity; loudness. **6.** a book, esp. one of a series. **7.** a set of issues of a periodical.

vo•lu•mi•nous (və lōō′mə nəs), *adj.* **1.** filling or sufficient to fill a volume. **2.** of great volume, size, or extent. —**vo•lu′mi•nous•ly,** *adv.*

vol•un•tar•y (vol′ən ter′ē), *adj.* **1.** done, made, given, or undertaken of one's own free will. **2.** depending on voluntary action: *voluntary hospitals.* **3.** done by or composed of volunteers. **4.** *Law.* done by intention and not by accident. **5.** controlled by the will. **6.** having the power of willing. —**vol′un•tar′i•ly** (-târ′ə lē), *adv.*

vol′un•teer′ *n.* **1.** a person who voluntarily offers himself or herself for a service or undertaking. —*v.i.* **2.** to offer oneself for a service or undertaking. —*v.t.* **3.** to offer, give, or perform voluntarily.

vo•lup•tu•ous (və lup′chōō əs), *adj.* **1.** derived from, affording, or marked by gratification of the senses. **2.** full and shapely. —**vo•lup′tu•ous•ly,** *adv.*

vo•lute (və lōōt′), *n.* a spiral or twisted object or ornament.

vom•it (vom′it), *v.i., v.t.* **1.** to eject (the contents of the stomach) through the mouth. **2.** to eject or be ejected forcefully. —*n.* **3.** the act of vomiting. **4.** the matter ejected in vomiting.

voo•doo (vōō′dōō), *n., pl.* **-doos. 1.** a polytheistic religion deriving principally from African cult worship. **2.** a person who practices voodoo. **3.** an object of voodoo worship, as a fetish.

vo•ra•cious (vô rā′shəs, və-), *adj.* **1.** craving or consuming large quantities of food. **2.** exceedingly eager. —**vo•ra′cious•ly,** *adv.* —**vo•rac′i•ty** (-ras′i-tē), *n.*

vor•tex (vôr′teks), *n., pl.* **-tex•es, -ti•ces** (-tə sēz′). **1.** a whirling mass of water; whirlpool. **2.** something like a whirlpool: *was drawn into the vortex of the controversy.*

vo•ta•ry (vō′tə rē), *n., pl.* **-ries. 1.** a devoted worshiper. **2.** a devout adherent. **3.** a person bound by religious vows.

vote (vōt), *n., v.,* **vot•ed, vot•ing.** —*n.* **1.** a formal expression of opinion or choice, as in an election. **2.** a means, as a ballot, of indicating a vote. **3.** suffrage: *gave women the vote.* **4.** the number of votes cast. **5.** a group of voters. —*v.i.* **6.** to cast a vote. —*v.t.* **7.** to enact, establish, or determine by vote. **8.** to declare by general consent. [< L *vōtum* a vow] —**vot′er,** *n.*

vouch (vouch), *v.i.* **1.** to provide proof, supporting evidence, or assurance. **2.** to give a guarantee; take personal responsibility.

vouch′er *n.* **1.** one that vouches. **2.** a document, receipt, etc., that constitutes evidence, as of an expenditure.

vouch′safe′ *v.t.,* **-safed, -saf•ing.** to grant or give, esp. in a condescending manner.

vow (vou), *n.* **1.** a solemn promise, pledge, or commitment. **2.** a solemn or earnest declaration. —*v.t.* **3.** to promise by a vow. **4.** to declare solemnly or earnestly. —*v.i.* **5.** to make a vow. —*Idiom.* **6.** take vows, to enter a religious order.

vow•el (vou′əl), *n.* **1.** a speech sound produced without obstructing the flow of air from the lungs. **2.** a letter representing a vowel.

voy•age (voi′ij), *n., v.,* **-aged, -ag•ing.** —*n.* **1.** a journey, esp. a long journey by water. **2.** a journey through air or space. —*v.i., v.t.* **3.** to make, take, or traverse by a voyage.

vo•yeur (vwä yûr′, voi ûr′), *n.* a person who obtains sexual gratification by looking at sexual objects or acts. [< F] —**vo•yeur′ism,** *n.*

V.P. or **VP,** Vice President.

vs. or **vs,** versus.

VT or **Vt.,** Vermont.

v.t. transitive verb.

vul•can•ize (vul′kə nīz′), *v.t.,* **-ized, -iz•ing.** to treat (rubber) with sulfur and heat to impart greater strength, elasticity, and durability. —**vul′can•i•za′tion,** *n.*

vul•gar (vul′gər), *adj.* **1.** characterized by lack of good breeding, refinement, or taste. **2.** indecent; obscene. **3.** of or constituting the ordinary people in a society. **4.** spoken by or expressed in the language of ordinary people; vernacular. —**vul•gar′i•ty** (-gar′i tē), *n., pl.* **-ties.** —**vul′gar•ly,** *adv.*

Vul•gate (vul′gāt, -git), *n.* the Latin version of the Bible used in the Roman Catholic Church.

vul•ner•a•ble (vul′nər ə bəl), *adj.* **1.** capable of or susceptible to being wounded. **2.** open to or defenseless against criticism or attack. **3.** having won one game of a rubber of bridge. —**vul′ner•a•bil′i•ty,** *n.*

vul•ture (vul′chər), *n.* **1.** any of several large birds of prey that feed on carrion. **2.** a greedy or unscrupulous person.

vul•va (vul′və), *n., pl.* **-vae** (-vē), **-vas.** the external female genitalia.

vy•ing (vī′ing), *v.* pres. part. of VIE.

WXYZ
abcdefghijklmnopqrstuv

W, w (dub′əl yōō′, -yōō), *n., pl.* **Ws** or **W's, ws** or **w's.** the 23rd letter of the English alphabet, a semivowel.

W 1. watt. **2.** west. **3.** western. **4.** wide. **5.** width.

W *Chem. Symbol.* tungsten. [< G *Wolfram*]

w 1. watt. **2.** with.

W. 1. Wales. **2.** watt. **3.** Wednesday. **4.** weight. **5.** Welsh. **6.** west. **7.** western. **8.** width.

w. 1. watt. **2.** week. **3.** weight. **4.** west. **5.** western. **6.** wide. **7.** width. **8.** wife. **9.** with. **10.** *Physics.* work.

w/ with.

WA Washington.

wack•y (wak′ē), *adj.,* **-i•er, -i•est.** *Slang.* odd or irrational.

wad (wod), *n., v.,* **wad•ded, wad•ding.** —*n.* **1.** a small mass, as of cotton, used esp. for padding and packing. **2.** a roll of bank notes. **3.** a large stock or quantity, as of money. **4.** a plug used to hold the powder or shot in place in a gun or cartridge. —*v.t.* **5.** to form into a wad. **6.** to stuff or hold in place with a wad.

wad•dle (wod′l), *v.,* **-dled, -dling,** *n.* —*v.i.* **1.** to walk with short steps, swaying from side to side in the manner of a duck. —*n.* **2.** a waddling gait.

wade (wād), *v.i.,* **wad•ed, wad•ing. 1.** to walk

through a substance, as water or snow, that impedes motion. **2.** to make one's way laboriously.

wa•fer (wā′fər), *n.* **1.** a thin, crisp cake, cookie, biscuit, or candy. **2.** a thin disk of unleavened bread used in the Eucharist.

waf•fle¹ (wof′əl), *n.* a batter cake baked in a hinged appliance **(waf′fle i′ron)** that forms a gridlike pattern on each side.

waf•fle² (wof′əl), *v.i., v.t.* **-fled, -fling.** to speak or write equivocally.

waft (wäft, waft), *v.t., v.i.* **1.** to carry or float lightly and smoothly through or as if through the air. —*n.* **2.** a faintly perceived sound or odor. **3.** a light current or gust. **4.** the act of wafting.

wag (wag), *v.,* **wagged, wag•ging,** *n.* —*v.t., v.i.* **1.** to move up and down or from side to side. **2.** to move (the tongue) in idle chatter. —*n.* **3.** the act of wagging. **4.** a witty person.

wage (wāj), *n., v.,* **waged, wag•ing.** —*n.* **1.** Often, **wages.** money paid or received for work or services. **2. wages,** recompense; return: *the wages of sin.* —*v.t.* **3.** to carry on (a battle, argument, etc.).

wa•ger (wā′jər), *n.* **1.** something risked or staked on an uncertain event; bet. **2.** the act of betting. —*v.t., v.i.* **3.** to bet.

wag′gish *adj.* **1.** full of roguish good humor. **2.** characteristic of or befitting a wag.

wag•gle (wag′əl), *v.,* **-gled, -gling,** *n.* —*v.i., v.t.* **1.** to move up and down or from side to side. —*n.* **2.** a waggling motion.

wag•on (wag′ən), *n.* **1.** a four-wheeled vehicle, esp. one for the transport of heavy loads. **2.** STATION WAGON. —*Idiom.* **3. on the wagon,** *Informal.* abstaining from alcoholic beverages.

wag′on train′ *n.* a train of wagons and horses, as one transporting settlers in the westward migration.

waif (wāf), *n.* **1.** a person, esp. a child, who has no home. **2.** a stray animal.

wail (wāl), *v.i.* **1.** to express sorrow with a prolonged cry. **2.** to make mournful sounds, as the wind. —*n.* **3.** a wailing cry or any similar sound. —**wail′er,** *n.*

wain•scot (wān′skət, -skot, -skōt), *n., v.,* **-scot•ed, -scot•ing** or *(esp. Brit.)* **-scot•ted, -scot•ting.** —*n.* **1.** a paneling of wood on an interior wall, often only the lower portion. —*v.t.* **2.** to panel with wainscot.

waist (wāst), *n.* **1.** the narrow part of the human body between the ribs and the hips. **2.** the part of a garment covering the waist. **3.** BLOUSE (def. 1). **4.** the narrow central or middle part of something.

waist′band′ *n.* a band, as on a skirt, encircling the waist.

waist•coat (wes′kət, wāst′kōt′), *n. Chiefly Brit.* VEST (def. 1).

waist•line (wāst′līn′), *n.* **1.** the circumference of the body at the waist. **2.** the seam where the skirt and bodice of a dress are joined. **3.** an imaginary line encircling the waist.

wait (wāt), *v.i.* **1.** to remain inactive until something expected happens. **2.** to be available or in readiness. **3.** to be postponed or delayed. **4.** to work or serve as a waiter. —*v.t.* **5.** to await. **6.** to postpone or delay. **7.** to serve as waiter for. **8. wait on, a.** to attend to the needs of (a customer). **b.** to be an attendant or servant for. **9. ~ up, a.** to postpone going to bed to await a person or event. —*n.* **10.** an act or period of waiting. —*Idiom.* **11. lie in wait,** to wait in ambush.

wait′er *n.* a person, esp. a man, who waits on tables, as in a restaurant.

wait′ing list′ a list of persons waiting, as for reservations or admission.

wait•ress (wā′tris), *n.* a woman who waits on tables, as in a restaurant.

waive (wāv), *v.t.,* **waived, waiv•ing. 1.** to refrain from claiming or insisting on. **2.** to relinquish (a right) intentionally. **3.** to put off; defer.

waiv′er *n.* **1.** the intentional relinquishment of a right. **2.** a written statement containing a waiver.

wake¹ (wāk), *v.,* **waked** or **woke, waked** or **wok•en, wak•ing,** *n.* —*v.i.* **1.** to become roused

from sleep; awake. **2.** to become aware of something. **3.** to be or continue to be awake. —*v.t.* **4.** to rouse from or as if from sleep; awaken. —*n.* **5.** a vigil by the body of a dead person before burial.

wake² (wāk), *n.* **1.** the track of waves left by a moving ship or boat. **2.** the path or course of something that has passed or preceded. —*Idiom.* **3. in the wake of, a.** as a result of. **b.** close behind.

wake′ful *adj.* **1.** unable to sleep. **2.** sleepless. —**wake′ful•ness,** *n.*

wak′en *v.t., v.i.* to awake; awaken.

wale (wāl), *n., v.,* **waled, wal•ing.** —*n.* **1.** a stripe produced on the skin by a rod or whip. **2.** a vertical rib or cord in woven cloth. **3.** the texture of a fabric. —*v.t.* **4.** to mark with wales.

Wales (wālz), *n.* a division of the United Kingdom, in SW Great Britain.

walk (wôk), *v.i.* **1.** to move on foot at a moderate pace. **2.** (in baseball) to receive a base on balls. **3.** to conduct one's life in a particular manner. —*v.t.* **4.** to proceed along, through, or over on foot. **5.** to cause or help to walk. **6.** to accompany on foot. **7.** (of a baseball pitcher) to give a base on balls to. **8. walk off** or **away with, a.** to steal. **b.** to win (a prize, competition, etc.), esp. with ease. **9. ~ out, a.** to go on strike. **b.** to leave in protest. **10. ~ out on,** to desert; forsake. —*n.* **11.** an act or instance of walking. **12.** a distance walked or to be walked: *a ten-minute walk from here.* **13.** a characteristic manner of walking. **14.** BASE ON BALLS. **15.** a place or path for walking. **16.** a branch of activity, line of work, or position in society: *in every walk of life.* —**walk′er,** *n.*

walk′a•way′ *n., pl.* **-ways.** an easy victory or conquest.

walk•ie-talk•ie (wô′kē tô′kē), *n., pl.* **-talk•ies.** a portable combined voice transmitter and receiver.

walk′ing stick′ *n.* **1.** a stick used for support in walking. **2.** any of several insects with a long, slender, twiglike body.

walk′out′ *n.* a strike by workers.

wall (wôl), *n.* **1.** an upright structure, as of brick, serving to shelter, divide, or protect. **2.** an immaterial or intangible barrier or obstruction. **3.** a walllike part, thing, or mass. **4.** Usu., **walls.** a defensive rampart. —*v.t.* **5.** to enclose, border, or surround with or as if with a wall. **6.** to seal or fill (an opening) with a wall. —*Idiom.* **7. climb the walls,** *Informal.* to be frantic. **8. drive** or **push to the wall,** to force into a desperate situation. **9. off the wall,** *Slang.* **a.** unreasonable; crazy. **b.** eccentric; bizarre. **10. up the wall,** *Informal.* into a state of frantic frustration. —**walled,** *adj.*

wall′board′ *n.* material manufactured in large sheets for use in covering walls and ceilings.

wal•let (wol′it, wôl′it), *n.* a flat, folding case with compartments, as for paper money and credit cards.

wall′eye′ *n., pl.* **-eyes,** for 1 also **-eye. 1.** Also called **wall′eyed pike′.** a North American game fish with large eyes. **2.** a condition in which the eye or eyes are turned outward. —**wall′eyed′,** *adj.*

wall′flow′er *n.* **1.** a person who remains at the side at a party or dance, esp. from shyness. **2.** a European plant of the mustard family, bearing sweetscented yellow or orange flowers.

wal•lop (wol′əp), *v.t.* **1.** to beat soundly; thrash. **2.** to strike hard; sock. —*n.* **3.** a hard blow. **4.** the ability to deliver hard blows. **5.** *Informal.* a forceful impression; impact.

wal′lop•ing *Informal. adj.* **1.** very large; whopping. **2.** very fine; impressive.

wal•low (wol′ō), *v.i.* **1.** to roll around, as in mud. **2.** to indulge oneself; luxuriate. —*n.* **3.** an act or instance of wallowing. **4.** a place in which animals wallow.

wall′pa′per *n.* **1.** paper, usu. with decorative patterns, for covering walls or ceilings. —*v.t.* **2.** to put wallpaper on or in.

wal•nut (wôl′nut′, -nət), *n.* **1.** a meaty, edible nut with a hard, wrinkled shell. **2.** a tree bearing walnuts. **3.** the wood of a walnut, used esp. in making furniture.

wal•rus (wôl′rəs, wol′-), *n., pl.* **-rus•es, -rus.** a large mammal of arctic seas, having large tusks and a tough, wrinkled hide. [< D: lit., whale-horse]

waltz (wôlts), *n.* **1.** a ballroom dance in moderately fast triple meter. **2.** music for or in the rhythm of the waltz. —*v.i., v.t.* **3.** to dance a waltz (with). **4.** to move or progress easily.

wam•pum (wom′pəm, wôm′-), *n.* beads made of pierced and strung shells, once used by North American Indians as a medium of exchange.

wan (won), *adj.*, **wan•ner, wan•nest. 1.** unnaturally pale; ashen. **2.** showing ill health or fatigue: *a wan smile.* —**wan′ly,** *adv.*

wand (wond), *n.* **1.** a slender rod, esp. one used by a magician or conjurer. **2.** a staff carried as an emblem of office or authority.

wan•der (won′dər), *v.i.* **1.** to move around without a definite purpose or objective; roam. **2.** to go or extend in an irregular course or direction. **3.** to stray, as from a path or subject. **4.** to deviate in conduct or belief; go astray. —*v.t.* **5.** to travel about, on, or through. —**wan′der•er,** *n.*

wan′der•lust′ *n.* a strong desire to travel.

wane (wān), *v.*, **waned, wan•ing,** *n.* —*v.i.* **1.** to decrease, as in strength or intensity. **2.** to decline in power or importance. **3.** to draw to a close. **4.** (of the moon) to decrease periodically in brightness and roundness after the full moon. —*n.* **5.** an act or period of waning.

wan•gle (wang′gəl), *v.t.,* **-gled, -gling. 1.** to bring about or obtain by scheming or underhand methods. **2.** to manipulate for dishonest ends.

wan•na•be (won′ə bē′, wô′nə-), *n.,* *pl.* **-bes.** *Informal.* one who aspires, often vainly, to emulate another's success or attain eminence in some area.

want (wont, wônt), *v.t.* **1.** to feel a need for; wish or desire. **2.** to request the presence of. **3.** to be deficient in. **4.** to require. —*v.i.* **5.** to feel inclined. **6.** to have need. **7.** to be in a state of poverty. —*n.* **8.** something wanted or needed. **9.** deficiency; lack. **10.** a state of destitution; poverty.

want′ing *adj.* **1.** lacking or absent. **2.** deficient. —*prep.* **3.** lacking; without. **4.** less; minus.

wan•ton (won′tn), *adj.* **1.** malicious or unjustifiable; inhumane: *wanton cruelty.* **2.** without motive; unprovoked: *a wanton attack.* **3.** sexually unrestrained; lascivious. **4.** extravagant or excessive: *wanton luxury.* —*n.* **5.** a wanton person, esp. a lascivious woman.

war (wôr), *n., v.,* **warred, war•ring.** —*n.* **1.** armed conflict between nations or factions. **2.** the science or profession of armed fighting. **3.** any conflict or struggle. —*v.i.* **4.** to make or carry on war.

war•ble (wôr′bəl), *v.,* **-bled, -bling,** *n.* —*v.i., v.t.* **1.** to sing or whistle with trills or melodic embellishments. —*n.* **2.** a warbled song or trill.

war′bler *n.* **1.** any of numerous small New World songbirds, often brightly colored. **2.** any of numerous small, chiefly Old World songbirds.

ward (wôrd), *n.* **1.** an administrative or electoral division of a city or town. **2.** a division of a hospital. **3.** a division of a prison. **4.** a person, esp. a minor, under the care of a legal guardian or a court. **5.** the state of being under guard. **6.** the act of keeping guard. —*v.t.* **7.** to turn aside; avert: *to ward off a blow.*

-ward a suffix meaning in or toward a specified spatial or temporal direction (*backward*). Also, **-wards.**

war•den (wôr′dn), *n.* **1.** the chief administrative officer of a prison. **2.** an official charged with the enforcement of regulations: *a fire warden.*

ward′er *n.* a person who guards something; watchman.

ward′ heel′er *n.* a minor politician who does chores for a political machine.

ward′robe′ *n.* **1.** a collection of clothes or costumes. **2.** a piece of furniture or closet in which to keep clothes.

ware (wâr), *n.* **1.** Usu., **wares.** merchandise; goods. **2.** a particular kind of merchandise: *glassware.* **3.** pottery: *delft ware.*

ware•house (*n.* wâr′hous′; *v.* -houz′, -hous′), *n., v.,* **-housed, -hous•ing.** —*n.* **1.** a building for the

storage of goods or merchandise. **2.** a large and usu. public custodial institution, as for the mentally ill. —*v.t.* **3.** to place, deposit, or store in a warehouse.

war′fare′ *n.* **1.** armed conflict between enemies. **2.** conflict, esp. when unrelenting, between competitors or rivals.

war′head′ *n.* the section of a missile, as a bomb, containing the explosive or payload.

war′-horse′ *n.* **1.** a horse used in war. **2.** *Informal.* a veteran of many conflicts, as a soldier or politician.

war′like′ *adj.* **1.** fond of war; bellicose. **2.** threatening war. **3.** of or used in war.

war•lock (wär′lok′), *n.* a male witch.

warm (wôrm), *adj.,* **-er, -est,** *v.* —*adj.* **1.** having or giving out moderate heat. **2.** having a sensation of bodily heat. **3.** conserving warmth: *warm clothes.* **4.** suggestive of warmth; friendly, affectionate, sympathetic, or hearty: *a warm welcome.* **5.** heated or angry. **6.** strong or fresh: *a warm scent.* **7.** close to something sought, as in a game. **8.** uncomfortable or unpleasant. —*v.t., v.i.* **9.** to make or become warm. **10. warm up, a.** to prepare for strenuous exercise by engaging in moderate exercise. **b.** to increase in excitement, intensity, or violence. —**warm′er,** *n.* —**warm′ly,** *adv.* —**warmth,** *n.*

warm′-blood′ed *adj.* of or designating an animal, as a mammal, having a relatively constant body temperature that is independent of the environment.

warmed′-o′ver *adj.* **1.** reheated: *warmed-over stew.* **2.** lacking freshness; stale: *a warmed-over plot.*

warm′heart′ed *adj.* having or showing emotional warmth.

war′mon′ger *n.* a person who advocates war.

warn (wôrn), *v.t.* **1.** to give advance notice to, esp. of impending danger or possible harm. **2.** to advise to be careful; admonish. **3.** to direct to go or stay away. —*v.i.* **4.** to give a warning.

warn′ing *n.* **1.** the act of one that warns. **2.** something that serves to warn. —*adj.* **3.** being a warning: *a warning bell.*

warp (wôrp), *v.t.* **1.** to bend or twist out of shape. **2.** to turn away from what is right or proper. —*v.i.* **3.** to become warped. —*n.* **4.** a bend or twist in something formerly straight or flat. **5.** a mental bias or quirk. **6.** the lengthwise threads in a loom or woven fabric.

war•rant (wôr′ənt, wor′-), *n.* **1.** authorization, sanction, or justification. **2.** something providing formal assurance; guarantee. **3.** a writ authorizing an officer to make an arrest or search or seize property. —*v.t.* **4.** to authorize. **5.** to be sufficient reason for; justify. **6.** to vouch for. **7.** to give a formal assurance or guarantee of. **8.** to guarantee (something sold) to be as represented.

war′rant of′ficer *n.* an officer in the armed forces ranking below a commissioned officer.

war•ran•ty (wôr′ən tē, wor′-), *n.,* *pl.* **-ties.** a written guarantee given to a purchaser specifying that the manufacturer will make repairs or replace defective parts free of charge for a stated period of time.

war•ren (wôr′ən, wor′-), *n.* **1.** a place where rabbits breed or abound. **2.** a crowded building or area.

war•ri•or (wôr′ē ər, wor′-), *n.* a person engaged or experienced in warfare; soldier.

war′ship′ *n.* a ship armed for combat.

wart (wôrt), *n.* **1.** a small, often hard growth on the skin, usu. caused by a virus. **2.** a small protuberance, as on the surface of certain plants. —**wart′y,** *adj.,* **-i•er, -i•est.**

war•y (wâr′ē), *adj.,* **-i•er, -i•est. 1.** being on guard; watchful. **2.** characterized by caution. —**war′i•ly,** *adv.*

was (wuz, woz; *unstressed* wəz), *v.* 1st and 3rd pers. sing. past indic. of BE.

wash (wosh, wôsh), *v.t.* **1.** to cleanse by dipping, rubbing, or scrubbing in liquid, esp. water. **2.** to remove by or as if by the action of water. **3.** to moisten or wet. **4.** to flow through, over, or against. **5.** to carry or deposit by the action of water. **6.** to overlay with a thin coat, as of metal. —*v.i.* **7.** to wash oneself. **8.** to wash clothes. **9.** to undergo washing without damage. **10.** *Informal.* to prove true when subjected to testing: *His alibi simply won't wash.* **11.** to be carried or driven by water. **12.** to move along in or as if in waves. **13.** to be removed by the action of water. —*n.* **14.** the act or process of washing. **15.** items, as clothes, washed or to be washed at one time. **16. a.** the dash or breaking of water. **b.** the sound made by this. **17.** water moving in waves or with a rushing movement. **18.** the wake of a moving boat. **19.** a disturbance in the air caused by a moving airplane. **20.** a liquid for grooming or medicinal purposes. **21.** Also, **washing.** a thin coat, as of color or metal. **22.** waste liquid matter, as for hogs; swill. —*adj.* **23.** capable of being washed. —**wash′a•ble,** *adj.*

Wash. Washington.

wash′board′ *n.* a board with a corrugated metal surface on which clothes are scrubbed.

washed′-out′ *adj.* **1.** faded, esp. from washing. **2.** *Informal.* weary or tired-looking.

washed′-up′ *adj. Informal.* done for; having failed.

wash′er *n.* **1.** one that washes. **2.** an apparatus, esp. a household appliance, for washing clothing, linens, etc. **3.** a flat ring used, as under a bolt, to give tightness to a joint, prevent leakage, etc.

wash′out′ *n.* **1.** a washing out of earth by water, as from an embankment. **2.** *Informal.* a complete failure.

wash′room′ *n.* a room with washbowls and toilet facilities.

was•n't (wuz′ənt, woz′-), contraction of *was not.*

wasp (wosp), *n.* a slender winged insect with a narrowed abdomen, the female inflicting a painful sting.

WASP or **Wasp** (wosp), *n.* a white Anglo-Saxon Protestant.

wasp′ish *adj.* **1.** like or suggesting a wasp. **2.** snappish or peevish; testy.

was•sail (wos′əl, wo säl′), *n.* **1.** a former English toast to a person's health. **2.** liquor used in such a toast. **3.** a festivity with much drinking. —*v.i., v.t.* **4.** to drink a toast.

waste (wāst), *v.,* **wast•ed, wast•ing,** *n., adj.* —*v.t.* **1.** to consume, spend, or use to no avail or profit; squander. **2.** to fail to use: *Never waste an opportunity.* **3.** to consume gradually; wear away. **4.** to make feeble or thin: *wasted by disease.* **5.** to devastate or ruin. **6.** *Slang.* to murder. —*v.i.* **7.** to be consumed, spent, or used uselessly or carelessly. **8.** to become gradually used up or worn away. **9.** to become emaciated or enfeebled. —*n.* **10.** an act or instance of wasting. **11.** devastation or ruin. **12.** a devastated area. **13.** desolate country, as desert. **14.** something left over or superfluous: *factory wastes.* **15.** garbage; refuse. **16. wastes,** excrement. —*adj.* **17.** wild; desolate. **18.** left over; superfluous. **19.** rejected as useless or worthless. **20.** unused by or unusable to the organism. **21.** designed to receive or carry away waste. —**waste′ful,** *adj.*

waste′land′ *n.* uncultivated or barren land.

wast•rel (wā′strəl), *n.* a wasteful person; spendthrift.

watch (woch), *v.i.* **1.** to look attentively; observe. **2.** to wait attentively and expectantly: *We watched for the signal.* **3.** to be careful or cautious. **4.** to keep awake; stay vigilant. —*v.t.* **5.** to view attentively or with interest. **6.** to wait attentively and expectantly for. **7.** to guard or tend: *Watch the baby.* **8. watch out,** to be cautious. —*n.* **9.** close, continuous observation. **10.** vigilant guard. **11.** a keeping awake. **12.** a portable timepiece, as a wristwatch. **13. a.** a period of time, usu. four hours, during which a part of a ship's crew is on duty. **b.** the crew on duty during this time. **14.** a lookout, guard, or sentinel. —**watch′ful,** *adj.*

watch′dog′ *n.* **1.** a dog kept to guard property. **2.** a watchful guardian, as against illegal or unethical conduct.

watch′man *n., pl.* **-men.** a person who keeps watch, esp. at night.

watch′tow′er *n.* a tower for a sentinel or guard.

watch′word′ *n.* **1.** a password. **2.** a slogan or rallying cry.

wa•ter (wô′tər, wot′ər), *n.* **1.** an odorless, tasteless liquid compound of hydrogen and oxygen that constitutes rain, oceans, lakes, and rivers. **2.** Often, **waters.** water obtained from a mineral spring. **3.** a body of water, as an ocean. **4. waters,** the sea bordering on and controlled by a country. **5.** a liquid or aqueous organic secretion, as urine. **6.** a wavy, lustrous pattern, as on silk. —*v.t.* **7.** to sprinkle or drench with water. **8.** to supply (animals) with drinking water. **9.** to dilute or weaken with or as if with water. **10.** to produce a wavy, lustrous pattern on. —*v.i.* **11.** to fill with or secrete water or liquid: *Her eyes watered.* **12.** to drink water. —*Idiom.* **13. hold water,** to be capable of being substantiated or defended.

wa′ter•bed′ *n.* a bed with a liquid-filled mattress.

wa′ter buf′falo *n.* a widely domesticated Asian buffalo with large, curved horns.

wa′ter chest′nut *n.* **1.** an Old World aquatic plant with an edible, nutlike fruit. **2.** the fruit itself.

wa′ter clos′et *n.* a room or compartment containing a toilet bowl with a mechanism for flushing.

wa′ter•col′or *n.* **1.** a pigment for which water and not oil is the vehicle. **2.** the art of painting with watercolors. **3.** a picture done with watercolors.

wa′ter•course′ *n.* **1.** a stream of water. **2.** the bed of a stream.

wa′ter•cress′ *n.* a plant that grows in clear, running streams and bears pungent leaves used esp. in salads.

wa′ter•fall′ *n.* a steep fall of water from a height, as over a precipice.

wa′ter•fowl′ *n., pl.* **-fowl, -fowls. 1.** an aquatic bird. **2.** aquatic birds collectively.

wa′ter•front′ *n.* a part of a city or town on the edge of a body of water, esp. an ocean.

wa′ter gap′ *n.* a transverse gap in a mountain ridge, giving passage to a stream or river.

wa′ter•ing place *n.* a vacation or health resort by water or having mineral springs.

wa′ter lil′y *n.* an aquatic plant with large, disklike floating leaves and showy flowers.

wa′ter line′ *n.* one of a series of lines on a ship's hull indicating the level to which it is immersed.

wa′ter•logged′ *adj.* so filled with water as to be heavy or unmanageable.

wa′ter•mark′ *n.* **1.** a design impressed on paper that is visible when the paper is held to the light. **2.** a line indicating the height to which water has risen. —*v.t.* **3.** to mark with a watermark.

wa′ter•mel′on *n.* a large melon with a hard, green rind and sweet, juicy, usu. red pulp.

wa′ter moc′casin *n.* the cottonmouth.

wa′ter•proof′ *adj.* **1.** impervious to water. —*v.t.* **2.** to make waterproof.

wa′ter rat′ *n.* any of various aquatic rodents, as the muskrat.

wa′ter-repel′lent *adj.* repelling water but not entirely waterproof.

wa′ter•shed′ *n.* **1.** a region or area drained by a river or stream. **2.** a ridge dividing two drainage areas. **3.** an important point of division or transition.

wa′ter ski′ *n.* a short, broad ski on which to glide over water while being towed by a speedboat. —**wa′ter-ski′,** *v.i.,* **-skied, -ski•ing.** —**wa′ter-ski′er,** *n.*

wa′ter•spout′ *n.* **1.** a spout, duct, or pipe from which water is discharged. **2.** a whirling, funnel-shaped cloud that touches the surface of a body of water, drawing upward spray and mist.

wa′ter ta′ble *n.* the underground level beneath which soil and rock are saturated with water.

wa′ter•tight′ *adj.* **1.** constructed or fitted so tightly as to be impervious to water. **2.** incapable of being nullified or discredited: *a watertight alibi.*

wa′ter•way′ *n., pl.* **-ways.** a body of water serving as a travel or transport route.

wa′ter wheel′ *n.* a wheel turned by the weight or momentum of water and used to operate machinery.

wa′ter·works′ *n., pl.* **-works.** (*used with a sing. or pl. v.*) a system, as of reservoirs, pipelines, and conduits, by which water is collected, purified, stored, and pumped to urban users.

wa′ter·y *adj.* **1.** of, consisting of, or full of water. **2.** containing too much water. **3.** resembling water. —**wa′ter·i·ness,** *n.*

watt (wot), *n.* a unit of power equal to the power in a circuit in which a current of one ampere flows across a potential difference of one volt. [after J. Watt (1736–1819), Scottish engineer and inventor]

wat·tle[1] (wot′l), *n.* Often, **-tles.** rods interwoven with twigs or branches and used esp. for making fences and walls. —**wat′tled,** *adj.*

wat·tle[2] (wot′l), *n.* a fleshy lobe hanging down from the head or neck of certain birds, as the turkey.

wave (wāv), *n., v.,* **waved, wav·ing.** —*n.* **1.** a moving ridge or swell on the surface of water. **2.** a movement or part resembling a wave: *waves of grain; a wave in her hair.* **3.** a swell, surge, or rush: *a wave of disgust.* **4.** an outward curve, as in a surface. **5.** an act or instance of waving. **6.** a period of unusually hot or cold weather. **7.** *Physics.* a progressive disturbance propagated from point to point in a medium or space, as in the transmission of sound or light. —*v.i.* **8.** to move back and forth or up and down: *flags waving in the wind.* **9.** to curve alternately in opposite directions. **10.** to signal by moving the hand to and fro. —*v.t.* **11.** to cause to wave. **12.** to signal or express by a waving movement: *We all waved good-bye.* —*Idiom.* **13.** make waves, *Informal.* to disturb the status quo. —**wav′y,** *adj.,* **-i·er, -i·est.**

wave′length′ *n.* the distance, measured in the direction of propagation of a wave, between two successive points in the wave.

wa·ver (wā′vər), *v.i.* **1.** to sway to and fro. **2.** to flicker or quiver, as light. **3.** to be unsteady; falter. **4.** to tremble, as the voice. **5.** to feel or show doubt or indecision. —*n.* **6.** an act of wavering.

wax[1] (waks), *n.* **1.** a solid, yellowish substance secreted by bees in constructing their honeycomb. **2.** any of various similar substances, esp. ones composed of hydrocarbons. **3.** earwax. —*v.t.* **4.** to rub, polish, or treat with wax. —**wax′en,** *adj.* —**wax′y,** *adj.,* **-i·er, -i·est.**

wax[2] (waks), *v.i.* **1.** to increase, as in extent or intensity. **2.** (of the moon) to increase gradually in brightness and roundness before the full moon. **3.** to become: *waxing resentful.*

wax′ muse′um *n.* a museum in which wax effigies of famous persons are exhibited.

wax′ myr′tle *n.* a bayberry of the southeastern U.S. bearing waxy berries used in candlemaking.

wax′ pa′per *n.* paper made moisture-resistant by a paraffin coating.

wax′wing′ *n.* a crested songbird having wing feathers tipped with a red, waxy substance.

way[1] (wā), *n.* **1.** manner, mode, or fashion. **2.** a characteristic or habitual manner of acting, living, etc. **3.** a method or means for attaining a goal. **4.** a respect or particular: *defective in several ways.* **5.** a direction or vicinity: *He went that way.* **6.** passage or progress on a course: *Lead the way.* **7.** Often, **ways.** distance: *a long way from home.* **8.** a path or course: *the shortest way to town.* **9.** one's preferred manner of acting or doing: *He always gets his own way.* **10.** condition; state: *He's in a bad way.* **11.** space for passing or advancing: *cleared a way through the crowd.* —*Idiom.* **12. by the way,** incidentally. **13. by way of,** by the route of; through. **14. give way, a.** to withdraw or retreat. **b.** to break down; collapse. **15. under way, a.** in motion; traveling. **b.** in progress; proceeding.

way[2] (wā), *adv.* to a great degree or at quite a distance: *way too heavy; way down the road.*

way′bill *n.* a list of goods with shipping directions.

way′far′er *n.* a traveler, esp. on foot. —**way′far′ing,** *adj., n.*

way·lay (wā′lā′, wā lā′), *v.t.,* **-laid, -lay·ing. 1.** to intercept or attack from ambush. **2.** to await and accost unexpectedly.

way′-out′ *adj. Informal.* very unconventional.

ways′ and means′ *n.pl.* methods of raising revenue, esp. for the use of a government.

way′side′ *n.* land adjacent to a road or highway.

way′ward (-wərd), *adj.* **1.** stubbornly willful; disobedient. **2.** capricious or erratic.

we (wē), *pron.pl., poss.* **our** or **ours,** *obj.* **us. 1.** nominative plural of *I.* **2.** (used to denote oneself and another or others): *We attended a concert.* **3.** (used in place of *I* by a sovereign, an editor, or a writer).

weak (wēk), *adj.,* **-er, -est. 1.** liable to give way under pressure or strain. **2.** lacking in strength or vigor; feeble. **3.** lacking in force, intensity, or efficacy: *a weak president.* **4.** lacking in logical or legal force: *a weak argument.* **5.** deficient in intelligence or judgment: *a weak mind.* **6.** lacking in moral strength or force of character: *too weak to resist temptation.* **7.** deficient in ability or skill: *weak in spelling.* **8.** deficient in the essential or usual properties or ingredients: *weak tea.* —**weak′en,** *v.t., v.i.* —**weak′ly,** *adv.*

weak′-kneed′ *adj.* yielding readily to opposition, pressure, or intimidation.

weak′ling (-ling), *n.* a person who is physically or morally weak.

weak′ly *adj.,* **-lier, -liest,** *adv.* —*adj.* **1.** sickly. —*adv.* **2.** in weak manner.

weak′ness *n.* **1.** the state or quality of being weak. **2.** a slight fault or defect. **3.** a special fondness.

weal[1] (wēl), *n.* well-being, prosperity, or happiness.

weal[2] (wēl), *n.* WHEAL.

wealth (welth), *n.* **1.** abundance of money, property, or possessions. **2.** plentiful amount; abundance: *a wealth of imagery.* **3.** all things with monetary or exchange value. **4.** valuable contents or produce. —**wealth′y,** *adj.,* **-i·er, -i·est.**

wean (wēn), *v.t.* **1.** to accustom (a child or young animal) to food other than the mother's milk. **2.** to rid of an undesirable object or practice.

weap·on (wep′ən), *n.* **1.** an instrument or device used for attack or defense. **2.** something used against an opponent or adversary. —**weap′on·less,** *adj.*

weap′on·ry *n.* weapons collectively.

wear (wâr), *v.,* **wore, worn, wear·ing.** —*v.t.* **1.** to have on the body as clothing, covering, or ornament. **2.** to bear or have in one's aspect or appearance: *wore a big smile.* **3. a.** to cause to deteriorate by a constant or repetitive action. **b.** to make (a hole, channel, etc.) by such action. **4.** to weary; fatigue: *worn by illness.* —*v.i.* **5.** to deteriorate from or as if from use. **6.** to withstand continued use or strain: *fabric that wears well.* **7.** (of time) to pass slowly or tediously. **8. wear down,** to overcome by persistence. **9. ~ off,** to diminish slowly or gradually. —*n.* **10.** the act of wearing or state of being worn. **11.** clothing of a particular kind: *winter wear.* **12.** gradual deterioration, as from use. **13.** the quality of withstanding use; durability. —**wear′a·ble,** *adj.*

wea·ri·some (wēr′ē səm), *adj.* causing weariness; tedious. —**wea′ri·some·ly,** *adv.*

wea′ry *adj.,* **-ri·er, -ri·est,** *v.,* **-ried, -ry·ing.** —*adj.* **1.** physically or mentally exhausted. **2.** characterized by or causing fatigue. **3.** impatient or dissatisfied: *weary of excuses.* —*v.t., v.i.* **4.** to make or become weary. —**wea′ri·ly,** *adv.* —**wea′ri·ness,** *n.*

wea·sel (wē′zəl), *n., pl.* **-sels, -sel. 1.** a small carnivore, as a ferret or mink, having a long, slender body. —*v.i.* **2.** to evade an obligation or duty. **3.** to be evasive or ambiguous.

weath·er (weth′ər), *n.* **1.** the state of the atmosphere with respect to wind, temperature, moisture, etc. **2.** a strong wind or storm. —*v.t.* **3.** to expose to or affect by exposure to the weather. **4.** to come safely through. —*v.i.* **5.** to endure or resist exposure to the weather.

weath′er-beat′en *adj.* **1.** worn or damaged by exposure to the weather. **2.** tanned and toughened by exposure to the weather.

weath′er•ing *n.* the action of natural agents, as wind and water, on exposed rock.

weath′er•ize′ *v.t.,* **-ized, -iz•ing.** to make (a building) secure against cold weather, as by adding insulation.

weath•er•proof (weᵺ′ər pro͞of′), *adj.* **1.** able to withstand exposure to all kinds of weather. —*v.t.* **2.** to make weatherproof.

weath′er vane′ *n.* a rod to which a freely rotating pointer is attached, for indicating the direction of the wind.

weave (wēv), *v.,* **wove** or (*esp. for 6, 8*) **weaved; wo•ven** or **wove; weav•ing;** *n.* —*v.t.* **1.** to interlace (threads, strands, etc.) so as to form a fabric. **2.** to form by weaving: *to weave a basket.* **3.** (of a spider or larva) to spin (a web or cocoon). **4.** to combine into a connected whole. **5.** to introduce as an element. **6.** to make or move by winding or zigzagging. —*v.i.* **7.** to form or construct something by weaving. **8.** to move in a winding or zigzagging course. —*n.* **9.** a pattern of or method for weaving. —**weav′er,** *n.*

web (web), *n., v.,* **webbed, web•bing.** —*n.* **1.** a fabric formed by weaving. **2.** a cobweb. **3.** something that snares or entangles: *a web of lies.* **4.** a membrane connecting the digits of an animal, as an aquatic bird. **5.** an intricate network: *a web of tiny wrinkles.* **6.** (*usu. cap.*) World Wide Web (usu. prec. by *the*). —*v.t.* **7.** to cover with or as if with a web. —**webbed,** *adj.*

web′foot′ *n., pl.* **-feet.** a foot with the toes joined by a web. —**web′-foot′ed,** *adj.*

Web•ster (web′stər), *n.* Also, **Web′ster's.** *Informal.* a dictionary of the English language.

wed (wed), *v.t., v.i.,* **wed•ded** or **wed, wed•ding. 1.** to marry. **2.** to unite.

we'd (wēd), contraction of *we had, we should,* or *we would.*

Wed. Wednesday.

wed′ding *n.* **1.** the act or ceremony of marrying. **2.** the anniversary of a marriage or its celebration.

wedge (wej), *n., v.,* **wedged, wedg•ing.** —*n.* **1.** a tapered triangular piece of hard material used for raising, holding, or splitting objects. **2.** something shaped like a wedge. **3.** something that serves to part, split, or divide. —*v.t.* **4.** to split with or as if with a wedge. **5.** to insert or fix firmly with a wedge. **6.** to pack tightly into a narrow space. —*v.i.* **7.** to force a way like a wedge.

wed′lock′ *n.* the state of being married; matrimony.

Wednes•day (wenz′dā, -dē), *n.* the fourth day of the week.

wee (wē), *adj.,* **we•er, we•est. 1.** very small; tiny. **2.** very early: *the wee hours of the morning.*

weed (wēd), *n.* **1.** an undesirable plant growing wild, esp. to the disadvantage of a crop, lawn, or flower bed. —*v.t.* **2.** to free from weeds. **3.** to remove as being undesirable or superfluous: *weeded out inexperienced players.* —*v.i.* **4.** to remove weeds. —**weed′y,** *adj.,* **-i•er, -i•est.**

weeds (wēdz), *n.pl.* black mourning garments.

week (wēk), *n.* **1.** a period of seven successive days, usu. beginning with Sunday. **2.** the working portion of a week: *a 35-hour week.*

week′day′ *n.* any day of the week except Sunday or, often, Saturday and Sunday.

week′end′ (-end′, -end′), *n.* **1.** the end of a week, esp. the period between Friday evening and Monday morning. —*v.i.* **2.** to pass the weekend.

week′ly *adj., adv., n., pl.* **-lies.** —*adj.* **1.** done, happening, or appearing once a week. **2.** computed or determined by the week: *the weekly rate.* —*adv.* **3.** once a week. —*n.* **4.** a publication appearing weekly.

weep (wēp), *v.i., v.t.,* **wept, weep•ing. 1.** to shed (tears) from any overwhelming emotion. **2.** to mourn or grieve. **3.** to exude (liquid, as water).

wee•vil (wē′vəl), *n.* any of numerous beetles with a long snout that are destructive to nuts, grain, and fruit.

weft (weft), *n.* woof (def. 1).

weigh (wā), *v.t.* **1.** to determine the heaviness of,

esp. by use of a scale. **2.** to evaluate in the mind; consider carefully. —*v.i.* **3.** to have weight or a specified weight. **4.** to have importance or consequence. **5.** to bear down as a burden. **6. weigh down,** to lower the spirits of; depress. —*Idiom.* **7. weigh anchor,** to raise up a ship's anchor.

weight (wāt), *n.* **1.** the amount something weighs. **2.** gravitational force exerted upon a body. **3.** a system of units for expressing heaviness or mass. **4.** a unit of heaviness or mass. **5.** a body of determinate mass for use in weighing on a balance or scale. **6.** a specific quantity determined by weighing. **7.** a heavy load, mass, or object. **8.** a heavy object used to hold something open or down. **9.** a burden, as of responsibility. **10.** importance, consequence, or influence: *an opinion of great weight.* **11.** a heavy apparatus lifted or held for exercise, body building, or in athletic competition. —*v.t.* **12.** to add weight to. **13.** to burden with or as if with weight. —**weight′less,** *adj.* —**weight′y,** *adj.,* **-i•er, -i•est.**

weir (wēr), *n.* **1.** a dam in a stream. **2.** a fence, as of brush, set in a stream for catching fish.

weird (wērd), *adj.,* **-er, -est. 1.** suggesting the supernatural; unearthly. **2.** strange; peculiar.

weird•o (wēr′dō), *n., pl.* **-os.** *Slang.* an odd, eccentric, or abnormal person.

wel•come (wel′kəm), *n., v.,* **-comed, -com•ing,** *adj.* —*n.* **1.** a kindly greeting or reception. —*v.t.* **2.** to greet with pleasure or courtesy. **3.** to receive or accept with pleasure: *to welcome a change.* —*adj.* **4.** gladly received: *a welcome visitor.* **5.** given permission or consent: *She is welcome to try it.* **6.** (used as a conventional response to thanks): *You're welcome.*

weld (weld), *v.t.* **1.** to unite (metal or plastic pieces) by hammering or compressing, esp. after applying heat. **2.** to bring into complete union or harmony. —*v.i.* **3.** to undergo welding. —*n.* **4.** a welded joint. **5.** the act of welding. —**weld′er,** *n.*

wel•fare (wel′fâr′), *n.* **1.** health, happiness, and prosperity; well-being. **2.** organized efforts to improve the living conditions of needy persons. **3.** assistance given to those in need; public relief.

well¹ (wel), *adv., adj., compar.* **bet•ter,** *superl.* **best.** —*adv.* **1.** in a good or satisfactory manner: *Our plans are going well.* **2.** thoroughly or carefully: *Shake well before using.* **3.** in a proper manner: *behaves well.* **4.** commendably or excellently: *a difficult task well handled.* **5.** with justice or reason: *I couldn't very well refuse.* **6.** with favor or approval: *thinks well of her.* **7.** comfortably or prosperously: *to live well.* **8.** to a considerable degree: *well below average.* **9.** in a close way; intimately: *know her well.* **10.** without doubt; certainly: *I cry easily, as you well know.* —*adj.* **11.** in good health: *not a well man.* **12.** satisfactory or good: *All is well.* **13.** proper, fitting, or prudent: *It is well that you didn't go.* —*Idiom.* **14. as well,** in addition; also. **15. as well as,** equally as.

well² (wel), *n.* **1.** a hole drilled or bored into the earth to obtain a natural deposit, as water or petroleum. **2.** a natural source of water, as a spring. **3.** an abundant source: *a well of compassion.* **4.** a container, receptacle, or reservoir, as for ink. **5.** an enclosed space, as for air, stairs, or an elevator, extending vertically through the floors of a building. —*v.i.* **6.** to rise, spring, or gush, as from a well: *Tears welled up in my eyes.*

we'll (wēl; *unstressed* wil), contraction of *we shall* or *we will.*

well′-advised′ *adj.* **1.** acting with caution, care, or wisdom. **2.** based on or showing wise consideration.

well′-appoint′ed *adj.* attractively or properly equipped or furnished.

well′-be′ing *n.* a state characterized by health, happiness, and prosperity; welfare.

well′born′ *adj.* born of a good, noble, or highly esteemed family.

well′-bred′ *adj.* showing good breeding, as in behavior.

well′-disposed′ *adj.* feeling favorable, sympathetic, or kind.

well′-done′ *adj.* **1.** performed accurately and skillfully. **2.** (of meat) thoroughly cooked.

well′-found′ed *adj.* having or based on good reasons, sound information, etc.

well′-ground′ed *adj.* **1.** WELL-FOUNDED. **2.** thoroughly instructed in the basic principles of a subject.

well′-heeled′ *adj.* well-off.

well′-informed′ *adj.* having extensive knowledge, as in a variety of subjects.

well′-man′nered *adj.* polite; courteous.

well′-mean′ing *adj.* having or based on good intentions.

well′-nigh′ *adv.* very nearly; almost.

well′-off′ *adj.* **1.** well-to-do; prosperous. **2.** in a favorable position or condition.

well′-round′ed *adj.* **1.** having desirably varied abilities or attainments. **2.** desirably varied.

well′spring′ *n.* **1.** the source of a spring, stream, or river. **2.** a continuous, seemingly inexhaustible supply.

well′-to-do′ *adj.* wealthy; prosperous.

well′-worn′ *adj.* **1.** showing the effects of extensive use or wear. **2.** trite; hackneyed.

welsh (welsh, welch), *v.i. Often Offensive.* **1.** to fail to pay what is owed. **2.** to go back on one's word.

Welsh (welsh, welch), *n.* **1.** (*used with a pl. v.*) the inhabitants of Wales. **2.** the Celtic language of Wales. —*adj.* **3.** of Wales, its inhabitants, or their language.

welt (welt), *n.* **1.** a ridge on the surface of the body, as from a blow. **2.** a strip, esp. of leather, to which the edges of the insole and upper of a shoe are attached. **3.** a strip or cord sewn along a seam for strength or as decoration. —*v.t.* **4.** to beat soundly. **5.** to furnish with a welt.

wel•ter (wel′tər), *v.i.* **1.** to toss or heave, as ocean waves. **2.** to roll around; wallow. **3.** to lie drenched in something, as blood. —*n.* **4.** a confused mass; jumble. **5.** a state of commotion, turmoil, or upheaval.

wen (wen), *n.* a cyst containing sebaceous matter.

wench (wench), *n.* **1.** a girl or young woman. **2.** *Archaic.* a strumpet.

wend (wend), *v.t.,* **wend•ed, wend•ing.** to travel on or direct (one's way).

went (went), *v.* **1.** pt. of GO. **2.** *Archaic.* a pt. and pp. of WEND.

were (wûr; *unstressed* wər), *v.* a 2nd pers. sing. past indic., pl. past indic., and past subj. of BE.

we're (wēr), contraction of *we are.*

were•n′t (wûrnt, wûr′ənt), contraction of *were not.*

were•wolf (wâr′wŏŏlf′, wēr′-, wûr′-), *n., pl.* **-wolves.** (in folklore) a person who has assumed the form of a wolf.

west (west), *n.* **1.** the cardinal point of the compass 90° to the left of north. **2.** the direction in which west lies. **3.** (*usu. cap.*) a region in the west. **4. the West, a.** the western part of the world as distinguished from the East; the Occident. **b.** the western part of the U.S. —*adj.* **5.** lying toward or situated in the west. **6.** coming from the west. —*adv.* **7.** to, toward, or in the west.

west′er•ly *adj., adv.* toward or from the west.

west′ern *adj.* **1.** of, toward, or in the west. **2.** coming from the west. **3.** (*usu. cap.*) of the West. —*n.* **4.** (*often cap.*) a story, movie, or radio or television program about the U.S. West of the 19th century. —**west′ern•er,** *n.*

West′ern Hem′isphere *n.* the half of the globe that includes North and South America.

west•ern•ize (wes′tər nīz′), *v.t.,* **-ized, -iz•ing.** to influence or convert to western ideas, customs, and practices.

West′ern Samo′a *n.* a country on a group of islands in the S Pacific.

west•ward (west′wərd), *adj.* **1.** moving, facing, or situated toward the west. —*adv.* **2.** Also, **west′-wards.** toward the west.

wet (wet), *adj.,* **wet•ter, wet•test,** *n., v.,* **wet** or **wet•ted, wet•ting.** —*adj.* **1.** moistened, covered, or soaked with liquid, as water. **2.** in a liquid state:

wet paint. **3.** rainy or misty. **4.** allowing the sale of alcoholic beverages. —*n.* **5.** something wet, as water. **6.** liquid; moisture. **7.** damp weather; rain. **8.** a person in favor of allowing the sale of alcoholic beverages. —*v.t., v.i.* **9.** to make or become wet. —*Idiom.* **10. all wet,** completely mistaken.

wet′ blan′ket *n.* one that dampens or discourages enthusiasm or enjoyment.

wet′ nurse′ *n.* a woman hired to suckle another's infant.

wet′ suit′ *n.* a close-fitting rubber suit worn for body warmth, as by scuba divers.

whack (hwak, wak), *v.t., v.i.* **1.** to strike with a smart, resounding blow. —*n.* **2.** a smart, resounding blow. **3.** an attempt: *took a whack at the job.* —*Idiom.* **4. out of whack,** out of order.

whale¹ (hwāl, wāl), *n., pl.* **whales, whale,** *v.,* **whaled, whal•ing.** —*n.* **1.** one of the larger marine mammals with a fishlike body. **2.** something big, great, or fine of its kind: *I had a whale of a time in Europe.* —*v.i.* **3.** to engage in whaling.

whale² (hwāl, wāl), *v.t., v.i.,* **whaled, whal•ing.** to thrash or beat soundly.

whale′bone′ *n.* **1.** a flexible, horny substance hanging from the upper jaws of certain whales. **2.** something, esp. corset stays, made of whalebone.

wharf (hwôrf, wôrf), *n., pl.* **wharves** (hwôrvz, wôrvz), **wharfs.** a structure next to which ships moor to load or unload.

wharf′age *n.* **1.** the use of a wharf. **2.** the charge for such use.

what (hwut, hwot, wut, wot; *unstressed* hwət, wət), *pron.* **1.** (used interrogatively as a request for information): *What is the matter?* **2.** (used interrogatively to inquire about the character, origin, identity, or worth of a person or thing): *What is wealth without friends?* **3.** how much?: *What does it cost?* **4.** that which: *I will send what was promised.* **5.** whatever: *come what may.* **6.** as much or as many as: *Give what you can.* —*adj.* **7.** (used interrogatively before nouns): *What clothes shall I pack?* **8.** whatever or whichever: *Take what supplies you need.* —*adv.* **9.** to what extent or degree?: *What does it matter?* —*Idiom.* **10. what for,** why.

what•ev′er *pron.* **1.** anything that: *Do whatever you like.* **2.** no matter what: *Do it, whatever happens.* **3.** what (used interrogatively): *Whatever do you mean?* —*adj.* **4.** no matter what: *whatever problems you might have.* **5.** of any kind: *no friends whatever.* —*interj.* **6.** (used to indicate indifference to a state of affairs, situation, previous statement, etc.)

what′not′ *n.* a stand with shelves, esp. for bric-a-brac.

what′so•ev′er *pron., adj.* (an intensive form of WHATEVER).

wheal (hwēl, wēl), *n.* **1.** a burning or itching swelling on the skin. **2.** a wale or welt.

wheat (hwēt, wēt), *n.* **1.** the grain of a cereal grass used esp. in the form of flour. **2.** the plant itself.

whee•dle (hwēd′l, wēd′l), *v.t., v.i.,* **-dled, -dling.** **1.** to influence (a person) by flattering or beguiling. **2.** to obtain by or use artful persuasion.

wheel (hwēl, wēl), *n.* **1.** a circular frame or disk that can revolve on an axis. **2.** something like a wheel in shape or function. **3.** the steering wheel of a vehicle. **4. wheels, a.** propelling or animating agencies: *the wheels of commerce.* **b.** *Slang.* a car. **5.** someone powerful and influential. —*v.t., v.i.* **6.** to turn, rotate, or revolve. **7.** to move or convey on wheels. **8.** to change direction by or as if by turning around.

wheel′bar′row *n.* a small cart for conveying a load that is supported at one end by a wheel and pushed at the other by two handles.

wheel′base′ *n.* the distance from the front-wheel spindle of a motor vehicle to the rear-wheel axle.

wheel′chair′ *n.* a chair mounted on wheels for use by persons who cannot walk.

wheeze (hwēz, wēz), *v.,* **wheezed, wheez•ing,** *n.* —*v.i.* **1.** to breathe with difficulty and with a whistling sound. —*n.* **2.** a wheezing breath or sound.

whelp (hwelp, welp), *n.* **1.** the young of such

mammals as the dog or the wolf. **2.** an impudent youth. —*v.t., v.i.* **3.** to give birth to (whelps).

when (hwen, wen; *unstressed* hwən, wən), *adv.* **1.** at what time or period?: *When are the guests to arrive?* **2.** under what circumstances?: *When is an apology in order?* —*conj.* **3.** at what time: *knows when to be silent.* **4.** at the time that: *when we were young.* **5.** whenever: *The dog barks when the doorbell rings.* **6.** upon or after which: *Stop the car when the light turns red.* **7.** whereas: *Why are you here when you should be in school?* —*pron.* **8.** what or which time: *Since when have you been teaching?* —*n.* **9.** the time of something.

whence (hwens, wens), *adv.* **1.** from what place?: *Whence comest thou?* **2.** from what source, origin, or cause?: *Whence came his wisdom?*

when•ev′er *adv., conj.* at whatever time; when.

where (hwâr, wâr), *adv.* **1.** in, at, or to what place?: *Where is he? Where are you going?* **2.** in what position, circumstances, respect, or way: *Where do you stand on this question?* **3.** from what source?: *Where did you get such a notion?* —*conj.* **4.** in or at what place, part, or point: *Find where the trouble is.* **5.** in or at the place, part, or point in or at which: *The cup is where you left it.* **6.** in a position or situation in which: *He's useless where tact is needed.* **7.** to what or whatever place: *I will go where you go.* **8.** in or at which place: *They pitched a tent, where they slept.* —*pron.* **9.** what place?: *Where are you from?* **10.** the place in or point at which: *This is where the boat docks.* —*n.* **11.** a place; location.

where′a•bouts′ *adv.* **1.** about where? —*n.* **2.** (*used with a sing. or pl. v.*) the place where a person or thing is.

where•as′ *conj.* **1.** while on the contrary. **2.** it being the case that.

where•by′ *conj.* by what or which; under the terms of which.

where′fore′ *adv.* **1.** for that cause or reason. **2.** *Archaic.* for what reason? why? —*n.* **3.** a cause or reason.

where•in′ *conj.* **1.** in what or in which. —*adv.* **2.** in what way or respect?

where•of′ *adv., conj.* of what, which, or whom.

where′up•on′ *conj.* **1.** upon what or which. **2.** at or after which.

wher•ev′er *conj., adv.* in, at, or to whatever place or circumstance.

where′with•al′ *n.* means, esp. money, with which to do something.

whet (hwet, wet), *v.t.,* **whet•ted, whet•ting. 1.** to sharpen by grinding or friction. **2.** to make keen or eager; stimulate.

wheth•er (hweth′ər, weth′-), *conj.* **1.** (used to introduce the first of two or more alternatives): *I don't care whether we go or stay.* **2.** (used to introduce a single alternative, the other being implied): *See whether she has come.*

whet′stone′ *n.* a stone for sharpening cutlery or tools by friction.

whey (hwā, wā), *n.* the liquid that separates from the curd in coagulated milk.

which (hwich, wich), *pron.* **1.** what one or ones?: *Which of these do you want?* **2.** whichever: *Choose which appeals to you.* **3.** (used in relative clauses to represent a specified antecedent): *This book, which I read last night, was exciting.* **4.** (used after a preposition to represent an antecedent): *the house in which I lived.* —*adj.* **5.** what one or ones of a number or group: *Which book do you want?* **6.** whichever: *Go which way you please.*

which•ev′er *pron.* **1.** any one that: *Take whichever you like.* **2.** no matter which: *Whichever you choose, the others will be offended.* —*adj.* **3.** no matter which.

whiff (hwif, wif), *n.* **1.** a slight gust or puff, as of wind or smoke. **2.** a slight trace, as of an odor; hint: *a whiff of onions; a whiff of scandal.* **3.** a single inhalation, as of tobacco smoke. —*v.i., v.t.* **4.** to blow or drive in whiffs.

while (hwīl, wīl), *n., conj., v.,* **whiled, whil•ing.** —*n.* **1.** an interval of time: *a long while ago.* —*conj.*

2. during the time that: *He read the paper while he waited.* **3.** as long as: *While there's quiet I can sleep.* **4.** even though: *While they are related, they don't get along.* —*v.t.* **5.** to cause (time) to pass, esp. pleasantly: *whiling away the hours.*

whim (hwim, wim), *n.* a capricious notion; fancy.

whim•per (hwim′pər, wim′-), *v.i., v.t.* **1.** to cry with or utter in low plaintive sounds. —*n.* **2.** a whimpering sound.

whim•sy or **-sey** (hwim′zē, wim′-), *n., pl.* **-sies** or **-seys. 1.** playful or fanciful humor. **2.** an odd or fanciful notion. —**whim′si•cal,** *adj.*

whine (hwīn, wīn), *v.,* **whined, whin•ing,** *n.* —*v.i.* **1.** to utter a low, usu. nasal complaining sound. **2.** to complain in a peevish, self-pitying way. —*v.t.* **3.** to utter with a whine. —*n.* **4.** a whining utterance, sound, or complaint.

whin•ny (hwin′ē, win′ē), *n., pl.* **-nies,** *v.,* **-nied, -ny•ing.** —*n.* **1.** a subdued gentle neigh of a horse. —*v.i.* **2.** to utter a whinny.

whip (hwip, wip), *v.,* **whipped** or **whipt, whip•ping,** *n.* —*v.t.* **1.** to beat with a flexible implement, as a lash, esp. as punishment. **2.** to spank. **3.** to urge on by or as if by whipping. **4.** to train forcefully: *trying to whip the team into shape.* **5.** to defeat; overcome. **6.** to move, pull, or seize suddenly: *She whipped out her camera.* **7.** to beat to a froth: *whipped cream.* —*v.i.* **8.** to go quickly and suddenly. **9.** to lash about: *flags whipping in the wind.* **10. whip up, a.** to prepare quickly. **b.** to incite; arouse. —*n.* **11.** a flexible implement for whipping. **12.** a whipping stroke or motion. **13.** a dessert of beaten egg whites or cream. **14.** a party manager in a legislative body who secures attendance and directs other members.

whip′cord′ *n.* **1.** a fabric with a diagonally ribbed surface. **2.** a strong, hard-twisted cord, esp. of catgut.

whip′lash′ *n.* **1.** the lash of a whip. **2.** a neck injury caused by a sudden jerking of the head.

whip•per•snap•per (hwip′ər snap′ər, wip′-), *n.* an unimportant but presumptuous person.

whip•pet (hwip′it, wip′-), *n.* a slender swift dog resembling a small greyhound.

whip•poor•will (hwip′ər wil′, wip′-), *n.* a nocturnal North American bird with an insistently repeated call.

whir or **whirr** (hwûr, wûr), *v.,* **whirred, whir•ring,** *n.* —*v.i., v.t.* **1.** to move, revolve, or transport quickly with a humming sound. —*n.* **2.** an act or sound of whirring.

whirl (hwûrl, wûrl), *v.i.* **1.** to turn around, spin, or rotate rapidly. **2.** to move or be carried rapidly along. **3.** to experience dizziness: *My head is whirling.* —*v.t.* **4.** to cause to whirl. —*n.* **5.** the act of whirling. **6.** a whirling movement. **7.** a rapid round of events: *a whirl of parties.* **8.** a state of dizziness. **9.** an attempt; trial: *gave the diet a whirl.*

whirl•i•gig (hwûr′li gig′, wûr′-), *n.* **1.** something that whirls. **2.** a merry-go-round. **3.** a whirling or spinning toy.

whirl′pool′ *n.* water in swift circular motion producing a downward spiraling action.

whirl′wind′ *n.* **1.** a small, rapidly rotating mass of air, as a tornado. **2.** something resembling a whirlwind, as in destructive force. —*adj.* **3.** like a whirlwind, as in speed or force.

whisk (hwisk, wisk), *v.t.* **1.** to move with a rapid brushing or sweeping stroke. **2.** to carry or move rapidly. **3.** to whip or blend with a whisk. —*n.* **4.** the act of whisking. **5.** whisk broom. **6.** an implement, usu. of wire, for beating or whipping food.

whisk′ broom′ *n.* a small short-handled broom used chiefly to brush clothes.

whisk′er *n.* **1.** Usu. **-kers.** the hair growing on the sides of a man's face. **2.** a single hair of the beard. **3.** one of the long bristly hairs growing near the mouth of certain animals, as the cat.

whis•key (hwis′kē, wis′-), *n., pl.* **-keys.** an alcoholic liquor distilled from a fermented mash of grain, as barley.

whis•per (hwis′pər, wis′pər), *v.i., v.t.* **1.** to speak or utter with soft hushed sounds, esp. with no vibration of the vocal cords. **2.** to talk or tell softly and privately. **3.** to make a soft rustling sound. —*n.* **4.** an act or instance of whispering. **5.** a whispered word or remark. **6.** a rumor or insinuation. **7.** a soft rustling sound. —**whis'per•er,** *n.*

whist (hwist, wist), *n.* a card game that is an early form of bridge.

whis•tle (hwis'əl, wis'-), *v.,* **-tled, -tling,** *n.* —*v.i.* **1.** to make a high clear sound by forcing the breath through puckered lips or through the teeth. **2.** to produce a sound or call resembling a whistle. **3.** to move with a whistling sound, as a bullet. —*v.t.* **4.** to produce by whistling. **5.** to call or signal by whistling. —*n.* **6.** an instrument for producing whistling sounds. **7.** a whistling sound.

whis'tle-blow'er *n.* a person who informs on another or discloses corruption or wrongdoing.

whis'tle stop' *n.* **1.** a small town, esp. one along a railroad line. **2.** a short talk from the rear platform of a train during a political campaign.

whit (hwit, wit), *n.* the smallest amount: *I don't care a whit.*

white (hwīt, wīt), *adj.,* **whit•er, whit•est,** *n.* —*adj.* **1.** of the color of pure snow. **2.** light in color; pale. **3.** marked by little skin pigmentation. **4.** for, limited to, or predominantly consisting of Caucasians. **5.** silvery; gray: *white hair.* **6.** snowy: *a white Christmas.* **7.** lacking color. **8.** morally pure; innocent. —*n.* **9.** a color without hue that is the opposite of black. **10.** a person of Caucasian racial heritage. **11.** a white material, substance, or part: *the white of an egg.* **12. whites,** white clothing. —**whit'en,** *v.t., v.i.*

white' blood' cell' *n.* any of various nearly colorless blood cells of the immune system.

white'-bread' *adj.* **1.** *Disparaging.* of or characteristic of the white middle class. **2.** bland; conventional.

white'-col'lar *adj.* of or designating professional or clerical workers whose jobs do not usu. involve manual labor.

white' el'ephant *n.* **1.** a possession unwanted by the owner but of use to another. **2.** a possession entailing expense out of proportion to its value. **3.** an albino Indian elephant.

white'fish' *n., pl.* **-fish, -fish•es.** any of several freshwater food fishes resembling the trout.

white' gold' *n.* a gold alloy colored white esp. by the presence of nickel.

white' goods' *n.pl.* **1.** household linens, as sheets and towels. **2.** white fabrics, esp. of cotton or linen.

white' lie' *n.* a harmless lie; fib.

white'wash' *n.* **1.** a composition, as of lime and water, for whitening walls and woodwork. **2.** a concealment of faults or errors or exoneration from blame. —*v.t.* **3.** to whiten with whitewash. **4.** to conceal the faults or errors of; absolve from blame.

white' wa'ter *n.* frothy water, as in rapids.

whith•er (hwith'ər, with'-), *adv.* **1.** to what place; where? **2.** to what end, point, or action? —*conj.* **3.** to which place. **4.** to whatever place.

whit•ing¹ (hwī'ting, wī'-), *n., pl.* **-ings, -ing.** any of several marine food fishes.

whit•ing² (hwī'ting, wī'-), *n.* pure-white chalk powder used esp. in making putty and whitewash.

whit'low (hwit'lō, wit'-) *n.* an inflammation of a finger or toe, usu. near the nail.

Whit•sun•day (hwit'sun'dā, -dē, -sən dā', wit'-), *n.* PENTECOST.

whit•tle (hwit'l, wit'l), *v.,* **-tled, -tling.** —*v.t.* **1.** to cut, trim, or shape (wood) by carving off bits with a knife. **2.** to form by whittling. **3.** to reduce gradually. —*v.i.* **4.** to whittle wood. —**whit'tler,** *n.*

whiz or **whizz** (hwiz, wiz), *v.,* **whizzed, whiz•zing,** *n.* —*v.i.* **1.** to make or move with a humming, buzzing, or hissing sound, as of an object flying swiftly through the air. —*n.* **2.** *Informal.* a very skillful person; expert: *a whiz at math.* **3.** a whizzing sound.

who (hōō), *pron., possessive* **whose,** *objective* **whom. 1.** what person or persons?: *Who is he?* **2.** the person or persons that: *Do you know who called?* **3.** (used in relative clauses to represent an

antecedent): *The woman who called this morning is here.*

WHO World Health Organization.

whoa (hwō, wō), *interj.* a command, esp. to an animal, to stop.

who•dun'it (-dun'it), *n.* a detective story.

who•ev'er *pron.* whatever person; anyone that: *Whoever did it should be proud.*

whole (hōl), *adj.* **1.** comprising the full quantity, extent, or duration; entire or total. **2.** lacking nothing; complete: *a whole set of china.* **3.** not divided: *a whole cheese.* **4.** *Math.* not fractional. **5.** not broken or damaged; intact. **6.** not injured or hurt; sound. —*n.* **7.** the entire quantity, number, extent, or duration. **8.** a thing complete in itself. —*Idiom.* **9. on the whole, a.** taking everything into consideration. **b.** in general. —**whole'ness,** *n.* —**whol'ly,** *adv.*

whole'heart'ed *adj.* completely sincere or enthusiastic.

whole'sale' *n., adj., adv., v.,* **-saled, -sal•ing.** —*n.* **1.** the sale of goods in quantity, as to retailers. —*adj.* **2.** of or engaged in sale by wholesale. **3.** extensive; broadly indiscriminate: *wholesale firings.* —*adv.* **4.** in a wholesale way. —*v.t., v.i.* **5.** to sell by wholesale. —**whole'sal'er,** *n.*

whole'some (-səm), *adj.* **1.** conducive to well-being; healthful. **2.** suggestive of health, esp. in appearance. **3.** healthy or sound. —**whole'some•ly,** *adv.*

whole'-wheat' *adj.* prepared with the complete wheat kernel.

whom (hōōm), *pron.* the objective case of WHO.

whom•ev'er *pron.* the objective case of WHOEVER.

whoop (hwōōp, hwōōp, wōōp, wōōp; *esp. for 2* hōōp, hōōp), *n.* **1.** a loud cry or shout, as of excitement. **2.** a deep intake of air with a hollow gasping sound following a fit of coughing. —*v.i., v.t.* **3.** to utter or utter with a loud cry or shout.

whoop'ing cough' (hōō'ping, hōōp'ing), *n.* an infectious disease characterized by a series of short, convulsive coughs followed by a whoop.

whop•per (hwop'ər, wop'-), *n. Informal.* **1.** something uncommonly large. **2.** a big lie.

whop'ping *adj. Informal.* uncommonly large.

whore (hôr; *often* hōōr), *n.* a prostitute. —**whor'ish,** *adj.*

whorl (hwûrl, hwôrl, wûrl, wôrl), *n.* **1.** a circular arrangement of like parts, as leaves or flowers. **2.** one of the central ridges of a fingerprint. —**whorled,** *adj.*

whose (hōōz), *pron.* **1.** the possessive case of WHO or WHICH used as an adjective: *someone whose faith is strong; a word whose meaning escapes me.* **2.** the one or ones belonging to what person or persons: *Whose umbrella is that?*

who'so•ev'er *pron.* whoever.

why (hwī, wī), *adv., conj., n., pl.* **whys,** *interj.* —*adv.* **1.** for what reason or purpose?: *Why do you ask?* —*conj.* **2.** for what cause or reason: *I don't know why he left.* **3.** on account of which: *the reason why she refused.* **4.** the reason for which: *That is why he returned.* —*n.* **5.** the cause or reason. —*interj.* **6.** an exclamation of surprise, hesitation, or impatience.

WI Wisconsin.

W.I. 1. West Indian. **2.** West Indies.

wick (wik), *n.* a twist of soft threads that in a candle or oil lamp draws up the flammable liquid to be burned.

wick•ed (wik'id), *adj.* **1.** evil or morally bad; sinful. **2.** playfully mischievous. **3.** harmful; dangerous: *wicked roads.* **4.** unpleasant; foul: *a wicked odor.* **5.** *Slang.* wonderful; great; masterful. —**wick'ed•ly,** *adv.* —**wick'ed•ness,** *n.*

wick'er *n.* **1.** a slender, pliant twig. **2.** wickerwork. —*adj.* **3.** made of wicker. —**wick'er•work',** *n.*

wick•et (wik'it), *n.* **1.** a window or opening, often with a grating, as in a ticket office. **2.** a small door or gate, esp. one beside or forming part of a larger one. **3.** (in croquet) a hoop or arch. **4.** (in cricket) either of the two frameworks at which the bowler aims the ball.

wide (wīd), *adj.* and *adv.*, **wid·er, wid·est.** —*adj.*
1. of great extent from side to side; broad. **2.** having a specified measurement from side to side: *three feet wide.* **3.** of great range or scope: *wide experience.* **4.** fully opened: *stared with wide eyes.* **5.** far from an objective: *wide of the truth.* —*adv.* **6.** to the utmost; fully: *wide open.* **7.** away from a target or objective: *The shot went wide.* **8.** over an extensive area: *scattered far and wide.* —**wide′ly,** *adv.* —**wid′en,** *v.t., v.i.*

wide′-awake′ *adj.* **1.** fully awake. **2.** alert or observant.

wide′-eyed′ *adj.* having the eyes open wide, as in amazement or innocence.

wide′spread′ *adj.* **1.** spread over a wide area. **2.** occurring in many places or among many persons.

wid·ow (wid′ō), *n.* **1.** a woman who has lost her husband by death and has not remarried. —*v.t.* **2.** to make (someone) a widow. —**wid′ow·hood′,** *n.*

wid′ow·er *n.* a man who has lost his wife by death and has not remarried.

width (width, witth), *n.* **1.** extent from side to side; breadth. **2.** something, as a piece of cloth, of a particular width.

wield (wēld), *v.t.* **1.** to exercise (power, influence, etc.). **2.** to use (a weapon, instrument, etc.) effectively; handle.

wie·ner (wē′nər), *n.* FRANKFURTER.

wife (wīf), *n., pl.* **wives** (wīvz). a married woman. —**wife′ly,** *adj.*

wig (wig), *n., v.,* **wigged, wig·ging.** —*n.* **1.** a covering of natural or artificial hair for the head. **2.** a toupee. —*v.t.* **3.** to furnish with a wig.

wig·gle (wig′əl), *v.,* **-gled, -gling,** *n.* —*v.i., v.t.* **1.** to move with quick, irregular side-to-side movements. —*n.* **2.** a wiggling movement or course. —**wig′gler,** *n.* —**wig′gly,** *adj.,* **-gli·er, -gli·est.**

wig·wag (wig′wag′), *v.,* **-wagged, -wag·ging,** *n.* —*v.t., v.i.* **1.** to signal by waving a flag or lantern according to a code. —*n.* **2.** the act or process of wigwagging. **3.** a wigwagged message.

wig·wam (wig′wom, -wôm), *n.* a North American Indian dwelling, typically rounded in shape, formed of poles overlaid with bark, mats, or skins.

wild (wīld), *adj.,* **-er, -est,** *adv., n.* —*adj.* **1.** living in a state of nature; not tamed or domesticated. **2.** growing or produced without cultivation, as flowers. **3.** not inhabited; undeveloped: *wild country.* **4.** not civilized; barbarous. **5.** characterized by violence or intensity: *a wild storm.* **6.** characterized by violent feelings: *a wild look.* **7.** frantic; distracted: *drove me wild.* **8.** not disciplined; unruly: *wild children.* **9.** wide of the mark: *a wild pitch.* **10.** (of a card) having its value decided by the wishes of the players. —*adv.* **11.** in a wild manner. —*n.* **12.** Often, **wilds.** an uncultivated region or tract; wilderness or wasteland. —**wild′ly,** *adv.* —**wild′ness,** *n.*

wild′cat′ *n., pl.* **-cats,** also **-cat** for 1, *adj., v.,* **-cat·ted, -cat·ting.** —*n.* **1.** any of several medium-sized cats, as the bobcat, related to the domestic cat. **2.** a quick-tempered or savage person. **3.** an exploratory well drilled in an effort to discover deposits of oil or gas. —*adj.* **4.** characterized by or proceeding from unsafe business methods: *wildcat stocks.* **5.** not sanctioned by a labor union: *a wildcat strike.* —*v.i., v.t.* **6.** to search (an area of unknown productivity) for oil, gas, or ore.

wil·de·beest (wil′də bēst′, vil′-), *n., pl.* **-beests, -beest.** GNU.

wil·der·ness (wil′dər nis), *n.* a wild, uncultivated, uninhabited region.

wild′-eyed′ *adj.* **1.** having a wild expression in the eyes. **2.** extreme or radical.

wild′fire′ *n.* a large fire that spreads rapidly and is hard to extinguish.

wild′flow′er *n.* the flower of a plant that grows wild.

wild′-goose′ chase′ *n.* a senseless search for something nonexistent or unobtainable.

wild′life′ *n.* undomesticated animals living in the wild.

wile (wīl), *n., v.,* **wiled, wil·ing.** —*n.* **1.** a trick or stratagem meant to fool, trap, or entice. **2.** wiles, artful or beguiling behavior. —*v.t.* **3.** to beguile, entice, or lure. **4. wile away,** to pass (time), esp. in a pleasurable fashion.

will¹ (wil), *auxiliary v.* and *v., pres.* **will;** *past* **would.** —*auxiliary verb.* **1.** (used to express simple futurity): *I will be there tomorrow.* **2.** (used to express willingness): *Nobody will help us.* **3.** (used to express a command): *You will report to the principal at once.* **4.** (used to express probability): *They will be asleep by this time.* **5.** (used to express customary action): *She will write for hours at a time.* **6.** (used to express capability): *This couch will seat four.* —*v.t., v.i.* **7.** to wish; like: *Take what you will.*

will² (wil), *n.* **1.** the faculty of conscious and deliberate action. **2.** the power of choosing or deciding: *a strong will.* **3.** wish or desire: *went against his will.* **4.** purpose or determination: *the will to succeed.* **5.** disposition toward another: *ill will.* **6.** a legal document specifying the disposition of a person's property after death. —*v.t.* **7.** to decide upon or bring about by an act of the will. **8.** to dispose of by a will; bequeath. **9.** to influence by the power of the will. —*v.i.* **10.** to exercise the will. —**willed,** *adj.*

will′ful *adj.* **1.** deliberate; intentional. **2.** unreasonably stubborn or headstrong. —**will′ful·ly,** *adv.* —**will′ful·ness,** *n.*

wil·lies (wil′ēz), *n.pl.* nervousness; jitters (usu. prec. by *the*).

will′ing *adj.* **1.** disposed or consenting; inclined. **2.** cheerfully consenting or ready. **3.** done, given, borne, or used with cheerful readiness. —**will′ing·ly,** *adv.* —**will′ing·ness,** *n.*

will-o'-the-wisp (wil′ə thə wisp′), *n.* **1.** a flickering light seen at night over marshy ground, believed to be due to the burning of marsh gas. **2.** an elusive thing or person.

wil·low (wil′ō), *n.* **1.** a tree or shrub with lance-shaped leaves and tough, pliable twigs used esp. for wickerwork. **2.** the wood of a willow tree.

wil′low·y *adj.,* **-i·er, -i·est. 1.** pliant; lithe. **2.** slender and graceful.

wil·ly-nil·ly (wil′ē nil′ē), *adv.* whether one wishes or not.

wilt¹ (wilt), *v.i.* **1.** to become limp and drooping, as a fading flower. **2.** to lose strength, vigor, or courage. —*v.t.* **3.** to cause to wilt.

wilt² (wilt), *v. Archaic.* second pers. sing. pres. indic. of WILL¹.

wil·y (wī′lē), *adj.,* **-i·er, -i·est.** full of or marked by wiles; cunning. —**wil′i·ness,** *n.*

wimp (wimp), *n. Informal.* a weak, ineffectual person. —**wimp′y,** *adj.,* **-i·er, -i·est.**

win (win), *v.,* **won, win·ning,** *n.* —*v.i.* **1.** to finish first, as in a race. **2.** to succeed by effort. **3.** to overcome an adversary. —*v.t.* **4.** to succeed in reaching, esp. by great effort. **5.** to get by effort, as through labor or competition. **6.** to be victorious in (a game, battle, etc.). **7.** to gain the favor, consent, or support of. **8.** to persuade (someone) to marry oneself. —*n.* **9.** a victory, as in a horse race.

wince (wins), *v.,* **winced, winc·ing,** —*v.i.* **1.** to draw back, as from a blow; flinch. —*n.* **2.** a wincing movement.

winch (winch), *n.* **1.** the crank or handle of a revolving machine. **2.** a windlass for hoisting or hauling.

wind¹ (*n.* wind, *Literary* wīnd; *v.* wind), *n.* **1.** air in natural motion. **2.** a stream of air, as that produced by a bellows. **3. winds, a.** wind instruments collectively. **b.** players of wind instruments. **4.** breath or breathing. **5.** an influential force or trend. **6.** a hint or intimation: *caught wind of a scandal.* **7.** air carrying an animal's scent. **8.** gas generated in the stomach and intestines. —*v.t.* **9.** to follow by scent. **10.** to make short of breath. **11.** to allow to recover breath, as after exertion. —**Idiom. 12. in the wind,** about to occur. —**wind′y,** *adj.,* **-i·er, -i·est.**

wind² (wīnd), *v.,* **wound** (wound) or (*Rare*) **wind·ed** (wīn′did); **wind·ing;** *n.* —*v.i.* **1.** to have or take a curving course; meander. **2.** to coil or twine around something. —*v.t.* **3.** to wrap around; encircle or wreathe. **4.** to roll (thread, string, etc.) into a ball or on a spool. **5.** to tighten the spring of: *wound the clock.* **6.** to make (one's way) in a curving course. **7. wind up, a.** to bring or come to a conclusion. **b.** to make tense or nervous; excite. —*n.* **8.** the act of winding. **9.** a single turn, twist, or bend. —**wind′er,** *n.*

wind′bag′ (wind′-), *n.* a voluble, often pompous talker.

wind′break′ (wind′-), *n.* something, as a growth of trees, serving as a shelter from the wind.

wind′chill fac′tor (wind′chil′), *n.* the apparent temperature felt on the exposed human body owing to the combination of temperature and wind speed.

wind•ed (win′did), *adj.* out of breath.

wind′fall′ (wind′-), *n.* **1.** an unexpected gain or piece of good fortune. **2.** something, as fruit, blown down by the wind.

wind′ing sheet′ (wīn′ding), *n.* SHROUD (def. 1).

wind′ in′strument (wind), *n.* a musical instrument, as the trumpet or flute, sounded by an air current, esp. the breath.

wind•lass (wind′ləs), *n.* a device for hauling or hoisting, commonly having a horizontal drum on which a rope attached to the load is wound.

wind′mill′ (wind′-), *n.* a machine for grinding or pumping that is driven by the wind acting on vanes or sails.

win•dow (win′dō), *n.* **1.** an opening in a building, vehicle, etc., for admitting air or light. **2.** a window with its frame, sashes, and panes of glass. **3.** a windowpane. **4.** something resembling a window in appearance or function. **5.** a period of time available or highly favorable for doing something. **6. a.** a portion of a computer screen on which data can be displayed independently of the rest of the screen. **b.** a view of a portion of a document bounded by the borders of a computer's display screen.

win′dow dress′ing *n.* **1.** the art, act, or technique of trimming the display windows of a store. **2.** something done solely to create a favorable impression.

win′dow-pane′ *n.* a pane of glass for a window.

win′dow-shop′ *v.i.,* **-shopped, -shop•ping.** to look at articles in store windows without making purchases. —**win′dow shop′per,** *n.*

wind′pipe′ (wind′-), *n.* the trachea of an air-breathing vertebrate.

wind′shield′ (wind′-, win′-), *n.* a shield of glass above the dashboard of an automobile.

wind′sock′ (wind′-), *n.* a mounted cloth cone that catches the wind to indicate wind direction.

wind′storm′ (wind′-), *n.* a storm with heavy wind but little or no precipitation.

wind′surf′ing (wind′-), *n.* the sport of riding on a surfboard mounted with a sail. —**wind′surf′,** *v.i.* —**wind′surf′er,** *n.*

wind′-swept′ (wind), *adj.* exposed to or blown by the wind.

wind′up′ (wīnd′-), *n.* **1.** the conclusion of an action or activity. **2.** *Baseball.* the movement of a pitcher's arm before throwing the ball.

wind•ward (wind′wərd), *adv.* **1.** toward the wind. —*adj.* **2.** of, situated in, or moving toward the quarter from which the wind blows. —*n.* **3.** the point or quarter from which the wind blows.

wine (wīn), *n., v.,* **wined, win•ing.** —*n.* **1.** the fermented juice of grapes, used esp. as a beverage. **2.** the often fermented juice of another fruit or plant. —*v.t., v.i.* **3.** to supply with or drink wine. —*Idiom.* **4. wine and dine,** to entertain lavishly. [< L *vīnum*]

win′er•y *n., pl.* **-ies.** an establishment where wine is made.

wing (wing), *n.* **1.** either of the two forelimbs or appendages of birds, insects, and bats that are specialized for flight. **2.** a means or instrument of flight, travel, or progress. **3.** the act or manner of flying. **4.** something, as the vane of a windmill, that resembles a wing. **5.** one of a pair of airfoils on the fuselage of an aircraft that provides lift. **6.** a part of

a building projecting from a central or main part. **7.** a flank of an army or fleet. **8.** a unit of the U.S. Air Force. **9.** an often extreme faction within an organization: *the liberal wing.* **10.** *Sports.* a position or player on the far side of the center, as in hockey. **11.** Usu., **wings.** the space at the side of a stage, usu. not seen by the audience. —*v.t.* **12.** to equip with wings. **13.** to transport on or as if on wings. **14.** to accomplish by flight. **15.** to traverse in flight. **16.** to wound in the wing or arm. —*v.i.* **17.** to travel on or as if on wings. —*Idiom.* **18. on the wing,** in flight; flying. **19. under one's wing,** under one's protection, care, or patronage. **20. wing it,** to improvise. —**winged,** *adj.*

wing′ding′ *n. Slang.* a noisy, exciting party.

wink (wingk), *v.i.* **1.** to close and open the eyes quickly. **2.** to close and open one eye quickly as a hint or signal. **3.** to twinkle. —*v.t.* **4.** to make (one or both eyes) wink. **5. wink at,** to ignore (wrongdoing) deliberately. —*n.* **6.** the act of winking. **7.** a hint or signal given by winking. **8.** an instant. **9.** the least bit: *didn't sleep a wink.*

win′ner *n.* one that wins; victor.

win′ning *n.* **1.** the act of one that wins. **2.** Usu., **-nings.** something won, esp. money. —*adj.* **3.** successful or victorious. **4.** engaging; pleasing: *a winning personality.* —**win′ning•ly,** *adv.*

win•now (win′ō), *v.t.* **1.** to free (grain) of chaff with a forced current of air. **2.** to drive or blow (chaff, dirt, etc.) away by fanning. **3.** to separate, distinguish, or sift.

win•o (wī′nō), *n., pl.* **-os.** a person who is addicted to wine.

win•some (win′səm), *adj.* sweetly or innocently charming; winning.

win•ter (win′tər), *n.* **1.** the cold season between autumn and spring. **2.** a year: *a man of 60 winters.* **3.** a period of decline or adversity. —*adj.* **4.** of or characteristic of winter. **5.** planted in the autumn to be harvested in the spring or summer: *winter rye.* —*v.i.* **6.** to spend the winter. —*v.t.* **7.** to keep, feed, or manage during winter. —**win′try,** *adj.,* **-tri•er, -tri•est.**

win′ter•green′ *n.* **1.** a creeping evergreen shrub bearing white flowers, red berries, and leaves that yield an aromatic oil. **2.** the oil of the wintergreen.

wipe (wīp), *v.,* **wiped, wip•ing,** *n.* —*v.t.* **1.** to clean or dry by patting or rubbing: *Wipe your hands.* **2.** to rub or draw (something) over a surface, as in cleaning or drying. **3.** to remove by or as if by rubbing. **4. wipe out, a.** to destroy completely. **b.** to murder. —*n.* **5.** the act of wiping. —**wip′er,** *n.*

wire (wīʳr), *n., adj., v.,* **wired, wir•ing.** —*n.* **1.** a slender piece or filament of metal. **2.** a length of wire used as a conductor of current in electrical, cable, telegraph, or telephone systems. **3. a.** a telegram. **b.** a telegraphic system. **4.** the finish line of a racetrack. —*adj.* **5.** made of wire. —*v.t.* **6.** to equip, furnish, or connect with wire. **7.** to send by telegraph. **8.** to send a message to by telegraph. —*v.i.* **9.** to telegraph.

wire′less *adj.* **1.** having no wire. **2.** operated with or actuated by electromagnetic waves. —*n.* **3.** wireless telegraphy or telephony. **4.** a wireless telegraph or telephone. **5.** *Chiefly Brit.* radio.

wire′ serv′ice *n.* an agency that sends syndicated news by wire to its subscribers.

wire′tap′ *n., v.,* **-tapped, -tap•ping.** —*n.* **1.** an act or instance of tapping a telephone or telegraph wire for information. —*v.t.* **2.** to listen in on by means of a wiretap. —*v.i.* **3.** to tap a telephone or telegraph wire.

wir′ing *n.* a system of electric wires, as in a building.

wir′y *adj.,* **-i•er, -i•est. 1.** resembling wire. **2.** lean and sinewy. —**wir′i•ness,** *n.*

Wis. or **Wisc.,** Wisconsin.

wis•dom (wiz′dəm), *n.* **1.** the quality or state of being wise. **2.** scholarly knowledge or learning. **3.** a wise act.

wis′dom tooth′ *n.* the third molar on each side of the upper and lower jaws.

wise[1] (wīz), *adj.*, **wis•er**, **wis•est**. **1.** having or showing discernment and good judgment. **2.** having or showing scholarly knowledge or learning; erudite. **3.** knowing; informed. —**wise′ly**, *adv.*

wise[2] (wīz), *n.* way; manner: *in no wise.*

-wise a suffix meaning: in a particular manner, position, or direction (*clockwise*); with reference to (*timewise*).

wise′a′cre (-ā′kər), *n.* a conceited, often insolent person.

wise′crack′ *n.* **1.** a smart or facetious remark. —*v.i., v.t.* **2.** to make or say as a wisecrack.

wish (wish), *v.t.* **1.** to want; desire. **2.** to desire (a person or thing) to be as specified: *We wished the matter settled.* **3.** to express a hope or desire for: *Wish me well.* **4.** to bid, as in greeting: *I wished her a good morning.* **5.** to request or charge: *I wish him to come.* —*v.i.* **6.** to desire; yearn. **7.** to make a wish. —*n.* **8.** an act or instance of wishing. **9.** a request or command. **10.** an expression of a wish. **11.** something wished or desired. —**wish′ful**, *adj.* —**wish′ful•ly**, *adv.*

wish′bone′ *n.* a forked bone in front of the breastbone in most birds.

wish•y-wash•y (wish′ē wosh′ē, -wô′shē), *adj.* **1.** lacking strength or character; ineffectual. **2.** watery, as a liquid; thin and weak.

wisp (wisp), *n.* **1.** a small bundle of straw or hay. **2.** a thin tuft, lock, or mass: *wisps of hair.* **3.** a thin puff or streak, as of smoke. **4.** a person or thing that is small or delicate. —**wisp′y**, *adj.*, -**i•er**, -**i•est**.

wis•te•ri•a (wi stēr′ē ə) also **wis•tar′i•a** (wistēr′-, -stâr′-), *n.*, *pl.* -**as**. a climbing shrub with flower clusters in white, pale purple, blue-violet, or pink.

wist•ful (wist′fəl), *adj.* characterized by pensive longing. —**wist′ful•ly**, *adv.* —**wist′ful•ness**, *n.*

wit[1] (wit), *n.* **1.** the keen perception and clever expression of those connections between ideas that awaken amusement. **2.** a person having or noted for wit. **3.** Usu., **wits. a.** resourcefulness; ingenuity. **b.** mental faculties; senses. —*Idiom.* **4. at one's wit's** or **wits' end**, drained of all ideas or mental resources.

wit[2] (wit), *v.t., v.i.*, **wist** (wist), **wit•ting**. **1.** *Archaic.* to know. —*Idiom.* **2. to wit,** that is to say.

witch (wich), *n.* **1.** a person believed to practice magic, esp. black magic. **2.** an ugly or mean old woman; hag. —*v.t.* **3.** to bewitch.

witch′craft′ *n.* the art or practices of a witch; sorcery.

witch′ doc′tor *n.* a person in some societies who uses magic esp. to cure illness.

witch′er•y *n.*, *pl.* -**ies**. **1.** witchcraft; magic. **2.** fascination; charm.

witch ha•zel (wich′ hā′zəl; *for 2 also* wich′ hā′-), *n.* **1.** a shrub that bears small yellow flowers. **2.** an alcoholic solution made from witch hazel leaves or bark and used as an astringent.

with (with, wiŧħ), *prep.* **1.** accompanied by: *I will go with you.* **2.** in relation to: *dealt with the problem.* **3.** characterized by or having: *a person with initiative.* **4.** by means of; using: *cut with a knife.* **5.** in a manner showing: *working with diligence.* **6.** in comparison or proportion to: *How does their plan compare with ours?* **7.** in regard to: *was pleased with the gift.* **8.** owing to: *shaking with rage.* **9.** from: *hated to part with the book.* **10.** against: *Don't fight with your brother.* **11.** in the keeping of: *left her cat with a friend.* **12.** in the judgment or estimation of: *Her argument carried weight with the trustees.* **13.** at the same time as or immediately after: *With that last remark, she left.* **14.** of the same opinion as: *Are you with me on this issue?* **15.** in the same household as: *He lives with his parents.*

with•draw (with drô′, wiŧħ-), *v.*, -**drew**, -**drawn**, -**draw•ing**. —*v.t.* **1.** to draw back, away, or aside. **2.** to remove, retract, or recall. —*v.i.* **3.** to move back, away, or aside. **4.** to remove oneself from participation, as in an activity.

with•draw′al *n.* **1.** the act of withdrawing or state

of being withdrawn. **2.** the act or process of ceasing to use an addictive drug.

with•drawn′ *v.* pp. of WITHDRAW. —*adj.* **2.** removed, as from circulation. **3.** shy and introverted; retiring.

with•er (wiŧħ′ər), *v.i.* **1.** to shrivel; fade. **2.** to lose freshness. —*v.t.* **3.** to cause to shrivel or fade. **4.** to make powerless, as by a scathing glance.

with•ers *n.* (*used with a pl. v.*) the highest part of the back at the base of the neck of a horse.

with•hold (with hōld′, wiŧħ-), *v.t.*, -**held**, -**hold•ing**. **1.** to hold back; restrain or check. **2.** to refrain from giving or granting.

withhold′ing tax′ *n.* that part of an employee's tax liability withheld by the employer from wages or salary.

with•in (wiŧħ in′, with-), *prep.* **1.** in or into the interior of: *within city walls.* **2.** in the compass or limits of; not beyond: *within view.* **3.** in the field, sphere, or scope of: *within the family.* —*adv.* **4.** in or into an interior or inner part. **5.** in the mind, heart, or soul; inwardly. —*n.* **6.** the inside of a place.

with•out (wiŧħ out′, with-), *prep.* **1.** with no or none of; lacking: *without help; without shoes.* **2.** free from; excluding: *a world without hunger.* **3.** not accompanied by: *Don't go without me.* **4.** at, on, or to the outside of: *both within and without the city.* —*adv.* **5.** outside. **6.** outdoors. **7.** lacking something: *had to go without.*

with•stand (with stand′, wiŧħ-), *v.t.*, -**stood**, -**stand•ing**. to resist or oppose, esp. successfully.

wit′less *adj.* lacking wit or intelligence; stupid. —**wit′less•ly**, *adv.*

wit•ness (wit′nis), *v.t.* **1.** to see, hear, or know by personal presence and experience. **2.** to be present at as a legal witness. **3.** to give or be evidence of. **4.** to attest by one's signature. —*n.* **5.** one who has witnessed something, esp. one who is able to attest to what took place. **6.** one who gives testimony. **7.** something serving as evidence. **8.** testimony or evidence: *bore witness to her suffering.*

wit•ti•cism (wit′ə siz′əm), *n.* a witty remark.

wit′ting *adj.* knowing; aware.

wit′ty *adj.*, -**ti•er**, -**ti•est**. having or showing wit; amusingly clever. —**wit′ti•ly**, *adv.* —**wit′ti•ness**, *n.*

wiz•ard (wiz′ərd), *n.* **1.** a magician or sorcerer. **2.** a person of amazing skill or accomplishment. —**wiz′ard•ry**, *n.*

wiz•ened (wiz′ənd, wē′zənd), *adj.* withered; shriveled.

wk. **1.** week. **2.** work.

w/o without.

wob•ble (wob′əl), *v.*, -**bled**, -**bling**, *n.* —*v.i.* **1.** to move unsteadily with a side-to-side motion. **2.** to be unsteady; tremble. **3.** to vacillate; waver. —*v.t.* **4.** to cause to wobble. —*n.* **5.** a wobbling movement. —**wob′bly**, *adj.*, -**bli•er**, -**bli•est**.

woe (wō), *n.* **1.** grievous distress or trouble. **2.** an affliction. —**woe′ful**, *adj.* —**woe′ful•ly**, *adv.*

woe′be•gone′ (-bi gôn′, -gon′), *adj.* feeling or showing woe; forlorn.

wok (wok), *n.* a large bowl-shaped pan used esp. in cooking Chinese food.

wolf (wŏŏlf), *n.*, *pl.* **wolves** (wŏŏlvz). **1.** any of several carnivorous predatory mammals resembling and related to the dog. **2.** a cruelly rapacious person. **3.** a man who makes amorous advances to women. —*v.t.* **4.** to devour voraciously. —**wolf′ish**, *adj.*

wolf′hound′ *n.* any of several large dogs once used in hunting wolves.

wolfs′bane′ *n.* a plant yielding a poisonous alkaloid used medicinally.

wol•ver•ine (wŏŏl′və rēn′), *n.* a strong, stocky Northern Hemisphere carnivore of the weasel family.

wom•an (wŏŏm′ən), *n.*, *pl.* **wom•en** (wim′in). **1.** an adult female person. **2.** a female servant or attendant. **3.** women collectively; womankind. **4.** feminine nature, characteristics, or feelings. —**wom′an•hood′**, *n.* —**wom′an•ly**, *adj.*

womb (wo͞om), *n.* **1.** UTERUS. **2.** the place in which something is formed or produced.

wom•bat (wom′bat), *n.* a burrowing, herbivorous Australian marsupial about the size of a badger.

won•der (wun′dər), *v.i.* **1.** to think or speculate curiously and sometimes doubtfully. **2.** to be filled with awe; marvel. —*v.t.* **3.** to be curious about. —*n.* **4.** a cause of surprise, astonishment, or admiration. **5.** a feeling of amazement, puzzled interest, or reverent admiration. —**won′der•ment,** *n.*

won′der•ful *adj.* **1.** excellent; marvelous. **2.** exciting wonder; extraordinary.

won′drous *adj.* wonderful; remarkable.

wont (wônt, wōnt, wunt), *adj.* **1.** accustomed; used: *She is wont to rise at dawn.* —*n.* **2.** custom; habit: *It was his wont to meditate daily.*

won′t (wōnt), contraction of *will not.*

woo (wo͞o), *v.t.* **1.** to seek the love of, esp. with a view to marriage. **2.** to seek or invite: *to woo fame.* —*v.i.* **3.** to court a woman. —**woo′er,** *n.*

wood (wo͝od), *n.* **1.** the hard, fibrous substance composing most of the stem and branches of a tree or shrub beneath the bark. **2.** timber or lumber. **3.** FIREWOOD. **4.** Often, **woods.** a thick growth of trees; forest. **5.** any of a set of four golf clubs that orig. had wooden heads. —*adj.* **6.** made of wood; wooden. **7.** used to store, work, or carry wood. **8.** dwelling or growing in woods. —*v.t.* **9.** to cover or plant with trees. —**wood′y,** *adj.,* **-i•er, -i•est.**

wood′bine′ (-bīn′), *n.* any of several climbing vines, as the Virginia creeper.

wood′chuck′ *n.* a stocky North American burrowing rodent that hibernates in the winter.

wood′cut′ *n.* **1.** a block of wood engraved in relief from which prints are made. **2.** a print or impression from a woodcut.

wood′ed *adj.* covered with woods or trees.

wood′en *adj.* **1.** consisting or made of wood. **2.** stiff, ungainly, or awkward. **3.** lacking animation; spiritless.

wood′land′ (-land′, -lənd), *n.* land covered with woods or trees.

wood′peck′er *n.* a climbing bird with a chisellike bill that it hammers repeatedly into wood in search of insects.

wood′pile′ *n.* a pile or stack of firewood.

wood′ruff (-rəf, -ruf′), *n.* a fragrant plant with small white flowers.

wood′shed′ *n.* a shed for storing firewood.

woods′man *n., pl.* **-men.** a person accustomed to life in the woods and skilled in the arts of the woods.

woods′y *adj.,* **-i•er, -i•est.** of or suggestive of woods.

wood′wind′ *n.* a musical wind instrument of the group comprising the flutes, clarinets, oboes, bassoons, and saxophones.

wood′work′ *n.* **1.** objects or parts made of wood. **2.** interior wooden fittings, as doors or moldings. —**wood′work′er,** *n.*

woof (wo͝of, wo͞of), *n.* **1.** the threads interlacing at right angles with the warp in a woven fabric. **2.** texture; fabric.

woof•er (wo͝of′ər), *n.* a loudspeaker to reproduce low-frequency sounds.

wool (wo͝ol), *n.* **1.** the fine, soft, curly hair that forms the fleece of some animals, esp. sheep. **2.** yarn, a fabric, or a garment of wool. **3.** something resembling the wool of sheep: *steel wool.* —**wool′en** or *(esp. Brit.)* **wool′len,** *adj., n.*

wool′gath•er•ing *n.* indulgence in idle fancies and daydreaming.

wool′ly or **wool′y,** *adj.,* **-li•er** or **-i•er, -li•est** or **-i•est,** *n., pl.* **-lies** or **-ies.** —*adj.* **1.** of or resembling wool. **2.** rough, vigorous, and lacking in order: *the wild and woolly West.* **3.** unclear; disorganized: *woolly thinking.* —*n.* **4.** *Western U.S.* a wool-bearing animal; sheep. **5.** a woolen garment, esp. a knitted undergarment.

wool′ly bear′ *n.* any of several caterpillars with woolly hairs.

word (wûrd), *n.* **1.** a linguistic unit consisting of one or more spoken sounds or their written repre-

sentation and functioning as a carrier of meaning. **2. words, a.** the text or lyrics of a song. **b.** a quarrel. **3.** a short talk. **4.** something said; expression or utterance. **5.** assurance or promise. **6.** news; information. **7.** a verbal signal, as a password. **8.** an authoritative command. **9.** *(cap.)* **a.** the Scriptures; Bible. **b.** the message of the gospel of Christ. —*v.t.* **10.** to express in words. —**Idiom. 11. in a word,** in short. **12. in so many words,** in unequivocal terms; explicitly. —**word′less,** *adj.*

word•age (wûr′dij), *n.* **1.** words collectively. **2.** number of words. **3.** choice of words; wording.

word′ing *n.* choice of words to express something.

word′ of mouth′ *n.* oral communication.

word′play′ *n.* witty repartee, esp. a play on words.

word′ proc′essing *n.* the automated production and storage of documents using computers, electronic printers, and text-editing software.

word processor *n.* a computer program or computer system designed for word processing.

word′y *adj.,* **-i•er, -i•est.** characterized by or given to the use of too many words; verbose. —**word′i•ness,** *n.*

work (wûrk), *n., adj., v.,* **worked** or *(Archaic except in some senses, esp.* **22, 23, 25)** **wrought; work•ing.** —*n.* **1.** exertion or effort to produce or accomplish something; labor. **2.** a task or undertaking. **3.** productive activity, esp. employment: *looking for work.* **4.** a place of employment. **5.** something, as material, on which work is being or is to be done. **6.** the result of exertion, labor, or activity. **7.** an engineering structure, as a bridge. **8.** something, as a wall, constructed as a means of fortification. **9. works, a.** *(used with a sing. or pl. v.)* a place or establishment for manufacturing. **b.** the working parts of a machine. **10.** *Physics.* the transfer of energy measured by the scalar product of a force and the distance through which it acts. **11. the works, a.** everything: *a hamburger with the works.* **b.** unpleasant or abusive treatment: *gave him the works.* —*adj.* **12.** of, for, or concerning work: *work clothes.* —*v.i.* **13.** to do work. **14.** to be employed. **15.** to be functional, as a machine; operate. **16.** to prove effective: *This plan works.* **17.** to come to be, as by repeated movement: *The nails worked loose.* **18.** to have an effect, as on a person's feelings. **19.** to make way with effort or under stress. **20.** to ferment, as a liquid. —*v.t.* **21.** to use or operate (an apparatus, machine, etc.). **22.** to bring about by or as if by work. **23.** to put into or keep in operation. **24.** to carry on operations in (a region). **25.** to make or fashion by work. **26.** to cause to work: *He works his employees hard.* **27.** to solve (a puzzle or problem). **28.** to cause a strong emotion in: *to work a crowd into a frenzy.* **29.** to make or decorate by needlework or embroidery. **30. work off,** to get rid of. **31. ~ on,** to try to influence or persuade. **32. ~ out, a.** to bring about. **b.** to solve, as a problem. **c.** to arrive at by or as if by calculation. **d.** to have a result. **e.** to evolve; elaborate. **f.** to amount. **g.** to prove effective or successful. **h.** to exercise or train, esp. in an athletic sport. **33. ~ through,** to deal with successfully. **34. ~ up, a.** to stir the feelings of; excite. **b.** to prepare; elaborate. **c.** to cause to develop by exertion. —**Idiom. 35. in the works,** in preparation. **36. out of work,** not employed. —**work′a•ble,** *adj.* —**work′er,** *n.*

work•a•day (wûr′kə dā′), *adj.* **1.** characteristic of or befitting working days. **2.** ordinary; everyday.

work•a•hol•ic (-hô′lik, -hol′ik), *n.* a person who works compulsively. [*work* + -AHOLIC]

work′bench′ *n.* a sturdy table at which an artisan works.

work′horse′ *n.* **1.** a horse used for heavy labor. **2.** a person who works tirelessly.

work′house′ *n.* **1.** a house of correction in which the prisoners are required to work. **2.** *Brit.* a poorhouse.

work′ing class′ *n.* the social or economic class composed of persons working for wages, esp. in manual labor.

work′load′ *n.* the amount of work that a machine, employee, or group of employees can be or is expected to perform.

work′man *n., pl.* **-men.** a man employed or skilled in manual, mechanical, or industrial work.

work·man·like′ *adj.* well executed; skillful.

work′man·ship′ *n.* **1.** the art or skill of a workman. **2.** the quality or mode of execution of work done.

work′out′ *n.* **1.** practice or a test to maintain or determine physical ability or endurance. **2.** a structured regime of physical exercise.

work′shop′ *n.* **1.** a room or building in which work, esp. mechanical work, is carried on. **2.** a seminar that meets to explore a subject or develop a skill or technique.

work′sta′tion *n.* **1.** a work area for one person that often accommodates a computer terminal or microcomputer connected to a mainframe, minicomputer, or data-processing network. **2.** a powerful microcomputer used for graphics-intensive processing.

work′up′ *n.* a thorough medical diagnostic examination.

world (wûrld), *n.* **1.** the earth considered as a planet. **2.** (*often cap.*) a particular division of the earth: *the Western world.* **3.** the human race; humanity. **4.** the general public. **5.** a class of people with common interests: *the literary world.* **6.** a sphere, realm, or domain: *the world of dreams.* **7.** everything that exists; the universe. **8.** one of the general groupings of physical nature: *the animal world.* **9.** Often, **worlds.** a great deal: *a world of problems.* **10.** a heavenly body. —*Idiom.* **11. for all the world,** in every respect; precisely. **12. out of this world,** extraordinary; wonderful.

world′-class′ *adj.* being among the world's best; of the highest caliber.

world′ly *adj.,* **-li·er, -li·est. 1.** of this world as contrasted with heaven or spiritual life. **2.** experienced; sophisticated. —**world′li·ness,** *n.*

world′ly-wise′ *adj.* wise as to the affairs of this world.

world′-wea′ry *adj.* weary of the world; blasé.

World′ Wide′ Web′ *n.* a system of extensively interlinked hypertext documents: a branch of the Internet.

worm (wûrm), *n.* **1.** any of numerous long, softbodied, legless invertebrates, as the earthworm. **2.** something resembling a worm in appearance or movement. **3.** a groveling or contemptible person. **4. worms,** (*used with a sing. v.*) a disorder caused by parasitic worms in the intestines. —*v.i.* **5.** to creep, crawl, or advance slowly, stealthily, or insidiously. —*v.t.* **6.** to cause to move deviously or stealthily. **7.** to get by persistent, insidious efforts: *He wormed the secret out of his sister.* **8.** to insinuate (oneself) into another's favor or confidence. **9.** to free from intestinal worms. —**worm′y,** *adj.,* **-i·er, -i·est.**

worm′wood′ *n.* a bitter aromatic plant used esp. as an ingredient in the licorice-flavored liqueur absinthe.

worn (wôrn), *v.* **1.** pp. of WEAR. —*adj.* **2.** diminished in value or usefulness through wear or use. **3.** exhausted; spent.

worn′-out′ *adj.* **1.** worn or used beyond repair. **2.** depleted of energy or strength; exhausted.

wor′ry *v.,* **-ried, -ry·ing,** *n., pl.* **-ries.** —*v.i.* **1.** to feel uneasy or anxious. —*v.t.* **2.** to make uneasy or anxious. **3.** to disturb with annoyances; plague. **4.** to seize with the teeth and shake or mangle. **5.** to touch or adjust repeatedly. —*n.* **6.** uneasiness or anxiety. **7.** a cause of worry. —**wor′ri·er,** *n.* —**wor′ri·some,** *adj.*

worse (wûrs), *adj., comparative of* **bad** *and* **ill. 1.** bad or ill to a greater extent; inferior. **2.** more unfavorable or injurious. **3.** in poorer health. —*n.* **4.** something that is worse. —*adv.* **5.** in a worse manner. **6.** to a worse degree. —**wors′en,** *v.t., v.i.*

wor·ship (wûr′ship), *n., v.,* **-shiped** or **-shipped, -ship·ing** or **-ship·ping.** —*n.* **1.** reverence for God, a sacred personage, or a sacred object. **2.** a formal or ceremonious expression of worship. **3.** adoring

reverence or regard. **4.** (*cap.*) *Brit.* a title of honor for certain magistrates and others of high rank or station. —*v.t.* **5.** to render religious worship to. **6.** to feel an adoring reverence or regard for. —*v.i.* **7.** to engage in religious worship. —**wor′ship·er,** *n.* —**wor′ship·ful,** *adj.*

worst (wûrst), *adj., superlative of* **bad** *and* **ill. 1.** bad or ill in the most extreme degree. **2.** most faulty or unsatisfactory. **3.** most unfavorable or injurious. **4.** in the poorest condition. **5.** most unpleasant, unattractive, or disagreeable. **6.** least skilled. —*n.* **7.** something that is worst. —*adv.* **8.** in the worst manner. **9.** in the greatest degree. —*v.t.* **10.** to defeat; beat. —*Idiom.* **11. at (the) worst,** under the worst conditions. **12. if worst comes to worst,** if the very worst happens. **13. in the worst way,** very much; extremely.

wor·sted (wŏŏs′tid, wûr′stid), *n.* **1.** a firmly twisted yarn or thread spun from wool fibers. **2.** wool cloth woven from worsted.

worth (wûrth), *prep.* **1.** good or important enough to justify: *a place worth visiting.* **2.** having a value of: *a vase worth 20 dollars.* **3.** having property to the value of: *They are worth millions.* —*n.* **4.** excellence, as of character; merit. **5.** value, as in money. **6.** a quantity of something of a specified value: *50 cents' worth of candy.* **7.** property or possessions; wealth. —**worth′less,** *adj.* —**worth′less·ness,** *n.*

worth′while′ *adj.* worthy of the time, work, trouble, or money spent.

wor·thy (wûr′thē), *adj.,* **-thi·er, -thi·est,** *n., pl.* **-thies.** —*adj.* **1.** having merit, character, or value. **2.** deserving; meritorious: *an effort worthy of praise.* —*n.* **3.** a person of worth. —**wor′thi·ly,** *adv.* —**wor′thi·ness,** *n.*

would (wŏŏd; *unstressed* wəd), *v.* **1.** pt. of WILL¹. **2.** (used to express the future): *He said he would go tomorrow.* **3.** (used in place of *will* to soften a statement or question): *Would you be so kind?* **4.** (used to express habitual action in the past): *We would take the train every morning.* **5.** (used to express a wish, intention, or inclination): *Nutritionists would have us all eat whole grains.* **6.** (used to express uncertainty): *It would appear that he is guilty.* **7.** (used to express choice or possibility): *They would come if they had the fare.*

would′-be′ *adj.* wishing or pretending to be.

wound¹ (wŏŏnd), *n.* **1.** an injury, usu. involving the cutting or tearing of tissue. **2.** an injury or hurt to feelings, sensibilities, or reputation. —*v.t.* **3.** to inflict a wound upon; injure.

wound² (wound), *v.* a pt. and pp. of WIND².

wrack (rak), *n.* **1.** damage or destruction: *wrack and ruin.* **2.** a trace of something destroyed.

wraith (rāth), *n.* an apparition; ghost.

wran·gle (rang′gəl), *v.,* **-gled, -gling,** *n.* —*v.i.* **1.** to argue or dispute, esp. noisily or angrily. —*v.t.* **2.** to tend or round up (livestock, as cattle). **3.** to obtain by badgering. —*n.* **4.** a noisy or angry dispute. —**wran′gler,** *n.*

wrap (rap), *v.,* **wrapped** or **wrapt, wrap·ping.** —*v.t.* **1.** to enclose or cover in something wound or folded about. **2.** to enclose and make fast within a covering, as of paper. **3.** to wind or fold (something) around as a covering. **4.** to surround, envelop, or hide. **5.** to cover (fingernails) with a sheer fabric to repair or strengthen them. —*v.i.* **6.** to become wrapped. **7. a. wrap up,** to finish work on; conclude. **b.** to give a summary of. —*n.* **8.** something, as a shawl, to be wrapped around a person, esp. for warmth. **9.** a wrapper. **10.** a sheer fabric glued to the fingernails to repair or strengthen them. **11.** a beauty treatment in which part of the body is covered with lotion, herbs, or the like and then wrapped snugly with cloth. **12.** a piece of thin, flat bread wrapped around a filling and eaten as a sandwich. —*Idiom.* **13. under wraps,** *Informal.* secret. **14. wrapped up in,** intensely absorbed in.

wrap′per *n.* **1.** one that wraps. **2.** something in which a thing is wrapped. **3.** a loose garment, esp. a woman's bathrobe or negligee.

wrath (rath, räth), *n.* **1.** fierce anger; ire. **2.** punishment for sins; retribution. —**wrath′ful,** *adj.*

wreak (rēk), *v.t.* **1.** to inflict (punishment, vengeance, etc.). **2.** to carry out the promptings of (rage, ill humor, etc.), as on a victim.

wreath (rēth), *n., pl.* **wreaths** (rēthz, rēths). **1.** a circular band, as of flowers, used for decorative purposes. **2.** a ringlike, curving, or curling mass or formation.

wreathe (rēth), *v.t.,* **wreathed, wreath•ing. 1.** to encircle or adorn with or as if with a wreath. **2.** to form as a wreath by twisting or twining. **3.** to envelop: *a face wreathed in smiles.*

wreck (rek), *n.* **1.** a building, structure, or object reduced to ruin. **2. a.** wreckage remaining after a shipwreck, esp. when cast ashore. **b.** a shipwreck. **3.** ruin; destruction. **4.** a person of ruined physical or mental health. —*v.t.* **5.** to cause the wreck of. **6.** to tear down; demolish.

wreck′age (-ij), *n.* **1.** the act of wrecking or state of being wrecked. **2.** the remains of something that has been wrecked.

wreck′er *n.* **1.** one that wrecks. **2.** a vehicle equipped to tow wrecked or disabled automobiles. **3.** a person or business that demolishes and removes buildings. **4.** a person or ship employed in recovering salvage from wrecks.

wren (ren), *n.* any of various small songbirds with streaked or spotted brown-gray plumage.

wrench (rench), *v.t.* **1.** to pull, jerk, or force with a violent twist. **2.** to injure (the ankle, knee, etc.) by a sudden, violent twist. **3.** to affect distressingly as if by a wrench. —*n.* **4.** a sudden, violent twist. **5.** a sharp, distressing strain, as to the feelings. **6.** a tool for gripping and turning or twisting a bolt, nut, etc.

wrest (rest), *v.t.* **1.** to take away by force. **2.** to get by effort. **3.** to twist or turn from the proper course or meaning. —*n.* **4.** a twist or wrench.

wres•tle (res′əl), *v.,* **-tled, -tling,** *n.* —*v.i.* **1.** to engage in wrestling. **2.** to struggle, as for mastery. —*v.t.* **3.** to contend with in wrestling. **4.** to force by or as if by wrestling. —*n.* **5.** an act or bout of wrestling. —**wres′tler,** *n.* —**wres′tling,** *n.*

wretch (rech), *n.* **1.** a very unfortunate or unhappy person. **2.** a despicable or base person.

wretch′ed *adj.* **1.** very unfortunate; pitiable. **2.** characterized by or causing misery and sorrow. **3.** contemptible or mean. **4.** worthless; inferior.

wrig•gle (rig′əl), *v.,* **-gled, -gling,** *n.* —*v.i.* **1.** to twist to and fro; writhe. **2.** to move along by twisting and turning the body, as a worm. **3.** to make one's way by shifts or expedients. —*v.t.* **4.** to cause to wriggle. —*n.* **5.** the act or motion of wriggling. —**wrig′gly,** *adj.,* **-gli•er, -gli•est.**

wring (ring), *v.,* **wrung, wring•ing,** *n.* —*v.t.* **1.** to twist forcibly. **2.** to twist or compress to force out a liquid. **3.** to extract by or as if by wringing. **4.** to affect painfully. **5.** to clasp tightly, usu. with twisting: *She wrung her hands in anguish.* —*n.* **6.** the act of wringing. —**wring′er,** *n.*

wrin•kle¹ (ring′kəl), *n., v.,* **-kled, -kling.** —*n.* **1.** a small crease in the skin, as from aging. **2.** a slight ridge in a fabric, as from folding. **3.** a problem; fault: *still a few wrinkles to be worked out.* —*v.t., v.i.* **4.** to form wrinkles (in). —**wrin′kly,** *adj.,* **-kli•er, -kli•est.**

wrin•kle² (ring′kəl), *n.* a creative innovation.

wrist (rist), *n.* **1.** the part of the forearm where it joins the hand. **2.** the joint between the forearm and the hand.

writ (rit), *n.* **1.** a court order directing a person to do or refrain from doing something specified. **2.** something written.

write (rīt), *v.,* **wrote, writ•ten, writ•ing.** —*v.t.* **1.** to form (letters, words, etc.), esp. on paper, with a pen or pencil. **2.** to express or communicate in writing. **3.** to communicate with by letter. **4.** to be the author or composer of. **5.** to transfer (data, text, etc.) from computer memory to an output medium. —*v.i.* **6.** to express ideas in writing. **7.** to write a letter. **8. write in,** to vote for (a candidate not listed) by writing his or her name on the ballot. **9. ~ off, a.** to cancel (an unpaid or uncollectible debt). **b.** to amortize. **10. ~ out,** to write in full. **11. ~ up,** to put into writing, esp. in full detail.

write′-in′ *n.* a candidate or vote for a candidate not listed on a ballot but written in by the voter.

write′-off′ *n.* something written off.

writ′er *n.* a person engaged in writing, esp. as an occupation.

writhe (rīth), *v.,* **writhed, writh•ing,** *n.* —*v.i.* **1.** to twist and turn, as in pain. **2.** to suffer acute embarrassment. —*n.* **3.** a twisting of the body.

writ′ing *n.* **1.** the act of one that writes. **2.** written matter. **3.** written form: *Put the agreement in writing.* **4.** handwriting. **5.** the style, form, or quality of a composition: *stilted writing.* **6.** the profession of a writer.

wrong (rông, rong), *adj.* **1.** not in accordance with what is morally right. **2.** deviating from truth or fact; incorrect. **3.** being in error; mistaken. **4.** not proper; unsuitable. **5.** out of order; amiss. **6.** of or being a surface or side ordinarily kept inward or under. —*n.* **7.** something improper, immoral, unjust, or harmful. —*adv.* **8.** in a wrong manner. —*v.t.* **9.** to do wrong to; harm. **10.** to impute evil to (someone) unjustly; malign. —*Idiom.* **11. in the wrong,** being in error. [< Scand] —**wrong′do′er,** *n.* —**wrong′do′ing,** *n.* —**wrong′ful,** *adj.* —**wrong′ly,** *adv.*

wrong′head′ed *adj.* misguided and stubborn; perverse.

wrought (rôt), *v.* **1.** *Archaic except in some senses.* a pt. and pp. of **WORK.** —*adj.* **2.** worked; formed. **3.** embellished. **4.** shaped by being beaten with a hammer.

wrought′-up′ *adj.* stirred up; excited.

wry (rī), *adj.,* **wri•er, wri•est. 1.** contorted; lopsided: *a wry grin.* **2.** abnormally bent or turned to one side; twisted. **3.** bitingly ironic or amusing. —**wry′ly,** *adv.* —**wry′ness,** *n.*

WV or **W.V.,** West Virginia.

WWW World Wide Web.

WY or **Wy.,** Wyoming.

WYSIWYG (wiz′ē wig′), *adj.* of or being a computer screen display that shows text exactly as it will appear when printed. [*w*(*hat*) *y*(*ou*) *s*(*ee*) *i*(*s*) *w*(*hat*) *y*(*ou*) *g*(*et*)]

X, x (eks), *n., pl.* **Xs** or **X's, xs** or **x's. 1.** the 24th letter of the English alphabet, a consonant. **2.** something that is shaped like an X.

X *Symbol.* **1.** the Roman numeral for 10. **2.** a motion-picture rating applied to sexually graphic or explicit films. **3.** a person or thing of unknown identity.

x *Symbol.* **1.** an unknown quantity; variable. **2.** times: $8 \times 8 = 64$. **3.** a person or thing of unknown identity.

X′ chro/mosome *n.* a sex chromosome that determines femaleness when paired with another X chromosome and that occurs singly in males.

xen•o•pho•bi•a (zen′ə fō′bē ə, zē′nə-), *n.* an unreasonable fear or hatred of foreigners or strangers or of anything foreign or strange. —**xen′o•pho′bic,** *adj.*

xe•rog•ra•phy (zi rog′rə fē), *n.* a copying process in which areas on a sheet of paper corresponding to those on an original are sensitized by static electricity and sprinkled with resin that is fused to the paper. —**xe•ro•graph•ic** (zēr′ə graf′ik), *adj.*

Xe•rox (zēr′oks), **1.** *Trademark.* a brand name for a copying machine using xerography. —*n.* **2.** (*sometimes l.c.*) a copy made on a Xerox. —*v.t., v.i.* **3.** (*sometimes l.c.*) to print or reproduce by Xerox.

Xmas (kris′məs; *often* eks′məs), Christmas.

X-rat•ed (eks′rā′tid), *adj.* sexually explicit; obscene.

x-ray or **X-ray,** *n., v.,* **-rayed, -ray•ing.** —*n.* Also, **x ray, X ray. 1.** Often, **x-rays.** electromagnetic radiation having very short wavelengths and capable of penetrating solids. **2.** a photograph made by x-rays. —*v.t.* **3.** to photograph, examine, or treat with x-rays.

xy•lo•phone (zī′lə fōn′), *n.* a musical instrument consisting of a graduated series of wooden bars struck with small wooden hammers. —**xy′lo•phon′ist,** *n.*

Y, y (wī), *n., pl.* **Ys** or **Y's, ys** or **y's. 1.** the 25th letter of the English alphabet, a semivowel. **2.** something shaped like a Y.

Y *Chem. Symbol.* yttrium.

y *Math. Symbol.* an unknown quantity; variable.

-y¹, an adjective suffix meaning: characterized by or like (*cloudy*); inclined to (*squeaky*).

-y², a noun suffix meaning: dear (*granny*); little (*kitty*).

-y³, a noun suffix meaning: action of (*inquiry*); quality or state (*victory*); goods or business establishment specified (*bakery*).

yacht (yot), *n.* **1.** a boat or ship used for private cruising or racing. —*v.i.* **2.** to cruise, race, or sail in a yacht. —**yacht′ing,** *n.* —**yachts′man,** *n.,* *pl.* **-men.**

ya·hoo (yä′hōō), *n.,* *pl.* **-hoos.** an uncultivated or boorish person; lout.

yak¹ (yak), *n.* a large, shaggy-haired wild ox of the Tibetan highlands.

yak² (yak), *v.,* **yakked** or **yacked,** **yak·king** or **yack·ing,** *n. Slang.* —*v.i.* **1.** to gab; chatter. —*n.* **2.** incessant idle or gossipy talk.

yam (yam), *n.* **1.** the starchy, tuberous root of an African climbing vine resembling but unrelated to the sweet potato. **2.** the sweet potato.

yam·mer (yam′ər), *Informal.* —*v.i.* **1.** to whine or complain. **2.** to talk loudly and persistently. —*n.* **3.** the act or noise of yammering. —**yam′mer·er,** *n.*

yank (yangk), *v.i., v.t.* **1.** to pull or tug sharply. —*n.* **2.** an abrupt, sharp pull.

Yank (yangk), *n., adj. Informal.* Yankee.

Yan·kee (yang′kē) *n.* **1.** a native or inhabitant of the United States. **2.** a native or inhabitant of New England. **3.** a native or inhabitant of a Northern state. —*adj.* **4.** of or characteristic of a Yankee.

yap (yap), *v.,* **yapped,** **yap·ping,** *n.* —*v.i.* **1.** to bark sharply; yelp. **2.** *Slang.* to talk noisily or foolishly. —*n.* **3.** a sharp bark; yelp. **4.** *Slang.* **a.** noisy or foolish talk. **b.** the mouth.

yard¹ (yärd), *n.* **1.** a unit of linear measure equal to 3 feet or 36 inches (0.9144 meter). **2.** a long spar, supported at its center, by which the head of a sail is supported.

yard² (yärd), *n.* **1.** the ground that adjoins or surrounds a building. **2.** an outdoor space surrounded by buildings, as on a college campus. **3.** an enclosure for livestock. **4.** an enclosed area set aside for particular use: *lumberyard.* **5.** a system of railroad tracks where trains are made up and rolling stock is stored.

yard·age (yär′dij), *n.* measurement or an amount measured in yards.

yard′arm′ *n.* either of the yards of a square sail.

yard′stick′ *n.* **1.** a measuring stick a yard long. **2.** a standard of measurement or judgment.

yar·mul·ke (yär′məl kə, -mə-, yä′-), *n., pl.* **-kes.** a skullcap worn by Jewish males, esp. during prayer.

yarn (yärn), *n.* **1.** a continuous strand or thread made of fibers and used for knitting and weaving. **2.** a long tale, esp. of adventure or incredible happenings.

yar·row (yar′ō), *n.* a plant with flat-topped clusters of white-to-yellow flowers.

yaw (yô), *v.i.* **1.** to deviate from a straight course, as a ship. **2.** (of an aircraft) to turn around a vertical axis. —*n.* **3.** the movement of yawing.

yawl (yôl), *n.* **1.** a ship's small boat. **2.** a two-masted fore-and-aft-rigged sailing ship with a large mainmast.

yawn (yôn), *v.i.* **1.** to open the mouth wide, usu. involuntarily, as from drowsiness or boredom. **2.** to stretch wide open: *a yawning pit.* —*n.* **3.** an act or instance of yawning. —**yawn′er,** *n.*

Y′ chro′mosome *n.* a sex chromosome present only in males and paired with an X chromosome.

ye¹ (yē), *pron. Archaic.* you (def. 1).

ye² (t͡hē; *spelling pron.* yē), *definite article. Archaic.* THE¹.

yea (yā), *adv., n., pl.* **yeas.** —*adv.* **1.** yes (used in affirmation or assent). **2.** indeed. —*n.* **3.** an affirmative vote. **4.** a person who votes in the affirmative.

year (yēr), *n.* **1.** a period in the Gregorian calendar of 365 or 366 days divided into 12 calendar months,

reckoned as beginning Jan. 1 and ending Dec. 31. **2.** a division of time equal to the time it takes the earth to complete one revolution around the sun. **3.** a part of the year devoted to a certain pursuit or activity: *the academic year.* **4. years, a.** age: *a person of advanced years.* **b.** a long time: *We haven't spoken in years.* —**year′ly,** *adv., adj.*

year′book′ *n.* **1.** a book published annually that contains information about the past year. **2.** a commemorative book published by a graduating class.

year′ling (-ling), *n.* **1.** an animal in its second year. **2.** a horse one year old.

yearn (yûrn), *v.i.* **1.** to have a strong desire; long. **2.** to feel tenderness.

year′-round′ *adj.* continuing, available, or used throughout the year.

yeast (yēst), *n.* **1.** any of various small single-celled fungi capable of fermenting carbohydrates into alcohol and carbon dioxide. **2.** any of several yeasts used in brewing alcoholic beverages and as a leaven in baking breads. **3.** something that causes ferment or agitation.

yell (yel), *v.i.* **1.** to cry out; shout. **2.** to scream, as with pain. —*v.t.* **3.** to say by yelling. —*n.* **4.** a cry uttered by yelling. **5.** a cheer used esp. to encourage a team.

yel·low (yel′ō), *n.* **1.** the color of an egg yolk or a ripe lemon. **2.** something yellow, as the yolk of an egg. —*adj.* **3.** of the color yellow. **4.** having a somewhat yellow complexion. **5.** cowardly. **6.** emphasizing sensational or lurid details: *yellow journalism.* —*v.t., v.i* **7.** to make or become yellow. —**yel′low·ish,** *adj.*

yel′low fe′ver *n.* an acute, infectious viral disease of warm climates that is transmitted by a mosquito and characterized by fever and jaundice.

yelp (yelp), *v.i., v.t.* **1.** to give or utter with a sharp, shrill cry or bark. —*n.* **2.** a sharp, shrill cry or bark.

Yem·en (yem′ən, yā′mən), *n.* **Republic of,** a country in S Arabia.

yen¹ (yen), *n., pl.* **yen.** the basic monetary unit of Japan.

yen² (yen), *n.* a desire or craving. [prob. < dial. Chinese]

yeo·man (yō′mən), *n., pl.* **-men. 1.** an enlisted person in the U.S. Navy whose duties are chiefly clerical. **2.** *Brit.* a farmer who cultivates his own land. **3.** (formerly, in England) **a.** one of a class of lesser freeholders below the gentry. **b.** an attendant in a royal household.

yes (yes), *adv.* **1.** (used to express affirmation or agreement or to emphasize a previous statement): *Do you want that? Yes, I do.* —*n.* **2.** an affirmative reply or vote.

ye·shi·va or **-vah** (yə shē′və), *n., pl.* **-vas** or **-vahs. 1.** an Orthodox Jewish school for the religious and secular education of children. **2.** an Orthodox Jewish school of higher instruction in Jewish learning.

yes′-man′ *n., pl.* **-men.** a person who always agrees with superiors.

yes·ter·day (yes′tər dā′, -dē), *adv.* **1.** on the day before this day. **2.** in the recent past. —*n.* **3.** the day before this day. **4.** the recent past.

yet (yet), *adv.* **1.** at the present time; now. **2.** up to a particular time; thus far. **3.** in the time remaining. **4.** as previously; still. **5.** in addition; again. **6.** even: *yet greater power.* **7.** nevertheless. —*conj.* **8.** still; nevertheless.

yew (yōō), *n.* **1.** an evergreen tree or shrub with needlelike foliage. **2.** the fine-grained elastic wood of a yew.

Yid·dish (yid′ish), *n.* a language of esp. central and E European Jews that is based on German and written in the Hebrew alphabet.

yield (yēld), *v.t.* **1.** to give forth by a natural process; bear. **2.** to produce or furnish (profit). **3.** to give up, as to superior power; surrender. **4.** to relinquish or resign. **5.** to give as due or required. —*v.i.* **6.** to give a return; produce or bear. **7.** to surrender. **8.** to give way, as to entreaty. **9.** to give place or

precedence. 10. to give way to force or pressure; collapse. —*n.* **11.** a quantity yielded or produced.

yip (yip), *v.*, **yipped, yip•ping,** *n.* —*v.i.* **1.** to bark sharply. —*n.* **2.** a sharp bark.

yo•del (yōd′l), *v.*, **-deled, -del•ing** or (*esp. Brit.*) **-delled, -del•ling,** *n.* —*v.t., v.i.* **1.** to sing or call out with frequent changes from the ordinary voice to falsetto and back again. —*n.* **2.** a yodeled song or refrain.

yo•ga (yō′gə), *n.* (*sometimes cap.*) **1.** a series of postures and breathing exercises practiced to attain physical and mental control and tranquillity. **2.** a school of Hindu philosophy using yoga to unify the self with the Supreme Being. [< Skt]

yo•gi (yō′gē) also **-gin** (-gin), *n., pl.* **-gis** also **-gins.** a person who practices yoga.

yo•gurt or **-ghurt** (yō′gərt), *n.* a tart, custardlike food made from milk curdled by the action of bacterial cultures.

yoke (yōk), *n., pl.* **yokes** for 1, 3–7, **yoke** for 2; *v.*, **yoked, yok•ing.** —*n.* **1.** a crosspiece or frame for joining together a pair of draft animals, esp. oxen, at the neck. **2.** a pair of draft animals joined by a yoke. **3.** a frame resting on a person's shoulders to carry two loads, as a pair of buckets, one at each end. **4.** an agency or symbol of oppression, subjection, or servitude. **5.** something that binds; bond or tie. **6.** a viselike piece for gripping two parts firmly together. **7.** a shaped and fitted piece in a garment, esp. at the shoulders. —*v.t.* **8.** to put a yoke on. **9.** to attach (a draft animal) to. **10.** to join, couple, link, or unite.

yo•kel (yō′kəl), *n.* a country bumpkin; rustic.

yolk (yōk), *n.* the yellow and principal substance of an egg. —**yolked,** *adj.*

yon•der (yon′dər), *adj.* **1.** being in that place. **2.** being more distant. —*adv.* **3.** at, in, or to that place.

yore (yôr), *n. Chiefly Literary.* time past: *knights of yore.*

you (yo̅o̅; *unstressed* yo̅o̅, yə), *pron.* **1.** the person or persons being addressed. **2.** anyone; one: *a tiny mark you can't even see.*

young (yung), *adj.*, **young•er** (yung′gər), **young•est** (yung′gist), *n.* —*adj.* **1.** being in an early period of life or growth. **2.** having qualities, as freshness, associated with youth. **3.** not far advanced in experience. **4.** being in an early stage: *a young nation.* —*n.* **5.** young persons collectively. **6.** young offspring. —**young′ish,** *adj.*

young′ster (-stər), *n.* **1.** a child. **2.** a young person.

your (yo̅o̅r, yôr; *unstressed* yər), *pron.* **1.** a form of the possessive case of **you** used as an attributive adjective: *I like your idea.* **2.** (used to indicate that one belonging or relevant to oneself or to any person): *The library is on your left.*

you're (yo̅o̅r; *unstressed* yər), contraction of *you are.*

your•self′ *pron., pl.* **-selves. 1.** a reflexive form of you: *You can think for yourself.* **2.** an intensive form of you: *a letter you yourself wrote.* **3.** your normal or customary self: *Be yourself at the party.*

youth (yo̅o̅th), *n., pl.* **youths** (yo̅o̅ths, yo̅o̅thz). **1.** the condition of being young. **2.** qualities, as freshness and vigor, characteristic of the young. **3.** the time of being young. **4.** the period of life from puberty to adulthood. **5.** a first or early period of something. **6.** young persons collectively. **7.** a young person, esp. a young man. —**youth′ful,** *adj.*

yowl (youl), *v.i.* **1.** to utter a long, dismal cry; howl. —*n.* **2.** a yowling cry.

yo-yo (yō′yō), *n., pl.* **-yos,** *v.*, **-yoed, -yo•ing.** —*n.* **1.** a spoollike toy that is spun out and reeled in by an attached string that loops around the player's finger. —*v.i.* **2.** to move up and down or back and forth; fluctuate.

yr. 1. year. **2.** your.

yuc•ca (yuk′ə), *n., pl.* **-cas.** a New World plant with rigid sword-shaped leaves and white flowers.

yuck (yuk), *interj. Slang.* an exclamation of disgust or repugnance. —**yuck′y,** *adj.*, **-i•er, -i•est.**

Yu•go•sla•vi•a (yo̅o̅′gō slä′vē ə), *n.* a republic in SE Europe. —**Yu′go•sla′vi•an,** *adj., n.*

yule (yo̅o̅l), *n.* Christmas.

yule′tide′ *n.* the Christmas season.

yum•my (yum′ē), *adj.*, **-mi•er, -mi•est.** very pleasing, esp. to the taste.

yup•pie or **-py** (yup′ē), *n., pl.* **-pies.** (*sometimes cap.*) a young, ambitious, and affluent professional who lives in or near a city.

Z, z (zē; *esp. Brit.* zed), *n., pl.* **Zs** or **Z's, zs** or **z's.** the 26th letter of the English alphabet, a consonant.

zaf′tig (zäf′tik, -tig), *adj. Slang.* (of a woman) pleasantly plump.

Zam•bi•a (zam′bē ə), *n.* a republic in S Africa. —**Zam′bi•an,** *adj., n.*

za•ny (zā′nē), *adj.*, **-ni•er, -ni•est,** *n., pl.* **-nies.** —*adj.* **1.** absurdly or whimsically comical; clownishly crazy. —*n.* **2.** a comically wild or eccentric person. **3.** a buffoon; clown. [orig. the name for a character in early Italian comedy; perh. a form of *Gianni* John] —**za′ni•ness,** *n.*

zap (zap), *v.*, **zapped, zap•ping,** *n. Informal.* —*v.t.* **1.** to attack, destroy, or kill with sudden speed and force. **2.** to bombard with or as if with electrical current. —*v.i.* **3.** to move quickly, forcefully, or destructively. —*n.* **4.** force, energy, or drive.

zeal (zēl), *n.* eager desire or interest; fervor. —**zeal•ous** (zel′əs), *adj.*

zeal•ot (zel′ət), *n.* a person who shows zeal, esp. to an excessive degree. —**zeal′ot•ry,** *n.*

ze•bra (zē′brə), *n., pl.* **-bras, -bra.** a horselike African mammal with a characteristic pattern of dark stripes on a whitish body.

Zen (zen), *n.* a Buddhist movement that emphasizes enlightenment by means of meditation and direct, intuitive insights. [< Japn < Chinese < Skt: meditation, thought]

ze•nith (zē′nith), *n.* **1.** the point on the celestial sphere that is directly overhead. **2.** the highest point or state; acme.

zeph•yr (zef′ər), *n.* **1.** a gentle breeze. **2.** a fine, light fabric or yarn.

zep•pe•lin (zep′ə lin), *n.* (*often cap.*) a rigid airship consisting of a long cylindrical covered framework supported by gas, esp. helium. [after Count Ferdinand von *Zeppelin* (1838–1917), German designer]

ze•ro (zēr′ō), *n., pl.* **-ros, -roes,** *v.*, *adj.* —*n.* **1.** the figure or numerical symbol 0. **2.** an origin from which values are calibrated, as on a thermometer. **3.** nothing; naught. **4.** the lowest point or degree. —*v.t.* **5.** to adjust (an instrument or apparatus) to a zero point. **6. zero in, a.** to aim at the precise center, as of a target. **7. ~ in on, a.** to aim at, focus on, or converge on. **b.** to direct one's attention to; focus on. —*adj.* **8.** amounting to zero. **9.** having no measurable quantity or magnitude: *zero economic growth.*

ze′ro hour′ *n.* the time set for the beginning of any event or action, esp. a military attack.

ze′ro popula′tion growth′ *n.* a condition in which population remains constant because of a balance between the number of births and deaths.

zest (zest), *n.* **1.** hearty enjoyment; gusto. **2.** something added to impart flavor or relish. **3.** piquancy. **4.** a strip of citrus peel, esp. lemon, used for flavoring. —**zest′ful,** *adj.* —**zest′y,** *adj.*, **-i•er, -i•est.**

zig•zag (zig′zag′), *n., adj., adv., v.*, **-zagged, -zag•ging.** —*n.* **1.** a line, course, or progression characterized by sharp turns first to one side and then to the other. **2.** one of a series of zigzags. —*adj.* **3.** proceeding or formed in a zigzag. —*adv.* **4.** in a zigzag manner. —*v.t., v.i.* **5.** to make into or proceed in a zigzag.

zilch (zilch), *n. Slang.* zero; nothing.

zil•lion (zil′yən), *n., pl.* **-lions, -lion.** *Informal.* an extremely large, indeterminate number.

Zim•bab•we (zim bäb′wā, -wē), *n.* a republic in S Africa. —**Zim•bab′we•an,** *adj., n.*

zinc (zingk), *n., v.*, **zincked** or **zinced, zinck•ing** or **zinc•ing.** —*n.* **1.** a ductile, bluish white metallic element used in making galvanized iron and alloys. *Symbol:* Zn; *at. wt.:* 65.37; *at. no.:* 30. —*v.t.* **2.** to coat or cover with zinc.

zinc′ ox′ide *n.* a white powder used as a pigment and in ointments and cosmetics.

zing (zing), *n.* **1.** a sharp singing or whining sound. **2.** vitality or zest. —*v.i., v.t.* **3.** to move or cause to move with a zing. —**zing′y**, *adj.,* **-i•er, -i•est.**

zin•ni•a (zin′ē ə), *n., pl.* **-ni•as.** a New World plant with dense, colorful flower heads.

Zi•on (zī′ən), *n.* **1.** the Jewish people. **2.** Palestine as the Jewish homeland and symbol of Judaism. **3.** heaven as the final gathering place of true believers.

Zi′on•ism *n.* a worldwide Jewish movement for the establishment and development of the state of Israel. —**Zi′on•ist,** *n., adj.*

zip¹ (zip), *n., v.,* **zipped, zip•ping.** —*n.* **1.** a sudden brief hissing sound. **2.** energy; vigor. —*v.i.* **3.** to act or move with speed and energy.

zip² (zip), *v.t., v.i.,* **zipped, zip•ping.** to fasten or unfasten with a zipper.

ZIP′ code′ *Trademark.* a system to facilitate mail delivery by assigning a numerical code to every postal area in the U.S. [*Z(one) I(mprovement) P(rogram)*]

zip′per *n.* a fastening device consisting of two parallel tracks of teeth or coils that can be interlocked by pulling a sliding piece.

zip′py *adj.,* **-pi•er, -pi•est.** full of energy.

zir•con (zûr′kon), *n.* a mineral that is used as a gem when transparent.

zir•co•ni•um (zûr kō′nē əm), *n.* a metallic element used esp. in metallurgy and ceramics. *Symbol:* Zr; *at. wt.:* 91.22; *at. no.:* 40.

zit (zit), *n. Slang.* a pimple.

zith•er (zith′ər, zith′-), *n.* a musical instrument with numerous strings that is played with a plectrum and the fingertips.

zo•di•ac (zō′dē ak′), *n.* **1.** an imaginary belt in the heavens that contains the apparent paths of the sun, moon, and principal planets and is divided into 12 divisions or signs, each named after a constellation. **2.** a diagram representing the zodiac.

zom•bie (zom′bē), *n., pl.* **-bies. 1.** (in voodoo) a corpse supernaturally imbued with the semblance of life. **2.** a person whose behavior or responses are wooden, listless, or mechanical.

zone (zōn), *n., v.,* **zoned, zon•ing.** —*n.* **1.** an area that differs or is distinguished in some respect from adjoining areas. **2.** any of five divisions of the earth's surface bounded by lines parallel to the equator and named according to the prevailing temperature. **3.** an area or district in which certain circumstances exist or restrictions apply. —*v.t.* **4.** to divide into, mark with, or surround with zones. [< L < Gk *zṓnē*] —**zon′al,** *adj.* —**zoned,** *adj.*

zonked (zongkt, zôngkt), *adj. Slang.* stupefied from or as if from alcohol or drugs.

zoo (zōō), *n., pl.* **zoos.** a parklike area in which live animals are kept for public exhibition.

zo•ol•o•gy (zō ol′ə jē), *n.* the scientific study of animals. —**zo′o•log′i•cal** (-ə loj′i kəl), *adj.* —**zo•ol′o•gist,** *n.*

zoom (zōōm), *v.i.* **1.** to move with a loud humming or buzzing sound. **2.** to fly a plane suddenly and sharply upward. **3.** to focus a camera with a zoom lens. **4.** to rise suddenly and sharply. —*v.t.* **5.** to cause to zoom. —*n.* **6.** the act or process of zooming. **7.** a zooming sound.

zoom′ lens′ *n.* a camera lens whose focal length can be continuously adjusted to change magnification with no loss of focus.

zo•o•phyte (zō′ə fīt′), *n.* any of various invertebrate animals resembling a plant, as a coral.

zuc•chi•ni (zōō kē′nē), *n., pl.* **-nis, -ni. 1.** a cucumber-shaped summer squash with a smooth, dark green skin. **2.** a plant bearing zucchini.

Zu•ni (zōō′nē) also **Zu•ñi** (zōōn′yē), *n., pl.* **-ni, -nis** also **-ñi, -ñis. 1.** a member of a Pueblo Indian people of W New Mexico. **2.** the language of the Zuni.

zwie•back (zwī′bak′, -bäk′, swē′-), *n.* an egg bread that is baked, sliced and dried, then baked again.

zy•gote (zī′gōt), *n.* a cell produced by the union of two gametes. —**zy•got′ic** (-got′ik), *adj.*

Business Dictionary

A b c d e f g h i j k l m n o p q r s t u v w x y z

AAA 1. See **American Academy of Advertising**. 2. See **American Accounting Association**. 3. See **American Arbitration Association**.

AAAA See **American Association of Advertising Agencies**.

abandonment 1. The relinquishing of real property with no intention of repossessing it. 2. The withdrawing of a claim or legal action.

abatement Cancellation or reduction of an expenditure, tax, charge, or levy.

abatement clause A section of a lease that releases the tenant from the obligation to pay rent when an event classifiable as an act of God prevents occupancy.

ABC analysis See **ABC inventory management**.

ABC Data Bank Also called **ABC Newspaper Audience Research Data Bank**. A research service that provides demographic data about the readership of all daily and Sunday newspapers belonging to the Audit Bureau of Circulation.

ABC inventory management Also called **ABC analysis**. A system used to track and control inventory selectively by dividing it into three categories of use or value: A (high), B (medium), and C (low).

ABC Newspaper Audience Research Data Bank See **ABC Data Bank**.

abnormal spoilage A deterioration of inventory or raw materials that exceeds the level expected during normal or efficient business operations and sales (generally considered an expense rather than a product cost).

aboriginal cost The price paid for an asset by the first company to use it for public service, calculated by a formula in general use among public utilities and used in the calculation of expenses in order to prevent the increased prices paid in subsequent exchanges from increasing the expenses (and rates) of other utilities.

above-the-line 1. Referring to an expense or source of income that is current or routine. 2. (*motion pictures*) Referring to the creative costs of a film (e.g., story, stars, director, producer). See also **below-the-line**.

abrogation of agreement The cancellation of a contract or of a section of a contract.

absentee management Ownership of property or of a business by a person who does not reside on the property or hires someone else to manage the business.

absolute frequency The number of data units in a category used for statistical measurement.

absolute liability. See **strict liability**.

absolute sale A nonconditional sale in which neither buyer nor seller imposes obstacles to or delays in the completion of the transaction. See also **conditional sale**.

absolute threshold The lowest level of intensity at which a stimulus can be detected. See also **just noticeable difference**.

absolute title Ownership with no conditions or reservations.

absorbable risk A risk or potential loss that a corporation is confident it can cover either with current capital or with amounts set aside in a self-insurance fund. See also **self-insurance**.

absorption costing Also called **full costing**. The practice of allocating all manufacturing costs (including materials, labor, and overhead) in relation to the number of units produced. See also **direct costing**.

abstract of title A detailed outline of all legal actions that have taken place in regard to a piece of land, including transfers of title, mortgages, and liens.

accelerated depreciation Depreciation of an as-

set at a higher rate in early years than in later years, for the purpose of reducing tax liability. See also **sum-of-the-years'-digits method; units-of-production method**.

acceleration clause A contractual agreement that specifies that an entire debt becomes due immediately if the debtor fails to pay according to contract.

acceptance needs See **need for acceptance**.

acceptance sampling The use of a sample of items from an incoming shipment to indicate the acceptability of the shipment as a whole.

acceptance theory of authority A management theory that stresses the placing of much decision making in the hands of subordinates rather than the reserving of all decisions to top management, and that for the theory to succeed in practice, subordinates must resolve their conflicts without recourse to higher authority.

access To gain entry to (data stored in a computer, etc.).

accessing Internal processing of information by means of the pictures, sounds, words, and feelings that make up an individual's memories.

accommodation endorsement An endorsement made by one individual to another in order to add his or her credit to the second individual's commercial paper or negotiable instrument.

accord An agreement between a debtor and a creditor or between persons engaged in a controversy as to the way in which an obligation is to be discharged. See also **satisfaction**.

account 1. A chronological record of debits and credits kept in a ledger to account for transactions involving a class of items (e.g., notes receivable) or a particular person or company. 2. A person, company, or class of items assigned a page in a ledger for the recording of pertinent transactions. 3. A customer or client.

accountability 1. The condition of being liable for the performance of tasks for which one has the necessary authority and for which one accepts responsibility. 2. The procedure for reporting up through the chain of command the results of tasks accomplished within or by a work group or subsystem.

accountancy (*chiefly British*) The practice and profession of accounting.

accountant A person skilled in the practice of accounting. See also **accounting; certified public accountant; chartered accountant; independent accountant**.

Accountant's Index A periodical published by the American Institute of Certified Public Accountants, listing in detail all accounting literature published since the last issue.

accountant's report See **audit report**.

account debtor An individual who is obligated to pay.

account executive Also called **account supervisor; contact person**. A person in an advertising or public relations agency who is responsible for executing agency services for a client, and who may assume as much authority over the creation of a product as is required by the client.

account form A common balance sheet format, with assets on the left and liabilities and owners' equity on the right. See also **report form**.

accounting A system and process of gathering and recording financial information that provides a continuous balance between assets on the one hand and liabilities and equity on the other; also provides a record of property owned, liabilities, investments, etc., and facilitates the preparation of financial reports.

accounting equation Also called **accounting identity**. A transaction expressed in the form of debits and credits in a double-entry bookkeeping system.

accounts payable Liabilities to creditors, carried on open account, usually for purchases of goods and services.

accounts receivable Claims against debtors, carried on open account, usually limited to debts due from the sale of goods or services.

account supervisor See **account executive.**

accrual A debt that has been incurred or an asset that has been generated but that has not been paid, received, or recorded. See also **accrued expense; accrued income; accrued interest.**

accrual accounting The recording of expenses along with the revenues they ultimately generate rather than at the time when they are paid, based on the reasoning that expenses are incurred in order to generate revenues. See also **cash accounting.**

accrued depreciation See **accumulated depreciation.**

accrued expense Also called **accrued liability.** An expense incurred and still owed, such as unpaid wages, salaries, interest, utility bills, insurance premiums, and other expenses normally scheduled to be paid within 30 days.

accrued income Income due to be received, reflected in an accounting system by a debit to an asset and a credit to an income account.

accrued interest Interest payable on a bond that has accrued since the issuer last paid interest (an amount added to the market price of the bond if it is sold before maturity).

accrued liability See **accrued expense.**

accumulated depreciation Also called **accrued depreciation.** The total depreciation taken on an asset from the time of original purchase to the present (a contra asset normally deducted from an asset account to derive net book value).

accumulated earnings tax A federal tax on retained earnings beyond a reasonable amount for anticipated needs, imposed as a means of preventing principal stockholders from avoiding the tax on accumulated business income.

accumulation plan A systematic program to buy an investment at regular intervals and reinvest the dividends and capital gains earned from the amounts previously invested.

ACE See **Active Corps of Executives.**

achievement needs See **need for achievement.**

achievement-oriented leadership A style of leadership in which the leader sets high standards, shows a high degree of confidence, and provides stimulating goals for subordinates to strive for.

acid-test ratio Also called **quick ratio.** Current liabilities divided by total cash, receivables, and marketable securities; a rough and conservative indication of a company's ability to meet its obligations. See also **liquidity ratio.**

ACME (*acronym for a*im, *c*ontent, *m*ethod, *e*xpectation) A format used by professional sales trainers to evaluate the effectiveness of each sales training program they consider for use within a given context.

acquisition cost Also called **historical cost; original cost.** The net invoice price of an asset.

across-the-board 1. Embracing all categories or classes. **2.** Appearing (as a television program) at the same time of day every day of the week (the weekend usually excepted). **3.** Uniformly affecting an entire population (e.g., a uniform salary increase granted to all employees regardless of position or seniority).

action-event area Also called **area of choice and chance.** A critical point in a decision tree, representing a proposed course of action and the probable consequences that may be expected to flow from it. See also **decision tree.**

action maze A pattern of simulated actions developed to improve decision-making skills by requiring a trainee to select one alternative response to an incident and follow it through alternative avenues of decision making, each response leading to additional information and new consequences.

action planning The use of surveys and group

process activities with the objective of improving motivational levels, internal communications, and general cooperation among employees: a human resource technique.

action research 1. The use of innovative ideas of proactive members of an organization to motivate a research team to investigate new ideas on an ongoing basis. See also **proactive. 2.** See **data-based intervention.**

Active Corps of Executives (*acronym* ACE) An advisory group of business executives who work with the Small Business Administration to provide assistance to small firms. See also **Service Corps of Retired Executives.**

active income 1. Salary or wages. **2.** Income from engaging in a trade or owning or managing a business.

activity ratio Any of four formulas used to measure the efficiency with which assets are being used. See also **average collection period ratio; fixed asset turnover ratio; inventory turnover ratio; total asset turnover ratio.**

act of bankruptcy Any action within the legal definition of bankruptcy that results in an individual's or corporation's qualifying as bankrupt.

act of God (*insurance*) An event of natural origin (e.g., flood, earthquake) that causes property loss and can be neither foreseen nor prevented by reasonable care.

actual authority The authority given to an agent by a principal.

actual damages The damages caused by failure to fulfill the terms of a contract, exclusive of incidental damages.

actuary An expert in pension and life insurance plans, trained to calculate expected liabilities and the income that must be generated to cover them, taking into consideration the costs of premiums, the cost of operations, and earnings on the company's reserve funds.

additional paid-in capital See **capital surplus.**

add-on A purchase added to a charge account in a retail store, which generally follows a standard procedure to determine the amount of such purchases that may be added to a customer's previous balance before the recorded amount has been fully paid.

address A number or other code that identifies the physical location of data stored in a computer's memory.

ad hoc (*Latin*) For this; for the particular purpose at hand.

ad hoc committee A temporary committee created to deal with a specific situation.

adjustable-rate mortgage (*abbr* ARM) Any mortgage whose interest rate may increase or decrease periodically, along with monthly payments: usually offered at a rate lower than that of the fixed-rate mortgage. See also **renegotiable-rate mortgage; variable-rate mortgage.**

adjusted book value The value of inventory adjusted to reflect the current actual worth of the items.

adjusted gross income Actual money received less allowable deductions and exclusions.

adjusting entry Also called **adjustment.** A final journal entry made at the end of an accounting period to reflect a change in assets, liabilities, expenses, or revenues that was not recognized or was not calculable at the time the change occurred (e.g., an adjustment for ending inventory, uncollected accounts receivable, depreciation, accrued amounts).

adjustment 1. A change in an account to correct an erroneous entry. **2.** See **adjusting entry. 3.** The determination of the amount of indemnity an insured will receive.

administrative assistant A person employed to aid an executive, as by coordinating office services and supervising the flow of work.

administrative expense Generally, the cost of running an administrative office or department (e.g., salaries of office personnel, rent, legal services), in contrast to manufacturing or sales expense: an allowable deduction from income for tax purposes.

administrative intensity The size of an organization's administrative staff in relation to the size of its production staff, a ratio that changes in accordance with changes in the size of the organization. Growth leads to increased need for coordination and for administrators to deal with problems; conversely, when growth leads to an increase in specialization, resulting efficiency in the use of administrative skills leads to a decrease in administrative personnel.

administrative ratio The ratio of managers to subordinates in an organization.

admiralty law The body of law dealing with maritime matters.

admission of partner The legal introduction of an individual into a partnership and thus the creation of a new partnership, which must be reflected in entries recording how the new partner joined and the assets and/or liabilities that that partner contributed.

admitted company A company licensed to do business within a state.

adoption notice A notification that a carrier accepts the obligations of its predecessor.

adoption process The process by which an individual or organization acquires psychological acceptance of a new product or innovation, from first awareness of the product to the final decision to purchase it. See also **AIDA process; AIDCAS process; diffusion process.**

ADP See **automatic data processing.**

ad referundum (*Latin*) To be referred; an indication that although a contract has been signed, certain issues remain to be clarified.

ad valorem tax A tax, such as the typical property tax, based on appreciated value or cost.

advance dating The application of a code to goods shipped by sea that are on their way to but have not yet cleared an inland customs point.

advance from (by) customer Also called **deferred income; deferred revenue.** A liability incurred when a customer pays for goods or services that he or she has not yet received (often recorded under accounts payable).

adverse opinion An opinion rendered by a certified public accountant (usually an external auditor) or by a lawyer that a company's financial statements do not accurately or fairly reflect its financial position or history, the results of its operations, or changes in its financial position, or the opinion that generally accepted accounting principles have been breached or used inconsistently.

adverse possession Acquisition of property to which one does not have a legal right or clear title.

advertisement A public message paid for by a sponsor and appearing in print or in the broadcast media for the purpose of promoting a product, service, or idea. See also **announcement.**

advertising The use of sales messages paid for by a sponsor and communicated through the mass media, as on a television broadcast or in a magazine, usually on a repeated basis to an audience of potential buyers or consumers.

advertising agency A company that specializes in creating and developing advertisements for clients, and whose services include preparation of layouts and copy, media selection, and marketing research.

advertising theme The pivotal concept of an advertisement or ad campaign, often used to specify and amplify the differences between one product and another in the minds of the target audience.

advisory relationship A balanced relationship between a line manager and a general staff involving an exchange of information for the purpose of identifying and solving staff problems, such that specialists, via the manager, provide enough information and assistance to the general staff to enable them to solve their problems without overstepping the boundaries of their responsibilities.

affidavit A written statement that has been signed before a person who is legally authorized to administer oaths and that is usually legally binding.

affiliate 1. A (usually independent) television or radio station that contracts to broadcast programs provided by a major network on a regular basis. **2.** A business that contracts to work with another business.

affinity card A credit card issued in conjunction with an organization, as a university, sports club, or corporation.

affirmative action Active recruitment of members of all social groups without discrimination on the basis of race, religion, sex, age, or national origin, for the purpose of promoting equal employment and educational opportunities.

affirmative action program A program of active recruitment of women and minority employees, mandated by the Civil Rights Act of 1964 for companies that employ more than 50 people and have government contracts.

AFL-CIO See **American Federation of Labor; Congress of Industrial Organizations.**

after cost An expense incurred after the revenue that the expense generated has been received (e.g., the expense of repairing or servicing a machine that was sold under warranty or leased under a service contract).

aftermarket 1. The market for replacement parts, accessories, etc., as for an automobile, after its sale to the consumer. **2.** See **secondary market.**

AFTRA See **American Federation of Television and Radio Artists.**

Age Discrimination in Employment Act An act of Congress that prohibits job discrimination on the basis of age by employment agencies, labor unions with more than 25 members, and companies that employ more than 20 people.

agency 1. A legally binding association that exists when a principal party authorizes another (the agent) to act on his or her behalf, either orally, in writing, or (as in the transfer of real property) by power of attorney. See also **agent** (def. 2); **principal** (def. 2). **2.** A company, organization, or business whose primary activity is the provision of services to other companies (e.g., an advertising, public relations, real estate, or insurance agency).

agency of record The principal advertising agency chosen by an advertiser to coordinate and manage the activities of a media project involving a number of subordinate agencies.

agency recognition A written or oral statement given to an advertising agency by appropriate officials of a client company testifying that the agency meets required standards and is entitled to agency commissions.

agency shop A unionized workplace that collects union dues from union members and also from nonunion employees who benefit from any agreements that result from negotiations between employer and union.

agent 1. A person who acts as an intermediary in a business transaction and for such service receives a percentage (generally from 10 to 25%) of the fee negotiated. **2.** Any person who acts for another (as a broker for an investor, a trustee for a bondholder, a fiduciary for an heir).

age of majority The age (varying among states) at which an individual acquires full legal rights and responsibilities (e.g., to sue and be sued).

aggregate demand 1. The total dollars spent on goods and services in an economy during a specified period of time. **2.** The total demand for all of a firm's products and services during a specified period of time.

aggregate planning Preparation of an intermediate-range production schedule, together with a plan for providing the capacity needed to meet that schedule.

aggregate supply The total amount of goods and services produced in an economy during a specified period of time.

aggressive Emphasizing maximum growth and capital gains over quality, security, and income.

aging schedule A list, often issued quarterly, of outstanding accounts receivable, in which accounts are grouped according to the age of overdue amounts: a "strong" aging schedule indicates a lower percentage of accounts receivable on old sales than on recent sales.

AIA See **Business and Professional Advertisers Association.**

AIDA process (*acronym for* attention, interest, desire, action) The process of increasing involvement through which prospective customers go while being influenced to buy a product.

AIDCAS process (*acronym for* attention, interest, desire, conviction, action, satisfaction) An expansion of the AIDA process to include the customer's conviction that the product's benefits are better than those offered by other products and satisfaction with the purchased product.

algorithm A series of instructions to be followed or steps to be taken to solve a particular problem.

alien corporation A corporation chartered in a foreign country but operating in the United States (e.g., Toyota, Volkswagen).

allocation 1. Dispersal of a supply of a product in multiple small containers for transporting. See also **bulk breaking. 2.** The assignment of a frequency and broadcast signal to a radio or television station by the Federal Communications Commission.

allonge A separate form attached to a negotiable instrument to provide space for multiple endorsements.

allowance for doubtful accounts Also called **allowance for bad debts; reserve for bad debts.** A contra asset account in which the amounts of accounts receivable that may not be collected are recorded (the balance thus deducted from accounts receivable yields the net book value of receivables).

allowed time The amount of time that hourly and part-time employees are permitted to absent themselves from the job on personal breaks.

all-purpose revolving account See **revolving charge account.**

alphanumeric Consisting of both numbers and letters (e.g., "x305PS6").

alternate sponsorship 1. Sponsorship of a television program by two advertisers on alternate weeks. **2.** The sharing of commercial time by two advertisers who provide programs on alternate weeks during the same time slot.

AMA 1. See **American Management Associations.** **2.** See **American Marketing Association.**

amalgamation A merger of two or more companies brought together by an outside interest, such as an investment bank.

American Academy of Advertising (*abbr* ACA) An organization composed of individuals in the advertising field who are interested in furthering their own and other members' education in advertising.

American Accounting Association (*abbr* AAA) An association of accountants, accounting teachers, and accounting researchers formed to develop accounting theory and techniques, conduct research, and promote understanding of accounting principles; publishes *Accounting Review.*

American Arbitration Association (*abbr* AAA) A nongovernmental, nonprofit organization founded in 1926 to promote the use of arbitration in the settlement of disputes.

American Association of Advertising Agencies (*abbr* AAAA) An organization founded in 1917 to foster, strengthen, and improve the advertising agency business, and to aid its members in operating more effectively and profitably.

American College of Life Underwriters A professional organization that awards certification to practice insurance underwriting, upon the passing of examinations and fulfillment of experience requirements.

American Federation of Labor (*abbr* AFL) A national federation of craft unions, which joined in 1955 with the CIO to become the AFL-CIO. See also **Congress of Industrial Organizations.**

American Federation of Television and Ra-

dio Artists (*acronym* AFTRA) A performers' union that lobbies for improvements in benefits and working conditions for its members and offers standard union services.

American Institute of Certified Public Accountants (*abbr* AICPA) An association of CPAs that carries on wideranging programs encompassing professional development, the establishment of accounting standards and procedures, continuing education, publication of the *Journal of Accountancy*, and administration of the uniform CPA examination (though each state sets its own requirements for certification).

American Management Associations (*abbr* AMA) A professional nonprofit organization of business professionals that conducts study courses, training programs, and management seminars, conducts research, and issues numerous publications on business subjects.

American Marketing Association (*abbr* AMA) A professional organization devoted to its members' continued improvement in the marketing arena and to the setting and upholding of ethical standards for the marketing profession as a whole; publishes *Journal of Marketing, Journal of Marketing Research*, and other periodicals.

American Production and Inventory Control Society (*acronym* APICS) A society of professionals in production and inventory management who have joined together to establish professional standards, research new ways to improve production and inventory management, develop and offer educational programs, publish journals, and provide research grants.

American Society of Woman Accountants (*abbr* ASWA) An association of female accountants; joint publisher, with the American Women's Society of Certified Public Accountants, of *The Woman CPA*, a bimonthly journal.

American Stock Exchange (*abbr* ASE) Also called **AMEX.** The second largest stock exchange in the U.S., located in New York City.

American Women's Economic Development Corporation (*abbr* AWED) A corporation set up by the federal government to train women entrepreneurs in basic business practices.

American Women's Society of Certified Public Accountants (*abbr* AWSCPA) An association of female certified public accountants; joint publisher, with the American Society of Woman Accountants, of *The Woman CPA*, a bimonthly journal.

AMEX See **American Stock Exchange.**

amortization The scheduled periodic repayment of a debt or loan at a rate sufficient to meet current interest and to extinguish the debt at the point of maturity; interest is usually charged only on the unpaid balance of the loan, though generally all payments are equal.

analytic process The process of breaking down a raw material into its component parts in order to extract one or more products, which may or may not resemble the original material in form and function. See also **synthetic process.**

anchor 1. A catchy phrase used by consumers as a rule of thumb to guide purchasing decisions (e.g., "You get what you pay for"). **2.** A major store in a shopping center.

announcement Also called **commercial.** A sponsor's message broadcast by television or radio, either between programs or during a brief break in a program, for the purpose of advertising a product, service, or idea. See also **advertisement.**

annual percentage rate (*abbr* APR) The annual rate of interest; the total interest to be paid in a year divided by the balance due.

annual report A corporation's financial and organizational report prepared by its officers on a yearly basis, as required by law, stating the corporation's assets, liabilities, earnings, general financial condition, profits, and losses and other information that may provide evidence to shareholders, customers, and creditors of the corporation's ability to pay its debts, and indicating the officers' goals and assessment of performance potential.

annuitant A person who receives an annuity.

annuity An income payable in equal installments at fixed intervals, either for life or for a specified number of years.

annuity depreciation Depreciation of an asset by a method that allows for a return of imputed interest on the undepreciated balance of the value of the asset, such interest being subtracted from the amount of current depreciation before that amount is credited to the accumulated depreciation accounts.

anthropometric data Data on the physical dimensions of various parts of the human body that serve as a basis for the design of products and tools.

anticipation The payment of an account before the due date, normally for the purpose of receiving a discount.

anticipatory breach The breaching of a contract before the time specified for performance, as by notifying the other party that the terms of the contract will not be fulfilled, such that the other party to the contract has the legal right to sue for damages.

Antitrust Improvement Act An act of Congress passed in 1976 requiring companies to give advance notice of planned mergers and empowering state attorneys general to bring suit on behalf of state residents harmed by failure to comply with its provisions.

antitrust laws The body of legislation passed by Congress to maintain competition, prevent monopoly, and outlaw price discrimination. See also **Antitrust Improvement Act; Antitrust Procedures and Penalties Act; Celler-Kefauver Act; Clayton Act; Federal Trade Commission; Robinson-Patman Act; Sherman Antitrust Act; Wheeler-Lea Act.**

Antitrust Procedures and Penalties Act An act of Congress passed in 1974 to increase the penalties for failure to comply with the provisions of the Sherman Antitrust Act to a maximum fine of $100,000 for an individual or $10 million for a corporation.

appellate court A court that has the power to affirm, repeal, or modify a decision of a lower court upon appeal by either plaintiff or defendant on any of various grounds (e.g., denial of fair trial, judicial error).

application 1. The use of concepts and/or devices, such as those of science and technology, to define and solve real problems (e.g., engineering is the application of science, technology, art, and economics for practical ends). **2.** A computer program designed for a specific kind of task, such as word processing.

applied behavior analysis A behavior-change technique characterized by a functional combination of systems analysis, feedback systems, and reinforcement (e.g., analysis of a worker's job performance, decision-making ability, and competence to evaluate situations carried out by the worker's peers and/or supervisors for the purpose of determining any need for further training of the individual).

applied cost A cost allocated to a certain department or project before the expense has been incurred.

applied overhead Overhead costs for a specific department.

applied research Investigation or experimentation with the aim of developing practical applications of the knowledge thus gained.

appraisal 1. A professional estimate of the market value of an asset or liability. **2.** Evaluation of an employee's job performance.

appreciation An increase in the value of an asset, the amount being listed on the balance sheet as a capital gain or other form of income only when the asset is sold. See also **capital appreciation.**

apprenticeship A system by which a novice learns a skill while practicing it under the guidance of an experienced person.

appropriated retained earnings Also called

surplus revenue; suspense reserve. A portion of retained earnings that a board of directors has designated for a special purpose and that thus is not available for dividends or other purposes.

appropriation An amount of money designated for the payment of known or anticipated costs.

APR See **annual percentage rate.**

a priori (*Latin*) From the former; based on accepted definitions or assumptions rather than on factual evidence.

arb (*informal*) Arbitrageur.

arbitrage 1. The simultaneous purchase and sale of the same security or of equivalent securities for the purpose of profiting from differences in market prices (as between New York and Paris). The practice tends to equalize prices by boosting them in the depleted cheaper markets and driving them down in the glutted expensive markets. **2.** See **risk arbitrage.**

arbitrageur Also called **arbitrager.** A person who engages in arbitrage. Also known, familiarly, as an "arb."

arbitration Also called **mediation.** Mediation of a dispute by a person chosen by the parties to the dispute or appointed under statutory authority: a right guaranteed by most union contracts. See also **compulsory arbitration; conciliation.**

arbitrator A disinterested person who individually or as a member of a group mediates a dispute between labor and management, with powers defined by contract and whose ruling is the final resolution of the conflict.

area of choice and chance See **action-event area.**

Area Redevelopment Program A federal program initiated under the Area Redevelopment Act of 1961 to stimulate business growth and employment in depressed areas.

arithmetic mean The sum of all items divided by the number of items.

ARM See **adjustable-rate mortgage.**

ARO After receipt (of) order.

array (*statistics*) An arrangement of items by value, size, etc., from either smallest to largest or largest to smallest.

arrears 1. The state of a bill or invoice unpaid past its due date, which may be subject to interest or the loss of any discount allowed for prompt payment. **2.** The state of an as yet undeclared dividend on cumulative preferred stock.

arrival rate The average rate at which customers arrive for service, expressed in terms of customers per time period.

articles of association A written affiliation agreement entered into by a nonprofit organization.

articles of copartnership A written partnership agreement that includes the names of the parties; the specific business and its intended duration; the amounts of the original investments; any arrangements concerning future investments, salaries, profits, and other financial matters; and procedures to be followed in the event that a partner wishes to withdraw from the agreement.

articles of incorporation A written agreement embodying the terms and conditions of the incorporation of a business entity in accordance with the laws of the state in which the entity seeks to be incorporated: upon approval by the state becomes the corporation's charter.

artificial intelligence (*abbr* AI) The capacity of a computer to perform operations similar to the learning and decision-making abilities of human beings. Advances in AI have led to the increased use of computers in product design and in the manufacturing process.

artisan's lien Also called **mechanic's lien.** A legal claim against property pending payment to a worker for services rendered or materials supplied.

ASCII (*acronym for* American Standard Code for Information Interchange) A standardized code in which characters are represented for computer storage and transmission by the numbers 0 through 127.

ASE See **American Stock Exchange.**

asked price The lowest price a securities dealer will accept for a given stock. See also **bid and asked; bid price.**

assemble-to-order A type of manufacturing in which standard-design components or modules are produced for stock and subsequently assembled to meet the specific needs of each customer.

assembly line An arrangement of tools, machines, and workers, as in a manufacturing plant, so that a product can be assembled as it passes through a succession of workers and work stations.

assertiveness training A developmental program designed to help participants to experience and diagnose their own behavior for the purpose of improving their ability to influence other individuals and groups by stating their ideas and opinions with assurance.

assessment 1. An official valuation of property for the purpose of levying a tax; an assigned value. **2.** An amount assessed as payable.

assessment center A place where individuals are brought together, either voluntarily or at the request of an organization seeking to fill a position, and administered a series of tests and simulations to determine their mode of reaction in certain situations for the purpose of assessing their appropriateness for a given position.

asset Anything owned that has a value. See also **liability.**

asset accounting The total resources and property of a person or organization, as listed on a balance sheet.

asset allocation The apportioning of investments among broad categories of investments, such as stocks and bonds.

asset depreciation range (*abbr* ADR) The length of time within high and low limits established by the Internal Revenue Service for the useful life of an asset, within which the owner of the asset may depreciate it without offering evidence in justification.

assignee An individual or organization to whom property or a right under a contract has been transferred. See also **assignment.**

assignment The transfer of property or a right, as to collect money or to receive a performance, specified by the terms of a contract, such transfer being exercisable only after the assignee has given the party who owes money or services written notification of the assignment.

assignor An individual or organization that transfers property or a right under a contract. See also **assignment.**

associated buying office A cooperatively supported resident buying office established in a central buying area.

associated independent An independent retail store associated with other stores for the purpose of gaining merchandising benefits.

Association of Industrial Advertisers (*abbr* AIA) Former name of the Business and Professional Advertisers Association.

assortment plan A merchandising strategy whereby a carefully selected variety of merchandise is held by a retail store to meet its customers' needs. See also **basic stock; model stock.**

ATM (*abbr for* automated-teller machine) An electronic machine that provides banking services when activated by insertion of a plastic card.

attached Subject to a security interest; seized by virtue of a writ to be held to satisfy a judgment. See also **perfected.**

attachment The seizure of an asset by a legal process to satisfy a judgment against a debtor who has failed to discharge an obligation.

at-the-market price A retail price generally agreed upon by area store owners. See also **market-minus pricing; market-plus pricing; price leader.**

attitude survey 1. A questionnaire used to gather data on the opinions of individuals or groups for any legitimate purpose. **2.** A survey of employees' opinions about the organization that employs them,

intended to reveal trends in such variables as feelings toward supervisor, pay, and work itself.

attrition Staff reduction due to the customary causes of resignation, firing for cause, retirement, transfers, etc. **2.** Forcing the resignation of an undesirable employee by constant criticism, pressure, etc.

audimeter A mechanical device that records the amount of time a radio is operated and the station or stations to which it is tuned.

audit 1. A review of the accuracy and validity of the financial and/or operations records, reports, and statements of a company for the purpose of verifying that the firm has conformed to established accounting procedures and principles. **2.** To conduct such a review.

Audit Bureau of Circulation (*abbr* ABC) An independent organization that collects and provides data on the number of copies of U.S. publications distributed at each printing.

audit committee A group appointed by a board of directors to select an external auditor and to serve as liaison between the auditor selected and the board, handling such problems as audit procedures and differences of opinion between the auditor and management.

audit opinion Also called **auditor's opinion.** Part of an audit report in which the auditor states whether or not the financial statement was prepared according to generally accepted accounting principles and is consistent with previous financial statements.

auditor An individual, group, or company qualified to perform an audit. See also **external auditor; internal auditor.**

audit program A description, agreed upon by management and auditor, of the objective of an audit and the procedures to be followed to reach those objectives.

audit report Also called **auditor's report; accountant's report.** A written statement by the outside auditor, accompanying a financial statement and addressed to the executives, board members, shareholders, etc., expressing his or her opinion as to the accuracy of the statement in setting forth the company's financial position for the period specified.

audit trail A sequence of financial evidence, consisting of codes, cross-references, documentation, account balances, and previous calculations, which an auditor follows in order to verify balances and to locate and correct errors.

authoritative leadership Leadership that depends on formal authority backed by the power of the organization.

authoritative power See **legitimate power.**

authority 1. The legitimate power attached to position, office, or rank. **2.** The right granted by an organization and acknowledged by its employees to issue orders, make decisions, and command the activities of subordinates. See also **functional authority (def. 2); line authority; staff authority.**

authorized dealership A retail outlet that has been given exclusive right by a manufacturer to sell a specific item or line of goods in a defined geographical area (akin to a franchise on a manufacturer's product).

authorized stock The maximum number of shares a corporation is entitled to issue, as stated in the corporate charter.

autocratic style A management style characterized by the direct exercise of authority over subordinates.

automated-teller machine See **ATM.**

automatic data processing (*abbr* ADP) The systematic and orderly analysis, sorting, gathering, and processing of data by a mechanical or electrical device, with little human intervention. See also **electronic data processing.**

automatic markdown A price reduction based on the length of time merchandise has been in stock in a retail store.

automatic reorder The ordering of goods or

materials in accordance with a system based on levels of stock on hand.

automatic selling Retailing by vending machine.

automation The efficient use of mechanical or electrical devices to perform tasks previously accomplished by human action. See also **robotics.**

autonomous work group A group of workers given total responsibility to meet a specific level of production, its members determining and therefore handling much of the management activity involved in their work. See also **job enrichment.**

autonomy 1. Freedom from arbitrary control. **2.** A quality of freedom evident in the performance of individuals with well-defined job activities and relationships.

auxiliary memory Also called **secondary storage.** Computer memory, as on disk or tape, supplemental to and slower than main memory, and not under the direct control of the CPU.

average collection period ratio Total accounts receivable divided by average daily sales: a formula used to determine the amount of daily sales revenue locked up in unreceived payments. See also **activity ratio.**

average cost The sum of the costs of beginning inventory and subsequent additions to inventory divided by the total number of units available during the time period.

average gross sales The dollar amount of all sales divided by the number of sales transactions.

average tax rate Allowable expenses divided by pretax net income.

avoidable cost A variable cost that can be avoided if production is not permitted to reach the level at which additional expenses will be incurred.

awareness (*marketing research*) The level of information about a product possessed by individuals being researched. See also **perceptions.**

a B c d e f g h i j k l m n o p q r s t u v w x y z

backdating The practice of placing on a statement, order, or check a date earlier than that on which the document is prepared.

back-door financing The financing of a program of a governmental agency by borrowing from the U.S. Treasury when Congress fails to appropriate the requested funds.

back-haul allowance A price reduction granted to customers who pick up their goods from a seller's warehouse to reflect the seller's savings in freight costs.

backlog The aggregate of production orders that have been processed through a company's records as sales but have not been shipped to customers.

back office Functions performed in a service organization by personnel who have little or no contact with customers.

back order An order or part of an order waiting to be filled.

backup stock Merchandise in excess of that needed for retail display, usually kept in an easily accessible stockroom.

backward integration The acquisition by a firm of ownership or control of facilities that provide raw materials or parts for products that the firm produces and sells.

backward scheduling A method of preparing a schedule by starting with the desired completion date and working backward to schedule earlier activities in time to meet the completion date.

backward vertical merger See **vertical merger.**

bad check A check written either against a bank balance that is insufficient to cover the amount specified or against a bank in which the drawer has no account. See also **NSF check.**

bad title A legal document assigning ownership of land or goods which is in some way improperly executed.

bafflegab Unintelligible, often deliberately confusing jargon.

bailment lease A security agreement by which a buyer rents goods from a seller with the understanding that when the sum paid for rental equals the purchase price, the buyer may take possession of the item for an additional nominal sum.

bailout period The time until the total net cash inflows accumulated from a project, including the potential salvage value of all assets at periodic points in time and the present value of cash to be received after the termination date of the project, equal the total cash spent on the project. See also **payback period.**

bait and switch A system of publicizing exceptional prices or terms in a deceptive effort to attract customers; the advertised product (the bait) is either unavailable or disparaged to the customer, who

is encouraged to buy a more expensive product (the switch).

balance 1. The remainder; the part left untouched or unpaid. **2.** The sum of all debits less the sum of all assets in an account. See **credit balance; debit balance. 3.** The book value of an asset or liability. **4.** The total to date of a revenue or expense account. **5.** The amount in a checking or savings account. **6.** To calculate any difference between debits and credits in an account. **7.** To cause debits and credits in an account to be equal.

balanced economy An economy in which the value of imports equals the value of exports in monetary terms.

balanced fund A mutual fund that must keep a certain percentage of its assets invested in senior securities.

balanced scale (*marketing research*) A questionnaire design that includes categories calling for equal numbers of favorable and unfavorable responses.

balanced stock A stock of goods at all prices sufficient to meet customers' demands, maintained as a long-range inventory strategy.

balanced tenancy A mix of stores in a geographical area adequate to meet the needs of the population of the area, as determined by a needs assessment.

balance of payments The net flow of money in and out of a country, including the value of imports and exports, loans and investments, foreign aid, income from tourism, deposits of foreign currency in domestic banks, and withdrawals of such deposits.

balance of trade 1. The net value of a country's total imports and exports. **2.** The net value of a country's import and export transactions with a given country. See also **favorable balance of trade; unfavorable balance of trade.**

balance sheet Also called **statement of financial position.** A statement of a company's financial position on a given date, usually at the end of a calendar or business year, including all of the elements in the accounting equation and the details of the financial transactions that back it up, specifying the type and amount of assets, liabilities, and owners' equity on the given date.

balloon loan Also called **balloon mortgage.** A relatively short-term loan, usually at a fixed rate of interest, in which the entire balance is due at the end of the term. Attractive because of generally low monthly payments, though these may pay off only the interest, with all or most of the principal coming due with the final payment.

ballpark pricing The practice of estimating a dollar value or price for a product to be produced or a job to be done by comparing the prices of similar projects or by adding the estimated costs of completing the project.

bandwagon effect An infectious buying climate in which the buying enthusiasm of some people spreads to others.

bangtail A detachable offer of merchandise on the back of a self-addressed envelope accompanying a monthly billing statement, usually supplied by a merchandise syndicator. See also **syndicator.**

Bank Deposit Insurance Act of 1934 Federal legislation enacted to protect depositors against loss in the event of bank failure by insuring bank deposits for amounts up to a specified maximum.

bank draft A check drawn by a bank on funds deposited to its account in another bank.

banker's acceptance A promissory note drawn on and accepted by a bank (commonly used in import/export transactions involving foreign banks and currencies), which by its endorsement accepts the obligation to pay the note on the due date, drawing the amount of the note plus interest from a deposit made by the debtor.

Banking Act of 1933 The first major banking legislation leading to significant changes in banking law, including the creation of commercial banking loans and credits, with or without collateral, and the development of branch banking services.

bank reconciliation An analysis that brings into agreement the amount in a bank account, as calculated by the depositor on the basis of canceled checks and stubs, and a different amount reported on the bank's statement; lists outstanding checks, deposits recorded after the statement date, bank service charges, and any other items that explain the difference.

bankruptcy A court action that cancels the debts of an individual, business, or corporation whose liabilities exceed its assets or that is otherwise unable to meet its financial obligations by dividing the debtor's available assets among the creditors. See also **Chapter 11; involuntary bankruptcy; voluntary bankruptcy.**

Bank Secrecy Act of 1970 Federal legislation requiring banks to maintain records of all transactions with depositors, and to report transactions over $10,000 to the Treasury Department.

bantam store Also called **vest-pocket supermarket.** A small convenience store generally open 24 hours a day.

bar chart A graph consisting of bars of uniform width but varying lengths proportional to the numbers they represent, permitting comparison of amounts of items or variables.

bar code A series of lines of varying width, printed on a product, package, etc., that can be read by an optical scanner to determine charges for purchases, destinations for letters, etc. See also **Universal Product Code.**

bargain and sale deed A deed transferring title to real property with no guarantee of the title or of the use of the property.

bargaining strategy A plan devised to permit two negotiating parties with differing opinions to reach agreement within the limits imposed by their organizational objectives.

bargaining unit A group of employees within an organization who are represented by a particular labor union.

barter An exchange of goods and/or services by two or more parties without the use of money, credit, or formal documents.

barter plan A trading arrangement (often found in the communications industry) by which advertising time on television or space in a publication may be paid for in merchandise or services rather than money.

base pay Pay received for a given work period, as an hour or week, but not including additional pay, as for overtime work.

base period A period of time selected as a reference point to define a time frame, so that changes in prices or other economic indicators over the designated interval can be assessed.

base-point pricing The calculation of freight charges on the basis of distance from a geographical location that differs from the point of origin of the goods shipped (often a place within a state where a major competitor is located) for the purpose of reducing freight fees charged and thus enhancing the shipper's competitive position or of charging customers for freight costs not paid by the seller. See also **phantom freight.**

base-stock method A method of costing inventory (no longer acceptable for tax purposes) which assumes a minimum inventory that must be kept on hand, valued at its acquisition cost; items added to this base stock are valued on the basis of last in, first out.

BASIC (*acronym for* Beginners' All-Purpose Symbolic Instruction Code) An easy-to-use computer programming language, developed in the 1960's. See also **COBOL.**

basic research Investigation or experimentation for the purpose of increasing knowledge or understanding. See also **applied research.**

basic stock A retail store's stock of merchandise consisting of items that the store intends to keep on hand for approximately a year and lists in a form that indicates when stock is nearly depleted and should be reordered.

basis The acquisition cost or book value of an asset, which is subtracted from the selling price of that asset to determine capital gain or loss.

basis point One hundredth of one percent, as of interest rates or investment yields.

basket purchase Also called **lump-sum purchase.** The purchase of several assets for a single price; for accounting purposes, each asset is assigned a cost to be entered into the proper account, the sum of all such costs equaling the cost of the basket purchase.

batch processing The processing of all related materials or documents at one time; in computers, the execution of programs by sets, so that each program within a set is completed before the next is begun.

battleground map A map designating all branch stores and competitive stores within a retailer's trading area.

bean counter (*informal*) A person who makes judgments chiefly on the basis of numerical calculations.

bearer bond A bond payable to any person who presents it, such person being presumed to be its owner. See **bond** (def. 1).

bearer instrument A legal instrument that is not registered and is negotiated merely by delivery.

bear hug A takeover offer in which a company is willing to pay a price significantly higher than the target company's market value.

bearish **1.** Pessimistic, especially about stock prices. **2.** (of stock prices) Generally declining.

bear market A stock market characterized by a general decline in prices. See also **bull market.**

BE cluster See **belief-evaluation cluster.**

beginning inventory The value of an inventory at the beginning of an accounting period.

behavioral modeling A training technique in which a trainee role-plays a situation calling for particular skills; a trainer then evaluates the effectiveness of the skills demonstrated and shows the trainee how to adopt a new pattern of behavior demonstrated by a model, in the hope that the new behaviors can be transferred to the individual's work situation.

behavioral science **1.** The body of disciplines (psychology, sociology, anthropology) encompassing the study of human behavior. **2.** A branch of experimental psychology that emphasizes the influence of the immediate consequences of actions on subsequent learning and performance.

behavior analysis See **applied behavior analysis.**

behavior modification A program of systematic reward for desired behavior and withholding of reward for undesired behavior, for the purpose of increasing desired behavior and reducing or eliminating undesired behavior. See also **coercive reward and punishment system.**

belief-evaluation cluster (*abbr* BE cluster) The collection of impressions, ideas, and judgments, subject to change with new information and experience, which make up an individual's attitude toward a subject.

below par Below face value; (a stock) offered for sale at a price lower than the amount appearing on the face.

below-the-line 1. Referring to an expense or source of income that is unique or unusual. 2. (*motion pictures*) Referring to the production costs of a film (e.g., settings and costumes, camera crews, sound effects). See also **above-the-line.**

benchmark Also called **yardstick.** 1. Anything that serves as a standard against which other things are compared and measured; a reference point. 2. (*advertising, marketing research*) A variable (e.g., brand awareness) that is measured before and after an advertising campaign to help determine the campaign's effectiveness in influencing the target audience to buy the product.

beneficial interest The right to receive a benefit from property that one does not own.

beneficiary 1. A person who receives benefits or income. 2. A person who will legally receive an amount of money or property at the death of another person, as stipulated by a contract or will. 3. One who benefits from the act of another.

benefit 1. Financial or other assistance offered to employees in addition to salaries and wages. See also **compensation; employee benefit plan; fringe benefit.** 2. A significant advantage that a customer can expect to enjoy as a result of purchasing a product (emphasized in consumer-oriented selling).

benevolent leadership Also called **system 2 management.** A style of leadership that emphasizes the formal roles of superiors and subordinates, discourages interaction between them, maintains strict control, and initiates any communication, while fostering a psychological closeness to subordinates that maintains discipline through apprehension and sometimes fear.

bequest A gift of property bestowed by a will.

best-case scenario The best possible outcome of a situation.

beta Also called **Beta Factor.** A measure of a stock's volatility, based on the volatility of the market as a whole. A stock having a beta of 1.1 would be considered 10 percent more volatile than the market average.

Better Business Bureau A nonprofit organization established by business leaders to promote ethical business practices, investigate complaints of unethical practices, and expose unethical businesses to the public: branches in most major cities.

betterment An improvement made to an asset in order to enhance its performance or productivity or to prolong its useful life, the cost of which is added to the asset account for later depreciation.

bid 1. To elicit prices from a number of competitive vendors. 2. To offer a price or prices for a job to be done for a potential client or for a stock.

bid and asked The amount offered (bid) for a stock by a prospective buyer and the amount asked for that stock by a prospective seller, reported in over-the-counter stock quotations. See also **asked price; bid price.**

bid peddling The practice of reporting a low bid to potential suppliers of goods or services in an attempt to elicit an offer lower than the one reported.

bid price Also called **quoted bid.** The highest price a securities dealer will pay for a given stock. See also **asked price.**

big bath A write-off of extensive asset costs for the purpose of shedding an unprofitable line of business or of eliminating the need for gradual write-offs in future periods.

big board The enormous wall of the New York Stock Exchange where quotations and other information are displayed; by extension, the New York Stock Exchange itself.

big-ticket item An item that commands a very high price.

big-ticket sales Sales of big-ticket items. See also **megaselling.**

bilateral Affecting two parties reciprocally.

bilateral contract A contract by whose terms two parties are bound by reciprocal obligations. See also **unilateral contract.**

bill An invoice submitted to a purchaser detailing the costs of products sold or services rendered, applicable taxes, total amount due, and due date.

billing cycle See **cycle billing.**

bill of exchange Also called **draft.** A written order (e.g., a check) signed by one person (the drawer) requiring that a sum of money be paid to a second person (the payee) by a third party (the drawee), who indicates his or her willingness to pay by writing "Accepted" on it and signing it.

bill of labor A list of the standard times required in each work center to produce one unit of a specific product.

bill of lading A receipt for goods accepted for shipment given by a transportation company to a shipper. See also **order bill of lading.**

bill of materials A list of the quantities of all parts and material needed to complete the production of one unit of a specific product.

bill of sale A written statement of the transfer of ownership of personal property or of the rendering of services, proving past title to property transferred but not proving present ownership.

binary system A system consisting of two components or offering two alternatives (e.g., yes/no, go/no-go). See also **bit.**

binder 1. A temporary insurance policy that extends coverage to an applicant for a policy until the regular policy can be issued, such coverage generally being in effect from the moment that the insurance agent accepts the application. 2. Money or a receipt for money paid to the owner of real estate for the exclusive right to purchase the property at terms agreed upon or to be agreed upon by buyer and seller.

bingo card A prepaid postcard inserted in a magazine by its publisher that a reader can return to order free information about advertisers' products.

bird dog A person who is paid by a salesperson to identify prospective customers (a practice considered all but unethical in some industries).

birdyback The transportation of goods by truck in a trailer that is then loaded directly onto an air carrier for delivery to an airport near its destination.

bit (*from* binary dig*it*) A single digit, either 0 or 1, used in a binary system of numeration; the smallest unit of information storage for a computer.

blacklist A secret list circulated among employers to prevent union organizers and other antagonistic employees from obtaining work.

black market 1. The illicit buying and selling of goods in violation of legal price controls, rationing, etc. 2. A place where such activity is carried on.

Black Monday October 19, 1987, when the Dow Jones Industrial Average fell a record 508 points in trading on the New York Stock Exchange.

Black Tuesday October 29, 1929, when stock values on the New York Stock Exchange collapsed and, after frantic selling, many shares became virtually worthless.

blad (*informal*) A flier or other promotional piece distributed by a company to sell a product.

blank endorsement An endorsement of an instrument (e.g., a check) which does not specify any person to whom payment is to be made, thus making the amount named in the instrument payable to any person who presents it without further endorsement.

blanket agreement An agreement reached by collective bargaining that applies to workers throughout an organization, industry, or geographical area.

blanket lien A lien that gives a creditor the right to seize any or all of a debtor's real property in

business

order to cover an unpaid loan. See also **lien** (def. 2); **specific lien.**

blanket order Also called **open-end order; yearly order.** A purchase order issued by a buyer to cover a year or some other specified period, eliminating the need to issue routine releases and redundant purchase orders throughout the time frame covered.

blanket policy An insurance policy that covers multiple properties, locations, or shipments under one contract.

blind check A system in which a form used for verifying invoice data is circulated between the receiving clerk and the accounting department as a systematic way of double-checking inventory.

blind entry An accounting entry that indicates only the accounts and the amounts debited and credited, without supporting information or explanation.

blister packaging A type of clear packaging that forms a protective bubble of plastic about a product while permitting visual inspection.

block A large holding of stock, commonly considered to be more than 10,000 shares.

blocked need satisfaction Inability to satisfy a need or reach a desired goal, resulting in a state of tension which the individual attempts to reduce by coping behavior that others may interpret as trial-and-error problem-solving behavior. See also **need satisfaction.**

blow-in A piece of advertising inserted in but not attached to a magazine or newspaper, usually printed on stiff card stock.

blowout A quick sellout of securities being offered to the public due to heavy demand.

blue chip A stock issue of a company with a consistent history of earnings and dividend payments, leadership in an established industry, and good prospects of future stability and growth, such that its stock tends not to be subject to sudden or great changes in price and is generally expensive.

blue-collar Belonging or relating to wage-earning workers who wear work clothes or other specialized clothing on the job, as mechanics, longshoremen, and miners.

blue-sky Unsound or of no value; applied to ideas that are beyond the realm of the possible (sometimes interpreted as ideas that are ahead of their time).

blue-sky laws Federal laws designed to protect investors from investing in securities that have no value by empowering such federal agencies as the Securities and Exchange Commission and the U.S. Postal Service to enforce state laws requiring public disclosure of the issuing corporation's financial status and the way in which the money collected from the sale of stocks is to be used.

blurb A brief advertisement or notice, as on a book jacket, especially one expressing praise.

board of directors The group of persons (at least three in most states) at the highest level of organizational responsibility in the modern corporation, with the authority to guide corporate affairs and make general policies.

board of governors The governing body of the Federal Reserve System.

bodily injury liability insurance Insurance that protects the insured against claims and lawsuits resulting from accidental injury or death caused by the insured person's negligence, as in the operation of a motor vehicle.

boiler room A slang term for a roomful of telephone operators who phone prospects, giving sales pitches for investments and investment schemes.

bond 1. An interest-bearing instrument issued by a corporation or governmental body as evidence of a long-term debt, usually incurred for a specific purpose. See also **bearer bond; convertible bond; corporate bond; coupon bond; government bond; municipal bond. 2.** An agreement under which an insurer agrees to indemnify the insured for losses caused by the act, negligence, or default of a third party, or by circumstances over which the third party has no control. **3.** The state of goods being

manufactured, transported, or held in the care of an agency covered by such a bond pending payment of taxes ("in bond").

bonded warehouse 1. A warehouse in which goods stored are insured against loss or damage. **2.** A warehouse in which goods stored are in bond to the government pending payment of taxes. See also **bond** (def. 3).

bond fund A mutual fund that invests primarily in specialized corporate bonds or in municipal bonds, usually charging an initial sales fee (included in the offering price) plus an annual management fee that seldom exceeds 1 percent of the fund's net asset value. See also **bond** (def. 1).

bondholder The current owner of a bond.

bonding company An organization that insures a party against loss caused by a third party. See also **bond** (def. 2).

bond rating Evaluation of a corporation's or state or local government's ability to honor the debt represented by the bonds it issues, made on the basis of the issuer's debt level and past payment record, the coupon rate, the security of the assets backing the bonds, and any other relevant data. Bond ratings are usually classified as follows: AAA (highest quality), AA (high quality), A (upper medium grade), BBB (medium grade), BB (mostly speculative), B (low grade, speculative), CCC (poor), CC (highly speculative), C (lowest quality), D (in default).

bond refunding Issuance of additional bonds (and thus the incurring of additional debt) for the purpose of acquiring the funds needed to redeem outstanding bonds.

bond table A schedule for determination of the current value of bonds as a function of their coupon rates, times to maturity, and effective yields until maturity.

bonus A payment to an employee in addition to the regular wage or salary, intended as motivation for increased productivity, an incentive to remain with the company, or as a supplemental reward.

bonus circulation Copies of a publication distributed in excess of the number guaranteed to advertisers by the publisher.

bonus method A method of calculating partners' shares in a business whereby a new partner is credited with an amount in excess of the capital he or she has actually contributed by transfer of capital from the accounts of the old partners to that of the new. See also **goodwill method.**

book inventory The amount of stock shown to be on hand by a perpetual inventory method; total purchases to date less sales, markdowns, and discounts.

bookkeeping The keeping of account books or systematic records of money transactions: distinguished from accounting, which is the analysis of such records. See also **double-entry bookkeeping; single-entry bookkeeping.**

book of original entry See **journal.**

books The financial records of a business.

book value 1. The value of a share of common stock calculated by subtracting all liabilities (including liquidation value of outstanding preferred stock) from total assets and dividing the result by the number of outstanding common shares. See also **market value. 2.** The current value of equipment or other depreciable capital asset after all accumulated depreciation has been subtracted from its acquisition cost.

book-value shares Shares of stock offered to executives at a price equal to their book value rather than at their market price, with the understanding that when the book value has risen, the company will buy back the stock at the increased book-value price or will make payments in stock equal to the appreciation in book value.

boom Any period of economic prosperity (opposite of *bust*).

boondoggle Any wasteful, inefficient, and generally useless program or activity.

booster A shoplifter.

boot Also called **boot money.** An amount of cash paid along with an asset traded for another, more valuable asset.

bootlegging 1. Illegal movement of goods and materials for the purpose of avoiding payment of taxes. **2.** Movement of illegal goods.

borrow to carry inventory To borrow money in order to pay the costs of seasonal inventories that must be purchased substantially in advance of sales.

bottleneck Any operation whose capacity is insufficient to meet requirements, resulting in reduced system output and often the buildup of inventory prior to that operation.

bottom line 1. The sum or result of all items listed above the last line of a balance sheet or financial statement; thus, final profit or loss. **2.** The final result. **3.** The ultimate objective or the critical issue.

bottom management Collectively the people who hold lower-level supervisory positions in a company but do not become directly involved in major corporate decision-making, marketing, or forecasting activities. See also **management pyramid; top management.**

boundary-spanning unit An informally organized group created to meet a short-term objective or to work on a special problem unique to the organization that called it into being. See also **ad hoc committee.**

bounded rationality A tendency to choose facile and easily workable solutions to problems over more difficult courses of action that might be of greater long-term value but that would be more immediately costly in time and money.

bourse A stock exchange, esp. the stock exchange of certain European cities.

boutique agency An advertising agency that specializes in a specific service or phase of advertising (e.g., copywriting).

boycott 1. An organized refusal to buy or handle a company's products or use its services, as well as an attempt to persuade others not to do so in order to express disapproval or exert pressure. **2.** To engage in such a concerted action.

BPI (*abbr for* buying-power *index*) See **consumer price index.**

bracket creep Also called **tax-bracket creep.** The gradual movement of a wage earner into a higher federal income-tax bracket as a result of wage increases intended to offset inflation. Since tax rates also tend to increase during inflation, the individual is often left with no corresponding increase in real income.

brainstorming A technique for solving a specific problem by which group members gather together and spontaneously offer as many ideas as possible in a nonthreatening atmosphere, each idea offered generating others.

branch accounting The keeping of records by a branch office, until they are combined with those of all other branches and of the main office in a single financial statement.

brand The name or symbol of a product or service; an identifying mark intended to differentiate a product or line of products from those offered by competitors. See also **trademark.**

brand awareness Conscious knowledge by consumers that a particular brand of merchandise is available.

brand image The impression of a brand held in the minds of consumers or conveyed by the physical and qualitative characteristics of the product or products with which it is associated and by advertising and publicity.

brand leader A brand that is the leading seller in its field.

brand loyalty Marked preference for a product of a particular brand over similar brands of other brands.

brand name 1. A word, name, symbol, etc., especially one legally registered as a trademark, used by a manufacturer or merchant to identify its products distinctively from others of the same type and usu-

ally prominently displayed on its goods, in advertising, etc. **2.** A product, line of products, or service bearing a widely known brand name.

brand switching Ceasing to buy a product of a brand that one has been accustomed to using and shifting to another, similar product of a different brand.

breach of contract Failure to carry out the terms of a contract without legal justification, or compliance in an unsatisfactory manner, such that the injured party may sue for damages or for specific performance. See also **anticipatory breach.**

break-even analysis Calculation of the relationship between production costs, both fixed and variable, and income (revenue) generated by that production. See also **break-even point.**

break-even point 1. The amount of sales a business must generate in order to cover the costs of operation. **2.** The point on a graph at which the vector for total revenues (usually plotted against the horizontal axis) meets the vector for total costs (usually plotted against the vertical axis).

breaking bulk The process of dividing a large shipment into smaller lots. See also **bulk breaking.**

bribery The act of promising or giving a monetary or other reward to gain an improper advantage.

bridge loan Also called **swing loan.** A temporary, short-term loan, as for making the down payment on a new house while one's present house is being sold.

broadcast 1. To transmit television or radio signals from a transmitting station to remote terminals. **2.** A television or radio program as it is received by an audience. **3.** To mail promotional material to all dealers simultaneously.

broad-form insurance Insurance that provides more comprehensive coverage than the ordinary policy.

broadside A promotional advertisement, usually very large and inexpensively printed, distributed in quantity as handouts or from door to door.

brochure A pamphlet designed to promote a company's products or services.

broken lot 1. A quantity of manufactured goods insufficient to fill a boxcar or standard container. **2.** See **odd lot.**

broker 1. Also called **registered representative.** An agent, especially a stockbroker, who for a fee or commission negotiates a transaction between a buyer and seller of securities, commodities, or real estate without personally taking title to or possession of the subject of the transaction. **2.** A person who acts as an agent to negotiate on behalf of a principal in the making of a contract with a third party.

brood hen A buyer employed by the main store of a retail chain who buys merchandise for all stores in the chain.

bubble diagram A graphic plan designed for use in structuring environmental space allocated to a department of a company, which may be manipulated before actual construction in order to determine the most desirable locations of line officers and staff.

bucket shop 1. The illegal practice by a broker of accepting an order for stock but not executing the order until the price is more advantageous to the broker. **2.** The practice of selling stocks, usually by phone, but never actually placing the orders. **3.** Any overaggressive brokerage house dealing usually in highly speculative stocks.

budget A plan or schedule detailing income and allocation of expenses, which when complete includes a production budget, a materials budget, a cash budget derived from the production and materials budgets, and pro forma accrual-based income statements and balance sheets.

budget variance 1. The difference between the amount budgeted and the net amount of actual expenditures and receipts. **2.** In a standard cost system, the amount by which overhead exceeds the amount budgeted for it.

buffer stock See **safety stock.**

bug An error in a computer software program. See also **debug**.

built-in obsolescence. See **planned obsolescence.**

bulk breaking The dividing up of large quantities of goods for sale.

bulk discount A price reduction based on volume of purchases.

bulk freight A large quantity of items transported uncrated or unpackaged.

bullion Gold or silver that has been processed, refined, and formed into bars or ingots.

bullish Optimistic.

bull market A stock market characterized by generally rising prices. See also **bear market.**

bundle To offer or supply related products or services in a single transaction at one all-inclusive price.

burden The portion of the cost of manufacturing or business that does not contribute directly to production or operations (e.g., employee fringe benefits, overhead).

bureaucracy An administrative system characterized by diffusion of authority among many departments or divisions and strict adherence to inflexible rules and procedures.

bureaucrat A manager who demonstrates strict conformity to rules and prescribed routines, characterized by a lack of flexibility and initiative, indifference to the needs of others, and a proclivity for referring decisions to superiors.

Bureau of Labor Statistics (*abbr* BLS) A research agency of the U.S. Department of Labor that develops and disseminates statistics on a variety of matters related to employment.

buried position A position in a publication considered unfavorable for an advertisement because the surrounding material either has little attraction to the target audience or distracts attention from the ad.

burn-rate The rate at which start-up capital is used to bring a product to market, usually budgeted to carry over until the product begins to show a profit.

burst A graphic design, usually a notched circle, printed on a product package, cover, or label, or on a direct-mail envelope, and bearing a brief sales pitch.

business Any activity, enterprise, or transaction designed to provide consumers with goods or services for a profit.

Business and Professional Advertisers Association An association of marketing and advertising executives in the industrial goods field.

business cycle A fluctuating pattern of business conditions characterized by successive periods of prosperity, crisis, recession, and recovery which cannot be predicted with assurance by any theory.

business development center A local office of a federally funded program that provides research and consulting services to small businesses.

business environment All of the phenomena and conditions that directly or indirectly influence business.

business ethics A set of principles that guides business practices to reflect a concern for society as a whole while pursuing profits.

business film A film or tape conveying information on a product, service, or other subject of interest to business, professional, or technical audiences. See also **sponsored film; training film.**

business game A training and educational technique designed to improve participants' business skills, incorporating such activities as simulations, action mazes, in-basket experiences, card-sort and functional games concentrating on management principles, long-range planning, decision making, and time management, in which participants engage either individually or as members of a team, the particular activity engaged in being determined by the objectives sought.

business indicator See **economic indicator.**

business interruption insurance Insurance that protects a business against loss in the event of a fire, flood, or other disaster that forces it to suspend operations temporarily.

business market A sphere of business activity in which goods and services are sold to businesses rather than to the general public.

business park 1. See **office park. 2.** See **industrial park.**

business plan A proposal prepared by an entrepreneur for prospective investors, explaining a new business idea, indicating why it represents an attractive investment opportunity, and often outlining ideas for marketing, financing, and operations.

business reply A form of mail, usually sent as an enclosure, which can be mailed back by respondents without their having to pay postage. Business reply cards are often used for sales promotions. Business reply envelopes are used for orders, payments, etc.

business year See **fiscal year.**

bust A sudden severe decline in business and economic activity (opposite of *boom*).

buyback The buying back by a company of its own stock (a) when the market price is low or (b) usually at an inflated price, in an attempt to thwart a takeover.

buyer 1. Any person who makes or seeks to make a purchase. **2.** A person employed by a department store to select, purchase, and price merchandise to be sold in a specific department of the store, and often to supervise the personnel of the department.

buyer's market A market in which goods are available in large quantities and in great variety, so that prices tend to fall as sellers compete for buyers. See also **seller's market.**

buyer's wheel A pocket-size disk marked with figures representing costs, attached to another disk marked with figures representing selling prices, such that when a specific cost is aligned with a specific selling price, the resulting profit margin is shown.

buying by specification Purchasing materials or goods in accordance with requirements precisely described in writing.

buying committee A group of buyers who jointly select products to be purchased, usually for sale in a retail store.

buying on margin Purchasing securities by paying half or more of the purchase price, the remainder being financed as a loan by the broker.

buying power Also called **purchasing power.** The total amount of money available for spending and consumption (liquid assets plus available credit).

buying-power index (*abbr* BPI) See **consumer price index.**

buy out To purchase all of the assets of an existing business or partner.

buzzing Brainstorming as a training technique.

by-bidder An individual who deceptively bids at an auction for the purpose of generating higher bids.

bylaws Rules and regulations devised by a corporation to specify and govern its methods of doing business, generally dealing with matters not covered by local, state, or federal statutes and more unchanging than policies and general operating procedures.

by-product A product created incidentally while manufacturing the main product (e.g., sawdust as a by-product of lumbering), with a sales value insignificant compared with that of the main product; no value is attached to the anticipated sale of a by-product, but for accounting purposes, any income realized from its sale is deducted from the cost of the main product.

Byrnes Act Federal legislation enacted in 1936 to prohibit the use of strikebreakers.

byte A string of eight binary digits (bits) that are processed as a unit by a computer: one byte equals one alphanumeric character. See also **bit.**

CA See **chartered accountant.**

CAA See **Civil Aeronautics Administration.**

cable television A system of transmission of television signals from distant stations via a master antenna and thence by a cable to the television sets of individual subscribers.

CAD See **computer-aided design.**

cafeteria plan A group benefit plan under which employees may choose among various benefits offered those that best fit their own individual needs and situations, up to a specified maximum dollar value. See also **fringe benefit.**

CAI (*abbr for* computer-*assisted* instruction) See **programmed instruction.**

call 1. a. Also called **call option.** An option to buy a stock or commodity at a specified price (call price) within a specified period, purchasable for a premium of a percentage of the current market price of the stock or commodity; if the price rises during the option period, the owner of the option can either buy the shares or commodity for the (lower) price specified or sell the option at a profit. See also **put. b.** To exercise such an option. **2. a.** A notice to a holder of a bond or of preferred stock that the issue is to be redeemed before its normal maturity. See also **callable bond. b.** To issue such a notice. **3. a.** A notice to a stockholder or subscriber that an assessment or subscription to capital is to be paid. **b.** To issue such a notice.

callable bond Also called **redeemable bond.** A bond that the issuing corporation reserves the right to redeem before maturity, as when the general market interest rate has dropped below the interest rate payable on the bond.

callback pay A premium wage paid to a worker who is called back to work after completion of his or her regular work shift.

call option See **call** (def. 1a).

call premium The percentage of a bond's face value that a company must pay in addition to the face value in order to redeem (call) a callable bond.

call price 1. Call premium plus face value. **2.** The specified price at which the owner of a call option may buy stock during a specified period.

CAM See **computer-aided manufacturing.**

cancel 1. To close an account by crediting or paying all outstanding charges. **2.** To eliminate or offset a debit or credit with an entry for an equal amount on the opposite side of a ledger, as when a payment is received on a debt.

canceled check A check that has been redeemed by a bank and then usually returned to the issuer.

cancellation 1. Termination of a contract. **2.** Elimination of a particular business activity.

cap 1. A maximum limit set by law or agreement on prices, wages, spending, interest rates, etc. **2.** See **capitalization.**

capacity The number of units that can be processed in a unit of time; for accounting purposes, capacity can be used to allocate fixed costs for normal amounts of goods to be produced.

capacity costs Fixed costs, consisting of standby costs and enabling costs, incurred to give a company the capacity to produce or operate.

capital 1. a. Long-term assets in which a corporation has invested for the production of goods or services. **b.** The money raised to invest in such assets. **c.** Funds in the form of investments, profits, or loans necessary to finance the operation of a business. **2.** The equity interest of the owners in a company.

capital appreciation An increase in the value of capital assets, usually reflected in the market value of a corporation's securities.

capital assets Land, buildings, machinery, and other major items owned by a business for use in its operations.

capital budget A budget that lists the amount needed to purchase capital items and indicates the source from which the money is to be obtained.

capital expenditure An addition to the value of fixed assets, as by the purchase of a new building.

capital gains Income from the sale of capital assets, formerly subject to special tax breaks, but now taxed as ordinary income. See also **capital losses.**

capital goods Items that usually are treated as long-term investments because of their substantial value and life.

capital-intensive Requiring a greater expenditure for capital assets per unit of production than for labor. See also **labor-intensive.**

capital investment Funds that have been invested in capital goods.

capitalism An economic system, first defined by Adam Smith in 1776, that is based on the law of supply and demand and relies on the institutions of private property, competitive markets, free consumer choice, and minimal government interference. See also **classical economics; invisible hand; law of supply and demand.**

capitalization 1. The total amount of long-term debt (preferred and common stock, bonds, promissory notes, debentures, etc.) and owners' equity. **2.** See **market capitalization.**

capitalization rate The interest rate used to calculate a single present value of a series of future payments, receipts, or earnings or to evaluate the worth of an asset on the basis of its income stream.

capitalize To record as a capital or long-term asset an expenditure that will benefit future periods, permitting depreciation of the asset thus created.

capital lease Also called **financing lease; sales-type lease.** A lease agreement extending over at least 75 percent of the leased asset's useful life and allowing the lessee to buy the asset either for a bargain price or by assuming ownership at the end of the lease period.

capital losses Losses resulting from the sale of capital assets. See also **capital gains.**

capital market A securities market in which securities with maturities of more than one year are traded, so called because such securities (most corporate, municipal, and government bonds, mortgages, and some preferred stocks) ultimately represent claims against capital assets.

capital rationing A capital budgeting measure used to constrain or restrict the total amounts of capital expenditures.

capital shares Shares of stock in a dual-type closed-end investment company which earn no dividends but gain or lose value as the net assets of the company rise or fall. See also **dual distribution.**

capital stock The entire stated value of the shares of stock issued by a corporation.

capital structure The long-term financial foundation of a corporation, consisting of long-term debt, preferred stock, and the net worth of common stock and retained earnings.

capital surplus Also called **additional paid-in capital; paid-in surplus.** The money that comes into a corporation beyond the amount raised by the par or stated value of common and preferred stock issued; the difference between the par value of shares issued and the price actually paid for them plus capital otherwise contributed, as by gifts or donations (part of owners' equity).

capital turnover The rate at which the assets of a business are converted into cash.

captive insurance company An insurance

company established by a business or a group of businesses for the purpose of providing low-cost coverage to the organizations involved.

cardmember A person authorized to use a credit card.

career development See **life planning.**

career-path planning A technique for motivating an employee to consider the company's long-range goals in concert with his or her expectations of personal growth and occupational desires, for the purpose of clarifying the relationship between the employee's chosen career steps and increased responsibility within the organization.

carload lot A shipment of goods that completely fills a rail freight car (and usually costs less per unit of goods to send than a partial carload).

carrier's lien A legal claim against goods pending payment to a carrier for transportation of the goods.

carry-over Also called **carry-back; carry-forward.** Deduction of corporate operating losses from taxable income during the past three years (carry-back) or the next five years (carryforward) in order to reduce overall taxable income when income fluctuates drastically: not applicable if 50 percent of the corporation's securities have changed hands in the last two years or if the corporation changes the business in which it engages.

carry-over effects The long-range effects of a short-term advertising campaign.

cartel 1. A group of people, organizations, or nations joined to limit competition and regulate prices. **2.** A written agreement of trust between two dispassionate parties.

cartouche A decorative frame, frequently oval, enclosing a brand name or symbol.

case divider A divider strip used to organize food sections in a store display, often designed to allow an advertising message to be carried on it.

case method A teaching method that presents for discussion and analysis actual instances of the problem being studied and encourages students to arrive at practical solutions.

case study An intensive analysis of a person, group, community, or other social unit stressing the interaction of developmental and environmental factors.

cash accounting The recording of expenses when they are actually paid and of revenues when they are actually received. See also **accrual accounting.**

cash-and-carry wholesaler A wholesaler who provides goods from a warehouse but no transportation, credit, or other services, and whose prices reflect the savings in expenses thus effected.

cash audit An examination and analysis to determine that all cash has been properly accounted for.

cashbook A journal or ledger used in a simple accounting system to record and keep a balance of all receipts and disbursements of cash.

cash budget A projection indicating expected receipts and expenditures and consequent anticipated need for or surplus of cash.

cash cow A slow-growth company that invests little money in research and development because its existing product lines sell steadily and produce a good profit. See also **dog; star.**

cash discount A deduction from the selling price offered for prompt payment.

cash flow Also called **gross received.** The amount of money generated by a special activity after payment of expenses.

cash-flow cycle The financial process from the time a company buys raw materials until the finished goods have been sold and payment for them has been received.

cashier's check A check issued by a bank, usually in exchange for cash, that is signed by the cashier or other official and that represents an obligation of the bank. See also **certified check.**

cash machine. See **ATM.**

cash surrender value Also called **surrender value.** The actual value of a life insurance policy; the money that the insured will receive if the policy

is canceled or cashed in, which increases with the age of the policy as long as the premiums are paid.

cash trading See **futures trading.**

cash up To total up receipts at closing time, the end of a shift, etc.

casualty insurance Insurance that protects the policyholder against losses resulting from accidents or from such disasters as fire, flood, and wind.

casualty loss A financial loss caused by an unexpected or unusual disaster, such as fire or flood.

catalyst A person who provokes or precipitates action without exercising direct control or influence over the outcome.

causal model A model used in business forecasting, as in regression analysis, that describes the reaction of a variable factor to changes in one or more explanatory variables.

cause-and-effect diagram A diagram that graphically shows the relationship between a problem and its major potential causes as well as the contributory causes: often used in an effort to improve quality.

caveat emptor (*Latin*) Let the buyer beware.

caveat venditor (*Latin*) Let the seller beware.

CD See **certificate of deposit.**

Celler-Kefauver Act An act of Congress passed in 1950 to close loopholes in the Clayton Act by forbidding mergers through the acquisition of a competitor's assets and by other means not covered by the Clayton Act, and authorizing the Federal Trade Commission to approve or deny proposed mergers before they occur.

centerfold Also called **center spread.** An advertisement or other material that occupies the two facing pages at the center of a magazine. See also **double-page spread; double-truck spread.**

central corporate expenses The overhead expenses of operating a corporate headquarters and its activities, exclusive of manufacturing overhead.

centralization Concentration of power in the hands of executives, who delegate only limited decision-making authority to lower-level managers.

centralized functional design An organizational design in which decision-making power is concentrated at the top of the system, with each department or division (e.g., marketing, production, sales, personnel) headed by an executive, usually a vice president, who is accountable to a chief executive officer, who in turn is responsible for strategic planning and coordination of the divisions or subsystems of the organization.

central limit theorem An important statistical theorem that the distribution of the sums of a large number of samples of random variables will, when plotted, fit a normal, or bell-shaped, curve, regardless of the type of distribution from which the samples were obtained.

central processing unit (*abbr* CPU) The main internal part of a computer, encompassing a control unit, an arithmetic-logic unit, and a main or internal memory, which controls all operations of the system, provides primary storage of data, and transfers data

cents-off promotion A promotion of merchandise through a price reduction of less than $1, advertised on the product's package either alone or in combination with other advertising.

CEO chief executive officer (of a company).

Certificate in Management Accounting (*abbr* CMA) A certificate awarded by the National Association of Accountants' Institute of Management Accounting after the candidate has passed an examination and met other requirements.

certificate of deposit (*abbr* CD) A deposit account in a bank or savings and loan association, usually for a minimum of $1000 and with a maturity of from 30 days to several years, from which money usually cannot be withdrawn without loss of interest or other penalty and which earns interest at a rate established by law for accounts of less than $100,000 or at a rate that may be negotiable for larger accounts.

certificate of incorporation A document issued

by a state government authorizing an organization to operate as a corporation.

certificate of indebtedness A note that specifies the amount of a debt and the time limit or repayment schedule.

certified check A depositor's check drawn on a bank and bearing the words "certified" or "accepted" and the signature of a bank official; in effect, the bank certifies that money to cover the check is on deposit and will be set aside until the check is presented by the payee. See also **cashier's check.**

certified financial statement A set of financial papers that generally carry a CPA's acknowledgment that they are fairly presented, usually as a result of extensive review and testing.

certified internal auditor (*abbr* CIA) An auditor who has satisfied the experience, ethics, educational, and examination requirements established by the Institute of Internal Auditors.

certified public accountant (*abbr* CPA) A person who has satisfied the requirements for education and/or experience established by the state in which he or she practices and who has passed the Uniform Certified Public Accountants' Examination and met other statutory requirements, and thus is authorized to express an audit opinion on the fairness of corporate financial statements and to perform other work reserved to CPAs.

CFO chief financial officer (of a company).

CFP Certified Financial Planner. See also **financial planner.**

chain of command The path of authority from the lowest-ranking worker to the highest-ranking supervisor/manager; a pattern of authority and responsibility.

chairman of the board The presiding officer of a corporation's board of directors, who manages its activities and delegates responsibilities to its top officers (i.e., the president and/or the chief executive officer), on either a full-time or a part-time basis.

change agent A person who is responsible for mobilizing an organization's resources; an expediter or facilitator.

channels of distribution The paths goods follow from the producer through intermediaries, if any, to the consumer, including all transportation systems and storage facilities used.

Chapter 11 A section of the Bankruptcy Reform Act of 1978, under which a company unable to pay its debts may petition a court for permission to retain its assets while reorganizing in an effort to regain profitability; continued failure to pay debts following reorganization may result in liquidation of the company by distribution of its assets first to its creditors and then, if any assets remain, to its common stockholders.

charge 1. (*bookkeeping*) **a.** A debit to an account. **b.** To enter such a debit. **2.** To buy on credit, thus incurring a debit in one's charge account in the seller's ledger.

charge and discharge statement A trustee or fiduciary's periodic report on the resources received and their disposition.

charge card See **credit card.**

charge off To treat what was originally assumed to be an asset as a loss or expense: usually an indication that the charge (debit) is not equal to its earlier stated value.

charismatic power Power derived from the ability to inspire and motivate by force of personality. See also **expert power; legitimate power.**

charter A written instrument of a state government granting an organization the rights, privileges, and immunities of a corporation. See also **articles of incorporation.**

chartered accountant (*abbr* CA) The British equivalent of the certified public accountant in the United States.

chartered financial analyst (*abbr* CFA) An individual who has passed a series of examinations and demonstrated expertise in securities investing.

chartered life underwriter (*abbr* CLU) An indi-

vidual who has met the standards established by the American College of Life Underwriters.

chart of accounts A company's list of all bookkeeping accounts and their assigned codes.

chattel mortgage An agreement by which a car, truck, agricultural machine, or other movable equipment becomes collateral for a loan of money to purchase it; until or unless the lender must seize the property for nonpayment, the borrower retains ownership of it with attendant risk of damage or loss.

checking account A bank deposit against which checks can be drawn by the depositor. Cf. **savings account.**

checking copy A copy of a magazine supplied to an advertiser for the purpose of gaining approval of the position and appearance of the advertiser's ad.

checkoff The authorized withholding of union dues and assessments from employees' wages for transmittal to the union that represents them.

check register 1. A written record of issued checks detailing check number, date, payee, amount, and purpose of payment, with a running balance maintained for the account. **2.** A format for the keeping of such records, as a series of check stubs or journals or a program for computer printouts.

cherry picking Selection by a buyer of only a few items out of a vendor's complete line.

chief executive officer (*abbr* CEO) A manager (usually chairman of the board or president) who occupies the most powerful position in a corporation, with responsibility for setting company policies under the guidance of the board of directors and for supervising the executives who carry out those policies.

chief financial officer (*abbr* CFO) The company executive empowered to make the financial decisions necessary to carry out company policy.

chief operating officer (*abbr* COO) A manager responsible for administering and supervising the day-to-day operations of a company under the direction of the chief executive officer and/or the board of directors.

chip Also called **microchip.** A tiny slice of semiconducting material (usually silicon) on which an integrated circuit is formed.

chronological stabilization Also called **spread-loss plan.** Periodic repayment to an insurance company of a sum received under the terms of a policy; a method of risk management that allows an insurer to assume a higher degree of risk than would be the case under regular insurance.

churn (*stock market*) To trade a customer's securities excessively in order to earn more commissions.

CIF (*abbr for* cost, insurance, freight) An indication that the price quoted in a shipping contract includes the cost of freight and insurance until delivery at the port whence the goods will be shipped.

CIM See **computer-integrated manufacturing.**

circularization An auditor's confirmation of the validity of accounts payable and receivable by direct contact of customers and suppliers involved in those accounts.

circulation 1. The approximate number of copies of a newspaper or magazine that are distributed at each printing. **2.** The number of homes in which a particular television show is regularly viewed.

civil action A lawsuit filed by an individual who seeks to recover damages resulting from an invasion of his or her personal rights.

Civil Aeronautics Administration (*abbr* CAA) A governmental agency established in 1940 to regulate nonmilitary aviation.

Civil Rights Act of 1964 Federal legislation enacted to promote equal opportunity by prohibiting discrimination against any individual on the basis of race, creed, or national origin.

claim 1. A demand for payment, reimbursement, or compensation, as under the terms of contract or an insurance policy. **2.** A statement, usually included as the final paragraph of a patent specification, that clearly explains and describes the unique nature of an invention as created by the applicant, and which ultimately serves as the protection conferred by the patent.

classical administrative theory A theory of high-level management functions that emphasizes five fundamental components of managerial activity (planning, organizing, commanding, coordinating, controlling), each subdivided into a specialization of tasks, chain of command, unity of direction, tenure, and centralization of authority.

classical economics The economic concepts developed in 18th and 19th-century England by Adam Smith, David Ricardo, and John Stuart Mill, which constituted the first formulation of the capitalist system and were generally held in England and the United States until the Great Depression of the 1930s demonstrated a lack of correspondence between the theory and reality. See also **Keynesian economics.**

classical theory of motivation The theory that the individual worker is motivated primarily by money and therefore will perform tasks according to company standards only if payment is made contingent on performance.

classification 1. Collectively, all items of a given category or use or sharing common characteristics. **2.** A system, method, or act of categorizing.

classified ad Also called **classified advertisement, want ad.** A brief advertisement in a newspaper, magazine, or the like, dealing with offers of or requests for jobs, houses, apartments, used cars, etc.

Clayton Act An act of Congress passed in 1914 to discourage monopolies by declaring illegal such business practices as tying contracts, interlocking directorates, purchase of large quantities of a competitor's stock, and discriminatory pricing.

Clean Air Act Federal legislation enacted in 1970 to require emission controls on sources of air pollution and to establish air-quality standards that the states must meet within a specified time limit.

clearing account An account (e.g., an income summary account) in which money accumulates until it is transferred to another account (e.g., retained earnings) at the end of the fiscal year or accounting period.

clearinghouse An institution where representatives of member banks meet to exchange checks, drafts, notes, and other instruments drawn on each other's banks.

client bank A treasury of customers or users of one's services or products, related or unrelated, which encompasses the total inventory of accounts of the organization or individual providing such services or products.

client rough A preliminary layout of an ad or other promotional material that is shown to a client for approval before the material is prepared in final form.

client system A system (organization, unit, group) that is the object of a change strategy by a consultant or other professional.

close 1. The end of the selling process; the conversion of a prospect into a customer. See also **objection. 2.** To finalize the transaction in which a property is sold to a new customer.

closed corporation A corporation owned by a few individuals who seldom sell their stock and so retain control.

closed display A merchandising display case, usually covered by glass, that permits no access to goods by customers. See also **open display.**

closed-end credit 1. Credit, such as a bank loan, that is limited to a specified amount, so that any further money sought can be obtained only in the form of a new loan. **2.** A loan payable in monthly installments or by a specified date. See also **open-end credit.**

closed-end investment company An investment company that is capitalized by a public offering of usually common stock, which is traded on an exchange or over the counter. See also **open-end investment company.**

closed-end mortgage bond A corporate bond backed by property that is guaranteed not to back

another bond issue or otherwise be used as collateral. See also **open-end mortgage bond.**

closed shop A place of business where by agreement with a union the employer hires only union members and keeps in employment only union members in good standing (illegal under the provisions of the Taft-Hartley Act). See also **union shop.**

closed system A method of decision making that takes into account only the system under observation, without regard to the influence of environmental factors on its activity.

closely held Referring to a corporation whose stock is held by a few individuals. See also **closed corporation.**

closing 1. The accounting activities performed at the end of a period of time, generally one year, including the preparation of closing entries and financial statements. **2.** The final act in securing a sale or purchase: the delivery of final payments and the transfer of title.

closing date 1. The latest date on which an advertisement can arrive at a publisher or broadcaster to be eligible for appearance in the next scheduled issue or program. **2.** The date on which a real estate transaction is to be finalized.

closing inventory See **ending inventory.**

closure 1. An act or instance of finishing or bringing to a conclusion. **2.** Perception of incomplete figures, objects, or situations as though they were complete by the process of ignoring missing parts or filling them in from experience, whether consciously or unconsciously; a manifestation of the human tendency to seek wholeness.

cluster analysis A marketing procedure involving the sorting through of quantities of information on consumer behavior and the grouping of similar behaviors and attitudes in regard to a product, with the object of identifying patterns that may indicate typical responses to a product among various population segments.

cluster sampling A random sampling method involving the grouping (clustering) of items according to time period, type, or some other identifiable characteristic, the random selection of some of those clusters, and the subsequent analysis or examination of the clusters chosen.

CMA See **Certificate in Management Accounting.**

coalition bargaining Negotiation with an employer by two or more unions acting in concert, with the expectation that together they will have greater bargaining strength than any one of them alone.

COBOL (acronym for Common Business-Oriented Language) A computer programming language that uses common English business terms. See also **BASIC.**

COBRA (acronym for Consolidated Omnibus Budget Reconciliation Act) See **continuation of benefits.**

c.o.d. (abbr for cash on delivery) A method of purchasing goods whereby the customer agrees to pay for the purchase in full when it is delivered.

codetermination Participation by workers in such decision-making activities as planning for modernization and expansion, selection of production methods, hiring and firing of management personnel, and planning of mergers, layoffs, investments, and declaration of dividends.

codicil A formal addendum to a legal document, usually a will, which may take the form of an addition to the original document or a separate paper, and which must be developed with all the formalities of the original document.

coercive power The capacity to dominate others by controlling punishment, withholding information or membership, and demoting or firing.

coercive reward and punishment system A motivational technique that employs coercion in the form of punishment for objectionable behavior and rewards for acceptable behavior. See also **behavior modification.**

c.o.g. (abbr for customer-owned goods) Goods already paid for.

cognitive approach An approach to the acquisition of knowledge characterized by the gathering of facts and the application of logic.

cognitive dissonance Incongruity between two related perceptions or opinions, resulting in a state of tension that the individual tries to reduce by altering one of the perceptions.

cognitive style A style of learning based on teacher-directed activities, lectures, and readings. See also **experimental learning.**

coinsurance 1. A form of casualty insurance in which the insured is required to maintain coverage on the property insured at a certain minimum percentage of its estimated replacement value in order to avoid a penalty in the event of loss. **2.** The percentage of total property value covered by fire insurance, agreed upon and maintained by the insured, which the insurer will pay in the event of loss by fire. **3.** A form of major medical insurance in which payments for hospital and medical treatment for illness or injury are shared by the insurer and the insured in a prescribed ratio.

COLA (*acronym for* cost-of-living adjustment) See **cost-of-living escalator.**

cold call A visit or phone call to a prospective customer without an appointment or a previous introduction.

cold canvassing Systematic coverage by cold calls of a geographical area by a salesperson.

Colgate doctrine A Supreme Court decision incorporated in the Robinson-Patman Act (1936), acknowledging the seller's right to conduct business or to refuse to conduct business with any dealer or other person.

collar (*stock exchange slang*) Official restrictions imposed on computerized program trading when the Dow Jones rises or falls 50 points or more in one day's trading.

collateral Also called **collateral security.** An asset that a lender is entitled by law to seize from a borrower if the loan is not repaid in accordance with the terms agreed upon.

collection 1. The presentation of a draft, check, etc., for payment. **2.** The process of receiving or compelling payment of a debt.

collective bargaining Negotiation by representatives of an employer and a union of the terms of a contract covering wages and working conditions of union members.

comaker A person who formally agrees to repay a loan made to another person if the borrower fails to pay.

COMEX Commodity Exchange, New York.

comfort letter A CPA's letter to an underwriter or legal counsel attesting that financial statements submitted in regard to a securities offering are not false or misleading.

commercial See **announcement.**

commercial bank A bank chartered by a state government or by the federal government to offer a full range of financial services, including checking and savings accounts, short-term business and personal loans, foreign currency exchange, and the discounting of promissory notes and drafts.

commercial goods Goods and services used by companies in carrying on their businesses.

commercial paper 1. Collectively, negotiable instruments in the form of drafts or notes. **2.** Collectively, short-term notes with maturities of less than a year, usually in amounts of $15,000 or more, issued by corporations to provide working capital and purchasable at a discount (below face value) or on an interest-bearing basis and sellable before maturity.

commercial paper house A company that buys commercial paper from corporations for resale, either on order from a customer or on its own account.

commercial protection See **product protection.**

commission A percentage of the price charged for a good or service paid to a salesperson or agent.

commission house An agency that negotiates the sale of goods and receives payment on the basis of volume of goods sold.

committed cost The fixed, long-term cost incurred when an asset is bought, leased, or modified, which cannot be readily reduced or liquidated and is not affected by short-term fluctuations in production levels.

committee An advisory group, ideally made up of people with a vested interest in the organization, responsible for identifying the needs of a unit or subsystem. See also **ad hoc committee.**

committee buying Selection of merchandise to be ordered for sale in a retail store by a group rather than by an individual buyer. See also **buying committee.**

committee organization An organizational structure in which authority and responsibility are held jointly by a group, usually consisting of high-level officers of the corporation, rather than by one executive.

Commodities Futures Trading Commission (*abbr* CFTC) An independent federal agency that regulates the commodities futures markets in the United States.

commodity A product of agriculture, animal husbandry, lumbering, or mining, in contrast to services, and usually excluding manufacturing.

commodity approach A method of studying marketing that focuses on the means by which products move from producers to consumers. See also **functional approach; institutional approach.**

commodity exchange A trading facility similar to a stock exchange, such as the Chicago Board of Trade or the New York Mercantile Exchange, where members meet to trade commodities up to a year or more in advance of their delivery dates.

common carrier A company that offers transportation services for goods or people to the general public at uniform rates.

common cost See **joint cost.**

common law The system of unwritten law governing the rights and duties of individuals, based on principles established by judicial decisions, such that all new decisions or interpretations set precedents for future decisions, but which in the absence of a precedent is capable of being modified and adapted to new circumstances. See also **public law.**

common market 1. An economic alliance that provides for common tariffs and attempts to bring the trade rules of all participating governments into agreement. **2. Common Market** See **European Economic Community.**

common share See **common stock.**

common-size statement A financial statement in which amounts are expressed in percentages of some base figure, usually total assets or revenues, which is listed as equaling 100 percent.

common stock Stock issued by a corporation with no guarantee of dividends, which if declared are distributed after the holders of preferred stock have received their guaranteed share of corporate profits, but with the right to vote on matters presented at the corporation's annual meeting. See also **preferred stock.**

common stock fund A mutual fund that invests only in common stock, as a result of either a decision made or a policy set forth in its charter.

community-planning legislation Legislation empowering a local government to develop and implement plans to control community growth.

comp (*abbr for* comprehensive layout) A presumably final version of a printed advertisement presented to the client for approval.

company loan A loan or guarantee of a bank loan, often at a low interest rate and with generous repayment terms, made by a company to an executive, usually to enable the executive to exercise a stock option.

company-sponsored tax shelter A limited partnership organized usually by a privately held company to provide its executives with a means of sheltering income from taxes.

comparable worth The belief or practice that (1)

employees having identical responsibilities or performing identical tasks should receive comparable or identical wages, and (2) that women should receive comparable wages to men for the same work. See also **two-tier wage plan.**

comparative advantage theory A theory of foreign trade that holds that all trading partners would benefit if each country were to specialize in the products that it can produce most cheaply (those in which it has a comparative advantage) and trade them for the specialized products of other nations (in which they have a comparative advantage).

comparative financial statement A comprehensive financial statement that provides detailed figures for both the current and preceding periods, so that they may be compared. See also **historical summary.**

compensating balance The minimum amount of a line of credit that a customer of a bank is expected to maintain.

compensation A benefit in the form of money or an equivalent beyond the basic salary or wage paid for time on the job (e.g., employee services, health insurance, time off with pay, retirement benefits).

competition Also called **competitive market.** A market condition in which a large number of independent buyers and sellers vie with each other for identical goods and services, trade with each other without restriction, and freely enter and leave the market.

compiler A computer translation program that converts programs from the programmer's language (e.g., BASIC, FORTRAN) into a language of binary numbers (machine language).

complementary products Products that are generally used in combination (e.g., shampoo and hair conditioner, razors and blades).

completed-contract method An accounting method in which the profits from a long-term project are not entered on the books until the project is completed.

composite estimate A prediction of total sales based on the collective estimates of all district managers, each assessing future sales in his or her own territory on the basis of past events. See also **correlation; time series analysis.**

compound interest Interest calculated on the basis of principal plus interest previously credited.

compound journal entry A journal entry that requires more than one debit and one credit, as in the instance of revenue received partly in cash and partly in securities.

comprehensive advertising Advertising in which the advertised brand is compared with competitive brands.

comprehensive insurance Insurance that covers loss of or damage (e.g., to a motor vehicle) as a result of theft, fire, flood, windstorm, vandalism, rain, or lightning.

comprehensive major medical insurance Employee health insurance characterized by high maximum benefits, a low deductible, and a coinsurance feature.

comp time Time off from work, granted to an employee in lieu of overtime pay; compensatory time.

comptroller See **controller.**

compulsory arbitration Mediation of a labor dispute, initiated by the federal government or another outside agency with the power to require both labor and management to accept the arbitrator's decisions. See also **arbitration.**

computer A complex electronic machine that can be programmed to perform computations and to analyze, sort, compare, store, and edit huge quantities of information. See also **hardware; software.**

computer-aided design (*abbr* CAD) The use of computers, especially computer graphics, to develop new products, packaging, manufacturing processes, etc.

computer-aided manufacturing (*abbr* CAM) The use of computers in the manufacturing process, especially to control the operation of an assembly line. See also **robotics.**

computer-assisted fraud (*abbr* CAF) Illegal entry into and use of a confidential data base. See also **fraud.**

computer graphics Images created on a display screen by the use of a computer linked with additional electronic devices.

computer-integrated manufacturing (*abbr* CIM) The use of computers to control, on a real-time basis, the complete manufacturing cycle, including design, planning, and manufacture.

computer-output microfilm (*abbr* COM) Microfilm in either roll or card form on which materials are printed by computer to reduce the amount of space required to store them.

COMSAT (*acronym for Com*munications and *Satel*lite Corporation) A cooperative communications network of businesspeople who supply management and satellite expertise to government representatives upon request.

concentration A clustering of production plants, factories, or warehouses within a designated geographical area. See also **dispersion.**

conciliation Intervention in a labor dispute by a third party who has no power to compel the opposing parties to reach agreement but relies on persuasion.

conditional sale A sale that is subject to the fulfillment of a stated condition (e.g., full payment of the selling price) before title to the merchandise is passed from seller to buyer.

condition precedent A condition that must be fulfilled before title to merchandise can pass from seller to buyer.

condition subsequent A condition that must be fulfilled after title to merchandise has passed from seller to buyer (e.g., a warranty).

condominium 1. An apartment house, office building, or other multiple-unit complex, the units of which are individually owned, with each owner receiving a deed to the unit purchased, including the right to sell or mortgage that unit, and sharing in joint ownership of any common grounds, passageways, etc. 2. A unit in such a building.

conduit A channel through which something is transmitted, such as untaxed dividends passed along to investors by an investment organization. Fannie Mae Remics, for example, are "real estate mortgage-investment conduits."

conference call A telephone call that interconnects three or more phones simultaneously.

confidential disclosure Divulgation of information under the terms of a disclosure agreement.

confirmation A detailed description of the terms of a securities transaction supplied by a broker to a customer.

conflict management Judicious use of disagreements between individuals or factions to produce beneficial results in place of an attempt to eliminate disagreement.

conflict resolution Management of interpersonal conflict by either (*a*) adoption of a passive role, (*b*) facilitation of a win-lose situation, or (*c*) facilitation of a win-win or integrative solution.

confrontation Face-to-face opposition as a method of resolving an issue or difference.

conglomerate A corporation made up of companies that produce significant quantities of output in several industries.

conglomerate merger Absorption by a corporation of another in an industry distinct from that of the parent company.

Congress of Industrial Organizations (*abbr* CIO) A national federation of labor unions organized according to industry, formed in 1935 by a dissident faction of the American Federation of Labor to represent unskilled and semiskilled workers; merged with the AFL in 1955 to become the AFL-CIO.

congruent innovation Also called **me-too.** Imitation of an innovation already introduced.

connect time The time that elapses between the signing on of a computer user and the moment of that user's signing off.

consent order An order issued by a government agency by whose terms a respondent agrees not to engage in a specified business practice proscribed by statute and/or regulation, without admitting to having actually engaged in such activities previously.

conservative focus An orientation to problem solving characterized by a tendency to identify alternative solutions to a problem one at a time and to alter one's views accordingly.

consideration Anything of value, including the relinquishing of a legal right, exchanged as a binder between parties to a contract.

consignment A quantity of goods delivered to a dealer with the agreement that title remains with the shipper until the goods are sold and that the dealer will remit the proceeds of sales less a commission and return goods unsold.

consolidated financial statement A financial statement in which information in regard to a parent company and its subsidiaries is presented as a unified whole, with like accounts combined and some eliminated as balances offset each other.

consolidation The combining of the accounts of a parent company and all subsidiaries into a consolidated financial statement.

consortium An international business or banking combination organized to carry out a large project.

conspicuous consumption The purchase of goods and services well beyond basic material needs.

constant dollars Current dollars valued as a percentage of their buying power in a specified previous year, as determined by the net change in the consumer price index.

constraint Any restriction imposed on the decision-making process that eliminates certain alternatives. See also **feasible solution.**

constructive receipt A ruling by the Internal Revenue Service specifying that receivable but unreceived income (e.g., reinvested dividends from mutual funds) is taxable in the year in which it could have been received if the taxpayer had elected to receive it.

consultant See **external consultant; internal consultant.**

consultative leadership Also called **system 3 management.** A leadership style characterized by discussion with subordinates for the purpose of giving them a sense of responsibility for productivity and decision making.

consumer advisory board A group of consumers whose opinions and advice are sought by a company in the early stages of marketing a new product or service, which need not be of potential use or interest to the consumers consulted. See also **consumer panel; idea-development interview.**

consumer credit Credit extended to an individual for the purchase of personal products or services.

Consumer Credit Protection Act Federal legislation that releases consumers from obligations under contracts with obscure credit terms and affords other protections of their rights.

consumer jury See **consumer panel.**

consumer movement Also called **consumerism.** A movement begun in the 1960s for passage of laws to protect consumers against unsafe and misrepresented products, unfair and misrepresented credit terms, and other business abuses. See also **consumer rights.**

consumer-oriented marketing See **target marketing.**

consumer panel A carefully selected group of people, representative of a population of potential users of a product or service, who are hired on an ad hoc basis to help advertising and marketing research companies pretest and evaluate products or ads before they are presented to the public.

consumer price index (*abbr* CPI) Also called **cost-of-living index.** An index issued periodically by the Bureau of Labor Statistics that expresses the cost of goods and services purchased by typical wage earners as a percentage of the cost of the same goods and services in some base period.

Consumer Product Safety Act Federal legislation enacted in 1972 requiring that manufacturers (1) have documented proof that their products have been tested for reliability before being placed on the market, (2) have means of recalling their products if necessary, and (3) reply to valid customer complaints.

Consumer Product Warranties Act See **Magnuson-Moss Act.**

consumer rights A concept, put forward by President John F. Kennedy and subsequently enacted into law by Congress, that encompasses consumers' rights to safety, to be heard, to choose, and to be informed. See also **Consumer Product Safety Act; Magnuson-Moss Act; Truth-in-Lending Act; Wheeler-Lea Act.**

consumer sovereignty The economic power exercised by consumers in the marketplace by virtue of their ability to select or reject products and services.

consumer's risk The risk run by a consumer that a defective item from a lot will be accidentally purchased. See also **producer's risk.**

contact person See **account executive.**

containerization Packaging of goods in sealed containers before shipment for the purpose of minimizing damage and transportation costs. See also **birdyback; fishyback; piggyback.**

contingency approach A method of analyzing the activity of an organization that focuses on the causal relationships of four factors: (*a*) the degree of openness of the system, (*b*) the system as the sum of its parts, (*c*) the boundaries of the system, and (*d*) the various paths by which the system can reach its goals.

contingency management See **situational management.**

contingency theory An organizational theory that seeks to explain the idiosyncratic nature of each organization's response to similar situations by focusing on organizational patterns and the degree to which management methods are appropriate to specific situations.

contingent business-interruption insurance Insurance that covers the risk of a business loss resulting from interruption in the delivery of supplies necessary to the conduct of business.

contingent liability A possible or likely liability that will be incurred only in the event of some specific occurrence (e.g., an unfavorable court decision) and that is noted in parentheses or footnoted in financial statements but is not added to total liabilities unless the unfavorable event is fully expected to occur.

continuation of benefits The right of an employee and his or her spouse and dependents to continue participation in an employee health plan after coverage has been terminated due to layoff, divorce, etc. This right was conferred by a federal law commonly referred to by the acronym COBRA, which stands for Consolidated Omnibus Budget Reconciliation Act.

continuous compounding The calculation of compound interest on an ongoing basis rather than at specific points in time. See also **compound interest; discrete compounding.**

continuous innovation A gradual improvement in a product already in the marketplace, usually with little measurable effect on established buying patterns.

continuous inventory See **perpetual inventory.**

continuous process A production operation that turns out finished products with little or no change in procedures or equipment over a period of days, months, or years, as in the production of steel and the refining of petroleum.

contra account A separate bookkeeping account in which sums are accumulated for eventual subtraction (deduction) from a main account, with attendant elimination of the need for constant subtractions from the main account (e.g., discounts on

business

bonds payable, allowance for doubtful accounts, accumulated depreciation).

contra asset An account balance that is deducted from an asset account to arrive at a net book value.

contract A legally enforceable agreement, either oral or in writing, between two or more mentally competent adults, one or more of whom voluntarily accept a legitimate offer voluntarily made, and who exchange something of value (e.g., money, goods, services, or the relinquishing of a legal right).

contract carrier A person or company that enters into a contract with an individual shipper or other person to transport goods or people.

contraction 1. A restriction or withdrawal of currency or funds available to be lent. **2.** A decrease in economic and industrial activity.

contracts administration Management of purchase orders and other contracts involved in procurement, including maintenance of contract files and oversight of the carrying out of the terms of such agreements.

contract to sell A contract to sell goods at a future date. See also **future goods.**

contractual liability An obligation assumed under the terms of a contract.

contrarian A person who rejects the majority opinion. This term is often applied to an investor who buys when others are selling, and vice versa.

contributed capital See **paid-in capital.**

contribution income statement An operations report in which the contribution margin is determined by subtraction of variable costs from revenues and the further subtraction of fixed costs to yield net income.

contribution margin The amount by which the revenues of a given company, branch, department, or project exceed its total variable costs; the unit's contributions to profit and fixed costs.

contributory pension plan A pension plan financed by contributions from both employees and employer. See also **noncontributory pension plan.**

control account An account that contains the total of transactions that are recorded in detail in a subsidiary ledger (e.g., the accounts receivable account contains the total of the balances of all subsidiary accounts receivable).

control chart A graph used for plotting the measured quality of samples of completed work and comparing these observed quality levels against predetermined limits (**control limits**) to decide whether the process quality is acceptable or indicates the need for corrective action.

controllable cost A cost that to some extent is under the control of a manager or otherwise affected by the way business operations are conducted.

controlled-circulation publication A periodical publication consisting of no less than 25 percent editorial material sent free of charge to members of an association by virtue of their paid membership.

controller Also called **comptroller.** The chief accounting officer or financial vice president of a company, in charge of designing and directing the accounting information system, including such matters as internal control, cost accounting, financial accounting, tax planning, and financial reporting.

control limits See **control chart.**

controlling interest Ownership of enough stock in a company to exert control over policy and management.

convenience goods Products, generally moderately priced, that can frequently be purchased in conveniently located outlets (convenience stores).

convergent marketing The marketing of all of a company's products by a single marketing team. See also **divergent marketing.**

convertible bond A corporate bond that the holder can at any time exchange for shares of the corporation's common stock at a specified ratio of shares per bond.

convertible preferred stock Preferred stock that the holder can at any time exchange for shares of the corporation's common stock at a specified ratio.

COO chief operating officer (of a company).

cooling-off law An FTC ruling that allows customers to cancel sales contracts with door-to-door salespeople within three days.

cooling-off period 1. A period of 80 days during which, under the terms of the Taft-Hartley Act, a strike that endangers the national health or safety may be halted by an injunction obtained by the president of the United States. **2.** A period of 60 days following submission by an employer or a union of a notice of termination of contract, mandated by the TaftHartley Act, before a strike or lockout may be called.

co-op See **cooperative.**

cooperative 1. An association of people or small companies, predominantly in the agricultural field, who join together in order to increase their bargaining power in the marketplace and divide profits among members. **2.** Also called **co-op.** A building or apartment owned and managed by a corporation in which shares are sold, entitling the shareholders to occupy individual units in the building.

cooperative advertising Also called **dealer tie-in.** The sharing by local merchants and national advertisers of the costs of product promotions appearing locally.

cooperative buying Purchasing by customers or buyers who have joined together to increase their bargaining power.

copay Also called **copayment.** A fixed amount, or a percentage of the usual and customary fee for a medical service, required by a health insurer to be paid by the patient to the health-care provider.

coping behavior Behavioral adjustment to an unsatisfied need, usually in the form of a trial-and-error search for an alternative goal that is more realistically attainable than that to which access has been blocked.

copy 1. The part of an advertisement that delivers the advertiser's message, exclusive of illustrations. **2.** See **transfer** (def. 4).

copyright Legal protection offered for a fee by the Library of Congress to the creator of any printed, taped, filmed, or recorded material against infringement of the exclusive right of the creator or of his or her heirs to copy or adapt the material during the creator's lifetime and for fifty years thereafter.

copywriter A writer of copy for advertisements, news releases, etc.

corporate bond A promissory note issued by a corporation, usually in multiples of $1000 and bearing a specified rate of interest until a specified expiration date, at which time the corporation must return the loan represented by the bond. See also **bond** (def. 1); **convertible bond; coupon bond; government bond; municipal bond.**

corporate purpose A corporation's stated goals, objectives, quality of management, community responsibility, and manner of doing business.

corporate raider See **raider.**

corporate welfare Financial assistance, as tax breaks or subsidies, given by the government esp. to large companies.

corporation An entity formed and authorized by a state charter to act as an individual (i.e., to own, buy, and sell property, to enter into contracts, and to sue and be sued), with the right of succession; to issue shares of stock, which represent shares of ownership of the corporation; and to have legal liability for damages and debt only to the limit of the stockholders' investments.

correction A reversal of the trend of stock prices, especially temporarily, as after a sharp advance or decline in the previous trading sessions.

correlation The relationship or interdependence between two random variables, used in predicting or forecasting events.

correspondent bank A bank that acts on behalf of another bank in a business transaction.

cost A (usually initial or long-term) payment or sacrifice, direct or indirect, tangible or intangible, that is incurred or will be incurred to acquire, produce, or provide goods or services. See also **acquisition cost; expense; fixed cost; incremental cost.**

cost accounting **1.** A branch of management accounting that clarifies, summarizes, measures, accumulates, controls, allocates, and reports on current or predicted costs, especially those of production. **2.** The recording, reporting, and allocation of current and forecast expenses for labor, equipment, supplies, and utilities.

cost basis The original cost of an asset, used in calculating depreciation and capital gains or losses.

cost-benefit analysis A financial management technique developed to explore alternative courses of action in order to determine the one that will produce the optimum benefit at the minimum cost.

cost-benefit worksheet A worksheet used by a project team to compute the costs and benefits of its recommendations in regard to materials, work force, machines, reduction of error, time needed for processing, etc.

cost center A part of a company (division, department, branch, plant, territory, project, product) that is important enough to accumulate its own accountable costs.

cost depletion The depletion of a natural resource calculated by multiplying the estimated total value of the resource by a fraction representing the amount consumed during a certain period. See also **percentage depletion.**

cost-effective Also called **cost-efficient.** Producing benefits or revenues in excess of the total cost.

costly time Work time for which the employer must pay a premium wage or otherwise divert resources in order to complete a task. See also **crash time; expediting time.**

cost of goods manufactured The total cost of producing goods during a certain accounting period, including materials, labor, and overhead, but excluding the ending work-in-progress inventory.

cost of goods sold The sum of all expenses incurred in the manufacturing and/or purchasing and selling of goods that were actually sold during an accounting period, calculated by adding beginning inventory and cost of goods purchased or manufactured and from that sum subtracting ending inventory adjustment.

cost-of-living escalator Also called **COLA** (*cost-of-living adjustment*). A clause in a union contract guaranteeing that wages will be adjusted to reflect changes in the consumer price index whenever inflation reaches a specified rate, so that employees' buying power will be maintained.

cost-of-living index See **consumer price index.**

cost overrun Cost in excess of that originally estimated or budgeted, especially in a government contract. Often caused by delays in starting, resulting in higher costs of labor, materials, etc. Such costs are usually borne by the client.

cost per minute (*abbr* cpm) The cost charged advertisers per 1000 viewers of a television program or 1000 listeners to a radio program divided by the number of minutes of commercial time made available on the program.

cost per thousand (*abbr* cpt) The cost charged advertisers for each 1000 homes reached by a television or radio program or for each 1000 copies of a publication distributed.

cost-plus pricing The practice of basing the selling price of an item on its cost plus a percentage of that cost, so as to recover selling expenses and make a reasonable profit.

cost-push inflation Inflation due to increased production costs, such as labor and parts, although demand remains the same. See also **demand-pull inflation.**

cost sheet See **job cost sheet.**

cost trade-off The allocation of more money for some marketing activities than for others, with the goal of creating the most effective overall campaign.

cost-volume-profit analysis (*abbr* CVP analysis) A form of break-even analysis in which the effect on cost of changes in volume are compared with consequent changes in profit: done for the purpose of evaluating the possibility of a change of price, introducing a new product, or expanding capacity or sales territory.

Council of Economic Advisers (*abbr* CEA) A group of economists who advise the President of the United States on matters pertaining to the economy.

counteradvertising FTC-approved advertising by a public group warning consumers of potential harm that can result from the use of a product or class of products.

counterdependent One who continually resists the authority and leadership of others, creating a lack of unity in an organization or subsystem.

countervailing powers Two opposing authorities (as of big business, labor, or government) that are equally strong and mutually influential.

coupon bond A corporate bond from which coupons entitling the bearer to payment of interest may be detached for presentation to the issuing company at the specified time.

couponing The practice of offering a discount on or partial refund of the purchase price of a product upon presentation of a coupon clipped from a publication, received through the mail, or acquired with a previous purchase.

coupon rate The rate of interest designated on a bond certificate.

covenant A provision or reservation specified in a legal agreement restricting the actions of one or both parties.

CPA See **certified public accountant.**

CPI See **consumer price index.**

cpm See **cost per minute.**

cpt See **cost per thousand.**

CPU See **central processing unit.**

craft union A labor union that represents skilled artisans of a particular trade, who band together to establish a fair price for their services, regulate working hours, and restrict entry into the trade in order to maximize their bargaining power.

crash A sudden general collapse of a business enterprise, the stock market, etc.

crashing Shortening the time it takes to complete an activity by assigning additional resources to it.

crash time Also called **red rush.** Work time during which a product or service is rushed to completion with special handling or attention.

credit **1.** The dollar amount of goods or services a person may receive for payment in the future. See also **closed-end credit; line of credit; open-end credit. 2.** The balance in a person's account. **3.** An amount of money placed at a person's disposal by a bank or other lending institution. **4.** (*abbr* cr.) An entry on the right side of a balance sheet, indicating a decrease in assets (in asset accounting) or an increase in equity (in equity accounting). See also **debit.**

credit balance **1.** An excess of credits over debits in an account. **2.** The amount by which the sum of credit entries in an account exceeds the sum of debit entries in that account. See also **debit balance.**

credit card A plastic card bearing a customer's name and account number and usually an expiration date evidencing a firm's willingness to extend credit to the customer named for the purchase of goods or services.

credit life insurance Insurance on the life of a borrower that guarantees payment of the amount due on a loan installment contract in the event of the borrower's death.

credit line **1.** A line of type accompanying a photograph, illustration, published article, or television program acknowledging its source. **2.** See also **line of credit.**

creditor An individual or organization that is owed money by a borrower or customer.

credit rating An estimate of the amount of credit that may safely be extended to an individual or a company, usually made by an agency that specializes in such services on the basis of financial resources and responsibilities and history of repayment of past loans.

credit sale A sale of goods or services for which the purchaser agrees to pay in the future in accordance with specified terms.

credit union A cooperative group that makes loans to its members at low rates of interest.

crime insurance Insurance that covers losses resulting from the commission of a crime by a person other than the insured.

criminal law The body of laws and court decisions dealing with violations of public law.

crisis management The techniques used to deal with or avert crisis situations, especially strikes or violence.

critical incident An incident or experience that constitutes a turning point in one's life or way of thinking about a subject (the recall and description of which are thought to be helpful in management training). See also **incident pattern.**

critical path Also called **critical activity.** The order of operations in a manufacturing process, usually expressed in a diagram using arrows to indicate the flow: used as a basis for scheduling. See also **PERT.**

critical path method (*abbr* CPM) A project-planning method by which the sequence of activities involved in a planned project is plotted and timed for the purpose of determining the minimum time the project can be expected to require for completion.

cross-elasticity of demand A relationship between two products, often those that are substitutes for each other, such that a change in the price of one product affects the sales of the other.

crossfoot To add figures across a row rather than up and down. See also **foot.**

cross-ruff promotion A coupon, premium, or cents-off promotion in which products of two or more companies are promoted jointly.

cross-train To train (an employee) to be proficient at different, usually related, skills, tasks, etc.

culture The body of beliefs, attitudes, values, patterns of behavior, social forms, language, and material adjuncts of a social group; by extension, the consistent habits, values, and customs of an organizational environment.

cum dividend With dividend: applied to shares of stock traded when payment of a declared dividend is pending, indicating that the price of the stock includes the value of the declared dividend, to which the buyer is entitled. See also **ex dividend.**

Cummins Amendment An amendment to the Interstate Commerce Act of 1877, affecting the liability of carriers for loss or damage of freight transported across state lines.

cumulative preferred stock Stock that carries with it a guarantee that in the event that a dividend is not declared in any year, such dividend will be added to the next dividend declared and paid before the holders of common stock receive any dividend.

cumulative voting 1. The practice of combining stockholders' votes in elections of members of a board of directors, thus increasing the influence of small holders. 2. The practice (required in 22 states and permissible in 18 others) of multiplying the number of shares owned by one stockholder by the total number of candidates for membership in a board of directors to determine the number of votes that may be cast by the stockholder, who may divide them among the candidates in any proportion he or she wishes or cast them all for one candidate.

current assets All assets currently owned, including cash and that which can or will become cash within a year (e.g., cash on hand and in checking and savings accounts, inventories, prepaid expenses, marketable securities, accounts receivable, notes receivable).

current liabilities Money owed by a company and payable within one year.

current ratio Current assets divided by current liabilities; a rough indication of a company's ability to meet its obligations. See also **liquidity ratio.**

current value 1. The value of an asset estimated by reference to recent transactions involving similar assets, as by reference to market value or replacement cost. 2. The value of a long-term asset or inventory calculated as replacement cost multiplied by the fraction of acquisition cost not yet depreciated.

current yield The ratio of the annual interest or dividend to the actual market price of a bond or stock.

curriculum vitae (*abbr* CV) See **résumé.**

custodian A bank or corporation authorized to safeguard the securities and other properties of an investment portfolio.

customer A person who buys or leases some product or employs some service, especially one who does so frequently or regularly.

customer's man See **broker** (def. 1).

custom manufacturing The production of goods in accordance with customers' orders, with resultant short production runs and frequent shutdown of machinery. See also **assemble-to-order; intermittent process; make-to-order.**

customs Duties or taxes imposed by a government on goods imported from foreign countries.

customs union An economic alliance of nations that establish a free-trade area for members and place uniform tariffs on trade with nonmember nations.

cutoff test An audit procedure to ascertain whether transactions executed shortly before or after the closing of an accounting period have been recorded consistently and in the correct period.

CV See curriculum vitae.

CVP analysis See **cost-volume-profit analysis.**

cybernetics The study of control systems, especially the analogy between human reasoning processes and mechanical and electronic systems designed to replace them.

cycle billing The practice of billing a portion of a firm's customers on each working day of the month, the specific day for each customer being determined by the initial of the last name, to equalize the work involved.

cycle stock Inventory resulting from periodic replenishment or production of an item in batches or lots.

cycle time The time allotted to each work station on an assembly line to perform the assigned tasks for each successive unit.

cyclical stock A security that rises and falls in value in accordance with business fluctuations.

cyclical unemployment Unemployment attributable to a temporary disruption of the economy (as during the energy crisis of the 1970s) or to a low level of aggregate demand (as during a recession).

cyclical variation A fluctuation in business conditions seen as part of a recurrent cycle characterized by initial prosperity followed by crisis, recession, and recovery.

data (*Latin, plural; sing. datum*) Individual facts, statistics, or items of information. See **primary data; secondary data.**

database 1. A body of information, usually factual and from a primary source, which serves as a foundation for future decisions, discussions, or operations. **2.** Also called **data bank.** Information entered and stored in a computer to serve as the primary data source for other operations.

data-based intervention Also called **action research.** The gathering and evaluation of information for the purpose of formulating appropriate plans to improve the operations of an organization.

database management system (*abbr* DBMS) A set of software programs for controlling the storage, retrieval, and modification of organized data in a computerized database.

DBMS See **database management system.**

DDB See **double-declining-balance depreciation.**

dead-cat bounce (*slang*) A temporary recovery in stock prices after a steep decline, often resulting from the purchase of securities that have been sold short.

deadhead To move an empty truck, rail car, airplane, or the like, to a destination to pick up freight, passengers, etc.

deadline A time limit set on the completion of a project; the time by which a product must be finished or material for publication must reach the publisher. See also **closing date** (def. 1).

dealer brand See **private brand.**

dealer tie-in See **cooperative advertising.**

death benefit 1. An amount of money paid to a beneficiary upon the death of a person covered by life insurance. **2.** An amount of money paid from Social Security funds to a spouse or child to help pay for the funeral expenses of a person who has been receiving Social Security benefits.

debenture A corporate bond or long-term loan that is secured only by the general credit rating of the issuing company. See also **mortgage bond.**

debit (*abbr* dr.) An entry on the left side of a balance sheet, indicating an increase in assets or expenses and a decrease in liabilities or income accounts (depending on the accounting system used). See also **credit.**

debit balance 1. An excess of debits over credits in an account. **2.** The amount by which the total debits in an account exceed the sum of the credits in that account (asset, expense, and some contra accounts normally have debit balances). See also **credit balance.**

debit card A plastic card through which payments for purchases are made electronically from the bank account of the cardholder.

debt See **liability.**

debt capital Capital raised by the sale of bonds or the borrowing of money. See also **equity capital.**

debt-equity ratio The ratio of either total liabilities or long-term debt (depending on context) to owners' equity: an indication of the extent to which investors or lenders are financing a company's assets.

debtor An individual or organization that is obligated either to repay money borrowed or to make payment for goods or services received on credit.

debt-service cost The amount that must be paid annually for the use of borrowed money, including interest, required payments of principal, and contributions to sinking funds.

debt-to-assets ratio A measure of a company's ability to sustain debt, determined by dividing its total liabilities by its total assets.

debt-to-equity ratio A measure of a company's ability to sustain debt, determined by dividing the total liabilities by the owner's equity.

debug To locate an error in a software program and make the appropriate corrections; by extension, to eliminate any technical problem.

decapitalize To withdraw financing from (a company).

decay rate The approximate percentage of customers who cease to buy a product in the course of a year.

decentralization Delegation to middle and supervisory managers of authority to make decisions in regard to financial, production, and personnel matters. See also **centralization.**

decentralized divisional design An organizational structure in which each division of a company is semiautonomous, specializing in a particular product or responsible for a regional market, and whose head is given all but total authority to coordinate operations within the division, to make decisions, and to establish strategy under the overall coordination of the chief executive officer at the organization's headquarters.

decertification Revocation of a labor union's authorization to serve as bargaining agent as a result of a vote conducted among workers under the supervision of the National Labor Relations Board.

decision-making process A rational thought process involving the identification and evaluation of two or more alternatives, selection and implementation of one, and evaluation of the effectiveness of the alternative chosen.

decision rule A guideline selected to express the conditions under which a decision to proceed with a recommended course of action will be made (e.g., "If 55 percent of our test market favor the new design, we'll go ahead with it.").

decision tree A graphic representation of a network of hypothetical actions and events indicating the probabilities of success and failure of each action that might be taken in the situation under study, designed to facilitate the decision-making process. See also **action-event area.**

declaration 1. Disclosure of income, property, or items to customs agents or other governmental or legal authorities. **2.** A written but unsworn statement, as by an applicant for a patent.

declining-balance depreciation A method of accelerated depreciation by which each year's depreciation is calculated as a percentage of current book value. See also **double-declining-balance depreciation.** The calculation is made by means of the following formula, in which L is the useful life, s is the salvage value, and c is the acquisition cost:

$$1 - \frac{L}{s/c}$$

deductible A specified amount of a loss that an insurance policy does not cover (e.g., a $100 deductible policy means that the insurance company deducts $100 from each claim that is paid).

deed A legal document by which title to real property is passed to a new owner. See also **quitclaim deed; warranty deed.**

deed of trust A deed transferring ownership of property to a third party, such as a bank, until a mortgage or other indebtedness is fully discharged, at which time the trustee transfers the deed to the purchaser.

deep discount A discount far larger than normally offered.

default Failure to fulfill a contract or other obligation, especially to pay a debt or interest due.

defendant A person who must answer a criminal

charge or a civil action in a court of law. See also **plaintiff.**

deferred annuity An annuity providing for payments to begin at some specified future date.

deferred charge Also called **deferred cost; deferred debit; deferred expense.** An expenditure, as for an advance payment or an insurance premium, which is regarded as an asset to be depreciated over future periods rather than as a charge in the period in which it is made.

deferred compensation Payment made to an employee in the form of a stock option or by other means designed to bring the employee income in the future and encourage long-term commitment to the employer.

deferred income See **advance from (by) customer.**

deferred income-tax liability See **interperiod income-tax allocation.**

deferred revenue See **advance from (by) customer.**

deficit 1. The amount by which a sum of money falls short of the required amount. 2. A loss, as in the operation of a business. 3. The amount by which liabilities exceed assets.

deficit financing Expenditures, especially by a government, in excess of public revenues, usually made possible by borrowing.

deficit spending The practice, especially by a government, of spending funds in excess of income, usually financed by borrowing.

deflation 1. A decline in the general price level, or an increase in the value of money; a reversal of inflation. 2. (*economics*) A decrease in the amount of money in circulation. See also **disinflation.**

defraud Deceptively or improperly to take or withhold something that belongs to another.

dehire A euphemism for "discharge" or "dismiss": often used of executive layoffs.

Delaney Amendment A 1958 amendment to the Food, Drug, and Cosmetics Act of 1938 authorizing the Food and Drug Administration to remove from the market any food or food additive that has been shown to cause cancer in animals or humans.

delegate To assign, commit, or entrust to another, as authority, responsibility, or a task.

delivered cost The price at which goods are billed, including the cost of transportation.

Delphi technique The practice of seeking the opinions of experts on likely future events and trends that would affect business.

demand 1. The desire to purchase a particular product or service by those who have the means to do so. 2. The quantity of a good or service that buyers will take at a particular price. See also **law of demand; law of supply and demand.**

demand-backward pricing See **market-minus pricing.**

demand curve A graphic representation of the quantities of a good or service that will be purchased at various prices at a specific time.

demand deposit A checking account in a bank.

demand loan A loan that has no specified maturity date but is payable whenever the lender demands payment.

demand-pull inflation Inflation resulting from increased demand. See also **cost-push inflation.**

demarketing A temporary reduction in purchasing activity in the marketplace resulting from a supply of goods inadequate to meet the demand for them.

democratic leadership Also called **participative leadership; system 4 management.** A style of leadership characterized by group involvement in decision making, a free flow of information and communications, and delegation of authority to qualified members of the group.

demographics The study or aggregate of definable characteristics of a population, including sex, race, religion, health, age, income, education, and home-ownership. See also **RACORNOS.**

demotion Reassignment of an employee to a position of lesser status and responsibility than the position the employee previously held.

demotivator Also called **demotivating factor.** An aspect of one's employment that, if diminished or downgraded, tends to inhibit peak performance.

demurrage The holding of a rail car, barge, or ship beyond the time allowed for loading and unloading.

demurrer A plea that a legal action be dismissed on the grounds that although the facts presented by the opposing side are true, either they are insufficient to support the claim based on them or the pleadings suffer from some other defect in law sufficient to call for a judgment that the case should not proceed further.

denominator value The expected volume of units to be produced in the current period, which when used as the figure by which budgeted fixed costs are divided yields fixed cost per unit of production.

dental and vision insurance Insurance covering a percentage of an employee's expenditures for eyeglasses, contact lenses prescribed by a physician, and dentistry, often excluding bridgework and children's braces.

department A group or section of employees who work together in a specific area of a company. See also **departmentation.**

departmentation Also called **departmentalization.** The grouping or departmentalizing of employees in accordance with type of work done, territory served, product produced, type of customer dealt with, etc.

dependency The state of an organization, subsystem, or individual that requires support from other organizations or persons.

dependent demand Demand for component parts and raw materials that is determined by or dependent upon requirements for products and can therefore be calculated rather than forecast.

dependent variable (*statistics*) A value that can be predicted as a result of knowing the value of one or more independent variables.

depletion The reduction in value of capital that results from the exhaustion or using up of an asset. See also **amortization; depreciation** (def. 1).

depletion allowance The amount by which the Internal Revenue Service permits taxable income to be reduced to reflect the exhaustion of such assets as oil wells, mines, and quarries.

deposit in transit A bank deposit made and recorded but not yet reported on a bank statement.

deposition Written testimony given under oath by a witness for use in a court trial.

depreciation 1. A decline in the value of an asset attributable to wear, use, or the passage of time. 2. The amount by which taxable income is or may be reduced to reflect such a decline in value, based on the asset's estimated or allowable useful life. 3. A fall in the value of one currency in relation to another. See also **devaluation.**

depression 1. A drastic drop in business with resultant high rates of unemployment and business failure; the bottom of a business cycle. 2. A severe and long-term recession during which unemployment exceeds 10 percent of the work force and profits drop sharply enough to cause widespread bankruptcy; a chronic aberration in the normal business cycle, not easily rectified by the normal dynamics of supply and demand.

deregulation The removal of existing state or federal regulations governing such industries as airlines, railroads, and trucking, with the objective of stimulating business competition and lowering consumer costs. See also **price war.**

derivative A financial contract whose value derives from the value of underlying stocks, bonds, currencies, commodities, etc.

derived demand Demand for a product that is directly or indirectly related to the demand for another product, as the demand for tires is related to the demand for automobiles.

descriptive billing A billing system that incorporates a description of the charges rather than copies of the original invoices.

designated market-area rating (*abbr* DMA

rating) The number of homes in which a television program is being viewed in a defined market area at a given time.

design review Inspection of a completed or planned product design by representatives of each segment of the operation for the purpose of confirming the producibility of the product and of identifying errors that may be rectified.

desktop publishing The design and production of publications by means of specialized software enabling a microcomputer to generate typeset-quality text and graphics.

devaluation A reduction in the exchange value of a currency by a lessening of its equivalency in gold or in some other currency, with resultant decreases in the prices of the country's goods in foreign markets. See also **depreciation** (def. 3).

developing Designating a nation or region having a standard of living or level of industrial production well below that possible with financial or technical aid; not yet highly industrialized.

development 1. The process of making usable and commercially available a product or process discovered or perfected by applied research. **2.** The process of mutual adaptation by which an individual pursues his or her career goals within an organization that guides the individual's training and performance in light of its own objectives.

development training Training in skills required for job performance and advancement appropriate to an individual's motivation and capabilities.

diagnosis Assessment of strengths and weaknesses, dependent on the perceptions and interpretations of those reviewing the data.

Dictionary of Occupational Titles (*abbr* DOT) A reference book published by the U.S. Department of Labor that lists and describes 20,000 jobs.

die-cut Cut by a set of tools or devices that produce a desired form, usually for assembly with other components into a more complex product (e.g., an automobile).

differential advantage An advantage enjoyed by one marketer, retailer, or nation over competitors (e.g., lower cost, better product features, location).

differential cost See **incremental cost** (def. 2).

differential threshold See **just noticeable difference.**

diffusion process The process by which a new product or service comes into general use.

digital Involving the use of a code consisting of numerical digits, recognized and read by a computer or other electronic device.

Dilbert A syndicated 1990's comic strip character created by Scott Adams. The comic strip satirizes business activities and management techniques.

dilution A decrease in the percentage of ownership of a corporation represented by a quantity of stock resulting from issuance of additional shares.

diminishing returns A rate of return on investment that at some future date fails to increase in proportion to additional investment. See also **law of diminishing returns.**

direct-action advertising Advertising designed to elicit some action from the target audience (e.g., sending money for a sample, writing for additional information).

direct confrontation An aggressive strategy to limit reliance on other organizations by seeking a monopolistic position or by initiating an exchange of services.

direct cost Also called **direct expense.** The costs of overhead, materials, and labor that can be directly attributed to the production of a specific number of units of product, an organizational unit, or a project.

direct costing Also called **marginal costing.** The charging of variable manufacturing costs only (the costs of labor, materials, and variable factory overhead costs) to the cost of a product. See also **absorption costing.**

direct deposit The use of electronic funds transfer to deposit wages directly to an employee's bank account each payday.

directed interview A structured interview in which the interviewer follows a prepared form or list of questions (often used to select a candidate for a specific job).

direct expense See **direct cost.**

direct exporting The shipping of goods from a company in one country directly to a company in another country, without the use of intermediaries.

direct labor Factory labor that is clearly responsible for the production of a specific number of units or batches of product. See also **indirect labor.**

direct mail Mail, usually consisting of advertising matter, appeals for donations, or the like, sent to large numbers of people.

direct marketing Marketing direct to the consumer, as by direct mail or coupon advertising. Also called **direct selling.**

direct materials Raw materials that can be associated with an identifiable amount of units or batches manufactured.

direct posting The making of accounting entries directly in ledger accounts without prior entry in journals.

direct supervision Management characterized by direct interaction between supervisor and subordinates.

disability benefit An insurance payment made to an employee who is unable to work as a result of illness or injury.

disability income insurance Insurance that protects an employee against loss of income while partially or totally disabled by illness or injury.

disbursement A payment made by cash or check, often recorded in a separate cash disbursements account.

discharge 1. Permanent involuntary termination of employment. **2.** To pay (a debt) or perform (an obligation).

disciplinary action A penalty (e.g., loss of privileges, a fine, demotion, suspension, oral or written reprimand, discharge) imposed on an employee whose behavior on the job is unacceptable to management, illegal, or contrary to union regulations.

disciplinary practices Formal procedures to be followed in the taking of disciplinary action, specified in a document that outlines offenses that warrant disciplinary action and stipulates the sequence of penalties and the steps to be taken in carrying them out.

disclaimer Refusal of a certified public accountant to permit an audit opinion to be included in a financial statement because (1) he or she was not independent of the company, (2) the information available was insufficient to support an opinion, or (3) the outcome of the audit was too inconclusive to justify an opinion.

disclosure agreement A written agreement whereby one party promises to keep secret information that is to be divulged by another.

discount 1. A price reduction given to a customer in the form of cash, a reduction of the list price, or merchandise. See also **cash discount; quantity discount; trade discount. 2.** The percentage by which a price is reduced. **3.** To purchase a promissory note before its due date for the face value of the note less a service charge. **4.** To take into account the present value of a sum of money or other asset having a known value at a certain time in the future.

discount broker 1. An agent who discounts commercial paper. **2.** A stockbroker who charges discount commission fees.

discount rate 1. The rate of interest charged in discounting commercial paper. **2.** The interest rate charged by Federal Reserve Banks on loans to their member banks, usually against government securities as collateral.

discount store A store that sells a variety of goods below market price, usually because of large volume of sales and a small profit margin.

discrete compounding The periodic calculation of compound interest at specific points in time. See

business

also **compound interest; continuous compounding.**

discretionary account An investor's account with a broker or agent who, within specified limitations, is free to buy, sell, or retain securities at times and in amounts the agent deems to be in the best interest of the investor.

discretionary income Also called **discretionary spending power.** The amount of money remaining after essential expenses are met. See also **disposable income.**

discretionary order An order to buy issued with the proviso that the broker is to judge whether to execute the transaction immediately or to wait for a better price.

diseconomy 1. A lack of economy. **2.** Something that adds costs, as opposed to something that contributes to economy or efficiency.

disemploy To cause to be unemployed: often a tactful reference to large-scale layoffs.

disinflation A slowing down of the inflation rate, when prices are still going up, but at a lesser rate than before. See also **deflation.**

disinvestment The withdrawal of invested funds or the cancellation of subsidies or other financial aid.

disk Any of several types of media for storing electronic data consisting of thin, round plates of plastic or metal. See also **floppy disk; hard disk.**

diskette See **floppy disk.**

dispatcher A person who is responsible for issuing work orders to all people working together on a job on the basis of a list prepared by a supervisor or department head. See also **dispatching.**

dispatching A phase of production control, usually managed by supervisors and department heads, in which tasks required to be completed in a work center are listed, assigned priorities, and routed; from this list a dispatcher in each work area issues work orders to employees.

dispersion The degree to which plants, factories, or warehouses are scattered over a large geographical area. See also **concentration.**

display 1. (*data processing*) **a.** The visual representation of the output of an electronic device. **b.** The portion of the device, such as a screen, that shows this representation. **2.** (*advertising*) A presentation of promotional material in a store.

display ad An advertisement in a newspaper, magazine, or on a billboard that includes a picture or special graphics in addition to a verbal message.

disposable income Personal income after income and social security taxes have been withheld; the amount that a person has available for living expenses, clothing, entertainment, etc. See also **discretionary income.**

dissatisfier Also called **hygiene factor.** A factor whose presence, according to Frederick Herzberg's motivation/hygiene theory, does not motivate an employee but whose absence leads to employee dissatisfaction (e.g., attractive work space, well-kept washrooms).

dissolution The liquidation and disbanding of a corporation, usually as a result of bankruptcy, as a consequence of which all stock is rendered valueless except for shareholders' claims against residual assets.

distressed Designating merchandise that is damaged, out-of-date, or used, or real estate that is foreclosed and offered for sale.

distribution 1. The marketing, transporting, merchandising, and selling of any item. **2.** The division of the aggregate income of any society among its members. **3.** The parceling out of a decedent's estate to the beneficiaries. **4.** The paying out of corporate profits to shareholders in the form of dividends, or the total amount of money involved. **5.** The sale of a large block of stock. **6.** The allocation of a bankrupt's assets to creditors.

distribution expense The expense of sales, marketing, and delivery of goods to the marketplace.

distributor Also called **service wholesaler.** An independent wholesaler who sells assorted goods to all users, including other wholesalers, retailers, and the industrial market, and provides such services as displays, delivery, and extension of credit.

divergent marketing The marketing of each line of a company's products by a separate marketing team. See also **convergent marketing.**

diversification 1. The act or process of increasing the variety of products manufactured or of services offered. See also **merger. 2.** The process of spreading investments among various kinds of securities.

diversified investment company An investment company that is required by law to invest 75% of its assets in such a way that no more than 5% is invested in any one company and that it holds no more than 10% of the voting securities of any one company.

divestiture The process of selling one or more small companies (usually companies that bear only a tenuous relationship to the parent organization's primary business or that have been marginally profitable) in order to raise cash or increase borrowing capacity.

dividend A distribution of a corporation's earnings to its shareholders.

divisible contract A document specifying two or more dissimilar obligations that are unrelated to each other.

divisionalization The dividing of an organization into separate sections that operate in an autonomous or semiautonomous manner. See also **decentralized divisional design.**

document of title A written document, either negotiable or nonnegotiable, signed by a titleholder and certifying to legal ownership of property specified (e.g., a car).

dog A company or product whose prospects are poor. See also **cash cow; star.**

dollar averaging Also called **dollar-cost averaging.** An investment technique whereby an investor invests a fixed number of dollars in stocks at regular intervals, so that more shares are bought when the price is low than when the price is high, with the expectation of profiting by selling all stock when the price is above the average cost paid per share.

domestic corporation A corporation that conducts its business in the state in which it was incorporated. See also **foreign corporation.**

dominant coalition An informal structure within an organization made up of top-level management, such as the chief executive and others in strategic decision-making positions. See also **inner circle.**

dormant partner A business partner who takes no active role in running a business and whose association with the firm is not public knowledge. See also **silent partner.**

DOS (*acronym for* disk-operating system) A computer cataloging device that provides the user with a directory of information or programs on a disk and also acts as the mechanism by which these data may be accessed.

double-bill To bill two different customers for the same charge.

double-declining-balance depreciation (*abbr* DDB) A method of accelerated depreciation by which the annual depreciation charge is a percentage of the remaining book value equal to twice the percentage that would be calculated under the straight-line method; thus an asset bought for $1000 with a useful life of 10 years, which would be depreciated at a rate of 10% a year under the straight-line method, would be depreciated at a rate of 20% of recent book value under the double-declining-balance method.

double-entry bookkeeping A bookkeeping system that recognizes both what is received and what is given up in each business transaction by crediting one account and debiting another, the total debits always balancing the total credits.

double indemnity A provision in a life or accident insurance policy that entitles the beneficiary of the policy to receive double the face value of the policy if the insured dies an accidental death.

double-page spread Also called **double spread.** An advertisement or other material that occupies two facing pages of a magazine. See also **centerfold; double-truck spread.**

double T-account A T-account with double horizontal lines, used to record a change in an account balance during the preparation of a statement of change in financial position.

double taxation The taxation of a corporation's profit twice, once under the corporate income tax and again under the personal income tax levied against stockholders to whom that profit has been distributed in the form of dividends.

double-truck spread An advertisement or other related material that occupies two facing pages of a newspaper. See also **double-page spread.**

Dow Jones average An index of the relative price of securities based on the average daily prices of common stocks issued by selected companies in the fields of industry and transportation and selected public utilities.

down payment An initial amount given as partial payment at the time of purchase, as in installment buying.

downsize To reduce a labor force in size or number; to cut back.

downstream 1. In the future. **2.** Concerning a lower level of business activity or authority, such as a subordinate or a subsidiary.

downtick (*stock exchange*) A closing price slightly below that of the previous day or trading period.

downtime Time when workers are idle because machinery is shut down for some cause, such as equipment failure, routine maintenance, or a temporary plant closing.

Dow theory A market analysis theory that predicts that if either the Dow Jones industrial or Dow Jones transportation average exceeds a previous significant high or low price, a general market trend will follow in the same direction.

draft See **bill of exchange; trade draft.**

drawee A person who must pay another the amount specified on a bill of exchange or a trade draft.

drawer A person who draws up a bill of exchange or trade draft specifying an amount payable by the drawee.

drive time The rush hour, when commuters listen to car radios: perceived as a source of increased ratings for programs and a consequent increase in advertising revenue.

drop shipper A wholesaler who deals in ship-

ments of goods sent directly to a retailer by a manufacturer without passing through the hands of the wholesaler who negotiated the transaction.

dry goods Fabrics, clothing, and the like, as distinguished from hardware and groceries.

dual distribution Sale of a product or service through more than one marketing channel.

dub See **transfer** (def. 4).

due bill A statement of charges for services rendered, specifying the nature and date of the services, the terms of payment, and the date by which payment is due.

due date The day by which a debt is to be paid.

due process of law The proceedings and limitations set forth in the U.S. Constitution and in state constitutions to protect the rights of individuals against incursions by branches and agents of government and before courts of law.

dues checkoff See **checkoff.**

dummy Also called **mockup.** A preliminary layout of a publication showing the intended concept and design.

dump bin A jumble display in which all products are alike. See also **jumble basket.**

dumping The practice of selling goods in a foreign market at a price lower than that charged in the domestic market.

Du Pont system A system by which the relationship of a corporation's activity ratio and profit margin is analyzed in order to determine the relationship of profitability and assets. A simplified formula expressing this relationship is

$$\frac{\text{Net profit}}{\text{Sales}} \times \frac{\text{Sales}}{\text{Total investment}}$$

$$= \text{Return on investment}$$

durable goods Also called **hard goods.** Automobiles, machinery, refrigerators, jewelry, etc., designed to be used over a period of time, usually at least three years.

Dutch auction A method of selling, in which the price of an item is gradually reduced until a buyer is found.

duty-free Exempt from customs.

dyad Any two individuals who have a close personal relationship, such as husband and wife.

dynamics The pattern of interaction and response between two people or among members of a group.

business

---

a b c d **E** f g h i j k l m n o p q r s t u v w x y z

---

early retirement benefits Pension benefits received by an employee who retires before the age of 65, usually reduced in amount from benefits receivable at age 65.

earned income Income from wages, salaries, fees, or the like, accruing from labor or services performed by the earner. Cf. **unearned income.**

earned surplus (*obsolete*) See **retained earnings.**

earnings before interest and taxes (*acronym* EBIT) See **net operating income.**

earnings per share (*abbr* EPS) Net revenues for a specific period divided by the number of shares of common stock issued.

easement A legal right to use or have access to property belonging to another (e.g., the right of a public utility to install and service pipes or wires running under private property.)

EBCDIC (*acronym for* extended binary-coded decimal interchange code) An eight-bit code with 256 character combinations used on large computers for data representation and transfer.

EBIT (*acronym for* earnings before interest and taxes) See **net operating income.**

echelon A steplike formation of units or individuals; thus, a level of decision-making responsibility and power.

econometrician A specialist in econometrics.

econometrics The use of scientific techniques, especially of mathematics and statistics, to support or test economic theories, solve economic problems, etc.

economic externalities Costs (or benefits) of a market activity borne by a third party (e.g., the costs of air and water pollution, which do not appear on the financial statement of the polluting firm but are borne by society at large).

economic growth An increase in production of goods and services as indicated by real GNP.

economic indicator Also called **business indicator.** An economic factor that is considered to signal the general direction of economic activity by fluctuating either in advance of, concurrently with, or after the aggregate of economic activity. See also **lagging indicator; leading indicator; roughly coincident indicator.**

economic life The period over which an asset is expected to yield benefits.

economic order quantity (*abbr* EOQ) The most economically efficient amount of stock to order or produce when inventory must be replenished. This is calculated by the following formula, in which *D* is the amount needed for a given period, *P* is the cost of placing one order, and *C* is the cost of carrying one unit for the period, including lost return on investment:

$$EOQ = \sqrt{\frac{2DP}{C}}$$

Economic Recovery Act An act of Congress passed in 1981 to cut federal taxes for individuals and businesses in order to encourage business investment.

economics The science that deals with the production, distribution, and consumption of goods and services, or the material welfare of humankind.

economic system 1. A system devised to establish the nature and quantity of goods and services to be produced, the means by which they should be produced, and the means by which they should be allocated. 2. A system by which limited resources are allocated among competing uses.

economies of scale Reductions in minimum average costs that result from increases in the size of plant and equipment.

economy 1. The management of the resources of a community, country, etc., especially with a view to its productivity. 2. The prosperity or earnings of a place.

EDP See **electronic data processing.**

effective interest method Also called **scientific method.** A method of amortizing a bond discount or premium so that at the beginning of each period the interest expense for that period (calculated by multiplying the bond's original yield rate by the net liability at the beginning of the period) divided by the bond's net liability (its face amount plus premium or minus discount) is equal to the bond's yield rate as of its issue date.

effective interest rate 1. Also called **effective yield.** The yield to maturity of a bond as of its date of issue. See also **coupon rate.** 2. The simple annual interest rate that would yield the same amount as a stated compound interest rate, equal to $(1 + r/m)\ m - 1$, where r is the compound rate and m is the number of compoundings per year.

EFT See **electronic funds transfer.**

EFTA See **European Free Trade Association.**

e.g. (*Latin abbr for* exempli gratia) For example.

ego motive An incentive to performance provided by assurance of one's importance and self-worth.

elasticity See **price elasticity of demand; price elasticity of supply.**

electronic data processing (*abbr* EDP) Collection, storage, and processing of information in a computer and retrieval of that information from any connecting terminal. See also **automatic data processing.**

electronic funds transfer (*abbr* EFT) The transfer of funds by debiting a bank account and crediting another account in the same or another bank by means of a computer.

electronic mail Also called **e-mail.** A system for sending messages via telecommunications links between computers.

electronic point of sale An automatic data-processing station located at a cashier's station in a retail store that enables a clerk or operator to verify customers' charge accounts, record sales, and process other information.

elimination An entry made on a worksheet used in preparing a consolidated statement in order to avoid a duplication of recorded assets, liabilities, owners' equity, revenues, or expenses in the summation of the records of a parent company and its subsidiaries.

e-mail Also, **E-mail.** 1. See **electronic mail.** 2. A message sent by e-mail.

embargo A prohibition of trade in either certain specified products or all products of a foreign country.

embezzlement The act of appropriating for one's own use property entrusted to one's care by its owner (e.g., the theft of money by a bank employee).

emergent factor An informal condition or element in a work situation (e.g., consistency) that over time serves to indicate the nature and effectiveness of group interactions.

emerging market A market in a less developed country whose economy is just beginning to grow.

eminent domain The legal right of the government to appropriate property for public use.

empathy 1. Projection in imagination of a subjective mental or emotional state onto another person or an object. 2. The capacity to experience vicariously another person's feelings, wishes, or thoughts.

employee benefit plan A plan encompassing pension, insurance, and other benefits offered employees. See also **cafeteria plan; compensation; fringe benefit.**

employee communications Company or departmental memos, newsletters, etc., circulated between departments and between management and staff as a means of keeping employees informed of new policies, promotions, hirings, and the like.

employee counseling The assessment and improvement of employees' skills and competencies as a means of enhancing job performance, production levels, morale, etc.

employee insurance Insurance coverage for life, accident, major medical, etc., usually provided by management as an employee benefit. See also **disability income insurance; employee life insurance.**

employee life insurance Insurance providing for payment of a specified multiple of an employee's annual salary to a surviving beneficiary upon the death of the employee. Usually paid for entirely by the employer.

employee maintenance A program for keeping able employees within the organization, as by insuring that wages and benefits are competitive.

Employee Retirement Income Security Act (*acronym* ERISA) An act of Congress passed in 1974, establishing the Pension Guaranty Corporation to insure the assets of pension plans, requiring disclosure of the provisions of employee pension and welfare plans, establishing standards of conduct for the trustees and administrators of such plans, and establishing requirements for funding of and participation and vesting in pension plans.

employee stock ownership plan (*acronym* ESOP) A program to encourage and aid employees to become shareholders in the corporation that employs them, thus contributing capital to the corporation, sharing in profits, and acquiring an incentive to help it reach its goals.

employers' association A cooperative alliance of employers (e.g., National Association of Manufacturers, U.S. Chamber of Commerce) who publicize the views of members on issues of concern to them and negotiate with labor unions on behalf of individual employers.

employment 1. Work performed for pay. 2. The number or percentage of people who are employed of the nation's total work force. See also **unemployment.** 3. The process of recruiting and selecting qualified job applicants.

employment agency An independently owned agency that recruits and screens job applicants for employers for a variable fee (from 7% to 25% of the annual salary of the position filled) payable within a specified time of hiring by either the employer or the applicant in accordance with terms agreed upon, which vary over time with the state of the job market. See also **executive search firm.**

employment taxes See **payroll taxes.**

enabling costs Capacity costs incurred to permit production or operations to take place, and which cease when production ceases. See also **standby costs.**

encounter group An unstructured group in which members are encouraged to confront one another directly and express their feelings for the purpose of developing emotional ties and promoting understanding of themselves and others; a device used in organizational development.

ending inventory Also called **closing inventory.** The cost of inventory on hand at the end of an accounting period: generally carried into the following period as beginning inventory and shown on the balance sheet as an asset at the end of the reporting period.

endorsement 1. Writing on the back of a negotiable instrument that transfers the property named in the instrument to a person specified or to the bearer. **2.** See **testimonial.**

endowment insurance Insurance that will pay the face value of the policy to a named beneficiary if the insured dies within a stated length of time, generally 20 or 30 years, or to the insured if he or she is still alive at the end of that time.

end user The ultimate user for whom a machine, product, or service is designed. Also called **end consumer.**

Engel's law The economic principle, proposed by Ernst Engel, that the lower a person's income, the greater the proportion of it he or she must spend on food and other necessities.

enterprise 1. Any corporation, public utility, firm, partnership, company, or other business organization. **2.** An investment venture or project.

enterprise fund A government fund used to support and account for the acquisition, operation, and maintenance of a government service intended to be self-supporting through payments and charges collected from users, such as those paid to water companies and airports.

entrepreneur A person who plans, organizes, manages, and owns a business and assumes the attendant risks of the enterprise.

entropy 1. The degree to which effort is determined to be lacking at the management and production levels of an organization. **2.** A tendency of a subsystem or work unit to remain stable and unchanging, especially at a low or unproductive level.

entry level The lowest position within a job category; usually the lowest job from which one can be promoted.

entry process 1. The series of events that take place when a new employee enters an organization to begin work. **2.** The process by which the expectations of a new employee and of the employing organization are adapted to the realities of the situation.

entry value The current fair-market acquisition cost of an asset, usually equal to replacement cost.

envelope stuffer A promotional piece (e.g., a printed announcement, a product sample) sent to customers along with an invoice or other correspondence at no additional mailing cost.

environment See **business environment.**

environmental impact statement A study detailing the possible effect on the environment of a specific proposed activity and discussing alternatives to the proposed action, required to be disseminated to federal agencies, state and local governments, and the public under the provisions of the National Environmental Policy Act before any process that might have undesirable environmental effects may proceed.

environmentally adaptive design An organizational plan that identifies potentially adverse conditions and proposes longand short-range activities responsive to and contingent on such conditions.

Environmental Protection Agency (*abbr* EPA) A federal agency created in 1970 to execute the policies of the Council on Environmental Quality, which conducts research studies and coordinates all federal programs dealing with industrial pollution.

environmental protection legislation A series of acts passed by Congress beginning in 1970 to regulate the use of air pollutants, water pollutants,

pesticides, and other toxic chemicals. See also **Clean Air Act; Federal Insecticide, Fungicide, and Rodenticide Act; Federal Water Pollution Control Act; Toxic Substances Control Act.**

environmental turbulence An upheaval created by a change in the status of interacting dependent environmental systems (e.g., an increase in the relevance of one department to an organization's goals at the expense of other departments).

EOM dating (*abbr for* end-of-month dating) The practice of stating credit terms as of the end of the month in which the transaction occurred (e.g., "2/20 EOM" indicates that a 2 percent cash discount is given if the bill is paid within 20 days of the end of the month).

EPA See **Environmental Protection Agency.**

EPS See **earnings per share.**

Equal Credit Opportunity Act Federal legislation passed in 1975 prohibiting discrimination on account of sex or marital status in any transaction involving credit. See also **Regulation B.**

Equal Employment Opportunity Commission. An agency of the U.S. government instituted to establish guidelines for hiring and recruitment practices in order to reduce discrimination against members of minority groups and to encourage such people to apply for jobs they are qualified to fill.

equal opportunity Policies and practices in employment and other areas that do not discriminate against persons on the basis of race, color, religion, sex, age, mental or physical handicap, or national origin.

Equal Pay Act A 1963 amendment to the Fair Labor Standards Act of 1938, which provides that any employer who engages in business activities involved in interstate' commerce or who receives federal funds must give women employees the same pay as men who perform the same job.

equity 1. An interest in the net assets of a corporation. **2.** The percentage of investment that an investor has contributed in a margin transaction. **3.** The value of a property in excess of the amount that the owner still owes on a mortgage or debt secured by a lien.

equity accounting The right of ownership to securities and investments made by an individual or organization, listed on a balance sheet.

equity capital Funds raised through the sale of stock or the conversion of one or more stock issues into a single new issue. See also **debt capital.**

equity real estate investment trust (*abbr* equity REIT) A mutual fund that buys real estate and distributes at least 90 percent of its income as dividends, issuing shares to meet demand at a low price per share and offering a choice of automatic reinvestment or periodic payment of dividends, thus permitting greater flexibility than a mortgage real estate investment trust.

equity turnover A ratio that indicates the relationship between sales and stockholders' equity.

ergonomics Also called **human engineering.** An aspect of technology that studies the application of engineering and biological data to the mutual adjustment of machines and the people who operate them, and seeks to improve physical working conditions.

ERISA See **Employee Retirement Income Security Act.**

escalator clause A contract provision calling for increased charges, wages, or other payments, based on increased production costs, the cost of living, etc.

escape clause A provision in a contract that enables a party to terminate contractual obligations in specified circumstances.

escheat The reversion to the state of property left by a deceased person who has no legal heirs at the time of death.

escrow 1. A bond, deed, sum of money, or article of property left in the care of a third party to be held until specified conditions are fulfilled. **2. in escrow** In trust as surety for payment or performance.

ESOP See **employee stock ownership plan.**

business

esprit de corps (*French*) Group spirit; a feeling among peers of satisfaction in group membership and enthusiasm for and commitment to the group's goals: the end product of team building.

estimation sampling Random selection of facts or examples in order to derive an estimated characteristic of the large group that includes those facts or examples (e.g., by checking at random 100 of every 100,000 invoices for arithmetic correctness, one can calculate an estimated percentage of incorrect invoices among all invoices).

estoppel A legal bar against making a statement of affirmation or denial that will contradict a statement one has previously made.

et al. (*Latin abbr for et al*ii) And (all the) others.

ethical pricing The practice of charging less than the maximum price for products or services subject to price elasticity.

ethics A set of moral principles and values that govern one's actions. See also **business ethics.**

et seq. (*Latin abbr for et seq*uens) And the following (one or ones).

euro A proposed single monetary unit for all European countries.

Eurocurrency Money and negotiable instruments of non-European countries held outside their countries of origin for use in European money markets.

Eurodollars U.S. dollars held in European banks and used as a medium of international credit, especially for foreign trade.

European Economic Community (*abbr* EEC) Also called **Common Market.** An economic alliance established in 1958 by Belgium, France, Italy, Luxembourg, the Netherlands, and West Germany (since joined by Great Britain, Ireland, Denmark, Greece, Spain, and Portugal) to adopt common import duties and expedite trade among member nations.

European Free Trade Association (*abbr* EFTA) An economic association established in 1960 and originally composed of Austria, Denmark, Britain, Norway, Portugal, Sweden, and Switzerland, that maintains free trade in industrial products among member countries.

evoked set (*marketing research*) The limited number of brand items that a consumer can mentally recall before making a product selection. See also **span of recall.**

Excel A powerful spreadsheet program developed by Microsoft Corporation for personal computers. It is known for its ease of use and its built-in routines for producing charts and graphs from the data.

excessive trading The practice of churning.

exchange See **stock exchange.**

exchange controls Regulations imposed by some governments to allocate, expand, or restrict the exchange of their national currencies into foreign currencies as a means of regulating foreign trade.

exchange gain (loss) 1. a. A difference caused by the translation of a financial statement from one unit of currency to another when the exchange rate has changed during the period of that statement. **b.** An entry item that reconciles the difference caused by the translation. **2.** An amount gained or lost on foreign currency held when the exchange rate changes.

exchange rate The price at which a nation's money can be exchanged for another currency or for gold.

excise tax A tax on certain items or services, payable by manufacturers or consumers or both, imposed by a state or by the federal government in order to control the traffic in potentially harmful goods or to subsidize services related to the items so taxed.

exclusion clause A clause in an insurance policy detailing specific risks not covered by the policy.

exclusion ratio The portion of an annuity that is made up of nondeductible contributions and is therefore nontaxable.

exclusive marketing plan A business strategy whereby a product is offered to a limited number of

retail firms in exchange for their agreement not to stock competitive products.

ex dividend (*abbr* ex div; XD) Exclusive of dividend: applied to a stock traded when payment of a dividend is pending to indicate that the price of the security does not include any dividend declared. See also **cum dividend.**

executive A person who assumes responsibility for the performance of others within a corporation. See also **middle management; top management.**

executive park See **office park.**

executive search firm An independently owned agency that recruits and screens top-level executives for prospective employers, who are charged a fee consisting of a percentage of the annual salary of the position filled.

executor A person named in a will to administer the estate of the deceased.

exemption An amount that an individual (noncorporate) taxpayer may deduct from his or her gross income before calculating income tax owed, based on the number of dependents claimed (including oneself).

exempt personnel An employee or the group of employees who are exempted from the provisions of the Fair Labor Standards Act, and thus are not required to be paid for overtime work: in general, administrative, executive, professional, and outside sales employees.

exercise price (*stock trading*) The price at which an open order is executed. See also **limit order.**

exit interview A meeting between resigning or terminated employees and a representative of the personnel department to determine employee perceptions and reasons for leaving, to settle final payments and disposition of benefits, and to ensure the return of company property.

expansion An increase in economic and industrial activity.

expected return The amount that is expected to be earned from an investment in securities or from a business venture.

expected value The weighted average outcome for a specific decision alternative, where the weights are the probabilities associated with each possible outcome.

expected yield The ratio of the expected return to the total amount invested.

expediting time Work time spent in locating a misplaced order and carrying out the tasks necessary for its fulfillment.

expense 1. A current charge incurred in order to generate revenues and sustain operations. **2.** A charge incurred by an employee in the course of conducting business outside the office, typically for transportation, meals, and lodging.

expense account An account of business-related expenses incurred outside the office by an employee and reimbursable by the employer. See also **expense** (def. 2).

experience curve See **learning curve.**

experience rating A determination of current charges on the basis of past costs and risks, used in insurance, especially unemployment insurance.

experimental learning A proactive method of learning whereby learners develop their own understandings of concepts on the basis of personal experience; learning by doing. See also **cognitive style.**

expert power Power derived from technical or professional expertise that is recognized by others. See also **charismatic power; legitimate power.**

exploitive leadership Also called **system 1 management.** A style of leadership that emphasizes the formal roles of superiors and subordinates, discourages interaction between them, leaves it to management to control all activities and initiate all communication, and makes no provision for teamwork, thus eliminating any possibility of influence by subordinates on the goals of the organization or the methods and activities of their work group and generating fear and distrust.

exponential smoothing A forecasting procedure

that uses an exponentially weighted average of past observations as a basis for forecasts.

export 1. To sell goods or raw materials to a foreign country. **2.** A product sold to a foreign country.

express warranty A promise or statement of fact concerning goods made by a seller as part of a bargain with a buyer. See also **implied warranty.**

ex rights Without the right, enjoyed by current shareholders, to purchase a new issue at a special subscription price: applied to previously issued shares that are traded during the period when the special price is being offered to shareholders.

ex-rights date The date after which shares of stock are sold ex rights. See also **rights on.**

external auditor Also called **independent auditor.** An independent auditor engaged to scrutinize a company's accounting data and financial statements in order to determine whether the firm has conformed to accepted accounting practices and principles. See also **internal auditor.**

external consultant Also called **outside consultant.** An adviser who is hired by a company on a temporary basis to analyze a specific problem and suggest a solution.

external control The management and regulation of people within an organization by those to whom power has been formally delegated. See also **first-order controls.**

external data Facts generated outside a company, as by surveys or by government or private sources.

externalities See **economic externalities.**

external reporting The reporting of a company's financial situation to shareholders, the public at large, or any audience outside the company (e.g., annual report, 8-K report). See also **internal reporting.**

external storage Computer memory storage not part of the computer but connected to it in such a way that it is accessible by the central processing unit.

extra dating Extension of time beyond the established limit for payment of an invoice.

extra dividend Also called **extra.** A dividend in cash or in additional shares paid in addition to regular dividends.

extra-expense insurance Insurance that covers the extra expenses of carrying on business in temporary quarters after a fire or other disaster.

extraordinary item Also called **extraordinary gain (loss).** An accounting entry or tax item reflecting a material expense or revenue that is neither frequent nor normal (e.g., a gain generated by the sale of a significant portion of the company at a profit, a loss incurred as a result of an earthquake).

extraordinary repair An accounting entry reflecting the cost of repairs not frequently or normally made (e.g., reconditioning or overhaul of a major piece of equipment to extend its useful life or utility).

extrapolation Projection or extension of known facts to an unknown situation.

extra terms Provisions of an agreement that allow a credit customer extra time for payment for a product or service.

extrinsic reward Satisfaction derived from salary, status, job title, and other recompense for work performed. See also **intrinsic reward.**

business

---

a b c d e **F** g h i j k l m n o p q r s t u v w x y z

---

fabricating material A raw material (e.g., wood, cotton) that is processed into usable forms (e.g., lumber, fabric).

fabrication A form of manufacturing that involves machining, finishing, weaving, or some other treatment of raw materials.

face value The amount designated on the face of an instrument that is to be paid by the issuer or that represents its book value (e.g., the principal amount of a bond, the maturity value of a life insurance policy, the par value of a municipal bond).

facilitation 1. Provision of clear objectives to be attained in the accomplishment of a task. **2.** Coordination of assigned tasks and direction of effective performance in light of the goals to be achieved.

facsimile See **fax.**

factor 1. An agent who buys or sells goods for other persons on commission. **2.** A finance company or commercial bank that discounts accounts receivable for dealers and producers.

factoring 1. The practice of lending money on the basis of a company's accounts receivable. **2.** The purchase by a bank or other financial institution or group of a company's accounts receivable, after which customers make payments directly to the institution or group holding the accounts.

factor of production A resource used in the production of goods and services: land, labor, or capital.

factory outlet A store, operated by a manufacturer, that sells quality merchandise directly to consumers for less than current retail prices.

factory overhead Also called **manufacturing overhead.** Charges incurred in the manufacturing process exclusive of charges for raw materials and direct labor.

fact sheet A printed sheet listing all features of a product, intended to accompany the product when it is sold.

Fair Credit Reporting Act Federal legislation enacted in 1970 that includes among its provisions (enforced by the Federal Trade Commission) the requirement that consumers be permitted access to their personal credit records and given an opportunity to correct inaccurate data, and specifies the conditions under which such records will be maintained and disseminated.

Fair Labor Standards Act Also called **Wage and Hour Law.** An act of Congress passed in 1938 that regulates minimum wages, compensation for overtime work, and employment of minors, and designates employees exempt from its provisions.

fair market value The fair price that is likely to be paid for stock, real estate, or any other asset offered for sale on the open market when all existing factors are taken into consideration. See also **market value.**

fair-trade agreement An agreement or contract between a manufacturer and a retailer to sell a brand product at no less than a specified price: declared illegal in 1975.

false drop A descriptor or term that fails to describe the concept one is attempting to identify by means of a computer search of related terms.

family brand A brand name that is used on two or more products.

family group A group of individuals who are part of the same organization or are closely associated as an integral work group: applied to such a group undergoing training to improve interpersonal relationships with the aim of forming a cohesive unit.

Fannie Mae See **Federal National Mortgage Association.**

farming See **prospecting.**

f.a.s. (*abbr for* *f*ree *a*longside *s*hip) An indication that the cost of transporting goods to a ship is borne by the seller, but that thereafter the transportation costs are to be paid by the buyer.

FASB statement An official decision policy or pronouncement issued by the Financial Accounting Standards Board that establishes a particular financial accounting practice as a standard and acceptable accounting principle.

fast track A career track in which a person advances more rapidly than usual.

favorable balance of trade An excess in value of exports over imports.

fax 1. Also called **facsimile. a.** A method or device **(fax machine)** for transmitting documents, drawings, photographs, or the like by telephone or radio for exact reproduction elsewhere. **b.** An exact copy or reproduction so transmitted. **2.** To transmit documents or the like by fax.

FCC See **Federal Communications Commission.**

FDA See **Food and Drug Administration.**

FDIC See **Federal Deposit Insurance Corporation.**

feasibility study Any of a series of studies, conducted principally by systems analysts, to determine the advisability of manufacturing a new product, revising a manufacturing process, etc., and if recommended, the steps necessary to implement such a course of action.

feasible solution A decision alternative that satisfies all constraints.

featherbedding The practice of requiring an employer to retain union members on a job when their skills are no longer needed, to hire more workers than are needed for an operation, or otherwise to pay full wages for unnecessary or nonproductive labor.

Fed See **Federal Reserve system.**

federal agency obligations Bonds or notes issued by the Federal National Mortgage Association, the Federal Home Loan Bank, the Government National Mortgage Association, and other federal agencies to finance their operations and available through commercial banks, generally at minimum values of $1000 to $5000 and at yields slightly higher than those of bills, notes, and bonds issued by the U.S. Treasury.

Federal Communications Commission (abbr FCC) A federal agency empowered to grant licenses to commercial broadcasters, assign frequencies, regulate interstate communications by radio, television, telephone, and telegraph, and set rates for wire communications.

Federal Deposit Insurance Corporation (abbr FDIC) A federal agency that insures up to a maximum amount deposits in all banks that belong to the Federal Reserve system.

Federal Energy Administration (abbr FEA) A federal agency instituted in 1973 to establish and implement a federal energy policy.

Federal Home Loan Mortgage Corporation A federally sponsored private corporation that purchases mortgages from banks, repackages them as securities, and sells them to private investors: primary purpose is to provide funds for residential mortgages.

Federal Housing Administration (abbr FHA) A federal agency established in 1934, now part of the Department of Housing and Urban Development, that insures mortgages on private and multifamily houses, housing for the elderly, nursing homes, and housing in urban renewal areas, and insures loans for property improvement.

Federal Insecticide, Fungicide, and Rodenticide Act An act of Congress passed in 1972 requiring that before a pesticide may be sold to the public it must be registered with the Environmental Protection Agency, which may refuse registration or restrict the sale of the product to specified types of customers.

Federal Insurance Contributions Act (acronym FICA) Also called **Social Security Act.** Federal legislation passed in 1935 to institute the social security system, under whose provisions a percentage of each worker's salary or wages is deducted by the employer and credited to the individual's social security account in order to create a fund for the provision of monthly benefits to retired and disabled workers and their dependents or survivors.

Federal Mediation and Conciliation Service

A federal agency that may be called upon for aid in settling a labor dispute. See also **arbitration.**

Federal National Mortgage Association (abbr FNMA) A federally sponsored private corporation that purchases mortgages from banks for resale to investors, the purpose being to maintain a steady supply of funds for home mortgages.

Federal Reserve system (abbr Fed) A federal banking system created by the Federal Reserve Act of 1913 to set monetary policy and control the amount of cash and credit available by establishing reserve requirements, buying and selling government bonds, and setting the interest rates charged its member banks (now numbering 6000) in its 12 geographical districts when they borrow money from it.

Federal Trade Commission (abbr FTC) A federal agency created by the Federal Trade Commission Act (1914) with powers to enforce legislation banning unfair competitive practices among businesses and to guide businesses in avoidance of activities in restraint of trade. See also **Magnuson-Moss Act; Wheeler-Lea Act.**

Federal Water Pollution Control Act An act of Congress passed in 1972 establishing limits on the discharge of pollutants into national waterways.

federal withholding tax (abbr FWT) A percentage of an employee's gross earnings that is deducted from each paycheck and deposited with the federal government to offset the employee's income-tax liability, the percentage being dependent on the employee's income and number of exemptions.

fee A sum of money, either fixed by prior agreement or negotiated, paid by a client to cover the provision of services and materials used in the completion of a job.

feedback 1. Information on the results of any action, considered as influencing future decisions or performance. **2.** Reintroduction of part of the output of a computer system as input, especially for purposes of correction or control. **3.** Continuous, automatic furnishing of data concerning the output of a machine to an automatic control device so that errors may be corrected.

feedback system 1. A system of regular (daily or weekly) reports on production performance generated by computerized monitoring and/or supervisors. **2.** A system for continuous, automatic furnishing of data concerning the output of a machine to an automatic control device.

FHA See **Federal Housing Administration.**

FICA See **Federal Insurance Contributions Act.**

fidelity bond An insurance agreement providing for indemnification of an employer against losses sustained as a result of the dishonesty of an employee (as by embezzlement or theft).

fiduciary A person who has the legal power to act for another; a trustee (as of a pension fund or an investment plan).

fiduciary management system A formal system whereby an individual employee, work group, or supervisor can bring to management's attention any issue considered dysfunctional to the organization as a whole.

Fiedler's leadership contingency model A group contingency or interaction model developed by Fred E. Fiedler to measure leadership styles and permit evaluation of the effectiveness of a leader's style in relation to the makeup of the group.

Fiedler's LPC scale (abbr for least preferred co-worker scale) An eight-point scale developed by Fred E. Fiedler for evaluation of behaviors that either help or hinder successful completion of group tasks, the least preferred co-worker being rated low on such qualities as pleasantness, friendliness, helpfulness, enthusiasm, warmth, harmoniousness, and efficiency.

field salesperson A salesperson who visits clients and prospective clients at their business establishments.

field warehousing Storage of inventories used as collateral in a warehouse or area set apart on the borrower's property, usually to avoid the cost and difficulties of transporting awkward materials.

FIFO (*acronym for* first *in*, first *out*) A method of costing inventory that assumes that the stock acquired first will be sold first. Goods sold are therefore costed at the price of the earliest stock, and ending inventory is costed at the price of the most recent purchases (opposite of LIFO). See also **weighted average cost.**

file maintenance The process of periodically updating the information in computer memory files.

file wrapper A folder containing an application for a patent and all other documents pertaining to it.

final-goods recession Long-term erosion of consumer purchasing power due to a combination of inflation, increases in taxes and interest rates, and other factors. See also **inventory recession.**

finance 1. The management function of raising and using moneys. 2. To supply with money or capital; obtain money or credit for a purchase or enterprise.

finance charge, interest or a fee charged for borrowing money or buying on credit.

finance company An institution engaged in such specialized forms of financing as extending credit to retailers and lending money with goods as security.

financial accounting The area of accounting concerned with external reporting, as with financial statements and reports to government agencies.

Financial Accounting Standards Board (*abbr* FASB) An independent organization established by the certified public accounting profession to create and confirm accounting principles and financial reporting practices for adoption by the profession. See also **FASB statement; generally accepted accounting principles.**

financial lease A noncancelable lease that includes no maintenance service and is fully amortized (i.e., total payments equal or exceed the value of the property).

financial leverage The extent to which assets are supported or generated by debt, which acts as a sort of lever to raise income by providing funds for investment. See also **leverage.**

financial planner A professional who devises a program for the allocation of personal finances and capital through budgeting, investments, etc.

financial ratio A ratio expressing the relationship of any of various financial factors, including income, sales, expenses, and stock turnover, used as an indicator of a firm's economic condition and operating efficiency.

financial responsibility law A state law requiring automobile owners to provide evidence that they can pay for damages caused by accidents in which they are legally at fault.

financial risk Also called **speculative risk.** The probability that the return on an investment or the value of an asset will be unpredictably negative. See also **pure risk.**

financial statement Any of five reports on the operations or financial position of a business organization on a certain date or during a certain period, often in comparison with prior periods. See also **balance sheet; income statement; statement of changes in financial position; statement of changes in owners' equity; statement of retained earnings.**

financing lease See **capital lease.**

finder's fee 1. Payment to one who brings a buyer and seller together. 2. Payment to one who secures a mortgage for a buyer, or who arranges a merger, finds an underwriter for a company issuing stock, etc.

finished goods inventory 1. The stock of finished products ready for sale. 2. The dollar value of finished products ready for sale (a current asset).

firm order A written or verbal order that cannot be canceled by either buyer or seller without payment of a substantial penalty.

first in, first out See **FIFO.**

first-line management The lowest level of supervisory position in an organization, with responsibility for supervision of hourly production workers.

first-order controls Rules and regulations formally recognized by an organization and used to restrain or modify employees' behavior. See also **external control.**

first proof The first print of an advertisement, made for examination and correction.

fiscal policy The financial policy of a government, particularly in regard to debt and budgetary matters.

fiscal year Also called **business year.** The period of time, which may be less than 12 months but not more, and which may but usually does not coincide with a calendar year, from one balancing of accounts to the next; the period covered by an annual report.

fishbowl A training technique whereby participants take turns acting out solutions to organizational problems and observing and analyzing the solutions acted out by others.

fishyback Transportation of goods by truck in a trailer that is then loaded directly onto a ship for delivery to the port of their destination. See also **birdyback.**

five m's *M*anpower, *m*aterials, *m*oney, *m*achinery, *m*anagement: the basic resources of any organization.

fixed asset Also called **long-term asset; noncurrent asset.** A tangible asset with a useful life of more than one year (e.g., a building, land, furniture, manufacturing or transportation equipment) used in running a business and not usually converted into cash.

fixed asset turnover ratio Sales divided by fixed assets. See also **activity ratio.**

fixed cost Also called **fixed charge.** A cost that does not fluctuate with variation in production (e.g., interest, rent, payment to a sinking fund). See also **fixed overhead.**

fixed expense An expenditure (usually in connection with administration rather than manufacturing) that does not vary with short-term changes in production or sales.

fixed-income Gaining or yielding a more or less uniform rate of income, such as bonds that pay a fixed rate of interest until maturity or preferred stock that pays a fixed dividend.

fixed liability Also called **long-term liability; noncurrent liability.** An obligation that will not come due for a relatively long time, usually more than a year.

fixed overhead Factory overhead that does not change with normal increases or decreases in production (e.g., rent, most wages, utility costs).

fixed-rate mortgage A home mortgage for which equal monthly payments of interest and principal are made over the life of the loan, usually for a term of 30 years.

fixture An attachment to a building (e.g., a lavatory, a lighting fixture) that, though permanently installed, could be removed (a depreciable fixed asset).

flash sales report A daily report of the dollar value of sales made by each department of a retail store.

flat organization An organizational hierarchy that has relatively few levels and consequently is characterized by wide spans of management with a high degree of authority delegated to middle managers.

flat rate A standard or uniform rate charged for a product or service, with no discount given for any reason.

flat tax A tax applied at the same rate to all levels of taxable income.

flexdollars Money given by an employer that an employee can apply to any of various employee benefits.

flexible budget Also called **variable budget.** A budget in which alternative expense allowances are provided in conjunction with alternative levels of production and/or sales.

flexible manufacturing system (*abbr* FMS) A grouping of machines with reprogrammable controllers linked by an automated materials-handling system and integrated through a central computer, so

business

that the system can produce a variety of parts that have similar processing requirements.

flexible-rate mortgage 1. See **variable-rate mortgage.** 2. See **renegotiable-rate mortgage.**

flextime Also called **flexitime.** A flexible schedule of work hours for employees, permitting them to arrive and depart within specified limits so long as they complete the required number of hours per day, week, etc.

flexweek Also called **flexiweek.** A four-day workweek.

flier A sales-promotion announcement, usually of one page, distributed to regular and prospective customers; a handbill.

flighting Also called **pulsing.** An advertising strategy that alternates periods of highly concentrated advertising with periods of no advertising at all.

float 1. To lay out an advertisement on a sheet much larger than any on which it will appear in print, leaving a large border. 2. To offer (an issue of stock) for sale. 3. The amount of money represented by checks that have been deposited in a bank but not yet collected from the banks on which they are drawn. The interest thus earned is often a bank's prime source of revenue. 4. Also called **slack.** The amount of time an activity can be delayed beyond its earliest possible starting time without delaying the completion of a project. 5. (*stock exchange*) The part of a new stock issue that has not been bought by the public. 6. To let a currency or interest rate fluctuate in the foreign-exchange or money market.

floater An insurance policy to cover personal property taken with one, as on vacation.

floating rate note A note whose interest rate fluctuates in line with the money market, prime rate, etc.

floppy disk A thin plastic disk coated with magnetic material, for storing computer data and programs; diskette.

flow chart 1. A detailed diagram of the operations and equipment used to complete a manufacturing process. 2. A graphic representation, using symbols interconnected with lines, used to show the successive steps in any procedure or system.

flow process chart A chart listing in detail each element involved in each step of a process, for use in analyzing and simplifying procedures.

fluid cash The cash and checks that are gathered by a company in the course of daily business.

FNMA See **Federal National Mortgage Association.**

f.o.b. (*abbr for* f*ree on* b*oard*) An indication that a seller will deliver goods to a shipper but thereafter freight charges are borne by the buyer.

f.o.b. destination (*abbr for* f*ree on* b*oard and to* d*estination*) An indication that a seller bears the cost of transporting goods to a buyer and retains title to them until they are delivered.

focus gambling The process of focusing on alternative solutions to a problem or on alternative strategies for solving a problem. See also **scanning.**

focus group A representative group of people questioned together, usually in a controlled setting, about their opinions on product marketing or other issues.

follow-on experience An activity designed to reinforce concepts introduced in a training session and to support the lessons taught.

follow-up 1. A process of or system for taking additional action after an initial effort. 2. The process of examining a past effort for any insights it may yield.

Food and Drug Administration (*abbr* FDA) A division of the U.S. Department of Health and Human Services that protects the public against impure and unsafe foods, drugs, and cosmetics.

Food, Drug, and Cosmetic Act An act of Congress passed in 1938 to prohibit the manufacture and interstate shipment of any food, drug, cosmetic, or health device that is mislabeled (bears a label that includes any false or misleading statement), adulterated (contains an admixture of another substance sufficient to dilute its strength), or injurious to health. See also **Delaney Amendment.**

foot To add figures in a vertical column. See also **crossfoot.**

forbearance The act of abstaining from doing or promising not to do something one has the legal right to do (e.g., the collecting of a debt).

forecasting The process of predicting future business conditions on the basis of study and analysis of available data for the purpose of making intelligent decisions in regard to promotions, advertising, plant expansion, development of new products, and other activities.

foreclosure The process of depriving a mortgagor of the right to own mortgaged property as a consequence of failure to pay by the due date, title to the property then passing to the mortgagee.

foreign corporation A corporation that conducts its business in a state other than the one in which it was incorporated. See also **domestic corporation.**

Foreign Corrupt Practices Act (*abbr* FCPA) An act of Congress passed in 1977 to outlaw payments of bribes to foreign officials for the opportunity to obtain lucrative contracts.

foreign exchange 1. The process of balancing accounts in transactions between individuals or firms in different countries. 2. The currency of a foreign country or negotiable instruments payable in such currency.

foreign-exchange contract A contract by which two parties agree to an exchange of currencies on a specified future date at a specified rate, both parties thereby seeking to protect themselves against unforeseeable fluctuations in the exchange rate.

foreign-exchange rate The rate at which the currency of one country may be exchanged for another currency at a given time.

foreign-exchange service (*abbr* FX) Long-distance telephone service by means of a special (trunk) line run from a foreign or distant exchange to the subscriber's phone, on which calls may be placed at the rate in effect in the distant community.

foreign licensing A process by which a company authorizes a firm in a foreign country to produce and market its products in that country for a fee.

foreign-trade zone See **free-trade zone.**

forestalling The process of including anticipated objections in a formal sales presentation to a client, thereby retaining control over the presentation.

formal group A group of people, usually consisting of a supervisor and subordinates, assembled on a permanent or ad hoc basis to work toward common organizational goals and objectives. See also **ad hoc committee; informal group.**

formal integrative unit A group designated to facilitate and coordinate efforts to integrate various organizational units with specialized functions to meet the organization's specific goals.

formalization The process of establishing organizational standards to govern the behavior of employees.

formal leader A person selected by management to assume a position of leadership in the organization.

formal organization A company organized in accordance with a formal structural plan. See also **organization chart.**

formal search Systematized information retrieval through a process of data-based intervention.

format 1. The arrangement of data for computer input or output, such as the number of fields in a database record or the margins in a report. 2. The programming featured by a radio or television station, such as talk show or classical music. 3. **a.** To set the format of computer data input or output. **b.** To prepare a computer disk as required by the software that will be used.

form utility The value created through the transformation of raw materials and other inputs into finished goods.

FORTRAN (*acronym for* For*mula* Tran*slation*) A

computer programming language designed for use in solving mathematical and scientific problems.

Fortune 500 An annual list compiled by Fortune magazine of the 500 largest industrial corporations in the U.S.

forward buying The practice of purchasing raw materials or other items required in manufacturing in large quantities far in advance of need for the purpose of securing a discount, ensuring needed supplies, and facilitating analysis of costs.

forward scheduling A method of preparing a schedule by starting with the first activity and working forward in sequence to schedule the later activities and derive a completion date.

forward vertical merger See **vertical merger.**

four-day week Also called **flexweek.** A workweek consisting of four days, usually of ten hours each.

401(k) A savings plan that allows employees to contribute a fixed amount of income to a retirement account and to defer taxes until withdrawal.

FPA See **Freight Paid Allowance.**

FPT See **freight-pass-through.**

franchise A right granted by a producer to sell or distribute the producer's products and use the producer's name, patents, trademarks, and processes in a specified location or territory in exchange for an initial fee plus royalties or commissions.

franchisee A person who has been granted a franchise.

franchisor Also called **franchiser.** A person who grants a franchise to another person.

fraud An act of trickery, deceit, or breach of confidence committed to gain an unfair or dishonest advantage.

Freddie Mac See **Federal Home Loan Mortgage Corporation.**

free enterprise Also called **private enterprise.** An economic system that operates in accordance with the law of supply and demand, private businesses competing to satisfy consumers' demands, and government acting only to protect individual rights, not to regulate commercial activity.

freelance A self-employed specialist in some (usually creative) field who works on a temporary basis for various employers.

free-market system Also called **market economy.** An economic system that operates by free competition, the merchant setting his or her own prices and selling to anyone who will pay those prices, the consumer purchasing from any seller in accordance with his or her needs, desires, and ability to pay.

free-rein leader A manager who practices a policy of minimal supervision while delegating most decision making to subordinates.

free trade International trade unhampered by tariffs or other governmental restrictions. Free traders advocate the removal of all existing tariffs and restrictions on trade between countries.

free-trade area A geographical area consisting of nations (not necessarily contiguous) that agree to permit unrestricted trade in each other's products and commodities, with tariffs, if any, used only as a source of revenue and not as a means of limiting access to foreign goods or influencing their prices.

free-trader A person who opposes any restriction on foreign trade.

free-trade zone Also called **foreign trade zone.** A designated industrial area into which foreign goods (usually raw materials or parts) can be imported without payment of customs until the goods leave the zone as finished products, or with no such payment at all if the finished products are exported to a third country.

freeze **1.** To fix rents, prices, etc., at a specific amount, usually by government order. **2.** To prevent assets from being liquidated or collected.

freeze rate Also called **rate stop.** A minimum rate established by a trucking company for transportation of goods that is essentially independent of the distance traveled.

freight allowed See **postage-stamp pricing.**

freight forwarder Also called **package-consol-**

idating agency. An independent person or company that arranges for transportation of goods within a country or between countries.

freight in See **transportation in.**

freight out See **transportation out.**

Freight Paid Allowance (*abbr* FPA) An agreement whereby the shipper pays a specified percent or part of shipping costs, such as an agreement between publisher and bookstores.

freight-pass-through (*abbr* FPT) A special discount given a retailer for paying the freight charge on a shipment of merchandise: the charge is then passed along to the consumer by an increase in the product's suggested retail price.

frequency distribution An arrangement of a set of statistical data showing the number of times each item appears in each of the categories, intervals, or values into which the data are classified.

frictional unemployment Brief periods of unemployment, unrelated to basic inadequacies of supply or demand, experienced by people entering the job market or moving between jobs.

friendship, commerce, and navigation treaty (*abbr* FCN treaty) An international agreement by which each signatory nation permits nationals of the treaty partner to conduct business in its domestic market under conditions specified.

fringe benefit Compensation extended to employees (e.g., a pension plan, health and life insurance, vacations and sick leave with pay) in addition to basic salaries and wages. See also **cafeteria plan.**

front end Any location inside or outside a store where customers pay for goods.

front-end bonus A payment made usually to an executive at the time of hiring to compensate for bonuses or other payments the individual would have received in the job he or she is leaving and as an incentive, in preference to a higher salary, which might cause resentment among company veterans.

front-end checkout The placement of checkout counters near store exits rather than near sales areas.

front-end load The sales commission and other fees taken out of the initial payments when an investor contracts to purchase shares of certain mutual funds.

front money **1.** Money paid in advance, as for goods or services, to a commission agent or the like. **2.** Capital necessary to begin a business enterprise. **3.** Money furnished by a company to a financier under a promise to procure funds for it.

front office Collectively, the offices of top management within a company.

frozen See **freeze.**

FTC See **Federal Trade Commission.**

fulfillment The process or business of handling and executing customer orders, as packing, shipping, or processing checks.

full costing See **absorption costing.**

full employment The lowest rate of unemployment compatible with price stability, variously estimated at between 5 and 6 percent.

full endorsement Also called **special endorsement.** Writing on the back of a negotiable instrument, consisting of the name of the person or persons to whom it is being transferred and, underneath, the signature of the payee.

full-service agency An advertising agency that provides accounting and marketing services, does product research and development, and works with clients from product conceptualization to market testing and full-scale launching, in addition to creating and placing advertisements.

full warranty A manufacturer's guarantee that a defective product will be repaired free of charge within a specified time after purchase, and that after a reasonable number of attempts to repair the product, the purchaser may elect either a refund (less an amount for depreciation) or replacement. See also **limited warranty; Magnuson-Moss act.**

fully diluted earnings per share The smallest earnings per share of common stock that would be paid if all convertible bonds and preferred stock and other convertible securities were converted to common stock, and which must be reported on the company's income statement if the figure represents less than 97 percent of total earnings available to an average number of outstanding common stocks.

fully managed fund A mutual fund with an investment policy that allows the fund's management to act with reasonable discretion in the buying and selling of any securities in any combination or quantity.

functional authority 1. The formal power exercised by the manager of a specific unit or subsystem of an organization. 2. A right to direct the activities of others based on possession of specialized knowledge, skill, or ability. See also **authority.**

functional departmentalization A homogeneous grouping of jobs into a single department, major division, or subsystem.

functional discount See **trade discount.**

functional management The administration and control of a specific unit of an organization.

functional organization An organizational structure (common today only in the film industry) in which direct authority over each task or function resides in a manager who is considered a specialist, and each employee below the level of top management reports to more than one superior in accordance with a specific phase of his or her activity.

fund 1. funds **a.** Money; working capital. **b.** Assets, especially cash or marketable securities, set aside for a specific purpose. See also **sinking fund.** 2. A mutual fund. See also **closed-end investment com-**

pany. 3. A self-balancing account, as requested by a donor to a nonprofit organization or as required of a governmental agency by policy restrictions.

fund accounting A system of accounting in which each account is self-balancing. See also **fund** (def. 3).

fund balance In the fund accounting system of a nonprofit organization or governmental agency, the difference between assets and liabilities (including any reserves).

funding The acquisition and allocation of money needed to operate a business or to finance a venture.

funds statement See **statement of changes in financial position.**

fungible goods Products that consist of like units that can be replaced by other units similar in weight and number.

furlough 1. A temporary layoff, usually due to lack of business. 2. A leave of absence from work or other duties due to an employee's desire for time to take care of personal business.

future goods Products that are allocated for sale before they have been manufactured, as crops that are not yet grown. See also **contract to sell; identified goods.**

futures trading Also called **cash trading.** Contract agreements that promise the buying and selling of commodities or securities for delivery at a later date, often a year or more in the future.

FWT See **federal withholding tax.**

FX See **foreign-exchange service.**

a b c d e f G h i j k l m n o p q r s t u v w x y z

game plan A strategy or design for the achievement of an objective or goal.

game theory A mathematical theory that deals with strategies for maximizing gains and minimizing losses within prescribed constraints, applied to the solution of business problems and to the training of employees to deal with conflict, the decision-making process, leadership struggles, and group norms.

Gantt chart A chart on which work activities are plotted against a time scale.

garbage in, garbage out See GIGO.

garnishment A legal notice requiring the person addressed to hold money or property of another person in his or her possession pending the outcome of litigation over an unpaid debt owed by the owner of the money or property.

gatefold A magazine cover or page that is larger than the regular pages, being folded so as not to extend beyond the edges. Gatefolds are used for advertisement.

gatekeeping Regulation of communication patterns among individuals by a group facilitator, who encourages some to speak and others to listen.

gateway The point at which a shipment is transferred from one carrier to another or at which goods enter the transportation system.

GDP See **gross domestic product.**

General Agreement on Tariffs and Trade (*abbr* GATT) An international treaty and the autonomous agency established in 1967 to administer its provisions, with headquarters in Geneva, Switzerland, which provides a forum for settlement of trade disputes and negotiation of trade liberalization among nearly 90 signatory nations plus 30 de facto members.

generally accepted accounting principles (*abbr* GAAP) Standards, conventions, and rules established by the Financial Accounting Standards Board (in FASB Opinions), by the Accounting Principles Board (in APB Opinions), and by the American Institute of Certified Public Accountants to be followed in the preparation of financial statements.

generally accepted accounting standards (*abbr* GAAS) Rules established by the American Institute of Certified Public Accountants to be followed in audits of financial statements.

general partner A partner in a firm who plays an active role in management of the company, is publicly known as a partner, and has unlimited liability for the company's financial commitments. See also **dormant partner; limited partner; secret partner; silent partner.**

generic product A product that bears no brand name, is packaged inexpensively, is not advertised, and generally is priced lower than comparable brand-name products.

gentrification The buying and renovation of houses and stores in deteriorated urban neighborhoods by upper- or middle-income families or individuals, thus improving property values but often displacing low-income families and small businesses.

GERT (*acronym for* graphical evaluation and review technique) A method of network planning, introduced in 1966 to overcome shortcomings of the PERT method, encompassing activities that have probability of occurrence, an option of being performed, and variable completion times.

gestalt theory A theory that views the human mind as having the capacity to perceive an event or occurrence as a unified whole having specific qualities that cannot be derived from the sum of its component parts or individual elements.

gift tax A federal tax on gifts above $10,000. Gifts up to this amount may be given annually to a child of any age.

GIGO (*acronym for* garbage in, garbage out) Data that are incorrect or incorrectly entered in a computer will yield useless results.

gilt-edged security Any security, especially a blue-chip bond, that has a good record of regular interest payments and redemption and a high likelihood of continued high performance. United States Treasury bonds are the best examples of gilt-edged securities.

Ginnie Mae See **Government National Mortgage Association**.

giveback A concession by unions that represents a cut in wages or benefits, usually demanded by a management in order to avoid large-scale layoffs, factory closings, etc.

glamour stock A stock, as in a new or rapidly developing industry, that captures investors' fancy and tends to rise quickly in price.

glass ceiling An upper limit to professional advancement, especially as imposed upon women, that is not readily perceived or openly acknowledged.

global firm, A business that has production and distribution facilities, as well as R & D and strategic decision-making authority, in more than one country.

GNMA See **Government National Mortgage Association**.

GNP See **gross national product**.

goal An objective of a system, subsystem, or group established to give its members direction, a common purpose, and a unique position in their environment, to facilitate accountability and resolution of conflicts, to provide a means of measuring performance and rating success, and to challenge and motivate individuals by stimulating commitment and involvement in a mutually beneficial direction.

goal setting The process of creating and revising realistic objectives for a system, subsystem, or group.

goal succession The process of establishing a set of new organizational goals or objectives to replace those goals that have been achieved or abandoned.

going concern A company expected to continue its business operations into the indefinite future, paying its debts on time and generating revenues at profitable levels.

golden handcuffs A succession of raises, bonuses, perks, etc., given or promised at specified future intervals or tied to length of employment, so that an executive would find it extremely difficult to leave a company.

golden handshake Dismissal of an employee with generous benefits, cash bonus, etc.

golden parachute A package of benefits, as severance pay and bonuses, guaranteed a key executive in case of job loss due to a merger or takeover. See also **tin parachute**.

gold fixing Also called **gold fix. 1.** The procedure by which the price of gold is established. **2.** The price itself, esp. as established daily in the gold market.

go/no-go gauge A standard by which defective products or parts are distinguished from those that are acceptable.

good A product or commodity that is manufactured or otherwise made available for sale (distinguished from *service*): usually used in plural.

good delivery A correct, legal transaction of an order involving a security in accordance with the terms agreed upon (usually a precondition of payment).

good faith Absence of intent to deceive; a belief in the honesty of one's purposes and actions.

good-till-canceled order See **open order**.

goodwill 1. The business advantage acquired by a firm as a result of reputation for good business dealings. **2.** The excess in purchase price for a firm over the value of its net assets. **3.** The capitalized value of a firm's anticipated profits in excess of the rate of return considered normal in the industry in which the firm operates.

goodwill method A method of calculating partners' shares of a business whereby the capital account of a new partner is credited with an amount of goodwill equal to the amount of money he or she has contributed to the partnership. See also **goodwill** (def. 3).

go public To abandon the policy or position of having a limited number of stockholders and issue shares of stock for sale to the general public.

government bond A promissory note issued by the U.S. government (i.e., a Series E or Series H bond, a bill, note, or bond issued by the U.S. Treasury, or an obligation of a federal agency), technically not guaranteed but considered to be the highest quality bond available. See also **bond** (def. 1); **municipal bond**.

Government National Mortgage Association (*abbr* GNMA) A federally owned corporation that buys mortgages, especially those on low-rent housing, and raises funds by selling bonds guaranteed by the Veterans Administration and the Federal Housing Administration.

grace period A period of time after a payment becomes due, as of a loan or life-insurance premium, before one is subject to penalties or late charges or before the loan or policy is canceled.

graduated tax See **progressive tax**.

grandfather clause A clause exempting certain people or firms from a regulation by reason of circumstances or conditions that existed before the regulation went into effect.

grant A transfer of real property from one owner to another by means of a deed.

grapevine An informal communication system that is present in all organizations and that operates outside the formal communication channels.

graphical evaluation and review technique See **GERT**.

graveyard shift A work shift, usually from midnight until 8 a.m.

gravure A printing process whereby a desired design is cut into a metal plate, ink rolled onto the plate fills the grooves, and the design is transferred to paper. See also **intaglio**.

gray market 1. A market in which scarce goods (e.g., computer chips) are traded at above-market prices through irregular channels or by methods not explicitly illegal but usually not considered ethical. **2.** The selling at bargain prices of goods one has bought covertly at an abnormally large discount. **3.** The market provided by senior citizens for special products and services.

greenmail The purchase, usually surreptitiously, of a large bloc of a company's stock, thereby signaling a possible takeover attempt, and ultimately forcing the company to try to thwart the attempt by buying back its stock at a much higher price.

Green River ordinance A local regulation that establishes standards for allowable door-to-door selling practices.

grid See **managerial grid**.

grievance A complaint of an employee or group of employees that an injustice is being suffered in a job-related matter.

grievance committee A group of representatives of employees, or of management and employees jointly, formed to discuss and seek to eliminate employees' grievances.

gross annual wages See **guaranteed annual wage**.

gross audience 1. The total number of households that tune in to a television show for at least six minutes, as measured by a random sample. **2.** The total number of people who are exposed to a publication at any time and in any manner, as measured by a random sample.

gross domestic product (*abbr* GDP) Gross national product excluding payments on foreign investments.

gross national product (*abbr* GNP) The total market value of all final goods and services produced in a country in a given period of time (usually a year).

gross profit Also called **gross margin**. Net sales less cost of goods sold.

gross profit method Evaluation of ending inventory by means of the estimated gross profit ratio.

gross profit ratio Gross profit (net sales less cost of goods sold) divided by net sales.

gross rating points (*abbr* GRP) A percentage of homes containing television sets where sets are tuned to a specific program at a designated time,

business

used as a measure of the number of people reached by the program.

gross received See **cash flow.**

gross sales The dollar amount of all sales before deduction of discounts, returns, and allowances.

gross weight The total weight of a shipment, including the item shipped, the packing material, and the container.

gross working capital The capital available for ongoing operations of a business, calculated by determining the excess of current assets over liabilities.

group See **formal group; informal group.**

group depreciation Accounting for the simultaneous loss in value of several assets that have similar useful lives by a single figure representing their combined loss of value in each accounting period.

group development 1. A process for increasing the effectiveness of a team or work group. 2. Establishment of a working team through a process designed to bring the group closer together in commitment to goals and objectives.

group discount A special discount given in connection with the purchase of large quantities of an item or service at one time or of air time on several radio or television stations simultaneously.

grouping Perception of clusters of figures, objects, or facts as related rather than as discrete units. See also **closure.**

group maintenance The arrangement of individuals in a group, with either a centralized or decentralized leader, in such a way that work flow and satisfactory performance are established and continued.

group process The process by which such intangible elements of a work group as morale, tone, participation, competition, and cooperation interact and coalesce into a working force of high motivation and productivity striving toward a common goal.

group structure An arrangement of individuals within a particular framework that varies in degree of openness and centralization in proportion to size.

group technology (*abbr* GT) The grouping of items into families with similar characteristics and manufacturing requirements and the arrangement of equipment into cells or work stations for efficient processing of these families.

growth fund 1. A mutual fund whose net asset value has been rising at a rate greater than that of business as a whole. 2. A mutual fund whose net asset value has been rising at a rate of 10 percent or more.

growth stock A stock that is expected to increase in value as its issuing corporation grows in size and earnings.

GTC (*abbr for* good till canceled) See **open order.**

guarantee An assurance, written or implied, that a product is as represented and will perform satisfactorily. See also **express warranty; full warranty; implied warranty; limited warranty.**

guaranteed annual wage (*abbr* GAW) Also called **gross annual wages.** A minimum income guaranteed to employees by agreement between union and management.

guaranteed position An assurance given by a publisher that an advertisement will be displayed in a specific location in each edition printed. See also **run-of-paper.**

guaranty 1. An agreement to pay a debt or perform a duty owed by another person if that person fails to do so. 2. Something given or possessed as security for the fulfillment of some action.

a b c d e f g H i j k l m n o p q r s t u v w x y z

half-life (*marketing*) The estimated time required for half of the total number of responses to a mailing to be received.

halo effect 1. A tendency to permit a high rating on one aspect of an employee's performance or of a job applicant's personality or background to exert undue influence on one's overall evaluation of the individual. 2. The high regard for one brand name that is shared by a new product marketed under the same brand.

hand-to-mouth buying The practice of maintaining only enough stock to meet short-term basic business needs.

hangup An unintentional stoppage or closing down of a computer, generally caused by miscoded information in the software.

hard copy Text material in printed form, as in a manuscript or a computer printout. See also **soft copy.**

hard currency Money that is backed by gold reserves and thus is easily convertible into the currency of another country. See also **soft currency.**

hard disk A rigid disk coated with magnetic material, for storing computer programs and relatively large amounts of data.

hard goods See **durable goods.**

hard sell Forceful, aggressive, high-pressure salesmanship. See also **soft sell.**

hardware The electronic, mechanical, electrical, and magnetic components of a computer system. See also **software.**

hash total A sum (as of serial numbers of products) that has no meaning except as a control that can ascertain if any item has been omitted, as from a list or inventory.

Hawthorne studies A series of motivational studies conducted at a Western Electric Company plant (the Hawthorne Works) in Illinois that revealed the extraordinary autonomous power of the informal group to motivate workers' behavior.

head An electronic device in a computer or an audiotape or videotape machine that is responsible for recording, reading, and erasing incoming and outgoing messages.

headhunter See **executive search firm; recruiter.**

health-maintenance organization (*abbr* HMO) An organization of physicians and other health-care professionals that offers a prepaid medical plan entitling its members to unlimited access to medical and other health-care services.

hedge 1. To protect oneself against a possible loss (in an investment, in financial position, etc.) by diversifying one's investments, buying or selling commodity futures, etc. 2. An act or means of protecting oneself against loss on an investment with a partially counterbalancing one.

helping relationship A client-centered therapeutic relationship, introduced by Carl Rogers, in which the professional is supportive of the client's self-discovery and personal growth.

Herzberg two-factor theory A theory introduced by Frederick Herzberg that bases employee satisfaction and motivation on factors intrinsic to the work itself and on a work environment in which employees can be entrusted with responsibility and achieve recognition. See also **extrinsic reward; intrinsic reward.**

heuristic Something that serves as a guide (as a rule of thumb) or that stimulates thought or research in the absence of known facts or proof. Such a procedure can be used to generate satisfactory solutions to decision problems but cannot guarantee that such solutions are optimal.

hiatus A temporary suspension of a regularly broadcast television or radio program (usually in the summer) because of reduced audience interest or because the number of programs prepared is insufficient to fill a full year's schedule.

hidden reserves The amount of understated value on a balance sheet, resulting from overvaluation of liabilities or undervaluation of assets.

hidden tax A tax that is included in the price of goods or services but is not separately stated.

hierarchy A management structure that has graduated top, middle, and lower levels, with the majority of employees occupying the bottom level and each successive higher level occupied by progressively fewer employees. See also **management pyramid.**

hierarchy of needs A five-step system of human needs proposed by Abraham Maslow, ranging from basic survival needs upward through needs for security, social interaction, self-esteem, and self-actualization, such that each successive level of need becomes dominant as the need at the preceding level is satisfied.

high-tech Related to or making use of high technology.

high technology Scientific technology involving advanced, sophisticated electronic devices, particularly for use in computers and in machines controlled by computers.

hiring hall A union-operated placement office where members are referred to available jobs.

histogram A graph of a frequency distribution in which the widths of rectangles based on the horizontal axis are equal to class intervals and their heights are equal to the corresponding frequencies.

historical cost See **acquisition cost.**

historical summary A selected list, usually part of an annual report, itemizing such significant financial figures as net income, total revenues, assets, liabilities, and earnings per share in each of the past five or ten fiscal years, including the current year. See also **comparative financial statement.**

HMO See **health-maintenance organization.**

holder A person who owns and is entitled to payment of a negotiable instrument (e.g., a promissory note).

holder in due course A person other than the original owner who holds a negotiable instrument and is entitled to payment.

holder-of-record date The final date on which stockholders can register with a corporation in order to receive future dividends, vote at shareholders' meetings, and be entitled to certain other benefits and rights.

hold-harmless agreement A contractual agreement that provides that one party will not hold the other liable for any damages that may result from the performance of the contract.

holding company A corporation that controls or is in a position to control one or more other companies by virtue of ownership of stock in those companies, usually without direct participation in productive activities.

holding cost Those costs incurred as a result of carrying inventory, usually expressed as a percentage of dollar value.

holding gain (loss) The difference between the price or value of an asset at the beginning of a period in which it is held and its value at the end of that period.

holding power (*marketing*) The ability of a television program to hold an audience for a full season.

home-industry argument The argument that competition in the domestic markets of any industry is increased by foreign imports, to the detriment of domestic firms.

home office 1. The main office of a company; headquarters. **2.** A work or office space set up in a worker's home.

homeowner's policy Also called **homeowner's insurance.** A form of home insurance that provides compensation for damage, loss, or injury of property, personal belongings, or persons due to fire, theft, accidents, etc.

homeshopping The purchase, usually by a phone call to an 800 number, of products displayed on television.

horizontal buying The practice of purchasing advertising space in a wide variety of publications as a way of reaching many target audiences with a wide diversity of interests.

horizontal integration The acquisition of one company by another in the same line of business.

horizontal merger Absorption of a company by another in the same field for the purpose of achieving economies of scale and lessening competition. See also **conglomerate merger; vertical merger.**

hospitalization insurance Insurance covering a specified percentage of hospital costs related to covered illnesses and injuries.

hostile takeover The act of taking control of a company by buying up, often surreptitiously, enough of its stock to gain a controlling interest.

house shop An advertising agency owned or controlled by an advertiser.

human assets accounting See **human resources accounting.**

human engineering See **ergonomics.**

human factors engineering Management of the work of industrial workers with a view to minimizing the physical actions required to perform a task and maximizing efficiency.

human relations A field of management study concerned with problems arising from the interactions of people in organizations, specifically the relationship of managers and subordinates and its contribution to productive efficiency and work satisfaction.

human resources accounting Also called **human assets accounting.** Evaluation of the productive capacity of a company's employees by consideration of such variables as aptitude and intellect, training, quality of leadership, morale, communications, and decision making.

human resources forecast Prediction of future personnel needs based on analysis of the numbers and skills of current employees and the numbers and skills required to meet anticipated levels of production under anticipated economic and technological conditions.

human resources management Also called **personnel administration.** The recruitment, assessment, hiring, training, and counseling of employees at all levels within a company, and administration of employee benefit programs, health and safety programs, and labor relations.

human resources planning Establishment of schedules designed to facilitate the provision and maintenance of an efficient work force capable of meeting current objectives and anticipated future production requirements.

hygiene factor See **dissatisfier.**

hyperinflation Extreme or excessive inflation.

hypothecation The securing of a loan by a pledge of property that does not involve the transfer of title or possession.

business

IC See **integrated circuit.**

ICC **1.** See **International Chamber of Commerce. 2.** See **Interstate Commerce Commission.**

idea-development interview (*abbr* IDI) (*marketing research*) A technique for eliciting product and advertising ideas from groups of consumers through the use of questions skillfully designed to tap consumer attitudes and perceptions of new products and advertising concepts. See also **consumer advisory board; consumer panel.**

identified goods Existing products that are allocated for sale under contract, thereby meeting the legal requirement for transfer of title to goods under a sales contract.

IDP See **integrated data processing.**

i.e. (*abbr for id est*) That is; in other words.

image The impression of a product, service, or company held in the minds of consumers or conveyed by its physical and qualitative characteristics or by advertising and publicity. See also **brand image; product position.**

image building (*public relations*) The process by which an organization tries to influence the public's attitude toward the firm and its products or services.

IMF See **International Monetary Fund.**

immaterial Not substantive; not large enough to count, to record, to affect decisions, or to require adjustment.

implicit cost A cost that is involved in the conduct of business and that is the responsibility of the owner.

implied warranty A guarantee assumed to have been given in connection with a transaction, though not expressly stated, and arguable at law for reasons of public policy (as that an automobile sold is safe to drive). See also **express warranty.**

import **1.** To purchase goods or raw materials in one country and bring them or cause them to be brought to another country. **2.** A product brought into a country from another country.

import quota A limitation on the number of products in a specific category that can be brought into a country from another country. See also **embargo.**

imprest fund Also called **imprest account.** An account or fund (such as a petty-cash account) that is constantly diminished but periodically replenished to an established amount.

impulse item A product that customers are likely to buy impulsively rather than as a result of advance planning.

imputed interest Estimated interest due and assumed to be included in a single repayment of a loan, as the difference between the face value of a note upon maturity and the price actually paid for it.

inactive stock A stock for which there is little demand.

in-basket exercise A training exercise in which participants simulate the handling of messages, reports, memos, and other communications that may come to their attention during the course of a business day.

in bond See **bond** (def. 3).

Inc. See **incorporated.**

incidental damages Any expenses incurred in the process of gaining redress for failure to fulfill the terms of a contract. See also **actual damages.**

incident pattern Also called **critical incidence.** A behavioral pattern that emerges in the course of observations of individuals as they perform various tasks, which serves to indicate areas of strength and weakness.

income from continuing operations All revenues less all expenses, exclusive of gains or losses on the sale of business segments and extraordinary items (including tax effects), cumulative accounting charges, and the results of operations that have been or soon will be discontinued.

income from discontinued operations Net income, after taxes, from business segments or lines that have been or soon will be sold or otherwise discontinued.

income fund A mutual fund that invests in stocks that have a good record of dividend payments and high likelihood of continued and increasing dividends.

income statement Also called **profit and loss statement; statement of operations.** A concise financial statement that reports a company's revenues, associated expenses and losses, and the resulting net income over a specified period, and that may also include earnings per share and a reconciliation of beginning and ending retained earnings balances.

income summary (*bookkeeping*) A temporary account representing an income statement, to which revenue closing entries are transferred as credits and expenses are closed as debits; after all other closing entries are made, the closing balance is transferred to the retained earnings account, where it represents net income for the period.

income-tax expense Also called **provision for income tax.** An estimated charge for a company's income tax, considered part of operating expense.

incorporated (*abbr* Inc.) Chartered by a state as a corporation and thus as an entity burdened with certain obligations and freed from certain liabilities. See also **corporation.**

incorporation The process of forming or being formed as a legally chartered corporation, with legal rights to make contracts, to own, buy, and sell property, and to sue and be sued. See also **corporation.**

incremental budgeting The practice, followed by most organizations, of basing each period's budget on that of the previous period, with increases to keep pace with inflation or to permit expansion. See also **zero-based budgeting.**

incremental cost **1.** A cost incurred by the exercise of one option rather than another. **2.** Also called **differential cost; marginal cost.** The cost of producing each additional unit.

incremental revenue Also called **marginal revenue.** The additional net or gross income (depending on context) that would come from the sale of one more unit.

indemnity **1.** Protection or security against loss or damage. **2.** Compensation for damage or loss. **3.** Protection (as by insurance for a private individual or by law for a public officer) against liabilities and penalties otherwise incurred by one's actions.

indenture A contract between a bond issuer and a bondholder specifying the form of the bond, any property that backs it, the authorized amount of bonds issued, restrictions on the issuer's indebtedness and dividend payments, provisions for a sinking fund and premature redemption, and other pertinent facts.

independent accountant An accountant temporarily employed by an organization to conduct public accounting, who is financially and familially detached from the audited organization and whose only nonremunerative interest in the task is impartial fairness, accuracy, and honesty.

independent auditor See **external auditor.**

independent contractor A person or firm hired to do a specific task or to provide a specific service but not as an employee under the control of an employer. See also **freelance.**

independent variable (*statistics*) A variable

whose value is known and which can be used to predict the value of a dependent variable.

index See **index number**.

index arbitrage An attempt by stock traders, especially those representing large institutions, to lock in profits by selling off the more expensive futures and buying those that are less expensive.

indexation The practice of adjusting salaries or other payments to some index of inflation. See also **consumer price index**.

index fund A fund, as a mutual fund or pension fund, with a portfolio that contains many of the securities listed in a major stock index in order to match the performance of the stock market generally.

index number A quantity whose variation from one day to the next or over a period of time measures the change in relative value of prices or some other phenomenon. See also **Dow Jones average; Standard & Poor's 500**.

indirect action advertising Advertising activities designed to give a product or brand significant exposure for the purpose of generating favorable attitudes and long-term commitment to it.

indirect cost An expense that cannot readily be charged to a particular product or project. See also **factory overhead; overhead**.

indirect labor Factory labor that cannot readily be charged to the production of specific units, and whose costs are therefore recorded as part of factory overhead. See also **direct labor**.

indirect materials Raw materials that are consumed in the production process but that cannot readily be charged to the production of specific units, and whose costs are therefore recorded as part of factory overhead. See also **direct materials**.

indirect supervision Management characterized by adherence to guidelines and policies established at higher levels of the organizational hierarchy and significantly influenced by the overall climate of the organization.

individual retirement account See **IRA**.

industrial democracy A participative method of management that involves workers in company decision making, exemplified in the United States by cooperatives, in Israel by the kibbutz and moshav movements, in Peru by industrial communities, and in Yugoslavia and Jamaica by the self-management system.

industrial espionage The stealing of research data, blueprints, technological secrets, etc., especially by an employee in the hire of a competing company.

industrial goods Items, sometimes raw materials, used to make other goods and sold to manufacturers rather than consumers.

industrial humanism A philosophy of human resources management and related practices designed to alter the conventional complex structure of work relationships and the content of work itself by special attention to staffing and supervising.

industrial park Also called **business park**. An industrial complex of buildings and offices set in parklike surroundings, usually in a suburban or rural area.

industrial psychology A branch of psychology concerned with the behavior and motivation of individual workers in industrial organizations.

industrial-revenue bond A tax-exempt municipal bond sold to help finance local private industry, on which the interest rate is typically 3 percent lower than that of the average corporate bond.

industrial spy A person who engages in industrial espionage.

industrial union A labor union representing both skilled and unskilled workers in a particular industry. See also **Congress of Industrial Organizations**.

industry 1. The aggregate of manufacturing or technically productive enterprises in a particular field. **2.** Manufacture or trade in general. **3.** The ownership or management of factories.

inelastic demand A demand for a product or

service that remains more or less constant despite changes in its price.

inelastic supply A supply of a product or service that remains more or less constant despite changes in its price.

in escrow See **escrow** (def. 2).

infant-industry argument The argument that in the absence of protective tariffs a new domestic industry can lose its market to foreign imports before it has time to develop sufficiently in technology, skill, and size to compete effectively with them.

inflation A general increase in consumer prices over time, usually expressed as an annual percentage rate.

Infomaster A computer service of Western Union consisting of translation of TWX messages into Telex and vice versa (so that the user needs only one dispatching teleprinter), the sending of messages to multiple addresses, storage of mailing lists, and the sending of collect messages.

infomercial A program-length television commercial that is cast in a standard format so as to disguise the fact that it is an advertisement.

informal group A group of people (in a business organization usually consisting of co-workers) who identify themselves as part of a system and create objectives and standards of behavior for themselves without the support of formal guidelines or leadership. See also **Hawthorne studies**.

informal leader Also called **peer leader**. A nonsupervisory employee who is recognized as a leader by members of his or her work group by reason of demonstrated influence, knowledge, or power. See also **formal leader**.

informal organization 1. An interconnection of managers and subordinates not specified by the formal structure of an organization. **2.** The personal and social level at which members of the organization interact. See also **grapevine**.

informal search An active effort to gather information from a limited and unstructured base of resources, as through discussion with co-workers or colleagues.

informal structure A set of objectives, duties, and behaviors that is not formally acknowledged but that influences and directs the actions of group members.

in good faith See **good faith**.

in-house 1. Employed on the staff of a company. **2.** Utilizing an organization's own staff or resources rather than external facilities.

in-house course Instruction offered by management to members of its staff.

initialize 1. To set variables, switches, etc., to their starting values at the beginning of a computer program. **2.** To prepare a computer or printer for reuse by clearing previous data from memory. **3.** To format a computer disk.

initial markup Also called **initial mark-on**. The amount by which the purchase price of a product is first raised to establish a selling price.

initial public offering, See **IPO**.

injunction A court order either directing someone to do something or prohibiting an activity or practice, often issued to restrain violence, restrict picketing, and prevent damage to property.

inner circle A small coalition of individuals within a larger dominant coalition formed to work out the plans and strategies of the organization. See also **dominant coalition**.

innovation 1. Introduction of something new; alteration of an existing situation; a change. **2.** A goal for organizational development that can be directed from outside or within the organization.

innovative design A formally designated framework of activities and relationships created for an organization and subdivided into project groups to meet the specific goals of the organization in a unique manner.

input 1. See also **output. a.** Data entered into a computer for processing. **b.** To enter data into a computer. **2.** An idea or suggestion made as part of the group process.

insert 1. An announcement usually printed by an advertiser and delivered to a publisher for insertion in a magazine or newspaper during the production process, either loose or bound into the publication. **2.** A clip added to a videotape program after the program has been assembled.

in-service training See **on-the-job training.**

inside out Proceeding from inside an organization to the outside, as when the publisher of a newspaper or magazine supplies demographic data about its readers to a potential advertiser. See also **outside in.**

insider trading The illegal practice of using inside information (e.g., merger agreements not yet made public) as a basis for trading stocks.

insolvency Inability to pay debts. See also **bankruptcy.**

installment sale A sales agreement allowing for periodic partial payments (installments) by the buyer, who receives conditional title or ownership of the goods purchased until all payments have been made.

Institute of Internal Auditors An organization of professional accounting auditors that maintains and develops standards of practice in the profession, and awards certification to practice professionally upon completion of examination requirements.

institutional advertising Advertising designed to establish a favorable image for an organization by emphasizing the quality of its products or services, its role in the community, etc.

institutional approach A method of studying marketing that focuses on the means by which middlemen can facilitate marketing functions.

institutional investor An organization that invests large sums of money in the securities market, such as a bank, mutual fund, insurance company, or pension fund.

institutional level The executive management level in an organization.

instrument A legal document (e.g., a bond, lease, note, check, ticket, agreement) giving evidence of rights and responsibilities between two parties.

insurable risk A loss that an insurance company will insure against, especially a common one (e.g., fire) beyond the control of the insured and of a major monetary value that can be calculated in such a way as to arrive at an economically acceptable premium.

insurance Protection purchased from an insurance company against losses of property or earning power or losses due to liability or to a disbarred or nonperforming employee.

insurance policy A written contract between an insured person and an insurance company specifying the exact losses to be covered and the costs to the insured person.

intaglio A printing process in which images etched or otherwise incised in a hard surface are transferred to paper by ink applied to the sunken design. See also **gravure.**

intangible asset Any nonphysical property (e.g., a patent, copyright, trademark, and such other nonphysical assets as goodwill and credit rating). See also **tangible asset.**

intangible property Property not physical in nature and usually consisting of legal rights. See also **intangible asset.**

integrated circuit (*abbr* IC) A network of many electronic circuits and transistors pressed into a small silicon chip that functions as the memory storage for a computer.

integrated data processing (*abbr* IDP) Coordination of all steps required to process data by computer.

integrated work team A group of workers whose jobs and tasks are interrelated and rotated among group members.

intensive marketing plan A marketing plan designed to offer a product in as many outlets as possible. See also **exclusive marketing plan.**

interactive Designating a computer system or program that allows users to enter commands or data,

allowing immediate communication between computer and user.

interactive videodisk A videodisk system that permits the operator to branch off or access a prerecorded program by means of a hand-operated device.

interdependency A relationship between an organization and its environment, two or more organizations, or two or more people, such that neither can survive without the help of the other.

interest 1. A sum paid or charged for the use of money or for borrowing money; such a sum expressed as a percentage of money borrowed to be paid over a given period, usually one year. **2.** A business in which a person has a share, right, or title.

interface 1. A surface or general area regarded as the boundary between two diverse and independent systems, where certain aspects of those systems interconnect. **2.** To connect with (another independent system). **3.** Computer hardware or software designed to communicate information between hardware devices, between software programs, between devices and programs, or between computer and user.

interlocking directorate A board of directors one or more of whose members are simultaneously directors of one or more other corporations, especially those that are in direct competition.

intermerchant A specialist in foreign trade who arranges the payments for goods sold between a country with hard currency and a country with soft currency.

intermittent process Also called **job-order production.** A manufacturing operation involving frequent alterations in equipment setup and materials for the production of different products, as in the manufacture of clothing and in custom manufacturing.

internal accounting See **management accounting.**

internal administration The aggregate of procedures required for the proper functioning of an organization, including the keeping of records on losses and values, communications involving claims and loss-prevention techniques, preparation of manuals and administration of company policies, maintenance of paperwork dealing with insurance purchases, and distribution of risk costs among organizational units.

internal audit An analysis of records, reports, policies, and procedures that is regularly performed by the organization itself. See also **internal auditor.**

internal auditor A person permanently employed by a company to scrutinize its accounting data and financial statements in order to determine whether operations and managerial practices conform to company policy and the law, and to find opportunities to decrease costs and improve efficiency.

internal consultant An adviser permanently employed to determine by surveys, interviews, and observations practical means of improving the effectiveness of an organization's personnel and practices.

internal control Modification of the behavior of employees in order to increase willingness to accept company standards.

internal rate of return (*abbr* IRR) Also called **time-adjusted rate of return. 1.** The effective yield of an investment project, calculated annually over the life of the project. **2.** The discount rate used to evaluate a proposed long-term project, derived by equating the present value of the cash outlays needed to start and maintain the project and the expected cash receipts and payments. **3.** The interest rate on an amount to be invested in a project that, if it were paid on an equal amount otherwise invested, would be equal to the expected future cashflow rate to be generated by that project.

internal reporting Also called **management reporting.** The reporting of a company's financial situation to management or any other audience inside the firm. See also **external reporting.**

Internal Revenue Service (*abbr* IRS) The agency of the U.S. Treasury Department charged with administering the Internal Revenue Code and collecting income, excise, and other federal taxes.

International Chamber of Commerce (*abbr* ICC) An international organization that seeks to improve trading conditions among nations by supporting free movement of people, goods, and services and by sponsoring a court of arbitration, a service to help standardize business practices and documents, and a publication.

international firm A company that produces goods in one country for distribution in other countries. See also **multinational firm.**

international law The body of rules developed to guide and control nations in their conduct toward each other.

International Monetary Fund (*abbr* IMF) A fund established by the U.S. government to promote international trade by making loans to countries that require assistance and by promoting stability in foreign exchange, orderly markets, and international liquidity.

international trade The profitable interchange of goods and raw materials between countries. See also **export; import.**

Internet A large computer network linking smaller computer networks worldwide.

interperiod income-tax allocation Also called **deferred income-tax liability.** Allocation of one year's income-tax liability to two or more years' operations so that those liabilities are deducted from the revenues of those years, sometimes used as a means of reconciling differences of timing in the recording of transactions and charges for purposes of financial reporting.

interpersonal relationship A social relationship characterized by distinctive styles of expression and behavior and by a pattern of shared expectations.

interrole conflict Disagreement between individuals based on a variance in their expectations and preconceived perceptions of each other's role or the procedures that each is to follow.

Interstate Commerce Commission (*abbr* ICC) The first independent regulatory agency established (1887) by the federal government, now authorized to regulate the rates charged for transporting goods by rail, ship, and motor vehicle across state lines and other matters concerning public transport.

interstate traffic The movement of goods across state lines.

intervening variable An incidental element (e.g., group loyalty, conflict, technological assistance, attitude) that influences performance.

intervention **1.** A change in action or behavior from accepted ways of doing things with an anticipated new end result. **2.** The process of interceding in aspects of an organization's management operations for the purpose of increasing effectiveness and work output.

interview A consultative meeting between people in which information is gathered, shared, or evaluated. See also **directed interview; exit interview; nondirected interview; stress interview.**

intestate **1.** Having made no valid will. **2.** Not disposed of by a valid will.

in toto (*Latin*) Totally; entirely.

intranet A computer network with restricted access, as within a corporation, that uses software and protocols developed for the Internet.

in-transit storage Temporary storage of cargo or goods at some point between producer and customer.

intrapreneur An employee of a large corporation who is given the freedom and financial support to create new products, services, systems, etc., free of the corporation's usual routines and restrictions.

intrasender role conflict Discomfort produced within a superior by the need to give directions that conflict with a personal concept of his or her proper role or behavior.

intrastate traffic Movement of goods within the boundaries of a state.

intrinsic reward Satisfaction derived from work itself or from the results of work accomplished. See also **extrinsic reward.**

invention An original or improved design of a process, product, or idea, for which the law provides ownership protection upon the filing and acceptance of an application for a patent.

inventory Goods on hand, particularly finished products that have not been sold or raw materials that have not gone through the manufacturing process.

inventory control Any system designed to determine the economic order quantity, the reorder point, and the proper quantity of safety stock that should be maintained in order to minimize the cost of ordering and carrying an inventory.

inventory equation Ending inventory equals beginning inventory plus net additions (usually net purchases) less withdrawals (cost of goods sold).

inventory profit The amount by which the current replacement cost or selling price of an inventory exceeds the amount carried in the company's accounting records.

inventory recession A slump in business caused by increased production and decreased consumer spending, resulting in a rapid buildup of inventories followed by employee layoffs. See also **final-goods recession; recession.**

inventory turnover The number of times an inventory as a whole has been sold or consumed during a period, as calculated by the inventory turnover ratio.

inventory turnover ratio Sales divided by average inventory for the period. See also **activity ratio.**

inverse demand pattern A pattern of consumer buying habits associated with some status goods and characterized by an increase in demand for a product as its price rises (but only to a certain point, after which demand drops).

inverted-U hypothesis The hypothesis that at low levels of stress, performance is low; with moderate stress (perceived as challenge), performance increases; at very high levels of stress, performance deteriorates.

investment bank An intermediary institution that underwrites (buys complete issues of) securities and then sells them in smaller units to individual investors.

investment company Also called **investment fund.** A company or trust (such as a mutual fund) that invests in other companies the capital contributed by investors, who buy shares that rise and fall in value with the average price of the company's investment. See also **closed-end investment company; Investment Company Act of 1940; open-end investment company.**

Investment Company Act of 1940 Federal legislation providing that an investment company cannot invest more than 5 percent of its capital in any one company or own more than 10 percent of any one company.

investment counsel One whose business is to advise investors and supervise their investments.

investment fund See **investment company.**

investment grade Designating bonds with ratings from AAA to BBB. See also **bond rating.**

investment tax credit A corporate tax credit obtainable through investments in certain categories of long-term assets, equal to a percentage of the value of the asset. See also **tax credit.**

invisible hand The underlying principle (in the economics of Adam Smith) that ensures the optimum level of economic welfare of a society when each person acts out of self-interest.

invoice A printed acknowledgment of a sale from the seller, usually accompanying a shipment of goods, giving a description of the merchandise supplied, the quantity, etc., as well as the terms of the sale, total charges, and amount due.

involuntary bankruptcy Bankruptcy initiated by a court action brought by a creditor. See also **voluntary bankruptcy.**

business

IPO (*abbr for* initial public offering) A company's first stock offering to the public.

ipso facto (*Latin*) By the fact itself; by the very nature of the case.

IRA (*abbr for* Individual Retirement Account) A plan that permits individuals to set aside savings that are tax free until retirement. See also **Keogh account.**

IRS See **Internal Revenue Service.**

issue 1. To create or sell shares or bonds. **2.** Shares or bonds created and offered for sale at one time. See also **primary offering.**

itemized deductions A list of allowable expenses (e.g., unreimbursed medical expenses) that can be deducted from gross income to determine taxable income. See also **standard deduction.**

itemized statement A detailed list specifying all expenses and costs involved in an individual purchase.

item validity (*employment testing*) The extent to which an item (question) on a test measures what it is intended to measure.

a b c d e f g h i J K l m n o p q r s t u v w x y z

Java (*trademark*) A computer programming language used to create interactive applications running over the Internet.

JCL See **job control language.**

J hook Also called **spindle.** A small shelf mount, usually shaped like the letter J, extending from a supermarket shelf for the display of impulse items.

j.i.t. See **just-in-time manufacturing.**

job 1. A task or group of tasks performed as part of one's occupation or for a specific price. **2.** Those operations and activities performed by the members of a work group, and an integral part of the design and structure of an organization.

job analysis A description of the standards for effective performance of a job and the responsibilities and necessary skills expected of the jobholder.

jobber A person who buys from manufacturers or importers and sells to retailers; a wholesaler.

job bidding A procedure that allows present workers to be considered for future job openings.

job control language (*abbr* JCL) A computer language used to construct statements that identify a particular job to be run and specify the job's requirements to the operating system under which it will run.

job cost sheet A record or schedule of accumulated costs incurred in the production of a single unit, batch, or lot, such costs usually being divided into direct labor and direct materials with a special allocation for factory overhead.

job description A detailed written account of the tasks, responsibilities, skills, and environmental dynamics of a job.

job design Those aspects of a job that influence employee attitudes, satisfaction, and motivation.

job enlargement An increase in the horizontal scope of a job, with a concomitant increase in responsibility but not in authority.

job enrichment An increase in the vertical scope of a lower-level job, with a concomitant increase in the areas of responsibility, authority, and recognition: the employee is allowed to plan work schedules to fit overall deadlines. See also **autonomous work group.**

job evaluation Assessment of the specific tasks involved in the various jobs in an organization for the purpose of establishing a scale on which their relative worth may be measured.

job involvement The personal commitment of an individual to a job, including his or her involvement with the growth, importance, and value of the job.

job-order costing A cost accounting system in which costs are categorized, assigned, and accumulated in accordance with the units or batches that incurred them. See also **process costing.**

job-order production See **intermittent process.**

job rotation 1. Movement of employees into a variety of jobs in one organization for the purpose of filling vacancies or for acclimating and motivating new employees. See also **job enlargement. 2.** Movement within an organization which can lead to promotion. See also **job enrichment.**

job safety training (*abbr* JST) Instruction in safe work practices and in their importance.

job satisfaction 1. Gratification derived from one's job or from evaluation of work accomplished. **2.** The difference between an individual's feeling about a particular job situation and the general purpose and goals of the organization. **3.** The fit between an individual's qualifications and the requirements of a specific job.

job scope The number of measurable skills and tasks required by a specific job.

job security Protection of a worker's job, usually by a clause in a union contract.

job sharing The sharing of one full-time job by two persons, each working half time.

job specification A detailed description of the duties of a particular job, the skills and experience necessary, the salary range, etc.

job tension The degree of stress that an individual experiences in the performance of a task, such stress generally being related to the individual's ability to meet internal or external expectations in regard to performance.

joint and several liability Responsibility held by two or more persons, both together and individually.

joint contract A written agreement by which two or more persons are responsible for fulfilling the terms specified.

joint cost Also called **common cost.** A cost that confers benefits on two or more departments, projects, or products (e.g., rent, utilities).

joint estate Property owned by two or more persons; the survivor or survivors receive the interest of the first to die, with full title going to the last survivor.

joint liability The responsibility of two or more persons (as partners) for the actions of any one of them taken in connection with a project or business in which all are contractually engaged.

joint tenancy A form of co-ownership of real property in which the owners agree that at the death of one of them, the interest of the deceased will pass to the survivors, full title finally passing to the last survivor. See also **tenancy in common.**

joint tenant A co-owner of an estate in joint tenancy.

joint venture A partnership entered into by two or more people or companies to accomplish a specific task or engage in a specific undertaking.

journal A book in which transactions not entered in specialized books are recorded.

journal voucher A document supporting the validity or accuracy of an accounting entry.

journeyman A union craftworker who has successfully completed an apprenticeship and is recognized as fully qualified to practice a particular specialty.

judgment sample A sample of a population selected at least in part on the basis of a personal judgment as to those persons who would constitute the best, fairest, most representative or equitable sample.

jumble basket A jumble display, such as a large basket, that holds an assortment of usually unrelated products. See also **dump bin.**

jumbo Referring to certificates of deposit having a denomination of $100,000 or more, traded by large institutional investors.

jumbo certificate A type of certificate of deposit issued in denominations of $100,000 or more; usually pays an interest rate above 10 percent.

junior security Also called **subordinate security.** A security (as common stock) that represents a claim to dividends or assets of lower priority than the claims of other securities (as preferred stock and bonds).

junk bond Slang term for a high-risk bond rated BB or lower. It offers a high return but is considered to have dubious backing; sometimes offered to shareholders in lieu of cash in takeover bids.

jurisdiction 1. The authority given to a court or judge to hear and decide a legal case. **2.** The limits within which authority (as of a labor union) may be exercised.

jurisdictional strike A strike caused by conflict between two or more labor unions over the right of one of them to organize the workers in an organization, trade, or industry, to control certain work, or to operate in a certain territory.

just-in-time The practice of manufacturing and shipping products only as they are required.

just-in-time inventory Inventory on hand to support just-in-time manufacturing.

just-in-time manufacturing (*abbr* j.i.t.) A production control method that authorizes the manufacture of components, subassemblies, etc., or the receipt of raw materials, only when needed and in the quantities needed to support specific downstream activities.

just noticeable difference (*abbr* j.n.d.) Also called **differential threshold.** The smallest increase in the intensity of a stimulus that can be detected.

kanban A method of inventory control, similar to just-in-time procedures, originally developed by Japanese automobile manufacturers.

keiretsu A loose coalition of business groups, especially in Japan.

Keogh account A type of retirement account for self-employed persons, providing income-tax deductions and tax-deferred income.

key A code number or letter printed on coupons, orders, or consumer inquiries which when returned indicates to the advertiser the mailing list that generated the response.

key-executive insurance Also called **key-man insurance.** Insurance that protects a business against financial loss in the event of the death of an important executive.

Keynesian economics The economic concepts advanced by John Maynard Keynes in the 1930s, emphasizing the role of expectations in investment decisions and advocating governmental fiscal and monetary programs to increase employment. See also **classical economics.**

keynote idea The most important idea presented in an advertisement or in any document.

keystone To set the retail price of an item at double the manufacturer's price.

kickback A rebate given (usually secretively) by a seller to a buyer, a supplier to a contractor, etc.: usually considered an unethical practice.

kite To create a false bank balance by depositing a check for nonexistent funds, which may then be covered by another check written against an overdrawn account.

knockoff An unlicensed copy of something, especially fashion clothing, intended to be sold at a lower price than the original.

business

L

abcdefghijk **L** mnopqrstuvwxyz

label A piece of paper or other material affixed to a product, especially food or medicine, and stating its contents, the name of the manufacturer, and other information as required by law.

labor 1. Physical or mental work done for pay. **2.** The body of people who perform work for wages, as distinguished from entrepreneurs and managers.

labor arbitration See **arbitration.**

laboratory training Training in which participants are helped to experience and diagnose their own behavior and relationships in a specially designed environment and are both experimenters and subjects in joint learning. See also **sensitivity training.**

labor-efficiency variance See **labor-rate variance.**

labor-intensive Requiring a greater expenditure for labor per unit of production than for capital assets. See also **capital-intensive.**

Labor-Management Reporting and Disclosure Act. Also called **Landrum-Griffin Act.** An act of Congress passed in 1959 in response to evidence of collusion between some employers and union officials and misuse of funds by certain union officials: provides for the regulation of internal union affairs, restricts secondary boycotts and organizational and recognition picketing, and protects union members against abuses by a bill of rights that guarantees freedom of speech and periodic secret elections. See also **National Labor Relations Act; Taft-Hartley Act.**

labor-rate variance In a standard cost accounting system, the difference between the standard or normal labor cost of producing a certain number of units and the actual cost of producing those units, attributable to a difference in the average hourly wages paid: arrived at by multiplying the difference in wage rates by the number of hours worked.

labor relations Relations between management and labor, especially as conducted by a business organization in regard to collective bargaining and fulfillment of the terms of a union contract.

labor union An organization of workers that bargains with management on the part of its members over wages, hours, working conditions, etc.

lagging indicator An economic factor that is considered to respond to an economic trend after the aggregate of economic activity, as measured by the National Association of Business Research. See also **business cycle; leading indicator; roughly coincident indicator.**

laissez faire (*French*) Allow to act; the economic theory that government should intervene as little as possible in the direction of economic affairs. See also **classical economics; invisible hand.**

laissez-faire style A management style found mainly in organizations that emphasize high levels of creativity, whereby the manager permits subordinates to exercise a high degree of autonomy and acts largely as a consultant.

LAN See **local-area network.**

landlord A person who owns and leases apartments, buildings, land, etc. See also **lease.**

Landrum-Griffin Act See **Labor-Management Reporting and Disclosure Act.**

lapping (*accounting*) Embezzlement carried out by an employee who steals payments made to accounts receivable, covering the theft by using a second customer's payment to pay the account of the first, a third customer's payment to cover the account of the second, and so on until the thefts are repaid or discovered or the accounts are thoroughly muddled.

laptop A type of microcomputer that is portable and so compact that it can be operated while resting on the user's lap.

large-cap Designating a stock with a market capitalization of $1 billion or more.

large-scale integration Location on a single computer chip of many thousands of electronic circuits, each having a distinct function.

last in, first out See LIFO.

late charge A penalty charge in addition to the regularly scheduled payment, as of a loan, if such payment has not been made when due.

latent demand (*marketing*) Desire for or willingness to buy a certain type of product that has not yet been manufactured, often increased by offering discount coupons for such products.

lateral leadership Interaction of formal leaders with their peers outside their specific work groups, occasioned by a need to influence other members of an organization in order to complete a work assignment.

lateral reasoning Thought processes that permit a person to adapt the procedures used in the creation of one product or service as tools for the creation of a second, unrelated product or service.

launder To disguise the source of illegal or secret funds or profits, usually by transmittal through a foreign bank or a complex network of intermediaries.

lawful purpose Legally acceptable intent (an element necessary for the validity of a contract).

law of demand The assumption that the quantity of a good demanded at any particular time increases as its price falls and decreases as the price rises. See also **law of supply and demand.**

law of diminishing returns The assumption that at any given stage of technology, there is a point at which additional inputs of capital or labor fail to yield a proportional increase in production.

law of effect The assumption that feelings associated with a situation have a powerful effect on the recurrence or nonrecurrence of that situation.

law of supply and demand The assumption that the competitive price that prevails in a market is determined by the interaction of the supply of products and services for sale and consumers' willingness to buy.

layaway plan See will-call.

layoff A temporary or permanent involuntary termination of work, usually resulting from a cutback in production.

layout A composition or arrangement of elements in an advertisement (text, headlines, trademark, illustrations) designed to communicate a message effectively.

LBO See **leveraged buyout.**

LDC less developed country.

leader An individual who by virtue of his or her superior ideas, forceful personality, etc., is able to direct and control the attitudes and actions of others.

leadership 1. The capacity to inspire in others a willingness to accept one's direction. 2. Influence acquired by a person above and beyond that which is bestowed by the position he or she occupies. See also **achievement-oriented leadership; authoritative leadership; benevolent leadership; democratic leadership; exploitive leadership; lateral leadership; multiple-influence approach; participative leadership; situational approach; trait approach.**

leadership contingency model See **Fiedler's leadership contingency model.**

leading indicator An economic factor, such as interest rates or housing starts, that is considered to signal the general direction of economic activity. See also **business cycle; lagging indicator; roughly coincident indicator.**

lead system One's primary representational system, or the form one uses for storing and recalling experiences (e.g., a visual orientation to experience).

lead time 1. The time between the placement of a purchase order and the receipt of materials from a supplier. 2. The time between the beginning of a production run and the completion of either the first product or the entire run.

learning curve Also called **experience curve. 1.** A graphic representation of the sharp increase in proficiency demonstrated by an individual, group, or organization in the course of learning a new task or procedure, followed by a leveling off. **2.** The relationship between production labor or cost per unit and cumulative production volume, often resulting in a constant proportional decline in effort per unit for each doubling of cumulative volume.

lease A document evidencing an agreement allowing one party (a tenant or lessee) to rent real estate, equipment, or some other asset from a second party (a landlord or lessor) for a specified time in exchange for specified periodic payments. See also **financial lease; leaseback; operating lease.**

leaseback The sale of property to a buyer who then leases it back to the seller. The seller often becomes the principal tenant, and both benefit from tax savings.

lease-based arrangement An arrangement whereby a franchisor maintains primary control on property to be used by a franchisee by signing the primary lease on the property and subleasing it to the franchisee.

leasehold Property used, rented, or otherwise held under a lease.

leasehold improvement An improvement made to leased property by the lessee (e.g., a new parking lot, building, landscaping), which is considered a long-term asset that depreciates over the term of the lease or the life of the improvement, whichever is shorter.

leave Permission to be absent from work, as to care for a new baby; leave of absence.

ledger (*bookkeeping*) A book containing accounts of a specialized nature (e.g., sales, overhead), usually posted from a journal of chronological transactions.

legal capital Also called **stated capital.** The par value of a corporation's outstanding stock, an amount usually required by state law to be retained for the protection of creditors, and thus unavailable for return to stockholders as dividends, the repurchase of outstanding stock, or other uses as long as the corporation has outstanding debts.

legal list A document drawn up by a state listing corporations, funds, and other investment possibilities in which fiduciaries, banks, insurance companies, and certain other organizations are allowed to invest for the reason that they meet certain high standards and are unlikely to breach the responsibilities of those entrusted with other people's money. See also **prudent man rule.**

legal tender The amount of currency that may be lawfully tendered or offered in payment of a debt and that a creditor may not lawfully refuse.

legitimate power Authority attached to a position, office, or rank and recognized by others as conferring upon its holder the right to command. See also **charismatic power; expert power.**

lessee A person who rents property owned by another. See also **lease.**

lessor A person who permits another the use of property under a lease. See also **lease.**

less than carload lot (*abbr* LCL lot) A shipment of goods that does not completely fill a freightcar, and therefore requires a scheduler (freight forwarder) to combine lots in order to complete a shipment to a destination.

letter of credit 1. A document issued by a banker allowing the person named to draw money to a specified amount. 2. A letter from a bank notifying a person that drafts on the issuer have been authorized up to a specified amount.

level playing field A state of equality, as between business competitors; an equal opportunity to achieve or succeed.

leverage The increased strength an investor musters by using borrowed funds to finance a portion of an investment (as in a margin transaction). See also **financial leverage.**

leveraged buyout (*abbr* LBO) A procedure by which an investor or group of investors borrows money to purchase enough of a company's assets to gain a controlling interest, using the assets of the targeted firm as collateral, with the expectation of increasing the firm's profits sufficiently to repay the debt plus high interest charges quickly and realize a profit (often by liquidating the company).

leveraged marketing The process of expanding a manufacturing business by diversifying a product's use, as from an industrial use to a consumer use.

levy 1. To seize or attach property by judicial order. **2.** An assessment (as of taxes or contributions).

liability Anything that is owed, whether money, a product or commodity, or a service. See also **asset.**

liability insurance Insurance that protects the insured against losses arising from injury to or death of another or from damage to another's property.

libel A false written or printed statement that causes injury to another's reputation. See also **slander.**

licensee A person, company, etc., to whom a license is granted.

lien 1. A claim made on property as security for a debt owed. See also **artisan's lien; carrier's lien. 2.** A contracted claim to a piece of property that has been specified as collateral for a loan. See also **blanket lien; specific lien.**

life estate An interest in property held only during the lifetime of the holder, who must maintain the property, make mortgage and tax payments, and use the property's natural resources only for its maintenance, and who may sell or mortgage the interest in the property only under the same terms as those under which he or she holds it.

life insurance Insurance providing for payment of a specified sum to a beneficiary upon the death of the insured. See also **employee life insurance.**

life interest Interest on property that is payable during the owner's lifetime but cannot be passed on to another or others after his or her death.

life planning Also called **career development.** An organic approach to organizational renewal by which employees can review, evaluate, and examine their organizational roles and determine the congruence of those roles with their life plans and career goals.

LIFO (*acronym for* last *in,* first *out*) A method of costing inventory that assumes that the stock acquired most recently will be sold first. Goods sold are therefore costed at the price of the latest stock, and ending inventory is costed at the price of the earliest purchases (opposite of FIFO). See also **weighted average cost.**

limited company A company (usually British) whose owners are liable for its debts only to the extent of the par value of their stock.

limited liability The responsibility of shareholders in a corporation for the corporation's debts only to the amount invested by each. See also **unlimited liability.**

limited-line store A relatively small retail store that carries a narrow line of goods (e.g., women's apparel, men's haberdashery).

limited partner An investor whose liability is limited to the amount of his or her investment and who makes no management decisions. See also **silent partner.**

limited partnership A partnership in which the liability of at least one of the partners for the debts of the firm is limited to the extent of that partner's capital contribution, and in which at least one partner does not enjoy such limited liability.

limited warranty A written statement accompanying a product specifying what the manufacturer will do in the event of a defect or malfunction, for what period of time, and other pertinent information, but not guaranteeing free repair, replacement, or refund of the purchase price. See also **full warranty; Magnuson-Moss Act.**

limit order A market order to a broker that specifies the highest buying price or lowest selling price (exercise price) the investor is willing to accept for a given stock, and which normally expires if not executed by the end of the day.

Lincoln incentive management plan An incentive plan, developed by J. F. Lincoln, by which exempt as well as nonexempt employees share in the firm's profits on the basis of their merit ratings, and which provides a guaranteed 32-hour workweek and three weeks of vacation each year.

line 1. Collectively, those employees who are directly responsible for the company's profit and loss. See also **staff. 2.** A stock of commercial goods of the same general class but including a variety of styles, colors, sizes, etc.

linear programming A method used to solve decision problems, usually involving resource allocation, that can be represented by linear relationships among the objective, the decision variables, and the constraints.

line authority The power vested in management personnel to make decisions and give orders to subordinates in the chain of command.

line balancing Design of a production line so that work flows evenly and without delay from one work station to the next, accomplished by assigning approximately equal tasks to each and allowing adequate time for each to meet the desired production rate.

line of balance (*abbr* LOB) A charting device, containing elements of the PERT method, for planning and monitoring the progress of an order, project, or program to be completed by a specific date.

line of credit The maximum amount that a bank or other lending institution is willing to lend a given customer or the extent to which he or she may make charges over a specified period.

line organization An organizational system in which the line of authority is clearly defined from the top positions down to the lower management positions (e.g., shop foremen). See also **chain of command.**

linking-pin concept A concept developed by Rensis Likert that holds that every manager is a subordinate to the person or group to whom he or she is responsible, and that effective supervision of one's work group depends to a great extent on one's ability to exert influence upward, and thus on the skill with which one plays the subordinate role.

links and role indicators Elements of a method of information retrieval designed to eliminate false drops, in which groups of words or ideas that are linked in the original material are linked in the computer, which is also programmed to show the role that each term plays in the concept of the original material.

liquid asset See **quick asset.**

liquidation 1. The general conversion of a firm's assets into cash (often as a result of bankruptcy). **2.** Conversion of a (usually short-term) asset into cash.

liquidation damages An amount that parties to a contract agree in advance will be payable by any party who breaches the contract.

liquidation value 1. The price an asset can bring if it is liquidated (i.e., converted into cash). **2.** The value of a share of a mutual fund when it is redeemed (normally equal to the net asset value).

liquidity The extent to and ease with which a given asset can be converted into cash.

liquidity ratio Any of several ratios taken to indicate a company's ability to meet its obligations if it should be subjected to stress. See also **acid-test ratio; current ratio.**

list broker A person or firm that buys mailing lists from companies and sells them to other organizations.

listed stock A stock that is traded at a regional or national stock exchange, and thus one that has been shown to meet the standards of the exchange and is subject to certain government regulations.

list price The advertised retail price of an item, usually suggested or determined by the manufacturer.

lithography A printing process by which ink impressions of a picture or design are taken from a stone or metallic surface prepared with a greasy or oily substance.

load fund A mutual fund sold by a broker or other salesman that carries a sales charge or commission deducted from the amount invested or the net asset value.

local advertising Advertising intended to reach only a defined regional area and designed to attract customers to a local retail store, restaurant, or other place of business.

local-area network Also called **LAN.** A computer network confined to a limited area, linking personal computers so that programs, data, peripheral devices, and processing tasks can be shared.

local private line (*abbr* LPL) A line connecting two telephones in such a way that one phone rings as soon as the receiver of the other is picked up, without the need for dialing or operator assistance.

location habit (*marketing*) A customer's tendency to shop at a certain store, usually because of special treatment or service or some other appeal that the establishment has over other local stores.

lock-box plan The use by a company of a post-office box to which remittances are sent and collected by a bank for immediate deposit: expedites collection and availability of funds.

locked in 1. Obligated, contracted, finalized, or otherwise beyond the possibility of change. **2.** Unable or unwilling to sell a security that could render profit because of the wish to avoid payment of tax on capital gains.

lockout The closing of a plant or other means taken to prevent workers from entering a workplace in an effort to force a union to accept management's last contract proposal.

locus sigilli (*Latin; abbr* LS) The place of the seal; the place on a legal document where a seal required by law is to be affixed.

logical task A task requiring logical reasoning, such as comparing one item with another or categorizing items according to a predetermined set of characteristics, which a computer is programmed to perform.

logo (*abbr for* logotype) A design incorporating words, letters, and/or symbols and used as an identifying mark. See also **brand; trademark.**

logotype See **logo.**

long 1. Referring to a bond that matures in more than ten years. **2.** Holding or accumulating stocks, futures, commodities, etc., with the expectation of a rise in prices.

long-form report An external audit report that includes explanations in addition to a basic financial statement and audit opinion, specifying whether the

audit opinion covers the explanations as well as the financial statement.

longitudinal study A series of observations of a subject or subjects over a long period of time and under a variety of conditions, used to supplement survey research.

long-range plan A plan setting forth an organization's goals, objectives, and policies to be pursued over an extended period of time, usually two to five years and sometimes longer.

long-term asset See **fixed asset.**

long-term capital gains Capital gains resulting from the sale of assets held more than six months, formerly subject to special tax breaks, but now taxed as ordinary income. See also **short-term capital gains.**

long-term liability See **fixed liability.**

long-term performance bonus A bonus in the form of stock offered to an executive, its dollar value hinging on the attainment of a designated long-term performance objective.

long-term variation A pattern of increased or decreased activity in a specific industry over a long period of time, usually 20 or 30 years.

loss 1. The amount by which expenses exceed revenues for a given transaction, project, investment, period, etc. **2.** A consumption of assets that does not generate minimal income. **3.** The assessed damages caused by a disaster, accident, etc.

loss control The deterrent means taken, under the supervision of a risk manager, to curb or minimize all accidental losses (as by fire protection, a security program, regulation of claims adjusting). See also **risk management.**

loss leader An item offered for sale by a retail store at or below cost as a means of attracting customers, many of whom will presumably make impulse purchases while in the store.

loss ratio The total amount of claims paid by an insurance company divided by the total amount of premiums received.

Lotus 1-2-3 A computer program developed by the Lotus Development Corporation, combining spreadsheet, data management, and graphics capabilities.

lower of cost or market The valuation of an asset (usually an inventory) in accordance with either its original cost or its current market value (replacement cost or quoted selling price), whichever is lower.

low-margin retailing The selling of merchandise at low prices (and presumably in large quantities).

low-pressure selling See **soft sell.**

lump-sum purchase See **basket purchase.**

luxury tax A tax levied on items that are not considered essential for daily living.

a b c d e f g h i j k l **M** n o p q r s t u v w x y z

ma-and-pa store See **mom-and-pop store.**

machine language Instructions encoded in a form that can be understood and used by a computer. See also **programming language.**

macroeconomics The study of an entire economic system, with focus on such broad issues as money flow, growth in gross national product, national inflation rate, and general factors of production rather than on individual components of the system. See also **microeconomics.**

MAD See **mean absolute deviation.**

Madison Avenue A street in New York City that was once a center of the advertising and public relations industries and remains a symbol of their attitudes, methods, and practices.

magazine concept A strategy by which commercial sponsors select television advertising time on the basis of the known buying habits of the audiences that watch particular shows.

magnetic disk A floppy disk or hard disk.

magnetic tape Magnetized plastic tape on which data and programs are stored for use in a computer but can be retrieved only sequentially.

Magnuson-Moss Act Also called **Consumer Products Warranties Act.** An act of Congress that became law in 1975 and that, while not requiring manufacturers to give any warranties on their products, requires that all warranties that are given must set forth 13 specific pieces of information (among them the products or parts covered, the steps the warrantor will take in the event of defect or malfunction, and the steps the consumer must take) and distinguishes between full and limited warranties. See also **full warranty; limited warranty.**

mailgram A telegraph-type message sent overnight by Telex or TWX teleprinter for delivery with the first mail distribution the following day, through a joint venture of the U.S. Postal Service and Western Union.

mailing list A list of names and addresses of actual and potential buyers of a product or service, available for purchase, often from the company itself or from companies that compile and deal in such lists, or sometimes created by in-house research.

mail merge A word-processing feature that allows the user to create a form letter by storing lists of names and addresses in one file and the text of the letter in another file. The merge command is used to generate the personalized letter.

mail-order sales Generation of mail or telephone orders for products to be sent directly to consumers by means of catalogs, brochures, fliers, sales letters, and other forms of advertising.

mainframe 1. The largest category of computer on the market, to which terminals in distant locations may be linked. **2.** Historically, the physical casing around a central processing unit.

main memory Also called **primary storage.** See **RAM.** See also **auxiliary memory.**

maintained mark-on The difference between the amount paid for goods and the amount actually received when they are sold.

maintenance factor A characteristic of a job (e.g., salary, job security) that must be present in order to prevent employee dissatisfaction and that serves as a strong motivator when it is present in an adequate amount.

maintenance management Regulation and adjustment of the organizational system to ensure its survival through disciplinary measures, advertising and public relations, and lobbying.

maintenance requirement Reimbursement required by a broker from an investor who has bought stock on margin or sold short and seems to be losing money.

major medical insurance Insurance that pays for a percentage of medical costs not covered by either hospitalization or surgical/medical plans, usually subject to a deductible clause.

make-or-buy A decision to make an item or buy it from some other organization.

maker A person who signs a promissory note and thus incurs the debt that the note represents.

make-to-order Customized manufacturing, in which products are built to meet unique customer specifications.

make-to-stock Manufacture of standardized products for inventory in anticipation of future customer demands.

mall 1. A large retail complex containing stores and restaurants in adjacent buildings or in a single large building. **2.** An urban street lined with shops and closed off to motor vehicles.

malpractice insurance Insurance protecting a professional person against liability claims arising from alleged negligence or improper performance of professional activities.

Malthusian Referring to the theories of T. R. Malthus, an English economist, which state that population tends to increase faster than the means of subsistence, and that this will result in an inadequate supply of the goods supporting life unless war, famine, or disease intervenes or the increase of population is checked.

managed care Comprehensive health care provided by a health maintenance organization or similar system.

management 1. The process of setting an organization's goals and directing the activities by which they may be achieved. **2.** The functions of planning, organizing, directing, and controlling an organization's resources. See also **five m's.**

management accounting Also called **internal accounting.** Accumulation of financial data needed for use by managers, for financial control reports, and for accounting reports intended for external audiences (e.g., stockholders, Securities and Exchange Commission) by the tracing of all costs and revenues to the specific managers responsible for them.

management audit A review, evaluation, and/or financial audit, internal or external, of management performance and its proper execution of company policies, procedures, and objectives, usually taking into account such qualitative factors as decisions made, results obtained, and physical and psychological work environment.

management by exception A type of management control system in which measured results of performance and productivity are compared with the expected outputs in order to establish a balance between them, and only exceptions from the expected outputs are brought to the attention of higher levels of management.

management by objectives (*abbr* MBO) A process whereby the manager and the subordinates of an enterprise jointly identify common goals, define each individual's major areas of responsibility as well as the results expected of him or her, and use these measures as guides for operating the unit and assessing the contributions of its members.

management consultant A professional in any area of management activity who for a fee lends his or her experience, expertise, and objectivity to client organizations to aid in analyzing management problems, propose solutions, and if necessary carry out the activities suggested.

management control system A system by which managers determine the organization's objectives, measure performance in light of those objectives, and take any corrective steps found to be necessary.

management development The organization, direction, and control of an organization's tangible resources and the provision of opportunities for training, education, experience, and growth for its employees.

management fee An annual fee charged to a mutual fund (about 0.5 percent of the fund's net asset value) for the service of maintaining the fund's portfolio.

management information system (*abbr* MIS) A computer-based system that links the divisions within a company and can furnish any information needed for decision making.

management pyramid The structure formed by the various levels of management, generally divided into three categories: top, middle, and supervisory management.

management reporting See **internal reporting.**

management science A technique for developing and using computer-based mathematical aids for decision making.

managerial grid A technique for assessing a manager's leadership style, by which the degrees of the individual's concern for production and concern for interpersonal relationships are plotted on a grid measuring nine squares both horizontally and vertically.

M & A Mergers and acquisitions.

mandatory subject A topic (e.g., wages, hours) that the National Labor Relations Board rules must be discussed during the negotiation of a labor contract. See also **permissive subject.**

manifest 1. A shipping document that itemizes the contents, value, point of origin, destination, and other important information concerning a shipment of goods. **2.** A list of passengers and cargo carried on an airplane.

manipulation An illegal attempt to generate an erroneous and general impression of a trend in securities prices by buying or selling large numbers of securities and thus deceptively inducing other investors to follow suit, thereby altering prices in a way beneficial to oneself.

manufacturer's agent Also called **manufacturer's representative.** A person who acts as a broker between wholesaler and retailer, offering no credit or storage services to clients.

manufacturer's brand Also called **name brand.** A trade name owned by the maker of a particular item.

manufacturing cell A grouping of equipment organized specifically to perform a sequence of operations common to a family of parts.

business

manufacturing cost Any cost incurred in the production of goods, normally within the categories of direct materials, factory overhead, and sometimes indirect costs.

manufacturing overhead See **factory overhead.**

margin 1. The amount of an investor's equity in an investment made in part with money borrowed from a broker. See also **margin transaction. 2.** The difference between cost and selling price.

marginal analysis Decision analysis that determines the best trade-off between two marginal costs.

marginal cost See **incremental cost** (def. 2).

marginal costing See **direct costing.**

marginal customer A customer who is on the borderline between being profitable and unprofitable to a seller.

marginal revenue See **incremental revenue.**

marginal tax rate The change in total personal income tax divided by the change in total taxable income.

marginal utility The extra utility or satisfaction derived by a consumer from the consumption of the last unit of a commodity.

margin call Notification that the price of stock bought on margin has dropped to a value below which the buyer's equity in the investment fails to equal a specified minimum percentage, and that the buyer must therefore invest further or accept the loss by allowing the broker to sell the stock and to keep the part of the proceeds that represents the money borrowed from the broker plus interest.

margin of safety The amount by which sales exceed the break-even point.

margin rate Also called **margin requirement.** The minimum percentage an investor must personally invest in a stock transaction (a figure that can vary from 50 to 100 percent), as established by the Federal Reserve Board.

margin transaction A purchase of stock in which the investor uses a broker's capital, in effect borrowing it, as part of the investment. See also **margin call; margin rate.**

markdown A reduction in the originally established selling price of an item.

market 1. A specific place where things are bought and sold. **2.** A region (e.g., Latin America, United Kingdom) where things are traded. **3.** The stock market. **4.** The sphere of commercial activity in general.

marketable securities 1. Corporate stocks and government, municipal, and corporate bonds that can be readily converted into cash. **2.** Short-term investments in such securities intended to provide cash as needed without disruption of normal business operations, considered as current assets and part of working capital.

market analysis Systematic gathering and processing of data related to consumer needs for the purpose of designing a product to meet those needs and developing market strategies to minimize the impact of competing products on a target audience.

market atomization A market segmentation strategy that addresses the needs of consumers individually rather than grouping them into segments.

market capitalization The total market value of a company, computed by multiplying the number of outstanding shares of its common stock by the current share price.

market development The process of reaching new target markets with existing products by placing stock in new territories or redesigning advertising to attract a new audience. See also **market share; product development.**

market economy See **free-market system.**

marketing The aggregate of strategies developed and activities performed before the actual selling of goods, including market research, product positioning, packaging, pricing, selling, distribution, publicity, and advertising and sales promotion.

marketing mix The elements of product, price, distribution, and promotion considered in relation to ongoing market conditions and the company's market position.

marketing research Also called **market research.** The gathering of data on consumer needs through needs assessment, economic forecasts, and motivation studies for the purpose of developing product ideas and marketing strategies.

marketing risk A factor that produces a loss in anticipated profit from the production of goods (e.g., damage, waste, theft, declining demand, obsolescence).

Marketing Science Institute (*abbr* MSI) A non-profit marketing research organization made up of academics, professionals, and companies that conducts research projects, workshops, and conferences, publishes newsletters and marketing reports, and issues statement papers.

market-minus pricing The practice of estimating the maximum cost-to-produce allowance for a product by subtracting middleman fees from the anticipated retail price. Also called **demand-backward pricing.**

market order An investor's instruction to a broker to execute a transaction at the best price possible at the moment.

market penetration See **market share.**

market-plus pricing The practice of setting the prices of some goods (e.g., gourmet foods) higher than those commanded by similar products.

market power Ability to control trade channels (i.e., suppliers, delivery services, outlets) so that one's products have a competitive advantage.

market price 1. The price or value of a product or service determined by the operation of an uncontrolled open market, in which price varies directly with demand and inversely with supply. **2.** The price at which supply and demand are in a state of equilibrium.

market profile An analysis of present or potential customers for a particular good or service in terms of age, sex, income level, and other characteristics.

market research See **marketing research.**

market segmentation Division of the total market into consumer subgroups on the basis of age, income, and/or other characteristics for the purpose of identifying and matching particular consumer groups with potential products or services.

market share Also called **market penetration.** The percentage of total sales in a particular market segment represented by the sales of a particular product.

market timing An investment strategy in which decisions to buy or sell securities are made by analyzing economic indicators such as the direction of interest rates or stock prices.

market value. The price at which a seller is willing to sell and a buyer is willing to buy.

Markov chain analysis A technique developed by Andrei A. Markov for studying the movement of individuals within an organization from one job to another in a specified time frame, used to determine probable positions available at various levels of an organization, numbers of people in other positions available to fill vacancies, career planning contingencies, and turnover rates.

markup 1. An amount, stated either in dollars or as a percentage, added to the estimated cost of an item in order to determine its selling price. **2.** The difference between the cost of an item and the manufacturer's suggested retail price.

Maslow's hierarchy of needs See **hierarchy of needs.**

master agreement A union agreement that covers several companies or multiple locations of a single firm.

master budget A plan projecting the financial statements for an entire organization and its individual components, often including details of component budgets (e.g., cash, factory overhead, finished goods).

master production schedule (*abbr* MPS) A schedule of all items to be produced by manufacturing, indicating both the quantity and timing of production.

materiality 1. The quality of being significant enough to affect decisions and require adjustment. **2.** The principle that requires or allows only important financial events (i.e., material events) to be disclosed in accounting records.

material price variance In a standard cost system of accounting, the difference between prices actually paid for materials and the current prices of those materials, calculated by multiplying the per-unit differences by the number of units used or purchased.

materials budget A budget based on the cost of materials needed to fulfill a production plan.

materials flow The pattern of materials movement from one operation to the next throughout a manufacturing facility.

materials handling Methods and equipment (e.g., conveyors, fork lifts, cranes) for physically moving materials from one location to another.

materials management The organizational unit that oversees purchasing, production control, and physical distribution of materials.

materials requirements planning (*abbr* MRP) A computerized manufacturing planning-and-control system used to schedule production, determine when to order materials from suppliers, and prioritize work on the shop floor.

mathetics The study of techniques for reinforcing and programming behavior responses by which the concepts of behavioral science are adapted to the practices and procedures of organizational personnel.

matrix design Also called **matrix structure.** A rectangular grid used to plot the interaction of a function manager and a program manager.

maturity The date stated on a bond, bill, note, or other instrument as that on which it must be or can be redeemed by its issuer, after which no further interest is payable.

maturity yield See **yield to maturity.**

M.B.A. Master of Business Administration.

MBO See **management by objectives.**

mean Average; having a value midway between extremes. See also **median; mode.**

mean absolute deviation (*abbr* MAD) A common measure of forecast error, computed by determining the average error without regard to whether the error was positive or negative.

means-end chain A linkage of organizational subgoals such that each is seen as a means toward the accomplishment of another and the entire series as a means toward the achievement of the organization's major goals.

mean square error (*abbr* MSE) A measure of forecast error, computed by averaging the square of the errors.

Mechanic's lien See **artisan's lien.**

mechanistic system A corporate management system that relies heavily on the strict hierarchical structure of obedience to authority, narrow specialization, and internal communications that take the form of rules and directions. See also **organic system.**

media buying service An independent firm that buys broadcast time on television and space in publications as a service to advertisers, and sometimes also advises them on the selection of media, the presentation of messages, and the frequency of their appearance.

median Having a value that is midway between the extremes of high and low. See also **mean; mode.**

media support The aggregate of media advertising and publicity that occurs in the course of the launching of a new product or service.

media survey A series of interviews or written questionnaires administered for the purpose of measuring the effectiveness of a medium in selling and promoting a product.

mediation See **arbitration.**

megaselling Also called **big-ticket sales.** The sell-

ing of items that command very high prices (big-ticket items).

meltdown (*stock market*) A sudden and catastrophic collapse in stock prices (as on Oct. 19, 1987), causing large losses to most investors.

memory The capacity of a computer to store and process data. See also **RAM; ROM.**

mental health insurance Insurance that covers a percentage (generally 50 percent) of the costs of psychiatric counseling and hospitalization in excess of an amount specified in a deductible clause.

mercantile Of or relating to merchants or trade; commercial.

merchandise inventory The aggregate of finished products in a manufacturer's warehouses and stockrooms.

merchandise mart A building devoted to the display of merchandise to retailers (not to the general public).

merchandiser A product display unit provided (usually at no charge) by a manufacturer to a retailer.

merchandising The totality of activities designed to stimulate and encourage interest in a product or service. See also **promotion.**

merchandising group A group of people who join together to take advantage of the benefits of cooperative advertising.

merchant wholesaler A distributor of products who carries both full lines and specialty lines of merchandise, extends credit to clients, provides transportation and storage services, and takes title to the products carried.

mergee The object of a merger; a company acquired by merger.

merger A consolidation of two or more companies, effected by the sale of one company's assets and liabilities to another, with the result that the identity of only one of the companies remains or an entirely new company is created. See also **amalgamation; conglomerate merger; horizontal merger; vertical merger.**

merit rating See **performance rating.**

method analysis Study of existing operations so as to improve them through simplification, specialization, mechanization, etc.

me-too See **congruent innovation.**

Michigan Four-Factor Scale A method of measuring (on an ascending scale of 1 to 5) a leader's (*a*) support (use of ego motives), (*b*) interaction facilitation (encouragement of close relationships among group members), (*c*) goal emphasis (maintenance of high standards of performance), and (*d*) work facilitation (provision of resources to employees and coordination of activities).

microchip See **chip.**

microcomputer A computer smaller than a minicomputer and with less capacity to store and process data.

microeconomics The study of economics in terms of individual components (e.g., the family, consumers, industries, retailers, local employment). See also **macroeconomics.**

microfiche Also called **micropublisher.** A film bearing a photographic image, greatly reduced in size, of printed material (e.g., documents, books), for storage in a file, archive, or library.

micromanage To manage or control with excessive attention to minor details.

microprocessor An integrated computer circuit that performs all the functions of a CPU.

micropublisher See **microfiche.**

mid-cap Designating a stock with a market capitalization of between $500 million and $5 billion.

middleman A person who plays an economic role intermediate between producer and retailer or consumer.

middle management Collectively the people (middle managers) who manage particular operations within an organization, developing detailed plans and procedures to carry out the directives of top management.

military-preparedness argument The argu-

business

ment that imports of certain goods should be restricted for the protection of industries that are critical to national defense.

minicomputer A computer with processing and storage capabilities smaller than those of a mainframe but larger than those of a microcomputer.

minimum-maximum inventory system An inventory control method that reviews items at fixed intervals and places a replenishment order if the on-hand inventory is below the minimum, the quantity ordered being sufficient to increase inventory to the maximum level.

minimum planning horizon The cumulative time needed to manufacture a product, including the time required for procurement of needed materials and for all steps to be completed in the manufacturing process.

minimum wage the lowest hourly wage that may be paid to an employee, as fixed by law or by union contract.

minority group A segment of a population consisting of people who share a cultural or racial background, physical handicap, or other characteristic that historically has deprived them of economic advancement.

minority interest The number or percentage of shares in a subsidiary company not owned by that company, its parent company, or related subsidiaries, and reported in a balance sheet account or a consolidated statement reporting the owners' equity of a subsidiary.

MIS See management information system.

mixed cost Also called **semivariable cost**. A cost that includes both variable and fixed costs (e.g., the part of a utility bill not attributable to an increase in production).

mixed economy Also called **modified capitalism**. An economy based on the private enterprise system but influenced by nonmarket (chiefly governmental) forces.

MNE multinational enterprise.

mockup 1. A life-size facsimile or model of a product or an environment used to simulate reality for television or filming. **2.** See **dummy.**

mode The value that occurs with greatest frequency in a series of observations. See also **mean; median.**

model stock An ideal inventory expected to be maintained when a wide variety of goods is sold rapidly, in order to keep inventory and sales in relative balance.

modem (*acronym for mo*dulator/*dem*odulator) An electronic device that makes possible the transmission of data to or from a computer via telephone or other communication lines.

modified capitalism See **mixed economy.**

mom-and-pop store Also called **ma-and-pa store. 1.** A small retail business, as a grocery or candy store, usually owned and operated by members of a family. **2.** Any small, independent modestly financed business.

mommy track A path of career advancement for women who are willing to forgo some promotions and pay increases so that they can spend more time with their children.

M-1B The total supply of money in circulation in the United States, defined as the total of all cash, demand deposits, NOW accounts, checks, and other drafts that entitle the bearer to a designated sum.

monetarism A theory that the direction of a nation's economy is determined by changes in its money supply. Monetarists believe that steady economic growth is achieved only when the increase in the money supply is commensurate with the increase in a nation's ability to produce.

Monetary Control Act of 1980 Federal legislation providing for the phasing out, over a six-year period, of the ceilings on bank interest rates required by Regulation Q, permitting savings and loans associations and savings banks to perform many of the services previously reserved for commercial banks, and extending the federal government's control of nonbanking financial institutions.

money Currency plus demand deposits. See also **M-1B.**

money market The aggregate of financial institutions that buy, sell, and transfer the short-term, higher-interest securities and other credit instruments.

money-market fund A mutual fund that invests in short-term corporate and government securities, including bonds, stocks, Treasury bills, and commercial paper, permitting small investors access to high-interest securities that would otherwise require an investment of more than $10,000.

money order An order for the payment of money, as one issued by one bank or post office and payable at another.

money-purchase plan A type of pension plan to which the employer contributes a specified sum each year, the total benefits depending upon the amount such invested sums have earned.

money supply The sum of demand or checking-account deposits and currency in circulation.

monopoly Exclusive control of a market for a product or service, or sufficient control to permit manipulation of prices.

monopsony The market condition that exists when there is only one buyer for a product or service from a large number of sellers.

mooch A slang term in telephone sales for the name of a prospect, who is given a sales pitch, often for a phony investment scheme.

moonlight To work at an additional job after one's regular, full-time employment, as at night.

moratorium 1. Legal authorization to defer payment of a debt or performance of an obligation. **2.** The period during which such deferment is in effect.

mortgage 1. A long-term loan backed by real estate or valuable equipment (often the item bought with the money borrowed), which the creditor can seize if the borrower fails to make all payments when they are due; listed under long-term liabilities on a balance sheet, with the possible exception of payments due within the next year. **2.** To pledge property as security for a loan.

mortgage bond A corporate bond backed by real estate, machinery, equipment, or other property to which the holder is entitled in whole or in part should the issuer of the bond fail to pay the principal and interest to which the bond entitles the bondholder. See also **closed-end mortgage bond; debenture; open-end mortgage bond.**

mortgagee A person who holds a mortgage.

mortgage real estate investment trust (*abbr* mortgage REIT) A mutual fund that makes loans secured by real estate and distributes at least 90 percent of its income as dividends. See also **equity real estate investment trust.**

mortgagor A person who mortgages his or her property.

motivation See classical theory of motivation.

motivational research A multiphase investigation that seeks to discover why consumers choose one product rather than another.

motivator Also called **motivating factor.** A factor, such as the likelihood of advancement or the prospect of a wage increase, that motivates an employee to produce more work or work of higher quality.

moving-average method 1. An inventory costing method in which an average is computed over time by periodically adding the value of purchased items, subtracting the value of goods sold, and dividing the running total by the number of units currently in inventory. **2.** A forecasting procedure that uses either a weighted or unweighted average of a limited set of past observations.

MPS See master production schedule.

MSE See mean square error.

multiemployer bargaining Collective bargaining between a union and two or more employers negotiating jointly.

multinational firm A business that has both production and distribution facilities in more than one country. See also **international firm.**

multiple-influence approach A contingency approach to leadership in which the leadership role is seen as directly or indirectly influenced by the environment and structure of the group and by the leader's own behavior, which in combination affect the leader's ability to balance the requirements and outcomes of performance on the one hand and employees' desires and present level of satisfaction on the other.

multiple listing, the listing of a home for sale with a number of real-estate brokers who participate in a shared listing service.

multiple management plan A plan whereby employee advisory boards pass on new ideas and proposed policy changes and thus develop management potential by taking part in decision making.

multiplier The multiple by which an initial change in spending will alter aggregate demand after an infinite number of spending cycles.

multiplier effect A sequence of adjustments initiated by a reduction in total income, which leads to cutbacks in consumer spending, which cause a further decrease in income, leading to additional spending reductions, and so on, until an increase in income causes the process to reverse direction.

municipal bond Also called **municipal note.** A promissory note issued by a state or local government or by an authority established by such a government and yielding interest at a rate determined by current interest rates at the time of issuance, the credit rating of the issuer, and relevant tax laws. See also **corporate bond; government bond.**

mutual fund See **open-end investment company.**

mutual insurance company An insurance company cooperatively owned by its policyholders, who usually receive dividends or reductions in premiums.

mutual savings bank A noncapitalized bank that distributes its available net earnings to its depositors.

N

abcdefghijklm **N** opqrstuvwxyz

NAFTA North American Free Trade Agreement.

name brand See **manufacturer's brand; national brand.**

NARB See **National Advertising Review Board.**

NASDAQ (*acronym for* National Association of Securities Dealers Automated Quotations) A computerized communication system that transmits over-the-counter price quotations to terminals in dealers' offices.

National Advertising Review Board (*abbr* NARB) A national organization whose purpose is to help regulate advertisers by reviewing problems of disclosure, deception, truth, and accuracy brought to its attention and to encourage advertisers' compliance with FTC rules.

National Alliance of Businessmen A federally financed organization of businessmen offering job training and placement assistance to the unemployed.

National Association of Accountants (*abbr* NAA) A national society of managerial and cost accountants that oversees the CMA examinations and publishes the periodical *Management Accounting.*

National Association of Securities Dealers (*abbr* NASD) A private organization created by and reporting to the Securities and Exchange Commission that establishes self-regulatory rules for brokers and enables the SEC to exercise some authority regarding over-the-counter transactions.

National Association of Securities Dealers Automated Quotations See **NASDAQ.**

National Association of Wholesaler-Distributors (*abbr* NAW) An association of wholesalers that publishes newsletters and research findings affecting the wholesaling industry, represents the industry in legislative matters, and works with other groups to solve mutual problems.

national brand Also called **name brand.** A brand that is privately owned and advertised and distributed throughout the country.

National Bureau of Economic Research (*abbr* NBER) A nonprofit organization that reports on economic indicators.

National Industrial Conference Board (*abbr* NICB) An organization founded in 1916 for the purpose of collecting and disseminating information of importance to business and industry.

National Labor Relations Act Also called **Wagner Act.** An act of Congress passed in 1935 requiring employers to negotiate in good faith with any union chosen by a majority of their employees and prohibiting blacklisting, yellow-dog contracts, and other tactics directed against the formation of unions.

National Labor Relations Board (*abbr* NLRB) A five-member board appointed by the president of the United States to enforce the provisions of the National Labor Relations Act and to investigate complaints of violations.

National Training Laboratory Former name of **NTL / Institute of Applied Behavioral Sciences.**

natural monopoly A business that provides services thought to be too expensive to duplicate locally (e.g., utilities).

NC See **network computer.**

near money Any asset that is easily converted into cash, such as government bonds or savings deposits.

need for acceptance The desire to be liked and approved by peers, subordinates, and authority figures.

need for achievement The desire to perform work successfully and to receive recognition for it.

needle trades Businesses involved in the production of wearing apparel.

needs assessment Also called **needs analysis. 1.** An analysis of a company's strengths and weaknesses regarding skilled workers in order to determine whether present workers can be retrained or new workers must be hired. **2.** The use of marketing research to determine potential markets for a new product. **3.** A marketing analysis of a community to determine which kinds of stores, as in a shopping mall, would best serve the area.

need satisfaction Fulfillment of a want or desire, such that a new need arises to serve as motivation for behavior. See also **blocked need satisfaction; hierarchy of needs.**

needs hierarchy See **hierarchy of needs.**

negative amortization An increase in the principal of a loan by the amount by which the regular payment falls short of the interest due, usually the result of an adjustable rate loan whose interest rate increases after the loan is taken out.

negative assurance An auditor's report that nothing emerged in the course of an audit to indicate any irregularities or noncompliance with acceptable policies, principles, standards, or contractual conditions.

negative confirmation (*accounting*) A customer's failure to respond to a letter requesting that he or she notify the designated auditor if the account balance stated in the letter is incorrect. See also **positive confirmation.**

negative float A reduction of cash flow attributable to payments by check that have been received and deposited but have not yet been cleared by a bank. See also **lock-box plan.**

negative income Invested income that has produced a loss and may be used as a tax deduction.

negative income tax A system of income subsidy through which persons having less than a certain annual income receive money from the government rather than pay taxes to it.

negative option A clause in a sales contract, as for books or recordings, stating that merchandise will be sent periodically to the subscriber unless the company is notified in writing that the item or items are not wanted.

negotiable Capable of being converted into cash or transferred to a new owner.

negotiable instrument A written document signed by the maker representing an unconditional promise to pay a stated amount of money to the bearer either on demand or at a specified time.

negotiate To bring about (a labor agreement, etc.) by discussion and settlement of terms, usually by means of mutual compromise.

net A value reduced by all applicable deductions (e.g., net income is total or gross income reduced by the expenses incurred in the generation or earning of that income).

net asset value The price of a share in a mutual fund, equal to the total value of the fund's securities divided by the number of shares outstanding.

net capital gains Capital gains less capital losses.

net change 1. The difference between the closing price of a security on one day and its closing price on the following day. 2. A change in price after all other factors have been accounted for (e.g., a dividend included one day but not the next is computed as part of the net change).

net current assets See **working capital.**

net income Also called **net earnings; profit.** The amount by which revenues exceed expenses or the amount of earnings remaining after all operating expenses, interest on debt, and taxes are deducted from gross income.

net operating income (*abbr* NOI) Also called **earnings before interest and taxes.** A company's earnings before payment of taxes and interest on debt.

net present value (*abbr* NPV) The present value of foreseen returns from an investment less the initial outlay for the investment.

net realizable value Estimated selling price less estimated costs of completion and disposal.

net sales Gross sales less all discounts, exchanges, and returns effected in the course of normal business transactions.

net weight The weight of an item shipped exclusive of packing material and container.

network 1. A group of television or radio stations physically linked by lines, coaxial cables, or microwave relays so that they may simultaneously broadcast the same programs. 2. A series of planned activities organized in the order in which they must occur. 3. A group of college alumni or professional people from diverse organizations who meet regularly to pool job tips, business contacts, and other knowledge for the benefit of the individual members. 4. A computer or telecommunications system linked to permit exchange of information.

network computer (*abbr* NC) A relatively inexpensive computer with minimal processing power, designed primarily to provide access to computer networks, as corporate intranets or the Internet.

network promo (*abbr for* network promotion) A series of announcements provided by a network, without cost to advertisers, to promote a program.

network time A guarantee that a sponsor's advertisement will be broadcast at a particular time on a very large number of network-affiliated television stations.

net worth The excess of the book value of all assets over liabilities.

news release Also called **press release.** A news or publicity story or announcement sent to publications or to radio and television stations for dissemination to the public for the purpose of publicizing an event, an individual, a company, or a product.

New York Stock Exchange (*abbr* NYSE) The largest stock exchange in the U.S., located in New York City.

New York Stock Exchange Index (*abbr* NYSE Index) A continuously computed index reported by the New York Stock Exchange every half hour during the working day, indicating the average price per share of a large number of stocks considered to be representative of the market.

niche A distinct segment of a market.

Nielsen rating Also called **program rating; rating.** A rating of a television program made by the A. C. Nielsen Company indicating the percentage of television homes in which the program was viewed. See also **share** (def. 2).

night differential An addition to the regular pay rate offered for work during evening and early-morning hours.

Nikkei An index showing the average closing prices of 225 stocks on the Tokyo Stock Exchange.

NLRB See **National Labor Relations Board.**

no-fault insurance A type of auto insurance in which the insurer of each car involved in an accident pays for damages and injuries up to a specified amount regardless of who is at fault.

no-frills See **plain-vanilla.**

NOI See **net operating income.**

no-load fund A mutual fund not sold by a broker or other salesperson and therefore free of any sales charge.

nolo contendere (*Latin*) No contest; a defendant's pleading that does not admit guilt but subjects the individual to punishment as though he or she had pleaded guilty.

nominal Referring to money or income measured in an amount rather than in real value.

nominal account Also called **temporary proprietorship account.** A temporary account (e.g., income statement account, dividends account, special closing account) opened for use during one accounting period and then closed to owners' equity.

nominal capital The total par value of a company's issued stock: of little practical significance, since a stock's par value has no exact or permanent relationship to its book value or market value.

nominal group technique A group decision-making technique whereby participants write their ideas and potential solutions to problems on a sheet of paper and all ideas contributed are then listed on a chart pad. The listed contributions are discussed and ideas clarified or modified, after which participants rank the ideas in order of preference, and the results are mathematically evaluated to arrive at a group decision.

noncontributory pension plan A company pension plan financed entirely by the employer.

noncumulative preferred stock Preferred stock on which dividends unpaid in any year are not carried over to be paid in a subsequent year.

noncurrent asset See **fixed asset.**

noncurrent liability See **fixed liability.**

nondirected interview A free-flowing interview in which the interviewer's questions and the interviewee's comments are unstructured, conducted for the purpose of ascertaining the interviewee's work methods, attitudes, and ambitions.

nonnotification plan A method of pledging accounts receivable, often as collateral, to a bank or other creditor, whereby the creditor has the right to receive and keep, without notification to the company's customers, the payments made on those accounts, which are sent to the company as usual and forwarded to the creditor institution. See also **notification plan.**

nonoperating expenses/revenues 1. (*income statement*) Those revenues or expenses generated by transactions not related to the company's normal line of business. 2. (*statement of changes in financial position*) All uses of working capital other than operations.

nonprofit corporation An organization whose prime reason for operating is not to make economic gain but rather to provide a needed public service (e.g., a hospital, church, school).

nonprogrammed decision A decision concerning an unstructured problem that involves no specific objective, only general elements difficult to measure; a decision arrived at through personal judgment, intuition, and creativity.

nonqualified pension plan A deferred compensation plan whereby each year an executive can increase his or her retirement benefits by additional contributions to the company's basic plan (so called because such plans exceed the maximum amount imposed by ERISA on qualified pension plans). See also **qualified pension plan.**

nonqualified stock option A stock-option plan that does not qualify for tax treatment as capital gains, permitting an executive to buy stock during a period of up to ten years at the market price or lower. See also **qualified stock option.**

nonrecurring charge A cost or expense that is not likely to occur again.

normal spoilage The level or extent of deterioration of inventories or materials that is expected even under efficient business operations and optimum sales (usually allocated to product cost rather than to expenses).

normative reward and punishment system A system for regulating an individual's behavior that involves rewards for acceptable performance and punishment for unacceptable performance.

note See **instrument; negotiable instrument.**

notebook A small, lightweight laptop computer.

notes receivable Promissory notes that must be paid on or before a specified date, often with accumulated interest (considered current assets, as they are routinely collected before that date by being discounted at a bank).

notification plan A method of factoring accounts receivable whereby a company's customers are notified that their accounts have been sold to a financial institution (a factor), and that payment on those accounts should be made directly to that institution. See also **nonnotification plan.**

novation The substitution of a new agreement or contract for an old one, usually following the substitution of a new debtor or a new creditor.

NOW account (*acronym for n*egotiable *o*rder of *w*ithdrawal account) An interest-paying savings account offered by savings banks and savings and loan associations, on which the depositor may write checks as on a checking account.

NSF check (*abbr for n*ot-sufficient-*f*unds check) A check written against a bank account that has insufficient funds to cover the amount named. See also **bad check.**

NTL/Institute of Applied Behavioral Sciences A private, academically oriented consulting organization that provides nationally known speakers and training activities for business groups.

numbered account A confidential bank account whose owner is identified only by a serial number.

NYSE See **New York Stock Exchange.**

NYSE Index See **New York Stock Exchange Index.**

a b c d e f g h i j k l m n **O** p q r s t u v w x y z

O & O (*abbr for o*wned *and o*perated) A designation for a facility that is owned and operated by another company.

oath A sworn statement signed before a notary public affirming that all information given in a document is true to the best knowledge of the signer. See also **declaration** (def. 2).

objection (*sales training*) A statement made by a prospective customer or client in opposition to some aspect of a salesperson's presentation, which the salesperson tries to turn into a reason for buying.

objectives Broad, long-range organizational goals that provide direction in the areas of profitability, customer service, and social responsibility.

obligee A person to whom a bond is given. See also **bond** (def. 2); **surety bond.**

obligor A person who gives a bond. See also **bond** (def. 2); **surety bond.**

Occupational Safety and Health Administration (*acronym* OSHA) An agency of the U.S. Department of Labor established by Congress in 1970 to set and enforce health and safety standards for the protection of workers, to train workers and employers in proper health and safety practices, and also to conduct field investigations of alleged violations.

OD See **organization development.**

odd-even pricing Also called **psychological pricing.** The setting of prices slightly below a full dollar value (e.g., $5.95 rather than $6.00).

odd lot Also called **broken lot.** A number of shares of stock smaller than the standard 100-share unit normally exchanged in a single transaction (fewer than 10 if the stock is inactive), costing a premium of $1/8$ of a point above the market price to buy.

OEM See **original equipment manufacturer.**

offering price The price quoted when something is offered for sale, especially the price per share, as of an investment security or mutual fund available for purchase by the public.

office park Also called **business park; executive park.** An office building containing commercial offices and set in parklike surroundings, usually in a suburban area.

officers of the board The chairman of the board, assistant chairman of the board, chairpersons of various committees, and secretary.

off-line Also, **offline.** Operating independently of, or disconnected from, an associated computer.

off-peak Of or relating to a period of less than maximum frequency, demand, intensity, or use, such as the off-peak travel season or off-peak train fares.

off-price Offering or dealing in goods, esp. brand-name apparel, at prices lower than those at regular retail stores or discount stores.

off-shore Registered, located, conducted, or operated in a foreign country, such as an off-shore investment company.

off-the-books Not recorded in account books or not reported as taxable income.

Old Age and Survivors Insurance (*abbr* OASI) The part of the federal social security program that provides income for retired people and for surviving dependents of deceased covered workers.

oligopoly A market condition that exists when a few large companies dominate an industry.

oligopsony The market condition that exists when there are few buyers, who can thereby greatly influence price and other market factors.

ombudsman An individual who hears and investigates complaints and problems and assists in their resolution.

one-time rate The highest rate charged for the running of an advertisement, because the advertiser is buying insufficient space or air time to qualify for a volume discount.

on-line Also, **online. 1.** Operating under the direct control of, or connected to, a main computer. **2.** Connected by computer to one or more other computers or networks, as through a commercial electronic information service or the Internet. **3.** Using a computer.

on spec (*abbr for* on *spec*ulation) Executed (as a creative effort) with the hope that the work will be accepted and paid for by a client, but with no actual commission to do the work.

on-the-job training (*abbr* OJT) Also called **in-**

service training. Instruction in skills required to perform a job by a supervisor or experienced worker in the actual work environment rather than in a simulated work site.

open account A mutual fund account that allows the investor to buy or redeem shares at will, to receive dividends in cash, or to have them automatically reinvested.

open-book credit An informal agreement whereby a customer may obtain goods with a promise to pay later, usually within 30 to 120 days.

open corporation A large corporation whose stock is owned by many stockholders, so that it is usually possible to buy shares from existing shareholders.

open-date labeling The practice of printing the last date on which a product should be sold on the package of a perishable product. See also **shelf life.**

open display A merchandising display case that permits access to goods by customers. See also **closed display.**

open-end credit Also called **revolving credit.** A credit agreement that permits the incurrence of additional debt, as for goods purchased, up to a specified limit before the original debt is canceled. See also **closed-end credit.**

open-end investment company Also called **mutual fund.** An investment company that is capitalized by the continuous sale of its stock, which it may eventually buy back at the current value. See also **closed-end investment company.**

open-end mortgage bond A corporate bond backed by property that may be used to back other bond issues or may otherwise be used as collateral. See also **closed-end mortgage bond.**

open-end order See blanket order.

open-market operations Buying and selling of government securities by the Federal Reserve system to control the money supply and thus the availability of credit.

open order 1. Also called **good-till-canceled (GTC) order.** An instruction to a broker to buy or sell securities until the investor issues contrary instructions. **2.** An order placed with a supplier for items that have not yet been delivered.

open shop A workplace where a union represents all employees in negotiations with the employer but where membership in the union is not a condition of employment.

open-systems planning Study of an organization by an outside consultant who identifies its objectives and analyzes all relevant variables outside as well as within the organization.

open-to-buy The amount of money or goods to which a retailer's purchases from suppliers are limited, or the amount of money allocated for such purchases remaining to be spent.

operating expenses Either (broadly) those expenses incurred in normal business activities or (more narrowly) selling, general, and administrative expenses only, exclusive in either case of the cost of goods sold, interest, income tax, and the costs of financing the organization.

operating income The amount by which revenues exceed operating expenses, i.e., income from normal operations before the addition or subtraction of income and expenses not associated with normal operations.

operating lease Also called **service lease.** A rental agreement that obliges the lessor to maintain and service the leased property (usually equipment) and may allow the lessee to return the property and terminate the lease at any time.

operating leverage The extent to which fixed costs affect net income in a company's expense structure: the greater the revenues and net income in relation to variable costs, the greater the leverage.

operating period The time between the purchase of materials or merchandise and the collection of payment from the sale of the finished products.

operating system The software that directs a computer's operations, as by controlling and sched-

uling the execution of other programs and managing storage and input/output.

operational auditing Extension of the internal auditing function into the areas of finance, production, marketing, and personnel management, undertaken by either a task force composed of people within the company or by external independent analysts.

operational goals 1. The significant goals and behavioral objectives that actually direct and modify the conduct of employees. **2.** Organizational standards of performance for marketing, sales, manufacturing, finance, research and development, and other operations.

opportunity fund An investment fund specializing in buying distressed companies at bargain prices and applying more skillful methods of management to make them profitable.

optical coincidence system Also called **peek-a-boo.** A filing system in which holes punched in large cards correspond to documents in which a particular word or term is used or concept discussed; when several cards are juxtaposed it is easy to see which documents contain the terms or words.

optical scanner See scanner.

option 1. The right to buy or sell a security at a specified price within a specified period of time. See also **call** (def. 1a); **put** (def. 1). **2.** The right, as granted in a contract or upon an initial payment, to buy or sell a property or a service at a stated price within a specified time.

order bill of lading A receipt for goods shipped which provides that the shipped articles can be delivered only upon presentation to the transportation company of the original bill of lading. See also **straight bill of lading.**

order cycle Also called **lead time.** The time interval between the placement of an order with a vendor and the order's delivery to a customer.

ordinary income Income generated by a firm's normal business operations, exclusive of capital gains realized through the sale of capital assets that are not normally sold by that business; revenue.

ordinary life insurance Life insurance with premiums paid throughout the lifetime of the insured. Also called **straight life insurance; whole life insurance.**

organic system A corporate management system that emphasizes decisions based on group interaction, individual choice of methods, group goals, etc., and has the flexibility to adjust to changes inside and outside the organization. See also **mechanistic system.**

organizational analysis and planning A long-range design for an organization's structure that takes into account such variables as turnover and anticipated environmental changes.

organizational development specialist A change agent, consultant, or behavioral science professional who employs behavioral theory and technology as well as action research to instruct trainees in effective functioning within the context of the organization.

organizational picketing The picketing of an employer in order to encourage union membership.

organization chart A formal plan in graphic form indicating the formal chain of command in an organization and identifying major departments, staff and line relationships, and permanent committees.

organization cost The cost of planning, incorporating, and setting up an organization, including legal and incorporation fees and the costs of issuing stock.

organization development (abbr OD) A process for improvement of an organization that involves philosophies, concepts, techniques, and procedures that influence the progress and betterment of individuals performing within the system.

original cost See acquisition cost.

original entry An entry in a journal, as opposed to an entry posted to a ledger.

original equipment manufacturer (abbr OEM)

A company that produces items that are products in themselves and are also used as components of larger products (e.g., batteries, carburetors).

OSHA See **Occupational Safety and Health Administration.**

ostensible partner An individual who is represented as a business partner with his or her knowledge and consent and who therefore may be held liable for company loans (and for whose actions the firm may be held liable) although he or she has no real business function in the company.

OTC stock See **over-the-counter stock.**

OTO (abbr for one time only) A designation for a commercial that runs only once.

outlet See **factory outlet.**

outplacement The process of aiding a newly separated executive in finding a new job (as through the company-paid services of a counselor or placement agency).

output 1. a. Production; amount manufactured. **b.** The amount produced by one person in a specified time period. **2. a.** The information fed out by a computer, either as hard copy (a printout) or soft copy (an image on a screen). **b.** To produce by a computer. See also **input** (def. 1).

outside consultant See **external consultant.**

outside director A member of the board of directors of a corporation who takes an active part in the company's affairs but who is not an employee of the corporation.

outside in Proceeding (as information about magazine readers' tastes and habits) from persons outside the organization (as subscribers) to a person inside the organization (as an advertising director who asks readers to reply with that information). See also **inside out.**

outsource To buy or hire from an outside supplier (e.g., a car manufacturer may outsource a substantial percentage of its parts).

outstanding check A check that has been written, signed, and released by a maker but not yet cleared (paid) by the bank holding the account.

outstanding shares Shares of stock that have been issued and are still in the open market or in the possession of individuals or organizations not of the issuing corporation; does not include treasury

stock or stock that has been authorized and registered but not issued.

over and short Any expense account used to reconcile or account for differences between book balances and actual balances of receipts and remaining cash in petty cash or change funds.

overapplied overhead An amount of factory overhead charged to a particular product in excess of the actual overhead incurred during the period; the amount of the credit balance of an overhead account at the end of the period.

overbought 1. (stock trading) Having an artificially and temporarily high price as a result of unusually active trading, most of which has consisted of more offers to buy than to sell. **2.** (retailing) Having stocked more goods than can be sold by normal methods.

overdraft 1. The overdrawing of a checking account. **2.** A check overdrawn on an account. **3.** The amount overdrawn.

overdraw To draw upon an account, allowance, etc., in excess of the balance standing to one's credit or at one's disposal.

overhead Charges that cannot be assigned exclusively to any particular product or project (e.g., rent, taxes, office expenses). See also **fixed overhead.**

overhead rate A predetermined rate at which overhead costs are charged or applied to units of production.

overtapping See **telescoping.**

over-the-counter stock (abbr OTC stock) Stock issued by a company that has insufficient earnings or shares outstanding to be listed by a stock exchange, or by a bank or insurance company, and which is traded between brokers acting either as principals or as agents for customers.

overtime Time worked in excess of the hours stipulated by union contract or by agreement and for which a worker may receive additional payment (usually 1½ to 2 times the normal wage). See also **straight time.**

owners' equity Also called **shareholders' equity.** The portion of a company's assets that represents shareholders' investments, after all liabilities have been settled.

a b c d e f g h i j k l m n o P q r s t u v w x y z

PA See **public accountant.**

package 1. (television) **a.** A program or other production ready for broadcast or publication, exclusive of commercials or advertising. **b.** A group of such productions sold as a unit. **c.** To produce such programs or other productions. **2.** To design or produce a protective container for a product.

package-consolidating agency See **freight forwarder.**

packager 1. A person or firm that packages a product or merchandise for commercial sale. **2.** A person or firm that creates and assembles a television show, book, or other product and offers it for sale, use, exhibition, etc., in a completed form.

Pac-Man defense A tactic, named after the video game, in which a targeted company tries to avert a hostile takeover by taking over the acquirer.

paid-in capital Also called **contributed capital.** The capital that a corporation has raised through the issuance of common and preferred stock; that part of owners' equity which does not include retained earnings. See also **capital surplus.**

paid-in surplus See **capital surplus.**

paired comparison questions Duplicative multiple-choice questions on a questionnaire designed to reveal respondents' overall rankings of subjective items.

palmtop A battery-powered microcomputer small enough to fit in the palm.

P. & L. profit and loss. See **profit and loss statement.**

panel See **consumer panel.**

panic A sudden widespread fear concerning financial affairs leading to credit contraction and widespread sale of securities at depressed prices in an effort to acquire cash.

paper profit A profit that one has in theory because a stock or other investment has increased in price but remains unrealized until the holding is sold.

par See **par value.**

pareto analysis An approach that determines the relative frequency of various problems or causes for problems so that primary attention can be focused on the most important ones. See also **80-20 rule.**

parking An accommodation employed especially in covert takeover attempts, whereby an agent buys shares of stock for the client for future delivery, usually at purchase price plus a commission; allows a client to accumulate shares without having to report them.

Parkinson's law Any of various facetious statements about business and office management expressed as if a law of physics, such as the statement that work expands to fill the time allotted for its completion. These rules were proposed by the English historian C. Northcote Parkinson.

parliamentary procedure The procedure followed in conducting a meeting or conference, conforming to the rules, usages, and precedents that govern proceedings of legislative and deliberative assemblies.

parol evidence rule A legal rule stating that parties to a written contract are bound by its terms and are debarred from offering proof of an oral agreement that contradicts or is not specified by those terms.

participant observer An investigator who studies a group engaged in work-related problem solving by taking part in its activities.

participating preferred stock Stock that carries with it the right not only to its fixed dividend but to additional dividends on a specified basis after payment of dividends on common stock.

participation show A television show with many sponsors, whose commercials appear before, during, and after the program. See also **magazine concept.**

participative leadership See **democratic leadership.**

partner A person associated with one or more others as a contributor of capital in a joint enterprise who shares in its risks and profits. See **dormant partner; general partner; limited partner; ostensible partner; secret partner; silent partner.**

partnership A legal association of two or more persons who share in the risks of financing and managing a business and in its profits.

party plan Also called **party selling.** An arrangement whereby a consumer, in exchange for either a gift or a discount on items purchased, gives a party at which a salesperson demonstrates and sells a line of products to the guests.

par value The face value of a stock or bond (e.g., a $100 savings bond that sells for $75 is selling *below par:* a bond that sells at its face value is selling *at par*).

passbook savings account A type of savings account in which transactions are entered into a passbook in the possession of the account holder. Cf. **statement savings account.**

passive income Income from an activity in which one does not actively participate (e.g., limited partnerships, research and experimentation projects).

pass-through Also called **passalong.** The additional amount charged in a price increase.

patent An exclusive right granted by a government to an inventor to make, use, license, or sell a new device, process, material, or other innovation for a specified period of time (currently 17 years in the United States).

path-goal approach The technique of motivating a subordinate by indicating the relationship between work goals and the employee's personal goals.

patronage discount See **quantity discount.**

payable A liability; a debt. See also **accounts payable.**

payback period The time until the net cash flow from a project equals the amount invested in it, calculated as the net operating income less taxes and depreciation, exclusive of potential salvage value of assets and the present value of cash to be received after the termination date of the project. See also **bailout period.**

payee A person to whom money is paid or is to be paid.

payer The person named in a bill or note as obligated to pay.

payout The amount of dividend paid by a company on each share of common stock.

pay-per-view A pay television service in which a subscriber pays for each program viewed.

payroll costs Wages, salaries, and payroll taxes.

payroll taxes Also called **employment taxes.** Federal, state, and local taxes levied on salaries and wages paid to employees, the employers' share of social security taxes, and unemployment compensation insurance taxes.

PC 1. See **personal computer. 2.** See **professional corporation.**

PDA See **personal digital assistant.**

p/e See **price-earnings ratio.**

peek-a-boo See **optical coincidence system.**

peer leader See **informal leader.**

penetration pricing A strategic pricing approach by which a company prices a new product below its anticipated normal price during its introduction to the marketplace in order to discourage competition and in the hope of recouping its initial investment quickly. See also **skimming.**

penny stock A low-priced stock of a small company, sold on a local stock exchange but usually not traded on the major exchanges and not officially indexed: so named because the price of such shares was formerly (especially in the 1930s) less than $1.

pension A fixed amount paid at regular intervals to a retired person in consideration of past services.

pension plan A benefit plan by which an employer, alone or jointly with employees, makes regular contributions to a fund that will provide income to employees after their retirement. See **contributory pension plan; noncontributory pension plan.**

per capita output The output by or for each person; the value of a nation's output divided by its population: a commonly used measure of a country's standard of living.

percentage depletion Depletion of a natural resource calculated as a percentage of the gross income earned from the resource during a certain period: often used as a tax-deductible expense. See also **cost depletion.**

percentage-of-completion method A method of accounting used for a long-term project by which revenues and expenses are entered in proportion to either (*a*) the costs incurred during the period divided by the total estimated costs or (*b*) an estimate of the percentage of job completion.

percentage-of-last-year's-sales method A budgeting technique applicable to any aspect of business by which the current year's budget for a specific area (e.g., advertising, marketing) is based on a percentage of the previous year's sales.

percentage-of-next-year's-sales method A budgeting technique applicable to any aspect of business by which the current year's budget in a specific area (e.g., advertising, marketing) is based on a percentage of the expected sales for the following year.

perceptions (*marketing*) Those features and benefits recognized by a prospective customer as critical to a purchase.

perceptual defense The mind's ability to block out certain stimuli that, if acknowledged, could be threatening to one's deepest values or ideas.

perceptual distortion The tendency to interpret reality in a subjective way consistent with one's personal value system.

perceptual map (*marketing*) A graph or visual diagram used to demonstrate how consumers perceive each attribute of a product in terms of its relevance and importance to them, or to measure the relative importance of a product's benefits to a consumer.

per diem (*Latin*) By the day; for each day.

perfect competition A hypothetical market condition in which a large number of small businesses produce the same products. Since none can independently influence prices, buyers and sellers are well informed about prices and resources, and all are free to enter and leave the market as they wish, with little effect on the general economy.

perfected Brought to a state of completion by the fulfillment of all conditions stipulated by the Uniform Commercial Code: said of a security interest in goods pledged by a debtor as security for a loan. The secured party (the lender) has greater legal rights to the goods than any other party.

performance plan A bonus arrangement whereby executives are paid extra compensation on the basis of the growth of the company, measured by increases in capital spending, earnings per share of stock, return on assets, and other figures.

performance rating Also called **merit rating.** A systematized evaluation of an employee's performance as to quantity and quality, usually used as a basis for promotions, salary increases, and the like.

performance shares Shares of common stock given to executives when a designated corporate performance objective is attained.

per inquiry advertising A form of television advertising in which the price the advertiser pays to the station for air time is based on the number of inquiries about the advertised product received as a result of the advertising.

period An accounting period; a fiscal year or portion thereof.

periodic expense Also called **periodic cost.** An expense normally incurred in order to stay in business during a period of time (e.g., rent and insurance); a fixed cost: charged to the operating expenses of that period.

periodic inventory A system that records changes in inventory that have occurred over a period of time, noting the total purchases and uses during that period (and sometimes during previous periods) rather than noting each transaction as it occurs: frequently used by companies that sell large numbers of small items. See also **perpetual inventory.**

perk (*abbr for perq*uisite) An extra benefit, often not taxable, that forms part of a job and is often used to entice a coveted executive into accepting a company's job offer. Perks may consist of chauffeured limousines, all-expense vacations, luxury living accommodations, and club memberships.

permissive subject A topic (e.g., retirees' benefits) that may arise during negotiation of a labor contract but that one side prefers not to discuss, and that the National Labor Relations Board rules may be omitted from consideration. See also **mandatory subject.**

perpetual inventory Also called **continuous inventory.** A system that accounts for every purchase or use of raw materials or goods as it occurs, often on a perpetual stock record: frequently used by manufacturing firms that sell limited numbers of expensive items or wholesale shipments. See also **periodic inventory.**

perpetual stock record A list of materials on hand that is changed daily as items are received or issued.

personal computer (*abbr* PC) A type of microcomputer designed for individual use, as at home or in an office.

personal digital assistant (*abbr* PDA) A handheld computer that provides organizational software, such as an appointment calendar, and communications hardware, such as a fax modem. Most of these devices use a stylus rather than a keyboard for input, so that they can recognize handwriting.

personal information manager (*acronym* PIM) A type of computer program that allows the user to enter reminders, lists, appointments, etc., and link the information in useful ways. Most of these programs offer scheduling and calculating capabilities.

personal property Anything owned other than land.

personnel administration See **human resources management.**

PERT (*acronym for* program *e*valuation and review *technique*) A technique for project scheduling and cost control, originally developed for the U.S. Navy, that incorporates uncertainty concerning activity times and costs.

PERT cost method A technique for controlling the cost of a large project that uses the critical path method to compute the estimated completion time and costs associated with scheduling an early start or a late start.

Peter Principle A principle set forth by Laurence J. Peter to explain humorously "why things always go wrong": "In a hierarchy every employee tends to rise to his level of incompetence."

petrodollars Surplus revenues in dollars accumulated by petroleum-exporting countries, such as

those of the Middle East, especially when used for foreign investments.

petty cash 1. A small amount of cash kept on hand for minor expenditures. **2.** (*accounting*) An imprest fund that is continually depleted and periodically replenished to an established level; a current asset account with a normal debit balance.

phantom diagram A cutaway diagram or drawing of a product, showing its internal construction or composition.

phantom freight A freight cost not paid by the seller but charged to the buyer, calculated by the addition of a base-point charge to the unit price. See also **base-point pricing.**

phantom stock Units of company stock to be granted as part of an incentive program to executives, who may be told that, should business conditions continue to improve, they will receive a bonus equal to the value of a specified number of shares on a certain date.

physical distribution The movement of goods from the point of origin to the consumer.

physical inventory The procedure of physically counting the number of items in an inventory.

pictogram A chart in which figures, such as simple line drawings, are used to indicate the relative values of the variables being compared.

piecemeal opinion An auditor's opinion on certain identified individual items on a financial statement rather than on the statement as a whole, submitted when a disclaimer or adverse opinion has been rendered on the financial statement (not a generally accepted auditing practice).

piecework system An incentive procedure whereby each employee's pay is based on the number of units he or she produces.

pie chart A circle diagram that is divided into sectors, each representing the relative value of a variable to the whole.

piggyback Also called **trailer-on-flatcar.** Transportation of goods in a truck that is then driven onto a railroad flatcar for delivery to the destination.

PIM See **personal information manager.**

pioneering stage (*marketing*) The first stage in the life cycle of a product, when the marketer places emphasis on building demand for the product.

pirate To appropriate and reproduce (a videotape, phonograph record, etc.) without legal authorization.

pit The physical area of a commodities market where traders conduct their business. See also **ring.**

place utility (*marketing*) A value added to a product by a consumer on the basis of its convenience and accessibility.

plaintiff 1. A person who brings a lawsuit against another person in an effort to recover the value of injury to his or her rights. See also **defendant. 2.** The complaining party in any litigation.

plain-vanilla Also called **no-frills.** A product or service whose features are limited to those considered basic or standard.

planned obsolescence (of a manufactured product) The condition of becoming unusable or outmoded by the deliberate design of the manufacturer, so that every few years consumers will be — or will feel themselves to be — obliged to buy a new model of the product.

planning horizon An arbitrary time frame specified for the achievement of a goal or the accomplishment of a course of action.

plug An unsubstantiated amount added to or subtracted from a verified total to obtain agreement with a target amount.

PM See **push money.**

PO See **purchase order.**

point A unit of price change: (*stocks*) $1, usually expressed as a fraction of a dollar (e.g., $+\frac{1}{8}$ or $-\frac{1}{8}$, a gain or loss of 12.5 cents); (*bonds, real estate*) 1 percent of $1000, or $10 per $1000.

point of origin The location at which goods are received into the physical distribution system.

point-of-purchase advertising (*abbr* POP advertising) Also called **point-of-sale advertising.** A display, usually provided by a product manufacturer to promote the sale of a new or specialty item, placed strategically in a store, usually near a sales counter, as a means of influencing consumers to buy.

poison pill Any of various methods devised by a company to thwart a hostile takeover attempt, as by issuing new stock or instituting a generous package of employee bonuses, any of which would prove costly to a potential acquirer.

pollution-control bonds Bonds authorized by Congress (and exempted from taxes) in 1968 to help companies finance activities or devices to control the emission of pollutants.

Ponzi scheme A type of swindle in which new investors are lured by quick profit on small sums invested and are soon enticed into investing large sums, which are not returned.

pooling-of-interest method An accounting method for combining the assets, liabilities, and owners' equity of two or more previously distinct companies. See also **purchase method.**

POP (*abbr for* point of purchase) See **point-of-purchase advertising.**

population An aggregate of people or items of any sort from which a sample is to be taken for statistical measurement.

portability Capable of being transferred, as pension benefits, from one company plan to another employer's plan, to an individual IRA, or from an IRA to a company pension plan.

portfolio 1. A collection of securities and other investments (e.g., real estate, precious metals, collectibles) held by or managed for a company or individual. **2.** A collection of samples of a freelancer's work (e.g., writing, artwork) for presentation to a prospective employer.

POS (*abbr for* point of sale) See **point-of-purchase advertising.**

positioning The technique of influencing the way a product is perceived by consumers through the effective use of advertising, promotion, and selling techniques.

positive confirmation A customer's written response to a letter requesting confirmation of an account balance, indicating to the institution that the stated balance is correct. See also **negative confirmation.**

post 1. To transfer accounting information from a journal to a ledger. **2.** A place in the stock exchange where a particular stock is traded.

postage-stamp pricing Also called **freight allowed.** The practice of including delivery costs in the prices of goods quoted to customers, such costs not being based on the destination of the goods.

potential-competition doctrine The principle that one company may not legally acquire another company in order to eliminate a potential competitor but may do so for other reasons, such as to expand its business base.

potential demand The anticipated market for a particular item predicted on the basis of economic and demographic projections.

power of attorney A notarized document specifying the manner in which an agent may act for a principal.

PPI (*abbr for* producer price index) See **wholesale price index.**

preapproach The totality of strategic planning and development work done before a client is approached for a sales presentation.

predatory pricing The practice of reducing prices so as to lure customers from one's competitors.

predictive behavior sample A selection of job-related events involving an individual, used to predict the individual's future actions and conduct.

preemptive pricing The practice of setting prices so low that potential competitors are kept out of the market. See also **predatory pricing.**

preemptive right The right of current shareholders to have a first option on the purchase of new issues of the same stock, such that corporate man-

agement is prevented from issuing new shares at below-market value for the purpose of either diluting the value of issued shares or of immediately buying them up and thus acquiring the voting control they could represent.

preferred stock Also called **preferred issue.** A share of the ownership of a corporation that entitles the holder to a fixed dividend that must be paid before any dividend is paid on common stock. See **convertible preferred stock; cumulative preferred stock; noncumulative preferred stock.**

premium 1. The difference between par value and the market value of a preferred stock. **2.** The periodic fee paid to an insurance company for coverage of risks. **3.** A free or reduced-price product offered to consumers as a means of stimulating interest in a company's products or services.

premium pay A rate of pay that is higher than the amount paid for work performed during normal hours or under normal conditions.

prepaid expense A stock of supplies on hand or a service paid for but not yet used or expired (e.g., an insurance policy, prepaid utilities), included among current assets because it will not reduce cash in the future.

preretailing The affixing of retail prices to merchandise by its manufacturer or wholesaler.

presentation graphics A kind of computer software that allows users to create charts, graphs, and other graphic images for business presentations and reports.

present value Also called **present discounted value; present worth.** The amount of money that must be invested at a specified rate of interest for a specified length of time to yield a specified sum (e.g., the present value of $100, invested for 5 years at 6 percent interest, is $75).

press release See **news release.**

prestige pricing The marketing strategy of increasing the price of an item for the purpose of establishing an image of high quality for the product or for the firm that sells it.

pretest (*marketing*) A procedure by which prospective customers are asked detailed questions about a new product's strengths and weaknesses for the purpose of fashioning selling strategies.

preventive maintenance Those maintenance activities performed before equipment breaks down, intended to increase operating performance and reduce the likelihood of breakdown. See also **remedial maintenance.**

price-earnings ratio (*abbr* p/e) The price of a share of stock divided by earnings per share for a 12-month period (e.g., a stock selling for $10 a share and earning $1 has a priceearnings ratio of 10).

price elasticity of demand The responsiveness of demand to a change in price, measured by the formula

$$\text{elasticity} = \frac{\text{Percentage change in quantity demanded}}{\text{Percentage change in price per unit}}$$

price elasticity of supply The responsiveness of price to a change in demand, measured by the formula

$$\text{elasticity} = \frac{\text{Percentage change in quantity supplied}}{\text{Percentage change in price per unit}}$$

price guarantee Also called **price protection.** A seller's guarantee that if a product's price is reduced within a specified period of time, a buyer of a large amount of that product will be refunded the difference between the price paid and the new (lower) price.

price leader A company whose pricing strategy influences the prices set by competing companies.

price lining (*marketing*) The practice of varying the features of a basic product slightly in order to offer high-, medium-, and low-priced versions of the product for different target audiences.

price point The price for which something is sold on the retail market, especially in contrast to competitive prices.

price protection See price guarantee.

price war A market characterized by repeated price cutting by competitors for the purpose of capturing each other's customers.

prima facie (*Latin*) At first view; based on first impression; self-evident.

primary boycott Refusal by union members to purchase goods or services from a company against which their union is conducting a strike.

primary data Information gathered directly from the original source, as from original documents or research. See also **secondary data.**

primary distribution See primary offering.

primary earnings per share (*abbr* primary EPS) Total corporate earnings available to holders of common stock divided by the number of outstanding shares: so called because the value does not reflect unexercised warrants and unconverted convertible bonds and preferred stock.

primary liability An absolute obligation to pay, with no conditions.

primary offering Also called **primary distribution.** An issue of shares or bonds. See also **issue** (def. 2).

primary storage See main memory.

prime rate Also called **prime interest rate.** The interest rate that banks charge for loans to their biggest and highest rated customers, which fluctuates in accordance with the corporate demand for money and with the discount rate that the Federal Reserve Bank charges for loans to banks: used as a major economic indicator.

prime time The hours, generally between 7 and 11 P.M., considered to have the largest television audience of the day.

principal 1. An original amount of money, without accumulated interest. **2.** A person who acts for himself or herself, or who is represented by an agent.

printer A computer output device that produces a paper copy of data or graphics. Dot-matrix printers form characters by dot configurations. Laser printers use lasers to form dot-matrix patterns and an electrostatic process to produce a page at a time. Ink-jet printers spray droplets of ink through nozzles. Line printers print an entire line at one time.

private brand Also called **dealer brand; private label.** A brand owned by a retailer or wholesaler.

private carrier A transportation company that carries goods exclusively for the owner or leaser of the transportation equipment, providing no service to the public.

private enterprise See free enterprise.

private label The label of a product, or the product itself, sold under the name of a wholesaler or retailer, by special arrangement with the manufacturer or producer.

private sector Economic activities that do not directly involve the government, including those of nonprofit corporations, private firms, and individuals. See also **public sector.**

proact To take active measures to influence future events rather than simply to react to events as they occur.

proactive Tending to initiate change and to influence events rather than reacting passively; enterprising.

probability assessment method The forecasting of sales volume and market size on the basis of the subjective opinions of experts.

problem clinic A training session at which groups of employees discuss various alternative solutions to common problems, thereby revealing any needs for further training.

procedural audit A planned evaluation or inspection that involves subjective analysis of a process for the purpose of quality control.

procedure The precise sequence of steps to be taken to accomplish a given end (e.g., to move raw materials from a receiving platform to an assembly line).

procedure flow chart A chart that shows the precise sequence of steps for a procedure, including the routing of all documents involved.

process approach An effort to increase productivity by the imposition of fixed conditions and job standards by which performance may be measured.

process audit Chemical analysis of fluids or substances used in the production process for the purpose of quality control.

process consumable Any material that must be bought for and is subsequently consumed in the manufacturing process.

process costing A cost accounting method in which costs are categorized, assigned, and accumulated in accordance with the departments, processes, or products that incurred them (used for assembly-line processes that produce continuously). See also **job-order costing.**

process layout A method of production in which personnel and equipment are grouped by function or process. See also **product layout.**

producer goods Such goods as raw materials and machinery that are used in the making of consumer goods.

producer price index (*abbr* PPI) See wholesale price index.

producer's risk The risk run by a producer that an acceptable lot will be accidentally rejected due to a sampling error. See also **consumer's risk.**

product Something made to be sold; a good or service that is or can be marketed.

product audit Measurement of individual components and parts of a product for the purpose of quality control.

product cost A cost associated with the manufacture of a product. See also **period cost.**

product development The process of improving existing products and creating new products, product lines, and product applications.

production The process of converting raw materials into finished goods by human labor and machinery.

production budget A budget based on forecasts of sales and production costs.

production control The function of coordinating people, materials, and machinery to provide maximum efficiency during the assembly of products, generally involving five basic steps: planning, routing, scheduling, dispatching, and follow-up.

production era In the United States, the early twentieth century, when business managers focused mainly on production rather than marketing: an era characterized by specialization and the introduction of assembly lines.

production management Control of quality, the setting of completion and delivery dates, and the making of decisions in regard to the most economical way of carrying out the production process.

production method 1. Also called **service basis.** A method of depreciation whereby the cost of an asset is depreciated over its useful life in accordance with units of production consumed or created by the asset. **2.** The technological steps used to manufacture a product.

production planning Estimating how much goods and services must be produced in order to meet anticipated demand and determining the most efficient way to accomplish this in order to maximize profits while maintaining quality.

production schedule A detailed chart showing the manufacturing procedures to be carried out on a product, the time required for each, the expected completion date, etc.

productivity Economic output per unit of labor, expressed as revenue per employee, units produced per labor hour, etc. It is a measure of the amount and quality of the finished product against the amount of resources required to accomplish this, and can be regarded as measuring the efficiency of a company, a worker or workstaff, or production methods.

product layout A method of production in which personnel and equipment are arranged in a manner consistent with the sequence of steps necessary to manufacture a specific product. See also **process layout.**

product liability A manufacturer's legal responsibility for injuries suffered by consumers as a result of defective, dangerous, or unhealthful products, whether or not the manufacturer was aware of the defect or danger.

product life cycle The commercial life of a product from introduction, maturity, and peak through decline and disappearance from the market.

product line A group of related products (e.g., cosmetics) produced by a manufacturer.

product manager The company executive responsible for developing new products, from the idea stage through marketing.

product market A market in which finished goods are bought and sold.

product mix The variety of products offered by a company to consumers.

product-oriented marketing Marketing efforts that do not rely on feedback from consumers.

product planning The aggregate of activities engaged in before the actual production of a new product, which may include an assessment of the original product idea, an analysis of market conditions, the creation of a prototype, and product testing.

product position Also called **product space.** The relative standing of a product with regard to its competition, as perceived by consumers.

product protection Also called **commercial protection.** A television network's guarantee to an advertiser that no other commercial advertising a similar product will be scheduled during the program on which the advertiser has bought time.

product research 1. In general, scientific or market research into ways of perfecting or popularizing a manufactured product; also, determining the feasibility of manufacturing new products. **2.** Systematic gathering and analysis of consumers' responses to polls, panel discussions, and questionnaires as a means of directing product design and packaging; also, test-marketing of new products in selected areas prior to general distribution.

product safety The professional area dealing with the continuous inspection of products for the purpose of identifying and eliminating features that may cause harm to the user and with the recall of products so identified that have already been sold.

product space See **product position.**

professional corporation *(abbr PC)* A corporation formed by one or more licensed practitioners, especially medical or legal, to operate their practices on a corporate plan.

profile A list of the distinguishing characteristics of a human population or a segment of it, a new product, etc. See also **demographics.**

profit See **net income.**

profitability ratio A measure of the extent to which a company is making a profit.

profit and loss statement See **income statement.**

profit center A self-contained unit within a business organization that has or may develop a profitable base independent of the larger system.

profit corporation A private organization operated for gain.

profit margin on sales Net income as a percent of total sales.

profit sharing 1. A compensation plan whereby employees receive a fixed share of any profits made by the employer. **2.** An incentive plan whereby each employee receives as a bonus the portion of the company's profits that represents his or her productivity.

profit squeeze A decline in profit resulting from declining prices, intense competition, or increasing costs.

profit taking The selling of stocks or other securities for the purpose of gaining the additional value that has resulted from rising prices.

pro forma *(Latin)* For the sake of form.

pro forma financial statement A statement that projects the financial position of a company under certain hypothetical conditions or assumptions (e.g., a possible merger, expansion, retrenchment).

pro forma invoice An invoice sent to a customer before shipment of goods as a memorandum specifying goods to be shipped, means of shipment, and terms.

programmed instruction Presentation of information in a structured format such that each step of the learning process is mastered before advancing to the next.

programmer 1. A person who programs a computer. **2.** A person who schedules radio and television programs. **3.** A person who inculcates new behavior in another person.

programming language The artificial language in which computer programs are written, such as COBOL or BASIC. See also **machine language.**

program rating See **Nielsen rating; share** (def. 2).

program trader A specialist in program trading.

program trading The often computerized trading by large institutions of vast quantities of stocks, sometimes blamed for the instability of the stock market.

progressive tax Also called **graduated tax.** A tax structured so that the rate increases as taxable income increases.

project management Direction by a team brought together to carry out research on and development of a specific project within a specified time limit.

promissory note A borrower's written promise to pay a specified amount plus interest at a specified rate on a designated date in the future.

promotion 1. An advancement to a position with higher status and greater responsibility, usually with an increase in salary. **2.** The totality of communications designed to sell a product, service, or idea, including personal selling, advertising, publicity, and public relations.

property Anything of value that is owned. See also **personal property; real estate.**

property dividend A dividend paid in resources, assets, goods, etc., rather than cash.

property insurance Insurance that protects the insured against losses resulting from damage to or destruction of property as a result of unavoidable risks.

proprietary information Information about a company or about an aspect of its business that should be known only to a limited number of people involved in the relevant activities.

proprietorship An ownership interest in a company, equal to assets less liabilities or contributed capital plus retained earnings.

pro rata *(Latin)* In proportion; proportionately determined.

prorate To calculate on a proportionate basis; to divide or distribute proportionately.

pro se *(Latin)* For himself/herself/oneself/ themselves.

prospect A potential customer.

prospecting *(sales)* Also called **farming.** The totality of activities designed to identify legitimate prospects and eliminate those unlikely to become customers.

prospective planning Planning to meet the needs of an organization's employees that takes into account their long-range expectations as well as their present needs.

prospectus A published summary of a corporation's earnings, financial condition, product lines, and the qualifications and salaries of its officers, required by the Securities Exchange Act of 1934 to be provided to all potential investors in the corporation's securities.

protectionism The protection of domestic industries against foreign competition by enacting high tariffs and/or restrictions on imports. Advocates of such procedures are called *protectionists.*

protective tariff A tariff imposed on a class of

imports for the purpose of protecting a domestic industry against foreign competition.

prototype A model of a product prepared for testing, evaluation, and possible modification before the product is mass-produced.

provision for income tax See **income-tax expense.**

proxy Written authorization for one person to act for another, as to vote one's shares of stock.

proxy fight A competition between management and disagreeing shareholders for control of the company, each group attempting to secure the major portion of shareholders' proxies.

prudent man rule A rule adopted by states that lack a legal list, indicating that a fiduciary has wide discretion in investment decisions, provided only that they be such as would conceivably be made by any prudent investor.

psychographics Also called **psychographic segmentation.** A market-segmentation strategy by which consumers are grouped according to their behavior patterns and lifestyles, as indicated by responses to questionnaires.

psychological pricing See **odd-even pricing.**

public accountant (*abbr* PA) An independent accountant who offers his or her professional services to the public for a fee. See also **certified public accountant.**

public corporation A corporation owned and operated by a government, established to administer a designated governmental program and managed in accordance with business principles.

public domain The rights belonging to the public at large; the status of properties (as writings, music, or inventions) on which copyright or patent protection has expired or which have been issued without such protection, and which may be used by any person.

public good A product or service whose consumption by one person does not exclude consumption by others (e.g., fire and police protection).

publicity Information designed to appear in any medium of communication for the purpose of keeping the name of a person or company before the public or of creating public interest in their activities.

public law A law enacted by a legislative body, applicable throughout the geographical area over which the legislature has jurisdiction. See also **common law.**

public-liability insurance Insurance that provides coverage against claims by the public for damages arising from negligence.

public offering An issuance of a security for sale to the public.

public relations Promotion of a favorable image for a company through particular attention to how, when, why, and what information is given to customers, employees, stockholders, and the general public.

public sector That part of the economy which is considered to be the government's domain, involving such activities and decisions as have an effect on the society at large. See also **private sector.**

public warehouse A warehouse in which storage space is rented to any person.

puffery 1. Undue or extravagantly flattering praise issued for promotional purposes. **2.** Also called **puff piece.** An example of this in the form of a newspaper or magazine article, usually commissioned and placed by a hired public-relations specialist.

pull distribution strategy A marketing strategy based on efforts to induce consumers to ask retailers for a product they have seen advertised, so that retailers will then order the product. See also **push distribution strategy.**

pulsing See **flighting.**

pump priming Government spending designed to stimulate the economy.

purchase journal An accounting journal used to record purchases of merchandise, the total being posted as a credit to accounts payable and a debit to the purchases account.

purchase method An accounting method whereby two previously distinct companies are combined by adding the value of one company's assets to the total assets of the other. See also **pooling-of-interest method.**

purchase order (*abbr* PO) A printed agreement to buy a product, indicating the quantity of goods desired, delivery dates, order number, and other relevant information.

purchasing agent A person who has the authority to select and buy supplies for a company.

purchasing power See **buying power..**

push distribution strategy A marketing strategy based on efforts to place a product with wholesalers, who will then make an effort to place it with retailers, who will make an effort to sell it to customers. See also **pull distribution strategy.**

push money (*abbr* PM) Commissions, bonuses, etc., paid to retail sales personnel for selling specified items.

put 1. Also called **put option.** An option to sell a stock or commodity at a specified (put) price within a specified period, purchased from a broker for a premium based on a percentage of the current market price of the stock or commodity; if the price falls during the option period, the owner of the option can sell the shares or commodity at the (higher) price specified. See also **call. 2.** To exercise such an option.

pyramid selling An illegal marketing scheme whereby an initial investor recruits and establishes subordinate distributors, each of whom recruits additional distributors, and so on, each distributor to receive a commission on the sales of all subordinate distributors recruited by him or her and by those recruited by subordinates.

business

a b c d e f g h i j k l m n o p **Q R** s t u v w x y z

qualified endorsement An endorsement that limits the liability of the endorser by specific words added above the signature (e.g., "Without recourse").

qualified opinion Also called **qualified report.** An auditor's report that includes a statement that the auditor has been unable to examine all relevant documents or has some doubts about the impact of some information on the financial report.

qualified pension plan A pension plan that conforms to the provisions of the Employee Retirement Income Security Act and so qualifies the employee to receive tax benefits for tax-deducted contributions and tax-free investment growth (e.g., a profit-sharing plan or a money-purchase plan).

qualified prospect A prospective buyer who has the financial ability and authority to buy the product being offered.

qualified report See **qualified opinion.**

qualified stock option A once popular but now rarely used plan by which executives could buy stock during a five-year period at the market price, with appreciation in value being taxed as capital gains. See also **nonqualified stock option.**

quality assurance Any steps taken to improve and maintain the quality performance of an organization.

quality circle A group of workers (typically 5 to 12) who meet regularly to identify, analyze, and solve work-related problems, such as quality improvement.

quality control Spot checking of goods after manufacture, before assembly, or through lab testing, in order to eliminate defective products or improve performance standards and practices.

quality of work life (*abbr* QWL) Employee involvement in the making of decisions involving the organization as a whole, instituted to increase morale and individual productivity. See also **quality circle.**

quant A slang term for a specialist in quantitative analysis (quantitative analyst).

quantitative analysis Also called **quantitative research.** The use of statistical data, usually computerized, to support management decision making, make business forecasts or recommendations to investors, etc.

quantity discount Also called **patronage discount.** A price reduction offered for purchases of large quantities of a product.

quasi contract An obligation imposed by law in the absence of a contract in order to prevent one person from being unjustly enriched at the expense of another.

quasi-public corporation A corporation created jointly by public and private funds.

quasi reorganization A reorganization of a company effected by court intervention following bankruptcy or near bankruptcy in which no new company has been formed. See also **Chapter 11.**

QUBE (*trademark*) A device that enables television viewers to answer questions, order merchandise, or otherwise respond to information projected on their television screens.

queuing theory Analytical models used to describe customer service systems with waiting lines, or queues, and to provide various performance measures, such as average waiting time and expected line length.

quick asset Also called **liquid asset.** An asset that can be quickly converted to cash (e.g., a marketable security, current accounts receivable).

quick ratio See **acid-test ratio.**

quitclaim deed A legal instrument transferring any interest, claim, or title that a person may have in real property, normally with no warranty in regard to rights others may have in the property.

quorum The minimum number of people whose presence is considered necessary before business may be conducted.

quota 1. The quantity of goods that an employee is expected to produce or sell within a given time span. **2.** A government-imposed restriction on imports of a specified product or on the amount or number imported from a particular country, often on a par with exports. **3.** A percentage of minority or handicapped workers hired by a company.

quotation (*abbr* quote) The highest bid price a dealer offers for a given stock and the lowest asked price that a seller is willing to accept for that stock.

quoted bid See **bid price.**

QWL See **quality of work life.**

rabble hypothesis The hypothesis that employees are motivated by self-interest: a principle of early management theorists who believed that no employee could be expected to cooperate with management for any reason other than monetary reward.

rack jobber A wholesaler (usually in the food business) who provides goods and then stacks, arranges, and displays them in retail stores.

RACORNOS (*acronym for* race, color, religion, national origin, sex) A term that first appeared in the Civil Rights Act of 1964 as part of the text defining and outlawing discrimination in employment.

raider Also called **corporate raider.** A person, company, etc., that attempts to take over another company, especially by surreptitiously buying up the target company's stock.

rail average The average price per share of 30 transportation stocks as calculated by the Dow Jones transportation index. See also **Dow Jones average.**

rainmaker An employee who generates money for a firm, as by bringing in new clients.

rainmaking The act of generating revenue for a firm, especially by bringing in new clients, as in a law firm or advertising agency.

rally A sudden reversal of a downward trend in the prices of all stocks or a particular stock.

RAM (*acronym for* random access memory) Also called **main memory.** Computer memory used for creating, running, and loading programs and for manipulating and temporarily storing data. See also ROM.

R & D (*abbr for* research and development) See **development; research.**

random sampling Selection of a small portion of a population, group of products, etc., in such a way that the response, quality, etc., of the sampling can be considered typical of the whole.

rate Charge per unit (e.g., a price for advertising time or space based on the average number of viewers or readers or a premium cost per $1000 of insurance).

rate base An amount of circulation guaranteed to advertisers by a publisher and used as the basis for the charge per unit of advertising space.

rate card A printed statement distributed to purchasers of media space indicating advertising rates and technical requirements for use of each medium.

rate cutting An employer-initiated reduction in employee wage rates.

rate of exchange See **exchange rate.**

rate of return The profit shown by an investment, expressed as a percentage of the total money invested in it.

rate protection A guarantee that advertising rates will not be increased during a specified time period.

rate stop See **freeze rate.**

rating See **Nielsen rating; share** (def. 2).

ratio analysis An analysis of the various elements that make up a financial statement, with their relationships expressed either as percentages of the whole or as ratios.

reacquired stock See **treasury stock.**

real account A permanent balance-sheet account, as opposed to a nominal account.

real earnings The actual value of earnings after adjustment for inflation, deflation, or devaluation of the currency.

real estate Also called **real property.** Land and anything permanently attached to it.

real estate investment trust (*abbr* REIT) A mutual fund that invests only in real estate and must distribute at least 90 percent of its income as dividends. See also **equity real estate investment trust; mortgage real estate investment trust.**

real GNP (*abbr for* real gross national product) The value of the output of a nation's goods and services in a given period measured in the prices of a previous period.

real income The total purchasing power of an individual or a nation.

realizable value Market value; the amount that can be obtained on the open market for a given asset.

realization The final earning of revenues and subsequent recognition of them in bookkeeping accounts.

real property See **real estate.**

real-time Of or relating to computer programs or processes that respond immediately to user input.

rearrangement costs Costs incurred in the reinstallation of an asset either after maintenance work or for the purpose of relocating it.

reasonable value A value placed on an asset that accurately reflects its worth on the open market.

reassessment An official reevaluation of the value of real property.

rebate A return of part of the original payment for some service or merchandise.

recall 1. To summon laid-off employees back to work. **2.** To cause defective or unsafe products to be returned to the manufacturer for repair, replacement, or refund.

receipt-of-goods dating See **ROG dating**.

receivable A claim against a customer or debtor, listed as an asset on a balance sheet. See also **accounts receivable**.

receiver A person with the legal authority to receive and to hold in trust property that is or could be involved in a lawsuit.

receiving apron A document used by retailers to account for incoming shipments of merchandise.

recession 1. A period when business production, employment, and earnings fall below normal levels. **2.** A period when real GNP declines for two consecutive quarters. See also **final-goods recession; inventory recession**.

reciprocity Mutual exchange of trade between two parties, such that trade with nonparticipating parties is virtually eliminated.

recognition 1. The entering of the amount of a transaction into a bookkeeping account. **2.** Formal acknowledgment of the right of a union to act as bargaining agent for employees.

recognition picketing Picketing by union members of a company where a rival union is already recognized in an effort to replace that union as bargaining agent for the employees of the company.

reconciliation 1. The act of calculating or analyzing how the balance of one account was derived from another. Also called **reconcilement.** The act of accounting for differences between two financial balances. **3.** See **bank reconciliation**.

record The documents that must be processed during the filing of a patent and that remain a permanent part of the application.

record date See **holder-of-record date**.

recovery A turnaround in economic conditions following a recession or depression.

recruiter A staffing specialist employed by a company or by an outside agency to find qualified persons, especially executives, for specific positions. See also **executive search firm**.

redeemable bond See **callable bond**.

redemption price 1. The price a corporation must pay to redeem (buy back) its preferred stock or a bond before its maturity date. **2.** The price a mutual fund must pay to redeem an outstanding share, usually the fluctuating net asset value.

red herring An unofficial prospectus distributed to potential investors for the purpose of ascertaining the extent of their interest in a new issue of stock.

red rush See **crash time**.

reentry An employee's return to work after a training program, a leave of absence, etc.

reference column Also called **ref.** The column in an accounting journal in which is recorded the account number of the ledger to which the journal data were posted, or the column in a ledger in which is recorded the page number of the journal from which the ledger data were posted.

reference group A group with which an individual identifies and whose opinions, attitudes, and values strongly influence the individual's decisions.

referral scheme A sales technique whereby the seller promises to give the purchaser a monetary rebate or free products if a certain number of the buyer's friends buy the item also.

refinance 1. To finance again. **2.** To satisfy a mortgage or other debt by making another loan on new terms. **3.** To increase or change the financing of, as by selling stock or obtaining additional credit.

refinancing 1. Satisfying a mortgage or other debt by making another loan on new terms. **2.** Changing the financing of a debt, as by selling stock or obtaining additional credit.

reflective listening An interpersonal problem-solving technique that requires those individuals involved in conflict to restate the assertions of the other party before answering them.

reframing A training technique whereby a person is encouraged to view a commonplace event from a new vantage point that is useful or enjoyable, with the expectation that when the frame of reference of the event changes, the person's responses and behavior will likewise change.

refreeze To strengthen, support, and routinize newly established behavior patterns within a work group, usually as the final phase of a planned intervention program. See also **intervention** (def. 2).

refusal to deal A refusal to do business with a particular company; a right recognized by the Supreme Court so long as there is no indication of conspiracy, price fixing, restraint of trade, or racial or religious discrimination. See also **Colgate doctrine**.

registered representative (*abbr* RR) See **broker** (def. 1).

registrar An outside agent, usually a bank or trust company, that approves the issuance of stock, authenticates stock certificates, keeps track of registered stockholders and dividend distributions, and sometimes also serves as a transfer agent.

registration The formal recording of a stock issue by the Securities and Exchange Commission, required by the Securities Act of 1933 for all public offerings of more than $1.5 million within 20 days of issuance, with financial, legal, and technical information about the company.

regression analysis A statistical technique used to describe the relationship between two variables, so that if the value of one variable is known, the value of the other can be predicted.

regressive tax A tax structured so that the tax rate decreases as taxable income increases. An example is the Social Security tax.

Regulation B A regulation of the Federal Reserve Board issued to carry out the provisions of the Equal Credit Opportunity Act, limiting the kind of information that a credit applicant may be required to supply, in particular a woman of childbearing age or one who is widowed or divorced.

Regulation S-X A regulation of the Securities and Exchange Commission specifying the form and content of reports that must be filed with the Commission.

Regulation T A regulation of the Federal Reserve Board that sets the maximum amount of credit that a broker or dealer can extend to customers for the purchase of securities.

Regulation U A regulation of the Federal Reserve Board that sets the maximum amount a bank may loan a customer for the purchase of listed securities when such a loan is to be secured by listed securities.

Regulation Z A regulation of the Federal Reserve Board issued to carry out the provisions of the Truth-in-Lending Act, requiring that borrowers be informed of the exact costs of credit offered up to $25,000 for personal, family, household, or farming purposes.

Rehabilitation Act An act of Congress passed in 1973 requiring that any employer who has a government contract take affirmative action to employ and promote the handicapped.

reinvestment rate The rate at which the cash generated by a project before its completion is reinvested.

REIT See **real estate investment trust**.

relative advantage (*marketing*) The advantage that one product has over another or over competing products, as viewed by consumers.

release A signed authorization for the use of a photo, name, property, film or tape clip, or testimonial for commercial purposes.

relevant costs Differing future costs of alternative courses of action.

relevant environment The individuals outside an organization who directly affect its operations and sales (e.g., suppliers, customers, competitors, regulatory agencies).

reliability The degree to which an experiment, test, or survey will repeatedly yield the same results. See also **validity**.

remainder A future estate that takes effect at the termination of another estate, as when property is conveyed to one person for life and thereafter to another.

remedial maintenance Those maintenance activ-

business

ities performed to restore equipment to an acceptable operating condition after a breakdown has occurred. See also **preventive maintenance.**

remedy A legal means of correcting a wrong or recovering a legal right or privilege.

remittance Money forwarded from one person or firm to another as payment for goods or services.

renegotiable-rate mortgage Also called **flexible rate mortgage; rollover mortgage.** A federally sponsored loan that requires the holder to renegotiate its terms every three to five years, when interest rates are subject to increase or decrease, depending upon market conditions. See also **adjustable-rate mortgage; variable-rate mortgage.**

rent 1. A periodic payment made by a tenant to a landlord in return for the use of property. **2.** A series of payments made by a lessee to an owner in return for the use of equipment, machinery, etc. **3.** Profit or return derived from land or from any differential advantage in production.

reopener clause A contractual provision that allows a current contract to be renegotiated for specified reasons.

reorder point The quantity of materials or merchandise on hand that signals the need to reorder.

reorganization A reconstruction of a business corporation, including a marked change in capital structure and reporting structure.

replacement cost The actual cost to a company to replace an item or piece of machinery.

repo See repurchase agreement.

report form The standard form of a balance-sheet presentation, in which assets less liabilities are shown as one total in the top portion, often with a subtotal for current assets and current liabilities and a subtotal for noncurrent assets and liabilities, followed by the components of owners' equity. See also **account form.**

repossession The reclaiming of items that were sold on an installment sales contract but not paid for in accordance with the contractual terms.

representation election An election conducted by the National Labor Relations Board to determine whether a particular labor union is to represent workers in a designated bargaining unit.

repressive tax A government levy that discourages production and productivity.

reproduction cost The cost of acquiring an asset with physical characteristics similar to those of an asset already owned and for which a current value must be determined.

repurchase agreement Also called **repo. 1.** A contract between a dealer, such as a bank, and an investor, whereby the investor purchases securities with the promise that they will be bought back by the dealer on a designated date, for which the investor receives a fixed return. **2.** A contract between a buyer and a seller whereby the seller agrees to repurchase the item sold after a specified length of time or amount of use.

requisition A written authorization issued by one department of a company to another (e.g., supply department) for the release of goods.

rescission Revocation or abrogation of a contract, either by consent of the parties involved or by court order, as when one party has breached the contract or has signed it under fraudulent terms.

research Purposeful and methodical investigation or experimentation. See also **applied research; basic research.**

research and development (*abbr* R&D) See **development; research.**

reserve A special account (e.g., reserve for contingencies, reserve for warranty claims, reserve for income taxes) that appropriates retained earnings and limits dividend distributions in anticipation of likely future costs.

reserve for bad debts See allowance for doubtful accounts.

reserve requirement A percentage of the total amount of a bank's demand deposits that the Federal Reserve Board requires to be kept on hand as cash or on deposit with a federal bank.

resident buyer An individual located in a particular geographical area who provides services and assistance to retail buyers who wish to buy merchandise in that location.

residual income Income to be distributed to holders of common stock after the senior claims of bonds and preferred stock are paid.

residual value The net realizable value of a depreciable asset: the market or salvage value less the cost of removing and/or delivering the asset.

resource decision A euphemism often employed when a company is forced to scrap a project, close down one of its plants, and lay off a number of employees.

restraining order A court order that prohibits certain actions until all parties in a dispute can be officially heard.

restraint of trade Illegal restriction or impeding of competition or unfair imposition of limits on the right to do business.

restricted stock Company stock granted to an executive, often subject to forfeiture and with the right to sell limited.

restrictive covenant 1. An agreement accompanying a conveyance of land and restricting the use to which the land may be put. **2.** An agreement accompanying an employment contract whereby the employee promises not to work for anyone else in the same business or to form a competing business in a specified area for a specified number of years.

restrictive endorsement An endorsement that transfers an instrument for a particular purpose only (e.g., "Pay to the order of...," "For deposit only"), after which the instrument is no longer negotiable.

résumé Also, **resume.** A descriptive listing of one's job experience, education, and training, used in seeking employment: usually sent to a prospective employer prior to a job interview.

retailing The activities involved in selling goods or services directly to people for their own use.

retail inventory method A method commonly used by large retail stores to determine inventory cost for interim statements, in which total sales are subtracted from the total retail value of the goods available for sale during the specified period in order to determine the retail value of the inventory, the result being reduced by an estimated (or average) markup rate.

retained earnings 1. (*income statement*) The portion of a corporation's recent net profit that is reinvested in the business rather than distributed as dividends. **2.** (*balance sheet*) A corporation's total earnings in the current and previous periods reduced by the amounts distributed as dividends.

retainer A fee paid to secure the services of an individual with a particular skill or knowledge (e.g., lawyer, auditor).

retentive stage The point in the life cycle of a product where the brand has so much consumer acceptance that promotional activities can be kept to a minimum without loss of consumer loyalty.

retirement 1. (*accounting*) The disposal of an asset at the end of its useful life. **2.** Voluntary or involuntary withdrawal from active employment.

retroactive pay Delayed payment for services rendered in the past.

retrospective planning Organizational planning by which past errors in judgment are assessed and rectified before new objectives are set.

return 1. See yield. **2.** See tax return.

return on investments (*abbr* ROI) Net income divided by total assets: expressed as a percentage.

revaluation surplus Part of owners' equity created by the upward revaluation of fixed assets.

revenue Incoming assets in the form of cash and other receivables resulting from sales of products or services and returns on investments, exclusive of borrowed assets and income from sales of capital stock.

revenue bond A municipal bond backed by the income-producing project it finances, as a toll road.

revenue tariff A tax levied on imported products for the sole or primary purpose of raising revenue.

reversal entry A journal entry usually made to reverse or undo the effects of an adjusting entry of a previous period.

reverse-annuity mortgage An income plan whereby homeowners may borrow against their equity in a house or other property, the loan providing them with a monthly income that is deducted from the amount of their equity.

reverse split Also called **reverse stock split**. The recalling of shares of stock by the issuer and the subsequent issuance of one new share for two or more old shares.

reversion The return of an estate to the original owner or to that owner's successor after the interest granted expires.

revolving charge account A type of retail charge account by whose terms no service charge is imposed if the customer pays the full amount owed within a given period of time after the billing date, usually 30 days; otherwise a specified percentage of the amount owed will be added as a service charge.

revolving credit See **open-end credit**.

revolving loan A loan expected to be renewed upon maturity.

reward See **extrinsic reward; intrinsic reward.**

reward/punishment system See **utilitarian reward/punishment system.**

rider An addition to a standard insurance policy offering further coverage.

rights See **ex-rights; preemptive right.**

rights on With the right to purchase a new issue of stock at a special subscription price offered to current shareholders: applied to shares of stock traded before the ex-rights date.

right-to-work law A state law that prohibits the practice of requiring a worker to join a union as a condition of employment.

ring The area of a commodities market, usually ring-shaped, where traders conduct their business. See also **pit.**

risk The possibility or probability of an unfavorable occurrence. See also **absorbable risk; financial risk; insurable risk; pure risk; systematic risk; uninsurable risk; unsystematic risk.**

risk analysis Analysis of the possible outcomes of a management decision and the probability that such outcomes will occur.

risk arbitrage A high-risk type of trading in which the investor buys up large blocks of stock in a company rumored to be on the verge of expanding its operations, targeted for takeover, etc.

risk capital See **venture capital.**

risk finance The totality of procedures (e.g., insurance, bank lines of credit, pooling of risks among members of a particular industry) used to fund known or anticipated losses.

risk management The reduction of the risk of financial loss caused by unpredictable events by (1) avoidance of risk, (2) preparation to accept or absorb it without permanent financial injury, (3) minimization of the threat of risk or the extent of damages, or (4) purchase of insurance to guarantee full or partial recovery.

risk premium The difference in interest rates between a low- or no-risk security (e.g., a short-term government security) and a security of high risk (e.g., a corporate bond or stock).

risky-shift phenomenon A tendency to venture a more hazardous solution to a problem when the responsibility is shared with others.

road warrior (*slang*) A person who travels extensively on business.

Robinson-Patman Act An act of Congress passed in 1936 to amend the Clayton Act by reducing the amount of proof needed to show anticompetitive effects of price discrimination. See also **Colgate doctrine.**

robotics The use of computer-controlled robots to perform mechanical tasks previously done by humans, as on an assembly line.

ROG dating (*abbr for* receipt-of-goods dating) The setting of the due date and the calculation of any

discount in accordance with the date goods are actually received by the buyer.

role indicators See **links and role indicators.**

role playing A training technique whereby individuals behave realistically in simulated situations, thus experimenting with new behaviors and new attitudes in a low-risk situation.

roll-in A film or tape commercial inserted into a television program for broadcast.

rollout 1. The inauguration of a new service, product, production method, etc. **2.** Specification of the most economical sequence of operations for work to be done during the manufacturing process.

rollover The reinvestment of funds, as from one stock or bond into another.

rollover mortgage See **renegotiable-rate mortgage.**

ROM (*acronym for* read-only memory) A form of computer memory in which operating procedures and programmed instructions to the system are permanently stored, usually imprinted on electronic chips during manufacture and which generally cannot be changed. See also **RAM.**

rough cut A method of capacity planning that roughly estimates the feasibility of a proposed production schedule, especially in determining the ability of the known bottlenecks to fulfill their part of the requirements.

round lot An even 100 shares of an active stock or a multiple thereof.

route sheet A document that specifies for a part, component, or product the sequence of operations in the production process, the amount of time each operation should take, and the work center or machine that will accomplish each task.

routing Determination of the path that work will take through the production process.

royalty Compensation in the form of a percentage of revenues payable for the use of property protected by a patent or copyright or of a natural resource.

RR (*abbr for* registered representative) See **broker** (def. 1).

rubber check See **NSF check.**

rule of 69 A formula used to calculate the number of periods it will take an amount invested to double in value at a particular compound interest rate, accurate to $1/10$ of a period. In the following formula, X is the percentage of compound interest per period:

$$69/X + 0.35 = \text{Number of periods}$$

rule of 72 A formula used to calculate the approximate number of periods it will take an amount invested to double at a given compound interest rate. In the following formula, X is the compound interest rate per period:

$$72/X = \text{Number of periods}$$

rule of 78 A method used by finance companies to allocate earnings on loans among the 12 months of the year when all monthly payments are equal, based on the sum-of-the-years'-digits concept: the sum of the digits 1 through 12 (for the 12 months) equals 78; $12/78$ of annual earnings are allocated to the first month, $11/78$ to the second month, and so on to the end of the year.

runoff election A second election conducted by the National Labor Relations Board when the first does not determine a clear majority of votes in favor of one of two labor unions.

run of paper (*abbr* ROP) An arrangement whereby an advertiser leaves the position of an ad to the discretion of the publisher. See also **guaranteed position.**

Russell Index One of several U.S. stock indexes maintained by the Frank Russell Company. The Russell 3000 is comprised of the largest U.S. companies, and the Russell 2000 is comprised of small companies. Each stock is weighted according to its market capitalization.

business

safety engineering Examination and analysis of potentially hazardous conditions in a plant or other industrial environment so that measures can be taken to prevent accidents.

safety stock Also called **buffer stock.** An extra supply of materials kept on hand to complete a production run or for use in the event that abovenormal needs occur during the time required to receive new materials.

salary Payment to an employee for work done, based on a weekly, monthly, or annual rate rather than on an hourly rate.

sale 1. The delivery of goods in exchange for some resource, most commonly cash or a promise to pay cash. **2.** An agreement or contract to transfer title or ownership of property or movable goods from one individual, the seller, to another, the buyer, for a specified price.

sale and leaseback See **leaseback.**

sales (*accounting*) A revenue account with a normal credit balance that reflects revenues from the sale of goods for the period to date.

sales agent A marketing agent who handles all of the production of a manufacturer and acts as the firm's marketing department.

sales forecast A prediction of the sales of a product in an area, based on knowledge of past buying habits of the target audience plus identified and calculated environmental influences.

sales journal A special accounting journal used to record sales on credit, the total being posted as a credit to sales and a debit to accounts receivable.

sales promotion The aggregate of carefully and persuasively designed events, activities, and products (e.g., contests, coupons, direct mail, point-of-purchase displays, sales meetings, samples, sweepstakes, trade shows) used by an advertiser to encourage sales.

sales quota The amount of sales expected to be made by a salesperson, based on the number of stores in the territory and factors influencing buying patterns.

sales returns and allowances An account with a normal debit balance in which are recorded refunds and credit given to customers who have returned goods and the cost of goods damaged in shipment, which can be a contra account deducted from gross sales or can be treated as a selling expense.

sales tax A tax on a purchase, added to the total sale.

sales-type lease See **capital lease.**

salvage value Also called **scrap value.** The value of an asset that has been fully depreciated, i.e., the market price of an asset that is to be replaced.

sample A section or part of a larger group of people or items selected for statistical measurement. See also **random sampling.**

S & L See **savings and loan association.**

S & P 500 See **Standard & Poor's 500.**

satisfaction Execution of an accord; settlement of a claim or discharge of a legal obligation.

saturation 1. Frequent repetition of an advertising message. **2.** A stage of marketing at which a product or line of products has achieved as great a share of the market as can be expected.

Saturday-night special A buyout offer made directly to the shareholders of a company and which expires in one week.

savings account A bank account on which interest is paid, traditionally one for which a bankbook is used to record deposits, withdrawals, and interest payments. Cf. **checking account.**

savings and loan association (*abbr* S & L) An institution, organized either as a cooperative or a

corporation, that uses deposits to finance loans, primarily those to homebuyers.

savings bond A U.S. government bond, sold in two forms: (1) **Series EE,** available in denominations of $50 up to $10,000 and sold at half the face value, to mature in 8 years, and (2) **Series HH,** sold at face value in denominations beginning at $500 and usually paying 6 to 8 percent interest.

scab 1. A union member who refuses to strike or goes back to work before a strike is ended. **2.** A person who is hired to replace a striking worker.

scalar chain of command A graduated or steplike pattern of authority and responsibility.

Scanlon plan A group incentive program in which an entire work group is rewarded for a suggestion by any member that, when implemented, increases productivity.

scanner Also called **optical scanner.** A device that scans and identifies data in printed, handwritten, bar-code, or other visual form. A type of handheld scanner is commonly used at retail checkout counters.

scanning The process of examining the elements of a problem in a patterned way, which varies from individual to individual. See also **conservative focus; focus gambling; simultaneous scanning; successive scanning.**

scenario 1. The plans made for dealing with an upcoming event. **2.** An imagined sequence of events, especially those resulting from an intended or possible course of action, as a *best-case scenario* or a *worst-case scenario.*

schedule (*accounting*) A display of the calculations used to arrive at the figures in a tax report or financial statement.

scheduling The phase of production control in which timetables for production operations are developed.

scientific management A concept popularized by Frederick Taylor, who developed the systematic use of time-and-motion studies to maximize efficiency.

scientific method See **effective interest method.**

scorched earth A tactic in which a targeted company divests itself of its most attractive assets, in an attempt to avert a hostile takeover.

SCORE See **Service Corps of Retired Executives.**

S corporation See **Subchapter S corporation.**

scrambled merchandising A profit-seeking strategy by which retailers add lines of goods unrelated to their basic categories of merchandise (e.g., children's underwear in a supermarket) as a way of stimulating sales.

scrap allowance The amount by which a second or subsequent batch must be increased to compensate for rejects considered unavoidable in the processing.

scrap value See **salvage value.**

search 1. A researched analysis of existing and filed patents conducted for the purpose of determining the position and validity of a new patent. **2.** Also called **title search.** A search of recorded deeds to a property, as by a lawyer, to make certain there are no encumbrances against it and that the present owner is free to transfer title.

search and recruitment executive A personnel specialist, usually the vice president of personnel, who is responsible for selecting the strategies for finding and hiring new employees.

search firm See **executive search firm.**

seasonal employment pool The aggregate of workers who do seasonal work and are let go when they are no longer needed (e.g., migrant farm workers, construction workers, store clerks employed for the Christmas season).

seasonal unemployment Unemployment due to seasonal changes in the number of workers required (as at Cape Cod resorts in winter) or in the number looking for jobs (as in summer, when students seek temporary work).

seasonal variation A regularly occurring annual change, such as the increase in sales that occurs before Christmas.

seat A paid membership on a stock exchange and the accompanying right to buy and sell securities there.

SEC See **Securities and Exchange Commission.**

secondary boycott A boycott of an employer by unionized employees for the purpose of inducing the employer to bring pressure to bear on another employer involved in a labor dispute with the union.

secondary data Information collected from a source other than original documents or research, as from a book. See also **primary data.**

secondary distribution Also called **secondary offering.** The sale by a stockholder of a large block of shares previously issued, usually offered at a fixed price.

secondary market Also called **aftermarket.** The market, as a stock exchange or over-the-counter sales, for trading securities after they have been issued.

secondary stock A relatively inexpensive stock issued by a small company; regarded as somewhat less risky than a penny stock and traded on the major exchanges.

secondary storage See **auxiliary memory.**

secret partner A partner who is not publicly known to be a partner but who is active in management decision making and is equally liable with other partners for the company's financial obligations.

sector A distinct part of a nation's economy.

secured loan A loan whose repayment is guaranteed by a pledge of something of value. See also **unsecured loan.**

secured party A lender who is assured of payment by a pledge of or a mortgage on property.

Securities Act of 1933 An act of Congress passed in response to the collapse of the stock market in 1929, regulating the interstate sale of newly issued investment securities valued at more than $1.5 million by requiring them to be registered 20 days before they can be offered to the public. See also **registration.**

Securities and Exchange Commission (*abbr* SEC) A five-member board appointed by the president of the United States to regulate and oversee all trading in stocks, oversee proxy voting, analyze market aberrations and the financial reports of corporations listed on American stock exchanges, and enforce the provisions of the Securities Exchange Act of 1934 and later legislation bearing on securities, corporate reorganizations, and holding companies.

Securities Exchange Act of 1934 Federal legislation enacted to regulate the sale of previously issued securities by establishing the Securities and Exchange Commission to analyze financial and other information in regard to the issuing corporations and their officers.

Securities Investor Protection Corporation (*abbr* SIPC) A public corporation created by Congress to insure investors against the loss of cash and securities held by a brokerage house that goes bankrupt or engages in fraudulent practices.

securitization The packaging by banks of traditional loans (e.g., mortgages, car loans) into bond-like securities for resale to other investors: benefits consumer by lower interest rates and frees institutional capital for other investments.

security 1. Any evidence of debt or ownership (e.g., stock certificate, bond, promissory note). **2.** Property pledged as collateral to guarantee payment of a debt or of a potential debt.

security agreement An agreement by which a borrower guarantees payment to a creditor by pledging or mortgaging property.

security analyst Also called **securities analyst.** A financial expert, often employed by a brokerage firm, who specializes in evaluating information regarding stocks and bonds, as by measuring the ratio of their prices to their dividends and earnings.

security interest A right or share in the ownership of property pledged as security for a debt.

seed money Capital for the first stages of a new business or other enterprise, especially for the initial setup and operating costs.

segment A component part of a business organization whose activities can be financially and operationally distinguished from the organization's other activities, owing to a difference in assets, products, geographical location, or type of customers.

segment margin The amount that a segment of a business contributes to the profits of the entire organization; the amount by which that segment's revenues exceed its expenses.

segment reporting Financial reporting of the income and assets of an identified segment of a business.

selective marketing system A marketing plan whereby a manufacturer chooses retail dealers who will, in the manufacturer's estimation, best represent the manufacturer's products in a particular area.

selective retention (*marketing*) A tendency to recall information and events that are consistent with one's value system, feelings, and beliefs and to forget the rest.

self-actualization process An approach to employee development by which individuals are encouraged to analyze their needs and assume responsibility for the direction and extent of personal development.

self-employed Earning one's living directly from one's own profession or business, as a freelance writer or artist, rather than as an employee earning salary or commission from another.

self-insurance Money set aside to cover potential losses and permitted to accumulate interest; in time the maintenance of such a fund may cost less than a conventional insurance policy.

self-liquidating 1. (of an asset) Capable of being converted into cash quickly. **2.** (of an investment, project, loan, etc.) Generating enough cash to repay the funds invested.

self-mailer A direct-mail piece that can be sent without an envelope.

seller's market A market in which goods are scarce and variety is limited, so that prices tend to rise as buyers compete for the available supply. See also **buyer's market.**

sell-in Strategies used by a manufacturer to improve retail sales of its products, as by offering trade discounts.

sell-off 1. A sudden and marked decline in stock or bond prices resulting from widespread selling. **2.** Liquidating of assets or subsidiaries, as by divestiture.

sell short See **short selling.**

sell-through 1. The characteristic of a product to continue selling in different media (e.g., a motion picture with sell-through is released in theaters, then repackaged as a videocassette, and finally shown on television). **2.** The process through which a product is sold, from manufacturer to wholesaler to retailer and ultimately to consumer.

semifixed cost See **stepped cost.**

semivariable cost See **mixed cost.**

senior security A security whose claims on dividends or assets have priority over those of another security (e.g., bonds are senior to preferred stock, which is senior to common stock).

sensitivity analysis Testing of a decision to determine the impact of changes or potential errors in the data on which that decision was based.

sensitivity training A series of training sessions, usually in the form of discussion groups, in which trainees are encouraged to develop sensitivity not only to their own needs and emotions but to those of the other participants. See also **laboratory training**.

SEP Also called **SEP-IRA**. Simplified Employee Pension: A tax-deferred pension plan in which an IRA is funded by employer and employee contributions. SEPs are for companies with 25 or fewer employees, or for self-employed persons.

separation Termination of employment. See also **discharge** (def. 1); **layoff**; **retirement** (def. 2).

sequencer See **sorter.**

sequential processing Processing of data in a computer in sequence, such as alphabetical.

sequential sampling Testing of randomly selected units from a lot, one by one, until the proportion of defects found is either below an acceptance limit (in which case the lot is accepted) or above a rejection limit (in which case the lot is rejected) or until the entire lot has been tested.

serial bond One of an issue of bonds that have progressive or otherwise differing maturity dates, such that the issuing corporation has several years in which to redeem the bonds.

service A useful labor (e.g., dry cleaner, car wash, watch repair) performed directly for others, usually on demand and for a specified fee. See also **good.**

service basis See **production method.**

service business Also called **service establishment.** A company that provides useful work on behalf of the public, such as a barbershop, exterminator, or taxi service.

service center A company that makes repairs, usually on its own products or those of a particular manufacturer.

Service Corps of Retired Executives (*acronym* SCORE) A group of volunteer retired men and women, sponsored by the Small Business Administration, who offer free management advice to those managing small businesses and to people interested in starting a small business: supplemented in 1969 by Active Corps of Executives.

service lease See **operating lease.**

service level A performance measure for an activity showing the proportion of output meeting a target criterion, such as the proportion of customers served in two minutes or less or the proportion of demand satisfied from inventory.

service mark (*abbr* SM) A proprietary term, such as American Express, that is registered with the Patent and Trademark Office.

service potential The future benefits to be derived from an asset.

service rate The capacity of a service operation stated in terms of customers per unit of time (e.g., customers per hour).

service wholesaler See **distributor.**

settlement option Any of several alternative methods by which the benefits of an insurance policy, annuity contract, or pension plan may be paid to the person entitled to receive them, as described in the policy or contract.

setup costs The labor costs involved in setting up machines for a production run, either at the start of a workday or at the inauguration of a new product, machine, or method.

setup time The time necessary to prepare for a manufacturing operation and to clean up after it is completed.

severance pay Money, exclusive of wages, back pay, etc., paid to an employee who has tenure and who is dismissed because of lack of work or other reasons beyond the employee's control.

severance tax A tax levied by a state on the extraction of a natural product (e.g., oil, coal) sold outside the state.

sexual harassment Unwelcome sexual advances, especially when made by an employer or superior, usually with compliance as a condition of continued employment or promotion.

shadow price The value per unit of a specific resource based on the increased profit generated by one additional unit of the resource: used in decisions affecting resource allocation.

shakeout A mild recession or other decline or setback within an industry that forces out the weaker competitors.

share 1. One of the equal fractional parts into which the capital stock of a corporation is divided. **2.** Also called **program rating; share rating.** The percentage of television homes with sets turned on that were tuned to a particular program. See also **Nielsen rating. 3.** See **market share.**

shared-appreciation mortgage A type of mortgage, usually extended for 10 years, that carries a lower down payment or lower interest rate than customary in return for the lender's sharing in the appreciation of the property when sold or when the loan comes due, whichever occurs first.

shareholder Also called **stockholder.** A person who owns shares of stock in a corporation.

shareholders' equity See **owners' equity.**

share of market See **market share.**

share rating See **share** (def. 2).

shark repellent Any methods used by a company to prevent a hostile takeover, as by changing bylaws to require approval by 75 percent of the company's shareholders before a merger can take effect.

shelf life The length of time that a product can hold its chemical stability and therefore can be sold without fear of decomposition or harm to a consumer.

shelf talker A cardboard, paper, or plastic advertisement of a product designed to be attached to a shelf on which the product is exhibited for sale.

Sherman Antitrust Act An act of Congress passed in 1890 to discourage the formation of monopolies, subsequently strengthened by the Clayton Act, the Federal Trade Commission Act, and the Robinson-Patman Act.

shift differential Additional compensation provided to employees who work during hours not considered part of the normal workday.

shop committee A group of union members who are authorized to speak for the entire membership of a particular bargaining unit.

shop floor control Procedures or systems used to establish priorities for tasks assigned to production work centers.

shopping goods Items (e.g., furniture, major appliances) that are purchased infrequently and usually only after comparison of features and prices offered by various manufacturers and stores.

shop steward Also called **union steward.** A union member who is elected by other union members to discuss grievances with the foreman or employer.

short-form opinion See **standard opinion.**

short-range planning Identification and implementation of specific strategies to influence an organization's daily, weekly, or monthly performance (e.g., budgeting procedures for action in a given situation, rules and detailed methods for handling problems).

short selling A transaction whereby a speculator, expecting a given stock to decline in price, borrows some shares from a broker, sells them at the current high price, waits for the price to fall, then buys new shares at the lower price and returns them to the broker, keeping the price difference (less interest to the broker) as profit. The transaction, though regulated, is extremely risky, since the speculator must return the shares at the stipulated time, regardless of their price.

short-term capital gains Capital gains resulting from the sale of assets held less than six months, formerly subject to special tax breaks, but now taxed as ordinary income. See also **long-term capital gains.**

short-term debt Indebtedness incurred to cover operating expenses, meet payrolls, etc., and scheduled to be repaid within a year.

shotgun approach An advertiser's attempt to reach a great many people with a message by placing a large number of untargeted advertisements in various media, especially mass-circulation magazines.

shrinkage Reduction in inventory value caused by theft, waste, breakage, water damage, etc.

shrink-wrap A flexible film of plastic used to wrap and seal a book, food product, etc. The plastic film is exposed to a heating process and shrinks to the contour of the merchandise.

SIC See **standard industrial classification system**.

sight draft A trade draft that is payable on demand.

signature loan A loan requiring no collateral.

silent partner A partner who is publicly known to be a partner and who is liable for the partnership's financial obligations but who takes no management role. See also **dormant partner**.

simple interest An amount or rate of interest calculated as a percentage of the principal only, exclusive of interest earned in past periods.

simplification A reduction without specific cause in the number of items offered for sale by a company.

simplified employee pension See **SEP**.

simulation 1. A re-creation or model of a real-world situation or event (e.g., a problem in queuing theory to be solved by computer). 2. A training technique whereby individuals act out scenarios in artificial settings simulating the work environment, where they can safely practice skills and behaviors demanded of them on the job.

simultaneous scanning An orientation to problem solving characterized by a tendency to take an overall view of the situation rather than to focus on any one element. See also **scanning**.

single-entry bookkeeping A simple accounting system in which each transaction is recorded in a single entry in a single account, as in a checkbook or simple list of accounts receivable, with no balancing of debits and credits.

single-line retailer A retail store that concentrates on one type of goods or line of merchandise.

single-step statement An income statement that shows first the total of all ordinary revenues and gains and then the total of all ordinary expenses and losses, with the difference between the two, adjusted for income from discontinued operations and extraordinary items, shown as net income.

sinking fund A quantity of money that is set aside, usually in annual installments, for the purpose of satisfying a debt, replacing equipment, etc.

sinking-fund depreciation A method of depreciating an asset whereby periodic allocations of money to a hypothetical sinking fund are considered to be an annuity whose value at the end of the depreciation life is equal to the replacement cost of the asset, each periodic charge including the imputed interest on the accumulated depreciation.

sin tax A tax levied against liquor, cigarettes, racetrack betting, and other items or activities considered by some to be sinful.

SIPC See **Securities Investor Protection Corporation**.

situational approach A hypothetical approach to leadership based on the supposition that in a given situation a variety of individuals would be equally effective in the leadership role.

situational management Also called **contingency management**. A style of management whereby the theories and general practices of management are adapted to the needs of the company.

skeleton account See **T-account**.

skills inventory A list of qualifications and aptitudes necessary for the successful completion of a job.

skimming 1. A strategic pricing approach by which a company prices a new product above its expected normal level during its introduction to the marketplace, hoping to appeal to the consumers who are the least price conscious, then reducing the price when the market competition appears to be growing. See also **penetration pricing**. 2. The removing of profits from a business and concealing the evidence from shareholders, tax authorities, or partners.

skip loss A cash loss resulting when a credit customer permanently leaves an unpaid balance in an account.

SKU (*pronounced* "skyōō") (*acronym for* stockkeeping unit) A retailer-defined coding system used to distinguish individual items within a retailer's accounting, warehousing, and POS systems.

slack See **float** (def. 4).

slander A false oral statement that causes injury to the reputation of another. See also **libel**.

slide A bookkeeping error in which all the digits of an entry are correct and in order but rendered incorrect by a misplaced decimal point.

sliding scale 1. A variable scale, especially of industrial costs, as wages, that may be adapted to changes in demand. 2. A wage scale varying with the selling price of goods produced, the cost of living, or profits. 3. A price scale, as of medical fees, in which prices vary according to the ability of individuals to pay. 4. A tariff scale varying according to changing prices.

slowdown A planned lessening of effort in performance by workers for the purpose of securing concessions from management.

slump Any mild recession in the economy as a whole or in a particular industry.

SM See **service mark**.

small business Typically, a business that is independently owned and managed, operates in a local area (often a neighborhood), and does not dominate its field.

Small Business Administration (*abbr* SBA) A federal agency created in 1953 to help, counsel, and protect the interests of small business operations; to make and guarantee loans to small businesses; to conduct courses in management and special programs for minority-owned small businesses; and to assist small businesses in securing government contracts.

Small Business Institute An independent organization established in 1953 to help small businesses by issuing surety bonds and loans, by offering management assistance, and by counseling small businesses that wish to secure SBA loans and government contracts.

small-cap Designating a stock with a market capitalization of under $500 million: these small companies are considered to have more growth potential and higher investment risk.

small office/home office (*acronym* SOHO) Referring to small offices or home offices that have limited space. Some manufacturers design space-saving office equipment for this market.

smart money 1. Money invested or wagered by experienced investors or bettors. 2. Such knowledgeable investors or bettors.

smoothing See **exponential smoothing**.

snapper An incentive (e.g., a discount coupon) used to encourage customers to buy a product that is the subject of a big advertising campaign.

sniffer An advertising display in which fragrance is used to draw attention to the product.

snob effect Evidence of the desirability of a unique product in the form of less expensive imitations marketed by other manufacturers, so that the unique product has proportionately less appeal to the elite shopper.

Social Security Act See **Federal Insurance Contributions Act**.

sociotechnical systems Manufacturing operations that combine the technology required to perform tasks and the social organization in which the tasks are performed.

soft copy Readable material in the form of images created electronically on a computer screen. See also **hard copy**.

soft currency Currency that is subject to sharp fluctuations in value. See also **hard currency**.

soft goods Goods made of textiles, such as clothing, linens, and towels. See also **durable goods**.

soft sell Also called **low-pressure selling**. A selling technique that is low-keyed, persuasive, and indirect. See also **hard sell**.

business

software Any computer program or set of instructions for a computer. See also **hardware.**

SOHO See **small office/home office.**

sole proprietorship An unincorporated business owned and usually operated by one individual.

S-1 A standardized statement that a company must file with the Securities and Exchange Commission before it may list and trade securities on a national exchange, including such information as the company's business, its capital structure, financial statements, major contracts, the salaries of its directors and officers, and details regarding the stock it will trade.

sort A process that arranges items in accordance with a set of given rules.

sorter Also called **sequencer.** An automatic data-processing machine that can order data or items as directed.

source marketing The practice of setting a retail price for an item before it is shipped, generally accompanied by a price label for the retailer to apply to the product before displaying it.

space buyer A media consultant whose services to clients include recommendations concerning where, how, and when to advertise as well as the placement of ads.

space sales The business of selling advertising in either print or broadcast media.

span of management The number of people, departments, etc., that report to one manager.

span of recall (*marketing research*) The number of items, especially brand items, that a person can recall when asked to do so. See also **evoked set.**

spec See **on spec.**

special endorsement See **full endorsement.**

special identification method A method of evaluating cost of goods sold and ending inventory by which the costs of specifically identified individual items sold or in inventory (usually large or expensive items not sold in great quantities or lots, such as jewelry or cars) are added together.

special journal An accounting journal in which frequently occurring transactions of a similar nature are recorded (e.g., sales, cash disbursements).

special-revenue debt (*government accounting*) The debt of a specific governmental unit or agency that is paid by the revenues of a specific source, such as a bridge toll.

specialty goods Products whose distinctive qualities make consumers reluctant to accept substitutes (e.g., designer jeans, French champagne).

specification A detailed explanation of an invention, either with or without a claim. See also **claim** (def. 2).

specific lien A claim against a specific piece of property that has been pledged as security for an unpaid loan. See also **blanket lien; lien** (def. 2).

specific performance The carrying out of the terms of a contract exactly as they are specified: used chiefly in regard to the fulfillment of a contract ordered by a court in cases where damages would be inadequate compensation to the complaining party.

specific price changes Changes in the market prices of specific goods or services, either individually or on average.

speculative presentation A formal, no-fee demonstration sometimes made by an individual or company to a prospective client showing how a job would be approached.

speculative risk See **financial risk.**

speedup An effort by management to increase production by increasing the speed of an assembly line, often without a simultaneous increase in wages or other employee benefits.

spindle See **J hook.**

spin-off **1.** A process of reorganizing a corporate structure whereby the capital stock of a division or subsidiary of a corporation or of a newly affiliated company is transferred to the stockholders of the parent corporation without an exchange of any part of the stock of the latter. **2.** A product that is an adaptation, outgrowth, or development of another similar product.

spiral The evolution of a product's acceptance in the marketplace, often marked by three stages: pioneering, competitive, and retentive.

split Also called **stock split.** A division of the existing shares of a corporation's stock into a greater number of shares, so that the value of each share is proportionally reduced (e.g., a 2–1 split doubles the number of shares owned by each shareholder, each worth half of its previous value): often done to attract new shareholders. See also **reverse split.**

split-dollar insurance Insurance on the life of a key executive for which the company pays the amount of premium equal to the annual increase in the policy's cash value and the executive pays the remainder, the company to receive the cash value of the policy and the executive's beneficiaries to receive any additional benefits if the executive should die.

split-off A process of reorganizing a corporate structure whereby the capital stock of a division or subsidiary of a corporation or of a newly affiliated company is transferred to the stockholders of the parent corporation in exchange for part of the stock of the latter.

split shift The standard number of working hours divided into two or more working periods per day.

split-up A process of reorganizing a corporate structure whereby all the capital stock and assets are exchanged for those of two or more newly established companies, resulting in the liquidation of the parent corporation.

sponsor **1.** An advertiser who pays for the broadcast of a program as well as for the commercial messages that appear before, during, and after it. **2.** An advertiser whose commercial messages appear along with those of other advertisers during a broadcast program. See also **participation show.**

sponsored film A film created or financed by a company and containing an educational message rather than product information, often made available to any interested audience. See also **business film; training film.**

spot broadcasting Also called **spot buy.** Placement of a commercial by a national advertiser on local rather than network television for the purpose of reaching a selected market.

spot time A time period of 30 to 60 seconds purchased by an advertiser from a television network and its affiliates for the purpose of airing a commercial message before, during, or after a program at a rate that varies in accordance with the size of the viewing audience.

spot trading Buying or selling of a commodity, such as grain or crude oil, usually for cash and for immediate delivery. See also **futures trading.**

spread **1.** The difference between bid (offered) and asked prices. **2.** A combined put and call order, used to take advantage of either rising or falling stock prices.

spread-loss plan See **chronological stabilization.**

spreadsheet **1.** (*accounting*) A multicolumn worksheet for analyzing several related entries. **2.** (*computers*) A visual display of a simulated worksheet for use in financial planning, records, etc.

staff The aggregate of employees who have no direct responsibility for profit and loss but who provide services for people who do (e.g., market researcher, accountant). See also **line** (def. 1).

staff authority The right to advise or assist those with line authority or other staff personnel.

staffing **1.** The hiring of people to run a company, operate a factory, etc. **2.** The aggregate functions of recruitment, training, selection, and evaluation of personnel, determination of compensation, and management of health and safety measures.

stagflation A combination of persistent inflation, stagnant consumer demand, and high unemployment.

Standard & Poor's 500 A group of 500 common stocks considered to be representative of the market, and whose average daily prices form the basis for an index of the day's security prices.

standard cost system An accounting method of production costing by which standard costs, estimated on the basis of a good but not perfect production run, are later compared with actual costs so that any variance can be determined and investigated.

standard cost variance The difference between actual and estimated costs for materials and labor, quantities of materials, labor hours, etc.

standard deduction A certain amount of income that a taxpayer can deduct from gross income to determine taxable income. The amount is adjusted yearly for inflation. See also **itemized deductions.**

standard industrial classification system (*abbr* SIC) A numerical system developed by the Bureau of the Budget to classify business establishments in accordance with the type of activity they perform in order to facilitate the collection and tabulation of business information.

standardization The mass production of uniform or identical goods, the same in weight, color, quality, etc.

standard labor hours The estimated number of hours that will be worked during production.

standard labor rate The estimated hourly labor rate that will be paid during production.

standard material price Also called **standard purchase price.** The estimated cost assigned to one unit of raw material.

standard material quantity Also called **standard quantity.** The estimated amount of a raw material that will be needed to produce one finished unit.

standard opinion Also called **short-form opinion.** An auditor's statement testifying that financial statements are fairly and consistently presented, that no excessive uncertainties were involved in the audit, and that the auditor adhered to generally accepted auditing standards.

standard price The estimated price of a unit of production.

standard purchase price See **standard material price.**

standard quantity See **standard material quantity.**

standards 1. The criteria by which performance is to be measured. **2.** Standard costs. See also **standard cost system. 3.** Generally accepted auditing standards.

standard time The amount of time an average employee takes to complete a particular task or job under normal work conditions. See also **allowed time.**

standby costs Capacity costs incurred even if operations are shut down, such as property taxes. See also **enabling costs.**

standing order An order for repeated shipment of goods over a specified time period, eliminating the necessity to reorder the items.

star A fast-growing product or company with good potential. See also **cash cow; dog.**

start-up Also called **start-up time.** The time needed to begin production or to reach full capacity after a contract is signed or a project is approved; the time needed for hiring new staff, procuring additional equipment, training staff, etc.

stated capital See **legal capital.**

stated value A value assigned, usually for legal purposes only, to common stock that does not have a par value.

statement of affairs A financial statement showing the immediate liquidation values rather than the historical costs of the assets of a company filing for or approaching bankruptcy.

statement of cash receipts and disbursements Also called **statement of cash flow.** A list of cash receipts and expenditures and the beginning and ending balances of a past or future period.

statement of changes in financial position Also called **funds statement.** A financial statement that shows or explains changes in the working capi-

tal (cash) balances during a stated period by showing the sources and uses of the working capital and changes in the working capital accounts.

statement of changes in owners' equity A financial statement that explains any change or changes in owners' equity during a fiscal period, that is the sum represented by paid-in capital plus retained earnings.

statement of financial position See **balance sheet.**

statement of operations See **income statement.**

statement of policy A statement issued by the Securities and Exchange Commission specifying what it has interpreted as misleading information in an open-end investment company's offer of shares.

statement of retained earnings A statement setting forth a company's net profit minus whatever dividends were paid to shareholders during the year.

statement savings account A savings account in which transactions are confirmed periodically by a bank statement. Cf. **passbook savings account.**

state of the art The highest level of current knowledge or development in a particular field, especially those areas associated with modern technologies.

statistical quality control The use of carefully selected samplings during the production process to determine the overall quality of a product and to quickly identify any deterioration in that quality so that corrective action may be taken.

statistics 1. The gathering, analysis, and interpretation of numerical data. **2.** The data itself.

statute of limitations A statute designating a period of time beyond which a legal action may not be brought.

statutory tax rate The tax rate for each type of income, such as ordinary income and capital gains.

stepped cost Also called **semifixed cost.** A cost that rises in steps with increased levels of production.

sticker price 1. The dealer's full asking price of a new automobile as shown on an attached sticker that gives an itemized list of basic and optional equipment and other charges. **2.** Any retailer's asking price or list price.

stock A share in the ownership of a corporation. See also **common stock; preferred stock; stock certificate.**

stock allowance A percentage of production above normal needs that is held in inventory for use in case of unforeseen need.

stock appreciation right The right to receive payment of all or part of the appreciation on a stock option rather than to exercise the option; a nonqualified stock option.

stock average The average price per share of diverse stocks that are considered to be representative of either a given industry or the entire market, calculated by adding the closing prices of the sample stocks and dividing by a Dow Jones divisor that accounts for such factors as dividends and splits. See also **Dow Jones average; New York Stock Exchange Index; Standard & Poor's 500.**

stockbroker See **broker.**

stock certificate A certificate providing evidence of stock ownership, showing the name of the stockholder, the name of the corporation, the number of shares the certificate represents, whether the stock is common or preferred, the par value, and the rate of preferred dividends.

stock dividend A dividend paid in additional shares of stock (up to 25 percent of shares outstanding) rather than in cash.

stock exchange A market where securities are traded, such as the New York Stock Exchange and the American Stock Exchange.

stockholder See **shareholder.**

stock market 1. A particular market where stocks and bonds are traded; stock exchange. **2.** The market for stocks throughout a nation.

stock option See **option** (def. 1).

business

stockout An instance of an item normally carried in stock not being available.

stock split See **split.**

stock table Also called **stock quotation.** A list of (1) all stocks with their high and low prices for the year to date; (2) special information, such as whether the stock is preferred or exdividend; (3) dividends paid per share in the last 12 months; price-earnings ratio; (4) high, low, and closing prices; and (5) the changes in price since the previous day.

stop order A market order to buy a security above the current market price (usually to prevent further loss or reduction of paper profits incurred through a short sell) or to sell below the current price (usually to protect diminishing paper profits or to prevent further loss on securities currently held).

stop payment A bank depositor's request that the bank refuse payment on a check issued by the depositor.

stop price The price at which a stop order is activated.

store brand An item offered for sale under a store's own label. See also **private label.**

straddle A combination of a put option and a call option, primarily used when the investor expects a large change in a stock's price but is unsure which direction the price will move.

straight bill of lading A simple receipt for goods accepted for shipment given by the transportation company to the shipper. See also **order bill of lading.**

straight life insurance. See **ordinary life insurance.**

straight-line depreciation The simplest method of depreciation, by which the value of a capital asset is reduced at a uniform rate throughout the projected useful life of the asset. See also **declining-balance depreciation.**

straight time 1. The time or number of hours established as standard for a specific work period in a particular industry, usually computed on the basis of a work week and fixed variously from 35 to 40 hours. **2.** The rate of pay established for the period. See also **overtime.**

strategic plan (*marketing*) A plan spelling out what a company hopes to do in the marketplace and how it proposes to do it, including marketing mix and needed resources.

strategic product-line adjustment Also called **tactical product-line adjustment.** The making of additions to and/or subtractions from the assortment of like products offered by a company, determined in part by the amount of capital available to produce the variations and in part by potential market interest.

street name The broker in whose name stocks purchased are registered, although the investor is entitled to all dividends, corporate reports, and voting rights.

stress interview A simulated interview in which the interviewer is openly hostile and deliberately irritating to the interviewee (used in police, sales, and investigative work).

strict liability Also called **absolute liability.** Liability without fault; the obligation of an insurer to pay damages without assessing blame or proving responsibility.

strike A temporary work stoppage by union members designed to force settlement of a dispute with management or the signing of a contract with the union.

strikebreaker 1. A person employed to replace a striking worker; a scab. **2.** Any person who crosses a picket line to work.

strike fund A special fund collected by a union to provide benefits to members who are on strike.

strike price The price at which an employee's stock option may be exercised, usually the market price at the time the option was granted.

strip mall A retail complex consisting of stores or restaurants in adjacent spaces in one long building, typically having a narrow parking area directly in front of the stores.

stripping The practice of splitting bonds, especially mortgage-backed securities, into two parts, one paying interest and the other paying principal, and selling the parts to different investors. See also **zero-coupon bond.**

structural analysis An analytical approach to understanding the group process that focuses on the interdepartmental and intergroup differences of the members' orientations, interpersonal relations, and goals. See also **group process.**

structural unemployment Unemployment caused by a mismatch between the skills (or location) of job seekers and the requirements (or location) of available jobs.

SUB See **supplemental unemployment benefits.**

subassembly A component of a finished product that is itself assembled from other parts and components.

Subchapter S corporation Also called **tax-option corporation.** A corporation with ten or fewer stockholders, who are permitted by a section of the Internal Revenue Code to report the corporation's profits as though they were partners rather than shareholders, and thus avoid paying taxes twice, once on corporate income and again on dividends.

sublicense A license or contract granted to a third party by a licensee for specified rights or uses of a product.

sublicensee A person, company, etc., to whom a sublicense is granted.

subordinate security See **junior security.**

subscription price (*finance*) A special price offered to shareholders for the purchase of a new issue of stock.

subsequent event (*accounting*) An event that follows the date of a balance sheet but precedes the issuance of a financial statement that is affected by the event.

subsidiary A corporation all or a large part of whose stock is owned by another corporation and whose management is usually chosen by the parent company's chief executive with the approval of the parent's board of directors.

subsidiary account An account that supports or contributes to the balance of a control account (e.g., the accounts receivable account contains the total of the balances of all subsidiary accounts receivable).

subsidiary rights Rights to publish or produce in different formats works based on the original work under contract, as a paperback edition of a hardcover book or a television series based on a novel.

subsidy 1. A direct financial aid furnished by a government to a private industrial undertaking, a charitable organization, or the like. **2.** A sum paid, often in accordance with a treaty, by one government to another to secure some service in return.

substantial performance The carrying out of all essential terms of a contract, which entitles the contractor to payment. See also **specific performance.**

substitution goods Two products or services so related that an increase in the demand for one is followed by an increase in the price of the other. See also **cross-elasticity of demand.**

successful-efforts method (*gas and oil industries*) An accounting method that capitalizes only the costs of drilling wells that actually produce oil or gas, while costs of unsuccessful efforts are recorded as expenses.

successive scanning An orientation to problem solving characterized by a tendency to start with an overall view of a situation and then to narrow one's focus to those elements that appear to confirm one's theories. See also **scanning.**

suggestion selling A sales strategy by which a person who has bought an item is encouraged to buy complementary items.

suitor An individual or company that expresses interest in acquiring another company.

sum-of-the-years'-digits method A method of depreciating an asset whereby depreciation is accelerated in the early years of the asset's useful life by means of a fraction in which all the years of useful life (n) are added together ($1 + 2 + 3...$ etc.); for an asset with a useful life of six years ($n = 6$), the denominator is 21 and depreciation is $^6/_{21}$ the first year, $^5/_{21}$ the second year, $^4/_{21}$ the third year, and so on.

sunk cost An expenditure or outlay made in the past that cannot be affected by present or future decisions except for income-tax effects (e.g., a decision on whether or not to sell a piece of equipment may depend on the imputed cost of continuing to own it, not on the sunk cost of acquiring it).

sunrise industry A new industry that is gaining in importance, especially in the field of advanced technology (e.g., microcircuitry).

sunset industry An older industry regarded as being in decline because of obsolete technology, decreased demand for products, etc.

superstore A very large store, especially one stocking a wide variety of merchandise.

supervisory management See **first-line management.**

supplemental unemployment benefits (*abbr* SUB) Benefits beyond the legislated unemployment insurance payments made to workers who are laid off, paid by the employer.

supply 1. The quantity of a product, service, or resource available on the open market. See also **law of supply and demand. 2.** The specific quantity of a product that a manufacturer or retailer can supply at a given time.

supply-side economics An approach to the management of the national economy that advocates a reduction in taxes on corporate and personal income, which is believed will stimulate investment in private industry.

support consumables Expense items, such as stationery, typewriter ribbons, and cleaning service, necessary to the day-to-day operation of a business.

suprasystem A system composed of interdependent subsystems (e.g., the suprasystem of which a motor company is a part consists of other motor companies, subsidiaries, and dependent industries).

surety bond A three-way contract by which the first party (the obligor) agrees to be responsible to the second party (the obligee) for the obligations of the third party, the obligee being protected by an insurer (surety) who promises to cover any default on the part of the obligor.

surplus revenue See **appropriated retained earnings.**

surrender value See **cash surrender value.**

survey A questionnaire administered to respondents either in person, by mail, or by telephone to determine their attitudes and opinions.

survey feedback Information acquired from completed questionnaires or from systematic interviews. See also **attitude survey.**

suspense account An account in which accounting items of undetermined destination are temporarily recorded pending a decision as to where they should be posted.

suspense reserve See **appropriated retained earnings.**

suspension A disciplinary action taken against an employee who has violated an established company rule, requiring the employee to absent himor herself from the job without pay for a period of time depending on the severity of the infraction.

sustainable income The portion of distributable income earned in the current period that can be expected to be earned in the next period if operations continue at the same level.

sweat equity Unreimbursed labor that results in the increased value of a property in which one

shares or that is invested to establish or expand an enterprise.

sweep account An interest-earning checking account from which money over a certain minimum balance is transferred to another account earning a higher rate of interest.

sweetheart agreement Also called **sweetheart contract.** An agreement between an employer and a union on terms especially favorable to the employer, often arranged through bribery or management's promise not to eliminate jobs and usually put into effect without a vote by the workers.

swing loan See **bridge loan.**

swing shift A work shift, usually from 4 p.m. until midnight.

symbiotic marketing The marketing of a product with the assistance of a company that offers a generally unrelated product for mutual benefit (e.g., the offer of a free airline ticket to anyone who buys a car during a limited time period).

syndicate Also called **venture management.** A temporary association of two or more individuals or companies formed to take part in a joint venture or business undertaking for profit, the members generally sharing in gains or losses in proportion to their individual investments.

syndicated program 1. An independently produced television program sold to individual stations for broadcast. **2.** A successful network program purchased for rerun by local stations.

syndicator A company that provides other companies with fliers and brochures offering products for sale that can be sent to customers with monthly bills.

synectics A brainstorming or creative problem-solving technique that presents problems to group participants in such a generalized way that they are stimulated to achieve highly original solutions through the use of analogies, figurative comparisons, and speculative thought.

synergy The action or interaction of two separate enterprises that when combined produce superior results, as in the case of a corporate merger.

synthetic process A production process by which raw materials or parts are combined to form a finished product that differs from any of its components.

system A group of constituent parts functioning in unison for a common purpose.

system 1 management See **exploitive leadership.**

system 2 management See **benevolent leadership.**

system 3 management See **consultative leadership.**

system 4 management See **democratic leadership.**

systematic risk Risk that cannot be eliminated through diversification. See also **unsystematic risk.**

systems analyst A data-processing specialist whose job (systems analysis) is to identify business problems and to formulate solutions that lead to better ways of organizing, planning, and controlling activities in a company.

systems contract A buyer's agreement to make a blanket order of a product or products from a catalog supplier at a fixed markup in order to minimize administrative costs, all orders being made directly from the buyer's departments to the supplier.

system software See **software.**

systems selling The retail merchandising of a group of items that have a functional relationship in a single package rather than as individual items (e.g., the selling of microcomputers, disk drives, monitors, printers, and some software programs as a complete package).

business

T-account Also called **skeleton account.** (*bookkeeping*) Any account in the standard form of a T, with the title above a horizontal line at the top, the debits listed on the left side of a vertical line below, and the credits on the right side of that line.

tactical planning Planning of the activities of subgroups within an organization to meet short-range objectives.

tactical product-line adjustment See **strategic product-line adjustment.**

Taft-Hartley Act An act of Congress passed in 1947 to amend the National Labor Relations Act by (1) authorizing the president of the United States to obtain an 80-day injunction against a strike that endangers the national health or safety, so that mediators may attempt to bring labor and management to agreement; (2) prohibiting the closed shop; and (3) permitting the union shop in states that have not passed right-to-work laws.

take-home pay The amount of salary remaining after deductions, as of taxes, have been made.

takeover An acquisition or gaining control of a corporation through the purchase or exchange of stock.

taking An action by the federal government, as a regulatory ruling, that imposes a restriction on the use of private property for which the owner must be compensated; an exercise of the power of eminent domain.

tangible asset Any physical asset (e.g., building, piece of equipment, share of stock). See also **intangible asset.**

tangible value The worth of a physical asset to the public.

tare weight The weight of the packing material and container in which an item is shipped.

target marketing Also called **consumer-oriented marketing.** The methods used to (1) identify those consumers most likely to want a product or to benefit from it, (2) create an image for a product that will appeal to such consumers, and (3) inform them of it via the most appropriate media.

tariff Duties or customs imposed by a government on imported or exported products to raise revenue, protect domestic industries, or exert pressure on foreign governments that impose high duties on domestic products.

task cycle The amount of time necessary to complete an assignment, activity, etc., from beginning to end.

task force A committee formed to investigate problem areas and generate workable solutions.

tax-bracket creep See **bracket creep.**

tax credit A reduction of taxes payable, allowed to certain classes of taxpayers for reasons of public policy. See also **tax deduction.**

tax deduction An expenditure or a certain amount that a taxpayer can deduct from taxable income. See also **tax credit.**

tax-deferred annuity (*abbr* TDA) Also called **tax-sheltered annuity.** An annuity to which teachers, college professors, and other employees of nonprofit organizations may contribute to supplement their pension programs, taxes on contributions and income payments being deferred until retirement.

tax-free bond A bond, usually a municipal or pollution-control bond, on which interest is legally exempt from all federal taxes.

tax lien A formal claim by a governmental body against property for taxes due.

tax-option corporation See **Subchapter S corporation.**

tax return A statement, on an officially prescribed form, of income, deductions, exemptions, etc., and taxes due.

tax shelter An investment in certain businesses, activities, or items that legally entitles the investor to avoid, reduce, or defer income taxes.

tax-sheltered annuity See **tax-deferred annuity.**

tax shield An expense that reduces taxable income, either without consuming working capital (e.g., depreciation) or otherwise (e.g., research and development).

T-bill See **Treasury bill.**

TDA See **tax-deferred annuity.**

team building Group learning activities moderated by a trainer for the purpose of identifying and changing patterns of behavior that interfere with group productivity or with relations with superiors.

teaser 1. An advertisement that attempts to stimulate the reader's or viewer's curiosity by withholding certain facts or information of interest. **2.** A short clip shown before the start of a television program for the purpose of gaining audience attention.

technical core The organizational structure that encompasses lower-level subordinates, most often people whose expertise lies in technical rather than managerial or administrative areas.

technical partnership A situation in which one company purchases stock in another company so that the two of them can collaborate as partners on new products and technologies.

technician An individual (e.g., electrician, plumber, computer programmer) with specific knowledge about and skill in the use of a technology.

technobandit A person who steals technological secrets, as from a place of employment, and sells them to agents from competing firms, a foreign government, etc.

technological unemployment Unemployment that results from the introduction of new equipment, methods, or procedures.

technology The aggregate of knowledge and methods used to transform raw materials into a useful product or other improved output.

telecommunications The science and technology dealing with communications at a distance.

telecommuting Working at home using a computer terminal electronically linked to one's place of employment.

teleconference A business meeting, educational session, etc., conducted among participants in different locations via telecommunications equipment.

telemarketing The use of telephoning to make a sales presentation and attempt to sell a product or service.

teleprinter Also called **teletypewriter.** A machine that operates like a typewriter and is capable of transmitting messages over telephone lines.

telescoping Also called **overlapping.** Splitting a production lot into smaller lots so that one operation can be performed on some of the units while another is being performed on the remainder, thereby reducing the total elapsed time to process the original lot.

Teletypewriter Exchange See **TWX.**

television homes Homes that have television sets. See also **Nielsen rating; share** (def. 2).

telex An electronic system by which written words are transmitted over Western Union lines from one teleprinter to another at a rate of 66 words per minute, used for short messages.

temporary investment An investment in a marketable security expected to be sold within a year and treated as a current asset.

temporary proprietorship account See **nominal account.**

temporary system An organization of formal groups created to investigate and perform specific tasks. See also **ad hoc committee; task force.**

tenancy in common A form of co-ownership of real estate in which the interest of each owner passes at death to his or her heirs rather than to a surviving co-owner. See also **joint tenancy.**

tenant 1. A person who holds property by any kind of right, temporary or permanent. **2.** A person who has the temporary right to occupy property belonging to another; a lessee.

tender offer An offer by one corporation to the stockholders of another to buy their shares for a specified price above the market value so that the offering corporation can gain quick control of the company.

term bond A bond that has the same maturity date as all other bonds of the same issue. See also **serial bond.**

terminal A hardware device, usually including a keyboard and a video display unit, for entering information into a computer or receiving information from it. A terminal may adjoin a computer, or be located at some distance from it.

term insurance Insurance that gives protection for a stated number of years and has no cash surrender or loan value.

terms of sale Conditions for the payment of an amount due for a sale (e.g., "5/10, n/30" indicates a 5 percent reduction in amount payable if paid within 10 days; net amount is due within 30 days).

test campaign A series of activities focused on an advertisement or promotion that is subject to alterations that may increase its effectiveness.

testimonial Also called **endorsement.** A statement, usually made by a well-known personality, claiming satisfaction with a product, publicized by an advertiser to persuade other consumers to purchase the product: subject to guidelines issued by the Federal Trade Commission for honest use of such endorsements.

test marketing The offering for sale of a new product in one or more preselected markets, for the purpose of assessing customer response before the product is mass-marketed.

test of compliance An audit procedure to determine whether a corporation is adhering to its internal control policies.

test of transactions A detailed audit procedure that determines the accuracy and fairness of account balances by recalculating arithmetic, verifying consistency with supporting documents, and tracing the movements of balances from original transactions to final financial statements.

TF (*abbr for* till forbid) The indication that an advertisement is to be run until it is canceled.

t-group A training group presided over by a trainer, with the objective of behavior modification within a social context. See also **encounter group; sensitivity training.**

theory X An authoritarian approach to management by which the average worker is regarded as disliking work, having little ambition, and requiring threats and coercion to perform satisfactorily.

theory Y An approach to management by which the average worker is regarded as seeking responsibility and being motivated by rewards.

theory Z An approach to management by which employees at all levels are involved in the decision-making process, employment is guaranteed for life, and jobs are varied to avert boredom.

therblig (*backward spelling—more or less—of* [Frank B.] Gilbreth, *founder of time-and-motion study*) A basic indivisible physical movement involved in a manual operation or task.

third-party beneficiary A person who benefits by a legal agreement between two other persons.

thrift institution A savings bank or savings and loan association, which caters primarily to the individual depositor and prospective homebuyer in search of financing.

tickler file A chronological collection of vouchers, memorandums, or bills used to remind someone to make timely payments or perform certain tasks on schedule.

tick mark A symbolic notation (e.g., asterisk,

checkmark, number) used by an auditor to indicate a footnote that provides information regarding the amount thus indicated.

tie-in 1. Designating a sale or advertisement in which the buyer, in order to get the item desired, must also purchase one or more other items. **2.** Relating to two or more products advertised or sold together. **3.** A marketing strategy or campaign in which related products are promoted or sold together. **4.** An item in a tie-in sale or advertisement.

tie-line service A circuit that connects two or more telephone systems.

time-adjusted rate of return See **internal rate of return.**

time-and-motion study The systematic investigation and analysis of the motions and the time required to perform a specific task with a view to devising more efficient methods of production and setting time standards. See also **therblig.**

time deposit Money deposited in an interest-bearing account in a bank that cannot be withdrawn without penalty before the expiration of a specified time period, usually a minimum of three months.

time discount A discount extended to an advertiser who purchases television time in quantity.

time draft A trade draft payable by a specified date.

time management Regulation of tasks and activities according to a specific schedule.

time-series analysis Also called **trend analysis.** Analysis of statistical data collected or recorded at successive intervals over a period of time long enough to permit patterns to be identified that can be used as a basis for business forecasting.

time sharing The sharing of use of a central processing unit by two or more companies or subdivisions of a company, each user being allotted a proportionate amount of operating time.

time study See **time-and-motion study.**

time to maturity The amount of time remaining before a note or other obligation becomes due.

time utility The enhanced value of any product that is available in the marketplace when requested, especially a new product whose availability coincides with the initial barrage of publicity.

tin parachute A guaranteed package of bonuses and benefits for workers in the event of job loss due to a merger or takeover. See also **golden parachute.**

title 1. Legal, registered ownership. **2.** A document certifying such ownership.

title search See **search** (def. 2).

T-note See **Treasury note.**

TOFC (*abbr for* trailer-on-flat car) See **piggyback.**

tombstone advertising Advertising placed by an underwriter, broker, investment banker, etc., usually a boxed ad, very simple in format, with no graphics.

top management Also called **upper management.** The level of professional management at which major policy decisions and long-range plans are made, including such positions as chief executive officer and president.

total advertising The total number of standard lines (or pages) available for advertising in a newspaper (or magazine).

total asset turnover ratio Sales divided by total assets. See also **activity ratio.**

total cost approach An approach to decision making that relies on a formal comparative cost analysis of alternate channels of distribution before commitment to one of them.

total quality management (*abbr* TQM) A philosophy that emphasizes the broad involvement of the entire organization in achieving standards of quality.

total return The percentage gain or loss on an investment over a specific period, including income and price appreciation or depreciation.

total system concept The study of the relationships of all interacting parts of a complex whole

business

and of that of the system and the environment in which it operates.

Toxic Substances Control Act An act of Congress passed in 1976 to empower the Environmental Protection Agency to regulate the production, use, marketing, and disposal of toxic chemicals.

TQM See **total quality management.**

tracer A procedure used to locate a shipment, parcel, or letter that fails to arrive at its proper destination within the normal time period.

trade acceptance A trade draft signed by a customer.

trade association A nonprofit organization of professionals in related businesses and industries, established to serve the common interests of its members.

trade credit Short-term credit issued to a business for the purchase of goods; the most substantial form of short-term liability for most businesses.

trade deficit An imbalance of trade, occurring when a nation buys more goods from abroad than it sells; an excess of imports over exports. Such a deficit is usually expressed in dollars. See also **balance of payments.**

trade discount Also called **trade allowance.** A percentage taken off the selling price for certain dealers who make a large volume of purchases. Discounts often vary, as between wholesalers and retailers or between small and large retailers (functional discount).

trade draft A document drawn up by a supplier to be signed by a customer, who is then obligated to pay the supplier a stated amount in exchange for goods or services within a specified period. See also **sight drafts; time drafts; trade acceptance.**

trade dress In legal parlance, the visual concept and presentation of a product, especially the design of the product itself and its packaging.

trade-in An asset given as full or partial payment for another asset taken in exchange.

trade journal A periodical published for members of a specific profession or trade.

trademark A distinguishing symbol, device, and/or term used in connection with a product or service and whose exclusive use is legally reserved to the owner.

trade name 1. The name used by a manufacturer, merchant, service company, farming business, etc., to identify itself individually as a business. **2.** A word or phrase used in a trade to designate a business, service, or particular class of goods, but that is not technically a trademark, either because it cannot be exclusively appropriated as a trademark or because it is not affixed to goods sold in the market. **3.** The name by which an article or substance is known to the trade.

trade-off A gain in benefits in one area at the expense of a loss in benefits in another area.

trade secret A secret process, technique, method, etc., used to advantage in a trade, business, profession, etc.

trade show An exhibition and demonstration of new products (e.g., automobiles, boats) held to promote sales.

trade union A voluntary affiliation of workers, usually within the same or similar occupational specialties, to further their mutual interests in regard to wages, job security, and working conditions.

trading on equity Investing with borrowed money, on the expectation of a return greater than the cost of the borrowed funds.

traffic manager 1. A person who supervises the transportation of goods for an employer. **2.** An employee responsible for routing items of business within a company for appropriate action by various departments.

trailer-on-flatcar (*abbr* TOFC) See **piggyback.**

trainer An individual who conducts training programs within an organization and selects outside training resources for specialized studies.

training director An individual who establishes and implements training programs for the employ-

ees of an organization, generally under the supervision of the personnel officer.

training film A film or videotape created for use in an employee training program.

training manual A printed guide or outline for use in a training program or course of instruction.

trait approach An approach to leadership based on the assumption that effective leaders share a set of personality traits and can be distinguished from other people early on.

transactional analysis (*abbr* TA) A framework for analyzing interpersonal communications that assumes there are three ego states (Parent, Adult, Child) that alternate in each individual.

transaction cost The commission plus tax that an investor must pay for the services of a broker in buying or selling securities.

transaction document An invoice, check, requisition, or purchase order testifying to a transaction.

transaction worksheet A record in which every change in assets (cash, accounts receivable, inventory, real estate, etc.) and equities (accounts payable, salaries payable, capital stock, retained earnings, etc.) is recorded and explained.

transfer 1. The placement of an employee in another position of equal status but often with different tasks to perform. **2.** The delivery of a security certificate from the selling broker to the purchasing broker. **3.** To record a change in the ownership of a security. Also called **copy; dub.** To duplicate a videotaped program.

transfer agent An agent responsible for recording changes of ownership of securities, canceling obsolete certificates of ownership, and issuing new ones.

transfer line Automated materials-handling equipment with which individual parts are moved from one machine to another where they are properly positioned for processing without the need for manual intervention.

transfer price (*bookkeeping*) A value assigned to an asset transferred from one unit (division, department, subsidiary, etc.) of an organization to another, for purposes of accounting and internal control.

transloading A loading site where incoming goods are repackaged and shipped to other destinations, customers, etc.

transportation in Also called **freight in.** The transportation expense incurred to effect delivery of inventory items purchased.

transportation out Also called **freight out.** The charges paid to transport inventory items sold.

transshipping Also called **transshipment. 1.** The transfer of goods from one ship, freight car, etc., to another so as to reach a final destination. **2.** The practice of ordering abnormally large amounts of a high-demand product, so as to obtain the most advantageous discount, then reselling the excess to another dealer or dealers who sell it at bargain prices.

treasurer An officer of an organization who is responsible for obtaining and managing corporate capital, cash, and investments.

Treasury bill (*abbr* T-bill) A short-term investment issued weekly by the U.S. Treasury and available from any of the 12 Federal Reserve banks, commercial banks, and brokers, with a face value of $10,000 or more payable upon maturity, usually in 13, 26, or 52 weeks.

Treasury note (*abbr* T-note) A note issued by the U.S. Treasury with a fixed maturity of one to seven years and a fixed interest rate payable semiannually, available from a commercial bank or broker in an amount of $1000 or more.

treasury stock Also called **reacquired stock.** Common stock that the issuing corporation has purchased from its holders as an alternative to paying dividends, such that the earnings per share of outstanding shares are increased, with an expected concomitant rise in the market price of the stock.

trend analysis See **time-series analysis.**

trespass Unlawful or unauthorized entry onto the property of another.

trial-and-error pricing The setting of different prices for the same item in separate markets in an effort to determine which price will produce the desired sales volume and profit.

trial balance (*bookkeeping*) A listing of account balances in debit and credit columns so that they may be totaled separately and checked for arithmetical accuracy.

trickle-down theory A theory of federal economic policies that providing generous benefits to business and industry will eventually benefit the lower and middle classes.

triple-tax-free (*bonds*) Not subject to federal, state, or local income taxes.

triple witching hour (*stock exchange*) The hour of closing on a particular day when stock index futures, stock index options, and individual stock options simultaneously expire: regarded as a time of extreme volatility in trading.

troubled debt restructuring The granting by a creditor of changes in the terms of a previously contracted debt repayment such that the borrower can repay the debt under easier terms, usually undertaken in the hope that the borrower will not go bankrupt and default on all payments.

troubleshooting The process of locating, diagnosing, and eliminating the source of a problem within a particular activity or operation.

trough The lowest point in an economic cycle.

truck jobber A wholesaler who uses trucks for storage and selling as well as for delivery of goods (generally nationally advertised specialty goods) sold for cash.

trunk show A vendor's display of merchandise offerings to one or more retail buyers.

trust 1. An illegal combination of companies whose stock is controlled by a central board of trustees, so that prices may be controlled and competition eliminated. **2.** A fiduciary relationship in which one person (the trustee) holds title to property (the trust estate) for the benefit of another (the beneficiary).

trust company An institution whose financial staff manages the financial affairs of trust beneficiaries as fiduciaries or trustees. See also **trust** (def. 2).

trust deed See **deed of trust**.

trustee 1. A person who holds property in trust for another person (the beneficiary). See also **trust** (def. 2). **2.** An individual or company (often the commercial branch of a bank) appointed to act on

behalf of several bondholders in such matters as certifying the validity of the bond issue, observing the legal and financial behavior of the issuing corporation, and taking steps to handle corporate default on payment of interest or principal.

trust estate Property held by one person for the benefit of another. See also **trust** (def. 2).

trust receipt A document signed by a borrower giving a lender a security interest in an inventory (usually of valuable, nonperishable, and easily marketable goods) stored in a warehouse as collateral for a loan.

Truth-in-Lending Act An act of Congress passed in 1968 requiring that before a loan agreement is signed, the borrower must be fully informed of the interest charges, both simple and compound, attached to the loan. See also **Regulation Z**.

turnaround 1. A reversal, especially in business sales, from loss to profit. **2.** The time between the making of an investment and receiving a return.

turnkey operation An operation that is so well supported and self-contained that one need only "turn a key" in the front door to get the operation running, often used to describe equipment whose purchase cost includes everything necessary to make the equipment operational, such as delivery, installation, training, and maintenance.

turnover 1. The aggregate of worker replacements in an organization in a given time period. **2.** The rate at which items are sold in a given period, especially with reference to depletion of stock and replacement of inventory.

two-bin system An inventory control method that physically segregates normal working stock from the reorder-level stock so that the need to replenish is signaled visually whenever normal working stock has been exhausted.

two-tier wage plan A policy or practice of paying new employees on a lower pay scale than that of longtime employees, though all have identical responsibilities. See also **comparable worth**.

TWX (*abbr for* Teletypewriter Exchange) An electronic system by which written words are transmitted over Western Union lines from one teleprinter to another at a rate of 100 words per minute, used when messages uniformly exceed 100 words.

tying contract An agreement by which a purchaser is required to buy goods he or she does not want in order to get goods he or she does want.

business

a b c d e f g h i j k l m n o p q r s t U V w x y z

UGMA See **Uniform Gifts to Minors Act**.

ultimate consumer A person who buys goods or services for his or her own use or for use in the buyer's household.

ultra vires (*Latin*) Beyond the scope of the legal power or authority of a corporation or official (indicating that a contract so designated is not binding).

umbrella policy A type of insurance that provides businesses with more extensive coverage than that provided in a general liability policy.

unconscionable agreement An agreement or contract that a court would refuse to enforce, either in part or in its entirety, because of the inadequacy of the benefits received by one party and unfair advantage to the other.

underdeveloped See **developing**.

underemployment The aggregate of people who are employed at jobs that do not require the full range of their skills or education, or who are working part-time but would take full-time work if it were available.

underlying Referring to a claim, mortgage, etc., that takes precedence over another.

underwater option A situation in which the employee's stock-option price is higher than the market value of the stock.

underwriter 1. An investment firm that acquires new issues of stocks and bonds from a corporation and sells them to individual investors, thus assuming all the risks of ownership unless the arrangement is on a best-effort basis, in which case the underwriter acts merely as a broker. **2.** (*insurance*) An employee who evaluates risks and decides how large a policy is to be granted and at what premiums.

underwriting syndicate A loosely associated group of investment institutions that share the cost and risk of underwriting a new issue of a security.

undirected viewing The viewing of a situation or of data with an open mind rather than with the intention of proving a point.

unearned income Income received from property, as interest, dividends, or the like. Cf. **earned income**.

unemployment 1. The aggregate of people over the age of 16 who are not working. **2.** The aggregate of people over the age of 16 who have no jobs, are available for work, and are actively seeking work. **3.** The number of people in the labor force who do not have jobs divided by the number of those who do. See also **cyclical unemployment;**

frictional unemployment; seasonal unemployment; structural unemployment.

unemployment insurance Also called **unemployment compensation.** Insurance that provides monetary benefits to workers who become unemployed for reasons unrelated to job performance, administered by the individual states and financed by payroll taxes levied on employers.

unfair labor practice An illegal activity engaged in by an employer (as set forth in the National Labor Relations Act) or by a union (as set forth in the Taft-Hartley Act).

unfavorable balance of trade An excess in value of imports over exports.

Uniform Commercial Code (*abbr* UCC) The body of laws concerning business transactions adopted by the several states, governing sales, bills of lading, bulk transfers, commercial paper, bank deposits and collections, and letters of credit.

uniform delivery price A price to all buyers for delivered goods, regardless of transportation costs. See also **postage-stamp pricing; zone pricing.**

Uniform Gifts to Minors Act (*abbr* UGMA) A law that provides a means to transfer money or securities to a minor without establishing a formal trust. The assets are managed by a a custodian and turned over to the minor when he or she reaches the age of 18 or 21.

Uniform Transfers to Minors Act (*abbr* UTMA) A law that is similar to the Uniform Gifts to Minors Act, but covers gifts of real estate, works of art, etc., as well as money and securities.

unilateral contract An agreement by which one party (the offeree) performs a certain action in exchange for a promise by another person (the offerer), the offeree being under no obligation to perform the action, and the offerer, once the act is performed, being obliged to keep the promise made. See also **bilateral contract.**

uninsurable risk A risk not usually covered by insurance, such as a decline in economic conditions, a climatic change (e.g., drought), or business losses attributable to poor management or to changes in the law.

union See **trade union.**

union recognition An employer's acceptance, either voluntary or as a result of a representational election, of a particular union as the bargaining agent or representative for the company's employees.

union shop A place of business where by agreement with a union the employer may hire nonunion personnel as well as union members but may not retain such nonunion personnel beyond a specified period, usually 30 days, unless they join the union. See also **closed shop; Taft-Hartley Act.**

union steward See **shop steward.**

unit cost The cost of a single unit of production, calculated by dividing total cost (either actually incurred, predicted, or assigned) by total number of units produced.

United States Employment Service (*abbr* USES) A federal-state system that refers job-seekers to available jobs and provides employment counseling.

United States Trademark Association (*abbr* USTA) A national organization, founded in 1878, that provides information on the use and registration of trademarks in the United States and abroad.

unit pricing 1. The posting of the price per unit (e.g., per ounce or per pound) of goods offered for sale in packages of varying quantities. 2. The price per item, when several items are offered at one price.

units-of-production method A method of calculating annual depreciation by which an asset's depreciable cost (original cost less salvage value) is divided by its useful life, expressed in hours of use or units of production, the resulting hourly or per-unit depreciation cost then being multiplied by the hours or units actually used or produced in a given year.

unity-of-command principle A management principle that specifies that each employee should be accountable to only one superior.

universal life insurance A type of insurance in which the insured deposits money in a money-market fund, earnings from which pay the premiums on term life insurance, while any remainder continues to earn interest.

Universal Product Code (*abbr* UPC) A type of bar code that indicates number of articles, weight, price, inventory number, etc., and is widely used at supermarket checkout counters.

unlimited liability 1. The legal responsibility of each partner in an unincorporated business for all of the company's liabilities, even if such liabilities exceed the partners' individual or combined investments. 2. The legal responsibility of a sole proprietor of a business for any money owed by the business or for damages done in the process of conducting the business by the proprietor or any employee. See also **limited liability.**

unsecured loan A loan for which no collateral or other security is demanded from the borrower, usually because of an excellent credit rating.

unsystematic risk A risk that is subject to the influence of predictably random events and that can be minimized by diversification. See also **systematic risk.**

UPC See **Universal Product Code.**

upper management See **top management.**

upscale Also called **upmarket.** Of high or luxurious quality; catering to high-income consumers.

uptick (*stock exchange*) A closing price slightly above that of the previous trading period.

uptime The time during which employees are working or machines are operating or can be operating.

useful life The estimated length of time an asset will be used by its owner, in contrast to its physical life, or the length of time the asset will be of use to anyone at all.

use tax A tax levied by a state on goods purchased outside the state.

USTA See **United States Trademark Association.**

utilitarianism The concept that decision making must be based on what will benefit the greatest number of people.

utilitarian reward/punishment system A method of increasing employee productivity by the promise of rewards (e.g., raises, bonuses, promotions) for superior performance and the threat of penalties (e.g., docking wages, demotion) for unsatisfactory performance.

utility The capacity of a product or service to satisfy some human want.

UTMA See **Uniform Transfers to Minors Act.**

validation The function of a computer program that compares one computer file against another to check the accuracy and program content (raw data, codes, format) of the original file.

validity The degree to which a test, experiment, or survey actually measures what it is intended to measure. See also **reliability.**

value 1. **a.** The monetary worth or utility of an item, service, claim, product, asset, or right. **b.** To assign such a worth. 2. The estimated fair-market worth of real estate to a buyer.

value added The additional value that raw materials or components take on as they proceed through the processes of refining, manufacturing, assembly, packaging, etc.

value-added tax (*abbr* VAT) A tax levied on the value of a product at each stage of its manufacturing and distribution processes, each such tax being added to the price of the product as it passes to each successive processor and ultimately to the consumer.

value fund A mutual fund that invests in stocks that are considered to be undervalued by the market and whose share price is expected to rise.

variable annuity A contract that provides lifetime retirement payments to an individual, the amounts of the payments varying with the earnings of the funds that provide the income.

variable base salary A salesperson's salary that rises in regular increments with increases in performance.

variable budget See **flexible budget.**

variable cost An expense that increases or decreases according to the volume of production.

variable life A type of life insurance whose premiums are invested in stocks and whose death benefits depend on the performance of such stocks during the insured's lifetime, though a minimum death benefit is guaranteed.

variable overhead Overhead costs that vary with volume of production.

variable-rate mortgage Also called **flexible-rate mortgage.** A type of mortgage whose interest rate may fluctuate according to current rates, but may rise no more than 2.5 percent during the life of the mortgage. Changes in interest are usually put into effect annually and, by law, no oftener than every six months. See also **adjustable-rate mortgage, renegotiable-rate mortgage.**

variance (*accounting*) The difference between budgeted and actual amounts, or between standard and actual costs, hours, units, etc.

variety store A retail store that carries a wide selection of household and personal items, most of which are relatively inexpensive.

VAT See **value-added tax.**

VDT See **video display terminal.**

venture capital Also called **risk capital.** Money invested by professional investors (venture capitalists) in a new company with perceived potential for great growth but without a record of proven performance.

venture management See **syndicate.**

venture team A group of specialists assembled from various divisions of a company and guided by a team manager to brainstorm ideas for a highly innovative product designed for a specialized market.

vertical merger Also called **vertical acquisition.** Absorption by a company of one of its suppliers (backward vertical merger) or one of its customers (forward vertical merger). See also **horizontal merger.**

vertical split A division of the formal structure of responsibility of an organization between top management, middle management, and technical staff.

vested benefit A financial benefit that is guaranteed and cannot be canceled.

vestibule training Training in skills in a simulated work environment.

vest-pocket supermarket See **bantam store.**

viatical Of or pertaining to a form of insurance business that pays off on the insurance policies of the terminally ill.

video display terminal (*abbr* VDT) A computer device with a keyboard for input and a screen for the display of images called up from the computer's memory.

videotex A system by which potential customers are linked via computers and telephones with retail merchants, who can display their wares on the home screen and accept on-the-spot orders.

vision insurance See **dental and vision insurance.**

voice mail An electronic communications system that routes voice messages interactively to appropriate recipients, stores the messages in digitized form, and notifies the recipients that the messages are available for playback through the system.

voice-over 1. The voice of an offscreen narrator or announcer, as in a television commercial. **2.** a televised sequence, as in a commercial, narrated by voice-over.

volatile stock Also called **yo-yo stock.** A highly speculative stock whose value tends to fluctuate drastically.

voluntary arbitration Arbitration of unresolved differences by an unbiased third party, agreed to by labor and management.

voluntary bankruptcy Bankruptcy effected by a legal procedure initiated by a debtor. See also **involuntary bankruptcy.**

voluntary chain A confederation of independent retailers who join together in order to obtain such benefits as group purchasing power unavailable to individual businesses.

voluntary deferral plan A plan by which executives (usually at a specified position or earnings level) postpone accepttance of a portion of their income or annual bonus until retirement, after which the deferred amounts plus earnings (at a fixed interest rate) are paid out over 10 to 15 years.

voting rights The rights of shareholders to elect the corporation's board of directors and to vote on certain resolutions at the annual shareholders' meeting.

voting security A stock that entitles the holder to vote on board members, new issues of stock, and other major corporate decisions at the annual shareholders' meeting.

voucher A document that controls and/or separates expenditures by authorizing and/or recording them.

vulture fund See **opportunity fund.**

abcdefghijklmnopqrstuv **WXYZ**

wage Payment for work performed based on the number of hours or days worked or the number of items produced.

Wage and Hour Law See **Fair Labor Standards Act.**

wage and price control Also called **wage and price stabilization.** A legislative measure that freezes wages and prices at existing levels in an effort to combat inflation.

wage and salary administration The function of human resource management to establish wages and salaries that conform to the overall policies of the organization.

wage incentive plan A method of remuneration by which employees' wages, individually or as a group, are at least partly based on the number of units produced.

wage-push inflation An inflationary trend caused by wage increases that trigger a rise in production costs and prices.

Wagner Act See **National Labor Relations Act.**

waiting-line theory See **queuing theory.**

waiver The relinquishing of a right or presumed right to a piece of property or other asset that is owned or controlled by another.

walkout See **strike.**

Wall Street 1. A street in New York City, in downtown Manhattan: the major financial center of the United States. **2.** The money market or the financiers of the United States.

WAN See **wide-area network.**

want ad See **classified ad.**

want-slip system A system by which retail stores record out-of-stock or unstocked items requested by customers.

warehouse 1. A facility where goods are stored until they are distributed to retailers or consumers. See also **bonded warehouse; public warehouse. 2.** To keep apartments in a building vacant in order to receive additional tax benefits for depreciation on unrented units or, when a building is going co-op, to sell such apartments to nonresidents at inflated prices.

warehouse receipt A written record of items stored in a particular warehouse, often used to prove ownership of goods that the owner wishes to use as collateral for a loan.

warrant A certificate entitling its holder to buy a specified security at a specified price within a specified period.

warrantor A person or firm that gives a warranty.

warranty See **express warranty; full warranty; limited warranty.**

warranty deed A legal instrument transferring title to real property and certifying that the property is free of all liens and encumbrances and that the warrantor will defend the buyer against all claims in regard to it.

watered stock Capital stock that is intentionally assigned a par value greater than the market value of the assets of the issuing company.

waybill A document prepared by a carrier of cargo that describes the shipment, states the charges, names the consignee and consignor, and specifies the origin, route, and destination. See also **bill of lading.**

Web site A connected group of pages on the World Wide Web regarded as a single entity, usually maintained by one person or organization and devoted to one topic or several related topics.

wedding A slang term for a business merger.

weighted average 1. Also called **weighted average cost.** The average cost of a unit of inventory, calculated by dividing the total cost of all items (even if they were bought at various costs) by the total number of units. See also **FIFO; LIFO. 2.** The average value for a group of items, where one or more of the individual items are assigned an extra degree of importance.

Wheeler-Lea Act An act of Congress passed in 1938 to amend the Federal Trade Commission Act by extending the power of the Federal Trade Commission to move against firms that engage in practices harmful to the public (e.g., deceptive advertising of foods, drugs, and cosmetics) as well as those that injure competitors.

wheel of retailing A business cycle in which a store featuring low-priced merchandise gradually upgrades or is forced by economic conditions to raise its prices until it is no longer competitive with other stores in its original price range.

when-issued Relating to a transaction involving securities expected to be issued and for which payment is not required until the securities are actually registered and issued.

where-used The identification of those products or customer orders for which a specific batch of parts will ultimately be used.

whiplash effect The effect of unusual and unexpected changes in the demand for a product, resulting in either excessive or inadequate inventory at various points in the channel of distribution.

whisper stock The stock of a company rumored to be the target of a takeover attempt.

white-collar Belonging or relating to the ranks of office and professional workers whose jobs generally do not involve manual labor or the wearing of a uniform or work clothes.

white-collar crime Any of various crimes, as embezzlement, fraud, or stealing office equipment, committed by business or professional people while working at their occupations.

white knight A friendly company that attempts to forestall a hostile takeover by outbidding the raider for the fellow company's stock.

whole life insurance See **ordinary life insurance.**

wholesale price index Also called **producer price index.** An index that measures the average change in prices paid by wholesalers and manufacturers for 2000 selected goods.

wholesaler A seller of merchandise and/or services to commercial, industrial, and institutional users for use in their operations or for resale.

wide-area network Also called **WAN.** A computer network that spans a relatively large geographical area.

wildcat strike A work stoppage that is not author-

ized by the union representing the striking workers and that is in violation of the labor contract.

will-call Also called **layaway plan.** A method of purchasing by which the customer reserves an article with a down payment and takes possession of the article when payments have been completed.

Wilshire 5000 An index of U.S. stocks traded on the New York Stock Exchange and American Stock Exchange, as well as actively traded OTC stocks. The index is actually comprised of over 6000 stocks, each weighted according to its market capitalization.

Windows (*trademark*) Any of several microcomputer operating systems or environments featuring a graphical user interface.

wire transfer An order transmitted by telephone, telegraph, or electronically from one bank to another to pay or credit money to a payee designated by a payer.

withdrawal plan A system allowing periodic withdrawal of specified amounts of interest and/or principal from a mutual fund, or of a fluctuating amount determined by the periodic redemption of a fixed number of shares.

withholding tax That part of an employee's tax liability withheld by the employer from wages or salary and paid directly to the government.

word processing Writing, editing, production, and storage of documents, as letters, reports, and books, through the use of a computer program or a complete computer system designed to facilitate rapid and efficient manipulation of text.

word processor A computer program or computer system designed for word processing.

work design A scientific approach to effective performance by which some work is divided into small task segments and other work is subjected to job enlargement and enrichment in order to meet the individual needs of employees with different attitudes, abilities, and goals.

worker buyout A method of reducing a company's payroll by offering older employees bonuses (e.g., one or two years' salary) and other incentives to resign or take early retirement.

workers' compensation Insurance benefits that cover lost wages and medical costs of employees who become ill or are injured in the course of their work, such benefits not being dependent on a showing of negligence on the part of the employer.

workfare A government plan requiring welfare recipients to accept public-service jobs or enroll in vocational training.

work-flow integration A sequencing of technological activities to be carried out by employees in a work environment, with much thought given to the order of events in terms of ease or difficulty, degree of automation, and interdependence of tasks.

work force 1. The total number of people in a country who are employed or are looking for work and are considered employable. **2.** The number of people employed by a company or in a particular industry or occupation.

working asset Invested capital that is comparatively liquid.

working capital Also called **net current assets.** The excess of current assets over current liabilities.

working control Control of voting at a shareholders' meeting achieved by ownership of more than 50 percent of the corporation's voting securities or by acquisition of a greater number of proxies than any other group or individual has secured.

work-in-process inventory Also called **work-in-progress inventory.** (*abbr* WIP) The aggregate of products entered into the manufacturing process (i.e., all those started but not yet finished); a current asset account with a normal debit balance.

work measurement The evaluation of employee performance based on predetermined standards for effective work output.

work papers Also called **working papers.** An auditor's schedules and analysis of work done and conclusions drawn before the issuance of an opinion on a financial statement.

work rules Policies and regulations regarding the work required of employees and the working conditions that management will provide, usually arrived at by collective bargaining between unions and management.

work sharing A reduction in the number of hours worked per week by each employee, with a concomitant reduction in wages, instituted to avoid the necessity of laying off some workers.

workshop A course of instruction or a seminar in which management skills are developed through group practice in such skills as planning, decision making, and report writing.

work station also **workstation 1.** A work or office area assigned to one person, often one accommodating a computer terminal or other electronic equipment. **2.** A computer terminal or microcomputer connected to a mainframe, minicomputer, or data-processing network. **3.** A powerful microcomputer, often with a high-resolution display, used for computer-aided design, electronic publishing, or other graphics-intensive processing.

work stoppage The collective stoppage of work by employees in a business or an industry to protest working conditions.

World Wide Web (*abbr* WWW) A system of extensively interlinked electronic documents: a branch of the Internet.

worst-case scenario The worst possible outcome of a situation.

wraparound mortgage (*abbr* WAM) A second mortgage that includes payments on the first mortgage, usually assumable at a considerably lower rate of interest.

write-off 1. A reduction of an amount in an account as required by abnormal or unfavorable circumstances (e.g., uncollectible receivables, unsalable assets or inventory). **2.** Reduction of book value; depreciation.

written-down value The value of an asset reduced by the depreciation already taken.

W-2 A standard tax form showing the total wages paid to an employee and the taxes withheld during the calendar year: prepared by an employer for each employee.

WWW See **World Wide Web.**

WYSIWYG (*acronym for* What you see is what you get) The capacity of a computer to print out what is shown on the display screen.

XD See **ex dividend.**

yardstick See **benchmark.**

yearly order See **blanket order.**

yellow-dog contract A contract between a worker and an employer whereby the worker promises, if hired, not to join or remain in a union (a practice prohibited by the National Labor Relations Act).

yield Also called **return.** The dividends or interest paid to shareholders and bondholders, expressed as a percentage of the current price of the security in question.

yield management A management concept that attempts to respond realistically to a variety of market factors (e.g., demand, season, competition) that constantly fluctuate. One such response is to maintain flexible price structures based on one or more of these factors.

yield to maturity Also called **maturity yield.** (*bonds*) The return on an investment expressed as a percentage of its cost, if held until it can or must be redeemed by its issuer.

yo-yo stock See **volatile stock.**

YTD (*accounting*) year to date.

YTM See **yield to maturity.**

zero-balance account An accommodation by a bank allowing a commercial customer to write checks on a subsidiary account in which no funds are maintained. Checks are paid when presented, after which funds are transferred from the master account to bring the subsidiary account back to zero.

zero-based budgeting (*abbr* ZBB) The practice, followed only by governmental and some nonprofit organizations, of assuming that budgets for all programs, activities, and projects are zero at the beginning of each financial period and basing their budgets on an analysis of past performance and probable future costs and benefits, for the purpose of trimming or shedding projects that are marginally profitable or no longer useful. See also **incremental budgeting.**

zero-coupon bond A type of bond having no coupons. It is sold at a discount and redeemed after a specified period at face value, the profit being the difference between purchase price and selling price.

zero-salvage value A salvage value of a depreciable asset that is less than 10 percent of the asset's cost and that is assumed to be zero for purposes of tax and financial reporting.

zero-sum Denoting an economy or other system or situation in which gains equal losses.

zone of acceptance The area within which subordinates accept and comply with the majority of orders and requests received from superiors without considering other options.

zone of indifference The area within which subordinates follow orders and are indifferent to a superior's right to exert authority over them.

zone pricing The practice of pricing goods to be distributed on the basis of a customer's location in relation to the distribution point, each customer being charged a base price plus a standard rate for the zone in which he or she is located. See also **base-point pricing; phantom freight.**

zoning ordinance A local ordinance that regulates and prescribes the kinds of buildings and businesses that can be established in specific locations.

business

Computer Dictionary

abort *v.t.* **1.** to stop (a program or function) before it has finished naturally: *to abort a print job; to abort a search.* —*v.i.* **2.** to terminate before completion: *The program aborted because of a bug in the software.*
⇒ See also BOMB; CRASH; HANG; QUIT.

absolute address *n.* a fixed address in memory. Also called **real address, machine address.**
⇒ See also ADDRESS; RELATIVE ADDRESS.

absolute cell reference *n.* in spreadsheet applications, a reference, to a particular cell or group of cells, that never changes.
⇒ See also CONSTANT; RELATIVE CELL REFERENCE; SPREADSHEET.

AC-3 the coding system used by Dolby Digital.
⇒ See also DOLBY DIGITAL.

Accelerated Graphics Port *n.* See AGP.

accelerator board *n.* **1.** GRAPHICS ACCELERATOR. **2.** a type of expansion board that makes a computer faster by adding a faster CPU or FPU.
⇒ See also BUS; COPROCESSOR; CPU; EXPANSION BOARD; FLOATING-POINT NUMBER; FPU; GRAPHICS ACCELERATOR; MAIN MEMORY; MOTHERBOARD; RAM; ZERO INSERTION FORCE (ZIF) SOCKET.

access *v.t.* **1.** to retrieve data from; to use. Programs can read data from or write data to main memory. A user can access files, directories (or folders), databases, computers, or peripheral devices. **2.** to read (data) from or write (data) to a mass storage device. —*n.* **3.** the act of accessing data. **4.** a privilege to use computer information in some manner. For example, a user who is granted only *read access* to a file can read the file but cannot modify or delete it.
⇒ See also ACCESS TIME; MASS STORAGE; MEMORY; RANDOM ACCESS; READ; WRITE.

Access.bus *n.* a serial communications protocol developed by Philips Semiconductors and Digital Equipment (DEC) for connecting relatively low-speed peripheral devices to a computer. Access.bus uses a bus topology, which enables it to support up to 125 devices.
⇒ See also BUS; SERIAL PORT; USB.

access code *n.* PASSWORD.
⇒ See also ACCESS; LOG ON; PASSWORD.

access control *n.* the mechanisms and policies that restrict access to computer resources. An *access control list* specifies which operations different users can perform on specific files and directories.
⇒ See also AUTHORIZATION; SECURITY.

accessory slot *n.* EXPANSION SLOT.

access time *n.* the time required to locate a piece of information and make it available to the computer. Ideally, the access time of memory chips should be fast enough to keep up with the CPU. Access time is also frequently used to describe the speed of disk drives.
⇒ See also ACCESS; CLOCK SPEED; CPU; CYCLE TIME; DATA TRANSFER RATE; DISK CACHE; INTERLEAVE; WAIT STATE.

accounting software *n.* computer programs that perform accounting operations.
⇒ See also PERSONAL FINANCE MANAGER; YEAR 2000 PROBLEM.

ACM Association for Computing Machinery: an organization composed of U.S. computer professionals. The ACM publishes information relating to computer science, holds seminars, and creates and promotes computer standards.
⇒ See also STANDARD.

acoustic coupler *n.* a device onto which a telephone handset is placed to connect a computer with a network. Acoustic couplers are no longer widely used because current modems usually connect via modular telephone connectors. However, acoustic couplers are useful in some situations, as in hotel rooms where the telephone cable is anchored to the wall.
⇒ See also MODEM; NETWORK.

ACPI Advanced Configuration and Power Interface: a power management specification developed by Intel, Microsoft, and Toshiba. ACPI, which is included in Windows 98, enables the operating system to control the amount of power given to each device attached to the computer, which permits the operating system to turn off peripheral devices when they are not in use.
⇒ See also APM; POWER MANAGEMENT; SLEEP MODE.

Acrobat *n.* a suite of programs developed by Adobe Systems, Inc., for creating and distributing electronic documents. A user can create and distribute the PDF file electronically. People viewing a PDF file (or document) with Acrobat Reader see the document with the exact layout and typography intended by the author.
⇒ See also PDF.

acronym *n.* a word formed by combining some parts (usually the first letters) of other terms. For example, *modem* is an acronym derived from *mod(ulator)/dem(odulator).* An acronym is pronounced as if it were a word rather than just a series of individual letters.

active *adj.* referring to objects currently displayed or used on a computer. For example, in graphical user interfaces, the *active window* is the window currently receiving mouse and keyboard input. In spreadsheet applications, the *active cell* is the cell, usually highlighted, in which data can be entered or modified. The *active program* is the program currently running.
⇒ See also CELL; GRAPHICAL USER INTERFACE; SPREADSHEET; WINDOW.

active backplane *n.* See under BACKPLANE.

Active Directory *n.* a new directory service from Microsoft; part of Windows NT 5.0.
⇒ See also DIRECTORY SERVICE; LDAP; NDS; WINDOWS NT; X.500.

active matrix *n.* See under ACTIVE-MATRIX DISPLAY.

active-matrix display *n.* a type of flat-panel display in which the screen is refreshed more frequently than in conventional passive-matrix displays and is therefore sharper and brighter. The terms *TFT* and *active-matrix* are often used interchangeably.
⇒ See also FLAT-PANEL DISPLAY; LCD; TFT.

ActiveMovie *n.* a new multimedia streaming technology developed by Microsoft. It is built into the Internet Explorer browser and will be part of future versions of the Windows operating system. Supporting most multimedia formats, ActiveMovie enables users to view multimedia content distributed over the Internet or on CD-ROM.
⇒ See also MULTIMEDIA; QUICKTIME; STREAMING.

Active Server Pages *n.* a specification for a dynamically created Web page with a *.ASP* extension that contains either Visual Basic or Jscript code. When a browser requests an ASP page, the Web server generates a page with HTML code and sends it back to the browser.
⇒ See also CGI; VISUAL BASIC.

ActiveX *n.* a loosely defined set of technologies developed by Microsoft for sharing information among different applications.
⇒ See also ACTIVEX CONTROL; ADO; COMPONENT OBJECT MODEL; DIRECTX; JAVA; MICROSOFT; OLE; WINDOWS DNA.

ActiveX control *n.* a control using ActiveX technologies. An ActiveX control can be automatically downloaded and executed by a Web browser. Programmers can develop ActiveX controls in a variety of languages, including C, C++, Visual Basic, and Java. An ActiveX control is similar to a Java applet.

computer

⇒ See also ACTIVEX; BROWSER; DYNAMIC HTML; IN-TERNET EXPLORER; JAVABEANS; OCX; SHOCKWAVE.

ActiveX Data Objects *n.* See ADO.

Ada *n.* a high-level, general-purpose programming language developed for the U.S. Defense Department. It incorporates modular techniques that make it easy to build and maintain large systems. Ada is the mandatory development language for most U.S. military applications. It is often the language of choice for large systems that require real-time processing. [named after Augusta Ada Byron (1815–52), Countess of Lovelace and daughter of Lord Byron, who is considered by many to be the world's first programmer]
⇒ See also HIGH-LEVEL LANGUAGE; MODULAR ARCHITEC-TURE; REAL TIME.

adapter *n.* **1.** EXPANSION BOARD. **2.** the circuitry required to support a particular device. For example, *video adapters* enable a computer to support graphics monitors, and *network adapters* enable a computer to attach to a network.
⇒ See also CONTROLLER; EXPANSION BOARD; VIDEO ADAPTER.

adaptive differential pulse-code modulation *n.* See ADPCM.

ADB Apple Desktop Bus: a type of communications pathway built into all versions of the Apple Macintosh computer and used to connect low-speed input devices such as the keyboard and mouse.
⇒ See also BUS; MACINTOSH COMPUTER; PORT.

add-in *n.* **1.** a component added to a computer or other device to increase its capabilities. Add-ins can increase memory or add graphics or communications capabilities to a computer. They come in the form of expansion boards, cartridges, or chips. **2.** a software program that extends the capabilities of larger programs.
⇒ See also ADD-ON; CARTRIDGE; EXPANSION BOARD; OLE.

add-on *n.* a product designed to complement another product. Add-ons usually refer to an entire circuit board, cartridge, or software program, although they can also be individual chips that are inserted into boards.
⇒ See also ADD-ON BOARD; ADD-IN; CARTRIDGE; EXPAN-SION BOARD; EXPANSION SLOT; PRINTED CIRCUIT BOARD.

add-on board *n.* EXPANSION BOARD.

address *n.* **1.** a location of data, usually in main memory or on disk. Computer memory may be thought of as an array of storage boxes, each of which is one byte in length and has a unique number. By specifying an address, programmers can access a particular byte of data. Disks are divided into tracks and sectors, each with a unique address. **2.** a name or token that identifies a network component. In local-area networks (LANs), every node has a unique address. On the Internet, every file has a unique address, called a URL.
⇒ See also ABSOLUTE ADDRESS; ADDRESS BUS; ADDRESS SPACE; BASE ADDRESS; DISK; E-MAIL ADDRESS; MAC AD-DRESS; MACHINE ADDRESS; MAIN MEMORY; MEMORY; OFF-SET; RELATIVE ADDRESS; SECTOR; TRACK; URL.

address bus *n.* a collection of wires connecting the CPU with main memory that is used to identify particular locations (addresses) in main memory. The width of the address bus (that is, the number of wires) determines how many unique memory locations can be addressed.
⇒ See also ADDRESS; BUS; CPU; MAIN MEMORY.

Address Resolution Protocol *n.* See ARP.

address space *n.* the set of all legal addresses in memory for a given application. The address space represents the amount of memory available to a program.
⇒ See also ADDRESS; MAIN MEMORY; MEMORY; THUNK; VIRTUAL MEMORY.

ADO ActiveX Data Objects: Microsoft's newest high-level interface for data objects. ADO is designed eventually to replace *Data Access Objects (DAO)* and *Remote Data Objects (RDO)*. ADO is more general and can be used to access many different types of data, including Web pages and spreadsheets.
⇒ See also ACTIVEX; DAO; ODBC.

Adobe Acrobat *n.* ACROBAT.

Adobe Photoshop *n.* a leading paint program from Adobe Systems, Inc. Photoshop runs on both Macintoshes and Windows PCs.
⇒ See also DESKTOP PUBLISHING; IMAGE ENHANCEMENT; PAINT PROGRAM.

Adobe PostScript *n.* POSTSCRIPT.

ADPCM Adaptive Differential Pulse-Code Modulation: a form of *pulse-code modulation (PCM)* that produces a digital signal with a lower bit rate than standard PCM. ADPCM records only the difference between samples and adjusts the coding scale dynamically to accommodate large and small differences.
⇒ See also MODULATE; PCM; SAMPLING.

ADSL asymmetric digital subscriber line: a technology that allows more data to be sent over existing copper telephone lines, known as POTS. ADSL supports data rates of from 1.5 to 9 Mbps when receiving data and from 16 to 640 Kbps when sending data. ADSL requires a special ADSL modem. It is not currently available to the general public except in trial areas.
⇒ See also ISDN; POTS; SDSL.

Advanced Differential Pulse-Code Modulation *n.* See ADPCM.

Advanced Graphics Port *n.* See AGP.

Advanced Micro Devices *n.* See AMD.

Advanced Power Management *n.* See APM.

Advanced SCSI Programming Interface *n.* See ASPI.

AFC Application Foundation Classes: a set of Microsoft foundation classes written entirely in Java. The AFC sits on top of the Java Development Kit (JDK) and extends Sun's Abstract Windows Toolkit (AWT).
⇒ See also AWT; CLASS; IFC; JAVA; JDK; MFC.

agent *n.* a program that performs some information-gathering or information-processing task in the background. Typically, an agent is given a very small and well-defined task. Special software, for example, enables a user to configure an agent to search the Internet for certain types of information.
⇒ See also ARTIFICIAL INTELLIGENCE; DAEMON.

aggregate function *n.* a function that performs a computation on a set of values rather than on a single value. For example, finding the average or mean of a list of numbers is an aggregate function. All database management and spreadsheet systems support a set of aggregate functions that can operate on a set of selected records or cells.
⇒ See also DATABASE MANAGEMENT SYSTEM; FUNCTION; SPREADSHEET.

AGP *n.* Accelerated Graphics Port: an interface specification developed by Intel Corporation. AGP is based on PCI but is designed especially for the throughput demands of 3-D graphics. AGP introduces a dedicated point-to-point channel so that the graphics controller can directly access main memory.
⇒ See also 3-D GRAPHICS; 3-D SOFTWARE; GRAPHICS AC-CELERATOR; NLX; PCI; TEXTURE.

AI ARTIFICIAL INTELLIGENCE.

AIFF Audio Interchange File Format: a common format for storing and transmitting sampled sound. The format was developed by Apple Computer and is the standard audio format for Macintosh computers. It is also used by Silicon Graphics, Incorporated (SGI).

AIX Advanced Interactive eXecutive: a version of UNIX produced by IBM. AIX runs on a variety of computers, including PCs and workstations.
⇒ See also UNIX.

alert box *n.* a small box that appears on the display screen to give information or to warn about a potentially damaging operation. For example, it might warn that the system is deleting one or more files. Unlike dialog boxes, alert boxes do not require any user input. Also called **message box.**
⇒ See also BOX; DIALOG BOX; GRAPHICAL USER INTER-FACE; WINDOW.

algorithm *n.* a formula or set of steps for solving a particular problem. The set of rules must be unambiguous and have a clear stopping point. Algorithms

can be expressed in any language, from natural languages like English to programming languages like FORTRAN.
⇒ See also ARTIFICIAL INTELLIGENCE; BUBBLE SORT; HEAP SORT; HEURISTIC PROGRAMMING; PROGRAM; PROGRAMMING LANGUAGE; PSEUDOCODE.

alias *n.* an alternative name for an object, such as a variable, file, or device.
⇒ See also DEVICE; FILE; NAME; VARIABLE.

aliasing *n.* **1.** in computer graphics, the process by which smooth curves and other lines become jagged because the resolution of the graphics device or file is not high enough to represent a smooth curve. **2.** in digital sound, a static distortion resulting from a low sampling rate—below 40 kilohertz (Khz).
⇒ See also ANTIALIASING; JAGGIES; RESOLUTION; SMOOTHING.

alignment *n.* **1.** the arrangement of text or graphics relative to a margin. **2.** the relative positions of graphical objects.
⇒ See also DRAW PROGRAM; JUSTIFICATION; MARGINS.

alpha blending *n.* See under ALPHA CHANNEL.

alpha channel *n.* in graphics, a portion of each pixel's data that is reserved for transparency information. A 32-bit graphics system contains four channels—three 8-bit channels for red, green, and blue (RGB) and one 8-bit alpha channel. The alpha channel specifies how the pixel's colors should be merged with another pixel when the two are overlaid. Rendering overlapping objects that include an alpha value is called *alpha blending*.
⇒ See also ANIMATION; GRAPHICS; MASK; PIXEL; RGB MONITOR.

alphanumeric *adj.* utilizing the combined set of all letters in the alphabet and the numbers 0 through 9. Most operating systems allow the use of any letters or numbers in filenames but prohibit the use of many punctuation characters.
⇒ See also CHARACTER; SPECIAL CHARACTER.

Alpha Processor *n.* a powerful RISC processor developed by Digital Equipment Corporation and used in its line of workstations and servers. It is the only microprocessor, other than x86 microprocessors, that runs Windows NT.
⇒ See also MICROPROCESSOR; RISC; WINDOWS NT; WORKSTATION.

alpha testing *n.* See under ALPHA VERSION.

alpha version *n.* a very early version of a software product. Typically, software goes through two stages of testing. The first stage, called *alpha testing*, is often performed by users within the organization developing the software. The second stage, called *beta testing*, generally involves a limited number of external users.
⇒ See also BETA TEST; DEBUG.

Alta Vista *n.* a software firm associated with Digital Equipment Corporation (DEC) that offers products used to locate and manage information on the Internet or an intranet. The Alta Vista search service contains one of the largest Web indices.
⇒ See also DEC; EXCITE; HOTBOT; INFOSEEK; LYCOS; MAGELLAN; OPEN TEXT; SEARCH ENGINE; SPIDER; WEBCRAWLER; WORLD WIDE WEB; YAHOO!.

Alt key *n.* Alternate key: a key that is similar to a second Control key. It is held down while pressing another key. The meaning of any Alt key combination depends on which application is running.
⇒ See also CONTROL CHARACTER; KEYBOARD; OPTION KEY.

ALU arithmetic logic unit: the part of a computer that performs all arithmetic computations and all comparison operations. The ALU is one component of the CPU.
⇒ See also CPU.

AMD Advanced Micro Devices: a manufacturer of chips for personal computers. AMD is challenging Intel with a set of Intel-compatible microprocessors.
⇒ See also CYRIX; INTEL; INTEL MICROPROCESSORS; K6; MICROPROCESSOR; MMX; PENTIUM MICROPROCESSOR.

American National Standards Institute *n.* See ANSI.

American Standard Code for Information Interchange *n.* See ASCII.

America Online *n.* a popular online service. *Abbr.:* AOL
⇒ See also COMPUSERVE INFORMATION SERVICE; MSN; ONLINE SERVICE.

Amiga *n.* a family of personal computers originally produced by Commodore Business Machines and built around the Motorola 680x0 line of microprocessors. Amigas are powerful computers that have extra microprocessors to handle graphics and sound generation. Although the Amiga operating system is not compatible with other PC operating systems, emulation programs enable the Amiga to run PC, Macintosh, and even UNIX programs.
⇒ See also GRAPHICS; MICROPROCESSOR; MIDI; PERSONAL COMPUTER.

analog *adj.* of or being a mechanism that represents data by measurement to a continuous physical variable. Early attempts at building computers used analog techniques, but today almost all computers are digital.
⇒ See also DAC; DIGITAL.

analog monitor *n.* the traditional type of color display screen that has been used for years in televisions.
⇒ See also ANALOG; CRT; DIGITAL; DIGITAL MONITOR; FLAT-PANEL DISPLAY; MONITOR; MULTISCANNING MONITOR; VIDEO ADAPTER.

anchor *v.t.* in desktop publishing, to fix (a graphical object) so that its position relative to some other object remains the same during repagination: *to anchor a picture next to a piece of text.*
⇒ See also DESKTOP PUBLISHING.

AND operator *n.* a Boolean operator that returns a value of TRUE if both its operands are TRUE, and FALSE otherwise.
⇒ See also BOOLEAN OPERATOR; OPERAND; OPERATOR.

animated GIF *n.* a type of GIF image that can be animated by combining several images into a single GIF file. Applications that support the animated GIF standard, *GIF89A*, cycle through each image.
⇒ See also ANIMATION; GIF.

animation *n.* a simulation of movement created by displaying a series of pictures, or frames. Many software applications enable the user to create animations that can be displayed on a computer monitor.
⇒ See also VIDEO; 3-D GRAPHICS; 3-D SOFTWARE; ALPHA CHANNEL; ANIMATED GIF; MODELING; MORPHING; MULTIMEDIA; SGI; SPRITE; TWEENING.

annotation *n.* a comment attached to a particular section of a document. Many applications enable the user to enter annotations on text documents, spreadsheets, presentations, and other objects. This is a particularly effective way to use computers to edit and review work in a workgroup environment.
⇒ See also WORKGROUP COMPUTING.

anonymous FTP *n.* a method for downloading public files using the File Transfer Protocol (FTP). The user types the word *anonymous* or the abbreviation *ftp* as a username; the password can be anything, as an e-mail address or simply the word *guest.*
⇒ See also DOWNLOAD; FTP.

ANSI (an′sē), *n.* American National Standards Institute: a voluntary organization that creates standards for the computer industry. In addition to programming languages, ANSI sets standards for a wide range of technical areas, from electrical specifications to communications protocols.
⇒ See also FDDI; PORTABLE; STANDARD.

ANSI Character Set *n.* a collection of special characters (including many foreign characters, special punctuation, and business symbols) and associated codes adopted by the ANSI standards organization.
⇒ See also ASCII; ISO LATIN 1.

ANSI.SYS (an′sē dot′sis′), *n.* a DOS device driver that makes a monitor conform to the ANSI standard, which specifies a series of escape sequences that cause the monitor to behave in various ways.
⇒ See also ANSI; BIOS; CONFIG.SYS; DRIVER; ESCAPE SEQUENCE.

answer-only modem *n.* a modem that can receive messages but cannot send them. Only the

computer

most inexpensive modems are answer-only.

⇒ See also MODEM.

antialiasing *n.* in computer graphics, a software technique for diminishing jaggies by surrounding the stairsteps with intermediate shades of gray (for gray-scaling devices) or color (for color devices). Although this reduces the jagged appearance of the lines, it also makes them fuzzier.

⇒ See also JAGGIES; RESOLUTION; SMOOTHING.

antistatic mat *n.* a mat on which one can stand while repairing a computer or adding expansion cards. The mat absorbs static electricity, which might otherwise damage electronic components. Another way to eliminate damage caused by static electricity is to wear an antistatic wristband.

antivirus program *n.* a utility that searches a hard disk and memory for viruses and removes them. Most antivirus programs include an update feature that enables the program to download profiles of new viruses and thereby detect and destroy them.

⇒ See also MACRO VIRUS; VIRUS.

AOL AMERICA ONLINE.

Apache Web server *n.* a public-domain Web server developed by a loosely knit group of programmers. Because it was developed from existing NCSA code plus various patches, it was called *a patchy server* — hence the name *Apache server*. By some estimates, it is used to host more than 50 percent of all Web sites in the world.

⇒ See also LINUX; WEB SERVER.

API application program interface: a set of routines, protocols, and tools for building software applications. A good API makes it easier to develop a program by providing all the building blocks. A programmer puts the blocks together.

⇒ See also APPLICATION; HLLAPI; INTERFACE; OPERATING ENVIRONMENT; ROUTINE; RPC; SDK; TAPI; TSAPI; WIN32.

APM Advanced Power Management: an API developed by Intel and Microsoft that allows developers to include power management in BIOSes. APM defines a layer between the hardware and the operating system that effectively shields the programmer from hardware details.

⇒ See also ACPI; POWER MANAGEMENT.

app *n.* *Informal.* an application program; application software. A *killer app* is an application that surpasses its competitors.

⇒ See also APPLICATION.

append *v.t.* to add (something) at the end: *to append a field to a record.*

⇒ See also CONCATENATE; INSERT.

Apple Computer *n.* a personal-computer company founded in 1976 by Steven Jobs and Steve Wozniak. In addition to inventing new technologies, Apple has often been the first to bring sophisticated technologies to the personal computer.

⇒ See also GRAPHICAL USER INTERFACE; LOCALTALK; MACINTOSH COMPUTER; NEXTSTEP; PLUG-AND-PLAY; POWERPC; QUICKTIME; RISC.

Apple Desktop bus *n.* See ADB.

Apple key *n.* a special key on Macintosh computers labeled with the Apple logo. On all but the oldest Apple computers the Apple key serves as the Command key.

⇒ See also COMMAND KEY.

Apple Macintosh computer *n.* MACINTOSH COMPUTER.

AppleScript *n.* a scripting language developed by Apple Computer that is integrated into the MacOS starting with System 7.5. AppleScript provides an easy way to automate common tasks and is powerful enough to automate complex tasks and customize applications.

⇒ See also MACOS; MACRO; SCRIPT.

applet *n.* a program designed to be executed from within another application. Applets cannot be executed directly from the operating system. A well-designed applet can be invoked from many different applications.

⇒ See also APPLICATION; COMPONENT; JAVA; OLE; SERVLET.

AppleTalk *n.* an inexpensive local-area network (LAN) architecture built into all Apple Macintosh computers and laser printers.

⇒ See also LOCAL-AREA NETWORK; LOCALTALK; MACINTOSH COMPUTER; TOPOLOGY.

application *n.* a program or group of programs designed for end users. Application software includes database programs, word processors, and spreadsheets.

⇒ See also APPLET; APPLICATION SHARING; END USER; LEGACY APPLICATION; SYSTEMS SOFTWARE; UTILITY.

Application Foundation Classes *n.* See AFC.

Application Program Interface *n.* See API.

application sharing *n.* a feature of many video-conferencing applications that enables the conference participants to run the same application simultaneously. The application itself resides on only one of the machines connected to the conference.

⇒ See also APPLICATION; VIDEOCONFERENCING; WHITEBOARD.

application software *n.* See under APPLICATION.

Application Specific Integrated Circuit *n.* See ASIC.

applications software *n.* See under APPLICATION.

ARC (ärk), *n.* a data compression format, popular among bulletin board systems (BBSs), that produces files with names ending in a *.arc* extension.

⇒ See also DATA COMPRESSION; ZIP.

Archie *n.* a program that allows the user to search for files anywhere on the Internet by filename.

⇒ See also FILENAME; GOPHER; INTERNET.

architecture *n.* a fundamental underlying design of hardware, software, or both. The architecture of a system always defines its broad outlines and may also define precise mechanisms.

⇒ See also CLIENT/SERVER ARCHITECTURE; FUNCTIONAL SPECIFICATION; MODULAR ARCHITECTURE; OPEN ARCHITECTURE; STANDARD.

archival backup *n.* a type of backup in which all files are copied to a backup storage device. Also called **full backup**.

⇒ See also ARCHIVE; BACKUP; INCREMENTAL BACKUP.

archive *v.t.* **1.** to copy (files) to a long-term storage medium for backup. Large computer systems often have two layers of backup, the first of which is a disk drive. Periodically, the files on the disk are then archived to a second storage device, usually a tape drive. **2.** to compress (a file). —*n.* **3.** a disk, tape, or directory that contains files that have been backed up. **4.** a file that contains one or more files in a compressed format.

⇒ See also ARC; ARCHIVAL BACKUP; ATTRIBUTE; BACKUP.

ARCnet *n.* Attached Resource Computer network: one of the oldest, simplest, and least expensive types of local-area network.

⇒ See also ETHERNET; LOCAL-AREA NETWORK; TOKEN-RING NETWORK.

area chart *n.* a type of presentation graphic that emphasizes a change in values by filling in the portion of the graph beneath the line connecting various data points.

⇒ See also PRESENTATION GRAPHICS.

areal density *n.* the amount of data that can be packed onto a storage medium. Areal densities are generally measured in gigabits per square inch. The term is useful for comparing different types of media, such as magnetic disks and optical disks.

⇒ See also DENSITY; DISK; OPTICAL DISK.

argument *n.* a variable to which a value will be assigned when a program is run. It is given in parentheses following a function name and used to calculate the function.

⇒ See also OPTION; PARAMETER; ROUTINE.

arithmetic expression *n.* an expression that represents a numeric value. Other types of expressions can represent character or Boolean values.

⇒ See also EXPRESSION.

arithmetic logic unit *n.* See ALU.

arithmetic operator *n.* See under OPERATOR.

ARP Address Resolution Protocol: a TCP/IP protocol used to convert an IP address into a physical address, such as an Ethernet address.

⇒ See also DLC; IP ADDRESS; TCP/IP.

ARPANET *n.* a large wide-area network created by the U.S. Defense Advanced Research Project Agency (ARPA). In 1969 it served as a testbed for new networking technologies, linking many universities and research centers.
⇒ See also INTERNET; NSFNET.

array *n.* in programming, a series of objects that are all of the same size and type, such as a series of integers or characters.
⇒ See also DATA STRUCTURE; DATA TYPE; MATRIX; SUBSCRIPT; VECTOR.

arrow key *n.* one of usually four keys for moving the cursor or insertion point right, left, up, or down. When combined with the Shift, Function, Control, or Alt keys (on PCs), the arrow keys can have different meanings. For example, pressing Ctrl + Right arrow might move the cursor to the right one word at a time. On Macintoshes, the arrow keys can be combined with the Shift, Option, and Command keys.
⇒ See also KEYBOARD.

artificial intelligence (AI) *n.* the branch of computer science concerned with making computers behave like humans. The term was coined in 1956 by John McCarthy at the Massachusetts Institute of Technology. The greatest advances in artificial intelligence have occurred in the field of game playing. The best computer chess programs are now capable of beating humans. In the area of robotics, computers are now widely used in assembly plants, but they are capable only of very limited tasks. Natural-language processing offers the greatest potential rewards because it would allow people to interact with computers without specialized knowledge.
⇒ See also COMPUTER SCIENCE; CYBERNETICS; EXPERT SYSTEM; FUZZY LOGIC; GENETIC PROGRAMMING; HEURISTIC PROGRAMMING; LISP; PROLOG; ROBOTICS; VOICE RECOGNITION.

AS/400 Application System/400: a line of IBM minicomputers introduced in 1988 and still popular today.
⇒ See also IBM; MINICOMPUTER.

ascender *n.* in typography, the portion of a lowercase letter that rises above the main body of the letter. For example, the letter *t*'s ascender is the part of the vertical line above the horizontal line.
⇒ See also BASELINE; DESCENDER; X-HEIGHT.

ASCII (as′kē), *n.* American Standard Code for Information Interchange: a code for representing English characters as numbers, with each letter assigned a number from 0 to 127. Most computers use ASCII codes to represent text, which makes it possible to transfer data from one computer to another.
⇒ See also ANSI CHARACTER SET; ASCII FILE; CHARACTER SET; EBCDIC; EXTENDED ASCII; ISO LATIN 1; TEXT FILE; UNICODE.

ASCII file *n.* a text file in which each byte represents one character according to the ASCII code. ASCII characters include spaces and punctuation, but an ASCII, or *plain text*, file will not include the kind of formatting, like bolded text, normally present in a word-processed file.
⇒ See also ASCII; PLAIN TEXT; BINARY FILE.

ASIC (ā′sik), *n.* Application Specific Integrated Circuit: a chip designed for a particular application. ASICs are built by connecting existing circuit building blocks in new ways.
⇒ See also CHIP; INTEGRATED CIRCUIT.

ASP ACTIVE SERVER PAGES.

aspect ratio *n.* in computer graphics, the relative horizontal and vertical sizes. For example, if a graphic has an aspect ratio of 2:1, the width is twice as large as the height. When resizing graphics, it is important to maintain the aspect ratio.
⇒ See also AUTOSIZING; GRAPHICS.

ASPI Advanced SCSI Programming Interface: an interface specification for sending commands to a SCSI host adapter. ASPI has become a de facto standard.
⇒ See also SCSI.

assembler *n.* a program that translates programs from assembly language to machine language.
⇒ See also ASSEMBLY LANGUAGE; MACHINE LANGUAGE.

assembly language *n.* a programming language

that is once removed from a computer's machine language. Assembly languages have the same structure and set of commands as machine languages, but they enable a programmer to use names instead of numbers. Most programs are now written in a high-level language, but assembly language is used when speed is essential or an operation is required that is impossible in a high-level language.
⇒ See also ASSEMBLER; COMPILE; LOW-LEVEL LANGUAGE; MACHINE LANGUAGE; PROGRAMMING LANGUAGE.

assign *v.t.* to give (a value) to a variable. In many languages, a value is assigned by using the equal sign (=), as in the statement x = 5.
⇒ See also OPERATOR; STATEMENT; VARIABLE.

associate *v.t.* to link (a certain type of file) to a specific application. In MS-DOS and Microsoft Windows environments, the file's type is specified by its three-character extension, such as the .DOC extension, which identifies Microsoft Word documents. Once a file type has been associated with an application, selecting any file of that type automatically starts its associated application.
⇒ See also EXTENSION; FILENAME.

Association for Computing Machinery *n.* See ACM.

asterisk *n.* a punctuation mark denoted by a snowflake shape (*). In many operating systems and applications, the asterisk is used as a wildcard symbol to represent any string of characters. It is also used to denote multiplication, as in n * 2.5.
⇒ See also WILDCARD CHARACTER.

asymmetric digital subscriber line *n.* See ADSL.

asymmetric encryption *n.* See under PUBLIC-KEY ENCRYPTION.

async *adj.* ASYNCHRONOUS.

asynchronous *adj.* not synchronized; not occurring at predetermined or regular intervals. This term is usually used to describe communications in which data can be transmitted intermittently rather than in a steady stream. Most communications between computers and devices are asynchronous.
⇒ See also COMMUNICATIONS; FLOW CONTROL; ISOCHRONOUS; START BIT; STOP BIT.

Asynchronous Transfer Mode *n.* See ATM.

AT advanced technology: an IBM PC model that includes an Intel 80286 microprocessor, a 1.2-MB floppy drive, and an 84-key AT keyboard. Today the term is used more generally to refer to any PC with an 80286 processor.
⇒ See also INTEL MICROPROCESSORS; PC.

ATA AT Attachment: a disk drive implementation that integrates the controller on the disk drive itself. There are several versions of ATA.
⇒ See also CONTROLLER; DISK DRIVE; EIDE; IDE INTERFACE; PIO; ULTRA ATA.

AT bus *n.* the expansion bus on the IBM PC/AT and compatible computers. The AT bus, which runs at 8 megahertz and has a 16-bit data path, is the de facto standard for PCs.
⇒ See also BACKWARD COMPATIBLE; BUS; EISA; EXPANSION BOARD; IBM PC; INDUSTRY STANDARD ARCHITECTURE (ISA) BUS; LOCAL BUS; MICRO CHANNEL ARCHITECTURE (MCA); PCI; VL-Bus.

AT command set *n.* the de facto standard language for controlling modems. The AT command set is recognized by virtually all personal computer modems.
⇒ See also HAYES COMPATIBLE; MODEM.

AT keyboard *n.* an 84-key keyboard introduced with the PC/AT. It was later replaced with the 101-key Enhanced Keyboard.
⇒ See also ENHANCED KEYBOARD.

ATM Asynchronous Transfer Mode: a network technology based on transferring data in cells or packets of a fixed size. The small, constant cell size allows ATM equipment to transmit video, audio, and computer data over the same network.
⇒ See also CELL RELAY; ETHERNET; FDDI; FRAME RELAY; INTERNET; IP SWITCHING; QoS; TCP/IP.

Attached Resource Computer Network *n.* ARCNET.

attachment *n.* a file attached to an e-mail mes-

sage. Many e-mail systems support only text files as e-mail. If the attachment is a binary file or formatted text file, it must be encoded before it is sent and decoded once it is received.
⇒ See also E-MAIL.

Attachment Unit Interface *n.* See AUI.

attribute *n.* **1.** a property or characteristic. In a word processing application, an underlined word is said to have the *underline attribute*. In database systems, a field can have various attributes. **2.** in DOS systems, every file has *file attributes* that indicate, for example, whether the file is read-only, whether it needs to be backed up, and whether it is visible or hidden.
⇒ See also DOS; FIELD; FILE; HIDDEN FILE.

ATX the modern shape and layout of PC motherboards. It improves on the previous standard, the *Baby AT form factor*, by rotating the orientation of the board 90 degrees. This allows for a more efficient design.
⇒ See also ATX; BABY AT; FORM FACTOR; MOTHERBOARD.

.au See under AU.

AU audio: a common format for sound files on UNIX machines. It is also the standard audio file format for the Java programming language. AU files generally end with a *.au* extension.
⇒ See also DIGITAL AUDIO; MIDI; WAV.

audio card *n.* SOUND CARD.

Audio Interchange File Format *n.* See AIFF.

audit trail *n.* a record showing who has accessed a computer system and what operations he or she has performed during a given period of time. Audit trails are useful both for maintaining security and for recovering lost transactions.
⇒ See also LOG FILE; SECURITY.

AUI Attachment Unit Interface: the portion of the Ethernet standard that specifies how a cable is to be connected to an Ethernet card.
⇒ See also COAXIAL CABLE; ETHERNET; NETWORK INTERFACE CARD.

authentication *n.* the process of identifying an individual, usually based on a username and password.
⇒ See also AUTHORIZATION; BIOMETRICS; CHALLENGE-RESPONSE; CHAP; DIGITAL SIGNATURE; KERBEROS; PAP; PASSWORD; RADIUS; USERNAME.

authoring tool *n.* a program used to write hypertext or multimedia applications. Authoring tools usually enable the author to create a final application by linking objects, such as a paragraph of text and an illustration.
⇒ See also HYPERTEXT; MULTIMEDIA; PROGRAMMING LANGUAGE; SCRIPT.

authorization *n.* the process of granting or denying access to a network resource.
⇒ See also ACCESS CONTROL; AUTHENTICATION; EXTRANET; SECURITY.

authorware *n.* AUTHORING TOOL.

auto-answer *n.* a feature supported by many modems that enables a computer to accept incoming calls even if no one is present. All fax machines are auto-answer.
⇒ See also FAX MACHINE; FAX MODEM; MODEM.

autoexec.bat *n.* automatically executed batch file: the file that DOS automatically executes when a

computer boots up.
⇒ See also BATCH FILE; BOOT.

automatic acceleration *n.* DYNAMIC ACCELERATION.

automatic recalculation *n.* in spreadsheets, a mode in which all cells are recalculated whenever a value changes in one. Alternatively, if *manual recalculation* is specified, the user must instruct the application to recalculate.
⇒ See also RECALCULATE; SPREADSHEET.

auto-redial *n.* a feature supported by many modems that allows the modem to continue redialing a number until it makes a connection.
⇒ See also MODEM.

auto-repeat *n.* a feature of some keys on computer keyboards that causes them to repeat as long as they are held down.
⇒ See also KEYBOARD.

autosave *n.* a feature supported by many applications in which the program automatically saves data files at predetermined intervals.
⇒ See also CRASH; SAVE; WORD PROCESSING.

autosizing *n.* a monitor's ability to automatically adjust the raster, depending on the resolution of signals being received.
⇒ See also ASPECT RATIO; MONITOR; RASTER; RESOLUTION; SVGA; VGA; VIDEO ADAPTER.

autosync monitor *n.* MULTISCANNING MONITOR.

autotracing *n.* the process of converting a bit-mapped image (or raster image) into a vector image. In a bit-mapped image, each object is represented by a pattern of dots, whereas in a vector image every object is defined geometrically.
⇒ See also BIT MAP; BIT-MAPPED GRAPHICS; EPS; OPTICAL SCANNER; PCX; PostScript; TIFF; VECTOR GRAPHICS.

AUX *n.* Auxiliary port: the logical name in DOS systems for the standard communications port.
⇒ See also COM; PORT.

A/UX (ôks, oks), *n.* Apple's version of UNIX, which runs on some versions of the Macintosh.
⇒ See also UNIX.

auxiliary storage *n.* MASS STORAGE.

avatar *n.* **1.** a graphical icon that represents a real person in a cyberspace system. 3-D avatars even change shape, depending on what they are doing (for example, walking or sitting). **2.** a common name for the superuser account on UNIX systems.
⇒ See also CHAT; CYBERSPACE; MUD; VIRTUAL REALITY.

AVI Audio Video Interleave: the file format for Microsoft's Video for Windows standard.
⇒ See also VIDEO FOR WINDOWS.

awk *n.* an interpreted programming language that is included in most versions of UNIX. The name is derived from the initials of its creators—Alfred A(ho), Peter W(einberger), and Brian K(ernighan).
⇒ See also PERL; PROGRAMMING LANGUAGE.

AWT Abstract Windows Toolkit: the Java API that enables programmers to develop Java applications with GUI components, such as windows, buttons, and scroll bars. Ideally, the AWT should enable any Java application to appear the same in a Windows, Macintosh, and UNIX environment. In practice, however, most Java applications look slightly different on each platform.
⇒ See also AFC; GRAPHICAL USER INTERFACE; IFC; JAVA; VIRTUAL MACHINE.

a B c d e f g h i j k l m n o p q r s t u v w x y z

Baby AT, *n.* the form factor used by most PC motherboards prior to 1998, replaced by the ATX form factor.
⇒ See also ATX; FORM FACTOR; LPX; NLX.

backbone, *n.* another term for *bus*, the main wire that connects nodes: often used to describe the main network connections composing the Internet.
⇒ See also BUS; HIPPI; MAE; NAP; NETWORK; NODE; NSP; T-3 CARRIER; vBNS.

back end, *n.* See under FRONT END.

background *n.* **1.** in a multitasking computer system, a process that can access data stored on a disk and write data to the video display but that cannot accept interactive output from a user. **2.** the area of a display screen not covered by characters and graphics.
⇒ See also DISPLAY SCREEN; FOREGROUND; MONITOR; MULTITASKING.

backlighting, *n.* a technique used to make flat-panel displays easier to read.
⇒ See also BACKGROUND; FLAT-PANEL DISPLAY; NOTEBOOK COMPUTER; SUPERTWIST.

backplane, *n.* a circuit board containing sockets into which other circuit boards can be plugged. *Active backplanes* contain logical circuitry that performs computing functions. *Passive backplanes* contain almost no computing circuitry.
⇒ See also MOTHERBOARD; PRINTED CIRCUIT BOARD; VME BUS.

backslash, *n.* the *backslash* character is \, as against the simple *slash* or *forward slash* character, which is /. The backslash represents the root directory in DOS and Windows systems and is also used to separate directory names and filenames in a pathname.
⇒ See also PATHNAME; ROOT DIRECTORY.

backspace, *n.* a character that causes the cursor to move backward one character space, possibly deleting the preceding character.
⇒ See also ASCII; BACKSPACE KEY; CURSOR; KEYBOARD; POINTER.

Backspace key, *n.* a key that moves the cursor or insertion point backward one character space and usually deletes the character to the left of the cursor or insertion point.
⇒ See also ARROW KEYS; BACKSPACE; DELETE KEY; KEYBOARD.

back up *v.t.* to copy (files) to a second medium (a disk or tape) as a precaution in case the first medium fails.
⇒ See also 3480, 3490; ARCHIVAL BACKUP; ARCHIVE; DATA COMPRESSION; DATA INTEGRITY; DMA; HSM.

backup *n.* **1.** the act of backing up. **2.** a substitute or alternative: usu. refers to a disk or tape that contains a copy of data.

backward compatible *adj.* **1.** of a program, able to use files and data created with an older version of the same program. **2.** of a computer, able to run the same software as the previous model of the computer. Also called **downward compatible**.
⇒ See also COMPATIBLE; UPWARD COMPATIBLE.

bad sector *n.* a portion of a disk that cannot be used because it is flawed.
⇒ See also DISK; FORMAT; SECTOR.

BAK file *n.* in DOS systems, a file with a .BAK extension, indicating that it is a backup.
⇒ See also AUTOSAVE; EXTENSION.

ballistic tracking *n.* DYNAMIC ACCELERATION.

banding *n.* the presence of extraneous lines in a printed page.
⇒ See also COLOR PRINTER.

bandwidth *n.* the amount of data that can be transmitted in a fixed amount of time: usu. expressed in bits per second (bps) or bytes per second for digital devices and in cycles per second or Hertz (Hz) for analog devices.
⇒ See also BUS; CIR; EISA; I/O; LATENCY; PCI.

bar chart *n.* in presentation graphics, a type of graph in which different values are represented by rectangular bars.
⇒ See also PRESENTATION GRAPHICS.

barrel distortion *n.* See under PINCUSHION DISTORTION.

base address *n.* an address that serves as a reference point for other addresses.
⇒ See also ADDRESS; OFFSET; RELATIVE ADDRESS.

baseband transmission *n.* a type of digital data transmission in which each medium (wire) carries only one signal, or channel, at a time: used for communications from the computer to devices (printers, monitors, and so on), communications via modems, and most networks.
⇒ See also 10BASE-2; BROADBAND ISDN (B-ISDN); BROADBAND TRANSMISSION; CHANNEL; COMMUNICATIONS; ISDN; LOCAL-AREA NETWORK; NETWORK.

baseline *n.* in typography, the imaginary line on which characters sit.
⇒ See also ASCENDER; DESCENDER; FONT; TYPEFACE; X-HEIGHT.

base memory *n.* CONVENTIONAL MEMORY.

BASIC *n.* Beginner's All-purpose Symbolic Instruc-
tion Code: one of the earliest and simplest high-level programming languages, used for a wide variety of business applications: developed by John Kemeney and Thomas Kurtz at Dartmouth College.
⇒ See also GW-BASIC; HIGH-LEVEL LANGUAGE; INTERPRETER; MUMPS; PROGRAMMING LANGUAGE; QBASIC; VISUAL BASIC.

basic input/output system *n.* See BIOS.

Basic-Rate Interface *n.* See BRI.

batch file *n.* a file that contains a sequence, or batch, of commands that are always executed together: ends with a .BAT extension in DOS systems. Also called **command file**, **shell script**.
⇒ See also AUTOEXEC.BAT; BAT FILE; BATCH PROCESSING; DOS.

batch processing *n.* executing a series of noninteractive jobs all at one time.
⇒ See also BATCH FILE; INTERACTIVE; TRANSACTION PROCESSING.

BAT file *n.* a batch file, so called because the filename ends with a .BAT extension in DOS systems.
⇒ See also BATCH FILE; EXTENSION; FILENAME.

battery pack *n.* a rechargeable battery used in portable computer devices, such as notebook computers, often containing nickel cadmium (NiCad), nickel metal hydride (NiMH), or lithium-ion batteries.
⇒ See also LITHIUM-ION BATTERY; NiCad BATTERY PACK; NiMH BATTERY PACK; POWER MANAGEMENT.

baud (bôd), *n.* the number of signaling elements or bits that occur each second in transmitting data, as over a phone line. [named after J. M. E. Baudot, the inventor of the Baudot telegraph code]
⇒ See also BPS; MODEM.

baud rate *n.* BAUD.

bay *n.* a site in a personal computer where a hard or floppy disk drive, CD-ROM drive, or tape drive can be installed. Also called **drive bay**.
⇒ See also DISK DRIVE; EXPANSION BOARD; MASS STORAGE; SLOT.

BBS BULLETIN BOARD SYSTEM.

BCD binary-coded decimal: a format for representing decimal numbers (integers) in which each digit is represented by four bits (a nibble).
⇒ See also BINARY; BINARY FORMAT; DECIMAL; HEXADECIMAL; NIBBLE.

B-channel *n.* Bearer-Channel: the main data channel in an ISDN connection.
⇒ See also BRI; CHANNEL; ISDN.

BEDO DRAM *n.* Burst EDO DRAM: a type of EDO DRAM that can process four memory addresses in one burst but stay synchronized with the CPU clock for short periods (bursts) only and cannot keep up with processors whose buses run faster than 66 MHz.
⇒ See also BURST MODE; DRAM; EDO DRAM; PIPELINE BURST CACHE; RDRAM; SDRAM; SLDRAM.

Bell 103 *n.* the de facto standard protocol in the United States for transmitting data over telephone lines at transmission rates of 300 baud.
⇒ See also ASYNCHRONOUS; BAUD; CCITT; COMMUNICATIONS PROTOCOL; FULL DUPLEX; PROTOCOL.

Bell 212A *n.* the de facto standard protocol in the United States for transmitting data over telephone lines at transmission rates of 1,200 baud.
⇒ See also ASYNCHRONOUS; BAUD; CCITT; COMMUNICATIONS PROTOCOL; FULL DUPLEX; PROTOCOL.

bells and whistles *n.pl.* extra, often unnecessary, features provided by an application.
⇒ See also FEATURE.

benchmark *n.* a test used to compare performance of hardware and/or software.
⇒ See also FLOPS; SPEC.

BeOS *n.* an operating system developed by Be, Inc., that runs on the PowerPC platform and Intel x86 processors and provides a modern graphical user interface (GUI), preemptive multitasking, multithreading, and built-in support for symmetric multiprocessing (SMP).
⇒ See also MAC OS; OPERATING SYSTEM; POWERPC; SMP.

Berkeley Internet Name Domain *n.* See BIND.

Bernoulli disk drive *n.* a special type of floppy

disk drive from Iomega Corporation that was faster and had greater storage capacity than traditional floppy drives: no longer being produced.
⇒ See also DISK; HARD DISK DRIVE; MASS STORAGE.

beta *n.* BETA TEST.

beta test *n.* the last stage of testing for a computer product prior to commercial release, usually involving sending the product to various beta test sites outside the company for real-word exposure to situations that would be encountered by users: often preceded by a round of testing called alpha testing, conducted inside the company.
⇒ See also ALPHA VERSION; APPLICATION.

Bézier curve (bez/ē ā′), *n.* curved lines (splines) defined by mathematical formulas. Nearly all draw programs support Bézier curves.
⇒ See also DRAW PROGRAM; GRAPHICS; NURBS; SPLINE; VECTOR GRAPHICS.

BFT BINARY FILE TRANSFER.

BGP Border Gateway Protocol: an Internet protocol that enables groups of routers (called autonomous systems) to share routing information so that efficient, loop-free routes can be established.
⇒ See also ROUTER; ROUTING.

Big Blue *n.* an informal name for International Business Machines Corporation (IBM). Blue is IBM's corporate color.
⇒ See also IBM PC.

big-endian *adj.* denoting the most significant bytes in multibyte data types. In *big-endian* architectures, the leftmost bytes (those with a lower address) are most significant. In *little-endian* architectures, the rightmost bytes are most significant. Many mainframe computers use a big-endian architecture. Most modern computers, including PCs, use the little-endian system. The PowerPC system, however, is *bi-endian* because it can understand both.
⇒ See also BYTE; DATA TYPE.

bilevel printer *n.* a type of printer that can print only two levels of intensity for each dot—on or off. Shading is created by varying the position of the dots, or dithering.
⇒ See also COLOR PRINTER; CONTINUOUS TONE; CONTONE PRINTER; DITHERING; PRINTER.

binary *adj.* pertaining to a system of numerical rotation to the base 2 in which each place of a number, expressed as 0 or 1, corresponds to a power of 2. Computers are based on a binary number system.
⇒ See also BINARY FORMAT; DECIMAL; HEXADECIMAL; OCTAL.

binary-coded decimal *n.* See BCD.

binary compatible *adj.* having exactly the same data format, down to the binary level. Two files that are binary compatible have the same pattern of zeroes and ones in the data portion of the file and are therefore interchangeable.
⇒ See also BINARY FILE; COMPATIBLE; CROSS-PLATFORM; EXPORT; HETEROGENEOUS NETWORK; IMPORT.

binary digit *n.* BIT.

binary file *n.* a file stored in binary format that is computer-readable but not human-readable.
⇒ See also ASCII FILE; BINARY FORMAT; COFF; EXECUTABLE FILE.

Binary File Transfer *n.* a standard for transmitting data files using fax modems. *Abbr.*: BFT
⇒ See also CCITT.

binary format *n.* a format for representing data used by some applications for executable programs and numeric data.
⇒ See also BCD; BINARY; BINARY FILE.

binary tree *n.* a special type of tree structure in which each node has at most two leaves: often used for sorting data, as in a heap sort.
⇒ See also HEAP; HEAP SORT; TREE STRUCTURE.

BIND *n.* Berkeley Internet Name Domain: a domain name server (DNS) designed for UNIX systems based on BSD, the version of UNIX developed at the University of California's Berkeley campus.
⇒ See also DNS; DOMAIN NAME.

bind *v.t.* to assign a value to (a symbolic placeholder). The moment at which binding occurs is called *bind time* or *link time.*
⇒ See also ADDRESS; COMPILE; LINK.

binder *n.* LINKER.

BinHex *n.* an encoding scheme that can convert binary data from any type of file into ASCII characters. Encoded files generally have a .hqx extension.
⇒ See also E-MAIL; MIME; UUENCODE.

biometrics *n.* **1.** generally, the study of measurable biological characteristics. **2.** in computer security, authentication techniques that rely on measurable physical characteristics that can be automatically checked, such as computer analysis of fingerprints or speech.
⇒ See also AUTHENTICATION; ELECTRONIC COMMERCE; SECURITY.

BIOS (bī′ōs), *n.* basic input/output system: built-in software that determines what a computer can do without accessing programs from a disk: contains all the code required to control the keyboard, display screen, disk drives, etc.
⇒ See also BOOT; CMOS; ESCD; FLASH MEMORY; I/O; PNP; POST; SHADOWING.

B-ISDN BROADBAND ISDN.

bisync *adj.* binary synchronous: referring to a type of synchronous communications used primarily in mainframe networks.
⇒ See also ASYNCHRONOUS; SYNCHRONOUS.

bit *n.* binary digit: the smallest unit of information on a machine. A single bit can hold only one of two values, 0 or 1.
⇒ See also 32-BIT; ADDRESS SPACE; KILOBIT; MEGABIT; NIBBLE; REGISTER.

bit block transfer *n.* a transformation of a rectangular block of pixels, as by changing the color or shade of all pixels or rotating the entire rectangle.
⇒ See also GRAPHICS; PIXEL; VIDEO ADAPTER.

bitblt (bit′blit′), *n.* Short for BIT BLOCK TRANSFER.

bit map *n.* a representation, consisting of rows and columns of dots, of a graphics image in computer memory. The density of the dots, known as the resolution, determines how sharply the image is represented. The computer translates the bit map into pixels to display it on a monitor or ink dots to print it. Bit-mapped graphics are also called **raster graphics.**
⇒ See also BIT-MAPPED GRAPHICS; PIXEL; RESOLUTION; VECTOR GRAPHICS.

bit-mapped font *n.* See under FONT.

bit-mapped graphics *n.* the representation of graphics images as bit maps. Also called **raster graphics.**
⇒ See also BIT MAP; COMPUTER IMAGING; GRAPHICS; PNG; VECTOR GRAPHICS.

BITNET *n.* Because It's Time Network: one of the oldest and largest wide-area networks, used extensively by universities.
⇒ See also INTERNET; NETWORK; WIDE-AREA NETWORK.

bits per second *n.* See BPS.

bitwise operator *n.* an operator that manipulates individual bits rather than bytes or groups of bytes.
⇒ See also OPERATOR.

blank character *n.* the character produced when the space bar is pressed. Also called **space character.**

bleed *n.* **1.** text or graphics extending all the way to the edge of the paper, used for graphical effect and for printed tabs. —*v.i.* **2.** to run to the edge of the paper, thereby producing a bleed.

bloatware *n. Informal.* software that has many features and requires a great deal of disk space and RAM.
⇒ See also VAPORWARE.

BLOB *n.* binary large object: a collection of binary data used primarily to hold multimedia objects as a single entity in a database management system (DBMS).
⇒ See also DATABASE MANAGEMENT SYSTEM; FIELD; OBJECT.

block *n.* **1.** in word processing, a group of characters that has been highlighted for some action, such as deleting or changing the font. **2.** in data management, a group of records on a storage device. **3.** in communications, a fixed-size chunk of data that is transferred as a unit. —*v.t.* **4.** in word processing, to specify or highlight (a section of text). See

definition (1) above. Some applications call this *se-lecting*.
⇒ See also COMMUNICATIONS; SELECT; WORD PROCESS-ING; XMODEM.

block graphics *n.* graphical images created in character mode.
⇒ See also CHARACTER MODE.

BMP the standard bit-mapped graphics format used in the Windows environment. BMP files, which conventionally have names that end in a .BMP extension, store graphics in a format called *device-independent bit map (DIB)*.
⇒ See also BIT MAP; DIB; GRAPHICS FILE FORMATS.

BNC BNC CONNECTOR.

BNC connector *n.* British Naval Connector or Bayonet Nut Connector or Bayonet Neill Concelman: a type of connector used with coaxial cables and to connect some monitors.
⇒ See also 10BASE-2; COAXIAL CABLE; CONNECTOR;

board *n.* EXPANSION BOARD; PRINTED CIRCUIT BOARD.

boilerplate *n.* phrases, units of text, or graphics elements designed to be used repeatedly.
⇒ See also TEMPLATE.

boldface *n.* thick, heavy type. **This is an example of boldface**.
⇒ See also FONT.

bomb *v.i.* (of a program) to hang or end prematurely.
⇒ See also ABORT; BUG; CRASH; HANG.

bookmark *v.t.* **1.** to mark (a document, a place in a document, or the address of a Web page) for later retrieval. —*n.* **2.** a marker or address that identifies a document or a place in a document.
⇒ See also BROWSER.

Boolean expression *n.* an expression that results in a value of either TRUE or FALSE. Also called **comparison expression, conditional expression, relational expression.**
⇒ See also BOOLEAN LOGIC; BOOLEAN OPERATOR; EXPRESSION; RELATIONAL OPERATOR.

Boolean logic *n.* a form of algebra in which all values are reduced to either TRUE or FALSE: important for computer science because it fits with the binary numbering system, in which each bit has a value of either 1 or 0. [named after the 19th-century British mathematician George Boole]
⇒ See also BINARY; BOOLEAN EXPRESSION; BOOLEAN OPERATOR.

Boolean operator *n.* an operator that can be used to manipulate TRUE/FALSE values. There are five Boolean operators: AND, OR, XOR, NOR, NOT. Boolean operators are widely used in programming and in forming database queries.
⇒ See also AND OPERATOR; BOOLEAN EXPRESSION; BOOLEAN LOGIC; OR OPERATOR; NOR OPERATOR; NOT OPERATOR; XOR OPERATOR.

boot *v.t.* **1.** to start (a computer) by loading the operating system, which is essential for running all other programs. —*n.* **2.** the starting up of a computer by loading the operating system and other basic software. Turning the computer on from an off position is a *cold boot*. Resetting a computer that is already on is a *warm boot*.
⇒ See also BIOS; BOOTABLE DISKETTE; BOOTP; CLEAN BOOT; COLD BOOT; MBR; OPERATING SYSTEM; POST; WARM BOOT.

bootable diskette *n.* a diskette from which a computer can be booted if the hard disk is damaged, as by a virus. Also called **bootable floppy, boot disk, startup disk.**
⇒ See also BOOT; MBR; VIRUS.

bootable floppy *n.* BOOTABLE DISKETTE.

boot disk *n.* BOOTABLE DISKETTE.

BOOTP Bootstrap Protocol: an Internet protocol that enables a diskless workstation to boot without requiring a hard or floppy disk drive. ⇒ See also BOOT; DISKLESS WORKSTATION.

boot sector *n.* See under MBR.

Border Gateway Protocol *n.* See BGP.

Borland International *n.* a company in Scotts Valley, Calif., that provides programming and database tools.
⇒ See also C++; PASCAL; RDBMS; SPREADSHEET.

bot *n.* robot: a computer program that runs automatically.
⇒ See also ROBOT.

box *n.* **1.** in graphical user interfaces, an enclosed area, resembling a window, that appears on the screen. A *dialog box*, for example, requests some type of input or information from the user. An *alert box* appears on the screen when it is necessary to give information immediately to the user. **2.** *Informal.* a personal computer or workstation.
⇒ See also ALERT BOX; BUTTON; DIALOG BOX; GRAPHICAL USER INTERFACE; ICON; WINDOW; ZOOM.

bps bits per second: the standard measure of data transmission speeds.
⇒ See also BAUD; CCITT; COMMUNICATIONS; MODEM.

branch *n.* in tree structures, a single line of the tree that ends with a leaf.
⇒ See also DIRECTORY; TREE STRUCTURE.

Break key *n.* a key on computer keyboards that temporarily interrupts the computer's communications line.
⇒ See also KEYBOARD.

BRI Basic-Rate Interface: the basic ISDN configuration.
⇒ See also B-CHANNEL; ISDN.

bridge *n.* a protocol-independent device that connects two local-area networks (LANs) or two segments of the same LAN.
⇒ See also BROUTER; HUB; INTERNETWORKING; LOCAL-AREA NETWORK; REPEATER; ROUTER; WIDE-AREA NETWORK.

British Naval Connector *n.* BNC CONNECTOR.

broadband ISDN (B-ISDN) *n.* a standard for transmitting voice, video, and data at the same time over fiber optic telephone lines. *Abbr.:* B-ISDN
⇒ See also BPS; BROADBAND TRANSMISSION; FIBER OPTICS; ISDN; SONET.

broadband transmission *n.* a type of data transmission in which a single medium (wire) can carry several channels at once.
⇒ See also BASEBAND TRANSMISSION; BROADBAND ISDN (B-ISDN); CHANNEL; COMMUNICATIONS; LOCAL-AREA NETWORK; NETWORK.

broadcast *v.t.* to send (the same message) simultaneously to multiple recipients.
⇒ See also E-MAIL; FAX; MULTICAST; RTSP; WEBCASTING.

brouter (brou′tər), *n.* bridge router: a device that functions as both a router and a bridge.
⇒ See also BRIDGE; ROUTER.

browse *v.i.* **1.** in database systems, to look through data quickly without being able to modify it. Many database systems support a special *browse mode*, in which users can flip through fields and records quickly. Usually, data cannot be modified in browse mode. **2.** in object-oriented programming languages, to examine data structures. **3.** to view formatted documents.
⇒ See also BROWSER; DATA STRUCTURE; DATABASE MANAGEMENT SYSTEM; FIELD; RECORD; SURF.

browser *n.* Web browser: a software application used to locate and display Web pages.
⇒ See also ACTIVEX CONTROL; BROWSE; HTML; INTERNET EXPLORER; MOSAIC; NAVIGATOR; WORLD WIDE WEB; XML.

BSDI Berkeley Software Design, Inc.: a commercial supplier of Internet and networking software based on the BSD (Berkeley) version of UNIX.
⇒ See also UNIX; WEB SERVER.

bubble memory *n.* a type of nonvolatile memory composed of a thin layer of material that can be easily magnetized in only one direction. The application of a magnetic field to a circular area of this substance that is not magnetized in the same direction reduces the area to a smaller circle, or bubble.
⇒ See also EEPROM; NONVOLATILE MEMORY.

bubble sort *n.* a simple but popular sorting algorithm: used frequently as a programming exercise because it is relatively easy to understand.
⇒ See also ALGORITHM; HEAP SORT; PSEUDOCODE.

buffer *n.* **1.** a temporary storage area, usually in RAM, that holds data until the computer is ready to process it. Many programs keep track of data on a buffer and then copy the buffer to disk. —*v.t.* **2.** to move (data) into a temporary storage area.

⇒ See also CACHE; COMMAND BUFFER; DISK CACHE; SAVE; SPOOLING.

bug *n.* an error or defect in software or hardware that causes a program to malfunction.

⇒ See also BOMB; CRASH; GLITCH; HANG; MEMORY LEAK.

built-in font *n.* RESIDENT FONT.

built-in function *n.* a function that is built into an application and can be accessed by end users.

⇒ See also FUNCTION.

bullet *n.* a small graphical element used to highlight or itemize a list.

⇒ See also DINGBAT.

bulletin board system *n.* an electronic facility for collecting and relaying messages.

⇒ See also COMMUNICATIONS SOFTWARE; E-MAIL; ONLINE SERVICE.

bundled software *n.* software that is sold as part of a package with a computer or other hardware component or with other software.

⇒ See also HARDWARE; SOFTWARE.

burst mode *n.* a transmission mode in which data is sent faster than normal for a limited period of time and under special conditions.

⇒ See also BEDO DRAM; DATA TRANSFER RATE; PIPELINE BURST CACHE; WAIT STATE.

bus *n.* **1.** a collection of wires through which data is transmitted from one part of a computer to another. **2.** in networking, a central cable that connects all devices on a local-area network (LAN). Also called **backbone.**

⇒ See also 32-BIT; ACCESS.BUS; ADB; ADDRESS BUS; BUS MASTERING; CHANNEL; CLOCK SPEED; CONTROLLER; EXPANSION BUS; LOCAL BUS; PCI; USB; VME BUS.

business graphics *n.* PRESENTATION GRAPHICS.

bus mastering *n.* a feature supported by some bus architectures that enables a controller connected to the bus to communicate directly with other devices on the bus without going through the CPU.

⇒ See also BUS; PCI.

bus mouse *n.* an obsolete kind of mouse that connects to a computer via an expansion board.

⇒ See also BUS; MOUSE; SERIAL PORT.

bus network *n.* a network in which all nodes are connected to a single wire (the bus) that has two endpoints.

⇒ See also ETHERNET; RING NETWORK; STAR NETWORK; TOKEN BUS NETWORK; TOPOLOGY.

bus topology *n.* See under TOPOLOGY.

button *n.* **1.** in graphical user interfaces, a small outlined area in a dialog box that the user can click on to select an option or command. **2.** a button on a mouse that the user clicks to perform various functions, such as selecting an object.

⇒ See also CLICK; DIALOG BOX; GRAPHICAL USER INTERFACE; MOUSE; RADIO BUTTONS.

byte *n.* binary term: a unit of storage capable of holding a single character: equal to 8 bits.

⇒ See also BIG-ENDIAN; GIGABYTE; KILOBYTE; MEGABYTE; NIBBLE.

bytecode *n.* the compiled format for Java programs.

⇒ See also COMPILE; JAVA; JIT.

a b C d e f g h i j k l m n o p q r s t u v w x y z

C a programming language developed at Bell Labs in the mid-1970s: used for a variety of applications, from business programs to engineering.

⇒ See also ASSEMBLY LANGUAGE; C++; EIFFEL; HIGH-LEVEL LANGUAGE; MACHINE LANGUAGE; PROGRAMMING LANGUAGE; UNIX; VISUAL C++.

C++ a programming language developed at Bell Labs that adds object-oriented features to its predecessor, C.

⇒ See also C; HIGH-LEVEL LANGUAGE; JAVA; MFC; OBJECT-ORIENTED; PROGRAMMING LANGUAGE; SMALLTALK; VISUAL C++.

CA CERTIFICATE AUTHORITY.

cable modem *n.* a modem, designed to operate over cable TV lines, that can achieve very fast access to the World Wide Web.

⇒ See also WEBTV.

cache (kash), *n.* a special high-speed storage mechanism, either a reserved section of main memory or an independent high-speed storage area. A *memory cache* is a section of high-speed static ram (SRAM). A *disk cache* uses conventional main memory to speed access to data stored on the hard disk.

⇒ See also BUFFER; DISK CACHE; MAIN MEMORY; PIPELINE BURST CACHE; RAM DISK; TAG RAM; WRITE-BACK CACHE.

cache memory *n.* CACHE.

CAD *n.* computer-aided design: a combination of hardware and software that enables an engineer or an architect to view a design from any angle and to zoom in or out for close-ups and long-distance views. The computer also keeps track of design dependencies and changes the values of linked quantities automatically.

⇒ See also CAD/CAM; CAE; CAM; DIGITIZING TABLET; GRAPHICS; LIGHT PEN; MONITOR; MOUSE; PLOTTER; WORKSTATION.

CAD/CAM *n.* computer-aided design/computer-aided manufacturing: computer systems that can be used to design a product and to control its manufacture.

⇒ See also 3-D SOFTWARE; CAD; CADD; CAM; MODELING.

CADD computer-aided design and drafting: a CAD system with drafting features, as one that enables an engineer or an architect to insert size annotations and other notes into a design.

⇒ See also CAD; CAD/CAM.

CAE computer-aided engineering: a computer system that analyzes engineering designs. CAE systems can simulate a design under a variety of conditions to see how it works.

⇒ See also CAD; CASE.

calculator *n.* **1.** a small hand-held computer that performs mathematical calculations. **2.** a program on a computer that simulates a hand-held calculator.

⇒ See also DESK ACCESSORY (DA).

calendar *n.* a program that enables the user to record events and appointments on an electronic calendar: part of a more general category of software known as PIMs (personal information managers).

⇒ See also PIM; SCHEDULER; UTILITY.

call *v.t.* **1.** to invoke (a routine). —*n.* **2.** an invocation of a routine.

⇒ See also FUNCTION; ROUTINE.

CAM *n.* computer-aided manufacturing: the use of computer systems to help automate a factory, including real-time control, robotics, or materials requirements.

⇒ See also CAD; CAD/CAM; ROBOTICS.

camera-ready *adj.* in desktop publishing, referring to the final state of a publication before it is printed. The term arises from the old method of making a film image of pages to transfer to printing plates.

⇒ See also DESKTOP PUBLISHING; IMAGESETTER; ISP; OFFSET PRINTING.

caps *n.pl.* capital letters.

⇒ See also CASE SENSITIVE; UPPERCASE.

Caps Lock key *n.* a key on computer keyboards that, when activated, causes all subsequent alphabetic characters to be uppercase but has no effect on other keys.

⇒ See also KEYBOARD; TOGGLE; UPPERCASE.

capture *v.t.* **1.** to save (the output of a program) as the information currently visible on a display screen either to a printer or to a file. **2.** to record (keystrokes during the definition of a macro).

⇒ See also LEARN MODE; SCREEN CAPTURE.

card *n.* **1.** EXPANSION BOARD. **2.** in hypertext systems, a single page of information.

⇒ See also HYPERCARD; HYPERTEXT.

CardBus *n.* the 32-bit version of the PCMCIA PC Card standard.

⇒ See also PC CARD; PCMCIA.

caret *n.* a wedge-shaped symbol (^) generally found above the 6 on computer keyboards, sometimes used to indicate the Control key. Also called **hat.**

⇒ See also CONTROL KEY.

carpal tunnel syndrome *n.* a common form of repetitive strain injury (RSI) produced by repeating the same small movements many times.

⇒ See also ERGONOMICS.

carriage *n.* the mechanism on a printer that feeds paper.

⇒ See also PAPER FEED; PRINTER.

carriage return *n.* a special code that moves the cursor (or print head) to the beginning of the current line. *Abbr.*: cr

⇒ See also LINE FEED; RETURN.

carrier *n.* CARRIER SIGNAL, CARRIER SYSTEM, CARRIER SERVICE PROVIDER.

⇒ See also FDM; MULTIPLEX; T-1 CARRIER; T-3 CARRIER.

Carrier Sense Multiple Access/Collision Detection *n.* See CSMA/CD.

carrier service provider *n.* a company offering telephone and data communications between points in a state or in one or more countries.

carrier signal *n.* a frequency in a communications channel modulated to carry analog or digital information.

carrier system *n.* a communications system providing a number of point-to-point channels through some type of multiplexing.

cartridge *n.* **1.** a removable storage medium (tape, disk, or memory chip). **2.** for laser and ink jet printers, a container that holds the toner or ink.

⇒ See also FONT CARTRIDGE; LASER PRINTER; REMOVABLE HARD DISK; SLOT; TONER.

cartridge font *n.* FONT CARTRIDGE.

cascading delete *n.* in relational database management systems, a *referential integrity* rule specifying that when a record is deleted from one table, any linked records in a related table will also be deleted.

Cascading Style Sheets *n.* See CSS.

cascading update *n.* in relational database management systems, a *referential integrity* rule specifying that if a value in a field in one table is modified, all linked records containing that same field, with the same information, in a related table will also be modified accordingly.

cascading windows *n.pl.* windows arranged so that they overlap one another with the title bar always visible. Also called **overlaid windows.**

⇒ See also TILED WINDOWS; WINDOW.

CASE *n.* Computer Aided Software Engineering: a category of software that provides tools to automate, manage, and simplify the development process for programming teams.

⇒ See also CAE; PROGRAM.

case sensitive *adj.* referring to a program that distinguishes between uppercase (capital) and lowercase (small) letters.

⇒ See also LOWERCASE; UPPERCASE.

cathode-ray tube *n.* See CRT.

CAV Constant Angular Velocity: a technique for reading data from rotating disks in which the disk rotates at a constant number of revolutions per second regardless of what area of the disk is being accessed.

⇒ See also CD-ROM; CD-ROM PLAYER; CLV.

CBT computer-based training: a type of education in which the student learns to use computer applications by executing special training programs.

⇒ See also COURSEWARE; DISTANCE LEARNING.

CCD charge-coupled device: a chip containing semi-

conductor elements connected so that the output of one serves as the input of the next. CCDs are often used as image-detectors.

⇒ See also DIGITAL CAMERA; OPTICAL SCANNER.

CCITT Comité Consultatif International Téléphonique et Télégraphique: an organization that sets international communications standards; now known as ITU (the parent organization).

⇒ See also BAUD; BPS; COMMUNICATIONS PROTOCOL; DATA COMPRESSION; E-MAIL; FAX MACHINE; FAX MODEM; FULL DUPLEX; HALF DUPLEX; ISDN; ITU; MNP; MODEM; PROTOCOL; STANDARD; X.400; X.500.

CD COMPACT DISC.

CD-DA RED BOOK.

CDDI Copper Data Distribution Interface: a network technology capable of carrying data at 100 Mbps over unshielded twisted-pair (UTP) cable.

⇒ See also FDDI; LOCAL-AREA NETWORK; TWISTED-PAIR CABLE; UTP.

cdev (sē′dev′), *n.* control panel device: a type of Macintosh utility that enables the user to adjust basic system parameters. Also called **control panel.**

⇒ See also CONTROL PANEL.

CDF channel definition format: a specification developed by Microsoft that allows Web publishers to *push* content at users. Once a user subscribes to a CDF channel, any software that supports the CDF format will automatically receive new content posted on the channel's Web server.

⇒ See also INTERNET EXPLORER; POINTCAST; PUSH.

CDFS CD-ROM File System: the Windows 95 and 98 driver for CD-ROM players, replacing MSCDEX.

⇒ See also CD-ROM PLAYER; MSCDEX; VCACHE.

CD-I Compact Disc–Interactive: a software and hardware standard developed jointly by Philips International and Sony Corporation for storing video, audio, and binary data on compact optical disks. Also called **Green Book standard.**

⇒ See also CD-ROM; CD-ROM/XA; DVD; DVI; GREEN BOOK; OPTICAL DISK; OS/9.

CDMA Code-Division Multiple Access: a digital cellular technology in which every transmission channel varies its frequency according to a predetermined pattern to avoid interference.

⇒ See also CELLULAR; GSM; MULTIPLEX; PCS; TDM; TDMA.

CDPD Cellular Digital Packet Data: a data transmission technology developed for use on cellular phone frequencies that offers data transfer rates of up to 19.2 Kbps.

⇒ See also CELL; PACKET SWITCHING.

CD-R CD-R DRIVE.

CD-R drive *n.* Compact Disc-Recordable drive: a type of disk drive that can create CD-ROMs and audio CDs allowing users to "master" a CD-ROM or audio CD for publishing.

⇒ See also CD-ROM; CD-ROM PLAYER; CD-RW DISK; ORANGE BOOK.

CD-recordable drive *n.* CD-R DRIVE.

CD-ROM (sē′dē′rom′), *n.* Compact Disc–Read-Only Memory: a type of optical disk capable of storing large amounts of data.

⇒ See also CAV; CD-I (COMPACT DISC-INTERACTIVE); CD-ROM PLAYER; CD-ROM/XA; CD-RW DISK; CLV; COMPACT DISC; DISK; ERASABLE OPTICAL DISK; MASS STORAGE; MULTIMEDIA; OPTICAL DISK; YELLOW_BOOK.

CD-ROM drive *n.* CD-ROM PLAYER.

CD-ROM player *n.* an internal or external device in a computer that can read information from a CD-ROM. Also called **CD-ROM drive.**

⇒ See also ACCESS TIME; BAY; CAV; CD-ROM; CDFS; CLV; IDE INTERFACE; MPC; MSCDEX; MULTIMEDIA KIT; MULTIREAD; PARALLEL PORT; PHOTOCD; SCSI.

CD-ROM/XA *n.* CD-ROM/extended architecture: a specification developed by Sony, Philips, and Microsoft that enables many different types of data—audio, video, compressed video, and graphics—to be stored on a single CD-ROM.

⇒ See also CD-I (COMPACT DISC-INTERACTIVE); CD-ROM; YELLOW_BOOK.

CD-RW disk *n.* CD-Rewritable disk: a type of CD disk that can be written, erased, and rewritten.

⇒ See also CD-R DRIVE; CD-ROM; DVD+RW; DVD-RAM; DVI; MULTIREAD.

cell *n.* **1.** in spreadsheet applications, a box in which one can enter a single piece of data, text, a numeric value, or a formula. **2.** in communications and networking, a fixed-size packet of data. **3.** in cellular telephone systems, a geographic area.
⇒ See also CDPD; CELL RELAY; CELLULAR; FIELD; FORMULA; SPREADSHEET.

cell relay *n.* a system that transmits data in small, fixed-size packets or cells containing only basic path information that allows switching devices to route each cell quickly.
⇒ See also ATM; CELL; FRAME RELAY; PACKET; PACKET SWITCHING.

Cells in Frames *n.* a specification that enables ATM cells to be carried in
Ethernet packets.
⇒ See also ATM; ETHERNET.

cellular *adj.* referring to communications systems that divide a geographic region into sections, called cells, to make the most use of a limited number of transmission frequencies.
⇒ See also CDMA; CELL; GSM; PCS; TDMA.

cellular digital packet data *n.* See CDPD.

central processing unit *n.* See CPU.

centrex *n.* central office exchange service: a type of PBX service in which switching occurs at a local telephone station instead of at the company premises.
⇒ See also PBX.

Centronics interface *n.* a standard interface for connecting printers and other parallel devices.
⇒ See also ECP; EPP; INTERFACE; PARALLEL INTERFACE; STANDARD.

CERN (sûrn), *n.* European Laboratory for Particle Physics [Conseil Europeen pour le Recherche Nucleaire in French]: a research laboratory headquartered in Geneva, Switzerland, and funded by many different countries.
⇒ See also WEB SERVER; WORLD WIDE WEB.

Certificate Authority *n.* a trusted third-party organization or company that issues digital certificates used to create digital signatures and public-private key pairs: a critical component in data security and electronic commerce.
⇒ See also DIGITAL CERTIFICATE; DIGITAL SIGNATURE; ELECTRONIC COMMERCE; PKI; PUBLIC-KEY ENCRYPTION.

CGA color/graphics adapter: a graphics system for PCs introduced in 1981 by IBM: superseded by VGA systems.
⇒ See also BACKWARD COMPATIBLE; EGA; GRAPHICS MODE; IBM PC; MCGA; PALETTE; RESOLUTION; SVGA; TEXT MODE; VGA; VIDEO ADAPTER; XGA.

CGI Common Gateway Interface: a specification for transferring information between a World Wide Web server and a program. A CGI program is any program designed to accept and return data that conforms to the CGI specification.
⇒ See also ACTIVE SERVER PAGES; DYNAMIC HTML; FORM; ISAPI; JAVA; NSAPI; PERL; SERVLET; WORLD WIDE WEB.

CGM *n.* Computer Graphics Metafile: a file format designed to be the standard vector graphics file format and supported by a wide variety of software and hardware products.
⇒ See also ANSI; GRAPHICS FILE FORMATS; VECTOR GRAPHICS.

Challenge Handshake Authentication Protocol *n.* See CHAP.

challenge-response *adj.* describing authentication techniques in which an individual is prompted (the challenge) to provide some private information (the response) that depends on the challenge. It is thus resistant to eavesdropping.
⇒ See also AUTHENTICATION; CHAP; SMART CARD.

channel *n.* **1.** in communications, a path between two computers or devices: *TV channels; IRC channels.* **2.** for IBM PS/2 computers, EXPANSION BUS. **3.** in sales and marketing, the way in which a vendor communicates with and sells products to consumers.
⇒ See also B-CHANNEL; BUS; COMMUNICATIONS; IRC.

channel bonding *n.* a technology that combines two telephone lines into a single channel, effectively doubling data transfer speeds.
⇒ See also ISDN; K56FLEX; MODEM; X2.

channel definition format *n.* See CDF.

CHAP *n.* Challenge Handshake Authentication Protocol: a type of authentication in which the authentication agent (typically a network server) sends the client program a key to be used to encrypt the username and password as protection against eavesdropping.
⇒ See also AUTHENTICATION; CHALLENGE-RESPONSE; PAP.

character *n.* in the C language, any symbol that requires one byte of storage.
⇒ See also ALPHANUMERIC; ASCII; CHARACTER BASED; CPI; EXTENDED ASCII; GRAPHICS BASED.

character based *adj.* referring to programs capable of displaying only ASCII and extended ASCII characters. Character-based programs treat a display screen as an array of boxes, each of which can hold one character.
⇒ See also CHARACTER MODE; EXTENDED ASCII; GRAPHICAL USER INTERFACE; GRAPHICS BASED; TEXT MODE.

character mode *n.* a mode of resolution in which the display screen is treated as an array of blocks, each of which can hold one ASCII character. Programs that run entirely in character mode are called *character-based* programs.
⇒ See also ASCII; BLOCK GRAPHICS; CHARACTER BASED; PIXEL; VIDEO ADAPTER.

character recognition *n.* OPTICAL CHARACTER RECOGNITION.

character set *n.* a defined list of characters recognized by computer hardware and software. Each character is represented by a number.
⇒ See also ASCII; CHARACTER; CONTROL CHARACTER; UNICODE.

characters per inch *n.* See CPI.

characters per second *n.* See CPS.

character string *n.* a series of characters manipulated as a group, often specified by enclosing the characters in single or double quotes: 'WASHINGTON' and "WASHINGTON".
⇒ See also DATA TYPE; NAME.

charge-coupled device *n.* See CCD.

chassis *n.* a metal frame that serves as the structural support for electronic components, as circuit boards, wiring, and slots for expansion boards.
⇒ See also DESKTOP MODEL COMPUTER; EXPANSION BOARD; PRINTED CIRCUIT BOARD; SLOT; TOWER MODEL.

chat *n.* real-time communication between two users via computer offered by most networks and online services.
⇒ See also AVATAR; CHAT ROOM; E-MAIL; INSTANT MESSAGING; IRC; NETMEETING; ONLINE SERVICE.

chat room *n.* a virtual room, actually a channel, where a chat session takes place.
⇒ See also ACRONYM; CHAT; IRC; LURK; MUD.

check box *n.* in graphical user interfaces, a box that can be clicked to turn an option on or off. When the option is on, an *x* appears in the box.
⇒ See also BOX; DIALOG BOX; GRAPHICAL USER INTERFACE; OPTION.

checksum *n.* a method of error detection in which each transmitted message is accompanied by a numerical value based on the number of "1" or "0" bits in the message.
⇒ See also COMMUNICATIONS; CRC; ECC MEMORY; ERROR DETECTION.

chip *n.* a small piece of semiconducting material (usually silicon) on which an integrated circuit is embedded. A typical chip is less than ¼ square inches and can contain millions of electronic components (transistors).
⇒ See also ASIC; CHIPSET; CONTROLLER; CPU; INTEGRATED CIRCUIT; MICROPROCESSOR; MOORE'S LAW; PGA; PINOUT; PLD; PRINTED CIRCUIT BOARD; SEMICONDUCTOR; SIMM; TRANSISTOR.

chipset *n.* a number of integrated circuits designed to work together to perform one or more related functions. The term is often used to refer to the main chips (other than CPU and memory) on a motherboard.

⇒ See also CHIP; CONTROLLER; MICROPROCESSOR; TRITON.

choose *v.t.* to pick (a command or option), as by clicking on a menu command or command button.

⇒ See also CLICK; COMMAND; COMMAND KEY; GRAPHICAL USER INTERFACE; MENU; OPTION; SELECT.

Chooser *n.* a Macintosh desk accessory (DA) that enables the user to select and configure printers and network devices, such as file servers.

⇒ See also DESK ACCESSORY (DA).

CHRP (chûrp), *n.* Common Hardware Reference Platform: a specification for PowerPC-based machines that can run the MacOS, Windows NT, or AIX. Also called **PowerPC Platform (PPCP)**.

⇒ See also MacOS; MACINTOSH COMPUTER; POWERPC; PPCP.

CICS Customer Information Control System: a mainframe program from IBM that controls the interaction between applications and users and lets programmers develop screen displays without detailed knowledge of the terminals being used.

⇒ See also COBOL; TP MONITOR; TRANSACTION PROCESSING.

CIDR *n.* Classless Inter-Domain Routing: an IP addressing scheme in which a single IP address can be used to designate many unique IP addresses.

⇒ See also IP ADDRESS; ROUTING.

CIE color model *n.* a color model based on human perception developed by the CIE (Commission Internationale de l'Eclairage) committee.

⇒ See also CMYK; COLOR MATCHING; RGB MONITOR.

CIF 1. Cells in Frames. **2.** Common Intermediate Format.

Cinepak *n.* a popular codec (compression/decompression technology) for computer video developed by SuperMac Inc.

⇒ See also CODEC; INDEO.

cipher text *n.* data that has been encrypted and is therefore unreadable until it has been converted into plain text (decrypted) with a key.

⇒ See also ENCRYPTION; PLAIN TEXT.

CIR *n.* committed information rate: a specified amount of guaranteed bandwidth (measured in bits per second) on a Frame Relay service.

⇒ See also BANDWIDTH; FRAME RELAY; QoS.

circuit board *n.* PRINTED CIRCUIT BOARD.

circuit switching *n.* a type of communications in which a dedicated channel (or circuit) is established for the duration of a transmission. The telephone system is a *circuit-switching network*.

⇒ See also PACKET SWITCHING; PSTN.

CIS *n.* CompuServe Information Service. See under CompuServe.

CISC (sisk), *n.* complex instruction set computer: an architecture in which the CPU supports many multistep instructions.

⇒ See also ARCHITECTURE; CPU; MACHINE LANGUAGE; RISC.

Cisco Systems *n.* one of the leading manufacturers of network equipment.

⇒ See also 3COM; BRIDGE; INTERNETWORKING; LAYER Two Forwarding; ROUTER; SWITCH; VLAN.

class *n.* in object-oriented programming, a category that defines all the common properties of the different objects that belong to it.

⇒ See also AFC; IFC; MFC; OBJECT-ORIENTED PROGRAMMING; OVERLOADING; POLYMORPHISM.

Classless Inter-Domain Routing *n.* See CIDR.

clean boot *n.* starting (booting) a computer in a manner that loads only those files and programs absolutely required.

⇒ See also BOOT; OPERATING SYSTEM.

clear *v.t.* to erase. *Clear the screen*, for example, means to erase everything on the display screen. *Clear a variable* means to remove whatever data is currently stored in the variable. *Clear memory* means to erase all data currently stored in memory.

⇒ See also DISPLAY SCREEN; MEMORY; VARIABLE.

click *v.i.* to tap on a mouse button, pressing it down and then immediately releasing it. The phrase *to click on* means to select (a screen object) by moving the mouse pointer to the object's position

and clicking a mouse button. —*n.* **2.** the pressing down and rapid release of a mouse button. **3.** in the World Wide Web advertising industry, the selection of a banner ad by a user. The effectiveness of Web advertisements is measured by their *click-through rate*—how often people who see the ad click on it.

⇒ See also CHOOSE; DOUBLE CLICK; DRAG; MOUSE; SHIFT CLICKING.

client *n.* an application that runs on a personal computer or workstation and relies on a server to perform some operations. An *e-mail client* is an application that enables the user to send and receive e-mail.

⇒ See also CLIENT-SIDE; CLIENT/SERVER ARCHITECTURE; E-MAIL CLIENT; SERVER; THIN CLIENT.

client/server architecture *n.* a network architecture in which each computer or process on the network is either a client or a server. Also called **two-tier architecture**.

⇒ See also ARCHITECTURE; CLIENT; CLIENT-SIDE; LOCAL-AREA NETWORK; NETWORK; NODE; PEER-TO-PEER ARCHITECTURE; PROCESS; SERVER; SERVER-SIDE; SYBASE; THIN CLIENT; THREE-TIER; TWO-TIER.

client-side *adj.* occurring on the client side of a client-server system, as JavaScript scripts, which are executed by the browser (the client).

⇒ See also CLIENT; CLIENT/SERVER ARCHITECTURE; SERVER-SIDE.

clip *v.t.* in computer graphics, to cut off (a portion of a graphic) at a defined boundary.

⇒ See also CROP; GRAPHICS; WINDOW.

clip art *n.* electronic illustrations that can be inserted into a document.

⇒ See also DESKTOP PUBLISHING.

clipboard *n.* a special memory area (*buffer*) where data is stored temporarily before being copied to another location. Cutting and pasting in word-processing programs is done by means of a clipboard.

⇒ See also COPY; CUT; PASTE.

Clipper chip *n.* an encryption chip designed under the auspices of the U.S. government with the intention of enforcing its use in all devices that might use encryption, including computers, modems, telephones, and televisions. Clipper chips send information with each message that would allow government officials to decrypt it.

⇒ See also CRYPTOGRAPHY; ELECTRONIC FRONTIER FOUNDATION; ENCRYPTION; SECURITY.

clock rate *n.* CLOCK SPEED.

clock speed *n.* the speed, expressed in megahertz, at which a microprocessor executes instructions. Also called **clock rate**.

⇒ See also BUS; CPU; INSTRUCTION; MICROPROCESSOR; OVERCLOCK; SUPERSCALAR; WAIT STATE.

clone *n.* a computer, software product, or device that functions exactly like another, better-known product.

⇒ See also COMPATIBLE; IBM PC; PC.

close *v.t.* **1.** to finish work on (a data file) and save it. **2.** in graphical user interfaces, to remove (a window) from the screen.

⇒ See also GRAPHICAL USER INTERFACE; OPEN; SAVE; WINDOW.

cluster *n.* a group of disk sectors to which the operating system assigns numbers that it uses to keep track of files. DOS and Windows keep track of clusters with the file allocation table (FAT).

⇒ See also FILE ALLOCATION TABLE; FRAGMENTATION; PARTITION; ScanDisk; SECTOR; SLACK SPACE.

clustering *n.* connecting two or more computers together in such a way that they behave like a single computer: used for parallel processing, load balancing, and fault tolerance.

⇒ See also FAULT TOLERANCE; LOAD BALANCING; MSCS; PARALLEL PROCESSING; WOLFPACK.

CLUT *n.* color look-up table: same as PALETTE (def. 1).

CLV Constant Linear Velocity: a method by which CD-ROM players access data.

⇒ See also CAV; CD-ROM; CD-ROM PLAYER.

CMIP (sē′mip′), *n.* Common Management Information Protocol: an OSI protocol used with the Common Management Information Services (CMIS) that provides improved security and better reporting of unusual network conditions.

⇒ See also ISO; NETWORK MANAGEMENT.

CMOS (sē′môs′, -mos′), *n.* complementary metal oxide semiconductor: a widely used type of semiconductor that uses both NMOS (negative polarity) and PMOS (positive polarity) circuits and requires less power than chips using just one type of transistor.

⇒ See also BIOS; SEMICONDUCTOR.

CMS COLOR MANAGEMENT SYSTEM.

CMYK Cyan-Magenta-Yellow-Black: a color model in which all colors are described as a mixture of these four process colors: CMYK is the standard color model used in offset printing for full-color documents.

⇒ See also COLOR MATCHING; COLOR SEPARATION; DESKTOP PUBLISHING; INTEL MICROPROCESSORS; OFFSET PRINTING; RGB MONITOR; SPOT COLOR; WYSIWYP.

coaxial cable *n.* a type of wire that consists of a center wire surrounded by insulation and a grounded shield of braided wire that minimizes electrical and radio frequency interference. It is the primary type of cabling used by the cable television industry and widely used for computer networks.

⇒ See also 10BASE-2; 10BASE5; AUI; BNC CONNECTOR; INFORMATION SUPERHIGHWAY; NETWORK; UTP.

COBOL *n.* common business oriented language: a high-level programming language developed in the late 1950s and early 1960s that is very popular for business applications that run on large computers. It is the most widely used programming language in the world.

⇒ See also CICS; CODASYL; HIGH-LEVEL LANGUAGE; PROGRAMMING LANGUAGE.

CODASYL (kō′də sil), *n.* Conference on Data Systems Languages: an organization founded in 1957 by the U.S. Department of Defense to develop computer programming languages. Although the organization no longer exists, the term CODASYL is still used sometimes to refer to COBOL, which it developed.

⇒ See also COBOL.

code *n.* **1.** a set of symbols for representing something: *ASCII code.* **2.** written computer instructions. —*v.i.* **3.** *Informal.* to program; to write source code.

⇒ See also ASCII; COMPILE; EXECUTABLE FILE; MACHINE LANGUAGE; OBJECT CODE; PROGRAM; PSEUDOCODE; SOURCE CODE.

codec 1. compressor/decompressor: any technology for compressing and decompressing data, as MPEG, Indeo, Cinepak. **2.** in telecommunications, a device that encodes or decodes a signal. **3.** the translation of a binary value into a voltage that can be transmitted over a wire.

⇒ See also CINEPAK; INDEO; MPEG; QUICKTIME; VIDEO FOR WINDOWS.

Code Division Multiple Access *n.* See CDMA.

coff *n.* Common Object File Format: a binary file format used in UNIX System V and Windows.

⇒ See also BINARY FILE; UNIX.

cold boot *n.* the start-up of a computer from a powered-down state.

⇒ See also BOOT.

collapse *v.t.* to compress (a view of a hierarchy) so that only the roots of each branch are visible.

⇒ See also BRANCH; HIERARCHICAL; ROOT DIRECTORY.

color depth *n.* the number of distinct colors that can be represented by a piece of hardware or software, expressed in bits. Also called **bit depth.**

⇒ See also OPTICAL SCANNER; TRUE COLOR; VIDEO ADAPTER.

color/graphics adapter *n.* See CGA.

Color Look-Up Table *n.* PALETTE (def. 1).

color management system *n.* a system for ensuring that colors remain the same regardless of the device or medium used to display the colors. *Abbr.:* CMS

⇒ See also CIE COLOR MODEL; CMYK; COLOR MATCHING; PANTONE MATCHING SYSTEM (PMS); PROCESS COLORS; RGB MONITOR; WYSIWYP.

color matching *n.* the process of ensuring that a color displayed in one medium remains the same when converted to another medium.

⇒ See also CIE COLOR MODEL; CMYK; COLOR MANAGEMENT SYSTEM (CMS); RGB MONITOR.

color monitor *n.* a display monitor capable of displaying many colors.

⇒ See also CRT; DEGAUSS; DOT PITCH; LCD MONITOR; MASK PITCH; MONITOR; RGB MONITOR; VIDEO ADAPTER.

color printer *n.* a printer capable of printing more than one color, usually based on the CMYK color model.

⇒ See also BANDING; BILEVEL PRINTER; CMYK; COLOR SEPARATION; CONTONE PRINTER; INK-JET PRINTER; LASER PRINTER; PRINTER; PROCESS COLORS; SNAPSHOT PRINTER.

color separation *n.* the separation of a color graphic or photo into single layers of the four basic ink colors (cyan, magenta, yellow, and black) in order to print the picture on an offset press.

⇒ See also CMYK; COLOR MANAGEMENT SYSTEM (CMS); COLOR PRINTER; DESKTOP PUBLISHING; PROCESS COLORS.

Color Super-Twist Nematic *n.* See CSTN.

column *n.* **1.** (on a display screen in character mode) a vertical line of characters extending from the top to the bottom of the screen. **2.** (in spreadsheets) a vertical row of cells, usu. identified by letters. **3.** (in database management systems) *field.* **4.** (in documents) a vertical area reserved for text.

⇒ See also CELL; CHARACTER MODE; DATABASE MANAGEMENT SYSTEM; DESKTOP PUBLISHING; DISPLAY SCREEN; FIELD; SPREADSHEET; WORD PROCESSING.

column graph *n.* a type of presentation graphic in which numerical values are illustrated with horizontal columns.

⇒ See also PRESENTATION GRAPHICS.

COM 1. in DOS systems, the name of a serial communications port. **2.** COMPONENT OBJECT MODEL.

⇒ See also AUX; COMMUNICATIONS; PORT; SERIAL; WINDOWS DNA.

COM file *n.* in DOS environments, an executable command file with a .COM filename extension and a maximum size of 64K.

⇒ See also COMMAND; DOS; EXE FILE; EXECUTABLE FILE; EXTENSION; FILE.

Comité Consultatif International Téléphonique et Télégraphique *n.* See CCITT.

comma-delimited *adj.* referring to a format in which each piece of data is separated by a comma: a popular format for transferring data from one application to another.

⇒ See also EXPORT; IMPORT.

command *n.* an instruction to a computer or device to perform a specific task. Commands can be given by special words (keywords), function keys, choices in a menu, buttons or other graphical objects on the screen. Also called **directive.**

⇒ See also BAT FILE; COM FILE; COMMAND DRIVEN; COMMAND LANGUAGE; COMMAND LINE; DOS; EXE FILE; EXTERNAL COMMAND; FUNCTION KEYS; INSTRUCTION; INTERNAL COMMAND; KEYWORD; MENU; USER INTERFACE.

command buffer *n.* a temporary storage area where commands are kept.

⇒ See also BUFFER; COMMAND; UNDO.

COMMAND.COM *n.* the DOS file that contains the DOS command processor.

⇒ See also COMMAND PROCESSOR; INTERNAL COMMAND.

command driven *adj.* referring to programs and operating systems that accept commands in the form of special words or letters.

⇒ See also COMMAND; MENU DRIVEN; USER INTERFACE.

Command key *n.* on a Macintosh computer, a special command key marked by a four-leaf clover or an apple: similar to a PC's Alt key. Also called **Apple key, Open Apple.**

⇒ See also APPLE KEY; CONTROL KEY; KEYBOARD.

command language *n.* the programming language through which a user communicates with the operating system or an application. The DOS command language includes the commands DIR, COPY, and DEL. With graphical user interfaces, the command language consists of operations performed with a mouse or similar input device.

⇒ See also COMMAND; COMMAND PROCESSOR; GRAPHICAL USER INTERFACE; OPERATING SYSTEM; SHELL.

command line *n.* the line on the display screen where a command is expected.
⇒ See also COMMAND; PROMPT.

command-line interpreter *n.* COMMAND PROCESSOR.

command processor *n.* the part of the operating system that receives and executes operating system commands. In operating systems with a graphical user interface, the command processor interprets mouse operations and executes the appropriate command. Also called **command-line interpreter**.
⇒ See also COMMAND LANGUAGE; OPERATING SYSTEM.

Commodore Amiga *n.* AMIGA.

common carrier *n.* PUBLIC CARRIER.

Common Gateway Interface *n.* See CGI.

Common Hardware Reference Platform *n.* See CHRP.

Common Intermediate Format *n.* a format used in videoconferencing systems that easily supports both NTSC and PAL signals. *Abbr.:* CIF
⇒ See also NTSC; PAL; QCIF; VIDEOCONFERENCING.

Common Management Information Protocol *n.* See CMIP.

Common Object Request Broker Architecture *n.* See CORBA.

Common User Access *n.* See CUA.

communications *n.* the transmission of data from one computer to another, or from one device to another. A *communications device* is any machine that assists data transmission, as a modem, cable, or a port. *Communications software* refers to programs that make it possible to transmit data.
⇒ See also BASEBAND TRANSMISSION; COMMUNICATIONS PROTOCOL; COMMUNICATIONS SOFTWARE; FLOW CONTROL; MODEM; NETWORK; PORT.

communications protocol *n.* the set of rules defining a format for data that is to be transmitted. Protocols also include techniques for detecting and recovering from transmission errors and for encoding and decoding data.
⇒ See also ASYNCHRONOUS; BELL 103; BELL 212A; BPS; CCITT; COMMUNICATIONS; FULL DUPLEX; HALF DUPLEX; HDLC; IPX; PROTOCOL.

communications software *n.* software that makes it possible to send and receive data over telephone lines through modems.
⇒ See also AUTO-ANSWER; BATCH FILE; BULLETIN BOARD SYSTEM; COMMUNICATIONS; COMMUNICATIONS PROTOCOL; EDITOR; EMULATION; KERMIT; LOG ON; MACRO; MAINFRAME; MODEM; MULTITASKING; QUEUE; SCRIPT.

compact disc *n.* a polycarbonate platter with one or more metal layers capable of storing digital information. *Abbr.:* CD
⇒ See also CD-ROM; DVD; ERASABLE OPTICAL DISK; MASS STORAGE; MULTIREAD; OPTICAL DISK; RED BOOK; WORM.

Compaq *n.* one of the leading PC manufacturers, based in Houston, Texas, and founded in 1982 by Rod Canion, Bill Murto, and Jim Harris.
⇒ See also DEC; DELL COMPUTER; IBM; PC.

comparison operator *n.* RELATIONAL OPERATOR.

compatible *n.* **1.** a product that can work with or is equivalent to another, better-known product; an IBM-compatible PC. Also called **clone**. —*adj.* **2.** referring to the ability of one device or program to work with another device or program.
⇒ See also BACKWARD COMPATIBLE; BINARY COMPATIBLE; CLONE; COMPATIBLE; DBASE; EMULATION; FONT CARTRIDGE; IBM PC; PC; PLUG COMPATIBLE; STANDARD; UPWARD COMPATIBLE.

compile *v.t.* to transform (a program written in a high-level programming language) from source code into object code so that the program can run.
⇒ See also ASSEMBLY LANGUAGE; BIND; BYTECODE; COMPILER; HIGH-LEVEL LANGUAGE; INTERPRETER; LINK; OBJECT CODE; PARSE; PROGRAMMING LANGUAGE; RUNTIME; SOURCE CODE.

compiler *n.* a program that translates source code into object code.
⇒ See also ASSEMBLY LANGUAGE; COMPILE; INTERPRETER;

JIT; LINK; OBJECT CODE; PARSE; PROGRAMMING LANGUAGE; SOURCE CODE.

complementary metal oxide semiconductor *n.* See CMOS.

complex instruction set computer *n.* See CISC.

component *n.* **1.** a small binary object or program that performs a specific function and operates easily with other components and applications. **2.** a part of a device.
⇒ See also APPLET; COMPONENT OBJECT MODEL; COMPONENT SOFTWARE; OCX; VBX.

Component Object Model *n.* a model for binary code developed by Microsoft that enables programmers to develop software objects that can be accessed by any COM-compliant application.
⇒ See also ACTIVEX; COMPONENT; COMPONENT SOFTWARE; DCOM; OLE; OPENDOC; SOM.

component software *n.* software designed to work as a component of a larger application. Also called **componentware**.
⇒ See also COMPONENT; COMPONENT OBJECT MODEL; OBJECT-ORIENTED PROGRAMMING; OLE; OPENDOC; PLUG-IN.

componentware *n.* COMPONENT SOFTWARE.

COM port *n.* See COM.

composite video *n.* a type of video signal in which all information—the red, blue, and green signals (and sometimes audio signals as well)—is mixed together: used by televisions in the United States.
⇒ See also NTSC; RGB MONITOR; S-VIDEO.

compound document *n.* a document that contains elements from a variety of computer applications, such as text from a word processor, graphics from a draw program, and a chart from a spreadsheet application, all stored in such a way that each piece of data can be manipulated by the application that created it.
⇒ See also DOCUMENT; OLE; OPENDOC.

compression *n.* DATA COMPRESSION.

CompuServe Information Service *n.* one of the first and largest online services, CompuServe supports a wide array of *forums* and provides many types of electronic-mail services. In addition, it is connected to hundreds of different database systems. In 1997, the content portion of CompuServe was acquired by America Online and the network service was acquired by WorldCom.
⇒ See also AMERICA ONLINE; MSN; ONLINE SERVICE.

computer *n.* a programmable machine that responds to a specific set of instructions in a well-defined manner and can execute a prerecorded list of instructions (a program). The actual machinery—wires, transistors, and circuits—is called *hardware;* the instructions and data are called *software.*
⇒ See also CPU; HARDWARE; MAINFRAME; MICROPROCESSOR; MINICOMPUTER; PERSONAL COMPUTER; SOFTWARE; SUPERCOMPUTER; WORKSTATION.

computer-aided design *n.* See CAD.

computer-aided engineering *n.* See CAE.

computer-aided instruction *n.* COMPUTER-BASED TRAINING. See CBT.

computer-aided manufacturing *n.* See CAM.

Computer-Aided Software Engineering *n.* See CASE.

Computer-Aided Systems Engineering *n.* See CASE.

computer-based training *n.* See CBT.

Computer Graphics Metafile *n.* See CGM.

computer imaging *n.* a field of computer science covering images that can be stored on a computer (digital images). Also called **digital imaging**.
⇒ See also BIT-MAPPED GRAPHICS; DIGITAL PHOTOGRAPHY; OPTICAL SCANNER.

computer literacy *n.* a person's level of expertise and familiarity with computers and his or her ability to use applications.
⇒ See also POWER USER.

computer science *n.* the study of computers, including hardware design, artificial intelligence, and software engineering.
⇒ See also ARTIFICIAL INTELLIGENCE; IT; PROGRAM; SOFTWARE ENGINEERING.

computer

computer system n. a complete, working computer including any software and peripheral devices that are necessary to make it function.
⇒ See also COMPUTER; OPERATING SYSTEM.

computer-telephony-integration n. See CTI.

computer virus n. VIRUS.

concatenate v.t. to link together or join (a series of characters or a group of files).
⇒ See also APPEND; CHARACTER STRING.

concatenation n. the act of linking together two or more objects.
⇒ See also CONCATENATE.

concentrator n. a device that combines multiple communication channels onto a single transmission medium in such a way that all the individual channels can be simultaneously active.
⇒ See also HUB; MULTIPLEXOR.

conditional adj. referring to an action that takes place only if a specific condition is met. Conditional expressions enable a program to act differently each time it is executed, depending on the input.
⇒ See also EXPRESSION; PROGRAMMING LANGUAGE.

conference n. an area in a bulletin board or online service in which participants can discuss a topic of common interest. Also called **forum**.
⇒ See also BULLETIN BOARD SYSTEM; FORUM; LURK; ONLINE SERVICE.

CONFIG.SYS n. the configuration file for DOS systems.
⇒ See also BOOT; CONFIGURATION; DRIVER; HIMEM.SYS.

configuration n. the way a system is set up, or the assortment of components such as main memory, floppy drive, hard disk, monitor, modem, etc., that make up the system. Configuration can refer to either hardware or software, or the combination of both.
⇒ See also CONFIG.SYS; CONFIGURATION FILE; CONTROL PANEL; DIP SWITCH; JUMPER; MIF; PARAMETER; REGISTRY.

configuration file n. a file that contains configuration information.
⇒ See also .INI FILE; CONFIG.SYS; CONFIGURATION.

configure v.t. to set up (a program or computer system) for a particular application.
⇒ See also CONFIGURATION.

connectionless adj. referring to network protocols in which a host can send a message without establishing a connection with the recipient. Ethernet, IPX, and UDP are connectionless protocols.
⇒ See also CONNECTION-ORIENTED; IPX; PROTOCOL; UDP.

connection-oriented adj. referring to a protocol that requires a channel to be established between the sender and receiver before any messages are transmitted. The telephone, TCP, and HTTP are connection-oriented protocols.
⇒ See also CONNECTIONLESS.

connectivity n. the ability of a program or device to link with other programs and devices. A program that can *import* data from a wide variety of other programs and can *export* data in many different formats is said to have *good connectivity*.
⇒ See also EXPORT; IMPORT.

connector n. the part of a cable that plugs into a port or interface to connect one device to another.
⇒ See also BNC CONNECTOR; DIN CONNECTOR; INTERFACE; PINOUT; PORT; RJ-45.

connect time n. the amount of time a computer is logged in to a remote computer.
⇒ See also ONLINE SERVICE.

console n. **1.** the combination of display monitor and keyboard (or other device that allows input). The term *console* usually refers to a dedicated terminal attached to a minicomputer or mainframe and used to monitor the status of the system. Also called **terminal**. **2.** MONITOR or DISPLAY SCREEN. **3.** a bank of meters and lights indicating a computer's status, with switches that allow an operator to control the computer.
⇒ See also DISPLAY SCREEN; KEYBOARD; TERMINAL.

constant n. in programming, a value that never changes, as a number, a character, or a character string.

⇒ See also ABSOLUTE CELL REFERENCE; CHARACTER STRING; FORMULA; LITERAL; VARIABLE.

Constant Linear Velocity n. See CLV.

contact manager n. an application that enables the user to store and find contact information, such as names, addresses, and telephone numbers.
⇒ See also PIM.

contention n. **1.** competition for resources, as in a situation where two or more computers attempt to transmit a message across the same wire at the same time. **2.** a type of network protocol that defines what happens when two or more nodes try to send messages across a network simultaneously.
⇒ See also CSMA/CD; ETHERNET.

context sensitive adj. referring to a program feature that changes depending on what the user is doing in the program. *Context-sensitive help* provides documentation for the particular feature that is being used.
⇒ See also HELP.

context switching n. TASK SWITCHING.

contiguous adj. immediately adjacent, as sectors on a disk that come one after the other.
⇒ See also FRAGMENTATION.

continuous-form paper n. a type of printing paper that consists of a single roll of paper, perforated at regular intervals so that sheets can be separated.
⇒ See also PAPER FEED; TRACTOR FEED.

continuous tone adj. (of an image) having an almost unlimited range of color or shades of gray, as photographs and television images.
⇒ See also BILEVEL PRINTER; CONTONE PRINTER; DIGITAL; GRAY SCALING; HALFTONE.

contone printer n. a type of printer that uses a combination of dithering and printing at different levels of intensity to produce different colors and different shades of light and dark.
⇒ See also BILEVEL PRINTER; COLOR PRINTER; CONTINUOUS TONE; DITHERING.

control n. **1.** an object in a window or dialog box, as a push-button, scroll bar, radio button, or pull-down menu. **2.** an OLE or ActiveX object.
⇒ See also ACTIVEX CONTROL; GRAPHICAL USER INTERFACE; OCX; OLE; VBX.

control character n. a special, nonprinting character, used to control display monitors, printers, etc.
⇒ See also ASCII; BREAK KEY; CONTROL KEY; KEYBOARD.

Control key n. a key on PC keyboards labeled *Ctrl*, used in combination with other characters. Many Apple keyboards have both Ctrl and Cmd keys.
⇒ See also APPLE KEY; COMMAND KEY; CONTROL KEY COMBINATION.

Control key combination n. a command issued by pressing a keyboard character in conjunction with the Control key.
⇒ See also COMMAND; CONTROL KEY.

controller n. a device that controls the transfer of data between a computer and a peripheral device, as a disk drive, display screen, keyboard, or printer.
⇒ See also ADAPTER; ATA; BUS; CHIP; CPU; DRIVER; EISA; EXPANSION BOARD; MICROCONTROLLER; PCI; PERIPHERAL DEVICE; PRINTED CIRCUIT BOARD; SCSI.

control panel n. a utility on both Macintoshes and Windows operating systems that permits the user to set such system parameters as the sensitivity of the mouse.
⇒ See also CDEV.

control panel device n. See CDEV.

control program n. **1.** a program that enhances another system by creating an environment in which other programs can be run. **2.** OPERATING SYSTEM.
⇒ See also GRAPHICAL USER INTERFACE; MICROSOFT WINDOWS; OPERATING ENVIRONMENT; OPERATING SYSTEM.

conventional memory n. on DOS systems, the portion of memory that is available to standard DOS programs.
⇒ See also EXPANDED MEMORY; EXTENDED MEMORY; MAIN MEMORY.

convergence n. **1.** the coming together of two or more disparate disciplines or technologies. **2.** in

graphics, the degree of sharpness of an individual color pixel on a monitor.
⇒ See also GRAPHICS; MONITOR; PIXEL; RGB MONITOR.

convert *v.t.* to change (data) from one format to another.
⇒ See also EXPORT; IMPORT.

cookie *n.* a message to identify users that is given to a Web browser by a Web server.
⇒ See also BROWSER; DYNAMIC HTML; LOG FILE; STATELESS; WEB SERVER; WORLD WIDE WEB.

CoolTalk *n.* an Internet telephone (Voice on the Net) tool built into Netscape Navigator 3.0 that supports audio conferencing, a whiteboard, and a chat tool.
⇒ See also INTERNET TELEPHONY; NETMEETING.

cooperative multitasking *n.* a type of multitasking in which the process currently controlling the CPU must offer control to other processes: all programs must cooperate for it to work.
⇒ See also MICROSOFT WINDOWS; MULTITASKING; UNIX.

Copper Distributed Data Interface *n.* See CDDI.

coprocessor *n.* a special-purpose processing unit that assists the CPU in performing certain types of operations. A *math* (or *numeric*) coprocessor performs mathematical computations, particularly floating-point operations. A *graphics coprocessor* is specially designed for handling graphics computations.
⇒ See also ACCELERATOR BOARD; CPU; FLOATING-POINT NUMBER.

copy *v.t.* **1.** to copy (a piece of data) to a temporary location, as to duplicate a section of a document and place it in a *buffer* (sometimes called a *clipboard*) from which it can be retrieved and pasted somewhere else. **2.** in file management, to make a duplicate of (a file). —*n.* **3.** a duplicate of a piece of data, such as a file or a directory.
⇒ See also BUFFER; CLIPBOARD; CUT; FILE MANAGEMENT SYSTEM; PASTE.

copy protection *n.* any of the programming techniques used to prevent the unauthorized copying of software.
⇒ See also DIGITAL WATERMARK; DONGLE; DVD-VIDEO; SHAREWARE; SOFTWARE LICENSING; SOFTWARE PIRACY; WAREZ.

CORBA *n.* Common Object Request Broker Architecture: an architecture that enables objects written in different programming languages and running on different systems to communicate with one another: developed by the Object Management Group (OMG).
⇒ See also DCOM; DISTRIBUTED COMPUTING; IIOP; OBJECT; OMG; ORB; RMI; RPC; SOM.

core memory *n.* an obsolete term for RAM, which was composed of doughnut-shaped magnets called *cores.*
⇒ See also MAIN MEMORY.

corrupted *adj.* referring to data that have been damaged in some way.

Courier font *n.* a common monospaced (fixed-pitch) font, supported by most printers and most word-processing software.
⇒ See also FIXED PITCH; FONT; MONOSPACING.

courseware *n.* software designed to be used in an educational program.
⇒ See also CBT.

cpi characters per inch: a typographic measurement specifying the number of characters that can fit on a printed line one inch long.
⇒ See also CHARACTER; FIXED PITCH; FONT; MONOSPACING; PITCH; PROPORTIONAL SPACING.

CP/M Control Program for Microprocessors: an obsolete operating system for personal computers created by Digital Research Corporation.
⇒ See also DOS; OPERATING SYSTEM.

cps characters per second: a unit of measure used to describe the speed of dot-matrix and daisy-wheel printers.
⇒ See also PRINTER.

CPU central processing unit: the most important element of a computer system. It includes an arithmetic-logic unit for calculations and a control unit for

sequencing operations and transferring data between the CPU and memory. The CPU also issues instructions to I/O devices.
⇒ See also ALU; CHIP; CISC; CLOCK SPEED; COPROCESSOR; INTEL MICROPROCESSORS; MICROPROCESSOR; MMU; POWERPC; RISC.

CPU time *n.* the amount of time the CPU is actually executing instructions, used to compare the speed of two different processors, to gauge how CPU-intensive a program is, and to measure the amount of processing time being allocated to different programs in a multitasking environment.
⇒ See also CPU; MULTITASKING.

crack *v.t.* **1.** to break into (a computer system). **2.** to copy (commercial software) illegally by breaking protection techniques.
⇒ See also HACKER; PHREAKING; SMURF.

cracker *n.* a person who cracks computer systems or software.

crash *n.* **1.** a serious computer failure in which a computer stops working or a program suddenly aborts as the result of a hardware malfunction or software bug. —*v.i.* **2.** to fail or break.
⇒ See also ABORT; BOMB; BUG; FATAL ERROR; GPF; HANG; HEAD CRASH; INVALID PAGE FAULT; SMART.

CRC cyclic redundancy check: a common technique for detecting data transmission errors.
⇒ See also CHECKSUM; COMMUNICATIONS PROTOCOL; ERROR DETECTION; ZMODEM.

crippled version *n.* a demonstration version of a piece of software that has one or more critical features disabled.
⇒ See also BETA TEST.

crop *v.t.* in computer graphics, to cut off the edges of (an image) to make it the proper size or to remove unwanted parts.
⇒ See also CLIP.

crop marks *n.pl.* printed or drawn lines indicating where the paper on which a composed page has been printed should be cut to produce the correct page size.
⇒ See also CAMERA-READY; DESKTOP PUBLISHING; OFFSET PRINTING.

cross-platform *adj.* referring to the capability of software or hardware to run identically on different platforms, as Windows and Macintosh.
⇒ See also BINARY COMPATIBLE; LOCAL-AREA NETWORK; PLATFORM.

CRT cathode-ray tube: the technology used in most televisions and computer display screens.
⇒ See also COLOR MONITOR; DEGAUSS; DISPLAY SCREEN; LCD MONITOR; MONITOR; PINCUSHION DISTORTION; REFRESH.

cryptography *n.* the art of protecting information by transforming or encrypting it into an unreadable format called *cyphertext.*
⇒ See also CLIPPER CHIP; DES; PRETTY GOOD PRIVACY; PUBLIC-KEY ENCRYPTION; SECURITY; SYMMETRIC-KEY CRYPTOGRAPHY.

CSMA/CD Carrier Sense Multiple Access/Collision Detection: a set of rules determining how to avoid network deadlock when two devices attempt to use a data channel simultaneously: a type of contention protocol.
⇒ See also 100BASE-T; CONTENTION; ETHERNET.

CSS Cascading Style Sheets: a feature added to HTML that enables both Web site developers and users to create style sheets that define how different elements, such as headers and links, appear. These style sheets can then be applied to any Web page.
⇒ See also HTML; STYLE SHEET.

CSTN color super-twist nematic: an LCD technology developed by Sharp Electronics Corporation. It is based on a passive matrix, which is less expensive to produce than an active-matrix (TFT) display.
⇒ See also DSTN; LCD; PASSIVE-MATRIX DISPLAY; SUPER-TWIST; TFT.

CSU See under CSU/DSU.

CSU/DSU Channel Service Unit/Data Service Unit: a device that performs protective and diagnostic functions for a telecommunications line.
⇒ See also SMDS; T-1 CARRIER; T-3 CARRIER; V.35.

CTI computer-telephony-integration: systems that

computer

enable a computer to accept incoming calls and route them to the appropriate device or person.
⇒ See also TELEPHONY.

Ctrl CONTROL KEY.

CUA Common User Access: a set of standards for user interfaces developed by IBM: one component of the *System Application Architecture (SAA)* standards introduced in 1987.
⇒ See also SAA; USER INTERFACE.

current *adj.* referring to an object that is active or acting as a reference point: *current directory; current drive; current cell.*
⇒ See also ACTIVE; DEFAULT; WORKING DIRECTORY.

cursor *n.* **1.** a special symbol, usually a solid rectangle or a blinking underline character, that signifies where the next character will be displayed on the screen. **2.** Also called **puck.** a device, similar in appearance to a mouse, that is used to sketch lines on a digitizing tablet. **3.** in some database languages, short for *cur(rent) s(et) o(f) r(ecords)*, the currently selected set of records.
⇒ See also ARROW KEYS; DIGITIZING TABLET; MOUSE; POINTER.

cursor control keys *n.pl.* special keys on computer keyboards that move the cursor, such as arrow keys, *End, Home, Page Up, Page Down*, and *Backspace* keys.
⇒ See also ARROW KEYS; CURSOR; KEYBOARD.

cursor position *n.* the position of the cursor on the display screen.
⇒ See also CURSOR; DISPLAY SCREEN; TEXT MODE.

CU-SeeMe *n.* a videoconferencing program that uses the Internet to transmit audio and video signals.
⇒ See also VIDEOCONFERENCING.

Customer Information Control System *n.* See CICS.

customer support *n.* service that computer and software manufacturers, and third-party service companies offer to customers, as mail-in or carry-in service, on-site contract, etc. Also called **technical support.**
⇒ See also BULLETIN BOARD SYSTEM; DOWNLOAD.

cut *v.t.* in word processing, to remove (a section of text) from a document to a temporary buffer, from which it can be moved to another place.
⇒ See also BUFFER; CLIPBOARD; COPY; DELETE; PASTE.

cut-sheet feeder *n.* SHEET FEEDER.

cyber- a prefix used to describe new things that are being made possible by the spread of computers: *cyberphobia; cyberpunk; cyberspace.* ⇒ See also CYBERSPACE; VIRTUAL REALITY.

cybernetics *n.* originally the study of biological and artificial control systems, now concerned with discovering what mechanisms control systems and, in particular, how systems regulate themselves.
⇒ See also ARTIFICIAL INTELLIGENCE; ROBOTICS.

cyberspace *n.* a metaphor for describing the non-physical terrain created by computer systems, within which people can communicate with one another.
⇒ See also AVATAR; INFORMATION SUPERHIGHWAY; MUD; ONLINE SERVICE; VIRTUAL REALITY; VRML.

cycle time *n.* a measurement of how quickly two successive pieces of data can be fetched from a memory chip.
⇒ See also ACCESS TIME; DRAM; SRAM.

cyclic redundancy check *n.* See CRC.

cylinder *n.* a single track location on all the platters making up a hard disk.
⇒ See also HARD DISK; PLATTER; TRACK.

Cyrix *n.* a U.S. corporation founded in 1988 that manufactures Intel-compatible microprocessors: acquired by National Semiconductor in 1997.
⇒ See also AMD; INTEL; INTEL MICROPROCESSORS; MICROPROCESSOR; PENTIUM MICROPROCESSOR.

a b c D e f g h i j k l m n o p q r s t u v w x y z

D3D DIRECT3D.

DA DESK ACCESSORY.

DAC digital-to-analog converter: a device (usually a single chip) that converts digital data into analog signals that can be carried by telephone signals or processed by a monitor.
⇒ See also ANALOG; DIGITAL; RAMDAC.

daemon (dē′mən, dā′-), *n.* a process, such as a print spooler or an e-mail handler, that runs in the background and performs a specified operation at predefined times or in response to certain events. Also called **System Agent; service.**
⇒ See also AGENT; PROCESS; UNIX.

daisy chain *n.* **1.** a hardware configuration in which devices are connected in a series. —*v.t.* **2.** to connect (devices) in a daisy chain pattern.
⇒ See also SCSI.

daisy-wheel printer *n.* an obsolete type of printer in which letters are mounted on spokes, rotated into position, and struck by a hammer to produce text.
⇒ See also IMPACT PRINTER; PRINTER.

DAO 1. data access objects: software objects that work with Microsoft's Jet database engine, generally created with Visual Basic and including all of the applications in Microsoft Office, such as MS-Word, MS-Access, and Excel. **2.** disk at once: a method of recording to CD-R disks in which all data are written in a single session.
⇒ See also ADO; JET; VISUAL BASIC.

DASD (daz′dē), *n.* Direct Access Storage Device: another name for disk drive in the world of mainframes.
⇒ See also DISK DRIVE; RANDOM ACCESS.

DAT *n.* digital audio tape: a type of magnetic tape that uses helical scan to record data and can hold from 2 to 24 GB of data in a cartridge about the size of a credit card.
⇒ See also DDS; GIGABYTE; HELICAL-SCAN CARTRIDGE; MASS STORAGE; MEGABYTE; SEQUENTIAL ACCESS; TAPE.

data *n.pl.* or *n.* **1.** distinct pieces of information, usually formatted in a special way. Strictly speaking, data is the plural of *datum*, a single piece of information. When used as a singular noun, it means "information." **2.** binary machine-readable information as distinguished from textual human-readable information. —*adj.* **3.** in database management systems, referring to the files that store the database information, as opposed to index files and data dictionaries, which store administrative information.
⇒ See also ASCII; BINARY; DATA DICTIONARY; DATA INTEGRITY; DATABASE MANAGEMENT SYSTEM; METADATA; PROGRAM; SOFTWARE.

database *n.* **1.** a collection of information in electronic form that is organized in such a way that a computer program can quickly select desired pieces of data. Traditional databases are organized by *fields, records,* and *files.* A field is a single piece of information; a record is one complete set of fields; and a file is a collection of records. For example, a telephone book is analogous to a file. It contains a list of records, each of which consists of three fields: name, address, and telephone number. An alternative concept in database design is known as *Hypertext.* In a Hypertext database, any object, whether it be a piece of text, a picture, or a film, can be linked to any other object. Hypertext databases are particularly useful for organizing large amounts of disparate information, but they are not designed for numerical analysis. **2.** DATABASE MANAGEMENT SYSTEM.
⇒ See also DATA MINING; DATA WAREHOUSE; DATABASE MANAGEMENT SYSTEM; DISTRIBUTED DATABASE; FIELD; FILE;

HYPERTEXT; METADATA; OLAP; RDBMS; RECORD; REPLICATION.

DATABASE 2 *n*. See DB2.

database management system *n*. a collection of programs for storing, modifying, and extracting information from a database, as a computerized library system, an automated teller machine, a flight reservation system, or a computerized parts inventory system.
⇒ See also BLOB; DATA DICTIONARY; DATA MART; DATABASE; DB2; DISTRIBUTED DATABASE; FLAT-FILE DATABASE; FOURTH-GENERATION LANGUAGE; HYPERTEXT; INFORMIX; ISAM; MULTIDIMENSIONAL DBMS; OLAP; ORACLE; PROGRESS SOFTWARE; QUERY; RDBMS; REPORT WRITER; SQL; STORED PROCEDURE.

data bus *n*. BUS.

data communications *n*. COMMUNICATIONS.

data compression *n*. the storage of data in a format that requires less space than usual: used esp. in backup utilities, spreadsheet applications, and database management systems.
⇒ See also ARC; CCITT; DCT; DISK COMPRESSION; DSP; JPEG; LOSSLESS COMPRESSION; LOSSY COMPRESSION; LZW; MNP; MP3; MPEG; ZIP.

data dictionary *n*. in database management systems, a file that defines the basic organization of a database, containing a list of all files in the database, the number of records in each file, and the names and types of each field.
⇒ See also DATABASE MANAGEMENT SYSTEM.

data encryption *n*. ENCRYPTION.

Data Encryption Standard *n*. See DES.

data entry *n*. the process of entering data into a computerized database or spreadsheet, either by an individual typing at a keyboard or by a machine entering data electronically.
⇒ See also DATABASE; SPREADSHEET.

datagram *n*. PACKET.

data integrity *n*. the validity of data. ⇒ See also BACKUP; DATA; ERROR DETECTION.

data mart *n*. a database, or collection of databases, focused on a particular subject and designed to help managers make decisions about their business.
⇒ See also DATA WAREHOUSE; DATABASE MANAGEMENT SYSTEM.

data mining *adj*. referring to a class of database applications that look for hidden patterns in a collection of data.
⇒ See also DATABASE.

data processing *n*. **1.** the organization and manipulation of data, usu. large amounts of numeric data. **2.** INFORMATION TECHNOLOGY (IT).
⇒ See also ACCOUNTING SOFTWARE; APPLICATION.

data rate *n*. DATA TRANSFER RATE.

data recovery *n*. salvaging data stored on damaged media, such as magnetic disks and tapes.
⇒ See also HEAD CRASH; VIRUS.

data structure *n*. in programming, a scheme for organizing related pieces of information.
⇒ See also ARRAY; FILE; HEAP; LIST; RECORD; STACK; TREE STRUCTURE.

data transfer rate *n*. the speed with which data can be transmitted from one device to another, typically measured in megabits (million bits) or megabytes (million bytes) per second. Also called **throughput.**
⇒ See also ACCESS TIME; BURST MODE; KBPS; MBPS; MBPS; STREAMING.

data type *n*. in programming, the classification of a particular piece of information, as integer, string, and so forth.
⇒ See also BIG-ENDIAN; CHARACTER; DATABASE; DECLARE; FIELD; FLOATING-POINT NUMBER; INTEGER; OVERLOADING; POLYMORPHISM; VARIABLE.

data warehouse *n*. a combination of many databases across an entire enterprise that presents a coherent picture of business conditions at a single point in time and is designed to support management decision-making.
⇒ See also DATA MART; DATABASE; METADATA.

data warehousing *n*. DATA WAREHOUSE.

daughtercard *n*. a printed circuit board that plugs into another circuit board (usu. the motherboard) and accesses motherboard components (memory and CPU) directly instead of sending data through the slower expansion bus. Also called **daughterboard.**
⇒ See also EXPANSION BOARD; MOTHERBOARD; PRINTED CIRCUIT BOARD.

DB2 Database 2: a group of relational database products offered by IBM that provides an open database environment that runs on a wide variety of computing platforms.
⇒ See also DATABASE MANAGEMENT SYSTEM; RDBMS.

dBASE *n*. a database management system produced by Ashton-Tate Corporation: a de facto standard supported by nearly all database management and spreadsheet systems.
⇒ See also DATABASE MANAGEMENT SYSTEM; EXPORT; IMPORT.

DBMS DATABASE MANAGEMENT SYSTEM.

DCC Direct Cable Connection: a Windows 95 feature that enables two computers to be connected via a serial or parallel cable and to access each other's files, functioning as if they were on a local-area network (LAN).
⇒ See also ECP; LOCAL-AREA NETWORK; NETWORK NEIGHBORHOOD; NULL-MODEM CABLE.

DCE 1. Distributed Computing Environment: a suite of technology services developed by The Open Group for creating distributed applications that run on different platforms. **2.** Data Communications Equipment: a device that communicates with a Data Terminal Equipment (DTE) device in RS-232C communications.
⇒ See also DISTRIBUTED PROCESSING; DTE; FAULT TOLERANCE; MIDDLEWARE; MODEM; OSF; THE OPEN GROUP.

DCI DIRECTDRAW.

DCOM *n*. Distributed Component Object Model: an extension of the Component Object Model (COM) to support objects distributed across a network.
⇒ See also COMPONENT OBJECT MODEL; CORBA; DISTRIBUTED COMPUTING; DSOM; RMI.

DCT Discrete Cosine Transform: a technique used for data compression.
⇒ See also DATA COMPRESSION; JPEG; LOSSY COMPRESSION.

DDC Display Data Channel: a VESA standard for communication between a monitor and a video adapter.
⇒ See also MONITOR; VESA; VIDEO ADAPTER.

DDE Dynamic Data Exchange: an older interprocess communication (IPC) system built into the Macintosh, Windows, and OS/2 operating systems, replaced by OLE, which provides greater control over shared data.
⇒ See also INTERPROCESS COMMUNICATION (IPC); OLE.

DDR-SDRAM *n*. Double Data Rate-Synchronous DRAM: a type of SDRAM that supports data transfers on both edges of each clock cycle, effectively doubling the memory chip's data throughput. Also called **SDRAM II.**
⇒ See also SDRAM.

DDS Digital Data Storage: the industry standard for digital audio tape (DAT) formats.
⇒ See also DAT.

deadlock *n*. a condition that occurs in multitasking and client/server environments when two processes are each waiting for the other to proceed, with the result that neither process responds to input. Also called **deadly embrace.**
⇒ See also HANG.

deadly embrace *n*. DEADLOCK.

debug *v.t.* to find and remove errors, or bugs, from (a program or design).
⇒ See also ALPHA VERSION; BUG; TWEAK.

debugger *n*. a special program used to find errors, or bugs, in other programs by allowing a programmer to stop a program at any point and examine and change the values of variables.
⇒ See also BUG.

DEC (dek), *n*. Digital Equipment Corporation: one of the leading producers of workstations, servers, and high-end PCs and also the developer of Alta Vista. It was acquired by Compaq in 1998.

⇒ See also ALTA VISTA; COMPAQ; IBM; SERVER; SGI; SUN MICROSYSTEMS; VAX; WORKSTATION.

decimal *n.* any number in base 10 (the numbers used in everyday life).
⇒ See also BCD; BINARY; FLOATING-POINT NUMBER; HEXADECIMAL; INTEGER; OCTAL.

declare *v.t.* in programming, to define the name and data type of (a variable or other programming construct).
⇒ See also DATA TYPE; PROGRAMMING LANGUAGE; VARIABLE.

decrement *n.* **1.** the act or process of decreasing. **2.** the amount lost by decreasing. —*v.t.* **3.** to decrease (the value of a variable).
⇒ See also INCREMENT.

decryption *n.* the process of decoding data, which has previously been encrypted into a secret format, by means of a secret *key* or password.
⇒ See also CRYPTOGRAPHY; ENCRYPTION; SECURITY.

dedicated *adj.* reserved for a specific use: *dedicated channel; dedicated server.*
⇒ See also CHANNEL; EXPANSION SLOT; NETWORK; SERVER.

de facto standard *n.* a format, language, or protocol that has become a standard as a result of its wide use and recognition by the industry, as Kermit communications protocol or PostScript page description language.
⇒ See also HAYES COMPATIBLE; KERMIT; PCL; POSTSCRIPT; STANDARD; XMODEM.

default *n.* a preset value or setting that a device or program automatically selects if no substitute is specified: *default margins, default directory.* For example, word processors have default margins and default page lengths that the user can override or reset. The *default drive* is the disk drive the computer accesses unless a different one is specified. Likewise, the *default directory* (or *folder*) is the directory the operating system searches unless a different one is specified. The default can also be an action that a device or program will take. For example, some word processors generate backup files *by default.*
⇒ See also MODE.

Defrag *n.* a DOS and Windows utility for defragmenting the hard disk.
⇒ See also DISK OPTIMIZER; FRAGMENTATION; SCANDISK.

defragment *v.t.* to optimize (a disk) by unfragmenting files—that is, by putting scattered pieces of a file together in a contiguous sequence.
⇒ See also FRAGMENTATION.

defragmentation *n.* See under DEFRAGMENT.

degauss *v.t.* to remove magnetism from (a device). The term is usually used in reference to color monitors and other display devices that use a cathode-ray tube (CRT).
⇒ See also COLOR MONITOR; CRT; MONITOR; PINCUSHION DISTORTION.

degausser *n.* a device for degaussing magnetic tape, disks, or other objects.

delete *v.t.* to remove or erase (data or images), as from a file, a display screen, or a disk.
⇒ See also CUT; RECYCLE BIN.

Delete key *n.* a key used to remove characters and other objects.
⇒ See also BACKSPACE; BACKSPACE KEY; INSERTION POINT; KEYBOARD.

delimiter *n.* a punctuation character, as a backslash, comma, semicolon, or quotation mark, that separates two characters or two pieces of data or marks the beginning or end of a programming construct.
⇒ See also PATHNAME.

Dell Computer *n.* the world's largest mail-order computer vendor, founded by Michael Dell in 1984.
⇒ See also COMPAQ; PC.

Delphi *n.* a rapid application development (RAD) system, based on Pascal, developed by Borland International, Inc.
⇒ See also PASCAL; RAPID APPLICATION DEVELOPMENT; VISUAL BASIC.

demand paging *n.* in virtual memory systems, a type of swapping in which pages of data are not copied from disk to RAM until they are needed, as opposed to anticipatory paging, in which the operating system attempts to anticipate which piece of data will be needed next and copies it to RAM before it is actually required.
⇒ See also PAGING; RAM; SWAP; VIRTUAL MEMORY.

demodulate *v.t.* to convert (received modulated carrier signals) into a form that can be used by a computer.
⇒ See also MODULATE.

demodulation *n.* the act or process, performed by a modem, of demodulating received carrier signals.
⇒ See also MODULATE.

density *n.* a measure of how much data can be stored in a given amount of space on a disk or tape: *double density; high density.*
⇒ See also AREAL DENSITY; DISK; DISK DRIVE; DOUBLE-DENSITY DISK; FDHD; FLOPPY DISK; HIGH-DENSITY DISK.

DES Data Encryption Standard: a popular symmetric-key encryption method, developed in 1975 and standardized by ANSI in 1981 as ANSI X.3.92. It uses a 56-bit key and may not be exported from the U.S. or Canada.
⇒ See also CRYPTOGRAPHY; SYMMETRIC-KEY CRYPTOGRAPHY.

descender *n.* in typography, the portion of a lowercase letter that falls below the baseline.
⇒ See also ASCENDER; BASELINE; X-HEIGHT.

Deschutes *n.* one of Intel's Pentium II microprocessors having transistor sizes of 0.25 microns.
⇒ See also PENTIUM II; PENTIUM MICROPROCESSOR.

desk accessory (DA) *n.* on Apple Macintoshes, a small, stand-alone program designed to perform a single task.
⇒ See also UTILITY.

desktop *n.* **1.** in graphical user interfaces, the primary display screen, consisting of icons representing files, folders, programs, etc. **2.** DESKTOP MODEL COMPUTER.
⇒ See also GRAPHICAL USER INTERFACE; SHORTCUT.

Desktop Management Interface *n.* See DMI.

desktop model computer *n.* a computer designed to fit comfortably on top of a desk, typically with the monitor sitting on top of the computer.
⇒ See also CHASSIS; PERSONAL COMPUTER; TOWER MODEL.

desktop publishing *n.* the use of a personal computer or workstation to produce high-quality printed documents, using different typefaces and creating or inserting illustrations.
⇒ See also ADOBE PHOTOSHOP; COLOR SEPARATION; ISP; OFFSET PRINTING; PAGE LAYOUT PROGRAM.

desktop system *n.* DESKTOP MODEL COMPUTER.

destination *n.* **1.** the file storage device to which data is moved from the source. —*adj.* **2.** indicating the file or device to which data is moved.
⇒ See also SOURCE.

device *n.* any machine or component, as a disk driver, printer, or modem, that attaches to a computer.
⇒ See also COMPUTER; CONFIG.SYS; DRIVER; INPUT DEVICE.

Device Bay *n.* a specification developed by Intel, Compaq, and Microsoft to standardize the size, shape, and connection of computer components, such as disk drives, modems, and audio devices.
⇒ See also IEEE 1394; PCMCIA; USB.

device dependent *adj.* referring to programs that can run only on a certain type of hardware.
⇒ See also MACHINE DEPENDENT.

device driver *n.* DRIVER.

DHCP Dynamic Host Configuration Protocol: a protocol for assigning IP addresses to devices on a network and keeping track of such addresses.
⇒ See also WINS.

DHTML DYNAMIC HTML.

dialog box *n.* in a graphical user interface, a box that appears on a display screen to present information or request input.
⇒ See also BOX; GRAPHICAL USER INTERFACE; POP-UP WINDOW; WINDOW.

dial-up access *n.* the connection of a device to a computer network via a modem and a telephone.

⇒ See also DIAL-UP NETWORKING; FRACTIONAL T-1; INTERNET; ISP; L2TP; LEASED LINE; MODEM; POP; RADIUS.

Dial-Up Networking *n.* a component in Windows 98 that allows a computer to be connected to a network via a modem. *Abbr.:* DUN

⇒ See also DIAL-UP ACCESS; POP; RAS; WINDOWS 95.

DIB *n.* **1.** Dual Independent Bus: a bus architecture that is part of Intel's Pentium Pro and Pentium II microprocessors and enables the processor to access cache and main memory simultaneously, which increases throughput. **2.** device-independent bitmap: the bit-mapped graphics format used by Windows in which colors are represented in a format independent of the final output device.

⇒ See also BIT-MAPPED GRAPHICS; BMP; GRAPHICS FILE FORMATS; NETWORK MANAGEMENT; PENTIUM PRO; RMON.

digital *adj.* describing any system based on discontinuous data or events. Computers are digital machines because at their most basic level they can distinguish between just two values, 0 and 1, or off and on.

⇒ See also ANALOG; DAC; DIGITAL AUDIO; DIGITIZE; MODEM.

digital audio *n.* the reproduction and transmission of sound stored in a digital format: includes CDs and any sound files stored on a computer.

⇒ See also AU; DIGITAL; DIGITAL VIDEO; DOLBY DIGITAL; MIDI; MP3; WAV.

digital audio tape *n.* See DAT.

digital camera *n.* a camera that stores images digitally rather than recording them on film. Pictures may then be downloaded to a computer system and manipulated with a graphics program.

⇒ See also DIGITAL; DIGITAL PHOTOGRAPHY; FLASHPIX; OPTICAL RESOLUTION; PHOTOCD.

digital cash *n.* a system that permits people to pay for goods or services by means of encrypted serial numbers that are transferred from one computer to another.

⇒ See also ELECTRONIC COMMERCE; INTERNET; SMART CARD.

digital certificate *n.* an attachment to an electronic message that verifies the identity of the user sending the message and enables the receiver to encode a reply: used for security purposes.

⇒ See also CERTIFICATE AUTHORITY; ENCRYPTION; PUBLIC-KEY ENCRYPTION; SSL; X.509.

Digital Data Storage *n.* See DDS.

digital envelope *n.* a type of security that uses a fast but less-secure code to encrypt a message, and then a slow but highly-secure code to protect the encryption key.

⇒ See also ENCRYPTION; PUBLIC-KEY ENCRYPTION; SYMMETRIC ENCRYPTION.

Digital Equipment Corporation *n.* See DEC.

digital imaging *n.* COMPUTER IMAGING.

Digital Light Processing *n.* See DLP.

digital monitor *n.* a monitor that accepts digital rather than analog signals.

⇒ See also ANALOG; ANALOG MONITOR; DIGITAL; MONITOR; VIDEO ADAPTER.

digital nervous system *n.* See DNS.

digital photography *n.* the art and science of producing and manipulating photographs that are represented as bit maps. They are produced directly with a digital camera, by capturing a frame from a video, or by scanning a conventional photograph.

⇒ See also COMPUTER IMAGING; DIGITAL CAMERA; FLASHPIX; IMAGE ENHANCEMENT; IMAGE PROCESSING; SNAPSHOT PRINTER.

Digital Service Unit/Channel Service Unit *n.* See CSU/DSU.

digital signal processing *n.* See DSP.

digital signature *n.* a digital code that can be attached to a message to identify the sender.

⇒ See also AUTHENTICATION; CERTIFICATE AUTHORITY; ELECTRONIC COMMERCE; SSL.

Digital Simultaneous Voice and Data *n.* See DSVD.

digital-to-analog converter *n.* See DAC.

digital versatile disk *n.* See DVD.

digital video *n.* the capturing, manipulation, and storage of video in digital formats.

⇒ See also DIGITAL AUDIO; DIGITAL PHOTOGRAPHY; DOLBY DIGITAL; MOTION-JPEG; VIDEO CAPTURE; VIDEO EDITING.

Digital Video Interactive *n.* See DVI.

digital watermark *n.* a pattern of bits inserted into a digital image or an audio or video file that identifies the file's copyright information (author, rights, etc.).

⇒ See also COPY PROTECTION; FlashPix; SOFTWARE PIRACY.

digitize *v.t.* to convert (data) into a digital form.

⇒ See also BIT MAP; DIGITAL; OPTICAL SCANNER; PCM; SAMPLING.

digitizing tablet *n.* an input device, consisting of an electronic tablet and a special cursor or pen, that enables the user to enter drawings and sketches into a computer. The tablet is able to detect movement of the cursor or pen and translate the movements into digital signals.

⇒ See also CURSOR; INPUT DEVICE; MOUSE.

DIMM *n.* dual in-line memory module: a small circuit board that holds memory chips.

⇒ See also DRAM; SIMM.

DIN connector *n.* a connector, as the keyboard connector for PCs, that conforms to one of the many standards defined by the Deutsche Industrienorm, the standards-setting organization for Germany.

⇒ See also CONNECTOR.

dingbat *n.* a small picture, such as a star or a pointing finger, that can be inserted into a document.

⇒ See also BULLET; FONT.

DIP *n.* dual in-line package: a type of chip housed in a rectangular casing with two rows of connecting pins on either side.

⇒ See also CHIP; PGA.

DIP switch *n.* any in a series of tiny toggle switches built into a *DIP* on a circuit board.

⇒ See also CHIP; CONFIGURATION; EXPANSION BOARD; PRINTED CIRCUIT BOARD; TOGGLE.

DirecPC *n.* a service offered by Hughes Network Systems that provides Internet access through private satellite dishes.

⇒ See also ISDN; ISP.

Direct3D *n.* an Application Programming Interface (API) developed by Microsoft for manipulating and displaying three-dimensional objects.

⇒ See also 3-D SOFTWARE; DIRECTDRAW; DIRECTX; GRAPHICS ACCELERATOR; OPENGL.

direct access *n.* RANDOM ACCESS.

Direct Access Storage Device *n.* See DASD.

Direct Cable Connection *n.* See DCC.

direct-connect modem *n.* a modem that connects directly to a telephone line via modular connectors rather than requiring an acoustic coupler.

⇒ See also ACOUSTIC COUPLER; MODEM.

DirectDraw *n.* a software interface standard for transferring video processing from a PC's CPU to the video adapter.

⇒ See also DIRECT3D; GDI; GRAPHICS ACCELERATOR; VIDEO ADAPTER.

directive *n.* COMMAND.

direct memory access *n.* See DMA.

directory *n.* **1.** a special kind of file used to organize other files into a hierarchical structure. To access a file, you may need to specify the names of all the directories above it. You do this by specifying a path containing these names in order, separated from each other by a delimiter. The topmost directory in any file is called the *root directory*. A directory that is below another directory is called a *subdirectory*. A directory above a subdirectory is called the *parent directory*. Under UNIX, the root directory is represented by a forward slash (/); under DOS and Windows by a backslash (\). Some graphical user interfaces use the term *folder* instead of *directory*. **2.** in networks, a database of network resources, such as e-mail addresses. See under DIRECTORY SERVICE.

⇒ See also FILE; FILE MANAGEMENT SYSTEM; FOLDER; HIERARCHICAL; PATH; ROOT DIRECTORY; TREE STRUCTURE.

directory service *n.* a network service that identi-

computer

fies all resources, as e-mail addresses, computers, and peripheral devices, on a network and makes them accessible to users and applications.

⇒ See also ACTIVE DIRECTORY; LDAP; NDS; UNC; X.500.

DirectX *n.* a set of APIs developed by Microsoft that enables programmers to write programs that access hardware features of a computer without knowing exactly what hardware will be installed on the machine on which the program eventually runs.

⇒ See also ACTIVEX; DIRECT3D; GRAPHICS ACCELERATOR.

disc *n.* DISK. The spelling *disc* is often used for optical discs, whereas *disk* generally refers to magnetic disks, but there is no real rule.

⇒ See also DISK; OPTICAL DISK.

discretionary hyphen *n.* a hyphen that is inserted automatically by a hyphenation utility to split a word that would otherwise extend beyond the right margin. If the document is edited so that the word no longer requires hyphenating, the hyphen disappears.

⇒ See also HARD HYPHEN.

disk *n.* a round plate of plastic or metal, coated with magnetically or optically active material, on which data can be encoded.

⇒ See also AREAL DENSITY; CD-ROM; DISK DRIVE; ERASABLE OPTICAL DISK; FLOPPY DISK; FORMAT; HARD DISK; HEAD; MASS STORAGE; OPTICAL DISK; REMOVABLE HARD DISK.

disk cache *n.* a portion of RAM used to speed up access to data on a disk.

⇒ See also ACCESS TIME; BUFFER; CACHE; DISK DRIVE; RAM; SMARTDRIVE; VCACHE.

disk compression *n.* a type of data compression utility that works by storing compressed versions of files on the hard disk.

⇒ See also DATA COMPRESSION; HARD DISK DRIVE; PACKED FILE.

disk controller *n.* a chip and associated circuitry that is responsible for controlling a disk drive.

⇒ See also CONTROLLER; DISK DRIVE; EISA; IDE INTERFACE; SCSI.

disk crash *n.* HEAD CRASH.

disk drive *n.* a machine that reads data from and writes data onto a disk. A disk drive rotates the disk very fast and has one or more heads that read and write data.

⇒ See also ATA; DISK; DISK STRIPING; FLOPPY DISK; HARD DISK; MASS STORAGE; OPTICAL DISK; RAID; SMART.

diskette *n.* FLOPPY DISK.

diskless workstation *n.* a workstation or PC on a local-area network (LAN) that stores files on a network file server instead of having its own disk.

⇒ See also BOOTP; DISK DRIVE; LOCAL-AREA NETWORK; NET PC; NETWORK COMPUTER; SERVER; WORKSTATION.

disk mirroring *n.* a technique in which data is written to two duplicate disks simultaneously so that the system can instantly switch to the other disk without any loss of data or service if one of the disk drives fails.

⇒ See also FAULT TOLERANCE; RAID; SERVER MIRRORING.

disk operating system *n.* See DOS.

disk optimizer *n.* a program that uses a variety of techniques to make a disk more efficient.

⇒ See also DEFRAG; FRAGMENTATION.

disk pack *n.* a stack of removable hard disks for a mainframe, encased in a metal or plastic container.

⇒ See also HARD DISK; REMOVABLE HARD DISK.

disk striping *n.* a technique for spreading data over multiple disk drives to speed up operations that retrieve data from disk storage.

⇒ See also RAID.

dispatch table *n.* INTERRUPT VECTOR TABLE.

display *v.t.* **1.** to make (data or images) appear on a monitor. —*n.* **2.** DISPLAY SCREEN or MONITOR.

display adapter *n.* VIDEO ADAPTER.

Display Control Interface *n.* DIRECTDRAW.

Display Data Channel *n.* See DDC.

display screen *n.* the part of a monitor on which information is displayed.

⇒ See also CAD/CAM; DESKTOP PUBLISHING; FLAT-

PANEL DISPLAY; GRAPHICS; MONITOR; NOTEBOOK COMPUTER; PINCUSHION DISTORTION; RASTER; RESOLUTION.

distance learning *n.* a type of education in which students work on their own at home or at the office and communicate with faculty and other students via computer.

⇒ See also CBT; FORUM; VIDEOCONFERENCING.

Distributed Component Object Model *n.* See DCOM.

distributed computing *n.* a type of computing in which different components and objects constituting an application can be located on different computers connected to a network.

⇒ See also CORBA; DCOM; OBJECT-ORIENTED PROGRAMMING; OMG.

Distributed Computing Environment *n.* See DCE.

distributed database *n.* a database that consists of two or more data files located at different sites on a computer network.

⇒ See also DATABASE; DATABASE MANAGEMENT SYSTEM; DISTRIBUTED PROCESSING; NETWORK; TWO-PHASE COMMIT.

distributed processing *n.* any of a variety of computer systems that use more than one computer, or processor, to run an application.

⇒ See also DATABASE MANAGEMENT SYSTEM; DCE; DISTRIBUTED DATABASE; LOCAL-AREA NETWORK; PARALLEL PROCESSING.

Distributed System Object Model *n.* See DSOM.

dithering *n.* creating the illusion of new colors and shades by varying the pattern of dots. Newspaper photographs, for example, are dithered; different shades of gray are produced by varying the patterns of black and white dots.

⇒ See also BILEVEL PRINTER; CONTONE PRINTER; GRAY SCALING; HALFTONE.

Divx (div′iks), *n.* Digital video express: a DVD-ROM format being promoted by several large Hollywood companies, including Disney, Dreamworks SKG, Paramount, and Universal, in which a movie (or other data) loaded onto a DVD-ROM is playable only during a specific time frame.

⇒ See also DVD; DVD-ROM.

DLC Data Link Control: the second lowest layer in the OSI Reference Model.

⇒ See also ARP; IEEE 802 STANDARDS; MAC ADDRESS; NETWORK INTERFACE CARD; NODE; OSI.

DLL Dynamic Link Library: a library of executable functions or data that can be used by a Windows application.

⇒ See also LIBRARY; LINK; OLE; VBX.

DLP Digital Light Processing: a technology developed by Texas Instruments, used for projecting images from a monitor onto a large screen for presentations.

⇒ See also LCD; MONITOR; TEXAS INSTRUMENTS.

DLT Digital Linear Tape: a type of magnetic tape storage device that is faster than most other types of tape drives, achieving transfer rates of 2.5 MBps.

⇒ See also TAPE; TAPE DRIVE.

DMA direct memory access: a technique for transferring data from main memory to a device without passing it through the CPU.

⇒ See also BACKUP; CHANNEL; CPU; DIP SWITCH; EXPANSION BOARD; MAIN MEMORY; REAL TIME.

DMI Desktop Management Interface: an API to enable software to collect information about a computer environment, such as what software and expansion boards are installed.

⇒ See also MIF.

DNA WINDOWS DNA.

DNS 1. Domain Name System (or Service): an Internet service that translates domain names, which are alphabetic, into IP addresses, which are composed of numbers. **2.** digital nervous system: a term coined by Bill Gates to describe a network of personal computers that make it easier to obtain and understand information.

⇒ See also BIND; DOMAIN; DOMAIN NAME; IAHC; INTERPROCESS COMMUNICATION (IPC); WINS.

docking station *n.* a platform into which a portable computer can be installed, usu. containing slots for expansion cards, bays for storage devices, and connectors for peripheral devices, such as printers and monitors.

⇒ See also BAY; DESKTOP MODEL COMPUTER; EXPANSION BOARD; NOTEBOOK COMPUTER; PORT REPLICATOR; PORTABLE; SLOT.

document *n.* **1.** a file created with a word processor that can contain graphics, charts, and other objects in addition to text. —*v.t.* **2.** to enter written explanations into (a program's source code or a similarly opaque text).

⇒ See also COMPOUND DOCUMENT; DOCUMENTATION; FILE.

documentation *n.* instructions for using a computer device or program.

⇒ See also HELP; MAN PAGE; README FILE.

document management *n.* the computerized management of electronic as well as paper-based documents. A document-management system generally includes an optical scanner and OCR system, a database system, and a search mechanism.

⇒ See also OPTICAL CHARACTER RECOGNITION; PAPERLESS OFFICE.

Document Object Model *n.* See DOM.

Dolby Digital *n.* a standard for high-quality digital audio that is used for the sound portion of video stored in digital format, especially videos stored on DVD-ROMs.

⇒ See also AC-3; DIGITAL AUDIO; DIGITAL VIDEO; DVD.

DOM *n.* Document Object Model: the specification for the representation of the objects in a Web page (text, images, headers, links, etc.) that defines what attributes are associated with each object and how the objects and attributes can be manipulated.

⇒ See also DYNAMIC HTML; HTML; JAVASCRIPT; WEB PAGE; XML.

domain *n.* a group of computers and devices on a network that are administered as a unit with common rules and procedures: defined within the Internet by the *IP address*.

⇒ See also DNS; DOMAIN NAME; INTERNET.

domain name *n.* a name that identifies one or more IP addresses and is used in a URL, usually along with the name of a particular host computer, to identify a particular Web page. Every domain name has a suffix that indicates which top-level domain (TLD) it belongs to, as *gov* for government agencies, *edu* for educational institutions, and *org* for organizations.

⇒ See also DNS; DOMAIN; IAHC; InterNIC; IP ADDRESS; TLD; WHOIS.

Domain Name Server *n.* See DNS.

Domain Name Service *n.* See DNS.

dongle *n.* a device that attaches to a computer to control access to a particular application as a means of copy protection.

⇒ See also COPY PROTECTION.

DOS (dôs *or* dos *or as initials*), *n.* disk operating system: any operating system, but most often MS-DOS (Microsoft disk operating system). Originally developed by Microsoft for IBM, MS-DOS was the standard operating system for IBM-compatible personal computers.

⇒ See also MICROSOFT; MICROSOFT WINDOWS; OPERATING SYSTEM; OS/2; PC; PIF FILE.

dot *n.* **1.** same as the period character (.): used in DOS, Windows, and OS/2 systems to separate a file-name from its extension or in URLs to separate the parts of a host name. **2.** in bit-mapped representations, a single point, the smallest identifiable part of an image.

⇒ See also BIT MAP; DPI; EXTENSION; FILENAME; RESOLUTION.

dot-matrix printer *n.* a type of printer that produces characters and illustrations by striking pins against an ink ribbon to print closely spaced dots in the appropriate shape.

⇒ See also IMPACT PRINTER; OKIDATA; PRINTER.

dot pitch *n.* a measurement that indicates the distance between like-colored phosphor dots on a display screen, measured in millimeters.

⇒ See also COLOR MONITOR; MASK PITCH; MONITOR; PIXEL.

dots per inch *n.* See DPI.

double click *v.i.* to tap a mouse button twice in rapid succession, as to open a file.

⇒ See also CLICK; MOUSE.

double-density disk *n.* an obsolete kind of floppy disk that has twice the storage capacity of a single-density floppy.

⇒ See also DENSITY; FLOPPY DISK.

double precision *adj.* referring to a type of floating-point number that has more precision (that is, more digits to the right of the decimal point) than a single-precision number. It uses twice as many bits as a regular floating-point number.

⇒ See also FLOATING-POINT NUMBER; IEEE.

double-scan display *n.* DUAL-SCAN DISPLAY.

double-sided disk *n.* a floppy disk with both sides prepared for recording data.

⇒ See also DISK DRIVE; FLOPPY DISK.

double-speed CD-ROM *n.* a CD-ROM drive that transfers data at about 300Kbp/sec.

double supertwist *n.* See DSTN.

down *adj.* of a computer system, not working or not available to users, either because it has crashed or because routine servicing is taking place.

⇒ See also CRASH.

download *v.t.* to copy (data or software) from a main source to a peripheral device, as from an on-line service to one's own computer, or from a computer into a laser printer.

⇒ See also ANONYMOUS FTP; BULLETIN BOARD SYSTEM; FONT; ONLINE SERVICE; UPLOAD.

downloadable font *n.* SOFT FONT.

downward compatible *adj.* BACKWARD COMPATIBLE.

DP DATA PROCESSING.

dpi dots per inch: a measure of resolution used for images. The more dots per inch, the higher the resolution. A resolution of 600 dots per inch means 600 dots across and 600 dots down, or 360,000 dots per square inch.

⇒ See also DOT; LASER PRINTER; RESOLUTION.

draft mode *n.* a printing mode in which the printer prints text as fast as possible without regard to print quality.

⇒ See also DOT-MATRIX PRINTER; LETTER QUALITY (LQ); NEAR LETTER QUALITY.

draft-quality *adj.* referring to or producing print whose quality is less than near-letter-quality.

⇒ See also DOT-MATRIX PRINTER; DRAFT MODE; LETTER QUALITY (LQ); NEAR LETTER QUALITY.

drag *v.t.* **1.** in graphical user interfaces, to move (an icon or other image) on a display screen, esp. by using a mouse. More generally, to perform any operation, such as moving a block of text from one part of a document to another, in which the mouse button is held down while the mouse is moved. **2.** to move (the mouse) while holding down the button, as to select a block of text.

⇒ See also DRAG-AND-DROP; GRAPHICAL USER INTERFACE; MOUSE; SELECT.

drag-and-drop *adj.* describing an application that allows the user to drag objects to specific locations on the screen to perform actions on them.

⇒ See also DRAG; GRAPHICAL USER INTERFACE.

drag-n-drop *adj.* DRAG-AND-DROP.

DRAM (dē′ram′), *n.* dynamic random access memory: a type of memory used in most personal computers.

⇒ See also BEDO DRAM; DIMM; DYNAMIC RAM; EDO DRAM; MDRAM; PIPELINE BURST CACHE; RDRAM; SDRAM; SGRAM; SLDRAM.

drawing tablet *n.* DIGITIZING TABLET.

draw program *n.* a graphics program that uses vector graphics and enables the user to draw pictures, then store the images in files, merge them into documents, and print them.

⇒ See also GRAPHICS; PAINT PROGRAM; VECTOR GRAPHICS.

drive *n.* DISK DRIVE.

drive bay *n.* an area of reserved space in a personal computer case where hard or floppy disk drives (or tape drives) can be installed.

⇒ See also BAY; DISK DRIVE; MASS STORAGE.

computer

driver *n.* a program that controls a device, as a printer, disk drive, or keyboard.
⇒ See also CONFIG.SYS; CONTROLLER; DEVICE; ODI; VIRTUAL DEVICE DRIVER.

drop cap *n.* in desktop publishing, the first letter of a paragraph that is enlarged to "drop" down two or more lines.
⇒ See also DESKTOP PUBLISHING.

drop-down menu *n.* PULL-DOWN MENU.

DS-1 See T-1.

DS-3 See T-3.

DSL See xDSL.

DSOM *n.* Distributed System Object Model: a version of **SOM** that supports sharing binary objects across networks.
⇒ See also CORBA; DCOM; SOM.

DSP **1.** digital signal processing: the process of using a data compression technique to manipulate analog information, such as sound or photographs, that has been converted into a digital form. **2.** digital signal processor: a special type of coprocessor designed for performing the mathematics involved in DSP. Most DSPs are programmable, which means that they can be used for manipulating different types of information, including sound, images, and video.
⇒ See also COPROCESSOR; DATA COMPRESSION; DIGITIZE; GRAPHICS ACCELERATOR; MMX; SOUND CARD.

DSS digital satellite system: a network of satellites that broadcast digital data.
⇒ See also HDTV.

DSTN double-layer supertwist nematic: a passive-matrix LCD technology that uses two display layers to counteract the color shifting that occurs with conventional supertwist displays.
⇒ See also CSTN; LCD; PASSIVE-MATRIX DISPLAY; SUPERTWIST.

DSU See CSU/DSU.

DSVD Digital Simultaneous Voice and Data: an all-digital technology for concurrent voice and data (SVD) transmission over a single analog telephone line.
⇒ See also ITU; MODEM; POTS.

DTE Data Terminal Equipment: a device that controls data flowing to or from a computer.
⇒ See also DCE; RS-232C; UART.

DTMF Dual Tone Multi-Frequency: the signaling system used by touchtone telephones. Each key produces a sound consisting of two specific frequencies (tones).
⇒ See also TELEPHONY.

DTP DESKTOP PUBLISHING.

dual in-line memory module *n.* See DIMM.

dual in-line package *n.* See DIP.

dual-scan display *n.* a type of passive-matrix LCD display that provides faster refresh rates than conventional passive-matrix displays by dividing the screen into two sections that are refreshed simultaneously.
⇒ See also ACTIVE-MATRIX DISPLAY; FLAT-PANEL DISPLAY; LCD; PASSIVE-MATRIX DISPLAY.

dual supertwist *n.* See under SUPERTWIST.

Dual Tone Multi-Frequency *n.* See DTMF.

dumb terminal *n.* a display monitor and keyboard with no processing capabilities.
⇒ See also DISPLAY SCREEN; INTELLIGENT TERMINAL; SMART TERMINAL; TERMINAL; WINDOWS TERMINAL.

dummy *adj.* referring to a placeholder. A *dummy variable* is a variable that does not contain any useful data, but does reserve space that a real variable will use later.
⇒ See also VARIABLE.

dump *v.t.* **1.** to output (computer data), esp. in order to diagnose a failure. **—***n.* **2.** the result of copying raw data from one place to another with little or no formatting for readability.

DUN DIAL-UP NETWORKING.

duplex *n.* FULL DUPLEX.

DV DIGITAL VIDEO.

DVD digital versatile disc or digital video disc: a type of CD-ROM that holds a minimum of 4.7GB, enough for a full-length movie.
⇒ See also CD-I (COMPACT DISC–INTERACTIVE); CD-ROM; COMPACT DISC; DIVX; DOLBY DIGITAL; DVD+RW; DVD-RAM; DVD-ROM; DVD-VIDEO; DVI; MPEG; MULTIMEDIA.

DVD-RAM *n.* a type of rewritable DVD disc.
⇒ See also CD-RW DISK; DVD; DVD+RW; DVD-ROM; DVD-VIDEO.

DVD-ROM *n.* a type of read-only DVD disc.
⇒ See also DVD; DVD-RAM; MPEG.

DVD+RW a standard for rewritable DVD disks being promoted by Hewlett-Packard, Philips, and Sony. It is competing with another standard, called DVD-RAM, developed by the DVD Consortium. The two standards are incompatible.
⇒ See also CD-RW DISK; DVD; DVD-RAM.

DVD-Video *n.* a video format for displaying full-length digital movies on a player that attaches to a television like a videocassette player.
⇒ See also COPY PROTECTION; DVD; DVD-ROM.

DVI **1.** Digital Video Interactive: a technology developed by General Electric that enables a computer to store and display moving video images like those on television by using specialized processors to compress and decompress the data. **2.** Device Independent: a file format used by the TeX typography system.
⇒ See also CD-I (COMPACT DISC–INTERACTIVE); CD-RW DISK; CODEC; DVD; INDEO; INTEL; MPEG.

Dvorak keyboard *n.* a keyboard on which the middle row of keys includes the most common letters, and common letter combinations are positioned in such a way that they can be typed quickly. [named after August Dvorak, who invented it with his brother-in-law, William Dealy]
⇒ See also KEYBOARD; MACRO; QWERTY KEYBOARD.

DW DATA WAREHOUSING.

DXF Data Exchange File: a two-dimensional graphics file format supported by most PC-based CAD products.
⇒ See also CAD; GRAPHICS; GRAPHICS FILE FORMATS.

dynamic *adj.* referring to actions that take place at the moment they are needed rather than in advance: *dynamic memory allocation.*
⇒ See also DYNAMIC VARIABLE; STATIC VARIABLE.

dynamic acceleration *n.* a feature that causes the mouse resolution to depend on how fast the mouse is moved. When it is moved fast, the cursor moves proportionally farther. Also called **ballistic tracking, automatic acceleration, variable acceleration.**
⇒ See also MOUSE; RESOLUTION.

Dynamic Data Exchange *n.* See DDE.

Dynamic Host Configuration Protocol *n.* See DHCP.

dynamic HTML *n.* **1.** in contrast to static HTML pages, Web content that changes each time it is viewed, depending on such factors as time of day and profile of the reader. **2. Dynamic HTML,** extensions that enable a Web page to react to user input without sending requests to the Web server.
⇒ See also ACTIVEX CONTROL; CGI; COOKIE; DOM; JAVA; JAVASCRIPT; SSI; W3C; WINDOWS DNA.

dynamic link library *n.* See DLL.

dynamic RAM *n.* a type of physical memory that must be constantly refreshed to avoid losing its contents: used in most personal computers.
⇒ See also MAIN MEMORY; RAM; REFRESH; SRAM.

dynamic variable *n.* in programming, a variable whose storage is allocated when the program is run.
⇒ See also STATIC VARIABLE; VARIABLE.

easter egg *n.* a secret message or screen buried in an application, made visible only through an elaborate sequence of keystrokes not revealed in the documentation. Usually easter eggs are used to display the credits for the development team, or a humorous message.
⇒ See also APPLICATION; PROGRAM.

EBCDIC (eb′si dik), *n.* Extended Binary-Coded Decimal Interchange Code: an IBM code for representing characters as numbers. Although it is widely used on large IBM computers, most other computers, including PCs and Macintoshes, use ASCII codes.
⇒ See also ASCII.

ECC Error-Correcting Code: a technique for adding redundant bits to detect and correct errors in blocks of binary data.
⇒ See also PARITY.

ECC memory *n.* Error-Correcting Code memory: a type of memory that includes special circuitry for ensuring the accuracy of data as it passes in and out of memory.
⇒ See also CHECKSUM; MEMORY.

e-commerce *n.* ELECTRONIC COMMERCE.

ECP Extended Capabilities Port: a parallel-port standard for PCs that supports bi-directional communication between the PC and peripheral devices such as a printer.
⇒ See also CENTRONICS INTERFACE; DCC; EPP; PARALLEL PORT.

edge connector *n.* the part of a printed circuit board that plugs into a computer or device. The edge connector usually has a row of metallic tracks that provide the electrical connection.
⇒ See also PRINTED CIRCUIT BOARD.

EDI Electronic Data Interchange: the transfer of data between different companies through the use of networks, such as the Internet. EDI is becoming increasingly important as a way for companies to buy, sell, and trade information.
⇒ See also ELECTRONIC COMMERCE.

editor *n.* a program used to create and edit text files. A *line editor* is a primitive form of editor that requires the user to specify a particular line of text before making changes to it. A *screen-oriented editor* lets the user modify any text that appears on the display screen by moving the cursor to the desired location. In general, editors provide fewer formatting features than word processors. The term *editor* usually refers to source code editors.
⇒ See also SOURCE CODE; WORD PROCESSING.

EDO DRAM *n.* Extended Data Output Dynamic Random Access Memory: a type of DRAM that is faster than conventional DRAM. EDO DRAM can start accessing the next block of memory at the same time that it sends the previous block to the CPU.
⇒ See also ACCESS TIME; BEDO DRAM; CYCLE TIME; DRAM; FPM RAM; RDRAM; SDRAM; SLDRAM.

EEMS Enhanced Expanded Memory Specification: an enhanced version of the original EMS, which enables DOS applications to use more than 1MB (megabyte) of memory.
⇒ See also EXPANDED MEMORY; LIM MEMORY.

EEPROM (dub′əl ē′prom′, ē′ē′prom′), *n.* electrically erasable programmable read-only memory: a special type of PROM that can be erased by exposing it to an electrical charge. EEPROM retains its contents even when the power is turned off.
⇒ See also EPROM; FLASH MEMORY; MEMORY; NVRAM; PROM; RAM; ROM.

EGA enhanced graphics adapter: a now obsolete graphics display system for PCs introduced by IBM in 1984. EGA supports 16 colors from a palette of 64 and provides a resolution of 640 by 350.
⇒ See also CGA; VGA; VIDEO ADAPTER.

EIA ELECTRONIC INDUSTRIES ASSOCIATION.

EIA (Electronic Industries Association) interface *n.* See RS-232C.

EIDE enhanced IDE: a newer version of the IDE mass storage device interface standard. It supports data rates up to at least 16.6 MBps. EIDE has replaced SCSI in many areas. For historical reasons it is also known as Fast ATA or Fast IDE.
⇒ See also ATA; ESDI; IDE INTERFACE; SCSI.

Eiffel *n.* an advanced programming language introduced in 1986. A basic Windows compiler is available at no charge. Eiffel encourages object-oriented program development and supports a systematic approach to software development.
⇒ See also C; OBJECT-ORIENTED PROGRAMMING.

8088 an early Intel microprocessor, used in the original IBM PC and PC/XT.

8086 an early Intel microprocessor.

8514/A a high-resolution video standard for PCs developed by IBM in 1987. It is designed to extend the capabilities of VGA. The 8514/A standard provides a resolution of 1,024 by 768 pixels, and a palette of 262,000 colors.
⇒ See also INTERLACING; MONOCHROME; PALETTE; RESOLUTION; SVGA; VIDEO ADAPTER; XGA.

80486 an early Intel microprocessor, faster than an 80386 but slower than a Pentium.

80386 an early Intel microprocessor, faster than an 80286 but slower than an 80486.

80286 an early Intel microprocessor, faster than an 8086 but slower than an 80386.

EISA *n.* Extended Industry Standard Architecture: a bus architecture designed for PCs using an Intel 80386, 80486, or Pentium microprocessor. EISA buses are 32 bits wide and support multiprocessing. Computers with an EISA bus can use new EISA expansion cards as well as old AT expansion cards. EISA and MCA are not compatible with each other.
⇒ See also BUS; EXPANSION BOARD; INDUSTRY STANDARD ARCHITECTURE (ISA) BUS; LOCAL BUS; MICRO CHANNEL ARCHITECTURE (MCA); MULTIPROCESSING; PCI.

ELD ELECTROLUMINESCENT DISPLAY.

electrically erasable programmable read-only memory *n.* See EEPROM.

electroluminescent display (ELD) *n.* a technology used in some notebook computers to produce a flat-panel display. It works by sandwiching a thin film of phosphorescent substance between two plates coated with wire at right angles. When an electrical current is passed through wire on each plate, the phosphorescent film at the intersection glows, creating a pixel.
⇒ See also ACTIVE-MATRIX DISPLAY; FLAT-PANEL DISPLAY; GAS-PLASMA DISPLAY; LCD; NOTEBOOK COMPUTER.

electronic commerce *n.* the conducting of business on-line. This includes, for example, buying and selling products with digital cash and via Electronic Data Interchange (EDI).
⇒ See also BIOMETRICS; CERTIFICATE AUTHORITY; DIGITAL CASH; DIGITAL SIGNATURE; EDI; ESD; PKI; SET.

Electronic Data Interchange *n.* See EDI.

Electronic Frontier Foundation *n.* a nonprofit organization dedicated to protecting civil liberties in the modern communications age.
⇒ See also CLIPPER CHIP.

Electronic Industries Association *n.* a trade association representing the U.S. high technology community. It began in 1924 as the Radio Manufacturers Association.
⇒ See also RS-232C; RS-422 AND RS-423; RS-485; STANDARD.

electronic mail *n.* E-MAIL.

electronic publishing *n.* the publishing of information in an electronic form. This includes publishing CD-ROMs as well as making information available through online services.

⇒ See also CD-ROM; MULTIMEDIA; ONLINE SERVICE.

electrostatic discharge *n.* See ESD.

elevator *n.* a scroll box. See under SCROLL BAR.

ELF emission *n.* extremely low frequency emission: a magnetic field generated by common electrical appliances, such as computer monitors.

⇒ See also MPR II; MONITOR.

e-mail or email *n.* **1.** the transmission of messages over communications networks. Some e-mail systems are confined to a single computer system or network, but others have gateways to other computer systems. **2.** a message sent by such a system. Messages can be notes entered from the keyboard or files stored on disk. Sent messages are stored in electronic mailboxes.

⇒ See also ACRONYM; ATTACHMENT; BROADCASTING; BinHex; CCITT; E-MAIL ADDRESS; FINGER; GATEWAY; IMAP; INSTANT MESSAGING; MAILBOX; MAILING LIST; MAPI; MIME; NETWORK; ONLINE SERVICE; POP; SNAIL-MAIL; SNMP; SPAM; USERNAME; UUENCODE; WORKGROUP COMPUTING.

e-mail address *n.* a name that identifies an electronic post office box on a network where e-mail can be sent. Different types of networks have different formats for e-mail addresses. Every user on the Internet has a unique e-mail address.

⇒ See also ADDRESS; E-MAIL; X.400.

e-mail client *n.* an application that runs on a personal computer or workstation and enables the user to send, receive, and organize e-mail. E-mail is sent from many clients to a server, which re-routes the mail to its intended destination.

⇒ See also CLIENT; EUDORA; FINGER; MAILING LIST; PINE; TNEF.

embedded command *n.* in word processing, a sequence of special characters inserted into a document that affects the formatting of the document when it is printed. Embedded commands are usually invisible when the file is being edited.

⇒ See also COMMAND; FONT; WORD PROCESSING.

embedded computer *n.* EMBEDDED SYSTEM.

embedded object *n.* a reference to an object created by one application, embedded (rather than just inserted or pasted) in a document created by another application in such a way that changes made to the object by the first application automatically appear in the embedded version.

⇒ See also DOCUMENT; OLE.

embedded system *n.* a specialized computer system that is part of a larger system or machine. Virtually all appliances that have a digital interface, such as watches, microwaves, VCRs, and cars, contain embedded systems.

⇒ See also MICROCONTROLLER; SYSTEM.

emoticon *n.* a small symbol formed with punctuation characters: used to communicate humor, sarcasm, etc., within an e-mail message. For example, a :-) emoticon indicates that the previous statement is meant as a joke and should not be taken seriously.

⇒ See also E-MAIL; SMILEY.

EMS EXPANDED MEMORY SPECIFICATION.

⇒ See also EXPANDED MEMORY.

emulation *n.* the ability of a program or device to imitate another program or device. Emulation can make one printer accept formatting codes meant for a printer of some other type. It is also possible for a computer to emulate another type of computer.

⇒ See also COMMUNICATIONS SOFTWARE; COMPATIBLE; LOG ON; MAINFRAME; TERMINAL.

Encapsulated PostScript *n.* See EPS.

encapsulation *n.* **1.** (in programming) the process of combining elements to create a new entity. For example, a complex data type such as a record or structure encapsulates a collection of simpler pieces of data. **2.** (in networking) TUNNELING.

encryption *n.* the translation of data into a secret code. To read an encrypted file, one must have access to a secret key or password. Encryption is the most effective way to achieve data security.

⇒ See also CIPHER TEXT; CLIPPER CHIP; CRYPTOGRAPHY; DECRYPTION; DIGITAL CERTIFICATE; DIGITAL ENVELOPE;

PASSWORD; PLAIN TEXT; PUBLIC-KEY ENCRYPTION; RSA; SECURITY; SYMMETRIC ENCRYPTION.

endian *n.* See under BIG-ENDIAN.

End key *n.* a special cursor control key on PC keyboards and Macintosh extended keyboards. The End key might move the cursor to the end of the line, the end of the page, or the end of the file, depending on which program is running.

⇒ See also KEYBOARD.

end of file *n.* EOF MARK..

end of line *n.* EOL MARK.

end user *n.* the final or ultimate user of a computer system. The end user is the individual who uses the product after it has been fully developed and marketed.

⇒ See also EULA; USER.

Energy Star *n.* a voluntary labeling program of the U.S. Environmental Protection Agency (EPA) and the U.S. Department of Energy that identifies energy efficient products.

⇒ See also GREEN PC.

Enhanced Data Output DRAM *n.* EDO DRAM.

Enhanced Expanded Memory Specification *n.* See EEMS.

enhanced graphics adapter *n.* See EGA.

Enhanced IDE *n.* See EIDE.

Enhanced Keyboard *n.* a 101- or 102-key keyboard from IBM that supersedes the keyboard for the PC/AT computer. The Enhanced Keyboard has a row of 12 function keys at the top instead of 10 function keys grouped on the left side of the keyboard.

⇒ See also EXTENDED KEYBOARD; FUNCTION KEYS; KEYBOARD.

Enhanced Small Device Interface *n.* See ESDI.

Enter key *n.* a key that informs the currently running program that the user has finished with a line of input. In some programs, the Enter key causes whatever option or action has been selected to be executed.

⇒ See also RETURN KEY.

enterprise *n.* in the computer field, any large organization. An intranet is an example of an enterprise computing system.

⇒ See also ERP; INTRANET.

enterprise resource planning *n.* See ERP.

environment *n.* **1.** the state of a computer, usually determined by which programs are running and basic hardware and software characteristics. One ingredient of an environment is the operating system. **2.** in DOS and UNIX systems, an area in memory that the operating system and other programs use to store various types of miscellaneous information.

⇒ See also DOS; OPERATING SYSTEM; PLATFORM.

EO ERASABLE OPTICAL DISK.

EOF mark *n.* end-of-file mark: a special character or sequence of characters that marks the end of a file. Operating systems need to keep track of where every file ends.

⇒ See also EOL MARK.

EOL mark *n.* end-of-line mark: a special character or sequence of characters that marks the end of a line.

⇒ See also EOF MARK.

EPOC *n.* an operating system from Psion Software, designed specifically for mobile, ROM-based computing devices.

⇒ See also HAND-HELD COMPUTER; OPERATING SYSTEM; PDA; WINDOWS CE.

EPP *n.* Enhanced Parallel Port: a parallel port standard for PCs that supports bi-directional communication between the PC and attached devices, such as a printer.

⇒ See also CENTRONICS INTERFACE; ECP; PARALLEL PORT.

EPROM (ē′prom′), *n.* erasable programmable read-only memory: a special type of memory that retains its contents until it is exposed to ultraviolet light. The ultraviolet light clears its contents, making it possible to reprogram the memory. A special device called a *PROM programmer* or *PROM burner* is needed to write to and erase an EPROM. EPROMs are used widely in personal computers because they

enable the manufacturer to update the contents of the memory until the computer is shipped.
⇒ See also EEPROM; MEMORY; PROM.

EPS Encapsulated PostScript: the graphics file format used by the PostScript language. EPS files can be either binary or ASCII.
⇒ See also GRAPHICS; GRAPHICS FILE FORMATS; POST-SCRIPT.

erasable optical disk *n.* a type of optical disk that can be erased and loaded with new data. In contrast, most optical disks, called CD-ROMs, are read-only.
⇒ See also ACCESS TIME; CD-ROM; DISK; FLOPPY DISK; MASS STORAGE; OPTICAL DISK.

erasable programmable read-only memory *n.* See EPROM.

ergonomics *n.* the science concerned with designing safe and comfortable machines for use by humans. In the computer field, ergonomics plays an important role in the design of monitors and keyboards.
⇒ See also CARPAL TUNNEL SYNDROME.

ERP enterprise resource planning: a business management system that integrates all facets of the business, including planning, manufacturing, sales, and marketing. Software applications are available to help business managers implement ERP.
⇒ See also ENTERPRISE.

error checking and correcting *n.* See ECC.

Error-Correcting Code memory *n.* ECC MEMORY.

error detection *n.* in communications, a class of techniques for detecting garbled messages.
⇒ See also CCITT; CHECKSUM; CRC; DATA INTEGRITY; KERMIT; MNP; XMODEM.

ESC *n.* ESCAPE KEY.
⇒ See also ESCAPE CHARACTER.

escape character *n.* a special character that can have many different functions. It is often used to abort the current command and return to a previous place in the program. It is also used to send special instructions to printers and other devices. An escape character is generated with the *Escape key.*
⇒ See also ESCAPE SEQUENCE; KEYBOARD.

Escape key *n.* a key on computer keyboards, usually labeled *Esc.* In DOS and Windows environments, pressing the Escape key usually cancels or aborts the current operation.
⇒ See also ABORT; ESC; KEYBOARD.

escape sequence *n.* a sequence of special characters that sends a command to a device or program. Typically, an escape sequence begins with an *escape character,* but this is not universally true.
⇒ See also ESCAPE CHARACTER.

ESCD Extended System Configuration Data: a format for storing information about Plug-and-Play (PnP) devices in the BIOS.
⇒ See also BIOS; PLUG-AND-PLAY; PNP.

ESD 1. Electronic Software Distribution: a system for selling software over a network. ESD systems provide secure communications that customers use to download and pay for software. **2.** electrostatic discharge: the rapid discharge of static electricity from one object to another of a different potential. An electrostatic discharge can damage integrated circuits in computer and communications equipment.
⇒ See also ELECTRONIC COMMERCE; UPGRADE.

ESDI (ez/dē *or as initials*), *n.* Enhanced Small Device Interface: an obsolete interface standard developed by a consortium of the leading personal-computer manufacturers for connecting disk drives to PCs.
⇒ See also DISK DRIVE; EIDE; IDE INTERFACE; SCSI; ST-506 INTERFACE.

Ethernet *n.* a local-area network (LAN) protocol developed by Xerox Corporation in cooperation with DEC and Intel in 1976. Ethernet uses a bus or star topology and supports data transfer rates of 10 Mbps or 100 Mbps. It is one of the most widely implemented LAN standards.
⇒ See also 10BASE-T; 10BASE-2; 10BASE5; 10BASET; ATM; AUI; BUS NETWORK; CSMA/CD; GIGABIT ETHERNET; IEEE; IEEE 802 STANDARDS; LOCAL-AREA NETWORK;

NETWORK; PROTOCOL; SHARED ETHERNET; SWITCHED ETHERNET; TOPOLOGY.

Eudora *n.* a popular e-mail client now owned by QUALCOMM, Inc.
⇒ See also E-MAIL CLIENT.

EULA End-User License Agreement: the type of license used for most software.
⇒ See also END USER; SOFTWARE LICENSING.

even header *n.* in word processing, a header that appears only on even-numbered pages.
⇒ See also HEADER.

even parity *n.* the parity-checking mode in which each set of transmitted bits must have an even number of set bits. The parity-checking system on the sending side ensures even parity by setting the extra *parity bit* if necessary.
⇒ See also PARITY CHECKING.

event *n.* an action or occurrence detected by a program. Events can be user actions, such as clicking a mouse button or pressing a key, or system occurrences, such as running out of memory.
⇒ See also INTERRUPT.

exabyte *n.* 2^{60} (1,152,921,504,606,846,976) bytes. An exabyte is equal to 1,024 petabytes.
⇒ See also PETABYTE; TERABYTE; YOTTABYTE; ZETTABYTE.

Excite *n.* a World Wide Web search engine developed by Excite, Inc. It provides a full-text index of approximately 50 million Web pages.
⇒ See also ALTA VISTA; HOTBOT; INFOSEEK; LYCOS; MAGELLAN; OPEN TEXT; SEARCH ENGINE; WEBCRAWLER; YAHOO!.

exclusive OR *n.* a Boolean operator that returns a value of TRUE only if both its operands have different values. Conversely, an *inclusive OR operator* returns a value of TRUE if *either* of its operands is TRUE. Whereas an inclusive OR can be translated "this, that, or both," an exclusive OR means "this or that, but not both." An exclusive OR is often called an *XOR* or *EOR.*
⇒ See also BOOLEAN OPERATOR.

executable file *n.* a file in a format that the computer can directly execute. Unlike source files, executable files cannot be read by humans.
⇒ See also ASSEMBLER; BINARY FILE; BINARY FORMAT; COM FILE; COMPILER; EXE FILE; FILE; SOURCE CODE.

execute *v.t.* to run (a program) or perform (a command).
⇒ See also LAUNCH.

EXE file (ē/eks'ē/) *n.* in DOS and Windows systems, an executable file with a .EXE extension.
⇒ See also COM FILE; EXECUTABLE FILE; EXTENSION; PROGRAM.

expanded memory *n.* a technique for utilizing more than 1MB (megabyte) of main memory in DOS-based computers. Also called **EMS (Expanded Memory Specification).**
⇒ See also CONVENTIONAL MEMORY; EEMS; EXTENDED MEMORY; LOW MEMORY; MAIN MEMORY; RAM DISK.

expansion board *n.* a printed circuit board that can be inserted into a computer to give it added capabilities. Sound cards and graphics accelerators are examples of expansion boards.
⇒ See also ACCELERATOR BOARD; ADAPTER; ADD-IN; ADD-ON; CPU; DAUGHTERCARD; EXPANSION SLOT; GRAPHICS ACCELERATOR; PCI; PRINTED CIRCUIT BOARD; SOUND CARD; TELEVISION BOARD; VIDEO ADAPTER.

expansion bus *n.* a collection of wires and protocols that allows the expansion of a computer by the insertion of printed circuit boards. Nearly all new PCs have a PCI bus for performance as well as an ISA bus for backward compatibility.
⇒ See also BUS; EISA; EXPANSION BOARD; EXPANSION SLOT; LOCAL BUS; PCI; PROTOCOL; VL-Bus.

expansion card *n.* EXPANSION BOARD.

expansion slot *n.* an opening in a computer where an expansion board can be inserted to add new capabilities to the computer.
⇒ See also EXPANSION BOARD; LOCAL BUS; PRINTED CIRCUIT BOARD.

expert system *n.* a computer application that performs a task that would otherwise be performed by a human expert. Expert systems are part of a general category of computer applications known as

artificial intelligence.
⇒ See also ARTIFICIAL INTELLIGENCE; HEURISTIC PROGRAMMING; PROLOG.

exploded view *n.* a picture or diagram that shows the components of an object slightly separated, as if there had been a neat explosion in the middle of the object. Many spreadsheet applications can automatically create simple exploded diagrams such as exploded pie charts.
⇒ See also SPREADSHEET.

export *v.t.* to format (data) in such a way that it can be used by another application. An application that can export data can create a file in a format that another application understands, enabling the two programs to share the same data.
⇒ See also EXPORT; COMMA-DELIMITED; CONVERT; FILTER; IMPORT; MIDDLEWARE.

expression *n.* in programming, an expression is any legal combination of symbols that represents a value. Each programming language and application has its own rules for what is legal and illegal.
⇒ See also ARITHMETIC EXPRESSION; BOOLEAN EXPRESSION; CHARACTER STRING; DATA TYPE; FLOATING-POINT NUMBER; FORMULA; INTEGER; OPERAND; OPERATOR; QUERY.

extended ASCII *n.* a set of codes that extends the basic ASCII set. The basic ASCII set uses 7 bits for each character, giving it a total of 128 unique symbols. The extended ASCII character set uses 8 bits, which gives it an additional 128 characters. The extra characters can represent characters from foreign languages and special symbols for drawing pictures.
⇒ See also ASCII; CHARACTER BASED; ISO LATIN 1.

Extended Binary-Coded Decimal Interchange Code *n.* See EBCDIC.

Extended Capabilities Port *n.* See ECP.

extended graphics array *n.* See XGA.

Extended Industry Standard Architecture *n.* See EISA.

extended keyboard *n.* a keyboard for Macintosh computers that contains up to 15 function keys above the alphanumeric keys, and a numeric keypad.
⇒ See also ENHANCED KEYBOARD.

extended memory *n.* memory above and beyond the standard 1MB (megabyte) of main memory that

DOS supports. Extended memory is generally only usable with the Windows and OS-2 operating systems.
⇒ See also CONVENTIONAL MEMORY; EXPANDED MEMORY; HIGH MEMORY AREA; LOW MEMORY; PROTECTED MODE; RAM DISK; VCPI; XMS.

Extended Memory Specification *n.* See XMS.

extended VGA *n.* See SVGA.

eXtensible Markup Language *n.* See XML.

extension *n.* **1.** an extra feature added to a standard programming language or operating system. **2.** in DOS and some other operating systems, one or several letters at the end of a filename. Filename extensions usually follow a period (dot) and indicate the type of information stored in the file. **3.** in Macintosh environments, a program that extends the system's capabilities. **4.** PLUG-IN.
⇒ See also ASSOCIATE; DOT; FTS FILE; GID FILE; INIT; MEMORY RESIDENT.

external bus *n.* a bus that connects a computer to peripheral devices.
⇒ See also IEEE 1394; PERIPHERAL DEVICE.

external cache *n.* L2 CACHE.

external command *n.* in DOS systems, any command that does not reside in the COMMAND.COM file. This includes all other COM files, as well as EXE and BAT files.
⇒ See also COMMAND; COMMAND.COM; INTERNAL COMMAND.

external modem *n.* a modem that resides in a self-contained box outside the computer system.
⇒ See also INTERNAL MODEM; MODEM.

extranet *n.* an intranet that is partially accessible to authorized persons outside of a company or organization.
⇒ See also AUTHORIZATION; FIREWALL; INTRANET.

extremely low-frequency (ELF) emission *n.* ELF EMISSION.

e-zine *n.* electronic magazine: a Web site that is modeled after a print magazine. Some e-zines are simply electronic versions of existing print magazines, whereas others exist only in their digital form.
⇒ See also WEB SITE.

abcde**F**ghijklmnopqrstuvwxyz

F1, F2 . . . F15 *n.* the names of the function keys. See under FUNCTION KEYS.

facsimile machine *n.* FAX MACHINE.

FAQ (ef/ā/kyōō/ *or* fak), *n.* frequently asked questions: an electronic document that contains answers to the most commonly asked questions about some topic, often a technical one.
⇒ See also HELP.

Fast ATA *n.* See EIDE.

Fast Ethernet *n.* See 100BASE-T.

fast IDE *n.* See EIDE.

Fast Page Mode RAM *n.* See FPM RAM.

FAT *n.* FILE ALLOCATION TABLE.

fatal error *n.* an error that causes a program to abort. When a fatal error occurs, whatever data the program was currently processing may be lost.
⇒ See also ABORT; CRASH; GPF; RUNTIME ERROR.

FAT32 *n.* a new version of the file allocation table (FAT) available in Windows 95 OSR 2 and in Windows 98. It can support larger disks (up to 2 terabytes) and stores files with less wasted space.
⇒ See also CLUSTER; FILE ALLOCATION TABLE; FILE MANAGEMENT SYSTEM; OSR 2; SLACK SPACE.

fault tolerance *n.* the ability of a system to respond to an unexpected hardware or software failure. There are many levels of fault tolerance, the lowest being the ability to continue operation in the event of a power failure.
⇒ See also CLUSTERING; DISK MIRRORING; RAID; SERVER MIRRORING.

fax *v.t.* **1.** to send (a document) by fax machine or fax modem. —*n.* **2.** a document that has been faxed or is about to be faxed. **3.** FAX MACHINE.

fax board *n.* FAX MODEM.

fax machine *n.* a device that can send or receive documents, drawings, photographs, etc., over a telephone line. Fax machines work by digitizing an image—dividing it into a grid of dots. Electronically, each dot is represented by a bit that has a value of either 0 (off) or 1 (on), depending on whether it is black or white. In this way, the fax machine translates a picture into a bit map that can be transmitted like computer data. The receiving fax machine reads the data, translates the zeros and ones back into dots, and reprints the picture.
⇒ See also BPS; DIGITIZE; FAX MODEM; MFP; OPTICAL SCANNER; THERMAL PRINTER.

fax modem *n.* a device that can be attached to a personal computer to transmit and receive electronic documents as faxes. A fax modem is designed to transmit documents to a fax machine or to another fax modem. Documents sent through a fax modem must already be in an electronic form (that is, in a disk file). The principle disadvantage of fax modems is that a separate optical scanner is needed if a user wants to fax paper documents.
⇒ See also BROADCAST; FAX MACHINE; MODEM; OPTICAL SCANNER.

FC-AL Fibre Channel Arbitrated Loop: a standard for

high-speed optical communication.

⇒ See also FIBRE CHANNEL.

FCC Federal Communications Commission: a U.S. government agency that regulates interstate and foreign communications. Among other duties, the FCC is responsible for rating personal computers according to how much radiation they emit.

FCIF Full Common Intermediate Format: same as COMMON INTERMEDIATE FORMAT.

FDC floppy disk controller: a chip and associated circuitry for controlling a floppy disk drive.

FDD FLOPPY DISK DRIVE.

FDDI Fiber Distributed Data Interface: a set of ANSI standards for sending digital data over fiber optic cable. FDDI networks are token-passing networks and support data rates of up to 100 Mbps (100 million bits) per second. They are typically used as backbones for wide-area networks.

⇒ See also ATM; CDDI; FIBER OPTICS; NETWORK.

FDHD (fud′hud′), *n.* floppy drive, high density: a 3½-inch disk drive for Macintosh computers that can accept double-density or high-density 3½-inch floppy disks. FDHDs can also read DOS-formatted floppy disks, which enables Macintosh computers and PCs to share data.

⇒ See also DENSITY; DOS; FLOPPY DISK; MACINTOSH COMPUTER; SUPERDRIVE.

fdisk *n.* a DOS and Windows utility that prepares a hard disk for formatting by creating one or more partitions on the disk.

⇒ See also FORMAT; PARTITION.

FDM Frequency Division Multiplexing: a multiplexing technique that uses different frequencies to combine multiple streams of data for transmission over a communications medium.

⇒ See also CARRIER; MULTIPLEX; TDM; WDM.

feathering *n.* in desktop publishing, the process of adding space between all lines on a page or in a column to force vertical justification.

⇒ See also JUSTIFICATION; VERTICAL JUSTIFICATION.

feature *n.* a notable property of a device or software application.

⇒ See also BELLS AND WHISTLES; BLOATWARE; OVERHEAD; VANILLA.

Federal Communications Commission *n.* See FCC.

female connector *n.* a connector, as at the end of a cable or on a port, containing holes into which a male connector can be inserted.

FF FORM FEED.

Fiber Distributed Data Interface *n.* See FDDI.

fiber optics *n.* a technology that uses glass or plastic fibers to transmit data, video and voice signals, etc. A fiber optic cable consists of a bundle of glass threads, each of which is capable of transmitting messages modulated onto light waves.

⇒ See also FDDI; ISDN; LOCAL AREA NETWORK; SDH; SONET; UTP; WDM.

Fibre Channel *n.* a high-speed serial data transfer architecture for optical fibers, developed by a consortium of computer and mass storage device manufacturers and now being standardized by ANSI.

⇒ See also BUS; HIPPI; SCSI.

field *n.* a unit of information, such as a person's name, that combines with related fields, such as an official title or company name, to form one complete record in a computerized database.

⇒ See also ATTRIBUTE; BLOB; CELL; DATA TYPE; DATABASE; DATABASE MANAGEMENT SYSTEM; FORM; RECORD.

file *n.* a collection of data or information that has a name. Different types of files store different types of information. For example, program files store programs, whereas text files store text.

⇒ See also DIRECTORY; DOCUMENT; EXECUTABLE FILE; FILENAME; FOLDER; LIBRARY.

file allocation table *n.* a table that the operating system uses to locate files on a disk. Because of fragmentation, a file may be divided into many sections that are scattered around the disk. *Abbr.:* FAT

⇒ See also CLUSTER; DISK; FAT32; FILE; FILE MANAGEMENT SYSTEM; FRAGMENTATION; PARTITION; SLACK SPACE; VFAT.

file attribute *n.* See under ATTRIBUTE (def. 2).

file compression *n.* storing a file in a standard format, such as ARC or ZIP, that takes up less space than the file's native format. File compression is useful for conserving storage space and for facilitating electronic transmission.

⇒ See also PACKED FILE.

file defragmentation *n.* the automated process of taking scattered parts of a file and placing them in contiguous locations on a disk.

file extension *n.* EXTENSION.

file format *n.* a format for encoding information in a file. Each type of file has a different file format. It specifies first whether the file is a binary or ASCII file, and second, how the information is organized.

⇒ See also FILE; FORMAT; GRAPHICS FILE FORMATS; PDF.

file fragmentation *n.* FRAGMENTATION.

file locking *n.* See under LOCK.

file management system *n.* FILE SYSTEM.

filename *n.* the name of a file. Most operating systems prohibit the use of certain characters in a filename and impose a limit on its length. In addition, many systems allow a filename extension that consists of one or more characters following the proper filename.

⇒ See also ALIAS; DIRECTORY; EXTENSION; FILE; WILDCARD CHARACTER.

filename extension *n.* EXTENSION.

file server *n.* See under SERVER.

file system *n.* the system that an operating system or program uses to organize and keep track of files. For example, a *hierarchical file system* is one that uses directories to organize files into a tree structure.

⇒ See also DIRECTORY; FAT32; FILE ALLOCATION TABLE; HIERARCHICAL; NFS; NTFS; VFAT; VSAM.

File Transfer Protocol *n.* See FTP.

File Transport Protocol *n.* See FTP.

fill *v.t.* **1.** in graphics applications, to paint the inside of (an enclosed object) with a single color or texture. **2.** in spreadsheet applications, to copy the contents of one cell to (an entire range of cells).

⇒ See also GRAPHICS; SPREADSHEET.

filter *n.* **1.** a program that accepts a certain type of data as input, transforms it, and then outputs the transformed data. For example, a program that sorts names is a filter. **2.** a pattern through which data is passed. Only data that match the pattern are allowed to pass through the filter. **3.** in paint programs and image editors, an effect that can be applied to a bit map. Some filters mimic conventional photographic filters, but others transform images in unusual ways.

⇒ See also EXPORT; IMAGE EDITOR; IMAGE ENHANCEMENT; IMPORT; PHOTO ILLUSTRATION.

Finder *n.* the desktop management system for Macintosh computers.

⇒ See also CLIPBOARD; DESKTOP; FILE MANAGEMENT SYSTEM; MACOS; MULTIFINDER; MULTITASKING.

finger *n.* a UNIX program that takes an e-mail address as input and returns information about the user who owns that e-mail address.

⇒ See also E-MAIL; E-MAIL CLIENT; INSTANT MESSAGING; WHOIS.

firewall *n.* a system designed to prevent unauthorized access to or from a private network, esp. an intranet connected to the Internet. A firewall is considered a first line of defense in protecting private information. For greater security, data can be encrypted.

⇒ See also EXTRANET; INTRANET; IP SPOOFING; NAT; NETWORK; PROXY SERVER; SECURITY.

FireWire *n.* See IEEE 1394.

firmware *n.* software (programs or data) that has been written onto read-only memory (ROM, EPROM, EEPROM, etc.).

⇒ See also HARDWARE; PROM; ROM; SOFTWARE.

fixed disk *n.* HARD DISK.

fixed-frequency monitor *n.* a monitor that can accept signals in only one frequency range.

⇒ See also MONITOR; MULTISCANNING MONITOR.

fixed-length *adj.* having a set length that never varies. In database systems, a fixed-length field is one whose length is the same in each record. A

fixed-length record is one in which every field has a fixed length.
⇒ See also DATABASE MANAGEMENT SYSTEM; FIELD; RECORD; VARIABLE LENGTH.

fixed-pitch *adj.* referring to fonts in which every character has the same width. Most typewriters and inexpensive printers use fixed-pitch fonts.
⇒ See also COURIER FONT; CPI; FONT; MONOSPACING; PITCH; PROPORTIONAL SPACING.

fixed-width *adj.* FIXED-PITCH.

flag *n.* **1.** a software or hardware mark that signals a particular condition or status. The flag is said to be *set* when it is turned on. **2.** a special mark indicating that a piece of data is unusual. For example, a record might contain an *error flag* to indicate that the record consists of unusual, probably incorrect, data. —*v.t.* **3.** to mark (an object) to indicate that a particular event has occurred or that the object marked is unusual in some way.
⇒ See also SEMAPHORE.

flame *n.* **1.** an e-mail or newsgroup message in which the writer attacks another participant in overly harsh, and often personal, terms. —*v.i.* **2.** to post a flame. —*v.t.* **3.** to attack (a person) on-line.
⇒ See also CONFERENCE; E-MAIL; FORUM; MODERATED NEWSGROUP; ONLINE SERVICE.

flash BIOS *n.* BIOS that has been recorded on an updatable flash memory chip.

flash EEPROM *n.* FLASH MEMORY.

flash memory *n.* a special type of *EEPROM* that can be erased and reprogrammed in blocks instead of one byte at a time. Many modern PCs have their BIOS stored on a flash memory chip so that it can easily be updated if necessary. Flash memory is also used by modem manufacturers.
⇒ See also BIOS; EEPROM.

FlashPix *n.* a format for storing digital images, especially digital photographs, developed by Eastman Kodak Company.
⇒ See also COMPUTER IMAGING; DIGITAL CAMERA; DIGITAL PHOTOGRAPHY; DIGITAL WATERMARK.

flash ROM *n.* FLASH MEMORY.

flatbed scanner *n.* a type of optical scanner that consists of a flat surface on which documents are placed.
⇒ See also OPTICAL SCANNER.

flat-file database *n.* a relatively simple database system in which each database is contained in a single file. Flat databases are adequate for many small applications.
⇒ See also RELATIONAL DATABASE; DATABASE MANAGEMENT SYSTEM; RDBMS.

flat-panel display *n.* a very thin display screen used in portable computers and increasingly as a replacement for a CRT with desktop computers. Nearly all flat-panel displays use LCD technologies.
⇒ See also ACTIVE-MATRIX DISPLAY; BACKLIGHTING; DISPLAY SCREEN; DUAL-SCAN DISPLAY; ELECTROLUMINESCENT DISPLAY (ELD); GAS-PLASMA DISPLAY; LCD; LCD MONITOR; NOTEBOOK COMPUTER; TFT; VIRTUAL DESKTOP.

flat screen *n.* FLAT-PANEL DISPLAY.

flat technology monitor *n.* a monitor that has a flat display screen to reduce glare. Conventional display screens are curved, which makes them more susceptible to reflections from external light sources.
⇒ See also CRT; FLAT-PANEL DISPLAY; MONITOR.

flicker *n.* SCREEN FLICKER.

floating *adj.* (in graphical user interfaces) referring to an element that can be moved to different places. Many applications support *floating toolbars*, which are collections of icons that represent tools. They can be moved on the screen to create a customized working environment.
⇒ See also PALETTE.

floating point *n.* See under FLOATING-POINT NUMBER.

floating-point number *n.* a number with no fixed number of digits before and after the decimal point (hence the term *floating point*). Such numbers are used in most computer calculations.
⇒ See also DATA TYPE; DOUBLE PRECISION; FLOPS; FPU; NORMALIZATION; PRECISION; SCIENTIFIC NOTATION.

floating-point unit *n.* See FPU.

floppy *n.* FLOPPY DISK.

floppy disk *n.* a soft magnetic disk. It comes in two basic sizes: 3½-inch disks (encased in a rigid envelope) and 5¼-inch disks (a common size for PCs made before 1987). Floppy disks are slower to access than hard disks and have less storage capacity, but they are portable and much less expensive.
⇒ See also DENSITY; DISK; FDHD; FLOPPY DRIVE; HIFD; SUPERDISK; ZIP DRIVE.

floppy disk drive *n.* FLOPPY DRIVE.

floppy drive *n.* short for floppy disk drive (FDD), a disk drive that can read and write to floppy disks.
⇒ See also DISK DRIVE; FLOPPY DISK; HIFD; ZIP DRIVE.

FLOPS *n.* floating point operations per second: a common benchmark measurement for rating the speed of computers.
⇒ See also MEGAFLOPS; GIGAFLOPS; BENCHMARK; FLOATING-POINT NUMBER; FPU; MIPS; SPEC.

floptical *adj.* designating a type of disk drive technology that uses a combination of magnetic and optical techniques to achieve greater storage capacity than normal floppy disks.
⇒ See also OPTICAL DISK.

flow *v.t.* in desktop publishing, to insert (a body of text) into a document such that it wraps (or *flows*) around any objects on the page.
⇒ See also DESKTOP PUBLISHING.

flow control *n.* in communications, the process of adjusting the speed of transmission to ensure that the receiving device can handle all of the incoming data. This is particularly important where the sending device is capable of sending data much faster than the receiving device can receive it.
⇒ See also ASYNCHRONOUS; COMMUNICATIONS; LOOP; PROGRAM; PROGRAMMING LANGUAGE.

flush *adj.* **1.** aligned along a margin. For example, text that is *flush left* is aligned along the left margin. *Flush-right* text is aligned along the right margin. —*v.t.* **2.** to move (data) from a temporary storage area such as RAM to a more permanent storage medium such as a disk.
⇒ See also JUSTIFY; MARGINS; RAGGED.

folder *n.* in graphical user interfaces such as Windows and the Macintosh environment, an object that can contain multiple documents or other folders. Folders are used to organize information.
⇒ See also DESKTOP; DIRECTORY; FILE; GRAPHICAL USER INTERFACE.

font *n.* a design for a set of characters. A font is the combination of typeface and other qualities, such as size, pitch, and spacing. For example, within Times Roman, there are many fonts to choose from. More loosely, a font can refer to a typeface. In this sense, computers and display or output devices use two methods to represent fonts. In a *bit-mapped font*, every character is represented by an arrangement of dots. A font of a different size requires a different set of bit maps. In the other method, a *vector graphics system*, the outline of each character is defined geometrically. Such fonts are *scalable* and the same outline can be any size.
⇒ See also BIT-MAPPED GRAPHICS; CPI; FIXED PITCH; FONT CARTRIDGE; FONT FAMILY; KERNING; PAGE DESCRIPTION LANGUAGE (PDL); PITCH; POINT; POSTSCRIPT; PROPORTIONAL SPACING; SCALABLE FONT; SOFT FONT; TRUETYPE; TYPEFACE; VECTOR GRAPHICS.

font card *n.* FONT CARTRIDGE.

font cartridge *n.* a ROM cartridge that contains one or more fonts. The cartridge is inserted into a printer to give the printer the ability to print different fonts. Another way to load fonts into a printer is to download them from the computer's storage device.
⇒ See also CARTRIDGE; DOWNLOAD; FONT; LASER PRINTER; SOFT FONT.

font family *n.* a set of fonts all with the same typeface, but with different sizes, weights, and slants.
⇒ See also FONT; TYPEFACE.

footer *n.* one or more lines of information repeated at the bottom of every page of a document. Once the user specifies what text should appear in the

footer, the application automatically inserts it. Most applications allow the use of special symbols in the footer that represent changing values. For example, if a symbol is entered for the page number, the application will replace the symbol with the correct number on each page.
⇒ See also HEADER.

footprint *n.* the amount of floor or desk space occupied by a device. A *small-footprint* computer is one whose width and depth are relatively small.
⇒ See also DESKTOP MODEL COMPUTER; TOWER MODEL.

forced page break *n.* a special code that directs an application to start a new page when printing, regardless of whether or not it has reached the bottom of the current page.
⇒ See also HARD; PAGE BREAK; SOFT.

foreground *n.* **1.** in multiprocessing systems, the process that is currently accepting input from the keyboard or other input device is sometimes called the *foreground process.* **2.** on display screens, the characters and pictures that appear on the screen. The background is the uniform canvas behind the characters and pictures.
⇒ See also BACKGROUND; MULTIPROCESSING.

foreign key *n.* See under KEY.

form *n.* a formatted document containing blank fields that users can fill in with data. The form appears on the display screen and the user fills it in by selecting options with a pointing device or typing in text from the keyboard. The data is then sent directly to a forms processing application, which enters the information into a database.
⇒ See also CGI; FIELD; OPTICAL CHARACTER RECOGNITION.

format *v.t.* **1.** to prepare (a storage medium, usually a disk) for reading and writing. The operating system erases all existing information on the disk, tests the disk to make sure all sectors are reliable, marks bad sectors, and creates internal address tables that it later uses to locate information. —*n.* **2.** a particular arrangement. Almost everything associated with computers has a format.
⇒ See also CONTROLLER; DISK; FDISK; HARD DISK; INITIALIZE; INTERLEAVE; LOW-LEVEL FORMAT; MFM; RLL; SECTOR; TAG.

form factor *n.* the physical size and shape of a device. It is often used to describe the size of circuit boards.
⇒ See also ATX; BABY AT; LPX; NLX; PRINTED CIRCUIT BOARD.

form feed *n.* **1.** the process that advances the paper in a printer to the beginning of the next page. **2.** a special character that causes the printer to advance one page length or to the top of the next page.
⇒ See also ASCII.

forms software *n.* a type of program used for designing and filling in forms on a computer. Most forms software packages contain a number of sample forms that can be modified.

formula *n.* **1.** an equation or expression. **2.** in spreadsheet applications, an expression that defines how one cell relates to other cells.
⇒ See also CELL; CONSTANT; EXPRESSION; SPREADSHEET.

FORTRAN *n.* the oldest high-level programming language. Designed for IBM in the late 1950s, it is still popular today, particularly for scientific applications that require extensive mathematical computations.
⇒ See also HIGH-LEVEL LANGUAGE; PROGRAMMING LANGUAGE.

forum *n.* an online discussion group. Online services and bulletin board services (BBSs) provide a variety of forums, in which participants with common interests can exchange open messages.
⇒ See also BULLETIN BOARD SYSTEM; CONFERENCE; DISTANCE LEARNING; NEWSGROUP; ONLINE SERVICE; USENET.

486 short for the *Intel 80486 microprocessor.*
⇒ See also INTEL MICROPROCESSORS.

4GL FOURTH-GENERATION LANGUAGE.

fourth-generation language *n.* a programming language that is closer to human languages than typical high-level programming languages. Most fourth-generation languages are used to access databases. The other three generations of computer languages are: *first generation* (machine language); *second generation* (assembly language); and *third generation* (high-level programming language).
⇒ See also DATABASE MANAGEMENT SYSTEM; NATURAL LANGUAGE; PROGRAMMING LANGUAGE; QUERY; QUERY LANGUAGE.

FPM RAM *n.* Fast Page Mode RAM: a type of Dynamic RAM (DRAM) that allows faster access to data in the same row or page.
⇒ See also CPU; EDO DRAM; INTERLEAVED MEMORY; MEMORY; RAM; RDRAM; SLDRAM; WAIT STATE.

fps frames per second: a measure of how much information is used to store and display motion video. The term applies equally to film video and digital video. The more frames per second (fps), the smoother the motion appears.
⇒ See also AVI; NTSC.

FPU floating-point unit: a specially designed chip that performs *floating-point* calculations. Computers equipped with an FPU perform certain types of applications much faster than computers that lack one. In particular, graphics applications are faster with an FPU.
⇒ See also COPROCESSOR; FLOATING-POINT NUMBER; FLOPS.

fractal *n.* a shape that is "self-similar", that is, a shape that looks the same at different magnifications. Many of the computer-generated images that appear in science fiction films utilize fractals.
⇒ See also GRAPHICS.

fractional T-1 *n.* one or more channels of a T-1 long-distance data transmission line. A full T-1 contains 24 channels of 64 Kbps each.
⇒ See also DIAL-UP ACCESS; LEASED LINE; T-1 CARRIER.

FRAD *n.* Frame Relay Assembler/Disassembler: a communications device that breaks a data stream into frames for transmission over a Frame Relay network and recreates a data stream from incoming frames.

fragmentation *n.* **1.** the condition of a disk in which files are divided into pieces scattered around the disk, slowing access to them. Fragmentation occurs naturally when a disk is used frequently; at some point, the layout of available space will force the operating system to store parts of a file in non-contiguous locations. **2.** a similar condition for RAM. *External fragmentation* occurs when RAM has small, unused regions scattered throughout it. *Internal fragmentation*, which is more common, arises when memory is allocated in frames of fixed size, but the frame size is larger than the amount that programs request.
⇒ See also CLUSTER; DEFRAG; DISK OPTIMIZER; FILE ALLOCATION TABLE.

frame *n.* **1.** in graphics and desktop publishing applications, a rectangular area in which text or graphics can appear. **2.** in communications, a packet of transmitted information. **3.** in video and animation, a single image in a sequence of images. **4.** in HTML, a subdivision of a Web browser's display area. See FRAMES.
⇒ See also FPS.

Frame Relay *n.* a packet-switching protocol for connecting devices on a Wide-Area Network (WAN).
⇒ See also ATM; CELL RELAY; CIR; FRAD; PACKET SWITCHING; PVC.

Frame Relay Assembler/Disassembler *n.* See FRAD.

frames *n.pl.* a feature supported by most modern Web browsers that enables the Web author to divide the browser display area into two or more sections (frames). The contents of each frame are taken from a different Web page.
⇒ See also HTML.

frames per second *n.pl.* See FPS.

FreeBSD *n.* a popular and free version of UNIX that runs on Intel microprocessors.
⇒ See also LINUX; UNIX.

freeware *n.* software given away by the author, for use by others, although the author retains the copyright.

computer

⇒ See also PUBLIC-DOMAIN SOFTWARE; SHAREWARE; WAREZ.

Frequency Division Multiplexing *n.* See FDM.

friction feed *n.* a method of feeding paper through a printer. Friction-feed printers use plastic or rubber rollers to squeeze a sheet of paper and pull it through the printer.

⇒ See also PRINTER; SHEET FEEDER; TRACTOR FEED.

front end *n.* **1.** for software applications, the user interface. **2.** in client/server applications, the client part of the program. The server part is called the *back end.* **3.** for compilers, the part responsible for checking syntax and detecting errors. The *back end* performs the actual translation into object code.

⇒ See also CLIENT/SERVER ARCHITECTURE; COMPILER; DISTRIBUTED PROCESSING; USER INTERFACE.

frozen *adj.* unresponsive. The term is used to describe a monitor, keyboard, or the entire computer system when it no longer reacts to input because of a malfunction.

⇒ See also CRASH.

FTM FLAT TECHNOLOGY MONITOR.

FTP File Transfer Protocol or File Transport Protocol: the protocol used on the Internet for sending files.

⇒ See also ANONYMOUS FTP; COMMUNICATIONS; INTERNET; TFTP; UUCP.

.fts extension *n.* FTS FILE.

FTS file *n.* a hidden index file ending in a .FTS (full-text search) extension used by the Windows 95 and NT Help system.

⇒ See also EXTENSION; GID FILE; HELP.

full duplex *n.* the transmission of data in two directions simultaneously. When a terminal is used in full-duplex mode, a user's keystrokes do not appear on the screen until they have been received

and sent back by the computer at the other end of the line.

⇒ See also COMMUNICATIONS; HALF DUPLEX; MODEM; SIMPLEX.

full-length *adj.* referring to full-sized, 16-bit expansion boards, such as video adapters and graphics accelerators, that can be inserted into a computer and to the full-length expansion slots that can accept them.

function *n.* **1.** in programming, a named section of a program that performs a specific task. **2.** an operation or command.

⇒ See also COMMAND; LIBRARY; PROCEDURE; PROGRAM; ROUTINE.

functional spec *n.* FUNCTIONAL SPECIFICATION.

functional specification *n.* a formal description of a software system that is used as a blueprint for implementing the program. At minimum, a functional specification should precisely state the purpose or function of the software.

⇒ See also ARCHITECTURE; SOFTWARE ENGINEERING; USER INTERFACE.

function keys *n.pl.* special keys on the keyboard that have different meanings depending on which program is running. Function keys are normally labeled F1 to F10 or F12 (or F15 on Macintoshes).

⇒ See also ALT KEY; ENHANCED KEYBOARD; F1, F2... F15; KEYBOARD.

fuzzy logic *n.* a type of logic that recognizes more than simple true and false values. Fuzzy logic has proved to be particularly useful in expert system and other artificial intelligence applications. It is also used in some spell checkers to suggest a list of probable words to replace a misspelled one.

⇒ See also ARTIFICIAL INTELLIGENCE; BOOLEAN LOGIC; EXPERT SYSTEM; SPELL CHECKER.

---

a b c d e f G h i j k l m n o p q r s t u v w x y z

G GIGA; GIGABYTE.

garbage in, garbage out a well-known computer axiom meaning that if invalid data is entered into a system, the resulting output will be invalid regardless of the sophistication with which it is processed. *Abbr.:* GIGO.

gas-plasma display *n.* a type of thin display screen, called a *flat-panel display,* used in some older portable computers. It works by sandwiching neon gas between two plates.

⇒ See also FLAT-PANEL DISPLAY; LCD; NOTEBOOK COMPUTER.

gateway *n.* in networking, a combination of hardware and software that links two different types of networks.

⇒ See also NETWORK.

GB GIGABYTE.

Gbps gigabits per second: a data transfer speed measurement for high-speed networks such as Gigabit Ethernet.

⇒ See also GIGABIT; GIGABIT ETHERNET; MBPS.

GDI Graphical Device Interface: a Windows standard for representing graphical objects and transmitting them to output devices, such as monitors and printers.

⇒ See also DIRECTDRAW; GDI PRINTER; HOST-BASED PRINTER.

GDI printer *n.* a printer that has built-in support for Windows Graphical Device Interface (GDI), which is used by most Windows applications to display images on a monitor. Also called **host-based printer.**

⇒ See also GDI; HOST-BASED PRINTER; PCL; POSTSCRIPT; PRINTER; WINDOWS.

geek *n.* computer geek: an individual with a passion for computers, to the exclusion of other human interests.

⇒ See also HACKER.

GEM *n.* **1.** a graphical user interface developed by Digital Research. It is built into personal computers

made by Atari and is also used as an interface for some DOS programs. **2.** a special graphics file format used in GEM-based applications.

⇒ See also GRAPHICAL USER INTERFACE; MACINTOSH COMPUTER; MICROSOFT WINDOWS.

general protection fault *n.* See GPF.

genetic programming *n.* a type of programming that utilizes the same properties of natural selection found in biological evolution.

⇒ See also ARTIFICIAL INTELLIGENCE; LISP.

genlock *n.* generator locking device: a device that enables a composite video machine, such as a TV, to accept two signals simultaneously by locking their vertical and horizontal synchronization signals together.

⇒ See also COMPOSITE VIDEO.

Geoport *n.* a serial port for Apple computers, now obsolete, that provides an interface between a telephone line and the computer.

⇒ See also SERIAL PORT; VIDEOCONFERENCING.

GFLOPS *n.* GIGAFLOPS.

⇒ See also FLOPS.

.gid extension *n.* See under GID FILE.

GID file *n.* a hidden Windows 95 configuration file, ending with a .GID extension, used by the Windows Help system to speed up access to help file topics.

⇒ See also EXTENSION; FTS FILE; HELP.

GIF (jif, gif), *n.* graphics interchange format: a bit-mapped graphics file format used by the World Wide Web, CompuServe, and many BBSs. It supports color and various resolutions and includes data compression.

⇒ See also ANIMATED GIF; DATA COMPRESSION; GRAPHICS FILE FORMATS; IMAGE MAP; LZW; PNG.

giga *n.* **1.** in decimal notation, 10^9. For example, a *gigavolt* is 1,000,000,000 volts. **2.** in referring to computers, which use the binary notation system, 2^{30} or 1,073,741,824, a little more than 1 billion.

⇒ See also BINARY; MASS STORAGE; MEGABYTE.

gigabit *n.* **1.** in describing data storage, 1,024 megabits. **2.** in describing data transfer rates, one 10^9 (1,000,000,000) bits.
⇒ See also GBPS; GIGABYTE; MEGABIT.

Gigabit Ethernet *n.* a version of Ethernet that supports data transfer rates of 1 gigabit (1,000 megabits) per second.
⇒ See also 100BASE-T; ETHERNET; HIPPI; IEEE.

gigabyte *n.* 2^{30} (1,073,741,824) bytes: equal to 1,024 megabytes. *Abbr.:* G, GB.
⇒ See also BYTE; GIGA; GIGABIT; MEGABYTE; PETABYTE.

GigaFLOPS *n.* one billion *FLOPS.*

GIGO (gī′gō *or as separate letters*), *n.* GARBAGE IN, GARBAGE OUT.

glitch *n.* a malfunction, as of hardware.
⇒ See also BUG.

GNU (nōō *or as separate letters*), *n.* GNU's not UNIX: a non-proprietary UNIX-compatible software system developed by the Free Software Foundation (FSF).
⇒ See also LINUX; UNIX.

Gopher *n.* a system that predates the World Wide Web for organizing and displaying files on Internet servers. [named after the mascot of the University of Minnesota, where it was developed]
⇒ See also ARCHIE; INTERNET; JUGHEAD; VERONICA; WORLD WIDE WEB.

GPF General Protection Fault: a computer condition that causes a Windows application to crash, as when one application tries to use memory assigned to another.
⇒ See also CRASH; FATAL ERROR; INVALID PAGE FAULT; RUNTIME ERROR.

gppm graphics pages per minute: the speed with which laser printers can print nontext pages.
⇒ See also LASER PRINTER; PPM.

grabber *n.* **1.** a device that captures data, as one that can capture full-motion video from a television or video camera and convert it to digital form for storage on a computer's disk. **2.** in some applications, a special tool or cursor that enables the user to grab objects on the screen and move them or manipulate them: often represented by a hand icon.
⇒ See also CURSOR.

Graphical Device Interface *n.* See GDI.

graphical user interface *n.* a program interface, as Microsoft Windows and that used by the Apple Macintosh, that takes advantage of the computer's graphics capabilities to free the user from having to learn complex command languages. It makes the computer easier to use. Also called **GUI.**
⇒ See also AWT; CHARACTER BASED; DESKTOP; DRAG-AND-DROP; ICON; MACINTOSH COMPUTER; MDI; MICROSOFT WINDOWS; POINTER; POINTING DEVICE; USER INTERFACE; XEROX.

graphics *n.* **1.** pictorial computer output. —*adj.* **2.** pertaining to any computer device or program that makes a computer capable of displaying and manipulating pictures: *graphics applications; a graphics monitor.* Software applications that include graphics are said to *support* graphics. For example, certain word processors let the user draw or import pictures. All CAD/CAM systems support graphics. Some database management systems and spreadsheet programs support graphics because they let users display data in the form of graphs and charts. Such simple displays are often referred to as *business graphics.*
⇒ See also ALPHA CHANNEL; BIT MAP; BIT-MAPPED GRAPHICS; CAD; CAD/CAM; CHARACTER BASED; CLIP ART; CPU; DESKTOP PUBLISHING; DISPLAY SCREEN; GRAPHICS FILE FORMAT; IMAGE PROCESSING; LASER PRINTER; MICROSOFT WINDOWS; MONITOR; PERSONAL COMPUTER; PLOTTER; 3-D GRAPHICS.

graphics accelerator *n.* a type of video adapter that contains its own processor. A graphics accelerator is specialized for computing graphical transformations and therefore achieves better results than the general-purpose CPU used by the computer. It also has its own memory for storing screen images.
⇒ See also 3-D GRAPHICS; ACCELERATOR BOARD; AGP; CPU; Direct3D; DirectDraw; DirectX; DRAM; GRAPH-

ICS; MDRAM; MULTIMEDIA; PCI; SGRAM; VIDEO ADAPTER; VIDEO MEMORY; VRAM.

graphics adapter *n.* VIDEO ADAPTER.

graphics based *adj.* referring to software and hardware that treat objects on a display screen as bit maps or geometrical shapes rather than as characters.
⇒ See also CHARACTER BASED.

graphics card *n.* VIDEO ADAPTER.

graphics character *n.* a character whose displayed image is a shape rather than a letter, number, or punctuation mark.
⇒ See also BLOCK GRAPHICS; CHARACTER MODE; EXTENDED ASCII.

graphics coprocessor *n.* See under COPROCESSOR.
⇒ See also GRAPHICS ACCELERATOR.

graphics display system *n.* the combination of monitor and video adapter that makes a computer capable of displaying graphics.
⇒ See also GRAPHICS; MONITOR; VIDEO ADAPTER.

graphics file format *n.* a file format, either bit-mapped or vector, that is designed specifically for representing graphical images.
⇒ See also BMP; CGM; DIB; DXF; EPS; GEM; GIF; GRAPHICS; HPGL; IGES; PCX; PIC; PICT FILE FORMAT; TIFF; WMF.

graphics mode *n.* a sophisticated mode of resolution in which the display screen is treated as an array of pixels, and characters and other shapes are formed by turning on combinations of pixels. Programs that run entirely in graphics mode are called *graphics-based* programs.
⇒ See also CHARACTER BASED; GRAPHICS BASED; PIXEL; VIDEO ADAPTER.

graphics monitor *n.* a monitor capable of displaying graphics.
⇒ See also GRAPHICS; MONITOR.

graphics pages per minute *n.* See GPPM.

graphics tablet *n.* DIGITIZING TABLET.

gray scaling *n.* the use of many shades of gray to represent an image.
⇒ See also CONTINUOUS TONE; DATA COMPRESSION; DITHERING; MONITOR; OPTICAL SCANNER.

greeking *n.* **1.** the approximation of text characters on a screen display to show what a document will look like when printed: used by word processors that support a preview function. **2.** nonsense text inserted in a document to allow a layout artist to concentrate on the overall appearance of a page without being concerned about the text to be inserted later.
⇒ See also LAYOUT; PREVIEW.

Green Book *n.* the specification covering CD-I.
⇒ See also CD-I (Compact Disc–Interactive); ORANGE BOOK; RED BOOK; WHITE BOOK; YELLOW BOOK.

green PC *n.* a PC specially designed to minimize power consumption.
⇒ See also ENERGY STAR; SLEEP MODE.

Group 3 protocol *n.* the universal protocol defined by the CCITT for sending faxes.
⇒ See also CCITT; FAX MACHINE.

Group 4 protocol *n.* a protocol defined by CCITT for sending faxes over ISDN networks.
⇒ See also CCITT; FAX MACHINE; ISDN.

groupware *n.* a class of software that helps colleagues (workgroups) attached to a network organize their activities by supporting such operations as telephone utilities, e-mail, and file distribution. Also called **workgroup productivity software.**
⇒ See also E-MAIL; LOTUS NOTES; SCHEDULER; TEAMWARE; WORKGROUP COMPUTING.

GSM Global System for Mobile Communications: one of the leading digital cellular systems, and the de facto standard in Europe and Asia.
⇒ See also CDMA; CELLULAR; PCS; TDMA.

GUI (gōō′ē), *n.* GRAPHICAL USER INTERFACE.

gutter *n.* in desktop publishing, the space between columns in a multiple-column document.
⇒ See also DESKTOP PUBLISHING.

GW-BASIC *n.* a dialect of the BASIC programming language that comes with many versions of the DOS operating system.
⇒ See also BASIC; QBASIC.

computer

H.323 a standard approved by the International Telecommunication Union (ITU) that defines how audiovisual conferencing data is transmitted across networks.
⇒ See also H.324; ITU; RTSP; VIDEOCONFERENCING.

H.324 a suite of standards approved by the International Telecommunications Union (ITU) that defines videoconferencing over analog telephone lines.
⇒ See also H.323; ITU; STREAMING; VIDEOCONFERENCING.

hack n. **1.** an inelegant and usually temporary solution to a problem. —v.t. **2.** to modify (a program), often in an unauthorized manner. —v.i. **3.** to write or explore software systems.
⇒ See also HACKER; KLUDGE.

hacker n. Slang. **1.** a computer enthusiast, esp. an amateur or a programmer who lacks formal training. **2.** an individual who gains unauthorized access to computer systems.
⇒ See also CRACK; GEEK; IP SPOOFING; PHREAKING; PROGRAMMER; SNIFFER.

half duplex adj. referring to the transmission of data in just one direction at a time, as on a walkie-talkie.
⇒ See also COMMUNICATIONS; FULL DUPLEX; MODEM; SIMPLEX.

half height adj. referring to a type of bay for disk drives and other mass storage devices.
⇒ See also BAY.

halftone n. in printing, a continuous-tone image, such as a photograph, that has been converted into a black-and-white image. Halftones are created through a process in which the density and pattern of black-and-white dots are varied to simulate different shades of gray. In conventional printing, halftones are created by photographing an image through a *screen*. Modern desktop publishing systems can create halftones by simulating this process.
⇒ See also CONTINUOUS TONE; DESKTOP PUBLISHING; DITHERING; MOIRÉ.

hand-held computer n. a portable computer that is small enough to be held in one's hand, as one designed to provide personal information manager (PIM) functions such as a calendar and address book.
⇒ See also HANDWRITING RECOGNITION; NOTEBOOK COMPUTER; PALMTOP; PDA; PIM; WINDOWS CE.

Handheld PC n. See HPC.

handle n. **1.** any of the small boxes that appear with a selected graphical object and that can be dragged to change the size and shape of the object. **2.** in programming, an address datum that enables the program to access a resource, such as a library function. **3.** in an online service, the name employed by a user to identify him or herself.
⇒ See also CHAT; GRAPHICS; ONLINE SERVICE; POINTER.

handshaking n. the process by which two devices initiate communications.
⇒ See also COMMUNICATIONS; PROTOCOL.

handwriting recognition n. the technique by which a computer system can recognize characters and other symbols written by hand.
⇒ See also HAND-HELD COMPUTER; PDA; PEN COMPUTER.

hang v.i. to crash in such a way that the computer does not respond to input from the keyboard or mouse.
⇒ See also ABORT; BOMB; BUG; CRASH; DEADLOCK.

hanging indent n. in word processing, a paragraph that has all lines but the first indented.
⇒ See also WORD PROCESSING.

hanging paragraph n. HANGING INDENT.

hard adj. referring to anything that is permanent or that physically exists, as opposed to "soft" concepts, symbols, and other intangible and changeable objects.
⇒ See also HARDWARE; HARDWIRED; SOFTWARE.

hard card n. a hard disk drive and controller on an expansion card.
⇒ See also BAY; CONTROLLER; EXPANSION BOARD; EXPANSION SLOT; HARD DISK.

hard coded adj. unchangeable, such as features built into hardware or software in such a way that they cannot be modified.
⇒ See also HARD.

hard copy n. a printout of data stored in a computer.
⇒ See also HARD; SOFT.

hard disk n. a rigid magnetic disk on which computer data can be stored, usu. consisting of several platters with read/write heads.
⇒ See also CACHE; CYLINDER; DISK DRIVE; DISK PACK; EIDE; FLOPPY DISK; HARD CARD; HARD DISK TYPE; IDE INTERFACE; INTERLEAVE; MASS STORAGE; PLATTER; REMOVABLE HARD DISK; SCANDISK; SMART; TRACK.

hard disk drive n. the mechanism that reads and writes data on a hard disk.
⇒ See also DISK COMPRESSION; DISK DRIVE; HARD DISK.

hard disk type n. a number that indicates important features of a hard disk, such as the number of platters and cylinders.
⇒ See also BIOS; HARD DISK.

hard drive n. HARD DISK DRIVE.

hard hyphen n. a hyphen, usually part of the spelling, that is deliberately inserted in data and that will appear regardless of whether or not it occurs at the end of a line.
⇒ See also DISCRETIONARY HYPHEN.

hard return n. a return that causes the word processor to start a new line regardless of how margins are set.
⇒ See also RETURN; SOFT RETURN.

hardware n. objects that can be touched, such as disks, disk drives, display screens, keyboards, printers, boards, and chips.
⇒ See also FIRMWARE; HARD; SOFTWARE.

hardwired adj. referring to elements of a program or device that cannot be changed.
⇒ See also CONSTANT; HARD.

hash n. **1.** HASH VALUE. —v.t. **2.** to engage in hashing of (a particular input).

hashing n. producing hash values for accessing data or for security.
⇒ See also INDEX; KEY.

hash search n. the process of searching a hash table.

hash table n. an index of records to which hash values have been assigned.

hash value n. a number generated from a string of text in such a way that it is unlikely that some other text will produce the same number: used in security systems and in accessing data. Also called **hash.**

Hayes compatible adj. referring to any modem that recognizes modem commands in the AT command set developed by Hayes Microcomputer Products.
⇒ See also AT COMMAND SET; COMMUNICATIONS; DE FACTO STANDARD; MODEM.

HDC hard disk controller: a chip and associated circuitry for controlling a hard disk drive.

HDD HARD DISK DRIVE.

HDLC High-level Data Link Control: a transmission protocol that is used at the data link layer (layer 2) of the OSI seven-layer model for data communications and that embeds information in a data frame that allows devices to control data flow and correct errors.
⇒ See also COMMUNICATIONS PROTOCOL; FRAME; OSI.

HDTV High-Definition Television: a type of television that provides much better resolution than televisions based on the NTSC standard by compressing images before they are transmitted and decompressing them when they reach the TV.

⇒ See also DSS; NTSC.

head *n.* the mechanism that reads data from or writes data to a magnetic disk or tape. Also called **read/write head.**

⇒ See also DISK DRIVE; HEAD CRASH; PLATTER.

head crash *n.* a serious disk drive malfunction, usu. caused when the head has scratched or burned the disk as the result of a misalignment or the presence of dust particles. Also called **disk crash.**

⇒ See also CRASH; DATA RECOVERY; DISK; DISK DRIVE; HEAD.

header *n.* **1.** Also called **running head.** In word processing, one or more lines of text set up to appear at the top of each page of a document and automatically inserted by the program. **2.** in many disciplines of computer science, a unit of information that precedes a data object.

⇒ See also FOOTER; WORD PROCESSING.

head-mounted display *n.* See HMD.

heap *n.* **1.** in programming, an area of memory reserved for data that is created when a program actually executes. **2.** a special type of binary tree in which the value at each node is greater than the values at its leaves.

⇒ See also BINARY TREE; DATA STRUCTURE; STACK.

heap sort *n.* a sorting algorithm that works by first organizing the data to be sorted into a special type of binary tree called a *heap* that has the largest value at the top of the tree.

⇒ See also ALGORITHM; BINARY TREE; BUBBLE SORT.

heat sink *n.* a component, usu. made of a zinc alloy, that is designed to lower the temperature of an electronic device by dissipating heat into the surrounding air. A heat sink without a fan is called a *passive heat sink;* a heat sink with a fan is called an *active heat sink.*

⇒ See also MOTHERBOARD; VOLTAGE REGULATOR.

helical-scan cartridge *n.* a type of magnetic tape that uses the same technology as VCR tapes.

⇒ See also DAT; MASS STORAGE; TAPE.

Help *n.* online documentation, accessed by pressing a designated key, as F1 in Windows, or entering a "Help" command.

⇒ See also CONTEXT SENSITIVE; DOCUMENTATION; FAQ; FTS FILE; GID FILE; HELP DESK; MAN PAGE.

help desk *n.* a department within a company that responds to user's technical questions by telephone, e-mail, BBS, or fax.

⇒ See also HELP.

Hercules graphics *n.* an obsolete graphics display system for PCs developed by Van Suwannukul, founder of Hercules Computer Technology, in 1982.

⇒ See also MDA; VIDEO ADAPTER.

heterogeneous network *n.* a network that includes computers and other devices from different manufacturers, as local-area networks (LANs) that connect PCs with Apple Macintosh computers.

⇒ See also LOCAL-AREA NETWORK; NETWORK.

heuristic programming *n.* a branch of artificial intelligence that uses heuristics, or common-sense rules drawn from experience, to solve problems.

⇒ See also ALGORITHM; ARTIFICIAL INTELLIGENCE; EXPERT SYSTEM.

Hewlett-Packard *n.* See HP.

Hewlett-Packard Graphics Language *n.* See HPGL.

hex *adj.* HEXADECIMAL.

hexadecimal *adj.* referring to the base-16 number system, which consists of 16 unique symbols: the numbers 0 to 9 and the letters A to F.

⇒ See also BCD; BINARY; DECIMAL; NIBBLE; OCTAL.

hidden file *n.* a file with a special hidden attribute turned on, so that the file is not normally visible to users.

⇒ See also ATTRIBUTE; FILE MANAGEMENT SYSTEM.

hierarchical *adj.* referring to systems that are organized so that each row of objects is linked to objects directly beneath it.

⇒ See also DIRECTORY; FILE MANAGEMENT SYSTEM; TREE STRUCTURE.

Hierarchical Storage Management *n.* See HSM.

HiFD *n.* High Floppy Disk: a type of high-density floppy disk developed by Sony that can hold 200 MB of data.

⇒ See also FLOPPY DISK; FLOPPY DRIVE; SUPERDISK; ZIP DRIVE.

high ASCII *n.* EXTENDED ASCII.

High Definition Television *n.* See HDTV.

high-density disk *n.* a high-quality floppy disk capable of holding more data than a double-density disk.

⇒ See also DENSITY; FLOPPY DISK.

High-level Data Link Control *n.* See HDLC.

high-level language *n.* a programming language such as C, FORTRAN, or Pascal that enables a programmer to write programs that are more or less independent of a particular type of computer. High-level languages are closer to human language and easier to read, write, and maintain than low-level languages.

⇒ See also ADA; ASSEMBLY LANGUAGE; BASIC; C; C++; COBOL; COMPILE; FORTRAN; LISP; LOW-LEVEL LANGUAGE; MACHINE LANGUAGE; OBJECT-ORIENTED PROGRAMMING; PASCAL; PROGRAMMING LANGUAGE.

High Level Language Application Program Interface *n.* See HLLAPI.

highlight *v.t.* to make (an object on a display screen) stand out by displaying it in a different mode from that of other objects.

⇒ See also SELECT.

high memory *n.* in DOS-based systems, the memory area between the first 640K and 1 megabyte. Also called **upper memory area (UMA).**

⇒ See also CONVENTIONAL MEMORY; DOS; EXPANDED MEMORY; EXTENDED MEMORY; LOW MEMORY; TSR.

high memory area *n.* in DOS-based systems, the first 64K of extended memory.

⇒ See also EXTENDED MEMORY.

High Performance Computing *n.* a branch of computer science that concentrates on developing supercomputers and software to run on them.

⇒ See also HPCC; PARALLEL PROCESSING; SUPERCOMPUTER.

High Performance Computing and Communications *n.* See HPCC.

high resolution *n.* See under RESOLUTION.

himem.sys *n.* an extended memory (XMS) driver included with DOS, Windows 3.1, Windows for Workgroups, Windows 95, and Windows 98, loaded automatically during start-up by the newer version of Windows.

⇒ See also CONFIG.SYS; EXTENDED MEMORY; XMS.

HIPPI *n.* High Performance Parallel Interface: a standard technology for connecting devices at short distances and high speeds: an official ANSI standard since 1990 and used primarily to connect supercomputers and to provide high-speed backbones for local-area networks (LANs).

⇒ See also BACKBONE; FIBRE CHANNEL; GIGABIT ETHERNET; SUPERCOMPUTER.

HLLAPI *n.* High Level Language Application Program Interface: an IBM API that allows a PC application to communicate with a mainframe computer.

⇒ See also API; MAINFRAME; TERMINAL; TERMINAL EMULATION.

HMD *n.* head-mounted display: a headset, either a pair of goggles or a full helmet, used with virtual reality systems.

⇒ See also VIRTUAL REALITY.

home computer *n.* a personal computer specially configured for use in a home rather than an office, usu. having medium-power microprocessors and equipped with a full complement of multimedia devices.

⇒ See also MULTIMEDIA; PERSONAL COMPUTER.

Home key *n.* a key on PC and newer Macintosh keyboards that controls cursor movement.

⇒ See also KEYBOARD.

home page *n.* the main page of a Web site usu. serving as an index or table of contents for other

computer

documents at the site.
⇒ See also WEB SITE.

home PC *n.* HOME COMPUTER.

hop *n.* an intermediate connection in a string of connections linking two network devices. The more hops, the longer it takes for data to go from source to destination.
⇒ See also PING; ROUTER; TRACEROUTE; TTL.

host *n.* **1.** a computer system that is accessed by a user working at a remote location. **2.** a computer that is connected to a TCP/IP network, including the Internet. —*v.t.* **3.** to provide the infrastructure for (a computer service).
⇒ See also HOST-BASED; REMOTE CONTROL; REMOTE CONTROL SOFTWARE; TELNET.

host-based *adj.* referring to any device that relies on the host computer (the computer the device is attached to) to handle some operations.
⇒ See also HOST; HOST-BASED MODEM; HOST-BASED PRINTER.

host-based modem *n.* a modem that uses the computer's processor to handle some operations. Also called **Win-modem**.
⇒ See also HOST-BASED; MODEM; SOFTWARE MODEM.

host-based printer *n.* a printer that relies on the host computer's processor to generate printable pages.
⇒ See also GDI; GDI PRINTER; HOST-BASED; PRINTER.

HotBot *n.* a World Wide Web search engine developed collaboratively by Inktomi Corporation and HotWired, Inc.
⇒ See also ALTA VISTA; EXCITE; INFOSEEK; LYCOS; SEARCH ENGINE; YAHOO!.

HotJava *n.* a set of products developed by Sun Microsystems that utilize Java technology.
⇒ See also BROWSER; JAVA.

hot key *n.* a user-defined key sequence that executes a command or causes the operating system to switch to another program.
⇒ See also CONTROL CHARACTER; FUNCTION KEYS; MEMORY RESIDENT; TSR.

hot link *n.* **1.** a link between two applications such that changes in one affect the other. —*v.t.* **2.** to establish a link between (two applications).
⇒ See also DATABASE; LINK; OLE; SPREADSHEET.

hot plugging *n.* the ability to add to and remove devices from a computer while the computer is running and have the operating system automatically recognize the change. Also called **hot swapping**.
⇒ See also IEEE 1394; PCMCIA; PLUG-AND-PLAY; USB.

hot spot *n.* an area of a graphics object, or a section of text, that activates a function when selected.
⇒ See also IMAGE MAP; MULTIMEDIA.

hot swap *n.* the act of hot swapping.

hot swapping *n.* HOT PLUGGING.

HP Hewlett-Packard: one of the world's largest computer and electronics companies, founded in 1939 by William Hewlett and David Packard.
⇒ See also HP-COMPATIBLE PRINTER; PCL; PRINTER.

HPC 1. HIGH PERFORMANCE COMPUTING. **2.** Handheld PC: Microsoft's name for a personal digital assistant (PDA).
⇒ See also PDA; WINDOWS CE.

HPCC the U.S. government's term for HIGH PERFORMANCE COMPUTING.

HP-compatible printer *n.* a laser printer that understands the printer control language (PCL) used by Hewlett-Packard Printers.
⇒ See also COMPATIBLE; DRIVER; EMULATION; FONT CARTRIDGE; HP; LASER PRINTER; PCL; POSTSCRIPT.

HPGL Hewlett-Packard Graphics Language: a set of commands for controlling plotters and printers.
⇒ See also PCL; PLOTTER.

.hqx See under BINHEX.

hqx See under BINHEX.

HSM Hierarchical Storage Management: a data storage system that automatically moves data between high-cost and low-cost storage media, effectively turning fast disk drives into caches for slower mass storage devices.
⇒ See also BACKUP; MASS STORAGE; STORAGE; STORAGE DEVICE.

HTML HyperText Markup Language: the authoring language used to create documents on the World Wide Web.
⇒ See also BROWSER; CSS; DOM; FRAMES; HTTP; HYPERTEXT; JAVASCRIPT; SGML; SSI; TAG; VRML; W3C; WORLD WIDE WEB; XML.

HTTP HyperText Transfer Protocol: the underlying protocol used by the World Wide Web that defines how messages are formatted and transmitted, and what actions Web servers and browsers should take in response to various commands.
⇒ See also HTML; S-HTTP; W3C; WORLD WIDE WEB.

hub *n.* a common connection point for devices in a network, commonly used to connect segments of a LAN.
⇒ See also 10BASET; 3COM; BRIDGE; CONCENTRATOR; MAU; REPEATER; STAR NETWORK; SWITCHING HUB.

human engineering *n.* ERGONOMICS.

HyperCard *n.* a hypertext programming environment for the Macintosh, introduced by Apple in 1987.
⇒ See also AUTHORING TOOL; HYPERTEXT.

hyperlink *n.* an element in an electronic document that links to another place in the same document or in an entirely different one.
⇒ See also HYPERMEDIA; HYPERTEXT.

hypermedia *n.* an extension to hypertext that supports linking graphics, sound, and video elements in addition to text elements.
⇒ See also HYPERLINK; HYPERTEXT; MULTIMEDIA; WORLD WIDE WEB.

Hypertext *n.* a special type of database system, invented by Ted Nelson in the 1960s, in which objects (text, pictures, music, programs, and so on) can be creatively linked to each other.
⇒ See also AUTHORING TOOL; HELP; HTML; HYPERCARD; HYPERLINK; HYPERMEDIA; MULTIMEDIA; SGML.

Hypertext Markup Language *n.* See HTML.

HyperText Transfer Protocol *n.* See HTTP.

HyperText Transport Protocol *n.* See HTTP.

hyphenation *n.* in word processing, splitting a word that would otherwise extend beyond the right margin.
⇒ See also WORD PROCESSING; WORD WRAP.

abcdefgh**I**jklmnopqrstuvwxyz

I2 Internet 2: a global network being developed cooperatively by about 100 universities. It will support high bandwidths required by such applications as live video and is expected to be 100 to 1,000 times faster than the current Internet.
⇒ See also INTERNET; NGI INITIATIVE; vBNS.

I2O I/O architecture being developed by a consortium of computer companies called the I2O Special Interest Group (SIG). It is designed to eliminate I/O bottlenecks by utilizing special I/O processors (IOPs) that handle the details of interrupt handling, buffering, and data transfer. Also called

Intelligent I/O.
⇒ See also I/O; PCI.

IA-64 See under MERCED.

IAB INTERNET ARCHITECTURE BOARD.

IAC Internet Access Coalition: a consortium of companies involved in the Internet—including AT&T, Microsoft, and MCI—whose stated purpose is to maintain the affordability of Internet access over telephone lines and accelerate the availability of inexpensive digital telephone network connections to the Internet.
⇒ See also INTERNET.

IAHC Internet International Ad Hoc Committee: the international organization responsible for managing the Internet's domain name system (DNS).
⇒ See also DNS; DOMAIN NAME.

IANA Internet Assigned Numbers Authority: an organization working under the auspices of the Internet Architecture Board (IAB) that is responsible for assigning new Internet-wide Internet Protocol (IP) addresses.
⇒ See also INTERNET ARCHITECTURE BOARD; IP ADDRESS.

I-beam pointer *n.* a pointer shaped like a capital I, used in graphics-based text-processing applications.
⇒ See also INSERTION POINT; POINTER.

IBM International Business Machines: the largest computer company in the world. IBM started in 1911 as a producer of punch card tabulating machines, introduced its first computer in 1953, dominated the field of mainframe and minicomputers in the 1960s and 1970s, and launched its first personal computer in 1981.
⇒ See also AS/400; IBM PC; MAINFRAME.

IBM compatible *n.* IBM PC.

IBM PC *n.* **1.** one of a family of personal computers produced by IBM. **2.** Also called **IBM clone, IBM compatible.** a computer that conforms to a set of loosely controlled industry standards that originally reflected those of IBM but are now somewhat more independent.
⇒ See also COMPATIBLE; IBM; PC.

ICC See under SMART CARD.

ICMP Internet Control Message Protocol: an extension to the Internet Protocol (IP) defined by RFC 792. It supports packets containing error, control, and informational messages.
⇒ See also IP; PING.

icon *n.* a small picture that represents an object or program: a principal feature of graphical user interfaces.
⇒ See also GRAPHICAL USER INTERFACE.

IDE 1. See under IDE INTERFACE. **2.** See under INTEGRATED DEVELOPMENT ENVIRONMENT.
⇒ See also IDE INTERFACE; INTEGRATED; VISUAL C++.

IDE interface *n.* Intelligent Drive Electronics or Integrated Drive Electronics: an interface for mass storage devices in which the controller is integrated into the disk or CD-ROM drive.
⇒ See also ATA; EIDE; INTERFACE; SCSI; ST-506 INTERFACE.

identifier *n.* NAME.
⇒ See also VARIABLE.

IE INTERNET EXPLORER.

IEEE (ī′ trip/əl ē′), *n.* Institute of Electrical and Electronics Engineers: an organization of engineers, scientists, and students founded in 1884 and best known for developing standards for the computer and electronics industry.
⇒ See also ETHERNET; GIGABIT ETHERNET; IEEE 802 STANDARDS; TOKEN-RING NETWORK.

IEEE 1394 *n.* a very fast external bus standard that supports data transfer rates of up to 400 Mbps (400 million bits per second).
⇒ See also DEVICE BAY; HOT PLUGGING; PCMCIA; PLUG-AND-PLAY; USB.

IEEE 802 IEEE 802 STANDARDS.

IEEE 802 standards *n.pl.* a set of network standards developed by the IEEE.
⇒ See also DLC; ETHERNET; IEEE; LOCAL-AREA NETWORK; MAN; TOKEN BUS NETWORK; TOKEN-RING NETWORK.

IETF Internet Engineering Task Force: the main standards organization for the Internet, open to any interested individual.
⇒ See also INTERNET; INTERNET ARCHITECTURE BOARD; INTERNET SOCIETY; RFC; SSL; STANDARD.

IFC Internet Foundation Classes: a set of Java classes developed by Netscape that enables programmers to easily add GUI elements, such as windows, menus, and buttons.
⇒ See also AFC; AWT; CLASS; JAVA; JDK.

IGES Initial Graphics Exchange Specification: an ANSI graphics file format for three-dimensional wire frame models.
⇒ See also ANSI; GRAPHICS FILE FORMATS.

IIOP Internet Inter-ORB Protocol: a protocol developed by the Object Management Group (OMG) to implement CORBA solutions over the World Wide Web, enabling browsers and servers to exchange integers, arrays, and more complex objects.
⇒ See also CORBA; OMG.

IIS Internet Information Server: Microsoft's Web server that runs on Windows NT platforms.
⇒ See also ISAPI; WEB SERVER.

illegal page fault *n.* See under PAGING.

image editor *n.* a graphics program that provides a variety of special features for altering bit-mapped images, such as filters and image transformation algorithms, and the ability to create and superimpose layers.
⇒ See also IMAGE ENHANCEMENT; PAINT PROGRAM; PHOTO ILLUSTRATION.

image enhancement *n.* in computer graphics, the process of improving the quality of a digitally stored image by manipulating the image with software.
⇒ See also ADOBE PHOTOSHOP; DIGITAL PHOTOGRAPHY; IMAGE EDITOR; IMAGE PROCESSING; PHOTO ILLUSTRATION; PHOTO SCANNER.

image map or **imagemap** *n.* a single graphic image containing more than one hot spot: used extensively on the World Wide Web.
⇒ See also GIF; HOT SPOT.

image processing *n.* analysis and manipulation of images with a computer.
⇒ See also DIGITAL PHOTOGRAPHY; GRAPHICS; IMAGE ENHANCEMENT; PHOTO SCANNER.

imagesetter *n.* a typesetting device that produces very-high-resolution output on paper or film.
⇒ See also DESKTOP PUBLISHING; ISP; LaTeX; LINOTRONIC; POSTSCRIPT.

ImageWriter *n.* any in a family of dot-matrix printers that Apple offers for the Macintosh computer.
⇒ See also DOT-MATRIX PRINTER; LASERWRITER; MACINTOSH COMPUTER; PRINTER.

IMAP *n.* Internet Message Access Protocol: a protocol for retrieving e-mail messages, developed at Stanford University in 1986.
⇒ See also POP; SMTP.

impact printer *n.* a class of printers, as dot-matrix printers, daisy-wheel printers, and line printers, that work by striking a hammer or pin against an ink ribbon, or against an object that in turn strikes the ink ribbon, to make a mark on the paper.
⇒ See also DAISY-WHEEL PRINTER; DOT-MATRIX PRINTER; INK-JET PRINTER; LINE PRINTER; PRINTER.

import *v.t.* to bring (documents, data, etc.) into one application program from another.
⇒ See also COMMA-DELIMITED; CONVERT; EXPORT; FILTER; MIDDLEWARE.

in-betweening *n.* TWEENING.

inclusive OR operator *n.* a Boolean operator that returns a value of TRUE if either or both of its operands is TRUE.
⇒ See also BOOLEAN OPERATOR.

increment *n.* **1.** the act or process of increasing. **2.** the amount added by increasing.
⇒ See also DECREMENT; LOOP.

incremental backup *n.* a procedure that backs up only those files that have been modified since the previous backup.
⇒ See also ARCHIVAL BACKUP; BACKUP.

Indeo *n.* a codec (compression/decompression technology) for computer video developed by Intel Corporation.
⇒ See also CINEPAK; CODEC; DVI; MPEG.

index *n.* **1.** in database design, a list of keys (or keywords), each of which identifies a unique record. —*v.i.* **2.** to create an index for a database, or to find records using an index.
⇒ See also HASHING; ISAM; KEY; KEYWORD.

Indexed Sequential Access Method *n.* See ISAM.

Industry Standard Architecture (ISA) bus *n.* the bus architecture used in the IBM PC/XT and

PC/AT. *Abbr.:* ISA bus
⇒ See also AT BUS; BUS; EISA; LOCAL BUS; PCI; PLUG-AND-PLAY.

Information Services *n.* See IS.

information superhighway *n.* a term used to describe the Internet, bulletin board services, online services, and other services that enable people to obtain information from telecommunications networks.
⇒ See also BULLETIN BOARD SYSTEM; ONLINE SERVICE; TELECOMMUNICATIONS.

Information Systems *n.* See IS.

Information Technology *n.* See IT.

Informix *n.* one of the fastest-growing DBMS software companies.
⇒ See also DATABASE MANAGEMENT SYSTEM; ORACLE; SYBASE.

Infoseek *n.* a World Wide Web search engine developed by Infoseek Corporation that provides categorized lists of Web sites.
⇒ See also ALTA VISTA; EXCITE; HOTBOT; LYCOS; OPEN TEXT; SEARCH ENGINE; WEBCRAWLER; YAHOO!.

Infrared Data Association *n.* See IRDA.

INI *n.* See under .INI FILE.

.INI file (dot′ in′ē fīl′), *n.* a file that has a .INI extension and contains configuration information for MS-Windows.
⇒ See also EXTENSION.

init *n.* **1.** on Macintoshes, an old term for SYSTEM EXTENSIONS. —*v.t.* **2.** INITIALIZE.
⇒ See also EXTENSION.

Initial Graphics Exchange Specification *n.* See IGES.

initialize *v.t.* **1.** on Apple Macintosh computers, to format (a disk). **2.** in programming, to assign a starting value to (a variable). **3.** to start up (a program or system).
⇒ See also ASSIGN; FORMAT; VARIABLE.

ink-jet printer *n.* a type of printer that has magnetized plates that direct a spray of ionized ink onto the paper in the desired shapes.
⇒ See also COLOR PRINTER; FONT; FONT CARTRIDGE; LASER PRINTER; PRINTER; SOLID INK-JET PRINTER.

input *n.* **1.** whatever goes into the computer, as commands entered from the keyboard or data from another computer or device. —*v.t.* **2.** to enter (data) into a computer.
⇒ See also I/O; OUTPUT.

input device *n.* any instrument that feeds data into a computer, as a keyboard, a mouse, or a trackball.
⇒ See also DEVICE; I/O; LIGHT PEN; MOUSE; OUTPUT; TRACKBALL.

input/output *n.* See I/O.

insert *v.t.* to place (an object) between two other objects.
⇒ See also APPEND; INS KEY; INSERT MODE.

insertion point *n.* in graphics-based programs, the point where the next characters typed from the keyboard will appear on the display screen, usually represented by a blinking vertical line.
⇒ See also I-BEAM POINTER; INSERT MODE; POINTER.

Insert key *n.* a key on computer keyboards that turns insert mode on and off.
⇒ See also INSERT MODE.

insert mode *n.* a text-entry mode in the editor that inserts all characters typed at the cursor position (or to the right of the insertion point).
⇒ See also INSERT KEY; INSERTION POINT; OVERSTRIKE.

Ins key *n.* INSERT KEY.

instant messaging *n.* a type of communications service that enables the user to create a private chat room with another individual.
⇒ See also CHAT; E-MAIL; FINGER.

Institute of Electrical and Electronics Engineers *n.* See IEEE.

instruction *n.* a basic command.
⇒ See also CISC; COMMAND; MACHINE LANGUAGE; MICROCODE; RISC; SUPERSCALAR.

integer *n.* a whole number.
⇒ See also CHARACTER STRING; DATA TYPE; FLOATING-POINT NUMBER.

integrated *adj.* **1.** referring to two or more compo-

nents merged together into a single system. **2.** referring to applications that combine word processing, database management, spreadsheet functions, and communications into a single package.
⇒ See also IDE; MIDDLEWARE.

integrated circuit *n.* a small electronic device made out of a semiconductor material, used in microprocessors, audio and video equipment, automobiles, etc. Also called **chip**.
⇒ See also ASIC; CHIP; PLD; SEMICONDUCTOR; TRANSISTOR.

integrated development environment (IDE) *n.* a programming environment integrated into an application.
⇒ See also POWERBUILDER.

Integrated Drive Electronics *n.* See IDE.

integrated services digital network *n.* See ISDN.

Intel *n.* the world's largest manufacturer of computer chips.
⇒ See also AMD; CYRIX; DVI; INTEL MICROPROCESSORS; NEC; PCI; WINTEL.

Intellifont *n.* a scalable font technology that is part of Hewlett-Packard's PCL 5 page description language (PDL).
⇒ See also PAGE DESCRIPTION LANGUAGE (PDL); PCL; SCALABLE FONT.

Intelligent Drive Electronics *n.* See IDE.

Intelligent I/O *n.* See I2O.

intelligent terminal *n.* a terminal (monitor and keyboard) with processing power.
⇒ See also DUMB TERMINAL; SMART TERMINAL; TERMINAL.

Intel microprocessor *n.* a microprocessor made by Intel Corporation: the basic chip in all PCs.
⇒ See also ALPHA PROCESSOR; MICROPROCESSOR; MULTITASKING; PENTIUM II; PENTIUM MICROPROCESSOR; PENTIUM PRO; REGISTER; RISC.

interactive *adj.* accepting input from a human; allowing users to enter data or commands. Most popular programs, such as word processors, are interactive.

interface *n.* **1.** something that connects two separate entities, as a user interface that connects the computer with a human operator (user). —*v.i.* **2.** to communicate, as two devices that transmit data between each other.
⇒ See also USER INTERFACE.

interlacing *n.* **1.** a display technique in which the electron guns draw only half the horizontal lines on each pass, enabling a monitor to provide more resolution inexpensively but resulting in a slower reaction time. **2.** preparing a graphic image so that alternating rows are displayed in separate passes: esp. prevalent on the World Wide Web.
⇒ See also CRT; MONITOR; REFRESH; RESOLUTION.

interleave *v.t.* to arrange (data) in a noncontiguous way, as on a disk drive to make the drive more efficient and thus increase performance, or as in memory.
⇒ See also DISK; DISK DRIVE; INTERLEAVED MEMORY; SECTOR; TRACK.

interleaved memory *n.* main memory divided into two or more sections so that the CPU can access alternate sections immediately, without waiting for memory to catch up (through wait states).
⇒ See also ACCESS TIME; CACHE; CLOCK SPEED; DYNAMIC RAM; FPM RAM; MEMORY; WAIT STATE.

internal bus *n.* EXPANSION BUS.

internal cache *n.* L1 CACHE.

internal command *n.* in DOS systems, any command that resides in the COMMAND.COM file, such as COPY and DIR.
⇒ See also COMMAND; DOS; EXTERNAL COMMAND.

internal font *n.* RESIDENT FONT.

internal modem *n.* a modem on an expansion board that plugs into a computer.
⇒ See also EXPANSION BOARD; EXTERNAL MODEM; MODEM.

International Business Machines *n.* See IBM.

International Standards Organization *n.* See ISO.

International Telecommunication Union *n.* See ITU.

Internet *n.* a decentralized global network connecting millions of computers worldwide.
⇒ See also ARPANET; ATM; DIAL-UP ACCESS; FTP; GOPHER; I2; IAC; IETF; InterNIC; INTRANET; IP ADDRESS; MBONE; MOSAIC; NAP; NGI INITIATIVE; ONLINE SERVICE; USENET; vBNS; WORLD WIDE WEB.

Internet2 *n.* See I2.

Internet Access Coalition *n.* See IAC.

Internet Ad Hoc Committee *n.* See IAHC.

Internet appliance *n.* NETWORK COMPUTER.

Internet Architecture Board *n.* a technical advisory group of the Internet Society.
⇒ See also IANA; IETF; INTERNET SOCIETY; RFC.

Internet Assigned Numbers Authority *n.* See IANA.

Internet box *n.* NETWORK COMPUTER.

Internet Engineering Task Force *n.* See IETF.

Internet Explorer *n.* Microsoft's Web browser.
⇒ See also ACTIVEX CONTROL; BROWSER; CDF; NAVIGATOR; VBSCRIPT; WINDOWS 98.

Internet Foundation Classes *n.* See IFC.

Internet Information Server *n.* See IIS.

Internet Inter-ORB Protocol *n.* See IIOP.

Internet Message Access Protocol *n.* See IMAP.

Internet Phone *n.* either of two popular Voice on the Net products, one produced by Intel and the other developed by VocalTec Ltd.
⇒ See also INTERNET TELEPHONY; NetMeeting; TELEPHONY.

Internet Protocol *n.* See IP.

Internet Relay Chat *n.* See IRC.

Internet Service Provider *n.* See ISP.

Internet Society *n.* a nongovernmental, nonprofit organization dedicated to maintaining and enhancing the Internet by means of committees such as the Internet Advisory Board and the Internet Engineering Task Force.
⇒ See also IETF; INTERNET ARCHITECTURE BOARD; STANDARD.

Internet telephony *n.* a category of hardware and software that enables people to use the Internet as the transmission medium for telephone calls.
⇒ See also CoolTalk; INTERNET; INTERNET PHONE; TELEPHONY.

internetworking *n.* the art and science of connecting individual local-area networks (LANs) to create wide-area networks (WANs), and connecting WANs to form even larger WANs, accomplished by means of routers, bridges, and gateways.
⇒ See also BRIDGE; CISCO SYSTEMS; LOCAL-AREA NETWORK; ROUTER; WIDE-AREA NETWORK.

Internetwork Packet eXchange *n.* See IPX.

InterNIC *n.* a collaborative project between AT&T and Network Solutions, Inc. (NSI), supported by the National Science Foundation, that offers services to users of the Internet.
⇒ See also DOMAIN NAME; INTERNET; IP ADDRESS.

interpolated resolution *n.* See under OPTICAL RESOLUTION.

interpreter *n.* a program that translates high-level instructions into an intermediate form, which it then executes.
⇒ See also BASIC; BYTECODE; COMPILE; COMPILER; JAVA; LISP; PAGE DESCRIPTION LANGUAGE (PDL); PERL; POSTSCRIPT; PROGRAMMING LANGUAGE; TCL.

interprocess communication *n.* a capability supported by some operating systems that allows one process to communicate with another process. The processes can be running on the same computer or on different computers connected through a network. *Abbr.:* IPC
⇒ See also DDE; MULTIPROCESSING; NAMED PIPES; NETWORK; OPERATING SYSTEM; PROCESS; SEMAPHORE.

interrupt *n.* **1.** a signal, as one generated by a keystroke or by a printer, informing a program that an event has occurred. —*v.i.* **2.** to send an interrupt signal.
⇒ See also EVENT; INTERRUPT VECTOR TABLE; IRQ.

interrupt request line *n.* See IRQ.

interrupt vector table *n.* a table of *interrupt vec-*tors (pointers to routines that handle interrupts). Also called **dispatch table.**
⇒ See also INTERRUPT; IRQ.

intranet *n.* a network, based on TCP/IP protocols developed for the Internet, belonging to an organization, usually a corporation, accessible only to the organization's members, employees, or others with authorization. An intranet's Web sites look and act just like other Web sites, but the firewall surrounding an intranet prevents unauthorized access.
⇒ See also ENTERPRISE; EXTRANET; FIREWALL; INTERNET; LOTUS NOTES; NETWORK.

invalid page fault *n.* a page fault that produces an error, as instability of the virtual memory system due to shortage of RAM or of free disk space. Also called **page fault error (PFE).**
⇒ See also CRASH; GPF; PAGE FAULT.

inverse video *n.* REVERSE VIDEO.

inverted tree *n.* See under TREE STRUCTURE.

invisible file *n.* HIDDEN FILE.

invocation *n.* the execution of a program or function.
⇒ See also INVOKE.

invoke *v.t.* to activate (a function or routine) in a program.
⇒ See also CALL; FUNCTION; ROUTINE.

I/O (ī′ō′), input/output: any operation, program, or device whose purpose is to enter data into a computer or to extract data from a computer.
⇒ See also I2O; INPUT; OUTPUT.

IP Internet Protocol: a set of rules that specifies the format of packets (also called **datagrams**) and the addressing scheme.
⇒ See also ICMP; IPng; IPsec; PACKET; TCP; TCP/IP; UDP.

IP address *n.* an identifier for a computer or device on a TCP/IP network. The format of an IP address is a 32-bit numeric address written as four numbers separated by periods. Each number can be from 0 to 255.
⇒ See also ARP; CIDR; DNS; DOMAIN NAME; IANA; INTERNET; InterNIC; IP SPOOFING; NAT; PING; ROUTING; SUBNET; TCP/IP; TLD; WHOIS; WINS.

IPC *n.* INTERPROCESS COMMUNICATION.

IP Multicast *n.* sending out data to distributed servers on the MBone (Multicast Backbone): more efficient than normal Internet transmissions because the server can broadcast a message to many recipients simultaneously.
⇒ See also MBONE; MULTICAST; REALVIDEO.

IPng *n.* Internet Protocol next generation: a version of the Internet Protocol (IP) currently being reviewed in IETF standards committees.
⇒ See also IP.

IPsec *n.* IP Security: a set of protocols being developed by the IETF to support secure exchange of packets at the IP layer.
⇒ See also IP; L2TP; SSL.

IP spoofing *n.* a technique used to gain unauthorized access to computers, whereby the intruder sends messages to a computer with an IP address indicating that the message is coming from a trusted port.
⇒ See also FIREWALL; HACKER; IP ADDRESS; ROUTER; SMURF; SPOOF.

IP switch *n.* See under IP SWITCHING.

IP switching *n.* a type of IP routing, developed by Ipsilon Networks, Inc., that uses ATM hardware to speed packets through networks.
⇒ See also ATM; ROUTER; ROUTING; ROUTING SWITCH.

IPX Internetwork Packet Exchange: a networking protocol used by the Novell NetWare operating systems.
⇒ See also COMMUNICATIONS PROTOCOL; CONNECTIONLESS; NETWARE; SPX; UDP.

IPX/SPX See under SPX.

IRC Internet Relay Chat: a chat system developed by Jarkko Oikarinen in Finland in the late 1980s that enables people connected anywhere on the Internet to join in live discussions.
⇒ See also CHANNEL; CHAT; CHAT ROOM; INTERNET.

IrDA Infrared Data Association: a group of device manufacturers that developed a standard for trans-

computer

mitting data from one device to another via infrared light waves rather than cables.
⇒ See also PARALLEL PORT.

IRMA board *n.* an expansion board for PCs and Macintoshes that enables them to emulate IBM 3278 and 3279 mainframe terminals.
⇒ See also EMULATION; EXPANSION BOARD; STAND-ALONE; TERMINAL.

IRQ (*pronounced as separate letters*), interrupt request line: a hardware line over which devices can send interrupt signals to the microprocessor.
⇒ See also DIP SWITCH; EXPANSION BUS; INDUSTRY STANDARD ARCHITECTURE (ISA) BUS; INTERRUPT; INTERRUPT VECTOR TABLE.

IS (*pronounced as separate letters*), Information Systems *or* Information Services: the name of the department responsible for computers, networking, and data management. Also called **IT (Information Technology), MIS (Management Information Services).**
⇒ See also IT; MIS; SYSTEM MANAGEMENT.

ISA (ī/sə), *n.* Industry Standard Architecture. See INDUSTRY STANDARD ARCHITECTURE (ISA) BUS.

ISA bus *n.* INDUSTRY STANDARD ARCHITECTURE (ISA) BUS.

ISAM *n.* Indexed Sequential Access Method: a method for managing the way a computer accesses records and files stored on a hard disk.
⇒ See also DATABASE MANAGEMENT SYSTEM; INDEX; RANDOM ACCESS; SEQUENTIAL ACCESS.

ISAPI *n.* Internet Server API: an API for Microsoft's IIS (Internet Information Server) Web server that enables programmers to develop Web-based applications that run much faster than conventional CGI programs because they are more tightly integrated with the Web server.
⇒ See also CGI; IIS; NSAPI; STATELESS.

ISDN integrated services digital network: an international communications standard for sending voice, video, and data over digital telephone lines.
⇒ See also ADSL; B-CHANNEL; BRI; BROADBAND ISDN (B-ISDN); CHANNEL BONDING; DIRECPC; FDDI; FIBER OPTICS; GROUP 4 PROTOCOL; NDIS; SDSL; SPID; TERMINAL ADAPTER; xDSL.

ISO *n.* International Organization for Standardization: an international organization composed of national standards bodies from more than 75 countries. It has defined important computer standards, as OSI (Open Systems Interconnection), a standardized architecture for designing networks. [< Gk

isos equal]
⇒ See also ANSI; CMIP; ISO 9000; NETWORK; OSI; STANDARD.

ISO 9000 *n.* a family of standards approved by the International Organization for Standardization (ISO) that define a quality assurance program.
⇒ See also ISO; STANDARD.

ISOC INTERNET SOCIETY.

isochronous (ī sok/rə nəs), *adj.* time dependent: referring to processes where data must be delivered within certain time constraints.
⇒ See also ASYNCHRONOUS; ATM; IEEE 1394; REAL TIME; SYNCHRONOUS; THROUGHPUT.

ISO Latin 1 *n.* officially named ISO-8859-1, a standard character set developed by the International Organization for Standardization (ISO).
⇒ See also ANSI CHARACTER SET; ASCII; EXTENDED ASCII.

ISP Internet Service Provider: a company that provides access to the Internet for a monthly fee. Also called **IAP (Internet Access Provider).**
⇒ See also DIAL-UP ACCESS; DIRECPC; E-MAIL; INTERNET; MAE; NAP; NSP; RADIUS; T-1 CARRIER; T-3 CARRIER; USENET; WORLD WIDE WEB.

ISV Independent Software Vendor: a company that produces software.
⇒ See also SOFTWARE.

IT (*pronounced as separate letters*), Information Technology: the broad subject concerned with all aspects of managing and processing information, especially within a large organization or company. Also called **IS (Information Services), MIS (Management Information Services).**
⇒ See also COMPUTER SCIENCE; IS; MIS; SYSTEM MANAGEMENT.

italic *adj.* in typography, referring to fonts with characters slanted to the right.
⇒ See also FONT.

iteration *n.* a single pass through a group of instructions.
⇒ See also LOOP.

ITU International Telecommunication Union: an intergovernmental organization through which public and private organizations develop telecommunications: founded in 1865, United Nations agency since 1947.
⇒ See also CCITT; DSVD; H.323; STANDARD; TELECOMMUNICATIONS; V.35; V.90; X.500.

IVT INTERRUPT VECTOR TABLE.

a b c d e f g h i J K l m n o p q r s t u v w x y z

jaggies *n.pl.* stairlike lines that appear on a display monitor or on printed output where there should be smooth curves or smooth, straight diagonal lines.
⇒ See also ANTIALIASING; SMOOTHING.

Java *n.* a high-level general purpose programming language developed by Sun Microsystems and used to create interactive applications that can run over the Internet.
⇒ See also ACTIVEX; APPLET; AWT; BYTECODE; C++; CGI; DYNAMIC HTML; HOTJAVA; IFC; INTERPRETER; JAVABEANS; JAVASCRIPT; JDBC; JDK; JIT; OBJECT-ORIENTED PROGRAMMING; PROGRAMMING LANGUAGE; RMI; SMALLTALK; SUN MICROSYSTEMS; THIN CLIENT; VIRTUAL MACHINE.

JavaBeans *n.* a specification developed by Sun Microsystems that defines how Java objects interact. Java program fragments that conform to it can work together on any platform.
⇒ See also ACTIVEX CONTROL; JAVA; JDK.

Java Database Connectivity *n.* See JDBC.

Java Development Kit *n.* See JDK.

JavaScript *n.* a scripting language for Netscape's Web browser that helps Web authors design interactive sites.

⇒ See also DOM; DYNAMIC HTML; HTML; JAVA; JSCRIPT; SCRIPT; VBSCRIPT.

JavaSoft *n.* the business unit of Sun Microsystems that is responsible for Java technology.
⇒ See also HOTJAVA; JAVA; JDBC; JDK; SUN MICROSYSTEMS.

Java VM *n.* See under VIRTUAL MACHINE.

Jaz drive *n.* a removable disk drive developed by Iomega Corporation, that has a 12-ms average seek time and a transfer rate of 5.5 Mbps.
⇒ See also REMOVABLE HARD DISK.

JDBC Java Database Connectivity: a Java API that enables Java programs to interact with any SQL-compliant database.
⇒ See also JAVA; JAVASOFT; JDK; ODBC; SQL.

JDK Java Development Kit: a software development kit (SDK) for producing Java programs.
⇒ See also AFC; IFC; JAVA; JAVABEANS; JAVASOFT; JDBC; SDK.

Jet *n.* Joint engine technology: the database engine used by Microsoft Office and Visual Basic.
⇒ See also DAO; VISUAL BASIC.

JIT just-in-time compiler: a code generator that converts Java bytecode into machine language instructions.

⇒ See also BYTECODE; COMPILER; JAVA; VIRTUAL MACHINE.

job *n.* a task performed by a computer system, as printing a file.
⇒ See also PROGRAM; TASK.

join *v.t.* in relational databases, to match (tables that have a common field, called a *join field*). The process is called a *join operation.*
⇒ See also DATABASE; FIELD; QUERY; RDBMS.

Joint Photographic Experts Group *n.* See JPEG.

joystick *n.* a lever that moves in all directions and controls the movement of a pointer or some other display symbol, as for use in computer games, CAD/CAM systems, etc.
⇒ See also MOUSE; POINTER.

JPEG (jā′peg′), *n.* Joint Photographic Experts Group: a lossy compression technique for color images that can reduce files to about 5 percent of their normal size.
⇒ See also DATA COMPRESSION; DCT; MOTION-JPEG; MPEG.

.jpg the file extension for a JPEG-encoded image.

JScript *n.* Microsoft's version of NetScape's JavaScript, which is built into Internet Explorer (IE) browsers: not fully compatible with JavaScript.
⇒ See also JAVASCRIPT; VBSCRIPT.

Jughead *n.* a search engine for Gopher sites.
⇒ See also GOPHER; SEARCH ENGINE; VERONICA.

jumper *n.* a metal bridge that closes an electrical circuit to enable a hardware option, usu. consisting of a plastic plug that fits over a pair of protruding pins.
⇒ See also CONFIGURATION; CONFIGURE; EXPANSION BOARD.

justification *n.* alignment of text along a margin.
⇒ See also ALIGNMENT; FEATHERING; LEADING; MICROSPACING; VERTICAL JUSTIFICATION.

justify *v.t.* in word processing, to align (text) along the left and right margins.
⇒ See also FLUSH; JUSTIFICATION.

just-in-time compiler *n.* See JIT.

K kilo: 1,000 for communications purposes, as 56 Kbps (56,000 bits per second); 1,024 when discussing memory and file sizes, as 64 KB (65,536 bytes).
⇒ See also KB; M.

K56flex *n.* a technology developed by Lucent Technologies and Rockwell International for delivering data rates up to 56 Kbps over plain old telephone service (POTS) by taking advantage of high-speed digital lines by which most phone switching stations are connected.
⇒ See also CHANNEL BONDING; MODEM; V.90; X2.

K6 a microprocessor from AMD that supports the MMX instruction set and is completely compatible with Intel's Pentium processors.
⇒ See also AMD; MMX; PENTIUM MICROPROCESSOR; SOCKET 7.

KB kilobyte: in reference to data storage, 1,024 bytes; In reference to data transfer rates, 1,000 bytes.
⇒ See also KILOBYTE.

Kbps kilobits per second: a measure of data transfer speed, as by a modem. One Kbps is 1000 bits per second.
⇒ See also DATA TRANSFER RATE; KILOBIT; MODEM.

Kerberos (kûr′bə ros′), *n.* an authentication system developed at the Massachusetts Institute of Technology (MIT) that is designed to enable two parties to exchange private information across an otherwise open network by means of a unique key,

called a *ticket.*
⇒ See also AUTHENTICATION; SECURITY.

Kermit *n.* a communications protocol and set of associated software utilities developed at Columbia University that can be used to transfer files or for terminal emulation. It is frequently used with modem connections but also supports communications via other transport mechanisms.
⇒ See also CCITT; COMMUNICATIONS; COMMUNICATIONS SOFTWARE; FTP; FULL DUPLEX; MNP; MODEM; PROTOCOL; TERMINAL EMULATION; XMODEM; ZMODEM.

kernel *n.* the central module of an operating system, responsible for memory management, process and task management, and disk management.
⇒ See also OPERATING SYSTEM.

kerning *n.* in typography, adjusting the space between characters, esp. by placing two characters closer together than normal, so as to make them look better.
⇒ See also DESKTOP PUBLISHING; FONT; WORD PROCESSING.

key *n.* **1.** a button on a keyboard. **2.** Also called **key field, sort key, index, keyword.** in database management systems, a field used to sort data, as an age field, a data field, or the like. **3.** a password or table needed to decipher encoded data.
⇒ See also DATABASE MANAGEMENT SYSTEM; ENCRYPTION; FIELD; HASHING; INDEX; NORMALIZATION; PASSWORD; REFERENTIAL INTEGRITY; SYMMETRIC-KEY CRYPTOGRAPHY.

keyboard *n.* the set of typewriter-like keys used to enter data into a computer: includes alphanumeric keys, punctuation keys, and special keys that perform a variety of functions.
⇒ See also ADB; ALPHANUMERIC; ALT KEY; ARROW KEYS; BACKSPACE KEY; BREAK KEY; CAPS LOCK KEY; CONTROL KEY; CURSOR; DELETE KEY; DVORAK KEYBOARD; END KEY; ENHANCED KEYBOARD; ENTER KEY.

keyboard buffer *n.* a memory area where data about which keys have been pressed is stored prior to processing.

keyboard template *n.* TEMPLATE (def. 1).

key field *n.* KEY (def. 1).

keypad *n.* NUMERIC KEYPAD.

keystroke *n.* the pressing of a key on a keyboard or keypad.
⇒ See also KEY; KEYBOARD.

keyword *n.* **1.** in text editing and database management systems, an index entry that identifies a specific record or document. **2.** in programming, a word that has a special meaning in a particular programming language, as for a command or parameter, and is therefore reserved by the program. Also called **reserved name.**
⇒ See also COMMAND; INDEX; PARAMETER; VARIABLE.

killer app *n.* See under APP.
⇒ See also APPLICATION.

kilobit *n.* 1,024 bits for data storage; 1,000 bits for data transmission.
⇒ See also BIT; KBPS; MEGABIT.

kilobyte *n.* **1.** 1,024 bytes. **2.** loosely, 1,000 bytes: a computer that has 256K main memory can store approximately 256,000 bytes (or characters).
⇒ See also BINARY; BYTE; GIGA (G); MEGABYTE; MEMORY.

kiosk *n.* a booth providing a computer-related service, as an automated teller machine (ATM).
⇒ See also TOUCH SCREEN.

kludge (klōōj), *n.* a derogatory term for a poor design.
⇒ See also HACK.

computer

L1 cache *n.* Level 1 cache: a memory cache generally built into the microprocessor. Also called **primary cache**.
⇒ See also CACHE.

L2 cache *n.* Level 2 cache: cache memory that is generally external to the microprocessor. Also called **secondary cache**.
⇒ See also CACHE; L1 CACHE; PENTIUM MICROPROCESSOR; PENTIUM PRO; TAG RAM.

L2F LAYER TWO FORWARDING.

L2TP Layer Two Tunneling Protocol: an extension to the PPP protocol that enables ISPs to operate Virtual Private Networks (VPNs).
⇒ See also DIAL-UP ACCESS; IPSEC; LAYER TWO FORWARDING; PPTP; TUNNELING; VPN.

label *n.* **1.** a name. **2.** for mass storage devices, the name of a storage volume. **3.** in spreadsheet programs, any descriptive text placed in a cell. **4.** in programming languages, a particular location in a program, usu. a particular line of source code. **5.** a small, sticky piece of paper placed on an object to identify it.
⇒ See also CELL; DISK; MASS STORAGE; NAME; SPREADSHEET; VOLUME.

LAN *n.* LOCAL-AREA NETWORK.

landscape *adj.* in word processing and desktop publishing, pertaining to or producing output with lines of data parallel to the two longer sides of a page.
⇒ See also MONITOR; PORTRAIT; PRINTER; WORD PROCESSING.

language *n.* a set of characters and syntactic rules for their combination and use, by means of which a computer can be given directions: *machine language; programming language; fourth-generation language.*
⇒ See also ARTIFICIAL INTELLIGENCE; FOURTH-GENERATION LANGUAGE; MACHINE LANGUAGE; NATURAL LANGUAGE; PROGRAMMING LANGUAGE; SYNTAX.

laptop computer *n.* a small, flat portable computer, shaped like a briefcase and typically weighing around 7 pounds. Also called **notebook computer**.
⇒ See also NOTEBOOK COMPUTER; PORTABLE.

large-scale integration *n.* the placement of thousands of electronic components on a single integrated circuit. *Abbr.:* LSI.
⇒ See also CHIP; INTEGRATED CIRCUIT; VLSI.

laser printer *n.* a high-speed, high-resolution printer that utilizes a laser beam to form dot-matrix patterns and an electrostatic process to print a page at a time.
⇒ See also COLOR PRINTER; INK-JET PRINTER; LCD PRINTER; OFFSET PRINTING; OKIDATA; PAGE DESCRIPTION LANGUAGE (PDL); PCL; POSTSCRIPT; PRINTER; RESIDENT FONT; RESOLUTION ENHANCEMENT; SMOOTHING; SOFT FONT; TONER.

LaserWriter *n.* a family of Apple laser printers designed to run with a Macintosh computer.
⇒ See also IMAGEWRITER; LASER PRINTER; MACINTOSH COMPUTER; POSTSCRIPT; PRINTER; QUICKDRAW.

latency *n.* **1.** in general, the period of time that one component in a system must wait after requesting a particular action or piece of information from another component. **2.** in networking, the amount of time it takes a packet to travel from source to destination.
⇒ See also BANDWIDTH; QOS; WAIT STATE.

LaTeX *n.* a typesetting system based on the TeX text-formatting language that provides high-level macros.
⇒ See also MACRO; MUTEX; TEX.

launch *v.t.* to start (an application or a program).
⇒ See also EXECUTE; LOAD; RUN.

LAWN *n.* LOCAL-AREA WIRELESS NETWORK.

layer-3 switch *n.* ROUTING SWITCH.

Layer Two Forwarding *n.* a tunneling protocol

developed by Cisco Systems that enables organizations to set up virtual private networks (VPNs) that use the Internet backbone to move packets.
⇒ See also CISCO SYSTEMS; L2TP; PPTP; TUNNELING; VPN.

layout *n.* **1.** in word processing and desktop publishing, the arrangement of text and graphics, as on a page or display screen. **2.** in database management systems, the way information is displayed.
⇒ See also DATABASE MANAGEMENT SYSTEM; DESKTOP PUBLISHING; FIELD; REPORT WRITER; WORD PROCESSING; WYSIWYG.

LBA logical block addressing: a method used in DOS and Windows to translate the cylinder, head, and sector specifications of a SCSI or IDE disk drive that is larger than 528 MB into addresses that can be used by an enhanced BIOS.
⇒ See also CYLINDER; DISK DRIVE; HEAD; SECTOR.

LCD liquid crystal display: an information display, as on digital watches, calculators, and portable computers, that uses a liquid-crystal film that changes its optical properties when a voltage is applied.
⇒ See also ACTIVE-MATRIX DISPLAY; BACKLIGHTING; CSTN; DLP; DSTN; ELECTROLUMINESCENT DISPLAY (ELD); FLAT-PANEL DISPLAY; GAS-PLASMA DISPLAY; LCD MONITOR; LCD PRINTER; LED; NOTEBOOK COMPUTER; SUPERTWIST; TFT.

LCD monitor *n.* a monitor that uses LCD technologies rather than the conventional CRT technologies used by most desktop monitors.
⇒ See also COLOR MONITOR; CRT; FLAT-PANEL DISPLAY; LCD; MONITOR.

LCD printer *n.* a type of printer, similar to a laser printer, that shines a light through a liquid crystal panel to form dot-matrix patterns.
⇒ See also LASER PRINTER; LCD; PIXEL.

LDAP *n.* Lightweight Directory Access Protocol: a set of protocols for accessing information directories.
⇒ See also ACTIVE DIRECTORY; DIRECTORY SERVICE; NDS; PUBLIC-KEY ENCRYPTION; TCP/IP.

leader *n.* a row of dots, dashes, or other characters that leads the eye from one text element to another, as in a table of contents.

leading (led′ing), *n.* a typographical term that refers to the vertical space between lines of text. Also called **line spacing**.
⇒ See also FONT; JUSTIFICATION; POINT; VERTICAL JUSTIFICATION.

leading zero (lē′ding), *n.* a zero that appears in the leftmost digit(s) of a number.

leaf *n.* an item, as a file, at the very bottom of a hierarchical tree structure.
⇒ See also HIERARCHICAL; NODE; TREE STRUCTURE.

learn mode *n.* a mode in which a program records a user's keystrokes and other actions, as when defining a macro.
⇒ See also MACRO.

leased line *n.* a permanent telephone or data connection between two points set up by a telecommunications common carrier and used by businesses to connect geographically distant offices.
⇒ See also DIAL-UP ACCESS; FRACTIONAL T-1; T-1 CARRIER; T-3 CARRIER; TDM; TELECOMMUNICATIONS.

LED light emitting diode: an electronic device that lights up when electricity is passed through it: used for displaying readings on digital watches, calculators, etc.
⇒ See also LASER PRINTER; LCD.

LED printer *n.* a type of printer, similar to a laser printer, that uses an array of LEDs to form patterns on the page.

left justify *v.t.* to align (text) along the left margin.
⇒ See also FLUSH; JUSTIFY.

legacy application *n.* an application in which a company or organization has already invested considerable time and money, as a database management system running on a mainframe or minicomputer. It is important that new software products be compatible with a company's legacy applications because these programs can be very difficult to modify or replace.
⇒ See also APPLICATION; MAINFRAME; MINICOMPUTER.

legend *n.* in presentation graphics, text that describes the meaning of colors and patterns used in the chart.
⇒ See also PRESENTATION GRAPHICS.

letter-quality *adj.* referring to or producing print that has the same quality as that produced by a typewriter.
⇒ See also DAISY-WHEEL PRINTER; DOT-MATRIX PRINTER; DRAFT QUALITY; INK-JET PRINTER; LASER PRINTER; NEAR LETTER QUALITY; PRINTER.

Level 2 cache *n.* L2 CACHE.

library *n.* **1.** a collection of files. **2.** in programming, a collection of precompiled routines, or modules, that a program can use.
⇒ See also DLL; LINKER; MODULE; OBJECT CODE; ROUTINE; RUNTIME.

light bar *n.* on a display screen, a highlighted region that indicates a selected component in a menu.
⇒ See also HIGHLIGHT; MENU; REVERSE VIDEO.

light-emitting diode *n.* See LED.

light pen *n.* an input device analogous to a mouse that utilizes a light-sensitive detector to select objects on a display screen.
⇒ See also CAD/CAM; DISPLAY SCREEN; INPUT DEVICE; MOUSE; PIXEL; POINTER.

Lightweight Directory Access Protocol *n.* See LDAP.

Li-ion *n.* LITHIUM-ION (BATTERY).

LIM *n.* LIM MEMORY.

LIM memory *n.* an obsolete technique for adding memory to DOS systems: superseded by extended memory.
⇒ See also EEMS; EXPANDED MEMORY; EXTENDED MEMORY.

line *n.* **1.** a hardware circuit connecting two devices. **2.** in programming, a single program statement. **3.** in caches, a single data entry.
⇒ See also CHANNEL.

line art *n.* a type of graphic without any shading.
⇒ See also GRAPHICS.

line editor *n.* a primitive type of editor that allows only one line of a file to be edited at a time.
⇒ See also EDITOR.

line feed *n.* **1.** a code that moves the cursor on a display screen down one line. **2.** on a printer, a code that advances the paper one line. *Abbr.:* LF
⇒ See also ASCII; CARRIAGE RETURN.

line graph *n.* a type of graph that highlights trends by drawing connecting lines between data points.
⇒ See also BAR CHART; PIE CHART; PRESENTATION GRAPHICS.

line-interactive UPS *n.* a type of UPS that switches a computer to battery power when it detects a power problem, sometimes leaving the computer without power for several milliseconds before the switch can be effected. Also called **standby power system.**

line printer *n.* a high-speed printer capable of printing an entire line at one time but not capable of printing graphics.
⇒ See also IMPACT PRINTER; PRINTER.

line spacing *n.* LEADING.

lines per inch *n.* a measurement of the fineness of a halftone image.
⇒ See also HALFTONE.

link *v.t.* **1.** to bind (software or hardware objects) together. **2.** to paste (a copy of an object) into a document in such a way that it retains its connection with the original object. **3.** in spreadsheet programs, to take (data for particular cells) from another worksheet. —*v.i.* **4.** to execute a linker. —*n.* **5.** in communications, a line or channel over which data is transmitted. **6.** in data management systems, a pointer to another record. **7.** in some operating systems, such as UNIX, a pointer to a file. **8.** in hypertext systems, such as the World Wide Web, a reference to another document.
⇒ See also CHANNEL; COMMUNICATIONS; COMPILE; DATABASE MANAGEMENT SYSTEM; DLL; FILENAME; HOT LINK; LINKER; OLE; PATH; SPREADSHEET.

link edit *v.i.* to run a linker.
⇒ See also LINKER.

linker *n.* a program that combines object modules to form an executable program. Also called **link editor; binder.**
⇒ See also ADDRESS; COMPILE; EXECUTABLE FILE; MODULE; OBJECT CODE.

Lino *n.* LINOTRONIC.
⇒ See also IMAGESETTER; LINOTRONIC.

Linotronic *n.* a type of high-quality printer, also called an imagesetter, capable of printing at resolutions of up to 2,540 dots per inch.
⇒ See also IMAGESETTER.

Linux (lin′əks, lē′nəks), *n.* a freely distributable implementation of UNIX that runs on a number of hardware platforms, including Intel and Motorola microprocessors.
⇒ See also APACHE WEB SERVER; FREEBSD; GNU; UNIX.

liquid crystal display *n.* See LCD.

liquid crystal shutter printer *n.* LCD PRINTER.

LISP (lisp), *n.* list processor: a high-level programming language especially popular for artificial intelligence applications, developed in the early 1960s at MIT.
⇒ See also ARTIFICIAL INTELLIGENCE; GENETIC PROGRAMMING; HIGH-LEVEL LANGUAGE; PROGRAMMING LANGUAGE; PROLOG.

list *v.t.* **1.** to display (data) in an ordered format. —*n.* **2.** any ordered set of data.
⇒ See also DATA; DATA STRUCTURE.

listing *n.* a printout of text, usually a source program.
⇒ See also PRINTOUT; SOURCE CODE.

LISTSERV *n.* an automatic mailing list server developed by Eric Thomas for BITNET in 1986.
⇒ See also MAILING LIST SERVER; MAJORDOMO.

list server *n.* MAILING LIST SERVER.

literal *n.* in programming, a value, such as a number, a character, or a string, written exactly as it is meant to be interpreted.
⇒ See also CONSTANT; NAME; VARIABLE.

Lithium-Ion battery *n.* a type of battery containing Lithium: used for portable devices such as notebook computers.
⇒ See also BATTERY PACK; NICAD BATTERY PACK; NIMH BATTERY PACK.

little-endian *n.* See under BIG-ENDIAN.

load *v.t.* **1.** to install (software). **2.** to copy (a program) from a storage device into memory. **3.** in programming, to copy (data) from main memory into a data register. —*n.* **4.** in networking, the amount of traffic—that is, the data being carried by the network.
⇒ See also MAIN MEMORY; OPERATING SYSTEM; PROGRAM; REGISTER; TRAFFIC.

load balancing *n.* distributing processing and communications activity evenly across a computer network so that no single device is overwhelmed.
⇒ See also CLUSTERING; SERVER; THREE-TIER; TP MONITOR.

loader *n.* a component of an operating system that copies programs from a storage device to main memory, and also replaces the addresses where they can be executed.
⇒ See also LOAD; MAIN MEMORY; PROGRAM; VIRTUAL MEMORY.

local *adj.* in networks, referring to files, devices, and other resources at the user's workstation.
⇒ See also LOCAL-AREA NETWORK; NETWORK; REMOTE; WORKSTATION.

local-area network *n.* a computer network confined to a limited area, as a single building or group of buildings, linking workstations and personal computers so that data and devices such as printers can be shared.
⇒ See also APPLETALK; ARCNET; BRIDGE; CLIENT/

SERVER ARCHITECTURE; DCC; E-MAIL; ETHERNET; IEEE 802 STANDARDS; INTERNETWORKING; MAN; NETWARE; NETWORK; NETWORK INTERFACE CARD; NETWORK OPERATING SYSTEM; NODE; NOVELL; PEER-TO-PEER ARCHITECTURE; PERSONAL COMPUTER; SNMP; SWITCHING HUB; TOKEN BUS NETWORK; TOKEN-RING NETWORK; TOPOLOGY; TOPS; VLAN; WIDE-AREA NETWORK.

local-area wireless network *n.* a type of local-area network that uses radio waves or infrared transmissions rather than wires to communicate between nodes. *Abbr.:* LAWN
⇒ See also LOCAL-AREA NETWORK.

local bus *n.* a data bus that connects directly, or almost directly, to the microprocessor.
⇒ See also BUS; EXPANSION BUS; PCI; VL-BUS.

local echo *n.* HALF DUPLEX.

LocalTalk *n.* the cabling scheme supported by the AppleTalk network protocol for Macintosh computers.
⇒ See also APPLETALK; ETHERNET; LOCAL-AREA NETWORK; MACINTOSH COMPUTER.

lock *v.t.* **1.** to make (a file, a database record, or other piece of data) inaccessible for writing so that two or more users do not attempt to modify the same file simultaneously. **2.** in Macintosh environments, to write-protect (a diskette).
⇒ See also DATABASE MANAGEMENT SYSTEM; FILE; LOCAL-AREA NETWORK; MULTI-USER; OPERATING SYSTEM; RECORD; WRITE-PROTECT.

log *v.t.* **1.** to record (an action), as to enter a record into a log file. —*n.* **2.** LOG FILE.

log file *n.* a file that lists actions that have occurred, as requests made to a Web server.
⇒ See also AUDIT TRAIL; COOKIE; LOG.

logical *adj.* **1.** referring to a user's view of the way data or systems are organized, as opposed to the physical, or actual, organization of a system. **2.** referring to any Boolean logic operation.
⇒ See also BOOLEAN LOGIC; PHYSICAL.

logical block address *n.* See LBA.

logical operator *n.* BOOLEAN OPERATOR.

log in *v.i.* LOG ON.

login *v.i.* LOG ON.

log off *v.i.* LOG OUT.

log on *v.i.* to gain access to a computer system or on-line service by entering some kind of personal identifier. Also, **log in, login.**
⇒ See also ACCESS CODE; LOG OUT; PASSWORD; USER-NAME.

log out *v.i.* to terminate a session on a computer or on-line service. Also, **log off.**
⇒ See also LOG ON.

look-and-feel *n.* the general appearance and operation of a user interface.
⇒ See also USER INTERFACE.

loop *n.* in programming, a series of instructions that is repeated until a certain condition is met. Each pass through the loop is called an *iteration*.
⇒ See also FLOW CONTROL; ITERATION.

lossless compression *n.* any of the data compression techniques in which the original data can be recovered exactly. Lossless compression generally saves less space than lossy compression.
⇒ See also DATA COMPRESSION; LOSSY COMPRESSION; PKZIP.

lossy compression *n.* any of the data compression techniques, such as those used for video, in which some amount of data is lost because unnecessary information is eliminated.
⇒ See also DATA COMPRESSION; DCT; JPEG; LOSSLESS COMPRESSION.

Lotus 1-2-3 *n.* a spreadsheet program designed for IBM-compatible personal computers by Lotus Corporation in 1982: combines graphics, spreadsheet functions, and data management.
⇒ See also SPREADSHEET; VISICALC.

Lotus Notes *n.* a groupware application developed by Lotus (now part of IBM) that enables users to work with local copies of documents and have their modifications propagated throughout an entire Notes network.
⇒ See also GROUPWARE; INTRANET; REPLICATION.

lowercase *adj.* referring to small letters, as opposed to capital letters.
⇒ See also CASE SENSITIVE; UPPERCASE.

low-level format *n.* the first format of a hard disk, usu. performed at the factory, that sets the interleave factor and prepares the disk for a particular type of disk controller. Also called **physical format.**
⇒ See also CONTROLLER; FORMAT; INTERLEAVE.

low-level language *n.* a machine language or an assembly language.
⇒ See also ASSEMBLY LANGUAGE; HIGH-LEVEL LANGUAGE; LANGUAGE; MACHINE LANGUAGE; PROGRAMMING LANGUAGE.

low memory *n.* in DOS systems, the first 640K of memory, reserved for applications, device drivers, and memory-resident programs (TSRs). Also called **conventional memory.**
⇒ See also EXPANDED MEMORY; EXTENDED MEMORY; HIGH MEMORY; TSR.

low resolution *n.* See under RESOLUTION.

LPT a name frequently used by operating systems to identify a printer: an abbreviation for line printer terminal, now used to identify any type of printer.
⇒ See also PRINTER.

LPX a kind of motherboard used in some desktop model PCs in which expansion boards are inserted into a riser that contains several slots.
⇒ See also ATX; BABY AT; FORM FACTOR; MOTHERBOARD; NLX.

LQ LETTER-QUALITY.

LS-120 SUPERDISK.

LSI LARGE-SCALE INTEGRATION.

luggable *adj.* TRANSPORTABLE.

lurk *v.i.* to read messages in a chat room, newsgroup, or other on-line forum without posting messages in public.
⇒ See also CHAT ROOM; CONFERENCE; NEWSGROUP; SURF.

Lycos *n.* a popular World Wide Web search engine and directory.
⇒ See also ALTA VISTA; EXCITE; HOTBOT; INFOSEEK; OPEN TEXT; SEARCH ENGINE; WEBCRAWLER; YAHOO!.

LZW Lempel-Ziv-Welsh: a popular data compression technique developed in 1977 by J. Ziv and A. Lempel, and later refined by T. Welsh. It is the compression algorithm used in the GIF graphics file format, one of the standard graphics formats used by CompuServe and the World Wide Web.
⇒ See also DATA COMPRESSION; GIF; PNG; ZIP.

a b c d e f g h i j k l **M** n o p q r s t u v w x y z

M 1. mega or megabyte. **2.** MUMPS.
⇒ See also K; MEGABYTE.

Mac *n.* MACINTOSH COMPUTER.

MAC address *n.* Media Access Control address: a hardware address that uniquely identifies each node of a network.
⇒ See also ADDRESS; DLC; NETWORK INTERFACE CARD; NODE.

machine address *n.* ABSOLUTE ADDRESS.
⇒ See also ADDRESS.

machine code *n.* MACHINE LANGUAGE.

machine dependent *adj.* referring to a software application that runs only on a particular type of computer.
⇒ See also APPLICATION.

machine independent *adj.* able to run on a variety of computers.

machine language *n.* the lowest-level programming language (except for computers that utilize programmable microcode), consisting entirely of

numbers. Machine language is the only language computers understand and is almost impossible for humans to use for programming. Therefore, programmers use either a high-level programming language or an assembly language; their programs are then translated into machine language.
⇒ See also ASSEMBLY LANGUAGE; INSTRUCTION; LOW-LEVEL LANGUAGE; MICROCODE.

machine readable *adj.* presented in a form that a computer can accept, as files stored on disk or tape, or data that comes from a device connected to a computer.
⇒ See also OPTICAL CHARACTER RECOGNITION.

Macintosh computer *n.* a computer made by Apple Computer, introduced in 1984 and featuring a graphical user interface (GUI) that utilizes windows, icons, and a mouse.
⇒ See also APPLE COMPUTER; CHRP; GRAPHICAL USER INTERFACE; POWERPC.

MacOS *n.* the official name of the Macintosh operating system.
⇒ See also APPLESCRIPT; BeOS; CHRP; FINDER; MULTI-FINDER; OPERATING SYSTEM; SYSTEM.

macro *n.* **1.** a symbol, name, or key that represents a list of commands, actions, or keystrokes. **2.** in dBASE programs, a variable that points to another variable where the data is actually stored.
⇒ See also APPLESCRIPT; BATCH FILE; COMMAND; DBASE; LINK; LOOP; MACRO VIRUS; PROGRAM.

macro virus *n.* a type of computer virus that is encoded as a macro embedded in a document.
⇒ See also ANTIVIRUS PROGRAM; MACRO; VIRUS.

MAE *n.* Metropolitan Area Ethernet: a Network Access Point (NAP) where Internet Service Providers (ISPs) can connect with each other.
⇒ See also BACKBONE; ISP; NAP.

Magellan *n.* a Web directory published by the McKinley Group, now owned by Excite, Inc. [named after the explorer Ferdinand Magellan]
⇒ See also ALTA VISTA; EXCITE; YAHOO!

magic cookie *n.* a UNIX object; any of a group of tokens that are attached to files belonging to a user or program and change depending on the areas entered by the user or program.

magnetic disk *n.* a disk on which data is encoded as microscopic magnetized needles on the disk's surface, allowing the data to be erased and recorded any number of times.

magnetic tape *n.* TAPE.

magneto-optical (MO) drive *n.* a type of disk drive that combines magnetic disk technologies with CD-ROM technologies and that has a storage capacity of more than 200 megabytes.
⇒ See also CD-ROM; HARD DISK; MASS STORAGE; PHASE CHANGE DISK.

mail *n.* E-MAIL.

mailbox *n.* an area in memory or on a storage device where e-mail is placed.

mail client *n.* E-MAIL CLIENT.

mailing list *n.* a list of e-mail addresses identified by a single name, so that an e-mail message sent to the mailing list name is automatically forwarded to all the addresses in the list.
⇒ See also E-MAIL; E-MAIL CLIENT; MAILING LIST SERVER.

mailing list server *n.* a server that manages mailing lists for groups of users.
⇒ See also LISTSERV; MAILING LIST; MAJORDOMO.

mail merge *n.* a feature supported by many word processors that permits the user to personalize form letters by extracting specific information, such as a person's name, from a separate file of data. Also called **print merge**.
⇒ See also MERGE.

mainboard *n.* MOTHERBOARD.

mainframe *n.* a very large and expensive computer capable of supporting hundreds, or even thousands, of users simultaneously.
⇒ See also COMPUTER; HLLAPI; IBM; LEGACY APPLICATION; MICROPROCESSOR; MINICOMPUTER; MVS; SNA; SUPERCOMPUTER; VSAM.

main memory *n.* physical memory that is internal to the computer, as opposed to memory available on external mass storage devices such as disk

drives. Also called **RAM**.
⇒ See also ADDRESS SPACE; CACHE; CHIP; CONVENTIONAL MEMORY; EXPANSION BOARD; EXTENDED MEMORY; LOADER; MEMORY; RAM; SWAP.

Majordomo *n.* a free mailing list server that runs under UNIX.
⇒ See also LISTSERV; MAILING LIST SERVER.

male connector *n.* a connector, as at the end of a cable or on a port, containing one or more exposed pins for inserting into a female connector.

MAN *n.* Metropolitan Area Network: a data network designed for a town or city usu. characterized by very-high-speed connections using fiber optical cable or other digital media.
⇒ See also IEEE 802 STANDARDS; LOCAL-AREA NETWORK; NETWORK; WIDE-AREA NETWORK.

Management Information Base *n.* See MIB.

management information system *n.* See MIS.

man page *n.* manual page: a page of on-line documentation in UNIX systems.
⇒ See also DOCUMENTATION; HELP.

manual recalculation *n.* in spreadsheet programs, a mode in which formulas are not recalculated until the user explicitly (manually) runs the recalculation function.
⇒ See also AUTOMATIC RECALCULATION; RECALCULATE.

map *n.* **1.** a file that shows the structure of a program after it has been compiled and lists every variable in the program along with its memory address. —*v.t.* **2.** to make logical connections between (two entities). **3.** to copy (a set of objects) from one place to another while preserving the objects' organization.
⇒ See also COMPILE; DEBUG; PROGRAMMING LANGUAGE.

map file *n.* See MAP (def. 1).

MAPI *n.* Messaging Application Programming Interface: a system built into Microsoft Windows that enables different e-mail applications to work together to distribute mail.
⇒ See also API; E-MAIL.

margins *n.pl.* in word processing, the strips of white space around the edge of the paper and the analogous strips of space shown on screen.
⇒ See also FLUSH; WORD PROCESSING; WORD WRAP.

marquee *n.* **1.** on Web pages, a scrolling area of text. **2.** in graphics software, a sizable and movable frame that identifies a selected portion of a bit-mapped image.
⇒ See also PAINT PROGRAM; SCROLL; SELECT; TAG.

mask *n.* a filter that selectively includes or excludes certain values, as in defining a database field.
⇒ See also FIELD; SUBNET MASK.

mask pitch *n.* in color monitors, the distance between holes in the shadow mask, usu. about .30 millimeters (mm). The tighter the mask pitch, the sharper the image.
⇒ See also COLOR MONITOR; DOT PITCH; RGB MONITOR.

massively parallel processing *n.* See MPP.

mass storage *n.* various techniques and devices, as floppy disks, hard disks, optical disks, and tapes, for storing large amounts of data. Unlike main memory, mass storage devices retain data even when the computer is turned off. Also called **auxiliary storage**.
⇒ See also DAT; ERASABLE OPTICAL DISK; FLOPPY DISK; HARD DISK; HSM; MAGNETO-OPTICAL (MO) DRIVE; MEMORY; OPTICAL DISK; RANDOM ACCESS; STORAGE DEVICE; TAPE.

Master Boot Record *n.* See MBR.

master/slave *adj.* referring to an architecture in which one device (the master) controls one or more other devices (the slaves).

math coprocessor *n.* See under COPROCESSOR.

mathematical expression *n.* any expression that represents a numeric value.
⇒ See also EXPRESSION.

matrix *n.* **1.** a two-dimensional array; that is, an array of rows and columns. **2.** the background area of color display.
⇒ See also ARRAY; BACKGROUND.

MAU *n.* **1.** Media Access Unit: an Ethernet transceiver. **2.** Also, **MSAU.** Multistation Access Unit: a token-ring network device that connects network computers in a star topology while retaining the logical ring structure.

⇒ See also HUB; TOKEN-RING NETWORK; TRANSCEIVER.

maximize *v.t.* in graphical user interfaces, to enlarge (a window) to maximum size.

⇒ See also GRAPHICAL USER INTERFACE; WINDOW; ZOOM.

MB *n.* megabyte (1,000,000 or 1,048,576 bytes, depending on the context).

⇒ See also MEGABYTE.

Mbone (em′bōn′), *n.* Multicast Backbone: an extension to the Internet to support IP multicasting—two-way transmission of data between multiple sites.

⇒ See also INTERNET; IP MULTICAST; MULTIMEDIA.

MBps megabytes per second: a measure of data transfer speed. Mass storage devices are generally measured in MBps.

⇒ See also DATA TRANSFER RATE.

Mbps megabits per second: a measure of data transfer speed. Networks, for example, are generally measured in Mbps.

⇒ See also DATA TRANSFER RATE; GBPS; MEGABIT.

MBR Master Boot Record: a small program that resides on the first sector of the hard disk and is executed when a computer boots up.

⇒ See also BOOT; BOOTABLE DISKETTE; PARTITION; VIRUS.

Mbyte *n.* MEGABYTE.

MCA MICRO CHANNEL ARCHITECTURE.

MCGA multicolor/graphics array *or* memory controller gate array: the graphics system built into some older PCs.

⇒ See also CGA; EGA; GRAPHICS; MDA; MONITOR; VGA; VIDEO STANDARDS.

MCI 1. Media Control Interface: a high-level API developed by Microsoft and IBM for controlling multimedia devices, such as CD-ROM players and audio controllers, and supported by both OS/2 and Windows. **2.** a large telecommunications company.

⇒ See also API; MULTIMEDIA.

MDA monochrome display adapter: an old monochrome video standard for PCs that supports high-resolution monochrome text but does not support graphics or colors.

⇒ See also GRAPHICS; HERCULES GRAPHICS; MONITOR; MONOCHROME; PIXEL; RESOLUTION; VGA; VIDEO STANDARDS.

MDI Multiple Document Interface: a Windows API that enables programmers to easily create applications with multiple windows.

⇒ See also GRAPHICAL USER INTERFACE; WINDOW.

MDRAM (em′dē′ram′), *n.* Multibank DRAM: a memory technology developed by MoSys, Inc., that utilizes small banks of DRAM (32 KB each) in an array, where each bank has its own I/O port that feeds into a common internal bus. Because of this design, data can be read or written to multiple banks simultaneously, which makes it much faster than conventional DRAM.

⇒ See also DRAM; GRAPHICS ACCELERATOR; MEMORY; SDRAM; VIDEO ADAPTER; VRAM.

mean time between failures *n.* See MTBF.

media *n.pl.* **1.** objects on which data can be stored, as hard disks, floppy disks, CD-ROMs, and tapes. **2.** in computer networks, the cables linking workstations together, as twisted-pair wire (normal electrical wire), coaxial cable (the type of cable used for cable television), and fiber optic cable (glass cables). **3.** the form and technology used to communicate information, as sound, pictures, and videos.

⇒ See also DISK; FIBER OPTICS; LOCAL-AREA NETWORK; MASS STORAGE; MULTIMEDIA; NETWORK.

Media Control Interface *n.* See MCI.

meg *n.* MEGABYTE.

mega *n.* **1.** in decimal systems, one million. **2.** in binary systems, 2^{20}, or 1,048,576.

⇒ See also GIGA (G); KILOBYTE; MEGABYTE.

megabit *n.* **1.** when used to describe data storage, 1,024 kilobits. **2.** when used to described data transfer rates, one million bits.

⇒ See also BIT; GIGABIT; KILOBIT; MBPS.

megabyte *n.* **1.** when used to describe data storage, 1,048,576 (2^{20}) bytes. *Abbr.:* M; MB **2.** when used to describe data transfer rates, one million

bytes.

⇒ See also BYTE; GIGABYTE; KILOBYTE.

megaflop *n.* See MFLOP.

megaFLOPS *n.* one million *FLOPS.*

megahertz *n.* See MHz.

membrane keyboard *n.* a type of keyboard in which the keys are covered by a transparent, plastic shell so that they have very little movement but are sensitive to pressure.

memory *n.* **1.** internal storage areas in the computer. **2.** physical memory, or the actual chips capable of holding data.

⇒ See also ADDRESS; CHIP; EEPROM; EPROM; MAIN MEMORY; MDRAM; MEMORY LEAK; NVRAM; PROM; RAM; RDRAM; ROM; VIRTUAL MEMORY; VRAM.

memory cache *n.* See under CACHE.

memory controller gate array *n.* See MCGA.

memory dump *n.* See under DUMP.

memory effect *n.* the property of nickel-cadmium (NiCad) batteries that causes them to lose their capacity for full recharging if they are discharged repeatedly the same amount and then recharged without overcharge before they have fully drained. The term derives from the fact that the battery appears to have a *memory* for the amount of charging it can sustain.

⇒ See also NiCad BATTERY PACK.

memory leak *n.* a bug in a program that prevents it from freeing up memory it no longer needs and finally causes it to crash because it is out of memory.

⇒ See also BUG; MEMORY.

memory management unit *n.* See MMU.

memory resident *adj.* permanently in memory. Also called **RAM resident.**

⇒ See also MEMORY; OPERATING SYSTEM; SWAP; TSR.

menu *n.* a list of commands or options from which one can choose by highlighting the item and then pressing the Enter or Return key, or by simply pointing to the item with a mouse and clicking one of the mouse buttons.

⇒ See also CHOOSE; COMMAND DRIVEN; GRAPHICAL USER INTERFACE; MOVING-BAR MENU; POP-UP MENU, PULL-DOWN MENU; TEAR-OFF MENU; USER INTERFACE.

menu bar *n.* a horizontal menu that appears on top of a window. Usually, each option in a menu bar is associated with a pull-down menu.

⇒ See also MENU; WINDOW.

menu driven *adj.* referring to programs whose user interface employs menus.

⇒ See also COMMAND DRIVEN; MENU; USER INTERFACE.

Merced (mər sed′), *n.* the code name for a 64-bit microprocessor developed jointly by Intel and Hewlett-Packard that is designed primarily for use in servers and workstations. It uses a new architecture, officially known as *Intel Architecture-64 (IA-64)*, that employs cutting-edge microprocessor techniques.

⇒ See also INTEL MICROPROCESSORS; MICROPROCESSOR; PENTIUM MICROPROCESSOR.

merge *v.t.* **1.** to combine (two files) in such a way that the resulting file has the same organization as the two individual files. **2.** in word processing, to generate form letters by combining one file containing a list of names, addresses, and other information with a second file containing the text of the letter.

⇒ See also MAIL MERGE.

message box *n.* ALERT BOX.

Messaging Application Programming Interface *n.* See MAPI.

meta- in computer science, a prefix that means "about": *metadata; metalanguage; metafile.*

⇒ See also META TAG; METADATA.

metadata *n.* data about data. Metadata describes how and when and by whom a particular set of data was collected, and how the data is formatted.

⇒ See also DATA; DATA WAREHOUSE; DATABASE; META.

meta tag *n.* a special HTML tag that provides information about a Web page, such as who created the page, how often it is updated, what the page is about, and which keywords represent the page's content.

⇒ See also META; SEARCH ENGINE; TAG.

MFC Microsoft Foundation Classes: a large library of C++ classes developed by Microsoft.
⇒ See also AFC; C++; CLASS; VISUAL C++.

MFLOP n. mega floating-point operations per second: a common measure of the speed of computers used to perform floating-point calculations.
⇒ See also FLOATING-POINT NUMBER; MIPS.

MFLOPS n. See under FLOPS.

MFM modified frequency modulation: an encoding scheme used by PC floppy disk drives and older hard drives.
⇒ See also CONTROLLER; DISK DRIVE; MODULATE; RLL; ST-506 INTERFACE.

MFP multifunction peripheral: a single device that serves as a printer, a scanner, a fax machine, and a photocopier. Also called **multifunction printer**.
⇒ See also FAX MACHINE; OPTICAL SCANNER; PRINTER; SOHO.

MHz megahertz: one million cycles per second. The speed of microprocessors, called the clock speed, is measured in megahertz. For example, a microprocessor that runs at 200 MHz executes 200 million cycles per second.
⇒ See also BUS; CLOCK SPEED; OVERCLOCK.

MIB Management Information Base: a database of objects that can be monitored by a network management system.
⇒ See also NETWORK MANAGEMENT; SNMP.

micro n. **1.** MICROPROCESSOR. **2.** PERSONAL COMPUTER. **3.** a prefix meaning *one millionth*. **4.** a prefix meaning something very small: *microfloppy*.
⇒ See also MICROFLOPPY DISK.

Micro Channel Architecture n. a bus architecture for older PCs. *Abbr.:* MCA
⇒ See also AT BUS; BUS; LOCAL BUS.

microcode n. **1.** the lowest-level instructions that directly control a microprocessor. A single machine-language instruction typically translates into several microcode instructions. **2.** FIRMWARE.
⇒ See also INSTRUCTION; MACHINE LANGUAGE; MICRO-PROCESSOR.

Microcom Networking Protocol n. See MNP.

microcomputer n. PERSONAL COMPUTER.

microcontroller n. a highly integrated chip that contains all the components making up a controller, a CPU, RAM, some form of ROM, I/O ports, and timers.
⇒ See also CONTROLLER; EMBEDDED SYSTEM; MICROPROCESSOR.

microfloppy disk n. an old name for the small, 3.5-inch floppy disks.
⇒ See also DENSITY; DISK; FLOPPY DISK.

microjustification n. the use of microspacing to justify text.
⇒ See also MICROSPACING.

microprocessor n. a silicon chip that contains a CPU.
⇒ See also ALPHA PROCESSOR; BANDWIDTH; CHIP; CISC; CLOCK SPEED; CPU; CYRIX; MOORE'S LAW; OVERCLOCK; PENTIUM MICROPROCESSOR; POWERPC; SUPERSCALAR.

Microsoft n. the largest company in the personal computer industry, founded in 1975 by Paul Allen and Bill Gates. In addition to developing the de facto standard operating systems—DOS and Windows—Microsoft has a strong presence in almost every area of computer software, from programming tools to end-user applications.
⇒ See also ACTIVEX; DOS; INTERNET EXPLORER; MICROSOFT WORD; NETSCAPE; ODBC; WINDOWS; WINDOWS NT; WINTEL.

Microsoft Cluster Server n. See MSCS.

Microsoft Foundation Classes n. See MFC.

Microsoft Internet Explorer n. INTERNET EXPLORER.

Microsoft Network n. See MSN.

Microsoft Windows n. a family of operating systems for personal computers that provides a graphical user interface (GUI), virtual memory management, multitasking, and support for many peripheral devices.
⇒ See also DOS; INTEL MICROPROCESSORS; OPERATING SYSTEM; OS/2; WINDOWS 98; WINDOWS NT.

Microsoft Word n. a popular word processor

from Microsoft.
⇒ See also MICROSOFT; WORD PROCESSING.

microspacing n. the insertion of variable-sized spaces between letters to justify text.
⇒ See also JUSTIFICATION; PRINTER.

middleware n. software that connects two otherwise separate applications, as a database system and a Web server. This allows users to request data from the database using forms displayed on a Web browser, and it enables the Web server to return dynamic Web pages based on the user's requests and profile.
⇒ See also DCE; EXPORT; IMPORT; INTEGRATED; ORB; RPC; THREE-TIER; TP MONITOR.

MIDI (mid′ē), n. musical instrument digital interface: a standard adopted by the electronic music industry for controlling devices, such as synthesizers and sound cards, that emit music.
⇒ See also AMIGA; AU; MACINTOSH COMPUTER; SOUND CARD; WAVE TABLE SYNTHESIS.

MIF Management Information Format: a format used to describe a hardware or software component. MIF files are used by DMI to report system configuration information. Although MIF is a system-independent format, it is used primarily by Windows systems. To install a new device in a Windows 95 system, the corresponding MIF file is needed.
⇒ See also CONFIGURATION; DMI.

millennium bug n. YEAR 2000 PROBLEM.

million instructions per second n. See MIPS.

millisecond n. one thousandth of a second. *Abbr.:* ms ⇒ See also ACCESS TIME.

MIME (mīm), n. Multipurpose Internet Mail Extensions: a specification for formatting non-ASCII messages so that they can be sent over the Internet.
⇒ See also BINHEX; E-MAIL; S/MIME; UUENCODE.

mini n. MINICOMPUTER.

minicomputer n. a midsized computer, usu. capable of supporting from 4 to about 200 users simultaneously.
⇒ See also AS/400; COMPUTER; LEGACY APPLICATION; MAINFRAME; MULTI-USER; VAX; WORKSTATION.

minifloppy n. a 5¼-inch floppy disk.
⇒ See also FLOPPY DISK.

minimize v.t. in graphical user interfaces, to convert (a window) into an icon.
⇒ See also GRAPHICAL USER INTERFACE; ICON; WINDOW.

minitower n. a type of computer somewhat smaller than a *tower model* but with the same sort of configuration, including vertically stacked power supply, motherboard, and mass storage devices.

MIPS n. million instructions per second: an old measure of a computer's speed and power.
⇒ See also CPU; FLOPS; MFLOP; SPEC.

MIS management information system or management information services: a class of software that provides managers with tools for organizing and evaluating their department. Typically, MIS systems are written in COBOL and run on mainframes or minicomputers. Also called **IS (Information Services; IT (Information Technology).**
⇒ See also COBOL; IS; IT; MAINFRAME; MINICOMPUTER; SYSTEM ADMINISTRATOR; SYSTEM MANAGEMENT.

M-JPEG MOTION-JPEG.

MMU memory management unit: the hardware component that manages virtual memory systems and includes a small amount of memory that holds a table matching virtual addresses to physical addresses.
⇒ See also CPU; PAGE FAULT; VIRTUAL MEMORY.

MMX a set of 57 multimedia instructions built into Intel's newest microprocessors and other x86-compatible microprocessors.
⇒ See also AMD; DSP; INTEL MICROPROCESSORS; K6.

MMX processor n. See MMX.

MMX Technology n. See MMX.

MNP Microcom Networking Protocol: a communications protocol developed by Microcom, Inc., that is used by many high-speed modems and that supports several different classes of communication, with each higher class providing additional features.

computer

⇒ See also COMMUNICATIONS PROTOCOL; DATA COMPRESSION; ERROR DETECTION; KERMIT; MODEM; XMODEM.

mode *n.* the state or setting of a program or device: *insert mode; overstrike mode.*

⇒ See also INSERT MODE; OVERSTRIKE.

modeling *n.* **1.** the process of representing a real-world object or phenomenon as a set of mathematical equations. **2.** the process of representing three-dimensional objects in a computer.

⇒ See also 3-D SOFTWARE; ANIMATION; CAD/CAM; NURBS; RENDER; TEXTURE; VRML.

modem *n.* modulator-demodulator: a device or program that enables a computer to transmit data over telephone lines. Computer information is stored digitally, whereas information transmitted over telephone lines is in the form of analog waves. A modem converts between these two forms.

⇒ See also BPS; CCITT; CHANNEL BONDING; COMMUNICATIONS; COMMUNICATIONS PROTOCOL; COMMUNICATIONS SOFTWARE; DATA COMPRESSION; DIAL-UP ACCESS; DSVD; FLASH MEMORY; HOST-BASED MODEM; K56FLEX; MNP; MODULATE; RJ-11; RS-232C; SOFTWARE MODEM; TERMINAL ADAPTER; V.90; WIRELESS MODEM; X2.

moderated newsgroup *n.* a newsgroup monitored by an individual or group (the moderator) who has the authority to block messages deemed inappropriate.

⇒ See also FLAME; NEWSGROUP; SPAM.

moderator *n.* See under MODERATED NEWSGROUP.

modified frequency modulation *n.* See MFM.

modifier key *n.* a key on a keyboard that has a meaning only when combined with another key, as the Shift, Control, and Alt keys.

MO drive *n.* MAGNETO-OPTICAL (MO) DRIVE.

Modula-2 *n.* a programming language designed by Niklaus Wirth, the author of Pascal, that addresses Pascal's lack of support for separate compilation of modules and multitasking.

⇒ See also COMPILE; MULTITASKING; PASCAL; PROGRAMMING LANGUAGE.

modular architecture *n.* the design of any system composed of separate components that can be connected so that any one component (module) can be added or replaced without affecting the rest of the system.

⇒ See also ARCHITECTURE; INTEGRATED; MODULE.

modulate *v.t.* to blend (data) into a carrier signal.

⇒ See also ADPCM; MFM; MODEM; PCM; TDM.

module *n.* **1.** in software, a part of a program. **2.** in hardware, a self-contained component.

⇒ See also LINK; MODULAR ARCHITECTURE; PROGRAM; ROUTINE.

moiré *n.* an undesirable pattern that appears when a graphic image is displayed or printed with an inappropriate resolution.

⇒ See also HALFTONE.

monitor *n.* **1.** a display screen. **2.** the entire box of which the display screen is a part. **3.** a program that observes a computer. For example, some monitor programs report how often another program accesses a disk drive or how much CPU time it uses.

⇒ See also ANALOG MONITOR; BANDWIDTH; COLOR MONITOR; CONVERGENCE; DDC; DIGITAL MONITOR; DLP; DOT PITCH; DPI; ELF EMISSION; FIXED-FREQUENCY MONITOR; FLAT TECHNOLOGY MONITOR; GRAY SCALING; INTERLACING; LCD MONITOR; MULTISCANNING MONITOR; PINCUSHION DISTORTION; PIXEL; RAMDAC; RASTER; REFRESH.

monochrome *adj.* referring to monitors or printers that display the foreground in one color or shades of one color and the background in a second color.

⇒ See also BACKGROUND; FOREGROUND; GRAPHICS; GRAY SCALING; MONITOR.

monochrome display adapter *n.* See MDA.

monospacing *n.* the use of the same width for different characters. In a monospaced font, *W* has the same width as the letter *I*. Courier is an example of a monospaced font.

⇒ See also COURIER FONT; CPI; FONT; PROPORTIONAL SPACING.

MOO (mōō), *n.* Mud, Object Oriented: a specific implementation of a MUD system developed by Stephen White. MOO is in the public domain and can

be freely downloaded and executed.

⇒ See also MUD; OBJECT ORIENTED.

Moore's Law *n.* the observation made in 1965 by Gordon Moore, cofounder of Intel, that the number of transistors per square inch on integrated circuits had doubled every year since the integrated circuit was invented. Moore's law has been updated to reflect the fact that data density now doubles approximately every 18 months.

⇒ See also CHIP; INTEGRATED CIRCUIT; MICROPROCESSOR; NANOTECHNOLOGY; TRANSISTOR.

morphing *n.* metamorphosing: an animation technique in which one image is gradually turned into another.

⇒ See also ANIMATION.

Mosaic *n.* an application that simplifies accessing documents on the World Wide Web.

⇒ See also BROWSER; INTERNET; WORLD WIDE WEB.

motherboard *n.* the main circuit board of a microcomputer containing the CPU, BIOS, memory, mass storage interfaces, serial and parallel ports, expansion slots, and all the controllers required to control standard peripheral devices, such as the display screen, keyboard, and disk drive.

⇒ See also ADD-ON; ATX; BACKPLANE; BIOS; BUS; CONTROLLER; CPU; DAUGHTERCARD; EXPANSION BOARD; EXPANSION SLOT; HEAT SINK; LPX; NLX; OVERCLOCK; PORT; PRINTED CIRCUIT BOARD; VOLTAGE REGULATOR.

motion-JPEG *n.* Joint Photographic Experts Group standard: a standard for storing and compressing digital images.

⇒ See also JPEG; MPEG.

Motorola microprocessors *n.pl.* the microprocessors used in all Apple Macintosh computers and in many workstations until the early 1990s. In 1993, Motorola joined Apple Computer and IBM in designing a new RISC architecture, an effort that culminated in the introduction of the PowerPC architecture in 1994.

⇒ See also CISC; MICROPROCESSOR; PowerPC; RISC.

mount *v.t.* **1.** to make (a mass storage device) available. **2.** to install (a device).

⇒ See also MASS STORAGE.

mouse *n.* a small object that is connected to the CPU by a wire and is rolled along a hard, flat surface to control the movement of the cursor or pointer on a display screen.

⇒ See also ADB; BUS; BUS MOUSE; CLICK; CURSOR; DOUBLE CLICK; EXPANSION BOARD; GRAPHICAL USER INTERFACE; MENU DRIVEN; POINTER; SERIAL PORT; TRACKBALL.

mousepad *n.* a pad over which a mouse can be moved. Mousepads provide more traction than smooth surfaces such as glass and wood, so they make it easier to move a mouse accurately.

⇒ See also MOUSE.

mouse pointer *n.* POINTER (def. 1).

mouse port *n.* PS/2 PORT.

moving-bar menu *n.* a common type of menu in which options are selected by moving a highlighted bar over them by means of a mouse, arrow keys, or the Tab key.

⇒ See also MENU.

Moving Picture Experts Group *n.* See MPEG.

Mozilla *n.* the original name for Netscape's browser, now called Navigator.

MP3 MPEG Layer 3: a type of audio data compression that can reduce digital sound files by a 12:1 ratio with virtually no loss in quality.

⇒ See also DATA COMPRESSION; DIGITAL AUDIO; MPEG.

MPC Multimedia Personal Computer: a software and hardware standard developed by a consortium of computer firms led by Microsoft.

⇒ See also CD-ROM; CD-ROM PLAYER; INTEL MICROPROCESSORS; MULTIMEDIA.

MPEG (em′peg′), *n.* **1.** Moving Picture Experts Group: a working group of ISO. **2.** the family of digital video compression standards and file formats developed by the group.

⇒ See also CODEC; DATA COMPRESSION; DVD; DVD-ROM; DVI; FPS; INDEO; JPEG; MP3; QUICKTIME; VIDEO EDITING.

MPP massively parallel processing: a type of computing that uses many separate CPUs, each having

its own memory, running in parallel to execute a single program.
⇒ See also NUMA; SMP.

ms millisecond: one thousandth of a second. Access times of mass storage devices are often measured in milliseconds.
⇒ See also MASS STORAGE.

MSAU See MAU.

MSCDEX Microsoft CD-ROM Extension: a driver that enables DOS and Windows 3.x systems to recognize and control CD-ROM players.
⇒ See also CD-ROM PLAYER; CDFS.

MSCS Microsoft Cluster Server: a clustering technology built into Windows NT 4.0 and later versions that supports clustering of two NT servers to provide a single fault-tolerant server.
⇒ See also CLUSTERING; WINDOWS NT.

MS-DOS (em′es dôs′, -dos′), n. See under DOS.

MSN Microsoft Network: Microsoft's online service.
⇒ See also AMERICA ONLINE; COMPUSERVE INFORMATION SERVICE; ONLINE SERVICE.

MS-TNEF See TNEF.

MS-Windows (em′es win′dōz), n. MICROSOFT WINDOWS.

MS-Word (em′es wûrd′), n. MICROSOFT WORD.

MTBF mean time between failures: a rating that is measured in hours and indicates the sturdiness of hard disk drives and printers.
⇒ See also DISK DRIVE; SMART.

MTU Maximum Transmission Unit: the largest physical packet size, measured in bytes, that a network can transmit. Any messages larger than the MTU are divided into smaller packets before being sent.
⇒ See also PACKET; WINSOCK.

MUCK (muk), n. Multi-User Chat Kingdom: a text-based MUD system. MUCK is similar to MUSH, though it uses different software.
⇒ See also MUD; MUSH.

MUD (mud), n. Multi-User Dungeon or Multi-User Dimension: a cyberspace where users can take on an identity in the form of an avatar and interact with one another. Also called **3-d world; chat world.**
⇒ See also AVATAR; CHAT ROOM; CYBERSPACE; MOO; MUCK; MUSH; VIRTUAL REALITY.

multicast v.i. to transmit a message to a select group of recipients, as to send an e-mail message to a mailing list.
⇒ See also BROADCAST; IP MULTICAST; RTSP; TELECONFERENCE.

Multicast Backbone n. See MBONE.

multicolor/graphics array n. See MCGA.

multidimensional DBMS n. a database management system (DBMS) organized around large groups of records that share a common field value.
⇒ See also DATABASE MANAGEMENT SYSTEM; OLAP; RDBMS.

MultiFinder n. the multitasking version of Finder for Apple Macintosh computers. This is the part of the operating system responsible for managing the desktop—locating documents and folders and handling the Clipboard and Scrapbook.
⇒ See also CLIPBOARD; DESKTOP; FINDER; MACOS; MACINTOSH COMPUTER; MULTITASKING; OPERATING SYSTEM.

multifrequency monitor n. a type of video monitor capable of accepting signals at more than one frequency range, which enables the monitor to support several different resolutions.
⇒ See also MONITOR; MULTISCANNING MONITOR; VIDEO ADAPTER.

multifunction peripheral n. See MFP.

multifunction printer n. MULTIFUNCTION PERIPHERAL (MFP).

multilevel printer n. CONTONE PRINTER.

multimedia n. the use of computers to present text, graphics, video, animation, and sound in an integrated way.
⇒ See also 3DO; ACTIVEMOVIE; ANIMATION; AUTHORING TOOL; CD-ROM; HYPERMEDIA; HYPERTEXT; MBONE; MEDIA; MMX; MPC; SHOCKWAVE; STREAMING; WAV.

multimedia kit n. a package of hardware and software that adds multimedia capabilities to a computer, usu. including a CD-ROM or DVD player, a sound card, speakers, and a bundle of CD-ROMs.
⇒ See also CD-ROM; MULTIMEDIA.

Multimedia Personal Computer n. See MPC.

Multiple Document Interface n. See MDI.

multiplex v.t. to combine (multiple analog or digital signals) for transmission over a single line or medium. A common type of multiplexing combines several low-speed signals for transmission over a single high-speed connection.
⇒ See also CARRIER; CDMA; FDM; MULTIPLEXOR; TDM; WDM.

multiplexor n. a communications device that multiplexes (combines) several signals for transmission over a single medium. A demultiplexor completes the process by separating multiplexed signals from a transmission line. Also called **mux.**
⇒ See also CONCENTRATOR; MULTIPLEX.

multiprocessing n. **1.** a computer system's ability to support more than one process (program) at the same time, as UNIX or OS/2. **2.** the utilization of multiple CPUs in a single computer system. Also called **parallel processing.**
⇒ See also CPU; DISTRIBUTED PROCESSING; INTERPROCESS COMMUNICATION (IPC); MULTITASKING; OS/2; PARALLEL PROCESSING; PROCESS; SMP; UNIX.

Multipurpose Internet Mail Extensions n. See MIME.

MultiRead n. a specification for CD-ROM and compact disc players that enables them to read discs created by CD-RW drives, developed jointly by Philips Electronics and Hewlett-Packard.
⇒ See also CD-ROM PLAYER; CD-RW DISK; COMPACT DISC.

multiscanning monitor n. a type of monitor that automatically adjusts to the signal frequency of the video display board to which it is connected and that can display images based on almost any graphics display system, including MDA, Hercules, EGA, VGA, and SVGA.
⇒ See also ANALOG MONITOR; DIGITAL MONITOR; FIXED-FREQUENCY MONITOR; MULTIFREQUENCY MONITOR; VIDEO ADAPTER; VIDEO STANDARDS.

Multi-station Access Unit n. See MAU.

Multistation Access Unit n. See MAU.

multisync monitor n. MULTISCANNING MONITOR.

multitasking n. the ability of a computer to execute more than one task, or program, at the same time.
⇒ See also COOPERATIVE MULTITASKING; MULTIFINDER; MULTIPROCESSING; OPERATING SYSTEM; OS/2; UNIX.

multithreading n. the ability of an operating system to execute different parts of a program, called threads, simultaneously.
⇒ See also MULTITASKING; SMP.

multi-user adj. referring to computer systems that support two or more simultaneous users, as mainframes and minicomputers.
⇒ See also MAINFRAME; MINICOMPUTER; TIME SHARING.

MUMPS (mumps), n. Massachusetts General Hospital Utility Multi Programming System: a general-purpose programming language developed in the late 1960s.
⇒ See also BASIC; FORTRAN.

MUSH (mush), n. Multi-User Shared Hallucination: a text-based MUD system.
⇒ See also MUCK; MUD.

musical instrument digital interface n. See MIDI.

MuTeX n. a package of macros for the TeX typesetting system that supports musical notation.
⇒ See also LaTeX; MACRO; TeX.

mux n. MULTIPLEXOR.

MVS Multiple Virtual Storage: the operating system for older IBM mainframes. It has been largely superseded by IBM's newer operating system, OS/390.
⇒ See also MAINFRAME; OPERATING SYSTEM; VSAM.

computer

name *n.* a sequence of one or more characters that uniquely identifies a file, variable, account, or other entity.
⇒ See also ALIAS; DOMAIN NAME; EXTENSION; FILENAME; IDENTIFIER; LABEL; LITERAL; VARIABLE.

Named Pipes *n.* an interprocess control (IPC) protocol for exchanging information between two applications, possibly running on different computers in a network.
⇒ See also INTERPROCESS COMMUNICATION (IPC).

name server *n.* a program that translates names from one form into another, such as domain name servers (DNSs) that translate domain names into IP addresses.
⇒ See also DNS; SERVER.

nanosecond *n.* a billionth of a second. Many computer operations, such as the speed of memory chips, are measured in nanoseconds. *Abbr.:* ns
⇒ See also ACCESS TIME.

nanotechnology *n.* a field of science whose goal is to control individual atoms and molecules to create computer chips and other devices that are thousands of times smaller than current technologies permit.
⇒ See also INTEGRATED CIRCUIT; MOORE'S LAW.

NAP Network Access Point: a public network exchange facility where Internet service providers (ISPs) can connect with one another in *peering* arrangements.
⇒ See also BACKBONE; INTERNET; ISP; MAE; NSP.

NAT Network Address Translation: an Internet standard that enables a local-area network (LAN) to use one set of IP addresses for internal traffic and a second set of addresses for external traffic. A NAT provides a type of firewall by hiding internal IP addresses and allows a company to use more internal IP addresses.
⇒ See also FIREWALL; IP ADDRESS.

National Television Standards Committee *n.* See NTSC.

native *adj.* referring to an original form. For example, an application's *native file format* is the one it uses internally. For all other formats, the application must first convert the file to its native format.
⇒ See also EXPORT; IMPORT.

natural language *n.* a human language. Probably the single most challenging problem in computer science is to develop computers that can understand natural languages.
⇒ See also ARTIFICIAL INTELLIGENCE; FOURTH-GENERATION LANGUAGE; LANGUAGE.

navigation keys *n.pl.* CURSOR CONTROL KEYS.

Navigator *n.* Netscape Communication's Web browser. There are many versions of Navigator, and it runs on all the major platforms.
⇒ See also BROWSER; INTERNET EXPLORER; NETSCAPE.

NC a type of network computer designed to execute Java programs locally. NCs must be connected to a network server that holds the data to be processed.
⇒ See also NET PC; NETWORK COMPUTER; THIN CLIENT; WINDOWS TERMINAL.

NDIS Network Device Interface Specification: a Windows device driver interface that enables a single network interface card (NIC) to support multiple network protocols.
⇒ See also ISDN; NETWORK INTERFACE CARD; PROTOCOL.

NDS Novell Directory Services: the directory services for Novell NetWare networks. NDS provides a logical tree-structure view of all resources on the network.
⇒ See also ACTIVE DIRECTORY; DIRECTORY SERVICE; LDAP; NETWARE; X.500.

near-letter-quality *adj.* referring to or producing print that is not quite letter quality but is better than draft quality. Many dot-matrix printers produce near-letter-quality print.

⇒ See also DOT-MATRIX PRINTER; DRAFT MODE; DRAFT QUALITY; LETTER QUALITY (LQ); PRINTER.

NEC one of the world's largest computer and electronics manufacturers.
⇒ See also INTEL; MONITOR; SEMICONDUCTOR.

nesting *n.* the embedding of one object in another object of the same type. Many word processing applications allow users to embed (nest) one document inside another.

Net *n.* the Internet.

Netbeui (net′bōō/ē), *n.* NetBios Enhanced User Interface: an enhanced version of the NetBIOS protocol used by network operating systems such as LAN Manager, Windows 95, Windows 98, and Windows NT.
⇒ See also NETBIOS.

NetBIOS *n.* Network Basic Input/Output System: an application programming interface (API) that augments the DOS BIOS by adding special functions for local-area networks (LANs).
⇒ See also API; BIOS; LOCAL-AREA NETWORK; NETBEUI; SMB.

netiquette *n.* the etiquette guidelines for posting messages to on-line services, particularly Internet newsgroups. Netiquette covers not only rules to maintain civility in discussions but also guidelines unique to the electronic nature of forum messages.
⇒ See also FORUM; INTERNET.

NetMeeting *n.* a product developed by Microsoft Corporation that enables groups to teleconference using the Internet as the transmission medium.
⇒ See also CHAT; COOLTALK; INTERNET PHONE; TELECONFERENCE.

Net PC *n.* a type of network computer designed cooperatively by Microsoft and Intel.
⇒ See also DISKLESS WORKSTATION; NC; NETWORK COMPUTER; SMS; WINDOWS TERMINAL; ZAW.

Netscape *n.* officially called *Netscape Communications Corporation,* Netscape was founded in 1994. In addition to its Web browsers, Netscape produces Web servers and tools for building intranets.
⇒ See also MICROSOFT; NAVIGATOR; SUN MICROSYSTEMS.

Netscape Navigator *n.* NAVIGATOR.

Netscape Server API *n.* See NSAPI.

NetShow *n.* a specification developed by Microsoft for streaming multimedia content over the World Wide Web.
⇒ See also RTSP; STREAMING.

NetWare *n.* a popular local-area network (LAN) operating system developed by Novell Corporation.
⇒ See also ETHERNET; IPX; LOCAL-AREA NETWORK; NDS; NOVELL; OPERATING SYSTEM; SAP; SPX; TOKEN-RING NETWORK.

NetWare Loadable Module *n.* software that enhances or provides additional functions in a NetWare 3.x or higher server. *Abbr.:* NLM

network *n.* a group of two or more computer systems linked together. There are many types of computer networks, including local-area networks (LANs) and wide-area networks (WANs).
⇒ See also BACKBONE; CLIENT/SERVER ARCHITECTURE; COMMUNICATIONS; ETHERNET; FIREWALL; HETEROGENEOUS NETWORK; INTRANET; LOCAL-AREA NETWORK; MAN; NETWORK MANAGEMENT; SNA; SNMP; TOKEN-RING NETWORK; WIDE-AREA NETWORK.

network adapter *n.* NETWORK INTERFACE CARD.

Network Address Translation *n.* See NAT.

Network Basic Input/Output System *n.* See NETBIOS.

network card *n.* NETWORK INTERFACE CARD.

network computer *n.* a computer with minimal memory, disk storage, and processor power designed to connect to a network, especially the Inter-

net. Network computers rely on the power of the network servers.
⇒ See also DISKLESS WORKSTATION; INTERNET; NC; NET PC; ORACLE; SMS; SUN MICROSYSTEMS; TCO; THIN CLIENT; WINDOWS TERMINAL; WORKSTATION; ZAW.

Network Device Interface Specification *n.* See NDIS.

Network Directory Services *n.* See NDS.

Network File System *n.* See NFS.

network interface card *n.* an expansion board inserted into a computer so the computer can be connected to a network. *Abbr.:* NIC
⇒ See also AUI; BNC CONNECTOR; DLC; EXPANSION BOARD; LOCAL-AREA NETWORK; MAC ADDRESS; NDIS; NETWORK; ODI; PROTOCOL; PROTOCOL STACK; TRANSCEIVER.

network management *n.* the management of computer networks.
⇒ See also CMIP; DIB; MIB; NETWORK; RMON; SECURITY; SNIFFER; SNMP; SPOOF.

Network Neighborhood *n.* a Windows 95 and 98 folder that lists computers, printers, and other resources connected to a user's local-area network (LAN).
⇒ See also DCC; LOCAL-AREA NETWORK; WINDOWS 95.

Network News Transfer Protocol *n.* See NNTP.

network operating system (NOS) *n.* an operating system that includes special functions for connecting computers and devices into a local-area network (LAN). For example, some popular NOSs for DOS and Windows systems include Novell Netware, Artisoft's LANtastic, Microsoft LAN Manager, and Windows NT.
⇒ See also LOCAL-AREA NETWORK; OPERATING SYSTEM.

network PC *n.* NETWORK COMPUTER.

Network Service Provider *n.* See NSP.

network topology *n.* TOPOLOGY.

neural network *n.* a type of artificial intelligence that attempts to imitate the way a human brain works. A neural network works by creating connections between *processing elements*, the computer equivalent of neurons.
⇒ See also ARTIFICIAL INTELLIGENCE; DIGITAL; VOICE RECOGNITION.

newbie *n. Slang.* someone who is a new user on an online service, particularly the Internet.
⇒ See also ONLINE SERVICE.

newsgroup *n.* an on-line discussion group. On the Internet, there are literally thousands of newsgroups covering every conceivable interest.
⇒ See also ACRONYM; FORUM; LURK; MODERATED NEWSGROUP; NEWS READER.

news reader *n.* an application for reading messages from and posting messages to Internet newsgroups.
⇒ See also NEWSGROUP; NNTP.

Next Generation Internet Initiative *n.* NGI INITIATIVE.

NEXTSTEP *n.* an object-oriented operating system developed by Next, Inc. In 1997, Apple Computer acquired Next with the idea of making NEXTSTEP the foundation of its new Macintosh operating system.
⇒ See also APPLE COMPUTER; OBJECT ORIENTED; OPERATING SYSTEM.

NFS Network File System: an open operating system designed by Sun Microsystems that allows all network users to access shared files stored on computers of different types.
⇒ See also FILE MANAGEMENT SYSTEM; UNIX.

NGI Initiative Next Generation Internet Initiative: a U.S. program designed to fund and coordinate federal agencies and academia to design and build the next generation of Internet services.
⇒ See also I2; INTERNET; vBNS.

nibble *n.* half a byte; four bits. Nibbles are important in hexadecimal and BCD representations.
⇒ See also BCD; BIT; BYTE; HEXADECIMAL.

NIC NETWORK INTERFACE CARD.

NiCad battery pack *n.* the battery pack for many notebook computers. Nickel-cadmium batteries can provide considerable power, but they need to be recharged every three or four hours.

⇒ See also BATTERY PACK; LITHIUM-ION BATTERY; MEMORY EFFECT; NiMH BATTERY PACK; NOTEBOOK COMPUTER.

NiMH battery pack *n.* a type of battery pack that is made of nickel-metal hydroxide and can store up to 50 percent more power than NiCad batteries.
⇒ See also BATTERY PACK; LITHIUM-ION BATTERY; MEMORY EFFECT; NiCad BATTERY PACK.

NLM NETWARE LOADABLE MODULE.

NLQ NEAR-LETTER-QUALITY.

NLX a form factor designed by Intel for PC motherboards. It features a number of improvements over the current LPX form factor.
⇒ See also AGP; BABY AT; FORM FACTOR; MOTHERBOARD; LPX.

NNTP Network News Transfer Protocol: the protocol used to post, distribute, and retrieve USENET messages.
⇒ See also NEWS READER; USENET.

node *n.* **1.** in networks, a processing location. A node can be a computer or some other device, such as a printer. **2.** in tree structures, a point where two or more lines meet.
⇒ See also DLC; LEAF; MAC ADDRESS; NETWORK; TREE STRUCTURE.

noise *n.* **1.** in communications, interference (static) that destroys the integrity of signals on a line. Noise can come from radio waves, nearby electrical wires, lightning, and bad connections. **2.** anything that prevents a clear signal or message from being transmitted.
⇒ See also COMMUNICATIONS; FIBER OPTICS.

nonimpact printer *n.* a type of printer that does not operate by striking a head against a ribbon. Examples of nonimpact printers include laser and ink-jet printers.
⇒ See also IMPACT PRINTER; INK-JET PRINTER; LASER PRINTER; PRINTER.

noninterlaced *adj.* referring to monitors and video standards that do not use interlacing techniques to improve resolution. Although interlacing increases resolution, it also increases screen flicker and reduces reaction time.
⇒ See also INTERLACING; MONITOR; SCREEN FLICKER.

Non-Uniform Memory Access *n.* See NUMA.

nonvolatile memory *n.* any of various types of memory that retain their contents when power is turned off. ROM is nonvolatile.
⇒ See also BUBBLE MEMORY; MEMORY; NVRAM; RAM; ROM.

normalization *n.* **1.** in relational database design, the process of organizing data to minimize duplication. Normalization usually involves dividing a database into two or more tables and defining relationships between the tables. **2.** in data processing, a process applied to all data in a set that produces a specific statistical property. **3.** in programming, changing the format of a floating-point number so the left-most digit in the mantissa is not a zero.
⇒ See also FLOATING-POINT NUMBER; KEY; RDBMS; REFERENTIAL INTEGRITY.

NOR operator *n.* a Boolean operator that returns a value of TRUE only if both operands are FALSE.
⇒ See also BOOLEAN OPERATOR.

NOS NETWORK OPERATING SYSTEM.

notebook computer *n.* an extremely lightweight personal computer weighing typically less than 6 pounds and small enough to fit easily in a briefcase. Many notebook display screens are limited to VGA resolution. Active-matrix screens produce very sharp images but do not refresh as rapidly as full-size monitors. In terms of computing power, modern notebook computers are nearly equivalent to personal computers.
⇒ See also ACTIVE-MATRIX DISPLAY; BACKLIGHTING; BATTERY PACK; HAND-HELD COMPUTER; LAPTOP COMPUTER; PDA; PORT REPLICATOR; SLATE PC; SUBNOTEBOOK COMPUTER; VGA; VIRTUAL DESKTOP; ZV PORT.

Notes *n.* Short for LOTUS NOTES.

NOT operator *n.* a Boolean operator that returns TRUE if its operand is FALSE, and FALSE if its operand is TRUE.
⇒ See also BOOLEAN OPERATOR.

Novell *n.* the world's largest network software

computer

company.
⇒ See also LOCAL-AREA NETWORK; NETWARE.

Novell NetWare *n.* NETWARE.

ns nanosecond.

NSAPI Netscape Server API: an API for Netscape's Web servers. NSAPI enables programmers to create sophisticated Web-based applications.
⇒ See also CGI; ISAPI; STATELESS.

NSFnet *n.* a wide-area network developed as the main government network linking universities and research facilities. In 1995 NSFnet was dismantled and replaced with a commercial Internet backbone.
⇒ See also ARPANET; NETWORK; WIDE-AREA NETWORK.

NSP Network Service Provider: a company that provides Internet access to ISPs.
⇒ See also BACKBONE; ISP; NAP.

NT *n.* Short for WINDOWS NT.

NT File System *n.* See NTFS.

NTFS NT file system: one of the file systems for the Windows NT operating system.
⇒ See also FILE MANAGEMENT SYSTEM; UNICODE; VOLUME; WINDOWS NT.

NTSC National Television Standards Committee: an organization responsible for setting television and video standards in the United States.
⇒ See also COMMON INTERMEDIATE FORMAT; COMPOSITE VIDEO; HDTV; INTERLACING; PAL; QCIF; RGB MONITOR; S-VIDEO; SAP; TELEVISION BOARD; VIDEO ADAPTER; VIDEO OVERLAY.

NuBus *n.* the expansion bus for versions of Macintosh computers starting with the Macintosh II and ending with the Performa. Current Macs use the PCI bus.
⇒ See also EXPANSION BUS; MACINTOSH COMPUTER; PCI.

null character *n.* a character that has all its bits set to 0. A null character has a numeric value of 0. In some programming languages, a null character is used to mark the end of a character string. In database and spreadsheet applications, null characters are often used as padding.
⇒ See also CHARACTER STRING; PADDING.

null modem *n.* NULL-MODEM CABLE.

null-modem cable *n.* a specially designed cable that connects two computers directly to each other

via their communications ports. Null modems are particularly useful with portable computers.
⇒ See also DCC; MODEM; PORT; RS-232C.

NUMA Non-Uniform Memory Access: a type of parallel processing architecture in which each processor has its own local memory but can also access memory owned by other processors.
⇒ See also MPP; PARALLEL PROCESSING; SMP.

number cruncher *n.* **1.** a computer whose dominant characteristic is its ability to perform large amounts of numerical computations quickly. **2.** a program whose main task is to perform mathematical calculations. **3.** an individual who uses a computer primarily for analyzing numbers.
⇒ See also SUPERCOMPUTER; WORKSTATION.

numeric coprocessor *n.* See under COPROCESSOR.

numeric keypad *n.* a separate set of keys on some keyboards that contains the numbers 0 through 9 and a decimal point arranged as on an adding machine. Numeric keypads make it easier to enter large amounts of numeric data.
⇒ See also ARROW KEYS; KEYBOARD; MODE; NUM LOCK KEY.

Num Lock key *n.* a key that switches the numeric keypad from numeric mode to cursor control mode, and vice versa. In numeric mode, the keys represent numbers even when they are combined with the Shift key, Function key, or Control key.
⇒ See also CURSOR CONTROL KEYS; NUMERIC KEYPAD; TOGGLE.

NURBS Non-Uniform Rational B-Spline: a mathematical representation of a three-dimensional object. Most CAD/CAM applications support NURBS, which can be used to represent analytic shapes, such as cones, as well as free-form shapes, such as car bodies.
⇒ See also 3-D SOFTWARE; BÉZIER CURVE; MODELING; SPLINE.

NVRAM *n.* Non-Volatile Random Access Memory: a type of memory that retains its contents when power is turned off.
⇒ See also EEPROM; MEMORY; NONVOLATILE MEMORY; RAM; SRAM.

a b c d e f g h i j k l m n **O** p q r s t u v w x y z

OA OFFICE AUTOMATION.

object *n.* any item that can be individually selected and manipulated. This can include pictures on a display screen as well as software entities. In object-oriented programming, an object is a self-contained entity that consists of both data and procedures to manipulate the data.
⇒ See also BLOB; CORBA; OBJECT ORIENTED; OBJECT-ORIENTED GRAPHICS; OBJECT-ORIENTED PROGRAMMING; OLE; OMG.

object code *n.* the code produced by a compiler. Programmers write programs in a form called source code. To get from source code to machine language, the programs must be transformed by a compiler. The compiler produces an intermediary form called object code.
⇒ See also ASSEMBLER; ASSEMBLY LANGUAGE; CODE; COMPILE; LIBRARY; LINK; LOAD; MACHINE LANGUAGE.

Object Linking and Embedding *n.* See OLE.

Object Management Group *n.* See OMG.

object-oriented *adj.* **1.** referring to a special type of programming that combines data structures with functions to create reusable objects. **2.** describing a system that deals with different types of objects and in which actions depend on the type of object being manipulated.
⇒ See also OBJECT-ORIENTED PROGRAMMING; SMALLTALK; VECTOR GRAPHICS.

object-oriented graphics *n.* the representation of graphical objects, such as lines, circles, and rectangles, with mathematical formulas. This enables

the system to manipulate the objects more freely. Also, object-oriented images profit from high-quality output devices. One of the most widely used formats for object-oriented graphics is PostScript.
⇒ See also BIT-MAPPED GRAPHICS; GRAPHICS; POST-SCRIPT; SCALABLE FONT; VECTOR GRAPHICS.

object-oriented programming *n.* a type of programming in which programmers define the data type of a data structure and the types of operations (functions) that can be applied to the data structure. The data structure becomes an *object* that includes both data and functions. Programmers can create relationships between one object and another. When a new type of object is added, it inherits many of its features from existing objects. This makes object-oriented programs easier to modify.
⇒ See also C++; CLASS; COMPONENT SOFTWARE; DISTRIBUTED COMPUTING; EIFFEL; ENCAPSULATION; JAVA; OBJECT ORIENTED; OMG; OVERLOADING; POLYMORPHISM; SMALLTALK; UML; VISUAL C++.

Object Request Broker *n.* See ORB.

OC Optical Carrier: used to specify the speed of fiber-optic networks conforming to the SONET standard.
⇒ See also SDH; SONET; T-1 CARRIER; T-3 CARRIER.

OCR OPTICAL CHARACTER RECOGNITION.

octal *adj.* referring to the base-8 number system, which uses just eight unique symbols (0, 1, 2, 3, 4, 5, 6, and 7). Programs often display data in octal format because it is relatively easy for humans to read and can easily be translated into binary format.

⇒ See also BINARY; DECIMAL; HEXADECIMAL.

OCX OLE Custom control: an independent program module that can be accessed by other programs in a Windows environment. OCX controls have now been superseded by ActiveX controls. However, ActiveX is backward compatible with OCX controls.

⇒ See also ACTIVEX CONTROL; COMPONENT; CONTROL; OLE; VBX.

ODBC Open Data Base Connectivity: a standard database access method developed by Microsoft Corporation. The goal of ODBC is to make it possible to access any data from any application, regardless of which database management system (DBMS) is handling the data.

⇒ See also ADO; DATABASE MANAGEMENT SYSTEM; DRIVER; JDBC; QUERY; SQL.

odd header *n.* in word processing, a header that appears only on odd-numbered pages.

⇒ See also HEADER.

odd parity *n.* the mode of parity checking in which each 9-bit combination of a data byte plus a parity bit contains an odd number of set bits.

⇒ See also PARITY CHECKING.

ODI Open Data-link Interface: an application programming interface (API) developed by Novell for writing network drivers.

⇒ See also API; DRIVER; NETWORK INTERFACE CARD; OSI.

OEM original equipment manufacturer: a company that has a special relationship with computer producers. OEMs buy computers in bulk and customize them for a particular application. They then sell the customized computer under their own name.

⇒ See also VAR.

office automation *n.* the use of computer systems to execute a variety of office operations, such as word processing, accounting, and e-mail. Office automation almost always implies a network of computers with a variety of available programs.

⇒ See also E-MAIL; NETWORK; WORD PROCESSING.

off-line *adj.* **1.** not connected. For example, when a printer is off-line, it can advance the paper (*form feed*) but cannot print documents sent from the computer. **2.** describing events that occur outside of a standard procedure. For example, if someone says, "Let's continue this discussion off-line," it means, "Let's discuss it informally at another time."

⇒ See also FORM FEED; ON-LINE.

offset *n.* **1.** a value added to a base address to produce a second address. Specifying addresses using an offset is called *relative addressing* because the resulting address is relative to some other point. **2.** in desktop publishing, the amount of space along the edge of the paper. Its purpose is to allow room for the binding.

⇒ See also ADDRESS; BASE ADDRESS; DESKTOP PUBLISHING; GUTTER; RELATIVE ADDRESS.

offset printing *n.* a printing technique whereby ink is spread on a metal plate with etched images, then transferred to an intermediary surface such as a rubber blanket, and finally applied to paper by pressing the paper against the intermediary surface.

⇒ See also DESKTOP PUBLISHING; POSTSCRIPT.

Okidata *n.* one of the leading producers of printers, especially dot-matrix and LED printers.

⇒ See also DOT-MATRIX PRINTER; LASER PRINTER.

OLAP Online Analytical Processing: a category of software tools for analyzing data stored in a database. OLAP tools enable users to study different dimensions of multidimensional data.

⇒ See also DATABASE; DATABASE MANAGEMENT SYSTEM; MULTIDIMENSIONAL DBMS; OLTP.

OLE (ō lā′ *or as separate letters*), *n.* Object Linking and Embedding: a compound document standard that enables the user to create objects with one application and link or embed them in a second application.

⇒ See also ACTIVEX; APPLET; COMPONENT OBJECT MODEL; COMPONENT SOFTWARE; DDE; DLL; EMBEDDED OBJECT; HOT LINK; LINK; OBJECT ORIENTED; OCX; OPEN-Doc.

OLTP On-Line Transaction Processing. See TRANSAC-TION PROCESSING.

⇒ See also OLAP.

OMG Object Management Group: a consortium of companies that provide a common framework for developing applications using object-oriented programming techniques.

⇒ See also CORBA; DISTRIBUTED COMPUTING; IIOP; OBJECT; OBJECT-ORIENTED PROGRAMMING.

on-board *adj.* literally, on a circuit board. *On-board memory*, for example, refers to memory chips on the motherboard. *On-board modems* are modems that are on expansion boards.

⇒ See also EXPANSION BOARD; MOTHERBOARD; ON-BOARD MODEM; PRINTED CIRCUIT BOARD.

on-board modem *n.* a modem that comes as an expansion board that can be inserted into a computer. Also called **internal modem.**

⇒ See also MODEM.

100Base-T *n.* a networking standard that supports data transfer rates up to 100 Mbps (100 megabits per second). 100Base-T is based on the older Ethernet standard. Because it is 10 times faster than Ethernet, it is often referred to as *Fast Ethernet.*

⇒ See also 10BASET; CSMA/CD; ETHERNET; GIGABIT ETHERNET; SWITCHED ETHERNET.

on-line or **online** *adj.* **1.** turned on and connected. For example, printers are on-line when they are ready to receive data from the computer. **2.** (of a user) connected to a host computer through a modem.

⇒ See also OFF-LINE; PRINTER.

OnLine Analytical Processing *n.* See OLAP.

online help *n.* See under HELP.

online service *n.* a business that provides its subscribers with a wide variety of data transmitted over telecommunications lines. Online services provide an infrastructure in which subscribers can communicate with one another by exchanging e-mail messages or by participating in online conferences (forums). In addition, the service can connect users with an almost unlimited number of third-party information providers. Three of the largest online services are America Online, CompuServe, and MSN.

⇒ See also AMERICA ONLINE; BULLETIN BOARD SYSTEM; CHAT; COMPUSERVE INFORMATION SERVICE; FORUM; INTERNET; MSN.

On-Line Transaction Processing *n.* See OLTP.

OOP OBJECT-ORIENTED PROGRAMMING.

OOPL object-oriented programming language.

open *v.t.* **1.** to make (an object) accessible. Whenever the user accesses a file, the operating system opens the file. In a multiprocessing operating system, the operating system must decide whether the file can be accessed simultaneously by more than one user, and, if so, it must ensure that different users do not try to modify the file's contents at the same time. —*adj.* **2.** (of designs or architectures) accessible; public. See under OPEN ARCHITECTURE.

⇒ See also CLOSE; FILE; OPERATING SYSTEM.

open architecture *n.* an architecture whose specifications are public. This includes officially approved standards as well as privately designed architectures whose specifications are made public.

⇒ See also ADD-ON; ARCHITECTURE; CLONE; PROPRIETARY; STANDARD; THE OPEN GROUP.

Open Data-Link Interface *n.* See ODI.

OpenDoc *n.* a standard application programming interface (API) that makes it possible to design independent programs (components) that can work together on a single document.

⇒ See also COMPONENT OBJECT MODEL; COMPONENT SOFTWARE; COMPOUND DOCUMENT; OLE.

OpenGL *n.* a 3-D graphics language developed by Silicon Graphics. There are two main implementations: Microsoft OpenGL is built into Windows NT and is designed to improve performance on hardware that supports the OpenGL standard; Cosmo OpenGL is a software-only implementation specifically designed for machines that do not have a graphics accelerator.

⇒ See also 3-D SOFTWARE; DIRECT3D; SGI.

Open Graphics Language *n.* OPENGL.

Open Shortest Path First *n.* See OSPF.

Open Software Foundation (OSF) *n.* See under THE OPEN GROUP.

Open System Interconnection *n.* See OSI.

Open Text *n.* a popular Internet search engine developed by Open Text Corporation. Open Text provides powerful ways to fine-tune a query.

⇒ See also ALTA VISTA; EXCITE; INFOSEEK; LYCOS; SEARCH ENGINE; WEBCRAWLER.

operand *n.* in all computer languages, an object that is manipulated.

⇒ See also EXPRESSION; OPERATOR; OVERLOADING.

operating environment *n.* the environment in which users run programs. For example, the DOS environment consists of all the DOS commands available to users. The Macintosh environment, on the other hand, is a graphical user interface that uses icons and menus instead of commands.

⇒ See also CONTROL PROGRAM; ENVIRONMENT; GRAPHICAL USER INTERFACE; MICROSOFT WINDOWS; OPERATING SYSTEM; SHELL; VIRTUAL MACHINE.

operating system *n.* the program that performs such basic tasks as recognizing input from the keyboard, sending output to the display screen, keeping track of files and directories on the disk, and controlling peripheral devices such as disk drives and printers. This is the most important program that runs on computers. For large systems, the operating system makes sure that different programs and users running at the same time do not interfere with each other. The operating system is also responsible for security.

⇒ See also APPLICATION; BeOS; BIOS; COMMAND PROCESSOR; DOS; FILE MANAGEMENT SYSTEM; KERNEL; MacOS; MICROSOFT WINDOWS; MULTI-USER; MULTIPROCESSING; MULTITASKING; MULTITHREADING; MVS; OS/2; UNIX; VMS; WINDOWS CE.

operator *n.* **1.** a symbol that represents a specific action. For example, a plus sign (+) is an *arithmetic operator* that represents addition. **2.** an individual responsible for mounting tapes and disks, making backups, and generally ensuring that a computer runs properly.

⇒ See also BITWISE OPERATOR; BOOLEAN OPERATOR; EXPRESSION; OPERAND; OVERLOADING; PRECEDENCE; RELATIONAL OPERATOR.

optical character recognition (OCR) *n.* the branch of computer science that involves reading text from paper and translating the images into a form that the computer can manipulate, such as ASCII codes. For example, images from pages of a book or a magazine article can be fed directly into an electronic computer file, translated by an OCR system, and then edited with a word processor. All OCR systems include an optical scanner for reading text, and sophisticated software for analyzing images.

⇒ See also ASCII; DOCUMENT MANAGEMENT; FONT; FORM; OPTICAL SCANNER; PRINTED CIRCUIT BOARD.

optical disk *n.* a storage medium from which data is read and to which it is written by lasers. Optical disks can store much more data—up to 6 gigabytes (6 billion bytes)—than most portable magnetic media. The three basic types of optical disks are: **CD-ROM, WORM,** and **erasable.**

⇒ See also AREAL DENSITY; CD-I (COMPACT DISC-INTERACTIVE); CD-ROM; COMPACT DISC; ERASABLE OPTICAL DISK; MASS STORAGE; PHASE CHANGE DISK; ROM; WORM.

optical fiber *n.* See under FIBER OPTICS.

optical resolution *n.* the degree of detail with which a device can capture an image. The term is used most frequently with reference to optical scanners and digital cameras. In contrast, the *interpolated resolution* indicates the resolution that the device can yield through *interpolation* —the process of generating intermediate values based on known values.

⇒ See also DIGITAL CAMERA; OPTICAL SCANNER; RESOLUTION.

optical scanner *n.* a device that can read text or illustrations printed on paper and translate the information into a form the computer can use. A scanner digitizes the image—dividing it into a grid of boxes and representing each box with either a zero or a one, depending on whether the box is filled in. The resulting bit map can be stored in a file, displayed on a screen, and manipulated by programs. Some scanners are small, hand-held devices that are moved across the paper. Larger scanners include machines into which sheets of paper are fed. These are called *sheet-fed* scanners. A second type of large scanner, called a *flatbed scanner,* is like a photocopy machine. It consists of a board on which books, magazines, and other documents are placed.

⇒ See also BIT MAP; CCD; COLOR DEPTH; COMPUTER IMAGING; FAX MACHINE; FLATBED SCANNER; FONT; GRAY SCALING; MFP; OPTICAL CHARACTER RECOGNITION; OPTICAL RESOLUTION; PHOTO SCANNER; RESOLUTION; TWAIN.

optimize *v.t.* **1.** in programming, to fine-tune (a program) so that it runs more quickly or takes up less space. **2.** (of a disk) to defragment. **3.** to configure (a device or application) so that it performs better.

⇒ See also DEFRAGMENT; FRAGMENTATION; PROGRAM.

option *n.* **1.** in command-driven interfaces, an addition to a command that changes or refines the command in a specified manner. **2.** in graphical user interfaces, a choice in a menu or dialog box.

⇒ See also COMMAND; COMMAND DRIVEN; DIALOG BOX; GRAPHICAL USER INTERFACE; MENU.

Option key *n.* a key on Macintosh keyboards used with other keys to generate special characters and commands.

⇒ See also ALT KEY; KEYBOARD; MACINTOSH COMPUTER.

Oracle *n.* the largest software company whose primary business is database products.

⇒ See also DATABASE MANAGEMENT SYSTEM; INFORMIX; NETWORK COMPUTER; SQL; SYBASE.

Orange Book *n.* the specification covering writable CDs, including CD-R.

⇒ See also CD-R DRIVE; GREEN BOOK; RED BOOK; WHITE BOOK; YELLOW_BOOK.

ORB Object Request Broker: a component in the CORBA programming model that acts as the middleware between clients and servers. The various ORBs receive the requests, forward them to the appropriate servers, and then hand the results back to the client.

⇒ See also CORBA; MIDDLEWARE.

orientation *n.* See under LANDSCAPE and PORTRAIT.

original equipment manufacturer *n.* See OEM.

OR operator *n.* a Boolean operator that returns a value of TRUE if either (or both) of its operands is TRUE. This is called an *inclusive OR operator.* There is also an *exclusive OR operator* (often abbreviated *XOR*) that returns a value of TRUE only if just one of the operands is TRUE.

⇒ See also BOOLEAN OPERATOR.

orphan *n.* in word processing, the first line of a paragraph that appears as the last line of a page, or the last line of a paragraph that appears as the first line of a page (this is sometimes called a *widow*). Orphans are considered bad form in page layout.

⇒ See also PAGINATION; WIDOW; WORD PROCESSING.

OS OPERATING SYSTEM.

OS/2 *n.* an operating system for PCs developed originally by Microsoft Corporation and IBM but sold and managed solely by IBM. OS/2 is compatible with DOS and Windows programs. However, programs written specifically to run under OS/2 will not run under DOS or Windows.

⇒ See also DOS; GRAPHICAL USER INTERFACE; MICROSOFT WINDOWS; MULTITASKING; OPERATING SYSTEM; PC.

OS-9 *n.* a real-time, multi-user, multitasking operating system developed by Microware Systems Corporation.

⇒ See also CD-I (COMPACT DISC-INTERACTIVE); REAL TIME; WEBTV.

OSF Open Software Foundation: now part of *The Open Group.*

⇒ See also DCE.

OSI Open System Interconnection: an ISO standard for worldwide communications that defines a networking framework for implementing protocols in

seven layers. Control is passed from one layer to the next.
⇒ See also DLC; ISO; PROTOCOL STACK.

OSI Reference Model *n.* See OSI.

OSPF Open Shortest Path First: a protocol that defines how routers share routing information. OSPF transfers only routing information that has changed since the previous transfer.
⇒ See also ROUTER; ROUTING; ROUTING INFORMATION PROTOCOL.

OSR 2 OEM Service Release 2: a version of Windows 95 released at the end of 1996. Also called **Windows 95b.**
⇒ See also FAT32; WINDOWS 95.

outline font *n.* a scalable font in which the outlines of each character are geometrically defined. The most popular languages for defining outline fonts are *PostScript* and *TrueType.*
⇒ See also BIT MAP; FONT; POSTSCRIPT; RESOLUTION; SCALABLE FONT; TRUETYPE; TYPEFACE; VECTOR GRAPHICS.

output *n.* **1.** anything that comes out of a computer. Output can be meaningful information or gibberish, and it can appear in a variety of forms—as binary numbers, as characters, as pictures, and as printed pages. Output devices include display screens, loudspeakers, and printers. —*v.t.* **2.** to give out. For example, display screens output images and printers output print.
⇒ See also I/O.

output device *n.* any machine capable of representing information from a computer. This includes display screens, printers, plotters, and synthesizers.
⇒ See also DEVICE; OUTPUT.

overclock *v.t.* to run (a microprocessor) faster than the speed for which it has been tested and approved. Overclocking is a popular technique for ek-

ing out a little more performance from a system.
⇒ See also CLOCK SPEED; MHz; MICROPROCESSOR; MOTHERBOARD.

OverDrive *n.* a user-installable microprocessor from Intel for the 486 microprocessor.
⇒ See also INTEL MICROPROCESSORS.

overflow error *n.* an error that occurs when the computer attempts to handle a number that is too large for it.
⇒ See also FLOATING-POINT NUMBER.

overhead *n.* the use of computer resources for performing a specific feature. Typically, the term is used to describe a function that is optional, or an enhancement to an existing application. Programmers often need to weigh the overhead of new features before implementing them.
⇒ See also FEATURE.

overlaid windows *n.pl.* CASCADING WINDOWS.

overloading *n.* in programming languages, a feature that allows an object to have different meanings, depending on its context. It is a feature of most object-oriented languages.
⇒ See also CLASS; DATA TYPE; OBJECT-ORIENTED PROGRAMMING; OPERAND; OPERATOR; POLYMORPHISM.

oversampling *n.* ANTIALIASING.

overstrike *v.t.* to print (one character) directly on top of another. In older printers, this was one way to create unusual characters or bold characters, but it is not necessary with modern printers.

overwrite mode *n.* one of two modes in word processors and text editors. In overwrite mode, every character typed is displayed at the cursor position. If a character is already at that position, it is replaced.
⇒ See also INSERT MODE.

computer

a b c d e f g h i j k l m n o **P** q r s t u v w x y z

pack *v.t.* to compress (data).
⇒ See also DATA COMPRESSION; PACKED FILE.

packed file *n.* a file in a compressed format. Many operating systems and applications contain commands used to pack a file so that it takes up less memory.
⇒ See also DATA COMPRESSION; DISK COMPRESSION; MODEM.

packet *n.* a piece of a message transmitted over a packet-switching network. A packet contains the destination address in addition to the data.
⇒ See also CELL RELAY; IP; MTU; PACKET SWITCHING; ROUTER; ROUTING; TRACEROUTE.

packet switching *n.* protocols in which messages are divided into a series of packets before they are sent. Each packet is then transmitted individually. Once all the packets arrive at the destination, they are recompiled into the original message.
⇒ See also CDPD; CELL RELAY; CIRCUIT SWITCHING; FRAME RELAY; NETWORK; SVC; TCP/IP; WIDE-AREA NETWORK; X.25.

pad character *n.* a character used to fill empty space. Many applications have fields that must be a particular length. If all the allotted characters are not used, the program must fill in the remaining ones with pad characters.
⇒ See also DATABASE; FIELD; NULL CHARACTER.

padding *n.* filling in unused space.
⇒ See also PAD CHARACTER.

page *n.* **1.** a fixed amount of data. **2.** in word processing, a page of text. **3.** in virtual memory systems, a fixed number of bytes recognized by the operating system. **4.** WEB PAGE. —*v.t., v.i.* **5.** to display one page or screenful of (a document) at a time. **6.** to copy a page of (data) from main memory to a mass storage device, or vice versa.
⇒ See also FPM RAM; MAIN MEMORY; PAGING; SEGMENT; SWAP; VIRTUAL MEMORY.

page break *n.* the end of a page of text. In word processing, the user enters special codes, called

hard page breaks or *forced page breaks*, that cause the printer to advance to the next page. Otherwise, the word processor begins a new page after a page has been filled; this is called a *soft page break.*
⇒ See also HARD; SOFT; WORD PROCESSING.

Page Description Language *n.* a language for describing the layout and contents of a printed page. *Abbr.:* PDL
⇒ See also LASER PRINTER; OBJECT ORIENTED; PCL; POSTSCRIPT.

Page Down key *n.* a key that is standard on PC and Macintosh keyboards. Its meaning differs from one program to another, but it usually moves the cursor down a set number of lines.
⇒ See also KEYBOARD.

page eject *n.* FORM FEED.

page fault *n.* an interrupt that occurs when a program requests data not currently in virtual memory. The interrupt triggers the operating system to retrieve the data from a storage device and load it into RAM.
⇒ See also INVALID PAGE FAULT; MMU; PAGING; VIRTUAL MEMORY.

page fault error *n.* INVALID PAGE FAULT.

page layout program *n.* a program enabling the user to format pages of text and graphics.
⇒ See also DESKTOP PUBLISHING; KERNING; TEXT WRAP; WORD PROCESSING.

page-mode memory *n.* a type of memory that works by eliminating the need for a row address if data is located in the row previously accessed.

page preview *n.* See under PREVIEWING.

page printer *n.* a printer that processes an entire page at one time. All laser and ink-jet printers are page printers.
⇒ See also LASER PRINTER; PAGE DESCRIPTION LANGUAGE (PDL); PRINTER.

pages per minute *n.* See PPM.

Page Up key *n.* a standard key on PC and Macintosh keyboards. Its meaning differs from one pro-

gram to another, but it usually scrolls the document up one screenful.
⇒ See also KEYBOARD.

page-white display *n.* a special type of LCD display screen that uses supertwist technology to produce a high contrast between the foreground and background.
⇒ See also FLAT-PANEL DISPLAY; LCD; SUPERTWIST.

pagination *n.* **1.** the numbering of pages in a document. **2.** the division of a document into pages.
⇒ See also ORPHAN; WIDOW; WORD PROCESSING.

paging *n.* a technique used by virtual memory operating systems to help ensure that needed data is available as quickly as possible. When a program needs a page that is not in main memory, the operating system copies the required page into memory and copies another page back to the disk. One says that the operating system *pages* the data. Each time a page is needed that is not currently in memory, a *page fault* occurs.
⇒ See also DEMAND PAGING; MAIN MEMORY; OPERATING SYSTEM; PAGE; PAGE FAULT; SEGMENT; SWAP; THRASH; VIRTUAL MEMORY.

paint program *n.* a graphics program that enables the user to draw pictures on the display screen that are represented as bit maps (bit-mapped graphics).
⇒ See also ADOBE PHOTOSHOP; BIT-MAPPED GRAPHICS; DRAW PROGRAM; GRAPHICS; MARQUEE; VECTOR GRAPHICS.

PAL 1. Phase Alternating Line: the dominant television standard in Europe. PAL delivers 625 lines at 50 half-frames per second. **2.** Programmable Array Logic: a type of Programmable Logic Device (PLD).
⇒ See also COMMON INTERMEDIATE FORMAT; NTSC; QCIF; VIDEO ADAPTER.

palette *n.* **1.** in computer graphics, the set of available colors. For a given application, the palette may be only a subset of all the colors that can be physically displayed. **2.** in paint and illustration programs, a collection of symbols that represent drawing tools. For example, a simple palette might contain a paintbrush, a pencil, and an eraser.
⇒ See also DRAW PROGRAM; EGA; GRAPHICS; PAINT PROGRAM; VIDEO ADAPTER.

palmtop *n.* a small computer that literally fits in the palm. Compared with full-size computers, palmtops are severely limited. Those that use a pen rather than a keyboard for input are often called *hand-held computers* or *PDAs.*
⇒ See also HAND-HELD COMPUTER; NOTEBOOK COMPUTER; PDA; PORTABLE; WINDOWS CE.

Pantone Matching System *n.* a popular color matching system used by the printing industry to print spot colors. *Abbr.:* PMS
⇒ See also CMYK; COLOR MANAGEMENT SYSTEM (CMS); PROCESS COLORS; SPOT COLOR.

PAP Password Authentication Protocol: the most basic form of authentication, in which a user's name and password are transmitted over a network and compared with a table of name–password pairs.
⇒ See also AUTHENTICATION; CHAP.

paper feed *n.* the mechanism or method that moves paper through a printer.
⇒ See also PRINTER; TRACTOR FEED.

paperless office *n.* the idealized office in which paper is absent because all information is stored and transferred electronically.
⇒ See also DOCUMENT MANAGEMENT; FAX MACHINE; OPTICAL CHARACTER RECOGNITION; WORKGROUP COMPUTING.

paper-white display *n.* a high-quality monochrome monitor that displays characters in black against a white background. Such monitors are popular for desktop publishing.
⇒ See also DISPLAY SCREEN; MONITOR.

parallel *adj.* referring to processes that occur simultaneously. *Parallel* means that the printer or other device is capable of receiving more than one bit at a time (that is, it receives several bits *in parallel*).
⇒ See also PARALLEL PORT; PORT; PRINTER; SERIAL.

parallel computing *n.* PARALLEL PROCESSING.

parallel interface *n.* a channel capable of transferring more than one bit simultaneously.

⇒ See also CENTRONICS INTERFACE; CHANNEL; PARALLEL; PARALLEL PORT; SERIAL PORT.

parallel port *n.* a parallel interface for connecting an external device such as a printer. Most personal computers have both a parallel port and at least one serial port.
⇒ See also CENTRONICS INTERFACE; ECP; EPP; IrDA; LOCALTALK; PARALLEL; PORT; SCSI; SERIAL PORT; USB.

parallel processing *n.* the simultaneous use of more than one CPU to execute a program. Single-CPU computers can process data in a parallel way when they are connected in a network.
⇒ See also CLUSTERING; CPU; DISTRIBUTED PROCESSING; HIGH PERFORMANCE COMPUTING; MPP; MULTITASKING; NUMA; SUPERSCALAR.

parameter *n.* **1.** a characteristic used to customize a program, such as filenames, page lengths, and font specifications. **2.** (in programming) ARGUMENT.

parameter RAM *n.* See PRAM.

parent directory *n.* the directory (or folder) above another directory (or folder). The lower directory is called a subdirectory. In DOS and UNIX systems, the parent directory is identified by two dots (..).
⇒ See also DIRECTORY; ROOT DIRECTORY.

parity *n.* the quality of being either odd or even. The fact that all numbers have a parity is commonly used in data communications to ensure the validity of data.
⇒ See also PARITY CHECKING.

parity bit *n.* See under PARITY CHECKING.

parity checking *n.* in communications, the use of *parity bits* to check that data has been transmitted accurately. The parity bit is added to every data unit that is transmitted. The parity bit for each unit is set so that all bytes have either an odd number or an even number of set bits. Parity checking is used not only in communications but also in the testing of memory storage devices.
⇒ See also CCITT; COMMUNICATIONS; COMMUNICATIONS PROTOCOL; MNP; MODEM.

park *v.t.* to lock the *read/write head* of (a hard disk drive) in a safe position so that the disk will not be damaged while the drive is being moved.
⇒ See also DISK DRIVE; HEAD; HEAD CRASH.

parse *v.t.* to divide (language) into small components that can be analyzed. Compilers must parse source code to be able to translate it into object code. Similarly, any application that processes complex commands must be able to parse the commands.
⇒ See also COMPILE; COMPILER; SEMANTICS.

partition *v.t.* **1.** to divide (memory or mass storage) into isolated sections. In DOS systems, each partition of a disk will behave like a separate disk drive. —*n.* **2.** a section of main memory or mass storage that has been reserved for a particular application.
⇒ See also CLUSTER; DISK DRIVE; FDISK; FILE ALLOCATION TABLE; FINDER; MBR; SLACK SPACE.

Pascal (pa skal′) *n.* a high-level programming language developed in the late 1960s. Pascal is best known for its affinity to structured programming techniques. Despite its success in academia, it has had only modest success in the business world. [named after Blaise Pascal, a 17th-century mathematician who constructed one of the first adding machines]
⇒ See also BORLAND INTERNATIONAL; DELPHI; HIGH-LEVEL LANGUAGE; MODULA-2; PROGRAMMING LANGUAGE.

passive backplane *n.* See under BACKPLANE.

passive-matrix display *n.* a type of flat-panel display consisting of a grid of horizontal and vertical wires. At the intersection of each grid is an LCD element that constitutes a single pixel, either letting light through or blocking it.
⇒ See also ACTIVE-MATRIX DISPLAY; CSTN; DSTN; FLAT-PANEL DISPLAY; LCD; PIXEL; TFT.

password *n.* a secret series of characters that enables a user to access a file, computer, or program. The password helps ensure that unauthorized users do not access the computer. In addition, data files and programs may require a password.

⇒ See also ACCESS CODE; AUTHENTICATION; KEY; LOG ON; SECURITY.

Password Authentication Protocol *n.* See PAP.

paste *v.t.* to copy (an object) from a buffer or clipboard to a file. In word processing, blocks of text can be cut (removed) from a file and placed in a temporary buffer. The material can then be pasted somewhere else. It is also possible to cut an object from one application and paste it into another.
⇒ See also BUFFER; CLIPBOARD; COPY; CUT; EMBEDDED OBJECT; LINK; OLE.

patch *n.* a temporary fix to a program bug. A patch is an actual piece of object code that is inserted into an executable program.
⇒ See also BUG; EXECUTABLE FILE; OBJECT CODE.

path *n.* **1.** in DOS and Windows systems, a list of directories where the operating system looks for executable files if it is unable to find the file in the working directory. **2.** PATHNAME.
⇒ See also DIRECTORY; DOS; EXECUTABLE FILE; PATHNAME; WORKING DIRECTORY.

pathname *n.* a sequence of symbols and names that identifies a file. The operating system finds the directory containing a particular file by following the specified path.
⇒ See also DIRECTORY; FILENAME; ROOT DIRECTORY; UNC; WORKING DIRECTORY.

pattern recognition *n.* an important field of computer science concerned with recognizing patterns, particularly visual and sound patterns. It is central to optical character recognition (OCR), voice recognition, and handwriting recognition.
⇒ See also HANDWRITING RECOGNITION; OPTICAL CHARACTER RECOGNITION; VOICE RECOGNITION.

Pause key *n.* a key used to temporarily halt the display of data.
⇒ See also SCROLL.

PBX private branch exchange: a private telephone network used within a company. PBX users share outside lines for external telephone calls.
⇒ See also CENTREX; POTS; TELEMATICS.

PC **1.** personal computer or IBM PC. The first personal computer produced by IBM was called the *PC;* increasingly, the term came to mean IBM or IBM-compatible personal computers. In recent years, the term *PC* has been applied to any personal computer based on an Intel or Intel-compatible microprocessor. **2.** printed circuit.
⇒ See also CLONE; COMPAQ; COMPATIBLE; DELL COMPUTER; EXPANSION BUS; IBM; IBM PC; LOCAL BUS; MACINTOSH COMPUTER; OPERATING SYSTEM; PERSONAL COMPUTER; PRINTED CIRCUIT BOARD; VIDEO STANDARDS.

PC/AT See under AT.

PCB PRINTED CIRCUIT BOARD.

PC card *n.* a computer device packaged in a small card about the size of a credit card and conforming to the PCMCIA standard.
⇒ See also CARDBUS; PCMCIA; ZV PORT.

PC-DOS *n.* the name IBM uses to market its version of the DOS operating system.
⇒ See also DOS.

PC fax *n.* FAX MODEM.

PCI Peripheral Component Interconnect: a local bus standard developed by Intel Corporation. PCI is a 64-bit bus, though it is usually implemented as a 32-bit bus. It can run at clock speeds of 33 or 66 MHz.
⇒ See also AGP; BUS; BUS MASTERING; CONTROLLER; EXPANSION BUS; I2O; INDUSTRY STANDARD ARCHITECTURE (ISA) BUS; INTEL; LOCAL BUS; NUBUS.

PCL Printer Control Language: the page description language (PDL) developed by Hewlett-Packard and used in many of its laser and ink-jet printers.
⇒ See also HP; HP-COMPATIBLE PRINTER; HPGL; INTELLIFONT; LASER PRINTER; PAGE DESCRIPTION LANGUAGE (PDL); POSTSCRIPT; SCALABLE FONT.

PCM Pulse Code Modulation: a sampling technique for digitizing analog signals, especially audio signals.
⇒ See also ADPCM; DIGITIZE; MODULATE; SAMPLING; TDM.

PCMCIA Personal Computer Memory Card International Association: an organization that has developed a standard for PC cards. Originally designed for adding memory to portable computers, the PCMCIA standard is now suitable for many types of devices. There are three types of PCMCIA cards. Type I cards are used primarily for adding more ROM or RAM to a computer. Type II cards are often used for modem and fax modem cards. Type III cards can hold portable disk drives.
⇒ See also CARDBUS; DEVICE BAY; HOT PLUGGING; IEEE 1394; PLUG-AND-PLAY; USB; ZV PORT.

PCS Personal Communications Service: the U.S. Federal Communications Commission (FCC) term used to describe a set of digital cellular technologies being deployed in the U.S.
⇒ See also CDMA; CELLULAR; GSM; TDMA.

PC/TV a combination of a personal computer and television.
⇒ See also TELEVISION BOARD; WEBTV.

PCX a graphics file format for graphics programs running on PCs.
⇒ See also BIT-MAPPED GRAPHICS; BMP; GRAPHICS FILE FORMATS; TIFF.

PDA personal digital assistant: a hand-held device that combines computing, telephone/fax, and networking features. Most PDAs are pen-based, using a stylus rather than a keyboard for input.
⇒ See also APPLE COMPUTER; EPOC; HAND-HELD COMPUTER; HANDWRITING RECOGNITION; HPC; PALMTOP; VOICE RECOGNITION; WINDOWS CE.

PDF Portable Document Format: a file format developed by Adobe Systems. PDF captures formatting information from desktop publishing applications, making it possible to send formatted documents and have them appear on the recipient's monitor or printer as they were intended.
⇒ See also ACROBAT; FILE FORMAT.

PDL PAGE DESCRIPTION LANGUAGE.

peer-to-peer architecture *n.* a type of network in which each workstation has equivalent capabilities and responsibilities.
⇒ See also CLIENT/SERVER ARCHITECTURE; LOCAL-AREA NETWORK.

pel PIXEL.

pen computer *n.* a computer that utilizes an electronic pen (called a *stylus*) rather than a keyboard for input. Pen computers generally require special operating systems that support handwriting recognition.
⇒ See also HAND-HELD COMPUTER; HANDWRITING RECOGNITION; PALMTOP; PDA.

Pentium 2 *n.* PENTIUM II.

Pentium II *n.* Intel's Pentium chip that builds on the design of the Pentium Pro. Current versions run at speeds of from 233 to 450 MHz.
⇒ See also DESCHUTES; INTEL MICROPROCESSORS; PENTIUM MICROPROCESSOR; PENTIUM PRO; SLOT 1.

Pentium microprocessor *n.* a 32-bit microprocessor introduced by Intel in 1993. Though still in production, it has been superseded by the Pentium Pro and Pentium II microprocessors.
⇒ See also AMD; CYRIX; DESCHUTES; INTEL MICROPROCESSORS; K6; MERCED; MICROPROCESSOR; PENTIUM II; PENTIUM PRO; SOCKET 7; TILLAMOOK; TRITON.

Pentium MMX *n.* See MMX.

Pentium Pro *n.* Intel's sixth-generation microprocessor (P6). The Pentium Pro can perform at nearly twice the speed of previous Pentium microprocessors.
⇒ See also DIB; INTEL MICROPROCESSORS; MICROPROCESSOR; PENTIUM II; PENTIUM MICROPROCESSOR; SOCKET 8.

peripheral *n.* PERIPHERAL DEVICE.

Peripheral Component Interconnect *n.* See PCI.

peripheral device *n.* any external device attached to a computer. Examples include printers, disk drives, monitors, keyboards, and mice.
⇒ See also CONTROLLER; DEVICE; EXTERNAL BUS.

Perl Practical Extraction and Report Language: a programming language developed by Larry Wall, especially designed for processing text.
⇒ See also AWK; CGI; INTERPRETER; TCL.

Permanent Virtual Circuit *n.* See PVC.

persistent cookie *n.* Another name for *cookie,* so

called because cookies typically stay in a user's browser for long periods of time.

persistent URL *n.* See PURL.

Personal Communications Service *n.* See PCS.

personal computer *n.* a small, relatively inexpensive computer designed for an individual user. One of the first personal computers was the Apple II, introduced in 1977 by Apple Computer. The IBM PC, introduced in 1981, quickly became the personal computer of choice. Other companies adjusted to IBM's dominance by building IBM clones. Today, the world of personal computers is basically divided between Apple Macintoshes and PCs. The principal characteristics of personal computers are that they are single-user systems and are based on microprocessors.
⇒ See also AMIGA; CLONE; COMPUTER; HOME COMPUTER; MACINTOSH COMPUTER; MICROPROCESSOR; PC; WORKSTATION.

Personal Computer Memory Card International Association *n.* See PCMCIA.

Personal Digital Assistant *n.* See PDA.

personal finance manager *n.* a simple accounting program that helps individuals manage their finances.
⇒ See also ACCOUNTING SOFTWARE.

personal information manager *n.* See PIM.

petabyte *n.* 2^{50} (1,125,899,906,842,624) bytes. A petabyte is equal to 1,024 terabytes.
⇒ See also EXABYTE; GIGABYTE; TERABYTE.

PFE INVALID PAGE FAULT.

PGA **1.** pin grid array: a type of chip package in which the connecting pins are located on the bottom in concentric squares. **2.** Professional Graphics Adapter: a video standard developed by IBM that supports 640 by 480 resolution.
⇒ See also CHIP; DIP; SIP.

PgDn key *n.* PAGE DOWN KEY.

PGP PRETTY GOOD PRIVACY.

PgUp key *n.* PAGE UP KEY.

phase change disk *n.* a type of rewritable optical disk that employs the phase change recording method. The disk drive writes data with a laser that changes spots on the disk between amorphous and crystalline states. An optical head reads data by detecting the difference in reflected light from amorphous and crystalline spots. A medium-intensity pulse can then restore the original crystalline structure.
⇒ See also MAGNETO-OPTICAL (MO) DRIVE; OPTICAL DISK; SOLID INK-JET PRINTER; WORM.

phase-change printer *n.* SOLID INK-JET PRINTER.

Phoenix BIOS *n.* a common version of the PC BIOS developed by Phoenix Corporation.
⇒ See also BIOS; CLONE.

phosphor pitch *n.* DOT PITCH.

PhotoCD *n.* a file format for storing digital photographs developed by Eastman Kodak Co.
⇒ See also PHOTO ILLUSTRATION.

photo illustration *n.* a type of computer art that begins with a digitized photograph. Using special image-enhancement software, an artist can then apply a variety of special effects.
⇒ See also IMAGE ENHANCEMENT; PHOTOCD.

photo scanner *n.* a type of high-resolution optical scanner designed for scanning photographs.
⇒ See also IMAGE ENHANCEMENT; IMAGE PROCESSING; OPTICAL SCANNER; SNAPSHOT PRINTER.

Photoshop *n.* ADOBE PHOTOSHOP.

phreaking *n.* using a computer or other device to trick a phone system. Phreaking is used to make free calls or to have calls charged to a different account.
⇒ See also CRACK; HACKER.

physical *adj.* pertaining to hardware. For example, *physical memory* refers to the actual RAM chips installed in a computer. A *physical data structure* refers to the actual organization of data on a storage device.
⇒ See also FRAGMENTATION; HARDWARE; LOGICAL; SOFTWARE; VIRTUAL MEMORY.

PIC Lotus Picture File: the graphics file format used to represent graphics generated by Lotus 1-2-3.

⇒ See also GRAPHICS; GRAPHICS FILE FORMATS; LOTUS 1-2-3.

pica *n.* in typesetting, a unit of measurement equal to 1/6 of an inch, or 12 points.
⇒ See also POINT.

PICT file format *n.* a file format developed by Apple Computer in 1984. PICT files are encoded in QuickDraw commands and can hold both object-oriented images and bit-mapped images.
⇒ See also GRAPHICS; GRAPHICS FILE FORMATS; MACINTOSH COMPUTER; OBJECT ORIENTED; QUICKDRAW.

pie chart *n.* a type of presentation graphic in which percentage values are represented as proportionally sized slices of a pie.
⇒ See also PRESENTATION GRAPHICS.

PIF *n.* program information file: a type of file that holds information about how Windows should run a non-Windows application. These instructions can include the amount of memory to use, the path to the executable file, and what type of window to use.
⇒ See also DOS; EXECUTABLE FILE; WINDOWS.

PIM (*usually pronounced as separate letters*), *n.* personal information manager: a type of software application designed to help users organize random bits of information. Most PIMs are used to enter various kinds of textual notes—reminders, lists, dates—and to link this information in useful ways. Many PIMs also include calendar, scheduling, and calculator programs.
⇒ See also CALCULATOR; CALENDAR; CONTACT MANAGER; SCHEDULER.

pin *n.* **1.** in dot-matrix printers, the device that presses on the ink ribbon to make dots on the paper. Dot-matrix printers can have anywhere from 9 to 24 pins. A 24-pin printer can produce letter-quality print. **2.** a male lead on a connector. **3.** one of an array of thin metal feet (pins) on the underside of silicon chips that enables them to be attached to a circuit board.
⇒ See also CHIP; CONNECTOR; DOT-MATRIX PRINTER; LETTER QUALITY (LQ); NEAR LETTER QUALITY; PINOUT; PRINTER.

pincushion distortion *n.* a common type of distortion in CRT monitors in which horizontal and vertical lines bend inward toward the center of the display. The opposite of pincushion distortion is *barrel distortion*, in which horizontal and vertical lines bend outward toward the edge of the display. A third type of distortion, called *trapezoid distortion*, occurs when vertical lines are straight but not parallel with one another.
⇒ See also CRT; DEGAUSS; DISPLAY SCREEN; MONITOR.

pincushioning *n.* See under PINCUSHION DISTORTION.

PINE (pīn), *n.* pine is not elm (or Program for Internet News and E-Mail): a character-based e-mail client for UNIX systems. Developed at the University of Washington, PINE replaces an older e-mail program called *elm*.
⇒ See also E-MAIL CLIENT.

pin feed *n.* TRACTOR FEED.

PING Packet Internet Groper: a utility to determine whether a specific IP address is accessible. It works by sending a packet to the specified address and waiting for a reply.
⇒ See also HOP; ICMP; IP ADDRESS; SMURF; TRACEROUTE.

pin grid array *n.* See PGA.

pinout *n.* a diagram or table that describes the purpose of each pin in a chip or connector, or each wire in a cable.
⇒ See also CHIP; CONNECTOR; PIN.

PIO Programmed Input/Output: a method of transferring data between two devices that uses the computer's main processor as part of the data path.
⇒ See also ATA; DATA TRANSFER RATE.

pipe *n.* a temporary software connection between two programs or commands. Sometimes it is useful to use the output from one command as the input for a second command, without passing the data through the keyboard or display screen. Pipes were invented for these situations.
⇒ See also INPUT; OUTPUT.

pipeline *n.* See under PIPELINING.

pipeline burst *n.* See under PIPELINE BURST CACHE.

pipeline burst cache *n.* a type of memory cache built into many DRAM controller and chipset designs. Pipeline burst caches use two techniques—a burst mode that pre-accesses memory contents before they are requested, and pipelining, so that one memory value can be accessed in the cache at the same time that another memory value is accessed in DRAM.
⇒ See also BEDO DRAM; BURST MODE; CACHE; DRAM; PIPELINING; SDRAM; WAIT STATE.

pipeline processing *n.* See under PIPELINING.

pipelining *n.* **1.** a technique used in advanced microprocessors where the microprocessor begins executing a second instruction before the first has been completed. When a segment of the pipeline completes an operation, it passes the result to the next segment and fetches the next operation from the preceding segment. The final results of each instruction emerge at the end of the pipeline in rapid succession. **2.** a similar technique used in DRAM, in which the memory loads the requested memory contents into a small cache composed of SRAM and then immediately begins accessing the next memory contents.
⇒ See also INTEL MICROPROCESSORS; MICROPROCESSOR; PIPELINE BURST CACHE; RISC; SUPERSCALAR.

piracy *n.* SOFTWARE PIRACY.

pitch *n.* **1.** (for fixed-pitch fonts) the number of characters printed per inch. Pitch is one characteristic of a monospaced font. Common pitch values are 10 and 12. **2.** in graphics, *dot pitch* refers to the spacing between pixels on a monitor. The smaller the dot pitch, the sharper the image.
⇒ See also CPI; DOT PITCH; FIXED PITCH; FONT; MONITOR; PROPORTIONAL SPACING.

pixel *n.* Picture Element: a single point in a graphic image. Graphics monitors display pictures by dividing the display screen into thousands (or millions) of pixels, arranged in rows and columns. The pixels are so close together that they appear connected. The quality of a display system largely depends on its resolution, how many pixels it can display, and how many bits are used to represent each pixel.
⇒ See also ALPHA CHANNEL; CONVERGENCE; GRAPHICS; GRAY SCALING; MONITOR; RESOLUTION; TRUE COLOR.

PKI public-key infrastructure: a system of digital certificates, Certificate Authorities, and other registration authorities that verify and authenticate the validity of each party involved in an Internet transaction.
⇒ See also CERTIFICATE AUTHORITY; ELECTRONIC COMMERCE.

PKZIP *n.* a widely used file compression method. Files that have been compressed using PKWARE are said to be *zipped*. Decompressing them is called *unzipping*.
⇒ See also DATA COMPRESSION; SHAREWARE; TAR; ZIP.

plain text *n.* **1.** textual data in ASCII format. Plain text is supported by nearly every application on every machine, regardless of operating system. It is quite limited, however, because it cannot contain any formatting commands. **2.** (in cryptography) any message that is not encrypted.
⇒ See also ASCII FILE; CIPHER TEXT; ENCRYPTION.

plasma display *n.* a type of flat-panel display that works by sandwiching an ionized gas between two wired panels. In one panel the wires are in vertical rows, and in the other they are in horizontal rows. The two panels form a grid. An individual pixel can then be charged by passing a current through the appropriate *x*-coordinate and *y*-coordinate wires. When the gas is charged, it glows a bright orange. Plasma displays are not often used today.
⇒ See also FLAT-PANEL DISPLAY; PIXEL.

platform *n.* the underlying hardware or software for a system. For example, the platform might be an Intel 80486 processor running DOS Version 6.0. Once the platform has been defined, software developers can produce appropriate software and managers can purchase appropriate hardware and applications. The term *cross-platform* refers to applications,

formats, or devices that work on different platforms.
⇒ See also ENVIRONMENT; PPCP; SDK.

platter *n.* a round magnetic plate that constitutes part of a hard disk. Hard disks typically contain up to a dozen platters. Most platters require two read/write heads, one for each side.
⇒ See also HARD DISK.

PLD Programmable Logic Device: an integrated circuit that can be programmed in a laboratory to perform complex functions. A PLD consists of arrays of AND and OR gates. A system designer implements a logic design with a device programmer that blows fuses on the PLD to control gate operation.
⇒ See also CHIP; INTEGRATED CIRCUIT; PROM.

plot *v.t.* to produce (an image) by drawing lines. A computer can be programmed to plot images on a display screen or on paper.
⇒ See also PLOTTER.

plotter *n.* a device that draws pictures on paper based on commands from a computer. Plotters draw lines using a pen and can produce continuous lines. In general, plotters are considerably more expensive than printers. They are used in engineering applications, where precision is mandatory.
⇒ See also CAD; PRINTER.

plug *n.* a connector used to link devices.
⇒ See also CONNECTOR.

plug-and-play *adj.* denoting a computer system's ability to configure expansion boards and other devices automatically. Since the introduction of the NuBus, the Apple Macintosh has been a plug-and-play computer. The Plug and Play (PnP) specification has made PCs more plug-and-play.
⇒ See also HOT PLUGGING; IEEE 1394; PnP; SCAM.

plug-compatible *adj.* able to replace another product without any alterations. Two devices are plug-compatible if either one can be plugged into the same interface. The term is sometimes used to describe software modules that interface with an application in the same way.
⇒ See also COMPATIBLE; EXPANSION BOARD.

plug-in *n.* a hardware or software module that adds a specific feature or service to a larger system.
⇒ See also COMPONENT SOFTWARE; MODULAR ARCHITECTURE; SHOCKWAVE.

PMS PANTONE MATCHING SYSTEM (PMS).

PNG (ping), *n.* Portable Network Graphics: a new bit-mapped graphics format similar to GIF. In contrast to GIF, PNG is completely patent- and license-free.
⇒ See also BIT-MAPPED GRAPHICS; GIF; LZW.

PnP Plug and Play: a technology developed by Microsoft and Intel that supports plug-and-play installation.
⇒ See also BIOS; ESCD; EXPANSION BOARD; PLUG-AND-PLAY; SCAM.

point *v.i.* **1.** to move the pointer on a display screen to select an item. Graphical user interfaces are often called *point-and-click* interfaces because a user typically points to an object on the screen and then clicks a button on the mouse. —*n.* **2.** in typography, 1/72 of an inch used to measure the height of characters. The height of the characters is one characteristic of fonts.
⇒ See also FONT; GRAPHICAL USER INTERFACE; LEADING; MOUSE; POINTER; SCALABLE FONT.

PointCast *n.* a company founded in 1992 to deliver news and other information over Internet connections.
⇒ See also CDF; PUSH; WEBCASTING.

pointer *n.* **1.** in graphical user interfaces, a small arrow or other symbol on the display screen that moves as the mouse is moved. Commands and options are selected by positioning the tip of the arrow over the desired choice and clicking a mouse button. **2.** in programming, a special type of variable that holds a memory address (that is, it *points* to a memory location).
⇒ See also ADDRESS; GRAPHICAL USER INTERFACE; I-BEAM POINTER; VARIABLE.

pointing device *n.* a device with which a user can control the movement of the pointer to select items on a display screen. Examples include mice,

trackballs, joysticks, touchpads, and light pens.
⇒ See also INPUT DEVICE; JOYSTICK; LIGHT PEN; MOUSE; POINTER; POINTING STICK; PUCK; TOUCHPAD; TRACKBALL.

pointing stick *n.* a pointing device first developed by IBM for its notebook computers. It consists of a miniature joystick, usually with a rubber eraser-head tip, positioned somewhere between the keys on the keyboard.
⇒ See also JOYSTICK; POINTING DEVICE; TRACKBALL.

Point of Presence *n.* See POP.

Point-to-Point Protocol *n.* See PPP.

Point-to-Point Tunneling Protocol *n.* See PPTP.

polling *n.* making continual requests for data from another device. For example, modems that support polling can call another system and request data.
⇒ See also MODEM.

polyline *n.* in computer graphics, a continuous line composed of one or more line segments.
⇒ See also DRAW PROGRAM.

polymorphism *n.* in object-oriented programming, a programming language's ability to process objects differently, depending on their data type or class. For example, given a base class *shape*, polymorphism enables the programmer to define different *circumference* methods for any number of derived classes, such as circles and triangles. Polymorphism is considered to be a requirement of any true object-oriented programming language (OOPL).
⇒ See also CLASS; DATA TYPE; OBJECT-ORIENTED PROGRAMMING; OVERLOADING.

POP or **pop 1.** Post Office Protocol: a protocol used to retrieve e-mail from a mail server. The first version, called *POP2*, became a standard in the mid-1980s and requires SMTP to send messages. The newer version, *POP3*, can be used with or without SMTP. **2.** Point of Presence: a telephone number that gives a user dial-up access. Internet service providers (ISPs) generally provide many POPs so that users can make a local call to gain Internet access.
⇒ See also DIAL-UP ACCESS; DIAL-UP NETWORKING; E-MAIL; IMAP; SMTP; SNMP.

pop *v.t.* to pull (an item) off a stack of items. Although originally coined to describe manipulation of data stacks, the term is often used in connection with popping a display window so that it is the topmost window.
⇒ See also POP-UP WINDOW; PUSH; WINDOW.

POP3 See under POP.

pop-up menu *n.* a menu that appears temporarily when the user clicks the mouse button on a selection.
⇒ See also MENU.

pop-up utility *n.* a program installed to be memory resident. When the hot key is pressed, the pop-up utility appears, regardless of which application is currently running.
⇒ See also HOT KEY; MEMORY RESIDENT; TSR.

pop-up window *n.* a window that suddenly appears when a user selects an option with a mouse or presses a special function key. Usually, the pop-up window contains a menu of commands and stays on the screen only until one of the commands is selected.
⇒ See also GRAPHICAL USER INTERFACE; PULL-DOWN MENU; WINDOW.

port *n.* **1.** an interface on a computer to which a device can be connected. Internally, there are several ports for connecting disk drives, display screens, and keyboards. Externally, there are ports for connecting modems, printers, mice, and other peripheral devices. **2.** in TCP/IP and UDP networks, an endpoint to a logical connection. The port number identifies the type of port. —*v.t.* **3.** to move (a program) from one type of computer to another. Sections that are machine dependent are rewritten, and the program is recompiled on the new computer.
⇒ See also CENTRONICS INTERFACE; COM; COMPILE; CONNECTOR; INTERFACE; MACHINE DEPENDENT; PARALLEL PORT; PORT REPLICATOR; PORTABLE; PS/2 PORT; SERIAL PORT.

portable *adj.* **1.** (of hardware) small and light-weight. Portable computers include notebook and subnotebook computers, hand-held computers, palmtops, and PDAs. **2.** (of software) having the ability to run on a variety of computers.
⇒ See also DOCKING STATION; HAND-HELD COMPUTER; MACHINE INDEPENDENT; NOTEBOOK COMPUTER; PALMTOP; PDA; POSIX; SUBNOTEBOOK COMPUTER.

Portable Document Format *n.* See PDF.

Portable Network Graphics *n.* See PNG.

portrait *adj.* referring to a vertical orientation of the paper. A page with portrait orientation, typical for letters and other text documents, is taller than it is wide. Orientation is also a characteristic of monitors.
⇒ See also LANDSCAPE; MONITOR; PRINTER.

port replicator *n.* a device containing common PC ports, such as serial and parallel ports, that plugs into a notebook computer.
⇒ See also DOCKING STATION; NOTEBOOK COMPUTER; PORT.

port-switching hub *n.* SWITCHING HUB.

POSIX (pŏ/sĭks, -zĭks), *n.* Portable Operating System Interface for UNIX: a set of IEEE and ISO standards that define an interface between programs and operating systems.
⇒ See also PORTABLE; UNIX; WINDOWS NT.

POST or **post** power-on self test: a series of diagnostic tests that run automatically when a computer is turned on. Usually the POST tests the RAM, the keyboard, and the disk drives.
⇒ See also BIOS; BOOT; POWER UP.

post *v.t.* **1.** to publish (a message) in an on-line forum or newsgroup. —*n.* **2.** a message published in an on-line forum or newsgroup.
⇒ See also FORUM; USENET.

Post Office Protocol *n.* See POP.

PostScript *n.* a page description language (PDL) developed by Adobe Systems. PostScript is primarily a language for printing documents on laser printers. It is the standard for desktop publishing because it is supported by *imagesetters*, the very-high-resolution printers used to produce camera-ready copy. PostScript is an object-oriented language, meaning that it treats images, including fonts, as collections of geometrical objects rather than as bit maps. There are three basic versions of PostScript: Level 1, Level 2, and PostScript 3.
⇒ See also DESKTOP PUBLISHING; EPS; ISP; LASER PRINTER; OBJECT-ORIENTED GRAPHICS; PAGE DESCRIPTION LANGUAGE (PDL).

PostScript 3 *n.* See under POSTSCRIPT.

POTS plain old telephone service: the standard telephone service that most homes use. The main distinctions between POTS and non-POTS services are speed and bandwidth.
⇒ See also ADSL; COMMUNICATIONS; DSVD; IAC; ISDN; K56FLEX; PBX; PSTN; X2; xDSL.

PowerBuilder *n.* one of the leading client/server development environments. PowerBuilder supports all the leading platforms.
⇒ See also CLIENT/SERVER ARCHITECTURE; INTEGRATED DEVELOPMENT ENVIRONMENT; SYBASE.

power down *v.i.* to turn a computer or other machine off.
⇒ See also POWER UP; SHUT DOWN.

power management *n.* the directing of power to different components of a system in an efficient manner. Power management is especially important for portable devices that rely on battery power.
⇒ See also ACPI; APM; BATTERY PACK.

power-on self test *n.* See POST.

PowerPC *n.* a RISC-based computer architecture developed jointly by IBM, Apple Computer, and Motorola Corporation. The name is derived from IBM's name for the architecture, *Performance Optimization With Enhanced RISC*. There are already a number of different operating systems that run on PowerPC-based computers, including the Macintosh operating system (System 7.5 and higher), Windows NT, and OS/2.
⇒ See also BeOS; CHRP; INTEL MICROPROCESSORS;

MACINTOSH COMPUTER; MICROPROCESSOR; MOTOROLA MICROPROCESSORS; PPCP; RISC.

PowerPC Platform *n.* See PPCP.

power supply *n.* the component that supplies power to a computer. Most personal computers can be plugged into standard electrical outlets. The power supply then pulls the required amount of electricity and converts the AC current to DC current. It also regulates the voltage to eliminate spikes and surges.
⇒ See also UPS; VOLTAGE REGULATOR; VRM.

power up *v.i.* to turn a computer or other machine on.
⇒ See also POST; POWER DOWN.

power user *n.* a sophisticated and experienced user of personal computers.
⇒ See also USER.

PPCP PowerPC Platform: a computer hardware specification that allows a computer to run multiple operating systems.
⇒ See also CHRP; PLATFORM; PowerPC; RISC.

ppm pages per minute: the speed of certain types of printers, particularly laser and ink-jet printers.
⇒ See also GPPM; LASER PRINTER; PRINTER.

PPP Point-to-Point Protocol: a method of connecting a computer to the Internet. PPP is more stable than the older SLIP protocol.
⇒ See also INTERNET; PPTP; PROTOCOL; SLIP.

PPTP Point-to-Point Tunneling Protocol: a technology for creating *Virtual Private Networks (VPNs)*, developed jointly by Microsoft Corporation, U.S. Robotics, and several remote-access vendor companies. A VPN is a private network of computers that uses the public Internet to connect some nodes. The Point-to-Point Tunneling Protocol (PPTP) is used to ensure that messages transmitted from one VPN node to another are secure.
⇒ See also L2TP; LAYER TWO FORWARDING; PPP; TUNNELING; VPN; WINDOWS NT.

PRAM (pē′ram′), *n.* parameter RAM: (on Macintosh computers) a small portion of RAM used to store information about the way the system is configured.
⇒ See also CONFIGURE; CONTROL PANEL; MACINTOSH COMPUTER; MEMORY; RAM.

precedence *n.* a characteristic of operators that indicates when they will be evaluated when they appear in complex expressions. Operators with high precedence are evaluated before operators with low precedence.
⇒ See also EXPRESSION; OPERAND; OPERATOR.

precision *n.* (of floating-point numbers) the number of bits used to hold the fractional part. A double-precision floating-point number uses twice as many bits as a single-precision value, so it can represent fractional quantities much more exactly.
⇒ See also DOUBLE PRECISION; FLOATING-POINT NUMBER.

preemptive multitasking *n.* a type of multitasking in which the operating system parcels out CPU time slices to each program.

prepress service bureau *n.* SERVICE BUREAU.

presentation graphics *n.* a type of business software that enables users to create highly stylized images for slide shows and reports, such as charts and graphs. Also called **business graphics.**
⇒ See also BAR CHART; GRAPHICS; LINE GRAPH; PIE CHART; SCATTER DIAGRAM; SPREADSHEET.

Pretty Good Privacy *n.* a technique for encrypting messages. It is one of the most common ways to protect messages on the Internet because it is effective, easy to use, and free.
⇒ See also CRYPTOGRAPHY; PUBLIC-KEY ENCRYPTION; RSA.

previewing *n.* in word processing, formatting a document for the printer but then displaying it on the display screen instead of printing it. Previewing shows exactly how the document will appear when printed.
⇒ See also GREEKING; THUMBNAIL; WORD PROCESSING; WYSIWYG.

primary cache *n.* L1 CACHE.

primary key *n.* a field in a database upon which records can be sorted, which—unlike other key fields in that database, upon which records can also

be sorted—holds a unique, nonduplicable value for each record.

primary storage *n.* a somewhat dated term for *main memory.* Mass storage devices, such as disk drives and tapes, are sometimes called *secondary storage.*
⇒ See also MAIN MEMORY; MASS STORAGE.

printed circuit board *n.* a thin plate on which chips and other electronic components are placed. Computers consist of one or more boards, often called *cards* or *adapters.*
⇒ See also BACKPLANE; CHIP; CONTROLLER; DAUGHTERCARD; EXPANSION BOARD; EXPANSION SLOT; FORM FACTOR; LOCAL-AREA NETWORK; MOTHERBOARD; VIDEO ADAPTER.

printer *n.* a device that prints text or illustrations on paper. There are many different types of printers.
⇒ See also BILEVEL PRINTER; DAISY-WHEEL PRINTER; DOT-MATRIX PRINTER; DRAFT QUALITY; FONT; GRAPHICS; HOST-BASED PRINTER; HP; IMPACT PRINTER; INK-JET PRINTER; LASER PRINTER; LCD; LCD PRINTER; LED; LETTER QUALITY (LQ); LINE PRINTER; MFP; NEAR LETTER QUALITY; PAGE PRINTER.

Printer Control Language *n.* See PCL.

printer driver *n.* a program that controls a printer.
⇒ See also DRIVER.

printer engine *n.* the main component of a printer that actually performs the printing. The printer engine determines how fast and at what resolution the printer can print.
⇒ See also PRINTER.

print merge *n.* MAIL MERGE.

printout *n.* a printed version of text or data. Also called **hard copy.**

Print Screen key *n.* a key on most PCs. In DOS, pressing this key causes the computer to send whatever images and text are currently on the display screen to the printer. Some graphical user interfaces, including Windows, use this key to obtain screen captures.
⇒ See also CAPTURE; HARD COPY.

print server *n.* See under SERVER.

print spooling *n.* See under SPOOLING.

procedure *n.* **1.** a section of a program that performs a specific task; a routine, subroutine, or function. **2.** an ordered set of tasks for performing some action.
⇒ See also FUNCTION; ROUTINE.

process *n.* **1.** an executing program. The term is used loosely as a synonym of *task.* —*v.t.* **2.** to perform some useful operations on (data).
⇒ See also DAEMON; TASK.

process colors *n.pl.* the CMYK color model used in offset printing.
⇒ See also CMYK; COLOR SEPARATION; OFFSET PRINTING.

processor *n.* MICROPROCESSOR.
⇒ See also CPU.

processor unit *n.* CENTRAL PROCESSING UNIT.

Prodigy *n.* an online service developed jointly by IBM and Sears.
⇒ See also ONLINE SERVICE.

program *n.* **1.** an organized list of instructions that, when executed, causes the computer to behave in a predetermined manner. A program is like a recipe. It contains a list of ingredients (called *variables*) and a list of directions (called *statements*) that tell the computer what to do with the variables. The variables can represent numeric data, text, or graphical images. —*v.t.* **2.** to write programs for (a computer).
⇒ See also ALGORITHM; ASSEMBLER; ASSEMBLY LANGUAGE; CASE; CODE; COMPILER; EXECUTABLE FILE; FLOW CONTROL; HIGH-LEVEL LANGUAGE; INSTRUCTION; INTERPRETER; LANGUAGE; LOW-LEVEL LANGUAGE; MACHINE LANGUAGE; MODULE; PROGRAMMING LANGUAGE; PSEUDOCODE; SOFTWARE.

Programmable Logic Device *n.* See PLD.

programmable read-only memory *n.* See PROM.

programmer *n.* **1.** an individual who writes programs. **2.** a device that writes a program onto a

computer

PROM chip.

⇒ See also HACKER; PROGRAM; PROM; SOFTWARE ENGINEER.

programming language *n.* a vocabulary and set of grammatical rules for instructing a computer to perform specific tasks. The term *programming language* usually refers to high-level languages. Each language has a unique set of keywords (words that it understands) and a special syntax for organizing program instructions. The choice of which language to use depends on the type of computer the program is to run on, what sort of program it is, and the expertise of the programmer.

⇒ See also ADA; ASSEMBLY LANGUAGE; AWK; BASIC; C; C++; COBOL; COMPILER; FLOW CONTROL; FORTRAN; FOURTH-GENERATION LANGUAGE; HIGH-LEVEL LANGUAGE; INTERPRETER; JAVA; LANGUAGE; LISP; LOW-LEVEL LANGUAGE; MACHINE LANGUAGE; MODULA-2; OBJECT-ORIENTED PROGRAMMING; PASCAL; PROLOG; TCL; VBSCRIPT; VISUAL BASIC.

Progress Software *n.* a leading software company in the DBMS field. Although Progress Software has its own DBMS system, it also provides tools to develop applications that can interact with any DBMS.

⇒ See also DATABASE MANAGEMENT SYSTEM.

Prolog *n.* Programming Logic: a high-level programming language based on defining and then solving logical formulas. Prolog is used for artificial intelligence applications, particularly expert systems.

⇒ See also ARTIFICIAL INTELLIGENCE; EXPERT SYSTEM; LISP; PROGRAMMING LANGUAGE.

PROM (prom), *n.* programmable read-only memory: a memory chip on which data can be written only once. PROMs retain their contents when the computer is turned off. The difference between a PROM and a ROM is that a PROM is manufactured as blank memory, whereas a ROM is programmed during the manufacturing process. The process of programming a PROM is sometimes called *burning* the PROM.

⇒ See also EEPROM; EPROM; MAIN MEMORY; MEMORY; PLD; ROM.

prompt *n.* a symbol on a display screen indicating that the computer is waiting for input.

⇒ See also TIME-OUT.

property *n.* a characteristic of an object. In many programming languages, the term is used to describe attributes associated with a data structure.

⇒ See also ATTRIBUTE.

proportional font *n.* a font in which different characters have different *pitches* (widths). Also called **proportional-pitch font.**

⇒ See also FIXED PITCH; FONT; PITCH; PROPORTIONAL SPACING.

proportional pitch *adj.* proportionally spaced. See under PROPORTIONAL SPACING.

proportional spacing *n.* the use of different widths for different characters. In a proportionally spaced font, the letter *i* is narrower than the letter *q*, and the letter *m* is wider. Most books, magazines, and newspapers use a proportionally spaced font.

⇒ See also CPI; FIXED PITCH; FONT; MONOSPACING; PITCH.

proprietary *adj.* privately owned and controlled. A proprietary design or technique is one that is owned by a company; it implies that the company has not divulged specifications. Consumers prefer open and standardized architectures, which allow them to mix and match products from different manufacturers.

⇒ See also ARCHITECTURE; OPEN ARCHITECTURE; STANDARD.

protected mode *n.* a type of memory utilization available on Intel 80286 and later-model microprocessors. In protected mode, these processors provide the following features: **protection** (each program is allocated a section of memory, so it is protected from interference), **extended memory, virtual memory,** and **multitasking.**

⇒ See also DOS; EXTENDED MEMORY; INTEL MICROPROCESSORS; MICROSOFT WINDOWS; MULTITASKING; OS/2; UNIX; VIRTUAL MEMORY.

protocol *n.* an agreed-upon format for transmitting data between two devices. There are a variety of standard protocols from which programmers can choose. From a user's point of view, the computer or device must support the right protocols to communicate with other computers.

⇒ See also CCITT; COMMUNICATIONS; COMMUNICATIONS PROTOCOL; CONNECTIONLESS; HANDSHAKING; MODEM; PROTOCOL STACK.

protocol stack *n.* a set of network protocol layers that work together. The OSI Reference Model that defines seven protocol layers is often called a stack, as is the set of TCP/IP protocols that define communication over the Internet. The term *stack* also refers to the actual software that processes the protocols.

⇒ See also NETWORK INTERFACE CARD; OSI; PROTOCOL; TCP/IP; WINSOCK.

proxy *n.* See under PROXY SERVER.

proxy server *n.* a server that sits between a client application, such as a Web browser, and a real server. It intercepts all requests to the real server to see if it can fulfill the requests itself. If not, it forwards the request to the real server.

⇒ See also FIREWALL; SERVER; SOCKS; WEB SERVER.

Prt Scr key *n.* PRINT SCREEN KEY.

PS/2 port *n.* a type of port developed by IBM for connecting a mouse or keyboard to a PC.

⇒ See also PORT; SERIAL MOUSE; SERIAL PORT.

pseudocode *n.* an outline of a program, written in a form that can easily be converted into real programming statements.

⇒ See also ALGORITHM; BUBBLE SORT; CODE; PROGRAM.

PSTN Public Switched Telephone Network: the international telephone system based on copper wires carrying analog voice data. Telephone service carried by the PSTN is often called POTS.

⇒ See also CIRCUIT SWITCHING; POTS.

public carrier *n.* any of the government-regulated organizations that provide telecommunications services to the public. These include AT&T, MCI, and Western Union.

⇒ See also E-MAIL.

public-domain software *n.* any program that is not copyrighted. Public-domain software is free and can be used without restrictions.

⇒ See also FREEWARE; SHAREWARE.

public key *n.* See under PUBLIC-KEY ENCRYPTION.

public-key encryption *n.* a cryptographic system that uses two keys—a *public key* known to everyone and a *private* or *secret key* known only to the recipient of the message. Public-key systems, such as Pretty Good Privacy (PGP), are becoming popular for transmitting information via the Internet. This kind of encryption is also called *asymmetric encryption* because it uses two keys instead of one key (*symmetric encryption*).

⇒ See also CERTIFICATE AUTHORITY; CRYPTOGRAPHY; DIGITAL CERTIFICATE; DIGITAL ENVELOPE; ENCRYPTION; LDAP; PRETTY GOOD PRIVACY; RSA; S/MIME; SYMMETRIC-KEY CRYPTOGRAPHY.

public-key infrastructure *n.* See PKI.

puck *n.* CURSOR (def. 2).

⇒ See also POINTING DEVICE.

pull *v.t.* to request (data) from another program or computer. The World Wide Web is based on pull technologies, where a page is not delivered until a browser requests it. Increasingly, however, information services are harnessing the Internet to broadcast information using push technologies.

⇒ See also PUSH.

pull-down menu *n.* a menu of commands or options that appears when an item is selected with a mouse. The item selected is generally at the top of the display screen, and the menu appears just below it.

⇒ See also COMMAND; MENU; OPTION; POP-UP WINDOW.

pulse code modulation *n.* See PCM.

punctuation *n.* (in programming languages) special characters that serve to separate words and phrases. Unlike human language punctuation, which is often optional, computer punctuation is strictly required.

⇒ See also SPECIAL CHARACTER.

purge *v.t.* to remove (old and unneeded data) systematically and permanently. It is often possible to regain deleted objects by *undeleting* them, but purged objects are gone forever.

⇒ See also DELETE; RECYCLE BIN.

PURL persistent URL: a type of URL that acts as an intermediary for a real URL. When a user enters a PURL, the browser sends the page request to a PURL server, which then returns the real URL of the page. Once a PURL is established, it never needs to change.

⇒ See also URL.

push *v.t.* **1.** in client/server applications, to send

(data) to a client without the client's requesting it. Broadcast media are push technologies because they send information out regardless of whether anyone is tuned in. Increasingly, companies are using the Internet to deliver information push-style. **2.** in programming, to place (a data item) onto a stack.

⇒ See also CDF; POINTCAST; POP; PULL; WEBCASTING.

push-button *n.* a button in a dialog box. See under BUTTON.

⇒ See also DIALOG BOX.

PVC permanent virtual circuit: a virtual circuit that is permanently available. PVCs are more efficient than SVCs for connections between hosts that communicate frequently.

⇒ See also FRAME RELAY; SVC; VIRTUAL CIRCUIT.

abcdefghijklmnop QR stuvwxyz

QBASIC *n.* an interpreter for the BASIC programming language, at one time provided by Microsoft with the DOS operating system.

⇒ See also BASIC; GW-BASIC.

QBE QUERY BY EXAMPLE.

QCIF *n.* Quarter Common Intermediate Format: a videoconferencing format that specifies data rates of 30 frames per second (fps), with each frame containing 144 lines and 176 pixels per line. This is one fourth the resolution of Full CIF. QCIF support is required by the ITU H.261 videoconferencing standard.

⇒ See also COMMON INTERMEDIATE FORMAT; NTSC; PAL; VIDEOCONFERENCING.

QIC (kwik), *n.* quarter-inch cartridge: a standard for magnetic tape drives. QIC tapes are among the most popular tapes used for backing up personal computers. They are divided into two general classes: full-size (also called *data-cartridge*) and minicartridge.

⇒ See also MASS STORAGE; TAPE; TRAVAN.

QoS Quality of Service: a networking term that specifies a guaranteed throughput level.

⇒ See also ATM; CIR; LATENCY; RSVP.

QTVR QUICKTIME VR.

quad-speed CD-ROM drive *n.* a CD-ROM drive designed to run four times as fast as original models.

⇒ See also CD-ROM PLAYER.

Quality of Service *n.* See QoS.

quarter-inch cartridge *n.* See QIC.

query *n.* **1.** a request for information matching certain criteria from a database. —*v.t.* **2.** to make a request for information from (a database).

⇒ See also DATABASE MANAGEMENT SYSTEM; FIELD; QUERY BY EXAMPLE; QUERY LANGUAGE; RECORD.

query by example *n.* in database management systems, a method of forming queries in which the database program displays a blank record with a space for each field. A user can then enter conditions for each field.

⇒ See also DATABASE MANAGEMENT SYSTEM; FIELD; QUERY; QUERY LANGUAGE; RECORD.

query language *n.* a specialized language for requesting information from a database.

⇒ See also DATABASE MANAGEMENT SYSTEM; QUERY; SQL.

queue *v.t.* **1.** to line up (jobs) for a computer or device. For example, the operating system (or a print spooler) queues documents to be printed by placing them in a special area called a *print buffer* or *print queue.* —*n.* **2.** a group of jobs waiting to be executed. **3.** in programming, a data structure in which elements are removed in the same order in which they were entered. This is often referred to as FIFO (first in, first out). In contrast, a *stack* is a data structure in which elements are removed in the reverse order from which they were entered. This is referred to as LIFO (last in, first out).

⇒ See also BUFFER; DATA STRUCTURE; JOB; OPERATING SYSTEM; SPOOLING.

QuickDraw *n.* the underlying graphics display system for Apple Macintosh computers. The QuickDraw system enables programs to create and manipulate graphical objects.

⇒ See also GRAPHICS; MACINTOSH COMPUTER; PIXEL; POSTSCRIPT.

QuickTime *n.* a video and animation system developed by Apple Computer. QuickTime is built into the Macintosh operating system and is used by most Mac applications that include video or animation. PCs with appropriate software can also run files in QuickTime format.

⇒ See also ANIMATION; AVI; CINEPAK; CODEC; INDEO; MPEG; MULTIMEDIA; QUICKTIME VR.

QuickTime Virtual Reality *n.* QUICKTIME VR.

QuickTime VR *n.* an enhanced version of the QuickTime standard developed by Apple for displaying multimedia content. This enhanced version allows a user to move through a three-dimensional scene.

⇒ See also QUICKTIME; VIRTUAL REALITY; VRML.

quit *v.t.* to exit (a program) in an orderly way.

⇒ See also ABORT.

QWERTY keyboard (kwûr′tē, kwer′-), *n.* a standard English computer or typewriter keyboard layout. The name derives from the first six characters on the top alphabetic line of the keyboard.

⇒ See also DVORAK KEYBOARD; KEYBOARD.

RAD *n.* RAPID APPLICATION DEVELOPMENT.

radio buttons *n.pl.* in graphical user interfaces, groups of buttons, of which only one can be on at a time.

⇒ See also BUTTON; CHECK BOX; GRAPHICAL USER INTERFACE; SELECT.

RADIUS *n.* Remote Authentication Dial-In User Service: an authentication and accounting system used by many Internet service providers (ISPs).

⇒ See also AUTHENTICATION; DIAL-UP ACCESS; ISP.

ragged *adj.* in text processing, not aligned along a margin, esp. the right margin.

⇒ See also FLUSH; JUSTIFY.

RAID *n.* Redundant Array of Independent (or Inexpensive) Disks: a category of disk subsystems that employ two or more drives in combination for fault tolerance and performance, used frequently on servers.

⇒ See also DISK DRIVE; DISK MIRRORING; DISK STRIPING; FAULT TOLERANCE.

RAM (ram), *n.* random-access memory: a type of computer memory that can be accessed randomly; that is, any byte of memory can be accessed without touching adjacent bytes. RAM is the most common type of memory found in computers and other devices.

⇒ See also DYNAMIC RAM; MAIN MEMORY; MEMORY; NVRAM; ROM; SRAM; TAG RAM; VRAM; WRAM.

Rambus memory *n.* See RDRAM.

RAM cache *n.* **1.** L2 CACHE. **2.** on Apple Macintosh computers, a disk cache.

⇒ See also CACHE; DISK CACHE; L2 CACHE.

computer

RAMDAC (ram′dak′), *n.* Random Access Memory Digital-to-Analog Converter: a chip on video adapter cards that converts digitally encoded images into analog signals that can be displayed by a monitor.
⇒ See also DAC; MONITOR; VIDEO ADAPTER; VIDEO MEMORY.

RAM disk or **drive** *n.* RAM that has been configured to simulate a disk drive. Faster than hard disk drives, RAM disks are useful for applications that require frequent disk access.
⇒ See also DISK; EXTENDED MEMORY; RAM.

RAM resident *n.* MEMORY RESIDENT.

random access *n.* the ability to access data at random. Disks are effectively random-access media; tape drives are not. A random-access data file enables users to read or write information anywhere in the file.
⇒ See also ACCESS; RAM; SEQUENTIAL ACCESS.

random-access memory *n.* See RAM.

range *n.* in spreadsheet applications, one or more contiguous cells. For example, a range could be an entire row or column, or multiple rows or columns.
⇒ See also CELL; EXPRESSION; FUNCTION; SPREADSHEET.

rapid application development *n.* a programming system that enables programmers to build working programs quickly. Among other things, RAD systems provide tools to help build graphical user interfaces.
⇒ See also DELPHI; PROGRAMMING LANGUAGE; VISUAL BASIC.

RAS Remote Access Services: a feature built into Windows NT that enables users to log into an NT-based LAN using a modem, X.25 connection, or WAN link.
⇒ See also DIAL-UP NETWORKING; REMOTE ACCESS; REMOTE CONTROL; WINDOWS NT.

raster *n.* the rectangular area in which images are displayed on a monitor or LCD display.
⇒ See also AUTOSIZING; BIT-MAPPED GRAPHICS; DISPLAY SCREEN; MONITOR; RASTER IMAGE PROCESSOR; RESOLUTION.

raster graphics *n.* BIT-MAPPED GRAPHICS.

raster image processor *n.* a hardware-software combination that converts a vector image into a bit-mapped image, often for printing.
⇒ See also BIT MAP; POSTSCRIPT; RASTER; VECTOR GRAPHICS.

raw data *n.* information that has not been organized, formatted, or analyzed.
⇒ See also DATA.

ray tracing *n.* in computer graphics, an advanced technique for adding realism to an image.
⇒ See also 3-D GRAPHICS; GRAPHICS; TEXTURE.

RDBMS relational database management system: a type of database management system (DBMS) that stores data in the form of related tables. Relational databases are powerful because they require few assumptions about how data is related or how it will be extracted from the database. As a result, the same data can be viewed in many different ways.
⇒ See also BORLAND INTERNATIONAL; DATABASE; DATABASE MANAGEMENT SYSTEM; DB2; FLAT-FILE DATABASE; MULTIDIMENSIONAL DBMS; NORMALIZATION; QUERY; REFERENTIAL INTEGRITY; SQL SERVER.

RDRAM *n.* Rambus DRAM: a type of memory (DRAM) developed by Rambus, Inc. RDRAM can transfer data at up to 600 MHz, much faster than SDRAM.
⇒ See also DRAM; EDO DRAM; MEMORY; SDRAM; VIDEO MEMORY.

read *v.t.* **1.** to copy (data) to a place where it can be used by a program. The term is commonly used to describe copying data from a storage medium, such as a disk, to main memory. —*n.* **2.** the act of reading: *A fast disk drive performs 100 reads per second.*
⇒ See also ACCESS.

readme file *n.* a small text file that comes with many software packages and contains information not included in other documentation.
⇒ See also DOCUMENTATION.

read-only *adj.* capable of being displayed, but not modified or deleted. All operating systems allow users to protect disks, files, and directories with a

read-only attribute that prevents other users from modifying them.
⇒ See also ATTRIBUTE; CD-ROM; READ/WRITE; ROM.

read-only memory *n.* See ROM.

read/write *adj.* capable of being displayed (read) and modified (written to). Most disks, files, and directories are read/write, but operating systems also allow users to prevent other users from modifying them.
⇒ See also READ-ONLY.

read/write head *n.* HEAD.

real address *n.* ABSOLUTE ADDRESS.

RealAudio *n.* the de facto standard for streaming audio data over the World Wide Web. A RealAudio player or plug-in program is needed to hear a RealAudio sound file.
⇒ See also REALVIDEO; STREAMING.

real mode *n.* an execution mode supported by the Intel 80286 and later processors. In real mode, these processors imitate the Intel 8088 and 8086 microprocessors, although they run much faster.
⇒ See also DOS; INTEL MICROPROCESSORS; MICROSOFT WINDOWS; MULTITASKING; OS/2; PROTECTED MODE.

real time *adj.* describing immediate response by a computer system. Most general-purpose operating systems are not real-time because they can take a few seconds, or even minutes, to react to input. *Real time* can also refer to events simulated by a computer at the same speed that they would occur in real life.
⇒ See also ISOCHRONOUS; OPERATING SYSTEM; OS/9.

real-time clock *n.* a clock that keeps track of the time even when the computer is turned off.
⇒ See also CLOCK SPEED.

Real Time Streaming Protocol *n.* See RTSP.

Real-Time Transport Protocol *n.* See RTP.

RealVideo *n.* a streaming technology for transmitting live video over the Internet.
⇒ See also IP MULTICAST; REALAUDIO; STREAMING.

reboot *v.t., v.i.* to restart (a computer), as by pressing the Alt, Control, and Delete keys simultaneously or by turning the computer off and then on again. On Macs, the user reboots by selecting the "Restart" option from the Special menu or pushing the reset button.
⇒ See also BOOT.

recalculation *n.* in spreadsheet programs, the computing of the values of cells in a spreadsheet. Recalculation is necessary whenever a formula is changed or new data is entered into one or more cells.
⇒ See also AUTOMATIC RECALCULATION; BACKGROUND; CELL; FORMULA; SPREADSHEET.

record *n.* **1.** in database management systems, a complete set of information. Records are composed of *fields*, each of which contains one item of information. A set of records constitutes a *file*. **2.** in some programming languages, a special data structure. Generally, a record is a combination of other data objects.
⇒ See also DATA STRUCTURE; DATA TYPE; DATABASE; DATABASE MANAGEMENT SYSTEM; FIELD; FILE.

record locking *n.* See under LOCK.

recursion *n.* a programming method in which a routine calls itself.
⇒ See also PROGRAM; PROGRAMMING LANGUAGE.

Recycle Bin *n.* an icon on the Windows 95 and Windows 98 desktops that represents a directory where deleted files are temporarily stored.
⇒ See also DELETE.

Red Book *n.* the standard for audio CDs, developed by Philips and Sony.
⇒ See also CD-ROM; COMPACT DISC; GREEN BOOK; ORANGE BOOK; WHITE BOOK.

red-green-blue monitor *n.* RGB MONITOR.

redirection *n.* the diversion of input and output to files and devices other than the default I/O devices (usually the keyboard and screen respectively).
⇒ See also DEFAULT; DEVICE; FILE; I/O; OPERATING SYSTEM; SHELL; UNIX.

redlining *n.* in word processing, the marking of text that has been edited, as with a change in font or color, to enable the next person in the editorial

process to track changes.
⇒ See also WORD PROCESSING.

reduced instruction set computer n. See RISC.

Redundant Array of Independent Disks n. See RAID.

referential integrity n. a feature of relational database management systems (RDBMSs) that prevents users or applications from entering inconsistent data.
⇒ See also KEY; NORMALIZATION; RDBMS.

refresh v.t. **1.** generally, to update (something) with new data. For example, some Web browsers have a refresh button that updates the currently displayed Web pages. **2.** to recharge (a device) with power or information. For example, *dynamic RAM* needs to be refreshed thousands of times per second. Similarly, display monitors must be refreshed many times per second. The faster this refresh rate, the less the monitor flickers.
⇒ See also DYNAMIC RAM; INTERLACING; MONITOR; SCREEN FLICKER.

refresh rate n. See under REFRESH.

register n. **1.** a special high-speed storage area within the CPU. All data must be represented in a register before it can be processed. —v.i., v.t. **2.** to notify the manufacturer after purchasing (a product). Registering a product is often a prerequisite to receiving customer support, and it is one of the ways that software producers control software piracy.
⇒ See also CPU; MICROPROCESSOR; SOFTWARE PIRACY.

Registry n. a database used by the Windows operating system (Windows 95, 98, and NT) to store configuration information.
⇒ See also CONFIGURATION; WINDOWS 95.

relational database n. See RDBMS.

relational expression n. RELATIONAL OPERATOR.

relational operator n. an operator that compares two values. For example, the expression x < 5 means x *is less than 5*. This expression will have a value of TRUE if the variable x is less than 5; otherwise the value will be FALSE.
⇒ See also BOOLEAN LOGIC; EXPRESSION; OPERATOR.

relative address n. an address specified by indicating its distance from another address, called the *base address*.
⇒ See also ABSOLUTE ADDRESS; ADDRESS; BASE ADDRESS; CELL; MEMORY; OFFSET.

relative cell reference n. in spreadsheet applications, a reference to a cell or group of cells by indicating how far away it is from some other cell. For example, the cell reference "C2" points to the cell in the third column and second row. If this reference is inserted in cell A1, the program can translate it to "2 columns right and 1 row down."
⇒ See also ABSOLUTE CELL REFERENCE; CELL; SPREADSHEET.

remote adj. in networks, referring to files, devices, and other resources that are not connected directly to a workstation.
⇒ See also LOCAL; LOCAL-AREA NETWORK; NETWORK; REMOTE ACCESS; REMOTE CONTROL SOFTWARE; WORKSTATION.

remote access n. the ability to log onto a network from a distant location either by telephone or by an internetwork connection. The remote computer becomes a full-fledged host on the network.
⇒ See also RAS; REMOTE; REMOTE CONTROL.

remote control n. a program's ability to control a computer system from a remote location. Only keystrokes and screen updates are transmitted between the two machines as all processing takes place in the controlled computer.
⇒ See also HOST; LOCAL; RAS; REMOTE; REMOTE ACCESS; REMOTE CONTROL SOFTWARE.

remote control software n. software, installed in both machines, that allows a user at a local computer to have control of a remote computer via modem or other connection.
⇒ See also HOST; REMOTE CONTROL.

remote procedure call n. See RPC.

removable cartridge n. REMOVABLE HARD DISK.

removable drive n. REMOVABLE HARD DISK.

removable hard disk n. a type of disk drive system in which hard disks are enclosed in plastic or metal cartridges so that they can be inserted into and removed from an accessible drive bay like floppy disks.
⇒ See also CARTRIDGE; DISK; DISK PACK; HARD DISK; JAZ DRIVE; MASS STORAGE.

render v.t. to create (a computer graphics image) from a file containing descriptions of the objects in a scene.
⇒ See also 3-D GRAPHICS; 3-D SOFTWARE; CAD/CAM; MODELING; RAY TRACING; TEXTURE.

repaginate v.i. to recalculate page breaks. Most systems automatically repaginate whenever a document is modified.
⇒ See also ORPHAN; PAGE BREAK; WIDOW.

repeater n. a network device used to regenerate or replicate a signal. Repeaters are used to regenerate signals distorted by transmission loss.
⇒ See also 10BASET; BRIDGE; HUB; ROUTER.

replace v.t. to insert (a new object) in place of an existing object.
⇒ See also SEARCH AND REPLACE.

replication n. the process of creating and managing duplicate versions of a database. Replication enables many users to work with their own local copy of a database but have the database updated as if they were working on a single, centralized database.
⇒ See also DATABASE; LOTUS NOTES.

report n. a formatted and organized presentation of data.
⇒ See also REPORT WRITER; RPG.

report generator n. REPORT WRITER.

report writer n. a program, usually part of a database management system, that extracts information from one or more files and presents the information in a specified format.
⇒ See also DATABASE MANAGEMENT SYSTEM; FIELD; RECORD; REPORT; RPG.

Request for Comments n. See RFC.

reserved word n. a special word reserved by a programming language or by a program. Reserved words cannot be used as variable names.
⇒ See also KEYWORD; VARIABLE.

reset button n. a button or switch that is used to reset the computer. The computer will enter its start-up procedure as if the power had been turned off and then on again. Generally, the reset button is used only when a program error has caused the computer to hang.
⇒ See also BOOT; HANG; REBOOT.

resident adj. **1.** permanently available to a user, as a font in a printer's ROM or software on a CD-ROM. **2.** of a computer program, currently in RAM.

resident font n. a font built into the hardware of a printer. Additional fonts can be added by inserting font cartridges or downloading soft fonts.
⇒ See also DOWNLOAD; FONT; FONT CARTRIDGE; PRINTER; SOFT FONT.

resize v.t. SIZE.

resolution n. the sharpness and clarity of an image. The term is most often used to describe the potential performance of given monitors and printers, and the achieved fineness of bit-mapped graphic images. Printers, monitors, scanners, and other I/O devices are often classified as *high resolution, medium resolution,* or *low resolution*.
⇒ See also BIT MAP; DPI; MONITOR; OPTICAL RESOLUTION; PIXEL; PRINTER; RASTER; VIDEO ADAPTER.

resolution enhancement n. a collection of techniques used in many laser printers to enable the printer to print at a higher resolution than normal.
⇒ See also LASER PRINTER; PRINTER ENGINE; RESOLUTION.

resource n. **1.** generally, any item that can be used, such as memory or a disk drive. **2.** in an operating system, a routine or data available to a program.

Resource Reservation Setup Protocol n. See RSVP.

restore v.t. in graphical user interfaces, to return (a window) to its original size.
⇒ See also GRAPHICAL USER INTERFACE; SIZE; WINDOW; ZOOM.

return *n.* a special code that marks the end of a line.
⇒ See also CARRIAGE RETURN; HARD RETURN; RETURN KEY; SOFT RETURN.

Return key *n.* a key marked *Return* or *Enter*: in text entry, this key moves the cursor (or insertion point) to the beginning of the next line. During other program activity, pressing the Return key may signal that the program's requests for information from the user have been responded to, thus returning control to the program. In word-processing programs, pressing the Return key inserts a hard return into a document.
⇒ See also CURSOR; ENTER KEY; HARD RETURN; INSERTION POINT; KEYBOARD; PROMPT.

reverse engineering *n.* the process of recreating a software or hardware design by analyzing a final product.
⇒ See also SOFTWARE ENGINEER.

reverse video *n.* a display method that causes a portion of the display to appear like a negative of the regular display. If the display screen normally displays light images against a dark background, *reverse video mode* will cause it to display dark images against a light background.
⇒ See also BACKGROUND; DISPLAY SCREEN; FOREGROUND.

RFC Request for Comments: a series of notes about the Internet. An RFC can be submitted by anyone. If it gains enough interest, it may evolve into an Internet standard.
⇒ See also IETF; INTERNET ARCHITECTURE BOARD.

RGB monitor *n.* red, green, blue monitor: a monitor that requires separate signals for each of the three colors. This differs from color televisions, in which all the colors are mixed together. Almost all color computer monitors are RGB monitors.
⇒ See also COLOR MONITOR; COMPOSITE VIDEO; CONVERGENCE; MASK PITCH; MONITOR; S-VIDEO.

rich text format *n.* a standard developed by Microsoft Corporation for specifying formatting of documents. *Abbr.:* RTF
⇒ See also HTML; SGML; WORLD WIDE WEB.

right justify *v.t.* to align (text) along the right margin.

ring network *n.* a local-area network (LAN) whose topology is a ring; all of the nodes are connected in a closed loop.
⇒ See also BUS NETWORK; LOCAL-AREA NETWORK; TOKEN-RING NETWORK; TOPOLOGY.

RIP (rip) *n.* **1.** RASTER IMAGE PROCESSOR **2.** ROUTING INFORMATION PROTOCOL.

RISC (risk), *n.* reduced instruction set computer: a type of microprocessor that recognizes a relatively limited number of instructions. One advantage of RISC computers is that they can execute their instructions very fast. Another advantage is that RISC chips require fewer transistors.
⇒ See also ALPHA PROCESSOR; CISC; CPU; INSTRUCTION; MICROPROCESSOR; SPARC.

RJ-11 Registered Jack-11: a four- or six-wire modular connector used primarily to connect telephone equipment in the United States.
⇒ See also MODEM; RJ-45.

RJ-45 Registered Jack-45: an eight-wire modular connector used commonly to connect computers to local-area networks (LANs), especially Ethernets.
⇒ See also 10BASET; CONNECTOR; RJ-11.

RJ45 See RJ-45.

RLL run length limited: an encoding scheme used to store data on newer PC hard disks. RLL produces fast data access times and increases a disk's storage capacity over the older MFM encoding.
⇒ See also DISK DRIVE; MFM.

RMI a set of protocols being developed by Sun's JavaSoft division that enables Java objects to communicate remotely with other Java objects.
⇒ See also CORBA; DCOM; JAVA.

RMON remote monitoring: a network management protocol that allows network information to be gathered from a single workstation.
⇒ See also NETWORK MANAGEMENT; SNMP.

robot *n.* **1.** a device that can move and respond to sensory input. **2.** a program that runs automatically

on a networked computer, without human intervention.
⇒ See also ROBOTICS; SPIDER.

robotics *n.* the field of computer science and engineering concerned with creating robots, devices that can move and react to sensory input. Robotics is one branch of artificial intelligence.
⇒ See also ARTIFICIAL INTELLIGENCE; CAM; CYBERNETICS.

ROM (rom), *n.* read-only memory: computer memory on which data have been prerecorded. ROM retains its contents even when the computer is turned off; it is nonvolatile. Most personal computers contain a small amount of ROM that stores critical low-level programs. ROM is used extensively in calculators and peripheral devices such as laser printers.
⇒ See also BIOS; BOOT; EEPROM; FIRMWARE; MEMORY; PROM; RAM.

roman *adj.* referring to fonts with characters whose ascending and descending parts are straight up and down rather than slanted.
⇒ See also FONT; ITALIC.

ROM-BIOS *n.* See BIOS.

root directory *n.* the top directory in a file system. The root directory is provided by the operating system and has a special name; for example, in DOS systems the root directory is given the name of the backslash character (\).
⇒ See also DIRECTORY; FILE MANAGEMENT SYSTEM; HIERARCHICAL.

router *n.* a device that connects two or more networks. Routers are similar to the bridges that connect LANs but provide additional functionality, such as the ability to filter messages and forward them to different places. The Internet uses routers to forward packets from one host to another.
⇒ See also 3COM; BGP; BRIDGE; BROUTER; GATEWAY; HOP; INTERNETWORKING; IP SPOOFING; IP SWITCHING; OSPF; PACKET; REPEATER; ROUTING; ROUTING INFORMATION PROTOCOL; ROUTING SWITCH.

routine *n.* a section of a program that performs a particular task. Also called **procedure, function, subroutine.**
⇒ See also FUNCTION; MODULE; PROGRAM.

routing *n.* in internetworking, the process of moving a packet of data from source to destination. Routing is a key feature of the Internet. Part of this process involves analyzing a *routing table* to determine the best path.
⇒ See also BGP; BRIDGING; CIDR; IP ADDRESS; IP SWITCHING; OSPF; PACKET; ROUTER; ROUTING INFORMATION PROTOCOL; ROUTING SWITCH.

Routing Information Protocol *n.* a protocol defined by RFC 1058 that specifies how routers exchange routing table information. *Abbr.:* RIP
⇒ See also OSPF; ROUTER; ROUTING.

routing switch *n.* a switch that also performs routing operations. Routing switches perform many of the layer 3 (Network layer) functions usually reserved for routers.
⇒ See also IP SWITCHING; ROUTER; ROUTING; SWITCH.

RPC remote procedure call: a type of protocol that allows a program on one computer to execute a program on another computer.
⇒ See also API; CORBA; MIDDLEWARE; PROTOCOL; REMOTE.

RPG **1.** Report Program Generator: a programming language developed by IBM in the mid-1960s for developing business applications, especially generating reports from data. The newest version, RPG 400, is still widely used on AS/400 systems. **2.** role-playing game: a computer game in which one or more players adopt a role and act it out.
⇒ See also REPORT; REPORT WRITER.

RS-232C or RS-232 recommended standard-232C: a standard interface approved by the Electronic Industries Association (EIA) for connecting serial devices. In 1987, the EIA released a new version of the standard and changed the name to *EIA-232-D.* And in 1991, they issued a new version of the standard called *EIA/TIA-232-E.*
⇒ See also CONNECTOR; DTE; ELECTRONIC INDUSTRIES ASSOCIATION (EIA); INTERFACE; MODEM; RS-422 AND RS-423; SERIAL PORT.

RS-422 and RS-423 standard interfaces approved by the Electronic Industries Association (EIA) for connecting serial devices. RS-422 supports multipoint connections whereas RS-423 supports only point-to-point connections.
⇒ See also COMMUNICATIONS; CONNECTOR; ELECTRONIC INDUSTRIES ASSOCIATION (EIA); INTERFACE; MODEM; PORT; RS-232C; RS-485.

RS-485 an Electronic Industries Association (EIA) standard for multipoint serial communications. It supports several types of connectors.
⇒ See also ELECTRONIC INDUSTRIES ASSOCIATION (EIA); RS-422 and RS-423.

RSA a public-key encryption technology developed by RSA Data Security, Inc. The abbreviation stands for Rivest, Shamir, and Adelman, the inventors. The RSA algorithm is the de facto standard for industrial-strength encryption, especially for data sent over the Internet, but software containing it is not generally exportable from the U.S.
⇒ See also ENCRYPTION; PRETTY GOOD PRIVACY; PUBLIC-KEY ENCRYPTION; S/MIME; SECURITY.

RSVP Resource Reservation Setup Protocol: an Internet protocol being developed to enable the Internet to support specified Qualities-of-Service (QoSs). RSVP is a chief component of a new type of Internet, known broadly as an *integrated services Internet*. The idea is to enhance the Internet to support transmission of real-time data.
⇒ See also QoS.

RTF RICH TEXT FORMAT.

RTP Real-Time Transport Protocol: an Internet protocol for transmitting real-time data such as audio and video. It provides mechanisms for the sending and receiving of applications to support streaming data.
⇒ See also RTSP; STREAMING; UDP; VIDEOCONFERENCING.

RTSP Real-Time Streaming Protocol: a proposed standard for controlling streaming data over the Internet.
⇒ See also BROADCAST; H.323; MULTICAST; NetShow; RTP; STREAMING.

rule *n.* **1.** in word processing and desktop publishing, a straight line that separates columns of text or illustrations. **2.** in expert systems, a conditional statement that tells the system how to react to a particular situation.
⇒ See also EXPERT SYSTEM.

ruler *n.* in word processing, a line running across the display screen. It measures the printed-page layout, as measured on paper, in points, picas, inches, or centimeters, and is useful for setting margins and tabs. It is also used in graphics programs.
⇒ See also DESKTOP PUBLISHING; MARGINS; PAGE LAYOUT PROGRAM.

run *v.t.* **1.** to execute (a program). —*v.i.* **2.** to operate. For example, a device that is *running* is one that is turned on and operating properly.
⇒ See also LAUNCH; RUNTIME.

run length limited *n.* See RLL.

running head *n.* HEADER (def. 1).

runtime *adj.* occurring while a program is executing.
⇒ See also COMPILE; LIBRARY; RUN; RUNTIME ERROR; RUNTIME VERSION.

runtime error *n.* an error that occurs during the execution of a program. Runtime errors indicate bugs in the program or operating system, or hardware failures.
⇒ See also BOMB; BUG; COMPILER; CRASH; FATAL ERROR; GPF; RUNTIME.

runtime version *n.* a limited version of one program that enables a user to run programs written in a high-level language but not necessarily to write them. To run a program written in Visual Basic, for example, the runtime version of Visual Basic is needed.
⇒ See also RUNTIME; SOFTWARE LICENSING.

a b c d e f g h i j k l m n o p q r S t u v w x y z

SAA System Application Architecture: a set of architecture standards developed by IBM for program, user, and communications interfaces on various IBM platforms.
⇒ See also CUA; STANDARD; USER INTERFACE.

sampling *n.* a technique used to capture continuous phenomena, whereby periodic snapshots are taken. Music CDs are produced by sampling live sound at frequent intervals and then digitizing each sample. The term sampling is also used to describe a similar process in digital photography.
⇒ See also ADPCM; ANALOG; DIGITAL; DIGITAL CAMERA; DIGITIZE; PCM.

sans serif (san′ser′if, sans′-), *n.* a category of typefaces that do not use *serifs*, small lines at the ends of characters. Popular sans serif fonts include Helvetica, Avant Garde, Arial, and Geneva.
⇒ See also FONT.

SAP 1. Service Advertising Protocol: a NetWare protocol used to identify the services and addresses of servers attached to the network. **2.** Secondary Audio Program: an NTSC audio channel used for auxiliary transmission in television broadcasting, such as foreign language dialog or teletext. **3.** (*SAP America, Inc., Lester, PA*) the U.S. branch of the German software company SAP AG.
⇒ See also NetWare; NTSC.

save *v.t., v.i.* to copy (data) from a temporary area to a more permanent storage medium. For example, in word processing, in order to record modifications made to a file, the file must be saved. To do this, the word processor copies the contents of its working buffer back to the file on the disk, replacing the previous version of the file.
⇒ See also AUTOSAVE; CLOSE.

scalability *n.* the quality of being scalable.

scalable *adj.* **1.** referring to how well a hardware or software system can adapt to increased demands. **2.** referring to anything whose size can be changed.
⇒ See also ARCHITECTURE; SCALABLE FONT.

scalable font *n.* a font represented in an object-oriented graphics language such as PostScript or TrueType. The representation of the font defines the shape of each character (the typeface) but not the size. A scalable font system can produce well-formed characters at any size.
⇒ See also FONT; INTELLIFONT; OUTLINE FONT; POSTSCRIPT; TRUETYPE; TYPEFACE; VECTOR GRAPHICS.

scale *v.t.* to change the size of (an object) while maintaining its shape. Most graphics software, particularly vector-based packages, allow users to scale objects freely.
⇒ See also GRAPHICS; SCALABLE FONT; VECTOR GRAPHICS.

SCAM *n.* SCSI Configuration Automatically: a subset of the PnP specification that provides plug-and-play support for SCSI devices.
⇒ See also PLUG-AND-PLAY; PnP; SCSI.

scan *v.t.* to digitize (an image) by passing it through an optical scanner.
⇒ See also OPTICAL SCANNER.

ScanDisk *n.* a DOS and Windows utility that finds different types of errors on hard disks and is able to correct some of them.
⇒ See also CLUSTER; DEFRAG; HARD DISK.

scanner *n.* OPTICAL SCANNER.

scatter diagram *n.* a type of diagram used to show the relationship between data items that have two numeric properties, one represented along the x-axis and the other along the y-axis. Each item is then represented by a single point. Scatter diagrams are used frequently by computer publications to compare categories of hardware and software products. One axis represents price, while the other represents performance.

⇒ See also PRESENTATION GRAPHICS.

scheduler *n.* **1.** a software product designed to help a group of colleagues schedule meetings and other appointments. The scheduler program allows members of a group to view one anothers' calendars. **2.** in operating systems, a program that coordinates the use of shared resources, such as a printer.

⇒ See also CALENDAR; GROUPWARE; OPERATING SYSTEM; WORKGROUP COMPUTING.

scientific notation *n.* a format for representing real (floating-point) numbers. Instead of writing the full number, it represents values as a number between 1 and 10 multiplied by 10 to some power. The 10 is often replaced by an *e.* Most programming languages, and many numeric applications, use scientific notation.

⇒ See also FLOATING-POINT NUMBER.

scissoring *n.* CLIPPING. See under CLIP.

Scrapbook *n.* in Macintosh environments, a desk accessory (DA) that enables users to store objects for future use. It retains its contents when the computer is turned off.

⇒ See also CLIPBOARD; DESK ACCESSORY (DA).

screen *n.* **1.** DISPLAY SCREEN. **2.** in offset printing, a mesh used to create halftones. See under HALFTONE.

screen capture *n.* the act of copying what is currently displayed on a screen to a file or printer.

⇒ See also CAPTURE; PRINT SCREEN KEY.

screen dump *n.* SCREEN CAPTURE.

screen flicker *n.* the phenomenon whereby a display screen appears to flicker. This phenomenon may occur if the image on the screen is refreshed too slowly, so that the phosphors in the screen cease glowing between refreshes.

⇒ See also INTERLACING; MONITOR; REFRESH.

screen font *n.* a font designed especially for a display screen. Typically, display fonts are bit-mapped and must be specially designed to compensate for the relatively low resolution of display screens.

⇒ See also FONT; RESOLUTION.

screen resolution *n.* See under RESOLUTION.

screen saver *n.* a small program that takes over the display screen if there are no keystrokes or mouse movements for a specified duration. Screen savers were originally developed to prevent *ghosting,* the permanent etching of a pattern on a display screen. Modern display screens do not suffer so much from this problem. Today, therefore, screen savers are mostly an adornment.

⇒ See also DISPLAY SCREEN; MONITOR.

screen shot *n.* SCREEN CAPTURE.

script *n.* a list of commands that can be executed without user interaction. A *script language* is a simple programming language in which scripts can be written. Apple Computer uses the term *script* to refer to programs written in its HyperCard or AppleScript language.

⇒ See also APPLESCRIPT; BATCH FILE; HYPERCARD; JAVASCRIPT; MACRO.

scroll *v.i.* to view more data than fits in a display window. When a user scrolls down, each new line appears at the bottom of the screen and all the other lines move up one row, so that the top line disappears. The term *vertical scrolling* refers to the ability to scroll up or down. *Horizontal scrolling* means that the image moves sideways.

⇒ See also PAGE; SCROLL BAR.

scroll bar *n.* a bar that appears on the side or bottom of a window to control which part of a list or document is currently in the window's frame. Typically, a scroll bar has arrows at either end, and a *scroll box* (or *elevator*) that moves from one end to the other to reflect position in the document. Clicking on the arrows causes the document to scroll in the indicated direction.

⇒ See also CLICK; DRAG; GRAPHICAL USER INTERFACE; WINDOW.

scroll box *n.* See under SCROLL BAR.

Scroll Lock key *n.* a key on PC and enhanced Macintosh keyboards that controls the way the cursor control keys work for some programs.

⇒ See also CURSOR CONTROL KEYS; SCROLL.

SCSI (skuz′ē), *n.* Small Computer System Interface: a parallel interface standard used by Apple Macintosh computers, PCs, and many UNIX systems for attaching peripheral devices to computers. SCSI interfaces provide for faster data transmission rates (up to 80 megabytes per second) than standard serial and parallel ports. In addition, many devices can be attached to a single SCSI port.

⇒ See also BUS; DAISY CHAIN; FIBRE CHANNEL; INTERFACE; PORT.

SDH Synchronous Digital Hierarchy: an international standard for synchronous data transmission over fiber optic cables.

⇒ See also FIBER OPTICS; OC; SONET.

SDK software development kit: a programming package that enables a programmer to develop applications for a specific platform. Typically, an SDK includes one or more APIs, programming tools, and documentation.

⇒ See also API; JDK; PLATFORM.

SDLC Synchronous Data Link Control: a protocol used in IBM's SNA networks.

⇒ See also HDLC; SNA.

SDRAM *n.* Synchronous DRAM: a new type of DRAM that can run at much higher clock speeds than conventional memory. SDRAM actually synchronizes itself with the computer's bus and is capable of running about three times faster than conventional FPM RAM, and about twice as fast as EDO DRAM and BEDO DRAM.

⇒ See also BEDO DRAM; DDR-SDRAM; DRAM; EDO DRAM; MDRAM; PIPELINE BURST CACHE; RDRAM; SGRAM; SLDRAM; WAIT STATE.

SDRAM II *n.* DDR-SDRAM.

SDSL symmetric digital subscriber line: a new technology that allows more data to be sent over existing copper telephone lines (POTS). SDSL is called symmetric because, unlike ADSL, it supports the same data rate in both directions.

⇒ See also ADSL; ISDN; xDSL.

search and replace *n.* a feature supported by most word processors that lets a user replace a character string (a series of characters) with another string wherever the first string appears in the document.

⇒ See also CHARACTER STRING; WORD PROCESSING.

search engine *n.* a program that searches one or more documents, as on the World Wide Web, for specified keywords and returns a list of locations where those keywords were found. Although *search engine* designates a general type of program, such as one that enables a user to find information in an electronic book, the term is most often used to refer to such Internet services as Alta Vista and Excite.

⇒ See also ALTA VISTA; EXCITE; HOTBOT; INFOSEEK; JUGHEAD; LYCOS; META TAG; OPEN TEXT; SPIDER; VERONICA; WEBCRAWLER; YAHOO!.

secondary cache *n.* L2 CACHE.

secondary storage *n.* MASS STORAGE.

sector *n.* the smallest unit that can be accessed on a disk. When a disk undergoes a low-level format, it is divided into tracks and sectors. The tracks are concentric circles around the disk, and the sectors are segments within each circle. The operating system and disk drive keep tabs on where information is stored on the disk by noting its track and sector number.

⇒ See also BAD SECTOR; DISK; FORMAT; INTERLEAVE; TRACK.

Secure Electronic Transactions *n.* See SET.

Secure HTTP *n.* See S-HTTP.

Secure Socket Layer *n.* See SSL.

security *n.* any of several techniques for ensuring that data stored in a computer cannot be read or compromised, usually involving data encryption and passwords.

⇒ See also ACCESS CONTROL; AUDIT TRAIL; AUTHENTICATION; AUTHORIZATION; BIOMETRICS; CLIPPER CHIP; CRYPTOGRAPHY; ENCRYPTION; FIREWALL; KERBEROS; NETWORK MANAGEMENT; PASSWORD; RSA; SNIFFER; SSL.

seek time *n.* the time a program or device takes to

locate a particular piece of data. For disk drives, the terms *seek time* and *access time* are often used interchangeably. Technically speaking, however, the access time is often longer than the seek time because it includes a brief latency period until disk rotation brings the desired sector under the read-write head.
⇒ See also ACCESS TIME; DISK DRIVE.

segment *n.* **1.** in networks, a section of a network that is bounded by bridges, routers, hubs, or switches. Dividing an Ethernet into multiple segments is one of the most common ways of increasing bandwidth on the LAN. If segmented correctly, most network traffic will remain within a single segment. Hubs and switches are used to connect each segment to the rest of the LAN. **2.** in virtual memory systems, a variable-sized portion of data that is swapped in and out of main memory. **3.** in graphics, a piece of a polyline.
⇒ See also MAIN MEMORY; PAGE; SWAP; SWITCHING HUB; VIRTUAL MEMORY.

select *v.t.* to choose (an object) so that it can be manipulated in some way. To select an object, such as an icon or file, the user moves the pointer to the object and clicks a mouse button. In many applications, blocks of text are selected by positioning the pointer at an end-point of the block and then dragging it over the block.
⇒ See also BLOCK; CHOOSE; DRAG; GRAPHICAL USER INTERFACE; HIGHLIGHT; ICON; MARQUEE; POINTER.

semantics *n.* the meaning of an instruction or command. If a user enters a legal command that does not make sense in the current context, that is a semantic error. If the command is misspelled, or has the wrong parameters, that is a syntax error.
⇒ See also PARSE; PROGRAMMING LANGUAGE; SYNTAX.

semaphore *n.* a hardware or software flag. In multitasking systems, a semaphore is a variable with a value that indicates the status of a common resource. It is used to lock a resource that is being used.
⇒ See also FLAG; INTERPROCESS COMMUNICATION (IPC); MULTITASKING.

semiconductor *n.* a material that is neither a good conductor of electricity (like copper) nor a good insulator (like rubber). The most common semiconductor materials are silicon and germanium. Computer chips, both for CPU and memory, are composed of semiconductor materials.
⇒ See also CHIP; CMOS; INTEGRATED CIRCUIT; NEC; TEXAS INSTRUMENTS; TRANSISTOR.

sequential access *n.* reading or writing data records in sequential order—that is, one after another. Some programming languages and operating systems distinguish between sequential-access data files and random-access data files, allowing a choice between the two types. Devices can also be classified as sequential access or random access. For example, a tape drive is a sequential-access device and a disk drive is a random-access device.
⇒ See also ISAM; RANDOM ACCESS.

serial *adj.* one by one. *Serial data transfer* refers to transmitting data one bit at a time.
⇒ See also COMMUNICATIONS; PARALLEL; SERIAL PORT.

serial interface *n.* See SERIAL PORT.

Serial Line Internet Protocol *n.* See SLIP.

serial mouse *n.* a mouse that connects to a computer via a serial port.
⇒ See also MOUSE; PORT; PS/2 PORT; SERIAL; SERIAL PORT.

serial port *n.* a port that can be used for serial communication, in which only one bit is transmitted at a time.
⇒ See also ACCESS.BUS; COMMUNICATIONS; GEOPORT; IEEE 1394; INTERFACE; PARALLEL PORT; PS/2 PORT; RS-232C; RS-422 AND RS-423; UART; USB.

serif *n.* a small decorative line added as embellishment to the basic form of a character. The most common serif typeface is Times Roman.
⇒ See also FONT; SANS SERIF; TYPEFACE.

server *n.* a computer or device on a network that manages network resources. For example, a *file server* is a computer and storage device dedicated to storing files. A *network server* is a computer that manages network traffic. A *print server* is a computer that manages one or more printers, allowing access from the rest of the network.
⇒ See also CLIENT; CLIENT/SERVER ARCHITECTURE; DEC; LOAD BALANCING; LOCAL-AREA NETWORK; NETWORK; PROXY SERVER; SERVER MIRRORING; SERVER-SIDE; SGI; SUN MICROSYSTEMS; VIRTUAL SERVER.

server mirroring *n.* utilizing a backup server that duplicates all the processes and transactions of the primary server. Server mirroring is an expensive but effective strategy for achieving fault tolerance.
⇒ See also DISK MIRRORING; FAULT TOLERANCE; SERVER.

server-side *adj.* occurring on the server side of a client/server system. For example, on the World Wide Web, CGI scripts are server-side applications because they run on the Web server rather than in the browser.
⇒ See also CLIENT-SIDE; CLIENT/SERVER ARCHITECTURE; SERVER; SSI.

Server-Side Include *n.* See SSI.

service *n.* **1.** CUSTOMER SUPPORT. **2.** ONLINE SERVICE.

Service Advertising Protocol *n.* See SAP.

service bureau *n.* a company that provides a variety of desktop publishing services. In addition to providing high-resolution output with imagesetters, many service bureaus also offer scanning services.
⇒ See also DESKTOP PUBLISHING; IMAGESETTER; LINOTRONIC; OFFSET PRINTING; POSTSCRIPT.

Service Profile Identifier *n.* See SPID.

service provider *n.* INTERNET SERVICE PROVIDER.

servlet *n.* an applet that runs on a server. The term usually refers to a Java applet that runs within a Web server environment.
⇒ See also APPLET; CGI.

SET *n.* Secure Electronic Transaction: a standard intended to enable secure credit card transactions on the Internet.
⇒ See also ELECTRONIC COMMERCE.

setup *v.t.* **1.** to install and configure (hardware or software). Most Windows applications come with a program called SETUP.EXE or INSTALL.EXE, which installs the software on the computer's hard disk. —*n.* **2.** the configuration of hardware or software.
⇒ See also CONFIGURATION.

SGI Silicon Graphics Incorporated: a company based in Mountain View, California, that provides computer hardware and software.
⇒ See also ANIMATION; DEC; IBM; OPENGL; SERVER; SUN MICROSYSTEMS; VIDEO EDITING; WORKSTATION.

SGML Standard Generalized Markup Language: a system for organizing and tagging elements of a document. SGML specifies the rules for tagging elements. These tags can then be interpreted to format elements in different ways. SGML is used widely to manage large documents that are revised frequently and need to be printed in different formats.
⇒ See also HTML; HYPERTEXT; ISO; RICH TEXT FORMAT; TAG; WORLD WIDE WEB; XML.

SGRAM *n.* Synchronous Graphic Random Access Memory: a type of DRAM used increasingly on video adapters and graphics accelerators.
⇒ See also DRAM; GRAPHICS ACCELERATOR; SDRAM; VIDEO ADAPTER; VIDEO MEMORY; VRAM; WRAM.

shadowing *n.* a technique used to increase a computer's speed by using RAM in place of slower ROM. On PCs all code to control hardware devices is normally executed from a ROM chip called the *BIOS ROM.* However, many manufacturers configure their PCs to copy the BIOS code into RAM when the computer boots. The RAM used to hold the BIOS code is called *shadow RAM.*
⇒ See also BIOS; BOOT; MAIN MEMORY; RAM; ROM.

shared Ethernet *n.* the traditional type of Ethernet, in which all hosts are connected to the same bus and compete with one another for bandwidth.
⇒ See also ETHERNET; SWITCHED ETHERNET.

shareware *n.* software that, although copyrighted, is usually distributed free of charge. The author requests that users pay a small fee if they like the program and use it regularly.
⇒ See also BULLETIN BOARD SYSTEM; FREEWARE; ONLINE

computer

SERVICE; PUBLIC-DOMAIN SOFTWARE; SOFTWARE LICENSING; SOFTWARE PIRACY; WAREZ.

sheet feeder *n.* a mechanism that holds a stack of paper and feeds each sheet into a printer, fax machine, or scanner one at a time.
⇒ See also DOT-MATRIX PRINTER; FAX MACHINE; LASER PRINTER; OPTICAL SCANNER; PRINTER.

shell *n.* **1.** Also called **user interface.** the outermost layer of a program. **2.** Also called **command shell.** the command processor interface. The command processor is the program that executes operating system commands directly in response to user input.
⇒ See also COMMAND DRIVEN; COMMAND LANGUAGE; COMMAND PROCESSOR; INTERFACE; MENU DRIVEN; OPERATING ENVIRONMENT; OPERATING SYSTEM; UNIX; USER INTERFACE.

shift clicking *n.* clicking a mouse button while holding the Shift key down. In Microsoft Windows and Macintosh systems, shift clicking enables the user to select multiple items.
⇒ See also CLICK; GRAPHICAL USER INTERFACE; MACINTOSH COMPUTER; MICROSOFT WINDOWS; MOUSE; SELECT.

Shift key *n.* a key on computer keyboards. When combined with alphabetic keys, the Shift key causes the system to output a capital letter. The Shift key can also be combined with other keys to produce program-dependent results.
⇒ See also ALT KEY; CONTROL KEY; KEYBOARD.

Shockwave *n.* a technology developed by Macromedia, Inc., that enables Web pages to include multimedia objects. Shockwave supports audio, animation, and video.
⇒ See also ACTIVEX CONTROL; MULTIMEDIA; PLUG-IN.

shortcut *n.* in Windows 95 and Windows 98, a special type of file that points to another file or device. A user can place shortcuts on the desktop to conveniently access files that may be stored deep in the directory structure.
⇒ See also ALIAS; DESKTOP; LINK; SHORTCUT KEY.

shortcut key *n.* a special key combination that causes a specific command to be executed. Typically, shortcut keys combine the Ctrl or Alt keys with some other keys.
⇒ See also ALT KEY; COMMAND; CONTROL KEY; SHORTCUT.

shtml See under SSI.

S-HTTP an extension to the HTTP protocol to support sending data securely over the World Wide Web. Not all Web browsers and servers support S-HTTP.
⇒ See also HTTP; SSL.

shut down *v.t., v.i.* **1.** to turn (a device's) power off. **2.** in Windows 95 and Windows 98, to turn (a computer) off by selecting **Start→Shut Down...**
⇒ See also POWER DOWN.

SIG (sig) *n.* special interest group: a group of users interested in a particular subject who discuss the subject at meetings or via an online service. Online SIGs are sometimes called *forums.*
⇒ See also BULLETIN BOARD SYSTEM; FORUM; ONLINE SERVICE.

sign *n.* a symbol that identifies a number as being either positive or negative. A positive sign is +; a negative sign is -. These two signs are also used to indicate addition and subtraction, respectively.
⇒ See also OPERATOR.

Silicon Graphics *n.* See SGI.

Silicon Valley *n.* a nickname for the region south of San Francisco that contains an unusually high concentration of computer companies. Silicon is the most common semiconductor material used to produce chips.
⇒ See also CHIP; SEMICONDUCTOR.

SIMM (sim), *n.* single in-line memory module: a small circuit board that can hold a group of memory chips. Unlike memory chips, SIMMs are measured in bytes rather than bits.
⇒ See also CHIP; DIMM; RAM.

Simple Mail Transfer Protocol *n.* See SMTP.

Simple Network Management Protocol *n.* See SNMP.

simplex *adj.* referring to transmission in only one

direction. Simplex refers to *one-way* communications where one party is the transmitter and the other is the receiver. An example is a radio broadcast.
⇒ See also FULL DUPLEX; HALF DUPLEX.

simulation *n.* the process of imitating a real phenomenon with a set of mathematical formulas. Advanced computer programs can simulate weather conditions, chemical reactions, atomic reactions, even biological processes.

single-density disk *n.* a low-density floppy disk. All modern floppies are double-density or high-density.
⇒ See also FLOPPY DISK.

single in-line memory module *n.* See SIMM.

single in-line package *n.* See SIP.

single-sided disk *n.* a floppy disk with only one side prepared for storing data. All modern floppies are double-sided.
⇒ See also FLOPPY DISK.

SIP (sip) *n.* single in-line package: a type of housing for electronic components in which the connecting pins protrude from one side. Also called **Single In-line Pin Package (SIPP).**
⇒ See also DIP; PGA.

site *n.* WEB SITE.

680x0 See under MOTOROLA MICROPROCESSORS.

16-bit *adj.* referring to the number of bits that can be processed or transmitted in parallel, or the number of bits used for a single element in a data format. The term is often applied to microprocessors, buses, graphics devices, operating systems, applications, and expansion boards.
⇒ See also 32-BIT; BIT; BUS.

size *v.t.* to set the dimensions of (an object).
⇒ See also GRAPHICAL USER INTERFACE; SCALE; WINDOW.

slack space *n.* the unused space in a disk cluster. The DOS and Windows file systems use fixed-size clusters. Even if the actual data being stored require less storage than the cluster size, an entire cluster is reserved for the file.
⇒ See also CLUSTER; FAT32; FILE ALLOCATION TABLE; PARTITION.

slate PC *n.* a class of notebook computer that accepts input from an electronic pen rather than from a keyboard. Typically, slate PCs can decipher clearly written block letters and translate them into their ASCII equivalents.
⇒ See also HAND-HELD COMPUTER; HANDWRITING RECOGNITION; NOTEBOOK COMPUTER; PDA; PEN COMPUTER.

slave *n.* any device that is controlled by another device, called the *master.*
⇒ See also MASTER/SLAVE.

SLDRAM *n.* SyncLink DRAM: a new type of memory being developed by a consortium of computer manufacturers. SLDRAM is competing with Rambus memory (RDRAM).
⇒ See also BEDO DRAM; DRAM; EDO DRAM; FPM RAM; RDRAM; SDRAM.

sleep mode *n.* an energy-saving mode of operation in which all unnecessary components are shut down. Many battery-operated devices, such as notebook computers, support a sleep mode.
⇒ See also GREEN PC.

slimline model *n.* a small desktop model computer.
⇒ See also DESKTOP MODEL COMPUTER.

SLIP *n.* Serial Line Internet Protocol: a method of connecting to the Internet via telephone line. SLIP is an older protocol than PPP.
⇒ See also INTERNET; ISP; PPP; PROTOCOL.

slot *n.* an opening in a computer in which to insert a printed circuit board. Also called **expansion slot.**
⇒ See also BAY; CARTRIDGE; CHASSIS; EXPANSION BOARD; EXPANSION SLOT; PRINTED CIRCUIT BOARD.

Slot 1 *n.* the form factor for Intel's Pentium II processors. The Slot 1 package replaces the Socket 7 and Socket 8 form factors.
⇒ See also FORM FACTOR; PENTIUM II; SOCKET 7.

small computer system interface *n.* See SCSI.

Smalltalk *n.* an object-oriented operating system and programming language. It was the first object-oriented programming language, although it never achieved the commercial success of other languages such as C++ and Java.

⇒ See also C++; JAVA; OBJECT ORIENTED; OBJECT-ORIENTED PROGRAMMING.

SMART (smärt), *n.* Self-Monitoring, Analysis and Reporting Technology: an open standard for developing disk drives and software systems that automatically monitor a disk drive's health and report potential problems.

⇒ See also CRASH; DISK DRIVE; HARD DISK; MTBF.

smart battery *n.* See under BATTERY PACK.

smart card *n.* a small electronic device about the size of a credit card that contains an integrated circuit (IC). Such devices are sometimes called *Integrated Circuit Cards (ICCs).* Smart cards are used for a variety of purposes, including storing medical records, storing digital cash, and generating network IDs.

⇒ See also CHALLENGE-RESPONSE; DIGITAL CASH; TOKEN.

Smartdrive *n.* a disk-caching system provided by Microsoft with later versions of DOS and used with Windows 3.1. Starting with Windows 95, Smartdrive was replaced by *VCACHE.*

⇒ See also DISK CACHE; VCACHE.

smart terminal *n.* a terminal that has some processing capabilities. Smart terminals have built-in logic for performing simple display operations, such as blinking and boldface.

⇒ See also DUMB TERMINAL; INTELLIGENT TERMINAL; TERMINAL.

SMB Server Message Block: a message format used by DOS and Windows to share files, directories and devices. NetBIOS is based on the SMB format, and many network products use SMB.

⇒ See also NETBIOS.

SMDS Switched Multimegabit Data Services: a high-speed switched data communications service offered by telephone companies that enables organizations to connect geographically separate local-area networks (LANs) into a single wide-area network (WAN).

⇒ See also CSU/DSU; WIDE-AREA NETWORK.

SMIL Synchronized Multimedia Integration Language: a new markup language now being developed. It would enable Web developers to divide multimedia content into separate files and streams (audio, video, text, and images), send them to a user's computer, and then have them displayed together as if they were a single multimedia stream. SMIL is based on the eXtensible Markup Language (XML).

⇒ See also MULTIMEDIA; RTSP; STREAMING; XML.

smiley *n.* EMOTICON.

S/MIME *n.* Secure/MIME: a new version of the MIME protocol that supports encryption of messages. S/MIME is based on RSA's public-key encryption technology.

⇒ See also MIME; PUBLIC-KEY ENCRYPTION; RSA.

smoothing *n.* a technique used by some printers to make curves look smoother. Most printers that support smoothing implement it by reducing the size of the dots that make up a curved line.

⇒ See also ANTIALIASING; JAGGIES; LASER PRINTER.

SMP 1. Symmetric Multiprocessing: a computer architecture that provides fast performance by making multiple CPUs work together as peers. **2.** Simple Management Protocol: another name for SNMP2. See under SNMP.

⇒ See also BEOS; MPP; MULTIPROCESSING; MULTITHREADING; NUMA; SNMP; SOLARIS.

SMS Systems Management Server: a set of tools from Microsoft that assists network administrators in managing PCs connected to a local-area network (LAN).

⇒ See also NET PC; NETWORK COMPUTER; SYSTEM MANAGEMENT; SYSTEMS ADMINISTRATOR.

SMTP Simple Mail Transfer Protocol: a protocol for sending e-mail messages between servers. The messages can then be retrieved with an e-mail client using either POP or IMAP. In addition, SMTP is generally used to send messages from a mail client to a mail server.

⇒ See also POP.

smurf *n.* a type of network security breach in which a network connected to the Internet is swamped with replies to ICMP echo (PING) requests. Smurfing is a *Denial of Service attack*—it doesn't try to steal information, but instead tries to disable a computer or network.

⇒ See also CRACK; IP SPOOFING; PING.

SNA Systems Network Architecture: a set of network protocols originally designed for IBM's mainframe computers. SNA now also supports peer-to-peer networks of workstations.

⇒ See also MAINFRAME; NETWORK; SDLC; VTAM.

snailmail or **snail mail** *n.* normal postal mail, where an actual physical letter or package is delivered. The term is a retronym; that is, it did not exist until electronic mail (e-mail) became so prevalent that there was a requirement to differentiate the two.

⇒ See also E-MAIL.

snapshot printer *n.* a color printer designed to print photographic-quality snapshots.

⇒ See also COLOR PRINTER; DIGITAL PHOTOGRAPHY; PHOTO SCANNER.

sniffer *n.* a program and/or device that monitors data traveling over a network. Sniffers can be used both for legitimate network management functions and for stealing information from a network.

⇒ See also HACKER; NETWORK MANAGEMENT; SECURITY.

SNMP Simple Network Management Protocol: a set of protocols for managing complex networks. SNMP 1 reports only whether a device is functioning properly. The industry has attempted to define a new set of protocols called *SNMP 2* that would provide additional information. However, network managers have turned to a related technology called *RMON* that provides more detailed information about network usage.

⇒ See also LOCAL-AREA NETWORK; MIB; NETWORK; NETWORK MANAGEMENT; RMON.

socket *n.* **1.** in UNIX and some other operating systems, a software object that connects an application to a network protocol. The programmer need only manipulate the socket and can rely on the operating system to transport messages across the network. **2.** a receptacle into which a plug can be inserted. **3.** a receptacle for a microprocessor or other hardware component.

⇒ See also SOCKET 8; SOCKET 7; TCP/IP; WINSOCK.

Socket 7 *n.* the form factor for fifth-generation CPU chips from Intel, Cyrix, and AMD. All Pentium chips, except Intel's Pentium Pro (Socket 8) and Pentium II (Slot 1), conform to the Socket 7 specifications.

⇒ See also FORM FACTOR; K6; PENTIUM MICROPROCESSOR; SLOT 1; SOCKET 8; ZERO INSERTION FORCE (ZIF) SOCKET.

Socket 8 *n.* the form factor for Intel's Pentium Pro microprocessors.

⇒ See also PENTIUM PRO; SOCKET; SOCKET 7; ZERO INSERTION FORCE (ZIF) SOCKET.

SOCKS *n.* a protocol for handling TCP traffic through a proxy server. It provides a simple firewall because it checks incoming and outgoing packets and hides the IP addresses of client applications.

⇒ See also PROXY SERVER; TCP.

soft *adj.* in computer science, describing things that are intangible. For example, you cannot touch *software. Soft* is also used to describe things that are easily changed or impermanent.

⇒ See also HARD; HARDWARE; SOFTWARE.

soft font *n.* a font that is copied from a computer's disk to a printer's memory. Soft fonts require a lot of disk space and printer memory. Also called **downloadable font.**

⇒ See also DOWNLOAD; FONT; FONT CARTRIDGE; LASER PRINTER; RESIDENT FONT.

soft hyphen *n.* DISCRETIONARY HYPHEN.

soft return *n.* a set of special codes inserted into a document to cause the display screen, printer, or other output device to advance to the next line if necessary. Soft returns are inserted automatically by some word processors as part of their word wrap capability.

⇒ See also HARD RETURN; MARGINS; WORD WRAP.

software *n.* computer instructions and associated data. Software is often divided into two categories: systems software and applications software.
⇒ See also APPLICATION; BLOATWARE; DATA; FIRMWARE; HARDWARE; PROGRAM; SYSTEMS SOFTWARE; VAPORWARE.

software development kit *n.* See SDK.

software engineer *n.* a programmer. The term implies that the individual is more involved with design and management than with actual coding.
⇒ See also PROGRAMMER; SOFTWARE ENGINEERING.

software engineering *n.* the computer science discipline concerned with developing large applications. Software engineering covers not only the technical aspects of building software systems but also management issues, such as directing programming teams, and budgeting.
⇒ See also COMPUTER SCIENCE; FUNCTIONAL SPECIFICATION; SOFTWARE ENGINEER; UML.

software licensing *n.* allowing an individual or group to use a piece of software. Nearly all applications are licensed rather than sold. Some licenses are based on the number of machines on which the licensed program can run, whereas others are based on the number of users that can use the program.
⇒ See also APPLICATION; COPY PROTECTION; EULA; SHAREWARE.

software modem *n.* a modem implemented entirely in software. Software modems rely on the computer's processor to modulate and demodulate signals.
⇒ See also HOST-BASED MODEM; MODEM.

software piracy *n.* the unauthorized copying of software. Most retail programs are licensed for use at just one computer site or for use by only one user at any time. Originally, companies tried to stop software piracy by copy-protecting their software. Most software now requires some sort of registration, which may discourage piracy.
⇒ See also COPY PROTECTION; DIGITAL WATERMARK; REGISTER; SHAREWARE; SOFTWARE; WAREZ.

SOHO (sō'hō), *n.* Small Office/Home Office: the fastest-growing market for computer hardware and software. SOHO products are specifically designed to meet the needs of professionals who work at home or in small offices.
⇒ See also MFP.

Solaris *n.* a UNIX-based operating environment developed by Sun Microsystems. Originally developed to run on Sun's SPARC workstations, Solaris now runs on many workstations from other vendors.
⇒ See also SMP; SUN MICROSYSTEMS; UNIX; X-WINDOW.

solid ink-jet printer *n.* a type of color printer that works by melting wax-based inks and then spraying them on paper. Solid ink-jet printers produce vivid colors and can print on nearly any surface, but they are relatively slow and expensive.
⇒ See also COLOR PRINTER; INK-JET PRINTER; PHASE CHANGE DISK.

SOM System Object Model: an architecture developed by IBM that allows binary code to be shared by different applications. It serves the same purpose as Microsoft's competing COM standard.
⇒ See also COMPONENT OBJECT MODEL; CORBA; DSOM.

SONET Synchronous Optical Network: a standard for connecting fiber-optic transmission systems. SONET is now an ANSI standard.
⇒ See also BROADBAND ISDN (B-ISDN); FIBER OPTICS; OC; SDH; T-1 CARRIER; T-3 CARRIER.

sound card *n.* an expansion board that enables a computer to output sounds through speakers connected to the board, to record sound input from a microphone connected to the computer, and to manipulate sound stored on a disk.
⇒ See also 3-D AUDIO; CD-ROM; MIDI; MULTIMEDIA; WAVE TABLE SYNTHESIS.

source *n.* a place from which data is taken. The place from which the data is moved is called the *source*, whereas the place it is moved to is called the *destination* or *target*. The source and destination can be files, directories, or devices.
⇒ See also COPY; DESTINATION.

source code *n.* program instructions in their origi-

nal form. A programmer writes a program in a particular programming language. This form of the program is called the *source program* or, more generically, the *source code*. To execute the program, it must be translated into machine language.
⇒ See also ASSEMBLER; CODE; COMPILER; EDITOR; MACHINE LANGUAGE; OBJECT CODE; PROGRAM; PROGRAMMING LANGUAGE.

spam *n.* **1.** electronic junk mail or junk newsgroup postings. Spam is generally e-mail advertising for some product sent to a mailing list or newsgroup. In addition to wasting people's time with unwanted e-mail, spam also eats up a lot of network bandwidth. —*v.t.*, *v.i.* **2.** to send spam (to). [term derives from a comedy routine on *Monty Python's Flying Circus*, a British TV series]
⇒ See also E-MAIL; MODERATED NEWSGROUP.

SPARC *n.* Scalable Processor Architecture: a RISC technology developed by Sun Microsystems. The term *SPARC*® itself is a trademark of SPARC International, an independent organization that licenses the term to Sun.
⇒ See also RISC; SUN MICROSYSTEMS; WORKSTATION.

SPEC *n.* **1.** Standard Performance Evaluation Corporation: a nonprofit corporation set up by computer and microprocessor vendors to create a standard set of benchmark tests. **2.** Also **spec.** a functional or other specification.
⇒ See also BENCHMARK; FLOPS; MIPS.

special character *n.* a character that is not a letter, number, symbol, or punctuation mark. Control characters, for example, are special characters, as are special formatting characters such as paragraph marks.
⇒ See also CONTROL CHARACTER; PUNCTUATION.

special interest group *n.* See SIG.

speech recognition *n.* VOICE RECOGNITION.

speech synthesis *n.* computerized production of sound that resembles human speech. Speech synthesis systems can read text files and output them in a very intelligible, if somewhat dull, voice.
⇒ See also VOICE RECOGNITION.

spell checker *n.* a program that checks the spelling of words in a text document. Many word processors come with a built-in spell checker, but standalone utilities can be purchased.
⇒ See also WORD PROCESSING.

spelling checker *n.* SPELL CHECKER.

SPID Service Profile Identifier: a number that identifies a specific ISDN line. Part of the ISDN initialization procedure is to configure the terminal adapter to use this SPID.
⇒ See also ISDN; TERMINAL ADAPTER.

spider *n.* a program that automatically retrieves Web pages. Spiders are used to feed pages to search engines. Also called **webcrawler.**
⇒ See also ALTA VISTA; ROBOT; SEARCH ENGINE.

spline *n.* in computer graphics, a smooth curve that passes through two or more points. Splines are generated with mathematical formulas.
⇒ See also BÉZIER CURVE; NURBS.

split screen *n.* division of the display screen into separate parts, each of which displays a different document, or different parts of the same document.
⇒ See also WINDOW.

spoof *v.t.*, *v.i.* to fool or trick (hardware or software). IP spoofing, for example, involves trickery that makes a message appear as if it came from an authorized IP address. Spoofing is also used as a network management technique to reduce traffic. Routers and other network devices can be programmed to *spoof* replies from distant nodes. Rather than sending the packets to the remote nodes and waiting for a reply, the devices generate their own *spoofed* replies.
⇒ See also IP SPOOFING; NETWORK MANAGEMENT.

spool *v.i.* See under SPOOLING.

spooler *n.* a program that controls spooling. Most operating systems come with one or more spoolers. In addition, some applications include spoolers.
⇒ See also QUEUE; SPOOLING.

spooling *n.* simultaneous peripheral operations online: the loading of jobs into a buffer, a special area

in memory or on a disk where a device can access them when it is ready. In print spooling, documents are loaded into a buffer and the printer pulls them off the buffer at its own rate. Spooling also lets the user place a number of print jobs on a queue.
⇒ See also BACKGROUND; BUFFER; QUEUE.

spot color *n.* a method of specifying and printing colors in which each color is printed with its own ink. Spot color printing is effective when the printed matter contains only one to three different colors, but it becomes prohibitively expensive for more colors.
⇒ See also COLOR SEPARATION; PANTONE MATCHING SYSTEM (PMS); PROCESS COLORS.

spreadsheet *n.* a table of values arranged in rows and columns. Each value can have a predefined relationship to the other values. If one value is changed, other values may need to be changed as well. *Spreadsheet applications* (sometimes referred to as *spreadsheets*) are computer programs that let the user create and manipulate spreadsheets electronically. Most spreadsheet applications are *multidimensional*, meaning that the user can link one spreadsheet to another.
⇒ See also BORLAND INTERNATIONAL; CELL; EXCEL; FORMULA; LABEL; LOTUS 1-2-3; RECALCULATION; THREE-DIMENSIONAL SPREADSHEET; VISICALC.

sprite *n.* a graphic image that can move within a larger graphic. Animation software that supports sprites enables the designer to develop independent animated images that can then be combined in a larger animation.
⇒ See also ANIMATION.

SPX Sequenced Packet Exchange: a transport layer protocol used in Novell NetWare networks. The SPX layer sits on top of the IPX layer. SPX is used primarily by client/server applications.
⇒ See also IPX; NETWARE; TCP.

SQL (sē′kwal *or as separate letters*), *n.* structured query language: a standardized query language for requesting information from a database. SQL has been the favorite query language for database management systems running on minicomputers and mainframes. Increasingly, however, SQL is being supported by PC database systems because it supports distributed databases.
⇒ See also DATABASE MANAGEMENT SYSTEM; DISTRIBUTED DATABASE; JDBC; ORACLE; QUERY; QUERY LANGUAGE; SQL SERVER.

SQL server *n.* generically, any database management system (DBMS) that can respond to queries from client machines formatted in the SQL language. When capitalized, the term generally refers to either of two database management products from Sybase and Microsoft.
⇒ See also RDBMS; SQL; SYBASE.

SRAM (es′ram′), *n.* static random access memory: a type of memory that is generally faster than the more common DRAM (dynamic RAM). The term *static* is derived from the fact that it does not need to be refreshed like dynamic RAM.
⇒ See also ACCESS TIME; CACHE; CYCLE TIME; DYNAMIC RAM; NVRAM; RAM.

SSI server-side include: a type of HTML comment that directs the Web server to dynamically generate data for the Web page whenever it is requested. The basic format for SSIs is:
   < !—#command tag = 'value'... > , where #command can be any of various commands supported by the Web server. SSIs can also be used to execute programs and insert the results. They therefore represent a powerful tool for Web developers.
⇒ See also DYNAMIC HTML; HTML; SERVER-SIDE.

SSL Secure Sockets Layer: a protocol developed by Netscape for transmitting private documents via the Internet. SSL works by using a private key to encrypt data that is transferred over the SSL connection.
⇒ See also DIGITAL CERTIFICATE; DIGITAL SIGNATURE; IETF; IPSEC; S-HTTP; SECURITY; X.509.

ST-412 interface *n.* ST-506 INTERFACE.

ST-506 interface *n.* an old standard interface for hard disks. Newer standards, such as enhanced IDE and SCSI, support faster data transfer rates.

⇒ See also HARD DISK; IDE INTERFACE; INTERFACE; MFM; RLL; SCSI.

stack *n.* **1.** in programming, a special type of data structure in which items are removed in the reverse order from that in which they are added, so the most recently added item is the first one removed. This is also called *last-in, first-out* (LIFO). Adding an item to a stack is called *pushing.* Removing an item from a stack is called *popping.* **2.** in networking, short for *protocol stack.* **3.** in Apple Computer's HyperCard software system, a collection of cards.
⇒ See also DATA STRUCTURE; HEAP.

standalone *adj.* referring to a device that is self-contained, or one that does not require any other devices to function. For example, a fax machine is a standalone device. A printer, on the other hand, is not a standalone device because it requires a computer to feed it data.

standard *n.* a definition or format that has been approved by a recognized standards organization or is accepted as a de facto standard by the industry. Standards exist for programming languages, operating systems, data formats, communications protocols, and electrical interfaces.
⇒ See also ACM; ANSI; ARCHITECTURE; CCITT; COMPATIBLE; DE FACTO STANDARD; ELECTRONIC INDUSTRIES ASSOCIATION (EIA); IEEE; IETF; INTERNET SOCIETY; ISO; ITU; OPEN ARCHITECTURE; SAA; VESA.

Standard Generalized Markup Language *n.* See SGML.

standard input *n.* the place from which input comes unless the user specifies a different input device. The standard input device is usually the keyboard.
⇒ See also INPUT.

standard output *n.* the place where output goes unless the user specifies a different output device. The standard output device is usually the display screen.
⇒ See also OUTPUT.

standby power system LINE-INTERACTIVE UPS.

star network *n.* a local-area network (LAN) that uses a star topology in which all nodes are connected to a central point.
⇒ See also 10BASET; BUS NETWORK; HUB; LOCAL-AREA NETWORK; TOPOLOGY.

start bit *n.* in asynchronous communications, the bit that signals the receiver that data is coming. Every byte of data is preceded by a start bit and followed by a stop bit.
⇒ See also ASYNCHRONOUS; BIT; BYTE.

start-stop transmission *n.* asynchronous communication, which distinguishes between noise and valid data by placing a *start bit* and a *stop bit* at the beginning and end of each piece of data.

startup disk *n.* BOOTABLE DISKETTE.

stateless *adj.* having no information about what occurred previously. Most modern applications *maintain state*, which means they remember what the user was doing last time he or she interacted with the application. The World Wide Web, on the other hand, is intrinsically stateless.
⇒ See also COOKIE; HTTP; ISAPI; NSAPI.

statement *n.* an instruction written in a high-level language. A statement directs the computer to perform a specified action. A single statement in a high-level language can represent several machine-language instructions.
⇒ See also EXPRESSION; PROGRAMMING LANGUAGE.

static RAM *n.* See SRAM.

static variable *n.* a variable that retains the same data throughout the execution of a program.
⇒ See also DYNAMIC VARIABLE; VARIABLE.

station *n.* WORKSTATION.

STN supertwist nematic. See under SUPERTWIST.

stop bit *n.* in asynchronous communications, a bit that indicates that a byte has just been transmitted. Every byte of data is preceded by a start bit and followed by a stop bit.
⇒ See also ASYNCHRONOUS; BIT; BYTE.

storage *n.* **1.** the capacity of a device to hold and retain data. **2.** MASS STORAGE.
⇒ See also HSM; STORAGE DEVICE.

storage device *n.* a device capable of storing data. The term usually refers to mass storage devices, such as disk and tape drives.
⇒ See also DISK DRIVE; HSM; MASS STORAGE; STORAGE; TAPE DRIVE.

store *v.t.* **1.** to copy (data) from a CPU to memory, or from memory to a mass storage device. —*n.* **2.** a storage device.
⇒ See also SAVE.

stored procedure *n.* in database management systems (DBMSs), an operation that is stored with the database server. Typically, stored procedures are written in SQL. They are especially important for client/server database systems because storing the procedure on the server side means that it is available to all clients. When the procedure is modified, all clients automatically get the new version.
⇒ See also DATABASE MANAGEMENT SYSTEM; SQL.

streamer *n.* TAPE.

streaming *n.* a technique for transferring data such that it can be processed as a steady and continuous stream. Streaming technologies are becoming increasingly important because most users do not have fast enough access to download large multimedia files quickly. With streaming, the client browser or plug-in can start displaying the data before the entire file has been transmitted.
⇒ See also ACTIVEMOVIE; H.324; MULTIMEDIA; NET-SHOW; REALAUDIO; REALVIDEO; RTP; RTSP; SMIL.

strikeout *n.* a method of marking text by drawing a horizontal line through the characters. Many word processors support edit modes in which deleted sections are displayed with strikeouts.
⇒ See also WORKGROUP COMPUTING.

strikethrough *n.* STRIKEOUT.

string *n.* CHARACTER STRING.

Structured Query Language *n.* See SQL.

stub *n.* a routine that does nothing other than declare itself and the parameters it accepts. Stubs are used commonly as placeholders for routines that still need to be developed.
⇒ See also DECLARE; ROUTINE.

style *n.* in word processing, a named set of formatting parameters. By applying the style name to a section of text, many formatting properties may be changed at once.
⇒ See also FORMAT; STYLE SHEET.

style sheet *n.* in word processing and desktop publishing, a file or form that defines the layout of a document, such as the page size, margins, and fonts. Also called **template**.
⇒ See also CSS; DESKTOP PUBLISHING; FONT; LAYOUT; MARGINS; STYLE; WORD PROCESSING.

stylus *n.* a pointing and drawing device shaped like a pen. It is used with a digitizing tablet or touch screen.
⇒ See also DIGITIZING TABLET; TOUCH SCREEN.

subdirectory *n.* a directory below another directory. Every directory except the root directory is a subdirectory.
⇒ See also DIRECTORY; FOLDER; ROOT DIRECTORY.

subnet *n.* a portion of a network that shares a common address component. On TCP/IP networks, subnets are defined as all devices whose IP addresses have the same prefix. Dividing a network into subnets is useful for both security and performance reasons.
⇒ See also IP ADDRESS; SUBNET MASK.

subnet mask *n.* a mask used to determine what subnet an IP address belongs to. An IP address has two components, the network address and the host address. Subnetting divides the host address further into two or more subnets by reserving a part of the host address to identify the particular subnet. The subnet mask indicates which bits in the host address are used for subnetting: all the bits in the network-address part and the subnetting part are set to 1.
⇒ See also MASK; SUBNET.

subnotebook computer *n.* a portable computer that is slightly lighter and smaller than a full-sized notebook computer.

⇒ See also HAND-HELD COMPUTER; NOTEBOOK COMPUTER; PORTABLE.

subroutine *n.* ROUTINE.

subscript *n.* **1.** in programming, a symbol or number used to identify an element in an array. Usually, it is placed in brackets following the array name. For example, AR[5] identifies element number 5 in an array called AR. **2.** in word processing, a character that appears slightly below the line, as in this example: H_2O.
⇒ See also ARRAY; SUPERSCRIPT; WORD PROCESSING.

Sun Microsystems *n.* a company that builds computer hardware and software. The firm is best known for developing workstations and operating environments for UNIX, and for developing the Java programming language.
⇒ See also DEC; IBM; JAVA; JAVASOFT; MICROSOFT; NETSCAPE; NETWORK COMPUTER; SERVER; SGI; SOLARIS; SPARC; UNIX; WORKSTATION.

supercomputer *n.* the fastest type of computer, used for applications that require immense amounts of mathematical calculations. A supercomputer executes a few programs as fast as possible, whereas a mainframe uses its power to execute many programs concurrently.
⇒ See also COMPUTER; HIGH PERFORMANCE COMPUTING; HIPPI; MAINFRAME.

supercomputing *n.* HIGH PERFORMANCE COMPUTING.

SuperDisk *n.* a disk storage technology that supports very high-density diskettes. A SuperDisk diskette can have 2,490 tracks. This higher density translates into 120 MB capacity per diskette.
⇒ See also FLOPPY DISK; HiFD; ZIP DRIVE.

SuperDrive *n.* another name for the *FDHD (floppy disk, high density)* disk drive. The SuperDrive can read and write to all Macintosh disk sizes as well as the two PC 3½-inch disk sizes.
⇒ See also FDHD; FLOPPY DISK; MACINTOSH COMPUTER.

super-programmer *n.* WIZARD (def. 2).

superscalar *adj.* referring to microprocessor architectures that enable more than one instruction to be executed per clock cycle.
⇒ See also CLOCK SPEED; INSTRUCTION; MICROPROCESSOR; PARALLEL PROCESSING; PIPELINING.

superscript *n.* a symbol or character that appears slightly above a line, such as a footnote number.
⇒ See also SUBSCRIPT; WORD PROCESSING.

supertwist *n.* a technique for improving LCD display screens by increasing the helicity of their liquid crystals. In general, the more twists, the higher the contrast, and double-twist (or *dual supertwist*) and triple-twist displays are common. Supertwist displays are also called supertwist nematic (STN) displays.
⇒ See also BACKGROUND; BACKLIGHTING; CSTN; DSTN; FLAT-PANEL DISPLAY; LCD; NOTEBOOK COMPUTER.

Super VGA *n.* See SVGA.

Super-Video *n.* See S-VIDEO.

support *v.t.* **1.** to have (a specific functionality). For example, a word processor that *supports* graphics is one that has a graphics component. —*n.* **2.** the assistance that a vendor offers to customers.
⇒ See also CUSTOMER SUPPORT.

surf *v.t., v.i.* to move from place to place on (the Internet or Web) searching for topics of interest. The term generally describes an undirected type of Web browsing as opposed to searching for specific information.
⇒ See also BROWSE; LURK; WORLD WIDE WEB.

surge protector *n.* a device that protects a power supply and communications lines from electrical surges. All computers come with some built-in surge protection, but this separate device offers added protection. Also called **surge suppressor.**
⇒ See also UPS.

surround sound *n.* DOLBY DIGITAL.

SVC switched virtual circuit: a temporary virtual circuit that is set up and used only as long as data is being transmitted.
⇒ See also PACKET SWITCHING; PVC; VIRTUAL CIRCUIT.

SVGA Super VGA: a set of graphics standards designed to offer greater resolution than VGA. There are several varieties of SVGA, each providing a dif-

ferent resolution. All SVGA standards support a palette of 16 million colors.
⇒ See also 8514/A; PALETTE; RESOLUTION; VESA; VGA; VIDEO STANDARDS.

S-Video *n.* Super-Video: a technology for transmitting video signals over a cable by dividing the video information into two separate signals: one for color (*chrominance*), and the other for brightness (*luminance*). Most digital video devices, such as digital cameras, produce video in RGB format. The images look best, therefore, when output on a computer monitor. When output on a television, however, they look better in S-Video format than in composite format.
⇒ See also COMPOSITE VIDEO; NTSC; RGB MONITOR; VIDEO.

swap *v.i.* **1.** to replace pages or segments of data in memory. Swapping enables a computer to execute programs and manipulate data files larger than main memory. The operating system copies as much data as needed into main memory and leaves the rest on the disk. When the operating system needs data from the disk, it exchanges a portion of data in main memory with a portion of data on the disk. **2.** in UNIX systems, to move entire processes in and out of main memory.
⇒ See also DEMAND PAGING; MAIN MEMORY; MEMORY; OPERATING SYSTEM; PAGE; PAGING; PROCESS; SEGMENT; THRASH; UNIX; VIRTUAL MEMORY.

swap file *n.* a file used by the operating system for swapping.
⇒ See also SWAP.

switch *n.* **1.** in networks, a device that forwards packets between LAN segments. LANs that use switches to join segments are called *switched LANs*. **2.** a small lever or button. The switches on the back of printers and on expansion boards are called DIP switches. **3.** OPTION; PARAMETER.
⇒ See also 3COM; DIP SWITCH; ROUTING SWITCH; SWITCHED ETHERNET; TOGGLE.

switched Ethernet *n.* an Ethernet LAN that uses switches to connect individual hosts or segments. Switched Ethernets are becoming very popular because they are an effective and convenient way to extend the bandwidth of existing Ethernets.
⇒ See also 100BASE-T; ETHERNET; SHARED ETHERNET; SWITCH; SWITCHING HUB.

switched virtual circuit *n.* See SVC.

switching hub *n.* a special type of network hub that forwards packets to the appropriate port based on the packet's address. Because switching hubs forward each packet only to the required port, they provide much better performance than conventional hubs.
⇒ See also HUB; LOCAL-AREA NETWORK; SEGMENT; SWITCHED ETHERNET.

Sybase *n.* a software company. Its DBMS products are branded with the Sybase name, whereas its client/server products, chiefly PowerBuilder, are branded with the name *PowerSoft*.
⇒ See also INFORMIX; ORACLE; POWERBUILDER; SQL SERVER.

symmetric digital subscriber line *n.* See SDSL.

symmetric encryption *n.* a type of encryption where the same key is used to encrypt and decrypt the message. This differs from asymmetric (or public-key) encryption.
⇒ See also ENCRYPTION.

symmetric-key cryptography *n.* an encryption system in which the sender and receiver of a message share a single key that is used to encrypt and decrypt the message. Contrast this with public-key cryptology, which utilizes a public key to encrypt messages and a private key to decrypt them.
⇒ See also CRYPTOGRAPHY; DES; KEY; PUBLIC-KEY ENCRYPTION.

Symmetric Multiprocessing *n.* See SMP.

synchronous *adj.* occurring at regular intervals. Communication within a computer is usually synchronous and is governed by the microprocessor clock.
⇒ See also ASYNCHRONOUS; BISYNC; BUS; CLOCK SPEED; ISOCHRONOUS.

Synchronous Digital Hierarchy *n.* See SDH.
synchronous DRAM *n.* See SDRAM.
Synchronous Optical Network *n.* See SONET.
SyncLink memory *n.* See SLDRAM.
syntax *n.* the spelling and grammar of a programming language. Each program defines its own syntactical rules that control which words the computer understands, which combinations of words are meaningful, and what punctuation is necessary.
⇒ See also LANGUAGE; SEMANTICS.

sysadmin *n.* SYSTEM ADMINISTRATOR.

sysop (sis/op′), *n.* system operator: an individual who manages a bulletin board system (BBS), online service, or special interest group (SIG).
⇒ See also BULLETIN BOARD SYSTEM; NETWORK; SIG.

System *n.* System File: an essential program that runs whenever a Macintosh is started up. The System provides information to all other applications that run on a Macintosh.
⇒ See also FINDER; MACOS; MACINTOSH COMPUTER; OPERATING SYSTEM.

system *n.* **1.** a combination of components working together. For example, a *computer system* includes both hardware and software. A *Windows system* is a personal computer running the Windows operating system. **2.** COMPUTER SYSTEM. **3.** OPERATING SYSTEM **4.** an organization or methodology.
⇒ See also COMPUTER SYSTEM; EMBEDDED SYSTEM; OPERATING SYSTEM; SYSTEM MANAGEMENT.

system administrator *n.* an individual responsible for maintaining a multi-user computer system, often including a local-area network (LAN). Also called **systems administrator, sysadmin.**
⇒ See also MIS; SYSTEM MANAGEMENT.

System Application Architecture *n.* See SAA.

system board *n.* MOTHERBOARD.

system call *n.* the invocation of an operating system routine.
⇒ See also INVOKE; OPERATING SYSTEM; ROUTINE.

System folder *n.* a standard folder on Macintoshes that contains the System and Finder programs, as well as other resources needed by the operating system.
⇒ See also FINDER; FOLDER; MACINTOSH COMPUTER; SYSTEM.

system management *n.* the general area of Information Technology (IT) that concerns configuring and managing computer resources, especially network resources.
⇒ See also IS; IT; MIS; SMS; SYSTEM; SYSTEM ADMINISTRATOR.

System Object Model *n.* See SOM.

system prompt *n.* See under PROMPT.

systems administrator *n.* SYSTEM ADMINISTRATOR.

systems analyst *n.* a programmer or consultant who designs and manages the development of business applications. Typically, systems analysts are more involved in design issues than in day-to-day coding.
⇒ See also PROGRAMMER; SYSTEMS INTEGRATOR.

systems integrator *n.* an individual or company that specializes in building complete computer systems by putting together components from different vendors.
⇒ See also PROGRAMMER; SYSTEMS ANALYST.

Systems Management Server *n.* See SMS.
Systems Network Architecture *n.* See SNA.
system software *n.* SYSTEMS SOFTWARE.

systems software *n.* the operating system and all utility programs that manage computer resources at a low level. Software is generally divided into systems software and applications software. Systems software includes compilers, loaders, linkers, and debuggers.
⇒ See also APPLICATION; END USER; SOFTWARE; UTILITY.

system unit *n.* the main part of a personal computer. The system unit includes the chassis, microprocessor, main memory, bus, and ports but does not generally include the keyboard or monitor, or any peripheral devices other than disk drives.
⇒ See also CHASSIS; MAIN MEMORY; MICROPROCESSOR; PORT.

computer

T-1 carrier *n.* a dedicated phone connection supporting data rates of 1.544 Mbps. Most telephone companies sell individual channels, known as *fractional T-1* access. T-1 lines are a popular option for businesses connecting to the Internet and for Internet Service Providers (ISPs) connecting to the Internet backbone.
⇒ See also CARRIER; CSU/DSU; FRACTIONAL T-1; ISP; LEASED LINE; OC; SONET; T-3 CARRIER; TDM.

T-3 carrier *n.* a dedicated phone connection supporting data rates of about 43 Mbps. T-3 lines are used mainly by Internet Service Providers (ISPs) connecting to the Internet backbone and for the backbone itself.
⇒ See also BACKBONE; CARRIER; CSU/DSU; ISP; LEASED LINE; OC; SONET; T-1 CARRIER; TDM.

TA TERMINAL ADAPTER.

tab character *n.* a special character that can be inserted into a text document. Most word processors move the cursor or insertion point to the next tab stop, and most printers move the print head to the next tab stop as well.
⇒ See also TAB KEY; TAB STOP.

Tab key *n.* a key on computer keyboards that inserts a tab character or moves the insertion point to the next tab stop. Spreadsheet and database management applications usually respond to the Tab key by moving the cursor to the next field or cell. In dialog boxes and menus, pressing the Tab key highlights the next button or option.
⇒ See also CELL; CURSOR; FIELD; INSERTION POINT; TAB CHARACTER; TAB STOP.

table *n.* data arranged in rows and columns, such as a spreadsheet. In relational database management systems, all information is stored in the form of tables.
⇒ See also DATABASE MANAGEMENT SYSTEM; RDBMS; SPREADSHEET.

tablet *n.* DIGITIZING TABLET.

tab stop *n.* a stop point for tabbing. In word processing, each line generally contains a number of tab stops placed at regular intervals. When the Tab key is pressed, the cursor or insertion point jumps to the next tab stop.
⇒ See also TAB CHARACTER; TAB KEY.

tag *n.* **1.** a command inserted in a document that specifies how the document, or a portion of the document, should be formatted. Tags are used by all format specifications that store documents as text files. This includes SGML, XML, and HTML, although the tags in SGML and XML do not directly specify formatting, but indicate the content or structure of what is tagged. —*v.t.* **2.** to mark a section of (a document) with a formatting command.
⇒ See also FORMAT; HTML; META TAG; SGML; XML.

Tagged Image File Format *n.* See TIFF.

tag RAM *n.* the area in an L2 cache that identifies which data from main memory is currently stored in each *cache line*. The actual data is stored in a different part of the cache, called the *data store*. The values stored in the tag RAM determine whether a cache lookup results in a *hit* or a *miss*.
⇒ See also CACHE; L2 CACHE; RAM.

tape *n.* a magnetically coated strip of plastic on which data can be encoded. Storing data on tapes is considerably cheaper than storing data on disks. Tapes also have large storage capacities. Tapes are sequential-access media, and because they are so slow, they are generally used only for long-term storage and backup. They are also used for transporting large amounts of data.
⇒ See also 3480, 3490; BACKUP; DAT; DISK DRIVE; DLT; HELICAL-SCAN CARTRIDGE; MASS STORAGE; QIC; SEQUENTIAL ACCESS; TRAVAN.

tape drive *n.* a device, like a tape recorder, that reads data from and writes it onto a tape. Data ca-

pacities and transfer speeds of tape drives vary considerably. They are sequential-access devices, which makes them too slow for general-purpose storage. Therefore, they are used for making backups.
⇒ See also BACKUP; DLT; SEQUENTIAL ACCESS; TAPE; TRAVAN.

TAPI Telephony Application Programming Interface: an API for connecting a PC running Windows to telephone services.
⇒ See also API; TELEPHONY; TSAPI.

tar *n.* **1.** tape archive: a UNIX utility that combines a group of files into a single file. The resulting file has a .TAR extension. Frequently, a tar file is compressed with the *compress* or *gzip* commands to create a file with a .TAR.GZ or .TAR.Z extension. —*v.t.* **2.** to combine (files) with the **tar** command.
⇒ See also PKZIP.

target *n.* a file, device, or any type of location to which data is moved or copied. The computer copies from the source to the target (or destination).
⇒ See also SOURCE.

task *n.* the combination of a program being executed and bookkeeping information used by the operating system. The task is like an envelope for the program. The terms *task* and *process* are often used interchangeably, although some operating systems make a distinction between the two.
⇒ See also JOB; MULTITASKING; MULTITHREADING; OPERATING SYSTEM.

taskbar *n.* in Windows 95 and 98, a graphical list of active applications. If the application window is minimized, it can be restored by clicking on its button in the taskbar. By default, the taskbar appears on the bottom of the screen.

task switching *n.* the ability of operating systems or operating environments to enable a user to switch from one program to another without quitting the spot in the first program.
⇒ See also DOS; MULTITASKING; OPERATING ENVIRONMENT; OPERATING SYSTEM.

Tcl (tik′əl *or as separate letters*), *n.* tool command language: a powerful interpreted programming language. Tcl can be easily extended through the addition of custom libraries. It is used for prototyping applications as well as for developing CGI scripts.
⇒ See also INTERPRETER; Perl; PROGRAMMING LANGUAGE.

TCO Total Cost of Ownership: a popular buzzword representing how much it actually costs to own a PC. Most estimates place the TCO at about three to four times the actual purchase cost of the PC.
⇒ See also NETWORK COMPUTER; UPGRADE; ZAW.

TCP Transmission Control Protocol: one of the main protocols in TCP/IP networks. TCP enables two hosts to establish a connection and exchange streams of data. TCP guarantees delivery of data in order.
⇒ See also IP; SOCKS; SPX; TCP/IP.

TCP/IP Transmission Control Protocol/Internet Protocol: the suite of communications protocols used to connect hosts on the Internet. TCP/IP is built into the UNIX operating system and is the fundamental standard of the Internet.
⇒ See also INTERNET; IP; IP ADDRESS; PACKET SWITCHING; PROTOCOL; SOCKET; TCP; UDP.

TDM Time Division Multiplexing: a type of multiplexing that combines data streams by assigning each stream a different time slot in a set. TDM repeatedly transmits a fixed sequence of time slots over a single transmission channel.
⇒ See also CDMA; FDM; LEASED LINE; MODULATE; MULTIPLEX; PCM; T-1 CARRIER; T-3 CARRIER; TDMA; WDM.

TDMA Time Division Multiple Access: a technology for delivering digital wireless service using time-division multiplexing (TDM). TDMA works by dividing a radio frequency into time slots and then allocating slots to multiple calls. In this way, a single frequency can support multiple, simultaneous data channels.

⇒ See also CDMA; CELLULAR; GSM; PCS; TDM.

teamware *n.* GROUPWARE.

tear-off menu *n.* a pop-up menu that can be moved around the screen like a window.

⇒ See also MENU.

technical support *n.* CUSTOMER SUPPORT.

telecommunications *n.* all types of long-distance data transmission, from voice to video.

⇒ See also COMMUNICATIONS; ITU; TELEMATICS; TELEPHONY.

telecommuting *n.* working at home on a computer and transmitting data and documents to a central office via telephone lines.

⇒ See also E-MAIL; NETWORK; WORKGROUP COMPUTING.

teleconference *v.i.* to hold a conference via a telephone or network connection.

⇒ See also MULTICAST; NETMEETING; VIDEOCONFERENCING; WHITEBOARD; WORKGROUP COMPUTING.

telecopy *v.t.* to send (a document) from one place to another via a fax machine.

⇒ See also FAX MACHINE.

telematics *n.* the broad industry related to using computers in concert with telecommunications systems. This includes dial-up service to the Internet as well as all types of networks that rely on a telecommunications system to transport data.

⇒ See also PBX; TELECOMMUNICATIONS; TELEPHONY.

Telenet *n.* one of the largest public data networks (PDNs) in the United States, owned by U.S. Sprint Communications Corporation.

⇒ See also ONLINE SERVICE; WIDE-AREA NETWORK.

telephony *n.* the science of translating sound into electrical signals, transmitting them, and then converting them back to sound. The term is used frequently to refer to computer hardware and software that perform functions traditionally performed by telephone equipment, such as voice mail.

⇒ See also CTI; DTMF; INTERNET TELEPHONY; MODEM; TAPI; TELECOMMUNICATIONS; TELEMATICS; TSAPI.

Telephony API *n.* See TAPI.

Telephony Server API *n.* See TSAPI.

television board *n.* an expansion board that enables a computer monitor to function as a television screen. Most television boards support windowed as well as full-screen viewing.

⇒ See also EXPANSION BOARD; NTSC; PC/TV.

Telnet *n.* a terminal emulation protocol for TCP/IP networks such as the Internet. The Telnet client runs on a PC and connects it to a server on the network. Telnet is a common way to control Web servers remotely.

⇒ See also HOST; INTERNET; TERMINAL EMULATION.

template *n.* **1.** Also called **keyboard template.** a plastic or paper diagram placed on a keyboard to indicate the meanings of different keys, esp. the function keys, for a particular program. **2.** a sheet of plastic with menus and command boxes drawn on it that is placed on top of a digitizing tablet. Commands are selected by pressing the digitizing tablet's pen against a command box or by positioning the cursor over a box and pressing one of the cursor keys. **3.** in spreadsheet and database applications, a blank form that shows which fields exist, their locations, and their length. **4.** (in some word processing applications) STYLE SHEET. **5.** (in DOS) COMMAND BUFFER.

⇒ See also BOILERPLATE; COMMAND BUFFER; CURSOR; DIGITIZING TABLET.

10Base-2 *n.* one of several adaptations of the Ethernet standard for local-area networks (LANs). The 10Base-2 standard uses 50 ohm coaxial cable with maximum lengths of 185 meters. This cable is thinner and more flexible than that used for the 10Base-5 standard. The 10Base-2 system operates at 10 Mbps and uses baseband transmission methods. Also called **Thin Net.**

⇒ See also 10BASE5; 10BASET; BASEBAND TRANSMISSION; BNC CONNECTOR; COAXIAL CABLE; ETHERNET.

10Base5 *n.* the original cabling standard for Ether-

net that uses coaxial cables. The name derives from the fact that the maximum data transfer speed is 10 Mbps, it uses baseband transmission, and the maximum length of cables is 500 meters. Also called **thick Ethernet, ThickNet.**

10BaseT *n.* one of several adaptations of the Ethernet standard for local-area networks (LANs). The 10Base-T standard uses a twisted-pair cable with maximum lengths of 100 meters. The cable is thinner and more flexible than that used for the 10Base-2 or 10Base-5 standards.

⇒ See also 100BASE-T; 10BASE-2; 10BASE5; ETHERNET; HUB; REPEATER; RJ-45; STAR NETWORK; TWISTED-PAIR CABLE.

terabyte *n.* **1.** 2^{40} (1,099,511,627,776) bytes. This is approximately 1 trillion bytes. **2.** 10^{12} (1,000,000,000,000) bytes.

⇒ See also EXABYTE; GIGABYTE; MEGABYTE; PETABYTE.

terminal *n.* **1.** a device that enables a user to communicate with a computer. Generally, a terminal is a combination of keyboard and display screen. **2.** in networking, a personal computer or workstation connected to a mainframe. The personal computer usually runs terminal emulation software.

⇒ See also CONSOLE; DISPLAY SCREEN; DUMB TERMINAL; EMULATION; HLLAPI; INTELLIGENT TERMINAL; KEYBOARD; MONITOR; NETWORK; SMART TERMINAL.

terminal adapter *n.* a device that connects a computer to an external digital communications line, such as an ISDN line. A terminal adapter is analogous to a modem (which is used for analog lines).

⇒ See also ISDN; MODEM; SPID.

terminal emulation *n.* making a computer respond like a particular type of terminal. Terminal emulation programs allow users to access a mainframe computer or bulletin board service with a personal computer.

⇒ See also BULLETIN BOARD SYSTEM; EMULATION; MAINFRAME; TELNET; TERMINAL.

terminate and stay resident *n.* See TSR.

TeX (tek), *n.* a typesetting language that provides complete control over formatting. Most people who use TeX, however, utilize one of several macro packages that provide an easier interface.

⇒ See also LaTeX; MuTeX.

Texas Instruments *n.* a large electronics company. In 1958, a TI researcher demonstrated the first integrated circuit (IC), and in 1967, TI introduced the first hand-held calculator. Today, its core business is in producing semiconductors.

⇒ See also DLP; INTEGRATED CIRCUIT; SEMICONDUCTOR; TEXAS INSTRUMENTS GRAPHICS ARCHITECTURE (TIGA); TI 34010.

Texas Instruments Graphics Architecture (TIGA) *n.* a high-resolution graphics specification designed by Texas Instruments. TIGA does not specify a particular resolution or number of colors. Instead, it defines an interface between software and graphics processors.

⇒ See also 8514/A; GRAPHICS; SVGA; TEXAS INSTRUMENTS; TI 34010; VESA; VIDEO STANDARDS; XGA.

text *n.* words, sentences, and paragraphs. *Text processing* refers to the ability to manipulate information consisting only of printable ASCII characters and intended to be readable. Typically, the term *text* refers to text stored as text files, usually documents. Objects that are *not* text include graphics, numbers, and machine code.

⇒ See also ASCII.

text editor *n.* EDITOR.

text file *n.* a file that holds text. The term *text file* is often used as a synonym for *ASCII file,* a file in which characters are represented simply by their ASCII codes.

⇒ See also ASCII; FILE; TEXT.

text flow *n.* TEXT WRAP.

text mode *n.* a video mode in which a display screen is divided into rows and columns of boxes. Each box can contain one character. Also called **character mode.**

⇒ See also CHARACTER BASED; GRAPHICS BASED; GRAPHICS MODE; VIDEO MODE; VIDEO STANDARDS.

computer

texture *n.* in 3-D graphics, the digital representation of the surface of an object. In addition to two-dimensional qualities, such as color and brightness, a texture is also encoded with three-dimensional properties, such as how transparent and reflective the object is. Once a texture has been defined, it can be wrapped around any three-dimensional object. This is called *texture mapping.* Well-defined textures are very important for rendering realistic 3-D images. However, they also require a lot of memory.
⇒ See also 3-D GRAPHICS; 3-D SOFTWARE; AGP; MODELING; RAY TRACING; RENDER.

texture mapping *n.* See under TEXTURE.

text wrap *n.* a feature supported by many word processors that enables a user to surround a picture or diagram with text. The text wraps around the graphic. Also called **text flow.**
⇒ See also WORD PROCESSING.

TFT thin film transistor: the basis for a type of LCD flat-panel display screen in which each pixel is controlled by from one to four transistors. The TFT technology provides the best performance of all the flat-panel techniques, but it is also the most expensive.
⇒ See also ACTIVE-MATRIX DISPLAY; CSTN; FLAT-PANEL DISPLAY; LCD.

TFTP Trivial File Transfer Protocol: a simple form of the file transfer protocol (FTP). It is often used by servers to boot diskless workstations, X-terminals, and routers.
⇒ See also FTP.

The Open Group *n.* an international consortium of computer and software manufacturers and users dedicated to advancing multivendor technologies. The Open Group was formed in 1996 by merging two previously independent groups— the *Open Software Foundation (OSF)* and *X/Open Company Ltd.*
⇒ See also DCE; OPEN ARCHITECTURE.

thermal printer *n.* a type of printer that produces images by electrically heating pins in contact with special heat-sensitive paper. Thermal printers are inexpensive; they are used in most printing calculators and many fax machines.
⇒ See also FAX MACHINE; PRINTER.

thin client *n.* in client/server applications, a client designed to be especially small so that the bulk of the data processing occurs on the server. The term *thin client* usually refers to software, but it is used for hardware designed to run thin-client software. A thin client is a network computer without a hard disk drive, whereas a fat client includes a disk drive.
⇒ See also CLIENT; CLIENT/SERVER ARCHITECTURE; JAVA; NC; NETWORK COMPUTER; WinFrame.

thin film transistor *n.* See TFT.

ThinNet *n.* See 10BASE2.

1394 short for *IEEE 1394.*

3480, 3490 the IBM designation for families of half-inch magnetic tape drives typically used on mainframes and AS/400s.
⇒ See also BACKUP; TAPE.

32-bit *adj.* referring to the number of bits processed or transmitted in parallel, or the number of bits used for a single element in a data format. The term is often applied to microprocessors (indicating the width of the registers), buses (indicating the number of data wires), graphics devices (indicating the number of bits used to represent a pixel), operating systems (indicating the number of bits used to represent memory addresses), and applications (indicating how a program is compiled).
⇒ See also 16-BIT; BIT; BUS; REGISTER.

thrash *v.i.* (of virtual memory operating systems) to spend too much time moving data in and out of virtual memory (swapping pages) rather than executing programs. A computer is often thrashing when an application stops responding but the disk drive light keeps blinking on and off.
⇒ See also PAGING; SWAP; VIRTUAL MEMORY.

thread *n.* **1.** in on-line discussions, a series of messages that have been posted as replies to one another. A single forum or conference typically contains many threads covering different subjects. **2.** in

programming, a part of a program that can execute independently of other parts. Operating systems that support multithreading enable programmers to design programs whose parts can execute concurrently.
⇒ See also FORUM; MULTITHREADING; ONLINE SERVICE.

3COM *n.* one of the largest networking companies in the world. The name is derived from the prefixes of three terms—com(puter), com(munication), and com(patibility).
⇒ See also CISCO SYSTEMS; HUB; ROUTER; SWITCH.

3-D audio *n.* a technique for giving more depth to traditional stereo sound. Typically, 3-D audio is produced by placing a device in a room with stereo speakers. The device analyzes the sound coming from the speakers and sends feedback to the sound system so that it can readjust the sound. 3-D audio devices are particularly popular for improving computer audio where the speakers tend to be small and close together.
⇒ See also MULTIMEDIA; SOUND CARD.

3-D graphics *n.* the field of computer graphics concerned with generating and displaying 2-D images of three-dimensional objects. Whereas pixels in a two-dimensional graphic have the properties of position, color, and brightness, 3-D pixels include a depth property.
⇒ See also 3-D SOFTWARE; ANIMATION; GRAPHICS; GRAPHICS ACCELERATOR; RAY TRACING; RENDER; TEXTURE; Z-BUFFER.

three-dimensional spreadsheet *n.* a spreadsheet program that allows the user to arrange data as a stack of identically-formatted tables.
⇒ See also SPREADSHEET.

3DO a technology that supports photo-realistic graphics, full-motion video, and CD-quality sound.
⇒ See also EXPANSION BOARD; MULTIMEDIA.

3-D software *n.* the category of software that represents three-dimensional objects on a computer. This includes CAD/CAM, computer games, and animation packages.
⇒ See also 3-D GRAPHICS; ANIMATION; Direct3D; MODELING; NURBS; OpenGL; RENDER; TEXTURE.

3-D sound *n.* 3-D AUDIO.

3-D spreadsheet *n.* THREE-DIMENSIONAL SPREADSHEET.

386 short for the *Intel 80386 microprocessor.*
⇒ See also INTEL MICROPROCESSORS.

386DX See under INTEL MICROPROCESSORS.

386SX short for the *Intel 80386SX microprocessor.*
⇒ See also INTEL MICROPROCESSORS.

three-tier *adj.* referring to a special type of client/server architecture consisting of three well-defined and separate processes, each running on a different platform. The first tier is the user interface, which runs on the user's computer (the *client*). Next are the functional modules that actually process data. This middle tier runs on a server and is often called the *application server.* The third tier is a database-management system (DBMS) that stores the data required by the middle tier. This tier runs on a second server called the *database server.* The three-tier design has many advantages over traditional two-tier or single-tier designs.
⇒ See also CLIENT/SERVER ARCHITECTURE; LOAD BALANCING; MIDDLEWARE; TP MONITOR; TWO-TIER.

throughput *n.* the amount of data transferred from one place to another or processed in a specified amount of time. Typically, throughputs are measured in FLOPS, MIPS, Kbps, Mbps, and Gbps.
⇒ See also DISK DRIVE; ISOCHRONOUS; NETWORK.

thumbnail *n.* a miniature display of a page to be printed. Thumbnails make it possible to see the layout of many pages on the screen at once.
⇒ See also DESKTOP PUBLISHING; GREEKING; LAYOUT.

thunk *v.i.* **1.** in PCs, to convert a 16-bit memory address to a 32-bit address, and vice versa. Windows 95 supports a thunk mechanism to enable 32-bit programs to call 16-bit DLLs. This is called a *flat thunk.* On the other hand, 16-bit applications running under Windows 3.x and Windows for Workgroups cannot use 32-bit DLLs unless the 32-bit addresses are converted to 16-bit addresses. This is

the function of Win32s and is called a *universal thunk.* —*n.* **2.** the operation of converting between a segmented memory address space and a flat address space.
⇒ See also ADDRESS SPACE; WIN32s.

TI TEXAS INSTRUMENTS.

TI 34010 *n.* a video standard from Texas Instruments that supports a resolution of 1,024 by 768 pixels.
⇒ See also TEXAS INSTRUMENTS GRAPHICS ARCHITECTURE (TIGA); VIDEO STANDARDS.

TIF *n.* See under TIFF.

TIFF (tif), *n.* tagged image file format: one of the most widely supported file formats for storing bitmapped images on personal computers. TIFF graphics can be any resolution, and they can be black and white, gray-scaled, or color. Files in TIFF format often end with a .TIF extension.
⇒ See also BIT MAP; GRAPHICS; GRAPHICS FILE FORMATS; GRAY SCALING.

TIGA *n.* TEXAS INSTRUMENTS GRAPHICS ARCHITECTURE.

tiled windows *n.pl.* windows arranged so that they do not overlap one another.
⇒ See also CASCADING WINDOWS; OVERLAID WINDOWS; WINDOW.

Tillamook *n.* the codename for a low-power version of the Pentium microprocessor designed especially for portable devices.
⇒ See also PENTIUM MICROPROCESSOR.

Time Division Multiple Access *n.* See TDMA.

Time Division Multiplexing *n.* See TDM.

time-out *n.* a signal generated by a program or device that has waited a certain length of time for some input but has not received it.
⇒ See also INTERRUPT.

time sharing *n.* the concurrent use of a computer by more than one user. Almost all mainframes and minicomputers are time-sharing systems, but most personal computers and workstations are not.
⇒ See also MAINFRAME; MINICOMPUTER; MULTITASKING; MULTI-USER.

title bar *n.* a bar on top of a window that contains the name of the file or application. In many graphical user interfaces, a user moves (drags) a window by grabbing the title bar.
⇒ See also DRAG; WINDOW.

TLD top-level domain: the suffix attached to Internet domain names. There are a limited number of predefined suffixes, and each one represents a top-level domain. Current top-level domains include: com (commercial businesses); gov (government agencies); and edu (educational institutions).
⇒ See also DOMAIN NAME; IP ADDRESS.

TNEF (tě′nef), *n.* Transport Neutral Encapsulation Format: a proprietary format used by the Microsoft Exchange and Outlook e-mail clients when sending messages in rich text format (RTF). Because of the proprietary nature of TNEF encoding, most non-Microsoft e-mail clients cannot decifer such a message, which usually appears as an attached file named WINMAIL.DAT.
⇒ See also E-MAIL CLIENT; RICH TEXT FORMAT.

toggle *v.t.* to switch (a parameter) from one setting to another. A *toggle switch* is a switch that has just two positions: pressing it once turns it on; pressing it again turns it off. On computer keyboards, the Caps Lock key is a toggle switch. Toggle switches exist in software too. For example, a check box in a dialog box is a toggle switch.
⇒ See also DIP SWITCH; KEYBOARD; SWITCH.

token *n.* **1.** in programming languages, a single element of a programming language, such as a keyword, an operator, or a punctuation mark. **2.** in networking, a special series of bits that travels around a token-ring network. As the token circulates, computers attached to the network can capture it. The token acts like a ticket, enabling its owner to send a message across the network. **3.** in security systems, a small device the size of a credit card that displays a constantly changing ID code. A user first enters a password and then the card displays an ID that can be used to log into a network.
⇒ See also KEYWORD; OPERATOR; PROGRAMMING LAN-

GUAGE; SMART CARD; TOKEN BUS NETWORK; TOKEN-RING NETWORK.

token bus network *n.* a type of local-area network (LAN) that has a bus topology and uses a token-passing mechanism to regulate traffic on the bus.
⇒ See also BUS NETWORK; IEEE 802 STANDARDS; LOCAL-AREA NETWORK; TOKEN; TOKEN-RING NETWORK; TOPOLOGY.

Token Ring *n.* See under TOKEN-RING NETWORK.

token-ring network *n.* **1.** a type of computer network in which all the computers are arranged (schematically) in a circle. A *token,* which is a special bit pattern, travels around the circle. To send a message, a computer catches the token, attaches a message to it, and then lets it continue to travel around the network. **2.** (*caps.*) the PC network protocol developed by IBM. The Token-Ring specification has been standardized as the IEEE 802.5 standard.
⇒ See also ARCNET; IEEE; IEEE 802 STANDARDS; LOCAL-AREA NETWORK; NETWORK; TOKEN; TOKEN BUS NETWORK.

toner *n.* a special type of ink used by copy machines and laser printers. Toner consists of a dry, powdery substance that can be electrically charged so that it adheres to a drum, plate, or piece of paper charged with the opposite polarity.
⇒ See also LASER PRINTER.

Top-Level Domain *n.* See TLD.

topology *n.* the shape of a local-area network (LAN) or other communications system. There are three principal topologies used in LANs. In a *bus topology,* all devices are connected to a central cable, called the *bus* or *backbone.* In a *ring topology,* all devices are connected to one another in the shape of a closed loop, so that each device is connected directly to two other devices. In a *star topology,* all devices are connected to a central *hub.*
⇒ See also BUS NETWORK; ETHERNET; LOCAL-AREA NETWORK.

TOPS *n.* transparent operating system: a type of local-area network that can combine Macintosh computers, PCs, and Sun workstations on the same network. TOPS uses the Macintosh computer's built-in AppleTalk protocol. It is a peer-to-peer network.
⇒ See also APPLETALK; LOCAL-AREA NETWORK; PEER-TO-PEER ARCHITECTURE; SUN MICROSYSTEMS.

Total Cost of Ownership *n.* See TCO.

touchpad *n.* a small touch-sensitive pad used as a pointing device on some portable computers.
⇒ See also DIGITIZING TABLET; POINTING DEVICE.

touch screen *n.* a type of display screen that has a touch-sensitive transparent panel covering the screen.
⇒ See also DISPLAY SCREEN; KIOSK; LIGHT PEN; MOUSE; POINT.

touch tablet *n.* DIGITIZING TABLET.

tower model *n.* a computer in which the power supply, motherboard, and mass storage devices are stacked on top of one another in a case.
⇒ See also CHASSIS; DESKTOP MODEL COMPUTER.

TPI tracks per inch: the density of tracks on a disk. For example, high-density 3.5-inch diskettes are formatted with 135 TPI. Hard disks have TPIs in the thousands.
⇒ See also DISK; TRACK.

TP monitor *n.* transaction processing monitor: a program that monitors a transaction as it passes from one stage in a process to another. TP monitors are especially important in three-tier architectures that employ load balancing because a transaction may be forwarded to any of several servers.
⇒ See also CICS; LOAD BALANCING; MIDDLEWARE; THREE-TIER; TRANSACTION PROCESSING.

traceroute *n.* a utility that traces a packet from a computer to an Internet host, showing how many hops the packet requires to reach the host and how long each hop takes.
⇒ See also HOP; PACKET; PING.

track *n.* an annular region on a disk where data can be written. A typical floppy disk has 80 (double-density) or 160 (high-density) tracks. The

computer

operating system remembers where information is stored by noting its track and sector numbers. The density of tracks (how close together they are) is measured in terms of tracks per inch (TPI).

⇒ See also CYLINDER; FORMAT; HARD DISK; INTERLEAVE; SECTOR.

trackball *n.* a pointing device. Essentially, a trackball is a mouse lying on its back. To move the pointer, the ball is rotated with a finger or the palm. There are usually one to three buttons next to the ball, which are used like mouse buttons. The trackball is stationary, so not much space is required to use it.

⇒ See also MOUSE; POINTING DEVICE.

tracks per inch *n.* See TPI.

tractor feed *n.* a method of feeding paper through an impact printer. Tractor-feed printers have two sprocketed wheels on either side of the printer that fit into holes in the paper. As the wheels revolve, the paper is pulled through the printer.

⇒ See also FRICTION FEED; IMPACT PRINTER.

traffic *n.* the load on a communications device or system. One of the principal jobs of a system administrator is to monitor traffic levels and take appropriate actions when traffic becomes heavy.

⇒ See also LOAD.

transaction processing *n.* a type of computer processing in which the computer responds to requests individually. ATMs for banks are an example of transaction processing. The opposite of transaction processing is batch processing.

⇒ See also BATCH PROCESSING; CICS; TP MONITOR; TWO-PHASE COMMIT.

transceiver *n.* transmitter-receiver: a device that both transmits and receives analog or digital signals. The term is used most frequently to describe the component in local-area networks (LANs) that actually applies signals onto the network wire and detects signals passing through the wire.

⇒ See also LOCAL-AREA NETWORK; NETWORK; NETWORK INTERFACE CARD.

transfer rate *n.* DATA TRANSFER RATE.

transistor *n.* a device composed of semiconductor material that amplifies a signal or opens or closes a circuit. Invented in 1947 at Bell Labs, transistors have become the key ingredient of all digital circuits, including computers. Today's microprocessors contain tens of millions of microscopic transistors. Prior to the invention of transistors, digital circuits were composed of vacuum tubes.

⇒ See also CHIP; INTEGRATED CIRCUIT; MOORE'S LAW; SEMICONDUCTOR.

Transmission Control Protocol/Internet Protocol *n.* See TCP/IP.

transparent *adj.* in computer software, referring to complex action (such as converting data from one format to another) that takes place without any visible effect on the user. Transparency is usually considered to be a good characteristic.

transportable *n.* a large portable computer (over 15 pounds). Also called **luggable.**

⇒ See also LAPTOP COMPUTER; NOTEBOOK COMPUTER; PORTABLE.

trap *n.* an interrupt signal initiated by a software program.

trapezoid distortion *n.* See under PINCUSHION DISTORTION.

Travan *n.* a magnetic tape technology that allows for higher data densities. Travan tape drives can read and write older QIC tapes as well as the newer high-capacity Travan tapes.

⇒ See also QIC; TAPE; TAPE DRIVE.

tree structure *n.* a type of data structure in which each element is attached to one or more elements directly *beneath* it. The connections between elements are called branches. Trees are often called *inverted trees* because they are normally drawn with the *root* at the top. The elements at the very bottom of an inverted tree (that is, those that have no elements below them) are called *leaves.* Inverted trees are used to represent hierarchical file structures.

⇒ See also BINARY TREE; BRANCH; DATA STRUCTURE; DIRECTORY; HIERARCHICAL; LEAF.

Triton *n.* the Intel 430 family of Pentium chipsets. The first in the family, the 430FX, is called the *Triton;* the 430 HX is called *Triton 2.* The VX model is sometimes called *Triton-2* or *Triton-3.*

⇒ See also CHIPSET; INTEL MICROPROCESSORS; PENTIUM MICROPROCESSOR.

Trivial File Transfer Protocol *n.* See TFTP.

Trojan horse *n.* a destructive program that masquerades as a benign application. Unlike viruses, Trojan horses do not replicate themselves.

⇒ See also VIRUS.

true color *adj.* referring to any graphics device or software that uses at least 24 bits to represent each dot or pixel. Using 24 bits means that more than 16 million unique colors can be represented.

⇒ See also COLOR DEPTH.

TrueType *n.* an outline font technology developed jointly by Microsoft and Apple. Anyone using Windows or Macintosh operating systems can create documents using TrueType fonts.

⇒ See also FONT; OUTLINE FONT; POSTSCRIPT.

truncate *v.t.* to cut off the end of. Usually, the term is used to describe a type of rounding of floating-point numbers. For example, if there is too little space to print or store a long floating-point number, a program may truncate the number by lopping off the decimal digits that do not fit. Truncation always rounds toward zero: 1.199 truncated to two digits yields 1.1.

⇒ See also FLOATING-POINT NUMBER.

trust hierarchy *n.* PUBLIC-KEY INFRASTRUCTURE (PKI).

TSAPI Telephony Server API: an API developed by Novell and AT&T that enables programmers to build telephony and CTI applications. TSAPI runs on NetWare applications, whereas TAPI has been implemented for the Windows operating system. Another difference is that TSAPI is strictly a server API, whereas TAPI can be used for client- and server-based applications.

⇒ See also API; TAPI; TELEPHONY.

TSR terminate and stay resident: a DOS program that can be memory resident (remaining in memory at all times) regardless of whether it is currently running. Calendars, calculators, spell checkers, thesauruses, and notepads are often set up as TSRs so that they can be instantly accessed from within another program. TSRs are sometimes called *pop-up programs* because they can pop up in applications.

⇒ See also HOT KEY; LOW MEMORY; MEMORY RESIDENT; MULTITASKING; OPERATING SYSTEM.

TTL **1.** transistor-transistor logic: a common type of digital circuit in which the output is derived from two transistors. The term is commonly used to describe any system based on digital circuitry, as in *TTL monitor.* **2.** Time to Live: a field in the Internet Protocol (IP) that specifies how many more hops a packet can travel before being discarded or returned.

⇒ See also HOP; IP; SEMICONDUCTOR; TTL MONITOR.

TTL monitor *n.* a computer display, mostly obsolete, that accepts digital inputs rather than analog ones.

⇒ See also ANALOG MONITOR; DIGITAL MONITOR; MDA; TTL.

tunneling *n.* a technology that enables one network to send its data via another network's connections. Tunneling works by encapsulating a network protocol within packets carried by the second network.

⇒ See also L2TP; LAYER TWO FORWARDING; PPTP; VPN.

turnkey system *n.* a computer system that has been customized for a particular application. Turnkey systems include all the hardware and software necessary for the application.

⇒ See also OEM; VAR.

TWAIN (twān), *n.* Technology [or Toolkit] Without An Interesting Name: a de facto interface standard for scanners. Nearly all scanners come with a TWAIN driver, which makes them compatible with any TWAIN-supporting software.

⇒ See also DRIVER; OPTICAL SCANNER.

tweak *v.t., v.i.* to make small changes that fine-tune (a piece of software or hardware). Tweaking sometimes refers to changing the values of underlying variables slightly to make the results of a program coincide with desired results.
⇒ See also DEBUG.

tweening *n.* in-betweening: the process of generating intermediate frames between two images to give the appearance that the first image evolves smoothly into the second image. Tweening is a key process in all types of animation.
⇒ See also ANIMATION.

TWIP *n.* twentieth of a point: a typographical measurement.
⇒ See also POINT.

twisted-pair cable *n.* a type of cable that consists of two independently insulated wires twisted around each other. One wire carries the signal while the other wire is grounded and absorbs signal interference. Twisted-pair cable is used by older telephone networks and is the least expensive type of local-area network (LAN) cable.
⇒ See also 10BASET; CDDI; COAXIAL CABLE; FIBER OPTICS; LOCAL-AREA NETWORK.

286 short for the *Intel 80286 microprocessor*.
⇒ See also INTEL MICROPROCESSORS.

two-phase commit *n.* a feature of transaction processing systems that enables databases to be returned to the pre-transaction state if some error condition occurs. A single transaction can update many different databases. The two-phase commit strategy is designed to ensure that either all the databases are updated or none of them, so that the databases remain synchronized.
⇒ See also DISTRIBUTED DATABASE; TRANSACTION PROCESSING.

two-tier *adj.* referring to client/server architectures in which the user interface runs on the client and the database is stored on the server. The actual application logic can run on either the client or the server.
⇒ See also CLIENT/SERVER ARCHITECTURE; THREE-TIER.

Tymnet (tīm′net′), *n.* one of the largest public data networks (PDNs) in the United States, owned by MCI.
⇒ See also NETWORK; TELENET.

type *v.i., v.t.* **1.** to enter (characters) by pressing keys on the keyboard. **2.** in DOS, OS/2, and many other operating systems, the TYPE command causes a file to appear on the display screen. —*n.* **3.** DATA TYPE.

typeface *n.* a design for a set of characters. Popular typefaces include Times Roman, Helvetica, and Courier. The typeface is one aspect of a font.
⇒ See also FONT; FONT FAMILY; SERIF; SANS SERIF.

typesetter *n.* IMAGESETTER.

---

abcdefghijklmnopqrst **UV** wxyz

computer

UART (yōō′ärt′), *n.* universal asynchronous receiver-transmitter: a computer component that handles asynchronous serial communication. Every computer contains a UART to manage the serial ports, and all internal modems have their own UART.
⇒ See also ASYNCHRONOUS; DTE; SERIAL PORT.

UDMA ULTRA DMA.

UDP User Datagram Protocol: a connectionless protocol that, like TCP, runs on top of IP networks. UDP/IP provides very few error recovery services, offering instead a direct way to send and receive individual datagrams over an IP network. It is used primarily for broadcasting messages over a network.
⇒ See also CONNECTIONLESS; IP; IPX; RTP; TCP/IP.

UDP/IP See under UDP.

UIDE Ultra IDE: See ATA-3.

ULSI ultra large scale integration: referring to technology that places more than about one million circuit elements on a single chip. The Intel 486 and Pentium microprocessors use ULSI technology.
⇒ See also CHIP; PENTIUM MICROPROCESSOR.

Ultra2 SCSI *n.* a type of SCSI interface that uses an 8-bit bus and supports data rates of 40 MBps.

Ultra ATA *n.* the newest version of the AT Attachment (ATA) standard, which supports burst mode data transfer rates of 33.3 MBps.
⇒ See also ATA; ULTRA DMA.

Ultra DMA *n.* a protocol developed by Quantum Corporation and Intel that supports burst mode data transfer rates of 33.3 MBps, which is twice as fast as the previous disk drive standard for PCs and is necessary to take advantage of Ultra ATA disk drives. The official name for the protocol is Ultra DMA/33. Also called **UDMA; UDMA/33; DMA mode 33.**
⇒ See also ULTRA ATA.

ultra large scale integration *n.* See ULSI.

Ultra SCSI *n.* a type of SCSI interface that uses an 8-bit bus and supports data rates of 20 MBps.

UML Unified Modeling Language: a general-purpose notational language for specifying and visualizing complex software, esp. large, object-oriented projects.
⇒ See also OBJECT-ORIENTED PROGRAMMING; SOFTWARE ENGINEERING.

UNC Universal Naming Convention *or* Uniform Naming Convention: a PC format for specifying the location of resources on a local-area network (LAN). UNC uses the following format:
\\server-name\shared-resource-pathname
⇒ See also DIRECTORY SERVICE; PATHNAME; RESOURCE.

underflow *n.* the condition that occurs when a computer attempts to represent a number that is too small for it (that is, a number too close to zero).
⇒ See also FLOATING-POINT NUMBER; OVERFLOW ERROR.

undo *v.t.* to reverse (a command) and return to a previous state.
⇒ See also COMMAND.

undocumented *adj.* referring to features that are not described in the official documentation of a product, as features that were useful to the programmers developing the product but were deemed unnecessary to end users.
⇒ See also DOCUMENTATION.

Unicode *n.* a standard for representing characters as integers that uses 16 bits, which means that it can represent more than 65,000 unique characters: necessary for languages such as Chinese and Japanese. Many analysts believe that as the software industry becomes increasingly global, Unicode will eventually supplant ASCII as the standard character coding format.
⇒ See also ASCII; CHARACTER; CHARACTER SET; NTFS.

Unified Modeling Language *n.* See UML.

Uniform Naming Convention *n.* See UNC.

Uniform Resource Identifier *n.* See URI.

Uniform Resource Locator *n.* See URL.

uninterruptible power supply *n.* See UPS.

universal asynchronous receiver-transmitter *n.* See UART.

Universal Naming Convention *n.* See UNC.

Universal Serial Bus *n.* See USB.

UNIX (yōō′niks), *n.* a widely-used multi-user, multi-tasking operating system. Developed at Bell Labs in the early 1970s, it was one of the first operating systems to be written in a high-level programming language.
⇒ See also A/UX; AIX; BSDI; C; DAEMON; FREEBSD; GNU; LINUX; MULTITASKING; NFS; OPERATING SYSTEM; OS/2; POSIX; SOLARIS; SUN MICROSYSTEMS; VMS.

Unix-to-Unix Copy *n.* See UUCP.

unpack *v.t.* to convert (a packed file) into its original form. A packed file is a file that has been

compressed to take up less storage area.
⇒ See also DATA COMPRESSION.

Unshielded Twisted Pair *n.* See UTP.

upgrade *n.* a new version of a software or hardware product designed to replace an older version of the same product, often sold at a discount to owners of the older version.
⇒ See also ESD; TCO.

upload *v.t.* to transmit (data) from a computer to a bulletin board service, mainframe, or network.
⇒ See also BULLETIN BOARD SYSTEM; DOWNLOAD; NETWORK; ONLINE SERVICE.

uppercase *adj.* referring to capital letters.
⇒ See also CAPS LOCK KEY; CASE SENSITIVE; LOWERCASE.

upper memory *n.* HIGH MEMORY.

UPS uninterruptible power supply: a power supply that can maintain power temporarily in the event of a power outage. This enables the user to save data and shut down the computer safely.
⇒ See also POWER SUPPLY.

upward compatible *adj.* referring to software that runs not only on the computer for which it was designed but also on newer and more powerful models. Also called **forward compatible**.
⇒ See also BACKWARD COMPATIBLE; COMPATIBLE; DOS.

URI Uniform Resource Identifier: the generic term for all types of names and addresses that refer to objects on the World Wide Web. A URL is one kind of URI.
⇒ See also URL.

URL Uniform Resource Locator: the global address of documents and other resources on the World Wide Web. The first part of the address indicates what protocol to use, and the second part specifies the location of the resource.
⇒ See also ADDRESS; INTERNET; PURL; URI; WORLD WIDE WEB.

USB Universal Serial Bus: an external bus standard that supports data transfer rates of 12 Mbps (12 million bits per second). A single USB port can be used to connect up to 127 peripheral devices, such as mice, modems, and keyboards.
⇒ See also BUS; DEVICE BAY; HOT PLUGGING; IEEE 1394; PARALLEL PORT; PCMCIA; SERIAL PORT.

USENET *n.* a worldwide discussion system that contains more than 14,000 forums, called newsgroups.
⇒ See also BULLETIN BOARD SYSTEM; FORUM; INTERNET; NNTP.

user *n.* an individual who uses a computer.
⇒ See also APPLICATION; END USER.

User Datagram Protocol *n.* See UDP.

user-friendly *adj.* referring to anything that makes it easier for people to use a computer, as a menu-driven program or an on-line help system.
⇒ See also GRAPHICAL USER INTERFACE.

user group *n.* a group of individuals with common interests in some aspect of computers.
⇒ See also SIG.

user interface *n.* the set of commands or menus through which a user communicates with a program. A *command-driven interface* is one in which the user enters commands. A *menu-driven interface* is one in which the user selects command choices from various menus displayed on the screen.
⇒ See also COMMAND DRIVEN; CUA; FUNCTIONAL SPECIFICATION; GRAPHICAL USER INTERFACE; LOOK-AND-FEEL; SAA; XEROX.

username *n.* a name used to gain access to a computer system.
⇒ See also AUTHENTICATION; BULLETIN BOARD SYSTEM; MULTI-USER; ONLINE SERVICE; PASSWORD.

utility *n.* a program that performs a very specific task, usually related to managing system resources such as disk drives, printers, etc.
⇒ See also APPLICATION; TSR.

UTP Unshielded Twisted Pair: a type of cable that consists of two unshielded wires twisted around each other that is used extensively for local-area networks (LANs).
⇒ See also CDDI; COAXIAL CABLE; ETHERNET; FIBER OPTICS; LOCAL-AREA NETWORK.

UUCP UNIX-to-UNIX Copy: a UNIX utility and protocol that enables one computer to send files to another.
⇒ See also FTP; UNIX.

Uudecode *n.* See under UUENCODE.

Uuencode *n.* a set of algorithms for converting files on any platform into a series of 7-bit ASCII characters that can be transmitted over the Internet: esp. popular for sending e-mail attachments. Files are Uudecoded at the receiving end.
⇒ See also BINHEX; E-MAIL; MIME.

V.22 (vē′dot twen′tē too′), *n.* the CCITT *V.22* communications standard.
⇒ See also CCITT.

V.22bis (vē′dot twen′tē too′bis′), *n.* the CCITT *V. 22bis* communications standard.
⇒ See also CCITT.

V.32 (vē′dot thûr′tē too′), *n.* the CCITT *V.32* communications standard.
⇒ See also CCITT.

V.34 (vē′dot thûr′tē fôr′), *n.* the CCITT *V.34* communications standard.
⇒ See also CCITT.

V.35 (vē′dot thûr′tē fīv′), an ITU standard for high-speed synchronous data exchange that is used by most routers and DSUs that connect to T-1 carriers in the U.S.
⇒ See also CSU/DSU; ITU.

V.42 (vē′dot fôr′tē too′), *n.* the CCITT *V.42* communications standard.
⇒ See also CCITT.

V.90 (vē′dot nīn′tē) *n.* a standard for 56 Kbps modems that resolved the battle between the two competing 56 Kbps technologies—X2 from 3COM and K56flex from Rockwell Semiconductor.
⇒ See also K56FLEX; MODEM; X2.

value-added reseller *n.* See VAR.

vanilla *adj.* without added features: *a vanilla PC.*
⇒ See also FEATURE.

vaporware *n.* a sarcastic term used to designate software and hardware products that have been announced and advertised but are not yet available or may never become available.
⇒ See also BLOATWARE; SOFTWARE.

VAR (*pronounced as separate letters*), *n.* value-added reseller: a company that integrates hardware and software from multiple sources and sells them as a single package to customers.
⇒ See also OEM.

variable *n.* a symbol or name that stands for a value, as x and y in the expression $x + y$.
⇒ See also CHARACTER STRING; CONSTANT; DATA; DATA TYPE; EXPRESSION; LITERAL.

variable-length *adj.* referring to anything whose length can vary: *a variable-length field in a database.*
⇒ See also DATABASE MANAGEMENT SYSTEM; FIELD; FIXED LENGTH; RECORD.

variable-length record *n.* a record that has at least one variable-length field. The length of the entire record, therefore, varies according to what data are placed in the variable-length field.
⇒ See also FIELD; FIXED LENGTH; RECORD; VARIABLE LENGTH.

VAX *n.* Virtual Address eXtension: Digital Equipment Corporation's successor to its PDP-11 line of minicomputers, featuring an operating system, VMS, that supports virtual memory.
⇒ See also DEC; MINICOMPUTER; VMS.

VB Visual Basic.

vBNS very high-speed Backbone Network Service: an experimental wide-area network backbone, sponsored by the National Science Foundation (NSF) and implemented by MCI, that is designed to serve as a platform for testing new, high-speed Internet technologies and protocols.
⇒ See also BACKBONE; I2; INTERNET; NGI INITIATIVE.

VBScript *n.* Visual Basic Scripting Edition: a scripting language, developed by Microsoft and supported by Microsoft's Internet Explorer Web browser, that is based on the Visual Basic programming language but is much simpler.
⇒ See also INTERNET EXPLORER; JAVASCRIPT; JSCRIPT; VISUAL BASIC.

VBX Visual Basic custom control: a reusable software component designed for use in many different applications.

⇒ See also COMPONENT; CONTROL; DLL; OCX; VISUAL BASIC.

VCACHE *n.* the 32-bit disk cache system in Windows 95/98 that replaced the Smartdrive system used in older versions of Windows.

⇒ See also CDFS; DISK CACHE; SMARTDRIVE.

VCPI Virtual Control Program Interface: a specification for managing memory beyond the first megabyte on PCs with 80386 or later processors.

⇒ See also EXTENDED MEMORY; XMS.

VDT video display terminal. See under MONITOR.

VDT radiation *n.* the radiation emitted by video display terminals.

⇒ See also ELF EMISSION; MONITOR.

VDU visual display unit: an obsolete term for a display monitor.

⇒ See also CRT; MONITOR.

vector *n.* **1.** in computer programming, a one-dimensional array or a pointer. **2.** in computer graphics, a line that is defined by its start and end point.

⇒ See also ARRAY; VECTOR GRAPHICS.

vector font *n.* SCALABLE FONT.

vector graphics *n.* software and hardware that use geometrical expressions to represent images. Also called **object-oriented graphics.**

⇒ See also AUTOTRACING; BÉZIER CURVE; BIT MAP; BITMAPPED GRAPHICS; DRAW PROGRAM; GRAPHICS; GRAPHICS FILE FORMATS.

Veronica *n.* a search engine for Gopher sites.

⇒ See also GOPHER; JUGHEAD; SEARCH ENGINE.

VersaModule Eurocard bus *n.* VME BUS.

vertical frequency *n.* See under REFRESH.

vertical justification *n.* a feature supported by some word processors and desktop publishing systems in which the system automatically adjusts the vertical space between lines (the leading) so that columns and pages have an even top and bottom margin. Also called **feathering.**

⇒ See also JUSTIFICATION; LEADING; WORD PROCESSING.

vertical refresh rate *n.* See under REFRESH.

vertical scrolling *n.* See under SCROLL.

very large-scale integration *n.* See VLSI.

VESA Video Electronics Standards Association: a consortium of video adapter and monitor manufacturers whose goal is to standardize video protocols.

⇒ See also DDC; SVGA; VL-BUS.

VESA Local Bus *n.* VL-Bus.

VFAT Virtual File Allocation Table: the 32-bit file system used in Windows for Workgroups and Windows 95/98.

⇒ See also FILE ALLOCATION TABLE; FILE MANAGEMENT SYSTEM; WINDOWS 95.

VGA video graphics array: a graphics display system developed by IBM that has become one of the de facto standards for PCs.

⇒ See also SVGA; VIDEO ADAPTER; ZV PORT.

VGA Plus *n.* See under SVGA.

video *adj.* **1.** referring to recording, manipulating, and displaying moving images, esp. in a format that can be presented on a television. **2.** referring to displaying images and text on a computer monitor. **—***n.* **3.** a recording produced with a video recorder (camcorder) or some similar device.

⇒ See also DVI; INDEO; QUICKTIME; REALVIDEO; S-VIDEO; SHOCKWAVE; VIDEO CAPTURE; VIDEO EDITING; VIDEO FOR WINDOWS; VIDEO OVERLAY; VIDEO STANDARDS; VIDEOCONFERENCING.

video accelerator *n.* GRAPHICS ACCELERATOR.

video adapter *n.* a board that plugs into a personal computer to give it display capabilities. Most modern video adapters contain memory, so that the computer's RAM is not used for storing displays. In addition, most adapters have their own graphics coprocessor for performing graphics calculations. These adapters are often called *graphics accelerators.* Also called **video card, video board, video display board, graphics card, graphics adapter.**

⇒ See also 8514/A; ADAPTER; COLOR DEPTH; DDC; DirectDRAW; GRAPHICS ACCELERATOR; MDRAM; MONITOR;

PAL; RAMDAC; SGRAM; VIDEO MEMORY; VIDEO MODE; VIDEO STANDARDS; VRAM; WRAM.

video capture *n.* the conversion of analog video signals, such as those generated by a video camera, into a digital format that is then stored on a computer's mass storage device.

⇒ See also DIGITAL VIDEO; VIDEO EDITING.

video card *n.* VIDEO ADAPTER.

videoconferencing *n.* conducting a conference between two or more participants at different sites by using computer networks to transmit audio and video data.

⇒ See also APPLICATION SHARING; COMMON INTERMEDIATE FORMAT; CU-SeeMe; DISTANCE LEARNING; H.323; H.324; QCIF; RTP; TELECONFERENCE; WORKGROUP COMPUTING.

video display board *n.* VIDEO ADAPTER.

video editing *n.* the process of manipulating video images by cutting segments (trimming), resequencing clips, and adding transitions and other special effects.

⇒ See also DIGITAL VIDEO; MPEG; SGI; VIDEO CAPTURE.

Video Electronics Standards Association *n.* See VESA.

Video for Windows *n.* a format developed by Microsoft Corporation for storing video and audio information.

⇒ See also CODEC; MPEG; QUICKTIME.

Video Graphics Array *n.* See VGA.

video memory *n.* RAM installed on a video adapter. The amount of video memory dictates the maximum resolution and color depth available.

⇒ See also BIT MAP; GRAPHICS ACCELERATOR; MAIN MEMORY; RAMDAC; RDRAM; SGRAM; VIDEO ADAPTER; VRAM; WRAM.

video mode *n.* the setting of a video adapter. Most video adapters can run in either *text mode* or *graphics mode.*

⇒ See also GRAPHICS MODE; TEXT MODE; VIDEO ADAPTER.

Video-on-Demand *n.* See VoD.

video overlay *n.* the placement of a full-motion video window on the display screen.

⇒ See also NTSC; VIDEO ADAPTER.

video RAM *n.* See VRAM.

video standard *n.* any of the standards that defines the resolution and colors for displays on a monitor.

⇒ See also 8514/A; MCGA; MDA; SVGA; TI 34010; VGA; VIDEO ADAPTER; XGA.

view *n.* in database management systems, a particular way of looking at the records in a database. A single database can support numerous different views. Typically, a view arranges the records in some order and makes only certain fields visible.

⇒ See also DATABASE; DATABASE MANAGEMENT SYSTEM; FIELD.

viewer *n.* a utility program that enables the user to read a file.

⇒ See also FILE MANAGEMENT SYSTEM; FORMAT; SHELL.

virtual *adj.* not real; referring to something that behaves in some ways like the object in question, but without physical reality: *virtual memory.*

⇒ See also VIRTUAL MACHINE; VIRTUAL MEMORY; VIRTUAL SERVER; VLAN.

virtual circuit *n.* a permanent or temporary connection between two devices that acts as though it is a direct physical connection: used to describe certain connections between two hosts in a packet-switching network.

⇒ See also PACKET SWITCHING; PVC; SVC.

Virtual Control Program Interface *n.* See VCPI.

virtual desktop *n.* **1.** a feature supported by some notebook computers that enables them to display images on an external monitor at a higher resolution than is supported by the built-in flat-panel display. **2.** a feature supported by some video adapters that enables them to provide a desktop larger than what is actually displayed. The user scrolls the display to see hidden areas.

⇒ See also FLAT-PANEL DISPLAY; NOTEBOOK COMPUTER.

virtual device driver *n.* in Windows systems, a special type of device driver that has direct access

to the operating system. In Windows 95, virtual device drivers are often called *VxDs* because the file-names end with the .vxd extension.
⇒ See also DRIVER.

virtual disk *n.* RAM DISK.

Virtual File Allocation Table *n.* See VFAT.

virtual LAN *n.* See VLAN.

virtual machine *n.* **1.** a self-contained operating environment that behaves as if it is a separate computer. **2.** a specification for a computing system that can then be instantiated by many different kinds of hardware or software.
⇒ See also JAVA; JIT; OPERATING ENVIRONMENT; VIRTUAL.

virtual memory *n.* a conceptual view of memory supported by some operating systems, as UNIX, in conjunction with the hardware in order to increase the amount of instructions and data that can be stored. When the program is actually executed, the virtual addresses are converted into real memory addresses.
⇒ See also ADDRESS SPACE; MAIN MEMORY; MEMORY; MMU; OPERATING SYSTEM; PAGE; PAGE FAULT; PAGING; SWAP; THRASH; VIRTUAL.

Virtual Memory System *n.* See VMS.

virtual private network *n.* See VPN.

virtual reality *n.* **1.** an artificial environment created with computer hardware and software and presented to the user in such a way that it appears and feels like a real environment. To "enter" a virtual reality, a user dons special gloves, earphones, and goggles, all of which receive their input from the computer system. **2.** any virtual world represented in a computer as a text-based or graphical representation.
⇒ See also AVATAR; CYBERSPACE; HMD; MUD; QUICK-TIME VR; VIRTUAL; VRML.

Virtual Reality Modeling Language *n.* See VRML.

virtual server *n.* a server, usually a Web server, that shares computer resources with other virtual servers.
⇒ See also SERVER; VIRTUAL; WEB SERVER.

virus *n.* a program or piece of code that is loaded onto a computer without the user's knowledge and runs against the user's wishes. Most viruses can also replicate themselves and are capable of using all available memory and bringing the entire system to a halt.
⇒ See also ANTIVIRUS PROGRAM; ARPANET; BOOTABLE DISKETTE; DATA RECOVERY; HACKER; MACRO VIRUS; MBR; NETWORK; TROJAN HORSE.

VisiCalc *n.* the first electronic spreadsheet application, introduced in the late 1970s.
⇒ See also LOTUS 1-2-3; SPREADSHEET.

Visual Basic *n.* a programming language and environment developed by Microsoft. Based on the BASIC language, Visual Basic was one of the first products to provide a graphical programming environment and a paint metaphor for developing user interfaces.
⇒ See also BASIC; DAO; DELPHI; JET; MICROSOFT; PROGRAMMING LANGUAGE; RAPID APPLICATION DEVELOPMENT; VBSCRIPT; VBX.

Visual Basic custom control *n.* See VBX.

Visual Basic Scripting Edition *n.* VBSCRIPT.

Visual C++ *n.* an application development tool, developed by Microsoft for C++ programmers, that supports object-oriented programming of 32-bit Windows applications.
⇒ See also C; C++; IDE; MFC; OBJECT-ORIENTED PROGRAMMING.

visual display unit *n.* See VDU.

VLAN virtual LAN: a network of computers that behave as if they were connected to the same wire even though they may actually be physically located on different segments of a LAN.
⇒ See also LOCAL-AREA NETWORK; VIRTUAL.

VLB VESA LOCAL-BUS.

VL-Bus VESA Local-Bus: a local bus architecture created by the Video Electronics Standards Association (VESA).
⇒ See also EXPANSION BUS; LOCAL BUS; PCI.

VLSI very large-scale integration: the process of placing hundreds of thousands of electronic components on a single chip.
⇒ See also CHIP; INTEGRATED CIRCUIT; ULSI.

VM VIRTUAL MACHINE.

VME See under VME BUS.

VME bus *n.* Versa Module Eurocard bus: a 32-bit bus developed by Motorola, Signetics, Mostek, and Thompson CSF that is widely used in industrial, commercial, and military applications.
⇒ See also BACKPLANE; BUS.

VMS Virtual Memory System: a multi-user, multitasking, virtual memory operating system that runs on DEC's VAX and Alpha lines of minicomputers and workstations.
⇒ See also MULTI-USER; MULTITASKING; OPERATING SYSTEM; UNIX; VAX; VIRTUAL MEMORY.

VoD Video-on-Demand: an umbrella term for a wide set of technologies and companies whose common goal is to enable individuals to select videos from a central server for viewing on a television or computer screen.
⇒ See also VIDEO.

VOI Voice over the Internet: See INTERNET TELEPHONY.

voice mail *n.* a voice message held on a central server for later retrieval.
⇒ See also E-MAIL.

Voice over the Internet *n.* INTERNET TELEPHONY.

voice recognition *n.* the field of computer science that deals with designing computer systems that can recognize spoken words.
⇒ See also ARTIFICIAL INTELLIGENCE; NATURAL LANGUAGE.

VOIP Voice Over IP: See INTERNET TELEPHONY.

volatile memory *n.* memory, as most RAM, that loses its contents when the power is turned off.
⇒ See also MEMORY; RAM; ROM.

voltage regulator *n.* a small device or circuit that regulates the voltage fed to the microprocessor.
⇒ See also HEAT SINK; MICROPROCESSOR; MOTHERBOARD; POWER SUPPLY; VRM.

voltage regulator module *n.* See VRM.

volume *n.* a fixed unit of disk or tape storage.
⇒ See also DISK; MASS STORAGE.

volume label *n.* in DOS systems, the name of a volume, as a disk or tape.
⇒ See also DISK; LABEL; VOLUME.

VON Voice on the Net: a coalition of Internet telephony software producers whose main goal is to ensure that the telephone companies do not succeed in their bid to outlaw Internet telephony.

VPN virtual private network: a network that is constructed by using public links, as the Internet, to connect nodes.
⇒ See also L2TP; LAYER TWO FORWARDING; PPTP; TUNNELING.

VRAM (vē′ram′), *n.* video RAM: special-purpose memory used by video adapters.
⇒ See also GRAPHICS; GRAPHICS ACCELERATOR; MDRAM; MEMORY; MONITOR; PROCESSOR; RAM; VIDEO MEMORY.

VRM voltage regulator module: a small module that installs on a motherboard to regulate the voltage to the microprocessor.
⇒ See also POWER SUPPLY; VOLTAGE REGULATOR.

VRML (vûr′məl), *n.* Virtual Reality Modeling Language: a specification for displaying three-dimensional objects on the World Wide Web.
⇒ See also BROWSER; CYBERSPACE; HTML; MODELING; QUICKTIME VR; VIRTUAL REALITY; WORLD WIDE WEB.

VSAM Virtual Sequential Access Method: a file management system used on IBM mainframes that speeds up access to data by using an inverted index of all records added to each file.
⇒ See also FILE MANAGEMENT SYSTEM; LEGACY APPLICATION; MAINFRAME; MVS.

VTAM Virtual Telecommunications Access Method: the software component that controls communications in Systems Network Architecture (SNA) networks.
⇒ See also SNA; TOKEN-RING NETWORK.

VxD See under VIRTUAL DEVICE DRIVER.

W3C World Wide Web Consortium: an international consortium of companies involved with the Internet and the Web whose purpose is to develop open standards so that the Web evolves in a single direction rather than being splintered among competing factions.
⇒ See also HTML; HTTP; WORLD WIDE WEB.

WAIS (wās) *n.* Wide Area Information Server: a program for retrieving documents on the Internet.
⇒ See also GOPHER; INTERNET.

wait state *n.* a period during which a CPU or bus lies idle to enable a component that functions at a slower speed to catch up.
⇒ See also BURST MODE; CACHE; CLOCK SPEED; FPM RAM; INTERLEAVE; LATENCY; PIPELINE BURST CACHE; SDRAM.

WAN *n.* WIDE-AREA NETWORK.

warez (wârz, wârs) *n.* commercial software that has been pirated and made available to the public via a BBS or the Internet.
⇒ See also COPY PROTECTION; FREEWARE; SHAREWARE; SOFTWARE PIRACY.

warm boot *n.* the process of resetting a computer that is already turned on: sometimes necessary when a program encounters an error from which it cannot recover.
⇒ See also BOOT; COLD BOOT.

WAV *n.* the format for storing sound in files, developed jointly by Microsoft and IBM.
⇒ See also AU; MULTIMEDIA.

Wavelength Division Multiplexing *n.* See WDM.

wavetable *n.* the stored samples for WAVE TABLE SYNTHESIS.

wave table synthesis *n.* a technique that stores digital samples of sound from various instruments, which can then be combined, edited, and enhanced to reproduce sound defined by a digital input signal.
⇒ See also MIDI; SOUND CARD.

WDM Wavelength Division Multiplexing: a type of multiplexing developed for use on optical fiber that modulates each of several data streams onto a different part of the light spectrum.
⇒ See also FDM; FIBER OPTICS; MULTIPLEX; TDM.

Web *n.* WORLD WIDE WEB.

Web browser *n.* BROWSER.

webcasting *n.* the use of the World Wide Web to broadcast information.
⇒ See also BROADCAST; PointCast; PUSH.

webCrawler *n.* a popular Web search engine run by America Online.
⇒ See also ALTA VISTA; EXCITE; INFOSEEK; LYCOS; OPEN TEXT; SEARCH ENGINE.

webcrawler *n.* SPIDER.

Webmaster *n.* an individual who manages a Web site, performing tasks such as creating and updating Web pages, monitoring traffic through the site, etc.
⇒ See also CGI; WEB PAGE; WEB SITE.

Web page *n.* a document on the World Wide Web.
⇒ See also DOM; HOME PAGE; URL; WEB SERVER; WEBMASTER; WORLD WIDE WEB.

Web server *n.* a computer that delivers Web pages to machines that request them.
⇒ See also APACHE WEB SERVER; IIS; PROXY SERVER; SERVER; VIRTUAL SERVER; WEB PAGE; WEB SITE; WORLD WIDE WEB.

Web site *n.* a coherent collection of one or more pages (URLs) on the World Wide Web, usually under a single domain or username.
⇒ See also E-ZINE; HOME PAGE; WEB SERVER; WEBMASTER; WORLD WIDE WEB.

WebTV *n.* a category of products and technologies that enable users to surf the Web on a TV. WebTV products make a connection to the Internet via telephone service.

⇒ See also CABLE MODEM; OS/9; PC/TV; WORLD WIDE WEB.

what-you-see-is-what-you-get *adj.* WYSIWYG.

whiteboard *n.* **1.** an area on a display screen on which multiple users can write or draw: a principal component of teleconferencing applications. **2.** a large, smooth, glossy sheet of white plastic used in offices for making presentations with markers.
⇒ See also APPLICATION SHARING; TELECONFERENCE.

White Book *n.* the specification covering the video CD format.
⇒ See also YELLOW BOOK.

whitespace *n.* all characters that appear as blanks on a display screen or printer, such as the space character and the tab character.
⇒ See also NULL CHARACTER.

whois (hōō'iz'), *n.* an Internet utility that returns information about a domain name or IP address.
⇒ See also DOMAIN NAME; FINGER; IP ADDRESS.

Wide Area Information Server *n.* See WAIS.

wide-area network *n.* a computer network that spans a relatively large geographical area usu. consisting of two or more local-area networks (LANs).
⇒ See also BRIDGE; INTERNET; INTERNETWORKING; LOCAL-AREA NETWORK; MAN; NETWORK; PACKET SWITCHING; SMDS.

wide SCSI *n.* See under SCSI.

widow *n.* **1.** in word processing, the last line of a paragraph that appears as the first line of a page. **2.** the last line of a paragraph that is much shorter than all the other lines in the paragraph.
⇒ See also ORPHAN; PAGINATION; WORD PROCESSING.

wildcard character *n.* a special symbol that stands for one or more characters, used for identifying files and directories, and enabling the user to select multiple files with a single specification, as the asterisk (*) in UNIX.
⇒ See also FILENAME.

Win32 *n.* the Windows API for developing 32-bit applications.
⇒ See also API; WIN32s; WINDOWS; WINDOWS 95; WINDOWS NT.

Win32s *n.* WIN32 subset: a software package that can be added to Windows 3.1 and Windows for Workgroups systems to give them the ability to run some 32-bit applications.
⇒ See also THUNK; WIN32; WINDOWS.

Win95 *n.* WINDOWS 95.

Winchester disk drive *n.* HARD DISK DRIVE.
⇒ See also DISK DRIVE; HARD DISK.

window *n.* **1.** an enclosed, rectangular area on a display screen. Most modern operating systems and applications have graphical user interfaces that allow the user to divide the display into several windows. Within each window, it is possible to run a different program or display different data. **2.** a logical view of a file.
⇒ See also DIALOG BOX; GRAPHICAL USER INTERFACE; ICON; MDI; MICROSOFT WINDOWS.

Windows *n.* MICROSOFT WINDOWS.
⇒ See also MICROSOFT; WIN32s; WINDOWS 98; WINDOWS CE; WINFRAME; WINTEL.

Windows 95 *n.* a major release of the Microsoft Windows operating system released in 1995.
⇒ See also DIAL-UP NETWORKING; MICROSOFT WINDOWS; OSR 2; REGISTRY; VFAT; WIN32; WINDOWS 98; WINDOWS CE; WINDOWS NT.

Windows 98 *n.* the successor to Windows 95, released in mid-1998.
⇒ See also INTERNET EXPLORER; WINDOWS; WINDOWS 95; WINDOWS NT.

Windows CE *n.* a version of the Windows operating system designed for small devices such as personal digital assistants (PDAs).

computer

⇒ See also HAND-HELD COMPUTER; HPC; PALMTOP; PDA; WINDOWS.

Windows DNA *n.* Windows Distributed (Inter)Net Applications Architecture: a marketing name for a collection of Microsoft technologies that enables the Windows platform to work with the Internet.
⇒ See also ACTIVEX; COM; DYNAMIC HTML.

Windows Internet Naming Service *n.* See WINS.

Windows Metafile Format *n.* See WMF.

Windows NT *n.* a 32-bit operating system that supports preemptive multitasking.
⇒ See also MICROSOFT WINDOWS; MULTITASKING; OPERATING SYSTEM; WINDOWS TERMINAL; WINFRAME.

Windows terminal *n.* a terminal that is connected to a Windows NT server through a network and that sends the user's input (keystrokes and mouse movements) to the server and displays the results on the display screen but does not process or store data.
⇒ See also DUMB TERMINAL; NC; NET PC; NETWORK COMPUTER; WINDOWS NT; WINFRAME.

WinFrame *n.* a technology developed by Citrix Systems that turns Windows NT into a multi-user operating system.
⇒ See also THIN CLIENT; WINDOWS; WINDOWS NT; WINDOWS TERMINAL; X-WINDOW.

WINMAIL.DAT *n.* See under TNEF.

WINS *n.* Windows Internet Naming Service: a Windows system that determines the IP address associated with a particular network computer.
⇒ See also DHCP; DNS; IP ADDRESS.

Winsock *n.* Windows Socket: an Application Programming Interface (API) for developing Windows programs that can communicate with other machines via the TCP/IP protocol.
⇒ See also API; MTU; PROTOCOL STACK; SOCKET; TCP/IP.

Wintel *adj. Informal.* of or designating a computer that uses an Intel microprocessor and any of the Windows operating systems.
⇒ See also INTEL; INTEL MICROPROCESSORS; MICROSOFT; WINDOWS.

wireless modem *n.* a modem that accesses a private wireless data network or a wireless telephone system, such as the CDPD system.
⇒ See also CDPD; MODEM.

wizard *n.* **1.** a utility within an application that assists in the use of the application to perform a particular task. **2.** Also called **super-programmer.** an outstanding programmer. **3.** the system administrator for a chat room or MUD.
⇒ See also UTILITY.

WMF *n.* Windows Metafile Format: a graphics file format used to exchange graphics information between Microsoft Windows applications.
⇒ See also GRAPHICS; GRAPHICS FILE FORMATS.

Wolfpack *n.* the codename for Microsoft's clustering solution, Microsoft Cluster Server (MSCS).
⇒ See also CLUSTERING; MSCS; WINDOWS NT.

word *n.* **1.** in word processing, any group of characters separated by spaces or punctuation on both sides. **2.** in programming, the natural data size, such as 32 bits, that can be handled by a computer processor. **3.** MICROSOFT WORD.
⇒ See also BIT; BYTE; CPU.

WordPerfect *n.* one of the most popular word processors for PCs and Apple Macintoshes.
⇒ See also WORD PROCESSING.

word processing *n.* the use of a computer to create, edit, and print documents.
⇒ See also COPY; CUT; DELETE; DESKTOP PUBLISHING; EDITOR; FONT; FOOTER; GRAPHICS; HEADER; HYPHENATION; INSERT; JUSTIFY; LAYOUT; MACRO.

word processor *n.* a program or computer that enables the user to perform word processing functions.
⇒ See also WORD PROCESSING.

word wrap *n.* in word processing, a feature that causes the word processor to force all text to fit within the defined margins by moving automatically to the next line, observing appropriate word breaks, when the right margin is reached. The user is not

required to insert hard returns manually within a paragraph of continuous text.
⇒ See also HARD RETURN; HYPHENATION; MARGINS; SOFT RETURN; WORD PROCESSING.

workflow *n.* the defined series of tasks within an organization to produce a final outcome. Sophisticated workgroup computing applications allow the user to define different workflows for different types of jobs.
⇒ See also WORKGROUP COMPUTING.

workgroup *n.* a collection of individuals working together on a task.

workgroup computing *n.* the connection to a network by all the individuals in a workgroup that allows them to send e-mail to one another, share data files, and schedule meetings.
⇒ See also E-MAIL; GROUPWARE; TELECONFERENCE; WORKFLOW; WORKGROUP.

workgroup productivity package *n.* a software package that includes e-mail, calendar programs, scheduling programs, and other utilities that promote communication between users on a local-area network.
⇒ See also CALENDAR; E-MAIL; LOCAL-AREA NETWORK; SCHEDULER; WORKGROUP COMPUTING.

working directory *n.* the directory in which one is currently working.
⇒ See also DIRECTORY; PATHNAME; ROOT DIRECTORY.

worksheet *n.* SPREADSHEET.

workstation *n.* **1.** a type of computer used for engineering applications (CAD/CAM), desktop publishing, software development, and other types of applications that require a moderate amount of computing power and relatively high-quality graphics capabilities. **2.** in networking, any computer connected to a local-area network.
⇒ See also CAD/CAM; COMPUTER; DESKTOP PUBLISHING; DISKLESS WORKSTATION; GRAPHICS; LOCAL-AREA NETWORK; NETWORK; NETWORK COMPUTER; PERSONAL COMPUTER; SGI; UNIX.

World Wide Web *n.* the system of Internet servers that delivers documents formatted in a language called HTML (HyperText Markup Language). It supports links to other documents, as well as graphics, audio, and video files.
⇒ See also BROWSER; CERN; CGI; HTML; HTTP; HYPERMEDIA; HYPERTEXT; INTERNET; MOSAIC; surf; W3C; WEB SITE; WEBTV.

WORM *n.* write once, read many (times): an optical disk technology that allows the user to write data onto a disk only once. After that, the data are permanent and can be read any number of times.
⇒ See also CD-ROM; ERASABLE OPTICAL DISK; MASS STORAGE; OPTICAL DISK; PHASE CHANGE DISK.

WRAM *n.* Windows RAM: a type of RAM developed by Samsung Electronics that supports two ports, enabling a video adapter to fetch the contents of memory for display at the same time that new bytes are being written.
⇒ See also RAM; SGRAM; VIDEO ADAPTER; VIDEO MEMORY; VRAM.

write *v.t.* to copy (data) from main memory to a storage device, such as a disk.
⇒ See also ACCESS; READ; WRITE-BACK CACHE.

write-back cache *n.* a caching method in which modifications to data in the cache are not copied to the cache source until the cache line is replaced by an unrelated one. Also called **copy-back cache.**
⇒ See also CACHE; WRITE.

write once/read many *n.* See WORM.

write-protect *v.t.* to mark (a file or disk) so that the contents cannot be modified or deleted.
⇒ See also FLOPPY DISK; LOCK.

write-through cache *n.* a cache in which modifications to cached data are simultaneously written to main memory.

WWW *n.* WORLD WIDE WEB.

WYSIWYG (wiz/ē wig′) *adj.* What You See Is What You Get: referring to an application that shows on the screen exactly what will appear when the document is printed.
⇒ See also COLOR MATCHING; DESKTOP PUBLISHING;

FONT; POSTSCRIPT; RESOLUTION; WORD PROCESSING; WYSI-WYP.

WYSIWYP (wiz′ē wip′) *adj.* What You See Is What You Print: referring to the ability of a computer system to print colors exactly as they appear on a monitor.
⇒ See also COLOR MANAGEMENT SYSTEM (CMS); COLOR MATCHING; WYSIWYG.

X2 a technology developed by U.S. Robotics (now 3COM) for delivering data rates up to 56 Kbps over analog telephone lines.
⇒ See also K56FLEX; MODEM; V.90.

X.25 a popular standard for packet-switching networks.
⇒ See also CCITT; PACKET SWITCHING.

X.400 an ISO and ITU standard for addressing and transporting e-mail messages.
⇒ See also CCITT; E-MAIL ADDRESS; X.500.

X.500 an ISO and ITU standard that defines how global directories should be structured.
⇒ See also ACTIVE DIRECTORY; CCITT; DIRECTORY SERVICE; ITU; NDS; X.400.

X.509 the most widely used standard for defining digital certificates.
⇒ See also DIGITAL CERTIFICATE; SSL.

x86 See under INTEL MICROPROCESSORS.

xDSL the collective term for all types of digital subscriber lines, which use sophisticated modulation schemes to jam data through copper wires.
⇒ See also ADSL; ISDN; POTS; SDSL.

Xenix *n.* a version of UNIX that runs on PCs.
⇒ See also OPERATING SYSTEM; UNIX.

Xerox *n.* a company that is best known for its photocopiers. Xerox Corporation also has conducted pioneering work on user interfaces and document management. Modern GUIs trace their inspiration to Xerox's Palo Alto Research Center.
⇒ See also GRAPHICAL USER INTERFACE; LASER PRINTER; USER INTERFACE.

XGA extended graphics array: a high-resolution graphics standard introduced by IBM in 1990.
⇒ See also 8514/A; INTERLACING; RESOLUTION; SVGA; VGA; VIDEO STANDARDS.

x-height *n.* in typography, the height of a lowercase *x* in a specific font. Also called **body height.**
⇒ See also ASCENDER; BASELINE; DESCENDER; TYPEFACE.

XML eXtensible Markup Language: a pared-down, simplified version of SGML, designed especially for Web documents, that enables designers to create their own customized tags to provide functionality not available with HTML.
⇒ See also DOM; HTML; SGML; TAG.

Xmodem *n.* one of the most popular non-Internet file transfer protocols.
⇒ See also COMMUNICATIONS PROTOCOL; COMMUNICATIONS SOFTWARE; KERMIT; MODEM; PROTOCOL; YMODEM; ZMODEM.

XMS Extended Memory Specification: a procedure for using extended memory and DOS's high memory area, a 64K block just above 1 MB.
⇒ See also EXPANDED MEMORY; EXTENDED MEMORY; HIGH MEMORY AREA.

XOR operator *n.* exclusive OR operator: a Boolean operator that returns a value of TRUE only if just one of its operands is TRUE.
⇒ See also BOOLEAN OPERATOR.

XT form factor *n.* BABY AT.

X-Window *n.* a windowing and graphics system developed at the Massachusetts Institute of Technology (MIT), which has placed the X-Window source code in the public domain, making it a particularly attractive system for UNIX vendors.
⇒ See also GRAPHICAL USER INTERFACE; PUBLIC-DOMAIN SOFTWARE; SOLARIS; UNIX.

Y2K YEAR 2000 PROBLEM.

Yahoo! Yet Another Hierarchical Officious Oracle: a World Wide Web directory started by David Filo and Jerry Yang at Stanford University. It is the leading Web portal (the starting location for Web activities).
⇒ See also ALTA VISTA; EXCITE; HOTBOT; INFOSEEK; LYCOS; MAGELLAN.

Y/C video *n.* See under S-VIDEO.

Year 2000 problem *n.* the pervasive problem caused by the fact that many applications are designed to assume that all years begin with '19'. Also called **millennium bug, Y2K problem.**
⇒ See also ACCOUNTING SOFTWARE.

Yellow Book *n.* the specification for CD-ROMs and CD-ROM/XA.
⇒ See also CD-ROM; CD-ROM/XA; GREEN BOOK; ORANGE BOOK; RED BOOK; WHITE BOOK.

Ymodem *n.* an asynchronous communications protocol that extends Xmodem by increasing the number of bytes transferred between acknowledgments and by supporting batch file transfers.
⇒ See also BATCH PROCESSING; COMMUNICATIONS PROTOCOL; XMODEM; ZMODEM.

yottabyte *n.* 2^{80} bytes, which is approximately 10^{24} (1,000,000,000,000,000,000,000,000) bytes. A yottabyte is equal to 1,024 zettabytes. [*yotta* is the second-to-last letter of the Latin alphabet and it sounds like the Greek letter *iota*]
⇒ See also EXABYTE; ZETTABYTE.

ZAW *n.* Zero Administration for Windows: a collection of utilities developed by Microsoft that enables administrators to centrally manage and update software on PCs connected to a LAN.
⇒ See also NET PC; NETWORK COMPUTER; TCO.

Z-buffer *n.* an area in graphics memory reserved for storing the Z-axis value of each pixel.
⇒ See also 3-D GRAPHICS; Z-BUFFERING.

Z-buffering *n.* an algorithm used in 3-D graphics to determine which objects, or parts of objects, are visible and which are hidden behind other objects.
⇒ See also 3-D GRAPHICS; Z-BUFFER.

Zero Administration for Windows *n.* See ZAW.

Zero Insertion Force (ZIF) socket *n.* a chip socket that allows the user to insert and remove a chip without special tools.
⇒ See also CHIP.

zero wait state *adj.* referring to systems that have no *wait states*—that is, they allow the microprocessor to run at its maximum speed without waiting for the memory chips.
⇒ See also WAIT STATE.

zettabyte *n.* 2^{70} bytes, which is approximately 10^{21} (1,000,000,000,000,000,000,000) bytes. A zettabyte is equal to 1,024 exabytes. [*zetta* is the last letter of the Latin alphabet]
⇒ See also EXABYTE; YOTTABYTE.

ZIF socket *n.* ZERO INSERTION FORCE (ZIF) SOCKET.

zine *n.* E-ZINE.

ZIP *n.* a popular data compression format. Files that have been compressed with the ZIP format are called *ZIP files* and usually end with a *.zip* extension.
⇒ See also ARC; DATA COMPRESSION; LZW.

Zip drive *n.* a high-capacity floppy disk drive developed by Iomega Corporation. Zip disks are slightly larger than conventional floppy disks and can hold 100 MB of data. New generations of Zip drives and disks hold more.
⇒ See also FLOPPY DISK; FLOPPY DRIVE; HIFD; SUPERDISK.

Zmodem *n.* an asynchronous communications protocol that provides faster data transfer rates and better error detection than Xmodem.
⇒ See also COMMUNICATIONS PROTOCOL; KERMIT; XMODEM; YMODEM.

zoom *v.i.* in graphical user interfaces, to make a window larger. Many applications also provide a zoom feature, which enlarges the view of an object, such as a portion of text, enabling you to see more detail.
⇒ See also BOX; GRAPHICAL USER INTERFACE; MAXIMIZE.

zoomed video *n.* See under ZV PORT.

ZV Port *n.* zoomed video port: a port that enables data to be transferred directly from a PC card to a VGA controller.
⇒ See also BUS; LAPTOP COMPUTER; NOTEBOOK COMPUTER; PC CARD; PCMCIA; VGA.

computer

Legal Dictionary

ab initio *Latin.* from the beginning; see, for example, *void ab initio* (under VOID).

abandon *v.* **1.** to give up a right, claim, or interest without specifically transferring it to someone else. **2.** to desert a child or spouse. See also DESERTION. —**abandonment,** *n.*

abate *v.* **1.** to reduce or eliminate: *to abate taxes; to abate rent; to abate a nuisance.* **2.** to diminish or be extinguished: *The action abated because the plaintiff failed to serve the defendant with a summons.* —**abatable,** *adj.* —**abatement,** *n.*

abduction *n.* **1.** KIDNAPPING, especially of a child, ward, or spouse. **2.** the tort of luring away, carrying off, or concealing another's spouse or child. When no force is involved, also called **enticement.** The tort has its origins in a man's ownership of his wife and children and his right to compensation for being deprived of their services. The modern scope of the tort varies from state to state.

abet *v.* to incite, encourage, instigate, or support, especially something bad. In legal contexts, used almost exclusively in, or as short for, the phrase AID AND ABET. —**abettor, abetter,** *n.*

abide *v.* **1.** to await. For example, see *costs to abide the event* (under COSTS). **2.** to accept and obey: *a law-abiding citizen.*

abnormally dangerous activity an activity, such as blasting, that is regarded as so inherently dangerous that anyone who engages in it should be held strictly liable for any damage it causes to person or property. Also called **ultrahazardous activity.** See also *strict liability* (under LIABILITY).

abortion *n.* the intentional termination of a pregnancy other than by live birth. A limited right of a woman to decide for herself whether to seek an abortion is included in the RIGHT TO PRIVACY protected by *substantive due process* (see under DUE PROCESS).

about. See ON OR ABOUT.

above *adv.* previously in the same document: *the authorities cited above.* See also SUPRA.

abridge *v.* to restrict or diminish a legal right: *The First Amendment prohibits Congress from abridging freedom of speech.* —**abridgment,** *n.*

abrogate *v.* to annul, repeal, overturn, supersede, or cancel by some legally effective means: *to abrogate a statute, an order, a contract, a will.* —**abrogation,** *n.*

abscond *v.* to depart from a jurisdiction or secrete oneself in order to avoid arrest, service of a summons or other process, or action by creditors. —**absconding, abscondence,** *n.*

absolute *adj.* unrestricted; unencumbered; unconditional. A term used to distinguish an unqualified right, interest, duty, privilege, order, transaction, document, or the like from one that is qualified in some way. See, for example, *absolute discretion* (under DISCRETION); *absolute immunity* (under IMMUNITY); *absolute privilege* (under PRIVILEGE); *fee simple absolute* (under FEE¹).

abstention *n.* the act of a federal court in refusing to exercise its jurisdiction over a case on the ground that the issues would be better dealt with by a state court or an administrative agency. —**abstain,** *v.*

abstract of title a summary of the history of ownership of a parcel of land, with a list of encumbrances on the land. An abstract of title is typically prepared in connection with a proposed sale of land, by a company in the business of ferreting out such information from public records.

abuse *n.* **1.** mistreatment of a person: *physical abuse; psychological abuse;* SPOUSAL ABUSE; CHILD ABUSE. **2.** wrongful or unwarranted exercise of a right or power: ABUSE OF DISCRETION; ABUSE OF PROCESS.

abuse of discretion an unsound or illogical ruling by a court or administrative body on a matter within its DISCRETION. A discretionary ruling will not be reversed simply because the reviewing court would have decided the matter differently, but only if the decision is found to be so unreasonable as to constitute an "abuse of discretion." The phrase does not imply wrongdoing; it simply indicates that the tribunal committed an error. Also called **improvident exercise of discretion.**

abuse of process the tort of instituting a judicial proceeding or otherwise using judicial PROCESS for an improper purpose. Essentially it is the use of an otherwise justifiable judicial procedure as a form of extortion to gain some advantage or benefit unrelated to the legitimate objective of the judicial proceeding. This tort differs from MALICIOUS PROSECUTION in that there may have been a legally sufficient basis for instituting such a proceeding, but the actual purpose to which the proceeding is put is wrongful.

accelerate *v.* **1.** to cause a legal right, duty, or interest that was to arise or vest in the future to do so immediately. **2.** in particular, to cause a debt that was to be repaid in the future to become immediately due: *Under the terms of the automobile loan, his failure to pay one installment accelerated the entire debt.* —**acceleration,** *n.*

acceleration clause a clause in a credit agreement providing that upon the occurrence of specified events the party extending credit may declare the entire outstanding balance immediately due. The purpose of such clauses is to enable the creditor to take immediate legal action to recover the amount loaned if it appears that the debtor is in financial difficulty.

accept *v.* to manifest satisfaction with or assent to a transaction, proposal, or state of affairs, thereby becoming legally bound. For example: (a) in property law, to take delivery of property or otherwise give formal assent to becoming the owner; (b) in contract law, to agree to an offer (this is the final step in forming a legally binding contract); (c) in the case of a bank or other entity upon which a check or other draft is drawn, to indicate on the instrument that it will be paid; for example, to certify a check. —**acceptance,** *n.*

accessory *n.* **1.** one who assists a criminal in connection with a crime, especially a felony, without being present when the crime is committed. **2. accessory after the fact,** one who knowingly assists a person who has committed a felony to avoid or hinder capture, prosecution, conviction, or punishment. This conduct is usually treated as an offense of less severity than the felony itself, often under the name **hindering.** See also OBSTRUCTION OF JUSTICE. **3. accessory before the fact,** one who encourages or assists in the planning or commission of a felony without being present. An accessory before the fact is an *aider and abettor* (see under AID AND ABET) and is ordinarily regarded by the law as equally culpable with the person who directly commits the felony.

accommodation *n.* **1.** something done as a favor rather than for consideration, especially acting as a SURETY: *The mother signed the car loan as an accommodation to her son.* **2. accommodation party,** a person who adds her name to a negotiable instrument or credit agreement as an accommodation to the principal obligor and so becomes liable on it. This is often done when the person taking the instrument or extending the credit is not satisfied with the creditworthiness of the principal obligor. See also PUBLIC ACCOMMODATION.

accomplice *n.* one who, for the purpose of promoting or facilitating a crime, solicits or encourages another to commit it, assists or attempts to assist in its planning or commission, or in some situations simply fails to make an attempt to prevent it. An

legal

accomplice is normally equal in culpability to the person who directly commits the crime.

accord n. 1. an agreement to settle a claim for a sum of money to be paid in the future, or occasionally for some other performance. 2. **accord and satisfaction,** an accord that has been satisfied by rendering the promised payment or performance. A claim that is the subject of an accord and satisfaction can never again be raised in court.

account n. 1. a list of financial transactions between two parties, typically a buyer and seller of goods or services, showing amounts of money paid and to be paid as a result of their business with each other. 2. Also called **bank account.** a deposit of money in a bank, pursuant to an agreement with the bank as to services it will provide (such as payment of checks), interest to be paid by the bank for the use of the money, and fees to be paid by the depositor. 3. **individual account,** a bank account held by one person only. 4. **joint account,** a bank account held by two or more people, each of whom may withdraw funds without the consent of the other. Such an account usually entails a RIGHT OF SURVIVORSHIP, so that any balance in the account when one holder dies becomes the property of the surviving holders. See also *Totten trust* (under TRUST).

account stated 1. a statement of account upon which the parties agree; typically it is prepared by the party to whom money is owed and submitted to the debtor, who indicates assent. 2. a common law action for the balance due upon such an account.

accounting n. 1. a detailed description of how the assets in an estate or trust fund have been managed and disposed of. 2. an action, which originated in courts of equity, to compel a FIDUCIARY to account for all assets handled in a fiduciary capacity and to turn over any profits received.

accrue v. 1. (of a financial right or obligation) to come into existence, mature, or accumulate: *accrued interest.* 2. (of a legal claim) to arise; to come into existence or mature so that it can be sued upon: *The statute of limitations begins to run when the cause of action accrues.* —**accrual,** n.

accusatorial system the Anglo-American system of criminal prosecution, in which the government, having accused the defendant, must prove its allegations by the adversary process, with the judge acting only as a neutral referee. Same as ADVERSARY SYSTEM, except that the latter term applies to both civil and criminal cases. Cf. INQUISITORIAL SYSTEM.

accusatory instrument a formal document accusing a person of a crime and initiating a criminal prosecution, such as an INFORMATION or INDICTMENT.

accused n. a person arrested, indicted, or otherwise formally charged with a crime; the defendant or prospective defendant in a criminal case: *The Sixth Amendment guarantees the accused the right to a speedy and public trial.*

acknowledgment n. 1. an admission of the truth of a fact or the existence of an obligation, by which one accepts civil legal responsibility. This may be by words ("I am the father of that child") or by action (e.g., signifying acknowledgment of a debt by making a partial payment). 2. an individual's declaration that she is the one who executed a particular deed or other instrument, and that she did so for the purposes stated in the instrument. Such an acknowledgment is made before a notary public or similar officer, who is responsible for confirming the individual's identity, and who puts a formal notation of the acknowledgment on the instrument. —**acknowledge,** v.

acquaintance rape. See under RAPE.

acquit[1] v. to release a criminal defendant from a charge, either upon a finding of NOT GUILTY by the jury or because the court or the prosecution determined that the case should not go forward after the trial was commenced. So far as the law is concerned, an acquitted defendant is innocent. —**acquittal,** n.

acquit[2] v. to release a person from a contractual obligation (especially an obligation to pay money)

or acknowledge that the obligation has been fulfilled, as by giving a receipt. —**acquittance,** n.

act n. 1. a statute: *act of Congress; legislative act; the Civil Rights Act of 1964.* 2. something done (an **affirmative act** or **act of commission**) or under some circumstances not done (a **negative act** or **act of omission**) by a person. See also ACTUS REUS; OMISSION; OVERT ACT; VERBAL ACT.

act of God a natural event such as lightning, a hurricane, an earthquake, or some other natural catastrophe beyond human causation or control. Sometimes such events provide an excuse for nonperformance of an obligation, either because a contract specifically so provides or as a matter of law.

act of state an official act of a foreign government. Under the **act of state doctrine,** American courts will not question the validity of such an act (for example, the expropriation of American property) by a recognized foreign government within its own territory.

action n. 1. any conduct; an act or series of acts by a person or entity. See also STATE ACTION. 2. a court case, especially a civil case; the procedure by which a legal dispute, claim, or accusation is resolved. 3. **civil action,** an action brought for any purpose other than punishment of a crime. This is the usual meaning of the word "action." 4. **class action,** an action brought on behalf of, or occasionally against, a class of persons having a common interest but too numerous to be conveniently joined as individual parties in the case. 5. **criminal action,** a case brought by the government to punish a person or entity for a crime; more often called a criminal case, a criminal proceeding, or a prosecution. 6. **damage action.** See under DAMAGES. 7. **derivative action,** an action brought on behalf of a corporation by one of its shareholders, to protect a right of the corporation. Also called **shareholder derivative action** or **stockholder derivative action.** 8. **equitable action,** an action of a type traditionally maintainable only in courts of EQUITY. Also called **action in equity** or, more traditionally, SUIT in equity. 9. **in personam action** or **action in personam,** an action in which the plaintiff seeks damages or other relief against a specific person or entity. It must be based upon *in personam jurisdiction* (see under JURISDICTION[1]) over the defendant. Most lawsuits are of this type. See also IN PERSONAM. Cf. *in rem action; quasi in rem action.* 10. **in rem action** or **action in rem,** an action in which the plaintiff seeks judgment declaring the status or disposition of property or a relationship within the jurisdiction of the court. For examples, see *in rem jurisdiction* (under JURISDICTION[1]). See also IN REM. Cf. *in personam action; quasi in rem action.* 11. **legal action, a.** broadly, any court case. **b.** Also called **common law action** or **action at law.** An action of a type traditionally maintained in courts of LAW as distinguished from courts of EQUITY. See also FORM OF ACTION, CAUSE OF ACTION, EX CONTRACTU, EX DELICTO, and MERGER OF LAW AND EQUITY. 12. **quasi in rem action** or **action quasi in rem,** an action against an out-of-state defendant, typically commenced by ATTACHMENT of property of the defendant located within the state, in which the plaintiff seeks judgment on a claim unrelated to the property and seeks to use the seized property to satisfy that judgment if payment is not made. This was formerly a device by which a claim could be litigated against a defendant who was not personally subject to the jurisdiction of the court, but the modern view is that the court must have *in personam jurisdiction,* not just *quasi in rem jurisdiction* (see both under JURISDICTION[1]), to render such a judgment. See also QUASI IN REM. Cf. *in personam action; in rem action.* 13. **third-party action.** See under THIRD PARTY.

actionable adj. describing an act or situation that could be the basis for a lawsuit: *Defamatory speech is actionable, but not speech that is merely offensive.*

actual adj. real; existing in fact: a word used to distinguish something known to have happened or to exist from something that the law simply deems to have happened or to exist. The opposite of CONSTRUCTIVE, IMPUTED, APPARENT, and *implied in law* (see under IMPLIED). See *actual* AUTHORITY[1], DAMAGES, EVICTION, FRAUD, KNOWLEDGE, MALICE, NOTICE under those words.

actus reus *Latin.* (lit. "guilty act") a voluntary act or omission to which criminal responsibility can attach. Without such an act there can be no crime, for a fundamental principle of Anglo-American law is that one cannot be punished for bad thoughts alone. See also MENS REA.

ad damnum *Latin.* (lit. "to the loss") the amount of money sought as damages in a complaint. The **ad damnum clause** is the part of a complaint in which that amount is specified. If judgment is obtained by default, it cannot exceed that amount; if the defendant does not default, then the judgment will be for whatever amount of damages the plaintiff proves at trial, whether higher or lower than the ad damnum.

ad litem *Latin.* (lit. "for the case") for purposes of a particular case. Used primarily in the phrase GUARDIAN AD LITEM.

ad testificandum *Latin.* for the purpose of testifying. See *subpoena ad testificandum* (under SUBPOENA).

ad valorem *Latin.* (lit. "according to the worth") **1.** in proportion to the value of something. **2. ad valorem tax,** a tax or duty calculated as a percentage of the stated or assessed value of the thing taxed.

additur *n. Latin.* (lit. "it is added") an order increasing the amount of damages awarded by a jury. The defendant must either agree to the higher figure or submit to a new trial. Cf. REMITTITUR.

ademption *n.* the reduction or extinguishment of a legacy because, by the time of the testator's death, some or all of the money or property needed to satisfy the legacy has been destroyed, disposed of, or already given to the legatee. Cf. ADVANCEMENT. —**adeem,** *v.*

adequate remedy at law. See under REMEDY.

adhesion contract. See under CONTRACT.

adjective law. Same as PROCEDURE (def. 2).

adjourn *v.* to suspend or postpone a proceeding, either temporarily or indefinitely. —**adjournment,** *n.*

adjudge *v.* to render a judicial decision or judgment to a certain effect: *The will was adjudged void. It is adjudged that the plaintiff shall recover the sum of $3,500.*

adjudicate *v.* to hear and resolve a case in a court or administrative agency: *The matter was adjudicated in the Court of Common Pleas.* —**adjudication,** *n.*

adjudicated *adj.* determined by adjudication: *an adjudicated incompetent; an adjudicated matter.*

administer *v.* to take charge of the estate of a decedent, marshal and manage the assets, see to the paying of the estate's debts and taxes, and distribute whatever is left in accordance with the terms of the will or, if there is no will, the laws of INTESTATE SUCCESSION. See also ADMINISTRATOR; EXECUTOR. —**administration,** *n.*

administrative *adj.* pertaining to an ADMINISTRATIVE AGENCY or to the work of such agencies in general: *administrative officer; administrative order; administrative function.* See also *administrative procedure* (under PROCEDURE); *administrative review* (under REVIEW).

administrative agency a federal, state, or local governmental unit with responsibility for administering and enforcing a particular body of law; for example, the Internal Revenue Service, a state power commission, or a city human rights department. Also called **agency.** See also REGULATORY AGENCY.

administrative law 1. the body of law that deals with the duties and operations of administrative agencies. **2.** a body of law on a particular subject created by an administrative agency through its regulations and decisions.

administrative law judge an official of an administrative agency who hears, weighs, and decides on evidence in administrative proceedings. In some states called a **hearing examiner** or **hearing officer.**

administrator *n.* a person appointed by a court to ADMINISTER the estate of a person who dies without a will. It is still common to refer to a female administrator by the archaic term **administratrix.** Cf. EXECUTOR.

admiralty. See under MARITIME.

admissible *adj.* **1.** (of evidence) permitted by the rules of evidence to be considered by the judge or jury in a case. Evidence that is admissible may nevertheless not be admitted by the judge if, for example, it is CUMULATIVE or unduly inflammatory. See also PREJUDICIAL EFFECT. **2. admissible for a limited purpose,** describing evidence that may be considered for one purpose or on one issue, but not another. —**admissibility,** *n.*

admission *n.* **1.** any words or acts of a party to a case offered as evidence by that party's opponent. Admissions are usually allowed into evidence as an exception to the *hearsay rule* (see under HEARSAY) on the ground that the party whose admission is being offered can take the stand and explain or dispute it if it is misleading. **2.** a defendant's failure to deny an allegation in a complaint, counterclaim, or *request for admissions.* The usual consequence is that the allegation in question is deemed true and may no longer be contested in the case. **3.** the act of a judge in allowing proffered evidence to be considered by the jury. See also RECEIVE. Cf. EXCLUSION. **4. admission to the bar,** the granting or obtaining of a license from the state, or permission from a court, to practice law in that state or before that court. When an out-of-state lawyer, or a lawyer not admitted to the bar of a particular court, is given special permission to appear in a particular case, that is called **admission pro hac vice.** See also PRO HAC VICE. **5. request for admissions,** a paper served by one party upon another in a case, demanding that an adversary admit or deny certain facts; often served shortly before a trial to narrow the issues and eliminate the need to spend court time proving things that are not in dispute. —**admit,** *v.*

admonition *n.* a judge's courtroom direction, advice, or warning to a jury, witness, lawyer, or even spectator, regarding any matter arising during a case. —**admonish,** *v.*

adoption *n.* the legal procedure by which an adult acquires the rights, duties, and status of a parent with respect to a child who is not the adult's natural offspring. —**adopt,** *v.*

adultery *n.* sexual intercourse by a married person with someone other than that person's spouse. This was traditionally regarded as a crime, at least when committed by a woman, and as a ground for divorce. Most states have abolished the crime and eliminated the requirement of an accusation of wrongdoing in order to obtain a divorce. Cf. CRIMINAL CONVERSATION; FORNICATION.

advance directive a LIVING WILL, a HEALTH CARE PROXY, or a combination of the two.

advancement *n.* an advance payment or transfer of a portion of one's estate to an heir (usually a child) while one is still alive, with the understanding that this is in place of a share of the estate after death. The effect is to extinguish, to the extent of the advancement, that heir's claim to a share of the estate under the laws of INTESTATE SUCCESSION. Cf. ADEMPTION.

adventure. See JOINT VENTURE.

adversary system the Anglo-American method of adjudication, in which the responsibility for ferreting out the truth in a case rests almost exclusively on the opposing parties and their lawyers, through examination and cross-examination of witnesses of their choosing. With reference to criminal cases, also called ACCUSATORIAL SYSTEM. Cf. INQUISITORIAL SYSTEM.

adverse possession a method of acquiring title to real estate, accomplished by openly occupying the property to the exclusion of everyone else and in defiance of the rights of the real owner for a period of time set by statute, typically ten to twenty years. If the owner fails to take appropriate action to oust you within that time, the property is yours.

legal

adverse witness. Same as *hostile witness* (see under WITNESS).

advisory opinion an opinion by a court on a hypothetical legal question posed by a legislative or executive body or official, as distinguished from a question arising in an actual case; for example, a question about the constitutionality of a proposed law or the legality of a proposed transaction. The Constitution bars federal courts from issuing advisory opinions, but some state courts are authorized to render such advice in certain circumstances.

affiant *n.* the person who makes an AFFIDAVIT.

affidavit *n.* **1.** a formal written statement affirming or swearing to the truth of the facts stated, signed before a notary public or similar officer. Dishonesty in an affidavit is FALSE SWEARING or PERJURY. In a narrow sense, "affidavit" refers to a sworn statement (see SWEAR) and so is distinguished from AFFIRMATION (def. 2); in a broader sense it includes affirmations. **2. affidavit (or affirmation) of service,** an affidavit or affirmation stating the time and manner in which a summons or other court paper was served in a case.

affirm¹ *v.* **1.** to declare solemnly that certain statements are true, or that one will testify truthfully. **2.** to make a solemn promise, particularly to carry out one's duties as a citizen or officeholder and to obey or uphold the law. See also SWEAR; SWEAR OR AFFIRM; OATH. —**affirmation,** *n.*

affirm², *v.* to uphold the judgment of a lower tribunal in a case that has been appealed. Cf. REVERSE; REMAND; VACATE. —**affirmance,** *n.*

affirmation *n.* **1.** the act of affirming something (see AFFIRM¹), or the words recited in doing so. An affirmation has exactly the same legal effect as an OATH. **2.** a formal written statement affirming certain facts subject to the penalties for false swearing and perjury, sometimes required to be executed before a notary public and sometimes not. This is substantially the same in form, and exactly the same in legal effect, as an AFFIDAVIT. See also *affirmation of service* (under AFFIDAVIT); OATH; OATH OR AFFIRMATION.

affirmative act. See under ACT.

affirmative action any step by a public or private employer, school, institution, or program, beyond the mere cessation of intentional discrimination, to promote diversity, provide opportunities, and alleviate the effects of past discrimination on the basis of race, sex, national origin, or disability.

affirmative defense. See under DEFENSE.

affirmative easement. See under EASEMENT.

affirmative relief. See under RELIEF.

affirmative warranty. See under WARRANTY.

after-acquired property property acquired by a debtor after the debtor's existing property has been pledged as collateral for a loan. The security agreement with the lender may provide that any after-acquired property will automatically become part of the collateral.

against the weight of the evidence. See *verdict against the weight of the evidence* (under VERDICT).

age *n.* **1. age of consent, a.** the age below which one may not get married without a parent's consent. **b.** the age below which a person is deemed incapable of consenting to sexual intercourse. Sexual intercourse with a person below that age is *statutory rape* (see under RAPE). In many states the age of consent depends upon the age of the other party to the sexual act; for example, a 14-year-old might be regarded by the law as capable of consenting to intercourse with a 17-year-old but not with an 18-year-old. **2. age of majority,** the age at which an otherwise competent person acquires the power to make binding contracts, along with most of the other legal rights and responsibilities of adulthood. Traditionally 21, the age of majority has generally been reduced to 18 in the wake of ratification of the Twenty-Sixth Amendment (see Appendix). Also called **majority; full age.** See also *legal age.* **3. age of reason,** the age below which a child cannot be found guilty of a crime or, in some states, liable for a tort; most commonly, the age of seven. **4. legal**

age, the age at which a person becomes legally capable of exercising certain rights or assuming certain responsibilities. For most purposes, same as *age of majority;* but it may be younger (e.g., driving age) or older (e.g., drinking age). See also UNDERAGE.

age discrimination discrimination on the basis of a person's age. Federal law protects most workers between the ages of 40 and 70 from age discrimination in employment; other federal and local laws provide varying degrees of protection from age discrimination in such areas as credit, housing, and public accommodations. See also BONA FIDE OCCUPATIONAL QUALIFICATION; SENIORITY SYSTEM.

agency *n.* **1.** a relationship between two people or entities whereby one (the AGENT) is authorized to act on behalf of the other (the PRINCIPAL). For legal purposes, the acts of the agent within the SCOPE OF AUTHORITY are generally deemed to be acts of the principal, and the agent is a FIDUCIARY of the principal. **2.** Short for ADMINISTRATIVE AGENCY.

agent *n.* a person or entity authorized to act on behalf of another in some matter or range of matters. For example, an insurance agent is authorized by one or more insurance companies to sell their insurance; an ATTORNEY IN FACT is an agent. See also AGENCY.

aggravated *adj.* (of a crime) characterized by some element that makes the crime more serious, such as the use of a deadly weapon, the seriousness of the injury caused or intended, or the youthfulness of the victim: *aggravated assault, aggravated rape.* Aggravated offenses are subject to more serious penalties than unaggravated forms of the same offense.

aggrieved *adj.,* adversely affected by an act or a situation, or perceiving oneself to be so affected: *A party aggrieved by a trial court's judgment may appeal.*

agreed case. See under CASE¹

agreement *n.* **1.** a manifestation of assent by two or more people to a course of action. An agreement is normally enforceable only if it meets the requirements of a CONTRACT, in which case the terms "agreement" and "contract" are interchangeable. **2. agreement to agree,** a preliminary agreement that the parties will enter into a contract along certain lines, the exact terms of which have not yet been entirely worked out. Whether the agreement to agree is itself a contract, and thus enforceable, depends upon how definite or INDEFINITE it is. See also *collective bargaining agreement* (under COLLECTIVE BARGAINING); GENTLEMEN'S AGREEMENT.

aid and abet 1. to order, encourage, or knowingly assist or attempt to assist a person who commits a crime. Aiding and abetting a crime is normally punishable to the same extent as committing the crime directly. **2.** to assist another in the commission of a tort. Ordinarily this results in joint liability with the primary actor. See also *joint tortfeasor* (under TORTFEASOR). —**aider and abettor** (or **abetter**). —**aiding and abetting.**

alibi *n.* in a criminal case, a defense that the accused was somewhere else when the crime was committed. In the federal and most state systems, the defendant must notify the prosecution in advance if she intends to use such a defense.

alien *n.* **1.** a person who is not a citizen or national of the United States. **2. nonresident alien,** an alien whose permanent residence is in another country; for example, a tourist or seasonal worker. **3. resident alien,** an alien who has lawfully established a permanent residence in the United States. Such persons are entitled to full constitutional protection, and may not be discriminated against in employment on the basis of citizenship. See also ALIENAGE. **4. undocumented alien,** an alien who has entered or remained in the United States without government authorization. Also called **illegal alien.** Although it is illegal for an employer to hire such a person, the Supreme Court has held that the public schools may not exclude children for being undocumented.

alienage *n.* the state of being an alien. For EQUAL PROTECTION purposes, alienage is a SUSPECT CLASSIFICA-

TION, so that laws and public policies discriminating between citizens and *resident aliens* (see under AL-IEN) are subject to STRICT SCRUTINY.

alienate *v.* to transfer property to another by gift, sale, or will. See also RESTRAINT ON ALIENATION. —**alienation,** *n.*

alienation of affections a tort consisting of conduct by a third party intentionally causing one spouse in a married couple to become disaffected with the other. The tort has been abolished in many states.

alimony *n.* money that one divorced spouse must pay to the other for support during or after the divorce, pursuant to a court order or an agreement between the parties. Also called **maintenance; spousal support.**

all the world everyone in the world. Often referred to simply as **the world.** Whereas an IN PERSO-NAM action normally determines only the relative rights of the particular parties before the court, an IN REM action, being directed at a piece of property rather than a particular person, typically seeks to establish the plaintiff's rights with respect to that property as against "(all) the world."

allegation *n.* an assertion that one intends to prove at trial, especially such an assertion as set forth formally in a complaint, indictment, or the like. —**allege,** *v.*

Allen charge. See under CHARGE.

allocution *n.* **1.** the process by which a guilty plea is made and accepted in a criminal case, typically involving a series of questions and answers through which the judge seeks assurance that the defendant understands the charges, understands the consequences of the plea and the rights that are being given up, and is pleading guilty of his own free will. **2.** the procedure by which a criminal defendant who is about to be sentenced is given an opportunity to make a personal statement to the judge. Typically, the judge, having heard argument from both the prosecution and the defendant's lawyer, addresses the defendant by name and says, "Is there anything that you would like to say before I pronounce sentence?" **3.** a similar procedure by which the victim of a crime is sometimes given an opportunity to address the court personally before sentence is pronounced on the person convicted of the crime.

alternative pleading. See under PLEADING.

ameliorating waste. See under WASTE.

amenable *adj.* reachable; subject to the court's power: *amenable to suit; amenable to process.* —**amenability,** *n.*

amend *v.* to revise, correct, add to, or subtract from a document of legal significance such as a constitution, a legislative bill, an executive order, a tax return, or a corporation's bylaws. Virtually any paper submitted to or issued by a court may be amended if prompt action is taken and no undue prejudice results: *amended complaint; amended offer of proof; amended reply; amended order.*

amendment *n.* **1.** the act or process of amending something. **2.** the words added to, or other changes made in, a document that has been amended; especially, an addition to the Constitution of the United States. The term is usually capitalized when referring to a specific amendment to the Constitution: *the Fifth Amendment; the Prohibition Amendment.* For a summary of all U.S. constitutional amendments to date, see Appendix.

amicus curiae *pl.* **amici curiae.** *Latin.* (lit. "friend of the court") a nonparty that volunteers or is invited by the court to submit its views on the issues presented in a case, because it has an interest in or perspective on the matter that may not be adequately represented by the parties. Usually the amicus curiae (or **amicus** for short) only submits a BRIEF (called a **brief amicus curiae** or **amicus brief**), but sometimes the amicus is also allowed to participate in oral argument. Also called **friend of the court,** but only by nonlawyers or by lawyers addressing nonlawyers.

amnesty *n.* a government's forgiveness of past offenses for a class of people, as when a state or city declares that for a period of time anyone who turns in an illegal weapon will not be prosecuted for illegal possession, or when President Ford declared an amnesty for Vietnam War deserters and draft evaders on the condition that they perform alternative public service. Amnesties may be granted either by executive decree or by legislative act, and have the effect of a PARDON for each individual covered. Cf. COMMUTE; REPRIEVE. See also CLEMENCY.

amortize *v.* **1.** to pay off a debt in regular installments over a specific period of time. **2.** to write off or deduct for income tax purposes a portion of the cost of an intangible asset each year until the entire cost has been used up. —**amortization,** *n.*

amount *n.* See JURISDICTIONAL AMOUNT.

ancillary jurisdiction. See under JURISDICTION[1].

annotated *adj.* describing a compilation of statutes to which ANNOTATIONS have been added for the benefit of legal researchers; a typical title is *United States Code Annotated.* Cf. UNITED STATES CODE.

annotation *n.* **1.** Also called **case note.** a one-paragraph summary of the holding of a case applying or interpreting a particular statutory provision, appended to the statute in question by the editors of a set of ANNOTATED statutes. An important statute may have hundreds, even thousands, of annotations in such a book. **2.** a COMMENT.

annuity *n.* **1.** a regular income paid out at fixed intervals for a certain period of time, often beginning at a certain age and continuing for the life of the recipient (the **annuitant**), usually in consideration of a PREMIUM paid by the annuitant either in a lump sum or in installments. **2.** the right to receive such income.

annulment *n.* **1.** a judicial declaration that something is legally VOID, either as of the date of the declaration or AB INITIO. **2.** in particular, a judicial declaration that a marriage is void because of some defect dating back to the time of the marriage, such as the fact that one of the partners was already married. —**annul,** *v.*

answer *v.* **1.** to respond to a complaint, motion, discovery request, or other procedural step in a case. **2.** to account for one's actions; put up a defense: *We will answer the allegations in court.* **3.** to assume responsibility or liability: *to answer for the debt of another.* **4.** to suffer the consequences for: *answer for one's crimes.* **5.** to respond to a question: *The witness is directed to answer.* —*n.* **6.** a response to a procedural step, allegation, or question: *Our answer to the motion will be filed on Friday.* **7.** in particular, the pleading filed in a civil case in response to the COMPLAINT. In the answer, the defendant must admit or deny each allegation in the complaint except for those as to which she lacks sufficient information to respond. The answer must also contain any *affirmative defense* (see under DE-FENSE) that the defendant wishes to raise, and may contain COUNTERCLAIMS, to which the plaintiff must then file a REPLY.

answering brief. See under BRIEF.

antenuptial agreement. Same as PRENUPTIAL AGREEMENT.

anticipatory breach (or **repudiation**). See under BREACH. See also REPUDIATION.

antilapse statute a statute that protects the family of a person named in a will from losing the legacy if that person dies before the will takes effect. For example, if a testator names his sister in his will but then the sister dies before the testator, at common law the bequest to the sister would LAPSE and the sister's family might end up with nothing. Under antilapse statutes in most states, the bequest to the sister would remain valid and be distributed to her own heirs.

antitrust *adj.* relating to the body of law—primarily federal law—intended to foster vigorous competition among businesses by outlawing such practices as price fixing and monopolization. The principal antitrust laws are the SHERMAN ANTI-TRUST ACT and the CLAYTON ACT. See also TRADE REGU-LATION.

apparent *adj.* **1.** obvious, or at least deducible from the facts available: *It is apparent from the re-*

cord that the defendant failed to exercise due care. **2.** seeming, but not ACTUAL; for example, see *apparent authority* (under AUTHORITY¹).

appeal *n.* **1.** the process by which one obtains review of a judicial decision by a higher court, or of an administrative decision by a court or by a higher authority within the administrative agency: *The case is on appeal.* **2. appeal as of right, a.** an appeal that the higher tribunal is required by law to consider. **b.** to file or pursue such an appeal: *The defendant appealed as of right to this court.* **3. appeal by permission, a.** Also called **discretionary appeal.** an appeal that may be pursued only if specific permission is granted by a court. **b.** to file or pursue such an appeal. **4. interlocutory appeal,** an appeal from an interim order in a case that is still proceeding in the lower tribunal. Most jurisdictions permit interlocutory appeals only under limited circumstances. —*v.* **5.** to seek or pursue review by a higher authority: *If we lose, we will appeal. They are appealing the order.* —**appealable,** *adj.* —**appealability,** *n.*

appeal bond. See under BOND².

appealable order. See under ORDER¹.

appear *v.* **1.** (of a person) to come before a court or file a formal paper announcing that one will participate in a case: *The defendant appeared voluntarily; the attorney appeared on behalf of the defendant; the witness appeared pursuant to subpoena.* For many purposes a party need not appear personally but may send a lawyer instead **(appear by counsel). 2.** (of a fact) to be found in or deducible from the record in a case, so that it can be considered by an appellate court: *The defendant's age does not appear in the record.*

appearance *n.* **1.** the act of coming before a court or of formally notifying the court that one will participate in a case as a party, lawyer, or witness. **2. general appearance,** an appearance in which a party consents to the court's jurisdiction and agrees to participate in a case for all purposes. **3. special appearance,** an appearance for the limited purpose of contesting the court's jurisdiction. Also called **limited appearance.**

appellant *n.* the party who files an appeal.

appellate *adj.* relating to appeals or an appeal: *appellate judge; appellate decision.* See also *appellate* BRIEF, JURISDICTION¹, REVIEW under those words.

appellee *n.* the adversary of the party who files an appeal.

appoint *v.* to designate who shall receive property that is the subject of a POWER OF APPOINTMENT.

appraisal rights the rights of corporate shareholders, granted by statutes which vary from state to state, to dissent from certain extraordinary corporate actions such as a merger, have the value of their stock prior to such an action appraised in a judicial proceeding, and compel the corporation to buy the stock back at the appraised value.

appraise *v.* to determine the MARKET VALUE of something. Cf. ASSESS. —**appraisal,** *n.*

appropriation *n.* **1.** the taking of anything; for example, the government's TAKING of private property for public use: *appropriation of land for construction of a school.* **2.** the act of a legislative body in setting aside a sum of money from public funds for a particular use: *appropriation of $1,000,000 for construction of a school.* —**appropriate,** *v.*

appurtenant *adj.* describing a right or thing attached to or associated with a parcel of land in such a way that it normally passes with title to the land. For example, buildings on land are appurtenant to it, and an easement to pass over a neighbor's land to reach one's own land is appurtenant to one's own land.

arbitrary *adj.* completely unreasonable; lacking a rational basis. Often used in the phrase **arbitrary and capricious,** which means the same thing.

arbitration *n.* **1.** a process for resolution of disputes without resort to the courts, through submission of the dispute to a private individual (the **arbitrator**), or a panel of arbitrators, selected jointly by the parties. Arbitration can sometimes be cheaper and quicker than litigation and have the advantage of utilizing arbitrators who are specialists in the field involved in the dispute. It can also be amazingly expensive and time-consuming, and result in decisions biased in favor of the industry with which the specialist arbitrators are associated. Cf. MEDIATION. **2. compulsory arbitration,** arbitration required by law, rather than submitted to by mutual agreement. —**arbitrable,** *adj.* —**arbitrate,** *v.*

arguable *adj.* capable of being supported by respectable argument, though not necessarily a winning argument.

argue *v.* to present an ARGUMENT on a matter: *argue the motion; argue the appeal; argue the issue;* or simply *argue.*

arguendo *Latin.* (lit. "in arguing") hypothetically; for purposes of argument; a term used in assuming a fact for the purpose of argument without waiving the right to question its truth later: *Assuming arguendo that the plaintiff's allegations are true, the complaint nevertheless fails to state a claim.*

argument *n.* **1.** the reasons supporting a conclusion or proposed conclusion, or the formal presentation of such reasons to a person or body that one hopes to convince. **2.** the section of a BRIEF in which a party presents its analysis of the law pertaining to a motion or appeal. This follows a section in which the pertinent facts are outlined, and explains why the party contends that, upon those facts, the law requires a particular decision. **3.** Also called **oral argument. a.** an oral presentation to a court of the reasons—both legal and factual—why a party contends that the court should reach a particular conclusion or take a particular action. **b.** the procedure in which a court hears such arguments from both sides on a motion or appeal, often questioning the lawyers on various details as they argue. Cf. *take on submission* (under SUBMIT). **4.** Also called **closing argument.** a SUMMATION.

argumentative *adj.* (of a statement or question) suggesting that the facts support a particular inference or conclusion. See also *argumentative question* (under QUESTION¹).

arm's length referring to dealings between unrelated parties, each motivated solely by its own self-interest: *The parties dealt at arm's length. It was an arm's-length transaction.* See also MARKET VALUE.

arraignment *n.* the proceeding in which a criminal defendant is brought before the court, formally advised of the charges, and required to enter a PLEA. —**arraign,** *v.*

array. Same as VENIRE.

arrest *n.* **1.** any significant deprivation of an individual's freedom of action, especially the taking of an individual into custody for the purpose of transporting him to a police station and charging him with a crime. Cf. STOP. **2. citizen's arrest,** an arrest made by a private citizen rather than a law enforcement officer, as when bystanders tackle a purse-snatcher. Such arrests are lawful only under narrow circumstances. **3. false arrest.** See under FALSE IMPRISONMENT. **4. warrantless arrest,** an arrest made without a warrant (see WARRANT¹). As a general rule, a police officer may arrest a person for a felony without a warrant if she has PROBABLE CAUSE and the arrest is made in a public place, but a warrant is required to enter a person's home. —*v.* **5.** to make an arrest of a person.

arrest warrant. See under WARRANT¹.

arson *n.* the crime of intentionally causing a dangerous fire or explosion, especially for the purpose of destroying a building of another or of damaging property in order to collect insurance.

articles of impeachment the formal written instrument that forms the basis for an IMPEACHMENT proceeding against a public officer, listing the charges against the officer.

articles of incorporation a document setting forth the basic structure of a corporation, including its name and purposes and the number of shares of stock that it will be authorized to issue, which must be filed with a state government in order to bring the corporation into existence. See also CERTIFICATE OF INCORPORATION; CHARTER¹.

artificial person See under PERSON.

as a matter of law (of a legal conclusion) compelled by principles of law and justice; said particularly of factual findings that a court takes out of the hands of the jury: *The judge directed a verdict for the defendant in the personal injury case because the plaintiff deliberately ignored a warning sign and therefore assumed the risk of injury as a matter of law.* See also BY OPERATION OF LAW.

as applied. See *unconstitutional* (or *invalid*) *as applied* (under UNCONSTITUTIONAL).

as is without any express or implied warranty. The words "as is," "with all faults," or the like in a contract for sale of goods mean that the buyer assumes the risk of any defects or malfunctions.

assault *n.* **1.** in tort law, an act putting another person in apprehension of imminent BATTERY, done either with intent actually to cause a battery (as by taking a swing at someone) or simply with intent to cause the apprehension (as by shaking your fist under someone's nose). If in either case the act results in physical contact, then there has been both an assault and a battery. **2.** in criminal law, a term used in different states to mean one or more of the following crimes: **a.** BATTERY. **b.** attempted battery. **c.** conduct inducing a reasonable fear of battery or immediate bodily harm. **3. assault and battery.** Another term for the crime of battery. **4. sexual assault,** the crime of intentionally touching another person in a sexual way without that person's consent, or when that person lacks the capacity to give legally effective consent. Also called **indecent assault.**

assembly. See FREEDOM OF ASSEMBLY; UNLAWFUL ASSEMBLY.

assess *v.* **1.** to set the amount of, and impose, a tax, fine, or damages: *Damages were assessed at $1.5 million. The Liquor Authority assessed a fine of $10,000.* **2.** to establish the value of real estate for property tax purposes (the **assessed value**). Typically the assessed value is lower than the MARKET VALUE. Cf. APPRAISE. **3.** to require stockholders to make additional contributions to the corporation, or partners to make additional contributions to the partnership, to fill a need for additional capital. See also *assessable stock* and *nonassessable stock* (under STOCK). —**assessment,** *n.*

assessable stock. See under STOCK.

asset *n.* **1.** any property or right of a person or entity that has monetary value, such as land, an automobile, stock, a copyright, money, or a right to payment for goods sold (if payment is a realistic possibility). Cf. LIABILITY (def. 3). **2. assets,** all such property and rights collectively, or their total value; the total resources of a person, estate, business, etc. If assets exceed liabilities, the excess is the entity's **net assets:** *The company has assets of $1,000,000, liabilities of $900,000, and net assets of $100,000.* **3. capital asset,** for income tax purposes, virtually all property except certain business assets and certain other property excluded by the Internal Revenue Code. The tax treatment of a sale or exchange of property depends in part upon whether the property was a capital asset. **4. liquid asset,** an asset readily convertible into cash, such as shares of publicly traded stock.

assign *v.* **1.** to transfer an interest, right, or duty; to substitute another person for oneself in a contract: *The company assigned its accounts receivable to the bank. I assigned my lease to someone else and moved to San Francisco.* **2.** to appoint: *The judge assigned counsel for the defendant.* **3.** to identify, point out: *The appellant assigns numerous alleged errors by the trial judge.* —*n.* **4. assigns,** persons to whom an interest, right, or duty might be assigned. Used principally in the phrase *heirs and assigns* (see under HEIR); in most other contexts, and whenever the singular is called for, the term used is ASSIGNEE. —**assignment,** *n.*

assignable *adj.* capable of being assigned. Some rights and most duties are not assignable, at least without the permission of other parties involved; for example, an opera star cannot unilaterally assign her contract to sing in an opera to an inferior per-

former. But a right to receive a payment is normally freely assignable.

assigned counsel. See under COUNSEL.

assigned risk a risk that, under state law, is assigned to an insurer chosen from a pool of insurers who otherwise would not accept it.

assignee *n.* the person or entity to which an interest, right, or duty is assigned.

assignment for the benefit of creditors an assignment, by an entity overwhelmed with debts, of substantially all of its assets to a trustee, to be liquidated and used to satisfy the debts to the extent possible.

assignment of error a specification, in appellate papers, of a ruling by the court below that the appellant contends was improper and requires reversal.

assignor *n.* the person or entity that assigns an interest, right, or duty to another.

Assistant United States Attorney. See under UNITED STATES ATTORNEY.

assisted suicide. See under SUICIDE.

associate *n.* the usual title for an attorney in a law firm who works on salary but does not share in the firm's profits. Most attorneys in large law firms are associates rather than partners or owners.

association *n.* **1.** Also called **unincorporated association.** any group of people organized for a common purpose and not formed as a corporation. **2.** for income tax purposes, an unincorporated organization having characteristics that make it more like a corporation than like a partnership or trust. Such an association is taxed as a corporation. **3. joint stock association.** The name used in some states for *joint stock company* (see under COMPANY). **4. professional association.** The name used in some states for *professional corporation* (see under CORPORATION). See also *cooperative association* (under COOPERATIVE).

assume *v.* to take on or accept responsibility for; especially, to take over an obligation of another. For example, the purchaser of a house with a mortgage may assume the mortgage; the purchaser of a business may assume the debts of the business. —**assumption,** *n.*

assumption of risk the doctrine that one who voluntarily enters into a situation known to be dangerous may not recover from someone else for any resulting injury; the injured party is said to have "assumed the risk" of being injured. The defense of assumption of risk has been modified or abolished in many states. Cf. *comparative negligence* (under NEGLIGENCE).

assure *v.* to provide INSURANCE, act as a SURETY, or put up collateral (see COLLATERAL¹). —**assurance,** *n.* —**assured,** *adj.*, *n.*

asylum *n.* refuge granted by a country to a person who is wanted for prosecution in another country; especially, such refuge for a person wanted for exercising political, civil, or human rights such as speaking or running for office (**political asylum**). Cf. EXTRADITE.

at *prep.* **1.** the word customarily used instead of "in," "under," or "by" in referring to modern or ancient COMMON LAW (often shortened to "law"): *Commercial bribery was not a crime at common law, but is a crime under modern criminal statutes. We are seeking relief in equity because we do not have an adequate remedy at law.* **2.** the word usually used by lawyers to refer to a page number: *You'll find the citation at page 33, Your Honor, and the discussion begins at 35.*

at bar. See under BAR.

at will describing or referring to a status or relationship that can be terminated at any time for any reason: *tenancy* (or *estate*) *at will* (see under TENANCY); *employee at will.*

attach *v.* to effect an ATTACHMENT: *The plaintiff attached the defendant's car and bank account.*

attachment *n.* **1.** the seizing or freezing of property by court order in order to subject the property to the jurisdiction of the court, either so that a dispute as to ownership of it can be resolved or so that it will be available to satisfy a judgment against the owner. **2.** the writ or other document authorizing or effecting such a seizure.

attachment bond. See under BOND².

attack. See *direct attack* (under DIRECT¹); *collateral attack* (under COLLATERAL²).

attainder. See BILL OF ATTAINDER.

attempt *n.* the taking of a substantial step toward the commission of a crime, beyond mere preparation. Attempt is itself a crime, sometimes punishable to the same extent as the crime that was attempted, sometimes (especially in the case of more serious crimes such as murder) treated as a slightly lower grade of offense. In a prosecution for attempt, it does not matter whether the attempt was successful or not. —**attempted,** *adj.*

attest *v.* **1.** to sign a document as a witness to its execution by someone else. **2.** to CERTIFY the authenticity of a document or the accuracy of a copy. **3.** attested copy. Same as *certified copy* (see under CERTIFY). —**attestation,** *n.*

attesting witness. See under WITNESS.

attorney *n.* **1.** Also called **attorney at law.** A slightly pretentious word for LAWYER. **2.** Also called **attorney in fact.** A person who acts on behalf of another pursuant to a POWER OF ATTORNEY. **3. attorney of record,** the attorney or law firm listed in court as representing a particular party in a case. All papers and communications in a case intended for that party must go to the attorney of record. Cf. PRO SE.

attorney-client privilege. See under PRIVILEGE.

Attorney General 1. the chief legal officer of the federal government or of a state; the head of the United States Department of Justice or of a state's legal department. Cf. *Solicitor General* (under SOLICITOR); UNITED STATES ATTORNEY. **2. private attorney general,** *Informal.* a private person who brings a civil case to draw attention to unlawful conduct and force compliance with or punish noncompliance with a law, not only for personal satisfaction or compensation but also in the hope that the public at large will ultimately benefit. The term is rather subjective; what one person might hail as the action of a private attorney general another might condemn as a *strike suit* (see under SUIT).

attorney work product. Same as WORK PRODUCT.

attorney's lien. See under LIEN.

attractive nuisance a condition existing on private property, but in a place where children are likely to trespass, that poses an unreasonable danger to such children. In general, property owners will be held liable to children injured by such conditions if the danger could have been prevented by reasonable measures. For example, a homeowner would be expected to take strong precaution-

ary measures to make sure that children cannot get in and play near his uncovered swimming pool without supervision.

authenticate *v.* **1.** to introduce evidence to show that a document or other item offered as evidence in a case is in fact what the proponent claims it to be. Some authenticating evidence is ordinarily required before an exhibit can be admitted into evidence. **2. self-authenticating,** showing on its face that it is authentic, or otherwise presumed to be authentic, so that no other authenticating evidence is required unless the authenticity of the item is called into question; for example, a certified copy of a public document. —**authentication,** *n.*

authority¹ *n.* **1.** the legal power of a public official or body to act in an official capacity. **2.** the power to act on behalf of another and bind the other by such actions; the power of an AGENT to act on behalf of the PRINCIPAL. See also SCOPE OF AUTHORITY. **3. actual authority,** authority intentionally granted by a principal to an agent. Such authority may be granted explicitly **(express authority)** or simply understood as necessary or proper in order to carry out expressly authorized tasks **(implied authority). 4. apparent authority,** authority of an agent reasonably inferred from conduct of the principal, even if the principal did not intend the agent to have such authority.

authority² *n.* a source of information or insight on how to interpret and apply the law in a particular situation. The term includes judicial decisions, legislative history, and scholarly writing. A clearly applicable HOLDING by a higher court in the same jurisdiction must be followed by a lower court **(binding authority);** all other authority is at best **persuasive authority,** which need not be followed by a court.

automatic stay. See under STAY.

automobile guest statute a statute providing that a nonpaying passenger in an automobile (a "guest" of the driver) who is injured in an accident caused by the driver's negligence may not recover damages from the driver, and hence from the driver's insurance company, unless the driver's negligence was extreme. At one time over half the states had such statutes, largely as a result of insurance industry lobbying. In recent years the tide has turned, and now only a few states still have such statutes.

avoid *v.* to nullify, upon some legal ground, an obligation or transaction to which one is a party; especially, in a situation where one party to a contract lacked the capacity to contract (e.g., because of infancy), to render the contract void by disaffirming it. See also VOIDABLE. Cf. RATIFY. —**avoidance,** *n.*

award *n.* **1.** a grant of damages or other relief by a court, jury, or administrative tribunal. —*v.* **2.** to grant such relief: *The plaintiff was awarded $5,000.*

a B c d e f g h i j k l m n o p q r s t u v w x y z

bad *adj.* generally, not favored by the law or acceptable in the marketplace. The specific legal meaning varies from phrase to phrase; see the entries directly below and *bad* CHECK, DEBT, TITLE under those words.

bad faith absence of GOOD FAITH; lack of overall fairness and honesty in a transaction; especially, an intent to deceive others or to evade one's own obligations.

bad law 1. a judicial opinion or decision that misconstrues or misapplies a legal principle, producing erroneous or misleading results. **2.** any statute or ruling regarded by the speaker as unwise. Cf. GOOD LAW.

bail¹ *n.* **1.** money or other property pledged to a court by or on behalf of a person accused of a crime to assure her appearance in court. Cf. PREVENTIVE DETENTION; RELEASE ON OWN RECOGNIZANCE. **2. bail bond,** the document in which bail is pledged by the

accused. Typically a third party acceptable to the court (traditionally called a **bail bondsman**) must also sign as a SURETY, so that the court will not have to try to collect forfeited bail from a missing defendant. **3. cash bail,** bail posted entirely in cash. If the accused satisfies all bail conditions, the cash is eventually returned. **4. excessive bail,** bail set in an amount higher than is reasonably necessary to secure the defendant's presence at trial. The Eighth Amendment (see Appendix) prohibits the government from demanding excessive bail and thereby keeping people not convicted of a crime in jail unnecessarily. **5. jump bail,** to flee while free on bail. **6. make bail,** to secure one's own release from custody by posting the required bail or having someone else do so. **7. on bail** or **out on bail,** free from custody because bail has been posted. **8. post bail,** to provide the required cash or bond for bail, either for oneself or for someone else. **9. stand bail,** to post bail for someone else. —*v.* **10.** to secure the release of a person by posting bail (usually with *out*): *My sister bailed me out.*

bail² *v.* to transfer possession of personal property temporarily. See also BAILMENT.

bailable offense a charged offense for which the accused may be released on bail. Cf. PREVENTIVE DETENTION.

bailiff *n.* a court officer charged with managing the courtroom and taking care of the jury.

bailment *n.* an arrangement in which one person (the **bailor**) transfers possession (but not ownership) of personal property to another (the **bailee**) for storage, use, or some other temporary purpose. The legal rights and duties of the parties depend upon the purpose and terms of the bailment. The bailee may be storing the bailor's goods for a fee **(bailment for hire)**, or working on them, as in the case of a car in a repair shop **(bailment for mutual benefit)**, or simply borrowing them **(gratuitous bailment)**; in each case, the bailor and bailee may be referred to according to type of bailment: *gratuitous bailee, bailor for mutual benefit,* etc. If one person is renting property from the other, the arrangement is usually referred to as a LEASE rather than a bailment.

bait and switch the practice of drawing customers into a store by advertising a product at a low price and then inducing them to purchase a more expensive product by disparaging the advertised product or saying that it is not available. This is usually a crime. See also FALSE ADVERTISING.

balancing of the equities a court's weighing of all factors favoring each side in order to determine the overall fairness of granting or denying an injunction or other equitable relief. Also called **balancing of the hardships.**

balancing test any decision-making process that involves the weighing of competing values and interests.

banc. See EN BANC.

bank account. See under ACCOUNT.

bank check. See under CHECK.

bankrupt *n.* a person or entity that is the subject of BANKRUPTCY proceedings.

bankruptcy *n.* **1.** a judicial proceeding under federal law (the **Bankruptcy Code**) by which a person or corporation unable to pay its debts can have the debts adjusted and get a fresh start. The entity that is the subject of such proceedings is referred to as the DEBTOR or the BANKRUPT, and is said to be "in bankruptcy." The proceedings are often identified by the chapter of the Bankruptcy Code under which they are brought: **Chapter 7 bankruptcy** (also called **straight bankruptcy**), in which most of the debtor's remaining assets are sold outright, the court distributes the proceeds among the creditors, and the debts are extinguished; **Chapter 11 bankruptcy** (also called REORGANIZATION), in which the debtor, usually a corporation, is allowed to continue operating its business in the hope of making more money with which to pay creditors, and a plan **(reorganization plan** or **plan of reorganization)** is worked out under which creditors agree to reduce the amount of the debts or extend the payment schedule; **Chapter 12 bankruptcy,** a proceeding analogous to Chapter 11, designed specifically for farmers going through hard times to enable them to keep their farms and keep farming; **Chapter 13 bankruptcy** (also called REHABILITATION), a proceeding analogous to Chapter 11, designed specifically for individuals with a steady income and involving a plan **(wage earner's plan)** under which they agree to pay off at least a specified portion of their debts over time. **2. involuntary bankruptcy,** a bankruptcy proceeding initiated by a creditor. **3. voluntary bankruptcy,** a bankruptcy proceeding initiated by the debtor. See also *bankruptcy estate* (under ESTATE²); *bankruptcy trustee* (under TRUSTEE); *discharge in bankruptcy* (under DISCHARGE).

bar *n.* **1.** the legal profession generally, or all lawyers whose practice shares a common element: *the Houston bar; the plaintiffs' bar; the Tax Court bar.* See also *admission to the bar* (under ADMISSION); DIS-

BAR. Cf. BENCH. **2.** a legal impediment or barrier, especially to the formation of a valid contract or the pursuit or defense of a case. **3. at bar,** currently before the court: *the case at bar; the plaintiff at bar.* **4. in bar,** as a bar to an action: *Because the defendant in the contract action was a minor when she signed the contract, she pleaded legal incapacity in bar.* —*v.* **5.** to prohibit or act as a bar to: *The statute of limitations bars the action.*

bare. Same as NAKED.

bargain *v.* **1.** to negotiate terms of a contract; to haggle. —*n.* **2.** a negotiated contract. Cf. *adhesion contract* (under CONTRACT).

bargained for 1. describing a contract term that was subject to negotiation or for which some concession or return benefit is deemed to have been given. If placed before the noun, requires a hyphen: *The term was bargained for; a bargained-for term.* Cf. BOILERPLATE. **2. bargained-for exchange,** a classic definition of CONTRACT, reflecting the ideal that a contract represents a mutually satisfactory exchange of benefits resulting from genuine bargaining between parties of equal BARGAINING POWER. The reality is often very different. Cf. *adhesion contract* (under CONTRACT).

bargaining. See COLLECTIVE BARGAINING.

bargaining power the ability of a party to a proposed contract to influence the terms of the contract. Two successful corporations negotiating a joint venture typically have equal bargaining power; an individual seeking coverage from an insurance company typically has no bargaining power at all.

barratry *n.* persistently stirring up litigation or quarrels. This was an offense at common law. Initiating groundless litigation may still be an offense in some states. See also CHAMPERTY; MAINTENANCE; ABUSE OF PROCESS; MALICIOUS PROSECUTION.

barrister *n.* **1.** in England, a lawyer who is a courtroom advocate. Cf. SOLICITOR. **2.** in America, occasionally and informally, another word for lawyer.

barter *n.* **1.** an exchange of goods or services without using money. Such transactions are normally subject to the same income and sales taxes as money transactions, but are sometimes employed to avoid taxes because they are difficult to trace. —*v.* **2.** to effect or engage in a barter.

basis *n.* the amount of money that one has invested in a piece of property. The gain or loss on sale of the property is calculated for tax purposes as the amount by which the value received for the property exceeds or falls short of the basis.

bastard *n.* formerly the standard legal term for a child born out of wedlock.

bastardy action (or **proceeding**), the older legal term for a PATERNITY SUIT.

battered person syndrome a psychological condition said to result from persistent physical abuse, regularly invoked in recent years as a proposed JUSTIFICATION for homicide. The argument has had a mixed reception from courts and scholars, but often finds favor with juries. Also called **battered woman syndrome, battered child syndrome,** etc., according to the circumstances.

battery *n.* harmful or offensive touching of another person, either intentionally or as a byproduct of some other intentional wrong. The touching may be either direct or indirect, as by grabbing clothes, using a stick, or launching a projectile. Battery is usually both a tort and a crime. Cf. ASSAULT.

battle of the experts *Informal.* a trial whose outcome depends in large part on a choice between the conflicting opinions of expert witnesses hired by the opposing sides. In the federal courts and in most states the court can appoint a neutral expert, but this is seldom done.

bearer *n.* a person in possession of a negotiable instrument or other document, especially one made out or indorsed to "bearer" or in some other way that does not designate a specific payee or person entitled to enforce it, such as a check made out to "cash" or indorsed IN BLANK. Such a document is called a **bearer instrument, bearer bond,** or the like, depending upon its na-

legal

ture; and if it is an instrument for the payment of money, such as a check or note, it is **payable to bearer.** Bearer paper must be carefully safeguarded, since anyone who comes into possession of it may NEGOTIATE it. Cf. *order instrument* (under ORDER²).

below *adv.* **1.** in the lower court from which an appeal was taken (the **court below**): *The decision below should be affirmed.* **2.** later on in the same document: *As we will explain below, the decision should be affirmed.* See also INFRA.

bench *n.* **1.** the judge's seat and desk in a courtroom: *Instead of issuing a written opinion, the judge ruled from the bench.* **2.** the judicial profession; judges collectively, as distinguished from practicing lawyers: *The conference provided an opportunity for the bench and the bar to meet informally.* **3. bench conference.** Same as SIDEBAR. See also *bench trial* (under TRIAL); *bench warrant* (under WARRANT¹). Cf. BAR.

beneficial *adj.* referring to rights that derive from something other than legal title to property, particularly rights of a trust beneficiary. See *beneficial ESTATE¹, INTEREST¹, OWNER* under those words. See also EQUITABLE.

beneficiary *n.* **1.** a person for whose benefit a trust is established, and for whose benefit the trustee must manage the trust property. **2.** the person to whom benefits are to be paid under an insurance policy. **3. third-party beneficiary.** See under CONTRACT.

bequeath *v.* **1.** to give personal property by will. Cf. DEVISE. **2.** broadly, to give any property by will.

bequest *n.* **1.** a gift of personal property by will, or the property so given. Also called **legacy,** especially in reference to gifts of money. Cf. DEVISE. **2.** broadly, any testamentary gift of property, whether real or personal. *Legacy* is also used in this broad sense. **3. general bequest** (or **legacy**), a bequest to be paid out of the general assets of the estate, that is, out of whatever is left after payment of debts and expenses and distribution of specific bequests. **4. residuary bequest** (or **legacy**), the final bequest in a typical will, disposing of any assets left over after payment of all debts and expenses and satisfaction of all other bequests. **5. specific bequest** (or **legacy**), a bequest of a specific item or items of property.

best evidence rule the principle that in order to prove the contents of a writing, photograph, or the like, one must produce the original unless it is unavailable through no serious fault of one's own. Modern evidence rules, however, permit the use of a duplicate, such as a photocopy, in most circumstances.

best use or **best and highest use.** See under USE.

beyond a reasonable doubt the highest STANDARD OF PROOF; the degree of certainty necessary to convict a defendant of a crime. It does not mean beyond all possible doubt, but beyond any doubt based upon reason and common sense.

beyond the scope. Short for **beyond the scope of the direct (cross, redirect, recross) examination.** The objection raised at a trial or hearing when a person examining a witness (other than on direct examination) attempts to delve into matters that were not asked about in the immediately preceding examination. See also EXAMINATION; SCOPE OF EXAMINATION; OPEN THE DOOR. Cf. SCOPE OF EXPERTISE.

BFOQ. See BONA FIDE OCCUPATIONAL QUALIFICATION.

bias crime. Same as HATE CRIME.

bilateral contract. See under CONTRACT.

bill *n.* **1.** a formal document, often one containing a list of items. **2.** a proposed statute filed in Congress or a state or local legislature by one or more members for consideration by the whole body. **3.** the initial pleading in courts of EQUITY. In modern practice this has been replaced by the COMPLAINT. **4. no bill,** the outcome of a grand jury's deliberations when it refuses to issue a proposed INDICTMENT. **5. true bill,** words endorsed on a proposed indictment to indicate that the grand jury has approved of it; hence, an INDICTMENT.

bill of attainder a law imposing a punishment on someone, or on a class of people, without a trial. Bills of attainder are prohibited by the Constitution.

bill of exchange. Same as DRAFT.

bill of lading 1. a document issued by a person or entity in the business of transporting or forwarding goods, identifying goods received for shipment and designating who is entitled to delivery of them. **2. order bill of lading,** or **order bill,** a bill of lading stating that the goods are to be delivered to the order of a named party. This is a *negotiable document of title* (see under DOCUMENT OF TITLE). **3. straight bill of lading,** or **straight bill,** a bill of lading stating that the goods are to be delivered to a specific named party. This is a *nonnegotiable document of title* (see under DOCUMENT OF TITLE). **4. through bill of lading,** or **through bill,** a bill of lading issued by the first of a series of connecting carriers, assuming responsibility for the entire shipment.

bill of particulars a written statement setting forth the details of a civil claim or a criminal charge.

Bill of Rights 1. the first ten amendments to the Constitution, added to the Constitution shortly after its adoption as a formal statement of fundamental rights of Americans. See Appendix for summary. Originally intended only as a limitation on the powers of the federal government (not state governments), most of the Bill of Rights has now been extended to the states, so that, for example, a law restricting freedom of speech would be unconstitutional whether adopted by Congress or by a state legislature. See INCORPORATION DOCTRINE. **2.** (*sometimes l.c.*) by extension, a name given to any formal list of rights of a group, enacted as a law or adopted by an organization or institution: *patients' bill of rights; victim's bill of rights; consumer bill of rights.*

bill of sale a document transferring title in personal property from seller to buyer.

bind *v.* to put under a legal obligation. See also *binding authority* (under AUTHORITY²).

bind over to order that a person accused of a crime be subjected to a trial, as a result of a finding of PROBABLE CAUSE at a *bindover hearing* (see under HEARING): *The defendant was bound over to the Superior Court for trial.*

binder *n.* a document granting a person who has applied for an insurance policy temporary coverage until the policy is issued or the application is rejected.

black letter law. Same as HORNBOOK LAW.

blackmail *n.* **1.** EXTORTION, especially extortion by means of threats to reveal injurious truths about a person. —*v.* **2.** to extort money from a person, especially by threatening to reveal an injurious truth.

blank indorsement. See under INDORSEMENT.

blind trust. See under TRUST.

blockbusting *n.* inducing people to sell their homes by spreading stories about ethnic minorities moving into the neighborhood. This once common device used by real estate agents to induce panic selling by white homeowners—generating commissions for the agents—was outlawed in 1968 by the federal Fair Housing Act.

blue law a law of Puritan origin or inspiration regulating conduct for essentially religious reasons, especially a SUNDAY CLOSING LAW.

blue sky law any of the state statutes, which exist in all fifty states, regulating the issuance of securities within the state; the state counterparts of the federal SECURITIES ACTS.

Bluebook, The The most commonly used reference work on how cases, statutes, and other authorities are cited in legal writing. Formerly titled, and now subtitled, **A Uniform System of Citation.**

board of directors the governing body of a corporation, elected by the shareholders to set policy, select officers to carry it out, monitor the corporation's operations, and make major decisions regarding the corporation's business and finances.

boiler room sales high-pressure selling of securities by telephone.

boilerplate *n.* standardized language usually included in legal documents of a certain type, such as contracts, wills, or deeds, or in a particular class of such documents, such as apartment leases or bank loan agreements. In a printed contract, boilerplate often appears in fine print and represents terms that are either noncontroversial (such as a clause specifying which state's law governs the contract) or nonnegotiable. See also *adhesion contract* (under CONTRACT).

bona fide *Latin.* (lit. "in good faith") **1.** describing a thing done or a person acting in GOOD FAITH: *bona fide purchaser.* **2.** genuine: *bona fide occupational qualification.*

bona fide occupational qualification (BFOQ) a qualification reasonably necessary to the normal operation of a particular business or enterprise. The federal civil rights laws outlawing discrimination in employment provide exceptions for situations in which a particular religion, sex, national origin, or age range (but not race or color) is a bona fide occupational qualification. In addition, a special exception allows religious organizations and schools to discriminate on the basis of religion even when hiring people for positions for which religion is not a bona fide occupational qualification, such as janitor in a church-owned building in which no religious activities take place.

bona fide purchaser or **bona fide purchaser for value.** Same as GOOD FAITH PURCHASER.

bona fides *Latin.* good faith: *His bona fides was proved at trial.* Because the *s* in this Latin phrase makes it look like an English plural, one occasionally sees it with a plural verb (*"His bona fides were proved"*); more often the phrase is used in a way that avoids the issue: *He proved his bona fides at trial.* In modern legal writing, the phrase is usually rejected entirely in favor of the English GOOD FAITH.

bond¹ *n.* a kind of security (see SECURITY²) issued by a corporation or governmental body in order to borrow money from the public. It is in the form of a certificate evidencing the issuer's obligation to repay the debt in full on or by a specific date, and usually to make regular interest payments until then. Unlike a stockholder, the owner of a bond (the **bondholder**) has no ownership interest in the issuing corporation, but is simply a CREDITOR of the issuer. See also *bearer bond* (under BEARER); DEBENTURE.

bond² *n.* **1.** a written obligation to pay or forfeit a sum of money, or occasionally to perform some other act, upon the occurrence of a specified event—particularly some default by the person or entity by or for which the bond is issued. The bond may be issued by the person or entity whose default is being guarded against **(personal bond)**, but in most situations it is provided—for a fee—by a third party such as an insurance company **(surety bond** or **suretyship bond).** See also SURETY; SURETYSHIP. **2. appeal bond,** a bond required of a losing party in a civil case who wishes to appeal, to assure that the winning party's costs will be paid if the appeal is dropped or is unsuccessful. **3. attachment bond,** a bond posted by a person whose property has been attached, as a substitute for the attached property. This frees the property while providing the same protection for the attacher. See also ATTACH; ATTACHMENT. **4. bail bond.** See under BAIL¹. **5. completion bond,** a bond posted to provide money to complete a construction project if the construction contractor fails to do so in accordance with the terms of the contract. Also called **performance bond. 6. fidelity bond,** insurance against loss due to embezzlement or other dishonest conduct by an employee, particularly one whose position deals with the employer's financial affairs. **7. fiduciary bond,** a bond issued to protect against misappropriation or misapplication of property under the control of a FIDUCIARY such as a trustee, a guardian, or the executor or administrator of an estate. **8. payment bond,** a bond issued to guarantee that funds will be available to pay workers, subcontractors, and suppliers of materials for a construction project if the general contractor fails to pay them, so that their claims will not be a lien on the property. **9.**

supersedeas bond, a bond required of a losing party in a case as a condition for obtaining a delay in execution of the judgment while the judgment is appealed. The purpose is to assure that there will be money available to satisfy the judgment if the appeal is unsuccessful. See also SUPERSEDEAS.

bondholder. See under BOND¹.

border search. See under SEARCH.

boycott *n.* **1.** concerted action by two or more people or entities not to buy from, sell to, work for, or in some other way deal with a company, or an effort to induce others to engage in such conduct. The legality of a boycott depends upon the circumstances. **2. group boycott,** concerted action by a group of business competitors to boycott a business that they otherwise might do business with, for example a boycott of a supplier to pressure it into lowering its prices. Group boycotts are a violation of the SHERMAN ANTITRUST ACT. **3. primary boycott,** a union-organized boycott of an employer with which the union is engaged in a labor dispute; for example, urging shippers to refuse to ship the employer's goods or consumers not to buy them. Primary boycotts are permitted by the National Labor Relations Act. **4. secondary boycott,** a boycott or other coercive tactics directed at an employer other than the one with which a union has a grievance, for the purpose of inducing that employer to refrain from dealing with the one with which the union does have a grievance. Secondary boycotts are forbidden by federal law. —*v.* **5.** to engage in a boycott directed against a particular company, group of companies, or product: *to boycott a store; to boycott grapes.*

Brady material any evidence known to the prosecution that is favorable to the defendant in a criminal case. Under a rule laid down in the 1963 Supreme Court case of Brady v. Maryland (the **Brady rule**), such evidence must be disclosed to the defendant if requested; a later modification of the rule requires it to be disclosed even if not requested, if it is obviously helpful to the defendant's case.

brain death irreversible cessation of brain functioning. In an age when heart and lung functioning can often be maintained indefinitely by machines, this is increasingly used as the legal definition of death, though the details of the definition vary from state to state.

breach *n.* **1.** a violation of a legal duty. Usually the term refers to wrongful conduct viewed as the basis for a civil remedy rather than a criminal penalty: *Embezzlement is both a crime and a breach of the employee's duty of loyalty to the employer.* **2. anticipatory breach,** a statement or action showing that a party to a contract does not intend or will not be able to perform when the time comes to do so. Most jurisdictions allow the other party to treat that as a *breach of contract* even though, technically, no obligation has yet been breached because the performance is not yet due. Also called **anticipatory repudiation. 3. breach of fiduciary duty,** an intentional or unintentional failure by a FIDUCIARY to live up to the duty of utmost care and loyalty in dealing with matters that are the subject of a FIDUCIARY RELATIONSHIP. See also FIDUCIARY DUTY. **4. breach of contract,** any failure, without legal justification, to perform as promised in a contract, or any act hindering another party from performing as promised; for example, after contracting for certain repairs to your house, not allowing the contractor in to do the work. **5. breach of promise.** Short for **breach of promise of marriage** or **breach of promise to marry;** the breaking off of an engagement to be married. The common law action for damages for breach of promise has been abolished in many states. **6. breach of the peace, a.** broadly, any conduct, especially criminal conduct, tending to provoke violence or disrupt public tranquility. **b.** in some jurisdictions, a specifically defined offense; see under DISORDERLY CONDUCT. **7. breach of trust,** a *breach of fiduciary duty,* especially by a TRUSTEE and especially if it is intentional: *It was a breach of trust for the guardian of the child's property to borrow money from the child's bank account to pay a* *personal debt.* **8. breach of warranty,** any falsehood in a WARRANTY; any failure of a product, instrument, or transaction to conform to a warranty made with respect to it. **9. immaterial** (or **partial**) **breach,** a minor breach of contract, entitling the aggrieved party to damages or some other appropriate remedy, but not entitling that party to cancel the contract. **10. material** (or **total**) **breach,** a breach of contract so serious that it destroys the value of the contract for the other party, entitling that party to call off the deal and refuse any further performance of its own obligations under the contract. —*v.* **11.** to violate a legal duty: *By driving when he was too tired, he breached the duty of due care.*

breaking and entering two of the elements of the crime of BURGLARY. At common law, breaking and entering required forcible entry into the premises of another; under modern statutes, it is usually enough simply to enter or remain without authorization, as by crawling in an open window or hiding in a store until it closes. See also *criminal trespass* (under TRESPASS).

bribery *n.* **1.** the crime of giving or receiving, or offering or requesting, something of value to influence the official conduct of a public official. **2. commercial bribery,** the giving or receiving of something of value to influence the business conduct of an employee or agent of a company. This is usually both a crime and a tort against the company, as well as a form of UNFAIR COMPETITION. See also COMPOUNDING A CRIME; KICKBACK.

brief *n.* **1.** a written argument submitted to a court, outlining the facts and presenting the legal authorities upon which a party relies in a case. In addition to briefs stating the parties' overall positions on a case, submitted at major stages (**trial brief** often submitted just before a trial, **appellate brief** submitted when the case is on appeal**),** briefs are submitted in connection with motions, evidentiary issues, and other matters as they arise during the course of a case. On most motions and on appeal, three briefs are normally submitted: a **brief in support** or **main brief** by the party making the motion or taking the appeal; a **brief in opposition** or **answering brief** by the opposing party; and a **reply brief** by the first party. Occasionally a court will give special permission for the opposing party to put in a **surreply brief** responding to new arguments made in the reply brief. In some courts, a brief is customarily referred to as a **memorandum of law, memorandum of points and authorities,** or simply **memorandum:** See also *brief amicus curiae* (under AMICUS CURIAE). **2.** a digest of a judicial opinion, prepared by a law student or junior lawyer. —*v.* **3.** to prepare or submit a brief on a matter: *The judge asked us to brief the issue* (or *brief her on the issue*) *of the plaintiff's standing to sue. Beginning law students are required to brief each case they read.*

bring *v.* **1.** to initiate; file in court: *to bring suit; bring a complaint; bring a motion.* **2. bring on,** to call a case or motion for trial, hearing, or argument, or cause it to be called: *The motion for a preliminary injunction was brought on by order to show cause. After several months of discovery, the case was brought on for trial.*

broad construction. See under CONSTRUCTION.

broker *n.* a middleman; a person or entity that puts together a buyer and seller of property or services, acting as an AGENT for one or both of the parties and taking a COMMISSION on the transaction. Examples include a broker who arranges insurance coverage for people or companies (**insurance broker**), a broker who arranges sales of real property (**real estate broker**), and a broker who arranges purchases and sales of stocks and bonds (**securities broker** or **stockbroker**).

broker-dealer *n.* a company that acts both as a securities broker, taking commissions on securities transactions in which it is merely a middleman, and as a securites dealer, buying and selling securities in its own name and taking a profit, or occasionally a loss, on the change in price.

brother *n., pl.* **brethren.** a traditional term by

which one lawyer or judge referred to another. The customary use of the archaic plural "brethren" (instead of "brothers") shows how up-to-date this terminology is.

burden[1] *n.* **1.** an obligation to take some action to protect one's own rights: *The burden was on the insurance company, as drafter of the policy, to make sure that the language was unambiguous; therefore the ambiguous clause will be construed against the company.* **2. burden of persuasion,** the requirement that a party to a case introduce sufficient evidence of a fact to persuade the jury (or judge in a bench trial) of it by the applicable STANDARD OF PROOF. Also called **risk of nonpersuasion.** See also *burden of proof.* **3. burden of pleading,** the requirement that a party seeking to raise a particular issue in a case include allegations about it in the pleadings. **4. burden of producing evidence,** the requirement that a party to a case introduce evidence to support a claim or defense in order to have that issue considered by the judge or jury. Also called **burden of going forward (with evidence), burden of introducing evidence, burden of proceeding, burden of production.** See also *burden of proof;* PRIMA FACIE CASE. **5. burden of proof, a.** usually, same as *burden of persuasion.* **b.** occasionally, same as *burden of producing evidence.* In most situations, the same party will have both the initial burden of producing evidence and the ultimate burden of persuasion on a particular issue, so that *burden of proof* can be used to refer to both simultaneously. **6. burden shifting,** the shifting of the *burden of producing evidence* on a particular issue from one party to another as the evidence unfolds at trial. See also *affirmative defense* (under DEFENSE) (for defs. 2–5).

burden[2] *n.* **1.** a restriction upon the uses that an owner may make of a piece of land, resulting from an EASEMENT, a *covenant running with the land* (see under COVENANT), or the like. It is not the owner, but the land itself, that is said to be under a burden. —*v.* **2.** to impose or constitute a burden upon a piece of land; for example, if Jones has an easement to walk across Smith's land in order to reach his own land, Smith's land is "burdened" by the easement.

burglary *n.* the crime of BREAKING AND ENTERING with intent to commit a crime in the place entered.

business. See DOING BUSINESS; TRANSACTION OF BUSINESS.

business corporation. See under CORPORATION.

business judgment rule the rule of corporate law that directors and officers cannot be held liable to investors for business decisions that turn out to have been bad for the corporation, so long as the decisions were within their power to make, were made in good faith, and had a reasonable basis.

business record. See under RECORD.

business trust. See under TRUST.

buy-sell agreement an agreement among shareholders in a *close corporation* (see under CORPORATION) that if any one of them leaves the business or dies, her shares will be sold to, and bought by, the remaining shareholders or the corporation itself, so as to keep the business in the hands of the original group.

buyer in the ordinary course of business a buyer of some product who buys it in the normal way from a person in the business of selling goods of that kind and buys it in good faith, without knowledge that the sale is a violation of someone else's rights in the goods. Such a buyer will get good title to the thing bought even if the thing was in fact pledged to a lender as security for a loan.

by operation of law as a result of application of legal rules, rather than the action or intent of a person: *Upon her death, the property that she did not dispose of by will went to her children by operation of law.* See also AS A MATTER OF LAW.

by the entirety words used to describe ownership of an interest in real property granted to a married couple as a unit, with each spouse having RIGHT OF SURVIVORSHIP: *estate by the entirety; ownership by the entirety; tenants by the entirety.* At common law the husband had exclusive control over all property held by the entirety so long as he lived, on the theory that "the husband and wife are one, and that one is the husband." This form of ownership has been abolished in the majority of states; where it still exists, the husband and wife now have equal rights with respect to the property, making owner-ship by the entirety substantially identical to joint ownership. Cf. JOINT; IN COMMON; IN SEVERALTY. See also COMMUNITY PROPERTY.

bylaw *n.* any rule in the set of rules (**bylaws**) adopted collectively by an association, corporation, or other entity to govern itself.

a b C d e f g h i j k l m n o p q r s t u v w x y z

© copyright; a symbol giving notice that COPYRIGHT protection is claimed for the work upon which it appears. If the copyright is valid, the work may not be copied without permission of the copyright owner, whose name ordinarily appears with this symbol, along with the year from which the copyright runs.

calendar *n.* **1.** a court's list of cases scheduled for argument, hearing, or trial on a particular day or over a certain time period. Sometimes called a DOCKET. **2. calendar call,** a courtroom procedure in which a court officer calls out the names of cases on the calendar and lawyers or litigants respond by saying whether they are ready to proceed or desire an adjournment. The officer is said to **call the calendar.**

call *n.* **1.** a demand for payment, or for delivery of a bond (see BOND[1]) or other instrument in exchange for payment, by one having a right to make such a demand. —*v.* **2. call the calendar.** See under CALENDAR.

callable security. Same as *redeemable security* (see under SECURITY[2]).

camera. See IN CAMERA.

canon *n.* a rule or principle, particularly one regarded as fundamental: *a canon of statutory construction; the canons of ethics.*

canon law the internal rules of the Roman Catholic Church, or a similar body of religious rules in certain other Christian denominations.

capacity *n.* the legal ability to perform an act having legal consequences, such as entering into a contract, making a will, suing or being sued, committing a crime, or getting married. Also called **legal capacity.** See also DIMINISHED CAPACITY.

capita. See PER CAPITA.

capital[1] *n.* **1.** broadly, any form of wealth used or capable of being used for the production of more wealth. **2.** money and property owned or employed in business by a corporation or other enterprise. Sometimes refers to a company's total *assets,* sometimes to *net assets* (see both under ASSET). See also *capital stock* (under STOCK). **3. capital gain** (or **loss),** the GAIN or LOSS incurred by a taxpayer upon the sale or exchange of a *capital asset* (see under ASSET). **4. capital gains tax,** income tax on a capital gain, such as an investor's profit on sale of stock; often this is taxed at lower rates than wages and other ordinary income. See also *holding period* (under HOLDING).

capital[2], *adj.* punishable by death, or involving the death penalty: *capital case; capital crime.*

capital asset. See under ASSET.

capital punishment the killing of a person by the government as punishment for a crime. Also called **death penalty.**

capital stock. See under STOCK.

capricious *adj.* arbitrary; unreasonable. Usually used in the phrase *arbitrary and capricious* (see under ARBITRARY).

caption *n.* the heading on a court paper, containing such information as the name and number of the case, the name of the court, and the nature of the paper. The exact form of the caption in each court is a matter of local custom.

care *n.* **1.** the exercise of caution and prudence in one's conduct so as to avoid causing injury or loss. **2. ordinary care,** the degree of care that a person of ordinary intelligence and prudence would exercise under the given circumstances. This is the standard of care expected of virtually everyone at all times; a failure to exercise ordinary care is NEGLIGENCE. Also called **due care** or **reasonable care.** See also MALPRACTICE. **3. utmost care,** the standard of care that must be exercised by a trustee or other FIDUCIARY in matters relating to her fiduciary responsibilities; also called **extraordinary care** or **highest degree of care.** A fiduciary's failure to exercise such care is a *breach of fiduciary duty* (see under BREACH).

carnal knowledge an old term for sexual intercourse.

carrier. See COMMON CARRIER.

case[1] *n.* **1.** all proceedings with respect to a charge, claim, or dispute filed with a court: *criminal case; civil case; contract case.* **2. agreed case,** a civil case in which the parties stipulate to the facts and submit them to the judge for a ruling upon their legal effect instead of having a trial. Also called **case stated. 3. case in point,** a previously decided case involving facts or issues that are similar or analogous to those currently under consideration, cited as a precedent. **4. case of first impression,** a case raising a significant legal issue that has not previously been ruled upon by any court. **5. companion case,** one of a pair or group of separate cases raising related issues, dealt with at the same time by a court, especially the Supreme Court. **6. consolidated case,** two or more separately filed cases involving common issues, combined into a single case for efficient treatment. **7. diversity case,** a federal civil suit between citizens of different states. See also *diversity jurisdiction* (under JURISDICTION[1]). **8. federal case,** a case filed in federal court, especially one involving FEDERAL LAW. A federal case is not necessarily big or important, and you cannot "make a federal case out of" a case that does not fall within the *limited jurisdiction* (see under JURISDICTION[1]) of the federal courts. **9. landmark case,** a case whose decision established a new legal principle of historic importance; a case viewed as representing a great stride forward for the law. For example, Marbury v. Madison (the 1803 decision establishing the doctrine that courts may strike down laws as unconstitutional) or Brown v. Board of Education (the 1954 decision holding racial segregation of public schools unconstitutional). **10. leading case,** a case that is generally regarded as the first example of a particular legal principle, or whose decision is an especially influential early exposition of a principle; for example, the 1863 English case of Byrne v. Boadle, in which the phrase RES IPSA LOQUITUR was first used. **11. test case,** a case instituted or continued for the purpose of testing the constitutionality of a law or establishing a new legal principle.

case[2] *n.* the totality of evidence presented by a party in support of its position in a case: *plaintiff's case; defendant's case; prosecution case.* In a typical trial, the plaintiff or prosecution first presents what it regards as sufficient evidence to prove its claims (the **case in chief**), then the defendant puts on its case, then the plaintiff responds with further evidence (the **rebuttal case,** or simply **rebuttal**). Sometimes the defendant then puts in still more evidence (a **surrebuttal case,** or **surrebuttal**) to rebut the rebuttal, but the alternation seldom goes beyond this. The party that ultimately prevails is said to have "proved (or sustained) its case." See also *prima facie case* (under PRIMA FACIE).

case law 1. law created by judicial decision rather than by statute, including decisions interpreting statutes. **2.** the body of published judicial opinions in cases dealing with a particular point or kind of issue: *The case law under this statute generally adopts a narrow construction.* Also called **decisional law.**

case method (or **system**), the general method by which most legal subjects are taught in most law schools today, in which students' primary reading material consists of judicial opinions in actual cases, which are analyzed in class by use of the SOCRATIC METHOD. See also CASEBOOK.

case note. Same as ANNOTATION (def. 1).

case or controversy an actual dispute over legal rights. Under the Constitution, the federal courts may consider only cases or controversies, not hypothetical questions. See also ADVISORY OPINION.

casebook *n.* a collection of judicial opinions in a particular area of law, edited, organized, and supplemented with questions and commentary for use in the CASE METHOD of legal instruction.

cash bail. See under BAIL¹.

cashier's check. See under CHECK.

casual *adj.* occasional; irregular; out of the ordinary: *casual employee; casual sale.*

casualty *n.* harm to person or property caused by a sudden, unexpected, or unusual event such as an automobile accident or a natural disaster.

causa mortis *Latin.* (lit. "because of [impending] death") describing something done by a person in the belief that she is about to die. See also *gift causa mortis* (under GIFT).

causation *n.* the fact that a certain action or event produced a certain result. This is an essential element to be proved in many kinds of cases; for example, to convict a defendant of murder the prosecution must prove that the victim's death actually resulted from the defendant's conduct; to recover damages in a tort or contract action the plaintiff must prove that the claimed loss was actually caused by defendant's wrongful conduct **(causation of loss** or **loss causation).**

cause *n.* **1.** an action or event that brings about or contributes to a particular outcome. See also PROXIMATE CAUSE. **2.** a reason for taking certain action, especially a good or legally sufficient reason. See also FOR CAUSE; GOOD CAUSE; INSUFFICIENT CAUSE; PROBABLE CAUSE. **3.** a somewhat formal or flowery term for case (see CASE¹), especially a civil case: *The cause was tried in Superior Court, County of Los Angeles.*

cause of action 1. facts which, if proved, would entitle a party to relief in a lawsuit on some legal theory: *The complaint was dismissed for failure to state a cause of action.* In the federal courts and many states, this terminology has been replaced for many purposes by *claim for relief* (see under CLAIM). **2.** a right of recovery arising from such facts: *The seller has a cause of action for breach of contract against the purchaser, who failed to pay for the goods.*

cautionary instruction. See under INSTRUCTION.

cease and desist order an order of an administrative agency requiring a person or entity to refrain from specified unlawful conduct. If issued by a court, such an order is more often called an INJUNCTION.

censure *n.* **1.** a formal statement issued by a body such as a legislature or a bar disciplinary committee condemning the behavior of one of its own members or a member of a group whose conduct it is legally charged with monitoring. —*v.* **2.** to issue such a statement.

cert. See under CERTIORARI.

certificate *n.* **1.** a formal document, typically a single sheet of paper, evidencing some right, interest, or permission granted to the person or entity to which it was issued. **2.** Also called **certification.** a written statement confirming that certain facts are true, that certain acts have been performed, or that something is authentic.

certificate of deposit (CD) an acknowledgment by a bank of receipt of money with a promise to repay it upon specified terms as to interest rate and time of repayment.

certificate of incorporation 1. in some states, same as ARTICLES OF INCORPORATION. **2.** in most states, a document issued by the state certifying that articles of incorporation have been filed and the named corporation has come into existence; essentially a fancy receipt for the articles and the filing fee.

certificate of title 1. an official certificate that a certain person is the owner of a particular motor vehicle. **2.** in jurisdictions with a TITLE REGISTRATION SYSTEM for land, a certificate issued by the state or local government identifying the owner or owners of interests in specified real estate and listing any easements, mortgages, covenants, or other encumbrances on the property. **3.** a certificate issued by a title insurance company expressing its professional opinion, after diligent examination, that a person has good title to certain land, except as specifically noted. This does not constitute a guarantee or insurance of good title.

certification *n.* **1.** the act of certifying or issuing a certificate. **2.** the fact or state of being certified. **3.** CERTIFICATE (def. 2). **4.** the word for CERTIORARI in some state court systems.

certify *v.* **1.** to make a written representation or guarantee that something is authentic, acceptable, or true, or that certain acts have been or will be performed. **2.** to issue a CERTIFICATE. **3. certified check.** See under CHECK. **4. certified copy,** a copy of a document to which a statement has been affixed swearing or affirming that it has been compared with the original and is a true copy. Also called **verified copy** or **attested copy. 5. certified question,** under procedures permitted in some jurisdictions, a question of law posed by a lower court to a higher court, or a question of state law posed by a federal court to the appropriate state court, so that the answer can be applied in resolving a pending case. **6. certify the record,** to transmit documents constituting the record in a case to a higher court for appellate review, with a certification that this is in fact the record.

certiorari *n. Latin.* (lit. "to be informed," "to be assured") a writ issued by an appellate court as a matter of discretion, directing a lower court to *certify the record* (see under CERTIFY) in a case that was not appealable as of right. The usual route by which a case reaches the Supreme Court of the United States is by a petition for certiorari from the party on the losing end of a decision of a United States Court of Appeals or a state's highest court; the Supreme Court grants only about one percent of such petitions. In informal speech, certiorari is typically referred to by its abbreviation: **cert.**

cestui que trust *Law French.* (lit. "the one who trusts") the BENEFICIARY of a trust. Often shortened to *cestui;* more often not used at all, since "beneficiary" means the same thing and is pronounceable.

chain of custody the sequence of places where, and persons with whom, a piece of physical evidence was located from the time of its gathering to its introduction at a trial. Establishing the chain of custody is essential to proof of authenticity of the evidence.

chain of title the sequence of owners and transfers of a parcel of real property. Any gap in the recorded chain of title casts doubt upon the validity of a present claim of title to the property.

challenge *n.* **1.** a party's rejection of a potential juror, either because of an obvious bias or interest in the case **(challenge for cause)** or simply because of a belief that the juror may not be receptive to that party's arguments **(peremptory challenge).** In selecting a jury, each party is allowed unlimited challenges for cause and a limited number of peremptory challenges. **2. challenge to the array,** a party's objection to the manner in which the entire array of potential jurors was selected from the population at large.

chambers *n.pl.* a judge's office. Depending upon the court, it may be a single room or a suite of two or three rooms for the judge, one or more law clerks, and a secretary. See also ROBING ROOM.

champerty *n.* an agreement to finance someone else's lawsuit in return for a share of the proceeds. Prohibitions on champerty are the reason that lawyers working for a **contingency fee** (see under CONTINGENCY) usually insist that filing fees and other expenses of a suit be paid by the client. See also MAINTENANCE; BARRATRY. —**champertous,** *adj.*

chance verdict. See under VERDICT.

Chancellor *n.* the traditional title of judges in courts of EQUITY or CHANCERY.

chancery *n.* the traditional name for a court of EQUITY. Also called **chancery court** or **court of chancery.**

Chapter 7 11, 12, or **13.** See under BANKRUPTCY.

character *n.* the general disposition of a person, particularly with respect to some trait that is relevant in a case, such as honesty or propensity for violence. See also **character evidence** (under EVIDENCE); **character witness** (under WITNESS).

charge *n.* **1.** a formal allegation that a person has violated a specific criminal law; a COUNT in an indictment or information. **2.** a judge's INSTRUCTION to the jury on a particular point of law, or her *instructions* collectively (see under INSTRUCTION). **3. Allen charge,** a charge to a jury that has declared itself unable to reach a verdict, urging it to try harder. The Allen charge is prohibited in some states because of its tendency to coerce holdout jurors to go along with the majority despite genuine doubts. —*v.* **4.** to make or deliver a charge.

charter¹ *n.* **1.** a formal grant of rights and powers from a sovereign, or the document embodying such a grant; for example, the MAGNA CARTA, or **Great Charter. 2.** the basic set of governing principles of an organization: the *United Nations Charter.* **3.** Also called **corporate charter. a.** a legislative act establishing a corporation and setting forth its purposes and basic structure. **b.** a CERTIFICATE OF INCORPORATION or other document issued by the state granting corporate status to an entity. **c.** a corporation's ARTICLES OF INCORPORATION. —*v.* **4.** to establish, or grant a corporate charter to, an entity: *The United Nations was chartered in 1945.*

charter² *n.* **1.** the rental of a ship, airplane, or bus. **2.** Also called **charter party.** A written contract for the hire of such a vessel, especially a ship. —*v.* **3.** to rent such a vessel to or from someone: *We chartered a bus for the company picnic.*

chattel *n.* an item of personal property, especially tangible personalty.

chattel mortgage. See under MORTGAGE.

check *n.* **1.** an instrument by which a person (the drawer) directs a bank (the drawee) to pay a specified sum of money to the order of another person (the payee), or to the bearer of the instrument, upon demand. Normally the payment is made out of funds that the drawer has on deposit with the bank. A check is a special kind of DRAFT. **2. bank check,** a check drawn by a bank upon another bank. **3. bad check,** a check that is forged, drawn upon insufficient funds, or in some other way defective, so that payment is properly refused by the drawee bank. **4. cashier's check,** a check drawn by a bank on itself; it amounts to a promise to pay if the payee makes a proper demand. **5. certified check,** a check on which the bank has written a notice (usually just the word "certified") signifying that the funds necessary to pay it have been set aside so that payment will definitely be made upon proper demand by the payee. **6. NSF check,** a check that the drawee bank may refuse to pay because the drawer does not have sufficient funds on deposit to cover it when it is presented to the bank for payment. NSF stands for "not sufficient funds" or "nonsufficient funds." See also KITE.

child *n.* **1.** a person deemed by the law to require special protection or treatment because of youth. The age below which one is regarded as a child depends upon the particular statute or legal doctrine at issue. **2.** an offspring or a person treated as such. Depending upon the context, the term may or may not include an illegitimate child or a stepchild, but would almost always include an adopted child.

child custody. See under CUSTODY.

child neglect. See under NEGLECT.

child pornography. See under PORNOGRAPHY.

chilling effect a tendency to inhibit the exercise of constitutional rights, especially those protected by the First Amendment (see Appendix). Statutes that unnecessarily create such an effect are often held unconstitutional.

choice of evils. Same as NECESSITY.

choice of law the problem of deciding which law to apply when an action involves events that took place or have an impact in two or more jurisdictions having different laws. This is the central concern of the field of CONFLICT OF LAWS.

chose in action a right to obtain money or personal property by bringing a legal action; a claim for such a thing. For example, a right to recover a debt. "Chose" (pronounced "shows") is Law French for "thing," and the entire phrase is sometimes rendered in English as **thing in action.**

churning *n.* a stockbroker's excessive and inappropriate trading of securities in a customer's account for the purpose of generating extra commissions for the broker. This is made illegal by the securities laws.

circuit *n.* a geographic division established by some states or by the United States for purposes of judicial administration, with a court in each circuit. At the federal level, the United States is divided geographically into twelve circuits for appellate purposes, with the United States Court of Appeals for each such circuit handling appeals from all federal district courts within its area. In addition, a special circuit covering the entire country, called the **Federal Circuit,** has been established in order to funnel all appeals on a number of subjects, such as patents and international trade, to a single specialized court, the **United States Court of Appeals for the Federal Circuit.** See also UNITED STATES COURT OF APPEALS. Cf. DISTRICT.

circumstantial evidence. See under EVIDENCE.

citation *n.* **1.** a written notice to appear in court (or sometimes to respond by mail) to answer a charge; for example, a traffic ticket. Citations are a substitute for arrest in minor offenses. **2.** a reference to a statute, previous judicial decision, or other writing as authority for a fact or legal proposition. Standard abbreviations and formats for citing common sources minimize the space required and are recognized by all lawyers. See also BLUEBOOK. —**cite,** *v.*

citizen *n.* **1.** a person who owes allegiance to a government and is entitled to its protection. Under the Fourteenth Amendment (see Appendix), virtually all persons born or naturalized in the United States are citizens of the United States and of the state where they reside. In addition, by statute, persons born in Puerto Rico, the U.S. Virgin Islands, Guam, and the Northern Mariana Islands are citizens of the United States. See also NATIONAL; NATURALIZE. **2.** for purposes of determining whether a suit by or against a corporation or a resident alien falls within the *diversity jurisdiction* (see under JURISDICTION¹) of the federal courts, an alien admitted to the United States for permanent residence is deemed to be a "citizen" of the state where the alien is domiciled, and a corporation is deemed to be a "citizen" both of the state where it was incorporated and of the state where it has its principal place of business.

citizen's arrest. See under ARREST.

civil *adj.* **1.** pertaining to all aspects of law other than those dealing with criminal or military matters: *civil court; civil case.* See also *civil* ACTION, COMMITMENT, CONTEMPT, LIABILITY, PENALTY, PROCEDURE, PROSECUTION under those words. Cf. CIVIL LAW. **2.** pertaining generally to the rights, duties, and status of people as members of society. See CIVIL RIGHTS; CIVIL DISOBEDIENCE.

civil disobedience open and nonviolent refusal to obey certain laws, and acceptance of punishment,

legal

for the purpose of influencing public opinion, legislation, or governmental policy.

civil law the prevailing system of law in continental Europe, derived from Roman law. In contrast to the traditional COMMON LAW system of England and America, the basic source of law in the civil law system is organized codes rather than case-by-case judicial decisions. In the United States, Louisiana stands out as the state whose law is most heavily influenced by civil law, because of its origins as a French territory. See also COMMUNITY PROPERTY; INQUISITORIAL SYSTEM.

civil liberties. See under CIVIL RIGHTS.

civil rights 1. Also called **civil liberties.** governmentally recognized and legally protected rights and liberties of people in areas of personal autonomy, personal welfare, and participation in the political, business, and social life of the nation. In the United States, these include political and personal liberties protected by the Constitution (see FUNDAMENTAL RIGHT) and freedom from private and governmental discrimination on the basis of characteristics such as race, sex, religion, or disability. **2.** more narrowly, the phrase "civil rights" is sometimes distinguished from "civil liberties," with the former phrase referring to freedom from discrimination, especially on the basis of race, and the latter referring to rights of personal autonomy and political expression and participation.

Civil War amendments the Thirteenth, Fourteenth, and Fifteenth Amendments to the Constitution (see Appendix), adopted in the wake of the Civil War to bring a permanent end to slavery and extend basic rights of citizenship and equal treatment to people of color. Unfortunately, the Supreme Court construed these amendments so narrowly (see SEPARATE BUT EQUAL) that legally endorsed public and private discrimination were permitted to continue for almost a century more, and became so entrenched that the nation is still struggling with the consequences.

claim *n.* **1.** an assertion that one is entitled to something. **2.** Also called **claim for relief.** in the federal courts and many states, an assertion of facts that, if true, would legally entitle the claimant to judgment in a civil case. A plaintiff's complaint must allege such facts or suffer dismissal for "failure to state a claim." See also CAUSE OF ACTION. **3.** an apparent or actual right to receive something by way of a lawsuit: *The person injured in the automobile accident has a tort claim against the negligent driver.*

claim joinder. See under JOINDER.

claimant *n.* one who has a claim; one who asserts a claim.

class action. See under ACTION.

classification *n.* **1.** in a regulation or statute, a division of people into different classes subject to different legal treatment. This may occur intentionally and explicitly, as when a legislature decrees that only citizens (not aliens) shall receive certain benefits, or simply as a practical consequence of application of the law, as when a fee requirement effectively excludes the poor (but not the wealthy) from some opportunity. For the purpose of assessing the constitutionality of such laws under the EQUAL PROTECTION clause, the Supreme Court has created two special categories of classifications, known as SUSPECT CLASSIFICATION and QUASI-SUSPECT CLASSIFICATION. **2.** in modern criminal codes, the categorizing of offenses according to severity, with a specified range of punishments for each class of offense.

Clayton Act a federal ANTITRUST law prohibiting a range of business activities that may substantially lessen competition, such as a corporate merger between two dominant companies in the same business, where the effect would be to eliminate competition between them and enable them to use their combined strength against smaller competitors.

clean hands the quality of having acted fairly and properly in a matter over which one is suing someone else. Cf. UNCLEAN HANDS; see also *clean hands doctrine* and *clean hands defense* (under UNCLEAN HANDS).

clear and convincing evidence an intermediate STANDARD OF PROOF, more stringent than PREPONDERANCE OF THE EVIDENCE but less than BEYOND A REASONABLE DOUBT. It requires that the factfinder be persuaded that the fact to be proved is highly probable. This standard is used in various types of noncriminal proceeding in which public policy requires an extra level of proof, such as a deportation hearing.

clear and present danger an imminent risk of harm of a type that the government may legitimately protect against; a phrase sometimes used to describe the circumstances under which the government may prohibit or punish SPEECH.

clear title. Same as *marketable title* (see under TITLE).

clearly erroneous the STANDARD OF REVIEW by which a trial judge's findings of fact are normally tested in the appeal of a civil case that was tried without a jury. The appellate court may not reverse simply because it would have reached a different conclusion on the same evidence, but it may reverse a judge's findings more easily than a jury's.

clemency *n.* the exercise by a President or governor of the power to grant an AMNESTY, PARDON, or REPRIEVE, or to COMMUTE a sentence. Also called **executive clemency.**

clergy-communicant privilege. See under PRIVILEGE.

clerk *n.* **1.** Also called **court clerk.** a court official charged with the overall administration of the court's operations or with some aspect of administration, particularly the processing and maintenance of court papers and records. **2.** Also called **law clerk.** a recent law graduate employed as an assistant to a judge for one or two years. —*v.* **3.** to serve as a law clerk.

close (or **closely held**) **corporation.** See under CORPORATION.

closing *n.* **1.** the completion of a transaction, especially a real estate transaction or major corporate transaction, usually at a meeting attended by counsel for all parties. A detailed written summary of the financial aspects of the transaction being closed is called a **closing statement. 2.** Also called **closing statement** or **closing argument.** a SUMMATION.

cloud on title a claim with respect to land that casts doubt on the validity or completeness of the owner's title to the land. The legal mechanism for removing such a cloud is an action to QUIET TITLE.

co-conspirator. See under CONSPIRACY.

code *n.* **1.** an organized compilation of statutes or rules: *Code of Federal Regulations*; UNITED STATES CODE. **2.** a coherent and comprehensive statute dealing with a major area of law: INTERNAL REVENUE CODE; UNIFORM COMMERCIAL CODE.

codicil *n.* an addition to or amendment of an existing will. To be valid it must be executed with all the formalities of a will.

codify *v.* **1.** to enact a statute embodying a principle of common law or a particular judicial interpretation of the law. **2.** to organize existing statutes or an existing body of law into a CODE. —**codification,** *n.*

coercion. Same as DURESS.

cognizable *adj.* **1.** within the jurisdiction of a court; capable of being considered: *Divorce actions are not cognizable in federal court.* **2.** describing a claim for which a court could provide relief: *Mere disagreement by a taxpayer with the way tax revenues are spent does not give rise to a cognizable claim.*

cognovit *n.* Latin. (lit. "he has recognized") an instrument containing a CONFESSION OF JUDGMENT. See also *cognovit note* (under NOTE[1]).

cohabit *v.* **1.** of unmarried couples, to live together in an intimate relationship similar to that of husband and wife. Viewed until recently as a crime or at least evidence of a crime (see FORNICATION), cohabitation has begun to emerge as a legally protected relationship (see PALIMONY). See also DOMESTIC PARTNERSHIP. Cf. *common law marriage* (under MARRIAGE). **2.** of unrelated people generally, to live together. Zoning ordinances may restrict the number of unrelated people who can cohabit in single-family residential areas. —**cohabitation,** *n.*

coinsurance *n.* a form of insurance in which the insurance company pays only a certain percentage of any loss, the balance being paid by the policyholder personally or by other insurance purchased by the policyholder; for example, medical insurance under which the insurer pays 80% of covered expenses and the policyholder pays 20%.

collateral¹ *n.* property in which someone has a *security interest* (see under INTEREST¹), especially property pledged as security for a loan (see PLEDGE).

collateral² *adj.* **1.** indirect; off to the side. Often used in contrast to DIRECT¹. **2. collateral attack,** an attack on a judgment or judicial proceeding that is made in a different proceeding. For example, if A obtains a default judgment against B in New York and then attempts to seize B's property in California to satisfy the judgment, B might attack the New York judgment in California on the ground that the New York court did not have jurisdiction over him. Cf. *direct attack* (under DIRECT¹). **3. collateral estoppel.** See under ESTOPPEL. **4. collateral heir,** an heir who is not a direct ancestor or descendant of the deceased, but is descended from a common ancestor; for example, a sister, cousin, uncle, or nephew. Cf. *direct heir* (under DIRECT¹). **5. collateral source rule,** the principle of tort law that compensation for an injured party from a source other than the tortfeasor (e.g., from the injured party's insurance company) does not reduce the amount that can be collected from the wrongdoer. See also SUBROGATE.

collective bargaining 1. negotiation between an employer and a union representing employees with regard to wages and other conditions of employment. **2. collective bargaining agreement,** a contract between an employer and a union representing employees with regard to the terms and conditions of employment.

colloquy *n.* discussion among lawyers, or between the lawyers and the judge, in the course of a judicial proceeding.

color *n.* **1.** appearance; especially, appearance without reality: *color of authority; color of title.* See also UNDER COLOR OF LAW. **2.** skin complexion. Constitutional provisions and civil rights statutes prohibiting discrimination on the basis of RACE customarily add "color" as well, to eliminate legalistic arguments over the exact basis upon which someone is wrongfully discriminating.

color of law. See UNDER COLOR OF LAW.

colorable *adj.* **1.** superficially, and perhaps actually, valid; possibly valid. **2.** seemingly, but not actually, valid or authentic; deceptive.

combat zone. See under ZONE.

comity *n.* the principle under which the courts of one jurisdiction will recognize and defer to the decisions, proceedings, and laws of another jurisdiction, not out of obligation but out of mutual respect. For example, American courts will ordinarily extend comity to a decision of a court in another country if it is convinced that the procedures in the other country were fundamentally fair. Cf. FULL FAITH AND CREDIT.

comment *n.* an article, usually written by a student and published in a law review, analyzing a particular judicial decision and placing it in a larger legal context. Sometimes called an **annotation.** Cf. NOTE²

commerce *n.* trade, business, and travel, especially across state lines (**interstate commerce**) or between the United States and other countries (**foreign commerce**). The powerlessness of the new national government to prevent trade wars between the states following independence from Britain was a principal motivating factor behind the adoption of the Constitution, with a clause (the **Commerce Clause**) giving Congress the power to regulate interstate and foreign commerce (the **commerce power**). This power forged the United States into a powerful economic unit and has also enabled Congress to adopt laws in such diverse fields as guaranteeing civil rights, protecting the environment, and

attacking organized crime, since these are matters seen as affecting interstate commerce.

commercial bribery. See under BRIBERY.

commercial paper NEGOTIABLE INSTRUMENTS, especially short-term promissory notes (see NOTE¹) issued by corporations to investors and traded among investors as securities. Also called **paper.**

commercial speech. See under SPEECH.

compensation *n.* **1.** compensation for services rendered in facilitating a transaction, or for acting as a trustee, executor, or the like, calculated as a percentage of the value of the transaction or of the property involved. See also KICKBACK. **2.** authority to hold an appointive office or perform delegated duties. **3.** the act of committing a crime. **4.** a name sometimes given to an administrative agency: *Interstate Commerce Commission.*

commissive waste. See under WASTE.

commit *v.* **1.** to do something wrong: *The witness committed perjury. The judge committed error by admitting hearsay testimony.* See also COMMISSION. **2.** to place a person in a prison, hospital, or other institution, especially by court order. See also COMMITMENT.

commitment 1. imprisonment or institutionalization of a person, especially by order of a court. **2. civil commitment, a.** commitment of a person to a mental hospital or other treatment facility upon a court's finding that the person poses a danger to himself or others. **b.** the jailing of a person for *civil contempt* (see under CONTEMPT) to induce compliance with a court order. **3. voluntary commitment,** commitment to a treatment facility upon the request or with the consent of the person in need of care.

committee *n.* **1.** a small group of members of a larger organization, established to carry out specific duties delegated ("committed") to it by the organization. Virtually all bills in Congress or a state legislature are considered by a committee before being voted on by the entire legislative body. **2.** the word used in some states for a GUARDIAN of an incompetent adult (the person into whose care the incompetent is committed). See also CONSERVATOR.

common. See IN COMMON.

common carrier a company in the business of transporting people or goods, or sometimes messages or information, and offering this service to the public at large.

common law 1. the legal system that evolved over many centuries in England and is the foundation of law in Great Britain and many of its former possessions, including the United States. In contrast to the CIVIL LAW system of continental Europe, the basic source of common law is judicial decisions rather than codes, with judges seeking in each new case to adapt the principles worked out in previous cases to new facts and circumstances in such a way as to achieve justice. See also ADVERSARY SYSTEM. **2.** judge-made law, as distinguished from STATUTORY law. Although large areas of earlier common law have now been codified, including criminal law and commercial law, there remain other large areas, notably tort law, contract law, and property law, that are still predominantly governed by common law rather than statutes. See also *common law crime* (under CRIME). **3.** Often shortened to **law.** legal principles that originated in the procedures and decisions of England's LAW courts as distinguished from its courts of EQUITY: *Damages are a common law remedy* (or *remedy at law*), *whereas the injunction is a form of equitable relief.* See also AT; MERGER OF LAW AND EQUITY. **4.** all of the law of England at the time when America achieved its independence. That law, whether judge-made or statutory, was generally regarded as the common law of the United States after independence. **5. federal common law,** law made by federal court judges with respect to subjects of uniquely federal concern under the Constitution, such as admiralty law and law pertaining to rights of action under the Constitution. With respect to matters of general law traditionally regulated by the states, such as torts and contracts, the federal courts may not develop a uniform national

legal

body of common law, but instead must follow state law. See also FEDERAL LAW.

common law action. See under ACTION.

common law crime. See under CRIME.

common law marriage. See under MARRIAGE.

common law state or **common law property state.** See under COMMUNITY PROPERTY.

common stock. See under STOCK.

community property a system of property ownership and distribution for married couples, derived from Spanish civil law and followed in California and a few other western and southwestern states (called **community property states;** all other states, having property systems derived from English common law, being referred to for this purpose as **common law states** or **common law property states**). Under this system, most income or property obtained by either spouse during marriage belongs to the "marital community." Each spouse may distribute half of the community property by will; in the event of divorce, the community property is divided either equitably (in certain states) or equally (in certain states, including California). See also EQUITABLE DISTRIBUTION. Cf. BY THE ENTIRETY.

commute v. to reduce a convicted criminal's sentence by executive action: *The governor commuted the death sentence to life imprisonment.* Cf. PARDON, REPRIEVE. See also CLEMENCY. —**commutation,** *n.*

compact *n.* a contract or treaty, especially an agreement between two states **(interstate compact)** to resolve a dispute or cooperate in a matter of mutual concern.

companion case. See under CASE[1].

company *n.* 1. a business enterprise, especially one owned or carried on by a group of people; an association, partnership, or corporation. 2. **holding company,** a company, usually a corporation, formed to hold stock in other companies, and often to control those other companies through ownership of large amounts of their stock. 3. **joint stock company,** an unincorporated company with ownership interests represented by shares of stock, in which owners share the profits in proportion to their holdings of stock but, unlike corporate stockholders, are personally liable to the company's creditors if the company's assets prove insufficient to pay its debts. Also called **stock association** or **joint stock association.** See also PARENT COMPANY.

comparative negligence. See under NEGLIGENCE.

compelling interest an extremely important governmental interest, important enough to justify a law that limits a FUNDAMENTAL RIGHT or treats people differently on the basis of a SUSPECT CLASSIFICATION. Also called **compelling governmental interest** or, in the case of a state law, **compelling state interest.**

compensation *n.* 1. payment for services rendered. 2. payment for injury or loss sustained. See also *compensatory damages* (under DAMAGES); JUST COMPENSATION.

compensatory damages. See under DAMAGES.

competent[1] *adj.* possessing sufficient mental capacity to make rational decisions about a legal matter and understand the consequences, so that the law will permit one to proceed and will give legal effect to one's actions: *competent to make a will; competent to stand trial; competent to act as one's own lawyer.* —**competency;** occasionally **competence,** *n.*

competent[2] *adj.* 1. (of a person) possessing the legal or other qualifications necessary to perform a task. For example, to be competent to serve as a witness to the execution of a will one must ordinarily be over a certain age and not a beneficiary under the will. 2. (of a court or other official body) possessing jurisdiction or authority to deal with a matter. Such a court is often referred to as a "court of competent jurisdiction." 3. (of evidence or of a witness in a proceeding) admissible, or possessing information that would be admissible. A person whose only knowledge about an issue is hearsay would ordinarily not be competent to testify on that

issue. —**competence;** (for defs. 1,3) sometimes **competency,** *n.*

competent evidence. See under EVIDENCE.

complaint *n.* 1. the initial PLEADING in a civil case, in which the plaintiff states the facts that she contends entitle her to relief and states what relief she seeks. See also *verified complaint* (under VERIFY). 2. the initial instrument charging a person with a crime, sworn to by a witness or police officer (the **complainant**) and describing the alleged crime.

completion bond. See under BOND[2].

compound question. See under QUESTION[1].

compounding a crime the offense of accepting something of value from a person known to have committed a crime, and agreeing in return not to report or prosecute the crime. If the crime in question is a felony, this offense is also called **compounding a felony.** In some states an exception is made for victims who agree not to prosecute if the criminal restores what was taken or compensates them for their injury or loss. Cf. MISPRISION OF FELONY.

compromise verdict. See under VERDICT.

compulsory arbitration. See under ARBITRATION.

compulsory counterclaim. See under COUNTERCLAIM.

compulsory joinder. See under JOINDER.

concealed weapon. See under WEAPON.

conclusion of law in a nonjury trial, a judge's decision on a legal issue (e.g., whether the court has jurisdiction or which state's law applies to the case) or conclusion based upon the application of law to the facts (e.g., that the defendant is or is not liable for negligence). See also FINDING OF FACT; FINDINGS OF FACT AND CONCLUSIONS OF LAW.

conclusive presumption. See under PRESUMPTION.

conclusory *adj.* stating a conclusion without supporting facts: *a conclusory allegation; a conclusory affidavit.*

concur v. 1. (of one or more judges on a panel) to agree with the decision being made by the court; to agree with the conclusion, though not necessarily with all of the reasoning, of the majority or plurality opinion. 2. **concurring in the result** or **concurring in the judgment,** a phrase used to emphasize that a particular judge on a panel agrees with the outcome in a case but in no way endorses the reasoning in the majority or plurality opinion. See also *concurring opinion* (under OPINION). —**concurrence,** *n.*

concurrent *adj.* 1. occurring or existing simultaneously: *concurrent jurisdiction* (see under JURISDICTION[1]); *concurrent sentences* (see under SENTENCE). 2. acting together: *concurrent causes; concurrent tortfeasors.* —**concurrently,** *adv.*

condemn v. 1. to take property for public use; exercise the power of EMINENT DOMAIN. 2. to order something destroyed because it is illegal or poses a hazard to the public. 3. to adjudge a person guilty or impose sentence, especially a very severe sentence such as death or life imprisonment. —**condemnation,** *n.*

condition 1. a future event which is possible but not certain, upon the occurrence of which a right, interest, or obligation under a contract, deed, will, or other instrument is made to depend. 2. **condition precedent,** (pronounced preSEEdent), a condition that must occur in order for such a right, interest, or obligation to arise. 3. **condition subsequent,** a condition whose occurrence extinguishes such a right, interest, or obligation. —**conditional,** *adj.*

condition of bail. See under BAIL[1].

conditional fee. Same as **fee simple defeasible** (see under FEE[1]).

conditional privilege. See under PRIVILEGE.

condominium *n.* a form of ownership of real property in which several owners each own a separate residential or commercial unit within the property and all of them together own the common areas, such as lobbies and recreational areas, as tenants in common. Cf. COOPERATIVE (def. 2).

confession *n.* 1. a statement admitting that one has committed a crime. 2. **involuntary confession, a.** narrowly, a confession obtained by physical or psychological coercion. **b.** broadly, a confession obtained by such coercion or in violation of the MI-RANDA RULE. A confession that is involuntary in this broad sense may not be used in a criminal case against the person who makes it. **3. voluntary confession,** a confession that is not involuntary.

confession of judgment an acknowledgment by a defendant that the plaintiff is right and that judgment should be entered in favor of the plaintiff. Transactions in which a party is required to provide such a confession in advance, so that in the event of any default by that party the other one can go straight into court and get a judgment without allowing any opportunity for presentation of a defense, are restricted or prohibited in many states. For example, see *cognovit note* (under NOTE¹). See also COGNOVIT.

confidentiality stipulation a STIPULATION by the parties in a case, usually so ORDERED by the judge (turning it into a **confidentiality order**), that information obtained during pretrial discovery, or the terms of a settlement, will be kept confidential. Sometimes the purpose is to protect legitimate confidential information, such as trade secrets or employee medical records; sometimes it is simply to prevent public access to damaging information that might assist other injured parties in seeking justice.

conflict of interest 1. a situation in which one has both a personal interest in a matter and some duty to another, or to the general public, with respect to that same matter, so that one's personal interest could potentially influence the way one carries out the duty. For example, a judge presiding over a suit against a company in which she owns stock, or an office manager asked to hire the best candidate for a position for which his brother is one of the applicants, would have a conflict of interest. **2.** a situation in which one owes duties to two different people whose interests in a matter may not be compatible, as when an attorney undertakes to represent two different defendants in the same case, or both the husband and the wife in an uncontested divorce. The law tolerates some conflicts of interest if the interested parties are informed of them and have no objection; in other situations, the law requires a person with a conflict of interest to withdraw from the matter.

conflict of laws the field of law that deals with the problems arising from application of the laws of different states or countries to events and transactions affecting two or more jurisdictions. These problems include CHOICE OF LAW and the question whether a judgment rendered in one jurisdiction will be recognized in another. In most countries this conflict of laws is primarily a branch of IN-TERNATIONAL LAW, but because law in the United States is a patchwork of more than fifty independent legal systems, it is a subject that pervades all areas of American law. See also COMITY; FULL FAITH AND CREDIT; UNIFORM LAWS.

conformed copy a copy of a document on which changes or insertions have been made to make it an accurate copy of the original. When a proposed order is submitted to a judge, the judge typically writes in various changes before signing it; then the party who submitted it "conforms" a copy of the proposed order by copying in the judge's changes and writing the judge's name on the signature line, and serves that conformed copy on the person to whom the order is directed. The original piece of paper signed by the judge stays on file with the court. See also /s/.

conforming use. See under USE.

confrontation *n.* the right of a criminal defendant, under the Sixth Amendment (see Appendix), to be confronted in open court by the witnesses against him so that they can be cross-examined and the jury can evaluate their demeanor. The Supreme Court has held, however, that a child may be permitted to testify by closed circuit television upon a finding that face-to-face confrontation with an alleged abuser would cause the child serious emotional distress.

congressional intent. See under LEGISLATIVE IN-TENT.

connect up to introduce evidence showing that previously offered evidence was admissible. A judge may permit evidence to be presented to a jury "subject to connection" or "subject to connecting up"; if the necessary connection to the case is never shown, the jury will be instructed to disregard that evidence.

conscientious objector 1. a person whose religion or sincere personal belief system forbids participation as a combatant in any war. By statute, conscientious objectors may provide an alternative form of service to the country if drafted in time of war. **2. selective conscientious objector,** a person opposed not to all wars, but only to those he regards as unjust. The law does not give such a person the status of a conscientious objector.

consecutive sentences. See under SENTENCE.

consent *n.* **1.** acquiescence in a course of action. **2. age of consent.** See under AGE. **3. informed consent,** consent given after receiving sufficient information about the nature, costs, risks, and benefits of a proposed course of action to make an intelligent decision. In the absence of such information, one's "consent" may not be legally valid. For example, surgery upon a person who was not informed of the nature of the procedure may make the surgeon liable for the tort of BATTERY. **4. on consent,** describing a judicial action taken because all parties agree to it, or at least none objects: *The injunction was entered on consent.* —*v.* **5.** to give consent or manifest acquiescence: *The defendant consented to the entry of a preliminary injunction.* —*adj.* **6.** describing action taken with the consent of those affected: *consent decree; consent order.* See also *consent search* (under SEARCH).

consequential damages. See under DAMAGES.

conservator *n.* the term used in some states for a court-appointed GUARDIAN for an incompetent adult. See also COMMITTEE. —**conservatorship,** *n.*

consideration *n.* **1.** that which is given or promised by a party to a CONTRACT in exchange for the other's promise. Unless something is given up by the promisee or some benefit is conferred on the promisor in exchange for the promise, the promise is merely GRATUITOUS and ordinarily will be unenforceable for *want of consideration* (see under WANT). See also FAILURE OF CONSIDERATION. **2. nominal consideration,** consideration recited in the contract but of no meaningful value, as in a contract to sell a parcel of land for one dollar. Although under traditional contract law courts do not pass judgment on the fairness of consideration, a court today might conclude that such a contract is unenforceable because of UNCONSCIONABILITY, or on the ground that the transaction is not a contract at all, but merely an unenforceable promise of a gift. **3. past consideration,** conduct in the past that is recited as "consideration" for a new promise; for example, "In consideration of the years of faithful service that you have given me, I promise to leave you my house." In most situations, traditional contract law regarded such a promise as unenforceable because nothing was actually demanded or given in exchange for it, but in sympathetic cases modern courts sometimes find a way to enforce such promises despite the lack of real consideration.

consign *v.* to place goods into the hands of a carrier for delivery to another person (the **consignee**), or to place goods in the hands of a merchant (the **consignee**) for sale to others. In both cases, the original owner (the **consignor**) retains title to the goods until the ultimate delivery or sale occurs. Goods that have been consigned to a merchant and are awaiting sale are said to be "on consignment." —**consignment,** *n.*

consolidate *v.* to put two or more things together; particularly, to combine two or more cases into one for administrative convenience. See also *consolidated case* (under CASE¹). Cf. SEVER. —**consolidation,** *n.*

consortium *n.* **1.** the companionship, affection, services, and sexual attention of a spouse. In some states, for some purposes, the concept has been extended to include the affection and companionship between parent and child. **2. loss of consortium,** the loss of such companionship by reason of wrongful conduct of another. This is commonly an element of damages for which recovery is sought in a tort action, usually an action against someone who has negligently or intentionally injured or killed one's spouse. See also SERVICES.

conspiracy *n.* an agreement among two or more persons (each referred to as a **conspirator** or **co-conspirator**) to do an unlawful act, or to achieve a lawful end by unlawful means; often described informally as a "partnership in crime." Conspiracy is a separate offense from the one it is formed to accomplish, and is a crime even if the contemplated acts are never performed, although in most states the agreement itself is not a crime until there has been some OVERT ACT by one of the conspirators in furtherance of the conspiracy.

constitution *n.* **1.** the fundamental law of a nation or state, providing a framework against which the validity of all other laws is measured; the system of fundamental principles according to which the nation or state is governed. **2. Constitution,** a particular constitution. Unless the context indicates otherwise, in American legal writing this always refers to the **Constitution of the United States.**

constitutional *adj.* **1.** (of a law, policy, or action) in harmony with or not forbidden by a constitution, especially the Constitution of the United States. Cf. UNCONSTITUTIONAL. **2.** pertaining or pursuant to a constitution, especially the Constitution of the United States. **3. constitutional issue** (or **question**), an issue in a case that requires resort to the Constitution and cases interpreting it for resolution. See also *constitutional right* (under RIGHT); *constitutional tort* (under TORT).

constitutionality *n.* the quality or state of being CONSTITUTIONAL: *A case was instituted to test the constitutionality of the statute.*

construction *n.* **1.** the process of determining the meaning of a constitution, statute, or instrument and its legal effect in a particular situation, or the meaning and effect so determined. Often interchangeable with **interpretation,** although "construction" is the more common term with respect to constitutions, rules, and statutes **(statutory construction),** and "interpretation" is more commonly used with respect to private instruments such as contracts, wills, and deeds. **2. liberal construction,** construction of a statute or constitutional provision that considers the overall purposes for which it was enacted and interprets it in such a way as to further those purposes. This approach, also called **broad construction,** recognizes that words are always an imperfect tool and that not all possible circumstances to which a provision might apply can be anticipated and specifically addressed by the language used. As a general rule, statutes granting rights, benefits, and protections are construed liberally. **3. strict construction,** construction of a statute or constitutional provision that focuses on the specific words used and tends to reject application to circumstances not clearly within the ordinary meaning of those words. Also called **narrow construction.** Criminal statutes are usually construed strictly, on the ground that no one should be punished for conduct that the legislature has not clearly and specifically made a crime. See also LEGISLATIVE HISTORY; LEGISLATIVE INTENT; ORIGINAL INTENT; PLAIN MEANING. —**construe,** *v.*

construction warranty. See under WARRANTY.

constructive *adj.* having the legal effect of; deemed by the law to exist or to have occurred even though that is not actually true. For example, a person who says "I'm giving you the contents of my safe; here's the key," would probably be held to have made "constructive delivery" of the contents of the safe (or to have "constructively delivered" them) by delivering the key, even though the contents have actually not been moved. See also *constructive* EVICTION, FRAUD, NOTICE, SERVICE, TRUST, TRUSTEE under those words. Cf. ACTUAL. —**constructively,** *adv.*

construe. See under CONSTRUCTION.

consumer *n.* a person who purchases or leases goods, services, or real property primarily for personal, family, household, or other nonbusiness purposes. See also *consumer goods* (under GOODS).

contemnor. See under CONTEMPT.

contemplation of death. See *gift in contemplation of death* (under GIFT).

contempt *n.* **1.** a judicial or legislative finding of willful disobedience of an order, or other willful conduct disrupting the procedures of a court **(contempt of court)** or legislature (e.g., **contempt of Congress).** Unless otherwise specified, "contempt" alone usually means contempt of court. The person or entity guilty of contempt is called a **contemnor.** See also CONTUMACIOUS; CONTUMACY. **2. civil contempt,** continuing contempt for which the court imposes a sanction that is to be lifted as soon as the contempt ends. The usual case is refusal to comply with a court order, for which the court places a person in jail or imposes a daily fine with the understanding that the fine or jailing will end as soon as steps are taken to comply with the order. **3. criminal contempt,** contempt that is not continuing, for which a fixed sanction is imposed as a penalty. For example, in a courtroom proceeding a judge may impose an instant fine upon a lawyer who does something in front of the jury that the lawyer was told not to do, or even send a disruptive person directly to jail.

contingency *n.* **1.** a future event or circumstance that may or may not arise, upon the occurrence of which something else depends. See also CONTINGENT. **2.** Short for **contingency fee,** also called **contingent fee.** An arrangement under which the amount of an attorney's fee in a civil case will depend upon the outcome of the case, usually being a percentage of the amount recovered: *The law firm took the case on contingency.*

contingent *adj.* uncertain; subject to future events. Said of something that will or will not occur, come into existence, or become definite, depending upon circumstances in the future. See *contingent* ESTATE[1], INTEREST[1], LIABILITY under those words, and *contingent fee* (under CONTINGENCY). Cf. VESTED.

continuance *n.* an order suspending or postponing a proceeding: *The defendant's new attorney moved for a 30-day continuance to allow her time to become familiar with the case.*

continue *v.* to grant or order a CONTINUANCE of: *The judge refused to continue the case, and instead ordered the parties to proceed as scheduled.*

continuing jurisdiction. See under JURISDICTION[1].

continuing objection. See under OBJECTION.

contraband *n.* illegal goods; goods that it is illegal to possess, sell, or transport; e.g., illegal drugs, smuggled goods.

contract *n.* **1.** broadly, any legally enforceable promise: *A bank's signature on a check that it has certified represents its contract to honor the check when it is presented for payment.* **2.** in its usual sense, an agreement among two or more persons or entities (the parties to the contract; see PARTY) whereby at least one of them promises to do (or not to do) something in exchange for something done or promised by the others. Such a contract typically comes into existence when one party accepts (see ACCEPT) another's OFFER, provided that there is CONSIDERATION for the promises in the agreement. See also *breach of contract* (under BREACH); *option contract* (under OPTION); QUASI CONTRACT; SUBCONTRACT. **3.** a document embodying such an agreement. **4. adhesion contract,** a preprinted contract that is not subject to negotiation, offered to a consumer on a "take it or leave it" basis; e.g., an automobile rental agreement or apartment lease. Also called **contract of adhesion.** If the terms are extremely oppressive, enforcement may be denied on the ground of UNCONSCIONABILITY. **5. bilateral contract,** a contract in which promises are made on both sides. The consideration for each party's promise is the return promise made by the other. Cf. *unilateral contract.* **6. contract under seal,** an old form of contract in which the promise is embodied in a *sealed instru-*

ment (see under SEAL[1]) delivered to the promisee. At common law such a promise was enforceable even if there was no consideration for it. In most states the role of the contract under seal has been modified or eliminated by statute. **7. express contract,** a contract expressed in words, whether spoken **(oral contract)** or reduced to writing **(written contract). 8. implied contract, a.** Also called **contract implied in fact.** a contract manifested by conduct. For example, if you sit down in a barber's chair and allow your hair to be cut, it is understood that this amounts to an agreement to pay for the haircut, even though nothing is said about it. **b.** Also called **contract implied in law.** a contract-like obligation imposed by law to do justice in a situation where there is no enforceable contract. For example, if a doctor provides necessary care to an unconscious accident victim, the law will "imply" an obligation to pay a reasonable amount for those services, even though the patient obviously never agreed to do so. See also QUASI CONTRACT. **9. third-party beneficiary contract,** a contract made for the purpose of conferring a benefit on someone other than the parties to the contract (the **third-party beneficiary**). For example, suppose A and B agree that A will plow B's field, in return for which B will permit C to grow his own crops on a portion of the field. If A plows the field but then B refuses to let C plant on it, C, as a third-party beneficiary, has an action against B for breach of the contract even though C was not a party to the contract. **10. unilateral contract,** a contract in which there is a promise on only one side, the consideration for which is not a return promise but the doing of some act. For example, an offer of a reward for return of a lost dog is an offer of a unilateral contract: if someone who has seen the offer returns the dog, the offeror is contractually obligated to pay the reward. Cf. *bilateral contract.* —*v.* **11.** to enter into a contract; make a contractual promise. —**contractual,** *adj.*

contractor *n.* **1.** a party who contracts to provide goods or services, especially on a large scale. **2. general contractor,** a company that undertakes contractual responsibility for completion of a large project, especially a construction project, by hiring and coordinating the work of specialized *subcontractors* (see under SUBCONTRACT) for different facets of the project. Also called **prime contractor. 3. government contractor,** a company, or occasionally an individual, hired by the government to furnish goods (such as airplanes or toilet seats for the military) or services (such as construction or consulting). **4. independent contractor,** an individual who contracts to provide services to others but, unlike an employee, retains significant autonomy in deciding how to carry out the work; e.g., a plumber, a management consultant, a freelance editor.

contribution *n.* **1.** the principle that when one of several people liable for the same judgment or obligation is called upon to satisfy it, the others may be required to reimburse her ("make contribution") to the extent of their share of the total liability. The principle is often applied in tort cases, where it is called **contribution among joint tortfeasors. 2.** a payment or reimbursement under the principle of contribution, or the amount paid, or a claim or cause of action for such reimbursement.

contributory negligence. See under NEGLIGENCE.

controlled substance a drug whose addicting, intoxicating, or mood-altering qualities have led Congress and state legislatures to make its production, possession, importation, and distribution for all but very limited purposes a crime. Examples include narcotics, amphetamines, barbiturates, tranquilizers, hallucinogens, and marijuana. America's traditional addictive and intoxicating recreational substances—tobacco and alcohol—are not included.

controversy. See CASE OR CONTROVERSY.

contumacious *adj.* describing behavior that would justify a finding of CONTEMPT, or a person who engages in such behavior: *The lawyer's conduct was contumacious. The lawyer was contumacious.*

contumacy *n.* disruptive or disrespectful behavior that would justify a finding of CONTEMPT.

conversation. See CRIMINAL CONVERSATION.

conversion *n.* **1.** the tort of intentionally depriving another of the use or benefit of her personal property, as by taking it, seriously damaging it, or exercising control over it. One who does this is said to "convert (the property) to his own use." **2.** the exchange of a *convertible security* (see under SECURITY[2]) for another security in accordance with the terms of the convertible security. —**convert,** *v.*

convertible security. See under SECURITY[2].

conveyance *n.* **1.** a transfer of an interest in property, especially real estate, by means of a deed or other instrument other than a will. **2.** the instrument by which a conveyance is accomplished. **3. voluntary conveyance,** a GRATUITOUS conveyance. —**convey,** *v.*

convict *v.* to prove or officially declare someone GUILTY of an offense, especially after a trial. —**conviction,** *n.*

cooperative *n.* **1.** a jointly owned enterprise carrying out purchasing, distribution, management, or other activities on behalf of its members, not for profit but to achieve economies of scale and other benefits of combined rather than individual efforts and resources. A cooperative may be organized as an association **(cooperative association)** or a corporation **(cooperative corporation). 2.** an apartment building owned by a cooperative corporation whose shareholders are the building's tenants, all of whom lease their apartments from the corporation. Cf. CONDOMINIUM.

copy. See *certified copy* (under CERTIFY); conformed copy; courtesy copy; examined copy.

copyright *n.* **1.** the exclusive right, granted by federal statute to the creator of a written, musical, artistic, or similar work, to control the reproduction and exploitation of the work for a considerable period of time, usually the life of the author plus 50 years. It is not the ideas and facts in a work that are protected, but the way in which they are expressed. See also ©; FAIR USE; WORK MADE FOR HIRE. —*v.* **2.** to take such steps as are necessary to secure or register a copyright. —**copyrightable,** *adj.* —**copyrighted,** *adj.*

coram nobis *Latin.* (lit. "before us," "in our presence") a writ under which a court may review one of its own judgments for errors of fact and, if necessary, change the judgment in light of facts that were not and could not have been known when the judgment was rendered.

corporate *adj.* **1.** pertaining to a corporation, to corporations generally, or, in some broad contexts, to business matters generally. **2. corporate law,** broadly, the area or type of legal practice that deals with business organizations and transactions rather than personal legal matters; sometimes the term includes corporate LITIGATION, and sometimes it refers only to counseling and assistance with business matters rather than court-related work. **3. corporate veil,** the legal distinction between a corporation and its owners; the recognition of a corporation as a distinct legal entity for whose acts and debts its owners (the shareholders) are not personally responsible. In rare cases, a court may find that a corporation is essentially a sham or that the corporate form is being used for improper purposes, and will therefore disregard the corporate form **(pierce the corporate veil)** and hold the owner or owners (often a PARENT COMPANY) liable for its debts. See also *corporate* CHARTER[1], INCOME TAX, SEAL[1], SECURITY[2] under those words.

corporation *n.* **1.** a legally recognized entity formed by legislative act, or by individuals pursuant to general legislative authorization, with ownership ordinarily represented by shares of stock owned in varying quantities by anywhere from one to millions of stockholders. Corporations are typically characterized by LIMITED LIABILITY of stockholders, separation of ownership and management (in that the stockholders usually have no day-to-day role in management of the company, but merely vote once a year for directors), and treatment for most legal purposes as a distinct entity or "person" separate from its owners. **2. business corporation,** a corporation organized to carry out activities for profit. Also called **for-profit corporation.** Cf. *nonprofit corporation.* **3. close corporation,** a corporation owned by a single shareholder or a small group of shareholders, who typically are all personally active in the business of the corporation or are related to each other, and ordinarily are not allowed to sell their shares to anyone else without approval of the group. Also called **closely held corporation; privately held corporation.** See also *private corporation.* Cf. *publicly held corporation.* **4. domestic corporation, a.** usually, a corporation incorporated in one's own state. **b.** sometimes (e.g., for federal income tax purposes), any corporation incorporated within the United States. Cf. *foreign corporation.* **5. foreign corporation, a.** usually, a corporation incorporated in another state. For example, in a Maryland court or a discussion of Maryland law, a Delaware corporation would be referred to as a "foreign corporation." **b.** sometimes (e.g., for federal income tax purposes), a corporation or similar entity organized under the laws of another country. Cf. *domestic corporation.* **6. nonprofit** (or **not-for-profit**) **corporation,** a corporation organized for charitable, religious, educational, cultural, or similar purposes, and not to generate profits for the shareholders. Cf. *business corporation.* **7. nonstock corporation,** a corporation that does not issue stock. **8. parent corporation.** Same as PARENT COMPANY. **9. private corporation, a.** a corporation established for nongovernmental purposes. Cf. *public corporation.* **b.** sometimes, a *close corporation.* **10. professional corporation (P.C.),** a form of business organization allowed to individuals or groups practicing professions such as law or medicine, having some characteristics of corporations but not affording LIMITED LIABILITY to the members. In some states, called **professional association (P.A.). 11. public corporation, a.** a corporation established by legislative act to carry out specified governmental purposes. Cf. *private corporation.* **b.** sometimes, short for *publicly held corporation.* **12. publicly held corporation,** a corporation owned by a diverse group of shareholders, with stock freely traded among members of the public. See also *public corporation.* Cf. *close corporation.* **13. S corporation,** a small business corporation whose shareholders have elected, under Subchapter S of Chapter 1 of the Internal Revenue Code, to have the corporation's income treated as personal income to them and taxed as part of their personal income taxes, thus avoiding normal corporate income taxes. **14. shell corporation,** a corporation having no business or ongoing activity of its own, and sometimes lacking any substantial assets as well. **15. sister corporations,** corporations that are subsidiaries of the same parent corporation. **16. subsidiary corporation.** Same as SUBSIDIARY. See also *cooperative corporation* (under COOPERATIVE); MUNICIPAL CORPORATION.

corpus *n. Latin.* (lit. "body") **1.** the property of a trust; all of the assets under administration by a trustee pursuant to a particular trust instrument. See also PRINCIPAL; RES. **2.** any collection of things viewed as a unit.

corpus delicti *Latin.* (lit. "the body of the crime") the fact that a crime under discussion did occur—that there was in fact a crime. In general, American law does not allow a person to be convicted of a crime solely on the basis of his own confession, absent some independent evidence of the corpus delicti, that is, some evidence that the crime for which he claims responsibility actually happened.

corroborate *v.* to provide support or confirmation from an independent source for testimony or other evidence already introduced; to back up independently. **—corroborating, corroborative,** *adj.*

costs *n.* **1.** filing fees and certain other expenses necessarily incurred in pursuing or defending a civil case. The losing party is usually required to pay the winner's costs. Since "costs" does not include attorneys' fees, this is often a rather insignificant amount. Also called **court costs. 2. costs to abide the event,** a phrase appearing in appellate decisions indicating that a decision on which party must pay the other's costs must await the outcome of further proceedings, usually a new trial.

counsel *n.* **1.** a lawyer or lawyers, particularly in the role of advisor to or representative of a particular client: *Upon the advice of counsel, he canceled the interview.* **2.** a collective term for the lawyers representing parties in a case or present for a proceeding: *Copies of the scheduling order were sent to all counsel. Will counsel please approach the bench?* **3. assigned counsel,** counsel appointed by a court to represent a criminal defendant who cannot afford to hire a lawyer. See also RIGHT TO COUNSEL. **4. general counsel,** a company's chief legal officer. **5. house counsel, a.** a company's regular lawyer or law firm. **b.** Also called **in-house counsel.** a lawyer or lawyers who are employees of a company and do legal work only for that company. **6. independent counsel,** counsel hired or appointed to handle a matter because the lawyers who would normally do so have a CONFLICT OF INTEREST. **7. local counsel,** an attorney admitted to practice in the court in which a case is pending, who assists an attorney not so admitted (usually from out of state) in representing a client in the proceeding. See also PRO HAC VICE. **8. outside counsel,** any counsel performing services for a company other than *in-house counsel.* **9. special counsel,** counsel hired or appointed to assist in a matter because of special expertise, or to act as *independent counsel.* **10. standby counsel,** counsel appointed by a court to stand by and lend such assistance as she can to a criminal defendant who insists on representing himself, and to take over the representation if the defendant changes his mind. See also OF COUNSEL.

counselor *n.* a lawyer. The word is used only in two contexts: (a) in letterheads, usually in the form **counselor at law** or the plural **counselors at law.** The British spelling **counsellor** is also seen. (b) as a form of oral address in a judicial proceeding: *Counselor, please sit down.* For the plural, only COUNSEL is used in this context, never "counselors."

count *n.* each of several distinct claims or causes of action in a civil complaint, or charges in a criminal information or indictment.

counterclaim *n.* **1.** a CAUSE OF ACTION or *claim for relief* (see under CLAIM) asserted by a defendant against the plaintiff in a civil case. It is asserted in the ANSWER to the complaint. **2. compulsory counterclaim,** any claim that the defendant has against the plaintiff arising out of the same events that are the subject of the plaintiff's complaint. As a general rule, failure to assert such a counterclaim constitutes a waiver of it. **3. permissive counterclaim,** any other claim that the defendant has against the plaintiff, regardless of what it relates to. The defendant may assert such a claim as a counterclaim or hold it for a separate action, as she chooses.

counteroffer *n.* a response to an OFFER of a contract that does not accept the offer as stated, but instead proposes different terms.

course of business. See ORDINARY COURSE OF BUSINESS.

course of dealing a sequence of previous dealings between the parties to a particular transaction, to which courts will refer, in the event of a dispute about the latest transaction, as evidence of how the parties intended it to be carried out. Cf. COURSE OF PERFORMANCE; USAGE.

course of performance the carrying out of some recurring contractual obligation, such as the making of installment payments, in substantially the same way several times without objection from the other party to the contract. In the event of a dispute over a subsequent performance of that obligation, the previously established course of performance will normally be taken by the court as showing how the parties intended that step to be performed. Cf. COURSE OF DEALING; USAGE.

court *n.* **1.** an institution of government whose function is to interpret and apply the law to specific cases within its jurisdiction. Within a judicial system, a court is referred to as a **lower court** or **higher court** in relation to others, as determined by the fact that decisions of the lower courts are subject to review by those above, and decisions of the higher courts are binding upon those below. In the basic three-tier judicial system of the United States and most states, the first level is primarily a trial court and the next two are primarily or exclusively appellate courts; the middle level is thus the lowest appellate court for most cases, but is usually referred to as the **intermediate appellate court**. See also CHANCERY; *court below* (under BELOW); INFERIOR COURT; INTERNATIONAL COURT OF JUSTICE; KANGAROO COURT; STAR CHAMBER; SMALL CLAIMS COURT; SUPERIOR COURT; SUPREME COURT; UNITED STATES COURT OF APPEALS; UNITED STATES DISTRICT COURT. **2.** the judges, collectively, of a court. **3.** the judge or panel of judges sitting on a particular case. **4.** (*cap.*) **a.** a particular court, especially the Supreme Court of the United States or the court in which a specific case is pending. **b.** a form of address commonly used in addressing or referring to the judge or panel of judges in a case: *May it please the Court... As the Court will recall...* **5. court of law** or **court of record**, phrases that formerly had specialized meanings but now are rather formal ways of referring to almost any court, especially a trial court.

court clerk. See under CLERK.

court costs. Same as COSTS.

court-martial *n.* **1.** a military court; a court of military personnel convened to try a member of the military for an offense against military law. **2.** a trial or conviction in or by such a court. —*v.* **3.** to charge, try, or convict a person in such a court.

court reporter a person who makes a word-forword record of what is said in a trial or similar proceeding, and if requested (and paid) by the litigants, produces a typed or printed transcript.

court rules. See under RULE.

courtesy copy an extra copy of a motion, brief, or other document being filed in a case, delivered directly to the judge's chambers "as a courtesy." Some judges find the extra copy so convenient that they require it; some find the extra paper such a nuisance that they forbid it.

covenant *n.* **1.** a legally enforceable promise, especially a promise that a particular state of affairs will be maintained during the term of a contract or that certain actions will or will not be taken with respect to land. **2.** a WARRANTY, especially in connection with a transfer of land. **3. covenant not to compete**, a promise in an employment contract or contract for the sale of a business, that the employee or seller will not subsequently go into competition with the employer or buyer. Such covenants are enforceable only if limited in duration and geographic scope. **4. covenant not to sue**, in an agreement settling a claim, dispute, or lawsuit, a promise not to pursue the matter in court. **5. covenant running with the land**, a promise with respect to land that survives transfers of the land; it is binding on and enforceable by subsequent owners. Also called **running covenant**. **6. covenants** (or **warranties**) **of title**, a set of covenants, including the *covenant of quiet enjoyment* or *covenant of warranty* (see under QUIET ENJOYMENT), usually insisted upon by a buyer of real estate as assurance that she will receive good and unencumbered title to the property. Often referred to in negotiations as the **usual covenants**. Cf. *warranty of title* (under WARRANTY). **7. restrictive covenant**, **a.** a covenant limiting the use or disposition that an owner may make of land. A covenant forbidding transfer of property to anyone of a particular race or ethnic group **(racially restrictive covenant)** was formerly a tool for maintaining segregated housing; such covenants are no longer enforceable. **b.** Another term for *covenant not to compete*.

covenantee *n.* one to whom a covenant is made or who has a right to enforce it.

covenantor *n.* one who makes or is bound by a covenant.

cover *v.* **1.** (of a buyer of goods) to buy substitute goods from another source when a seller under contract to provide certain goods fails to make delivery. If the reasonable cost of "cover" exceeds the original contract price, the buyer may recover the difference from the original seller as part of the damages for breach of the contract. **2.** (of an insurer or insurance policy) to protect a certain person or protect against a certain risk: *My health insurance policy covers my children but does not cover cosmetic surgery.* —*n.* **3.** the purchase of substitute goods elsewhere when a seller fails to deliver as promised.

craft union. See under UNION.

credible *adj.* worthy of belief: *credible testimony; credible evidence; a credible witness; a credible defense.* —**credibility,** *n.*

credit *n.* **1.** trust in the ability and intention of a person or entity to repay a loan or to pay for goods or services provided without immediate payment, or the quality of a person or entity that inspires such trust: *to extend credit to a purchaser; to make a purchase on credit.* **2.** the amount of money loaned or made available, or of payments deferred or that a vendor is willing to defer, by reason of such credit: *We have used $1,500 of credit on our credit card and have $500 of credit left for additional purchases.* **3.** a reduction in an amount owed, by reason of a payment or correction or for some other reason. See also TAX CREDIT. **4.** respect; deference. See also FULL FAITH AND CREDIT. —*v.* **5.** to believe: *The jury credited the witness's testimony on the issue of self-defense.*

creditor *n.* **1.** a person to whom money is owed. Cf. DEBTOR. **2. judgment creditor,** a person who obtained a money judgment in a civil case which has not yet been fully paid. See also *secured creditor* (under SECURE).

crime *n.* **1.** an act or omission contrary to laws established for the welfare of the public at large, for which the law provides a punishment. Especially, an act or omission punishable by a sentence of incarceration; a FELONY or MISDEMEANOR. See also INFRACTION; OFFENSE; VIOLATION. **2. common law crime,** an offense that was a crime at common law, before criminal laws were generally written into statutes. Most acts that were crimes at common law are also crimes under modern statutes. Because of the constitutional problem of vagueness (see VAGUE), it is doubtful that any common law crime not embodied in a statute could now be enforced. **3. statutory crime, a.** an act that was not a crime at common law, but has been made a crime by statute. **b.** broadly, any crime defined by statute, whether or not it was a crime at common law. See also *crime against nature* (under UNNATURAL ACT); HATE CRIME; HIGH CRIMES AND MISDEMEANORS; VICTIMLESS CRIME; WHITE-COLLAR CRIME.

criminal *adj.* **1.** constituting an offense or an element of an offense. See CRIMINAL CONVERSATION, and *criminal* CONTEMPT, HOMICIDE, NEGLIGENCE, TRESPASS under those words. **2.** pertaining to crime and criminal law: *criminal case; criminal law.* See also *criminal* ACTION, LIABILITY, PROCEDURE, PROSECUTION under those words. —*n.* **3.** a person who commits a crime.

criminal conversation the tort of engaging in sexual intercourse with another person's spouse. Like many legal concepts having their origin in the concept of wife as chattel, this tort has been abolished in many states. Cf. ADULTERY.

criminalist *n.* a specialist in the collection and scientific analysis of physical evidence of crimes **(criminalistics)**.

criminally negligent homicide. See under HOMICIDE.

criminologist *n.* a person engaged in the sociological study of crime and criminals **(criminology)**.

cross *Informal.* —*n.* **1.** Same as *cross examination* (see under EXAMINATION). —*v.* **2.** Same as *cross-examine* (see under EXAMINE).

cross-appeal *n.* **1.** an appeal filed by the appellee in a case in which an appeal has already been filed, challenging the same judgment that is the subject of the first appeal but on a different ground. For example, a losing defendant might appeal a decision on the ground that the damage award was too high,

legal

then the plaintiff might cross-appeal on the ground that the damage award was too low. —*v.* **2.** to file a cross-appeal.

cross-claim *n.* in a civil action against two or more defendants, a CLAIM or CAUSE OF ACTION asserted by one of the defendants against one or more of the other defendants. For example, in a tort case against several people alleged to have harmed the plaintiff jointly, the defendants often assert cross-claims against each other, each claiming a right of CONTRIBUTION from the others. In rare cases, a cross-claim might be asserted by one plaintiff against another in the same case.

cross-complaint *n.* the pleading in which one asserts a CROSS-CLAIM.

cross examination. See under EXAMINATION.

cross-examine. See under EXAMINE.

cruel and unusual punishment punishment of a person convicted of a crime in a manner that fails to meet minimal contemporary standards of decency, or that is grossly disproportionate to the crime. The Eighth Amendment (see Appendix) forbids such punishments.

cruelty *n.* a traditional ground for divorce, consisting of a pattern of physical or psychological abuse by one spouse rendering married life intolerable for the other. The level of abuse that a married woman was formerly expected to tolerate from her husband is illustrated by the names given to this ground for divorce ("cruelty," "extreme cruelty," "cruel and inhuman treatment," and the like), and the fact that a single instance of cruelty was normally not considered sufficient to entitle one to a divorce.

culpable *adj.* blameworthy; meriting imposition of liability or punishment. —**culpability,** *n.*

cumulative evidence. See under EVIDENCE.

cumulative sentences. See under SENTENCE.

cumulative zoning. See under ZONING.

curative instruction. See under INSTRUCTION.

custodial interrogation. See under INTERROGATION.

custody *n.* **1.** immediate possession and control over a thing, with responsibility for its care. **2.** any significant restraint on a person's freedom of action imposed by law enforcement authorities. **3.** Also called **child custody.** the right and responsibility of determining the residence, care, and education of a minor child. **4. joint custody,** an arrangement whereby divorced parents continue to share responsibility for raising their children. **5. sole custody,** custody of a child by one adult only. This is the most common arrangement for custody of a child following divorce of the parents.

custom *n.* **1.** in older law, a traditional business practice of such ancient origin and universal application as to have acquired the status of a legal requirement. **2.** Also called **custom and usage.** in modern contexts, same as USAGE.

customs *n.* **1.** taxes imposed by the federal government on goods imported into or exported from the country. Also called **duties,** except that "duties" has a singular form (see DUTY) but "customs" does not. **2.** the agency or procedure by which, or the place where, such taxes are collected.

cy pres *Law French.* (lit. "as near") the doctrine under which a court confronted with a deed or will whose terms cannot be carried out exactly may modify it so as to carry out the intent of the maker as nearly as possible, especially in the case of charitable bequests and trusts.

a b c **D** e f g h i j k l m n o p q r s t u v w x y z

damages *n.pl.* **1.** a sum of money asked for by a plaintiff or awarded by a court in a civil action, to be paid by the defendant because of the wrong that gave rise to the suit. An action seeking an award of damages is called a **damage action. 2.** sometimes, the injuries for which the plaintiff seeks an award of damages. **3. compensatory damages,** damages awarded to compensate for the harm resulting from the defendant's wrong, including actual financial loss and intangible harm such as pain and suffering. These are the damages to which a plaintiff is normally entitled upon proving her case. Also called **actual damages.** For some purposes, compensatory damages are subdivided into **general damages,** which compensate for losses of a sort that would normally be expected to follow from the nature of the wrong, and **special (or consequential) damages,** which arise from the unique circumstances of the case. **4. liquidated damages,** damages for breach of contract in an amount stated in the contract, where the parties agreed at the time of contracting on a reasonable figure or formula for determination of the compensation to be paid in the event of a breach. Also called **stipulated damages.** Unlike the payment provided for in a *penalty clause* (see under PENALTY), agreements for payment of liquidated damages are normally enforceable. **5. nominal damages,** an award of a token amount, such as $1.00, indicating that the defendant did do the wrong alleged but that no significant measure of damages was established by the plaintiff. In certain kinds of DEFAMATION action, such an award can be made to vindicate the honor of the plaintiff. **6. punitive damages,** damages awarded in excess of actual damages in tort cases in which the defendant's conduct is deemed especially egregious. Punitive damages are awarded to punish the defendant, discourage repetition of such conduct, and set an example for others who might be tempted to engage in similar conduct. Also called **exemplary**

damages. 7. speculative damages, claimed damages for injury or loss that may occur in the future but cannot be predicted or evaluated on any reasonable basis. Speculative damages are not allowed. **8. treble damages,** damages in an amount equal to three times the *actual damages,* awarded in cases under certain statutes specifically providing for such an award, notably the ANTITRUST laws and the RACKETEER INFLUENCED AND CORRUPT ORGANIZATIONS ACT.

dangerous weapon. See under WEAPON.

date rape. See under RAPE.

de facto *Latin.* (lit. "arising from that which has been done") existing in fact, without regard to legal requirements or formalities; said of things that came into being without legal blessing, but that the law chooses to take cognizance of for practical reasons: *de facto segregation; the de facto government of a foreign country.* Cf. DE JURE.

de jure *Latin.* (lit. "arising from law") existing by reason of law; brought into existence and maintained in accordance with legal requirements and formalities. Sometimes the existence is more theoretical than real, as in the case of a *de jure government* that has been ousted by war or revolution; sometimes it is all too real, as in the case of *de jure segregation* in the old South. Cf. DE FACTO.

de minimis *Latin.* (lit. "concerning trifles") insignificant; too small to merit attention: *The plaintiff suffered only de minimis damages. The chilling effect on speech, if any, is de minimis.* The phrase comes from the maxim **de minimis non curat lex** ("the law does not concern itself with trifles").

de novo *Latin.* (lit. "anew") from the beginning; all over again. See *de novo review* (under REVIEW); *de novo trial* (under TRIAL).

deadly weapon. See under WEAPON.

dealer *n.* a person who buys and resells things as a business. See also BROKER-DEALER.

death. See BRAIN DEATH.

death penalty. Same as CAPITAL PUNISHMENT.
death warrant. See under WARRANT[1].
deathbed declaration. See under DECLARATION.
debenture *n.* a corporate debt obligation, usually a long-term bond or note, that is not secured or guaranteed, but depends solely upon the company's continued financial well-being for payment.
debt *n.* **1.** an unconditional obligation to pay a sum of money, either at present or in the future. **2. bad debt,** a debt owed to a taxpayer that the taxpayer will be completely unable to collect. The taxpayer usually may deduct all or part of a bad debt for income tax purposes in the year in which the debt becomes worthless.
debt security. See under SECURITY[2].
debtor *n.* **1.** a person who owes money. Cf. CREDITOR. **2.** a person or entity that is the subject of a bankruptcy action. **3. debtor in possession,** a debtor in bankruptcy who is allowed to continue to control his business during REORGANIZATION. **4. judgment debtor,** a person who owes money pursuant to a judgment entered against him in a civil case. **5. principal debtor.** See under PRINCIPAL.
decedent *n.* a person who has died. This is the term used in the law of trusts, wills, intestate succession, administration of estates, and the like; in a murder case or wrongful death action, "deceased" would be the more common term. See also *decedent's estate* (under ESTATE[2]).
deceit *n.* an older, but still often used, term for FRAUD.
decision *n.* **1.** the determination of a court, jury, or administrative tribunal on how a case should come out. **2.** a judicial or administrative OPINION.
decisional law. Same as CASE LAW.
declarant *n.* the person who makes a DECLARATION; particularly, in discussions of the *hearsay rule* (see under HEARSAY), the maker of an out-of-court statement whose admissibility is under discussion.
declaration *n.* **1.** an oral or written assertion; a statement. **2.** a formal announcement: *Declaration of Independence; declaration of war.* **3.** a word used in some jurisdictions for AFFIRMATION (def. 2). **4.** an old word for the initial pleading in a case at law; now called a COMPLAINT. **5. declaration against interest,** a statement that is so strongly contrary to the interests of the declarant at the time it is made that a reasonable person in the declarant's position would not have made it unless he believed it to be true; e.g., "I owe her $1,000," "I shouldn't have been driving so fast." Such statements are generally admissible under an exception to the *hearsay rule* (see under HEARSAY). **6. declaration of trust,** a document in which a property owner declares that she holds the property in trust for the benefit of someone else, thereby creating a TRUST with herself as trustee. Cf. DEED OF TRUST. **7. dying (or deathbed) declaration,** a statement made in the belief that one is about to die, particularly about the circumstances of the impending death; e.g., "Joe shot me." Such statements are often admitted into evidence as an exception to the *hearsay rule* (see under HEARSAY), on the quaint assumption that no one would dare "go to his death with a lie upon his lips." **8. spontaneous declaration.** Same as EXCITED UTTERANCE.
declaratory judgment. See under JUDGMENT.
decree *n.* **1.** a JUDGMENT. Before the MERGER OF LAW AND EQUITY, the final order disposing of a case was called a "judgment" at law but a "decree" in equity. Now "judgment" is the usual term for most cases, but "decree" is often used as a synonym and is the usual term in certain contexts: *bankruptcy decree, divorce decree.* **2. consent decree,** a court order entered by agreement between a federal agency and a party accused of illegal conduct in the field regulated by the agency, resolving the case and typically including a promise by the party not to engage in certain activities in the future. —*v.* **3.** to ORDER or ADJUDGE.
decriminalize *v.* to repeal a criminal law or otherwise make conduct that previously was a crime no longer a crime; sometimes distinguished from LEGALIZE in that conduct that has been "legalized" might

still be subject to extensive special regulation, whereas conduct that has been "decriminalized" would be regulated primarily by the general laws applicable to all conduct. For example, to "legalize" prostitution might mean to require prostitutes to have special licenses and practice in specific areas; to "decriminalize" prostitution might mean to remove the government from involvement with exchanges of money for sex except for enforcement of general rules regarding fraud, public decency, exploitation of minors, and the like.
dedication *n.* a gift or abandonment of an interest in land, in a copyrightable work, or in some other property, by the owner or creator to a governmental entity or to the public at large.
deductible *adj.* **1.** qualifying as a DEDUCTION for income tax purposes: *a deductible contribution to charity; a deductible trip to a business conference in Hawaii.* —*n.* **2.** the amount for which the insured is liable on covered losses before the insurance company must begin paying under a policy: *a medical insurance policy with a $500 annual deductible.*
deduction *n.* **1.** a portion of income or an item of expense that a taxpayer may subtract from income for purposes of calculating income tax. Cf. TAX CREDIT. **2. itemized deduction,** any of a number of specific types of expense that must be specifically listed on a tax return to be claimed as deductions; e.g., medical expenses, mortgage interest. **3. standard deduction,** a fixed amount that may be claimed as a deduction instead of claiming separate itemized deductions.
deed *n.* **1.** a formal instrument by which a living person or an entity conveys an interest in property, especially real property. **2. quitclaim deed,** a deed conveying to someone else whatever interest one has in a piece of real property, without any promise that the title one is purporting to convey is any good. Typically used for gifts of property. **3. warranty deed,** a deed conveying title to real property and containing *covenants of title* (see under COVENANT), making the grantor liable to the grantee for losses caused by undisclosed defects in the title. —*v.* **4.** to convey property by deed.
deed of trust 1. an instrument by which the owner of certain property conveys it to another to be held in trust for the benefit of someone, thereby creating a TRUST with the person receiving the property as trustee. Cf. *declaration of trust* (under DECLARATION). **2.** specifically, in some states, a deed conveying title to real property to a trustee to hold as security until the transferor repays a loan; similar to a MORTGAGE except that the mortgage is given directly to the creditor to hold. Also called **trust deed.**
defalcation *n.* **1.** misuse, misappropriation, or loss of funds over which one has fiduciary responsibility as a trustee, a corporate or public official, or the like. **2.** the sum taken or lost.
defamation *n.* the communication to a third person of a falsehood that is injurious to the reputation of a living individual, or of a corporation or other organization. Defamation is the basis for the torts of libel (see LIBEL[1]) and SLANDER. —**defamatory,** *adj.* —**defame,** *v.*
default *n.* **1.** failure to fulfill a legal obligation, such as performing a contract, paying a debt, or responding to a properly served summons. —*v.* **2.** to fail to perform a legal obligation.
default judgment. See under JUDGMENT.
defeasance *n.* the termination or nullification of a fee interest in real property. See *fee simple defeasible* (under FEE[1]).
defeasible fee. Same as *fee simple defeasible* (see under FEE[1]).
defeat *v.* to cause to be void or ineffective; to bar: *The original owner's title was defeated by adverse possession. The statute of frauds defeats the plaintiff's contract claim.*
defect *n.* **1.** a flaw in design or manufacture that renders a product ineffective or dangerous. **2.** a circumstance that defeats a legal transaction, claim, or right. See also *defective title* (under TITLE). —**defective,** *adj.*

defendant *n.* **1.** the person against whom a lawsuit is brought. **2.** a person against whom a criminal COMPLAINT or other charging instrument has been filed with a court in a criminal case.

defendant in error the APPELLEE in a case where the appeal is commenced by *writ of error* (see under WRIT).

defense *n.* **1.** the facts and legal theories relied upon, or the evidence and argument presented, in opposition to a civil claim or criminal charge. **2.** a legal justification for conduct that otherwise appears to be wrongful, or a legal principle that renders one immune from liability for wrongful conduct: *the defense of duress; the defense of statute of limitations.* See also TWINKIE DEFENSE. **3.** the defendant and attorneys representing the defendant in a case. **4.** **affirmative defense,** a defense that, rather than simply showing that a claim or charge is untrue or arguing that it is legally insufficient, presents additional facts to defeat the claim or charge. For example, the defense of RES JUDICATA in a civil case; the INSANITY DEFENSE in a criminal case; or the defense that one was acting in SELF-DEFENSE in a tort case or criminal case. In most situations the defendant who relies upon such a defense has the *burden of pleading* and *burden of proof* (see under BURDEN[1]) regarding the facts necessary to establish it. **5. equitable defense,** in a civil suit, a defense based upon principles that originated in courts of EQUITY; e.g., *fraud in the inducement* (see under FRAUD) or UNCLEAN HANDS.

deficiency judgment. See under JUDGMENT.

defined-benefit plan. See under PENSION PLAN.

defined-contribution plan. See under PENSION PLAN.

definite failure of issue. See under ISSUE[2].

defraud *v.* to obtain money or property from a person by FRAUD.

degree *n.* the GRADE of an offense.

degree of care. Same as STANDARD OF CARE.

degree of proof. Same as STANDARD OF PROOF.

dehors *prep. Law French.* outside; beyond the scope of: *facts dehors the record; evidence dehors the contract.*

delegated power. See under POWER.

delict *n.* a civil or criminal wrong, especially a tort.

delinquent *n.* Same as *juvenile delinquent* (see under JUVENILE).

delivery *n.* the voluntary transfer of possession of property, or handing over of a piece of paper, with intent thereby to consummate a legal transaction. For example, a conveyance of land by DEED normally requires delivery of the deed. Delivery may be ACTUAL or CONSTRUCTIVE; see discussion under CONSTRUCTIVE. See also GIFT; *personal service* (under SERVICE).

demand *n.* **1.** a call for someone to perform a legal obligation. **2.** a request for payment of a check or other instrument for the payment of money. **3.** an assertion of legal right in a complaint or lawsuit. **4.** **demand deposit,** money deposited with a bank which can be withdrawn at any time. An ordinary checking or savings account is a demand deposit. Cf. *time deposit* (under TIME). **5. demand for relief.** Same as PRAYER FOR RELIEF. **6. demand letter,** a letter making a formal demand for payment of money owed, or for satisfaction of some other legal obligation. A demand letter is sent partly to lay the groundwork for a lawsuit, and partly in the hope that the recipient will perform as requested or work out a settlement so that a suit will not be necessary. **7. due demand,** demand that must be made before it can be said that a party has failed to perform a legal obligation. Usually this is made by means of a *demand letter.* For example, before suing to evict a tenant for nonpayment of rent, a landlord normally must make a formal demand for payment. Complaints seeking performance of a contract or remedy for breach typically recite that the defendant failed to perform "despite due demand," "due demand having been made," or the like. **8. on demand,** upon request; whenever requested. A negotiable instrument that does not specify a time for payment,

such as a check, is **payable on demand,** and is referred to as a **demand instrument, demand note,** or the like. Cf. TIME.

demise *n.* **1.** the transfer of an estate in land, especially one for a limited time, particularly by lease or by will or intestacy. **2.** death. —*v.* **3.** to bring about a demise of real property, especially by renting out the property: *The tenant is required to maintain the demised premises.*

demonstrative evidence. See under EVIDENCE.

demur *v.* **1.** to file a DEMURRER. **2.** broadly, to raise any objection to a claim or procedure, especially on the ground that it is legally irrelevant or insufficient.

demurrer *n.* a motion or pleading in response to a complaint or counterclaim, taking the position that the facts alleged, even if true, would not entitle the claimant to relief on any theory of law. In most American jurisdictions the demurrer has been replaced by the motion to dismiss for failure to state a claim (see discussion under CLAIM), but "demurrer" is sometimes used as an informal term for such a motion.

deny *v.* **1.** to assert, in response to a complaint, counterclaim, or *request for admissions* (see under ADMISSION), that a particular allegation is untrue, or that the party responding lacks sufficient knowledge or information to form a belief as to its truth or falsity. All allegations not denied in one of these manners are deemed admitted and, absent special circumstances, can no longer be contested in the case. **2.** (of a court) to refuse to grant a motion, petition, or other request for judicial action. Opposite of GRANT. —**denial,** *n.*

dependent *n.* an individual who depends upon another for financial support. For income tax purposes, a taxpayer may claim an EXEMPTION for each dependent who meets certain tests, including receiving over half of his support from the taxpayer and either being a close relative of the taxpayer or living as a member of the taxpayer's household.

deponent *n.* a person who makes a written statement or gives testimony under oath or affirmation, especially the witness in a DEPOSITION.

deportation *n.* the expulsion of an ALIEN from the country. DUE PROCESS requires that a person believed to be subject to deportation be allowed a hearing before an impartial tribunal before being deported.

depose *v.* **1.** to give a sworn statement or testimony. **2.** to say under oath or affirmation. **3.** to ask questions of the deponent in a deposition; also referred to as "taking the deposition": *The lead attorney for the defense will depose the plaintiff.*

deposit. See CERTIFICATE OF DEPOSIT; *demand deposit* (under DEMAND); *time deposit* (under TIME).

deposition *n.* **1.** a DISCOVERY procedure in which a witness testifies under oath in response to questions from the lawyer for one of the parties to a case. It is usually conducted much like a regular courtroom proceeding, complete with a court reporter and cross examination by the opposing lawyer, but it normally takes place outside the courtroom and without a judge present. The purpose is partly to discover information and partly to have the testimony available on record in case the witness is no longer available when the trial is finally held. **2.** the testimony, or the transcript of the testimony, given at a deposition. **3. deposition in aid of execution,** a posttrial deposition of a party against whom a money judgment has been entered, for the purpose of identifying assets that could be seized to satisfy the judgment.

depreciation *n.* **1.** the gradual decrease in the value of tangible property that occurs because of wear and tear and obsolescence. **2.** a DEDUCTION allowed for income tax purposes because of depreciation in the value of property used in business or held for production of income. Ordinarily, a portion of the original cost of the property may be deducted each year for a number of years, until all or most of the original cost has been deducted.

derivative action. See under ACTION.

derogation *n.* limitation on the scope of something; partial repeal. Statutes on subjects that traditionally were governed by common law are said to be "in derogation of the common law."

descend v. **1.** (of property of a decedent, especially real property) to pass to one's heirs by INTESTATE SUCCESSION. **2.** loosely, to pass by intestate succession or by will, especially if the person who takes by will is a child or other relative who would have received property by intestate succession if there had been no will. —**descent,** n.

descent and distribution 1. the principles by which the property of a person who dies without a will is distributed. Also called INTESTATE SUCCESSION. **2.** broadly, the principles by which the property of a decedent is distributed, whether by intestate succession or by will. See also DISTRIBUTION.

desertion n. **1.** the breaking off of marital cohabitation, unprovoked by any wrongdoing by one's spouse, with the intent not to return and not to fulfill marital responsibilities. Desertion is one of the traditional grounds for divorce. **2.** the military crime of abandoning one's post to avoid danger or of leaving one's unit with the intent of staying away permanently.

desuetude n. the state of being no longer used or enforced. Statutes that have not been enforced for a great many years, or that linger on the books even though the subject they address or the reason for their enactment no longer exists, are said to have "fallen into desuetude." Nevertheless, if they are on the books and circumstances arise to which they are applicable, they can be enforced. See the case discussed under SODOMY.

detain v. **1.** to keep a person in CUSTODY for a limited time for an official purpose: *detain for questioning.* See also PREVENTIVE DETENTION. **2.** to retain possession of another's property. —**detention,** n.

detainer n. **1.** a WRIT calling for continued detention of a person about to be released from custody, as when a prisoner is wanted for another crime. **2.** Also called **unlawful detainer.** Wrongfully retaining possession of property of another, as by refusing to vacate an apartment upon expiration of the lease. **3.** any detention of person or property. (See DETAIN.)

detention n. See under DETAIN. See also PREVENTIVE DETENTION.

determinable adj. See *fee simple determinable* (under FEE¹).

determinate sentence. See under SENTENCE.

determine v. **1.** to reach a DECISION on a matter. See also *hear and determine* (under HEAR). **2.** (of an interest in real property) to terminate; come to an end; expire.

detrimental reliance. See under RELIANCE.

devise v. **1.** to dispose of real property by will. Cf. BEQUEATH, GRANT. —n. **2.** a gift of real property by will, or the property interest so given. Cf. BEQUEST. Note that although the very influential Uniform Probate Code uses *devise* in reference to personal as well as real property, that broader usage does not appear to have caught on among practicing lawyers generally.

devisee n. the recipient of a DEVISE. Cf. LEGATEE.

devisor n. one who makes a DEVISE.

devolve v. to pass from one person to another, especially BY OPERATION OF LAW: *Upon President Lincoln's death, the Presidency devolved on Vice President Johnson. When the corporations merged, their debts devolved upon the successor corporation.* —**devolution,** n.

dictum n., pl. **dicta.** *Latin.* (lit. "a remark") short for OBITER DICTUM; a legal assertion in a court's opinion that is peripheral to its main argument and unnecessary to the actual HOLDING. Because it may not have received the court's fullest consideration, dictum is regarded as less persuasive in a precedent than a fully considered holding. Note that "dictum" is used to refer either to a single such assertion or to a number of them collectively; "dicta" can properly be used only if two or more discrete passages are being referred to: *In support of its position, plaintiff cites only dictum. The defendant points to several dicta in older cases, but we find them unpersuasive.*

digest n. a book or series of volumes in which HEADNOTES or other summaries of the holdings of cases are collected and arranged by subject matter for ease of reference by lawyers or others doing legal research.

diligence n. serious and persistent attention and effort. In many contexts the law requires people to exercise diligence in regard to a matter in order to preserve their rights or avoid liability. —**diligent,** adj.

diminished capacity (or **responsibility**), mental retardation or other mental condition, sometimes including intoxication, that is not the kind or degree of impairment necessary to establish the INSANITY DEFENSE, but that calls into question whether a defendant could have had the necessary STATE OF MIND to commit a particular crime. In some jurisdictions this may be considered as a factor reducing the degree of the crime for which a defendant may be convicted.

diplomatic immunity. See under IMMUNITY.

direct¹ adj. **1.** proximate; straightforward; without intervening events. Often distinguished from collateral; for example, a **direct attack** on a judgment is one made in the same case, as by an appeal or motion for a new trial, and a **direct heir** is a direct descendent or ancestor (compare *collateral attack* and *collateral heir,* under COLLATERAL²). See also *direct examination* vs. *cross examination* (under EXAMINATION); *direct evidence* vs. *circumstantial evidence* (under EVIDENCE). —n. **2.** Short for *direct examination* (see under EXAMINATION).

direct² v. (of a judge or court) to instruct or order someone to do something; a gentle way of saying "order": *The jury is directed to disregard the answer. The plaintiff is directed to produce the documents requested by the defendant forthwith. Would Your Honor please direct the witness to answer the question?* In such contexts, "direct" is interchangeable with INSTRUCT. See also *directed verdict* (under VERDICT). —**direction,** n.

director n. one of the persons elected by the stockholders of a corporation to manage its affairs. The directors together constitute the BOARD OF DIRECTORS. Cf. OFFICER.

disability n. **1.** for purposes of insurance, unemployment compensation, social security, and the like, a disease or injury that renders one unable to perform one's usual occupation, or a physical or mental condition making it impossible to engage in any substantial gainful employment. **2.** for purposes of the federal law against DISABILITY DISCRIMINATION, a physical or mental impairment that substantially limits one or more of the major life activities of an individual. **3.** Also called **legal disability.** Same as INCAPACITY.

disability discrimination discrimination against, or failure to provide reasonable accommodation for, people with disabilities or people who have been disabled or are perceived as being disabled, in such areas as employment, public accommodations, transportation, and communications. Such discrimination is prohibited by the federal Americans with Disabilities Act of 1990.

disbar v. to take away an attorney's right to practice law, usually for criminal or unethical conduct.

discharge v. **1.** to release a person from an obligation, or to satisfy or extinguish an obligation. —n. **2.** the release of a person from an obligation or the satisfaction or extinguishment of an obligation. **3.** **discharge in bankruptcy,** the discharge of all or most of a bankrupt's remaining debts at the conclusion of a BANKRUPTCY proceeding.

disclaim v. **1.** to renounce or disavow a right, interest, or claim. **2.** to renounce or disavow a duty or liability. —**disclaimer,** n.

disclosure. See under DISCOVERY.

discontinuance n. DISMISSAL of a suit, especially *voluntary dismissal* (see under DISMISSAL), which is also called **voluntary discontinuance.** —**discontinue,** v.

discovery n. the set of procedures by which each side in a case may obtain pertinent information from the other. The most common discovery techniques are the DEPOSITION, *interrogatories* (see under INTERROGATORY), and PRODUCTION OF DOCUMENTS. Modern practice permits liberal discovery in order to prevent TRIAL BY AMBUSH. Discovery is primarily of use in the period leading up to the trial, and thus is often referred to as **pretrial discovery;** but in some situations it is also conducted during or even after a trial. In some jurisdictions discovery is usually referred to as **disclosure,** which is just the same thing from the point of view of the giver of the information rather than the receiver. Information, documents, or other things that may be obtained through discovery are said to be **discoverable.** See also FISHING EXPEDITION.

discredit *v.* to introduce evidence, by cross examination or otherwise, casting doubt upon the believability of a witness or authenticity of a document.

discretion *n.* **1.** the power to exercise one's own judgment in a matter and choose among various options in dealing with it. **2. absolute discretion,** theoretically unlimited discretion, so that any choice among available options, however unreasonable it might appear, would be immune from challenge. For example, a will might give the executor "absolute discretion" to decide how certain property should be distributed among the testator's children. Even so, a court might set aside a distribution upon a showing that the decision was not made in good faith. **3. judicial discretion,** the power of a judge to make any reasonable ruling on matters with respect to which there is no single "right answer." A court's decision on such a matter may be reversed only for ABUSE OF DISCRETION. **4. prosecutorial discretion,** the discretion of prosecutors in choosing cases to prosecute and accepting or rejecting plea bargains. Not every violation of law can be prosecuted, and prosecutors have wide discretion in deciding which to pursue and which to drop, so long as their decisions are not discriminatory or vindictive.

discretionary appeal. See under APPEAL.

discrimination *n.* **1.** treating some people differently from others for reasons that are extraneous to the matter at hand, especially because of some group membership or characteristic such as race, sex, religion, or national origin. **2.** Also called **illegal discrimination.** discrimination in violation of a state or federal constitution, statute, or regulation. **3. invidious discrimination,** illegal discrimination, especially discrimination on the basis of a SUSPECT CLASSIFICATION. See also AFFIRMATIVE ACTION; AGE DISCRIMINATION; DISABILITY DISCRIMINATION; PREGNANCY DISCRIMINATION; RACIAL DISCRIMINATION; SEPARATE BUT EQUAL; SEX DISCRIMINATION; SEX-PLUS DISCRIMINATION.

dishonor *v.* **1.** to fail or refuse to HONOR an instrument for the payment of money when presented for payment or acceptance. —*n.* **2.** the act of dishonoring an instrument.

disinterested *adj.* lacking in bias or interest (see INTEREST²) in a case. The judge and jurors in a case must be disinterested. Cf. INTERESTED.

dismissal *n.* **1.** an order or judgment in favor of a defendant, throwing a case out of court without a trial, or without completing a trial. **2.** the act of issuing such an order or judgment. **3. dismissal with leave to replead,** dismissal of a civil case because of some inadequacy in the complaint, with permission to file an amended complaint to try to cure the defect. Plaintiffs are normally given at least one chance to replead when their first complaint is inadequate. **4. dismissal with prejudice,** a dismissal barring the plaintiff or prosecution from ever reinstituting the case. **5. dismissal without prejudice,** a dismissal leaving the plaintiff or prosecutor free to try again later if circumstances change. For example, a dismissal for lack of personal jurisdiction would normally be without prejudice to the filing of a new case upon the same claims if jurisdiction can be obtained over the defendant. **6. involuntary dismissal,** dismissal upon motion of the defendant or upon the court's own motion, without the consent of the plaintiff. **7. voluntary dismissal,** dismissal at the request of the plaintiff, or with the plaintiff's consent. —**dismiss,** *v.*

disorderly conduct a term used in some states for

such minor offenses as public drunkenness, public fighting, making too much noise, urinating in public, or other conduct that is mildly dangerous or disturbing to the public. The particular conduct covered by the term must be clearly defined by statute; otherwise the statute making it an offense would be *void for vagueness* (see under VAGUE). Other terms sometimes used for the same general range of offenses include **breach of the peace** and **disturbing the peace.**

disparagement *n.* the communication to third parties of false and derogatory information about a person's property, products, or business, such as to discourage others from doing business with the person or otherwise cause economic and personal injury. Disparagement, also called **injurious falsehood,** is a tort akin to DEFAMATION.

dispossess *v.* to put someone out of possession of real property; for example, to evict a tenant. Cf. QUIT.

dissent *v.* **1.** to declare formally that one disagrees with a course of action being taken by a body of which one is a member, as when a stockholder dissents from a corporate action in order to pursue her APPRAISAL RIGHTS. **2.** specifically, of one or more members of a panel of judges, to put on record the fact that they voted against the decision of the majority. —*n.* **3.** the act of dissenting or the fact that one dissents. **4.** a *dissenting opinion* (see under OPINION).

dissolve *v.* to terminate a legal relationship or bring the legal existence of an entity to an end: *dissolve a marriage; dissolve a partnership; dissolve a corporation.* —**dissolution,** *n.*

distinguish *v.* to recognize or point out differences between a previous case and a case currently under consideration that make it appropriate to reach a different result in the current case. A precedent that can be distinguished in this manner is said to be **distinguishable:** *The cases cited by the plaintiff are distinguishable in that they all involved fiduciary relationships rather than arm's-length contracts.*

distrain *v.* to seize a person's goods as security for an obligation, as when a landlord changes the locks on property upon which the rent has not been paid so that the lessee cannot remove the things inside until the rent has been paid, and if necessary they can be sold for back rent. Distraint is now regulated by statute in all or nearly all states.

distress or **distraint,** *n.* the act of distraining, or the state of being distrained: *The landlord resorted to distraint. The goods are under distress.* The terms are interchangeable.

distributee *n.* **1.** a person entitled to share in the DISTRIBUTION of an intestate's estate or, more broadly, of any decedent's estate. **2.** generally, anyone who shares in any DISTRIBUTION of money or property.

distribution *n.* **1. a.** the parceling out of the property (especially the personal property) of a person who died without a will, to those entitled to it under the rules of INTESTATE SUCCESSION. **b.** more broadly, the parceling out of any decedent's estate, whether by the rules of intestate succession or under a will. See also ADMINISTER, ADMINISTRATOR, EXECUTOR. **2.** generally, any allocation and dispensing of money or property in which a number of people are entitled to share; e.g., a distribution of corporate profits to shareholders in the form of dividends, or the distribution of a bankrupt's assets to creditors. **3.** the total amount of money subject to such a distribution. **4.** Also called **distributive share.** the portion of an estate or other aggregate of property received by a particular DISTRIBUTEE. —**distribute,** *v.*

district *n.* **1.** generally, any geographic division established by a government for administrative convenience: *school district; election district.* **2.** Also called **judicial district.** a geographic division established for purposes of organizing a court system. For federal judicial purposes, the United States is divided into over ninety such districts, with at least one for every state or other federal political subdivision, and from two to four in each of the larger states: *District of Delaware; District of Guam; West-*

ern District of Texas. See also UNITED STATES ATTORNEY; UNITED STATES DISTRICT COURT. Cf. CIRCUIT.

district attorney the public official responsible for managing the prosecution of criminal offenses under state law in a particular locality.

disturbing the peace. See under DISORDERLY CONDUCT.

diversity case. See under CASE¹.

diversity jurisdiction. See under JURISDICTION¹.

diversity of citizenship the situation that exists when a plaintiff and defendant in a federal case are citizens of different states. Often called **diversity** for short. Diversity is one of the two major grounds upon which a federal court can exercise jurisdiction over a case. See *subject matter jurisdiction* and *diversity jurisdiction* (under JURISDICTION¹).

dividend *n.* a portion of the earnings and profits of a corporation distributed to the shareholders in proportion to their holdings: *The company paid a year-end dividend of $1.25 per share.*

divorce *n.* **1.** the termination of a marriage other than by death. This can be accomplished in the United States only by obtaining a judgment (typically called a **divorce decree**) from a court in accordance with state law. The divorce decree typically includes provisions regarding division of property, custody of children, and alimony and child support. **2.** **no-fault divorce,** a divorce obtained without assessing blame on either party for the breakdown of the marriage. Traditionally, divorce was permitted only if one party proved wrongdoing by the other, such as ADULTERY, CRUELTY, or DESERTION. Now most divorces are granted without any showing of fault, and many states have completely abolished the concept of fault as a basis for divorce. —*v.* **3.** to obtain a divorce.

docket *n.* **1.** a chronological record of steps taken in a case—papers filed, orders entered, trial days held, etc.—maintained by a court clerk. **2.** sometimes, a court CALENDAR. —*v.* **3.** to record on a docket.

doctrine *n.* a legal principle. The term sometimes connotes a firm rule, sometimes a general guideline to be applied flexibly and judiciously.

document *n.* anything upon which information is recorded; most often a writing (including telephone message slips, checks, grocery lists), but also, in some contexts, photographs, audio tapes, computer files, or any other form in which information can be preserved. See also PRODUCTION OF DOCUMENTS.

document of title 1. a document, such as a BILL OF LADING or WAREHOUSE RECEIPT, issued by or addressed to a person or entity entrusted with goods for storage or shipment, identifying the goods and serving as evidence of the right of the person with the document to receive the goods or direct their delivery. **2.** **negotiable document of title,** a document of title stating that the specified goods are to be delivered either to the order of a named person or simply to whoever presents the document. Title to the goods covered by such a document can be transferred from a seller to a buyer simply by indorsing and handing over the document. The buyer then presents the document to receive the goods. **3.** **nonnegotiable document of title,** a document of title that provides for delivery of the goods covered by it only to a specific named person, who need not present the document to receive the goods.

documentary evidence. See under EVIDENCE.

doing business (of a corporation) conducting regular activity within a particular state, of a nature sufficient to justify holding the corporation subject to suit in the state even on causes of action that are unrelated to any particular business transacted there. An out-of-state corporation found to be "doing business" in the state is deemed to be present in the state and subject to the jurisdiction of its courts for all purposes. Cf. TRANSACTION OF BUSINESS.

domain. See EMINENT DOMAIN; PUBLIC DOMAIN.

domestic *adj.* pertaining to the internal workings of the United States, a particular state, or a family. See, for example, *domestic corporation* (under CORPORATION); *domestic relations* (under FAMILY LAW).

domestic partnership a committed relationship between two unmarried people, of the same or opposite sex, analogous to a marriage. Some municipalities and some private companies formally recognize such relationships, particularly for same-sex couples, granting them the same status and employment benefits as married couples.

domicile *n.* the place where one has one's permanent and primary home, or where a corporation has its headquarters or principal place of business; the place with which one is associated for taxing and voting purposes. One can have many residences, but only one domicile. One whose domicile is in a particular place is said to be **domiciled** there or to be a **domiciliary** of that place: *a person domiciled in Paris; an Idaho domiciliary.* See also RESIDENCE; RESIDENT.

donee *n.* **1.** the recipient of a gift. **2.** the person designated to exercise a POWER OF APPOINTMENT.

donor *n.* **1.** a person who makes a gift. **2.** one who confers a POWER OF APPOINTMENT. **3.** the SETTLOR of a trust.

double jeopardy being put in JEOPARDY twice for the same offense. This is prohibited by the Fifth Amendment (see Appendix), so that a defendant who has been acquitted may not be tried again in the hope of a conviction, a defendant who has been convicted may not be tried again to increase the punishment, and the government, seeing that a trial is going badly, may not ask for a mistrial in the hope of doing better with a new jury and a fresh start. On the other hand, a defendant may be retried if a conviction is overturned on appeal, if a mistrial is declared at the request of the defendant or because of a hung jury or other circumstance beyond the control of the prosecution, or if the same conduct also constitutes an offense in another jurisdiction.

doubt *n.* See BEYOND A REASONABLE DOUBT.

draft *n.* **1.** an instrument by which one person (the drawer) orders another (the drawee) to pay a specified sum of money to the order of someone else (the payee), or to the bearer. Also (but no longer commonly) called a **bill of exchange.** The most common form of draft is an ordinary check. See also NEGOTIABLE INSTRUMENT. **2.** **time draft,** a draft that is not payable until a specified time in the future. **3.** **sight draft,** a draft payable on demand.

draw *v.* **1.** to prepare a legal instrument: *draw a contract; draw a will.* **2.** to prepare and sign an instrument for the payment of money, especially a DRAFT. The person who draws a draft is called the **drawer,** the person ordered by the draft to pay money (often a bank) is the **drawee,** and the person designated to receive the money is the PAYEE; the draft is said to be drawn "on" the drawee and "to" or "payable to" the payee. Cf. MAKE. **3.** to withdraw money from a fund or account.

driving while intoxicated (DWI) the offense of driving a motor vehicle while intoxicated by alcohol or other drugs that impair driving ability. Also referred to in various jurisdictions as **driving under the influence (DUI), driving while impaired (DWI),** or **driving while ability impaired (DWAI),** and commonly known everywhere as **drunk driving.** In some jurisdictions several such terms are used to designate varying degrees of intoxication.

drug *n.* **1.** a substance intended to affect the structure or function of the body of humans or animals, or intended for use in the diagnosis, treatment, or prevention of disease in humans or animals. Such substances are subject to regulation by the federal Food and Drug Administration. **2.** a CONTROLLED SUBSTANCE.

drunk driving *Informal.* Same as DRIVING WHILE INTOXICATED.

duces tecum *Latin.* (lit. "you will bring with you") See *subpoena duces tecum* (under SUBPOENA).

due *adj.* **1.** appropriate to the circumstances; such as is required to fulfill legal obligations or satisfy legal standards: *due care* (see under CARE); *due diligence; due demand* (see under DEMAND); *due delivery;* DUE PROCESS. **2.** owing; supposed to be paid or performed now; to be paid or performed at the time

legal

specified: *The rent is due. The account is past due. Payment is due upon delivery.*

due process 1. fair administration of law in accordance with established procedures and with due regard for the fundamental rights and liberties of people in a free society. The concept is embodied in the Fifth and Fourteenth Amendments to the Constitution, which prohibit the federal government and state governments, respectively, from depriving any person "of life, LIBERTY, or PROPERTY, without due process of law." These provisions are interpreted as dealing primarily with the PROCEDURE by which law is administered (see *procedural due process*), but also as having some smaller and less well defined role in assessment of the SUBSTANCE of laws whose effect would be to deprive people of FUNDAMENTAL RIGHTS (see *substantive due process*). **2. procedural due process,** the concept that in administering a system of justice, and in taking any official action aimed at depriving a particular person of life, liberty, or property, the government must follow, and require individual litigants to follow, established and known rules, and that those rules must be fundamentally fair. At a minimum, the persons directly affected must be given NOTICE and an OPPORTUNITY TO BE HEARD; at the maximum, in criminal cases, a wide array of due process protections comes into play, from the MIRANDA RULE to proof BEYOND A REASONABLE DOUBT. **3. substantive due process,** the concept that there are some freedoms so fundamental that any law taking them away, absent a COMPELLING INTEREST, must be struck down as a deprivation of liberty without due process. Some such freedoms, notably the First Amendment freedoms of speech, press, religion, and assembly, are specified in the Constitution (see INCORPORATION DOCTRINE); others, including the RIGHT TO TRAVEL and the RIGHT OF PRIVACY in areas of marriage and childbearing, are regarded as inherent in the concept of LIBERTY. See also SCRUTINY.

durable power of attorney. See under POWER OF ATTORNEY.

durable power of attorney for health care. Same as HEALTH CARE PROXY.

duress *n.* the use of force, or the threat of force or of other unlawful acts, to induce someone to do something that she otherwise would not do, such as sign an instrument or commit a crime. Conduct that is induced by duress of such a nature that a person of reasonable firmness would not have been able to resist it is usually relieved of its normal legal effect; for example, a will signed under duress may be void, a contract signed under duress is usually voidable, and duress can constitute a complete defense to a criminal charge. Also called **coercion.**

duty *n.* **1.** a legal obligation, whether imposed by operation of law (e.g., the duty to pay one's taxes or to exercise due care so as to avoid unnecessary injury to others) or assumed voluntarily (e.g., the duty to perform a contract or repay a debt). See also FIDUCIARY DUTY; OBLIGATION. **2.** a tax on imports or exports.

dying declaration. See under DECLARATION.

E

abcd **E** fghijklmnopqrstuvwxyz

earned income. See under INCOME.

easement *n.* **1.** an interest in land belonging to another, consisting of a right to use it or control its use for some purpose, but not to take anything from it or possess it. **2. affirmative easement,** an easement allowing the holder of the easement to go on the land; for example, a right to use a path across the land. **3. easement appurtenant,** an easement in one piece of land specifically for the benefit of another; for example, a right to cross someone else's land in order to reach one's own, which otherwise would be inaccessible (**easement of access**). Such an easement passes automatically with any transfer of title to the benefited land. **4. easement in gross,** an easement whose benefit is unrelated to specific other land; for example, an easement granted to a public utility company to run wires over or pipes under the property burdened with the easement. **5. negative easement,** an easement whose only effect is to limit the use that the owner of the burdened property can make of that land; for example, an easement in a neighbor's property prohibiting its owner from spoiling one's view by building above a certain height. **6. public easement,** an easement for the benefit of the public at large, such as a street across private land. See also BURDEN². Cf. PROFIT (def. 2).

eavesdropping *n.* **1.** the act of listening in on conversations or activities of others without their knowledge. If done without any trespass and without electronic or other artificial assistance, this in itself normally has no legal consequences. **2. electronic eavesdropping,** eavesdropping by means of hidden microphones or other electronic aids. This is severely restricted by law; see WIRETAP. See also SURVEILLANCE.

effective assistance of counsel. See under RIGHT TO COUNSEL.

effective tax rate. See under TAX RATE.

ejectment *n.* the traditional name for an action to obtain possession of land from another person, such as a holdover tenant or a person claiming ownership of the land, by establishing paramount title to the property.

elect *v.* to make a choice in a situation where the law presents two permissible alternatives but allows only one to be selected: *The couple elected to file income tax returns separately rather than jointly. Since Congress does not allow immigrants to have dual citizenship, an immigrant must elect between becoming a United States citizen and retaining her original citizenship.*

election *n.* **1.** the act of making a legally required choice, or the choice made. **2. election of remedies,** a plaintiff's choice among available remedies for the same wrong; e.g., between return of an item of property wrongfully taken and payment for the loss. **3. election under the will,** an election by a person named in a will either to be bound by all of the terms of a will or to give up all rights under the will and pursue independent claims to property in the estate. One cannot ordinarily take what one is given under a will and also assert claims to property that the will left to someone else. **4. spouse's** (or **widow's** or **widower's**) **election,** the election of a surviving spouse either to take the property left to her under the decedent's will or to take her ELECTIVE SHARE of the estate.

elective share the share of a decedent's estate that the surviving spouse is entitled to under state law when a married person dies and leaves a will. If the will leaves a different amount, the survivor may (but need not) choose to take the elective share instead of what the will provides. Also called **statutory share; spouse's** (or **widow's** or **widower's**) **elective** (or **statutory**) **share.** See also *spouse's election* and *election under the will* (both under ELECTION).

electronic eavesdropping. See under EAVESDROPPING.

electronic surveillance. See under SURVEILLANCE.

element *n.* a constituent part of something; especially, one of the components of a crime or cause of action that must be proved to sustain a charge or claim. For example, the usual elements of a claim for fraud are: (1) a false representation by the defendant, (2) knowledge by the defendant of the falsity, (3) intent by the defendant to induce some conduct by the plaintiff, (4) reasonable reliance by the plaintiff, and (5) resulting damage to the plaintiff.

emancipation *n.* **1.** the freeing of slaves in the United States by the Emancipation Proclamation issued by President Lincoln during the Civil War, confirmed after the war by the Thirteenth Amendment (see Appendix). **2.** the freeing of a minor from parental control (and of parents from their duties toward the child), giving the child the right to keep and control her own earnings and make decisions with regard to such matters as her own medical care. This may occur by agreement of parent and child, by order of a court upon petition of the child, or automatically upon marriage. A minor after emancipation is called an **emancipated minor.**

embezzlement *n.* the crime of converting to one's own use property of another that is lawfully within one's possession. The usual case involves the taking of money over which one gains control in the course of one's job.

embracery *n.* an old word for the crime of improperly attempting to influence a jury, now usually dealt with in statutes on bribery and obstruction of justice.

eminent domain the inherent power of a government to take private property for public purposes, e.g., to build a road or reservoir. See also TAKING; JUST COMPENSATION.

emolument *n.* anything received as compensation for services, especially by a public or corporate official.

Employee Retirement Income Security Act of 1974 (ERISA). See under PENSION PLAN.

employee stock option. See under STOCK OPTION.

employers' liability act. See under WORKERS' COMPENSATION.

employers' liability insurance. See under WORKERS' COMPENSATION.

employment. See SCOPE OF EMPLOYMENT.

en banc *Law French.* (lit. "as a bench") referring to consideration of a matter by all of the judges of a court together, as distinguished from a single judge or a panel. Some courts, including the Supreme Court, normally sit en banc; other courts, notably the United States Courts of Appeals, do so only in special situations. See also PANEL; REARGUMENT.

enabling *adj.* **1.** (in reference to a statute) authorizing an official or agency to take the necessary steps to carry out a law or policy: *enabling clause; enabling legislation.* **2.** broadly, authorizing any particular conduct by anyone.

encouragement *n.* conduct by a law enforcement officer creating an opportunity for a suspect to commit a crime and encouraging the suspect to do it. The fact that a crime was induced by such encouragement is not a defense in a subsequent prosecution for that crime. Cf. ENTRAPMENT.

encumbrance *n.* any interest, right, or obligation with respect to property that reduces the value or completeness of the property owner's title; for example, a mortage, lease, easement, or covenant.

endorse *v.* **1.** to show support for or approval of: *to endorse a candidate; to endorse another court's interpretation of the law.* **2.** to write something on a document, as in the margin or on the back: *Instead of issuing a typed opinion regarding the motion, the judge endorsed her two-sentence decision on the notice of motion.* **3.** (in the law of negotiable instruments) to INDORSE. In this field, the spelling "indorse" has become standard in American (but not British) legal writing, although "endorse" is acceptable and is still preferred in nonlegal writing. —**endorsement,** *n.*

English-only law a popular name for any of a variety of laws in a number of states, and of proposed federal laws, that designate English as the "official" language, require the use of English for various governmental purposes, and the like. These laws do not appear to have deterred lawyers and judges from using Latin locutions like CORPUS DELICTI, EX POST FACTO, and IN LOCO PARENTIS in official proceedings.

enjoin *v.* to issue an INJUNCTION against; to forbid by court order: *The judge enjoined the sale of the land* (or *enjoined the parties from selling the land*).

enjoy *v.* to possess or exercise a right or interest: *Americans enjoy the right of trial by jury in criminal cases.* See also QUIET ENJOYMENT.

enlarge *v.* **1.** to expand: *The statute enlarged the rights of judgment creditors.* **2.** especially, to extend a procedural time limit: *Defendant moved for an enlargement of the time to respond to the complaint.* —**enlargement,** *n.*

enter *v.* **1.** to go onto or into real property. **2.** to place formally in the record, especially a court record, as by adding to the court file or making a notation in a docket, judgment book, or the like: *enter an appearance; enter an order; enter judgment for the defendant.* See also ENTRY.

enticement *n.* **1.** Also called enticement of a child. the crime of luring a child into a secluded place for sexual purposes. **2.** For the meaning in tort law, see under ABDUCTION.

entirety *n.* See BY THE ENTIRETY.

entitlement *n.* a legislatively created right or benefit, such as a driver's license or welfare benefits, which, once granted to a person, cannot be taken away without a fair hearing to make sure that the recipient is no longer entitled to the benefit. Entitlements are sometimes regarded as PROPERTY and sometimes as a LIBERTY; either way, the Supreme Court holds that they cannot be taken away from an individual without *procedural due process* (see under DUE PROCESS).

entrapment *n.* the planning of a crime by law enforcement agents and their procuring of its commission by a person who had no predisposition to do it and would not have done so but for the trickery of the officers. Entrapment is a defense in a subsequent prosecution for the crime, but the police conduct must be extreme for the defense to succeed. Cf. ENCOURAGEMENT.

entry *n.* **1.** the act of entering (see ENTER). **2.** a notation entered in a record.

enumerated power. See under POWER.

equal protection the principle that law should be even-handed in its application and that people should be free from irrational and invidious discrimination at the hands of the government. Under the Fourteenth Amendment (see Appendix), a state government may not "deny to any person within its jurisdiction the equal protection of the laws," and the DUE PROCESS clause of the Fifth Amendment has been interpreted as extending the principle of equal protection to the federal government as well. Thus any law or governmental practice having a discriminatory purpose or effect is subject to challenge in the courts to determine whether it meets constitutional standards. See also SCRUTINY; SEPARATE BUT EQUAL.

equitable *adj.* **1.** pertaining to, enforceable under, or derived from principles of EQUITY as distinguished from LAW (def. 4). See, for example, *equitable* ACTION, DEFENSE, ESTOPPEL, REMEDY, RIGHT under those words. **2.** in particular, describing property rights and interests deriving from something other than legal title, including the rights of a trust beneficiary with respect to the property held in trust. See, for example, *equitable* ESTATE¹, OWNER, INTEREST¹, TITLE under those words. **3.** fair; consistent with fundamental justice. See, for example, EQUITABLE DISTRIBUTION.

equitable action. See under ACTION.

equitable distribution a method of dividing property in a divorce case, authorized by statute in most states, under which the court allocates property acquired by the couple during marriage according to what seems fair, without regard to whether *legal title* (see under TITLE) is in the name of the husband or the wife. The court takes into account a wide range of factors, such as the relative earning capacity of the parties and the role that each played in the family as an economic unit, including a homemaker's contribution to overall family welfare.

equity *n.* **1.** one of the two systems of justice that grew up side by side in England and together gave rise to the present-day system of justice in both

England and the United States. Equity was a flexible system in which judges were able to fashion remedies for situations that did not fit within principles followed in the courts of LAW (def. 4); it was less concerned with technicalities and more concerned with reaching a fair result—"doing equity." Its most notable power was the power to issue INJUNCTIONS. See also MERGER OF LAW AND EQUITY. **2.** overall fairness; justice in a moral as well as legal sense. See also BALANCING OF THE EQUITIES. **3.** the net value of an owner's interest in property; the market value of the property minus amounts still owed on debts secured by mortgages or liens on the property. **4.** the *net assets* (see under ASSET) of an enterprise, representing the value of the owners' interest in the business.

equity of redemption a statutory right to avoid losing one's property through foreclosure of a mortgage by paying off the mortgage in full, with interest and costs, within a specified time after default.

equity security. See under SECURITY².

ERISA. See under PENSION PLAN.

error *n.* **1.** an incorrect ruling by a judge in a case, as determined by a higher court on appeal. In a nonjury trial, there can be error in the judge's findings of fact (see CLEARLY ERRONEOUS); however, the word is most often used in reference to rulings on matters of law, as in admitting or excluding certain evidence or giving certain instructions to the jury. **2. harmless error,** an error that did not affect the outcome of the case or prejudice a substantial right of a party. Reversal will not be granted on the basis of errors deemed to be harmless. **3. plain error,** an error so obviously prejudicial to substantial rights of a party that it amounts to an affront to the judicial system. Such an error will result in reversal even if the party adversely affected by it failed to object to it. Also called **fundamental error. 4. reversible error,** an error that prejudiced the appellant in a way that could have affected the outcome of the trial. Such an error, if properly objected to when the ruling was made, requires modification or reversal of the judgment. Also called **prejudicial error.** See also STANDARD OF REVIEW. **—erroneous,** *adj.*

escheat *n.* **1.** the reverting of property to the state if no claimant with a right to it can be found, especially upon the death of an owner who leaves no will and no known heirs. **—v. 2.** to revert to the state by escheat.

escrow *n.* **1.** money or a deed or other instrument deposited with a third person for delivery to a given party upon the fulfillment of some condition. While in the keeping of the third party, the money or instrument is said to be "in escrow." **—v. 2.** to place into escrow.

Esq. abbreviation of *Esquire,* a title often appended (usually in abbreviated form) to the names of American lawyers (instead of putting Mr. or Ms. in front of the name) in addressing letters or in certain other formal contexts.

esse. See IN ESSE.

essence. See OF THE ESSENCE.

establishment of religion governmental sponsorship of religion, including financial support for a religion or religions at public expense. This is prohibited by the **Establishment Clause** of the First Amendment to the Constitution. Under current Supreme Court doctrine, a government program having the effect of providing public financial support for religion does not violate the Establishment Clause if it is regarded as (1) having a secular purpose, (2) having a primary effect that neither aids nor inhibits religion, and (3) not involving "excessive entanglement" of government and religion. See also SEPARATION OF CHURCH AND STATE.

estate¹ *n.* **1.** an interest in real property which is or may become possessory; that is, it either confers upon the owner of the interest a current right to exclusive possession of the property for some period of time or embodies at least the possibility that the owner will have such a right in the future. An estate may be designated as JOINT, BY THE ENTIRETY, IN COMMON, or IN SEVERALTY, depending upon the ownership arrangement, and as either a **legal estate** or

a **beneficial** (or **equitable**) **estate,** depending upon whether it is viewed from the perspective of a *legal owner* or, in the case of property held in trust, a *beneficial owner* (see both phrases under OWNER). Because an estate is a form of property interest and a tenancy is a form of estate, the words "estate," "interest," and "tenancy" are interchangeable in many contexts. See INTEREST¹; TENANCY. **2. contingent estate,** an estate that is not yet possessory, and in which the owner's right of exclusive possession in the future depends upon circumstances that are not certain to occur. For example, if A grants land "to B so long as the property is used for church purposes," then A retains a contingent estate in the land, called a POSSIBILITY OF REVERTER, because it is possible (but not certain) that the condition for continuation of B's estate will be violated and the land will revert to A's possession. Cf. *vested estate.* **3. estate** (or **tenancy**) **in fee.** Same as FEE¹. **4. future estate,** an estate which has not yet become possessory. For example, a grant of property "to A for life, then to B" gives B a future estate (called a REMAINDER), because B's right of possession will not arise until A dies. For types of future estate, see *executory interest* (under INTEREST¹); POSSIBILITY OF REVERTER; REMAINDER; REVERSION. Cf. *possessory estate.* **5. life estate** (or **tenancy**), an estate whose duration is measured by the life of some person or group of people (the MEASURING LIFE or lives); for example, the estates granted by the words "to A for life," "to B during the life of his mother," or "to C Church so long as any of its present parishioners remain alive." Also called **estate** (or **tenancy**) **for life** or, when the measuring life is not the grantee's own, **estate** (or **tenancy**) **pur autre vie** (*Law French.* lit. "for another life"). **6. possessory estate,** an estate whose owner has a current right to exclusive possession of the property, at least for a while. Also called **present estate** or **present possessory estate.** Cf. *future estate.* A possessory estate may be classified as either a **freehold estate** (same as FREEHOLD) or a **leasehold estate** (same as LEASEHOLD). For types of leasehold estate, see under TENANCY. **7. vested estate,** an estate that is either possessory or certain to become so in due course; the owner's right to eventual possession is not subject to a contingency. For example, if land has been granted "to A for life, then to B," both A's present estate (a *life estate*) and B's future estate (a REMAINDER) are vested estates: A's because it is already possessory, and B's because it will become possessory upon A's death, which is certain to occur. If B is no longer alive at that point, B's heirs or other successors will possess the property. Cf. *contingent estate.*

estate² *n.* **1.** an aggregate of money and property administered as a unit. **2. bankruptcy estate,** the total assets of a person or entity in bankruptcy. Also called **estate in bankruptcy. 3. decedent's estate,** all money and property owned by a decedent at the time of death. **4. residuary estate,** in the case of a decedent who left a will, whatever is left of the decedent's estate after payment of debts and expenses and distribution of all bequests save the *residuary bequest* (see under BEQUEST). Also called the **residue** of the estate.

estate tax a tax imposed on large estates left by decedents, based upon the value of the estate and required to be paid out of estate funds before the estate is distributed to heirs or takers under a will. Cf. INHERITANCE TAX.

estimated tax an advance on income taxes that must be paid approximately quarterly by taxpayers whose income is not subject to WITHHOLDING TAX, or whose withholding will not substantially cover their tax liability for the year.

estop *v.* to hinder or prevent by ESTOPPEL. When the doctrine of estoppel bars a litigant from taking a position at trial contrary to a prior assertion, he is said to be "estopped to deny" or "estopped from denying" the truth of the assertion.

estoppel *n.* **1.** a bar or impediment preventing a litigant in certain situations from asserting facts or claims inconsistent with facts previously established or with his own prior assertions or conduct. **2. col-lateral estoppel,** the doctrine that a person who has had a full and fair opportunity to litigate an issue of importance to a case and had the issue resolved against him may not relitigate the issue in a subsequent case involving the same parties. Sometimes the estoppel extends to subsequent cases against other parties as well. Also called **issue preclusion. 3. equitable estoppel,** the doctrine that one who makes an assertion (or by conduct creates an impression) upon which another relies may not turn around and assert the opposite to gain advantage in subsequent litigation against the other person. The doctrines of LACHES and *apparent authority* (see under AUTHORITY[1]) are essentially special applications of equitable estoppel. **4. promissory estoppel,** the doctrine under which a promise that is not enforceable under traditional principles of contract law (for example, for lack of consideration) may nevertheless be enforced to the extent necessary to prevent injustice if the promisor should reasonably have expected that the promisee would take substantial action in reliance upon the promise, and the promisee did so.

et al. *Latin.* abbreviation for *et alius* ("and another") or *et alii* ("and others"); used primarily as a stand-in for the names of all parties except the first on each side of a case in the CAPTION on court papers. In citations to cases, even this is usually left out, and only the last name of the first party on each side is listed unless there is a special reason for indicating that there were others involved.

et seq. *Latin.* abbreviation for *et sequentia* ("and those following"); used in citations to include a number of pages or sections beyond the one listed: *appellant's brief at page* (or *pages) 34 et seq.*

et ux. *Latin.* abbreviation for *et uxor* ("and wife"); formerly used instead of the wife's name in case names and legal documents involving a husband and wife jointly: *Smith et ux. v. Jones.*

ethics *n.pl.* **1.** standards of honesty and fairness in the conduct of a business or profession, often embodied in written rules adopted by professional associations. See also UNETHICAL CONDUCT. **2.** moral principles generally.

eviction *n.* **1.** a landlord's exclusion of a tenant from possession of leased premises, either by legal proceedings or by personal action. **2. actual eviction,** physically excluding a tenant, as by changing the lock while the tenant is out. **3. constructive eviction,** conduct by a landlord rendering leased premises unfit for use and thus, as a practical matter, forcing the tenant out.

evidence *n.* **1.** information and things pertaining to the events that are the subject of a case, especially the testimony or objects (but not the questions or comments of the lawyers) offered at a trial or hearing for the judge or jury to consider in deciding the issues in the case. **2. character evidence,** evidence pertaining to the CHARACTER of a party or a witness. **3. circumstantial evidence,** evidence of a fact that makes the existence of another fact—one that actually must be decided in the case—more or less likely. Circumstantial evidence is not second-class evidence; it is as valid, as admissible, and as acceptable a basis for a verdict as *direct evidence.* Most evidence in most cases is circumstantial, and many kinds of issues, such as intent and good faith, depend upon a SUBJECTIVE TEST that cannot be satisfied in any other way. **4. competent evidence,** evidence that is ADMISSIBLE. **5. cumulative evidence,** additional evidence introduced to prove a fact for which there has already been considerable evidence, adding little to what has already been admitted. A trial judge has discretion to draw the line at a reasonable point and preclude further evidence on a particular issue, or of a particular type, on the ground that it is cumulative. **6. demonstrative evidence,** evidence that the jury can perceive directly instead of just being told about it by a witness, including documents and objects involved in the incident giving rise to a case, lawyers' charts and diagrams admitted into evidence, courtroom demonstrations, site visits, and the demeanor of

witnesses. **7. direct evidence,** evidence purportedly showing the existence or nonexistence of a fact that must be decided in a case without the need for any application of reasoning or linking of related facts; sometimes a document or other *real evidence,* most often the testimony of an eyewitness. See EYEWITNESS for discussion of reliability. Cf. *circumstantial evidence.* **8. documentary evidence,** *real evidence* in the form of a DOCUMENT. **9. extrinsic evidence,** evidence pertaining to a written instrument such as a deed, contract, or will, beyond what is contained in the writing itself. See also PAROL EVIDENCE. **10. hearsay evidence.** See under HEARSAY. **11. opinion evidence,** testimony as to what a witness believes or concludes about a situation as distinguished from what the witness personally observed. Except for opinions on matters within common experience ("He sounded angry." "She acted drunk."), opinion evidence may be given only by an *expert witness* rather than a *fact witness* (see both under WITNESS). **12. real evidence,** broadly, any *demonstrative evidence;* specifically, a document or other object offered as having been involved in the events that are the subject of the case, such as a murder weapon, a ransom note, or a bloody glove. See also BEST EVIDENCE RULE; *burden of producing evidence* (under BURDEN[1]); EXHIBIT; IN EVIDENCE; MATERIAL; PAROL EVIDENCE; PREPONDERANCE OF THE EVIDENCE; *prima facie evidence* (under PRIMA FACIE); RELEVANT; STATE'S EVIDENCE; SUBSTANTIAL EVIDENCE; *weight of the evidence* (under WEIGHT); WITNESS.

evidentiary fact. See under FACT.

ex contractu *Latin.* (lit. "arising from a contract") based upon a contract: *a right ex contractu; an action ex contractu.*

ex delicto *Latin.* (lit. "arising from a wrong") based upon a breach of duty other than a contractual promise, as a tort or a crime: *an action ex delicto; a trust ex delicto.*

ex officio *Latin.* (lit. "by virtue of office") describing a position or power that comes automatically with a particular office: *As chairman of the board, she sits ex officio on the executive committee.*

ex parte *Latin.* (lit. "from a side") done by, for, or with one side of a case or dispute without notice to the other side: *an ex parte application for a restraining order; an order granted ex parte; an ex parte conversation between the judge and the plaintiff's attorney.* The situations in which ex parte proceedings are allowed are very limited. See, for example, *temporary restraining order* (under RESTRAINING ORDER). Cf. ON NOTICE.

ex post facto *Latin.* (lit. "from what is done afterward") retroactive; retroactively; after the fact. The Constitution prohibits the states and the federal government from passing any "ex post facto Law"—that is, any law that criminalizes conduct that was legal at the time it was done, or increases the penalty for a crime after it was committed. Laws affecting civil rights and duties can be made retroactive, however, as frequently occurs when tax laws are changed.

ex rel. *Latin.* abbreviation for *ex relatione* (lit. "on the proposal of"); an abbreviation appearing in the names of certain kinds of proceedings brought by a state or the United States on behalf of a private party (the RELATOR): *State of New York ex rel. Smith v. Jones* (Smith is the relator at whose request or for whose benefit the state instituted the action against Jones). Some courts and lawyers use English equivalents such as "on behalf of," "for the use of," or, most commonly, **on the relation of.** All such phrases are usually shortened to "ex rel." in citations.

examination *n.* **1.** the questioning of a witness at a trial, hearing, or deposition. Examination of a witness begins with **direct examination,** also called **examination in chief,** by the side that called the witness, followed by **cross examination** by the other side. Then each side in turn may ask follow-up questions, called **redirect examination** and **recross examination** respectively, alternating back and forth until both sides run out of questions. Informally, these stages are called **direct, cross, redi-**

legal

rect, and **recross,** without the word "examination." Ordinarily, only subjects that were raised on direct may be inquired about on cross. Each redirect and recross is strictly limited to follow-up on the testimony in the immediately preceding examination, so these are quite brief. See also SCOPE OF EXAMINATION; BEYOND THE SCOPE; OPEN THE DOOR; SCOPE OF EXAMINATION. **2. examination before trial,** a pretrial DEPOSITION. **3. examination in aid of execution.** Same as a *deposition in aid of execution* (see under DEPOSITION).

examine *v.* **1.** to ask questions of a witness at a trial, hearing, or deposition: *The lawyers for both sides examined the chauffeur at length.* **2. cross-examine,** to conduct the cross examination of a witness: *After Mr. Jones examined the chauffeur, Miss Smith cross-examined her.* Also, very informally, **cross.** Note that there are no parallel expressions "to direct-examine" or "to direct." —**examiner,** *n.*

examined copy a copy of a document that has been compared with the original and found to be accurate. See also CERTIFIED COPY

exception *n.* **1.** a special situation excluded from coverage of an otherwise applicable rule, principle, contract, insurance policy, etc.; e.g., *hearsay exception* (see under HEARSAY). **2.** a formal objection to a judge's overruling of an objection or denial of a motion at a trial, formerly required in order to preserve the issue for appeal. Modern rules of practice do away with the tedious and silly requirement of taking exception every time a trial judge makes an adverse ruling.

excess insurance supplemental insurance to cover a portion of potential loss in excess of the limits of other policies; essentially a policy with a large deductible. A company with large risks might have a basic insurance policy and several layers of excess insurance from different insurers, with coverage under each policy picking up where the previous one leaves off.

excessive bail. See under BAIL¹.

excessive verdict. See under VERDICT.

excise or **excise tax, 1.** a tax on products manufactured, sold, or used within the country; e.g., a gasoline tax, liquor tax, or tobacco tax. **2.** a tax paid for the privilege of carrying on certain transactions or activities; e.g., a FRANCHISE TAX.

excited utterance a statement about a startling event or condition made in the excitement caused by the situation. Such utterances are usually admitted into evidence as an exception to the rule against HEARSAY on the theory that people cannot make up lies under such circumstances. (Of course, their perceptions may be distorted.) Also called **spontaneous declaration** (or **statement** or **exclamation**).

exclusion *n.* **1.** the act of a judge in refusing to allow proffered evidence to be considered in a case. Cf. ADMISSION; RECEIVE. See also EXCLUSIONARY RULE. **2.** the act of a judge in barring certain people, especially prospective witnesses in a case, from the courtroom during a trial. See also SEQUESTER. **3.** the omission of a particular class of people, property, transactions, or events from coverage of a statute or of a contract or other instrument, or a provision expressly rejecting such coverage. In particular, **a.** the specification in an insurance policy of particular risks not covered by the policy. **b.** the specification in a tax law of particular kinds of income, property, or transactions that will not be subject to the tax; for example, the exclusion of most municipal bond interest from income subject to the federal income tax. —**exclude,** *v.*

exclusionary rule the principle that the prosecution in a criminal case may not use evidence obtained in violation of the Constitution, particularly evidence derived from an illegal search and seizure in violation of the Fourth Amendment (see Appendix). In recent years the Supreme Court has created several exceptions to this rule, including the GOOD FAITH EXCEPTION and the INEVITABLE DISCOVERY EXCEPTION. See also FRUIT OF THE POISONOUS TREE.

exclusionary zoning. See under ZONING.

exclusive jurisdiction. See under JURISDICTION¹.

exclusive zoning. See under ZONING.

exculpatory statement. See under STATEMENT.

excusable neglect. See under NEGLECT.

execute *v.* **1.** to sign a legal instrument such as a deed, will, or contract, and sometimes to take additional steps necessary to put the instrument into effect, such as delivering a deed or acknowledging a will. **2.** to carry out an obligation fully; to complete performance. **3.** to carry out a court order or judgment; especially, to seize and, if necessary, sell property of a *judgment debtor* (see under DEBTOR) to satisfy a money judgment. **4.** to put a person to death pursuant to a death sentence. —**execution,** *n.*

executed *adj.* **1.** complete; fully performed; leaving no uncertainty to be resolved. In this sense, an "executed contract" is one that has been performed by both parties, leaving nothing for either side to do. Opposite of EXECUTORY. **2.** signed; fully effective: *executed will; executed deed.*

executive *adj.* pertaining to the branch of government charged with implementing the law, headed at the state level by the governor of each state and at the national level by the President, and operating through executive departments and administrative agencies. See also SEPARATION OF POWERS.

executive agreement an agreement between the United States and one or more other countries, entered into by the President but not submitted to the Senate for ratification as a TREATY. Such agreements are sometimes negotiated pursuant to specific statutory authority, but even when they are not they are generally regarded as binding upon the United States so long as Congress does not specifically act to overrule them.

executive clemency. Same as CLEMENCY.

executive order an order issued by the President or a state governor on a matter within the scope of executive authority, having the force of law. For example, the desegregation of America's armed forces after World War II came about not by any action of Congress or the courts, but by an executive order of President Truman.

executive privilege the right of the President, founded in the constitutional principle of SEPARATION OF POWERS, to refuse to disclose to the courts or Congress confidential communications within the executive branch. This is a *qualified privilege* (see under PRIVILEGE), so that a strong need for the information can outweigh the privilege when there is no strong need to keep the information secret.

executor *n.* a person designated in a will, or appointed by a court if necessary, to ADMINISTER the estate of a decedent who left a will in accordance with the terms of the will. The archaic term **executrix** is still often used to refer to an executor who is a woman. Cf. ADMINISTRATOR.

executory *adj.* not yet fully performed or fully resolved. For example, an "executory contract" is one under which at least one side has not completed performance. Opposite of EXECUTED (def. 1). See also *executory interest* (under INTEREST¹).

exemplar *n.* a typical specimen or example, especially a sample of a criminal suspect's handwriting, voice, fingerprints, hair, or other identifying information taken under controlled conditions for analysis and subsequent use as evidence. The compelled production of such exemplars does not violate the constitutional ban on compulsory SELF-INCRIMINATION because an exemplar is not a statement or testimony by the suspect.

exemplary damages. Same as *punitive damages* (see under DAMAGES).

exempt. See *exempt property* (under EXEMPTION); TAX EXEMPT.

exemption *n.* **1.** the relieving of a particular person or class of persons from a legal duty: *exemption of conscientious objectors from combat duty; exemption of an individual from jury duty on the ground of hardship.* **2.** statutory protection of certain property of a debtor **(exempt property)** from attachment by creditors. See also HOMESTEAD EXEMPTION. **3.** an income tax DEDUCTION, in an amount fixed by statute, for each taxpayer who is not claimed as a dependent on someone else's return and for each DEPENDENT claimed by the taxpayer.

exhaustion of administrative remedies the general rule that where the law provides an administrative procedure for dealing with a particular kind of matter, a person must pursue all possible avenues for redress within the administrative agency before resorting to the courts.

exhaustion of state remedies the general rule that a state prisoner who feels that he is being held in violation of the Constitution must pursue all possible avenues for redress in the state courts before seeking a writ of HABEAS CORPUS in federal court.

exhibit *n.* **1.** a document referred to in an affidavit, contract, or other instrument and attached to the instrument. Such exhibits are regarded as an intrinsic part of the instrument to which they are attached. **2.** a document or object sought to be used as evidence at a trial. Each party's proposed exhibits are numbered or lettered sequentially ("marked") for ease of identification, and until they are admitted into evidence they are referred to as "Plaintiff's Exhibit C for identification," "Defendant's Exhibit 3 for identification," and the like. If the judge admits an exhibit into evidence, it is thereafter referred to as "Plaintiff's Exhibit C in evidence," "Defendant's Exhibit 3 in evidence," or the like.

exigent circumstances special circumstances under which law enforcement officers who have probable cause to conduct a search may do so without waiting to get a search warrant. These include, among others, any situation involving the search of an automobile on a roadway and any situation in which the police reasonably believe that the search is necessary to protect life or prevent serious injury. See also FRESH PURSUIT.

expectancy *n.* a property interest that may or may not come into existence in the future; a hoped-for property right but not one that exists at present: *Her uncle has made a will leaving her the house, but he can always change his will, so all she has now is a mere expectancy.*

expert witness. See under WITNESS. See also BATTLE OF THE EXPERTS; *qualify as an expert* (under QUALIFY[1]).

expertise. See SCOPE OF EXPERTISE.

express *adj.* explicit; set forth in words; oral or written. Opposite of IMPLIED. See *express* AUTHORITY[1], CONTRACT, REPEAL, TRUST, WAIVER, WARRANTY under those words. For a somewhat broader use of the term, see def. b of *express warranty* (under WARRANTY).

expropriation *n.* a TAKING of private property by a government under the power of EMINENT DOMAIN.

extortion *n.* the crime of obtaining money or property from a person by threat of harmful conduct in the future (e.g., killing, injuring, destroying property, disclosing embarrassing information) or threat of imminent harm falling short of the kinds of threatened harm necessary for ROBBERY (e.g., a threat to destroy property other than a home). See also KICKBACK (def. 2); BLACKMAIL. —**extort,** *v.*

extradition *n.* **1.** the handing over by one state to another of a suspect wanted for criminal prosecution in the second state. The Constitution requires the states of the United States to honor each other's requests for extradition if the suspect has been formally charged with a crime in the requesting state and was in that state at the time the crime was committed. The suspect may, however, be required to serve out a current sentence in the sending state before being handed over. **2.** the handing over of a criminal suspect from one country to another. Such extraditions are provided for by treaties between the United States and many other countries. Cf. ASYLUM.

extrajudicial *adj.* not part of court proceedings or not within the authority of a court.

extraordinary care. See under CARE.

extraordinary remedy (or **relief**). See under REMEDY.

extraordinary writ. See under WRIT.

extrinsic evidence. See under EVIDENCE.

eyewitness *n.* **1.** a person who saw an event under discussion. **2.** broadly, a person who directly perceived an event under discussion, whether by seeing, hearing, or otherwise. Eyewitness testimony, or the lack of it, is often viewed as crucial in a case, despite scientific studies consistently showing that such testimony is very unreliable and despite repeated accounts of people convicted on the basis of eyewitness identification who are later released from prison when the real criminal comes to light. Cf. *circumstantial evidence* (under EVIDENCE).

a b c d e **F** g h i j k l m n o p q r s t u v w x y z

face *n.* **1.** the front of an instrument. **2.** the obvious meaning of a statement or a writing; the explicit provisions of a writing: *The legislature's discriminatory purpose is clear from the face of the statute.* **3.** the outward appearance as distinguished from the real significance: *Although the minimum height requirement for employees is facially neutral, in practice it discriminates against women.* **4. on its face, a.** obviously and without qualification: *unconstitutional* (or *invalid*) *on its face* (see under UNCONSTITUTIONAL). **b.** apparently; superficially: *The statement that one can buy bacon at a certain butcher shop, though innocent on its face, amounts to defamation when made in reference to a kosher butcher shop.* —**facial,** *adj.* —**facially,** *adv.*

face amount (or **value**), the sum shown on the face of an instrument; the principal amount of an obligation, not taking into account interest, deductions, or other adjustments: *The face amount of the mortgage is $60,000, but only $25,000 remains to be paid. The face value of the life insurance policy is $100,000, but with dividends it will pay $120,000.*

fact *n.* **1.** an event or circumstance; an aspect of reality. As distinguished from LAW, a matter ascertained by consideration of evidence; as distinguished from OPINION, a matter directly observed by a witness. **2. evidentiary fact,** a fact that is itself evidence of another fact at issue in a case; a fact providing a basis for determination of an *ultimate fact.* **3. ultimate fact,** one of the facts so basic to a claim, charge, or defense that their determination is the ultimate objective of a trial. See also *fact witness* (under WITNESS); *finding of fact; implied in fact* (under IMPLIED); *stipulated fact* (under STIPULATION); *question of fact* and *mixed question of fact and law* (both under QUESTION[2]); TRIER OF FACT.

factfinder. Same as TRIER OF FACT.

factor *n.* **1.** a merchant who, instead of buying goods and reselling at a profit, receives goods on *consignment* (see under CONSIGN) and sells them for a commission. **2.** a company that lends money to merchants or manufacturers, taking an assignment of their accounts receivable as security.

fail *v.* **1.** (of a contract) to be unenforceable—for example, because the terms are too INDEFINITE, or a party lacked CAPACITY to contract, or the contract is against PUBLIC POLICY. **2.** (of a gift or bequest) to be ineffective—for example, because the property no longer exists or the donee is deceased.

failure of consideration a situation in which the CONSIDERATION agreed upon in a contract does not materialize or ceases to exist or becomes worthless. In some cases this renders the promise or the negotiable instrument given in exchange for that consideration unenforceable, or justifies other relief. The most common example of failure of consideration is simply the failure of a party to do whatever was promised in the contract. Cf. *want of consideration* (under WANT).

failure of issue. See under ISSUE².

failure to prosecute in either a civil or criminal case, the failure of the plaintiff or prosecutor to pursue the case diligently once it has been commenced. Also called **want of prosecution.** In extreme cases, a civil case may be dismissed for failure to prosecute; criminal cases will be so dismissed if there is a violation of the requirement of a *speedy trial* (see under TRIAL).

fair comment the right to express one's opinion on matters of public interest, such as the conduct of a public official, the conduct of a private person in a matter affecting the community at large, or the contents of a book or other published work. As long as the comment is not completely unreasonable, the person making it may not be held liable for DEFAMATION on account of it.

fair market value. Same as MARKET VALUE.

fair preponderance of the evidence. Same as PREPONDERANCE OF THE EVIDENCE.

fair use reasonable and limited use of a copyrighted work without permission of the owner, as in quoting a few lines from a book in a review of the book. Such use is not an infringement of the copyright.

faith. See GOOD FAITH; BAD FAITH.

false *adj.* **1.** untrue: *false representation.* **2.** misleading: FALSE ADVERTISING. **3.** unlawful: FALSE IMPRISONMENT.

false advertising advertising that is materially misleading about the nature, origin, or quality of a product or the training or skill of a provider of service. It is illegal. See also BAIT AND SWITCH.

false arrest. See under FALSE IMPRISONMENT.

false exculpatory statement. See under STATEMENT.

false imprisonment the tort and crime of restricting a person to a particular area without legal justification, whether by means of physical restraints (as in a prison, a locked room, or a speeding automobile) or through force or threat of immediate harm to one's person or valuable property. Also called **false arrest,** especially when done by one falsely claiming to have law enforcement authority, or by a law enforcement officer who lacks probable cause or other legal grounds for detaining the arrestee.

false pretenses the crime of obtaining title to property, especially personal property, by means of false representations, as by swindling someone out of money or tricking someone into selling something. If only possession, rather than title, is obtained by trick, the crime is LARCENY.

false swearing the crime of making a false statement under oath or affirmation, other than in the belief that what is being said is true. A broader and less serious offense than PERJURY.

falsus in uno, falsus in omnibus *Latin.* (lit. "deceitful in one thing, deceitful in all things") the doctrine that a witness who is shown to have deliberately lied on a material issue in a case may be regarded by the jury as generally unworthy of belief.

family *n.* a group of people related by blood, marriage, or adoption, or in an analogous relationship linked by bonds of affection and commitment. The exact scope of the term varies with the context.

family law the area of law dealing with marriage, separation, and divorce; adoption, custody, and support of children; DOMESTIC PARTNERSHIP; and related matters. Also called **domestic relations.**

fatal *adj.* causing invalidity; describing an error or legal defect that renders a transaction or interest void, an argument ineffective, a trial invalid, or the like: *A new trial was ordered because of the judge's fatal error in excluding certain evidence at the first trial.*

fatal variance. See under VARIANCE.

fault *n.* wrongfulness; blameworthiness; broadly, the doing of anything that provides a basis for a suit or criminal action against oneself; narrowly, the

element—often called STATE OF MIND or MENS REA—that makes an act a tort or crime. Cf. NO-FAULT DIVORCE; NO-FAULT INSURANCE; STRICT LIABILITY.

federal *adj.* relating to the United States, and especially to the government and law of the United States, as distinguished from a state: *federal crime; federal income tax; federal government; federal judge.*

federal case. See under CASE¹.

Federal Circuit. See under CIRCUIT.

Federal Insurance Contributions Act (FICA). See under SOCIAL SECURITY.

federal law law adopted or recognized by the government of the United States with respect to matters within its constitutional powers, uniformly applicable throughout the nation. It includes the Constitution; statutes adopted by Congress; executive orders of the President; regulations and rulings of federal agencies; treaties and executive agreements to which the United States is a party; international law, at least to the extent that the courts choose to recognize it and Congress has not acted to the contrary; judicial interpretations and rulings with respect to all of the foregoing matters; and *federal common law* (see under COMMON LAW).

federal question an issue requiring the application or interpretation of FEDERAL LAW in a case. See also *federal question jurisdiction* (under JURISDICTION¹).

federal statute. See under STATUTE.

fee¹ *n.* **1.** Also called **estate** (or **tenancy**) **in fee; fee estate.** a possessory interest in real estate of potentially infinite duration. (See *possessory interest,* under INTEREST¹.) If not sold or given away during the owner's life or by will, and so long as no condition specified for its continued existence is violated, a fee descends automatically to the owner's heirs upon the owner's death, and then to their heirs, and so on indefinitely. **2. fee simple,** a fee which is inheritable by any heir of the owner. Older forms of fee in which the property was restricted to certain heirs, such as male descendants only, have been abolished, so that now every fee is a fee simple, and those two terms are often used interchangeably. **3. fee simple absolute,** a fee simple that is not subject to any condition on its continuation in the hands of the present owner and his heirs so long as they do not transfer it to someone else. (Even a fee simple absolute, however, is subject to the state and federal governments' power of EMINENT DOMAIN.) Cf. *fee simple defeasible.* **4. fee simple defeasible,** a fee simple estate that is subject to termination (DEFEASANCE) upon the occurrence of some future event. Upon defeasance, the current owner loses the property and the fee vests in someone else. Also called **defeasible fee; conditional fee.** Cf. *fee simple absolute.* **5. fee simple determinable,** a defeasible fee which is to continue only so long as a certain state of affairs continues, or only until a certain event occurs. Such fees are most often created in gifts to charity, as when real estate is left by will to a university "so long as the property is used for educational purposes." If the deed or will creating such a fee specifies who should get the property if the fee is terminated, that person has an EXECUTORY INTEREST in the property; otherwise the transferor and his heirs retain a POSSIBILITY OF REVERTER. In either case, if the condition for continuation of the present fee is violated, the person next in line will automatically get the property in *fee simple absolute.*

fee² *n.* **1.** compensation for services rendered by an *independent contractor* (see under CONTRACTOR), especially professional services by a lawyer, doctor, or the like. See also *contingency fee* (under CONTINGENCY). **2.** a sum paid for a LICENSE or privilege, such as a fee paid to the government for a driver's license or for admission to a national park. See also *filing fee* (under FILE). Cf. TAX.

felon *n.* a person who commits a FELONY.

felony *n.* a serious crime, usually defined as one punishable by death or by imprisonment for more than one year. Cf. MISDEMEANOR. **—felonious,** *adj.*

felony murder the commission or attempted commission of a felony that unintentionally results in a death. Felony murder is punishable as MURDER. The felony murder doctrine in its most extreme form holds a peripheral participant in a minor felony guilty of murder if an accidental and unforeseeable death occurs in the course of the crime, even if that participant had essentially nothing to do with the death. Most states limit the doctrine in various ways, as by applying it only to serious felonies and allowing a defendant to show as an *affirmative defense* (see under DEFENSE) that she was not involved in the killing and had no reason to believe that such a thing might occur.

FICA. See under SOCIAL SECURITY.

fiction. See LEGAL FICTION.

fidelity bond. See under BOND².

fidelity insurance insurance against loss due to dishonest or unfaithful conduct by an employee. A fidelity insurance contract is also called a *fidelity bond* (see under BOND²).

fiduciary *n.* **1.** a trustee or a person in a position analogous to that of a trustee, whereby another person or persons must rely upon the fiduciary to exercise special care, good faith, and loyalty in dealing with money and property. For example, an attorney is a fiduciary of her client, a corporate director is a fiduciary of the corporation, and each general partner in a business is a fiduciary of the other partners. See also FIDUCIARY DUTY. —*adj.* **2.** pertaining to a fiduciary or a FIDUCIARY RELATIONSHIP.

fiduciary bond. See under BOND².

fiduciary duty the duty of utmost good faith, loyalty, and care that the law imposes upon every FIDUCIARY in dealing with matters that are the subject of a FIDUCIARY RELATIONSHIP. See also *breach of fiduciary duty* (under BREACH); *utmost care* (under CARE); SELF-DEALING.

fiduciary relationship a legal relationship in which one party necessarily reposes special trust and confidence in the other, so that the other is held to be a FIDUCIARY of the first.

fighting words words spoken directly to a person that are of a sort likely to provoke violent retaliation. Such people may be outlawed as a *breach of the peace* (see under BREACH). See also FREEDOM OF SPEECH; *hate speech* (under SPEECH).

file *v.* **1.** to commence an action by depositing a copy of the complaint, indictment, or other initial court paper with the court: *to file suit; file charges*. **2.** to deposit a copy of each successive court paper with the court clerk for notation on the docket, for transmittal to the judge if it is a matter requiring the judge's attention, and ultimately for placement in the court's official file on the case: *to file a motion for summary judgment*. See also COURTESY COPY. **3.** to deposit any legal document with an appropriate governmental agency: *to file a tax return; file an application for a liquor license; file a registration statement for an issue of preferred stock*. **4. file under seal,** to file papers with a court in a sealed envelope to be opened only by the judge and not made available to the public, usually pursuant to a CONFIDENTIALITY STIPULATION. **5. filing fee,** a fee that must be paid to a court in order to commence an action in that court, or a fee required by any other government office upon the filing of certain kinds of papers. Cf. IN FORMA PAUPERIS. —*n.* **6.** the complete set of documents pertaining to a matter kept by a court or other government or private office.

final order. See under ORDER¹.

financial statement. See under STATEMENT.

find *v.* to make a determination of any kind in the course of a case: *The appellate court found the cases cited by the appellant unpersuasive. The jury found the defendant guilty.*

finding of fact in a nonjury trial, a judge's decision on a purely factual issue (e.g., whether the light was red or green; whether the purchaser was acting in good faith). See also CONCLUSION OF LAW; FINDINGS OF FACT AND CONCLUSIONS OF LAW.

findings of fact and conclusions of law the form in which a judge's decision is rendered in a civil suit tried without a jury in the federal courts

and many state courts. This full statement of the factual and legal bases for the court's decision provides a clear record for appellate review. Also called, informally, **findings and conclusions.** See also FINDING OF FACT; CONCLUSION OF LAW.

fine *n.* **1.** a sum of money required to be paid as a civil or criminal PENALTY. —*v.* **2.** to impose a fine upon a person; to sentence a person to pay a fine.

first impression describing a legal issue not previously considered by the courts: *question of first impression; matter of first impression*. See also *case of first impression* (under CASE¹).

first mortgage. See under MORTGAGE.

fishing expedition *Informal.* a derogatory term applied to requests from an adversary for wide-ranging DISCOVERY. In general, the purpose of discovery is to obtain evidence, or information leading to evidence, pertaining to a known cause of action, not to "fish around" in the hope of stumbling upon a basis for maintaining a suit.

fitness. See *warranty of fitness for a particular purpose* (under WARRANTY).

fixture *n.* an article that is attached to real property in such a way that its removal would damage the property, such as a furnace or a built-in bookcase. Ordinarily such fixtures are regarded as part of the real property.

flat tax. See under TAX.

floating zone. See under ZONE.

FOIA. See FREEDOM OF INFORMATION ACT.

follow *v.* (of a court) to adhere to a PRECEDENT; to apply the principles articulated or used in a particular precedent to the case at hand.

for cause for a legally sufficient reason logically related to the action being taken, not for arbitrary, whimsical, or irrelevant reasons; for example, the firing of an employee because of inadequate performance would be a "termination for cause." See also *challenge for cause* (under CHALLENGE).

for the record. See under RECORD.

for-profit corporation. See under CORPORATION.

force majeure *French.* (lit. "superior force") an unforeseeable natural or human event beyond the control of the parties to a contract, rendering performance of a contract impossible. A "force majeure clause" in a contract relieves a party from the duty to perform if performance is rendered impossible by force majeure.

foreclosure *n.* **1.** the termination of a property owner's rights in property that is subject to a mortgage or other *security interest* (see under INTEREST¹) when the owner has failed to pay the debt secured by the property, so that the property can be sold to pay off the debt. **2.** the entire procedure (normally a court action) by which foreclosure is accomplished, the property is sold (normally auctioned off), the proceeds are applied to the debt, and any money left over is refunded to the debtor. —**foreclose,** *v.*

foreign *adj.* referring to another jurisdiction—sometimes another country (see *foreign commerce,* under COMMERCE), but often just another state (see *foreign corporation,* under CORPORATION). To avoid confusion, the phrase "foreign country" is often used when that is what is meant: *a foreign country judgment; a foreign country divorce.*

forensic *adj.* for law enforcement and courtroom purposes: *forensic medicine; forensic chemistry; forensic anthropolgy.*

foreperson *n.* a jury member selected either by lot or by vote of the jury to coordinate deliberations and render the jury's verdict in court.

forfeiture *n.* the loss of a right, license, or property as a civil or criminal penalty; e.g., the loss of a fishing license as a penalty for taking fish that are too small or the loss of an automobile because it was used in a crime. —**forfeit,** *v.*

forgery *n.* the crime of making or altering a writing, recording, coin, or other document that is to be passed off as genuine and authorized when it is not, or of attempting to pass off such a document. See also *uttering a forged instrument* (under UTTER). —**forge,** *v.*

legal

form *n.* **1.** the superficial appearance of a transaction as distinguished from the underlying reality. See example under SUBSTANCE. **2.** Also called **legal form.** a model or preprinted document containing standard legal language for accomplishing a particular kind of transaction. Such forms can often be purchased in stationery and office supply stores.

form of action any of the dozen or so specific categories into which every action at law traditionally was required to fit. Each form of action had a special name, could be used only in certain types of cases, had its own highly technical pleading rules, and provided only a specific kind of remedy. The rigidity of this system was the main reason for the growth of EQUITY. Under modern rules of civil procedure, there is but one form of action—the civil action—and the plaintiff may request and obtain any relief warranted by the facts. The common law forms of action are still often referred to, however, because of their influence in shaping English and American law over the centuries.

forma pauperis. See IN FORMA PAUPERIS.

fornication *n.* the crime of engaging in sexual intercourse while unmarried. The crime has been abolished in most states; in the states where it has not been abolished, there are a lot of criminals. Cf. ADULTERY.

forum *n.* the court or jurisdiction in which an action is pending. See also LEX FORI; PUBLIC FORUM.

forum non conveniens *Latin.* (lit. "an inappropriate forum") the doctrine that a court in which an action has properly been filed may decline to exercise jurisdiction over it if the case has no significant relationship with that jurisdiction and would be more suitably litigated in another state or another country.

forum shopping the choosing of a forum expected to be sympathetic to one's case; for example, the choice of a tobacco state for a suit by a tobacco company, of a nontobacco state for a suit against a tobacco company, or of a Bible Belt state for a pornography prosecution.

foundation *n.* **1.** evidence establishing the admissibility of an exhibit or other evidence. For example, in order to introduce testimony that the plaintiff made a certain out-of-court statement about the defendant, it would usually be necessary to "lay a foundation" by establishing that the party testifying was in a position to hear the statement, to know who was making it, and perhaps to know whom it referred to. See also AUTHENTICATE; CONNECT UP. **2.** an institution established, usually by means of a large donation or legacy, to support research, the arts, or charitable activities.

franchise *n.* **1.** a right or license granted by a company (the **franchisor**) to an individual or group (the **franchisee**) to market its goods or services and use its trademark in a specific territory, usually pursuant to a detailed agreement requiring operation of the business in accordance with the franchisor's standards and setting forth the financial terms of the arrangement. **2.** a privilege granted by the government, such as the right to operate in the form of a corporation or to operate a bus company. **3.** the right to vote.

franchise tax a tax imposed upon a corporation for the privilege of doing business in a state.

fraud *n.* **1.** Also called **actual fraud** or **fraud in fact.** the tort of obtaining money or property by means of a false portrayal of facts, either by words or by conduct. For a list of the elements of fraud, see ELEMENT. In criminal law, fraudulent conduct may be classified as larceny, forgery, theft, or other crimes depending upon the circumstances. **2. constructive fraud,** conduct viewed by a court as having the same effect as actual fraud though not involving any false representation of fact. This usually occurs when a FIDUCIARY abuses the trust and confidence of the person to whom she owes a fiduciary duty, profiting by keeping silent about matters that should have been disclosed to that person. (In a nonfiduciary relationship, as between an ordinary buyer and seller, there is no general duty to speak about things one is not asked about.) Also called le-

gal fraud or fraud in law. **3. fraud in the factum,** a misrepresentation as to the fundamental nature of a contract, will, or other instrument being signed, as in a classic case in which a wife was told that a certain legal document was just a formality for tax purposes and it turned out to be a separation agreement. Such fraud renders an instrument VOID. Also called **fraud in the execution. 4. fraud in the inducement,** misrepresentation upon which a person relies in entering into a contract, not about the terms of the contract itself but about the subject of the contract or the surrounding circumstances, as when a seller conceals a serious defect in a product with a coat of paint. Such fraud renders the contract VOIDABLE. Also called **fraudulent inducement. 5. mail fraud,** the federal crime of using the mails in connection with a scheme to defraud. **6. wire fraud,** the federal crime of using interstate telephone or telegraph wires in connection with a scheme to defraud. See also SECURITIES FRAUD; TAX FRAUD.

frauds, statute of. See STATUTE OF FRAUDS.

fraudulent *adj.* **1.** pertaining to or constituting a FRAUD. **2.** intentionally wrongful; dishonest; unfair.

fraudulent conveyance a transfer of property by a debtor for less than its full value, in an effort to put it into friendly hands where it cannot be attached by creditors, or to favor one creditor over others. A court will usually set aside such a conveyance.

fraudulent inducement. Same as *fraud in the inducement* (see under FRAUD).

free exercise of religion the practice of one's religion and observance of its tenets without government interference—a right guaranteed by the **Free Exercise Clause** of the First Amendment to the Constitution. This right may be limited by laws of general applicability not targeted at religion, however; for example, in the 1980's and 1990's the Supreme Court upheld military regulations preventing Orthodox Jewish servicemen from wearing yarmulkes and criminal laws barring the sacramental use of peyote in Native American religious ritual.

freedom *n.* absence of legal restraint; the RIGHT to do or not do something without governmental interference. The conventional term used to describe a number of constitutional rights, including those referred to in the next few entries.

freedom of assembly the right of people to gather peacefully for political or other purposes. This is guaranteed by the First Amendment (see Appendix), subject only to the government's right to impose reasonable restrictions on the time, place, and manner of such assembly. Cf. UNLAWFUL ASSEMBLY.

freedom of association the constitutional right to join with others for lawful purposes, derived primarily from a combination of First Amendment rights (assembly, religion, etc.).

freedom of contract the name given to a now discredited constitutional doctrine, which the Supreme Court followed from 1897 to 1937, holding that the government has only very limited power to regulate contractual relationships, especially in regard to conditions of employment. It is now accepted that federal and state governments have wide powers to dictate reasonable terms for employment relationships, consumer transactions, and other contracts, which no claim of "freedom of contract" can overcome.

freedom of expression a general term for FREEDOM OF SPEECH and FREEDOM OF THE PRESS; sometimes used broadly to include FREEDOM OF RELIGION also.

Freedom of Information Act (FOIA) a federal statute, widely imitated at the state level, requiring most government documents and records to be made available to the public on request and specifying procedures for requests and disclosure.

freedom of religion the freedom to hold and practice one's religious beliefs and freedom from government involvement in religious matters, guaranteed by the First Amendment clauses protecting FREE EXERCISE OF RELIGION and prohibiting ESTABLISH-

MENT OF RELIGION. See also SEPARATION OF CHURCH AND STATE.

freedom of speech the First Amendment right to express oneself. It covers any form or medium of SPEECH, not just speaking and writing, and generally prohibits the government from restricting expression on the basis of content or viewpoint. As interpreted by the Supreme Court, however, the degree of freedom depends upon the category of speech. It is greatest for speech conveying ideas about such matters as politics, art, religion, or science. It is lower for such categories as *commercial speech* and *indecent speech* (see under SPEECH). And some categories, most notably OBSCENITY, are completely unprotected—not regarded as "speech" at all within the meaning of the Constitution.

freedom of the press the First Amendment right to publish books, newspapers, and magazines and otherwise distribute and broadcast information, opinion, and expression, largely free from government censorship. See also PRIOR RESTRAINT.

freehold *n.* a possessory interest in real property amounting to an *estate in fee* or *life estate* (see under ESTATE¹). Also called **freehold estate** or **freehold interest.** Cf. LEASEHOLD.

fresh pursuit pursuit by a law enforcement officer of a suspected felon who is fleeing and may escape if the pursuit is abandoned. An officer in fresh pursuit may usually follow the suspect across jurisdictional lines to make the arrest, or pursue a suspect into a building and search for him there without a search warrant. Also called **hot pursuit.** See also EXIGENT CIRCUMSTANCES.

friend of the court. See under AMICUS CURIAE.

frisk. See STOP AND FRISK.

frivolous *adj.* describing an action or procedural step that clearly has no basis in law or in any reasonable argument for a change in the law: *a frivolous action; a frivolous motion; a frivolous appeal.* A court may SANCTION an attorney or party who takes frivolous action, as by requiring him to pay the attorneys' fees incurred by his adversary in opposing it.

frolic of one's own conduct by an employee outside the SCOPE OF EMPLOYMENT. The employer is not liable for the acts of an employee under such circumstances. The classic example is a company driver who, when sent to make a delivery, makes a detour to visit his mistress and causes an accident while on the detour. The company will not be liable

for the damages because the employee was on "a frolic of his own." Cf. RESPONDENT SUPERIOR.

fruit of the poisonous tree evidence derived from information obtained through an illegal search or other illegal investigative technique. Such evidence is generally subject to the EXCLUSIONARY RULE to the same extent as the illegally obtained information that led to it.

frustration *n.* an unforeseen circumstance that destroys the purpose of a contract. Under the "doctrine of frustration," further performance of the contract is excused. For example, if an agreement is reached to rent a room overlooking a parade, and then the parade is unexpectedly cancelled, the would-be renter need not go through with the contract.

full age. See under AGE.

full faith and credit deference given by the courts of one state to the laws and judicial proceedings of another state. The Constitution requires the states to give full faith and credit to each other's laws and judgments; thus a judgment obtained in one state is generally enforceable in every other state, and may generally be attacked in another state only upon grounds that would have been allowed in the state where the judgment was rendered. Cf. COMITY.

full partner. See under PARTNER.

full warranty. See under WARRANTY.

fully paid stock. See under STOCK.

fundamental error. See under ERROR.

fundamental right any right expressly guaranteed by the Constitution, or deemed by the Supreme Court to be so basic to the concept of liberty as to be protected from government restriction (except to the extent necessary to serve a COMPELLING INTEREST) by the DUE PROCESS clause of the Fourteenth Amendment (see Appendix). Areas now deemed fundamental include voting and running for office, access to the courts, freedom of travel, freedom of association, and decision making in matters of marriage and procreation. See also RIGHT OF PRIVACY; *substantive due process* (under DUE PROCESS); STRICT SCRUTINY.

future estate. See under ESTATE¹.

future interest. See under INTEREST¹.

futuro. See IN FUTURO.

abcdef **G** hijklmnopqrstuvwxyz

gag order a judge's order to parties and attorneys in a sensational case not to discuss the case publicly, issued in the hope of avoiding publicity regarded as damaging to the fairness and dignity of the proceedings. Cf. CONFIDENTIALITY STIPULATION.

gain *n.* the profit on a sale or exchange of property; generally, the amount by which the value received in exchange for the property exceeds the owner's BASIS in the property. Ordinarily, the gain is subject to income tax. See also *capital gain* and *capital gains tax* (both under CAPITAL¹); REALIZE; RECOGNIZE. Cf. LOSS.

garnish *v.* to serve a GARNISHMENT; to attach wages or other money or property owed to or held for a debtor, so that those assets can be redirected to the debtor's creditor.

garnishee *n.* **1.** a person or entity served with a GARNISHMENT; for example, the employer of a judgment debtor whose wages are being garnished. —*v.* **2.** to GARNISH.

garnisher or **garnishor,** *n.* the creditor for whose benefit a garnishment is effected.

garnishment *n.* **1.** the ATTACHMENT of wages or other money or property owed to or held for a debtor, usually a judgment debtor, so that they can be used to satisfy the debtor's obligation. For example, the wages of a divorced parent who has failed

to pay court-ordered child support may be subject to garnishment by the custodial parent to satisfy the child support obligation. **2.** a judicial proceeding to effect such a garnishment. **3.** the formal document which must be served on the employer or other person being garnished in order to effect a garnishment.

general *adj.* describing the most usual, basic, comprehensive, or undifferentiated form or application of something, as distinguished from specialized forms, which are often characterized by such terms as "specific," "special," "limited," or "qualified." See *general* APPEARANCE, BEQUEST, CONTRACTOR, COUNSEL, DAMAGES, JURISDICTION¹, partner, partnership, power of attorney, release, verdict under those words.

generation-skipping trust a trust created, usually by will, in such a way that one's children will have the use and benefit (but not ownership) of certain property during their lives, and then ownership of the property will pass to their children. Formerly this saved the family one round of estate taxes because actual ownership of the property skipped over one generation. That tax loophole was plugged by the **generation-skipping transfer tax,** which is collected upon expiration of the beneficial interests of the first generation of children.

gentlemen's agreement an agreement not intended by the parties to be enforced by legal action, but expected to be performed or adhered to solely as a matter of personal friendship or honor. Sometimes this is because the agreement is in fact illegal, as to fix prices or pay a bribe.

geographic jurisdiction. Same as JURISDICTION².

gerrymander *n.* **1.** a voting district of seemingly illogical shape created in order to achieve a political purpose, such as diluting the votes of the opposing political party, protecting incumbents, or increasing the chance that a member of a racial or ethnic minority group will be elected to legislative office. The Supreme Court has been loath to upset gerrymanders created for the first two reasons, but has been strongly critical of "bizarre" district lines drawn in an effort to increase minority representation in Congress. —*v.* **2.** to create such a district; to draw irregular district lines for such purposes.

gift *n.* **1.** Also called **inter vivos gift** or **gift inter vivos. a.** a voluntary transfer of money or property, completed during one's lifetime, without expecting anything in return. For such a gift to be effective, the DONOR must understand and intend the consequences of the act, and the property must be delivered to and accepted by the DONEE. **b.** the property so transferred. See also DELIVERY; INTER VIVOS. **2.** Also called **testamentary gift. a.** a transfer of property by will; a BEQUEST or DEVISE. **b.** property so transferred. **3. gift causa mortis**, a conditional gift of personal property by a person who is ill or injured and expects to die. To be legally effective it must satisfy all the requirements of other inter vivos gifts, and in addition the donor must die of the illness or injury. If the donor recovers, the property must be returned. See also CAUSA MORTIS. **4. gift in contemplation of death, a.** a *gift causa mortis.* **b.** for tax purposes, a gift made within three years of death. Ordinarily the value of the gift is included in the donor's estate for estate tax purposes.

gift over a transfer of a future interest in property to one person in connection with the transfer of a present interest in the same property to someone else. For example, if property is granted "to A for life, then to B," the grant to B is a "gift over." The word *gift* is used even if the future interest being transferred was paid for.

gift tax a tax imposed by the federal government on very large gifts made during a person's lifetime. Payment of the tax is the obligation of the donor, not the recipients.

give *v.* to make a GIFT.

gloss *n.* **1.** an explanation or interpretation of a statute, constitutional provision, or judicial ruling, especially one that adds or makes explicit some qualification that is not expressly stated in the statute or ruling. **2. judicial gloss, a.** a court's gloss on a statutory or constitutional provision or prior court ruling, usually made in a discussion of its applicability or inapplicability to a particular case. **b.** the accumulated interpretations of a number of courts over a period of years; a judicial consensus on interpretation of a statutory or constitutional provision or a significant earlier ruling.

go forward or **go forward with evidence,** to introduce evidence on an issue in a case, thereby placing the issue before the factfinder. See also *burden of going forward* (under BURDEN¹).

go private to cease to be a *publicly held corporation* and become a *closely held corporation* (see both under CORPORATION) through a transaction by which most shareholders are forced to accept money for their shares and the business is left in the hands of a few officers, directors, or major shareholders. Cf. GO PUBLIC.

go public (of a corporation) to issue shares to the general public for the first time, thereby becoming a *publicly held corporation* (see under CORPORATION) Cf. GO PRIVATE.

go to to bear upon; be relevant to the issue of: *That evidence is admissible because it goes to the witness's credibility. Point 3 of their brief goes to the constitutionality of the statute.*

going concern an enterprise that is carrying on its

normal business and is expected to continue indefinitely. Cf. WIND UP.

golden parachute a contract between a corporation and any of its high executives promising the executive extremely generous financial compensation in the event that he loses his job or resigns because of a merger or takeover. This assures that regardless of what happens to ordinary employees who lose their jobs as a result of such corporate changes, the top executives will be amply rewarded.

good *adj.* generally, of a type approved or favored by law, or regarded as acceptable in the marketplace or by society at large. The specific legal significance of the word varies greatly from phrase to phrase.

good cause 1. a legally sufficient reason or excuse, especially for taking or omitting some procedural step in a case. Cf. INSUFFICIENT CAUSE. **2. for good cause shown** or **good cause having been shown,** expressions often used by a court in issuing an order, indicating that the party seeking the order has made a sufficient showing of facts warranting its issuance.

good faith the quality of mind and heart possessed by a person who is acting with sincerity and honesty, and without intent to cheat or take unfair advantage of another. Cf. BAD FAITH.

good faith exception an exception to the EXCLUSIONARY RULE, whereby evidence found in an illegal search may be used against a defendant if the police made the search in good faith reliance upon a search warrant issued by a neutral magistrate, which turned out to be invalid through no fault of the police.

good faith purchaser a purchaser of property who acts in good faith in making the purchase and has no reason to suspect that someone else might have a right to the property. Unless the property was stolen, a good faith purchaser will ordinarily get to keep the purchased property even if it turns out that the seller did not have the right to sell it. Also called **good faith purchaser for value** or **bona fide purchaser (for value).**

good law in accord with current law. The phrase is used mostly in discussing the status of past judicial decisions or statements of legal principle in light of subsequent evolution of the law: *The much criticized rule that property owners owe a higher duty of care to business invitees than to social guests is still good law in most states; but in at least thirteen states it is no longer good law.* Cf. BAD LAW.

good title. Same as *marketable title* (see under TITLE).

good will 1. the benefit to a business of customer loyalty, brand name recognition, reputation for quality and honesty, and the like. Wrongful conduct injurious to a company's good will may be the basis of an action for damages. **2.** in the purchase of an existing business, the excess of the price paid over the net asset value of the company. Now often written **goodwill**, but always pronounced as if two separate words, with the stress on *will.*

goods *n.pl.* **1.** virtually any *tangible personal property* (see under PROPERTY); movable things. **2. consumer goods,** goods used primarily for personal, family, or household purposes.

government *n.* **1.** the ruling authorities of a city, state, nation, or other political unit; the body of officials that makes and enforces the laws. **2.** (*sometimes cap.*) the prosecuting authority in a federal criminal case. Such cases are captioned United States v. So-and-So, but in court and in court papers the prosecution is typically referred to as "the Government": *The Government argues that the search was reasonable.* Cf. STATE; PEOPLE. **3. federal government,** the national government of the United States. **4. republican form of government,** government by the people, through their elected representatives. According to the Constitution, the federal government is required to guarantee that the states will maintain a republican form of government.

government contractor. See under CONTRACTOR.

government security. See under SECURITY².

grade *v.* **1.** to categorize offenses according to their degree of seriousness, setting more serious penalties for more serious crimes; for example, criminal homicide is typically graded into several levels, such as first degree murder, second degree murder, voluntary manslaughter, involuntary manslaughter, and criminally negligent homicide. —n. **2.** Also called **degree.** the level of a particular offense in such a grading system.

grand adj. Law French. (lit. "large") large, major, greater. Used in certain phrases, usually in contrast to PETIT or PETTY; e.g., *grand jury* (see under JURY), *grand larceny* (see under LARCENY).

grandfather v. **1.** to exempt a person or entity from a new law: *Existing buildings were grandfathered by the new zoning law, so they can remain even if they are nonconforming.* —adj. **2. grandfather clause,** a clause in a statute that exempts a class of persons or entities established and operating under prior law from new requirements.

grant v. **1.** broadly, to transfer or bestow property or a right of any kind: *The inventor granted his patent to a university. The Fifth Amendment grants to all property owners the right of just compensation if the government takes their property.* **2.** specifically, to convey an interest in real property. **3.** to accede to a motion, petition, or other request for judicial action, by issuing the requested order or taking the requested action; opposite of DENY: *The judge granted our motion for a protective order.* —n. **4.** the act of granting something. **5.** the thing granted.

grantee n. a person or entity to which something is granted, especially an interest in real property.

grantor n. **1.** a person or entity that grants something, particularly an interest in real property. **2.** The SETTLOR of a trust. See also *grantor trust* (under TRUST).

gratuitous adj. **1.** given, said, or done without an obligation to do so and without receiving or expecting anything in return; without CONSIDERATION. See, for example, *gratuitous* BAILMENT, PROMISE under these words. **2.** describing a party to a gratuitous transaction; for example, a *gratuitous bailee* (see under BAILMENT).

gravamen n. the fundamental or material part of an accusation; the essence of a complaint or charge. Lawyers who do not understand the full meaning of this word sometimes use it to mean the essence or gist of anything (the gravamen of my argument; the gravamen of the expert's report), thereby using the wrong word in the wrong place in an effort to sound professional.

Great Charter the MAGNA CARTA.

Great Writ the writ of HABEAS CORPUS. Also called the **great writ of liberty.**

green card Informal. an identification card—formerly colored green—issued to foreign nationals who have been granted permanent resident status in the United States and thus have full employment rights in the country. See also *resident alien* (under ALIEN).

grievance n. **1.** in a unionized workplace, a formal complaint by an employee, the union, or the employer, alleging a violation of the *collective bargaining agreement* (see under COLLECTIVE BARGAINING) or complaining about working conditions. **2.** a similar internal complaint concerning some condition in a nonunionized workplace, school, prison, or other institution with formal procedures for dealing with such complaints. **3. grievance committee,** a committee provided for by union contract or otherwise established to evaluate and attempt to remedy grievances. **4. grievance procedure,** a formal procedure for dealing with grievances.

gross adj. **1.** (of a sum of money) total before taking account of deductions or adjustments: *gross income* (see under INCOME). See also *gross lease* (under LEASE). **2.** flagrant or extreme (as distinguished from SIMPLE or ORDINARY): *gross negligence* (see under NEGLIGENCE).

ground lease. See under LEASE.

group boycott. See under BOYCOTT.

group insurance. See under INSURANCE.

guarantee v. **1.** to give a GUARANTY or become a SURETY; to act as a surety or GUARANTOR of someone else's obligation: *The bank would give me a loan only if my parents guaranteed it.* **2.** to assure: *The purpose of the program is to guarantee access to medical care.* **3.** Informal. to issue or stand behind a WARRANTY on a product. —n. **4.** a guaranty or suretyship agreement. **5.** any assurance: *The Fifth Amendment guarantee of due process.* **6.** Informal. a nonlawyer's term for a warranty on a product.

guaranteed security. See under SECURITY[2].

guarantor n. a person or entity that issues or is obligated under a GUARANTY.

guaranty n. **1.** in the strictest sense, a promise or contract to make someone whole if a third person fails to fulfill an obligation; that is, a promise by A to B that if C fails to pay a debt or perform some other obligation owed to B, then A will pay the debt or otherwise compensate B. **2.** any promise to answer for the debt, default, or miscarriage of another. In this broader sense, guaranty includes SURETYSHIP. Under the STATUTE OF FRAUDS, any such promise must be in writing and signed to be enforceable. **3.** in the broadest sense, any GUARANTEE. —v. **4.** to GUARANTEE anything.

guardian n. **1.** a person, especially one appointed by a court, with responsibility for the care of a child or an incompetent adult (the WARD) and legal control of the ward's affairs. Sometimes one person, such as a relative, is designated to take personal care of the ward, and another individual or a financial institution is designated to manage the ward's money and property; the former is then referred to as the **guardian of the person** and the latter as the **guardian of the property.** See also COMMITTEE; CONSERVATOR. **2. guardian ad litem,** a person, usually a lawyer, appointed by the court to represent the interests of an infant or incompetent person or a class of such people in a case. Of course, in some cases opinions might vary as to what those interests really are. See also AD LITEM. **3. testamentary guardian,** a guardian for a minor child, designated in the parent's will. —**guardianship,** n.

guest statute. See AUTOMOBILE GUEST STATUTE.

guilty adj. **1.** (of a criminal defendant) adjudged by a court to have committed an offense, either on the basis of a finding or verdict at trial, or because the defendant admitted or did not contest the charge. See also ADJUDGE; JUDGMENT. Cf. NOT GUILTY; INNOCENT. **2.** designating a PLEA entered by a criminal defendant, admitting the charge. This is usually the result of a PLEA BARGAIN. Cf. NOLO CONTENDERE; NOT GUILTY. **3.** having committed a tort, a breach of contract, or an act damaging to one's position in a civil case: *guilty of breach of contract; guilty of contributory negligence.*

gun control legal restrictions on the manufacture, importation, distribution, or possession of guns. Despite arguments that gun control laws violate the Second Amendment (see Appendix), no gun control law has ever been struck down under the Second Amendment. See also RIGHT TO BEAR ARMS.

habeas corpus *Latin.* (lit. "have the body") **1.** an ancient English writ commanding an official holding someone in custody to have the "body" (that is, the person) of the prisoner brought before the court so that the lawfulness of the imprisonment can be inquired into and the prisoner set free if not being held legally. **2.** a modern procedure or writ for testing the legality of custody, usually of a criminal defendant or suspect, but sometimes of a child or civil detainee, such as a person committed to a mental hospital. **3.** particularly, the constitutionally guaranteed procedure by which the constitutionality of a state conviction and imprisonment can be tested in federal court **(federal habeas corpus).** Habeas corpus is sometimes referred to as the **great writ of liberty,** or simply the **Great Writ.**

habitable *adj.* **1.** fit to live in; in compliance with building codes and free of dangers to health and safety. See also TENANTABLE. **2. warranty of habitability,** a landlord's WARRANTY, regarded by law in most states as inherent in every residential lease, that the premises are habitable and will be kept that way.

habitual criminal or **habitual offender,** a person previously convicted of several crimes, and thus subject to a more severe sentence for any subsequent crime. See also REPEAT OFFENDER, THREE STRIKES LAW.

haec verba. See IN HAEC VERBA.

halfway house a residence for individuals who have been in prison, providing a supervised and structured environment to help them adjust to outside life. Cf. WORK RELEASE.

hand *n.* **1.** Same as SIGNATURE. **2. hand and seal,** one's signature and seal (see SEAL¹) placed together on a document. —*v.* **3. hand down,** to render a judicial opinion, ruling, sentence, etc. This phrase is used whether the decision is rendered orally or in writing, and whether rendered from the bench or from chambers. See also ISSUE⁴. **4. hand up,** to pass a document or exhibit up to the judge in court. This phrase is used whether the object is handed directly to the judge or simply given to a bailiff or clerk to hand up.

handicap *n.* Same as DISABILITY, which is generally the preferred term today. —**handicapped,** *adj.*

hang *v.* **1.** (of a jury) to be unable to agree upon a decision; to be deadlocked. Past tense: **hung. 2.** (of a condemned person) to be suspended by the neck until dead. Past tense: **hanged.**

harassment *n.* **1.** the crime of deliberately and repeatedly annoying or interfering with a person, as by telephoning repeatedly, sending anonymous messages, following, taunting, etc. See also INTENTIONAL INFLICTION OF MENTAL DISTRESS; STALKING. **2.** annoying or offensive conduct in the workplace, directed toward an employee or group of employees because of their race, color, religion, sex, or national origin. Such harassment, when engaged in or tolerated by an employer, constitutes unlawful employment discrimination. See also HOSTILE WORKING ENVIRONMENT; SEXUAL HARASSMENT.

hardships, balancing of. See BALANCING OF THE EQUITIES.

harmless *adj.* **1.** not harmful or prejudicial; inconsequential. **2.** unharmed; safe from harm or prejudice. **3. harmless error.** See under ERROR. **4. hold** (or **save**) **harmless, a.** to release from liability or responsibility for loss or damage; to abandon any claim that one might have against someone. **b.** to indemnify; to promise to compensate someone for any loss that might be incurred by reason of claims asserted later by others.

hate crime a crime motivated by bias against a group identified by race, religion, sexual orientation, or other group characteristic, or a crime in which the victim is chosen because of perceived membership in such a group. States may impose extra penalties for such crimes. Also called **bias crime.**

hate speech. See under SPEECH.

head of household an unmarried person (or married person living separately from his or her spouse and filing a separate tax return) who lives with and maintains a household for an unmarried child or a dependent relative. Under the Internal Revenue Code, such a person qualifies for special income tax rates.

headnote *n.* a capsule summary, usually in one sentence, of a legal point in a judicial opinion, inserted by an editor at the head of the published version of the opinion as an aid to legal research. Most published opinions are preceded by several headnotes. Cf. DIGEST; SYLLABUS.

health care proxy a document, provided for by statute in some states, authorizing another person to make medical decisions for the signer if the signer is unable to do so. Also called DURABLE POWER OF ATTORNEY FOR HEALTH CARE. See also *durable power of attorney* (under POWER OF ATTORNEY); LIVING WILL; RIGHT TO DIE.

hear *v.* **1.** (of a court or judge) **a.** to handle a case. **b.** to receive evidence and argument, usually orally and without a jury: *to hear a motion; to hear an appeal; to hear a case without a jury.* Cf. TRY (def. 1); *take on submission* (under SUBMIT). See also OPPORTUNITY TO BE HEARD. **2. hear and determine,** to hear and reach a decision on. **3. hear and report,** to hear and make a recommendation on. In the federal courts, certain matters may be referred by a judge to a magistrate to hear and determine or hear and report.

hear ye a phrase often called out (usually two or three times) at the opening of court proceedings, to get the undivided attention of everyone present and impress upon them the seriousness and importance of the proceedings about to commence. Means the same thing as the Law French OYEZ, which is still used in many courts. Cf. KNOW ALL MEN BY THESE PRESENTS.

hearing *n.* **1.** any factfinding proceeding at which testimony is taken, except a full-scale court trial; for example, a hearing by a court on a motion for a preliminary injunction, a trial before an administrative tribunal or arbitration panel, or a hearing before a legislative committee. **2.** loosely, any proceeding at which legal matters are presented for consideration or decision, including full-scale court trials, appellate arguments, and even matters submitted entirely on papers. **3. hearing examiner** (or **officer**). Same as ADMINISTRATIVE LAW JUDGE. **4. preliminary hearing,** an early stage in a felony prosecution, in which the prosecutor must show a court that there is sufficient evidence to justify a trial. Also called **probable cause hearing, bindover hearing. 5. public hearing,** a hearing held by an administrative agency at which the general public is invited to comment on proposed rules or actions of the agency.

hearsay *n.* **1.** (in a courtroom proceeding) any assertion, other than one made on the witness stand in that very proceeding, that is offered as evidence of the matter asserted; often loosely summarized as "an out-of-court declaration offered for its truth." For example, the statement "I saw my husband shoot Smith," made by a suspect's wife to police shortly after an incident, is hearsay if offered by the prosecution at the husband's trial to help prove that he is the person who shot Smith; but a testator's statement "I am Napoleon," if offered at the trial of a challenge to the will to show that the testator was of unsound mind, is *nonhearsay,* because it is not offered as evidence that the declarant truly was

Napoleon. A hearsay assertion may be either oral or written, or even nonverbal (such as a nod of the head). **2. hearsay evidence,** any testimony or document offered in court that contains hearsay; for example, a police officer's testimony, "She told me she saw her husband shoot Smith," or a letter written by the defendant's wife containing the sentence, "I saw my husband shoot Smith." **3. hearsay exception,** any of the numerous exceptions to the *hearsay rule* under which hearsay evidence is deemed admissible, usually because the circumstances under which the hearsay assertion was made are thought to provide reasonable assurance of its reliability. See, for example, PRESENT SENSE IMPRESSION; EXCITED UTTERANCE; *dying declaration* and *declaration against interest* (under DECLARATION); *business record* and *public record* (under RECORD); *unavailable witness* (under WITNESS). **4. hearsay rule,** the American rule of evidence under which hearsay is generally deemed inadmissible because the assertion presented as "truth" is usually not made under oath and is not subject to cross examination under the scrutiny of the judge and jury.

heat of passion extreme anger or other emotional disturbance provoked by circumstances that the law regards as sufficient to make a reasonable person lose control. The classic example is the man who discovers his wife in bed with another man, goes and gets his gun, and deliberately shoots them to death "in the heat of passion." (His, not theirs.) It is still the law in nearly all American jurisdictions that this is not murder, but merely *voluntary manslaughter* (see under MANSLAUGHTER).

heightened scrutiny a test of constitutionality applied by the Supreme Court to laws that are alleged to violate EQUAL PROTECTION because they treat people differently on the basis of a QUASI-SUSPECT CLASSIFICATION, usually sex. This test is stricter than the RATIONAL BASIS TEST but less demanding than STRICT SCRUTINY. Under heightened scrutiny, a law will be upheld only if it is found to serve an "important governmental objective" and to be "substantially related" to the achievement of that objective. Also called **intermediate scrutiny.** See also SCRUTINY.

heir *n.* **1.** the person, or one of the people, to whom one's property passes by operation of law if one dies without leaving a will. Also called **legal heir, heir at law.** See also *direct heir* (under DIRECT[1]); *collateral heir* (under COLLATERAL[2]); PRETERMITTED HEIR; INTESTATE SUCCESSION. Cf. LEGATEE; DEVISEE. **2. and his heirs,** at common law, words that had to be included in any grant of real property to someone if the intent was to convey the property permanently—that is, to convey a *fee simple* (see under FEE[1]), so that the new owner could pass it on to his heirs or otherwise dispose of it. If the property was conveyed only to "John Smith," rather than to "John Smith and his heirs," Smith received only a *life estate* (see under ESTATE[1]), and upon his death the property reverted to the original owner (or his successors). Although this rule has been abolished nearly everywhere, these traditional words are still found in many deeds. **3. heirs and assigns,** everyone to whom one might leave, give, or sell property; a standard phrase covering anyone who might succeed to one's interest in a piece of property or rights in a matter. For example, a defendant who gives a plaintiff money to settle a case will normally receive in return a RELEASE against any further claims in the matter, executed by the plaintiff "for herself and her heirs and assigns"; this precludes anyone else from coming along and asserting a new claim as her successor. See also ASSIGN.

high crimes and misdemeanors the phrase used in the Constitution to denote misconduct by the President or another federal officer of sufficient gravity to warrant impeachment and removal from office. Whenever impeachment is considered, arguments arise over just what kind of crime meets this test, or whether conduct within the scope of this phrase necessarily must be punishable as a crime at all. The Supreme Court has never had occasion to construe the phrase.

high treason. See under TREASON.

higher court. See under COURT.

highest and best use. See under USE.

highest degree of care. See under CARE.

hindering. See under ACCESSORY.

His (or **Her**) **Honor.** See under HONOR.

hold *v.* **1.** (of a judge, court, or judicial opinion) to state the court's conclusion in a case, or on a particular issue in a case, especially an issue of law (as distinguished from fact). See also HOLDING. **2. hold harmless.** See under HARMLESS. **3. hold out,** to act in such a way as to create the impression—especially a false impression—that something or someone (often oneself) has certain qualities or status: *He held himself out as a qualified lawyer.* Depending upon the circumstances, this may lead to criminal penalties, civil liability for FRAUD, or an application of the doctrine of ESTOPPEL. **4. hold over,** to continue to occupy rented premises after the lease expires or the tenancy is legally terminated. The tenant who does this is commonly called a **holdover tenant.** See also *tenancy at sufferance* (under TENANCY).

holder *n.* **1.** a person in possession of a *bearer instrument* (see under BEARER), or a person in possession of an instrument issued or indorsed to him or to his order. **2. holder in due course,** a holder who gives value for an instrument and takes it in an honest transaction in the normal course of the transferor's business, without knowledge of any facts that might make it unenforceable. The right of a holder in due course to receive payment on an instrument is often stronger than that of an ordinary holder.

holding *n.* **1.** the ruling of a court in a case, or upon a particular issue in a case, especially an issue of law (as distinguished from fact). Cf. DICTUM. **2. holding company.** See under COMPANY. **3. holding period, a.** the period of time that a taxpayer keeps a piece of property before selling it. **b.** the length of time that a taxpayer must keep a piece of property before selling it in order to qualify for special reduced tax rates on the gain realized on the sale. See also *capital gains tax* (under CAPITAL[1]).

holdover tenancy. Same as *tenancy at sufferance* (see under TENANCY).

holdover tenant. See under HOLD.

holographic will. See under WILL.

home owner's warranty. Same as *construction warranty* (see under WARRANTY).

home rule the right of a city, town, or other local government to make its own laws on matters of local concern to the extent permitted by the state constitution or statutes.

homestead *n.* **1.** a dwelling and surrounding land occupied by the owner as a home. **2. homestead exemption,** the principle that property designated as one's homestead in accordance with a state statute (generally called the **homestead law, homestead exemption statute,** or the like) may not be seized by creditors to satisfy one's debts. The scope of such laws varies from state to state; under the most generous, a debtor can sometimes live quite luxuriously while leaving his creditors unpaid.

homicide *n.* **1.** an act or omission resulting in the death of another person. Also called **criminal homicide.** The crime of causing of another's death through conduct that was intentional, knowing, reckless, or extremely negligent, without JUSTIFICATION. All states recognize several degrees of the crime depending on the circumstances and the actor's STATE OF MIND. The major categories of homicide are usually called MURDER, MANSLAUGHTER, and *negligent homicide.* **3. justifiable homicide,** homicide committed under circumstances regarded by the law as justification for such an extreme act, the most common of which is SELF-DEFENSE. Justifiable homicide is not a crime. **4. negligent homicide,** the crime of causing another's death through *criminal negligence* (see under NEGLIGENCE); the lowest degree of criminal homicide. Called **criminally negligent homicide** in some states; in others, included in *involuntary manslaughter* (see under MANSLAUGHTER). **5. vehicular homicide,** a special category of homicide recognized in some states for dealing with

legal

homicides by careless and drunk drivers. Also called **homicide by automobile.**

honor *v.* **1.** to pay, or to ACCEPT and pay, a check, note, or other instrument for the payment of money. —*n.* **2. Your** (or **His** or **Her**) **Honor,** a respectful form of address or reference for a judge.

Honorable *adj.* the title accorded to judges; used with either the full name or an additional title, or both: *the Honorable Samuel S. Smith; the Honorable Samuel S. Smith, Judge; the Honorable Judge Smith.*

horizontal price fixing. See under PRICE FIXING.

horizontal union. See under UNION.

hornbook *n.* **1.** a one-volume text or treatise organizing and summarizing a significant area of law, such as torts or corporation law. Cf. CASEBOOK; TREATISE. **2. hornbook law,** a legal principle regarded as so basic and well established as to require no citation to case authority: *"It is hornbook law that a principal is bound by the act of an agent within the scope of the agent's authority."* Also called **black letter law.**

hostile environment harassment. See under SEXUAL HARASSMENT.

hostile witness. See under WITNESS.

hostile working environment working conditions in which an employee is subjected to HARASSMENT because of the employee's race, color, religion, sex, or national origin. The maintenance of such an environment constitutes unlawful employment discrimination. See also SEXUAL HARASSMENT.

hot blood. Colloquial expression for HEAT OF PASSION.

hot pursuit. Same as FRESH PURSUIT.

house counsel. See under COUNSEL.

HR-10 plan. See under PENSION PLAN.

hung jury. See under JURY. See also HANG.

hypnotically refreshed recollection. See under RECOLLECTION; see also RECOVERED MEMORY.

hypothecate *v.* to pledge property (either tangible or intangible) as collateral to secure a debt, especially without giving up possession of the property.

hypothetical *adj.* **1.** assumed for purposes of discussion: *hypothetical facts; hypothetical case.* **2.** based upon or relating to facts assumed for purposes of discussion: *hypothetical question* (see under QUESTION¹). —*n.* **3.** *Informal.* (used especially in law schools) short for hypothetical case or *hypothetical question* (see under QUESTION¹).

a b c d e f g h I j k l m n o p q r s t u v w x y z

id. *Latin.* abbreviation for *idem* (lit. "the same one") (in citations) the case or other writing just mentioned. A term used for all but the first of a series of citations to the same source. For example, three successive references to an appellant's brief (the first two to page 25 and the third to page 27) might read: "Appellant's Brief at 25," "id.," "id. at 27."

illegal *adj.* contrary to law; a term usually applied to conduct that is criminal or directly contrary to a specific statute or court order, or to a person engaged in such conduct. See *illegal* ALIEN, DISCRIMINATION under those words. Cf. the more general term UNLAWFUL.

illusory promise. See under PROMISE.

immaterial *adj.* not MATERIAL. See, for example, *immaterial breach* (under BREACH).

immigrant *n.* a person who enters a country intending to reside there permanently.

immigration *n.* the entry of people into a country for the purpose of establishing permanent residence. The Supreme Court has interpreted the Constitution as conferring upon Congress virtually unlimited power to regulate immigration into the United States.

immunity *n.* **1.** exemption from civil suit or criminal prosecution for allegedly wrongful acts, granted by law to certain classes of persons or by prosecutorial discretion to certain individuals, either by constitutional mandate or for reasons of public policy. In most cases the exemption is unqualified (**absolute immunity**), but sometimes it applies only if the wrongful acts were done in the good-faith (albeit erroneous) belief that they were legally justified (**qualified immunity**). **2. diplomatic immunity,** immunity from civil and criminal liability granted to foreign diplomats by the United States and most or all other countries. **3. judicial immunity,** immunity from tort liability for any official act of a judge within the scope of judicial functions. **4. legislative immunity,** constitutionally granted immunity from tort liability, and to a limited extent from criminal liability, for acts by members of Congress and their aides in carrying out legislative functions, including particularly the absolute right to speak freely in House and Senate debates without fear of liability for defamation. State legislators generally enjoy similar immunity. **5. official immunity,** a general term for immunity of governmental officials of all sorts from liability for acts within the scope of their duties. Such immunity may be absolute or qualified,

depending upon the official and the nature of the alleged wrong. **6. sovereign immunity,** the traditional immunity of the government itself from any suit at all—derived from the notion that "the King can do no wrong." The federal government and most states now have statutes permitting the assertion of most tort and contract claims against them. In addition, in certain kinds of cases sovereign immunity can be circumvented by seeking an injunction against a specific state officer rather than against the state itself. **7. transactional immunity,** immunity granted by a prosecutor to a witness, guaranteeing that the witness will not be prosecuted in connection with any event ("transaction") testified about. A witness who has been granted such immunity cannot refuse to testify on the basis of the Fifth Amendment privilege against SELF-INCRIMINATION. Cf. *use immunity.* **8. use immunity,** immunity granted by a prosecutor to a witness, guaranteeing that neither the witness's testimony nor any information derived from it will be used in any future prosecution against the witness. Although this does not preclude prosecution of the witness for involvement in the events testified about, any such case must be based entirely upon independently derived evidence. Therefore, like *transactional immunity,* use immunity makes it impossible for a witness to claim a Fifth Amendment privilege not to testify.

impanel *v.* to select and seat the jury for a case.

impeachment *n.* **1.** the instituting of formal misconduct charges against a government officer as a basis for removal from office. Under the Constitution, the House of Representatives has exclusive power to impeach federal officers, including the President, which it does by voting for ARTICLES OF IMPEACHMENT. A trial is then held in the Senate, and if convicted of an impeachable offense by the Senate, the officer may be removed from office. See also HIGH CRIMES AND MISDEMEANORS. **2.** the introduction of evidence calling into question the credibility of a witness; for example, a *prior inconsistent statement* (see under STATEMENT), evidence of interest (see INTEREST²) or bias; evidence that the witness has been convicted of crimes involving dishonesty; or simply evidence contradicting the witness's testimony. This is referred to as "impeaching the credibility of the witness," or simply "impeaching the witness." See also *hostile witness* and *interested witness* (both under WITNESS). Cf. REHABILITATION. —**impeach,** *v.*

impediment *n.* a legal bar; especially a circumstance rendering one legally incapable of making a contract or entering into a legal relationship; for example, being underage is an impediment to marriage.

impertinent *adj.* not pertinent to the case at hand. A court may order impertinent matter stricken from a pleading so that a party will not have to respond to allegations that have no place in the case.

implead *v.* to serve a complaint on a third party alleging that the third party should be held liable for all or part of any damages one is required to pay in a lawsuit; that is, to initiate a *third-party action* (see under THIRD PARTY): *The injured pedestrian sued the driver of the car, and the driver impleaded the auto mechanic, claiming that the accident was caused by the mechanic's poor work on the car's brakes.*

impleader *n.* the act of impleading and the procedures for third-party actions.

implied *adj.* **1.** suggested by conduct or circumstances rather than explicitly stated; describing a right, interest, obligation, authority, or status recognized by law even though not put into words—and perhaps not even intended—by the parties involved; opposite of EXPRESS. See *implied* CONTRACT, REPEAL, RIGHT OF ACTION under those words. **2.** Also called **implied in fact.** inferred from what a person has said or done; recognized by law because evidently reflecting a party's actual intent, even though nothing was specifically said about it. See *implied* AUTHORITY[1], waiver under those words, and *contract implied in fact* (under CONTRACT). **3.** Also called **implied in law.** imposed by law without regard to the intent of the parties; CONSTRUCTIVE. In essence, this means that in the eyes of the law, if the parties did not intend a certain result, they should have. See *implied warranty* (under WARRANTY); *contract implied in law* (under CONTRACT).

imply *v.* to impose an obligation or status, or declare it to exist, by operation of law: *The law implies duty of good faith in all contracts. The judge implied a contract to pay for life-saving medical treatment given while the defendant was unconscious, even though the defendant's intent was to commit suicide.*

impossibility *n.* the occurrence of an unforeseen circumstance rendering performance of a contract impossible. For example, a building to be rented might burn down, or a transaction to be completed might be made illegal, or the person whose services were contracted for might die. Under modern principles of contract law, further performance of the contract is usually excused in such cases (that is, the party whose performance became impossible will not have to pay damages for breach of contract), so long as this would not be unfair to the other party. Cf. IMPRACTICABILITY.

impost *n.* a tax; especially a duty on goods imported from another country.

impound *v.* to take property into custody of a court or law enforcement agency for such purposes as testing, use as evidence, possible forfeiture, or holding pending a decision as to its proper disposition. —**impoundment,** *n.*

impracticability *n.* an unforeseen circumstance that renders performance of a contract far more difficult and expensive than either party had reason to expect when the contract was entered into. Except in limited circumstances (notably contracts for the sale of goods), the law has not yet recognized impracticability as providing an excuse for nonperformance of a contract in most situations. Cf. IMPOSSIBILITY.

impress *v.* to impose a *constructive trust* (see under TRUST) upon property; that is, to deem or declare property in the hands of one person to be held, as a matter of equity, in trust for another: *The judge impressed a trust on the property obtained by fraud. Equity deems misdelivered property to be impressed with a trust for the benefit of the intended recipient.* —**impressment,** *n.*

impression. See FIRST IMPRESSION.

imprisonment *n.* the placing or keeping of a person in jail or prison as punishment for a crime. Cf. DETAIN; FALSE IMPRISONMENT.

improvement *n.* a permanent change in real property that increases its value, prolongs its useful life, or adapts it to a new use, and is more than a repair or maintenance.

improvident *adj.* unwise, ill-considered, or based upon inadequate information. A term often used by courts in explaining a change of mind: *The injunction is vacated as improvidently granted.*

improvident exercise of discretion. Same as ABUSE OF DISCRETION.

imputed *adj.* describing an act, fact, or state of mind attributed to a person by operation of law, often because of that person's relationship to a person more directly involved, as in the case of negligence of a driver imputed under the law of many states to the owner of the vehicle, or knowledge of an employee imputed to the employer. See also *imputed knowledge* (under KNOWLEDGE).

in bar. See under BAR.

in blank describing an indorsement that does not specify a particular *indorsee* (see under INDORSE). See also *blank indorsement* (under INDORSEMENT).

in camera *Latin.* (lit. "in the chamber") (of judicial business or proceedings) in private; not in open court. Usually referring to something that takes place in CHAMBERS, in the ROBING ROOM, or in a courtroom from which spectators have been excluded: *The judge met with the lawyers in camera. The judge ordered that the disputed documents be submitted to her for in camera inspection.*

in common signifying ownership of an interest in property by two or more people or entities with *undivided interests* (see under INTEREST[1]) in the whole, responsibility for expenses and a right to profits from the property in proportion to their interests, and no RIGHT OF SURVIVORSHIP. For example, one co-owner might own a one-half undivided interest in an apartment building while two others each own a one-fourth interest; upon the death of one, that owner's interest would pass to her heirs or to a taker designated in her will, instead of vesting in the surviving co-owners as in the case of joint ownership or ownership by the entirety: *estate in common; ownership in common; tenancy in common; tenant in common.* Cf. JOINT; BY THE ENTIRETY; IN SEVERALTY. See also COMMUNITY PROPERTY.

in esse *Latin.* in being; existing at the time under consideration. See example under IN POSSE.

in evidence 1. describing an EXHIBIT that the judge has admitted into evidence: *Exhibits 1 and 3 are in evidence; Exhibit 2 is not.* **2.** describing a fact for which testimony or other evidence has been introduced that, if believed, establishes the fact: *That the defendant owned a gun is already in evidence.*

in forma pauperis *Latin.* (lit. "in the character of a poor person") a method of proceeding in court under which filing fees and certain other requirements, such as the filing of multiple copies of printed briefs, are waived for indigent litigants. In certain situations indigent parties have a constitutional right to proceed in forma pauperis, but in most civil cases (including, ironically, petitions for bankruptcy) they do not.

in futuro *Latin.* in the future; taking effect at a future date. Cf. IN PRAESENTI.

in haec verba *Latin.* (lit. "in these words") using exactly the same words; verbatim: *The court's opinion sets forth the allegedly indecent material in haec verba.*

in house 1. (of a company's legal work) handled by lawyers and paralegals who are salaried employees of the company, rather than by an outside lawyer or law firm: *We saved money by drafting the brief in house.* **2. in-house,** designating such work or the lawyers who do it: *an in-house project; the in-house staff.* See also *in-house counsel* (under COUNSEL).

in kind 1. referring to a payment made in goods or services rather than money. See also BARTER. **2.** not the same, but of the same kind. For example, a neighbor who borrows a cup of sugar for baking

legal

will return it in kind—that is, will return a similar cup of sugar but not the same sugar that was borrowed.

in limine *Latin.* (lit. "at the threshold") at the outset; before beginning a trial or other proceeding. A "motion in limine" is one filed before a trial begins in order to get an issue that is bound to arise resolved in advance.

in loco parentis *Latin.* (lit. "in the position of a parent") describing a person or institution that has assumed, at least for some purposes, the rights and responsibilities of a parent toward a child: *For purposes of consenting to emergency treatment when the parents could not be located, the school acted in loco parentis.*

in pari delicto *Latin.* (lit. "in equal fault") **1.** a defense sometimes available in a civil case, in which it is argued that the plaintiff should not be permitted to complain of wrongful conduct by the defendant because the plaintiff's conduct in the matter was equally wrongful; it applies particularly to situations in which the plaintiff and defendant were involved together in some unlawful activity. **2.** describing participants in a crime whose roles make them guilty in the same degree: *The person who robbed the bank and the person who stood watch during the robbery are in pari delicto.*

in pari materia *Latin.* (lit. "in regard to the same matter") referring to statutes, passages of a contract, clauses of an instrument, or the like that deal with the same matter. In general, writings that are in pari materia are to be construed to the extent possible as consistent with each other, each being interpreted in light of the other.

in personam *Latin.* (lit. "directed at the person") describing the fundamental nature of a legal proceeding as focused on a person or entity rather than a piece of property. For details, see under JURISDICTION[1], action, and JUDGMENT. Cf. IN REM; QUASI IN REM.

in point. Same as ON POINT. See also *case in point* (under CASE[1]).

in posse *Latin.* (lit. "in potentiality") potential; not yet existing at the time under discussion. *The term "grandchildren" in the will was interpreted as meaning grandchildren in esse and in posse* (i.e., not only grandchildren existing at the time of the testator's death but also any future grandchildren). Cf. IN ESSE.

in praesenti *Latin.* in the present; effective immediately, Cf. IN FUTURO.

in propria persona *Latin.* (lit. "in one's own person") personally; in person; especially, not represented by an attorney; PRO SE. Abbreviated **in pro. per.**

in re *Latin.* in the matter of. This introductory phrase appears in certain case names; it is also used in citations as a concise substitute for such introductory phrases as "petition of" and "application of." Thus a case captioned "Petition of John J. Smith for a Writ of Habeas Corpus" would most likely be cited as "In re Smith." See also IN THE MATTER OF.

in rem *Latin.* (lit. "directed at the thing") describing the fundamental character of a legal proceeding as focused on a piece of property (real or personal, tangible or intangible) or occasionally on a legal relationship (e.g., a marriage), rather than on a particular person or entity. For details, see under JURISDICTION[1], action, and JUDGMENT. See also ALL THE WORLD. Cf. IN PERSONAM; QUASI IN REM.

in severalty signifying ownership of an interest in property by one person or entity only, with no co-owners: *estate in severalty; ownership in severalty; tenancy in severalty; tenant in severalty.* Cf. JOINT; BY THE ENTIRETY; IN COMMON. See also COMMUNITY PROPERTY.

in specie *Latin.* (lit. "in kind") **1.** in original form: *Some of the decedent's property was distributed to the heirs in specie; the rest was sold and the proceeds distributed.* **2.** of the kind or in the manner specified: *performance of the contract in specie.*

in terrorem *Latin.* (lit. "for the purpose of fear") describing anything intended as a threat; especially a clause in a will ("in terrorem clause"), permitted

in some states, that nullifies any bequest to a beneficiary who unsuccessfully contests the will.

in the matter of an introductory phrase in certain case names, often shortened to **matter of** or IN RE in citations

in toto *Latin.* (lit. "in the entirety") completely; in its entirety; as a whole: *The statute was repealed in toto.*

in trust. See under TRUST.

inadmissible *adj.* (of evidence) not ADMISSIBLE.

inapposite *adj.* describing a PRECEDENT that is regarded as not sufficiently similar to the present case to provide much guidance; *distinguishable* (see under DISTINGUISH).

incapacity *n.* the absence of legal CAPACITY to perform an act; for example, if a party to a marriage is underage or already married, the marriage will be void on the ground of incapacity.

incest *n.* the crime of having sexual intercourse, or living as husband and wife, with a close relative, such as an ancestor, descendant, or sibling. The exact list of prohibited relationships varies from state to state.

inchoate *adj.* incipient; commenced but not yet completed or matured. For example, an "inchoate lien" is one agreed to by a debtor and creditor but not yet recorded in accordance with laws requiring filing of liens in a public office; the crimes of ATTEMPT, SOLICITATION, and CONSPIRACY are sometimes classified as "inchoate crimes."

included offense. See LESSER INCLUDED OFFENSE.

inclusionary zoning. See under ZONING.

income *n.* **1.** money received, or the value of property or services received. **2. earned income,** income derived from working for another **(wages)** or in one's own business **(self-employment income).** Cf. *unearned income.* **3. gross income,** total income potentially subject to income tax and required to be reported on an income tax return, before subtraction of any deductions. **4. net income,** in a business, the excess of total income over expenses; profit. **5. ordinary income,** income subject to taxation at ordinary rates; that is, all income reportable on income tax returns except *capital gain* (see under CAPITAL[1]), which is subject to special lower tax rates. **6. taxable income, a.** any type of income subject to income tax; e.g., wages or alimony, but not gifts (usually) or child support. **b.** the portion of a taxpayer's income upon which income tax is based, consisting of *gross income* minus DEDUCTIONS. **7. unearned income,** income derived from investments and other sources other than employment or self-employment. Cf. *earned income.*

income tax a federal, state, or local tax on the annual INCOME of an individual or married couple **(personal income tax),** a corporation **(corporate income tax),** or a trust or estate. See also *capital gains tax* (under CAPITAL[1]); *flat tax* and *progressive tax* (under TAX); *marginal tax rate* and *effective tax rate* (under TAX RATE).

incompetent *adj.* **1.** not competent (see COMPETENT[1] and COMPETENT[2]). —*n.* **2.** an individual who is not mentally competent (see COMPETENT[1]): *a law protecting infants and incompetents.*

inconsistent statement. See *prior inconsistent statement* (under STATEMENT).

inconsistent verdict. See under VERDICT.

incorporate *v.* **1.** to organize as a corporation; to attain the status of a corporation by going through the formalities required by state law. **2.** to include as a part of: *Please incorporate these changes and additions into a revised draft of the legislation.* **3. incorporate by reference,** to make one document a part of another, not by physically reproducing the first in the second (although it typically would be attached for ease of reference), but by means of a statement in the second document simply declaring the first to be part of it. —**incorporation,** *n.*

incorporated *adj.* formed as a corporation. This word (or its abbreviation, **inc.**) in an entity's name indicates that the entity is a corporation; not all corporate names include this word, however.

incorporation doctrine the principle by which

most of the BILL OF RIGHTS, which originally operated only as a limitation on the power of the federal government, has been made binding upon state governments as well. The key to the process is the Fourteenth Amendment to the Constitution, which was adopted after the Civil War and provided, for the first time, that no *state* may deprive any person of life, liberty, or property without DUE PROCESS of law. Over time, the Supreme Court decided that most of the protections in the Bill of Rights—including both procedural protections (such as the right to a jury trial in criminal cases) and substantive rights (such as the right to speak one's mind or practice one's religion)—are inherent in the concept of due process, and hence protected from state governmental interference by the due process clause of the Fourteenth Amendment. Thus almost the entire Bill of Rights was ultimately "incorporated" or "absorbed" into the Fourteenth Amendment.

indecent *adj.* **1.** offensive to generally accepted standards of propriety in matters relating to sex, bodily functions, and display of the human body. **2. indecent exposure,** the crime of exposing one's genitals under circumstances likely to cause alarm or offense. See also *indecent* ASSAULT, SPEECH under those words. —**indecency,** *n.*

indefinite *adj.* (of a contract) not sufficiently certain to be enforceable. If the material terms of a purported contract are so indefinite that a court cannot reasonably ascertain who is to do what, the contract "fails for indefiniteness."

indefinite failure of issue. See under ISSUE[2].

indemnify *v.* to compensate or reimburse a person for loss or liability, or agree to do so if a loss or liability arises in the future.

indemnity *n.* **1.** a right to receive compensation for a loss from someone other than a wrongdoer who caused the loss, or to receive reimbursement for a payment that one has had to make to someone else to compensate that other person for a loss. A right of indemnity can arise in two ways: (a) by contract. An insurance policy is a contract by which the insurance company agrees (for consideration in the form of payment of premiums) to indemnify the insured against losses or liabilities specified in the policy. (b) by operation of law. In certain situations a person held liable for a tort is entitled to indemnity from another tortfeasor regarded as more directly at fault. For example, if the owner of a car is held liable under state law for injury caused by negligence of the driver, or an employer is held liable for the tort of an employee under the doctrine of RESPONDEAT SUPERIOR, the owner or employer is entitled to reimbursement from the driver or employee whose tortious conduct actually caused the injury. **2.** the compensation or reimbursement received pursuant to a right of indemnity.

indemnity insurance insurance that protects the insured against injury or loss suffered by the insured directly, as distinguished from losses to others for which the insured might be held liable. For example, automobile collision insurance is a form of indemnity insurance that compensates the insured for damage to his own automobile in an accident. Cf. LIABILITY INSURANCE.

indenture *n.* **1.** an old term for a deed or written contract, especially one under seal (see SEAL[1]). **2.** Also called **trust indenture.** an instrument stating the terms and conditions governing an issue of bonds, setting forth the rights of bondholders and providing various measures for the protection of those rights, including appointment of a trustee to handle necessary transfers of money and to look out for the interests of bondholders.

independent *adj.* free, or at least relatively free, from control by others; autonomous. See *independent* CONTRACTOR, COUNSEL, PROSECUTOR, UNION under those words.

indeterminate sentence. See under SENTENCE.

indicium *n., pl.* **indicia.** an indicator; a clue which by itself might not justify a conclusion, but may be persuasive when viewed together with other indicia pointing to the same conclusion. Often used in the plural, since it is only when several indicia are present that they are of much significance: *indicia of reliability; indicia of apparent authority.*

indict *v.* to issue an INDICTMENT against a person.

indictment *n.* the act of a *grand jury* (see under JURY) in formally charging a person with a crime, or the written instrument setting forth the charge. The written indictment is typically drawn up by the prosecutor, voted on by the grand jury after hearing evidence, endorsed with the words "a *true bill* " if approved by the jury (see under BILL), and then filed with the court, where it becomes the instrument upon which the rest of the case is based. Cf. INFORMATION.

indispensable party. See under PARTY.

individual *n.* **1.** a human being as distinguished from an entity such as a corporation; a *natural person* (see under PERSON). —*adj.* **2.** involving only one individual or entity; not JOINT: *individual account* (see under ACCOUNT); *individual return* (see under RETURN). See also SEVERAL.

individual retirement account (or **arrangement**) **(IRA),** an arrangement under which an individual can save or invest a certain amount of each year's earned income for retirement and not be taxed on it until then.

indorse *v.* to sign one's name, sometimes with additional instructions or conditions, on the back of a NEGOTIABLE INSTRUMENT for the purpose of assigning the rights under it to someone else. The person whose name is signed is the **indorser;** the person (if any) named in the indorsement to receive the rights is the **indorsee.** Ordinarily the indorser will be liable to the indorsee or any subsequent holder of the instrument if the instrument is ultimately dishonored. See also NEGOTIATE; RECOURSE; and see discussion under ENDORSE (def. 3).

indorsement *n.* **1.** the act of indorsing an instrument, or the signature and accompanying writing indorsed on the instrument. Also called *endorsement* (see ENDORSE). **2. blank indorsement,** an indorsement that does not name a specific person to receive rights under the instrument, usually consisting of a signature alone; for example, John Smith's signature (without more) on the back of a check made out to the order of John Smith. This turns the instrument into a *bearer instrument* (see under BEARER). Also called **indorsement in blank.** Cf. *special indorsement.* **3. qualified indorsement,** an indorsement that includes the words "without recourse." See RECOURSE for discussion. **4. restrictive indorsement,** an indorsement that limits or purports to limit the instrument in some way; for example, a signature with the phrase "for deposit," which forbids further negotiation except through banking channels. **5. special indorsement,** an indorsement that specifies the person to whose order it makes the instrument payable. This turns the instrument into an *order instrument* (see under ORDER[2]). Cf. *blank indorsement.*

inducement. See *fraud in the inducement* (under FRAUD).

industrial performance zoning. See under ZONING.

industrial union. See under UNION.

inevitable discovery exception an exception to the EXCLUSIONARY RULE under which evidence obtained through an illegal search may be used against a defendant in a criminal case if the prosecution can show that it would have found the evidence sooner or later even without the illegal search.

infancy *n.* the state or period of being an INFANT; MINORITY: *Since the actress was 17 when she signed the $3.5 million movie contract, the contract was voidable on the ground of infancy.*

infant *n.* a person under the *age of majority* (see under AGE); a MINOR.

inferior court a court from which appeals may be taken to a higher court within the same judicial system. Especially, a court of *limited jurisdiction* (see under JURISDICTION[1]) such as a probate court, family court, justice of the peace court, or municipal court,

infliction of mental distress. See INTENTIONAL INFLICTION OF MENTAL DISTRESS.

information *n.* a formal instrument charging a person with a crime, filed by a prosecutor instead of an INDICTMENT in cases where the law does not require involvement of a *grand jury* (see under JURY). In the federal courts this is possible only for misdemeanors.

information and belief a basis for including facts in a pleading or in an affidavit, verification, or other sworn statement, even though one cannot claim personal knowledge of them. If one has received what one reasonably regards as reliable information, on the basis of which one believes a certain fact to be true, one can include that fact in the pleading or other writing, introduced by the phrase "On information and belief." Cf. *personal knowledge* (under KNOWLEDGE).

informed consent. See under CONSENT.

infra *adv.* Latin. (lit. "below") later in the same document. Opposite of SUPRA.

infraction *n.* **1.** the violation of a rule or law; especially a minor violation. **2.** the name given in some states to an offense below the level of MISDEMEANOR, punishable only by a fine or forfeiture and not classified as a crime: *a traffic infraction.*

infringe *v.* to violate another's COPYRIGHT, PATENT, or TRADEMARK by copying or using the protected work, invention, or mark without permission from the owner. —**infringement,** *n.*

inherit *v.* **1.** strictly, to receive property by INTESTATE SUCCESSION; to take as an HEIR. **2.** broadly, to receive property from the estate of a decedent either by intestate succession or by will.

inheritance *n.* **1.** the act or fact of inheriting. **2.** property that one has inherited: *an inheritance worth $150,000.*

inheritance tax a tax upon the recipient of money or property under a will or by intestate succession, based upon the value received. Cf. ESTATE TAX.

initiative *n.* a lawmaking procedure, available in some states, that bypasses the state legislature. Under this procedure, if a certain number of citizens sign a petition calling for it, a proposed statute must be put to a vote at a general election, and becomes law if a majority of the voters vote for it. Cf. REFERENDUM.

injunction *n.* **1.** a court order directing a person to do or refrain from doing some act. **2. mandatory injunction,** an injunction requiring a person to do some affirmative act. **3. permanent injunction,** an injunction granted as part of the judgment at the end of a case, directing a party forever to refrain from certain conduct. **4. preliminary injunction,** an injunction granted shortly after the beginning of a case, to maintain the status quo while the case proceeds. A preliminary injunction will be issued only after a hearing. If, for example, the plaintiff initiates an action to prevent an owner from tearing down a landmark building, the typical sequence of events would be (1) a *temporary restraining order* (see under RESTRAINING ORDER) preventing the owner from tearing down the building until a hearing can be held; (2) if the hearing convinces the judge that the plaintiff may be right, a *preliminary injunction* prohibiting the owner from tearing down the building until a trial can be held; and (3) if the trial persuades the judge that it would be illegal for the owner to tear down the building, a *permanent injunction* against tearing down the building. **5. prohibitory injunction,** an injunction prohibiting a person from taking certain action. This is the most common kind of injunction. Also called a RESTRAINING ORDER.

injurious falsehood. Same as DISPARAGEMENT.

injury *n.* **1.** any harm to an individual or entity through conduct regarded by the law as wrongful, including bodily injury, mental suffering, harm to reputation, property damage, financial loss, or deprivation of a legal right. **2. irreparable injury,** injury of a sort that cannot be suitably remedied by an award of damages, and for which a superior remedy exists in the form of equitable relief such as an INJUNCTION or SPECIFIC PERFORMANCE. In general, a party must show irreparable injury, or the prospect of irreparable injury, in order to obtain equitable relief. **3. personal injury, a.** narrowly, physical harm to an individual, as through disease, bodily injury, or death. **b.** broadly, any harm or loss suffered by an individual as a result of a tort.

innocent *adj.* **1.** acting without knowledge of circumstances making an act or transaction legally defective or wrongful, and without reason to have such knowledge; acting in good faith. For example, a purchaser of property who has no reason to know that the seller had no right to sell it is an innocent purchaser; a person who wanders onto another's land while lost in the dark is an innocent trespasser. **2.** done in good faith: *an innocent trespass.* **3.** (in criminal cases) genuinely free from guilt, even if convicted of a crime and thus guilty in the eyes of the law: *Newly discovered evidence indicates that the prisoner is innocent of the crime for which he was convicted.* "Innocent" is not used in law as a synonym for NOT GUILTY; a defendant cannot "plead innocent" or be "found innocent."

inquest *n.* a name given to certain kinds of factfinding proceedings, including a proceeding in which the plaintiff in an action in which the defendant has failed to appear presents evidence to the court to establish the damages to be awarded in a default judgment. The traditional "coroner's inquest"—a hearing conducted by a coroner to inquire into the cause and circumstances of a suspicious death—has largely been supplanted by a combination of autopsy to determine the cause and police investigation to determine the circumstances.

inquire *v.* to ask questions; largely restricted to the formal phrase "You may inquire," sometimes said by a judge to a lawyer to grant permission for the lawyer to begin questioning a witness.

inquiry notice. See under NOTICE.

inquisitorial system a method of adjudication in which judges play a prominent role in investigating facts and questioning witnesses; used in CIVIL LAW countries. Cf. ADVERSARY SYSTEM; ACCUSATORIAL SYSTEM.

insanity defense an *affirmative defense* (see under DEFENSE) to a criminal charge, under which a defendant who proves that he was insane at the time of the crime is held not to be responsible for the crime. The verdict then is NOT GUILTY BY REASON OF INSANITY, and the usual consequence is incarceration in a mental institution. Most states (but not all) recognize some type of insanity defense, applying a variety of rules or tests as to what constitutes insanity, usually some form of the M'NAGHTEN RULE, the IRRESISTIBLE IMPULSE TEST, or the SUBSTANTIAL CAPACITY TEST.

insider trading buying or selling stock in a publicly held corporation on the basis of "inside information"—that is, information that is known only to people inside the company (or outsiders who have been told privately) and has not yet been disclosed to the general public. Insider trading is illegal.

insolvent *adj.* **1.** usually, unable to pay one's debts in the ordinary course of business as they become due. **2.** for some purposes, having liabilities exceeding assets. Opposite of SOLVENT. —**insolvency,** *n.*

installment *n.* **1.** one of a series of payments, deliveries, or other steps required of a party by a contract, all of which together constitute the complete performance called for. —*adj.* **2.** describing a contract calling for performance in installments, or referring to some aspect of such a transaction: *installment note* (see under NOTE[1]); *installment contract; installment loan.*

instant *adj.* referring to that which is currently under consideration; at hand; current: *the instant case; the instant decision; the instant crime.*

instanter *adv.* immediately; forthwith; usually used in connection with a court order, and often suggesting that the limits of the judge's patience have been reached: *The Court will brook no further delay; the documents are to be produced instanter. So ordered.*

instruct *v.* **1.** Same as DIRECT[2]. **2.** to issue an IN-STRUCTION or set of instructions to the jury: *The judge will instruct the jury tomorrow afternoon.*

instruction *n.* **1.** a judge's explanation and direction to a jury concerning a particular legal principle or duty of the jury: *The plaintiff objected to the court's instruction as to the inference that may be drawn from the plaintiff's failure to call his wife as a witness.* **2. instructions,** the comprehensive explanation of the applicable law and duties of the jury given by the judge to the jury at the end of a trial, just before the jury begins to deliberate. Also called the CHARGE to the jury. **3. cautionary instruction,** any warning, reminder, or admonishment to the jury; for example, not to commence deliberations until after all the evidence is in, or not to consider anything that a lawyer says as evidence. **4. curative instruction,** an instruction directing the jury to disregard certain inadmissible testimony, statements of counsel, or other potentially prejudicial events that occurred in their presence.

instrument *n.* **1.** a formal legal document, especially one that embodies legal rights or a legal interest (such as a stock certificate), or one that operates to cause legal consequences (such as a deed or will). See also *sealed instrument* (under SEAL[1]); AC-CUSATORY INSTRUMENT. **2.** a NEGOTIABLE INSTRUMENT or NONNNEGOTIABLE INSTRUMENT.

insufficient cause a legally insufficient reason for taking a particular action or seeking a particular court order. Cf. GOOD CAUSE.

insurable interest an interest in person or property justifying one in obtaining insurance on that person or that property. For example, since a company might suffer financially if its chief executive dies, the company has an "insurable interest" that it may protect by purchasing a life insurance policy under which the company will be compensated if the executive dies. The law prohibits people from taking out insurance on lives or property in which they have no insurable interest, since that amounts to nothing more than a gambling contract, and moreover would put the policyholder in the unseemly position of hoping that harm will befall someone else so that the policyholder can obtain a windfall.

insurable title. See under TITLE.

insurance *n.* **1.** a contractual arrangement whereby a company (the **insurer**), in consideration for a payment or periodic payments of money (the **premium**), agrees to compensate its customer (the **insured**) in the event that the insured suffers some loss or injury (in the case of INDEMNITY INSURANCE) or liability (in the case of LIABILITY INSURANCE) of a kind specified in the written contract (the POLICY). **2. group insurance,** insurance covering an identified group of people, such as employees of a company or members of an association, upon terms agreed to between the insurance company and the employer, association, or the like. **3. mutual insurance,** insurance provided by a company that is owned solely by its policyholders in proportion to the amount of insurance they have purchased from the company, rather than by stockholders. Since a mutual insurance company is not in business to make profits for stockholders, it can offer insurance at cost. See also COINSURANCE; *employers' liability insurance* (under WORKERS' COMPENSATION); EXCESS INSURANCE; FIDELITY INSURANCE; NO-FAULT INSURANCE; LIFE INSURANCE; REINSURANCE; *term insurance* (under LIFE INSURANCE); TITLE INSURANCE; *unemployment insurance* (under UNEMPLOYMENT COMPENSATION); *workers' compensation insurance* (under WORKERS' COMPENSATION). Cf. SELF-INSURANCE.

insurance broker. See under BROKER.

intangible property. See under PROPERTY.

intellectual property. See under PROPERTY.

intent *n.* **1.** broadly, a STATE OF MIND in which one either desires to achieve a certain result by one's conduct (even if that result is unlikely to occur) or knows that such a result is practically certain to occur (even if that is not what is desired). This is the usual meaning of "intent" in tort law and the traditional meaning in criminal law. See, for example,

intentional tort (under TORT); *intent to kill* (under MURDER). **2.** narrowly, a conscious objective of causing a certain result. This is the usual meaning of the term under modern criminal codes, which classify KNOWLEDGE of likely results without an actual intent to achieve them as a separate state of mind. See also PURPOSELY. **3.** Also called **intention.** the purpose or design underlying a statute, contract, will, or other instrument: LEGISLATIVE INTENT; *intent of the parties; the testator's intent.* —**intentional,** *adj.* —**intentionally,** *adv.*

intentional infliction of mental distress the tort of intentionally causing serious emotional distress to a person by means of conduct of an extremely outrageous nature.

inter alia *Latin.* among other things: *The contract provides, inter alia, that the parties will submit any dispute to binding arbitration.*

inter se *Latin.* among themselves; between themselves.

inter vivos *Latin.* (lit. "among the living") describing a transaction completed during one's lifetime, as distinguished from one occurring at death or effected by will or intestacy: *inter vivos gift* (see under GIFT); *inter vivos trust* (see under TRUST). Cf. TESTAMENTARY.

interest[1] **1.** a legally enforceable right with respect to real or personal property. An interest may be designated as either a **legal interest** or a **beneficial** (or **equitable**) **interest**, depending upon whether it is viewed from the perspective of the *legal owner* or, in the case of property held in trust, the *beneficial owner* (see both phrases under OWNER). See also ESTATE[1]; TENANCY. **2. contingent interest,** an interest which may give the holder a right of possession, use, or enjoyment of the property at some time in the future, but only upon the occurrence of specific circumstances which are possible but not certain to arise; for example, a *contingent estate* (see under ESTATE[1]). Cf. *vested interest.* **3. executory interest,** a *future estate* (see under ESTATE[1]) which will become possessory only upon termination of a fee simple, and which is held by someone other than the person (or the successors of the person) who transferred the fee to its present owner. See also *fee simple determinable* (under FEE[1]). Cf. POSSIBILITY OF REVERTER. **4. future interest,** an interest which does not confer a present right of possession, use, or enjoyment of property, but may do so in the future; for example, a REMAINDER or a POSSIBILITY OF REVERTER. Cf. *present interest.* **5. possessory interest,** a present right to possession of property, particularly real property. **6. present interest, a.** (in personal property) a present right to possession, use, or enjoyment of property. For example, the current beneficiary of a trust fund has a present interest in the fund. **b.** (in real property) Same as *possessory interest.* Present interests in real property may be classified as either a **freehold interest** (same as FREEHOLD) or a **leasehold interest** (same as LEASEHOLD). **7. security interest,** an interest in the property of another consisting of the right to sell that property in order to satisfy some obligation of the owner if the owner defaults; for example, the right of an automobile dealer or financer to take back your car and sell it to someone else if you do not keep up the payments. See also LIEN; MORTGAGE. **8. undivided interest,** the rights of each of two or more co-owners of a single interest in property when, instead of dividing the property up physically, they all share the right to use the whole property. Also called **undivided fractional interest. 9. vested interest,** a legally enforceable right to possession, use, or enjoyment of property which either exists at present or is certain to arise in the future; a present interest or a future interest that is not subject to any contingency. Cf. *contingent interest.* See also INSURABLE INTEREST; *successor in interest* (under SUCCESSOR).

interest[2] *n.* **1.** a financial or other direct legal stake in a matter, such that one's pocketbook or legal rights are directly affected. For example, a shareholder has an interest in a suit by or against the corporation; a child has an interest in a custody dispute between the parents. See also *real party in interest* (under PARTY). **2.** broadly, any close personal stake in a matter; for example, one's interest in a suit against a friend, a relative, or a personal enemy. See also CONFLICT OF INTEREST.

interest³ *n.* **1.** a sum paid or charged for the use of money or for the privilege of deferring a payment, expressed either as a dollar amount or as a percentage of the principal amount involved in the transaction. **2. legal interest, a.** the rate of interest set by law for certain kinds of debts, such as an unpaid judgment. **b.** the maximum rate of interest that can be charged without violating laws against USURY.

interested *adj.* having an *interest* (see INTEREST²) in a matter: *interested person* (see under PERSON); *interested witness* (see under WITNESS). Cf. DISINTERESTED.

interlocutory *adj.* interim; describing an order or other step occurring in the course of a case but not ending the case: *interlocutory order* (see under ORDER¹); *interlocutory appeal* (see under APPEAL).

intermeddler. See OFFICIOUS INTERMEDDLER.

intermediate appellate court. See under COURT.

intermediate scrutiny. Same as HEIGHTENED SCRUTINY.

Internal Revenue Code (I.R.C.) the portion of the UNITED STATES CODE that contains all federal tax laws.

Internal Revenue Service (I.R.S.) the federal agency that administers most federal tax laws.

International Court of Justice the chief judicial agency of the United Nations, based in the Hague, Netherlands. It is authorized to render advisory opinions to the United Nations and to decide disputes between nations voluntarily submitted to it by the nations involved.

international law 1. Also called **public international law** or the **law of nations.** a body of principles that are generally accepted among the nations of the world as governing their dealings with each other and each other's citizens or subjects. It is a combination of long-established custom and specific treaty obligations, depending for its vitality largely upon each nation's good will or desire for international acceptance. See also FEDERAL LAW. **2.** **private international law,** the branch of CONFLICT OF LAWS that deals with the application of potentially conflicting national laws to transactions, events, or litigation concerning two or more countries.

interpleader *n.* a type of action that may be commenced by a STAKEHOLDER in possession of property or funds known to belong to someone else but claimed by more than one other person, so that a court can determine which claimant should get the property. This procedure permits the stakeholder to deposit the property with the court and leave it to the competing claimants to plead their claims against each other (to **interplead**), freeing the stakeholder both of the burden of litigating over the property and of the risk of turning it over to the wrong claimant.

interpretation. See under CONSTRUCTION.

interrogation *n.* **1.** the questioning of a criminal suspect by law enforcement authorities. **2. custodial interrogation,** the questioning of a suspect who has been arrested or otherwise deprived of his freedom of action in any significant way. This is the situation to which the MIRANDA RULE applies. —**interrogate,** *v.*

interrogatory *n.* one of a set of written questions about the facts and contentions in a case **(interrogatories)** submitted to an adversary as part of the DISCOVERY process. Interrogatories are required to be answered in writing under oath. See also *special interrogatories* (under VERDICT).

interstate commerce. See under COMMERCE.

interstate compact. See under COMPACT.

intervene *v.* to insert oneself as a party in a lawsuit that is already pending between other parties, in order to assert or protect some interest that one has in the subject matter of the case. Depending upon the extent of an intervenor's need to be involved and the extent to which intervention would contribute to or detract from efficient dispute reso-

lution, intervention might or might not be allowed. See also *proper party* (under PARTY). —**intervener, intervenor,** *n.* —**intervention,** *n.*

intestacy *n.* the fact or state of being INTESTATE at death.

intestate *adj.* **1.** lacking a valid will, especially at the time of one's death: *to die intestate.* —*n.* **2.** a person who dies without leaving a valid will.

intestate succession taking as an HEIR; succeeding to property of a decedent by operation of law, either because the decedent left no valid will or because the will did not effectively dispose of all of the decedent's property. Each state has laws dictating how such property is to be distributed among surviving relatives, generally referred to as laws of intestate succession or laws of DESCENT AND DISTRIBUTION.

invalid. See *invalid as applied* and *invalid on its face* (both under UNCONSTITUTIONAL).

invasion of privacy the tort of unreasonable and highly offensive publicity about an individual or intrusion into an individual's private life and personal affairs. The contours of the tort vary from state to state, but in general it includes improper intrusions by such means as wiretapping, peeping, searching an individual's property and effects, or persistent telephoning; public disclosure of personal information about a private person without a legitimate news purpose; placing a person in a false public light (as by associating her with ideas or events with which she has no connection); and use of a person's name or image without consent for advertising or other commercial purposes.

investigative privilege. See under PRIVILEGE.

invidious discrimination. See under DISCRIMINATION.

invitee *n.* a person invited to enter real property to conduct business with the occupier or as a member of the general public invited for a public function. In tort law, the property owner owes a higher degree of care to an invitee than to a mere LICENSEE. But in most states an invited social guest is usually deemed to be a licensee rather than an invitee, on the theory that such a guest is like "one of the family" and thus is owed no special duty of care.

involuntary *adj.* **1.** compelled by law, by duress, by necessity, or otherwise. See *involuntary* BANKRUPTCY, CONFESSION, DISMISSAL, SERVITUDE under those words. **2.** unintentional; accidental. For example, *involuntary manslaughter* (see under MANSLAUGHTER). Cf. VOLUNTARY.

irrebuttable presumption. See under PRESUMPTION.

irrelevant *adj.* not RELEVANT.

irreparable injury. See under INJURY.

irresistible impulse test the principle that an INSANITY DEFENSE may be established by evidence that the crime was committed under the influence of a mental disease that made it impossible for the defendant to control her behavior, even if she knew that what she was doing was wrong. This test, also called **uncontrollable impulse test,** is recognized in a few states as a supplement to the M'NAGHTEN RULE.

issue¹ *n.* **1.** a disputed proposition presented in a case; any material fact or legal principle upon which the two sides disagree. Same as QUESTION², although many standard legal phrases customarily employ only one or the other of the two words. **2. constitutional issue.** See under CONSTITUTIONAL. **3. issue of fact** or **factual issue.** See under QUESTION². **4. issue of law** or **legal issue.** See under QUESTION². **5. issue preclusion.** Same as *collateral estoppel* (under ESTOPPEL). **6. join issue,** to file papers denying or contradicting an allegation in a case, thereby creating an issue for judicial determination. The point in a case where this occurs is called **joinder of issue.**

issue² *n.* **1.** descendants (children, grandchildren, etc.); normally construed to include generations yet unborn, not just those descendants existing at a particular time. **2. failure of issue,** the absence of surviving issue. **a. definite failure of issue,** the absence of surviving issue at the moment when property would have passed to them under the terms of a deed or will. This is the modern interpretation of the phrase *failure of issue.* **b. indefinite failure of issue,** the ultimate dying out of a person's line of descendants, which may (or may not) occur at an unknown time in the future. This older interpretation of the phrase *failure of issue* has been largely abandoned.

issue³ *v.* **1.** (of a corporation or other entity) to sell or put on the market a block of one's stock or other securities. —*n.* **2.** an entire class or block of securi-

ties sold or offered for sale at the same time. See also ISSUER.

issue⁴ *v.* **1.** to formally announce an order, rule, decision, etc., either orally or in writing. **2.** (of such an order, rule, etc.) to come forth; be announced: *The writ of mandamus issued from the Court of Appeals at 4:30 p.m.*

issuer *n.* the corporation or other entity that issued a particular security; the entity in which one is investing if one purchases a security.

itemized deduction. See under DEDUCTION.

a b c d e f g h i **J K** l m n o p q r s t u v w x y z

J. *pl.* **JJ.** abbreviation for Judge or Justice, always placed after the name: *The majority opinion was by White, J.; Brennan and Marshall, JJ., filed dissents.*

jail *n.* an institution, usually run by a county or municipality, for locking up offenders serving short sentences and accused people awaiting trial. Cf. PRISON.

Jane Doe. See under JOHN DOE.

J.D. *Latin.* abbreviation for *Juris Doctor* (lit. "doctor of law," "teacher of law"), the lowest law degree; the degree granted to everyone who graduates from law school. The degree was formerly called LL.B., for Bachelor of Laws, but the name was changed in the 1960's because lawyers felt that "J.D." made them sound more important. Cf. LL.M.

jeopardy *n.* risk of punishment for an offense. A criminal defendant is put in jeopardy when the jury is sworn in or, in a nonjury trial, when the first witness is sworn in. See also DOUBLE JEOPARDY.

JJ. See J.

j.n.o.v. See under JUDGMENT.

John (or **Jane**) **Doe,** a fictitious name used, sometimes with slight variations, in case names and in legal documents such as warrants and summonses, either to conceal a person's identity, or because the person's real name is not known, or because it is not yet known whether the person exists.

join *v.* to bring an additional claim or party into a case. See also *join issue* (under ISSUE¹). Cf. SEVER.

joinder *n.* **1.** the joining together in one action of more than one plaintiff or defendant **(party joinder** or **joinder of parties)** or more than one claim or charge **(claim joinder** or **joinder of claims).** Modern practice generally encourages joinder in the interest of resolving all aspects of a complex dispute in a single trial. **2. compulsory joinder,** joinder of a *necessary party* or *indispensable party* (see under PARTY). Such a party must be joined in the action if possible; and if a party found by the judge to be indispensable cannot be joined, the action will be dismissed. **3. permissive joinder,** joinder of a *proper party* (see under PARTY). The court will allow, but not require, the joinder of such a party. See also MISJOINDER; NONJOINDER. Cf. CONSOLIDATION; *joinder of issue* (under ISSUE¹); SEVER.

joint *adj.* **1.** collective; involving two or more people or entities acting or being dealt with together. See, for example, joint ACCOUNT, CUSTODY, LIABILITY, OBLIGATION, OWNER, TORTFEASOR, WILL under those words. Cf. SEVERAL; JOINT AND SEVERAL. **2.** referring to concurrent ownership of an interest in property by two or more people with equal *undivided interests* (see under INTEREST¹) in the whole, equal rights to possession and use of the property, and RIGHT OF SURVIVORSHIP: *joint estate; joint owner; joint ownership; joint tenancy; joint tenant.* Cf. BY THE ENTIRETY; IN COMMON; IN SEVERALTY. See also COMMUNITY PROPERTY. —**jointly,** *adv.*

joint and several susceptible of being treated legally either as JOINT or as SEVERAL—that is, as either collective or individual—at the option of the person initiating an action: *joint and several liability* (see under LIABILITY); *joint and several obligation* (see

under OBLIGATION). Cf. JOINT; SEVERAL. —**jointly and severally.**

joint stock company (or **association**). See under COMPANY.

joint venture an arrangement between two or more people or entities to work together on a specific project. Joint ventures are usually entered into because each participant **(venturer** or **joint venturer)** possesses some necessary skill or resource that the other lacks. Also called **joint adventure.**

journalists' shield law. See under SHIELD LAW.

judge *n.* **1.** a public official whose function is to hear and decide legal disputes, preside over trials, and generally monitor the conduct of cases presented to a court or administrative body and move the cases toward a final settlement or decision. **2.** (*cap.*) the title accorded to judges in many courts, including the United States District Courts and United States Courts of Appeals. See also ADMINISTRATIVE LAW JUDGE. Cf. MAGISTRATE; JUSTICE.

judge trial. Same as *bench trial* (see under TRIAL).

judgment *n.* **1.** a court's final decision in a case, or occasionally on a particular aspect of a case. **2.** the formal document embodying such a judgment, usually written in very formal and turgid prose. Cf. OPINION. **3. declaratory judgment,** a judgment resolving a dispute about legal rights or status but not awarding any relief. For example, two parties with conflicting claims to the same land might ask a court simply to declare which claim is valid. **4. default judgment,** a judgment against a party for failing to appear or to proceed with a case. Also called **judgment by default. 5. deficiency judgment,** in a case in which property of a debtor was sold at a court-supervised auction to satisfy a debt but failed to bring in enough money, a judgment against the debtor for the balance still owed. **6. in personam judgment** or **judgment in personam,** a judgment against a specific person or entity. If a money judgment against a party goes unpaid, any available property of that party may be seized to satisfy the judgment. Also called **personal judgment.** See also IN PERSONAM. **7. in rem judgment** or **judgment in rem,** a judgment determining the status or disposition of an item of property or a legal relationship. See also IN REM. **8. judgment notwithstanding the verdict,** a judgment contrary to the jury's findings in a case, entered by the judge on the ground that the jury's verdict lacked evidentiary support or was contrary to law. Also called **judgment n.o.v.** or, informally, **j.n.o.v.,** from the Latin *non obstante veredicto* (lit. "notwithstanding the verdict"). **9. judgment on the pleadings,** judgment granted to one side or the other even before the parties have commenced pretrial discovery, because the pleadings themselves contain admissions that, as a matter of law, permit only one possible outcome. **10. judgment on the verdict,** judgment in accordance with the jury's findings. See also *judgment notwithstanding the verdict.* See also *verdict against the weight of the evidence* (under VERDICT). **11. summary judgment,** judgment entered without a full trial because the evidence (or lack of evidence) brought out in pretrial discovery makes it clear which side must prevail as a matter of law. See also *judgment* CREDI-TOR, DEBTOR, LIEN under those words.

judgment proof describing a person or entity without assets that could be seized to satisfy a money judgment, making such a judgment worthless.

judicial *adj.* **1.** relating to a court or the courts. **2.** relating to a judge or judges: *judicial convention; judicial ethics.* **3. judicial economy,** efficiency in the management of judicial business; conservation of court resources: *The court consolidated the two related cases for trial in the interest of judicial economy.* **4. judicial notice,** acceptance of a fact by the judge in a case without requiring it to be proved. This is permitted when a fact is beyond reasonable dispute—either because it is generally known (the White House is located in Washington, D.C.) or because it is ascertainable from standard sources (on the night of the crime, the moon was 93% full). See also judicial DISCRETION, GLOSS, IMMUNITY, LEGISLATION, REVIEW, SALE, under those words.

judiciary *n.* **1.** the judicial branch of government; the system of courts. **2.** judges collectively.

jump bail. See under BAIL[1].

junior. Same as **subordinate.**

juridical *adj.* pertaining to law or legal proceedings. See also *juridical person* (under PERSON).

Juris Doctor. See J.D.

jurisdiction[1] *n.* **1.** the power and authority of a court or administrative tribunal to decide legal issues and disputes. The scope of a particular court's jurisdiction is determined by a combination of constitutional and statutory provisions. **2. ancillary jurisdiction, a.** broadly, the power of a court to decide issues incidental to a case properly within its jurisdiction, when those issues standing alone would have been beyond its jurisdiction. **b.** specifically, in a case that is properly before a federal court because the plaintiffs and defendants are from different states, the power to dispose at the same time of a releated claim between two parties from the same state. See also *diversity jurisdiction; supplemental jurisdiction.* **3. appellate jurisdiction,** jurisdiction to review orders and judgments of a lower tribunal. Cf. *original jurisdiction.* **4. concurrent jurisdiction,** jurisdiction of more than one court or agency with respect to the same type of case. For example, the state and federal courts have concurrent jurisdiction to enforce many federal laws. Cf. *exclusive jurisdiction.* **5. continuing jurisdiction,** jurisdiction over a case retained by the court even after final judgment has been rendered, for the purpose of dealing with any problems that arise in implementing the judgment. **6. diversity jurisdiction,** the jurisdiction of federal courts to entertain controversies between citizens of different states. See also CITIZEN; JURISDICTIONAL AMOUNT. **7. exclusive jurisdiction,** jurisdiction with respect to a type of case that may not be brought in any other tribunal. Specialized tribunals such as probate court or traffic court often have exclusive jurisdiction over cases within their specialty, and the federal courts have exclusive jurisdiction over cases in certain areas of federal law. Cf. *concurrent jurisdiction.* **8. federal question jurisdiction,** the jurisdiction of federal courts to decide cases arising under FEDERAL LAW. **9. general jurisdiction,** jurisdiction to hear any kind of case except one restricted to some specialized court. Cf. *limited jurisdiction.* **10. in personam jurisdiction** or **jurisdiction in personam,** jurisdiction to render a judgment that will be binding upon a particular person or entity. In a civil case, in personam jurisdiction exists over a party if that party either has appeared voluntarily in the case or has been properly served with a summons within the state or (in cases where *long-arm jurisdiction* applies) elsewhere. Also called **jurisdiction of** (or **over**) **the person.** See also *personal jurisdiction;* IN PERSONAM. **11. in rem jurisdiction** or **jurisdiction in rem,** jurisdiction to render a judgment with respect to property or a relationship located within the state in an action concerning the property or relationship itself, such as an action to QUIET TITLE to land or to

condemn contraband goods intercepted by federal agents at the border. See also *personal jurisdiction;* IN REM. **12. jurisdiction of** (or **over**) **the case,** jurisdiction to entertain a particular case; a court has jurisdiction over a case if it has both *subject matter jurisdiction* and *personal jurisdiction.* **13. limited jurisdiction,** jurisdiction to deal only with a particular category of cases; for example, the jurisdiction of a family court or a small claims court. Unlike some state courts, all federal courts are courts of limited jurisdiction, because they may hear only certain categories of cases specified in the Constitution and authorized by Congress. Also called **special jurisdiction.** Cf. *general jurisdiction.* See also *subject matter jurisdiction.* **14. long-arm jurisdiction,** jurisdiction to render a judgment binding upon a person or entity outside the state in a case arising out of conduct by that person or entity, either in person or through an agent, that either occurred within the state or occurred elsewhere and had an impact within the state. **15. original jurisdiction,** jurisdiction to give a case its first hearing and issue a judgment. Every new case must be filed in a court or agency that has original jurisdiction with respect to such cases. Cf. *appellate jurisdiction.* **16. pendent jurisdiction,** in a case that is properly before a federal court because it arises under federal law, the power to dispose at the same time of related state-law claims. See also *federal question jurisdiction; supplemental jurisdiction.* **17. personal jurisdiction,** jurisdiction to render a binding decision with respect to a particular person or thing. Traditional analysis divides personal jurisdiction in civil cases into three categories: *in personam jurisdiction, in rem jurisdiction,* and *quasi in rem jurisdiction.* Cf. *subject matter jurisdiction.* **18. quasi in rem jurisdiction** or **jurisdiction quasi in rem,** jurisdiction to render judgment upon a claim against a person who has property within the state to the extent of the value of that property, even when the dispute in the case has nothing to do with the property. Traditionally this has been used as a device for initiating actions against people over whom *in personam jurisdiction* could not be obtained, but this would now generally be considered unconstitutional. See also *personal jurisdiction;* QUASI IN REM. **19. subject matter jurisdiction,** jurisdiction to hear and decide cases of a particular type. The two major categories of subject matter jurisdiction in the federal courts are *diversity jurisdiction* and *federal question jurisdiction.* Cf. *personal jurisdiction.* **20. supplemental jurisdiction,** the name now used in the federal courts for *ancillary jurisdiction* (def. a). The principal categories of supplemental jurisdiction are *ancillary jurisdiction* (def. b) and *pendent jurisdiction* (def. a). —**jurisdictional,** *adj.* —**jurisdictionally,** *adv.*

jurisdiction[2] *n.* the geographic area throughout which the authority of a court, legislative body, law enforcement agency, or other governmental unit extends. "Jurisdiction" is a convenient shorthand for "a state, the District of Columbia, or the federal government": *Most jurisdictions today have the death penalty for at least some crimes.*

jurisdictional amount the amount of money or the value of property that must be at stake in order for a case to be within the jurisdiction of a particular court. For example, Congress has decided that the federal courts should not be available to hear cases founded upon *diversity jurisdiction* (see under JURISDICTION[1]) unless there is a lot of money at stake—currently more than $50,000. Diversity cases involving less than this jurisdictional amount must be brought in state court.

jurisprudence *n.* **1.** the philosophy of law; the consideration of broad questions relating to such matters as the sources, functions, and meaning of law. **2.** a body of judicial opinions: *the civil rights jurisprudence of the Supreme Court from 1954 to 1969.*

juristic person. See under PERSON.

juror *n.* **1.** a member of a jury. **2.** loosely, a member of a jury array; a person who has appeared in response to a summons for jury duty.

jury *n.* **1.** Also called **petit** (or **petty**) **jury.** a group of citizens called upon to hear the evidence at a trial, decide the facts, and render a verdict in accordance with the judge's instructions on the law. Traditionally this was a group of twelve men, often all white, required to reach a unanimous verdict. Under current interpretations of the Sixth and Seventh Amendments (see Appendix), people may not be excluded from a jury solely on the basis of race or sex; states may provide for six-member juries or nonunanimous verdicts in state criminal cases; and six-member juries may be used in civil cases in the federal courts. See also *jury trial* (under TRIAL); PETIT; PETTY. Cf. *grand jury*. **2. grand jury,** a group of citizens summoned to hear evidence presented by a prosecutor and issue an INDICTMENT if they find sufficient evidence to warrant trying a particular person for a particular crime. The Fifth Amendment (see Appendix) requires such screening of accusations by a grand jury before anyone can be prosecuted on a serious federal criminal charge. Federal grand juries are made up of 16 to 23 people, and it takes a vote of twelve to authorize an indictment. The constitutional requirement of indictment by grand jury has never been extended to state prosecutions; and since in practice grand juries seldom amount to more than a rubber stamp for prosecutors, they have been abolished, reduced in size, or given a reduced role in most states. **3. hung jury,** a jury unable to reach a verdict. This usually results, first, in an *Allen charge* (see under CHARGE), and if that fails, then a MISTRIAL. **4. jury array.** Same as VENIRE. **5. jury duty,** service as a JUROR. **6. jury nullification,** the power, and occasional practice, of a jury in a criminal case to ignore the judge's instructions on the law and acquit a defendant despite overwhelming evidence of guilt and absence of reasonable doubt. Because of the constitutional protection against DOUBLE JEOPARDY, the jury's acquittal must stand. Depending upon one's view of a particular case, jury nullification is either a gross injustice or the final safeguard against callous and overzealous prosecution. **7. jury panel.** Also called **panel. a.** the jury in a particular case. **b.** sometimes, the entire VENIRE from which a jury is to be chosen. See also IMPANEL. **8. jury trial.** See under TRIAL.

just compensation the compensation that the Fifth Amendment (see Appendix) requires the state or federal government to pay to a property owner whose property is taken for *public use* (see under USE). In general, it is the MARKET VALUE of the property at the time of the taking, taking into account the *best and highest use* (see under USE) to which a private buyer could have put the property. See also TAKING; EMINENT DOMAIN.

justice *n.* **1.** the ideal of fair and beneficent treatment of all people by each other and by their governments, which law in a democratic society attempts to serve. **2.** the system of law and administration of law: *administration of justice;* OBSTRUCTION OF JUSTICE. **3.** (*cap.*) the title given to judges in certain courts, particularly those designated "supreme" courts (most notably the Supreme Court of the United States) and inferior courts at the very lowest level of the judicial system (such as justice of the peace courts and police courts). Cf. JUDGE; MAGISTRATE.

justiciable *adj.* appropriate for adjudication; suitable for resolution by a court. In general, to be justiciable a case must involve a genuine dispute over legal rights or interests, resolution of which will have some real effect beyond satisfying the litigants' curiosity. In addition, the issue involved must not be one that, under the Constitution, lies within the exclusive province of the legislative or executive branch of government. Cases that might be dismissed as nonjusticiable include a case seeking an ADVISORY OPINION, a *collusive suit* (see under SUIT), a case that is MOOT, and a case raising a *political question* (see under QUESTION²). —**justiciability,** *n.*

justifiable homicide. See under HOMICIDE.

justification *n.* a legally sufficient excuse for having done something that otherwise would constitute a tort or a crime; for example, ENTRAPMENT, DURESS, or NECESSITY.

juvenile *n.* **1.** a person not yet old enough to be treated as an adult by the criminal justice system. The ages and circumstances under which a young person in trouble with the law will be treated as a juvenile vary from state to state; typically, state statutes set one age below which a youngster must be treated as a juvenile and a higher age above which a person must be treated as an adult, with treatment between those ages depending upon the circumstances of the case. **2. juvenile court,** a special court established in some states to handle criminal matters in which the accused is treated as a juvenile, and sometimes also child protection proceedings. As compared with criminal courts for adult offenders, the emphasis in juvenile courts is upon rehabilitation of youthful offenders rather than punishment. **3. juvenile offender,** a young person who violates a criminal law but is dealt with as a juvenile rather than as an adult. Also called **youthful offender** and sometimes **delinquent** or **juvenile delinquent,** although the latter two terms are often used more broadly to include young people who engage in troublesome or antisocial conduct that falls short of criminality.

kangaroo court *Slang.* **1.** a mock court set up by criminals or vigilantes to reach a predetermined verdict of guilty. **2.** a highly derogatory term for an actual judicial proceeding regarded as outrageously improper or manifestly unfair. See also STAR CHAMBER.

Keogh plan. See under PENSION PLAN.

kickback *n.* **1.** a form of BRIBERY in which a company that is awarded a contract, or from which a purchase is made, turns over a portion of the money received to an official or employee of the other party to the transaction, as a reward for helping to bring about the transaction or as an incentive to exercise such influence in the future. **2.** a form of EXTORTION in which an employer, supervisor, or union official demands a portion of a worker's rightful wages as a condition of continued employment.

kidnapping *n.* the crime of carrying off or isolating a person for the purpose of demanding money (**ransom**) for his release, using him as a hostage, harming or terrorizing him or others, or the like. Despite the allusion to "kids," the victim may be either a child or an adult. See also ABDUCTION; PARENTAL KIDNAPPING. —**kidnap,** *v.*

kind. See IN KIND.

King's Bench an English court of general jurisdiction for both civil and criminal cases. The court goes back centuries and is the source of much of the common law still in effect in America today. When a queen is on the throne, the court is called **Queen's Bench.**

kite *v.* to write a check knowing that there are not yet sufficient funds in the account to cover it. Depending upon the circumstances, check kiting may be a crime, especially where such a check is deposited in another bank account to create a false balance which is then withdrawn.

knock and announce rule the general rule that police officers must knock and announce themselves before breaking into a place to make an arrest or execute a search warrant.

knock off to make unlicensed copies of someone else's trademark or copyrighted design (for example, of clothing, fabric, watches, or furniture), usually for sale at a substantially lower price than the original. The copy is called a **knockoff.**

know all men by these presents an ancient but still quite common formulaic expression that may be placed at the beginning of a legal instrument, meaning essentially, "Let the world be put on notice by this instrument." The purpose is to impress upon both the person who signs the document and anyone who reads it the seriousness and legally binding nature of the instrument. Thus it serves for legal writings much the same function that HEAR YE or OYEZ does for courtroom proceedings.

knowledge *n.* **1.** Also called **actual knowledge.** awareness of a fact. "Knowledge" that a certain

legal

result will follow from certain action means awareness that the result is practically certain to occur. Knowledge is a crucial element in many tort cases and criminal cases, since assessment of culpability often depends upon what the people involved knew; for example, in a homicide case, the degree of guilt might depend in part on whether the defendant knew the gun was loaded. See also STATE OF MIND. Cf. *constructive knowledge; imputed knowledge.* **2.** Also called **personal knowledge.** awareness of a fact gained from direct observation or experience, as distinguished from a belief based upon what others have said or upon a less-than-certain chain of reasoning from other information. In general, witnesses are allowed to testify only to matters within their personal knowledge, and statements in affidavits and pleadings, unless expressly made upon INFORMATION AND BELIEF, should be based upon personal knowledge. Cf. HEARSAY; OPINION; *opinion evidence* (under EVIDENCE). **3. constructive knowledge,** knowledge that the law attributes to a person regardless of whether that person has actual knowledge of the matter, usually because the circumstances are such that a failure to know a fact is regarded as inexcusable. For example, an individual who was personally served with a court order but failed to read it would be said to have constructive knowledge of its contents despite the lack of actual knowledge. **4. imputed knowledge,** in a relationship of principal and agent, employer and employee, or the like, the superior's constructive knowledge of facts of which the subordinate was made aware in the course of the subordinate's duties. See also CARNAL KNOWLEDGE. **—know,** *v.* **—knowing,** *adj.* **—knowingly,** *adv.*

abcdefghijk L mnopqrstuvwxyz

labor organization the term used in the National Labor Relations Act for a UNION. It is defined very broadly to include any group of employees whose purposes include dealing with employers with regard to grievances or terms and conditions of employment.

labor union. Same as UNION.

laches *n.* unreasonable delay in pursuing a known right against someone. Laches is an *equitable defense* (see under DEFENSE) that may be raised in a case in which the defendant's position has been prejudiced by the plaintiff's delay in taking legal action. In cases at law, a plaintiff ordinarily may wait until the last day before expiration of the STATUTE OF LIMITATIONS to sue; but if an injunction or other equitable relief is sought, the court may take laches into account. For example, a landowner may not sit back and watch a building being built knowing that it encroaches on his land, and then expect a sympathetic hearing in a suit to have the building torn down, although he might still be entitled to compensatory damages for the loss of a little piece of his land.

lading. See BILL OF LADING.

land. Same as *real property* (see under PROPERTY). Although the term is sometimes used in the narrow sense of earth or soil, in law it is usually used as a shorthand for real property in general.

landlord *n.* the person who grants a LEASEHOLD interest in real property to a TENANT. See also LEASE.

landmark case. See under CASE[1].

lapse *v.* **1.** to expire because of the passage of time or be extinguished by the happening of some event. For example, an OFFER of a contract will lapse if not accepted within the time specified in the offer (or within a reasonable time, if no time is specified); a BEQUEST or DEVISE will lapse if the taker named in the will dies before the testator (unless the bequest is saved by an ANTILAPSE STATUTE); a statute enacted with an expiration date will lapse if not renewed. **—n. 2.** such expiration or extinguishment.

larceny *n.* the crime of wrongfully taking possession of personal property from another with intent to convert it to one's own use. Often designated as **grand larceny** if the value of the property exceeds a certain amount, and **petit** (or **petty**) **larceny** otherwise. The term has been abandoned in many modern criminal codes in favor of the broader concept of THEFT. See also GRAND; PETIT; PETTY.

last clear chance a doctrine under which, as between two people whose negligence contributed to an accident, the one who clearly had the last opportunity to avoid the accident may be held liable for injuries to the other. Thus a person who negligently placed himself in a dangerous situation might nevertheless be able to recover in full from another who should have realized the danger and avoided the accident. In most states this principle has been abandoned in favor of the more flexible doctrine of *comparative negligence* (see under NEGLIGENCE).

last will and testament a WILL. Sometimes called **last will.** The word "testament" adds nothing. In fact, the word "last" adds nothing; you can make a new "last will" every day.

latent *adj.* not obvious; present but not such as would be discovered in an inspection made with reasonable care: *latent ambiguity; latent defect.* Allocation of liability for defects in products or property sometimes depends upon whether the problem was latent or PATENT.

law *n.* **1.** the body of rules and principles for human behavior and the conduct of government in an organized community, state, or nation, created or recognized by custom or by government institutions and implemented or enforced by the government. **2.** a body of law relating to a subject: *constitutional law; the law of evidence.* **3.** a STATUTE. **4.** one of the two systems of justice—to some extent competing and to some extent complementary—that existed side by side in England prior to the MERGER OF LAW AND EQUITY. The law courts enforced criminal laws and granted awards of money damages for torts and breaches of contract. See also COMMON LAW (def. 3). Cf. EQUITY. **5.** the profession that deals with law and legal procedures: *the practice of law.* See also ADMINISTRATIVE LAW; AS A MATTER OF LAW; BAD LAW; BY OPERATION OF LAW; CASE LAW; CIVIL LAW; CONCLUSION OF LAW; CONFLICT OF LAWS; *corporate law* (under LAW); federal law; good law; *implied in law* (under IMPLIED); INTERNATIONAL LAW; *maritime law* (under MARITIME); POSITIVE LAW; PROCEDURE; PUBLIC INTEREST LAW; *question of law* and *mixed question of fact and law* (both under QUESTION[2]); SUBSTANCE. Cf. CANON LAW; NATURAL LAW; PARLIAMENTARY LAW.

law clerk. See under CLERK.

law of nations. Same as *public international law* (see under INTERNATIONAL LAW).

law of the case the principle that once an issue has been decided by one judge or panel of judges in a case, it will not be reconsidered if the case comes before a new judge or panel at the same level; except in special circumstances, the subsequent judges will adhere to the prior decision as the "law of the case" even if they disagree with it.

law review a journal for scholarly writing on legal topics. Most law schools publish one or more such periodicals, usually with the word "Review" or "Journal" in the title.

lawful *adj.* **1.** authorized or permitted by law; in harmony with law: *lawful conduct; a lawful enterprise.* **2.** recognized or sanctioned by law: *lawful marriage; lawful money.* Cf. LEGAL.

lawsuit *n.* a SUIT.

lawyer *n.* a person whose profession is to advise

or act for clients in legal matters; a person licensed by a state to practice law.

leading case. See under CASE¹.

leading question. See under QUESTION¹.

lease *n.* **1.** the grant of a LEASEHOLD interest in real property, usually in the form of a contract under which the person receiving possession of the property (the TENANT or **lessee**) agrees to pay rent to the grantor (the LANDLORD or **lessor**). **2.** a contract temporarily conveying the right to exclusive possession and use of tangible personal property from one person (the **lessor**) to another (the **lessee**). **3.** the instrument embodying such a grant or contract. **4. gross lease,** a lease at a fixed rate of rent. Cf. *net lease; percentage lease.* **5. ground lease,** a long-term lease (typically for 99 years) on the ground upon which a large commercial building sits or is to be built. **6. net lease,** a lease under which the rent consists of a fixed minimum amount plus a variable sum to cover specified expenses of the landlord, such as taxes and maintenance. **7. percentage lease,** a lease of real property for commercial use in which the rent is based at least in part upon a percentage of the lessee's sales. —*v.* **8.** to convey property rights by lease. **9.** to take or hold by lease.

leaseback. See *sale and leaseback* (under SALE).

leasehold *n.* a right to temporary possession of real property by agreement with the owner of the FREEHOLD or of a superior leasehold on the same property. Also called **leasehold estate; leasehold interest.** For types of leasehold, see TENANCY. See also ESTATE¹; LANDLORD; TENANT; LEASE.

leave *n.* permission from a court to take some action. Also called **leave of court.** See also *dismissal with leave to replead* (under DISMISSAL).

legacy *n.* Same as BEQUEST. See also LEGATEE.

legal *adj.* **1.** not against the law; not a crime: *Although it was legal to publish the defamatory statement, the publisher was ordered to pay damages for libel.* **2.** satisfying requirements or formalities of the law; sufficient under the law: *legal consideration; legal demand.* **3.** created, recognized, or imposed by law: LEGAL TENDER; *legal separation* (see under SEPARATION); *legal duty.* **4.** pertaining generally to law or the practice of law: *legal theory; legal ethics.* **5.** pertaining to law as distinguished from fact: *legal question.* **6.** pertaining to, enforceable under, or derived from principles of LAW (def. 4) as distinguished from EQUITY: *legal title* (see under TITLE); *legal remedy* (see under REMEDY). **7.** CONSTRUCTIVE: *legal fraud* (see under FRAUD). See also *legal* ACTION, AGE, CAPACITY, DISABILITY, ESTATE¹, FORM, HEIR, INTEREST¹, INTEREST³, OWNER, PERSON, RIGHT under those words, and *legal relief* (under REMEDY).

legal assistant. Same as PARALEGAL.

legal fiction a court's assumption of a fact known to be untrue in order to fit a case into a category recognized by the law, so that relief can be granted and justice done. Legal fictions have been an important mechanism in the evolution of common law. For example, "larceny" is traditionally defined as wrongfully taking property from another's possession; to cover situations in which a wrongdoer steals property that someone has accidentally left behind, the courts adopted the fiction that lost property is still in the "possession" of the person who lost it. See also CONSTRUCTIVE.

legal tender currency that may lawfully be used in payment of debts and may not be deemed inadequate by a creditor to whom it is tendered in the proper amount; the ordinary money of a country.

legalize *v.* to adopt legislation making conduct that formerly was unlawful lawful. See discussion under DECRIMINALIZE.

legatee *n.* **1.** a recipient of a BEQUEST. Cf. DEVISEE. **2. residuary legatee,** a person designated by will to receive or share in the *residuary estate* (see under ESTATE²).

legislation *n.* **1.** the enactment of statutes by a LEGISLATURE. **2.** a statute or body of statutes enacted or proposed. **3. judicial legislation,** a disparaging term for a court decision that interprets or applies the law in a way that the speaker disagrees with, suggesting that the court has usurped the function

of the legislature. It is usually used in situations where the court has extended some right to a class of people. But if a court seriously misreads the will of the legislature and the people, the legislature can always pass a law overruling the court—even amending the Constitution if necessary.

legislative *adj.* **1.** pertaining to the making of law or having the function of making law: *legislative power; legislative proceedings.* **2.** pertaining to a LEGISLATURE: *legislative hearings; legislative salaries.*

legislative history the process that a bill went through to become a law, often looked to by the courts as an aid in CONSTRUCTION of the statute that finally emerged. For example, if at some point a particular provision was removed from the bill, that may indicate the legislature's desire to limit the scope of the statute. Of course, it could also indicate the legislature's belief that other parts of the statute already cover that provision, so drawing conclusions from legislative history requires caution.

legislative immunity. See under IMMUNITY.

legislative intent the purpose of a legislature in enacting a particular statute. In the case of federal legislation, also called **congressional intent.** Legislative intent is looked to by the courts for assistance in such matters as CONSTRUCTION of a statute, determination of whether a federal statute preempts local legislation (see PREEMPTION), and determination of whether a superficially neutral statute was enacted for a discriminatory purpose. Sometimes courts attempt to glean intent solely from the words of the statute (see PLAIN MEANING); often they resort to LEGISLATIVE HISTORY.

legislature *n.* a deliberative body elected and authorized to write laws; the lawmaking branch of government: *state legislature; county legislature.* Congress is the national legislature. See also SEPARATION OF POWERS.

lemon law a statute that entitles the purchaser of a car that turns out to have substantial defects to return it for a refund or replacement.

lessee. See under LEASE (defs. 1 and 2).

lesser included offense an offense whose definition is included within the definition of a more serious crime, so that one cannot commit the more serious offense without also committing the lesser; for example, LARCENY is a lesser included offense of ROBBERY, and ATTEMPT to commit a crime is always a lesser included offense of the crime attempted. It is proper to charge a jury that if it fails to find that all the elements of the crime charged have been proved, it may nevertheless convict on a lesser included offense.

lessor. See under LEASE (defs. 1 and 2).

let *v.* **1.** to LEASE real property to someone. **2.** to award a contract for the performance of certain work, especially to one of several bidders for it.

lethal weapon. See under WEAPON.

letter of credit a letter in which a bank or other person, at the request of a customer, promises a third person (the beneficiary) that it will honor demands by the beneficiary for payment of drafts drawn or sums owed by the customer upon satisfaction of specified conditions, such as presentation of documents proving that goods shipped to the customer have arrived and payment is due. The letter of credit facilitates long-distance commercial transactions by assuring the seller that payment will be made when the goods arrive while assuring the buyer that payment will not be made if the goods do not arrive.

letter of intent a letter confirming an *agreement to agree* (see under AGREEMENT). See also *memorandum of understanding* (under MEMORANDUM).

letters *n.pl.* **1.** a formal document granting a right, privilege, or authorization, or conveying an official request. **2. letters of administration,** a document issued by a court appointing someone as ADMINISTRATOR of an estate. **3. letters patent,** a document issued by the government granting some right; in particular, letters granting a PATENT (a term derived from the phrase "letters patent") to an inventor. **4. letters rogatory,** a formal request by a court in one country to a court in another, asking the second

legal

court to take the testimony of a certain witness and transmit it to the first court for use in a case. **5. letters testamentary,** a document issued by a court formally authorizing someone to act as EXECUTOR under a will.

levy *v.* **1.** to impose a tax or fine: *The court levied a $500 fine for contempt.* **2.** to collect or seize property in accordance with legal authority; especially, to attach or seize property of a judgment debtor in order to satisfy a judgment **(levy execution):** *The plaintiff levied on the defendant's car and bank account.* —*n.* **3.** the act of levying.

lex *n. Latin.* law; a term that shows up in countless Latin legal maxims and phrases, especially in older writing. (See, for example, **de minimis non curat lex,** under DE MINIMIS.) The following three phrases are still seen in discussions of CONFLICT OF LAWS: **lex fori,** the law of the forum; that is, the law of the state in which a case is pending; **lex loci contractus,** the law of the place of the contract; that is, the law of the state or country where the agreement at issue in a contract case was entered into; and **lex loci delicti,** the law of the place of the wrong; that is, the law of the state or country where the conduct complained of in a tort case took place.

liability *n.* **1.** legal responsibility for a crime **(criminal liability)** or, more commonly, for a tort or breach of contract **(civil liability). 2.** the sum that one might be or has been ordered to pay in damages or fines because of such responsibility. **3.** any debt or other financial obligation of a person or entity. Cf. ASSET. **4. contingent liability,** a specific financial obligation that may or may not arise or become payable, depending upon future events. **5. joint and several liability,** liability for damages caused by the combined action of two or more persons, or for an obligation undertaken by two or more persons, under circumstances in which the law permits the plaintiff to proceed either against the whole group or against any member individually. Cf. *joint liability; several liability.* **6. joint liability,** liability of two or more persons as a group, as for a tort in which they all participated or for repayment of a loan made to them collectively. Cf. *several liability; joint and several liability.* **7. primary liability,** liability of a person directly responsible for an obligation, in a situation where another person has *secondary liability.* **8. secondary liability,** liability that arises only if another person (the one with *primary liability*) defaults in an obligation. In a GUARANTY arrangement, the principal debtor is primarily liable and the guarantor is secondarily liable. **9. several liability, a.** liability of each individual member of a group for damages caused, or an obligation owed, by all of them together. **b.** liability of a member of a group for damages caused or an obligation undertaken by that member separately from the others. Cf. *joint liability; joint and several liability.* **10. strict liability,** civil or criminal liability imposed upon a person without regard to whether the person intentionally or knowingly did anything wrong or was in any way reckless or negligent. In tort law, also called **liability without fault.** Typical examples in tort law include PRODUCTS LIABILITY and liability for ABNORMALLY DANGEROUS ACTIVITY; in criminal law, *statutory rape* (see under RAPE) and speeding. **11. vicarious liability,** liability imposed by law upon one person for acts of another; for example, the liability of an employer, under the doctrine of RESPONDEAT SUPERIOR, for acts committed by an employee, or the liability of all partners in a law firm for malpractice committed by one of them. See also LIMITED LIABILITY; PRODUCTS LIABILITY.

liability insurance insurance that protects the insured against liability to third persons. For example, automobile liability insurance covers (up to the maximum amounts specified in the policy) damages assessed against the insured for personal injuries or property damage suffered by others in an automobile accident for which the insured is held responsible. Cf. INDEMNITY INSURANCE.

liable *adj.* legally responsible; subject to liability. One is said to be "strictly liable," "jointly and sever-

ally liable," "vicariously liable," etc., according to the nature of the LIABILITY.

libel[1] *n.* **1.** the form of DEFAMATION in which the defamatory statement is communicated in writing or another medium having a degree of permanence, such as film. In some states, libel also includes defamatory statements broadcast on radio or television. Cf. SLANDER. —*v.* **2.** to publish a libel against a person. —**libelous,** adj.

libel[2] *n.* the former name for the complaint in an ADMIRALTY case. The plaintiff was called the **libelant;** the defendant was called the **libelee.** This terminology, still encountered in legal research, has nothing to do with defamation.

liberal construction. See under CONSTRUCTION.

liberty *n.* freedom of action. As used in the constitutional provisions protecting people from deprivation of "liberty" without DUE PROCESS, the term is interpreted as including not only freedom from physical restraint (as by being put in jail or deported), but also, at least in a few basic areas, the broader freedom to control one's own life and engage in pursuits of one's choosing (as by traveling, pursuing an education, or deciding for oneself whether to bear a child). See also ENTITLEMENT; FUNDAMENTAL RIGHT; RIGHT OF PRIVACY; RIGHT TO TRAVEL; *substantive due process* (under DUE PROCESS).

license *n.* **1.** government permission for a person to do something otherwise forbidden, such as practice medicine, drive a car, or sell liquor. **2.** a certificate evidencing such permission. **3.** permission given by the owner of a patent, copyright, or trademark for another to exploit it. Such licenses are usually embodied in detailed licensing agreements. **4.** consent of the owner or tenant of real property for another's entry upon the property, especially when the person entering is doing so solely for her own purposes (e.g., to take a shortcut or solicit for charity) or as a social guest. See also discussion under INVITEE. —*v.* **5.** to grant a license.

licensee *n.* a person to whom a LICENSE has been granted. Cf. INVITEE.

licensor *n.* a person who grants a LICENSE.

lie *v.* (of a cause of action or procedural right) to exist; to be sustainable: *The action lies in tort. Since the order was nonfinal, an appeal will not lie.*

lie detector. Same as POLYGRAPH.

lien *n.* **1.** a *security interest* (see under INTEREST[1]) in property of a debtor or other obligor. Liens may arise either by agreement between the parties or, very often, by operation of law—especially in various commercial situations where they serve to ensure payment of a supplier of goods or services, as in the case of an *attorney's lien, mechanic's lien,* or *warehouser's lien.* **2. attorney's lien,** a lien on money, papers, and property of a client in the hands of an attorney, or a lien that an attorney may request from a court on a fund or judgment obtained for the client by the attorney's efforts, to secure payment of attorney's fees. **3. judgment lien,** a lien that a judgment creditor may obtain on property of the judgment debtor, so that the property may be seized if the debtor fails to pay the judgment. **4. mechanic's lien,** the lien of one who works on, or supplies materials for use in, construction or repair of property (e.g., a house or automobile), imposed upon the property to secure payment for the work and materials. **5. tax lien,** a lien placed by the government on specific property to secure payment of back taxes on that property, or upon a taxpayer's property in general to secure payment of back income taxes. **6. warehouser's (or warehouseman's) lien,** the right of a warehouse to refuse to return a customer's goods until the storage bill is paid, and if necessary to sell them for payment.

life estate (or tenancy). See under ESTATE[1].

life in being. See under PERPETUITY.

life insurance 1. insurance under which the insurance company's undertaking is to pay out a specified sum of money upon the death of the insured person, either to the estate of the insured or to a beneficiary designated in the policy. **2. straight life insurance,** life insurance for which the annual premium never increases, and which remains in effect as long as the insured individual lives, provided that the premiums are paid. Also called **whole life insurance**. **3.** **term life insurance,** life insurance that remains in effect only for a specified period of time, after which the policy usually may be renewed for another term, but at a higher premium. Also called **term insurance.**

limine. See IN LIMINE.

limitation (or **limitations**) **period.** See under STATUTE OF LIMITATIONS.

limitations. See STATUTE OF LIMITATIONS.

Limited (Ltd.) *adj.* at the end of a company name, indicates that the company is a corporation. (Short for "limited company"—a reference to the LIMITED LIABILITY of the shareholders.)

limited appearance. See under APPEARANCE.

limited jurisdiction. See under JURISDICTION[1].

limited liability **1.** the characteristic of corporations and certain other forms of organization that insulates investors from liability for debts or other obligations of the company, so that the most a shareholder can lose is the value of her shares. **2.** a contractual arrangement by which one party agrees to a ceiling on the other's liability in case something goes wrong; for example, a commercial film processor usually accepts film only upon the customer's agreement that if the film is lost or destroyed, the processor's liability will be limited to the cost of a new roll of film.

limited liability partnership. See under PARTNERSHIP.

limited partner. See under PARTNER.

limited partnership. See under PARTNERSHIP.

limited warranty. See under WARRANTY.

lineup *n.* a police procedure in which a number of individuals, including a criminal suspect, are displayed to a witness to see if the witness identifies the suspect as the perpetrator. Unduly suggestive lineups, as when the suspect is the only individual resembling the witness's description, violate due process. Cf. SHOWUP.

liquid asset. See under ASSET.

liquidate *v.* **1.** to fix with certainty the amount of a debt or other liability, either because the obligation is certain by nature (e.g., a promissory note), or by agreement between the debtor and creditor or by judgment of a court. See also *liquidated damages* (under DAMAGES). **2.** to eliminate a debt or claim by paying or settling it. **3.** to sell assets for cash, especially other than in the ordinary course of business. **4.** to WIND UP an enterprise. —**liquidation,** *n.*

lis pendens *Latin.* (lit. "a pending suit") the name of a notice that must be recorded in some jurisdictions to warn that certain real estate is the subject of pending litigation. A buyer of such property would be subject to the court's ultimate decision about the property.

litigant *n.* a party to a lawsuit.

litigate *v.* **1.** to make something the subject of a lawsuit or to contest an issue in a judicial proceed-

ing: *My client will not hesitate to litigate her claim. Since the legality of the search and seizure was fully litigated in the pretrial hearing, the issue will not be reopened at the trial.* **2.** to perform all the tasks entailed in the pursuit of a court case—filing papers, taking discovery, making motions, questioning witnesses, arguing appeals, etc.: *The suit was litigated in the federal courts.*

litigation *n.* **1.** the process of litigating. **2.** a case or a set of cases discussed collectively. See also VEXATIOUS LITIGATION.

litigator *n.* a lawyer who specializes in litigation.

litigious *adj.* readily or excessively inclined to litigate: *America is a litigious society.*

living trust. Same as *inter vivos trust* (see under TRUST).

living will a formal instrument in which an individual states what medical measures he wants taken or withheld in the event of terminal illness or permanent unconsciousness. It will theoretically be followed if it is executed in conformity with state law, if those into whose hands the maker falls know about it and are sympathetic, and if the requests made are not contrary to public policy (see *physician-assisted suicide,* under SUICIDE); the maker should also execute a HEALTH CARE PROXY so that somebody will have clear authority to insist that the living will be obeyed.

LL.B. See J.D.

LL.M. abbreviation for Master of Laws, a degree typically requiring one year of study beyond law school. Such degrees are most often sought by lawyers who plan to concentrate their practice in a specialized field, such as taxation. Cf. J.D.

local *adj.* **1.** referring to a jurisdiction smaller than a state, such as a city, county, town, or village: *a local ordinance; federal, state, and local taxes.* **2.** sometimes, referring to a state and its subdivisions, as distinguished from the federal government: *In deciding the case, the federal court looked to local law.* **3.** any small region: *local custom; the local economy.* —*n.* **4.** Short for *local union* (see under UNION).

local counsel. See under COUNSEL.

local rules. See under RULE.

lockout *n.* the temporary closing of a business or refusal of an employer to allow employees to come to work, in order to pressure workers into accepting the employer's conditions. Cf. STRIKE[1].

loco parentis. See IN LOCO PARENTIS.

long-arm jurisdiction. See under JURISDICTION[1].

loss *n.* **1.** in a sale or exchange of property, the amount by which the value received for the property falls short of the owner's BASIS in the property. See also *capital loss* (under CAPITAL[1]). Cf. GAIN. **2.** any injury to person or property for which damages might be awarded in a civil action or payment obtained under an insurance contract.

loss causation. See under CAUSATION.

loss of consortium. See under CONSORTIUM.

lower court. See under COURT.

L.S., See under SEAL[1].

a b c d e f g h i j k l **M** n o p q r s t u v w x y z

magistrate *n.* **1.** broadly, any JUDGE. **2.** specifically, a judge of an inferior court such as a police court, town court, or justice of the peace court, with limited jurisdiction to deal with minor offenses and sometimes some minor civil matters. **3.** in federal district courts, an officer authorized to carry out a wide range of judicial functions that otherwise would have to be performed by judges. **4.** (*cap.*) the title accorded to some magistrates, though others have titles such as Justice of the Peace or Town Justice. Cf. JUDGE; JUSTICE.

Magna Carta *Latin.* (lit. "great charter") a document executed by King John of England in 1215, recognizing certain rights of English subjects and es-

tablishing the principle that came to be known as DUE PROCESS, under which even the sovereign is required to follow the law in taking action against a subject. The Magna Carta, often referred to as the **Great Charter,** is the source for many concepts embodied in the United States Constitution, and is still referred to in judicial opinions. Sometimes spelled "Magna Charta," but always pronounced "magna karta."

mail fraud. See under FRAUD.

main brief. See under BRIEF.

maintenance *n.* **1.** money for basic living expenses paid to a spouse from which one is separated or divorced. See also ALIMONY. **2.** giving financial or other assistance to a litigant in a case in which one has no interest. Instead of praising this as charity toward poor people who otherwise would be unable to obtain justice, English and American law have traditionally frowned upon it, and even to-day there is a strong current of opinion against support for legal services for the poor. See also BARRATRY; CHAMPERTY.

majority. See under AGE.

majority opinion. See under OPINION.

make *v.* to execute an instrument: *make a contract; make a will; make a promissory note.* Although the term can be applied to any instrument for the payment of money (e.g., *to make a check*), in strict usage one "draws" a check or other draft but "makes" a note. The person who promises payment in a promissory note is thus the **maker** of the note, not the "drawer." Cf. DRAW.

make a record. See under RECORD.

make bail. See under BAIL¹.

make law (of a court) to decide a significant issue on which the courts have not previously spoken, or announce a significant new principle of law.

make whole to compensate a person fully for injury or loss; to award or pay *compensatory damages* (see under DAMAGES).

malfeasance *n.* the doing of an unlawful act; especially, misconduct by a public official, corporate officer, or other person in a position of trust. Cf. MISFEASANCE; NONFEASANCE.

malice *n.* **1.** (in criminal law) **a.** any of the mental states required for the different kinds of MURDER: intent to kill or knowledge that one's conduct is substantially certain to cause death, intent to do serious bodily injury, extreme indifference to human life, or willing participation in a felony. **b.** generally, criminal intent; a purpose to perform an act that is a crime. **2.** (in tort law) improper purpose or lack of legally recognized justification. Such "malice" is often said to be an element of such torts as ABUSE OF PROCESS, DEFAMATION, DISPARAGEMENT, and MALICIOUS PROSECUTION. **3.** spite or ill will. Occasionally courts or lawyers use "malice" in this ordinary (nonlegal) meaning. Since the legal and nonlegal meanings of the word tend to get mixed up, the modern trend in law is to avoid the word altogether in defining torts and crimes. See STATE OF MIND. **4. actual malice,** (in defamation cases) knowledge that a statement one is publishing is false, or reckless disregard of its truth or falsity. The Supreme Court has held that a PUBLIC FIGURE cannot recover damages for defamation unless the person who uttered the defamatory words (usually a newspaper or other news medium) knew that they were false, or did not know one way or the other and recklessly plunged ahead with the comments anyway. Although the Court designates this as "actual malice," no actual spite or ill will is required; the publisher's feelings toward the subject of the comments are completely irrelevant. **5. malice aforethought, a.** strictly, an intent to kill formulated in advance. See also PREMEDITATION. **b.** broadly, a term applied to any form of murder, whether premeditated or not and with or without intent to kill (see def. 1a above). —**malicious,** *adj.* —**maliciously,** *adv.*

malicious prosecution the tort of initiating or continuing a criminal prosecution or civil case without probable cause and for an improper purpose. Cf. ABUSE OF PROCESS.

malpractice negligence or other failure by a professional, such as a lawyer, doctor, or accountant, to live up to reasonable professional standards in the peformance of services for a client. The client may sue in tort to recover resulting damages.

mandamus *n. Latin.* (lit. "we command") a writ by which a court directs a public or corporate body or officer, or a lower court or judge, to perform an official duty. This is a discretionary writ issued only in rare cases to remedy an injustice that otherwise might not be curable. Cf. PROHIBITION.

mandate *n.* **1.** an order from an appellate court to the lower court from which a case was appealed, communicating the higher court's decision as to

how the case should be dealt with. **2.** loosely, any court order or legal requirement.

mandatory injunction. See under INJUNCTION.

mandatory presumption. See under PRESUMPTION.

manipulation. See STOCK MANIPULATION.

manslaughter *n.* **1.** the crime of causing the death of another person under circumstances falling short of MURDER. Some states recognize different grades of manslaughter. **2. involuntary manslaughter,** causing death through RECKLESSNESS or, in some states, *criminal negligence* (see under NEGLIGENCE). In addition, some states include the unintentional causing of another's death while performing an unlawful act other than a felony, such as speeding or trespassing. (Cf. FELONY MURDER.) The most common occasion for involuntary manslaughter is reckless driving. See also *vehicular homicide* (under HOMICIDE). **3. voluntary manslaughter,** conduct that would be regarded as murder but for the fact that the killing, though not legally justified, occurred under extenuating circumstances. The most common example is killing in the HEAT OF PASSION.

marginal tax rate. See under TAX RATE.

marital rape. See under RAPE.

maritime *adj.* **1.** pertaining to navigation and commerce by water, both at sea and on inland waters. **2.** Also, **admiralty.** pertaining to *maritime law* or its administration: a *maritime* (or *admiralty*) *case; maritime* (or *admiralty*) *jurisdiction.* **3. maritime law,** the body of law governing maritime matters, including contracts relating to shipping by water, torts occurring at sea, property rights in vessels and freight, and the labor of ship and harbor workers. Maritime law is made and administered primarily by the federal government and the federal courts. Also called **admiralty law.**

mark *n.* **1.** a distinctive word, phrase, logo, or design, or even a sound or musical motif, used to identify products or services made, provided, or certified by a particular company or organization. See also **Ó** and TRADEMARK. **2.** a design—usually an X—used as a signature by someone who does not know how to write. See also X. —*v.* **3.** to place a letter or number on a document or other article used at a trial, hearing, or deposition, so that it can be referred to unambiguously in testimony and colloquy. See also EXHIBIT.

market *n.* **1.** a place where people come together to buy and sell things, or a mechanism (such as a computer network or informal network of buyers, sellers, and agents) that puts people in touch with each other for that purpose: *stock market; real estate market.* **2.** a geographic area where goods or services are sold: *the domestic market; the Los Angeles market.* **3.** demand for goods or services, or a body of existing or potential buyers: *the market for personal computers.* **4.** the level of prices prevailing in a market: *a rising market for shoes.* —*v.* **5.** to sell or offer for sale in a market.

market manipulation. Same as STOCK MANIPULATION.

market value the price that a willing purchaser would pay and a willing seller would accept for a particular item in an ARM'S-LENGTH transaction in an open market, where both are acting with full information and neither is under particular pressure to buy or sell. Also called **fair market value.**

marketable *adj.* suitable for sale; readily salable.

marketable security. See under SECURITY².

marketable title. See under TITLE.

marriage *n.* **1.** the legal relationship of husband and wife, entered into in conformity with state law and carrying various rights and duties imposed by law. **2.** a formal ceremony in which a marriage relationship is entered into. **3. common law marriage,** a marriage entered into without the usual ceremony; it is effected by an agreement to be married, followed by living together as husband and wife. The common law recognized such do-it-yourself marriages if the parties had the legal capacity to marry, but this method of marrying is no longer permitted in most states. Simply cohabiting has never been sufficient to create a marriage.

marshal *n.* **1.** a federal officer who serves summonses, executes writs, escorts criminal defendants between court and jail, and otherwise assists in the functioning of a federal court. **2.** the name given to certain state or local law enforcement or other officials in various localities. —*v.* **3.** to gather up the assets of a trust, estate, corporation, or the like and put them in order for distribution.

martial law government by the military, using military law and institutions in place of civilian. The Supreme Court has interpreted the Constitution as permitting martial law in the United States only in wartime and only if civilian courts are no longer able to function.

Massachusetts trust or **Massachusetts business trust.** Same as *business trust* (see under TRUST).

master *n.* **1.** the traditional common law term for an employer (the employee being referred to as a SERVANT). **2.** Also called **special master.** an individual appointed by a court to assist it in handling particular aspects of a case. See also REFEREE.

master and servant the traditional phrase for the area of common law concerned with the employment relationship and the rights and duties of employer and employee. This terminology is still in common use.

material *n.* **1.** important; of consequence; potentially dispositive; such as a reasonably prudent person would take into account in making a decision. To say that something is "material" usually simply means that it matters: *material fact, issue, mistake, variance, representation, misrepresentation, omission,* etc. **2.** essential; describing a component without which the whole will fail: *material allegation in a complaint; material element of a tort or crime; material term of a contract.* **3.** logically related to a material fact or issue: *material evidence.* —**materiality,** *n.*

material breach. See under BREACH.

material witness. See under WITNESS.

matter of. See under IN THE MATTER OF.

matter of law. See AS A MATTER OF LAW.

mature *adj.* **1.** due; presently payable or enforceable. Said of any right, claim, or obligation, but especially of bonds, notes, or other financial instruments. —*v.* **2.** to become mature.

maturity *n.* **1.** the state of being mature. **2.** the date upon which, or the time within which, a bond or negotiable instrument becomes due: *bonds with a maturity of 30 days.*

maxim *n.* a saying that expresses a general principle of law. See examples under DE MINIMIS and UNCLEAN HANDS.

mayhem *n.* the crime of maiming—that is, disabling, dismembering, or disfiguring—a person, either intentionally or, in some states, by any conduct intended to cause serious injury. This was a special offense at common law because it deprived the victim of the ability to fight; the modern trend is to include it in the general crime of assault and battery.

means test a requirement that people receiving a particular public benefit show that their income and assets are below a certain level.

measuring life **1.** the lifetime, or one of the lifetimes, determining the duration of a *life estate* (see under ESTATE[1]). **2.** the lifetime of the person, or of the longest survivor of the group of persons, identified for purposes of applying the *rule against perpetuities* (see under PERPETUITY).

mechanic's lien. See under LIEN.

mediation *n.* a procedure in which a neutral outsider (a **mediator**) assists the parties to a dispute in reaching a settlement. Mediation differs from ARBITRATION in that the purpose of mediation is to facilitate an agreement rather than to impose a decision on the parties.

meeting of the minds a misleading phrase sometimes used to signify the making of a contract, derived from an earlier view that there is no contract unless the parties share the same understanding of the deal. The contemporary view is that people are entitled to rely upon the normal and reasonable meaning of each other's words and actions; thus a party can generally enforce a contract on certain terms if a reasonable person in her position would have understood it that way, even if the other party can show that he had something different in mind, or did not intend to enter into a contract at all.

Megan's Law a New Jersey statute requiring registration by prior sex offenders whenever they take up residence in the state and prior to any subsequent change of address, and providing for official notification regarding their past records to the police, and sometimes to community groups and the general public, in the areas where they reside or intend to reside. The name has also been applied to similar legislation in other states providing various mechanisms by which law enforcement officials or private persons can monitor the whereabouts of such prior offenders.

memorandum *n., pl.* **memoranda. 1.** a brief written record or communication. **2.** a *memorandum of law* or *memorandum of points and authorities* (see under BRIEF). **3.** Also called **memorandum decision, memorandum order,** or **memorandum opinion.** a brief judicial decision, usually ranging in length from two words (e.g., "Motion denied.") to a long paragraph. When cited, such decisions are usually indicated by the abbreviation "mem." **4. memorandum of understanding,** a writing memorializing an *agreement to agree* (see under AGREEMENT). See also LETTER OF INTENT.

memorialize *v.* to make a written record of; confirm in writing: *Their telephone agreement was memorialized in an exchange of letters.* —**memorial,** *n.*

memory. See RECOLLECTION; RECOVERED MEMORY.

mens rea *Latin.* (lit. "guilty mind") the STATE OF MIND that makes the performance of a particular act a crime, or a crime of a particular degree; the element of fault that makes an otherwise innocent act or omission punishable. For example, a careful driver who hits a child who darts out from between parked cars may be guilty of no crime, whereas a driver who had time to avoid the child but carelessly failed to do so may be guilty of homicide. See also ACTUS REUS.

mental state. Same as STATE OF MIND.

merchantable *adj.* **1.** (of goods) fit for the ordinary purposes for which such goods are used, and of a quality that would be acceptable to merchants who regularly deal in goods of that kind. **2. warranty of merchantability,** in a sale of goods by a merchant who regularly deals in goods of that kind, an implied WARRANTY that the goods are merchantable. —**merchantability,** *n.*

merchantable title. Same as *marketable title* (see under TITLE).

meretricious *adj.* describing a relationship or contract having a sexual component unblessed by law, such as a living-together arrangement. Because "meretricious" contracts are contrary to PUBLIC POLICY, plaintiffs seeking PALIMONY upon the breakup of a relationship must be careful not to allege that sex was any part of the consideration for the relationship.

merger *n.* the absorption of one entity, right, interest, claim, agreement, or other thing into another, so that the first ceases to have independent existence and is superseded by the second. For example, one corporation may merge into another; a debt upon which a plaintiff sued and won is merged into the judgment, so that the debt no longer exists as an obligation distinct from the debtor's obligation to pay the judgment; and a **merger clause** in a contract provides that all prior negotiations and agreements between the parties are merged into the new contract, so that neither party can claim that the other has any obligation other than those expressed in the current contract. —**merge,** *v.*

merger of law and equity the blending of the two systems of justice that evolved side by side in England—LAW and EQUITY—into a single legal system. For centuries these systems dispensed different kinds of remedies in different kinds of cases from separate courts, using different procedures and even different basic vocabularies. It was not until 1937 that the federal courts in the United States adopted a unified procedure for law and equity cases, and provided that both legal and equitable relief can be sought in a single action. Although the formal separation of law and equity is now largely a thing of the past, substantive and procedural distinctions between "legal" and "equitable" principles still pervade American law.

merits *n.pl.* the substance of a case, claim, controversy, or the like, as distinguished from procedural or technical aspects; the heart of a matter. A decision, judgment, opinion, trial, or the like is said to be **on the merits** if it disposes of or is based upon the actual claim or charge presented in a case.

military law the rules and procedures governing conduct in the armed forces. The Constitution gives Congress the power to enact such law for the American military, and it has done so in the UNIFORM CODE OF MILITARY JUSTICE.

militia *n.* a military body with officers appointed by a state and members trained by the state. The Constitution gives Congress the power to organize, arm, and discipline the militia, making it primarily an arm of the federal government. The principle unit of the militia is the National Guard. See also RIGHT TO BEAR ARMS.

ministerial *adj.* done in accordance with specific instructions or requirements; carrying out a delegated task; nondiscretionary: *ministerial act; ministerial function.*

minor *n.* a person who has not yet reached the *age of majority* (see under AGE). See also *emancipated minor* (under EMANCIPATION).

minority *n.* **1.** the state or period of being a MINOR. **2.** Also called **minority group. a.** a group of people sharing a characteristic that distinguishes them from the majority; e.g., a racial or religious minority. **b.** a group identified for protection by civil rights laws or the Constitution. In this sense the term includes women even though they are a numerical majority.

minority opinion. See under OPINION.

Miranda rule the rule that criminal suspects must be informed of certain basic constitutional rights before being questioned. In the 1966 case of Miranda v. Arizona, the Supreme Court held that police who detain a person for questioning must inform him of his right to remain silent, his right to have a lawyer present, his right to have a lawyer appointed if he cannot afford one, and the fact that anything he says may be used against him. This information is referred to as the **Miranda warning.** See also *custodial interrogation* (under INTERROGATION).

misbranding *n.* placing a false or misleading label on a product.

misdemeanant *n.* a person who commits a MISDEMEANOR.

misdemeanor *n.* a crime less serious than a FELONY, usually one punishable by incarceration for up to one year. In some states misdemeanors include some offenses punishable only by a fine. See also HIGH CRIMES AND MISDEMEANORS; INFRACTION; OFFENSE; VIOLATION.

misfeasance *n.* **1.** the negligent or otherwise improper performance of an otherwise permissible act. Cf. MALFEASANCE, NONFEASANCE. **2.** broadly, any wrongful affirmative act.

misjoinder *n.* inappropriate JOINDER into a single action of unrelated parties, claims, or charges.

misprision of felony failure to report a known felony, in the absence of any agreement with or assistance to the felon. This was a misdemeanor under English common law, but absent some affirmative act to conceal the felony it is not a crime in the United States. Cf. *accessory after the fact* (under ACCESSORY); COMPOUNDING A CRIME.

misrepresentation *n.* **1.** a false or misleading REPRESENTATION, or words or conduct having the effect of preventing another's discovery of material facts. In this usual sense, misrepresentation is an element of the tort of FRAUD. **2.** sometimes, another name for FRAUD.

mistake *n.* an erroneous belief about a material

fact **(mistake of fact)** or about the legal effect or significance of known facts **(mistake of law).** When a contract is entered into on the basis of mistake, it may be a misconception of one party only **(unilateral mistake)** or one shared and relied upon by both parties **(mutual mistake).** The legal effect or status of an act or transaction (e.g., a contract, a marriage, an alleged crime) may be altered if the parties were acting under the influence of mistake, depending upon such factors as the nature of the mistake, the reasonableness of the mistake, the mutuality of the mistake, and whether one party knew that the other was acting under a mistaken impression.

mistrial *n.* a trial that ends without a verdict, decision, or settlement. The most common cause of a mistrial is a *hung jury* (see under JURY), but sometimes a mistrial is precipitated by an error so serious that no instruction to the jury can cure it (such as seriously prejudicial remarks by a lawyer) or by circumstances such as the death of a juror or a natural disaster. The usual result is a new trial. See also DOUBLE JEOPARDY.

mitigate *v.* **1.** to ameliorate; make less serious or severe. **2. mitigating circumstances,** circumstances reducing or limiting (but not eliminating) the liability of a person for a crime or tort; e.g., DIMINISHED CAPACITY. **3. mitigation of damages,** the use of reasonable efforts by the victim of another's breach of contract to limit the adverse consequences of the breach. As a general rule, the plaintiff in an action for breach of contract may not recover for any portion of the damages that could have been avoided by reasonable effort; this is often referred to as the "duty to mitigate damages" or just "duty to mitigate." —**mitigation,** *n.*

mixed nuisance. See under NUISANCE.

mixed question of fact and law. See under QUESTION².

M'Naghten rule (or **test**), the traditional test used in determining whether an INSANITY DEFENSE has been established, under which a defendant is not responsible for a crime if, because of a disease of the mind, he did not know the nature of his act or did not know that it was wrong. This is the test used in most American jurisdictions, augmented in a few jurisdictions by the IRRESISTIBLE IMPULSE TEST.

model law (or **act** or **statute**), any proposed statute drafted by anyone and promoted for adoption by state legislatures. Two of the most successful such proposals, upon which statutes in a great many states have been based, are the American Bar Association's Model Business Corporation Act, which provides a general framework for regulating corporations, and the MODEL PENAL CODE. See also UNIFORM LAWS.

Model Penal Code a comprehensive model statute organizing, rationalizing, and unifying the basic areas of state criminal law. The Model Penal Code was drafted over a number of years by the American Law Institute and finally promulgated in 1962; it provides the underlying theoretical framework, the overall approach, and a great deal of the exact language for the modern criminal codes that have been enacted in most states since then.

moiety *n.* half; a one-half interest. Sometimes used to mean any portion or fractional interest.

money had and received an action to compel payment of money received by another that should have gone to the plaintiff.

money order an instrument similar to a check, which is purchased from a bank, post office, or other institution by a person wishing to make a payment or transfer money to another, naming the other as payee and entitling the payee to payment, by the issuer, of the sum specified in the instrument.

monopolization *n.* the intentional acquisition or maintenance by a company or group of cooperating companies of a monopoly in the market for a product or service—that is, of such dominance of the market that it can fix prices and exclude competition. See also ANTITRUST; SHERMAN ANTITRUST ACT.

month-to-month tenancy. See under TENANCY.

moot *adj.* **1.** (of a claim, issue, case, etc.) dead; no longer a real controversy with practical consequences for the parties. For example, a constitutional challenge to a law would become moot if the law is repealed while the case is pending. Cases that become moot are usually dismissed as no longer presenting a JUSTICIABLE controversy; but exceptions can be made for cases that are "capable of repetition, yet evading review" because they become moot too quickly, such as a case brought by a pregnant woman with regard to rights of pregnant women. —*v.* **2.** to make moot: *The parties' stipulation mooted the motion for a protective order.*

moot court a mock court proceeding in which law students or lawyers practice argument or trial techniques in hypothetical cases.

moral turpitude dishonesty or immorality. Statutes providing special penalties or disadvantages (e.g., deportation or ineligibility for a professional license) for people convicted of a "crime involving moral turpitude," though notoriously vague, generally refer to more serious, intentional crimes as distinguished from less serious, technical crimes.

mortgage *n.* **1.** a *security interest* (see under INTEREST[1]) in real property, usually to secure repayment of a substantial debt—often the debt incurred in borrowing the money to buy the property. The debtor whose land is subject to the mortgage is called the **mortgagor**; the creditor who holds the mortgage is the **mortgagee**. **2.** the instrument evidencing a mortgage. **3. chattel mortgage,** a similar security interest in personal property, **4. second mortgage,** an additional mortgage on property that is already subject to a mortgage (the **first mortgage**). If the debtor defaults and the property is sold in a FORECLOSURE proceeding, the debt to the first mortgagee is paid off first, and the second mortgagee is entitled to repayment only to the extent that there are proceeds left over.

motion *n.* an application to a court for an order, made while a case is pending. Motions may be made orally or in writing, and ON NOTICE or EX PARTE, depending upon the circumstances. See also *motion*

papers (under PAPERS); *on its own motion* (under SUA SPONTE).

movant *n.* the party or lawyer who makes a motion.

move *v.* to make a motion: *The attorney moved to strike the witness's answer. The defendant moved for judgment notwithstanding the verdict.*

municipal *adj.* relating to a MUNICIPALITY or to local governments in general.

municipal corporation a city, town, village, or other local governmental unit that operates under a corporate charter granted by the state legislature.

municipal security. See under SECURITY[2].

municipality *n.* a MUNICIPAL CORPORATION or other local governmental unit.

murder *n.* **1.** the most serious form of *criminal homicide* (see under HOMICIDE). The exact scope of the crime varies from state to state, but always includes unjustified conduct resulting in a person's death and undertaken with **intent to kill**—that is, either a conscious purpose to kill or knowledge that death is substantially certain to result; depending upon the state, murder may also include one or more of the following: (1) causing death by unjustified conduct intended to cause serious bodily injury, (2) causing death by extremely negligent or reckless conduct that creates a very high risk of death or serious bodily injury to others or manifests extreme indifference to human life, or (3) FELONY MURDER. Murder is usually divided into two or more degrees depending upon factors that vary from state to state. See also MALICE; PREMEDITATION. —*v.* **2.** to commit murder; to kill by an act constituting murder.

mutiny *n.* **1.** a concerted refusal by two or more members of the military or of the crew of a ship to obey officers or perform duties. —*v.* **2.** to engage in mutiny.

mutual fund a company whose sole business is to invest in securities and return the profit to its own shareholders.

mutual insurance. See under INSURANCE.

mutual mistake. See under MISTAKE.

mutual releases. See under RELEASE.

N

a b c d e f g h i j k l m **N** o p q r s t u v w x y z

nail and mail a form of *substituted service* of process (see under SERVICE) consisting of affixing the process to the door of the person to be served and sending a follow-up copy by mail.

naked *adj.* mere; simple; unsupported; and nothing more. Thus "naked possession" is possession without ownership or authority; a "naked promise" is one unsupported by consideration; a "naked licensee" is a person permitted, but not invited, to be on another's land (see LICENSE, def. 4). Used interchangeably with **bare.**

narrow construction. See under CONSTRUCTION.

national *n.* **1.** a person who owes allegiance to a government and is entitled to its protection, but not necessarily to full citizenship status. All United States citizens are also nationals of the United States; however, persons born in American Samoa are United States nationals but not citizens. See also CITIZEN. —*adj.* **2.** pertaining or belonging to the nation as a whole: *national affairs; a national park.*

natural law a hypothetical body of fundamental principles of ethics and government supposedly inherent in nature. Natural law is a philosophical and religious concept rather than a scientific or legal one. Cf. POSITIVE LAW.

natural person. See under PERSON.

naturalize *v.* to confer citizenship upon an individual who was not a citizen. Congress has virtually unlimited power to establish the criteria and procedures for naturalization; once naturalized, however, such a citizen has the same status and rights as a natural born citizen in almost all respects, a notable

exception being that, under the Constitution, only a natural born citizen may become President. See also CITIZEN. —**naturalization,** *n.*

necessaries *n.pl.* basic goods and services needed by a child, dependent person, or family. Most or all states make both spouses liable for debts incurred by either one for necessaries for the children or family, though the range of goods and services covered usually depends upon the financial circumstances of the particular family; what is "necessary" for a rich family might be a luxury for a poor family.

Necessary and Proper Clause the clause of the Constitution that authorizes Congress to enact all laws "necessary and proper" to carry out the powers of the federal government under the Constitution. It is not limited to laws that are essential or indispensable; rather, it gives Congress discretion to adopt any convenient or appropriate means for accomplishing any constitutionally permissible objective.

necessary party. See under PARTY.

necessity *n.* a circumstance leaving a person no reasonable choice but to do something that normally would be a tort or crime in order to avoid a greater evil. Where a person's conduct is reasonable under the circumstances, necessity (also called **choice of evils**) generally affords a defense to a tort action or criminal prosecution, especially if the harm avoided would have affected the public at large **(public necessity)** rather than only the individual interests of the person sued **(private ne-cessity)**.

negative act. See under ACT.

negative easement. See under EASEMENT.

negative pregnant a denial that leaves open the possibility that the proposition being denied may be partly or even substantially true; for example, "Defendant denies that he recklessly drove the car onto the sidewalk, striking the plaintiff and injuring her." Such a denial is said to be "pregnant with an admission." (In the example, the defendant may be denying only that he was reckless, or only that the plaintiff was injured, or only that she was on the sidewalk when his car struck and injured her.) Under flexible modern pleading rules this might not have serious adverse consequences, but it is still bad form.

neglect *n.* **1.** failure to perform some act or fulfill some duty specifically required by law. **2. child neglect,** failure of a parent to support a child or to safeguard a child's health and well-being. Also called **parental neglect. 3. excusable neglect,** a failure to perform some procedural step or court-ordered act in a case, for which there is an excuse that the law will recognize and the judge deems adequate. **4. neglect of duty,** failure of a public official or a member of the military to carry out official or military duties. **5. willful neglect,** intentional, knowing, or reckless failure to fulfill a legal duty, especially with respect to the care of a child.

negligence *n.* **1.** (in tort law) conduct involving an unreasonable risk of injury or loss to others; conduct that falls short of the degree of care that a *reasonable person* (see under REASONABLE) would have exercised in the same circumstances. Negligence is determined by an OBJECTIVE TEST: a person who considered a situation thoroughly and took what he genuinely regarded as a reasonable risk would nevertheless properly be found negligent if the jury concludes that a person of ordinary intelligence and prudence in that situation would not have done what the defendant did. Negligence is a tort; the wrongdoer is generally liable for any injury to person or property directly resulting from it. See also PROXIMATE CAUSE. Cf. *intentional tort* (under TORT); RECKLESSNESS. **2.** Also called **criminal negligence.** (in criminal law) a gross deviation from the standard of care that a reasonable person would observe, under circumstances posing a substantial and unjustifiable risk of which the actor should have been aware. Except for relatively rare STRICT LIABILITY offenses, this is usually the minimum level of fault that will subject a person to criminal liability; *ordinary negligence* is normally insufficient. See also *negligent homicide* (under HOMICIDE); STATE OF MIND. **3. comparative negligence,** the modern doctrine that as between a plaintiff and a defendant in a tort case, and sometimes as among several defendants, fault (and liability for damages) should be allocated in proportion to each party's contribution to the injury or loss complained of. Cf. *contributory negligence.* **4. contributory negligence, a.** negligence by a plaintiff contributing to the injury or loss that is the subject of a tort case, as when a plaintiff sues over an automobile accident that was primarily caused by the defendant but was also partly caused or made worse by inattentiveness on the part of the plaintiff. **b.** the traditional doctrine that any contributory negligence by a plaintiff, however slight, bars the plaintiff from recovering in a negligence case. In most states this harsh common law doctrine has been superseded by some form of *comparative negligence.* **5. gross negligence,** highly unreasonable conduct; a term used primarily in civil contexts, sometimes interpreted as RECKLESSNESS but more often representing essentially the same degree of fault as *criminal negligence.* In most civil contexts it does not matter whether negligence is "gross" or "slight"; often the phrase "gross negligence" is used just for rhetorical effect. **6. ordinary** (or **simple**) **negligence,** conduct falling short of the standard of *ordinary care* (see under CARE); negligence as described in def. 1 above. **7. willful** (or **wanton**) **negligence,** in theory, RECKLESSNESS. In practice, these concepts tend to shade into *gross negligence.* **—negligent,** *adj.* **—negligently,** *adv.*

negligent homicide. See under HOMICIDE.

negotiable *adj.* (of an instrument evidencing certain rights) transferable by INDORSEMENT and delivery. The concept of negotiability applies particularly to three kinds of instruments: a DOCUMENT OF TITLE; a security evidenced by a certificate, such as a STOCK CERTIFICATE (see SECURITY[2] and BOND[1]); and a check or other "negotiable instrument" in the narrow sense of that phrase (see NEGOTIABLE INSTRUMENT, def. 2). In each case, if the instrument satisfies certain requirements specified in the UNIFORM COMMERCIAL CODE, then ownership of the instrument and the rights it represents may be transferred simply by indorsing it and delivering it to the transferee—and sometimes even the indorsement is unnecessary (see NEGOTIATE). See also *negotiable document of title* (under DOCUMENT OF TITLE). **—negotiability,** *n.*

negotiable instrument 1. broadly, any document that is NEGOTIABLE, including a negotiable document of title or a security. **2.** specifically and usually, a financial instrument that (1) contains an unconditional promise or order to pay a specific sum of money, but (with certain exceptions) no other promise, order, power, or obligation; (2) is payable on demand or at a definite time; (3) is payable to order or to bearer; and (4) is signed by the issuer. If it is a promise it is usually called a note (see NOTE[1]); if it is an order it is a DRAFT, the most common example of which is an ordinary CHECK. See also BEARER; DEMAND; ORDER[2]; TIME.

negotiate *v.* **1.** to transfer a check or other negotiable instrument or document in such a way that the transferee becomes a HOLDER. In the case of a *bearer instrument* (see under BEARER), this can be done simply by handing over the instrument. In the case of an *order instrument* (see under ORDER[2]), it is done by indorsing the instrument and then delivering it. For example, a check may be negotiated by cashing it, depositing it, or signing it over to someone else. Negotiation transfers ownership of the instrument and the rights it represents to the person to whom the instrument is delivered. **2.** to bargain or haggle: *to negotiate a contract.* **—negotiation,** *n.*

net assets. See under ASSET.

net income. See under INCOME.

net lease. See under LEASE.

next friend a person who files a lawsuit on behalf of a minor or incompetent who lacks legal capacity to sue or be sued, and stands in for that person as a party in the case.

no bill. See under BILL.

no contest. Same as NOLO CONTENDERE.

no-fault divorce. See under DIVORCE.

no-fault insurance a type of automobile insurance required in some states, under which compensation for minor personal injuries incurred in an accident is made by the insurance company covering the car in which the injured person was riding (or, in the case of pedestrian injuries, the car that struck the pedestrian), regardless of which driver involved in the accident was more at fault. The purpose of no-fault insurance laws is to spare everyone involved the time and expense of lawsuits to apportion blame for relatively minor accidents.

no-par stock. Same as *stock without par value* (see under STOCK).

nolle prosequi *Latin.* (lit. "to be unwilling to pursue") the formal abandonment of a criminal charge by the prosecuting attorney. If the trial has not begun and the statute of limitations has not expired, the defendant can be reindicted on the same charge. Often shortened informally to **nolle** or **nol pros** and used as a verb: *Counts 12 and 13 of the indictment were nollied* (or *nol prossed*).

nolo contendere *Latin.* (lit. "I will not contest") a PLEA to a criminal charge, permitted in the federal courts and in many states (subject to the judge's consent), whereby the defendant states that he will not contest the charge. The result of such a plea is a conviction on the charge, and for sentencing purposes it is the same as a guilty plea. Unlike a guilty plea, however, it may not be used in a subsequent civil case as proof of guilt. Also called **non vult contendere** or **no contest**.

nominal *adj.* **1.** in name only; in form rather than in substance. For example, a nominal party is one (such as a NEXT FRIEND) named as a plaintiff or defendant only to satisfy technical requirements. **2.** symbolic, token: *nominal consideration* (see under CONSIDERATION); *nominal damages* (see under DAMAGES).

nominate *v.* to select or appoint as one's agent, representative, or designee: *The powers granted to my executor by this will are to be exercised by her or by such other person as she may nominate.* A person so selected is called a **nominee**.

non compos mentis *Latin.* (lit. "not in possession of the mental faculties") insane or incompetent.

non obstante veredicto (n.o.v.) *Latin.* (lit. "notwithstanding the verdict") See *judgment notwithstanding the verdict* (under JUDGMENT).

non prosequitur *Latin.* (lit. "he/she does not pursue") an older term for a judgment against a plaintiff who stops pursuing a case at some point after filing it. Shortened informally to **non pros.** Today this would usually take the form of a dismissal for FAILURE TO PROSECUTE or a *default judgment* (see under JUDGMENT).

non vult contendere *Latin.* (lit. "he/she will not contest") Same as NOLO CONTENDERE.

nonage *n.* the state of being under the *age of majority* or *legal age* (see both under AGE).

nonassessable stock. Opposite of *assessable stock* (see under STOCK).

nonconforming use. See under USE.

nonfeasance *n.* unjustified failure to perform a required act or carry out an official duty. Cf. MALFEASANCE; MISFEASANCE.

nonjoinder *n.* the failure of a party asserting a claim in a case to JOIN a *necessary* or *indispensable party* (see under PARTY). See also JOINDER.

nonjury trial. Same as *bench trial* (see under TRIAL).

nonnegotiable document of title. See under DOCUMENT OF TITLE.

nonnegotiable instrument an instrument that is substantially in the form of a NEGOTIABLE INSTRUMENT, but fails in some particular respect to meet the exact requirements for negotiability; for example, an unsigned check, or a note that says "I promise to pay to Mary Jones" instead of "I promise to pay *to the order of* Mary Jones" (see under ORDER²).

nonpar stock. Same as *stock without par value* (see under STOCK).

nonprofit describing an organization or institution organized for purposes other than to make a profit, such as an educational, charitable, or cooperative organization; for example, a *nonprofit corporation* (see under CORPORATION).

nonrecourse *adj.* lacking the right to proceed against a particular obligor personally in the event of nonpayment or default. See examples under RECOURSE.

nonresident alien. See under ALIEN.

nonresponsive *adj.* (of a witness's answer to a lawyer's question) avoiding the question, answering some other question, or including commentary beyond what was asked for. Depending upon strategic considerations, a lawyer might "move to strike" the answer or the nonresponsive portion of the answer (see STRIKE²), request the judge to instruct the witness to answer, repeat the question, or simply move on. If the judge strikes an answer or part of an answer, she will usually specifically instruct the jury to disregard it, although just saying "it is stricken" amounts to such an instruction.

nonstock corporation. See under CORPORATION.

nonsuit *n.* **1.** an older term for DISMISSAL of a civil case. —*v.* **2.** to issue a nonsuit against: *The judge nonsuited the plaintiff.*

nonsupport *n.* the crime of failing to provide needed financial support that one has the resources

to provide to one's child, spouse, or other dependent where there is a duty to provide such support.

not found. Same as *no bill* (see under BILL).

not guilty 1. acquitted of a criminal charge; tried and not proved guilty. Cf. INNOCENT. **2.** a PLEA by which a criminal defendant preserves the right to a trial to determine guilt. Cf. GUILTY; NOLO CONTENDERE.

not guilty by reason of insanity deemed not legally responsible for a criminal act on the ground that the actor was insane at the time. See also INSANITY DEFENSE and specific tests listed there.

not-for-profit corporation. See under CORPORATION.

notarial *adj.* pertaining to or done by a NOTARY PUBLIC.

notarize *v.* to authenticate a document or attest to the performance of some other notarial act by affixing the signature and seal of a notary public.

notary public a person authorized by the government to administer oaths and affirmations, take acknowledgments, authenticate signatures, and tend to various other formalities relating to legal documents and transactions. Often shortened to **notary.**

note¹ *n.* **1.** an instrument representing a promise to pay a sum of money, and often interest, to (or to the order of) the bearer or a named PAYEE. A note is a NEGOTIABLE INSTRUMENT if it meets the requirements listed under that entry. Also called **promissory note.** See also MAKE; *to the order of* (under ORDER²). **2. cognovit note,** a note in which the maker's promise to pay is coupled with a confession of judgment, so that the payee can automatically obtain a judgment against the maker if a payment is missed. See discussion under CONFESSION OF JUDGMENT. See also COGNOVIT. **3. installment note,** a note promising payments at fixed intervals over a period of time, or one of a set of notes each of which provides for one such payment.

note² *n.* an article on a legal topic, typically written by a law student and published in a law review, and usually quite comprehensive. Cf. *case note* (under ANNOTATION); COMMENT.

notice *n.* **1.** the act of conveying information of legal significance to a person, or, when such information is conveyed in writing, the document itself: *notice of deposition; notice of increase in rent.* See also ON NOTICE; SERVICE. **2.** information of legal significance to a person that is known to, or at least available to, that person. **3.** for purposes of satisfying DUE PROCESS, **a.** the publication of laws and regulations, so that no one will be charged with a crime for conduct that they had no way of knowing was illegal. **b.** formal warning of proposed action to be taken against a person (such as a criminal charge, a civil suit, or termination of welfare benefits), so as to advise the person of the nature of the charges, allegations, or proposed action and provide an OPPORTUNITY TO BE HEARD. In civil cases this is normally accomplished by service of a SUMMONS and COMPLAINT; in criminal cases, by ARRAIGNMENT. **4. actual notice,** notice actually received by, or information actually known to, a person. **5. constructive notice,** information that a person could have or should have known, or information conveyed in a way that was reasonably calculated to give actual notice. **6. inquiry notice,** notice of facts sufficient to cause a reasonably prudent person to make further inquiry with regard to a matter if she wishes to safeguard her rights or avoid liability. **7. judicial notice.** See under JUDICIAL. **8. notice by publication,** publication of a notice in a newspaper in the hope of reaching persons affected by a matter who cannot otherwise be identified or located. Such notice is allowed or required in certain legal situations, but only as a last resort. **9. notice pleading.** See under PLEADING. —*v.* **10.** to give formal legal notice of or to: *The judge noticed the hearing for Wednesday. Each of the defendants has been noticed for a deposition.*

notorious *adj.* open; well known; not concealed: *notorious possession; notorious cohabitation.*

n.o.v. see *judgment notwithstanding the verdict* (under JUDGMENT).

novation *n.* the substitution of a new contract for

an old one, extinguishing all rights and obligations under the old one, by agreement of all parties to both contracts. For example, the new contract might substitute new terms for the terms of the original contract, or substitute a new party for one of the original parties.

NSF check. See under CHECK.

nuisance *n.* **1.** Also called **private nuisance.** the tort of engaging in conduct, or maintaining a condition on one's property, that substantially and unreasonably interferes with another's use and enjoyment of her own property; for example, activities that create unreasonable noise, vibrations, foul odors, or a health or fire hazard. **2.** Also called **public nuisance.** conduct, especially in the use of one's own land, that unreasonably interferes with the health, safety, welfare, comfort, or rights of the public at large, or of a large number of people. Examples include extending a building so that it encroaches on a public sidewalk; maintenance of an illegal estab-lishment, such as a brothel or gambling house; violating zoning restrictions; or any kind of conduct that might constitute a private nuisance but is severe enough to interfere with more than a few immediate neighbors. Conduct amounting to a public nuisance is usually a crime, and may independently constitute a private nuisance with respect to certain individuals particularly affected, in which case it may be called a **mixed nuisance.** Cf. ATTRACTIVE NUISANCE.

null or **null and void.** Same as VOID.

nullification. See *jury nullification* (under JURY).

nunc pro tunc *Latin.* now for then; a phrase making an order retroactive to a certain date. For example, an order correcting an error in a previous order would normally be made "nunc pro tunc" to make it clear that the first order should be regarded as having said what was originally intended all along.

nuncupative will. See under WILL.

a b c d e f g h i j k l m n **O** p q r s t u v w x y z

oath *n.* **1.** a solemn declaration that certain facts are true or that one will speak the truth, faithfully carry out one's official duties, uphold the law, or the like. The taking of an oath to tell the truth renders any dishonest statement punishable as FALSE SWEARING or PERJURY. In its traditional and strict sense, an oath is an invocation of God, as distinguished from an AFFIRMATION (def. 1), which lacks religious content. Broadly, an oath may take any suitably solemn form and need not refer to God; in this sense "oath" includes affirmations. See also OATH OR AFFIRMATION; SWEAR. **2.** the words recited in giving or taking an oath. **3. oath of office,** the oath or affirmation of a person elected or appointed to public office, undertaking to support the Constitution and to perform the duties of the office faithfully.

oath or affirmation a phrase used to avoid the religious issues raised by the use of OATH alone: *The application must be accompanied by a statement made upon oath or affirmation.* The Constitution states that all state and federal officeholders must "be bound by Oath or Affirmation, to support this Constitution." See also SWEAR or AFFIRM.

obiter dictum *pl.* **obiter dicta.** *Latin.* (lit. "a thing said in passing") Same as DICTUM (see discussion there). Occasionally shortened instead to **obiter** (lit. "in passing," "by the way"): *Although the court's remark was obiter in the context of that case, we believe that it correctly states the rule applicable here.*

objection *n.* **1.** a formal statement or notice that one regards a claim or procedural step as impermissible or invalid; a request that a particular course of action not be permitted or pursued. **2.** especially, such a statement or request in regard to a question asked, evidence sought to be admitted, or other conduct at a trial or hearing. It is made by saying "Objection" or "I object" and, if necessary, adding just enough explanation to make clear what is being objected to and the legal grounds for the objection. If testimony and other evidence is not objected to at the time it is sought to be introduced, it cannot be complained about on appeal. For some types of questions likely to be objected to, see QUESTION¹ (defs. 3–6). The court's response to an objection is to SUSTAIN or OVERRULE it. **3. continuing objection,** a single objection applicable to all questions in a line of questioning. If an attorney regards an entire area of questioning as improper but the judge disagrees, then instead of requiring the attorney to object to each question in turn in order to preserve the issue for appeal, the judge may grant the attorney a "continuing objection" to the entire line of inquiry. **4. speaking objection,** an objection in a jury trial that contains more than the minimum necessary information for the judge to rule, often in an attempt to sway the jury. Many judges forbid lawyers to give any grounds for their objection unless specifically requested to do so, and some require lawyers to give their reasons by citing sections of a state evidence code or the federal rules of evidence by number, so that the jury will not understand what they are talking about. —**object**, *v.*

objective test a legal test that does not depend upon what is in someone's mind, but on external criteria. For example, any legal principle that depends upon whether someone's conduct was REASONABLE involves an objective test, because what matters is not how the person involved viewed the situation, but how a reasonable person in that situation would have viewed it. Cf. SUBJECTIVE TEST.

obligation *n.* **1.** a legal requirement that one perform or refrain from performing some act, or the act that one is required to perform. **2. joint and several obligation,** a contractual obligation undertaken by two or more persons with the understanding that performance may be sought in court either from all of them collectively or from any one of them individually. **3. joint obligation,** a contractual obligation for which two or more persons have agreed to be liable as a group but not individually.

obligee *n.* a person or entity owed an obligation under a contract or negotiable instrument, especially an obligation to pay money.

obligor *n.* **1.** a person or entity owing an obligation under a contract or negotiable instrument, especially an obligation to pay money. **2. principal obligor.** See under PRINCIPAL.

obscenity *n.* any form of expression, such as a book, painting, photograph, movie, or play, that deals with sex in a way that is regarded as so offensive as to be beyond the protection of the constitutional guarantee of FREEDOM OF SPEECH. Under the most recent of the Supreme Court's efforts to define obscenity, the term applies to material that appeals to PRURIENT INTEREST, depicts or describes sexual conduct in a way that is PATENTLY OFFENSIVE, and lacks "serious literary, artistic, political, or scientific value." See also PORNOGRAPHY; PRIOR RESTRAINT; SPEECH. —**obscene**, *adj.*

obstruction of justice the crime of attempting to impede or pervert the administration of justice, as by concealing or falsifying evidence, or by bribing, threatening, or otherwise attempting to influence witnesses, jurors, or court officials improperly. The term is sometimes extended to acts that impede police or other law enforcement activities as well. The exact terminology and classification scheme for such offenses varies from state to state.

occupancy *n.* *actual possession* (see under POSSESSION), or the act of taking actual possession, of real property. This does not require physical presence on the property at all times, but at the very least diligence in keeping others out except with one's own permission. Also called **occupation**. —**occupy,** *v.*

occupy the field. See under PREEMPTION.

of age having reached the *age of majority*, or *legal age* for a particular activity (see both under AGE). Cf. UNDERAGE.

of counsel 1. referring to a lawyer who assists the *attorney of record* (see under ATTORNEY) in a trial or appeal; a member of a legal team other than the leader. **2.** a lawyer associated in some way with a law firm, but not as a member or employee; for example, one retained to assist in a particular matter, or a retired member of the firm who consults with it on specific matters when called upon.

of record. See under RECORD.

of the essence 1. essential; said of contract terms whose exact performance is so central to the purposes of the contract that any failure by a party to adhere to them would be deemed a *material breach* (see under BREACH), justifying cancellation of the contract by the other party. **2. time is of the essence,** a phrase signifying that any failure to perform within the time specified in the contract will constitute a material breach, even if the delay is slight.

off the record. See under RECORD.

offender *n.* a person who commits an OFFENSE.

offense *n.* **1.** any CRIME or other violation of law for which a penalty is prescribed. **2. petty offense,** a very minor offense, defined in some jurisdictions to include any misdemeanor for which the possible sentence does not exceed six months, in others as an offense below the level of misdemeanor, for which no jail sentence can be imposed. See also BAILABLE OFFENSE; LESSER INCLUDED OFFENSE.

offer *n.* **1.** a proposal to enter into a CONTRACT upon specified terms. A proposal is an offer if it is made in such a way that the person to whom it is made has only to ACCEPT it to bring the contract into existence. See also TENDER OFFER. **2.** any PROFFER. **3. firm offer,** an offer to buy or sell goods, made by a merchant in a signed writing that includes an assurance that the offer will be held open. Contrary to the usual rule that an offer may be withdrawn at any time before acceptance, an offer meeting these requirements is irrevocable for the period of time stated in the offer, or for a reasonable time if no specific time is stated. —*v.* **4.** to make an offer. **5.** to request admission of an exhibit into evidence: *"I offer this as Plaintiff's Exhibit 57."*

offer of proof a brief statement by a lawyer to a judge, out of the hearing of the jury, of the testimony that a particular witness is expected to give in response to a particular question or line of questioning. A lawyer may request permission to make an offer of proof, also called a **proffer,** in response to a judge's initial ruling sustaining an objection to a question, and to try to persuade the judge that the testimony is admissible and to make a record for arguing on appeal that the judge was wrong to exclude it.

offeree *n.* a person to whom an offer is made.

offeror *n.* a person who makes an offer.

officer *n.* **1.** a person appointed or elected to a position of responsibility or authority in government or a private organization. **2.** in a corporation, **a.** strictly, one of the handful of individuals selected by the board of directors to have overall responsibility for day-to-day management of the corporation's business. **b.** loosely, anyone in a management position to which an impressive title has been assigned, partly for their own satisfaction and partly to give them credibility in dealing with the public. A corporation may have thousands of such officers.

officer of the court any employee of a court or any lawyer involved in a matter before the court. The phrase is used to emphasize the responsibility of all such individuals to conduct themselves with utmost honesty and good faith in all matters involving the court.

official immunity. See under IMMUNITY.

officious intermeddler a person who intrudes into the business of others without an invitation or a reasonable basis for believing that his involvement is needed. Even if the officious intermeddler's motives are good, he generally receives little sympathy from the law if, for example, he subsequently seeks payment for his services or compensation for an injury sustained.

offset. Same as *setoff* (see under SET OFF).

omission *n.* a failure to do something that one should have done. An omission may be viewed as a type of act (see *act of omission*, under ACT), or as failure to act (often appearing in the phrase "act or omission").

on all fours a perfect fit. A phrase describing a PRECEDENT that is claimed to be so similar in its facts to the case at hand as to be legally indistinguishable.

on bail. See under BAIL[1].

on consent. See under CONSENT.

on demand. See under DEMAND.

on its (his, her, their) own motion. Same as SUA SPONTE.

on its (his, her, their) own motion. Same as SUA SPONTE.

on its face. See under FACE.

on notice 1. with advance notice; describing a procedural step taken after all concerned parties have been given sufficient notice, usually in writing, to allow them an opportunity to argue against the step: *The plaintiff moved on notice for summary judgment. The injunction was issued on notice. The judge ordered the defendant to submit a proposed order on three days' notice to the plaintiff.* Procedural rules dictate how many days' notice must normally be given for most steps in a case. **2.** having received sufficient information so that one should be aware of a certain fact: *The owner was on notice of the dog's dangerous disposition, because the dog had already bitten the letter carrier.*

on or about on approximately the date specified; a phrase often used to qualify a date when the exact date is not important, to avoid petty and irrelevant disputes over the accuracy of the date specified and allow for the possibility of a slight error.

on papers. See under PAPERS.

on point referring to a precedent or authority regarded as particularly relevant or instructive with respect to an issue under discussion: *The remarks of Smythe, J., dissenting in Cox v. Swaine, are on point.* Also called **in point.** See also *case in point* (under CASE[1]).

on the merits. See under MERITS.

on the record. See under RECORD.

on the relation of. Same as EX REL.

open *v.* **1.** to reconsider a matter that once was regarded as closed: *open a judgment.* **2.** to deliver an OPENING STATEMENT: *Ms. Smith will open for the prosecution.* —*adj.* **3.** accessible to public view or knowledge; not private or concealed: *After the plea bargain was worked out in chambers, the judge took the guilty plea in open court.*

open the door to raise an issue at a trial or hearing by asking questions or submitting evidence about it, or sometimes just by commenting on the subject to the jury, thereby entitling the other side to introduce additional or contrary evidence or make adverse comment that otherwise would not have been allowed.

opening statement a lawyer's address to the judge or jury in advance of presenting evidence, to outline the case. Often described informally as a "road map of the case." Also called **opening.** Cf. SUMMATION.

operation of law. See BY OPERATION OF LAW.

opinion *n.* **1.** the beliefs, conclusions, and inferences one draws from observation of an incident or from scientific or other specialized knowledge and experience, as distinguished from a mere description of what one has observed. See also *opinion evidence* (under EVIDENCE); *expert witness* (under WITNESS). Cf. FACT. **2.** Also called **opinion of counsel.** a formal document (sometimes in the form of a letter) called an **opinion letter**) setting forth an attorney's conclusions about the legality of a transaction or the legal aspects of a situation. **3.** a court's explanation of how it reached a particular decision in a matter; its analysis and resolution of the legal issues involved in a motion or appeal. If the case was heard by a panel of judges (for example, the nine justices of the Supreme Court), there may be several opinions: Usually a majority of judges will agree upon both the result and most of the reasoning, which they give in a **majority opinion,** sometimes referred to as the **opinion for the court.** Judges who wish to add something to the majority opinion or express some disagreement with it may issue a **separate opinion,** which is also referred to as a **concurring opinion** or **concurrence** if it reaches the same result as the majority opinion, and as a **minority opinion** or **dissenting opinion** or **dissent** if it advocates a different result. If no reasoning commands a majority of the court, the largest group that agrees upon the result reached may issue a **plurality opinion.** If all judges are in accord, they may issue a **unanimous opinion** or **opinion for a unanimous court.** Each of the foregoing opinions would normally be issued under the name of the judge who principally authored it, with a listing of other judges who have added their names to it. In cases not regarded as meriting elaborate discussion, a court may issue a short, unsigned opinion called a **per curiam opinion** or **opinion by the court,** or issue a decision with no opinion at all. See also ADVISORY OPINION; *concurring in the result* (or *judgment*) (under CONCUR); FINDINGS OF FACT AND CONCLUSIONS OF LAW; *memorandum opinion* (under MEMORANDUM); PER CURIAM; *reported opinion* (under REPORT); SLIP OPINION.

opportunity to be heard 1. the DUE PROCESS right to present evidence and argument to a neutral decision maker in a fair proceeding when the government or a private person takes judicial or administrative action intended to affect one's legal rights. **2.** an opportunity often granted by a legislature or administrative agency, but not constitutionally required, for members of the public at large to comment formally on proposed legislation or administrative action at a public hearing or in writing.

option *n.* **1.** a contractual right, good for a specified length of time, to go through with a certain transaction on specified terms or to cancel it. **2.** Also called **option contract.** a contract that gives one such a right; for example, a contract under which A, in exchange for a certain payment to B, is given the right for 60 days to purchase ten tons of wheat from B at a specified price. The decision whether to go ahead with the purchase during that time is entirely A's, because A has paid for the privilege of keeping the choice open. See also STOCK OPTION.

oral *adj.* spoken rather than written; see *oral* ARGUMENT, CONTRACT, WILL under those words. Cf. VERBAL.

order[1] *n.* **1.** a ruling or direction of a court, administrative tribunal, or legislative or executive body or official. Willful violation of a court order directing a person to do or not to do something is punishable as CONTEMPT. **2. appealable order, a.** a court order from which an immediate appeal can be taken. As a general rule in most jurisdictions, only a *final order,* such as an order granting a motion to dismiss the case, is immediately appealable. **b.** a court order that can be challenged in connection with an ultimate appeal of the entire case, but must be complied with in the meantime. For example, an order denying a motion to dismiss a case ordinarily cannot be appealed at once, but can be challenged on appeal if the case eventually goes to judgment and the judgment is appealed. See also *interlocutory appeal* (under APPEAL). **3. consent order,** an order entered with the consent of all parties to a case. **4. final order,** a JUDGMENT or other order disposing of a case; one that leaves nothing for the litigants to do except comply with the order or take an appeal. **5. interlocutory order,** an order that concerns some matter connected with a case but does not end the case, such as an order granting or denying tempo-

rary alimony in a divorce case. **6. order to show cause,** a court order directing a party to appear and present reasons why a certain order, such as an injunction or an order of contempt, should not be issued. If the party to whom the order to show cause is directed fails to appear or appears but fails to make a sufficient showing, the threatened order will be issued. An order to show cause is usually an emergency measure, issued because there is reason to believe that a party is doing something or about to do something that routine court procedures would be too slow to deal with adequately. It is often issued EX PARTE, usually accompanied by a *temporary restraining order* (see under RESTRAINING ORDER), and almost always RETURNABLE on very short notice. See also *confidentiality order* (under CONFIDENTIALITY STIPULATION); EXECUTIVE ORDER; INJUNCTION; PROTECTION ORDER; PROTECTIVE ORDER; *stipulation and order* (under STIPULATION). —*v.* **7.** to issue an order; to direct that something be done or not done. See also SO ORDERED.

order[2] *n.* **1.** a written direction to pay money. For example, a check is an order addressed to one's bank, directing it to pay out a certain sum of money from one's account. See also NEGOTIABLE INSTRUMENT; MONEY ORDER. **2. to the order of,** to the person named or a subsequent HOLDER. The use of these words is one way of signifying that a document or instrument is intended to be NEGOTIABLE. For example, an instrument that just says "pay to John Jones" may normally be enforced only by Jones, but if it says "pay to the order of John Jones," then Jones may sign it over to anyone else, making it payable to that person instead. Such an instrument is said to be **payable to order** and referred to as an **order instrument.** See also *order bill of lading* (under BILL OF LADING). Cf. **bearer instrument** (under BEARER).

ordinance *n.* a municipal law; a law adopted by a city, town, county, or other local government with respect to a matter permitted by the state to be regulated at the local level.

ordinary *adj.* describing the normal, usual, or common, as against the unusual or exceptional. For example, compare *ordinary care* with *utmost care* (under CARE); *ordinary negligence* with *gross negligence* (under NEGLIGENCE); *ordinary income* (under INCOME) with *capital gain* (under CAPITAL[1]).

ordinary course of business the routine activities of one's business as distinguished from extraordinary events. For example, maintaining routine records as distinguished from writing a special report on a unique occurrence, or selling inventory piece by piece to different customers over time as distinguished from suddenly selling one's entire remaining stock of goods to a single purchaser at a discount.

original intent a theory of constitutional interpretation under which it has been suggested that the meaning and proper application of constitutional provisions should be determined from the intent of the Constitution's framers. But there were at least a hundred people involved in the Constitutional Convention of 1787 and the first United States Congress (which put forth the Bill of Rights), and just about the only thing that can be said with certainty about how they would want their broad language to be applied today is that they would disagree among themselves as much as constitutional scholars and Supreme Court Justices do today.

original jurisdiction. See under JURISDICTION[1].

out on bail. See under BAIL[1].

outside *prep.* not covered by; not governed by: *outside the statute.* Cf. WITHIN.

outside counsel. See under COUNSEL.

overbreadth *n.* a constitutional doctrine applicable to laws that are intended to forbid certain impermissible conduct but are drafted so broadly that they also forbid a good deal of constitutionally protected conduct; for example, a law that attempts to deal with violent picketing by prohibiting all picketing, even if it is peaceful. Under the overbreadth doctrine, the Supreme Court will usually strike down such a law in its entirety and leave it to the legislature to draft a narrower law.

overreaching *n.* taking advantage of trickery or superior knowledge or bargaining power to obtain a contract that is grossly unfair to the other party, especially in a consumer transaction. A contract resulting from such overreaching may be voided by a court on the ground of UNCONSCIONABILITY.

overrule *v.* **1.** (of a trial court) to rule unfavorably upon a motion or, especially, an objection raised at trial; to refuse to sustain an objection. **2.** (of an appellate court) to nullify a legal principle announced or relied upon in a previous case by reaching a result inconsistent with it in a subsequent case; for example, a state supreme court, by issuing an opinion adopting the principle of comparative negligence, might overrule its prior cases holding that contributory negligence is a complete bar to recovery by the plaintiff in a negligence case. Sometimes courts overrule a prior case expressly; on other occasions they do so SUB SILENTIO. Direct overruling of precedents is rather unusual, because it violates the principle of STARE DECISIS.

overt act an act in furtherance of a criminal purpose. As an element in a prosecution for CONSPIRACY, the overt act need not itself be illegal, but it must constitute a step toward attainment of the unlawful objective. To convict a person of TREASON the Constitution requires "Testimony of two Witnesses to the same overt Act," and this has been construed as meaning an actual act of treason. Thus in the United States merely speaking out against government policy, without an intent to aid the enemy, is not treason.

owner *n.* **1.** a person or entity with a right to control and dispose of an interest in real or personal property, or for whose benefit such a right must be exercised. **2. beneficial owner,** a person for whose benefit another (the *legal owner*) holds property. Also called **equitable owner. 3. joint owner, a.** one of the owners of equal undivided interests in property with right of survivorship, as described under JOINT (def. 2). **b.** informally, any co-owner; a person who shares ownership of something with another person upon any legally feasible terms. **4. legal owner,** a person with the actual legal right to control or dispose of an interest in property, either for his own benefit or as a trustee or constructive trustee for the benefit of another (the *beneficial* or *equitable owner*). **5. record owner,** the person whose name appears in a public record as the owner of land and thus as the person liable for property taxes, or in the records of a corporation as the owner of stock and thus as the person entitled to receive dividends and vote on corporate matters. Also called **owner of record.**

ownership *n.* the status or rights of an owner regarding an interest in property. In addition to the types of ownership described under OWNER (*beneficial* or *equitable, joint,* etc.), ownership may be characterized as BY THE ENTIRETY, IN COMMON, or IN SEVERALTY, as appropriate.

oyez *interj. Law French.* hear ye. In many courts, this is called out (usually two or three times) at the opening of each session to impress upon those present the solemnity of the proceedings. See also HEAR YE; KNOW ALL MEN BY THESE PRESENTS. —**Pronunciation.** Pronounced "oh yes" or "oh yez." The pronunciation "oh yay," which is sometimes heard, is inauthentic—an effort to pronounce this as if it were a modern French word.

a b c d e f g h i j k l m n o **P** q r s t u v w x y z

paid-up stock. See under STOCK.

pain and suffering physical and mental suffering caused by another's tortious conduct, as when one has suffered a personal injury or emotional loss. The compensatory damages awarded in a tort case may include a sum of money for the plaintiff's pain and suffering.

palimony *n.* an ALIMONY-like financial provision upon the breakup of an unmarried couple who lived together. The courts in some states have expressed a willingness to make such awards in limited circumstances, but few if any separated lovers have actually received such an award. See also MERETRICIOUS.

palming off. Same as PASSING OFF.

pandering. Same as PROMOTING PROSTITUTION.

panel *n.* **1.** the set of judges hearing a case. For example, appeals in the United States Courts of Appeals are normally heard by a panel of three judges selected at random from among the several judges assigned to the court. Cf. EN BANC. **2.** Same as *jury panel* (see under JURY).

paper. See COMMERCIAL PAPER; PAPERS.

papers *n.pl.* **1.** the lawyer-generated documents in a case; for example, pleadings, affidavits, briefs. Occasionally a single such document is referred to as a **paper. 2. motion papers,** the set of papers submitted to a court in support of or in opposition to a motion. **3. on papers,** the manner of submission of a matter to a court when no oral argument or testimony is offered or is allowed.

par value 1. the face value of a share of STOCK or of a bond (see BOND¹). In the case of a bond or preferred stock, the par value is the basis upon which dividends and interest are calculated. In the case of common stock, par value used to represent the original selling price of the stock, but now is an arbitrary and largely meaningless figure, typically $1.00. Many states have eliminated the requirement that corporations assign a par value to stock. **2. par value stock.** Same as *stock with par value* (see under STOCK).

paralegal *n.* a nonlawyer employed to assist a lawyer or lawyers by performing, subject to supervision by the lawyers, a variety of legal tasks requiring less than a full legal education. Also called **legal assistant.**

paramount title. See under TITLE.

pardon *n.* **1.** the release of a person from penalties for a past offense or alleged offense. For federal offenses a pardon can be issued only by the President; for state offenses, usually only by the governor. A pardon may be granted before or after an arrest or conviction, and even after death. It bars any further prosecution or punishment, but it does not remove a conviction from one's record. **2.** the document in which a pardon is declared. —*v.* **3.** to grant a pardon to someone: *President Ford pardoned ex-President Nixon for all crimes that he may have committed as President.* Cf. AMNESTY, COMMUTE, REPRIEVE. See also CLEMENCY.

parens patriae *Latin.* (lit. "parent of the country," originally a reference to the King or Queen) a state government in its role as protector of the people, and especially of children and the mentally infirm. In this role, the state may initiate certain civil actions to protect the interests of the state on behalf of all its people, or to protect people who lack the legal capacity to protect their own interests, as by taking children away from abusive parents or institutionalizing incompetents who pose a danger to themselves or others.

parent company *n.* a corporation that owns more than 50% of the voting stock of another corporation. Also called **parent corporation** or simply **parent.** Cf. SUBSIDIARY.

parental kidnapping the taking or secreting of a child by one parent in violation of the custody or visitation rights of the other parent.

parental liability liability of parents for damages

caused by tortious conduct of their children, imposed to varying extents by statutes in some states. Extensions of this concept to the criminal law, so that parents can be fined for offenses committed by their children, have been tried, but are of uncertain constitutionality.

parental neglect. See under NEGLECT.

pari delicto. See IN PARI DELICTO.

pari materia. See IN PARI MATERIA.

parliamentary law rules of procedure for meetings of organizations. Parliamentary "law" is not part of federal or state law except in the peripheral sense that Congress and state legislatures necessarily adopt certain rules for the orderly conduct of their own debates and business.

parol *adj.* **1.** oral: *parol promise; parol statement.* Cf. PAROL EVIDENCE. —*n.* **2.** an oral declaration or communication.

parol evidence 1. literally, either evidence of oral communications or evidence given orally. **2.** in its customary use, any oral or written information about a written contract, or a transaction involving a written contract, apart from the language of the instrument itself; for example, prior correspondence in which the contract was negotiated. **3. parol evidence rule,** the rule of contract law that generally prohibits the use of extrinsic evidence, whether written or oral, to contradict contract terms that have been reduced to writing; in addition, if the writing was intended by the parties to embody their entire agreement, extrinsic evidence may not be used to add terms to it.

parole *n.* **1.** release of a convicted criminal from jail or prison after serving part of a sentence, on the condition that he stay out of trouble with the law and comply with other requirements, such as meeting regularly with a parole officer. If parole conditions are violated, parole can be revoked and the parolee returned to confinement. Cf. PROBATION. —*v.* **2.** to release on parole.

partial breach. See under BREACH.

particulars. See BILL OF PARTICULARS.

partition *v.* **1.** to divide property up among its co-owners, either physically or, more often, by selling it and dividing the proceeds. —*n.* **2.** such a division, or a civil action seeking such a division by court order.

partner *n.* **1.** a member of a PARTNERSHIP. **2. general** (or **full**) **partner, a.** a partner in a *general partnership* (see under PARTNERSHIP). **b.** one of the partners in a *limited partnership* (see under PARTNERSHIP) having responsibility for operation of the business and unlimited liability for its debts; a partner other than a *limited partner.* Unless otherwise specified, "partner" normally means general partner. **3. limited partner,** a partner in a limited partnership who merely invests money in the enterprise; one who does not participate in its management or operation and whose liability is limited to the amount invested. **4. silent partner,** a partner whose involvement in the partnership is kept secret, or at least is not generally known. Referred to in England as a **sleeping partner** —a term that might be misunderstood in America.

partnership *n.* **1.** an association of two or more people or entities to carry on a business for profit. Profits and losses are shared by the partners and taxed to them directly; the partnership as an entity does not pay income taxes. See also DOMESTIC PARTNERSHIP. **2. general partnership,** an ordinary partnership, in which each partner is personally liable for the acts of every other partner in the conduct of the business and has unlimited personal liability for the debts of the partnership, and usually all partners participate in the management and conduct of the business. Unless otherwise specified, "partnership" means general partnership. **3. limited liability partnership (L.L.P.),** a form of partnership in which individual partners are not subject to personal liability for claims against the partnership. **4. limited partnership (L.P.),** a partnership consisting of one or more *general partners* and one or more *limited partners* (see under PARTNER).

party *n.* **1.** a person or entity directly and officially involved in a transaction; especially, one of those bound by a contract. **2.** a person or entity by or against whom a claim or charge is asserted in a case, especially one who has appeared or been served in the action. **3. indispensable party,** a person or entity whose rights are so bound up in a matter in suit that the case will not be allowed to proceed unless that person or entity is joined as a party. See also *compulsory joinder* (under JOINDER). Cf. *necessary party; proper party.* **4. necessary party,** a person or entity whose rights are sufficiently involved in an action to require joinder as a party if that is possible; but if it is not possible, the action will be allowed to proceed without that additional party. See also *compulsory joinder* (under JOINDER). Cf. *indispensable party; proper party.* **5. party of the first part,** in old drafting syle, the first party named in a contract or other instrument, often the maker or drafter; subsequently named parties were identified as "party of the second part," "party of the third part," and so on. This terminology is no longer used, but shows up in old legal instruments, old judicial opinions, old movies, and old and new works of all kinds satirizing lawyers. **6. proper party,** a person or entity with a sufficient interest in a matter in suit to justify inclusion in the case, but whose absence would not hinder a just adjudication. A person bringing a case need not join every proper party in the action, although a proper party who is left out normally has a right to INTERVENE. See also *permissive joinder* (under JOINDER). Cf. *indispensable party; necessary party.* **7. real party in interest,** the person or entity possessing the legal right sued upon, or having a direct *interest* in the outcome of a case (see INTEREST², def. 1). Under old procedural rules, actions sometimes had to be brought in the name of someone other than the real party in interest; modern rules eliminate such technicalities. See also THIRD PARTY; *charter party* (under CHARTER²).

party joinder. See under JOINDER.

passing off marketing one thing as if it were another; for example, a counterfeit as an original, another's product as one's own, or, particularly, one's own inferior product as if it were the superior product of a better-known company. Also called **palming off.**

passport *n.* a document issued by a national government to one of its citizens, subjects, or nationals, authorizing travel out of the country and requesting other countries to permit entry and grant legal protection to the person.

past consideration. See under CONSIDERATION.

past recollection recorded. See under RECOLLECTION.

patent *n.* **1.** the exclusive right to exploit an invention for a number of years, granted by the federal government to the inventor if the inventor applies for it and the invention qualifies (is **patentable**). —*v.* **2.** to apply for and receive a patent on one's invention. —*adj.* **3.** open to public inspection; intended for public view: *letters patent* (see under LETTERS). **4.** obvious; apparent at a glance or upon reasonable inspection: *patent defect; patent ambiguity.* Cf. LATENT. —**patently,** *adv.* —**Pronunciation.** For the noun and the verb, the first syllable rhymes with *hat.* For the adjective and the adverb, the first syllable rhymes with *hate.*

patently offensive obviously offensive. For purposes of an OBSCENITY prosecution, a depiction of sexual conduct is patently offensive if the jury regards it as patently offensive, unless the highest court to which the case is appealed subsequently decides that it is clearly not patently offensive.

paternity suit (or **action** or **proceeding**), an action to establish that a particular man is the father of a child born out of wedlock. The action may be brought, for example, by the mother, in order to obtain child support payments; by the state, in order to compel such payments; or by the putative father himself, in order to obtain parental rights.

pawn *n.* **1.** the deposit of goods as security for a loan or other obligation, especially an individual's deposit of personal possessions to secure a personal loan. **2.** an item so deposited; the collateral for the loan. **3.** the state of being deposited or held as security: *His television set is in pawn.* —*v.* **4.** to make such a deposit: *She pawned her wedding ring.*

pawnbroker *n.* a person in the business of making loans secured by pawns of personal property.

payable *adj.* supposed to be paid; now due or to become due: *accounts payable; a check payable to the order of Jane Smith.* See also *payable on demand* (under DEMAND); *payable to bearer* (under BEARER); *payable to order* (under ORDER²).

payee *n.* a person to whom, or to whose order, money is paid or is supposed to be paid; especially, the person so named in an instrument, such as the person or entity to which a check is made out.

payment bond. See under BOND².

payor *n.* the person who makes, or is supposed to make, a payment; especially, the person or entity so designated in a negotiable instrument, such as the bank upon which a check or other draft is drawn **(payor bank).**

payroll tax any of several kinds of tax collected from employers on the basis of employee count or employee salaries. Some such taxes are paid by the employer in addition to the employees' salaries; others are paid by the employees through withholding from their salaries. See SOCIAL SECURITY TAX for an example.

penal *adj.* **1.** pertaining to a penalty or to penalties generally. **2.** pertaining to crime and punishment.

penalty *n.* **1.** a punishment for a crime; e.g., the *death penalty* (see under CAPITAL PUNISHMENT). **2.** a sum specified in a contract to be paid, beyond or instead of payment of damages, in the event of a breach, or agreed to as the price of being excused from an obligation. Cf. *liquidated damages* (under DAMAGES). **3. civil penalty,** a fine or forfeiture provided for by statute or regulation, not for commission of a crime but for failure to fulfill a legal obligation or adhere to regulations. Civil penalties are often imposed by administrative agencies. Examples: a percentage added to one's income tax bill as a penalty for failure to pay on time; removal of one's license to conduct a food business for persistent failure to maintain health standards. **4. penalty clause,** a contract clause requiring payment of a specific sum of money, unrelated to and usually greater than anticipated damages, as a penalty in the event of breach. As a general rule, such clauses are unenforceable. Cf. *liquidated damages* (under DAMAGES). **5. prepayment penalty,** in connection with a mortgage or other loan agreement, a penalty that the debtor must pay if the debt is repaid early. Prepayment penalties are often enforceable because they compensate the lender for loss of interest.

pendent jurisdiction. See under JURISDICTION¹.

pendente lite *Latin.* (lit. "with a lawsuit pending") during litigation; while a case is in progress: *injunction pendente lite.*

penitentiary. Same as PRISON.

pension *n.* **1.** regular payments to a retired employee from a fund **(pension fund)** created by the employer or by a combination of employer and employee contributions, or the right to receive such payments. **2. vested pension,** a pension to which an employee will become entitled upon retirement even if she quits or loses her job before then. Ordinarily an employee must stay with a particular employer for five to seven years for a pension associated with that position to become fully vested.

pension plan 1. a program established by an employer for the provision of pensions to employees. The standards for such plans are set by the **Employee Retirement Income Security Act of 1974 (ERISA). 2. defined-benefit plan,** a pension plan that guarantees a certain level of pension payments after retirement, based upon the employee's length of employment, salary, and age at retirement. **3. defined-contribution plan,** a pension plan under which the level of employer and employee contributions is fixed, and the level of benefits ultimately received may be higher or lower depending upon how successful the pension fund's investments have been. **4. qualified pension plan,** a pension plan conforming to certain provisions of the Internal

Revenue Code, making the employer's contributions tax deductible and deferring income tax for the employee until benefits are actually received, after retirement. A qualified pension plan set up by a self-employed individual, a sole proprietor, or a partnership is called a **Keogh plan** or **HR-10 plan. 5. simplified employee pension (SEP),** a pension plan affording most of the tax advantages of other qualified plans, under which the employer simply makes contributions to each employee's INDIVIDUAL RETIREMENT ACCOUNT. See also RETIREMENT PLAN.

people *n.pl.* **1.** human beings; especially, the inhabitants of a state or nation collectively. **2.** *cap.* in many states, the name by which the state government and the prosecution are identified in criminal cases under state law. See also STATE. Cf. GOVERNMENT.

per capita *Latin.* (lit. "by the heads") **1.** per person; divided equally among all the people in a defined group. **2.** a principle for distributing a decedent's estate under which all takers of a particular portion of the estate, or at least all takers at the same generational level, receive equal shares without regard to what branch of the family they belong to. Cf. PER STIRPES.

per curiam *Latin.* by the court. See also *per curiam opinion* (under OPINION).

per se *Latin.* (lit. "by itself") intrinsically; without more. Said of acts that constitute such strong evidence of wrongdoing that no further evidence is needed. For example, under the law forbidding UNREASONABLE RESTRAINT OF TRADE, price fixing is regarded as "unreasonable per se," and certain kinds of insult are regarded as so inherently defamatory as to constitute "slander per se."

per stirpes *Latin.* (lit. "by the stems"; "by the branches") describing a principle for distributing a decedent's estate under which the descendants of any person who would have received a share of the estate if he had still been alive at the time of the decedent's death divide up that person's share. Thus the portion left to each branch of the family is divided and subdivided only within that branch. Cf. PER CAPITA.

percentage lease. See under LEASE.

peremptory challenge. See under CHALLENGE.

perfect *v.* to take all legal steps necessary to secure or put on record a claim, right, or interest: *perfect a security interest; perfect title to land; perfect an appeal.*

perform *v.* to carry out a legal duty; to fulfill one's obligations, especially under a contract. See also SPECIFIC PERFORMANCE; SUBSTANTIAL PERFORMANCE. —**performance,** *n.*

performance bond. See under BOND².

periodic tenancy (or **estate**). See under TENANCY.

perjury *n.* the crime of making a false statement under oath or affirmation on a material issue in a judicial or administrative proceeding, other than in the belief that what is being said is true. Cf. FALSE SWEARING.

permanent injunction. See under INJUNCTION.

permissive *adj.* permitted but not required; opposite of compulsory or mandatory. See *permissive* COUNTERCLAIM, JOINDER, PRESUMPTION under those words.

perpetuate *v.* to obtain and preserve testimony in a form suitable for later use at a trial, in case the witness is unavailable. See also DEPOSITION.

perpetuity *n.* a *contingent interest* in real property (see under INTEREST¹) that might remain contingent for a length of time regarded by the law as excessive; that is, the contingency that would cause the interest to VEST might remain unresolved—not having occurred, but still possible—for a longer time than permitted by law. At common law, the maximum time limit was the lifetime of someone alive (or at least conceived) at the time the interest was created and identified in the instrument creating the interest (a **life in being**), plus 21 years. This allowed, for example, a testator to leave his estate to his children for as long as they live, then finally "to

legal

such of my grandchildren as reach the age of 21." Under the **rule against perpetuities**, any interest that might remain contingent longer than lives in being plus 21 years was just too uncertain, and was declared void. Some version of the rule against perpetuities exists in all or virtually all states, but the details vary from state to state. See also RESTRAINT ON ALIENATION.

person *n., pl.* **persons. 1.** a human being **(natural person)** or an organization or entity **(juridical person, juristic person, artificial person,** or **legal person)** such as a corporation, recognized by the law as capable of performing legal acts (such as entering into a contract) and having legal rights and responsibilities (such as the right to due process and liability for torts). The exact scope of the term depends upon the context. In this dictionary, the phrase "person or entity" is often used to emphasize that a definition applies to juridical as well as natural persons, and the nonlegalistic plural "people" is sometimes used to indicate that a concept applies exclusively or primarily to natural persons rather than juridical persons. See also INDIVIDUAL. **2.** the human body: *injury to person and property.* **3. interested person,** a person with an interest (see INTEREST²) in a matter; particularly a person whose legal and financial rights will be directly affected by the outcome of a case or the disposition of a decedent's estate. Persons having such an interest will normally be allowed to INTERVENE in a case or otherwise assert their claims and rights in a matter if their interest is not already adequately represented. **4. protected person,** an individual, especially an incompetent person, for whom a court has appointed a GUARDIAN or made some other order of protection. **5. reasonable person.** See under REASONABLE.

personal. See *personal* BOND², INCOME TAX, INJURY, JUDGMENT, JURISDICTION¹, KNOWLEDGE, PROPERTY, SERVICE under those words, and *release on personal recognizance* (under RELEASE ON OWN RECOGNIZANCE).

personalty. Same as *personal property* (see under PROPERTY).

personam. See IN PERSONAM.

persuasion. See *burden of persuasion* (under BURDEN¹).

persuasive authority. See under AUTHORITY².

petit *adj. Law French.* (lit. "small") small, minor, lesser. Used in certain legal phrases of ancient origin, usually in contrast to GRAND; e.g., *petit jury* (see under JURY), *petit larceny* (see under LARCENY). Pronounced, and often written, "petty."

petition *n.* **1.** a formal request, addressed to a person or body in a position of authority, soliciting some benevolent exercise of power. The right to present such petitions to the government is one of the rights guaranteed by the First Amendment (see Appendix). **2.** the name given to the initial pleading in certain kinds of judicial or administrative proceedings, and to certain requests for special permission or relief from appellate courts: *petition for a writ of habeas corpus; petition in bankruptcy; petition for leave to appeal.* —*v.* **3.** to present or file a petition: *to petition the governor for a pardon; to petition the legislature for a change in the law; to petition for a writ of mandamus.* —**petitioner,** *n.*

petty *adj.* small, minor, lesser. See *petty* JURY, LARCENY, OFFENSE under those words. In certain phrases, often rendered in the original French form: PETIT. Cf. GRAND.

physician-assisted suicide. See under SUICIDE.

physician-patient privilege. See under PRIVILEGE.

picket *v.* **1.** to stand or parade in front of a place of employment carrying signs, in order to publicize a labor grievance and discourage customers and other employees from entering or patronizing the establishment until the dispute is resolved. **2.** to engage in any similar demonstration in front of a government or private building or site for the purpose of publicizing a cause, protesting conduct, or petitioning for action. Since picketing is *speech plus* (see under SPEECH), it is subject to greater regulation than pure speech. —*n.* **3.** an individual engaged in picketing.

pierce the corporate veil. See under CORPORATE.

piracy *n.* **1.** plundering, violence, or other criminal acts on a ship or airplane, or the stealing or highjacking of such a vessel. **2.** the unauthorized reproduction, imitation, or use of a copyrighted work, patented invention, or trademarked product; especially, unauthorized reproduction of copyrighted books, records, tapes, videotapes, and software on a large scale for commercial purposes. —**pirate,** *v., n.*

plagiarize *v.* to present another's ideas, words, or other form of expression as if they were one's own. This may or may not be unlawful, depending upon whether it involves unauthorized use of copyrighted work and other factors, but in academic and scholarly contexts it is always unethical and may lead to disciplinary proceedings. —**plagiarism,** *n.*

plain error. See under ERROR.

plain meaning the apparent meaning of a statutory or constitutional provision as gleaned solely from the words of the provision itself, without consideration of other factors, such as the context in which the words were written and the objective the writers were trying to achieve. The **plain meaning rule** is a theory of statutory and constitutional CONSTRUCTION that regards the "plain meaning" of a provision as dispositive. This theory disregards the fact that writing is an inherently inexact activity, that reasonable people can reach very different conclusions as to what a particular provision "plainly means," and that the "plain meaning" found by a judge is often as much a reflection of what the judge wants to find in the provision as of what the drafter put there. Cf. LEGISLATIVE INTENT.

plain view doctrine the principle that police who are lawfully in a place do not need a search warrant to seize evidence of crime that is in plain view; similarly, an officer may seize evidence obvious to the touch in the conduct of a lawful patdown for weapons.

plaintiff *n.* the person who starts a lawsuit by serving or filing a complaint.

plaintiff in error the APPELLANT in a case in which the appeal is commenced by *writ of error* (see under WRIT).

plan of reorganization. See under BANKRUPTCY.

plea *n.* **1.** a criminal defendant's formal response to the charges: GUILTY, NOT GUILTY, or NOLO CONTENDERE. At ARRAIGNMENT, the usual plea is "not guilty," but this is often changed later, usually as the result of a PLEA BARGAIN. **2.** any of a considerable number of specific pleadings and motions that were used in civil cases prior to the adoption of modern rules of procedure, seldom referred to in modern cases.

plea bargain a negotiated agreement between the prosecution and a criminal defendant whereby the prosecution grants some concessions in exchange for the defendant's plea of guilty to at least one charge. Typical concessions include dropping certain charges, especially the most serious ones, and agreeing to make a particular sentencing recommendation. Most criminal cases end in a plea bargain.

plead *v.* to enter a PLEA or file a PLEADING, or to assert in a pleading: *He pleaded the defense of statute of limitations.* "Pleaded" is the conventional past tense; "pled," though increasingly common in the United States, still carries for traditionalists an overtone of uneducated speech.

pleading *n.* **1.** the formal document in which a party to a civil case sets out or responds to a claim or defense. Under modern rules, the principal pleadings are the COMPLAINT, the ANSWER, and if the answer contains counterclaims, a REPLY. **2.** the act of asserting or filing a claim, defense, or plea. **3. alternative pleading,** the inclusion in a pleading of allegations or defenses based upon varying—or even conflicting—interpretations of the facts or the law. For example, "Defendant either negligently failed to see a red light or, in the alternative, saw the red light and deliberately ignored it"; "Defendant's conduct constitutes a fraud, or alternatively a breach of contract." Such pleading was formerly disfavored, but under modern procedure is freely allowed. **4. notice pleading,** the modern philosophy that the function of pleadings is simply to give reasonable notice of the nature of one's claims or defenses, the details of which can be developed through DISCOVERY. This is in contrast to earlier practice, in which pleading was a highly technical exercise and cases could easily be lost because of minor pleading defects even if the facts supported the pleader. See also *burden of pleading* (under BURDEN[1]); *judgment on the pleadings* (under JUDGMENT).

pledge *n.* **1.** a deposit of personal property, or of documents (such as stock certificates) representing intangible property, with a lender or other person as security for a loan or other obligation. —*v.* **2.** to make such a pledge.

plenary *adj.* **1.** full, complete, sufficient, unqualified: *plenary jurisdiction over a case; plenary trial.* **2.** involving all members of a body: *a plenary session of the legislature.*

plurality opinion. See under OPINION.

pocket part a common form of supplement to a book of statutes or a treatise or other legal reference work, in which updated portions are tucked into a pocket in the back of the book.

point *n.* **1.** a proposition of fact or law. **2.** a section of a brief devoted to argument in support of a particular point of significance in the case. See also *case in point* (under CASE[1]); *memorandum of points and authorities* (under BRIEF); ON POINT.

poisonous tree. See FRUIT OF THE POISONOUS TREE.

police power state legislative power; the inherent power of state governments, and of local governments to the extent delegated by the state, to enact laws safeguarding the health, safety, morals, convenience, and general welfare of people in the state, subject only to the constraints of the Constitution and the supremacy of federal law in matters within its purview.

policy *n.* **1.** Also called **insurance policy.** the written instrument embodying a contract of INSURANCE. **2.** See PUBLIC POLICY.

political asylum. See under ASYLUM.

political question. See under QUESTION[2].

poll tax a "head tax"; a fixed tax imposed on everyone regardless of income. After the Civil War, poll taxes were enacted in many states as a condition of being allowed to vote, making it difficult for the poor, and in particular the black populace, to vote. In 1964 this requirement was eliminated in elections for national office by the Twenty-fourth Amendment (see Appendix); two years later the Supreme Court abolished it for state and local elections, on the ground that it denied impoverished voters equal protection of the laws.

poll the jury to require the jurors in a case in which a verdict has just been announced to declare in open court, usually one by one, whether that is, in fact, their verdict. This is done by the judge or a court officer if requested by a party.

polygraph *n.* a device for measuring certain involuntary bodily responses, such as blood pressure and perspiration, from which an opinion is drawn as to whether or not the person being tested is telling the truth. Also called, somewhat optimistically, a **lie detector.** The problem with it is that while it may yield accurate opinions in many cases, it can make nervous or confused truth-tellers look like liars and amoral or self-deluding liars look like truth-tellers, and there is no way to know which results are accurate and which are not. Accordingly, polygraph results are excluded from evidence under most circumstances in most jurisdictions, and federal law prohibits employers, except in very limited circumstances, from using the device on employees and applicants for employment.

pornography *n.* **1.** broadly, any sexually explicit material intended primarily to provide sexual entertainment and arousal to those who read or view it for that purpose. **2.** narrowly, sexual material satisfying the constitutional test for OBSCENITY. In general, any commercial, and sometimes noncommercial, involvement with such pornography is a crime. **3. child pornography,** any sexually explicit visual depiction of an individual under the age of 18. Courts have held that such material may be banned

even if it is not obscene and does not involve nudity.

positive law human-made law as distinguished from so-called NATURAL LAW; the actual rules of behavior and government enforced by a society.

posse. See IN POSSE; POSSE COMITATUS.

posse comitatus *Latin.* (lit. "force of the county") a group of people who may be called upon to assist law enforcement authorities in preserving the peace, making an arrest, or the like; or a group actually called upon and assembled for such a purpose. Also called a **posse.** It is in the tradition of the posse comitatus that the National Guard may be called out for such purposes as enforcing school integration, quelling riots, or maintaining order after a natural disaster.

possession *n.* **1.** occupation or control of real property to the exclusion of others (save with permission of the possessor), or knowing dominion and control over personal property. **2. actual possession,** direct or immediate physical occupation or control of property. See also ADVERSE POSSESSION; OCCUPANCY. **3. constructive possession,** the power and intention of exercising control over property that is in the hands of someone else. For example, the owner of a house currently occupied by a lessee, or of furniture stored in a warehouse, has constructive possession of the house or furniture, while the tenant or the warehouser has actual possession. To sustain a charge of "criminal possession" of contraband, such as illegal drugs or stolen property, it is usually sufficient to show constructive possession.

possession is nine-tenths of the law a somewhat overstated adage reflecting two realities: (1) that in disputes over real property, a person in possession can only be ousted by one with a superior right; a person with no right or a lesser right has no standing to complain, even if the present occupant's possession is wrongful; and (2) that because of the expense, uncertainty, and difficulty of obtaining and enforcing legal judgments, a person in possession of disputed property or a disputed sum of money has a strategic advantage over an adverse claimant. Sometimes, especially in England, the idiom is **possession is nine points of the law.** See also *paramount title* (under TITLE).

possessory action an action to recover or maintain possession of real or personal property, such as an action to evict a holdover tenant or for REPLEVIN.

possessory estate. See under ESTATE[1].

possessory interest. See under INTEREST[1].

possibility of reverter the *future estate* (see under ESTATE[1]) retained by the owner of a fee (see FEE[1]) in real property (or her heirs) when she transfers the entire fee to someone else but imposes a condition on its continued existence so that, upon violation of the condition, the fee will revert to the original owner or her heirs. See also *fee simple determinable* (under FEE[1]). Cf. *executory interest* (under INTEREST[1]).

post bail. See under BAIL[1].

power *n.* **1.** legal authority to perform acts affecting legal rights and relationships, especially the authority of a legislative body to make laws on certain subjects (e.g., *commerce power,* under COMMERCE; POLICE POWER), the authority of other governmental bodies or officers to perform their respective duties (*e.g., executive power; judicial power*), or specific authority granted to a private person to take actions having legal consequences (e.g., POWER OF APPOINTMENT; POWER OF ATTORNEY). See also SEPARATION OF POWERS. **2. delegated power, a.** power granted by one person or body to another, to do something that the first could have done; especially, regulatory power conferred upon an administrative agency by Congress. **b.** Another name for *enumerated power.* **3. enumerated power,** a power conferred upon the federal government by the Constitution, such as the commerce power. The United States government is a "government of enumerated powers," having only those powers provided for in the Constitution. **4. reserved power,** a governmental power left to the states by the Constitution—that is, any governmental power that the Constitution neither grants to the federal government nor denies to state governments.

power of appointment the authority, granted by the owner of property (the DONOR of the power) to a person (the DONEE), to designate (APPOINT) the person or persons who are to receive the property upon the death of the donor, the death of the donee, or the termination of some intervening interest in the property.

power of attorney 1. an instrument by which one individual (the PRINCIPAL) confers upon another (the *attorney in fact*; see under ATTORNEY) the power to perform specified acts or kinds of acts on behalf of the principal. 2. the power possessed by an attorney in fact by reason of such an instrument. 3. **durable power of attorney,** a form of power of attorney allowed by statute, which remains effective if the principal becomes incompetent to perform or consent to the acts delegated. At common law, the power of attorney was automatically revoked upon incapacity of the principal. 4. **durable power of attorney for health care.** Same as HEALTH CARE PROXY. 5. **general power of attorney,** a power of attorney granting wide power to perform any act of a specified kind or of a range of kinds, such as handling all business and financial matters for the principal. 6. **special power of attorney,** a power of attorney to perform a certain act, such as signing a particular document or purchasing a particular parcel of land.

practice *n.* 1. the procedural aspects of law; the presentation of matters to courts and the manner in which cases are handled: *civil practice; rules of practice; Supreme Court practice.* 2. the pursuit of a profession: *the practice of law; the practice of architecture.* 3. one's usual way of dealing with a particular kind of situation: *Her practice is to have her secretary open her mail. The practice in our industry is to ship by truck unless another method is specified.* —*v.* 4. to engage in a profession.

praesenti. See IN PRAESENTI.

prayer for relief the portion at the end of a COMPLAINT in which the plaintiff states the damages or other remedy being sought in the action. Also called **demand for relief.**

preamble *n.* an introduction to a constitution, statute, contract, or other instrument, stating the reasons for enacting or writing it. It is usually not regarded as a part of the instrument, but is sometimes looked to for help in construing the instrument.

precatory *adj.* expressing or reflecting a hope, desire, or preference, but not a direction or command.

precatory language language in a trust instrument or will that indicates the maker's desire but is not legally binding; for example, "It is my hope that these funds will be used for educational purposes." Also called **precatory words.** Often it is difficult to know whether such language was intended to be mandatory or merely precatory. See also WISH.

precedent *n.* 1. a judicial decision cited as authority by an attorney or court in a subsequent case involving similar or analogous facts and issues. Virtually all judicial decisions are based upon precedent, which is central to the doctrine of STARE DECISIS. —*adj.* 2. condition precedent. See under CONDITION. —**Pronunciation.** The noun is PRESSedent; the adjective is more appropriately preSEEDent.

preclusion *n.* being prevented from making certain arguments or contesting certain issues in a case, either because one has already litigated them in an earlier case and lost, or because one has failed to provide information on the issue to the other side in compliance with discovery requirements, as a result of which the judge has issued a **preclusion order.** See also *issue preclusion* (under ESTOPPEL).

predator. See SEXUAL PREDATOR.

predatory pricing selling goods or services at an unreasonably low price in the hope of driving competitors out of business and then raising the price. This is a violation of ANTITRUST laws.

predecessor *n.* one who previously possessed a right, interest, or duty now belonging to another (a SUCCESSOR). Also called **predecessor in interest.**

preemption *n.* 1. the doctrine that a comprehen-

sive federal regulatory scheme in a field of federal interest may be held to preclude any state regulation whatever in that field. In such a situation federal law is said to **occupy the field** and to **preempt** state law. 2. the enactment of a federal law that preempts state law, or the preemptive effect of a federal law. See also SUPREMACY.

preference *n.* 1. a payment or transfer of property or of an interest in property by an insolvent debtor to a creditor in such a way that the creditor gets more than its share of the debtor's property as compared with other creditors. 2. **voidable preference,** a preference shortly before the debtor formally goes into bankruptcy, under circumstances permitting the bankruptcy court to recover whatever was given from the creditor who received it, so that it can be distributed fairly among all creditors.

preferred stock. See under STOCK.

pregnancy discrimination discrimination in employment on the basis of pregnancy, childbirth, or related medical conditions. After the Supreme Court held that this does not constitute discrimination against women, Congress in 1978 adopted a statute making it clear that pregnancy discrimination is to be regarded as a form of illegal sex discrimination.

prejudice *n.* 1. bias or prejudgment in a case; a tendency to favor one side over the other. See also INTEREST². 2. adverse effect on, or loss of, a legal right, particularly a procedural right in a lawsuit or criminal case. 3. **with prejudice,** having the effect of precluding a party from asserting a particular claim or right or contesting a particular issue in the future. 4. **without prejudice,** preserving a party's right to assert a particular claim or right or contest a particular issue in the future. See also *dismissal with prejudice* and *dismissal without prejudice* (under DISMISSAL). —*v.* 5. to cause prejudice to a party or to a specified right of a party.

prejudicial effect the tendency of a piece of evidence to inflame the jury unduly or to divert its attention to irrelevant matters. Relevant evidence in a case may be excluded if the judge concludes that its PROBATIVE VALUE is outweighed by its prejudicial effect.

prejudicial error. See under ERROR.

preliminary hearing. See under HEARING.

preliminary injunction. See under INJUNCTION.

premarital agreement. Same as PRENUPTIAL AGREEMENT.

premeditation *n.* contemplating something with a cool mind before doing it, if only briefly and on the spot. Premeditation is an element of the highest degree of MURDER in some states. —**premeditated,** *adj.*

premium *n.* 1. money paid to an insurance company for insurance coverage or for an annuity. 2. an extra amount paid or received for something; especially the amount by which the market value of a bond exceeds its face value if the bond carries interest at a higher rate than the current rate for newly issued bonds.

prenuptial agreement a contract between two people who are about to marry regarding their respective property and support rights upon termination of the marriage by divorce or death, and sometimes regarding property rights during the marriage as well. Such agreements are generally enforceable, and supersede otherwise applicable rules. Also called **antenuptial agreement** or **premarital agreement.**

prepayment penalty. See under PENALTY.

preponderance of the evidence the lowest STANDARD OF PROOF; the degree of persuasion necessary to find for the plaintiff in most civil cases. It requires just enough evidence to persuade the jury that a fact is more likely to be true than not true. If the evidence is equally balanced, then the party with the *burden of persuasion* (see under BURDEN¹) loses. Sometimes called **preponderance of the credible evidence** or **fair preponderance of the evidence.**

prerogative writ. Same as *extraordinary writ* (see under WRIT).

prescription *n.* a method of obtaining an EASEMENT over real property belonging to someone else, such as the right to use a path across it, consisting of openly and consistently using it for a period of time set by statute, usually ten to twenty years. Acquisition of an easement by prescription is analogous to acquisition of title by ADVERSE POSSESSION.

present estate or **present possessory estate.** Same as *possessory estate* (see under ESTATE¹).

present interest. See under INTEREST¹.

present recollection refreshed. See under RECOLLECTION.

present sense impression a statement describing an event or situation, or the declarant's own physical condition or state of mind, made by a person while actually observing or experiencing the thing being described or immediately thereafter. Statements of present sense impression are commonly admitted into evidence as an exception to the rule against HEARSAY.

presentence report a background report on a convicted defendant, prepared by a probation department to assist the judge in deciding upon a sentence.

presentment *n.* **1.** the act of presenting an instrument for the payment of money, such as a check or promissory note, to the payor for acceptance or payment. **2.** a written statement of an offense prepared by a grand jury on its own initiative, as distinguished from an INDICTMENT requested by the prosecutor. **3.** the formal act of presenting a matter to a body or official for legal action.

presents *n.pl.* the present writings; the contents of this legal instrument. Now limited almost exclusively to the phrase KNOW ALL MEN BY THESE PRESENTS or some minor variation of it.

press. See FREEDOM OF THE PRESS.

presumption *n.* **1.** a legal assumption that if one fact or group of facts exists, then another fact must also exist, so that the second can sometimes be proved in a court case simply by introducing evidence of the first. **2. conclusive presumption,** a rule of law under which once one set of facts is established, the facts that normally follow from it must be found to be true, and no evidence to the contrary will be permitted; for example, the presumption that if a driver's blood alcohol content was above a certain level, then the driver was drunk. Also called **irrebuttable presumption. 3. mandatory presumption,** a presumption that the factfinder in a criminal case must accept unless the defendant produces some evidence to rebut it. **4. permissive presumption,** a presumption that the factfinder in a criminal case may, but need not, accept in the absence of evidence to rebut it. **5. rebuttable presumption,** a presumption that can be defeated by introduction of sufficiently persuasive contrary evidence.

presumption of innocence the principle that a criminal defendant need not introduce evidence of innocence to be found not guilty; rather, the prosecution must prove each element of the crime in order to convict.

pretermitted heir a child or other heir omitted from mention in a will, usually because the will was made before the heir was born. A pretermitted heir—at least one who is a child of the testator—is entitled to a share of the estate by statute in most states.

pretrial conference a conference among the judge and the lawyers for all parties in a case, convened by the judge at any time after the pleadings have been filed and before the trial, to discuss discovery issues, scheduling, and the general status of the case, and usually to discuss the possibility of settlement.

pretrial discovery. See under DISCOVERY.

pretrial order an order issued by a judge just before a trial, usually reflecting things discussed or agreed upon at a final PRETRIAL CONFERENCE, setting forth ground rules for the trial.

preventive detention keeping a criminal defendant in jail before trial; not allowing release on bail.

This is permitted in serious felony cases upon a finding that it is necessary to protect individuals or the community at large.

price discrimination selling goods or services at different prices to different customers. This can be a violation of ANTITRUST laws if done in such a way as to harm competitors and reduce competition.

price fixing the setting of prices at which goods or services are to be sold, by means of an agreement or understanding between competing sellers **(horizontal price fixing)** or an agreement or arrangement between the seller and the producer or wholesaler who provided the product in question **(vertical price fixing).** Price fixing is a violation of the SHERMAN ANTITRUST ACT.

prima facie *Latin.* (lit. "at first appearance") **1.** so far as it appears; subject to further evidence; unless the contrary is shown: *The deed is in proper form, and so is prima facie valid.* **2. prima facie case** (or **evidence** or **proof**), evidence sufficient to justify submitting a party's claim or affirmative defense to a jury, and to support a verdict in favor of that party on that issue, if the jury so finds; that is, evidence sufficient to satisfy a party's *burden of producing evidence* (see under BURDEN¹).

primary boycott. See under BOYCOTT.

primary liability. See under LIABILITY.

prime contractor. Same as *general contractor* (see under CONTRACTOR).

principal *n.* **1.** a person who authorizes another to act as her AGENT. If the agent does not disclose to those he deals with that he is acting on behalf of someone else, the principal is called an **undisclosed principal.** See also AGENCY. **2.** Also called **principal debtor** or **principal obligor.** the person whose debt or other obligation is the subject of a SURETYSHIP contract or a GUARANTY. If the SURETY or GUARANTOR is required to pay or perform, that person normally has a right of reimbursement from the principal. **3.** a direct participant in a crime; either an actual perpetrator or an aider and abettor who is present (personally or through an innocent agent) when the crime is committed. **4.** a basic sum of money upon which interest or profit is calculated; e.g., the face amount of a bond (see BOND¹). **5.** the CORPUS of a trust, especially if the trust property consists almost entirely of money or securities. —*adj.* **6.** primary; most important.

prior inconsistent statement. See under STATEMENT.

prior restraint a ban on publishing something. The First Amendment (see Appendix) has been construed as prohibiting most prior restraints, allowing publishers to publish even wrongful or potentially wrongful material (e.g., LIBEL¹) if they are willing to take the risk of resulting liability or punishment. The primary exception to this rule is OBSCENITY, which may be censored in advance.

priority *n.* **1.** the right to satisfaction of one's claim against some property, such as the estate of a decedent or a bankrupt, ahead of someone else. **2.** the order in which the law ranks claims to property.

prison *n.* a state or federal facility in which people convicted of serious crimes and given long sentences are incarcerated. Also called **penitentiary.** Cf. JAIL.

privacy *n.* freedom from unwarranted intrusion into one's personal life and unwanted publicity about oneself. Various types of privacy interest are protected from private interference by tort law (see INVASION OF PRIVACY) and from governmental interference by statutes and by the Constitution (see RIGHT OF PRIVACY).

private *adj.* **1.** pertaining or belonging to one person or a limited group of persons rather than to the government or the public at large: *private property.* Cf. PUBLIC. **2.** pertaining to a person acting other than as a government official: *private attorney general* (see under ATTORNEY GENERAL); *private discrimination.* **3.** kept away from the public at large: *private information; private conduct.* See also *private* CORPORATION, INTERNATIONAL LAW, NECESSITY, NUISANCE, RIGHT OF ACTION, WRONG under those words.

privately held corporation. See under CORPORATION.

privilege *n.* **1.** in general, a special right or exemption that the law allows to a person or class of persons, or to people under certain circumstances, for reasons of public policy. Some privileges cannot be taken away under any circumstances (**absolute privilege**); others may be relied upon only if certain conditions are met, or may be defeated under certain circumstances (**qualified privilege** or **conditional privilege**). **2.** in tort law, the right to take actions that are necessary and reasonable under the circumstances even if they injure the person, property, or reputation of another; for example, the right to use reasonable force in SELF-DEFENSE (constituting a defense to a claim of BATTERY), or the absolute privilege of legislators to speak freely in legislative debate or of persons involved in court cases to speak freely in court (rendering them immune from any claim of DEFAMATION). **3.** Also called **testimonial privilege.** an absolute or qualified right to withhold certain evidence in judicial proceedings. The public policy reason for such privileges is usually to protect confidential relationships. The number, scope, and even names of such privileges vary from state to state; among the most common are the following: **a. attorney-client privilege,** the privilege of a client to prevent disclosure of confidential communications to her lawyer. **b. clergy-communicant privilege,** the privilege protecting confidential communications to one's spiritual advisor. **c. investigative privilege,** the privilege of law enforcement agencies to keep information gathered for law enforcement purposes secret. **d. physician-patient privilege,** the privilege of a patient to prevent her doctor from disclosing medical records and information obtained from her in connection with medical services. **e. spousal privilege,** the privilege to prevent disclosure of confidential communications to one's spouse. See also EXECUTIVE PRIVILEGE; SHIELD LAW.

privileged communication a communication that may be withheld from evidence because of a *testimonial privilege* (see under PRIVILEGE).

privileges and immunities fundamental rights associated with state citizenship. The Constitution requires each state in the United States to accord citizens of other states the same privileges and immunities as its own citizens.

privity *n.* the relationship between two or more persons participating in, or having related interests in, a transaction, proceeding, or piece of property. For example, there is **privity of contract** between the parties to a contract; and the grantor and grantee, lessor and lessee, or co-owners of an estate in land are in **privity of estate**. Persons in privity with each other are called **privies**; each one is the other's **privy.**

pro bono publico *Latin.* for the public good. A phrase (usually shortened to **pro bono**) signifying that legal services are being provided without charge: *The firm is handling the matter pro bono.*

pro hac vice *Latin.* (lit. "for this turn") for a single case or occasion only; a phrase used in reference to a lawyer—usually from out of state—who is given special permission to represent a client in a court to which the lawyer has not been admitted. The attorney is said to "appear pro hac vice." When this is permitted, the court invariably requires that *local counsel* (see under COUNSEL) also be retained, so that there will be an attorney involved who is close by and familiar with the court's rules. See also *admission pro hac vice* (under ADMISSION).

pro se *Latin.* for himself or herself; relating to a party who acts as his or her own lawyer in a case: *The plaintiff is appearing pro se. This is a pro se case.*

pro tanto *Latin.* (lit. "for so much") to that extent; proportionately.

probable cause. 1. reasonable grounds, based on substantial evidence, for believing a fact to be true. Under the Fourth Amendment (see Appendix), a person cannot be arrested for a crime unless there is probable cause to believe she committed it, and

one's person and property cannot be searched unless there is probable cause to believe that evidence of a crime will be found. **2. probable cause hearing.** See under HEARING.

probate *n.* a judicial proceeding in which a will is proved to be genuine and distribution of the estate is monitored.

probation *n.* a sentence allowing a convicted criminal to remain free instead of going to jail or prison, or to go free after serving a brief period of confinement, provided that certain conditions are met, including staying out of trouble with the law and reporting regularly to a probation officer. If the conditions of probation are violated, probation can be revoked and the probationer sent to prison.

probative value usefulness and persuasiveness of a piece of evidence in establishing a relevant fact. Cf. PREJUDICIAL EFFECT. See also WEIGHT.

procedural due process. See under DUE PROCESS.

procedure *n.* **1.** the methods used in investigating, presenting, managing, and deciding legal cases. **2.** Also called **procedural law** or **adjective law.** The body of law that determines which of these methods will be allowed and governs how they will be used: *appellate procedure; California procedure.* Cf. SUBSTANCE (def. 2). **3. administrative procedure,** the body of law applicable to the procedures used by adminstrative agencies in carrying out all of their rulemaking, regulatory, and adjudicative functions. **4. civil procedure,** the procedural aspects of a *civil action* (see under ACTION), including principles of jurisdiction, pleading, discovery, conduct of trials, and enforcement of judgments. **5. criminal procedure,** the body of law—much of it based directly on the Constitution—governing all aspects of criminal law enforcement, including not only judicial proceedings but also police procedures and post-sentencing procedures such as probation, imprisonment, and parole.

proceed *v.* to take action in court; to file or pursue a case: *The tenants voted to proceed against the landlord.*

proceeding *n.* any matter handled by or filed with a court or administrative tribunal; a case or some aspect of a case.

process *n.* **1.** a formal document through which a court obtains jurisdiction over a person or property, or compels a person to appear in court or participate in a proceeding; e.g., a SUMMONS, a writ of ATTACHMENT, or a SUBPOENA. See also *service of process* (under SERVICE); ABUSE OF PROCESS. **2.** Same as PROCEDURE. The term "process" in this sense is used almost exclusively in connection with the concept of DUE PROCESS.

production of documents a DISCOVERY procedure in which a party is required, upon request from the other side, to produce potentially relevant DOCUMENTS for inspection and copying.

products liability 1. the liability—usually strict liability—of manufacturers for damage caused by defects in their products. In cases dealing with a particular product, sometimes referred to as "product liability." **2.** the area of tort law dealing with such liability. See also *strict liability* (under LIABILITY).

professional corporation (or **association**). See under CORPORATION.

proffer *v.* **1.** to present or put forth for acceptance; to offer. Said especially of evidence, explanation, or argument: *The court excluded the proffered testimony as cumulative. The jury apparently accepted the explanation proffered by the defendant.* —*n.* **2.** the act of proffering, or the thing proffered. **3.** an OFFER OF PROOF.

profit *n.* **1.** financial gain from an investment, enterprise, or transaction. **2.** Short for **profit à prendre,** *Law French.* (lit. "benefit for the taking") **a.** an interest in land owned by another, consisting of a right to take something of value from it; e.g., mining rights, fishing rights, or timber rights. **b.** the thing taken pursuant to such a right. Cf EASEMENT.

progressive tax. See under TAX.

prohibition *n.* **1.** a writ by which a court directs a lower court or public agency to cease all proceedings with respect to a particular matter over which it has no jurisdiction. Cf. MANDAMUS. **2.** a ban on manufacture, distribution, and consumption of alcoholic beverages. **3. Prohibition Amendment,** the Eighteenth Amendment to the United States Constitution, ratified in 1919 and repealed by the Twenty-First Amendment in 1933 (see Appendix).

prohibitory injunction. See under INJUNCTION.

promise *n.* **1.** a commitment to perform, or refrain from performing, some act in the future. The person who makes a promise is the **promisor;** the person to whom it is made is the **promisee. 2. gratuitous promise,** a promise for which nothing is given or promised in return; e.g., "When I die I will leave you my fortune." As many have learned the hard way, most such promises are unenforceable. See also CONSIDERATION. **3. illusory promise,** a statement that sounds like a promise but actually promises nothing; e.g., "For $25,000, I will give such assistance to your project as I deem appropriate for one year." Traditionally such promises, and "contracts" based upon them, were unenforceable; the modern trend is to read into them a duty to act in GOOD FAITH and enforce them. —*v.* **4.** to make a promise.

promissory estoppel. See under ESTOPPEL.

promissory note. Same as NOTE[1].

promissory warranty. See under WARRANTY.

promoter *n.* **1.** a person involved in arranging a business transaction or launching a business venture. **2.** a person who sets up a corporation.

promoting prostitution the crime of inducing someone to become a prostitute, soliciting customers for a prostitute, or otherwise assisting in or benefiting from another's prostitution. Also called **pandering.**

proof *n.* **1.** the persuasive effect of evidence in the mind of a factfinder. **2.** the evidence submitted to establish a fact or support a position. **3.** the presentation of evidence. See also *burden of proof* (under BURDEN[1]); *prima facie proof* (under PRIMA FACIE;) STANDARD OF PROOF.

proper party. See under PARTY.

property *n.* **1.** a thing, interest, or right that is capable of being owned and, usually, transferred. See also ENTITLEMENT. **2. intangible property,** a property right in something that does not have physical existence, such as a copyright or trademark, a contract right or CHOSE IN ACTION, or an insurance policy or an ownership interest in a corporation (although the documents representing such interests are tangible property). **3. intellectual property,** copyrights, patents, and other rights in creations of the mind; also, the creations themselves, such as a literary work, painting, or computer program. **4. personal property,** all property other than *real property;* movable things (including animals in captivity, trees that have been cut down, coal that has been mined) and all intangible property. For historical reasons, a LEASEHOLD interest is often classified as personal property as well, even though it is an interest in land. Also called **personalty.** See also CHATTEL. **5. real property,** an interest in land or things attached to it, including buildings or other structures and substantial vegetation. Also called **realty** or **real estate,** and very often referred to simply as LAND. See also FIXTURE. **6. tangible property,** physical property; property you can touch.

property tax a state or local tax imposed annually on owners of real or personal property within the state or municipality, based upon the value of the property. See also *assessed value* (under ASSESS).

proponent *n.* one who offers or proposes something; in particular, one who offers or presents evidence in a case, or offers a will for PROBATE.

propria persona. See IN PROPRIA PERSONA.

proprietary *adj.* **1.** pertaining to ownership: *proprietary rights; proprietary interest.* **2.** owned by someone; describing something with respect to which a particular person or entity has the right to control use or access: *proprietary drug; proprietary information.*

proprietorship. See SOLE PROPRIETORSHIP.

prosecute *v.* to pursue a civil or criminal action

against someone: *The plaintiff prosecuted her case with vigor. The state prosecuted the young defendant as an adult.*

prosecution *n.* **1.** the act of prosecuting a case: *The prosecution went smoothly.* **2.** the attorney or group of attorneys involved in prosecuting a criminal case, or the party they represent (e.g., the STATE or the PEOPLE): *The prosecution moved for a restraining order.* **3.** Also called **criminal prosecution.** A criminal case. **4. civil prosecution,** the bringing of a civil case by a private party, particularly under the RACKETEER INFLUENCED AND CORRUPT ORGANIZATIONS ACT, to remedy what the party (often a business entity) believes to be illegal conduct (often by a competitor) that has resulted in damage to the plaintiff.

prosecutor *n.* **1.** a public official whose job it is to oversee the prosecution of criminal cases in a particular jurisdiction; for example, a county attorney, DISTRICT ATTORNEY, or UNITED STATES ATTORNEY. **2.** an attorney prosecuting a particular criminal case. **3. independent** (or **special**) **prosecutor,** an outside person appointed to investigate and, if necessary, prosecute a case in which there has been an allegation of criminal conduct, when the prosecutor who would normally handle it has a CONFLICT OF INTEREST. This occurs most commonly in cases of wrongdoing in high state or federal office.

prosecutorial discretion. See under DISCRETION.

prospectus *n.* a document prepared by the issuer of a security giving detailed information about the security and the issuer, including information bearing upon the riskiness of the security as an investment. Federal regulations determine what information must be included in a prospectus, require it to be accurate, and require the prospectus to be provided to each prospective purchaser of a new security being offered to the public.

prostitution *n.* the crime of engaging in sexual intercourse or other sexual activity for hire. See also PROMOTING PROSTITUTION.

protected person. See under PERSON.

protected speech. See under SPEECH.

protection order a court order that one person keep away from another, to protect the other from harassment and threatened harm—a difficult kind of order to enforce, as attested by repeated reports of women murdered by present or former husbands or lovers who had been ordered to stay away. Also called **order of protection.**

protective order a court order prohibiting a party to a case from engaging in procedures that unnecessarily annoy, burden, or embarrass the adversary. Such orders are usually granted to limit DISCOVERY that exceeds the needs of a case.

protest *n.* a formal written statement objecting to some action of another, made to preserve one's rights, lay the groundwork for a suit, and avoid any contention that by not speaking up one in effect consented to the action. See also UNDER PROTEST.

provisional remedy (or **relief**). See under REMEDY.

proximate cause in tort cases, wrongful conduct by a defendant leading to the injury complained of in a sufficiently direct way to justify holding the defendant liable for the plaintiff's damages. To recover for a tort, it is not enough to show that the defendant did something wrong and that the plaintiff suffered some injury; it must also be shown that the wrong was a proximate cause of the injury.

proxy *n.* **1.** an instrument authorizing one person to act on behalf of another, especially by voting or otherwise participating in a meeting. **2.** the authority given by such an instrument. **3.** Also called **proxy holder.** The person to whom the instrument and the authority are given.

prurient interest an unacceptable interest in sex. The Supreme Court has said that, for purposes of its current test of OBSCENITY, material appeals to prurient interest if it has "a tendency to excite lustful thoughts," that is, "sexual responses over and beyond those that would be characterized as normal."

public *adj.* **1.** pertaining, belonging, or available generally to the people of a municipality, a state, or

legal

the United States, or to the government on their behalf, rather than to a specific and limited group of persons: *public record* (see under RECORD); *public property; public office.* Cf. PRIVATE. **2.** occurring in a place open to the public or to public view: *public intoxication; public lewdness.* —*n.* **3.** the people of a community, state, or nation, collectively.

public accommodation a place offering services to the general public, such as a hotel, restaurant, gas station, or theater. Federal civil rights laws prohibit discrimination on the basis of race, color, religion, or national origin in places of public accommodation.

public corporation. See under CORPORATION.

public defender a lawyer whose job is to represent indigent defendants in criminal cases. See also RIGHT TO COUNSEL.

public domain 1. the status of a work or invention upon which the copyright or patent has expired, or which never was protected by a copyright or patent; such a work is said to be "in the public domain" and may be copied or used by anyone. **2.** land owned by the government.

public easement. See under EASEMENT.

public figure a public official or any other individual who has intentionally assumed a prominent role in matters of public importance or interest. In part because such individuals have intentionally subjected themselves to public attention, and in part because of the importance of the First Amendment right to publish facts and opinions on matters of public interest, the law makes it more difficult for public figures than for ordinary people to recover for INVASION OF PRIVACY or DEFAMATION. See also *actual malice* (under MALICE).

public forum a public place of a sort where people traditionally gather to express views and exchange ideas, such as a park, street, or sidewalk, or which the government has opened to such uses, such as a school that is open after hours for community activities. The Supreme Court has held that the First Amendment (see Appendix) precludes the government from banning speech or assembly in such areas, although the time, place, and manner of such activities can be regulated so long as the regulations do not restrict the content of the speech.

public hearing. See under HEARING.

public interest law an area of legal practice that emphasizes the handling of cases of importance to the public at large rather than just to the individual litigants, such as cases concerning civil rights, the environment, or the political process. A commonly used procedure in such a practice is the *class action* (see under ACTION).

public international law. See under INTERNATIONAL LAW.

public necessity. See under NECESSITY.

public nuisance. See under NUISANCE.

public policy a general concept of public good that colors judicial decisions in every field; in interpreting statutes, extending the common law, and enforcing (or refusing to enforce) private instruments, courts strive to do so in ways that conform to "public policy" as they perceive it. The concept arises particularly in contract law, because for most pur-

poses a contract that violates "public policy" is void. This includes contracts whose performance would be criminal or tortious, and occasionally other contracts that the courts regard as immoral, unconscionable, or otherwise unworthy of enforcement.

public trial. See under TRIAL.

public use. See under USE.

public wrong. See under WRONG.

publicly held corporation. See under CORPORATION.

publicly traded stock. See under STOCK.

publish *v.* **1.** generally, and of a copyrightable work, to make public; to offer or distribute to the general public. See also *service by publication* (under SERVICE). **2.** to communicate a defamatory statement to a person other than the subject of the statement. There is no cause of action for libel or slander if the defamatory statement has not been "published" to a third person. **3.** to declare formally to witnesses that a document one is signing is one's will. "Publishing" one's will to the witnesses who sign it is one of the formalities that the law usually requires in an effort to eliminate disputes after a person is dead over whether a document is in fact her will. **4.** to pass an instrument, especially a forged instrument, or present it for payment; to UTTER. —**publication,** *n.*

puffing *n.* conventional sales talk expressing a high opinion of a product but not intended to be taken too literally; for example, "It's a great little car. You won't find a better one. You can't beat the price. I'm sure you'll be completely satisfied." The law does not regard such talk as legally binding. Cf. WARRANTY.

punishment. See SENTENCE; CAPITAL PUNISHMENT.

punitive damages. See under DAMAGES.

pur autre vie. See *estate* (or *tenancy*) *pur autre vie* (under ESTATE[1]).

purchase *n.* **1.** in the most common usage, to acquire rights or property of any kind, or an interest in property, by promising or giving something in exchange. See also GOOD FAITH PURCHASER. **2.** as used in the UNIFORM COMMERCIAL CODE, the term also includes receipt of a negotiable instrument or a gift. **3.** in its most general and traditional legal sense, "purchase" means any acquisition of an interest in property other than by INTESTATE SUCCESSION, and thus includes acquisition by gift or by will as well as by giving value.

purge *v.* to remedy a CONTEMPT. For example, after a person has been jailed for refusing to testify in a case despite a court order to do so, she can change her mind and obey the order to testify; this is said to "purge the contempt" or "purge her of the contempt," and secures her release from jail.

purposely *adv.* with INTENT (def. 2).

pursuit of happiness a phrase from the Declaration of Independence, often erroneously thought to appear in the Constitution. The phrase is often used for rhetorical effect in legal arguments and occasionally appears in judicial opinions, but it has no specific or generally agreed-upon legal meaning.

putative *adj.* alleged; supposed; seeming: *putative father; putative marriage.*

a b c d e f g h i j k l m n o p Q R s t u v w x y z

quaere *Latin.* (lit. "You should ask," "you should question") a word used to cast doubt on, or raise a question about, a stated or suggested proposition of law. Pronounced, and now often spelled, the same as the English word **query,** which is derived from this Latin word: *Quaere* (or *query*) *the court's statement that a husband can never be guilty of raping his wife. Quaere* (or *query*) *whether the decision would have been the same if the husband and wife had been separated.*

qualification[1] *n.* **1.** the act of taking those steps required by law to acquire some legally recognized power or status. **2.** a quality required by law for a person or organization to hold a certain status or power. See also BONA FIDE OCCUPATIONAL QUALIFICATION; VOTER QUALIFICATION.

qualification[2] *n.* **1.** a limitation or condition. **2.** the process of limiting or imposing a condition.

qualified[1] *adj.* officially recognized as having a certain legal status as a result of possessing the legal qualifications and taking the legally required actions: *qualified pension plan* (see under PENSION PLAN).

qualified[2] *adj.* limited, conditional. See *qualified* IMMUNITY, INDORSEMENT, PRIVILEGE under those words.

qualify[1] *v.* **1.** to take the steps required by law to acquire some legally recognized power or status. **2. qualify as an executor**, to post a bond or take such other steps as a state requires before a person designated in a will as an executor may begin managing and distributing the decedent's property. **3. qualify as an expert** (or **expert witness**), to demonstrate to the satisfaction of the court that one has sufficient training and experience to be permitted to express expert opinions on a particular issue in a trial. See also VOIR DIRE (def. 2). **4. qualify for tax-exempt status,** to file necessary documents and obtain certification from the Internal Revenue Service showing that a non-profit organization is not subject to taxation under the Internal Revenue Code. **5. qualify to do business,** (of a corporation) to register with the Secretary of State of a state other than the state of incorporation, so as to be authorized to do business in the new state.

qualify[2] *v.* to limit; place conditions on.

quantum meruit *Latin.* (lit. "so much as he deserved") **1.** a cause of action for the reasonable value of services rendered, or occasionally of goods or materials provided, under circumstances in which there was no enforceable contract to pay for them but it would be unfair to leave the plaintiff uncompensated. **2.** the measure of recovery in such an action; that is, the reasonable value of the services or goods provided as found by the court. See also QUASI CONTRACT; RESTITUTION; UNJUST ENRICHMENT.

quash *v.* to nullify a previously issued legal process or order, such as a summons, warrant, or injunction. See also SET ASIDE; VACATE.

quasi *Latin.* (lit. "as if," "a sort of") a word or prefix placed in front of a legal term to mean "resembling, but different from in some legally insignificant respect."

quasi contract 1. a *contract implied in law* (see under CONTRACT). **2.** a name for any claim for RESTITUTION, particularly a claim in QUANTUM MERUIT.

quasi in rem *Latin.* (lit. "as if directed at the thing") describing the fundamental character of a legal proceeding as being, in form, directed at a piece of property, but in substance, directed at the owner of the property. For details, see under JURISDICTION[1] and ACTION. Cf. IN PERSONAM; IN REM.

quasi-suspect classification a law's CLASSIFICATION of people into categories regarded by the Supreme Court as requiring HEIGHTENED SCRUTINY, but not STRICT SCRUTINY, under the EQUAL PROTECTION clause of the Fourteenth Amendment (see Appendix). So far, the only classifications deemed to call for this level of SCRUTINY are those that discriminate on the basis of sex or illegitimacy. Cf. SUSPECT CLASSIFICATION.

Queen's Bench. See under KING's BENCH.

query *n.* **1.** a question. —*v.* **2.** to raise a question. **3.** to call into question. See also QUAERE.

question[1] *n.* **1.** something asked at a trial, hearing, or deposition, or in investigating an incident or crime. Cf. INTERROGATORY. **2. argumentative question,** a question that asks a fact witness to agree with an inference or conclusion favorable to the lawyer's case rather than merely eliciting facts. This is improper. **3. compound question,** a combination of two or more questions into one; for example, "Did she speed through a red light?" instead of "Did she go through a red light? Was she speeding?" Compound questions can be confusing and misleading, and are therefore objectionable. **4. hypothetical question, a.** a question in which a witness is asked to assume certain facts and express an opinion based upon that assumption. This is permitted with expert witnesses if the assumed facts are related to the evidence in the case and the opinion sought is within the scope of the witness's expertise, but it is generally not allowed with fact witnesses. **b.** such a question as posed by a law pro-

fessor to law students, to make them think about how slight changes in the facts of a case can alter the legal principles that apply and the legal conclusions that follow; referred to informally as "a hypothetical. " See also SOCRATIC METHOD. **5. leading question,** a question phrased so as to suggest the desired answer. Except for routine preliminary questions intended to introduce a topic, this is generally forbidden in direct examination but allowed in cross examination and in examining a *hostile witness* (see under WITNESS). Examples: "What color was the light?" is nonleading; "The light was red, wasn't it?" is leading. "Was the light red?" might be either, depending on the context. **6. special questions.** See under VERDICT. —*v.* **7.** to ask questions of anyone: *to question a witness; to question a suspect.* Cf. the more specialized terms EXAMINE; INQUIRE; *interrogate* (under INTERROGATION).

question[2] *n.* **1.** Same as ISSUE[1] (see discussion under that word). **2. mixed question of fact and law,** an issue in which facts and law are intertwined; for example, whether the defendant's conduct, as to which witnesses gave varying accounts, was "negligent" as that term is defined in law. In a jury case, such questions are typically submitted to the jury, but with careful instructions from the judge as to the law. **3. political question,** an issue that the courts will refuse to decide on the ground that it is of a type committed by the Constitution to the legislative or executive branch of government, rather than the judicial branch. **4. question** (or **issue**) **of fact,** a dispute over what circumstances and events have actually occurred or are likely to occur. In a jury trial, such questions are submitted to the jury for decision. **5. question** (or **issue**) **of law,** an issue concerning interpretation of law. These questions are decided by the judge rather than the jury. **6. questions presented,** a formal section in an appellate brief or petition, stating the precise issues that the appellate court is being asked to consider. See also constitutional question (under CONSTITUTIONAL); FEDERAL QUESTION.

qui tam *Latin.* (lit. "who both") a civil action brought by a private citizen pursuant to a statute that defines certain conduct as illegal and authorizes private suits against violators to collect a penalty, which is to be divided between the plaintiff (also called the RELATOR) and for the state. Thus the relator brings the action both for herself and for the state.

quid pro quo *Latin.* (lit. "What for what?") **1.** an informal expression, used more by nonlawyers than by lawyers, for CONSIDERATION in a contract. **2.** something demanded or expected, legally or illegally, in exchange for a favor, concession, or performance; for example, ransom demanded by a kidnapper in exchange for release of the victim, or a favorable vote expected from a corrupt legislator in exchange for a bribe. See also *quid pro quo harassment* (under SEXUAL HARASSMENT).

quiet enjoyment 1. the use and possession of real property free from interference or dispossession by someone with a superior right to the property. **2. covenant** (or **warranty**) **of quiet enjoyment,** the express or implied promise of a landlord or grantor of real property that no one with superior title will come along and put the lessee or grantee out of possession. Also called **covenant of warranty.**

quiet title to remove uncertainties about one's title to real property by bringing an action (called an "action to quiet title") against others who may have some claim to the property, challenging them to prove any claim they have or be forever barred from asserting any claim to the property. See also CLOUD ON TITLE.

quit *v.* to remove oneself from real property; vacate the premises. Cf. DISPOSSESS.

quitclaim *n.* **1.** abandonment of a claim (for example, to land, or against another person), or a document given as evidence of such abandonment. —*v.* **2.** to abandon a claim. See also *quitclaim deed* (under DEED).

quo warranto *Latin.* (lit. "by what authority") **1.** a judicial proceeding brought by the state to determine whether a person or entity purporting to act in a public capacity has the legal authority to do so. **2.** a writ by which such a proceeding traditionally was commenced, directing the defendant to appear and produce evidence of his authority.

quotient verdict. See under VERDICT.

⑨ a symbol used to identify a name or design as a *registered trademark* (see under TRADEMARK) or other MARK registered with the United States Patent and Trademark Office. This serves both as an assurance to consumers that the product or service with which the mark is associated is made or provided or approved by the company or organization identified with the mark, and as a warning to other companies that they may not use that mark. Cf. TM.

race *n.* as used in the Constitution and civil rights laws, a term generally applicable to any grouping on the basis of race, ancestry, or ethnicity. As used in the Fifteenth Amendment (see Appendix), the term also includes national origin.

racial discrimination discrimination on the basis of racial or ethnic identification or ancestry. See also SEPARATE BUT EQUAL; STRICT SCRUTINY.

racially restrictive covenant. See under COVENANT.

Racketeer Influenced and Corrupt Organizations Act (RICO) a federal statute enacted in 1970 and subsequently copied in many state statutes (informally called "Little Rico" statutes), designed to attack organized crime by providing special criminal penalties and civil liabilities for persons who engage in, or derive money from, repeated instances of certain types of crime. The statute permits persons who are injured by such conduct to sue the wrongdoers for *treble damages* (see under DAMAGES); this has provided an opportunity for many plaintiffs, with a little artful pleading, to turn what used to be routine tort claims for fraud into treble damage actions for "racketeering," much to the dismay of mainstream corporate defendants who chafe at being labled as "racketeers."

raise *v.* **1.** to invoke or bring into being: *to raise a defense; to raise the bar of statute of limitations; circumstances sufficient to raise a presumption of knowledge.* **2.** to increase fraudulently the face amount of a financial instrument: *a raised check.*

ransom *n.* **1.** money paid to secure the release of a kidnapped person. —*v.* **2.** to secure the release of a kidnapped person by paying ransom. See also KIDNAPPING.

rape *n.* **1.** generally, the crime of forcing or causing a person to submit to sexual intercourse (whether vaginal, oral, or anal) against his or her will, or when consent is obtained by unfair and unlawful means (as by putting a drug in a drink), or under circumstances in which the person is incapable of giving legally valid consent (as with a person who is unconscious or UNDERAGE). The terminology for such offenses, and the exact range of conduct covered by each term used (such as "rape," "sexual imposition," or "sexual assault") varies from state to state. **2. acquaintance rape,** rape by someone known to the victim, such as a friend of the family or a former lover. **3. date rape,** rape by a person with whom the victim is on a date. Like *acquaintance rape,* this term was coined to draw attention to the fact that such rapes are more frequent than previously recognized, and traditionally prosecuted less consistently and with less vigor than rapes by strangers. **4. marital rape,** rape by one's spouse. Rape has traditionally been regarded as a crime committed by a man against a woman other than his wife. In recent years, many states have eliminated the exception for forced sex with one's wife and made marital rape a crime; the modern view, though not yet universally adopted, is that if one spouse finds the other's refusal to have sex intolerable, the remedy is not force, but divorce. Also called **spousal rape. 5. statutory rape,** the crime of having sexual intercourse, even with consent, with a person (or at least with a female) below the AGE OF CONSENT. In 1981 the Supreme Court held that statutory rape laws may constitutionally discriminate on the basis of sex, upholding the convic-

tion of a 17½-year-old male for having sex with a 16½-year-old female under a statutory rape law that made sexual intercourse by an unmarried couple under the age of 18 a crime for the male but not for the female. See also *strict liability* (under LIABILITY). —*v.* **6.** to commit a rape upon someone.

rape shield law. See under SHIELD LAW.

ratify *v.* to manifest approval of a previous action by oneself or another so as to make it legally binding. Treaties negotiated by the President must be ratified by the Senate; constitutional amendments adopted by Congress must be ratified by three-quarters of the states; a contract entered into by a party under legal age may be ratified by that party after reaching legal age; a contract entered into on behalf of a principal by an agent who lacked authority to do so may be ratified by the principal. In the contract situations, ratification may be either express (by announcing one's intent to adhere to the contract) or implied (by continuing to perform under the contract or by accepting benefits under it). Cf. AVOID▷. —**ratification,** *n.*

rational basis test the level of SCRUTINY applied to a law whose constitutionality is challenged as a violation of due process when NO FUNDAMENTAL RIGHT is at stake, or as a violation of EQUAL PROTECTION when the challenged CLASSIFICATION is not one that the Supreme Court has recognized as meriting HEIGHTENED SCRUTINY or STRICT SCRUTINY. Under this test, the Supreme Court has said, "A statutory discrimination will not be set aside if any state of facts reasonably may be conceived to justify it." Findings of unconstitutionality under this test are extremely rare.

re *prep.* regarding; concerning: *Memo to Mr. Smith re year-end inventory.* See also IN RE.

real estate. Same as *real property* (under PROPERTY).

real estate broker. See under BROKER.

real evidence. See under EVIDENCE.

real party in interest. See under PARTY.

real property. See under PROPERTY.

realize *n.* to receive something of value from a transaction, especially from a sale or exchange of property. For income tax purposes, the amount realized includes the money received plus the market value of any property or services received. The amount by which this exceeds or falls short of the taxpayer's BASIS in the property transferred is the realized gain or loss. See also RECOGNIZE.

realty. Same as *real property* (under PROPERTY).

reargument *n.* **1.** a second round of argument, or sometimes of briefing and argument, held by a court on a matter previously argued and submitted. Occasionally this is requested by the court because it wants further discussion of certain points before deciding a motion or appeal; more often (but still rarely) it is permitted at the request of the losing party after the matter has been decided, upon a showing that the court may have misunderstood or overlooked an important point. Also called **rehearing** or, in cases where the court rendered a decision after its first argument, **reconsideration. 2. reargument** (or **rehearing** or **reconsideration**) **en banc,** reargument before all the judges of a court, of a matter previously heard and decided by a panel of some of them. This is occasionally permitted in matters of particular importance. See also EN BANC.

reasonable *adj.* **1.** appropriate in view of the circumstances; legally sufficient: *reasonable care* (see under CARE); *reasonable notice; reasonable reliance* (see under RELIANCE). **2.** having a basis in fact or evidence; sensible; not arbitrary and capricious or purely speculative: *reasonable belief; reasonable exercise of discretion.* See also BEYOND A REASONABLE DOUBT. **3. reasonable person,** a person of ordinary intelligence and prudence. Traditionally referred to as a **reasonable man,** this is an imaginary person who sets the standard by which the defendant's conduct is evaluated in a negligence case: If a reasonable person would have done the same thing the defendant did in the same situation, then the defendant was not negligent. See also OBJECTIVE TEST.

reasonable doubt. See BEYOND A REASONABLE DOUBT.

rebut *v.* **1.** to present evidence or argument to overcome or weaken the evidence or argument previously presented by an adversary. **2.** to present evidence to overcome a *rebuttable presumption* (see under PRESUMPTION). —**rebuttable,** *adj.*

rebuttal *n.* **1.** broadly, the presentation of any evidence or argument in response to that of an adversary, or to overcome a PRESUMPTION. **2.** specifically, a *rebuttal case* (see under CASE²). —*adj.* **3.** presented for purposes of rebuttal: *rebuttal case; rebuttal evidence; rebuttal witness.*

recall *v.* **1.** to vacate a previous order or judgment of the same court, especially because of a factual error. **2.** to call a witness who previously testified in a case back to the stand for further testimony. **3.** to remove an elected official from office before expiration of her term, by a special vote of the people.

receive *v.* to admit into evidence, especially in a nonjury case: *Exhibit 12 will be received.*

receiver *n.* a person appointed by a court to take over and manage property that is the subject of judicial proceedings—often the property or business of an insolvent debtor—and ultimately to dispose of it in accordance with the court's judgment.

receivership *n.* a proceeding in which a RECEIVER is appointed to preserve and distribute assets of an insolvent debtor.

receiving stolen property the crime of receiving, retaining, or disposing of property that one knows was stolen. It includes purchase, fencing, and receipt by gift.

recess *n.* **1.** a brief break in a trial or hearing: *a 15-minute recess.* **2.** a lengthy period during which a court holds no sessions: *The Supreme Court is in recess from July through September.* —*v.* **3.** to take a recess: *We will recess for the weekend.*

recidivist *n.* a person who, after being convicted of a crime and serving a sentence or being released, commits the same kind of crime again. —**recidivism,** *n.*

reciprocity *n.* a relationship between two entities, especially two states of the United States, in which each grants certain rights to the other, or to people from the other, in exchange for equivalent rights for itself and its own people. For example, two states might agree to share certain kinds of information with each other, or to allow each other's lawyers to be admitted to their own bar without having to take a second bar examination.

recital *n.* a formal statement of fact or of a reason or purpose for taking certain action, typically appearing at the beginning of a contract or other instrument and introduced by the word "Whereas." An instrument may have many recitals or none; they are not an operative part of an instrument, but may help in understanding and interpreting it.

recklessness *n.* conscious disregard of the safety or the rights of others. Sometimes the term is used as just another word for NEGLIGENCE, but usually it signifies a higher degree of culpability. To be negligent, it is enough that one fail to perceive a risk that a reasonably careful person would have perceived; to be reckless is to be aware of a significant risk to others and proceed anyway. But recklessness is a less culpable mental state than KNOWLEDGE, which requires not just awareness of a risk that something bad might happen, but awareness of the near certainty of such an outcome. See also *actual malice* (under MALICE); STATE OF MIND. —**reckless,** *adj.* —**recklessly,** *adv.*

recognizance *n.* See RELEASE ON OWN RECOGNIZANCE.

recognize *v.* to include, or be required to include, a gain or loss in one's income tax calculations. Usually a gain or loss is recognized in the year in which it is received (see REALIZE), but in special circumstances a gain may be realized in one year but not recognized until a later year, or perhaps never recognized at all.

recollection *n.* **1.** memory; ability to remember; remembered facts. **2.** **hypnotically refreshed recollection,** facts supposedly brought forth from a witness's repressed or forgotten memory through hypnosis. Since hypnosis is as likely to create a memory as to refresh it, testimony based upon such

a procedure is normally inadmissible. But see RECOVERED MEMORY. **3.** **past recollection recorded,** a written record of an event, prepared or reviewed by a witness while the event was fresh in her mind. If the witness can no longer recall the details of the event by the time of the trial, but can recall writing or reviewing that record and for that reason can swear that it is true, then the contents of the writing may be admitted into evidence and read to the jury. Also called **recorded recollection.** **4.** **present recollection refreshed,** facts about an event that a witness at the trial cannot recall when first asked, but can recall when shown something that jogs her memory. Anything at all can be used to refresh a witness's memory, but the most common item is a writing containing the details she could not remember. If after seeing the item as a refresher the witness recalls the details, she can then testify to her recollection. The material used to jog her memory does not come into evidence. Also called **refreshed recollection.**

reconsideration. See under REARGUMENT.

reconsideration en banc. See under REARGUMENT.

record *n.* **1.** generally, any writing or set of writings setting forth the facts of an event or series of events, made as the events happen or shortly thereafter and intended to be preserved as a reliable account for future reference. **2.** in a judicial or administrative action, **a.** the transcript of a deposition, trial, hearing, or argument. **b.** a full set of the papers, orders, and judgments filed, transcripts made, and evidence offered in a case. **c.** Also called **record on appeal.** those portions of the full record of a case that may be considered by the reviewing court in connection with an appeal. See also DEHORS. **3.** **business record,** a record made and kept in accordance with the normal practice of a business or organization, from information provided by an individual with personal knowledge of the event recorded. Such records are normally admissible into evidence under a *hearsay exception* (see under HEARSAY). **4.** **for the record,** describes something said or done, especially in a case, not in the expectation that it will produce any immediate benefit, but in order to preserve a right or argument for the future. **5.** **make a record,** to say or do something *for the record.* Failure to make a record on an issue may constitute an *implied waiver* (see under WAIVER). **6.** **of record,** recorded; contained in a record: *attorney of record* (see under ATTORNEY); *owner of record* (see under OWNER). See also *court of record* (under COURT). **7.** **off the record,** describing informal discussion that the court reporter in a proceeding is requested not to take down. **8.** **on the record,** describing anything said in a proceeding that is taken down by the court reporter. **9.** **public record,** any record, investigative report, or compilation of information or data created by a public office or agency pursuant to its legal authority or duties. Such records are usually admitted into evidence under a *hearsay exception* (see under HEARSAY). **10.** **spread upon the record,** to include something in the record of a case; to make sure something is clear from the record. —*v.* **11.** to make a record of; especially, to file a deed, security agreement, or other instrument creating or transferring an interest in property with a county clerk or other designated public official so as to put the general public on notice of it. See also TITLE RECORDING SYSTEM.

record owner. See under OWNER.

recorded recollection. Same as *past recollection recorded* (see under RECOLLECTION).

recourse *n.* **1.** resort or access to a person or thing for help, or the person or thing resorted to. **2.** the right to receive payment on a negotiable instrument from the drawer or any previous indorser if the instrument is dishonored. For example, if A draws a check payable to the order of B, who indorses it to the order of C, and the check bounces when C deposits it, C ordinarily has a right of recourse against both A and B. A negotiable instrument confers no such liability upon a drawer or indorser who adds the words "without recourse" to her signature; the instrument is then a NONRECOURSE instrument and

legal

subsequent holders are said to take it **without recourse. 3.** the right to repayment of a loan from the borrower personally, out of any available assets she has. If a secured loan is made with the understanding that in the event of default the lender will look only to the collateral (see COLLATERAL¹) or to the GUARANTOR or SURETY for compensation, it is a NONRECOURSE loan.

recover v. to obtain through litigation—usually by way of judgment, but sometimes through settlement; usually money or property, but sometimes other relief; usually compensation for what has been lost, but sometimes punitive damages: *Plaintiff A recovered $1,000 in a settlement; plaintiff B went to trial and recovered a judgment for $1,000 actual damages, $10,000 punitive damages, and injunctive relief.* —**recoverable,** *adj.* —**recovery,** *n.*

recovered memory the theory that a victim's entire memory of systematic, long-term physical and sexual abuse during childhood can be repressed for many years and then "recovered" in adulthood. Although there is as yet no scientific evidence that this can happen, and the techniques by which such material is recovered often have much in common with hypnosis (see *hypnotically refreshed recollection,* under RECOLLECTION), in recent years recovered memory has been a popular basis for legal actions and has been admitted into evidence in some courts.

recross or **recross examination.** See under EXAMINATION.

recuse v. to remove oneself from participation in a matter because of an actual or apparent CONFLICT OF INTEREST. Said especially of judges. —**recusal,** *n.*

redact v. to cover up or white out portions of a document; for example, to delete nondiscoverable information from a document being produced in DISCOVERY.

redeem v. **1.** to buy back or reacquire; especially, to reacquire property pledged as security for a loan by repaying the loan, or to extinguish a bond or other debt instrument by payment in accordance with its terms. See also *redeemable security* (under SECURITY²). **2.** to turn in a bond or other certificate for cash or property in accordance with its terms. —**redeemable,** *adj.* —**redemption,** *n.*

redirect or **redirect examination.** See under EXAMINATION.

redlining *n.* refusal by a financial institution to make mortgage loans on property in certain neighborhoods. Redlining is an illegal discriminatory practice.

reentry *n.* taking back possession of real property pursuant to a right reserved when possession was transferred to someone else, as in a lease.

referee *n.* a MASTER to whom a court refers a case for certain purposes, especially for the taking of testimony and reporting of proposed findings of fact.

referendum *n.* a procedure existing in most states by which certain proposed statutes or constitutional amendments may or must be put to a vote of the people before becoming effective. In some states, a statute adopted by the legislature must also be put to such a vote if a certain number of citizens sign a petition requesting it.

reform *n.* **1.** a change or proposed change in the law regarded by its proponents as an improvement. Since people never propose changes that they regard as detrimental, all proposed change is called "reform." Unfortunately, calling something an improvement does not always mean that it *is* an improvement. —*v.* **2.** to bring about a reform of: *The bill reforms the rules of civil procedure.* **3.** to effect a REFORMATION of: *Plaintiff asks the court to reform the contract.*

reformation *n.* **1.** judicially ordered interpretation or rewriting of a written instrument, usually a contract, which through fraud, mistake, or other circumstances failed to reflect the actual intent or agreement of the parties, so as to make it reflect what was originally intended or agreed upon. **2.** a proceeding or decree by which reformation is accomplished.

refresh *v.* to jog memory. See also *refreshed recol-*

lection or *present recollection refreshed* (under RECOLLECTION).

register *n.* **1.** an official list, file, or record, such as a corporation's list of stockholders or a municipality's list of eligible voters. **2.** the official who maintains such records. —*v.* **3.** to cause to be listed in such a record.

registered trademark. See under TRADEMARK.

registration statement a statement containing detailed information about the issuer of a security and the security itself, which in most cases must be filed with the federal Securities and Exchange Commission before a security can be issued to the public.

regressive tax. See under TAX.

regular *adj.* **1.** normal, usual, customary. **2.** in conformity, or apparently in conformity, with law, particularly with legal requirements as to form; not such as would arouse suspicion: *The check was regular on its face.*

regular course of business. Same as ORDINARY COURSE OF BUSINESS.

regulation *n.* **1.** a directive adopted by an administrative agency, either for its own internal procedures or to govern public behavior in matters over which it has authority, and having the force of law: *income tax regulations; regulations of the city Department of Buildings.* See also RULE; rulemaking. **2.** broadly, any rule or statute, or the act of controlling or attempting to control conduct by rules and laws.

regulatory agency an ADMINISTRATIVE AGENCY to which Congress or a legislature has delegated the power to adopt regulations governing public conduct; e.g., the federal Food and Drug Administration; a state Department of Motor Vehicles.

regulatory taking. See under TAKING.

rehabilitation *n.* **1.** questioning of a witness or introduction of evidence designed to restore the credibility of a witness whose credibility has been attacked. Cf. IMPEACHMENT. **2.** resolving an insolvent debtor's financial situation in bankruptcy court, especially through a *Chapter 13 bankruptcy* proceeding (see under BANKRUPTCY). —**rehabilitate,** *v.*

rehearing or **rehearing en banc.** See under REARGUMENT.

reinsurance *n.* insurance purchased by one insurance company from another, under which the second company agrees to cover all or part of a risk insured by the first company.

relation *n.* See *on the relation of* (under EX REL.).

relation back the principle applied in various situations under which an act is deemed effective as of a date earlier than when it actually took place. For example, a new claim added in an amended complaint but arising from the same events that are the subject of the original complaint "relates back" to the date of the original complaint, so that expiration of the statute of limitations during the period between the two pleadings does not operate to bar the claim.

relator *n.* person at whose request, or for whose benefit, certain kinds of actions are brought. See also EX REL.; QUI TAM.

release *n.* **1.** the relieving of another person from an obligation or liability, or alleged obligation or liability, to oneself; the formal, permanent abandonment of a claim. **2.** a formal document embodying such a release, given to the person being released. When a case is settled, it is usual for the parties to exchange **mutual releases** whereby each assures the other that no further claim will be asserted with respect to the matter being settled. Often a release given in connection with a settlement is a **general release,** which bars any claim by the releasor against the releasee in connection with anything that has happened "from the beginning of time to the date of this release." —*v.* **3.** to give someone a release.

release on own recognizance (ROR) pretrial release of a criminal defendant upon his promise to appear in court as needed, without any requirement of bail. Also called **release on personal recognizance.**

relevant *adj.* tending to make the existence of a fact that is of consequence in a case more probable or less probable. Relevant evidence includes evidence bearing on the credibility of a witness. Evidence must be relevant to be admissible at a trial, but even relevant evidence may be excluded by the rules of evidence (see, for example, HEARSAY; *testimonial privilege*, under PRIVILEGE) or as a matter of judicial discretion (see, for example, *cumulative evidence*, under EVIDENCE; PREJUDICIAL EFFECT). —**relevance,** *n.*

reliance *n.* **1.** the taking of or failure to take some action because of trust in what someone else has said or done. Reliance is an element of certain causes of action, such as FRAUD and PROMISSORY ESTOPPEL. **2.** detrimental reliance, reliance that results in a loss; an expenditure of time, effort, or money; or a change for the worse in one's legal position. **3.** reasonable reliance, conduct such as a reasonable person might have undertaken under the circumstances in light of another's words or actions. To support a claim for fraud or promissory estoppel, reliance must have been reasonable and detrimental.

relief *n.* **1.** the remedy or totality of remedies sought or awarded in a proceeding. See discussion and additional entries under REMEDY. **2. affirmative relief, a.** relief awarded to a plaintiff beyond payment of damages, especially relief that requires the defendant to perform some specific action. **b.** any relief granted to a defendant against a plaintiff beyond simple dismissal of the plaintiff's case. **3. specific relief,** any type of *equitable remedy* (see under REMEDY) that requires a party to take specified steps or that affects interests in specified property; for example, a judgment ordering *specific restitution* (see under RESTITUTION) or SPECIFIC PERFORMANCE.

religion. See FREEDOM OF RELIGION.

rem. See IN REM.

remainder *n.* **1.** the *future estate* (see under ESTATE[1]) created by a GIFT OVER of the balance of an estate in connection with a transfer of an estate of shorter duration, as when the owner of a fee grants a life estate in the property to A and the remainder to B. Cf. REVERSION. **2.** a right to receive trust property upon expiration of the trust, as when a will specifies that certain assets are to be held in trust with the income to be used for the benefit of the testator's children until they reach the age of 21, then given to a particular charity. The charity has a remainder interest in the trust assets.

remand *v.* **1.** to send a case back from an appellate court to the lower court from which it was appealed, for further proceedings in accordance with the appellate court's instructions. **2.** to send a criminal defendant back into custody. —*n.* **3.** the act of remanding or the state of being remanded. A case in a lower court after remand is said to be "on remand."

remedy *n.* **1.** redress sought from or awarded by a court; any type of judgment that can be issued by a court in a civil action. Before the MERGER OF LAW AND EQUITY, the conventional terminology was "a remedy at law" or "relief in equity." Now the terms "remedy" and "relief" are largely interchangeable, although the former is more often used in reference to damages and the latter in reference to other kinds of relief. In addition, one uses "a" or "the" with "remedy," but not with "relief." See also RELIEF. **2.** a right of action or a procedure for obtaining satisfaction of a claim or grievance: *If the car payments are not kept up, the lender has a remedy either in court or through repossessing the car.* **3. adequate remedy at law,** a *legal remedy* (almost always damages) that the law deems sufficient to compensate a plaintiff, making an *equitable remedy* (such as specific performance) unnecessary. **4. equitable remedy** (or **relief**), relief of a type traditionally available only in courts of EQUITY, such as SPECIFIC PERFORMANCE, an INJUNCTION, or REFORMATION of a contract. Also called **relief in equity.** Cf. *legal remedy.* **5. extraordinary remedy** (or **relief**), relief of a sort traditionally available only by *extraordinary writ* (see under WRIT). **6. legal remedy** (or **re-**

lief), a remedy of a type traditionally available in the law courts (rather than the equity courts), the most common of which is DAMAGES. Also called **remedy at law.** See LAW (def. 4). Cf. *equitable remedy.* **7. provisional** (or **temporary**) **remedy** (or **relief**), an order issued during the course of an action to protect the interests of a party while the action proceeds; e.g., a *preliminary injunction* (see under INJUNCTION), temporary alimony, or appointment of a RECEIVER.

remittitur *Latin.* (lit. "it is given back") an order reducing the amount of damages awarded by a jury. If the plaintiff does not accept the reduced amount, the defendant will not be granted a new trial. Cf. ADDITUR.

remove *v.* **1.** to move or transfer a person or thing; to change the location of: *to remove a person from office; to remove property from the state.* **2.** to take away; to eliminate: *to remove a cloud on title.* **3.** to transfer a case from one court to another; especially, to transfer a case, upon motion of the defendant, from a state court to a federal court of appropriate jurisdiction. —**removal,** *n.*

render *v.* **1.** to issue or announce: *render a judgment; render a verdict.* **2.** to give or perform: *render payment; render the performance called for by the contract.* —**rendition,** *n.*

renew *v.* **1.** to begin again: *renew a lease; renew a contract.* **2.** to repeat or revive a request previously denied, in light of subsequent developments: *renew a motion; renew an objection.* —**renewal,** *n.*

renounce *v.* **1.** to give up a right, interest, or claim. **2.** to abandon a criminal enterprise voluntarily and absolutely, before the crime is committed. In some jurisdictions renunciation is an affirmative defense to a criminal charge of ATTEMPT, SOLICITATION, or the like. —**renunciation,** *n.*

reorganization *n.* **1.** Also called **corporate reorganization.** Any substantial restructuring of a corporation's financial structure. **2.** Also called **bankruptcy reorganization.** The restructuring, and usually reduction, of a corporation's debt in a *Chapter 11 bankruptcy* proceeding (see under BANKRUPTCY).

reorganization plan. See under BANKRUPTCY.

repeal *n.* the nullification of a statute, constitutional provision, or regulation by subsequent enactment. Usually the subsequent enactment explicitly states that the earlier is repealed (**express repeal**), but sometimes the earlier provision is regarded as null simply because the later enactment is inconsistent with it (**implied repeal**).

repeat offender. 1. a person convicted more than once of the same kind of offense. Many laws and regulations provide more severe penalties for a second or third violation. **2.** a person convicted more than once of different crimes. See also HABITUAL CRIMINAL; THREE STRIKES LAW.

replevin *n.* **1.** an action to recover possession of tangible personal property wrongfully withheld by another. **2.** to return goods to a prior possessor who seeks them in an action for replevin.

replevy *v.* to recover goods by means of an action of REPLEVIN.

reply *n.* **1.** a plaintiff's PLEADING in response to a COUNTERCLAIM asserted by the defendant. A reply to a counterclaim is exactly like an ANSWER to a complaint. **2.** generally, any response to an adversary's submission in opposition to one's own motion, argument, or appeal in a case. See, for example, *reply brief* (under BRIEF). —*v.* **3.** to make or serve a reply.

report *n.* **1.** a written account of something based upon the writer's observation, investigation, or analysis: *a master's report; a police report.* **2. reports,** a published compilation of opinions of a particular court, agency, or set of courts, usually in an unending succession of volumes. Sometimes called a *reporter.* A **reported opinion** (**case, decision,** etc.) is one that has thus been published. Cf. SLIP OPINION. —*v.* **3.** to issue a report. See also *hear and report* (under HEAR).

reporter *n.* **1.** a person, sometimes a court official, who compiles and supervises publication of the decisions of a court or set of courts. **2.** the *reports*

legal

(see under REPORT) so published. **3.** a COURT REPORTER.

repossess *v.* to take back property in which one has retained a security interest upon failure of the buyer to keep up with the payments. —**repossession,** *n.*

represent *v.* **1.** to act on behalf of another or take over the position of another in a matter: *The lawyer represents the client. The executor represents the decedent.* **2.** to assert as a fact, particularly in a context in which others may rely upon the assertion: *Counsel represented to the court that her client was on his way. The seller represented that the paint contained no lead.*

representation *n.* **1.** the act of representing or state of being represented. **2.** words or conduct amounting to an assertion of fact, particularly one that others may rely upon. See also FRAUD.

reprieve *n.* **1.** the postponement of execution of a criminal sentence by executive order. The classic situation for a reprieve occurs when a person is about to be put to death for a capital crime; a reprieve does not necessarily mean that the prisoner will not be executed, but it does give her some extra time to make arguments. See also *stay of execution* (under STAY). **2.** the document in which a reprieve is granted. —*v.* **3.** to grant a reprieve to someone. Cf. COMMUTE; PARDON. See also CLEMENCY.

republican form of government. See under GOVERNMENT.

repudiation *n.* **1.** refusal to carry out a duty, or denial that a duty exists. Repudiation may be rightful or wrongful, depending upon the circumstances. **2.** especially, refusal to perform, or to continue performing, a contract. If a party repudiates a contract before any performance is due, that may be called *anticipatory repudiation* (see under BREACH).

request for admissions. See under ADMISSION.

requests for instructions a party's list of proposed instructions for the jury, with citations to authority, usually submitted to the judge shortly before the end of the case. Also called **requests to charge.** See also INSTRUCTION.

res *n., pl.* **res.** *Latin.* (lit. "thing," "matter," "property," "case") **1.** generally, a thing under discussion: *Whether property can be taxed by a state or seized by a sheriff depends upon the location of the res.* **2.** the tangible or intangible property or relationship that is the subject of an IN REM or QUASI IN REM action. **3.** the CORPUS of a trust; the property of a trust or estate.

res gestae *Latin.* (lit. "things done," "deeds," "exploits") an entire occurrence that is the subject of a legal action, including particularly the words spoken by participants and bystanders. The concept of res gestae is a traditional exception to the *hearsay rule* (see under HEARSAY), on the theory that the jury is entitled to learn about the entire event in dispute, including words as well as actions. Modern rules of evidence shun the term as vague, and substitute such concepts as PRESENT SENSE IMPRESSION and EXCITED UTTERANCE.

res ipsa loquitur *Latin.* (lit. "the thing itself speaks," "the situation speaks for itself") the doctrine that the plaintiff in a negligence case need not show exactly how the defendant caused an accident if the accident was of a type that normally could not have occurred but for some negligence by the defendant. For example, if a sponge was left in the plaintiff's body after surgery, the plaintiff can prevail in a malpractice case against the surgeon even though the plaintiff cannot describe how the incident happened, because "the thing speaks for itself." Such a case is said to be a res ipsa loquitur case, or "res ipsa case" for short.

res judicata *Latin.* (lit. "an adjudicated matter," "a decided case") the doctrine that prevents relitigation of a claim that has been fully considered and finally decided in the courts.

rescission *n.* the cancellation of a contract and restoration of the parties to the positions they held before the contract was made. Rescission may be agreed to by the parties or sought in a judicial action as an equitable remedy when a contract was entered into as a result of fraud, mutual mistake, or the like. —**rescind,** *v.*

reserve *v.* **1.** to retain specified rights or interests in a transaction otherwise disposing of property or rights. **2.** to set aside funds for a particular purpose or contingency. **3.** to withhold for the time being; specifically, a judge or panel that does not rule from the bench upon a matter that has been argued is said to "reserve decision" or "reserve judgment." —*n.* **4.** a fund set aside for a particular purpose or for future contingencies.

reserved power. See under POWER.

residence *n.* **1.** in some contexts, same as DOMICILE. **2.** usually, any place where one has a home, even if one's domicile is elsewhere.

residency *n.* **1.** the state of being a RESIDENT—that is, of having a residence or domicile within a jurisdiction. **2. residency requirement, a.** any legal requirement that a person have a residence or domicile within a particular state or local jurisdiction in order to vote, hold office, hold public employment, or receive public benefits in that jurisdiction. **b.** a state or municipal regulation that denies certain benefits or status, such as welfare or voting rights, to newcomers until they have resided within the jurisdiction for a specified length of time. Many such waiting periods have been struck down as unconstitutional infringements on the RIGHT TO TRAVEL. Also called **waiting period.**

resident *n.* one who has a RESIDENCE, or sometimes his DOMICILE, in a specified place: *a noted resident of Newport, Palm Beach, Aspen, and Monte Carlo, domiciled in Monaco.* See also *resident alien* (under ALIEN).

residuary bequest (or **legacy**). See under BEQUEST.

residuary estate. See under ESTATE².

residuary legatee. See under LEGATEE.

residue *n.* Same as *residuary estate* (see under ESTATE²).

resolution *n.* an expression of sentiment or opinion adopted by vote of a legislative body, not having the force of law.

respondeat superior *Latin.* (lit. "let the superior answer") the doctrine that an employer is liable for the torts of an employee acting within the SCOPE OF EMPLOYMENT, and in many situations a principal of any kind is liable for the torts of an agent arising from conduct within the agent's SCOPE OF AUTHORITY. See also *vicarious liability* (under LIABILITY).

respondent *n.* the name given in certain situations to the party who must respond to a procedural step in a case, such as a petition, motion, or appeal. In the case of an appeal, some courts use the term "respondent" and others APPELLEE.

responsive *adj.* **1.** describing papers, evidence, or argument offered in answer or opposition to something submitted by an adversary: *responsive pleading; responsive brief.* **2.** describing a witness's answer to a lawyer's question that gives the information requested rather than avoiding the question or adding unsolicited information. See discussion under NONRESPONSIVE.

restitution *n.* **1.** any remedy or order for the prevention of UNJUST ENRICHMENT, usually involving the defendant's giving up some benefit that in justice should have gone to the plaintiff or paying for some benefit received from the plaintiff. It may also involve giving back some piece of property (**specific restitution**), or other forms of relief tailored to the case at hand. **2.** in criminal law, giving back ill-gotten gains or paying for property damage as part of one's sentence, as a condition of probation, or as part of a plea bargain.

restraining order 1. an INJUNCTION that prohibits someone from taking some action. **2. temporary restraining order (TRO),** an injunction granted for a very short time, just to keep things as they are until a hearing can be held to determine whether it would be appropriate to issue a *preliminary injunction* (see under INJUNCTION). A TRO may be granted EX PARTE to avoid tipping off the person to whom it is directed and thus giving that person a chance to hurry up and do the act in question before being ordered not to.

restraint of trade. See UNREASONABLE RESTRAINT OF TRADE.

restraint on alienation 1. a provision in an instrument transferring land which forbids the taker from subsequently transferring the land to anyone else. Such provisions are usually unenforceable. **2.** the practical effect of a transfer creating interests in land that may or may not vest for many years to come, making the future status of the land so uncertain that the property is unlikely to be marketable. A primary purpose of the *rule against perpetuities* (see under PERPETUITY) is to limit such de facto restraints on alienation.

restricted stock. See under STOCK.

restrictive covenant. See under COVENANT.

restrictive indorsement. See under INDORSEMENT.

resulting trust. See under TRUST.

retainer *n.* **1.** the act of contracting for someone's services—especially a lawyer's—or the fact of being so retained. **2.** an initial fee paid to a lawyer upon being retained by a new client or for a new matter, usually viewed as a deposit on fees to be incurred.

retirement plan an arrangement by which money is set aside during an individual's working years for use after retirement, especially a PENSION PLAN.

retreat *v.* to withdraw from a confrontation rather than fighting back. In general, American law, in the spirit of the Wild West, holds that a person who is attacked need not retreat even if that can be done safely, but may stand his ground and use reasonable force in SELF-DEFENSE. Some jurisdictions make an exception for situations in which it appears that the only sufficient force to avoid death or serious bodily harm would be deadly force, requiring a person to withdraw (except from his own home or place of business) if it is clear that he can do so in complete safety, rather than use deadly force against the attacker. This is colloquially called a duty to "retreat to the wall."

retrial. Same as *de novo trial* (see under TRIAL).

return *v.* **1.** to submit to a court an account of action taken in a judicial matter, particularly action by an officer or official body: *The grand jury returned an indictment. The jury returned its verdict. The sheriff returned an affidavit of service of the writ of attachment.* —*n.* **2.** the act of returning such an account, or the written document itself: *Return was made last week. The return of service was filed last week.* **3.** Also called **tax return.** the document in which a taxpayer reports to the government on matters having tax consequences: *income tax return; estate tax return.* **4.** **individual return,** an income tax return filed by a person who is single, divorced, or legally separated pursuant to a judicial decree. **5.** **joint return,** an income tax return filed by a husband and wife together for the purpose of reporting and paying tax on their combined income. **6.** **return date,** the date upon which a return is due, a motion is to be argued or submitted, or a person is to appear or otherwise respond to a court order or PROCESS. See also RETURNABLE. **7.** **separate return,** an income tax return filed by a married person for the purpose of reporting and paying tax only upon his or her own income.

returnable *adj.* required to be submitted to the court or appropriately responded to; a term usually used in connection with the *return date* (see under RETURN): *The summons is returnable in twenty days. The order to show cause is returnable at 9:00 a.m. on Monday in Courtroom 23.*

reverse *v.* (of an appellate court) to nullify the judgment of a lower court in a case on appeal because of some ERROR in the court below. Sometimes a reversal disposes of the entire case; in other situations it requires further proceedings on REMAND. Cf. AFFIRM². —**reversal,** *n.*

reversible error. See under ERROR.

reversion *n.* the *future estate* (see under ESTATE¹) retained by the owner of an estate in real property (or his heirs) when the owner transfers an estate of shorter duration than the one he owns and does not dispose of the balance, as when the owner of a fee simple absolute conveys a life estate or a one-year tenant conveys the property to another for one week. Cf. REMAINDER.

reverter *n.* See POSSIBILITY OF REVERTER.

review *n.* **1.** Also called **appellate review.** examination of the proceedings and decision in a court case by a higher court or, in an administrative matter, by a court or a higher authority or tribunal within the same agency, to determine if the result should be affirmed. **2.** **administrative review,** review of an administrative decision, especially by a higher authority or tribunal within the agency itself. **3.** **de novo review,** review in which the reviewing court or authority may completely disregard the findings of the original factfinder and draw its own conclusions from the evidence. See also DE NOVO. **4.** **judicial review, a.** the power of the courts to declare laws unconstitutional. **b.** review by a court of an administrative decision. See also SCOPE OF REVIEW; STANDARD OF REVIEW. Cf. LAW REVIEW.

revoke *v.* **1.** to nullify something one has done: *revoke a will; revoke an offer of contract.* **2.** to take away a previously granted right or privilege by judicial or administrative action: *revoke a driver's license; revoke parole.* —**revocable,** *adj.* —**revocation,** *n.*

RICO. See RACKETEER INFLUENCED AND CORRUPT ORGANIZATIONS ACT.

rider *n.* a separate sheet of paper or set of pages containing one or more additions or amendments to a legal document such as a contract or an insurance policy, attached to and intended to be read as if integrated with the main document. See also CODICIL.

right *n.* **1.** a freedom, interest, power, protection, or immunity to which a person is entitled by reason of law, and for which one ordinarily may look to the government, and particularly the courts, for protection, enforcement, or, if a violation has already occurred, compensation or other remedy. **2.** a term used by advocates to describe something that they believe should be a legally protected right, or that they claim as a right even if the law is otherwise. **3.** **constitutional right,** a right protected by a constitution; unless the context clearly indicates otherwise, the constitution referred to is that of the United States. See also FREEDOM; LIBERTY; FUNDAMENTAL RIGHT. **4.** **equitable right,** a right or interest of a *beneficial owner* of property (see under OWNER), or a right for the violation of which one would be entitled to *equitable relief* (see under REMEDY). **5.** **legal right, a.** broadly, any right protected by law; same as def. 1 above. **b.** in a narrow sense, a right or interest of a *legal owner* of property (see under OWNER), or a right for the violation of which one would be entitled to a *legal remedy* (see under REMEDY). **6.** **vested right, a.** a VESTED property interest. **b.** in constitutional law, a contract right that cannot be interfered with by a state, a property right that cannot be taken away by the government without just compensation, or an ENTITLEMENT. See also BILL OF RIGHTS; CIVIL RIGHTS; VICTIMS' RIGHTS.

right of action 1. a right to sue; a CAUSE OF ACTION or *claim for relief* (see under CLAIM). **2.** **private right of action,** a right to sue for damages caused by another's violation of a criminal or regulatory law. A statute outlawing certain conduct may expressly provide that persons injured by such conduct may sue the violator for damages. In the absence of language expressly creating such a right, under traditional principles of tort law an **implied right of action** nevertheless exists under a statute or regulation that was designed to protect people in certain situations from a certain kind of harm, if the defendant's violation in fact caused such harm.

right of (or to) privacy, 1. in tort law, the complex of interests protected by the tort of INVASION OF PRIVACY. **2.** under the federal Privacy Act and similar state statutes, the right to have personal information that is on file with the government kept confidential and used only for authorized purposes. **3.** in constitutional law, **a.** the Fourth Amendment right to be free from unreasonable searches and seizures by the government, which the Supreme Court has held applicable in any area or situation in which the target would have a reasonable "expectation of privacy." **b.** the limited right to make decisions about marriage and procreation, including contraception or abortion, free from government interference, which the Supreme Court has found to be included in the concept of LIBERTY protected by the Fourteenth Amendment. The Court has been reluctant to expand this right to other areas of personal decision making and conduct; for example, under recent rulings the government still has the right to specify what sexual acts consenting adults may legally engage in in private. See also *substantive due process* (under DUE PROCESS); SODOMY.

right of survivorship the characteristic of JOINT ownership of property (as distinguished from ownership IN COMMON) whereby, upon the death of any co-owner, that owner's interest passes automatically to the surviving owners, until finally the last survivor owns the entire property alone.

right to bear arms a popular phrase taken from the Second Amendment, which states: "A well regulated Militia, being necessary to the security of a free State, the right of the people to keep and bear Arms, shall not be infringed." This amendment applies only to the federal government, and so is not a hindrance to state or local GUN CONTROL legislation. Since Congress has never enacted significant restrictions on gun ownership, the potential effect of the Second Amendment at the federal level remains a matter of debate. The Supreme Court's few comments on the amendment, however, suggest that the right to bear arms may extend only so far as necessary to enable the government to maintain a well regulated MILITIA.

right to counsel the right of a criminal defendant to have a lawyer, guaranteed by the Sixth Amendment (see Appendix). It includes the right to have a lawyer present at any significant step of a criminal prosecution, including custodial questioning, plea bargaining, and lineups; the right to a lawyer at government expense if the defendant cannot afford one; and the right of a mentally competent defendant to represent himself. It also includes the right to a lawyer with some minimal level of professional competence, for which reason it is also called the **right to effective assistance of counsel.** The right does not extend to civil cases.

right to die a phrase of varying scope, referring at a minimum to the right of a competent adult to refuse medical care that would prolong life, which is generally recognized by law, and at a maximum to a purported right to *physician-assisted suicide* (see under SUICIDE), which is generally not recognized in the United States. The Supreme Court has yet to find any such right in the Constitution. See also HEALTH CARE PROXY; LIVING WILL.

right to travel the constitutional right of Americans to travel freely from state to state and somewhat less freely to foreign countries. The right of interstate travel includes not only the right to go to another state, but also the right of a newcomer to a state to be treated equally with those already there. The right of foreign travel can be restricted to some extent on national security or foreign policy grounds. See also FUNDAMENTAL RIGHT; *residency requirement* (under RESIDENCY).

right to work laws anti-union legislation enacted in many states, protecting the right of workers to gain and keep employment without joining or contributing to a union.

ripe *adj.* (of a case) ready for the next procedural step: *ripe for decision; ripe for review.* Under the doctrine of **ripeness,** a court may decline to entertain a case that it feels is still speculative and has not "matured" into a real controversy, as when a plaintiff seeks to challenge the constitutionality of a law on the ground that it might be used against her when it has not yet been used in that way.

risk *n.* **1.** the potential injury or loss covered by an insurance policy. **2.** any possibility of harm or loss. See also ASSUMPTION OF RISK.

risk of nonpersuasion. Same as *burden of persuasion* (see under BURDEN[1]).

robbery *n.* the crime of taking someone's money or other personal property from the victim's person or in the victim's presence by force or threat of imminent harm. Robbery is essentially LARCENY with the added factor of personal danger. In general, the kinds of threat that suffice as an element of robbery are threat of imminent bodily harm to the victim or to another, or threat to destroy the victim's home (but not other property).

robing room a room just off a courtroom, where the judge can put on and take off the robe worn on the bench, meet with clerks or study papers during breaks in the proceedings, or meet with the lawyers out of public hearing and without the formality of a courtroom.

royalty *n.* **1.** a sum paid to the creator of a copyrighted work or the inventor of a patented invention, or to the holder of a copyright or patent, for the right to exploit the creation. Such royalties are usually based on the number of units sold, such as copies of a book or units of machinery. **2.** a sum paid to the owner of land for the privilege of extracting oil, gas, or minerals, based on the number of barrels, tons, or other units extracted.

rule *n.* **1.** any of a set of principles and directives formally adopted by or imposed upon a body for its own administration, the governance of its members, or the guidance of those dealing with it. **2.** especially, a regulation governing procedures in the courts: *rules of civil procedure; rules of criminal procedure; rules of appellate procedure; rules of evidence.* In addition to such generally applicable bodies of law, every court has a set of its own rules (**court rules, rules of court,** or, especially in the federal district courts, **local rules**) detailing how matters in that court are to be presented and handled. **3.** an administrative REGULATION. **4.** a legal principle, especially one of common law; e.g., the *rule against perpetuities* (see under PERPETUITY). **5.** an old word for a court order. —*v.* **6.** to decide an issue in a case; to issue a RULING: *The court will rule on our motion after lunch.*

rule against perpetuities. See under PERPETUITY.

rulemaking *n.* the enactment by an administrative agency of REGULATIONS governing conduct in those industries or areas of activity over which it has authority; the LEGISLATIVE function of an administrative agency.

ruling *n.* a judicial or administrative decision or order.

running covenant. See under COVENANT.

S

a b c d e f g h i j k l m n o p q r **S** t u v w x y z

/s/ or **s/,** signed; a symbol sometimes placed before the name of the signer of a document on a copy of the document, or put on the copy in place of the signer's name, to make it clear that the original (but not the copy) was actually signed by that person. For example, this symbol typically appears before the judge's name on the signature line of a CONFORMED COPY of an order signed by the judge.

S corporation. See under CORPORATION.

safe harbor in a statute or regulation governing some activity (usually a business activity) in broad terms, a provision setting forth specific steps that, if taken, will guarantee that one is in compliance with the law. The safe harbor is not the only way to comply, but if followed it eliminates all doubt about whether one is in compliance.

said *adj.* previously referred to; mentioned above; aforesaid: *Said defendant there and then took said gun and shot said victim.* Though still common in formal documents such as wills and indictments, this classic mark of the lawyer is now generally recognized as completely unnecessary: *The defendant then shot the victim with the gun.*

sale *n.* **1.** a transfer of title to property for money or its equivalent, or a contract for such a transfer. See also BILL OF SALE; BOILER ROOM SALES. Cf. BARTER. **2. sales,** income received from the sale of goods: *The company had sales of $350,000 last year.* **3. judicial sale,** a sale of property ordered by a court, either to satisfy a debt of the owner or to effect a PARTITION of the property. **4. sale and leaseback,** a contract in which one party buys property from the other and simultaneously agrees to rent it back to the seller for a period of time; in effect, the buyer is lending money to the seller and holding title to the property as security for repayment, which is made in the form of "rent." **5. tax sale,** a *judicial sale* of property to satisfy back taxes. **6. wash sale,** a sale, especially of stocks or bonds, entered into at about the same time as a purchase of the same thing, leaving the seller in the same position as if the transactions had never occurred. Tax law prohibits the taking of tax benefits from such a transaction, and the securities laws prohibit such transactions as a means of creating a false impression of market activity.

sales tax a tax imposed by many states and municipalities on purchasers of goods and services, consisting of a fixed percentage added to the selling price in each retail transaction. It is a *regressive tax* (see under TAX), since people with modest incomes must spend proportionately more of their income on taxable goods and services, and have proportionately less left over for investments that are not subject to sales tax, than people with high incomes.

sanction *v.* **1.** occasionally, to manifest approval of something, either in advance or after the fact: *The court sanctioned the defendant's conduct* (i.e., approved of it). **2.** usually, to punish someone or impose a punishment for something: *The court sanctioned the defendant's conduct* (i.e., imposed a penalty for it); *the court sanctioned the defendant* (i.e., punished her). —*n.* **3.** permission or approval. **4.** penalty or punishment. **5.** Often, **sanctions.** punitive measures taken by one or more countries toward another to force it to comply with international law.

satisfaction *n.* **1.** full performance of an obligation; especially, payment of a debt in full: *satisfaction of a mortgage; satisfaction of a judgment.* **2.** discharge of an obligation or undertaking by a performance or payment accepted in lieu of what was originally contemplated or agreed to: *satisfaction of a legacy by transfer of the property to the legatee prior to the testator's death.* **3.** a document or notation by an obligee that an obligation, especially a judgment, has been satisfied. **4.** fulfillment of a description, requirement, or set of requirements. See also *accord and satisfaction* (under ACCORD). —**satisfy,** *v.*

save harmless. See under HARMLESS.

saving clause **1.** in a legislative enactment that repeals a previous statute, a clause that continues the previous law's effectiveness for certain purposes, such as for purposes of any lawsuit initiated prior to the effective date of the repeal. **2.** Also called **separability clause** or **severability clause.** a clause in a statute or contract providing that if any part of the statute or contract is found to be void or unenforceable, that part will be carved out and the balance enforced to the extent possible.

scienter *Latin.* (lit. "knowingly") guilty knowledge; in a fraud case, the element of intent to defraud, or knowledge of the falsity of one's representations. The term is used particularly in connection with SECURITIES FRAUD.

scope of authority the range of an agent's duties or permitted activities on behalf of a principal. The principal is normally bound by and liable for the acts of an agent within the scope of the agent's ac-

tual or *apparent authority* (see under AUTHORITY[1]). Also called **scope of agency.** See also RESPONDEAT SUPERIOR.

scope of employment any job-related activity by an employee. The employer is normally liable for torts committed by an employee acting within the scope of employment, as when a company driver causes an accident while making a delivery. See also RESPONDEAT SUPERIOR. Cf. FROLIC OF ONE'S OWN.

scope of examination the range of subjects inquired into in the questioning of a witness at a hearing or trial. See also EXAMINATION; BEYOND THE SCOPE.

scope of expertise the area of an expert witness's specialized knowledge. An expert witness may not testify to opinions on matters beyond the scope of her expertise. See also *expert witness* (under WITNESS).

scope of review the extent of a court's power to review a decision of a lower court or of an administrative agency. Such power is usually limited by a combination of constitutional provisions, statutory provisions, judicial policy, and the court's own discretion. See also STANDARD OF REVIEW.

scrutiny *n.* judicial consideration of the purposes and effects of an administrative regulation or a state or federal law or policy in order to determine whether it is valid, especially under the DUE PROCESS and EQUAL PROTECTION clauses of the Constitution. In constitutional challenges under those clauses, the Supreme Court has defined three levels of scrutiny, the choice of which depends upon the nature of the rights at stake or the CLASSIFICATION involved: RATIONAL BASIS TEST; HEIGHTENED SCRUTINY; STRICT SCRUTINY.

seal[1] *n.* **1.** originally, an impression made in melted wax on a document such as a contract, deed, or will, containing the unique mark of the maker of the document and signifying the maker's intent to be bound by it. **2.** today, any mark on the paper intended to represent such a seal, most commonly the word "seal" or the letters **L.S.** (for the Latin "locus sigilli," lit. "the place of the seal") placed next to the maker's signature. **3. corporate seal,** an identifying design adopted by a corporation, embossed on legal documents executed by the corporation to authenticate them and to act as a seal. **4. sealed instrument** or **instrument under seal,** an INSTRUMENT to which the SIGNATURE and seal of the maker have been affixed. At common law, such an instrument became legally effective upon delivery to the person benefited by it (hence the phrase "signed, sealed, and delivered"). The legal significance of the seal has been modified by statutes which vary from state to state, and in some states it no longer has any significance at all. See also *hand and seal* (under HAND); *contract under seal* (under CONTRACT). —*v.* **5.** to affix a seal to; to execute with a seal.

seal[2] *v.* to place or keep items or records relating to a case in a sealed envelope, or otherwise shield them from public access. See also *file under seal* (under FILE); CONFIDENTIALITY STIPULATION.

search *n.* **1.** inspection by law enforcement officials of a person's body, home, or any area that the person would reasonably be expected to regard as private, for weapons, contraband, or evidence of criminal activity. Under the Fourth Amendment (see Appendix), a search ordinarily may not be conducted without PROBABLE CAUSE. Cf. STOP AND FRISK. **2. border search,** a search of a person or property coming into the country. If not unduly intrusive, this is permitted without any reason to suspect wrongdoing; strip searches and body cavity searches require an objective basis for suspicion of smuggling, but less than probable cause. **3. consent search,** a search conducted with the consent of the subject, or of a person with control over the area searched. This is legal even in the absence of probable cause, and even if the consent was given only because the subject did not know and was not told that she had any choice in the matter, so long as the consent was not the product of duress. **4. unreasonable search,** a search conducted without probable cause and in the absence of other consid-

legal

erations making it constitutionally permissible, such as consent or protection of the nation's borders. See also EXCLUSIONARY RULE. **5. warrantless search,** a search conducted without a warrant (see WARRANT¹). This is permissible under EXIGENT CIRCUMSTANCES requiring prompt action. —*v.* **6.** to conduct a search.

search and seizure 1. a SEARCH leading to a SEIZURE of property. Because searches and seizures are often linked in practice and are governed by the same body of law, they are often discussed jointly by use of this phrase. **2. unreasonable search and seizure,** an *unreasonable search* (see under SEARCH) leading to a seizure of property.

search warrant. See under WARRANT¹.

seasonable *adj.* timely; within the time agreed upon; within a reasonable time.

second mortgage. See under MORTGAGE.

secondary boycott. See under BOYCOTT.

secondary liability. See under LIABILITY.

section *n.* a subdivision of a statute or document, represented by the symbol + (or ++ for "sections"). Most statutes and codes are divided into sections.

secure *v.* **1.** to provide assurance that a debt will be paid or that funds will be available to pay damages if an obligation is not performed, particularly by giving the obligee a lien, mortgage, or other *security interest* (see under INTEREST¹) in property. Lawyers speak interchangeably of securing the obligee (who is then a **secured creditor**) or securing the obligation (which is then a **secured debt**). **2. secured transaction,** any transaction which has as one of its elements the creation of a security interest in favor of one of the parties. —**secured,** *adj.*

securities acts statutes regulating the issuance and marketing of stocks, bonds, and other securities (see SECURITY²) to the public. They seek to avoid the conditions that led to the stock market crash of 1929 by assuring that investors will have access to full and accurate information and will be treated fairly. The principal federal securities acts are the **Securities Act of 1933,** which regulates the initial distribution of a new security to the public, and the **Securities Exchange Act of 1934,** which regulates all subsequent trading of a security. See also BLUE SKY LAW.

securities broker. See under BROKER.

securities fraud the tort and crime of knowingly making any materially misleading statement, or failing to disclose a material fact, in connection with the purchase or sale of a security.

security¹ *n.* **1.** something given or deposited to provide assurance of payment of a debt or fulfillment of an obligation; especially, a *security interest* (see under INTEREST¹) in property. **2. security deposit,** money set aside and held as security; particularly, money paid by a tenant at the beginning of a lease and held by the landlord in case the tenant damages the property or leaves without paying rent.

security² *n.* **1.** an ownership interest in an enterprise (the ISSUER) or a right to share in profits from it or a debt owed by it, deriving from an investment in the enterprise rather than from participation in it. Most commonly, a bond (see BOND¹) or shares of STOCK. **2.** a certificate evidencing such an interest or right. **3. convertible security,** a security that can be exchanged for another kind of security from the same issuer upon specified conditions; e.g., a bond convertible into stock, or preferred stock convertible into common stock. **4. corporate security,** a security issued by a corporation. **5. debt security,** a bond or other security representing a right to receive a share of each payment of interest or principal made by an enterprise in connection with a particular debt owed by it. **6. equity security,** stock or another security representing an ownership interest in an enterprise, or carrying a right to acquire such an interest; e.g., a warrant (see WARRANT²). **7. government security,** a security issued by the federal government or a federal agency; sometimes, a security guaranteed by the federal government. **8. guaranteed security,** a security in which the issuer's obligation to make payments is guaranteed by an entity other than the issuer. **9. marketable secu-**

rity, a security that can easily be sold if the present owner needs cash or no longer wants the security. **10. municipal security,** a security issued by, or sometimes guaranteed by, a state or local government or governmental agency. **11. redeemable security,** a security that the issuer has a right to buy back (or, in the case of a *debt security,* to pay off prior to maturity) upon specified conditions. Also called **callable security.**

security interest. See under INTEREST¹.

seduction *n.* inducing a person, especially an unmarried woman, to engage in sexual intercourse. The term includes both honest and dishonest means of persuasion, but usually not force. Depending upon various factors such as the age of the person seduced, her previous chastity, the means used, and the state where the conduct occurred, seduction may be a crime, a tort for which the seduced person may sue, or a tort for which her father or mother may sue.

seizure *n.* **1.** (of a person) an ARREST. **2.** (of property in criminal matters) the taking of possession, by law enforcement officials, of a weapon, contraband, or evidence of a crime, usually pursuant to a SEARCH. The government's right to make such seizures is limited by the Fourth Amendment (see Appendix); a seizure resulting from an *unreasonable search* (see under SEARCH) is unlawful. See also SEARCH AND SEIZURE; EXCLUSIONARY RULE. **3.** (of property in civil cases) an ATTACHMENT or other procedure by which property is brought under the control of the court. —**seize,** *v.*

selective conscientious objector. See under CONSCIENTIOUS OBJECTOR.

self-authenticating. See under AUTHENTICATE.

self-dealing *n.* transactions by a trustee or other FIDUCIARY in which the fiduciary has a personal interest that might conflict with the interest of the party to whom she owes a fiduciary duty. Self-dealing usually constitutes a *breach of fiduciary duty* (see under BREACH).

self-defense *n.* the use of reasonable force against an aggressor by one who reasonably believes it necessary to avoid imminent bodily harm. Self-defense is a justification for conduct that would otherwise be a crime or tort. See also RETREAT.

self-employment income. See under INCOME.

self-employment tax a tax on self-employed individuals requiring them to make a double contribution to the SOCIAL SECURITY system, paying both the employer's share and the employee's share. See also SOCIAL SECURITY TAX.

self-help *n.* the taking of action to remedy a wrong without calling upon the police or initiating legal proceedings. Some kinds of self-help are permitted by law, such as (usually) the repossession of an automobile whose buyer has fallen behind in installment payments.

self-incrimination *n.* the making of a statement that may expose the speaker to criminal penalties. Under the Fifth Amendment (see Appendix), the government may not require people to make such statements or penalize them for refusing to do so. See also *transactional immunity* and *use immunity* (under IMMUNITY).

self-insurance *n.* the setting aside of funds to cover certain potential risks or losses instead of purchasing insurance for those particular risks.

senior *adj.* having priority among potential recipients of payment or benefits in the event that resources run short and a conflict arises among claimants with similar interests: *senior creditor; senior lien; senior security.* Opposite: JUNIOR; SUBORDINATE; SUBORDINATED. —**seniority,** *n.*

seniority system an employment policy, often required by union contract, under which workers who have worked for the same employer for longer periods are entitled to better benefits and more protection against firing than workers who have been there a shorter time. Although such policies perpetuate racial and other imbalances due to past discrimination in hiring, they are expressly permitted by most civil rights laws.

sentence *n.* **1.** a court's JUDGMENT imposing a penalty upon a person convicted of an offense, or the penalty imposed, such as imprisonment, a fine, community service, or death. See also CAPITAL PUNISHMENT. **2. concurrent sentences,** sentences on different charges to be served simultaneously. Concurrent sentences are often imposed so that if the defendant obtains a reversal of conviction on one or more counts, but less than all, it will not affect the length of time spent in prison. **3. consecutive sentences,** sentences on different charges to be served one after the other. Consecutive sentences may be imposed when a defendant's conduct constituted several distinct crimes, in order to maximize the total time of imprisonment. Also called **cumulative sentences. 4. determinate sentence,** a sentence setting a definite term of incarceration. **5. indeterminate sentence,** a sentence specifying minimum and maximum terms of imprisonment, with exact date of release between those limits to be determined by the parole board. **6. suspended sentence,** a sentence that the defendant will not be required to serve unless she commits another crime or violates some other condition imposed by the court. —**sentence,** *v.*

separability clause. See under SAVING CLAUSE.

separate but equal the doctrine, formally adopted by the Supreme Court in 1896 in the infamous case of Plesssy v. Ferguson, holding that legally mandated racial segregation does not violate the constitutional requirement of EQUAL PROTECTION, so long as the law contemplates the provision of "separate but equal" facilities for people of color. In the 1954 case of Brown v. Board of Education, the Supreme Court finally recognized that separate facilities are "inherently unequal" as well as demeaning, and took the first step away from this doctrine by declaring racially segregated public schools unconstitutional. But the doctrine may still be alive in slightly altered form: In 1977 the Court affirmed a decision permitting a city to maintain two separate high schools for academically gifted students—"Central High" for boys and "Girls High" for girls—upon a finding that "the academic facilities are comparable, with the exception of those in the scientific field where Central's are superior."

separate opinion. See under OPINION.

separate return. See under RETURN.

separation *n.* **1.** the termination of cohabitation of a husband and wife, or the status of a husband and wife who are living apart, either preliminary to a divorce or instead of divorcing. **2. legal separation,** separation of spouses pursuant to a court order or, sometimes, a *separation agreement.* **3. separation agreement,** a formal agreement between spouses stating that they will live apart and setting forth the terms of their separation.

separation of church and state a phrase commonly used to summarize the purpose of the First Amendment's guarantee of FREEDOM OF RELIGION. The phrase has been in use at least since 1802, when President Thomas Jefferson described the First Amendment as creating "a wall of separation between church and state."

separation of powers the theory that government should have three separate branches: a legislative branch to make laws, an executive branch to administer them, and a judicial branch to interpret them and resolve disputes arising under them. For the national government of the United States, the first three articles of the Constitution define the powers of each of these three branches in turn. In practice there is much overlap and interplay among the three branches.

sequester *v.* to segregate, isolate, or set apart, especially by court order. To sequester property is to hold it aside pending a decision on its disposition; to sequester witnesses is to keep them from talking to each other or listening to testimony during a trial; to sequester a jury is to shield it from outside influence. —**sequestration,** *n.*

servant *n.* an employee; a person hired to perform services for another (the MASTER) and subject to the other's control both as to what work is done and

how it is done (in contrast to an INDEPENDENT CONTRACTOR, who has more autonomy). See also MASTER AND SERVANT.

serve *v.* to effect SERVICE of papers or process. One can speak of serving either the person or the papers: *The marshal served the defendant with the summons. The marshal served the summons on* (or *upon*) *the defendant.*

service *n.* **1.** Also called **service of process.** the giving of formal notice of judicial proceedings or a judicial act to a person involved, by delivering a copy of the PROCESS to the person or following some other procedure prescribed by law. **2.** the act of providing a copy of any paper filed with the court, such as a motion or affidavit, to the other parties or attorneys in the case. Normally a court will reject the paper if this has not been done. Cf. EX PARTE. **3. personal service,** hand delivery of a copy of the process directly to the intended recipient or to an agent authorized to accept process. **4. service by publication,** the printing of notice of an action in a newspaper in the hope that the person affected by it will see it. This is the least effective method of service, allowed only in certain situations and only as a last resort. **5. substituted service,** any of several methods of service permitted in place of personal service under certain circumstances, such as service by mail. Also called **constructive service.** See also NAIL AND MAIL.

services *n.pl.* originally, the labor of a wife or child contributing to the economic welfare of a man's household. The common law recognized a man's right to recover damages for the loss of such services from anyone who injured or enticed away his wife or child. Since the husband owed no services to his wife, she had no such right of action. To the extent that loss of economic services of a family member is recognized as giving rise to a tort claim today, it applies without regard to the sex of the spouse or the parent. See also CONSORTIUM.

servitude *n.* **1.** Also called **involuntary servitude.** forced labor; working for another against one's will, whether for pay or not. This includes not only SLAVERY but also such schemes as requiring a person to work for one to whom he is indebted in order to work off the debt. It is outlawed by the Thirteenth Amendment (see Appendix), except as punishment for a crime. Public responsibilities such as jury duty and military service for draftees are not barred by the Thirteenth Amendment. **2.** a right to use another's land for a particular purpose, and the corresponding burden upon the land (see BURDEN²); for example, an EASEMENT OT PROFIT.

set aside to nullify a judgment, verdict, or court order. See also QUASH; VACATE.

set off to balance two opposing claims against each other, eliminating the smaller and reducing the larger by that amount. The reduction is called a **set-off** or **offset:** *The landlord's claim against the tenant for $1000 in property damage was set off against the tenant's claim for refund of the $3000 security deposit, and the landlord was ordered to refund the remaining $2000.*

settle *v.* **1.** to reach agreement resolving a dispute: *settle a case.* **2.** to pay in full: *settle a bill.* **3.** to complete all the tasks of administration and distribution of a decedent's property: *settle an estate.* **4.** to transfer title to property; especially, to create a TRUST by placing money or property in the hands of a TRUSTEE for administration: *settle a trust.* **5.** to submit to a court for approval: *settle an order.* —**settlement,** *n.*

settlor *n.* the person who creates a TRUST by transferring money or property to a TRUSTEE for administration. Also called the DONOR or GRANTOR of the trust.

sever *v.* to split off a part of a case and make it a separate case, in order to avoid prejudice or for administrative convenience: *to sever a claim; to sever a party; to sever the case.* Cf. CONSOLIDATE; JOIN. —**severance,** *n.*

severability clause. See under SAVING CLAUSE.

several *adj.* separate; individual, independent of

others in a group: *several liability* (see under LIABIL-ITY). Cf. JOINT; JOINT AND SEVERAL. **—severally,** *adv.*

severalty *n.* the condition of being under individual ownership. See also IN SEVERALTY.

sex discrimination discrimination against women for not being men, or occasionally against men for not being women. Sex discrimination permeated American law at every level until the 1960's, when statutes and constitutional decisions limiting such discrimination began to appear. See also BONA FIDE OCCUPATIONAL QUALIFICATION; HEIGHTENED SCRUTINY; PREGNANCY DISCRIMINATION; SEPARATE BUT EQUAL; SEXUAL HARASSMENT; STATUTORY RAPE.

sex-plus discrimination discrimination based upon a combination of sex and other factors; for example, refusing to hire married women while hiring men without regard to marital status, or harassing young female employees but not older ones. For purposes of laws against employment discrimination, such conduct constitutes sex discrimination.

sexual assault. See under ASSAULT.

sexual harassment a form of unlawful employment discrimination consisting of HARASSMENT of an employee or group of employees, usually women, because of their sex. This may take the form of requiring or seeking sexual favors as a condition of employment **(quid pro quo harassment)** or otherwise subjecting an employee to intimidation, ridicule, or insult because of her sex, whether or not the harassing conduct is sexual in nature **(hostile environment harassment).** See also HOSTILE WORKING ENVIRONMENT.

sexual predator a person with a history of sexual offenses against others, who is regarded as unlikely to be able to control the impulse to commit more such crimes in the future. Also called **sexually dangerous person.**

share *n.* a partial right or interest allotted to one of several people who together have the whole right or interest; in particular, a unit of ownership of a CORPORATION or *joint stock company* (see under COMPANY) —that is, one of the equal fractional parts into which a class of STOCK of such an entity is divided. See also ELECTIVE SHARE.

shareholder. Same as STOCKHOLDER.

shareholder derivative action. See under ACTION.

shell corporation. See under CORPORATION.

Sherman Antitrust Act the first federal ANTITRUST law. It prohibits MONOPOLIZATION, attempted monopolization, and any concerted action in UNREASONABLE RESTRAINT OF TRADE. Also called **Sherman Act.**

shield law a statute creating a *testimonial privilege* (see under PRIVILEGE). This phrase is most commonly used to describe laws protecting reporters from having to disclose news sources **(journalists' shield law)** or victims in rape cases from unnecessary inquiry into the sexual history of the victim **(rape shield law).**

shift. See *burden shifting* (under BURDEN[1]).

shop *n.* **1.** a business or place of employment, especially one in which the workers have a UNION. **2. agency shop,** a shop in which workers are required to pay union dues whether they join the union or not. **3. closed shop,** a shop in which one must be a union member to get a job, and must remain a member to keep it. Although federal labor law forbids closed shops, as a practical matter one cannot get work in some fields except through a union. **4. open shop,** a shop in which union and nonunion workers are treated equally. **5. preferential shop,** a shop in which union members are given preferential treatment over nonmembers. **6. union shop,** a shop in which nonunion workers may be hired but must then join and remain a member of a union. See also RIGHT TO WORK LAWS.

shoplifting *n.* the crime of taking possession of merchandise in a store with the intention of keeping or using it without paying for it. Shoplifting is a form of LARCENY.

show *v.* **1.** to convince or try to convince a court of something by evidence and legal argument: *The plaintiff failed to show a need for an injunction; an*

injunction will issue only upon a showing that without it the applicant will suffer irreparable harm. **2. show cause,** to present reasons why a court should issue, or refuse to issue, a particular order. See also *order to show cause* (under ORDER[1]). **—showing,** *n.*

showup *n.* the displaying of a criminal suspect singly to a witness for the purpose of identification, usually within a few hours after the crime; an inherently suggestive procedure that is nevertheless common. Cf. LINEUP.

sidebar *n.* in a jury trial, a brief courtroom conference among the judge and the lawyers, either on or off the record, conducted at or to the side of the bench so that the jury cannot hear it. Also called **bench conference.**

sight draft. See under DRAFT.

sign *v.* to affix a SIGNATURE to a document. See also SEAL[1].

signatory *n.* **1.** a person or entity whose SIGNATURE appears on a document. **2.** a nation that has agreed to a treaty.

signature *n.* the name or mark of a person or entity placed on a document to authenticate it. It need not be written by hand, and it need not be placed there by the person named so long as it is authorized or adopted by that person. See also HAND; seal[1]; X.

silent partner. See under PARTNER.

simple *adj.* **1.** describing the basic form of something; lacking special or complicating features. See *fee simple* (under FEE[1]). **2.** (of a tort or crime) unaggravated; often used to describe the lowest grade of an offense: *simple negligence* (see under NEGLIGENCE); *simple assault.*

simplified employee pension. See under PENSION PLAN.

sinking fund money or other assets set aside and accumulated to meet a future need, particularly the paying of a debt.

sister corporations. See under CORPORATION.

sit *v.* **1.** (of a court or other official body) to hold a formal session for the conduct of business: *The Supreme Court normally sits from October to June.* **2.** to preside over a particular case: *The appeal was decided by the Court of Appeals sitting en banc.*

situate *adj.* situated; located. A term found in descriptions of real property.

situs *n.* Latin. (lit. "site") the place where a thing (tangible or intangible) is deemed to be located for legal purposes. For example, the situs of personal property for tax purposes is usually the domicile of the owner; the situs of a debt is generally deemed to be wherever the debtor is at the moment.

slander *n.* **1.** the form of DEFAMATION in which the defamatory statement is communicated orally. Cf. LIBEL[1]. **—** *v.* **2.** to utter a slander against a person; to defame orally. **—slanderous,** *adj.*

slavery *n.* the ownership of one person by another, outlawed by the Thirteenth Amendment (see Appendix). See also SERVITUDE.

sleeping partner. See under PARTNER.

slip opinion a judicial OPINION in the form in which it is first issued, typed or printed on slips of paper; cited as "slip op." Cf. *reported opinion* (under REPORT).

small claims court a state or municipal court established to handle certain civil cases involving very small sums of money, using informal, streamlined procedures and often dispensing with lawyers.

smuggling *n.* the crime of importing or exporting prohibited matter, or importing or exporting permitted matter without paying required DUTY. **—smuggle,** *v.*

so ordered a formal expression often used by judges, both orally and in writing, to make it clear that a pronouncement is an official order of the court. See the example under INSTANTER.

social security a federal program designed to provide some continuing income to most workers after they retire or become disabled, and under some circumstances to their surviving spouse or children when they die. The program was established by the **Federal Insurance Contributions Act (FICA)** in 1935.

social security tax a payroll tax, paid one-half by the employee and one-half by the employer, to help fund the social security and Medicare programs; usually identified on pay stubs as "FICA" (see under SOCIAL SECURITY). It is a *regressive tax* (see under TAX), because it is paid only on *earned income* (see under INCOME) and not on income from investments, and also because most of it applies only to wages up to a certain maximum amount each year, so that employees with very high salaries (usually executives) pay the full tax only on a portion of their salary, whereas most ordinary workers pay it on their entire salary. Moreover, individuals without a regular employer to pay the employer's share must pay double on whatever they earn, in the form of SELF-EMPLOYMENT TAX.

Socratic method a teaching method heavily used in law schools today, based upon the technique used by Socrates in ancient Greece, in which students are led to analyze legal issues and principles through a series of *hypothetical questions* (see under QUESTION¹) from the teacher. See also CASE METHOD.

sodomy *n.* a term varying in meaning from state to state, but generally referring to any type of sex act disapproved by the legislature. At a minimum it includes oral and anal sexual intercourse between men, but it may extend to those or other acts between men and women (sometimes exempting married couples, sometimes not), or women and women, or people and animals. Sodomy is still a crime in many states, and as recently as 1986 the Supreme Court upheld a law providing for 20 years' imprisonment for either heterosexual or homosexual sodomy, as applied to a man who was found in bed with another man in his own home by police who entered to serve an arrest warrant for public drinking. Cf. RIGHT TO PRIVACY.

sole custody. See under CUSTODY.

sole proprietorship ownership of an unincorporated business by one individual, or the business so owned. For income tax purposes, the profits of such a business are taxed directly to the individual.

solicitation *n.* **1.** the crime of asking, advising, encouraging, or ordering another person to commit a crime, whether or not the offense solicited is then committed. This is usually punishable as a crime one degree lower in severity than the offense solicited. **2.** the offense of offering to engage in sexual activity with a person for money or of attempting to entice a person to patronize a prostitute.

solicitor *n.* **1.** in England, a lawyer who gives legal advice and performs general legal services outside the courtroom, including preparing cases for a BARRISTER to present in court, but who normally does not appear in court personally except in certain lower courts. **2.** in America, a title sometimes given to the chief legal officer of a municipality or governmental department: *county solicitor; town solicitor.* **3. Solicitor General,** the officer who oversees all legal representation of the United States government before the Supreme Court.

solvent *adj.* **1.** usually, able to pay one's debts in the ordinary course of business as they become due. **2.** for some purposes, having assets greater than liabilities. Opposite of INSOLVENT. —**solvency,** *n.*

sound *adj.* **1.** (of body or mind) healthy, fit, normal. **2. sound mind** or **sound and disposing mind and memory,** the mental CAPACITY necessary to make a valid will; having a reasonable understanding of what property one has, what options for it one has, and what one is doing with it.

sound in (of a civil action) to have its basis in; to have as its fundamental nature: *To determine which statute of limitations applies, the court must decide whether the action sounds in tort or in contract.*

sovereign immunity. See under IMMUNITY.

speaking objection. See under OBJECTION.

special *adj.* describing a form of something that is distinctive, particularized, limited, expanded, or otherwise worthy of separate consideration, often calling into play particular legal rules. Sometimes contrasted with GENERAL. See *special* APPEARANCE, COUNSEL, DAMAGES, INDORSEMENT, JURISDICTION¹, MASTER, POWER OF ATTORNEY, PROSECUTOR, VERDICT under those

words, and *special questions* (or *interrogatories*) (under VERDICT).

special circumstances aggravating or mitigating circumstances affecting the degree of a crime or the severity of punishment; especially, aggravating circumstances that justify a prosecutor in seeking or a jury in imposing the death penalty for a murder, such as a defendant's infliction of torture on the victim or commission of multiple murders.

specie. See IN SPECIE.

specific *adj.* **1.** particular or special; not vague or general: *specific bequest* (or *legacy*) (see under BEQUEST). **2.** as specified; in the manner or of the kind agreed to: SPECIFIC PERFORMANCE. **3.** referring to a particular thing: *specific restitution* (see under RESTITUTION). See also *specific relief* (under RELIEF).

specific performance an *equitable remedy* (see under REMEDY) in which a party is ordered to perform a contract according to its terms. The usual remedy for breach of contract is damages (a legal remedy), but in cases where money is not a satisfactory substitute for the thing contracted for, as in a contract for the sale of land or of a unique article such as a painting, the breaching party may be ordered to "perform specifically."

specification *n.* a detailed listing or description, such as a litigant's listing of errors in appellate papers, the prosecution's listing of charges in a court martial, or an inventor's detailing of an invention in a patent application.

speculate *v.* **1.** to guess; to reach conclusions not based on knowledge or evidence. Testimony based on speculation is ordinarily not admissible. See also *speculative damages* (under DAMAGES). **2.** to make risky investments. The purpose of the SECURITIES ACTS is to make it possible for investors to know to what extent they are speculating. —**speculation,** *n.* —**speculative,** *adj.*

speech *n.* **1.** within the meaning of the First Amendment (see Appendix), any form of expression, including words (whether written or spoken), pictures or other visual devices, and expressive conduct. **2. commercial speech,** advertising or other speech promoting economic interests. Formerly regarded as constitutionally unprotected, commercial speech that is not false or misleading and does not promote illegal goods, services, or conduct is now given considerable protection under the First Amendment, though still not to the extent of noncommercial speech. **3. hate speech,** speech that grossly insults or demeans people because of a group characteristic such as race or religion. Such speech may not be censored or penalized by the government because of its group-related content, although FIGHTING WORDS may be outlawed. **4. indecent speech,** speech that does not amount to OBSCENITY, but uses vulgar words or deals with sex or bodily functions in a way that is regarded as PATENTLY OFFENSIVE. Unlike obscenity, speech that is merely indecent has been given considerable constitutional protection (for example, "dial-a-porn" services cannot be completely banned); at the same time, some restrictions that would not be allowed for "decent" speech have been upheld, particularly in regard to broadcasting. **5. protected speech,** speech held by the courts to be within the scope of the First Amendment's guarantee of FREEDOM OF SPEECH. **6. speech plus,** speech accompanied by conduct deemed nonexpressive. Conduct is not immune from reasonable regulation merely because it is accompanied by speech. **7. symbolic speech,** expression other than through words. The expression may be political (waving a flag or burning a flag), artistic (painting or dance), or anything else. In general, symbolic speech is constitutionally protected to the same extent as verbal speech. See also FREEDOM OF SPEECH.

speedy trial. See under TRIAL.

spendthrift trust. See under TRUST.

spontaneous declaration (or **statement** or **exclamation**). Same as EXCITED UTTERANCE.

spot zoning. See under ZONING.

spousal abuse physical or psychological ABUSE of one spouse by the other, more often of the wife by

legal

the husband **(wife abuse).** Traditionally viewed more as a ground for divorce than as a crime; now taken seriously as a crime. See also BATTERED PERSON SYNDROME; CRUELTY.

spousal privilege. See under PRIVILEGE.

spousal rape. Same as *marital rape* (see under RAPE).

spousal support. Same as ALIMONY.

spouse's election. See under ELECTION.

spouse's elective (or **statutory**) **share.** Same as ELECTIVE SHARE.

spread upon the record. See under RECORD.

squeeze-out *n.* any of a number of techniques permitted by law to force minority shareholders out of a corporation ("squeeze them out"). See also GO PRIVATE.

ss. an abbreviation of uncertain origin and no particular meaning, customarily placed at the top of an affidavit or affirmation beside the statement of VENUE and followed by a colon, thus serving as a kind of introduction to the instrument.

stakeholder *n.* a person in possession of money or property to which she herself has no claim, but to which two or more others may have competing claims, so that the stakeholder cannot turn over the property to any claimant without the risk of being sued by one or more of the others. For the way out of this dilemma, see INTERPLEADER.

stale *adj.* rendered ineffective or unenforceable by the passage of time: *stale check; stale claim; stale offer.*

stalking *n.* **1.** the crime of following a person about in such a way as to instill fear of bodily harm. This is typically dealt with as a form of criminal HARASSMENT. It may also give rise to a tort action for ASSAULT or INTENTIONAL INFLICTION OF MENTAL DISTRESS. **2.** secretly following a person about or lying in wait for the purpose of committing a crime. In most states this is punishable as an ATTEMPT to commit a crime. —**stalk,** *v.* —**stalker,** *n.*

stamp tax a tax imposed upon a product (e.g., liquor or cigarettes) or a transaction (e.g., a transfer of land) by requiring someone to purchase a stamp and affix it to the product or instrument.

stand *n.* **1.** in a trial, the place where a witness sits while testifying; short for **witness stand. 2. take the stand,** to go to the stand to testify.

stand bail. See under BAIL[1].

standard deduction. See under DEDUCTION.

standard of care the level or nature of conduct necessary to avoid liability for MALPRACTICE, NEGLIGENCE, or *breach of fiduciary duty* (see under BREACH). Also called **degree of care.** See details under CARE.

standard of proof the degree to which the TRIER OF FACT must be persuaded of a fact in order to find in favor of a party in a trial or hearing. Also called **degree of proof.** Depending upon the nature of the case or the issue, the standard may be proof by a PREPONDERANCE OF THE EVIDENCE, proof by CLEAR AND CONVINCING EVIDENCE, or proof BEYOND A REASONABLE DOUBT.

standard of review the test by which a court or administrative tribunal determines whether to uphold or reverse an administrative or judicial decision submitted to it for REVIEW. The applicable standard depends upon many factors, including whether the issue being reviewed is one of fact or of law, and whether it was decided by a judge or by a jury. The usual test for upholding a jury verdict is whether there was evidence in the case on the basis of which a reasonable jury, applying the proper STANDARD OF PROOF, could have arrived at that verdict. For other standards of review, see ABUSE OF DISCRETION; CLEARLY ERRONEOUS; *de novo review* (under REVIEW); SUBSTANTIAL EVIDENCE; and *harmless error, plain error,* and *reversible error* (all under ERROR).

standby counsel. See under COUNSEL.

standing *n.* the right to have a court adjudicate a matter in which one is interested. To have standing to bring an action or otherwise raise an issue in

court, one must have a legally cognizable interest in the matter (see INTEREST[1], def. 1).

Star Chamber 1. an English court, finally abolished in 1641, whose unfettered powers, lack of procedural safeguards, and arbitrary punishments made it a symbol of much that our constitutional protections and rules of criminal procedure seek to guard against. **2. star chamber proceeding,** a phrase used to characterize a legal proceeding as grossly unfair to the defendant. See also KANGAROO COURT.

stare decisis *Latin.* (lit. "to stand by the things decided") the doctrine that legal principles established in previous judicial decisions will normally be followed in subsequent cases. This doctrine lends stability and fairness to the law; without it, each judge could make up a new rule for each case. But it also makes the law slow to react to social and scientific change. The evolution of common law depends upon judicious application of this doctrine.

state *n.* **1.** a nation or national government. See also ACT OF STATE. **2.** one of the fifty states making up the United States, or the government of such a state. In many contexts, the word is used a little more broadly to include the District of Columbia. **3.** *(cap.)* the government of a particular state. In many states, this is how the government and the prosecution are identified in criminal cases under state law. See also PEOPLE. Cf. GOVERNMENT.

state action action taken by the government (especially a state government) or in which the government is intimately involved, as distinguished from purely private action. The constitutional guarantees of DUE PROCESS and EQUAL PROTECTION apply only to state action, not private action.

state of mind 1. generally, the condition of mind or the element or degree of fault or blameworthiness that accompanies an act or omission. **2.** particularly, the additional condition that is required in most crimes, beyond the mere fact that the defendant committed a certain act causing certain results, to make the act a particular crime; MENS REA. The common law used many overlapping and poorly defined terms to describe different states of mind; e.g., MALICE, WANTON, WILLFUL. Most states now have criminal codes that define most crimes in terms of four distinctly defined states of mind signifying successively greater levels of culpability: NEGLIGENCE, RECKLESSNESS, KNOWLEDGE, INTENT. See also STRICT LIABILITY.

state statute. See under STATUTE.

statement *n.* **1.** an oral or written assertion, or nonverbal conduct intended as an assertion. Often interchangeable with DECLARATION, though in most contexts one word is more common than the other. **2.** Also called **financial statement.** a concise and systematic presentation of the financial status of a person or entity. **3.** Also called **statement of account.** a summary of the status of an ACCOUNT, showing the balance due and usually listing recent transactions. **4. closing statement.** See different meanings under CLOSING (def. 1) and SUMMATION. **5. exculpatory statement,** a statement that, if true, tends to exonerate a suspect; e.g., "I was at home watching TV." If such a statement is shown to be untrue (a **false exculpatory statement**), a jury is permitted to look upon it as evidence of guilt, on the dubious theory that an innocent person would have no reason to lie. **6. opening statement.** Same as OPENING. **7. prior inconsistent statement,** an earlier statement by a witness which is inconsistent with the witness's testimony at a trial or hearing. It may be introduced as evidence, not for its truth (since that would violate the rule against HEARSAY), but to impeach the witness's credibility. See also *admissible for a limited purpose* (under ADMISSIBLE). **8. spontaneous statement.** Same as EXCITED UTTERANCE. **9. statement of claim,** a document, or portion of a document, formally setting forth the claim that one is making in a case. **10. statement of the case,** the portion of a brief summarizing the facts rather than arguing the law. Also called **statement of facts.**

state's evidence 1. evidence voluntarily given by

a participant or accomplice in a crime against others involved, usually in exchange for immunity or lenient treatment. A suspect or defendant who agrees to provide such evidence is said to **turn state's evidence. 2.** generally, any evidence offered by the prosecution in a state criminal case.

states' rights a slogan invoked by those who oppose the granting of rights, benefits, and protections to people by FEDERAL LAW, and argue that the various state governments should have the right to set their own standards on such matters as civil rights, environmental protection, and care for the poor. Cf. SUPREMACY.

status quo *Latin.* (lit. "the position in which") **1.** the way things are at the time of speaking: *to preserve the status quo.* **2.** Also called **status quo ante,** with *ante* ("before"). the way things were prior to some specific event in the past: *to restore the status quo (ante).*

statute *n.* a written law enacted by Congress **(federal statute)** or a state legislature **(state statute).** Often called an ACT or a LAW. Cf. COMMON LAW; ORDINANCE; REGULATION; RULE.

statute of frauds a statute requiring certain kinds of contracts to be written, or at least to be memorialized in some writing signed by the party against which the contract is to be enforced. A contract of the specified type is said to be "within" the statute, and if it is adequately memorialized and signed it is said to "satisfy" the statute. The most common kinds of contracts covered by such statutes are agreements to be responsible for someone else's debt, contracts for the sale of land, contracts for the sale of goods above a certain price, and contracts requiring performance more than a year after the making of the contract.

statute of limitations a statute setting the length of time after an event within which a civil or criminal action arising from that event must be brought (the **limitation period, limitations period,** or **statutory period**). Cf. LACHES.

Statutes at Large (abbr. **Stat.**) the official compilation of acts and resolutions of Congress, treaties ratified, constitutional amendments proposed or ratified, and presidential proclamations issued, printed in chronological order for each session of Congress. Although this compilation reproduces federal statutes in the exact form in which Congress enacted them, the organization of the UNITED STATES CODE and the annotations added to it by private publishers make that the preferred version for legal research. *Abbr.:* Stat.

statutory *adj.* **1.** relating to statutes or a statute: *statutory construction* (see under CONSTRUCTION); *statutory period* (see under STATUTE OF LIMITATIONS). **2.** created by or pertaining to statutes rather than the common law: *statutory crime* (see under CRIME). **3.** existing by virtue of a statute, without regard to the intent of the parties involved or any agreement or lack of agreement among them: *statutory rape* (see under RAPE), *statutory share* (same as ELECTIVE SHARE).

stay *n.* **1.** the postponement or temporary suspension of a proceeding or of the legal effect of a statute or court order. **2. automatic stay,** a stay imposed by statute, which takes effect automatically upon the occurrence of some event. **3. stay of execution, a.** a stay preventing a person who has won a money judgment from immediately seizing the judgment debtor's assets, usually to allow the debtor time to appeal. **b.** an order that a prisoner sentenced to death not be put to death just yet. Such an order might be issued either by a court or by the governor of the state; in the latter case, it is commonly called a REPRIEVE. —*v.* **4.** to order or cause a stay.

steal *v.* to obtain money or property by LARCENY or, more broadly, by larceny or other criminal means such as ROBBERY, EMBEZZLEMENT, or FALSE PRETENSES.

stipulation *n.* **1.** a representation or condition spelled out in a contract. **2.** an agreement between opposing lawyers with respect to some procedural step in a case, often altering normal time limits or other procedural requirements for mutual conven-

ience or as a matter of courtesy. Typically such a stipulation will be submitted to the judge to be so ORDERED, which turns it into a **stipulation and order.** See also CONFIDENTIALITY STIPULATION. **3.** an agreement between the parties in a case with respect to a fact or a legal issue, so as to simplify the case by eliminating issues that cannot reasonably be disputed. A fact thus agreed upon is a **stipulated fact,** which must be accepted as true by the judge and jury. See also *stipulated damages* (under DAMAGES). —**stipulate,** *v.*

stirpes. See PER STIRPES.

stock *n.* **1.** a security (see SECURITY²) issued by a CORPORATION or *joint stock company* (see under COMPANY), representing an ownership interest in the issuer. An entity may issue several classes of stock conferring on their owners (called stockholders or shareholders) varying rights with respect to participation in control of the company (through voting for DIRECTORS and on certain company matters), participation in earnings (through DIVIDENDS declared by the directors), and participation in *net assets* (see under ASSET) upon liquidation of the company. The total stock of any class is divided into equal fractional parts (SHARES), varying quantities of which may be held by different owners, who have greater or lesser rights in proportion to the number of shares that they own. **2. assessable stock,** stock whose owners may be required to make additional financial contributions to the issuer if needed. Most stock carries no such obligation, and so is **nonassessable stock. 3. capital stock, a.** broadly, any stock; the totality of a company's stock of all classes. **b.** narrowly, *common stock.* **4. common stock,** the lowest class of stock in a corporation. If the corporation has only one class of stock, it is common stock. In the event of liquidation, the common stockholders divide up anything that is left of the company after all obligations to creditors and preferred stockholders have been satisfied. Cf. *preferred stock.* **5. paid-up stock,** stock for which the corporation has been paid in full. Also called **fully paid stock. 6. preferred stock,** stock conferring preferential rights to dividends or to assets upon liquidation of the corporation, ahead of the rights of common stockholders. Cf. *common stock.* **7. publicly traded stock,** stock that is freely bought and sold among members of the general investing public; stock in a *publicly held corporation* (see under CORPORATION). **8. restricted stock,** stock that may not be transferred to a new owner except upon specified conditions. Stock in a *close corporation* (see under CORPORATION) is often restricted to prevent sale to an outsider who would not fit in with the small group of owners. **9. stock with par value,** a class of stock to which the issuer has assigned a PAR VALUE. Also called **par value stock. 10. stock without par value,** a class of stock to which the issuer has not assigned a par value. Also called **no-par** (or **nonpar**) **stock.**

stock association Same as *joint stock company* (see under COMPANY).

stock certificate an instrument representing a specified number of shares of a specific class of stock in a particular company.

stock manipulation. engaging in *wash sales* of stock (see under SALE) or other conduct in the stock market designed to create a false impression of widespread investor interest in a stock, usually in the hope of driving up the price. Also called **market manipulation.** This is a kind of *securities fraud* (see under FRAUD).

stock option 1. a right to purchase or sell a specified number of shares of a particular stock at a specified price some time in the future. **2.** Also called **employee stock option.** Such an option to purchase stock in a corporation, granted by the corporation to an employee as a form of compensation.

stock warrant. Same as WARRANT².

stockbroker. See under BROKER.

stockholder *n.* an owner of shares of STOCK. Also called **shareholder.**

stockholder derivative action. See under ACTION.

stop *n.* **1.** momentary detention of a person by law enforcement officials, falling short of an ARREST, as at a highway checkpoint for drunk drivers or to question a person acting suspiciously. **2. stop and frisk,** a stop accompanied by a pat-down for weapons. This may be done upon grounds falling somewhat short of PROBABLE CAUSE for arrest or a full search, if the officer can articulate a sound basis for the procedure. —*v.* **3.** to make a stop of a person.

straight bankruptcy. See under BANKRUPTCY.

straight bill of lading. See under BILL OF LADING.

straight life insurance. See under LIFE INSURANCE.

stranger *n.* a person with no legally recognized right or interest in the transaction, proceeding, relationship, or other matter under discussion; an outsider.

street name the name of a firm of stockbrokers acting as *record owner* (see under OWNER) of stock on behalf of one of the firm's customers. Holding stock in street name rather than in the names of individual stockholders facilitates the transfer of stock when it is bought and sold among customers of the various brokerage firms.

strict construction. See under CONSTRUCTION.

strict liability. See under LIABILITY.

strict scrutiny the standard by which the Supreme Court assesses the constitutionality of a law that limits a FUNDAMENTAL RIGHT (such as freedom of speech) or that treats people differently on the basis of a SUSPECT CLASSIFICATION (such as race). Under the strict scrutiny test, a law will be upheld only if it is found to serve a COMPELLING INTEREST of the government and to be "necessary" to the achievement of that interest. See also SCRUTINY. Cf. HEIGHTENED SCRUTINY; RATIONAL BASIS TEST.

strike¹ *n.* **1.** a concerted stopping of work by employees in a company or industry, in support of a demand for higher wayes or better conditions of employment, or in protest of some action of the employer. Cf. LOCKOUT. **2. wildcat strike,** a spontaneous strike not officially authorized by a union. —*v.* **3.** to engage in a strike.

strike² *v.* to delete or nullify words spoken or written or papers submitted in a case. Stricken material is officially disregarded at trial, but normally remains in the record for purposes of appellate review. See discussion under NONRESPONSIVE.

strike suit. See under SUIT.

sua sponte *Latin.* of its (his, her, their) own accord. Said of action taken by a court without being asked to do so by a party. Often expressed in English as **on its (his, her, their) own motion,** although technically a court cannot make a motion to itself: *The court dismissed the action sua sponte* (or *on its own motion*) *for lack of jurisdiction.*

sub judice *Latin.* (lit., "under the judge") submitted to a judge or court (but not to a jury) and awaiting decision. See also SUBMIT.

sub silentio *Latin.* (lit. "under silence") implicitly; without saying so: *The court's holding overruled its prior decision sub silentio.*

subcontract *n.* a contract by which a party who has been engaged to carry out a large project engages someone else (a **subcontractor**) to do some of the work. See also *general contractor* (under CONTRACTOR).

subject matter jurisdiction. See under JURISDICTION¹.

subjective test a legal standard that depends upon what is in someone's mind. For example, legal principles phrased in terms of INTENT, KNOWLEDGE, or GOOD FAITH involve a subjective test. Cf. OBJECTIVE TEST.

sublease *n.* **1.** a LEASE granted by one who is already a lessee of the property. The grantor of a sublease on real property is called the **sublandlord** or **sublessor,** and the person to whom it is granted is the **subtenant** or **sublessee;** in the rare sublease of personal property, only the terms "sublessor" and "sublessee" would be appropriate. —*v.* **2.** to convey, receive, or hold by sublease.

sublet *v.* **1.** to SUBLEASE real property to or from someone. —*n.* **2.** a subleasing arrangement or rela-

tionship with respect to real property, or the property itself.

submit *v.* **1.** to place a matter formally and finally into the hands of the proper body for decision; for example, to submit a case to a jury, a motion to a judge, a dispute to an arbitration panel, or a referendum to the voters. See also SUB JUDICE. **2.** to present evidence and argument to a court solely in writing, without oral argument or testimony. See also *on papers* (under PAPERS). **3. take on submission,** (of a judge or court) to receive or allow only written evidence and argument on a matter to be decided. Cf. HEAR. —**submission,** *n.* —**submitted,** *adj.*

subordinate or **subordinated,** *adj.* lower in priority than a competing right, claim, or claimant. Also called **junior.** Opposite of SENIOR. —**subordination,** *n.*

subornation of perjury the crime of inducing a person to commit PERJURY. The person who commits this crime is said to **suborn** the witness or to **suborn perjury.**

subpoena *n.* **1.** a PROCESS directing a witness to appear and give evidence in a court proceeding. **2. subpoena ad testificandum,** a subpoena requiring the person served to appear and testify. See also AD TESTIFICANDUM. **3. subpoena duces tecum,** a subpoena requiring the person served not only to testify but also to produce specified documents or other physical evidence. See also DUCES TECUM. —*v.* **4.** to serve a subpoena on a person.

subrogate *v.* to substitute a new person for the original claimant with regard to a right or claim. For example, if A's car is damaged in an accident caused by B and A's insurance company pays the repair bill, then the insurance company may take A's place in suing B to recover those expenses; the insurance company is said to be "subrogated to" A's damage claim against B. The original claimant is called the **subrogor;** the substituted claimant is the **subrogee.** —**subrogation,** *n.*

subscribe *n.* **1.** to sign a document, particularly a formal instrument such as a deed, will, or affidavit. **2.** to agree to contribute a certain amount of capital to a corporation in exchange for a certain amount of its stock, or to promise to contribute a certain sum to charity. —**subscription,** *n.*

subsequent. See *condition subsequent* (under CONDITION).

subsidiary *n.* **1.** a corporation more than 50% of whose voting stock is owned by another corporation. Also called **subsidiary corporation.** Cf. PARENT COMPANY. **2. wholly owned subsidiary,** a corporation all of whose voting stock is owned by another corporation.

substance *n.* **1.** the real or underlying nature of a transaction, claim, law, or other matter, as distinguished from its FORM. For example, an exchange of valuable real estate for one dollar is a gift in form, but in substance a gift. **2.** Also called **substantive law.** the entire body of law that establishes and defines those rights and duties that the legal system exists to protect and enforce; distinguished from PROCEDURE. For example, in an automobile accident, the questions of whether a driver was responsible and should pay damages or be fined or imprisoned are matters of substance, whereas the steps that must be gone through to determine responsibility and assess damages or a penalty are matters of procedure. **3.** See CONTROLLED SUBSTANCE. —**substantive,** *adj.*

substantial capacity test the principle that a criminal defendant may establish an INSANITY DEFENSE by showing that as a result of mental disease or defect he lacked "substantial capacity" either to appreciate the wrongfulness of his conduct or to conform his conduct to the requirements of law. This test has been adopted in a substantial number of states.

substantial evidence the STANDARD OF REVIEW usually used by courts in reviewing administrative determinations. It requires considerable deference to the agency, whose decision will be affirmed so long as there was more than a minimal amount of evidence to support it, even if the reviewing court believes that the preponderance of the evidence pointed to the opposite conclusion.

substantial performance performance of a party's obligations under a contract that complies with what was required in all but minor respects; performance in such a way that there has been no *material breach* (see under BREACH).

substantive due process. See under DUE PROCESS.

substantive law. Same as SUBSTANCE (def. 2).

substituted service. See under SERVICE.

subtenant. See under SUBLEASE.

succeed *v.* to take over a right, interest, or duty of another; to take the place of another with respect to some matter: *When Company A was taken over by Company B, Company B succeeded to all the rights and obligations of Company A.*

succession *n.* **1.** broadly, any acquisition or taking over of another's right, interest, or duty. **2.** narrowly, the acquisition of rights or property of another upon the other's death, especially by INTESTATE SUCCESSION.

successor *n.* one who succeeds to the right, interest, or duty of another (the PREDECESSOR). Also called **successor in interest.**

sue *v.* to file a SUIT against a person: *The injured passenger sued. The injured passenger sued the driver.*

sufferance. See *tenancy at sufferance* (under TENANCY).

suicide *n.* killing oneself. Attempted suicide is a crime in some states; aiding and abetting a suicide (making the death what is commonly referred to as an **assisted suicide** or, if a physician renders the assistance, a **physician-assisted suicide**) is a crime in all or virtually all states. See also LIVING WILL.

suit *n.* **1.** a *civil action* (see under ACTION) brought by one person or entity against another. **2. collusive suit,** an improper type of suit in which the parties pretend to be adverse in order to present a hypothetical question to the court or obtain a mutually desired outcome. **3. strike suit,** a disparaging term for a large-scale *class action* or *derivative action* (see under ACTION) that is viewed by the defendants as unfounded and intended solely to induce them to agree to a settlement (usually including payment of attorneys' fees to the plaintiff's attorneys) in order to avoid the expense of litigating the case on the merits.

summary *adj.* describing proceedings conducted in a simplified or abbreviated manner because the issues and circumstances do not require more extended or elaborate treatment; for example, *summary judgment* (see under JUDGMENT). —**summarily,** *adv.*

summation *n.* a lawyer's address to the judge or jury after all evidence has been presented, summarizing the case and attempting to convince them to find in favor of her client. Also called **argument, closing argument, closing statement,** or just **closing.** Cf. OPENING STATEMENT.

summons *n.* a PROCESS directing a defendant to appear in court to answer a civil complaint or a criminal charge.

Sunday closing law a law forbidding certain otherwise legal activities on Sunday. See also BLUE LAW.

sunset law a statute that expires automatically after a certain period of time.

sunshine law a statute requiring that official meetings of governmental agencies be open to the public.

Superior Court the name given in some states to the lowest court of *general jurisdiction* (see under JURISDICTION[1]), and in a few states to the first level of appellate court. Cf. INFERIOR COURT.

supersedeas *Latin.* (lit. "You shall desist.") a stay of execution of a judgment to allow appellate review. See also *supersedeas bond* (under BOND[2]).

supervised visitation. See under VISITATION.

supplemental jurisdiction. See under JURISDICTION[1].

suppress *v.* **1.** (of a court in a criminal case) to prohibit the prosecution from introducing evidence

obtained in violation of the Constitution, such as evidence derived from an unlawful search and seizure or an involuntary confession. See also EXCLUSIONARY RULE; MIRANDA RULE. **2.** (of a party in a civil or criminal case) to withhold evidence that should have been produced. **3. suppression hearing,** a hearing held in advance of a criminal trial to determine whether evidence objected to by the defendant should be suppressed. —**suppression,** *n.*

supra *adv. Latin.* (lit. "above") earlier in the same document. Used particularly in a second or later reference to an authority already cited in full: *In Doe v. Bolton, supra, the court found the law unconstitutional.* Opposite of INFRA.

supremacy *n.* the principle, set forth in the Constitution, that FEDERAL LAW is the "supreme Law of the Land," so that any conflicting state law is invalid.

Supreme Court 1. Short for **Supreme Court of the United States.** The highest court in the federal judicial system, with final say in interpretation of FEDERAL LAW and jurisdiction to resolve controversies between states. Unless the context makes it clear that a state court is being referred to, in American legal writing the phrase "Supreme Court" always means the Supreme Court of the United States. **2.** in most states, the highest court of the state, with final say in the interpretation of state law. In some states, the highest court has a different name or there may be more than one highest court handling different types of cases; in at least one state (New York) the Supreme Court is the lowest court of general jurisdiction, equivalent to what some states call the SUPERIOR COURT. **3.** (*l.c.*) loosely, the highest court of any jurisdiction: *The final authority on interpretation of state law is the state's supreme court.*

surety *n.* a person who joins in a contract as a co-obligor in order to assure the obligee of an additional (usually more creditworthy) source for performance of the obligation. For example, when an automobile dealer insists that a young buyer get her father's signature on a car loan contract, the father becomes a surety; the daughter is called the **principal obligor** or **principal debtor,** or simply the **principal,** but the dealer (the **creditor** or **obligee**) may look to either the principal or the surety for payment.

surety bond. See under BOND[2].

suretyship *n.* **1.** strictly, the three-way contract or relationship among a SURETY, a principal obligor, and their obligee. **2.** broadly, any arrangement or undertaking by which one becomes answerable for the debt, default, or miscarriage of another, including a GUARANTY (def. 1). See also GUARANTY (def. 2).

suretyship bond. See under BOND[2].

surrebuttal *n.* **1.** the presentation of evidence or argument in response to a REBUTTAL. **2.** specifically, a *surrebuttal case* (see under CASE[2]). —*adj.* **3.** presented in response to a rebuttal: *surrebuttal case; surrebuttal argument.*

surreply brief. See under BRIEF.

Surrogate *n.* in some states, the title given (instead of Judge or Justice) to the judge of a probate court or other court dealing with decedents' estates.

surrogate mother a woman who bears a child for a couple when the wife is unable to do so, having agreed to relinquish parental rights to the couple upon the birth of the child. The child is usually conceived with the husband's sperm, either through artificial insemination of the surrogate mother or through in vitro fertilization of an egg from the wife, which is then implanted in the surrogate mother's uterus. As a general rule, courts and state legislatures have not been supportive of such arrangements.

surveillance *n.* **1.** covert monitoring of a person's movements and activities or of people and activities at a specific location, especially by law enforcement authorities; often includes EAVESDROPPING. **2. electronic surveillance,** the use of video cameras, radio transmitters, and other electronic devices in surveillance. See also *electronic eavesdropping* (under EAVESDROPPING); WIRETAP.

survive *v.* of a cause of action, to remain in existence ("alive") after the death of the plaintiff or de-

legal

fendant. At common law, most tort claims did not survive the death of either the injured party or the tortfeasor; most states have adopted "survival statutes" permitting most such actions to continue, with a representative of the decedent's estate substituted for the decedent as a party. —**survival,** *n.*

survivorship. See RIGHT OF SURVIVORSHIP.

suspect classification a law's CLASSIFICATION of people into categories regarded by the Supreme Court as requiring STRICT SCRUTINY under the EQUAL PROTECTION clause of the Constitution. So far, the only classifications deemed to merit this highest level of SCRUTINY are those based on race, ethnicity, national origin, and ALIENAGE. Cf. QUASI-SUSPECT CLASSIFICATION.

suspended sentence. See under SENTENCE.

sustain *v.* **1.** to rule favorably upon: *The court sustained the objection (the motion, the appeal).* **2.** to satisfy: *The plaintiff sustained her burden of proof.* **3.** to justify; to warrant: *The evidence sustained the verdict.*

swear *v.* **1.** to take an OATH or state under oath. Sworn statements are subject to the penalties for FALSE SWEARING and PERJURY. In its narrow and traditional sense, swearing is an explicit or implicit invocation of God; in a loose sense, it is simply a solemn promise or statement (backed up by the law of

perjury), and so includes affirming (see under AFFIRM[1]). To avoid religious implications that are offensive both to some very religious and to some nonreligious people, the word "affirm" may always be used instead of "swear." See also SWEAR OR AFFIRM. **2.** (sometimes followed by *in*) to administer an oath to a person: *swear the witness; swear in the new Chief Justice.* **3. swearing contest,** *Slang.* a situation in which the only evidence on an issue in a case is the conflicting testimony of opposing witnesses, each of whom swears (or affirms) that his version is correct and the opposing version is a lie.

swear or affirm a phrase used to avoid the religious issues raised by the use of SWEAR alone: *Do you swear or affirm that the testimony you give will be the truth, the whole truth, and nothing but the truth?* The Constitution requires that the President of the United States take an oath or affirmation that begins: "I do solemnly swear (or affirm) that I will faithfully execute the Office of President... " See also OATH OR AFFIRMATION.

syllabus *n.* a brief summary of the facts and holdings in a case, prepared or authorized by the court and printed at the top of the court's opinion for the convenience of readers, but not forming part of the official opinion. Cf. HEADNOTE.

symbolic speech. See under SPEECH.

a b c d e f g h i j k l m n o p q r s **T** u v w x y z

take on submission. See under SUBMIT.

take the stand. See under STAND.

taking *n.* **1.** the act of a state or federal government in depriving a property owner of the use of her property in order to serve a public purpose; an exercise of the power of EMINENT DOMAIN. This may occur through a formal proceeding to take title to the land and oust the owner, or by any law or government activity that substantially destroys the usefulness or economic value of the land. If a taking has occurred, the property owner has a constitutional right to JUST COMPENSATION. **2. regulatory taking,** a statute or regulation that destroys the value of land and thus amounts to a taking.

tangible property. See under PROPERTY.

tax *n.* **1.** a sum of money required to be paid to the federal, state, or local government for the support of government activities and services to the public at large; distinguished from a fee (see FEE[2]) in that taxes are collected from a broad class of persons without regard to their use of a particular government service or exercise of a particular privilege. **2. flat tax,** a tax, particularly an INCOME TAX, set at a fixed percentage of the amount being taxed, so that those with low taxable incomes are taxed at the same rate as those with high incomes. Most so-called "flat tax" proposals, however, would tax only earned income (primarily wages), and make unearned income (interest, dividends, capital gains) entirely exempt from income taxes. Since the rich derive a much higher proportion of their income from investments than do people of ordinary means, the overall effect of many such proposals would actually be regressive, not "flat." **3. progressive tax,** a tax with rates that increase as the amount subject to the tax increases, so that taxpayers with more money pay proportionately higher taxes. The basic design of the federal income tax has traditionally been progressive, at least in theory, although over a 30-year period beginning in the 1960's the top marginal tax rate—the rate paid on the top portion of the taxable income of taxpayers with the very highest incomes—has been lowered over and over again, from 91 percent to less than 40 percent, making the system much "flatter" than was contemplated when the current Internal Revenue Code was adopted in 1954. See also TAX

BRACKET; TAX RATE. **4. regressive tax,** a tax structured so that the effective tax rate decreases as income or value of the kind subject to the tax increases (e.g., the SOCIAL SECURITY TAX), or any other tax whose practical effect is to tax the poor more heavily in proportion to their incomes than the rich (e.g., the SALES TAX). —*v.* **5.** to impose a tax on or by reason of: *to tax an individual or corporation; to tax income, imports, or property.* **6.** to require the losing party to pay the winner's COSTS in a court case: *costs were taxed to the plaintiff.* See also *ad valorem tax* (under AD VALOREM); *capital gains tax* (under CAPITAL[1]); DUTY (def. 2); ESTATE TAX; ESTIMATED TAX; EXCISE; FRANCHISE TAX; *generation-skipping transfer tax* (under GENERATION-SKIPPING TRUST); GIFT TAX; IMPOST; INCOME TAX; INHERITANCE TAX; PAYROLL TAX; POLL TAX; PROPERTY TAX; SALES TAX; SELF-EMPLOYMENT TAX; SOCIAL SECURITY TAX; STAMP TAX; USE TAX; VALUE ADDED TAX; WITHHOLDING TAX.

tax avoidance the structuring of transactions and choosing of options in filling out tax forms so as to minimize one's taxes by lawful means. Cf. TAX EVASION; TAX FRAUD.

tax bracket an income range to which a specific TAX RATE is applied for income tax purposes. In a progressive income tax structure (see *progressive tax,* under TAX), the portion of a taxpayer's taxable income that falls within the lowest bracket is taxed at the lowest rate, and the portions in higher brackets are taxed at successively higher rates. A taxpayer is said to be "in the X% bracket" if the highest bracket into which her income reaches is taxed at the indicated rate; it does *not* mean that the taxpayer's entire taxable income is taxed at that rate. See also *marginal tax rate* and *effective tax rate* (under TAX RATE).

tax credit a reduction in a tax allowed to certain classes of taxpayers for reasons of public policy. A tax credit is a direct subtraction from the tax itself, in contrast to an income tax DEDUCTION, which only reduces the income upon which the tax is calculated and so has less impact on the actual tax bill.

tax evasion the crime of contriving in any way not to pay the amount that one is legally obligated to pay in taxes. Cf. TAX AVOIDANCE.

tax exempt 1. not required to pay taxes: *Qualified charitable organizations are tax exempt.* See also *qualify for tax-exempt status* (under QUALIFY[1]). **2. a.**

not taxable to the recipient or owner: *tax-exempt interest; tax-exempt property.* **b.** producing income that is not taxable: *tax-exempt municipal bonds.*

tax fraud the crime of intentionally filing a false tax return or making other false statements under penalties of perjury to taxing authorities. Cf. TAX AVOIDANCE.

tax free *Informal.* Same as TAX EXEMPT (def. 2).

tax lien. See under LIEN.

tax rate **1.** the percentage of taxable income or of the value of taxable property that must be paid as tax. **2. effective tax rate,** the actual percentage of one's taxable income that is owed as income taxes; in a progressive tax system, this is always lower than the *marginal tax rate* except for taxpayers in the lowest income bracket, because all taxable income below the taxpayer's top bracket is taxed at less than the marginal rate. **3. marginal tax rate,** in a progressive income tax system, the tax rate applicable to the portion of a taxpayer's income that exceeds the threshold for that taxpayer's top tax bracket. Cf. *effective tax rate.* See also *progressive tax* (under TAX); TAX BRACKET.

tax return. See under RETURN.

tax sale. See under SALE.

tax shelter an investment or other financial arrangement that serves to reduce taxes or to generate both income and offsetting deductions and credits so as to minimize tax on the income.

taxable *adj.* subject to being taxed: *taxable income* (see under INCOME); *taxable property; taxable gain; taxable costs.*

temporary remedy (or **relief**). See under REMEDY.

temporary restraining order (TRO). See under RESTRAINING ORDER.

tenancy *n.* **1.** broadly, any *possessory estate* in real property, including *tenancy in fee* and *life tenancy.* (See all three phrases under ESTATE¹.) A tenancy may be designated as BY THE ENTIRETY, IN COMMON, IN SEVERALTY, or JOINT, depending upon the ownership arrangement. **2.** specifically, a LEASEHOLD or landlord-tenant relationship. See defs. 3, 5, and 6 for types of leasehold. **3. periodic tenancy** (or **estate**), a tenancy which runs for successive fixed periods of time such as a month or a year, continuing indefinitely but terminable at will by either the landlord or the tenant upon reasonable notice at the end of any period. Also called **month-to-month tenancy, tenancy** (or **estate**) **from year to year,** or the like. **4. tenancy** (or **estate**) **at sufferance,** the interest of a person who wrongfully continues to occupy property after the right to possession has ended; this is not a real tenancy or estate because it is not a possessory interest. Also called **holdover tenancy.** **5. tenancy** (or **estate**) **at will,** a tenancy of indefinite duration terminable by either the landlord or the tenant upon reasonable notice at any time. **6. tenancy** (or **estate**) **for years,** tenancy for a specific length of time, not necessarily measured in years; for example, a one-week tenancy. Also called a **term of years.**

tenant *n.* a holder of a TENANCY; a person with a present right to possession of real property, especially the holder of a LEASEHOLD. A tenant is designated as a *periodic tenant, tenant in common, tenant in fee,* etc., according to the nature of the tenancy; see classifications under TENANCY and ESTATE¹. See also *holdover tenant* (under HOLD). Cf. LANDLORD.

tenantable *adj.* (of leased premises) in sufficiently good repair to be usable for the intended purpose. In the case of a residential lease, "tenantable" is the same thing as HABITABLE.

tender *v.* **1.** to offer something formally, in a way that makes it clear that the thing offered will be given, done, or effective immediately upon acceptance: *to tender payment; to tender performance; to tender one's resignation.* —*n.* **2.** the act of tendering or the thing tendered. See also LEGAL TENDER.

tender offer a public offer to buy up a specified amount of stock in a particular corporation at a particular price if shares are tendered by the current stockholders on or before a particular date, made in an effort to take over control of the corporation.

tender years extreme youthfulness: *a child of tender years.*

tenement *n.* **1.** any property of a permanent nature, especially an interest in land. **2.** a run-down or overcrowded apartment house in a poor section of a city.

tenor *n.* **1.** the exact words or terms of an instrument: *The defendant offered a compromise, but the plaintiff seeks to enforce the contract according to its tenor.* **2.** the general meaning or course of thought in an informal communication: *The tenor of our conversation was that there is still ground for compromise.*

term *n.* **1.** a specific, finite period of time during which an agreement is operative or an interest remains good, or at the end of which an obligation matures: *the term of a lease; the term of a bond.* **2.** (of a court) **a.** the period of time during which the court has sessions: *The October Term of the Supreme Court runs from October to June.* **b.** in some courts, a sitting of the court for a particular type of business: *trial term.* **3.** a portion of an instrument dealing with a certain matter, or the provision it makes for a particular matter: *The contract includes a cancellation term permitting either party to terminate the arrangement on 60 days' notice.* **4.** a word or phrase. See also TERM OF ART. —*adj.* **5.** lasting only for a specified term or maturing at a specified time: *term insurance; term loan.*

term life insurance or **term insurance.** See under LIFE INSURANCE.

term of art a word or phrase having a special meaning in a particular field, different from or more precise than its customary meaning.

term of years. Same as *tenancy* (or *estate*) *for years* (see under TENANCY).

terms and conditions all of the provisions of a contract or other instrument; another way of saying "terms."

terrorem. See IN TERROREM.

test case. See under CASE¹.

testament *n.* a WILL. In previous centuries, sometimes a technical distinction was drawn between "will" and "testament." In modern usage, " "testament" is almost never used except in the phrase LAST WILL AND TESTAMENT.

testamentary *adj.* **1.** pertaining to a will or wills: *The will was declared void because the decedent lacked testamentary capacity.* **2.** established or accomplished by will: *testamentary gift* (see under GIFT); *testamentary guardian* (see under GUARDIAN); *testamentary trust* (see under TRUST). Cf. INTER VIVOS.

testator *n.* a person, especially a man, who makes a will. When the maker of a will is a woman, it is still usual to refer to her by the old-fashioned word **testatrix.**

testify *v.* to give evidence under oath or affirmation at a trial, hearing, or deposition.

testimonial privilege. See under PRIVILEGE.

testimony *n.* statements made under oath or affirmation by a witness at a trial, hearing, or deposition.

theft *n.* a broad term for crimes involving the wrongful taking or keeping of money or property of another. The exact scope of the term varies from state to state, but it typically includes LARCENY, FALSE PRETENSES, EXTORTION, EMBEZZLEMENT, and RECEIVING STOLEN PROPERTY, but not ROBBERY, BURGLARY, or FORGERY.

thing in action. Same as CHOSE IN ACTION.

third party a person who is not a party—or at least not initially or directly a party—to a transaction, proceeding, or other matter under discussion, but who may be affected by it: *The court considered the potential effect of its injunction on third parties.*

third-party *adj.* **1.** involving or pertaining to a third party, or to a *third-party action.* See also *third-party beneficiary contract* and *third-party beneficiary* (under CONTRACT). **2. third-party action,** an action by which the defendant in a civil case files a complaint against a person who was not initially a party to the case, claiming a right of INDEMNITY or CONTRIBUTION from that third party in the event that the defendant is found liable to the plaintiff. The third-party action is an extension of the main action, and the issues in both actions are litigated together in one big case. See also IMPLEAD.

three strikes law a law providing for life imprisonment for anyone convicted of a third crime of a particular type; for example, a third violent crime.

through bill of lading. See under BILL OF LADING.

ticket *n.* **1.** a piece of paper evidencing a contractual right to goods or services: *movie ticket; pawn ticket.* **2.** a simple form of SUMMONS or CITATION issued for minor traffic and motor vehicle violations.

time *adj.* **1.** lasting until, maturing on, or payable only on or after, a specific date in the future; not payable on demand: *time loan; time instrument.* See also *time draft* (under DRAFT). Cf. *payable on demand* (under DEMAND). **2. time deposit,** money deposited with a bank which the depositor does not have the right to withdraw until a specific length of time has passed; for example, an account represented by an ordinary CERTIFICATE OF DEPOSIT. Cf. *demand deposit* (under DEMAND).

time is of the essence. See under OF THE ESSENCE.

time, place, and manner, a phrase describing the kinds of restrictions that a government may place on SPEECH without violating the First Amendment. Restrictions may be placed on the time, place, and manner of speech if they are narrowly tailored to serve legitimate governmental interests and are not based on the content of the speech. For example, to prevent chaos a city may prohibit marching in the streets without a parade permit, but the granting or denial of a permit may not depend upon the message the marchers seek to convey.

title *n.* **1.** ownership of property, or of a *possessory interest* (see under INTEREST¹) in property; the right to possess or control possession of property. **2.** *Informal.* a document evidencing such ownership, such as a DEED or BILL OF SALE or, especially, a CERTIFICATE OF TITLE (defs. 1 and 2). **3.** a portion of a statute or codification: *Employment discrimination is prohibited by Title VII of the Civil Rights Act of 1964.* See also UNITED STATES CODE. **4. defective title,** title that, because of a gap in records or for some other reason, is too uncertain to qualify as *marketable title.* Also called **bad title** or **unmarketable title. 5. equitable title, a.** the ownership interest of a person who has a right to have title conveyed to her but to whom legal title has not yet been formally conveyed, especially a person who has entered into a specifically enforceable contract to purchase land but has not yet received the deed. **b.** the right of the beneficiary of a trust with respect to trust property of which the trustee is the legal owner. Cf. *legal title.* **6. insurable title,** title that a reputable insurance company would be willing to insure. Insurable title may contain minor defects that would make it unmarketable, but that are too remote to cause an insurance company to refuse to insure it. See also TITLE INSURANCE. **7. legal title,** actual title to property as recognized under traditional principles of law without consideration of equitable rights, including a seller's title in land as to which a deed has not yet been delivered to the buyer, and a trustee's title to property held in trust for the benefit of another. Cf. *equitable title;* EQUITABLE DISTRIBUTION. **8. marketable title,** title that is free of any reasonable risk of successful challenge by an outsider claiming *paramount title* to the same property. Also called **clear title, good title,** or **merchantable title.** If a person who has contracted to sell land proves unable to deliver marketable title, the purchaser ordinarily may cancel the deal. **9. paramount title,** as between competing claims to possession of the same property, the superior claim. A person in possession of real property may be evicted only by one with paramount title; for example, although a holdover tenant has no right to possession of the premises, he cannot be evicted by an outsider who has no better right, but can be evicted by the landlord. **10. Torrens title system.** Same as TITLE REGISTRATION SYSTEM. See also ABSTRACT OF TITLE; CHAIN OF TITLE; CLOUD ON TITLE; COLOR; *covenants* (or *warranties*) *of title* (under COVENANT); DOCUMENT OF TITLE; *try title* (under TRY); QUIET TITLE; *warranty of title* (under WARRANTY).

title insurance insurance purchased by a buyer of real estate to protect herself or the bank that is taking a mortgage on the property from loss due to previously unrecognized encumbrances on the property or competing claims to title. See also TITLE RECORDING SYSTEM.

title recording system the only mechanism made available by most state governments for keeping track of ownership of real estate. It consists of a public office in which copies of documents affecting title to land—such as deeds and mortgages—may be (but often are not) filed. To attempt to determine the status of title to a parcel, one must hire someone familiar with these records to do a TITLE SEARCH. But since the system is too haphazard to be reliable, anyone actually spending or lending money for the land must also purchase TITLE INSURANCE to be protected from loss due to unexpected claims or encumbrances upon the land. Cf. TITLE REGISTRATION SYSTEM.

title registration system an alternative to the TITLE RECORDING SYSTEM made available in a few states, under which title to land can be registered in a state or local government office and evidenced by an official certificate (see CERTIFICATE OF TITLE, def. 2), which is conclusive evidence of title for most purposes. Also called **Torrens title system.**

title search the process of searching through public records in an effort to assess the status of a claimed title to real property by tracing the CHAIN OF TITLE, noting mortgages or other encumbrances on the property, and the like. See also TITLE RECORDING SYSTEM.

TM an abbreviation indicating that the word or design it accompanies is claimed or sought to be established as a TRADEMARK, although it is not a *registered trademark* (see under TRADEMARK). Cf. ®.

to the order of. See under ORDER².

toll *v.* to suspend the running of the STATUTE OF LIMITATIONS under circumstances where the law recognizes that a plaintiff or prosecutor was prevented, through no fault of her own, from commencing an action. One speaks of circumstances that "toll the statute" or "toll the limitations period."

Torrens title system. Same as TITLE REGISTRATION SYSTEM.

tort *n.* **1.** a wrongful act, other than a breach of contract, that results in injury to another's person, property, reputation, or some other legally protected right or interest, and for which the injured party is entitled to a remedy at law, usually in the form of damages. **2. constitutional tort,** unconstitutional conduct by a public official causing injury to a private individual. The Supreme Court has held that under certain constitutional provisions—notably the Fourth Amendment ban on unreasonable searches and seizures—a person harmed by offical conduct in violation of her constitutional rights may sue the official for damages. **3. intentional tort,** a tort committed by one who intends by his action to bring about a wrongful result or knows that that result is substantially certain to occur; e.g., BATTERY or TRESPASS. Cf. NEGLIGENCE; STRICT LIABILITY. —**tortious,** *adj.*

tortfeasor *n.* **1.** a person or entity that commits a tort. **2. joint tortfeasor,** one of a number of individuals or entities whose tortious conduct contributed to an injury.

total breach. See under BREACH.

toto. See IN TOTO.

Totten trust. See under TRUST.

trade regulation the body of law that deals with government regulation of competitive business activities; it includes ANTITRUST law and laws dealing with unfair competition, false advertising, and the like.

trade secret confidential information used in a company's business, such as a secret formula or process or a database of client information, that gives the company an advantage over competitors and would be helpful to competitors if they learned of it. Trade secrets are valuable property of a company and courts are very protective of them.

trade union 1. broadly, a labor UNION of any kind. **2.** narrowly, a *craft union* (see under UNION).

trade usage. See under USAGE.

trademark *n.* a name, symbol, or other MARK used by a company to identify its products and distinguish them from goods produced or sold by others. Such a mark may be registered with the United States Patent and Trademark Office, making it a **registered trademark;** unless the registrant's right to use the mark is successfully challenged within five years after registration, the registrant normally has the exclusive right to use the mark from then on. See also **Ⓡ**.

transaction of business any activity of a corporation within a particular state or having an impact within the state. Such transaction of business provides a sufficient basis for a court to exercise jurisdiction over the corporation in a suit arising out of that specific activity, even if the corporation does not engage in regular activity in that state and thus is not generally subject to suit there. Cf. DOING BUSINESS.

transactional immunity. See under IMMUNITY.

travel. See RIGHT TO TRAVEL.

treason *n.* **1.** the crime of committing acts of war against the United States or intentionally giving aid and comfort to its enemies. See also OVERT ACT. **2. high treason,** in early English law, treason against the Crown, as distinguished from "petty treason," which included a wife's killing of her husband or a servant's killing of his master.

treatise *n.* a book or, especially, a multivolume work, systematically and exhaustively discussing and analyzing an area of law, such as contracts, evidence, or federal procedure. Treatises are a major research tool for lawyers and are often cited as authority by judges. See also HORNBOOK.

treaty *n.* a formal agreement between two or more nations on matters of international concern. Treaties of the United States are negotiated by the President and ratified by a two-thirds vote of the Senate. They are part of FEDERAL LAW and thus supersede any contrary state law and any prior federal statute; but Congress may negate or abrogate a treaty simply by refusing to enact any necessary implementing legislation or by enacting a subsequent statute inconsistent with the treaty. See also EXECUTIVE AGREEMENT.

treble damages. See under DAMAGES.

trespass *n.* **1.** Also called **trespass to land.** intentional or knowing conduct that directly results in invasion of land possessed by another, such as walking on it without permission, chopping down a tree onto it, tunneling under it, shooting a bullet over it, or staying on it after being asked to leave. Trespass is a tort against the person entitled to exclusive possession of the land. **2. criminal trespass,** the crime of entering or remaining upon another's land, structure, or vehicle after being notified (orally or by posting of signs or enclosure with fencing) to keep out or to leave. **3. trespass to chattels,** the tort of intentionally interfering with another's possession of goods, as by using, moving, or damaging the property. This tort is confined to relatively minor interference; serious interference with personal property is regarded as CONVERSION. —*v.* **4.** to commit a trespass.

trial *n.* **1.** the procedure by which evidence is presented in court under the supervision of a judge and the ultimate factual issues in a case are decided. **2. bench trial,** a trial in which no jury is present and all factual issues are decided by the judge. Also called **nonjury trial; judge trial;** trial (or **by) the court. 3. de novo trial,** a new trial, granted by the trial judge or ordered by an appellate court in a case because of some error or injustice in the first trial. Also called **trial de novo; retrial;** or simply a new trial. See also DE NOVO. **4. jury trial,** a trial in which the facts are determined by a JURY. Under the Sixth Amendment (see Appendix), state or federal criminal defendants facing potential sentences in excess of six months' imprisonment are

entitled to demand a jury trial. The Seventh Amendment (see Appendix) gives litigants in the federal courts a right of jury trial in civil damage actions that would have been submitted to a jury in traditional common law courts; in the state courts, juries in civil actions are usually allowed by state law but are not required by the United States Constitution. Also called **trial by jury. 5. public trial,** a trial open to observation by members of the public. The Sixth Amendment (see Appendix) gives state and federal criminal defendants the right to such a trial, and in 1980 the Supreme Court held that the First Amendment gives the press and public a general right to attend such proceedings. However, proceedings may be closed in rare cases in which a judge finds an overriding interest such as protection of a juvenile witness, and cameras may be banned from the courtroom. **6. speedy trial,** a criminal trial commencing without unreasonable delay after arrest or indictment. The Sixth Amendment guarantees this right, and all jurisdictions have statutes or court rules setting standards for moving criminal cases to trial in a timely fashion.

trial brief. See under BRIEF.

trial by ambush *Informal.* a disparaging term for trial procedures or strategies that involve withholding relevant information from the other side and then presenting it under circumstances in which the other side does not have a reasonable opportunity to investigate and rebut it. Modern procedural rules, especially those providing for DISCOVERY, seek to minimize opportunities for trial by ambush. Also called **trial by surprise.**

tribunal *n.* any court or body established to decide disputes: *administrative tribunal; disciplinary tribunal; judicial tribunal.*

trier of fact the person or group charged with deciding the factual issues in a proceeding; the jury in a jury trial or judge in a nonjury trial. Also called **factfinder.**

TRO. See *temporary restraining order* (under RESTRAINING ORDER).

true bill. See under BILL.

trust *n.* **1.** an arrangement in which one person (the TRUSTEE) holds property for the benefit of another (the BENEFICIARY or CESTUI QUE TRUST), to whom the trustee owes a FIDUCIARY DUTY in regard to the safeguarding, management, and disposition of the trust property and income. See also *breach of trust* (under BREACH). **2.** broadly, any FIDUCIARY RELATIONSHIP. **3.** a cartel or other monopolistic business arrangement or enterprise. This is the kind of trust for which the ANTITRUST laws were named. **4. blind trust,** a trust in which assets of a public official are managed without disclosing to the official (who is the beneficiary) how they are invested; established to minimize CONFLICTS OF INTEREST. **5. business trust,** an unincorporated association serving the same general purposes as a business corporation and subject to the same taxes, but organized as a trust. Instead of shareholders it has beneficiaries, whose investments constitute the trust property and are usually represented by transferrable certificates. Also called **Massachusetts trust** or **Massachusetts business trust. 6. constructive trust,** a trust that arises by OPERATION OF LAW, without any intention by the parties to create a trust, when through fraud, duress, mistake, or the like, property, or legal title to property, falls into the hands of a person who has no right to it. Under principles of EQUITY, the person with the property is deemed to hold it in trust for the person who should have received it, with an obligation to turn it over in full and intact. See also IMPRESS. **7. express trust,** a trust established intentionally (unlike a *constructive trust*) and explicitly (unlike a *resulting trust*). It may be created orally, but usually is set up in a written TRUST INSTRUMENT, by which the person setting it up (the grantor or donor or settlor) transfers property to the trustee with instructions as to how and for whose benefit it is to be managed and used. **8. grantor trust,** a trust in which the grantor conveys property to a trustee to be held or managed for the grantor's own benefit; for example, a *blind trust.* **9. in trust,** sub-

legal

ject to a trust: *He left $100,000 to his brother in trust for his brother's children, to be distributed to them when they reach the age of 21.* **10. inter vivos trust,** a trust established and effective during the grantor's lifetime. Also called **living trust.** Cf. *testamentary trust.* **11. resulting trust,** a trust inferred from a transaction or conduct of a sort that normally evidences an intent that property in the hands of one person be held for the benefit of another. **12. spendthrift trust,** a trust created to provide some income to the beneficiary while preventing both the beneficiary and the beneficiary's creditors from having access to the money or property held in trust except to the extent that the trustee doles it out. **13. testamentary trust,** a trust established by will or taking effect only upon the grantor's death. Cf. *inter vivos trust.* **14. Totten trust,** a bank account in which a beneficiary is named to receive any funds that happen to be left in the account if the account holder dies. Although the beneficiary is said to be "in trust for" the beneficiary, no trust arises so long as the account holder remains alive. **15. voting trust,** an arrangement by which a number of shareholders in a corporation transfer their voting stock to a trustee for a period of time to hold and vote in accordance with an agreement among them, thereby concentrating their voting power and avoiding dissension.

trust deed. Same as a DEED OF TRUST.

trust indenture. See under INDENTURE.

trust instrument an instrument creating a TRUST, such as a *trust indenture* (see under INDENTURE), dec-

laration of trust (see under DECLARATION), DEED OF TRUST, or will. The instrument must identify the trust property, the trustee, and the beneficiaries and state the terms of the trust.

trustee *n.* **1.** the person who holds the property in a trust and administers it for the benefit of the beneficiaries. **2.** very loosely, anyone with a FIDUCIARY DUTY to another. **3. bankruptcy trustee,** a person appointed by a court to administer the property of a debtor. Also called **trustee in bankruptcy. 4. constructive trustee,** the person in possession of property subject to a *constructive trust* (see under TRUST).

try *v.* **1.** (of a judge) to conduct the trial of a case, either with or without a jury. **2.** (of a lawyer) **a.** to present or defend a case in court, through witnesses and other evidence. **b. try to the court** (or **to the judge**), to try a case without a jury. **c. try to a jury,** to try a case with a jury. **3. try title,** to test the validity of title to property in a judicial proceeding.

turn state's evidence. See under STATE'S EVIDENCE.

Twinkie defense the popular name given to the defense raised by the assassin of two San Francisco government officials in the 1970's. The jury accepted the killer's argument that eating junk food had corrupted his mind, and convicted him of involuntary manslaughter instead of murder. The defense has become a symbol of what many regard as the inventiveness of attorneys in devising excuses for criminal conduct and the credulousness of juries in accepting them.

a b c d e f g h i j k l m n o p q r s t **UV** w x y z

ultimate fact. See under FACT.

ultra vires *Latin.* (lit. "beyond the powers") describing an act that is beyond the scope of authority of the actor, especially an action taken by a corporation that is not authorized by its articles of incorporation. Under traditional doctrine, any ultra vires contract or other act of a corporation was void. Modern articles of incorporation typically authorize the corporation to do "anything a natural person might do," making ultra vires corporate acts almost impossible.

ultrahazardous activity. Same as ABNORMALLY DANGEROUS ACTIVITY.

unanimous opinion. See under OPINION.

unavailable witness. See under WITNESS.

unclean hands 1. the quality of having acted unfairly in regard to the very matter with respect to which one is seeking relief in court. Cf. CLEAN HANDS. **2.** the doctrine, derived from England's courts of EQUITY, that one who comes into court complaining of another's unfairness will be denied relief unless he himself acted fairly in the matter; expressed in such maxims as: "He who seeks equity must come into court with clean hands." Referred to equally as the **clean hands doctrine** and the **unclean hands doctrine. 3.** a defense often raised in response to claims for *equitable relief* (see under REMEDY), based upon the plaintiff's own improper and unjust conduct in the matter. Referred to as the **unclean hands defense** or somewhat less commonly as the **clean hands defense.** See also IN PARI DELICTO.

unconscionability *n.* the doctrine that a contract that is so unfair and one-sided as to "shock the conscience of the court" need not be enforced by the court. The doctrine is most often applied to consumer transactions in which the court believes that the consumer was taken advantage of. See also *adhesion contract* (under CONTRACT); BARGAINING POWER. **—unconscionable,** *adj.*

unconstitutional *adj.* **1.** in conflict with some provision of a constitution; said particularly of state or federal statutes that violate the United States Constitution. Cf. CONSTITUTIONAL. **2. unconstitu-**

tional (or **invalid**) **as applied,** unconstitutional in its impact upon a specific individual or class of individuals, but otherwise enforceable. For example, a public school dress code prohibiting the wearing of hats in class might be held unconstitutional as applied to children whose religions require head covering. **3. unconstitutional** (or **invalid**) **on its face,** unconstitutional in its entirety and hence not enforceable at all. **—unconstitutionality,** *n.*

uncontrollable impulse test. Same as IRRESISTIBLE IMPULSE TEST.

under color of law (of improper conduct by a state official) with the appearance of legal authority; in actual or purported performance of one's duties as a state official. In some circumstances the phrase also applies to private conduct that is specifically authorized or approved by state law. Under the Civil Rights Act of 1871, anyone who has been deprived of federal civil rights under color of state law may sue the wrongdoer.

under protest an expression signifying that in complying with some demand or performing some action one is not conceding that the action is legally required and reserves the right to contest the issue in court. A particularly common example is the payment of a tax bill under protest, in order to preserve the right to question its amount or validity while avoiding penalties for late payment should the tax be upheld.

under seal. See *contract under seal* (under CONTRACT); *instrument under seal* (under SEAL¹).

under the influence. See DRIVING WHILE INTOXICATED.

underage *adj.* describing a person who has not yet reached the minimum age set by law for a specified activity, such as consumption of alcohol or engaging in sexual activity. See also *statutory rape* (under RAPE); AGE.

undersigned *n., adj.* a term used in the body of a document to designate the person or persons whose signatures appear at the end. This expression is commonly used in preprinted form contracts to refer to anyone who might sign them.

understanding *n.* **1.** an agreement, particularly a

somewhat informal or preliminary one. It may or may not be sufficiently definite to be enforceable as a contract. See also INDEFINITE; *memorandum of understanding* (under MEMORANDUM). **2.** a party's interpretation of a contract term. If one party's understanding differs from another's, a court may have to interpret the contract.

undertaking *n.* **1.** a bond (see BOND²), PLEDGE, or promise given to guarantee performance or indemnify another against loss. **2.** any contractual or noncontractual promise.

underwrite *v.* **1.** to provide insurance; to guarantee payment under an insurance policy: *to underwrite insurance; underwrite an insurance policy.* **2.** to guarantee that an entire issue of securities will be sold, either by assisting in their sale to the public and agreeing to purchase any that remain unsold, or by buying up the entire issue for resale to the public: *to underwrite securities; underwrite an issue of securities.* —**underwriter,** *n.*

undisclosed principal. See under PRINCIPAL.

undivided interest or **undivided fractional interest.** See under INTEREST¹.

undocumented alien. See under ALIEN.

undue influence the use of a position of power or trust to induce a person to enter into a transaction that does not reflect his true wishes, or that he would not have entered into if given unbiased advice. This is a ground for rescinding or refusing to enforce wills, gifts, and contracts.

unearned income. See under INCOME.

unemployment compensation weekly payments made for a limited period of time to most workers who lose their jobs through no fault of their own, provided under a system of insurance (**unemployment insurance**) established by state law.

unethical *adj.* contrary to the generally accepted standards of honesty and fairness in the conduct of one's business or profession. **Unethical conduct,** also called **unprofessional conduct,** is not necessarily a crime, but is often the basis for a malpractice action or disciplinary proceeding.

unfair competition 1. the use of product names, packaging, or other devices similar to those of a competitor so as to confuse the public about whose product they are buying. **2.** Also called **unfair methods of competition.** any improper conduct by which a business might gain unfair advantage over competitors. See also PASSING OFF.

unfair labor practice any of a long list of coercive, discriminatory, or otherwise improper activities of employers or unions prohibited by the National Labor Relations Act.

Uniform Code of Military Justice the federal statute establishing a comprehensive system of justice applicable to members of the armed forces in their military capacity, complete with its own courts and judicial procedures.

Uniform Commercial Code (U.C.C.) a lengthy statute, adopted in substantially the same form in every state except Louisiana, establishing a uniform basic body of law governing sales of goods, negotiable instruments, bank deposits and collections, and various other commercial instruments and transactions. See under UNIFORM LAWS.

Uniform Laws (or **Acts**), a set of model statutes on a wide range of subjects, approved by the National Conference of Commissioners on Uniform State Laws (made up of representatives appointed by the governors of all states) and recommended to state legislatures for adoption. The purpose of the Uniform Laws is to mitigate the legal uncertainty and confusion that inevitably arises when fifty states adopt different and often conflicting laws on the same subjects, particularly with regard to transactions involving people and property in different states. Many of the Uniform Laws have been widely adopted, most notably the UNIFORM COMMERCIAL CODE. See also CONFLICT OF LAWS; MODEL LAW.

Uniform System of Citation. See BLUEBOOK.

unilateral contract. See under CONTRACT.

unilateral mistake. See under MISTAKE.

unincorporated association. See under ASSOCIATION.

union *n.* **1.** Also called **labor union.** an organization of workers formed for the purpose of bargaining collectively with employers over wages and working conditions. See also LABOR ORGANIZATION; TRADE UNION. **2. craft union,** a union composed only of people in the same trade or craft, regardless of the industry in which they work. Also called **horizontal union.** See also TRADE UNION. Cf. *industrial union.* **3. independent union,** a union of workers in a particular company, not affiliated with a larger union. **4. industrial union,** a union of workers in a particular industry, regardless of their individual trade or craft. Also called **vertical union.** Cf. *craft union.* **5. local union,** a local bargaining unit of a larger union. **6. union certification,** certification by the National Labor Relations Board of a particular union as the exclusive collective bargaining agent for a particular group of employees, upon a vote of the employees. **7. union shop.** See under SHOP.

United States Attorney the chief lawyer for the United States government within a federal *judicial district* (see under DISTRICT). Each United States Attorney is appointed by the President and is responsible for prosecuting federal crimes and representing the United States in all civil litigation within her district. Lawyers on the staff of a United States Attorney, who usually do most of the actual courtroom work, have the title **Assistant United States Attorney (AUSA).** Cf. ATTORNEY GENERAL; *Solicitor General* (under SOLICITOR).

United States Code (U.S.C.) the congressionally authorized codification of statutes enacted by Congress, organized into fifty broad subject areas, or "titles." See also ANNOTATED; STATUTES AT LARGE.

United States Court of Appeals one of the intermediate appellate courts in the federal judicial system, lying between the United States District Courts and the Supreme Court of the United States. There is one such court for each CIRCUIT in the federal system. Since very few cases are accepted for review by the Supreme Court, as a practical matter the Court of Appeals is the court of last resort for most federal litigants, and since the decisions of a Court of Appeals are binding upon all United States District Courts in its circuit, these decisions are extremely important in formulating federal law.

United States District Court the federal court of original jurisdiction for nearly all civil and criminal matters that can be brought in federal courts. There is one such court for each federal *judicial district* (see under DISTRICT), although each court has several judges and many have two or more courthouses located in different parts of the district.

United States Supreme Court an informal but generally accepted name for the *Supreme Court of the United States* (see under SUPREME COURT).

unjust enrichment any situation in which a person receives a benefit that properly belongs to another or retains, without paying for it, a benefit that in justice should be paid for; for example, receiving delivery of goods intended for another, or refusing to pay a doctor who provided necessary emergency care while one was unconscious. See also RESTITUTION.

unlawful *adj.* contrary to, unauthorized by, or disapproved of by law. Unlawful conduct need not be criminal; the term is broad enough to include torts, or conduct such as undue influence which might lead a court to declare a transaction void. Cf. ILLEGAL.

unlawful assembly the offense of the coming together as a group of three or more people in public for the purpose of engaging in a riot or some other openly violent activity. Cf. FREEDOM OF ASSEMBLY.

unlawful detainer. See under DETAINER.

unliquidated *adj.* **1.** uncertain, disputed, or not yet determined as to amount: *unliquidated claim; unliquidated damages.* **2.** not yet sold: *unliquidated assets; unliquidated inventory.* Cf. LIQUIDATE.

unmarketable title. Same as *defective title* (see under TITLE).

unnatural act oral or anal sex or sex with an animal—acts that the law traditionally regarded as so unspeakable that courts and legislatures literally would not speak their names, but instead condemned them under such names as "unnatural act" or "the crime against nature." See also SODOMY.

unprofessional conduct. Same as *unethical conduct* (see under UNETHICAL).

unreasonable restraint of trade business conduct which tends to reduce competition in the marketplace, and whose adverse effect is not outweighed by some permissible business justification. Concerted action that unreasonably restrains trade, such as PRICE FIXING or a *group boycott* (see under BOYCOTT), is outlawed by the SHERMAN ANTITRUST ACT.

unreasonable search. See under SEARCH.

unreasonable search and seizure. See under SEARCH AND SEIZURE.

usage *n.* **1.** a practice or method of doing business that is followed with such consistency by people engaged in transactions of a certain type in a particular place, vocation, or trade that the law will normally presume, with respect to a particular transaction of that type, that the parties intended that practice to be followed. See also CUSTOM. **2. usage of trade,** a usage followed in a particular vocation or trade. Also called **trade usage.** Cf. COURSE OF DEALING; COURSE OF PERFORMANCE.

use *n.* **1.** Also called **use and benefit.** benefit. For example, a case named *Smith for the use of Jones v. Lee* would be one brought for technical reasons by Smith although the person who would benefit from its success would be Jones. **2.** an old term for a *beneficial interest* (see under INTEREST[1]) in property, especially real property. **3.** the manner in which land that has been zoned is or could be utilized. **4. best use,** the most lucrative use that could be made of a parcel of land as currently zoned. The assessed value of land for property tax purposes may be based upon this hypothetical use rather than the actual use. Also called **best and highest use** or **highest and best use. 5. conforming use,** a use of land permitted by current zoning regulations. **6. nonconforming use,** a land use contrary to zoning regulations. Nonconforming uses typically exist because they were there before a zoning plan was adopted, and are usually permitted to continue for many years. **7. public use,** a use of land that benefits the public at large. Under the power of EMINENT DOMAIN, the state or federal government may take private property for any public use, provided that the owner is fairly compensated.

use immunity. See under IMMUNITY.

use tax a state tax on the purchase price of goods purchased outside the state for use within the state from a vendor who does business in the state. Use taxes are imposed in an effort to make up revenue lost when consumers avoid local sales taxes by shopping out of state.

usual covenants. See under COVENANT.

usury *n.* the crime of charging a higher rate of interest for a loan than is allowed by law. —**usurious,** *adj.*

utmost care. See under CARE.

utter *v.* **1.** to put an instrument into circulation or offer it to someone as what it purports to be. **2. uttering a forged instrument,** the crime of passing a counterfeit or forged instrument or attempting to do so by offering it as if it were genuine.

v. the abbreviation for *versus,* meaning "against," in case names; usually read as a letter rather than a word: *Roe v. Wade* (pronounced "Roe vee Wade").

vacate *v.* to nullify a judgment or court order. This may be done by the court that issued the original judgment or order, or by a higher court on appeal. See also QUASH; SET ASIDE.

vacatur *n.* Latin. (lit. "Let it be made void.") **1.** a court order vacating a previous judgment or order. **2.** Sometimes called **vacation.** the act of vacating a judgment or order.

vague *adj.* uncertain in meaning or scope. In a contract, a certain amount of vagueness is seldom a barrier to enforceability; the court will enforce the

contract in accordance with whatever it finds to be the most reasonable interpretation. Cf. INDEFINITE. A criminal law that is excessively vague may be held unconstitutional **(void for vagueness)** on the ground that it is a violation of due process to convict a person of a crime for behavior that was not clearly defined as criminal. —**vagueness,** *n.*

value. See *assessed value* (under ASSESS); MARKET VALUE.

value-added tax a tax, used in many countries and sometimes proposed for the United States, levied upon the increase in value of a product at each stage of production or distribution. The tax at each stage is paid by the seller and added to the price paid by the buyer, having much the same effect as a SALES TAX.

variance *n.* **1.** in zoning law, permission to use property in a particular way that is not generally allowed in that zone, granted to an individual property owner to prevent undue hardship. **2.** in procedure, a difference between what was originally alleged and what was actually shown at trial. This is seldom of much importance in civil cases. **3. fatal variance,** in criminal cases, so great a variance between what was charged and what was proved that the defendant was misled and deprived of a fair trial.

vehicular homicide. See under HOMICIDE.

veil *n.* See *corporate veil* (under CORPORATE).

vel non Latin. (lit. "or not") or the opposite; or the lack thereof: *The issue for decision is the adequacy, vel non, of notice.*

vendee *n.* a buyer.

vendor *n.* a seller.

venire *n.* a group of citizens called into court at the same time for jury duty, from which a jury or juries will be selected. An individual potential juror was traditionally called a **venireman,** but today **veniremember** is preferable. Also called **array** or **jury array,** or sometimes **panel** or **jury panel.** See also *jury panel* (under JURY).

venture *n.* See JOINT VENTURE.

venturer. See under JOINT VENTURE.

venue *n.* **1.** the county or judicial district where a case is maintained. When courts in more than one geographic area have jurisdiction to consider a case, rules of *venue* determine where the case should be filed. **2.** in an affidavit or affirmation, the part that tells where the instrument was executed. See also SS.

verbal *adj.* **1.** in words; spoken or written; expressed in words rather than implied by conduct: *An offer of contract may be accepted either verbally or by conduct manifesting agreement, such as commencement of performance.* The word "verbal" is sometimes confused with ORAL. **2. verbal act,** words (written or spoken) having legal effect; for example, a written consent or an oral contract. A verbal act is not regarded as a mere assertion of fact, and so is not excluded from evidence as HEARSAY.

verdict *n.* **1.** the jury's decision in a case. Traditionally required to be unanimous, but now in many cases permitted by a vote of 10 or 11 members of a 12-member jury or 5 members of a 6-member jury. Cf. JUDGMENT; FINDINGS OF FACT AND CONCLUSIONS OF LAW. **2. chance verdict,** one reached by flip of a coin or other process of chance. Obviously improper. **3. compromise verdict,** one arrived at as a compromise among conflicting views of jurors. Unless all jurors, after further deliberation, come to agree that the verdict is correct (i.e., consistent with the evidence and the judge's instructions), this is improper. **4. directed verdict,** one entered by the judge because, upon the evidence presented, the law permits only one outcome, so that there is nothing for the jury to decide. **5. excessive verdict,** one awarding damages grossly disproportionate to the plaintiff's injuries in light of the evidence and the nature of the case. A remedy for this is REMITTITUR. **6. general verdict,** one consisting of a single overall finding covering all issues; for example, "Guilty," "Not guilty," or "We find for the plaintiff in the amount of $60,000." Cf. *special verdict.* **7. inconsistent verdict,** one having two or more components that, under the judge's instructions, are logically inconsistent. If this is noticed in time, the jury may be sent back to reconsider, with clarifying instructions. **8. quotient verdict,** a type of *compromise verdict* in which the amount of damages is arrived at by averaging the amounts proposed by different jurors. **9. special verdict,** one in which the jurors are required to agree upon answers to a list of questions (called **special questions** or **special interrogatories**) about specific issues in the case. Used especially in complex civil cases. Cf. *general verdict.* **10. verdict against the weight of the evidence,** one found by the judge to be so clearly contrary to the credible evidence that it would be unjust to let it stand. The usual remedy in such a situation is to set aside the verdict and order a new trial.

verification n. **1.** the act of verifying a document. **2.** a statement affirming or swearing to the truth or authenticity of a document, written on the document itself or attached to it.

verify v. **1.** to swear to or affirm the authenticity of a document, or the truth of the statements it contains. **2. verified complaint,** a COMPLAINT to which a VERIFICATION has been affixed affirming or swearing to the truth of the facts alleged. (Other pleadings may likewise be verified.) **3. verified copy.** Same as *certified copy* (see under CERTIFY).

vertical price fixing. See under PRICE FIXING.

vertical union. See under UNION.

vest v. (of a power, right, or property interest) **1.** to come into being or become certain: *Your pension will vest when you have worked here for five years.* **2.** to attach to or reside in someone (used with *in*): *Upon the death of the parents, title to the farm will vest in the children.* **3.** to grant to or endow someone (used with *with*): *The deed vests the buyer with title to the property.*

vested adj. **1.** describing an interest in property that either confers a present right to possession, use, or enjoyment of the property or is certain to confer such a right in the future: *vested estate* (see under ESTATE[1]); *vested interest* (see under INTEREST[1]); *vested pension* (see under PENSION). **2.** (of rights generally) protected by the Constitution from being arbitrarily taken away or nullified. See also *vested right* (under RIGHT).

vexatious litigation baseless LITIGATION commenced only to annoy and harass the defendant.

vicarious liability. See under LIABILITY.

victim impact statement a report on the impact that a crime had on its victims, given to a judge for consideration in sentencing the convicted criminal. See also PRESENTENCE REPORT.

victimless crime conduct not in itself harmful to the person or property of anyone but consenting participants, but nevertheless defined as criminal; for example, gambling, drug use, or prostitution.

victims' rights rights of individuals who have been the victim of a crime to be informed of various stages of the criminal justice process concerning the crime of which they were a victim and to present their views, as by addressing the judge before sentencing and the parole board at any parole hearing.

Such rights are a relatively new concept enacted into law in some states.

video will. See under WILL.

violation n. **1.** a breach, infringement, or transgression of any rule, law, or duty. **2.** the name given in some states to an offense below the level of MISDEMEANOR, punishable only by a fine or forfeiture and not classified as a crime: *a littering violation.*

visa n. written authorization to enter a country, issued to an individual from another country and normally stamped into the individual's passport. Typically a visa states when entry may be made, how long the individual may stay, and the permitted purpose for the visit. See also GREEN CARD.

visitation n. **1.** a visit by a parent with a child who is in the custody of someone else, in a situation in which the parent has been deprived of custody, as through divorce or because of child neglect. **2. visitation rights,** authorization by court order for regular visitation, upon whatever terms the court decrees. **3. supervised visitation,** court-ordered visitation conditioned upon there being another adult present, in cases in which there is reason for concern regarding the safety of the child.

void adj. having no legal force or effect; not binding or enforceable because of a legal defect or for reasons of PUBLIC POLICY: *a void check, statute, contract, judgment, marriage,* etc. A transaction or instrument may be void from the outset **(void ab initio),** and thus never legally recognized at all, or it may become void at a later stage because of a change in circumstances. See also AB INITIO; VOIDABLE; *void for vagueness* (under VAGUE).

voidable adj. describing a contract, instrument, transaction, or relationship that may be rendered VOID at the option of one party: *voidable preference* (see under PREFERENCE); *voidable contract; voidable marriage.* For example, a transaction entered into as a result of fraud would normally be voidable at the option of the defrauded party. See also AVOID, RATIFY.

voir dire *Law French.* (lit. "to say truly") **1.** questioning of prospective jurors for possible sources of bias and for other information relevant to jury selection. See also CHALLENGE. **2.** preliminary questioning of a trial witness, usually outside the presence of the jury, to determine competency to testify, admissibility of proposed testimony, qualification as an expert, and the like. See also *qualify as an expert* (under QUALIFY[1]).

voluntary adj. **1.** done without compulsion or obligation. See *voluntary* BANKRUPTCY, COMMITMENT, CONFESSION, DISCONTINUANCE, DISMISSAL under those words. **2.** done intentionally rather than accidentally or reflexively. See *voluntary* MANSLAUGHTER, WASTE under those words. **3.** gratuitous; without consideration. See *voluntary conveyance* (under CONVEYANCE).

voter qualification a legal requirement for eligibility to vote in a public election, such as age or residence. Federal voting rights legislation has outlawed many such requirements, such as passing a literacy test, that tended to prevent disadvantaged minorities from voting. See also POLL TAX.

voting trust. See under TRUST.

legal

abcdefghijklmnopqrstuv WXYZ

wage earner's plan. See under BANKRUPTCY.

wait and see zoning. See under ZONING.

waiting period. See under RESIDENCY.

waive v. to abandon a right, privilege, or claim, intentionally and with knowledge of what you are giving up.

waiver n. **1.** the voluntary, intentional relinquishment of a right, privilege, or claim that you know you have. **2. express waiver,** a waiver expressed in words. **3. implied waiver,** a waiver indicated by

conduct. For mere conduct to be effective as a waiver, the circumstances must evidence the actor's awareness of her rights and intent to give them up.

want n. **1.** the absence of some necessary element or prerequisite: *The application for a search warrant was denied for want of probable cause. The fraud claim was dismissed for want of evidence of reliance.* **2. want of consideration,** the lack of CONSIDERATION for a promise, without which there is no enforceable contract: *The contract failed for want of* *consideration.* Cf. FAILURE OF CONSIDERATION. **3. want of jurisdiction, a.** a court's lack of *subject matter jurisdiction* (see under JURISDICTION[1]) over a particular case, making any decision it might render on the merits of the case void. **b.** a court's lack of *personal jurisdiction* (see under JURISDICTION[1]) over a party to a case, making any decision on the merits unenforceable as against that particular party unless the party appeared in the case without raising a prompt jurisdictional objection. **4. want of prosecution.** Same as FAILURE TO PROSECUTE.

wanton *adj.* an older term of somewhat vague scope, generally describing conduct characterized by INTENT, KNOWLEDGE, or RECKLESSNESS rather than mere negligence. (But see *wanton negligence,* under NEGLIGENCE.) The term is often thrown in to add a note of moral outrage to a description: *willful and wanton; recklessly and wantonly.* See also STATE OF MIND.

ward *n.* a person for whom a GUARDIAN has been appointed.

ward of the court *Informal.* any minor or incompetent person involved in legal proceedings. The common saying that "infants and incompetents are wards of the court" signifies that judges have a duty to make sure that the interests of litigants who are unable to look out for their own rights are adequately represented and well protected.

warehouse receipt a receipt issued by a warehouser identifying goods received for storage and evidencing the right of the person with the receipt to take possession of those goods. A warehouse receipt is a DOCUMENT OF TITLE.

warehouser *n.* a person or entity in the business of storing goods for others: still often referred to by the more cumbersome historical term **warehouseman**—an odd linguistic artifact since the warehouser is usually a company rather than an individual of either sex. See also *warehouser's* (or *warehouseman's) lien* (under LIEN).

warrant[1] *n.* **1.** a formal document, usually issued by a court, authorizing or directing an official to take a specific action. **2. arrest warrant,** a warrant directing or authorizing law enforcement officers to arrest an individual. It is issued upon a showing of PROBABLE CAUSE to believe that a crime has been committed and that the individual in question committed it. Also called **warrant of arrest.** Cf. SUMMONS; CITATION. **3. bench warrant,** a warrant issued by a judge from the bench, directing that an individual be brought before the court, usually because the individual has failed to appear in response to a summons or subpoena or has violated a court order. **4. death warrant,** a warrant signed by the governor of a state directing the warden of a prison or another appropriate official to carry out a death sentence at a specific time on a specific day. **5. search warrant,** a warrant, issued upon a showing of probable cause to believe that items connected with a crime will be found in a particular place, authorizing law enforcement authorities to search for those items in that place and seize them if found. **6. warrant of eviction,** a warrant directing a sheriff to put a person wrongfully in possession of property (usually a holdover tenant) out of the property.

warrant[2] *n.* a certificate issued by a corporation entitling the holder to purchase a specified number of shares of a specified class of the company's stock at a specified price, usually good until a specified date. Also called **stock warrant.**

warrant[3] *v.* to issue or become bound by an express or implied warranty.

warrantless *adj.* performed without a warrant. See *warrantless arrest* (under ARREST); *warrantless search* (under SEARCH).

warranty *n.* **1.** a legally binding representation made or implied in connection with a sale of goods, transfer of land, or other contract or financial transaction, ordinarily relating to the quality, integrity, or usefulness of the subject matter of the transaction (such as a product, a parcel of land, or a check); if the representation proves untrue, the person or company that made it (the **warrantor**) normally will be liable for any resulting loss or injury. Popularly called GUARANTEE, though in legal usage that

means something different. In some phrases, especially in real estate transactions, also called a COVENANT. **2.** a representation made by the purchaser of an insurance policy, incorporated into the policy and relied upon by the insurance company in issuing the policy; if it proves untrue, the policy will be void. **3. affirmative warranty,** in an insurance policy, a policy owner's warranty of existing or past fact, such as that he is 52 years old and has never been treated for heart disease. Cf. *promissory warranty.* **4. construction warranty,** a warranty by the builder or seller of a new house that it is free from basic structural defects. Also called **home owner's warranty. 5. express warranty, a.** a warranty expressed in words. **b.** in connection with a sale of goods, any words or conduct of the seller amounting to a representation about the quality or nature of the goods, such as the showing of a sample. Cf. *implied warranty;* PUFFING. **6. full warranty,** in the sale of a consumer product, a written warranty meeting certain federal standards. To qualify as a full warranty, the warranty must include a promise to remedy any defect or malfunction that occurs within a specified period of time without charge, and to permit the consumer to choose between a replacement and a refund if the product cannot be fixed. Cf. *limited warranty.* **7. implied warranty,** a warranty imposed by law in connection with a particular transaction, because the law regards such a warranty as inherent in that type of transaction unless the circumstances clearly indicate or the parties explicitly agree otherwise. For example, if you buy a painting at a gallery, the gallery impliedly warrants that it is theirs to sell; therefore, if it turns out to be stolen and the rightful owner traces it and takes it back from you, you can sue the seller to recover the value of the painting. Cf. *express warranty.* **8. limited warranty,** in the sale of a consumer product, any written warranty that falls short of the requirements for a **full warranty.** Under federal law, a limited warranty must be clearly labeled as such and must clearly state the scope of the warranty. **9. promissory warranty,** in an insurance policy, a policy owner's warranty that certain facts will continue to exist, or certain acts will or will not be done, during the term of the policy; for example, that she will not smoke. Cf. *affirmative warranty.* **10. warranty of fitness for a particular purpose,** the implied warranty of a seller of goods who has reason to know that the buyer needs the goods for a particular use and is relying upon the seller to furnish suitable goods, that the goods being furnished will in fact be suitable for that use. **11. warranty of title,** the implied warranty of a seller of goods that the title conveyed to the buyer will be good and unencumbered, and that its transfer is rightful. Cf. *warranties of title* (under COVENANT). See also *breach of warranty* (under BREACH); *warranty deed* (under DEED); *warranty of habitability* (under HABITABLE); *warranty of merchantability* (under MERCHANTABLE); *warranty of quiet enjoyment* or *covenant of warranty* (both under QUIET ENJOYMENT). Cf. COVENANT, GUARANTEE, GUARANTY.

waste *n.* **1.** substantial permanent change, beyond normal wear and tear, in the condition of real property while it is in possession of a tenant. A tenant who causes or permits waste is normally liable to the owner for damages. **2. ameliorating waste,** a substantial change that actually increases the value of the property. Normally this does not give rise to liability. **3. commissive waste,** waste caused by intentional conduct of the tenant. Also called **voluntary waste. 4. permissive waste,** waste that the tenant negligently allows to occur, as by failing to provide routine maintenance.

wasting *adj.* of such a nature as to be used up or dissipated over time: oil and coal are *wasting assets;* a trust in which funds are used for trust purposes faster than they accrue is a *wasting trust.*

weapon *n.* **1.** anything designed or used to cause bodily injury. **2. concealed weapon,** a weapon carried in such a way as not to be obvious. **3. deadly weapon,** anything which, either by design or by the way it is wielded in a particular case, could cause death or serious injury. Also called **dangerous weapon; lethal weapon.**

weight *n.* **1.** Same as PROBATIVE VALUE. **2.** of all the evidence on both sides of an issue, the more convincing body of evidence, as determined not by mere quantity but by its significance, coherence, and credibility. See also *verdict against the weight of the evidence* (under VERDICT).

whistleblower *n.* **1.** an employee who reports dangerous or illegal conduct of an employer to authorities. **2. whistleblower law,** a statute protecting whistleblowers from retaliatory firing or other action by the employer.

white-collar crime *Informal.* any business or financial crime of a type typically engaged in by executives and professional people, often involving very large sums of money to which they have access in the course of their business. Punishments for such crimes are sometimes thought to be disproportionately light when compared with those for nonviolent crimes, involving far less money, by people of lower social status.

white slavery until 1986, the statutory term for the federal crime of transporting a woman across state lines "for the purpose of prostitution or debauchery, or for any other immoral purpose." In 1986, the White-Slave Traffic Act was amended to sanitize it of sexist and racist terminology and make it as applicable to someone who takes a paid male companion on a trip as to one who takes a female.

whole life insurance. Same as *straight life insurance* (see under LIFE INSURANCE).

wholly owned subsidiary. See under SUBSIDIARY.

widow's (or **widower's**) **election.** See under ELECTION.

widow's (or **widower's**) **elective** (or **statutory**) **share.** See under ELECTIVE SHARE.

wife abuse. See under SPOUSAL ABUSE.

wildcat strike. See under STRIKE[1].

will *n.* **1.** a person's declaration of how she wants her property to be distributed when she dies. Because the maker of a will (the TESTATOR) is never available to testify to its authenticity, the law requires considerable formality in the execution of a will. The requirements vary from state to state, and not following them exactly will render the will invalid. **2. holographic will,** a will written out by hand, signed, and dated by the maker; recognized in a number of states as valid even if not witnessed like a normal will. **3. joint will,** the wills of two people, usually husband and wife, in a single document. **4. nuncupative will,** a will that is spoken, not written; allowed in a few states under special circumstances, notably when death is imminent. Also called **oral will. 5. video will,** a will read or recited by the testator on videotape, sometimes augmented by explanations of the reasons for certain gifts (or nongifts) and expressions of sentiment for those left behind. Videotape cannot take the place of formalities required for a valid will, but can be a useful supplement. **6. will contest,** a challenge to the validity of a will. See also CODICIL; *election under the will* (under ELECTION); TESTAMENT; LAST WILL AND TESTAMENT. Cf. AT WILL; LIVING WILL; INTESTATE SUCCESSION.

willful *adj.* describing wrongful conduct done with INTENT or KNOWLEDGE, sometimes RECKLESSNESS: *willful neglect* (see under NEGLECT); *willful negligence* (see under NEGLIGENCE); *willful violation of an injunction.* See also STATE OF MIND.

wind up to bring the affairs of a corporation, partnership, estate, or other enterprise to an end by fulfilling or settling remaining business obligations, liquidating and distributing any remaining assets, and dissolving the organization. Cf. GOING CONCERN.

wire fraud. See under FRAUD.

wiretap *n.* originally, the attachment of an extra wire to a telephone line to listen in on conversations. Now the term is used broadly and informally to cover any interception or recording of conversations or data transmissions by electronic or other artificial means without the consent of the participants. If done by a private individual, wiretapping is normally a crime, and may also give rise to a tort

claim for INVASION OF PRIVACY. If done by law enforcement authorities, it normally requires a search warrant. In most states, however, one participant in a conversation may record it without the knowledge of the others.

wish *n., v.* an ambiguous word in wills, sometimes construed as a directive and sometimes as a hope or suggestion. See PRECATORY LANGUAGE.

with all faults. See AS IS.

with prejudice. See under PREJUDICE.

withholding tax a sum of money required to be held back from an employee's wages, or in special circumstances from an investor's earnings, and sent directly to taxing authorities as an advance on the employee's or investor's taxes. Often simply called **withholding.**

within *prep.* covered by; governed by: *within the statute; within the usual meaning of the word; within the intent of the contract; within the language of Smith v. Jones.* Cf. OUTSIDE; DEHORS.

without prejudice. See under PREJUDICE.

without recourse. See under RECOURSE.

witness *n.* **1.** a person who has seen or heard something relevant to a case or an investigation. See also EYEWITNESS. **2.** a person who testifies in a legal or legislative proceeding. **3.** Also called **attesting witness.** a person who formally observes the execution of a document, especially a will, and signs it as evidence that it was duly executed. **4. character witness,** a witness called to testify about the CHARACTER of a party or of another witness. **5. expert witness,** a witness qualified by education or experience to testify about and render opinions on specialized subjects beyond the knowledge of average people. Unlike a *fact witness,* an expert witness need not have personal knowledge of the events or matters involved in the case. See also BATTLE OF THE EXPERTS; *qualify as an expert* (under QUALIFY[1]). **6. fact witness,** a witness called to testify about things she has personally done or observed. Unlike an *expert witness,* a fact witness ordinarily may not express opinions. See also *opinion evidence* (under EVIDENCE). **7. hostile witness,** a witness called by one side in a case but known to be friendly to the other side or found to be evasive in answering questions. If declared to be a hostile witness by the judge, such a witness may be asked leading questions even on direct examination and may be impeached even in states that normally do not allow impeachment of one's own witness. Also called **adverse witness. 8. interested witness,** a witness with an interest (see INTEREST[2]) in the case. That interest may be considered by the jury in assessing the witness's credibility. See also IMPEACHMENT. **9. material witness,** a witness whose testimony is essential to one side or the other in a criminal case. Such a witness may be required to travel from one state to another to testify, and in some circumstances may even be held in custody to assure that she will appear to testify. **10. unavailable witness,** a witness whose testimony cannot be obtained at a trial, for reasons ranging from outright refusal to answer questions while on the stand to being dead. In some circumstances, prior statements or testimony of such a witness may be admitted under a *hearsay exception* (see under HEARSAY). —*v.* **11.** to see or hear an event. **12.** to act as an attesting witness to the execution of a document: *to witness a will.*

witness stand. Same as STAND.

work made for hire any of a certain class of copyrightable works, specified by statute, with respect to which the copyright is usually owned not by the creator of the work, but by the company that hired the creator to do the work. The principal categories of such works are those created by an employee whose job it is to produce such works (as in the case of a newspaper article by a staff reporter), and those created by an *independent contractor* (see under CONTRACTOR) who was specially hired to produce a compilation, a contribution to a larger work, or an adjunct to a work created by someone else and who agreed in writing that the resulting work would be deemed a work made for hire. Often referred to informally as a **work for hire.**

legal

work product 1. Also called **attorney work product.** notes and other documents and materials prepared by or for an attorney in preparing for a case. **2. work product doctrine,** the principle that work product materials may not be demanded by the other side in pretrial DISCOVERY except upon a showing of special need, and that even then the attorney's analysis of the case need not be disclosed.

work release the release of a prisoner for a certain period of time each day to work at a job or participate in a training program. Cf. HALFWAY HOUSE.

workers' compensation payment to a worker as compensation for on-the-job injury. Most employees in America are covered by a state or federal law, often called a **workers' compensation act** or **employers' liability act,** requiring compensation for such injuries regardless of who was at fault, establishing the amount of compensation for different types of injuries, and dictating a funding mechanism, such as an insurance program **(workers' compensation insurance** or **employers' liability insurance)** paid for by employers.

world. See ALL THE WORLD.

World Court. Informal name for the INTERNATIONAL COURT OF JUSTICE.

writ *n.* **1.** any of a class of court orders derived from early English law, each having a specific name and purpose, by which a court commands a certain official or body to carry out a certain action. Only a few writs are still in use in the United States. Their formal names are always in the form "writ of..." (for example, "writ of habeas corpus"), but the words "writ of" are often omitted. **2. extraordinary writ,** any of a special class of writs whose effect is in some way to interfere with or open to question the proceedings of a court or other body. Most of the writs that survive in America today are extraordinary writs. Also referred to by the older name **prerogative writ. 3. Great Writ.** See HABEAS CORPUS. **4. writ of error,** a writ issued by an appellate court to a lower court in certain kinds of cases that may be appealed as a matter of right, directing that the record of a case be sent up for review of alleged errors of law. **5. writ of execution,** a writ directed to a sheriff or similar officer directing the officer to seize property of a *judgment debtor* (see under DEBTOR) or take other action to enforce or satisfy a judgment of the court. For writs of ATTACHMENT, CERTIORARI, CORAM NOBIS, HABEAS CORPUS, MANDAMUS, PROHIBITION, and QUO WARRANTO, see those words.

written contract. See under CONTRACT.

wrong *n.* **1.** the violation of or failure to perform a legal duty, or the infringement of another's legal rights. **2. private wrong,** a wrong that injures or interferes with the rights of a specific person or private entity, usually a basis for a tort or contract action. **3. public wrong,** a wrong that injures or interferes with the rights of the public at large, subject to civil or criminal proceedings brought by the state or its agencies or the federal government. —**wrongful,** *adj.*

wrongful birth a relatively new kind of tort action, usually brought by the parents of a newborn infant on their own behalf or on behalf of the child, alleging that the child would not have been born but for the medical malpractice of the defendant, such as an unsuccessful sterilization or abortion or bad advice that led the parents not to have an abortion. The damages sought typically include the costs of raising the child, and particularly the extra costs of caring indefinitely for a severely disabled child. Also called **wrongful life.**

wrongful death a tort action brought by or on behalf of close relatives or beneficiaries of someone who has died, alleging that the death was caused by a wrongful act of the defendant, such as medical malpractice, reckless driving, or murder. The damages claimed include the loss of future income that the deceased would have earned over a normal lifespan.

wrongful discharge the firing of an employee for a reason not permitted by law or in violation of contract. Depending upon the circumstances, this may give rise to a tort or contract claim, a union grievance, or a civil rights claim. Also called **wrongful termination.**

wrongful life. Same as WRONGFUL BIRTH.

wrongful termination. Same as WRONGFUL DISCHARGE.

X *n.* a mark traditionally used as a SIGNATURE by people who cannot write their names. Typically, the person's name and the words "his mark" or "her mark" would be printed near the X, and one or more neutral individuals would sign as witnesses.

X-rated *adj.* a lay term popularly applied to sexually oriented or pornographic entertainment in any form. The label has no legal significance. Cf. OBSCENE; INDECENT; PORNOGRAPHY.

year-and-a-day rule the common law rule, still followed in many states, that one cannot be found guilty of homicide if the victim lives for a year and a day after the act. Most states have abandoned the rule in light of modern medicine's ability to prolong dying in some cases for very long periods.

Your Honor. See under HONOR.

youthful offender. Same as *juvenile offender* (see under JUVENILE).

zone *n.* **1.** an area or district within a city, town, or county designated for a particular use or uses under a ZONING plan. **2. combat zone,** *Slang.* a zone in which sex-related businesses, such as "X-rated" video stores, are concentrated. This was once viewed as a way to allow some such businesses to exist while limiting their spread. In recent years, zoning plans that require dispersion of such businesses, rather than concentration of them in one zone, have been more popular with municipal governments. **3. floating zone,** a zone definition included in a municipality's zoning law but not assigned a specific location on the map until some real estate developer proposes to put a particular tract of land to the specified use. —*v.* **4.** to designate an area for particular uses under a zoning plan.

zone of employment for purposes of WORKERS' COMPENSATION laws, an employee's workplace. Any accidental injury to a worker within the employee's zone of employment entitles the worker to compensation from the employer.

zoning *n.* **1.** the division of a locality into geographic zones, pursuant to a plan under which the kinds of uses to which the land may be put, and the kinds of structures that may be built, vary from zone to zone. **2. cumulative zoning,** a zoning plan in which each successive zone definition merely adds to the list of permitted uses. Thus a zone might permit residential use only, or residential and trade use, or residential and trade and industrial use. Cf. *exclusive zoning.* **3. exclusionary zoning,** zoning that effectively keeps out low- and moderate-income families. For example, zoning in which all residential areas are restricted to single-family homes on large lots. Cf. *inclusionary zoning.* **4. exclusive zoning,** zoning in which each zone has its own distinct use; for example, residential only, trade only, or industrial only. Cf. *cumulative zoning.* **5. inclusionary zoning,** zoning that provides for a certain amount of low- and moderate-income housing. A few states have laws requiring that zoning plans be inclusionary. Cf. *exclusionary zoning.* **6. industrial performance zoning,** zoning in which the definition of permitted use depends upon the amount of noise, smoke, or other pollution generated, rather than upon general categorizations such as "industrial" vs. "non-industrial." This allows nonpolluting industries to exist in zones where more polluting industries would be disruptive. **7. spot zoning,** the zoning of a single lot or small tract to allow a particular use that is not permitted in the surrounding area. Often attacked as political favoritism inconsistent with the general zoning plan. **8. wait and see zoning,** a zoning plan in which undeveloped areas are not designated for any use until a developer comes forward and proposes a particular use for a particular area.

Abbreviations Dictionary

A **1.** *Cards.* ace. **2.** adulterer; adulteress. **3.** *Electricity.* ampere; amperes. **4.** *Physics.* angstrom. **5.** answer. **6.** *British.* arterial (used with a road number to designate a major highway).

A *Symbol.* **1.** the first in order or in a series. **2.** (in some grading systems) a grade or mark, indicating the quality of a student's work as excellent or superior. **3.** (in some school systems) a symbol designating the first semester of a school year. **4.** *Music.* **a.** the sixth tone in the scale of C major or the first tone in the relative minor scale, A minor. **b.** a string, key, or pipe tuned to this tone. **c.** a written or printed note representing this tone. **d.** (in the fixed system of solmization) the sixth tone of the scale of C major, called *la.* **e.** the tonality having A as the tonic note. **5.** *Physiology.* a major blood group, usually enabling a person whose blood is of this type to donate blood to persons of group A or AB and to receive blood from persons of O or A. **6.** (*sometimes lowercase*) the medieval Roman numeral for 50 or 500. **7.** *Chemistry.* (formerly) argon. **8.** *Chemistry, Physics.* mass number. **9.** *Biochemistry.* **a.** adenine. **b.** alanine. **10.** *Logic.* universal affirmative. **11.** *British.* a designation for a motion picture recommended as suitable for adults. **12.** a proportional shoe width size, narrower than B and wider than AA. **13.** a proportional brassiere cup size, smaller than B and larger than AA. **14.** a quality rating for a corporate or municipal bond, lower than AA and higher than BBB.

a *Measurements.* are; ares.

a *Symbol, Logic.* universal affirmative.

Å *Symbol, Physics.* angstrom.

A- atomic (used in combination): *A-bomb; A-plant.*

A. **1.** Absolute. **2.** Academy. **3.** acre; acres. **4.** America. **5.** American. **6.** angstrom. **7.** year. [from Latin *annō,* ablative of *annus*] **8.** answer. **9.** before. [from Latin *ante*] **10.** April. **11.** Artillery. **12.** Australia. **13.** Australian.

a. **1.** about. **2.** acre; acres. **3.** active. **4.** adjective. **5.** alto. **6.** ampere; amperes. **7.** year. [from Latin *annō,* ablative of *annus*] **8.** anonymous. **9.** answer. **10.** before. [from Latin *ante*] **11.** *Measurements.* are; ares. **12.** *Sports.* assist; assists. **13.** at.

AA **1.** administrative assistant. **2.** Alcoholics Anonymous. **3.** antiaircraft. **4.** author's alteration.

AA *Symbol.* **1.** a proportional shoe width size, narrower than A and wider than AAA. **2.** the smallest proportional brassiere cup size. **3.** a quality rating for a corporate or municipal bond, lower than AAA and higher than A. **4.** *Electricity.* a battery size for 1.5 volt dry cells: diameter, 0.6 in. (1.4 cm); length, 2 in. (5 cm). **5.** *British.* a designation for motion pictures certified as unsuitable for children under 14 unless accompanied by an adult. Compare **A** (def. 11), **U** (def. 5), **X** (def. 9).

A.A. **1.** Alcoholics Anonymous. **2.** antiaircraft. **3.** antiaircraft artillery. **4.** Associate in Accounting. **5.** Associate of Arts. **6.** author's alteration.

a.a. **1.** always afloat. **2.** author's alteration. Also, **aa**

AAA **1.** Agricultural Adjustment Administration. **2.** Amateur Athletic Association. **3.** American Automobile Association. **4.** antiaircraft artillery. **5.** Automobile Association of America.

AAA *Symbol.* **1.** a proportional shoe width size, narrower than AA. **2.** the highest quality rating for a corporate or municipal bond. **3.** *Electricity.* a battery size for 1.5 volt dry cells: diameter, 0.4 in. (1 cm); length 1.7 in. (4.3 cm).

A.A.A. **1.** Amateur Athletic Association. **2.** American Automobile Association. **3.** Automobile Association of America.

A.A.A.L. American Academy of Arts and Letters.

A.A.A.S. American Association for the Advancement of Science. Also, **AAAS**

A.A.E. American Association of Engineers.

A.Ae.E. Associate in Aeronautical Engineering.

A.A.E.E. American Association of Electrical Engineers.

AAES American Association of Engineering Societies.

AAF **1.** Allied Air Forces. **2.** (in the U.S., formerly) Army Air Forces. Also, **A.A.F.**

A.Agr. Associate in Agriculture.

AAM air-to-air missile.

a&b assault and battery.

A&E Arts and Entertainment (a cable television station).

a&h *Insurance.* accident and health.

a&i *Insurance.* accident and indemnity.

A&M Agricultural and Mechanical (college). Also, **A and M**

A&R (in the recording industry) artists and repertory. Also, **A. & R., A-and-R**

a&r assault and robbery.

a&s *Insurance.* accident and sickness.

AAP Association of American Publishers.

A.A.P.S.S. American Academy of Political and Social Science.

a.a.r. **1.** against all risks. **2.** average annual rainfall.

AARP (*pronounced as initials or*

ärp), American Association of Retired Persons.

A.A.S. **1.** Fellow of the American Academy. [from Latin *Academiae Americanae Socius*] **2.** American Academy of Sciences. **3.** Associate in Applied Science.

A.A.U. Amateur Athletic Union. Also, **AAU**

A.A.U.P. **1.** American Association of University Professors. **2.** American Association of University Presses. Also, **AAUP**

A.A.U.W. American Association of University Women.

AB **1.** *Nautical.* able seaman. **2.** airbase. **3.** airborne. **4.** *U.S. Air Force.* Airman Basic. **5.** Alberta, Canada (for use with ZIP code). **6.** antiballistic; antiballistic missile. **7.** assembly bill.

AB *Symbol, Physiology.* a major blood group usually enabling a person whose blood is of this type to donate blood to persons of type AB and to receive blood from persons of type O, A, B, or AB.

Ab *Symbol.* **1.** *Chemistry.* alabamine. **2.** *Immunology.* antibody.

ab. **1.** about. **2.** *Baseball.* (times) at bat.

A.B. **1.** *Nautical.* able seaman. **2.** Bachelor of Arts. [from Latin *Artium Baccalaureus*] **3.** *Baseball.* (times) at bat.

a.b. *Baseball.* (times) at bat.

ABA **1.** Amateur Boxing Association. **2.** American Badminton Association. **3.** American Bankers Association. **4.** American Bar Association. **5.** American Basketball Association. **6.** American Book Award. **7.** American Booksellers Association. **8.** Associate in Business Administration. Also, **A.B.A.**

abbr. **1.** abbreviate. **2.** abbreviated. **3.** abbreviation. Also, **abbrev.**

ABC **1.** American Broadcasting Company. **2.** atomic, biological, and chemical: *ABC warfare.*

A.B.C. **1.** Advance Booking Charter. **2.** Alcoholic Beverage Control.

abcb air-blast circuit breaker.

ABD All but dissertation: applied to a person who has completed all requirements for a doctoral degree except for the writing of a dissertation. Also, **abd.**

abd **1.** abdomen. **2.** abdominal.

abd. **1.** abdicated. **2.** abdomen. **3.** abdominal.

A.B.Ed. Bachelor of Arts in Education.

A.B.F.M. American Board of Foreign Missions.

abl. *Grammar.* ablative.

A.B.L.S. Bachelor of Arts in Library Science.

ABM antiballistic missile.

abn airborne.

ABO *Physiology.* ABO system (of blood classification).

A-bomb (ā′bom′), atomic bomb.
abp. archbishop.
abr. 1. abridge. **2.** abridged. **3.** abridgment.
ABRV Advanced Ballistic Reentry Vehicle.
ABS 1. *Chemistry.* ABS resin: a type of plastic. [(*a*)*crylanitrile,* (*b*)*utadiene,* and (*s*)*tyrene*] **2.** antilock braking system.
abs. 1. absent. **2.** absolute. **3.** abstract.
A.B.S. 1. American Bible Society. **2.** American Bureau of Shipping.
abs. re. *Law.* in the absence of the defendant. [from Latin *absente reo*]
abstr. 1. abstract. **2.** abstracted.
abt. about.
abv. above.
AC 1. *Real Estate.* air conditioning. **2.** *Electricity.* alternating current.
Ac *Chemistry.* **1.** acetate. **2.** acetyl.
Ac *Electricity.* alternating current.
Ac *Symbol, Chemistry.* actinium.
ac *Electricity.* alternating current.
A/C 1. *Bookkeeping.* **a.** account. **b.** account current. **2.** *Real Estate.* air conditioning. Also, **a/c**
A.C. 1. *Real Estate.* air conditioning. **2.** *Electricity.* alternating current. **3.** before Christ. [from Latin *ante Christum*] **4.** Army Corps. **5.** Athletic Club.
a.c. 1. *Real Estate.* air conditioning. **2.** *Electricity.* alternating current. **3.** (in prescriptions) before meals [from Latin *ante cibum*].
ACA 1. American Camping Association. **2.** American Canoe Association. **3.** American Casting Association.
ACAA Agricultural Conservation and Adjustment Administration.
acad. academy. Also, **Acad.**
AC and U Association of Colleges and Universities. Also, **AC&U**
acb air circuit breaker.
ACC Atlantic Coast Conference.
acc. 1. accelerate. **2.** acceleration. **3.** accept. **4.** acceptance. **5.** accompanied. **6.** accompaniment. **7.** accordant. **8.** according. **9.** account. **10.** accountant. **11.** accounted. **12.** accusative.
ACCD American Coalition of Citizens with Disabilities.
accel. *Music.* accelerando.
accom accommodate.
accomp. 1. accompaniment. **2.** accomplishment.
accrd. accrued.
acct. 1. account. **2.** accountant.
accum. 1. accumulate. **2.** accumulative.
accus. accusative.
ACDA Arms Control and Disarmament Agency.
AC/DC 1. *Electricity.* alternating current or direct current. **2.** *Slang.* sexually responsive to both men and women; bisexual. Also, **A.C./D.C., ac/dc, a-c/d-c, a.c.-d.c.**
acdt accident.
ACE 1. American Council on Education. **2.** Army Corps of Engineers.
acft aircraft.
ACH automated clearinghouse.
ACh *Biochemistry.* acetylcholine.

achiev. achievement.
ack. 1. acknowledge. **2.** acknowledgment.
A.C.L.S. American Council of Learned Societies.
ACLU 1. American Civil Liberties Union. **2.** American College of Life Underwriters. Also, **A.C.L.U.**
ACM Association for Computing Machinery.
ACOC Air Command Operations Center.
ACOG American College of Obstetricians and Gynecologists.
A.C.P. American College of Physicians.
acpt. acceptance.
acq acquisition.
A.C.S. 1. Advanced Communications System. **2.** American Cancer Society. **3.** American Chemical Society. **4.** American College of Surgeons. **5.** autograph card signed. Also, **ACS**
A.C.S.C. Association of Casualty and Surety Companies.
A/cs pay. accounts payable. Also, **a/cs pay.**
A/cs rec. accounts receivable. Also, **a/cs rec.**
acst acoustic.
acsy accessory.
ACT 1. American College Test. **2.** Association of Classroom Teachers. **3.** Australian Capital Territory.
act. 1. acting. **2.** action. **3.** active. **4.** actor. **5.** actual. **6.** actuary.
actg. acting.
ACTH *Biochemistry.* a polypeptide hormone that stimulates the cortex of adrenal glands. [*a*(*dreno*)*c*(*ortico*)*t*(*ropic*) *h*(*ormone*)]
ACTION (ak′shən), *U.S. Government.* an independent agency that administers domestic volunteer programs. [named by analogy with the acronymic names of other agencies, but itself not an acronym]
actl actual.
ACTP American College Testing Program.
actr actuator.
actvt activate.
ACV 1. Also, **A.C.V.** actual cash value. **2.** air cushion vehicle.
ACW *Radio.* alternating continuous waves.
AD assembly drawing.
Ad Alzheimer's Disease.
a-d *Electronics.* analog-to-digital.
ad. 1. adverb. **2.** advertisement.
A.D. 1. active duty. **2.** in the year of the Lord; since Christ was born. [from Latin *annō Dominī*] **3.** art director. **4.** assembly district. **5.** assistant director. **6.** athletic director. **7.** average deviation.
a.d. 1. after date. **2.** before the day. [from Latin *ante diem*] **3.** autograph document.
ADA 1. adenosine deaminase. **2.** American Dental Association. **3.** American Diabetes Association **4.** Americans for Democratic Action.
A.D.A. 1. American Dental Association. **2.** American Diabetes Association. **3.** Americans for Democratic Action.
ADAD (ā′dad), a coded card or

other device that when inserted into a telephone allows the user to reach a number without dialing. [*a*(*utomatic telephone*) *d*(*ialing-*)*a*(*nnouncing*) *d*(*evice*)]
ADAMHA Alcohol, Drug Abuse, and Mental Health Administration.
A.D.B. accidental death benefit. Also, **adb.**
ADC 1. advanced developing countries. **2.** Aid to Dependent Children. **3.** Air Defense Command.
A.D.C. aide-de-camp.
ADD attention deficit disorder.
addn. addition.
addnl. additional.
ADF automatic direction finder.
ad fin. to, toward, or at the end. [from Latin *ad finem*]
ADH *Biochemistry.* antidiuretic hormone.
ADHD attention deficit hyperactivity disorder.
ad inf. to infinity; endlessly; without limit. Also, **ad infin.** [from Latin *ad infinitum*]
ad init. at the beginning. [from Latin *ad initium*]
ad int. in the meantime. [from Latin *ad interim* for the time between]
adj. 1. adjacent. **2.** adjective. **3.** adjoining. **4.** adjourned. **5.** adjudged. **6.** adjunct. **7.** adjust. **8.** *Banking.* adjustment. **9.** adjutant.
Adj.A. Adjunct in Arts.
adjt. adjutant.
ADL Anti-Defamation League (of B'nai B'rith). Also, **A.D.L.**
ad lib. 1. at one's pleasure. **2.** *Music.* not obligatory. [from Latin *ad libitum*]
ad loc. at or to the place. [from Latin *ad locum*]
Adm. 1. admiral. **2.** admiralty. Also, **ADM**
adm. 1. administration. **2.** administrative. **3.** administrator. **4.** admission.
admin. administration.
admov. (in prescriptions) **1.** apply. [from Latin *admovē*] **2.** let it be applied. [from Latin *admoveātur*]
ADP 1. *Biochemistry.* an ester of adenosine and pyrophosphoric acid, $C_{10}H_{12}N_5O_3H_3P_2O_7$, serving to transfer energy during glycolysis. [*a*(*denosine*) *d*(*i*)*p*(*hosphate*)] **2.** automatic data processing.
ad part. dolent. (in prescriptions) to the painful parts. [from Latin *ad partēs dolentēs*]
adptr adapter.
adrs address.
ADS 1. Alzheimer's Disease Society. **2.** American Dialect Society.
a.d.s. autograph document, signed.
adst. feb. (in prescriptions) when fever is present. [from Latin *adstante febre*]
ADTS Automated Data and Telecommunications Service.
Adv. 1. Advent. **2.** Advocate.
adv. 1. in proportion to value. [from Latin *ad valorem*] **2.** advance. **3.** adverb. **4.** adverbial. **5.** adverbially. **6.** adversus. **7.** advertisement. **8.** advertising. **9.** adviser. **10.** advisory.

ad val. in proportion to value. [from Latin *ad valorem*]

advt. advertisement.

AE 1. account executive. **2.** Actors Equity. **3.** American English.

ae. at the age of. [from Latin *aetātis*]

A.E. 1. Agricultural Engineer. **2.** Associate in Education. **3.** Associate in Engineering.

a.e. *Math.* almost everywhere.

A.E.A. 1. Actors' Equity Association. **2.** Also, **AEA** *British.* Atomic Energy Authority.

A.E. and P. Ambassador Extraordinary and Plenipotentiary.

AEC Atomic Energy Commission.

A.E.C. *Insurance.* additional extended coverage.

A.Ed. Associate in Education.

Ae.E. Aeronautical Engineer.

A.E.F. American Expeditionary Forces; American Expeditionary Force. Also, **AEF**

A.Eng. Associate in Engineering.

aeq. equal. [from Latin *aequālis*]

aero. 1. aeronautic; aeronautical. **2.** aeronautics. **3.** aerospace.

aerodyn aerodynamic.

aeron. aeronautics.

aet. at the age of. Also, **aetat.** [from Latin *aetātis*]

AEW airborne early warning.

AF 1. Air Force. **2.** Anglo-French. **3.** Asian Female.

af 1. audiofidelity. **2.** audiofrequency. **3.** autofocus.

Af. 1. Africa. **2.** African.

A.F. 1. Air Force. **2.** Anglo-French. **3.** audio frequency.

a.f. audio frequency.

A.F.A. Associate in Fine Arts.

AFAIK as far as I know.

A.F.A.M. Ancient Free and Accepted Masons.

AFB Air Force Base.

A.F.B. American Federation for the Blind.

AFBF American Farm Bureau Federation.

AFC 1. American Football Conference. **2.** American Foxhound Club. **3.** Association Football Club. **4.** automatic flight control. **5.** automatic frequency control.

AFCS automatic flight control system.

AFDC Aid to Families with Dependent Children. Also, **A.F.D.C.**

aff. 1. affairs. **2.** affirmative. **3.** affix.

afft. affidavit.

AFGE American Federation of Government Employees.

Afgh. Afghanistan. Also, **Afg.**

A1c airman, first class.

AFL 1. American Federation of Labor. **2.** American Football League.

A.F.L. American Federation of Labor. Also, **A.F. of L.**

AFL-CIO American Federation of Labor and Congress of Industrial Organizations.

AFM 1. American Federation of Musicians. **2.** audio frequency modulation.

AFP *Biochemistry.* alphafetoprotein.

Afr African.

Afr. 1. Africa. **2.** African.

A.-Fr. Anglo-French.

AFS American Folklore Society.

A.F.S. American Field Service.

AFSCME American Federation of State, County, and Municipal Employees.

AFT American Federation of Teachers. Also, **A.F.T.**

aft. afternoon.

AFTRA (af′trə), American Federation of Television and Radio Artists. Also, **A.F.T.R.A.**

Ag *Symbol, Chemistry.* silver. [from Latin *argentum*]

Ag. August.

ag. 1. agricultural. **2.** agriculture.

A.G. 1. Adjutant General. **2.** Attorney General. Also, **AG**

AGA Amateur Gymnastics Association.

AGAC American Guild of Authors and Composers.

AGC 1. advanced graduate certificate. **2.** automatic gain control. Also, **A.G.C.**

AGCA automatic ground-controlled approach.

AGCL automatic ground-controlled landing.

agcy. agency.

Ag.E. Agricultural Engineer.

A.G.E. Associate in General Education.

Agh. (in Afghanistan) afghani.

AGI 1. Also, **agi.** adjusted gross income. **2.** American Geological Institute.

agit. (in prescriptions) shake, stir. [from Latin *agitā*]

AGM air-to-ground missile.

AGMA American Guild of Musical Artists. Also, **A.G.M.A.**

agr. 1. agricultural. **2.** agriculture.

agric. 1. agricultural. **2.** agriculture.

agron. agronomy.

AGS 1. American Gem Society. **2.** American Geographical Society. **3.** American Geriatrics Society.

A.G.S. Associate in General Studies.

agst. against.

Agt. agent. Also, **agt.**

AGU American Geophysical Union.

Ah ampere-hour. Also, **a.h.**

A.H. in the year of the Hegira; since the Hegira (A.D. 622). [from Latin *annō Hejirae*]

AHA American Heart Association.

A.H.A. 1. American Historical Association. **2.** American Hospital Association.

AHAUS Amateur Hockey Association of the United States.

AHE Association for Higher Education.

A.H.E. Associate in Home Economics.

AHF *Biochemistry.* antihemophilic factor.

AHL 1. American Heritage Foundation. **2.** American Hockey League.

AHQ 1. Air Headquarters. **2.** Army Headquarters.

AHRA American Hot Rod Association.

AHS American Humane Society.

AHSA American Horse Shows Association.

AI 1. Amnesty International. **2.**

artificial insemination. **3.** artificial intelligence. Also, **A.I.**

A.I.A. 1. American Institute of Architects. **2.** American Insurance Association.

A.I.C. 1. Army Intelligence Center. **2.** American Institute of Chemists.

AIChE American Institute of Chemical Engineers. Also, **A.I. Ch.E.**

AID (ād), *U.S. Government.* the division of the United States International Development Cooperation Agency that coordinates the various foreign aid programs with U.S. foreign policy. [*A(gency for) I(nternational) D(evelopment)*]

AID 1. American Institute of Decorators. **2.** American Institute of Interior Designers. **3.** Also, **A.I.D.** *British.* artificial insemination donor.

aid. acute infectious disease.

AIDS (ādz), Acquired Immune Deficiency Syndrome.

AILS automatic instrument landing system.

AIM (ām), American Indian Movement.

A.I.M.E. 1. American Institute of Mining Engineers. **2.** Association of the Institute of Mechanical Engineers.

A.I.M.U. American Institute of Marine Underwriters.

AInd Anglo-Indian.

AIP American Institute of Physics.

air. artist in residence.

AIS administrative and information services.

AISI American Iron and Steel Institute.

AK Alaska (for use with ZIP code).

a.k. *Slang (vulgar).* ass-kisser.

a.k.a. also known as: *Joe Smith a.k.a. Joseph Smathers.* Also, **AKA, aka**

A.K.C. American Kennel Club.

AL 1. Alabama (for use with ZIP code). **2.** Anglo-Latin.

Al *Symbol, Chemistry.* aluminum.

AL. Anglo-Latin.

al. 1. other things. [from Latin *alia*] **2.** other persons. [from Latin *aliī*]

A.L. 1. *Baseball.* American League. **2.** American Legion. **3.** Anglo-Latin.

a.l. autograph letter.

Ala *Biochemistry.* alanine.

Ala. Alabama.

A.L.A. 1. American Library Association. **2.** Associate in Liberal Arts. **3.** Authors League of America. **4.** Automobile Legal Association.

Alas. Alaska.

Alb. 1. Albania. **2.** Albanian. **3.** Albany. **4.** Alberta.

alb. (in prescriptions) white. [from Latin *albus*]

ALBM air-launched ballistic missile.

alc. alcohol.

alcd alcad: aluminum clad.

ALCM air-launched cruise missile. Also, **A.L.C.M.**

Ald. alderman. Also, **ald.**

A.L.E. *Insurance.* additional living expense.

abbrev.

Alg. 1. Algerian. 2. Algiers.

alg. algebra.

ALGOL (al′gol, -gôl), a computer language in which information is expressed in algebraic notation. [*algo(rithmic) l(anguage)*]

alk. 1. alkali. 2. alkaline.

allow. allowance.

ALM audio-lingual method.

Alp. alpine.

A.L.P. American Labor Party. Also, **ALP**

alpha alphabetical.

ALS amyotrophic lateral sclerosis.

a.l.s. autograph letter, signed.

alt. 1. alternate. 2. alternate. 3. altitude. 4. alto.

Alta. Alberta.

altm altimeter.

altn alternate.

altntr alternator.

altnv alternative.

altrd altered.

altrn alternation.

ALU *Computers.* arithmetic/logic unit.

Aly. alley.

AM 1. *Electronics.* amplitude modulation. 2. *Radio.* a system of broadcasting by means of amplitude modulation. 3. Asian male.

Am *Symbol, Chemistry.* americium.

Am. 1. America. 2. American.

am amber.

A/m ampere per meter.

A.M. 1. before noon. [from Latin *ante merīdiem*] 2. Master of Arts. [from Latin *Artium Magister*]

a.m. before noon.

A.M.A. 1. American Management Association. 2. American Medical Association. 3. American Motorcycle Association.

Amb. Ambassador. Also, **amb.**

AMC American Movie Classics (a cable channel).

A.M.D.G. for the greater glory of God: motto of the Jesuits. Also **AMDG** [from Latin *ad majōrem Deī glōriam*]

A.M.E. 1. Advanced Master of Education. 2. African Methodist Episcopal.

AMEDS Army Medical Service. Also, **AMedS**

Amer. 1. America. 2. Also, **Amer** American.

AmerSp American Spanish.

AMEX (am′eks), American Stock Exchange. Also, **Amex**

am/fm (ā′em′ef′em′), (of a radio) able to receive both AM and FM stations. Also, **AM/FM**

AMG Allied Military Government.

ami acute myocardial infarction.

A.M.L.S. Master of Arts in Library Science.

amm antimissile missle.

ammo ammunition.

Amn *Air Force.* airman.

AMNH American Museum of Natural History.

AMORC Ancient Mystic Order Rosae Crucis.

amort. amortization.

AMP *Biochemistry.* a white, crystalline, water-soluble nucleotide, $C_{10}H_{12}N_5O_3H_2PO_4$, obtained by the partial hydrolysis of ATP or of ribonucleic acid. [*a(denosine) m(-ono) p(hosphate)*]

amp. *Electricity.* 1. amperage. 2. ampere; amperes.

AMPAS Academy of Motion Picture Arts and Sciences.

ampl amplifier.

AMS 1. Agricultural Marketing Service. 2. American Mathematical Society. 3. American Meteorological Society. 4. American Musicological Society.

A.M.S. Army Medical Staff.

A.M.S.W. Master of Arts in Social Work.

AMT alternative minimum tax.

amt. amount.

A.M.T. 1. Associate in Mechanical Technology. 2. Associate in Medical Technology. 3. Master of Arts in Teaching.

amu atomic mass unit. Also, **AMU**

A.Mus. Associate in Music.

A.Mus.D. Doctor of Musical Arts.

AMVETS (am′vets′), an organization of U.S. veterans of World War II and more recent wars. [*Am(erican) Vet(eran)s*]

AN Anglo-Norman. Also, **A.-N.**

An *Symbol, Chemistry.* actinon.

an. 1. above named. 2. annual. 3. in the year. [from Latin *annō*]

A.N. 1. Anglo-Norman. 2. Associate in Nursing.

A.N.A. 1. American Newspaper Association. 2. American Nurses Association. 3. Association of National Advertisers. Also, **ANA**

anal analysis.

analyt. analytical.

anat. 1. anatomical. 2. anatomist. 3. anatomy.

ANBS Armed Nuclear Bombardment Satellite.

ANC 1. Also, **A.N.C.** African National Congress. 2. Army Nurse Corps.

anc automatic noise control.

anc. ancient.

andz anodize.

aner aneroid.

ANF *Biochemistry.* atrial natriuretic factor.

ANG 1. acute necrotizing gingivitis; trench mouth. 2. Air National Guard.

ang. 1. angiogram. 2. angle.

Angl. 1. Anglican. 2. Anglicized.

anglr angular.

anhyd. *Chemistry.* anhydrous.

ani *Telecommunications.* automatic number identification.

anim. *Music.* animato.

anl automatic noise limiter.

anlg analog.

anlr annular.

ann. 1. annals. 2. annuity. 3. years. [from Latin *annī*]

annot. 1. annotated. 2. annotation. 3. annotator.

ano alphanumeric output.

anon. 1. anonymous. 2. anonymously.

ANPA American Newspaper Publishers Association.

ANRC American National Red Cross.

ANS American Name Society.

ans. answer.

ANSI (an′sē), American National Standards Institute.

Ant. Antarctica.

ant. 1. antenna 2. antonym.

ANTA (an′tə), American National Theatre and Academy.

anthol. anthology.

anthrop. 1. anthropological. 2. anthropology.

anthropol. anthropology.

antiq. 1. antiquarian. 2. antiquary. 3. antiquity.

ANTU (an′tōō), *Trademark.* a brand of gray, water-insoluble, poisonous powder, $C_{11}H_{10}N_2S$, used for killing rodents; alpha-naphthylthiourea.

ANZUS (an′zəs), Australia, New Zealand, and the United States, especially as associated in the mutual defense treaty (**ANZUS Pact** or **ANZUS Treaty**) of 1952.

A/O 1. account of. 2. and others. Also, **a/o**

AOA Administration on Aging.

AOH Ancient Order of Hibernians.

aoi angle of incidence.

A-OK all OK; perfect. Also, **A-o.k.**, **A-okay.**

AOL *Computers.* America Online.

A-1 first class.

AOR 1. advice of rights. 2. album-oriented radio. 3. album-oriented rock.

aor angle of reflection.

AOS 1. American Opera Society. 2. American Orchid Society.

A.O.U. American Ornithologists′ Union.

AP 1. adjective phrase. 2. *Education.* Advanced Placement. 3. Air Police. 4. American plan. 5. antipersonnel. Also, **A.P.**

Ap. 1. Apostle. 2. Apothecaries′.

A/P 1. account paid. 2. accounts payable. 3. authority to pay or purchase. Also, **a/p**

a-p American plan.

a.p. 1. additional premium. 2. advanced placement. 3. as prescribed. 4. author′s proof.

APA 1. American Psychiatric Association. 2. American Psychological Association.

A.P.A. 1. American Philological Association. 2. American Protective Association. 3. American Protestant Association. 4. American Psychiatric Association. 5. American Psychological Association. 6. Associate in Public Administration.

a-part. alpha particle; alpha particles.

APB all-points bulletin.

APC 1. Also, **A.P.C.** *Pharmacology.* aspirin, phenacetin, and caffeine: a compound formerly used in headache and cold remedies. 2. armored personnel carrier.

APCB Air Pollution Control Board.

aper. aperture.

APEX (ā′peks), a type of international air fare offering reduced rates for extended stays that are booked in advance. [*A(dvance) P(urchase) Ex(cursion)*]

aph. *Linguistics.* aphetic.

APHIS Animal and Plant Health Inspection Service.

API American Petroleum Institute. Also, **A.P.I.**

APL 1. allowance parts list. **2.** *Computers.* an interactive programming language. [*A P(rogramming) L(anguage)*]

APLA American Patent Law Association.

A.P.O. Army & Air Force Post Office. Also, **APO**

app. 1. apparatus. **2.** apparent. **3.** appendix. **4.** *Computers.* application. **5.** applied. **6.** appointed. **7.** approved. **8.** approximate.

appar. 1. apparent. **2.** apparently.

appd. approved.

appl. 1. appeal. **2.** applicable. **3.** application. **4.** applied.

appmt. appointment.

approp. appropriation.

approx. 1. approximate. **2.** approximately.

apprp appropriate.

apprx approximate.

appt. 1. appoint. **2.** appointed. **3.** appointment.

apptd. appointed.

appx appendix.

APR annual percentage rate. Also, **A.P.R.**

Apr. April.

aprch approach.

aprt airport.

A.P.S. 1. American Peace Society. **2.** American Philatelic Society. **3.** American Philosophical Society. **4.** American Physical Society. **5.** American Protestant Society.

A.P.S.A. American Political Science Association.

apt. apartment. Also, **apt**

apu auxiliary power unit.

apv approve.

apvd approved.

apvl approval.

apx. appendix.

AQ *Psychology.* achievement quotient.

aq. water. [from Latin *aqua*]

AQAB Air Quality Advisory Board.

aq. bull. (in prescriptions) boiling water. [from Latin *aqua bulliēns*]

aq. comm. (in prescriptions) common water. [from Latin *aqua commūnis*]

aq. dest. (in prescriptions) distilled water. [from Latin *aqua dēstillāta*]

aq. ferv. (in prescriptions) hot water. [from Latin *aqua fervēns*]

AQL acceptable quality level.

aqstn acquisition.

AR 1. annual return. **2.** Arkansas (for use with ZIP code). **3.** Army Regulation; Army Regulations. **4.** as required.

Ar Arabic.

Ar *Symbol, Chemistry.* argon.

Ar. 1. Arabic. **2.** Aramaic.

ar. 1. arrival. **2.** arrive; arrived; arrives.

A/R account receivable; accounts receivable. Also, **a/r**

A.R. 1. annual return. **2.** Army Regulation; Army Regulations.

a.r. *Insurance.* all risks.

ARA Agricultural Research Administration.

A.R.A. 1. American Railway Association. **2.** Associate of the Royal Academy.

Aram Aramaic. Also, **Aram.**

ARC (ärk), *Pathology.* AIDS-related complex.

ARC American Red Cross. Also, **A.R.C.**

Arc. arcade (approved for postal use).

arc cos *Trigonometry.* arc cosine.

arc cot *Trigonometry.* arc cotangent.

arc csc *Trigonometry.* arc cosecant.

Arch. Archbishop.

arch. 1. archaic. **2.** archaism. **3.** archery. **4.** archipelago. **5.** architect. **6.** architectural. **7.** architecture. **8.** archive; archives.

archaeol. 1. archaeological. **2.** archaeology.

Archbp. Archbishop.

archd. 1. archdeacon. **2.** archduke. Also, **Archd.**

Arch. E. Architectural Engineer.

archt. architect.

ARCN *Computers.* Attached Resource Computer Network.

A.R.C.S. 1. Associate of the Royal College of Science. **2.** Associate of the Royal College of Surgeons.

ard acute respiratory disease.

ARDS *Pathology.* adult respiratory distress syndrome.

arf acute respiratory failure.

Arg *Biochemistry.* arginine.

Arg. Argentina.

argus advanced research on groups under stress.

arith. 1. arithmetic. **2.** arithmetical.

Ariz. Arizona.

Ark. Arkansas.

ARL Association of Research Libraries.

arl average remaining lifetime.

ARM adjustable-rate mortgage.

Arm Armenian.

Arm. 1. Armenian. **2.** Armorican.

Ar.M. Master of Architecture. [from Latin *Architecturae Magister*]

aro *Commerce.* after receipt of order.

ARP *Stock Exchange.* adjustable-rate preferred.

ARR American Right to Read.

arr. 1. arranged. **2.** arrangement. **3.** *Music.* arranger. **4.** arrival. **5.** arrive; arrived; arrives.

arrgt. arrangement.

ARS 1. advanced record system. **2.** Agricultural Research Service. **3.** American Rescue Service. **4.** American Rose Society.

ART *Linguistics.* article: often used to represent the class of determiners, including words such as *this, that,* and *some* as well as the articles *a, an,* and *the.*

art. 1. artificial. **2.** artillery. **3.** artist.

ARU *Computers.* audio response unit.

A.R.V. 1. AIDS-related virus. **2.** American Revised Version (of the Bible).

ARVN (är′vin), (in the Vietnam War) a soldier in the army of South Vietnam. [*A(rmy of the) R(epublic of) V(iet) N(am)*]

AS 1. American Samoa (for use with ZIP code). **2.** Anglo-Saxon. **3.** antisubmarine.

As *Symbol, Chemistry.* arsenic.

AS. Anglo-Saxon.

A.S. 1. Anglo-Saxon. **2.** Associate in Science.

A.-S. Anglo-Saxon.

ASA 1. Acoustical Society of America. **2.** American Standards Association. **3.** the numerical exposure index of a photographic film under the system adopted by the American Standards Association.

ASAP as soon as possible. Also, **A.S.A.P., a.s.a.p.**

ASAT (ā′sat′), antisatellite.

ASBM air-to-surface ballistic missile. Also, **A.S.B.M.**

ASC American Society of Cinematographers. Also, **A.S.C.**

ASCAP (as′kap), American Society of Composers, Authors, and Publishers.

ASCE American Society of Civil Engineers.

ASCII (as′kē), a standard code for characters stored in a computer or to be transmitted between computers. [*A(merican) S(tandard) C(ode for) I(nformation) I(nterchange)*]

ASCM antiship capable missile.

ASCP American Society of Clinical Pathologists.

ascr *Electronics.* asymmetrical semiconductor controlled rectifier.

ASCS Agricultural Stabilization and Conservation Service.

ASCU Association of State Colleges and Universities.

ASE American Stock Exchange. Also, **A.S.E.**

ASEAN Association of Southeast Asian Nations. Also, **A.S.E.A.N.**

asgd. assigned.

asgmt. assignment.

asgn assign.

ASHD arteriosclerotic heart disease.

ASI 1. *Aeronautics.* airspeed indicator. **2.** American Safety Institute.

ask amplitude shift keying.

ASL 1. American Shuffleboard League. **2.** American Sign Language. **3.** American Soccer League.

ASLA American Society of Landscape Architects.

ASM air-to-surface missile.

asm assemble.

ASME American Society of Mechanical Engineers.

ASN Army service number.

Asn *Biochemistry.* asparagine.

ASNE American Society of Newspaper Editors.

ASP American selling price.

Asp *Biochemistry.* aspartic acid.

A.S.P.C.A. American Society for the Prevention of Cruelty to Animals.

ASPCC American Society for the Prevention of Cruelty to Children.

ASR 1. airport surveillance radar. **2.** *U.S. Navy.* air-sea rescue.

asr *Teletype.* automatic send-receive.

ass. 1. assistant. **2.** association. **3.** assorted.

assn. association. Also, **Assn.**

assoc. 1. associate. **2.** associated. **3.** association.

ASSR Autonomous Soviet Socialist Republic. Also, **A.S.S.R.**

asst. 1. assistance. **2.** assistant.

asstd. assorted.

Assyr. Assyrian.

AST Atlantic Standard Time. Also, **A.S.T., a.s.t.**

astb *Electronics.* astable.

ASTM American Society for Testing Materials. Also, **A.S.T.M.**

Astronomy. 1. astronomer. **2.** astronomical. **3.** astronomy.

ASU American Students Union.

A.S.V. American Standard Version (of the Bible). Also, **ASV**

A.S.W. Association of Scientific Workers.

ASWG American Steel Wire Gauge.

asym assymmetric.

asymp *Math.* asymptote.

asyn asynchronous.

AT 1. achievement test. **2.** *Military.* antitank.

At ampere-turn.

At *Symbol, Chemistry.* astatine.

at. 1. atmosphere. **2.** atomic. **3.** attorney.

A.T. Atlantic time.

ATA Air Transport Association.

A.T.A. Associate Technical Aide.

atb *Telephones.* all trunks busy.

ATC 1. Air Traffic Control. **2.** Air Transport Command.

atch attach.

ATE equipment that makes a series of tests automatically. [*a(utomatic) t(est) e(quipment)*]

ATF (Bureau of) Alcohol, Tobacco, and Firearms.

ATLA American Trial Lawyers Association.

ATM automated-teller machine.

atm. 1. atmosphere; atmospheres. **2.** atmospheric.

At/m ampere-turns per meter.

at. m. atomic mass.

at. no. atomic number.

ATP *Biochemistry.* an ester of adenosine and triphosphoric acid, $C_{10}H_{12}N_5O_4H_4P_3O_9$. [*a(denosine) t(ri)p(hosphate)*]

atr antitransmit-receive.

ATS *British. Military.* Auxiliary Territorial Service.

A.T.S. 1. American Temperance Society. **2.** American Tract Society. **3.** American Transport Service.

att. 1. attached. **2.** attention. **3.** attorney.

att. gen. attorney general.

attn. attention.

attrib. 1. attribute. **2.** attributive. **3.** attributively.

atty. attorney.

Atty. Gen. Attorney General.

ATV all-terrain vehicle.

at. wt. atomic weight. Also, **at wt**

AU astronomical unit.

Au *Symbol, Chemistry.* gold. [from Latin *aurum*]

au. author.

A.U. *Physics.* angstrom unit. Also, **a.u.**

A.U.A. American Unitarian Association.

A.U.C. 1. from the founding of the city (of Rome in 753? B.C.). [from Latin *ab urbe conditā*] **2.** in the year from the founding of the city (of Rome). [from Latin *annō urbis conditae*]

aud. 1. audit. **2.** auditor.

Aug. August.

aug. 1. augmentative. **2.** augmented.

AUM air-to-underwater missile.

AUS Army of the United States. Also, **A.U.S.**

Aus. 1. Austria. **2.** Austrian.

Aust. 1. Austria. **2.** Austria-Hungary. **3.** Austrian.

Austral Australian.

Austral. 1. Australasia. **2.** Australia. **3.** Australian.

auth. 1. authentic. **2.** author. **3.** authority. **4.** authorized.

Auth. Ver. Authorized Version (of the Bible).

auto. 1. automatic. **2.** automobile. **3.** automotive.

AUTODIN (ô′tō din), automatic digital network.

autoxfmr autotransformer.

AUX *Linguistics.* auxiliary verb. Also, **Aux**

aux. auxiliary; auxiliaries. Also, **aux, auxil.**

AV 1. arteriovenous. **2.** atrioventricular. **3.** audiovisual.

av. 1. avenue. **2.** average. **3.** avoirdupois weight.

A-V 1. atrioventricular. **2.** audiovisual.

A/V 1. Also, **a.v.** ad valorem. **2.** audiovisual.

A.V. 1. Artillery Volunteers. **2.** audiovisual. **3.** Authorized Version (of the Bible).

A.V.C. 1. American Veterans' Committee. **2.** automatic volume control. Also, **AVC**

avdp. avoirdupois weight.

Ave. avenue. Also, **ave.**

AVF all-volunteer force.

avg. average.

avlbl available.

AVMA American Veterinary Medical Association.

avn. aviation.

avr automatic voltage regulator.

AW Articles of War.

a.w. 1. actual weight. **2.** (in shipping) all water. **3.** atomic weight. Also, **aw**

AWACS (ā′waks), a detection aircraft, fitted with radar and computers, capable of simultaneously tracking and plotting large numbers of low-flying aircraft. [*A(irborne) W(arning) A(nd) C(ontrol) S(ystem)*]

AWB air waybill.

AWG American Wire Gauge.

AWI Animal Welfare Institute.

AWIS Association of Women in Science.

A.W.L. absent with leave. Also, **a.w.l.**

AWOL (*pronounced as initials or* ā′wôl, ā′wol), away from military duties without permission, but without the intention of deserting. Also, **awol, A.W.O.L.,** a. **w.o.l.** [*A(bsent) W(ith)o(ut) L(e-ave)*]

AWS American Weather Service.

AWSA American Water-Skiing Association.

ax. 1. axial. **2.** axiom.

A.Y.H. American Youth Hostels.

AZ Arizona (for use with ZIP code).

az. 1. azimuth. **2.** azure.

AZT *Pharmacology, Trademark.* azidothymidine: an antiviral drug used in the treatment of AIDS.

---

a **B** c d e f g h i j k l m n o p q r s t u v w x y z

B 1. base: a semiconductor device. **2.** *Chess.* bishop. **3.** black. **4.** *Photography.* bulb. **5.** *Computers.* byte.

B *Symbol.* **1.** the second in order or in a series. **2.** (In some grading systems) a grade or mark, indicating the quality of a student's work as good or better than average. **3.** (In some school systems) a symbol designating the second semester of a school year. **4.** *Physiology.* a major blood group usually enabling a person whose blood is of this type to donate blood to persons of type B or AB and to receive blood from persons of type O or B. **5.** *Music.* **a.** the seventh tone in the scale of C major or the second tone in the relative minor scale, A minor. **b.** a string, key, or pipe tuned to this tone. **c.** a written or printed note representing this tone. **d.** (in the fixed system of solmization) the seventh note of the scale of C major, called *ti.* **e.** the tonality having B as the tonic note. **6.** (*sometimes lowercase*) the medieval Roman numeral for 300. **7.** *Chemistry.* boron. **8.** a proportional shoe width size, narrower than C and wider than A. **9.** a proportional brassiere cup size, smaller than C and larger than A. **10.** *Physics.* magnetic induction. **11.** bel. **12.** *Electricity.* susceptance. **13.** a designation for a motion picture made on a low budget and meant as the secondary part of a double feature. **14.** a quality rating for a corporate or municipal bond, lower than BB and higher than CCC.

b 1. *Physics.* **a.** bar; bars. **b.** barn; barns. **2.** *Computers.* bit. **3.** black.

B- *U.S. Military.* (in designations of aircraft) bomber: *B-29.*

B. 1. bachelor. **2.** bacillus. **3.** *Baseball.* base; baseman. **4.** bass.

5. basso. **6.** bay. **7.** Bible. **8.** bolivar. **9.** boliviano. **10.** book. **11.** born. **12.** breadth. **13.** British. **14.** brother. **15.** brotherhood.

b. **1.** bachelor. **2.** bale. **3.** *Baseball.* base; baseman. **4.** bass. **5.** basso. **6.** bay. **7.** billion. **8.** blend of; blended. **9.** book. .**10.** born. **11.** breadth. **12.** brother. **13.** brotherhood.

BA bank acceptance.

Ba *Symbol, Chemistry.* barium.

ba. **1.** bath. **2.** bathroom.

B.A. **1.** Bachelor of Arts. [from Latin *Baccalaureus Artium*] **2.** *Theater.* bastard amber. **3.** *Baseball.* batting average. **4.** British Academy. **5.** British America. **6.** British Association (for Advancement of Science). **7.** Buenos Aires.

B.A.A. Bachelor of Applied Arts.

B.A.A.E. Bachelor of Aeronautical and Astronautical Engineering.

Bab. Babylon; Babylonia.

BAC blood-alcohol concentration: the percentage of alcohol in the bloodstream.

bact. **1.** bacterial. **2.** bacteriology. **3.** bacterium.

BAE **1.** Bureau of Agricultural Economics. **2.** Bureau of American Ethnology.

B.A.E. **1.** Bachelor of Aeronautical Engineering. **2.** Bachelor of Agricultural Engineering. **3.** Bachelor of Architectural Engineering. **4.** Bachelor of Art Education. **5.** Bachelor of Arts in Education.

B.A.Ed. Bachelor of Arts in Education.

B.A.E.E. Bachelor of Arts in Elementary Education.

B.Ag. Bachelor of Agriculture.

B.Ag.E. Bachelor of Agricultural Engineering.

B.Agr. Bachelor of Agriculture.

B.Ag.Sc. Bachelor of Agricultural Science.

Ba. Is. Bahama Islands.

B.A.Jour. Bachelor of Arts in Journalism.

BAK file (bak), *Computers.* backup file.

BAL **1.** *Chemistry.* British Anti-Lewisite: dimercaprol. **2.** *Computers.* Basic Assembly Language.

bal blood alcohol level.

Bal. Baluchistan.

bal. **1.** balance. **2.** balancing.

Balt. Baltic.

balun balanced-to-unbalanced network.

B.A.M. **1.** Bachelor of Applied Mathematics. **2.** Bachelor of Arts in Music.

B.A.Mus.Ed. Bachelor of Arts in Music Education.

B and B **1.** *Trademark.* a brand of liqueur combining Benedictine and brandy. **2.** bed-and-breakfast. Also, **B&B**

B&D bondage and discipline: used in reference to sadomasochistic sexual practices. Also, **B and D**

B&S Brown and Sharp wire gauge.

Bap. Baptist. Also, **Bapt.**

bap. baptized.

B.A.P.C.T. Bachelor of Arts in Practical Christian Training.

B.App.Arts. Bachelor of Applied Arts.

BAR Browning automatic rifle.

Bar. *Bible.* Baruch.

bar. **1.** barometer. **2.** barometric. **3.** barrel. **4.** barrister.

B.Ar. Bachelor of Architecture.

B.Arch. Bachelor of Architecture.

B.Arch.E. Bachelor of Architectural Engineering.

barit. baritone.

baro barometer.

barr. barrister.

BART (bärt), Bay Area Rapid Transit.

Bart. Baronet.

B.A.S. **1.** Bachelor of Agricultural Science. **2.** Bachelor of Applied Science.

B.A.Sc. **1.** Bachelor of Agricultural Science. **2.** Bachelor of Applied Science.

BASIC (bā′sik), *Computers.* a programming language that uses English words, punctuation marks, and algebraic notation. [*B(eginner's)   A(ll-purpose)   S(ymbolic)   I(nstruction)   C(ode)*]

bat. **1.** battalion. **2.** battery.

BATF Bureau of Alcohol, Tobacco, and Firearms.

batt. **1.** battalion. **2.** battery.

Bav. **1.** Bavaria. **2.** Bavarian.

bay *Electronics.* bayonet.

bayc *Electronics.* bayonet candelabra.

bay cand dc *Electronics.* bayonet candelabra double-contact.

bay cand sc *Electronics.* bayonet candelabra single-contact.

BB a quality rating for a corporate or municipal bond, lower than BBB and higher than B.

bb. **1.** ball bearing. **2.** *Baseball.* base on balls; bases on balls. **3.** bulletin board.

B/B bottled in bond.

B.B. **1.** bail bond. **2.** Blue Book. **3.** B'nai B'rith. **4.** Bureau of the Budget.

b.b. **1.** bail bond. **2.** baseboard.

B.B.A. **1.** Bachelor of Business Administration. **2.** Big Brothers of America.

BBB Better Business Bureau.

BBB a quality rating for a corporate or municipal bond, lower than A and higher than BB.

B.B.C. British Broadcasting Corporation. Also, **BBC**

bbl. barrel.

bbq barbecue.

bbrg ball bearing.

BBS *Computers.* **1.** bulletin board service. **2.** bulletin board system.

BC **1.** British Columbia, Canada (for use with ZIP code). **2.** *Scuba Diving.* buoyancy compensator.

bc **1.** *Music.* basso continuo. **2.** between centers. **3.** Also, **bcc** blind carbon copy: used as a notation on the carbon copy of a letter or other document sent to a third person without the addressee's knowledge. **4.** broadcast.

B/C bills for collection.

B.C. **1.** Bachelor of Chemistry. **2.** Bachelor of Commerce. **3.** bass clarinet. **4.** battery commander. **5.** before Christ (used in indicating dates). **6.** British Columbia.

BCA Boys' Clubs of America.

bcc blind carbon copy.

BCD **1.** *Military.* bad conduct discharge. **2.** *Computers.* binary-coded decimal system.

B.C.E. **1.** Bachelor of Chemical Engineering. **2.** Bachelor of Christian Education. **3.** Bachelor of Civil Engineering. **4.** before Christian (or Common) Era.

B.Cer.E. Bachelor of Ceramic Engineering.

bcfsk binary-coded frequency-shift keying.

bch. bunch.

B.Ch. Bachelor of Chemistry.

B.Ch.E. Bachelor of Chemical Engineering.

bci binary-coded information.

B.C.L. Bachelor of Civil Law.

bcn beacon.

BCNU *Pharmacology.* carmustine. [abbreviation of the chemical name *1,3-bis   2-chloro-ethyl-1-nitrosourea*]

B.Com.Sc. Bachelor of Commercial Science.

B.C.P. **1.** Bachelor of City Planning. **2.** Book of Common Prayer.

B.C.S. **1.** Bachelor of Chemical Science. **2.** Bachelor of Commercial Science.

Bd *Symbol.* baud.

BD. (in Bahrain) dinar; dinars.

bd. **1.** board. **2.** bond. **3.** bound. **4.** bundle.

B/D **1.** bank draft. **2.** bills discounted. **3.** *Accounting.* brought down.

b/d barrels per day.

B.D. **1.** Bachelor of Divinity. **2.** bank draft. **3.** bills discounted.

B.D.A. **1.** Bachelor of Domestic Arts. **2.** Bachelor of Dramatic Art.

bdc bottom dead center.

bde *Military.* brigade.

bd elim band elimination.

B.Des. Bachelor of Design.

bd. ft. board foot; board feet.

bdg binding.

bdgh binding head.

bdl. bundle.

bdle. bundle.

bdrm. bedroom.

bdry boundary.

B.D.S. Bachelor of Dental Surgery.

b.d.s. (in prescriptions) twice a day. [from Latin *bis diē sūmendum*]

BDSA Business and Defense Services Administration.

Be *Symbol, Chemistry.* beryllium.

Bé. *Chemistry.* Baumé: calibrated according to a Baumé scale, used to measure specific gravity of liquids.

B/E bill of exchange. Also, **b.e.**

B.E. **1.** Bachelor of Education. **2.** Bachelor of Engineering. **3.** Bank of England. **4.** bill of exchange. **5.** Board of Education.

bec. because.

B.Ed. Bachelor of Education.

B.E.E. Bachelor of Electrical Engineering.

bef. before.

B.E.F. British Expeditionary Force; British Expeditionary Forces.

Bel. **1.** Belgian. **2.** Belgic. **3.** Belgium.

Belg. **1.** Belgian. **2.** Belgium.

B.E.M. **1.** Bachelor of Engineering

of Mines. **2.** British Empire Medal.

benef. beneficiary.

Beng. 1. Bengal. **2.** Bengali.

B. Engr. Bachelor of Engineering.

B.E.P. Bachelor of Engineering Physics.

ber bit error rate.

Ber. Is. Bermuda Islands.

B.E.S. Bachelor of Engineering Science.

BEShT *Judaism.* Baal Shem-Tov.

BET Black Entertainment Television.

bet. between.

betw between.

BeV (bev), *Physics.* billion electron-volts. Also, **Bev, bev**

BEW Board of Economic Warfare.

BF black female.

bf. *Law.* brief.

B/F *Accounting.* brought forward.

B.F. 1. Bachelor of Finance. **2.** Bachelor of Forestry.

b.f. *Printing.* boldface. Also, **bf**

B.F.A. Bachelor of Fine Arts.

B.F.A.Mus. Bachelor of Fine Arts in Music.

bfo *Electronics.* beat-frequency oscillator.

bfr 1. before. **2.** buffer.

B.F.S. Bachelor of Foreign Service.

BFT biofeedback training. Also, **bft**

B.F.T. Bachelor of Foreign Trade.

bg. 1. background. **2.** bag.

B.G. 1. Birmingham gauge. **2.** brigadier general. Also, **BG**

bge beige.

bGH *Biochemistry, Agriculture.* bovine growth hormone.

Bglr. bugler.

BHA *Chemistry, Pharmacology.* a synthetic antioxidant, $C_{11}H_{16}O_2$. [*b(utylated) h(ydroxy)a(nisole)*]

BHC *Chemistry.* a crystalline, water-soluble, poisonous solid, $C_6H_6Cl_6$. [*b(enzene) h(exa) c(hloride)*]

bhd. bulkhead.

B.H.L. 1. Bachelor of Hebrew Letters. **2.** Bachelor of Hebrew Literature.

Bhn *Metallurgy.* Brinell hardness number.

bhp brake horsepower. Also, **BHP, B.H.P., b.hp., b.h.p.**

BHT *Chemistry, Pharmacology.* an antioxidant, $C_{15}H_{24}O$. [*b(utylated) h(ydroxy)t(oluene)*]

BI *Real Estate.* built-in.

Bi *Symbol, Chemistry.* bismuth.

bi bisexual.

BIA Bureau of Indian Affairs.

BiAF bisexual Asian female.

BiAM bisexual Asian male.

Bib. 1. Bible. **2.** Biblical.

bib. (in prescriptions) drink. [from Latin *bibe*]

BiBF bisexual black female.

Bibl Biblical. Also, **Bibl.**

bibl. 1. biblical. **2.** bibliographical. **3.** bibliography.

BiblHeb Biblical Hebrew.

BiBM bisexual black male.

bicarb. 1. bicarbonate. **2.** bicarbonate of soda.

B.I.D. Bachelor of Industrial Design.

b.i.d. (in prescriptions) twice a day. [from Latin *bis in die*]

B.I.E. Bachelor of Industrial Engineering.

BiF bisexual female.

Big O *Slang.* orgasm.

BIL Braille Institute Library.

BiM bisexual male.

bin binary.

B.Ind.Ed. Bachelor of Industrial Education.

biog. 1. biographer. **2.** biographical. **3.** biography.

biol. 1. biological. **2.** biologist. **3.** biology.

BIOS (bī′ōs, -os), *Computers.* firmware that directs many basic functions of the operating system. [*B(asic) I(nput)/O(utput) S(ystem)*]

B.I.S. 1. Bank for International Settlements. **2.** British Information Services.

B.I.T. Bachelor of Industrial Technology.

BiWF bisexual white female.

BiWM bisexual white male.

B.J. Bachelor of Journalism.

Bk *Symbol, Chemistry.* berkelium.

bk 1. back. **2.** *Baseball.* balk; balks. **3.** black.

bk. 1. bank. **2.** book.

bkbndr. bookbinder.

bkcy. bankruptcy.

bkdn breakdown.

bkg. 1. banking. **2.** bookkeeping. **3.** breakage.

bkgd. background.

bklr. *Printing.* black letter.

bkpg. bookkeeping.

bkpr. bookkeeper.

bkpt. bankrupt.

bks. 1. banks. **2.** barracks. **3.** books.

bkt. 1. basket. **2.** bracket. **3.** bucket.

bl. 1. bale; bales. **2.** barrel; barrels. **3.** black. **4.** block. **5.** blue.

b/l *Commerce.* bill of lading. Also, **B/L**

B.L. 1. Bachelor of Laws. **2.** Bachelor of Letters. **3.** bill of lading.

b.l. 1. bill of lading. **2.** *Military.* breech loading.

B.L.A. 1. Bachelor of Landscape Architecture. **2.** Bachelor of Liberal Arts.

bldg. building.

Bldg.E. Building Engineer.

bldr. builder.

B.L.E. Brotherhood of Locomotive Engineers.

B.Lit. Bachelor of Literature.

B.Litt. Bachelor of Letters.

blk. 1. black. **2.** block. **3.** bulk.

blkg 1. blanking. **2.** blocking.

B.LL. Bachelor of Laws.

BLM Bureau of Land Management. Also, **B.L.M.**

blo blower.

BLS Bureau of Labor Statistics.

bls. 1. bales. **2.** barrels.

B.L.S. 1. Bachelor of Library Science. **2.** Bureau of Labor Statistics.

BLT a bacon, lettuce, and tomato sandwich. Also, **B.L.T.**

bltin built-in.

Blvd. boulevard. Also, **blvd.**

blw below.

blzd blizzard.

BM 1. basal metabolism. **2.** *Surveying.* bench mark. **3.** black

male. **4.** *Informal.* bowel movement.

bm *Electricity.* break-before-make: a relay contact.

B.M. 1. Bachelor of Medicine. **2.** Bachelor of Music. **3.** British Museum.

B.Mar.E. Bachelor of Marine Engineering.

B.M.E. 1. Bachelor of Mechanical Engineering. **2.** Bachelor of Mining Engineering. **3.** Bachelor of Music Education.

B.M.Ed. Bachelor of Music Education.

B.Met. Bachelor of Metallurgy.

B.Met.E. Bachelor of Metallurgical Engineering.

BMEWS (bē myōōz′), *U.S. Military.* Ballistic Missile Early Warning System.

B.Mgt.E. Bachelor of Management Engineering.

BMI Broadcast Music, Inc.

B.Min.E. Bachelor of Mining Engineering.

BMOC big man on campus. Also, **B.M.O.C.**

BMR basal metabolic rate.

B.M.S. Bachelor of Marine Science.

B.M.T. Bachelor of Medical Technology.

B.Mus. Bachelor of Music.

B.M.V. Blessed Mary the Virgin. [from Latin *Beāta Maria Virgō*]

bn brown.

Bn. 1. Baron. **2.** Battalion.

bn. battalion.

B.N. Bachelor of Nursing.

BNA British North America. Also, **B.N.A.**

BND Germany's national intelligence service. [from German *B(undes)n(achrichten)d(ienst)*]

bnls boneless.

bnr burner.

B.N.S. Bachelor of Naval Science.

bnsh burnish.

bnz bronze.

bo 1. blackout. **2.** *Electronics.* blocking oscillator.

B/o *Accounting.* brought over.

B.O. 1. Board of Ordnance. **2.** *Informal.* body odor. **3.** *Theater.* box office.

b.o. 1. back order. **2.** box office. **3.** branch office. **4.** broker's order. **5.** buyer's option.

BOB Bureau of the Budget.

BOD biochemical oxygen demand.

Bol. Bolivia.

bol. (in prescriptions) bolus (larger than a regular pill).

BOMFOG brotherhood of man, fatherhood of God.

BOQ *U.S. Military.* bachelor officers' quarters.

bor. borough.

bot. 1. botanic; botanical. **2.** botanist. **3.** botany. **4.** bottle.

B.O.T. Board of Trade.

BP 1. beautiful people; beautiful person. **2.** blood pressure.

bp 1. between perpendiculars. **2.** blueprint. **3.** boilerplate.

bp. 1. baptized. **2.** birthplace. **3.** bishop.

B/P *Commerce.* bills payable.

B.P. 1. Bachelor of Pharmacy. **2.** Bachelor of Philosophy. **3.**

Finance. basis point. **4.** *Archaeology.* before the present: (in radiocarbon dating) in a specified amount of time or at a specified point in time before A.D. 1950. **5.** *Commerce.* bills payable.

b.p. 1. *Finance.* basis point. **2.** below proof. **3.** *Commerce.* bills payable. **4.** *Physics, Chemistry.* boiling point. **5.** the public good [from Latin *bonum publicum*].

bpa bandpass amplifier.

B.P.A. Bachelor of Professional Arts.

BPD barrels per day. Also, **B.P.D.**

B.P.E. Bachelor of Physical Education.

B.Pet.E. Bachelor of Petroleum Engineering.

B.Ph. Bachelor of Philosophy.

B.P.H. Bachelor of Public Health.

B.Pharm. Bachelor of Pharmacy.

B.Phil. Bachelor of Philosophy.

BPI 1. Also, **bpi** *Computers.* **a.** bits per inch. **b.** bytes per inch. **2.** Bureau of Public Inquiries.

bpl. birthplace.

B.P.O.E. Benevolent and Protective Order of Elks.

bps *Computers.* bits per second. Also, **BPS**

BR 1. *Real Estate.* bedroom. **2.** Bureau of Reclamation.

Br *Symbol, Chemistry.* bromine.

Br. 1. branch (in place names). **2.** brick. **3.** Britain. **4.** British.

br. 1. bedroom. **2.** branch. **3.** brass. **4.** brig. **5.** bronze. **6.** brother. **7.** brown.

b.r. *Commerce.* bills receivable. Also, **B.R., B/R**

Braz. 1. Brazil. **2.** Brazilian.

B.R.C.A. Brotherhood of Railway Carmen of America.

B.R.C.S. British Red Cross Society.

brdg bridge.

B.R.E. Bachelor of Religious Education.

brg bearing.

Brig. 1. brigade. **2.** brigadier.

Brig. Gen. brigadier general.

Brit. 1. Britain. **2.** British.

brk brake.

brkg breaking.

brkr *Electricity.* breaker.

brkt bracket.

brng burning.

Bros. brothers. Also, **bros.**

brs brass.

Br. Som. British Somaliland.

BR STD British Standard.

brt 1. bright. **2.** brightness.

B.R.T. Brotherhood of Railroad Trainmen.

BRV Bravo (a cable television station).

brz braze.

BS 1. Bureau of Standards. **2.** *Slang (sometimes vulgar).* bullshit.

b/s 1. bags. **2.** bales. **3.** bill of sale.

B.S. 1. Bachelor of Science. **2.** Bachelor of Surgery. **3.** bill of sale. **4.** *Slang (sometimes vulgar).* bullshit.

b.s. 1. balance sheet. **2.** bill of sale. **3.** *Slang (sometimes vulgar).* bullshit.

B.S.A. 1. Also, **B. S. Agr.** Bachelor of Science in Agriculture. **2.**

Bachelor of Scientific Agriculture. **3.** Boy Scouts of America.

B.S.A.A. Bachelor of Science in Applied Arts.

B.S.Adv. Bachelor of Science in Advertising.

B.S.A.E. 1. Also, **B.S.Ae.Eng.** Bachelor of Science in Aeronautical Engineering. **2.** Also, **B.S. Ag.E.** Bachelor of Science in Agricultural Engineering. **3.** Also, **B.S. Arch.E., B.S.Arch.Eng.** Bachelor of Science in Architectural Engineering.

B.S.Arch. Bachelor of Science in Architecture.

B.S.Art.Ed. Bachelor of Science in Art Education.

B.S.B.A. Bachelor of Science in Business Administration.

B.S.Bus. Bachelor of Science in Business.

B.S.Bus.Mgt. Bachelor of Science in Business Management.

B.Sc. Bachelor of Science.

B.S.C. Bachelor of Science in Commerce.

B.S.C.E. Bachelor of Science in Civil Engineering.

B.S.Ch. Bachelor of Science in Chemistry.

B.S.Ch.E. Bachelor of Science in Chemical Engineering.

B.Sch.Music Bachelor of School Music.

B.S.Com. Bachelor of Science in Communications.

B.S.C.P. Brotherhood of Sleeping Car Porters.

B.S.D. Bachelor of Science in Design. Also, **B.S.Des.**

B.S.E. 1. Also, **B.S.Ed.** Bachelor of Science in Education. **2.** Also, **B. S.Eng.** Bachelor of Science in Engineering.

B.S.Ec. Bachelor of Science in Economics.

B.S.E.E. 1. Also, **B.S.E.Engr.** Bachelor of Science in Electrical Engineering. **2.** Bachelor of Science in Elementary Education.

B.S.El.E. Bachelor of Science in Electronic Engineering.

B.S.E.M. Bachelor of Science in Engineering of Mines.

B.S.E.P. Bachelor of Science in Engineering Physics.

B.S.E.S. Bachelor of Science in Engineering Sciences.

B.S.F. Bachelor of Science in Forestry. Also, **B.S.For.**

B.S.F.M. Bachelor of Science in Forest Management.

B.S.F.Mgt. Bachelor of Science in Fisheries Management.

B.S.F.S. Bachelor of Science in Foreign Service.

B.S.F.T. Bachelor of Science in Fuel Technology.

B.S.G.E. Bachelor of Science in General Engineering. Also, **B.S. Gen.Ed.**

B.S.G.Mgt. Bachelor of Science in Game Management.

bsh. bushel; bushels.

B.S.H.A. Bachelor of Science in Hospital Administration.

B.S.H.E. Bachelor of Science in Home Economics. Also, **B.S.H.Ec.**

B.S.H.Ed. Bachelor of Science in Health Education.

bshg bushing.

B.S.Hyg. Bachelor of Science in Hygiene.

B.S.I.E. 1. Also, **B.S.Ind.Ed.** Bachelor of Science in Industrial Education. **2.** Also, **B.S.Ind.Engr.** Bachelor of Science in Industrial Engineering.

B.S.Ind.Mgt. Bachelor of Science in Industrial Management.

B.S.I.R. Bachelor of Science in Industrial Relations.

B.S.I.T. Bachelor of Science in Industrial Technology.

B.S.J. Bachelor of Science in Journalism.

bskt. basket.

Bs/L bills of lading.

B.S.L. 1. Bachelor of Sacred Literature. **2.** Bachelor of Science in Law. **3.** Bachelor of Science in Linguistics.

B.S.L.A. and Nurs. Bachelor of Science in Liberal Arts and Nursing.

B.S.Lab.Rel. Bachelor of Science in Labor Relations.

B.S.L.Arch. Bachelor of Science in Landscape Architecture.

B.S.L.M. Bachelor of Science in Landscape Management.

B.S.L.S. Bachelor of Science in Library Science.

B.S.M. 1. Bachelor of Sacred Music. **2.** Bachelor of Science in Medicine. **3.** Bachelor of Science in Music.

B.S.M.E. 1. Bachelor of Science in Mechanical Engineering. **2.** Bachelor of Science in Mining Engineering. **3.** Also, **B.S.Mus.Ed.** Bachelor of Science in Music Education.

B.S.Met. Bachelor of Science in Metallurgy.

B.S.Met.E. Bachelor of Science in Metallurgical Engineering.

bsmt basement. Also, **Bsmt**

B.S.M.T. Bachelor of Science in Medical Technology. Also, **B.S. Med.Tech.**

B.S.N. Bachelor of Science in Nursing.

B.S.N.A. Bachelor of Science in Nursing Administration.

bsns business

BSO *Astronomy.* blue stellar object.

B.S.Orn.Hort. Bachelor of Science in Ornamental Horticulture.

B.S.O.T. Bachelor of Science in Occupational Therapy.

B.S.P. Bachelor of Science in Pharmacy. Also, **B.S.Phar., B.S. Pharm.**

B.S.P.A. Bachelor of Science in Public Administration.

B.S.P.E. Bachelor of Science in Physical Education.

B.S.P.H. Bachelor of Science in Public Health.

B.S.P.H.N. Bachelor of Science in Public Health Nursing.

B.S.P.T. Bachelor of Science in Physical Therapy. Also, **B.S. Ph.Th.**

B.S.Radio-TV. Bachelor of Science in Radio and Television.

B.S.Ret. Bachelor of Science in Retailing.

B.S.R.T. Bachelor of Science in Radiological Technology.

B.S.S. 1. Bachelor of Secretarial Science. **2.** Bachelor of Social Science.

B.S.S.A. Bachelor of Science in Secretarial Administration.

B.S.S.E. Bachelor of Science in Secondary Education.

B.S.S. 1. Bachelor of Science in Secretarial Studies. **2.** Bachelor of Science in Social Science.

B.S.T.&I.E. Bachelor of Science in Trade and Industrial Education.

bstb *Electricity, Electronics.* bistable.

B.S.Trans. Bachelor of Science in Transportation.

Bt. Baronet.

bt. 1. boat. **2.** bought.

B.T. 1. Bachelor of Theology. **2.** board of trade.

B.t. *Biology, Agriculture.* Bacillus thuringiensis.

B.T.Ch. Bachelor of Textile Chemistry.

B.T.E. Bachelor of Textile Engineering.

bth bathroom.

B.Th. Bachelor of Theology.

btl. bottle.

btn button.

btn. battalion.

btry. battery.

btry chgr battery charger.

B.T.U. *Physics.* British thermal unit; British thermal units. Also, **BTU, B.t.u., B.th.u., Btu**

BU *Numismatics.* brilliant uncirculated.

bu. 1. bureau. **2.** bushel; bushels.

Bulg. 1. Bulgaria. **2.** Bulgarian. Also, **Bulg**

bull. bulletin. Also, **bul.**

BUN blood urea nitrogen.

Bur. Burma.

bur. bureau.

bus. business.

bush. bushel; bushels.

B.V. 1. Blessed Virgin. [from Latin *Beāta Virgō*] **2.** farewell. [from Latin *bene valē*]

b.v. book value.

B.V.A. Bachelor of Vocational Agriculture.

B.V.D. *Trademark.* a brand of men's underwear. Also, **BVD's**

B.V.E. Bachelor of Vocational Education.

bvg beverage.

B.V.I. British Virgin Islands.

bvl bevel.

B.V.M. Blessed Virgin Mary. [from Latin *Beāta Virgō Marīa*]

bvt. 1. brevet. **2.** brevetted.

BW 1. bacteriological warfare. **2.** biological warfare. **3.** (in television, motion pictures, photography, etc.) black and white.

bw *Telecommunications.* bandwidth.

BWC Board of War Communications.

BWG Birmingham Wire Gauge.

B.W.I. British West Indies.

bx base exchange. Also, **BX**

bx. box.

By *Computers.* byte.

BYOB bring your own bottle (in an invitation, to indicate that the host will not provide liquor). Also, **BYO**

byp. bypass. Also, **Byp.**

Byz. Byzantine.

Bz. benzene.

bzr buzzer.

---

a b **C** d e f g h i j k l m n o p q r s t u v w x y z

C 1. cocaine. **2.** *Electronics.* collector: an electron device. **3.** *Electricity.* common (in diagrams). **4.** *Grammar.* complement. **5.** consonant. **6.** coulomb. **7.** county (used with a number to designate a county road).

C *Symbol.* **1.** the third in order or in a series. **2.** (in some grading systems) a grade or mark, indicating the quality of a student's work as fair or average. **3.** *Music.* **a.** the first tone, or keynote, in the scale of C major or the third tone in the relative minor scale, A minor. **b.** a string, key, or pipe tuned to this tone. **c.** a written or printed note representing this tone. **d.** (in the fixed system of solmization) the first tone of the scale of C major, called *do*. **e.** the tonality having C as the tonic note. **f.** a symbol indicating quadruple time and appearing after the clef sign on a musical staff. **4.** (*sometimes lowercase*) the Roman numeral for 100. **5.** Celsius. **6.** centigrade. **7.** *Electricity.* **a.** capacitance. **b.** a battery size for 1.5 volt dry cells: diameter, 1 in. (2.5 cm); length, 1.9 in. (4.8 cm). **8.** *Chemistry.* carbon. **9.** *Physics.* **a.** charge conjugation. **b.** charm. **10.** *Biochemistry.* **a.** cysteine. **b.** cytosine. **11.** Also, **C-note.** *Slang.* a hundred-dollar bill. **12.** a proportional shoe width size, narrower than D and wider than B. **13.** a proportional brassiere cup size, smaller than D and larger than B. **14.** the lowest quality rating for a corporate or municipal bond. **15.** *Computers.* a high-level programming language. **16.** coulomb.

c 1. calorie. **2.** *Optics.* candle; candles. **3.** carbohydrate; carbo-

hydrates. **4.** (with a year) about: *c1775.* [from Latin *circā, circiter, circum*] **5.** *Physics, Chemistry.* curie; curies. **6.** cycle; cycles.

c- *U.S. Military.* (in designations of aircraft) cargo: *C-124.*

C. 1. calorie. **2.** Cape. **3.** Catholic. **4.** Celsius. **5.** Celtic. **6.** Centigrade. **7.** College. **8.** (in Costa Rica and El Salvador) colon; colons. **9.** Congress. **10.** Conservative.

c. 1. calorie. **2.** *Optics.* candle; candles. **3.** carat. **4.** carbon. **5.** carton. **6.** case. **7.** *Baseball.* catcher. **8.** cathode. **9.** cent; cents. **10.** centavo. **11.** *Football.* center. **12.** centigrade. **13.** centime. **14.** centimeter. **15.** century. **16.** chairman; chairperson. **17.** chapter. **18.** chief. **19.** child. **20.** church. **21.** (with a year) about: *c. 1775.* [from Latin *circā, circiter, circum*] **22.** cirrus. **23.** city. **24.** cloudy. **25.** cognate. **26.** color. **27.** gallon. [from Latin *congius*] **28.** copper. **29.** copyright. **30.** corps. **31.** cubic. **32.** (in prescriptions) with. [from Latin *cum*] **33.** cycle; cycles.

C++ *Computers.* a programming language.

CA 1. cable. **2.** California (for use with ZIP code). **3.** chronological age.

Ca *Symbol, Chemistry.* calcium.

ca. 1. cathode. **2.** centiare. **3.** Also, **ca** (with a year) about: *ca. 476 B.C.* [def. 3 from Latin *circā*]

C/A 1. capital account. **2.** cash account. **3.** credit account. **4.** current account.

C.A. 1. Central America. **2.** chartered accountant. **3.** *Accounting.* chief accountant. **4.** Coast Artillery. **5.** commercial agent. **6.**

consular agent. **7.** controller of accounts. **8.** current assets.

CAA Civil Aeronautics Administration. Also, **C.A.A.**

CAB Civil Aeronautics Board. Also, **C.A.B.**

cab cabinet.

CAC *Real Estate.* central air conditioning.

C.A.C. Coast Artillery Corps.

CAD (kad), computer-aided design.

CAD/CAM (kad′kam′), computer-aided design and computer-aided manufacturing.

CADMAT (kad′mat), computer-aided design, manufacture, and test.

CAE computer-aided engineering.

C.A.F. 1. cost and freight. **2.** cost, assurance, and freight. Also, **c.a.f.**

CAFE (ka fā′, kə-), *n.* a U.S. standard of average fuel consumption for all the cars produced by one manufacturer in a given year. [*C(orporate) A(verage) F(uel) E(conomy)*]

C.A.G.S. Certificate of Advanced Graduate Study.

CAI computer-aided instruction; computer-assisted instruction. Also, **cai**

Cal kilocalorie.

cal 1. calibrate. **2.** calorie.

Cal. California.

cal. 1. calendar. **2.** caliber. **3.** calorie.

calc. calculate.

Calif. California.

CAM (kam), computer-aided manufacturing.

Cam. Cambridge.

cam. camber.

CAMA (kam′ə), *Telecommunica-*

tions. centralized automatic message accounting.

Camb. Cambridge.

camflg camouflage.

cAMP *Biochemistry.* cyclic AMP.

camr camera.

Can. 1. Canada. **2.** Canadian.

can. 1. canceled. **2.** canon. **3.** canto.

Canad. Canadian.

canc. 1. cancel. **2.** canceled. **3.** cancellation.

cand candelabra.

C. & F. *Commerce.* cost and freight.

C&I 1. commerce and industry. **2.** commercial and industrial.

c&sc *Printing.* capitals and small capitals.

cand scr candelabra screw.

C and W country-and-western. Also, **C&W**

CanF Canadian French.

Cant. 1. Canterbury. **2.** Cantonese.

cantil cantilever.

canv canvas.

CAP 1. Civil Air Patrol. **2.** Common Agricultural Policy. **3.** computer-aided publishing. **4.** *Stock Exchange.* convertible adjustable preferred (stock). Also, **C.A.P.** (for defs. 1, 2, 4).

cap. 1. capacitance, capacitor. **2.** capacity. **3.** (in prescriptions) let the patient take. [from Latin *capiat*] **4.** capital. **5.** capitalize. **6.** capitalized. **7.** capital letter. **8.** chapter. [from Latin *capitulum, caput*] **9.** computer-aided production.

cap. moll. (in prescriptions) soft capsule. [from Latin *capsula mollis*]

caps. 1. capital letters. **2.** (in prescriptions) a capsule [from Latin *capsula*].

cap scr cap screw.

capt. *Military.* captain. Also, **CPT**

CAR computer-assisted retrieval.

car. 1. carat; carats. **2.** cargo.

carb carburetor.

Card. Cardinal.

CARE (kâr), Cooperative for American Relief Everywhere. Also, **Care**

Caricom (kar′i kom′, kâr′-), an economic association formed in 1974 by ten Caribbean nations. Also, **CARICOM** [*Cari(bbean) com(munity)*]

Carol. Carolingian.

carp. carpentry.

carr carrier.

carr cur carrier current.

CAS collision-avoidance system.

cas 1. calculated airspeed. **2.** castle.

C.A.S. Certificate of Advanced Studies.

case computer-aided support equipment.

cas nut castle nut.

CAT 1. clear-air turbulence. **2.** *Medicine.* computerized axial tomography.

cat. 1. catalog; catalogue. **2.** catapult. **3.** catechism.

cate computer-aided test equipment.

cath *Electricity.* cathode.

Cath. 1. (*often lowercase*) cathedral. **2.** Catholic.

CATV community antenna television (a cable television system).

caus. causative.

cav. 1. cavalier. **2.** cavalry. **3.** cavity.

cax community automatic exchange.

CB 1. Citizens Band (radio). **2.** *Military.* construction battalion. **3.** continental breakfast.

Cb *Symbol, Chemistry.* columbium.

cb 1. *Electronics.* common base. **2.** *Telephones.* common battery.

C.B. 1. Bachelor of Surgery. [from Latin *Chīrurgiae Baccalaureus*] **2.** *British.* Companion of the Bath.

cbal counterbalance.

CBAT College Board Achievement Test.

CBC 1. Also, **C.B.C.** Canadian Broadcasting Corporation. **2.** *Medicine.* complete blood count.

C.B.D. 1. cash before delivery. **2.** central business district.

C.B.E. Commander of the Order of the British Empire.

C.B.E.L. Cambridge Bibliography of English Literature. Also, **CBEL**

CBI computer-based instruction.

CBO Congressional Budget Office.

cbore counterbore.

cboreo counterbore other side.

CBS Columbia Broadcasting System.

CBT 1. Chicago Board of Trade. **2.** computer-based training.

CBW chemical and biological warfare.

CC *Symbol.* a quality rating for a corporate or municipal bond, lower than CCC and higher than C.

Cc cirrocumulus.

cc 1. carbon copy. **2.** close-coupled. **3.** closing coil. **4.** *Electronics.* common collector. **5.** copies. **6.** crosscouple. **7.** cubic centimeter.

cc. 1. carbon copy. **2.** chapters. **3.** copies. **4.** cubic centimeter. Also, **c.c.**

C.C. 1. carbon copy. **2.** cashier's check. **3.** chief clerk. **4.** circuit court. **5.** city council. **6.** city councilor. **7.** civil court. **8.** company commander. **9.** county clerk. **10.** county commissioner. **11.** county council. **12.** county court. Also, **c.c.**

C.C.A. 1. Chief Clerk of the Admiralty. **2.** Circuit Court of Appeals. **3.** County Court of Appeals.

CCC 1. Civilian Conservation Corps. **2.** Commodity Credit Corporation. **3.** copyright clearance center.

CCD 1. *Electronics.* charge-coupled device. **2.** Confraternity of Christian Doctrine.

ccf hundred cubic feet (used of gas).

ccg *Electricity.* constant-current generator.

C.C.I.A. Consumer Credit Insurance Association.

CCITT Consultative Committee for International Telephony and Telegraphy.

CCK *Physiology.* cholecystokinin.

C.Cls. Court of Claims.

CCM counter-countermeasures.

ccm *Electricity.* constant-current modulation.

ccn contract change notice.

cco crystal-controlled oscillator.

CCP Chinese Communist Party.

C.C.P. 1. *Law.* Code of Civil Procedure. **2.** Court of Common Pleas.

CCR Commission on Civil Rights.

ccs 1. *Telephones.* common-channel signaling. **2.** continuous commercial service.

cct *Electricity.* constant-current transformer.

CCTV closed-circuit television.

CCU coronary-care unit.

ccu camera control unit.

ccw counterclockwise.

CD 1. *Finance.* certificate of deposit. **2.** Civil Defense. **3.** Community Development. **4.** compact disk.

Cd *Symbol, Chemistry.* cadmium.

cd 1. candela; candelas. **2.** card. **3.** circuit description. **4.** cold drawn. **5.** Also, **cd.** cord; cords. **6.** current density.

C/D certificate of deposit. Also, **c/d**

C.D. 1. *Finance.* certificate of deposit. **2.** Civil Defense. **3.** civil disobedience. **4.** Congressional District.

c.d. cash discount.

CDC Centers for Disease Control.

cdc cold-drawn copper.

cdel constant delivery.

cdf *Telephones.* combined distributing frame.

cdg coding.

CD-P compact disc-photographic.

cd pl cadmium plate.

Cdr. Commander. Also, **CDR**

cd rdr card reader.

cdrill counterdrill.

CD-ROM (sē′dē′rom′), a compact disk on which digitized read-only data can be stored. [*c(ompact) d(isk) r(ead-)o(nly) m(emory)*]

cds cold-drawn steel.

CDT Central daylight time. Also, **C.D.T.**

CDTA Capital District Transportation Authority.

cdx control-differential transmitter.

Ce *Symbol, Chemistry.* cerium.

ce 1. *Electronics.* common emitter. **2.** communications-electronics.

C.E. 1. Chemical Engineer. **2.** chief engineer. **3.** Christian Era. **4.** Church of England. **5.** Civil Engineer. **6.** common era. **7.** Corps of Engineers.

c.e. 1. buyer's risk. [from Latin *cáveat emptor* may the buyer beware] **2.** compass error.

CEA Council of Economic Advisers.

CEEB College Entrance Examination Board.

C.E.F. Canadian Expeditionary Force.

Cels. Celsius.

Celt. Celtic.

CEM communications electronics meteorological.

cem cement.

CEMA Council for Economic Mutual Assistance.

cemf counter electromotive force.

cen. 1. central. 2. century.

cent. 1. centigrade. 2. central. 3. centum. 4. century.

CEO chief executive officer. Also, **C.E.O.**

cephalom. cephalometry.

cer ceramic.

Cer.E. Ceramic Engineer.

cermet (sûr′met), ceramic-to-metal: a type of seal.

CERN (sârn, sûrn), European Laboratory for Particle Physics; formerly called European Organization for Nuclear Research. [from French *C(onseil) e(uropéen pour la) r(echerche) n(ucléaire)*]

cert. 1. certificate. 2. certification. 3. certified. 4. certify.

certif. 1. certificate. 2. certificated.

CETA (sē′tə), Comprehensive Employment and Training Act.

cet. par. other things being equal. [from Latin *ceteris paribus*]

CF 1. *Baseball.* center field. 2. *Baseball.* center fielder. 3. Christian female. 4. Also, **cf** cubic foot; cubic feet. 5. cystic fibrosis.

Cf *Symbol, Chemistry.* californium.

cf 1. cathode follower. 2. center field. 3. center fielder. 4. centrifugal force. 5. concrete floor.

cf. 1. *Bookbinding.* calf. 2. *Music.* cantus firmus. 3. compare [from Latin *confer*].

c.f. 1. *Baseball.* center field. 2. *Baseball.* center fielder. 3. cost and freight.

c/f *Bookkeeping.* carried forward.

C.F. cost and freight.

CFA chartered financial analyst.

CFAE contractor-furnished aircraft equipment.

cfd cubic feet per day.

CFE contractor-furnished equipment.

CFG Camp Fire Girls.

cfh cubic feet per hour.

C.F.I. cost, freight, and insurance. Also, **c.f.i.**

CFL Canadian Football League.

cfm cubic feet per minute.

CFNP Community Food and Nutrition Programs.

CFO chief financial officer. Also, **C.F.O.**

CFP 1. certified financial planner. 2. contractor-furnished property.

CFR Code of Federal Regulations.

cfr crossfire.

CFS chronic fatigue syndrome.

cfs 1. cold-finished steel. 2. cubic feet per second.

CFT *Medicine.* complement fixation test.

CFTC Commodity Futures Trading Commission.

CG Commanding General.

cg centigram; centigrams.

C.G. 1. Captain of the Guard. 2. center of gravity. 3. Coast Guard. 4. Commanding General. 5. Consul General.

c.g. 1. Captain of the Guard. 2. center of gravity. 3. Commanding General. 4. Consul General.

CGA *Computers.* color graphics adapter.

cgs centimeter-gram-second (system). Also, **CGS, c.g.s.**

ch 1. case harden. 2. *Surveying, Civil Engineering.* chain; chains. 3. channel. 4. chiffonier. 5. *Electricity.* choke.

Ch. 1. Chaldean. 2. Chaldee. 3. *Television.* channel. 4. chapter. 5. Château. 6. *Chess.* check. 7. China. 8. Chinese. 9. church.

ch. 1. chair. 2. chaplain. 3. chapter. 4. *Chess.* check. 5. chief. 6. child; children. 7. church.

c.h. 1. candle hours. 2. clearinghouse. 3. courthouse. 4. custom house.

chal challenge.

Chal. 1. Chaldaic. 2. Chaldean. 3. Chaldee.

Chald. 1. Chaldaic. 2. Chaldean. 3. Chaldee.

cham chamfer.

Chan. 1. Chancellor. 2. Chancery. Also, **Chanc.**

chan. channel.

chanc. 1. chancellor. 2. chancery.

chap. 1. Chaplain. 2. chapter. Also, **Chap.**

char. 1. character. 2. charter.

chart. (in prescriptions) paper. [from Latin *charta*]

chart. cerat. (in prescriptions) waxed paper. [from Latin *charta cērāta*]

chas chassis.

Chât. (especially in Bordeaux wines) Château.

Ch.B. Bachelor of Surgery. [from Latin *Chīrurgiae Baccalaureus*]

chc choke coil.

chd chord.

Ch.E. Chemical Engineer.

Chem. 1. chemical. 2. chemist. 3. chemistry.

Chem.E. Chemical Engineer.

chg. 1. change. 2. charge. Also, **chge.**

chgov changeover.

Chin. 1. China. 2. Chinese. Also, **Chin**

Ch. J. Chief Justice.

chk check.

chkb check bit.

chld chilled.

chm. 1. chairman. 2. checkmate.

chmbr chamber.

chmn. chairman.

chng change.

choc. chocolate.

chp 1. chairperson. 2. chopper.

CHQ Corps Headquarters.

chr chroma.

Chr. 1. Christ. 2. Christian.

Chron. *Bible.* Chronicles.

chron. 1. chronicle. 2. chronograph. 3. chronological. 4. chronology.

chrst characteristic.

chs. chapters.

chw chairwoman.

CI counterintelligence.

Ci curie; curies.

ci 1. cast iron. 2. circuit interrupter.

C.I. Channel Islands.

CIA Central Intelligence Agency. Also, **C.I.A.**

Cia. Company. Also, **cia.** [from Spanish *Compañía*]

cib. (in prescriptions) food. [from Latin *cibus*]

C.I.C. 1. Combat Information Center. 2. Commander in Chief. 3. Counterintelligence Corps.

cid component identification.

C.I.D. Criminal Investigation Department (of Scotland Yard).

c.i.d. *Automotive.* cubic-inch displacement: the displacement of an engine measured in cubic inches. Also, **cid, CID**

Cie. Company. Also, **cie.** [from French *Compagnie*]

C.I.F. *Commerce.* cost, insurance, and freight (the price quoted includes the cost of the merchandise, packing, and freight to a specified destination plus insurance charges). Also, **CIF, c.i.f.**

CIM 1. computer input from microfilm. 2. computer-integrated manufacturing.

C. in C. Commander in Chief. Also, **C-in-C**

cine cinematographic.

C.I.O. 1. chief investment officer. 2. Congress of Industrial Organizations. Also, **CIO**

CIP Cataloging in Publication: a program in which a partial bibliographic description of a work appears on the verso of its title page.

cip cast-iron pipe.

Cir. circle (approved for postal use).

cir. 1. about: *cir. 1800.* [from Latin *circā, circiter, circum*] 2. circle. 3. circular.

circ (sûrk), circular.

circ. 1. about: *circ. 1800.* [from Latin *circā, circiter, circum*] 2. circuit. 3. circular. 4. circulation. 5. circumference.

circum. circumference.

CIS *Computers.* CompuServe Information Services.

C.I.S. Commonwealth of Independent States.

CISC (sisk), complex instruction set computer.

cit. 1. citation. 2. cited. 3. citizen. 4. citrate.

C.I.T. counselor in training.

ciu computer interface unit.

Civ. 1. civil. 2. civilian.

CJ Chief Justice.

ck. 1. cask. 2. check. 3. cook. 4. cork.

ckb cork base.

ckbd corkboard.

ckpt cockpit.

ckt circuit.

ckt brkr circuit breaker.

ckt cl circuit closing.

ckt op circuit opening.

CL common law.

Cl *Symbol, Chemistry.* chlorine.

cl 1. center line. 2. centiliter; centiliters. 3. class. 4. closed loop. 5. clothing. 6. clutch.

cl. 1. carload. 2. claim. 3. clarinet. 4. class. 5. classification. 6. clause. 7. clearance. 8. clerk. 9. close. 10. closet. 11. cloth.

C/L 1. carload. 2. carload lot. 3. cash letter.

c.l. 1. carload. 2. carload lot. 3. center line. 4. civil law. 5. common law.

CLA College Language Association.

clar. clarinet.

class. **1.** classic. **2.** classical. **3.** classification. **4.** classified.

cld. **1.** *Stock Exchange.* (of bonds) called. **2.** cleared. **3.** cooled.

cldy cloudy.

clg **1.** ceiling. **2.** cooling.

CLI cost-of-living index. Also, **cli**

clin. clinical.

clk. **1.** clerk. **2.** clock.

clkg caulking.

clkj caulked joint.

cln clean.

clnc clearance.

clnt coolant.

clo. clothing.

clos *Real Estate.* closet.

clp clamp.

clpbd *Real Estate.* clapboard.

clpr clapper.

clp scr clamp screw.

clr. **1.** clear. **2.** color. **3.** cooler. **4.** current-limiting resistor.

clrg clearing.

cls classify.

clt cleat.

clthg clothing.

CLU Civil Liberties Union.

C.L.U. Chartered Life Underwriter.

clws. clockwise.

CM **1.** Christian male. **2.** Common Market. **3.** countermeasures.

Cm *Symbol, Chemistry.* curium.

cm **1.** Also, **cm.** centimeter; centimeters. **2.** *Computers.* core memory. **3.** corrective maintenance.

c/m (of capital stocks) call of more.

C.M. *Roman Catholic Church.* Congregation of the Mission.

c.m. **1.** church missionary. **2.** common meter. **3.** corresponding member. **4.** court martial.

cm³ *Symbol.* cubic centimeter.

CMA Canadian Medical Association.

C.M.A. certificate of management accounting.

CMC **1.** certified management consultant. **2.** Commandant of the Marine Corps.

cmd *Computers.* core-memory drive.

cmd. command.

cmdg. commanding.

Cmdr. Commander.

Cmdre Commodore.

CME Chicago Mercantile Exchange.

CMEA Council for Mutual Economic Assistance. See **COMECON.**

cmf coherent memory filter.

cmflr cam follower.

C.M.G. Companion of the Order of St. Michael and St. George.

CMI computer-managed instruction. Also, **cmi**

cmil circular Military.

CML current-mode logic.

cml. commercial.

cmnt comment.

CMOS (sē′môs′, -mos′), *Electronics.* complementary metal oxide semiconductor.

CMP *Biochemistry.* cytidine monophosphate.

cmpd compound.

cmplm complement.

cmplt complete.

cmpns compensate.

cmpnt component.

cmpr compare.

cmps compass.

cmpsg compensating.

cmpsn composition.

cmpst composite.

cmpt compute.

cmptg computing.

cmptr computer.

CMS *Printing.* color management system.

cms current-mode switching.

cmshft camshaft.

cmsn commission.

Cmsr Commissioner.

cmte committee.

CMV *Pathology.* cytomegalovirus.

CMYK *Computers, Printing.* cyan, magenta, yellow, black; used for color mixing for printing.

CN **1.** change notice. **2.** chloroacetophenone: used as a tear gas.

C/N **1.** circular note. **2.** credit note.

cna copper-nickel alloy.

cncl concealed.

cnctrc concentric.

cncv concave.

cnd conduit.

cndct *Electricity.* **1.** conduct. **2.** conductivity. **3.** conductor.

cnds condensate.

cndtn condition.

cnfig configuration.

CNM Certified Nurse Midwife.

CNN Cable News Network (a cable television channel).

CNO Chief of Naval Operations.

CNS central nervous system. Also, **cns**

cnsld consolidate.

cnsltnt consultant.

cnsp conspicuously.

cnstr canister.

cntbd centerboard.

cntd contained.

cntor *Electricity.* contactor.

cnvc convenience.

cnvr conveyor.

cnvt convert.

cnvtb convertible.

cnvtr converter.

cnvx convex.

CO **1.** change order. **2.** Colorado (for use with ZIP code). **3.** Commanding Officer. **4.** conscientious objector.

Co *Symbol, Chemistry.* cobalt.

co **1.** carbon monoxide. **2.** cardiac output. **3.** cutoff. **4.** cutout.

Co. **1.** Company. **2.** County. Also, **co.**

C/O **1.** cash order. **2.** *Commerce.* certificate of origin.

C/o **1.** care of. **2.** *Bookkeeping.* carried over.

c/o **1.** care of. **2.** *Bookkeeping.* carried over. **3.** cash order. **4.** consist of.

C.O. **1.** cash order. **2.** Commanding Officer. **3.** conscientious objector. **4.** correction officer.

c.o. **1.** care of. **2.** *Bookkeeping.* carried over.

COA change of address.

CoA *Biochemistry.* coenzyme A.

coam coaming.

coax (kō′aks), *Electronics.* coaxial (cable).

COBOL (kō′bôl), *Computers.* a programming language. [*Co(mmon) B(usiness-)O(riented) L(anguage)*]

coch. (in prescriptions) a spoonful. [from Latin *cochlear*]

coch. amp. (in prescriptions) a tablespoonful. [from Latin *cochlear amplum* large spoon(ful)]

coch. mag. (in prescriptions) a tablespoonful. [from Latin *cochlear magnum* large spoon(ful)]

coch. med. (in prescriptions) a dessertspoonful. [from Latin *cochlear medium* medium-sized spoon(ful)]

coch. parv. (in prescriptions) a teaspoonful. [from Latin *cochlear parvum* little spoon(ful)]

COD. codex. Also, **cod.**

C.O.D. *Commerce.* cash, or collect, on delivery (payment to be made when delivered to the purchaser). Also, **c.o.d.**

coef coefficient.

COFC container-on-flatcar.

C of C Chamber of Commerce.

coff cofferdam.

C. of S. Chief of Staff.

cog. **1.** cognate. **2.** cognizant.

coho coherent oscillator.

COIN (koin), counterinsurgency. [*co(unter) in(surgency)*]

COL **1.** Computer-Oriented Language. Also, **col** **2.** cost of living.

Col. **1.** Colombia. **2.** Colonel. **3.** Colorado. **4.** *Bible.* Colossians.

col. **1.** (in prescriptions) strain. [from Latin *colā*] **2.** collected. **3.** collector. **4.** college. **5.** collegiate. **6.** colonial. **7.** colony. **8.** color. **9.** colored. **10.** column.

COLA (kō′lə), a clause, especially in union contracts, that grants automatic wage increases to cover the rising cost of living due to inflation. [*c(ost) o(f) l(iving) a(djustment)*]

colat. (in prescriptions) strained. [from Latin *colātus*]

colent. (in prescriptions) let them be strained. Also, **colen.** [from Latin *colentur*]

colet. (in prescriptions) let it be strained. [from Latin *colētur*]

colidar coherent light detection and ranging.

coll. **1.** collateral. **2.** collect. **3.** collection. **4.** collective. **5.** collector. **6.** Also, **Coll.** college. **7.** collegiate. **8.** colloquial. **9.** (in prescriptions) an eyewash. [from Latin *collýrium*]

collab. **1.** collaboration. **2.** collaborator.

collat. collateral.

colloq. **1.** colloquial. **2.** colloquialism. **3.** colloquially.

collun. (in prescriptions) a nose wash. [from Latin *collunarium*]

collut. (in prescriptions) a mouthwash. [from Latin *collūtorium*]

collyr. (in prescriptions) an eyewash. [from Latin *collýrium*]

Colo. Colorado.

colog *Math.* cologarithm.

color. (in prescriptions) let it be colored. [from Latin *colōrētur*]

COM (kom), **1.** Comedy Central (a cable channel). **2.** computer output on microfilm.

Com. **1.** Commander. **2.**

Commission. **3.** Commissioner. **4.** Committee. **5.** Commodore. **6.** Commonwealth.

com. 1. comedy. **2.** comma. **3.** command. **4.** commander. **5.** commerce. **6.** commercial. **7.** commission. **8.** commissioner. **9.** committee. **10.** common. **11.** commonly. **12.** communications.

comb. 1. combination. **2.** combined. **3.** combining. **4.** combustion.

combl combustible.

comdg. commanding.

Comdr. commander. Also, **comdr.**

Comdt. commandant. Also, **comdt.**

COMECON (kom′i kon′), an economic association of Communist countries. Also, **Comecon, CMEA** [*Co(uncil for) M(utual) Econ(omic Assistance)*]

COMEX (kō′meks), Commodity Exchange, New York.

Com. in Chf. Commander in Chief.

coml. commercial.

comm 1. communication. **2.** commutator.

comm. 1. commander. **2.** commerce. **3.** commission. **4.** committee. **5.** commonwealth. Also, **Comm.**

comp. 1. companion. **2.** comparative. **3.** compare. **4.** compensation. **5.** compilation. **6.** compiled. **7.** compiler. **8.** complement. **9.** complete. **10.** composition. **11.** compositor. **12.** compound. **13.** comprehensive.

compander *Audio.* compressor-expander.

compar. comparative.

compass *Computers.* compiler-assembler.

compd. compound.

Comp. Gen. Comptroller General.

compl complete.

compn compensate.

compt. 1. compartment. **2.** Also, **Compt.** comptroller.

comptr comparator.

Comr. Commissioner.

Com•sat (kom′sat′), *Trademark.* a privately owned corporation servicing the global communications satellite system. Also, **Com**[*Com(munications) Sat(ellite Corporation)*]

Con. 1. *Religion.* Conformist. **2.** Consul.

con. 1. concerto. **2.** conclusion. **3.** connection. **4.** consolidated. **5.** consul. **6.** continued. **7.** against [from Latin *contrā*].

CONAD (kon′ad), Continental Air Defense Command.

conc. 1. concentrate. **2.** concentrated. **3.** concentration. **4.** concerning. **5.** concrete.

concl conclusion.

concr concrete.

cond. 1. condenser. **2.** condition. **3.** conditional. **4.** conductivity. **5.** conductor.

conf. 1. (in prescriptions) a confection. [from Latin *confectiō*] **2.** compare. [from Latin *confer*] **3.** conference. **4.** confessor. **5.** confidential. **6.** conformance.

confed. 1. confederacy. **2.** con-

federate. **3.** confederation. Also, **Confed.**

Cong. 1. Congregational. **2.** Congregationalist. **3.** Congress. **4.** Congressional.

cong. gallon. [from Latin *congius*]

congr congruent.

coni conical.

conj. 1. conjugation. **2.** conjunction. **3.** conjunctive.

conn connect, connector.

Conn. Connecticut.

conn diag connection diagram.

Cons. 1. Conservative. **2.** Constable. **3.** Constitution. **4.** Consul. **5.** Consulting.

cons. 1. consecrated. **2.** conservative. **3.** (in prescriptions) conserve; keep. [from Latin *conservā*] **4.** consolidated. **5.** consonant. **6.** constable. **7.** constitution. **8.** constitutional. **9.** construction. **10.** consul. **11.** consulting.

consec consecutive.

consol. consolidated.

conspec construction specification.

consperg. (in prescriptions) dust; sprinkle. [from Latin *consperge*]

Const. Constitution.

const. 1. constable. **2.** constant. **3.** constitution. **4.** constitutional. **5.** construction.

constr. 1. constraint. **2.** construction. **3.** construed.

cont 1. contact. **2.** continue. **3.** continued. **4.** continuous.

Cont. Continental.

cont. 1. containing. **2.** contents. **3.** continent. **4.** continental. **5.** continue. **6.** continued. **7.** contra. **8.** contract. **9.** contraction. **10.** control. **11.** (in prescriptions) bruised [from Latin *contūsus*].

contd. continued.

contemp. contemporary.

contg. containing.

contin. continued.

contr. 1. contract. **2.** contracted. **3.** contraction. **4.** contractor. **5.** contralto. **6.** contrary. **7.** contrasted. **8.** control. **9.** controller.

cont. rem. (in prescriptions) let the medicines be continued. [from Latin *continuāntur remedia*]

contrib. 1. contribution. **2.** contributor.

contro contracting officer.

conv. 1. convention. **2.** conventional. **3.** convertible. **4.** convocation.

convn convection.

COO chief operating officer.

coop. cooperative. Also, **co-op.**

coord coordinate.

COP *Thermodynamics.* coefficient of performance.

Cop. 1. Copernican. **2.** Coptic.

cop. 1. copper. **2.** copyright; copyrighted.

COPD chronic obstructive pulmonary disease.

cop pl copper plate.

Cor. 1. *Bible.* Corinthians. **2.** Coroner.

cor. 1. corner. **2.** cornet. **3.** coroner. **4.** corpus. **5.** correct. **6.** corrected. **7.** correction. **8.** correla-

tive. **9.** correspondence. **10.** correspondent. **11.** corresponding.

CORE (kôr, kōr), Congress of Racial Equality. Also, **C.O.R.E.**

Corn. 1. Cornish. **2.** Cornwall.

coroll. corollary. Also, **corol.**

corp. 1. corporal. **2.** corporation. Also, **Corp.**

corpl. corporal. Also, **Corpl.**

corpn. corporation.

corr. 1. correct. **2.** corrected. **3.** correction. **4.** correspond. **5.** correspondence. **6.** correspondent. **7.** corresponding. **8.** corrugated. **9.** corrupt. **10.** corrupted. **11.** corruption.

correl. correlative.

corresp. correspondence.

corspnd correspond.

cort. (in prescriptions) the bark. [from Latin *cortex*]

cos *Trigonometry.* cosine.

cos. 1. companies. **2.** consul. **3.** consulship. **4.** counties.

C.O.S. cash on shipment. Also, **c. o.s.**

cosh *Trigonometry.* hyperbolic cosine.

cot 1. *Trigonometry.* cotangent. **2.** cotter pin.

coth *Trigonometry.* hyperbolic cotangent.

cov cutoff valve.

covers *Trigonometry.* coversed sine.

cowl cowling.

COWPS Council on Wage and Price Stability.

CP 1. candlepower. **2.** *Pharmacology.* chemically pure.

cP *Physics.* centipoise. Also, **cp**

cp. 1. camp. **2.** center punch. **3.** cerebral palsy. **4.** clock pulse. **5.** command post. **6.** compare. **7.** constant pressure.

C.P. 1. Chief Patriarch. **2.** command post. **3.** Common Pleas. **4.** Common Prayer. **5.** Communist Party.

c.p. 1. chemically pure. **2.** circular pitch. **3.** command post. **4.** common pleas.

C.P.A. 1. certified public accountant. **2.** chartered public accountant.

CPB Corporation for Public Broadcasting. Also, **C.P.B.**

cpch prop controllable-pitch propeller.

CPCU *Insurance.* Chartered Property and Casualty Underwriter. Also, **C.P.C.U.**

cpd. compound.

CPFF cost plus fixed fee.

CPI 1. consumer price index. **2.** cost plus incentive.

cpi characters per inch.

cpl couple.

cpl. corporal. Also, **Cpl.**

cpld coupled.

cplg coupling.

cplr coupler.

cplry capillary.

CPM 1. *Commerce.* cost per thousand. **2.** Critical Path Method.

cpm 1. card per minute. **2.** *Commerce.* cost per thousand. **3.** critical-path method. **4.** cycles per minute.

CP/M *Trademark.* Control

Program/Microprocessors: a microcomputer operating system.

c.p.m. *Music.* common particular meter.

cpntr carpenter.

CPO chief petty officer. Also, **C. P.O., c.p.o.**

CPR cardiopulmonary resuscitation.

cprs compress.

cprsn compression.

cprsr compressor.

CPS certified professional secretary.

cps 1. *Computers.* characters per second. **2.** cycles per second.

cpse counterpoise.

cpt critical-path technique.

cpt. counterpoint.

CPU *Computers.* central processing unit.

cpunch counterpunch.

CQ 1. *Radio.* a signal sent at the beginning of radiograms. **2.** *Military.* charge of quarters.

CR 1. conditioned reflex; conditioned response. **2.** consciousness-raising. **3.** critical ratio.

Cr *Symbol, Chemistry.* chromium.

cr 1. cold rolled. **2.** controlled rectifier. **3.** control relay. **4.** crystal rectifier. **5.** current relay.

cr. 1. credit. **2.** creditor. **3.** crown.

C.R. 1. Costa Rica. **2.** *Banking.* credit report.

CRC Civil Rights Commission.

crc *Computers.* cyclical redundancy check.

crclt circulate.

crcmf circumference.

crctn correction.

cre corrosion-resistant.

Cres. crescent (in addresses).

cres corrosion-resistant steel.

CRF *Biochemistry.* corticotropin releasing factor.

crg carriage.

crim. criminal.

crim. con. *Law.* criminal conversation.

criminol. 1. criminologist. **2.** criminology.

crit. 1. critic. **2.** critical. **3.** criticism. **4.** criticized.

crk crank.

crkc crankcase.

CRM counter-radar measures.

crn 1. crane. **2.** crown.

crnmtr chronometer.

cro cathode-ray oscilloscope.

CRP *Biochemistry.* C-reactive protein.

crp crimp.

crpt carpet.

crs 1. coarse. **2.** cold-rolled steel.

crs. 1. creditors. **2.** credits.

crsn corrosion.

crsv corrosive.

crsvr crossover.

CRT cathode-ray tube.

crtg 1. cartridge. **2.** crating.

crv curve.

cryo cryogenic.

crypta cryptanalysis.

crypto cryptography.

cryst. 1. crystalline. **2.** crystallized. **3.** crystallography.

Cs *Symbol, Chemistry.* cesium.

cS *Physics.* centistoke; centistokes. Also, **cs**

cs 1. case; cases. **2.** cast steel. **3.**

control switch. **4.** *Computers.* core shift.

C/S cycles per second.

C.S. 1. chief of staff. **2.** Christian Science. **3.** Christian Scientist. **4.** Civil Service. **5.** Confederate States.

c.s. 1. capital stock. **2.** civil service.

CSA Community Services Administration.

C.S.A. Confederate States of America.

CSC Civil Service Commission.

csc *Trigonometry.* cosecant.

CSCE Conference on Security and Cooperation in Europe.

csch *Trigonometry.* hyperbolic cosecant.

csd *Computers.* core-shift drive.

CSEA Civil Service Employees Association.

CSF *Physiology.* cerebrospinal fluid.

csg casing.

cshaft crankshaft.

csk. 1. cask. **2.** countersink.

cskh countersunk head.

C.S.O. 1. Chief Signal Officer. **2.** Chief Staff Officer. Also, **CSO**

CSP C-SPAN (a cable channel).

C-SPAN (sē′span′), Cable Satellite Public Affairs Network (a cable channel).

CSR 1. Certified Shorthand Reporter. **2.** customer service representative.

csr customer signature required.

CST 1. Also, **C.S.T., c.s.t.** Central Standard Time. **2.** convulsive shock therapy.

cstl castellate.

CSW Certified Social Worker. Also, **C.S.W.**

Cswy. causeway.

CT 1. Central time. **2.** Connecticut (for use with ZIP code).

ct 1. control transformer. **2.** current transformer.

Ct. 1. Connecticut. **2.** Count.

ct. 1. carat; carats. **2.** cent; cents. **3.** centum; hundred. **4.** certificate. **5.** county. **6.** Also, **Ct.** court.

C.T. Central time.

CTA commodities trading adviser.

C.T.A. *Law.* with the will annexed. [from Latin *cum testāmentō annexō*]

CTC 1. centralized traffic control. **2.** Citizens' Training Corps.

ctd coated.

ctf certificate.

ctg. 1. Also, **ctge.** cartage. **2.** cartridge. **3.** coating. **4.** cutting.

CTL 1. *Computers.* complementary transistor logic. **2.** core transistor logic.

ctlst catalyst.

ct/m count per minute.

ctn *Trigonometry.* cotangent.

ctn. carton.

ctnr container.

c to c center to center.

ctr. 1. center. **2.** contour. **3.** cutter.

ctrfgl centrifugal.

ctrg centering.

ctrl central.

ctrlr controller.

ctrst contrast.

CTS Cleveland Transit System.

cts. 1. centimes. **2.** cents. **3.** certificates.

ct/s count per second.

ctshft countershaft.

CTU centigrade thermal unit. Also, **ctu**

ctwlk catwalk.

ctwt counterweight.

cty county.

CU close-up.

Cu *Symbol, Chemistry.* copper. [from Latin *cuprum*]

cu 1. cubic. **2.** *Electronics.* crystal unit.

Cu. cumulus.

cu. 1. cubic. **2.** cumulus.

cub. 1. cubic. **2.** cubicle.

cu. ft. cubic foot; cubic feet.

cu. in. cubic inch; cubic inches.

cuj. (in prescriptions) of which; of any. [from Latin *cūjus*]

culv culvert.

cu m cubic meter.

cum. cumulative.

cu mm cubic millimeter.

cuo copper oxide.

cur. 1. currency. **2.** current.

cust. 1. custodian. **2.** custody. **3.** customer.

cu yd cubic yard.

CV 1. cardiovascular. **2.** Also, **C.V.** curriculum vitae.

cv 1. continuously variable. **2.** Also, **cvt.** convertible. **3.** counter voltage.

CVA 1. *Pathology.* cerebrovascular accident. **2.** Columbia Valley Authority.

CVD *Commerce.* countervailing duty.

CVJ *Automotive.* constant-velocity joint.

cvntl conventional.

C.V.O. Commander of the Royal Victorian Order.

cvr cover.

cvrsn conversion.

CVT continuously variable transmission.

CW 1. chemical warfare. **2.** *Radio.* continuous wave.

cw 1. clockwise. **2.** continuous wave.

c/w complete with.

CWA 1. Civil Works Administration. **2.** Communications Workers of America.

CWO *Military.* chief warrant officer.

c.w.o. cash with order.

CWPS Council on Wage and Price Stability.

cwt hundredweight; hundredweights.

cx control transmitter.

CY calendar year.

Cy. county.

cy. 1. capacity. **2.** currency. **3.** cycle; cycles.

CYA *Slang (sometimes vulgar).* cover your ass.

CYC *Biochemistry.* cyclophosphamide.

cyc. cyclopedia.

cyl. 1. cylinder. **2.** cylindrical.

Cym. Cymric.

CYO Catholic Youth Organization.

Cys *Biochemistry.* cysteine.

cytol. 1. cytological. **2.** cytology.

C.Z. Canal Zone. Also, **CZ**

abbrev.

D

abc **D** efghijklmnopqrstuvwxyz

D 1. *Electricity.* debye. **2.** deep. **3.** depth. **4.** *Optics.* diopter. **5.** divorced. **6.** Dutch.

D *Symbol.* **1.** the fourth in order or in a series. **2.** (in some grading systems) a grade or mark, indicating the quality of a student's work as poor or barely passing. **3.** (*sometimes lowercase*) a classification, rating, or the like, indicating poor quality. **4.** *Music.* **a.** the second tone in the scale of C major, or the fourth tone in the relative minor scale, A minor. **b.** a string, key, or pipe tuned to this tone. **c.** a written or printed note representing this tone. **d.** (in the fixed system of solmization) the second tone of the scale of C major, called *re.* **e.** the tonality having D as the tonic note. **5.** (*sometimes lowercase*) the Roman numeral for 500. **6.** *Chemistry.* deuterium. **7.** *Electricity.* **a.** electric displacement. **b.** a battery size for 1.5 volt dry cells: diameter, 1.3 in. (3.3 cm); length, 2.4 in. (6 cm). **8.** *Biochemistry.* aspartic acid. **9.** a proportional shoe width size, narrower than E and wider than C. **10.** a proportional brassiere cup size, larger than C. **11.** *Physics.* darcy.

D- *Symbol, Biochemistry.* (of a molecule) having a configuration resembling the dextrorotatory isomer of glyceraldehyde: always printed as a small capital, roman character (distinguished from *l-*). Cf. **d-**.

d- *Symbol, Chemistry, Biochemistry.* dextrorotatory; dextro- (distinguished from *l-*). Cf. **D-**.

D. 1. day. **2.** December. **3.** Democrat. **4.** Democratic. **5.** *Physics.* density. **6.** Deus. **7.** *Bible.* Deuteronomy. **8.** Doctor. **9.** dose. **10.** Dutch.

d. 1. (in prescriptions) give. [from Latin *dā*] **2.** date. **3.** daughter. **4.** day. **5.** deceased. **6.** deep. **7.** degree. **8.** delete. **9.** *British.* pence. [from Latin *denāriī*] **10.** *British.* penny. [from Latin *denārius*] **11.** *Physics.* density. **12.** depth. **13.** deputy. **14.** dialect. **15.** dialectal. **16.** diameter. **17.** died. **18.** dime. **19.** dividend. **20.** dollar; dollars. **21.** dose. **22.** drachma.

DA 1. Department of Agriculture. **2.** *Dictionary of Americanisms.* **3.** a male hairstyle in which the hair is slicked back on both sides to overlap at the back of the head. [euphemistic abbreviation of *duck's ass*]

da *Telecommunications.* don't answer.

d-a *Electronics.* digital-to-analog.

DA. (in Algeria) dinar; dinars.

da. 1. daughter. **2.** day; days.

D/A *Commerce.* **1.** Also, **d/a.** days after acceptance. **2.** deposit account. **3.** documents against acceptance. **4.** documents for acceptance.

D.A. 1. delayed action. **2.** direct action. **3.** District Attorney. **4.** *Commerce.* documents against acceptance. **5.** *Commerce.* documents for acceptance. **6.** doesn't answer; don't answer.

DAB *Dictionary of American Biography.*

D.A.E. *Dictionary of American English.* Also, **DAE**

dag dekagram; dekagrams.

D.Agr. Doctor of Agriculture.

Dak. Dakota.

dal dekaliter; dekaliters.

dam dekameter; dekameters.

Dan. 1. *Bible.* Daniel. **2.** Also, **Dan** Danish.

D and C *Medicine.* a surgical method for the removal of diseased tissue or an early embryo from the lining of the uterus. [*d(ilation) and c(urettage)*]

D&D drug and disease free.

Danl. Daniel.

DAR Defense Aid Reports.

dar 1. *Military.* defense acquisition radar. **2.** digital audio recording.

D.A.R. Daughters of the American Revolution.

DARE (dâr), *Dictionary of American Regional English.*

DARPA (där′pə), Defense Advanced Research Projects Agency.

DAT digital audiotape.

dat. 1. dative. **2.** datum.

datacom (dā′tə kom′), data communication.

dau. daughter.

D.A.V. Disabled American Veterans. Also, **DAV**

DB *Radio and Television.* delayed broadcast.

dB *Physics.* decibel; decibels.

D.B. 1. Bachelor of Divinity. **2.** Domesday Book.

d.b. daybook.

DBA doing business as. Also, **dba, d.b.a.**

dBa decibels above reference noise, adjusted. Also, **dba**

d/b/a doing business as.

D.B.A. Doctor of Business Administration.

D.B.E. Dame Commander of the Order of the British Empire.

D.Bib. Douay Bible.

dbl. double.

dblr *Electronics.* doubler.

DBMS *Computers.* Data Base Management System.

DBS *Television.* direct broadcast satellite.

DC 1. dental corps. **2.** *Electricity.* direct current. **3.** District of Columbia (for use with ZIP code).

dc *Electricity.* **1.** Also, **d.c.** direct current. **2.** double contact.

D.C. 1. *Music.* da capo. **2.** *Dictionary of Canadianisms.* **3.** *Electricity.* direct current. **4.** District of Columbia. **5.** Doctor of Chiropractic.

dcd decode.

dcdr decoder.

DCF divorced Christian female.

D.Ch.E. Doctor of Chemical Engineering.

DCHP *Dictionary of Canadianisms on Historical Principles.*

dckg docking.

dcl door closer.

D.C.L. Doctor of Civil Law.

dclr decelerate.

DCM divorced Christian male.

D.C.M. *British.* Distinguished Conduct Medal.

D.Cn.L. Doctor of Canon Law.

DCPA Defense Civil Preparedness Agency.

D.Crim. Doctor of Criminology.

D.C.S. 1. Deputy Clerk of Sessions. **2.** Doctor of Christian Science. **3.** Doctor of Commercial Science.

DCTL *Computers.* direct-coupled transistor logic.

DD dishonorable discharge.

dd 1. *Law.* today's date. [from Latin *dē datō*] **2.** deep-drawn. **3.** degree-day. **4.** delayed delivery. **5.** delivered. **6.** *Banking.* demand draft. **7.** double deck. **8.** *Shipbuilding.* dry dock.

dd. delivered.

D/D *Commerce.* days after date.

D.D. 1. *Banking.* demand draft. **2.** Doctor of Divinity.

dda digital differential analyzer.

D-day (dē′dā′), **1.** a day set for beginning something. **2.** June 6, 1944, the day the Allies invaded W Europe. Also, **D-Day.**

DDD *Telecommunications.* direct distance dialing.

DDP *Computers.* distributed data processing.

DDR German Democratic Republic. [from German *D(eutsche) D(emokratische) R(epublik)*]

DDS *Pharmacology.* dapsone. [*d(iamino)d(iphenyl) s(ulfone)*]

D.D.S. 1. Doctor of Dental Science. **2.** Doctor of Dental Surgery.

D.D.Sc. Doctor of Dental Science.

DDT *Chemistry.* a white, crystalline, water-insoluble solid, $C_{14}H_9Cl_5$, used as an insecticide and as a scabicide and pediculicide. [*d(ichloro)d(iphenyl) t(richloroethane)*]

DE 1. Delaware (for use with ZIP code). **2.** destroyer escort.

de digital encoder.

D.E. 1. Doctor of Engineering. **2.** driver education.

DEA Drug Enforcement Administration.

Dec. December.

dec. 1. (in prescriptions) pour off. [from Latin *decantā*] **2.** deceased. **3.** decimal. **4.** decimeter. **5.** declension. **6.** decrease. **7.** *Music.* decrescendo.

decaf. decaffeinated.

decd. deceased.

decn decision.
decompn decompression.
decontn decontamination.
decr decrease.
ded. 1. dedicate. **2.** dedicated. **3.** deduct. **4.** deducted. **5.** deduction.
D.Ed. Doctor of Education.
de d in d (in prescriptions) from day to day. [from Latin *dē diē in diem*]
def. 1. defective. **2.** defense. **3.** definition. Also, **def.**
DEFCON (def′kon), any of several alert statuses for U.S. military forces. [*def(ense readiness) con(dition)*]
defl deflect.
defs. definitions.
deg. degree; degrees.
deglut. (in prescriptions) may be swallowed; let it be swallowed. [from Latin *dēglutiātur*]
D.E.I. Dutch East Indies.
Del. Delaware.
del. 1. delegate; delegation. **2.** delete; deletion. **3.** he or she drew this [from Latin *delineavit*].
dele delete.
dely. delivery.
dem demodulator.
Dem. 1. Democrat. **2.** Democratic.
dem. 1. demand. **2.** demonstrative. **3.** demurrage.
demod (dē′mod), demodulator.
demux (dē′muks), *Telecommunications.* demultiplexer.
den denote.
Den. Denmark.
deng diesal engine.
D.Eng. Doctor of Engineering.
D.Eng.S. Doctor of Engineering Science.
dens density.
dent. 1. dental. **2.** dentist. **3.** dentistry.
dep. 1. depart. **2.** department. **3.** departs. **4.** departure. **5.** deponent. **6.** deposed. **7.** deposit. **8.** depot. **9.** deputy.
depr. 1. depreciation. **2.** depression.
dept. 1. department. **2.** deponent. **3.** deputy.
der. 1. derivation. **2.** derivative. **3.** derive. **4.** derived.
deriv. 1. derivation. **2.** derivative. **3.** derive. **4.** derived.
DES *Pharmacology.* diethylstilbestrol.
des designation.
descr 1. describe. **2.** description.
D. ès L. Doctor of Letters. [from French *Docteur ès Lettres*]
D. ès S. Doctor of Sciences. [from French *Docteur ès Sciences*]
destn destination.
DET 1. Also, **Det** *Linguistics.* determiner. **2.** *Pharmacology.* diethyltryptamine.
det. 1. detach. **2.** detachment. **3.** detail. **4.** detector. **5.** determine. **6.** (in prescriptions) let it be given [from Latin *dētur*].
Deut. *Bible.* Deuteronomy.
dev. 1. development. **2.** deviation.
devel. development.
DEW (dōō, dyōō), distant early warning.
DF divorced female.

df 1. direction finder. **2.** dissipation factor.
D/F direction finding. Also, **DF**
D.F. 1. Defender of the Faith. [from Latin *Dēfēnsor Fideī*] **2.** Distrito Federal. **3.** Doctor of Forestry.
D.F.A. Doctor of Fine Arts.
D.F.C. Distinguished Flying Cross.
dfl deflating.
D.F.M. Distinguished Flying Medal.
dfr defrost.
dft drift.
dftg drafting.
dftr deflector.
dftsp draftsperson.
dg decigram; decigrams.
D.G. 1. by the grace of God. [from Latin *Deī grātiā*] **2.** Director General.
dgr degrease.
dgs degaussing system.
dgt digit.
dgtl digital.
DH 1. *Racing.* dead heat. **2.** *Baseball.* designated hitter. Also, **dh**
DH. (in Morocco) dirham; dirhams.
D.H. 1. Doctor of Humanics. **2.** Doctor of Humanities.
DHA *Biochemistry.* an omega-3 fatty acid present in fish oils. [*d(ocosa)h(exaenoic) a(cid)*]
D.H.L. 1. Doctor of Hebrew Letters. **2.** Doctor of Hebrew Literature.
dhmy dehumidify.
dhw double-hung window.
dhyr dehydrator.
DI 1. Department of the Interior. **2.** drill instructor.
Di *Symbol, Chemistry.* didymium.
di. diameter. Also, **dia.**
dia. diameter. Also, **dia.**
diag 1. diagonal. **2.** diagram.
Dial. 1. dialect. **2.** dialectal. **3.** dialectic. **4.** dialectical.
diaph diaphragm.
dict. 1. dictation. **2.** dictator. **3.** dictionary.
DID 1. data item description. **2.** *Telecommunications.* direct inward dialing.
dieb. alt. (in prescriptions) every other day. [from Latin *diēbus alternīs*]
dieb. secund. (in prescriptions) every second day. [from Latin *diēbus secundīs*]
dieb. tert. (in prescriptions) every third day. [from Latin *diēbus tertius*]
diel dielectric.
dif. 1. difference. **2.** different.
diff. 1. difference. **2.** different. **3.** differential.
dig. digest.
dil 1. dilute. **2.** diluted.
dim. 1. dimension. **2.** (in prescriptions) one-half. [from Latin *dīmidius*] **3.** diminish. **4.** *Music.* diminuendo. **5.** diminutive.
dimin. 1. diminish. **2.** *Music.* diminuendo. **3.** diminutive.
DIN (din), *Photography.* a designation, originating in Germany, of the speed of a particular film emulsion. [from German *D(eutsche) I(ndustrie) N(ormen) (German industrial standards (later construed as Das ist Norm that is*

(the) standard), registered mark of the German Institute for Standardization]
Din. (in Yugoslavia) dinar; dinars.
d. in p. aeq. (in prescriptions) let it be divided into equal parts. [from Latin *dīvidātur in partēs aequālēs*]
dio diode.
dioc. 1. diocesan. **2.** diocese.
diopt *Optics.* diopter.
DIP (dip), *Computers.* a packaged chip that connects to a circuit board by means of pins. [*d(ual) i(n-line) p(ackage)*]
dipl. 1. diplomat. **2.** diplomatic.
diplxr *Electronics.* diplexer.
dir. 1. direct. **2.** direction. **3.** directional. **4.** director. **5.** directory. **6.** direxit.
dir cplr *Electronics.* directional coupler.
direc. prop. (in prescriptions) with a proper direction. [from Latin *dīrectiōne prōpriā*]
DIS The Disney Channel (a cable channel).
dis. 1. distance. **2.** distant. **3.** distribute.
disassm disassemble.
disassy disassembly.
disc. 1. disconnect. **2.** discount. **3.** discovered.
disch discharge.
disp 1. dispatcher. **2.** dispenser.
displ displacement.
dist. 1. distance. **2.** distant. **3.** distinguish. **4.** distinguished. **5.** district.
Dist. Atty. district attorney.
Dist. Ct. District Court.
distn distortion.
distr. 1. distribute. **2.** distribution. **3.** distributor.
div 1. *Mathematics, Mechanics.* divergence. **2.** *Music.* divisi.
Div. 1. divine. **2.** divinity.
div. 1. diverter. **2.** divide. **3.** divided. **4.** dividend. **5.** division. **6.** divisor. **7.** divorced.
div. in par. aeq. (in prescriptions) let it be divided into equal parts. [from Latin *dīvidātur in partēs aequālēs*]
DIY *British.* do-it-yourself. Also, **D.I.Y., d.i.y.**
DIYer (dē′ī′wī′ər), *British.* do-it-yourselfer. Also, **DIY′er.**
D.J. 1. Also, **DJ, d.j.** disc jockey. **2.** District Judge. **3.** Doctor of Law [from Latin *Doctor Jūris*].
DJF divorced Jewish female.
DJM divorced Jewish male.
D.Journ. Doctor of Journalism.
D.J.S. Doctor of Juridical Science.
D.J.T. Doctor of Jewish Theology.
DK *Real Estate.* deck.
dk. 1. dark. **2.** deck. **3.** dock.
dkg dekagram; dekagrams.
dkl dekaliter; dekaliters.
dkm dekameter; dekameters.
DL diesel.
dl 1. data link. **2.** daylight. **3.** dead load. **4.** deciliter; deciliters. **5.** drawing list.
D/L demand loan.
dla data link address.
D. Lit. Doctor of Literature.
D. Litt. Doctor of Letters. [from Latin *Doctor Litterārum*]
D.L.O. dead letter office.

dlr. 1. dealer. 2. Also, **dlr** dollar.

dlrs. dollars. Also, **dlrs**

D.L.S. Doctor of Library Science.

dlvy delivery.

dlx deluxe.

dly 1. delay. 2. dolly.

DM 1. Deutsche mark. 2. divorced male.

dm 1. decimeter; decimeters. 2. demand meter.

DM. direct mail.

Dm. Deutsche mark.

DMA Computers. direct memory access.

dmd demodulate.

D.M.D. Doctor of Dental Medicine. [from Latin *Dentāriae Medicīnae Doctor* or *Doctor Medicīnae Dentālis*]

DMDT Chemistry. methoxychlor. [*d(i)m(ethoxy)d(iphenyl)-t(richloroethane)*]

D.M.L. Doctor of Modern Languages.

dmm Electricity. digital multimeter.

DMN Chemistry. dimethylnitrosamine. Also, **DMNA**

dmp Computers. dot-matrix printer.

dmpr damper.

dmr dimmer.

D.M.S. 1. Director of Medical Services. 2. Doctor of Medical Science.

DMSO a liquid substance, C₂H₆OS, used in industry as a solvent; proposed as an analgesic and anti-inflammatory. [*d(i)-m(ethyl) s(ulf)o(xide)*]

DMT Pharmacology. dimethyltryptamine.

D. Mus. Doctor of Music.

DMV Department of Motor Vehicles.

dmx data multiplex.

DMZ demilitarized zone.

dn. down.

DNA Genetics. deoxyribonucleic acid: an extremely long macromolecule that is the main component of chromosomes and is the material that transfers genetic characteristics.

dna does not apply.

DNase (dē'en/ās, -āz), deoxyribonuclease: any of several enzymes that break down the DNA molecule. Also, **DNAase**.

D.N.B. Dictionary of National Biography.

DNC Democratic National Committee.

DNR 1. Medicine. do not resuscitate (used in hospitals and other health-care facilities). 2. Also, **D.N.R.** do not return.

dntl dental.

do. ditto.

D/O delivery order. Also, **d.o.**

D.O. 1. Also, **DO, d.o.** direct object. 2. Doctor of Optometry. 3. Doctor of Osteopathy.

DOA dead on arrival. Also, **D.O.A.**

DOB date of birth. Also, **D.O.B., d.o.b.**

DOC Department of Commerce.

doc. 1. data output channel. 2. document. 3. Also, **doc** documentation.

DOD 1. Department of Defense.

2. Telecommunications. direct outward diaing.

DOE 1. Department of Energy. 2. Also, **d.o.e.** depends on experience; depending on experience (used in stating a salary range in help-wanted ads).

DOHC Automotive. double overhead camshaft.

DOI Department of the Interior.

DOJ Department of Justice.

DOL Department of Labor.

dol. 1. Music. dolce. 2. dollar.

dols. dollars.

Dom. 1. Dominica. 2. Dominican.

dom. 1. domain. 2. domestic. 3. dominant. 4. dominion.

D.O.M. to God, the Best, the Greatest. [from Latin *Deō Optimō Maximō*]

d.o.m. Slang. dirty old man.

D.O.P. Photography. developing-out paper.

Dor. 1. Dorian. 2. Doric.

DORAN (dôr'an, dōr'-), an electronic device for determining range and assisting navigation. [*Do(ppler) r(ange) a(nd) n(avigation)*]

DOS (dôs, dos), Computers. any of several operating systems, especially for microcomputers, that reside wholly on disk storage. [*d(isk) o(perating) s(ystem)*]

DOS Department of State.

DOT 1. Department of Transportation. 2. Dictionary of Occupational Titles.

DOVAP (dō'vap), Electronics. a system for plotting the trajectory of a missile or other rapidly moving object by means of radio waves bounced off it. [*Do(ppler) V(elocity) a(nd) P(osition)*]

Dow. dowager.

doz. dozen; dozens.

DP 1. data processing. 2. displaced person.

dp 1. dashpot: relay. 2. data processing. 3. deflection plate. 4. depth. 5. dial pulsing. 6. Baseball. double play; double plays. 7. Electricity. double-pole. 8. dripproof.

D/P documents against payment.

D.P. 1. data processing. 2. displaced person.

d.p. (in prescriptions) with a proper direction. [from Latin *dīrēctiōne prōpriā*]

D.P.A. Doctor of Public Administration.

DPC Defense Plant Corporation.

dpdt Electricity. double-pole double-throw.

dpg damping.

DPH Department of Public Health.

D. Ph. Doctor of Philosophy.

D.P.H. Doctor of Public Health.

dpi Computers. dots per inch.

DPL diplomat.

D.P.M. Doctor of Podiatric Medicine.

D.P.P. Insurance. deferred payment plan.

D.P.S. Doctor of Public Service.

dpst Electricity. double-pole single-throw.

dpstk dipstick.

DPT diphtheria, pertussis, and tet-

anus: a mixed vaccine used for primary immunization. Also, **DTP**

dpt. 1. department. 2. deponent.

D.P.W. Department of Public Works. Also, **DPW**

dpx duplex.

DQ disqualify.

DR Real Estate. dining room.

Dr Chiefly British. Doctor.

dr 1. dead reckoning. 2. door. 3. Electronics. drain. 4. dram; drams. 5. drill. 6. drive.

Dr. 1. Doctor. 2. Drive (used in street names).

dr. 1. debit. 2. debtor. 3. drachma; drachmas. 4. dram; drams. 5. drawer. 6. drum.

D.R. 1. Daughters of the (American) Revolution. 2. Navigation. dead reckoning. 3. Dutch Reformed.

dram detection-radar automatic monitoring.

dram. pers. Theater. dramatis personae.

drch. drachma; drachmas. Also, **dr.**

D.R.E. 1. Director of Religious Education. 2. Doctor of Religious Education.

dri dead-reckoning indicator.

drsg dressing.

DRTL Computers. diode resistor transistor logic.

D.R.V. (on food labels) Daily Reference Value: the amount of nutrients appropriate for one day.

drvr driver.

drzl drizzle.

Ds Symbol, Chemistry. (formerly) dysprosium.

ds 1. diode switch. 2. domestic service.

D.S. 1. Music. from the sign. [from Italian *dal segno*] 2. Doctor of Science.

d.s. 1. daylight saving. 2. Commerce. Also, **D/S** days after sight. 3. document signed.

DSA Medicine. digital subtraction angiography.

dsb Electronics. double sideband.

dsbl disable.

DSC 1. The Discovery Channel (a cable channel). 2. Defense Supplies Corporation.

D.Sc. Doctor of Science.

D.S.C. 1. Distinguished Service Cross. 2. Doctor of Surgical Chiropody.

dscc dessicant.

dscont. discontinue.

dscrm Electronics. discriminator.

dsd Computers. dual-scan display.

dsdd Computers. double-side, double-density.

dsgn design.

dshd Computers. double-side, high density.

dsl diesel.

dsltr desalter.

dslv dissolve.

D.S.M. 1. Distinguished Service Medal. 2. Doctor of Sacred Music.

DSNA Dictionary Society of North America.

D.S.O. Distinguished Service Order.

dsp Computers. digital signal processing.

D.S.P. died without issue. [from Latin *dēcessit sine prōle*]

dspec design specification.

dspl display.

dspo disposal.

DSR *Medicine.* dynamic spatial re-constructor.

D.S.S. Doctor of Social Science.

dssd *Computers.* double-side, single-density.

DST daylight-saving time.

D.S.T. 1. daylight-saving time. 2. Doctor of Sacred Theology.

dstlt distillate.

dstng distinguish.

DSU disk storage unit.

D. Surg. Dental Surgeon.

D.S.W. 1. Doctor of Social Welfare. 2. Doctor of Social Work.

DT *Slang.* detective. Also, **D.T.**

dt 1. decay time. 2. double throw.

dtd dated.

d.t.d. (in prescriptions) give such doses. [from Latin *dentur tālēs dosēs*]

D.Th. Doctor of Theology. Also, **D.Theol.**

DTL *Computers.* diode transistor logic.

dtl detail.

dtmf *Telecommunications.* dual-tone multifrequency.

DTP 1. desktop publishing. 2. diphtheria, tetanus, and pertussis. See **DPT.**

dtrbd *Computers.* daughterboard.

dtrs distress.

d.t.'s (dē′tēz′), *Pathology.* delirium tremens.

dtv digital television.

dty cy duty cycle.

Du. 1. Duke. 2. Dutch.

DUI driving under the influence.

dulc. (in prescriptions) sweet. [from Latin *dulcis*]

dupl duplicate.

duplxr duplexer.

dut *Electronics.* device under test.

D.V. 1. God willing. [from Latin *D(eo) v(olente)*] 2. Douay Version (of the Bible).

dvc device.

dvl develop.

D.V.M. Doctor of Veterinary Medicine. Also, **DVM**

D.V.M.S. Doctor of Veterinary Medicine and Surgery.

dvr diver.

D.V.S. Doctor of Veterinary Surgery.

dvt deviate.

DW *Real Estate.* dishwasher.

dw 1. dishwasher. 2. distilled water. 3. double weight.

D/W *Law.* dock warrant.

dwg drawing.

DWI driving while intoxicated.

dwl dowel.

DWM *Slang.* dead white male.

dwn drawn.

dwr drawer.

DWT deadweight tons; deadweight tonnage.

dwt 1. deadweight tons; deadweight tonnage. 2. pennyweight; pennyweights.

d.w.t. deadweight tons; deadweight tonnage.

DX *Radio.* distance. Also, **D.X.**

Dx diagnosis.

dx duplex.

Dy *Symbol, Chemistry.* dysprosium.

dyn 1. dynamic. 2. *Physics.* dyne; dynes.

dyn. dynamics. Also, **dynam.**

dynm dynamotor.

dynmm dynamometer.

dynmt dynamite.

DZ drop zone.

dz. dozen; dozens.

---

a b c d E f g h i j k l m n o p q r s t u v w x y z

E 1. east. 2. eastern. 3. English. 4. excellent. 5. Expressway.

E *Symbol.* 1. the fifth in order or in a series. 2. (in some grading systems) a grade or mark, indicating the quality of a student's work is in need of improvement in order to be passing. 3. *Music.* a. the third tone in the scale of C major or the fifth tone in the relative minor scale, A minor. b. a string, key, or pipe tuned to this tone. c. a written or printed note representing this tone. d. (in the fixed system of solmization) the third tone of the scale of C major, called *mi.* e. the tonality having E as the tonic note. 4. (*sometimes lowercase*) the medieval Roman numeral for 250. 5. *Physics, Electricity.* a. electric field. b. electric field strength. 6. *Physics.* energy. 7. *Biochemistry.* glutamic acid. 8. *Logic.* universal negative. 9. a proportional shoe width size, narrower than EE and wider than D.

e 1. electron. 2. *Physics.* elementary charge.

E. 1. Earl. 2. Earth. 3. east. 4. Easter. 5. eastern. 6. engineer. 7. engineering. 8. English.

e. 1. eldest. 2. *Football.* end. 3. engineer. 4. engineering. 5. entrance. 6. *Baseball.* error; errors.

ea. each.

E.A.A. Engineer in Aeronautics and Astronautics.

ead. (in prescriptions) the same. [from Latin *eādem*]

EAM National Liberation Front, a Greek underground resistance movement and political coalition of World War II. [from Modern Greek *E(thnikō) A(pelevtherōtikò) M(étōpo)*]

EAP employee assistance program.

eax electronic automatic exchange.

EB Epstein-Barr (syndrome).

EBCDIC (eb′sē dik′), *n. Computers.* a code used for data representation and transfer. [*e(xtended) b(inary-)c(oded) d(e-cimal) i(nterchange) c(ode)*]

EbN east by north.

EbS east by south.

EBV Epstein-Barr virus.

EC European Community.

E.C. 1. Engineering Corps. 2. Established Church.

e.c. for the sake of example. [from Latin *exemplī causā*]

ECA Economic Cooperation Administration. Also, **E.C.A.**

ECC *Computers.* error-correction code.

ecc eccentric.

Eccl. *Bible.* Ecclesiastes. Also, **Eccles.**

eccl. ecclesiastic; ecclesiastical. Also, **eccles.**

Ecclus. *Bible.* Ecclesiasticus.

ECCM *Military.* electronic countermeasures.

ecd estimated completion date.

ECF extended-care facility.

ECG 1. electrocardiogram. 2. electrocardiograph.

ech echelon.

ECL *Computers.* emitter-coupled logic.

ECM 1. electronic countermeasures. 2. European Common Market.

ecn engineering change notice.

eco 1. electron-coupled oscillator. 2. engineering change notice.

ecol. 1. ecological. 2. ecology.

E. co•li (ē′ kō′lī), *Escherichia coli,* an anaerobic bacterium.

econ. 1. economic. 2. economics. 3. economy.

ecp engineering change proposal.

ecr engineering change request.

ECT electroconvulsive therapy.

ECU (ā kōō′ *or, sometimes,* ē′sē′-yōō′), a money of account of the European Common Market used in international finance. [*E(uropean) C(urrency) U(nit),* perhaps with play on *écu,* an old French coin]

E.C.U. English Church Union.

ED Department of Education.

ED₅₀ *Pharmacology.* effective dose for 50 percent of the group.

ed. 1. edited. 2. edition. 3. editor. 4. education.

E.D. 1. Eastern Department. 2. election district. 3. *Finance.* ex dividend. 4. executive director.

EDA Economic Development Administration.

edac error detection correction.

EDB *Chemistry.* a colorless liquid, $C_2H_4Br_2$, used as an organic solvent, gasoline additive, pesticide, and soil fumigant. [*e(thylene) d(i)b(romide)*]

Ed.B. Bachelor of Education.

EDC European Defense Community.

Ed.D. Doctor of Education.

EDES Hellenic National Democratic army, a Greek resistance coalition in World War II. [from Modern Greek *E(thnikós)*

D(ēmokratikós) *E(llēnikós)* *S(yndésmos)*]

edit. **1.** edited. **2.** edition. **3.** editor.

Ed.M. Master of Education.

EDP *Computers.* electronic data processing.

eds. **1.** editions. **2.** editors.

Ed.S. Education Specialist.

EDT Eastern daylight time. Also, **E.D.T.**

EDTA *Chemistry., Pharmacology.* a colorless compound, $C_{10}H_{16}N_2O_8$, with a variety of medical and other uses. [*e(thylene)d(iamine)t(etraacetic) a(cid)*]

edtn edition.

edtr editor.

educ. **1.** educated. **2.** education. **3.** educational.

E.E. **1.** Early English. **2.** electrical engineer. **3.** electrical engineering.

e.e. errors excepted.

E.E. & M.P. Envoy Extraordinary and Minister Plenipotentiary.

EEC European Economic Community.

EEG **1.** electroencephalogram. **2.** electroencephalograph.

EENT *Medicine.* eye, ear, nose, and throat.

EEO equal employment opportunity.

EEOC Equal Employment Opportunity Commission.

eeprom *Electronics.* electronically erasable programmable read-only memory.

EER energy efficiency ratio.

ef emitter follower.

eff. **1.** effect. **2.** effective. **3.** efficiency.

EFI electronic fuel injection.

EFL English as a foreign language.

efl **1.** effluent. **2.** *Photography.* equivalent focal length.

EFM electronic fetal monitor.

efph equivalent full-power hour.

EFT electronic funds transfer. Also, **EFTS**

EFTA European Free Trade Association.

EFTS electronic funds transfer system.

Eg. **1.** Egypt. **2.** Egyptian.

e.g. for example; for the sake of example; such as. [from Latin *exemplī grātiā*]

EGA *Computers.* enhanced graphics adapter.

EGmc East Germanic.

EGR *Automotive.* exhaust-gas recirculation.

EHF extremely high frequency. Also, **ehf**

EHS Environmental Health Services.

EHV extra high voltage.

E.I. **1.** East Indian. **2.** East Indies.

EIA Electronic Industries Association.

E. Ind. East Indian.

EIR Environmental Impact Report.

EIS Environmental Impact Statement.

EISA *Computers.* extended industry standard architecture.

EJ (ē′jā′), **1.** electronic journalism. **2.** electronic journalist.

ejn ejection.

ejtr ejector.

EKG **1.** electrocardiogram. **2.** electrocardiograph. [from German *E(lectro)k(ardio)g(ramme)*]

el. **1.** electroluminescent. **2.** elevation.

E.L.A.S. Hellenic People's Army of Liberation, Greek resistance force in World War II. [from Modern Greek *E(thnikòs) L(aïkòs) A(peleutherōtikòs) S(tratós)*]

elb elbow.

elctd electrode.

elctlt electrolyte; electrolytic.

elctrn electron.

elctrochem electrochemical.

Elect. **1.** electric. **2.** electrical. **3.** electrician. **4.** electricity. Also, **elec.**

elek electronic.

elem. **1.** element; elements. **2.** elementary.

elev. **1.** elevation. **2.** elevator.

elex electronics.

ELF extremely low frequency. Also, **elf**

elim eliminate.

ELISA (i līz′ə, -sə), **1.** *Medicine.* a diagnostic test for past or current exposure to an infectious agent, as the AIDS virus. **2.** *Biology, Medicine.* any similar test using proteins as a probe for the identification of antibodies or antigens. [*e(nzyme-)l(inked) i(mmuno)s(orbent) a(ssay)*]

elix. (in prescriptions) elixir.

Eliz. Elizabethan.

elmech electromechanical.

elng elongate.

e. long. east longitude.

elp elliptical.

elpneu electropneumatic.

elvn elevation.

EM **1.** electromagnetic. **2.** electromotive. **3.** electronic mail. **4.** electron microscope. **5.** electron microscopy. **6.** end matched. **7.** Engineer of Mines. **8.** enlisted man; enlisted men.

Em *Symbol, Physical Chemistry.* emanation.

em **1.** electromagnetic. **2.** enlisted men.

E.M. **1.** Earl Marshal. **2.** Engineer of Mines.

e-mail (ē′māl′), electronic mail. Also, **E-mail.**

emb emboss.

embryol. embryology.

emer emergency.

E.Met. Engineer of Metallurgy.

emf electromotive force. Also, **EMF, E.M.F., e.m.f.**

EMG **1.** electromyogram. **2.** electromyograph. **3.** electromyography.

emi electromagnetic interference.

EMP *Physics.* electromagnetic pulse.

Emp. **1.** Emperor. **2.** Empire. **3.** Empress.

emp. (in prescriptions) a plaster. [from Latin *emplastrum*]

e.m.p. (in prescriptions) after the manner prescribed; as directed. [from Latin *ex mōdō praescrīptō*]

empl employee.

EMS **1.** emergency medical service. **2.** European Monetary System.

ems electromagnetic surveillance.

emsn emission.

EMT emergency medical technician.

emtr *Electronics.* emitter.

EMU **1.** Also, **emu** electromagnetic unit; electromagnetic units. **2.** *Aerospace.* extravehicular mobility unit.

emuls. (in prescriptions) an emulsion. [from Latin *ēmulsiō*]

enam enamel.

enbl enable.

enc. **1.** enclosed. **2.** enclosure. **3.** encyclopedia.

encap encapsulate.

encd encode.

encl. **1.** enclosed. **2.** enclosure.

encsd encased.

ency. encyclopedia. Also, **encyc., encycl.**

end. endorsed.

ENE east-northeast. Also, **E.N.E.**

ENG *Television.* electronic news gathering.

Eng. **1.** England. **2.** English.

eng. **1.** engine. **2.** engineer. **3.** engineering. **4.** engraved. **5.** engraver. **6.** engraving.

enga engage.

Eng. D. Doctor of Engineering.

engr. **1.** engineer. **2.** engraved. **3.** engraver. **4.** engraving.

engrg engineering.

engrv engrave.

engy energy.

enl. **1.** enlarge. **2.** enlarged. **3.** enlisted.

enlg enlarge.

enrgz energize.

Ens. Ensign.

ensi (en′sē), equivalent-noise-sideband-input.

ENT *Medicine.* ear, nose, and throat.

entomol. **1.** entomological. **2.** entomology. Also, **entom.**

entr **1.** enter. **2.** entrance.

enum enumerate, enumeration.

env. envelope.

envr **1.** environment. **2.** environmental.

EO executive order.

e.o. ex officio.

EOB Executive Office Building.

EOE **1.** equal-opportunity employer. **2.** *Disparaging.* an employee who is considered to have been hired only to satisfy equal-opportunity regulations.

EOF *Computers.* end-of-file.

EOG electrooculogram.

eolm electrooptical light modulator.

eom end of message.

e.o.m. *Chiefly Commerce.* end of the month. Also, **E.O.M.**

EOP Executive Office of the President.

eot end of tape.

EP **1.** European plan. **2.** extended play (of phonograph records).

Ep. *Bible.* Epistle.

EPA **1.** Environmental Protection Agency. **2.** an omega-3 fatty acid present in fish oils. [*e(icosa)p(en-taenoic) a(cid)*]

Eph. *Bible.* Ephesians. Also, **Ephes., Ephs.**

Epiph. Epiphany.

Epis. **1.** Episcopal. **2.** Episcopalian. **3.** *Bible.* Epistle.

Episc. 1. Episcopal. 2. Episcopalian.

Epist. *Bible.* Epistle.

epit. 1. epitaph. 2. epitome.

EPROM (ē′prom), *Computers.* a memory chip whose contents can be erased and reprogramed. [*e(rasable)* *p(rogrammable)* *r(ead)-o(nly)* *m(emory)*]

EPS earnings per share.

EPT excess-profits tax.

ept external pipe thread.

epu emergency power unit.

EQ educational quotient.

eq. 1. equal. 2. equation. 3. equivalent.

eql equal, equally.

eqlz 1. equalize. 2. equalizer.

eqpt. equipment.

equil equilibrium.

equip. equipment.

equiv. equivalent.

ER 1. efficiency report. 2. emergency room.

Er *Symbol, Chemistry.* erbium.

E.R. 1. East Riding (Yorkshire). 2. East River (New York City). 3. King Edward. [from Latin *Edwardus Rex*] 4. Queen Elizabeth. [from Latin *Elizabeth Regina*] 5. emergency room.

ERA 1. Also, **era** *Baseball.* earned run average. 2. Emergency Relief Administration. 3. Equal Rights Amendment.

ercg erecting.

erct erection.

ERG electroretinogram.

ERIC Educational Resources Information Center.

ERISA (ə ris′ə), Employee Retirement Income Security Act.

ERP European Recovery Program. Also, **E.R.P.**

errc error correction.

erron. 1. erroneous. 2. erroneously.

ERS Emergency Radio Service. Also, **E.R.S.**

ers 1. erase. 2. erased.

ERTS Earth Resources Technology Satellite.

E.R.V. English Revised Version (of the Bible).

Es *Symbol, Chemistry.* einsteinium.

es electrostatic.

E.S. Education Specialist.

ESA European Space Agency.

Esc. (in Portugal and several other nations) escudo; escudos.

esc. 1. escape. 2. escrow.

escl escalator.

esct escutcheon.

Esd. *Bible.* Esdras.

ESDI (es′dē), *Computers.* enhanced small device interface.

ESE east-southeast. Also, **E.S.E.**

esk engineering sketch.

Esk. Eskimo.

ESL English as a second language.

ESOL (ē′sôl, es′əl), English for speakers of other languages.

ESOP (ē′sop), a plan under which a company's stock is acquired by its employees or work-

ers. [*E(mployee)* *S(tock)* *O(wnership)* *P(lan)*]

ESP extrasensory perception.

esp. especially.

espec. especially.

ESPN the Entertainment Sports Network (a cable channel).

Esq. Esquire. Also, **Esqr.**

ESR 1. erythrocyte sedimentation rate: the rate at which red blood cells settle in a column of blood, serving as a diagnostic test. 2. electron spin resonance.

ess electronic switching system.

EST Eastern Standard Time. Also, E.S.T., e.s.t.

est. 1. established. 2. estate. 3. estimate. 4. estimated. 5. estuary.

estab. established.

Esth. 1. *Bible.* Esther. 2. Esthonia.

esu electrostatic unit.

Et *Symbol, Chemistry.* ethyl.

E.T. 1. Eastern time. 2. extraterrestrial. Also, **ET**

e.t. electrical transcription.

E.T.A. estimated time of arrival. Also, **ETA**

et al. (et al′, äl′, ôl′), 1. and elsewhere. [from Latin *et alibi*] 2. and others. [from Latin *et alii*]

etc. et cetera.

E.T.D. estimated time of departure. Also, **ETD**

Eth. Ethiopia.

ethnog. ethnography.

ethnol. 1. ethnological. 2. ethnology.

ethol. ethology.

ETI extraterrestrial intelligence.

eti elapsed-time indicator.

ETO (in World War II) European Theater of Operations. Also, E.T.O.

e to e end to end.

etr estimated time of return.

Etr. Etruscan.

ETS *Trademark.* Educational Testing Service.

et seq. *plural* et seqq., et sqq. and the following. [from Latin *et sequēns*]

et seqq. and those following. Also, **et sqq.** [from Latin *et sequentēs, et sequentia*]

et ux. *Chiefly Law.* and wife. [from Latin *et uxor*]

ETV educational television.

etvm electrostatic transistorized voltmeter.

ety. etymology.

etym. 1. etymological. 2. etymology. Also, **etymol.**

Eu *Symbol, Chemistry.* europium.

Eur. 1. Europe. 2. European.

eV *Physics.* electron-volt. Also, **ev**

E.V. English Version (of the Bible).

EVA *Aerospace.* extravehicular activity.

evac evacuation.

eval evaluation.

evap. 1. evaporate. 2. evaporation.

evg. evening.

evm electronic voltmeter.

evom electronic voltohmmeter.

EW 1. electronic warfare. 2. enlisted women.

Ex. *Bible.* Exodus.

ex. 1. examination. 2. examined. 3. example. 4. except. 5. exception. 6. exchange. 7. excursion. 8. executed. 9. executive. 10. express. 11. extra.

exam. 1. examination. 2. examined. 3. examinee. 4. examiner.

Exc. Excellency.

exc. 1. excellent. 2. except. 3. exception. 4. he or she printed or engraved (this). [from Latin *excudit*] 5. excursion.

exch. 1. exchange. 2. exchequer. Also **Exch.**

excl. 1. exclamation. 2. excluding. 3. exclusive.

exclam. 1. exclamation. 2. exclamatory.

excsv excessive.

exctr exciter.

excud. he or she printed or engraved (this). [from Latin *excudit*]

Ex. Doc. executive document.

exec. 1. executive. 2. executor.

exer exercise.

exh 1. exhaust. 2. exhibit.

ex int. *Stock Exchange.* ex interest.

ex lib. from the library of. [from Latin *ex libris*]

Exod. *Bible.* Exodus.

ex off. by virtue of office or position. [from Latin *ex officio*]

exor. executor.

exp 1. expand. 2. expansion. 3. experiment. 4. expose. 5. expulsion.

exp. 1. expenses. 2. experience. 3. expired. 4. exponential. 5. export. 6. exported. 7. exporter. 8. express.

exped expedite.

expen expendable.

exp jt expansion joint.

expl 1. explain. 2. explanation.

expld explode.

expln explosion.

expnt 1. exponent. 2. exponential.

expo exposition.

expr express.

expsr exposure.

expt. experiment.

exptl. experimental.

Expy. expressway.

exr. executor.

exstg existing.

ext. 1. extension. 2. exterior. 3. external. 4. extinct. 5. extinguish. 6. extra. 7. extract.

extd. 1. extended. 2. extrude.

extm extreme.

extn. 1. extension. 2. external.

extnr extinguisher.

extr. 1. exterior. 2. extract.

eylt eyelet.

eypc eyepiece.

Ez. *Bible.* Ezra. Also, **Ezr.**

Ezek. *Bible.* Ezekiel.

F 1. Fahrenheit. 2. female. 3. *Genetics.* filial. 4. firm. 5. franc; francs. 6. French.

F *Symbol.* 1. the sixth in order or in a series. 2. (in some grading systems) a grade or mark that indicates academic work of the lowest quality; failure. 3. *Music.* **a.** the fourth tone in the scale of C major or the sixth tone in the relative minor scale, A minor. **b.** a string, key, or pipe tuned to this tone. **c.** a written or printed note representing this tone. **d.** (in the fixed system of solmization) the fourth tone of the scale of C major, called *fa.* **e.** the tonality having F as the tonic note. 4. (*sometimes lowercase*) the medieval Roman numeral for 40. 5. *Math.* **a.** field. **b.** function (of). 6. (*sometimes lowercase*) *Electricity.* farad. 7. *Chemistry.* fluorine. 8. (*sometimes lowercase*) *Physics.* **a.** force. **b.** frequency. **c.** fermi. 9. *Biochemistry.* phenylalanine.

f 1. firm. 2. *Photography.* f-number. 3. *Music.* forte.

f *Symbol, Optics.* focal length.

F- *Military.* (in designations of aircraft) fighter: *F-105.*

F. 1. Fahrenheit. 2. February. 3. Fellow. 4. (in Hungary) forint; forints. 5. franc; francs. 6. France. 7. French. 8. Friday.

f. 1. (in prescriptions) make. [from Latin *fac*] 2. farad. 3. farthing. 4. father. 5. fathom. 6. feet. 7. female. 8. feminine. 9. (in prescriptions) let them be made. [from Latin *fīant*] 10. (in prescriptions) let it be made. [from Latin *fiat*] 11. filly. 12. fine. 13. fluid (ounce). 14. folio. 15. following. 16. foot. 17. form. 18. formed of. 19. franc. 20. from. 21. *Math.* function (of). 22. (in the Netherlands) guilder; guilders.

f/ *Photography.* f-number. Also, **f/, f:**

fa 1. final assembly. 2. forced air.

FAA Federal Aviation Administration.

F.A.A.A.S. 1. Fellow of the American Academy of Arts and Sciences. 2. Fellow of the American Association for the Advancement of Science.

fab fabricate.

fabx fire alarm box.

fac. 1. facsimile. 2. factor. 3. factory. 4. faculty.

facil facility.

F.A.C.P. Fellow of the American College of Physicians. Also, **FACP**

FACS 1. *Biology.* fluorescence-activated cell sorter. 2. Also, **F.A. C.S.** Fellow of the American College of Surgeons.

facsim. facsimile.

FAdm Fleet Admiral.

Fahr. Fahrenheit (thermometer). Also, **Fah.**

F.A.L.N. Armed Forces of National Liberation: a militant underground organization whose objective is independence for Puerto Rico. Also, **FALN** [from Spanish *F(uerzas) A(rmadas de) L(iberación) N(acional)*]

FAM The Family Channel (a cable television station).

fam. 1. familiar. 2. family.

F.A.M. Free and Accepted Masons. Also, **F. & A.M.**

F. & T. *Insurance.* fire and theft.

FAO Food and Agriculture Organization.

F.A.Q. *Australian.* fair average quality. Also, **f.a.q.**

f/a ratio fuel-air ratio.

FAS 1. fetal alcohol syndrome. 2. Foreign Agricultural Service.

F.A.S. *Commerce.* free alongside ship: without charge to the buyer for goods delivered alongside ship. Also, **f.a.s., fas**

FASB Financial Accounting Standards Board.

fath. fathom.

fax (faks), facsimile.

f.b. 1. freight bill. 2. *Sports.* fullback.

F.B.A. Fellow of the British Academy.

FBI *U.S. Government.* Federal Bureau of Investigation.

fbk firebrick.

fbm foot board measure.

FBO for the benefit of. Also, **F/B/O**

fbr fiber.

fbrbd fiberboard.

FC foot-candle; footcandles. Also, **fc**

fc 1. *Computers.* ferrite core. 2. file cabinet. 3. fire control.

f.c. 1. *Baseball.* fielder's choice. 2. *Printing.* follow copy.

FCA Farm Credit Administration.

FCC *U.S. Government.* Federal Communications Commission.

FCIA Foreign Credit Insurance Association.

FCIC Federal Crop Insurance Corporation.

fcp. foolscap.

fcr fuse current rating.

fcs. francs.

fcsg focusing.

fcsle forecastle.

fctn function.

fctnl functional.

fcty factory.

fcy. fancy.

fd feed.

F.D. 1. Defender of the Faith. [from Latin *Fidei Defensor*] 2. fire department. 3. focal distance.

fdb field dynamic braking.

fdbk feedback.

fdc 1. fire department connection. 2. *Computers.* floppy-disk controller.

fdd *Computers.* floppy-disk drive.

fddl frequency-division data link.

Fdg *Banking.* funding.

FDIC Federal Deposit Insurance Corporation.

fdm frequency-division multiplex.

fdn foundation.

fdp *Hardware.* full dog point.

FDR Franklin Delano Roosevelt.

fdr 1. feeder. 2. finder. 3. fire door.

fdry foundry.

fd svc food service.

fdx *Telecommunications.* full duplex.

Fe *Symbol, Chemistry.* iron. [from Latin *ferrum*]

fe. he or she has made it. [from Latin *fecit*]

FEB Fair Employment Board.

Feb. February.

Fed. Federal.

fed. 1. federal. 2. federated. 3. federation.

fedn. federation.

Fed. Res. Bd. Federal Reserve Board.

Fed. Res. Bk. Federal Reserve Bank.

felr feeler.

FeLV feline leukemia virus.

fem. 1. female. 2. feminine.

FEMA Federal Emergency Management Agency.

FEPA Fair Employment Practices Act.

FEPC Fair Employment Practices Commission.

FERA Federal Emergency Relief Administration.

FERC Federal Energy Regulatory Commission.

FET 1. *Banking.* federal estate tax. 2. *Electronics.* field-effect transistor.

F.E.T. Federal Excise Tax.

fext fire extinguisher.

ff 1. flip-flop. 2. folios. 3. (and the) following (pages, verses, etc.). 4. *Music.* fortissimo.

FFA Future Farmers of America.

F.F.A. *Commerce.* free from alongside (ship). Also, **f.f.a.**

FFC 1. Foreign Funds Control. 2. free from chlorine.

F.F.I. free from infection.

ffilh *Hardware.* flat fillister head.

ffrr full frequency-range recording.

F.F.V. First Families of Virginia.

ffwd fast forward.

f.g. *Basketball, Football.* field goal; field goals.

fgd forged.

fgn. foreign.

FGP Foster Grandparent Program.

FGT federal gift tax.

fgy foggy.

FH *Pathology.* familial hypercholesterolemia.

fh fire hose.

FHA 1. Farmers' Home Administration. 2. Federal Housing Administration. 3. Future Homemakers of America.

FHLB Federal Home Loan Bank.

FHLBA Federal Home Loan Bank Administration.

FHLBB Federal Home Loan Bank Board.

FHLBS Federal Home Loan Bank System.

FHLMC Federal Home Loan Mortgage Corporation.

FHWA Federal Highway Administration.

fhy fire hydrant.

F.I. Falkland Islands.

FIA Federal Insurance Administration.

fict. fiction.

fid. fiduciary.

FIDO (fī'dō), *Aeronautics*. a system for evaporating the fog above airfield runways. [f(og) i(nvestigation) d(ispersal) o(perations)]

FIFO (fī'fō), *n.* **1.** *Commerce*. first-in, first-out. **2.** *Computers*. a storage and retrieval technique, in which the first item stored is also the first item retrieved.

fig. **1.** figurative. **2.** figuratively. **3.** figure; figures.

FIIG (fig), Federal Item Identification Guide.

fil **1.** filament. **2.** *Hardware*. fillister.

filh *Hardware*. fillister head.

filt. (in prescriptions) filter. [from Latin *filtrā*]

Fin. **1.** Finland. **2.** Finnish.

fin. **1.** finance. **2.** financial. **3.** finish.

fin. sec. financial secretary.

F.I.O. *Commerce*. free in and out: a term of contract in which a ship charterer pays for loading and unloading.

FIT *Banking*. Federal Insurance Tax.

fk fork.

FL **1.** Florida (for use with ZIP code). **2.** foreign language.

fL *Optics*. foot-lambert.

fl **1.** *Sports*. flanker. **2.** flashing. **3.** flat. **4.** flush. **5.** focal length.

Fl. **1.** Flanders. **2.** Flemish.

fl. **1.** floor. **2.** florin; florins. **3.** flourished. [from Latin *flōruit*] **4.** fluid. **5.** (in the Netherlands) guilder; guilders. [from Dutch *florin*]

Fla. Florida.

flav. (in prescriptions) yellow. [from Latin *flāvus*]

F.L.B. Federal Land Bank.

fld. **1.** field. **2.** fluid.

fldg folding.

fl dr fluid dram; fluid drams.

fldt floodlight.

fldxt (in prescriptions) fluidextract. [from Latin *fluidextractum*]

FLETC Federal Law Enforcement Training Center.

flex flexible.

flg **1.** flange. **2.** flooring.

flh flathead.

fll frequency-locked loop.

flld full load.

flm flame.

flmb flammable.

flmt flush mount.

fln fuel line.

FLOPS (flops), *Computers*. floating-point operations per second.

flor. flourished. [from Latin *flōruit*]

flot flotation.

fl. oz. fluid ounce; fluid ounces.

flr **1.** failure. **2.** filler. **3.** floor.

FLRA Federal Labor Relations Authority.

flrt flow rate.

flry flurry.

flt **1.** flashlight. **2.** flight. **3.** float.

fltg floating.

fltr **1.** filter. **2.** flutter.

fluor fluorescent.

flusoch fluted socket head.

flv flush valve.

flw flat washer.

flwp followup.

flywhl flywheel.

FM **1.** Federated States of Micronesia (approved for postal use). **2.** *Electronics*. frequency modulation: a method of impressing a signal on a radio carrier wave. **3.** *Radio*. a system of radio broadcasting by means of frequency modulation.

Fm *Symbol, Chemistry*. fermium.

fm **1.** *Symbol, Physics*. femtometer. **2.** field manual.

fm. **1.** fathom; fathoms. **2.** from.

f.m. (in prescriptions) make a mixture. [from Latin *fiat mistūra*]

FMB Federal Maritime Board.

FMC Federal Maritime Commission.

FMCS Federal Mediation and Conciliation Service.

fmcw frequency-modulated continuous wave.

F.Mk. finmark; Finnish markka. Also, **FMk**

fmla formula.

fmr former.

fmw *Computers*. firmware.

fn footnote.

fnd found.

FNMA Federal National Mortgage Association.

fnsh finish.

fo. **1.** *Electricity*. fast-operate: a type of relay. **2.** foldout. **3.** folio.

F.O. **1.** field officer. **2.** foreign office. **3.** *Military*. forward observer.

f.o.b. *Commerce*. free on board: without charge to the buyer for goods placed on board a carrier at the point of shipment. Also, **F.O.B.**

FOBS fractional orbital bombardment system. Also, **F.O.B.S.**

foc focal.

F.O.E. Fraternal Order of Eagles.

FOIA Freedom of Information Act.

fol. **1.** folio. **2.** (in prescriptions) a leaf. [from Latin *folium*] **3.** followed. **4.** following.

foll. following.

For. Forester.

for. **1.** foreign. **2.** forester. **3.** forestry.

F.O.R. *Commerce*. free on rails. Also, **f.o.r.**

fort. **1.** fortification. **2.** fortified.

FORTRAN (fôr'tran), *Computers*. a programming language used mainly in science and engineering. [for(mula) tran(slation)]

F.O.S. *Commerce*. **1.** free on station. **2.** free on steamer. Also, **f.o.s.**

F.O.T. *Commerce*. free on truck. Also, **f.o.t.**

fouo for official use only.

4WD four-wheel drive.

fp **1.** faceplate. **2.** *Music*. forte-piano. **3.** *Football*. forward pass.

F.P. *Physics*. foot-pound; foot-pounds.

f.p. **1.** fireplug. **2.** foolscap. **3.** foot-pound; foot-pounds. **4.** *Music*. forte-piano. **5.** freezing point. **6.** fully paid.

FPC **1.** Federal Power Commission. **2.** fish protein concentrate.

FPHA Federal Public Housing Authority.

Fpl *Real Estate*. fireplace.

fpl fire plug.

fpm feet per minute. Also, **ft/min, ft./min.**

FPO *Military*. **1.** field post office. **2.** fleet post office.

fprf fireproof.

fps **1.** Also, **ft/sec** feet per second. **2.** *Physics*. foot-pound-second.

f.p.s. **1.** Also, **ft./sec.** feet per second. **2.** *Physics*. foot-pound-second. **3.** frames per second.

fpsps feet per second per second. Also, **ft/s²**

FPT freight pass-through.

fpt female pipe thread.

FR **1.** *Real Estate*. family room. **2.** freight release.

Fr *Symbol, Chemistry*. francium.

fr **1.** failure rate. **2.** *Electricity*. fast release: a type of relay. **3.** field reversing.

Fr. **1.** Father. **2.** franc; francs. **3.** France. **4.** *Religion*. frater. **5.** Frau: the German form of address for a married woman. **6.** French. **7.** Friar. **8.** Friday.

fr. **1.** fragment. **2.** franc; francs. **3.** from.

frac fractional.

frag fragment.

F.R.A.S. Fellow of the Royal Astronomical Society.

FRB **1.** Federal Reserve Bank. **2.** Federal Reserve Board. Also, **F.R.B.**

frbd freeboard.

FRC Federal Radio Commission.

FRCD *Finance*. floating-rate certificate of deposit.

F.R.C.P. Fellow of the Royal College of Physicians.

F.R.C.S. Fellow of the Royal College of Surgeons.

freq. **1.** frequency. **2.** frequent. **3.** frequentative. **4.** frequently.

freqm frequency meter.

frequ frequency.

fres fire-resistant.

F.R.G. Federal Republic of Germany.

F.R.G.S. Fellow of the Royal Geographical Society.

Fri. Friday.

frict friction.

Fris. Frisian. Also, **Fris**

Frl. Fräulein: the German form of address for an unmarried woman.

frm frame.

FRN *Finance*. floating-rate note.

frnc furnace.

frng fringe.

front. frontispiece.

frpl *Real Estate*. fireplace.

FRS Federal Reserve System.

Frs. Frisian.

frs. francs.

abbrev.

F.R.S. Fellow of the Royal Society.

F.R.S.L. Fellow of the Royal Society of Literature.

F.R.S.S. Fellow of the Royal Statistical Society.

frt. 1. freight. 2. front.

frwk framework.

frz freeze.

frzr freezer.

FS Federal Specification.

fs 1. field service. 2. fire station. 3. functional schematic.

f.s. foot-second; foot-seconds.

FSA Farm Security Administration

fsbl 1. feasible. 2. fusible.

fsc full scale.

FSH *Biochemistry.* follicle-stimulating hormone.

fsk frequency-shift keying.

FSLIC Federal Savings and Loan Insurance Corporation.

fsm field-strength meter.

FSN Federal Stock Number.

FSO foreign service officer.

FSR Field Service Regulations.

fssn fission.

fstnr fastener.

fsz full size.

FT full time.

Ft. (in Hungary) forint; forints.

ft. foot; feet.

ft³ *Symbol.* cubic foot; cubic feet.

FTC *U.S. Government.* Federal Trade Commission.

ftc fast time constant.

ftd fitted.

ftg 1. fitting. 2. footing.

fth. fathom; fathoms. Also, **fthm.**

ft./hr. feet per hour.

fthrd female thread.

ft-L *Optics.* foot-lambert.

ft-lb *Physics.* foot-pound.

ft./min. feet per minute.

FTP *Computers.* File Transfer Protocol.

ft-pdl *Physics.* foot-poundal.

ft./sec. feet per second.

FTZ free-trade zone.

fu fuse.

fuhld fuseholder.

ful fulcrum.

fund fundamental.

funl funnel.

fur. furlong; furlongs.

furl. furlough.

furn 1. furnish. 2. furniture.

fuslg fuselage.

fut. future.

fv flux valve.

f.v. on the back of the page. [from Latin *folió versó*]

FVC *Medicine.* forced vital capacity.

FWA Federal Works Agency.

FWD 1. Also, **4WD** four-wheel drive. 2. front-wheel drive.

fwd. 1. foreword. 2. forward.

F.W.I. French West Indies.

fwv full wave.

Fwy. freeway.

FX foreign exchange.

fx. 1. fracture. 2. fractured.

fxd fixed.

fxtr fixture.

FY fiscal year.

FYI for your information.

fz fuze.

---

a b c d e f **G** h i j k l m n o p q r s t u v w x y z

G 1. *Slang.* grand: one thousand dollars. 2. (*sometimes lowercase*) *Aerospace.* gravity: a unit of acceleration.

G 1. gay. 2. *Psychology.* general intelligence. 3. German. 4. good.

G *Symbol.* 1. the seventh in order or in a series. 2. *Music.* **a.** the fifth tone in the scale of C major or the seventh tone in the relative minor scale, A minor. **b.** a string, key, or pipe tuned to this tone. **c.** a written or printed note representing this tone. **d.** (in the fixed system of solmization) the fifth tone of the scale of C major, called *sol.* **e.** the tonality having G as the tonic note. 3. (*sometimes lowercase*) the medieval Roman numeral for 400. 4. *Electricity.* **a.** conductance. **b.** gauss. 5. *Physics.* constant of gravitation; law of gravity. 6. *Biochemistry.* **a.** glycine. **b.** guanine. 7. a rating assigned to a motion picture by the Motion Picture Association of America indicating that the film is suitable for general audiences, or children as well as adults.

g 1. *Psychology.* general intelligence. 2. good. 3. gram; grams. 4. *Electronics.* grid.

g *Symbol, Physics.* 1. acceleration of gravity. 2. gravity.

G. 1. General. 2. German. 3. (in Haiti) gourde; gourdes. 4. (specific) gravity. 5. Gulf.

g. 1. gauge. 2. gender. 3. general. 4. generally. 5. genitive. 6. going back to. 7. gold. 8. grain; grains. 9. gram; grams. 10. *Sports.* guard. 11. *British.* guinea; guineas. 12. gun.

GA 1. Gamblers Anonymous. 2. General American. 3. general of the army. 4. Georgia (for use with ZIP code).

Ga *Symbol, Chemistry.* gallium.

Ga. Georgia.

G.A. 1. General Agent. 2. General Assembly. 3. Also, **g.a.,** **G/A** *Insurance.* general average.

G.A.A. Gay Activists' Alliance.

GABA (gab′ə), *Biochemistry.* a neurotransmitter of the central nervous system that inhibits excitatory responses. [*g(amma-)a(mino)b(utyric) a(cid)*]

G/A con. *Insurance.* general average contribution.

G/A dep. *Insurance.* general average deposit.

GAE General American English.

GAI guaranteed annual income.

Gal. *Bible.* Galatians.

gal. gallon; gallons.

gal/h *Symbol.* gallons per hour.

gall gallery.

gal/min *Symbol.* gallons per minute.

gals. gallons.

gal/s *Symbol.* gallons per second.

galv galvanic.

galvnm galvanometer.

galvs galvanized steel.

galy galley.

GAM 1. graduate in Aerospace Mechanical Engineering. 2. ground-to-air missile.

G&AE *Accounting.* general and administrative expense.

G and T gin and tonic. Also, **g and t**

GAO General Accounting Office.

GAPL Ground-to-Air Data Link.

gar. garage. Also, **gar**

G.A.R. Grand Army of the Republic.

gas gasoline.

GASP Gravity-assisted Space Probe.

GAT 1. *Military.* Ground Attack Tactics. 2. Ground-to-Air Transmitter.

GATT (gat), General Agreement on Tariffs and Trade.

G.A.W. guaranteed annual wage.

gaz. 1. gazette. 2. gazetteer.

GB 1. *Computers.* gigabyte: 1000 megabytes. 2. *Finance.* Gold Bond. 3. (on CB radio) good-bye. 4. Great Britain.

Gb *Electricity.* gilbert.

G.B. Great Britain.

G.B.E. Knight Grand Cross of the British Empire or Dame Grand Cross of the British Empire.

GBF gay black female.

gbg garbage.

GBM gay black male.

GBO *Commerce.* goods in bad order.

GBS *Radiography.* Gall Bladder Series.

Gc 1. gigacycle; gigacycles. 2. gigacycles per second.

GCA Girls' Clubs of America.

g-cal gram calorie. Also, **g-cal.**

G.C.B. Grand Cross of the Bath.

GCC Gulf Cooperation Council.

G.C.D. 1. *Math.* greatest common denominator. 2. greatest common divisor. Also, **g.c.d.**

GCE *British.* General Certificate of Education.

G.C.F. *Math.* greatest common factor; greatest common divisor. Also, **g.c.f.**

GCG *Military.* Guidance Control Group.

G.C.M. *Math.* greatest common measure. Also, **g.c.m.**

GCPS gigacycles per second. Also, **Gc/s, Gc/sec**

GCR *Military.* ground-controlled radar.

G.C.T. Greenwich Civil Time.

GCU *Aerospace.* Ground Control Unit.

GD 1. *Real Estate.* garbage disposal. 2. General Delivery.

Gd *Symbol, Chemistry.* gadolinium.

gd. 1. good. **2.** guard.

G.D. 1. Grand Duchess. **2.** Grand Duke.

Gde. (in Haiti) gourde; gourdes.

GDI *Slang.* God Damned Independent.

gdlk grid leak.

Gdn guardian.

gdn garden.

gdnc guidance.

Gdns. gardens.

GDP gross domestic product.

GDR German Democratic Republic. Also, **G.D.R.**

gds. goods.

GE *Medicine.* gastroenterology.

Ge *Symbol, Chemistry.* germanium.

g.e. *Bookbinding.* gilt edges.

GEB Guiding Eyes for the Blind.

geb. born. [from German *geboren*]

GED 1. general educational development. **2.** general equivalency diploma.

GEF 1. Gauss Error Function. **2.** *Military.* ground equipment failure.

GEM giant earth mover.

Gen. 1. *Military.* General. **2.** Genesis. **3.** Geneva.

gen. 1. gender. **2.** general. **3.** generator. **4.** genitive. **5.** genus.

genit. genitive.

genl general.

Genl. General.

Gen. Mtg. *Banking.* general mortgage.

Gent. gentleman; gentlemen. Also, **gent.**

Geo. George.

geod. 1. geodesy. **2.** geodetic.

geog. 1. geographer. **2.** geographic; geographical. **3.** geography.

geol. 1. geologic; geological. **2.** geologist. **3.** geology.

geom. 1. geometric; geometrical. **2.** geometry.

GEOS Geodetic Earth Orbiting Satellite.

Ger. 1. German. **2.** Germany.

ger. 1. gerund. **2.** gerundive.

Gestapo (gə stä′pō), the German secret police under Hitler. [from German *Ge(heime) Sta(ats) po(lizei)* secret state police]

GeV *Physics.* gigaelectron volt. Also, **GeV**

GF gay female.

gfci ground-fault circuit interrupter.

GFE government-furnished equipment.

GFR German Federal Republic.

G.F.T.U. General Federation of Trade Unions.

GG 1. gamma globulin. **2.** great gross.

GGR great gross.

GH growth hormone.

GHA Greenwich hour angle.

GHF gay Hispanic female.

GHM gay Hispanic male.

GHz *Physics.* gigahertz; gigahertzes.

GI (jē′ī′), a member of the U.S. armed forces, especially an enlisted soldier. Also, **G.I.** [originally abbreviation of *galva-*

nized iron, used in U.S. Army bookkeeping in entering articles (e.g., trash cans) made of it; later extended to all articles issued (as an assumed abbreviation of *government issue*) and finally to soldiers themselves]

Gi *Electricity.* gilbert; gilberts.

gi. gill; gills.

G.I. 1. galvanized iron. **2.** gastrointestinal. **3.** general issue. **4.** government issue. Also, **GI, g.i.**

Gib. Gibraltar.

GIGO (gī′gō), *Computers.* a rule of thumb stating that when faulty data are fed into a computer, the information that emerges will also be faulty. [*g(arbage) i(n) g(arbage) o(ut)*]

GILMER guardian of impressive letters and master of excellent replies.

GIRLS (gûrlz), Generalized Information Retrieval and Listing System.

GI's (jē′īz′), **the GI's,** *Slang.* diarrhea. Also, **G.I.'s, G.I.s** [probably for *GI shits*]

GJ *Informal.* grapefruit juice.

GJF gay Jewish female.

GJM gay Jewish male.

Gk Greek. Also, **Gk.**

Gl *Symbol, Chemistry.* glucinum.

gl gold.

gl. 1. glass; glasses. **2.** gloss.

g/l grams per liter.

GLB gay, lesbian, bisexual.

glb *Math.* greatest lower bound.

Gld. guilder; guilders.

GLF Gay Liberation Front.

Gln *Biochemistry.* glutamine.

GLO *Slang.* get the lead out.

gloss. glossary.

GLOW Gross Lift-Off Weight.

GLP Gross Lawyer Product.

glpg glowplug.

glsry glossary.

Glu *Biochemistry.* glutamic acid.

glv globe valve.

Gly *Biochemistry.* glycine.

glyc. (in prescriptions) glycerite. [from Latin *glyceritum*]

glycn glycerine.

glz glaze.

GM 1. gay male. **2.** General Manager. **3.** General Medicine. **4.** Greenwich Meridian.

gm. 1. gram; grams. **2.** guided missile.

G.M. 1. General Manager. **2.** Grand Marshal. **3.** Grand Master. Also, **GM**

G.M.&S. general, medical, and surgical.

GMAT 1. *Trademark.* Graduate Management Admissions Test. **2.** Greenwich Mean Astronomical Time.

GMB *British.* Grand Master of the Bath.

gmbl gimbal.

Gmc Germanic. Also, **Gmc.**

GMP *Biochemistry.* a ribonucleotide constituent of ribonucleic acid. [*g(uanosine) m(ono) p(hosphate)*]

GMT Greenwich Mean Time. Also, **G.M.T.**

gmtry geometry.

gmv guaranteed minimum value.

GMW gram-molecular weight.

gn green.

G.N. Graduate Nurse.

gnd *Electricity.* ground.

GNI *Economics.* Gross National Income.

gnltd granulated.

GNMA Government National Mortgage Association.

GNP gross national product. Also, **G.N.P.**

GnRH gonadotropin releasing hormone.

G.O. 1. general office. **2.** general order. Also, **g.o.**

GOES Geostationary Operational Environmental Satellite.

G.O.K. *Medicine.* God Only Knows.

GOO Get Oil Out.

G.O.P. Grand Old Party (an epithet of the Republican party since 1880). Also, **GOP**

Goth. Gothic. Also, **Goth, goth.**

Gov. governor.

gov. 1. government. **2.** governor.

Govt. government. Also, **govt.**

GP 1. Galactic Probe. **2.** General Purpose.

gp 1. general purpose. **2.** glide path.

gp. group. Also, **Gp.**

G.P. 1. General Practitioner. **2.** General Purpose. **3.** Gloria Patri. **4.** Graduate in Pharmacy. **5.** Grand Prix.

GPA grade point average.

gpad gallons per acre per day.

gpcd gallons per capita per day.

gpd gallons per day.

gph 1. gallons per hour. **2.** graphite.

gpi ground-position indicator.

gpib *Computers.* general-purpose interface bus.

gpm 1. gallons per mile. **2.** gallons per minute.

G.P.O. 1. general post office. **2.** Government Printing Office. Also, **GPO**

GPRF gay Puerto Rican female.

GPRM gay Puerto Rican male.

GPS *Aerospace, Navigation.* Global Positioning System.

gps gallons per second.

GPU General Postal Union; Universal Postal Union.

GPU (gä′pā′ōō′, jē′pē′yōō′), (in the Soviet Union) the secret-police organization (1922–23) functioning under the NKVD. Also, **G.P.U.** [from Russian *G(o-sudárstvennoe) p(olitícheskoe) u(pravlénie)* state political directorate]

GQ General Quarters.

gr 1. gear. **2.** grain. **3.** gram; grams. **4.** gross.

Gr. 1. Grecian. **2.** Greece. **3.** Greek.

gr. 1. grade. **2.** grain; grains. **3.** gram; grams. **4.** grammar. **5.** gravity. **6.** great. **7.** gross. **8.** group.

G.R. King George. [from Latin *Geōrgius Rēx*]

grad. 1. *Math.* gradient. **2.** graduate. **3.** graduated.

gram. 1. grammar. **2.** grammarian. **3.** grammatical.

gran 1. granite. **2.** granular; granulated.

GRAS (gras), generally recognized as safe: a status label assigned by the FDA to a listing of substances not known to be hazardous and thus approved for use in foods.

Gr. Br. Great Britain. Also, **Gr. Brit.**

grbx gearbox.

grd 1. grind. 2. guard.

grdl griddle.

grdtn graduation.

GRE Graduate Record Examination.

GRF growth hormone releasing factor.

GRI Government Reports Index.

gro. gross.

grom grommet.

grp group.

grph graphic.

grs grease.

grshft gearshaft.

grtg grating.

grtr grater.

GRU (in the former Soviet Union) the Chief Intelligence Directorate of the Soviet General Staff, a military intelligence organization founded in 1920 and functioning as a complement to the KGB. Also, **G.R.U.** [from Russian G(l-ávnoe) r(azvédyvatel'noe) u(prav-lénie)]

Grv. grove.

grv groove.

gr. wt. gross weight.

GS 1. General Schedule (referring to the Civil Service job classification system). 2. general staff. 3. German silver.

gs ground speed.

G.S. 1. general secretary. 2. general staff. Also, **g.s.**

GSA 1. General Services Administration. 2. Girl Scouts of America. Also, **G.S.A.**

G.S.C. General Staff Corps.

GSE ground-support equipment.

Gsil German silver.

gskt gasket.

GSL Guaranteed Student Loan.

G spot (jē'spot'), Gräfenberg spot: a patch of tissue in the vagina purportedly excitable and erectile. Also, **G-spot.**

GSR 1. galvanic skin reflex. 2. galvanic skin response.

gsr glide slope receiver.

GST Greenwich Sidereal Time.

G-suit (jē'sōōt'), Aerospace. anti-G suit: a flier's or astronaut's suit. Also, **g-suit.** [g(ravity) suit]

GT 1. Game Theory. 2. gigaton; gigatons. 3. grand theft 4. Automotive. grand touring: a car type.

gt. 1. gilt. 2. great. 3. (in prescriptions) a drop [from Latin gutta].

Gt. Br. Great Britain. Also, **Gt. Brit.**

g.t.c. 1. good till canceled. 2. good till countermanded. Also, **G. T.C.**

gtd. guaranteed.

GTG ground-to-ground.

GTO Automotive. Gran Turismo Omologato: a car style (grand touring).

GTP Biochemistry. an ester that is an important metabolic cofactor and precursor in the biosynthesis of cyclic GMP. [g(uanosine) t(ri) p(hosphate)]

gtrb gas turbine.

GTS gas turbine ship.

gtt. (in prescriptions) drops. [from Latin guttae]

GU 1. genitourinary. 2. Guam (for use with ZIP code).

guar guarantee.

GUGB the Chief Directorate for State Security: the former Soviet Union's secret police organization (1934–1941) functioning as part of the NKVD. Also, **G.U.G.B.** [from Russian G(lávnoe) u(prav-lénie) g(osudárstvennoĭ) b(ezo-pásnosti)]

GUI (gōō'ē), Computers. graphical user interface.

Gui. Guiana.

Guin. Guinea.

gun. gunnery.

GUT Physics. grand unification theory.

gut gutter.

g.v. 1. gravimetric volume. 2. gigavolt; gigavolts.

gvl gravel.

GVW gross vehicle weight; gross vehicular weight.

GW gigawatt; gigawatts. Also, **Gw**

GWF gay white female.

GWh Gigawatt-hour.

GWM gay white male.

Gy Physics. gray: a measure of radiation absorption.

gy gray.

GYN 1. gynecological. 2. gynecologist. 3. gynecology. Also, **gyn.**

gyp gypsum.

GySgt Marine Corps. gunnery sergeant.

GZ ground zero.

Gz Graetz number.

---

a b c d e f g **H** i j k l m n o p q r s t u v w x y z

H 1. hard. 2. Grammar. head. 3. Electricity. henry. 4. Slang. heroin. 5. high.

H Symbol. 1. the eighth in order or in a series. 2. (sometimes lowercase) the medieval Roman numeral for 200. 3. Chemistry. hydrogen. 4. Biochemistry. histidine. 5. Physics. **a.** enthalpy. **b.** horizontal component of the earth's magnetic field. **c.** magnetic intensity. 6. Music. the letter used in German to indicate the tone B.

H¹ Symbol, Chemistry. protium. Also, **¹H, Hᵃ**

H² Symbol, Chemistry. deuterium. Also, **²H, Hᵇ**

H³ Symbol, Chemistry. tritium. Also, **³H, Hᶜ**

h hard.

h Symbol, Physics. Planck's constant.

H. (in prescriptions) an hour. [from Latin hōra]

h. 1. harbor. 2. hard. 3. hardness. 4. heavy sea. 5. height. 6. hence. 7. high. 8. Baseball. hit; hits. 9. horns. 10. hour; hours. 11. hundred. 12. husband. Also, **H.**

Ha Symbol, Chemistry. hahnium.

ha hectare; hectares.

h.a. 1. Gunnery. high angle. 2. in this year [from Latin hōc annō].

Hab. Bible. Habakkuk.

HAC House Appropriations Committee.

Hag. Bible. Haggai.

Hal Chemistry. halogen.

H&A Health and Accident.

haust. (in prescriptions) draught. [from Latin haustus]

Haw. Hawaii.

HAWK (hôk), 1. have alimony, will keep. 2. Homing All the Way Killer (small missile).

haz hazardous.

Hb Symbol, Biochemistry. hemoglobin.

h.b. Sports. halfback.

H.B.M. His Britannic Majesty; Her Britannic Majesty.

HBO Home Box Office (a cable television channel).

H-bomb (āch'bom'), hydrogen bomb.

HBP high blood pressure.

HBV hepatitis B.

H.C. 1. Holy Communion. 2. House of Commons.

h.c. for the sake of honor. [from Latin honōris causā]

hce human-caused error.

H.C.F. Math. highest common factor. Also, **h.c.f.**

hCG human chorionic gonadotropin.

H.C.M. His Catholic Majesty; Her Catholic Majesty.

H. Con. Res. House concurrent resolution.

HCR highway contract route.

hcs high-carbon steel.

hd. 1. hand. 2. hard. 3. head.

h.d. 1. heavy duty. 2. (in prescriptions) at bedtime [from Latin hōra dēcubitūs].

hdbk. handbook.

hdcp handicap.

hdd Computers. hard-disk drive.

hdg heading.

hdkf. handkerchief.

HDL high-density lipoprotein.

hdl handle.

hdlg handling.

hdlng headlining.

hdn harden.

hdns hardness.

H. Doc. House document.

HDPE high-density polyethylene.

hdqrs. headquarters.

hdr header.

hdshk Computers. handshake.

hdst headset.

HDTV high-definition television.

hdw. hardware. Also, **hdwe, hdwr.**

hdwd hardwood.

hdx *Telecommunications.* half duplex.

HE high explosive. Also, **he**

He *Symbol, Chemistry.* helium.

H.E. 1. high explosive. **2.** His Eminence. **3.** His Excellency; Her Excellency.

HEAO High Energy Astrophysical Observatory.

Heb Hebrew.

Heb. 1. Hebrew. **2.** *Bible.* Hebrews. Also, **Hebr.**

herp. herpetology. Also, **herpet.**

herpetol. 1. herpetological. **2.** herpetology.

het heterodyne.

HETP *Chemistry.* hexaethyl tetraphosphate.

HEW Department of Health, Education, and Welfare.

hex. 1. *Math.* hexadecimal (number system). **2.** hexagon. **3.** hexagonal.

hex hd hexagonal head.

hex soch hexagonal socket head.

HF 1. high frequency. **2.** Hispanic female.

Hf *Symbol, Chemistry.* hafnium.

hf. half.

hf. bd. *Printing.* half-bound.

hfe human-factors engineering.

HG 1. High German. **2.** *British.* Home Guard.

Hg *Symbol, Chemistry.* mercury. [from Latin *hydrargyrum,* from Greek *hydrárgyros* literally, liquid silver]

hg hectogram; hectograms.

H.G. 1. High German. **2.** His Grace; Her Grace.

hGH human growth hormone.

hgr hanger.

hgt. height.

hgwy. highway.

H.H. 1. His Highness; Her Highness. **2.** His Holiness.

hhd hogshead; hogsheads.

HH.D. Doctor of Humanities.

HHFA Housing and Home Finance Agency.

H-hour (āch′ou°r′, -ou′ər), the time, usually unspecified, set for the beginning of a planned attack.

HHS Department of Health and Human Services.

HI Hawaii (for use with ZIP code).

H.I. 1. Hawaiian Islands. **2.** *Meteorology.* heat index.

HIF human-initiated failure.

hi-fi (hī′fī′), high fidelity. Also, **hi fi**

H.I.H. His Imperial Highness; Her Imperial Highness.

H.I.M. His Imperial Majesty; Her Imperial Majesty.

Hind Hindustani.

Hind. 1. Hindi. **2.** Hindu. **3.** Hindustan. **4.** Hindustani.

hint high intensity.

HIP (āch′ī′pē′ *or, sometimes,* hip), Health Insurance Plan.

hipar high-power acquisition radar.

hipot high potential.

His *Biochemistry.* histidine.

hist. 1. histology. **2.** historian. **3.** historical. **4.** history.

HIV human immunodeficiency virus; AIDS virus.

H.J. here lies. [from Latin *hīc jacet*]

H.J. Res. House joint resolution.

H.J.S. here lies buried. [from Latin *hīc jacet sepultus*]

HK Hong Kong.

hksw *Telephones.* hookswitch.

hl 1. haul. **2.** hectoliter; hectoliters.

H.L. House of Lords.

HLA *Immunology.* human leukocyte antigen.

HLBB Home Loan Bank Board.

hlcl helical.

hlcptr helicopter.

hldg holding.

hldn holddown.

hldr holder.

hll *Computers.* high-level language.

hlpr helper.

HLTL *Computers.* high-level transistor logic.

HLTTL *Computers.* high-level transistor-transistor logic.

HM Hispanic male.

hm hectometer; hectometers.

H.M. Her Majesty; His Majesty.

hma *Computers.* high-memory area.

HMAS Her Majesty's Australian Ship; His Majesty's Australian Ship.

hmc harmonic.

HMCS Her Majesty's Canadian Ship; His Majesty's Canadian Ship.

hmd humidity.

HMF Her Majesty's Forces; His Majesty's Forces.

HMMV humvee: a military vehicle. Also, **HMMWV.** [*H*(*igh*)-*M*(*obility*) *M*(*ultipurpose*) *W*(*heeled*) *V*(*ehicle*)]

HMO health maintenance organization.

hmr hammer.

H.M.S. 1. Her Majesty's Service; His Majesty's Service. **2.** Her Majesty's Ship; His Majesty's Ship.

hnd cont hand control.

hndrl handrail.

hndst handset.

hndwl handwheel.

hng hinge.

hntg hunting.

HO (hō), (in police use) habitual offender.

Ho *Symbol, Chemistry.* holmium.

ho. house.

H.O. 1. Head Office. **2.** Home Office.

HOLC Home Owners' Loan Corporation. Also, **H.O.L.C.**

Hon. 1. Honorable. **2.** Honorary.

hon. 1. honor. **2.** honorable. **3.** honorably. **4.** honorary.

Hond. Honduras.

hor. 1. horizon. **2.** horizontal. **3.** horology.

hor. interm. (in prescriptions) at intermediate hours. [from Latin *hōrā intermediīs*]

horol. horology.

hor. som. (in prescriptions) at bedtime. [from Latin *hōrā somnī* at the hour of sleep]

hort. 1. horticultural. **2.** horticulture.

hor. un. spatio (in prescriptions) at the end of one hour. [from Latin *hōrae ūnius spatiō*]

horz horizontal.

Hos. *Bible.* Hosea.

hosp. hospital.

HOV high-occupancy vehicle.

hp 1. high pass. **2.** horsepower.

H.P. 1. *Electricity.* high power. **2.** high pressure. **3.** horsepower. Also, **h.p., HP**

HPER Health, Physical Education, and Recreation.

hpot helical potentiometer.

hps high-pressure steam.

HPV human papilloma virus.

H.Q. headquarters. Also, **h.q., HQ**

HR 1. *Baseball.* home run; home runs. **2.** House of Representatives.

Hr. Herr: the German form of address for a man.

hr. hour; hours. Also, **h.**

H.R. House of Representatives. Also, **HR**

h.r. *Baseball.* home run; home runs. Also, **hr**

HRA Health Resources Administration.

H-R diagram *Astronomy.* Hertzsprung-Russell diagram.

H.R.E. 1. Holy Roman Emperor. **2.** Holy Roman Empire.

H. Rept. House report.

H. Res. House resolution.

hrg hearing.

H.R.H. His Royal Highness; Her Royal Highness.

H.R.I.P. here rests in peace. [from Latin *hīc requiēscit in pāce*]

hrs. 1. hot-rolled steel. **2.** hours.

hrzn horizon.

HS 1. *Medicine.* Herpes Simplex. **2.** laid here. [from Latin *Hic sĭtus*]

hs high speed.

H.S. 1. High School. **2.** *British.* Home Secretary.

h.s. 1. in this sense. [from Latin *hōc sensū*] **2.** (in prescriptions) at bedtime. [from Latin *hōrā somnī* at the hour of sleep]

hse house.

hsg housing.

H.S.H. His Serene Highness; Her Serene Highness.

hshld household.

HSI heat stress index.

H.S.M. His Serene Majesty; Her Serene Majesty.

hss high-speed steel.

HST Hawaii Standard Time. Also, **H.S.T., h.s.t.**

hsth hose thread.

HSV-1 herpes simplex virus: usually associated with oral herpes. Also, **HSV-I.**

HSV-2 herpes simplex virus: usually causing genital herpes. Also, **HSV-II.**

HT 1. *Sports.* halftime. **2.** halftone. **3.** Hawaii time. **4.** *Electricity.* high tension. **5.** high tide. **6.** at this time. [from Latin *hōc tempŏre*] **7.** under this title. [from Latin *hōc titulō*]

ht. height.

h.t. at this time. [from Latin *hōc tempŏre*]

htd heated.

HTLV *Pathology.* human T-cell lymphotropic virus.

HTLV-1 *Pathology.* human T-cell lymphotropic virus type 1. Also, **HTLV-I.**

HTLV-2 *Pathology.* human T-cell lymphotropic virus type. Also, **HTLV-II.**

HTLV-3 *Pathology.* human T-cell lymphotropic virus type 3; AIDS virus. Also, **HTLV-III.**

HTML *Computers.* HyperText Markup Language.

htr heater.

Hts. Heights.

HUAC (hyo͞o′ak), House Un-American Activities Committee.

HUD (hud), Department of Housing and Urban Development.

HUM humanities.

huricn hurricane.

husb. husbandry.

H.V. 1. high velocity. **2.** Also, **h.v., hv** high voltage. **3.** high volume.

HVAC heating, ventilating, and air conditioning.

HVDC high-voltage direct current.

HVP hydrolyzed vegetable protein. Also, **H.V.P.**

hvps high-voltage power supply.

hvy. heavy.

HW 1. half wave. **2.** *Real Estate.* hardwood. **3.** high water. **4.** hot water (heat).

HWM high-water mark. Also, **H. W.M., h.w.m.**

hwy highway. Also, **Hwy, hwy.**

hy. *Electricity.* (formerly) henry.

hyb hybrid.

hyd. 1. hydrant. **2.** hydraulics. **3.** hydrostatics.

hydm hydrometer.

hydr hydraulic.

hydraul. hydraulics.

hydrelc hydroelectric.

HYDROPAC (hī′drə pak′), an urgent warning of navigational dangers in the Pacific Ocean, issued by the U.S. Navy Hydrographic Office.

hydros. hydrostatics.

hyp. 1. hypotenuse. **2.** hypothesis. **3.** hypothetical.

hypoth. 1. hypothesis. **2.** hypothetical.

Hz hertz; hertzes.

---

a b c d e f g h I j k l m n o p q r s t u v w x y z

I interstate (used with a number to designate an interstate highway): *I-95.*

I *Symbol.* **1.** the ninth in order or in a series. **2.** (*sometimes lowercase*) the Roman numeral for 1. **3.** *Chemistry.* iodine. **4.** *Biochemistry.* isoleucine. **5.** *Physics.* isotopic spin. **6.** *Electricity.* current. **7.** *Logic.* particular affirmative.

i *Symbol, Math.* **1.** the imaginary number. **2.** a unit vector on the *x*-axis of a coordinate system.

I. 1. Independent. **2.** Indian. **3.** Iraqi. **4.** Island; Islands. **5.** Isle; Isles. **6.** Israeli.

i. 1. imperator. **2.** incisor. **3.** interest. **4.** intransitive. **5.** island. **6.** isle; isles.

IA Iowa (for use with ZIP code).

ia 1. immediately available. **2.** impedance angle. **3.** international angstrom.

Ia. Iowa.

i.a. in absentia.

IAAF International Amateur Athletic Federation.

IAB 1. Industry Advisory Board. **2.** Inter-American Bank.

IAC Industry Advisory Commission.

IACA Independent Air Carriers Association.

IACB International Association of Convention Bureaus.

IADB 1. Inter-American Defense Board. **2.** Inter-American Development Bank.

IAEA International Atomic Energy Agency.

IAG International Association of Gerontology.

IAIA Institute of American Indian Arts.

IAMAW International Association of Machinists and Aerospace Workers.

IAS 1. *Aeronautics.* indicated air speed. **2.** Institute for Advanced Study.

ias indicate airspeed.

IAT international atomic time.

IATA International Air Transport Association.

IATSE International Alliance of Theatrical Stage Employees (and

Moving Picture Machine Operators of the U.S. and Canada).

iaw in accordance with.

ib. 1. in the same book, chapter, page, etc. [from Latin *ibidem*] **2.** instruction book.

IBA 1. Independent Bankers Association. **2.** International Bar Association.

IBC 1. International Broadcasting Corporation. **2.** international business company.

IBD inflammatory bowel disease.

IBEW International Brotherhood of Electrical Workers.

IBF international banking facilities.

ibid. (ib′id), in the same book, chapter, page, etc. [from Latin *ibidem*]

IBR infectious bovine rhinotracheitis.

I.B.T.C.W.H. International Brotherhood of Teamsters, Chauffeurs, Warehousemen, and Helpers of America.

IC 1. immediate constituent. **2.** *Computers, Electronics.* integrated circuit. **3.** intensive care.

I.C. Jesus Christ. [from Latin *I(ēsus) C(hrīstus)*]

ICA 1. International Communication Agency (1978–82). **2.** International Cooperation Administration.

ICAO International Civil Aviation Organization.

icas intermittent commercial and amateur service.

ICBM intercontinental ballistic missile. Also, **I.C.B.M.**

ICC Indian Claims Commission.

I.C.C. 1. International Control Commission. **2.** Interstate Commerce Commission. Also, **ICC**

Icel. 1. Iceland. **2.** Icelandic. Also, **Icel**

ICF *Physics.* inertial confinement fusion: an experimental method for producing controlled thermonuclear energy.

ICJ International Court of Justice.

ICM Institute of Computer Management.

icm 1. intercom. **2.** intercommunication.

ICR 1. Institute of Cancer Research. **2.** Institute for Cooperative Research.

ICRC International Committee of the Red Cross.

icrm ice cream.

ICS International College of Surgeons.

ICSE International Committee for Sexual Equality.

ICSH *Biochemistry, Pharmacology.* interstitial-cell stimulating hormone.

ICU intensive care unit.

icw interrupted continuous wave.

ID (ī′dē′), a means of identification, as a card or bracelet.

ID 1. Idaho (for use with ZIP code). **2.** Also, **i.d., id** inside diameter.

id 1. inside diameter. **2.** internal diameter.

ID. (in Iraq) dinar; dinars.

Id. Idaho.

id. idem: the same as previously given.

I.D. 1. identification. **2.** identity. **3.** *Military.* Infantry Division. **4.** Intelligence Department.

IDA 1. Industrial Development Agency. **2.** Institute for Defense Analysis.

IDB 1. Industrial Development Board. **2.** industrial development bond.

IDE *Computers.* integrated drive electronics: hard-drive interface.

ident 1. identical. **2.** identification.

idf *Telephones.* intermediate distributing frame.

IDP 1. integrated data processing. **2.** International Driving Permit.

IDR 1. Institute for Dream Research. **2.** international drawing rights.

idrty indirectly.

idx index.

IE Indo-European.

I.E. 1. Indo-European. **2.** Industrial Engineer.

i.e. that is. [from Latin *id est*]

IEC International Electrotechnical Commission.

I.E.E.E. (ī′ trip′əl ē′), Institute of

Electrical and Electronics Engineers. Also, **IEEE**

IEP Individualized Educational Program.

IES Illuminating Engineering Society.

if 1. inside frosted (of a light bulb). **2.** intermediate frequency.

IFA *Medicine.* immunofluorescence assay.

IFALP International Federation of Air Line Pilots Associations.

IFC 1. International Finance Corporation. **2.** International Fisheries Commission **3.** International Freighting Corporation.

IFF 1. *Military.* Identification, Friend or Foe: a system to distinguish between friendly and hostile aircraft. **2.** Institute for the Future.

iff *Math.* if and only if.

IFIP (ifʹip), International Federation for Information Processing.

I.F.L.W.U. International Fur and Leather Workers' Union.

IFN *Biochemistry, Pharmacology.* interferon.

ifr instrument flight rules.

IFS International Foundation for Science.

I.F.S. Irish Free State.

IG *Electronics.* ignitor: an electron device.

Ig *Immunology.* immunoglobulin.

I.G. 1. Indo-Germanic. **2.** Inspector General.

IgA *Immunology.* immunoglobulin A.

IgE *Immunology.* immunoglobulin E.

IGFET insulated-gate field-effect transistor.

IgG *Immunology.* immunoglobulin G.

IgM *Immunology.* immunoglobulin M.

ign. 1. ignition. **2.** unknown [from Latin *ignōtus*].

igt ingot.

IGY International Geophysical Year.

IHL International Hockey League.

ihp indicated horsepower. Also, **IHP**

IHS 1. Jesus. [from Latin, from Greek: partial transliteration of the first three letters of *Iēsoûs* Jesus] **2.** Jesus Savior of Men. [from Latin *Iēsus Hominum Salvātor*] **3.** in this sign (the cross) shalt thou conquer. [from Latin *In Hōc Signō Vincēs*] **4.** in this (cross) is salvation. [from Latin *In Hōc Salūs*]

IL Illinois (for use with ZIP code).

Il *Symbol, Chemistry.* illinium.

il. 1. illustrated. **2.** illustration.

ILA 1. International Law Association. **2.** International Longshoremen's Association. Also, **I.L.A.**

ILAS Instrument Landing Approach System.

I.L.G.W.U. International Ladies' Garment Workers' Union. Also, **ILGWU**

Ill. Illinois.

ill. 1. illustrated. **2.** illustration. **3.** illustrator. **4.** most illustrious [from Latin *illustrissimus*].

illum illuminate.

illus. 1. illustrated. **2.** illustration. Also, **illust.**

ILO International Labor Organization. Also, **I.L.O.**

I.L.P. Independent Labour Party.

ILS 1. *Aeronautics.* instrument landing system. **2.** Integrated Logistic Support.

ILTF International Lawn Tennis Federation.

I.L.W.U. International Longshoremen's and Warehousemen's Union.

im intermodulation.

I.M. Isle of Man.

imag imaginary.

IMCO Inter-Governmental Maritime Consultive Organization.

imd intermodulation distortion.

IMF International Monetary Fund. Also, **I.M.F.**

imit. 1. Also, **imit** imitation. **2.** imitative.

immed immediate.

immunol. immunology.

IMP *Bridge.* international match point.

Imp. 1. Emperor. [from Latin *Imperātor*] **2.** Empress. [from Latin *Imperātrīx*]

imp. 1. impact. **2.** imperative. **3.** imperfect. **4.** imperial. **5.** impersonal. **6.** implement. **7.** import. **8.** important. **9.** imported. **10.** importer. **11.** imprimatur. **12.** in the first place. [from Latin *imprīmīs*] **13.** imprint. **14.** improper. **15.** improved. **16.** improvement.

impd impedance.

imper. imperative.

imperf. imperfect.

impers. impersonal.

impf. imperfect.

imp. gal. imperial gallon.

impl implement.

implr impeller.

imprg impregnate.

impri imprint.

improv 1. improvement. **2.** improvisation.

imprsn impression.

impv. imperative.

imrs immersion.

IN Indiana (for use with ZIP code).

In *Symbol, Chemistry.* indium.

in. inch; inches.

in³ *Symbol.* cubic inch; cubic inches.

INA 1. international normal atmosphere. **2.** Israeli News Agency.

inbd inboard.

Inc. incorporated.

inc. 1. engraved. [from Latin *incīsus*] **2.** inclosure. **3.** included. **4.** including. **5.** inclusive. **6.** income. **7.** incorporated. **8.** increase. **9.** incumbent.

incand incandescent.

incin incinerator.

incl. 1. inclosure. **2.** including. **3.** inclusive.

incln inclined.

incls inclosure.

incm incoming.

incmpl incomplete.

incnd incendiary.

incog incognito.

incoh incoherent.

incor. 1. Also, **incorp.** incorporated. **2.** incorrect.

incorr. incorrect. Also, **incor.**

incpt intercept.

incr. 1. increase. **2.** increased. **3.** increasing. **4.** increment.

incrt increment.

IND *Pharmacology.* investigative new drug.

Ind. 1. India. **2.** Also, **Ind** Indian. **3.** Indiana. **4.** Indies.

ind. 1. independence. **2.** independent. **3.** index. **4.** indicate. **5.** indicated. **6.** indicative. **7.** indicator. **8.** indigo. **9.** indirect. **10.** industrial. **11.** industry.

in d. (in prescriptions) daily. [from Latin *in diēs*]

I.N.D. in the name of God. [from Latin *in nōmine Deī*]

Ind.E. Industrial Engineer.

indef. indefinite.

indep independent.

indic. 1. indicating. **2.** indicative. **3.** indicator.

individ. individual. Also, **indiv.**

indl industrial.

indn induction.

indt indent.

indtry industry.

induc. induction.

indus. 1. industrial. **2.** industry.

indv individual.

INF European-based U.S. nuclear weapons that were capable of striking the Soviet Union and Soviet ones that could hit Western Europe. [*I(ntermediate-range) N(uclear) F(orces)*]

inf 1. *Math.* greatest lower bound. [from Latin *infimum*] **2.** infinite. **3.** infinity.

Inf. 1. infantry. **2.** infuse [from Latin *infunde*].

in f. in the end; finally. [from Latin *in fīne*]

infin. infinitive.

info (inʹfō), information.

INH *Pharmacology, Trademark.* a brand of isoniazid.

inher. inheritance.

in. Hg *Meteorology.* inch of mercury.

init. Also, **init** initial.

inject. (in prescriptions) an injection. [from Latin *injectiō*]

inl inlet.

in loc. cit. in the place cited. [from Latin *in locō citātō*]

in mem. in memoriam.

inn. *Sports.* inning.

inop inoperative.

inorg. inorganic.

INP International News Photos.

inp input.

inq inquiry.

inr inner.

I.N.R.I. Jesus of Nazareth, King of the Jews. [from Latin *Iēsūs Nazarēnus, Rēx Iūdaeōrum*]

INS 1. Immigration and Naturalization Service. **2.** Also, **I.N.S.** International News Service. **3.** Integrated Navigation System.

ins. 1. inches. **2.** *Chiefly British.* inscribed. **3.** inside. **4.** inspector. **5.** insulated. **6.** insurance. **7.** insure.

in./sec. inches per second.

insep. inseparable. Also, **insep**

insol. insoluble.

insp. 1. inspection. **2.** inspector.

inst. 1. instant. 2. instantaneous. 3. Also, **Inst.** institute. 4. Also, **Inst.** institution. 5. instructor. 6. instrument. 7. instrumental.

instl 1. install. 2. installation.

instm instrumentation.

instr. 1. instruct. 2. instructor. 3. instrument. 4. instrumental.

insuf insufficient.

insul 1. insulate. 2. insulation.

int. 1. intelligence. 2. interest. 3. interim. 4. interior. 5. interjection. 6. internal. 7. international. 8. interpreter. 9. interval. 10. intransitive.

intchg interchangeable.

intcom intercommunication.

intcon interconnection.

integ 1. integral. 2. integrate.

integrg integrating.

intel intelligence.

INTELSAT (in tel′sat′, in′tel-), International Telecommunications Satellite Consortium.

inten intensity.

Intens *Grammar.* intensifier. Also, **intens**

intens. 1. intensifier. 2. intensive.

inter. 1. intermediate. 2. interrogation. 3. interrogative.

interj. interjection.

internat. international.

Interpol (in′tər pōl′), International Criminal Police Organization.

interrog. 1. interrogation. 2. interrogative.

intfc *Computers.* interface.

intk intake.

intl. 1. internal. 2. Also, **intnl.** international.

intlk interlock.

intlz initialize.

intmd intermediate.

intmt intermittent.

intpr interpret.

intr. 1. interior. 2. intransitive. 3. introduce. 4. introduced. 5. introducing. 6. introduction. 7. introductory.

intrans. intransitive.

in trans. in transit. [from Latin *in trānsitū*]

Int. Rev. Internal Revenue.

intrf interference.

intrg interrogate.

intro introduction.

intrpl interpolate.

intrpt interrupt.

intsct intersect.

intstg interstage.

intvl interval.

inv. 1. he or she invented it. [from Latin *invenit*] 2. invented. 3. invention. 4. inventor. 5. inventory. 6. investment. 7. invoice.

invs inverse.

invt. 1. inventory. 2. invert.

invtr inverter.

Io *Symbol, Chemistry.* ionium.

Io. Iowa.

I/O 1. inboard-outboard. 2. Also *i/o Computers.* input/output.

I.O. indirect object. Also, **IO, i.o.**

IOC International Olympic Committee. Also, **I.O.C.**

I.O.F. Independent Order of Foresters.

IOM interoffice memo.

I.O.O.F. Independent Order of Odd Fellows.

IOU a written acknowledgment of a debt, especially an informal one. Also, **I.O.U.** [representing *I owe you*]

IPA 1. International Phonetic Alphabet. 2. International Phonetic Association. 3. International Press Association. Also, **I.P.A.**

IPB illustrated parts breakdown.

i.p.h. 1. *Printing.* impressions per hour. 2. inches per hour. Also, **iph**

IPI International Patent Institute.

IPL information processing language. Also, **ipl**

IPM integrated pest management.

ipm inches per minute. Also, **i. p.m.**

IPO initial public offering.

ipr inches per revolution. Also, **i. p.r.**

ips inches per second. Also, **i.p.s.**

IQ *Psychology.* intelligence quotient.

i.q. the same as. [from Latin *idem quod*]

IR 1. information retrieval. 2. infrared. 3. intelligence ratio.

Ir Irish.

Ir *Symbol, Chemistry.* iridium.

ir 1. infrared. 2. insulation resistance.

Ir. 1. Ireland. 2. Irish.

I.R. 1. immediate reserve. 2. infantry reserve. 3. intelligence ratio. 4. internal revenue.

IRA 1. individual retirement account. 2. Irish Republican Army. Also, **I.R.A.**

IRB 1. Industrial Relations Bureau. 2. industrial revenue bond.

IRBM intermediate range ballistic missile. Also, **I.R.B.M.**

IRC 1. Internal Revenue Code. 2. International Red Cross.

Ire. Ireland.

IRO 1. International Refugee Organization. 2. International Relief Organization.

IRQ *Computers.* interrupt request.

irreg. 1. irregular. 2. irregularly.

irrglr irregular.

IRS Internal Revenue Service.

Is. 1. *Bible.* Isaiah. 2. Island; Islands. 3. Isle; Isles.

is. 1. island; islands. 2. isle; isles.

ISA Instrument Society of America.

Isa. *Bible.* Isaiah.

ISBA International Seabed Authority.

ISBN International Standard Book Number.

ISDN integrated-services digital network.

isgn insignia.

isl. 1. island. 2. isle. Also, **Isl.**

isln isolation.

isls. islands. Also, **Isls.**

ISO 1. incentive stock option. 2. in search of. 3. *Photography.* International Standardization Organization.

iso isometric.

isol isolate.

isos isosceles.

ISR Institute for Sex Research.

Isr. 1. Israel. 2. Israeli.

iss issue.

ISSN International Standard Serial Number.

IST 1. insulin shock therapy. 2. International Standard Thread (metric).

Isth. isthmus. Also, **isth.**

ISV International Scientific Vocabulary.

It Italian.

It. 1. Italian. 2. Italy.

I.T.A. Initial Teaching Alphabet. Also, **i.t.a.**

Ital. 1. Italian. 2. Italic. 3. Italy.

ital. 1. italic; italics. 2. italicized.

ITC 1. International Trade Commission. 2. investment tax credit.

ITO International Trade Organization.

ITU International Telecommunication Union.

I.T.U. International Typographical Union.

ITV instructional television.

IU 1. immunizing unit. 2. Also, **I.U.** international unit.

IUD intrauterine device.

IUS *Rocketry.* inertial upper stage.

IV (ī′vē′), *Medicine.* an intravenous device.

IV *Medicine.* 1. intravenous. 2. intravenous drip. 3. intravenous injection. 4. intravenously.

I.V. initial velocity.

i.v. 1. increased value. 2. initial velocity. 3. invoice value.

IVF in vitro fertilization.

I.W. Isle of Wight.

i.w. 1. inside width. 2. isotopic weight.

IWC International Whaling Commission.

I.W.W. Industrial Workers of the World. Also, **IWW**

J **1.** *Cards.* jack. Also, **J.** **2.** Jewish. **3.** *Physics.* joules.

J *Symbol.* **1.** the tenth in order or in a series, or, when *I* is omitted, the ninth. **2.** (*sometimes lowercase*) the medieval Roman numeral for 1. **3.** *Physics.* angular momentum.

j *Symbol.* **1.** *Math.* a unit vector on the y-axis of a coordinate system. **2.** *Engineering.* the imaginary number *A*.

J. **1.** *Cards.* jack. Also, **J** **2.** Journal. **3.** Judge. **4.** Justice.

JA **1.** joint account. **2.** Joint Agent. **3.** Judge Advocate. **4.** Junior Achievement. Also, **J.A.**

Ja. January.

J.A.C. Junior Association of Commerce.

J.A.G. Judge Advocate General. Also, **JAG**

Jam. Jamaica.

Jan. January.

Jap. **1.** Japan. **2.** Japanese.

Japn. **1.** Japan. **2.** Japanese. Also, **Japn**

Jas. *Bible.* James.

Jav. Javanese.

jb junction box.

JC **1.** junior college. **2.** juvenile court.

J.C. **1.** Jesus Christ. **2.** Julius Caesar. **3.** *Law.* jurisconsult. [from Latin *jūris cōnsultus*]

J.C.B. **1.** Bachelor of Canon Law. [from Latin *Jūris Canonicī Baccalaureus*] **2.** Bachelor of Civil Law. [from Latin *Jūris Civilis Baccalaureus*]

J.C.C. Junior Chamber of Commerce.

J.C.D. **1.** Doctor of Canon Law. [from Latin *Jūris Canonicī Doctor*] **2.** Doctor of Civil Law. [from Latin *Jūris Civilis Doctor*]

JCI Jaycees International.

JCL *Computers.* job control language.

J.C.L. Licentiate in Canon Law. [from Latin *Jūris Canonicī Licentiātus*]

J.C.S. Joint Chiefs of Staff. Also, **JCS**

jct. junction. Also, **jctn.**

JD *Informal.* **1.** juvenile delinquency. **2.** juvenile delinquent.

JD. (in Jordan) dinar; dinars.

J.D. **1.** *Astronomy.* Julian Day. **2.** Doctor of Jurisprudence; Doctor of Law. [from Latin *Jūris Doctor*] **3.** Doctor of Laws. [from Latin *Jūrum Doctor*] **4.** Justice Department. **5.** *Informal.* **a.** juvenile delinquency. **b.** juvenile delinquent.

JDC Juvenile Detention Center.

JDL Jewish Defense League.

Je. June.

Jer. **1.** *Bible.* Jeremiah. **2.** Jersey.

JFET (jā′fet), junction field-effect transistor.

JFK John Fitzgerald Kennedy.

jg junior grade. Also, **j.g.**

JHS IHS (defs. 1, 2).

J.H.S. junior high school.

JJ. **1.** Judges. **2.** Justices.

jk jack.

jkt jacket.

jl journal.

Jl. **1.** Journal. **2.** July.

jn join.

Jno. John.

jnr. junior.

jnt. joint.

Jo. Bapt. John the Baptist.

JOBS (jobz), Job Opportunities in the Business Sector.

Jo. Div. John the Divine.

Jo. Evang. John the Evangelist.

Josh. *Bible.* Joshua.

jour. **1.** journal. **2.** journeyman.

journ. journalism.

JP **1.** jet propulsion. **2.** Justice of the Peace.

J.P. Justice of the Peace. Also, **j.p.**

JPEG (jā′peg), Joint Photographic Experts Group.

Jpn. **1.** Japan. **2.** Japanese. Also, **Jpn**

Jr. **1.** Journal. **2.** Junior.

jr. junior.

JRC Junior Red Cross.

JSC Johnson Space Center.

J.S.D. Doctor of the Science of Law; Doctor of Juristic Science.

jt. joint.

Ju. June.

Jud. *Bible.* **1.** Judges. **2.** Judith (Apocrypha).

jud. **1.** judge. **2.** judgment. **3.** judicial. **4.** judiciary.

Judg. *Bible.* Judges.

Jul. July.

Jun. **1.** June. **2.** Junior.

Junc. Junction. Also, **junc.**

Jur. D. Doctor of Law. [from Latin *Jūris Doctor*]

jurisp. jurisprudence. Also, **juris.**

Jur. M. Master of Jurisprudence.

just. justification.

juv. juvenile.

JV **1.** joint venture. **2.** junior varsity. Also, **J.V.**

jwlr. jeweler.

J.W.V. Jewish War Veterans.

Jy jansky; janskies.

Jy. July.

K **1.** *Chess.* king. **2.** *Physics.* Kelvin. **3.** the number 1000: *The salary is $20K.* [abbreviation of *kilo-*] **4.** *Electronics.* cathode. **5.** *Music.* Köchel listing. **6.** kindergarten: *a K–12 boarding school.* **7.** *Real Estate.* kitchen.

K *Symbol.* **1.** the eleventh in order or in a series, or, when *I* is omitted, the tenth. **2.** *Chemistry.* potassium. [from Latin *kalium*] **3.** *Computers.* **a.** the number 1024 or 2^{10}. **b.** kilobyte. **4.** *Baseball.* strikeout; strikeouts. **5.** *Physics.* kaon. **6.** *Biochemistry.* lysine.

K *Ecology.* carrying capacity.

k *Symbol.* **1.** *Math.* a vector on the z-axis, having length 1 unit. **2.** *Physics.* Boltzmann constant.

K. **1.** kip; kips (monetary unit). **2.**

Knight. **3.** (in Malawi or Zambia) kwacha.

k. **1.** *Electricity.* capacity. **2.** karat. **3.** kilogram; kilograms. **4.** kindergarten. **5.** *Chess.* king. **6.** knight. **7.** knot. **8.** kopeck.

kA *Electricity.* kiloampere; kiloamperes.

Kan. Kansas. Also, **Kans., Kas.**

KB **1.** *Chess.* king's bishop. **2.** *Computers.* kilobyte; kilobytes.

Kb *Computers.* kilobit; kilobits.

kB *Computers.* kilobyte; kilobytes.

kb kilobar; kilobars.

K.B. **1.** King's Bench. **2.** Knight Bachelor.

kbar (kā′bär), kilobar; kilobars.

K.B.E. Knight Commander of the British Empire.

KBP *Chess.* king's bishop's pawn.

kc **1.** kilocycle; kilocycles. **2.** kilocurie; kilocuries.

K.C. **1.** Kansas City. **2.** King's Counsel. **3.** Knight Commander. **4.** Knights of Columbus.

K.C.B. Knight Commander of the Bath.

kCi kilocurie; kilocuries.

K.C.M.G. Knight Commander of the Order of St. Michael and St. George.

Kčs. koruna; korunas. [from Czech *k(oruna)* *č(esko)* *s(lovenská)*]

kc/s kilocycles per second. Also, **kc/sec**

K.C.S.I. Knight Commander of the Order of the Star of India.

K.C.V.O. Knight Commander of the (Royal) Victorian Order.

KD **1.** kiln-dried. **2.** Also, **k.d.** *Commerce.* knocked-down.

KD. (in Kuwait) dinar; dinars.

Ken. Kentucky.

kG kilogauss; kilogausses.

kg kilogram; kilograms.

kg. **1.** keg; kegs. **2.** kilogram; kilograms.

K.G. **1.** Knight of the Garter. **2.** (in police use) known gambler.

KGB Committee for State Security: the intelligence and internal-security agency of the former Soviet Union. Also, **K.G.B.** [from Russian *K(omitét)* *g(osudárstvennoĭ)* *b(ezopásnosti)*]

kgf kilogram-force.

kg-m kilogram-meter; kilogram-meters.

KGPS kilograms per second. Also, **kgps**

Kh Knoop hardness.

Khn Knoop hardness number.

kHz kilohertz.

Ki. *Bible.* Kings.

KIA killed in action. Also, **K.I.A.**

KIAS knot indicated airspeed.

kil. kilometer; kilometers.

kip-ft one thousand foot-pounds.

KISS (kis), keep it simple, stupid.

K.J.V. King James Version (of the Bible).

K.K.K. Ku Klux Klan. Also, **KKK**

KKt *Chess.* king's knight.

KKtP *Chess.* king's knight's pawn.

kl kiloliter; kiloliters. Also, **kl.**

km kilometer; kilometers.

km. **1.** kilometer; kilometers. **2.** kingdom.

kMc kilomegacycle; kilomegacycles.

km/sec kilometers per second.

KN *Chess.* king's knight.

kn knot; 1 nautical mile.

kn. (in Germany and Austria) kronen.

KNP *Chess.* king's knight's pawn.

kn sw knife switch.

Knt. Knight.

KO (kā′ō′, kā′ō′), *Slang.* a knockout, especially in boxing. Also, **ko, K.O., k.o., kayo.** [*k(nock) o(ut)*]

K. of C. Knights of Columbus.

K. of P. Knights of Pythias.

kop. kopeck.

KP *Chess.* king's pawn.

K.P. **1.** *Military.* kitchen police. **2.** Knight of the Order of St. Patrick. **3.** Knights of Pythias.

kpc kiloparsec; kiloparsecs.

kph kilometers per hour. Also, **k. p.h.**

KR *Chess.* king's rook.

Kr *Symbol, Chemistry.* krypton.

Kr. **1.** (in Sweden and the Faeroe Islands) krona; kronor. **2.** (in Iceland) króna; krónur. **3.** (in Denmark and Norway) krone; kroner.

kr. **1.** (in Germany and Austria) kreutzer. **2.** (in Sweden and the Faeroe Islands) krona; kronor. **3.** (in Iceland) króna; krónur. **4.** (in Denmark and Norway) krone; kroner.

KRP *Chess.* king's rook's pawn.

krs (in Turkey) kurus.

krsn kerosene.

KS Kansas (for use with ZIP code).

ksi one thousand pounds per square inch. [*k(ilo)* + *s(quare)* *i(nch)*]

ksr *Telecommunications.* keyboard send and receive.

Kt *Chess.* knight. Also, **Kt.**

Kt. knight.

kt. **1.** karat; karats. **2.** kiloton; kilotons. **3.** knot; knots.

K.T. **1.** Knights Templars. **2.** Knight of the Order of the Thistle.

Kt. Bach. knight bachelor.

kV kilovolt; kilovolts. Also, **kv**

K.V. *Music.* Köchel-Verzeichnis, the chronological listing of Mozart's works.

kVA kilovolt-ampere; kilovolt-amperes. Also, **kva**

kVAhm kilovolt-ampere hour meter.

kW kilowatt; kilowatts. Also, **kw.**

kWh kilowatt-hour. Also, **kwhr, K.W.H.**

KWIC (kwik), of or designating an alphabetical concordance of the principal terms in a text showing every occurrence of each term surrounded by a few words of the context. [*k(ey)-w(ord)-i(n)-c(ontext)*]

kwy keyway.

KY Kentucky (for use with ZIP code).

Ky. Kentucky.

kybd keyboard.

kypd keypad.

---

a b c d e f g h i j k **L** m n o p q r s t u v w x y z

L **1.** *Optics.* lambert; lamberts. **2.** language. **3.** large. **4.** Latin. **5.** left. **6.** length. **7.** *British.* pound; pounds. [from Latin *lībra*] **8.** long: denoting a size longer than regular, esp. for suits and coats. **9.** longitude. **10.** *Theater.* stage left.

L *Symbol.* **1.** the 12th in order or in a series, or, if *I* is omitted, the 11th. **2.** (*sometimes lowercase*) the Roman numeral for 50. **3.** *Electricity.* inductance. **4.** *Physics.* kinetic potential. **5.** *Biochemistry.* leucine. **6.** *Economics.* liquid assets. **7.** liter; liters.

l **1.** large. **2.** liter; liters. **3.** long.

L- **1.** *Chemistry.* levo-. **2.** *U.S. Military.* (in designations of light aircraft) liaison: *L-15.*

L- *Symbol, Biochemistry.* (of a molecule) having a configuration resembling the levorotatory isomer of glyceraldehyde: printed as a small capital, roman character. Compare **l-.**

l- *Symbol, Optics, Chemistry, Biochemistry.* levorotatory; levo-. Compare **L-.**

L. **1.** Lady. **2.** Lake. **3.** large. **4.** Latin. **5.** latitude. **6.** law. **7.** left. **8.** (in Honduras) lempira; lempiras. **9.** (in Romania) leu; lei. **10.** (in Bulgaria) lev; leva. **11.** book. [from Latin *liber*] **12.** Liberal. **13.** (in Italy) lira; lire. **14.** place. [from Latin *locus*] **15.** Lord. **16.** Low. **17.** lumen. **18.** *Theater.* stage left.

l. **1.** large. **2.** latitude. **3.** law. **4.** leaf. **5.** league. **6.** left. **7.** length. **8.** *plural* **ll.,** line. **9.** link. **10.** (in Italy) lira; lire. **11.** liter; liters. **12.** long.

LA Louisiana (for use with ZIP code).

La *Symbol, Chemistry.* lanthanum.

La. Louisiana.

l/a letter of authority.

L.A. **1.** Latin America. **2.** Law Agent. **3.** Library Association. **4.** Local Agent. **5.** Los Angeles.

Lab. **1.** Laborite. **2.** Labrador.

lab. **1.** labor. **2.** laboratory. **3.** laborer.

LAC leading aircraftsman.

LACW leading aircraftswoman.

LAD language acquisition device.

LaF Louisiana French.

lag lagging.

LAK cell *Immunology.* lymphokine-activated killer cell.

Lam. *Bible.* Lamentations.

lam. laminated.

LAN (lan), local area network.

lang. language.

laq lacquer.

laser (lā′zər), *Electronics.* light amplification by stimulated emission of radiation.

LASH (lash), an ocean-going vessel equipped with special cranes and holds for lifting and stowing cargo-carrying barges. [*l(ighter) a(board) sh(ip)*]

Lat. Latin.

lat. latitude.

latl lateral.

lau laundry.

LAV lymphadenopathy-associated virus.

lav lavatory.

LAWN (lôn), local-area wireless network.

lb *Telecommunications.* local battery.

lb. *plural* **lbs., lb.** pound. [from Latin *lībra,* plural *lībrae*]

L.B. **1.** landing barge. **2.** light bomber. **3.** bachelor of letters; bachelor of literature. [from Latin *Litterārum* *Baccalaureus*;

Līterārum Baccalaureus] **4.** local board.

lb. ap. *Pharmacology.* pound apothecary's.

L bar. angle iron. Also, **L beam.**

lb. av. pound avoirdupois.

lbf *Physics.* pound-force.

LBJ Lyndon Baines Johnson.

lbl label.

LBO *Finance.* leveraged buyout.

lbr lumber.

lbry library.

lb. t. pound troy.

lbyr labyrinth.

LC **1.** inductance-capacitance. **2.** landing craft.

L/C letter of credit. Also, **l/c**

L.C. Library of Congress.

l.c. **1.** left center. **2.** letter of credit. **3.** in the place cited. [from Latin *locō citātō*] **4.** *Printing.* lowercase.

l.c.a. lowercase alphabet.

LCD *Electronics.* liquid-crystal display.

L.C.D. *Math.* least common denominator; lowest common denominator. Also, **l.c.d.**

L.C.F. *Math.* lowest common factor. Also, **l.c.f.**

L chain *Immunology.* light chain.

LCI *Military.* a type of landing craft used in World War II. [*L(anding) C(raft) I(nfantry)*]

lcl local.

L.C.L. *Commerce.* less than carload lot. Also, **l.c.l.**

L.C.M. least common multiple; lowest common multiple. Also, **l. c.m.**

LCR inductance-capacitance-resistance.

LCT *Military.* a type of landing craft used in World War II. [*L(anding) C(raft) T(ank)*]

LD **1.** praise (be) to God. [from

Latin *laus Deō*] **2.** learning disability. **3.** learning-disabled. **4.** lethal dose. **5.** long distance (telephone call). **6.** Low Dutch.

LD. (in Libya) dinar; dinars.

Ld 1. limited. **2.** Lord.

ld 1. leading. **2.** line drawing.

ld. load.

L.D. Low Dutch.

LD₅₀ *Pharmacology.* median lethal dose.

LDC less developed country. Also, **L.D.C.**

ldg. 1. landing. **2.** loading.

LDH *Biochemistry.* lactate dehydrogenase.

LDL *Biochemistry.* low-density lipoprotein.

ldmk landmark.

Ldp. 1. ladyship. **2.** lordship.

LDPE *Chemistry.* low-density polyethylene.

ldr ladder.

L.D.S. 1. Latter-day Saints. **2.** praise (be) to God forever. [from Latin *laus Deō semper*] **3.** Licentiate in Dental Surgery.

l.e. *Football.* left end.

lect. 1. lecture. **2.** lecturer.

LED *Electronics.* light-emitting diode.

legis. 1. legislation. **2.** legislative. **3.** legislature.

LEM (lem), lunar excursion module.

LEP 1. *Physics.* large electron-positron collider. **2.** limited English proficiency.

Lett. Lettish.

Lev. *Bible.* Leviticus.

lex. 1. lexical. **2.** lexicon.

LF 1. *Baseball.* left field. **2.** *Baseball.* left fielder. **3.** low frequency.

lf 1. *Baseball.* left field. **2.** *Baseball.* left fielder. **3.** *Printing.* lightface. **4.** line feed.

l.f. *Baseball.* **1.** left field. **2.** left fielder.

lfb *Sports.* left fullback.

LG Low German. Also, **L.G.**

lg. 1. large. **2.** length. **3.** long.

l.g. *Football.* left guard.

lgc logic.

lge. large. Also, **lge**

L. Ger. 1. Low German. **2.** Low Germanic.

LGk Late Greek. Also, **LGk, L.Gk.**

lgsltd legislated.

lgsltr legislature.

lgstcs logistics.

lgth. length.

LH *Biochemistry, Physiology.* luteinizing hormone.

lh *Sports.* left halfback.

l.h. 1. left hand; left-handed. **2.** lower half. Also, **L.H.**

l.h.b. *Sports.* left halfback.

L.H.D. 1. Doctor of Humane Letters. **2.** Doctor of Humanities. [from Latin *Litterārum Humāniōrum Doctor*]

lhdr left-hand drive.

Li *Symbol, Chemistry.* lithium.

li *Surveying.* link; links.

L.I. 1. *British.* light infantry. **2.** Long Island.

Lib. Liberal.

lib. 1. book. [from Latin *liber*] **2.** librarian. **3.** library.

lic. 1. license. **2.** licensed.

Lieut. lieutenant.

Lieut. Col. lieutenant colonel.

Lieut. Comdr. lieutenant commander.

LIF Lifetime (a cable television channel).

LIFO (lī′fō), **1.** *Commerce.* last-in, first-out. **2.** *Computers.* a data storage and retrieval technique, in which the last item stored is the first item retrieved. [*l(ast) i(n) f(irst) o(ut)*]

lim. limit.

lin. 1. lineal. **2.** linear. **3.** liniment.

lin ft linear foot; linear feet.

liq. 1. liquid. **2.** liquor. **3.** (in prescriptions) solution. [from Latin *liquor*]

LISP (lisp), *Computers.* a programming language that processes data in the form of lists. [*lis(t) p(rocessing)*]

Lit. (in Italy) lira; lire.

lit. 1. liter; liters. **2.** literal. **3.** literally. **4.** literary. **5.** literature.

Lit.B. Bachelor of Letters; Bachelor of Literature. [from Latin *Lit(t)erārum Baccalaureus*]

Lit.D. Doctor of Letters; Doctor of Literature. [from Latin *Lit(t) erārum Doctor*]

Lith. 1. Lithuania. **2.** Also, **Lith** Lithuanian.

lith. 1. lithograph. **2.** lithographic. **3.** lithography.

lithol. lithology.

Litt. B. Bachelor of Letters; Bachelor of Literature. [from Latin *Lit(t)erārum Baccalaureus*]

Litt. D. Doctor of Letters; Doctor of Literature. [from Latin *Lit(t) erārum Doctor*]

Litt.M. Master of Letters. [from Latin *Lit(t)erārum Magister*]

Lk. *Bible.* Luke.

lkd locked.

lkg looking.

lkge linkage.

lknt locknut.

lkr locker.

LL 1. Late Latin. **2.** Low Latin. Also, **L.L.**

ll. 1. lines. **2.** low level.

l.l. 1. in the place quoted. [from Latin *locō laudātō*] **2.** loose-leaf.

L. Lat. 1. Late Latin. **2.** Low Latin.

LLB Little League Baseball.

LL.B. Bachelor of Laws. [from Latin *Lēgum Baccalaureus*]

LL.D. Doctor of Laws. [from Latin *Lēgum Doctor*]

LL.M. Master of Laws. [from Latin *Lēgum Magister*]

llti long lead-time item.

LM (*often* lem), lunar module.

lm 1. list of material. **2.** *Optics.* lumen; lumens.

L.M. 1. Licentiate in Medicine. **2.** Licentiate in Midwifery. **3.** Lord Mayor.

lm-hr *Optics.* lumen-hour; lumen-hours.

LMT local mean time.

lmtr limiter.

lm/W *Symbol.* lumen per watt.

Ln. lane.

ln logarithm (natural).

lndry rm *Real Estate.* laundry room.

LNG liquefied natural gas.

lnrty linearity.

lntl lintel.

LO lubrication order.

loc. locative.

loc. cit. (lok′ sit′), in the place cited. [from Latin *locō citātō*]

loep list of effective pages.

lof local oscillator frequency.

log. logarithm.

logamp logarithmic amplifier.

LOGO (lō′gō), *Computers.* a programming language widely used to teach children how to use computers. [from Greek *lógos* word, spelled as if an acronym]

lon. longitude.

Lond. London.

long. 1. longitude. **2.** longitudinal.

L.O.O.M. Loyal Order of Moose.

LOP *Navigation.* line of position.

loq. he speaks; she speaks. [from Latin *loquitur*]

loran (lôr′an, lōr′-), *Electronics.* long-range navigation.

lo-res (lō′rez′), *Computers.* low-resolution.

lot. (in prescriptions) a lotion. [from Latin *lōtiō*]

lox (loks), liquid oxygen.

LP long-playing: a phonograph record played at 33⅓ r.p.m.

L.P. *Printing.* **1.** long primer. **2.** low pressure. Also, **l.p.**

LPG liquefied petroleum gas. Also called **LP gas.**

LPGA Ladies Professional Golf Association.

lphldr lampholder.

lpm *Computers.* lines per minute. Also, **LPM**

LPN licensed practical nurse.

lprsvr life preserver.

L.P.S. Lord Privy Seal.

lptv low-power television.

lpw lumen per watt.

LQ letter-quality.

lqp *Computers.* letter-quality printer.

LR 1. *Real Estate.* living room. **2.** long range. **3.** lower right.

Lr *Symbol, Chemistry.* lawrencium.

L.R. Lloyd's Register.

LRAM long-range attack missile.

LRBM long-range ballistic missile.

lrg. large.

LRT light-rail transit.

LS 1. left side. **2.** letter signed. **3.** library science. **4.** lightship.

ls loudspeaker.

L.S. 1. Licentiate in Surgery. **2.** Linnaean Society. **3.** Also, **l.s.** the place of the seal, as on a document [from Latin *locus sigilli*].

LSA 1. Leukemia Society of America. **2.** Linguistic Society of America.

LSAT *Trademark.* Law School Admission Test.

lsb 1. least significant bit. **2.** lower sideband.

l.s.c. in the place mentioned above. [from Latin *locā suprā citātō*]

LSD 1. *U.S. Navy.* a seagoing amphibious ship capable of carrying and launching assault landing craft. [*l(anding) s(hip) d(eck)*] **2.** *Pharmacology.* lysergic acid diethylamide: a powerful psychedelic drug. **3.** *Math.* least significant digit.

abbrev.

L.S.D. *British.* pounds, shillings, and pence. Also, **£.s.d.**, **l.s.d.** [from Latin *librae, solidī, dēnāriī*]

LSI *Electronics.* large-scale integration.

LSM a type of military landing ship. [*l(anding) s(hip) m(edium)*]

L.S.S. Lifesaving Service.

LST an oceangoing military ship, used for landing troops and heavy equipment on beaches. [*l(anding) s(hip) t(ank)*]

l.s.t. local standard time.

lt 1. Also, **lt.** light. 2. *Electricity.* low-tension.

Lt. lieutenant.

L.T. 1. long ton. 2. *Electricity.* low-tension.

l.t. 1. *Football.* left tackle. 2. local time. 3. long ton.

LTA (of an aircraft) lighter-than-air.

Lt. Col. Lieutenant Colonel. Also **LTC**

Lt. Comdr. Lieutenant Commander. Also, **Lt. Com.**

Ltd. limited. Also, **ltd, ltd.**

ltg lighting.

Lt. Gen. Lieutenant General. Also, **LTG**

Lt. Gov. Lieutenant Governor.

L.Th. Licentiate in Theology.

lthr leather.

Lt. Inf. *Military.* light infantry.

LTJG *U.S. Navy.* Lieutenant Junior Grade.

LTL *Commerce.* less-than-truckload lot.

LTR long-term relationship.

ltr. 1. letter. 2. lighter.

ltrprs letterpress.

lt-yr light-year; light-years.

lub *Math.* least upper bound.

lub. 1. lubricant. 2. lubricating. 3. lubrication.

lubo lubricating oil.

lubt lubricant.

luf lowest usable frequency.

LULAC League of United Latin-American Citizens.

lum luminous.

Luth. Lutheran.

Lux. Luxembourg.

LV. (in Bulgaria) lev; leva.

lv. 1. leave; leaves. 2. (in France) livre; livres.

lvl level.

LVN licensed vocational nurse.

lvr 1. lever. 2. louver.

LW low water.

l/w lumen per watt; lumens per watt.

l.w.m. low water mark.

lwop leave without pay.

lwp leave with pay.

lwr lower.

LWV League of Women Voters. Also, **L.W.V.**

lwyr lawyer.

lx *Optics.* lux.

lyr layer.

lyt layout.

LZ landing zone.

a b c d e f g h i j k l **M** n o p q r s t u v w x y z

M 1. mach. 2. *Music.* major. 3. male. 4. married. 5. Medieval. 6. medium. 7. mega-: one million. [from Greek *mégas* large, great] 8. Middle. 9. modal auxiliary. 10. modifier. 11. *Economics.* monetary aggregate. 12. *British.* motorway (used with a road number).

M *Symbol.* 1. the thirteenth in order or in a series, or, when *I* is omitted, the twelfth. 2. (*sometimes lowercase*) the Roman numeral for 1,000. 3. *Electricity.* magnetization. 4. *Biochemistry.* methionine.

m 1. *Physics.* mass. 2. *Finance.* (of bonds) matured. 3. medieval. 4. medium. 5. meter; meters. 6. middle. 7. *Music.* minor.

m *Symbol, Electricity.* magnetic pole strength.

M- *U.S. Military.* (used to designate the production model of military equipment, as the M-1 rifle.)

m- *Chemistry.* meta-: used hydrated (of a series); designating the meta position in the benzene ring.

M. 1. Majesty. 2. Manitoba. 3. (in Finland) markka; markkaa. 4. Marquis. 5. *Music.* measure. 6. medicine. 7. medium. 8. meridian. 9. noon. [from Latin *merīdiēs*] 10. Monday. 11. *plural* **MM.** Monsieur. 12. mountain.

m. 1. male. 2. (in Germany) mark; marks. 3. married. 4. masculine. 5. *Physics.* mass. 6. medium. 7. noon. [from Latin *merīdiēs*] 8. meter. 9. middle. 10. mile. 11. minute. 12. (in prescriptions) mix. [from Latin *misce*] 13. modification of. 14. *Physics, Math.* modulus. 15. molar. 16. month. 17. moon. 18. morning. 19. mouth.

m³ *Symbol.* cubic meter.

MA 1. Massachusetts (for use

with ZIP code). 2. *Psychology.* mental age.

mA *Electricity.* milliampere; milliamperes.

ma master.

M.A. 1. Master of Arts. [from Latin *Magister Artium*] 2. *Psychology.* mental age. 3. Military Academy.

MAA master-at-arms.

M.A.Arch. Master of Arts in Architecture.

MAb *Immunology.* monoclonal antibody.

mac maintenance allocation chart.

Mac. *Bible.* Maccabees.

M.Ac. Master of Accountancy.

Macc. *Bible.* Maccabees.

Maced. Macedonia.

Mach *Physics.* mach number.

mach. 1. machine. 2. machinery. 3. machinist.

MAD (mad), Mutual Assured Destruction.

Mad. Madam.

MADD (mad), Mothers Against Drunk Driving.

Madm. Madam.

M.A.E. 1. Master of Aeronautical Engineering. 2. Master of Art Education. 3. Master of Arts in Education.

M.A.Ed. Master of Arts in Education.

M.Aero.E. Master of Aeronautical Engineering.

mag. 1. magazine. 2. magnet. 3. magnetic. 4. magnetism. 5. magneto. 6. magnitude. 7. (in prescriptions) large. [from Latin *magnus*]

magamp magnetic amplifier.

M.Ag.Ec. Master of Agricultural Economics.

M.Ag.Ed. Master of Agricultural Education.

magn *Electronics.* magnetron.

magtd magnitude.

mah mahogany.

maint maintenance.

Maj. Major.

Maj. Gen. Major General.

Mal. *Bible.* 1. Malachi. 2. Malayan.

M.A.L.D. Master of Arts in Law and Diplomacy.

malf malfunction.

M.A.L.S. 1. Master of Arts in Liberal Studies. 2. Master of Arts in Library Science.

mam milliammeter.

Man. 1. Manila. 2. Manitoba.

man. manual.

manf manifold.

MAO *Biochemistry.* monoamine oxidase.

MAOI *Biochemistry.* monoamine oxidase inhibitor.

MAO inhibitor *Biochemistry.* monoamine oxidase inhibitor.

MAP modified American plan.

MAPI *Computers.* Messaging Application Programming Interface.

Mar. March.

mar. 1. maritime. 2. married.

M.A.R. Master of Arts in Religion.

MARC (märk), a standardized system developed by the Library of Congress for producing and transmitting records. [*ma(chine) r(eadable) c(atologing)*]

March. Marchioness.

M.Arch. Master of Architecture.

M.Arch.E. Master of Architectural Engineering.

Mar.E. Marine Engineer.

marg. 1. margin. 2. marginal.

Mar.Mech.E. Marine Mechanical Engineer.

Marq. 1. Marquess. 2. Marquis.

MARS (marz), 1. Military Affiliated Radio System. 2. multiple-access retrieval system.

mas. masculine.

masc. masculine.

maser (mā′zər), *Electronics.*

microwave amplification by stimulated emission of radiation.

MASH (mash), mobile army surgical hospital.

mas. pil. (in prescriptions) a pill mass. [from Latin *massa pilulāris*]

Mass. Massachusetts.

mat. 1. *Ecclesiastical.* matins. **2.** *Finance.* maturity.

M.A.T. Master of Arts in Teaching.

Mat.E. Materials Engineer.

math 1. mathematical. **2.** mathematics.

matl material.

MATS (mats), Military Air Transport Service.

Matt. *Bible.* Matthew.

MATV master antenna television system.

MAX Cinemax (a cable television channel).

max. maximum.

MB 1. Manitoba, Canada (for use with ZIP code). **2.** *Computers.* megabyte; megabytes.

Mb *Computers.* megabit; megabits.

mb *Physics.* **1.** millibar; millibars. **2.** millibarn; millibarns.

M.B. *Chiefly British.* Bachelor of Medicine. [from Latin *Medicinae Baccalaureus*]

M.B.A. Master of Business Administration. Also, **MBA**

mbb *Electricity.* make-before-break.

mbd (of oil) million barrels per day.

MBE Multistate Bar Examination.

M.B.E. Member of the Order of the British Empire.

mbl mobile.

Mbm one thousand feet, board measure.

mbm *Computers.* magnetic bubble memory.

MBO management by objective.

mbr member.

MBTA Massachusetts Bay Transportation Authority.

MByte *Computers.* megabyte: 1 million bytes.

MC 1. Marine Corps. **2.** master of ceremonies. **3.** Medical Corps. **4.** Member of Congress.

Mc 1. *Physics, Chemistry.* megacurie; megacuries. **2.** *Electricity.* megacycle.

mC 1. *Electricity.* millicoulomb; millicoulombs. **2.** *Physics, Chemistry.* millicurie; millicuries.

mc 1. *Electricity.* megacycle. **2.** *Optics.* meter-candle. **3.** *Physics, Chemistry.* millicurie; millicuries. **4.** *Electricity.* momentary contact.

M.C. 1. Master Commandant. **2.** master of ceremonies. **3.** Medical Corps. **4.** Member of Congress. **5.** Member of Council. **6.** *British.* Military Cross.

MCAT Medical College Admission Test.

M.C.E. Master of Civil Engineering.

Mcf one thousand cubic feet. Also, **mcf, MCF**

Mcfd thousands of cubic feet per day.

M.Ch.E. Master of Chemical Engineering.

MChin Middle Chinese.

mchry machinery.

mCi *Physics, Chemistry.* millicurie; millicuries.

M.C.J. Master of Comparative Jurisprudence.

mcm 1. *Computers.* magnetic-core memory. **2.** thousand circular mils.

MCP male chauvinist pig.

M.C.P. Master of City Planning.

M.C.R. Master of Comparative Religion.

mcw *Electronics.* modulated continuous wave.

MD 1. Maryland (for use with ZIP code). **2.** Doctor of Medicine. [from Latin *Medicīnae Doctor*] **3.** Middle Dutch. **4.** months after date. **5.** muscular dystrophy.

Md *Music.* right hand. [from Italian *mano destra* or French *main droite*]

Md *Symbol, Chemistry.* mendelevium.

md mean deviation.

Md. Maryland.

M/D months after date. Also, **m/d**

M.D. 1. Doctor of Medicine. [from Latin *Medicīnae Doctor*] **2.** Middle Dutch.

MDA *Pharmacology.* an amphetamine derivative, $C_{10}H_{13}NO_2$. [*m(ethylene) d(ioxy)a(mphetamine)*]

MDAA Muscular Dystrophy Association of America.

MDAP Mutual Defense Assistance Program.

M.Des. Master of Design.

mdf *Telephones.* main distributing frame.

mdl 1. middle. **2.** minimum detectable level. **3.** module.

Mdlle. Mademoiselle.

mdm medium.

Mdm. Madam.

MDMA an amphetamine derivative, $C_{11}H_{15}NO_2$. [*m(ethylene) d(ioxy)m(eth)a(mphetamine)*]

Mdme. Madame.

mdn median.

mdnt. midnight.

mdnz modernize.

MDR minimum daily requirement.

mdse. merchandise.

MDT 1. mean downtime. **2.** Also, **M.D.T.** Mountain Daylight Time.

ME 1. Maine (for use with ZIP code). **2.** Middle East. **3.** Middle English.

Me *Chemistry.* methyl.

Me. Maine.

M.E. 1. (*often lowercase*) managing editor. **2.** Master of Education. **3.** Master of Engineering. **4.** Mechanical Engineer. **5.** Medical Examiner. **6.** Methodist Episcopal. **7.** Middle English. **8.** Mining Engineer.

meas. 1. measurable. **2.** measure. **3.** measurement.

mech. 1. mechanical. **2.** mechanics. **3.** mechanism.

med. 1. medical. **2.** medicine. **3.** medieval. **4.** medium.

M.Ed. Master of Education.

Medit. Mediterranean.

Med.Sc.D. Doctor of Medical Science.

MEG *Medicine.* magnetoencephalogram.

meg 1. *Electricity.* megacycle. **2.** megohm; megohms.

MEGO (mē′gō), my eyes glaze over.

MEK *Chemistry.* methyl ethyl ketone.

mem. 1. member. **2.** memoir. **3.** memorandum. **4.** memorial. **5.** memory.

M.Eng. Master of Engineering.

M.E.P. Master of Engineering Physics.

m.e.p. mean effective pressure.

M.E.P.A. Master of Engineering and Public Administration.

mEq milliequivalent.

mer. 1. meridian. **2.** meridional.

merc. 1. mercantile. **2.** mercurial. **3.** mercury.

Messrs. (mes′ərz), plural of **Mr.**

Met *Biochemistry.* methionine.

met. 1. metal. **2.** metallurgical. **3.** metaphor. **4.** metaphysics. **5.** meteorology. **6.** metropolitan.

metal. 1. metallurgical. **2.** metallurgy.

metall. 1. metallurgical. **2.** metallurgy.

metaph. 1. metaphysical. **2.** metaphysics.

metaphys. metaphysics.

Met.E. metallurgical engineer.

meteor. 1. meteorological. **2.** meteorology.

meteorol. 1. Also, **metrl** meteorological. **2.** meteorology.

Meth. Methodist.

MeV (mev), *Physics.* million electron volts; megaelectron volt. Also, **Mev, mev**

Mex. 1. Mexican. **2.** Mexico.

MexSp Mexican Spanish.

mez mezzanine.

MF 1. married female. **2.** medium frequency. **3.** Middle French.

mF *Electricity.* millifarad; millifarads.

mf 1. medium frequency. **2.** microfilm. **3.** *Electricity.* millifarad; millifarads.

mf. 1. *Music.* mezzo forte. **2.** *Electricity.* microfarad.

m/f male or female: used especially in classified ads. Also, **M/F**

M.F. 1. Master of Forestry. **2.** Middle French.

MFA Museum of Fine Arts.

M.F.A. Master of Fine Arts.

mfd. manufactured.

mfg. manufacturing.

m/f/h male, female, handicapped: used especially in classified ads. Also, **M/F/H**

M.F.H. master of foxhounds.

MFlem Middle Flemish.

MFM *Computers.* modified frequency modulation: hard-drive interface.

M.For. Master of Forestry.

mfr. 1. manufacture. **2.** manufacturer.

M.Fr. Middle French.

M.F.S. 1. Master of Food Science. **2.** Master of Foreign Service. **3.** Master of Foreign Study.

mfsk multiple-frequency shiftkeying.

M.F.T. Master of Foreign Trade.

MG 1. machine gun. **2.** major

general. **3.** military government. **4.** *Pathology.* myasthenia gravis.
Mg *Music.* left hand. [from French *main gauche*]
Mg *Symbol, Chemistry.* magnesium.
mg 1. milligram; milligrams. **2.** motor-generator.
mGal milligal; milligals.
MGB the Ministry of State Security in the U.S.S.R. (1946–53). [from Russian, for *Ministérstvo gosudárstvennoĭ bezopásnosti*]
mgd millions of gallons per day.
mgf magnify.
MGk. Medieval Greek. Also, **MGk**
mgl mogul.
mgmt management.
mgn 1. magneto. **2.** margin.
MGr. Medieval Greek.
mgr. 1. manager. **2.** Monseigneur. **3.** Monsignor. Also, **Mgr.**
mgt. management.
MGy Sgt master gunnery sergeant.
MH Marshall Islands (approved for postal use).
mH *Electricity.* millihenry; millihenries. Also, **mh**
M.H. Medal of Honor.
M.H.A. Master in Hospital Administration; Master of Hospital Administration.
MHC *Biochemistry.* major histocompatibility complex.
MHD *Physics.* magnetohydrodynamics.
mhd 1. magnetohydrodynamic. **2.** masthead.
M.H.E. Master of Home Economics.
MHG Middle High German. Also, **M.H.G.**
M.H.R. Member of the House of Representatives.
M.H.W. mean high water. Also, **MHW, mhw, m.h.w.**
MHz megahertz. Also, **mhz**
mHz millihertz.
MI Michigan (for use with ZIP code).
MI *Pathology.* myocardial infarction.
mi mile; miles.
mi. 1. mile; miles. **2.** *Finance.* mill; mills.
M.I. 1. Military Intelligence. **2.** Mounted Infantry.
MIA *Military.* missing in action.
M.I.A. 1. Master of International Affairs. **2.** *Military.* missing in action.
mic 1. micrometer. **2.** microphone.
Mic. *Bible.* Micah.
Mich. 1. Michaelmas. **2.** Michigan.
MICR *Electronics.* magnetic ink character recognition.
micr microscope.
micros. microscopy.
Mid. Midshipman.
mid. middle.
M.I.D. Master of Industrial Design.
midar (mīʹdär), microwave detection and ranging.
MIDI (midʹē), *Electronics.* Musical Instrument Digital Interface.
MIDN Midshipman.
Midn. Midshipman.

M.I.E. Master of Industrial Engineering.
MiG (mig), any of several Russian fighter aircraft. Also, **Mig, MIG** [named after Artem *Mi(koyan)* and Mikhail *G(urevich)*, aircraft designers]
mil. 1. military. **2.** militia.
milit. military.
M.I.L.R. Master of Industrial and Labor Relations.
MIL-STD military standard.
min minim; minims.
min. 1. mineralogical. **2.** mineralogy. **3.** minim. **4.** minimum. **5.** mining. **6.** minor. **7.** minuscule. **8.** minute; minutes.
M.Ind.E. Master of Industrial Engineering.
Min.E. Mineral Engineer.
mineral. 1. mineralogical. **2.** mineralogy.
Mining Eng. Mining Engineer.
Minn. Minnesota.
mintr miniature.
MIP monthly investment plan.
MIPS (mips), *Computers.* million instructions per second: a measure of computer speed.
mir mirror.
MIr. Middle Irish. Also, **M.Ir.**
MIRV (mûrv), multiple independently targetable reentry vehicle. Also, **M.I.R.V.**
MIS 1. management information system. **2.** *Electronics.* metal-insulated semiconductor.
misc. 1. miscellaneous. **2.** miscellany.
Misc. Doc. miscellaneous document.
Miss. Mississippi.
miss. 1. mission. **2.** missionary.
mist. (in prescriptions) a mixture. [from Latin *mistūra*]
MITC mortgage investment tax credit.
mitt. (in prescriptions) send. [from Latin *mitte*]
mixt. mixture.
M.J. Master of Journalism.
mk. 1. (in Germany) mark. **2.** (in Finland) markka.
mkr marker.
MKS meter-kilogram-second. Also, **mks**
MKSA meter-kilogram-second-ampere. Also, **mksa**
mkt. market.
mktg. marketing.
ML Medieval Latin. Also, **M.L.**
mL *Optics.* millilambert; millilamberts.
ml milliliter; milliliters.
ml. 1. mail. **2.** milliliter; milliliters.
MLA Modern Language Association.
M.L.A. 1. Master of Landscape Architecture. **2.** Modern Language Association.
M.L.Arch. Master of Landscape Architecture.
MLB Maritime Labor Board.
MLD 1. median lethal dose. **2.** minimum lethal dose.
mldg molding.
MLF Multilateral Nuclear Force.
MLG Middle Low German. Also, **M.L.G.**
Mlle. Mademoiselle. Also, **Mlle**
Mlles. Mesdemoiselles.

MLR minimum lending rate.
MLS *Real Estate.* Multiple Listing Service.
M.L.S. Master of Library Science.
MLU *Psycholinguistics.* mean length of utterance.
MLW mean low water.
MM married male.
mM millimole; millimoles.
mm millimeter; millimeters.
MM. Messieurs.
mm. 1. *Music.* measures. **2.** thousands. [from Latin *millia*] **3.** millimeter; millimeters.
M.M. 1. Master Mason. **2.** Master Mechanic. **3.** Master of Music.
mm³ *Symbol.* cubic millimeter.
MMA Metropolitan Museum of Art.
Mme. Madame.
M.M.E. 1. Master of Mechanical Engineering. **2.** Master of Mining Engineering. **3.** Master of Music Education.
Mmes. Mesdames.
M.Met.E. Master of Metallurgical Engineering.
mmf *Electricity.* magnetomotive force. Also, **m.m.f.**
M.Mgt.E. Master of Management Engineering.
mm Hg millimeter of mercury. Also, **mmHg**
mmho *Electricity.* millimho; millimhos.
MMPI *Psychology.* Minnesota Multiphasic Personality Inventory.
M.M.Sc. Master of Medical Science.
MMT 1. *Astronomy.* Multiple Mirror Telescope. **2.** *Chemistry.* $C_9H_7MnO_3$, a gasoline additive. [*m*(ethylcyclopentadienyl) *m*(anganese) *t*(ricarbonyl)]
mmu memory-management unit.
M.Mus. Master of Music.
M.Mus.Ed. Master of Music Education.
MN Minnesota (for use with ZIP code).
Mn *Symbol, Chemistry.* manganese.
mn main.
M.N. Master of Nursing.
M.N.A. Master of Nursing Administration.
M.N.A.S. Member of the National Academy of Sciences.
mncpl municipal.
M.N.E. Master of Nuclear Engineering.
mnfrm *Computers.* mainframe.
mng managing.
Mngr. Monsignor.
mngr. manager.
mnl manual.
Mnr. manor.
mnrl mineral.
M.N.S. Master of Nutritional Science.
mnstb *Electronics.* monostable.
M.Nurs. Master of Nursing.
MO 1. method of operation. **2.** Missouri (for use with ZIP code). **3.** mode of operation. **4.** modus operandi.
Mo *Symbol, Chemistry.* molybdenum.
Mo. 1. Missouri. **2.** Monday.
mo. month. Also, **mo**
M.O. 1. mail order. **2.** manually

operated. **3.** Medical Officer. **4.** method of operation. **5.** mode of operation. **6.** modus operandi. **7.** money order.

m.o. **1.** mail order. **2.** modus operandi. **3.** money order.

mod **1.** *Computers.* magneto-optical drive. **2.** model. **3.** modification. **4.** modulator.

modem (mō′dəm, -dem), an electronic device that makes possible the transmission of data to or from a computer via telephone or other communication lines. [*mo(dulator)-dem(odulator)*]]

MODFET (mod′fet′), *Electronics.* modulation-doped field effect transistor.

ModGk Modern Greek. Also, **Mod. Gk., Mod. Gr.**

ModHeb Modern Hebrew. Also, **Mod. Heb.**

modif. modification.

mod. praesc. (in prescriptions) in the manner prescribed; as directed. [from Latin *modō praescrīptō*]

Moham. Mohammedan.

M.O.I. *British.* **1.** Ministry of Information. **2.** Ministry of the Interior.

mol *Chemistry.* mole.

mol. **1.** molecular. **2.** molecule.

mol. wt. molecular weight.

mom momentary.

m.o.m. middle of month.

MOMA (mō′mə), Museum of Modern Art.

Mon. **1.** Monday. **2.** Monsignor.

mon. **1.** monastery. **2.** monetary. **3.** monitor. **4.** monument.

mono monophonic.

Mons. Monsieur.

Mont. Montana.

MOPED (mō′ped), motor-assisted pedal cycle.

M.Opt. Master of Optometry.

MOR *Music.* middle-of-the-road.

mor. morocco.

more dict. (in prescriptions) in the manner directed. Also, **mor. dict.** [from Latin *mōre dictū*]

more sol. (in prescriptions) in the usual manner. Also, **mor. sol.** [from Latin *mōre solitō*]

morphol. morphology.

mort morse taper.

MOS *Electronics.* metal oxide semiconductor.

mos. **1.** months. **2.** mosaic.

MOSFET (mos′fet′), *Electronics.* metal oxide semiconducter field-effect transistor.

MOST (mōst), *Electronics.* metal-oxide-semiconductor transistor.

mot motor.

MP **1.** Military Police. **2.** Military Policeman. **3.** Mounted Police. **4.** Northern Mariana Islands (approved for postal use).

mp **1.** melting point. **2.** melting pot. **3.** *Music.* mezzo piano.

M.P. **1.** Member of Parliament. **2.** Metropolitan Police. **3.** Military Police. **4.** Military Policeman. **5.** Mounted Police.

m.p. **1.** melting point. **2.** (in prescriptions) in the manner prescribed; as directed. [from Latin *modō praescrīptō*]

M.P.A. **1.** Master of Professional Accounting. **2.** Master of Public

Administration. **3.** Master of Public Affairs.

MPAA Motion Picture Association of America.

MPB Missing Persons Bureau.

MPC Multimedia PC: a system conforming to specifications covering audio, video, and other multimedia components, and able to run multimedia software.

M.P.E. Master of Physical Education.

MPEG (em′peg), Motion Picture Experts Group.

MPers Middle Persian.

mpg miles per gallon. Also, **mi/gal., m.p.g., M.P.G., MPG**

mph miles per hour. Also, **mi/h., m.p.h., MPH**

M.Ph. Master of Philosophy.

M.P.H. Master of Public Health.

M.Pharm. Master of Pharmacy.

mpl maintenance parts list.

mpt male pipe thread.

MR **1.** motivation research. **2.** Moral Re-Armament. Also, **M.R.**

mR *Physics.* milliroentgen; milliroentgens. Also, **mr**

Mr. (mis′tər), *plural* **Messrs.** (mes′ərz). mister: a title of respect prefixed to a man's name or position: *Mr. Lawson; Mr. President.*

MRA Moral Re-Armament.

MRBM medium-range ballistic missile. Also, **mrbm**

M.R.E. Master of Religious Education.

mrg mooring.

MRI *Medicine.* **1.** Also called **NMR.** magnetic resonance imaging. **2.** magnetic resonance imager.

mRNA *Genetics.* messenger RNA.

M.R.P. Master in Regional Planning; Master of Regional Planning.

Mrs. (mis′iz, miz′iz), *plural* **Mmes.** (mā däm′, -dam′). a title of respect prefixed to the name of a married woman: *Mrs. Jones.*

MRV *Military.* multiple reentry vehicle. Also, **M.R.V.**

MS **1.** Mississippi (for use with ZIP code). **2.** motorship. **3.** multiple sclerosis.

ms millisecond; milliseconds.

MS., *plural* **MSS.** manuscript.

Ms. (miz), *plural* **Mses.** (miz′əz). a title of respect prefixed to a woman's name or position: unlike *Miss* or *Mrs.,* it does not depend upon or indicate her marital status.

ms., *plural* **mss.** manuscript.

M/S **1.** *Commerce.* months after sight. **2.** motorship.

m/s meter per second; meters per second.

M.S. **1.** mail steamer. **2.** Master of Science. **3.** Master in Surgery. **4.** motorship.

m.s. **1.** *Grammar.* modification of the stem of. **2.** *Commerce.* months after sight.

M.S.A. Master of Science in Agriculture.

M.S.A.E. Master of Science in Aeronautical Engineering.

M.S.A.M. Master of Science in Applied Mechanics.

M.S.Arch. Master of Science in Architecture.

MSAT Minnesota Scholastic Aptitude Test.

M.S.B.A. Master of Science in Business Administration.

M.S.B.C. Master of Science in Building Construction.

M.S.Bus. Master of Science in Business.

MSC Manned Spacecraft Center.

M.Sc. Master of Science.

M.Sc.D. Doctor of Medical Science.

M.S.C.E. Master of Science in Civil Engineering.

M.S.Ch.E. Master of Science in Chemical Engineering.

M.Sc.Med. Master of Medical Science.

M.S.Cons. Master of Science in Conservation.

M.S.C.P. Master of Science in Community Planning.

mscr machine screw.

MSD **1.** mean solar day. **2.** *Math.* most significant digit.

M.S.D. **1.** Doctor of Medical Science. **2.** Master of Science in Dentistry.

M.S.Dent. Master of Science in Dentistry.

MS DOS (em′es′ dôs′, -dos′), *Trademark.* a microcomputer operating system. Also, **MS-DOS**

M.S.E. **1.** Master of Science in Education. **2.** Master of Science in Engineering.

msec millisecond; milliseconds.

m/sec meter per second; meters per second.

M.S.Ed. Master of Science in Education.

M.S.E.E. Master of Science in Electrical Engineering.

M.S.E.M. **1.** Master of Science in Engineering Mechanics. **2.** Master of Science in Engineering of Mines.

M.S.Ent. Master of Science in Entomology.

M.S.F. Master of Science in Forestry.

M.S.F.M. Master of Science in Forest Management.

M.S.For. Master of Science in Forestry.

MSG monosodium glutamate.

msg. message.

M.S.Geol.E. Master of Science in Geological Engineering.

M.S.G.M. Master of Science in Government Management.

M.S.G.Mgt. Master of Science in Game Management.

msgr messenger.

Msgr. **1.** Monseigneur. **2.** Monsignor.

M.Sgt. master sergeant.

MSH **1.** *Biochemistry.* melanocyte-stimulating hormone; melanotropin: a hormone that causes dispersal of the black pigment melanin of melanocytes. **2.** *Mineralogy.* Mohs scale.

M.S.H.A. Master of Science in Hospital Administration.

M.S.H.E. Master of Science in Home Economics. Also, **M.S. H.Ec.**

M.S.Hort. Master of Science in Horticulture.

M.S.Hyg. Master of Science in Hygiene.

MSI *Electronics.* medium-scale integration.

M.S.J. Master of Science in Journalism.

mskg masking.

msl missile.

M.S.L. **1.** Master of Science in Linguistics. **2.** Also, **m.s.l.** mean sea level.

msly mostly.

M.S.M. **1.** Master of Sacred Music. **2.** Master of Science in Music.

M.S.M.E. Master of Science in Mechanical Engineering.

M.S.Met.E. Master of Science in Metallurgical Engineering.

M.S.Mgt.E. Master of Science in Management Engineering.

M.S.N. Master of Science in Nursing.

msnry masonry.

msp *Printing.* manuscript page.

M.S.P.E. Master of Science in Physical Education.

M.S.P.H. Master of Science in Public Health.

M.S.Phar. Master of Science in Pharmacy. Also, **M.S.Pharm.**

M.S.P.H.E. Master of Science in Public Health Engineering.

M.S.P.H.Ed. Master of Science in Public Health Education.

MSS. manuscripts. Also, **MSS,** **Mss, mss.**

M.S.S. **1.** Master of Social Science. **2.** Master of Social Service.

M.S.Sc. Master of Social Science.

M.S.S.E. Master of Science in Sanitary Engineering.

MST **1.** mean solar time. **2.** Mountain Standard Time.

M.S.T. **1.** Master of Science in Teaching. **2.** Also, **m.s.t.** Mountain Standard Time.

mstr moisture.

MSTS *U.S. Military.* Military Sea Transportation Service.

M.S.W. **1.** Master of Social Welfare. **2.** Master of Social Work or Master in Social Work. Also, **MSW**

MT **1.** mean time. **2.** mechanical translation. **3.** *Physics.* megaton; megatons. **4.** Montana (for use with ZIP code). **5.** Mountain time.

mt mount.

Mt. **1.** mount: *Mt. Rainier.* **2.** Also, **mt.** mountain.

M.T. **1.** metric ton. **2.** Also, **m.t.** Mountain time.

MTA Metropolitan Transit Authority.

MTBF mean time between failures.

MTBI mean time between incidents.

MTCF mean time to catastrophic failure.

mtchd matched.

mtd **1.** mean temperature difference. **2.** mounted.

mtg. **1.** meeting. **2.** mortgage. **3.** mounting. Also, **mtg**

mtge. mortgage.

M.Th. Master of Theology.

mthbd *Computers.* motherboard.

mthd method.

MTI *Electronics.* moving target indicator. Also, **mti**

mtn **1.** motion. **2.** mountain.

MTO *Military.* (in World War II) Mediterranean Theater of Operations.

MTR mean time to restore.

mtr **1.** magnetic tape recorder. **2.** meter (instrument).

Mt. Rev. Most Reverend.

mtrg metering.

MTS *Broadcasting.* multichannel television sound.

Mts. mountains. Also, **mts.**

MTTF mean time to failure.

MTTFF mean time to first failure.

MTTM mean time to maintain.

MTTR mean time to repair.

mtu magnetic tape unit.

MTV Music Television (a cable television channel).

mtx matrix.

MUF material unaccounted for.

muf **1.** maximum usable frequency. **2.** muffler.

mult **1.** multiple. **2.** multiplication.

multr multiplier.

mun. **1.** municipal. **2.** municipality.

munic. **1.** municipal. **2.** municipality.

M.U.P. Master of Urban Planning.

Mus. Muslim.

mus. **1.** museum. **2.** music. **3.** musical. **4.** musician.

Mus.B. Bachelor of Music. Also, **Mus. Bac.** [from Latin *Mūsicae Baccalaureus*]

Mus.D. Doctor of Music. Also, **Mus.Doc., Mus.Dr.** [from Latin *Mūsicae Doctor*]

Mus.M. Master of Music. [from Latin *Mūsicae Magister*]

mut. **1.** mutilated. **2.** mutual.

muw music wire.

mux (muks), *Electronics.* **1.** multiplex. **2.** multiplexer.

MV **1.** main verb. **2.** *Electricity.* megavolt; megavolts. **3.** motor vessel.

Mv *Symbol, Chemistry.* mendelevium.

mV *Electricity.* millivolt; millivolts.

mv **1.** mean variation. **2.** *Electronics.* multivibrator.

m.v. **1.** market value. **2.** mean variation. **3.** *Music.* mezza voce.

mvbl movable.

M.V.Ed. Master of Vocational Education.

mvg moving.

MVP Most Valuable Player. Also, **M.V.P.**

mvt movement.

MW *Electricity.* megawatt; megawatts.

mW *Electricity.* milliwatt; milliwatts.

mw medium wave.

M.W.A. Modern Woodmen of America.

MWG music wire gauge.

mwo modification work order.

mwp maximum working pressure.

M.W.T. Master of Wood Technology.

mwv maximum working voltage.

MX missile experimental: a ten-warhead U.S. intercontinental ballistic missile.

Mx *Electricity.* maxwell; maxwells.

mxd mixed.

mxg mixing.

mxr mixer.

mxt mixture.

mycol. mycology.

M.Y.O.B. mind your own business.

myth. **1.** mythological. **2.** mythology.

mythol. **1.** mythological. **2.** mythology.

---

a b c d e f g h i j k l m **N** o p q r s t u v w x y z

N **1.** *Physics.* newton; newtons. **2.** north. **3.** northern.

N *Symbol.* **1.** the 14th in order or in a series, or, when *I* is omitted, the 13th. **2.** (*sometimes lowercase*) the medieval Roman numeral for 90. **3.** *Chemistry.* nitrogen. **4.** *Biochemistry.* asparagine. **5.** *Math.* an indefinite, constant whole number, esp. the degree of a quantic or an equation, or the order of a curve. **6.** *Chess.* knight. **7.** *Printing.* en. **8.** *Chem-*

istry. Avogadro's number. **9.** neutron number.

n *Symbol.* **1.** *Physics.* neutron. **2.** *Optics.* index of refraction.

n- *Chemistry.* an abbreviated form of *normal,* used in the names of hydrocarbon compounds.

N. **1.** Nationalist. **2.** Navy. **3.** New. **4.** Noon. **5.** *Chemistry.* normal (strength solution). **6.** Norse. **7.** north. **8.** northern. **9.** *Finance.* note. **10.** November.

n. **1.** name. **2.** born. [from Latin *nātus*] **3.** nephew. **4.** *Commerce.*

net. **5.** neuter. **6.** new. **7.** nominative. **8.** noon. **9.** *Chemistry.* normal (strength solution). **10.** north. **11.** northern. **12.** *Finance.* note. **13.** noun. **14.** number.

NA **1.** not applicable. **2.** not available.

Na *Symbol, Chemistry.* sodium. [from Latin *natrium*]

n/a **1.** no account. **2.** not applicable.

N.A. **1.** National Army. **2.** North America. **3.** not applicable. **4.** *Microscopy.* numerical aperture.

NAA National Aeronautic Association.

NAACP National Association for the Advancement of Colored People. Also, **N.A.A.C.P.**

NAB 1. Also, **N.A.B.** National Association of Broadcasters. 2. New American Bible.

NACA National Advisory Committee for Aeronautics. Also, **N.A.C.A.**

NAD *Biochemistry.* a coenzyme, $C_{21}H_{27}N_7O_{14}P_2$, involved in many cellular oxidation-reduction reactions. [*n(icotinamide) a(denine) d(inucleotide)*]

N.A.D. National Academy of Design.

NADH *Biochemistry.* an abbreviation for the reduced form of NAD in electron transport reactions. [NAD + *H*, for hydrogen]

NADP *Biochemistry.* a coenzyme, $C_{21}H_{28}N_7O_{17}P_3$, similar in function to NAD. [*n(icotinamide) a(denine) d(inucleotide) p(hosphate)*]

NAFTA (naf'tə), North American Free Trade Agreement. Also, **Nafta.**

Nah. *Bible.* Nahum.

NAHB National Association of Home Builders.

NAM National Association of Manufacturers. Also, **N.A.M.**

nar narrow.

narc. narcotics.

N.A.S. 1. National Academy of Sciences. 2. naval air station. Also, **NAS**

NASA (nas'ə), National Aeronautics and Space Administration.

NASCAR (nas'kär), National Association for Stock Car Auto Racing. Also, **N.A.S.C.A.R.**

NASD National Association of Securities Dealers. Also, **N.A.S.D.**

NASDAQ (nas'dak, naz'-), National Association of Securities Dealers Automated Quotations.

nat. 1. national. 2. native. 3. natural. 4. naturalist.

natl. national.

NATO (nā'tō), an organization formed in 1949, comprising the 12 nations of the Atlantic Pact together with Greece, Turkey, and the Federal Republic of Germany, for the purpose of collective defense. [*N(orth) A(tlantic) T(reaty) O(rganization)*]

naut. nautical.

nav. 1. naval. 2. navigable. 3. navigation.

Nav. Arch. Naval Architect.

Nav. E. Naval Engineer.

navig. navigation.

NAVSAT (nav'sat'), navigational satellite.

NB 1. New Brunswick, Canada (for use with ZIP code). 2. Also, **N.B.** note well; take notice. [from Latin *nota bene*]

Nb *Symbol, Chemistry.* niobium.

nb *Telecommunications.* narrowband.

N.B. New Brunswick.

NBA 1. National Basketball Association. 2. Also, **N.B.A.** 1. National Book Award. 3. National Boxing Association.

nba narrowband amplifier.

NBC National Broadcasting System.

NbE north by east.

NBIOS *Computers.* network basic input-output system.

nbr number.

NBS National Bureau of Standards. Also, **N.B.S.**

NbW north by west.

NC 1. National coarse (a thread measure). 2. no change. 3. no charge. 4. North Carolina (for use with ZIP code). 5. numerical control. 6. *Military.* Nurse Corps.

nc 1. no connection. 2. *Electricity.* normally closed (of contacts).

n/c no charge.

N.C. 1. no charge. 2. North Carolina.

NCA 1. National Council on the Aging. 2. National Council on the Arts.

nca nickel-copper alloy.

NCAA National Collegiate Athletic Association. Also, **N.C.A.A.**

N.C.C. National Council of Churches. Also, **NCC**

NCCJ National Conference of Christians and Jews.

ncd no can do.

N.C.O. Noncommissioned Officer.

NCTE National Council of Teachers of English.

ND North Dakota (for use with ZIP code).

Nd *Symbol, Chemistry.* neodymium.

nd *Stock Exchange.* (especially of bonds) next day (delivery).

n.d. no date.

NDAC National Defense Advisory Commission.

N.Dak. North Dakota. Also, **N.D.**

nde near-death experience.

ndf *Photography.* neutral-density filter.

ndro nondestructive readout.

NDSL National Direct Student Loan.

ndt nondestructive testing.

NE 1. Nebraska (for use with ZIP code). 2. northeast. 3. northeastern.

Ne *Symbol, Chemistry.* neon.

N.E. 1. naval engineer. 2. New England. 3. northeast. 4. northeastern.

n.e. 1. northeast. 2. northeastern.

N.E.A. 1. National Education Association. 2. National Endowment for the Arts. Also, **NEA**

Neb. Nebraska.

NEbE northeast by east.

NEbN northeast by north.

Nebr. Nebraska.

NEC National Electrical Code.

nec necessary.

n.e.c. not elsewhere classified.

N.E.D. *New English Dictionary.* Also, **NED**

NEF National extra fine (a thread measure).

neg. 1. Also, **neg** negative. 2. negatively.

NEH National Endowment for the Humanities.

Neh. *Bible.* Nehemiah.

nem. con. no one contradicting; unanimously. [from Latin *nemine contradicente*]

nem. diss. no one dissenting; unanimously. [from Latin *nemine dissentiente*]

N. Eng. Northern England.

NEP (nep), New Economic Policy. Also, **Nep, N.E.P.**

NES New England Sports Network (a cable television channel).

n.e.s. not elsewhere specified. Also, **N.E.S.**

NESC National Electrical Safety Code.

NET National Educational Television.

Neth. Netherlands.

n. et m. (in prescriptions) night and morning. [Latin *nocte et mane*]

neurol. neurology; neurological.

neut. 1. neuter. 2. neutral.

Nev. Nevada.

Newf. Newfoundland.

NF 1. National fine (a thread measure). 2. *Pharmacology.* National Formulary. 3. Newfoundland, Canada (for use with ZIP code). 4. no funds. 5. Norman French.

nf *Telecommunications.* noise figure.

n/f no funds. Also, **N/F**

N.F. 1. no funds. 2. Norman French.

NFC National Football Conference.

NFD. Newfoundland. Also, **Nfd., Nfld.**

NFL National Football League.

NFS not for sale. Also, **N.F.S.**

NG 1. *Chemistry.* nitroglycerin. 2. *Anatomy.* nasogastric.

ng nanogram; nanograms.

N.G. 1. National Guard. 2. New Guinea. 3. no good.

n.g. no good.

NGC *Astronomy.* New General Catalogue: a catalog of clusters, nebulae, and galaxies published in 1888.

NGF nerve growth factor.

NGk New Greek. Also, **N.Gk.**

NGNP nominal gross national product.

NGS National Geodetic Survey.

NGU *Pathology.* nongonococcal urethritis.

NH New Hampshire (for use with ZIP code).

nh nonhygroscopic.

NHA National Housing Agency. Also, **N.H.A.**

nha next higher assembly.

N. Heb. New Hebrides.

NHG New High German. Also, **NHG., N.H.G.**

NHI *British.* National Health Insurance.

NHL National Hockey League.

NHS 1. *British.* National Health Service. 2. National Honor Society.

NHSC National Highway Safety Council.

NHTSA National Highway Traffic Safety Administration.

Ni *Symbol, Chemistry.* nickel.

N.I. Northern Ireland.

NIA 1. National Intelligence Authority. 2. Newspaper Institute of America.

NIH National Institutes of Health.

NIK Nickelodeon (a cable television channel).

NIMBY (*usually* nim'bē), not in my backyard. Also, **Nimby.**

NIMH National Institute of Mental Health.

NiMH *Electricity.* nickel-metal hydride (battery).

nip nipple.

ni. pr. (in prescriptions) unless before. [from Latin *nisi prius*]

NIRA National Industrial Recovery Act. Also, **N.I.R.A.**

NIST (nist), National Institute of Standards and Technology.

NIT National Invitational Tournament.

NJ New Jersey (for use with ZIP code).

N.J. New Jersey.

NKGB in the U.S.S.R., a secret-police organization (1941–46). [from Russian *N(aródnyĭ) k(omissariát) g(osudárstvennoĭ) b(ezopásnosti)* People's Commissariat for State Security]

nkl nickel.

NKVD in the U.S.S.R., a secret-police organization (1934–46). [from Russian *N(aródnyĭ) K(omissariát) V(nútrennikh) D(el)* People's Commissariat of Internal Affairs]

NL 1. Also, **NL.** New Latin; Neo-Latin. 2. night letter.

nl nonleaded (of gasoline).

N.L. 1. *Baseball.* National League. 2. New Latin; Neo-Latin.

n.l. 1. *Printing.* new line. 2. *Law.* it is not allowed. [from Latin *non licet*] 3. *Law.* it is not clear or evident. [from Latin *non liquet*]

N. Lat. north latitude. Also, **N. lat.**

N.L.F. National Liberation Front.

nlnr nonlinear.

NLRB National Labor Relations Board. Also, **N.L.R.B.**

NM 1. New Mexico (for use with ZIP code). 2. *Grammar.* noun modifier.

nm 1. nanometer; nanometers. 2. nautical mile. 3. nonmetallic.

N.M. New Mexico. Also, **N. Mex.**

nmag nonmagnetic.

NMI no middle initial. Also, **nmi**

nmi *Symbol.* nautical mile.

nmlz normalize.

NMN no middle name.

NMR 1. *Physics.* nuclear magnetic resonance. 2. *Medicine.* magnetic resonance imaging.

nmr no maintenance required.

NMSQT National Merit Scholarship Qualifying Test.

NMSS National Multiple Sclerosis Society.

N.M.U. National Maritime Union. Also, **NMU**

NNE north-northeast. Also, **N.N.E.**

NNP net national product.

NNW north-northwest. Also, **N. N.W.**

No *Symbol, Chemistry.* nobelium.

no *Electricity.* (of contacts) normally open.

no. 1. north. 2. northern. 3. number. Also, **No.**

N/O *Banking.* registered.

NOAA National Oceanic and Atmospheric Administration.

N.O.C. *Insurance.* not otherwise classified.

n.o.i.b.n. not otherwise indexed by name.

nol. pros. *Law.* unwilling to prosecute. [from Latin *nolle prosequi*]

nom. *Grammar.* nominative.

Nom. Cap. *Finance.* nominal capital.

nomen nomenclature.

noncom. noncommissioned.

nonflm nonflammable.

non obst. *Law.* notwithstanding. [from Latin *non obstante*]

non pros. *Law.* a judgment against a plaintiff who does not appear in court. [from Latin *non prosequitur* he does not pursue]

non rep. (in prescriptions) do not repeat. [from Latin *non repetatur* it is not repeated]

non seq. *Logic.* a conclusion which does not follow from the premises. [from Latin *non sequitur* it does not follow]

nonstd nonstandard.

nonsyn nonsynchronous.

NOP not our publication. Also, **N. O.P.**

Nor. 1. Norman. 2. North. 3. Northern. 4. Norway. 5. Norwegian.

nor. 1. north. 2. northern.

NORAD (nôr'ad), a joint U.S.-Canadian air force command. [*Nor(th American) A(ir) D(efence Command)*]

norm normal.

Norw. 1. Norway. 2. Norwegian.

NOS *Computers.* network operating system.

nos. numbers. Also, **Nos.**

n.o.s. not otherwise specified.

NOTA none of the above.

Nov. November.

nov. novelist.

NOW (nou), 1. National Organization for Women. 2. *Banking.* negotiable order of withdrawal.

noz nozzle.

NP 1. National pipe (a thread measure). 2. noun phrase. 3. nurse-practitioner.

Np *Physics.* neper; nepers.

Np *Symbol, Chemistry.* neptunium.

N.P. 1. new paragraph. 2. *Law.* nisi prius. 3. no protest. 4. notary public.

n.p. 1. net proceeds. 2. new paragraph. 3. *Law.* nisi prius. 4. no pagination. 5. no place of publication. 6. no protest. 7. notary public.

NPK *Horticulture.* nitrogen, phosphorus, and potassium.

npl nameplate.

npn negative-positive-negative (transistor).

n.p. or d. no place or date.

NPR National Public Radio. Also, **N.P.R.**

nprn neoprene.

NPT 1. National (taper) pipe thread. 2. Nonproliferation Treaty.

n.p.t. normal pressure and temperature. Also, **npt**

nr 1. negative resistance. 2. nuclear reactor.

NRA 1. National Recovery Administration: a former federal agency (1933–36). 2. National Recreation Area. 3. National Rifle Association. Also, **N.R.A.**

NRAB National Railroad Adjustment Board.

NRC 1. National Research Council. 2. Nuclear Regulatory Commission.

NROTC Naval Reserve Officer Training Corps. Also **N.R.O.T.C.**

NRPB National Resources Planning Board.

NRTA National Retired Teachers Association.

nrtn nonreturn.

nrvsbl nonreversible.

nrz nonreturn-to-zero.

NS 1. not sufficient (funds). 2. Nova Scotia, Canada (for use with ZIP code). 3. nuclear ship.

Ns *Meteorology.* nimbostratus.

ns 1. Also, **nsec** nanosecond; nanoseconds. 2. nonserviceable.

N.S. 1. New Style. 2. Nova Scotia.

n.s. not specified.

NSA 1. National Security Agency. 2. National Shipping Authority. 3. National Standards Association. 4. National Student Association. Also, **N.S.A.**

NSC 1. National Safety Council. 2. National Security Council.

NSF 1. National Science Foundation. 2. not sufficient funds. Also, **N.S.F.**

N/S/F not sufficient funds.

N.S.P.C.A. National Society for the Prevention of Cruelty to Animals.

N.S.P.C.C. National Society for the Prevention of Cruelty to Children.

n.s.p.f. not specifically provided for.

NSU *Pathology.* nonspecific urethritis; nongonococcal urethritis.

N.S.W. New South Wales.

NT 1. New Testament. 2. Northwest Territories, Canada (for use with ZIP code).

Nt *Symbol, Chemistry.* niton.

nt *Physics.* nit; nits.

N.T. 1. New Testament (of the Bible). 2. Northern Territory. 3. Northwest Territories.

ntc negative temperature coefficient.

NTIA National Telecommunications and Information Administration.

ntp normal temperature and pressure.

nts not to scale.

NTSB National Transportation Safety Board.

ntwk network.

nt. wt. net weight. Also, **ntwt**

nuc nuclear.

NUCFLASH (nōōk'flash', nyōōk'-), a report of highest precedence notifying the president or deputies of an accidental or unauthorized nuclear-weapon launch or of a nuclear attack. [*nuc(lear) flash*]

NUL National Urban League. Also **N.U.L.**

Num. *Bible.* Numbers.

num. 1. number. 2. numeral; numerals.

numis. 1. numismatic. 2. numismatics. Also, **numism.**

N.U.T. *British.* National Union of Teachers.

N.U.W.W. British. National Union of Women Workers.
NV Nevada (for use with ZIP code).
N/V Banking. no value.
NW 1. net worth. 2. northwest. 3. northwestern. Also, **N.W.**, **n.w.**
NWbW northwest by west.
NWC Military. National War College.

NWLB National War Labor Board.
NWS National Weather Service.
nwt nonwatertight.
n. wt. net weight.
N.W.T. Northwest Territories.
NY New York (for use with ZIP code).
N.Y. New York.
NYA National Youth Administration. Also, **N.Y.A.**

N.Y.C. New York City. Also, **NYC**
NYCSCE New York Coffee, Sugar, and Cocoa Exchange.
nyl nylon.
NYME New York Mercantile Exchange.
NYP not yet published. Also, **N. Y.P.**
NYSE New York Stock Exchange. Also, **N.Y.S.E.**
N.Z. New Zealand. Also, **N. Zeal.**

---

abcdefghijklmn **O** pqrstuvwxyz

O 1. Old. 2. Grammar. object.
O Symbol. 1. the fifteenth in order or in a series. 2. the Arabic cipher; zero. 3. (sometimes lowercase) the medieval Roman numeral for 11. 4. Physiology. a major blood group, usually enabling a person whose blood is of this type to donate blood to persons of group O, A, B, or AB and to receive blood from persons of group O. 5. Chemistry. oxygen. 6. Logic. particular negative.
O. 1. Ocean. 2. (in prescriptions) a pint. [from Latin octārius] 3. octavo. 4. October. 5. Ohio. 6. Old. 7. Ontario. 8. Oregon.
o. 1. pint. [from Latin octārius] 2. Printing. octavo. 3. off. 4. old. 5. only. 6. order. 7. Baseball. out; outs.
OA office automation.
oa overall.
o/a 1. on account. 2. on or about.
OAO U. S. Aerospace. Orbiting Astronomical Observatory.
OAP British. old-age pensioner.
OAPC Office of Alien Property Custodian.
OAS Organization of American States.
O.A.S.I. Old Age and Survivors Insurance.
OAU Organization of African Unity. Also, **O.A.U.**
OB 1. Also, **ob** Medicine. **a.** obstetrical. **b.** obstetrician. **c.** obstetrics. 2. off Broadway. 3. opening of books. 4. ordered back. 5. outward bound.
ob. 1. he died; she died. [from Latin obiit] 2. incidentally. [from Latin obiter] 3. oboe. 4. Meteorology. observation.
O.B. 1. opening of books. 2. ordered back. Also, **O/B**
obb. Music. obbligato.
obdt. obedient.
O.B.E. 1. Officer (of the Order) of the British Empire. 2. Order of the British Empire.
OB-GYN Medicine. 1. obstetrician-gynecologist. 2. obstetrics-gynecology.
obit. obituary.
obj. 1. object. 2. objection. 3. objective.
objv objective.
obl. 1. oblique. 2. oblong.
oblg 1. obligate. 2. obligation. 3. oblige.
obs. 1. observation. 2. observatory. 3. obsolete. Also, **Obs.**
obsl obsolete.

obstet. 1. obstetric. 2. obstetrics.
obstn obstruction.
obsv observation.
OBulg. Old Bulgarian. Also, **OBulg**
obv obverse.
oc outside circumference.
Oc. ocean. Also, **oc.**
o/c overcharge.
O.C. Philately. original cover.
o.c. 1. Architecture. on center. 2. in the work cited. [from Latin opere citātō]
occ. 1. occasional. 2. occasionally. 3. occident. 4. occidental. 5. occupation. 6. occupy.
occas. 1. occasional. 2. occasionally.
OCD Office of Civil Defense.
OCDM Office of Civil and Defense Mobilization.
ocld oil-cooled.
OCR Computers. 1. optical character reader. 2. optical character recognition.
OCS 1. Military. officer candidate school. 2. Old Church Slavonic. 3. outer continental shelf.
ocsnl occasional.
Oct. October.
oct. 1. octagon. 2. octavo.
octl octal.
octn octane.
OD an overdose of a drug, especially a fatal one.
OD 1. officer of the day. 2. Old Dutch. 3. Ordnance Department. 4. outside diameter.
od 1. on demand. 2. outside diameter. 3. outside dimensions.
O.D. 1. Doctor of Optometry. 2. (in prescriptions) the right eye. [from Latin oculus dexter] 3. officer of the day. 4. Old Dutch. 5. (of a military uniform) olive drab. 6. ordinary seaman. 7. outside diameter. 8. Banking. overdraft. 9. Banking. overdrawn.
o.d. 1. (in prescriptions) the right eye. [from Latin oculus dexter] 2. olive drab. 3. on demand. 4. outside diameter.
odom odometer.
odpsk oil dipstick.
ODT Office of Defense Transportation.
OE Old English. Also, **OE.**
Oe Electricity. oersted; oersteds.
O.E. 1. Old English. 2. Commerce. omissions excepted.

o.e. Commerce. omissions excepted. Also, **oe**
OEC Office of Energy Conservation.
OECD Organization for Economic Cooperation and Development.
OED Oxford English Dictionary. Also, **O.E.D.**
OEEC Organization for European Economic Cooperation.
OEM original equipment manufacturer.
OEO Office of Economic Opportunity.
OES 1. Office of Economic Stabilization. 2. Order of the Eastern Star.
OF Old French. Also, **OF.**, **O.F.**
of outside face.
ofc office.
ofcl official.
ofcr officer.
ofl offline.
OFlem Old Flemish. Also, **OFlem.**
ofltr oil filter.
O.F.M. Order of Friars Minor (Franciscan). [from Latin Ōrdō Frātrum Minōrum]
OFr. Old French. Also, **OFr**
OFris. Old Frisian. Also, **OFris**
oft outfit.
OG officer of the guard.
O.G. 1. officer of the guard. 2. Architecture. ogee. 3. Philately. See **o.g.** (def. 1.)
o.g. 1. Also, **O.G.** Philately. original gum: the gum on the back of a stamp when it is issued. 2. Architecture. ogee.
OGO U.S. Aerospace. Orbiting Geophysical Observatory.
OGPU (og′pōō), (in the U.S.S.R.) the government's secret-police organization (1923–1934). Also, **Ogpu.** Cf. **KGB.** [from Russian Ogpu, for Ob″edinénnoe gosudárstvennoe politícheskoe upravlénie Unified State Political Directorate]
ogr Telephones. outgoing repeater.
ogt Telephones. outgoing trunk.
OH Ohio (for use with ZIP code).
OHC Automotive. overhead camshaft.
OHG Old High German. Also, **OHG.**, **O.H.G.**
O.H.M.S. On His Majesty's Service; On Her Majesty's Service.
OI opportunistic infection.
OIC officer in charge.
OIcel Old Icelandic.
OIr Old Irish. Also, **OIr.**
OIt Old Italian.

OJ *Informal.* orange juice. Also, O.J., **o.j.**

OJT on-the-job training. Also, **O. J.T.**

OK Oklahoma (for use with ZIP code).

OK (ō′kā′, ō′kā′, ō′kā′), all right; permissible or acceptable; satisfactory or under control. Also, **O.K., okay** [initials of a facetious folk phonetic spelling, e.g., *oll* or *orl korrect* representing *all correct*, first attested in Boston, Massachusetts, in 1839, then used in 1840 by Democrat partisans of Martin Van Buren during his election campaign, who allegedly named their organization, the *O.K. Club,* in allusion to the initials of *Old Kinderhook,* Van Buren's nickname, derived from his birthplace *Kinderhook,* New York]

Okla. Oklahoma.

OL Old Latin. Also, **OL.**

Ol. (in prescriptions) oil. [from Latin *oleum*]

O.L. 1. Also, **o.l.** (in prescriptions) the left eye. [from Latin *oculus laevus*] **2.** Old Latin.

Old Test. Old Testament (of the Bible).

OLE *Computers.* object linking and embedding.

OLG Old Low German. Also, **O. L.G.**

OLLA Office of Lend Lease Administration.

olvl oil level.

Om. (formerly, in East Germany) ostmark.

O.M. *British.* Order of Merit.

OMA orderly marketing agreement.

OMB Office of Management and Budget. Also, **O.M.B.**

OMBE Office of Minority Business Enterprise.

omn. bih. (in prescriptions) every two hours. [from Latin *omnī bihōriō*]

omn. hor. (in prescriptions) every hour. [from Latin *omnī hōra*]

omn. man. (in prescriptions) every morning. Also, **omn man** [from Latin *omnī māne*]

omn. noct. (in prescriptions) every night. Also, **omn noct** [from Latin *omnī nocte*]

omn. quadr. hor. (in prescriptions) every quarter of an hour. Also, **omn quadr hor** [from Latin *omnī quadrante hōrae*]

ON 1. Also, **ON., O.N.** Old Norse. **2.** Ontario, Canada (for use with ZIP code).

ONF Old North French.

ONFr. Old North French.

ONI Office of Naval Intelligence.

ONR Office of Naval Research.

Ont. Ontario.

O.O.D. 1. officer of the deck. **2.** officer of the day.

OOG *Computers.* object-oriented graphics.

OOP *Computers.* object-oriented programming.

OOT out of town. Also, **O.O.T.**

OP observation post. Also, **O.P.**

op (op), a style of abstract art. [from *op(tical)*]

Op. *Music.* opus.

op. 1. opera. **2.** operation. **3.** opposite. **4.** opus.

O.P. 1. observation post. **2.** *British Theater.* opposite prompt. **3.** Order of Preachers (Dominican). **4.** out of print. **5.** *Distilling.* overproof.

o.p. out of print.

OPA Office of Price Administration: the federal agency (1941–46) charged with regulating rents and the distribution and prices of goods during World War II.

opa opaque.

op. cit. (op′ sit′), in the work cited. [from Latin *opere citātō*]

OPEC (ō′pek), an organization founded in 1960 of nations that export large amounts of petroleum, to establish oil-exporting policies and set prices. [O(rganization of) P(etroleum) E(xporting) C(ountries)]

Op-Ed (op′ed′), a newspaper page devoted to signed articles of varying viewpoints. [op(posite) ed(itorial page)]

OPer. Old Persian.

OPers Old Persian.

ophthal. 1. ophthalmologist. **2.** ophthalmology.

OPM 1. Office of Personnel Management. **2.** operations per minute. **3.** *Slang.* other people's money.

opn operation.

opnr opener.

Opp. *Music.* opuses. [from Latin *opera*]

opp. 1. opposed. **2.** opposite.

opp hnd opposite hand.

OPr Old Provençal.

opr 1. operate. **2.** operator.

oprg operating.

oprs oil pressure.

OPruss Old Prussian.

OPS Office of Price Stabilization. Also, **O.P.S.**

opt 1. optical. **2.** optimum.

optl optional.

opty opportunity.

OR 1. *Law.* on (one's own) recognizance. **2.** operating room. **3.** operations research. **4.** Oregon (for use with ZIP code). **5.** owner's risk.

or outside radius.

O.R. 1. *Military.* orderly room. **2.** owner's risk.

O.R.C. Officers' Reserve Corps.

orch. orchestra.

ord. 1. Also, **ord** order. **2.** ordinal. **3.** ordinance. **4.** ordinary. **5.** ordnance.

ordn. ordnance.

Ore. Oregon.

Oreg. Oregon.

orf orifice.

org. 1. organic. **2.** organization. **3.** organized.

orig. 1. origin. **2.** original. **3.** originally.

orn orange.

ornith. 1. ornithological. **2.** ornithology.

ornithol. 1. ornithological. **2.** ornithology.

ORT Registered Occupational Therapist.

Orth. Orthodox.

orth. 1. orthopedic **2.** orthopedics.

ORuss Old Russian.

ORV off-road vehicle.

OS 1. Old Saxon. **2.** *Computers.* operating system.

Os *Symbol, Chemistry.* osmium.

O/S (of the calendar) Old Style.

o/s 1. (of the calendar) Old Style. **2.** out of stock. **3.** *Banking.* outstanding.

O.S. 1. (in prescriptions) the left eye. [from Latin *oculus sinister*] **2.** Old Saxon. **3.** Old School. **4.** old series. **5.** (of the calendar) Old Style. **6.** ordinary seaman.

o.s. 1. (in prescriptions) the left eye. [from Latin *oculus sinister*] **2.** ordinary seaman.

O.S.A. Order of St. Augustine.

O.S.B. Order of St. Benedict.

osc oscillator.

OSD Office of the Secretary of Defense.

O.S.D. Order of St. Dominic.

O.S.F. Order of St. Francis.

OSFCW Office of Solid Fuels Coordinator for War.

OSHA (ō′shə, osh′ə), the division of the Department of Labor that sets and enforces occupational health and safety rules. [O(ccupational) S(afety and) H(ealth) A(dministration)]

osl oil seal.

osmv *Electronics.* one-shot multivibrator.

OSO *U.S. Aerospace.* Orbiting Solar Observatory.

OSP died without issue. [from Latin *obiit sine prōle*]

OSp Old Spanish.

OSRD Office of Scientific Research and Development.

OSS Office of Strategic Services: a U.S. government intelligence agency during World War II. Also, **O.S.S.**

OT 1. occupational therapist. **2.** occupational therapy. **3.** *Bible.* Old Testament. **4.** overnight telegram. **5.** overtime.

O.T. Old Testament (of the Bible).

o.t. overtime.

OTA Office of Technology Assessment.

OTB offtrack betting.

OTC 1. Also, **O.T.C.** Officers' Training Corps. **2.** over-the-counter.

OTS Officers' Training School. Also, **O.T.S.**

OU (in prescriptions) **1.** both eyes. [from Latin *oculi uterque*] **2.** each eye. [from Latin *oculus uterque*]

out 1. outlet. **2.** output.

outbd outboard.

outg outgoing.

ov over.

ovbd overboard.

ovh oval head.

ovhd overhead.

ovhl overhaul.

OV language (ō′vē′), *Linguistics.* a type of language that has direct objects preceding the verb. [O(bject)-V(erb)]

ovld overload.

ovp oval point.

ovrd override.

ovsz oversize.

ovtr overtravel.

ovv overvoltage.

OW Old Welsh.

OWI 1. Office of War Information: the U.S federal agency (1942–45) charged with disseminating information about World War II. 2. operating (a motor vehicle) while intoxicated.

Ox. Oxford. [from Latin *Oxonia*]

oxd oxidized.

Oxon. 1. Oxford. [from Latin *Ox-onia*] 2. of Oxford. [from Latin *Oxoniēnsis*]

oz. ounce; ounces. [abbreviation of Italian *onza*]

oz. av. ounce avoirdupois.

ozs. ounces.

oz. t. ounce troy.

a b c d e f g h i j k l m n o **P** q r s t u v w x y z

P 1. (as a rating of student performance) passing. 2. *Chess.* pawn. 3. *Electronics.* plate. 4. poor. 5. *Grammar.* predicate. 6. Protestant.

P *Symbol.* 1. the 16th in order or in a series, or, when *I* is omitted, the 15th. 2. (*sometimes lowercase*) the medieval Roman numeral for 400. 3. *Genetics.* parental. 4. *Chemistry.* phosphorus. 5. *Physics.* **a.** power. **b.** pressure. **c.** proton. **d.** space inversion. **e.** poise. 6. *Biochemistry.* proline.

p 1. penny; pence. 2. *Music.* softly. [from Italian *piano*]

P- *Military.* (in designations of aircraft) pursuit: *P-38.*

p- *Chemistry.* designating the 1, 4 position on the benzene ring. [from Greek *para-* beside, by, beyond]

P. 1. pastor. 2. father. [from Latin *Pater*] 3. peseta. 4. peso. 5. post. 6. president. 7. pressure. 8. priest. 9. prince. 10. progressive.

p. 1. page. 2. part. 3. participle. 4. past. 5. father. [from Latin *pater*] 6. *Chess.* pawn. 7. penny; pence. 8. per. 9. *Grammar.* person. 10. peseta. 11. peso. 12. *Music.* softly. [from Italian *piano*] 13. pint. 14. pipe. 15. *Baseball.* pitcher. 16. pole. 17. population. 18. after. [from Latin *post*] 19. president. 20. pressure. 21. purl.

PA 1. paying agent. 2. Pennsylvania (for use with ZIP code). 3. physician's assistant. 4. press agent. 5. public-address system.

Pa *Physics.* pascal; pascals.

Pa *Symbol, Chemistry.* protactinium.

Pa. Pennsylvania.

P.A. 1. Also, **PA** Parents' Association. 2. *Insurance.* particular average. 3. passenger agent. 4. *Military.* post adjutant. 5. power of attorney. 6. press agent. 7. public-address system. 8. publicity agent. 9. purchasing agent.

p.a. 1. participial adjective. 2. per annum. 3. press agent.

p.-a. public-address system.

PABA (pä′bə), *Chemistry, Biochemistry.* a crystalline solid, $C_7H_7NO_2$, used especially in pharmaceuticals. [*p*(*ara-*)*a*(*mino*)*b*(*enzoic*) *a*(*cid*)]

PABX *Telephones.* an automatically operated PBX. Also, **pabx** [*p*(*rivate*) *a*(*utomatic*) *b*(*ranch*) *ex*(*change*)]

PAC (pak), political action committee.

Pac. Pacific.

P.A.C. political action committee.

pacm pulse amplitude code modulation.

PaD Pennsylvania Dutch; Pennsylvania German.

p. ae. (in prescriptions) equal parts. [from Latin *partēs aequā-lēs*]

PaG Pennsylvania German.

Pak. Pakistan.

PAL (pal), a special air service offered by the U.S. Postal Service for sending parcels. [*P*(*arcel*) *A*(*ir*) *L*(*ift*)]

PAL Police Athletic League. Also, **P.A.L.**

Pal. Palestine.

pal. 1. paleography. 2. paleontology.

paleog. paleography.

paleon. paleontology.

paleontol. paleontology.

PAM 1. *Aerospace.* payload assist module. 2. Also, **pam** *Telecommunications.* pulse amplitude modulation.

pam. pamphlet.

pamfm pulse amplitude modulation frequency modulation.

Pan (pan), an international distress signal used by shore stations to inform a ship, aircraft, etc., of something vital to its safety or that of one of its passengers. Also, **pan.**

pan panoramic.

Pan. Panama.

P. and L. profit and loss. Also, **P. & L., p. and l.**

par precision-approach radar.

par. 1. paragraph. 2. parallel. 3. parenthesis. 4. parish.

para paragraph.

Para. Paraguay.

par. aff. (in prescriptions) to the part affected. [from Latin *pars affecta*]

paren parenthesis.

Parl. 1. Parliament. 2. Parliamentary. Also, **parl.**

parl. proc. parliamentary procedure.

parsec (pär′sek′), *Astronomy.* parallax second.

part. 1. participial. 2. participle. 3. particular.

part. adj. participial adjective.

part. aeq. (in prescriptions) equal parts. [from Latin *partes aequales*]

part. vic. (in prescriptions) in divided doses. [from Latin *partibus vicibus*]

pas public address system.

pass. 1. passage. 2. passenger. 3. here and there throughout. [from Latin *passim*] 4. passive.

PAT 1. *Football.* point after touchdown; points after touchdown. 2.

Banking. preauthorized automatic transfer.

pat. 1. patent. 2. patented.

patd. patented.

path. 1. pathological. 2. pathology.

pathol. 1. Also, **pathol** pathological. 2. pathology.

Pat. Off. Patent Office.

pat. pend. patent pending. Also, **patpend**

P.A.U. Pan American Union.

PAX *Telephones.* private automatic exchange.

PAYE 1. pay as you enter. 2. pay as you earn.

PB power brakes.

Pb *Symbol, Chemistry.* lead. [from Latin *plumbum*]

pb pushbutton.

P.B. 1. British Pharmacopoeia. [from Latin *Pharmacopoeia Britannica*] 2. Prayer Book.

p.b. *Baseball.* passed ball; passed balls.

PBA 1. Professional Bowlers Association. 2. Public Buildings Administration.

P.B.A. Patrolmen's Benevolent Association.

PBB *Chemistry.* any of the highly toxic and possibly carcinogenic aromatic compounds consisting of two benzene rings in which bromine takes the place of two or more hydrogen atoms. [*p*(*oly*)*b*(*rominated*) *b*(*iphenyl*)]

pbd pressboard.

PBK Phi Beta Kappa.

pblg publishing.

pblr publisher.

PBS Public Broadcasting Service.

PBX a manually or automatically operated telephone facility that handles communications within an office, office building, or organization. [*P*(*rivate*) *B*(*ranch*) *Ex*(*change*)]

PC 1. Peace Corps. 2. personal computer. 3. politically correct. 4. printed circuit. 5. professional corporation.

pc 1. *Astronomy.* parsec. 2. parts catalog. 3. *Physics, Chemistry.* picocurie; picocuries.

pc. 1. piece. 2. prices.

P/C 1. petty cash. 2. price current. Also, **p/c**

P.C. 1. Past Commander. 2. *British.* Police Constable. 3. politically correct. 4. Post Commander. 5. *British.* Prince Consort. 6. *British.* Privy Council. 7. professional corporation.

p.c. 1. percent. 2. petty cash. 3. postal card. 4. (in prescriptions) after eating; after meals. [from

Latin *post cibōs*] **5.** price current. **6.** printed circuit.

PCB a family of highly toxic chemical compounds consisting of two benzene rings in which chlorine takes the place of two or more hydrogen atoms. [*p(oly)c(hlorinated) b(iphenyl)*]

pcb *Electronics.* printed-circuit board.

pcf pounds per cubic foot.

pchs purchase.

pchsg purchasing.

pcht parchment.

PCI *Computers.* peripheral component interconnect.

pci pounds per cubic inch.

PCL *Computers.* Printer Control Language.

pcl pencil.

PCM **1.** *Computers.* plug-compatible manufacturer. **2.** Also, **pcm** *Telecommunications.* pulse code modulation.

PCMCIA Personal Computer Memory Card International Association.

pcmd pulse code modulation digital.

pcmfm pulse code modulation frequency modulation.

PCNB *Chemistry.* a crystalline compound, $C_6Cl_5NO_2$, used as a herbicide and insecticide. [*p(enta)c(hloro)n(itro)b(enzene)*]

PCP **1.** *Slang.* phencyclidine; an anaesthetic drug. [perhaps *p(hen)c(yclidine)* + *(peace)* *p(ill)*, an earlier designation] **2.** *Pathology.* pneumocystis pneumonia.

pct. percent. Also, **pct**

pctm pulse count modulation.

PCV *Automotive.* positive crankcase ventilation.

pcv pollution-control valve.

Pd *Symbol, Chemistry.* palladium.

pd pitch diameter.

pd. paid.

P.D. **1.** per diem. **2.** Police Department. **3.** *Insurance.* property damage.

p.d. **1.** per diem. **2.** potential difference.

PDA *Computers.* personal digital assistant.

PDB *Chemistry.* a crystalline solid, $C_6H_4Cl_2$, used especially as a moth repellent. [*p(ara-)d(ichloro)b(enzene)*]

Pd.B. Bachelor of Pedagogy.

Pd.D. Doctor of Pedagogy.

pdl **1.** *Computers.* page description language. **2.** poundal.

pdm pulse duration modulation.

Pd.M. Master of Pedagogy.

pdmfm pulse duration modulation frequency modulation.

P.D.Q. *Informal.* immediately; at once. Also, **PDQ** [*p(retty) d(amn) q(uick)*]

PDR Physicians' Desk Reference.

pdr powder.

PDT Pacific daylight time. Also, **P. D.T.**

PE Prince Edward Island, Canada (for use with ZIP code).

pe probable error.

p/e price-earnings ratio. Also, **P/E, PE, P-E, p-e**

P.E. **1.** Petroleum Engineer. **2.** physical education. **3.** Presiding

Elder. **4.** printer's error. **5.** *Statistics.* probable error. **6.** Professional Engineer. **7.** Protestant Episcopal.

p.e. printer's error.

pec photoelectric cell.

ped. **1.** pedal. **2.** pedestal. **3.** pedestrian.

Ped.D. Doctor of Pedagogy.

P.E.Dir. Director of Physical Education.

P.E.F. *Insurance.* personal effects floater.

P.E.I. Prince Edward Island.

pelec photoelectric.

pem *Computers.* preemptive multitasking.

pen penetration.

Pen. peninsula. Also, **pen.**

P.E.N. International Association of Poets, Playwrights, Editors, Essayists, and Novelists.

Penn. Pennsylvania. Also, **Penna.**

Pent. Pentecost.

Per. **1.** Persia. **2.** Persian.

per. **1.** percentile. **2.** period. **3.** person.

per an. per annum.

perc percussion.

perf. **1.** perfect. **2.** perforated. **3.** performance.

perf. part. perfect participle.

perh. perhaps.

perm **1.** permanent. **2.** permission.

permb permeability.

perp. perpendicular.

per pro. *Law.* by one acting as an agent; by proxy. Also, **per proc.** [from Latin *per procurationem*]

Pers Persian.

Pers. **1.** Persia. **2.** Persian.

pers. **1.** person. **2.** personal. **3.** personnel.

persp perspective.

PERT (pûrt), a management method of controlling and analyzing a system or program. [*P(rogram) E(valuation and) R(eview) T(echnique)*]

pert. pertaining.

PET (pet), *Medicine.* positron emission tomography.

Pet. *Bible.* Peter.

pet. petroleum.

Pet.E. Petroleum Engineer.

PETN *Chemistry, Pharmacology.* a crystalline, explosive solid, $C_5H_8N_4O_{12}$. [*p(enta)e(rythritol) t(etra)n(itrate)*]

petro petroleum.

petrog. petrography.

petrol. petrology.

pF *Electricity.* picofarad; picofarads.

pf power factor.

pf. **1.** perfect. **2.** (in Germany) pfennig. **3.** *Music.* pianoforte; piano. **4.** *Finance.* (of stock) preferred. **5.** proof.

p.f. *Music.* louder. [from Italian *più forte*]

Pfc. *Military.* private first class. Also, **PFC**

PFD personal flotation device.

pfd. preferred. Also, **pfd**

pfg. (in Germany) pfennig.

PFM *Telecommunications.* pulse frequency modulation. Also, **P. F.M.**

PG *Informal.* pregnant.

PG parental guidance: a rating assigned to a motion picture by the Motion Picture Association of America. [*p(arental) g(uidance) advised*]

pg **1.** picogram; picograms. **2.** pulse generator.

Pg. **1.** Portugal. **2.** Also, **Pg** Portuguese.

pg. page.

P.G. **1.** Past Grand. **2.** paying guest. **3.** Postgraduate. **4.** Also, **p.g.** *Informal.* pregnant.

PGA **1.** Also, **P.G.A.** Professional Golfers' Association. **2.** *Biochemistry.* folic acid [*p(teroyl) + g(lutamic) a(cid)*].

pga *Computers.* pin-grid array.

pgmt pigment.

Ph *Chemistry.* phenyl.

pH *Chemistry.* the symbol for the logarithm of the reciprocal of hydrogen ion concentration in gram atoms per liter, used to express the acidity or alkalinity of a solution.

ph *Optics.* phot; phots.

ph. **1.** phase. **2.** phone.

P.H. Public Health.

PHA Public Housing Administration.

Phar. **1.** pharmaceutical. **2.** pharmacology. **3.** pharmacopoeia. **4.** pharmacy. Also, **phar.**

Phar.B. Bachelor of Pharmacy.

Phar.D. Doctor of Pharmacy.

pharm. **1.** pharmaceutical. **2.** pharmacology. **3.** pharmacopoeia. **4.** pharmacy.

Pharm.D. Doctor of Pharmacy.

Pharm.M. Master of Pharmacy.

Ph.B. Bachelor of Philosophy. [from Latin *Philosophiae Baccalaureus*]

Ph. C. Pharmaceutical Chemist.

Ph.D. Doctor of Philosophy. [from Latin *Philosophiae Doctor*]

Phe *Biochemistry.* phenylalanine.

P.H.E. Public Health Engineer.

phen phenolic.

Ph. G. Graduate in Pharmacy.

phh phillips head.

Phil. **1.** *Bible.* Philemon. **2.** Philip. **3.** *Bible.* Philippians. **4.** Philippine.

phil. **1.** philosophical. **2.** philosophy.

Phila. Philadelphia.

Philem. *Bible.* Philemon.

Phil. I. Philippine Islands.

philol. **1.** philological. **2.** philology.

philos. **1.** philosopher. **2.** philosophical. **3.** philosophy.

Ph.L. Licentiate in Philosophy.

phm **1.** phantom. **2.** phase modulation.

Ph.M. Master of Philosophy.

phofl photoflash.

phon. phonetics.

phonet. phonetics.

phono phonograph.

phonol. phonology.

phos phosphate.

phot. **1.** photograph. **2.** photographer. **3.** photographic. **4.** photography.

photog. **1.** photographer. **2.** photographic. **3.** photography.

photom. photometry.

phr. phrase.

phren. 1. phrenological. 2. phrenology.

phrenol. 1. phrenological. 2. phrenology.

phrm pharmacy.

phrmcol pharmacological.

PHS Public Health Service. Also, P.H.S.

phsk phase-shift keying.

phys. 1. physical. 2. physician. 3. physics. 4. physiological. 5. physiology.

phys. chem. physical chemistry.

phys ed (fiz′ ed′), *Informal.* physical education. Also, **phys. ed.**

phys. geog. physical geography.

physiol. 1. physiological. 2. physiologist. 3. physiology.

PI 1. *Law.* personal injury. 2. politically incorrect. 3. principal investigator. 4. private investigator. 5. programmed instruction.

Pi. (in Turkey and other countries) piaster. Also, **pi.**

P.I. 1. Philippine Islands. 2. Also, **p.i.** private investigator.

p.i. politically incorrect.

pias. (in Turkey and other countries) piaster.

PID *Pathology.* pelvic inflammatory disease.

PIE Proto-Indo-European.

PIK payment in kind. Also, **p.i.k.**

pil. (in prescriptions) pill. [from Latin *pilula*]

PIM personal information manager.

pim pulse-interval modulation.

PIN (pin), *Computers.* a number assigned to an individual, used to establish identity in order to gain access to a computer system. [*p(ersonal) i(dentification) n(umber)*]

pin positive-intrinsic-negative transistor.

PINS (pinz), a person of less than 16 years of age placed under the jurisdiction of a juvenile court. [*P(erson) I(n) N(eed of) S(upervision)*]

PIO *U.S. Military.* 1. public information office. 2. public information officer.

PIRG Public Interest Research Group.

piv peak inverse voltage.

pizz. *Music.* pizzicato.

p.j.'s (pē′jāz′), *Informal.* pajamas. Also, **P.J.'s**

pjtr projector.

PK 1. personal knowledge 2. psychokinesis.

pk. 1. pack. 2. park. 3. Also, **pk** peak. 4. peck; pecks.

pkg. package.

pkt. 1. packet. 2. pocket.

PKU *Pathology.* phenylketonuria.

pkwy. parkway.

PL Public Law.

pl 1. parts list. 2. place. 3. plain. 4. plug. 5. private line.

pl. 1. Also, **Pl.** place. 2. plate. 3. plural.

P/L profit and loss.

P.L. Poet Laureate.

PLA People's Liberation Army.

PLAM price-level adjusted mortgage.

plat. 1. plateau. 2. platinum. 3. platoon.

PLC *British.* public limited company.

plc power-line carrier.

pld payload.

plf pounds per linear foot.

plf. plaintiff. Also, **plff.**

plk *Machinery.* pillowblock.

pll 1. pallet. 2. *Electronics.* phase-locked loop.

plmg plumbing.

plmr plumber.

pln plane.

plnm plenum.

plnr planar.

plnt planet.

plnty planetary.

PLO Palestine Liberation Organization.

plo phase-locked oscillator.

PL/1 *Computers.* programming language one.

plq plaque.

PLR Public Lending Right.

plr 1. pillar. 2. pliers. 3. puller.

plrs *Navigation.* pelorus.

plrt polarity.

pls. 1. please. 2. pulse.

PLSS portable life support system.

plstc plastic.

plt 1. pilot. 2. plant.

pltf platform.

pltg 1. planting. 2. plating.

PLU price lookup.

plu. plural.

plupf. pluperfect. Also, **plup., pluperf.**

plur. 1. plural. 2. plurality.

plywd plywood.

Plz. plaza.

plzd polarized.

PM preventive maintenance.

Pm *Symbol, Chemistry.* promethium.

pm 1. permanent magnet. 2. *Computers.* primary memory. 3. *Electronics.* pulse modulation.

pm. premium.

P.M. 1. Past Master. 2. Paymaster. 3. p.m. 4. Police Magistrate. 5. Postmaster. 6. post-mortem. 7. Prime Minister. 8. Provost Marshal.

p.m. after noon. [from Latin *post merīdiem*]

pmflt pamphlet.

P.M.G. 1. Paymaster General. 2. Postmaster General. 3. Provost Marshal General.

pmk. postmark.

P.M.L. *Insurance.* probable maximum loss.

PMLA Publications of the Modern Language Association of America. Also, **P.M.L.A.**

PMS 1. *Printing.* Pantone matching system. 2. premenstrual syndrome.

PMT premenstrual tension.

pmt. payment.

PN 1. please note. 2. promissory note. 3. psychoneurotic.

pn 1. part number. 2. please note. 3. promissory note.

P/N promissory note. Also, **p.n.**

pneum. 1. Also, **pneu** pneumatic. 2. pneumatics.

pnh pan head.

pnl panel.

pnld paneled.

pnlg paneling.

pnnt pennant.

pnp positive-negative-positive transistor.

pnt paint.

pntgn pentagon.

pnxt. he or she painted it. [from Latin *pinxit*]

PO purchase order.

Po *Symbol, Chemistry.* polonium.

po. *Baseball.* put-out; put-outs.

p/o part of.

P.O. 1. parole officer. 2. petty officer. 3. postal (money) order. 4. post office.

p.o. (in prescriptions) by mouth. [from Latin *per ōs*]

POA primary optical area.

POB post-office box. Also, **P.O.B.**

POC port of call.

pocul. (in prescriptions) a cup. [from Latin *pōculum*]

POD port of debarkation.

p.o.'d (pē′ōd′), *Slang.* angry or annoyed. [*p(issed) o(ff)*]

P.O.D. 1. pay on delivery. 2. Post Office Department.

POE 1. port of embarkation. 2. port of entry. Also, **P.O.E.**

poet. 1. poetic; poetical. 2. poetry.

POGO (pō′gō), Polar Orbiting Geophysical Observatory.

POL petroleum, oil, and lubricants.

Pol. 1. Poland. 2. Also, **Pol** Polish.

pol. 1. political. 2. politics.

polit. econ. political economy.

pol. sci. political science.

polstr polystyrene.

polthn polyethylene.

poly. polytechnic.

POP proof-of-purchase.

pop. 1. popular. 2. popularly. 3. population.

P.O.P. 1. printout paper. 2. point-of-purchase.

p.o.p. point-of-purchase.

p.o.r. pay on return.

Port. 1. Portugal. 2. Portuguese.

pos. 1. position. 2. positive. 3. possession. 4. possessive.

P.O.S. point-of-sale; point-of-sales. Also, **POS**

posn position.

poss. 1. possession. 2. possessive. 3. possible. 4. possibly.

POSSLQ (pos′əl kyoo′), either of two persons, one of each sex, who share living quarters but are not related by blood, marriage, or adoption: a categorization used by the U.S. Census Bureau. [*p(erson of the) o(pposite) s(ex) s(haring) l(iving) q(uarters)*]

postop (pōst′op′), postoperative. Also, **post-op.**

pot. *Electricity.* 1. potential. 2. potentiometer.

POTS (pots), *Telecommunications.* plain old telephone service.

POV *Motion Pictures.* point of view: used especially in describing a method of shooting a scene or film.

POW prisoner of war. Also, **P. O.W.**

PP 1. parcel post. 2. prepositional phrase.

pp *Radio.* push-pull.

pp. 1. pages. 2. past participle. 3. *Music.* pianissimo. 4. privately printed.

p-p peak-to-peak.

P.P. 1. parcel post. **2.** parish priest. **3.** past participle. **4.** postpaid. **5.** prepaid.

p.p. 1. parcel post. **2.** past participle. **3.** per person. **4.** postpaid.

PPA *Pharmacology.* a substance, $C_9H_{13}NO$, used as an appetite suppressant. [*p(henyl)p(ropanol)a(mine)*]

PPB 1. Also, **P.P.B.** *Publishing.* paper, printing, and binding. **2.** provisioning parts breakdown.

ppb *Publishing.* **1.** paper, printing, and binding. **2.** parts per billion. Also, **p.p.b.**

ppd. 1. postpaid. **2.** prepaid.

p.p.d.o. per person, double occupancy.

PPE *British.* philosophy, politics, and economics.

P.P.F. *Insurance.* personal property floater.

PPH paid personal holidays. Also, **P.P.H.**

pph. pamphlet.

PPI *Pharmacology.* **1.** patient package insert. **2.** Also, **ppi** *Electronics.* plan position indicator. **3.** producer price index.

ppl. participle.

ppll programmable phase-locked loop.

PPLO *Pathology.* pleuropneumonialike organism.

PPM 1. *Computers.* pages per minute. **2.** Also, **ppm** *Telecommunications.* pulse position modulation.

ppm 1. *Computers.* pages per minute: a measure of the speed of a page printer. **2.** parts per million. **3.** pulse per minute.

p.p.m. parts per million. Also, **P. P.M., ppm, PPM**

PPO preferred-provider organization.

ppp 1. peak pulse power. **2.** *Music.* pianississimo; double pianissimo.

ppr. 1. paper. **2.** Also, **p.pr.** present participle.

pps pulse per second.

P.P.S. a second or additional postscript. Also, **p.p.s.** [from Latin *post postscrīptum*]

ppt. *Chemistry.* precipitate. Also, **ppt**

ppv *Television.* pay-per-view. Also, **p.p.v., PPV, P.P.V.**

PQ Quebec, Canada (for use with ZIP code).

p.q. previous question.

PR 1. payroll. **2.** percentile rank. **3.** public relations. **4.** *Slang (often disparaging and offensive).* Puerto Rican. **5.** Puerto Rico (for use with ZIP code).

Pr Provençal.

Pr *Symbol, Chemistry.* praseodymium.

Pr. 1. (of stock) preferred. **2.** Priest. **3.** Prince. **4.** Provençal.

pr. 1. pair; pairs. **2.** paper. **3.** power. **4.** preference. **5.** (of stock) preferred. **6.** present. **7.** price. **8.** priest. **9.** *Computers.* printer. **10.** printing. **11.** pronoun.

P.R. 1. parliamentary report. **2.** Roman people. [from Latin *populus Rōmānus*] **3.** press release. **4.** prize ring. **5.** proportional representation. **6.** public relations. **7.** Puerto Rico.

p.r. public relations.

PRA Public Roads Administration.

prand. (in prescriptions) dinner. [from Latin *prandium*]

prblc parabolic.

PRC 1. Also, **P.R.C.** People's Republic of China. **2.** Postal Rate Commission.

prcht parachute.

prcs process.

prcsr processor.

prcst precast.

prdn production.

prdr producer.

P.R.E. Petroleum Refining Engineer.

prec. 1. preceded. **2.** preceding.

precdg preceding.

precp precipitation.

pred. predicate.

pref. 1. preface. **2.** prefaced. **3.** prefatory. **4.** preference. **5.** preferred. **6.** prefix. **7.** prefixed. Also, **pref**

prefab prefabricated.

prelim. preliminary.

prem. premium.

pre•op (prē′op′), preoperative; preoperatively. Also, **pre′-op′.**

prep. 1. preparation. **2.** preparatory. **3.** prepare. **4.** preposition.

Pres. 1. Presbyterian. **2.** President.

pres. 1. present. **2.** presidency. **3.** president.

Presb. Presbyterian.

Presbyt. Presbyterian.

prescr prescription.

pres. part. present participle.

press pressure.

pret. *Grammar.* preterit.

prev. 1. previous. **2.** previously.

PRF 1. Puerto Rican female. **2.** Also, **prf** *Telecommunications.* pulse repetition frequency.

prf. proof. Also, **prf**

prfm performance.

prfrd *Printing.* proofread.

prfrdg *Printing.* proofreading.

prfrdr proofreader.

prft press fit.

prfx prefix.

prgm program.

prgmg *Computers.* programming.

prgmr *Computers.* programmer.

pri primary.

prin. 1. principal. **2.** principally. **3.** principle.

print. printing.

priv. 1. private. **2.** *Grammar.* privative.

priv. pr. privately printed.

prl parallel.

PRM Puerto Rican male.

prm pulse rate modulation.

prm. premium.

prmtr parameter.

prn pseudorandom noise.

p.r.n. (in prescriptions) as the occasion arises; as needed. [from Latin *prō rē nāta*]

prntg printing.

PRO public relations officer. Also, **P.R.O.**

Pro *Biochemistry.* proline.

prob. 1. probable. **2.** probably. **3.** problem.

prob cse probable cause.

proc. 1. procedure. **2.**

proceedings. **3.** process. **4.** proclamation. **5.** proctor.

Prod. *Computers.* Prodigy.

prod. 1. produce. **2.** produced. **3.** producer. **4.** product. **5.** production.

Prof. Professor.

Prof. Eng. Professional Engineer.

Prog. Progressive.

prog. 1. progress. **2.** progressive.

proj project.

PROM (prom), *Computers.* a memory chip whose contents can be programmed by a user or manufacturer. Also, **prom** [*p(rogrammable) r(ead)-o(nly) m(emory)*]

prom. promontory.

pron. 1. *Grammar.* pronominal. **2.** pronoun. **3.** pronounced. **4.** pronunciation.

prop. 1. properly. **2.** property. **3.** proposition. **4.** proprietary. **5.** proprietor.

propr. proprietor.

pros. 1. *Theater.* proscenium. **2.** prosody.

Pros. Atty. prosecuting attorney.

prot protective.

Prot. Protestant.

pro tem. for the time being. [from Latin *pro tempore*]

Prov. 1. Provençal. **2.** Provence. **3.** *Bible.* Proverbs. **4.** Province. **5.** Provost.

prov. 1. province. **2.** provincial. **3.** provisional. **4.** provost.

prox. the next month. [from Latin *proximo*]

prp. 1. present participle. **2.** purpose.

prphl peripheral.

prpsl proposal.

prs. pairs.

prsrz pressurize.

PRT personal rapid transit.

prt print.

prtg printing.

prtl partial.

prtr printer.

Prus. 1. Prussia. **2.** Prussian. Also, **Pruss., Pruss**

prv peak reverse voltage.

prvw preview.

prx prefix.

PS 1. *Linguistics.* phrase structure. **2.** power steering.

ps picosecond; picoseconds.

Ps. *Bible.* Psalm; Psalms. Also, **Psa.**

ps. 1. pieces. **2.** pseudonym.

P.S. 1. passenger steamer. **2.** permanent secretary. **3.** postscript. **4.** Privy Seal. **5.** *Theater.* prompt side. **6.** Public School.

p.s. postscript.

PSA 1. *Medicine.* prostatic specific antigen. **2.** public service announcement.

Psa. *Bible.* Psalms.

p's and q's manners; behavior; conduct. [perhaps from some children's difficulty in distinguishing the two letters]

PSAT Preliminary Scholastic Aptitude Test.

PSB *Printing.* prepress service bureau.

PSC Public Service Commission.

PSD prevention of significant deterioration: used as a standard of measurement by the U.S. Environmental Protection Agency.

PSE Pidgin Sign English.

psec picosecond; picoseconds. Also, **ps**

pseud. 1. pseudonym. 2. pseudonymous.

psf pounds per square foot. Also, **p.s.f.**

PSG 1. platoon sergeant. 2. *Medicine.* polysomnogram.

psgr passenger.

psi pounds per square inch. Also, **p.s.i.**

psia pounds per square inch, absolute.

psid pounds per square inch, differential.

psig pounds per square inch, gauge.

psiv passive.

psm prism.

psnl personal.

PSRO Professional Standards Review Organization. Also, **P.S.R.O.**

P.SS. postscripts. Also, **p.ss.** [from Latin *postscrīpta*]

PST Pacific Standard Time. Also, **P.S.T., p.s.t.**

pst paste.

pstl pistol.

pstn piston.

psvt *Metallurgy.* passivate.

psvtn preservation.

psych. 1. psychological. 2. psychologist. 3. psychology.

psychoanal. psychoanalysis.

psychol. 1. psychological. 2. psychologist. 3. psychology.

Pt *Symbol, Chemistry.* platinum.

pt 1. patient. 2. pint; pints.

Pt. 1. point. 2. port.

pt. 1. part. 2. payment. 3. pint; pints. 4. point. 5. port. 6. *Grammar.* preterit.

P/T part-time. Also, **p/t**

P.T. 1. Also, **PT** Pacific time. 2. Also, **PT** part-time. 3. physical

therapy. 4. physical training. 5. postal telegraph. 6. post town. 7. pupil teacher.

p.t. 1. Pacific time. 2. past tense. 3. post town. 4. for the time being [from Latin *pro tempore*].

PTA 1. Also, **P.T.A.** Parent-Teacher Association. 2. Philadelphia Transportation Authority.

Pta. peseta.

PTC *Biochemistry.* phenylthiocarbamide.

ptc positive temperature coefficient.

ptd painted.

ptfe polytetrafluoroethylene.

ptg. printing.

ptl patrol.

ptly partly.

PTM *Telecommunications.* pulse time modulation. Also, **ptm**

ptn 1. partition. 2. pattern.

PTO 1. Parent-Teacher Organization. 2. Patent and Trademark Office. 3. *Machinery.* power take-off.

P.T.O. 1. Parent-Teacher Organization. 2. Also, **p.t.o.** please turn over (a page or leaf).

pts. points.

PTSD posttraumatic stress disorder.

PTT Post, Telegraph, and Telephone (the government-operated system, as in France or Turkey).

ptt push-to-talk.

PTV public television.

Pty *Australian.* proprietary.

pty party.

Pu *Symbol, Chemistry.* plutonium.

pu 1. Also, **p/u** pick up. 2. power unit. 3. purple.

pub. 1. public. 2. publication. 3. published. 4. publisher. 5. publishing.

publ. 1. public. 2. publication. 3. publicity. 4. published. 5. publisher.

pubn publication.

PUC Public Utilities Commission. Also, **P.U.C.**

P.U.D. pickup and delivery.

pul pulley.

pulsar (pul'sär), pulsating star.

pulv. (in prescriptions) powder. [from Latin *pulvis*]

punc. punctuation.

PUVA (pōō'və), *Medicine.* a therapy for psoriasis combining the drug psoralen and ultraviolet light. [*p*(*soralen*) + *UV-A* ultraviolet light of a wavelength between 320 and 400 nanometers]

pv 1. *Finance.* par value. 2. plan view.

PVA polyvinyl acetate.

PVC polyvinyl chloride. Also, **pvc**

pvnt prevent.

pvntv preventive.

pvt. private.

PW Palau (approved for postal use).

pw 1. plain washer. 2. pulse width.

PWA 1. person with AIDS. 2. Also, **P.W.A.** Public Works Administration.

P wave a longitudinal earthquake wave that is usually the first to be recorded by a seismograph. [*p*(*rimary*) *wave*]

pwb printed-wiring board.

P.W.D. Public Works Department. Also, **PWD**

pwm pulse-width modulation.

pwr power.

pwt pennyweight. Also, **pwt.**

pwtr pewter.

PX post exchange.

P.X. post exchange.

pxt. he or she painted it. [from Latin *pinxit*]

pymt. payment.

PYO pick your own.

pyr pyramid.

---

a b c d e f g h i j k l m n o p **Q** r s t u v w x y z

Q 1. quarterly. 2. *Cards, Chess.* queen.

Q *Symbol.* 1. the 17th in order or in a series, or, when *I* is omitted, the 16th. 2. (*sometimes lowercase*) the medieval Roman numeral for 500. 3. *Biochemistry.* glutamine. 4. *Physics.* heat. 5. *Thermodynamics.* a unit of heat energy, equal to 10^{18} British thermal units (1.055 × 10^{21} joules). 6. *Electronics.* the ratio of the reactance to the resistance of an electric circuit or component. 7. *Biblical Criticism.* the symbol for material common to the Gospels of Matthew and Luke that was not derived from the Gospel of Mark.

Q. 1. quarto. 2. Quebec. 3. Queen. 4. question. 5. (in Guatemala) quetzal; quetzals.

q. 1. farthing. [from Latin *quadrāns*] 2. quart; quarts. 3. query. 4. question. 5. quintal. 6. *Bookbinding.* quire.

QA quality assurance.

Q and A (kyōō' ən ā', ənd), *Informal.* an exchange of questions and answers. Also, **Q&A**

QB 1. *Football.* quarterback. 2. *Chess.* queen's bishop.

Q.B. *British Law.* Queen's Bench.

q.b. *Football.* quarterback.

QBP *Chess.* queen's bishop's pawn.

Q.C. 1. quality control. 2. Quartermaster Corps. 3. Queen's Counsel. Also, **QC**

QCD *Physics.* quantum chromodynamics.

q.d. (in prescriptions) every day. [from Latin *quāque diē*]

qdisc quick disconnect.

qdrnt quadrant.

qdrtr quadrature.

q.e. which is. [from Latin *quod est*]

QED *Physics.* quantum electrodynamics.

Q.E.D. which was to be shown or demonstrated (used especially in

mathematical proofs). [from Latin *quod erat dēmōnstrandum*]

Q.E.F. which was to be done. [from Latin *quod erat faciendum*]

Q.F. quick-firing.

Q fever *Pathology.* an acute, influenzalike disease caused by rickettsia. [abbreviation of *query*]

q.h. (in prescriptions) each hour; every hour. [from Latin *quāque hōrā*]

q.i.d. (in prescriptions) four times a day. [from Latin *quater in diē*]

QKt *Chess.* queen's knight.

QKtP *Chess.* queen's knight's pawn.

ql. quintal.

q.l. (in prescriptions) as much as is desired. [from Latin *quantum libet*]

QLI quality-of-life index. Also, **qli**

qlty. quality.

QM 1. Also, **Q.M.** Quartermaster. 2. *Physics.* quantum mechanics.

q.m. (in prescriptions) every

morning. [from Latin *quoque ma-tutino*]

QMC *Military.* Quartermaster Corps. Also, **Q.M.C.**

QMG Quartermaster-General. Also, **Q.M.G., Q.M.Gen.**

QN *Chess.* queen's knight.

q.n. (in prescriptions) every night. [from Latin *quoque nocte*]

QNP *Chess.* queen's knight's pawn.

QP *Chess.* queen's pawn.

q.p. (in prescriptions) as much as you please. Also, **q. pl.** [from Latin *quantum placet*]

Qq. *Bookbinding.* quartos.

qq. questions.

qq. v. (in formal writing) which (words, things, etc.) see. [from Latin *quae vide*]

QR *Chess.* queen's rook.

qr. 1. farthing. [from Latin *quadrāns*] 2. quarter. 3. *Bookbinding.* quire.

QRP *Chess.* queen's rook's pawn.

qry quarry.

q.s. 1. (in prescriptions) as much

as is sufficient; enough. [from Latin *quantum sufficit*] 2. quarter section.

QSO *Astronomy.* quasi-stellar object.

QSS *Astronomy.* quasi-stellar radio source.

qstn question.

qt. 1. quantity. 2. *plural* **qt., qts.** quart.

q.t. *Informal.* quiet. Also, **Q.T.**

qto. *Bookbinding.* quarto.

qtr. 1. quarter. 2. quarterly.

qty quantity.

qu. 1. quart. 2. quarter. 3. quarterly. 4. queen. 5. query. 6. question.

quad quadrilateral.

quad. 1. quadrant. 2. quadratic.

quadr quadruple.

qual. 1. qualification. qualify. 2. qualitative; quality.

quant. quantitative.

quar. 1. quarter. 2. quarterly.

quart. 1. quarter. 2. quarterly.

quasar (kwā′zär), *Astronomy.* quasi-stellar radio source.

quat. (in prescriptions) four. [from Latin *quattuor*]

Que. Quebec.

ques. question.

quin quintuple.

quinq. (in prescriptions) five. [from Latin *quīnque*]

quint. (in prescriptions) fifth. [from Latin *quīntus*]

quor. (in prescriptions) of which. [from Latin *quōrum*]

quot. 1. quotation. 2. quotient. Also, **quot**

quotid. (in prescriptions) daily. [from Latin *quotīdiē*]

q.v. 1. (in prescriptions) as much as you wish. [from Latin *quantum vīs*] 2. *plural* **qq.v.** (in formal writing) which see. [from Latin *quod vidē*]

QWERTY (kwûr′tē, kwer′-), of or pertaining to a keyboard having the keys in traditional typewriter arrangement, with the letters *q, w, e, r, t,* and *y* being the first six of the top row of alphabetic characters, starting from the left side.

a b c d e f g h i j k l m n o p q R s t u v w x y z

R 1. *Chemistry.* radical. 2. *Math.* ratio. 3. regular: suit or coat size. 4. *Electricity.* resistance. 5. restricted: a rating assigned to a motion picture by the Motion Picture Association of America indicating that children under the age of 17 will not be admitted unless accompanied by an adult. 6. *Theater.* stage right. 7. *Physics.* roentgen. 8. *Chess.* rook.

R *Symbol.* 1. the 18th in order or in a series, or, when *I* is omitted, the 17th. 2. (*sometimes lowercase*) the medieval Roman numeral for 80. 3. *Biochemistry.* arginine. 4. *Physics.* universal gas constant. 5. registered trademark: written as superscript ® following a name registered with the U.S. Patent and Trademark Office.

r 1. radius. 2. *Commerce.* registered. 3. *Electricity.* resistance. 4. *Physics.* roentgen. 5. royal. 6. (in Russia) ruble. 7. *Baseball.* run; runs. 8. (in India, Pakistan, and other countries) rupee.

r *Ecology.* the theoretical intrinsic rate of increase of a population; Malthusian parameter.

R. 1. rabbi. 2. radical. 3. radius. 4. railroad. 5. railway. 6. (in South Africa) rand; rands. 7. Réaumur (temperature). 8. Also, **R** (in prescriptions) take. [from Latin *recipe*] 9. rector. 10. redactor. 11. queen. [from Latin *regina*] 12. Republican. 13. response. 14. king. [from Latin *rex*] 15. river. 16. road. 17. royal. 18. (in Russia) ruble. 19. (in India, Pakistan, and other countries) rupee. 20. *Theater.* stage right.

r. 1. rabbi. 2. railroad. 3. railway. 4. range. 5. rare. 6. *Commerce.* received. 7. recipe. 8. replacing. 9. residence. 10. right. 11. rises.

12. river. 13. road. 14. rod. 15. royal. 16. rubber. 17. (in Russia) ruble. 18. *Baseball.* run; runs. 19. (in India, Pakistan, and other countries) rupee.

RA regular army.

Ra *Symbol, Chemistry.* radium.

R.A. 1. rear admiral. 2. regular army. 3. *Astronomy.* right ascension. 4. royal academician. 5. Royal Academy.

R.A.A.F. Royal Australian Air Force.

rab rabbit.

rad 1. *Math.* radian; radians. 2. radiation absorbed dose. 3. radio. 4. radius.

rad. 1. *Math.* radical. 2. Also, **rd** *Chemistry.* radium. 3. radius. 4. radix.

radar (rā′där), radio detection and ranging.

RADINT radar intelligence.

RAdm rear admiral. Also, **RADM**

radn radiation.

rad opr radio operator.

RAF Royal Air Force. Also, **R.A.F.**

rall. *Music.* rallentando.

RAM (ram), volatile computer memory available for creating, loading, or running programs and for the temporary storage and manipulation of data. [*r(andom)-a(ccess) m(emory)*]

RAM reverse annuity mortgage.

R.A.M. Royal Academy of Music.

R&B rhythm-and-blues. Also, **r&b, R and B**

R&D research and development. Also, **R and D**

R&E research and engineering.

R. & I. 1. king and emperor. [from Latin *Rēx et Imperātor*] 2. queen and empress. [from Latin *Rēgīna et Imperātrīx*]

R and R 1. rest and recreation. 2. rest and recuperation. 3. rest and

rehabilitation. 4. rock-'n'-roll. Also, **R&R**

raser (rā′zər), radio-frequency amplification by stimulated emission of radiation.

RATO (rā′tō), *Aeronautics.* rocket-assisted takeoff.

RB 1. *Sports.* right back. 2. *Football.* right fullback. 3. *Football.* running back.

Rb *Symbol, Chemistry.* rubidium.

RBC red blood cell.

R.B.I. *Baseball.* run batted in; runs batted in. Also, **RBI, rbi, r. b.i.**

rbr rubber.

RC resistance-capacitance.

rc remote control.

R.C. 1. Red Cross. 2. Reserve Corps. 3. Roman Catholic. Also, **RC**

R.C.A.F. Royal Canadian Air Force. Also, **RCAF**

RCB 1. Retail Credit Bureau. 2. *Football.* right cornerback.

RCC Rape Crisis Center.

R.C.Ch. Roman Catholic Church.

rcd. received.

rcdr recorder.

rcht ratchet.

rcl recall.

rclm reclaim.

R.C.M.P. Royal Canadian Mounted Police. Also, **RCMP**

rcn recreation.

R.C.N. Royal Canadian Navy. Also, **RCN**

rcndt recondition.

R.C.P. Royal College of Physicians.

rcpt. 1. receipt. 2. receptacle.

rcptn reception.

R.C.S. Royal College of Surgeons.

Rct 1. receipt. 2. *Military.* recruit. Also, **rct**

RCTL resistor-capacitor-transistor logic.

rcv receive.
rcvd received.
rcvg receiving.
rcvr receiver.
RD 1. Registered Dietician. **2.** rural delivery.
Rd *Symbol, Chemistry.* (formerly) radium.
rd 1. read. **2.** rod; rods.
Rd. Road.
rd. 1. rendered. **2.** road. **3.** rod; rods. **4.** round.
R/D *Banking.* refer to drawer.
R.D. 1. registered dietitian. **2.** Rural Delivery.
RDA 1. (not in technical use) recommended daily allowance. Compare **U.S. RDA. 2.** recommended dietary allowance. Also, **R.D.A.**
RdAc *Symbol, Chemistry.* radioactinium.
RD&D research, development, and demonstration.
RD&E research, development, and engineering.
rdc reduce.
rdcr reducer.
RDD *Marketing.* random digit dialing.
RDF 1. Also, **rdf** radio direction finder. **2.** rapid deployment force.
rdg 1. reading. **2.** rounding.
rdh round head.
rdl radial.
rdm recording demand meter.
rdout readout.
rdr 1. radar. **2.** reader.
RDS *Pathology.* respiratory distress syndrome.
rdsd roadside.
RDT&E research, development, testing, and engineering.
rdtr radiator.
RDX a white, crystalline explosive, $C_3H_6N_6O_6$. [*R(esearch) D(epartment) (E)x(plosive)*, referring to such a department in Woolwich, England]
Re *Symbol, Chemistry.* rhenium.
Re. (in India, Pakistan, and other countries) rupee. Also, **re.**
R/E real estate. Also, **RE**
R.E. 1. real estate. **2.** Reformed Episcopal. **3.** *Football.* right end. **4.** Right Excellent.
r.e. *Football.* right end.
REA Rural Electrification Administration. Also, **R.E.A.**
Rear Adm. Rear Admiral.
reasm reassemble.
reassy reassembly.
Réaum. Réaumur (temperature).
reb. *Basketball.* rebounds.
rec. 1. receipt. **2.** (in prescriptions) fresh. [from Latin *recēns*] **3.** recipe. **4.** record. **5.** recorder. **6.** recording. **7.** recreation.
recalc recalculate.
recd. received. Also, **rec'd.**
recip. 1. reciprocal. **2.** reciprocity.
recirc recirculate.
recit. *Music.* recitative.
recl reclose.
recm recommend.
recog recognition.
recon reconnaissance.
recpt receipt.
Rec. Sec. Recording Secretary. Also, **rec. sec.**
rect. 1. receipt. **2.** rectangle. **3.** rectangular. **4.** (in prescriptions)

rectified. [from Latin *rēctificātus*] **5.** rectifier. **6.** rector. **7.** rectory.
redupl. reduplication.
ref. 1. referee. **2.** reference. **3.** referred. **4.** refining. **5.** reformation. **6.** reformed. **7.** *Music.* refrain. **8.** refund. **9.** refunding.
Ref. Ch. Reformed Church.
ref des reference designation.
refl. 1. reflection. **2.** reflective. **3.** reflex. **4.** reflexive.
Ref. Pres. Reformed Presbyterian.
refr 1. refrigerate. **2.** refrigerator.
Ref. Sp. reformed spelling.
refs. req. references required.
Reg. 1. regiment. **2.** queen [from Latin *rēgīna*].
reg. 1. regent. **2.** regiment. **3.** region. **4.** register. **5.** registered. **6.** registrar. **7.** registry. **8.** regular. **9.** regularly. **10.** regulation. **11.** regulator.
regd. registered.
regen regenerate.
regr. registrar.
regt. 1. regent. **2.** regiment.
reinf reinforce.
REIT (rēt), real-estate investment trust.
rej reject.
rel. 1. relating. **2.** relative. **3.** relatively. **4.** released. **5.** religion. **6.** religious.
relig. religion.
rel. pron. relative pronoun.
REM (rem), rapid eye movement.
rem (rem), *Nucleonics.* the quantity of ionizing radiation whose biological effect is equal to that produced by one roentgen of x-rays. [*r(oentgen) e(quivalent in) m(an)*]
rem remainder.
remitt. remittance.
rep (rep), *Physics.* a unit proposed but not adopted as a supplement to roentgen for expressing dosage of ionizing radiation. [*r(oentgen) e(quivalent) p(hysical)*]
Rep. 1. Representative. **2.** Republic. **3.** Republican.
rep. 1. repair. **2.** repeat. **3.** (in prescriptions) let it be repeated. [from Latin *repetātur*] **4.** report. **5.** reported. **6.** reporter.
repl. 1. replace. **2.** replacement.
repr. 1. represented. **2.** representing. **3.** reprint. **4.** reprinted.
repro 1. reproduce. **2.** reproduction.
rept. report.
Repub. 1. Republic. **2.** Republican.
req. 1. Also, **req** request. **2.** require. **3.** Also, **reqd** required. **4.** requisition.
reqn requisition.
reqt requirement.
RES *Immunology.* reticuloendothelial system.
res 1. resistance. **2.** resistor. **3.** resume.
res. 1. research. **2.** reserve. **3.** residence. **4.** resident; residents. **5.** residue. **6.** resigned. **7.** resolution.
resc rescind.
resid residual.
resln resolution.
resn resonant.

resp. 1. respective. **2.** respectively. **3.** respelled; respelling. **4.** respondent.
Res. Phys. Resident Physician.
restr. 1. restaurant. **2.** restorer.
ret. 1. retain. **2.** retired. **3.** return. **4.** returned.
retd. 1. retained. **2.** retired. **3.** returned.
retn retain.
retr retract.
retro 1. retroactive. **2.** retrograde.
Rev. *Bible.* **1.** Revelation; Revelations. **2.** Reverend.
rev. 1. revenue. **2.** reverse. **3.** review. **4.** reviewed. **5.** revise; revised. **6.** revision. **7.** revolution. **8.** revolving.
Rev. Stat. Revised Statutes.
Rev. Ver. Revised Version (of the Bible).
rew rewind.
RF 1. radiofrequency. **2.** *Baseball.* right field; right fielder.
rf *Baseball.* right field; right fielder.
R.F. Reserve Force.
r.f. 1. range finder. **2.** rapid-fire. **3.** reducing flame. **4.** *Baseball.* right field; right fielder.
R.F.A. Royal Field Artillery.
r.f.b. *Sports.* right fullback. Also, **R.F.B.**
RFC Reconstruction Finance Corporation.
rfc radio-frequency choke.
R.F.D. rural free delivery. Also, **RFD**
RFE Radio Free Europe. Also, **R. F.E.**
rfgt refrigerant.
RFI radio frequency interference.
RFLP (rif'lip'), restriction fragment length polymorphism: a fragment of DNA used to trace family relationships. Also called **riflip.**
rflx reflex.
RFQ *Commerce.* request for quotation.
r.g. *Football.* right guard.
RGB *Television.* red-green-blue.
rgd rigid.
rglr regular.
rglt regulate.
rgltd regulated.
rgltr regulator.
RGNP real gross national product.
rgtr register.
RH *Meteorology.* relative humidity. Also, **rh**
Rh 1. *Physiology.* Rh factor. **2.** *Metallurgy.* Rockwell hardness.
Rh *Symbol, Chemistry.* rhodium.
R.H. Royal Highness.
r.h. right hand. right-handed.
r.h.b. *Football.* right halfback. Also, **RHB, R.H.B.**
rhd railhead.
rheo rheostat.
RHIP rank has its privileges.
Rhn *Metallurgy.* Rockwell hardness number.
Rho. Rhodesia. Also, **Rhod.**
rhomb 1. rhombic. **2.** rhomboid.
RI Rhode Island (for use with ZIP code).
R.I. 1. Queen and Empress. [from Latin *Rēgīna et Imperātrix*] **2.** King and Emperor. [from Latin

Rēx et Imperātor] **3.** Rhode Island.

R.I.B.A. Royal Institute of British Architects.

RICO (rē′kō), Racketeer Influenced and Corrupt Organizations Act.

RIF (rif), **1.** *Military.* a reduction in the personnel of an armed service or unit. **2.** a reduction in the number of persons employed, especially for budgetary reasons. [*R(eduction) I(n) F(orce)*]

R.I.I.A. Royal Institute of International Affairs.

RIP *Computers.* raster image processor.

R.I.P. 1. may he or she rest in peace. [from Latin *requiēscat in pāce*] **2.** may they rest in peace. [from Latin *requiēscant in pāce*] Also, **RIP**

RISC (risk), *Computers.* reduced instruction set computer.

rit. *Music.* ritardando. Also, **ritard.**

riv. river.

RJ *Military.* road junction.

rkt rocket.

RL resistance-inductance.

RLB *Football.* right linebacker.

RLC resistance, inductance, capacitance.

rlct *Electricity.* reluctance.

rld rolled.

R.L.D. retail liquor dealer.

rlf relief.

RLL *Computers.* run-length limited.

R.L.O. returned letter office.

rloc relocate.

rlr roller.

rlse release.

rlt relate.

rltn relation.

rltv relative.

rlv relieve.

rlxn relaxation.

rly relay.

RM (in Germany) reichsmark.

rm. 1. ream. **2.** room.

r.m. (in Germany) reichsmark.

R.M.A. *British.* **1.** Royal Marine Artillery. **2.** Royal Military Academy.

R.M.C. *British.* Royal Military College.

rmd remedy.

rmdr remainder.

rms *Math.* root mean square. Also, **r.m.s.**

R.M.S. 1. Railway Mail Service. **2.** *British.* Royal Mail Service. **3.** *British.* Royal Mail Steamship.

rmt remote.

rmv remove.

rmvbl removable.

Rn *Symbol, Chemistry.* radon.

rn 1. radio navigation. **2.** rain.

R.N. 1. registered nurse. **2.** *British.* Royal Navy.

RNA *Genetics.* ribonucleic acid.

R.N.A.S. *British.* Royal Naval Air Service.

RNase (är′en′ās, -āz), *Biochemistry.* ribonuclease. Also, **RNAase** (är′en′ā′ās, -āz).

RNC Republican National Committee.

rnd. round.

rndm random.

rng range.

rnge range.

rngg ringing.

rngr *Telephones.* ringer.

rnl renewal.

RNP *Biochemistry.* a nucleoprotein containing RNA. [*r(ibo)n(ucleo)p(rotein)*]

R.N.R. *British.* Royal Naval Reserve.

rnwbl renewable.

R.N.W.M.P. *Canadian.* Royal Northwest Mounted Police.

rnwy runway.

rny rainy.

RO. (in Oman) rial omani.

ro. 1. *Bookbinding.* recto. **2.** roan. **3.** rood.

R.O. 1. Receiving Office. **2.** Receiving Officer. **3.** Regimental Order. **4.** *British.* Royal Observatory.

ROA *Accounting.* return on assets.

ROE *Accounting.* return on equity.

R.O.G. *Commerce.* receipt of goods. Also, **ROG, r.o.g.**

ROI return on investment. Also, **R.O.I.**

ROK Republic of Korea.

ROM (rom), computer memory in which program instructions, operating procedures, or other data are permanently stored. [*r(ead)-o(nly) m(emory)*]

Rom. 1. Roman. **2.** Romance. **3.** Romania. **4.** Romanian. **5.** Romanic. **6.** *Bible.* Romans. Also, **Rom** (for defs. 2, 5).

rom. *Printing.* roman.

Rom. Cath. Roman Catholic.

Rom. Cath. Ch. Roman Catholic Church.

RONA *Accounting.* return on net assets.

R.O.P. run-of-paper: a designation specifying that the position of a newspaper or magazine advertisement is to be determined by the publisher.

R.O.R. *Law.* released on own recognizance.

ROS *Computers.* read only storage.

ROT rule of thumb.

rot. 1. rotating. **2.** rotation.

R.O.T.C. (är′ō tē sē′, rot′sē), Reserve Officers Training Corps. Also, **ROTC**

rotr rotator.

Roum. 1. Roumania. **2.** Roumanian.

ROW right of way.

RP 1. *Linguistics.* Received Pronunciation. **2.** repurchase agreement. **3.** *Pathology.* retinitis pigmentosa.

Rp. (in Indonesia) rupiah; rupiahs.

R.P. 1. Reformed Presbyterian. **2.** Regius Professor.

RPG role-playing game.

rpg *Basketball.* rebounds per game.

rplr repeller.

rplsn repulsion.

rplt repellent.

rpm revolutions per minute. Also, **r/min., r.p.m.**

R.P.O. Railway Post Office. Also, **RPO**

RPQ request for price quotation.

rpr repair.

rprt report.

rps revolutions per second. Also, **r.p.s., r/s**

rpt. 1. repeat. **2.** report.

rptn repetition.

rptr repeater.

RPV *Military.* remotely piloted vehicle.

rpvntv rust preventive.

R.Q. *Physiology.* respiratory quotient.

R.R. 1. railroad. **2.** Right Reverend. **3.** rural route.

RRM renegotiable-rate mortgage.

rRNA *Biochemistry.* ribosomal RNA.

R.R.R. return receipt requested (used in registered mail). Also, **RRR**

RRT rail rapid transit.

R.R.T. registered respiratory therapist.

Rs. 1. (in Portugal) reis. **2.** (in India, Pakistan, and other countries) rupees.

R.S. 1. Recording Secretary. **2.** Reformed Spelling. **3.** Revised Statutes. **4.** Royal Society.

r.s. right side.

RSA Republic of South Africa.

rsc rescue.

rsch research.

RSE Received Standard English.

RSFSR Russian Soviet Federated Socialist Republic. Also, **R.S.F.S.R.**

rslvr resolver.

rspd respond.

rsps response.

rspsb responsible.

rspv 1. respective. **2.** responsive.

rsrc resource.

rss root sum square.

rst restore.

rstg roasting.

rstr 1. *Electronics.* raster. **2.** restrain. **3.** restrict.

RSV Revised Standard Version (of the Bible).

rsv reserve.

RSVP (used on invitations) please reply. Also, **R.S.V.P., rsvp, r.s.v.p.** [from French *r(épondez) s(′il) v(ous) p(laît)*]

rsvr reservoir.

RSWC right side up with care.

RT radiotelephone.

rt. 1. rate. **2.** right.

r.t. *Football.* right tackle.

rtcl reticle.

rte. route. Also, **Rte.**

RTF *Genetics.* resistance transfer factor; R factor.

rtf *Computers.* rich-text format.

rtg rating.

Rt. Hon. Right Honorable.

RTL resistor-transistor logic.

rtn return.

rtng retaining.

rtnr retainer.

rtr rotor.

rtrv retrieve.

rtry rotary.

Rts. *Finance.* rights.

rtty radio teletypewriter.

rtw ready-to-wear.

rtz return-to-zero.

Ru *Symbol, Chemistry.* ruthenium.

Rum. 1. Rumania. **2.** Also, **Rum** Rumanian.
Rus. 1. Russia. **2.** Russian.
Russ. 1. Russia. **2.** Russian. Also, **Russ**
RV 1. recreational vehicle. **2.** Revised Version (of the Bible).
rv rear view.
rvam reactive volt-ampere meter.
rvlg revolving.
rvlv revolve.
rvm reactive voltmeter.

RVN Republic of Vietnam.
rvrb reverberation.
rvs 1. reverse. **2.** revise.
rvsbl reversible.
rvs cur reverse current.
rvsn revision.
RVSVP (used on invitations) please reply quickly. Also, **R.V.S. V.P., rvsvp, r.v.s.v.p.** [from French *r(épondez) v(ite) s('il) v(ous) p(laît)*]
rvw review.

R/W right of way.
r/w read/write. Also, **r-w**
R.W. 1. Right Worshipful. **2.** Right Worthy.
Rwy. Railway.
Rx 1. prescription. **2.** (in prescriptions) take. [from Latin, representing an abbreviation of *recipe*] **3.** (in India, Pakistan, and other countries) tens of rupees.
Ry. Railway.

a b c d e f g h i j k l m n o p q r **S** t u v w x y z

S 1. *Baseball.* sacrifice. **2.** satisfactory. **3.** Saxon. **4.** sentence. **5.** short. **6.** *Electricity.* siemens. **7.** signature. **8.** single. **9.** small. **10.** soft. **11.** *Music.* soprano. **12.** South. **13.** Southern. **14.** state (highway). **15.** stimulus. **16.** *Grammar.* subject.
S *Symbol.* **1.** the 19th in order or in a series, or, when *I* is omitted, the 18th. **2.** (*sometimes lowercase*) the medieval Roman numeral for 7 or 70. **3.** second. **4.** *Biochemistry.* serine. **5.** *Thermodynamics.* entropy. **6.** *Physics.* strangeness. **7.** *Chemistry.* sulfur.
s 1. satisfactory. **2.** signature. **3.** small. **4.** soft. **5.** *Music.* soprano. **6.** south. **7.** stere.
s *Symbol.* second.
S. 1. Sabbath. **2.** Saint. **3.** Saturday. **4.** Saxon. **5.** (in Austria) schilling; schillings. **6.** School. **7.** Sea. **8.** Senate. **9.** September. **10.** *British.* shilling; shillings. **11.** (in prescriptions) **a.** mark; write; label. [from Latin *signa*] **b.** let it be written. [from Latin *signētur*] **12.** Signor: an Italian form of address for a man. **13.** Small. **14.** Socialist. **15.** Society. **16.** Fellow. [from Latin *socius*] **17.** (in Peru) sol. **18.** South. **19.** Southern. **20.** (in Ecuador) sucre; sucres. **21.** Sunday.
s. 1. saint. **2.** school. **3.** second. **4.** section. **5.** see. **6.** series. **7.** *British.* shilling; shillings. **8.** sign. **9.** signed. **10.** silver. **11.** singular. **12.** sire. **13.** small. **14.** society. **15.** son. **16.** south. **17.** southern. **18.** species. **19.** statute. **20.** steamer. **21.** stem. **22.** stem of. **23.** substantive.
Sa *Symbol, Chemistry.* (formerly) samarium.
Sa. Saturday.
S/A *Banking.* survivorship agreement.
S.A. 1. Salvation Army. **2.** seaman apprentice. **3.** South Africa. **4.** South America. **5.** South Australia. **6.** corporation [from French *société anonyme* or Spanish *sociedad anónima*].
s.a. 1. semiannual. **2.** sex appeal. **3.** without year or date. [from Latin *sine annō*] **4.** subject to approval.
S.A.A. Speech Association of America.
Sab. Sabbath.

SAC (sak), Strategic Air Command. Also, **S.A.C.**
SAD seasonal affective disorder.
SADD Students Against Drunk Drivers.
S.A.E. 1. self-addressed envelope. **2.** Society of Automotive Engineers. **3.** stamped addressed envelope. Also, **SAE; s.a.e.** (for defs. 1, 3).
SAF single Asian female.
saf safety.
S. Afr. 1. South Africa. **2.** South African.
S. Afr. D. South African Dutch. Also, **SAfrD**
SAG (sag), Screen Actors Guild.
sal. hist. salary history.
SALT (sôlt), Strategic Arms Limitations Treaty.
Salv. Salvador.
SAM, (sam), **1.** shared-appreciation mortgage. **2.** single Asian male. **3.** surface-to-air missile. **4.** Space Available Mail: a special air service for sending parcels to overseas members of the armed forces.
Sam. *Bible.* Samuel.
S. Am. 1. South America. **2.** South American.
S. Amer. 1. South America. **2.** South American.
Saml. Samuel.
san sanitary.
sand. sandwich.
S.&F. *Insurance.* stock and fixtures.
S and H shipping and handling (charges). Also, **S&H**
S&L *Banking.* savings and loan association. Also, **S and L**
S and M sadomasochism; sadism and masochism. Also, **S&M, s&m**
S.&M. *Insurance.* stock and machinery.
S&P Standard & Poor's.
s. & s.c. (of paper) sized and supercalendered.
SANE (sān), a private nationwide organization in the U.S. that opposes nuclear testing and advocates international peace. [official shortening of its by-name *Committee for a Sane Nuclear Policy*]
Sans. Sanskrit.
Sansk. Sanskrit.
Sar. Sardinia.
S.A.R. 1. South African Republic. **2.** Sons of the American Revolution.
SASE self-addressed stamped en-

velope. Also, **sase, S.A.S.E., s.a. s.e.**
Sask. Saskatchewan.
SAT *Trademark.* Scholastic Aptitude Test.
Sat. 1. Saturday. **2.** Saturn.
sat. 1. satellite. **2.** saturate. **3.** saturated.
SATB *Music.* soprano, alto, tenor, bass.
satcom communications satellite.
Sax. 1. Saxon. **2.** Saxony.
Sb *Symbol, Chemistry.* antimony. [from Latin *stibium*]
sb 1. service bulletin. **2.** sideband. **3.** *Optics.* stilb. **4.** stove bolt.
sb. *Grammar.* substantive.
S.B. 1. Bachelor of Science. [from Latin *Scientiae Baccalaureus*] **2.** South Britain (England and Wales).
s.b. *Baseball.* stolen base; stolen bases.
SBA Small Business Administration. Also, **S.B.A.**
SbE south by east.
SBF single black female.
SBIC Small Business Investment Company.
SBLI Savings Bank Life Insurance.
SBM single black male.
SBN *Publishing.* Standard Book Number.
sbstr *Electronics.* substrate.
SbW south by west.
SC 1. security council. **2.** signal corps. **3.** South Carolina (for use with ZIP code). **4.** SportsChannel New England (a cable television channel). **5.** supreme court.
Sc *Symbol, Chemistry.* scandium.
sc solar cell.
Sc. 1. Scotch. **2.** Scotland. **3.** Scots. **4.** Scottish.
sc. 1. scale. **2.** scene. **3.** science. **4.** scientific. **5.** namely. [from Latin *scilicet,* contraction of *scīre licet* it is permitted to know] **6.** screw. **7.** scruple. **8.** he or she carved, engraved, or sculpted it. [from Latin *sculpsit*]
S.C. 1. Sanitary Corps. **2.** Security Council (of the U.N.). **3.** Signal Corps. **4.** South Carolina. **5.** Staff Corps. **6.** Supreme Court.
s.c. *Printing.* **1.** small capitals. **2.** supercalendered.
Scan. Scandinavian.
Scand Scandinavian.
Scand. 1. Scandinavia. **2.** Scandinavian.

s. caps. *Printing.* small capitals.

scav scavenge.

Sc.B. Bachelor of Science. [from Latin *Scientiae Baccalaureus*]

Sc.B.C. Bachelor of Science in Chemistry.

Sc.B.E. Bachelor of Science in Engineering.

scd specification control drawing.

Sc.D. Doctor of Science. [from Latin *Scientiae Doctor*]

Sc.D.Hyg. Doctor of Science in Hygiene.

Sc.D.Med. Doctor of Medical Science.

scdr screwdriver.

sce source.

SCF single Christian female.

scf standard cubic foot.

scfh standard cubic feet per hour

scfm standard cubic feet per minute.

sch socket head.

Sch. (in Austria) schilling; schillings.

sch. 1. schedule. 2. school. 3. schooner.

SCHDM schematic diagram.

sched. schedule.

schem schematic.

Sch.Mus.B. Bachelor of School Music.

sci. 1. science. 2. scientific.

SCID *Pathology.* severe combined immune deficiency.

sci-fi (sī′fī′), science fiction.

scil. to wit; namely. [from Latin *scilicet*]

SCLC Southern Christian Leadership Conference. Also, **S.C.L.C.**

sclr scaler.

SCM single Christian male.

Sc.M. Master of Science. [from Latin *Scientiae Magister*]

scn specification change notice.

scng scanning.

scnr scanner.

S. Con. Res. Senate concurrent resolution.

SCORE (skôr), Service Corps of Retired Executives.

Scot 1. Scots. 2. Scottish.

Scot. 1. Scotch. 2. Scotland. 3. Scottish.

ScotGael Scots Gaelic.

SCOTUS Supreme Court of the United States. Also, **SCUS**

SCR *Electronics.* semiconductor controlled rectifier.

scr. 1. screw. 2. scruple.

Script. 1. Scriptural. 2. Scripture.

scrn screen.

SCS Soil Conservation Service.

SCSI (skuz′ē), a standard for computer interface ports. [*s(mall) c(omputer) s(ystem) i(nterface)*]

sctd scattered.

sctrd scattered.

scty security.

SCU Special Care Unit.

scuba (skōō′bə), self-contained underwater breathing apparatus.

sculp. 1. sculptor. 2. sculptural. 3. sculpture. Also, **sculpt.**

SD 1. sea-damaged. 2. South Dakota (for use with ZIP code). 3. *Statistics.* standard deviation. 4. the intelligence and counterespionage service of the Nazi SS [from German *S(icherheits)d(ienst)*].

sd side.

sd. sound.

S/D 1. school district. 2. *Commerce.* sight draft.

S.D. 1. doctor of science. [from Latin *Scientiae Doctor*] 2. sea-damaged. 3. senior deacon. 4. South Dakota. 5. special delivery. 6. *Statistics.* standard deviation.

s.d. 1. without fixing a day for further action or meeting. [from Latin *sine die*] 2. *Statistics.* standard deviation.

S.D.A. Seventh Day Adventists.

S. Dak. South Dakota.

sdg siding.

SDI Strategic Defense Initiative.

sdl saddle.

sdn sedan.

S. Doc. Senate document.

SDR *Banking.* special drawing rights. Also, **S.D.R.**

sdr sender.

SDS Students for a Democratic Society.

SE 1. southeast. 2. southeastern. 3. *Football.* split end. 4. Standard English. Also, **S.E.**

Se *Symbol, Chemistry.* selenium.

se special equipment.

SEATO (sē′tō), Southeast Asia Treaty Organization (1954–1977).

SEbE southeast by east.

SEbS southeast by south.

SEC Securities and Exchange Commission. Also, **S.E.C.**

sec 1. *Trigonometry.* secant. 2. second. 3. section.

sec⁻¹ *Symbol, Trigonometry.* arc secant.

sec. 1. second. 2. secondary. 3. secretary. 4. section. 5. sector. 6. according to [from Latin *secundum*].

sech *Math.* hyperbolic secant.

sec. leg. according to law. [from Latin *secundum lēgem*]

secs. 1. seconds. 2. sections.

sect. 1. section. 2. sector.

secy secretary. Also, **sec'y**

SEE Signing Essential English.

seg segment.

seismol. 1. seismological. 2. seismology.

SEIU Service Employees International Union.

sel. 1. select. 2. selected. 3. selection; selections. 4. selectivity. 5. selector.

selsyn self-synchronous.

SEM 1. *Optics.* scanning electron microscope. 2. shared equity mortgage.

Sem. 1. Seminary. 2. Semitic. Also, **Sem**

sem. 1. semicolon. 2. seminar. 3. seminary.

semicnd semiconductor.

semih. (in prescriptions) half an hour. [from Latin *sēmihōra*]

sen. 1. senate. 2. senator. 3. senior. Also, **sen**

sens 1. sensitive. 2. sensitivity.

SEP simplified employee pension.

Sep. 1. September. 2. *Bible.* Septuagint.

sep. 1. *Botany.* sepal. 2. separable. 3. separate. 4. separated. 5. separation.

Sept. 1. September. 2. *Bible.* Septuagint.

seq 1. sequence. 2. sequential.

seq. 1. sequel. 2. the following

(one). [from Latin *sequēns*] 3. that which follows. [from Latin *sequitur*]

seqq. the following (ones). [from Latin *sequentia*]

Ser *Biochemistry.* serine.

ser. 1. serial. 2. series. 3. sermon.

Serb. 1. Serbia. 2. Serbian.

serno serial number.

serr serrate.

serv. service.

SES socioeconomic status.

sess. session.

setg setting.

SETI search for extraterrestrial intelligence.

setlg settling.

sew sewer.

SF 1. *Baseball.* sacrifice fly. 2. science fiction. 3. single female. 4. *Finance.* sinking fund.

sf 1. science fiction. 2. *Music.* sforzando.

s-f science fiction.

S.F. 1. San Francisco. 2. senior fellow.

Sfc *Military.* sergeant first class.

sfm surface feet per minute.

SFr. (in Switzerland) franc; francs. Also, **Sfr.**

sft shaft.

sftw software.

sfx suffix.

sfz *Music.* sforzando.

SG 1. senior grade. 2. Secretary General. 3. Solicitor General. 4. Surgeon General.

sg *Grammar.* singular. Also, **sg.**

s.g. specific gravity.

sgd. signed.

sgl single.

SGML *Computers.* Standard Generalized Markup Language.

SGO Surgeon General's Office.

Sgt. Sergeant.

Sgt. Maj. Sergeant Major.

sh 1. sheet. 2. shower. 3. shunt.

s/h 1. shipping/handling. 2. shorthand.

SHA *Navigation.* sidereal hour angle.

Shak. Shakespeare.

Shaks. Shakespeare.

SHAPE (shāp), Supreme Headquarters Allied Powers, Europe. Also, **Shape.**

shcr shipping container.

SHF 1. single Hispanic female. 2. Also, **shf** superhigh frequency.

shl shellac.

shld shield.

shldr shoulder.

shltr shelter.

SHM single Hispanic male.

S.H.M. *Physics.* simple harmonic motion. Also, **s.h.m.**

SHO Showtime (a cable channel).

shp shaft horsepower. Also, **SHP, S.H.P., s.hp., s.h.p.**

shpng shipping.

shpt. shipment.

sht. sheet.

shtc short time constant.

shtdn shutdown.

shtg. shortage.

shthg sheathing.

shv sheave.

shwr shower.

SI International System of Units.

[from French *S(ystème)* *I(nternationale d'unités)*]
Si *Symbol, Chemistry.* silicon.
S.I. Staten Island.
SIC Standard Industrial Classification: a system used by the federal government to classify business activities.
Sic. 1. Sicilian. **2.** Sicily.
SIDS (sidz), sudden infant death syndrome.
SIG special-interest group.
Sig. 1. (in prescriptions) write; mark; label: indicating directions to be written on a package or label for the use of the patient. [from Latin *signā*] **2.** let it be written. [from Latin *signētur*] **3.** Signore; Signori: the Italian form of address for a man.
sig. 1. signal. **2.** signature. **3.** signore; signori: an Italian form of address for a man.
sil silence.
sils silver solder.
sim. 1. similar. **2.** simile. **3.** simulator.
simlt simultaneous.
SIMM (sim), *Computers.* single inline memory module.
sing. singular.
sinh *Math.* hyperbolic sine.
SINS (sinz), *Navigation.* a gyroscopic device indicating the exact speed and position of a vessel. [*s(hip's)* *i(nertial)* *n(avigation)* *s(ystem)*]
SIOP (sī′op), (formerly) the secret U.S. contingency plan for waging a nuclear war with the Soviet Union. [*s(ingle)* *i(ntegrated)* *o(perations)* *p(lan)*]
SIP (sip), **1.** *Computers.* single in-line package. **2.** supplemental income plan.
sit situation.
SI units International System of Units.
S.J. Society of Jesus.
S.J.D. Doctor of Juridical Science. [from Latin *Scientiae Jūridicae Doctor*]
SJF single Jewish female.
SJM single Jewish male.
S.J. Res. Senate joint resolution.
SK Saskatchewan, Canada (for use with ZIP code).
sk. 1. sack. **2.** sink. **3.** sketch.
sklt skylight.
sks seeks.
Skt Sanskrit. Also, **Skt., Skr., Skrt.**
skt 1. skirt. **2.** socket.
sktd skirted.
SL source language.
sl sliding.
s.l. 1. Also, **sl.** salvage loss. **2.** *Bibliography.* without place (of publication). [from Latin *sine locō*]
SLA Special Libraries Association.
S. Lat. south latitude.
Slav Slavic. Also, **Slav.**
slbl soluble.
SLBM 1. sea-launched ballistic missile. **2.** submarine-launched ballistic missile. Also, **S.L.B.M.**
slc slice.
SLCM sea-launched cruise missile. Also, **S.L.C.M.**
sld *Electricity.* single-line diagram.
sld. 1. sailed. **2.** Also, **sld** sealed.

sldr solder.
SLE *Pathology.* systemic lupus erythematosus.
slfcl self-closing.
slfcln self-cleaning.
slfcntd self-contained.
slfprop self-propelled.
slftpg self-tapping.
SLIC (Federal) Savings and Loan Insurance Corporation. Also, **S.L.I.C.**
SLMA Student Loan Marketing Association.
slp slope.
S.L.P. Socialist Labor Party.
SLR *Photography.* single-lens reflex camera.
sls sales.
slt sleet.
sltd slotted.
slv sleeve.
slvg 1. salvage. **2.** sleeving.
slvt solvent.
SM 1. service mark. **2.** single male.
Sm *Symbol, Chemistry.* samarium.
sm some.
sm. small.
S-M 1. Also, **S and M.** sadomasochism. **2.** sadomasochistic. Also, **s-m, S/M, s/m**
S.M. 1. Master of Science. [from Latin *Scientiae Magister*] **2.** sergeant major. **3.** State Militia.
SMA Surplus Marketing Administration.
s-mail (es′māl′), snail mail.
smat see me about this.
S.M.B. Bachelor of Sacred Music.
sm. c. small capital; small capitals. Also, **sm. cap.** or **sm. caps**
SMD *Pathology.* senile macular degeneration.
S.M.D. Doctor of Sacred Music.
smk smoke.
sml small.
smls seamless.
S.M.M. Master of Sacred Music.
S.M.O.M. Sovereign and Military Order of Malta.
SMPTE Society of Motion Picture and Television Engineers.
SMS Synchronous Meteorological Satellite.
SMSA Standard Metropolitan Statistical Area.
smy summary.
SN 1. Secretary of the Navy. **2.** serial number.
Sn *Symbol, Chemistry.* tin. [from Latin *stannum*]
sna•fu (sna fōō′, snaf′ōō), situation normal, all fouled up.
SNCC (snik), a U.S. civil-rights organization formed by students and active especially during the 1960s. [*S(tudent)* *N(onviolent)* *C(oordinating)* *C(ommittee)*]
snd sound.
SNG synthetic natural gas.
snkl snorkel.
snl standard nomenclature list.
sno 1. snow. **2.** stock number.
snr 1. signal-to-noise ratio. **2.** sonar.
sns sense.
snsr sensor.
sntr *Metallurgy.* sintered.
sntzd sensitized.
sny sunny.
SO *Baseball.* strikeout; strikeouts.

so *Electricity.* slow operate (a relay type).
So. 1. South. **2.** Southern.
s/o shipping order.
S.O. 1. Signal Officer. **2.** Special Order. **3.** Standing Order.
s.o. 1. seller's option. **2.** shipping order.
S.O.B. 1. (*sometimes lowercase*) *Slang.* son of a bitch. **2.** Senate Office Building. Also, **SOB**
Soc. 1. socialist. **2.** (*often lowercase*) society. **3.** sociology.
socd source control drawing.
sociol. 1. sociological. **2.** sociology.
socn source control number.
SOF sound on a film.
S. of Sol. *Bible.* Song of Solomon.
sol 1. solenoid. **2.** solid.
Sol. 1. Solicitor. **2.** Song of Solomon.
sol. 1. soluble. **2.** solution.
S.O.L. *Slang.* **1.** strictly out (of) luck. **2.** *Vulgar.* shit out (of) luck. Also, **SOL**
soln solution.
som start of message.
sonar (sō′när), sound navigation ranging.
SOP Standard Operating Procedure; Standing Operating Procedure. Also, **S.O.P.**
sop. soprano.
SOS 1. the letters represented by the radio telegraphic signal (••• – – – •••) used as an internationally recognized call for help. **2.** *Slang.* creamed chipped beef on toast. [*s(hit) o(n a) s(hingle)*]
s.o.s. (in prescriptions) if necessary. [from Latin *sī opus sit*]
SOV language *Linguistics.* a type of language that has basic subject-object-verb order.
Sov. Un. Soviet Union.
SP 1. Shore Patrol. **2.** Specialist. **3.** Submarine Patrol.
sp 1. spare. **2.** special-purpose. **3.** speed
Sp. 1. Spain. **2.** Spaniard. **3.** Also, **Sp** Spanish.
sp. 1. space. **2.** special. **3.** species. **4.** specific. **5.** specimen. **6.** spelling. **7.** spirit.
S.P. 1. Shore Patrol. **2.** Socialist party. **3.** Submarine Patrol.
s.p. without issue; childless. [from Latin *sine prōle*]
Sp. Am. 1. Spanish America. **2.** Spanish American.
Span. 1. Spaniard. **2.** Spanish.
SPAR (spär), (during World War II) a woman enlisted in the women's reserve of the U.S. Coast Guard. Also, **Spar.** [from Latin *S(emper) par(ātus)* "Always ready" the Coast Guard motto]
SpAr Spanish Arabic.
spat silicon precision alloy transistor.
S.P.C.A. Society for the Prevention of Cruelty to Animals.
S.P.C.C. Society for the Prevention of Cruelty to Children.
spchg supercharge.
spcl special.
spcr spacer.
SPDA single-premium deferred annuity.
sp. del. special delivery.

spdl spindle.

spdom speedometer.

spdt sw single-pole double-throw switch.

spec. 1. special. **2.** specially. **3.** specifically. **4.** specification. **5.** specimen.

specif. 1. specific. **2.** specifically.

SPECT (spekt), *Medicine.* single photon emission computed tomography.

Sp.Ed. Specialist in Education.

SPF sun protection factor.

spg spring.

sp. gr. specific gravity. Also, **spg.**

spher spherical.

sp.ht. *Physics.* specific heat.

spkl sprinkler.

spkr speaker.

spkt sprocket.

splc splice.

splt spotlight.

spltr splitter.

sply supply.

spmkt supermarket.

spnr spanner.

spp. species.

sp/ph split/phase.

sppl spark plug.

S.P.Q.R. the Senate and People of Rome. Also, **SPQR** [from Latin *Senātus Populusque Rōmānus*]

spr spring.

S.P.R. Society for Psychical Research.

sprdr spreader.

SPRF single Puerto Rican female.

sprl spiral.

SPRM single Puerto Rican male.

sprt support.

spst sw single-pole single-throw switch.

spt. seaport.

spvn supervision.

Sq. 1. Squadron. **2.** Square (of a city or town).

sq. 1. sequence. **2.** the following; the following one. [from Latin *sequēns*] **3.** squadron. **4.** square.

sqdn squadron.

sq. ft. square foot; square feet.

sq. in. square inch; square inches.

sq. km square kilometer; square kilometers.

SQL *Computers.* structured query language.

sq. m square meter; square meters.

sq. mi. square mile; square miles.

sq. mm square millimeter; square millimeters.

sqq. the following; the following ones. [from Latin *sequentia*]

sq. r. square rod; square rods.

sq. rt. square root.

SQUID (skwid), *Medicine.* superconducting quantum interference device.

sq. yd. square yard; square yards.

SR *Postal Service.* star route.

Sr *Symbol, Chemistry.* strontium.

sr 1. selenium rectifier. **2.** shift register. **3.** *Electricity.* slow release (a relay type). **4.** *Geometry.* steradian.

Sr. 1. Senhor: a Portuguese form of address for a man. **2.** Senior. **3.** Señor: a Spanish form of ad-

dress for a man. **4.** Sir. **5.** *Ecclesiastical.* Sister [from L *Soror*].

S-R stimulus-response.

S.R. Sons of the Revolution.

s.r. semantic reaction.

Sra. 1. Senhora: a Portuguese form of address for a woman. **2.** Señora: a Spanish form of address for a woman.

SRAM short-range attack missile.

SRB solid rocket booster.

SRBM short-range ballistic missile.

srch search.

S. Rept. Senate report.

S. Res. Senate resolution.

srng syringe.

SRO 1. single-room occupancy. **2.** standing room only. Also, **S.R.O.**

SRS air bag. [*s(upplemental) r(estraint) s(ystem)*]

Srta. 1. Senhorita: a Portuguese form of address for a girl or unmarried woman. **2.** Señorita: a Spanish form of address for a girl or unmarried woman.

srvln surveillance.

SS 1. an elite military unit of the Nazi party. [from German *S(c-hutz)s(taffel)*] **2.** *Baseball.* shortstop. **3.** social security. **4.** steamship. **5.** *Football.* strong safety. **6.** supersonic.

ss 1. same size. **2.** (in prescriptions) a half. Also, **ss.** [from Latin *sēmis*] **3.** single-shot.

SS. 1. Saints. [from Latin *sānctī*] **2.** See **SS** (def. 1). **3.** See **ss.** (def. 1).

ss. 1. to wit; namely (used especially on legal documents, to verify the place of action). [from Latin *scīlicet*] **2.** sections. **3.** *Baseball.* shortstop.

S.S. 1. See **SS** (def. 1). **2.** (in prescriptions) in the strict sense. [from Latin *sēnsū strictō*] **3.** steamship. **4.** Sunday School.

SSA 1. Social Security Act. **2.** Social Security Administration.

SSAE stamped self-addressed envelope.

SSB 1. Selective Service Board. **2.** Social Security Board.

ssb single sideband.

SSBN the U.S. Navy designation for the fleet ballistic missile submarine. [*S(trategic) S(ubmarine) B(allistic) N(uclear)*]

SSC *Banking.* small-saver certificate.

S.Sc.D. Doctor of Social Science.

sscr setscrew.

SS.D. Most Holy Lord: a title of the pope. [from Latin *Sānctissimus Dominus*]

S.S.D. Doctor of Sacred Scripture. [from Latin *Sacrae Scrīptūrae Doctor*]

ssdd *Computers.* single-side, double-density.

SSE south-southeast. Also, **S.S.E., s.s.e.**

sse solid-state electronics.

ssf saybolt second furol.

ssfm single-sideband frequency modulation.

sshd *Computers.* single-side, high-density.

SSI 1. *Electronics.* small-scale integration: the technology for concentrating semiconductor devices

in a single integrated circuit. **2.** Supplemental Security Income.

S sleep slow-wave sleep.

SSM surface-to-surface missile.

ssm 1. single-sideband modulation. **2.** solid-state materials.

SSN Social Security number.

SSPE *Pathology.* subacute sclerosing panencephalitis.

SSR Soviet Socialist Republic. Also, **S.S.R.**

ssr solid-state relay.

SSS Selective Service System.

sssd *Computers.* single-side, single-density.

SST supersonic transport.

ssu saybolt second universal.

SSW south-southwest. Also, **S.S.W., s.s.w.**

ST *Real Estate.* septic tank.

St *Physics.* stoke.

st 1. sawtooth. **2.** stere.

St., 1. Saint. **2.** statute; statutes. **3.** Strait. **4.** Street.

st. 1. stanza. **2.** state. **3.** statute; statutes. **4.** *Printing.* let it stand. **5.** stitch. **6.** *British.* stone (weight). **7.** strait. **8.** street.

s.t. short ton.

Sta. 1. station. [from Italian or Spanish *Santa*] **2.** Station.

sta. 1. station. **2.** stationary.

stab. 1. stabilization. **2.** stabilizer. **3.** stable.

stacc. *Music.* with disconnected notes. [from Italian *staccato*]

START (stärt), Strategic Arms Reduction Talks.

stat (stat), *Medicine.* immediately. [from Latin *statim*]

stat. 1. (in prescriptions) immediately. [from Latin *statim*] **2.** statuary. **3.** statue. **4.** status. **5.** statute.

S.T.B. 1. Bachelor of Sacred Theology. [from Latin *Sacrae Theologiae Baccalaureus*] **2.** Bachelor of Theology. [from Latin *Scientiae Theologicae Baccalaureus*]

stbd. starboard.

stbln stabilization.

stby. standby.

STC Society for Technical Communication.

stc sensitivity time control.

stch stitch.

STD sexually transmitted disease.

std. standard. Also, **std**

S.T.D. Doctor of Sacred Theology. [from Latin *Sacrae Theologiae Doctor*]

stdy steady.

stdzn standardization.

Ste. (referring to a woman) Saint. [from French *Sainte*]

sten stencil.

steno. 1. stenographer. **2.** stenographic. **3.** stenography. Also, **stenog.**

ster. sterling.

stereo. stereotype.

St. Ex. Stock Exchange.

stg. 1. stage. **2.** sterling.

stge. storage.

stif stiffener.

stk. stock.

stl 1. steel. **2.** studio-transmitter link.

S.T.L. Licentiate in Sacred Theology.

STM scanning tunneling microscope.

stm 1. steam. **2.** storm.

S.T.M. Master of Sacred Theology.

stmt statement.

stmy stormy.

stng sustaining.

STOL (es'tôl'), a convertiplane that can become airborne after a short takeoff run and has forward speeds comparable to those of conventional aircraft. [*s(hort) t(ake)o(ff and) l(anding)*]

stor storage.

STP 1. standard temperature and pressure. **2.** *Slang.* a potent long-acting hallucinogen. [def. 2 probably after *STP*, trademark of a motor-oil additive]

stp stamp.

stpd stripped.

stpg stepping.

stpr *Telephones.* stepper.

str 1. straight. **2.** strength.

str. 1. steamer. **2.** strait. **3.** *Music.* string; strings.

strat strategic.

stratig. stratigraphy.

strato stratosphere.

strg 1. steering. **2.** strong.

strk stroke.

strl structural.

strln streamline.

strm 1. storeroom. **2.** stream.

strn strainer.

sttg starting.

sttr stator.

stud. student.

STV subscription television; pay television.

stv satellite television.

Su. Sunday.

SUB supplemental unemployment benefits.

sub. 1. submissive. **2.** subordinated. **3.** subscription. **4.** substitute. **5.** suburb. **6.** suburban. **7.** subway.

subassy subassembly.

subch. subchapter.

subj. 1. subject. **2.** subjective. **3.** subjectively. **4.** subjunctive.

submin subminiature.

subq subsequent.

subsc subscription.

subst. 1. *Grammar.* substantive. **2.** substantively. **3.** substitute.

substa substation.

subtr subtract.

suc 1. succeeding. **2.** successor.

suct suction.

suf sufficient.

suf. suffix. Also, **suff.**

Suff. 1. Suffolk. **2.** *Ecclesiastical.* suffragan.

suff. 1. sufficient. **2.** suffix.

Suffr. *Ecclesiastical.* suffragan.

SUM surface-to-underwater missile.

Sun. Sunday. Also, **Sund.**

sup. 1. superior. **2.** superlative. **3.** supine. **4.** supplement. **5.** supplementary. **6.** supply. **7.** above. [from Latin *supra*]

super. 1. superintendent. **2.** superior.

superl. superlative.

supp. 1. supplement. **2.** supplementary. Also, **suppl.**

Supp. Rev. Stat. Supplement to the Revised Statutes.

supr. 1. superior. **2.** suppress. **3.** supreme.

supra cit. cited above. [from Latin *supra citato*]

supsd supersede.

Supt. superintendent. Also, **supt.**

supv supervise.

supvr. supervisor.

surf surface.

surg. 1. surgeon. **2.** surgery. **3.** surgical.

surv. 1. survey. **2.** surveying. **3.** surveyor.

survey. surveying.

susp suspend.

Sv *Physics.* sievert; sieverts.

S.V. Holy Virgin. [from Latin *Sāncta Virgō*]

s.v. 1. under the word (or heading). [from Latin *sub verbo*] **2.** under the word. [from Latin *sub voce*]

SV 40 *Microbiology.* simian virus 40. Also, **SV-40, SV40**

svc. service. Also, **svce.**

SVGA *Computers.* super video graphics adapter.

svgs. savings.

SVO language *Linguistics.* a type of language that has basic subject-verb-object word order.

svr (of weather) severe.

S.V.R. (in prescriptions) rectified spirit of wine (alcohol). [from Latin *spīritus vīnī rēctificātus*]

SVS still-camera video system.

SW 1. shipper's weight. **2.** southwest. **3.** southwestern.

sw 1. short wave. **2.** single weight. **3.** switch.

Sw. 1. Sweden. **2.** Swedish. Also, **Swed**

S/W *Computers.* software.

S.W. 1. South Wales. **2.** southwest. **3.** southwestern.

S.W.A. South West Africa.

Swab. 1. Swabia. **2.** Swabian.

S.W.A.K. sealed with a kiss. Also, **SWAK** (swak).

SWAT (swot), a special section of some law enforcement agencies trained and equipped to deal with especially dangerous or violent situations. Also, **S.W.A.T.** [*S(pecial) W(eapons) a(nd) T(actics)*]

Swazil. Swaziland.

swbd switchboard.

SWbS southwest by south.

SWbW southwest by west.

SWC Southwest Conference.

Swed. 1. Sweden. **2.** Swedish.

SWF single white female.

swg sewage.

S.W.G. standard wire gauge.

swgr switchgear.

Swit. Switzerland.

Switz. Switzerland.

SWM single white male.

SWP Socialist Workers Party.

swp sweep.

swr *Electronics.* standing-wave ratio.

Swtz. Switzerland.

swvl swivel.

sxs *Telephones.* step-by-step: switching system.

syll. 1. syllable. **2.** syllabus.

sym. 1. symbol. **2.** *Chemistry.* symmetrical. **3.** symphony. **4.** symptom.

symm symmetrical.

symp symposium.

syn. 1. synonym. **2.** synonymous. **3.** synonymy. **4.** synthetic.

sync 1. synchronize. **2.** synchronous.

synd. 1. syndicate. **2.** syndicated.

synop. synopsis.

synth synthetic.

synthzr synthesizer.

syr *Pharmacology.* syrup.

Syr. 1. Syria. **2.** Syriac. **3.** Syrian.

SYSOP (sis'op'), systems operator.

syst. system. Also, **sys**

sz. size.

T

T 1. tablespoon; tablespoonful. **2.** tera-; one trillion of a base unit. **3.** *Electricity.* tesla; teslas. **4.** *Physics.* temperature. **5.** time. **6.** (*sometimes lowercase*) T-shirt.

T *Symbol.* **1.** the 20th in order or in a series, or, when *I* is omitted, the 19th. **2.** (*sometimes lowercase*) the medieval Roman numeral for 160. **3.** surface tension. **4.** *Biochemistry.* **a.** threonine. **b.** thymine. **5.** *Photography.* T number. **6.** *Physics.* **a.** tau lepton. **b.**

time reversal. **7.** the launching time of a rocket or missile.

T₁ *Biochemistry.* triiodothyronine.

T₂ *Biochemistry.* thyroxine.

t *Statistics.* **1.** a random variable having Student's t distribution. **2.** the statistic employed in Student's t-test.

T- *U.S. Military.* (in designations of aircraft) trainer: *T-11.*

t- *Chemistry.* tertiary.

T. 1. tablespoon; tablespoonful. **2.** Territory. **3.** Thursday. **4.** Township. **5.** Tuesday.

t. 1. *Football.* tackle. **2.** taken from. **3.** *Commerce.* tare. **4.** teaspoon; teaspoonful. **5.** temperature. **6.** in the time of. [from Latin *tempore*] **7.** *Music.* tenor. **8.** *Grammar.* tense. **9.** territory. **10.** time. **11.** tome. **12.** ton. **13.** town. **14.** township. **15.** transit. **16.** *Grammar.* transitive. **17.** troy.

TA 1. transactional analysis. **2.** transit authority.

Ta *Symbol, Chemistry.* tantalum.

t-a *Immunology.* toxin-antitoxin.

tab 1. tabular. **2.** tabulate.

tab. 1. tables. **2.** (in prescriptions) tablet. [from Latin *tabella*]

tac tactical.

TACAN (tə kan′), tactical air navigation.

tach tachometer.

T/Agt transfer agent. Also, **T. Agt.**

tal. (in prescriptions) such; like this. [from Latin *tālis*]

TAN (tan), tax-anticipation note.

tan *Trigonometry.* tangent.

tan⁻¹ *Trigonometry.* arc tangent.

T&A 1. *Slang.* tits and ass. **2.** tonsillectomy and adenoidectomy. Also, **T and A**

t&a tonsils and adenoids.

T&E travel and entertainment. Also, **T and E**

Tang. Tanganyika.

tanh *Math.* hyperbolic tangent.

TAP Trans-Alaska Pipeline.

TAR (tär), terrain-avoidance radar.

tas true airspeed.

Tasm. Tasmania.

TAT *Psychology.* Thematic Apperception Test.

taut. *Logic.* tautological; tautology.

TB 1. technical bulletin. **2.** *Baseball.* **a.** times at bat. **b.** total bases. **3.** *Boxing.* total bouts. **4.** treasury bill. **5.** tubercle bacillus. **6.** tuberculosis. Also **T.B.**

Tb 1. tubercle bacillus. **2.** tuberculosis.

Tb *Symbol, Chemistry.* terbium.

tb terminal board.

T/B title block.

t.b. 1. tablespoon. **2.** tablespoonful. **3.** *Bookkeeping.* trial balance. **4.** tubercle bacillus. **5.** tuberculosis.

T.B.A. to be announced. Also, **TBA, t.b.a.**

TBD to be determined.

TBI *Automotive.* throttle-body injection.

T-bill (tē′bil′), a U.S. Treasury bill.

tblr tumbler.

tblsht troubleshoot.

T.B.O. *Theater.* total blackout.

T-bond (tē′bond′), a U.S. Treasury bond.

TBS 1. *Nautical.* talk between ships: a radiotelephone for short-range communication between vessels. **2.** Turner Broadcasting System (a cable television channel).

tbs. tablespoon; tablespoonful.

TC 1. Teachers College. **2.** technical circular. **3.** Trusteeship Council (of the United Nations).

Tc *Symbol, Chemistry.* technetium.

tc 1. thermocouple. **2.** time constant.

TCA *Chemistry.* trichloroacetic acid.

TCB taking care of business.

TCBM transcontinental ballistic missile.

TCDD *Pharmacology.* dioxin.

TCE *Chemistry.* trichloroethylene.

tchr. teacher.

tci terrain-clearance indicator.

TCL transistor-coupled logic.

TCP/IP *Computers.* Transfer Control Protocol/Internet Protocol.

TCS traffic control station.

TCTO time-compliance technical order.

TD 1. technical directive. **2.** *Football.* touchdown; touchdowns. **3.** trust deed.

td time delay.

T/D *Banking.* time deposit.

T.D. 1. Traffic Director. **2.** Treasury Department.

tdc 1. *Electricity.* time-delay closing (of contacts). **2.** top dead center.

TDD telecommunications device for the deaf.

tdg twist drill gauge.

TDI temporary disability insurance.

TDL tunnel-diode logic.

TDM *Telecommunications.* time-division multiplex. Also, **tdm**

tdm tandem.

TDN totally digestible nutrients. Also, **t.d.n.**

tdo *Electricity.* time-delay opening (of contacts).

TDOS tape disk operating system.

TDRS Tracking and Data Relay Satellite.

t.d.s. (in prescriptions) to be taken three times a day. [from Latin *ter die sumendum*]

TDTL tunnel-diode transistor logic.

TDY temporary duty.

TE *Football.* tight end.

Te *Symbol, Chemistry.* tellurium.

te thermoelectric.

T/E table of equipment.

tech. 1. technic. **2.** technical. **3.** technology.

technol. technology.

tech. sgt. technical sergeant.

TEE Trans-Europe Express. Also, **T-E-E**

TEFL teaching English as a foreign language.

TEL *Chemistry.* tetraethyl lead.

tel. 1. telegram. **2.** telegraph. **3.** telephone.

telecom telecommunications.

teleg. 1. telegram. **2.** telegraph. **3.** telegraphy.

teleph. telephony.

telesat (tel′ə sat′), telecommunications satellite.

temp. 1. temperature. **2.** temporary. **3.** in the time of [from Latin *tempore*]

ten. 1. tenor. **2.** *Music.* tenuto.

Tenn. Tennessee.

TENS (tenz), *Medicine.* a self-operated portable device used to treat chronic pain by sending electrical impulses through electrodes placed upon the painful area. [*t(ranscutaneous) e(lectrical) n(erve) s(timulator)*]

TEPP *Chemistry.* tetraethyl pyrophosphate.

ter tertiary.

term. 1. terminal. **2.** termination.

terr. 1. Also, **Ter** terrace. **2.** territorial. **3.** territory.

terz terrazzo.

TESL teaching English as a second language.

TESOL (tē′sôl, tes′əl), **1.** teaching English to speakers of other lan-

guages. **2.** Teachers of English to Speakers of Other Languages.

Test. Testament.

test. 1. testator. **2.** testimony.

tetfleyne tetrafluoroethylene.

Teut. 1. Teuton. **2.** Teutonic.

TeV *Physics.* trillion electron-volts. Also, **Tev, tev.**

Tex. 1. Texan. **2.** Texas.

t/f true/false.

TFE *Chemistry.* tetrafluoroethylene; Teflon.

TFN till further notice.

tfr. transfer.

TFT thin-film transistor.

TFX *Military.* (in designations of aircraft) tactical fighter experimental.

TG 1. transformational-generative (grammar). **2.** transformational grammar.

tg *Trigonometry.* tangent.

t.g. *Biology.* type genus.

TGG transformational-generative grammar.

TGIF *Informal.* thank God it's Friday. Also, **T.G.I.F.**

tgl toggle.

tgn *Trigonometry.* tangent.

tgt target.

TGV a high-speed French passenger train. [from French *t(rain à) g(rande) v(itesse)* high-speed train]

Th. Thursday.

T.H. Territory of Hawaii.

Th 227 *Symbol, Chemistry.* radioactinium. Also, **Th-227**

Thai. Thailand.

Th.B. Bachelor of Theology. [from Latin *Theologicae Baccalaureus*]

THC *Pharmacology.* a compound, $C_{21}H_{30}O_2$, the active component in cannabis preparations. [*t(etra)-h(ydro)c(annabinol)*]

thd 1. thread. **2.** total harmonic distortion.

Th.D. Doctor of Theology. [from Latin *Theologicae Doctor*]

theat. 1. theater. **2.** theatrical.

theol. 1. theologian. **2.** theological. **3.** theology.

theor. 1. theorem. **2.** theoretical.

theos. 1. theosophical. **2.** theosophy.

therm. thermometer.

thermodynam. thermodynamics.

Thes. *Bible.* Thessalonians. Also, **Thess.**

T.H.I. temperature-humidity index. Also, **thi**

thkf *Electronics.* thick film.

thkns thickness.

thm *Physics.* therm.

Th.M. Master of Theology.

thml thermal.

thmom thermometer.

thms *Electronics.* thermistor.

thnf *Electronics.* thin film.

thnr thinner.

Thr *Biochemistry.* threonine.

thr threshold.

3b *Baseball.* **1.** third base. **2.** triple (3-base hit).

thrmo thermostat.

throt throttle.

thrt throat.

thstm thunderstorm.

Thu. Thursday.

Thurs. Thursday.

thwr thrower.

thyr *Electronics.* thyristor.

THz terahertz.

Ti *Symbol, Chemistry.* titanium.

TIA *Medicine.* transient ischemic attack.

TIAA Teachers Insurance and Annuity Association of America.

t.i.d. (in prescriptions) three times a day. [from Latin *ter in die*]

tif telephone interference factor.

Tim. *Bible.* Timothy.

TIN (tin), taxpayer identification number.

tinct. *Pharmacology.* tincture.

tip. truly important person.

TIROS (tī′rōs), television and infrared observation satellite.

Tit. *Bible.* Titus.

tit. title.

TKO *Boxing.* technical knockout. Also, **T.K.O.**

tkt. ticket.

TL **1.** target language. **2.** trade-last. **3.** truckload.

Tl *Symbol, Chemistry.* thallium.

TL. (in Turkey) lira; liras.

T/L time loan.

T.L. **1.** Also, **t.l.** trade-last. **2.** *Publishing.* trade list.

TLC tender loving care. Also, **T. L.C., t.l.c.**

tlg telegraph.

tlld total load.

tlmy telemetry.

t.l.o. *Insurance.* total loss only.

TLR *Photography.* twin-lens reflex camera.

tlscp telescope.

TM **1.** technical manual. **2.** trademark. **3.** Transcendental Meditation.

Tm *Symbol, Chemistry.* thulium.

t.m. true mean.

tmbr timber.

TMC The Movie Channel (a cable television channel).

tmd timed.

TMF The Menninger Foundation.

tmfl time of flight.

tmg timing.

TMI Three Mile Island.

TMJ *Anatomy.* temporomandibular joint.

TML **1.** *Chemistry.* tetramethyllead. **2.** three-mile limit.

TMO telegraph money order.

tmpl template.

TMV tobacco mosaic virus.

TN **1.** technical note. **2.** Tennessee (for use with ZIP code).

Tn *Symbol, Chemistry.* thoron.

tn. **1.** ton. **2.** tone. **3.** town. **4.** train.

TNB *Chemistry.* trinitrobenzene, especially the 1,3,5- isomer.

TNF *Biochemistry.* tumor necrosis factor.

tng **1.** tongue. **2.** training.

tnk trunk.

tnl tunnel.

TNN The Nashville Network (a cable television channel).

tnpk. turnpike.

tnsl tensile.

tnsn tension.

TNT **1.** *Chemistry.* a crystalline solid, $C_7H_5N_3O_6$, a high explosive. Also, **tnt,** **T.N.T.** [*t(ri)n(itro)t(oluene)*] **2.** Turner

Network Television (a cable television channel).

tntv tentative.

TO technical order.

T/O table of organization.

T.O. telegraph office. Also, **TO**

t.o. **1.** turnover. **2.** turn over.

TOA time of arrival.

Tob. *Bible.* Tobit.

TOEFL (tō′fəl), Test of English as a Foreign Language.

TOFC trailer-on-flatcar.

tol tolerance.

tonn. tonnage.

TOP temporarily out of print.

topog. **1.** topographical. **2.** topography.

torentl torrential.

torndo tornado.

TOS tape operating system.

tot. total.

TOW (tō), a U.S. Army antitank missile, steered to its target by two thin wires connected to a computerized launcher. [*t(ube-launched,) o(ptically-guided,) w(ire-tracked missile)*]

tox. toxicology.

tp. **1.** telephone. **2.** test point. **3.** township. **4.** troop.

t.p. **1.** title page. **2.** *Surveying.* turning point.

TPA *Biochemistry.* tissue plasminogen activator.

TPC The Peace Corps.

tpd **1.** tapped. **2.** tons per day.

tpg tapping.

tph tons per hour.

tpi **1.** teeth per inch. **2.** turns per inch.

tpk. turnpike. Also, **Tpk**

tpl triple.

tpm tons per minute.

TPN *Medicine.* total parenteral nutrition.

TPR *Medicine.* temperature, pulse, respiration.

tpr **1.** taper. **2.** teleprinter.

tptg tuned-plate tuned-grid.

t quark *Physics.* top quark.

TR technical report.

tr. **1.** *Commerce.* tare. **2.** tincture. **3.** trace. **4.** train. **5.** transaction. **6.** *Grammar.* transitive. **7.** translated. **8.** translation. **9.** translator. **10.** transpose. **11.** transposition. **12.** treasurer. **13.** *Music.* trill. **14.** troop. **15.** trust. **16.** trustee.

T.R. **1.** in the time of the king. [from Latin *tempore rēgis*] **2.** Theodore Roosevelt. **3.** tons registered. **4.** trust receipt.

TRA Thoroughbred Racing Association.

TRACON (trā′kon), terminal radar approach control.

trad. tradition; traditional.

traj trajectory.

tranfd. transferred.

trans. **1.** transaction; transactions. **2.** transfer. **3.** transferred. **4.** transformer. **5.** transit. **6.** *Grammar.* transitive. **7.** translated. **8.** translation. **9.** translator. **10.** transparent. **11.** transportation. **12.** transpose. **13.** transverse.

transa transaction.

transl. **1.** translated. **2.** translation. **3.** translator.

transp transparent.

trav. **1.** traveler. **2.** travels.

trb treble.

trd tread.

treas. **1.** treasurer. **2.** treasury. Also, **Treas.**

treasr. treasurer.

TRF *Biochemistry.* thyrotropin-releasing factor.

trf **1.** transfer. **2.** tuned radio frequency.

trfc traffic.

TRH *Biochemistry.* thyrotropin-releasing hormone.

trh truss head.

trib. tributary.

trid. (in prescriptions) three days. [from Latin *trīduum*]

trig. **1.** trigger. **2.** trigonometric. **3.** trigonometrical. **4.** trigonometry.

trip. **1.** triple. **2.** triplicate.

trit. *Pharmacology.* triturate.

trk **1.** track. **2.** truck.

trkg tracking.

Trl. (used in addresses) trail.

trlg trailing.

trlr trailer.

trly trolley.

TRM trademark.

trm training manual.

trmr trimmer.

trn train.

tRNA *Genetics.* transfer RNA.

trnbkl turnbuckle.

trnd turned.

trngl triangle.

trnr trainer.

trnspn transportation.

trntbl turntable.

TRO *Law.* temporary restraining order.

troch. (in prescriptions) troche; tablet or lozenge.

trop. **1.** tropic. **2.** tropical.

tropo troposphere.

Trp *Biochemistry.* tryptophan.

trp *Military.* troop.

trq torque.

trsbr transcriber.

trscb transcribe.

trtd treated.

trtmt treatment.

trun trunnion.

trx triplex.

TS **1.** tool shed. **2.** top secret. **3.** Also, **t.s.** *Slang* (*vulgar*). tough shit. **4.** transsexual. Also, **T.S.**

T.Sgt. technical sergeant.

TSH *Biochemistry.* thyroid-stimulating hormone.

tsi tons per square inch.

TSO time-sharing option.

TSP *Chemistry.* sodium phosphate.

tsp. **1.** teaspoon. **2.** teaspoonful.

TSR a computer program with any of several ancillary functions, usually held resident in RAM for instant activation while one is using another program. [*t(erminate and) s(tay) r(esident)*]

TSS *Pathology.* toxic shock syndrome.

tsteq test equipment.

tstg testing.

tstr tester.

tstrz transistorize.

TSWG Television and Screen Writers' Guild.

TT Trust Territories.

TTL transistor-transistor logic.

ttl total.

TTL meter *Photography.* through-the-lens meter.

TTS teletypesetter.

TTY teletypewriter.

Tu *Chemistry.* (formerly) thulium.

Tu. Tuesday.

T.U. 1. thermal unit. **2.** toxic unit. **3.** Trade Union. **4.** Training Unit.

t.u. trade union.

Tue. Tuesday.

tun tuning.

Tun. Tunisia.

tung tungsten.

tur turret.

turb turbine.

turbo alt turbine alternator.

turbo gen turbine generator.

Turk. 1. Turkey. **2.** Also, **Turk** Turkish.

TV 1. Also, **tv** television. **2.** transvestite.

TVA 1. tax on value added: a sales tax imposed by member nations of the Common Market on imports from other countries. **2.** Tennessee Valley Authority.

tvi television interference.

tvl travel.

tvlg traveling.

tvlr traveler.

tvm transistor voltmeter.

TVP *Trademark.* a brand of textured soy protein.

tw typewriter.

T.W.I.M.C. to whom it may concern.

2b *Baseball.* **1.** double (2-base hit). **2.** second base.

2WD two-wheel drive.

twp. township. Also, **Twp.**

twr tower.

twt traveling-wave tube.

TWU Transport Workers Union of America.

TWX (*often* twiks), a teletypewriter service operating in the United States and Canada. [*t(eletype)w(riter)* *(e)x(change service)*]

twy taxiway.

TX Texas (for use with ZIP code).

txtl textile.

Ty. Territory.

typ. 1. typical. **2.** typographer. **3.** typographic; typographical. **4.** typography.

typo. 1. typographer. **2.** typographic; typographical. **3.** typographical error. **4.** typography.

typog. 1. typographer. **2.** typographic; typographical. **3.** typography.

typstg typesetting.

typw. 1. typewriter. **2.** typewritten.

tyvm thank you very much.

---

a b c d e f g h i j k l m n o p q r s t **U** v w x y z

U *Symbol.* **1.** the 21st in order or in a series, or, when *I* is omitted, the 20th. **2.** *Chemistry.* uranium. **3.** *Biochemistry.* uracil. **4.** *Thermodynamics.* internal energy. **5.** *British.* a designation for motion pictures determined as being acceptable for viewing by all age groups. **6.** kosher certification.

u (unified) atomic mass unit.

U. 1. uncle. **2.** and. [from German *und*] **3.** uniform. **4.** union. **5.** unit. **6.** united. **7.** university. **8.** unsatisfactory. **9.** upper.

u. 1. and. [from German *und*] **2.** uniform. **3.** unit. **4.** unsatisfactory. **5.** upper.

U.A.E. United Arab Emirates. Also, **UAE**

UAM underwater-to-air missile.

u. & l.c. *Printing.* upper and lowercase.

U.A.R. United Arab Republic.

UART (yōō′ärt), *Computers.* universal asynchronous receiver-transmitter.

UAW United Automobile Workers. Also, **U.A.W.**

U.B. United Brethren.

ubl unbleached.

U.C. 1. Upper Canada. **2.** under construction. **3.** undercover.

u.c. 1. *Music.* una corda: with the soft pedal depressed. **2.** *Printing.* upper case.

ucc Universal copyright convention.

UCR Uniform Crime Report.

U.C.V. United Confederate Veterans.

U/D under deed.

u.d. (in prescriptions) as directed. [from Latin *ut dictum*]

UDAG (yōō′dag), a federal program providing funds to local governments or private investors for urban redevelopment projects. [*U(rban) D(evelopment) A(ction) G(rant)*]

UDC Universal Decimal Classification.

U.D.C. United Daughters of the Confederacy.

udtd updated.

U.F.C. United Free Church (of Scotland).

UFD user file directory.

UFO (yōō′ef′ō′ *or, sometimes,* yōō′fō), unidentified flying object.

UFT United Federation of Teachers. Also, **U.F.T.**

UFW United Farm Workers of America.

ugnd underground.

UHF ultrahigh frequency. Also, **uhf**

UHT ultrahigh temperature.

UI unemployment insurance.

u.i. as below. [from Latin *ut infra*]

UIT unit investment trust.

UJT unijunction transistor.

U.K. United Kingdom.

UL Underwriters' Laboratories (used especially on labels for electrical appliances approved by this safety-testing organization).

ULCC a supertanker with a deadweight capacity of over 250,000 tons. [*u(ltra) l(arge) c(rude) c(arrier)*]

ulf ultralow frequency.

ULMS underwater long-range missile system.

ULSI *Computers.* ultra large-scale integration.

ult. 1. Also, **ult** ultimate. **2.** ultimately. **3.** Also, **ulto.** the last month. [from Latin *ultimo*]

umbc umbilical cord.

Umbr. Umbrian.

UMT universal military training.

umus unbleached muslin.

UMW United Mine Workers.

UN 1. unified. **2.** Also, **U.N.** United Nations.

un union.

unan. unanimous.

unauth unauthorized.

UNC 1. Unified coarse (a thread measure). **2.** Also, **U.N.C.** United Nations Command.

unc. *Numismatics.* uncirculated.

UNCF United Negro College Fund.

UNCIO United Nations Conference on International Organization.

unclas unclassified.

uncond unconditional.

und under.

undc undercurrent.

undef undefined.

undetm undetermined.

undf underfrequency.

undld underload.

undv undervoltage.

UNEF 1. Unified extra-fine (a thread measure). **2.** United Nations Emergency Force.

UNESCO (yōō nes′kō), United Nations Educational, Scientific, and Cultural Organization.

UNF Unified fine (a thread measure).

unfin unfinished.

ung. (in prescriptions) ointment. [from Latin *unguentum*]

ungt. (in prescriptions) ointment. [from Latin *unguentum*]

Unh *Symbol, Chemistry, Physics.* unnilhexium.

UNICEF (yōō′nə sef′), United Nations Children's Fund. [*U(nited) N(ations) I(nternational) C(hildren's) E(mergency) F(und)* (an earlier official name)]

unif uniform.

unifet unipolar field-effect transistor.

Unit. Unitarian.

Univ. 1. Universalist. **2.** University.

univ. 1. universal. **2.** universally. **3.** university.

UNIVAC (yōō′ni vak′), Universal Automatic Computer.

unk unknown.

unl unloading.

unlim unlimited.

unlkg unlocking.

unmkd unmarked.

unmtd unmounted.

Unp *Symbol, Chemistry, Physics.* unnilpentium.

Unq *Symbol, Chemistry, Physics.* unnilquadium.

unrgltd unregulated.

UNRRA (un′rə), United Nations Relief and Rehabilitation Administration. Also, **U.N.R.R.A.**

UNRWA United Nations Relief and Works Agency.

uns unserviceable.

UNSC United Nations Security Council.

unstpd. unstamped.

untrtd untreated.

u/o used on.

up. **1.** underproof (alcohol). **2.** Also, **upr** upper.

U.P. Upper Peninsula (of Michigan).

UPC Universal Product Code.

updt update.

UPI United Press International. Also, **U.P.I.**

uprt upright.

UPS **1.** *Computers.* uninterruptible power supply. **2.** *Trademark.* United Parcel Service.

UPSW Union of Postal Service Workers.

UPU Universal Postal Union.

U.P.W.A. United Packinghouse Workers of America.

upwd upward.

UR unsatisfactory report.

ur urinal.

Ur. Uruguay.

URE Undergraduate Record Examination.

urol. **1.** urological. **2.** urologist. **3.** urology.

Uru. Uruguay.

US **1.** *Psychology.* unconditioned stimulus. **2.** *Photography.* Uniform Systems: lens-stop marking. **3.** United States. **4.** United States highway (used with a number): *US 66.*

U.S. **1.** Uncle Sam. **2.** United Service. **3.** United States.

u.s. **1.** where mentioned above. [from Latin *ubi suprā*] **2.** as above: a formula in judicial acts, directing that what precedes be reviewed. [from Latin *ut suprā*]

USA **1.** United States of America. **2.** United States Army. **3.** USA Network (a cable television channel). **4.** United Steelworkers of America.

U.S.A. **1.** Union of South Africa. **2.** United States of America. **3.** United States Army.

USAEC United States Atomic Energy Commission.

U.S.A.F. United States Air Force. Also, **USAF**

USAFI United States Armed Forces Institute.

U.S.A.F.R. United States Air Force Reserve. Also, **USAFR**

USAID United States Aid for International Development.

USAR United States Army Reserve.

usb upper sideband.

USBC United States Bureau of the Census.

USBLS United States Bureau of Labor Statistics.

USBP United States Border Patrol.

U.S.C. **1.** United States Code. **2.** United States of Colombia. Also, **USC**

U.S.C.A. United States Code Annotated. Also, **USCA**

U.S.C.&G.S. United States Coast and Geodetic Survey.

USCC United States Chamber of Commerce.

USCG United States Coast Guard. Also, **U.S.C.G.**

USCRC **1.** United States Citizens Radio Council. **2.** United States Civil Rights Commission.

USCS United States Civil Service.

U.S.C. Supp. United States Code Supplement.

USDA United States Department of Agriculture. Also, **U.S.D.A.**

USDE **1.** United States Department of Education. **2.** United States Department of Energy.

USDHEW United States Department of Health Education and Welfare.

USDHUD United States Department of Housing and Urban Development.

USDI United States Department of the Interior.

USDJ United States Department of Justice.

USDL United States Department of Labor.

USDT United States Department of Transportation.

USECC United States Employees' Compensation Commission.

USES United States Employment Service. Also, **U.S.E.S.**

USG United States Gauge.

U.S.G.A. United States Golf Association. Also, **USGA**

USGPO United States Government Printing Office.

USGS United States Geological Survey.

USHA United States Housing Authority. Also, **U.S.H.A.**

USIA United States Information Agency. Also, **U.S.I.A.**

USIS United States Information Service. Also, **U.S.I.S.**

USITC United States International Trade Commission.

U.S.L.T.A. United States Lawn Tennis Association. Also, **USLTA**

USM **1.** underwater-to-surface missile. **2.** United States Mail. **3.** United States Marines. **4.** United States Mint. Also, **U.S.M.**

U.S.M.A. United States Military Academy. Also, **USMA**

USMC **1.** United States Marine Corps. **2.** United States Maritime Commission. Also, **U.S.M.C.**

USMS United States Maritime Service.

USN United States Navy. Also, **U. S.N.**

USNA **1.** United States National Army. **2.** United States Naval Academy. Also, **U.S.N.A.**

USNG United States National Guard. Also, **U.S.N.G.**

USNR United States Naval Reserve. Also, **U.S.N.R.**

USO United Service Organizations. Also, **U.S.O.**

USOC United States Olympic Committee.

U.S.P. United States Pharmacopeia. Also, **U.S. Pharm.**

uspd underspeed.

USPHS United States Public Health Service. Also, **U.S.P.H.S.**

USPO **1.** United States Patent Office. **2.** United States Post Office. Also, **U.S.P.O.**

USPS United States Postal Service. Also, **U.S.P.S.**

USR United States Reserves. Also, **U.S.R.**

USRC United States Reserve Corps. Also, **U.S.R.C.**

U.S. RDA *Nutrition.* United States recommended daily allowance.

U.S.S. **1.** United States Senate. **2.** United States Service. **3.** United States Ship. **4.** United States Steamer. **5.** United States Steamship. Also, **USS**

U.S.S.B. United States Shipping Board. Also, **USSB**

U.S.S.Ct. United States Supreme Court.

U.S.S.R. Union of Soviet Socialist Republics. Also, **USSR**

U.S.S.S. United States Steamship. Also, **USSS**

USTA United States Trademark Association.

USTC United States Tariff Commission.

USTS United States Travel Service: part of the Department of Commerce.

usu. **1.** usual. **2.** usually.

U.S.V. United States Volunteers. Also, **USV**

USW ultrashort wave.

usw and so forth; etc. Also, **u. s.w.** [from German *und so weiter*]

USWAC United States Women's Army Corps.

usz undersize.

UT **1.** Also, **u.t.** universal time. **2.** Utah (for use with ZIP code).

Ut. Utah.

U/T under trust.

UTC universal time coordinated.

utend. (in prescriptions) to be used. [from Latin *ütendum*]

UTI urinary tract infection.

util 1. Also, **util.** utility. **2.** utilization.

utn utensil.

U.T.W.A. United Textile Workers of America. Also, **UTWA**

UUM underwater-to-underwater missile.

UV ultraviolet. Also, **U.V.**

UV filter *Photography.* ultraviolet filter.

UVM universal vendor marking.

U/W under will.

U/w underwriter. Also, **u/w**

u/w used with.

uwtr underwater.

ux. *Chiefly Law.* wife. [from Latin *uxor*]

V 1. vagabond. 2. variable. 3. *Math.* vector. 4. velocity. 5. verb. 6. victory. 7. *Electricity.* volt; volts. 8. volume. 9. vowel.

V *Symbol.* 1. the 22nd in order or in a series, or, when *I* is omitted, the 21st. 2. (*sometimes lowercase*) the Roman numeral for five. 3. *Chemistry.* vanadium. 4. *Biochemistry.* valine. 5. *Physics.* electric potential. 6. (especially during World War II) the symbol of Allied victory.

v 1. variable. 2. velocity. 3. *Crystallography.* vicinal. 4. victory. 5. *Electricity.* volt; volts. 6. voltage.

V. 1. valve. 2. Venerable. 3. verb. 4. verse. 5. version. 6. versus. 7. very. 8. Vicar. 9. vice. 10. see. [from Latin *vidē*] 11. Village. 12. violin. 13. Virgin. 14. Viscount. 15. vision. 16. visual acuity. 17. *Grammar.* vocative. 18. voice. 19. volume.

v. 1. valve. 2. (in personal names) van. 3. vector. 4. vein. 5. ventral. 6. verb. 7. verse. 8. version. 9. *Printing.* verso. 10. versus. 11. very. 12. vicar. 13. vice. 14. see. [from Latin *vidē*] 15. village. 16. violin. 17. vision. 18. *Grammar.* vocative. 19. voice. 20. volt. 21. voltage. 22. volume. 23. (in personal names) von.

VA 1. Veterans Administration. 2. Virginia (for use with ZIP code). 3. Also, **va** *Electricity.* volt-ampere; volt-amperes.

Va. Virginia.

V.A. 1. Veterans Administration. 2. Vicar Apostolic. 3. Vice-Admiral. 4. (Order of) Victoria and Albert. 5. visual aid.

v.a. 1. verb active. 2. *Grammar.* verbal adjective.

vac. 1. vacant. 2. vacation. 3. vacuum.

vacc. vaccination.

V. Adm. Vice-Admiral.

Val *Biochemistry.* valine.

val. 1. valentine. 2. valley. 3. valuation. 4. value. 5. valued.

valdtn validation.

vam voltammeter.

var. 1. variable. 2. variant. 3. variation. 4. variety. 5. variometer. 6. various.

varhm var-hour meter.

variac (vâr′ē ak′), variable-voltage transformer.

varistor (vâr′ə stər), voltage-variable resistor.

varitran (vâr′ə tran′), variable-voltage transformer.

VAT (vē′ā′tē′, vat), value-added tax.

Vat. Vatican.

v. aux. auxiliary verb.

vb. 1. verb. 2. verbal.

VBE vernacular black English.

vbtm verbatim.

VC 1. venture capital. 2. Vietcong. 3. vital capacity.

V.C. 1. venture capital. 2. Veteri-

nary Corps. 3. Vice-Chairman. 4. Vice-Chancellor. 5. Vice-Consul. 6. Victoria Cross. 7. Vietcong.

vcl vehicle centerline.

vco voltage-controlled oscillator.

VCR videocassette recorder.

vctr vector.

VD venereal disease. Also, **V.D.**

vd void.

v.d. various dates.

V-Day (vē′dā′), a day of final military victory. [*V(ictory) Day*]

V.D.M. Minister of the Word of God. [from Latin *Verbī Deī Minister*]

vdr voltage-dependent resistor: varistor.

VDT *Computers.* 1. video display terminal. 2. *Chiefly British.* visual display terminal.

VDU *Computers.* visual display unit.

V-E Day (vē′ē′), May 8, 1945, the day of victory in Europe for the Allies. [*V(ictory in) E(urope) Day*]

veg. vegetable.

veh vehicle.

vel. *Printing.* 1. vellum. 2. velocity.

Ven. 1. Venerable. 2. Venice.

Venez. Venezuela.

vent. 1. ventilate. 2. ventilation. 3. ventilator. 4. venture.

ver. 1. verse; verses. 2. version.

verif verification.

vers. *Trigonometry.* versed sine.

verst versatile.

vert. 1. vertebra. 2. vertebrate. 3. vertical.

vet. 1. veteran. 2. veterinarian. 3. veterinary.

vet. med. veterinary medicine.

vet. sci. veterinary science.

VF 1. *Botany.* a designation applied to various plant varieties, indicating resistance to verticillium wilt and fusarium wilt. 2. *Numismatics.* very fine. 3. *Television.* video frequency. 4. visual field. 5. voice frequency.

vf 1. variable frequency. 2. voice frequency.

vfc voice-frequency carrier.

VFD volunteer fire department.

vfo variable-frequency oscillator.

VFR visual flight rules.

V.F.W. Veterans of Foreign Wars of the United States. Also, **VFW**

VG very good.

V.G. Vicar-General.

v.g. for example. [from Latin *verbī gratiā*]

VGA *Computers.* video graphics adapter.

VHF very high frequency. Also, **vhf, V.H.F.**

VHS *Trademark.* Video Home System: a format for recording and playing VCR tape, incompatible with other formats.

VI Virgin Islands (for use with ZIP code).

Vi *Symbol, Chemistry.* virginium.

vi variable interval.

V.I. 1. Vancouver Island. 2. Virgin Islands.

v.i. 1. intransitive verb. 2. see below. [from Latin *vidē infrā*]

Via. viaduct (in addresses).

vib vibration.

Vic. 1. Vicar. 2. Vicarage. 3. Victoria.

vic. vicinity.

vice pres. vice president. Also, **Vice Pres.**

Vict. 1. Victoria. 2. Victorian.

vid. 1. see. [from Latin *vidē*] 2. Also, **vid** video.

vidf video frequency.

vil. village.

v. imp. verb impersonal.

VIN vehicle identification number.

vin. (in prescriptions) wine. [from Latin *vīnum*]

VIP (vē′ī′pē′), *Informal.* very important person. Also, **V.I.P.**

Virg. Virginia.

v. irr. irregular verb.

Vis. 1. Viscount. 2. Viscountess. 3. vista (in addresses).

vis. 1. visibility. 2. visual.

visc viscosity

Visc. 1. Viscount. 2. Viscountess.

Visct. 1. Viscount. 2. Viscountess.

VISTA (vis′tə), a national program in the U.S., sponsored by ACTION, for sending volunteers into poor areas to teach various job skills. [*V(olunteers) i(n) S(ervice) t(o) A(merica)*]

vitr vitreous.

viz. (used to introduce examples, etc.) namely. [from Latin *videlicet*]

VJ (vē′jā′), *Informal.* 1. Also, **V.J.** video jockey. 2. a video journalist.

V-J Day (vē′jā′), August 15, 1945, the day Japan accepted the Allied surrender terms. [*V(ictory over) J(apan) Day*]

VL Vulgar Latin.

v.l. variant reading. [from Latin *varia lectio*]

VLA *Astronomy.* Very Large Array.

vla very low altitude.

VLBI *Astronomy.* very long baseline interferometry.

VLCC a supertanker with a deadweight capacity of up to 250,000 tons. [*V(ery) L(arge) C(rude) C(arrier)*]

VLDL *Biochemistry.* very-low-density lipoprotein.

VLF very low frequency. Also, **vlf**

vlmtrc volumetric.

vlr very long range.

VLSI *Electronics.* very large scale integration: the technology for concentrating many thousands of semiconductor devices on a single integrated circuit.

vm velocity modulation.

V.M.D. Doctor of Veterinary Medicine. [from Latin *Veterināriae Medicīnae Doctor*]

v.n. verb neuter.

vo. *Printing.* verso.

V.O. very old (used especially to indicate the age of whiskey or brandy, usually 6 to 8 years old).

VOA 1. Also, **V.O.A.** Voice of America. **2.** Volunteers of America.

voc. *Grammar.* vocative.

vocab. vocabulary.

voc. ed. vocational education.

vodat (vō′dat), voice-operated device for automatic transmission.

vogad (vō′gad), voice-operated gain-adjusting device.

vol. 1. volcano. **2.** volume. **3.** volunteer.

VO language *Linguistics.* a type of language that has direct objects following the verb. [*V(erb)-O(bject)*]

vom volt-ohm-milliammeter.

VOR *Navigation.* omnirange. [*v(ery high frequency) o(mni) r(ange)*]

vordme vhf omnirange distance-measuring equipment.

vou. voucher.

VOX (voks), a device in certain types of telecommunications equipment, that converts an incoming voice or sound signal into an electrical signal. [acronym from *voice-operated keying,* altered to conform to Latin *vōx* voice]

vox pop. the voice of the people. [from Latin *vox populi*]

VP 1. verb phrase. **2.** Also, **vp, v-p** vice president.

vp vapor pressure.

V.P. Vice President. Also, **V. Pres.**

v.p. passive verb. [from Latin *verbum passīvum*]

vprs voltage-regulated power supply.

vprz vaporize.

VR 1. virtual reality. **2.** voltage regulator.

vr 1. variable response. **2.** voltage regulator.

V.R. Queen Victoria. [from Latin *Victōria Rēgīna*]

v.r. reflexive verb. [from Latin *verbum reflexīvum*]

V region *Immunology.* variable region.

V. Rev. Very Reverend.

vrfy verify.

vris *Electricity.* varistor.

VRM variable-rate mortgage.

vs. 1. verse. **2.** versus.

V.S. Veterinary Surgeon.

v.s. see above. [from Latin *vide supra*]

vsb vestigial sideband.

vsbl visible.

vsd variable-speed drive.

vsm vestigial-sideband.

V. S. O. (of brandy) very superior old.

VSO language *Linguistics.* a type of language that has basic verb-subject-object word order.

V.S.O.P. very superior old pale (used especially to indicate a type of aged brandy).

VSR very special reserve (a classification of fortified wines).

vss. versions.

vstbl vestibule.

vstm valve stem.

V/STOL (vē′stôl′), *Aeronautics.*

vertical and short takeoff and landing.

VSWR *Electronics.* voltage standing-wave ratio. Also, **vswr**

VT Vermont (for use with ZIP code).

Vt. Vermont.

v.t. transitive verb. [from Latin *verbum trānsitīvum*]

V.T.C. 1. Volunteer Training Corps. **2.** voting trust certificate.

Vte. Vicomte.

Vtesse. Vicomtesse.

VT fuze a variable time fuze.

vtm voltage-tunable magnetron.

VTO *Aeronautics.* vertical takeoff.

VTOL (vē′tôl′), *Aeronautics.* a convertiplane capable of taking off and landing vertically, having forward speeds comparable to those of conventional aircraft. [*v(ertical) t(ake)o(ff and) l(anding)*]

VTR *Television.* videotape recorder.

vtvm vacuum-tube voltmeter.

vu *Audio.* volume unit. Also, **VU**

Vul. Vulgate (bible).

vulc vulcanize.

Vulg. Vulgate (bible).

vulg. 1. vulgar. **2.** vulgarly.

VU meter a meter used with sound-reproducing or recording equipment that indicates average sound levels.

vv. 1. verses. **2.** violins.

v.v. vice versa.

V. V. O. (of brandy) very, very old.

V. V. S. (of brandy) very very superior.

V.W. Very Worshipful.

a b c d e f g h i j k l m n o p q r s t u v **W** x y z

W 1. watt; watts. **2.** west. **3.** western. **4.** white. **5.** wide. **6.** widowed. **7.** width. **8.** withdrawn; withdrew. **9.** withheld.

W *Symbol.* **1.** the 23rd in order or in a series, or, when *I* is omitted, the 22nd. **2.** *Chemistry.* tungsten. [from German *Wolfram*] **3.** *Biochemistry.* tryptophan.

w 1. *Baseball.* walk. **2.** watt; watts. **3.** withdrawn; withdrew. **4.** withheld.

W. 1. Wales. **2.** warden. **3.** warehouse. **4.** Washington. **5.** watt; watts. **6.** Wednesday. **7.** weight. **8.** Welsh. **9.** west. **10.** western. **11.** width. **12.** *Physics.* work.

w. 1. warden. **2.** warehouse. **3.** water. **4.** watt; watts. **5.** week; weeks. **6.** weight. **7.** west. **8.** western. **9.** wide. **10.** width. **11.** wife. **12.** with. **13.** won. **14.** *Physics.* work. **15.** wrong.

w/ with.

WA 1. Washington (for use with ZIP code). **2.** *Banking.* withholding agent.

W.A. 1. West Africa. **2.** Western Australia. **3.** *Marine Insurance.* with average.

WAAC (wak), **1. a.** Women's

Army Auxiliary Corps: founded during World War II. **b.** a member of the Women's Army Auxiliary Corps. **2.** *British.* **a.** Women's Army Auxiliary Corps: founded in 1917. **b.** a member of the Women's Army Auxiliary Corps. Also, **W.A.A.C.**

WAAF Women's Auxiliary Air Force.

waf width across flats.

W. Afr. 1. West Africa. **2.** West African.

WAFS Women's Auxiliary Ferrying Squadron. Also, **W.A.F.S.**

WAIS (wās for def. 1), **1.** Wechsler Adult Intelligence Scale. **2.** *Computers.* wide-area information server.

WAIS-R (wās′är′), Wechsler Adult Intelligence Scale-Revised.

Wal. 1. Wallachian. 2. Walloon.

WAM wraparound mortgage.

WAN (wan), wide-area network.

w. & f. (in shipping) water and feed.

WAP Women Against Pornography.

war. warrant.

warrty. warranty. Also, **warr**

Wash. Washington.

WASP (wosp), **1.** *Sometimes Disparaging and Offensive.* white Anglo-Saxon Protestant. Also, **Wasp 2.** a member of the Women's Air Force Service Pilots (in World War II).

WATS (wots), a bulk-rate long-distance telephone service. [*W(ide) A(rea) T(elecommunications) S(ervice)*]

WAVAW Women Against Violence Against Women.

Wb *Electricity.* weber; webers.

wb 1. wet bulb. **2.** workbench.

W/B waybill. Also, **W.B.**

w.b. 1. warehouse book. **2.** water ballast. **3.** waybill. **4.** westbound.

WBA World Boxing Association.

wba wideband amplifier.

wbfp *Real Estate.* wood-burning fireplace.

wbg webbing.

WbN west by north.

WbS west by south.

WC water closet.

W.C. 1. water closet. **2.** west central.

w.c. 1. water closet. **2.** without charge.

W.C.T.U. Women's Christian Temperance Union.

WD wiring diagram.

wd 1. *Stock Exchange.* when distributed. **2.** width. **3.** wind. **4.** wood. **5.** word.

wd. 1. ward. **2.** word.

W/D *Banking.* withdrawal.

w/d withdrawn.

W.D. War Department.

WDC War Damage Corporation.

wdg winding.

wdo window.

wea weather.

WEAL Women's Equity Action League.

Wed. Wednesday.

West. western. Also, **west.**

Westm. Westminster.

WF 1. wind force. **2.** withdraw failing.

wf *Printing.* wrong font. Also, **w.f.**

wfr wafer.

WFTU World Federation of Trade Unions. Also, **W.F.T.U.**

wg 1. waveguide. **2.** wing.

W.G. 1. water gauge. **2.** *Commerce.* weight guaranteed. **3.** wire gauge. Also, **w.g.**

W. Ger. 1. West Germanic. **2.** West Germany.

WGmc West Germanic. Also, **W. Gmc.**

WH *Banking.* withholding. Also, **w/h**

Wh watt-hour; watt-hours. Also, **wh, whr**

WHA World Hockey Association.

whf. wharf.

whl wheel.

WHO World Health Organization.

whr. watt-hour; watt-hours.

whse. warehouse. Also, **whs.**

whsle. wholesale.

whs. stk. warehouse stock.

wht white.

WI Wisconsin (for use with ZIP code).

wi *Stock Exchange.* when-issued. Also, **w.i.**

W.I. 1. West Indian. **2.** West Indies.

WIA *Military.* wounded in action.

wid. 1. widow. **2.** widower.

WIMP (wimp), *Physics.* any of a group of weakly interacting elementary particles characterized by relatively large masses. [*W(eakly) I(nteracting) M(assive) P(article)*]

WIP 1. work in process. **2.** work in progress. Also, **W.I.P.**

wip work in progress.

Wis. Wisconsin. Also, **Wisc.**

WISC (wisk), Wechsler Intelligence Scale for Children.

WISC-R (wisk′är′), Wechsler Intelligence Scale for Children-Revised.

Wisd. *Bible.* Wisdom of Solomon.

wk. 1. week. **2.** work.

wkg working.

wkly. weekly.

wks workshop.

wl wavelength.

WLB War Labor Board.

wlb wallboard.

wld welded.

WLF Women's Liberation Front.

w. long. west longitude.

Wm. William.

w/m *Commerce.* weight and/or measurement.

WMC War Manpower Commission.

wmk. watermark.

WMO World Meteorological Organization.

wmwhl wormwheel.

wnd wound.

wndr winder.

WNW west-northwest.

WO 1. wait order. **2.** War Office. **3.** Warrant Officer. Also, **W.O.**

w/o without.

w.o.b. *Commerce.* washed overboard.

w.o.c. without compensation.

WP word processing.

wp waste pipe.

wp. *Baseball.* wild pitch; wild pitches.

W.P. 1. weather permitting. **2.** wire payment. **3.** working pressure. Also, **WP, w.p.**

WPA Work Projects Administration: a former federal agency (1935–43), originally, Works Progress Administration.

WPB War Production Board. Also, **W.P.B.**

WPBL Women's Professional Basketball League.

wpg waterproofing.

WPI wholesale price index.

wpm words per minute.

wpn weapon.

WPPSI (wip′sē), Wechsler Preschool and Primary Scale of Intelligence.

wps words per second.

Wr *Medicine.* Wassermann reaction.

wr 1. washroom. **2.** wrench. **3.** writer.

w.r. 1. warehouse receipt. **2.** *Insurance.* war risk.

WRA War Relocation Authority.

WRAC *British.* Women's Royal Army Corps. Also, **W.R.A.C.**

WRAF (raf), *British.* Women's Royal Air Force. Also, **W.R.A.F.**

wrb wardrobe.

wrk work.

wrkg wrecking.

wrn warning.

wrngr wringer.

W.R.N.S. *British.* Women's Royal Naval Service.

wrnt. warrant.

wrpg warping.

W.R.S.S.R. White Russian Soviet Socialist Republic.

W-R star *Astronomy.* Wolf-Rayet star.

wrtr writer.

WS weapon system.

W.S. West Saxon.

WSA War Shipping Administration.

wshg washing.

wshld windshield.

wshr washer.

WSW west-southwest.

wt. weight.

WTA 1. Women's Tennis Association. **2.** World Tennis Association.

wtd wanted.

wtg 1. waiting. **2.** weighting.

wtr water.

wtrprf waterproof.

wtrtt watertight.

wtrz winterize.

WV West Virginia (for use with ZIP code).

W.Va. West Virginia.

wvfm waveform.

W.V.S. *British.* Women's Voluntary Service.

WW 1. World War. **2.** *Real Estate.* wall-to-wall. Also, **W/W**

ww 1. wirewound. **2.** *Stock Exchange.* with warrants (offered to the buyer of a given stock or bond).

WWI World War I.

WWII World War II.

w/wo with or without.

WWW *Computers.* World Wide Web (part of Internet).

WY Wyoming (for use with ZIP code).

Wy. Wyoming.

Wyo. Wyoming.

WYSIWYG (wiz′ē wig′), *Computers.* of, pertaining to, or noting a screen display that shows text exactly as it will appear in printed output. [*w(hat) y(ou) s(ee) i(s) w(hat) y(ou) g(et)*]

---

abcdefghijk l m n o p q r s t u v w **X Y Z**

X 1. experimental. **2.** extra. **3.** extraordinary.

X *Symbol.* **1.** the 24th in order or in a series, or, when *I* is omitted, the 23rd. **2.** (*sometimes lowercase*) the Roman numeral for 10. **3.** Christ. **4.** Christian. **5.** cross. **6.** *Electricity.* reactance. **7.** *Slang.* a ten-dollar bill. **8.** (in the U.S.) a rating of the Motion Picture Association of America for movies with subject matter that is suitable for adults only. **9.** (in Great Britain) a designation for a film recommended for adults only. **10.** a person, thing, agency, factor, etc., of unknown identity. **11.** *Chemistry.* (formerly) xenon.

x 1. *Finance.* without. [from Latin *ex*] **2.** excess. **3.** *Stock Exchange.*

a. (of stock trading) ex dividend; without a previously declared dividend. **b.** (of bond trading) ex interest; without accrued interest. **4.** experimental. **5.** extra.

x *Symbol.* **1.** an unknown quantity or a variable. **2.** (used at the end of letters, telegrams, etc., to indicate a kiss.) **3.** (used to indicate multiplication) times: 8×8

= *64.* **4.** (used between figures indicating dimensions) by: *3" × 4".* **5.** power of magnification: *a 50x telescope.* **6.** (used as a signature by an illiterate person.) **7.** cross. **8.** crossed with. **9.** (used to indicate a particular place or point on a map or diagram.) **10.** out of; foaled by: *Flag-a-way x Merrylegs.* **11.** (used to indicate choice, as on a ballot, examination, etc.) **12.** (used to indicate an error or incorrect answer, as on a test.) **13.** *Math.* (in Cartesian coordinates) the x-axis. **14.** *Chess.* captures. **15.** a person, thing, agency, factor, etc., of unknown identity.

xarm crossarm.

xbar *Telephones.* crossbar.

xbra crossbracing.

xbt *Telecommunications.* crossbar tandem.

xc *Stock Exchange.* without coupon. Also, **xcp**

X-C cross-country.

xcl *Insurance.* excess current liabilities.

xconn *Telephones.* crossconnection.

xcvr transceiver.

xcy cross-country.

xd *Stock Exchange.* ex dividend. See **x** (def. 3a). Also, **xdiv.**

xdcr transducer.

Xe *Symbol, Chemistry.* xenon.

XF *Numismatics.* extra fine.

xfmr *Electronics.* transformer.

xfr transfer.

xhair crosshair.

xhd crosshead.

xhvy extra heavy.

x in *Stock Exchange.* ex interest. See **x** (def. 3b).

xing crossing.

XL 1. extra large. **2.** extra long.

xmsn transmission.

xmt transmit.

xmtd *Electronics.* transmitted.

xmtg *Electronics.* transmitting.

xmtr *Electronics.* transmitter.

Xn. Christian.

Xnty. Christianity.

xpl explosive.

xpndr transponder.

x pr *Stock Exchange.* without privileges.

xprt transport.

xpt *Electricity.* crosspoint.

xptn transportation.

XQ cross question. Also, **xq**

xr *Stock Exchange.* ex rights; without rights.

xref cross reference.

XS extra small.

xsect cross section.

xstg extra strong.

xstr transistor.

Xt. Christ.

xtal *Electronics.* crystal.

xtalk *Telephones.* crosstalk.

Xtian. Christian.

xtlo crystal oscillator.

Xty. Christianity.

xvs transverse.

XX powdered sugar.

XXL extra, extra large.

XXXX confectioners' sugar.

xya *Math.* x-y axis.

xyv *Math.* x-y vector.

Y (wī), *Informal.* YMCA, YWCA, YMHA, or YWHA.

Y (in Japan) yen.

Y *Symbol.* **1.** the 25th in order or in a series, or, when *I* is omitted, the 24th. **2.** (*sometimes lowercase*) the medieval Roman numeral for 150. **3.** (*sometimes lowercase*) *Electricity.* admittance. **4.** *Chemistry.* yttrium. **5.** *Biochemistry.* tyrosine.

y *Symbol, Math.* **1.** an unknown quantity. **2.** (in Cartesian coordinates) the y-axis.

y. 1. yard; yards. **2.** year; years.

YA young adult.

YAG (yag), a synthetic yttrium aluminum garnet, used for infrared lasers and as a gemstone. [y(*ttrium*) a(*luminum*) g(*arnet*)]

yap young aspiring professional.

Yb *Symbol, Chemistry.* ytterbium.

Y.B. yearbook. Also, **YB**

Y.C.L. Young Communist League.

ycw you can't win.

YD (in the People's Democratic Republic of Yemen) dinar; dinars.

yd. yard; yards.

yd³ *Symbol.* cubic yard.

yds. yards.

yel yellow.

yeo. yeomanry.

YHA Youth Hostels Association.

YHVH *Judaism.* a transliteration of the Tetragrammaton, the four-letter name of God. Also, **YHWH, JHVH, JHWH** [from Hebrew *yhwh* God]

YIG (yig), a synthetic yttrium iron garnet, used in electronics in filters and amplifiers. [y(*ttrium*) i(*ron*) g(*arnet*)]

YMCA Young Men's Christian Association. Also, **Y.M.C.A.**

Y.M.Cath.A. Young Men's Catholic Association.

YMHA Young Men's Hebrew Association. Also, **Y.M.H.A.**

y.o. year old; years old.

y.o.b. year of birth. Also, **YOB**

Y.P.S.C.E. Young People's Society of Christian Endeavor.

yr. 1. year; years. **2.** your.

yrbk. yearbook.

yrs. 1. years. **2.** yours.

YT Yukon Territory, Canada (for use with ZIP code).

Y.T. Yukon Territory.

YTD *Accounting.* year to date.

Yugo. Yugoslavia.

yuppie (yup′ē), (*sometimes capital*) a young, ambitious, educated city dweller who has a professional career and an affluent lifestyle. Also, **yuppy.** [y(*oung*) u(*rban*) p(*rofessional*) + -*ie*]

YWCA Young Women's Christian Association. Also, **Y.W.C.A.**

YWHA Young Women's Hebrew Association. Also, **Y.W.H.A.**

Z 1. *Astronomy.* zenith distance. **2.** zone.

Z *Symbol.* **1.** the 26th in order or in a series, or, when *I* is omitted, the 25th. **2.** (*sometimes lowercase*) the medieval Roman numeral for 2000. **3.** *Chemistry, Physics.* atomic number. **4.** *Electricity.* impedance.

z zone.

z *Symbol, Math.* **1.** an unknown quantity or variable. **2.** (in Cartesian coordinates) the z-axis.

z. zero.

Z⁰ *Symbol, Physics.* Z-zero particle.

ZBB zero-base budgeting.

Zech. *Bible.* Zechariah.

ZEG zero economic growth.

Zeph. *Bible.* Zephaniah.

ZI *Military.* Zone of the Interior.

ZIF (zif), *Computers.* zero insertion force.

ZIP code (zip), *Trademark.* a system used to facilitate delivery of U.S. mail, consisting of five or nine digits. [Z(*one*) I(*mprovement*) P(*lan*)]

ZIP + 4 (zip′ plus′ fôr′, fōr′), a ZIP code of nine digits.

Zn *Symbol, Chemistry.* zinc.

zn zone.

zod. zodiac.

zof zone of fire.

zoochem. zoochemistry.

zool. 1. zoological. **2.** zoologist. **3.** zoology.

ZPG zero population growth.

Zr *Symbol, Chemistry.* zirconium.

ZZ zigzag approach.

zz zigzag.

Zz. ginger. Also, **zz.** [from Latin *zingiber*]

abbrev.

Ready Reference Guide

World Time Differences[†]

Amsterdam	6:00 P.M.	London	5:00 P.M.
Athens	7:00 P.M.	Madrid	6:00 P.M.
Bangkok	12:00 Mid.	Manila	1:00 A.M.[*]
Berlin	6:00 P.M.	Mexico City	6:00 P.M.
Bombay	10:30 P.M.	Montreal	12:00 Noon
Brussels	6:00 P.M.	Moscow	8:00 P.M.
Buenos Aires	2:00 P.M.	Paris	6:00 P.M.
Cape Town	7:00 P.M.	Prague	6:00 P.M.
Dublin	5:00 P.M.	Rio de Janeiro	2:00 P.M.
Havana	12:00 Noon	Rome	6:00 P.M.
Istanbul	7:00 P.M.	Shanghai	1:00 P.M.[*]
Lima	12:00 Noon	Stockholm	6:00 P.M.
Sydney (N.S.W.)	3:00 A.M.[*]	Warsaw	6:00 P.M.

[†]at 12:00 noon Eastern Standard time
[*]morning of the following day

U.S. Time Differences[†]

Tokyo	2:00 A.M.[*]	Zurich	6:00 P.M.
Atlanta	12:00 Noon	Los Angeles	9:00 A.M.
Baltimore	12:00 Noon	Memphis	11:00 A.M.
Boston	12:00 Noon	Miami	12:00 Noon
Buffalo	12:00 Noon	Milwaukee	11:00 A.M.
Chicago	11:00 A.M.	Minneapolis	11:00 A.M.
Cincinnati	12:00 Noon	Nashville	11:00 A.M.
Cleveland	12:00 Noon	New York	12:00 Noon
Columbus	12:00 Noon	New Orleans	11:00 A.M.
Dallas	11:00 A.M.	Omaha	11:00 A.M.
Denver	10:00 A.M.	Philadelphia	12:00 Noon
Des Moines	11:00 A.M.	Phoenix	10:00 A.M.
Detroit	12:00 Noon	Pittsburgh	12:00 Noon
El Paso	10:00 A.M.	Salt Lake City	10:00 A.M.
Honolulu	7:00 A.M.	San Diego	9:00 A.M.
Houston	11:00 A.M.	San Francisco	9:00 A.M.
Indianapolis	12:00 Noon	Seattle	9:00 A.M.
Juneau	8:00 A.M.	St. Louis	11:00 A.M.

[†]at 12:00 noon Eastern Standard time

reference

Distances Between U.S. Cities

	Atlanta	Chicago	Dallas	Denver	Los Angeles	New York	St. Louis	Seattle
Atlanta	—	592	738	1,421	1,981	762	516	2,354
Boston	946	879	1,565	1,786	2,739	184	1118	2,831
Chicago	592	—	857	909	1,860	724	251	1,748
Cincinnati	377	255	870	1,102	1,910	613	550	2,003
Cleveland	587	307	1,080	1,216	2,054	458	558	2,259
Dallas	738	857	—	683	1,243	1,391	547	2,199
Denver	1,421	909	683	—	838	1,633	781	1,074
Detroit	619	247	1,045	1,156	2,052	486	463	1,947
El Paso	1,293	1,249	543	554	702	1,902	1,033	1,373
Kansas City	745	405	452	552	1,360	1,117	229	1,626
Los Angeles	1,981	1,860	1,243	838	—	2,624	1,589	956
Miami	614	1,199	1,405	1,911	2,611	1,106	1,123	2,947
Minneapolis	942	350	860	840	1,768	1,020	492	1,398
New Orleans	427	860	437	1,120	1,680	1,186	609	2,608
New York	762	724	1,381	1,633	2,624	—	888	2,418
Omaha	1,016	424	617	485	1,323	1,148	394	1,533
Philadelphia	667	671	1,303	1,578	2,467	95	841	2,647
Pittsburgh	536	461	1,318	1,349	2,157	320	568	2,168
St. Louis	516	251	547	781	1,589	888	—	1,890
San Francisco	2,308	1,856	1,570	956	327	2,580	1,916	687
Seattle	2,354	1,748	2,199	1,074	956	2,418	1,890	—
Washington, D.C.	547	600	1,183	1,519	2,426	215	719	2,562

Major American Holidays

New Year's Day	January 1	Labor Day	First Monday in September
Martin Luther King Day	January 15[1]	Columbus Day	October 12[4]
Inauguration Day	January 20	Veterans Day	November 11
Lincoln's Birthday	February 12[2]	Election Day	Tuesday after first Monday in November
Washington's Birthday	February 22[2]		
Good Friday	Friday before Easter	Thanksgiving Day	Fourth Thursday in November
Memorial Day	May 30[3]	Christmas Day	December 25
Independence Day	July 4		

[1]officially observed on 3rd Monday in January
[2]officially observed as Presidents' Day on 3rd Monday in February
[3]officially observed on last Monday in May
[4]officially observed on 2nd Monday in October

Guide to Punctuation

There is a considerable amount of variation in punctuation practices. At one extreme are writers who use as little punctuation as possible. At the other extreme are writers who use too much punctuation in an effort to make their meaning clear. The principles presented here represent a middle road. As in all writing, consistency of style is essential.

The punctuation system is presented in four charts. Since punctuation marks are frequently used in more than one way, some marks appear on more than one chart. Readers who are interested in the various uses of a particular mark can scan the left column of each chart to locate relevant sections.

1. Sentence-Level Punctuation

	Guidelines	Examples
.	Ordinarily an independent clause is made into a sentence by beginning it with a capital letter and ending it with a period.	Some of us still support the mayor. Others think he should retire. There's only one solution. We must reduce next year's budget.
,	Independent clauses may be combined into one sentence by using the words *and, but, yet, or, not, for,* and *so.* The first clause is usually, but not always, followed by a comma.	The forecast promised beautiful weather, but it rained every day. Take six cooking apples and put them into a flameproof dish.
. **,**	The writer can indicate that independent clauses are closely connected by joining them with a semicolon.	Some of us still support the mayor; others think he should retire. There was silence in the room; even the children were still.
. **.**	When one independent clause is followed by another that explains or exemplifies it, they can be separated by a colon. The second clause may or may not begin with a capital letter.	There's only one solution: we must reduce next year's budget. The conference addresses a basic question: How can we take the steps needed to protect the environment?
? **.**	Sentences that ask a question should be followed by a question mark.	Are they still planning to move to Houston? What is the population of Norway?
! **.**	Sentences that express strong feeling may be followed by an exclamation mark.	Watch out! That's a stupid thing to say!
. **?** **:** **!** **.**	End-of-sentence punctuation is sometimes used after groups of words that are not independent clauses. This is especially common in advertising and other writing that seeks to reflect the rhythms of speech.	Somerset Estates has all the features you've been looking for. Like state-of-the-art facilities. A friendly atmosphere. And a very reasonable price. Sound interesting? Phone today!

785

2. Separating Elements in Clauses

When one of the elements in a clause is compounded—that is, when there are two or more subjects, predicates, objects, and so forth—punctuation is necessary.

Guidelines	Examples
When two elements are compounded, they are usually joined together with a word such as *and* or *or* without any punctuation. Occasionally more than two elements are joined in this way.	Haiti and the Dominican Republic share the island of Hispaniola. Tuition may be paid by check or charged to a major credit card. I'm taking history and English and biology this semester.
) Compounds that contain more than two elements are called series. Commas are used to separate items in a series, with a word such as *and* or *or* usually occurring between the last two items.	England, Scotland, and Wales share the island of Great Britain. Environmentally conscious businesses use recycled paper, photocopy on both sides of a sheet, and use ceramic cups. We frequently hear references to government of the people, by the people, for the people.
• **)** When the items in a series are very long or have internal punctuation, separation by commas can be confusing, and semicolons may be used instead.	Next year, they plan to open stores in Pittsburgh, Pennsylvania; Cincinnati, Ohio; and Baltimore, Maryland. Students were selected on the basis of grades; tests of vocabulary, memory, and reading; and teacher recommendations.

Note: Some writers omit the final comma when punctuating a series, and newspapers and magazines often follow this practice. Book publishers and educators, however, usually follow the practice recommended above.

3. Quotations

Quotations are used for making clear to a reader which words are the writer's and which have been borrowed from someone else.

Guidelines	Examples
" " When writers use the exact words of someone else, they must use quotation marks to set them off from the rest of the text.	In 1841, Ralph Waldo Emerson wrote, "I hate quotations. Tell me what you know."
Indirect quotations—in which writers report what someone else said without using the exact words—should not be set off by quotation marks.	Emerson said that he hated quotations and that writers should instead tell the reader what they themselves know.
When quotations are longer than two or three lines, they are often placed on separate lines. Sometimes shorter line length and/or smaller type is also used. When this is done, quotation marks are not used.	In his essay "Notes on Punctuation," Lewis Thomas gives the following advice to writers using quotations: If something is to be quoted, the exact words must be used. If part of it must be left out because of space limitations, it is good manners to insert three dots to indicate the omission, but it is unethical to do this if it means connecting two thoughts which the original author did not intend to have tied together.

. . .
. . . .
	If part of a quotation is omitted, the omission must be marked with points of ellipsis. When the omission comes in the middle of a sentence, three points are used. When the omission includes the end of one or more sentences, four points are used.	Lewis Thomas offers this advice:
		    If something is to be quoted, the exact words must be used.
		    If part of it must be left out…insert three dots to indicate the omission, but it is unethical to do this if it means connecting two thoughts which the original author did not intend to have tied together.

	When writers insert something within a quoted passage, the insertion should be set off with brackets. Insertions are sometimes used to supply words that make a quotation easier to understand.	Lewis Thomas warns that "it is unethical to [omit words in a quotation]…if it means connecting two thoughts which the original author did not intend to have tied together."
[ ]	Writers can make clear that a mistake in the quotation has been carried over from the original by using the word *sic,* meaning "thus."	As Senator Claghorne wrote to his constituents, "My fundamental political principals [*sic*] make it impossible for me to support the bill in its present form."
,	Text that reports the source of quoted material is usually separated from it by a comma.	Mark said, "I've decided not to apply to law school until next year." "I think we should encourage people to vote," said the mayor.
	When quoted words are woven into a text so that they perform a basic grammatical function in the sentence, no introductory punctuation is used.	According to Thoreau, most of us "lead lives of quiet desperation."
' '	Quotations that are included within other quotations are set off by single quotation marks.	The witness made the same damaging statement under cross-examination: "As I entered the room, I heard him say, 'I'm determined to get even.'"
" "	Final quotation marks follow other punctuation marks, except for semicolons and colons.	Ed began reading Williams's "The Glass Menagerie"; then he turned to "A Streetcar Named Desire."
	Question marks and exclamation marks precede final quotation marks when they refer to the quoted words. They follow when they refer to the sentence as a whole.	Once more she asked, "What do you think we should do about this?" What did Carol mean when she said, "I'm going to do something about this"? "Get out of here!" he yelled.

4. Word-Level Punctuation

The punctuation covered so far is used to clarify the structure of sentences. There are also punctuation marks that are used with words.

Guidelines	Examples
' The apostrophe is used with nouns to show possession:	The company's management resisted the union's demands. She found it impossible to decipher the students' handwriting.
(1) An apostrophe plus *s* is added to all words—singular or plural—that do not end in *-s*.	the boy's hat children's literature a week's vacation
(2) Just an apostrophe is added at the end of plural words that end in *-s*.	the boys' hats two weeks' vacation
(3) An apostrophe plus *s* is usually added at the end of singular words that end in *-s*. Just an apostrophe is added to names of classical or biblical derivation that end in *-s*.	the countess's daughter Dickens's novels Achilles' heel Moses' brother
An apostrophe is used in contractions to show where letters or numerals have been omitted.	he's didn't let's ma'am four o'clock readin', writin', and 'rithmetic the class of '55
An apostrophe is sometimes used when making letters or numbers plural.	45's ABC's *or* 45s ABCs
• A period is used to mark shortened forms like abbreviations and initials.	Prof. M. L. Smith 14 ft. 4:00 p.m. U.S.A. or USA etc.
— A hyphen is used to end a line of text when part of a word must be carried over to the next line.	... insta- bility
Hyphens are sometimes used to form compound words.	twenty-five self-confidence
In certain situations, hyphens are used between prefixes or suffixes and root words.	catlike *but* bull-like preschool *but* pre-Christian recover *vs.* re-cover
Hyphens are often used to indicate that a group of words is to be understood as a unit.	a scholar-athlete hand-to-hand combat
When two modifiers containing hyphens are joined together, common elements are often not repeated.	The study included fourth- and twelfth-grade students.

Note: It is important not to confuse the hyphen (-) with the dash (—), which is more than twice as long. The hyphen is used to group words and parts of words together, while the dash is used to clarify sentence structure. With a typewriter, a dash is formed by typing two successive hyphens(--). Many word-processing programs will create a dash automatically.

Spelling Rules

1. **Silent E Dropped.** Silent *e* at the end of a word is usually dropped before a suffix beginning with a vowel: *abide, abiding; recite, recital.*
   Exceptions: Words ending in *ce* or *ge* retain the *e* before a suffix beginning with *a* or *o* to keep the soft sound of the consonant: *notice, noticeable; courage, courageous.*
2. **Silent E Kept.** A silent *e* following a consonant (or another *e*) is usually retained before a suffix beginning with a consonant: *late, lateness; spite, spiteful.*
   Exceptions: *fledgling, acknowledgment, judgment, wholly,* and others.
3. **Final Consonant Doubled.** A final consonant following a single vowel in one-syllable words, or in a syllable that will take the main accent when combined with a suffix, is doubled before a suffix beginning with a vowel: *begin, beginning; occur, occurred; bat, batted.*
   Exceptions: *h* and *x* in final position; *transferable, gaseous,* and others.
4. **Final Consonant Single.** A final consonant following another consonant, a double vowel or diphthong, or that is not in a stressed syllable, is not doubled before a suffix beginning with a vowel: *part, parting; remark, remarkable.*
   Exceptions: an unaccented syllable does not prevent doubling of the final consonant, especially in British usage: *traveller* for *traveler.*
5. **Double Consonants Remain.** Double consonants are usually retained before a suffix except when a final *l* is to be followed by *ly* or *less.* To avoid a triple *lll,* one *l* is usually dropped: *full, fully.*
   Exceptions: Usage is divided, with some preferring *skilful* over *skillful, instalment* over *installment,* etc.
6. **Final Y.** If the *y* follows a consonant, change *y* to *i* before all endings except *ing.* Do not change it before *ing* or if it follows a vowel: *bury, buried, burying; try, tries;* but *attorney, attorneys.*
   Exceptions: *day, daily; gay, gaily; lay, laid; say, said.*
7. **Final IE to Y.** Words ending in *ie* change to *y* before *ing: die, dying; lie, lying.*
8. **Double and Triple E Reduced.** Words ending in double *e* drop one *e* before an ending beginning in *e,* to avoid a triple *e.* Words ending in silent *e* usually drop the *e* before endings beginning in *e* to avoid forming a syllable. Other words ending in a vowel sound commonly retain the letters indicating the sound. *Free + ed = freed.*
9. **EI or IE.** Words having the sound of *ē* are commonly spelled *ie* following all letters but *c;* with a preceding *c,* the common spelling is *ei.* Examples: *believe, achieve, besiege;* but *conceit, ceiling, receive, conceive.* When the sound is *ā* the common spelling is *ei* regardless of the preceding letter. Examples: *eight, weight, deign.*
   Exceptions: *either, neither, seize, financier;* some words in which *e* and *i* are pronounced separately, such as *notoriety.*
10. **Words Ending in C.** Before an ending beginning with *e, i,* or *y,* words ending in *c* commonly add *k* to keep the *c* hard: *panic, panicky.*
11. **Compounds.** Some compounds written as a unit bring together unusual combinations of letters. They are seldom changed on this account: *bookkeeper, roommate.*
    Exceptions: A few words are regularly clipped when compounded, such as *full* in *awful, cupful,* etc.

reference

Forms of Address

Government (United States)

President
Address: The President
The White House
Washington, D.C. 20500
Salutation: Dear Mr. *or* Madam
President:

Vice President
Address: The Vice President
United States Senate
Washington, D.C. 20510
Salutation: Dear Mr. *or* Madam Vice
President:

Cabinet Member
Address: The Honorable *(full
name)*
Secretary of *(name of
Department)*
Washington, D.C. *(zip
code)*
Salutation: Dear Mr. *or* Madam
Secretary:

Attorney General
Address: The Honorable *(full name)*
Attorney General
Washington, D.C. 20530
Salutation: Dear Mr. or Madam
Attorney General:

Senator
Address: The Honorable *(full name)*
United States Senate
Washington, D.C. 20510
Salutation: Dear Senator *(surname):*

Representative
Address: The Honorable *(full name)*
House of Representatives
Washington, D.C. 20515
Salutation: Dear Mr. *or* Madam
(surname):

Chief Justice
Address: The Chief Justice of the
United States
The Supreme Court of the
United States
Washington, D.C. 20543
Salutation: Dear Mr. *or* Madam Chief
Justice:

Associate Justice
Address: Mr. *or* Madam Justice
(surname)
The Supreme Court of the
United States
Washington, D.C. 20543
Salutation: Dear Mr. *or* Madam
Justice:

Judge of a Federal Court
Address: The Honorable *(full name)*
Judge of the *(name of
court; if a district court,
give district)*
(Local address)
Salutation: Dear Judge *(surname):*

Religious Leaders

Minister, Pastor, or Rector
Address: The Reverend *(full name)*
*(Title), (name of
church)*
(Local address)
Salutation: Dear (Mr., Ms., Miss, *or*
Mrs.) *(surname):*

Rabbi
Address: Rabbi *(full name)*
(Local address)
Salutation: Dear Rabbi *(surname):*

Catholic Cardinal
Address: His Eminence *(Christian
name)* Cardinal
(surname)
Archbishop of *(province)*
(Local address)
Salutation: *Formal:* Your Eminence:
Informal: Dear Cardinal
(surname):

Catholic Archbishop
Address: The Most Reverend *(full
name)*

Archbishop of *(province)*
(Local address)
Salutation: *Formal:* Your Excellency:
Informal: Dear
Archbishop *(surname):*

Catholic Bishop
Address: The Most Reverend *(full name)*
Bishop of *(province)*
(Local address)
Salutation: *Formal:* Your Excellency:
Informal: Dear Bishop
(surname):

Catholic Monsignor
Address: The Right Reverend
Monsignor *(full name)*
(Local address)
Salutation: *Formal:* Right Reverend
Monsignor:
Informal: Dear Monsignor
(surname):

Catholic Priest
Address: The Reverend *(full name), (initials of order, if any)*
(Local address)
Salutation: *Formal:* Reverend Sir:
Informal: Dear Father
(surname):

Catholic Sister
Address: Sister *(full name)*
(Name of organization)
(Local address)
Salutation: Dear Sister *(full name):*

Catholic Brother
Address: Brother *(full name)*
(Name of organization)
(Local address)
Salutation: Dear Brother *(given name):*

Protestant Episcopal Bishop
Address: The Right Reverend *(full name)*
Bishop of *(name)*
(Local address)
Salutation: *Formal:* Right Reverend
Sir *or* Madam
Informal: Dear Bishop
(surname):

Protestant Episcopal Dean
Address: The Very Reverend *(full name)*
Dean of *(church)*
(Local address)
Salutation: *Formal:* Very Reverend
Sir *or* Madam
Informal: Dear Dean
(surname):

Methodist Bishop
Address: The Reverend *(full name)*
Methodist Bishop
(Local address)
Salutation: *Formal:* Reverend Sir or
Madam:
Informal: Dear Bishop
(surname):

Mormon Bishop
Address: Bishop *(full name)*
Church of Jesus Christ of
Latter-day Saints
(Local address)
Salutation: *Formal:* Sir:
Informal: Dear Bishop
(surname):

Miscellaneous
President of a university or college
Address: (Dr., Mr., Ms., Miss, *or* Mrs.) *(full name)*
President, *(name of institution)*
(Local address)
Salutation: Dear (Dr., Mr., Ms., Miss, or Mrs.) *(surname):*

Dean of a college or school
Address: Dean *(full name)*
School of *(name)*
(Name of institution)
(Local address)
Salutation: Dear Dean *(surname):*

Professor
Address: Professor *(full name)*
Department of *(name)*
(Name of institution)
(Local address)
Salutation: Dear Professor
(surname):

reference

Avoiding Insensitive and Offensive Language

This essay is intended as a general guide to language that can, intentionally or not, cause offense or perpetuate discriminatory values and practices by emphasizing the differences between people or implying that one group is superior to another.

Several factors complicate the issue. A group may disagree within itself as to what is acceptable and what is not. Many seemingly inoffensive terms develop negative connotations over time and become dated or go out of style as awareness changes. A "within the group" rule often applies, which allows a member of a group to use terms freely that would be considered offensive if used by an outsider.

While it is true that some of the more extreme attempts to avoid offending language have resulted in ludicrous obfuscation, it is also true that heightened sensitivity in language indicates a precision of thought and is a positive move toward rectifying the unequal social status between one group and another.

Suggestions for avoiding insensitive or offensive language are given in the following pages. The recommended terms are given on the right. While these suggestions can reflect trends, they cannot dictate or predict the preferences of each individual.

Sexism

Sexism is the most difficult bias to avoid, in part because of the convention of using *man* or *men* and *he* or *his* to refer to people of either sex. Other, more disrespectful conventions include giving descriptions of women in terms of age and appearance while describing men in terms of accomplishment.

Replacing *man* or *men*

Man traditionally referred to a male or to a human in general. Using *man* to refer to a human is often thought to be slighting of women.

Avoid This	Use This Instead
mankind, man	→ human beings, humans, humankind, humanity, people, society, men and women
man-made	→ synthetic, artificial
man in the street	→ average person, ordinary person

Using gender-neutral terms for occupations, positions, roles, etc.

Terms that specify a particular sex can unnecessarily perpetuate certain stereotypes when used generically.

Avoid This	Use This Instead
actress	→ actor
anchorman	→ anchor
bellman, bellboy	→ bellhop
businessman	→ businessperson, executive, manager, business owner, retailer, etc.
chairman	→ chair, chairperson
cleaning lady, girl, maid	→ housecleaner, housekeeper, cleaning person, office cleaner
clergyman	→ member of the clergy, rabbi, priest, etc.
clergymen	→ the clergy
congressman	→ representative, member of Congress, legislator
fireman	→ firefighter
forefather	→ ancestor
girl/gal Friday	→ assistant
housewife	→ homemaker
insurance man	→ insurance agent
layman	→ layperson, nonspecialist, nonprofessional

Avoid This	Use This Instead
mailman, postman →	mail or letter carrier
policeman →	police officer or law enforcement officer
salesman, saleswoman, saleslady, salesgirl →	salesperson, sales representative, sales associate, clerk
spokesman →	spokesperson, representative
stewardess, steward →	flight attendant
weatherman →	weather reporter, weathercaster, meteorologist
workman →	worker

Replacing the pronoun *he*

The generic use of *he* can also be seen to exclude women.

Avoid This	Use This Instead
When a driver approaches a red light, he must prepare to stop. →	When drivers approach a red light, they must prepare to stop.
When a driver approaches a red light, he or she must prepare to stop. →	When approaching a red light, a driver must prepare to stop.

Referring to members of both sexes with parallel names, titles, or descriptions

Don't be inconsistent unless you are trying to make a specific point.

Avoid This	Use This Instead
men and ladies →	men and women, ladies and gentlemen
Betty Schmidt, an attractive 49-year-old physician, and her husband, Alan Schmidt, a noted editor →	Betty Schmidt, a physician, and her husband, Alan Schmidt, an editor
Mr. David Kim and Mrs. Betty Harrow →	Mr. David Kim and Ms. Betty Harrow (unless *Mrs.* is her known preference)

Avoid This	Use This Instead
man and wife →	husband and wife
Dear Sir: →	Dear Sir/Madam: Dear Madam or Sir: To whom it may concern:
Mrs. Smith and President Jones →	Governor Smith and President Jones

Race, Ethnicity, and National Origin

Some words and phrases that refer to racial and ethnic groups are clearly offensive. Other words (e.g., Oriental, colored) are outdated or inaccurate. Hispanic is generally accepted as a broad term for Spanish-speaking people of the Western Hemisphere, but more specific terms (Latino, Mexican American) are also acceptable and in some cases preferred.

Avoid This	Use This Instead
Negro, colored, Afro-American →	black, African-American (generally preferred to Afro-American)
Oriental, Asiatic →	Asian, or more specific designation such as Pacific Islander, Chinese American, Korean
Indian →	*Indian* properly refers to people who live in or come from India. *American Indian, Native American,* and more specific designations (*Chinook, Hopi*) are usually preferred when referring to the native peoples of the Western Hemisphere.
Eskimo →	Inuit, Alaska Natives
native (*n.*) →	native peoples, early inhabitants, aboriginal peoples (but not *aborigines*)

reference

Age

The concept of aging is changing as people are living longer and more active lives. Be aware of word choices that reinforce stereotypes (*decrepit, senile*) and avoid mentioning age unless it is relevant.

Avoid This	Use This Instead
elderly, aged, old, geriatric, the elderly, the aged	→ older person, senior citizen(s), older people, seniors

Avoiding Depersonalization of Persons with Disabilities or Illnesses

Terminology that emphasizes the person rather than the disability is generally preferred. *Handicap* is used to refer to the environmental barrier that affects the person. (Stairs handicap a person who uses a wheelchair.) While words such as *crazy, demented,* and *insane* are used in facetious or informal contexts, these terms are not used to describe people with clinical diagnoses of mental illness. The euphemisms *challenged, differently abled,* and *special* are preferred by some people, but are often ridiculed and are best avoided.

Avoid This	Use This Instead
Mongoloid	→ person with Down syndrome
wheelchair-bound	→ person who uses a wheelchair
AIDS sufferer, person afflicted with AIDS, AIDS victim	→ person living with AIDS, P.W.A., HIV +, (one who tests positive for HIV but does not show symptoms of AIDS)
polio victim	→ has/had polio
the handicapped, the disabled, cripple	→ persons with disabilities *or* person who uses crutches *or* more specific description
deaf-mute, deaf and dumb	→ deaf person

Avoiding Patronizing or Demeaning Expressions

Avoid This	Use This Instead
girls (when referring to adult women), the fair sex	→ women
sweetie, dear, dearie, honey	→ (usually not appropriate with strangers or in public situations)
old maid, bachelorette, spinster	→ single woman, woman, divorced woman (but only if one would specify "divorced man" in the same context)
the little woman, old lady, ball and chain	→ wife
boy (when referring to or addressing an adult man)	→ man, sir

Avoiding Language That Excludes or Unnecessarily Emphasizes Differences

References to age, sex, religion, race, and the like should be included only if they are relevant.

Avoid This	Use This Instead
lawyers and their wives	→ lawyers and their spouses
a secretary and her boss	→ a secretary and boss, a secretary and his or her boss
the male nurse	→ the nurse
Arab man denies assault charge	→ Man denies assault charge
the articulate black student	→ the articulate student
Marie Curie was a great woman scientist	→ Marie Curie was a great scientist (unless the intent is to compare her only with other women in the sciences)